AF819776

Skills in Mathematics

JEE Main & Advanced

Differential Calculus

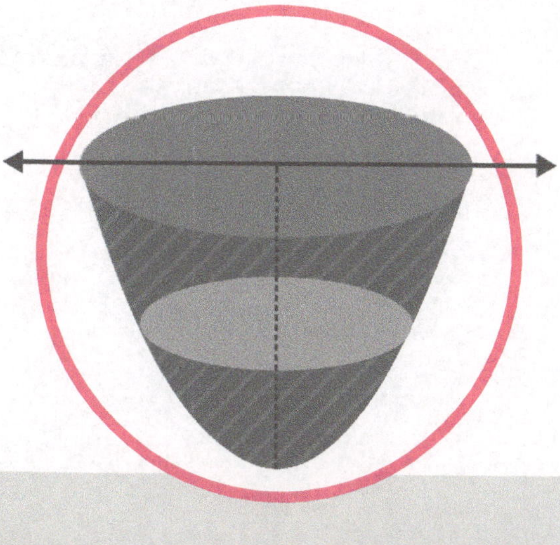

arihant

SUCCESS AND NOTHING LESS

ARIHANT PRAKASHAN (SERIES), MEERUT

Skills in Mathematics

JEE Main & Advanced

Differential Calculus

Amit M Agarwal

Supported by Girish Jain

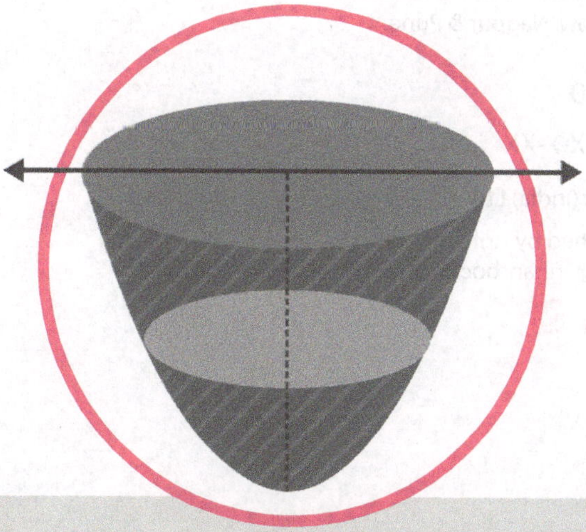

arihant
SUCCESS AND NOTHING LESS

Arihant Prakashan (Series), Meerut

卐 **Administrative & Production Offices**

Regd. Office

'Ramchhaya' 4577/15, Agarwal Road, Darya Ganj, New Delhi -110002
Tele: 011- 47630600, 43518550

卐 **Head Office**

Kalindi, TP Nagar, Meerut (UP) - 250002 Tel: 0121-7156203, 7156204

卐 **Sales & Support Offices**

Agra, Ahmedabad, Bengaluru, Bareilly, Chennai, Delhi, Guwahati, Hyderabad, Jaipur, Jhansi, Kolkata, Lucknow, Nagpur & Pune.

卐 **PRICE**: ₹ 665.00

卐 **PO No :** TXT-XX-XXXXXXX-X-XX

Published by Arihant Publications (India) Ltd.

For further information about the books published by Arihant, log on to www.arihantbooks.com or e-mail at info@arihantbooks.com

Follow us on

Preface

It is a matter of great pride and honour for me to have received such an overwhelming response to the previous editions of this book from the readers. In a way, this has inspired me to revise this book thoroughly as per the changed pattern of JEE Main & Advanced. I have tried to make the contents more relevant as per the needs of students, many topics have been re-written, a lot of new problems of new types have been added. All possible efforts are made to remove all the printing errors that had crept in previous editions. The book is now in such a shape that the students would feel at ease while going through the problems, which will in turn clear their concepts too.

A Summary of changes that have been made in Revised & Enhanced Edition

- Theory has been completely updated so as to accommodate all the changes made in JEE Syllabus & Pattern in recent years.
- The most important point about this new edition is, now the whole text matter of each chapter has been divided into small milestones with practice exercise in each milestones. This will help reader in step by step learning
- Theory of each milestone is more precise with **JEE focus Points** and **JEE Spike**.
- **JEE Scanners** are incorporated in theory for more synced learning with JEE Main and Advanced PYQs.
- Just after completion of theory, Solved Examples of all JEE types have been given, providing the students a complete understanding of all the formats of JEE questions & the level of difficulty of questions generally asked in JEE.
- Along with exercises given with each Milestone, following three exercises have been given at the end of each chapter.
- Practice Milestone 1- JEE Main Pattern Exercises.
- Practice Milestone 2- JEE Advanced Pattern Exercises.
- Practice Milestone 3- Challenging Problems Exercises.
- Previous Years questions asked in JEE Main and Advanced have been incorporated in all the exercises.

However I have made the best efforts and put my all teaching experience in revising this book. Still I am looking forward to get the valuable suggestions and criticism from my own fraternity i.e. the fraternity of JEE teachers. I strongly believe that

"YOU CAN DO ANYTHING IF YOU SET YOUR MIND FOR IT. I ALWAYS BELIEVE THE MOST IMPORTANT FORMULA IS

COURAGE + DREAMS = SUCCESS"

I would also like to motivate the students to send their suggestions or the changes that they want to be incorporated in this book. All the suggestions given by you all will be kept in prime focus at the time of next revision of the book.

Amit M Agarwal

Enhanced Features

JEE Focus Points

- $f(x) = a\sin x + b\cos x$
  $= \sqrt{a^2+b^2}\sin(x+\alpha)$, $\tan\alpha = \frac{b}{a}$
  $= \sqrt{a^2+b^2}\cos(x-\beta)$, $\tan\beta = \frac{a}{b}$

Proof $f(x) = a\sin x + b\cos x$

$$= \sqrt{a^2+b^2}\left(\frac{a}{\sqrt{a^2+b^2}}\sin x + \frac{b}{\sqrt{a^2+b^2}}\cos x\right)$$

[divide and multiply by $\sqrt{a^2+b^2}$]

$$= \sqrt{a^2+b^2}\,(\sin x\cos\alpha + \cos x\sin\alpha)$$

$$\left[\because \cos\alpha = \frac{a}{\sqrt{a^2+b^2}}, \sin\alpha = \frac{b}{\sqrt{a^2+b^2}}\right]$$

$$= \sqrt{a^2+b^2}\sin(x+\alpha), \text{ where } \tan\alpha = \frac{b}{a}$$

or $f(x) = \sqrt{a^2+b^2}\,(\sin x\sin\beta + \cos x\cos\beta)$

$$= \sqrt{a^2+b^2}\cos(x-\beta), \text{ where } \tan\beta = \frac{a}{b}$$

$$\left[\because \sin\beta = \frac{a}{\sqrt{a^2+b^2}}, \cos\beta = \frac{b}{\sqrt{a^2+b^2}}\right]$$

- $-\sqrt{a^2+b^2} \le a\sin x + b\cos x \le \sqrt{a^2+b^2}$

Concept Inside Video

A collection of Key Points/Results prime from JEE Preparation point of View. These are further elaborated with support videos.

JEE SPIKE

Vertical line test for f to be a function If graph of a function is cut a line parallel to Y-axis at more than one point, then it does not form a function.

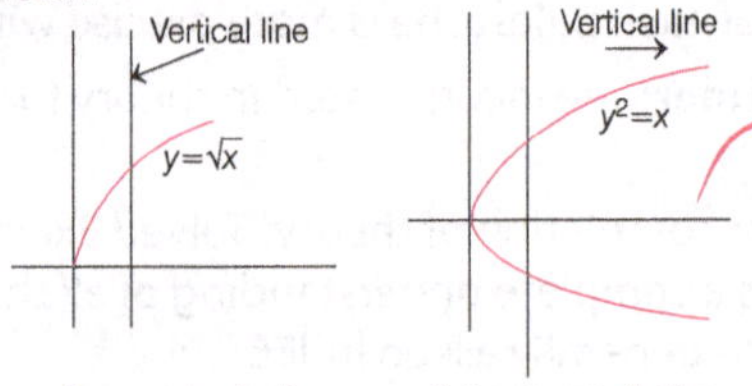

Represents a funtion **Not represent a funtion**

Concept Inside Video

Seggregated most valuable Pointers for JEE preparation

JEE SCANNER

Example Similar to PYQ Asked in JEE Main 2023

If $f(x) = \frac{9^x}{9^x+3}$, *then the value of*

$$f\left(\frac{1}{1996}\right)+f\left(\frac{2}{1996}\right)+f\left(\frac{3}{1996}\right)+\ldots+f\left(\frac{1995}{1996}\right) \text{ is}$$

(a) 997.5 (b) 979.5 (c) 597.9 (d) 959.7

Sol. (a) We have, $f(x) = \frac{9^x}{9^x+3}$

$$\therefore \quad f(1-x) = \frac{9^{1-x}}{9^{1-x}+3} = \frac{3}{3+9^x}$$

Skill Builder

If $f(x) = \frac{4^x}{4^x+2}$, then the value of $f\left(\frac{1}{20}\right)+f\left(\frac{2}{20}\right)$ $+f\left(\frac{3}{20}\right)+\ldots+f\left(\frac{19}{20}\right)$ is equal to

For Sol.

(a) 10.5 (b) 10
(c) 9 (d) 9.5

- **For more practice** See Q.5 of Milestone Practice 2.1.

Unmatched Concept elevation tool helpful in syncing recent JEE Main & Advanced PYQs with theory and provide additional practice through Skill Builders.

Contents

Syllabus

JEE Main

Limit, Continuity and Differentiability

Real valued functions, algebra of functions, polynomials, rational, trigonometric, logarithmic and exponential functions, inverse functions. Graphs of simple functions. Limits, continuity and differentiability.

Differentiation of the sum, difference, product and quotient of two functions. Differentiation of trigonometric, inverse trigonometric, logarithmic exponential, composite and implicit functions derivatives of order upto two. Applications of derivatives: Rate of change of quantities, monotonic - increasing and decreasing functions, Maxima and minima of functions of one variable.

JEE Advanced

Differential Calculus

Limit of a function at a real number, continuity of a function, limit and continuity of the sum, difference, product and quotient of two functions, L'Hospital rule of evaluation of limits of functions.

Continuity of composite functions, intermediate value property of continuous functions. Derivative of a function, derivative of the sum, difference, product and quotient of two functions, chain rule, derivatives of polynomial, rational, trigonometric, inverse trigonometric, exponential and logarithmic functions.

Tangents and normals, increasing and decreasing functions, derivatives of order two, maximum and minimum values of a function, Rolle's theorem and Lagrange's mean value theorem, geometric interpretation of the two theorems, derivatives up to order two of implicit functions, geometric interpretation of derivatives.

"A man is like a fraction whose numerator is what he is and whose denominator is what he thinks of himself. The larger the denominator, the smaller the fraction."

–Leo Tolstoy

1

Essential Tools of Mathematics

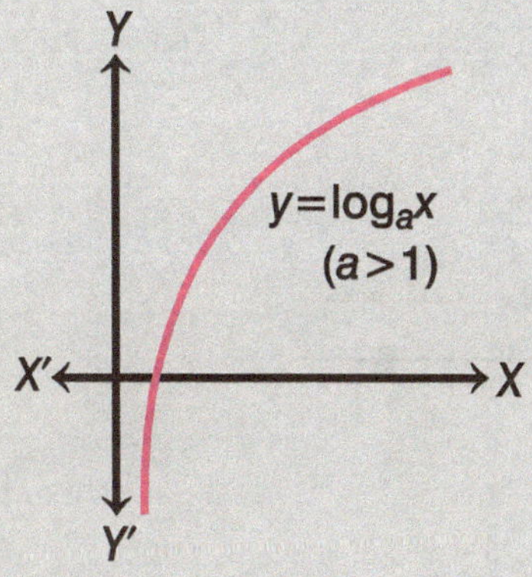

Learning Milestones

- Intervals
- Linear Inequalities
- Polynomial Inequality
- Rational Inequality
- Modulus Inequality
- Inequality Involving GIF and Fractional Part Function
- Trigonometric Inequality
- Logarithmic Inequality

Practice Milestones

Practice Milestone - JEE Main Pattern

Solving Inequality

1.1 Intervals

Intervals are the collections of all the numbers between any two real numbers. Interval is basically a subset of R (the set of all real numbers) and are commonly used in solving inequalities. If $a, b \in R$ such that $a < b$, then we can define four types of intervals as follows.

Name	Representation	Description
Open interval	(a, b)	all the numbers between a and b are included but a and b are not included $\{x : a < x < b\}$
Close interval	$[a, b]$	all the numbers between a and b including a and b are included $\{x : a \le x \le b\}$
Open-close interval	$(a, b]$	all the numbers between a and b including b, a is excluded $\{x : a < x \le b\}$
Close-open interval	$[a, b)$	all the numbers between a and b including a, b is excluded $\{x : a \le x < b\}$

Note Between any 2 real number, there exist infinite real numbers.

- The infinite intervals are defined as follows
  (i) $(a, \infty) = \{x : x > a\}$
  (ii) $[a, \infty) = \{x \mid x \ge a\}$
  (iii) $(-\infty, b) = \{x : x < b\}$
  (iv) $(-\infty, b] = \{x : x \le b\}$
  (v) $(-\infty, \infty) = \{x : x \in R\}$
- $x \in \{1, 2\}$ denotes some particular values of x, i.e. $x = 1, 2$.
- If there is no value of x, then we say $x \in \phi$ (i.e. null set or void set or empty set).

Note Here, we will discuss inequalities in one variable only and inequalities in two variables are solved by graphical approach.

1.2 Linear Inequalities

General form

$$ax + b \;>,\; <,\; \ge,\; \le$$

For solving, we take x in LHS remaining in RHS.

JEE SPIKE

Whenever we multiply or divide by '–' ve numbers sign of inequality will be changed

$$> \to <, \quad \ge \to \le$$
$$< \to >, \quad \le \to \ge$$

Example 1. Solve the following inequalities

(i) $5x + 7 \ge 17 - 3x$

(ii) $\dfrac{7x+2}{3} - \dfrac{2-3x}{5} < \dfrac{5-x}{3}$

(iii) $\dfrac{4x+7}{7} - \dfrac{3x-8}{2} \le \dfrac{5-3x}{14} + \dfrac{7-x}{7}$

(iv) $\dfrac{2-3x}{2} - \dfrac{x}{4} > \dfrac{5+11x}{6}$

Sol. (i) $5x + 7 \ge 17 - 3x$

$$5x + 3x \ge 17 - 7$$
$$8x \ge 10$$
$$x \ge \frac{10}{8} \text{ or } x \ge \frac{5}{4}$$

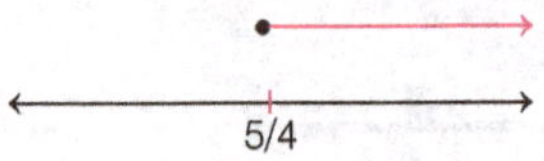

$$\therefore \quad x \in \left[\frac{5}{4}, \infty\right)$$

(ii) $\dfrac{7x+2}{3} - \dfrac{2-3x}{5} < \dfrac{5-x}{3}$

$$\frac{35x + 10 - 6 + 9x}{15} < \frac{5-x}{3}$$
$$44x + 4 < 5(5 - x)$$

$$44x + 4 < 25 - 5x$$
$$49x < 21$$
$$x < \frac{21}{49} \text{ or } x < \frac{3}{7}$$

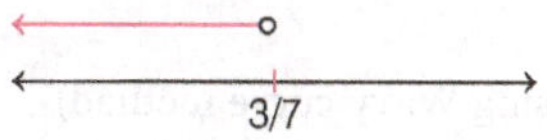

$$\therefore \quad x \in \left(-\infty, \frac{3}{7}\right)$$

(iii) $$\frac{4x+7}{7} - \frac{3x-8}{2} \le \frac{5-3x}{14} + \frac{7-x}{7}$$
$$\frac{8x + 14 - 21x + 56}{14} \le \frac{5 - 3x + 14 - 2x}{14}$$
$$-13x + 70 \le 19 - 5x$$
$$-13x + 5x \le 19 - 70$$
$$-8x \le -51 \Rightarrow x \ge \frac{51}{8}$$

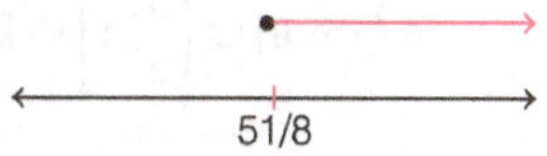

$$\therefore \quad x \in \left[\frac{51}{8}, \infty\right)$$

(iv) $$\frac{2-3x}{2} - \frac{x}{4} > \frac{5+11x}{6}$$
$$\frac{4 - 6x - x}{4} > \frac{5+11x}{6}$$
$$3(4-7x) > 2(5+11x)$$
$$12 - 21x > 10 + 22x$$
$$-21x - 22x > 10 - 12$$
$$-43x > -2 \Rightarrow x < \frac{2}{43}$$

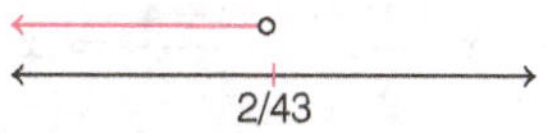

$$\therefore \quad x \in \left(-\infty, \frac{2}{43}\right)$$

1.3 Polynomial Inequality

General form

$$P(x) >, <, \ge, \le 0$$

where, $P(x)$ be any polynomial in x.

1.4 Rational Inequality

General form

$$\frac{P(x)}{Q(x)} >, <, \ge, \le 0$$

where, $P(x)$ and $Q(x)$ both are polynomial in x.

JEE SPIKE

Both polynomial and rational inequality solved by number line rule and wavy curve method.

Note For solving above inequalities first of all make RHS = 0 and then factorise the numerator and denominator (if available).

Method 1 : Number Line Rule

It is used to solve algebraic inequalities using following steps

(i) Factorise numerator as well as denominator.

(ii) Now, check the coefficients of x and make them positive.

(iii) Put only odd power factors in numerator and denominator and put them equal to zero separately and find the value of x.

(As for polynomial function only numerator = 0, denominator $\neq 0$).

(iv) Plot these points on number line in increasing order.

(v) Start number line from right to left taking sign of $f(x)$.

(vi) Check your answer, so that it should not contain a point for which $f(x)$ does not exist.

Method 2 : Wavy Curve Method

The method of intervals (or wavy curve) is used for solving inequalities of the form

$$f(x) = \frac{(x-a_1)^{n_1}(x-a_2)^{n_2}\ldots(x-a_k)^{n_k}}{(x-b_1)^{m_1}(x-b_2)^{m_2}\ldots(x-b_p)^{m_p}} > 0$$

$(< 0, \le 0 \text{ or } \ge 0)$

where, $n_1, n_2, \ldots, n_k$ and $m_1, m_2, \ldots, m_p$ are natural numbers.

$a_1, a_2, \ldots, a_k; b_1, b_2, \ldots, b_p$ are any real numbers such that $a_i \neq b_j$, where $i = 1, 2, 3, \ldots, k$ and $j = 1, 2, 3, \ldots, p$

It consists of the following statements

(i) All zeroes of the function $f(x)$ (the values of x corresponding to numerator = 0) contained on the left hand side of the inequality should be marked on the number line with inked (black) circles.

(ii) All points of discontinuities of the function $f(x)$ (the values of x corresponding to denominator = 0) contained on the left hand side of the inequality should be marked on the number line with uninked (white) circles.

(iii) Check the value of $f(x)$ for any real number greater than the rightmost marked number on the number line.

(iv) From right to left, beginning above the number line (in case of value of $f(x)$ is positive in step (iii) otherwise from below the number line), a wavy curve should be drawn to pass through all the marked points, so that when it passes through a simple point, the curve intersects the number line and when passing through a double point, the curve remains located on one side of the number line.

(v) The appropriate intervals are chosen in accordance with the sign of inequality (the function $f(x)$ is positive whenever the curve is situated above the number line, it is negative, if the curve is found below the number line). Their union just represents the solution of the inequality.

JEE Focus Points

- Points of discontinuity will never be included in the answers.
- If asked to find the intervals, where $f(x)$ is non-negative or non-positive, then make the intervals closed correspondingly.

Example 2. Let

$$f(x)=\frac{(x^2-5x+4)^{217}(5x-x^2)^{179}(x^2-4)^{420}}{(2x^2-7x+5)^{193}(7-x^2)^4}.$$

Then, solve the following.

(i) $f(x)>0$ (ii) $f(x)\geq 0$
(iii) $f(x)<0$ (iv) $f(x)\leq 0$

Sol. **Method 1** (Using number line rule)

$$f(x)=\frac{(x-4)^{217}(x-1)^{217}x^{179}(5-x)^{179}(x-2)^{420}(x+2)^{420}}{(2x-5)^{193}(x-1)^{193}(\sqrt{7}-x)^4(\sqrt{7}+x)^4}$$

After simplification,

$$f(x)=-\frac{(x-4)^{217}(x-1)^{24}x^{179}(x-5)^{179}(x-2)^{420}(x+2)^{420}}{(2x-5)^{193}(x-\sqrt{7})^4(x+\sqrt{7})^4}$$

where $x\neq 1$

Critical points

$x=4,1,0,5,2,-2\rightarrow$ numerator $=0$

$x=\frac{5}{2},\sqrt{7},-\sqrt{7}\rightarrow$ denominator $=0$

where $x=1,2,-2,\sqrt{7},-\sqrt{7}\rightarrow$ (even power)

Number line

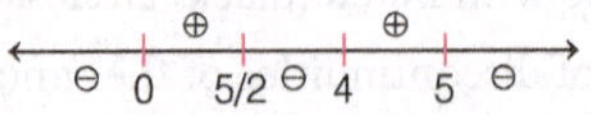

(i) $f(x)>0$ $\quad x\in\left(0,\frac{5}{2}\right)\cup(4,5)-\{1,2\}$

(ii) $f(x)\geq 0$ $\quad x\in\left[0,\frac{5}{2}\right)\cup[4,5]\cup\{-2\}-\{1\}$

(iii) $f(x)<0$ $\quad x\in(-\infty,0)\cup\left(\frac{5}{2},4\right)\cup(5,\infty)-\{-\sqrt{7},-2,\sqrt{7}\}$

(iv) $f(x)\leq 0$ $\quad x\in(-\infty,0]\cup\left(\frac{5}{2},4\right]\cup[5,\infty)\cup\{2\}-\{-\sqrt{7},\sqrt{7}\}$

Method 2 (Using Wavy curve method)

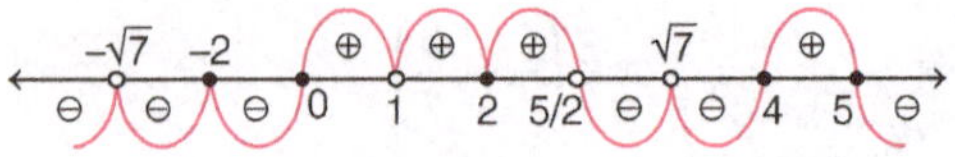

(i) $f(x)>0$ $\quad x\in\left(0,\frac{5}{2}\right)\cup(4,5)-\{1,2\}$

(ii) $f(x)\geq 0$ $\quad x\in\left[0,\frac{5}{2}\right)\cup[4,5]\cup\{-2\}-\{1\}$

(iii) $f(x)<0$ $\quad x\in(-\infty,0)\cup\left(\frac{5}{2},4\right)\cup(5,\infty)-\{-\sqrt{7},-2,\sqrt{7}\}$

(iv) $f(x)\leq 0$ $\quad x\in(-\infty,0]\cup\left(\frac{5}{2},4\right]\cup[5,\infty)\cup\{2\}-\{-\sqrt{7},\sqrt{7}\}$

Example 3. Solve the following inequalities.

(i) $x-\frac{1}{x}>2-\frac{x-4}{3}$

(ii) $\frac{2x^2-4x+7}{x^2-7x+5}\leq 2$

(iii) $\frac{(\sin x-1)(e^x-1)(4-x^2)(x^2-3x+2)^2}{(2\cos x+1)^2(\tan x-\sqrt{3})(x^3-1)}\geq 0$

where, $x\in[0,2\pi]$

Sol. (i)

$$x-\frac{1}{x}>2-\frac{x-4}{3}$$

$$x-\frac{1}{x}>\frac{6-x+4}{3}\Rightarrow x-\frac{1}{x}>\frac{10-x}{3}$$

$$x-\frac{1}{x}-\frac{10-x}{3}>0\Rightarrow\frac{3x^2-3-10x+x^2}{3x}>0$$

$$\frac{4x^2-10x-3}{3x}>0$$

Numerator $=0\Rightarrow 4x^2-10x-3=0$

$$x=\frac{10\pm\sqrt{100+48}}{8}=\frac{10\pm\sqrt{148}}{8}=\frac{5\pm\sqrt{37}}{4}$$

Denominator $=0\Rightarrow 3x=0\Rightarrow x=0$

Critical points, $x=\frac{5-\sqrt{37}}{4},0,\frac{5+\sqrt{37}}{4}$

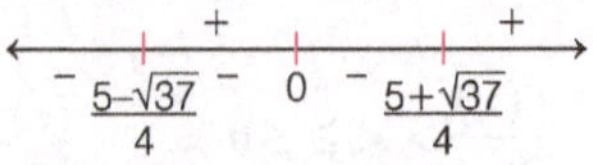

$$\therefore x\in\left(\frac{5-\sqrt{37}}{4},0\right)\cup\left(\frac{5+\sqrt{37}}{4},\infty\right)$$

(ii)
$$\frac{2x^2-4x+7}{x^2-7x+5}-2\le 0$$

$$\frac{2x^2-4x+7-2x^2+14x-10}{x^2-7x+5}\le 0$$

$$\frac{10x-3}{x^2-7x+5}\le 0$$

Numerator $=0 \Rightarrow x=\dfrac{3}{10}$

Denominator $=0 \Rightarrow x^2-7x+5=0$

$$x=\frac{7\pm\sqrt{49-20}}{2}$$
$$=\frac{7\pm\sqrt{29}}{2}$$

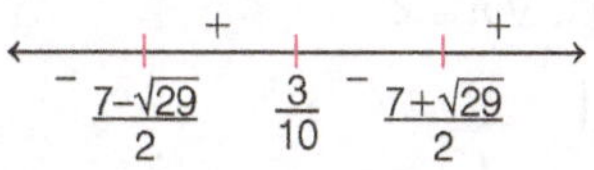

$$x\in\left(-\infty,\frac{7-\sqrt{29}}{2}\right)\cup\left[\frac{3}{10},\frac{7+\sqrt{29}}{2}\right)$$

(c)
$$\frac{(\sin x-1)(e^x-1)(4-x^2)(x^2-3x+2)^2}{(2\cos x+1)^2(\tan x-\sqrt{3})(x^3-1)}\ge 0$$

Simplifying

$$\frac{(\sin x-1)(e^x-1)(x-2)(x+2)(x-1)^2(x-2)^2}{(2\cos x+1)^2(\tan x-\sqrt{3})(x-1)(x^2+x+1)}\le 0$$

$$\frac{(\sin x-1)(e^x-1)(x-2)^3(x+2)(x-1)}{(2\cos x+1)^2(\tan x-\sqrt{3})(x^2+x+1)}\le 0\; x\ne 1$$

Numerator $=0$

$\sin x=1$	$e^x=1$	$x=2,-2,1$
$x=\dfrac{\pi}{2}$	$x=0$	

Denominator $=0$

$$\cos x=-\frac{1}{2}\Rightarrow x=\frac{2\pi}{3},\frac{4\pi}{3}\text{ (even power)}$$

$$x^2+x+1>0, \forall x\in R$$

No real values of x.

$$\tan x=\sqrt{3}\Rightarrow x=\frac{\pi}{3},\frac{4\pi}{3}$$

$\because$ $\tan x$ is not defined at $x=\dfrac{\pi}{2}$ and $x=\dfrac{3\pi}{2}$

So, we have to consider it also.

$\because x=\dfrac{4\pi}{3}$ is repeating odd number of times as if it is considered in $\cos x=-\dfrac{1}{2}$ and $\tan x=\sqrt{3}$.

$\therefore$ It will be plotted on number line.

$\because x=\dfrac{\pi}{2}$ is in numerator as well in denominator. So, it will create an even power.

So, does not plot it on the number line.

Plotting the points $\rightarrow$ $0, 2, 1, \dfrac{\pi}{3}, \dfrac{4\pi}{3}, \dfrac{3\pi}{2}$

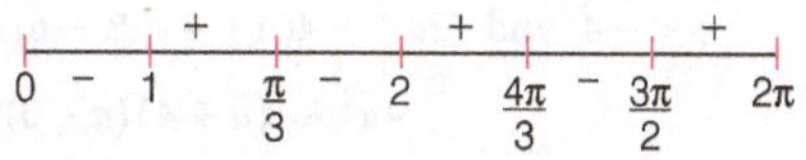

$\therefore f(x)\le 0$

$$x\in[0,1)\cup\left(\frac{\pi}{3},2\right]\cup\left(\frac{4\pi}{3},\frac{3\pi}{2}\right)-\left\{\frac{\pi}{2}\right\}$$

JEE SPIKE

Sometimes two parameters are involved in quadratic inequality, so in this situation we use the concept of nature of roots of quadratic expression.

Case I

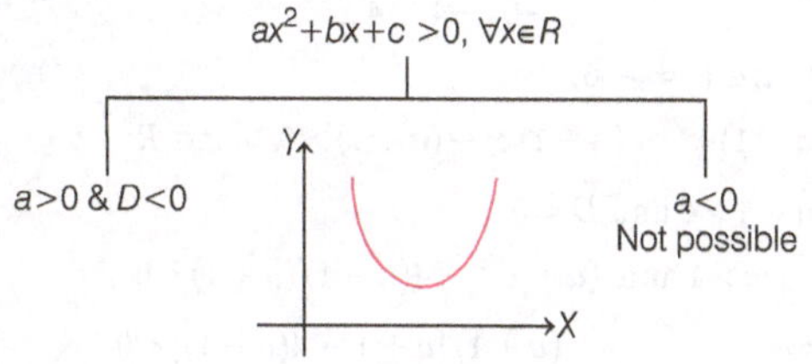

Case II

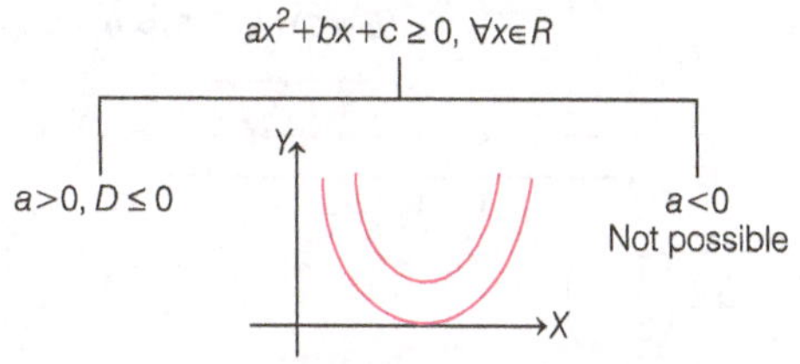

Case III

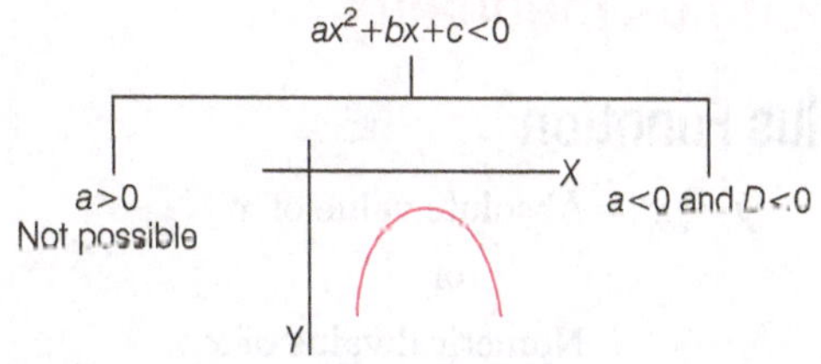

Case IV

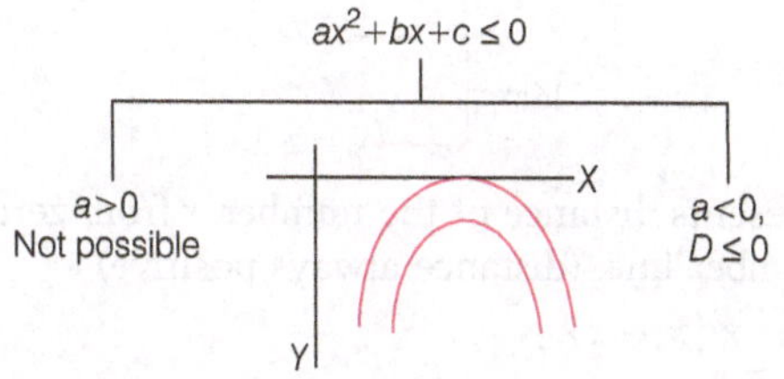

Example 4. Find the set of values of a for which the quadratic inequality holds

(i) $(a+4)x^2 - 2ax + 2a - 6 < 0, \forall x \in R$

(ii) $(a-1)x^2 - (a+1)x + (a+1) > 0, \forall x \in R$

Sol. (i) $(a+4)x^2 - 2ax + 2a - 6 < 0, \forall x \in R$

$\therefore (a+4) < 0$ and $D < 0$

$$a < -4 \text{ and } (2a)^2 - 4(a+4)(2a-6) < 0$$

$$\Rightarrow 4a^2 - 8(a+4)(a-3) < 0$$

$$\Rightarrow a^2 - 2(a^2 + a - 12) < 0$$

$$\Rightarrow a^2 - 2a^2 - 2a + 24 < 0$$

$$\Rightarrow -a^2 - 2a + 24 < 0$$

$$\Rightarrow a^2 + 2a - 24 > 0$$

$$\Rightarrow (a+6)(a-4) > 0$$

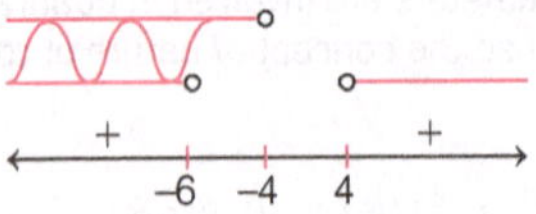

$\therefore a \in (-\infty, -6)$

(ii) $(a-1)x^2 - (a+1)x + (a+1) > 0, \forall x \in R$

$a - 1 > 0$ and $D < 0$

$$a > 1 \text{ and } (a+1)^2 - 4(a-1)(a+1) < 0$$

$$\Rightarrow (a+1)[a+1-4(a-1)] < 0$$

$$\Rightarrow (a+1)(-3a+5) < 0$$

$$\Rightarrow (a+1)(3a-5) > 0$$

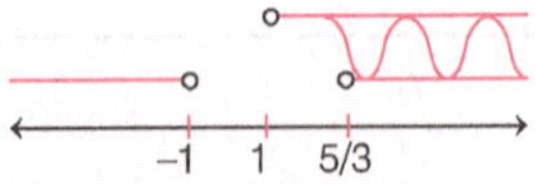

$\therefore a \in \left(\frac{5}{3}, \infty\right)$

1.5 Modulus Inequality

Modulus Function

$y = |x| =$ Absolute value of x

or

Numerical value of x

e.g. $|-3| = 3, |3| = 3$

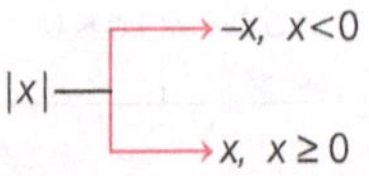

- It represents distance of the number x from zero on the number line. (distance always positive)
- $|x| = \max\{x, -x\}$
- $|x| = \sqrt{x^2}$
- Graph of $y = |x|$

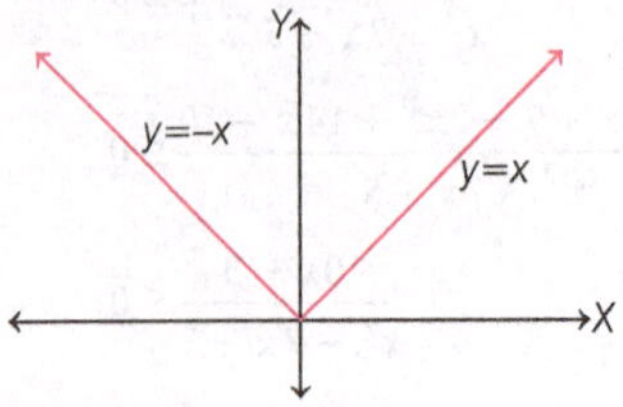

Properties of Modulus Function

(i) $||x|| = |x|$

(ii) $|x_1, x_2, \ldots, x_n| = |x_1||x_2|, \ldots, |x_n|$

(iii) $\left|\frac{x}{y}\right| = \frac{|x|}{|y|}, y \neq 0$

(iv) $|x^n| = |x|^n, \forall n \in Z$

(v) $|-x| = |x|$

(vi) $\sqrt{x^2} = |x|$

(vii) $|x| = a \Rightarrow x = \pm a$, where $a > 0$

(viii) $|x| \leq a \Rightarrow -a \leq x \leq a$

(ix) $|x| \geq a \Rightarrow x \leq -a$ or $x \geq a$

(x) Triangle inequalities, $||x| - |y|| \leq |x \pm y| \leq |x| + |y|$

JEE Focus Points

- **Triangle inequality** $|x + y| \leq |x| + |y|$ for all real x and y, inequality holds if $x \cdot y < 0$ i.e. x and y are of opposite signs, equality holds if $x \cdot y \geq 0$ i.e. x and y are of same sign or at least one of x and y is zero.
- $|x - y| \leq |x| + |y|$ for all real x and y, inequality holds if $x \cdot y > 0$, i.e. x and y are of same sign, equality holds if $x \cdot y \leq 0$ i.e. x and y are of opposite sign or at least one of x and y is zero.
- $||x| - |y|| \leq |x + y|$ for all real x and y. Equality holds if x and y are of opposite signs and for same sign inequality holds.
- $||x| - |y|| \leq |x - y|$ for all real x and y. Equality holds if x and y are of same sign and for opposite signs inequality holds.

Inequality Involving Modulus

(i) $|x| \leq a \Rightarrow -a \leq x \leq a$

(ii) $|x| \geq a \Rightarrow x \leq -a$ or $x \geq a$

(iii) We can define modulus after solving it.

(iv) Remember points of triangle inequality.

Example 5. Solve the following.

(i) $|x - 3| \geq 2$

(ii) $|x - 4| < 10$

(iii) $||3x - 9| + 2| > 2$

(iv) $|x^2 - 7x| + |6x - 2| > |x^2 - x - 2|$

Sol. (i) $|x-3| \geq 2$

$\Rightarrow \quad x-3 \leq -2 \text{ or } x-3 \geq 2$

$\Rightarrow \quad x \leq 1 \text{ or } x \geq 5$

$\Rightarrow \quad x \in (-\infty, 1] \cup [5, \infty)$

(ii) $|x-4| < 10$

$\Rightarrow \quad -10 < x-4 < 10$

$\Rightarrow \quad -6 < x < 14$

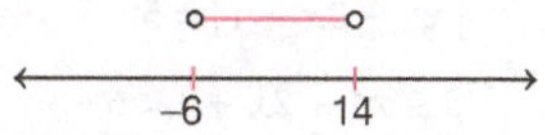

$x \in (-6, 14)$

(iii) $||3x-9|+2| > 2$

$|3x-9|+2 < -2 \text{ or } |3x-9|+2 > 2$

$|3x-9| < -4 \text{ or } |3x-9| > 0$

$|3x-9| < -4$ is not possible.

$\therefore \quad x \in R$

(iv) $|x^2-7x|+|6x-2| > |x^2-x-2|$

$= |(x^2-7x)+(6x-2)|$

$\because \quad |a|+|b| > |a+b|$

$\Rightarrow \quad a \cdot b < 0 \Rightarrow (x^2-7x)(6x-2) < 0$

$\Rightarrow x(x-7)(3x-1) < 0 \Rightarrow x \in (-\infty, 0) \cup (1/3, 7)$

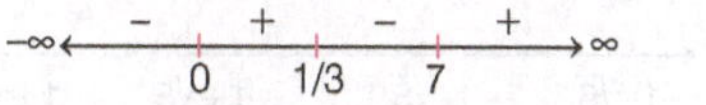

1.6 Inequality Involving GIF and Fractional Part Function

Greatest Integer Function (Bracket Function)

$y = [x] =$ Greatest integer of x

= largest integer less than or equal to x

= integral part of x

It pronounce as box of x or simply box x.

e.g. $[3.2] = 3, [-2.3] = -3, [5] = 5, [-5] = -5$

$$y = [x] = \begin{cases} \vdots & \vdots \\ -2, & -2 \leq x < -1 \\ -1, & -1 \leq x < 0 \\ 0, & 0 \leq x < 1 \\ 1, & 1 \leq x < 2 \\ 2, & 2 \leq x < 3 \\ \vdots & \vdots \end{cases}$$

Graph of $y = [x]$

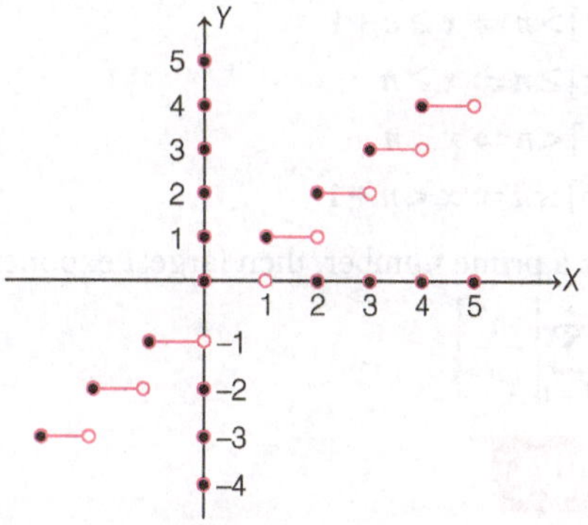

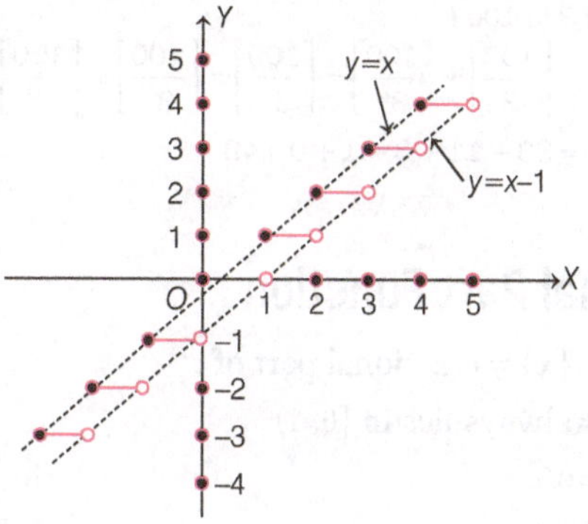

Properties

(i) $[[x]] = [x]$

(ii) $[x \pm I] = [x] \pm I$,

where I is any integer.

(iii) $[x] + [-x] = \begin{cases} 0 & \text{if } x \in I \\ -1 & \text{if } x \notin I \end{cases}$

(iv) $x - 1 < [x] \leq x$

(v) $[x] < x < [x] + I$

(vi) $\left[\frac{[x]}{n}\right] = \left[\frac{x}{n}\right]; n \in N$

(vii) $[x] + [y] \leq [x+y] \leq [x] + [y] + 1$

(viii) $[x] = \left[\frac{x}{2}\right] + \left[\frac{x+1}{2}\right]$

(ix) $\left[\frac{n+1}{2}\right] + \left[\frac{n+2}{4}\right] + \left[\frac{n+4}{8}\right] + \ldots = n, n \in N$

(x) $[x] + \left[x + \frac{1}{n}\right] + \left[x + \frac{2}{n}\right] + \ldots \left[x + \frac{n-1}{n}\right] = [nx]; n \in N$

(xi) If n is any integer

(a) $[x] > n \Rightarrow x \ge n+1$

(b) $[x] \ge n \Rightarrow x \ge n$

(c) $[x] < n \Rightarrow x < n$

(d) $[x] \le n \Rightarrow x < n+1$

(xii) If P is a prime number, then largest exponent of P in $n!$ is $\sum_{k=1}^{\infty}\left[\frac{n}{P^k}\right]$.

JEE SPIKE

Exponent of 3 in 100 !

$$= \left[\frac{100}{3}\right] + \left[\frac{100}{3^2}\right] + \left[\frac{100}{3^3}\right] + \left[\frac{100}{3^4}\right] + \left[\frac{100}{3^5}\right] + \ldots$$

$$= 33 + 11 + 3 + 1 + 0 = 48$$

Fractional Part Function

$y = \{x\} =$ Fractional part of x

$=$ always lies in $[0, 1)$

e.g. $\{1.3\} = 0.3$

$\{-1.3\} = 0.7$

For every real number x

$$x = [x] + \{x\}$$

Integeral part of x Fractional part of x

$$y = [x] = \begin{cases} \vdots & \vdots \\ x+2, & -2 \le x < -1 \\ x+1, & -1 \le x < 0 \\ x, & 0 \le x < 1 \\ x-1, & 1 \le x < 2 \\ x-2, & 2 \le x < 3 \\ \vdots & \vdots \end{cases}$$

Graph of $y = \{x\}$

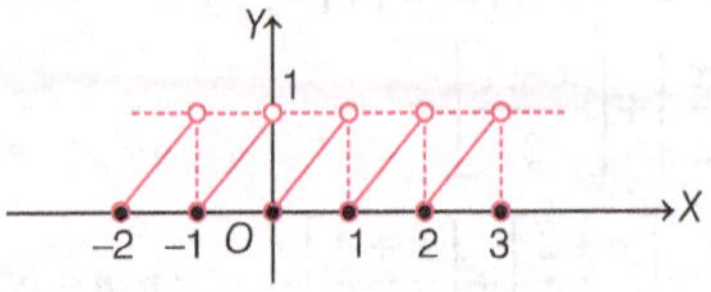

Properties

(i) $\{x + I\} = x$, $I =$ Integer

(ii) $[\{x\}] = 0$

(iii) $\{\{x\}\} = \{x\}$

(iv) $\{x\} + \{-x\} = \begin{cases} 0, & x \in z \\ 1, & x \notin z \end{cases}$

Example 6. Solve the following.

(i) $[x^2 + 2x + 1] = 5$

(ii) $\{\sin x\} + \{\cos x\} + \{x\} = 0$

(iii) $[x] - 8x + x^2 + 13 = 0$

(iv) $[x]^2 - 2[x] \ge 0$

(v) $2\{x\} - 1 < 0$

(vi) $[2x + 3] + [-2x + 5] > 0$

Sol. (i) We have, $[x^2 + 2x + 1] = 5$

$\therefore \quad 5 \le x^2 + 2x + 1 < 6$

When $\quad x^2 + 2x + 1 \ge 5$

$\Rightarrow \quad x^2 + 2x - 4 \ge 0$

Solution for $x^2 + 2x - 4 = 0$

$$x = -1 \pm \sqrt{5}$$

When $\quad x^2 + 2x + 1 < 6$

$\Rightarrow \quad x^2 + 2x - 5 < 0$

Solution for $x^2 + 2x - 5 = 0$

$$x = \frac{-2 \pm \sqrt{4 + 20}}{2} = -1 \pm \sqrt{6}$$

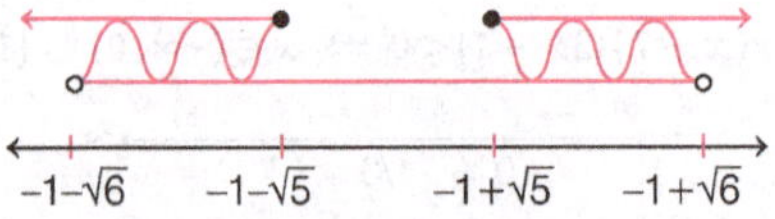

Hence, $x \in (-1 - \sqrt{6}, -1 - \sqrt{5}] \cup [-1 + \sqrt{5}, -1 + \sqrt{6})$

(ii) $\because \{x\} + \{\sin x\} + \{\cos x\} = 0$ ...(i)

$\because \{x\} \in [0, 1)$, which is positive.

$\therefore$ Eq. (i) only possible, when

$\{x\} = 0$ and $\{\sin x\} = 0$ and $\{\cos x\} = 0$

$x \in I$ and $\sin x = I$ and $\cos x = I$

$\sin x = \pm 1, 0$ and $\cos x = \pm 1, 0$

$$x = n\pi, (2n+1)\frac{\pi}{2}, x = n\pi, (2n+1)\frac{\pi}{2}$$

$\therefore$ Only one common solution i.e. $x = 0$.

(iii) $[x] - 8x + x^2 + 13 = 0$

$\Rightarrow x^2 - 8x + [x] + 13 = 0$ ...(i)

$\because \quad x = [x] + \{x\} \Rightarrow [x] = x - \{x\}$

Eq. (i) becomes

$$x^2 - 8x + x - \{x\} + 13 = 0$$

$\Rightarrow \quad x^2 - 7x + 13 = \{x\}$

$\because \{x\} \in [0, 1)$

$$0 \le x^2 - 7x + 13 < 1$$

Now, $\quad x^2 - 7x + 13$

$$D = 49 - 52 = -3 < 0$$

$\therefore x^2 - 7x + 13$ is always positive.

$\therefore \quad x \in R$

and $\quad x^2 - 7x + 13 < 1$

$$x^2 - 7x + 12 < 0$$

$$(x-3)(x-4) < 0$$

$\therefore \quad x \in (3, 4)$

Check $[x] = 3$

From Eq. (i), we get

$$x^2 - 8x + 16 = 0$$

$$x = \frac{8 \pm \sqrt{64 - 64}}{2} = 4$$

$$4 \notin (3, 4)$$

$\therefore$ No solution.

(iv) $[x]^2 - 2[x] \geq 0$

$\Rightarrow [x]([x] - 2) \geq 0$

$\Rightarrow \quad [x] \leq 0$ or $[x] \geq 2$

$\Rightarrow \quad x \in (-\infty, 0)$ or $x \in [2, \infty)$

$\therefore \quad x \in (-\infty, 0) \cup [2, \infty)$

(v) $2\{x\} - 1 < 0$

$\Rightarrow \{x\} < \frac{1}{2}$

$\Rightarrow \quad x \in \left[n, n + \frac{1}{2}\right)$, where $n \in I$

(vi) $[2x + 3] + [-2x + 5] > 0$

$\Rightarrow [2x] + [-2x] + 3 + 5 > 0$

$\Rightarrow \quad [2x] + [-2x] > -8$

$$\Rightarrow \quad [2x] + [-2x] = \begin{cases} 0, & 2x \in I \\ -1, & 2x \notin I \end{cases}$$

0 or -1 both are greater than -8.

$\therefore \quad x \in R$

1.7 Trigonometric Inequality

Trigonometric equation and inequation are deeply discussed in the unit of trigonometry but to solve trigonometric inequality we keep following points in our mind.

1. Trigonometric identities
2. For required interval we can use two approach
   (i) Graphical approach
   (ii) Algebraic approach

Example 7. Solve the following.

(i) $2\sin x - 1 \geq 0$

(ii) $\cos x - \sin x \geq 0$

(iii) $2\sin^2 x - 3\sin x + 1 > 0$

Sol. (i) $2\sin x - 1 \geq 0$

$$\sin x \geq \frac{1}{2}$$

Method 1 : Graphical Approach

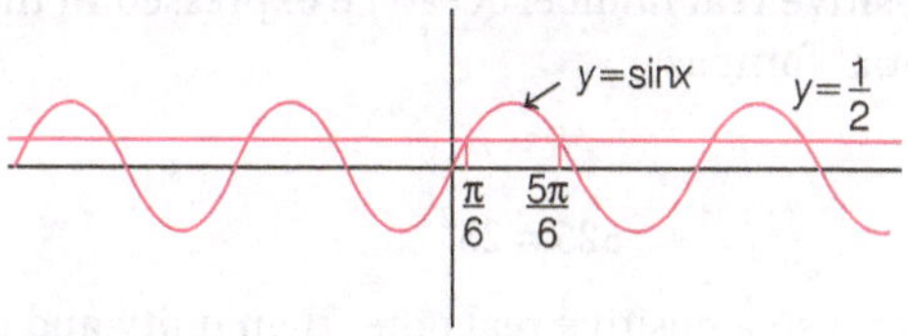

$x \in \left[\frac{\pi}{6}, \frac{5\pi}{6}\right] \rightarrow$ in $[0, 2\pi]$

General solution

$$x \in \left[2n\pi + \frac{\pi}{6}, 2n\pi + \frac{5\pi}{6}\right], n \in I$$

Method 2 $\quad 2\sin x - 1 \geq 0$

Critical points, $2\sin x - 1 = 0$

$$\Rightarrow \quad \sin x = \frac{1}{2} \Rightarrow x = \frac{\pi}{6}, \frac{5\pi}{6}$$

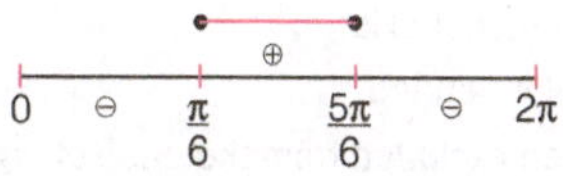

$$\therefore \; x \in \left[2n\pi + \frac{\pi}{6}, 2n\pi + \frac{5\pi}{6}\right], n \in I$$

(ii) $\cos x - \sin x \geq 0$

Critical points, $\cos x - \sin x = 0$

$$\Rightarrow \quad \cos x = \sin x$$

$$\Rightarrow \quad n = \frac{\pi}{4}, \frac{5\pi}{4}$$

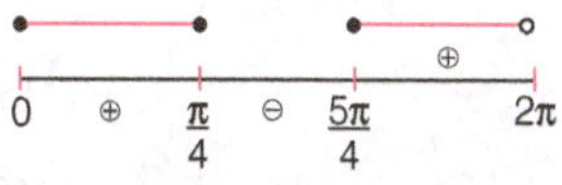

$$x \in \left[2n\pi, 2n\pi + \frac{\pi}{4}\right] \cup \left[2n\pi + \frac{5\pi}{4}, 2n\pi + 2\pi\right)$$

(iii) $$2\sin^2 x - 3\sin x + 1 > 0$$

$$\Rightarrow \quad 2\sin^2 x - 2\sin x - \sin x + 1 > 0$$

$$\Rightarrow 2\sin x(\sin x - 1) - 1(\sin x - 1) > 0$$

$$\Rightarrow \quad (2\sin x - 1)(\sin x - 1) > 0$$

Critical points, $2\sin x - 1 = 0, \sin x - 1 = 0$

$$\sin x = \frac{1}{2}, \sin x = 1$$

$$x = \frac{\pi}{6}, \frac{5\pi}{6}, x = \frac{\pi}{2}$$

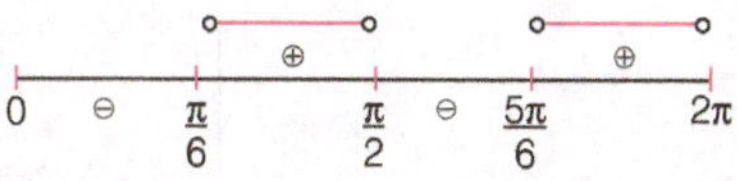

$$x \in \left(2n\pi + \frac{\pi}{6}, 2n\pi + \frac{\pi}{2}\right) \cup \left(2n\pi + \frac{5\pi}{6}, 2n\pi + 2\pi\right)$$

1.8 Logarithmic Inequality

Logarithm

Every positive real number R can be expressed in the exponential form as

$$R = b^a \quad \text{...(i)}$$

e.g. $625 = 25^2$,

where b is also a positive real other than unity and called 'base'.

a is called exponent.

Relation (i) can be written in logarithmic form

$$\log_b R = a \Leftrightarrow R = b^a,$$

where R(Index number) > 0, $b \in (0, \infty) - \{1\}$

JEE Focus Points

- log can be removed when its base take RHS as its power.
  $\log_b R = a \Rightarrow R = b^a$
- log (–ve) = Does not exist
- log (zero) = Not defined
- Unity has been excluded from the base of logarithm
- $2^9 = 512 \Rightarrow \log_2 512 = 9$
  Can be written $\Uparrow$ $\Downarrow$ Take antilog
  $512 = \log_2 9$

Graph of Logarithmic

$$y = \log_a x$$

Let $y = \log_{10} x$	$y = \log_{1/10} x$
$x = 10^{-2}, y = -2$	$x = 10^{-2}, y = 2$
$x = 10^{-1}, y = -1$	$x = 10^{-1}, y = 1$
$x = 1, y = 0$	$x = 1, y = 0$
$x = 10, y = 1$	$x = 10, y = -1$
$x = 10^2, y = 2$	$x = 10^2, y = -2$

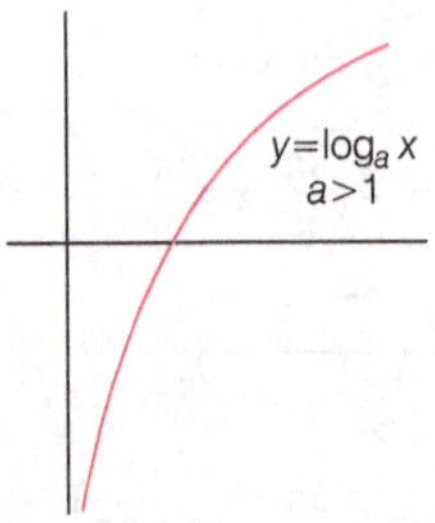

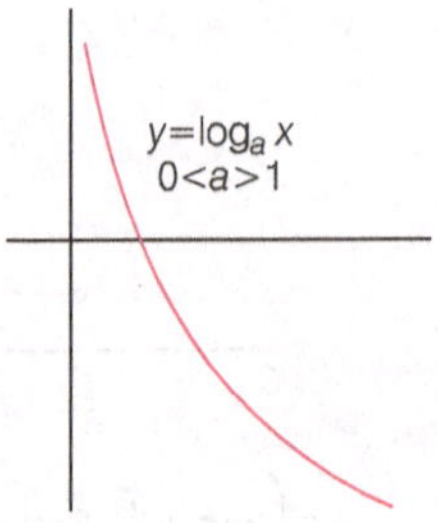

Properties of Logarithm

(i) $\log_b mn = \log_b m + \log_b n$

(ii) $\log_b \dfrac{m}{n} = \log_b m - \log_b n$

(iii) $\log_b m^n = n \log_b m$

(iv) $\log_{b^n} m = \dfrac{1}{n} \log_b m$

(v) $\log_b a = \dfrac{\log_c a}{\log_c b}$ [base changing property]

(vi) $\log_b a = \dfrac{1}{\log_a b}$ [reciprocal property]

(vii) $a^{\log_c b} = b^{\log_c a}$

(viii) $\log_a a = 1$

(ix) $\log_b 1 = 0$

(x) $a^{\log_a b} = b$

Logarithmic Equation and Inequation

(i) In logarithmic equation, first of all define the logarithm and try to remove logarithm to get unknown parameter.

(ii) In logarithmic inequation, first of all define logarithm and try to remove logarithm to get suitable interval.

JEE SPIKE

$\log_a x > \log_a y$ $\{x, y > 0, a > 0\}$

- If $a > 1$, then $x > y$ (a creates '+' ve sense)
- If $0 < a < 1$, then $x < y$
  (a creates (– ve) sense, so after removing logarithm inequality sign will reversed)

$\log_a x > b$

- If $a > 1$, then $x > a^b$
- If $0 < a < 1$, then $x < a^b$

Example 8. Solve the following inequality

(i) $\log_{0.5}(x^2 - 5x + 6) > -1$

(ii) $\log^2_{0.5} x + \log_{0.5} x - 2 \le 0$

(iii) $\log_x(x^3 - x^2 - 2x) < 3$

(iv) $\log_{2x}(x^2 - 5x + 6) < 1$

(v) $\log_{2x+3} x^2 < \log_{2x+3} 2x + 3$

Sol. (i) Expression inside log should be positive.

$$x^2 - 5x + 6 > 0 \Rightarrow (x-2)(x-3) > 0$$

$$\Rightarrow \quad x < 2 \text{ or } x > 3$$

$$\Rightarrow \quad x \in (-\infty, 2) \cup (3, \infty) \rightarrow \text{(initial condition)}$$

Now, $x^2 - 5x + 6 < (0.5)^{-1}$

[inequality is reversed since base is less than one]

$$x^2 - 5x + 6 < 2$$

$$\Rightarrow \quad x^2 - 5x + 4 < 0$$

$$\Rightarrow \quad (x-1)(x-4) < 0$$

$$\Rightarrow \quad 1 < x < 4 \rightarrow \text{(final condition)}$$

Taking intersection of initial condition and final condition, we get

$$x \in (1, 2) \cup (3, 4)$$

(ii) Put $\log_{0.5} x = t$

$$\Rightarrow \quad t^2 + t - 2 \le 0$$

$$\Rightarrow \quad (t+2)(t-1) \le 0$$

$$\Rightarrow \quad -2 \le t \le 1$$

$$\Rightarrow \quad -2 \le \log_{0.5} x \le 1$$

$$\Rightarrow \quad x > 0 \rightarrow \text{(initial condition)}$$

Now, since base is less than unity hence inequality will be reversed when log is removed.

$$(0.5)^{-2} \ge x \ge (0.5)^1$$

$$\Rightarrow \quad 4 \ge x \ge 0.5$$

$$\Rightarrow \quad x \in [0.5, 4] \rightarrow \text{(final condition)}$$

Taking intersection of initial and final condition, we get

$$x \in [0.5, 4]$$

(iii) Defining log

$$x^3 - x^2 - 2x > 0$$

$$\Rightarrow \quad x(x^2 - x - 2) > 0$$

$$\Rightarrow \quad x(x-2)(x+1) > 0$$

$$\Rightarrow \quad x \in (-1, 0) \cup (2, \infty)$$

Base > 0 and base ≠ 1

$$\Rightarrow \quad x > 0 \text{ and } x \ne 1$$

$$x \in (2, \infty) \rightarrow \text{(initial condition)}$$

Case I When base is greater than 1.

$$x > 1 \qquad \text{[condition I]}$$

$$x^3 - x^2 - 2x < x^3$$

$$x^2 + 2x > 0$$

$$x(x+2) > 0$$

$$x \in (-\infty, -2) \cup (0, \infty) \rightarrow \qquad \text{[condition I (a)]}$$

Taking intersection of initial condition, condition I and condition I(a), we get $x \in (2, \infty) \rightarrow$ (condition 'A').

Case II When base is less than 1.

$$0 < x < 1 \qquad \text{[condition II]}$$

$$\Rightarrow \quad \log_x(x^3 - x^2 - 2x) < 3$$

$$\Rightarrow \quad x^3 - x^2 - 2x > x^3$$

$$\Rightarrow \quad x^2 + 2x < 0$$

$$\Rightarrow \quad x(x+2) < 0$$

$$\Rightarrow \quad -2 < x < 0 \qquad \text{[condition II (a)]}$$

Taking intersection of initial condition, condition II and condition II(a), we get

$$x \in \phi \rightarrow \qquad \text{[condition 'B']}$$

Taking union of condition 'A' and condition 'B', we get

$$x \in (2, \infty)$$

(iv) $x^2 - 5x + 6 > 0$

$$\Rightarrow \quad (x-2)(x-3) > 0$$

$$\Rightarrow \quad x \in (-\infty, 2) \cup (3, \infty)$$

$$\Rightarrow \quad 2x > 0$$

$$\Rightarrow \quad x > 0$$

$$x \in (0, 2) \cup (3, \infty) \rightarrow \text{(initial conditon)}$$

Case I $1 < 2x$

$$\Rightarrow \quad \frac{1}{2} < x \rightarrow \qquad \text{[condition I]}$$

Since, base is greater than 1.

Inequality remains unchanged

$$x^2 - 5x + 6 < (2x)^1$$

$$\Rightarrow \quad x^2 - 7x + 6 < 0$$

$$\Rightarrow \quad (x-6)(x-1) < 0$$

$$\Rightarrow \quad 1 < x < 6 \rightarrow \text{condition I(a)}$$

Taking intersection of initial condition, condition I and condition I(a), we get

$$x \in (1, 2) \cup (3, 6) \rightarrow \text{condition (A)}$$

Case II $0 < 2x < 1$

$$0 < x < \frac{1}{2} \rightarrow \text{(condition II)}$$

$$x^2 - 5x + 6 > 2x$$

$$\Rightarrow \quad x^2 - 7x + 6 > 0$$

$$\Rightarrow \quad (x-6)(x-1) > 0$$

$$\Rightarrow \quad x \in (-\infty, 1) \cup (6, \infty) \rightarrow \text{(condition II(a))}$$

Taking intersection of initial condition, condition II and condition II(a), we get

$$x \in \left(0, \frac{1}{2}\right) \rightarrow \text{condition B}$$

Taking union of condition A and condition B, we get

$$x \in \left(0, \frac{1}{2}\right) \cup (1, 2) \cup (3, 6)$$

(v) For existence of logarithm

(i) $x^2 > 0$

(ii) $2x + 3 > 0$

(iii) $2x + 3 \neq 1 \Rightarrow x \in \left(-\frac{3}{2}, \infty\right) - \{-1, 0\}$ ...(i)

Now, on solving inequality

Case I $0 < 2x + 3 < 1$

$\Rightarrow \quad -\frac{3}{2} < x < -1$

$\because \quad \log_{2x+3} x^2 < \log_{2x+3} 2x + 3$

$\Rightarrow \quad x^2 > 2x + 3$

$\Rightarrow (x-3)(x+1) > 0$

$\Rightarrow \quad x \in (-\infty, -1) \cup (3, \infty);$

But $-\frac{3}{2} < x < -1$

$\Rightarrow x \in \left(-\frac{3}{2}, -1\right)$ intersection with (i)

$\Rightarrow x \in \left(-\frac{3}{2}, -1\right)$

Case II $2x + 3 > 1 \Rightarrow x > -1$

$\because \quad \log_{2x+3} x^2 < \log_{2x+3} 2x + 3$

$\Rightarrow \quad x^2 < 2x + 3$

$\Rightarrow \quad (x-3)(x+1) < 0$

$\Rightarrow \quad x \in (-1, 3)$; but $x > -1$

$\Rightarrow \quad x \in (-1, 3)$ intersection with (i)

$\Rightarrow \quad x \in (-1, 3) - \{0\}$

$\therefore \quad x \in$ Case I $\cup$ Case II

$\Rightarrow \quad x \in \left(-\frac{3}{2}, -1\right) \cup (-1, 0) \cup (0, 3)$

JEE Pattern EXAMPLES

Example 1 ■ *Solve the following.*

(i) $7 < \dfrac{5-3x}{2} < 12$

(ii) $5 - 2x < 7 + 3x \le \dfrac{8}{3} - x$

(iii) $\dfrac{7+x}{4} \le \dfrac{3-x}{3} + \dfrac{x}{2} < 5 - 2x$

Sol. (i) $7 < \dfrac{5-3x}{2} < 12$

does not contain x (variable)

$\Rightarrow \quad 14 < 5 - 3x < 24$ [multiply by 2]

$\Rightarrow \quad 14 - 5 < -3x < 24 - 5$ [subtract 5]

$\Rightarrow \quad 9 < -3x < 19$

$\Rightarrow \quad -3 > x > -\dfrac{19}{3}$ [divide by −3]

or $\quad -\dfrac{19}{3} < x < -3$

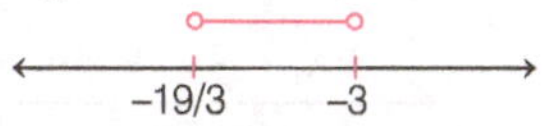

$\therefore \quad x \in \left(-\dfrac{19}{3}, -3\right)$

(ii) $5 - 2x < 7 + 3x \le \dfrac{8}{3} - x$

$\Rightarrow \quad 5 - 2x < 7 + 3x$ and $7 + 3x \le \dfrac{8}{3} - x$

$\Rightarrow \quad -5x < 2$ and $4x \le \dfrac{8}{3} - 7$

$\Rightarrow \quad x > \dfrac{-2}{5}$ and $4x \le \dfrac{-13}{3}$

$\Rightarrow \quad x > \dfrac{-2}{5}$ and $x \le \dfrac{-13}{12}$

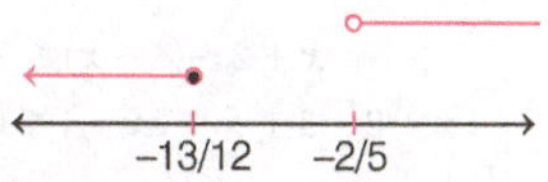

No common points.

$\therefore \quad x \in \phi$

(iii) $\dfrac{7+x}{4} \le \dfrac{3-x}{3} + \dfrac{x}{2} < 5 - 2x$

$\Rightarrow \quad \dfrac{7+x}{4} \le \dfrac{6-2x+3x}{6} < 5 - 2x$

$\Rightarrow \quad \dfrac{7+x}{4} \le \dfrac{6+x}{6} < 5 - 2x$

$\Rightarrow \quad \dfrac{7+x}{4} \le \dfrac{6+x}{6}$ and $\dfrac{6+x}{6} < 5 - 2x$

$\Rightarrow 3(7+x) \le 2(6+x)$ and $6 + x < 6(5-2x)$

$\Rightarrow 21 + 3x \le 12 + 2x$ and $6 + x < 30 - 12x$

$\Rightarrow \quad x \le -9$ and $13x < 24$

$\Rightarrow \quad x \le -9$ and $x < \dfrac{24}{13}$

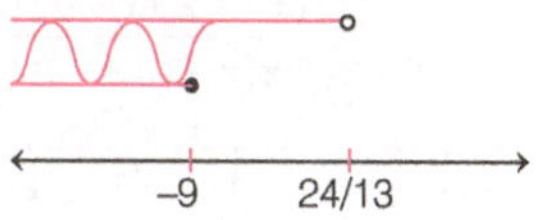

$\therefore x \in (-\infty, -9]$

Example 2 ■ *Solve following inequalities over the set of real numbers.*

(i) $\dfrac{x^2+1}{4x-3} > 2$

(ii) $\dfrac{20}{(x-3)(x-4)} + \dfrac{10}{x-4} + 1 > 0$

(iii) $\dfrac{1}{x-2} + \dfrac{1}{x-1} > \dfrac{1}{x}$

(iv) $\dfrac{x^1 - 3x^2 + 2x^2}{x^2 - x - 30} > 0$

(v) $\dfrac{2x}{x^2-9} \le \dfrac{1}{x+2}$

Sol. (i) $\dfrac{x^2+1}{4x-3} > 2$

$\Rightarrow \quad \dfrac{x^2+1-8x+6}{4x-3} > 0$

$\Rightarrow \quad \dfrac{x^2-8x+7}{4x-3} > 0$

$$\Rightarrow \frac{(x-7)(x-1)}{4x-3} > 0$$

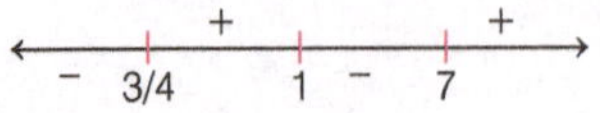

$$\therefore x \in \left(\frac{3}{4}, 1\right) \cup (7, \infty)$$

(ii) $\dfrac{20}{(x-3)(x-4)} + \dfrac{10}{x-4} + 1 > 0$

$$\Rightarrow (x-3)(x-4) + 10(x-3) + 20 > 0$$

$$\Rightarrow \quad x^2 - 7x + 12 + 10x - 30 + 20 > 0$$

$$\Rightarrow \quad x^2 + 3x + 2 > 0 \Rightarrow (x+2)(x+1) > 0$$

and at $x = 3$ and 4 original inequality denominator becomes zero

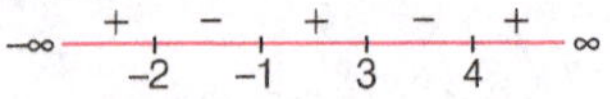

$$(-\infty, -2) \cup (-1, 3) \cup (4, \infty)$$

(iii) $\dfrac{1}{x-2} + \dfrac{1}{x-1} > \dfrac{1}{x}$

$$\Rightarrow \frac{x(x-1) + x(x-2) - (x-2)(x-1)}{(x-2)(x-1)x} > 0$$

$$\Rightarrow \quad \frac{x^2-2}{x(x-1)(x-2)} > 0$$

$$\Rightarrow \quad \frac{(x+\sqrt{2})(x-\sqrt{2})}{x(x-1)(x-2)} > 0$$

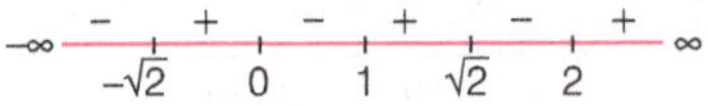

$$\therefore \quad x \in (-\sqrt{2}, 0) \cup (1, \sqrt{2}) \cup (2, \infty)$$

(iv) $\dfrac{x^4 - 3x^3 + 2x^2}{x^2 - x - 30} > 0$

or $\quad \dfrac{x^4 - 3x^3 + 2x^2}{(x-6)(x+5)} > 0 \Rightarrow \dfrac{x^4 - 3x^3 + 2x^2}{(x-6)(x+5)} > 0$

$$\Rightarrow \quad \frac{x^2(x^2 - 3x + 2)}{(x-6)(x+5)} > 0 \Rightarrow \frac{x^2(x-1)(x-2)}{(x-6)(x+5)} > 0$$

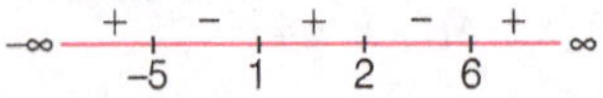

So, $x \in (-\infty, -5) \cup (1, 2) \cup (6, \infty)$

(v) $\dfrac{2x}{x^2 - 9} \le \dfrac{1}{x+2}$

$$\Rightarrow \quad \frac{2x(x+2) - x^2 - 9}{(x-3)(x+3)(x+2)} \le 0$$

$$\Rightarrow \quad \frac{x^2 + 4x + 9}{(x-3)(x+3)(x+2)} \le 0$$

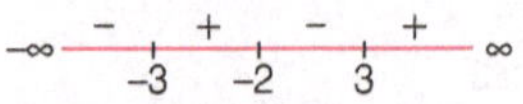

Hence, $x \in (-\infty, -3) \cup (-2, 3)$

Example 3 ■ *Solve the following inequality.*

(i) $\left|\dfrac{3x}{x^2 - 4}\right| < 1$

(ii) $|x+2| - |3-x| \le |2x-1|$

(iii) $|x^2 - 4x| + |x+6| > |x^2 - 5x - 6|$

Sol. (i) We know that if $|y| < 1$, then

$$-1 < y < 1 \Rightarrow -1 < \frac{3x}{x^2 - 4} < 1$$

Case I $\quad \dfrac{3x}{x^2-4} > -1 \Rightarrow \dfrac{3x}{x^2-4} + 1 > 0$

$$\Rightarrow \quad \frac{3x + x^2 - 4}{(x-2)(x+2)} > 0 \Rightarrow \frac{(x+4)(x-1)}{(x-2)(x+2)} > 0$$

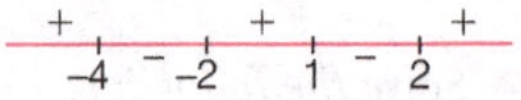

$\therefore \quad x \in (-\infty, -4) \cup (-2, 1) \cup (2, \infty)$ ...(i)

Case II $\quad \dfrac{3x}{x^2-4} < 1 \Rightarrow \dfrac{3x - x^2 + 4}{x^2 - 4} < 0$

$$\Rightarrow \quad \frac{x^2 - 3x - 4}{x^2 - 4} > 0 \Rightarrow \frac{(x-4)(x+1)}{(x-2)(x+2)} > 0$$

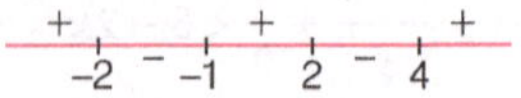

$\therefore x \in (-\infty, -2) \cup (-1, 2) \cup (4, \infty)$ ...(ii)

By intersection of Eqs. (i) and (ii),

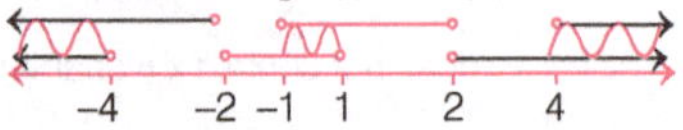

$$\therefore x \in (-\infty, -4) \cup (-1, 1) \cup (4, \infty)$$

(ii) $|x+2| - |3-x| \le |2x-1|$

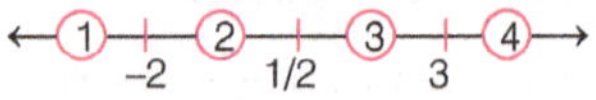

Case I $\quad x \le -2$

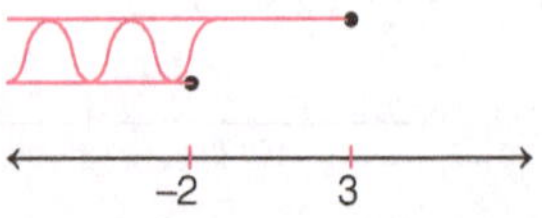

Inequality becomes

$$-(x+2) - (3-x) \le -(2x-1)$$

$$\Rightarrow \quad -x - 2 - 3 + x + 2x - 1 \le 0$$

$$\Rightarrow \quad 2x - 6 \le 0$$

$$\Rightarrow \quad x \le 3$$

$\therefore \quad x \in (-\infty, -2] \quad [\because x \le -2]$

Case II $\quad -2 < x \le \dfrac{1}{2}$

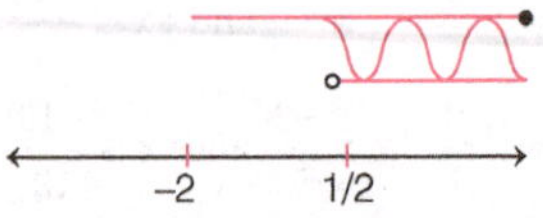

$$\Rightarrow \quad x + 2 - (3-x) \le -(2x-1)$$

$$\Rightarrow \quad x + 2 - 3 + x + 2x - 1 \le 0$$

$$\Rightarrow \quad 4x \le 2, x \le \frac{1}{2}$$

$$\Rightarrow \quad x \in \left(-2, \frac{1}{2}\right]$$

Case III $\frac{1}{2} < x < 3$

$\Rightarrow \quad x + 2 - (3 - x) \le 2x - 1$

$\Rightarrow \quad x + 2 - 3 + x - 2x + 1 \le 0$

$\Rightarrow \quad 0 \le 0$, which is true.

$\therefore \quad x \in \left(\frac{1}{2}, 3\right)$

Case IV $x \ge 3$

$\Rightarrow \quad x + 2 + (3 - x) \le 2x - 1$

$\Rightarrow \quad 5 - 2x + 1 \le 0$

$\Rightarrow \quad 2x \ge 6 \Rightarrow x \ge 3$

$\because \quad x \in [3, \infty)$

By cases I, II, III and IV

Solution is $x \in R$.

(iii) $|x^2 - 4x| + |x + 6| > |x^2 - 5x - 6| = |(x^2 - 4x) - (x + 6)|$

$\because \quad |a| + |b| > |a - b| \Leftrightarrow a \cdot b > 0$

$\Rightarrow \quad (x^2 - 4x)(x + 6) > 0$

$\Rightarrow \quad x(x - 4)(x + 6) > 0$

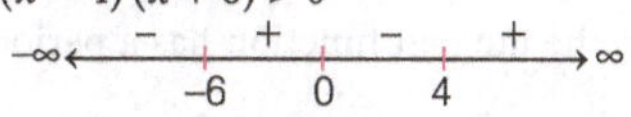

$\Rightarrow \quad x \in (-6, 0) \cup (4, \infty)$

Example 4 *Solve the following.*

(i) $[x]^2 - 7[x] + 6 \le 0$

(ii) $\frac{(2\{x\} - 1)(\{x\} - 2)}{(\{x\} + 3)(3 - 4\{x\})} \ge 0$

(iii) $5x + 3\{x\} = 4[2x + 2] - 5$

(iv) $4x + 5\{x\} = 3[x] - 1$

Sol.

Decoding the Question

When $[x] \in [a, b]$, where $a, b > 0$
then $x \in [a, b)$

(i) We have, $[x]^2 - 7[x] + 6 \le 0$

$\Rightarrow \quad ([x] - 6)([x] - 1) \le 0 \Rightarrow 1 \le [x] \le 6$

$\therefore \quad 1 \le x < 7$

(ii) We have, $\frac{(2\{x\} - 1)(\{x\} - 2)}{(\{x\} + 3)(3 - 4\{x\})} \ge 0$

Let $x \in (0, 1) \Rightarrow \frac{(2x - 1)(x - 2)}{(x + 3)(3 - 4x)} \ge 0$

$\therefore \quad x = \frac{1}{2}, 2, -3, \frac{3}{4}$

Now,

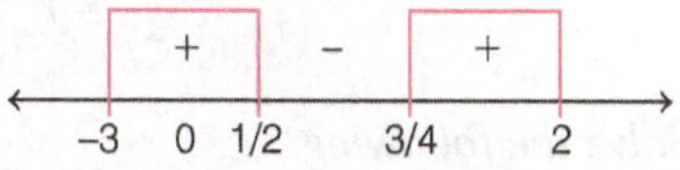

$\therefore \quad x \in \left(0, \frac{1}{2}\right) \cup \left(\frac{3}{4}, 1\right)$

$\Rightarrow x \in \left[n, n + \frac{1}{2}\right] \cup \left[n + \frac{3}{4}, n + 1\right]; n \in Z$

(iii) Given equation is $5x + 3\{x\} = 4[2x + 2] - 5$

$\Rightarrow \quad 5x + 3\{x\} = 4[2x] + 8 - 5$

$[\because [x + m] = [x] + m \text{ for } m \in Z]$

$\Rightarrow \quad 5x + 3\{x\} = 4[2x] + 3 \quad$ ...(i)

Now, $\quad 2x = 2([x] + \{x\})$

$\Rightarrow \quad 2x = 2[x] + 2\{x\}$

$\Rightarrow \quad [2x] = 2[x] + [2\{x\}] \quad$ ...(ii)

Using Eq. (ii) in Eq. (i), we get

$5x + 3\{x\} = 4(2[x] + [2\{x\}]) + 3$

$\Rightarrow \quad 5x + 3\{x\} = 8[x] + 4[2\{x\}] + 3 \quad$ ...(iii)

Let us deal with two cases

Case (i) When $0 \le \{x\} < \frac{1}{2}$

$\Rightarrow \quad 0 \le 2\{x\} < 1$

$\Rightarrow \quad [2\{x\}] = 0$

$\therefore$ From Eq. (iii),

$5x + 3\{x\} = 8[x] + 3$

$\Rightarrow \quad 5[x] + 5\{x\} + 3\{x\} = 8[x] + 3 \quad [\text{using } x = [x] = \{x\}]$

$\Rightarrow \quad 8\{x\} = 3[x] + 3$

$\Rightarrow \quad \{x\} = \frac{3[x] + 3}{8} \quad$ ...(iv)

Now, $\quad \{x\} \in [0, 1/2)$

$\Rightarrow \quad \frac{3[x] + 3}{8} \in \left[0, \frac{1}{2}\right)$

$\Rightarrow \quad 0 \le 3[x] + 3 < 4$

$\Rightarrow \quad -3 \le 3[x] < 1$

$\Rightarrow \quad -1 \le [x] < \frac{1}{3}$

$\Rightarrow \quad [x] = -1, 0$

Using these values of $[x]$ in Eq. (iv), we have

For $[x] = -1$; $\{x\} = 0 \Rightarrow x = -1$

For $[x] = 0$; $\{x\} = \frac{3}{8} \Rightarrow x = \frac{3}{8}$

$\therefore$ Solution set in this case is $\left\{-1, \frac{3}{8}\right\}$.

Case II When $\frac{1}{2} \le \{x\} < 1$

$\Rightarrow \quad 1 \le 2\{x\} < 2$

$\Rightarrow \quad [2\{x\}] = 1$

$\therefore$ From Eq. (iii),

$5x + 3\{x\} = 8[x] + 7$

$\Rightarrow \quad 5[x] + 5\{x\} + 3\{x\} = 8[x] + 7$

$\Rightarrow \quad 8\{x\} = 3[x] + 7$

$\Rightarrow \quad \{x\} = \frac{3[x] + 7}{8} \quad$ ...(v)

Now, $\quad \{x\} \in [1/2, 1)$

$\Rightarrow \quad \frac{3[x] + 7}{8} \in \left[\frac{1}{2}, 1\right)$

$\Rightarrow \quad 4 \le 3[x] + 7 < 8$

$$\Rightarrow \quad -3 \le 3[x] < 1$$

$$\Rightarrow \quad -1 \le [x] < \frac{1}{3}$$

$$\Rightarrow \quad [x] = -1, 0$$

Using these values of $[x]$ in Eq. (v), we have

For $[x] = -1, \{x\} = \frac{1}{2} \Rightarrow x = -\frac{1}{2}$

For $[x] = 0, \{x\} = \frac{7}{8} \Rightarrow x = \frac{7}{8}$

$\therefore$ Solution set in this case is $\left\{-\frac{1}{2}, \frac{7}{8}\right\}$.

Thus, the complete solution set is $\left\{-1, -\frac{1}{2}, \frac{3}{8}, \frac{7}{8}\right\}$.

(iv) Given equation is $4x + 5\{x\} = 3[x] - 1$

$$\Rightarrow \quad 4([x] + \{x\}) + 5\{x\} = 3[x] - 1$$

$$\Rightarrow \quad 4[x] + 9\{x\} = 3[x] - 1$$

$$\Rightarrow \quad 9\{x\} = -[x] - 1$$

$$\Rightarrow \quad \{x\} = \frac{-[x] - 1}{9} \quad \text{...(i)}$$

But $\{x\} \in [0, 1)$

$$\Rightarrow \quad 0 \le -\frac{-[x] - 1}{9} < 1$$

$$\Rightarrow \quad 0 \le -[x] - 1 < 9$$

$$\Rightarrow \quad 0 \ge [x] + 1 > -9$$

$$\Rightarrow \quad -1 \ge [x] > -10$$

$$\Rightarrow \quad -1 \ge [x] \ge -9 \quad \text{...(ii)}$$

Using values of $[x]$ from Eq. (ii) in Eq. (i), we have

For $[x] = -9; \Rightarrow \{x\} = \frac{8}{9} \Rightarrow x = -\frac{73}{9}$

For $[x] = -8; \Rightarrow \{x\} = \frac{7}{9} \Rightarrow x = -\frac{65}{9}$

For $[x] = -7; \Rightarrow \{x\} = \frac{2}{3} \Rightarrow x = -\frac{19}{3}$

For $[x] = -6; \Rightarrow \{x\} = \frac{5}{9} \Rightarrow x = -\frac{49}{9}$

For $[x] = -5; \Rightarrow \{x\} = \frac{4}{9} \Rightarrow x = -\frac{41}{9}$

For $[x] = -4; \Rightarrow \{x\} = \frac{1}{3} \Rightarrow x = -\frac{11}{3}$

For $[x] = -3; \Rightarrow \{x\} = \frac{2}{9} \Rightarrow x = -\frac{25}{9}$

For $[x] = -2; \Rightarrow \{x\} = \frac{1}{9} \Rightarrow x = -\frac{17}{9}$

For $[x] = -1; \Rightarrow \{x\} = 0 \Rightarrow x = -1$

$\therefore$ The set of solution is

$$\left\{-\frac{73}{9}, -\frac{65}{9}, -\frac{19}{3}, -\frac{49}{9}, -\frac{41}{9}, -\frac{11}{3}, -\frac{25}{9}, -\frac{17}{9}, -1\right\}.$$

Example 5 ■ *Solve the following.*

(i) $\tan x < 1$

(ii) $\sin x - \cos x > 0$

Sol. (i) We have, $\tan x < 1$

The corresponding trigonometric equation is

$$\tan x = 1 = \tan \frac{\pi}{4}$$

The other solution in $[0, 2\pi]$ is

$$x = \pi + \frac{\pi}{4} = \frac{5\pi}{4}$$

and corresponding negative angle

$$y = \frac{5\pi}{4} - 2\pi = -\frac{3\pi}{4}$$

However, the tangent function asymptotes at $\frac{\pi}{2}$.

Hence, the basic interval is $\left(-\frac{\pi}{2}, \frac{\pi}{4}\right)$.

Further, the tangent function has a period of π.

$$\therefore \quad n\pi - \frac{\pi}{2} < x < n\pi + \frac{\pi}{4}; n \in Z$$

or $x \in \left(n\pi - \frac{\pi}{2}, n\pi + \frac{\pi}{4}\right); n \in Z$

(ii) We have, $\sin x - \cos x > 0$

$$\Rightarrow \quad \sin x \cdot \cos \frac{\pi}{4} - \cos x \cdot \sin \frac{\pi}{4} > 0$$

$$\Rightarrow \quad \sin\left(x - \frac{\pi}{4}\right) > 0$$

Let $t = x - \frac{\pi}{4}$

Then, $\sin t > 0$

The solution of the corresponding equality is obtained as

$\Rightarrow \sin t = 0 = \sin 0 \Rightarrow t = 0$

The second angle between 0 and 2π is π.

$\therefore \quad x \in (0, \pi)$

The periodicity of sine is 2π. Hence, we add $2n\pi$ on either side of the base interval.

$$2n\pi < t < 2n\pi + \pi, n \in Z$$

or $$2n\pi < x - \frac{\pi}{4} < 2n\pi + \pi; n \in Z$$

$$\Rightarrow \quad 2n + \frac{\pi}{4} < x < 2n\pi + \frac{5\pi}{4}, n \in Z$$

$$\therefore \quad x \in \left(2n + \frac{\pi}{4}, 2n\pi + \frac{5\pi}{4}\right), n \in Z$$

Example 6 ■ *Solve the following.*

(i) $\log_4 (3^x - 1) \log_{1/4} \left(\frac{3^x - 1}{16}\right) \le \frac{3}{4}$

(ii) $\log_{1/3} \log_4 (x^2 - 5) > 0$

(iii) $\log_3(x+2)(x+4)+\log_{1/3}(x+2)<\frac{1}{2}\log_{\sqrt{3}}7$

(iv) $2^{x+2}>\left(\frac{1}{4}\right)^{1/x}$

(iv) $(1.25)^{1-x}<(0.64)^{2(1+\sqrt{x})}$

Sol. **Decoding the Question**

If $\log_a f(x)>0$, $a>1$, then $f(x)>1$
and $\log_a f(x)>0$, $0<a<1$, then $f(x)<1$

(i) Checking existence $3^x-1>0 \Rightarrow x>0$,

Now, solving inequality

$$\log_4(3^x-1)\log_{1/4}\left(\frac{3^x-1}{16}\right)\le\frac{3}{4}$$

$$\Rightarrow \log_4(3^x-1)\cdot[-\log_4(3^x-1)+\log_4 16]\le\frac{3}{4}$$

$$\Rightarrow \log_4(3^x-1)[-\log_4(3^x-1)+2]\le\frac{3}{4}$$

$$\Rightarrow -[\log_4(3^x-1)]^2+2[\log_4(3^x-1)]\le\frac{3}{4}$$

Put $\log_4(3^x-1)=t$

$$\Rightarrow -t^2+2t\le\frac{3}{4}$$

$$\Rightarrow -4t^2+8t-3\le 0$$

$$\Rightarrow 4t^2-8t+3\ge 0$$

$$\Rightarrow 4t^2-6t-2t+3\ge 0$$

$$\Rightarrow 2t(2t-3)-1(2t-3)\ge 0$$

$$\Rightarrow (2t-3)(2t-1)\ge 0$$

$$\Rightarrow \log_4(3^x-1)\le\frac{1}{2} \text{ or } \log_4(3^x-1)\ge\frac{3}{2}$$

$$\Rightarrow 0<3^x-1\le 4^{1/2} \text{ or } 3^x-1\ge 4^{3/2}$$

$$\Rightarrow 1<3^x\le 3 \text{ or } 3^x\ge 9$$

$$\Rightarrow 0<x\le 1 \text{ or } x\ge 2$$

$$\Rightarrow x\in(0,1]\cup[2,\infty)$$

(ii) Checking existence,

$$\log_4(x^2-5)>0$$

$$\Rightarrow x^2-5>1 \Rightarrow (x-\sqrt{6})(x+\sqrt{6})>0$$

$$\Rightarrow x\in(-\infty,-\sqrt{6})\cup(\sqrt{6},\infty) \quad \text{...(i)}$$

$$x^2-5>0$$

$$\Rightarrow x\in(-\infty,-\sqrt{5})\cup(\sqrt{5},\infty) \quad \text{...(ii)}$$

Solving inequality,

$$\log_{1/3}\log_4(x^2-5)>0$$

$$\Rightarrow \log_4(x^2-5)<1$$

$$\Rightarrow x^2-5<4 \Rightarrow x^2-9<0$$

$$\Rightarrow (x-3)(x+3)<0 \Rightarrow x\in(-3,3) \quad \text{...(iii)}$$

Ans. (i) $\cap$ (ii) $\cap$ (iii)

$\Rightarrow x\in(-3,-\sqrt{6})\cup(\sqrt{6},3)$

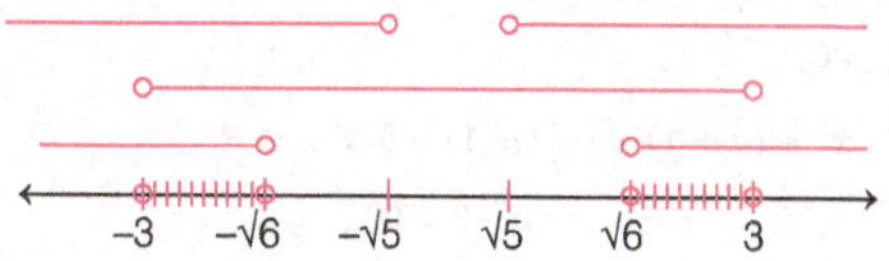

(iii) Checking existence,

$$(x+2)(x+4)>0 \text{ and } (x+2)>0$$

$$x<-4 \text{ or } x>-2 \text{ and } x>-2$$

Now solving inequality,

$$\log_3((x+2)(x+4))+\log_{1/3}(x+2)<\frac{1}{2}\log_{\sqrt{3}}7$$

$$\Rightarrow \log_3(x+2)(x+4)-\log_3(x+2)<\log_3 7$$

$$\Rightarrow \log_3(x+4)<\log_3 7$$

$$\Rightarrow x+4<7$$

$$\Rightarrow x<3$$

$$\Rightarrow -2<x<3$$

$$\Rightarrow x\in(-2,3)$$

(iv) We have, $2^{x+2}>2^{-2/x}$.

Since, the base $2>1$, we have $x+2>-\frac{2}{x}$

[the sign of the inequality is retained]

Now, $x+2+\frac{2}{x}>0$

$$\Rightarrow \frac{x^2+2x+2}{x}>0$$

$$\Rightarrow \frac{(x+1)^2+1}{x}>0$$

$$\Rightarrow x\in(0,\infty)$$

(v) We have, $\left(\frac{5}{4}\right)^{1-x}<\left(\frac{16}{25}\right)^{2(1+\sqrt{x})}$ or $\left(\frac{4}{5}\right)^{x-1}<\left(\frac{4}{5}\right)^{4(1+\sqrt{x})}$

Since, the base $0<\frac{4}{5}<1$, the inequality is equivalent to the inequality $x-1>4(1+\sqrt{x})$

$$\Rightarrow \frac{x-5}{4}>\sqrt{x}$$

Now, RHS is positive

$$\Rightarrow \frac{x-5}{4}>0$$

$$\Rightarrow x>5 \quad \text{...(i)}$$

We have, $\frac{x-5}{4}>\sqrt{x}$

Both sides are positive, so squaring both sides

$$\frac{(x-5)^2}{16}>x \text{ or } \frac{(x-5)^2}{16}-x>0$$

or $x^2-26x+25>0$ or $(x-25)(x-1)>0$

$$\Rightarrow x\in(-\infty,1)\cup(25,\infty) \quad \text{...(ii)}$$

Intersection (i) and (ii) gives $x\in(25,\infty)$.

Example 7 *Find the number of positive integral values of a for* $(a-2)x^2-(a+1)x-(a+1)>0 \ \forall\, x \in R$ *and* $a^2-100a>0$.

Sol. $(a-2)x^2-(a+1)x-(a+1)>0 \ \forall\, x \in R$

$\Rightarrow \quad a-2>0$

$\Rightarrow \quad a>2 \quad$ ...(i)

and $\quad D<0$

$\Rightarrow \quad (a+1)^2-4(a-2)(a+1)<0$

$\Rightarrow \quad (a+1)[(a+1)-4(a-2)]<0$

$\Rightarrow \quad (a+1)(-3a+9)<0$

$\Rightarrow \quad (a+1)(a-3)>0 \quad$ ...(ii)

Also, $\quad a^2-100a>0$

$a(a-100)>0 \quad$ ...(iii)

By intersection Eqs. (i), (ii) and (iii), we get

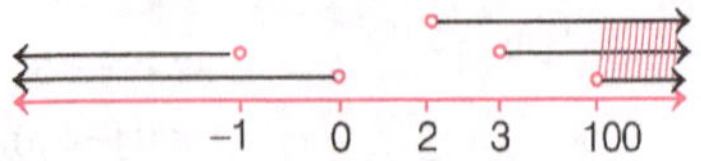

$\therefore \quad a \in (100, \infty)$

Example 8 *Find the number of the integral solutions of* $x^2+9<(x+3)^2<8x+25$.

Sol. We have, $x^2+9<(x+3)^2<8x+25$

Now, $\quad x^2+9<(x+3)^2$

$\Rightarrow \quad x^2+9<x^2+9+6x$

$\Rightarrow \quad 6x>0$

$\Rightarrow \quad x>0$

and $\quad x^2+9+6x<8x+25$

$\Rightarrow \quad x^2-2x-16<0$

$\Rightarrow \quad x=\dfrac{2\pm 2\sqrt{17}}{2}$

$\Rightarrow \quad x=1\pm\sqrt{17}$

So, $\quad 1-\sqrt{17}<x<1+\sqrt{17}$

$\Rightarrow \quad 0<x<1+\sqrt{17}$

$\Rightarrow \quad 0<x\le 5$

$\therefore \quad x=1,2,3,4,5$

Example 9 *Find the number of non-negative integral values of x satisfying the inequality*

$$\frac{2}{x^2-x+1}-\frac{1}{x+1}-\frac{2x-1}{x^3+1}\ge 0.$$

Sol. We have, $\quad \dfrac{2}{x^2-x+1}-\dfrac{1}{x+1}-\dfrac{2x-1}{x^3+1}\ge 0$

$$\Rightarrow \quad \frac{2}{x^2-x+1}-\frac{1}{x+1}-\frac{(2x-1)}{(x+1)(x^2-x+1)}\ge 0$$

$$\Rightarrow \quad \frac{2(x+1)-(x^2-x+1)-(2x-1)}{(x^2-x+1)(x+1)}\ge 0$$

$$\Rightarrow \quad \frac{2x+2-x^2+x-1-2x+1}{(x^2-x+1)(x+1)}\ge 0$$

$$\Rightarrow \quad \frac{2-x^2+x}{(x^2-x+1)(x+1)}\ge 0$$

$$\Rightarrow \quad \frac{(x^2-x-2)}{(x^2-x+1)(x+1)}\le 0$$

$$\Rightarrow \quad \frac{(x+1)(x-2)}{(x^2-x+1)(x+1)}\le 0$$

$$\Rightarrow \quad \frac{x-2}{(x^2-x+1)}\le 0$$

For x^2-x+1

$D=1-4$ i.e. $D<0$

$x^2-x+1>0$ and $x-2\le 0$

$x\le 2$

$\because \quad x\in(-\infty, 2]$

$\therefore$ Non-negative integers are 3.

Example 10 *Find the number of positive integeral solutions of the inequality* $\sqrt{\dfrac{1}{x^2}-\dfrac{3}{x}}<\dfrac{1}{x}-\dfrac{1}{2}$.

Sol. $\sqrt{\dfrac{1}{x^2}-\dfrac{3}{x}}<\dfrac{1}{x}-\dfrac{1}{2} \quad$ ...(i)

$\because \quad \dfrac{1}{x^2}-\dfrac{3}{x}\ge 0$

$\Rightarrow \quad \dfrac{1-3x}{x^2}\ge 0$

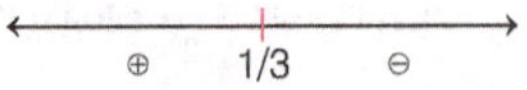

$x\in\left(-\infty, \dfrac{1}{3}\right]-\{0\}$

Case I $x\in(-\infty, 0)$ RHS will be –ve.

$\therefore \quad x\in\phi$

Case II $x\in\left(0, \dfrac{1}{3}\right]$ RHS will be +ve.

Then, $\quad \dfrac{1}{x^2}-\dfrac{3}{x}<\dfrac{1}{x^2}+\dfrac{1}{4}-\dfrac{1}{x}$

$\Rightarrow \quad -\dfrac{2}{x}-\dfrac{1}{4}<0$

$\Rightarrow \quad \dfrac{-8-x}{4x}<0 \Rightarrow \dfrac{x+8}{4x}>0$

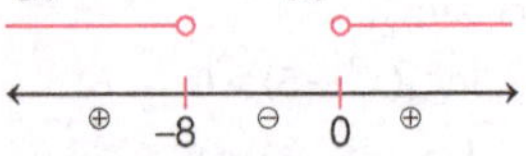

$\therefore$ Solution will be $x\in\left(0, \dfrac{1}{3}\right]$.

$\therefore$ Number of positive integral solution = 0

Example 11 *Find the set of values of λ for which the equation $|x^2-4|x|-12|=\lambda$ has 6 distinct real roots.*

Sol. $|x^2-4|x|-12|=\lambda$ has 6 distinct real roots.

$$|x^2-6|x|+2|x|-12|=\lambda$$

$$\Rightarrow \quad ||x|(|x|-6)+2(|x|-6)|=\lambda$$

$$\Rightarrow \quad |(|x|-6)(|x|+2)|=\lambda$$

Let $\quad |x|=t$

$$\Rightarrow \quad |(t-6)(t+2)|=\lambda$$

$$\Rightarrow \quad \lambda=|t^2-4t-12|$$

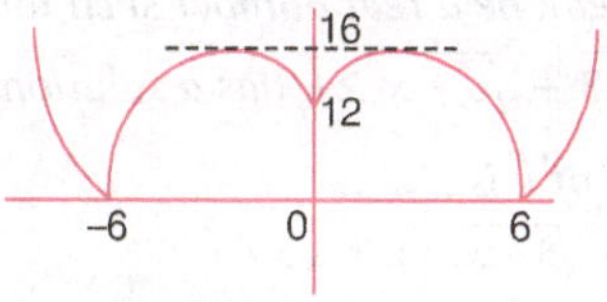

$$\lambda\in(12,16)$$

Example 12 *Find the number of real solution(s) of the equation $|x-3|^{3x^2-10x+3}=1$.*

Sol. We have, $\quad |x-3|^{3x^2-10x+3}=1$

$$\Rightarrow \quad |x-3|=1$$

$$\Rightarrow \quad x=2 \text{ or } 4$$

If $x-3\neq 0$, then

$$3x^2-10x+3=0$$

$$\Rightarrow \quad (3x-1)(x-3)=0$$

So $x=\frac{1}{3}, 3$

But $x\neq 3$, so $x=\frac{1}{3}$

Hence, the number of solution is 3 i.e. $\frac{1}{3}$, 2, 4.

Example 13 *If $(x^2-2|x|)(|2x|-2)-9\left(\frac{2|x|-2}{x^2-2|x|}\right)\leq 0$, then x is ....*

Sol. $(x^2-2|x|)(|2x|-2)-\frac{9(2|x|-2)}{x^2-2|x|}\leq 0$

$$\Rightarrow \quad (2|x|-2)\left(\frac{(x^2-2|x|)^2-9}{x^2-2|x|}\right)\leq 0$$

$$\Rightarrow \quad \frac{2(|x|-1)(x^2-2|x|+3)(x^2-2|x|-3)}{x^2-2|x|}\leq 0$$

$$\Rightarrow \quad \frac{2(|x|-1)[(|x|-1)^2+2][(|x|-3)(|x|+1)]}{|x|(|x|-2)}\leq 0$$

Critical point $|x|-1=0, |x|-3=0, |x|+1=0$

$|x|=1, |x|=3, |x|=-1$, not possible

$|x|=0, |x|=2\rightarrow\infty$

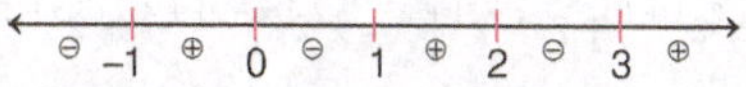

$$|x|\in(0,1]\cup(2,3]$$

$$\therefore x\in[-3,-2)\cup[-1,0)\cup(0,1]\cup(2,3]$$

Example 14 *Number of solution of pair of equations $y=|||x|-2|-2|$ and $y=\frac{x+2}{2}$ equals to ....*

Sol. The given equations are

$$y=|||x|-2|-2| \qquad \text{...(i)}$$

and $$y=\frac{x+2}{2} \qquad \text{...(ii)}$$

Case I When $x\geq 0$,

$$y=||x-2|-2|=\begin{cases}|x-4|, & x\geq 2\\ |x|, & x<2\end{cases}$$

and $$|x-4|=\begin{cases}x-4, & x\geq 4\\ 4-x, & x<4\end{cases} \qquad \text{...(iii)}$$

On solving Eqs. (ii) and (iii), we get

$$x=10,\ x\geq 4 \text{ and } x=2,\ x<4$$

Now, $$|x|=\begin{cases}x & x\geq 0\\ -x & x<0\end{cases} \qquad \text{...(iv)}$$

On solving Eqs. (ii) and (iv), we get

$$x=-\frac{2}{3},\ x<0$$

and $\quad x=2,\ x\geq 0$, Rejected $\quad [\because x<2]$

Case II When $x<0$

$$y=||-x-2|-2|=||x+2|-2|$$

$$=\begin{cases}|x| & x\geq -2\\ |4+x| & x<-2\end{cases}$$

Now, $$|x|=\begin{cases}x & x\geq 0\\ -x & x<0\end{cases} \qquad \text{...(v)}$$

On solving Eqs. (ii) and (v), we get

$$x=-\frac{2}{3},\ x<0$$

and $$x=2,\ x\geq 0$$

and $$|4+x|=\begin{cases}4+x & x\geq -4\\ -4-x & x<-4\end{cases} \qquad \text{...(vi)}$$

On solving Eqs. (ii) and (vi), we get

$$x=-6,\ x\geq -4$$

and $\quad x=-\frac{10}{3},\ x<-4$, Rejected $\quad [\because x<-2]$

Total number of solutions are 3.

Example 15 *The complete set of values of x satisfying the equation* $x^2 2^{x+1} + 2^{|x-3|+2} = x^2 \cdot 2^{|x-3|+4} + 2^{x-1}$ *is ......*

Sol. $x^2 2^{x+1} + 2^{|x-3|+2} = x^2 2^{|x-3|+4} + 2^{x-1}$

$\Rightarrow \quad x^2 \{2^{|x-3|+4} - 2^{x+1}\} = 2^{|x-3|+2} - 2^{x-1}$

$\Rightarrow \quad 4x^2 \{2^{|x-3|+2} - 2^{x-1}\} = \{2^{|x-3|+2} - 2^{x-1}\}$

$\Rightarrow \quad (2^{|x-3|+2} - 2^{x-1})(4x^2 - 1) = 0$

$\therefore \quad 2^{|x-3|+2} = 2^{x-1}$

$|x-3| + 2 = x - 1$

When $x \geq 3$,

$x - 3 + 2 = x - 1$

$-1 = -1$ always.

When $x < 3$,

$3 - x + 2 = x - 1$

$2x = 6$

$x = 3$

$\therefore \quad x \in [3, \infty)$

Also, $\quad 4x^2 - 1 = 0$

$x = \pm\frac{1}{2}$

$\therefore \quad x \in [3, \infty) \cup \left\{-\frac{1}{2}, \frac{1}{2}\right\}$

Example 16 *The number of solutions of the equation* $\frac{1}{[x]} + \frac{1}{[2x]} = \{x\} + \frac{1}{3}$*, is equal to ....*

(where [.] and {.} represent greatest integer and fractional part function)

Sol. (3) As, $x > 0$ $\quad$ [$\because$ RHS is positive]

Let $x = n + f$, where $n = [x]$ and $f = \{x\}$

Now, equation reduces to

$$\frac{1}{n} + \frac{1}{2n + [2f]} = f + \frac{1}{3}$$

Case I $0 \leq 2f < 1 \Rightarrow 0 \leq f \leq \frac{1}{2}$

which gives $\quad \frac{1}{n} + \frac{1}{2n} = f + \frac{1}{3} \Rightarrow 0 \leq \frac{3}{2n} - \frac{1}{3} < \frac{1}{2}$

$\Rightarrow \quad \frac{9}{5} < n \leq \frac{9}{2} \Rightarrow n = 2, 3, 4$

So, $x = \frac{29}{12}, \frac{19}{6}, \frac{97}{24}$

Case II $1 \leq 2f < 2 \Rightarrow \frac{1}{2} \leq f < 1$

Equation becomes

$$\frac{1}{n} + \frac{1}{2n+1} = f + \frac{1}{3}$$

If $n = 1 \Rightarrow f = 1$

$n = 2 \Rightarrow f = \frac{11}{30}$

$n = 3 \Rightarrow f = \frac{1}{7}$

$n = 4 \Rightarrow f = \frac{1}{36}$

$n = 5 \Rightarrow f < 0$

So, the value of f is in the interval $\left[\frac{1}{2}, 1\right)$.

So, the number of solution is 3.

Example 17 *Let k be a real number such that the inequality* $\sqrt{x-3} + \sqrt{6-x} \geq k$ *has a solution. The maximum value of k is ....*

Sol. $y = \sqrt{x-3} + \sqrt{6-x}, 3 \leq x \leq 6$

Then, $y^2 = (x-3) + (6-x) + 2\sqrt{(x-3)(6-x)}$

$\leq 2[(x-3) + (6-x)] = 6$

So, $0 < y \leq \sqrt{6}$ and the maximum value of k is $\sqrt{6}$.

Example 18 *The solution set of the inequality* $|x|^3 - 2x^2 - 4|x| + 3 < 0$ *is ....*

Sol. Notice that $|x| = 3$ is a root of the equation

$|x|^3 - 2x^2 - 4|x| + 3 = 0.$

Then, the original inequality can be rewritten as

$(|x| - 3)(|x|^2 + |x| - 1) < 0,$

i.e. $(|x| - 3)\left(|x| - \frac{-1+\sqrt{5}}{2}\right)\left(|x| - \frac{-1-\sqrt{5}}{2}\right) < 0$

$\because \quad |x| - \frac{-1-\sqrt{5}}{2} > 0$, then $\frac{-1+\sqrt{5}}{2} < |x| < 3$

So, the solution set is

$$\left(-3 - \frac{\sqrt{5}-1}{2}\right) \cup \left(\frac{\sqrt{5}-1}{2}, 3\right)$$

Example 19 *Suppose* $\frac{3}{2} \leq x \leq 5$*. Prove that* $2\sqrt{x+1} + \sqrt{2x-3} + \sqrt{15-3x} < 2\sqrt{19}$.

Sol. By Cauchy's inequality, we have

$2\sqrt{x+1} + \sqrt{2x-3} + \sqrt{15-3x}$

$= \sqrt{x+1} + \sqrt{x+1} + \sqrt{2x-3} + \sqrt{15-3x}$

$\leq \sqrt{[(x+1) + (x+1) + (2x-3) + (15-3x)](1^2 + 1^2 + 1^2 + 1^2)}$

$= 2\sqrt{x+14} \leq 2\sqrt{19},$

and the equality holds if and only if

$\sqrt{x+1} = \sqrt{2x-3} = \sqrt{15-3x}$ and $x = 5$.

But this is impossible.

So, $\quad 2\sqrt{x+1} + \sqrt{2x-3} + \sqrt{15-3x} < 2\sqrt{19}$

EXERCISE

JEE Pattern

Single Option Correct Type Questions

1. Complete set of solution of inequation $\frac{3}{\sqrt{2-x}} - \sqrt{2-x} < 2$ is

(a) $(-\infty, 1)$ (b) $(-\infty, 1]$ (c) $(1, \infty)$ (d) $[1, \infty)$

2. Complete set of solution of inequation $\sqrt{3x^2+5x+7} - \sqrt{3x^2+5x+2} > 1$ is $(-a, -b] \cup [-c, d)$ (where $a, b, c, d \in R^+$), then $a+b+c+d$ is equal to

(a) 4 (b) 3 (c) 2 (d) 1

3. Complete set of solution of a inequation $\sqrt{x+2\sqrt{x-1}} + \sqrt{x-2\sqrt{x-1}} > \frac{3}{2}$ is

(a) $(-\infty, 1)$ (b) $(-\infty, 1]$ (c) $[1, \infty)$ (d) $(1, \infty)$

4. The solution set of the inequality $|9^x - 3^{x+1} + 15| < 2 \cdot 9^x - 3^x$ is

(a) $(-\infty, 1)$ (b) $(1, \infty)$ (c) $(-\infty, 1]$ (d) $[2, \infty)$

5. If $f(x) = \{x\} + \left\{x + \left[\frac{x}{1+x^2}\right]\right\} + \left\{x + \left[\frac{x}{1+2x^2}\right]\right\} + \left\{x + \left[\frac{x}{1+3x^2}\right]\right\} \ldots + \left\{x + \left[\frac{x}{1+99x^2}\right]\right\}$,

then values of $[f(\sqrt{3})]$ is

(where [.] denotes greatest integer function and {.} represent fractional part function)

(a) 5050 (b) 4950 (c) 17 (d) 73

6. The complete set of value of x if $\log_{1/2} \frac{x^2+6x+9}{2(x+1)} < -\log_2(x+1)$, is

(a) $(-1, 1)$ (b) $(-1, 1+2\sqrt{2})$

(c) $(1, 1+2\sqrt{2})$ (d) None of these

7. If $\log_2(ax^2+x+a) \geq 1$, $\forall x \in R$, then exhaustive set of values of a is

(a) $\left(0, 1+\frac{\sqrt{5}}{2}\right)$ (b) $\left(1-\frac{\sqrt{5}}{2}, 1+\frac{\sqrt{5}}{2}\right)$

(c) $\left(0, 1-\frac{\sqrt{5}}{2}\right)$ (d) $\left(1+\frac{\sqrt{5}}{2}, \infty\right)$

8. If the inequality $\log_a(x^2-x-2) > \log_a(-x^2+2x+3)$ is known to be satisfied for $x = \frac{9}{4}$ in the interval (x_1, x_2), then the product (x_1x_2) is

(a) 3

(b) 4

(c) 2

(d) 5

9. Which of the following statements is correct?

(a) $[3x] = [x] + \left[x+\frac{1}{3}\right] + \left[x+\frac{2}{3}\right]$

(b) $[3x] = [2x] + \left[x+\frac{1}{2}\right] + \left[x+\frac{2}{3}\right]$

(c) Both (a) and (b)

(d) None of the above

Numerical Value Type Questions

10. If $[x] + \sum_{r=1}^{2024}\left(\frac{\{x+r\}}{2024}\right) = \frac{k}{2}x + n$, where $\{x\}$ and $[x]$ represent fractional and integral part of x respectively, then k^2+n^2 is ....

11. If x satisfies the equation

$$[x+0.19]+[x+0.20]+[x+0.21] + \ldots + [x+0.22] + \ldots + [x+0.91] = 542$$

Then, find the value of $[100x]$ is ....

12. Sum of integral values of k which satisfies $\left|\frac{x^2+kx+1}{x^2+x+1}\right| < 2 \,\forall\, x \in R$, is ....

13. The least positive value of x which satisfies the inequality $\log_{\log\left(\frac{x}{2}\right)}(x^2+10x+22) > 0$, $x \in I$ is ....

14. The number of integral values of a less then 11 for which exactly one solution of the equation $e^a x^2 - e^{2a} \cdot x + e^a - 1 = 0$ lies in the interval (1, 2) is ......

Answer Key

1. (a)	2. (a)	3. (c)	4. (b)	5. (d)	6. (b)	7. (d)	8. (d)	9. (a)
10. 4	11. 739	12. 6	13. 8	14. 0				

Solutions

1. $\sqrt{2-x}=t \Rightarrow \dfrac{3}{t}-t-2<0 \Rightarrow t^2+2t-3>0$

$t\in(-\infty,-3)\cup(1,\infty)$ $\quad$ $[\because t\neq 0 \text{ or } x\neq 2]$

$\Rightarrow \quad \sqrt{2-x}\in(1,\infty)$

$\Rightarrow \quad x\in(-\infty,2]\cap(-\infty,1)$

$\Rightarrow \quad x\in(-\infty,1)$

2. $3x^2+5x+2=t$

$\Rightarrow \quad \sqrt{t+5}>1+\sqrt{t}$

$\Rightarrow \quad t\geq 0 \text{ and } t+5>1+t+2\sqrt{t}$ $\quad$ [squaring]

$\Rightarrow \quad t\geq 0 \text{ and } t<4$

$\Rightarrow \quad 3x^2+5x+2>0$

and $\quad 3x^2+5x-2<0$

$\Rightarrow \quad (x+1)(3x+2)\geq 0$

and $\quad (x+2)(3x-1)<0$

$\Rightarrow x\in(-\infty,-1]\cup\left[\dfrac{-2}{3},\infty\right)$ and $x\in\left(-2,\dfrac{1}{3}\right)$

$\Rightarrow x\in(-2,-1]\cup\left[\dfrac{-2}{3},\dfrac{1}{3}\right)$

$\Rightarrow a+b+c+d=4$

3. $\sqrt{(x-1)+2\sqrt{x-1}+1}+\sqrt{(x-1)-2\sqrt{x-1}+1}>\dfrac{3}{2}$

$\Rightarrow \quad |\sqrt{x-1}+1|+|\sqrt{x-1}-1|>\dfrac{3}{2}$

$\Rightarrow \quad \sqrt{x-1}\in R$ $\quad$ [minimum value of LHS is 2]

$\Rightarrow \quad x\in[1,\infty)$

4. $(3^x)^2-3(3^x)+15<2(3^x)^2-3^x$ $\quad$ $[\because 9^x-3^{x+1}+15>0\ \forall\, x\in R]$

$\Rightarrow \quad (3^x)^2+2(3^x)-15>0$

$\Rightarrow \quad (3^x+5)(3^x-3)>0$

$\Rightarrow \quad x>1$

5. $f(x)=\{x\}\times 100$

$f(\sqrt{3})=\{\sqrt{3}\}\times 100$

$[f(\sqrt{3})]=[73.2\ldots]=73$

6. We have, $\dfrac{x^2+6x+9}{2(x+1)}>0$ and $(x+1)>0$

and $\log_{1/2}\dfrac{x^2+6x+9}{2(x+1)}<\log_{1/2}(x+1)$

$\Rightarrow x\in(-1,\infty)$ and $(x+3)^2>2(x+1)^2$

$\Rightarrow x\in(-1,\infty)$ and $x^2-2x-7<0$

$\Rightarrow x\in(-1,\infty)$ and $x\in(1-2\sqrt{2},1+2\sqrt{2})$

$\Rightarrow x\in(-1,1+2\sqrt{2})$

7. $\log_2(ax^2+x+a)\geq 1,\ \forall x\in R$

$\Rightarrow \quad ax^2+x+a\geq 2,\ \forall x\in R$

$\Rightarrow \quad ax^2+x+(a-2)\geq 0,\ \forall x\in R$

$\Rightarrow a>0,\ 1-4a(a-2)\leq 0 \Rightarrow 4a^2-8a-1\geq 0$

$\Rightarrow \quad a>0,\ a\in\left(-\infty,1-\dfrac{\sqrt{5}}{2}\right)\cup\left(1+\dfrac{\sqrt{5}}{2},\infty\right)$

$\Rightarrow \quad a\in\left(1+\dfrac{\sqrt{5}}{2},\infty\right)$

8. $x=\dfrac{9}{4}$ is a solution of the inequation,

$\log_a(x^2-x-2)>\log_a(-x^2+2x+3)$

$\Rightarrow \quad \log_a\left(\left(\dfrac{9}{4}\right)^2-\dfrac{9}{4}-2\right)>\log_a\left(-\left(\dfrac{9}{4}\right)^2+2\left(\dfrac{9}{4}\right)+3\right)$

$\Rightarrow \quad \log_a\left(\dfrac{13}{16}\right)>\log_a\left(\dfrac{39}{16}\right)$

$\Rightarrow \quad 0<a<1$

Now, $\log_a(x^2-x-2)>\log_a(-x^2+2x+3)$

if $0<a<1$

$\Rightarrow \quad x^2-x-2<-x^2+2x+3$

$\Rightarrow \quad 2x^2-3x-5<0 \Rightarrow (2x-5)(x+1)<0$

$\Rightarrow \quad x\in\left(-1,\dfrac{5}{2}\right)$ $\quad$ ...(i)

Also, $\quad x^2-x-2>0$ and $-x^2+2x+3>0$

$(x+1)(x-2)>0$ and $(x+1)(x-3)<0$

$\Rightarrow \quad x\in(-\infty,-1)\cup(2,\infty)$ and $x\in(-1,3)$

$\Rightarrow \quad x\in(2,3)$ $\quad$ ...(ii)

From Eqs. (i) and (ii), we get $x\in\left(2,\dfrac{5}{2}\right) \Rightarrow x_1\times x_2=5$

9. **Case I** When x is an integer

$\therefore \quad \text{LHS}=[3x]=3x$

and $\text{RHS}=[x]+\left[x+\dfrac{1}{3}\right]+\left[x+\dfrac{2}{3}\right]=x+x+x=3x$

$\therefore \quad$ LHS = RHS

Case II When x is not an integer

Let $x=m+f$

Now, $\text{LHS}=[3(m+f)]=[3m+3f]=3m+[3f]$

$$3m+[3f]=\begin{cases}3m; & 0\leq f<\dfrac{1}{3}\\[2mm] 3m+1; & \dfrac{1}{3}\leq f<\dfrac{2}{3}\\[2mm] 3m+2; & \dfrac{2}{3}\leq f<1\end{cases}$$

$$\text{RHS} = [m+f] + \left[m+f+\frac{1}{3}\right] + \left[m+f+\frac{2}{3}\right]$$

$$= 3m + [f] + \left[f+\frac{1}{3}\right] + \left[f+\frac{2}{3}\right]$$

$$= \begin{cases} 3m; & 0 \le f < \frac{1}{3} \\ 3m+1; & \frac{1}{3} \le f < \frac{2}{3} \\ 3m+2; & \frac{2}{3} \le f < 1 \end{cases}$$

10. We have, $[x] + \sum_{r=1}^{2024} \left(\frac{\{x+r\}}{2024}\right)$

$$= [x] + \left\{\left(\frac{\{x\}}{2024} + \frac{\{x\}}{2024} + \ldots \text{2024 times}\right\}$$

$[\because \{x+r\} = \{x\} \text{ as } x \in I]$

$$= [x] + \left[2024 \times \left(\frac{\{x\}}{2024}\right)\right]$$

$$= [x] + \{x\} = [x] + x - [x] = x$$

Hence, $[x] + \sum_{r=1}^{2024} \left(\frac{x+r}{2024}\right) = x$

$\Rightarrow \quad x = \frac{k}{2}x + n$

$\Rightarrow \quad \frac{k}{2} = 1 \Rightarrow k = 2$

and $\quad n = 0$

$\therefore \quad k^2 + n^2 = 4$

11. We have, $[x+0.19] + [x+0.20] + [x+0.21]$

$$+ \ldots + [x+0.22] + \ldots + [x+0.91] = 542$$

$$\Rightarrow \left[x+\frac{19}{100}\right] + \left[x+\frac{20}{100}\right] + \ldots + \left[x+\frac{91}{100}\right] = 542$$

$$\Rightarrow [100x] - \left([x] + \left[x+\frac{1}{100}\right] + \ldots + \left[x+\frac{18}{100}\right]\right)$$

$$- \left(\left[x+\frac{92}{100}\right] + \ldots + \left[x+\frac{99}{100}\right]\right) = 542$$

$\Rightarrow [100x] - 7 \times 19 - 8 \times 8 = 542 \qquad [\because 7.42 \le x < 8]$

$\Rightarrow [100x] = 542 + 133 + 64 = 739$

12. We have, $\left|\frac{x^2+kx+1}{x^2+x+1}\right| < 2 \Rightarrow -2 < \frac{x^2+kx+1}{x^2+x+1} < 2 \qquad$ ...(i)

$[\because |x| < a \Rightarrow -a < x < a]$

$\Rightarrow -2(x^2+x+1) < x^2+kx+1 < 2(x^2+x+1)$

$\Rightarrow -2x^2-2x-2 < x^2+kx+1 < 2x^2+2x+2$

$\Rightarrow \quad 3x^2+(k+2)+3 > 0$ and $x^2+(2-k)x+1 > 0$

For these quadratic expressions to be positive, for all values of x, discriminants must be negative.

$$(2+k)^2 - 36 < 0 \text{ and } (2-k)^2 - 4 < 0$$

$\therefore \quad -8 < k < 4$ and $0 < k < 4$

For both these conditions to be satisfied

$$0 < k < 4$$

Sum of integral value of $k = 1+2+3 = 6$

13. **Case I** $\log_2\left(\frac{x}{2}\right) > 1 \Rightarrow x^2 - 10x + 22 > 1$

$\Rightarrow \quad x > 4$ and $x \in (-\infty, 3) \cup (7, \infty)$

$\Rightarrow \quad x \in (7, \infty)$

Case II $0 < \log_2\left(\frac{x}{2}\right) < 1 \Rightarrow 0 < x^2 - 10x + 22 < 1$

$\Rightarrow \quad x \in (2, 4)$ and $x \in (3, 7)$ and $x^2 - 10x + 22 > 0$

$\Rightarrow$ No integer exist among above inequalities.

$\Rightarrow$ Least positive integral value of x is 8.

14. Let $f(x) = e^a x^2 - e^{2a} x + e^a - 1 = 0 \qquad$ ...(i)

Since, $f(x)$ is an upward opening parabola.

Exactly one root of (i) will lie in the interval (1, 2), if $f(1) \cdot f(2) < 0$.

We have, $f(1) = e^a - e^{2a} + e^a - 1 = -(e^a - 1)^2$

$\because \quad f(1) < 0$ if $a \ne 0$

Thus, we must have $f(2) > 0$

$\Rightarrow f(2) = e^a(2^2) - e^{2a}(2) + e^a - 1 > 0$

$\Rightarrow e^a$ lies between the roots of $2y^2 - 5y + 1 = 0$

i.e. between $\frac{5-\sqrt{17}}{4}$ and $\frac{5+\sqrt{17}}{4}$

Now, $\frac{5-\sqrt{17}}{4} < e^a < \frac{5+\sqrt{17}}{4}$

$$\Rightarrow \log_e\left(\frac{5-\sqrt{17}}{4}\right) < a < \log_e\left(\frac{5+\sqrt{17}}{4}\right)$$

As $a \ne 0$, we get

$$a \in \left(\log_e\left(\frac{5-\sqrt{17}}{4}\right), 0\right) \cup \left(0, \log_e\left(\frac{5+\sqrt{17}}{4}\right)\right)$$

$$\ln\frac{5+\sqrt{17}}{4} \le \ln\frac{5+4.2}{4}$$

$$\le \ln\frac{9.2}{4}$$

$$\le \ln 2.3$$

$$\le \log_e 2.3$$

$$< 1$$

$\therefore$ Number of integral values of a less than 11 is 0.

> “Mathematics is a more powerful instrument of knowledge than any other that has bequeathed to us by human agency.
>
> **-Rene Descartes**

2

Functions

Learning Milestones

Milestone 1 Introduction

- Definition of Function
- Representation of Function
- Algebra of Function
- Value of Function
- Number of Functions
- Domain, Codomain and Range of Function

Milestone 2 Types of Functions I

- Algebraic Function
- Non-algebraic Function (Transcendental Function)
- Piecewise Function

Milestone 3 Types of Functions II

- One-one (Injective) Function/Monomorphic
- Many-one Function
- Onto or Surjective Function
- Into Function
- One-one Onto/Bijective Function

Milestone 4 Types of Functions III (Some Special Types of Functions)

- Even and Odd Function
- Periodic Function
- Composite Function
- Inverse of a Function
- Equal or Identical Function
- Bounded Function
- Implicit and Explicit Function
- Homogeneous Function

Milestone 5 Some Special Points

- Functional Rule
- Functional Equation
- Miscellaneous Problems of Function

Practice Milestones

Practice Milestone 1- JEE Main Pattern

Practice Milestone 2 - JEE Advanced Pattern

Practice Milestone 3 - Challenging Problems

$y=|x|$

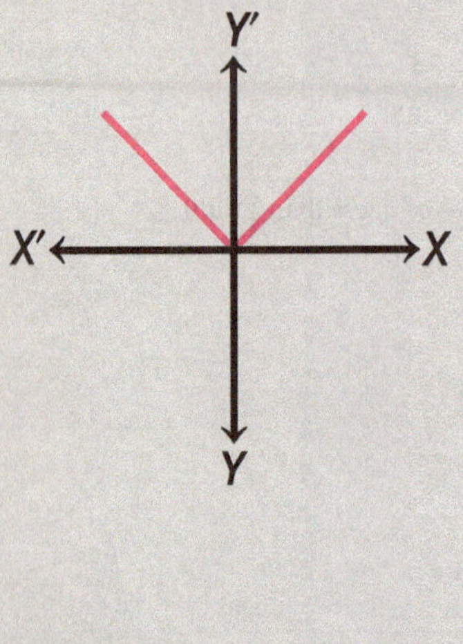

Milestone 1 Introduction

- Definition of Function • Representation of Function • Algebra of Function • Value of Function
- Number of Functions • Domain, Codomain and Range of Function

2.1 Definition of Function

The term function was firstly used by Leibnitz to denote dependent quantities to each other.

Definition I

Let A and B be two sets and let there exist a rule or manner or correspondence 'f', which associates to each element of A to a unique element in B, then f is called a **function** or **mapping** from A to B.

It is denoted by the symbol

$$f: A \to B \text{ or } A \xrightarrow{f} B$$

which reads 'f' is a function from A to B or 'f' maps A to B.

If an element $a \in A$ is associated with an element $b \in B$, then b is called 'the f image of a' or 'image of a under f' or 'the value of the function f at a'. Also, a is called the pre-image of b or argument of b under the function f.

We write it as

$$b = f(a) \text{ or } f: a \to b \text{ or } f:(a, b)$$

Definition II

A relation R from a set A to a set B is called a funciton if

(i) each element of A is associated with some element of B.

(ii) each element of A has unique image in B.

Thus, a function 'f' from a set A to a set B is a subset of $A \times B$ in which each 'a' belonging to A appears in one and only one ordered pair belonging to f.

Hence, a function f is a relation from A to B satisfying the following properties.

Every function from $A \to B$ satisfies the following conditions.

(i) $f \subset A \times B$

(ii) For all $a \in A \Rightarrow (a, f(a)) \in f$ and

(iii) $(a, b) \in f$ and $(a, c) \in f \Rightarrow b = c$.

Thus, the ordered pairs of f must satisfy the property that each element of A appears in some ordered pair and no two ordered pairs have same first element.

Note Every function is a relation but every relation is not necessarily a function.

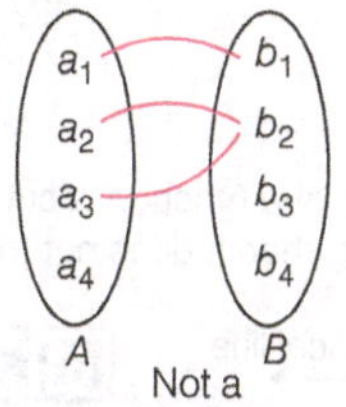

Not a function (a_4 does't have image)

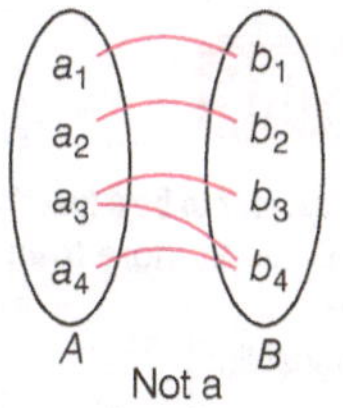

Not a function (a_3 have 2 images)

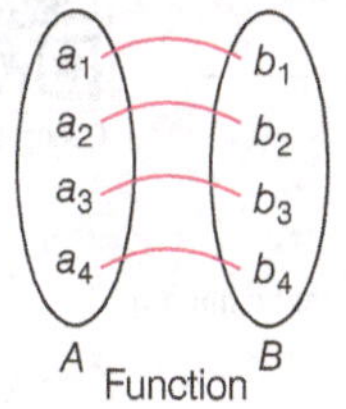

Function

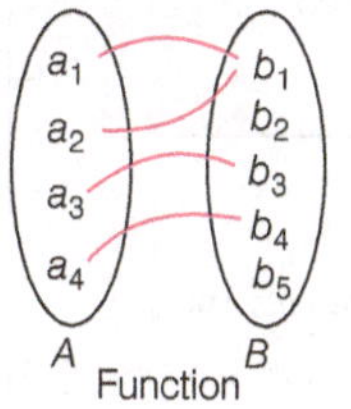

Function

2.2 Representation of Function

(1) In Roster Form

∵ In roster form the function is denoted by set of ordered pair (a, b) where a is functionally related to b, $a \in A, b \in B$.

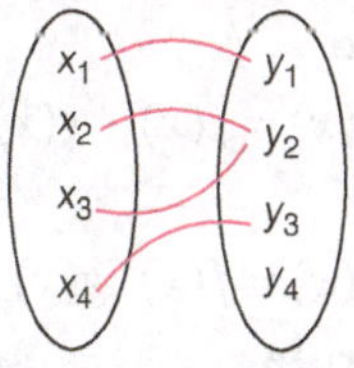

$$f = \{(x_1, y_1), (x_2, y_2), (x_3, y_2), (x_4, y_3)\}$$

(2) In Set Builder Form

$\because f = \{(a, b), a\, f\, b,\ a \in A, b \in B\}$

↳ functionally related to b.

(3) General Representation

$f: A \to B$, where $f(x) =$ expression in x.

(4) Analytical Representation

When a function is denoted as $y = f(x)$ or $f(x, y) = 0$, then it called analytical representation.

e.g. $y = \sqrt{x^2 + 1}, f(x) = \dfrac{\ln x + e^x}{\sin x}$ or $f(x) = \dfrac{ax^2 + bx + c}{e^{2x} \sin^{-1} x}$.

(5) Graphical Representation

The graph of $y = f(x)$, where f is a function, consists of points whose coordinates (x, y) satisfy $y = f(x)$.

Also, it is such that lines drawn parallel to the Y-axis **do not intersect the curve at more than one point.**

JEE SPIKE

Vertical line test for f to be a function If graph of a function is cut a line parallel to Y-axis at more than one point, then it does not form a function.

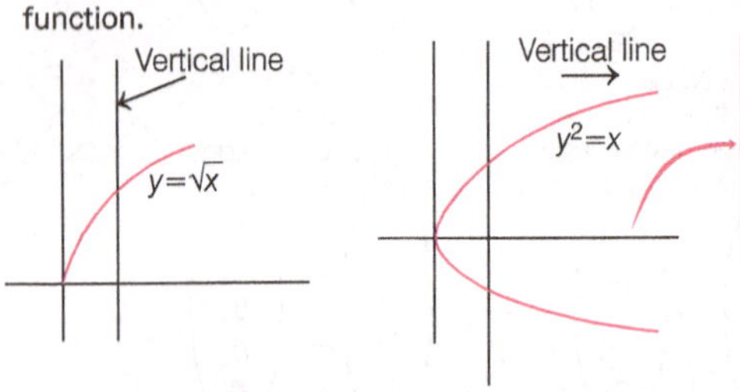

Represents a funtion **Not represent a funtion**

Concept Inside Video

2.3 Algebra of Function

Let $f: A \to B$ and $g: A \to C$ are two real valued functions, then

1. **Addition rule**
$$(f + g)(x) = f(x) + g(x)$$
2. **Subtraction rule**
$$(f - g)(x) = f(x) - g(x)$$
3. **Product rule**
$$(fg)(x) = f(x) \cdot g(x)$$
4. **Scalar Product rule**
$$(kf)(x) = kf(x)$$
5. **Quitent rule**
$$\left(\frac{f}{g}\right)(x) = \frac{f(x)}{g(x)} \text{ provided } g(x) \neq 0$$

Example 1. If $A = \{a, b, c, d, e\}$ and $B = \{p, q, r, s, t\}$, then which of the following subset(s) of $A \times B$ is/are function(s) from A to B.

(i) $f_1 = \{(a, r), (b, r), (b, s), (d, t), (e, q), (c, q)\}$
(ii) $f_2 = \{(a, r), (b, p), (c, t), (d, q)\}$
(iii) $f_3 = \{(a, p), (b, t), (c, r), (d, s), (e, q)\}$
(iv) $f_4 = \{(a, r), (b, r), (c, r), (d, r), (e, r)\}$

Sol. We check for the two conditions of the functions

(i) Since, b has two outputs (images) namely r and s, f_1 is not a function.
(ii) Since, e an element of A, does not have any image, it is also not a function.
(iii) Since, every element of A has only one output, it is a function.
(iv) Even, if every element's output is r, it is a function, as every element of A is participating and has a unique image r.

Example 2. Decide whether or not, the following are functions from A to B, where $A = \{1, 2, 3, 4, 5\}$ and $B = \{a, b, c, d, e\}$. If they are functions, give the range of each. If they are not, explain why?

(i) $f_1 = \{(1, a), (2, b), (3, b), (5, e)\}$
(ii) $f_2 = \{(1, e), (5, d), (3, a), (2, b), (1, d), (4, a)\}$

Sol. (i) Since, the element $4 \in A$ is not associated to any element of B, therefore f_1 is not a function from A to B.
(ii) The element $1 \in A$ is associated to two different element e and d of B. Therefore, f_2 is not a function from A to B.

Example 3. Let $A = \{1, 2, 4\}$ and $B = \{1, 3\}$. Let $R = \{(x, y): x + y$ is an even number, $x \in A, y \in B\}$. Does R represent a function?

Sol. We find all possible ordered pairs such that the sum of first element and second element is even $R = \{(1, 1), (1, 3)\}$

From the mapping, it is clear that R is a relation but not a function.

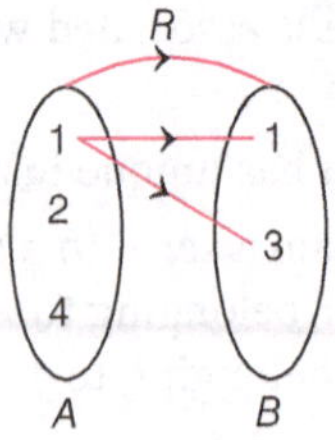

Example 4. If $A = \{2, 3, 4, 5\}$, then which of the following relations is a function from A to itself?

(a) $f_1 = \{(x, y): y = x + 1\}$
(b) $f_2 = \{(x, y): x + y > 6\}$
(c) $f_3 = \{(x, y): y < x\}$
(d) $f_4 = \{(x, y): x + y = 7\}$

Sol. Here, $f_1 = \{(2, 3), (3, 4), (4, 5)\}$

$$f_2 = \{(2, 5), (3, 4), (3, 5), (4, 3), (4, 4), (4, 5), (5, 2), (5, 3), (5, 4), (5, 5)\}$$

$$f_3 = \{(3, 2), (4, 2), (4, 3), (5, 2), (5, 3), (5, 4)\}$$

and $f_4 = \{(2, 5), (3, 4), (4, 3), (5, 2)\}$

Here, only f_4 is a function from A to itself.

Note that f_4 is a bijection

$[\because D_{f_1} \neq A; f_2(3), f_2(4), f_2(5)$ are not unique, $D_{f_3} \neq A]$

2.4 Value of Function

Let $f(x)$ be any real valued function and a be any real number the $f(a)$ denotes value of function at $x = a$, where x is replaced by a

e.g. $f(x) = x^3 - 4x^2 + 7x + 8$

$f(1) =$ value of $f(x)$ at $x = 1$

$$= (1)^3 - 4(1)^2 + 7(1) + 8 = 1 - 4 + 7 + 8 = 12$$

Note This point is important as per JEE Mains point of view. Some example are also discussed below. So, keep eyes on this topic.

Example 5. If $f(x) = \dfrac{ax - c}{cx - a} = y$, then find the value of $f(y)$ in terms of x.

Sol. Given, $f(x) = \dfrac{ax - c}{cx - a} = y$

Now, $f(y) = \dfrac{ay - c}{cy - a}$

$$= \frac{a\left(\dfrac{ax - c}{cx - a}\right) - c}{c\left(\dfrac{ax - c}{cx - a}\right) - a}$$

$$= \frac{a(ax - c) - c(cx - a)}{c(ax - c) - a(cx - a)}$$

$$= \frac{x(a^2 - c^2) - ac + ca}{x(ac - ac) - c^2 + a^2} = \frac{x(a^2 - c^2)}{(a^2 - c^2)} = x$$

Example 6. If $f(x) = \dfrac{x - 1}{x + 1}$, then show that

$$\frac{f\left(\dfrac{1}{x^2}\right) \cdot [1 + (f(x))^2]}{f(x)} = -2.$$

Sol. We have, $f(x) = \dfrac{x - 1}{x + 1}$

$$\Rightarrow \quad f\left(\frac{1}{x^2}\right) = \frac{\dfrac{1}{x^2} - 1}{\dfrac{1}{x^2} + 1} = \frac{1 - x^2}{1 + x^2}$$

$$\Rightarrow \quad \frac{f\left(\dfrac{1}{x^2}\right)[1 + (f(x))^2]}{f(x)} = \frac{\left(\dfrac{1 - x^2}{1 + x^2}\right)\left[1 + \left(\dfrac{x - 1}{x + 1}\right)^2\right]}{\left(\dfrac{x - 1}{x + 1}\right)}$$

$$= \frac{(1 - x^2)}{(1 + x^2)} \times \frac{2(x^2 + 1)}{(x + 1)^2} \times \frac{(x + 1)}{(x - 1)}$$

$$= \frac{2(1 - x)(1 + x)^2}{(x + 1)^2 (x - 1)} = -2$$

Hence proved.

Example 7. Let $f: R \to R$ be a function satisfying $f(3) = 2$ and $f(x + 3) = f(3) \cdot f(x)$, then find $(f(-3))$.

Sol. Since, we are interested in finding $f(-3)$, we first put $x = -3$ in the relation, obtaining $f(0) = f(3)(f(-3))$.

Thus, we must also known $f(0)$ in order to find $f(-3)$.

Put $x = 0$ in the relation,

$$f(3) = f(3)f(0)$$

$$\Rightarrow \quad f(0) = 1 \text{ as } f(3) = 2;$$

Thus, $\quad f(0) = f(3) \cdot f(-3)$

$$\Rightarrow \quad 1 = (2) \cdot f(-3)$$

$$\Rightarrow \quad f(-3) = \frac{1}{2}$$

Example 8. If $\dfrac{1}{a_1}, \dfrac{1}{a_2}, \dfrac{1}{a_3} \ldots \dfrac{1}{a_n}$ are in AP and function $f(k)$ is defined by $f(k) = \sum_{r=1}^{n} a_r - a_k$, then $\dfrac{f(1)}{a_1}, \dfrac{f(2)}{a_2}, \ldots, \dfrac{f(n)}{a_n}$ are in

(a) AP
(b) GP
(c) HP
(d) None of these

Sol. (a) $\dfrac{1}{a_1}, \dfrac{1}{a_2}, \dfrac{1}{a_3}, \ldots\ldots\ldots \dfrac{1}{a_n} \to$ AP

$$\therefore \quad f(k) = \sum_{r=1}^{n} a_r - a_k$$

Now, $f(1) = \sum_{r=1}^{n} a_r - a_1 \Rightarrow f(1) + a_1 = \sum_{r=1}^{n} a_r$

Similarly, $f(2) + a_2 = \sum_{r=1}^{n} a_r$

$$f(3) + a_3 = \sum_{r=1}^{n} a_r$$

$$\vdots$$

$$f(n) + a_n = \sum_{r=1}^{n} a_r$$

$\therefore \quad f(1) + a_1 = f(2) + a_2 = f(3) + a_3 \ldots$

$$= f(n) + a_n = \sum_{r=1}^{n} a_r = \lambda \text{ (say)} \quad \ldots\text{(i)}$$

$\because \quad \frac{1}{a_1}, \frac{1}{a_2}, \frac{1}{a_3}, \ldots \frac{1}{a_n} \rightarrow$ AP [given]

Now, each term is multiplied by λ to obtained a sequence which is also an AP.

$$\frac{\lambda}{a_1}, \frac{\lambda}{a_2}, \frac{\lambda}{a_3}, \ldots, \frac{\lambda}{a_n} \text{ are in AP}$$

By Eq. (i),

$$\frac{f(1)+a_1}{a_1}, \frac{f(2)+a_2}{a_2}, \frac{f(3)+a_3}{a_3}, \ldots, \frac{f(n)+a_n}{a_n}$$

are also in AP.

$$\Rightarrow \frac{f(1)}{a_1}+1, \frac{f(2)}{a_2}+1, \frac{f(3)}{a_3}+1 \ldots, \frac{f(n)}{a_n}+1$$

are also in AP.

On subtracting 1 from each term

$$\frac{f(1)}{a_1}, \frac{f(2)}{a_2}, \frac{f(3)}{a_3}, \ldots, \frac{f(n)}{a_n} \text{ also are in AP.}$$

Example 9. If a function is defined by $f(x)=\cos(\ln x)$, then the value of $f(x)(f(y))-\frac{1}{2}\left[f\left(\frac{x}{y}\right)+f(xy)\right]$ is equal to ....

Sol. (0) We have, $f(x)=\cos(\ln x)$

Now, $f(x)f(y)-\frac{1}{2}\left[f\left(\frac{x}{y}\right)+f(xy)\right]$

$$\Rightarrow \cos(\ln x)\cos(\ln y)-\frac{1}{2}\left[\cos\left(\ln\frac{x}{y}\right)+\cos(\ln(xy))\right]$$

$$\Rightarrow \cos(\ln x)\cos(\ln y)-\frac{1}{2}[\cos(\ln x-\ln y)+\cos(\ln x+\ln y)]$$

Let $\ln x=\theta$ and $\ln y=\phi$

$$\Rightarrow \cos\theta\cos\phi-\frac{1}{2}[\cos(\theta-\phi)+\cos(\theta+\phi)]$$

$$\Rightarrow \cos\theta\cos\phi-\frac{1}{2}[\cos\theta\cos\phi+\sin\theta\sin\phi + \cos\theta\cos\phi-\sin\theta\sin\phi]$$

$$= \cos\theta\cos\phi-\cos\theta\cos\phi$$

$$=0$$

$$\therefore f(x)f(y)-\frac{1}{2}\left[f\left(\frac{x}{y}\right)+f(xy)\right]=0$$

Example 10. Let $f:R\rightarrow\{0,1\}\rightarrow R$ be a function satisfies $f(x)+f\left(\frac{1}{1-x}\right)=1+x^2$. Then, $f(2)$ is equal to

(a) 0 (b) $\frac{19}{2}$ (c) $\frac{17}{8}$ (d) $\frac{11}{2}$

Sol. (c) We have, $f(x)+f\left(\frac{1}{1-x}\right)=1+x^2$

On putting $x=2$, we get

$$f(2)+f(-1)=5 \quad \ldots\text{(i)}$$

On putting $x=\frac{1}{2}$, we get

$$f\left(\frac{1}{2}\right)+f(2)=\frac{5}{4} \quad \ldots\text{(ii)}$$

On putting $x=-1$, we get

$$f(-1)+f\left(\frac{1}{2}\right)=2 \quad \ldots\text{(iii)}$$

On subtracting Eq. (iii) from Eq. (i), we get

$$f(2)-f\left(\frac{1}{2}\right)=3 \quad \ldots\text{(iv)}$$

Now, on adding Eqs. (ii) and (iv), we get

$$2f(2)=\frac{17}{4} \Rightarrow f(2)=\frac{17}{8}$$

JEE SCANNER

Example Similar to PYQ Asked in JEE Main 2023

If $f(x)=\frac{9^x}{9^x+3}$, then the value of $f\left(\frac{1}{1996}\right)+f\left(\frac{2}{1996}\right)+f\left(\frac{3}{1996}\right)+\ldots+f\left(\frac{1995}{1996}\right)$ is

(a) 997.5 (b) 979.5 (c) 597.9 (d) 959.7

Sol. (a) We have, $f(x)=\frac{9^x}{9^x+3}$

$$\therefore \quad f(1-x)=\frac{9^{1-x}}{9^{1-x}+3}=\frac{3}{3+9^x}$$

$$\Rightarrow \quad f(x)+f(1-x)=1$$

Let $S=f\left(\frac{1}{1996}\right)+f\left(\frac{2}{1996}\right)+\ldots+f\left(\frac{1995}{1996}\right)$

$$\Rightarrow S=f\left(\frac{1995}{1996}\right)+f\left(\frac{1994}{1996}\right)+\ldots+f\left(\frac{1}{1996}\right)$$

$$\Rightarrow 2S=f\left(\frac{1}{1996}\right)+f\left(\frac{1995}{1996}\right)+f\left(\frac{2}{1996}\right)+f\left(\frac{1994}{1996}\right)+\ldots+f\left(\frac{1995}{1996}\right)+f\left(\frac{1}{1996}\right)$$

$$=1+1+\ldots+1=1995$$

Hence, $S=\frac{1995}{2}=997.5$

Skill Builder

If $f(x)=\frac{4^x}{4^x+2}$, then the value of $f\left(\frac{1}{20}\right)+f\left(\frac{2}{20}\right)+f\left(\frac{3}{20}\right)+\ldots+f\left(\frac{19}{20}\right)$ is equal to

(a) 10.5 (b) 10
(c) 9 (d) 9.5

For Sol.

■ **For more practice** See Q.5 of Milestone Practice 2.1.

2.5 Number of Functions

Let a function $f = A \to B$ be a real valued function. If $n(A) = m$ and $n(B) = n$, then number of possible functions from A to B is given by

$$n \times n \times \ldots m \text{ times} = n^m$$

Example 11. Let $A = \{1, 2, 3, 4, 5\}$ and $B = \{1, 2, 3, 4, 5, 6\}$ be two sets and a function $f: A \to B$ such that $f(1) + 2f(2) - f(3) = 0$, then number of possible function are

(a) 144 (b) 216

(c) 72 (d) None of these

Sol. (b) $\because \; f(1) + 2f(2) - f(3) = 0 \Rightarrow f(3) = 2f(2) + f(1)$

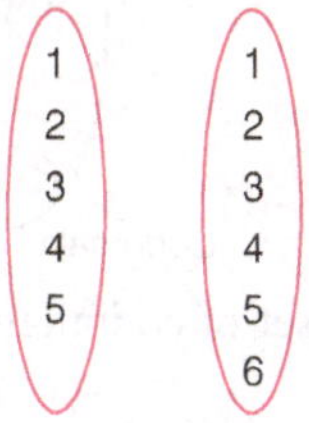

Case I Let $f(2) = 1 \Rightarrow f(3) = f(1) + 2$

$\therefore$ Possible values of $f(1) = 1, 2, 3, 4$

Corresponding $f(3) = 3, 4\; 5, 6$

$\therefore$ Choices of $f(4)$ and $f(5) = 6$

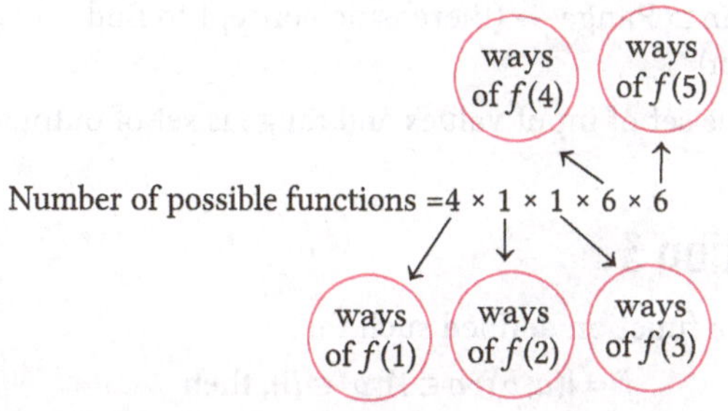

$= 144$

Case II $f(2) = 2 \Rightarrow f(3) = 4 + f(1)$

$f(1)$ can be $1, 2 \to 2$ ways

$f(3) \Rightarrow 5, 6$

$\therefore$ Number of possible functions $= 2 \times 1 \times 1 \times 6 \times 6 = 72$

Case III $f(2) = 3 \Rightarrow f(3) = 6 + f(1)$

Not possible

$\therefore$ Total number of possible functions $= 144 + 72 = 216$

Example 12. Let $f: \{1, 3, 4, 5, 6, 9\} \to \{1, 2, \ldots, 5\}$ be function such that $2f(1) - 3f(3) + f(4) + 2f(5) = 0$, then number of possible functions are

(a) 675 (b) 725 (c) 750 (d) 775

Sol. (a) $2f(1) - 3f(3) + f(4) + 2f(5) = 0$

$$2f(1) + f(4) + 2f(5) = 3f(3)$$

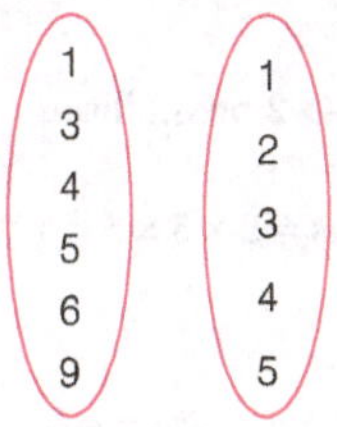

Case I For $f(3) = 1$

$2f(1) + f(4) + 2f(5) = 3, \; f(5) = 1$

$\therefore \quad 2f(1) + f(4) = 2$ [not possible]

Case II For $f(3) = 2$

$2f(1) + f(4) + 2f(5) = 6$

$f(5) = 1$

$\therefore \quad 2f(1) + f(4) = 4$

$f(1) = 1, \; f(4) = 2$

$f(6)$ and $f(9) = 5$ possibilities

Total functions $= 5 \times 5 = 25$

Now, $f(5) = 2$

$2f(1) + f(4) = 2$ [not possible]

Case III For $f(3) = 3$

$\therefore \quad 2f(1) + f(4) + 2f(5) = 9$

$f(5) = 1$

$\therefore \; 2f(1) + f(4) = 7$

$f(1) = 1 \,|\, 2 \,|\, 3$; $f(4) = 5 \,|\, 3 \,|\, 1$ $\to$ 3 possibilities

$f(6)$ and $f(9) \to 5$ possibilities

Number of functions $= 3 \times 5 \times 5 = 75$

Now, $f(5) = 2$

$2f(1) + f(4) = 5$

$f(1) = 1 \,|\, 2$; $f(4) = 3 \,|\, 1$ $\to$ 2 possibilities

Number of functions $= 2 \times 5 \times 5 = 50$

Now, $f(5) = 3$

$2f(1) + f(4) = 3$

$f(1) = 1$; $f(4) = 1$ $\to$ 1 possibility

Number of functions $= 5 \times 5 = 25$

Now, $f(5) = 4$

$2f(1) + f(4) = 1$ [not possible]

Case IV For $f(3) = 4$

$\therefore \quad 2f(1) + f(4) + 2f(5) = 12$

$f(5) = 1$

$\therefore \quad 2f(1) + f(4) = 10$

$f(1) = 3 \,|\, 4$; $f(4) = 4 \,|\, 2$ $\to$ 2 possibilities

Number of functions $= 2 \times 5 \times 5 = 50$

Now, $f(5) = 2$

$2f(1) + f(4) = 8$

$$\left.\begin{matrix} f(1) = 2 \\ f(4) = 4 \end{matrix}\right| \begin{matrix} 3 \\ 2 \end{matrix} \rightarrow 2 \text{ possibilities}$$

Number of functions $= 2 \times 5 \times 5 = 50$

Now, $f(5) = 3$

$2f(1) + f(4) = 6$

$$\left.\begin{matrix} f(1) = 1 \\ f(4) = 4 \end{matrix}\right| \begin{matrix} 2 \\ 2 \end{matrix} \rightarrow 2 \text{ possibilities}$$

Number of functions $= 50$

Now, $f(5) = 4$

$2f(1) + f(4) = 4$

$$\begin{matrix} f(1) = 1 \\ f(4) = 2 \end{matrix} \rightarrow 1 \text{ possibility}$$

Number of functions $= 5 \times 5 = 25$

Now, $f(5) = 5$

$2f(1) + f(4) = 2$ [not possible]

Case V For $f(3) = 5$

$\therefore \quad 2f(1) + f(4) + 2f(5) = 15$

$f(5) = 1$

$\therefore \quad 2f(1) + f(4) = 13$

$$\left.\begin{matrix} f(1) = 4 \\ f(4) = 5 \end{matrix}\right| \begin{matrix} 5 \\ 3 \end{matrix} \rightarrow 2 \text{ possibilities}$$

Number of functions $= 2 \times 5 \times 5 = 50$

Now, $f(5) = 2$

$2f(1) + f(4) = 11$

$$\begin{matrix} f(1) = 3, 4, 5 \\ f(2) = 5, 3, 1 \end{matrix} \rightarrow 3 \text{ possibilities}$$

Number of functions $= 3 \times 5 \times 5 = 75$

Now, $f(5) = 3$

$2f(1) + f(4) = 9$

$$\left.\begin{matrix} f(1) = 2 \\ f(4) = 5 \end{matrix}\right| \left.\begin{matrix} 3 \\ 3 \end{matrix}\right| \begin{matrix} 4 \\ 1 \end{matrix} \rightarrow 3 \text{ possibilities}$$

Number of functions $= 3 \times 5 \times 5 = 75$

Now, $f(5) = 4$

$2f(1) + f(4) = 7$

$$\left.\begin{matrix} f(1) = 1 \\ f(4) = 5 \end{matrix}\right| \left.\begin{matrix} 2 \\ 3 \end{matrix}\right| \begin{matrix} 3 \\ 1 \end{matrix} \rightarrow 3 \text{ possibilities}$$

Number of functions $= 3 \times 5 \times 5 = 75$

Now, $f(5) = 5$

$2f(1) + f(4) = 5$

$$\begin{matrix} f(1) \\ f(4) \end{matrix} = \left.\begin{matrix} 1 \\ 3 \end{matrix}\right| \begin{matrix} 2 \\ 1 \end{matrix} \rightarrow 2 \text{ possibilities}$$

Number of functions $= 2 \times 5 \times 5 = 50$

Therefore, total number of functions $= 675$

2.6 Domain, Codomain and Range of Function

Definition 1

Let a function $f: X \rightarrow Y$ be a real valued function, then

Set X is known as domain of function.

Set Y is known as codomain of function.

Set of elements in Y which are images of elements of X is known as range.

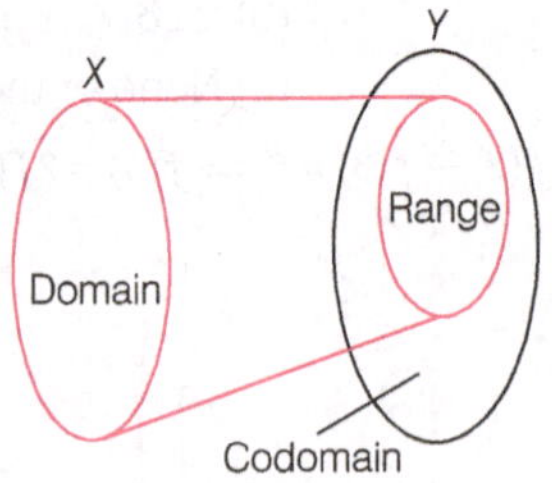

Range always be a subset of codomain

Definition 2

Let $y = f(x)$ be any real valued function, then

Domain set of values of x at which $f(x)$ is defined.

Range set of values of y corresponding to its domain.

Codomain $\supset$ Range $\rightarrow$ (there is no concept to find codomain)

Domain is set of input values and range is set of output values.

Definition 3

Let f be a function defined such that

$$f = \{(a, b) : a \in A, b \in B\}, \text{ then}$$

Domain $= \{a : a \in A\} = A$

Codomain $= B$.

Range $= \{b : (a, b) \in f, b \in B\}$.

Points for Finding Domain (when it is not given)

1. Set of values of x at which $y = f(x)$ is defined.
2. $\sqrt{f(x)}$ is defined when $f(x) \geq 0$ and $f(x)$ contain even roots also defines when $f(x) \geq 0$
3. $\dfrac{1}{f(x)}$ defines when $f(x) \neq 0$
4. Domain of $f(x) \pm g(x)$, $f(x) - g(x)$ are intersection of domain of $f(x)$ and $g(x)$.

5. Domain of $\dfrac{f(x)}{g(x)}$ is intersection of domain of $f(x)$ and $g(x)$ also $g(x) \neq 0$.

Example 13. Find the domain of following

(i) $f(x) = \dfrac{1}{x^2 - 3x + 2}$

(ii) $f(x) = \sqrt{5 - x}$

Sol. (i) $f(x) = \dfrac{1}{x^2 - 3x + 2}$

Domain, $x \in R - \{x^2 - 3x + 2 = 0\}$

$x \in R - \{1, 2\}$ $\quad [\because x^2 - 3x + 2 = 0 \Rightarrow x = 1, 2]$

(ii) $f(x) = \sqrt{5 - x}$

Domain, $5 - x \geq 0$

$\Rightarrow \quad x \leq 5$

$\therefore \quad x \in (-\infty, 5]$

Method for Finding Range

- **Method I** Standard approach
- **Method II** Using Restriction of function
- **Method III** Using Derivatives.

Method I - Standard Approach

Given $f(x) =$ expression in x

To find Range

Algorithm

1. Assume $f(x) = y$ and solve it for x
2. We get $x = g(y) =$ expression in y
3. Range is set of values of y for which $g(y)$ (i.e., x) is defined.

e.g. $f(x) = \dfrac{x}{x^2 + 1}$

Domain : $x \in R$

Range : $y = \dfrac{x}{x^2 + 1}$

$\Rightarrow \quad yx^2 - x + y = 0$

$\because \; x \in R \Rightarrow$ Roots are real

$D \geq 0$ and $(1) - 4(y)(y) \geq 0$

$\Rightarrow \quad y^2 \leq \dfrac{1}{4} \Rightarrow y \in \left[-\dfrac{1}{2}, \dfrac{1}{2}\right]$

Method II - Using Restriction of Function

There are many functions whose output values are restricted, so at that time we have to use these restrictions to calculate range.

e.g. $f(x) = \dfrac{3 \sin x + 4 \cos x - 4\sqrt{2}}{3}$

Domain $x \in R$

Range

We know that

$$-\sqrt{a^2 + b^2} \leq a \sin x + b \cos x \leq \sqrt{a^2 + b^2} \text{ (restriction)}$$

$$-\sqrt{3^2 + 4^2} \leq 3 \sin x + 4 \cos x \leq \sqrt{3^2 + 4^2}$$

$$-5 \leq 3 \sin x + 4 \cos x \leq 5$$

$$-5 - 4\sqrt{2} \leq 3 \sin x + 4 \cos x - 4\sqrt{2} \leq 5 - 4\sqrt{2}$$

$$\frac{-5 - 4\sqrt{2}}{3} \leq \frac{3 \sin x + 4 \cos x - 4\sqrt{2}}{3} \leq \frac{5 - 4\sqrt{2}}{3}$$

$$\therefore \; y \in \left[\frac{-5 - 4\sqrt{2}}{3}, \frac{5 - 4\sqrt{2}}{3}\right] \rightarrow \text{Range}$$

Method III - Using Derivatives

First of all find the domain of given function $y = f(x)$

(i) If domain contains finite number of points, range is the set of corresponding $f(x)$ values.

(ii) If domain is a finite interval, then find the least and the greatest values for range, using **monotonicity**.

e.g. If $f(x)$ is defined on $[a, b]$, then

Step I Put $f'(x) = 0 \Rightarrow x = \alpha_1, \alpha_2, \ldots, \alpha_n \in (a, b)$

Step II Find $\{f(a), f(\alpha_1), f(\alpha_2), \ldots, f(\alpha_n), f(b)\}$

The greatest and least values gives the range of $f(x)$.

JEE SPIKE

Monotonocity For a differentiable funtion $f(x)$, if its derivatives $f'(x) \geq 0$, then it is an increasing function and $f'(x) \leq 0$, then it is a decreasing function and $f'(x) = 0 \Rightarrow$ obtained x are the critical points, where function can occur its maximum and minimum value.

Concept Inside Video

e.g. $f(x) = \sqrt{x - 1} + \sqrt{5 - x}$.

Domain $x - 1 \geq 0$ and $5 - x \geq 0$

$x \geq 1$ and $x \leq 5$

$\therefore \quad x \in [1, 5]$

and domain is a finite interval.

Range $f'(x) = \dfrac{1}{2\sqrt{x - 1}} + \dfrac{1}{2\sqrt{5 - x}}(-1)$

$f'(x) = 0$

$$\frac{1}{2\sqrt{x - 1}} - \frac{1}{2\sqrt{5 - x}} = 0$$

$$\sqrt{x - 1} = \sqrt{5 - x}$$

On squaring both sides, we get

$$x-1=5-x$$

$$2x=6 \Rightarrow x=3$$

Now, $f(1)=\sqrt{1-1}+\sqrt{5-1}=2$

$$f(3)=\sqrt{3-1}+\sqrt{5-3}=\sqrt{2}+\sqrt{2}=2\sqrt{2}$$

$$f(5)=\sqrt{5-1}+\sqrt{5-5}=2$$

$\therefore \quad f\in[2,2\sqrt{2}]\rightarrow$ Range

JEE SPIKE

Some times the domain has two sub interval like $x\in[a, b)\cup(c, d]$, so at that time we calculate range correspondingly.

e.g. $f(x)=\sqrt{2x^2-3x-5}$

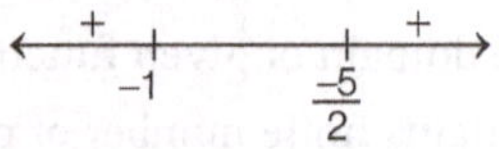

Domain $\quad 2x^2-3x-5\geq 0$

$$2x^2-5x+2x-5\geq 0$$

$$x(2x-5)+1(2x-5)\geq 0$$

$$(2x-5)(x+1)\geq 0$$

Range

$$f'(x)=\frac{(4x-3)}{2\sqrt{2x^2-3x-5}}$$

$$f'(x)=0$$

$$x=\frac{3}{4}\rightarrow \text{but not in domain}$$

$$f(-\infty)=\infty, \quad f\left(\frac{5}{2}\right)=0$$

$$f(-1)=0, \quad f(\infty)=\infty$$

$\therefore \quad y\in[0,\infty)$

Milestone Practice 2.1

1. Check whether the following relation represent function or no.

(i) $x^2+y^2=36, y\in[0,6]$

(ii) $x^2+y^2=36, x\in[0,1]$

(iii) $x^2+y^2=36, x\in[-6,6]$

(iv) $x^2+y^2=36$

2. Check which of the following represents a function from A to B, where

$$A=\{1,2,3,4,5,\ldots,10\},\ B=\{1,2,3,..,20\}$$

(i) $f=\{(a,b): a=2b+3;\ a\in A,\ b\in B\}$

(ii) $f=\{(a,b): a=b+1;\ a\in A,\ b\in B\}$

(iii) $f=\{(x,y): x^2=y;\ x\in A, y\in B\}$

3. Find the domain and range of following functions

(i) $f(x)=3\sin x-2\cos x+3$

(ii) $f(x)=\sqrt{x^2+4}$

(iii) $f(x)=\dfrac{x^2}{1+x^2}$

(iv) $f(x)=3x^2+5x-7$

(v) $f(x)=\dfrac{5x^2}{7x-1}$

4. Given the function $f(x)=\dfrac{a^x+a^{-x}}{2}$ (where $a>2$).

Then, $f(x+y)+f(x-y)=$

(a) $2f(x)\cdot f(y)$ (b) $f(x)\cdot f(y)$

(c) $\dfrac{f(x)}{f(y)}$ (d) None of these

5. Let $f(x)=\dfrac{4^x}{4^x+2}$. Then, the value of

$\dfrac{1}{499}\left[f\left(\dfrac{1}{1997}\right)+f\left(\dfrac{2}{1997}\right)+\ldots+f\left(\dfrac{1996}{1997}\right)\right]$ is given by ....

6. Let f be a function defined on $[0,2]$, then the function $g(x)=f(9x^2-1)$ has domain

(a) $[0,2]$

(b) $\left[-\dfrac{1}{3},\dfrac{1}{3}\right]$

(c) $[-3,3]$

(d) $\left[-\dfrac{1}{\sqrt{3}},-\dfrac{1}{3}\right]\cup\left[\dfrac{1}{3},\dfrac{1}{\sqrt{3}}\right]$

7. If $\alpha=e^{2\pi i/11}$ and $f(x)=5+\sum_{k=1}^{60}A_k x^k$, then find the value of $\dfrac{1}{11}\sum_{r=0}^{10}f(\alpha^r x)$.

8. Let $P_n(x)$ be a function satisfying

$$\sum_{n=0}^{\infty} h^n P_n(x) = (1 - 2hx + h^2)^{-1/2}, |x| \le 1, |h| < \frac{1}{3}.$$

Find $\frac{1}{355} P_3(10)$.

9. Let $f(n) = 1 + \frac{1}{2} + \frac{1}{3} + \dots + \frac{1}{n}$, then $f(1) + f(2) + f(3) + \dots + f(n)$ is equal to

(a) $nf(n) - 1$ (b) $(n + 1) f(n) - n$
(c) $(n + 1) f(n) + n$ (d) $nf(n) + n$

10. If $F(n + 1) = \frac{2F(n) + 1}{2}$, $n = 1, 2, \dots, 100$ and $F(1) = 2$, then $F(101)$ equals

(a) 52 (b) 49 (c) 48 (d) 51

11. Find the domain and range of the function $f(x)$ from a subset of set $A = \{x : x \text{ is a positive integral divisor of } 36\}$ to set of real numbers (R) defined by

$$f(x) = \frac{x}{(x-1)(x-2)(x-3)\dots(x-10)}.$$

12. Let $A = \{9, 10, 11, 12, 13\}$ and let $f : A \to N$ be defined by $f(n) =$ the highest prime factor of n. Find the range of f.

13. A cylinder is inscribed in a sphere of radius R. Express the volume V of the cylinder as a function of its height x. Indicate the domain of definition of this function.

14. O is a fixed point on a circle of unit radius whose centre is P. A chord perpendicular to OP at a distance x from O cuts the circle at A and B. Express the area of the segment AOB as a function of x.

15. In the figure, $BC = b$ and $AH = h$, where $AH \perp BC$. If $EF = x$, where $EF \perp BC$, then express the area and perimeter of the rectangle, $DEFG$ as function of x.

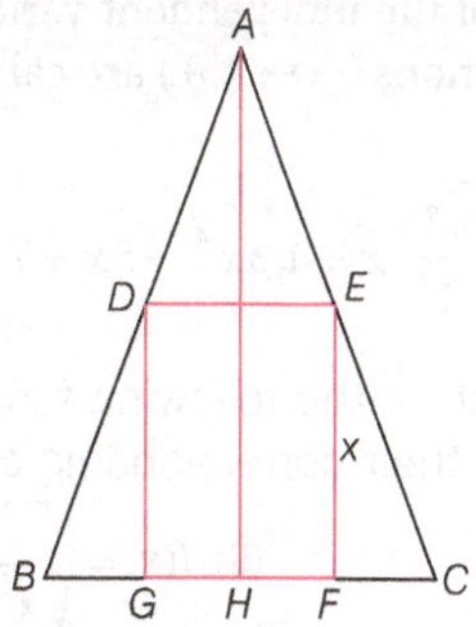

Answer Key

1. (i) Yes (ii) No (iii) No (iv) No **2.** (i) No (ii) No (iii) No

3. (i) Domain $= R$, Range $= [3 - \sqrt{13}, 3 + \sqrt{13}]$ (ii) Domain $= (-\infty, \infty)$, Range $= [2, \infty)$ (iii) Domain $= (-\infty, \infty)$, Range $= [0, 1)$ (iv) Domain $= (-\infty, \infty)$, Range $= \left[\frac{-109}{12}, \infty\right)$ (v) Domain $= (-\infty, \infty) - \left\{\frac{1}{7}\right\}$, Range $= (-\infty, 0] \cup \left[\frac{20}{49}, \infty\right)$

4. (a) **5.** 2 **6.** (d) **7.** 5 **8.** 7 **9.** (b)

10. (a) **11.** Domain $= \{12, 18, 36\}$, Range $= \left\{\frac{12}{11!}, \frac{18 \times 7!}{17!}, \frac{36 \times 25!}{35!}\right\}$ **12.** $\{3, 5, 11, 13\}$

13. $V = \pi x\left(R^2 - \frac{x^2}{4}\right)$, $(0, 2R)$ **14.** $\frac{1}{2}\left[\cos^{-1}(1 - x) - 2(1 - x)\sqrt{2x - x^2}\right]$

15. Perimeter $= 2\left(x + \frac{b(h - x)}{h}\right)$, Area $= \frac{bx(h - x)}{h}$

For Detailed Solution

Milestone 2 Types of Functions I

• Algebraic Function • Non-algebraic Function (Transcendental Function) • Piecewise Function

2.7 Algebraic Function

Functions consisting of finite number of terms involving powers and roots of the independent variable and the four fundamental operations (+, −, ×, ÷) are called algebraic functions.

e.g. $x^{3/2} + 5x, \dfrac{\sqrt{x+1}}{x-1}, x + 1, 3x^4 - 5x + 7$

Example 14. Which of the following functions are algebraic and find their corresponding domain.

(i) $f(x) = \dfrac{x^2+1}{x-1}$ (ii) $f(x) = \sqrt{\dfrac{x}{x^2-1}}$

(iii) $f(x) = \dfrac{\sqrt{\sin x + 1}}{x^2-1}$ (iv) $f(x) = \dfrac{x^2-5x+6}{(x-2)}$

(v) $f(x) = x \tan x$ (vi) $f(x) = \sin x + \cos^2 x$

Sol. (i), (ii), (iv) are algebraic function whereas (iii), (v) and (vi) are non-algebraic functions as they do not involve all terms containing powers of x.

(i) $f(x) = \dfrac{x^2+1}{x-1}, D = R - \{1\}$

(ii) $f(x) = \sqrt{\dfrac{x}{x^2-1}}, \dfrac{x}{x^2-1} \ge 0; x^2 - 1 \ne 0$

$\Rightarrow \quad x(x^2-1) \ge 0; \; x \ne \pm 1$

$\Rightarrow \quad (x+1)(x)(x-1) \ge 0, x \ne \pm 1$

$\Rightarrow \quad x \in (-1, 0] \cup (1, \infty) = D_f$

(iv) $f(x) = \dfrac{x^2 - 5x + 6}{(x-2)} = \dfrac{(x-2)(x-3)}{(x-2)} = x - 3$

for $x \ne 2$, $D_f = R \sim \{2\}$

Types of Algebraic Function

1. Polynomial Function

A function $f : R \to R$ is defined as

$f(x) = a_0 + a_1 x + a_2 x^2 + \ldots + a_n x^n$, where $n \in W$.

Degree of Polynomial

The highest index power of x having non-zero coefficient is called the degree of the polynomial.

The degree of the above polynomial is n, where $a_n \ne 0$.

e.g. The degree of the polynomials

1. $f(x) = 3$ is 0
2. $f(x) = 2x + 4$ is 1
3. $f(x) = x^2 + 3x + 2$ is 2
4. $f(x) = x^3 + 3x^2 + 5x + 6$ is 3
5. $f(x) = x^{2014} + 10x^{2000} + 5x^{199} + 6$ is 2014
6. $f(x) = 0$ is undefined.

JEE Focus Points

- The range of a polynomial depends on the degree of a polynomial.
- If the degree of a polynomial is odd, then its range is R.
- If the degree of a polynomial is even, then its range will not be all real number.

(i) Constant Function

A function $f : R \to R$ is defined as $f(x) = \text{constant} = c$

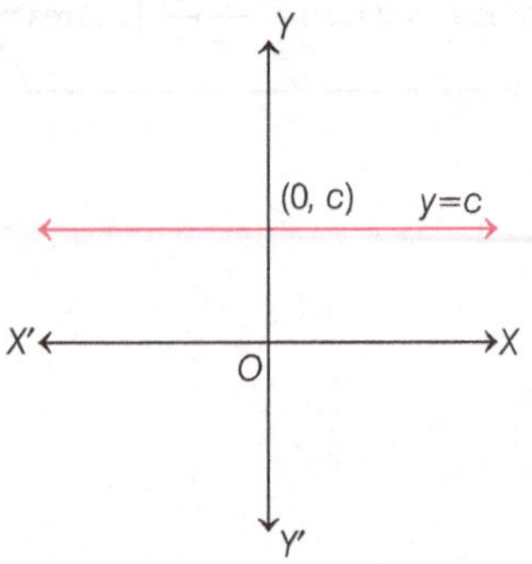

$D_f = R, R_f = \{c\}$

(ii) Identity Function

A function $f: R \to R$ is defined as $f(x) = x$

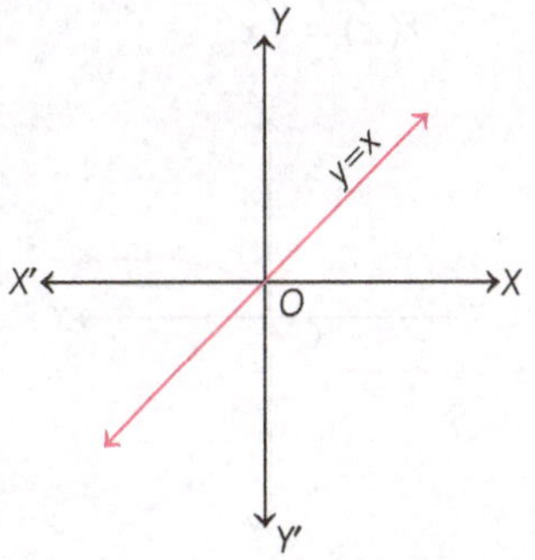

$D_f = R, R_f = R$

(iii) Parabolic Function

A function $f: R \to R$ is defined as $f(x) = x^2$

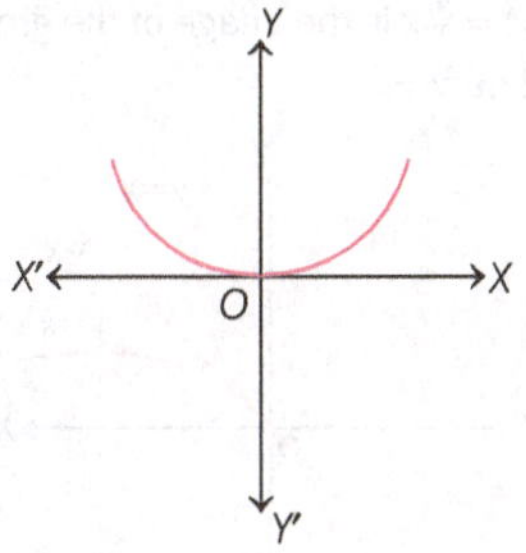

$D_f = R$ and $R_f = [0, \infty)$

(iv) Even Power Function

A function $f: R \to R$ is defined as

$$f(x) = x^{2n}, n \in N$$

i.e. $\quad f(x) = x^2, x^4, x^6, x^8, x^{10}, \ldots$

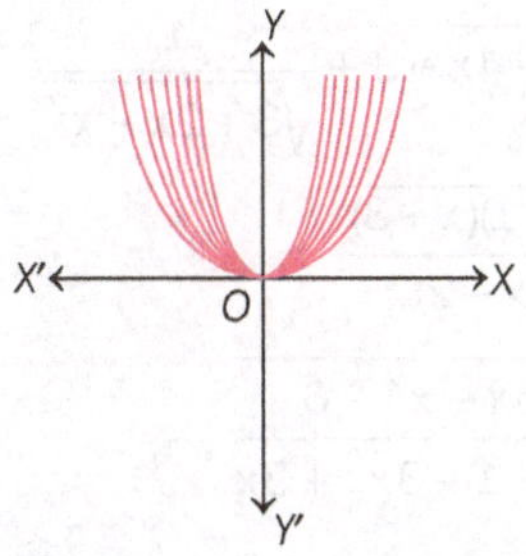

i.e. $D_f = R$ and $R_f = [0, \infty)$

(v) Odd Power function

A function $f: R \to R$ is defined as

$$f(x) = x^{2n+1}, n \in N$$

i.e. $\quad f(x) = x^3, x^5, x^7, x^9, x^{11}, \ldots$

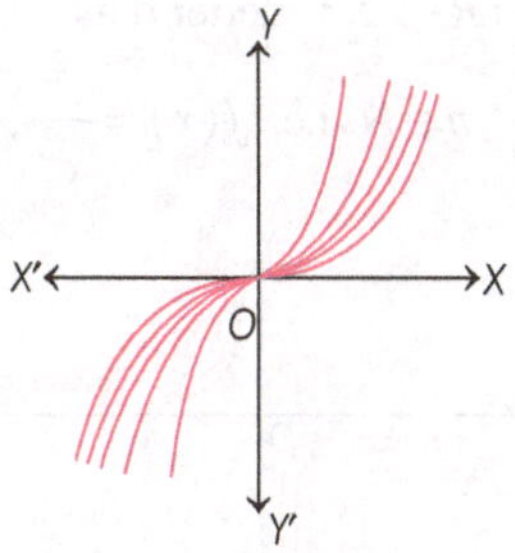

$D_f = R$ and $R_f = R$

2. Rational Functions

A function $f: R \to R$ is defined as

$f(x) = \dfrac{g(x)}{h(x)}, h(x) \neq 0, g(x)$ and $h(x)$ are two polynomial functions.

(i) Reciprocal Function

A function $f: R \to R$ is defined by $f(x) = \dfrac{1}{x}$ is known as reciprocal function.

$$f(x) = \frac{1}{x}$$

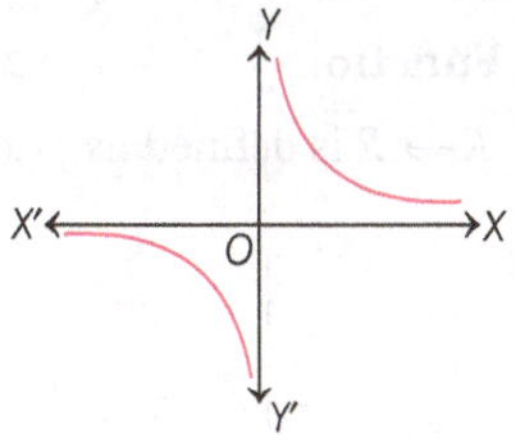

Domain $\to R - \{0\}$

Range $\to R - \{0\}$

(ii) Even Power Reciprocal Function

A function : $f: R \to R$ is defined as

$$f(x) = \frac{1}{x^2}$$

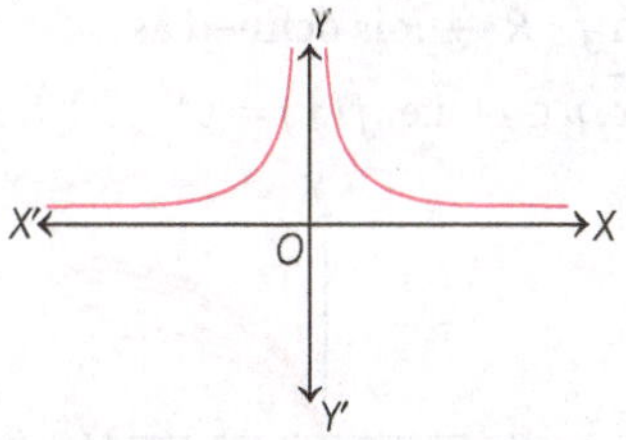

$D_f = R - \{0\}$ and $R_f = R^+$

(iii) Odd Power Reciprocal Functions

A function $f: R \to R$ is defiend as

$$f(x) = \frac{1}{x^{2n+1}}, n \in N \text{ i.e. } f(x) = \frac{1}{x^3}, \frac{1}{x^5}, \frac{1}{x^7}, \frac{1}{x^9}, \dots$$

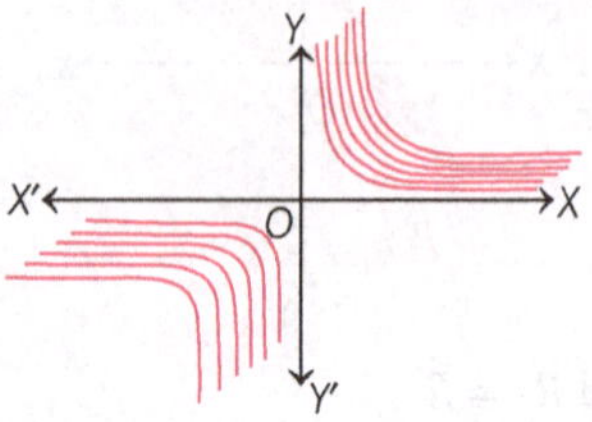

$D_f = R - \{0\} = R_f$

3. Irrational Function

The algebraic function containing one or more terms having non-integral rational powers of x are called irrational functions.

A function $f: R \to R$ is defined as

$$f(x) = (g(x))^{\frac{2p+1}{m}}; p, m \in N$$

It is undefined for $g(x) < 0$

More over these functions are also not defined when denominator is zero.

(i) Square root Function

A function $f: R \to R$ is defined as $f(x) = \sqrt{x}$

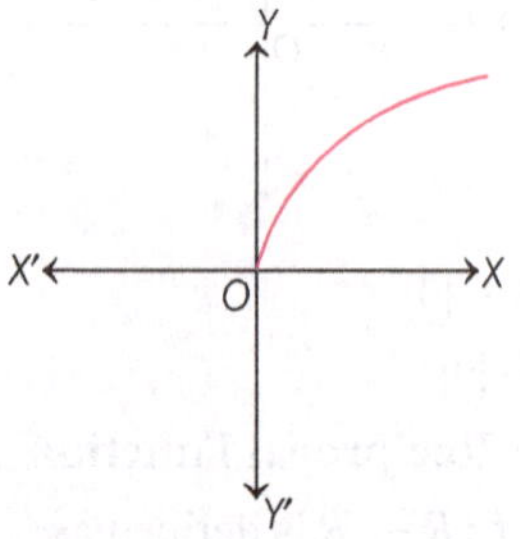

$D_f = [0, \infty)$ and $R_f = [0, \infty)$

(ii) Even root Function

A function $f: R \to R$ is defined as

$f(x) = \sqrt[2n]{x}, n \in N$ i.e. $f(x) = x^{1/2}, x^{1/4}, x^{1/6}, x^{1/8}, \dots$

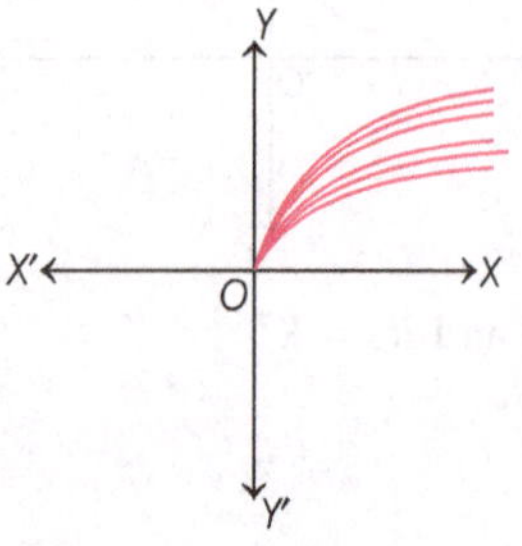

$D_f = [0, \infty)$ and $R_f = [0, \infty)$

(iii) Cube root Function

A function $f: R \to R$ is defiend as

$$f(x) = \sqrt[3]{x}$$

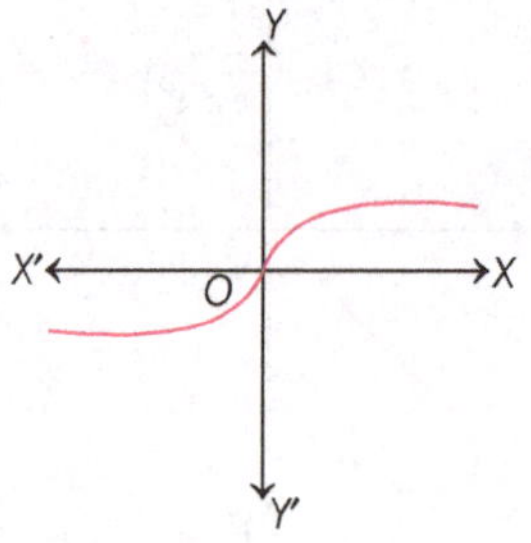

$D_f = R = R_f$

JEE SPIKE

The graph of $y = f(x) = \sqrt[3]{x}$ is the image of the graph of $y = f(x) = x^3$ with respect to the line $y = x$.

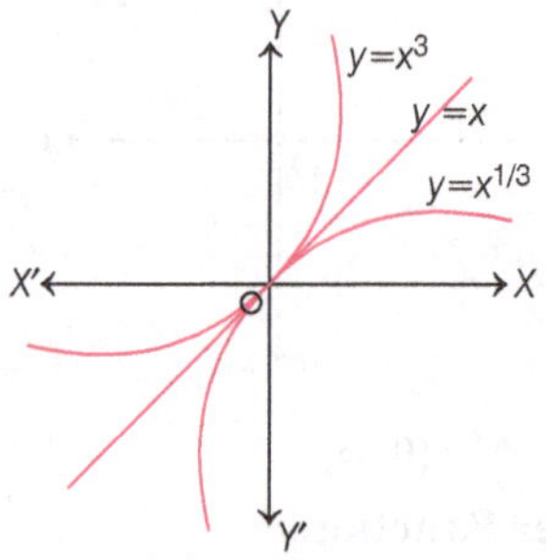

Note The graph of $y = f(x) = \sqrt[2n+1]{x}, n \in N$

i.e. $y = x^{1/3}, x^{1/5}, x^{1/7}, \dots$

Example 15. Find the domain of the following:

(i) $f(x) = \sqrt{x^2 - 4x + 3} + \dfrac{1}{\sqrt{3 + 2x - x^2}}$

(ii) $f(x) = \sqrt{\dfrac{(x+1)(x+3)}{(x-2)}}$

(iii) $f(x) = \sqrt{\dfrac{5x - x^2 - 6}{x^3 - 1 - 3x^2 + 3x}}$

Sol. (i) $f(x)$ is defined when

$x^2 - 4x + 3 \geq 0$ and $3 + 2x - x^2 > 0$

$(x-3)(x-1) \geq 0$ and $x^2 - 2x - 3 < 0$

$(x-3)(x-1) \geq 0$ and $(x-3)(x+1) < 0$

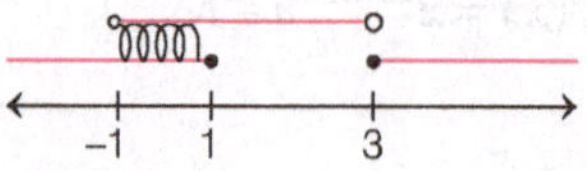

$\therefore$ Domain $x \in (-1, 1]$

(ii) $\dfrac{(x+1)(x+3)}{(x-2)} \geq 0$

Using wave curve method

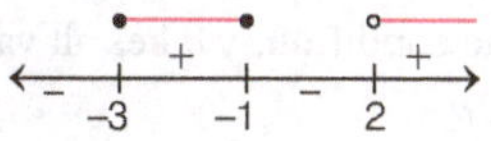

Domain $x \in [-3, -1] \cup (2, \infty)$

(iii) $\dfrac{5x - x^2 - 6}{x^3 - 1 - 3x^2 + 3x} \geq 0$

$$\frac{x^2 - 5x + 6}{(x^3 - 1^3 - 3x(x-1))} \leq 0$$

$$\frac{(x-2)(x-3)}{(x-1)^3} \leq 0$$

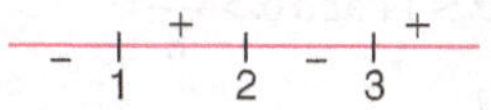

$x \in (-\infty, 1) \cup [2, 3]$

Example 16. Find the range of the follwoing

(i) $f(x) = \dfrac{x^2 + x + 1}{x^2 + x - 1}$ (ii) $f(x) = \dfrac{x^2}{x^4 + 1}$

(iii) $f(x) = 2^{\sqrt{x(x-1)}} + \sqrt{x(x-1)}$ (iv) $f(x) = \dfrac{x^2 - 2x - 8}{x^2 - 4x - 5}$

Sol. (i) $f(x) = \dfrac{x^2 + x + 1}{x^2 + x - 1}$

[$x^2 + x + 1$ and $x^2 + x - 1$ have no common factor]

Let $y = \dfrac{x^2 + x + 1}{x^2 + x - 1}$

$\Rightarrow \quad yx^2 + yx - y = x^2 + x + 1$

$\Rightarrow (y-1)x^2 + (y-1)x - y - 1 = 0$

If $y = 1$, then the above equation reduces to $-2 = 0$ which is not true.

Further if $y \neq 1$, then

$$(y-1)x^2 + (y-1)\,x - y - 1 = 0$$

is a quadratic and has real roots, if

$$(y-1)^2 - 4(y-1)(-y-1) \geq 0$$

i.e. if $y \leq -\dfrac{3}{5}$ or $y \geq 1$ but $y \neq 1$.

Thus, the range is $\left(-\infty, -\dfrac{3}{5}\right] \cup (1, \infty)$.

(ii) Clearly, $f(x) \geq 0$ for any $x \in R$.

For $x \neq 0$, $f(x) = \dfrac{x^2}{x^4 + 1}$.

Since, $x^2 + \dfrac{1}{x^2} \geq 2$, we have $f(x) \leq \dfrac{1}{2}$.

At $x = 0$, $f(x) = 0$.

Hence, the range of f is $[0, 1/2]$.

(iii) Let $t = x(x-1) \Rightarrow t \in \left[-\dfrac{1}{4}, \infty\right)$

Let $u = \sqrt{t}, t \in [0, \infty) \Rightarrow u \in [0, \infty)$

$\Rightarrow \; y = 2^u + u, u \in [0, \infty)$.

This is an increasing function.

The least value of y is obtained at $u = 0$,

and y approaches ∞ as u approaches ∞.

$\Rightarrow \; y \in [1, \infty)$.

(iv) We have, $x^2y - 4xy - 5y = x^2 - 2x - 8$

$$(y-1)x^2 + 2x(1-2y) + 8 - 5y = 0 \, (y \neq 1)$$

Since, $x \in R, D \geq 0$

$$4(1-2y)^2 - 4(y-1)(8-5y) \geq 0$$

$$(4y^2 - 4y + 1) - (13y - 8 - 5y^2) \geq 0$$

$$9y^2 - 17y + 9 \geq 0. \quad \text{...(i)}$$

Since, coefficient of $y^2 > 0$ and $D = 289 - 324 < 0$.

Eq. (i) is always true.

Also, if $y = 1$, we have $x = \dfrac{3}{2}$.

Hence, the range of y is $(-\infty, \infty)$.

Example 17. Let f be a function defined on $[0, 2]$, then the function $g(x) = f(9x^2 - 1)$ has domain

(a) $[0, 2]$ (b) $\left[-\dfrac{1}{3}, \dfrac{1}{3}\right]$

(c) $[-3, 3]$ (d) $\left[\dfrac{-1}{\sqrt{3}}, \dfrac{-1}{3}\right] \cup \left[\dfrac{1}{3}, \dfrac{1}{\sqrt{3}}\right]$

Sol. (d) g is meaningful if

$$0 \leq 9x^2 - 1 \leq 2$$

$\Rightarrow \quad 1 \leq 9x^2 \leq 3$

$\Rightarrow \quad \dfrac{1}{9} \leq x^2 \leq \dfrac{1}{3}$

$\Rightarrow \quad x^2 \geq \dfrac{1}{9}$ and $x^2 \leq \dfrac{1}{3}$

$\Rightarrow \quad x^2 - \dfrac{1}{9} \geq 0$ and $x^2 - \dfrac{1}{3} \leq 0$

$\Rightarrow \quad \left(x - \dfrac{1}{3}\right)\left(x + \dfrac{1}{3}\right) \geq 0$ and $\left(x - \dfrac{1}{\sqrt{3}}\right)\left(x + \dfrac{1}{\sqrt{3}}\right) \leq 0$

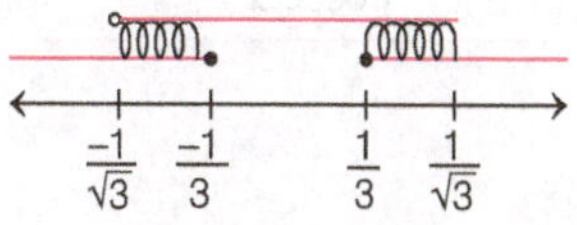

$\Rightarrow \quad x \in \left[-\dfrac{1}{\sqrt{3}}, \dfrac{-1}{3}\right] \cup \left[\dfrac{1}{3}, \dfrac{1}{\sqrt{3}}\right]$

Example 18. Find the complete set of values of a such that $\dfrac{x^2 - x}{1 - ax}$ attains all real values.

Sol. We have, $y = \dfrac{x^2 - x}{1 - ax} \Rightarrow x^2 - x = y - axy$

$\Rightarrow x^2 + x(ay - 1) - y = 0$

Since, x is real.

$\Rightarrow \quad (ay - 1)^2 + 4y \geq 0$

$\Rightarrow a^2y^2 + 2y(2 - a) + 1 \geq 0, \forall\ y \in R$

As, $\quad a^2 > 0, 4(2 - a)^2 - 4a^2 \leq 0 \Rightarrow 4 - 4a \leq 0 \Rightarrow a \in [1, \infty)$.

Example 19. Let $f: R \to R, f(x) = \dfrac{\alpha x^2 + 6x - 8}{\alpha + 6x - 8x^2}$. Then, find the value of α for $f(x)$ whose range is equal to codomain.

Sol. We have, $y = \dfrac{\alpha x^2 + 6x - 8}{\alpha + 6x - 8x^2}$

$\Rightarrow (\alpha + 8y)\, x^2 + 6(1 - y)x - (\alpha y + 8) = 0$

According to the condition, y takes all values for all real x i.e. $D \geq 0, \ \forall y \in R$.

$\Rightarrow \ 36(1 - y)^2 + 4(\alpha y + 8)(\alpha + 8y) \geq 0, \forall\ y \in R$

$\Rightarrow (9 + 8\alpha)y^2 + (\alpha + 46)y + (9 + 8\alpha) \geq 0, \forall\ y \in R$

i.e. $D \leq 0$ and coefficient of $y^2 > 0$

$\Rightarrow \quad (\alpha^2 + 46)^2 \leq 4(9 + 8\alpha)^2$ and $9 + 8\alpha > 0$

$\Rightarrow \alpha^2 - 16\alpha + 28 \leq 0$ and $\alpha > \dfrac{-9}{8}$

$\Rightarrow \quad 2 \leq \alpha \leq 14$ and $\alpha > \dfrac{-9}{8}$

Hence, $\alpha \in [2, 14]$.

2.8 Non-Algebraic Function (Transcendental Function)

A function which is not an algebraic function is known as non-algebraic or transcendental function. e.g. logarithmic function, trigonometric function etc.

Types of Non-algebraic Function

1. Trigonometric Function

There are six type for trigonometric functions, where angles are independent variable.

Trigonometric Function	Domain	Range	Period
$\sin x$	R	$[-1, 1]$	2π
$\cos x$	R	$[-1, 1]$	2π
$\tan x$	$R - \left\{\dfrac{(2n+1)\pi}{2}; n \in I\right\}$	R	π
$\cot x$	$R - \{n\pi : n \in I\}$	R	π
$\sec x$	$R - \left\{\dfrac{(2n+1)\pi}{2}; n \in I\right\}$	$(-\infty, -1] \cup [1, \infty)$	2π
$\text{cosec } x$	$R - \{n\pi : n \in I\}$	$(-\infty, -1] \cup [1, \infty)$	2π

Graph of Trigonometric Functions

(i) $y = \sin x$

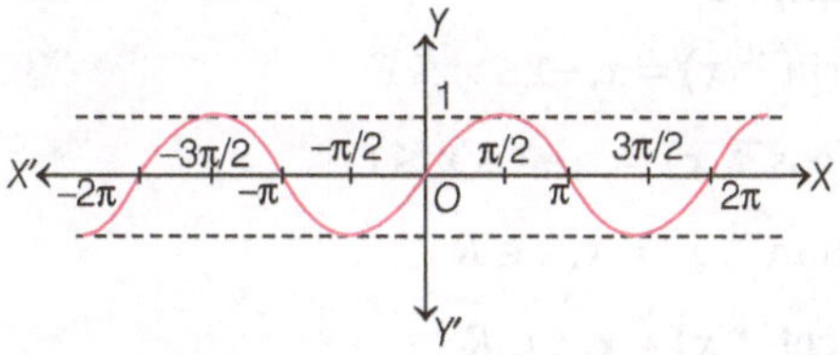

(ii) $y = \cos x$

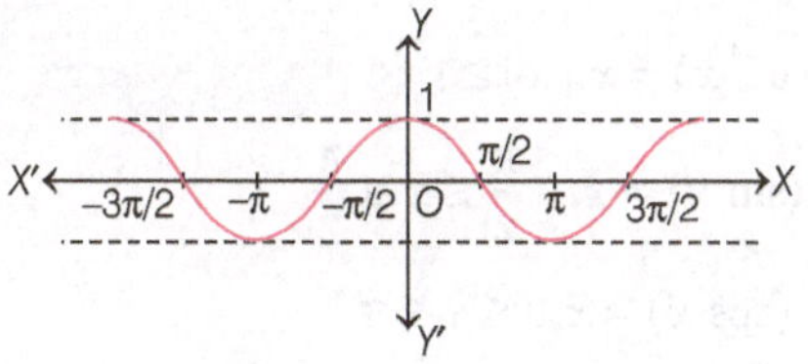

(iii) $y = \tan x$

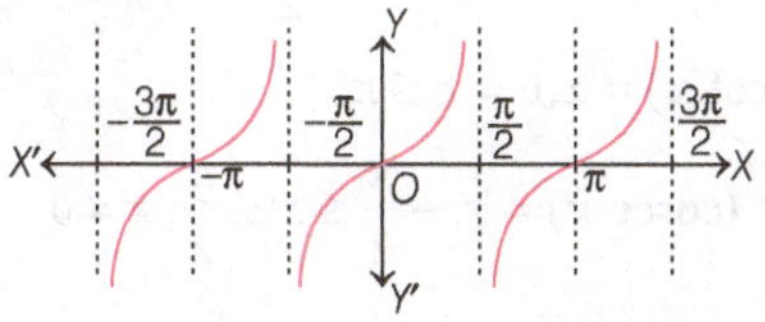

(iv) $y = \cot x$

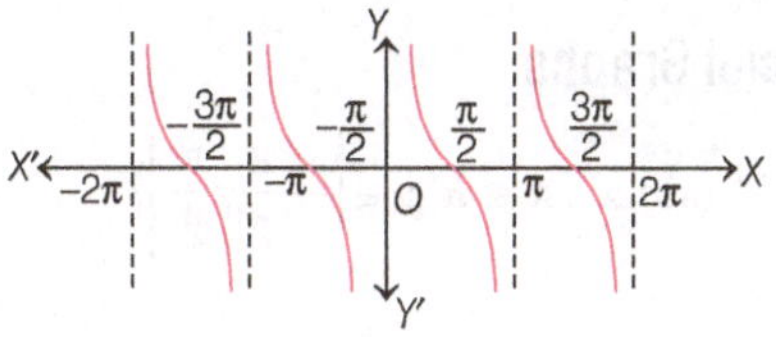

(v) $y = \sec x$

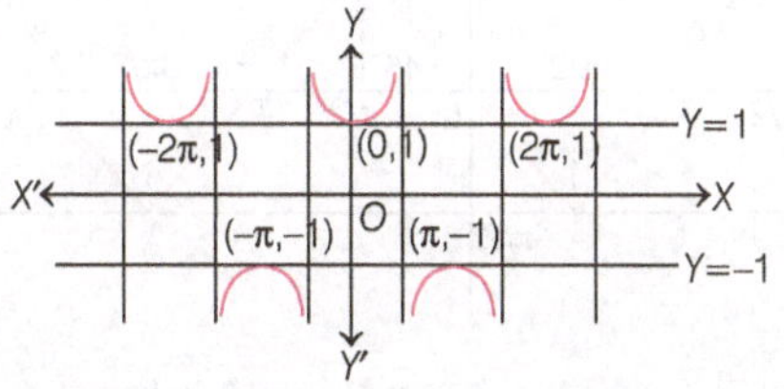

(vi) $y = \operatorname{cosec} x$

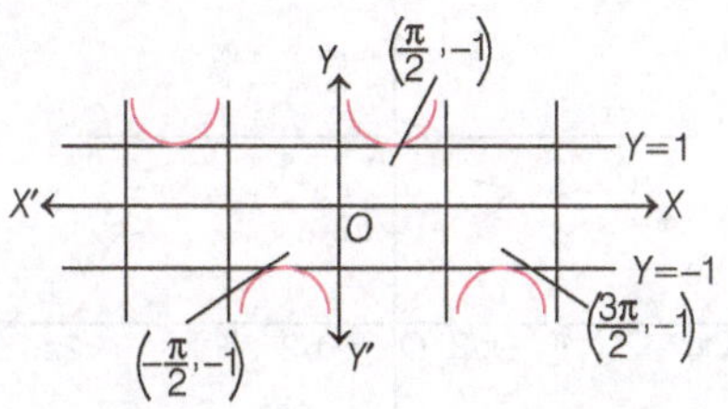

JEE Focus Points

- $f(x) = a\sin x + b\cos x$

$$= \sqrt{a^2+b^2}\,\sin(x+\alpha),\ \tan\alpha = \frac{b}{a}$$

$$= \sqrt{a^2+b^2}\,\cos(x-\beta),\ \tan\beta = \frac{a}{b}$$

Concept Inside Video

Proof $f(x) = a\sin x + b\cos x$

$$= \sqrt{a^2+b^2}\left(\frac{a}{\sqrt{a^2+b^2}}\sin x + \frac{b}{\sqrt{a^2+b^2}}\cos x\right)$$

[divide and multiply by $\sqrt{a^2+b^2}$]

$$= \sqrt{a^2+b^2}\,(\sin x\cos\alpha + \cos x\sin\alpha)$$

$$\left[\because \cos\alpha = \frac{a}{\sqrt{a^2+b^2}},\ \sin\alpha = \frac{b}{\sqrt{a^2+b^2}}\right]$$

$$= \sqrt{a^2+b^2}\,\sin(x+\alpha),\ \text{where } \tan\alpha = \frac{b}{a}$$

or $\quad f(x) = \sqrt{a^2+b^2}\,(\sin x\sin\beta + \cos x\cos\beta)$

$$= \sqrt{a^2+b^2}\,\cos(x-\beta),\ \text{where } \tan\beta = \frac{a}{b}$$

$$\left[\because \sin\beta = \frac{a}{\sqrt{a^2+b^2}},\ \cos\beta = \frac{b}{\sqrt{a^2+b^2}}\right]$$

- $-\sqrt{a^2+b^2} \le a\sin x + b\cos x \le \sqrt{a^2+b^2}$

Some useful properties of involving trigonometric function.

(i) $\sin(A \pm B) = \sin A\cos B \pm \cos A\sin B$

(ii) $\cos(A \pm B) = \cos A\cos B \mp \sin A\sin B$

(iii) $\tan(A \pm B) = \dfrac{\tan A \pm \tan B}{1 \mp \tan A\tan B}$

(iv) $\sin C + \sin D = 2\sin\left(\dfrac{C+D}{2}\right)\cos\left(\dfrac{C-D}{2}\right)$

(v) $\sin C - \sin D = 2\cos\left(\dfrac{C+D}{2}\right)\sin\left(\dfrac{C-D}{2}\right)$

(vi) $\cos C + \cos D = 2\cos\left(\dfrac{C+D}{2}\right)\cos\left(\dfrac{C-D}{2}\right)$

(vii) $\cos C - \cos D = 2\sin\left(\dfrac{C+D}{2}\right)\sin\left(\dfrac{D-C}{2}\right)$

(viii) $\sin 2\theta = 2\sin\theta\cos\theta = \dfrac{2\tan\theta}{1+\tan^2\theta}$

(ix) $\cos 2\theta = \cos^2\theta - \sin^2\theta = 2\cos^2\theta - 1$

$$= 1 - 2\sin^2\theta = \frac{1-\tan^2\theta}{1+\tan^2\theta}$$

(x) $1+\cos 2\theta = 2\cos^2\theta$ or $\cos\theta = \pm\sqrt{\dfrac{1+\cos 2\theta}{2}}$

(xi) $1-\cos 2\theta = 2\sin^2\theta$ or $\sin\theta = \pm\sqrt{\dfrac{1-\cos 2\theta}{2}}$

(xii) $\tan\theta = \dfrac{1-\cos 2\theta}{\sin 2\theta} = \dfrac{\sin 2\theta}{1+\cos 2\theta} = \pm\sqrt{\dfrac{1-\cos 2\theta}{1+\cos 2\theta}}$

(xiii) $\tan 2\theta = \dfrac{2\tan\theta}{1-\tan^2\theta}$

2. Inverse Trigonometric Functions

Some points and properties regarding ITF are given below

Function	Domain	Range
$y=\sin^{-1}x$	$-1\le x\le 1$	$-\dfrac{\pi}{2}\le y\le\dfrac{\pi}{2}$
$y=\cos^{-1}x$	$-1\le x\le 1$	$0\le y\le\pi$
$y=\tan^{-1}x$	$x\in R$	$-\dfrac{\pi}{2}<y<\dfrac{\pi}{2}$
$y=\cot^{-1}x$	$x\in R$	$0<y<\pi$
$y=\text{cosec}^{-1}x$	$x\le -1$ or $x\ge 1$	$-\dfrac{\pi}{2}\le y\le\dfrac{\pi}{2}, y\ne 0$
$y=\sec^{-1}x$	$x\le -1$ or $x\ge 1$	$0\le y\le\pi; y\ne\dfrac{\pi}{2}$

Graph of Inverse Trigonometric Functions

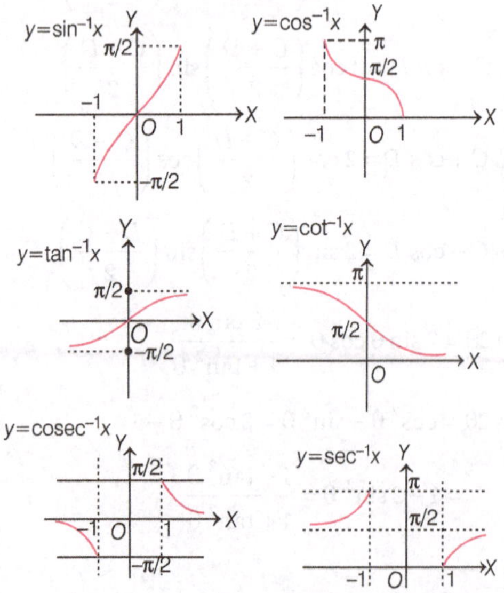

Properties Involving Inverse Trigonometric Function

PROPERTY 1

(i) $\sin(\sin^{-1}x)=x, -1\le x\le 1$

(ii) $\cos(\cos^{-1}x)=x, -1\le x\le 1$

(iii) $\tan(\tan^{-1}x)=x, x\in R$

(iv) $\cot(\cot^{-1}x)=x, x\in R$

(v) $\text{cosec}(\text{cosec}^{-1}x)=x, |x|\ge 1$

(vi) $\sec(\sec^{-1}x)=x, |x|\ge 1$

(vii) $\sin^{-1}(\sin x)=x, -\dfrac{\pi}{2}\le x\le\dfrac{\pi}{2}$

(viii) $\cos^{-1}(\cos x)=x, 0\le x\le\pi$

(ix) $\tan^{-1}(\tan x)=x, -\dfrac{\pi}{2}<x<\dfrac{\pi}{2}$

(x) $\cot^{-1}(\cot x)=x, 0<x\le\pi$

(xi) $\text{cosec}^{-1}(\text{cosec } x)=x, -\dfrac{\pi}{2}\le x\le\dfrac{\pi}{2}, x\ne 0$

(xii) $\sec^{-1}(\sec x)=x, 0\le x\le\pi, x\ne\dfrac{\pi}{2}$

Some Special Graphs

(i) $y=\sin^{-1}(\sin x), x\in R, y\in\left[-\dfrac{\pi}{2},\dfrac{\pi}{2}\right]$,

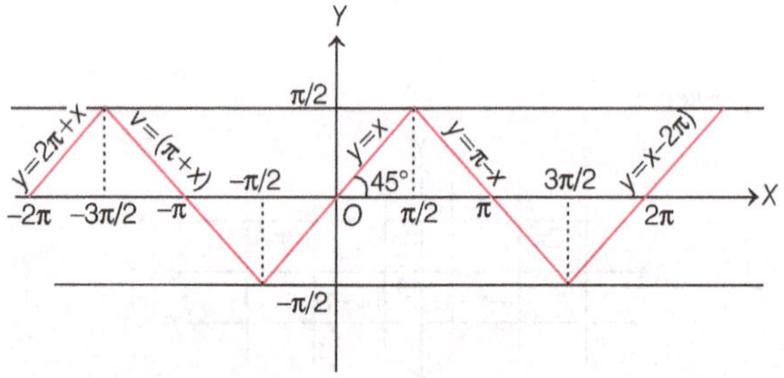

(ii) $y=\cos^{-1}(\cos x)=x, x\in R, y\in[0,\pi]$,

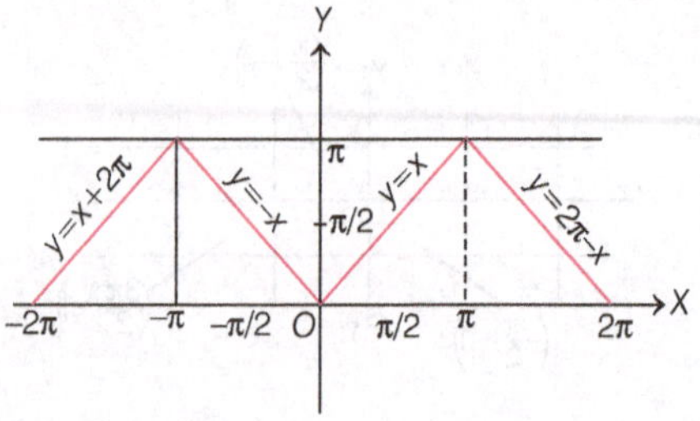

(iii) $y = \tan^{-1}(\tan x) = x,\ x \in R - \left\{(2n-1)\dfrac{\pi}{2}, n \in I\right\}$,

$y \in \left(-\dfrac{\pi}{2}, \dfrac{\pi}{2}\right)$,

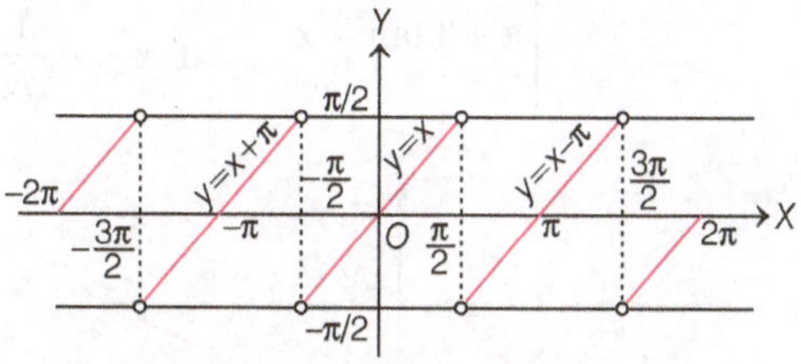

(iv) $y = \cot^{-1}(\cot x) = x,\ x \in R - \{n\pi\},\ y \in (0, \pi)$.

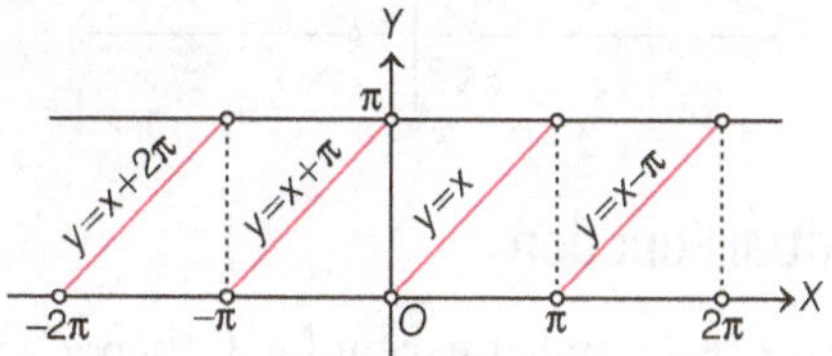

(v) $y = \operatorname{cosec}^{-1}(\operatorname{cosec} x),\ x \in R - \{n\pi, n \in I\}$,

$y \in \left[-\dfrac{\pi}{2}, 0\right) \cup \left(0, \dfrac{\pi}{2}\right]$

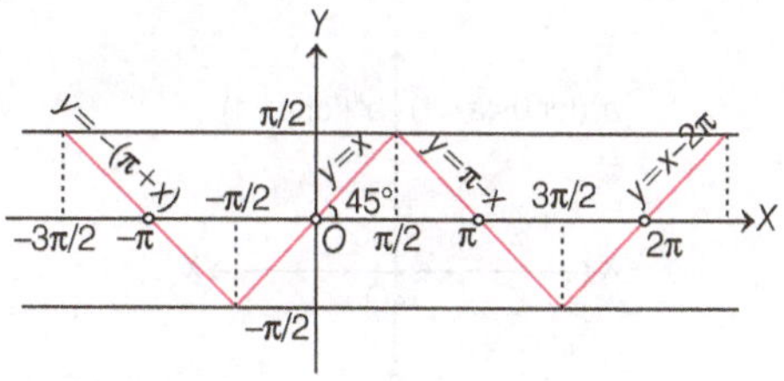

(vi) $y = \sec^{-1}(\sec x) = x$,

$x \in R - \left\{(2n-1)\dfrac{\pi}{2}\ n \in I\right\},\ y \in \left[0, \dfrac{\pi}{2}\right) \cup \left(\dfrac{\pi}{2}, \pi\right]$

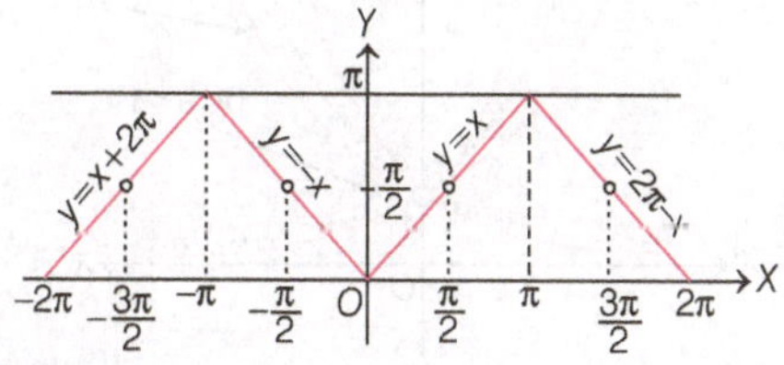

PROPERTY 2

(i) $\sin^{-1}(-x) = -\sin^{-1}x,\ -1 \le x \le 1$

(ii) $\tan^{-1}(-x) = -\tan^{-1}x,\ x \in R$

(iii) $\cos^{-1}(-x) = \pi - \cos^{-1}x,\ -1 \le x \le 1$

(iv) $\cot^{-1}(-x) = \pi - \cot^{-1}x,\ x \in R$

(v) $\operatorname{cosec}^{-1}(-x) = -\operatorname{cosec}^{-1}x,\ |x| \ge 1$

(vi) $\sec^{-1}(-x) = \pi - \sec^{-1}x,\ |x| \ge 1$

PROPERTY 3

(i) $\sin^{-1}x + \cos^{-1}x = \dfrac{\pi}{2},\ -1 \le x \le 1$

(ii) $\tan^{-1}x + \cot^{-1}x = \dfrac{\pi}{2},\ x \in R$

(iii) $\operatorname{cosec}^{-1}x + \sec^{-1}x = \dfrac{\pi}{2},\ |x| \ge 1$

PROPERTY 4

(i) $\tan^{-1}x + \tan^{-1}y$

$$= \begin{cases} \tan^{-1}\left(\dfrac{x+y}{1-xy}\right), & \text{if } xy < 1 \\ \pi + \tan^{-1}\left(\dfrac{x+y}{1-xy}\right), & \text{if } x > 0, y > 0 \text{ and } xy > 1 \\ -\pi + \tan^{-1}\left(\dfrac{x+y}{1-xy}\right), & \text{if } x < 0, y < 0, \text{ and } xy > 1 \end{cases}$$

(ii) $x > 0$ and $y > 0$, $\tan^{-1}x - \tan^{-1}y = \tan^{-1}\dfrac{x-y}{1+xy}$

(with no other restriction)

PROPERTY 5

(i) $$\sin^{-1}\frac{2x}{1+x^2} = \begin{cases} 2\tan^{-1}x, & \text{if } -1 \le x \le 1 \\ \pi - 2\tan^{-1}x, & \text{if } x \ge 1 \\ -\pi - 2\tan^{-1}x, & \text{if } x \le -1 \end{cases}$$

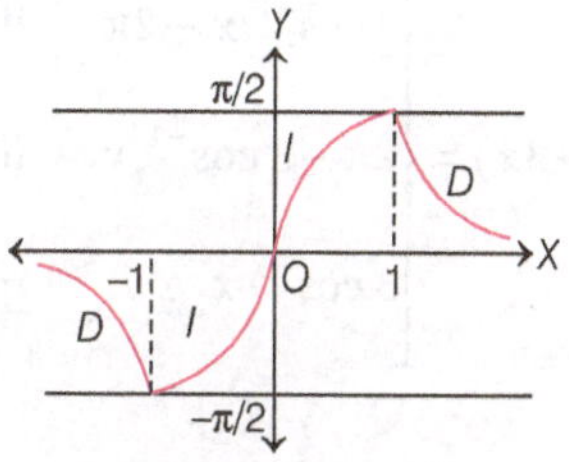

(ii) $$\cos^{-1}\frac{1-x^2}{1+x^2} = \begin{cases} 2\tan^{-1}x, & x \ge 0 \\ -2\tan^{-1}x, & x < 0 \end{cases}$$

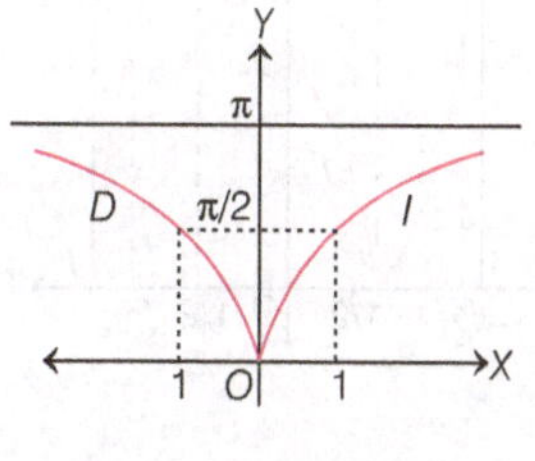

(iii) $\tan^{-1}\dfrac{2x}{1-x^2}=\begin{cases}\pi+2\tan^{-1}x, & x<-1\\ 2\tan^{-1}x, & -1<x<1\\ 2\tan^{-1}x-\pi, & x>1\end{cases}$

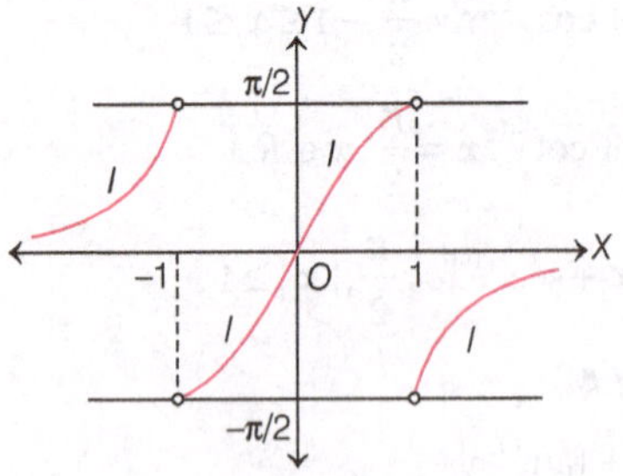

(iv) $\sin^{-1}(3x-4x^3)=\begin{cases}-(\pi+3\sin^{-1}x), & \text{if } -1\le x\le -\dfrac{1}{2}\\ 3\sin^{-1}x, & \text{if } -\dfrac{1}{2}\le x\le \dfrac{1}{2}\\ \pi-3\sin^{-1}x, & \text{if } \dfrac{1}{2}\le x\le 1\end{cases}$

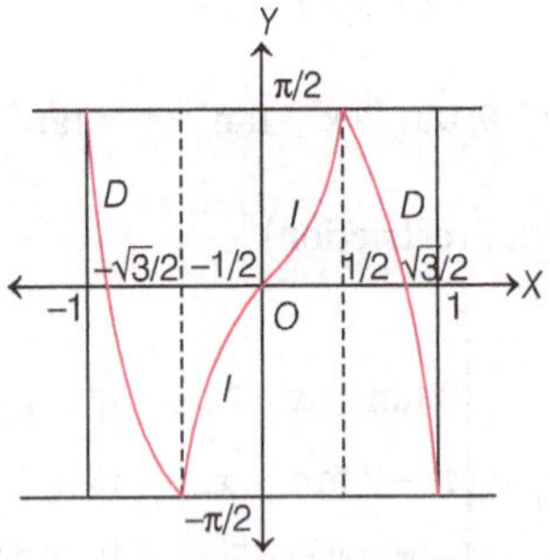

(v) $\cos^{-1}(4x^3-3x)=\begin{cases}3\cos^{-1}x-2\pi, & \text{if } -1\le x\le -\dfrac{1}{2}\\ 2\pi-3\cos^{-1}x, & \text{if } -\dfrac{1}{2}\le x\le \dfrac{1}{2}\\ 3\cos^{-1}x, & \text{if } \dfrac{1}{2}\le x\le 1\end{cases}$

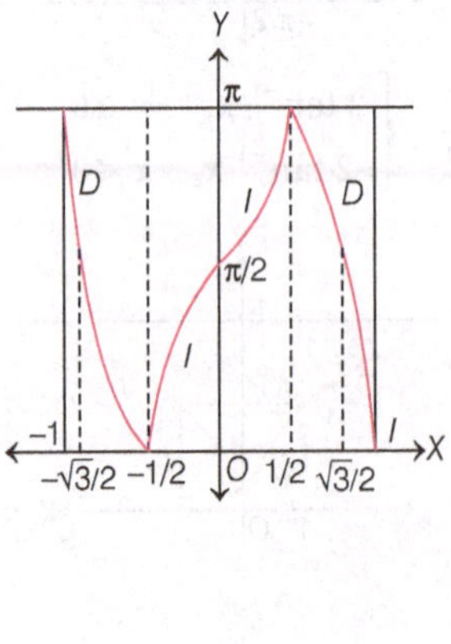

(vi) $\tan^{-1}\dfrac{3x-x^3}{1-3x^2}=\begin{cases}3\tan^{-1}x, & \text{if } -\dfrac{1}{\sqrt{3}}<x<\dfrac{1}{\sqrt{3}}\\ -\pi+3\tan^{-1}x, & \text{if } x>\dfrac{1}{\sqrt{3}}\\ \pi+3\tan^{-1}x, & \text{if } x<-\dfrac{1}{\sqrt{3}}\end{cases}$

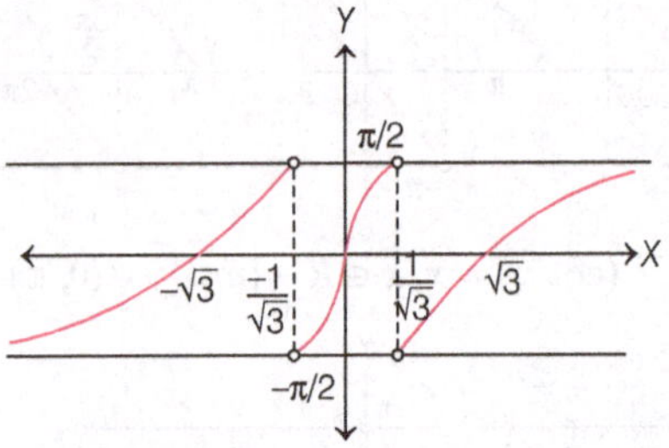

3. Exponential Function

If a is positive real number except for 1, then a^x, where $x\in R$ is always positive and it is called exponential function of x, a is called base and x is called index.

The graph of exponential functions are as shown in Figure.

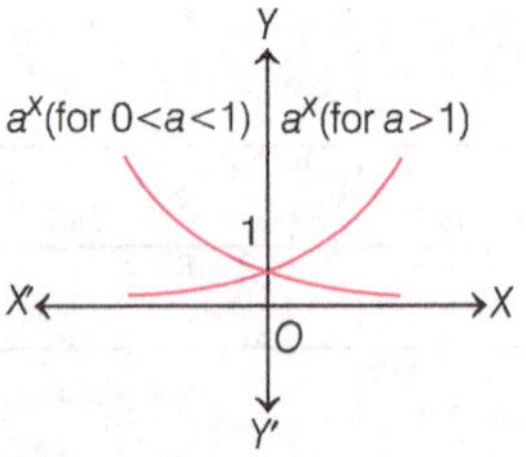

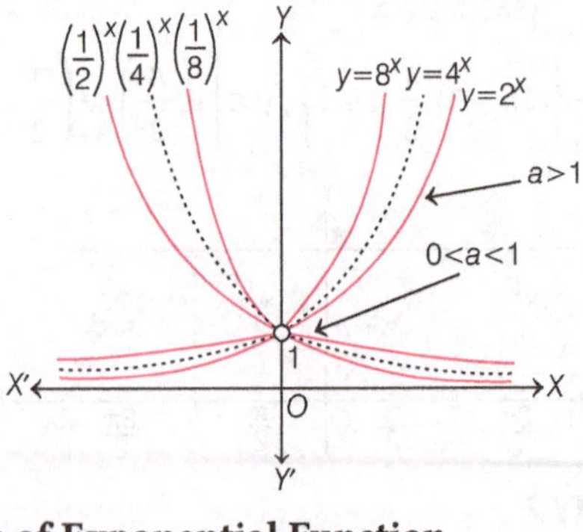

Properties of Exponential Function

(i) Domain of exponential function $y=a^x$; $D_f:(-\infty,\infty)$

Range of exponential function $=R_f:(0,\infty)$

$\because\ a^x$ is defined, $\forall\ x\in R$ and $a^x>0$

(ii) $\left.\begin{array}{l} f(x+y)=f(x)\cdot f(y) \\ f(x-y)=f(x)/f(y) \end{array}\right\}, \forall\, x, y \in R$

Proof $f(x)\cdot f(y)=a^x\cdot a^y=a^{x+y}=f(x+y)$

and $\dfrac{f(x)}{f(y)}=\dfrac{a^x}{a^y}=a^{x-y}=f(x-y)$

(iii) $a^x\cdot b^x=(ab)^x$ and $\dfrac{a^x}{b^x}=\left(\dfrac{a}{b}\right)^x$

(iv) $(a^x)^y=a^{xy}=(a^y)^x$

4. Logarithmic Function

Logarithm of a positive number x to the base a is defined as a number y, which when raised to base a the resulting number becomes equal to x.

i.e. $\log_a x=y \Leftrightarrow a^y=x$ when $a>0$ and $a\neq 1, x>0$ as a^y is positive.

e.g. $\log_7 49=2$ as $(7)^2=49$,

$\log_3 81=4$ as $(3)^4=81$,

Since, logarithmic function $y=\log_a x$ is defined only for positive real numbers and hence, its domain is $(0, \infty)$.

Its range is R, set of real numbers.

In general, $y=\log_a x$ is an increasing function for $a>1$ as it has been illustrated below for $y=\log_2 x$

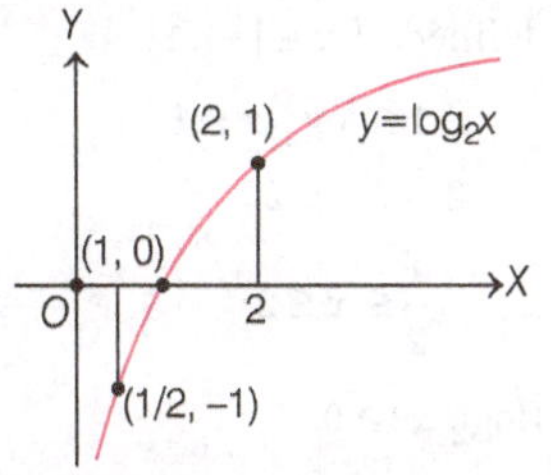

and in general, logarithmic function is a decreasing function for $a\in(0,1)$ as it has been illustrated below for $y=\log_{1/2} x$

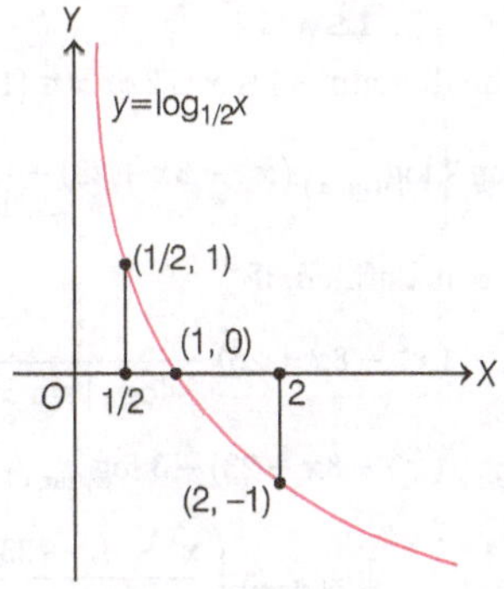

x	$\frac{1}{16}$	$\frac{1}{8}$	$\frac{1}{4}$	$\frac{1}{2}$	1	2	4	8
$\log_2 x$	–4	–3	–2	–1	0	1	2	3
$\log_{1/2} x$	4	3	2	1	0	–1	–2	–3

Example 20. Find the domain of definitions of the following functions.

(i) $f(x)=\cos^{-1}2x+\sqrt{16-x^2}$

(ii) $f(x)=\log_7\log_5\log_3\log_2(2x^3+5x^2-14x)$

(iii) $f(x)=\log(\sqrt{x^2-5x-24}-x-2)$

(iv) $f(x)=\sqrt{\dfrac{1-5^x}{7^{-x}-7}}$

(v) $y=\log_{10}\sin(x-3)+\sqrt{16-x^2}$

(vi) $f(x)=\sqrt{(x^2-3x-10)\cdot\ln^2(x-3)}$

(vii) $f(x)=\sqrt{\sin^{-1}(\log_2 x)}$

(viii) $f(x)=\log\left\{\log_{|\sin x|}(x^2-8x+23)-\dfrac{3}{\log_2|\sin x|}\right\}$

(ix) $f(x)=\log(\sqrt{10\cdot 3^{x-2}-9^{x-1}-1})+\sqrt{\cos^{-1}(1-x)}$

Sol. (i) $f(x)=\cos^{-1}2x+\sqrt{16-x^2}$

$\Rightarrow \quad -\dfrac{\pi}{2}\le 2x\le\dfrac{\pi}{2} \Rightarrow 2k\pi-\dfrac{\pi}{2}\le 2x\le\dfrac{\pi}{2}+2k\pi$

$\Rightarrow k\pi-\dfrac{\pi}{4}\le x\le\dfrac{\pi}{4}+k\pi, k\in I$

$D_2: 16-x^2>0, x\in[-4, 4]$

$\therefore \quad D_1\cap D_2$

$\Rightarrow\left[-\dfrac{\pi}{4},\dfrac{\pi}{4}\right]\cup\left[\dfrac{3\pi}{4},\dfrac{5\pi}{4}\right]\cup\left[-\dfrac{5\pi}{4},-\dfrac{3\pi}{4}\right]$

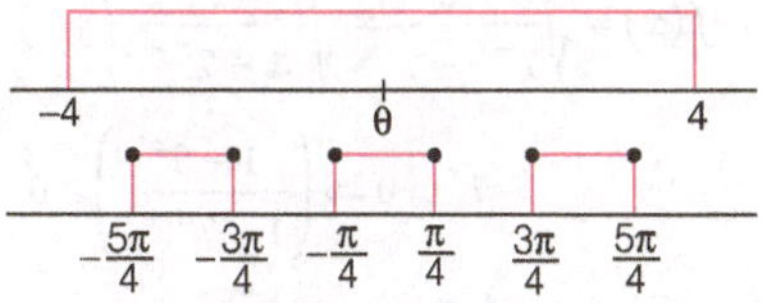

(ii) **Decoding the Question**

$\log_a x=y$

$a^y=x$, where $a>0$ and $a\neq 1, x>0$

$f(x)=\log_7\log_5\log_3\log_2(2x^3+5x^2-14x)$

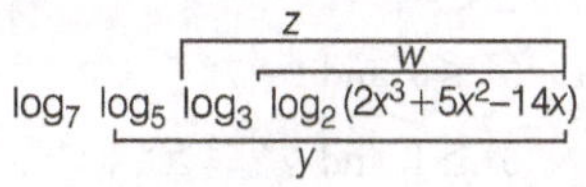

$\Rightarrow \log_3 \log_2 (2x^3 + 5x^2 - 14x) > 1$

$\Rightarrow \quad \log_2 (2x^3 + 5x^2 - 14x) > 3$

$\Rightarrow \quad 2x^3 + 5x^2 - 14x > 8$

$\Rightarrow \quad 2x^3 + 5x^2 - 14x - 8 > 0$

$\Rightarrow \quad (x-2)(2x+1)(x+4) > 0$

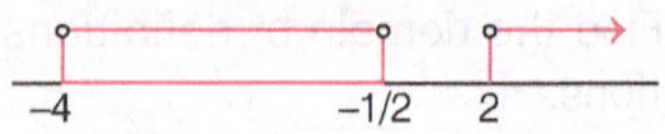

$\therefore \; x \in \left(-4, -\dfrac{1}{2}\right) \cup (2, \infty)$

(iii) $f(x) = \log(\sqrt{x^2 - 5x - 24} - x - 2)$

$\sqrt{x^2 - 5x - 24} > x + 2,$

if $x^2 - 5x - 24 \ge 0$ and $x + 2 < 0$

(1) $(x-8)(x+3) \ge 0$

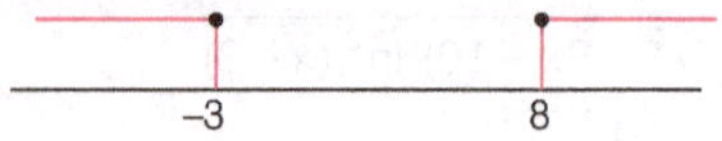

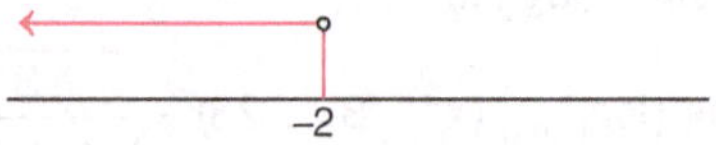

$x \in (8, \infty) \cup [-3, -\infty)$

and $x < -2 \Rightarrow (-\infty, -3]$

(2) $x^2 - 5x - 24 \ge 0$ and $x + 2 \ge 0$

and $x^2 - 5x - 24 > (x+2)^2$

$x^2 - 5x - 24 > x^2 + 4x + 4 \Rightarrow 9x + 28 < 0$

$x < -\dfrac{28}{9}$

$\therefore$ (1) $\cup$ (2) $\Rightarrow x \in (-\infty, -3]$

(iv) $f(x) = \sqrt{\dfrac{1 - 5^x}{7^{-x} - 7}}$

$(N^r \ge 0 \text{ and } D^r > 0) \cup (N^r \le 0 \text{ and } D^r < 0)$

$f(x) = \sqrt{\dfrac{1 - 5^x}{7^{-x} - 7}} = \sqrt{\dfrac{7^x(1 - 5^x)}{1 - 7^{x+1}}}$

$7^x > 0 \Rightarrow \left(\dfrac{1 - 5^x}{1 - 7^{x+1}}\right) \ge 0$

Case I $1 - 5^x \ge 0$ and $1 - 7^{x+1} > 0$

$5^x \le 1$ and $7^{x+1} < 1$

$x \le 0$ and $x + 1 < 0$ ...(i)

$x < -1$ ...(ii)

Eqs. (i) $\cap$ (ii), we get

$x < -1$

Case II $1 - 5^x \le 0$ and $1 - 7^{x+1} < 0$

$5^x \ge 1$ and $7^{x+1} \ge 1$

$x \ge 0$ ...(iii)

and $x + 1 > 0$

$\Rightarrow \quad x > -1$ ...(iv)

Eqs. (iii) $\cap$ (iv), we get

$x \ge 0$

$\therefore$ Case I $\cup$ Case II

$x \in (-\infty, -1) \cup [0, \infty)$

(v) $f(x) = \log_{10} \sin(x - 3) + \sqrt{16 - x^2}$

$D_1 : \sin(x-3) > 0 \Rightarrow 0 < x - 3 < \pi$

$\Rightarrow \quad 2k\pi < x - 3 < (2k+1)\pi$

$\Rightarrow 3 + 2k\pi < x < 3 + (2k+1)\pi$

$D_2 : x \in [-4, 4]$

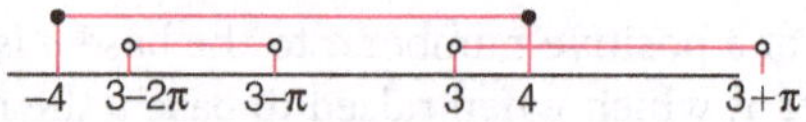

$(3 - 2\pi, 3 - \pi) \cup (3, 4]$

(vi) $f(x) = \sqrt{(x^2 - 3x - 10)\ln^2(x-3)}$

$f(x) = \sqrt{(x-5)(x+2)\ln^2(x-3)}$

$(x-5)(x+2)\ln^2(x-3) \ge 0$ and $x > 3$

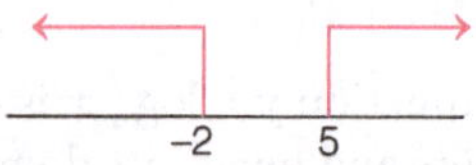

At $x = 4 \Rightarrow \ln(x-3) = 0$

$\therefore \quad [5, \infty) \cup \{4\}$

(vii) $f(x) = \sqrt{\sin^{-1}(\log_2 x)}$

$\sin^{-1} x$ is defined, if $x \in [-1, 1]$ ...(i)

$\therefore \quad -1 \le \log_2 x \le 1$

$\Rightarrow \quad 2^{-1} \le x \le 2$

$\Rightarrow \quad \dfrac{1}{2} \le x \le 2$ ...(ii)

and $\sin^{-1}(\log_2 x) \ge 0$ ...(iii)

$\Rightarrow \quad \log_2 x \ge 0 \Rightarrow x \ge 2^0$

$\Rightarrow \quad x \ge 1$ ...(iv)

From Eqs. (i), (ii) and (iv), we get

$1 \le x \le 2$

Hence, the domain is $1 \le x \le 2$ or $x \in [1, 2]$.

(viii) $f(x) = \log\left\{\log_{(\sin x)}(x^2 - 8x + 23) - \dfrac{3}{\log_2 |\sin x|}\right\}$

Here, $f(x)$ is defined, if

$\log_{|\sin x|}(x^2 - 8x + 23) - \dfrac{3}{\log_2 |\sin x|} > 0$

$\Rightarrow \log_{|\sin x|}(x^2 - 8x + 23) - 3\log_{|\sin x|} 2 > 0$

$\Rightarrow \quad \log_{|\sin x|}\left(\dfrac{x^2 - 8x + 23}{8}\right) > 0$

$$\Rightarrow \quad \frac{x^2 - 8x + 23}{8} < |\sin x|^0$$

and $|\sin x| \neq 0, 1$

$\Rightarrow \; x^2 - 8x + 23 < 8$ and $|\sin x| \neq 0, 1$

$\Rightarrow \; x^2 - 8x + 15 < 0$ and $\sin x \neq 0, \pm 1$

$\Rightarrow \; (x-3)(x-5) < 0$ and $x \neq n\pi, (2n+1)\frac{\pi}{2}$

$\Rightarrow \; x \in (3, 5)$ and $x \neq \pi, \frac{3\pi}{2}$ [using number line rule]

$\Rightarrow \; x \in (3, \pi) \cup \left(\pi, \frac{3\pi}{2}\right) \cup \left(\frac{3\pi}{2}, 5\right)$

Thus, domain of $f(x)$ is $(3, \pi) \cup \left(\pi, \frac{3\pi}{2}\right) \cup \left(\frac{3\pi}{2}, 5\right)$.

(ix) We have for $\cos^{-1}(1-x) \geq 0$

$\Rightarrow \quad -1 \leq (1-x) \leq 1 \Rightarrow -2 \leq -x \leq 0$

$\Rightarrow \quad 0 \leq x \leq 2$ ...(i)

Also, $10 \cdot 3^{x-2} - 9^{x-1} - 1 > 0$

$$10 \cdot 3^x - 9^x - 9 > 0$$

$$10 \cdot 3^x - 3^{2x} - 9 > 0$$

$$3^{2x} - 10 \cdot 3^x + 9 < 0$$

$$(3^x - 1)(3^x - 9) < 0$$

$1 < 3^x < 9 \Rightarrow 0 < x < 2$ ...(ii)

From Eqs. (i) and (ii), we get

$$0 < x < 2$$

Example 21. Find the range of following

(i) $f(x) = \dfrac{e^x (\log x) 5^{(x^2+2)} (x^2 - 7x + 10)}{2x^2 - 11x + 12}$

(ii) $f(x) = \sin^{-1} x^2 + [\{\log \sqrt{x - [x]}\}] + \cot^{-1}\left(\dfrac{1}{1 + \sqrt{2}x^2}\right)$

(iii) $f(x) = 3 - 4\sin x$

(iv) $f(x) = \dfrac{1}{2 - 5\sin x}$

(v) $f(x) = \cos^{-1}\left(\dfrac{\sqrt{2x^2+1}}{x^2+1}\right)$

(vi) $g(x) = \log_2(2 - \log_{\sqrt{2}}(4\cos^2 x + 1))$

(vii) $f(x) = \sin^{-1} x^4 + [\{\ln \sqrt{x - [x]}\}] + \cot^{-1}\left(\dfrac{1}{2 + \sqrt{3}x^2}\right)$,

where $\{\cdot\}$ and $[\cdot]$ are fractional part function and greatest integer function, respectively.

(viii) $f(x) = \dfrac{1}{x^5 - x^3 + x^2 - 1}$

(ix) $f(x) = \log_3 \{\log_{1/2}(x^2 + 4x + 4)\}$

(x) $f(x) = \sin^2 x - 5\sin x - 6$

Sol. (i) $f(x) = \dfrac{e^x (\log x) 5^{(x^2+2)} \cdot (x-2)(x-5)}{(2x-3)(x-4)}$

Note that at $x = \frac{3}{2}$ and $x = 4$ function is not defined and in open interval $\left(\frac{3}{2}, 4\right)$ function is continuous.

$$\lim_{x \to \frac{3}{2}^+} = \frac{(+\text{ve})(-\text{ve})(-\text{ve})}{(+\text{ve})(-\text{ve})} \to -\infty$$

$$\lim_{x \to 4^-} = \frac{(+\text{ve})(+\text{ve})(-\text{ve})}{(+\text{ve})(-\text{ve})} \to \infty$$

In the open interval $\left(\frac{3}{2}, 4\right)$, the function is continuous and takes up all real values from $(-\infty, \infty)$.

Hence, the range of the function is $(-\infty, \infty)$ or R.

(ii) Domain of function is $(-1, 1) - \{0\}$ because $x - [x] = 0$ for integral value of x, hence middle term will not be defined.

Also, $[\{f\}] = 0$, whenever f is meaningful.

$\therefore$ Value of $f(x) = \sin^{-1} x^2 + \tan^{-1}(1 + \sqrt{2}x^2)$

$\left(\cot^{-1} x = \tan^{-1}\frac{1}{x} \text{ when } x > 0\right)$

Function is continuous and is even for $x \in (-1, 1) - \{0\}$.

Also, $f(x)$ is decreasing on $(-1, 0)$ and increasing on $(0, 1)$

$\therefore$ Least value of the function will occur when $x \to 0$ and is $\frac{\pi}{4}$

and maximum value $= \lim_{x \to +1} f(x)$

$$= \sin^{-1} 1 + \tan^{-1}(1 + \sqrt{2})$$

$$= \frac{\pi}{2} + \frac{3\pi}{8} = \frac{7\pi}{8}$$

$\therefore$ Range of $f(x)$ is $\left(\frac{\pi}{4}, \frac{7\pi}{8}\right)$; Domain is $(-1, 1) - \{0\}$.

(iii) $f(x) = 3 - 4\sin x$ is defined for all those real values of x for which $\sin x$ is defined

$\Rightarrow$ Domain of function $- R - (-\infty, \infty)$

Also, $-1 \leq \sin x \leq 1 \Rightarrow -4 \leq -4\sin x \leq 4$

$\Rightarrow \quad -1 \leq 3 - 4\sin x \leq 7$

$\Rightarrow$ Range of $f(x) = [-1, 7]$

(iv) $f(x) = \dfrac{1}{2 - 5\sin x}$

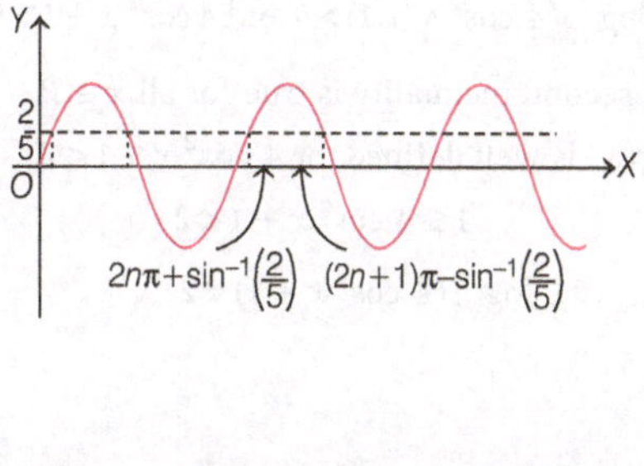

For $f(x)$ to be defined $\sin x \neq \frac{2}{5}$. From the graph of $\sin x$ given above, we conclude that $\sin x \neq \frac{2}{5}$

$\Rightarrow x \neq 2n\pi + \sin^{-1}\left(\frac{2}{5}\right), (2n+1)\pi - \sin^{-1}\left(\frac{2}{5}\right); n \in Z$

$\therefore$ Domain

$= R \sim \left\{2n\pi + \sin^{-1}\left(\frac{2}{5}\right), (2n+1)\pi - \sin^{-1}\left(\frac{2}{5}\right); n \in Z\right\}$

Clearly, $-1 \le \sin x \le 1$

$\Rightarrow \quad -5 \le -5\sin x \le 5 \Rightarrow -3 \le 2 - 5\sin x \le 7$

But $\sin x \neq \frac{2}{5}$

$\Rightarrow 2 - 5\sin x \in [-3, 7] \sim \{0\}$

$\Rightarrow \frac{1}{2 - 5\sin x} \in \left(-\infty, -\frac{1}{3}\right] \cup \left[\frac{1}{7}, \infty\right)$

$\therefore$ Range $= \left(-\infty, -\frac{1}{3}\right] \cup \left[\frac{1}{7}, \infty\right)$

(v) **Decoding the Question**

If $\sin\theta = x$, then $\cos\theta = \sqrt{1-x^2} \Rightarrow \sin^{-1} x = \cos^{-1}\sqrt{1-x^2}$

Given, $f(x) = \cos^{-1}\left(\frac{\sqrt{2x^2+1}}{x^2+1}\right)$

$= \sin^{-1}\left(\sqrt{1 - \frac{(2x^2+1)}{(x^2+1)^2}}\right)$

$= \sin^{-1}\left(\sqrt{\frac{x^4}{(x^2+1)^2}}\right) = \sin^{-1}\left(\frac{x^2}{1+x^2}\right)$

Now, $\frac{x^2}{x^2+1} = 1 - \frac{1}{x^2+1}$ and $x^2 + 1 \ge 1$

$\Rightarrow \quad \frac{1}{x^2+1} \in (0, 1] \Rightarrow 1 - \frac{1}{x^2+1} \in [0, 1)$

$\Rightarrow \quad 0 \le \sin^{-1}\left(\frac{x^2}{x^2+1}\right) < \frac{\pi}{2} \Rightarrow y \in \left[0, \frac{\pi}{2}\right)$

The range of $f(x) = \left[0, \frac{\pi}{2}\right)$

(vi) Given, $g(x) = \log_2(2 - \log_{\sqrt{2}}(4\cos^2 x + 1))$

Now, for $g(x)$ to be well defined,

$2 - \log_{\sqrt{2}}(4\cos^2 x + 1) > 0$ and $4\cos^2 x + 1 > 0$

The second inequality is true for all $x \in R$.

$\Rightarrow g(x)$ is well defined for $4\cos^2 x + 1 < 2$,

i.e. $\quad 1 \le 4\cos^2 x + 1 < 2$

$\Rightarrow \quad 0 \le \log_{\sqrt{2}}(4\cos^2 x + 1) < 2$

$\Rightarrow \quad -2 < -\log_{\sqrt{2}}(4\cos^2 x + 1) \le 0$

$\Rightarrow \quad 0 < 2 - \log_{\sqrt{2}}(4\cos^2 x + 1) \le 2$

$\Rightarrow \quad -\infty < g(x) \le \log_2 2$

$\Rightarrow \quad g(x) \in (-\infty, 1]$

Range of $g(x)$ is $(-\infty, 1]$.

(vii) $\sin^{-1} x^4$ is defined for $x^4 \in [-1, 1]$

$\Rightarrow x^4 \in [0, 1] \Rightarrow x \in [-1, 1]$

and $\cot^{-1}\left(\frac{1}{2+\sqrt{3}x^2}\right)$ is defined $\forall\ x \in R$ but

$\log\sqrt{x - [x]} = \log\sqrt{\{x\}}$ is not defined for $\{x\} = 0$ i.e. $x = -1, 0, 1$

Domain of given function is $(-1, 1) \sim \{0\}$

Now, $[\{\ln\sqrt{x - [x]}\}] = 0$, since $[\{k\}] = 0$ whenever k is defined.

$\therefore\ f(x) = \sin^{-1} x^4 + \cot^{-1}\left(\frac{1}{2+\sqrt{3}x^2}\right); x \in (-1, 1) \sim \{0\}$

or $f(x) = \sin^{-1} x^4 + \tan^{-1}(2 + \sqrt{3}x^2)$

$\left[\because \cot^{-1}\frac{1}{x} = \tan^{-1} x \text{ for } x > 0\right]$

Further $\sin^{-1} x^4$ and $\tan^{-1}(2 + \sqrt{3}x^2)$ are even continuous functions and decreasing for $x \in (-1, 0)$ and increasing for $x \in (0, 1)$.

Thus, $f(x)_{\min} \to f(0) = \sin^{-1}0 + \tan^{-1}2 = \tan^{-1}2$

and $f(x)_{\max} \to f(\pm 1) = \sin^{-1} 1 + \tan^{-1}(2 + \sqrt{3})$

$= \frac{\pi}{2} + \frac{5\pi}{12}$

$= \frac{11\pi}{12}$

$\therefore$ The range of $f(x)$ is $\left(\tan^{-1} 2, \frac{11\pi}{12}\right)$.

(viii) Given, function $f(x) = \frac{1}{x^5 - x^3 + x^2 - 1}$

$= \frac{1}{x^3(x^2-1) + 1(x^2-1)}$

$= \frac{1}{(x^2-1)(x^3+1)}$

$= \frac{1}{(x^2-1)(x+1)(x^2-x+1)}$

Therefore, domain of $f(x) = R - \{-1, 1\}$ as $x^2 - x + 1 > 0, \forall\ x \in R$

Also, range of $x^5 - x^3 + x^2 - 1$ is $(-\infty, \infty)$, therefore range $= (-\infty, \infty) - \{0\}$.

(ix) $f(x) = \log_3 \{\log_{1/2}(x^2 + 4x + 4)\}$

Firstly, finding the domain

$$\log_{1/2}(x^2 + 4x + 4) > 0$$

$$x^2 + 4x + 4 < 1$$

$$\Rightarrow \quad x^2 + 4x + 3 < 0$$

$$\Rightarrow \quad (x+1)(x+3) < 0$$

$$\Rightarrow \quad -3 < x < -1$$

Also, $x^2 + 4x + 4 > 0$

$$(x+2)^2 > 0$$

$$\Rightarrow \quad x \neq -2$$

Hence, $x \in (-3, -1) - \{2\}$

Since, $0 < \log_{1/2}(x^2 + 4x + 4) < \infty, \forall\ x \in$ domain, thus

Range $\in R$

(x) $f(x) = \sin^2 x - 5 \sin x - 6$

$$= \sin^2 x - 2\left(\frac{5}{2}\right)\sin x + \frac{25}{4} - 6 - \frac{25}{4}$$

$$= \left(\sin x - \frac{5}{2}\right)^2 - \frac{49}{4}$$

where, $\frac{9}{4} \le \left(\sin x - \frac{5}{2}\right)^2 \le \frac{49}{4}$

Hence, $f(x) \in [-10, 0]$.

2.9 Piecewise Function

A function is said to be piecewise function, if it defines differently for different interval of its domain.

Types of Piecewise Function

1. Modulus Function

A function $f : R \to R$ is defined as

$$f(x) = |x| = \begin{cases} x & : x \ge 0 \\ -x & : x < 0 \end{cases}$$

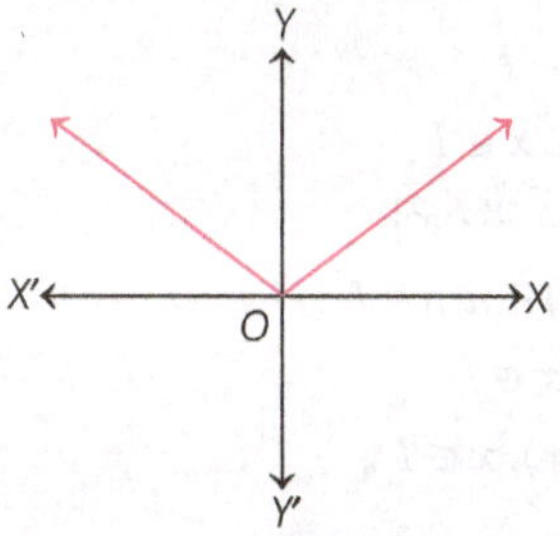

Note Properties of modulus already discussed.

$$D_f = R \text{ and } R_f = [0, \infty)$$

2. Signum Function (Sign function/sgn function)

A function $f : R \to R$ is defined as $f(x) = \text{sgn}(x)$

$$= \begin{cases} \frac{|x|}{x} & : x \ne 0 \\ 0 & : x = 0 \end{cases} \text{ or } \begin{cases} \frac{x}{|x|} & : x \ne 0 \\ 0 & : x = 0 \end{cases}$$

$$= \begin{cases} 1 & : x > 0 \\ 0 & : x = 0 \\ -1 & : x < 0 \end{cases}$$

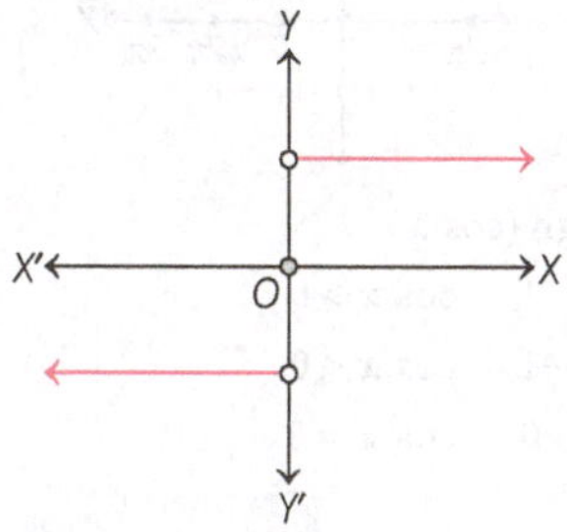

$$D_f = R \text{ and } R_f = \{-1, 0, 1\}$$

Example 22. Sketch the graph of

(i) $f(x) = \text{sgn}(x^2 + 1)$ (ii) $f(x) = \text{sgn}(\log_e x)$

(iii) $f(x) = \text{sgn}(\sin x)$ (iv) $f(x) = \text{sgn}(\cos x)$

Sol. (i) $f(x) = \text{sgn}(x^2 + 1) = \begin{cases} -1, & \text{if } x^2 + 1 < 0 \\ 0, & \text{if } x^2 + 1 = 0 \\ 1, & \text{if } x^2 + 1 > 0 \end{cases}$

$\therefore\ f(x) = 1, x \in R$

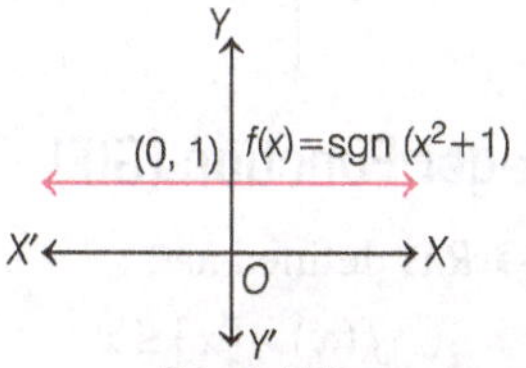

$f(x) = 1, \forall R$

(ii) $f(x) = \text{sgn}(\log_e x) = \begin{cases} 1, & \log_e x > 0 \\ -1, & \log_e x < 0 \\ 0, & \log_e x = 0 \end{cases}$

$$\therefore\ f(x) = \begin{cases} 1, & x > 1 \\ -1, & 0 < x < 1 \\ 0, & x = 1 \end{cases}$$

Graph for, $f(x) = \text{sgn}(\log_e x)$ is

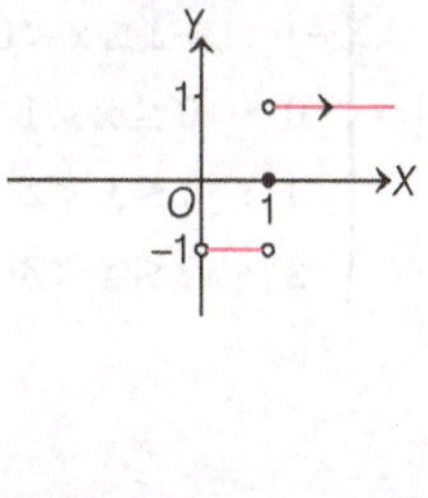

(iii) $f(x) = \text{sgn}(\sin x)$

$$f(x) = \begin{cases} 1, & \sin x > 0 \\ -1, & \sin x < 0 \\ 0, & \sin x = 0 \end{cases}$$

$$= \begin{cases} 1, & 2n\pi < x < (2n+1)\pi \\ -1, & (2n+1)\pi < x < (2n+2)\pi \\ 0, & x = n\pi \end{cases}$$

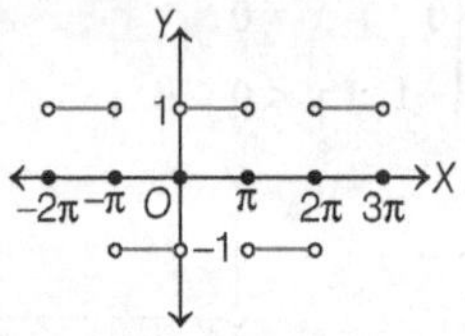

(iv) $f(x) = \text{sgn}(\cos x)$

$$f(x) = \begin{cases} 1, & \cos x > 0 \\ -1, & \cos x < 0 \\ 0, & \cos x = 0 \end{cases}$$

$$f(x) = \begin{cases} 1, & 2n\pi - \dfrac{\pi}{2} < x < 2n\pi + \dfrac{\pi}{2} \\ -1, & 2n\pi + \dfrac{\pi}{2} < x < 2n\pi + \dfrac{3\pi}{2} \\ 0, & x = \dfrac{(2n+1)\pi}{2} \end{cases}$$

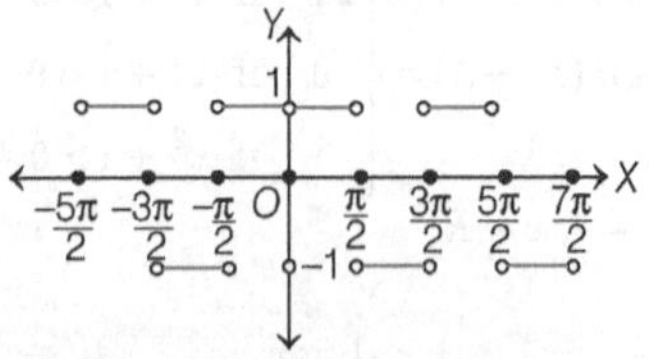

3. Greatest Integer Function (GIF)

A function $f : R \to R$ is defined as

$$f(x) = [x] \le x$$

Greatest integer of x means largest integer which is less than or equal to x.

i.e. any Real number = Integral + Fractional Part

$\Rightarrow$ Greatest integer of x = Integral part of x.

Thus, $[2.1] = 2, [3.5] = 3, [0.8] = 0, [1.9] = 1, [-0.7] = -1,$ $[-1.7] = -2, [-2.8] = -3$ etc.

Therefore, $[x] = n$, if $n \le x < n+1$.

$$\text{Thus, } y = f(x) = [x] = \begin{cases} -2 : & -2 \le x < -1 \\ -1 : & -1 \le x < 0 \\ 0 : & 0 \le x < 1 \\ 1 : & 1 \le x < 2 \\ 2 : & 2 \le x < 3 \end{cases}$$

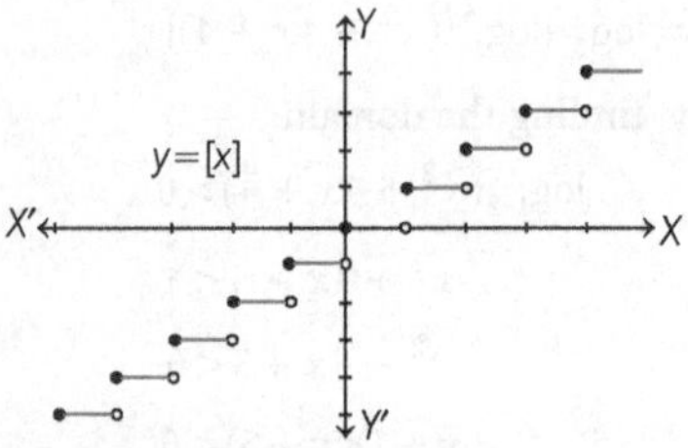

$D_f = R$ and $R_f = I$

4. Least Integer Function

A function $f : R \to R$ is defined as $f(x) = (x) \ge x$

The least integer of x means smallest integer which is more than or equal to x.

e.g. $(2.5) = 3,\ (3.1) = 4,\ (1.7) = 2,\ (0.5) = 1,\ (-1.4) = -1$ etc.

$$y = f(x) = \begin{cases} -2 : & -3 < x \le -2 \\ -1 : & -2 < x \le -1 \\ 0 : & -1 < x \le 0 \\ 1 : & 0 < x \le 1 \\ 2 : & 1 < x \le 2 \\ 3 : & 2 < x \le 3 \end{cases}$$

Thus, $y = (x) = n, n < x \le n+1$

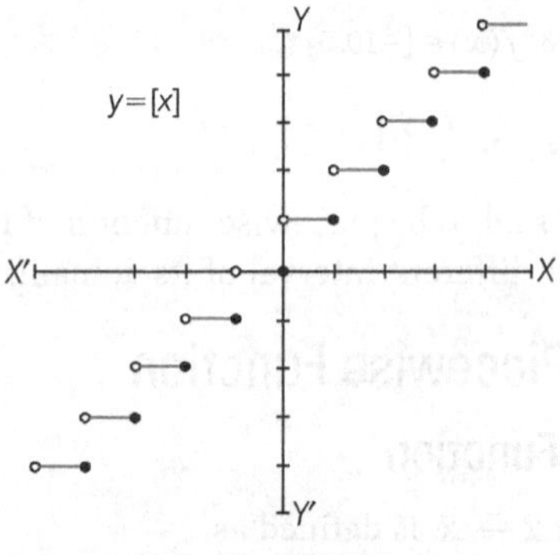

$D_f = R$ and $R_f = I$

Properties of Least Integer Function

(i) $(x) = x, x \in I$

(ii) $(x) = [x], x \in I$

(iii) $(x) = [x] + 1, x \notin I$

In fact, $(x) = -[-x]$

(iv) $(x + n) = (x) + n, n \in I$

(v) $(-x) = -x, x \in I$

(vi) $(-x) = 1 - (x), x \notin I$

5. Fractional Part Function

A function $f : R \to R$ is defined as

$$f(x) = \{x\} = x - [x]$$

e.g.

(i) If $x = 3.45, [x] = 3$

Thus, $\{x\} = x - [x] = 3.45 - 3 = 0.45$

(ii) If $x = 5$, then $[x] = 5$

Thus, $\{x\} = x - [x] = 5 - 5 = 0$

(iii) If $x = -2.75, [x] = -3$

Thus, $\{x\} = x - [x] = -2.75 + 3 = 0.25$

As we know that $x - 1 < [x] \le x$

$$\Rightarrow \quad -x \le -[x] < 1 - x$$
$$\Rightarrow \quad -x + x \le x - [x] < 1 - x + x$$
$$\Rightarrow \quad 0 \le x - [x] < 1$$
$$\Rightarrow \quad 0 \le \{x\} < 1$$

Though 0 is not a function, but fractional part function evaluates to zero for integral values. We should keep this exception in mind, while working with fractional part function.

$$y = f(x) = \begin{cases} x + 3 & : \ -3 \le x < -2 \\ x + 2 & : \ -2 \le x < -1 \\ x + 1 & : \ -1 \le x < 0 \\ x & : \ 0 \le x < 1 \\ x - 1 & : \ 1 \le x < 2 \\ x - 2 & : \ 2 \le x < 3 \end{cases}$$

Thus, $y = \{x\} = x - n, n \le x < n + 1$

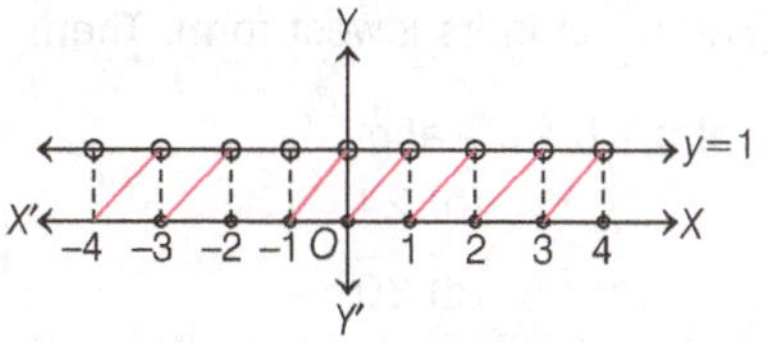

$D_f = R$ and $R_f = [0, 1)$.

Example 23. Find the domain of the function

(i) $f(x) = \log_3 \log_{(1/3)} (x^2 + 10x + 25) + \dfrac{1}{[x] + 5}$

(where [·] denotes greatest integer function.)

(ii) $f(x) = \dfrac{1}{\sqrt{[x]^2 - [x] - 6}}$

(iii) $f(x) = [\sin x] \cos\left(\dfrac{\pi}{[x - 1]}\right)$.

(iv) $f(x) = \dfrac{\log_4 (5 - [x - 1] - [x]^2)}{x^2 + x - 2}$

(where [x] denotes greatest integer function)

(v) $f(x) = \dfrac{1}{[|x - 1|] + [|7 - x|] - 6}$,

(where [·] denotes the greatest integer function)

(vi) $f(x) = \dfrac{1}{\sqrt[3]{[x] + [-x]} + 1}$

(vii) $f(x) = \dfrac{\log([x] + [-x] + 1)}{\sqrt{(x - 2)(6 - x)}}$

(viii) $f(x) = \dfrac{\sec^{-1} x}{\sqrt{x - [x]}}$,

Sol. (i) $f(x) = \log_3 \log_{(1/3)} (x^2 + 10x + 25) + \dfrac{1}{[x] + 5}$

$$x^2 + 10x + 25 > 0 \Rightarrow (x + 5)^2 > 0$$
$$\Rightarrow \quad x \ne -5 \quad \text{...(i)}$$

Also, $\log_{(1/3)}(x^2 + 10x + 25) > 0$

$$\Rightarrow \quad x^2 + 10x + 25 < 1$$
$$\Rightarrow \quad (x + 6)(x + 4) < 0$$
$$\Rightarrow \quad x \in (-6, -4) \quad \text{...(ii)}$$

From Eqs. (i) and (ii), we get

$$x \in (-6, -5) \cup (-5, -4)$$

Also, $[x] + 5 \ne 0, [x] \ne -5 \Rightarrow x \notin [-5, -4)$

Hence, the domain of $f(x) \in (-6, -5)$.

(ii) $f(x) = \dfrac{1}{\sqrt{[x]^2 - [x] - 6}}$

$$\Rightarrow \quad [x]^2 - [x] - 6 > 0$$
$$\Rightarrow \quad ([x] - 3)([x] + 2) > 0$$
$$\Rightarrow \quad [x] \in (3, \infty) \cup (-\infty, -2)$$
$$\Rightarrow \quad x \in [4, \infty)$$

Also, $[x] \in (-\infty, -2)$

$$\Rightarrow \quad x \in (-\infty, -2) \cup [4, \infty).$$

(iii) $[\sin x]$ is always defined, $\cos\left(\dfrac{\pi}{[x - 1]}\right)$ is also defined except when $[x - 1] = 0$

$$\Rightarrow \quad 0 \le x - 1 < 1$$
$$\Rightarrow \quad 1 \le x < 2$$

Hence, the domain of $f(x)$ is $R - [1, 2)$.

(iv) For domain of $f(x)$,

$$5 - [x - 1] - [x]^2 > 0$$

and $\quad x^2 + x - 2 \ne 0$

$$\Rightarrow \quad (x + 2)(x - 1) \ne 0$$
$$\Rightarrow \quad x \ne 1, -2$$

Now, $\quad 5 - [x] + 1 - [x]^2 > 0$

$$\Rightarrow \quad [x]^2 + [x] - 6 < 0$$
$$\Rightarrow \quad ([x] + 3)([x] - 2) < 0$$
$$\Rightarrow \quad -3 < [x] < 2$$
$$\Rightarrow \quad -2 \le x < 2$$

$\because \quad x \ne 1, -2$

$\therefore$ Domain $\in (-2, 1) \cup (1, 2)$

(v) $f(x)$ is defined when

$$[|x-1|]+[|7-x|]-6 \neq 0$$

$$\Rightarrow \begin{cases} [1-x]+[7-x] \neq 6, & \text{when } x \le 1 \quad \text{...(i)} \\ [x-1]+[7-x] \neq 6, & \text{when } 1 \le x \le 7 \quad \text{...(ii)} \\ [x-1]+[x-7] \neq 6, & \text{when } x \ge 7 \quad \text{...(iii)} \end{cases}$$

$$[1-x]+[7-x] \neq 6 \qquad \text{[from Eq. (i)]}$$

$$\Rightarrow 1+[-x]+7+[-x] \neq 6$$

$$\Rightarrow 2[-x] \neq -2 \Rightarrow [-x] \neq -1$$

$$\Rightarrow x \notin (0, 1] \qquad \text{...(a)}$$

From Eq. (ii), we get

$$[x-1]+[7-x] \neq 6$$

$$\Rightarrow [x]-1+7+[-x] \neq 6 \Rightarrow [x]+[-x] \neq 0$$

$\Rightarrow x \notin$ Integer

$$\Rightarrow x \notin \{1, 2, 3, 4, 5, 6, 7\} \qquad \text{...(b)}$$

From Eq. (iii), we get

$$[x-1]+[x-7] \neq 6$$

$$\Rightarrow [x]-1+[x]-7 \neq 6$$

$$\Rightarrow 2[x] \neq 14 \Rightarrow [x] \neq 7$$

$$\Rightarrow x \notin [7, 8) \qquad \text{...(c)}$$

(vi) $f(x) = \dfrac{1}{\sqrt[3]{[x]+[-x]+1}}$

For $f(x)$ to be defined $[x]+[-x]+1 \neq 0$

$$\Rightarrow [x]+[-x] \neq -1$$

But we know that $[x]+[-x] = \begin{cases} 0, & \text{for } x \in Z \\ -1, & \text{for } x \notin Z \end{cases}$

$\therefore$ For $f(x)$ to be defined, $x \in Z$

$\therefore$ $D_f = Z$ = set of all integers.

(vii) $f(x) = \dfrac{\log([x]+[-x]+1)}{\sqrt{(x-2)(6-x)}}$

For $f(x)$ to be defined

$[x]+[-x]+1 > 0$ and $(x-2)(6-x) > 0$

$[x]+[-x] = -1$, i.e. $[x]+[-x]+1 = 0$ for $x \notin Z$

and $[x]+[-x] = 0$, i.e. $[x]+[-x]+1 = 1 > 0$ for $x \in Z$

Thus, $[x]+[-x]+1 > 0$ for $x \in Z$

Also, $(x-2)(6-x) > 0 \Rightarrow x \in (2, 6)$

$\therefore$ x must be an integer in $(2, 6)$

$$\Rightarrow x \in \{3, 4, 5\}$$

Domain of function $f(x) = D_f = \{3, 4, 5\}$

(viii) $f(x) = \dfrac{\sec^{-1} x}{\sqrt{x-[x]}}$.

$\sec^{-1} x$ is defined for all $x \in R-(-1, 1)$ and $\dfrac{1}{\sqrt{x-[x]}}$ is defined for all $x \in R-I$.

So, the given function is defined for $x \in R - \{(-1, 1) \cup \{n, n \in I\}\}$.

JEE SCANNER

Example Similar to PYQ Asked in JEE Main 2019

If $[2\cos x]+[\sin x] = -3$, $x \in [0, 2\pi]$ (where [·] denotes greatest integer function), then the value of x lies in the interval is

(a) $x \in \left(\pi, \dfrac{4\pi}{3}\right)$ (b) $x \in \left(\dfrac{2\pi}{3}, \dfrac{4\pi}{3}\right)$

(c) $x \in \left(\dfrac{2\pi}{3}, \pi\right)$ (d) $x \in \left(\dfrac{4\pi}{3}, 2\pi\right)$

Sol. (a) $[2\cos x]+[\sin x] = -3$

Now, $-2 \le 2\cos x \le 2$

$\Rightarrow [2\cos x] \in (-2, -1, 0, 1, 2)$ and $-1 \le \sin x \le 1$

$\Rightarrow [\sin x] \in \{-1, 0, 1\}$

Now, equation holds true for $[2\cos x] = -2$ and $[\sin x] = -1$

$$\Rightarrow -1 \le \cos x < -\frac{1}{2} \text{ and } -1 \le \sin x < 0$$

$$\Rightarrow x \in \left(\frac{2\pi}{3}, \frac{4\pi}{3}\right) \text{ and } x \in (\pi, 2\pi) \Rightarrow x \in \left(\pi, \frac{4\pi}{3}\right)$$

Skill Builder

The set of real values of x satisfying the equality $\left[\dfrac{3}{x}\right]+\left[\dfrac{4}{x}\right] = 5$ (where [·] denotes the greatest integer function) belongs to the interval $\left(a, \dfrac{b}{c}\right]$, where $a, b, c \in N$ and $\dfrac{b}{c}$ is in its lowest form. Then, the value of $a+b+c+abc$ is

(a) 20 (b) 24

(c) 28 (d) 30

For Sol.

■ **For more practice** See Q.6 of Milestone Practice 2.2.

Example 24. A function f is defined as $f(x) = x^3 - 5x^2 + 15x + \sin^{-1}\left(\dfrac{x}{2}\right)$, then $(f_{max} - f_{min})$ is given by

(a) -40 (b) $\pi - 40$

(c) $76 + \pi$ (d) None of these

Sol. (c) $f'(x) = \underbrace{3x^2 - 10x + 15}_{\substack{a>0 \\ D<0}} + \dfrac{1}{2}\dfrac{1}{\sqrt{1-\dfrac{x^2}{4}}} > 0$

$\Rightarrow f(x)$ is monotonically increasing in its domain $[-2, 2]$

$$\therefore \quad f_{min} = f(-2) = -8 - 5(4) + 15(-2) + \left(-\frac{\pi}{2}\right)$$

$$= -\left(58 + \frac{\pi}{2}\right) = -\left(\frac{116+\pi}{2}\right)$$

and $f_{\max} = f(2)$

$$= 8 - 20 + 30 + \frac{\pi}{2}$$

$$= 18 + \frac{\pi}{2}$$

$$= \frac{36 + \pi}{2}$$

$$\Rightarrow f_{\max} - f_{\min} = 76 + \pi$$

Example 25. The range of $f(x) = |\sin x|^2 + 2|\sin x| - |\cos x|$ is given by

(a) $[-1, 2]$

(b) $[-1, 1]$

(c) $[-1, 3]$

(d) None of the above

Sol. (c) $f(x)$ is periodic with period π

$$\Rightarrow f(x) = \begin{cases} \sin^2 x + 2\sin x - \cos x, & \text{for } x \in \left[0, \frac{\pi}{2}\right] \\ \sin^2 x + 2\sin x + \cos x, & \text{for } x \in \left[\frac{\pi}{2}, \pi\right] \end{cases}$$

$\Rightarrow f(x)$ is increasing in the interval $\left[0, \frac{\pi}{2}\right]$

and decreasing in $\left[\frac{\pi}{2}, \pi\right]$.

Thus, if $0 \le x \le \frac{\pi}{2}$

$$\Rightarrow f(0) \le f(x) \le f\left(\frac{\pi}{2}\right)$$

$$\Rightarrow f(x) \in [-1, 3]$$

and if $\frac{\pi}{2} \le x \le \pi$

$$\Rightarrow f(\pi) \le f(x) \le f\left(\frac{\pi}{2}\right)$$

$$\Rightarrow f(x) \in [-1, 3]$$

JEE SCANNER

Example Similar to PYQ Asked in JEE Main 2023

The range of the expression $\frac{\tan^2\theta - 4\tan\theta - 2}{\tan^2\theta - 2\tan\theta - 5}$, *for all permissible value of* θ *is*

(a) $(-\infty, \infty)$ (b) $(0, \infty)$

(c) $(-\infty, 0)$ (d) None of these

Sol. (a) Let $x = \tan\theta$, where $x \in R$ for all permissible values of θ.

$$\Rightarrow y = \frac{x^2 - 4x - 2}{x^2 - 2x - 5}$$

$$\Rightarrow x^2y - 2xy - 5y = x^2 - 4x - 2$$

$\Rightarrow (y-1)x^2 + 2x(2-y) + 2 - 5y = 0$ as $x \in R$, hence, $D \ge 0$

$$\Rightarrow 4(2-y)^2 - 4(y-1)(2-5y) \ge 0$$

$$\Rightarrow 4(4 + y^2 - 4y) - 4(-5y^2 + 7y - 2) \ge 0$$

$$\Rightarrow 24y^2 - 44y + 24 \ge 0$$

$$\Rightarrow 6y^2 - 11y + 6 \ge 0 \quad \text{...(i)}$$

Since, coefficient of $y^2 > 0$

and $D = 121 - 144 < 0$

Hence, Eq. (i) is true for every real value of y.

Therefore, range of y is $(-\infty, \infty) = R$.

Skill Builder

Let $f: R \to R$ be defined as $f(x) = \frac{x^2 + 2x + \alpha}{x^2 + 4x + 3\alpha}$, where R and R denote the domain of f and the set of all real numbers, respectively, then the range of α is

For Sol.

(a) $0 \le \alpha \le 1$ (b) $0 < \alpha \le 1$

(c) $0 \le \alpha < 1$ (d) $0 < \alpha < 1$

■ **For more practice** See Q.9 of Milestone Practice 2.2.

Milestone Practice 2.2

1. The domain of

$$f(x) = \sqrt{\frac{[x]-2}{5-[x]}} + \log_{1/2}(\sqrt{x-1} + \sqrt{3-x}) \text{ is}$$

(a) $[2, 5)$
(b) $[2, 3)$
(c) $[2, 3]$
(d) None of the above

2. Minimum value of $f(x) = \dfrac{x^2 \sin^2 x + 4}{x \sin x}$, $x \in \left(0, \dfrac{\pi}{2}\right)$ is

(a) 3 (b) 2
(c) 5 (d) 4

3. The domain of $f(x) = \log_{10}(\log_{10}^2 x) - 5\log_{10} x + 6$
$+ \sqrt{2\{x\}^2 - 3\{x\} + 1}$, if $x \in [-1, 1]$, is

(a) $\left(0, \dfrac{1}{2}\right)$ (b) $\left(0, \dfrac{1}{2}\right) \cup \{1\}$
(c) $(0, 1)$ (d) $(0, 1) - \left\{\dfrac{1}{2}\right\}$

4. Let $g(x) \cdot (x^{(2^{2008}-1)} - 1) = (x+1)(x^2+1)(x^4+1)$
$\ldots (x^{2^{2007}} + 1) - 1$. Then, $g(2)$ is

(a) an odd prime number
(b) an even number
(c) a composite number
(d) None of the above

5. Domain of $f(x) = \log_e \dfrac{1}{\sqrt{[\cos x] - [\sin x]}}$ is

(a) $\bigcup_{n \in I} \left[2n\pi - \dfrac{\pi}{2}, 2n\pi\right]$
(b) $\bigcup_{n = I} \left[2n\pi + \dfrac{\pi}{2}, 2n\pi + \pi\right]$
(c) $\bigcup_{n \in I} \left[2n\pi - \dfrac{3\pi}{4}, 2n\pi\right]$
(d) $\bigcup_{n \in I} \left[2n\pi - \dfrac{5\pi}{6}, 2n\pi\right]$

6. The value of x for the function is

$$f(x) = \log_{\left[x + \frac{1}{x}\right]} |x^2 - x - 6| + {}^{16-x}C_{2x-1} + {}^{20-3x}P_{2x-5} \text{ is}$$

(where [·] denotes the greatest integer function)
(a) $(4, 5)$
(b) $\{4, 5\}$
(c) $[4, 5]$
(d) $\{3, 4, 5, 6\}$

7. Number of integer in the domain of
$f(x) = \sqrt{x^{14} - x^{11} + x^6 - x^3 + x^2 + 1}$ is

(a) 15 (b) 16
(c) 17 (d) Infinite

8. Range of $f(x) = 3\tan^2 x + 12\cot^2 x + 5$ is

(a) $[6, \infty)$ (b) $[12, \infty)$
(c) $[17, \infty)$ (d) $(15, \infty)$

9. Complete set of values of $f(x) = \dfrac{\{x\}}{1 + \{x\}}$ is

(a) $[0, 1)$ (b) $\left[0, \dfrac{1}{2}\right)$
(c) $\left[0, \dfrac{3}{4}\right)$ (d) $\left[0, \dfrac{1}{3}\right)$

10. Let $f(x) = \max\{\sin t : 0 \le t \le x\}$
$g(x) = \min\{\sin t : 0 \le t \le x\}$
and $h(x) = [f(x) - g(x)]$, [ ] denotes greatest integer function, then the number of possible values of $h(x)$

(a) 3 (b) 7
(c) 4 (d) 5

11. Let $f: R \to R$ be defined by $f(x) = \dfrac{x}{1 + x^2}$, $x \in R$, then the range of f is

(a) $\left[-\dfrac{1}{2}, \dfrac{1}{2}\right]$ (b) $(-1, 1) - \{0\}$
(c) $R - \left[-\dfrac{1}{2}, \dfrac{1}{2}\right]$ (d) $R - [-1, 1]$

Answer Key

1. (c)	2. (d)	3. (b)	4. (b)
5. (a)	6. (b)	7. (d)	8. (c)
9. (b)	10. (a)	11. (a)	

For Detailed Solution

Milestone 3 Types of Functions II

- One-one (Injective) Function/Monomorphic • Many-one Function • Onto or Surjective Function
- Into Function • One-one Onto/Bijective Function

Since, a function is mapping from set $x \to y$, where every element of x has one any only image in y.

Now, on the basis of this mapping we can categorised function into two categories.

Category I

1. One-One function/injective function/ Monomorophic
2. Many-one function

Category II

3. Onto/Surjective function
4. Into function

On the basis of these category we can also define

- One-one onto (bijective),
- One-one into
- Many-one onto
- Many-one into

2.10 One-One (Injective) Function/Monomorphic

$f: X \to Y$ is called injective when different elements in set X are related with different elements of set Y

i.e. no two elements of domain have same image in codomain.

In other words, we can also say that no element of codomain is related with two or more elements of domain. Consider the following mapping.

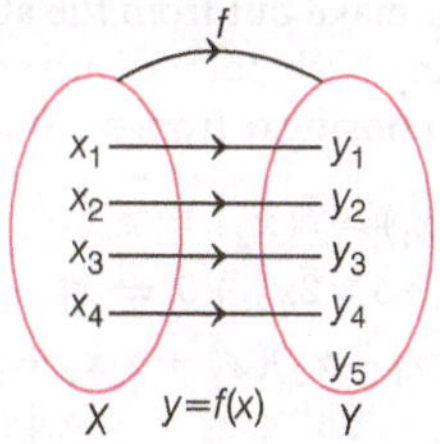

Clearly, it is one-one because each element x_i in X is associated with a distinct element y in Y.

2.11 Many-one Function

$f: X \to Y$ is many-one, when there exist at least two elements in the domain set X which are related with same element of codomain Y. e.g. consider a mapping.

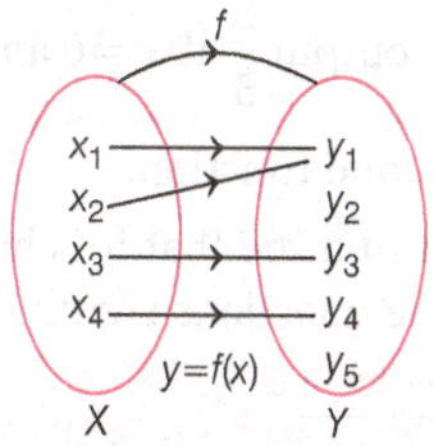

Clearly, it is a many-one mapping as $f(x_1) = f(x_2) = y_1$, whereas x_1 and x_2 are distinct elements.

A function which is not one-one, then it is many-one.

Methods to Check for One-one/Many-one

(a) **Checking algebraically (Using definition)**

(i) If $x_1 \neq x_2 \Rightarrow f(x_1) \neq f(x_2)$, then it is one-one function.

(ii) If $x_1 \neq x_2 \Rightarrow f(x_1) = f(x_2)$, then it is not a one-one function.

(b) **Checking geometrically** (Horizontal line test) Draw a system of lines parallel to X-axis on the given curve. If those lines intersects the curve in only one point, then it is one-one function otherwise many-one function.

(c) **Checking by Calculus** (Using monotonicity) If a function is either strictly increasing or strictly decreasing function, then it is one-one function. Otherwise function is many-one. i.e. either $f'(x) > 0$ or $f'(x) < 0$, then it is one-one function.

(d) **Hit and Trial method** (This method is used to check a function is many-one or not) Many a times by keen observation it is possible to find an element in the range of function which is f image of two or more than two elements in the domain of function thus, concluding the fact that the function being investigated in many-one function.

e.g. Let $f(x)=\dfrac{x^2-4x+3}{x^2+4x+5}$

Now, let us try $f(x)=f(\alpha)$ (where α is some fixed real number such that $f(\alpha)$ is simple fraction, say $\alpha=0$).

i.e. $f(x)=f(0)$

$\Rightarrow \dfrac{x^2-4x+3}{x^2+4x+5}=\dfrac{3}{5}$

$\Rightarrow 5x^2-20x+15=3x^2+12x+15$

$\Rightarrow 2x^2-32x=0$

$\Rightarrow 2x(x-16)=0 \Rightarrow x=0,16$

$\Rightarrow f(0)=f(16)=\dfrac{3}{5}$

It means it has some output $\dfrac{3}{5}$ at $x=0$ and 16.

Hence, $f(x)$ is many-one function.

But it should be kept in mind that it is hit and trial method and may fail to hit the questions rightly, for instance consider $f(x)=\dfrac{x^2-3x+4}{x^2+3x+4}$

On solving $f(x)=f(0)$, we get

$\dfrac{x^2-3x+4}{x^2+3x+4}=1 \Rightarrow 6x=0$, i.e. $x=0$

Thus, we can not arrive at any conclusion from the result, so f may or may not be many-one, to decide either we go by other method or try for some different real output of function say

Let $f(x)=f(1) \Rightarrow \dfrac{x^2-3x+4}{x^2+3x+4}=\dfrac{1}{4}$

$\Rightarrow 4x^2-12x+16=x^2+3x+4 \Rightarrow 3x^2-15x+12=0$,

i.e. $x^2-5x+4=0$ (which has $D>0$)

$\Rightarrow x=1,4$

Thus, $f(1)=f(4)=\dfrac{1}{4}$, and thus, f is many-one.

Example 26. Check whether following functions are one-one or many-one.

(i) Function $f:Z\to Z$ defined by $f(x)=x^2+x$, $\forall\, x\in Z$

(ii) $f(x)=e^{2x^3+5}$

(iii) $f(x)=\dfrac{x^2-x-2}{x^2-5x+6}$

(iv) $f(x)=\dfrac{2x-3}{2x+3}$

(v) $f(x)=\dfrac{ax^2-1}{ax^2+1}$, $(a>0)$

(vi) Function $f:R\to R$ is defined by $f(x)=\dfrac{e^x-e^{-x}}{e^x+e^{-x}}$

(vii) $f(x)=\dfrac{2\sin x-5}{2\sin x+5}$

(viii) $f(x)=\dfrac{a\log x^2-2}{a\log x^2+2}$, $(a, x>0)$

(ix) Function $f:R\to R$ defined as $f(x)=\dfrac{x^2-x+12}{x^2+x+8}$

(x) Function $f:[0,\infty)\to R$ is defined by $f(x)=\dfrac{e^{x^2}-e^{-x^2}}{e^{x^2}+e^{-x^2}}$.

Sol. (i) Let $x_1, x_2\in Z$ such that $f(x_1)=f(x_2)$, then

$f(x_1)=f(x_2)$

$\Rightarrow x_1^2+x_1=x_2^2+x_2$

$\Rightarrow (x_1^2-x_2^2)+(x_1-x_2)=0$

$\Rightarrow (x_1-x_2)(x_1+x_2+1)=0$

$\Rightarrow x_1=x_2$ or $x_1+x_2+1=0$

Since, $f(x_1)=f(x_2)$ does not provide a unique solution $x_1=x_2$ but it provides $x_2=-x_1-1$, this means there may arise a situation when $x_1\neq x_2$, but $f(x_1)=f(x_2)$. To verify the second situation, let us analyse the function further.

$$f(x)=x^2+x=\left(x+\frac{1}{2}\right)^2-\frac{1}{4}$$

$\Rightarrow f(x)=\dfrac{(2x+1)^2}{4}=-1$

It is very evident from above that $f(x)$, generates same output for $2x+1=\alpha$ or $-\alpha$, where $\alpha\in R$

i.e. for $x=-\dfrac{1}{2}-\dfrac{\alpha}{2}$ or $\dfrac{-1}{2}+\dfrac{\alpha}{2}$. For instance when $\alpha=1$, we get $x=-1$ or 0.

Clearly, $f(0)=f(-1)=0$.

Thus, for two distinct inputs $f(x)$ generates same output.

Hence, f is many-one function.

Also, one can make out from the above discussion that infinitely many such pairs of integer inputs are possible by choosing α from set $\{(2n+1); n\in Z\}$.

(ii) Consider, $f(x_1)=f(x_2) \Rightarrow e^{2x_1^3+5}=e^{2x_2^3+5}$

$\Rightarrow 2x_1^3+5=2x_2^3+5 \Rightarrow x_1^3-x_2^3=0$

$\Rightarrow (x_1-x_2)(x_1^2+x_1x_2+x_2^2)=0$

$[\because x_1^2+x_1x_2+x_2^2\geq 0]$

Consequently the only real solution is $x_1=x_2$.

Therefore, f is one-one function.

(iii) Given, function $f(x)=\dfrac{x^2-x-2}{x^2-5x+6}$

$$=\frac{(x+1)(x-2)}{(x-2)(x-3)}=\frac{x+1}{x-3}, x\neq 2,3$$

This is clearly a rational linear fractional function and we know that it is an injective function.

(iv) Given, $f(x)=\dfrac{2x-3}{2x+3}$

$$\therefore \quad f(x_1)=f(x_2)\Rightarrow\left(\frac{2x_1-3}{2x_1+3}\right)=\left(\frac{2x_2-3}{2x_2+3}\right)$$

On applying componendo and dividendo, we get

$$\frac{-4x_1}{6}=\frac{-4x_2}{6}\Rightarrow x_1=x_2.$$

$\Rightarrow f(x)$ is one-one function.

(v) Given, $f(x)=\dfrac{ax^2-1}{ax^2+1};(a>0)$

$$\therefore\ f(x_1)=f(x_2)\Rightarrow\left(\frac{ax_1^2-1}{ax_1^2+1}\right)=\left(\frac{ax_1^2-1}{ax_2^2+1}\right)$$

On applying componendo and dividendo, we get

$$-ax_1^2=-ax_2^2\Rightarrow x_1^2=x_2^2$$

$$\Rightarrow \quad x_1=x_2 \text{ or } x_1=-x_2$$

$\therefore\ f(x)$ is many-one function.

(vi) Given, $f(x)=\dfrac{e^x-e^{-x}}{e^x+e^{-x}}$

$$\Rightarrow \quad f'(x)=\frac{(e^x+e^{-x})^2-(e^x-e^{-x})^2}{(e^x+e^{-x})^2}$$

$$=\frac{4}{(e^x+e^{-x})^2}\geq 0, \forall\ x\in R.$$

Thus, $f(x)$ is strictly increasing and continuous function, consequently $f(x)$ is an injective function.

(vii) Given function is $f(x)=\dfrac{2\sin x-5}{2\sin x+5}$

$$\therefore\ f(x_1)=f(x_2)\Rightarrow\left(\frac{2\sin x_1-5}{2\sin x_1+5}\right)=\left(\frac{2\sin x_2-5}{2\sin x_2+5}\right)$$

On applying componendo and dividendo, we get

$$\frac{-4\sin x_1}{10}=\frac{-4\sin x_2}{10}$$

$$\Rightarrow \quad \sin x_1=\sin x_2$$

But we know that sin x is periodic function, and hence, is many-one function.

Thus, $\sin x_1=\sin x_2$ would occur at infinitely many pairs (x_1, x_2) such that $x_1\neq x_2$.

Hence, $f(x)$ is many-one function.

(viii) Given, $f(x)=\dfrac{a\log x^2-2}{a\log x^2+2}(a, x>0)$

$$\therefore \quad f(x_1)=f(x_2)\Rightarrow\left(\frac{a\log x_1^2-2}{a\log x_1^2+2}\right)=\left(\frac{a\log x_2^2-2}{a\log x_2^2+2}\right)$$

On applying componendo and dividendo, we get

$$\frac{-a\log x_1^2}{4}=\frac{-a\log x_2^2}{4}\Rightarrow \log x_1^2=\log x_2^2$$

But log x is a monotonic and continuous function on $(0,\infty)$, thus, log x is one-one function on $(0,\infty)$.

$\Rightarrow x_1^2=x_2^2\Rightarrow(x_1+x_2)(x_1-x_2)=0$

$\Rightarrow x_1=x_2$ or $x_1=-x_2$ but $x_1, x_2>0$

$\Rightarrow x_1\neq -x_2\Rightarrow x_1=x_2$

$\Rightarrow f(x)$ is one-one function.

(ix) **Method I. Analytically**

Let $f(x_1)=f(x_2)\Rightarrow\dfrac{x_1^2-x_1+12}{x_1^2+x_1+8}=\dfrac{x_2^2-x_2+12}{x_2^2+x_2+8}$

On applying componendo and dividendo, we get

$$\frac{4-2x_1}{2x_1^2+20}=\frac{4-2x_2}{2x_2^2+20}$$

$$\Rightarrow \quad (2-x_1)(x_2^2+10)=(2-x_2)(x_1^2+10)$$

$$\Rightarrow 2x_2^2+20-x_1x_2^2-10x_1=2x_1^2+20-x_2x_1^2-10x_2$$

$$\Rightarrow 2(x_2^2-x_1^2)-x_1x_2(x_2-x_1)+10(x_2-x_1)=0$$

$$\Rightarrow \quad (x_2-x_1)[2(x_1+x_2)-x_1x_2+10]=0$$

$$\Rightarrow \quad x_1=x_2 \text{ or } 2x_1+2x_2-x_1x_2+10=0$$

$$\Rightarrow \quad x_1=x_2 \text{ or } x_1=\frac{2(x_2+5)}{(x_2-2)}$$

Thus, evidently $f(x_1)=f(x_2)$ does not necessarily implying $x_1=x_2$.

For different inputs x_1 and x_2, $f(x_1)$ and $f(x_2)$ can be equal, consequently f is many-one function.

Method II. Monotonically

$f(x)$ is a continuous function because denominator is non-vanishing polynomial

Now,

$$f'(x)=\frac{(x^2+x+8)(2x-1)-(x^2-x+12)(2x+1)}{(x^2+x+8)^2}$$

$$=\frac{2x^2-8x-20}{(x^2+x+8)^2}=\frac{2(x^2-4x-5)}{(x^2+x+8)^2}$$

$\because$ Denominator is non-vanishing and perfect square thus, always positive, where as discriminant of numerator $=D=36>0$. Thus, has two real roots.

$$f'(x)=\frac{2(x-5)(x+1)}{(x^2+x+8)^2}$$

$$=\begin{cases}\text{positive for } x\in-(\infty,-1)\cup(5,\infty)\\ \text{negative for } x\in(-1,5)\end{cases}$$

Due to change in sign of derivative, $f(x)$ is clearly continuous but non-monotonic function, so it is non-injective function.

Method III. Using hit and trial

Let $\qquad f(x) = f(0)$

$\Rightarrow \qquad \dfrac{x^2 - x + 12}{x^2 + x + 8} = \dfrac{3}{2}$

$\Rightarrow \qquad 2x^2 - 2x = 3x^2 + 3x \Rightarrow x^2 + 5x = 0$

$\Rightarrow \qquad x = 0 \text{ or } -5$

So, for distinct inputs 0 and -5, $f(0) = f(-5) = \dfrac{3}{2}$.

Thus, $f(x)$ is many-one function.

(x) $f'(x) = \dfrac{e^{2x^2} 4x\,(e^{2x^2} + 1) - e^{2x^2} 4x\,(e^{2x^2} - 1)}{(e^{2x^2} + 1)^2}$

$= \dfrac{8xe^{2x^2}}{(e^{2x^2} + 1)^2} \geq 0, \forall\, x \in [0, \infty).$

Thus, $f(x)$ is strictly increasing and hence injective.

Example 27. Function $f : [-3, \infty) \to R$ is piecewise defined as $f(x) = \begin{cases} \sqrt{9 - x^2}, & -3 \leq x \leq 0 \\ \dfrac{2}{3^x} + k, & 0 < x < \infty \end{cases}$.

Determine the range of values of k for which the function f is (a) injective (b) many-one.

Sol. The function f represents quarter circle given by analytical formula $y = \sqrt{9 - x^2}$, i.e. $x^2 + y^2 = 9$ for $x \in [-3, 0]$ and $y \in [0, 3]$, as shown in figure, where as for the domain $(0, \infty)$ it is a decreasing exponential function such that $f(0) = k + 2$ and $f(\infty) \to k$, to remain injective, no horizontal line should intersect the graph more than once.

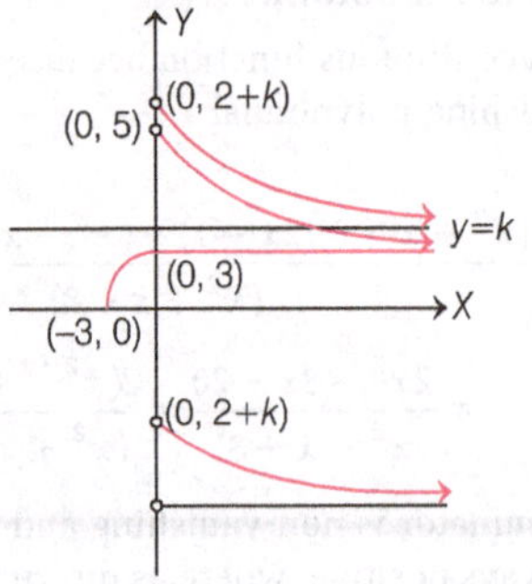

Therefore,

Case I Either $f(x) = \dfrac{2}{3^x} + k$ above the quarter circle

$\Rightarrow \qquad k \geq 3$

Case II Or it lies below the X-axis

$\Rightarrow 2 + k < 0 \Rightarrow k < -2$

Hence, if $k \in (-\infty, -2) \cup [3, \infty)$, $f(x)$ remains injective function but for $k \in [-2, 3)$, $f(x)$ becomes many-one function.

JEE SCANNER

Example Similar to PYQ Asked in JEE Main 2023

Let $f(x) = \dfrac{x^2 + 3x + a}{x^2 + x + 1}$, where $f : R \to R$. The value of parameter a, so that the given function is one-one

(a) for all values $\qquad$ (b) for all positive values

(c) for no values $\qquad$ (d) None of these

Sol. (c) $f(x) = \dfrac{x^2 + 3x + a}{x^2 + x + 1}$

$f'(x) = \dfrac{(x^2 + x + 1)(2x + 3) - (x^2 + 3x + a)(2x + 1)}{(x^2 + x + 1)^2}$

$= \dfrac{-2x^2 + 2x\,(1 - a) + (3 - a)}{(x^2 + x + 1)^2}$

Let $g(x) = -2x^2 + 2x\,(1 - a) + (3 - a)$

$g(x)$ will be negative for all x, if $4(1 - a)^2 + 8(3 - a) < 0$

$\Rightarrow \qquad 1 + a^2 - 2a + 6 - 2a < 0 \Rightarrow (a - 2)^2 + 3 < 0$

which is not possible.

Therefore, function is not monotonic.

Hence, no value of a is possible.

Skill Builder

If $f(x) = \dfrac{\sin([x]\pi)}{x^2 + x + 1}$, where [·] denotes the greatest integer function, then

(a) f is one-one

(b) f is not one-one and non-constant

(c) f is a constant function

(d) None of the above

For Sol.

■ **For more practice** See Q.1 of Milestone Practice 2.3.

Example 28. Find the set of all real values of parameter t for which the function $f : R \to R$ defined as $f(x) = 3\sin x - 4tx + 5$ is an injective function.

Sol. A continuous function $f(x)$ to be one-one it should be either monotonically increasing $(f'(x) \geq 0)$ or monotonically decreasing $(f'(x) \leq 0)$ in its entire domain.

Clearly, our function is continuous and $f'(x) = 3\cos x - 4t$ thus, for one-one either $f'(x) \geq 0$ $\forall\, x \in R$ or $f'(x) \leq 0, x \in R$

Case I $f'(x) \geq 0, \forall\, x \in R$

$\Rightarrow \qquad f'(x) = 3\cos x - 4t \geq 0, \forall\, x \in R$

$\Rightarrow \qquad t \leq \dfrac{3}{4}\cos x, \forall\, x \in R$

$\Rightarrow \qquad t \leq -\dfrac{3}{4}, \forall\, x \in R \text{ as } -\dfrac{3}{4} \leq \dfrac{3}{4}\cos x$

$\Rightarrow \qquad t \in \left(-\infty, -\dfrac{3}{4}\right]$

Case II $f'(x) = 3\cos x - 4t \le 0, \forall\, x \in R$

$\Rightarrow \quad t \ge \frac{3}{4}\cos x$

$\Rightarrow \quad t \ge \frac{3}{4}$

$\because \quad \frac{3}{4}\cos x \le \frac{3}{4}$

$\Rightarrow \quad t \in \left[\frac{3}{4}, \infty\right)$

Concluding the outcome of both the above cases, we conclude that f to be one-one function

$t \in \left(-\infty, \frac{-3}{4}\right] \cup \left[\frac{3}{4}, \infty\right)$.

Example 29. Let $y = \begin{cases} 2^x + a, & x < 0 \\ \sqrt{4 - x}, & 0 \le x < 4 \end{cases}$. Find a for which the function is one-one.

Sol. No horizontal line should intersect the graph more than once.

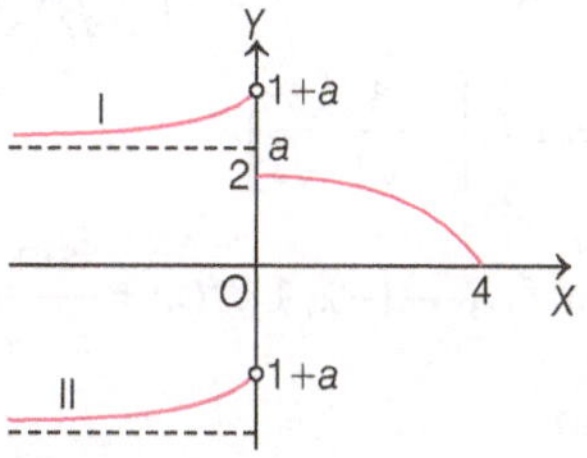

Case I $a \ge 2$

Case II $1 + a \le 0 \Rightarrow a \le -1$

Hence, $a \in (-\infty, -1] \cup [2, \infty)$

Example 30. A function $f: R \to R$ is given by $f(x) = \frac{ax^2 + 6x - 8}{a + 6x - 8x^2}$. Check whether $f(x)$ is not one-one function for $a = 3$.

Sol. The given function is a rational function.
Each of numerator and denominator of function is quadratic equation.

For $a = 3$, $f(x) = \frac{3x^2 + 6x - 8}{3 + 6x - 8x^2}$

In this case, on solving $f(x) = 0$ for x reveals the nature of function.

$$\frac{3x^2 + 6x - 8}{3 + 6x - 8x^2} = 0$$

$\Rightarrow \quad 3x^2 + 6x - 8 = 0$

$\Rightarrow \quad x = \frac{-6 \pm \sqrt{36 - 4 \cdot 3(-8)}}{6} = -1 \pm \frac{\sqrt{33}}{3}$

As x is not unique, the given function is not a one-one function. We should emphasize here that solution of function when equated to zero is not a full proof method.

In this particular case, it turns out that function value becomes zero for two values.

Example 31. Let $f: R \to R$ be defined as $f(x) = \begin{cases} x^2 + 2mx - 1, & x \le 0 \\ mx - 1 & x > 0 \end{cases}$. If $f(x)$ is one-one, then find all possible values of m.

Sol. Clearly, f is continuous at $x = 0$ and $f(0) = -1$.
For f to be one-one, $f'(x) > 0$ or $f'(x) < 0, \forall x$.
Assume that f is strictly increasing.
For $x > 0$, $f'(x) = m > 0$.
For $x < 0$, $f'(x) = 2(x + m)$ cannot be positive for all $x < 0$ when $m > 0$.
Now, assume that f is strictly decreasing.
For $x > 0$, $f'(x) = m < 0$.
For $x < 0$, $f'(x) = 2(x + m)$ is always negative for all $x < 0$, when $m < 0$.
$\therefore$ f is strictly decreasing and hence one-one, $\forall\, m < 0$.

2.12 Onto or Surjective Function

A function $f: X \to Y$ is called surjective only when each element in the codomain is f-image of at least one element in the domain, i.e. $f: X \to Y$ is onto iff $y \in Y$ there exists $x \in X$ such that $f(x) = y$, i.e. iff R_f = codomain (Y)

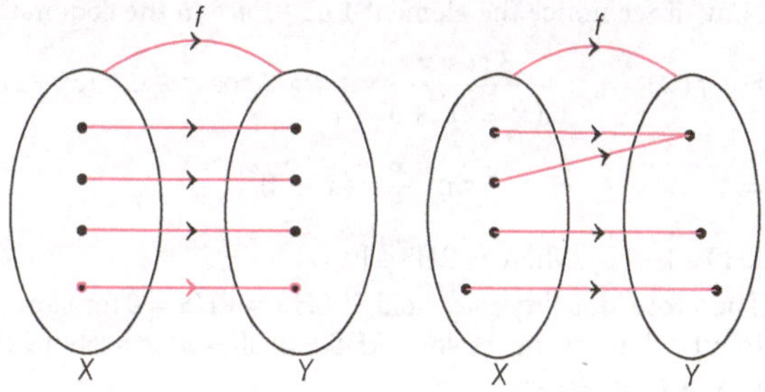

$\therefore$ Surjective $f: X \to Y$ reduce the codomain set of range of function.

2.13 Into Function

While defining function we have mentioned that there may exist some element in the codomain which are not related to any element in the domain.

$f: X \to Y$ is into iff there exists at least one $y \in Y$ which is not related with any $x \in X$.

Thus, the range of the into function is proper sub-set of the codomain. That is, Range $\subset$ Codomain (properly). The function which is not onto that is into.

Methods to Check for Onto Function/ Into Function

(i) If range = codomain, then f is onto. If range is a proper subset of codomain, then f is into.

(ii) Solve $f(x) = y$ for x, say $x = g(y)$.

Now, if $g(y)$ is defined for each $y \in$ codomain and $g(y) \in$ domain of f for all $y \in$ codomain, then $f(x)$ is onto. If this requirement is not met by at least one value of y in the codomain, then $f(x)$ is into.

JEE Focus Points

- An into function can be made onto, by redefining the codomain as the range of the original function.
- Any polynomial function $f: R \to R$ is onto if degree is odd; into if degree of f is even.

JEE SCANNER

Example Similar to PYQ Asked in JEE Main 2019

If $f: R \to [-1, 1]$; $f(x) = \dfrac{3\cos x}{x^2 - 4x + 7}$, then $f(x)$ is

(a) into function (b) bijective function
(c) surjective function (d) None of these

Sol. (a) Consider $f(x) = \dfrac{3\cos x}{x^2 - 4x + 7} = \dfrac{3\cos x}{(x-2)^2 + 3}$

Clearly, values of $f(x)$ cannot be out of the set $[-1, 1]$.

Now, if we notice the element 1 or -1 are in the codomain.

For $f(x) = 1$, $\dfrac{3\cos x}{(x-2)^2 + 3} = 1 \Rightarrow 3\cos x - 3 = (x-2)^2$

$$\Rightarrow \quad -6\sin^2 \frac{x}{2} = (x-2)^2$$

LHS $\in [-6, 0]$, whereas RHS $\in [0, \infty)$.

Therefore, equality may hold, if LHS = RHS = 0 for same input x, but it is never so as RHS vanishes at $x = 2$ but LHS is non-zero at $x = 2$.

$\Rightarrow f(x) \neq 1$, neither $f(x)$ can be -1. Clearly, it is an into function.

Skill Builder

If the function $f: R \to A$ given by $f(x) = \dfrac{x^2}{x^2 + 1}$ is surjective, then $A \in [k, m)$, then the value of $k + m$ is

(a) 1 (b) 2
(c) 3 (d) 4

For Sol.

■ **For more practice** See Q.8 of Milestone Practice 2.3.

Example 32. Find whether the following functions from $R \to R$ are onto or into?

(a) $f(x) = \dfrac{2x}{1 + x^2}$ (b) $y = x^3$

(c) $y = x|x|$ (d) $y = \sin \pi x$

Sol. (a) Since, range of function is $[-1, 1]$ therefore, range is subset of codomain (which is set of real number). Hence, $f(x)$ is into function.

(b) $y = x^3$ has range as set of real number, so it is onto function.

(c) $y = x^2$ when $x \geq 0$ and $y = -x^2$ when $x < 0$

$\Rightarrow$ Range is set of real numbers.

So, $f(x)$ is onto function.

(d) Range of $\sin \pi x$ is $[-1, 1]$ which is a proper subset of real numbers, so it is an into function.

Example 33. A function $f: X \to Y$ defined as $f(x) = x + \sqrt{3 - 2x^2}$ is onto. Find the set Y, if the set X is its natural domain.

Sol. As $f: X \to Y$ is given as onto, therefore Y must be range of the function. Now, to find range.

Let $\quad y = x + \sqrt{3 - 2x^2} \Rightarrow (y - x)^2 = 3 - 2x^2$

$$\Rightarrow \quad y^2 - 2xy + x^2 = 3 - 2x^2 \Rightarrow 3x^2 - 2xy + y^2 - 3 = 0$$

As, $x \in R$, $\quad D \geq 0 \Rightarrow y^2 - 3(y^2 - 3) \geq 0$

$$\Rightarrow \quad 2y^2 - 9 \leq 0 \Rightarrow y \in \left[-\frac{3}{\sqrt{2}}, \frac{3}{\sqrt{2}}\right]$$

Hence, the set Y is $\left[-\dfrac{3}{\sqrt{2}}, \dfrac{3}{\sqrt{2}}\right]$.

Example 34. Let $f: R \to [-1, 1]$, $f(x) = \dfrac{\sin x}{x^2 + 1}$. Find whether f is onto.

Sol. We note that 1 is an element of the codomain.

However, the function never attains the value 1.

We prove this as follows

Let $f(x) = \dfrac{\sin x}{x^2 + 1} = 1 \Rightarrow \sin x = x^2 + 1$

LHS ≤ 1 and RHS ≥ 1

The only possibility is that

$$\sin x = 1 \text{ and } x^2 + 1 = 1$$

The second equality holds at $x = 0$, but the first does not hold, then.

Thus, $f(x) \neq 1$ and hence, it is into.

Example 35. A function $f(x) = \sqrt{1 - 2x} + x$ is defined from $A \to B$ and is onto. If the set A is its natural domain, then find the set B.

Sol. B means range of the function.

Let $\quad y = \sqrt{1 - 2x} + x \Rightarrow (y - x)^2 = 1 - 2x$

$$\Rightarrow y^2 - 2xy + x^2 = 1 - 2x \Rightarrow x^2 + 2x(1 - y) + y^2 - 1 = 0$$

As, $x \in R$, $\quad D \geq 0$

$$\Rightarrow \quad 4(1 - y)^2 \geq 4(y^2 - 1)$$

$$\Rightarrow \quad 1 + y^2 - 2y \geq y^2 - 1 \Rightarrow -2y \geq -2$$

$$\Rightarrow \quad y \leq 1 \Rightarrow y \in (-\infty, 1]$$

Hence, the set B is $(-\infty, 1]$.

Example 36. Let a function f defined from $R \to R$ as

$$f(x) = \begin{cases} x + m & \text{for } x \le 1 \\ 2mx - 1 & \text{for } x > 1 \end{cases}$$. If the function is surjective, then find all values of m.

Sol. For f to be surjective, the range must be the set of all real numbers.

For $x \le 1$, $f'(x) = 1 \Rightarrow f$ increasing.

Hence, the maximum value of $f(x)$ for $x \le 1$ occurs at $x = 1$.

$\therefore$ The maximum value for $x \le 1$ is $m + 1$.

i.e. $f(x) \in (-\infty, m + 1]$ for $x \le 1$.

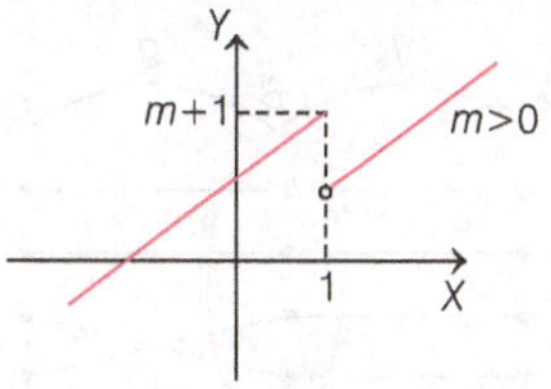

For range to be R, the minimum value of $f(x)$ for $x > 1$ must be less than or equal to $m + 1$.

Now, for $x > 1$, $\quad f'(x) = 2m$

Obviously $\quad m > 0 \quad$ ...(i)

[if $m < 0$, then the range cannot be R]

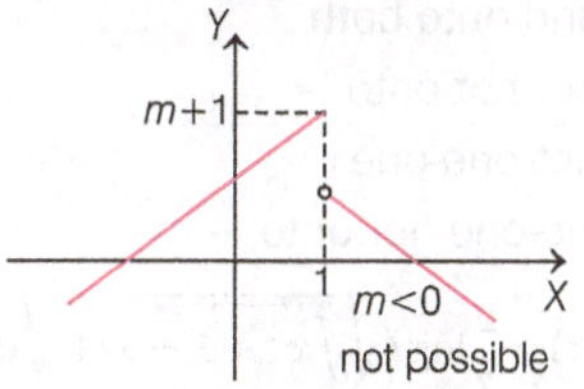

For $x > 1$, the function approaches the least level of $(2m - 1)$ at $x = 1$.

$$\therefore \quad 2m - 1 \le m + 1 \Rightarrow m \le 2 \quad \text{...(ii)}$$

From Eqs. (i) and (ii), we get

$$m \in (0, 2]$$

Example 37. Let $f : [0, \infty) - \{1\} \to B$, $f(x) = \dfrac{x+2}{x-1}$. Find B for which the function is onto.

Sol. $f(x) = \dfrac{x+2}{x-1} = \dfrac{(x-1)+3}{(x-1)} = 1 + \dfrac{3}{(x-1)}$

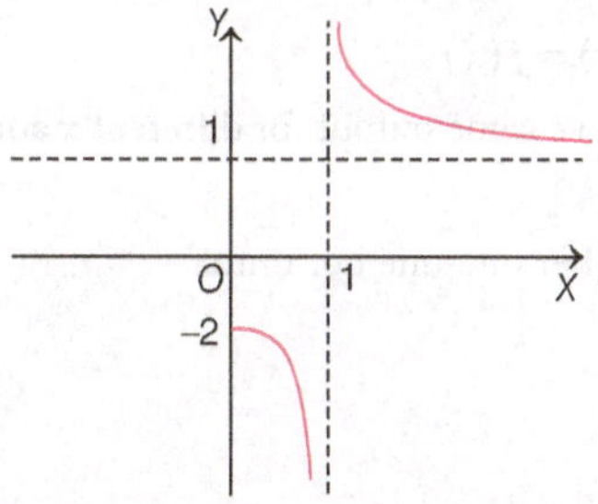

From the graph, the range is $(-\infty, -2] \cup (1, \infty)$. If we use this as the codomain B, then the function is onto.

Example 38. Let $f : R^+ \to [-2, \infty)$, $f(x) = x^2 + kx + k$. Find k such that f is onto.

Sol. We draw two possible graphs based on the position of the vertex with respect to the Y-axis.

Case I $-\dfrac{k}{2} \le 0$

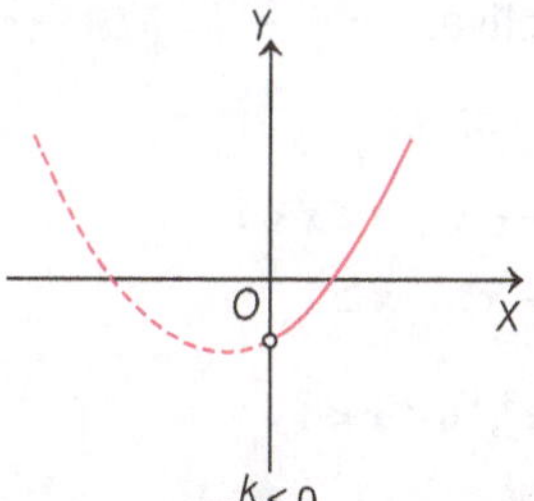

$-\dfrac{k}{2} \le 0$

Since, the function's value at $x = 0$ is not inclusive, the least value of -2 must be attained at the vertex. This is possible only when the vertex is on the right of Y-axis.

Case II $-\dfrac{k}{2} > 0 \Rightarrow k < 0$

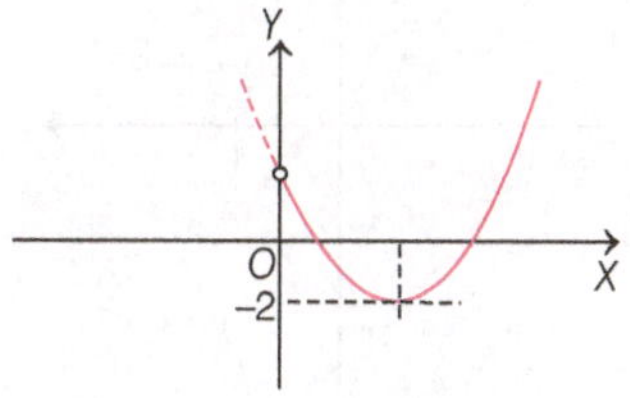

$$f\left(-\frac{k}{2}\right) = -2, \text{ for } k < 0$$

$$\Rightarrow \quad \frac{k^2}{4} - \frac{k^2}{2} + k = -2$$

$$\Rightarrow \quad \frac{k^2 - 2k^2 + 4k}{4} = -2$$

$$\Rightarrow \quad -k^2 + 4k = -8$$

$$\Rightarrow \quad k^2 - 4k - 8 = 0 \Rightarrow k = \frac{4 \pm \sqrt{48}}{2} = 2 \pm 2\sqrt{3}$$

We choose the negative value of k.

Hence, f is onto for $k = 2 - 2\sqrt{3}$.

Example 39. Find the linear function(s) which map the interval $[0, 2]$ onto $[1, 4]$.

Sol. Let $f(x) = ax + b$

If f is increasing, then $f(0) = 1$ and $f(2) = 4$

$$\Rightarrow \quad b = 1 \text{ and } a = \frac{3}{2}$$

If f is decreasing, then $f(0) = 4$ and $f(2) = 1$

$$\Rightarrow \quad b = 4 \text{ and } a = -\frac{3}{2}$$

Hence, $f(x) = \dfrac{3x}{2} + 1$ or $f(x) = 4 - \dfrac{3x}{2}$.

2.14 One-one Onto/Bijective Function

A function $f: X \to Y$ is said to be bijective function when it is one-one and onto both.

Example 40. Let $f: R^+ \to R$, $f(x) = e^{|\ln x|} - x^2$. Find whether f is bijective.

Sol. $f(x) = e^{|\ln x|} - x^2$

$$= \begin{cases} e^{-\ln x} - x^2, & 0 < x < 1 \\ e^{\ln x} - x^2, & x \ge 1 \end{cases}$$

$$= \begin{cases} \dfrac{1}{x} - x^2, & 0 < x < 1 \\ x - x^2, & x \ge 1 \end{cases}$$

We obtain the graph of f in (0, 1) by graphical addition.

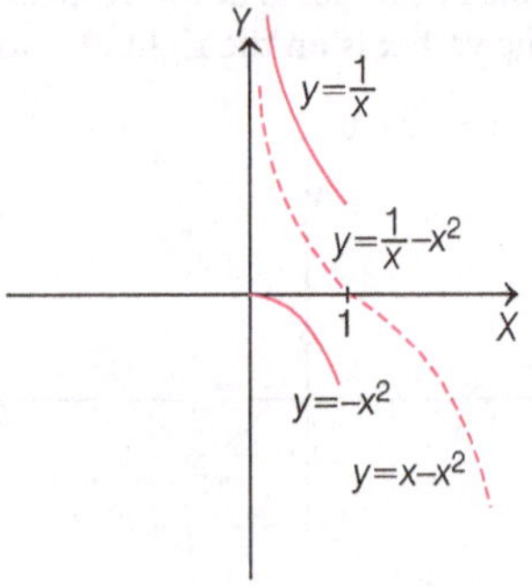

From the graph, we can see that f is one-one and onto.

Hence, f is bijective.

Note

(i) If $f: A \to B$ and $g: B \to C$ are one-one functions, then $gof: A \to C$ is also one-one.

(ii) If $f: A \to B$, $g: B \to C$, $gof: A \to C$ and gof is one-one, then f must be one-one.

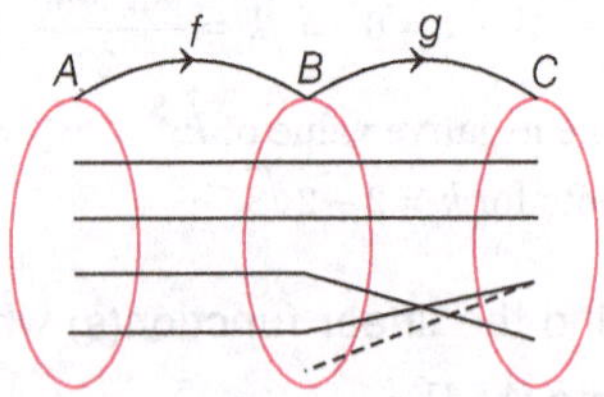

(iii) If $f: A \to B$ and $g: B \to C$ are onto, then $gof: A \to C$ is also one.

(iv) If $f: A \to B$, $g: B \to C$, $gof: A \to C$ and gof is onto, then g must be onto.

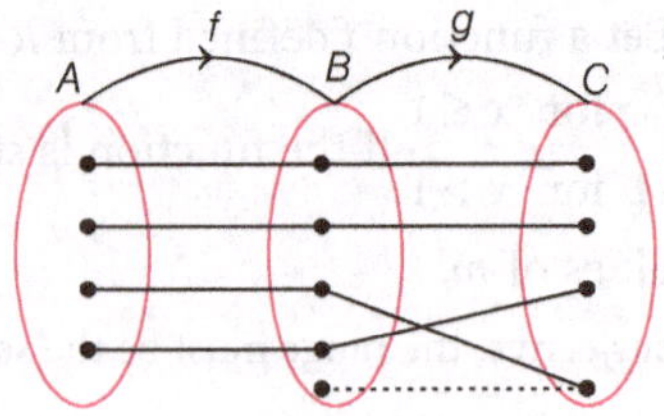

(v) If $f: A \to B$, $g: B \to C$ are bijective, then $gof: A \to C$ is also bijective.

(vi) If $f: A \to B$, $g: B \to C$, $gof: A \to C$ and gof is bijective, then f is one-one and g is onto.

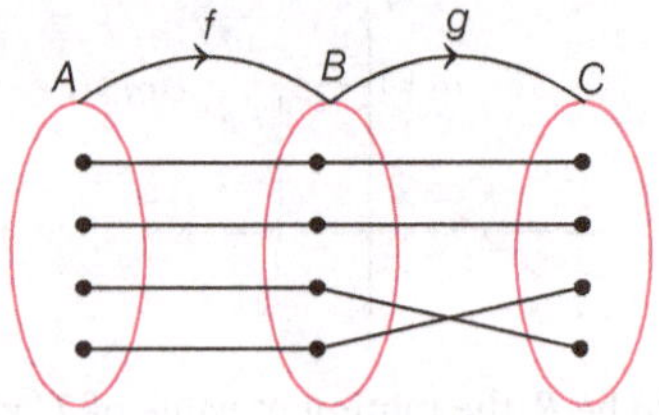

Example 41. The function $f: R \to R$ defined as

$f(x) = \log_e \left(\sqrt{\sqrt{x^2+1} + x} + \sqrt{\sqrt{x^2+1} - x}\right)$ is

(a) one-one and onto both

(b) one-one but not onto

(c) onto but not one-one

(d) Neither one-one nor onto

Sol. (d) Here, $f(x) = \dfrac{2}{2} \log \left(\sqrt{\sqrt{x^2+1} + x} + \sqrt{\sqrt{x^2+1} - x}\right)$

$$= \frac{1}{2} \log \left(\sqrt{\sqrt{x^2+1} + x} + \sqrt{\sqrt{x^2+1} - x}\right)^2$$

$$= \frac{1}{2} \log \left[\sqrt{x^2+1} + x + \sqrt{x^2+1} - x + 2\sqrt{(\sqrt{x^2+1})^2 - x^2}\right]$$

$$= \frac{1}{2} \log \left[2\sqrt{x^2+1} + 2\sqrt{x^2+1-x^2}\right]$$

$$= \frac{1}{2} \log \left[2\sqrt{x^2+1} + 2\right]$$

Now, $f(-x) = f(x)$

$\therefore$ It will have same output for different x and range $\neq$ codomain.

Hence, neither one-one nor onto.

Number of Function (Mapping)

Let a function $f: A \to B$, where A and B having n and m different elements respectively, then number of function is given by

	Description	Equivalent to number of ways in which n different balls can be distributed among r persons if	Number of functions
1.	Total number of functions	Any one can get any number of objects	$(m)^n$
2.	Total number of one-one functions	Each gets exactly 1 object or permutation of n different objects taken r at a time	$\begin{cases} {}^mP_n, & m \ge n \\ 0, & m < n \end{cases}$
3.	Total number of many one functions	At least one gets more than one ball	$\begin{cases} m^n - {}^mC_n \cdot n!, & m \ge n \\ m^n, & m < n \end{cases}$ (Total function − one-one function)
4.	Total number of onto functions	Each goes at least one ball **Note** Using principle of inclusion and exclusion	$\begin{cases} m^n - {}^mC_1(m-1)^n + {}^mC_2(m-2)^n - {}^mC_3(m-3)^n + \ldots, & m < n \\ m!, & m = n \\ 0, & m > n \end{cases}$
5.	Total number of into functions		$\begin{cases} {}^mC_1(m-1)^n - {}^mC_2(m-2)^n + {}^mC_3(m-3)^n - \ldots, & m \le n \\ (m)^n, & m > n \end{cases}$
6.	Total number of constant functions	All the balls are received by any one person	m
7.	Total number of bijective functions $(n = m)$	Permutation of n different objects taken all at a time	$n!$

Number of Into Functions and Onto Functions

Number of non-surjective Functions (Into-Functions)

Number of into functions (N) = Number of ways of distributing n different objects into m distinct boxes so that at least one box is empty.

$\Rightarrow N = n(A_1 \cup A_2 \cup A_3 \cup \ldots \cup A_m)$; where A_i denotes the distributions when ith box is empty

$= \Sigma n(A_i) - \Sigma n(A_i \cap A_j) + \Sigma n(A_i \cap A_j \cap A_k) - \ldots$

Now, $n(A_i) = (m-1)^n$; $n(A_i \cap A_j) = (m-2)^n$;

$n(A_i \cap A_j \cap A_{k)} = (m-3)^n$

$$\therefore\ {}^mC_1\,(m-1)^n - {}^mC_2(m-2)^n + {}^mC_3(m-3)^n - \ldots + (-1)^{m-2} \cdot {}^mC_{m-1}(1)^n$$

$$\Rightarrow \quad N = \sum_{r=1}^{m} {}^mC_r(-1)^{r-1}\,(m-r)^n]$$

Number of Surjective Functions

Number of surjective functions = Total number of functions − number of into functions

$$= m^n - \sum_{r=1}^{m} {}^mC_r\,(-1)^{r-1}\,(m-r)^n$$

$$= m^n + \sum_{r=1}^{m} {}^mC_r(-1)^r(m-r)^n = \sum_{r=0}^{m} {}^mC_r\,(-1)^r\,(m-r)^n$$

Conclusion In case when $n(A) = n(B)$, the onto functions will be bijection.

Number of onto functions = Number of one-one functions

$$\Rightarrow \sum_{r=0}^{n} {}^nC_r(-1)^r (n-r)^n = n!$$

Example 42. If $X = \{1, 2, 3, 4, 5\}$ and $Y = \{a, b, c, d, e, f\}$ and $f: X \to Y$, then find the total number of

(a) Functions (b) One to one function
(c) Many-one function (d) Constant function
(e) Onto function (f) Into function

Sol. (a) Total number of functions $= 6^5 = 7776$

(b) Total number of one to one function
$$= {}^6C_5 \cdot 5! = 6! = 720$$

(c) Total number of many-one function
$$= 6^5 - 6! = 7056$$

(d) Total number of constant function = 6

(e) Total number of onto function = 0 (as $r > n$)

(f) Total number of into function $= 6^5 = 7776$.

Example 43. Let $A = \{1, 2, 3\}$ and $B = \{4, 5, 6, 7\}$. How many functions are there from A to B? How many functions are there from B to A? How many injections are there from A to B? How many surjections are there from B to A.

Sol. Using formula

(1) Total number of function from A to $B = 3^4 = 81$

(2) Total number of function from B to $A = 4^3 = 64$

(3) Total number of injection from A to $B = {}^4P_3 = 4! = 24$

(4) Total number of surjection from B to A
$$= 3^4 - {}^3C_1 2^4 + {}^3C_2 - 0$$
$$= 81 - 48 + 3 = 36$$

Milestone Practice 2.3

1. If $f(x) = \dfrac{4\sin([x]\pi)}{2x^2 + 2\sqrt{2}x + 1}$, where [·] denotes the greatest integer function, then
(a) f is one-one
(b) f is not one-one and non-constant
(c) f is a constant function
(d) None of the above

2. Which of the following is true?
(a) $|x| = x \operatorname{sgn}(x)$ (b) $\operatorname{sgn}(\operatorname{sgn}(x)) = \operatorname{sgn}(x)$
(c) $x = |x| \operatorname{sgn}(x)$ (d) All of these

3. Let $f: A \to A$, where $A = \{x : -1 \le x \le 1\}$. Find whether the following functions are bijective.
(a) $x - \sin x$ (b) $x|x|$
(c) $\tan \dfrac{\pi x}{4}$ (d) x^4

4. Let a function $f: A \to B$, where $A = \{1, 2, 3\}$ and $B = \{6, 7, 8\}$ such that $a < b \Rightarrow f(a) < f(b)$, where $a \in A$ and $b \in B$, then find number of such functions.

5. Find the number of onto function between two sets A and B where, $A = \{1, 2, 3, 4, 5\}$ and $B = \{6, 7, 8\}$.

6. Find the number of bijective functions between two sets $A = \{1, 2, 3, 4\}$ and $B = \{5, 6, 7, 8\}$ such that $f(1) = 5$.

7. Let $f(x) = (x+1)(x+2)(x+3)(x+4) + 5$ where, $x \in [-6, 6]$. If the range of the function is $[a, b]$, where $a, b \in N$, then find the value of $(a + b)$.

8. Let $f: R \to R$ be defined as $f(x) = 3^{-|x|} - 3^x + \operatorname{sgn}(e^{-x}) + 2$ (where sgn x denotes signum function of x). Then, which one of the following is correct?
(a) f is injective but not surjective.
(b) f is surjective but not injective.
(c) f is injective as well as surjective.
(d) f is neither injective nor surjective.

9. The number of bijective functions of $f: A \to A$, where $A = \{1, 2, 3, 4, 5, 6\}$ such that $f(1) \ne 2$ is ......

Answer Key

1. (c)	2. (d)	3. (a) No (b) Yes (c) Yes (d) No		4. (3)
5. (150)	6. (24)	7. (5049)	8. (d)	9. (600)

For Detailed Solution

Milestone 4 Types of Functions III (Some Special Types of Functions)

• Even and Odd Function • Periodic Function • Composite Function • Inverse of a Function • Equal or Identical Function • Bounded Function • Implicit and Explicit Function • Homogeneous Function

2.15 Even and Odd Function

A function $f: X \rightarrow Y$ is said to be

(i) even function, if $f(-x) = f(x)\ \forall\ x, -x \in X$

(ii) odd function, if $f(-x) = -f(x)\ \forall\ x, -x \in X$

e.g. x^{2n}, $\cos x$, $\sin^2 x$, $|x|$ all are even and x^{2n+1}, $\sin x$, $x|x|$ all are odd functions.

Properties of Even and Odd Function

PROPERTY 1 Symmetricity

(a) Graph of even function is symmetric about Y-axis.

(b) Graph of odd function is symmetric about origin.

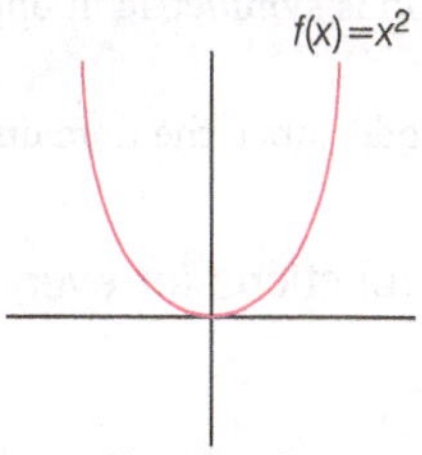

Even function

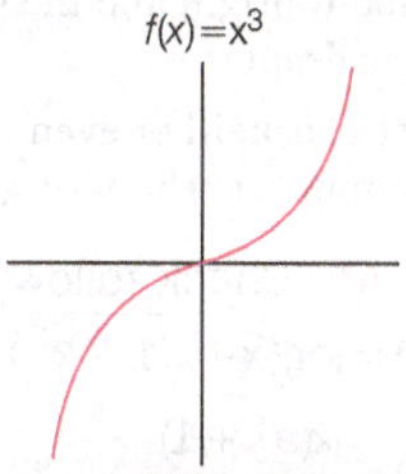

Odd function
Symmetric in opposite quadrants

JEE Focus Points

- $f(x) = f(-x) \rightarrow$ Graph of $y = f(x)$ is symmetric about Y-axis/$x = 0$
- $f(a + x) = f(a - x) \rightarrow$ Graph of $y = f(x)$ is symmetric about line $x = a$
- $f(x) + f(-x) = 0 \rightarrow$ Graph of $y = f(x)$ is symmetric about origin.
- $f(a + x) + f(a - x) = 0 \rightarrow$ Graph of $y = f(x)$ is symmetric about point $(a, 0)$

PROPERTY 2
Expressed any Function as sum of even and odd

Let $f(x)$ be any function, then $g(x) = f(x) + f(-x)$ is always even and $h(x) = f(x) - f(-x)$ is always odd.

$$\therefore\ f(x) = \frac{g(x) + h(x)}{2} = \underbrace{\frac{f(x) + f(-x)}{2}}_{\text{Even}} + \underbrace{\frac{f(x) - f(-x)}{2}}_{\text{Odd}}$$

PROPERTY 3 Domain

Domain of even and odd function must be symmetric about zero

i.e. $D_f \rightarrow [-a, a], (-a, a)$ or $(-a_2, -a_1) \cup (a_1, a_2)$

e.g. (a) $\cos x$ is even in $[-\pi, \pi]$ but not in $[0, \pi]$

(b) $\sin x$ is odd in $[-\pi, \pi]$ but not in $[-\pi, 2\pi]$

PROPERTY 4 Algebra of even and odd function

$f(x)$	$g(x)$	$f(x)+g(x)$	$f(x)-g(x)$	$f(x)g(x)$	$f(x)/g(x)$	$fog(x)$
Even	Even	Even	Even	Even	Even	Even
Even	Odd	Neither even nor odd	Neither even nor odd	Odd	Odd	Even
Odd	Even	Neither even nor odd	Neither even nor odd	Odd	Odd	Even
Odd	Odd	Odd	Odd	Even	Even	Odd

PROPERTY 5 Derivatives

First derivatives of odd function is even function and first derivative of even function is odd function but converse is not true.

PROPERTY 6
Even function is always many-one and non-invertible

PROPERTY 7 Constant function is always even

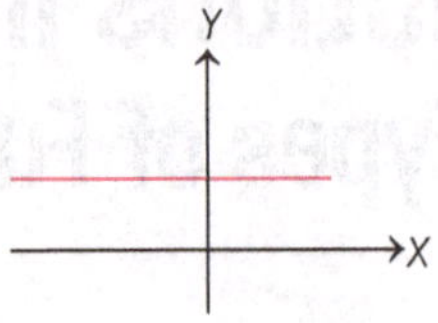

PROPERTY 8 $f(x) = 0 =$ Zero function

This is the only function which is defined on the entire number line is even and odd at the same time.

PROPERTY 9

A function can be either even or odd or neither

PROPERTY 10

If $x = 0 \in$ domain of f, then for odd function $f(x)$ which is continuous at $x = 0$, $f(0) = 0$

i.e. if for a function, $f(0) \neq 0$, then that function cannot be odd.

It follows that for a differentiable even function $f'(0) = 0$ i.e. if for a differentiable function $f'(0) \neq 0$, then the function f cannot be even.

Extension of Domain

Let a function be defined on a certain domain which is entirely non-negative (or non-positive). The domain of $f(x)$ can be extended to the set $X = \{-x : x \in \text{domain of } f(x)\}$ in two ways

(i) **Even extension** The even extension is obtained by defining a new function $f(-x)$ for $x \in X$, such that $f(-x) = f(x)$.

(ii) **Odd extension** The odd extension is obtained by defining a new function $f(-x)$ for $x \in X$, such that $f(-x) = -f(x)$.

Example 44. If $f(x) = \begin{cases} x^3 + x^2, & \text{for } 0 \le x \le 2 \\ x + 2, & \text{for } 2 < x \le 4 \end{cases}$. Then, find the even and odd extension of $f(x)$.

Sol. For even extension $f(x) = f(-x)$

$$f(x) = f(-x) = \begin{cases} (-x)^3 + (-x)^2 & , \ 0 \le -x \le 2 \\ -x + 2 & , \ 2 < -x \le 4 \end{cases}$$

$$= \begin{cases} -x + 2 & , \ -4 \le x < -2 \\ -x^3 + x^2 & , \ -2 \le x \le 0 \end{cases}$$

The odd extension of $f(x)$ is as follows

$$h(x) = \begin{cases} x - 2 & , \ -4 \le x < -2 \\ x^3 - x^2 & , \ -2 \le x \le 0 \end{cases}$$

Example 45. Identify whether the function graphically shown below are even or odd.

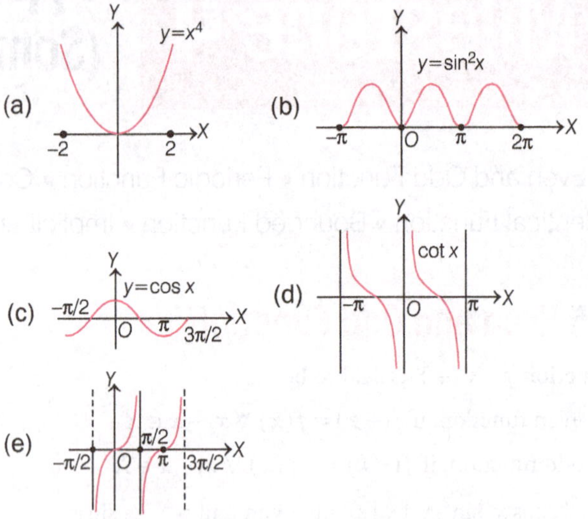

Sol. (a) $f(x)$ is an even function, since the domain is symmetric about origin and the graph is symmetric about Y-axis.

(b) $f(x)$ is neither even nor odd, since the domain is not symmetric about origin.

(c) $f(x)$ is neither even nor odd, since the domain is not symmetric about origin.

(d) $f(x)$ is an odd function, since the domain is symmetric about origin and the graph is symmetric in opposite quadrants.

(e) $f(x)$ is neither even nor odd, since the domain is not symmetric about origin.

Example 46. Check following functions for even or odd.

(a) $f(x) = \log(x + \sqrt{1 + x^2})$

(b) $f(x) = \dfrac{x(a^x + 1)}{a^x - 1}$

(c) $f(x) = \dfrac{(1 + 2^x)^2}{2^x}$

(d) $f(x) = \dfrac{x}{e^x - 1} + \dfrac{x}{2} + 1$

(e) $f(x) = [(x + 1)^2]^{1/3} + [(x - 1)^2]^{1/3}$

(f) $f(x) = \log\left(\dfrac{1 + \sin x}{1 - \sin x}\right)$

(g) $f(x) = x^3 \log\left(\dfrac{1 - x}{1 + x}\right)$

(h) $f(x) = x(e^x - e^{-x}) + \sqrt{\cot^{-1}(\sin(\sec^{-1} x))}$

(i) $f(x) = \tan^{-1}(\sin(\cos^{-1} x))$

(j) $f(x)=\dfrac{2(e^x-e^{-x})(\sin x+\tan x)}{2\left[\dfrac{x+2\pi}{\pi}\right]-3}$,

where [·] denotes the greatest integer function

(k) $f(x)=\begin{cases} x^2, & x\in Q \\ -2x^2, & x\notin Q \end{cases}$

(l) $f(x)=\begin{cases} x\cos x, & -\dfrac{\pi}{2}\le x\le\dfrac{\pi}{2} \\ 1-\sin^4 x, & x<-\dfrac{\pi}{2}, x>\dfrac{\pi}{2} \end{cases}$

(m) $f(x)=\begin{cases} e^{-\sqrt{|\ln\{x\}|}}-\{x\}^{\sqrt{\frac{1}{|\ln\{x\}|}}}, & \text{whenever it exists} \\ \{x\}, & \text{otherwise} \end{cases}$

(n) $f(x)=[x]+\dfrac{1}{2}, x\notin Z$

(o) $f(x)=\begin{cases} x|x|, & \text{if } x\le -1 \\ [1+x]+[1-x], & \text{if } -1<x<1 \\ -x|x|, & \text{if } x\ge 1 \end{cases}$

Sol. (a) Given, $f(x)=\log(x+\sqrt{1+x^2})$ ...(i)

$\Rightarrow\quad f(-x)=\log(-x+\sqrt{1+x^2})$ ...(ii)

On adding Eqs. (i) and (ii), we get

$$f(-x)+f(x)=\log(\sqrt{1+x^2}+x)+\log(\sqrt{1+x^2}-x)$$
$$=\log[(1+x^2)-x^2]$$

$\Rightarrow\quad f(-x)+f(x)=0$

$\Rightarrow\quad f(-x)=-f(x)$

$\therefore f(x)$ is an odd function.

(b) Given, $f(x)=\dfrac{x(a^x+1)}{a^x-1}$

$\Rightarrow\quad f(-x)=-\dfrac{x(a^{-x}+1)}{a^{-x}-1}$

$$=-\frac{x(1+a^x)}{1-a^x}=\frac{x(a^x+1)}{a^x-1}$$
$$=f(x)$$

$\therefore\ f(x)$ is an even function.

(c) Given, $f(x)=\dfrac{(1+2^x)^2}{2^x}$

$$\Rightarrow\quad f(-x)=\frac{(1+2^{-x})^2}{2^{-x}}=\frac{\left(1+\frac{1}{2^x}\right)^2}{\frac{1}{2^x}}=\frac{(2^x+1)^2}{2^{2x}\cdot\frac{1}{2^x}}$$
$$=\frac{(1+2^x)^2}{2^x}=f(x)$$

$\therefore f(x)$ is an even function.

(d) Given, $f(x)=\dfrac{x}{e^x-1}+\dfrac{x}{2}+1$ ...(i)

$$\Rightarrow\quad f(-x)=-\frac{x}{e^{-x}-1}-\frac{x}{2}+1$$
$$=\frac{-x}{\frac{1-e^x}{e^x}}-\frac{x}{2}+1$$

$\Rightarrow\quad f(-x)=\dfrac{xe^x}{e^x-1}-\dfrac{x}{2}+1$

On subtracting Eq. (i) from Eq. (ii), we get

$$f(-x)-f(x)=\frac{x(e^x-1)}{e^x-1}-x=0$$

$\Rightarrow\quad f(-x)=f(x)$

$\therefore f(x)$ is an even function.

(e) Given, $f(x)=[(x+1)^2]^{1/3}+[(x-1)^2]^{1/3}$

$$\Rightarrow\quad f(-x)=[(-x+1)^2]^{1/3}+[(-x-1)^2]^{1/3}$$
$$=[(1-x)^2]^{1/3}+[(1+x)^2]^{1/3}$$
$$=[(x-1)^2]^{1/3}+[(1+x)^2]^{1/3}$$
$$=f(x)$$

$\therefore f(x)$ is an even function.

(f) Given function is $f(x)=\log\left(\dfrac{1+\sin x}{1-\sin x}\right)$

$$\Rightarrow\quad f(-x)=\log\left(\frac{1-\sin x}{1+\sin x}\right)$$
$$=-\log\left(\frac{1+\sin x}{1-\sin x}\right)$$
$$=-f(x)$$

$\therefore f(x)$ is an odd function.

(g) Since, we have domain of $f(x)=(-1,1)$ which is symmetric about Y-axis and $f(x)=x^3\log\left(\dfrac{1-x}{1+x}\right)$

$$\Rightarrow\quad f(-x)=(-x)^3\log\left(\frac{1-(-x)}{1+(-x)}\right)$$
$$=-x^3\log\left(\frac{1+x}{1-x}\right)$$
$$=-x^3\log\left(\frac{1-x}{1+x}\right)^{-1}$$
$$=x^3\log\left(\frac{1-x}{1+x}\right)$$
$$=f(x)$$

Thus, $f(x)$ is clearly an even function.

(h) Now, $f(x) = x(e^x - e^{-x}) + \sqrt{\cot^{-1}(\sin(\sec^{-1} x))}$

$$\Rightarrow \quad f(-x) = -x(e^{-x} - e^x) + \sqrt{\cot^{-1}(\sin(\sec^{-1}(-x))}$$

$$= x(e^x - e^{-x}) + \sqrt{\cot^{-1}(\sin(\sec^{-1}(x)}) = f(x)$$

$\Rightarrow$ Indeed $f(x)$ is an even function.

(i) In order to determine the nature of the function, we check for $f(-x)$.

$$f(-x) = \tan^{-1}(\sin(\cos^{-1}(-x)))$$

$$= \tan^{-1}(\sin(\pi - \cos^{-1} x))$$

$$= \tan^{-1}(\sin(\cos^{-1} x))$$

$$= f(x)$$

Hence, the function is even.

(j) $$f(x) = \frac{2(e^x - e^{-x})(\sin x + \tan x)}{2\left[\frac{x}{\pi} + 2\right] - 3}$$

$$= \frac{2(e^x - e^{-x})(\sin x + \tan x)}{2\left[\frac{x}{\pi}\right] + 1}$$

Now, $$f(-x) = \frac{2(e^x - e^{-x})(\sin x + \tan x)}{2\left[\frac{-x}{\pi}\right] + 1}$$

Case I Let $x = n\pi, n \in I, \left[\frac{-x}{\pi}\right] = -\left[\frac{x}{\pi}\right]$ and the numerator of $f(-x)$ is zero.

$$\Rightarrow \quad f(-x) = 0 = -f(x)$$

Case II $x \neq n\pi, n \in I \Rightarrow \left[\frac{-x}{\pi}\right] = -\left[\frac{x}{\pi}\right] - 1$

$$\therefore f(-x) = \frac{2(e^x - e^{-x})(\sin x + \tan x)}{-2\left[\frac{x}{\pi}\right] - 1} = -f(x)$$

Hence, $f(x)$ is an odd function.

(k) $$f(x) = \begin{cases} x^2, & x \in Q \\ -2x^2, & x \notin Q \end{cases}$$

$$f(-x) = \begin{cases} (-x)^2, & -x \in Q, x \in Q \\ -2(-x)^2, & -x \notin Q, x \notin Q \end{cases}$$

$$= \begin{cases} x^2, & x \in Q \\ -2x^2, & x \notin Q \end{cases} = f(x)$$

Hence, the function is even.

(l) $$f(-x) = \begin{cases} -x\cos(-x), & -\frac{\pi}{2} \le -x \le \frac{\pi}{2} \\ 1 - \sin^4(-x), & -x < -\frac{\pi}{2}, -x > \frac{\pi}{2} \end{cases}$$

$$= \begin{cases} -x\cos x, & -\frac{\pi}{2} \le x \le \frac{\pi}{2} \\ 1 - \sin^4 x, & x < -\frac{\pi}{2}, x > \frac{\pi}{2} \end{cases}$$

This is neither equal to $f(x)$ nor $f(-x)$.

Hence, the function is neither even nor odd.

(m) Consider the following two cases as given below.

Case I Whenever the expression $e^{-\sqrt{|\ln\{x\}|}} - \{x\}^{\sqrt{\frac{1}{|\ln\{x\}|}}}$ exists.

Now, $\{x\} \in [0, 1)$ and $\ln\{x\}$ is defined for $\{x\} \in (0, 1)$.

Hence, $\forall x \in R - Z$

$$f(x) = \ln\{x\} < 0 \text{ for } \{x\} \in (0, 1) \Rightarrow |\ln\{x\}| = -\ln\{x\}$$

$$\therefore e^{\sqrt{|\ln\{x\}|}} - \{x\}^{\sqrt{\frac{1}{|\ln\{x\}|}}} = e^{(-\ln\{x\})^{1/2}} - e^{\ln\{x\}\left[\frac{1}{-\ln\{x\}}\right]^{\frac{1}{2}}}$$

$$= e^{-(-\ln\{x\})^{1/2}} - e^{\frac{1}{(-\ln\{x\})^{1/2}}\ln\{x\}}$$

$$= e^{-(-\ln\{x\})^{1/2}} - e^{-(-\ln\{x\})^{1/2}} = 0$$

Case II For $x \in Z$,

$$f(x) = \{x\} = 0 \quad [\because \{x\} \text{ equal to zero for } x \text{ an integer}]$$

Thus, $f(x) = 0, \forall x \in R$

$\Rightarrow f(x)$ is even as well as odd function.

(n) Given function is $f(x) = [x] + \frac{1}{2}, x \notin Z$

$$\Rightarrow f(-x) = [-x] + \frac{1}{2} = -[x] - 1 + \frac{1}{2}$$

$$= -\left([x] + \frac{1}{2}\right) = -f(x)$$

$$[\because [x] + [-x] = -1 \text{ for } x \notin Z]$$

$\therefore$ $f(x)$ is an odd function.

(o) Given function is

$$f(x) = \begin{cases} x|x|, & \text{if } x \le -1 \\ [1 + x] + [1 - x], & \text{if } -1 < x < 1, \\ -x|x|, & \text{if } x \ge 1 \end{cases}$$

$f(x)$ is graphically shown below.

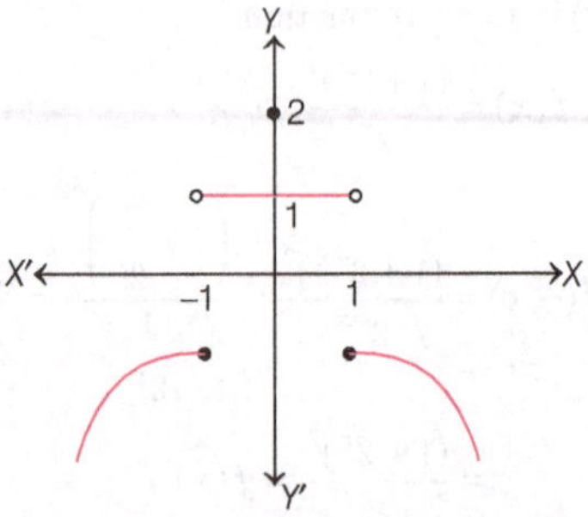

$$\Rightarrow f(-x)=\begin{cases}-(-x)|-x|, & \text{if } x\le -1\\ [1-x]+[1+x], & \text{if } -1<x<1\\ (-x)|-x|, & \text{if } x\ge 1\end{cases}$$

$$=\begin{cases}x|x|, & \text{if } x\le -1\\ [1-x]+[1+x], & \text{if } -1<x<1=f(x)\\ (-x)|x|, & \text{if } x\ge 1\end{cases}$$

Hence, $f(x)$ is an even function.

Example 47. Let $F(x)=\left[\dfrac{f(x)+f(-x)}{g(x)-g(-x)}\right]^n$. Show that $F(x)$ is even when n is even and is odd when n is odd.

Sol. Let $h(x)=f(x)+f(-x)$ and $k(x)=g(x)-g(-x)$

Then, $h(-x)=f(-x)+f(x)=h(x)$

and $k(-x)=g(-x)-g(x)=-k(x)$

So, $h(x)$ is even while $k(x)$ is odd.

Hence, $F(x)$ is an even function, when n is even and odd function, when n is odd.

Thus, $F(x)=\left[\dfrac{h(x)}{k(x)}\right]^n$

and $F(-x)=\left[\dfrac{h(-x)}{k(-x)}\right]^n=(-1)^n\left[\dfrac{h(x)}{k(x)}\right]^n=(-1)^n F(x)$

Example 48. Let $f(x)=|x-4|+|x-5|+|x-6|$ and $g(x)=f(x+k)$. Find k, so that $g(x)$ is an even function.

Sol. Given $f(x)=|x-4|+|x-5|+|x-6|$ and $g(x)=f(x+k)$

We observe that $x-4$, $x-5$ and $x-6$ are in an AP.

Since, the numbers are equally deviated from the AM of the numbers of the group.

So, let $y=$ AM of $(x-4, x-5, x-6)$

$\Rightarrow \quad y=x-5$

Replacing x by $y+5$ in $f(x)$, we get

$$f(y+5)=|y+1|+|y|+|y-1|$$
$$\Rightarrow f(-y+5)=|-y+1|+|-y|+|-y-1|$$
$$=|1-y|+|y|+|1+y|$$
$$=f(y+5)$$

$\therefore g(-y)=g(y)$ for $k=5$.

Hence, the value of k is 5.

Example 49. If $f(x)$ is a polynomial satisfying $f(x)\cdot f(y)-f(x)-f(y)-f(x\cdot y)+2=0$, $\forall\, x, y\in R$ and $f(3)=10$, then show that $f(x)$ is an even function.

Sol. Given, $f(x)\cdot f(y)-f(x)-f(y)-f(xy)+2=0$ ...(i)

On putting $x=1$ and $y=1$ in Eq. (i), we get

$$f(1)\cdot f(1)-f(1)-f(1)-f(1)+2=0$$
$$\Rightarrow \quad (f(1))^2-3(f(1))+2=0$$
$$\Rightarrow \quad f(1)=1 \text{ or } 2$$

Case I On putting $y=1$ and $f(1)=1$, we get

$$f(x)f(1)=f(x)+f(1)+f(x)-2$$
$$\Rightarrow \quad f(x)=1, \forall\, x\in R \quad [\text{rejected}, \because f(3)=10]$$

Case II On putting $y=1$ and $f(1)=2$, we get

$$f(x)\cdot f(1)=f(x)+f(1)+f(x)-2$$
$$\Rightarrow \quad 2f(x)=2f(x)+2-2$$

which is identically true.

Hence, $f(1)=2$

Now, given that $f(x)$ is a polynomial function, therefore on putting $y=1/x$, we get

$$f(x)f(1/x)=f(x)+f(1/x)+f(1)-2$$
$$\Rightarrow \quad f(x)\cdot f(1/x)=f(x)+f(1/x)$$
$$\Rightarrow \quad f(x)=1\pm x^n$$

Let $f(x)=1+x^n$ and $f(1)=2$, $f(3)=10$

$\Rightarrow \quad n=2$

$f(x)=1-x^n$ is rejected as it does not satisfy $f(1)=2$; $f(3)=10$ for any value of n

$\therefore f(x)=1+x^2$ and $f(-x)=1+(-x)^2$

$=1+x^2=f(x)$

$\Rightarrow f(x)$ is an even function.

Example 50. Prove that in the product $(1-x+x^2-x^3+\ldots-x^{49}+x^{50})$ $(1+x+x^2+x^3+\ldots+x^{49}+x^{50})$, after simplification there will be no term containing odd power of x and hence, show that the above product represents an even function.

Sol. Let $f(x)=(1-x+x^2-x^3+\ldots-x^{49}+x^{50})(1+x+x^2+\ldots+x^{50})$

$$=[(1+x^2+x^4+\ldots+x^{50})-(x+x^3+\ldots+x^{49})]\cdot[(1+x^2+x^4+\ldots+x^{50})+(x+x^3+\ldots+x^{49})]$$
$$=(1+x^2+x^4+\ldots+x^{50})^2-(x+x^3+\ldots+x^{49})^2$$
$$=(1+x^2+x^4+\ldots+x^{50})^2-x^2(1+x^2+\ldots+x^{48})^2$$

Now, we can observe that the above expression does not contain any term of x having odd degree. Hence, $f(x)$ is an even function.

Example 51. Let $f(x)=\begin{cases}0, & \text{if } x \text{ is rational}\\ x, & \text{if } x \text{ is irrational}\end{cases}$ and $g(x)=\begin{cases}x, & \text{if } x \text{ is rational}\\ 0, & \text{if } x \text{ is irrational}\end{cases}$, then find whether $f(x)-g(x)$ is even or odd.

Sol. $f(x)-g(x)=F(x)=\begin{cases}-x & \text{if } x \text{ is rational}\\ x & \text{if } x \text{ is irrational}\end{cases}$

$$F(-x)=\begin{cases}-(-x) & \text{if } -x \text{ is rational, } x \text{ is rational}\\ -x & \text{if } -x \text{ is irrational, } x \text{ is irrational}\end{cases}$$

$$F(-x)=\begin{cases}x & \text{if } x \text{ is rational}\\ -x & \text{if } x \text{ is irrational}\end{cases}$$
$$=-F(x)$$

Hence, $F(x)$ is odd.

Example 52. Let a function f satisfy $f(x+y)+f(x-y)=2f(x).f(y), \forall x, y \in R$, where $f(0) \neq 0$. Prove that f is even.

Sol. On putting $x=0$ in the given equation, we get

$$f(y)+f(-y)=2f(0)f(y) \quad \text{...(i)}$$

To obtain the value of $f(0)$, we put $y=0$ in Eq. (i), we get

$$\Rightarrow \quad 2f(0)=2f^2(0)$$

$$f(0)=0 \text{ or } 1, \text{ given } f(0) \neq 0$$

$$\Rightarrow \quad f(0)=1$$

From Eq. (i), we get $f(y)+f(-y)=2f(y)$

$$\Rightarrow \quad f(y)=f(-y)$$

Hence, the function is even.

Example 53. Let $f(x)=e^x+\sin x$ be defined on the interval $[-4, 0]$. Find the even and odd extension of $f(x)$ in the interval $[-4, 4]$.

Sol. Let $g_e(x)$ be the even extension of $f(x)$, then

$$g_e(x)=\begin{cases} f(x), & x \in [-4, 0] \\ f(-x), & x \in (0, 4] \end{cases}$$

$$=\begin{cases} e^x+\sin x, & x \in [-4, 0] \\ e^{-x}-\sin x, & x \in (0, 4] \end{cases}$$

We cannot have an odd extension of $f(x)$ because $f(0)=1 \neq 0$. An odd function must have $f(0)=0$.

Example 54. Define f for $x \in [-2, 0)$ so that

(i) f is an odd function

(ii) f is an even function

where $f(x)=\begin{cases} x\tan x, & 0 \le x \le \frac{\pi}{2} \\ \frac{\pi}{2}[x], & \frac{\pi}{2} < x \le 2 \end{cases}$ and $[\cdot]$ denotes the greatest integer function.

Sol. Since, $f(x)=\begin{cases} x\tan x, & 0 \le x \le \frac{\pi}{2} \\ \frac{\pi}{2}[x], & \frac{\pi}{2} < x \le 2 \end{cases}$

$$\therefore \quad f(-x)=\begin{cases} (-x)\tan(-x), & 0 < -x \le \frac{\pi}{2} \\ \frac{\pi}{2}[-x], & \frac{\pi}{2} < -x \le 2 \end{cases}$$

$$\text{or} \quad f(-x)=\begin{cases} x\tan x, & -\frac{\pi}{2} \le x < 0 \\ \frac{\pi}{2}[-x], & -2 \le x < -\frac{\pi}{2} \end{cases}$$

(i) If f is an odd function, then the extended definition in $[-2, 0]$ is

$$f(x)=\begin{cases} -x\tan x, & -\frac{\pi}{2} \le x < 0 \\ -\frac{\pi}{2}[-x], & -2 \le x < -\frac{\pi}{2} \end{cases}$$

Note that $f(0)=0$ for an odd function.

(ii) If f is an even function, then the extended definition in $[-2, 0]$ is

$$f(x)=\begin{cases} x\tan x, & -\frac{\pi}{2} \le x < 0 \\ \frac{\pi}{2}[-x], & -2 \le x < -\frac{\pi}{2} \end{cases}$$

2.16 Periodic Function

Periodic means the quantity which repeats after certain interval. In function, also it have same meaning.

A function $f: X \to Y$ is said to be periodic function, if there exists a real positive finite number T(independent of x) such that $f(x+T)=f(x), \forall x, x+T \in D_f$.

We can also conclude that

$$f(x)=f(x+T)=f(x+2T)=f(x+3T)=\ldots$$
$$=f(x-T)=f(x-2T)=f(x-3T)\ldots$$

Therefore, $f(x)=f(x+nT), \forall n \in Z$,

where $x, x+nT \in D_f$.

Period The least positive value of such T (if exists), is called the period, principal period or fundamental period of $f(x)$.

e.g. $f(x)=\tan x$ is periodic with period π.

(a) **Trigonometric Functions** The function $\sin x$, $\cos x$, $\sec x$, $\operatorname{cosec} x$ are periodic with period 2π, whereas $\tan x$, $\cot x$ are periodic functions with period π.

(b) **There may be Periodic Functions which have no Fundamental Period**

e.g.

(i) **Dirichlet Function**

$$f(x)=\begin{cases} 1, & \text{when } x \text{ is rational} \\ 0, & \text{when } x \text{ is irrational} \end{cases}$$

Let $\frac{p}{q}: p, q \in Z$, coprime to each other and $q \neq 0$ be period

$$\Rightarrow f\left(x+\frac{p}{q}\right)=\begin{cases} 1, & x+\frac{p}{q} \in Q \\ 0, & x+\frac{p}{q} \notin Q \end{cases}$$

$$\Rightarrow f\left(x+\frac{p}{q}\right)=\begin{cases} 1, & x \in Q \\ 0, & x \notin Q \end{cases}=f(x)$$

$\Rightarrow f(x)$ is periodic with $\frac{p}{q}$ but has no fundamental period, as it is impossible to find a least positive rational number p/q.

(ii) **Constant Function** Consider a function $f(x) = c$ Clearly, $f(x+T) = f(x) = c$ holds good for all positive values of T. Therefore, fulfilling the requirement of periodic function. Although any positive real number may be taken as period of constant function but indeed no such least real number can be predicted. Thus, constant function has no fundamental period.

(c) **No Rational Function (except constant function) can be a Periodic Function**

Let $F(x) = \dfrac{f(x)}{g(x)}$, where $f(x)$ and $g(x)$ are two polynomials and $g(x) \neq 0$ and $F(x)$ be periodic with period T.

$$\Rightarrow \quad F(x) = F(x+T) \quad \ldots(i)$$

$$\Rightarrow \quad \frac{f(x+T)}{g(x+T)} = \frac{f(x)}{g(x)}$$

$\Rightarrow f(x+T)\cdot g(x) - g(x+T) f(x) = 0$ is an identity in x therefore on substituting $x = 0$, we obtain

$$f(T)g(0) - g(T)f(0) = 0 \quad \ldots(ii)$$

It is clearly a polynomial in T of degree n (here n is degree of the polynomial having larger degree out of f and g). Now, since Eq. (ii) has degree n but can had $(n+1)$ roots for instance $0, T, 2T, 3T, \ldots nT$.

Consequently, by fundamental theorem of algebra, $f(x)$ must be identically equal to 0, $\forall\, x \in R$.

Therefore, $F(x)$ must be indeed a constant function.

(d) **Algebraic Function (Except Constant Function) Can Not be a Periodic Function.**

(e) **A Function Can be Periodic in a Bounded Subset of Its Natural Domain.**

We can discuss the periodicity of a function in an interval. For instance, $f(x) = \begin{cases} \cos\sqrt{-x}, & x < 0 \\ \cos \pi x, & 0 \le x \le 100 \\ 101 - x, & x > 100 \end{cases}$

is not a periodic function in its natural domain but it is clearly a periodic function in the interval [0,98]. Because $f(x+2) = f(x)$ holds good for all $x \in [0, 98]$

JEE Focus Points

Basic Concepts of LCM

- LCM of $\left[\dfrac{a}{b}, \dfrac{c}{d}, \dfrac{e}{f}, \ldots\right] = \dfrac{\text{LCM of } (a, c, e, \ldots)}{\text{HCF of } (b, d, f, \ldots)}$
- LCM of rational with rational is possible.
- LCM of irrational with irrational is also possible.
- But LCM of rational with irrational is not possible.
- Two important irrational number are π, e

The LCM of $\left(\dfrac{1}{2}, \dfrac{1}{3}, \dfrac{1}{4}\right) = \dfrac{\text{LCM of } (1, 1, 1)}{\text{HCF of } (2, 3, 4)} = \dfrac{1}{1} = 1$

Properties of Periodic Functions

PROPERTY 1

If $f(x)$ is a periodic function with period T, then the period of $f(a\,x)$, $f(ax+b)$, $f(ax+b)+c$, $df(ax+b)+c$ is $\dfrac{T}{|a|}$.

PROPERTY 2

If $f(x)$ and $g(x)$ are two periodic functions with periods T_1 and T_2, respectively, then the period of $f(x)+g(x)$, $f(x)-g(x)$, $f(x)\cdot g(x)$, $\dfrac{f(x)}{g(x)}$, $g(x) \neq 0$ is the LCM of $\{T_1, T_2\}$.

This is known as LCM rule.

Example 55. Find the period of $f(x) = \sin x + \sin 2x$.

Sol. Here, the period of $\sin x = 2\pi$ and the period of

$$\sin 2x = \frac{2\pi}{2} = \pi$$

Thus, the period of $f(x) = \text{LCM of } \{2\pi, \pi\} = 2\pi$

Example 56. Find the period of $f(x) = \sin 2x + \cos 3x$

Sol. Here, the period of $\sin 2x = \dfrac{2\pi}{2} = \pi$

and the period of $\cos 3x = \dfrac{2\pi}{3}$

$$\text{Thus, the period of } f(x) = \text{LCM of } \left\{\pi, \frac{2\pi}{3}\right\} = \frac{\text{LCM of } (\pi, 2\pi)}{\text{HCF of } (1, 3)} = \frac{2\pi}{1} = 2\pi$$

PROPERTY 3

If $f(x)$ and $g(x)$ both are periodic with periods T_1 and T_2 respectively and both are even and cofunction and pairwise comparable function, then the period of

(i) $f(x) + g(x)$

(ii) $f(x) - g(x)$

(iii) $f(x)\cdot g(x)$

(iv) $\dfrac{f(x)}{g(x)}$, $g(x) \neq 0$ is the $\dfrac{1}{2} \times \text{LCM of } \{T_1, T_2\}$

Example 57. Find the period of $f(x) = \sin^4 x + \cos^4 x$

Sol. Here, the period of $\sin^4 x = \pi$

and the period of $\cos^4 x = \pi$.

Since, both the functions are periodic, even, co-function as well as both are pairwise comparable function, so the period of $f(x)$ is

$$= \frac{1}{2} \times \text{LCM of } \{\pi, \pi\} = \frac{\pi}{2}$$

Example 58. Find the period of $f(x) = \cos(\cos x) + \cos(\sin x)$.

Sol. Here, the period of $\cos(\cos x)$ is π and the period of $\cos(\sin x)$ is also π.

Since, both the function are periodic, even, co-function as well as both are pairwise comparable function, so the period of $f(x)$ is

$$= \frac{1}{2} \times \text{LCM of } \{\pi, \pi\} = \frac{\pi}{2}$$

PROPERTY 4

If $f(x)$ is a periodic functions with period T, then the period of

(i) $\dfrac{1}{f(x)}$

(ii) $k^{f(x)}, k \in R^+ - \{1\}$

(iii) $(f(x))^{1/n}$ is also T.

Example 59. Find the period of $f(x) = \sqrt{\sin x}$

Sol. Since, the period of $\sin x$ is 2π, so the period of $f(x)$ is also 2π.

Example 60. Find the period of $f(x) = \dfrac{1}{\sin x}$

Sol. Since, the period of $\sin x$ is 2π, so the period of $f(x)$ is also 2π.

PROPERTY 5

If $f(x)$ is a periodic function with period T and $g(x)$ be non-periodic function, then $g(f(x))$ is periodic with period T and $f(g(x))$ is non-periodic.

Example 61. Find the period of $f(x) = \sin^{-1}(\sin x)$.

Sol. Let $h(x) = \sin x$ and $g(x) = \sin^{-1} x$

Thus, the period of $h(x)$ is 2π and $g(x)$ is non-periodic.

Therefore, the period of $f(x)$ is $= 2\pi$

Note The function $f(x) = \sin(\sin^{-1} x)$ is non-periodic, whereas $\sin x$ is periodic but $\sin^{-1} x$ is non-periodic.

PROPERTY 6

If $f(x)$ is a periodic function with period T, then $f'(x)$ is also periodic with period T.

Example 62. Find the period of $f(x) = \sin x$.

Sol. We have, $f'(x) = \cos x$

Thus, the period of $\cos x$ is 2π, whereas the period of $\sin x$ is also 2π.

PROPERTY 7

Constant function is periodic having no fundamental period.

PROPERTY 8

Algebraic function is non-periodic.

JEE Focus Points

- The functions $\sin^n x$, $\cos^n x$, $\text{cosec}^n x$, $\sec^n x$ are periodic with period 2π, when n is odd and π when n is even.
- The functions $\tan^n x$, $\cot^n x$ are periodic with periods π, whatever n may be.
- The functions $|\sin x|$, $|\cos x|$, $|\tan x|$, $|\cot x|$, $|\text{cosec } x|$, $|\sec x|$ are periodic with period π
- The functions $|\sin x| + |\cos x|$, $|\tan x| + |\cot x|$, $|\text{cosec } x| + |\sec x|$ are periodic with period $\frac{\pi}{2}$.
- The functions $|\sin x| - |\cos x|$, $|\tan x| - |\cot x|$, $|\text{cosec } x| - |\sec x|$ are periodic with period π.
- The function $\sqrt{\sin x}$, $\sqrt{\cos x}$, $\sqrt{\text{cosec } x}$ and $\sqrt{\sec x}$ are periodic with period 2π.
- The functions $\sin^{-1}(\sin x)$, $\cos^{-1}(\cos x) \sec^{-1}(\sec x)$, $\text{cosec}^{-1}(\text{cosec } x)$ are periodic with period 2π.
- The functions $\tan^{-1}(\tan x)$, $\cot^{-1}(\cot x)$ are periodic with period π.
- The functions $\sin^{-1} x$, $\cos^{-1} x$, $\tan^{-1} x$, $\cot^{-1} x$ are non-periodic.
- The function $x - [x]$ is periodic with period 1.

Example 63. Test the periodicity of the following functions and if periodic, find their fundamental period.

(i) $f(x) = a\cos(2x + c)$, $a \neq 0$ (ii) $f(x) = \sin\sqrt{x}$

Sol. As, we check periodicity by applying the definition of periodic function, assuming its period to be T and subsequently analysing equation $f(x + T) = f(x)$

(i) Given $f(x) = a\cos(2x + c)$ and $f(x) = f(x + T)$

$\Rightarrow \quad a\cos(2(x + T) + c) = a\cos(2x + c)$

$\Rightarrow \quad \cos(2(x + T) + c) - \cos(2x + c) = 0$

$\Rightarrow 2\sin\left(\dfrac{2(2x + T) + 2c}{2}\right)\sin\left(\dfrac{2(-T)}{2}\right) = 0$

$\Rightarrow \quad \sin(T) = 0 \text{ or } \sin\left(2\left(x + \dfrac{T}{2}\right) + c\right) = 0$

$\Rightarrow T = n\pi \text{ or } 2x + T + c = n\pi;\ n \in Z$

$\Rightarrow T = n\pi \text{ or } T = n\pi - 2x - c$ [rejected, as depends on x]

$\therefore\ T = n\pi,\ n \in Z$ which is constant $\quad [\because T > 0]$

$\Rightarrow T_{\min} = \pi \quad$ [fundamental period]

Therefore, $f(x) = a\cos(2x + c)$ is periodic function with fundamental period π.

(ii) Consider $f(x) = \sin\sqrt{x}$ be periodic with period T.

$\Rightarrow f(x) = f(x + T)$ i.e. $\sin\sqrt{(x + T)} = \sin\sqrt{x}$

$$\Rightarrow \quad \sin\sqrt{x+T} - \sin\sqrt{x} = 0$$

$$\Rightarrow 2\cos\left(\frac{\sqrt{x+T}+\sqrt{x}}{2}\right)\sin\left(\frac{\sqrt{x+T}-\sqrt{x}}{2}\right) = 0$$

$$\Rightarrow \quad \left(\frac{\sqrt{x+T}+\sqrt{x}}{2}\right) = \frac{(2n+1)\pi}{2}$$

or $$\left(\frac{\sqrt{x+T}-\sqrt{x}}{2}\right) = n\pi, n \in Z$$

$$\Rightarrow \quad \sqrt{x+T}+\sqrt{x} = (2n+1)\pi$$

or $$\sqrt{x+T}-\sqrt{x} = 2n\pi$$

Therefore, T can never be made independent of x, consequently $f(x)$ is a non-periodic function.

Alternate Solution

$$\sin\sqrt{(x+T)} = \sin\sqrt{x}$$

$$\Rightarrow \quad \sqrt{(x+T)} = n\pi + (-1)^n\sqrt{x}, n \in Z$$

On squaring both sides and solving for T, we get

$$(x+T) = (n\pi + (-1)^n\sqrt{x})^2$$

$$\Rightarrow \quad T = (n\pi + (-1)^n\sqrt{x})^2 - x$$

On expanding the right hand side, we observe that the expression of T is not independent of x.

Hence, our assumption is false and therefore the given function is not a periodic function.

Example 64. Using graphs, find whether the following functions are periodic and find the period

(i) $y = \dfrac{\sin 2x}{|\cos x|}$ (ii) $y = \sin x \operatorname{cosec} x$

Sol. (i) $y = \dfrac{\sin 2x}{|\cos x|} = \begin{cases} 2\sin x, & \cos x > 0 \\ -2\sin x, & \cos x < 0 \end{cases}$

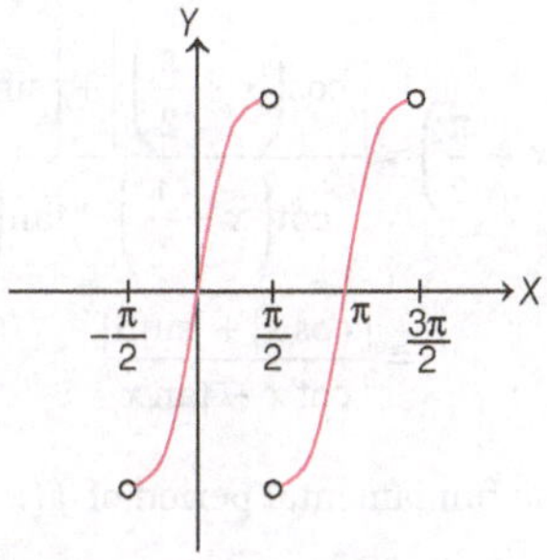

From the graph, we see that the period, $T = \pi$.

(ii) $y = \sin x \operatorname{cosec} x \Rightarrow y = 1, x \neq n\pi$

We see that the period, $T = \pi$

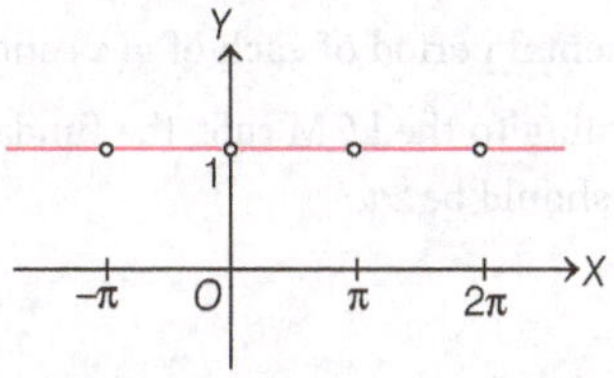

Example 65. Draw the graph of $f(x)$ defined as below in the domain $[-3, 9]$

$$f(x) = \begin{cases} x - 3n & \text{if } 3n \le x \le 3n+1 \\ 1 & \text{if } 3n+1 \le x \le 3n+2 \\ 3(n+1) - x & \text{if } 3n+2 \le x \le 3(n+1) \end{cases}$$ and state

whether the function $f(x)$ is periodic. If so, mention its domain of periodicity.

Sol. Consider the graph of function $f(x)$ in the interval $[-3, 9]$.

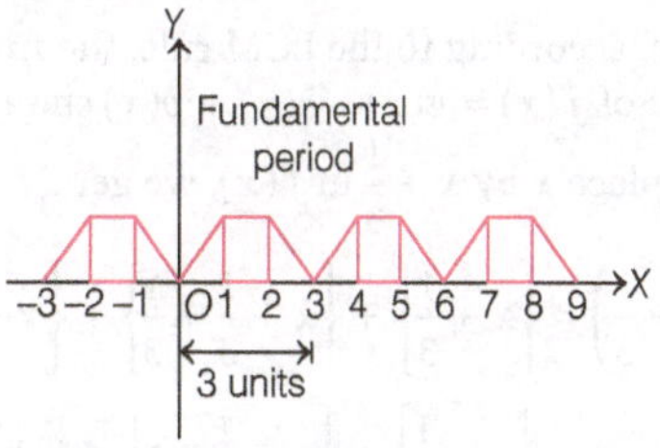

Clearly, $f(x+3) = f(x)$ holds $\forall\ x \in [-3, 9]$ for which $x + 3 \in [-3, 9]$.

Therefore, $f(x)$ is periodic with fundamental period 3 in the interval $[-3, 6]$.

Example 66. Find the fundamental period of following function

(i) $f(x) = \{x\} + \left\{x + \dfrac{1}{3}\right\} + \left\{x - \dfrac{1}{3}\right\}$

(ii) $f(x) = a|\tan mx| + b|\tan nx|$

(iii) $f(x) = 16(\sin^6 x + \cos^6 x) - 24(\sin^4 x + \cos^4 x) + 9$

(iv) $f(x) = \dfrac{|\cos x| + |\sin x|}{\cot x - \tan x}$

(v) $f(x) = \dfrac{\cos x - \cos 3x}{\sin x - \sin 3x}$

(vi) $\tan\left(\dfrac{\pi}{3} - x\right) \cdot \tan x \cdot \tan\left(\dfrac{\pi}{3} + x\right)$

(vii) $\dfrac{9\tan\theta - 84\tan^3\theta + 126\tan^5\theta - 36\tan^7\theta + \tan^9\theta}{1 - 36\tan^2\theta + 126\tan^4\theta - 84\tan^6\theta + 9\tan^8\theta}$

(viii) $f(x) = \operatorname{sgn}(e^{-x}) - \sin x + |\sin x| + \min(\sin x, |x|)$

(ix) $\left[x + \dfrac{1}{2}\right] + \left[x - \dfrac{1}{2}\right] + 2[-x]$, where $[x]$ denotes the greatest integer function

(x) Find the fundamental period of the function $f(x) = x + a - [x+b] + \sin \pi x + \cos 2\pi x + \sin 3\pi x + \cos 4\pi x + \ldots + \sin(2n-1)\pi x + \cos 2n\pi x$ for every $a, b \in R$ is (where [ ] denotes the greatest integer function).

Sol. (i) Let $f(x) = \{x\} + \left\{x + \dfrac{1}{3}\right\} + \left\{x - \dfrac{1}{3}\right\}$

Let $g(x)$, $h(x)$ and $p(x)$ be $\{x\}$, $\left\{x + \dfrac{1}{3}\right\}$ and $\left\{x - \dfrac{1}{3}\right\}$ respectively.

We observe that the fundamental period of each of $g(x)$, $h(x)$ and $p(x)$ is 1.

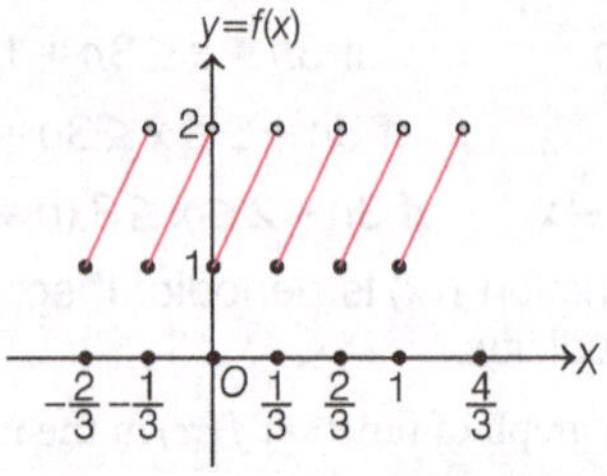

Hence, according to the LCM rule, the fundamental period of $f(x)=g(x)+h(x)+p(x)$ should be 1 but if we replace x by $x+\frac{1}{3}$ in $f(x)$, we get

$$f\left(x+\frac{1}{3}\right)=\left\{x+\frac{1}{3}\right\}+\left\{x+\frac{1}{3}+\frac{1}{3}\right\}+\left\{x+\frac{1}{3}-\frac{1}{3}\right\}$$

$$=\left\{x+\frac{1}{3}\right\}+\left\{x-\frac{1}{3}+1\right\}+\{x\}$$

$$=\{x\}+\left\{x+\frac{1}{3}\right\}+\left\{x-\frac{1}{3}\right\}=f(x)$$

Hence, fundamental period of $f(x)=\frac{1}{3}$. Same can be concluded from graph.

Here, $f(x)=\{x\}+\{x+1/3\}+\{x-1/3\}, \forall\, x\in[0,1/3)$

$$=x+x+1/3+x+2/3=3x+1$$

$\therefore f(x)$ is monotonic in $(0,1/3)$

$\Rightarrow f(x)$ cannot have any period smaller than 1/3.

(ii) Given, $f(x)=a|\tan mx|+b|\tan nx|$

Let $g(x)=a|\tan mx|$ and $h(x)=b|\cot nx|$

Now, period of $g(x)$ is $\frac{\pi}{m}$ and period of $h(x)$ is $\frac{\pi}{n}$,

For $(a\neq b, m=n)$; $(a=b, m\neq n)$; $(a\neq b, m\neq n)$, the fundamental period of $f(x)=\text{LCM of}\left\{\frac{\pi}{m}\text{ and }\frac{\pi}{n}\right\}$

$$=\frac{\pi}{\text{HCF }(m,n)}$$

But when $a=b$ and $m=n$, then $g(x)$ and $h(x)$ are inter convertible and hence the fundamental period of

$f(x)=\frac{1}{2}\left\{\text{LCM of }\frac{\pi}{m}\text{ and }\frac{\pi}{n}\right\}$ i.e. $\frac{\pi}{2m}$ or $\frac{\pi}{2n}$

(iii) Given, $f(x)=16(\sin^6 x+\cos^6 x)$
$-24(\sin^4 x+\cos^4 x)+9$

Let $g(x)=16(\sin^6 x+\cos^6 x)$

$$=16\{(\sin^2 x+\cos^2 x)^3-3\sin^2 x\cos^2 x(\sin^2 x+\cos^2 x)\}$$

$$=16\left\{1-\frac{3}{4}\sin^2(2x)\right\}$$

$\Rightarrow$ Fundamental period of $g(x)$ is $\frac{\pi}{2}$.

Let $h(x)=-24(\sin^4 x+\cos^4 x)$

$$=-24[(\sin^2 x+\cos^2 x)^2-2\sin^2 x\cos^2 x]$$

$$=-24\left(1-\frac{1}{2}\sin^2 2x\right)$$

Again, fundamental period of $h(x)=\frac{\pi}{2}$

and $p(x)=9$ is a constant function

[i.e. no fundamental period]

According to the LCM rule, fundamental period of $f(x)=\text{LCM of}\left(\frac{\pi}{2},\frac{\pi}{2}\right)=\frac{\pi}{2}$

But $f(x)=16(\sin^6 x+\cos^6 x)-24(\sin^4 x+\cos^4 x)$
$+9(\sin^2 x+\cos^2 x)$

$$=(16\sin^6 x-24\sin^4 x+9\sin^2 x)$$
$$+(16\cos^6 x-24\cos^4 x+9\cos^2 x)$$

$$=(4\sin^3 x-3\sin x)^2+(4\cos^3 x-3\cos x)^2$$

$$=(\sin 3x)^2+(-\cos 3x)^2=1$$

Hence, $f(x)$ is a constant function with no fundamental period.

(iv) Given, $f(x)=\frac{|\cos x|+|\sin x|}{\cot x-\tan x}$

Now, let $g(x)=|\cos x|+|\sin x|$ and $h(x)=\cot x-\tan x$ and the fundamental period of each of $g(x)$ and $h(x)$ is π.

$\therefore$ The fundamental period of $f(x)$ should be π

But if we replace x by $x+\frac{\pi}{2}$ in $f(x)$, we get

$$f\left(x+\frac{\pi}{2}\right)=\frac{\left|\cos\left(x+\frac{\pi}{2}\right)\right|+\left|\sin\left(x+\frac{\pi}{2}\right)\right|}{\cot\left(x+\frac{\pi}{2}\right)-\tan\left(x+\frac{\pi}{2}\right)}$$

$$=\frac{|\cos x|+|\sin x|}{\cot x-\tan x}$$

Hence, the fundamental period of $f(x)$ is $\frac{\pi}{2}$.

(v) Given, $f(x)=\frac{\cos x-\cos 3x}{\sin x-\sin 3x}$

Let $g(x)=\cos x-\cos 3x$ and $h(x)=\sin x-\sin 3x$

Fundamental period of each of $g(x)$ and $h(x)$ is 2π

$\therefore$ According to the LCM rule, the fundamental period of $f(x)$ should be 2π.

But $f(x)=\dfrac{-2\sin 2x\sin(-x)}{-2\sin x\cos 2x}=-\tan 2x$, $\sin x\neq 0$ and the period of $\tan 2x$ is $\dfrac{\pi}{2}$.

But as explained earlier, we need to be careful while dealing with domain.

$$\sin x\neq 0\Rightarrow x\neq n\pi,\ \forall\, n\in Z$$

Thus, the period of discontinuity of function is π.

$\therefore$ The fundamental period of $f(x)$ will be LCM of π and $\dfrac{\pi}{2}$ i.e. π.

(vi) Given, $f(x)=\tan\left(\dfrac{\pi}{3}-x\right)\cdot\tan x\cdot\tan\left(\dfrac{\pi}{3}+x\right)$

Let $g(x)=\tan\left(\dfrac{\pi}{3}-x\right)$, $h(x)=\tan x$ and $p(x)=\tan\left(\dfrac{\pi}{3}+x\right)$, respectively.

Fundamental period of each of $g(x)$, $h(x)$ and $p(x)$ is π.

$\therefore$ According to the LCM rule, the Fundamental period of $f(x)$ should be π.

But $f(x)=\tan\left(\dfrac{\pi}{3}-x\right)\cdot\tan x\cdot\tan\left(\dfrac{\pi}{3}+x\right)=\tan 3x$

$\therefore$ Fundamental period of $f(x)=\dfrac{\pi}{3}$

(vii) Given,

$$f(x)=\frac{9\tan\theta-84\tan^3\theta+126\tan^5\theta-36\tan^7\theta+\tan^9\theta}{1-36\tan^2\theta+126\tan^4\theta-84\tan^6\theta+9\tan^8\theta}$$

Let

$g(x)=9\tan\theta-84\tan^3\theta+126\tan^5\theta-36\tan^7\theta+\tan^9\theta$

and $h(x)=1-36\tan^2\theta+126\tan^4\theta-84\tan^6\theta+9\tan^8\theta$

Now, fundamental period of each of $g(x)$ and $h(x)=\pi$

$\therefore$ According to the LCM rule, fundamental period of $f(x)=\pi$

But

$$f(x)=\frac{9\tan\theta-84\tan^3\theta+126\tan^5\theta-36\tan^7\theta+\tan^9\theta}{1-36\tan^2\theta+126\tan^4\theta-84\tan^6\theta+9\tan^8\theta}=\tan 9\theta$$

Hence, the fundamental period of $f(x)=\dfrac{\pi}{9}$

(viii) Given, $\operatorname{sgn}(x)=\begin{cases}1, & x>0\\ 0, & x=0\\ -1, & x<0\end{cases}$

$\because\ e^{-x}>0\Rightarrow \operatorname{sgn}(e^{-x})=1$

$\therefore\ \operatorname{sgn}(e^{-x})$ is constant function which is periodic with no fundamental period.

$\therefore\quad f(x)=1-\sin x+|\sin x|+\sin x$

$\min(\sin x,|x|)=\sin x \qquad [\because \sin x\leq |x|]$

$\therefore\ f(x)=1-\sin x+|\sin x|+\sin x$

Hence, $f(x)=1+|\sin x|$ which is periodic with period π.

(ix) Given, $f(x)=\left[x+\dfrac{1}{2}\right]+\left[x-\dfrac{1}{2}\right]+2[-x]$

Case I If $x\in Z$, then $f(x)=[x]+\left[\dfrac{1}{2}\right]+[x]+\left[\dfrac{-1}{2}\right]+2(-[x])=0-1=-1$

Case II If $x\notin Z$

Sub-case (i) $x=k+\lambda$, where k is an integer and $\lambda\in(0,1/2)$.

Hence, $\left[k+\lambda+\dfrac{1}{2}\right]=k+\left[\lambda+\dfrac{1}{2}\right]$

and $k<k+\lambda+1/2<k+1\Rightarrow[x+1/2]=k$

Also, $[x-1/2]=[k+\lambda-1/2]$

and $k-1<k+\lambda-1/2<k$

$\therefore [x-1/2]=k-1$ and $[-x]=-[x]-1=-k-1$

$\therefore\ \left[x+\dfrac{1}{2}\right]+\left[x-\dfrac{1}{2}\right]+2[-x]$

$=(k)+(k-1)+2(-k-1)=-3$

Sub-case (ii) If $x=k+\lambda$, where k is an integer and $1/2\leq\lambda<1$

Hence, $x+1/2=k+\lambda+1/2$

and $k+1\leq k+\lambda+1/2<k+2$

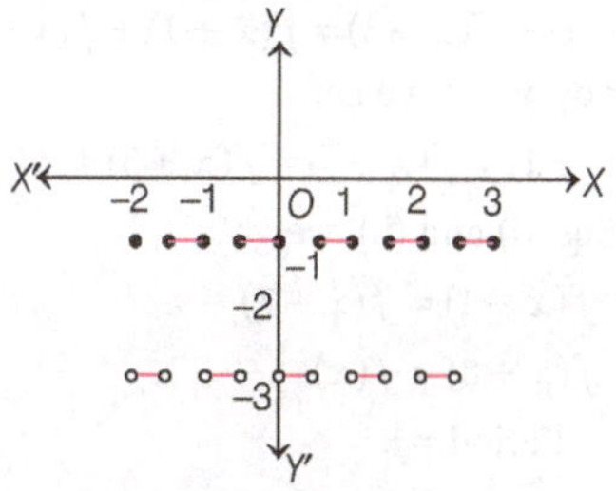

$\therefore\ \left[x+\dfrac{1}{2}\right]=k+1$

Also, $\left(x-\dfrac{1}{2}\right)=k+\lambda-\dfrac{1}{2}$ and $k\leq k+\lambda-\dfrac{1}{2}<k+1$

$\therefore\ [x-1/2]=k$ and $[-x]=-[x]-1=-k-1$

$\therefore\ [x+1/2]+[x-1/2]+2[-x]$

$=(k+1)+k+2(-k-1)=-1$

$\therefore$ The graph of $f(x)$ is as shown in figure.

Clearly, we can see that the function is periodic with a fundamental period 1.

(x) $f(x) = x + a - [x + b] + \sin \pi x + \cos 2\pi x + \sin(3\pi x) + \cos(4\pi x) + \dots + \sin(2n-1)\pi x + \cos(2n\pi x)$

$\Rightarrow f(x) = \{x + b\} + a - b + \sin(\pi x) + \cos(2\pi x) + \sin(3\pi x) + \cos(4\pi x) + \dots + \sin(2n-1)\pi x + \cos(2n\pi x)$

Period of $f(x) = \text{LCM}\left(1, 2, \frac{2}{3}, \frac{2}{4}, \dots, \frac{2}{2n-1}, \frac{2}{2n}\right) = 2$

$\therefore$ Fundamental period of $f(x) = 2$

Example 67. Prove that f is periodic, if it satisfies the condition.

$$f(x+p) = 1 + \{1 - 3f(x) + 3f^2(x) - f^3(x)\}^{1/3}.$$

Sol. We have,

$$[f(x+p) - 1]^3 = 1 - 3f(x) + 3f^2(x) - f^3(x) = [1 - f(x)]^3$$

$\Rightarrow f(x+p) - 1 = 1 - f(x)$

$\Rightarrow \quad f(x+p) + f(x) = 2 \quad \dots\text{(i)}$

Replacing x by $x + p$, Eq. (i) reduces to

$$f(x+2p) + f(x+p) = 2 \quad \dots\text{(ii)}$$

On subtracting Eq. (i) from Eq. (ii), we get

$$f(x+2p) - f(x) = 0$$

$\Rightarrow \quad f(x+2p) = f(x)$

Hence, f is periodic, having a period $2p$.

Example 68. Find the period of $f(x)$ satisfying the condition

$$f(x-1) + f(x+3) = f(x+1) + f(x+5)$$

Sol. Given, $f(x-1) + f(x+3) = f(x+1) + f(x+5) \quad \dots\text{(i)}$

Replacing x by $x + 2$, we get

$$f(x+1) + f(x+5) = f(x+3) + f(x+7) \quad \dots\text{(ii)}$$

On adding Eqs. (i) and (ii), we get

$$f(x-1) = f(x+7)$$

$\Rightarrow \quad f(x+8) = f(x)$

$\Rightarrow \quad \text{Period} = 8$

Example 69. Let f be a function that satisfies $f(x+6) + f(x-6) = f(x)$ for all real x. Prove that any such function is periodic with a common positive period p for all of them. Also, find the value of the period p.

Sol. Given, $f(x+6) + f(x-6) = f(x) \quad \dots\text{(i)}$

Replacing x by $x + 6$ in Eq. (i), we get

$$f(x+12) + f(x) = f(x+6) \quad \dots\text{(ii)}$$

On substituting the value of $f(x+6)$ from Eq. (i) in Eq. (ii), we get

$$f(x+12) + f(x) = f(x) - f(x-6) \quad \dots\text{(iii)}$$

Again, replacing x by $x + 6$ in Eq. (iii), we get

$$f(x+18) = -f(x)$$

Now, replacing x by $x + 18$, we get

$$f(x+36) = -f(x+18)$$

$\Rightarrow \quad f(x+36) = f(x)$

$\Rightarrow f(x)$ is periodic with period 36.

Example 70. Let $y = f(x)$, $x \in R$ be a function such that the graph of $f(x)$ is symmetrical about the lines $x = \alpha$ and $x = \beta$, where $\alpha < \beta$. Prove that $f(x)$ is periodic, also find the period of $f(x)$.

Sol. We have, $f(\alpha - x) = f(\alpha + x) \quad \dots\text{(i)}$

and $\quad f(\beta - x) = f(\beta + x) \quad \dots\text{(ii)}$

[$\because$ the function $f(x)$ is symmetrical about lines $x = \alpha$ and $x = \beta$]

Replacing x by $\alpha - x$ in Eq. (i), we get

$$f(x) = f(2\alpha - x) \quad \dots\text{(iii)}$$

Replacing x by $(\beta - x)$ in Eq. (ii), we get

$$f(x) = f(2\beta - x) \quad \dots\text{(iv)}$$

From Eq. (iii), we get

$$f(x) = f(2\alpha - x)$$
$$= f\{2\beta - (2\alpha - x)\}$$
$$= f\{x + 2(\beta - \alpha)\} \quad \text{[from Eq. (iv)]}$$

Hence, $f(x)$ is periodic, having a period $2(\beta - \alpha)$.

Example 71. Let f be real valued function defined for all real numbers x such that for some positive constant a, the equation $f(x+a) = \frac{1}{2} + \sqrt{f(x) - (f(x))^2}$ holds for all x. Prove that the function f is periodic.

Sol. Given, $f(x+a) = \frac{1}{2} + \sqrt{f(x) - (f(x))^2}$

or $f^2(x+a) + \frac{1}{4} - f(x+a) = f(x) - f^2(x)$

or $f^2(x) + f^2(x+a) + \frac{1}{4} = f(x) + f(x+a) \quad \dots\text{(i)}$

Replacing x by $x + a$, we have

$$f^2(x+a) + f^2(x+2a) + \frac{1}{4} = f(x+a) + f(x+2a) \quad \dots\text{(ii)}$$

On subtracting Eq. (ii) from Eq. (i), we get

(i) – (ii), gives $f^2(x) - f^2(x+2a) = f(x) - f(x+2a)$

$\Rightarrow \{f(x) - f(x+2a)\}\{f(x) + f(x+2a) - 1\} = 0$

$\Rightarrow f(x) = f(x+2a)$ or $f(x) = -f(x+2a) + 1$

(rejected, as by given equation, $f(x)$ is positive)

$\Rightarrow$ Period of $f(x) = 2a$

Example 72. A function $f(x)$ satisfies the equation $f(x+1) + f(x-1) = \sqrt{3}f(x)$ for all real x. Prove that f is periodic.

Sol. $f(x+1)+f(x-1)=\sqrt{3}f(x)$ ...(i)

Here, the main strategy is to replace x such that we get expression on RHS which is same as the expression on LHS. Replacing x by $x+1$ and replacing x by $x-1$ separately in the given equation, we get two equations

$$f(x+2)+f(x)=\sqrt{3}f(x+1)$$
$$f(x)+f(x-2)=\sqrt{3}f(x-1)$$

On adding these two equations, we get term on RHS, which is same as LHS.

$$f(x+2)+f(x-2)+2f(x)=\sqrt{3}\{f(x+1)+f(x-1)\}$$
$$=\sqrt{3}\{\sqrt{3}f(x)\} \quad \text{[using Eq. (i)]}$$
$$=3f(x)$$

$\Rightarrow \quad f(x+2)+f(x-2)=f(x)$ ...(ii)

Replacing x by $x+2$ in Eq. (ii), we get

$f(x+4)+f(x)=f(x+2)$ ...(iii)

Note that we have not replaced x by $x-2$ because that yields a relation which has argument form of $x-4$. As, definition of periodic function involves addition of a positive constant being added to independent variable, we replace x by $x+2$.

Now, on adding Eqs. (ii) and (iii), we get

$f(x+4)+f(x-2)=0$ ...(iv)

Replacing x by $x+2$ in Eq. (iv), so that one of the two terms becomes $f(x)$, we get

$f(x+6)+f(x)=0 \Rightarrow f(x+6)=-f(x)$ ...(v)

Replacing x by $x+6$ in Eq. (v), we have

$$f(x+12)=-f(x+6)$$

$\Rightarrow \quad f(x+12)=f(x)$ [using Eq. (v)]

Hence, the function is periodic and one of the period, $T=12$

2.17 Composite Function

Composition of function is a process of combining two or more function.

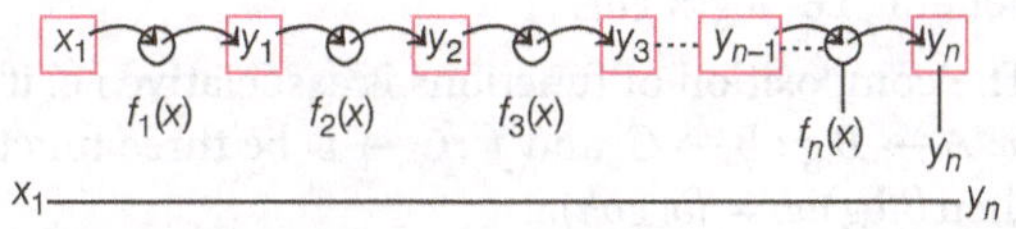

Composition of Two Functions

Case I

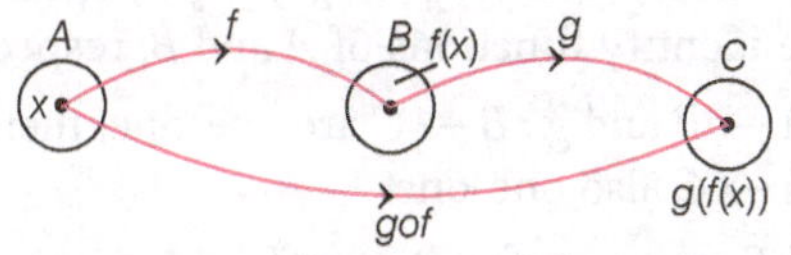

Let A, B and C be three non-empty sets.

Let $f: A \to B$ and $g: B \to C$ be two functions, then $gof: A \to C$.

This function is called composition of f and g, given by

$$gof(x)=g(f(x)), \forall x \in A$$

Thus, the image of every $x \in A$ under the function gof is the g-image of the f-image of x.

The gof is defined only if, $\forall x \in A$, $f(x)$ is an element of the domain of g, so that we can take its g-image.

The range of f must be a subset of the domain of g in gof.

Case II Let A, B, C and D be four non-empty sets.

Let $f: A \to B$ and $g: C \to D$ be two functions, then gof and fog is defined

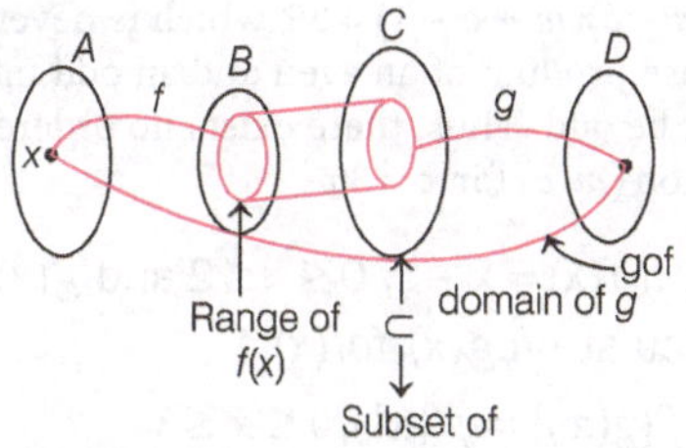

If the range of $f(x) \subseteq$ domain of $g(x)$

$\Rightarrow gof(x)$ exists.

Similarly, range of $g(x) \subseteq$ domain of $f(x)$

$\Rightarrow fog(x)$ exists.

Example 73. Let $f: \{1, 2, 3, 4\} \to \{2, 3, 5, 7, 11\}$ and $g: \{2, 3, 5, 7, 11\} \to \{5, 7, 9\}$ be function defined as $f(1)=2$, $f(2)=3$, $f(3)=5$, $f(4)=7$ and $g(2)=g(3)=5$ and $g(5)=7$, $g(7)=9$. Find gof.

Sol. We have,

$gof(1)=g(f(1))=g(2)=5$, $gof(2)=g(f(2))=g(3)=5$,
$gof(3)=g(f(3))=g(5)=7$ and $gof(4)=g(f(4))=g(7)=9$

Thus, gof, $\{1, 2, 3, 4\} \to \{5, 7, 9\}$ is given by

$$gof=\{(1, 5), (2, 5), (3, 7), (4, 9)\}$$

Example 74. Given two linear polynomial function f and g such that $f(x)=mx+c$ and $g(x)=cx+m$, where m and $c \in N$. If $f(g(5)-g(f(5))=k$, then find all possible ordered pairs (m, c) for

(i) $k=12$ (ii) $k=35$

Sol. From the definition of f and g,

$$f(g(x))=m(g(x))+c=m(cx+m)+c$$

$\Rightarrow \quad f(g(x))=cmx+m^2+c$ ...(i)

Similarly, $g(f(x))=c(mx+c)+m=cmx+c^2+m$ ...(ii)

Now, $f(g(x))-g(f(x))=m^2+c-c^2-m$

$$=(m^2-c^2)+(c-m)$$
$$=(m-c)(m+c-1)$$

(i) Now, since $f(g(5))-g(f(5))=12$

$\Rightarrow \quad (m-c)(m+c-1)=12$ ...(iii)

Since, $(m-c)$ and $(m+c-1)$ are of opposite parity and $m-c<m+c-1$ and $12=2^2 \times 3$.

$\Rightarrow$ Possible factorisations are 1×12 or 2×6 or 3×4

Case I $m-c=1$ and $m+c-1=12$

$\Rightarrow \quad c=6$ and $m=7$

Case II $m-c=2$ and $m+c-1=6$, not possible as $m-c$ and $m+c-1$ both cannot be even as they are of opposite parity

Case III $m-c=3$ and $m+c-1=4$

$\Rightarrow \quad c=1$ and $m=4$

Thus, the possible ordered pairs (m, c) are (7, 6), (4, 1)

(ii) If $f(g(5))-g(f(5))=35$

$\Rightarrow (m-c)(m+c-1)=35$, which is never possible because product of an even and an odd integer can never be odd. Thus, there exists no ordered pair solution (m, c) for $k=35$.

Example 75. If $f(x)=x+1$, $0\le x\le 2$ and $g(x)=|x|$, $0\le x\le 3$. Calculate $fog(x)$, $fof(x)$

Sol. $fog(x)=f\{g(x)\}=f(|x|), 0\le x\le 3$

$=|x|+1, 0\le |x|\le 2$ and $0\le x\le 3$

$=|x|+1, -2\le x\le 2$ and $0\le x\le 3$

$=|x|+1, 0\le x\le 2$

$fof(x)=f\{f(x)\}=f(x+1); 0\le x\le 2$

$=(x+1)+1, 0\le (x+1)\le 2$ and $0\le x\le 2$

$=(x+2), -1\le x\le 1$ and $0\le x\le 2$

$=(x+2), 0< x<1$

Example 76. Let $f(x)=\sin x$ and $g(x)=\sqrt{|1-x|}$. Find $gof(x)$, $fog(x)$, $gog(x)$ and $fof(x)$.

Sol. $gof(x)=g\{f(x)\}=g(\sin x)=\sqrt{|1-\sin x|}$

$fog(x)=f\{g(x)\}=f\{\sqrt{|1-x|}\}=\sin\sqrt{|1-x|}$

$gog(x)=g\{g(x)\}=g\{\sqrt{|1-x|}\}=\{\sqrt{|1-\sqrt{|1-x|}|}\}$

$fof(x)=f\{f(x)\}=f(\sin x)=\sin(\sin x)$

Example 77. Find fog and gof, if

(i) $f(x)=|x|$, $g(x)=\sin x$

(ii) $f(x)=\sin^{-1}x$, $g(x)=x^2$

(iii) $f(x)=x^2+2$, $g(x)=1-\dfrac{1}{1-x}$, $x\ne 1$

Sol. (i) $f(x)=|x|$ and $g(x)=\sin x$

$\Rightarrow \quad fog(x)=f(\sin x)=|\sin x|$

and $gof(x)=g(f(x))=g(|x|)=\sin|x|$

(ii) $f(x)=\sin^{-1}x$ and $g(x)=x^2$

$\Rightarrow \quad fog(x)=f(g(x))=\sin^{-1}(g(x))=\sin^{-1}x^2$

and $gof(x)=g(f(x))=(f(x))^2=(\sin^{-1}x)^2$

(iii) $f(x)=x^2+2$, $g(x)=\dfrac{x}{x-1}$

$\Rightarrow fog(x)=f(g(x))=(g(x))^2+2$

$$=\frac{x^2}{(x-1)^2}+2=\frac{3x^2-4x+2}{(x-1)^2}$$

and $gof(x)=g(f(x))=g(x^2+2)$

$$=\frac{x^2+2}{(x^2+2)-1}=\frac{x^2+2}{x^2+1}$$

Example 78. Let a and b real number and let $f(x)=a\sin x+b\sqrt[3]{x}+4$, $\forall x\in R$. If $f(\log_{10}(\log_3 10))=5$, then find the value of $f(\log_{10}(\log_{10} 3))$

Sol. Given, $f(x)=a\sin x+b\sqrt[3]{x}+4$

and $\quad f(\log_{10}(\log_3 10))=5$

Now, let $\log_{10}\log_3 10=k$, then

$$\log_{10}\log_{10}3=\log_{10}\left(\frac{1}{\log_3 10}\right)$$

$$=(\log_{10}1-\log_{10}\log_3 10)$$

$$=0-k=-k$$

Now, $f(k)=a\sin k+b(k)^{1/3}+4=5$

$\Rightarrow \quad a\sin k+b(k)^{1/3}=1$

$\therefore \quad f(-k)=a\sin(-k)+b(-k)^{1/3}+4$

$$=-(a\sin k+b(k)^{1/3})+4$$

$$=-1+4=3$$

Example 79. Let $f(x)=\dfrac{x+2}{3x-1}$, $g(x)=x^2$ and $h(x)=\sqrt{x}$.

Find $h(f(g(x)))$.

Sol. $h(f(g(x)))=h(f(x^2))$

$$=h\left(\frac{x^2+2}{3x^2-1}\right)=\sqrt{\frac{x^2+2}{3x^2-1}}$$

Properties of Composite Function

(i) The composition of functions is not commutative in general, i.e. $fog\ne gof$.

(ii) The composition of functions is associative i.e. if $h: A\to B, g: B\to C$ and $f: C\to D$ be three functions, then $(fog)oh=fo(goh)$.

(iii) The composition of any function with the identity function is the function itself

i.e. $f: A\to B$, then $foI_A=I_Bof=f$, where I_A and I_B are the identity functions of A and B, respectively.

(iv) If $f: A\to B$ and $g: B\to C$ are one-one, then $gof: A\to C$ also one-one.

Proof Suppose $gof(x_1)=gof(x_2)$

$\Rightarrow \quad g(f(x_1))=g(f(x_2))$

$\Rightarrow \quad f(x_1)=f(x_2)$, as g is one-one

$\Rightarrow \quad x_1=x_2$, as f is one-one

Hence, gof is one-one.

(v) If $f: A \to B$ and $g: B \to C$ are onto, then $gof: A \to C$ is also onto.

Proof Given an arbitrary element $z \in C$, there exists a pre-image y of z under g such that $g(y) = z$, since g is onto. Further, for $y \in B$, there exists an element x in A with $f(x) = y$, since f is onto.

Therefore, $gof(x) = g(f(x)) = g(y) = z$, showing that gof is onto.

(vi) If $gof(x)$ is one-one, then $f(x)$ is necessarily one-one but $g(x)$ may not be one-one.

Consider the function $f(x)$ and $g(x)$ as shown in the following figure.

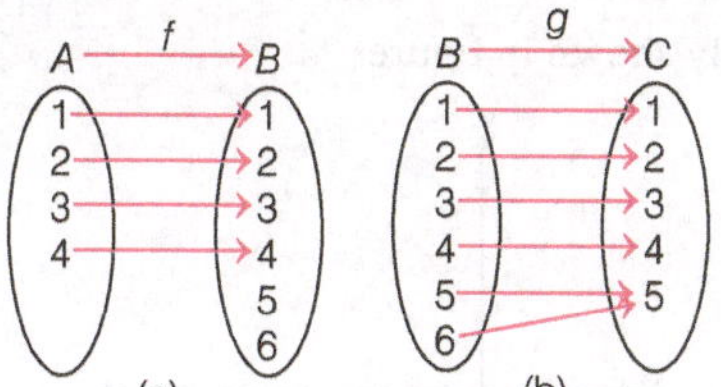

(a) (b)

Here, f is one-one but g is many-one. But $g(f(x))$: {(1, 1), (2, 2), (3, 3), (4, 4)} is one-one.

(vii) If $gof(x)$ is onto, then $g(x)$ is necessarily onto but $f(x)$ may not be onto.

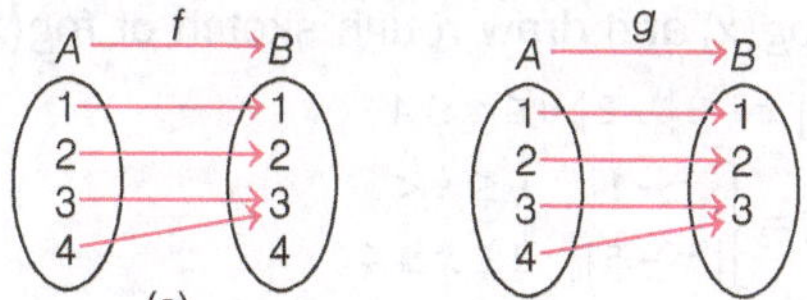

(a) (b)

Here, f is into and g is onto. But $gof(x)$: {(1, 1), (2, 2), (3, 3), (4, 3)} is onto.

Thus, it can be verified in general that gof is one-one implies that f is one-one.

Similarly, gof is onto implies that g is onto.

(viii) Algebra of composite function with reference of mapping

f	g	gof
one-one	one-one	one-one
many one	one-one	cannot say
one-one	many-one	cannot say
many-one	many-one	cannot say
onto-into	onto	cannot say
onto-into	into	into
bijective	bijective	bijective

(ix) Algebra of composite function reference of even/odd

f	g	gof	fog
Even	Even	Even	Even
Odd	Odd	Odd	Odd
Even	Odd	Even	Even
Odd	Even	Even	Even

Example 80. Suppose that $g(x) = 1 + \sqrt{x}$ and $f(g(x)) = 3 + 2\sqrt{x} + x$, then find the function $f(x)$.

Sol. $g(x) = 1 + \sqrt{x}$ and $f(g(x)) = 3 + 2\sqrt{x} + x$ ...(i)

$\Rightarrow f(1 + \sqrt{x}) = 3 + 2\sqrt{x} + x$

Put $1 + \sqrt{x} = y \Rightarrow x = (y - 1)^2$

Then, $f(y) = 3 + 2(y - 1) + (y - 1)^2 = 2 + y^2$

Therefore, $f(x) = 2 + x^2$

Example 81. A function $f: R \to R$ is such that $f\left(\dfrac{1 - x}{1 + x}\right) = x, \forall x \neq -1$. Then, prove that

(i) $f(f(x)) = x$ (ii) $f\left(\dfrac{1}{x}\right) = -f(x), x \neq 0$

(iii) $f(-x - 2) = -f(x) - 2$

Sol. (i) $f\left(\dfrac{1 - x}{1 + x}\right) = x$

Let $\dfrac{1 - x}{1 + x} = t \Rightarrow t + tx = 1 - x$

$\Rightarrow x(1 + t) = 1 - t$

$\Rightarrow x = \dfrac{1 - t}{1 + t}$

$f(t) = \dfrac{1 - t}{1 + t}$

$\therefore f(x) = \dfrac{1 - x}{1 + x}$ ...(i)

$\therefore f(f(x)) = \dfrac{1 - f(x)}{1 + f(x)} = \dfrac{1 - \dfrac{1 - x}{1 + x}}{1 + \dfrac{1 - x}{1 + x}}$

$= \dfrac{1 + x - 1 + x}{1 + x + 1 - x} = \dfrac{2x}{2}$

$\therefore f(f(x)) = x$

(ii) From Eq. (i), $f\left(\dfrac{1}{x}\right) = \dfrac{1 - (1/x)}{1 + (1/x)} = \dfrac{x - 1}{x + 1}$

$f\left(\dfrac{1}{x}\right) = -\left(\dfrac{1 - x}{1 + x}\right) = -f(x)$

(iii) Also, $f(-x-2)=\dfrac{1+(x+2)}{1-(x+2)}=-\left(\dfrac{x+3}{x+1}\right)$ ...(ii)

and $-f(x)-2=-\left(\dfrac{1-x}{1+x}+2\right)$

$$=-\left(\frac{1-x+2+2x}{1+x}\right)$$

$$=-\left(\frac{x+3}{x+1}\right) \quad \text{...(iii)}$$

From Eqs. (ii) and (iii), we get

$$f(-x-2)=-f(x)-2$$

Example 82. If $f(x)=-1+|x-2|$, $0\le x\le 4$ and $g(x)=2-|x|$, $-1\le x\le 3$, then find $fog(x)$ and $gof(x)$. Drawn rough sketches of the graphs of $fog(x)$ and $gof(x)$.

Sol. Given, $f(x)=\begin{cases}-1-(x-2), & 0\le x<2\\ -1+(x-2), & 2\le x\le 4\end{cases}$

$$\Rightarrow \quad f(x)=\begin{cases}1-x, & 0\le x<2\\ x-3, & 2\le x\le 4\end{cases}$$

and $g(x)=\begin{cases}2+x, & -1\le x<0\\ 2-x, & 0\le x\le 3\end{cases}$

$$fog(x)=f(g(x))$$

$$=\begin{cases}1-g(x), & 0\le g(x)<2\\ g(x)-3, & 2\le g(x)\le 4\end{cases}$$

$$=\begin{cases}1-(2+x), & 0\le 2+x<2, & -1\le x<0\\ 1-(2-x), & 0\le 2-x<2, & 0\le x\le 2\\ (2+x)-3, & 2\le 2+x\le 4, & -1\le x<0\\ (2-x)-3, & 2\le 2-x\le 4, & 0\le x\le 3\end{cases}$$

$$=\begin{cases}-1-x, & -2\le x<0, & -1\le x<0\\ x-1, & 0<x\le 2, & 0\le x\le 3\\ x-1, & 0\le x\le 2, & -1\le x<0\\ -1-x, & -2\le x\le 0, & 0\le x\le 3\end{cases}$$

$$f(g(x))=\begin{cases}-1-x, & -1\le x<0\\ x-1, & 0\le x\le 2\end{cases},$$

graphically shown in figure.

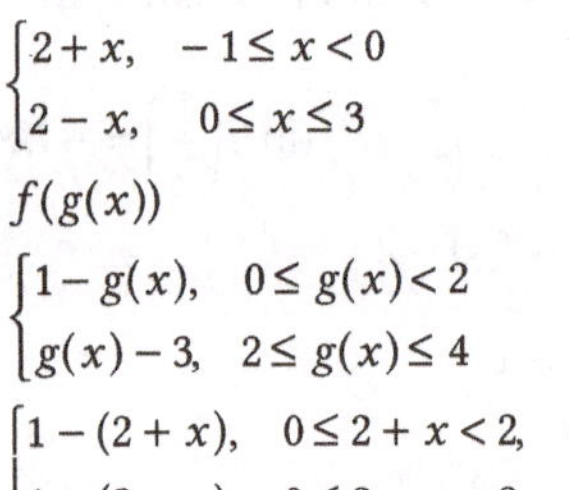

Next $(gof)(x)=g(f(x))=\begin{cases}2+f(x), & -1\le f(x)\le 0\\ 2-f(x), & 0\le f(x)\le 3\end{cases}$

$$=\begin{cases}2-(x-3), & 0\le (x-3)\le 3, & 2\le x\le 4\\ 2-(1-x), & 0\le (1-x)\le 3, & 0\le x<2\\ 2+(x-3), & -1\le (x-3)\le 0, & 2\le x\le 4\\ 2+(1-x), & -1\le (1-x)\le 0, & 0\le x<2\end{cases}$$

$$=\begin{cases}5-x, & 3\le x\le 6, & 2\le x<4\\ 1+x, & -2\le x\le 1, & 0\le x<2\\ x-1, & 2\le x\le 3, & 2\le x\le 4\\ 3-x, & 1\le x\le 2, & 0\le x<2\end{cases}$$

$$(gof)(x)=\begin{cases}1+x, & 0\le x<1\\ 3-x, & 1\le x<2\\ x-1;, & 2\le x<3\\ 5-x, & 3\le x\le 4\end{cases},$$

graphically shown in figure.

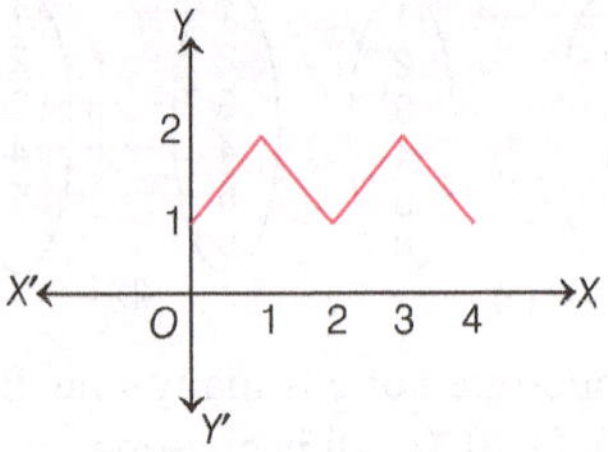

Example 83. If $f(x)=||x-3|-2|$, $0\le x\le 4$
$g(x)=4-|2-x|$, $-1\le x\le 3$,
then find $fog(x)$ and draw rough sketch of $fog(x)$.

Sol. $f(x)=||x-3|-2|; 0\le x\le 4$

$$\Rightarrow f(x)=\begin{cases}|x-1|, & 0\le x<3\\ |x-5|, & 3\le x\le 4\end{cases}$$

$$=\begin{cases}1-x, & 0\le x<1\\ x-1, & 1\le x<3\\ 5-x, & 3\le x\le 4\end{cases}$$

and $g(x)=4-|2-x|; -1\le x\le 3$

$$=\begin{cases}4-(2-x), & -1\le x<2\\ 4-(x-2), & 2\le x\le 3\end{cases}$$

$$=\begin{cases}2+x, & -1\le x<2\\ 6-x, & 2\le x\le 3\end{cases}$$

$$\therefore \quad fog(x)=\begin{cases}1-g(x), & 0\le g(x)<1\\ g(x)-1, & 1\le g(x)<3\\ 5-g(x), & 3\le g(x)\le 4\end{cases}$$

$$=\begin{cases}1-(2+x), & 0\le 2+x<1 & \text{and} & -1\le x<2\\ 2+x-1, & 1\le 2+x<3 & \text{and} & -1\le x<2\\ 5-(2+x), & 3\le 2+x\le 4 & \text{and} & -1\le x<2\\ 1-6+x, & 0\le 6-x<1 & \text{and} & 2\le x\le 3\\ 6-x-1, & 1\le 6-x<3 & \text{and} & 2\le x\le 3\\ 5-6+x, & 3\le 6-x\le 4 & \text{and} & 2\le x\le 3\end{cases}$$

$$= \begin{cases} -1-x, & -2 \le x < -1 \quad \text{and} \quad -1 \le x < 2 \\ 1+x, & -1 \le x < 1 \quad \text{and} \quad -1 \le x < 2 \\ 3-x, & 1 \le x \le 2 \quad \text{and} \quad -1 \le x < 2 \\ x-5, & -6 \le -x < -5 \quad \text{and} \quad 2 \le x \le 3 \\ 5-x, & -5 \le -x < -3 \quad \text{and} \quad 2 \le x \le 3 \\ x-1, & -3 \le -x \le -2 \quad \text{and} \quad 2 \le x \le 3 \end{cases}$$

$$= \begin{cases} -1-x, & -2 \le x < -1 \quad \text{and} \quad -1 \le x < 2 \\ 1+x, & -1 \le x < 1 \quad \text{and} \quad -1 \le x < 2 \\ 3-x, & 1 \le x \le 2 \quad \text{and} \quad -1 \le x < 2 \\ x-5, & 5 < x \le 6 \quad \text{and} \quad 2 \le x \le 3 \\ 5-x, & 3 < x \le 5 \quad \text{and} \quad 2 \le x \le 3 \\ x-1, & 2 \le x \le 3 \quad \text{and} \quad 2 \le x \le 3 \end{cases}$$

$$= \begin{cases} 1+x & . \quad -1 \le x < 1 \\ 3-x & . \quad 1 \le x < 2 \\ x-1 & . \quad 2 \le x \le 3 \end{cases}$$

Alternate Solution

$$g(x) = \begin{cases} 2+x, & -1 \le x < 2 \\ 6-x, & 2 \le x \le 3 \end{cases}$$

Graph of $g(x)$ is

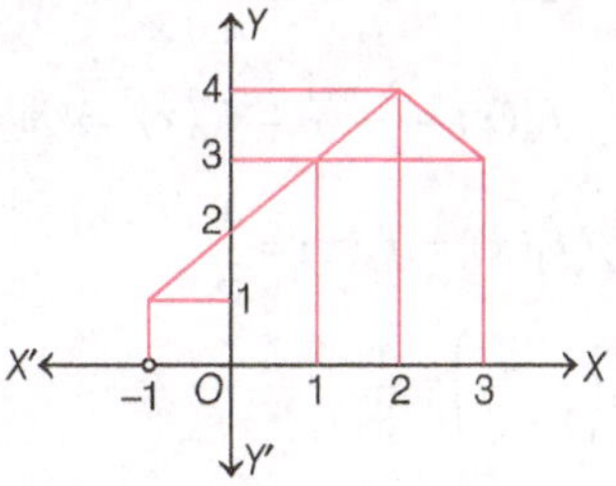

$$fog\,(x) = \begin{cases} 1-g(x) & , \quad 0 \le g(x) < 1 \\ g(x)-1 & , \quad 1 \le g(x) < 3 \\ 5-g(x) & , \quad 3 \le g(x) \le 4 \end{cases}$$

From the graph of $g(x)$, we note that no portion of graph of $g(x)$ lies in the interval $[0, 1)$.

Also, $g(x) \in [1, 3)$ for $x \in [-1, 1)$ and $g(x) \in [3, 4]$ for $x \in [1, 3]$

$$\therefore \quad fog(x) = \begin{cases} 1-g(x) & , \quad \text{for no value} \\ g(x)-1 & , \quad -1 \le x < 1 \\ 5-g(x) & , \quad 1 \le x \le 3 \end{cases} \quad \ldots \text{(i)}$$

Now, for $x \in [-1, 1)$, $g(x) = (2+x)$; for $x \in [1, 2)$, $g(x) = (2+x)$ and for $x \in [2, 3]$, $g(x) = (6-x)$.

Therefore, from Eq. (i), we get

$$fog(x) = \begin{cases} 2+x-1 & , \quad -1 \le x < 1 \\ 5-(2+x) & , \quad 1 \le x < 2 \\ 5-(6-x) & , \quad 2 \le x \le 3 \end{cases} = \begin{cases} x+1 & , \quad -1 \le x < 1 \\ 3-x & , \quad 1 \le x < 2\,; \\ x-1 & , \quad 2 \le x \le 3 \end{cases}$$

graphically shown in Figure.

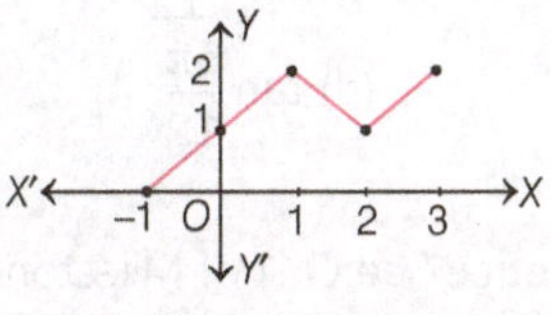

JEE SPIKE

Iteration/Repeated Composition Given a function $f(x)$, its iterate at x is $f(f(x))$, that is we use its value as the new input.

The iterates at x

$$x, f(x), f(f(x)), f(f(f(x))) \ldots$$

are called 0-th iterate, 1st iterate, 2nd iterate, 3rd iterate, etc. We denote the nth iterate by $f[n]$.

In some cases it is easy to find the nth iterate of a function,

Concept Inside Video

e.g. If $p(x) = x^t$, then $p^{[n]}(x) = x^{tn}$

If $q(x) = mx$ then $q^{[n]}(x) = m^n x$

If $r(x) = mx + k$, then $r^{[n]}(x) = m^n x + k\left(\dfrac{m^n - 1}{m-1}\right)$

The above examples are more an exception than the rule. Even, if it is possible to find a closed formula for the nth iterate in some cases it is very complicated.

Example 84. Let $f(x) = \dfrac{1}{1-x}$. Find the nth iterate of f at x and determine the set of values of x for which it is defined.

Sol. We have, $\quad f^{[2]}(x) = (fof)(x) = f(f(x))$

$$= \frac{1}{1 - \dfrac{1}{1-x}}$$

$$= \frac{x-1}{x}$$

$$f^{[3]}(x) = (fofof)(x) = f(f^{[2]}(x)))$$

$$= f\left(\frac{x-1}{x}\right)$$

$$= \frac{1}{1 - \dfrac{x-1}{x}} = x$$

Notice now that

$$f^{[4]}(x) = (fof^{[3]})(x) = f(x) = f^{[1]}(x).$$

We see, this is cyclic with period 3

i.e. $\quad f^{[1]}(x) = f^{[4]}(x) - f^{[7]}(x) = \ldots = \dfrac{1}{1-x}$

$$f^{[2]}(x) = f^{[5]}(x) = f^{[8]}(x) = \ldots = \frac{x-1}{x}$$

$$f^{[3]}(x) = f^{[6]}(x) = f^{[9]}(x) = \ldots = x$$

The formulae above hold for $x \notin \{0, 1\}$.

$$f^n(x) = \begin{cases} \dfrac{1}{1-x} & , \quad n = 3m+1 \\ \dfrac{x-1}{x} & , \quad n = 3m+2 \\ x & , \quad n = 3m, m \in I \end{cases}$$

Example 85. A function $f(x)$ is given as $f(x)=\{2-x^n\}^{1/n}$, where $x>0$ and n is a positive integer. Prove that $f(f(x))+f\left(f\left(\frac{1}{x}\right)\right)\geq 2$.

Sol. The domain of the given function is a positive number as $x>0$. In order to prove the inequality, we need to determine each composition on the left hand side of the given inequality.

If $f(x)=\{a-x^n\}^{1/n}$, then $f(f(x))=x$.

Hence, if $f(x)=\{2-x^n\}^{1/n}$, then $f(f(x))=x$.

Similarly, we determine $f(f(1/x))$.

Here, $f(f(1/x))=f(y)$

$$=\left[a-\left\{\left(a-\frac{1}{x^n}\right)^{1/n}\right\}^n\right]^{1/n}=\left(a-a+\frac{1}{x^n}\right)^{1/n}$$

$$\Rightarrow f\left(f\left(\frac{1}{x}\right)\right)=\left(\frac{1}{x^n}\right)^{1/n}=\frac{1}{x}$$

On substituting these values in the LHS of the inequality, we get

$$\text{LHS}=f(f(x))+f\left\{f\left(\frac{1}{x}\right)\right\}=x+\frac{1}{x}=\left(\sqrt{x}-\frac{1}{\sqrt{x}}\right)^2+2$$

But the square term is a non-negative number.

Hence, LHS ≥ 2

$\Rightarrow f(f(x))+f(f(1/x))\geq 2$

Example 86. Let $f(x)=\dfrac{x-1}{x+1}$, $f^2(x)=f(f(x))$, $f^3(x)=f(f^2(x))$, ... $f^{k+1}(x)=f(f^k(x))$ for $k\in N$. Find $f^{1998}(x)$.

Sol. $f(x)=\dfrac{x-1}{x+1}$,

$$f^2(x)=f(f(x))=\frac{f(x)-1}{f(x)+1}=\frac{\frac{x-1}{x+1}-1}{\frac{x-1}{x+1}+1}=\frac{-1}{x}$$

$$f^3(x)=f(f^2(x))=\frac{f^2(x)-1}{f^2(x)+1}=\frac{\frac{-1}{x}-1}{\frac{-1}{x}+1}=\frac{x+1}{1-x}$$

$$f^4(x)=f(f^3(x))=\frac{f^3(x)-1}{f^3(x)+1}=\frac{\frac{x+1}{1-x}-1}{\frac{x+1}{1-x}+1}=x$$

$$f^5(x)=f(f^4(x))=\frac{x-1}{x+1}=f(x).$$

Thus, we can see that $f^k(x)$ repeats itself at intervals of $k=4$.

Hence, we have $f^{1998}(x)=f^2(x)=-\dfrac{1}{x}$

$[\because 1998=499\times 4+2]$

JEE SCANNER

Example Similar to PYQ Asked in JEE Main 2023

Let $f_1(x)=x$, $f_2(x)=1-x$, $f_3(x)=\dfrac{1}{x}$, $f_4(x)=\dfrac{1}{1-x}$, $f_5(x)=\dfrac{x}{x-1}$, $f_6(x)=\dfrac{x-1}{x}$. Suppose that $f_6(f_m(x))=f_4(x)$ and $f_n(f_4(x))=f_3(x)$, then the value of m and n are

(a) 6 and 4 (b) 3 and 2

(c) 5 and 6 (d) 6 and 5

Sol. (d) Given, $f_6(x)=\dfrac{x-1}{x}$ ...(i)

$$f_6(f_m(x))=f_4(x)=\frac{1}{1-x} \quad \text{[given]}$$

$$\Rightarrow f_6(f_m(x))=\frac{f_m(x)-1}{f_m(x)}=\frac{1}{1-x}$$

[using given relation $f_6(x)=\dfrac{x-1}{x}$]

Put $f_m(x)=k$, we have $\dfrac{k-1}{k}=\dfrac{1}{1-x}$

$$\Rightarrow k-kx-1+x=k \Rightarrow k=\frac{x-1}{x}$$

$$\Rightarrow f_m(x)=\frac{x-1}{x}=f_6(x)\Rightarrow m=6$$

Again, $f_n(f_4(x))=f_3(x)=\dfrac{1}{x}$

$$f_n\left(\frac{1}{1-x}\right)=\frac{1}{x}$$

Let $\dfrac{1}{1-x}=t \Rightarrow t-tx=1$

$$\Rightarrow x=\frac{t-1}{t}\Rightarrow f_n(t)=\frac{t}{t-1}$$

$$\Rightarrow f_n(x)=\frac{x}{x-1}=f_5(x)$$

Hence, $n=5$

Skill Builder

For $x\in\left(0,\dfrac{3}{2}\right)$, let $f(x)=\sqrt{x}$, $g(x)=\tan x$ and $h(x)=\dfrac{1-x^2}{1+x^2}$. If $\phi(x)=((hof)og)(x)$, then $\phi\left(\dfrac{\pi}{3}\right)$ is equal to

(a) $\tan\dfrac{\pi}{12}$ (b) $\tan\dfrac{11\pi}{12}$

(c) $\tan\dfrac{7\pi}{12}$ (d) $\tan\dfrac{5\pi}{12}$

For Sol.

■ **For more practice** See Q.11 of Milestone Practice 2.4.

2.18 Inverse of a Function

Let $f: A \to B$ be a one-one and onto function, then there exists a unique function $g: B \to A$ such that $f(x) = y \Leftrightarrow g(y) = x, \forall x \in A$ and $y \in B$. Then, g is said to be inverse of f.

Thus, $g = f^{-1}: B \to A = ((f(x), x \mid (x, f(x)) \in f)$.

Consider a one-one onto function with domain $A = \{a, b, c\}$ and range $B = \{1, 2, 3\}$

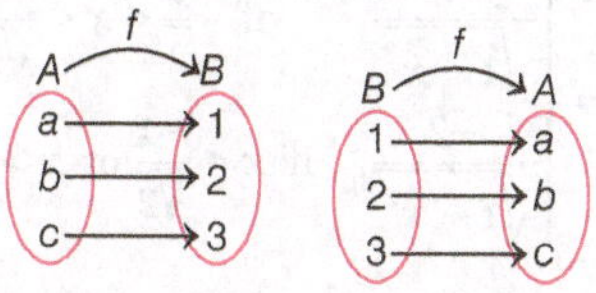

Domain of $f = \{a, b, c\} =$ Range of f^{-1}

Range of $f = \{1, 2, 3\} =$ Domain of f^{-1}

Properties of Inverse of a Function

1. Inverse of bijection is unique and bijection
2. $(f^{-1})^{-1} = f$
3. Let g be function exists in such a way that $gof(x) = x$ and $fog(x) = x$, then g is said to be inverse of f or *vice-versa*.

   $\Rightarrow f^{-1}of(x) = x$ and $fof^{-1}(x) = x$
4. $(gof)^{-1} = f^{-1}og^{-1}$
5. Since, to each $(x, y) \in f$, there exists $(y, x) \in f^{-1}$ and (y, x) and (x, y) are mirror images of each other in the line $y = x$, therefore the graph of $f^{-1}(x)$ is obtained by reflecting the graph of $f(x)$ in the line $y = x$ as

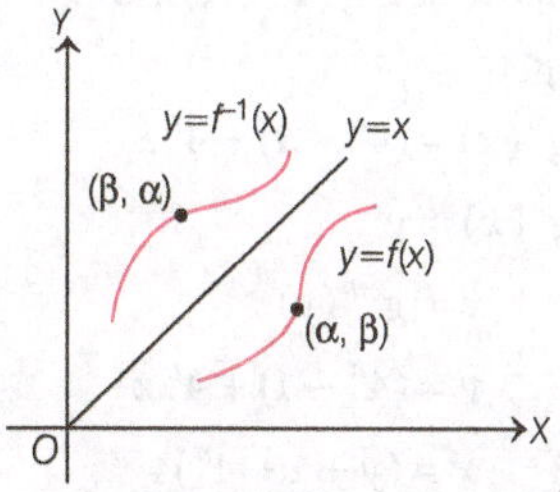

6. $f(x)$ and $f^{-1}(x)$ if intersect, then the point of intersection should be on line $y = x$ or $y = -x + k$ for some real value of k.

Example 87. If $f(x)$ is an invertible function and $g(x) = 2f(x) + 5$, then find the value of $g^{-1}(x)$.

Sol. Given equation is $g(x) = 2f(x) + 5$.

Replacing x by $g^{-1}(x)$, we get

$$g(g^{-1}(x)) = 2f(g^{-1}(x)) + 5$$

$$\Rightarrow \quad x = 2f(g^{-1}(x)) + 5$$

$$\Rightarrow \quad f(g^{-1}(x)) = \frac{x-5}{2}$$

$$\Rightarrow \quad g^{-1}(x) = f^{-1}\left(\frac{x-5}{2}\right)$$

Example 88. Compute the inverse of the following functions

(i) $f(x) = \ln(x + \sqrt{x^2 + 1})$

(ii) $f(x) = 2^{\frac{x}{x-1}}$

(iii) $y = \dfrac{10^x - 10^{-x}}{10^x + 10^{-x}}$

Sol. (i) Given, $f(x) = \ln(x + \sqrt{x^2 + 1})$

If $x \geq 0$, then $x + \sqrt{x^2 + 1} > 0$ and if $x < 0$, then

$$|x| = \sqrt{x^2} < \sqrt{x^2 + 1}$$

Thus, magnitude of x is less than the magnitude of $\sqrt{x^2 + 1} \Rightarrow x + \sqrt{x^2 + 1} > 0$

Thus, for every real values of x, $x + \sqrt{x^2 + 1} > 0$

$\Rightarrow$ Domain of $f(x)$ is R.

Also, $x + \sqrt{x^2 + 1}$ being the sum of two continuous functions is also continuous.

Further, $f'(x) = \dfrac{1}{\sqrt{x^2 + 1}} > 0, \forall x \in R$

$\Rightarrow f(x)$ is strictly increasing function. Thus, $f(x)$ is a bijective function from $R \to R$ (range)

Now, $\quad y = f(x) = \ln(x + \sqrt{x^2 + 1})$

$$\Rightarrow \quad e^y = x + \sqrt{x^2 + 1} \quad \text{...(i)}$$

Again, $y = \ln(x + \sqrt{x^2 + 1})$

$$\Rightarrow \quad -y = -\ln(x + \sqrt{x^2 + 1})$$

$$\Rightarrow \quad -y = \ln(x + \sqrt{x^2 + 1})^{-1}$$

$$\Rightarrow \quad -y = \ln\left(\frac{1}{x + \sqrt{x^2 + 1}}\right)$$

$$\Rightarrow \quad e^{-y} = \frac{1}{x + \sqrt{x^2 + 1}} \times \frac{x - \sqrt{x^2 + 1}}{x - \sqrt{x^2 + 1}} = -(x - \sqrt{x^2 + 1})$$

$$\Rightarrow -e^{-y} = x - \sqrt{x^2 + 1} \quad \text{...(ii)}$$

On adding Eqs. (i) and (ii), we get

$$e^y - e^{-y} = 2x \text{ or } x = \frac{e^y - e^{-y}}{2}$$

Thus, inverse function of $f(x)$ will be

$$y = \frac{e^x - e^{-x}}{2}$$

(b) Given, $f(x)=2^{\frac{x}{x-1}}$

Domain of $f(x)$ is $R-\{1\}$ and range of $\frac{x}{x-1}$ is $R-\{1\}$

Also, 2^x is continuous and increasing function, thus range of $f(x)$ will be $(2^{-\infty},2^{\infty})\sim\{2\}$.

i.e. $(0,\infty)\sim\{2\}$

Thus, $f(x)$ is a bijective function from $R\sim\{1\}$ to $(0,\infty)\sim\{2\}$ and hence is invertible when defined from set $R\sim\{1\}$ to set $(0,\infty)\sim\{2\}$

Now, $$y=2^{\frac{x}{x-1}}$$

$$\Rightarrow \log_2 y=\left(\frac{x}{x-1}\right)\log_2 2$$

$$\Rightarrow \log_2 y=\frac{x}{x-1}$$

$$\Rightarrow x(\log_2 y-1)-\log_2 y=0 \Rightarrow x=\frac{\log_2 y}{\log_2 y-1}$$

$$\Rightarrow f^{-1}(x)=\frac{\log_2 x}{\log_2 x-1}$$

(c) Given, $f(x)=\dfrac{10^x-10^{-x}}{10^x+10^{-x}}$

Clearly, $f(x)$ is defined for all real values x, hence, domain of $f(x)$ is R.

Further $f(x)=\dfrac{10^{2x}-1}{10^{2x}+1}=\left(1-\dfrac{2}{10^{2x}+1}\right)$ which is continuous and having greatest lower bound -1 and least upper bound 1.

Thus, the range of $f(x)$ is $(-1,1)$.

Further $f'(x)=\dfrac{4(10)^{2x}\log 10}{(10^{2x}+1)^2}>0, \forall\ x\in R$ which implies $f(x)$ is monotonically increasing and hence, is bijective when defined from R to $(-1,1)$.

Now, $y=\dfrac{10^x-10^{-x}}{10^x-10^{-x}} \Rightarrow y=\dfrac{10^{2x}-1}{10^{2x}+1}$

On applying componendo and dividendo, we get

$$\frac{y+1}{y-1}=\frac{10^{2x}-1+10^{2x}+1}{10^{2x}-1-10^{2x}-1} \Rightarrow \frac{y+1}{y-1}=\frac{2.10^{2x}}{-2}$$

$$\Rightarrow y+1=(1-y)10^{2x} \Rightarrow 10^{2x}=\frac{1+y}{1-y}$$

$$\Rightarrow 2x=\log_{10}\left(\frac{1+y}{1-y}\right) \Rightarrow x=\frac{1}{2}\log_{10}\left(\frac{1+y}{1-y}\right)$$

$$\Rightarrow f^{-1}(x)=\frac{1}{2}\log_{10}\left(\frac{1+x}{1-x}\right)$$

Example 89. Is the function $f:[-1,1]\to\left[-\frac{\pi}{2},\frac{\pi}{2}\right]$, where $f(x)=\sin^{-1}(2x\sqrt{1-x^2})$ invertible?

Sol. Given, $f(x)=\sin^{-1}(2x\sqrt{1-x^2})$

f is continuous.

$$f'(x)=\frac{2(1-2x^2)}{|1-2x^2|\sqrt{1-x^2}}$$

$$=\begin{cases}\dfrac{2}{\sqrt{1-x^2}}, & \text{if } \dfrac{-1}{\sqrt{2}}<x<\dfrac{1}{\sqrt{2}}\\[2ex] \dfrac{-2}{\sqrt{1-x^2}}, & \text{if } x<\dfrac{-1}{\sqrt{2}} \text{ or } x>\dfrac{1}{\sqrt{2}}\end{cases}$$

$\therefore f(x)$ is increasing in $\left(\frac{-1}{\sqrt{2}},\frac{1}{\sqrt{2}}\right)$ and is decreasing in each of the intervals $\left(-1,\frac{-1}{\sqrt{2}}\right)$ and $\left(\frac{-1}{\sqrt{2}},1\right)$

$\therefore$ $f(x)$ is not one-one, so it is not invertible.

Example 90. Let $g:R\to R$ be given by $g(x)=3+4x$. If $g^n(x)=gogo\ldots og(x)$, show that $g^n(x)=(4^n-1)+4^n x$. If $g^{-n}(x)$ denotes the inverse of $g^n(x)$, then find $g^{-n}(x)$.

Sol. Since, $g(x)=3+4x$

$$\therefore \quad g^2(x)=(gog)(x)=g(g(x))=g(3+4x)$$
$$=3+4(3+4x)$$

or $$g^2(x)=15+4^2x=(4^2-1)+4^2x$$

Now, $g^3(x)=(gogog)x$
$$=g(g^2(x))=g(15+4^2x)=3+4(15+4^2x)$$
$$=63+4^3x=(4^3-1)+4^3x$$

Similarly, we get
$$g^n(x)=(4^n-1)+4^nx$$

Now, let $\quad g^n(x)=y$

$$\Rightarrow \quad x=g^{-n}(y) \quad \ldots\text{(i)}$$

$$\therefore \quad y=(4^n-1)+4^nx$$

or $$x=(y+1-4^n)4^{-n} \quad \ldots\text{(ii)}$$

From Eqs. (i) and (ii), we get
$$g^{-n}(y)=(y+1-4^n)4^{-n}$$

Hence, $g^{-n}(x)=(x+1-4^n)4^{-n}$

Example 91. Let $f:[-\sqrt{2}+1,\sqrt{2}+1]\to\left[\frac{-\sqrt{2}+1}{2},\frac{\sqrt{2}+1}{2}\right]$ be a function defined by $f(x)=\dfrac{1-x}{1+x^2}$. Is f invertible? If yes, then find its inverse.

Sol. Domain of $f(x)=[-\sqrt{2}+1, \sqrt{2}+1]$ [given]

Here, $f(x)=\dfrac{1-x}{1+x^2} \Rightarrow f'(x)=\dfrac{x^2-2x-1}{(1+x^2)^2} \le 0$

For $x \in [-\sqrt{2}+1, \sqrt{2}+1]$

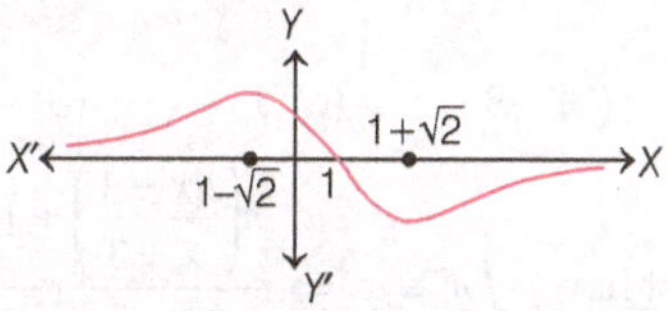

$\Rightarrow f(x)$ is a strictly decreasing function on $[-\sqrt{2}+1, \sqrt{2}+1]$ graphically as shown in figure.

$\Rightarrow f(x)$ is injective on $[-\sqrt{2}+1, \sqrt{2}+1]$

Also, $f(x)$ being a rational function is continuous on $[-\sqrt{2}+1, \sqrt{2}+1]$ as its denominator is non-vanishing.

Thus, $f(x)$ should have its range

$$(f(\sqrt{2}+1), f(-\sqrt{2}+1))=\left(\frac{-\sqrt{2}+1}{2}, \frac{\sqrt{2}+1}{2}\right)=\text{Codomain}$$

$\Rightarrow f(x)$ is surjective.

Thus, $f(x)$ is a bijective function and hence, is invertible.

Now, $$y=\frac{1-x}{1+x^2} \quad \text{...(i)}$$

$$\Rightarrow \quad x^2y+y=1-x$$

$$\Rightarrow x^2y+x+(y-1)=0$$

$$\Rightarrow \quad x=\frac{-1\pm\sqrt{1-4y(y-1)}}{2y}$$

$$=\frac{-1\pm\sqrt{4y-4y^2+1}}{2y}$$

$$=\frac{-1\pm\sqrt{-(4y^2-4y+1)+2}}{2y} \text{ for } y \ne 0$$

On taking negative sign, we get

$$x=\frac{-1-\sqrt{-(4y^2-4y+1)+2}}{2y} \text{ for } y \ne 0$$

Now, $\frac{1}{2} \in$ codomain of f(domain of f^{-1}), on substituting $y=\frac{1}{2}$, we get

$$x=-1-\sqrt{2}$$

Which does not belong to domain of f(range of f^{-1}),

Hence, rejecting negative sign, we get

$$x=\frac{-1+\sqrt{4y-4y^2+1}}{2y} \text{ for } y \ne 0 \text{ and for } y=0,\ x=1$$

[from Eq. (i)]

$$\therefore \quad f^{-1}(x)=\begin{cases}\dfrac{-1+\sqrt{4x-4x^2+1}}{2x}, & x \ne 0 \\ 1\quad, & x=0\end{cases}$$

Example 92. Let $f: N \to N$, where $f(x)=x+(-1)^{x-1}$. Find the inverse of f.

Sol. $$y=f(x)=\begin{cases}x+1; & x \text{ is an odd natural number} \\ x-1; & x \text{ is an even natural number}\end{cases} \quad \text{...(i)}$$

Injectivity

Let $x_1, x_2 \in N$ such that $f(x_1)=f(x_2)$

$\Rightarrow x_1+1=x_2+1$ if x_1, x_2 are odd natural numbers

$\Rightarrow x_1=x_2$

and $x_1-1=x_2-1$, if x_1, x_2 are even natural numbers

$\Rightarrow x_1=x_2$

If x_1 and x_2 are opposite in nature (say) x_1 odd and x_2 even, then $f(x_1)=f(x_2)$

$\Rightarrow x_1+1=x_2-1$

$\Rightarrow x_2-x_1=2$, which is a contradiction as difference of an odd and even integer can never be an even integer.

Similarly, x_1 even and x_2 odd is impossible. Thus, $f(x)$ is an injective function.

Surjectivity

Let n be any natural number.

Now, if n is odd say $n=2m-1$, $m \in N$; then

$$f(2m)=2m-1=n$$

and if n is even say $2m$, $m \in N$, then $f(2m-1)=2m=n$.

Thus, f is surjective function. Hence, f is an invertible function.

Now, from Eq. (i), we get

$$x=\begin{cases}y-1, & \text{if } x \text{ is an odd natural number} \\ y+1, & \text{if } x \text{ is an even natural number}\end{cases}$$

or $$x=\begin{cases}y-1, & \text{if } y \text{ is an even natural number} \\ y+1, & \text{if } y \text{ is an odd natural number}\end{cases}$$

$$\Rightarrow f^{-1}(x)=\begin{cases}x-1, & \text{if } x \text{ is an even natural number} \\ x+1, & \text{if } x \text{ is an odd natural number}\end{cases}$$

$$\Rightarrow f^{-1}(x)=(x)+(-1)^{x-1}=x+(-1)^{\pm(x\pm1)}$$

Example 93. Find the inverse of $f(x)=2^{\log_{10}x}+8$ and hence, solve the equation $f(x)=f^{-1}(x)$.

Sol. Given $y=2^{\log_{10}x}+8$

$\log_{10}x$ is defined for $x>0$, therefore domain of function $f(x)$ is $(0, \infty)$.

Also, range of $\log_{10}x$ is $(-\infty, \infty)$ and 2^x being continuous and increasing function, $2^{\log_{10}x}$ has its range $(0, \infty)$.

Thus, the range of function $f(x)=2^{\log_{10}x}+8$ is $(8, \infty)$.

Further $f(x)$ is monotonically increasing (sum of increasing and constant function) when defined from $(0, \infty)$ to set $(8, \infty)$ is bijective and hence, is invertible.

Now, $$y=2^{\log_{10}x}+8$$

$$\Rightarrow \quad \log_{10}x=\log_2(y-8) \Rightarrow x=10^{\log_2(y-8)}$$

$$\therefore \quad f^{-1}(x)=10^{\log_2(x-8)}$$

Now, to solve $f(x)=f^{-1}(x)$, we solve

$$f(x)=x \text{ and } f(x)=-x+k.$$

However, $f(x) = -x + k$ is taken if $f(x)$ has atleast two points of symmetric about the line $y = x$,

i.e. $(\alpha, \beta), (\beta, \alpha) \in f$ and $\alpha \neq \beta$.

Here, $f(x) = 2^{\log_{10} x} + 8$ is an increasing function, therefore it would not contain any two different points of symmetry.

Thus, $f(x)$ and $f^{-1}(x)$ can intersect only on line $y = x$.

Thus, $f(x) = f^{-1}(x)$ is equivalent to equation $f(x) = x$

$\therefore \quad 2^{\log_{10} x} + 8 = x$

$\Rightarrow \quad 2^{\log_{10} x} = x - 8 \Rightarrow \log_{10} x = \log_2(x-8)$

$\Rightarrow \quad \log_{x-8} x = \log_2 10 \Rightarrow x = 10$

Example 94. If $f(x) = \begin{cases} x, & \text{if } x < 1 \\ x^2, & \text{if } 1 \le x \le 4 \\ 8\sqrt{x}, & \text{if } x > 4 \end{cases}$, then find $f^{-1}(x)$, if $f(x)$ is invertible.

Sol. $y = f(x) = \begin{cases} x & \text{if } x < 1 \\ x^2, & \text{if } 1 \le x \le 4 \\ 8\sqrt{x}, & \text{if } x > 4 \end{cases}$ ...(i)

The graph of $f(x)$ is a shown below

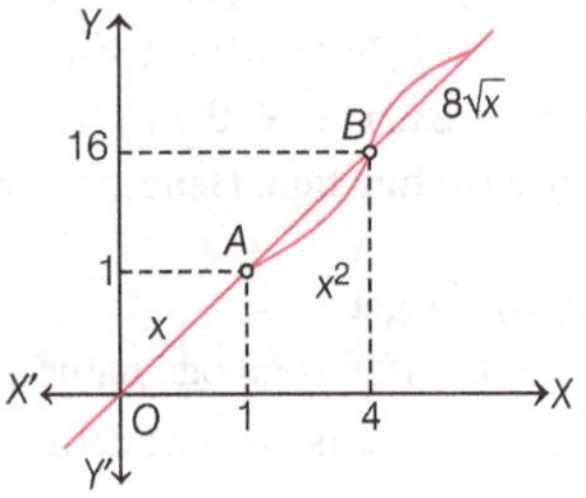

$\Rightarrow f'(x) = \begin{cases} 1, & \text{if } x < 1 \\ 2x, & \text{if } 1 \le x \le 4 \\ \frac{4}{\sqrt{x}}, & \text{if } x > 4 \end{cases}$

$\Rightarrow f'(x) > 0 \; \forall x \in R$

$\Rightarrow f(x)$ is strictly increasing $\forall \; x \in R$.

$\Rightarrow f(x)$ is injective function $\forall \; x \in R$.

$\Rightarrow f(x)$ is invertible from R to its range set.

Now, from Eq. (i), $x = \begin{cases} y, & \text{if } x < 1 \\ \sqrt{y}, & \text{if } 1 \le x \le 4 \\ \frac{y^2}{64}, & \text{if } x > 4 \end{cases}$

$\Rightarrow \quad x = \begin{cases} y, & \text{if } y < 1 \\ \sqrt{y}, & \text{if } 1 \le y \le 16 \\ \frac{y^2}{64}, & \text{if } y > 16 \end{cases}$

$\Rightarrow \quad f^{-1}(x) = \begin{cases} x. & \text{if } x < 1 \\ \sqrt{x}. & \text{if } 1 \le x \le 16 \\ \frac{x^2}{64}. & \text{if } x > 16 \end{cases}$

JEE SCANNER

Example Similar to PYQ Asked in JEE Main 2023

The value of a, so that $f(x) = \dfrac{ax+1}{x+3}$ is identical with $f^{-1}(x)$ is

(a) 3 (b) −3 (c) 1 (d) −1

Sol. (b) We must have, $fof \equiv x \Rightarrow \dfrac{a\left(\dfrac{ax+1}{x+3}\right)+1}{\dfrac{ax+1}{x+3}+3} \equiv x$

$\Rightarrow \quad a^2x + a + x + 3 \equiv x(ax + 1 + 3x + 9)$

$\Rightarrow \quad (a^2+1)x + a + 3 = (a+3)x^2 + 10x$

$\Rightarrow a + 3 = 0$ and $a^2 + 1 = 10$

$\Rightarrow \quad a = -3$ and $a = \pm 3$

$\Rightarrow \quad a = -3$

Time Saving Technique

In general, the function $f(x) = \dfrac{ax+b}{cx+d}$ is identical with its inverse, if $a + d = 0$.

Skill Builder

If $f: R \to R$, $g: R \to R$ defined as $f(x) = 3x - 4$ and $g(x) = 2 + 3x$, then $(g^{-1} o f^{-1})5$ is

(a) 1 (b) $\frac{1}{2}$

(c) $\frac{1}{3}$ (d) $\frac{1}{5}$

For Sol.

■ **For more practice** See Q.12 of Milestone Practice 2.4.

Example 95. Find the solution of the equation $x^2 - x + 1 = \dfrac{1}{2} + \sqrt{\left(x - \dfrac{3}{4}\right)}$.

Sol. Consider the function

$f: \left[\frac{1}{2}, \infty\right) \to \left[\frac{3}{4}, \infty\right)$, where $f(x) = x^2 - x + 1$

We note that f is one-one and onto.

Its inverse is $f^{-1}: \left[\frac{3}{4}, \infty\right) \to \left[\frac{1}{2}, \infty\right)$,

$$f^{-1}(x) = \frac{1}{2} + \sqrt{x - \frac{3}{4}}$$

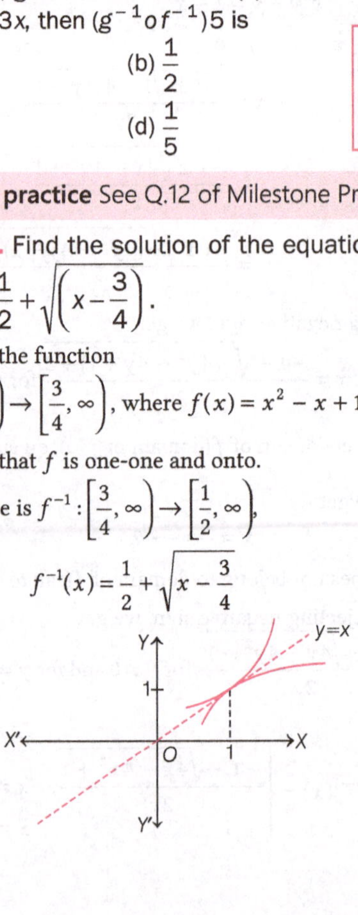

Hence, the two sides of the given equation are inverse of each other.

We draw the graphs of the given functions and observe that they intersect on line $y = x$ only.

Clearly, the intersection point is the solution of the equation,

$$f(x) = x$$

$$\Rightarrow \quad x^2 - x + 1 = x \Rightarrow x^2 - 2x + 1 = 0$$

$$\Rightarrow \quad (x-1)^2 = 0 \Rightarrow x = 1$$

This is the answer. It is interesting to know that we can also proceed to find the solution by working on the inverse function. This should also give the same result as given functions are inverse to each other.

$$f^{-1}(x) = x$$

$$\Rightarrow \quad \frac{1}{2} + \sqrt{\left(x - \frac{3}{4}\right)} = x$$

$$\Rightarrow \quad \sqrt{\left(x - \frac{3}{4}\right)} = x - \frac{1}{2}$$

On squaring both sides, we get

$$\left(x - \frac{3}{4}\right) = \left(x - \frac{1}{2}\right)^2 = x^2 + \frac{1}{4} - x$$

$$\Rightarrow \quad x^2 + \frac{1}{4} - x - x + \frac{3}{4} = 0$$

$$\Rightarrow \quad x^2 - 2x + 1 = 0 \Rightarrow x = 1$$

JEE SPIKE

Some points of intersection of f and f^{-1} lie on the line $y = x$. However, it must be noted that $f(x)$ and $f^{-1}(x)$ may intersect elsewhere also.

Example 96. If $f(x) = -x + \sin x$, solve the equation $f(x) = f^{-1}(x)$.

Sol. To solve the equation $f(x) = f^{-1}(x)$,

first we draw the graphs of both the functions to observe their points of intersection.

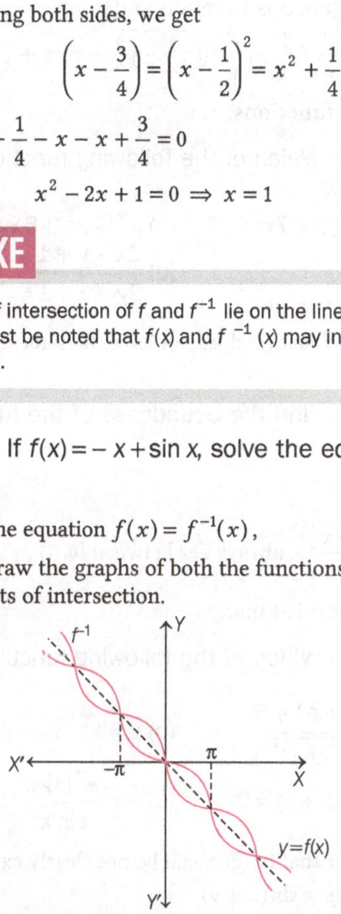

From, the graph, we realise that only the point (0, 0) lies on the line $y = x$. There are other points of intersection $(n\pi, n\pi)$, $n \in I$ which lie on the line $y = -x$.

Hence, the solution set is $\{n\pi, n \in I\}$.

2.19 Equal or Identical Function

Two functions f and g are said to be equal if

(i) The domain of f = The domain of g.

(ii) The range of f = The range of g.

(iii) $f(x) = g(x)$, for every x belonging to their common domain.

e.g. $f(x) = \dfrac{1}{x}$ and $g(x) = \dfrac{x}{x^2}$ are identical functions.

Functions are also equal if their graphs are same.

Examples of Equal or Identical Functions

(i) $f(x) = \ln x^2$, $g(x) = 2 \ln x$

$f(x) = \text{cosec } x$, $g(x) = \dfrac{1}{\sin x}$

(ii) $f(x) = \cot(\cot^{-1} x)$, $g(x) = x$

$f(x) = \tan x$, $g(x) = \dfrac{1}{\cot x}$

(iii) $f(x) = \sin^{-1}(3x - 4x^3)$, $g(x) = 3\sin^{-1} x$

(iv) $f(x) = sgn(x^2 + 1)$, $g(x) = \sin^2 x + \cos^2 x$

(v) $f(x) = \tan^2 x \cdot \sin^2 x$, $g(x) = \tan^2 x - \sin^2 x$

(vi) $f(x) = \sec^2 x - \tan^2 x$, $g(x) = 1$

(vii) $f(x) = \log_x e$, $g(x) = \dfrac{1}{\log_e x}$

(viii) $f(x) = \tan(\cot^{-1} x)$, $g(x) = \cot(\tan^{-1} x)$

(ix) $f(x) = \sqrt{x^2 - 1}$, $g(x) = \sqrt{x-1} \cdot \sqrt{x+1}$

(x) $f(x) = \tan x \cdot \cot x$, $g(x) = \sin x \cdot \text{cosec } x$

(xi) $f(x) = e^{\ln e^x}$, $g(x) = e^x$

(xii) $f(x) = \sqrt{\dfrac{1 - \cos 2x}{2}}$, $g(x) = \sin x$

(xiii) $f(x) = \sqrt{x^2}$, $g(x) = (\sqrt{x})^2$

(xiv) $f(x) = \log(x+2) + \log(x-3)$, $g(x) = \log(x^2 - x - 6)$

(xv) $f(x) = x\,|\,x\,|$, $g(x) = x^2 \text{ sgn } x$

(xvi) $f(x) = \lim\limits_{n \to \infty} \dfrac{x^{2n} - 1}{x^{2n} + 1}$, $g(x) = \text{sgn}(|x| - 1)$

(xvii) $f(x) = \sin(\sin^{-1} x)$, $g(x) = \cos(\cos^{-1} x)$

(xviii) $f(x)=\dfrac{1}{1+\dfrac{1}{x}}$, $g(x)=\dfrac{x}{1+x}$

(xix) $f(x)=e^{\ln \sec^{-1} x}$, $g(x)=\sec^{-1} x$

Identical, if $x\in(-\infty,-1]\cup[1,\infty)$

(xx) $F(x)=(fog)(x)$, $G(x)=(gof)(x)$,

where $f(x)=e^x$, $g(x)=\ln x$

Example 97. If $f(x)=\log_{x^2} 25$ and $g(x)=\log_x 5$, then $f(x)=g(x)$ holds, find the interval for x.

Sol. Domain of $f\in R-\{\pm1,0\}$

Domain of $g\in(0,\infty)-\{1\}$

For $f(x)=g(x)$, domain of f = domain of g.

i.e. $f(x)=g(x)$, if $x\in(0,\infty)-\{1\}$

Example 98. Let $A=\{1,2\}$, $B=\{3,6\}$ and $f:A\to B$ given by $f(x)=x^2+2$ and $g:A\to B$ given by $g(x)=3x$. Find whether they are equal or not.

Sol. $f(1)=3$, $f(2)=6$, $g(1)=3$, $g(2)=6$

which shows $f(x)$ and $g(x)$ have same domains and range, thus $f=g$.

Example 99. Which pair of functions is identical ?

(a) $\sin^{-1}(\sin x)$ and $\sin(\sin^{-1} x)$

(b) $\log_e e^x$, $e^{\log_e x}$

(c) $\log_e x^2$, $2\log_e x$

(d) None of the above

Sol. (d) Here, (a) $\sin^{-1}(\sin x)$ is defined for $x\in\left[-\dfrac{\pi}{2},\dfrac{\pi}{2}\right]$, while $\sin(\sin^{-1} x)$ is defined only for $x\in[-1,1]$

(b) $\log_e e^x$ is defined for all x,

while $e^{\log_e x}$ is defined for $x>0$

(c) $\log_e x^2$ is defined for all $x\in R-\{0\}$, while $2\log_e x$ is defined for $x>0$.

$\therefore$ None is identical.

2.20 Bounded function

A function is said to be bounded, if $f(x)\in[a,b]$, where a and b are finite number.

2.21 Implicit and Explicit Function

An equation $f(x,y)=0$ represents an implicit function, then y and x can not be easily expressed in terms of x and y respectively.

If y has been expressed in terms of x alone or *vice-versa*, then it is called explicit function.

e.g. 1. $x^3+y^3+xy=7\to$ Implicit function

2. $x\sqrt{1+y}+y\sqrt{1+x}=0\to$ Explicit

We get, $y=\dfrac{-x}{1+x}$

2.22 Homogeneous Functions

A function is said to be homogeneous with respect to any set of variables when each of its terms is of the same degree with respect to those variables.

e.g. $5x^2+3y^2-xy$ is homogeneous in x and y.

Symbolically, if $f(tx,ty)=t^n\cdot f(x,y)$, then $f(x,y)$ is a homogeneous function of degree n.

Examples of Homogeneous Functions

$$f(x,y)=\frac{x-y\cos x}{y\sin x+x}$$

is not a homogeneous function and

$f(x,y)=\dfrac{x}{y}\ln\dfrac{y}{x}+\dfrac{y}{x}\ln\dfrac{x}{y}$, $\sqrt{x^2-y^2}+x$, $x+y\cos\dfrac{y}{x}$ are homogeneous functions.

Example 100. Which of the following function is not homogeneous?

(a) $x^3+8x^2y+7y^3$

(b) y^2+x^2+5xy

(c) $\dfrac{xy}{x^2+y^2}$

(d) $\dfrac{2x-y+1}{2y-x+1}$

Sol. (d) It is clear that (d) does not have the same degree in each term.

Example 101. Find the boundness of the function $f(x)=\dfrac{x^2}{x^4+1}$.

Sol. $\because f(x)=\dfrac{x^2}{x^4+1}$ always lies between [0, 1)

$\therefore$ Boundness is 1 unit.

Example 102. Which of the following function is implicit function?

(a) $y=\dfrac{x^2+e^x+5}{\sqrt{1-\cos^{-1} x}}$

(b) $y=x^2$

(c) $xy-\sin(x+y)=0$

(d) $y=\dfrac{x^2\log x}{\sin x}$

Sol. (c) It is clear that in (c), y can be not clearly expressed in x.

$\because \quad xy=\sin(x+y)$

$\Rightarrow \quad xy=\sin x\cos y+\cos x\sin y$

$\Rightarrow \quad y=\dfrac{\sin x\cos y+\cos x\sin y}{x}$,

which is not expressed in terms of x.

Milestone Practice 2.4

1. Let $f(x) = 16\sin^2 x + 1$ and $g(x, y) = \log_x y$, then the range of $h(x) = g(\sqrt{2}, (2 - g(2, f(x))))$ is
   (a) $(-\infty, 1)$ (b) $(-\infty, 2)$
   (c) $(-\infty, 1]$ (d) $(-\infty, 2]$

2. Let $f(x) = ([a]^2 - 5[a] + 4)x^3 - (6\{a\}^2 - 5\{a\} + 1)x - (\tan x)\operatorname{sgn} x$, be an even function for all $x \in R - \left\{(2n+1)\frac{\pi}{2}; n \in Z\right\}$, then sum of all possible values of a is (where [] and {} denote greatest integer function and fractional part function, respectively)
   (a) $\frac{17}{6}$ (b) $\frac{53}{6}$
   (c) $\frac{35}{3}$ (d) None of these

3. Let f be a real valued function such that for any real x, $f(\lambda + x) = f(\lambda - x)$ and $f(2\lambda + x) = -f(2\lambda - x)$ for some $\lambda > 0$. Then,
   (a) f is even and non-periodic.
   (b) f is odd and periodic.
   (c) f is odd and non-periodic.
   (d) f is even and periodic.

4. The number of function f from the set $A = \{2, 3, 5\}$ into the set $B = \{1, 3, 5, 7, 9, 11, 13\}$ such that $f(i) \le f(j)$ for $i < j$ and $i, j \in A$
   (a) ${}^9C_3$ (b) ${}^9C_3 + 2({}^9C_2)$
   (c) ${}^8C_3 + {}^8C_2$ (d) None of these

5. Let $f : \{x, y, z\} \to \{a, b, c\}$ be a one-one function and only one of the following statements is true.
   (i) $f(x) \ne b$
   (ii) $f(y) = b$
   (iii) $f(z) \ne a$
   Determine $f^{-1}(b)$.

6. Solve $(x)^2 = [x]^2 + 2x$, where $[x]$ represents greatest integer less than or equal to x and (x) represents integer just greater than or equal to x.

7. Let $f : R - \{2\} \to R$ be a function satisfying the following functional equation
   $$2f(x) + 3f\left(\frac{2x+29}{x-2}\right) = 100x + 80, \forall x \in R - \{2\}$$
   Determine $f(x)$.

8. Determine all values of c, so that $f(x) = \frac{x-1}{c - x^2 + 1}$ does not take any value in the interval $\left[-1, -\frac{1}{3}\right]$.

9. Find the domain and range of $h(x) = g(f(x))$, where $f(x) = \begin{cases} [x], & -2 \le x \le -1 \\ |x| + 1, & -1 < x \le 2 \end{cases}$ and $g(x) = \begin{cases} [x], & -\pi \le x \le 0 \\ \sin x & 0 < x \le \pi \end{cases}$, where [·] denotes the greatest integer function.

10. Consider $f(x) = (1 - x^n)^{1/n}$ and $g(x) = x^2 + px + q$; $(p, q \in R)$. Let $g(x) = kx, (k > 0)$ has imaginary roots, then show that $g(g(g(x))) = k^3 f(f(f(f(x))))$ has no real solution.

11. Let $f_1(x) = \frac{1}{x}$, $f_2(x) = 1 - x$, $f_3(x) = \frac{x-1}{x}$. Suppose that $f_3(f_m(x)) = f_2(x)$, then the value of m is
    (a) 1 (b) 2
    (c) 3 (d) None of these

12. The value of β, so that $f(x) = \frac{\beta x + 1}{x + 4}$ is identical with $f^{-1}(x)$ is
    (a) 4 (b) −4
    (c) 1 (d) −1

Answer Key

1. (d) 2. (c) 3. (b) 4. (a) 5. x
6. $x = 0$ or $x = n + \frac{1}{2}, n \in Z$ 7. $16 - 40x + 60\left(\frac{2x+29}{x-2}\right)$ 8. $\left(-\infty, -\frac{1}{4}\right)$
9. Domain $= [-2, 2]$, Range $= [-2 \; -1] \cup [\sin 3, 1]$ 11. (a) 12. (b)

For Detailed Solution

Milestone 5 Some Special Points

• Functional Rule • Functional Equation • Miscellaneous Problems of Function

2.23 Functional Rule

If x and y are independent variables, then

(i) $f(xy) = f(x) + f(y) \Rightarrow f(x) = k \ln x$ or $f(x) = 0$

(ii) $f(xy) = f(x) \cdot f(y) \Rightarrow f(x) = x^n, n \in R$

(iii) $f(x+y) = f(x) \cdot f(y) \Rightarrow f(x) = a^{kx}$

$\Rightarrow f(x) = A^x, A > 0$

(iv) $f(x+y) = f(x) + f(y) \Rightarrow f(x) = kx$, where k is a constant.

(v) $f(x+y) = f(x) = f(y)$, then $f(x) = k$

(vi) If $P(x)$ is a polynomial function of degree n and $P(x) \cdot P\left(\frac{1}{x}\right) = P(x) + P\left(\frac{1}{x}\right)$ for $x \neq 0$.

Then, $P(x) = 1 + x^n$ or $1 - x^n$

(vii) $f(x+y) + f(x-y) = 2f(x) \cdot f(y)$, then $f(x) = \cos \lambda x$

(viii) $f(x-y) - f(x+y) = 2f(x)f(y)$, then $f(x) = \sin \lambda x$

2.24 Functional Equation

Functional equation is an equation, where the unknown is a function. A functional equation asks for a formula satisfying certain features. On solving such an equation, we obtain one or more functions as solutions.

Example 103. Find the natural number a for which $\sum_{k=1}^{n} f(a+k) = 16(2^n - 1)$, where f satisfies $f(x+y) = f(x) \cdot f(y), \forall\, x, y \in N$, and $f(1) = 2$.

Sol. Given, $f(1) = 2$

We put $x = 1$ and $y = 1$ in the given equation

$$f(1+1) = f(1) \cdot f(1) = 2^2$$

$\Rightarrow$ $f(2) = 2^2$

Now, $f(3) = f(2+1)$

$$= f(2) \cdot f(1) = 2^2 \cdot 2 = 2^3$$

We find that $f(n) = 2^n, n \in N$ and prove this using induction.

Now, $\sum_{k=1}^{n} f(a) \cdot f(k) = 16(2^n - 1)$

$\Rightarrow$ $f(a) \sum_{k=1}^{n} f(k) = 16(2^n - 1)$

$\Rightarrow$ $2^a(2^1 + 2^2 + \ldots + 2^n) = 16(2^n - 1)$

$\Rightarrow$ $2^a \cdot \frac{2(2^n - 1)}{2 - 1} = 16(2^n - 1)$

$\Rightarrow$ $a = 3$

Example 104. Let a polynomial function $f(x^2) = x^3 f(x) + x^3 - 1, \forall x \in R$, where $f(2) = 7$, then find $f(x)$.

Sol. Given, $f(x^2) = x^3 f(x) + x^3 - 1$ ...(i)

Let the degree of the polynomial $f(x)$ be n.

Then, the degree of LHS. of Eq. (i) is $2n$ and the degree of RHS is 0 or $n + 3$.

The degree is 0 when $f(x)$ is -1.

Since, $f(2) = 7$, this is not acceptable.

If the degree of RHS is $n + 3$, then

$$2n = n + 3 \Rightarrow n = 3$$

Let $f(x) = ax^3 + bx^2 + cx + d$

On placing $f(x)$ in Eq. (i), we get

$$ax^6 + bx^4 + cx^2 + d = ax^6 + bx^5 + cx^4 + dx^3 + x^3 - 1$$

On comparing the coefficients, we get

$$b = 0$$
$$b = c \Rightarrow c = 0$$
$$0 = d + 1 \Rightarrow d = -1$$

Hence, $f(x) = ax^3 - 1$

Since, $f(2) = 7 = 8a - 1$

$\Rightarrow$ $8a = 8 \Rightarrow a = 1, f(x) = x^3 - 1$

Example 105. Let $f: R - \{0\} \to R$ be any function such that $f(x) + 2f\left(\frac{1}{x}\right) = 3x$. Find the sum of the values of x for which $f(x) = 1$.

Sol. Given, $f(x) + 2f\left(\frac{1}{x}\right) = 3x$ ...(i)

Replacing x with $\left(\frac{1}{x}\right)$, we get

$$f\left(\frac{1}{x}\right)+2f(x)=\frac{3}{x} \quad \text{...(ii)}$$

On multiplying in Eq. (ii) by 2, we get

$$2f\left(\frac{1}{x}\right)+4f(x)=\frac{6}{x} \quad \text{...(iii)}$$

On subtracting Eq. (iii) from Eq. (i), we get

$$3f(x)=\frac{6}{x}-3x \Rightarrow f(x)=\frac{2}{x}-x$$

Solving $f(x)=1$, we get

$$2-x^2=x \Rightarrow x^2+x-2=0$$

$$\Rightarrow \quad x_1=-2, x_2=1 \Rightarrow x_1+x_2=-1$$

Thus, the sum of values of x for which $f(x)=1$ is -1.

JEE SCANNER

Example Similar to PYQ Asked in JEE Main 2023

$f(x)$ is a polynomial function of x, satisfying $f(x)\cdot f(y)=f(x)+f(y)+f(xy)-2$ and that $f(2)=5$. Then, the value of $f(3)$ is

(a) 9 (b) 8 (c) 10 (d) 7

Sol. (c) Given, $f(x)\cdot f(y)=f(x)+f(y)+f(xy)-2$

On putting $y=1/x$, we get

$$f(x)\cdot f\left(\frac{1}{x}\right)=f(x)+f\left(\frac{1}{x}\right)+f(1)-2$$

On putting $x=1$ and $y=1$, we get

$$f(1)\cdot f(1)=2f(1)+f(1)-2$$

$$f^2(1)-3f(1)+2=0$$

$$(f(1)-1)(f(1)-2)=0$$

$$\Rightarrow \quad f(1)=1 \text{ or } f(1)=2$$

But $f(1)\neq 1$, as in this case $f(x)=1, \forall x$.

$$\Rightarrow \quad f(1)=2$$

Hence, $f(x)\cdot f\left(\frac{1}{x}\right)=f(x)+f\left(\frac{1}{x}\right)$

$$\therefore \quad f(x)=\pm x^n+1$$

$$f(2)=\pm 2^n+1=5 \quad [n=2 \text{ using } (+) \text{ sign}]$$

$$\therefore \quad f(x)=x^2+1$$

$$\Rightarrow \quad f(3)=10$$

Skill Builder

Let $g(x)$ be a polynomial function satisfying $g(x)\,g(y)=g(x)+g(y)+g(xy)-2$ for all $x, y \in R$. If $g(2)=5$, then $g(5)$ is

(a) 26 (b) 28
(c) 25 (d) 27

For Sol.

■ **For more practice** See Q.1 of Milestone Practice 2.5.

Example 106. Let $f(\sin x)+2f(\cos x)=3, \forall x \in R$. Find $f(x)$.

Sol. $f(\sin x)+2f(\cos x)=3 \quad$ ...(i)

Replace x by $\frac{\pi}{2}-x$.

$$f(\cos x)+2f(\sin x)=3 \quad \text{...(ii)}$$

On putting the value of $f(\cos x)$ from Eq. (i) in Eq. (ii), we get

$$\frac{3-f(\sin x)}{2}+2f(\sin x)=3$$

$$\Rightarrow \quad 3+3f(\sin x)=6$$

$$\Rightarrow \quad f(\sin x)=1$$

Let $u=\sin x$

Then, $0<u<1$ for $0<x<\frac{\pi}{2}$

Hence, $f(u)=1, u\in(0,1)$

i.e. $\quad f(x)=1, x\in(0,1)$.

Example 107. Find all functions $f: R \to R$ such that $x^2 f(x)+f(1-x)=2x-x^4$.

Sol. From the given equation

$$f(1-x)=2x-x^4-x^2f(x)$$

Replacing x by $1-x$, we obtain

$$(1-x)^2f(1-x)+f(x)=2(1-x)-(1-x)^4$$

This implies that

$$f(x)=2(1-x)-(1-x)^4-(1-x)^2f(1-x)$$

$$=2(1-x)-(1-x)^4-(1-x)^2(2x-x^4-x^2f(x))$$

which in turn, gives

$$f(x)=2(1-x)-(1-x)^4-2x(1-x)^2+x^4(1-x)^2+x^2f(x)(1-x)^2$$

On solving, now for $f(x)$, we get

$$f(x)=\frac{2(1-x)-(1-x)^4-2x(1-x)^2+x^4(1-x)^2}{1-(1-x)^2x^2}$$

$$=\frac{(1-x)(2-(1-x)^3-2x(1-x)+x^4(1-x))}{(1-(1-x)x)(1+(1-x)x)}$$

$$=\frac{(1-x)(2-(1-3x+3x^2-x^3)-2x+2x^2+x^4-x^5)}{(1-x+x^2)(1+x-x^2)}$$

$$=1-x^2$$

We now check. If $f(x)=1-x^2$, then

$$x^2f(x)+f(1-x)=x^2(1-x^2)+1-(1-x)^2$$

$$=x^2-x^4+1-1+2x-x^2$$

$$=2x-x^4$$

Hence, $f(x)=1-x^2$ is the only solution.

Example 108. Let f be a function defined from $f: R^+ \to R^+$. If $(f(xy))^2 = x(f(y))^2$ for all positive numbers x and y and $f(2) = 6$, then find the value of $f(50)$.

Sol. On putting $x = 25$ and $y = 2$

$$(f(50))^2 = 25(f(2))^2 \Rightarrow (f(50))^2 = 25(6)^2 \qquad [\because f(2) = 6]$$

$$\Rightarrow f(50) = 30 \text{ or } -30 \qquad \text{[rejected]}$$

$$\therefore f(50) = 30$$

Alternate Solution

On putting $x = 1/y$, we get $f^2(1) = \frac{1}{y} f^2(y)$

Also, $f(2) = 6$, so putting $y = 2$, we get

$$f^2(1) = \frac{1}{2} f^2(2) = \frac{1}{2} \times 36 = 18 \Rightarrow f(1) = \sqrt{18} = 3\sqrt{2}$$

$$\therefore \quad f^2(y) = 18y \Rightarrow f(y) = 3\sqrt{2y} \Rightarrow f(50) = 3\sqrt{100} = 30$$

Example 109. If $f(x + y + 1) = (\sqrt{f(x)} + \sqrt{f(y)})^2$ and $f(0) = 1$, $\forall\, x, y \in W$. Determine $f(x)$.

Sol. Given, $f(x + y + 1) = (\sqrt{f(x)} + \sqrt{f(y)})^2$

On putting $x = y = 0$, we get

$$f(1) = (\sqrt{f(0)} + \sqrt{f(0)})^2 = (1 + 1)^2 = 2^2$$

Again, on putting $x = 0$ and $y = 1$, we get

$$f(2) = (\sqrt{f(0)} + \sqrt{f(1)})^2 = (1 + 2)^2 = 3^2$$

and for $x = 1$ and $y = 1$

$$f(3) = (\sqrt{f(1)} + \sqrt{f(1)})^2 = (2 + 2)^2 = 4^2$$

We assume that $f(x) = (x + 1)^2$ and prove this using induction.

The statement is true for $x = 1$.

Assume that it is true for $x = n$

We now prove that it is true for $x = n + 1$ also.

$$f(n + 1) = f(n + 0 + 1) = (\sqrt{f(n)} + \sqrt{f(0)})^2$$

$$= (\sqrt{(n + 1)^2} + \sqrt{1})^2 = (n + 1 + 1)^2$$

which is true.

Hence, $f(x) = (x + 1)^2$ for $x \in W$

Example 110. Let f be a function from the set of positive integers to the set of real numbers i.e. $f: N \to R$, such that.

(i) $f(1) = 1$

(ii) $f(1) + 2f(2) + 3f(3) + \ldots + nf(n) = n(n + 1)\, f(n)$ for $n \geq 2$, then find the value of $f(1994)$.

Sol. Given, $f(1) + 2f(2) + 3f(3) + \ldots + nf(n) = n(n + 1)f(n)$ ...(i)

Replacing n by $(n + 1)$, then

$$f(1) + 2f(2) + 3f(3) + \ldots + nf(n) + (n + 1)\, f(n + 1) = (n + 1)(n + 2)\, f(n + 1) \quad \text{...(ii)}$$

On subtracting Eq. (i) from Eq. (ii), we get

$$(n + 1)f(n + 1) = (n + 1)(n + 2)f(n + 1) - n(n + 1)\, f(n)$$

$$\Rightarrow \quad nf(n) = (n + 1)f(n + 1)$$

From which we conclude that

$$2f(2) = 3f(3) = 4f(4) = \ldots = nf(n)$$

On substituting the value of $2f(2), 3f(3)$, ... in terms of $nf(n)$ in Eq. (i), we have

$$f(1) + (n - 1)nf(n) = n(n + 1)f(n)$$

$$\Rightarrow \quad f(1) = 2nf(n)$$

$$\therefore \quad f(n) = \frac{f(1)}{2n} = \frac{1}{2n} \qquad [\because f(1) = 1]$$

$$\Rightarrow f(1994) = \frac{1}{2 \cdot 1994} = \frac{1}{3988}$$

Example 111. Let f be a function satisfying $2f(xy) = (f(x))^y + (f(y))^x$ and $f(1) = k \neq 1$. Prove that $(k - 1)\sum_{r=1}^{n} f(r) = k^{n+1} - k$.

Sol. Given that $2f(xy) = (f(x))^y + (f(y))^x$ ...(i)

Replacing y by 1, we get

$$2f(x) = f(x) + (f(1))^x \quad \text{...(ii)}$$

or

$$f(x) = (f(1))^x = k^x \qquad [\because f(1) = k]$$

$$\therefore \quad \sum_{r=1}^{n} f(r) = f(1) + f(2) + \ldots + f(n)$$

$$= k^1 + k^2 + k^3 + \ldots + k^n$$

$$= \frac{k(k^n - 1)}{(k - 1)} = \frac{k^{n+1} - k}{(k - 1)}$$

$$\text{or } (k - 1)\sum_{r=1}^{n} f(r) = (k^{n+1} - k)$$

2.25 Miscellaneous Problems of Functions

Functions of the form $f(x) = \max.(g_1(x), g_2(x), \ldots, g_n(x))$ or $f(x) = \min.(g_1(x), g_2(x), \ldots, g_n(x))$

Let's consider the function $f(x) = \max\{x, x^2\}$

To write the equivalent definition of the function, first draw the graph of $y = x$ and $y = x^2$.

Now, from the graph, we can see that

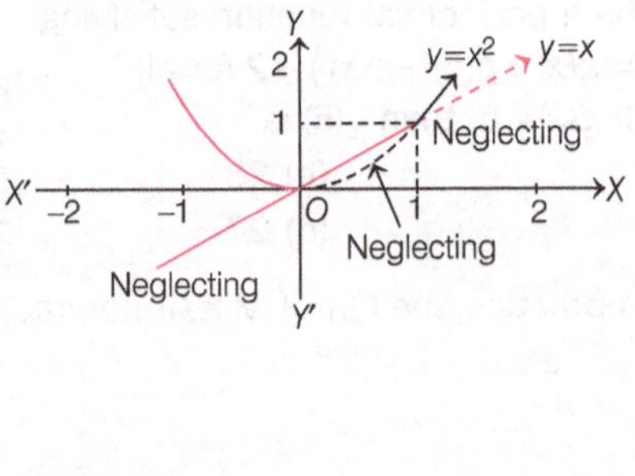

For $x \in (-\infty, 0)$, the graph of $y = x^2$ lies above the graph of $y = x$, or $x^2 > x$.

For $x \in (0, 1)$, the graph of $y = x$ lies above the graph of $y = x^2$ or $x > x^2$.

For $x \in (1, \infty)$, the graph of $y = x^2$ lies above the graph of $y = x$ or $x^2 > x$.

Hence, we have $f(x) = \begin{cases} x^2 & , \quad x < 0 \\ x & , \quad 0 \le x \le 1 \\ x^2 & , \quad x > 0 \end{cases}$

For $f(x) = \min\{x, x^2\}$, we have $f(x) = \begin{cases} x & , \quad x < 0 \\ x^2 & , \quad 0 \le x \le 1 \\ x & , \quad x > 0 \end{cases}$

In this situation, drawing graph of each function is better approach to redefine the function.

Milestone Practice 2.5

1. If $f(x)$ is a polynomial function of x, satisfying $f(x).f(y) = f(x) + f(y) + f(xy) - 2$ such that $f(1) = 2$ and $f(2) = 5$, then find the value of $f(6) + 2009$.
2. Let $P(x)$ be a polynomial satisfying the identity $P(x^2) + 2x^2 + 10x = 2x\,P(x+1) + 3$, then find the value of $P(x)$.
3. If $f(x)$ is a polynomial of degree 2 such that $f(0) = 1$ and $f(x+2) = f(x) + 4x + 2$, then find the polynomial $f(x)$.
4. If $f(2 + x) = f(2 - x)$ and $f(7 - x) = f(7 + x)$ and $f(0) = 0$, then find the minimum number of roots of $f(x) = 0$, where $20 \le x \le 20$.
5. If $a, b \in R^+$ and for all x in R, $f(a + x) = b + [b^3 + 1 - 3b^2 f(x) + 3b(f(x))^2 - (f(x))^3]^{1/3}$, then prove that $f(x)$ is periodic.
6. How many polynomials $p(x)$ of degree atleast one having integer coefficient satisfy $16p(x^2) = (p(2x))^2$, for all real numbers x?
7. If $f(x) + f(y) = f(x\sqrt{1-y^2} + y\sqrt{1-x^2})$, then prove that $f(4x^3 - 3x) + 3f(x) = 0$.

Answer Key

1. 2046	2. $2x + 3$	3. $x^2 - x + 1$
4. 5	6. 2	

For Detailed Solution

JEE Pattern EXAMPLES

Single Option Correct Type Questions

Example 1 *The set of exhaustive values of x satisfying the equation* $[\sin x]+[\cos x]=[4\sin x\cos x]$, $x\in[0, \pi/2]$ *is* $\left(0, \frac{p\pi}{r}\right)\cup\left(\frac{q\pi}{r}, \frac{\pi}{2}\right)$ *(where* $[\cdot]$ *represents greatest integer function, and p and r as well as q and r are coprime to each other). The value of* $|p+q-r|$ *is*

(a) 3

(b) 6

(c) 5

(d) 7

Sol. (b) As $x\in[0, \pi/2)$

$\Rightarrow\quad [\sin x]=0$

and $[\cos x]=\begin{cases}1, & \text{if } x=0\\ 0 & \text{if } x\in(0, \pi/2]\end{cases}$

If $x=0$, $[0]+[1]=[4\times0\times1]$

$1=0$ [not possible]

If $x\in(0, \pi/2)$, $0=[4\sin x\cos x]$

$\Rightarrow\quad 0\le 4\sin x\cos x<1$

$\Rightarrow\quad 0\le \sin 2x<\frac{1}{2}$

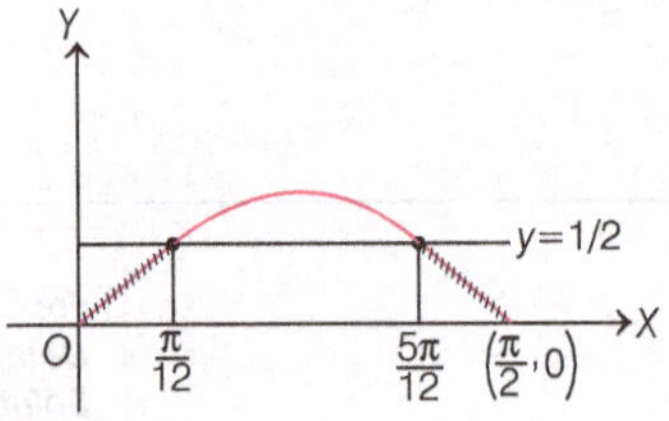

$\therefore\ x\in\left(0, \frac{\pi}{12}\right)\cup\left(\frac{5\pi}{12}, \frac{\pi}{2}\right)$

$\therefore\ p=1, q=5$ and $r=12$

Hence, $|p+q-r|=|1+5-12|=6$

Example 2 *Let*

$$f(x)=\sqrt{\sqrt{\cot(5+3x)(\cot(5)+\cot(3x))}-\sqrt{\cot 3x+1}},$$

then the domain of function $f(x)$ *is*

(a) $R-\bigcup_{n\in Z}\left[\frac{n\pi}{3}+\frac{1}{3}\cot^{-1}\left(\frac{2}{\cot 5-1}\right), \frac{1}{3}\left(n+\frac{3}{4}\right)\pi\right]$

(b) $\bigcup_{n\in Z}\left[\frac{n\pi}{3}+\frac{1}{3}\cot^{-1}\left(\frac{2}{\cot 5-1}\right), \frac{1}{3}\left(n+\frac{3}{4}\right)\pi\right]$

(c) $R-\left\{\frac{n\pi}{3}, \frac{n\pi-5}{3}\right\}, n\in Z$

(d) None of the above

Sol. (b) We have,

$$f(x)=\sqrt{\sqrt{\cot(5+3x)(\cot 5+\cot 3x)}-\sqrt{\cot 3x+1}}$$

For domain $\sqrt{\cot(5+3x)(\cot 5+\cot 3x)}\ge\sqrt{\cot(3x)+1}\ge 0$

$\Rightarrow\quad \cot(5+3x)(\cot 5+\cot 3x)\ge\cot 3x+1\ge 0$

$\Rightarrow\quad \cot(5+3x)\left[\frac{\sin 3x\cos 5+\cos 3x\sin 5}{\sin 5\sin 3x}\right]\ge\cot(3x)+1\ge 0$

$\Rightarrow\quad \cot(5+3x)\cdot\left[\frac{\sin(3x+5)}{\sin 5\cdot\sin 3x}\right]\ge\cot 3x+1\ge 0$

$\Rightarrow\quad \frac{\cos(5+3x)}{\sin 5\cdot\sin 3x}\ge\cot 3x+1\ge 0$

$\Rightarrow\quad \frac{\cos 5\cdot\cos 3x-\sin 5\cdot\sin 3x}{\sin 5\sin 3x}\ge\cot 3x+1\ge 0$

$\Rightarrow\quad (\cot 5)\cdot\cot 3x-1\ge\cdot\cot 3x+1\ge 0$

$\Rightarrow\quad (\cot 5-1)\cot 3x\ge 2,\ \cot 3x\ge -1$

$\because\quad 5\in\left(\frac{3\pi}{2}, 2\pi\right)\Rightarrow\cot 5<0$

$\Rightarrow\quad (\cot 5-1)<0$

$\Rightarrow\quad \cot 3x\le\frac{2}{\cot 5-1}$ and $\cot 3x\ge -1$

$\Rightarrow\quad -1\le\cot 3x\le\frac{2}{\cot 5-1}$

$\Rightarrow\quad \cot\frac{3\pi}{4}\le\cot 3x\le\cot\cot^{-1}\left(\frac{2}{\cot 5-1}\right)$

$\Rightarrow\quad n\pi+\cot^{-1}\left(\frac{2}{\cot 5-1}\right)\le 3x\le n\pi+\frac{3\pi}{4}, n\in Z$

$\Rightarrow\quad \frac{1}{3}\left[n\pi+\cot^{-1}\left(\frac{2}{\cot 5-1}\right)\right]\le x\le\frac{\pi}{3}\left(n+\frac{3}{4}\right), n\in Z$

$\Rightarrow\quad x\in\left[\frac{n\pi}{3}+\frac{1}{3}\cot^{-1}\left(\frac{2}{\cot 5-1}\right), \frac{1}{3}\left(n+\frac{3}{4}\right)\pi\right], n\in Z$

JEE SCANNER

Example 3 Similar to PYQ Asked in JEE Main 2022

The domain of the function

$f(x)=\sqrt{8-3^{x+1}-3^{1-x}}+\sqrt{\sin^{-1}(2x+1)}$ is $[a, b]$, then $|2a+b|$ is

(a) 1 (b) 0

(c) 2 (d) None of these

Sol. (a) We have, $f(x)=\sqrt{8-3^{x+1}-3^{1-x}}+\sqrt{\sin^{-1}(2x+1)}$

For domain of $f(x)$, $8-3(3^x)-\dfrac{3}{3^x}\geq 0$ and $\sin^{-1}(2x+1)\geq 0$

$\Rightarrow 8(3^x)-3(3^x)^2-3\geq 0$ and $(2x+1)\in[0,1]$

$\Rightarrow 3t^2-8t+3\leq 0$ and $x\in[-1/2, 0]$, when $t=3^x$

$\Rightarrow t\in\left[\dfrac{4-\sqrt{7}}{3},\dfrac{4+\sqrt{7}}{3}\right]$ and $x\in[-1/2, 0]$

$\Rightarrow 3^x\in\left[\dfrac{4-\sqrt{7}}{3},\dfrac{4+\sqrt{7}}{3}\right]$ and $x\in[-1/2, 0]$

$\Rightarrow x\in\left[\log_3\left(\dfrac{4-\sqrt{7}}{3}\right),\log_3\left(\dfrac{4+\sqrt{7}}{3}\right)\right]$ and $x\in[-1/2, 0]$

$\because \dfrac{4+\sqrt{7}}{3}>1\Rightarrow \log_3\left(\dfrac{4+\sqrt{7}}{3}\right)>0$

and $\dfrac{4+\sqrt{7}}{3}=\dfrac{9}{3(4-\sqrt{7})}=\dfrac{3}{4-\sqrt{7}}<\dfrac{3}{\sqrt{12}-\sqrt{3}}<\dfrac{1}{\sqrt{3}}$

$\Rightarrow \log_3\left(\dfrac{4-\sqrt{7}}{3}\right)<\log_3\left(\dfrac{1}{\sqrt{3}}\right)=-\dfrac{1}{2}$

$\Rightarrow \left[-\dfrac{1}{2},0\right]\subset\left[\log_3\left(\dfrac{4-\sqrt{7}}{3}\right),\log_3\left(\dfrac{4+\sqrt{7}}{3}\right)\right]$

$\Rightarrow$ Domain of $f(x)=[-1/2, 0]$

$\therefore a=-\dfrac{1}{2},\ b=0$

$\Rightarrow |2a+b|=|-1|=1$

Skill Builder

The domain of the function $f(x)=\sqrt{2\{x\}^2-3\{x\}+1}$, $x\in[-1, 1]$, where $\{\cdot\}$ denotes the fractional part function, is

(a) $\left(-1,-\dfrac{1}{2}\right)\cup\left(0,\dfrac{1}{2}\right)$

(b) $\left[-1,-\dfrac{1}{2}\right]\cup\left[0,\dfrac{1}{2}\right]$

(c) $\left(-1,-\dfrac{1}{2}\right)\cup\left[0,\dfrac{1}{2}\right]\cup\{1\}$

(d) $\left[-1,-\dfrac{1}{2}\right]\cup\left[0,\dfrac{1}{2}\right]\cup\{1\}$

For Sol.

Example 4 *The range of the function*

$f(x)=\sqrt{\cos^{-1}(\sqrt{\log_4 x})-\dfrac{\pi}{2}}+\sin^{-1}\left(\dfrac{1+x^2}{4x}\right)$ *is*

(a) empty set (b) singleton set

(c) infinite set (d) None of these

Sol. (b) We have, $f(x)=\sqrt{-\sin^{-1}(\sqrt{\log_4 x})}+\sin^{-1}\left(\dfrac{1+x^2}{4x}\right)$

Clearly, domain of $f(x)$ is $x=1$ only, so

$$f(1)=\sqrt{0}+\sin^{-1}\left(\frac{2}{4}\right)=\pi/6$$

Hence, range of $f(x)=\{\pi/6\}$

$\therefore$ It is a singleton set.

Example 5 *If* $2<x^2<3$, *then the number of positive roots of* $\{x^2\}-2=\left\{\dfrac{1}{x}\right\}$, *(where* $\{x\}$ *denotes the fractional part of x), is*

(a) 0 (b) 1 (c) 2 (d) 3

Sol. (a) We have, $2<x^2<3$

$\Rightarrow \{x^2\}=x^2-2$ $[\because 2<x^2<3]$

$\Rightarrow x\in(-\sqrt{3},-\sqrt{2})\cup(\sqrt{2},\sqrt{3})$

$\Rightarrow \dfrac{1}{x}\in\left(\dfrac{-1}{\sqrt{2}},\dfrac{-1}{\sqrt{3}}\right)\cup\left(\dfrac{1}{\sqrt{3}},\dfrac{1}{\sqrt{2}}\right)$

$\Rightarrow \left\{\dfrac{1}{x}\right\}=\dfrac{1}{x}-(-1)$ for $x\in(-\sqrt{3},-\sqrt{2})$

and $\left\{\dfrac{1}{x}\right\}=\dfrac{1}{x}-(0)$ for $x\in(\sqrt{2},\sqrt{3})$

For positive roots, $x\in(\sqrt{2},\sqrt{3})$

Given equation becomes, $x^2-2=\dfrac{1}{x}$

$\Rightarrow x^3-2x=0$

$\Rightarrow x(x^2-2)=0$

$\Rightarrow x=0$ or $x=\sqrt{2}$, but $x\in(\sqrt{2},\sqrt{3})$

There is no positive root.

Example 6 *Let* $f:R\to R$ *be an injective mapping and p, q, r are non-zero distinct quantities satisfying*

$$f\left(\frac{p}{r}\right)=f\left(\frac{p-q}{q-r}\right) \text{ and } f\left(\frac{q}{r}\right)=f\left(\frac{r}{p}\right)$$

If the graph of $g(x)=px^2+qx+r$ *passes through* $M(1, 6)$, *then find the value of q.*

(a) 3 (b) 8

(c) 1 (d) 4

Sol. (b) Since, f is injective, so

$$\frac{p}{r}=\frac{p-q}{q-r}$$

$$\Rightarrow \quad pq-pr=rp-rq$$

$$\Rightarrow \quad 2pr=q(p+r) \quad \text{...(i)}$$

Also, $\quad \dfrac{q}{r}=\dfrac{r}{p}$

$\Rightarrow p, r, q$ are in GP.

So, let $r=pa,\ q=pa^2$, where a is common ratio of GP.

Therefore, from Eq. (i), we get

$$2p\cdot pa=pa^2(p+pa)$$

$$\Rightarrow \quad 2=a^2+a$$

$$\Rightarrow \quad a^2+a-2=0$$

$$\Rightarrow \quad a=-2,1$$

So, $(p,-2p,4p)$ and (p,p,p).

[but common ratio $a=1$ is not possible as p, q, r are non-zero distinct quantities]

Also, $p+q+r=6$

[as $g(x)=px^2+qx+r$ passes through $M(1,6)$]

$\Rightarrow p+4p-2p=6$

$$\Rightarrow \quad p=2$$

$$\therefore \quad q=4p=4(2)=8$$

Example 7 *The set of all integral values of n for which the function $f(x)=\cos nx\cdot\sin\dfrac{5x}{n}$ is periodic with period 2π is*

(a) finite set having more than 5 elements

(b) finite set having less than 3 elements

(c) finite set having exactly 4 elements

(d) infinite set

Sol. (c) We have, $f(x)=\cos nx\cdot\sin\left(\dfrac{5x}{n}\right)$

Period of $\cos nx=\dfrac{2\pi}{|n|}$

and period of $\sin\dfrac{5x}{n}=\dfrac{2\pi}{|5/n|}=\dfrac{2|n|\pi}{5}$

$\therefore$ Period of $f(x)=\text{LCM}\left(\dfrac{2\pi}{|n|},\dfrac{2|n|\pi}{5}\right)=2\pi$

$$\Rightarrow \quad \text{LCM}\left(\frac{1}{|n|},\frac{|n|}{5}\right)=1$$

$$=\frac{\text{LCM}(1,|n|)}{\text{HCF}(|n|,5)}=1$$

$$\Rightarrow \quad \frac{|n|}{\text{HCF}(|n|,5)}=1$$

$$\Rightarrow \quad \text{HCF}(|n|,5)=|n|$$

If $\quad \text{GCD}(|n|,5)=1$

$$\Rightarrow \quad |n|=1$$

$$\Rightarrow \quad n=\pm 1$$

If $\quad \text{GCD}(|n|,5)\neq 1$

$$\Rightarrow \quad |n|=5m,\ m\in N$$

If $\quad \text{GCD}(5m,5)=5$

$$\Rightarrow \quad |n|=5$$

$$\Rightarrow \quad n=\pm 5$$

$$\therefore \quad n\in\{\pm 1,\pm 5\}$$

Example 8 *If range of expression $\dfrac{x^2-12}{2x-7}$ is $(-\infty,a]\cup[b,\infty)$ and the solution of $ax^{\log_a b}+b^{\log_a x}=b^3$ is say $x=c$, then*

(a) $(a+b)$ and c are both prime

(b) $(a+b)$ and c are both coprime

(c) $a+b+c$ is divisible by 5

(d) None of the above

Sol. (b) Let $y=\dfrac{x^2-12}{2x-7} \Rightarrow x^2-2xy+7y-12=0$

$$\therefore \quad D\ge 0 \Rightarrow 4y^2-4(7y-12)\ge 0$$

$$\Rightarrow \quad y\in(-\infty,3]\cup[4,\infty)$$

$$\therefore \quad a=3,\ b=4$$

Now, $\quad 3x^{\log_3 4}+4^{\log_3 x}=4^3$

$$\Rightarrow \quad 3x^{\log_3 4}+x^{\log_3 4}=4^3$$

$$\Rightarrow \quad 4\cdot x^{\log_3 4}=4^3$$

$$\Rightarrow \quad 4^{\log_3 x}=4^2 \Rightarrow x=9$$

Example 9 *Let $f: R\to R$ be defined by $f(x)=\dfrac{x}{1+x}$, $x\in R$. Then, the range of f is*

(a) $(-1,1)-\{0\}$ (b) $\left[-\dfrac{1}{2},\dfrac{1}{2}\right]$

(c) $R-\left[-\dfrac{1}{2},\dfrac{1}{2}\right]$ (d) $R-\{-1,1\}$

Sol. (b) $f(0)=0$

Further, if $x>0$, then $f(x)=\dfrac{1}{\dfrac{1}{x}+1}\in\left(0,\dfrac{1}{2}\right]$

and if $x<0$, then $f(x)=\dfrac{1}{\dfrac{1}{x}+1}\in\left[-\dfrac{1}{2},0\right)$

Hence, $\quad f(x)\in\left[-\dfrac{1}{2},\dfrac{1}{2}\right]$.

JEE SCANNER

Example 10 Similar to PYQ Asked in JEE Main 2023

If $g(x) = x^2 - 1$ and $g(f(x)) = 4x^2 + 5$, then the value of $f\left(\frac{1}{4}\right)$ is

(a) $\pm\frac{5}{2}$ (b) $\pm\frac{5}{4}$ (c) $\pm\frac{1}{3}$ (d) $\pm\frac{4}{3}$

Sol. (a) $g(f(x)) = [f(x)]^2 - 1$

$$\Rightarrow \quad g\left(f\left(\frac{1}{4}\right)\right) = 4\left(\frac{1}{4}\right)^2 + 5 = \frac{1}{4} + 5 = \frac{21}{4}$$

$$\Rightarrow \quad g\left(f\left(\frac{1}{4}\right)\right) = f^2\left(\frac{1}{4}\right) - 1$$

$$\Rightarrow \quad \frac{21}{4} = f^2\left(\frac{1}{4}\right) - 1$$

$$\Rightarrow \quad f^2\left(\frac{1}{4}\right) - \frac{25}{4} = 0$$

$$\Rightarrow \quad f\left(\frac{1}{4}\right) = \pm\frac{5}{2}$$

Skill Builder

Let $f(x) = \frac{kx}{x+1}$, $x \neq -1$, then the value of k is, where $f(f(x)) = x$

For Sol.

(a) 1 (b) −1

(c) 2 (d) 0

More than One Correct Option Type Questions

Example 11 *If* $f(n) = \frac{1}{n+1} + \frac{2}{n+2} + \frac{3}{n+3} + \ldots + \frac{1}{2}$, *where* $n \in N$, *then*

(a) $f(1000) < 500$ (b) $f(1000) < 250$

(c) $f(1000) > 200$ (d) $f(500) < 125$

Sol. (a, c) As, $\frac{1}{n+2} < \frac{1}{n+1}$

$$\Rightarrow \quad \frac{2}{n+2} < \frac{2}{n+1} \Rightarrow \frac{3}{n+3} < \frac{3}{n+1}$$

So, $$\sum_{r=1}^{r=n} \frac{r}{n+r} < \frac{n}{2}$$

Similarly, $$\frac{1}{n+1} > \frac{1}{n+n}$$

$$\Rightarrow \quad \frac{2}{n+2} > \frac{2}{n+n}$$

$$\vdots$$

$$\frac{n}{n+n} = \frac{n}{n+n}$$

$$\Rightarrow \quad \sum_{r=1}^{r=n} \frac{r}{n+r} > \frac{n+1}{4}$$

$$\therefore \quad \left(\frac{n+1}{4}\right) < f(n) < \frac{n}{2}$$

Put $n = 1000$

$$\frac{1001}{4} < f(1000) < 500$$

Example 12 *Let* f *be an injective function from domain* $\{1, i, \omega\}$ *to range* $\{5, 6, 7\}$. *If it is given that exactly one of the following statements is true and other two are false :* $f(1) = 5$, $f(i) \neq 5$, $f(\omega) \neq 7$, *then find the value of* $(f^{-1})^{2012}(6)$.

(when $i = \sqrt{-1}$, ω = cube root of unity)

(a) ω^2 (b) ω

(c) $-1-\omega$ (d) $-1-\omega^2$

Sol. (a, c) We have, $f: \{1, i, \omega\} \to \{5, 6, 7\}$

Case I $f(1) = 5$(true), $f(i) = 5$ (false), $f(\omega) = 7$ (false)

$\Rightarrow$ $f(1) = 5$, $f(i) = 5$, $f(\omega) = 7$ but it is many-one.

Case II $f(1) = 5$ (false), $f(i) = 5$

$\Rightarrow$ $f(\omega) = 7$, $f(1) = 5$, $f(i) = 5$

$\Rightarrow f(x)$ is not onto.

Case III $f(1) = 5$ (false), $f(i) = 5$ (false), $f(\omega) = 7$ (true)

$\Rightarrow$ $f(1) = 5$, $f(i) = 5$, $f(\omega) = 7$

$\Rightarrow$ $f(1) = 7$, $f(i) = 5$, $f(\omega) = 6$

$\Rightarrow$ $f^{-1}(6) = \omega$

$\Rightarrow$ $(f^{-1})^{2012}(6) = \omega^{2012} = (\omega^3)^{670}\,\omega^2 = \omega^2$

$\because$ $1 + \omega + \omega^2 = 0$

$\Rightarrow$ $\omega^2 = -1 - \omega$

Example 13 *Define functions* $f, g: R \to R$, $f(x) = 3x - 1 + |2x + 1|$ *and* $g(x) = \frac{1}{5}(3x + 5 - |2x + 5|)$, *then*

(a) $f(g(x)) = g(f(x))$ (b) $(f(f(x))) = g(g(x))$

(c) $f(g(x)) = x$ (d) for $x < -\frac{5}{2}$, $f(g(x)) = x$

Sol. (a, c, d) $f(x) = \begin{cases} 5x, & x \geq -\frac{1}{2} \\ x-2, & x < -\frac{1}{2} \end{cases}$ and $g(x) = \begin{cases} \frac{x}{5}, & x \geq -\frac{5}{2} \\ x+2, & x < -\frac{5}{2} \end{cases}$

For $x < \frac{-1}{2}$, $g(f(x)) = g(x-2) = (x-2) + 2 = x$

For $x \geq \frac{-1}{2}$, $g(f(x)) = g(5x) = \frac{1}{5}(5x) = x$

For $x < \frac{-5}{2}$, $f(g(x)) = f(x+2) = (x+2) - 2 = x$

For $x \geq \frac{-5}{2}$, $f(g(x)) = f\left(\frac{x}{5}\right) = 5\left(\frac{x}{5}\right) = x$

Example 14 *Let $f(x)=\sqrt{x-3r}$, where $3r \le x < 3(r+1)$, $r \in I$, then*

(a) The range of $f(x)$ is $[0, \sqrt{3})$

(b) $f(x)$ is periodic function with fundamental period 3

(c) $f(x)$ is one-one function

(d) $f(x)=\dfrac{|x|}{4}$ has 4 real solutions if $x \in (-6, 6)$

Sol. (a, b, d) Since, $f(x)=\sqrt{x-3r}=\begin{cases}\sqrt{x+3}, & -3 \le x < 0\\ \sqrt{x}, & 0 \le x < 3\\ \sqrt{x-3}, & 3 \le x < 6\end{cases}$

$\therefore f(x)$ is periodic with period 3.

Range of $f(x)$ is $[0, \sqrt{3})$.

$f(x)=\dfrac{|x|}{4}$ has exactly four real solutions in $(-6, 6)$.

Example 15 *If $(x^2-1)\,f(x)=\sqrt{x^2-4}+|f(x)|$, then*

(a) Domain of $f(x)$ is $R-(-2, 2)$

(b) $f(x)$ is an even function

(c) $f(x)=x-4$ has exactly one real solution

(d) $f(x)=1-x$ has exactly two real solutions

Sol. (a, b, c) Since, $x^2-4 \ge 0$

$\Rightarrow \quad x^2-1>0$

Now, $\quad (x^2-1)f(x)=\sqrt{x^2-4}+|f(x)|$

$\therefore \quad (x^2-1)f(x) \ge 0 \Rightarrow f(x) \ge 0$

$\Rightarrow \quad |f(x)|=f(x)$

$\therefore \quad (x^2-1)f(x)=\sqrt{x^2-4}+f(x)$

$\Rightarrow \quad f(x)=\dfrac{\sqrt{x^2-4}}{x^2-2}$

$\therefore$ Domain of $f(x)=(-\infty, -2] \cup [2, \infty)$

The graph of $f(x)$ is

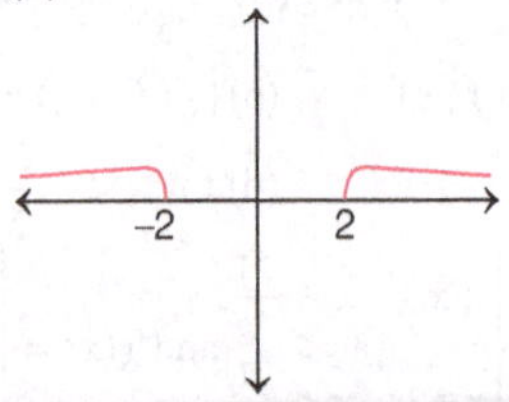

Example 16 *Which of the following functions are periodic?*

(a) $f(x)=\operatorname{sgn}(e^{-x})$

(b) $f(x)=\begin{cases} x & \text{if } x \text{ is a rational number}\\ -x & \text{if } x \text{ is an irrational number}\end{cases}$

(c) $f(x)=\sqrt{\dfrac{4}{1+\sin x}+\dfrac{4}{1-\sin x}}$

(d) $f(x)=x-[x]+1$, $[x]$ represents greatest integer function.

Sol. (a, c, d) Every constant function is periodic

(a) $e^{-x}>0, \forall\, x \in R$

$\therefore f(x)=\operatorname{sgn}(e^{-x})=1$

and every constant function is periodic.

$\therefore f(x)=\operatorname{sgn}(e^{-x})$ is a periodic function.

(b) Let $T>0$ be a rational number.

Then, $f(T+x)=\begin{cases} x, & \text{if } x \in Q\\ -x, & \text{if } x \notin Q\end{cases}=f(x)$

$\Rightarrow f(x)$ is a non-periodic function.

(c) $f(x)=\sqrt{\dfrac{4(1-\sin x+1+\sin x)}{1-\sin^2 x}}$

$=\sqrt{\dfrac{8}{\cos^2 x}}=2\sqrt{2}\,|\sec x|$,

which is a periodic function.

(d) $f(x)=\{x\}+1$

which is also a periodic function, since $\{x\}$ is a periodic function.

Example 17 *If $f(x)=2\tan 3x+5\sqrt{1-\cos 6x}$, $g(x)$ is a function having the same time period as that of $f(x)$, then which of the following can be $g(x)$?*

(a) $(\sec^2 3x+\operatorname{cosec}^2 3x)\tan^2 3x$

(b) $2\sin 3x+3\cos 3x$

(c) $2\sqrt{1-\cos^2 3x}+\operatorname{cosec} 3x$

(d) $3\operatorname{cosec} 3x+2\tan 3x$

Sol. (a) (a) $f(x)=2\tan 3x+5\sqrt{1-\cos 6x}$

$=2\tan 3x+5\sqrt{2\sin^2 3x}=2\tan 3x+5\sqrt{2}\,|\sin 3x|$

$\Rightarrow$ Period of $f(x)=\text{LCM}\,(\pi/3, \pi/3)=\pi/3$

Now, from (a),

$g(x)=(\sec^2 3x+\operatorname{cosec}^2 3x)\tan^2 3x$

$=\dfrac{1}{\cos^2 3x\sin^2 3x}\cdot\tan^2 3x$

$=\dfrac{1}{\cos^4 3x}=\sec^4 3x$, having period $\pi/3$

(b) $g(x)=2\sin 3x+3\cos 3x$

$\Rightarrow$ Period of $g(x)=\dfrac{2\pi}{3}$

(c) $k(x)=2\sqrt{1-\cos^2 3x}+\operatorname{cosec} 3x$

$=2\sqrt{\sin^2 3x}+\operatorname{cosec} 3x=2\,|\sin 3x|+\operatorname{cosec} 3x$

$\Rightarrow$ Period of $k(x)=\text{LCM}\left(\dfrac{\pi}{3}, \dfrac{2\pi}{3}\right)=\dfrac{2\pi}{3}$

(d) $P(x)=3\operatorname{cosec} 3x+2\tan 3x$

$\Rightarrow$ Period of $P(x)=\text{LCM}\left(\dfrac{2\pi}{3}, \dfrac{\pi}{3}\right)=\dfrac{2\pi}{3}$

Example 18 If $f(x)=4x^3-x^2-2x+1$ and

$$g(x)=\begin{bmatrix}\min\{f(t):0\le t\le x\} & , & 0\le x\le 1\\ 3x & , & 1<x\le 2\end{bmatrix},$$

$g\left(\frac{1}{4}\right)+g\left(\frac{3}{4}\right)+g(5/4)$ *is equal to P, then 2P is*

(a) a prime number (b) a composite number

(c) a factor of 200 (d) a factor of 55

Sol. (a, c, d) We have, $f(x)=4x^3-x^2-2x+1$

$\Rightarrow \quad f'(x)=12x^2-2x-2=2(6x^2-x-1)$

$\Rightarrow \quad x=\dfrac{1\pm\sqrt{1+4\times 6}}{2\times 6}$

$\Rightarrow \quad x=\dfrac{1\pm 5}{12}=\dfrac{6}{12},\dfrac{-4}{12}=\dfrac{1}{2},-\dfrac{1}{3}$

$\Rightarrow \quad f'(x)=2(2x-1)(3x+1)$

$\Rightarrow \quad f'(x)>0$ for $x>\dfrac{1}{2}$

$\Rightarrow \quad f'(x)<0$ for $0<x<\dfrac{1}{2}$

$\therefore f(x)$ is minimum at $x=\dfrac{1}{2}$ in (0, 1).

Also, in $\left(0,\dfrac{1}{2}\right)$, $f(x)$ is decreasing and in $\left(\dfrac{1}{2},1\right)$, $f(x)$ is increasing

$$g\left(\frac{1}{4}\right)=f\left(\frac{1}{4}\right)=4\times\left(\frac{1}{4}\right)^3-\left(\frac{1}{4}\right)^2-2\times\frac{1}{4}+1=\frac{1}{2}$$

$$g\left(\frac{3}{4}\right)=f\left(\frac{1}{2}\right)=4\times\left(\frac{1}{2}\right)^3-\left(\frac{1}{2}\right)^2-2\times\frac{1}{2}+1=\frac{1}{4}$$

$$g\left(\frac{5}{4}\right)=f\left(\frac{5}{4}\right)=3-\frac{5}{4}=\frac{7}{4}$$

$$\therefore g\left(\frac{1}{4}\right)+g\left(\frac{3}{4}\right)+g\left(\frac{5}{4}\right)=\frac{1}{2}+\frac{1}{4}+\frac{7}{4}=\frac{5}{2}=P$$

Hence, $2P=5$

Passage Based Questions

Passage I

(Ex. Nos. 19 to 20)

Let $f:[2,\infty)\to[1,\infty)$ defined by $f(x)=2^{x^4-4x^2}$ and $g:\left[\dfrac{\pi}{2},\pi\right]\to A$ defined by $g(x)=\dfrac{\sin x+4}{\sin x-2}$ be two invertible functions.

Example 19 $f^{-1}(x)$ *is equal to*

(a) $\sqrt{2+\sqrt{4-\log_2 x}}$ (b) $\sqrt{2+\sqrt{4+\log_2 x}}$

(c) $\sqrt{2-\sqrt{4+\log_2 x}}$ (d) None of these

Example 20 *The set A is equal to*

(a) $[-5,-2]$ (b) $[2,5]$

(c) $[-5,2]$ (d) $[-3,-2]$

Sol. (Ex. Nos. 19-20)

19. (b) Since, $ff^{-1}(x)=x$

$$2^{(f^{-1}(x))^4-4(f^{-1}(x))^2}=x$$

$\Rightarrow (f^{-1}(x))^4-4(f^{-1}(x))^2-\log_2 x=0$

$\therefore \quad (f^{-1}(x))^2=2+\sqrt{4+\log_2 x}$

$\therefore$Range of $f^{-1}(x)$ is $[2,\infty)$.

$\therefore \quad f^{-1}(x)=\sqrt{2+\sqrt{4+\log_2 x}}$

$\therefore \quad f^{-1}(x)>0$

20. (a) $g(x)=\dfrac{\sin x+4}{\sin x-2}$

$\Rightarrow g'(x)=\dfrac{-6\cos x}{(\sin x-2)^2}\ge 0 \qquad \left[\because x\in\left[\dfrac{\pi}{2},\pi\right]\right]$

$\Rightarrow g(x)$ is an increasing function, hence one-one function.

$\therefore$Range is $\left[g\left(\dfrac{\pi}{2}\right),g(\pi)\right]$ and lies in $[-5,-2]$.

Passage II

(Ex. Nos. 21 to 22)

Let $a_m\,(m=1,2,\dots p)$ be the possible integral values of a for which the graphs of

$$f(x)=ax^2+2bx+b \text{ and } g(x)=5x^2-3bx-a$$

meet at some points for all real values of b.

Let $t_r=\prod_{m=1}^{p}(r-a_m)$ and $S_n=\sum_{r=1}^{n}t_r,\ n\in N$

Example 21 *The minimum possible value of a is*

(a) $\dfrac{1}{5}$ (b) $\dfrac{5}{26}$ (c) $\dfrac{3}{28}$ (d) $\dfrac{2}{43}$

Example 22 *The sum of values of n for which S_n vanishes is*

(a) 8 (b) 9 (c) 10 (d) 15

Sol. (Ex. Nos. 21-22)

To find the point of intersection

$$ax^2+2bx+b=5x^2-3bx-a$$

$\Rightarrow \quad (a-5)x^2+5bx+(b+a)=0$

If $a\ne 5$, then since $x\in R$,

$D=25b^2-4(b+a)(a-5)\ge 0,\ \forall b\in R$

$\Rightarrow \quad 25b^2-4(a-5)b-4a(a-5)\ge 0,\ \forall b\in R$

$\therefore \quad 16(a-5)^2+16(25)a(a-5)\le 0$

$\Rightarrow \quad 16(a-5)(a-5+25a)\le 0\Rightarrow (a-5)(26a-5)\le 0$

$\therefore \quad a \in \left[\frac{5}{26}, 5\right)$

If $a = 5$, $5bx + (b+5) = 0$, is not satisfied for $b = 0$.

$\therefore\ a_m \in \{1, 2, 3, 4\}$; $t_r = (r-1)(r-2)(r-3)(r-4)$

$$S_n = \frac{1}{5}\sum_{r=1}^{n}(r-4)(r-3)(r-2)(r-1)(r-(r-5))$$

$$= \frac{1}{5}\sum_{r=1}^{n}[(r-4)(r-3)(r-2)(r-1)r - (r-5)(r-4)(r-3)(r-2)(r-1)]$$

$$= \frac{1}{5}n(n-1)(n-2)(n-3)(n-4)$$

$S_n = 0$

$\Rightarrow n = 1, 2, 3, 4$

$\therefore$ Sum of values of n for which S_n vanishes is

$1 + 2 + 3 + 4 = 10 \quad [n = 0 \text{ rejected}]$

21. (a) **22.** (c)

Stem Based Questions

Stem I

(Ex. Nos. 23 to 24)

Consider a quadratic function $f(x) = ax^2 + bx + c$, $(a, b, c \in R, a \neq 0)$ and satisfying the following conditions.

(i) $f(x-4) = f(2-x)$, $\forall x \in R$ and $f(x) \geq x$, $\forall\ x \in R$

(ii) $f(x) \leq \left(\frac{x+1}{2}\right)^2$, $\forall\ x \in (0, 2)$

(iii) The minimum value of $f(x)$ is zero

Example 23 *The value of the leading coefficient of the quadratic polynomial is ....*

Example 24 *$f'(1)$ has the value equals to ....*

Sol. (Ex. Nos. 23-24)

Since, minimum value is zero, hence $y = f(x)$ touches the X-axis and mouth opening upwards i.e. $a > 0$.

Given, $f(x-4) = f(2-x)$

$x \to x + 3$

$f(x-1) = f(-1-x)$

$f(-1+x) = f(-1-x)$

Hence, f is symmetric about the line $x = -1$

$\therefore\ f(x) = a(x+1)^2$

Now, given $f(x) \geq x$, $\forall\ x$

$f(1) \geq 1$ ...(i)

and $f(x) \leq \left(\frac{x+1}{2}\right)^2$ in (0, 2)

$f(1) \leq 1$ ...(ii)

From Eqs. (i) and (ii), we get

$f(1) = 1$

Now, $f(x) = a(x+1)^2$

$f(1) = 4a = 1$

$\Rightarrow \quad a = \frac{1}{4} = 0.25$

$\therefore \quad f(x) = \frac{(x+1)^2}{4}$

Now, $f'(x) = \frac{2(x+1)}{4} = \frac{x+1}{2}$

$f'(1) = \frac{1+1}{2} = 1$

23. (0.25) **24.** (1)

Stem II

(Ex. Nos. 25 to 26)

Consider the equation $x + y - [x][y] = 0$, where $[\cdot]$ is the greatest integer function.

Example 25 *The number of integral solutions to the equation is ....*

Example 26 *Equation of one of the lines on which the non-integral solution of given equation lies, is ....*

Sol. (Ex. Nos. 25-26)

25. (2) For integral solution,

$x + y - [x][y] = 0$

$\Rightarrow \quad x + y - xy = 0$

$\Rightarrow \quad -1 + x + y - xy = -1$

$\Rightarrow \quad (x-1)(y-1) = 1$

i.e. only possible if

$(x - 1 = 1, y - 1 = 1)$ or $(x - 1 = -1, y - 1 = -1)$

$\Rightarrow \quad x = 2, y = 2$ or $x = 0, y = 0$

$\therefore$ Solutions are (0, 0) or (2, 2).

$\therefore$ Number of integral solutions = 2

26. (2) For non-integral solution,

Let $x = [x] + f_1$ and $y = [y] + f_2$

$\therefore \quad [x][y] = [x] + f_1 + [y] + f_2$

$([x]-1)([y]-1) = f_1 + f_2 + 1$

Now, $0 \leq f_1 + f_2 < 2$

$\therefore \quad f_1 + f_2 = 1$

$\Rightarrow \quad ([x]-1)([y]-1) = 2$

Which is possible for

$[x] = 3$ and $[y] = 2$

$\Rightarrow \quad [x] = 2$ and $[y] = 3$

$\Rightarrow \quad [x] = -1$ and $[y] = 0$

$\Rightarrow \quad [x] = 0$ and $[y] = -1$

$\therefore \quad x + y = [x][y]$ becomes $x + y = 6$

or $\quad x + y = 0$

$\therefore$ Non-integer solution lies on $x + y = 6$

or $\quad x + y = 0$

Single Integer Answer Type Questions

Example 27 *If* $g(x)=\left(\dfrac{4\cos^4 x-2\cos 2x}{-\frac{1}{2}\cos 4x-x^7}\right)^{1/7}$*, then value of* $\dfrac{g(g(100))}{20}$ *is equal to ....*

Sol. (5) We have, $4\cos^4 x-2\cos 2x-\frac{1}{2}\cos 4x-x^7$

$$=4\cos^4 x-2(2\cos^2 x-1)-\frac{1}{2}(2\cos^2 2x-1)-x^7$$
$$=4\cos^4 x-4\cos^2 x+2-\cos^2 2x+\frac{1}{2}-x^7$$
$$=4\cos^4 x-4\cos^2 x+2-(2\cos^2 x-1)^2+\frac{1}{2}-x^7$$
$$=\frac{3}{2}-x^7$$

We get, $g(x)=\left(\frac{3}{2}-x^7\right)^{1/7}$

$$\Rightarrow g(g(x))=\left[\frac{3}{2}-(g(x))^7\right]^{1/7}=\left[\frac{3}{2}-\left(\frac{3}{2}-x^7\right)\right]^{1/7}=x$$

Hence, $g(g(100))=100$

$\therefore$ Required value $=\dfrac{100}{20}=5$

Example 28 *Let n be the number of values of x satisfying* $\left[\dfrac{3x^2-2x+1}{2}\right]=\dfrac{x+1}{2}$*. The value of*

$$\frac{1}{\pi}\left(\sin^{-1}\frac{1}{n}+\tan^{-1}\frac{1}{n}+\sec^{-1}\left(\frac{-1}{n}\right)+\frac{1}{2}\sin^{-1}\left(\frac{2n}{1+n^2}\right)\right) \text{ is ......}$$

([y] denotes the largest integer less than or equal to y)

Sol. (2) Since, $[x]$ is an integer.

$\therefore \quad x+1=2k;\ k\in I$

$$\Rightarrow \left[\frac{3(2k-1)^2-2(2k-1)+1}{2}\right]=k$$
$$\Rightarrow \left[\frac{12k^2-12k+3-4k+2+1}{2}\right]=k$$
$$\Rightarrow [6k^2-8k+3]=k \Rightarrow 6k^2-8k+3=k$$
$$\therefore \quad 6k^2-9k+3=0$$
$$\Rightarrow 2k^2-3k+1=0\Rightarrow (k-1)(2k-1)=0$$
$$\therefore \quad k=1,\ k=\frac{1}{2}\ [\text{reject as } k\in I]$$
$$\Rightarrow k=1$$
$$\therefore \quad x=1, \text{ so } n=1$$

Hence, $\dfrac{1}{\pi}\left(\dfrac{\pi}{2}+\dfrac{\pi}{4}+\pi+\dfrac{\pi}{4}\right)=2$

Example 29 *Suppose that f is a periodic function with period* $\frac{1}{2}$ *and that* $f(2)=5$ *and* $f\left(\frac{9}{4}\right)=2$*, then* $f(-3)-f\left(\frac{1}{4}\right)$ *has the value equals to ....*

Sol. (3) We have, $f\left(x+\frac{1}{2}\right)=f(x),\ f(2)=5,\ f\left(\frac{9}{4}\right)=2$

$\because f(x)$ is periodic with period $\frac{1}{2}$.

$$\Rightarrow f(x)=f\left(x+\frac{n}{2}\right),\ \forall n\in N$$
$$\Rightarrow f(-3)=f\left(-3+\frac{10}{2}\right)=f(2)=5$$
$$\text{and } f\left(\frac{1}{4}\right)=f\left(\frac{1}{4}+4\left(\frac{1}{2}\right)\right)=f\left(\frac{9}{4}\right)=2$$
$$\therefore \quad f(-3)-f\left(\frac{1}{4}\right)=5-2=3$$

Example 30 $f(x)=\left[\dfrac{x}{15}\right]\left[-\dfrac{15}{x}\right],\ \forall\, x\in(0,90)$,

(where [·] denotes greatest integer function)

Sol. (6) We have, $f(x)=\left[\dfrac{x}{15}\right]\left[-\dfrac{15}{x}\right],\ x\in(0,90)$

$f(x)=0,\quad 0\le x<15$
$f(x)=-1,\quad 15\le x<30$
$f(x)=-2,\quad 30\le x<45$
$f(x)=-3,\quad 45\le x<60$
$f(x)=-4,\quad 60\le x<75$
$f(x)=-5,\quad 75\le x<90$

Total integers in range $f(x)=\{0,-1,-2,-3,-4,-5\}$

Number of elements $=6$

Numerical Value Type Questions

Example 31 *It is given that polynomial* $P(x)=x^3+ax^2+bx+c$ *has three distinct positive integer roots and* $P(22)=21$*. Let* $Q(x)=x^2-2x+22$*. It is also given that* $P(Q(x))$ *has no real roots, then* $\dfrac{|a|}{10}$ *is equal to ....*

Sol. (5.5) We have, $Q(x)=(x-1)^2+21$, $Q(x)$ takes all values in interval $[21,\infty)$.

Since, $P(Q(x))$ has no real roots, all three roots of $P(x)$ must be less than 21.

$P(22)=21$ gives $(22-x_1)(22-x_2)(22-x_3)$
$=21=1\times 3\times 7$,

where x_1, x_2, x_3 are roots of $P(x)$.

So, $\{(22-x_1),(22-x_2),(22-x_3)\}=\{1,3,7\}$

So, $x_1=15, x_2=19, x_3=21$

Hence, $a=-(x_1+x_2+x_3)=-55$

$\therefore \quad \dfrac{|a|}{10}=\dfrac{55}{10}=5.5$

JEE SCANNER

Example 32 Similar to PYQ Asked in JEE Main 2024

Let $X=\{a_1, a_2, a_3, a_4, a_5\}$ and $Y=\{b_1, b_2, b_3, b_4, b_5\}$. Then, the number of one-one mappings from X to Y such that $f(a_i) \neq b_i$, $\forall\, i \in \{1,2,3,4,5\}$ is β, then β is ....

Sol. (44) We have, $X=\{a_1, a_2, a_3, a_4, a_5\}$, $Y=\{b_1, b_2, b_3, b_4, b_5\}$

$$f: X \to Y$$

Such that $f(x)$ is bijective and $f(a_i) \neq b_i$, then number of such functions will be equal to the number of ways of placing 5 letters into five envelops, so that no letter goes to its corresponding addressed envelope

$$=5!\left[1-\frac{1}{1!}+\frac{1}{2!}-\frac{1}{3!}+\frac{1}{4!}-\frac{1}{5!}\right]$$

$$=5!\left[\frac{1}{2}-\frac{1}{6}+\frac{1}{24}-\frac{1}{120}\right]=60-20+5-1=44$$

$\therefore \quad \beta = 44$

Skill Builder

Let x be a set with exactly 5 elements and y be a set with exactly 7 elements, if α is the number of one-one function from x to y and β is the number of onto function from y to x, then the value of $\frac{\beta-\alpha}{5!}$ is .....

For Sol.

Example 33 *If $(x-y) f(x+y)-(x+y) f(x-y) = 4xy(x^2-y^2)$, $\forall\, x, y \in R$ and $f(1)=-2$, then $f(-5)+f(-4)+f(0)+f(2)+f(3)+f(4)+f(5)-11$ is equal to α and the sum of its digit is β, then $\frac{\alpha+3\beta}{5}$ is ....*

Sol. (5.2) The given expression is equivalent to

$$\frac{f(x+y)}{x+y}-\frac{f(x-y)}{x-y}=4xy=(x+y)^2-(x-y)^2$$

$$\Rightarrow \quad \frac{f(x+y)}{x+y}-(x+y)^2=\frac{f(x-y)}{x-y}-(x-y)^2=c \text{ [constant]}$$

$$\Rightarrow \quad \frac{f(x)}{x}-x^2=c$$

$$\therefore \quad f(x)=x^3+cx$$

$$\because \quad f(1)=-2 \Rightarrow c=-3$$

$$\therefore \quad f(x)=x^3-3x$$

$$\therefore \quad f(x)+f(-x)=0$$

Thus, $f(-5)+f(-4)+f(0)+f(2)+f(3)+f(4)+f(5)$

$$=f(0)+f(2)+f(3)$$

$$=0+8-6+27-9=20$$

$$\therefore \quad \alpha=20$$

$$\beta=2+0=2$$

$$\therefore \quad \frac{\alpha+3\beta}{5}=\frac{26}{5}=5.2$$

Example 34 *Let f and g be real valued functions such that $f(x+2)=f(x-1)$, for each $x \in R$ and $g\left(x+\left[\frac{4x^2+13}{x^2+3}\right]\right) = g(x-2\pi-\sin^{-1}(\sin 7))$, for each $x \in R$, where $[\cdot]$ represents the greatest integer function, then the fundamental period of the function $h(x)=f(x)+g(x)$ is P, then $\frac{P}{99}$ equals ....*

Sol. (0.333) $f(x+2)=f(x-1) \Rightarrow f(x)=f(x+3)$

$\therefore$ Period of $f(x)$ is 3

and $g\left(x+\left[\frac{4x^2+13}{x^2+3}\right]\right)=g(x-2\pi-\sin^{-1}(\sin 7))$

$$\Rightarrow \quad g(x+4)=g(x-7)$$

$$\therefore \quad g(x)=g(x+11)$$

$\therefore$ Period of $g(x)$ is 11.

$\therefore$ Period of $h(x)$ is 33.

$$\therefore \quad P=33$$

$$\Rightarrow \quad \frac{P}{99}=\frac{33}{99}=\frac{1}{3}=0.333$$

Example 35 *Let $f(x)=(x+1)(x+2)(x+3)(x+4)+5$ where $x \in [-6, 6]$. If the range of the function is $[a, b]$ where $a, b \in N$, then the value of $\frac{(a+b)}{10098}$ is ....*

Sol. (0.5) We have, $f(x)=(x^2+5x+4)(x^2+5x+6)+5$

$$=[(x^2+5x+5)-1][(x^2+5x+5)+1]+5$$

$$f(x)=(x^2+5x+5)^2+4$$

Hence, $f(x)$ has minimum value 4 when $x^2+5x+5=0$

i.e. $x=\frac{-5\pm\sqrt{5}}{2}$

Hence, $x=\frac{-(5+\sqrt{5})}{2} \in [-6, 6]$

Also, maximum occurs at $x=6$

$$f(x)|_{\max}=(36+30+5)^2+4$$

$$=71^2+4=5045$$

$\therefore$ Range $[4, 5045]$

$$\therefore \quad a=4, b=5045$$

$$\Rightarrow \quad a+b=5049$$

$$\therefore \quad \frac{a+b}{10098}=\frac{5049}{10098}=\frac{1}{2}=0.5$$

Matching Type Questions

Example 36 *Match the entries of column I with one or more than one entries of column II. Note that* $[\cdot]$, $\{\cdot\}$ *and* $\text{sgn}(\cdot)$ *denote the greatest integer function, fractional part of and signum function respectively.*

Column I		Column II	
(A)	Let $f:[-1,1]\to R$ be defined by $f(x)=\sqrt[5]{x}+\sin^{-1}x$, then $f(x)$ is	(p)	Odd
(B)	Let $f:R\to\{-1,0,1\}$ is defined by $f(x)=\text{sgn}\left(\dfrac{1-\lvert x\rvert}{1+\lvert x\rvert}\right)$, then $f(x)$ is	(q)	Even
(C)	Let $f:(-\infty,0]\to[0,\infty)$ be defined by $f(x)=\dfrac{2^{-[x]}}{2^{\{x\}}}-2^{\lvert x\rvert}$, then $f(x)$ is	(r)	Onto
(D)	Let $f:(-4,2]\to[0,3]$ be defined by $f(x)=\sqrt{8-2x-x^2}$, then $f(x)$ is	(s)	One-one
		(t)	Many-one

Sol. A $\to$ p, s; B $\to$ q, r, t; C $\to$ t; D $\to$ r, t

(A) We have, $f(x)=\sqrt[5]{x}+\sin^{-1}x$

Clearly, domain of $f(x)=[-1,1]$

Also, $f(x)$ is increasing, so $f(x)$ is one-one function

and $f(-x)=-f(x)$

(B) $f(x)=\text{sgn}\dfrac{(1-\lvert x\rvert)}{(1+\lvert x\rvert)}$

Domain of $f(x)=R$ and range $=\{-1,0,1\}$, even function

Since, $f(-x)=f(x)$

(C) $f(x)=\dfrac{2^{-[x]}}{2^{\{x\}}}-2^{\lvert x\rvert}=2^{-([x]+\{x\})}-2^{\lvert x\rvert}$

$=2^{-x}-2^{\lvert x\rvert}=0,\ \forall x\le 0$

Hence, $f(x)$ is many-one.

(D) For domain of $f(x)$

$8-2x-x^2\ge 0 \Rightarrow (x+4)(x-2)\le 0 \Rightarrow x\in[-4,2]$

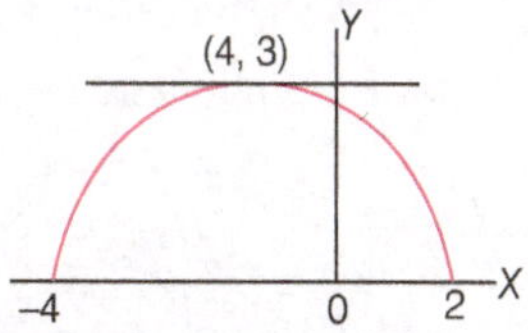

and range $=[0,3]=$ codomain

So, $f(x)$ is onto and many one.

Example 37 *Match the entries of column I with one or more than one entries of column II.*

Column I		Column II	
(A)	Let $f:[-1,\infty)\to(0,\infty)$ defined by $f(x)=e^{x^2+\lvert x\rvert}$, then $f(x)$ is	(p)	One-one
(B)	Let $f:(1,\infty)\to[3,\infty)$ defined by $f(x)=\sqrt{10-2x+x^2}$, then $f(x)$ is	(q)	Into
(C)	Let $f:R\to I$ defined by $f(x)=\tan^5\pi[x^2+2x+3]$ where $[\cdot]$ denotes GIF, then $f(x)$ is	(r)	Many one
(D)	Let $f:[3,4]\to[4,6]$ defined by $f(x)=\lvert x-1\rvert+\lvert x-2\rvert+\lvert x-3\rvert+\lvert x-4\rvert$, then $f(x)$	(s)	Onto
		(t)	Periodic

Sol. A $\to$ q, r; B $\to$ p, q; C $\to$ q, r, t; D $\to$ p, s

(A) $f(x)=e^{x^2+\lvert x\rvert}$

Clearly, function is many one as $f(1)=f(-1)$ into as minimum values of $f(x)=e^{x^2+\lvert x\rvert}$ is equal to 1 at $x=0$.

So, range is $[1,\infty)$.

(B) $f(x)=\sqrt{x^2-2x+10}$

$=\sqrt{(x-1)^2+9}$

For $x\in(1,\infty)$ range is $(3,\infty)$.

Hence, into, one-one as line drawn parallel to X-axis cuts graph at only one point.

Since, $x\in(1,\infty)$

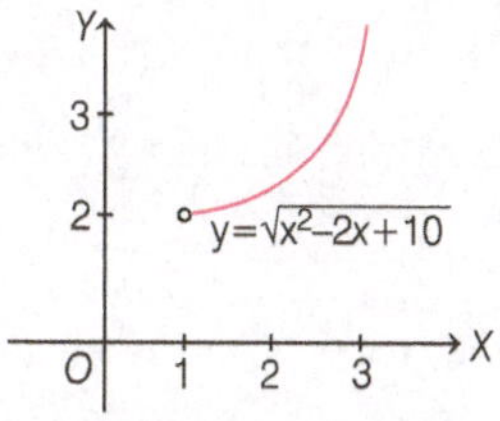

(C) $f:R\to I$

$f(x)=\tan^5\pi[x^2+2x+3]=0$

$[\because \tan\pi=0 \text{ and } [x^2+2x+3]\in I]$

Hence, function is into, many one and periodic.

(D) For $x\in[3,4]$ and $f(x)\in[4,6]$

As, $f(x)=2(x-1)$ for $x\in[3,4]$

Clearly, $f(x)$ is one-one and onto.

Example 38 *Consider the following table.*

	Column I		Column II
(A)	The set of possible values of λ for which $x^2 - (\lambda^2 - 5\lambda + 5) \cdot x + (2\lambda^2 - 3\lambda - 4) = 0$ has roots whose sum and product are both less than 1 is $(p, 2q)$, then	(p)	$p + q = 9$
(B)	If x satisfy the in equation $\dfrac{x^4 + x^2 + 1}{x^2 - 4x - 5} \le 0$, then x is (p, q), then	(q)	$p + q = 6$
(C)	If $(x^2 - 3x + 2)$ is a factor of $x^4 - px^2 + q = 0$, then	(r)	$p + q = 7$
(D)	A and B solved a quadratic equation with coefficient of $x^2 = 1$. In solving it, A made a mistake in the constant term only and got the roots as 5 and 2, while B made a mistake in the coefficient of x only and obtained 6 and 2 as roots. The correct roots are p and $q (p < q)$, then	(s)	$p + q = 4$
		(t)	$\lvert p - q \rvert = 1$

Sol. A $\to$ q; B $\to$ s; C $\to$ p, t; D $\to$ r, t

(A) Let α and β be roots of the equation

$$\alpha + \beta = (\lambda^2 - 5\lambda + 5) < 1$$

$$(\lambda^2 - 5\lambda + 4) < 0 \quad \text{...(i)}$$

$$\alpha\beta = (2\lambda^2 - 3\lambda - 4) < 1 \quad \text{...(ii)}$$

By Eq. (i), $(\lambda - 4) \cdot (\lambda - 1) < 0$

$$1 < \lambda < 4$$

By Eq (ii), $-1 < \lambda < \dfrac{5}{2}$

Required set $= \left(-1, \dfrac{5}{2}\right) \cap (1, 4) = \left(1, \dfrac{5}{2}\right)$

(B) $$\frac{x^4 + x^2 + 1}{x^2 - 4x - 5} \le 0,$$

$$\frac{x^4 + x^2 + 1}{(x - 5)(x + 1)} \le 0$$

$x^4 + x^2 + 1$ is always positive.

$$x \in (-1, 5)$$

(C) $x^2 - 3x + 2$ is a factor of $x^4 - px^2 + q = 0$,

Then, $x = 1$ and $x = 2$ are root's of the equation, then

$$1 - p + q = 0 \text{ ...(i) } (x = 1)$$

$$\underline{16 - 4p + q = 0 \text{ ...(ii) } (x = 2)}$$

we get, $p = 5, q = 4$

(D) $A \Rightarrow 5 + 2 = 7$ [correct sum]

$B \Rightarrow 6 \times 2 = 12$ [correct product]

$\therefore$ Equation is $x^2 - 7x + 12 = 0$

$\Rightarrow$ $x = 3, 4$

EXERCISE 1

JEE Main Pattern

Single Option Correct Type Questions

1. The domain of $f(x)=\sqrt{\dfrac{1-2^x}{5^{-x}-5}}$ is

(a) $(-\infty,-1)\cup[0,\infty)$ (b) $(-\infty,-1)$
(c) $[0,\infty)$ (d) $(-\infty,-1]$

2. The largest interval lying in $(-\pi/2, \pi/2)$ for which the function $f(x)=4^{-x^2}+\cos^{-1}\left(\dfrac{x}{2}-1\right)+\log(\cos x)$ is defined, is

(a) $[0,\pi]$ (b) $(-\pi/2,\pi/2)$
(c) $[-\pi/4,\pi/2)$ (d) $[0,\pi/2)$

3. If $f(x)=\dfrac{5^x}{5^x+\sqrt{5}}$, then $f\left(\dfrac{1}{3006}\right)+f\left(\dfrac{2}{3006}\right)+\ldots+f\left(\dfrac{3005}{3006}\right)$ is $\dfrac{m}{n}$, then sum of digits of $m+n$ is

(a) 9 (b) 10
(c) 11 (d) 12

4. If $f(x)=\pi\left(\dfrac{\sqrt{x+7}-4}{x-9}\right)$, then the range of function $y=\tan(2f(x))$ is

(a) $[0,1]$ (b) $\left(0,\dfrac{1}{\sqrt{2}}\right)$
(c) $(0,1)\cup(1,\infty)$ (d) $(0,\infty)$

5. Let $f(x)$ be a function such that $f(x+y)=f(x)\cdot f(y)$, $\forall\ x,y\in N$. If $f(1)=2$ and $\sum_{k=1}^{n} f(k)=510$, then the value of n is

(a) 6 (b) 7 (c) 8 (d) 9

6. The range of the function $f: R\to R$,
$f(x)=\dfrac{\sqrt{x^2+1}-3x}{\sqrt{x^2+1}+x}$ is

(a) $(0,\infty)$ (b) $(1,\infty)$
(c) $\left(\dfrac{1}{2},\infty\right)$ (d) $(-1,\infty)$

7. The domain of the function $f(x)=\ln\left(\ln\dfrac{x}{\{x\}}\right)$ is (where $\{\cdot\}$ denotes the fractional part function)

(a) $(1,\infty)$
(b) all integer
(c) $(1,\infty)-I$
(d) None of the above

8. The least integral values of x which can lie in the domain of the function
$f(x)=\log(ax^3+(a+b)x^2+(b+c)x+c)$, $a>0$ and $b^2-4ac<0$ is

(a) -4 (b) 0
(c) 1 (d) 2

9. The range of the function
$f(x)=\log_{\sqrt{2}}(2-\log_2(16\sin^2 x+1))$ is

(a) $(-\infty,1)$ (b) $(-\infty,3]$
(c) $(-\infty,2]$ (d) None of these

10. The domain of the function
$f(x)=\log_3(\log_3|\cos x|-\log_{x^2-4x+6}|\cos x|)$ contains which of the following intervals.

(a) $\left(1,\dfrac{\pi}{2}\right)$ (b) $\left(1,\dfrac{\pi}{2}\right)\cup\left(\dfrac{\pi}{2},3\right)$
(c) $\left(-1,\dfrac{\pi}{2}\right)\cup(2,3)$ (d) None of these

11. The maximum value of $\sec^{-1}\left(\dfrac{7-5(x^2+3)}{2(x^2+2)}\right)$ is

(a) $\dfrac{5\pi}{6}$ (b) $\dfrac{5\pi}{12}$
(c) $\dfrac{7\pi}{12}$ (d) $\dfrac{2\pi}{3}$

12. For $x,y\in R$, the maximum possible value of
$(\sin^{-1}x)^2+(\tan^{-1}y)^2+\pi\sin^{-1}x+\pi\tan^{-1}y+\dfrac{\pi^2}{2}$ is k, then the value of $\left[\dfrac{k}{2\pi^2}\right]$, where $[\cdot]$ represents greatest integer function, is

(a) 1 (b) 2 (c) 3 (d) 0

13. The function $f: R\to\left[-\dfrac{1}{2},\dfrac{1}{2}\right]$ defined as $f(x)=\dfrac{x}{1+x^2}$ is

(a) invertible
(b) injective but not surjective
(c) surjective but not injective
(d) neither injective nor surjective

14. The function $f:[0,3]\to[2,30]$ defined by $f(x)=2x^3-15x^2+36x+2$, is

(a) one-one and onto
(b) onto but not one-one
(c) one-one but not onto
(d) neither one-one nor onto

15. The function $f:R\to R$ defined as

$$f(x)=\frac{1}{2}\left(\sqrt{\sqrt{2x^2+3}-x+x^2}+\sqrt{\sqrt{2x^2+3}+x+x^2}\right)$$ is

(a) one-one and onto (b) one-one but not onto
(c) onto but not one-one (d) Neither one-one nor onto

16. Let $f:N\to Z$ and $f(x)=\begin{cases}\dfrac{x-1}{2}, & \text{when } x \text{ is odd}\\ \dfrac{-x}{2}, & \text{when } x \text{ is even}\end{cases}$

(a) $f(x)$ is bijective
(b) $f(x)$ is injective but not surjective
(c) $f(x)$ is not injective
(d) $f(x)$ is neither injective nor surjective

17. Let f and $g:N\to N$ such that $f(x+1)=f(x)+f(1)$, $\forall\ x\in N$ and g be any function. Which of the following is not true?

(a) f is one-one
(b) If fog is one-one, then g is one-one
(c) If g is onto, then fog is one-one
(d) If f is onto, then $f(x)=x$, $\forall\ x\in N$

18. The number of bijective function $f:\{1,3,5,7,\ldots,99\}\to\{2,4,6,8,\ldots,100\}$ Such that $f(5)\ge f(10)\ge f(15)\ge\ldots\ge f(100)$ is ......

(a) ${}^{50}P_{20}$ (b) ${}^{50}P_{30}$ (c) $50!\times 20!$ (d) $\dfrac{50!}{2}$

19. Let $f(x)=\dfrac{x-1}{x+1}$, $x\in R-\{0,-1,1\}$. If $f^{n+1}(x)=f(f^n(x))$, $\forall\ n\in N$, then $f^6(8)+f^7(9)$ is equal to

(a) $-3/2$ (b) $-7/2$ (c) $-11/3$ (d) $-11/8$

20. If $f(x)=\dfrac{(\tan 2^\circ)x+\log_e(124)}{x\log_e(144)-\tan 2^\circ}$, $x>0$, then the least value of $f(f(x))+f\left(f\left(\dfrac{2}{x}\right)\right)$ is

(a) 2 (b) 4 (c) 6 (d) 8

21. Let f be a function defined $f:\left[0,e^{-\frac{3}{2}}\right]\to[-1/4,\infty)$, $f(x)=(\ln x)^2+3\ln x+2$, then the inverse of f is

(a) $e^{\frac{-3-\sqrt{4x+1}}{2}}$ (b) $\log\left(\dfrac{-3-\sqrt{4x+1}}{2}\right)$
(c) $\log\left(\dfrac{-3+\sqrt{4x+1}}{2}\right)$ (d) $e^{\frac{-3+\sqrt{4x+1}}{2}}$

22. If the function $f(x)=ax+b$ has its own inverse, then the ordered pair (a,b) can be

(a) (1, 0) (b) (– 1, 0)
(c) (– 1, 1) (d) (2, 1)

23. Let $f(x)=(3x+2)^2-1$, $-\infty<x\le-2/3$. If $g(x)$ is the function whose graph is the reflection of the graph of $f(x)$ with respect to line $y=x$, then $g(x)$ equals

(a) $\dfrac{-2+\sqrt{x+1}}{3}$ (b) $\dfrac{-2-\sqrt{x+1}}{3}$
(c) $\dfrac{-2-\sqrt{x-1}}{3}$ (d) None of these

24. Let $f:\left[\dfrac{1}{2},1\right]\to[-1,1]$ is given by $f(x)=4x^3-3x$, then $f^{-1}(x)$ is given by

(a) $\cos\left(\dfrac{1}{3}\cos^{-1}x\right)$ (b) $3\cos(\sin^{-1}x)$
(c) $3\sin^{-1}(\cos x)$ (d) None of these

25. Let $f:[-\pi/3,2\pi/3]\to[0,4]$ be a function defined by $f(x)=\sqrt{3}\sin x-\cos x+2$, then $f^{-1}(x)$ is given by $\dfrac{a\pi}{b}-\cos^{-1}\left(\dfrac{x-d}{c}\right)$, then $a+b+c+d$ is

(a) 8 (b) 9 (c) 10 (d) 11

26. Let f be defined by $f(x)=\log_a(x+\sqrt{x^2+1})$, $a>0$ and f is onto function, then the inverse of $f(x)$ is

(a) $f^{-1}(x)=a^x-a^{-x}$ (b) $f^{-1}(x)=\dfrac{a^x-a^{-x}}{2}$
(c) $f^{-1}(x)=\dfrac{a^{\sqrt{x^2+1}}-1}{2}$ (d) $f^{-1}(x)=\dfrac{a^x+a^{-x}}{2}$

27. The inverse of function $f(x)=\dfrac{4^{2x}-4^{-2x}}{4^{2x}+4^{-2x}}$, $x\in(-1,1)$ is

(a) $\dfrac{1}{4\log_4 e}\log_e\left(\dfrac{1+x}{1-x}\right)$ (b) $\log_4\left(\dfrac{1+x}{1-x}\right)$
(c) $\dfrac{1}{2}\log_4\left(\dfrac{1-x}{1+x}\right)$ (d) $\dfrac{1}{4}\log_e\left|\dfrac{1+x}{1-x}\right|$

28. If f be a function $f(x+1)+f(x-1)=\sqrt{3}f(x)$ and $f(2)=4$, then $f(x)$ is

(a) $4\sin\left(\dfrac{\pi x}{6}\right)$ (b) $4\cos\left(\dfrac{\pi x}{6}\right)$
(c) $8\sin\left(\dfrac{\pi x}{6}\right)$ (d) $8\cos\left(\dfrac{\pi x}{6}\right)$

29. Let f be a real valued function defined $\forall\ x\in R$ and for $a>0$ such that $f(x+a)=\dfrac{1}{2}+\sqrt{f(x)-\{f(x)\}^2}\ \forall\ x$, then period of $f(x)$ is

(a) a (b) $2a$
(c) $3a$ (d) $a/2$

30. If $f(x+y)=f(x)+f(y)-xy-1, \forall\ x, y \in N$ and $f(1)=1$, then the value of $\sum_{r=1}^{4} f(r)$ is
(a) 6
(b) -6
(c) 7
(d) -8

Numerical Value Type Questions

31. Let $f(x)=-x^{100}$. If $f(x)$ is divided by x^2+x, then the remainder is $r(x)$. The value of $r(10)$ is ....

32. The number of integers belonging to the domain of the function $f(x)=\log_{(15-x)}(x-2)-\cos^{-1}\left[\frac{2x-26}{3}\right]$, where $[\cdot]$ represents the greatest integer function, is/are ......

33. If $f(x)=\sqrt{\left(\frac{2-|x|}{3-|x|}\right)}$ and domain of $f(x)$ is $(-\infty,-\beta)\cup[-\alpha,\alpha]\cup(\beta,\infty)$, then the value of $\alpha+\beta$ is ....

34. The range of a given real valued function can be obtained by expressing the given expression as a perfect square. Let us consider a real valued function f defined as $f(x)=x^2+2x+2$, then range of $f(\sec^2 x)$ and $\log(f(x))$ is $[a,\infty)$ and (b,∞), then number of prime factors of $2a+3b-4$ is ....

35. If the equation $(n^2-4)(n^2-9)x^3+\left[\frac{n-2}{2}\right]x^2+(n-4)(n^2-5n+6)x+\{2n-1\}=0$ is satisfied by all values of x in $(0, 3]$, then sum of all possible integral values of n is ....
(Note : $\{x\}$ and $[x]$ denote fractional part function and greatest integer function of x respectively)

36. Let $f(x)=\sin^{23}x-\cos^{22}x$ and $g(x)=1+\frac{1}{2}\tan^{-1}|x|$, then the number of values of x in interval $[-10\pi, 20\pi]$ satisfying the equation $f(x)=\text{sgn}(g(x))$, is ....

37. The set of real values of x satisfying the equation $\left[\frac{2}{x}\right]+\left[\frac{3}{x}\right]=4$, is interval I, then number of integers in that interval is ....

38. If a polynomial function f satisfies the relation
$$\log_2[f(x)]=\log_2\left[2+\frac{2}{3}+\frac{2}{9}+\ldots+\infty\right]\cdot\log_3\left(1+\frac{f(x)}{f\left(\frac{1}{x}\right)}\right)$$
and $f(10)=1001$, then the value of $f(5)$ is ....

39. If $f(x)=x^3+3x^2+4x+p\cos x+q\sin x, \forall x\in R$ is one-one function, then the maximum value of (p^2+q^2) is ....

40. Let $f(x)=ax^2+bx+c$, $(a<b)$ and $f(x)\geq 0, \forall x\in R$. Then, the minimum value of $\frac{a+b+c}{b-a}$ is ....

41. The function $f(x)$ is defined as
$$f(x)=\begin{cases}\frac{1}{2^x}, & \text{if } x\geq 4\\ f(x+1), & \text{if } x<4\end{cases}$$
Then, the value of $24f\left(2+\log_2\left(\frac{3}{2}\right)\right)$ is ....

42. The least integer a for which $1+\log_3(x^2+1)\leq\log_3(ax^2+4x+a)$ is true for all real values of x is ....

43. Let $f(x)=x+x^2+x^4+x^8+\ldots$ the coefficient of x^{10} in $f(f(x))$ is ....

44. A function $f: R\to R$ satisfies the equation $f(x)f(y)-f(xy)=x+y, \forall x, y\in R$ and $f(1)>0$, then $f(2)f^{-1}(2)=$ ....

45. If $f(x)=\cos 8\pi\{x\}+\sin 2\pi x\ \text{cosec}\ 2\pi x$ (where $\{\cdot\}$ represents fractional part function), the fundamental period of $f(x)$ is $\frac{a}{4}$, then $5a$ is ....

46. Period of function $f(x)=\min\{\sin x, |x|\}+\frac{x}{\pi}-\left[\frac{x}{\pi}\right]$ (where $[\cdot]$ denotes greatest integer function) is $k\pi$, then k^k is ....

47. The number of possible integral values of x such that $\frac{x}{x+4}=\frac{5}{7}\frac{[x]-7}{[x]-5}$ is ....
(where $[x]$ denotes greatest integer less than x)

48. Let f be real valued function satisfying $2f(\sin x)+f(\cos x)=x$, then the value of $f(1/2)$ is equal to ....

49. Let f be a function $f: R\to R$ such that $f(0)=4$ and $f(x+y)=2^x f(y)+4^y f(x), \forall\ x, y\in R$. If $f'(2)=2^a b\ln 2$, then the value of $(a+b)$ is ....

50. The function $f(x)$ satisfy the equation $f(1-x)+2f(x)=3x, \forall\ x\in R$, then $|f(0)|=$.........

Previous Year Questions

51. If the domain of the function

$f(x)=\dfrac{\sqrt{x^2-25}}{(4-x^2)}+\log_{10}(x^2+2x-15)$ is

$(-\infty,\alpha)\cup[\beta,\infty)$, then $\alpha^2+\beta^3$ is equal to

[Single Correct Type, 2024 Main]

(a) 175 (b) 150 (c) 125 (d) 140

52. If $S=\{a\in R:|2a-1|=3[a]+2\{a\}\}$, where $[t]$ denotes the greatest integer less than or equal to t and $\{t\}$ represents the fractional part of t, then $72\sum_{a\in S} a$ is equal to ....

[Numerical Value Type, 2024 Main]

53. Let $A=\{1, 2, 3, ..., 7\}$ and let $P(A)$ denote the power set of A. If the number of functions $f:A\to P(A)$ such that $a\in f(a), \forall\, a\in A$ is $m^n\cdot m$ and $n\in N$ and m is least, then $m+n$ is equal to .... **[Numerical Value Type, 2024 Main]**

54. The domain of the function $f(x)=\dfrac{1}{\sqrt{[x]^2-3[x]-10}}$ is (where, $[x]$ denotes the greatest integer less than or equal to x) **[Single Correct Type, 2023 Main]**

(a) $(-\infty,-2)\cup(5,\infty)$ (b) $(-\infty,-3]\cup[6,\infty)$
(c) $(-\infty,-3]\cup(5,\infty)$ (d) $(-\infty,-2)\cup[6,\infty)$

55. Let the sets A and B denote the domain and range respectively of the function $f(x)=\dfrac{1}{\sqrt{\lceil x\rceil-x}}$, where $\lceil x\rceil$ denotes the smallest integer greater than or equal to x. Then, among the statements (S1) : $A\cap B=(1,\infty)-N$ and (S2) : $A\cup B=(1,\infty)$

[Single Correct Type, 2023 Main]

(a) Both (S1) and (S2) are true.
(b) Neither (S1) nor (S2) is true.
(c) Only (S1) is true.
(d) Only (S2) is true.

56. Let $A=\{x\in R:\ [x+3]+[x+4]\le 3\}$,

$B=\left\{x\in R: 3^x\left(\sum_{r=1}^{\infty}\dfrac{3}{10^r}\right)^{x-3}<3^{-3x}\right\}$, where $[t]$ denotes greatest integer function. Then,

[Single Correct Type, 2023 Main]

(a) $A=B$ (b) $A\cap B=\phi$
(c) $B\subset C, A\ne B$ (c) $A\subset B, A\ne B$

57. Let $f:R-\{0,1\}\to R$ be a function such that $f(x)+f\left(\dfrac{1}{1-x}\right)=1+x$. Then, $f(2)$ is equal to

[Single Correct Type, 2023 Main]

(a) $\dfrac{9}{2}$ (b) $\dfrac{9}{4}$ (c) $\dfrac{7}{3}$ (d) $\dfrac{7}{4}$

58. If the domain of the function $f(x)=\dfrac{[x]}{1+x^2}$, where $[x]$ is greatest integer $\le x$, is $[2,6)$, then its range is

[Single Correct Type, 2023 Main]

(a) $\left(\dfrac{5}{37},\dfrac{2}{5}\right]-\left\{\dfrac{9}{29},\dfrac{27}{109},\dfrac{18}{89},\dfrac{9}{53}\right\}$

(b) $\left(\dfrac{5}{26},\dfrac{2}{5}\right]-\left\{\dfrac{9}{29},\dfrac{27}{109},\dfrac{18}{89},\dfrac{9}{53}\right\}$

(c) $\left(\dfrac{5}{26},\dfrac{2}{5}\right]$

(d) $\left(\dfrac{5}{37},\dfrac{2}{5}\right]$

59. Let $f:R-\{2,6\}\to R$ be real valued function defined as $f(x)=\dfrac{x^2+2x+1}{x^2-8x+12}$. Then, range of f is **[Single Correct Type, 2023 Main]**

(a) $\left(-\infty,-\dfrac{21}{4}\right]\cup[1,\infty)$ (b) $\left(-\infty,-\dfrac{21}{4}\right]\cup[0,\infty)$

(c) $\left(-\infty,-\dfrac{21}{4}\right]\cup\left[\dfrac{21}{4},\infty\right)$ (d) $\left(-\infty,-\dfrac{21}{4}\right)\cup(0,\infty)$

60. The domain of $f(x)=\dfrac{\log_{(x+1)}(x-2)}{e^{2\log x}-(2x+3)}$, $x\in R$ is

[Single Correct Type, 2023 Main]

(a) $R-\{3\}$ (b) $(2,\infty)-\{3\}$
(c) $(-1,\infty)-\{3\}$ (d) $R-\{-1,3)$

61. Consider a function $f:N\to R$, satisfying $f(1)+2f(2)+3f(3)+\ldots+xf(x)=x(x+1)f(x)$; $x\ge 2$ with $f(1)=1$. Then, $\dfrac{1}{f(2022)}+\dfrac{1}{f(2028)}$ is equal to

[Single Correct Type, 2023 Main]

(a) 8200 (b) 8000
(c) 8400 (d) 8100

62. Let $f(x)=2x^n+\lambda$, $\lambda\in R$, $n\in N$ and $f(4)=133$, $f(5)=255$. Then, the sum of all the positive integer divisors of $(f(3)-f(2))$ is **[Single Correct Type, 2023 Main]**

(a) 60 (b) 59 (c) 58 (d) 61

63. If $f(x)=\dfrac{2^{2x}}{2^{2x}+2}$, $x\in R$, then $f\left(\dfrac{1}{2023}\right)+f\left(\dfrac{2}{2023}\right)$ $+\ldots+f\left(\dfrac{2022}{2023}\right)$ is equal to

[Single Correct Type, 2023 Main]

(a) 2010 (b) 2011 (c) 1011 (d) 1010

64. The number of functions $f:\{1,2,3,4\}\to\{a\in Z\,|\,|a|\le 8\}$ satisfying $f(n)+\dfrac{1}{n}f(n+1)=1, \forall\, n\in\{1,2,3\}$ is

[Single Correct Type, 2023 Main]

(a) 3 (b) 2 (c) 1 (d) 4

65. Let $A=\{1, 2, 3, 5, 8, 9\}$. Then, the number of possible functions $f: A \to A$ such that $f(m \cdot n) = f(m) \cdot f(n), \forall\, m, n \in A$ with $m \cdot n \in A$ is equal to ....

[Numerical Value Type, 2023 Main]

66. Let $[x]$ denote the greatest integer $\le x$, where $x \in R$. If the domain of the real valued function $f(x)=\sqrt{\dfrac{|[x]|-2}{|[x]|-3}}$ is $(-\infty, a) \cup [b, c) \cup [4, \infty)$, $a<b<c$, then the value of $a+b+c$ is **[Single Correct Type, 2021 Main]**

(a) 8 (b) 1 (c) −2 (d) −3

67. If the functions are defined as $f(x)=\sqrt{x}$ and $g(x)=\sqrt{1-x}$, then what is the common domain of the following functions? $f+g$, $f-g$, f/g, g/f, $g-f$, where, $(f/g)(x)=\dfrac{f(x)}{g(x)}$

[Single Correct Type, 2021 Main]

(a) $0 \le x \le 1$ (b) $0 \le x < 1$
(c) $0 < x < 1$ (d) $0 < x \le 1$

68. Let $f: N \to N$ be a function such that $f(m+n)=f(m)+f(n)$ for every $m, n \in N$. If $f(6)=18$, then $f(2) \cdot f(3)$ is equal to **[Single Correct Type, 2021 Main]**

(a) 6 (b) 54 (c) 18 (d) 36

69. A function $f(x)$ is given by $f(x)=\dfrac{5^x}{5^x+5}$, then the sum of the series $f\left(\dfrac{1}{20}\right)+f\left(\dfrac{2}{20}\right)+f\left(\dfrac{3}{20}\right)+\ldots+f\left(\dfrac{39}{20}\right)$ is equal to **[Single Correct Type, 2021 Main]**

(a) 29/2 (b) 49/2
(c) 39/2 (d) 19/2

70. If $a+\alpha=1$, $b+\beta=2$ and $af(x)+\alpha f\left(\dfrac{1}{x}\right)=bx+\dfrac{\beta}{x}$, $x \ne 0$, then the value of expression $\dfrac{f(x)+f\left(\dfrac{1}{x}\right)}{x+\dfrac{1}{x}}$ is

[Single Correct Type, 2021 Main]

(a) −2 (b) 2 (c) 1 (d) −1

71. If $[x]$ be the greatest integer less than or equal to x, then $\sum_{n=8}^{100}\left[\dfrac{(-1)^n n}{2}\right]$ is equal to **[Single Correct Type, 2021 Main]**

(a) 0 (b) 4 (c) −2 (d) 2

72. Let $S=\{1, 2, 3, 4, 5, 6, 7\}$. Then, the number of possible functions $f: S \to S$ such that $f(m \cdot n)=f(m) \cdot f(n)$ for every $m, n \in S$ and $m \cdot n \in S$ is equal to ....

[Numerical Value Type, 2021 Main]

73. If $R=\{(x, y): x, y \in Z,\ x^2+3y^2 \le 8\}$ is a relation on the set of integers Z, then the domain of R^{-1} is

[Single Correct Type, 2020 Main]

(a) $\{-1, 0, 1\}$ (b) $\{-2, -1, 1, 2\}$
(c) $\{-2, -1, 0, 1, 2\}$ (d) $\{0, 1\}$

74. Let $f:(1, 3) \to R$ be a function defined by $f(x)=\dfrac{x[x]}{1+x^2}$, where $[x]$ denotes the greatest integer $\le x$. Then, the range of f is **[Single Correct Type, 2020 Main]**

(a) $\left(\dfrac{2}{5}, \dfrac{3}{5}\right] \cup \left(\dfrac{3}{4}, \dfrac{4}{5}\right)$ (b) $\left(\dfrac{2}{5}, \dfrac{4}{5}\right]$

(c) $\left(\dfrac{3}{5}, \dfrac{4}{5}\right)$ (d) $\left(\dfrac{2}{5}, \dfrac{1}{2}\right) \cup \left(\dfrac{3}{5}, \dfrac{4}{5}\right]$

EXERCISE 2

JEE Advanced Pattern

Single Option Correct Type Questions

1. The range of values of t for which $2\sin t = \dfrac{1-2x+5x^2}{3x^2-2x-1}, t \in \left[-\dfrac{\pi}{2}, \dfrac{\pi}{2}\right]$ is

(a) $\left[-\dfrac{\pi}{2}, -\dfrac{\pi}{10}\right] \cup \left[\dfrac{3\pi}{10}, \dfrac{\pi}{6}\right)$

(b) $\left[-\dfrac{\pi}{2}, \dfrac{-\pi}{6}\right] \cup \left[\dfrac{3\pi}{10}, \dfrac{\pi}{2}\right]$

(c) $\left[-\dfrac{\pi}{2}, \dfrac{-\pi}{10}\right] \cup \left[\dfrac{3\pi}{10}, \dfrac{\pi}{2}\right]$

(d) None of the above

2. The range of the function $f(x) = \dfrac{e^x - e^{|x|}}{e^x + e^{|x|}}$ is

(a) $(-1, 0)$ (b) $(-1, 2)$
(c) $(-1, 0]$ (d) $[-1, 0]$

3. If $f(x) = \dfrac{5^x}{5^x + \sqrt{5}}$, then $f\left(\dfrac{1}{3006}\right) + f\left(\dfrac{2}{3006}\right) + \ldots + f\left(\dfrac{3005}{3006}\right)$ is $\dfrac{m}{n}$, then sum of digits of $m+n$ is

(a) 9 (b) 10
(c) 11 (d) 12

4. If the domains of $f(x) = \sqrt{(0.625)^{4-3x} - (1.6)^{x(x+8)}}$ is $[a, b]$, then the value of $a^2 + b^2$ is

(a) 15 (b) 16
(c) 17 (d) 18

5. If the equation $|x-3| - |x+1| = P$ has exactly one solution, then number of integral values of P, is

(a) 6 (b) 5
(c) 7 (d) 8

6. If $f(x) = x^2 + bx + c$ and $f(3+t) = f(3-t)$ for all real numbers t, then which of the following is true?

(a) $f(6) < f(2) < f(1)$ (b) $f(2) < f(6) < f(1)$
(c) $f(2) < f(1) < f(6)$ (d) $f(1) < f(2) < f(6)$

7. Let f be a function $f: R \to R$ such that $f(1) = 18$ and $f(x+4) = 3^x f(y) + 9^y f(x) \forall x, y \in R$. If $f'(1) = 3^a \cdot b \cdot \ln 3$, then the value of $(a+b)$ is

(a) 4 (b) 5
(c) 7 (d) 8

8. The sum of all possible solution(s) of the equations $||x+3|-2| = \text{sgn}\left(1 - \left|\dfrac{(x-2)(x^2-x-6)}{(x^2+1)(x^2-5x+6)(x+2)}\right|\right)$ is

(a) 10 (b) -12 (c) 12 (d) -8

[sgn(x) denotes the signum function of x]

9. For $x \in R, x \neq 0, 1$, let $f_0(x) = \dfrac{1}{1-x}$ and $f_{n+1}(x) = f_0(f_n(x)), n = 0, 1, 2, \ldots$, then the value of $f_{100}(3) + f_1\left(\dfrac{2}{3}\right) + f_2\left(\dfrac{3}{2}\right)$ is equal to

(a) $\dfrac{4}{3}$ (b) $\dfrac{1}{3}$ (c) $\dfrac{5}{3}$ (d) $\dfrac{8}{3}$

10. If $f(x) = \{x\} + \left\{x + \left[\dfrac{x}{1+x^3}\right]\right\} + \left\{x + \left[\dfrac{x}{1+2x^3}\right]\right\} + \ldots + \left\{x + \left[\dfrac{x}{1+49x^3}\right]\right\}$, then the value of $[f(\sqrt{2})]$ is ([$\cdot$] and {$\cdot$} are GIF and fractional part of function respectively)

(a) 20.7 (b) 20 (c) 30.8 (d) 40

11. Let $f_n(x) = (1+x)(1+2x)(1+4x)\ldots(1+2^n x)$. If $f_n(x)$ can be expressed as $f_n(x) = a_n + a_{n-1}|x + \ldots + a_{n \cdot n} x^n$, then the value of a_{n_7} can be expressed as $a_{n,2} = \dfrac{(2^{n+1}-a)(2^{n+1}-b)}{c}$, where a, b and c are natural numbers. Then, value of $4a - b + 3c$ is equal to N, then sum of divisor of N.

(a) 27 (b) 28 (c) 29 (d) 30

12. Let f be a real valued periodic function defined for all real numbers such that for some fixed $a > 0$, $f(x+a) = \dfrac{1}{2} + \sqrt{f(x) - \{f(x)\}^2}$ for all x. Then, period of $f(x)$ is

(a) a (b) $2a$ (c) $3a$ (d) $4a$

13. If [$\cdot$] represents the greatest integer function and {$\cdot$} represents the fractional part function, then the domain of $f(x) = \sqrt{x^4 - x + 1} + \sqrt{[\sqrt{x^2}]} + \sqrt{\{\sqrt{x^2}\}}$ is

(a) Subset of real numbers except itself.
(b) Subset of rational numbers
(c) Set of real numbers
(d) None of the above

14. Let $f: R - \left\{\frac{3}{2}\right\} \to R, f(x) = \frac{3x+5}{2x-3}$. Let $f_1(x) = f(x)$, $f_n(x) = f(f_{n-1}(x))$ for $n \geq 2, n \in N$, then $f_{2008}(x) + f_{2009}(x) = \frac{ax^2+b}{cx+d}$, then $a+b+c+d=$

(a) 5 (b) 4
(c) 6 (d) 8

15. The number of solutions of the equation $[y+[y]] = 2\cos x$ is
(where $y = \frac{1}{3}[\sin x + [\sin x + [\sin x]]]$ and $[\cdot]$ = greatest integer function)

(a) 0 (b) 1
(c) 2 (d) infinite

16. Let f be a real valued function with domain R satisfying

$$f(x+k) = 1 + [2 - 5f(x) + 10\{f(x)\}^2 - 10\{f(x)\}^3 + 5\{f(x)\}^4 - \{f(x)\}^5]^{\frac{1}{5}}$$

For all real x and some positive constant k, then the period of the function $f(x)$ is

(a) k (b) $2k$
(c) $\frac{k}{2}$ (d) None of these

17. Let g be a function satisfying $g(x-2) + g(x+2) = \sqrt{3}g(x), \forall x \in R$. Then, g also satisfy the relation(s) given as

(a) $g(x-4) + g(x+8) = 0$ (b) $g(x) - g(x+12) = 0$
(c) $g(x-2) + g(x+4) = 0$ (d) $g(x) - g(x+24) = 0$

18. If $f: A \to B$ is a function, then A is called domain of $f(x)$ and range is the set $\{f(x): x \in A\}$. To find domain and range we may use the properties of different functions and also AM $\geq$ GM inequality. Then, domain and range of $y = f(x)$, where $e^{2x} - 2ye^x + 1 = 0$, is A and B, $A \cap B$ is

(a) $[1, \infty)$ (b) $[3, \infty)$
(c) $(2, \infty)$ (d) $[-1, \infty)$

19. If $A > 0$, c, d, u, v are non-zero constants and the graph of $f(x) = |Ax + c| + d$ and $g(x) = -|Ax + u| + v$ intersect exactly at two points (1, 4) and (3, 1), then the value of $\frac{u+c}{A}$ equals

(a) 4 (b) -4
(c) 2 (d) -2

20. Area bounded by the relation $[2x] + [y] = 5$, $x, y > 0$ is (where $[\cdot]$ represents the greatest integer function)

(a) 2 (b) 3
(c) 4 (d) 5

More than One Correct Option Type Questions

21. If $f(x) = \tan^2\left(\frac{\pi x}{n^2 - 5n + 8}\right) + \cot(n+m)\pi x, n \in N$, $m \in Q$ is a periodic function with 2 as its fundamental period, then

(a) $m \notin (-2, -1)$ (b) $m \notin (-3, -1)$
(c) $m \notin (-3, -2)$ (d) $m \notin (-4, 2)$

22. Let x and y be two non-empty set. Let $f: x \to y$ be a function. For $A \subset x$ and $B \subset y$, define $f(A) = \{f(x): x \in A\}$, $f^{-1}(B) = \{x \in x: f(x) \in B\}$, then

(a) $f^{-1}(f(A)) = A$ (b) $f^{-1}(f(A)) \neq A$
(c) $f^{-1}(f(B)) = B$ (d) $f^{-1}f(B) \neq B$

23. Which of the following inequalities are not equivalent.

(a) $|f(x)| \geq |g(x)|$ and $\sqrt{f^2(x)} \geq \sqrt{g^2(x)}$
(b) $\frac{x-3}{x^2-5x+6} < 2$ and $2x^2 - 11x + 15 > 0$
(c) $x + 3 - \frac{1}{x-1} > -x + 2 - \frac{1}{x-1}$ and $x + 3 > -x + 2$
(d) $\log_2(x^2-4) > \log_2(4x-7)$ and $x^2 - 4x + 3 > 0$

24. Consider a function defined by $f(x) = x + 1$, then identify the correct statement(s)

(a) $f(x) = 3$ has no solution
(b) If $f(x_1) = 3$ and $f(x_2) = 4$, then $x_1 + x_2 = 11$
(c) If $f(x_1) = 3$ and $f(x_2) = 4$, then $\frac{x_2}{x_1} = 2$
(d) $f^{-1}(1) + f^{-1}(2) = 3$

25. For the function $f(x) = \sqrt{\log_{\left(\frac{x-[x]}{1+x-[x]}\right)}([x]^2 - 3[x] + 3)}$

(a) Domain of $f(x)$ is $(1, 3) - \{2\}$
(b) Domain of $f(x)$ is $[0, 4]$
(c) Range of $f(x)$ is $[0, \infty)$
(d) Range of $f(x)$ is a singleton set

26. Let $f(x) = \begin{cases} x^2 - 4x + 3, & x < 3 \\ x - 4, & x \geq 3 \end{cases}$ and $g(x) = \begin{cases} x - 3, & x < 4 \\ x^2 + 2x + 2, & x \geq 4 \end{cases}$, which one of the following is/are true?

(a) $(f + g)(3.5) = 0$ (b) $f(g(3)) = 3$
(c) $f(g(2)) = 1$ (d) $(f - g)(4) = 0$

27. The function g defined by $g(x) = \sin\alpha + \cos\alpha - 1$; $\alpha = \sin^{-1}\sqrt{\{x\}}$, where $\{\cdot\}$ denotes the fractional part function, is

(a) an even function (b) periodic function
(c) odd function (d) neither even nor odd

28. If $f(x)$ is a polynomial of degree n such that $f(0) = 0$, $f(1) = \frac{1}{2}, \ldots, f(n) = \frac{n}{n+1}$, then the value of $f(n+1)$ is

(a) 1, when n is even (b) $\frac{n}{n+2}$, when n is odd

(c) 1, when n is odd (d) $\frac{n}{n+2}$, when n is even

29. Let $f(x) = 1 - x - x^3$. Then, the real values of x satisfying the inequality, $1 - f(x) - f^3(x) > f(1-5x)$, are

(a) $(-2, 0)$ (b) $(0, 2)$ (c) $(2, \infty)$ (d) $(-\infty, -2)$

30. Let $f : R \to R$ defined by $f(x) = \cos^{-1}(-\{-x\})$, where $\{x\}$ denotes fractional part of x. Then, which of the following is/are correct?

(a) f is many one but not even function
(b) Range of f contains two prime numbers
(c) f is non-periodic
(d) Graph of f does not lie below X-axis

31. Which of the following pair(s) of function have same graphs?

(a) $f(x) = \frac{\sec x}{\cos x} - \frac{\tan x}{\cot x}, g(x) = \frac{\cos x}{\sec x} + \frac{\sin x}{\operatorname{cosec} x}$

(b) $f(x) = \operatorname{sgn}(x^2 - 4x + 5)$,
$g(x) = \operatorname{sgn}\left(\cos^2 x + \sin^2\left(x + \frac{\pi}{3}\right)\right)$,
where sgn denotes signum function.

(c) $f(x) = e^{\ln(x^2 + 3x + 3)}, g(x) = x^2 + 3x + 3$

(d) $f(x) = \frac{\sin x}{\sec x} + \frac{\cos x}{\operatorname{cosec} x}, g(x) = \frac{2\cos^2 x}{\cot x}$

32. Consider the following statements:

S_1 : A function can never be odd and even simultaneously.
S_2 : Domain of the function $f(x) = \log x^2$ is R
S_3 : Period of $\sin^{99} x$ is 2π
S_4 : $\sin(e^x)$ is a periodic function

Which of the following option is/are correct?

(a) S_1 and S_2 is incorrect (b) Only S_3 is correct
(c) S_4 is incorrect (d) Only S_1 is incorrect

33. The function $f(x) = \cos^{-1}\left(\frac{2[|\sin x| + |\cos x|]}{\sin^2 x + 2\sin x + \frac{11}{4}}\right)$ is defined if x belongs to (where $[\cdot]$ denotes greatest integer function and $|\cdot|$ denotes absolute value)

(a) $\left[0, \frac{7\pi}{6}\right]$ (b) $\left[0, \frac{\pi}{6}\right]$

(c) $\left[\frac{11\pi}{6}, 2\pi\right]$ (d) $\left[\frac{7\pi}{6}, \frac{11\pi}{6}\right]$

34. A real valued function $f(x)$ satisfies $(f(x))^2 \cdot f(1-x) = x + 3, \forall x \in D_f$, given that $f(x) f(1-x) \neq 0$, $\forall x \in R - \{-4\}$, then

(a) The domain of $f(x)$ is R
(b) The domain of $f(x)$ is $R - \{4\}$
(c) $f(x) = 0$ at $x = -3$
(d) $f(0) = \left(\frac{3}{2}\right)^{\frac{2}{3}}$

35. Let $f : R \to R$ be a function defined by $f(x+1) = \frac{f(x) - 5}{f(x) - 3}, \forall x \in R$. Then, which of the following statement(s) is/are true?

(a) $f(2008) = f(2004)$ (b) $f(2006) = f(2010)$
(c) $f(2006) = f(2002)$ (d) $f(2006) = f(2018)$

Passage Based Questions

Passage I

(Q. Nos. 36 and 37)

■ A tower has the following shape a truncated right circular cone (one with radii $2R$ (the lower base) and R (the upper base) and the height R bears a right circular cylinder whose radius is R, the height being $2R$. Finally a semisphere of radius R is mounted on the cylinder. Suppose that the cross-sectional area S of the tower is given by $f(x)$, where x is the distance of the cross-section from the lower base of the cone.

36. The domain of the function $f(x)$ is

(a) $(-\infty, \infty)$ (b) $[0, 4R]$ (c) $[0, R]$ (d) $[R, 4R]$

37. For $0 \leq x \leq R$, the function $f(x)$ is given by

(a) $\pi(2R - x)^2$ (b) $\pi(R - x)^2$
(c) πR^2 (d) $4\pi x^2$

Passage II

(Q. Nos. 38 and 39)

■ If $y = \log_a x, x > 0, a > 0, a \neq 1$

38. For each ordered pairs of real number x, y satisfying $\log_2(2x + y) = \log_4(x^2 + xy + 7y^2)$ there is a real number k such that $\log_3(3x + y) = \log_9(3x^2 + 4xy + ky^2)$, then the product of all possible values of k is

(a) 179 (b) 180 (c) 182 (d) 189

39. There is a unique positive real x such that the three numbers $\log_8 2x, \log_4 x, \log_2 x$ in that order form a geometric progression with positive common ratio, if $x = \frac{m}{n}$ where m, n relative prime positive integer, then $m + n$ is

(a) 22 (b) 21 (c) 17 (d) 19

Passage III

(Q. Nos. 40 and 41)

- Let $f: R \to R$ be a function satisfying $f(2-x) = f(2+x)$ and $f(20-x) = f(x)$, $\forall x \in R$. For this function f answer the following questions.

40. If $f(0) = 5$, then minimum possible number of values of x satisfying $f(x) = 5$, $\forall x \in [0, 170]$, is

(a) 21 (b) 12 (c) 11 (d) 22

41. Graph of $y = f(x)$ is

(a) symmetrical about $x = 18$ (b) symmetrical about $x = 5$
(c) symmetrical about $x = 8$ (d) symmetrical about $x = 20$

Passage IV

(Q. Nos. 42 and 43)

- Let ω be non-real fifth root of 3 and $x = \omega^3 + \omega^4$. If $x^5 = f(x)$, where $f(x)$ is real quadratic polynomial, with roots α and β, $(\alpha, \beta, \in C)$, then determine $f(x)$ and answer the following questions.

42. Which of the following is not true?

(a) $\alpha + \beta = -3$ (b) $\alpha\beta = \frac{12}{5}$

(c) $|\alpha - \beta| = \sqrt{\frac{3}{5}}$ (d) $|\alpha| + |\beta| = 4\sqrt{\frac{3}{5}}$

43. If α and β are represented by points A and B in argand plane, then circumradius of ΔOAB, where O is origin, is

(a) $\frac{4}{5}$ (b) $\frac{8}{5}$ (c) $\frac{16}{5}$ (d) $\frac{32}{5}$

Stem Based Questions

Stem I

(Q. Nos. 44 and 45)

- Let $f: R - \{0, 1\} \to R$ be a function satisfying the relation $f(x) + f\left(\frac{x-1}{x}\right) = x, \forall x \in R - \{0, 1\}$.

Based on this, answer the following questions.

44. The value of $|f(-1)|$ is ....

45. The value of $f(3)$ is ....

Stem II

(Q. Nos. 46 and 47)

- The builders of the Trans-Alaska pipeline used insulted pads to keep the heat from the pipeline from melting the permanent frozen soil beneath. To design the pad, it was necessary to take into account the variation in air temperature through the year. The function fit into data was $f(x) = 37 \sin\left(\frac{2\pi}{365}(x - 101)\right) + 25$ where f is temperature in Fahrenheit and x is the number of the day counting from the beginning of the year.

46. The highest temperature will be ....

47. The lowest temperature will be ....

Single Integer Type Questions

48. Let $f(x) = \left| |x^2 - 4| - |x - a| \right|$, then the number of integers in the range of a so that $f(x) = 0$ has four distinct real roots is ....

49. If $x^2 + y^2 = 4$, then maximum value of $\left(\frac{x^3 + y^3}{x + y}\right)$ is ....

50. Let $f(n)$ denotes the square of the sum of the digits of natural number n, where $f^2(n)$ denotes $f(f(n))$, $f^3(n)$ denotes $f(f(f(n)))$ and so on. The value of $\frac{f^{2011}(2011) - f^{2010}(2011)}{f^{2013}(2011) - f^{2012}(2011)}$ is ....

51. The number of integral solutions of $\frac{1}{x} + \frac{1}{y} = \frac{1}{6}$ with $x \leq y$ is α. The value of $\alpha - 6$ is ....

52. If $f(x) = \frac{x^4 + x^2 + 1}{x^2 - x + 1}$, then value of $f(\omega^n)$ (where 'ω' is the non-real root of the equation $z^3 = 1$ and n is a multiple of 3), is ....

53. If $f^2(x) \cdot f\left(\frac{1-x}{1+x}\right) = x^3$, $[x \neq -1, 1$ and $f(x) \neq 0]$ the value of $|[f(-2)]|$ (where $[\cdot]$ is the greatest integer function), is ....

54. An odd function is symmetric about the vertical line $x = a (a > 0)$ and if $\sum_{r=0}^{\infty} [f(1 + 4r)]^r = 8$, then the numerical value of $8f(1)$ is ....

55. The period of the function $f(x)$ which satisfies the relation $f(x) + f(x+4) = f(x+2) + f(x+6)$ is ....

56. If a non-zero function $f(x)$ is symmetrical about $y = x$, then the value of p (constant) such that $f^2(x) = (f^{-1}(x))^2 - px \cdot f(x) \cdot f^{-1}(x) + 2x^2 f(x)$, $\forall x \in R^+$ is ....

57. Let $f: R \to R$ and $f(x) = \frac{3x^2 + mx + n}{x^2 + 1}$. If the range of this function is $[-4, 3]$, then the value of $\frac{m^2 + n^2}{4}$ is ....

Numerical Value Type Questions

58. $f(x)$ and $g(x)$ are linear function such that $\forall x$, $f(g(x))$ and $g(f(x))$ are identity functions. If $f(0) = 4$ and $g(5) = 17$, then compute $f(136)$.

59. Let $A=\{1, 2, 3, 4\}$ and $B=\{3, 4, 5, 6, 7\}$ are two sets. Let n be the number of one-one functions $f: A \to B$ such that $f(i) \neq i, \forall\, i \in A$ and m is the number of one-one functions $f: A \to B$ such that $|f(i)-i| \leq 3, \forall\, i \in A$, then the value of $n-m$ is ....

60. If $A_1=\{1, 2, 3, 4\}$ and $A_2=\{5, 6, 7, 8\}$; $A_3=\{9, 10\}$; $A_4=\{11, 12, 13, 14\}$. Let n_{ij} = Number of invertible function from A_i to A_j, then Σn_{ij} equals ....

61. Least value of the expression $\dfrac{1}{2bx-(x^2+b^2+\sin^2 x)}$, $x \in [-1, 0]$, $b \in [2, 3]$ is λ. The value of $\dfrac{1}{\lambda^2}$ is ....

62. Let $f: A \to B$ be any function where A is a set containing the positive integral solution of the inequality $\operatorname{cosec}^{-1}(\operatorname{cosec} 2) > x^2-3x$ and B is the set of all divisors of the natural number 2010. If $f(i) \leq f(j), \forall\, i < j$, then the total number of mappings from A to B is ....

63. The smallest value of a for which the inequality $(a-1)x^2-(a+1)x+(a-1) \geq 0$ holds, $\forall\, x > 2$ is $\dfrac{m}{n}$ (where m and n are coprime), then $m+n$ is equal to ....

64. Let $f(x, y)$ be defined for $x, y \in N$ and satisfy $f(x, x)=x$, $f(x, x+y)=\left(1+\dfrac{x}{y}\right) \cdot f(x, y)$, $f(x, y)=f(y, x)$. Then, $f(52, 14)$ is ....

65. Let $f:(-1, 1) \to R$ be such that $f(\cos 4\theta)=\dfrac{2}{2-\sec^2 \theta}$ for all $\theta \in \left(0, \dfrac{\pi}{4}\right) \cup \left(\dfrac{\pi}{4}, \dfrac{\pi}{2}\right)$. Then, the value of $f\left(\dfrac{1}{3}\right)$ is ......

66. The polynomial $R(x)$ is the remainder upon dividing x^{2007} by x^2-5x+6. If $R(0)$ can be expressed as $ab(a^c-b^c)$, then the value of $(a+b+c)$ ....

67. If f is a polynomial function satisfying $2+f(x) \cdot f(y)=f(x)+f(y)+f(xy), \forall\, x, y \in R$ and if $f(2)=5$, then $f(f(2))$ is equal to ....

Matching Type Questions

68. Match the following column.

	Column I		Column II
A.	Range of $\operatorname{sgn}\{x\}$ is (where $\{\cdot\}$ represents fraction part function)	p.	$\{1\}$
B.	Domain of $\sin^{-1} x+\sin^{-1}(1-x)$ is	q.	$[0, 1)$
C.	Range of $\sqrt{\dfrac{2\tan^{-1} x}{\pi}}$ is	r.	$\{0, 1\}$
D.	Range of $\dfrac{2}{\pi} \cdot \sin^{-1}[x^2+x+1]$ is (where $[\cdot]$ represents the greatest integer function)	s.	$[0, 1]$

69. Match the functions in Column I to the statement(s) in Column II, which hold true for that function.

	Column I		Column II
A.	$f(x)=\sin^2 2x-2\sin^2 x$	p.	Range contains no natural number
B.	$f(x)=\dfrac{4}{\pi}(\sin^{-1}(\sin \pi x))$	q.	Range contains atleast one integer
C.	$f(x)=\sqrt{\ln(\cos(\sin x))}$	r.	Many one but not even function
D.	$f(x)=\tan^{-1}\left(\dfrac{x^2+1}{x^2+\sqrt{3}}\right)$	s.	Both many one and even function
		t.	Periodic but not odd function

70. Match the functions Column I to in with Column II to correctly difine their nature.

	Column I		Column II
A.	$x^2 \sin\left\{\dfrac{1}{\left[\sin\left(\dfrac{1}{x}\right)\right]}\right\}$	p.	an odd function
B.	$\cos x \cdot \log \dfrac{1+\tan x}{1-\tan x}$	q.	an even function
C.	$\sqrt[3]{1+x+x^2}+\sqrt[3]{1-x+x^2}$	r.	neither odd nor even
D.	$\sqrt{1+2x+3x^2}-\sqrt{1-2x+3x^2}$	s.	cannot be said

71. Match the columns.

	Column I		Column II
A.	Let $x=\{a_1, a_2, \ldots a_6\}$ and $y=\{b_1, b_2, b_3\}$. The number of function f from x to y such that it is onto and there are exactly three elements x in X such that $f(x)=b_1$ is	p.	2
B.	The number of real solutions for x, y it $y=|\sin x|$ and $y=\sin^{-1}(\sin x)$ where $x \in [-2\pi, 2\pi]$ is	q.	5
C.	If a, b and c are distinct positive real numbers, such that $a+b+c=1$, then $\dfrac{(1+a)(1+b)(1+c)}{(1-a)(1-b)(1-c)}$ is greater than	r.	120
D.	Period of the function $[6x+7]+\cos x\pi-6x$, where $[\cdot]$ denotes the greater integer function is	s.	8
		t.	0

Previous Year Questions

72. Let $f: R \to R$ be a function such that $f(x+y) = f(x) + f(y)$ for all $x, y \in R$ and $g: R \to (0, \infty)$ be a function such that $g(x+y) = g(x)g(y)$ for all $x, y \in R$. If $f\left(\frac{-3}{5}\right) = 12$ and $g\left(\frac{-1}{3}\right) = 2$, then the value of $\left(f\left(\frac{1}{4}\right) + g(-2) - 8\right)g(0)$ is ....

[Numerical Value Type, 2024 Adv.]

73. Let the function $f: [0, 2] \to R$ be defined by $f(x) = \frac{4^x}{4^x + 2}$. Then, the value of

$f\left(\frac{1}{40}\right) + f\left(\frac{2}{40}\right) + f\left(\frac{3}{40}\right) + \ldots + f\left(\frac{39}{40}\right) - f\left(\frac{1}{2}\right)$ is ....

[Numerical Value Type, 2020 Adv.]

74. If the function $f: R \to R$ is defined by $f(x) = |x|(x - \sin x)$, then which of the following statements is true?

[Single Correct Type, 2020 Adv.]

(a) f is one-one, but not onto
(b) f is onto, but not one-one
(c) f is both one-one and onto
(d) f is neither one-one nor onto

EXERCISE 3

Challenging Problems

1. In which of the following cases there does not exist any function

(i) $f^2(x^2) + f(2^x) + 1 = 0, \ \forall x \in R$

(ii) $f^2(x^2 - x) - 4f(2x - 2) + x^2 + x = 0, \forall x \in R$

(iii) $f(x) + f\left(\frac{1}{x}\right) = 2x, \ \forall x \in R - \{0\}$

(iv) $f(\sin x) + f(\cos x) = x, \ \forall x \in R$

2. Find the domain and range of the function :

$$f(x) = \sin^{-1}[x^2] + [\{\ln \sqrt{x - [x]}\}] + \cot^{-1}\left(\frac{1}{1 + \sqrt{2}x^2}\right)$$

3. The domain of $f(x) = \frac{1}{\sqrt{\sin(\cos x)}} + \sin^{-1}\left(\frac{2x}{\pi}\right) + \frac{1}{\{-x\}} + \frac{1}{\ln\left(1 - \left[\tan\frac{x}{2}\right]\right) - \left[-\tan\frac{x}{2}\right]}$ is

4. Find the value of expression

$$\sqrt{1 + 2\sqrt{1 + 3\sqrt{1 + 4\sqrt{1 + 5\sqrt{\ldots \infty}}}}}.$$

5. If a, b, c, d, e are positive real numbers, such that $a + b + c + d + e = 8$ and $a^2 + b^2 + c^2 + d^2 + e^2 = 16$, then find the range of e.

6. Find the set of all solutions of the equation $2^{|y|} - |2^{y-1} - 1| = 2^{y-1} + 1$.

7. Find all possible values of x satisfying

$$\frac{[x]}{[x-2]} - \frac{[x-2]}{[x]} = \frac{8\{x\} + 12}{[x-2][x]}.$$

(where $[\cdot]$ denotes the greatest integer function and $\{\}$ is the fractional part)

8. If the equation $(a-2)(x - [x])^2 + 2(x - [x]) + a^2 = 0$, (where $[x]$ denotes the greatest integer $\le x$) has exactly one solution in $(2, 3)$, then find all possible values of a.

9. Solve the equation

$$10^{(x+1)(3x+4)} - 2 \cdot 10^{(x+1)(x+2)} = 10^{1-x-x^2}.$$

10. Find the real solution of $[x] + [5x] + [10x] + [20x] = 36K + 35$, $K \in$ integer, where $[\cdot]$ denotes the greatest integral function.

11. Let $f: N \to N$ be a function such that

$$x - f(x) = 19\left[\frac{x}{19}\right] - 90\left[\frac{f(x)}{90}\right], \forall x \in N,$$ where $[\cdot]$ denotes the greatest integer function.

If $1900 < f(1990) < 2000$, then find all the possible values of $f(1990)$.

12. Solve the system of equations $|x^2 - 2x| + y = 1$, $x^2 + |y| = 1$.

13. Solve $\sqrt{2+\sqrt{2+\sqrt{2+x}}} + \sqrt{3}\sqrt{2-\sqrt{2+\sqrt{2+x}}} = 2x$ for $x \geq 0$.

14. If $f(x)$ is a function such that $\dfrac{f(x-1)+f(x+1)}{2f(x)} = \sin 60°$ and $f(5) = 100$, then find $\sum_{r=0}^{99} f(5+12r)$.

15. Find the solution of the equation $2x^2 - 5x - 2 = \dfrac{5-\sqrt{9-8x}}{4}$, where $x < \dfrac{5}{4}$.

Answer Key

Exercise 1

1. (a)	2. (d)	3. (b)	4. (c)	5. (c)	6. (d)	7. (c)	8. (b)	9. (c)	10. (b)
11. (d)	12. (d)	13. (c)	14. (b)	15. (d)	16. (a)	17. (c)	18. (b)	19. (d)	20. (a)
21. (a)	22. (a)	23. (b)	24. (a)	25. (b)	26. (b)	27. (a)	28. (d)	29. (b)	30. (b)
31. (10)	32. (2)	33. (5)	34. (2)	35. (5)	36. (15)	37. (0)	38. (126)	39. (1)	40. (3)
41. (1)	42. (5)	43. (41)	44. (3)	45. (10)	46. (4)	47. (3)	48. (0)	49. (11)	50. (1)
51. (b)	52. (18)	53. (51)	54. (d)	55. (c)	56. (a)	57. (b)	58. (d)	59. (b)	60. (b)
61. (d)	62. (a)	63. (c)	64. (b)	65. (432)	66. (c)	67. (c)	68. (b)	69. (c)	70. (b)
71. (b)	72. (490)	73. (a)	74. (d)						

Exercise 2

1. (c)	2. (c)	3. (b)	4. (c)	5. (c)	6. (c)	7. (c)	8. (b)	9. (c)	10. (b)
11. (b)	12. (b)	13. (c)	14. (c)	15. (a)	16. (b)	17. (d)	18. (a)	19. (b)	20. (b)
21. (a,c)	22. (b,d)	23. (b,c,d)	24. (c,d)	25. (a,d)	26. (a,b)	27. (a,b)	28. (c,d)	29. (a,c)	30. (a,b,d)
31. (a,b,c,d)	32. (a,b,c)	33. (a,b,c)	34. (b,c,d)	35. (a,b,c)	36. (b)	37. (a)	38. (d)	39. (c)	40. (b)
41. (a)	42. (d)	43. (a)	44. (1.25)	45. (0.41)	46. (62)	47. (−12)	48. (7)	49. (6)	50. (1)
51. (4)	52. (3)	53. (2)	54. (7)	55. (8)	56. (2)	57. (4)	58. (12)	59. (62)	60. (144)
61. (16)	62. (816)	63. (10)	64. (364)	65. $\left(1 \pm \sqrt{\frac{3}{2}}\right)$	66. (2011)	67. (26)			

68. (A) → (r), (B) → (s), (C) → (q), (D) → (r)

69. (A) → (p,q,s,t), (B) → (q,r), (C) → (p,q,s), (D) → (p,s)

70. (A) → (p), (B) → (p), (C) → (q), (D) → (p)

71. (A) → (r), (B) → (q), (C) → (s), (D) → (p)

72. (51) 73. (19) 74. (c)

Solutions

Exercise 1 - JEE Main Pattern

1. For $f(x)$ to be defined $\dfrac{1-2^x}{5^{-x}-5} \geq 0$ and $5^{-x}-5 \neq 0$

$$\Rightarrow \quad \frac{2^x-1}{5^{-x}-5} \leq 0 \text{ and } 5^{-x}-5 \neq 0$$

Now, $\quad 2^x - 1 = 0 \Rightarrow x = 0$

and $\quad 5^{-x} - 5 = 0 \Rightarrow x = -1$

$$\underset{-1}{\overset{-}{}} \quad + \quad \underset{0}{\overset{-}{}}$$

(Sign scheme: $-$ for $x<-1$, $+$ on $(-1, 0)$, $-$ for $x>0$.)

The sign of $\dfrac{2^x-1}{5^{-x}-5}$ is positive in the interval $(-1, 0]$.

Hence, from the sign scheme $x \in (-\infty, -1) \cup [0, \infty)$

$\therefore$ Domain of $f(x)$ is $(-\infty, -1) \cup [0, \infty)$.

2. Given that $f(x) = 4^{-x^2} + \cos^{-1}\left(\dfrac{x}{2} - 1\right) + \log(\cos x)$

Here, 4^{-x^2} is defined for $(-\pi/2, \pi/2)$

$\cos^{-1}\left(\dfrac{x}{2}-1\right)$ is defined, if

$$-1 \leq \frac{x}{2} - 1 \leq 1$$

$$\Rightarrow \quad 0 \leq \frac{x}{2} \leq 2 \Rightarrow 0 \leq x \leq 4$$

and $\log(\cos x)$ is defined, if $\cos x > 0$

$$\Rightarrow \quad -\pi/2 < x < \pi/2$$

Hence, $f(x) = 4^{-x^2} + \cos^{-1}\left(\dfrac{x}{2}-1\right) + \log(\cos x)$ is defined,

if $x \in [0, \pi/2)$.

3. We have, $\quad f(x) = \dfrac{5^x}{5^x + \sqrt{5}}$

$$\therefore \quad f(1-x) = \frac{5^{1-x}}{5^{1-x}+\sqrt{5}} = \frac{5}{5+5^x\sqrt{5}} = \frac{\sqrt{5}}{\sqrt{5}+5^x}$$

$\therefore \; f(x) + f(1-x) = 1$

Let $S = f\left(\dfrac{1}{3006}\right) + f\left(\dfrac{2}{3006}\right) + \ldots + f\left(\dfrac{3005}{3006}\right)$

or $S = f\left(\dfrac{3005}{3006}\right) + f\left(\dfrac{3004}{3006}\right) + \ldots + f\left(\dfrac{1}{3006}\right)$

$$\Rightarrow 2S = \left(f\left(\frac{1}{3006}\right) + f\left(\frac{3005}{3006}\right)\right) + \left(f\left(\frac{2}{3006}\right) + f\left(\frac{3004}{3006}\right)\right) + \ldots + \left(f\left(\frac{3005}{3006}\right) + f\left(\frac{1}{3006}\right)\right)$$

$$\Rightarrow 2S = 1 + 1 + \ldots + 1 = 3005$$

$$\therefore \quad S = \frac{3005}{2} = \frac{m}{n}$$

$\therefore \quad m = 3005$ and $n = 2$

$$m + n = 3007$$

Sum of digits $= 10$

4. Given, $f(x) = \pi\left[\dfrac{\sqrt{x+7}-4}{x-9}\right]$

Clearly, domain of $f(x) = [-7, \infty) - \{9\}$

Now, $f(x) = \dfrac{\pi(x+7-16)}{(x-9)(\sqrt{x+7}+4)} = \dfrac{\pi}{\sqrt{x+7}+4}$

So, range of $f(x)$ is $\left(0, \dfrac{\pi}{4}\right] - \{\pi/8\}$.

Hence, the range of $y = \tan(2f(x))$ is $(0, \infty) - \{1\}$.

5.

> **Decoding the Question**
>
> The sum of n terms of a GP $= \dfrac{a(r^n-1)}{r-1}, r \neq 1$,
> where, a is first term and r is common ratio.

We have, $f(x+y) = f(x) \cdot f(y)$ and $f(1) = 2$

$$\therefore \quad f(1+1) = f(1) \cdot f(1) \Rightarrow f(2) = 2^2$$

$$f(2+1) = f(2) \cdot f(1) = 2^3$$

$$f(4) = f(2) \cdot f(2) = 2^4 \text{ and so on ......}$$

$\therefore \; 2, 2^2, 2^3, 2^4 \ldots$

$$\therefore \quad \sum_{k=1}^{n} f(k) = 510$$

$$\therefore \quad 2 + 4 + 8 + \ldots = 510 \Rightarrow \frac{2(2^n-1)}{1} = 510$$

$$\Rightarrow \quad 2^n = 256 \Rightarrow 2^n = 2^8 \Rightarrow n = 8$$

6. $\because f(x) = \dfrac{\sqrt{x^2+1}-3x}{\sqrt{x^2+1}+x} \Rightarrow \sqrt{x^2+1}+x \neq 0, x \in R$

$$\Rightarrow f'(x) = \frac{\left(\dfrac{2x}{2\sqrt{x^2+1}} - 3\right)(\sqrt{x^2+1}+x) - \left(\dfrac{2x}{2\sqrt{x^2+1}}+1\right)(\sqrt{x^2+1}-3x)}{(\sqrt{x^2+1}+x)^2}$$

$$\Rightarrow f'(x) = \frac{\dfrac{x-3\sqrt{x^2+1}}{\sqrt{x^2+1}}(\sqrt{x^2+1}+x) - \left(\dfrac{x+\sqrt{x^2+1}}{\sqrt{x^2+1}}\right)(\sqrt{x^2+1}-3x)}{(\sqrt{x^2+1}+x)^2}$$

$\Rightarrow f'(x) = 0$

$$x\sqrt{x^2+1} - x^2 - 3x^2 - 3 - 3x\sqrt{x^2+1}$$

$$\Rightarrow f'(x) = \frac{-x\sqrt{x^2+1} + 3x^2 - x^2 - 1 + 3x\sqrt{x^2+1}}{\sqrt{x^2+1}(\sqrt{x^2+1}+x)^2}$$

$\Rightarrow f'(x) = -2x^2 - 4 = 0$

$\Rightarrow f'(x) = -(2x^2+4) = 0$

$\Rightarrow f'(x) < 0$

So, $f(x)$ is always decreasing.

So, we will check function by putting the value from $(-\infty, \infty)$ to find its range.

$$\Rightarrow f(x)|_{x\to-\infty} = \frac{\sqrt{x^2+1} - 3x}{\sqrt{x^2+1} + x}$$

$$\Rightarrow f(x)|_{x\to-\infty} = \frac{x\sqrt{1+\frac{1}{x^2}} - 3x}{x\sqrt{1+\frac{1}{x^2}} + x} = \frac{1+3}{1-1} \to \infty$$

$$\Rightarrow f(x)|_{x\to\infty} = \frac{1-3}{1+1} = \frac{-2}{2} = -1$$

So, range $\in (-1, \infty)$

7.

> **Decoding the Question**
> Greatest integer function is denoted by $[x]$, gives the value round off the real number $[x] > 0$, if $x > 1$ and $[x] = x - \{x\}$.

We have, $f(x) = \ln\left(\ln\dfrac{x}{\{x\}}\right)$, $f(x)$ is defined

When $\ln\dfrac{x}{\{x\}} > 0$ and $\dfrac{x}{\{x\}} > 0$

$\Rightarrow \quad \dfrac{x}{\{x\}} > 1$ and $\dfrac{x}{\{x\}} > 0$ ...(i)

Here, $\quad 0 < \{x\} < 1$

$\Rightarrow \quad x \notin I$ ...(ii)

$\Rightarrow \quad x > \{x\}$ and $x > 0$

$\Rightarrow \quad x - \{x\} > 0$ and $x > 0$

$\Rightarrow \quad [x] > 0$ and $x > 0$

or $\quad x \ge 1$ and $x > 0$

or $\quad x \ge 1$

or $\quad x > 1$ ...(iii)

Hence, the domain of $f = (1, \infty) - I$

8. Given, $f(x) = \log[ax^3 + (a+b)x^2 + (b+c)x + c]$

$f(x)$ to be defined

$ax^3 + (a+b)x^2 + (b+c)x + c > 0$

$\Rightarrow \quad (ax^3 + bx^2 + cx) + (ax^2 + bx + c) > 0$

$\Rightarrow \quad x(ax^2 + bx + c) + (ax^2 + bx + c) > 0$

$\Rightarrow \quad (x+1)(ax^2 + bx + c) > 0$

$\Rightarrow \quad (x+1) > 0$

$\Rightarrow \quad x > -1$

$[\because b^2 - 4ac < 0$ and $a > 0]$

Hence, the domain of $f(x)$ is $(-1, \infty)$.

9. We have, $f(x) = \log_{\sqrt{2}}(2 - \log_2(16\sin^2 x + 1))$;

For domain, $\quad 2 - \log_2(16\sin^2 x + 1) > 0$

$\Rightarrow \quad \log_2(16\sin^2 x + 1) < 2$

$\Rightarrow \quad 16\sin^2 x + 1 < 4$

Also, $\quad 16\sin^2 x + 1 \ge 1$

$\Rightarrow \quad 1 \le 16\sin^2 x + 1 < 4$

$\Rightarrow \quad 0 \le \log_2(16\sin^2 x + 1) < 2$

$\Rightarrow \quad -2 < -\log_2(16\sin^2 x + 1) \le 0$

$\Rightarrow \quad -\infty < \log_{\sqrt{2}}(2 - \log_2(16\sin^2 x + 1)) \le 2$

$\therefore$ Range $= (-\infty, 2]$

10. $f(x) = \log_3(\log_3|\cos x| - \log_{x^2-4x+6}|\cos x|)$

$$= \log_3\left(\frac{1}{\log_{|\cos x|} 3} - \frac{1}{\log_{|\cos x|} x^2 - 4x + 6}\right)$$

For log to be defined $|\cos x| \ne 0, 1$

$$= \log_3\left(\frac{\log_{|\cos x|}(x^2-4x+6) - \log_{|\cos x|} 3}{\log_{|\cos x|} 3 \cdot \log_{|\cos x|} x^2 - 4x + 6}\right)$$

$$\therefore \quad \frac{\log_{|\cos x|}\left(\frac{x^2-4x+6}{3}\right)}{\log_{|\cos x|} 3 \cdot \log_{|\cos x|}(x^2-4x+6)} > 0 \Rightarrow \frac{x^2-4x+6}{3} < 1$$

$\Rightarrow \quad x^2 - 4x + 3 < 0 \Rightarrow x \in (1, 3)$

But $|\cos x| \ne 0 \Rightarrow x \ne \pi/2$

$\therefore \quad x \in (1, \pi/2) \cup (\pi/2, 3)$

11. We have, $\sec^{-1}\left[\dfrac{7 - 5(x^2+3)}{2(x^2+2)}\right]$

$$= \sec^{-1}\left[\frac{-5}{2} + \frac{2}{2(x^2+2)}\right] \quad [x^2 + 2 \ge 2]$$

$$= \sec^{-1}\left(\frac{-5}{2} + \frac{1}{x^2+2}\right) \quad \left[\because \frac{1}{x^2+2} \le \frac{1}{2}\right]$$

$$\le \sec^{-1}(-2) \quad \left[\because \frac{-5}{2} + \frac{1}{x^2+2} \le \frac{-5}{2} + \frac{1}{2} = -2\right]$$

$$\le \pi - \sec^{-1}(2) \le \frac{2\pi}{3}$$

12. The given expression can be written as

$$\left(\sin^{-1} x + \frac{\pi}{2}\right)^2 + \left(\tan^{-1} y + \frac{\pi}{2}\right)^2$$

Hence, the maximum value is less than $2\pi^2$

$\Rightarrow \quad k \in (0, 2\pi^2)$

$$\therefore \quad \left[\frac{k}{2\pi^2}\right] = 0$$

13. We have, $f(x) = \dfrac{x}{1+x^2}$

$$\therefore \quad f\left(\frac{1}{x}\right) = \frac{1/x}{1 + 1/x^2} = \frac{x}{1+x^2} = f(x)$$

$\therefore \quad f\left(\frac{1}{2}\right) = f(2), f\left(\frac{1}{3}\right) = f(3), f\left(\frac{1}{4}\right) = f(4)$

and so on.

So, $f(x)$ is many-one function

Again, let $\quad y = f(x) \Rightarrow y = \dfrac{x}{1+x^2}$

$\Rightarrow \quad y + x^2y = x \Rightarrow yx^2 - x + y = 0$

As, $x \in R$

$\therefore \quad D \geq 0$

$\therefore \quad (-1)^2 - 4y \times y \geq 0$

$\Rightarrow \quad 1 - 4y^2 \geq 0 \Rightarrow (1-2y)(1+2y) \geq 0$

$\Rightarrow \quad y \in \left[-1/2, \frac{1}{2}\right]$

Here, the range = codomain = $\left[\frac{-1}{2}, \frac{1}{2}\right]$

So, $f(x)$ is surjective function

Hence, $f(x)$ is surjective but not injective.

14. To find range in given domain $[a, b]$, put $f'(x) = 0$ and find $x = \alpha_1, \alpha_2, \ldots \alpha_n \in [a, b]$.

Now, find $\{f(a), f(\alpha_1), f(\alpha_2), \ldots f(\alpha_n), f(b)\}$ its greatest and least values gives you range

Now, $\quad f : [0, 3] \to [2, 30]$

$f(x) = 2x^3 - 15x^2 + 36x + 2$

$\therefore \quad f'(x) = 6x^2 - 30x + 36$

$= 6(x-2)(x-3)$

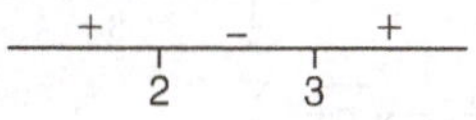

For given domain $[0, 3]$, $f(x)$ is increasing as well as decreasing.

$\Rightarrow f(x)$ is many-one.

Now, on putting $f'(x) = 0 \Rightarrow x = 2, 3$

This, for range $f(0) = 2$, $f(2) = 30$, $f(3) = 29$

$\Rightarrow \quad$ Range $\in [2, 30]$

$\therefore f(x)$ is onto but not one-one.

15. **Decoding the Question**

A function is called an even function, if its graph is unchanged under reflection.

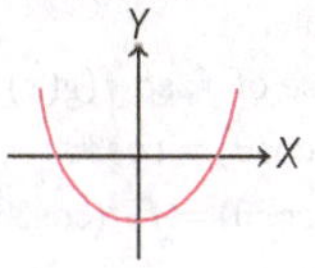

We have, $f(x) = \frac{1}{2}\left(\sqrt{\sqrt{2x^2+3} - x + x^2} + \sqrt{\sqrt{2x^2+3} + x + x^2}\right)$

Now, find $f(-x) = \frac{1}{2}\left(\sqrt{\sqrt{2(-x)^2+3} - (-x) + (-x)^2} + \sqrt{\sqrt{2(-x)^2+3} - x + (-x)^2}\right)$

$= \frac{1}{2}\left[\sqrt{\sqrt{2x^2+3} + x + x^2} + \sqrt{\sqrt{2x^2+3} - x + x^2}\right]$

$= \frac{1}{2}\left[\sqrt{\sqrt{2x^2+3} - x + x^2} + \sqrt{\sqrt{2x^2+3} + x + x^2}\right]$

$= f(x)$

So, $\quad f(-x) = f(x)$

Hence, $f(x)$ is an even function, so neither one-one nor onto.

16. We have, $f(x) = \begin{cases} \dfrac{x-1}{2}; & x = \text{odd} \\ \dfrac{-x}{2}; & x = \text{even} \end{cases} \quad f(x) : N \to Z$

Let $x = \text{odd} = (2n+1); n > 0$

$f(x) = \dfrac{2n+1-1}{2} = n \Rightarrow +$ ve integer

Let $x = \text{even} = 2m\,; m > 0$

$f(x) = \dfrac{-2m}{2} = -m \Rightarrow -$ ve integer

$\Rightarrow$ Range = codomain

$\Rightarrow$ onto and clearly $f(x)$ is one-one function.

Hence, $f(x)$ is bijective.

17. We have, $f(x+1) = f(x) + f(1)$

$\Rightarrow f(x+1) - f(x) = f(1)$

From an AP with common difference $f(1)$

and general term $T_n = f(1) + (x-1)f(1) = xf(1)$

$\Rightarrow \quad f(x) = xf(1)$

Clearly, f is one-one.

For fog to be one-one, g must be one-one.

For f to be onto, $f(x)$ should take all the values of natural number.

As, $f(x)$ is increasing, $f(1) = 1 \Rightarrow f(x) = x$

If g is many one, then fog is many one.

So, 'If g is onto, then fog is one-one' is not true.

18. A function is one-one and onto at 50 elements of domain set.

20 elements have following restriction

$f(5) \geq f(10) \geq f(10) \geq \ldots \geq f(100)$

So, all elements 5, 10, 15, ... 100

i.e. 20 elements have one choice.

Remaining $50 - 20 = 30$ elements has taken from 50 elements

$\therefore$ Number of ways ${}^{50}P_{30}$.

19. Given, $\quad f(x) = \dfrac{x-1}{x+1}$

$f(f(x)) = f\left(\dfrac{x-1}{x+1}\right) = \dfrac{\dfrac{x-1}{x+1} - 1}{\dfrac{x-1}{x+1} + 1}$

$\therefore \quad f^2(x) = -1/x$

Then, $f^3(x) = f(f^2(x)) = f\left(-\dfrac{1}{x}\right) \Rightarrow f^3(x) = \dfrac{-\dfrac{1}{x} - 1}{-\dfrac{1}{x} + 1}$

$\therefore \quad f^3(x) = \dfrac{x+1}{1-x}$

So, $\quad f^6(x) = f^3(f^3(x)) = \dfrac{\dfrac{x+1}{1-x} + 1}{1 - \dfrac{x+1}{1-x}} = \dfrac{-1}{x}$

and $f^7(x) = f(f^6(x)) = f\left(-\dfrac{1}{x}\right) = \dfrac{x+1}{1-x}$

$\therefore -f^6(8) + f^7(9) = -\dfrac{1}{8} + \dfrac{9+1}{1-9} = -\dfrac{1}{8} + \left(\dfrac{10}{-8}\right) = -\dfrac{11}{8}$

20. Given, $f(x) = \dfrac{(\tan 2°)x + \log_e(124)}{x\log_e(144) - \tan 2°}$.

Now, consider a similar function.

$\therefore \quad f(x) = \dfrac{Ax + B}{Cx - A}$

Now, $f(f(x)) = \dfrac{A\left(\dfrac{Ax+B}{Cx-A}\right) + B}{C\left(\dfrac{Ax+B}{Cx-A}\right) - A}$

$= \dfrac{A^2x + AB + BCx - AB}{ACx + BC - ACx + A^2} = \dfrac{x(A^2 + BC)}{(BC + A^2)} = x$

$\therefore \quad f(f(x)) = x$

Similarly, $f\left(f\left(\dfrac{2}{x}\right)\right) = \dfrac{2}{x}$

On applying, AM ≥ GM $\Rightarrow \left(x + \dfrac{2}{x}\right) \geq x \cdot \dfrac{2}{x} = 2 \qquad [\because x > 0]$

$\Rightarrow \quad f(f(x)) + f\left(f\left(\dfrac{2}{x}\right)\right) \geq 2$

Hence, the least value is 2.

21. We have, $f(x) = (\ln x)^2 + 3\ln x + 2$

Let $\ln x = t, \quad x \in (0, e^{-3/2}]$

$\Rightarrow \quad t \in (-\infty, -3/2]$

$\therefore \quad f(x) = t^2 + 3t + 2$

$f(x) = \left(t + \dfrac{3}{2}\right)^2 + 2 - 9/4$

$f(x) = \left[t + \dfrac{3}{2}\right]^2 - \dfrac{1}{4}$

$\therefore$ Range of $f(x)$ is $\left[\dfrac{-1}{4}, \infty\right)$.

$f(x) = -\dfrac{1}{4}$, when $t = \dfrac{-3}{2}$

$\Rightarrow \quad \ln x = \dfrac{-3}{2} \Rightarrow x = e^{-3/2}$

Now, $y = (\ln x)^2 + 3\ln x + 2$

$(\ln x)^2 + 3\ln x + 2 - y = 0$

$\ln x = \dfrac{-3 \pm \sqrt{9 - 4(2-y)}}{2} = \dfrac{-3 \pm \sqrt{4y+1}}{2}$

$\therefore \quad \ln x = \dfrac{-3 - \sqrt{4y+1}}{2} \Rightarrow x = e^{\frac{-3-\sqrt{4y+1}}{2}}$

$\therefore \quad f^{-1}(x) = e^{\frac{-3-\sqrt{4x+1}}{2}}$

22. Let $\quad y = f(x) \Rightarrow y = ax + b$

$\Rightarrow \quad x = \dfrac{y}{a} - \dfrac{b}{a}$

$\therefore \quad f^{-1}(x) = \dfrac{x}{a} - \dfrac{b}{a}$ ...(i)

and $\quad f(x) = ax + b$ ...(ii)

Now, from Eqs. (i) and (ii), we get

$\dfrac{1}{a} = a \Rightarrow a^2 = 1 \Rightarrow a = \pm 1$

and $\quad b = -\dfrac{b}{a}$

When $a = 1$, $2b = 0 \Rightarrow b = 0$

When $a = -1$, $b = b \Rightarrow b \in R$

Hence, $(-1, b)$ and $(1, 0)$, where $b \in R$.

23. **Decoding the Question**

The general equation of a parabola is $y = a(x-h)^2 + k$ or $x = a(y-k)^2 + h$, where (h, k) denotes the vertex.

We have, $f(x) = y = (3x+2)^2 - 1 \Rightarrow (3x+2)^2 = y + 1$

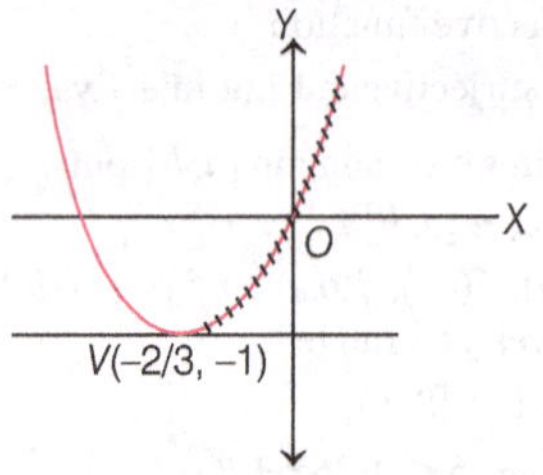

$3x + 2 = -\sqrt{y+1} \qquad [\text{as } x \leq -2/3]$

$\Rightarrow \quad x = \left(\dfrac{-2 - \sqrt{y+1}}{3}\right) = f^{-1}(y) = g(y)$

Hence, $g(x) = \left(\dfrac{-2 - \sqrt{x+1}}{3}\right)$

24. We have, $\quad f(x) = 4x^3 - 3x$

$\Rightarrow \quad f'(x) = 12x^2 - 3 \Rightarrow 3(2x+1)(2x-1) \geq 0$

For $x \in \left[-\infty, -\dfrac{1}{2}\right] \cup \left[\dfrac{1}{2}, \infty\right)$

$\Rightarrow f(x)$ is strictly increasing on $\left[\dfrac{1}{2}, 1\right]$ i.e. injective.

Also, range of function on $\left[\dfrac{1}{2}, 1\right]$ is $[-1, 1]$ = codomain

Thus, $f(x)$ is invertible.

Let $g(x)$ be the inverse of f, so $f(g(x)) = x, \forall x \in [-1, 1]$

Now, on putting $f(\cos\theta) = \cos 3\theta$

$f^{-1} f(\cos\theta) = f^{-1}(\cos 3\theta) \Rightarrow \cos\theta = f^{-1}(\cos 3\theta)$

On putting $\theta = \dfrac{1}{3}\cos^{-1} x$, we get

$f^{-1}(x) = \cos\left(\dfrac{1}{3}\cos^{-1} x\right)$

25. We have, $f(x) = \sqrt{3}\sin x - \cos x + 2$

Let $y = \sqrt{3}\sin x - \cos x + 2$

$\Rightarrow \quad y = 2\left(\dfrac{\sqrt{3}}{2}\sin x - \dfrac{1}{2}\cos x\right) + 2$

$$\Rightarrow \quad \frac{y}{2} - 1 = \frac{\sqrt{3}}{2}\sin x - \frac{1}{2}\cos x$$

$$\Rightarrow \quad \frac{y-2}{2} = -\cos\left(\frac{\pi}{3} + x\right)$$

$$\Rightarrow \quad \frac{y-2}{2} = \cos\left(\pi - \left(\frac{\pi}{3} + x\right)\right)$$

$$\Rightarrow \quad \frac{y-2}{2} = \cos\left(\frac{2\pi}{3} - x\right)$$

$$\therefore \quad \frac{2\pi}{3} - x = \cos^{-1}\left(\frac{y-2}{2}\right) \Rightarrow x = \frac{2\pi}{3} - \cos^{-1}\left[\frac{y-2}{2}\right]$$

$$\therefore \quad f^{-1}(x) = \frac{2\pi}{3} - \cos^{-1}\left(\frac{x-2}{2}\right)$$

$\therefore a = 2,\ b = 3,\ c = 2,\ d = 2$

$a + b + c + d = 9$

26. Given, $f(x) = \log_a(x + \sqrt{x^2 + 1})$

$$\therefore \quad f'(x) = \frac{\log_a e}{\sqrt{1 + x^2}} > 0$$

which is a strictly increasing function.

Thus, $f(x)$ is one-one and it is given $f(x)$ is onto.

So, $f(x)$ will be inversible.

Now, $y = \log_a(x + \sqrt{x^2 + 1})$

On taking antilog both sides, we get

$$a^y = x + \sqrt{x^2 + 1} \quad \text{...(i)}$$

and
$$a^{-y} = \sqrt{x^2 + 1} - x$$

$$\therefore \quad x = \frac{1}{2}(a^y - a^{-y}) \quad \text{...(ii)}$$

$$\therefore \quad f^{-1}(x) = \frac{1}{2}[a^x - a^{-x}]$$

27. Given, function, $f(x) = \dfrac{4^{2x} - 4^{-2x}}{4^{2x} + 4^{-2x}},\ x \in (-1, 1)$

$$= \frac{4^{4x} - 1}{4^{4x} + 1} = y$$

On applying componendo and dividendo law

$$4^{4x} = \frac{1 + y}{1 - y}$$

On taking log both sides having base 4

$$4x = \log_4\left(\frac{1+y}{1-y}\right) \Rightarrow x = \frac{1}{4}\log_4\left(\frac{1+y}{1-y}\right)$$

$$\therefore \quad f^{-1}(x) = \frac{1}{4\log_4 e}\log_e\left(\frac{1+x}{1-x}\right)$$

28. We have, $\quad f(x+1) + f(x-1) = \sqrt{3}f(x) \quad$ ...(i)

$$\Rightarrow \quad f(x+2) + f(x) = \sqrt{3}\ f(x+1) \quad \text{...(ii)}$$

$$\Rightarrow f(x+2) - \sqrt{3}f(x+1) + f(x) = 0 \quad \text{...(iii)}$$

On comparing Eq (iii) with $f(x+2) + pf(x+1) + qf(x) = 0$, we get

$$p = -\sqrt{3} \text{ and } q = 1$$

Let α and β be the roots of equation $x^2 - \sqrt{3}x + 1 = 0$

or $x = \dfrac{\sqrt{3} \pm \sqrt{3-4}}{2} = \dfrac{\sqrt{3} \pm i}{2} = \left(\cos\dfrac{\pi}{6} \pm i\sin\dfrac{\pi}{6}\right)$

$\therefore\ \alpha = \cos\dfrac{\pi}{6} + i\sin\pi/6,\ \beta = \cos\pi/6 - i\sin\pi/6$

$$\therefore\ f(x) = A\alpha^x + \beta\cdot\beta^x$$

$$= A(\cos\pi/6 + i\sin\pi/6) + B(\cos\pi/6 - i\sin\pi/6)$$

$\because\ f(x) = 4$

$$\Rightarrow A(\cos\pi/6 + i\sin\pi/6)^2 + B(\cos\pi/6 - i\sin\pi/6)^2 = 4$$

$$\Rightarrow \quad A(\cos\pi/3 + i\sin\pi/3) + B(\cos\pi/3 - i\sin\pi/3) = 4$$

$$\Rightarrow \quad A(1 + i\sqrt{3}) + B(1 - i\sqrt{3}) = 8$$

On comparing real and imaginary parts

$$A + B = 8 \text{ and } A - B = 0$$

$$\therefore \quad A = 4 \text{ and } B = 4$$

$$\therefore\ f(x) = 4\left[\left(\cos\pi/6 + i\sin\frac{\pi}{6}\right)^x + \left[\cos\frac{\pi}{6} - i\sin\frac{\pi}{6}\right]^x\right]$$

$$= 4\left[\left(\cos\frac{\pi x}{6} + i\sin\frac{\pi x}{6}\right) + \left(\cos\frac{\pi x}{6} - i\sin\frac{\pi x}{6}\right)\right]$$

$$= 4\left(2\cos\frac{\pi x}{6}\right)$$

$$\therefore\ f(x) = 8\cos\left(\frac{\pi x}{6}\right)$$

29. Given, $f(x+a) = \dfrac{1}{2} + \sqrt{f(x) - (f(x))^2}$ ...(i)

Replacing x by $x - a$ and $x + a$ in Eq. (i), we get

$$f(x) = \frac{1}{2} + \sqrt{f(x-a) - (f(x-a))^2} \geq \frac{1}{2}$$

$$\Rightarrow f(x+2a) = \frac{1}{2} + \sqrt{f(x+a) - (f(x+a))^2}$$

$$= \frac{1}{2} + \sqrt{f(x+a)(1 - f(x+a))}$$

$$= \frac{1}{2} + \sqrt{\left(\frac{1}{2} + \sqrt{f(x) - (f(x))^2}\right)\left(\frac{1}{2} - \sqrt{f(x) - (f(x))^2}\right)}$$

$$= \frac{1}{2} + \sqrt{\frac{1}{4} - f(x) + (f(x))^2}$$

$$= \frac{1}{2} + \sqrt{\left(f(x) - \frac{1}{2}\right)^2} = \frac{1}{2} + \left|f(x) - \frac{1}{2}\right|$$

$$= \frac{1}{2} + f(x) - \frac{1}{2} = f(x) \quad \left[\because f(x) > \frac{1}{2}\right]$$

$\therefore\ \ f(x+2a) = f(x)$

Hence, the period of $f(x)$ is $2a$.

30. We have, $f(x+y) = f(x) + f(y) - xy - 1$

When $x = 1 = y$

$$\therefore \quad f(1+1) = f(1) + f(1) - 1 - 1 \Rightarrow f(2) = 0$$

For $x = 2$, and $y = 1$

$$f(2+1) = f(2) + f(1) - 2 - 1 = 0 + 1 - 3 = -2$$

$$\therefore \quad f(3) = -2$$

For $x = 2 = y$,

$$f(2+2) = f(2) + f(2) - 4 - 1$$
$$f(4) = -5$$

Hence, $\sum_{r=1}^{4} f(r) = f(1) + f(2) + f(3) + f(4) = 1 + 0 - 2 - 5 = -6$

31. **Decoding the Question**

By remainder theorem,
Dividend = Divisor × Quotient + Remainder

We have, $f(x) = x(x+1)\underbrace{Q(x)}_{\text{Quotient}} + \underbrace{(ax+b)}_{r(x) = \text{remainder}}$ ...(i)

On putting $x = 0$ and $x = -1$ in Eq. (i), we get

$$b = 0 \quad \text{...(ii)}$$

and $-1 = -a + b$ ...(iii) $\begin{bmatrix} \text{as } f(0) = 0 \\ \text{and } f(-1) = -1 \end{bmatrix}$

$\therefore \quad a = 1$ and $b = 0$

So, $r(x) = ax + b = x$

Hence, $r(10) = 10$

32. For domain of $\log_{(15-x)}(x-2)$

$\Rightarrow \quad x - 2 > 0, 15 - x > 0$ and $15 - x \neq 1$

$\therefore \quad x \in (2, 15) - \{14\}$ ...(i)

For domain of $\cos^{-1}\left[\frac{2x-26}{3}\right]$

$$-1 \le \frac{2x-26}{3} < 2$$
$$-3 \le 2x - 26 < 6$$
$$\frac{23}{2} \le x < 16$$

$\therefore$ Domain of $f(x) = \left[\frac{23}{2}, 15\right) - \{14\}$

Number of integer = 2 i.e. 12, 13

33. Since, $f(x) = \sqrt{\left(\frac{2-|x|}{3-|x|}\right)}$

$\Rightarrow f(x)$ is defined when

$$\frac{2-|x|}{3-|x|} \ge 0 \Rightarrow \frac{|x|-2}{|x|-3} \ge 0$$

$\therefore$ Critical point of $|x|$ are 2 and 3.

$\therefore \quad |x| \le 2$ or $|x| > 3$

$\Rightarrow \quad -2 \le x \le 2$ or $x < -3$ or $x > 3$

$\Rightarrow \quad x \in (-\infty, -3) \cup [-2, 2] \cup (3, \infty)$

$\therefore \quad \alpha = 2$ and $\beta = 3$

So, $\alpha + \beta = 2 + 3 = 5$

34. We have, $f(\sec^2 x) = (\sec^2 x)^2 + 2\sec^2 x + 2 = (\sec^2 x + 1)^2 + 1$

Range is $[5, \infty)$

and $\quad fog(f(x)) = \log(x^2 + 2x + 2) = \log[(x+1)^2 + 1]$

$\therefore$ Range is $[0, \infty)$.

$$a = 5 \text{ and } b = 0$$
$$2a + 3b - 4 = 10 + 0 - 4 = 6$$

Number of prime factors = 2

35. We have, $(n^2 - 4)(n^2 - 9) = 0 \Rightarrow n = \pm 2, \pm 3$

$$\left[\frac{n-2}{2}\right] = 0 \Rightarrow 2 \le n < 4$$

$\Rightarrow \quad n - 4 = 0 \Rightarrow n = 4$

and $\quad n^2 - 5n + 6 = 0 \Rightarrow n = 2, 3$

and $\quad \{2n - 1\} = 0 \Rightarrow 2n - 1 = m, m \in I$

$\therefore \quad n = \frac{m+1}{2}$

$\therefore$ Possible values of n are 2 and 3.

$\therefore$ Sum of integral values of $n = 5$

36. We have, $\quad g(x) = \frac{1}{2}\tan^{-1}|x| + 1$

$\Rightarrow \quad \text{sgn}(g(x)) = 1$

$\Rightarrow \quad \sin^{23} x - \cos^{22} x = 1$

$\Rightarrow \quad \sin^{23} x = 1 + \cos^{22} x$

which is possible when

$$\sin x = 1 \text{ and } \cos x = 0$$
$$\sin x = 1 \Rightarrow x = 2n\pi + \pi/2$$

Hence, $-10\pi \le 2n\pi + \frac{\pi}{2} \le 20\pi$

$\Rightarrow \quad \frac{-21}{2} \le 2n \le \frac{39}{2}$

$\Rightarrow \quad \frac{-21}{4} \le n \le \frac{39}{4} \Rightarrow -5 \le n \le 9$

Hence, the number of values of x is 15.

37. **Case I** If $x < 0$, then $\left[\frac{2}{x}\right] + \left[\frac{3}{x}\right]$ is '–'ve.

Hence, $\left[\frac{2}{x}\right] + \left[\frac{3}{x}\right] = 4$

can never be equal to 5.

Case II If $x > 0$, we have

$$\frac{2}{x} < \frac{3}{x}$$

$\therefore \quad \left[\frac{2}{x}\right] \le \left[\frac{3}{x}\right]$

Since, each of $\left[\frac{2}{x}\right]$ and $\left[\frac{3}{x}\right]$ is an integer.

$\therefore$ 3 possibilities are there.

$$\left[\frac{2}{x}\right] = 0 \text{ and } \left[\frac{3}{x}\right] = 4$$
$$\left[\frac{2}{x}\right] = 1 \text{ and } \left[\frac{3}{x}\right] = 3$$
$$\left[\frac{2}{x}\right] = 2 \text{ and } \left[\frac{3}{x}\right] = 2$$

If $\quad \left[\frac{2}{x}\right] = 0 \Rightarrow 0 \le \frac{2}{x} < 1 \Rightarrow x > 2$

and $\quad \left[\frac{3}{x}\right] = 4 \Rightarrow 4 \le \frac{3}{x} < 5 \Rightarrow \frac{1}{5} < \frac{x}{3} \le \frac{1}{4} \Rightarrow \frac{3}{5} \le x < \frac{3}{4}$

These two equations are not possible simultaneously.

Hence, no solution in these cases.

Now, if $\left[\frac{2}{x}\right]=1 \Rightarrow 1 \le \frac{2}{x} < 2 \Rightarrow \frac{1}{2} < \frac{x}{2} < 1 \Rightarrow 1 < x < 2$

and $\left[\frac{3}{x}\right]=3 \Rightarrow 3 \le \frac{3}{x} < 4 \Rightarrow \frac{1}{4} < \frac{x}{3} \le \frac{1}{3} \Rightarrow \frac{3}{4} < x \le 1$

not possible simultaneously, no solution is available.

Now, if $\left[\frac{2}{x}\right]=2 \Rightarrow 2 \le \frac{2}{x} < 3 \Rightarrow \frac{1}{3} < \frac{x}{2} \le \frac{1}{2} \Rightarrow \frac{2}{3} < x \le 1$

and $\left[\frac{3}{x}\right]=2 \Rightarrow 2 \le \frac{3}{x} < 3 \Rightarrow \frac{1}{3} < \frac{x}{3} \le \frac{1}{2} \Rightarrow 1 < x \le 3/2$

Hence, no solution for the given equation. So, $x \in \phi$

$\therefore$ Number of integers = 0

38. We have, $\log_2(f(x)) = \log_2\left(\frac{2}{1-1/3}\right) \cdot \log_3\left[1 + \frac{f(x)}{f\left(\frac{1}{x}\right)}\right]$

$$= \log_2 3 \cdot \log_3\left(1 + \frac{f(x)}{f\left(\frac{1}{x}\right)}\right)$$

$$f(x) = 1 + \frac{f(x)}{f\left(\frac{1}{x}\right)}$$

$\Rightarrow \quad f(x)\, f\left(\frac{1}{x}\right) = f\left(\frac{1}{x}\right) + f(x)$

$\Rightarrow \quad f(x) = 1 \pm x^n$

$\Rightarrow \quad f(10) = 1 \pm 10^n = 1001$

$\Rightarrow \quad 10^n = 1000$

$\Rightarrow$ Positive sign must be taken and $n = 3$

$\therefore \quad f(x) = 1 + x^3$

$\therefore \quad f(5) = 1 + 5^3 = 126$

39. We have, $f(x) = x^3 + 3x^2 + 4x + p\cos x + q\sin x$

$\Rightarrow \quad f'(x) = 3x^2 + 6x + 4 + q\cos x - p\sin x$

Now, for $f(x)$ is to be one-one, then $f'(x) \ge 0,\ \forall\ x \in R$

$3x^2 + 6x + 4 + q\cos x - p\sin x \ge 0$

$$= 3x^2 + 6x + 4 \ge p\sin x - q\cos x$$

$$= 3x^2 + 6x + 4 \ge \sqrt{p^2 + q^2},\ \forall\ x \in R$$

$\Rightarrow \quad \sqrt{p^2+q^2} \le 3\,(x^2 + 2x + 1) + 1$

$\Rightarrow \quad \sqrt{p^2+q^2} \le 3(x+1)^2 + 1,\ \forall x \in R$

$\Rightarrow \quad \sqrt{p^2+q^2} \le 1,\ \forall\ x \in R$

$\Rightarrow \quad p^2 + q^2 \le 1,\ \forall\ x \in R$

Hence, the maximum value of $p^2 + q^2$ is 1.

40. We have, $f(x) = ax^2 + bx + c$

Now, $\quad f(1) = a + b + c$

and $\quad f(-2) = 4a - 2b + c$

Hence, $f(1) - f(-2) = 3(b - a)$

Now, $M = \frac{a+b+c}{b-a} = \frac{3f(1)}{f(1) - f(-2)} = \frac{3f(1)}{1 - \frac{f(-2)}{f(1)}}$

Hence, $M_{\min}$ occurs when $f(-2) = 0$

Hence, the minimum values of $\frac{a+b+c}{b-a}$ is 3.

41. **Decoding the Question**

$\log_a a = 1$

$\log_a xy = \log_a x + \log_a y$

We have, $f\left[2 + \log_2\left(\frac{3}{2}\right)\right] = f\left[\log_2 4 + \log_2 \frac{3}{2}\right]$

$$= f(\log_2 6) = f(\log_2 6 + 1)$$

$$= f(\log_2 12) = f(\log_2 12 + 1)$$

Hence, $f\left(2 + \log_2\left(\frac{3}{2}\right)\right) = f(\log_2 24) = \frac{1}{2^{\log_2 24}} = \frac{1}{24}$

$\therefore \quad 24 \cdot f\left(2 + \log_2\left(\frac{3}{2}\right)\right) = 1$

42. For $\log_3(ax^2 + 4x + a)$ to be valid

$$ax^2 + 4x + a > 0,\ \forall x \in R$$

$$a > 0 \text{ and } 4 - a^2 < 0 \in a > 2$$

Given, inequality $\log_3\left(\frac{ax^2 + 4x + a}{x^2 + 1}\right) \ge 1$

$$ax^2 + 4x + a \ge 3(x^2 + 1)$$

$$(a-3)x^2 + 4x + a - 3 \ge 0,\ \forall\ x \in R$$

For above expression to be true

$$a > 3 \text{ and } D \le 0$$

$$16 - 4(a-3)^2 \le 0$$

$$a > 3 \text{ and } a - 3 \ge 2 \Rightarrow a \ge 5$$

So, $\quad a \ge 5$

Least value of $a = 5$

43. We have, $f(f(x)) = f(x) + f^2(x) + f^4(x) + f^8(x) + \ldots$

Coefficient of x^{10} in $f(x) = 1$

Coefficient of x^{10} in $f^2(x) = 2$

Coefficients of x^{10} in $f^4(x) = {}^4C_2 + {}^4C_1 = 10$

Coefficient of x^{10} in $f^8(x) = {}^8C_2 = 28$

$\therefore$ Coefficient of x^{10} is $f(f(x)) = 1 + 2 + 10 + 28 = 41$

44. We have, $f(x)f(y) - f(xy) = x + y$ ...(i)

On putting $x = y = 1$, we get

$$f(1)f(1) - f(1) = 2$$

$$f(1)^2 - f(1) = 2$$

$$(f(1) + 1)(f(1) - 2) = 0$$

$\therefore \quad f(1) = 2 \qquad [\because f(1) > 0]$

On putting $y = 1$ in Eq. (i), we get

$$f(x) = x + 1$$

$\therefore \quad f^{-1}(x) = x - 1$

$\therefore \quad f^{-1}(x)\, f(x) = x^2 - 1$

$\Rightarrow \quad f(2) f^{-1}(2) = 2^2 - 1 = 3$

45. We have, $f(x) = \cos 8\pi\{x\}$

$$= \cos(8\pi x - 8\pi[x]) = \cos 8\pi x$$

Its period is 1/4 and period of $\sin 2\pi x \operatorname{cosec} 2\pi$ is 1/2.

Hence, the period of $f(x)$ is 1/2.

$$\frac{a}{4} = 1/2$$

$$a = 2$$

$$5a = 10$$

46. We have, $\min\{\sin x, |x|\} = \sin x$

Period '2π'

$$\frac{x}{\pi} - \left[\frac{x}{\pi}\right] = \left\{\frac{x}{\pi}\right\} \text{period '}\pi\text{'}$$

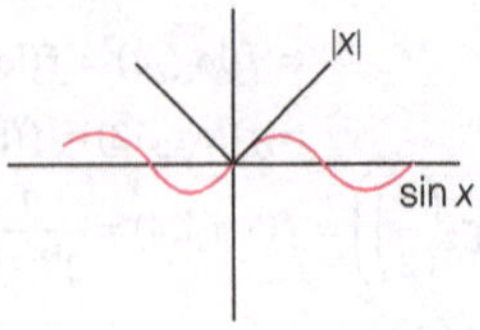

LCM of 2π and $\pi = 2\pi$

$\therefore \quad k = 2$

$$k^k = 2^2 = 4$$

47. Let $[x] = m$, then $\dfrac{x}{x+4} = \dfrac{5m-7}{7m-5}$

Rearranging, $x = \dfrac{10m - 14}{m+1}$

Now, we have $m \le x < m + 1$

$$\Rightarrow \quad m \le \frac{10m-14}{m+1} < m + 1$$

Simplify to get possible integral values of m to be 2, 6 and 7.

48. Given, $2f(\sin x) + f(\cos x) = x$ ...(i)

Replacing x by $\left(\dfrac{\pi}{2} - x\right)$ is Eq. (i), we get

$$\Rightarrow 2f\left[\sin\left(\frac{\pi}{2} - x\right)\right] + f\left[\cos\left(\frac{\pi}{2} - x\right)\right] = \frac{\pi}{2} - x$$

$$\Rightarrow \quad 2f(\cos x) + f(\sin x) = \pi/2 - x \quad \text{...(ii)}$$

Multiplying Eq. (i) by 2, and subtracting from Eq. (ii), we get

$$-3f(\sin x) = \pi/2 - x - 2x$$

$$\Rightarrow \quad 3f(\sin x) = 3x - \pi/2$$

$$\Rightarrow \quad f(\sin x) = x - \pi/6 \quad \text{...(iii)}$$

On putting $x = \pi/6$ in Eq. (iii), we get

$$f(\sin \pi/6) = 0$$

$$\therefore \quad f(1/2) = 0$$

49. We have, $f(x + y) = 2^x f(y) + 4^y f(x)$ ...(i)

and $f(y + x) = 2^y f(x) + 4^x f(y)$ ...(ii)

$$\Rightarrow \; 2^x f(y) + 4^y f(x) = 2^y f(x) + 4^x f(y)$$

$$\Rightarrow \quad \frac{f(x)}{4^x - 2^x} = \frac{f(y)}{4^y - 2^y} = k$$

$$\Rightarrow \quad f(x) = k \cdot (4^x - 2^x)$$

$$\Rightarrow \quad f(0) = k(4^\circ - 2^\circ)$$

$$\Rightarrow \quad k = 4$$

$$\therefore \quad f(x) = 4^{x+1} - 2^{x+2}$$

$$\Rightarrow \quad f'(x) = 4^{x+1}\ln 4 - 2^{x+2}\ln 2$$

$$\Rightarrow \quad f'(2) = 64\ln 4 - 16\ln 2$$

$$= 128\ln 2 - 16\ln 2 = 112\ln 2 = 2^4 \times 7\ln 2$$

$$\therefore \quad a = 4, \; b = 7$$

$$\Rightarrow \quad a + b = 11$$

50. We have, $f(1 - x) + 2f(x) = 3x, \; \forall \; x \in R$

Replacing x by $\dfrac{1}{2} + x$, we get

$$f\left(\frac{1}{2} - x\right) + 2f\left(\frac{1}{2} + x\right) = 3\left(\frac{1}{2} + x\right) \quad \text{...(i)}$$

Now, replacing x by $\dfrac{1}{2} - x$, we get

$$f\left(\frac{1}{2} + x\right) + 2f\left(\frac{1}{2} - x\right) = 3\left(\frac{1}{2} - x\right) \quad \text{...(ii)}$$

On adding Eqs. (i) and (ii), we get

$$3\left(f\left(\frac{1}{2} + x\right) + f\left(\frac{1}{2} - x\right)\right) = 3$$

$$f\left(\frac{1}{2} - x\right) = 1 - f\left(\frac{1}{2} + x\right)$$

$$1 + f\left(\frac{1}{2} + x\right) = \frac{3}{2} + 3x; \; f\left(\frac{1}{2} + x\right) = \frac{1}{2} + 3x$$

$$x = -\frac{1}{2}$$

$$\Rightarrow \quad f(0) = \frac{1}{2} - \frac{3}{2} = -1 \Rightarrow |f(0)| = 1$$

51. We have, $f(x) = \dfrac{\sqrt{x^2 - 25}}{4 - x^2} + \log_{10}(x^2 + 2x - 15)$

Now, for $\dfrac{\sqrt{x^2 - 25}}{4 - x^2}$,

$$x^2 - 25 \ge 0$$

$$(x - 5)(x + 5) \ge 0$$

$$\Rightarrow \quad x \in (-\infty, -5] \cup [5, \infty) \quad \text{...(i)}$$

and $\quad 4 - x^2 \ne 0$ ...(ii)

Now, for $\log_{10}(x^2 + 2x - 15)$

$$\Rightarrow \quad x^2 + 2x - 15 > 0$$

$$\Rightarrow \quad (x + 5)(x - 3) > 0$$

$$\Rightarrow \quad x \in (-\infty, -5) \cup [3, \infty) \quad \text{...(iii)}$$

From Eqs. (i), (ii) and (iii), we get

$$x \in (-\infty, -5) \cup [5, \infty)$$

So, $\alpha = -5, \beta = 5$, then

$$\alpha^2 + \beta^3 = 25 + 125 = 150$$

52. We have, $|2a - 1| = 3[a] + 2\{a\}$

$$\Rightarrow \quad |2a - 1| = 3[a] + 2(a - [a])$$

$$\Rightarrow \quad |2a - 1| = [a] + 2a$$

When $a > \frac{1}{2}$, then

$$2a - 1 = [a] + 2a$$

$\Rightarrow$ $[a] = -1$

$\Rightarrow$ $a \in [-1, 0)$, which is not satisfied.

When $a < \frac{1}{2}$, then

$$-2a + 1 = [a] + 2a$$

On putting $a = I + f$

$$-2(I + f) + 1 = I + 2(I + f)$$

$\Rightarrow$ $-2I - 2f + 1 = I + 2I + 2f$

$\Rightarrow$ $5I + 4f = 1$

$\Rightarrow$ $I = 0, f = \frac{1}{4}$

$\therefore$ $a = \frac{1}{4}$

$\therefore$ $72\ \Sigma a = 72 \times \frac{1}{4} = 18$

53. Given, $A = \{1, 2, 3, \ldots, 7\}$

Then, $n(P(A)) = 2^7 = 128$

$$f : A \to P(A)$$

So, number of function $= 128 \times 128 \times \ldots \times 128$

$$= 128^7 = (2^7)^7 = 2^{49}$$

$\Rightarrow$ $m^n = 2^{49}$

$\therefore$ $m = 2$ and $n = 49$

$\therefore$ $m + n = 51$

54. Given, $f(x) = \dfrac{1}{\sqrt{[x]^2 - 3[x] - 10}}$

For domain of $f(x)$,

$$[x]^2 - 3[x] - 10 > 0$$

Let $[x] = t$

Then, $t^2 - 3t - 10 > 0$

$\Rightarrow$ $(t - 5)(t + 2) > 0$

$\Rightarrow$ $t \in (-\infty, -2) \cup (5, \infty)$

$\Rightarrow$ $[x] < -2$ or $[x] > 5$

But $[x]$ is an integer value.

$\Rightarrow$ $x < -2$ or $x \geq 6$

Hence, domain is $x \in (-\infty, -2) \cup [6, \infty)$.

55. We have, $f(x) = \dfrac{1}{\sqrt{[x] - x}}$

$\therefore$ Domain of $f(x)$, $A = R - I$ and range of $f(x)$, $B = (1, \infty)$.

$\therefore$ $A \cap B = (1, \infty) - N$ and $A \cup B \neq (1, \infty)$

$\therefore$ Only S_1 is true.

56. We have, $A = \{x \in R : [x + 3] + [x + 4] \leq 3\}$

Here, $[x + 3] + [x + 4] \leq 3$

$\Rightarrow$ $[x] + 3 + [x] + 4 \leq 3$ $\quad [\because [x + n] = [x] + n, n \in I]$

$\Rightarrow$ $2[x] + 4 \leq 0$

$\Rightarrow$ $[x] \leq -2 \Rightarrow x \in (-\infty, -1)$

$A \equiv (-\infty, -1)$ ...(i)

Also, $B = \left\{x \in R : 3^x \left(\sum_{r=1}^{\infty} \frac{3}{10^r}\right)^{x-3} < 3^{-3x}\right\}$

Here, $3^x \left(\frac{3}{10} + \frac{3}{10^2} + \frac{3}{10^3} + \ldots\right)^{x-3} < 3^{-3x}$

$\Rightarrow$ $3^x \left(\dfrac{\frac{3}{10}}{1 - \frac{1}{10}}\right)^{x-3} < 3^{-3x} \Rightarrow 3^x \left(\frac{1}{3}\right)^{x-3} < 3^{-3x}$

$\Rightarrow$ $3^{x - x + 3} < 3^{-3x} \Rightarrow 3^3 < 3^{-3x}$

$\Rightarrow$ $-3x > 3 \Rightarrow x < -1$

$\Rightarrow$ $x \in (-\infty, -1)$

$\Rightarrow$ $B \equiv (-\infty, -1)$ ...(ii)

From Eqs. (i) and (ii), we get

$$A = B$$

57. We have, $f(x) + f\left(\frac{1}{1 - x}\right) = 1 + x$

Put $x = 2$, then $f(2) + f(-1) = 3$ ...(i)

Put $x = 1/2$, then $f\left(\frac{1}{2}\right) + f(2) = \frac{3}{2}$ ...(ii)

Put $x = -1$, then $f(-1) + f\left(\frac{1}{2}\right) = 0$ ...(iii)

On subtracting Eq. (iii) from Eq. (i), we get

$$f(2) - f\left(\frac{1}{2}\right) = 3 \quad \text{...(iv)}$$

On adding Eqs. (ii) and (iv), we get

$$2f(2) = \frac{3}{2} + 3 \Rightarrow 2f(2) = \frac{9}{2} \Rightarrow f(2) = \frac{9}{4}$$

Alternate Solution

We have, $f(x) + f\left(\frac{1}{1 - x}\right) = 1 + x$ ...(i)

Replacing x by $\frac{1}{1 - x}$ in Eq. (i), we get

$$f\left(\frac{1}{1 - x}\right) + f\left(\frac{1}{1 - \frac{1}{1 - x}}\right) = 1 + \frac{1}{1 - x}$$

$\Rightarrow$ $f\left(\frac{1}{1 - x}\right) + f\left(\frac{1 - x}{1 - x - 1}\right) = \frac{1 - x + 1}{1 - x}$

$\Rightarrow$ $f\left(\frac{1}{1 - x}\right) + f\left(\frac{1 - x}{-x}\right) = \frac{2 - x}{1 - x}$ ...(ii)

Now, replacing x by $\frac{x - 1}{x}$ in Eq. (i), we get

$$f\left(\frac{x - 1}{x}\right) + f(x) = \frac{2x - 1}{x} \quad \text{...(iii)}$$

Putting $x = 2$ in Eqs. (i), (ii) and (iii), we get

$f(2) + f(-1) = 3$ ...(iv)

$f(-1) + f\left(\frac{1}{2}\right) = 0$ ...(v)

and $f\left(\frac{1}{2}\right) + f(2) = \frac{3}{2}$ ...(vi)

On solving Eqs. (iv), (v) and (vi), we get

$$f(2) = \frac{9}{4}$$

58. We have, $f(x) = \dfrac{[x]}{1+x^2}, 2 \le x < 6$

$$= \begin{cases} \dfrac{2}{1+x^2}, & 2 \le x < 3 \\ \dfrac{3}{1+x^2}, & 3 \le x < 4 \\ \dfrac{4}{1+x^2}, & 4 \le x < 5 \\ \dfrac{5}{1+x^2}, & 5 \le x < 6 \end{cases}$$

Since, $f(x)$ is a decreasing function.

So, range of $f(x) = (f(6), f(2)]$

Now, $f(2) = \dfrac{2}{5}$ and $f(6) = \dfrac{5}{37}$

$\therefore$ Range of $f(x)$ is $\left(\dfrac{5}{37}, \dfrac{2}{5}\right]$.

59. Let $y = \dfrac{x^2+2x+1}{x^2-8x+12}$

$\Rightarrow (y-1)x^2 - (8y+2)x + 12y - 1 = 0$

Since, $x \in R$.

$\therefore \quad D \ge 0$

$\Rightarrow \quad (8y+2)^2 - 4(y-1)(12y-1) \ge 0$

$\Rightarrow 16y^2 + 8y + 1 - 12y^2 + 12y + y - 1 \ge 0$

$\Rightarrow \quad y(4y+21) \ge 0$

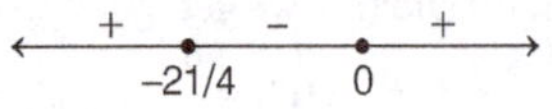

$\therefore y \in \left(-\infty, \dfrac{-21}{4}\right] \cup [0, \infty)$

So, range of f is $\left(-\infty, \dfrac{-21}{4}\right] \cup [0, \infty)$.

60. We have, $f(x) = \dfrac{\log_{(x+1)}(x-2)}{e^{2\log_e x} - 2x - 3}$

For domain, $x - 2 > 0$ ...(i)

$x + 1 > 0$ ...(ii)

$x + 1 \ne 1$ ...(iii)

$x > 0$ ...(iv)

$\Rightarrow \quad x > 2$ and $x > -1$ and $x > 0$

and $\quad x \ne 0$

$\Rightarrow \quad x \in (2, \infty)$ ...(v)

Also, $\quad f(x) = \dfrac{\log_{(x+1)}(x-2)}{e^{\log_e x^2} - 2x - 3}$

$[\because a \log x = \log x^a]$

$\Rightarrow \quad f(x) = \dfrac{\log_{(x+1)}(x-2)}{x^2 - 2x - 3} \quad [\because a^{\log_a x} = x]$

$\therefore \quad x^2 - 2x - 3 \ne 0$ for domain.

$\Rightarrow \quad (x+1)(x-3) \ne 0$

$\Rightarrow \quad x \ne -1, 3$ ...(vi)

From Eqs. (v) and (vi), we get

Required domain is $(2, \infty) - \{3\}$.

61. Let us consider a function $f : N \to R$ satisfying

$f(1) + 2f(2) + 3f(3) \ldots + xf(x) = x(x+1)f(x)$ ...(i)

We have for $x \ge 2$

$f(1) + 2f(2) + 3f(3) + \ldots + xf(x) = x(x+1)f(x)$ ...(ii)

Now, we will replace x by $(x+1)$

and subtract Eq. (i) from Eq. (ii), we get

$x(x+1)f(x) + (x+1)f(x+1) = (x+1)(x+2)f(x+1)$

$\Rightarrow \quad \dfrac{x}{f(x+1)} + \dfrac{1}{f(x)} = \dfrac{(x+2)}{f(x)}$

$\Rightarrow \quad xf(x) = (x+1)f(x+1)$ for $x \ge 2$

$f(2) = \dfrac{1}{4}; f(4) = \dfrac{1}{8}$

Now, $\quad f(2022) = \dfrac{1}{4044}$

Similarly, $\quad f(2028) = \dfrac{1}{4056}$

So, $\dfrac{1}{f(2022)} + \dfrac{1}{f(2028)} = 4044 + 4056 = 8100$

62. Given, $f(x) = 2x^n + \lambda, \ \lambda \in R, n \in N$

and put $x = 4$

$f(4) = 133, f(5) = 255$

$f(4) = 2x^n + \lambda$

So, $\quad 133 = 2(4)^n + \lambda$ ...(i)

and put $x = 5$

$255 = 2(5)^n + \lambda$ ...(ii)

On subtracting Eq. (i) from Eq. (ii), we get

$122 = 2[5^n - 4^n]$ or $5^n - 4^n = 61$

By hit and trial method for $n = 3$,

$5^3 - 4^3 = 61$

$n = 3$, satisfy the equation

Now, putting the value of n in Eq. (i), we get

$133 = 2(4)^3 + \lambda$

$\lambda = 133 - 128 \Rightarrow \lambda = 5$

Now, $\quad f(x) = 2x^3 + 5$

So, $\quad f(3) = 2(3)^3 + 5 = 59$

$f(2) = 2(2)^3 + 5 = 21$

So, $\quad f(3) - f(2) = 59 - 21 = 38$

Positive integer divisor of $38 = 1, 2, 19, 38$.

So, sum of positive integer divisors $= 1 + 2 + 19 + 38 = 60$

63. Given, $f(x) = \dfrac{2^{2x}}{2^{2x}+2}$

$\therefore \quad f(1-x) = \dfrac{2^{2(1-x)}}{2^{2(1-x)}+2} = \dfrac{\dfrac{2^2}{2^{2x}}}{\dfrac{2^2}{2^{2x}}+2} = \dfrac{4}{4 + 2\cdot 2^{2x}} = \dfrac{2}{2+2^{2x}}$

$\therefore f(x) + f(1-x) = \dfrac{2^{2x}}{2^{2x}+2} + \dfrac{2}{2+2^{2x}} = \dfrac{2^{2x}+2}{2^{2x}+2} = 1$

$\therefore f(x) + f(1-x) = 1$

$$\therefore \quad f\left(\frac{1}{2023}\right)+f\left(1-\frac{1}{2023}\right)=1$$

$$\Rightarrow \quad f\left(\frac{1}{2023}\right)+f\left(\frac{2022}{2023}\right)=1$$

$$\text{So, } \left\{f\left(\frac{1}{2023}\right)+f\left(\frac{2022}{2023}\right)\right\}+\left\{f\left(\frac{2}{2023}\right)+f\left(\frac{2021}{2023}\right)\right\}$$

$+ \ldots$ 1011 times

$= 1 + 1 + \ldots\ldots$ 1011 times $= 1011$

64. Given, $f:\{1, 2, 3, 4\} \to \{a \in Z\,; |a| \le 8\}$

And $f(n)+\frac{1}{n}f(n+1)=1, \forall\, n \in \{1, 2, 3\}$

So, let's suppose $A = a \in Z\,; |a| \le 8$

So, $\quad A = \{-8, -7, -6, \ldots, 7, 8\}$

Now, $f(n)+\frac{1}{n}f(n+1)=1$

On multiply n in above equation

$$nf(n)+f(n+1)=n$$

as, $\quad f(n+1)=n-nf(n)$

Now, for $n=1$, $\quad f(2)=1-f(1)$

For $n=2$, $\quad f(3)=2-2f(2)=2-2(1-f(1))$

or $\quad f(3)=2f(1)$

For $n=3$, $\quad f(4)=3-3f(3)=3-3(2f(1))$

or $\quad f(4)=3-6f(1)$

We know that

$$f(1) \in \{-8, -7, \ldots, 7, 8\} \quad \ldots\text{(i)}$$

Now, $\quad -8 \le f(2) \le 8$

$$-8 \le 1-f(1) \le 8$$

Subtract 1 from the inequality

$$-9 \le -f(1) \le 7$$

Now, multiply (-1) in the inequality

$$9 \ge f(1) \ge -7$$

or $\quad f(1) \in \{-7, -6 \ldots, 8, 9\} \quad \ldots\text{(ii)}$

Now, $-8 \le f(3) \le 8\,;\ -8 \le 2f(1) \le 8$

Divide the inequality by 2

$$-4 \le f(1) \le 4$$

or $\quad f(1) \in \{-4, -3, -2, -1, 0, 1, 2, 3, 4\} \quad \ldots\text{(iii)}$

Now, $\quad -8 \le f(4) \le 8$

$$-8 \le 3-6f(1) \le 8$$

Subtract 3 from inequality

$$-11 \le -6f(1) \le 5$$

Now, divide the inequality by (-6)

$$\frac{11}{6} \ge f(1) \ge \frac{-5}{6}$$

But, $f(1) \in I$

So, $\quad f(1) \in \{0, 1\} \quad \ldots\text{(iv)}$

From Eqs. (i), (ii), (iii) and (iv),

$$f(1) = 0, 1$$

If $f(1)=0$, then $f(2)=1$, $f(3)=0$, $f(4)=3$

If $f(1)=1$, then $f(2)=0$, $f(3)=2$, $f(4)=-3$

So, number of such functions $= 2$

65. $f(1 \cdot n) = f(1) \cdot f(n) \Rightarrow f(1) = 1$

$$f(3.3) = (f(3))^2$$

$\Rightarrow \quad f(9) = f(3) \times f(3)$

So, $\quad f(3) = 1$ or 3

$f(2)$, $f(5)$ and $f(8)$ can be chosen in 6 ways each.

Therefore, total number of functions

$$= 1 \times 6 \times 2 \times 6 \times 6 \times 1 = 432$$

66. $f(x) = \sqrt{\frac{|[x]|-2}{|[x]|-3}}, \frac{|[x]|-2}{|[x]|-3} \ge 0$

Let $|[x]| = t \Rightarrow \frac{t-2}{t-3} \ge 0$

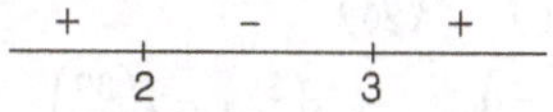

$t \in (-\infty, 2] \cup (3, \infty)$

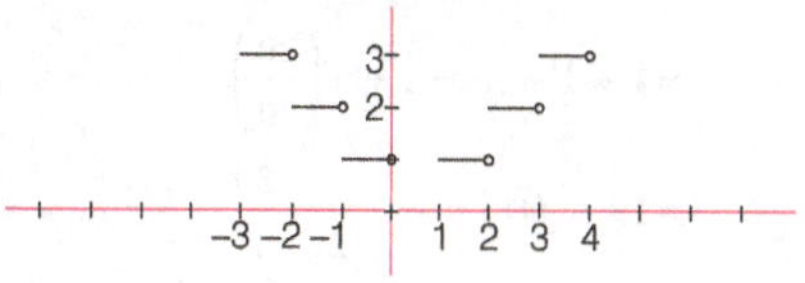

$$|[x]| = 3 \Rightarrow x \in [-3, -2) \cup [3, 4)$$

Domain of A

$$x = [-\infty, -3) \cup [-2, 3) \cup [4, \infty)$$

$$a = -3;\ b = -2;\ c = 3$$

$\therefore \ a + b + c = -3 + (-2) + 3 = -2$

Alternate Solution

$$\frac{|[x]|-2}{|[x]|-3} \ge 0$$

$|[x]| \le 2$ or $|[x]| > 3$

$\Rightarrow \quad -2 \le [x] \le 2$ or $[x] < -3$ or $[x] > 3$

$\Rightarrow \quad -2 \le x < 3$ or $x < -3$ or $x \ge 4$

$\Rightarrow \quad x \in (-\infty, -3) \cup [-2, 3) \cup [4, \infty]$

$\therefore \quad a = -3, b = -2, c = 3$

Therefore, $a + b + c = -2$

67. Given, $f(x) = \sqrt{x}$ and $g(x) = \sqrt{1-x}$

$\therefore$ Domain of $f(x) = D_1$ is $x \ge 0$

i.e. $\quad D_1 : x \in [0, \infty)$

and domain of $g(x) = D_2$ is $1 - x \ge 0 \Rightarrow x \le 1$

i.e. $\quad D_2 : x \in (-\infty\ 1]$

As, we know that, the domain of $f+g$, $f-g$, $g-f$ will be $D_1 \cap D_2$ as well as the domain for f/g is $D_1 \cap D_2$ except all those value(s) of x, such that $g(x) = 0$.

Similarly, for g/f is $D_1 \cap D_2$ but $f(x) \ne 0$.

Hence, common domain for $(f+g)$, $(f-g)$, $\left(\frac{f}{g}\right)$, $\left(\frac{g}{f}\right)$

and $(g-f)$ will be $0 < x < 1$.

68. $f(m+n) = f(m) + f(n)$, $m, n \in N$

$\therefore \quad f(3+3) = f(3) + f(3)$

$\Rightarrow \quad f(6) = 2f(3) = 18 \quad [\because\ f(6) = 18]$

Also, $f(3) = f(2+1) = f(2) + f(1) = f(1+1) + f(1)$

$f(3) = f(1) + f(1) + f(1)$

$\Rightarrow \quad 9 = 3f(1) \Rightarrow f(1) = 3$

$\therefore \quad f(2) = f(1+1) = f(1) + f(1) = 3 + 3 = 6$

Hence, $f(2) \cdot f(3) = 6 \cdot 9 = 54$

69. Given, $f(x) = \dfrac{5^x}{5^x + 5}$, then $f(2-x) = \dfrac{5^{2-x}}{5^{2-x}+5} = \dfrac{5}{5^x + 5}$

This gives, $f(x) + f(2-x) = \dfrac{5^x + 5}{5^x + 5} = 1$

$$\Rightarrow \quad f\left(\frac{1}{20}\right) + f\left(2 - \frac{1}{20}\right) = f\left(\frac{1}{20}\right) + f\left(\frac{39}{20}\right) = 1$$

Similarly, $f\left(\dfrac{2}{20}\right) + f\left(\dfrac{38}{20}\right) = 1$ and so on.

$$\therefore f\left(\frac{1}{20}\right) + f\left(\frac{2}{20}\right) + \ldots + f\left(\frac{38}{20}\right) + f\left(\frac{39}{20}\right)$$

$$= 1 + 1 + \ldots + 1 + f\left(\frac{20}{20}\right)$$

$$= 19 + f(1) = 19 + \frac{1}{2} = \frac{39}{2}$$

70. Given, $a + \alpha = 1$ and $b + \beta = 2$

$$\because \quad a \cdot f(x) + \alpha \cdot f\left(\frac{1}{x}\right) = bx + \frac{\beta}{x} \quad \ldots \text{(i)}$$

Replace x by $1/x$,

$$af\left(\frac{1}{x}\right) + \alpha f(x) = \frac{b}{x} + \beta x \quad \ldots \text{(ii)}$$

On adding Eqs. (i) and (ii), we get

$$(a+\alpha)\left[f(x) + f\left(\frac{1}{x}\right)\right] = \left(x + \frac{1}{x}\right)(b + \beta)$$

$$\therefore \quad \frac{f(x) + f\left(\frac{1}{x}\right)}{x + \frac{1}{x}} = \frac{b+\beta}{a+\alpha} = \frac{2}{1} = 2$$

71. We have, $\displaystyle\sum_{n=8}^{100}\left[\frac{(-1)^n n}{2}\right]$ [$\because [x]$ is the greatest integer function]

On substituting the values of n, we get

$[4] + [-4.5] + [5] + [-5.5] + \ldots + [-49.5] + [50]$

$= 4 - 5 + 5 - 6 + \ldots - 50 + 50$

$= 4$

72. $S = \{1, 2, 3, 4, 5, 6, 7\}$

$f : S \to S$

$f(m \cdot n) = f(m)\, f(n)$

$m, n \in S$

If $\quad mn \in S \Rightarrow mn \leq 7$

So, $\quad (1 \cdot 1, 1 \cdot 2, \ldots, 1 \cdot 7) \leq 7$

$(2 \cdot 2, 2 \cdot 3) \leq 7$

When, $m = 1$, $f(n) = f(1) \cdot f(n)$

$\Rightarrow \quad f(1) = 1$

When, $m = n = 2$, $f(4) = f(2)\, f(2)$

$$= \begin{cases} f(2) = 1 \Rightarrow f(4) = 1 \text{ or} \\ f(2) = 2 \Rightarrow f(4) = 4 \end{cases}$$

When $m = 2$, $n = 3$,

$$f(6) = f(2)\, f(3) \begin{cases} \text{When } f(2) = 1, \\ f(3) \;= 1 \text{ to } 7 \\ \text{When } f(2) = 2, \\ f(3) = 1 \text{ or } 2 \text{ or} 3 \end{cases}$$

And $f(5)$, $f(7)$ can take any value (1-7)

[$\because f(5) = f(1) \cdot f(5) \leq 7$ and $f(7) = f(1) \cdot f(7) \leq 7$]

The possible combination is

$f(1) = 1$	$f(1) = 1$
$f(2) = 1$	$f(2) = 2$
$f(3) = (1 \text{ to } 7)$	$f(3) = (1 \text{ to } 3)$
$f(4) = 1$	$f(4) = 4$
$f(5) = (1 \text{ to } 7)$	$f(5) = (1 \text{ to } 7)$
$f(6) = f(3)$	$f(6) = f(3)$
$f(7) = (1 \text{ to } 7)$	$f(7) = (1 \text{ to } 7)$

So, total $= (1 \times 1 \times 7 \times 1 \times 7 \times 1 \times 7) + (1 \times 1 \times 3 \times 1 \times 7 \times 1 \times 7)$

$= 490$

73. Given, $R = \{(x, y) | x, y \in z, x^2 + 3y^2 \leq 8\}$

For $x = 0$, $3y^2 \leq 8 \Rightarrow y^2 \leq \dfrac{8}{3} \Rightarrow y = 0, \pm 1$

For $x = \pm 1$, $1 + 3y^2 \leq 8 \Rightarrow y^2 \leq \dfrac{7}{3} \Rightarrow y = 0, \pm 1$

For $x = \pm 2$, $4 + 3y^2 \leq 8 \Rightarrow y^2 \leq \dfrac{4}{3} \Rightarrow y = 0$

$\therefore$ The relation, $R = \{(0, 0), (0, -1), (0, 1), (1, 0)(1, -1),$
$(1, 1), (-1, 0), (-1, 1), (2, 0), (-2, 0)\}$

Thus, R can be written as $\{-2, -1, 0, 1, 2\} \to \{-1, 0, 1\}$, where range of R is $\{-1, 0, 1\}$.

Since, the domain of R^{-1} is the range of R, then R^{-1} can be written as

$$\{-1, 0, 1\} \to \{-2, -1, 0, 1, 2\}$$

$\therefore$ Domain of R^{-1} is $\{-1, 0, 1\}$.

74. The given function $f : (1, 3) \to R$, defined by

$$f(x) = \frac{x[x]}{1+x^2} = \begin{cases} \dfrac{x(1)}{1+x^2}, & x \in (1, 2) \\ \dfrac{x(2)}{1+x^2}, & x \in [2, 3) \end{cases}$$

$$\because \quad f(x) = \begin{cases} \dfrac{x}{1+x^2}, & x \in (1, 2) \\ \dfrac{2x}{1+x^2}, & x \in [2, 3) \end{cases}$$

is a decreasing function,

so $\displaystyle\lim_{h \to 0} f(3-h) \longrightarrow \frac{2(3)}{1+9} = \frac{3}{5}$

$f(2) = 4/5$

Similarly, $f(x \to 2^-)$ tends to 2/5 and $f(x \to 1^+)$ tends to $\dfrac{1}{2}$.

So, range of the given function 'f' is $\left(\dfrac{2}{5}, \dfrac{1}{2}\right) \cup \left(\dfrac{3}{5}, \dfrac{4}{5}\right]$.

Exercise 2 - JEE Advanced Pattern

1. Given, $2\sin t = \dfrac{1-2x+5x^2}{3x^2-2x-1}, t \in \left[-\dfrac{\pi}{2}, \dfrac{\pi}{2}\right]$

On putting $2\sin t = y \Rightarrow -2 \le y \le 2$

$$\therefore \quad y = \frac{1-2x+5x^2}{3x^2-2x-1} \Rightarrow (3y-5)x^2 - 2x(y-1) - (y+1) = 0$$

Since, $x \in R - \left\{1, \dfrac{-1}{3}\right\}$

$$\left[\text{as } 3x^2 - 2x - 1 \ne 0 \Rightarrow (x-1)\left(3x+\frac{1}{3}\right) \ne 0\right]$$

$$\therefore \quad D \ge 0$$

$$\Rightarrow \quad 4(y-1)^2 + 4(3y-5)(y+1) \ge 0$$

$$\Rightarrow \quad y^2 - y - 1 \ge 0$$

$$\Rightarrow \quad \left(y-\frac{1}{2}\right)^2 - \frac{5}{4} \ge 0$$

$$\Rightarrow \left(y - \frac{1}{2} - \frac{\sqrt{5}}{2}\right)\left(y - \frac{1}{2} + \frac{\sqrt{5}}{2}\right) \ge 0$$

$$\Rightarrow \quad y \le \frac{1-\sqrt{5}}{2} \text{ or } y \ge \frac{1+\sqrt{5}}{2}$$

$$\Rightarrow \quad 2\sin t \le \frac{1-\sqrt{5}}{2} \text{ or } 2\sin t \ge \frac{1+\sqrt{5}}{2}$$

$$\Rightarrow \quad \sin t \le \sin\left(-\frac{\pi}{10}\right) \text{ or } \sin t \ge \sin\left(\frac{3\pi}{10}\right)$$

$$\Rightarrow \quad t \le -\frac{\pi}{10} \text{ or } t \ge \frac{3\pi}{10}$$

Hence, the range of t is $\left[\dfrac{-\pi}{2}, -\dfrac{\pi}{10}\right] \cup \left[\dfrac{3\pi}{10}, \dfrac{\pi}{2}\right]$.

2. We have, $f(x) = \dfrac{e^x - e^{|x|}}{e^x + e^{|x|}} = \begin{cases} 0, & x \ge 0 \\ \dfrac{e^x - e^{-x}}{e^x + e^{-x}}, & x < 0 \end{cases}$

When $x \ge 0$, so range of f is $\{0\}$ ...(i)

Now, when $x < 0$

Let $y = \dfrac{e^x - e^{-x}}{e^x + e^{-x}} \Rightarrow \dfrac{y+1}{1-y} = \dfrac{2e^x}{2e^{-x}} = e^{2x}$

$$\Rightarrow 0 < \frac{y+1}{1-y} < 1 \qquad [\because x < 0 \Rightarrow e^{2x} < 1 \quad \therefore 0 < e^{2x} < 1]$$

$$\Rightarrow 0 > \frac{y+1}{y-1} > -1 \Rightarrow \frac{y+1}{y-1} < 0$$

$$\Rightarrow \frac{y+1}{y-1} + 1 > 0$$

$$\Rightarrow \quad \frac{2y}{y-1} > 0$$

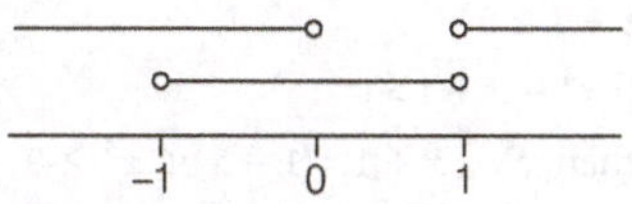

$\therefore y \in (-1, 0)$

$\therefore$ Range, $y \in (-1, 0]$

3. We have, $f(x) = \dfrac{5^x}{5^x + \sqrt{5}}$

$$\therefore \quad f(1-x) = \frac{5^{1-x}}{5^{1-x} + \sqrt{5}} = \frac{5}{5 + \sqrt{5}5^x} = \frac{\sqrt{5}}{\sqrt{5} + 5^x}$$

$\therefore f(x) + f(1-x) = 1$

Let $S = f\left(\dfrac{1}{3006}\right) + f\left(\dfrac{2}{3006}\right) + \dots + f\left(\dfrac{3005}{3006}\right)$

or $S = f\left(\dfrac{3005}{3006}\right) + f\left(\dfrac{3004}{3006}\right) + \dots + f\left(\dfrac{1}{3006}\right)$

$$\Rightarrow 2S = \left(f\left(\frac{1}{3006}\right) + f\left(\frac{3005}{3006}\right)\right) + \left(f\left(\frac{2}{3006}\right) + f\left(\frac{3004}{3006}\right)\right) + \dots + \left(f\left(\frac{3005}{3006}\right) + f\left(\frac{1}{3006}\right)\right)$$

$2S = 1 + 1 + \dots + 1 = 3005$

$$\therefore \quad S = \frac{3005}{2} = \frac{m}{n}$$

$\therefore \quad m = 3005$ and $n = 2$

$m + n = 3007$

Sum of digits $= 10$

4. We have, $f(x) = \sqrt{(0.625)^{4-3x} - (1.6)^{x(x+8)}}$

$$\Rightarrow \quad (0.625)^{4-3x} - (1.6)^{x(x+8)} \ge 0$$

$$\Rightarrow \quad \left(\frac{5}{8}\right)^{4-3x} \ge \left(\frac{8}{5}\right)^{x(x+8)}$$

$$\Rightarrow \quad \left(\frac{8}{5}\right)^{3x-4} \ge \left(\frac{8}{5}\right)^{x(x+8)}$$

$$\Rightarrow \quad 3x - 4 \ge x(x+8)$$

$$\Rightarrow \quad x^2 + 5x + 4 \le 0$$

$$\Rightarrow \quad (x+1)(x+4) \le 0$$

$$\therefore \quad x \in [-4, -1]$$

Hence, $a = -4, b = -1$

$\therefore a^2 + b^2 = 16 + 1 = 17$

5. Let $f(x) = |x-3| - |x+1| = \begin{cases} 4 & x < -1 \\ 2 - 2x & -1 \le x < 3 \\ -4 & x > 3 \end{cases}$

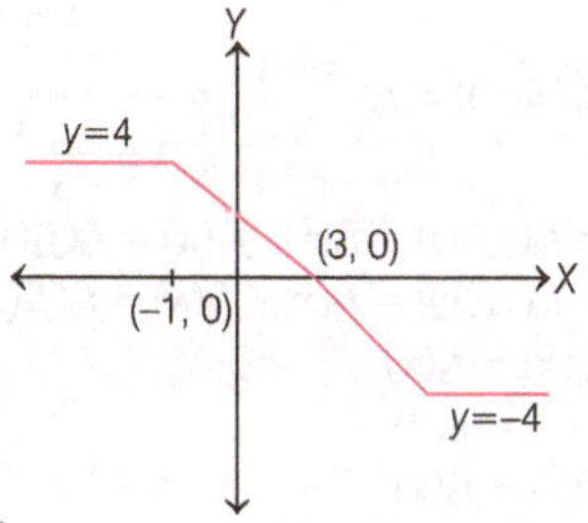

$\therefore P \in (-4, 4)$

So, integral value of P are $-3, -2, -1, 0, 1, 2, 3$.

Hence, total number of integral values of P is 7.

6. Since, $f(3+t) = f(3-t)$

$\Rightarrow$ function is symmetric about the line $x = 3$

Also, $x^2 + bx + c = 0$ is symmetric about $x = -\dfrac{b}{2}$

$\therefore \quad -\frac{b}{2}=3 \Rightarrow b=-6$

So, $\quad f(x)=x^2-6x+c$

Let c be positive.

$f(1)=c-5,\ f(2)=c-8,\ f(6)=c$

Let $\quad c=5$

$f(1)=0,\ f(2)=-3,\ f(6)=5$

$\therefore \quad f(2)<f(1)<f(6)$

7. We have, $f(x+y)=3^x f(y)+9^y f(x)$ ...(i)

$\Rightarrow \quad f(y+x)=3^y f(x)+9^x f(y)$ ...(ii)

From Eqs. (i) and (ii), we get

$3^x f(y)+9^y f(x)=3^y f(x)+9^x f(y)$

$\Rightarrow \quad (9^y-3^y)f(x)=(9^x-3^x)f(y)$

$\Rightarrow \quad \frac{f(x)}{9^x-3^x}=\frac{f(y)}{9^y-3^y}=k$ (let)

$\Rightarrow \quad f(x)=k(9^x-3^x)$

$\Rightarrow \quad f(1)=18=k(9^1-3^1) \Rightarrow k=3$

$\therefore \quad f(x)=3(9^x-3^x) \Rightarrow f'(x)=3(9^x \ln 9-3^x \ln 3)$

$f'(1)=3^2\cdot 5\cdot \ln 3 \Rightarrow a=2$ and $b=5$

$\therefore a+b=7$

8. We have,

$$||x+3|-2|=\operatorname{sgn}\left(1-\left|\frac{(x-2)(x-3)(x+2)}{(x^2+1)(x-2)(x-3)(x+2)}\right|\right)$$

$$=\operatorname{sgn}\left(1-\left|\frac{1}{1+x^2}\right|\right) x\neq 2, 3, -2$$

$||x+3|-2|=1 \Rightarrow |x+3|-2=\pm 1$

$\Rightarrow \quad |x+3|=3, 1 \Rightarrow x+3=\pm 3, \pm 1$

$\Rightarrow \quad x=0, -6, -2, -4$

$\therefore$ Sum of all possible solutions $=0-6-2-4=-12$

9. We have, $f_0(x)=\frac{1}{1-x}$ and $f_{n+1}(x)=f_0(f_n(x))$

$$\therefore \quad f_1(x)=f_0(f_0(x))=f_0\left(\frac{1}{1-x}\right)=\frac{1}{1-\frac{1}{1-x}}=\frac{x-1}{x}$$

and $f_2(x)=f_0(f_1(x))=f_0\left(\frac{x-1}{x}\right)=\frac{1}{1-\frac{x-1}{x}}=x$

Thus, $f_3(x)=f_0(f_2(x))=f_0(x),\ f_4(x)=f_0(f_3(x))=f_1(x)$

$f_5(x)=f_0(f_4(x))=f_2(x),\ f_6(x)=f_0(f_5(x))=f_3(x)$

In general $f_{3n}(x)=f_3(x)$

$f_{3n+1}(x)=f_1(x)$

$f_{3n+2}f(x)=f_2(x)$

$\therefore \quad f_{100}(x)=f_1(x)=\frac{x-1}{x}$

Hence, $f_{100}(3)+f_1\left(\frac{2}{3}\right)+f_2\left(\frac{3}{2}\right)=f_1(3)+f_1\left(\frac{2}{3}\right)+f_2\left(\frac{3}{2}\right)$

$$=\frac{3-1}{3}+\frac{\frac{2}{3}-1}{2/3}+\frac{3}{2}=\frac{2}{3}-\frac{1}{2}+\frac{3}{2}=\frac{5}{3}$$

10. We have, $f(x)=\{x\}+\left\{x+\left[\frac{x}{1+x^3}\right]\right\}+\left\{x+\left[\frac{x}{1+2x^3}\right]\right\}$

$$+\ldots+\left\{x+\left[\frac{x}{1+49x^3}\right]\right\}$$

$=5\{x\}$ $\quad [\because \{x+m\}=\{x\}, m\in I]$

$\therefore \quad f(\sqrt{2})=50\times\{1.414\}=50\times 0.414=20.7$

$\therefore [f(\sqrt{2})]=20$

11. We have, $f_n(x)=f_{n-1}(x)(1+2^n x)$

$=(1+(2^n-1)x+a_{n-1,2}x^2+\ldots)(1+2^n x)$

$=(1+(2^{n+1}-1)x+(a_{n-1,2}+2^{2n}-2^n)x^2+\ldots$

We have, $\quad a_{n,2}=a_{n-1,2}+2^{2n}-2^n$

$=a_{n-2,2}+2^{n-2}-2^{n-1}+2^{2n}-2^n$

$=a_{1,2}+(2^4+2^6+\ldots+2^{2n})-(2^2+2^3+\ldots+2^n)$

$=1+\frac{2^4(2^{n-2}-1)}{3}-4(2^{n-1}-1)$

$=\frac{2^{2n+2}-3\cdot 2^{n+1}+2}{3}=\frac{(2^{n+1}-1)(2^{n+1}-1)}{3}$

$\therefore \quad a=1, b=1$ and $c=3$

So, $4a-b+3c=4-1+9=12$

$N=12=2^2\times 3^1$

$\therefore$ Sum of $d_1=(2^0+2^1+2^2)(3^0+3^1)=28$

12. We have, $f(x+a)=\frac{1}{2}+\sqrt{f(x)-\{f(x)\}^2}$

$\therefore \quad f(x+a+a)=\frac{1}{2}+\sqrt{f(x+a)-\{f(x+a)\}^2}$

$\Rightarrow f(x+2a)=\frac{1}{2}+\sqrt{f(x+a)\{1-f(x+a)\}}$

$$\Rightarrow f(x+2a)=\frac{1}{2}+\sqrt{\left\{\frac{1}{2}+\sqrt{f(x)-\{f(x)\}^2}\right\}\left\{\frac{1}{2}-\sqrt{f(x)-\{f(x)\}^2}\right\}}$$

$\Rightarrow f(x+2a)=\frac{1}{2}+\sqrt{\frac{1}{4}-\{f(x)-\{f(x)\}^2\}}$

$\Rightarrow f(x+2a)=\frac{1}{2}+\sqrt{\frac{1}{4}-f(x)+(f(x))^2}$

$\Rightarrow f(x+2a)=\frac{1}{2}+\sqrt{\left\{f(x)-\frac{1}{2}\right\}^2}=\frac{1}{2}+\left|f(x)-\frac{1}{2}\right|$

$f(x+2a)=\frac{1}{2}+f(x)-\frac{1}{2}$ $\quad [\because f(x)\geq 1/2]$

$\Rightarrow f(x+2a)=f(x)$ for all x

Hence, $f(x)$ is a periodic function with period $2a$.

13. We have, $f(x)=\sqrt{x^4-x+1}+\sqrt{[|x|]}+\sqrt{\{|x|\}}$

Clearly, the domain of $\sqrt{[|x|]}+\sqrt{\{|x|\}}$ is $(-\infty, \infty)$

Also, $x^4-x+1\geq 0$

If $x\geq 1$, then $x^4-x+1>0$

If $x\in(0,1)$, then $x^4-x+1=(1-x)+x^4\geq 0$

If $x\in(-\infty, 0)$, then x^4-x

Hence, the domain of $f(x)$ is $(-\infty, \infty) \Rightarrow$ set of real numbers

14. We have, $f(x)=\dfrac{3x+5}{2x-3}$

Now, $f(f(x))=\dfrac{3\left[\dfrac{3x+5}{2x-3}\right]+5}{2\left[\dfrac{3x+5}{2x-3}\right]-3}=\dfrac{9x+15+10x-15}{6x+10-6x+9}=\dfrac{19x}{19}=x$

$\therefore f_{2008}(x)+f_{2009}(x)=x+f(x)=x+\dfrac{3x+5}{2x-3}=\dfrac{2x^2+5}{2x-3}$

$a=2, b=5, c=2, d=-3$

$a+b+c+d=6$

15. We have, $[y+[y]]=2\cos x$

$\Rightarrow \quad [y]+[y]=2\cos x \Rightarrow 2[y]=2\cos x;$

$[y]=\cos x$ ...(i)

When $y=\dfrac{1}{3}[\sin x+[\sin x+[\sin x]]]$

$=\dfrac{1}{3}[\sin x+[\sin x]+[\sin x]]=\dfrac{1}{3}([3[\sin x])$

$=[\sin x]$ ...(ii)

From Eqs. (i) and (ii), we get

$[\sin x]=\cos x \Rightarrow \cos x=0, 1, -1$

Hence, no solution.

16. We have, $f(x+k)=1+[1+\{1-f(x)\}^5]^{\frac{1}{5}}$

$\Rightarrow \quad f(x+k)-1=[1-(f(x)-1)^5]^{\frac{1}{5}}$

$\Rightarrow \quad \phi(x+k)=[1-\{\phi(x)\}^5]^{\frac{1}{5}}$

where $\phi(x)=f(x)-1$

$\Rightarrow \quad \phi(x+2k)=[1-\{\phi(x+k)\}^5]^{\frac{1}{5}}$

$\Rightarrow \quad \phi(x+2k)=[1-\{1-(\phi(x)^5\}]^{\frac{1}{5}}=\phi(x), \forall x\in R$

$\Rightarrow \quad f(x+2k)-1=f(x)-1$

$\Rightarrow \quad f(x+2k)=f(x), \forall x\in R$

$\therefore f(x)$ is periodic with $2k$ period.

17. We have, $g(x-2)+g(x+2)=\sqrt{3}g(x)$ ...(i)

Replace $x\to x+2$, $g(x)+g(x+4)=\sqrt{3}\,g(x+2)$ ...(ii)

Replace $x\to x-2$, $g(x-4)+g(x)=\sqrt{3}g(x-2)$ ...(iii)

On adding Eqs. (ii) and (iii), we get

$g(x-4)+g(x+4)+2g(x)=\sqrt{3}\,(g(x+2)+g(x-2))$

$=\sqrt{3}\,(\sqrt{3}g(x))=3g(x)$

So, $g(x-4)+g(x+4)=g(x)$ ...(iv)

In Eq. (iv), replace $x\to x+4$

$g(x)+g(x+8)=g(x+4)$ ...(v)

On adding Eqs. (iv) and (v), we get

$g(x-4)+g(x+8)=0$

$g(x-4)=-g(x+8)$

$x\to x+4$

$g(x)=-g(x+12)$

$x\to x+12$

$g(x+12)=-g(x+24)$

So, $g(x)=g(x+24)$

18. We have, $e^{2x}-2ye^x+1=0 \Rightarrow 2ye^x=1+e^{2x}$

$\Rightarrow \quad y=\dfrac{1}{2}(e^x+e^{-x})$

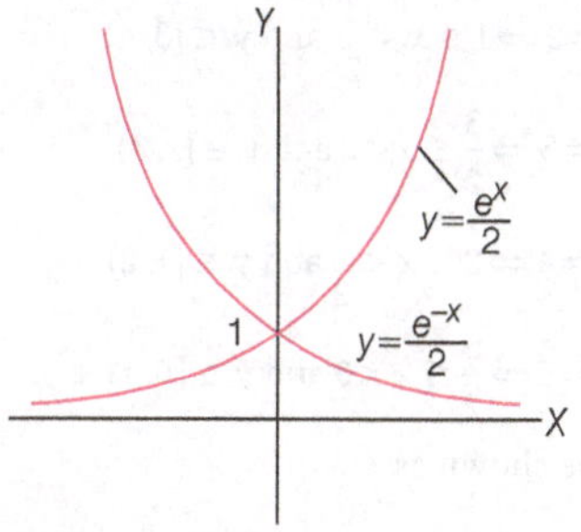

$\therefore$ Domain $=R$

Now, $y=\dfrac{1}{2}[e^x+e^{-x}]$

Hence, the range of $f(x)$ is

$y\in[1,\infty)$

$A\cap B=[1,\infty)$

19. In the figure, $4=A+u+v, 1=-3A-u+v$ ...(i)

and $1=3A+c+d, 4=-A-c+d$ ...(ii)

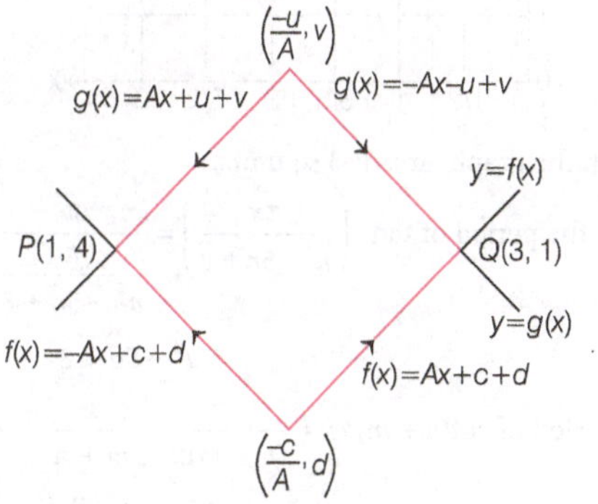

From Eq. (i), $3=4A+2u$ ...(iii)

From Eq. (ii), $-3=4A+2c$ ...(iv)

On adding Eqs. (ii) and (iv), we get

$8A+2u+2c=0$

$\therefore \quad \dfrac{u+c}{A}=-4$

Alternate Solution

$f(x)=|Ax+c|+d$

$g(x)=-|Ax+\mu|+v,$

which are sides of parallelogram and the diagonals bisect each other.

$\therefore \quad \left(\dfrac{-u}{A}\right)+\left(\dfrac{-c}{A}\right)=3+1\Rightarrow\dfrac{u+c}{A}=-4$

20. Here, $[2x]+[y]=5$

Let us consider $[2x]=0$

$\Rightarrow 0\le 2x<1$ and $[y]=5$

i.e. $x\in[0,1/2)$ and $y\in[5,6)$.

Similarly, we can consider $[2x] = 1, 2, 3, 4$ and 5.

when, $[2x] = 1 \Rightarrow \frac{1}{2} \le x < 1$ and $y \in [4, 5)$

$$[2x] = 2 \Rightarrow 1 \le x < \frac{3}{2} \text{ and } y \in [3, 4)$$

$$[2x] = 3 \Rightarrow \frac{3}{2} \le x < 2 \text{ and } y \in [2, 3)$$

$$[2x] = 4 \Rightarrow 2 \le x < \frac{5}{2} \text{ and } y \in [1, 2)$$

$$[2x] = 5 \Rightarrow \frac{5}{2} \le x < 3 \text{ and } y \in [0, 1)$$

which can be shown as

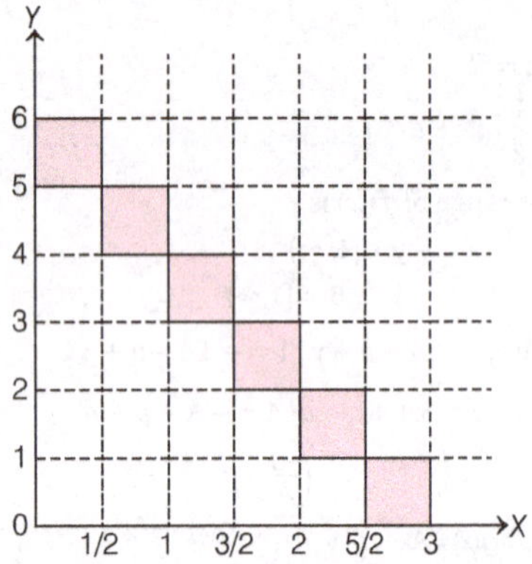

$\therefore$ From the graph, area is 3 sq units.

21. Since, the period of $\tan^2\left(\frac{\pi x}{n^2 - 5n + 8}\right) = \frac{\pi}{\frac{\pi}{n^2 - 5n + 8}}$

$$= n^2 - 5n + 8$$

and period of $\cot(n + m)\pi x = \frac{\pi}{(n + m)\pi} = \frac{1}{m + n}$

$\therefore$ Period of $f(x) =$ LCM of $\left(n^2 - 5n + 8, \frac{1}{n + m}\right) = 2$

Now,

Case I $n^2 - 5n + 8 = 1$ or $n^2 - 5n + 8 = 2$

$\Rightarrow \quad n^2 - 5n + 7 = 0$ or $n^2 - 5n + 6 = 0$

$\therefore \quad n = \frac{5 \pm \sqrt{3}i}{2}$ or $n = 2, 3$

But $n \in N$

$\therefore \quad n = 2, 3$

Case II $\left(\frac{1}{n + m}\right)\lambda = 2, \lambda \in I \Rightarrow \frac{1}{n + m} \not> 1$

For $n = 2$, $\frac{1}{2 + m} \not> 1 \Rightarrow \frac{1}{2 + m} - 1 \not> 0$

$\Rightarrow \quad \frac{-1 - m}{2 + m} \not> 0 \Rightarrow \frac{m + 1}{m + 2} \not< 0$

$\therefore \quad m \notin (-2, -1)$ ...(i)

and for $n = 3$, $\frac{1}{3 + m} \not> 0 \Rightarrow \frac{1}{3 + m} - 1 \not> 0$

$\Rightarrow \quad \frac{-2 - m}{3 + m} \not> 0 \Rightarrow \frac{m + 2}{m + 3} \not< 0$

$\therefore \quad m \notin (-3, -2)$ ...(ii)

Hence, from Eqs. (i) and (ii), we get

$$m \notin (-3, -2) \cup (-2, -1)$$

22. We have, $f(f^{-1}(B)) = (f(x) : x \in f^{-1}(B))$

$$= (f(x) : f(x) \in B)$$

$\Rightarrow \quad f(f^{-1}(B)) \subset B$

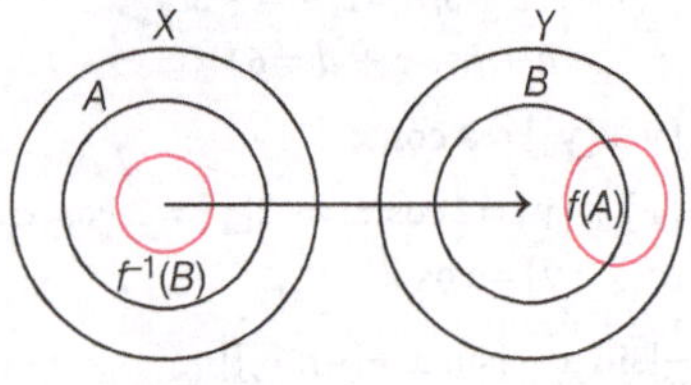

Now, if $x \in B \subset y \Rightarrow x \in y$

It may happen that $f^{-1}(x)$ does not exist in x as function is not given to be surjective.

$\therefore \quad f(f^{-1}(B)) \ne B$

Also, $f^{-1}(f(A)) = (x \in X : f(x) (- f(A))$

But $f(A) = (f(x) : x \in A)$

From above, we cannot conclude $f^{-1}(f(A)) \subset A$

If the function is non-injective, then it may happen that $x \notin A$ and $f(x) \in f(A)$

$\Rightarrow f^{-1}(f(A)) \not\subset A \Rightarrow f^{-1}(f(A)) \ne A$

23. (b) $\quad \frac{x - 3}{x^2 - 5x + 6} < 2$

$\Rightarrow \frac{-2x^2 + 11x - 15}{x^2 - 5x + 16} < 0$

$\Rightarrow \frac{(x - 3)(2x - 5)}{(x - 3)(x - 2)} > 0 \Rightarrow x < 2$ or $x > \frac{5}{2}, x \ne 3$

While $2x^2 - 11x + 15 > 0$, gives $x < \frac{5}{2}$ or $x > 3$

(c) $x + 3 - \frac{1}{x - 1} > -x + 2 - \frac{1}{x - 1}$

$\Rightarrow \quad x + 3 > -x + 2, x \ne 1$ or $x > -\frac{1}{2}, x \ne 1$

While $x + 3 > -x + 2$, gives $x > -\frac{1}{2}$

(d) $\log_2(x^2 - 4) > \log_2(4x - 7)$

$\Rightarrow \quad x^2 - 4 > 4x - 7, x^2 - 4 > 0, 4x - 7 > 0$

$\Rightarrow \quad x^2 - 4x + 3 > 0, x^2 - 4 > 0$ and $4x - 7 > 0$

or $(x - 3)(x - 1) > 0, (x - 2)(x + 2) > 0$ and $x > \frac{7}{4}$

$\Rightarrow x > 3$ or $x < 1$, $x > 2$ or $x < -2$ and $x > \frac{7}{4}$

$\Rightarrow x > 3$

While $x^2 - 4x + 3 > 0$, gives $x > 3$ or $x < 1$.

24. We have, $f(x) = x + 1$

On putting $2^x = t \Rightarrow x = \log_2 t$

$\Rightarrow f(t) = \log_2 t + 1 \Rightarrow f(x) = \log_2 x + 1$

Now, $f(x_1) = 3 \Rightarrow \log_2 x_1 + 1 = 3 \Rightarrow x_1 = 4$

Similarly, $f(x_2) = 4$

$\Rightarrow 1 + \log_2 x_2 = 4 \Rightarrow x_2 = 8$

So, option (c) is correct.

Now, $f^{-1}(x) = 2^{x-1} \Rightarrow f^{-1}(1) = 1, f^{-1}(2) = 2$

So, option (d) is also correct.

25. We have, $\dfrac{x-[x]}{1+x-[x]} = \dfrac{\{x\}}{1+\{x\}} \in \left[0, \dfrac{1}{2}\right)$

For domain $\dfrac{x-[x]}{1+x-[x]} > 0$ and $0 < [x]^2 - 3[x] + 3 \le 1$

$\Rightarrow x \notin I$ and $[x] = 1$ or $2 \Rightarrow x \in (1, 3) - \{2\}$

For range, if $x \in (1, 3) - \{2\}$

$f(x) = \log_{\frac{\{x\}}{1+\{x\}}}(1) = 0$

26. (a) $(f+g)(3.5) = f(3.5) + g(3.5) = (-0.5) + (0.5) = 0$ [true]

(b) $f(g(3)) = f(0) = 3$ [true]

(c) $f(g(2)) = f(-1) = 8$

(d) $(f-g)(4) = f(4) - g(4) = 0 - 26 = -26$

27. Here, $g(x) = \sin(\sin^{-1}\sqrt{\{x\}}) + \cos(\sin^{-1}\sqrt{\{x\}}) - 1$

$= \sqrt{\{x\}} + \cos(\cos^{-1}\sqrt{1-\{x\}}) - 1$

$= \sqrt{\{x\}} + \sqrt{1-\{x\}} - 1$

If $x \in I$, then $\{x\} = 0 \Rightarrow g(x) = 0$

Also, $g(-x) = g(x)$

$\Rightarrow$ $g(x)$ is even.

If $x \notin I$, then $\{-x\} = 1 - \{x\}$

$\Rightarrow g(-x) = \sqrt{1-\{x\}} + \sqrt{\{x\}} - 1 = g(x)$

$\Rightarrow g(x)$ is even function.

$\therefore$ $g(x) = 0, x \in I$ and $g(x) = g(-x), x \notin I$

$\Rightarrow g(x)$ is periodic function.

28. Here, $(x+1)\, f(x) = x$

$\Rightarrow (x+1)\, f(x) - x = 0$ is $(n+1)$th degree

$\Rightarrow (x+1) f(x) - x = (x-0)(x-1)(x-2)\ldots(x-n)\cdot k$

On putting $x = n+1$, we get

$(n+2) f(n+1) - (n+1) = (n+1)!\,(k)$ ...(i)

On putting $x = -1 \Rightarrow (-1)^{n+1}\cdot(n+1)!(k) = 1$ ...(ii)

From Eqs. (i) and (ii), we get

$$f(n+1) = \frac{(n+1)+(-1)^{n+1}}{(n+2)} = \begin{cases} 1, & \text{when } n \text{ is odd} \\ \dfrac{n}{n+2}, & \text{when } n \text{ is even} \end{cases}$$

29. $f(x) = 1 - x - x^3$

Replacing x by $f(x)$, $f(f(x)) = 1 - f(x) - f^3(x)$

Hence, the given equation is

$f(f(x)) > f(1-5x)$, $f(x) < 1 - 5x$

$f(x) = 1 - x - x^3$

$1 - x - x^3 < 1 - 5x$

$x^3 - 4x > 0$

$x(x-2)(x+2) > 0$

So, $x \in (-2, 0) \cup (2, \infty)$

30. We have, $f(x) = \cos^{-1}(-\{-x\})$

Domain of $f(x) \in R$.

As, $0 \le \{-x\} < 1, \forall x \in R \Rightarrow -1 < -\{-x\} \le 0$

So, the range of $f(x) \in \left[\dfrac{\pi}{2}, \pi\right)$.

$\therefore$Range of $f(x)$ contains two prime numbers 2 and 3. Graph of $f(x)$ does not lie below X-axis.

Clearly, f is neither even nor odd but many-one.

$\therefore f(x+1) = f(x) \Rightarrow f(x)$ is periodic.

31. (a) We have, $f(x) = \dfrac{\sec x}{\cos x} - \dfrac{\tan x}{\cot x}$,

$g(x) = \dfrac{\cos x}{\sec x} + \dfrac{\sin x}{\operatorname{cosec} x}$

Clearly, both $f(x)$ and $g(x)$ are identical functions as

$x \ne \dfrac{k\pi}{2}, \forall k \in I$.

(b) As $x^2 - 4x + 5 = (x-2)^2 + 1 > 0$

Hence, $f(x) = 1, \forall x \in R$.

Also, $\cos^2 x + \sin^2\left(x + \dfrac{\pi}{2}\right) > 0$

Hence, $g(x) = 1, \forall x \in R$ g

$\Rightarrow f(x)$ and $g(x)$ are identical.

(c) $f(x) = e^{\ln(x^2+3x+3)}$

As, $x^2 + 3x + 3 = \left(x + \dfrac{3}{2}\right)^2 + \dfrac{3}{4} > 0, \forall x \in R$.

Hence, $f(x) = x^2 + 3x + 3, \forall x \in R$,

$\Rightarrow f(x)k$ is identical to $g(x)$.

(d) We have, $f(x) = \dfrac{\sin x}{\sec x} + \dfrac{\cos x}{\operatorname{cosec} x}$, $g(x) = \dfrac{2\cos^2 x}{\cot x}$

Clearly, both $f(x)$ and $g(x)$ are identical functions as

$x \ne \dfrac{k\pi}{2}, \forall k \in I$.

32. S_1 is incorrect as zero function

i.e. $f(x) = 0$; $R \to R$ is both odd and even simultaneously

S_2 is incorrect as domain of $f(x)$ is $R \sim \{0\}$: $x = 0$ is not in domain, S_3 is correct as $f(x) = \sin^{99}(x)$

$\Rightarrow f(x + 2\pi) = \sin^{99}(x + 2\pi) = \sin^{99} x = f(x)$

$\therefore$ Period of $\sin^{99} x$ is 2π.

S_4 is false, since composition of a periodic function over a non-periodic and non-linear function is non periodic.

33. Since, $1 \le |\sin x| + |\cos x| \le \sqrt{2}$

$\Rightarrow [|\sin x| + |\cos x|] = 1$

For $f(x)$ to be defined

$\sin^2 x + 2\sin x + \dfrac{11}{4} \ge 2$

$$(\sin x + 1)^2 \geq \frac{1}{4}$$

$$\Rightarrow \quad \sin x + 1 \geq \frac{1}{2} \text{ or } \sin x + 1 \leq -\frac{1}{2}$$

$$\sin x \geq -\frac{1}{2} \text{ or } \sin x \leq -\frac{3}{2} \quad \text{[not possible]}$$

34. $(f(x))^2 f(1-x) = x + 3$ ...(i)

Replace x by $1 - x$, we get

$$(f(1-x))^2 f(x) = 4 - x \quad \text{...(ii)}$$

From Eqs. (i) and (ii), we get

$$f(x) = \left(\frac{x^2 + 6x + 9}{4 - x}\right)^{\frac{1}{3}}$$

$$f(x) = \frac{(x+3)^{2/3}}{(4-x)^{1/3}}$$

$\therefore \; D_f = R - \{4\}$

At $x = -3$, $\quad f(x) = 0$

$$f(0) = \frac{3^{2/3}}{(-4)^{1/3}} = \left(\frac{3}{2}\right)^{2/3}$$

35. $f(x+1) = \dfrac{f(x) - 5}{f(x) - 3}$ ...(i)

$$f(x) \cdot f(x+1) - 3f(x+1) = f(x) - 5$$

$$\Rightarrow \quad f(x) = \frac{3f(x+1) - 5}{f(x+1) - 1}$$

Replacing x by $(x - 1)$, we get

$$f(x-1) = \frac{3f(x) - 5}{f(x) - 1} \quad \text{...(ii)}$$

Using Eq. (i), we get

$$f(x+2) = \frac{f(x+1) - 5}{f(x+1) - 3} = \frac{\frac{f(x)-5}{f(x)-3} - 5}{\frac{f(x)-5}{f(x)-3} - 3} = \frac{2f(x) - 5}{f(x) - 2} \quad \text{...(iii)}$$

Using Eq. (ii), we get

$$f(x-2) = \frac{3f(x-1) - 5}{f(x-1) - 1}$$

$$= \frac{3\left(\frac{3f(x)-5}{f(x)-1}\right) - 5}{\frac{3f(x)-5}{f(x)-1} - 1} = \frac{2f(x) - 5}{f(x) - 2} \quad \text{...(iv)}$$

Using Eqs. (iii) and (iv), we get

$$f(x+2) = f(x-2) \Rightarrow f(x+4) = f(x)$$

$\therefore f(x)$ is periodic with period 4.

Sol. (Q.Nos. 36 to 37)

The function $f(x)$ is given by

$$f(x) = \begin{cases} \pi(2R - x)^2, & 0 \leq x \leq R \\ \pi R^2, & R \leq x \leq 3R \\ \pi(6Rx - x^2 - 8R^2), & 3R \leq x \leq 4R \end{cases}$$

f is not defined outside $[0, 4R]$.

36. (b) **37.** (a)

Sol. (Q.Nos. 38 to 39)

38. (d) Since, $(2x + y)^2 = x^2 + xy + 7y^2 \Rightarrow x = y$ or $x = -2y$

and for that $k = 9, 21$

Product $= 189$

39. (c) These form a GP, $\dfrac{\log_2 x}{\log_4 x}$ is common ratio $= 2$

Now, $\dfrac{\log_4 x}{\log_8 2x} = 2 \Rightarrow \log_4 x = 2 \log_8 2x$

$$\frac{1}{2}\log_2 x = 2\log_8 2 + 2\log_8 x; \frac{1}{2}\log_2 x = \frac{2}{3} + \frac{2}{3}\log_2 x$$

$$\left(\frac{1}{2} - \frac{2}{3}\right)\log_2 x = \frac{2}{3}, -\frac{1}{6}\log_2 x = \frac{2}{3},$$

$$\log_2 x = -\frac{2 \times 6}{3} = -4$$

$$\therefore \quad x = 2^{-4} = \frac{1}{16} = \frac{m}{n} \Rightarrow m = 1, n = 16$$

Hence, $m + n = 1 + 16 = 17$

Sol. (Q.Nos. 40 to 41)

$$f(2-x) = f(2+x) \quad \text{...(i)}$$

and $f(20 - x) - f(x) = 0, \forall x \in R$ ...(ii)

$$f(2-x) = f(2+x)$$

$f(x)$ is symmetric about the line $x = 2$

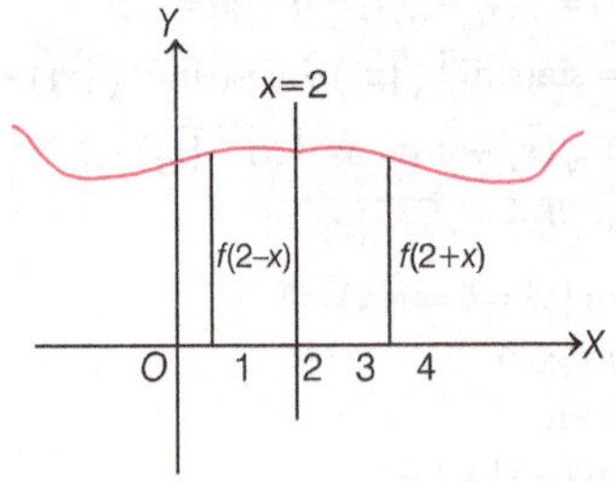

$$f(2-x) = f(20 - (2-x)) \quad \text{[using Eq. (ii)]}$$

$$= f(18 + x)$$

$$f(2+x) = f(18 - x) \quad \text{[using Eq. (i)]}$$

$$\Rightarrow \quad f(x) = f(x + 16)$$

$\Rightarrow f(x)$ is a function periodic with period 16.

Also, $f(2-x) = f(2+x) = f(0) = f(4)$ and the period of $f(x)$ is 16.

$\Rightarrow f(0) - f(4) - f(20) - f(36) = ... - f(4 + (n-1)(16))$,

where $4 + (n-1)(16) \leq 170$

$$\Rightarrow \quad 16n - 12 \leq 170 \Rightarrow 16n \leq 182$$

$$\Rightarrow \quad n \leq 11\frac{3}{8}$$

$\therefore f(x) = 5$ for $x \in \{0, 4, 20, ..., 176\}$ i.e. 12 values of x.

40. (b)

41. (a) Since, $f(x)$ is symmetrical about $x = 2$ and $f(x)$ is periodic with period 16.

$$\Rightarrow \quad f(2) = f(2 + 16) = f(18)$$

$\Rightarrow f(x)$ is also symmetrical about $x = 18$

Also, $\quad f(x-2) = f(2-x)$

$\Rightarrow f((20 - x) - 2) = f(2 - (20 - x)) \Rightarrow f(18 - x) = f(x - 18)$

Solutions (Q.Nos. 42 to 43)

Here, $x=\omega^3+\omega^4$

$$\Rightarrow \quad x^5=(\omega^2)^5(\omega+\omega^2)^5$$

$$=(\omega^5)^2[\omega^5+5\omega^4\cdot\omega^2+10\omega^3\cdot\omega^4+10\omega^2\cdot\omega^6+5\omega\cdot\omega^8+\omega^{10}]$$

Put $\omega^5=3$ and $\omega^{10}=9$

Now, $x^5=9[3+5\cdot(3\omega)+10\cdot(3\omega^2)+10\cdot3\omega^3+5\cdot(3\omega^4)+3^2]$

$$=9[12+15(\omega+\omega^2)+15(\omega^2+\omega^3)+15(\omega^3+\omega^4)]$$

$$=9\left[12+15\left(\frac{x}{\omega^2}\right)+15\cdot\left(\frac{x}{\omega}\right)+15x\right]$$

$$=9\left[12+15x\left(\frac{1}{\omega^2}+\frac{1}{\omega}\right)+15x\right]$$

$$=9\left[12+15x\cdot\frac{\omega+\omega^2}{\omega^3}\cdot\frac{\omega^2}{\omega^2}+15x\right]$$

$$=9\left[12+15x\cdot\frac{(\omega^3+\omega^4)}{\omega^5}+15x\right]$$

$$=9\left[12+15x\cdot\frac{x}{3}+15x\right]$$

$$=9[12+15x+5x^2]$$

$$=f(x)$$

Now, $f(x)=9(5x^2+15x+12)$

$\therefore \quad f(x)=0$

$$\Rightarrow \quad x=\frac{-15\pm\sqrt{-15}}{10}=\frac{-15\pm i\sqrt{15}}{10}=\alpha,\beta$$

42. (d) Clearly, $\alpha+\beta=-3, \alpha\beta=\frac{12}{5}, |\alpha-\beta|=\left|\frac{2i\sqrt{15}}{10}\right|=\sqrt{\frac{3}{5}}$

But $|\alpha|+|\beta|=2\left(\sqrt{\left(\frac{15}{10}\right)^2+\left(\frac{\sqrt{15}}{10}\right)^2}\right)=4\sqrt{\frac{3}{5}}$

43. (a) In argand plane, $OA=OB=\sqrt{\frac{12}{5}}$ and $AB=2\frac{\sqrt{15}}{10}=\sqrt{\frac{3}{5}}$

and area of ΔOAB, $\Delta=\frac{1}{2}AB(OM)=\frac{1}{2}\cdot\sqrt{\frac{3}{5}}\cdot\left(\frac{15}{10}\right)$

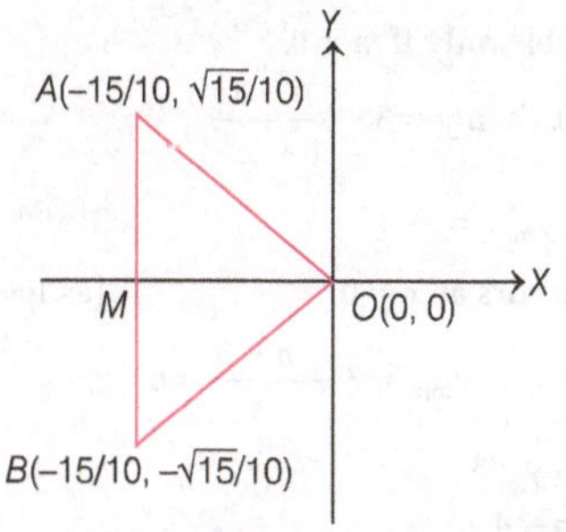

$$\therefore \text{Circumradius, } R=\frac{OA\cdot AB\cdot OB}{4\Delta}=\frac{\sqrt{\frac{12}{5}}\sqrt{\frac{3}{5}}\sqrt{\frac{12}{5}}}{4\cdot\frac{1}{2}\cdot\sqrt{\frac{3}{5}}\left(\frac{15}{10}\right)}=\frac{4}{5}$$

Solutions (Q.Nos. 44 to 45)

Given that $f(x)+f\left(\frac{x-1}{x}\right)=x$ for all $x\neq 0, 1$. Replacing x with $\frac{(x-1)}{x}$ both sides, we get

$$f\left(\frac{x-1}{x}\right)+f\left(\frac{\left[\frac{(x-1)}{x}\right]-1}{\frac{(x-1)}{x}}\right)=\frac{x-1}{x}$$

That is, $f\left(\frac{x-1}{x}\right)+f\left(\frac{1}{1-x}\right)=\frac{x-1}{x}$

Again, replacing x with $\frac{(x-1)}{x}$ in this, we get

$$f\left(\frac{1}{1-x}\right)+f(x)=\frac{1}{1-x}$$

Then, by taking Eq.(1.10) + Eq. (1.12) – Eq (1.11), we get

$$2f(x)=x+\frac{1}{1-x}-\frac{x-1}{x}$$

or $\quad f(x)=\frac{1}{2}\left[x+\frac{1}{1-x}-\frac{x-1}{x}\right]$

44. $f(-1)=\frac{1}{2}\left[-1+\frac{1}{1-(-1)}-\frac{(-1)-1}{-1}\right]$

$$=\frac{1}{2}\left[-1+\frac{1}{2}-2\right]$$

$$=\frac{1}{2}\left[\frac{1}{2}-3\right]$$

$$=\frac{1}{2}\times\frac{-5}{2}=\frac{-5}{4}$$

$$\therefore |f(-1)|=\left|\frac{-5}{4}\right|=\frac{5}{4}=1.25$$

45. $f(3)=\frac{1}{2}\left[3+\frac{3}{1-3}-\frac{(3-1)}{3}\right]$

$$=\frac{1}{2}\left[3-\frac{3}{2}-\frac{2}{3}\right]=\frac{1}{2}\left[\frac{18-9-4}{6}\right]=\frac{1}{2}\times\frac{5}{6}=\frac{5}{12}=0.41$$

Solutions (Q.Nos. 46 to 47)

Since, the maximum value of sine function is 1 and minimum value is –1, so the maximum temperature will be 62°F and minimum will be – 12°F.

46. 62 °F **47.** – 12 °F

48. We have, $|x^2-4|-|x-a|=0$

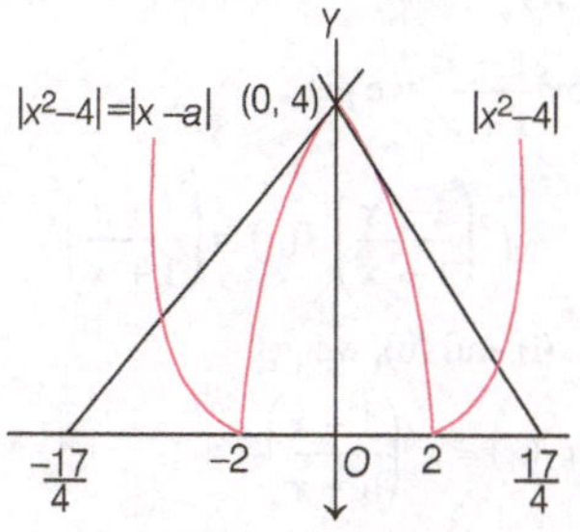

For tangency, $x^2 - 4 = x - a$

$\Rightarrow x^2 - x + a - 4 = 0$

Now, put $D = 0$

$\Rightarrow 1 - 4a + 16 = 0$

$\Rightarrow a = \frac{17}{4}$ and $a = \frac{-17}{4}$

$\therefore$ For 4 distinct solution,

$$a \in \left(\frac{-17}{4}, -2\right) \cup (-2, 2) \cup \left(2, \frac{17}{4}\right)$$

Hence, the number of integers is 7.

49. As $x^2 + y^2 = 4$

$\Rightarrow x = 2\cos\theta, y = 2\sin\theta$

$\therefore \frac{x^3 + y^3}{x + y} = x^2 + y^2 - xy = 4 - 2\sin 2\theta$

$\Rightarrow \left(\frac{x^3 + y^3}{x + y}\right)_{max} = (4 - 2(\sin 2\theta))_{min} = 4 + 2 = 6$

50. $f(2011) = (2 + 0 + 1 + 1)^2 = 16$

$f^2(2011) = (1 + 6)^2 = 49$

$f^3(2011) = (4 + 9)^2 = 169$

$f^4(2011) = (1 + 6 + 9)^2 = 256$

$f^5(2011) = (2 + 5 + 6) = 169$

$\vdots$

$f^{2n}(2011) = 256$

$\therefore f^{2n+1}(2011) = 169$

$\Rightarrow \frac{f^{2011}(2011) - f^{2010}(2011)}{f^{2013}(2011) - f^{2012}(2011)} = \frac{169 - 256}{169 - 256} = 1$

51. As $xy - 6(x + y) = 0 \Rightarrow (x - 6)(y - 6) = 36$

$\therefore (x - 6, y - 6) = (1, 36), (2, 18), (3, 12), (4, 9), (6, 6), (-36, -1),$
$(-18, -2), (-12, -3), (-4, -9), (-6, -6)$

$\because x \le y \Rightarrow \alpha = 10$

$\therefore (\alpha - 6) = 4$

52. Now, $f(x) = \frac{x^4 + x^2 + 1}{x^2 - x + 1} \Rightarrow f(x) = x^2 + x + 1$

Now, $f(\omega^n) = \omega^{2n} + \omega^n + 1 = 3$

$\because \omega^n = 1$, when n is a multiple of 3.

53. $f^2(x) \cdot f\left(\frac{1 - x}{1 + x}\right) = x^3$ ...(i)

Replacing x by $\frac{1 - x}{1 + x}$, we get

$$f^2\left(\frac{1 - x}{1 + x}\right) f(x) = \left(\frac{1 - x}{1 + x}\right)^3 \quad ...(ii)$$

By using Eqs. (i) and (ii), we get

$$f^3(x) = x^6\left(\frac{1 + x}{1 - x}\right)^3$$

$\Rightarrow f(x) = x^3\left(\frac{1 + x}{1 - x}\right) \Rightarrow f(-2) = \frac{8}{3}$

$\Rightarrow (f(-2)) = 2 \Rightarrow |(f(-2))| = 2$

54. $f(2a - x) = f(x) \Rightarrow f(2a - x) = -f(x)$

$\because f$ is odd $\Rightarrow f(x + 4a) = f(x)$

f is periodic with period $4a$.

$\Rightarrow f(1 + 4r) = f(1)$

Now, $\sum_{r=0}^{\infty} (f(1))^r = 8 \Rightarrow \frac{1}{1 - f(1)} = 8$

$\Rightarrow f(1) = \frac{7}{8} \Rightarrow 8f(1) = 7$

55. The period of the function is found as follows

Given, $f(x) + f(x + 4) = f(x + 2) + f(x + 6)$ ...(i)

$\therefore$ Replacing x by $x + 2$, we get

$f(x + 2) + f(x + 6) = f(x + 4) + f(x + 8)$ ...(ii)

From Eqs. (i) and (ii), we get

$f(x) + f(x + 4) = f(x + 4) + f(x + 8)$

$\Rightarrow f(x) = f(x + 8)$

Thus, 8 is the period.

56. Since, $f(x)$ is symmetric about $y = x$.

$\Rightarrow f^{-1}(x) = f(x)$

$\therefore f^2(x) = (f^{-1}(x))^2 - px \cdot f(x) f^{-1}(x) + 2x^2 f(x)$

$\Rightarrow f^2(x) = f^2(x) - px \cdot f(x) \cdot f(x) + 2x^2 f(x)$

$\Rightarrow f(x) \cdot (2x^2 - px \cdot f(x)\} = 0$

$\Rightarrow f(x) = \frac{2x^2}{px}$ [as $f(x) \ne 0$]

$\Rightarrow f(x) = \frac{2x}{p} \Rightarrow p = 2$

57. Here, $f(x) = \frac{3x^2 + mx + n}{x^2 + 1} = 3 + \frac{mx + n - 3}{x^2 + 1}$

$\therefore y = 3 + \frac{mx + n - 3}{1 + x^2}$

For y to lie in $[-4, 3)$.

$mx + n - 3 < 0, \forall x \in R.$

This is possible only if $m = 0$.

When $m = 0$, then $y = 3 + \frac{n - 3}{1 + x^2}$.

If $x \to \infty \Rightarrow y_{max} = \to 3^-$

Now, y_{min} occurs at $x = 0$ [as $1 + x^2$ is maximum]

$y_{min} = 3 + \frac{n - 3}{1} = n$ ...(i)

Since, $-4 \le y < 3$

$\therefore y_{min} = -4$ ...(ii)

From Eqs. (i) and (ii), we get

$n = -4$

$\therefore \frac{m^2 + n^2}{4} = \frac{16}{4} = 4$

58. Let $f(x) = ax + b$ and $g(x) = cx + d$

As, $f(g(x)) = x$ hold, $\forall x$, we get

$$f(g(x)) = a(g(x)) + b = a(cx + d) + b = acx + ad + b$$

$\therefore a(x + ad + b) = x$

On comparing coefficients, we get

$$ac = 1 \text{ and } ad + b = 0 \Rightarrow c = \frac{1}{a} \text{ and } d = -\frac{b}{a}$$

$\therefore \quad g(x) = \frac{x}{a} - \frac{b}{a}$

Also, $f(x) = ax + b$

Now, $f(0) = 4 \Rightarrow b = 4$

and $g(5) = 17 \Rightarrow \frac{5-4}{a} = 17 \Rightarrow a = \frac{1}{17}$

$\therefore \quad f(x) = \frac{x}{17} + 4$

Hence, $f(136) = \frac{136}{17} + 4 = 12$

59. We have, $n = {}^5C_4 \cdot 4! = 5!$

When exactly 2 elements of A maps to itself

$$f(3) = 3 \text{ and } f(4) = 4$$

$\therefore$From 5, 6, 7 select any 2 in ${}^3C_2 \times 2! = 6$ ways

When exactly one elements of A maps to itself say $f(3) = 3$

Now, 4 can be map in 3 ways and remaining elements $3 \times 2 = 6$ ways

$\therefore {}^2C_1 \times 3 \times 6 = 36$

Total $= 36 + 6 = 42 \Rightarrow 5! - 42 = 78 = n$

and $m = {}^2C_1 \cdot {}^2C_1 \cdot {}^2C_1 \cdot {}^2C_1 = 16$

$\therefore \quad n - m = 62$

60. We have, $A_1 = \{1, 2, 3, 4\}$, $A_2 = \{5, 6, 7, 8\}$, $A_3 = \{9, 10\}$

$A_4 = \{11, 12, 13, 14\}$

$n_{12} = 4!, n_{13} = 0, n_{14} = 4!, n_{21} = 4!, n_{23} = 0$

$n_{24} = 4!, n_{31} = 0, n_{32} = 0, n_{34} = 0, n_{41} = 4!$

$n_{42} = 4!, n_{43} = 0$

$\Rightarrow \Sigma n_{ij} = 6(4!) = 144$

61. Given expression $= \frac{1}{-f(x)}$,

where $f(x) = x^2 + b^2 + \sin^2 x - 2bx = (x - b)^2 + \sin^2 x$

Now, $x \in [-1, 0]$ and $b \in [2, 3]$

$\Rightarrow |x - b| \in [2, 4] \Rightarrow (x - b)^2 \in [4, 16]$ and $\sin^2 x \in [0, \sin^2 1]$

As x increases from -1 to 0; $\sin^2 x$ and $(x - b)^2$ both decreases from $\sin^2 1$ to 0 and $(1 + b)^2$ to b^2 respectively and $b \in [2, 3]$.

$$\Rightarrow f(x) \in [4, |6 + \sin^2|] \Rightarrow \frac{1}{f(x)} \in \left[\frac{1}{|6 + \sin^2|}, \frac{1}{4}\right]$$

$$\Rightarrow \frac{1}{-f(x)} \in \left[-\frac{1}{4}, -\frac{1}{|6 + \sin^2|}\right]$$

So, least value of expression is $-\frac{1}{4}$.

Here, $\lambda = -\frac{1}{4}$

$\therefore \frac{1}{\lambda^2} = (-4)^2 = 16$

62. We have, $\operatorname{cosec}^{-1}(\operatorname{cosec} 2) > x^2 - 3x$

$\Rightarrow \quad x^2 - 3x - (\pi - 2) < 0$

$$\Rightarrow \quad \frac{3 - \sqrt{1 + 4\pi}}{2} < x < \frac{3 + \sqrt{1 + 4\pi}}{2}$$

$\therefore$Positive integral solutions of above inequality are 1, 2, 3.

Now, $2010 = 2 \times 3 \times 5 \times 67$,

Total number of divisors of $2010 = 16$

So, A contains 3 elements and B contains 16 elements.

Number of mappings are as follows.

$$f(1) < f(2) < f(3) \Rightarrow {}^{16}C_3 = 560$$
$$f(1) = f(2) < f(3) \Rightarrow {}^{16}C_2 = 120$$
$$f(1) < f(2) = f(3) \Rightarrow {}^{16}C_2 = 120$$
$$f(1) = f(2) = f(3) \Rightarrow {}^{16}C_1 = 16$$

Hence, the total number of mappings $= 816$

63. $a(x^2 - x + 1) - (x^2 + x + 1) \geq 0$

$$\Rightarrow a \geq \frac{x^2 + x + 1}{x^2 - x + 1} \text{ or } a \geq \frac{(x^2 - x + 1) + 2x}{x^2 - x + 1}$$

$$\Rightarrow a \geq 1 + \frac{2x}{x^2 - x + 1} \text{ or } a \geq 1 + \frac{2}{\left(x + \frac{1}{x}\right) - 1}$$

Now, for $x \geq 2$, the minimum value of $x + \frac{1}{x}$ is $\frac{5}{2}$.

$\Rightarrow \quad a \geq \frac{7}{3}$

Here, $m = 7$ and $n = 3$

$\therefore m + n = 7 + 3 = 10$

64. $f(52, 14) = f(14, 52) = f(14, 14 + 38)$

$$= \left(1 + \frac{14}{38}\right) f(14, 38)$$
$$= \frac{52}{38} f(14, 14 + 24)$$
$$= \frac{26}{19}\left(1 + \frac{14}{24}\right) f(14, 24)$$
$$= \frac{26}{19} \times \frac{38}{24} f(14, 14 + 10)$$
$$= \frac{26}{19} \times \frac{19}{12}\left(1 + \frac{14}{10}\right) f(14, 10) = \frac{13}{6} \times \frac{24}{10} f(10, 14)$$
$$= \frac{52}{10} f(10, 10 + 4) = \frac{52}{10}\left(1 + \frac{10}{4}\right) f(10, 4)$$
$$= \frac{52}{10} \times \frac{14}{4} f(4, 10) = \frac{182}{10} f(4, 4 + 6)$$
$$= \frac{182}{10}\left(1 + \frac{4}{6}\right) f(4, 6) = \frac{182}{10} \times \frac{10}{6} f(4, 4 + 2)$$
$$= \frac{91}{3}\left(1 + \frac{4}{2}\right) f(4, 2) = \frac{91}{3} \times 3 f(2, 4)$$
$$= 91 f(2, 2 + 2) = 91\left(1 + \frac{2}{2}\right) f(2, 2)$$
$$= 91 \times 2 \times 2 = 364$$

65. We have, $\cos 4\theta = \dfrac{1}{3}$

$\Rightarrow 2\cos^2 2\theta - 1 = \dfrac{1}{3} \Rightarrow \cos^2 2\theta = \dfrac{2}{3} \Rightarrow \cos 2\theta = \pm\sqrt{\dfrac{2}{3}}$

But $\theta \in \left(0, \dfrac{\pi}{4}\right) \cup \left(\dfrac{\pi}{4}, \dfrac{\pi}{2}\right) \Rightarrow 2\theta \in \left(0, \dfrac{\pi}{2}\right) \cup \left(\dfrac{\pi}{2}, \pi\right)$

$$f(\cos 4\theta) = \frac{2\cos^2\theta}{2\cos^2\theta - 1}$$

$$= \frac{1+\cos 2\theta}{\cos 2\theta} = 1 + \sec^2\theta$$

$$f\left(\frac{1}{3}\right) = 1 + \frac{\sqrt{3}}{\sqrt{2}} \text{ or } 1 - \frac{\sqrt{3}}{\sqrt{2}}$$

66. We have, $x^{2007} = Q(x)\cdot(x^2 - 5x + 6) + ax + b$ ...(i)

On putting $x = 2$ in Eq. (i), we get

$$2a + b = 2^{2007} \quad \text{...(ii)}$$

On putting $x = 3$ in Eq. (i), we get

$$3a + b = 3^{2007} \quad \text{...(iii)}$$

On subtracting Eq. (ii) from Eq. (iii), we get

$$a = 3^{2007} - 2^{2007}$$

Now, $b = 2^{2007} - 2a = 2^{2007} - 2(3^{2007} - 2^{2007})$

$= 2^{2007} + 2\cdot 2^{2007} - 2\cdot 3^{2007}$

$= 3\cdot 2^{2007} - 2\cdot 3^{2007} = 6[2^{2006} - 3^{2006}]$

$= 2\cdot 3\,[2^{2006} - 3^{2006}] \equiv ab(a^c - b^c)$

Hence, $a = 2, b = 3$ and $c = 2006$

$\therefore\ a + b + c = 2 + 3 + 2006 = 2011$

67. Given, $2 + f(x)\,f(y) = f(x) + f(y) + f(xy)$

or $\quad 1 - f(x) - f(y) + f(x)\,f(y) = f(xy) - 1$

or $\quad (1 - f(x))\,(1 - f(y)) = f(xy) - 1$

The above result holds if and only if

$$f(x) = 1 + x^n$$

If $f(x) = a_n x^n + a_{n-1} x^{1-1} + \dots + a_0$

Then, consider $(1 + f(x))\,(1 - f(y)) = f(xy) - 1$

Compare constant term on either sides, we get

$1 - a_0 = a_0 - 1 \Rightarrow a_0 = 1$

Comparing coefficient of $x^n y^n$, we get

$a_n^2 = a_n \Rightarrow a_n = 1$ or otherwise polynomial would not be of n degree.

Comparing coefficient of $x, x^1, \dots, x^{n-1}$ on either sides, we get

$$a_1 = a_2 = \dots = a_{n-1} = 0$$

$\Rightarrow \quad a_n = 1$ and $f(x) = x^n + 1$

Given, $f(2) = 5$ i.e. $2^n + 1 = 5 \Rightarrow n = 2$

Thus, $f(x) = x^2 + 1$

$\Rightarrow f(f(2)) = f(5) = 5^2 + 1 = 26$

68. (A) When $\{x\} = 0$, then $\text{sgn}\{x\} = 0$

and when $0 < \{x\} < 1$, then $\text{sgn}\{x\} = 1$

$\Rightarrow$ Range of $\text{sgn}\{x\} = \{0, 1\}$

(B) For domain $-1 \le x \le 1$ and $-1 \le 1 - x \le 1$

$\Rightarrow -1 \le x \le 1$ and $0 \le x \le 2 \Rightarrow 0 \le x \le 1$

$\Rightarrow$ Domain of function $= [0, 1]$

(C) $-\dfrac{\pi}{2} < \tan^{-1} x < \dfrac{\pi}{2}, \forall\, x \in R$

$\Rightarrow -1 < \dfrac{2}{\pi}\tan^{-1} x < 1$

$\Rightarrow$ For $f(x) = \sqrt{\dfrac{2}{\pi}\tan^{-1} x}, \dfrac{2\tan^{-1} x}{\pi} \ge 0$

$\Rightarrow \qquad 0 \le \dfrac{2}{\pi}\tan^{-1} x < 1 \Rightarrow 0 \le \sqrt{\dfrac{2\tan^{-1} x}{\pi}} < 1$

$\Rightarrow$ Range of $f(x) = [0, 1)$

(D) $\dfrac{3}{4} \le x^2 + x + 1 < 0$ but for $\sin^{-1}[x^2 + x + 1]$;

$-1 \le [x^2 + x + 1] \le 1 \Rightarrow \dfrac{3}{4} \le x^2 + x + 1 < 2$

Case I When $\dfrac{3}{4} \le x^2 + x + 1 < 1$

$\Rightarrow [x^2 + x + 1] = 0 \Rightarrow \sin^{-1}[x^2 + x + 1] = 0$

$\Rightarrow \qquad f(x) = \dfrac{2}{\pi}\sin^{-1}[x^2 + x + 1] = 0$

Case II When $1 \le x^2 + x + 1 < 2, \Rightarrow [x^2 + x + 1] = 1$

$\Rightarrow \sin^{-1}[x^2 + x + 1] = \dfrac{\pi}{2} \Rightarrow f(x) = \dfrac{2}{\pi}\cdot\dfrac{\pi}{2} = 1$

$\therefore$ Range of given function is $\{0, 1\}$.

69. (A) We have, $f(x) = \sin^2 2x - 2\sin^2 x, x \in R$

$= 4\sin^2 x\cos^2 x - 2\sin^2 x$

$= 4\sin^2 x\,(1 - \sin^2 x)$

$\qquad - 2\sin^2 x = 2\sin^2 x - 4\sin^4 x$

$= -4\left[\sin^4 x - \dfrac{1}{2}\sin^2 x\right]$

$= -4\left[\left(\sin^2 x - \dfrac{1}{4}\right)^2 - \dfrac{1}{16}\right]$

$\therefore\ f(x) = \dfrac{1}{4} - 4\left(\sin^2 x - \dfrac{1}{4}\right)^2$

Clearly, range of $f = \left[-2, \dfrac{1}{4}\right]$

Also, $f(-x) = f(x)$

So, f is even function

Also, f is periodic with period π.

(B) We have, $f(x) = \dfrac{4}{\pi}\sin^{-1}(\sin \pi x), x \in R$

Clearly, f is periodic function with period '2' and also f is an odd function.

Clearly, $R_f = [-2, 2]$

(C) We have, $f(x)=\sqrt{\ln(\cos(\sin x))}$

For domain, $\ln(\cos(\sin x))\geq 0 : (\cos(\sin x))\geq 1$

$\Rightarrow \quad \cos(\sin x)=1,$

$\therefore\ \sin x=0 \Rightarrow x=n\pi, n\in I$

$R_f=\{0\}$

Since, $f(x)=0$

$\therefore f$ is both odd and even.

Also, f is periodic with period π.

(D) We have, $f(x)=\tan^{-1}\left(\dfrac{x^2+1}{x^2+\sqrt{3}}\right), x\in R$

Let $\quad y=\dfrac{x^2+1}{x^2+\sqrt{3}}$

$\Rightarrow \quad yx^2+\sqrt{3}y=x^2+1$

$\Rightarrow \quad (\sqrt{3}y-1)=(1-y)x^2$

$\therefore \quad x^2=\left(\dfrac{\sqrt{3}y-1}{1-y}\right)\geq 0$

So, $\dfrac{\sqrt{3}y-1}{y-1}\leq 0$

$\therefore$ Range of $f(x)=\left[\dfrac{\pi}{6},\dfrac{\pi}{4}\right)$

Also, $f(-x)=f(x),\ \forall\ x\in R$

$\therefore\ f$ is even function.

70. (A) $f(x)=x^2\sin\left\{\dfrac{1}{\sin\left(\dfrac{1}{x}\right)}\right\}$

$\Rightarrow\ f(-x)=x^2\sin\left\{\dfrac{1}{-\sin\left(\dfrac{1}{x}\right)}\right\}$

$\Rightarrow\ f(-x)=-x^2\sin\left\{\dfrac{1}{\sin\left(\dfrac{1}{x}\right)}\right\}=-f(x)$

$\Rightarrow f(x)$ is an odd function.

(B) $f(x)=\cos x\cdot\log\left(\dfrac{1+\tan x}{1-\tan x}\right)$

$\Rightarrow\ f(-x)=\cos x\cdot\log\left(\dfrac{1-\tan x}{1+\tan x}\right)$

$=-\cos x\cdot\log\left(\dfrac{1+\tan x}{1-\tan x}\right)$

$=-f(x)$

$\Rightarrow$ odd function

(C) $f(x)=\sqrt[3]{1+x+x^2}+\sqrt[3]{1-x+x^2}$

$\Rightarrow f(-x)=\sqrt[3]{1-x+x^2}+\sqrt[3]{1+x+x^2}$

$=f(x)$

$\Rightarrow$ even function

(D) $f(x)=\sqrt{1+2x+3x^2}-\sqrt{1-2x+3x^2}$

$\Rightarrow f(-x)=\sqrt{1-2x+3x^2}-\sqrt{1+2x+3x^2}$

$=-f(x)$

$\Rightarrow$ odd function

71. (A) We have, $x=\{a_1,a_2,\ldots a_6\}$ and $y=\{b_1,b_2,b_3\}$

Required number of functions $={}^6C_3(2^3-2)=120$

(B)

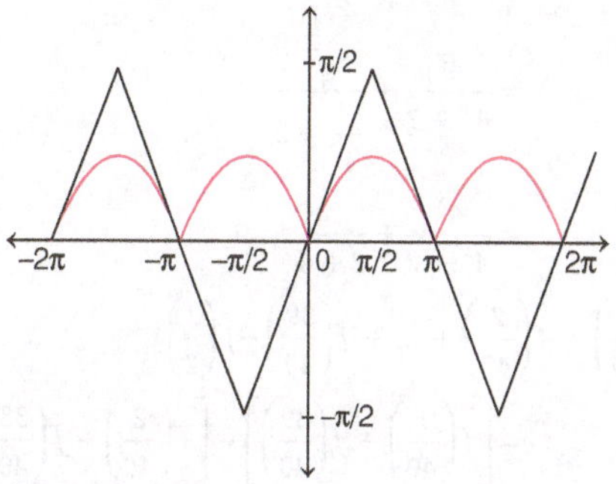

From figure, it is clear that number of solutions is 5.

(C) $a+b+c=1\Rightarrow a=1-b-c$

$\Rightarrow 1+a=(1-b)+(1-c)>2\sqrt{(1-b)(1-c)}$

[$\because$ AM $\geq$ GM]

Similarly, $1+b>2\sqrt{(1-a)(1-c)}$

$1+c>2\sqrt{(1-a)(1-b)}$

$\therefore\ (1+a)(1+b)(1+c)\geq 8(1-a)(1-b)(1-c)$

$\Rightarrow \dfrac{(1+a)(1+b)(1+c)}{(1-a)(1-b)(1-c)}\geq 8$

Required expression >8

(D) $[6x]+7+\cos\pi x-6x\Rightarrow\{6x\}+\cos\pi x$

Period of $\{6x\}$ is $\dfrac{1}{6}$ and period of $\cos\pi x$ is 2.

Hence, LCM of $\dfrac{1}{6}$, 2 is 2.

72. Given, $f(x+y)=f(x)+f(y)$

$\Rightarrow \quad f(x)=\lambda x$

Now, $\quad f\left(-\dfrac{3}{5}\right)=12$ (given)

$\Rightarrow \quad \lambda\left(\dfrac{-3}{5}\right)=12\Rightarrow\lambda=-20$

$\therefore \quad f(x)=-20x$

Also, given $g(x+y)=g(x)\cdot g(y)$

$\Rightarrow \quad g(x)=a^x$

On putting $x = -\frac{1}{3}$ in above, we get

$$g\left(-\frac{1}{3}\right) = a^{\frac{-1}{3}}$$

$$\Rightarrow \quad 2 = a^{\frac{-1}{3}} \quad \left[\because g\left(-\frac{1}{3}\right) = 2 \text{ (given)}\right]$$

$$\Rightarrow \quad a = 1/8$$

$$\therefore \quad g(x) = (1/8)^x$$

Hence, $\left(f\left(\frac{1}{4}\right) + g(-2) - 8\right) g(0) = (-5 + 64 - 8) \times 1 = 51$

73. Given, $f(x) + f(1-x)$

$$= \frac{4^x}{4^x + 2} + \frac{4^{1-x}}{4^{1-x} + 2}$$

$$= \frac{4^x}{4^x + 2} + \frac{\frac{4}{4^x}}{\frac{4}{4^x} + 2}$$

$$= \frac{4^x}{4^x + 2} + \frac{2}{2 + 4^x} = 1$$

$$\therefore f\left(\frac{1}{40}\right) + f\left(\frac{2}{40}\right) + \ldots + f\left(\frac{39}{40}\right) - f\left(\frac{1}{2}\right)$$

$$= \left[f\left(\frac{1}{40}\right) + f\left(\frac{39}{40}\right)\right] + \left[f\left(\frac{2}{40}\right) + f\left(\frac{38}{40}\right)\right] + \ldots + f\left(\frac{20}{40}\right) - f\left(\frac{1}{2}\right)$$

$$= \underbrace{(1 + 1 + 1 + \ldots + 1)}_{19 \text{ times}} + f\left(\frac{1}{2}\right) - f\left(\frac{1}{2}\right) = 19$$

74. The given function $f : R \to R$ is

$$f(x) = |x|(x - \sin x) \quad \ldots\text{(i)}$$

$\because$ The function f is a odd and continuous function and as $\lim_{x \to \infty} f(x) = \infty$ and $\lim_{x \to -\infty} = -\infty$,

so range is R, therefore

f is a onto function.

$$\because f(x) = \begin{bmatrix} x(x - \sin x), & x \geq 0 \\ -x(x - \sin x), & x < 0 \end{bmatrix}$$

$$\therefore f'(x) = \begin{bmatrix} 2x - \sin x - x\cos x, & x > 0 \\ -2x + \sin x + x\cos x, & x < 0 \end{bmatrix}$$

$$= \begin{bmatrix} (x - \sin x) + x(1 - \cos x), & x > 0 \\ (-x + \sin x) - x(1 - \cos x), & x < 0 \end{bmatrix}$$

For $x > 0$, $x - \sin x > 0$ and $x(1 - \cos x) > 0$

$\therefore f'(x) > 0, \forall x \in (0, \infty)$

$\Rightarrow f$ is strictly increasing function, $\forall x \in (0, \infty)$.

Similarly, for $x < 0$, $-x + \sin x > 0$

and $(-x)(1 - \cos x) > 0$

Therefore, $f'(x) < 0, \forall x \in (-\infty, 0)$

$\Rightarrow f$ is strictly increasing function, $\forall x \in (-\infty, 0)$.

Therefore, f is a strictly increasing function for $x \in R$ and it implies that f is one-one function.

Exercise 3 - Challenging Problems

1. (i) For $x = 2$, $f^2(4) + f(4) + 1 = 0$

which is not possible (as $D < 0$)

So, not valid, $\forall x \in R$

(ii) For $x = 1$, $f(0)$ has two value.

So, it is not function.

(iii) Replace $x \to \frac{1}{x}$, we get

$$x^2 = 1$$

$x = \pm 1$ only valid for two values of x.

So, not a function for given domain.

(iv) Replace $x \to \frac{\pi}{2} - x$, we get

$$x = \frac{\pi}{2} - x$$

$$x = \frac{\pi}{4}$$

So, not valid, $\forall x \in R$

2. $f(x) = \sin^{-1} x^2 + [\{\ln\sqrt{x - [x]}\}] + \cot^{-1}\left(\frac{1}{1 + \sqrt{2}x^2}\right)$

$$= \sin^{-1} x^2 + [\{\ln\sqrt{\{x\}}\}] + \cot^{-1}\left(\frac{1}{1 + \sqrt{2}x^2}\right)$$

If $x \notin Z$, then $f(x) = \sin^{-1} x^2 + 0 + \cot^{-1}\left(\frac{1}{1 + \sqrt{2}x^2}\right)$

$$= \sin^{-1} x^2 + \cot^{-1}\left(\frac{1}{1 + \sqrt{2}x^2}\right)$$

$\Rightarrow x \notin Z$ and $x^2 \in [-1, 1]$ and $x^2 \in [0, \infty)$

and $\frac{1}{1 + \sqrt{2}x^2} \in (-\infty, \infty)$

$\Rightarrow x \notin Z$ and $x^2 \in [0, 1]$ and $1 + \sqrt{2}x^2 \in (-\infty, 0) \cup (0, \infty)$

$\Rightarrow x \notin Z$ and $x \in [-1, 1]$ and $x^2 \in \left(-\infty, -\frac{1}{\sqrt{2}}\right) \cup \left(\frac{-1}{\sqrt{2}}, \infty\right)$

But $x^2 \geq 0$

$\Rightarrow x \in [-1, 1]$ and $x^2 \in [0, \infty)$ and $x \notin Z$

$\Rightarrow x \in [-1, 1]$ and $x \in R$ and $x \notin Z$

$\Rightarrow x \in [-1, 1]$ and $x \notin Z$

$\Rightarrow x \in (-1, 1) \sim \{0\}$

If $x \notin Z$, then function $f(x)$ will be undefined as ln 0 is not defined, therefore domain $(-1, 1) \sim \{0\}$.

$$f(x) = \sin^{-1} x^2 + [\{\ln\sqrt{x - \{x\}}\}] + \cot^{-1}\left[\frac{1}{1 + \sqrt{2}x^2}\right]$$

$$= \sin^{-1} x^2 + \cot^{-1}\left(\frac{1}{1 + \sqrt{2}x^2}\right)$$

$\Rightarrow$ Range of $f(x) = \left(\frac{\pi}{4}, \frac{7\pi}{8}\right)$

3. We have, $f(x)=\dfrac{1}{\sqrt{\sin(\cos x)}}+\sin^{-1}\left(\dfrac{2x}{\pi}\right)+\dfrac{1}{\{-x\}}$

$$+\frac{1}{\ln\left(\left(1-\left[\tan\frac{x}{2}\right]-\left[-\tan\frac{x}{2}\right]\right)\right)}$$

$\sin(\cos x)>0$ and $\dfrac{2x}{\pi}\in(-1,1)$ and $x\notin Z$

and $\ln\left(1-\left(\tan\dfrac{x}{2}\right)\right)-\left[-\tan\dfrac{x}{2}\right]\neq 0$ and $1-\left[\tan\dfrac{x}{2}\right]>0$

$\cos x\in(0,1]$ and $x\in\left(-\dfrac{\pi}{2},\dfrac{\pi}{2}\right)$ and $x\notin Z$

and $\ln\left(1-\left[\tan\dfrac{x}{2}\right]\right)-\left[-\tan\dfrac{x}{2}\right]\neq 0$ and $\tan\dfrac{x}{2}\in(-\infty,1)$

$\Rightarrow x\in\left(-\dfrac{\pi}{2},\dfrac{\pi}{2}\right)$ and $x\notin Z$ and $\ln\left(1-\left[\tan\dfrac{x}{2}\right]\right)+\left[-\tan\dfrac{x}{2}\right]\neq 0,$

$\tan\dfrac{x}{2}\in(-\infty,1)$

$\Rightarrow\ x\in\left(\dfrac{-\pi}{2},-1\right)\cup(-1,0)\cup(0,1)\cup\left(1,\dfrac{\pi}{2}\right)$ and P

$\ln\left(1-\left[\tan\dfrac{x}{2}\right]\right)+\left[-\tan\dfrac{x}{2}\right]\neq 0$

If $\quad x\in\left(\dfrac{-\pi}{2},\dfrac{\pi}{2}\right)$

$\Rightarrow\quad \dfrac{x}{2}\in\left(\dfrac{-\pi}{4},\dfrac{\pi}{4}\right)$

$\Rightarrow\quad \tan\dfrac{x}{2}\in(-1,1)$

$\quad \tan\dfrac{x}{2}\in(-1,1)$

$\Rightarrow\quad \left[\tan\dfrac{x}{2}\right]\in\{-1,0\}$

Case I $\dfrac{-\pi}{2}<x<-1$

$\Rightarrow\quad \dfrac{-\pi}{4}<\dfrac{x}{2}<\dfrac{-1}{2}$

$\Rightarrow\quad -1<\tan\dfrac{x}{2}<\tan\left(\dfrac{-1}{2}\right)$

$\Rightarrow\quad \left[\tan\dfrac{x}{2}\right]=-1$ and $\left[-\tan\dfrac{x}{2}\right]=0$

$\Rightarrow\quad \ln\left(1-\left[\tan\dfrac{x}{2}\right]\right)+\left[-\tan\dfrac{x}{2}\right]=\ln 2\neq 0$

Case II $-1<x<0\Rightarrow \ln\left(1-\left[\tan\dfrac{x}{2}\right]\right)+\left[-\tan\dfrac{x}{2}\right]=\ln 2$

Case III $0<x<1\Rightarrow \ln\left(1-\left[\tan\dfrac{x}{2}\right]\right)+\left[-\tan\dfrac{x}{2}\right]=-1\neq 0$

Case IV $1<x<\dfrac{\pi}{2}\Rightarrow \ln\left(1-\left[\tan\dfrac{x}{2}\right]\right)+\left[-\tan\dfrac{x}{2}\right]=-1\neq 0$

$\therefore D_f=\left(\dfrac{-\pi}{2},-1\right)\cup(-1,0)\cup(0,1)\cup\left(1,\dfrac{\pi}{2}\right)$

4. As, we can write

$$\begin{aligned}n&=\sqrt{n^2}=\sqrt{1+(n^2-1)}=\sqrt{1+(n-1)(n+1)}\\&=\sqrt{1+(n-1)\cdot\sqrt{(n+1)^2}}\\&=\sqrt{1+(n-1)\cdot\sqrt{1+(n+1)^2-1}}\\&=\sqrt{1+(n-1)\cdot\sqrt{1+(n)\cdot(n+2)}}\\&=\sqrt{1+(n-1)\cdot\sqrt{1+n\cdot\sqrt{(n+2)^2}}}\\&=\sqrt{1+(n-1)\cdot\sqrt{1+n\cdot\sqrt{1+(n+2)^2-1}}}\\&=\sqrt{1+(n-1)\cdot\sqrt{1+n\cdot\sqrt{1+(n+1)(n+3)}}}\\&=\sqrt{1+(n-1)\cdot\sqrt{1+n\cdot\sqrt{1+(n+1)\cdot\sqrt{(n+3)^2}}}}\ \text{... and so on.}\end{aligned}$$

$$\therefore\ \sqrt{1+2\cdot\sqrt{1+3\cdot\sqrt{1+4\cdot\sqrt{1+5\sqrt{.....\infty}}}}}=3$$

5. As we know that

$$\left(\frac{a+b+c+d}{4}\right)^2\leq\frac{a^2+b^2+c^2+d^2}{4}\quad\text{...(i)}$$

[using Tchebycheff's Inequality]

where, $a+b+c+d+e=8$

and $\quad a^2+b^2+c^2+d^2+e^2=16$

From Eq (i), reduces to

$$\left(\frac{8-e}{4}\right)^2\leq\frac{16-e^2}{4}$$

$\Rightarrow\quad 64+e^2-16e\leq 4(16-e^2)$

$\Rightarrow\quad 5e^2-16e\leq 0\Rightarrow e(5e-16)\leq 0$

$\Rightarrow\quad 0\leq e\leq\dfrac{16}{5}$ [using number line rule]

Thus, $e\in\left[0,\dfrac{16}{5}\right]$.

6. Here, $2^{|y|}-|2^{y-1}-1|=2^{y-1}+1$

We know that how to define modulus, we have three cases as

Case I $y<0$

$\Rightarrow 2^{-y}+(2^{y-1}-1)=2^{y-1}+1,\ \left\{\begin{array}{l}\text{as when } y<0\\ |y|=-y\\ \text{and } |2^{y-1}-1|=-(2^{y-1}-1)\end{array}\right.$

$\Rightarrow\quad 2^{-y}=2^1$

Hence, $y=-1$, which is true when $y<0$. ...(i)

Case II $0\leq y<1$

$\Rightarrow\ 2^y+(2^{y-1}-1)=2^{y-1}+1,\ \left\{\begin{array}{l}\text{as when } 0\leq y<1\\ |y|=y\\ \text{and } |2^{y-1}-1|=-(2^{y-1}-1)\end{array}\right.$

$\Rightarrow\quad 2^y=2$

$\Rightarrow\quad y=1$, which shows no solution

as $\quad 0\leq y<1$ ...(ii)

Case III $y \geq 1$

$$\Rightarrow \quad 2^y - (2^{y-1} - 1) = 2^{y-1} + 1, \begin{cases} \text{as when } y \geq 0 \\ |y| = y \\ \text{and } |2^{y-1} - 1| = (2^{y-1} - 1) \end{cases}$$

$$\Rightarrow \quad 2^y = 2^{y-1} + 2^{y-1}$$

$$\Rightarrow \quad 2^y = 2 \cdot 2^{y-1}$$

$$\Rightarrow \quad 2^y = 2^y,$$

which is an identity, therefore it is true,

$$\forall\, y \geq 1 \quad \text{...(iii)}$$

Hence, from Eqs. (i), (ii) and (iii) the solution set is $\{y : y \in [1, \infty) \cup \{-1\}\}$.

7. Here, $\dfrac{[x]}{[x-2]} - \dfrac{[x-2]}{[x]} = \dfrac{8\{x\} + 12}{[x-2][x]}$

$$\Rightarrow \quad \frac{[x]^2 - [x-2]^2}{[x-2][x]} = \frac{8\{x\} + 12}{[x][x-2]}$$

$$\Rightarrow \frac{([x] - [x-2])([x] + [x-2])}{[x-2][x]} = \frac{8\{x\} + 12}{[x][x-2]}$$

$$\Rightarrow ([x] - [x-2])([x] + [x-2]) = 8\{x\} + 12$$

$$\Rightarrow ([x] - [x] + 2)([x] + [x] - 2) = 8\{x\} + 12$$

$$[\because [x + I] = [x] + I]$$

$$\Rightarrow \quad 4([x] - 1) = 8\{x\} + 12$$

$$\Rightarrow \quad [x] - 4 = 2\{x\} \quad \text{...(i)}$$

Now, as we know $0 \leq \{x\} < 1 \Rightarrow 0 \leq 2\{x\} < 2$

$$\Rightarrow \quad 0 \leq [x] - 4 < 2 \Rightarrow 4 \leq [x] < 6$$

$$\Rightarrow \quad [x] = 4, 5$$

$$\left.\begin{aligned} &\text{if } [x] = 4 \Rightarrow 2\{x\} = [x] - 4 \\ &\text{becomes } \{x\} = 0 \end{aligned}\right\} \quad \text{...(ii)}$$

and $$\left.\begin{aligned} &\text{if } [x] = 5 \Rightarrow 2\{x\} = [x] - 4 \\ &\text{becomes } \{x\} = \frac{1}{2} \end{aligned}\right\} \quad \text{...(iii)}$$

Thus, from Eqs. (ii) and (iii), we get

$$x = [x] + \{x\}$$

i.e. $\quad x = 4 + 0 = 4 \quad$ [using Eq. (ii)]

and $\quad x = 5 + \dfrac{1}{2} = \dfrac{11}{2} \quad$ [using Eq. (iii)]

$$\Rightarrow \quad x \in \left\{4, \frac{11}{2}\right\}$$

8. Given, $(a-2)(x - [x])^2 + 2(x - [x]) + a^2 = 0 \quad$ ...(i)

Let $y = x - [x]$.

Then, Eq. (i) can be written as

$$f(y) = (a-2)y^2 + 2y + a^2 = 0 \quad \text{...(ii)}$$

As x cannot be an integer

$$y = x - [x] \neq 0$$

Thus, $a \neq 0$

When $2 < x < 3$, $[x] = 2$

$$\Rightarrow \quad 0 < x - [x] < 1$$

i.e. $\quad 0 < y < 1$.

Since, Eq. (i) has exactly one solution in the interval (2, 3) and Eq. (ii) has exactly one solution in the interval (0, 1).

This is possible if $f(0)\,f(1) < 0$, otherwise the Eq. (ii) has either no or two solutions in (0, 1).

$$\Rightarrow \quad a^2\{a - 2 + 2 + a^2\} < 0$$

$$\Rightarrow \quad a(a+1) < 0 \quad [\because a^2 > 0]$$

$$\Rightarrow \quad -1 < a < 0 \text{ or } a \in (-1, 0)$$

9. Given equation is

$$10^{3x^2 + 7x + 4} - 2.10^{x^2 + 3x + 2} = \frac{10}{10^{x + x^2}}$$

$$\Rightarrow \quad 10^{4x^2 + 8x + 4} - 2 \cdot 10^{2x^2 + 4x + 2} = 10$$

$$\Rightarrow \quad 10^{4(x^2 + 2x + 1)} - 2 \cdot 10^{2(x^2 + 2x + 1)} = 10$$

$$\Rightarrow \quad 10^{4(x+1)^2} - 2 \cdot 10^{2(x+1)^2} = 10$$

$$\Rightarrow \quad \{10^{2(x+1)^2}\}^2 - 2 \cdot \{10^{2(x+1)^2}\} = 10 \quad \text{...(i)}$$

Let $\quad 10^{2(x+1)^2} = y \quad$ ...(ii)

$$\Rightarrow \quad y^2 - 2y = 10$$

$$\Rightarrow \quad y^2 - 2y - 10 = 0$$

$$\Rightarrow \quad y = \frac{2 \pm \sqrt{4 + 40}}{2}$$

$$\Rightarrow \quad y = 1 \pm \sqrt{11}$$

$$\Rightarrow \quad y = 1 + \sqrt{11} \text{ [neglecting '–' ve sign as } y > 0]$$

$$\Rightarrow \quad 10^{2(x+1)^2} = 1 + \sqrt{11}$$

$$\Rightarrow \quad 2(x+1)^2 = \log_{10}(1 + \sqrt{11})$$

$$\Rightarrow \quad (x+1)^2 = \frac{1}{2}\log_{10}(1 + \sqrt{11})$$

$$\Rightarrow \quad x + 1 = \pm\sqrt{\frac{1}{2}\log_{10}(1 + \sqrt{11})}$$

Hence, $x = -1 \pm \sqrt{\dfrac{1}{2}\log_{10}(1 + \sqrt{11})}$

10. Let $x = a + r$, where $a \in$ integer and $r \in [0, 1)$. Then, there are four cases

(i) $0 \leq r < \dfrac{1}{20}$ (ii) $\dfrac{1}{20} \leq r < \dfrac{1}{10}$

(iii) $\dfrac{1}{10} \leq r < \dfrac{1}{5}$ (iv) $\dfrac{1}{5} \leq r < 1$

Case I If $0 \leq r < \dfrac{1}{20}$

$$\therefore \quad [x] + [5x] + [10x] + [20x] = 36K + 35$$

$$\Rightarrow [a + r] + [5a + 5r] + [10a + 10r] + [20a + 20r] = 36K + 35$$

$$\Rightarrow \quad a + 5a + 10a + 20a = 36K + 35$$

[by definition of the greatest integer function]

$$\Rightarrow \quad 36a = 36K + 35,$$

which is not possible for any values of a and K as they belong to integers. ...(i)

Case II If $\dfrac{1}{20} \leq r < \dfrac{1}{10}$

$$\therefore \quad [x] + [5x] + [10x] + [20x] = 36K + 35$$

$\Rightarrow [a+r]+[5a+5r]+[10a+10r]+[20a+20r]=36K+35$

$\Rightarrow \quad a+5a+10a+20a+1=36K+35$

$\Rightarrow \quad 36a+1=36K+35$

$\Rightarrow \quad 36a=36K+34,$

which is again not possible, $\forall\ a, K \in$ integers. ...(ii)

Case III If $\frac{1}{10} \le r < \frac{1}{5}$

$\therefore \quad [x]+[5x]+[10x]+[20x]=36K+35$

$\Rightarrow [a+r]+[5a+5r]+[10a+10r]+[20a+20r]=36K+35$

$\Rightarrow \quad a+5a+10a+1+20a+2=36K+35$

$\Rightarrow \quad 36a+3=36K+35$

$\Rightarrow \quad 36a=36K+32,$

which shows no value of a and K can be given. ...(iii)

Case IV If $\frac{1}{5} \le r < 1$

$\therefore \quad [x]+[5x]+[10x]+[20x]=36k+35$

$\Rightarrow [a+r]+[5a+5r]+[10a+10r]+[20a+20r]=36K+35$

$\Rightarrow \quad a+5a+1+10a+2+20a+4=36K+35$

$\Rightarrow \quad 36a+7=36K+35$

$\Rightarrow \quad 36a=36K+28$

Again, no solution is possible. ...(iv)

Hence, from Eqs. (i), (ii), (iii) and (iv), does not exist any real value of x.

11. Since, $1900 < f(1990) < 2000$

$$\Rightarrow \frac{1900}{90} < \frac{f(1990)}{90} < \frac{2000}{90}$$

$$\Rightarrow 21.1 < \frac{f(1990)}{90} < 22.2$$

$$\therefore \left[\frac{f(1990)}{90}\right] = 21.22 \quad \text{...(i)}$$

Given, $x - f(x) = 19\left[\frac{x}{19}\right] - 90\left[\frac{f(x)}{90}\right]$

Now, there are two cases arise.

Case I $\left[\frac{f(1990)}{90}\right] = 21$

We have, $1990 - f(1990) = 19\left[\frac{1990}{19}\right] - 90\left[\frac{f(1990)}{90}\right]$

$\Rightarrow \quad 1990 - f(1900) = 19\cdot(104) - 19\cdot(21)$

$\Rightarrow \quad f(1990) = 1904$ ...(ii)

Case II $\left[\frac{f(1990)}{90}\right] = 22$

We have, $1990 - f(1990) = 19\left[\frac{1990}{19}\right] - 90\left[\frac{f(1990)}{90}\right]$

$\Rightarrow \quad f(1990) = 1994$

From Eqs. (ii) and (iii), we get

$$f(1990) = 1904 \text{ or } 1994.$$

12. Here, $|x^2 - 2x| + y = 1$ and $x^2 + |y| = 1$ gives four cases as

Case I $x^2 - 2x \ge 0$ and $y \ge 0$ ...(i)

Equations are $x^2 - 2x + y = 1$ and $x^2 + y = 1$

$\Rightarrow \quad 1 - 2x = 1 \Rightarrow x = 0$ and $y = 1$ ...(ii)

From Eq. (i), $\quad x^2 - 2x \ge 0 \Rightarrow x \le 0, x \ge 2$ and $y \ge 0$

$x^2 - 2x \ge 0$ and $y \ge 0$

Thus, $x = 0$ and $y = 1$ is the only solution when

Case II $x^2 - 2x \ge 0$ and $y < 0$

$\Rightarrow \quad (x \le 0$ or $x \ge 2)$ and $(y < 0)$ ...(iii)

$\therefore$ Equations are $x^2 - 2x + y = 1$ and $x^2 - y = 1$.

On adding these equations, we get

$$2x^2 - 2x = 2$$

or $\quad x = \frac{1 \pm \sqrt{5}}{2}$ and $y = \frac{1 \pm \sqrt{5}}{2}$ ...(iv)

From Eqs. (iii) and (iv), we get

$$x = \frac{1-\sqrt{5}}{2} \text{ and } y = \frac{1-\sqrt{5}}{2}$$

Case III $x^2 - 2x \le 0$ and $y \ge 0$.

$\Rightarrow \quad (0 \le x \le 2)$ and $(y \ge 0)$ ...(v)

Equations are $-x^2 + 2x + y = 1$ and $x^2 + y = 1$, subtracting, we get

$$-2x^2 + 2x = 0$$

$\Rightarrow \quad x = 0, 1$

i.e. $\quad x = 0, y = 1$ or $x = 1, y = 0$ ...(vi)

which satisfy Eq. (v).

Case IV $x^2 - 2x \le 0$ and $y \le 0$.

$\Rightarrow \quad (0 \le x \le 2)$ and $(y \le 0)$ ...(vi)

$\therefore$ Equations are $-x^2 + 2x + y = 1$ and $x^2 - y = 1$, adding, we get

$$2x = 2$$

$\Rightarrow \quad x = 1$

and $y = 0$, which satisfy Eq. (vii).

Thus, solutions are

$$(x = 0, y = 1)\,(x = 1, y = 0)$$

and $\quad \left(x = y = \frac{1-\sqrt{5}}{2}\right)$

13. Since, $2 - \sqrt{2 + \sqrt{2 + x}} \ge 0$, we must have

$$0 \le x \le 2$$

Let $x = 2\cos\theta, \theta \in \left[0, \frac{\pi}{2}\right]$

The equation becomes

$$2\cos\frac{\theta}{8} + 2\sqrt{3}\sin\frac{\theta}{8} = 2 \times 2\cos\theta$$

$$\cos\left(\frac{\pi}{3} - \frac{\theta}{8}\right) = \cos\theta$$

Since, $0 < \frac{\pi}{3} - \frac{\theta}{8} < \frac{\pi}{3}$, we have

$$\frac{\pi}{3} - \frac{\theta}{8} = \theta$$

$\Rightarrow \quad \theta = \frac{8\pi}{27}$

$\therefore \quad x = 2\cos\frac{8\pi}{27}$

14. Given, $f(x-1)+f(x+1)=2f(x)\sin 60°$

$\Rightarrow \quad f(x-1)+f(x+1)=\sqrt{3}f(x)$ ...(i)

From Eq. (i), we get

$f(x+3)+f(x+1)=\sqrt{3}\,f(x+2)$

[replacing x by $x+2$] ...(ii)

On adding Eqs. (i) and (ii), we get

$f(x-1)+f(x+3)+2f(x+1)=\sqrt{3}(f(x)+f(x+2))$

$=\sqrt{3}\times\sqrt{3}\,f(x+1)$

[from Eq. (i), put $(x+1)$ in place of x]

$f(x-1)+f(x+3)=f(x+1)$ ...(iii)

and $\quad f(x+1)+f(x+5)=f(x+3)$ ...(iv)

On adding Eqs. (iii) and (iv), we get

$f(x-1)+f(x+1)+f(x+3)+f(x+5)=f(x+1)+f(x+3)$

$\Rightarrow \quad f(x-1)+f(x+5)=0$

$\Rightarrow \quad f(x-1)=-f(x+5)$

$\Rightarrow \quad f(x)=-f(x+6)$ ...(v)

From Eq. (v), $\quad f(x)=-(-f(x+2))$

$\Rightarrow \quad f(x+12)=f(x)$

Hence, $f(x)$ is a periodic function with period 12.

Now, $\sum_{r=0}^{99} f(5+12r)=f(5)+f(5+12)+f(5+2.12)$

$+\ldots+f(5+99.1)$

$=f(5)+f(5)+f(5)+\ldots+10100$ terms

$=100\,f(5)=100\times 100=10000$

15. $2x^2-5x+2=\dfrac{5-\sqrt{9+8x}}{4},\ x<\dfrac{5}{4}$ ...(i)

Let $y=2x^2-5x+2$

$\Rightarrow 2x^2-5x+(2-y)=0 \Rightarrow x=\dfrac{5\pm\sqrt{25-4(2)(2-y)}}{4}$

$\Rightarrow \quad x=\dfrac{5\pm\sqrt{9+8y}}{4}$

$\Rightarrow \quad x=\dfrac{5+\sqrt{9+8y}}{4}>\dfrac{5}{4}$

But $x<\dfrac{5}{4} \Rightarrow x=\dfrac{5-\sqrt{9+8y}}{4}$

$\Rightarrow \quad f^{-1}(x)=\dfrac{5-\sqrt{9+8x}}{4}$ ...(ii)

From Eqs. (i) and (ii), we get

$f(x)=f^{-1}(x)$

$\Rightarrow \quad f(x)=x$

$\Rightarrow \quad 2x^2-5x+2=x$

$\Rightarrow \quad 2x^2-6x+2=0$

$\Rightarrow \quad x^2-3x+1=0$

$\Rightarrow \quad x=\dfrac{3\pm\sqrt{9-4}}{2}=\dfrac{3\pm\sqrt{5}}{2}$ but $x<\dfrac{5}{4}$

$\Rightarrow \quad x=\dfrac{3-\sqrt{5}}{2}$

“

To not know math is a severe limitation to understanding the world.

–Richard Feynman

3 Limits

Learning Milestones

Milestone 1 Limits
- Definition of Limits
- Indeterminate Forms
- Algebra of Limits
- Evaluation of Limits
- Direct Substitution Method

Milestone 2 Limits of Algebraic Functions
- Factorisation Method
- Standard Formula
- Rationalisation Method
- Method of Substitution

Milestone 3 Limits of Transcendental Function
- Trigonometric Limits
- Logarithmic Limits
- Exponential Limits

Milestone 4 Some Special Limits
- Limits Using Expansion
- Evaluation of Limits of the form 0° and ∞°
- Limits of the Form 1^{∞}

Milestone 5 Use of Standard Theorem
- Use of Standard Theorems/Results
- L'Hospital Rule
- Newton Leibnitz's Theorem
- Limit Using Special Type of Function
- One Sided Limits
- Geometrical Limits

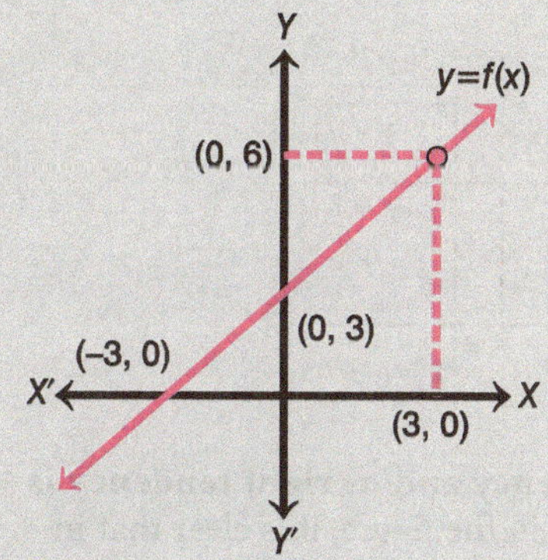

$$\lim_{x\to 3}\frac{x^2-9}{x-3}$$

Practice Milestones

Practice Milestone 1- JEE Main Pattern

Practice Milestone 2 - JEE Advanced Pattern

Practice Milestone 3 - Challenging Problems

Milestone 1 Limits

- Definition of Limits • Indeterminate Forms • Algebra of Limits • Evaluation of Limits
- Direct Substitution Method

Introduction

The concept of limit is developed to understand the behaviour of function.

e.g. Let us consider $f(x) = x^2 - 4$ and $g(x) = x - 2$ the value of $f(x)$ and $g(x)$ at $x = 2$ is $f(2) = 0$ and $g(2) = 0$

Now, consider $h(x) = \dfrac{f(x)}{g(x)} \Rightarrow h(x) = \dfrac{x^2 - 4}{x - 2}$

Now, $h(2) = \dfrac{0}{0}$

Here, we can say that $x = 2$ is not in domain of $h(x)$ but now we want to know the behaviour of $h(x)$ when we are approaching to $x = 2$, then in this situation we get another type of form i.e. indeterminate form.

In this we have to calculate these approaching value of function and this approaching value is known as limiting value of function.

3.1 Definition of Limits

Let $\lim_{x \to a} f(x) = l$. It would mean that when we approach the point $x = a$ from the values which are just greater than or smaller than $x = a$, $f(x)$ would have a tendency to move closer to the value l.

This is same as saying 'difference between $f(x)$ and l can be made as small as we feel like by suitably choosing x in the neighbourhood of $x = a$'.

Mathematically, we write this, as $\lim_{x \to a} f(x) = l$, which is equivalent of saying that, $|f(x) - l| < \varepsilon, \forall x$ **whenever** $0 < |x - a| < \delta$, **where** ε **and** δ **are sufficiently small negative numbers.**

It is clear from the above discussion that, if we are interested in finding the limit of $f(x)$ at $x = a$, the first thing we have to make sure that $f(x)$ is well defined in the neighbourhood of $x = a$ and not necessarily at $x = a$ (that means $x = a$ may or may not be in the domain of $f(x)$), because we have to examine its behaviour or tendency in the neighbourhood of $x = a$.

Following possibilities may arise :

(a) **Left tendency is same as its right tendency**
As shown in figure, when we approach $x = a$ from the values which are just less than a, $f(x)$ has a tendency to move towards the value l (**left tendency**).
Similarly, when we approach $x = a$ from the values which are just greater than a, $f(x)$ has a tendency to move towards the value l (**right tendency**).
In this case, we say $f(x)$ has limit l at $x = a$,
i.e. $\lim_{x \to a} f(x) = l$.

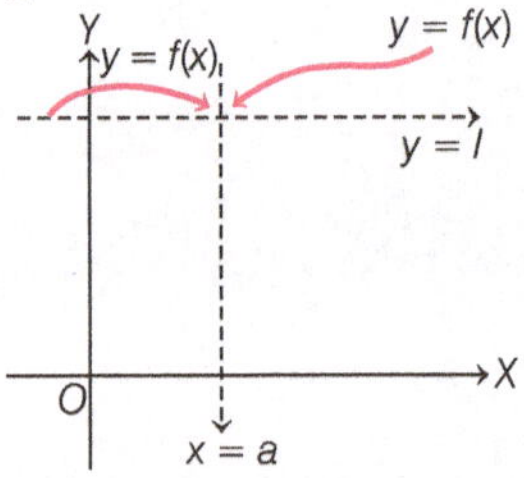

(b) **When the left tendency is not the same as its right tendency** Here, left tendency is l_1 and right tendency is l_2, clearly left tendency (l_1) is not same as right tendency (l_2).
In this case, we say that the limit of $f(x)$ at $x = a$ will not exist.
i.e. $\lim_{x \to a} f(x) =$ **Does not exist.**

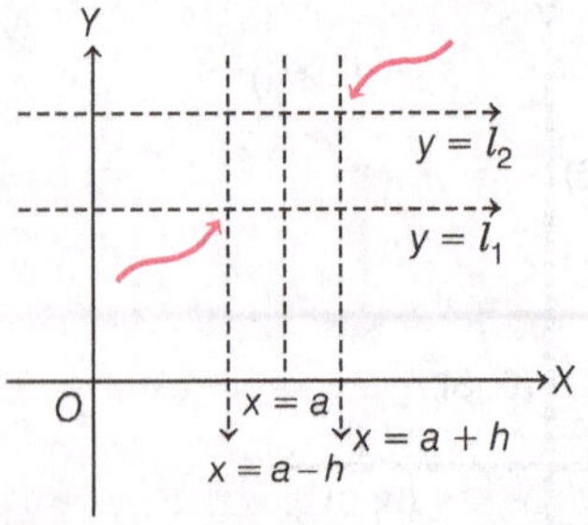

(c) **When the left tendency and/or right tendency is not fixed** As shown in the figure, it is clear that in this case, the function has **erratic** behaviour in the neighbourhood of $x = a$ and it will not be possible to talk about the left and right tendencies of the function in the neighbourhood of $x = a$.

In this case, we conclude that the limit of $f(x)$ at $x = a$ will not exist.

i.e. $\lim_{x \to a} f(x) =$ **Does not exist.**

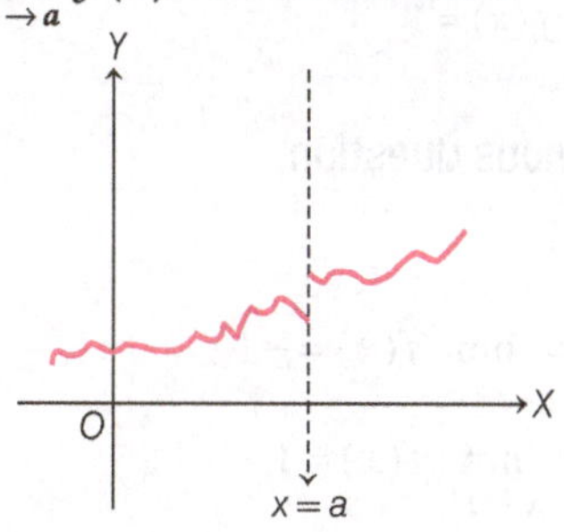

Conclusion

From above discussion, we can say that the value of limit of a function can be exists only. When the left tendency and right tendency both are same.

∴ These tendencies are known as left hand limit and right hand limit of a function.

Left hand limit = $\lim_{x \to a^-} f(x) = \text{LHL} = f(a^-)$

Right hand limit = $\lim_{x \to a^+} f(x) = \text{RHL} = f(a^+)$

(a) Existence of Limit

Limit of a function $f(x)$ at $x = a$ exist when LHL = RHL = Finite number

$$\lim_{x \to a^-} f(x) = \lim_{x \to a^+} f(x) = k$$

$$\Rightarrow \quad \lim_{h \to 0} f(a - h) = \lim_{h \to 0} f(a + h) = k$$

and $\quad \lim_{x \to a} f(x) = k$

(b) Non-Existence of Limit

Three of the most common types of behaviour associated with the non-existence of a limit.

1. $f(x)$ approaches a different number from the right side of a than it approaches from the left side.
2. $f(x)$ increases or decreases without bound as x approaches a.
3. $f(x)$ oscillates between two fixed values as x approaches a.

   There are many other interesting functions that have unusual limit behaviour. An often cited one is the Dirichlet function $f(x) = \begin{cases} 0, & \text{if } x \text{ is rational} \\ 1, & \text{if } x \text{ is irrational} \end{cases}$.

   This function has no limit at any real number a.

JEE Focus Points

Concept Inside Video

1. Normally, students have the perception that limit should be a finite number. But, it is not always so. It is quite possible that $f(x)$ has infinite limit at $x = a$.

   If $\lim_{x \to a} f(x) = \infty$, it would simply mean that function has tendency to assume very large positive values in neighbourhood of $x = a$ (as shown in figure).

   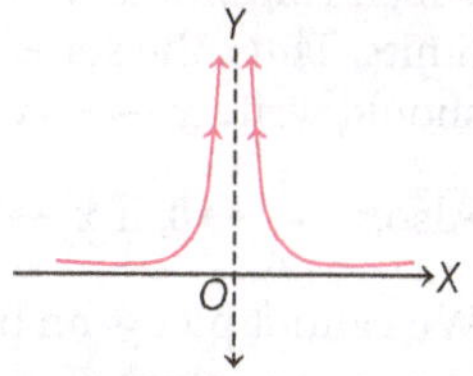

   e.g. $\lim_{x \to 0} \frac{1}{|x|} = \infty$

   which indicates the left tendency as well as right tendency are the same.

   Again, if $\lim_{x \to a} f(x) = -\infty$, it would simply mean that the function has tendency to assume very large negative values in the neighbourhood of $x = a$ as shown in figure.

   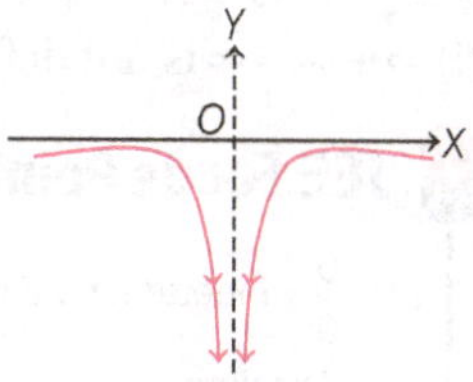

   e.g. $\lim_{x \to 0} \frac{-1}{|x|} = -\infty$

   At the end we discuss the case when left tendency is $(-\infty)$ and right tendency is $(+\infty)$ (i.e. $f(x)$ does not have unique tendency).

   Thus, in this case limit does not exist.

   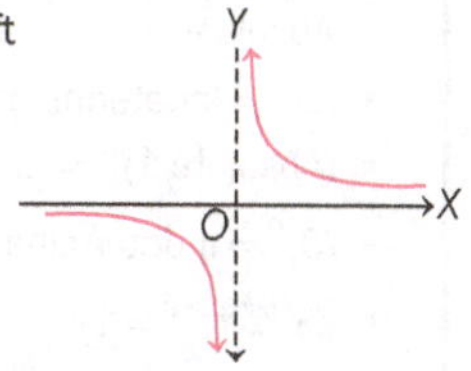

   e.g. $\lim_{x \to 0} \frac{1}{x}$ does not exist,

   since left tendency is $(-\infty)$ and right tendency is $(+\infty)$ as shown in figure.

2. If $f(x)$ is well defined at $x = a$, it does not imply that $\lim_{x \to a} f(x) = f(a)$. Because, it is quite possible that $f(x)$ is well defined at $x = a$ but not in the neighbourhood of $x = a$ or $f(x)$ is well defined in the neighbourhood of $x = a$, but does not have a unique tendency.

3.2 Indeterminate Forms

If direct substitution of $x = a$ while evaluating $\lim_{x \to a} f(x)$ leads to one of the following forms

$$\frac{0}{0}, \frac{\infty}{\infty}, \infty - \infty, 1^\infty, 0^0, \infty^0, \infty \times 0,$$

then it is called indeterminate form.

e.g. $\lim_{x \to 1} \frac{x^2 - 1}{x - 1} = \frac{0}{0}$ indeterminate form.

$\lim_{x \to a} \frac{x^n - a^n}{x - a} = \frac{0}{0}$ indeterminate form.

$\lim_{x \to 0} \frac{\sin x}{x} = \frac{0}{0}$ indeterminate form.

Infinity (∞) is a symbol and not a number. It is a symbol for the behaviour of a variable which continuously increases and passes through all limits. Thus, the statement $x = \infty$ is meaningless, we should write $x \to \infty$. Similarly, $-\infty$ is a symbol for the behaviour of a variable which continuously decreases and passes through all limits. Thus, the statement $x = -\infty$ is meaningless, we should write $x \to -\infty$.

Also, $\frac{1}{x} \to 0$, if $x \to +\infty$ and $\frac{1}{x} \to 0$, if $x \to -\infty$.

We cannot plot ∞ on paper. Infinity does not obey laws of elementary algebra.

(i) $\infty + \infty = \infty$ is not defined (ii) $\infty - \infty$ is indeterminate.

JEE Focus Points

Concept Inside Video

- $\frac{0}{0}$ = Indeterminate form
- $\frac{\text{Absolute } 0}{0} = 0$
- $\frac{0}{\text{Absolute } 0} = \infty / -\infty$
- $(1)^{\infty}$ = Indeterminate form
- $(\text{Absolute } 1)^{\infty} = 1$
- $(0)^0$ = Indeterminate form
- $(0)^{\text{Absolute } 0} = 1$
- $(\text{Absolute } 0)^0 = 0$

Example 1. Evaluate limits using graph given below.

(i) $\lim_{x \to -1^-} f(x)$ (ii) $\lim_{x \to 2^+} f(x)$

(iii) $\lim_{x \to -3^+} f(x)$ (iv) $\lim_{x \to 1^+} f(x)$

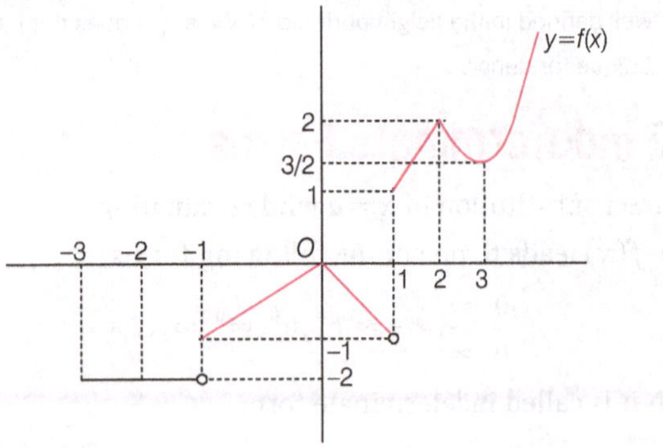

Sol. Using graph,

(i) When $x \to -1^-$, then $f(x) \to -1$

$\therefore \lim_{x \to -1^-} f(x) = -1$

(ii) When $x \to 2^+$, then $f(x) \to 2$

$\therefore \lim_{x \to 2^+} f(x) = 2$

(iii) When $x \to -3^+$, then $f(x) \to -2$

$\therefore \lim_{x \to -3^+} f(x) = -2$

(iv) $\lim_{x \to 1^+} f(x) = 1$

Again, In Previous Question

(a) $\lim_{x \to 1} f(x)$

$$\text{LHL} = \lim_{x \to 1^-} f(x) = -1$$

$$\text{RHL} = \lim_{x \to 1^+} f(x) = 1$$

$\therefore$ LHL $\neq$ RHL

$\therefore \lim_{x \to 1} f(x)$ does not exist.

(b) $\lim_{x \to 2} f(x)$

$$\text{LHL} = \lim_{x \to 2^-} f(x) = 2$$

$$\text{RHL} = \lim_{x \to 2^+} f(x) = 2$$

$\because$ LHL = RHL = 2

$\therefore \lim_{x \to 2} f(x)$ exists.

3.3 Algebra of Limits

Let $f(x)$ and $g(x)$ be two functions.

Case 1 Both limits exist

$$\lim_{x \to a} f(x) = l_1 \text{ and } \lim_{x \to a} g(x) = l_2$$

	Algebra	Result
(a)	$\lim_{x \to a} f(x) + g(x)$	$l_1 + l_2$
(b)	$\lim_{x \to a} f(x) - g(x)$	$l_1 - l_2$
(c)	$\lim_{x \to a} f(x) \cdot g(x)$	$l_1 \cdot l_2$
(d)	$\lim_{x \to a} \frac{f(x)}{g(x)}$	$\frac{l_1}{l_2}$, Provided $l_2 \neq 0$
(e)	$\lim_{x \to a} f(x)^{g(x)}$	$l_1^{l_2}$
(f)	$\lim_{x \to a} \log f(x)$	$\log l_1$
(g)	$\lim_{x \to a} \vert f(x) \vert$	$\vert l_1 \vert$
(h)	$\lim_{x \to a} e^{f(x)}$	e^{l_1}

Case 2 Exactly one limit exist say $\lim_{x \to a} f(x)$ does not exist and $\lim_{x \to a} g(x) = \text{L (finite)}$

(a) $\lim_{x \to a} f(x) \pm g(x) =$ Does not exists.

(b) $\lim_{x \to a} f(x) \cdot g(x) =$ May or may not exist.

Product of Two Functions : One with Defined Limit and One Without

When analyzing the product of two functions $f(x)$ and $g(x)$ as x approaches some value a, it is important to consider the behavior of each function near a.

1. **Limit of $f(x)$ is defined** Suppose $\lim(x \to a)$, $f(x) = L$, where L is a finite number.
2. **Limit of $g(x)$ is not defined** Suppose $\lim(x \to a)$ $g(x)$ does not exist. This can happen for several reasons, such as $g(x)$ oscillating indefinitely, approaching infinity or being undefined in some other way near a.

Now, consider the product $f(x) \cdot g(x)$ as x approaches a.

Cases to Consider

1. **$g(x)$ oscillates near a** If $g(x)$ oscillates indefinitely (e.g. $\sin(1/x)$ as $(x \to 0)$), then the product $f(x) \cdot g(x)$ may also oscillate unless $f(x)$ approaches 0. If $f(x)$ is a non-zero constant or does not approach 0, the limit of the product will generally not exist.

   e.g. $\lim_{x \to a} f(x) = 1$ **and** $g(x) = \sin\left(\frac{1}{x}\right)$

   $g(x)$ oscillates indefinitely as $x \to 0$. Thus, the product $f(x) \cdot g(x) = \sin\left(\frac{1}{x}\right)$ oscillates and does not have a limit as $x \to 0$.

2. **$g(x)$ approaches infinity or negative infinity**
   - If $g(x)$ approaches infinity (positive or negative), the behavior of the product $f(x) \cdot g(x)$ will depend on $f(x)$.
   - If $f(x)$ approaches 0, then the product $f(x) \cdot g(x)$ might approach 0 but this depends on the rate at which $f(x)$ approaches 0 relative to the rate at which $g(x)$ approaches infinity.
   - If $f(x)$ is a non-zero constant, then the product will approach infinity or negative infinity, based on sign of $f(x)$ and the behavior of $g(x)$.

   e.g. $\lim_{x \to 0} f(x) = 1$ **and** $g(x) = \frac{1}{x}$

   $g(x)$ approaches infinity as $x \to 0$. Therefore, the product $f(x) \cdot g(x) = \frac{1}{x}$ approaches infinity.

3. **$g(x)$ is undefined at a** If $g(x)$ is simply undefined at a (e.g. a discontinuity), then we need to look at the limit from both sides of a. If $g(x)$ has a well-defined limit from one side (e.g. $\lim_{x \to a^-} g(x)$ exists), the behavior of $f(x) \cdot g(x)$ will depend on this one-sided limit and $f(x)$.

   e.g. $\lim_{x \to 0} f(x) = 0$ **and** $g(x) = \frac{1}{x}$

   Here, the product $f(x) \cdot g(x)$ depends on how $f(x)$ approaches 0. If $f(x)$ approaches 0 faster than $g(x)$ approaches infinity, the product may approach a finite value or 0.

Conclusion

The limit of the product $f(x) \cdot g(x)$ when

$$\lim_{x \to a} f(x) = L$$

(a finite value) and $\lim_{x \to a} g(x)$ is undefined is not straightforward and depends heavily on the nature of $g(x)$ near a.

Each scenario requires careful analysis of the behaviour of both functions near the point.

$$\lim_{x \to a} \frac{f(x)}{g(x)} = \text{May or may not exist.}$$

Since, $\lim_{x \to a} f(x)$ does not exist and $\lim_{x \to a} g(x) = L$.

Then, $\lim_{x \to a} \frac{f(x)}{g(x)}$ may or may not exist.

e.g.

1. **Let $f(x) = \frac{1}{x}$ and $g(x) = x$**

   Then, $\lim_{x \to 0} f(x) = \lim_{x \to 0} \frac{1}{x}$ does not exist and $\lim_{x \to 0} g(x) = \lim_{x \to 0} x = 0$

   Now, $\lim_{x \to 0} \frac{f(x)}{g(x)} = \lim_{x \to 0} \frac{\frac{1}{x}}{x} = \lim_{x \to 0} \frac{1}{x^2}$

   = which does not exist.

   $\therefore \lim_{x \to 0} \frac{f(x)}{g(x)}$ does not exist.

2. Let $g(x)=\frac{1}{\sin x}$ and $f(x)=\tan x$

Then, $\lim_{x\to 0} g(x)=\lim_{x\to 0}\frac{1}{\sin 0}$ does not exist.

and $\lim_{x\to 0} f(x)=\lim_{x\to 0}\tan x=0$

Now, $\lim_{x\to 0}\frac{f(x)}{g(x)}=\lim_{x\to 0}\frac{\tan x}{\sin x}$

$$=\lim_{x\to 0}\frac{\sin x}{\sin x\cdot\cos x}=\lim_{x\to 0}\frac{1}{\cos x}=\frac{1}{\cos 0}=1$$

$\therefore \lim_{x\to 0}\frac{f(x)}{g(x)}=1$. So, it exists.

Case 3 Both limits do not exist.

In all cases we do not comment anything.

3.4 Evaluation of Limits

In this section, we will discuss that all the methods of evaluating the limiting value of any given function at any given point.

In better understanding we are categories in five subparts.

1. Limit of algebraic function
2. Trigonometric limits
3. Logarithmic limits
4. Exponential limits
5. Miscellaneous forms

Standard Approach

Two basic approach are discussed here which are used throughout the chapter.

By Definition

- $\lim_{x\to a} f(x)=?$

  If LHL = RHL = k (finite), then $\lim_{x\to a} f(x)=k$

  This concept is generally used when a function $f(x)$ is directly and indirectly changes its value in neighbourhood of $x=a$.

  e.g.

  (a) $f(x)=\begin{cases}3x+1 & x\le 1\\ 5x & x>1\end{cases}$, changes behaviour at $x=1$ directly

  (b) $f(x)=[x]\to\begin{cases}0 & 0\le x<1\\ 1 & 1\le x<2\end{cases}$, changes behaviour at $x=1$ indirectly, where $[\cdot]$ denotes the greatest integer function.

Example 2. Let $f(x)=\begin{cases}x^2+1 & x\le 0\\ 3x+1 & 0<x<1\\ [x] & x\ge 1\end{cases}$. Find

(i) $\lim_{x\to 0} f(x)$ (ii) $\lim_{x\to 1} f(x)$ (iii) $\lim_{x\to 2} f(x)$

where [·] denotes the greatest integer function.

Sol. (i) $\lim_{x\to 0} f(x)$

LHL = $\lim_{x\to 0^-} x^2+1=1$ and RHL = $\lim_{x\to 0^+} 3x+1=1$

$\because$ LHL = RHL = 1

$\therefore \lim_{x\to 0} f(x)=1$

(ii) $\lim_{x\to 1} f(x)$

LHL = $\lim_{x\to 1^-} 3x+1=4$ and RHL = $\lim_{x\to 1^+}[x]=1$

$\therefore$ LHL $\ne$ RHL

Limit does not exist.

(iii) $\lim_{x\to 2} f(x)=\lim_{x\to 2}[x]$ [indirectly]

LHL = $\lim_{x\to 2^-}[x]=1$

and RHL = $\lim_{x\to 2^+}[x]=2$

LHL = RHL

$\therefore \lim_{x\to 2} f(x)$ does not exist.

3.5 Direct Substitution Method

For $\lim_{x\to a} f(x)$ put $x=a$ directly, we get $f(a)$ if $f(a)$ is finite number, then $\lim_{x\to a} f(x)=f(a)$

[$\because$ provided $f(x)$ does not change at neighbourhood of $x=a$]

e.g. (a) $\lim_{x\to 1} 3x^2+4x-7=3(1)^2+4(1)-7=0$

(b) $\lim_{x\to\frac{\pi}{3}}\frac{\tan^2 x+\sin^2 x}{1+\cos^2 x}=\frac{(\sqrt{3})^2+\left(\frac{\sqrt{3}}{2}\right)^2}{1+\left(\frac{1}{2}\right)^2}$

$$=\frac{3+\frac{3}{4}}{1+\frac{1}{4}}=\frac{15}{5}=3$$

If $f(a)$ becomes indeterminate form, then we evaluate limit further using upcoming methods.

Milestone Practice 3.1

1. Evaluate the following limit ([·], {·} denotes greatest integer function and fractional part function respectively)

(i) $\lim\limits_{x \to n} [x]$, $\lim\limits_{x \to n} \{x\}$, $n \in I$ (ii) $\lim\limits_{x \to 0} \dfrac{|x|}{x}$

(iii) $\lim\limits_{x \to 0} \tan^{-1}\dfrac{1}{x}$ (iv) $\lim\limits_{x \to 0} \dfrac{1}{\ln|x|}$

(v) $\lim\limits_{x \to 0} \cot^{-1} x^2$ (vi) $\lim\limits_{x \to 0} [x] + \sqrt{\{x\}}$

(vii) $\lim\limits_{x \to 1} x\,\text{sgn}(x-1)$ (viii) $\lim\limits_{x \to 1} \dfrac{x}{[x]}$

(ix) $\lim\limits_{x \to 1} \dfrac{[x]}{x}$ (x) $\lim\limits_{x \to 0} \sin^{-1}[\sec x]$

2. Consider the graph of $y = f(x)$ given below, then find the following

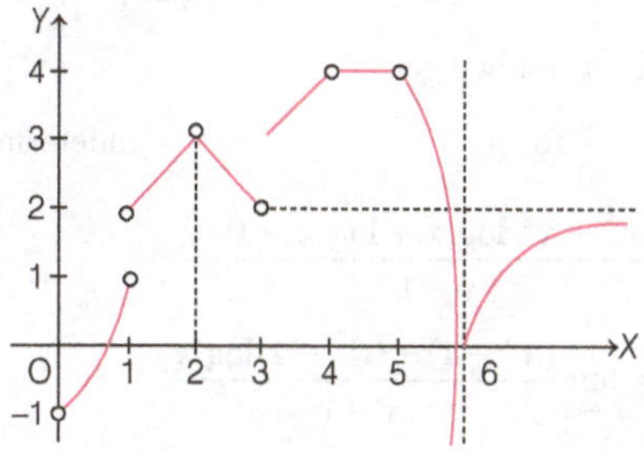

(i) $\lim\limits_{x \to 0^-} f(x)$ (ii) $\lim\limits_{x \to 0^+} f(x)$ (iii) $\lim\limits_{x \to 1^-} f(x)$

(iv) $\lim\limits_{x \to 1^+} f(x)$ (v) $\lim\limits_{x \to 2^-} f(x)$ (vi) $\lim\limits_{x \to 2^+} f(x)$

(vii) $\lim\limits_{x \to 3^-} f(x)$ (viii) $\lim\limits_{x \to 3^+} f(x)$ (ix) $\lim\limits_{x \to 4^-} f(x)$

(x) $\lim\limits_{x \to 4^+} f(x)$ (xi) $\lim\limits_{x \to \infty} f(x)$ (xii) $\lim\limits_{x \to 6^-} f(x)$

3. Consider the function

$$f(x) = \begin{cases} 1/x^2, & \text{if } x < -1 \\ 2, & \text{if } -1 \le x < 1 \\ 3, & \text{if } x = 1 \\ x+1, & \text{if } 1 < x \le 2 \\ -1/(x-2)^2, & \text{if } x > 2 \end{cases}$$

Sketch the graph of f.

Determine the following limits.

(i) $\lim\limits_{x \to -1^+} f(x)$ (ii) $\lim\limits_{x \to -1^-} f(x)$

(iii) $\lim\limits_{x \to -1} f(x)$ (iv) $\lim\limits_{x \to 1^+} f(x)$

(v) $\lim\limits_{x \to 1^-} f(x)$ (vi) $\lim\limits_{x \to 1} f(x)$

(vii) $\lim\limits_{x \to 2^+} f(x)$ (viii) $\lim\limits_{x \to 2^-} f(x)$

(ix) $\lim\limits_{x \to 2} f(x)$ (x) $\lim\limits_{x \to -3} f(x)$

(xi) $\lim\limits_{x \to 5} f(x)$ (xii) $\lim\limits_{x \to 1.5} f(x)$

4. Refer the figure, the value of λ for which

$2\left(\lim\limits_{x \to 0} f(x^3 - x^2)\right) = \lambda\left(\lim\limits_{x \to 0} f(2x^4 - x^5)\right)$ is

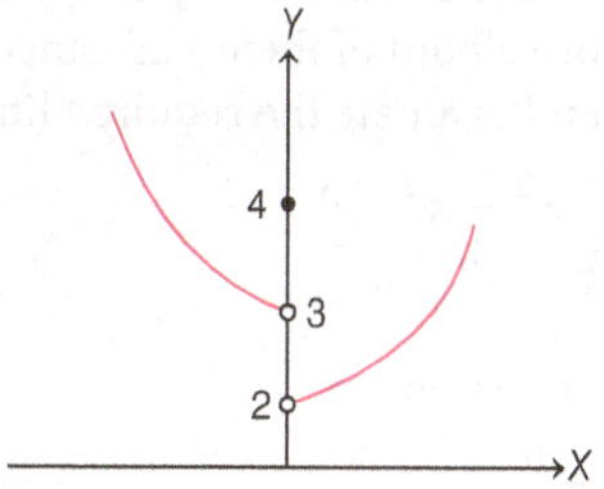

(a) $\dfrac{4}{3}$ (b) 2

(c) 3 (d) 5

5. Evaluate the left and right hand limits of the function $f(x) = \begin{cases} \dfrac{|x-4|}{x-4}, & x \ne 4 \\ 0, & x = 4 \end{cases}$.

6. Evaluate the left and the right hand limits of the function defined by $f(x) = \begin{cases} 1 + x^2, & \text{if } 0 \le x < 1 \\ 2 - x, & \text{if } x > 1 \end{cases}$

at $x = 1$. Also, show that $\lim\limits_{x \to 1} f(x)$ does not exist.

Answer Key

1. (i) Does not exist (ii) Does not exist (iii) Does not exist (iv) 0 (v) $\dfrac{\pi}{2}$ (vi) 0 (vii) Does not exist (viii) Does not exist (ix) Does not exist (x) $\dfrac{\pi}{2}$ **2.** (i) Does not exist (ii) – 1 (iii) 1 (iv) 2 (v) 3 (vi) 3 (vii) 2 (viii) 3 (ix) 4 (x) 4 (xi) 2 (xii) Does not exist **3.** (i) 2 (ii) 1 (iii) Does not exist (iv) 2 (v) 2 (vi) 2 (vii) Does not exist (viii) 3 (ix) Does not exist (x) $\dfrac{1}{9}$ (xi) $\dfrac{-1}{9}$ (xii) 2.5 **4.** (c) **5.** LHL = –1, RHL = 1 **6.** LHL = 2, RHL = 1

For Detailed Solution

Milestone 2 Limits of Algebraic Functions

• Factorisation Method • Rationalisation Method • Standard Formula • Method of Substitution

In this section, we will discuss the limiting value of different algebraic function. For evaluating algebraic limits we use algebraic methods like factorisation, rationalisation etc.

3.6 Factorisation Method

$$\lim_{x \to a} \frac{f(x)}{g(x)} = \frac{f(a)}{g(a)}$$

Where $f(x)$ and $g(x)$ are polynomial function or factorable expressions in such a way that $f(a) = g(a) = 0$. So, here we factorise both of them and cancel out the common factor and evaluate the required limit.

Example 3. $\lim_{x \to 2} \frac{x^3 - x^2 - 4}{x^2 - 4}$

Sol. On putting $x = 2$, we get

$$\frac{8 - 4 - 4}{4 - 4} = \frac{0}{0} \quad \text{[indeterminate form]}$$

Now, using factorisation

$$\lim_{x \to 2} \frac{(x-2)(x^2 + x + 2)}{(x-2)(x+2)}$$

$$= \lim_{x \to 2} \frac{x^2 + x + 2}{x + 2}$$

[cancel the common factor $(x - 2)$]

$$= \frac{4 + 2 + 2}{2 + 2} \quad \text{[using direct substitution]}$$

$$= \frac{8}{4} = 2$$

Example 4. Evaluate $\lim_{x \to 1} \left(\frac{1}{1 - x} - \frac{3}{1 - x^3} \right)$

Sol. On putting $x = 1$, we get

$$\lim_{x \to 1} \frac{1}{x - 1} - \lim_{x \to 1} \frac{3}{1 - x^3} = \infty - \infty \quad \text{[indeterminate form]}$$

$$\therefore \lim_{x \to 1} \frac{1}{1 - x} - \frac{3}{(1 - x)(1 + x^2 + x)}$$

$$= \lim_{x \to 1} \frac{x^2 + x - 2}{(1 - x)(1 + x^2 + x)}$$

$$= \lim_{x \to 1} \frac{(x + 2)(x - 1)}{(1 - x)(1 + x^2 + x)} = -\frac{3}{3} = -1$$

Example 5. Evaluate $\lim_{x \to 1} \frac{x^3 - x^2 \log x + \log x - 1}{x - 1}$

Sol. On putting $x = 1$, we get

$$\frac{0}{0} \text{ form} \quad \text{[indeterminate form]}$$

$$\therefore \lim_{x \to 1} \frac{x^3 - x^2 \log x + \log x - 1}{x - 1}$$

$$= \lim_{x \to 1} \frac{(x^3 - 1) - (x^2 - 1)\log x}{x - 1}$$

$$= \lim_{x \to 1} \frac{(x - 1)}{(x - 1)} [(x^2 + x + 1) - (x + 1)\log x] = 3$$

Example 6. Evaluate $\lim_{x \to \frac{\pi}{4}} \frac{(1 - \sin 2x)}{1 + \cos 4x}$.

Sol. On putting $x = \frac{\pi}{4}$, we get

$$\frac{0}{0} \text{ form} \quad \text{[indeterminate form]}$$

$$\therefore \lim_{x \to \frac{\pi}{4}} \frac{1 - \sin 2x}{1 + \cos 4x} = \lim_{x \to \frac{\pi}{4}} \frac{(\sin x - \cos x)^2}{2 \cos^2 2x}$$

$$= \lim_{x \to \frac{\pi}{4}} \frac{(\sin x - \cos x)^2}{2(\sin^2 x - \cos^2 x)^2} = \lim_{x \to \frac{\pi}{4}} \frac{1}{2(\sin x + \cos x)^2}$$

[cancel common factor]

$$= \frac{1}{2 \times 2} \quad \text{[direct substitution]}$$

$$= \frac{1}{4}$$

Example 7. Evaluate $\lim\limits_{x\to 2} \dfrac{2^x + 2^{3-x} - 6}{2^{-\frac{x}{2}} - 2^{1-x}}$

Sol. $\lim\limits_{x\to 2} \dfrac{2^x + 2^{3-x} - 6}{2^{-\frac{x}{2}} - 2^{1-x}}$ $\left[\dfrac{0}{0}\text{ form}\right]$

$$= \lim_{x\to 2} \frac{2^{2x} + 8 - 6\cdot 2^x}{2^{\frac{x}{2}} - 2} = \lim_{x\to 2} \frac{(2^x - 2)(2^x - 4)}{2^{\frac{x}{2}} - 2}$$

$$= \lim_{x\to 2} \frac{(2^x - 2)(2^{x/2} - 2)(2^{x/2} + 2)}{2^{x/2} - 2}$$

$$= 2 \times 4 = 8$$

Example 8. If the limit $\lim\limits_{x\to -2} \dfrac{3x^2 + ax + a + 3}{x^2 + x - 2}$ exists, then find a and the limit.

Sol. We see that the denominator $\to 0$. For the limit to be exist, we must have a finite value after substitution or indeterminate form i.e. $\left(\dfrac{0}{0}\right)$ form.

Hence, the numerator must $\to 0$,

i.e. $\lim\limits_{x\to -2} 3x^2 + ax + a + 3 = 0$

$\Rightarrow$ $12 - 2a + a + 3 = 0$

$\Rightarrow$ $a = 15$

Now, $\lim\limits_{x\to -2} \dfrac{3x^2 + ax + a + 3}{x^2 + x - 2}$

$$= \lim_{x\to -2} \frac{3x^2 + 15x + 18}{x^2 + x - 2}$$

$$= \lim_{x\to -2} \frac{3(x+2)(x+3)}{(x+2)(x-1)} = -1$$

3.7 Rationalisation Method

If in any limit, the denominator or numerator involves the radical sign, then we can rationalize the irrational expression by multiplying with their conjugates to remove the indeterminacy.

Example 9. Evaluate the following limits.

(i) $\lim\limits_{x\to 0} \dfrac{x}{\sqrt{1+x} - \sqrt{1-x}}$ (ii) $\lim\limits_{x\to 2} \dfrac{\sqrt{x^2 - 4} - \sqrt{x - 2}}{x - 2}$

Sol. (i) $\lim\limits_{x\to 0} \dfrac{x}{\sqrt{1+x} - \sqrt{1-x}}$ $\left[\dfrac{0}{0}\text{ form}\right]$

By rationalisation of denominator, we get

$$\lim_{x\to 0} \frac{x}{\sqrt{1+x} - \sqrt{1-x}} \times \frac{\sqrt{1+x} + \sqrt{1-x}}{\sqrt{1+x} + \sqrt{1-x}}$$

$$\Rightarrow \lim_{x\to 0} \frac{x(\sqrt{1+x} + \sqrt{1-x})}{2x} = \frac{2}{2} = 1$$

(ii) $\lim\limits_{x\to 2} \dfrac{\sqrt{x^2 - 4} - \sqrt{x - 2}}{(x - 2)}$ $\left[\dfrac{0}{0}\text{ form}\right]$

By rationalisation of numerator, we get

$$\lim_{x\to 2} \frac{\sqrt{x^2 - 4} - \sqrt{x - 2}}{x - 2} \times \frac{\sqrt{x^2 - 4} + \sqrt{x - 2}}{\sqrt{x^2 - 4} + \sqrt{x - 2}}$$

$$= \lim_{x\to 2} \frac{(x^2 - 4) - (x - 2)}{(x - 2)(\sqrt{x^2 - 4} + \sqrt{x - 2})}$$

$$= \lim_{x\to 2} \frac{(x - 2)(x + 2 - 1)}{(x - 2)(\sqrt{x^2 - 4} + \sqrt{x - 2})}$$

$$= \lim_{x\to 2} \frac{x + 1}{\sqrt{x^2 - 4} + \sqrt{x - 2}} = \frac{3}{0} = \infty$$

JEE SCANNER

Example Similar to PYQ Asked in JEE Main 2021

If $\lim\limits_{x\to 1} \dfrac{4 - \sqrt{15x + 1}}{2 - \sqrt{3x + 1}} = a$, *then a is equal to*

(a) $\dfrac{3}{2}$ (b) $\dfrac{1}{2}$ (c) $\dfrac{5}{2}$ (d) $\dfrac{9}{2}$.

Sol. (c) Given, $\lim\limits_{x\to 1} \dfrac{4 - \sqrt{15x + 1}}{2 - \sqrt{3x + 1}}$ $\left[\dfrac{0}{0}\text{ form}\right]$

Rationalisaing of numerator and denomenator both, we get

$$= \lim_{x\to 1} \frac{15 - 15x}{3 - 3x} \cdot \frac{(2 + \sqrt{3x + 1})}{(4 + \sqrt{15x + 1})}$$

$$= \lim_{x\to 1} 5\left(\frac{2 + \sqrt{3x + 1}}{4 + \sqrt{15x + 1}}\right) = 5 \times \frac{4}{8} = \frac{5}{2}$$

$\therefore$ $a = \dfrac{5}{2}$

Skill Builder

If $\lim\limits_{x\to 0} \dfrac{2 - \sqrt{2x + 4}}{3 - \sqrt{3x + 9}} = \alpha$, then α is equal to

(a) 1 (b) 5 (c) 3 (d) 2

For Sol.

■ **For more practice** See Q.4 of Milestone Practice 3.2.

Example 10. Evaluate $\lim\limits_{x\to 2a^+} \dfrac{\sqrt{x} - \sqrt{2a} + \sqrt{x - 2a}}{\sqrt{x^2 - 4a^2}}$

Sol. $\lim\limits_{x\to 2a^+} \dfrac{\sqrt{x} - \sqrt{2a} + \sqrt{x - 2a}}{\sqrt{x^2 - 4a^2}}$ $\left[\dfrac{0}{0}\text{ form}\right]$

$$= \lim_{x\to 2a^+} \frac{\sqrt{x} - \sqrt{2a}}{\sqrt{x^2 - 4a^2}} + \lim_{x\to 2a^+} \frac{\sqrt{x - 2a}}{\sqrt{x^2 - 4a^2}}$$

$$= \lim_{x \to 2a^+} \frac{(\sqrt{x} - \sqrt{2a})(\sqrt{x} + \sqrt{2a})}{\sqrt{x^2 - 4a^2}\,(\sqrt{x} + \sqrt{2a})} + \lim_{x \to 2a^+} \frac{(\sqrt{x - 2a})}{(\sqrt{x - 2a})(\sqrt{x + 2a})}$$

$$= \lim_{x \to 2a^+} \frac{x - 2a}{\sqrt{(x - 2a)(x + 2a)} \cdot (\sqrt{x} + \sqrt{2a})} + \frac{1}{\sqrt{4a}}$$

$$= \lim_{x \to 2a^+} \frac{\sqrt{x - 2a}}{\sqrt{x + 2a}\,(\sqrt{x} + \sqrt{2a})} + \frac{1}{2\sqrt{a}} = 0 + \frac{1}{2\sqrt{a}} = \frac{1}{2\sqrt{a}}$$

Example 11. $\lim_{t \to 0} \dfrac{\sqrt{1 + \sqrt{1 + t^4}} - \sqrt{2}}{t^4}$

Sol. $\lim_{t \to 0} \dfrac{\sqrt{1 + \sqrt{1 + t^4}} - \sqrt{2}}{t^4}$ $\left[\dfrac{0}{0} \text{ form}\right]$

By rationalisation of numerator, we get

$$\lim_{t \to 0} \frac{\sqrt{1 + t^4} - 1}{t^4 \cdot (\sqrt{1 + \sqrt{1 + t^4}} + \sqrt{2})}$$

Again, on rationalising the numerator, we get

$$\lim_{t \to 0} \frac{t^4}{t^4(\sqrt{1 + \sqrt{1 + t^4}} + \sqrt{2})(\sqrt{1 + t^4} + 1)} = \frac{1}{2\sqrt{2} \times 2} = \frac{1}{4\sqrt{2}}$$

JEE Focus Points

- $\left(x^{\frac{1}{n}} - a^{\frac{1}{n}}\right)\left(x^{\frac{n-1}{n}} + x^{\frac{n-2}{n}} a^{\frac{1}{n}} + x^{\frac{n-3}{n}} a^{\frac{2}{n}} + \ldots + a^{\frac{n-1}{n}}\right) = (x - a)$
- $\left(x^{\frac{1}{n}} + a^{\frac{1}{n}}\right)\left(x^{\frac{n-1}{n}} - x^{\frac{n-2}{n}} a^{\frac{1}{n}} + x^{\frac{n-3}{n}} a^{\frac{2}{n}} - \ldots\right) = (x + a)$, if n is odd

Example 12. Evaluate $\lim_{x \to -1} \dfrac{\sqrt[3]{(7 - x)} - 2}{(x + 1)}$

Sol. $\sqrt[3]{(7 - x)} - 2$

$$= \frac{(7 - x) - 8}{(7 - x)^{2/3} + (7 - x)^{1/3} \cdot 2 + 4}$$

$$= -\frac{(x + 1)}{(7 - x)^{2/3} + (7 - x)^{1/3} \cdot 2 + 4} \quad \text{...(i)}$$

$$\therefore \lim_{x \to -1} \frac{\sqrt[3]{(7 - x)} - 2}{(x + 1)}$$

$$= -\lim_{x \to -1} \frac{(x + 1)}{(x + 1)(7 - x)^{2/3} + (7 - x)^{1/3} \cdot 2 + 4}$$

[from Eq. (i)]

$$= -\lim_{x \to -1} \frac{1}{(7 - x)^{2/3} + (7 - x)^{1/3} \cdot 2 + 4}$$

$$= -\frac{1}{4 + 4 + 4} = -\frac{1}{12}$$

Limit when $x \to \infty$

In this section, we will discussion evaluation of limit of function $f(x)$ when $x \to \infty$ or $f\left(\dfrac{1}{x}\right)$ when $x \to 0$.

$x \to \infty$			
$x^n \to \infty$ where $n > 0$	$x^n \to 0$ where $n < 0$	$a^x \to \infty$ where $a > 1$	$a^x \to 0$ where $0 < a < 1$
e.g. $x^3, x^4 \to \infty$	e.g. $\left(\dfrac{1}{x}, \dfrac{1}{x^2} \to 0\right)$	e.g. $(2^x, 5^x \to \infty)$	e.g. $\left(\dfrac{1}{2}\right)^x \to 0$

TYPE 1 $\lim_{x \to \infty} \dfrac{f(x)}{g(x)}$, **where $f(x)$ and $g(x)$ both are function in exponent of x.**

In this situation, we take x^n as a common from numerator as well denominator, where n is corresponding highest exponent value.

Example 13. Evaluate following limits:

(i) $\lim_{x \to \infty} \dfrac{7x^4 + 3x^2 + 8x + 9}{9x^4 - 8x^3 + 3}$

(ii) $\lim_{x \to \infty} \dfrac{3x^4 - 2}{\sqrt{x^8 + 3x + 4}}$

(iii) $\lim_{x \to -\infty} \dfrac{4x + 3}{\sqrt{2x^2 + 5x - 7}}$

(iv) $\lim_{x \to -\infty} \sqrt{25x^2 - 3x} + 5x$

Sol. (i) $\lim_{x \to \infty} \dfrac{7x^4 + 3x^2 + 8x + 9}{9x^4 - 8x^3 + 3}$ $\left[\dfrac{\infty}{\infty} \text{ form}\right]$

$$= \lim_{x \to \infty} \frac{x^4\left(7 + \dfrac{3}{x^2} + \dfrac{8}{x^3} + \dfrac{9}{x^4}\right)}{x^4\left(9 - \dfrac{8}{x} + \dfrac{3}{x^4}\right)} = \frac{7}{9}$$

(ii) $\lim_{x \to \infty} \dfrac{3x^4 - 2}{\sqrt{x^8 + 3x + 4}}$ $\left[\dfrac{\infty}{\infty} \text{ form}\right]$

$$= \lim_{x \to \infty} \frac{x^4\left(3 - \dfrac{2}{x^4}\right)}{x^4\sqrt{1 + \dfrac{3}{x^7} + \dfrac{4}{x^8}}}$$

$$= \frac{3}{1} = 3$$

(iii) $\lim_{x \to -\infty} \frac{4x+3}{\sqrt{2x^2+5x-7}}$ $\left[\frac{\infty}{\infty}\text{form}\right]$

$$= \lim_{x \to -\infty} \frac{x\left(4+\frac{3}{x}\right)}{\sqrt{x^2}\sqrt{2+\frac{5}{x}-\frac{7}{x^2}}}$$

$$= \lim_{x \to -\infty} \frac{x\left(4+\frac{3}{x}\right)}{-x\sqrt{2+\frac{5}{x}-\frac{7}{x^2}}}$$

$[\because |x| = -x \text{ because } x \to -\infty \text{ (– ve)}]$

$$= -\frac{4}{\sqrt{2}} = -2\sqrt{2}$$

(iv) $\lim_{x \to -\infty} \sqrt{25x^2-3x}+5x$ $[\infty - \infty \text{ form}]$

By rationalisation, we get

$$\lim_{x \to -\infty} \frac{25x^2-3x-25x^2}{\sqrt{25x^2-3x}-5x}$$

$$= \lim_{x \to -\infty} \frac{-3x}{\sqrt{25x^2-3x}-5x}$$

$$= \lim_{x \to -\infty} \frac{-3x}{-x\left[\sqrt{25-\frac{3}{x}}+5\right]}$$

$[\because x \to -\infty \Rightarrow \sqrt{x^2} = -x]$

$$= \frac{3}{10}$$

TYPE 2 Function containing a^n type expression and $n \to \infty$

In this situation, we are try to make fraction which lies in between – 1 to 1 so that we can write their limiting value to zero when $n \to \infty$.

Example 14. Evaluate $\lim_{n \to \infty} (2^n + 5^n)^{\frac{1}{n}}$.

Sol. $\lim_{n \to \infty} (2^n + 5^n)^{\frac{1}{n}}$ $[\infty^0 \text{ form}]$

On taking 5^n common,

$$\Rightarrow \lim_{n \to \infty} 5\left[\left(\frac{2}{5}\right)^n + 1\right]^{\frac{1}{n}}$$

$$= 5(0+1)^0$$

$\left[\text{when } n \to \infty, \text{ then } \left(\frac{2}{5}\right)^n \to 0 \text{ and } \frac{1}{n} \to 0\right]$

$$= 5$$

Example 15. If $L = \lim_{n \to \infty} (2 \times 3^2 \times 2^3 \times 3^4 \ldots \times 2^{n-1} \times 3^n)^{\frac{1}{(n^2+1)}}$, then the value of L^4 is

(a) 6 (b) 4 (c) 8 (d) 5

Sol. (a) It is obvious that n is even. Then,

$$\lim_{n \to \infty} \left(2^{1+3+5+\ldots+n/2 \text{ terms}} \cdot 3^{2+4+6+\ldots+n/2 \text{ term}}\right)^{\frac{1}{(n^2+1)}}$$

$$= \lim_{n \to \infty} \left(2^{\frac{n^2}{4}} \cdot 3^{\frac{n(n+2)}{4}}\right)^{\frac{1}{(n^2+1)}}$$

$$= \lim_{n \to \infty} 2^{\frac{n^2}{4(n^2+1)}} \cdot 3^{\frac{n(n+2)}{4(n^2+1)}}$$

$$= 2^{\lim_{n \to \infty} \frac{1}{4\left(1+\frac{1}{n^2}\right)}} \cdot 3^{\lim_{n \to \infty} \frac{\left(1+\frac{2}{n}\right)}{4\left(1+\frac{1}{n^2}\right)}} = 2^{\frac{1}{4}} 3^{\frac{1}{4}} = (6)^{\frac{1}{4}}$$

$$\therefore \quad L^4 = (6)^{4 \times \frac{1}{4}} = 6$$

Example 16. Evaluate

$$\lim_{x \to 0} (1^{\text{cosec}^2 x} + 2^{\text{cosec}^2 x} + \ldots + 100^{\text{cosec}^2 x})^{\sin^2 x}.$$

Sol. Given, $\lim_{x \to 0} (1^{\text{cosec}^2 x} + 2^{\text{cosec}^2 x} + \ldots + 100^{\text{cosec}^2 x})^{\sin^2 x}$

On taking $100^{\text{cosec}^2 x}$ as common, $[\infty^0 \text{ form}]$

$$\lim_{x \to \infty} (100^{\text{cosec}^2 x})^{\sin^2 x} \left[\left(\frac{1}{100}\right)^{\text{cosec}^2 x} + \left(\frac{2}{100}\right)^{\text{cosec}^2 x} + \ldots 1\right]^{\sin^2 x}$$

$$= \lim_{x \to 0} 100 \left[\left(\frac{1}{100}\right)^{\text{cosec}^2 x} + \left(\frac{2}{100}\right)^{\text{cosec}^2 x} + \ldots + \left(\frac{99}{100}\right)^{\text{cosec}^2 x} + 1\right]^{\sin^2 x}$$

$$= 100$$

Example 17. Evaluate $\lim_{n \to \infty} \cos(\pi\sqrt{n^2+n})$, where n is an integer.

(a) 1 (b) – 1 (c) 0 (d) None of these

Sol. (c) $L = \lim_{n \to \infty} \cos(\pi\sqrt{n^2+n}) = \lim_{n \to \infty} \pm\cos(n\pi - \pi\sqrt{n^2+n})$

$$= \lim_{n \to \infty} \pm\cos(\pi(n - \sqrt{n^2+n}))$$

$$= \pm \lim_{n \to \infty} \cos\left(\frac{-n\pi}{n+\sqrt{n^2+n}}\right) = \pm \lim_{n \to \infty} \cos\left(\frac{n\pi}{n+n\sqrt{1+\frac{1}{n}}}\right)$$

$$= \pm \lim_{n \to \infty} \cos\left(\frac{\pi}{1+\sqrt{1+\frac{1}{n}}}\right) = \pm\cos\frac{\pi}{2} = 0$$

JEE SCANNER

Example Similar to PYQ Asked in JEE Main 2022

If $\lim_{n\to\infty}\sqrt{n^2-5n+7}-n\alpha+\beta=0$, then $2(\alpha+\beta)$ will be equal to, where α,β are finite numbers.

Sol. (7) $\because \lim_{n\to\infty}\sqrt{n^2-5n+7}-n\alpha=-\beta$

On putting $n=\infty$, we get

$\infty-\infty(\alpha)$, then limiting value 0 is only possible when $\alpha>0$, then we get $\infty-\infty$ form.

$\therefore$ After rationalisation, we get

$$\lim_{n\to\infty}\frac{n^2-5n+7-(n\alpha)^2}{\sqrt{n^2-5n+7}+n\alpha}=-\beta \quad \text{[finite]}$$

$$\Rightarrow \lim_{n\to\infty}\frac{n^2(1-\alpha^2)-5n+7}{\sqrt{n^2-5n+7}+n\alpha}=-\beta$$

Limit finitely exist when

$$1-\alpha^2=0\Rightarrow\alpha=\pm1(-1\text{ reject})\Rightarrow\alpha=1$$

$$\lim_{n\to\infty}\frac{n\left[-5+\frac{7}{n}\right]}{n\left[\sqrt{1-\frac{5}{n}+\frac{7}{n^2}}+\alpha\right]}=-\beta$$

$$\Rightarrow \frac{-5}{1+\alpha}=-\beta$$

$$\therefore\ \beta=\frac{5}{1+1}=\frac{5}{2}$$

Now, $2(\alpha+\beta)=7$

Skill Builder

If $\lim_{n\to\infty}\sqrt{n^2-6n+4}-n\alpha+\beta=0$, then the value of $(\alpha+\beta)$ is, where α,β are finite.

For Sol.

■ **For more practice** See Q.6 of Milestone Practice 3.2.

TYPE 3 Sum of series when number of terms tends to zero.

To understand this we are solving some examples below.

Example 18. If $a_1=1$ and $a_{n+1}=\dfrac{4+3a_n}{3+2a_n}$, $n\geq1$ and if $\lim_{n\to\infty}a_n=a$, then the value of a is

(a) $\sqrt{2}$ (b) $-\sqrt{2}$
(c) 2 (d) None of these

Sol. (a) We have, $a_{n+1}=\dfrac{4+3a_n}{3+2a_n}$

$$\Rightarrow \lim_{n\to\infty}a_{n+1}=\lim_{n\to\infty}\frac{4+3a_n}{3+2a_n}$$

$$\Rightarrow a=\frac{4+3a}{3+2a}\Rightarrow2a^2=4\Rightarrow a=\sqrt{2}$$

[where $\lim_{n\to\infty}a_n=a$]

[$a\neq-\sqrt{2}$ because each $a_n>0$, therefore $\lim_{n\to\infty}a_n=a>0$]

Example 19. For $n\in N$, let $a_n=\sum_{k=1}^{n}2k$ and $b_n=\sum_{k=1}^{n}(2k-1)$. Then, $\lim_{n\to\infty}(\sqrt{a_n}-\sqrt{b_n})$ is equal to

(a) 1 (b) $\frac{1}{2}$ (c) 0 (d) 2

Sol. (b) $a_n=\sum_{k=1}^{n}2k=n(n+1)$

$$b_n=\sum_{k=1}^{n}(2k-1)=n^2$$

$$\therefore \lim_{n\to\infty}(\sqrt{a_n}-\sqrt{b_n})=\lim_{n\to\infty}(\sqrt{n(n+1)}-n)$$

$$=\lim_{n\to\infty}\frac{n^2+n-n^2}{(\sqrt{n^2+n}+n)}$$

$$=\lim_{n\to\infty}\frac{n}{n\left(\sqrt{1+\frac{1}{n}}+1\right)}=\frac{1}{2}$$

Example 20. Let $U_n=\dfrac{n!}{(n+2)!}$, where $n\in N$. If $S_n=\sum_{n=1}^{n}U_n$, then $\lim_{n\to\infty}S_n$ equals

(a) 2 (b) 1
(c) 1/2 (d) Non-existent

Sol. (c) $U_n=\dfrac{n!}{(n+2)!}=\dfrac{1}{(n+2)(n+1)}$

$$S_n=\sum_{n=1}^{n}\frac{(n+2)-(n+1)}{(n+2)(n+1)}$$

$$S_n=\sum_{n=1}^{n}\left(\frac{1}{n+1}\right)-\left(\frac{1}{n+2}\right)$$

$$S_n=\left(\frac{1}{2}-\frac{1}{3}\right)+\left(\frac{1}{3}-\frac{1}{4}\right)+\left(\frac{1}{4}-\frac{1}{5}\right)+\ldots+\left(\frac{1}{n+1}-\frac{1}{n+2}\right)$$

$$S_n=\frac{1}{2}-\frac{1}{n+2}$$

$$\lim_{n\to\infty}S_n=\frac{1}{2}$$

Example 21. Let $f(x) = \lim_{n\to\infty} \sum_{n=1}^{n} 3^{n-1} \sin^3 \frac{x}{3^n}$, then find $f\left(\frac{\pi}{2}\right)$.

Sol. Using $\sin 3\theta = 3\sin\theta - 4\sin^3\theta$

$$T_1 = \sin^3 \frac{x}{3} = \frac{1}{4}\left(3\sin\frac{x}{3} - \sin x\right)$$

$$T_2 = 3\sin^3 \frac{x}{3^2} = \frac{3}{4}\left(3\sin\frac{x}{3^2} - \sin\frac{x}{3}\right)$$

and so on....

$$\because \quad T_1 = \frac{1}{4}\left(3\sin\frac{x}{3} - \sin x\right)$$

$$T_2 = \frac{1}{4}\left(3^2\sin\frac{x}{3^2} - 3\sin\frac{x}{3}\right)$$

$$\therefore \quad T_n = \frac{1}{4}\left(3^n\sin\frac{x}{3^n} - 3^{n-1}\sin\frac{x}{3^{n-1}}\right)$$

$$\therefore \quad f(x) = \lim_{n\to\infty}\frac{1}{4}\left(3^n\sin\frac{x}{3^n} - \sin x\right)$$

$$= \frac{1}{4}\left(\lim_{n\to\infty}\frac{x\sin\frac{x}{3^n}}{\frac{x}{3^n}} - \sin x\right)$$

$$= \frac{1}{4}(x - \sin x)$$

$$\therefore \quad f\left(\frac{\pi}{2}\right) = \frac{1}{4}\left(\frac{\pi}{2} - 1\right) = \frac{\pi - 2}{8}$$

Example 22. Evaluate

$$\lim_{n\to\infty}\sum_{r=1}^{n}\cot^{-1}\left(\frac{r^3 - r + \frac{1}{r}}{2}\right)$$

Sol. Here, $\lim_{n\to\infty}\sum_{r=1}^{n}\cot^{-1}\left(\frac{r^3 - r + \frac{1}{r}}{2}\right)$

$$= \lim_{n\to\infty}\sum_{r=1}^{n}\tan^{-1}\left(\frac{2r}{1 - r^2 + r^4}\right)$$

$$= \lim_{n\to\infty}\sum_{r=1}^{n}\tan^{-1}\left(\frac{2r}{1 + (r^2 - r)(r^2 + r)}\right)$$

$$= \lim_{n\to\infty}\sum_{r=1}^{n}\tan^{-1}\left(\frac{(r^2 + r) - (r^2 - r)}{1 + (r^2 + r)(r^2 - r)}\right)$$

$$= \lim_{n\to\infty}\sum_{r=1}^{n}\{\tan^{-1}(r^2 + r) - \tan^{-1}(r^2 - r)\}$$

$$= \lim_{n\to\infty}[(\tan^{-1}2 - \tan^{-1}0) + (\tan^{-1}6 - \tan^{-1}2) + (\tan^{-1}12 - \tan^{-1}6) + (\tan^{-1}(n^2 + n) - \tan^{-1}(n^2 - n))]$$

$$= \lim_{n\to\infty}\{\tan^{-1}(n^2 + n) - \tan^{-1}(0)\}$$

$$= \tan^{-1}(\infty) - \tan^{-1}(0) = \frac{\pi}{2}$$

$$\Rightarrow \quad \lim_{n\to\infty}\sum_{r=1}^{n}\cot^{-1}\left(\frac{r^3 - r + \frac{1}{r}}{2}\right) = \frac{\pi}{2}$$

Example 23. Evaluate

$\lim_{n\to\infty}\left(\frac{a_1 + 1}{a_1}\right)\left(\frac{a_2 + 1}{a_2}\right)\dots\left(\frac{a_n + 1}{a_n}\right)$, where $a_1 = 1$ and $a_n = n(1 + a_{n-1}), \forall\, n \ge 2$.

Sol. $\lim_{n\to\infty}\left(\frac{a_1 + 1}{a_1}\right)\left(\frac{a_2 + 1}{a_2}\right)\dots\left(\frac{a_n + 1}{a_n}\right)$

We know, $a_{n-1} + 1 = \frac{a_n}{n}$ ...(i)

$$\lim_{n\to\infty}\left(\frac{a_2}{2}\right)\left(\frac{a_3}{3}\right)\left(\frac{a_4}{4}\right)\dots\left(\frac{a_{n+1}}{n+1}\right)\frac{1}{a_1a_2\dots a_n}$$

$$= \lim_{n\to\infty}\frac{a_{n+1}}{(n+1)!} = \lim_{n\to\infty}\frac{1 + a_n}{n!} \quad \text{[using Eq. (i)]}$$

$$= \lim_{n\to\infty}\left(\frac{1}{n!} + \frac{a_n}{n!}\right)$$

$$= \lim_{n\to\infty}\left(\frac{1}{n!} + \frac{1}{(n-1)!} + \frac{a_{n-1}}{(n-1)!}\right) \quad \text{[using Eq. (i)]}$$

$$= \lim_{n\to\infty}\left(\frac{1}{n!} + \frac{1}{(n-1)!} + \frac{1}{(n-2)!} + \dots + \frac{1}{2!} + \frac{1}{1!} + \frac{a_1}{1!}\right) \quad [a_1 = 1, \text{given}]$$

$$= \lim_{n\to\infty}\left(\frac{1}{n!} + \frac{1}{(n-1)!} + \frac{1}{(n-2)!} + \dots + \frac{1}{(2)!} + \frac{1}{1!} + \frac{1}{1}\right)$$

$$= e$$

JEE Focus Points

Summation of series using definite integral as the limit

The expression of the form, $\lim_{n \to \infty} \frac{1}{n} \sum_{r=\phi(x)}^{\psi(x)} f\left(\frac{r}{n}\right) = \int_a^b f(x)dx$, where

- Σ is replaced by $\int$,
- $\frac{r}{n}$ is replaced by x,
- $\frac{1}{n}$ is replaced by dx,
- To obtain, $a = \lim_{n \to \infty} \frac{\phi(x)}{n}$ and $b = \lim_{n \to \infty} \frac{\psi(x)}{n}$

The value of obtained is the required sum of the given series.

Example 24. Evaluate $\lim_{n \to \infty} \frac{1}{n} \sum_{r=1}^{2n} \frac{r}{\sqrt{n^2 + r^2}}$.

Sol. Here, $\lim_{n \to \infty} \frac{1}{n} \sum_{r=1}^{2n} \frac{r}{\sqrt{n^2 + r^2}}$

Dividing numerator and denominator both by n, we get

$$\lim_{n \to \infty} \frac{1}{n} \sum_{r=1}^{2n} \frac{r}{\sqrt{n^2 + r^2}} = \lim_{n \to \infty} \frac{1}{n} \sum_{r=1}^{2n} \frac{\frac{r}{n}}{\sqrt{1 + \left(\frac{r}{n}\right)^2}}$$

On putting $\frac{r}{n} = x$; $\frac{1}{n} = dx$; $\lim_{n \to \infty} \sum_{r=1}^{2n} = \int_a^b$,

where $a = \lim_{n \to \infty} \frac{1}{n} = 0$ and $b = \lim_{n \to \infty} \frac{2n}{n} = 2$

$\therefore$ Required limit $= \int_0^2 \frac{x}{\sqrt{1 + x^2}} dx = [\sqrt{1 + x^2}]_0^2 = \sqrt{5} - 1$

This concept is discussed in detail in chapter definite integration.

3.8 Standard Formula

$$\lim_{x \to a} \frac{x^n - a^n}{x - a} = n \cdot a^{n-1}, \text{ where } n \in Q.$$

Proof We have, $\lim_{x \to a} \frac{x^n - a^n}{x - a}$

$$= \lim_{x \to a^+} \frac{x^n - a^n}{x - a} = \lim_{h \to 0} \frac{(a+h)^n - a^n}{a + h - a}$$

$$= \lim_{h \to 0} \frac{a^n \left\{\left(1 + \frac{h}{a}\right)^n - 1\right\}}{h}$$

[where $x \to 0, (1 + x)^n \to 1 + nx$]

$$= a^n \lim_{h \to 0} \frac{\left\{1 + n\frac{h}{a}\right\} - 1}{h} = a^n \frac{n}{a} = na^{n-1}$$

Example 25. Evaluate $\lim_{x \to 2} \frac{x^{10} - 1024}{x^5 - 32}$.

Sol. $\lim_{x \to 2} \frac{x^{10} - 1024}{x^5 - 32} = \lim_{x \to 2} \frac{x^{10} - 2^{10}}{x^5 - 2^5}$

$$= \frac{\lim_{x \to 2} \frac{x^{10} - 2^{10}}{x - 2}}{\lim_{x \to 2} \frac{x^5 - 2^5}{x - 2}} = \frac{10 \times 2^{10-1}}{5 \times 2^{5-1}} = 64$$

Example 26. Evaluate $\lim_{x \to 1} \frac{\sqrt[3]{x} + \sqrt{x} + x\sqrt{x} - 3}{x^3 - 1}$.

Sol. $\lim_{x \to 1} \frac{(\sqrt[3]{x} - 1) + (\sqrt{x} - 1) + (x^{3/2} - 1)}{(x - 1)(x^2 + x + 1)}$ $\left[\frac{0}{0} \text{ form}\right]$

$$= \lim_{x \to 1} \left\{\frac{\sqrt[3]{x} - 1}{x - 1} + \frac{(\sqrt{x} - 1)}{x - 1} + \frac{(x^{3/2} - 1)}{x - 1}\right\} \cdot \frac{1}{x^2 + x + 1}$$

$$= \left\{\left(\lim_{x \to 1} \frac{\sqrt[3]{x} - 1}{x - 1}\right) + \left(\lim_{x \to 1} \frac{\sqrt{x} - 1}{x - 1}\right) + \left(\lim_{x \to 1} \frac{(x^{3/2} - 1)}{x - 1}\right)\right\} \cdot \lim_{x \to 1} \frac{1}{x^2 + x + 1}$$

$$= \left\{\frac{1}{3}(1)^{1/3 - 1} + \frac{1}{2}(1)^{1/2 - 1} + \frac{3}{2}(1)^{3/2 - 1}\right\} \cdot \frac{1}{1^2 + 1 + 1}$$

$$= \left\{\frac{1}{3}(1)^{-2/3} + \frac{1}{2}(1)^{-1/2} + \frac{3}{2}(1)^{1/2}\right\} \cdot \frac{1}{3}$$

$$= \left(\frac{1}{3} + \frac{1}{2} + \frac{3}{2}\right) \cdot \frac{1}{3} = \left(\frac{2 + 3 + 9}{6}\right) \cdot \frac{1}{3} = \frac{7}{9}$$

Example 27. Evaluate $\lim_{x \to 1} \frac{x^{P+1} - (P+1)x + P}{(x - 1)^2}$.

Sol. $\lim_{x \to 1} \frac{x^{P+1} - (P+1)x + P}{(x - 1)^2}$ $\left[\frac{0}{0} \text{ form}\right]$

$$= \lim_{x \to 1} \frac{x^{P+1} - Px - x + P}{(x - 1)^2} = \lim_{x \to 1} \frac{x(x^P - 1) - P(x - 1)}{(x - 1)^2}$$

On dividing numerator and denominator by $(x - 1)$, we get

$$\lim_{x \to 1} \frac{x\frac{(x^P - 1)}{(x - 1)} - P}{(x - 1)} = \lim_{x \to 1} \frac{(x + x^2 + x^3 + \ldots + x^P) - P}{(x - 1)}$$

$$= \lim_{x \to 1} \frac{(x + x^2 + x^3 + \ldots + x^P) - (1 + 1 + 1 + \ldots \text{ upto } P \text{ times})}{(x - 1)}$$

$$= \lim_{x \to 1} \left\{\frac{(x - 1)}{(x - 1)} + \frac{(x^2 - 1)}{(x - 1)} + \frac{(x^3 - 1)}{(x - 1)} + \ldots + \frac{(x^P - 1)}{(x - 1)}\right\}$$

$$= 1 + 2(1)^{2-1} + 3(1)^{3-1} + \ldots + P(1)^{P-1}$$

$$= 1 + 2 + 3 + \ldots + P$$

$$= \frac{P(P + 1)}{2}$$ [using summation of P terms of AP]

3.9 Method of Substitution

In this method, we can simplify the limiting value of function by substitution. Here, we can use two types of substitution.

(a) Substitution of $x \to a$ in terms of h.

(b) Substitution in composite function.

(a) Substitution of $x \to a$ in terms of h

$$\lim_{x \to a} f(x) = \lim_{h \to 0} f(a+h)$$

or $$= \lim_{h \to 0} f(a-h)$$

Example 28. Evaluate $\lim_{x \to 2} \dfrac{x^4 - 16}{2 - x}$.

Sol. On putting $x = h + 2$

$\because x \to 2$, when $h \to 0$

$$= \lim_{h \to 0} \frac{(h+2)^4 - 16}{2-(h+2)}$$

$$= \lim_{h \to 0} \frac{h^4 + {}^4C_1 h^3 \cdot 2^1 + {}^4C_2 h^2 \cdot 2^2 + {}^4C_3 h\, 2^3 + {}^4C_4 \cdot 2^4 - 16}{2-h-2}$$

$$= \lim_{h \to 0} \frac{h^4 + 2\cdot {}^4C_1 h^3 + 4\cdot {}^4C_2 h^2 + 8\cdot {}^4C_3 h}{-h}$$

$$= -\lim_{h \to 0} h^3 + 2\cdot {}^4C_1 h^2 + 4\cdot {}^4C_2 \cdot h + 8\cdot {}^4C_3$$

$$= -8\cdot {}^4C_3 = -8 \times 4 = -32$$

(b) Substitution in composite function

$$\lim_{x \to a} f\{g(x)\} = \lim_{t \to b} f(t), \text{ where } g(x) = t, b = g(a)$$

Example 29. Evaluate $\lim_{x \to 2} \dfrac{\sqrt{(x+7)} - 3\sqrt{(2x-3)}}{\sqrt[3]{(x+6)} - 2\sqrt[3]{(3x-5)}}$

Sol. We have, $L = \lim_{x \to 2} \dfrac{\sqrt{(x+7)} - 3\sqrt{(2x-3)}}{\sqrt[3]{(x+6)} - 2\sqrt[3]{(3x-5)}}$ $\left[\dfrac{0}{0} \text{ form}\right]$

Let $x - 2 = t$ such that when $x \to 2, t \to 0$

Then, $L = \lim_{t \to 0} \dfrac{(t+9)^{\frac{1}{2}} - 3(2t+1)^{\frac{1}{2}}}{(t+8)^{\frac{1}{3}} - 2(3t+1)^{\frac{1}{3}}}$ $\left[\dfrac{0}{0} \text{ form}\right]$

$$= \frac{3}{2} \lim_{t \to 0} \frac{\left(1+\frac{t}{9}\right)^{\frac{1}{2}} - (2t+1)^{\frac{1}{2}}}{\left(1+\frac{t}{8}\right)^{\frac{1}{3}} - (3t+1)^{\frac{1}{3}}} \quad \left[\frac{0}{0} \text{ form}\right]$$

$$= \frac{3}{2} \lim_{t \to 0} \frac{\frac{1}{2}\frac{t}{9} - (2t)\frac{1}{2}}{\frac{t}{8}\frac{1}{3} - (3t)\frac{1}{3}} = \frac{3}{2} \frac{\left(\frac{1}{18} - 1\right)}{\left(\frac{1}{24} - 1\right)} = \frac{34}{23}$$

Example 30. Find $\lim_{x \to 0} \dfrac{\sqrt[5]{(1+x)^3} - 1}{x}$.

Sol. Let us put $1 + x = y^5$.

As $x \to 0, y \to 1$

Then, we have

$$\lim_{x \to 0} \frac{\sqrt[5]{(1+x)^3} - 1}{x} = \lim_{y \to 1} \frac{y^3 - 1}{y^5 - 1}$$

$$\lim_{y \to 1} \frac{y^2 + y + 1}{y^4 + y^3 + y^2 + y + 1} = \frac{3}{5}$$

Milestone Practice 3.2

1. If $\lim_{x \to \infty} \dfrac{x^2 + 3x + 5}{4x + 1 + x^k}$ exists, then

(a) $k = 2$ (b) $k < 2$
(c) $k > 2$ (d) $k \geq 2$

2. $\lim_{n \to \infty} \dfrac{1\cdot n + 2(n-1) + 3(n-2) + \ldots + n\cdot 1}{1^2 + 2^2 + 3^2 + \ldots + n^2}$ has the value

(a) $\dfrac{1}{2}$ (b) $\dfrac{1}{3}$ (c) $\dfrac{1}{4}$ (d) 1

3. If $\alpha = \lim_{n \to \infty} \left(\dfrac{1}{n^3+1} + \dfrac{4}{n^3+1} + \dfrac{9}{n^3+1} + \ldots + \dfrac{n^2}{n^3+1}\right)$ and $\beta = \lim_{x \to 0} \dfrac{\sin 2x}{\sin 8x}$, then the quadratic equation whose roots are α and β is

(a) $12x^2 - 7x + 1 = 0$ (b) $x^2 + 19x - 120 = 0$
(c) $x^2 - 17x + 66 = 0$ (d) $x^2 - 7x + 12 = 0$

4. The limit of $x^3\{\sqrt{x^2 + \sqrt{x^4+1}} - x\sqrt{2}\}$ as $x \to \infty$ equals

(a) $\dfrac{1}{2\sqrt{2}}$ (b) $\dfrac{1}{4\sqrt{2}}$ (c) zero (d) $\dfrac{1}{\sqrt{2}}$

5. $\lim_{x \to 0^+} \left(\dfrac{3\ln^2 x + 5\ln x + 6}{1 + \ln^2 x}\right)$ is equal to

(a) 0 (b) 3
(c) 1 (d) Does not exist

6. If $\lim_{n \to \infty} (\sqrt{n^2 - n - 1} + n\alpha + \beta) = 0$, then $8(\alpha + \beta)$ is equal to

(a) 4 (b) -8 (c) -4 (d) 8

7. Evaluate $\lim_{n\to\infty} \dfrac{1\cdot n + 2\cdot(n-1) + 3\cdot(n-2) \ldots + n\cdot 1}{n^3}$.

8. Find $\lim_{x\to\infty} \left(\sqrt[3]{x^3+x^2} - \sqrt[3]{x^3-x^2}\right)$.

9. If α and β are the roots of the equation $375x^2 - 25x - 2 = 0$, then $\lim_{n\to\infty} \sum_{r=1}^{n} \alpha^r + \lim_{n\to\infty} \sum_{r=1}^{n} \beta^r$ is equal to

(a) $\dfrac{21}{346}$ (b) $\dfrac{29}{358}$ (c) $\dfrac{1}{12}$ (d) $\dfrac{7}{116}$

10. If $\lim_{x\to 1} \dfrac{x^2 - ax + b}{x-1} = 5$, then $a+b$ is equal to

(a) -4 (b) 1 (c) -7 (d) 5

11. If $\lim_{x\to 1} \dfrac{x^4-1}{x-1} = \lim_{x\to k} \dfrac{x^3-k^3}{x^2-k^2}$, then k is

(a) $\dfrac{4}{3}$ (b) $\dfrac{3}{8}$ (c) $\dfrac{3}{2}$ (d) $\dfrac{8}{3}$

12. The value of

$$\lim_{x\to 2}\left(\left(\frac{x^3-4x}{x^3-8}\right)^{-1} - \left(\frac{x+\sqrt{2x}}{x-2} - \frac{\sqrt{2}}{\sqrt{x}-\sqrt{2}}\right)^{-1}\right)$$ is

(a) 1/2 (b) 2

(c) 1 (d) None of these

13. $\lim_{x\to\infty} \dfrac{(\sqrt{3x+1}+\sqrt{3x-1})^6 + (\sqrt{3x+1} - (3x-1)^6 x^3}{(x+\sqrt{x^2-1})^6 + (x-\sqrt{x^2-1})^6}$

(a) is equal to $\dfrac{27}{2}$ (b) Does not exist

(c) is equal to 27 (d) is equal to 9

14. The value of $\lim_{n\to\infty} \dfrac{(1+2-3)+(4+5-6)+\ldots+(3n-2)+(3n-1)-3n}{\sqrt{2n^4+4n+3}-\sqrt{n^4+5n+4}}$ is

(a) $\dfrac{3}{2}(\sqrt{2}+1)$ (b) $\dfrac{3}{2\sqrt{2}}$

(c) $3(\sqrt{2}+1)$ (d) $\sqrt{2}+1$

15. If $\lim_{x\to\infty} \left(\sqrt{a^2x^2+ax+1} - \sqrt{a^2x^2+1}\right) = K \cdot \lim_{x\to\infty} \left(\sqrt{x+\sqrt{x+\sqrt{x}}} - \sqrt{x}\right)$, then the value of K is

(a) 1 (b) a

(c) $2a$ (d) None of these

16. The limit $\lim_{n\to\infty} \left(1+\dfrac{1}{5}\right)\left(1+\dfrac{1}{5^2}\right)\left(1+\dfrac{1}{5^4}\right)\ldots\left(1+\dfrac{1}{5^{2^n}}\right)$ is equal to

(a) 0 (b) 5/4 (c) 4/5 (d) 1/5

17. Let $L = \lim_{x\to -2} \dfrac{3x^2+ax+a+1}{x^2+x-2}$. If L is finite, then

(a) $L = \dfrac{4}{3}$ (b) $L = 13$

(c) $L = -2$ (d) $L = \dfrac{-1}{3}$

18. If $\lim_{x\to 3} \left(\dfrac{\sqrt{2x+3}-x}{\sqrt{x+1}-x+1}\right)^{\frac{x-1-\sqrt{x^2-5}}{x^2-5x+6}}$ can be expressed in the form $\dfrac{a\sqrt{b}}{c}$, where $a, b, c \in N$, then find the least value of $(a^2+b^2+c^2)$.

19. Let $f(x) = \dfrac{ax^2+bx+c}{x+1}$ such that $\lim_{x\to 0} f(x) = 2$ and $\lim_{x\to\infty} f(x) = 1$, then find the value of $(a+b+c)$.

20. $\lim_{n\to\infty} \left(\dfrac{n!}{(mn)^n}\right)^{\frac{1}{n}}$ $(m \in N)$ is equal to

(a) $\dfrac{1}{em}$ (b) $\dfrac{m}{e}$ (c) em (d) $\dfrac{e}{m}$

Answer Key

1. (d)	2. (a)	3. (a)	4. (b)	5. (b)
6. (c)	7. (1/6)	8. (2/3)	9. (c)	10. (c)
11. (a)	12. (a)	13. (c)	14. (a)	15. (a)
16. (b)	17. (d)	18. (29)	19. (3)	20. (a)

For Detailed Solution

Milestone 3 Limits of Transcendental Functions

• Trigonometric Limits • Logarithmic Limits • Exponential Limits

In this section, we will discuss the evaluation of limits of non-algebraic functions like trigonometric, inverse trigonometric, exponential, logarithmic etc.

3.10 Trigonometric limits

Some standard results

(a) $\lim_{x \to 0} \frac{\sin x}{x} = 1$

(b) $\lim_{x \to 0} \frac{\tan x}{x} = 1$

(c) $\lim_{x \to 0} \frac{\sin^{-1} x}{x} = 1$

(d) $\lim_{x \to 0} \frac{\tan^{-1} x}{x} = 1$

(e) $\lim_{x \to 0} \frac{\sin x^\circ}{x} = \frac{\pi}{180^\circ}$

(f) $\lim_{x \to a} \frac{\sin(x-a)}{x-a} = 1$

(g) $\lim_{x \to a} \frac{\tan(x-a)}{x-a} = 1$

(h) $\lim_{x \to 0} \frac{1-\cos x}{x} = 0$

JEE SPIKE

$\lim_{x \to a} \frac{\sin[f(x)]}{f(x)} = 1$ provided $\lim_{x \to a} f(x) = 0$

This property also follow when sin is replaced by $\tan, \sin^{-1}$ and $\tan^{-1} x$.

Example 31. Evaluate following limit

(i) $\lim_{x \to 0} \frac{\sin^2 5x}{4x^2}$

(ii) $\lim_{x \to 0} \frac{\sin 5x \tan 3x}{7x^2}$

(iii) $\lim_{x \to 0} \frac{\sqrt{1-\cos x}}{x}$

(iv) $\lim_{x \to \frac{\pi}{2}} \frac{1-\sin x}{(\pi-2x)^2}$

Sol. (i) $\lim_{x \to 0} \frac{\sin^2 5x}{4x^2}$ $\left[\frac{0}{0} \text{ form}\right]$

$$= \lim_{x \to 0} \left(\frac{\sin 5x}{5x}\right)^2 \times \frac{(5x)^2}{4x^2}$$

{multiply and divide by $(5x)^2$}

$$= \lim_{x \to 0} \left(\frac{\sin 5x}{5x}\right)^2 \times \frac{25x^2}{4x^2} \quad \left[\because \lim_{x \to 0} \frac{\sin 5x}{5x} = 1\right]$$

$$= \frac{25}{4}$$

(ii) $\lim_{x \to 0} \frac{\sin 5x \cdot \tan 3x}{7x^2}$ $\left[\frac{0}{0} \text{ form}\right]$

$$= \lim_{x \to 0} \frac{\sin 5x}{5x} \cdot \frac{\tan 3x}{3x} \times \frac{5x \times 3x}{7x^2}$$

$$= 1 \times 1 \times \frac{15}{7} = \frac{15}{7}$$

(iii) $\lim_{x \to 0} \frac{\sqrt{1-\cos x}}{x}$ $\left[\frac{0}{0} \text{ form}\right]$

$$= \lim_{x \to 0} \frac{\sqrt{2\sin^2 \frac{x}{2}}}{x} \quad [\because 1-\cos 2A = 2\sin^2 A]$$

$$= \lim_{x \to 0} \frac{\sqrt{2}\left|\sin \frac{x}{2}\right|}{x}$$

$\because \left|\sin \frac{x}{2}\right|$ changes in the neighbourhood of $x = 0$

We have to check LHL and RHL.

$$\text{LHL} = \lim_{x \to 0^-} \frac{\sqrt{2}\left|\sin \frac{x}{2}\right|}{x} = \lim_{x \to 0^-} -\sqrt{2}\frac{\sin \frac{x}{2}}{x}$$

$$= \lim_{x \to 0^-} \frac{-\sqrt{2}\sin \frac{x}{2}}{\frac{x}{2}} \cdot \frac{1}{2} = -\frac{1}{\sqrt{2}}$$

$$\text{RHL} = \lim_{x \to 0^+} \frac{\sqrt{2}\left|\sin \frac{x}{2}\right|}{x}$$

$$= \lim_{x \to 0} \frac{\sqrt{2}\sin \frac{x}{2}}{\frac{x}{2} \cdot 2} = \frac{1}{\sqrt{2}}$$

LHL $\neq$ RHL

$\therefore$ Limit does not exist.

(iv) $\lim_{x \to \frac{\pi}{2}} \frac{1-\sin x}{(\pi-2x)^2}$

Using substitution

$$x = \frac{\pi}{2} + h$$

$$\lim_{h\to 0}\frac{1-\sin\left(\dfrac{\pi}{2}+h\right)}{\left[\pi-2\left(\dfrac{\pi}{2}+h\right)\right]^2}$$

$$=\lim_{h\to 0}\frac{1-\cos h}{4h^2}=\lim_{h\to 0}\frac{2\sin^2\dfrac{h}{2}}{4h^2}$$

$$\therefore\ \frac{1}{2}\lim_{h\to 0}\left(\frac{\sin\dfrac{h}{2}}{\dfrac{h}{2}}\right)^2\times\frac{\dfrac{h^2}{4}}{h^2}=\frac{1}{2}\times\frac{1}{4}=\frac{1}{8}$$

Example 32. Solve $\lim\limits_{x\to 0}\dfrac{1-\cos(1-\cos x)}{\sin^4 x}$

Sol. Here, $\lim\limits_{x\to 0}\dfrac{1-\cos(1-\cos x)}{\sin^4 x}$

$$=\lim_{x\to 0}\frac{1-\cos\left(2\sin^2\dfrac{x}{2}\right)}{x^4}\Bigg/\frac{\sin^4 x}{x^4}$$

$$=\lim_{x\to 0}\frac{1-\cos\left(2\sin^2\dfrac{x}{2}\right)}{x^4}\Bigg/\lim_{x\to 0}\frac{\sin^4 x}{x^4}$$

$$=\lim_{x\to 0}\frac{2\sin^2\left(\sin^2\dfrac{x}{2}\right)}{x^4}\Bigg/1$$

$$=\lim_{x\to 0}2\cdot\left(\frac{\sin\left(\sin^2\dfrac{x}{2}\right)}{\sin^2\dfrac{x}{2}}\cdot\frac{\sin^2\dfrac{x}{2}}{4\cdot\dfrac{x^2}{4}}\right)^2$$

$$=2\times\frac{1}{4^2}=\frac{1}{8}$$

Example 33. Evaluate $\lim\limits_{x\to 0}\dfrac{\sin(\pi\cos^2 x)}{x^2}$

Sol. $\lim\limits_{x\to 0}\dfrac{\sin(\pi\cos^2 x)}{x^2}=\lim\limits_{x\to 0}\dfrac{\sin\{\pi(1-\sin^2 x)\}}{x^2}$

$$=\lim_{x\to 0}\frac{\sin(\pi-\pi\sin^2 x)}{x^2}$$

$$=\lim_{x\to 0}\frac{\sin(\pi\sin^2 x)}{x^2}$$

$$=\lim_{x\to 0}\left\{\frac{\sin(\pi\sin^2 x)}{\pi\sin^2 x}\times\frac{\pi}{1}\times\frac{\sin^2 x}{x^2}\right\}$$

$$=\lim_{x\to 0}\frac{\sin(\pi\sin^2 x)}{\pi\sin^2 x}\times\pi\times\lim_{x\to 0}\frac{\sin^2 x}{x^2}$$

$$=1\times\pi\times 1$$

$$=\pi$$

JEE SCANNER

Example Similar to PYQ Asked in JEE Main 2023

$\lim\limits_{x\to 0}\left(\left(\dfrac{1-\cos^2(5x)}{\cos^3(6x)}\right)\left(\dfrac{\sin^3(6x)}{\tan^2(5x)}\right)\right)$ *is equal to ....*

Sol. (0) $\lim\limits_{x\to 0}\dfrac{1-\cos^2 5x}{\cos^3 6x}\times\dfrac{\sin^3 6x}{\tan^2 5x}$

$$=\lim_{x\to 0}\frac{\sin^2 5x}{\cos^3 6x}\times\frac{\sin^3 6x}{\tan^2 5x}$$

$$=\lim_{x\to 0}\frac{\sin^2 5x}{(5x)^2}\times\frac{(5x)^2}{\tan^2 5x}\times\frac{(\tan 6x)^3}{(6x)^3}\times(6x)^3$$

$$=\lim_{x\to 0}1\times 1\times 6x^3=0$$

Skill Builder

$\lim\limits_{x\to 0}\left(\dfrac{1-\cos^2(4x)}{\tan^3(x)}\right)\left(\dfrac{\sin^2(7x)}{\cos x}\right)$ is equal to λ.

Then, $\dfrac{\sqrt{\lambda}}{2}$ is ......

For Sol.

■ **For more practice** See Q.5 of Milestone Practice 3.3.

Example 34. Solve

(a) $\lim\limits_{x\to\frac{\pi}{4}}\dfrac{\sqrt{1-\sqrt{\sin 2x}}}{\pi-4x}$ (b) $\lim\limits_{x\to 0}\dfrac{\sqrt{1-\sqrt{\cos x}}}{x}$

Sol. (a) Here, $\lim\limits_{x\to\frac{\pi}{4}}\dfrac{\sqrt{1-\sqrt{\sin 2x}}}{\pi-4x}$

$$=\lim_{x\to\frac{\pi}{4}}\frac{\sqrt{1-\sqrt{\sin 2x}}}{\pi-4x}\cdot\frac{\sqrt{1+\sqrt{\sin 2x}}}{\sqrt{1+\sqrt{\sin 2x}}}$$

$$=\lim_{x\to\frac{\pi}{4}}\frac{\sqrt{1-\sin 2x}}{\pi-4x}\cdot\lim_{x\to\frac{\pi}{4}}\frac{1}{\sqrt{1+\sqrt{\sin 2x}}}$$

$$=\frac{1}{\sqrt{2}}\lim_{x\to\frac{\pi}{4}}\frac{\sqrt{\sin^2\left(\dfrac{\pi}{4}-x\right)}}{\pi-4x}$$

$$=\frac{1}{\sqrt{2}}\lim_{x\to\frac{\pi}{4}}\frac{\left|\sin\left(\dfrac{\pi}{4}-x\right)\right|}{4\left(\dfrac{\pi}{4}-x\right)}$$

Now, RHL at $x=\dfrac{\pi}{4}$

$$\frac{1}{\sqrt{2}}\lim_{x\to\frac{\pi}{4}^+}\frac{-\sin\left(\dfrac{\pi}{4}-x\right)}{4\left(\dfrac{\pi}{4}-x\right)}=-\frac{1}{4\sqrt{2}}$$

and LHL at $x = \frac{\pi}{4}$ is $\frac{1}{4\sqrt{2}}$

Thus, LHL = RHL

$\therefore$ Limit does not exist (as it is not unique).

(b) $\lim_{x \to 0} \frac{\sqrt{1-\sqrt{\cos x}}}{x}$

$$= \lim_{x \to 0} \frac{\sqrt{1-\cos x}}{x} \cdot \frac{1}{\sqrt{1+\sqrt{\cos x}}}$$

$$= \lim_{x \to 0} \frac{\sqrt{2}\left|\sin\left(\frac{x}{2}\right)\right|}{2\left(\frac{x}{2}\right)} \cdot \frac{1}{\sqrt{1+\sqrt{\cos x}}}$$

Now, we have

$$\text{LHL} = \lim_{x \to 0^-} \frac{-1}{\sqrt{2}} \cdot \frac{\sin\left(\frac{x}{2}\right)}{\frac{x}{2}} \cdot \frac{1}{\sqrt{1+\sqrt{\cos x}}}$$

$$= \frac{-1}{\sqrt{2}} \cdot \frac{1}{\sqrt{2}} = \frac{-1}{2}$$

$$\text{and RHL} = \lim_{x \to 0^+} \frac{1}{\sqrt{2}} \cdot \frac{\sin\left(\frac{x}{2}\right)}{\frac{x}{2}} \cdot \frac{1}{\sqrt{1+\sqrt{\cos x}}}$$

$$= \frac{1}{\sqrt{2}} \cdot \frac{1}{\sqrt{2}} = \frac{1}{2}$$

Hence, limit does not exist.

Example 35. Find $\lim_{x \to 0} \frac{\tan x - \sin x}{x^3}$

Sol. $\lim_{x \to 0} \frac{\tan x - \sin x}{x^3} = \lim_{x \to 0} \frac{\frac{\sin x}{\cos x} - \sin x}{x^3}$

$$= \lim_{x \to 0} \frac{\sin x(1-\cos x)}{x^3 \cos x} = \lim_{x \to 0} \frac{\sin x \cdot 2\sin^2 \frac{x}{2}}{x^3 \cos x}$$

$$= \lim_{x \to 0} \frac{2\left(\frac{\sin x}{x}\right) x \cdot \left(\frac{\sin \frac{x}{2}}{\frac{x}{2}}\right)^2 \left(\frac{x}{2}\right)^2}{x^3 \cos x}$$

$$= \lim_{x \to 0} \frac{2\left(\frac{\sin x}{x}\right) \cdot \left(\frac{\sin \frac{x}{2}}{\frac{x}{2}}\right)^2 \cdot \frac{1}{4}}{\cos x} = \frac{2 \cdot 1 \cdot 1^2 \cdot \frac{1}{4}}{1} = \frac{1}{2}$$

Example 36. Evaluate $\lim_{x \to \infty} x \sin \frac{1}{x}$

Sol. $\lim_{x \to \infty} x \sin \frac{1}{x}$

On putting $x = \frac{1}{t}$ as $x \to \infty, t \to 0^+$

$$= \lim_{t \to 0^+} \frac{\sin t}{t} = 1$$

Example 37. Evaluate $\lim_{\theta \to \frac{\pi}{4}} \frac{(1-\tan\theta)}{(1-\sqrt{2}\sin\theta)}$

Sol. Let $P = \lim_{x \to \frac{\pi}{4}} \frac{(1-\tan\theta)}{(1-\sqrt{2}\sin\theta)}$ $\left[\frac{0}{0}\text{form}\right]$

On putting $\theta = \frac{\pi}{4} + h$

$$\therefore \quad P = \lim_{h \to 0} \frac{1-\tan\left(\frac{\pi}{4}+h\right)}{1-\sqrt{2}\sin\left(\frac{\pi}{4}+h\right)}$$

$$= \lim_{h \to 0} \frac{1-\left(\frac{1+\tan h}{1-\tan h}\right)}{1-\sqrt{2}\left(\frac{1}{\sqrt{2}}\cos h + \frac{1}{\sqrt{2}}\sin h\right)} \quad \left[\frac{0}{0}\text{ form}\right]$$

$$= \lim_{h \to 0} \frac{-2\tan h}{(1-\tan h)\frac{(1-\cos h)(1+\cos h)}{(1+\cos h)} - \sin h}$$

$$= -2\lim_{h \to 0} \frac{\tan h}{(1-\tan h)\left(\frac{\sin^2 h}{1+\cos h} - \sin h\right)}$$

$$= -2\lim_{h \to 0} \frac{\sin h}{(\cos h - \sin h)\left(\frac{\sin^2 h}{1+\cos h} - \sin h\right)}$$

$$= -2\lim_{h \to 0} \frac{1}{(\cos h - \sin h)\left(\frac{\sin h}{1+\cos h} - 1\right)}$$

$$= -2 \cdot \frac{1}{(1-0)(0-1)} = 2$$

Example 38. Evaluate

$$\lim_{n \to \infty} n^2 \left\{\sqrt{\left(1-\cos\frac{1}{n}\right)\sqrt{\left(1-\cos\frac{1}{n}\right)\sqrt{\left(1-\cos\frac{1}{n}\right)..\infty}}}\right\}$$

Sol. Let

$$P = \lim_{n \to \infty} n^2 \left\{\sqrt{\left(1-\cos\frac{1}{n}\right)\sqrt{\left(1-\cos\frac{1}{n}\right)\sqrt{\left(1-\cos\frac{1}{n}\right)..\infty}}}\right\}$$

On putting $\frac{1}{n} = x$

$$\therefore \quad P = \lim_{x \to 0^+} \frac{\sqrt{(1-\cos x)\sqrt{(1-\cos x)\sqrt{(1-\cos x)\ldots\infty}}}}{x^2}$$

$$= \lim_{x \to 0^+} \frac{(1-\cos x)^{\frac{1}{2}+\frac{1}{2^2}+\frac{1}{2^3}-\ldots\infty}}{x^2}$$

$$= \lim_{x \to 0^+} \frac{(1-\cos x)}{x^2} \quad \left[\text{for GP, } S_\infty = \frac{a}{1-r}, |r|<1\right]$$

$$= \frac{2\sin^2 \frac{x}{2}}{\frac{x^2}{4} \times 4}$$

$$= \frac{2}{4} = \frac{1}{2}$$

Example 39. Evaluate $\lim_{x \to 0} \frac{\tan^{-1} x - \sin^{-1} x}{\sin^3 x}$.

Sol. $\lim_{x \to 0} \frac{\tan^{-1} x - \sin^{-1} x}{\sin^3 x}$

$$= \lim_{x \to 0} \frac{\tan^{-1} x - \tan^{-1}\left(\frac{x}{\sqrt{1-x^2}}\right)}{x^3 \left(\frac{\sin^3 x}{x^3}\right)}$$

$$= \lim_{x \to 0} \frac{\tan^{-1} x - \tan^{-1}\left(\frac{x}{\sqrt{1-x^2}}\right)}{x^3} \quad \left[\text{as } \lim_{x \to 0} \frac{\sin x}{x} = 1\right]$$

$$= \lim_{x \to 0} \frac{\tan^{-1}\left(\frac{x - \frac{x}{\sqrt{1-x^2}}}{1 + \frac{x \cdot x}{\sqrt{1-x^2}}}\right)}{x^3}$$

$$= \lim_{x \to 0} \frac{\tan^{-1}\left[\frac{x\sqrt{1-x^2} - x}{x^2 + \sqrt{1-x^2}}\right]}{x^3}$$

$$= \lim_{x \to 0} \frac{\tan^{-1}\left(\frac{x\sqrt{1-x^2} - x}{x^2 + \sqrt{1-x^2}}\right)}{x^3 \left(\frac{x\sqrt{1-x^2} - x}{x^2 + \sqrt{1-x^2}}\right)} \cdot \frac{x\sqrt{1-x^2} - x}{x^2 + \sqrt{1-x^2}}$$

$$= \lim_{x \to 0} \frac{x(\sqrt{1-x^2} - 1)}{x^3(x^2 + \sqrt{1-x^2})} \quad \left[\text{as } \lim_{x \to 0} \frac{\tan^{-1} x}{x} = 1\right]$$

$$= \lim_{x \to 0} \frac{x(\sqrt{1-x^2} - 1)}{x^3(x^2 + \sqrt{1-x^2})} \times \frac{\sqrt{1-x^2}+1}{\sqrt{1-x^2}+1}$$

$$= \lim_{x \to 0} \frac{-x^3}{x^3(x^2 + \sqrt{1-x^2})} \cdot \left[\frac{1}{\sqrt{1-x^2}+1}\right]$$

$$= -\frac{1}{2}$$

3.11 Logarithmic Limit

In this section, we will deal with the problems based on expansion of logarithmic series

i.e. $\log(1+x) = x - \frac{x^2}{2} + \frac{x^3}{3} + \ldots + \infty, -1 \le x \le 1$

To evaluate the logarithmic limit, we use

(a) $\lim_{x \to 0} \frac{\ln(1+x)}{x} = 1$

$$\because \lim_{x \to 0} \frac{\ln(1+x)}{x} = \lim_{x \to 0} \frac{x - \frac{x^2}{2} + \frac{x^3}{3} - \frac{x^4}{4} + \frac{x^5}{5} - \ldots}{x}$$

$$= \lim_{x \to 0} 1 - \frac{x}{2} + \frac{x^2}{3} - \frac{x^3}{4} + \frac{x^4}{5} - \ldots$$

$$= 1 - 0 = 1$$

(b) $\lim_{x \to 0} \frac{\ln(1-x)}{-x} = 1$

(c) $\lim_{x \to a} \frac{\ln(1+f(x))}{f(x)} = 1$, provided $\lim_{x \to a} f(x) = 0$.

Example 40. Evaluate $\lim_{x \to a} \frac{\log\{1+(x-a)\}}{(x-a)}$

Sol. Let $x - a = y$, when $x \to a, y \to 0$

$$\therefore \lim_{y \to 0} \frac{\log\{1+y\}}{y} = 1$$

Example 41. Evaluate $\lim_{h \to 0} \frac{\log_{10}(1+h)}{h}$

Sol. $\lim_{h \to 0} \frac{\log_{10}(1+h)}{h}$ $\left[\frac{0}{0}\text{ form}\right]$

$$= \lim_{h \to 0} \frac{\log_e(1+h) \times \log_{10} e}{h}$$

$$= \lim_{h \to 0} \frac{\log_e(1+h)}{h} \times \log_{10} e$$

$$= \log_{10} e \times 1 = \log_{10} e$$

Example 42. Evaluate $\lim\limits_{x\to 0}\dfrac{\log(5+x)-\log(5-x)}{x}$

Sol. $\lim\limits_{x\to 0}\dfrac{\log\left\{5\left(1+\dfrac{x}{5}\right)\right\}-\log\left\{5\left(1-\dfrac{x}{5}\right)\right\}}{x}$

$$=\lim_{x\to 0}\frac{\log 5+\log\left(1+\dfrac{x}{5}\right)-\log 5-\log\left(1-\dfrac{x}{5}\right)}{x}$$

$$=\lim_{x\to 0}\frac{\log\left(1+\dfrac{x}{5}\right)}{5\left(\dfrac{x}{5}\right)}-\frac{\log\left(1-\dfrac{x}{5}\right)}{-5\left(-\dfrac{x}{5}\right)}=\frac{1}{5}+\frac{1}{5}=\frac{2}{5}$$

Example 43. Evaluate $\lim\limits_{x\to e}\dfrac{\ln x-1}{x-e}$.

Sol. Limit $=\lim\limits_{x\to e}\dfrac{\ln\dfrac{x}{e}}{e\left(\dfrac{x}{e}-1\right)}=\lim\limits_{t\to 1}\dfrac{\ln t}{(t-1)e}$ [put $x/e=t$]

On putting $t=1+y$

$$\therefore \quad \lim_{y\to 0}\frac{\ln(1+y)}{ey}=\frac{1}{e}$$

Example 44. Evaluate $\lim\limits_{t\to 0}\dfrac{\ln\cos(\sin t)}{t^2}$

Sol. $\lim\limits_{t\to 0}\dfrac{\ln\cos(\sin t)}{t^2}$

$$=\lim_{t\to 0}\frac{\ln\left(1-2\sin^2\left(\dfrac{\sin t}{2}\right)\right)}{-2\sin^2\left(\dfrac{\sin t}{2}\right)}\cdot\frac{\left(-2\sin^2\left(\dfrac{\sin t}{2}\right)\right)}{t^2}\left[\frac{0}{0}\text{ form}\right]$$

$$=\lim_{t\to 0}-2\cdot\left(\frac{\sin\left(\dfrac{\sin t}{2}\right)}{\dfrac{\sin t}{2}}\right)^2\cdot\frac{\sin^2 t}{4\cdot t^2}=-\frac{1}{2}$$

Example 45. Find $\lim\limits_{x\to\frac{\pi}{4}}\dfrac{\ln\tan x}{1-\cot x}$

Sol. On putting $x=t+\dfrac{\pi}{4}$

$$\lim_{t\to 0}\frac{\ln\tan\left(t+\dfrac{\pi}{4}\right)}{1-\cot\left(t+\dfrac{\pi}{4}\right)}=\lim_{t\to 0}\frac{\ln\left[\dfrac{1+\tan t}{1-\tan t}\right]}{1-\left[\dfrac{\cot t-1}{\cot t+1}\right]}$$

$$=\lim_{t\to 0}\frac{\ln(1+\tan t)}{\dfrac{2\tan t}{1+\tan t}}+\lim_{t\to 0}\frac{\ln(1-\tan t)}{\dfrac{-2\tan t}{1+\tan t}}$$

$$=\frac{1}{2}[1\cdot 1+1\cdot 1]=\frac{2}{2}=1$$

Example 46. Let $f(x)=\lim\limits_{x\to\infty}\dfrac{\log(2+x)-x^{2n}\sin x}{1+x^{2n}}$, then

(a) f is continuous at $x=1$

(b) $\lim\limits_{x\to 1^+}f(x)\neq\lim\limits_{x\to 1^-}f(x)$

(c) $\lim\limits_{x\to 1^+}f(x)=2\sin 1$

(d) $\lim\limits_{x\to 1^-}f(x)$ does not exist

Sol. (b) For $|x|<1$, $x^{2n}\to 0$ as $n\to\infty$

and for $|x|>1$, $\dfrac{1}{x^{2n}}\to 0$ as $n\to\infty$

$$\text{Hence, } f(x)=\begin{cases}\log(2+x), & \text{if } |x|<1\\ \lim\limits_{x\to\infty}\dfrac{x^{-2n}\log(2+x)-\sin x}{x^{-2n}+1}, & \text{if } |x|>1\\ \dfrac{1}{2}(\log(2+x)-\sin x), & \text{if } |x|=1\end{cases}$$

$$\lim_{x\to 1^+}f(x)=\lim_{x\to 1}(-\sin x)=-\sin 1$$

[$\because x^{-2n}\to 0$ as $n\to\infty$]

$$\lim_{x\to 1^-}f(x)=\lim_{x\to 1}\log(2+x)=\log 3$$

$$\lim_{x\to 1^+}f(x)\neq\lim_{x\to 1^-}f(x)$$

3.12 Exponential limits

To evaluate the exponential limit, we use the following results.

(a) $\lim\limits_{x\to 0}\dfrac{e^x-1}{x}=1$ (b) $\lim\limits_{x\to 0}\dfrac{a^x-1}{x}=\ln a,\ a>0,\ a\neq 1$

JEE Focus Points

- $\lim\limits_{x\to a}\dfrac{e^{f(x)}-1}{f(x)}=1$, provided $\lim\limits_{x\to a}f(x)=0$
- $\lim\limits_{x\to c}\dfrac{a^{f(x)}-1}{f(x)}=\ln a$, provide $\lim\limits_{x\to c}f(x)=0$

Concept Inside Video

Example 47. Evaluate $\lim\limits_{x\to 0}\dfrac{a^x-b^x}{x}$.

Sol. $\lim\limits_{x\to 0}\dfrac{a^x-b^x}{x}=\lim\limits_{x\to 0}\dfrac{(a^x-1)-(b^x-1)}{x}$

$$=\lim_{x\to 0}\frac{a^x-1}{x}-\lim_{x\to 0}\frac{b^x-1}{x}$$

$$=\log a-\log b=\log\left(\frac{a}{b}\right)$$

Example 48. Evaluate $\lim_{x \to 0} \frac{(ab)^x - a^x - b^x + 1}{x^2}$.

Sol. $\lim_{x \to 0} \frac{(ab)^x - a^x - b^x + 1}{x^2} = \lim_{x \to 0} \frac{a^x b^x - a^x - b^x + 1}{x^2}$

$= \lim_{x \to 0} \frac{a^x(b^x - 1) - (b^x - 1)}{x^2}$

$= \lim_{x \to 0} \frac{(a^x - 1)}{x} \times \lim_{x \to 0} \frac{(b^x - 1)}{x}$

$= \log a \times \log b$

Example 49. Evaluate $\lim_{x \to 0} \frac{e^{\tan x} - e^x}{\tan x - x}$.

Sol. $\lim_{x \to 0} \frac{e^{\tan x} - e^x}{\tan x - x}$

$= \lim_{x \to 0} \frac{e^x \times e^{(\tan x - x)} - e^x}{(\tan x - x)}$

$= \lim_{x \to 0} \frac{e^x \{e^{\tan x - x} - 1\}}{(\tan x - x)}$

$= e^0 \times 1$ [as $x \to 0$, $\tan x - x \to 0$]

$= 1 \times 1 = 1$

Example 50. Show that $\lim_{x \to 0} \frac{e^{1/x} - 1}{e^{1/x} + 1}$ does not exist.

Sol. Let $f(x) = \frac{e^{1/x} - 1}{e^{1/x} + 1}$.

Then, LHL $= \lim_{x \to 0^-} f(x) = \lim_{h \to 0} f(0 - h)$

$= \lim_{h \to 0} \frac{e^{-1/h} - 1}{e^{-1/h} + 1}$

$= \lim_{h \to 0} \frac{(1/e^{1/h} - 1)}{(1/e^{1/h} + 1)} = \frac{0 - 1}{0 + 1} = -1$

[as $h \to 0 \Rightarrow \frac{1}{h} \to \infty \Rightarrow e^{\frac{1}{h}} \to \infty \Rightarrow \frac{1}{e^{1/h}} \to 0$] ...(i)

RHL $= \lim_{x \to 0^+} f(x) = \lim_{h \to 0} f(0 + h)$

$= \lim_{h \to 0} \frac{e^{1/h} - 1}{e^{1/h} + 1} = \lim_{h \to 0} \frac{\left(1 - \frac{1}{e^{1/h}}\right)}{\left(1 + \frac{1}{e^{1/h}}\right)}$

[dividing numerator and denominator both by $e^{1/h}$]

$= \frac{1 - 0}{1 + 0} = 1$ [using Eq. (i)]

Clearly, $\lim_{x \to 0^-} f(x) \neq \lim_{x \to 0^+} f(x)$

$\therefore$ Limit does not exist.

JEE SCANNER

Example Similar to PYQ Asked in JEE Main 2024

$\lim_{x \to 0} \frac{e - (1 + 5x)^{\frac{1}{5x}}}{x}$ *is equal to*

(a) $\frac{e}{2}$ (b) $\frac{3e}{2}$ (c) $\frac{5e}{2}$ (d) $\frac{7e}{2}$

Sol. (c) $\lim_{x \to 0} \frac{e - (1 + 5x)^{\frac{1}{5x}}}{x} = \lim_{x \to 0} \frac{e - e^{\frac{1}{5x}\ln(1 + 5x)}}{x}$

$= \lim_{x \to 0} \frac{(-e)\left(e^{\frac{\ln(1 + 5x)}{5x} - 1} - 1\right)}{x}$

$= \lim_{x \to 0} \frac{(-e)\, e^{\frac{\ln(1+5x)}{5x} - 1} - 1}{\frac{\ln(1 + 5x)}{5x} - 1} \cdot \frac{\frac{\ln(1 + 5x)}{5x} - 1}{x}$

$= \lim_{x \to 0} (-e) \frac{\ln(1 + 5x) - 5x}{5x^2}$ $\left[\because \lim_{x \to 0} \frac{e^x - 1}{x} = 1\right]$

$= \lim_{x \to 0} \frac{(-e)\left[\left(5x - \frac{(5x)^2}{2} + \ldots\right) - 5x\right]}{5x^2}$

$= e \times \frac{25}{2 \times 5} = \frac{5e}{2}$

Skill Builder

For Sol.

$\lim_{x \to 0} \frac{e - (1 + 7x)^{\frac{1}{7x}}}{3x}$ is equal to

(a) $\frac{e}{6}$ (b) $\frac{7e}{6}$ (c) $\frac{5e}{6}$ (d) $\frac{2e}{3}$

■ **For more practice** See Q.14 of Milestone Practice 3.3.

Example 51. Evaluate $\lim_{x \to 0} \frac{e^x - \ln(x + e)}{e^x - 1}$.

Sol. $\lim_{x \to 0} \frac{\left(e^x - \ln\left(e\left(1 + \frac{x}{e}\right)\right)\right)}{x\left(\frac{e^x - 1}{x}\right)}$

$= \lim_{x \to 0} \left[\frac{(e^x - 1)}{x} - \frac{\ln\left(1 + \left(\frac{x}{e}\right)\right)}{x}\right] = 1 - \lim_{x \to 0} \frac{\ln(1 + x/e)}{e \cdot \frac{x}{e}}$

$= 1 - \frac{1}{e}$

Example 52. $\lim_{x\to\infty} \frac{e^x\left(\left(2^{x^n}\right)^{\frac{1}{e^x}} - \left(3^{x^n}\right)^{\frac{1}{e^x}}\right)}{x^n}$, $n \in N$ is equal to

(a) 0 (b) 1 (c) $\ln\frac{2}{3}$ (d) $\ln\frac{3}{2}$

Sol. (c) We have,

$$\lim_{x\to\infty} \frac{e^x\left(2^{\left(\frac{x^n}{e^x}\right)} - 3^{\left(\frac{x^n}{e^x}\right)}\right)}{x^n} = \lim_{x\to\infty} \frac{2^{\left(\frac{x^n}{e^x}\right)} - 3^{\left(\frac{x^n}{e^x}\right)}}{\left(\frac{x^n}{e^x}\right)}$$

Now, we find $\lim_{x\to\infty} \frac{x^n}{e^x}$

Using L-Hospital rule, $\lim_{x\to\infty} \frac{n x^{n-1}}{e^x}$

Applying L-Hospital rule n times,

$$= \lim_{x\to\infty} \frac{n!}{e^x} = 0$$

So, $\lim_{x\to\infty} \frac{2^{\left(\frac{x^n}{e^x}\right)} - 3^{\left(\frac{x^n}{e^x}\right)}}{\left(\frac{x^n}{e^x}\right)}$ $\left[\frac{0}{0}\text{form}\right]$

$$= \lim_{x\to\infty} \left(\frac{2^{\left(\frac{x^n}{e^x}\right)} - 1}{\frac{x^n}{e^x}} - \frac{3^{\left(\frac{x^n}{e^x}\right)} - 1}{\left(\frac{x^n}{e^x}\right)}\right)$$

$$= \ln 2 - \ln 3 = \ln\frac{2}{3}$$

Example 53. Evaluate $\lim_{x\to 0} \frac{\ln(1 + x^2 + x^4)}{(e^x - 1)\cdot x}$

Sol. $\lim_{x\to 0} \frac{\ln(1+x^2+x^4)}{(e^x-1)x} = \lim_{x\to 0} \frac{\ln(1+x^2+x^4)}{\left(\frac{e^x-1}{x}\right)x^2}$

$$\therefore \lim_{x\to 0} \frac{\ln(1+x^2+x^4)}{x^2} = \lim_{x\to 0} \ln(1+x^2+x^4)^{\frac{1}{x^2}}$$

$$= \ln \lim_{x\to 0} e^{\frac{1}{x^2}(1+x^2+x^4-1)}$$

$$= \lim_{x\to 0} \frac{x^2+x^4}{x^2}$$

$$= \lim_{x\to 0} (1+x^2) = 1$$

Example 54. Evaluate $\lim_{x\to 0} \left(\frac{\ln(\cos 3x)}{x^2} \cdot \frac{2\sin x}{e^x - e^{-x}}\right)$.

Sol. $\lim_{x\to 0} \frac{\ln(\cos 3x)\cdot 2\sin x}{x^2(e^x - e^{-x})}$

$$= \lim_{x\to 0} \frac{\ln(\cos 3x)\cdot 2\sin x\cdot e^x}{x^2(e^{2x}-1)}$$

$$= \lim_{x\to 0} \left(\frac{\ln(1+\cos 3x - 1)}{(\cos 3x - 1)} \times (\cos 3x - 1) \times \frac{2\sin x}{x} \times \frac{1}{\left(\frac{e^{2x}-1}{2x}\right)2x^2}\right)$$

$$= \lim_{x\to 0} \left(\frac{\ln(1+\cos 3x - 1)}{(\cos 3x - 1)} \times \frac{\left(-2\sin^2\frac{3x}{2}\right)\times\frac{9}{4}}{2x^2\times\frac{9}{4}} \times \frac{2\sin x}{x} \times \frac{1}{\left(\frac{e^{2x}-1}{2x}\right)}\right)$$

$$= 1 \times (-1) \times \frac{9}{4} \times 2 \times 1$$

$$= -\frac{9}{2}$$

Example 55. Evaluate $\lim_{h\to 0} \frac{(x+h)^{\sqrt{x+h}} - x^{\sqrt{x}}}{h}$ $(x>0)$.

Sol. $\lim_{h\to 0} \frac{e^{\sqrt{x+h}\,\ln(x+h)} - e^{\sqrt{x}\,\ln x}}{h}$

$$= \lim_{h\to 0} e^{\sqrt{x}\ln x}\left[\frac{e^{\sqrt{x+h}\,\ln(x+h) - \sqrt{x}\ln x} - 1}{h}\right]$$

Let $s = \sqrt{x+h}\log(x+h) - \sqrt{x}\log x$

$$= x^{\sqrt{x}}\left[\lim_{s\to 0}\frac{e^s - 1}{s}\cdot\lim_{h\to 0}\frac{\sqrt{x+h}\,\ln(x+h) - \sqrt{x}\,\ln x}{h}\right]$$

$$= x^{\sqrt{x}} \lim_{h\to 0} \frac{\sqrt{x+h}\left(\ln x + \ln\left(1+\frac{h}{x}\right)\right) - \sqrt{x}\ln x}{h}$$

$$= x^{\sqrt{x}}\left[\lim_{h\to 0} \ln x \frac{(\sqrt{x+h} - \sqrt{x})}{h} + \lim_{h\to 0}\frac{\sqrt{(x+h)}}{x}\ln\left(1+\frac{h}{x}\right)^{\frac{x}{h}}\right]$$

$$= x^{\sqrt{x}}\left[\frac{\ln x}{2\sqrt{x}} + \frac{1}{\sqrt{x}}\right]$$

Milestone Practice 3.3

1. If $\lim_{x\to 0}\frac{\{(a-n)nx-\tan x\}\sin nx}{x^2}=0$, where n is non-zero real number, then a is equal to

(a) 0 (b) $\frac{n+1}{n}$
(c) n (d) $n+\frac{1}{n}$

2. The integer n for which $\lim_{x\to 0}\frac{(\cos x-1)(\cos x-e^x)}{x^n}$ is a finite non-zero number, is

(a) 1 (b) 2
(c) 3 (d) 4

3. $\lim_{x\to 0}\frac{x\tan 2x-2x\tan x}{(1-\cos 2x)^2}$ is

(a) 2 (b) -2
(c) $\frac{1}{2}$ (d) $-\frac{1}{2}$

4. If $\alpha>\beta>0$ are the roots of the equation $ax^2+bx+1=0$ and $\lim_{x\to\frac{1}{\alpha}}\left(\frac{1-\cos(x^2+bx+a)}{2(1-\alpha x)^2}\right)^{\frac{1}{2}}=\frac{1}{k}\left(\frac{1}{\alpha}-\frac{1}{\beta}\right)$, then k is equal to

(a) α (b) 2α
(c) 2β (d) β

5. $\lim_{x\to\infty}\left(\left(\frac{1-\cos^2(3x)}{\cos^3(4x)}\right)\left(\frac{\sin^3(4x)}{(\log_e(2x+1))^5}\right)\right)$ is equal to

(a) 24 (b) 9
(c) 18 (d) 15

6. $\lim_{x\to\infty}x\left[\tan^{-1}\left(\frac{x+1}{x+2}\right)-\tan^{-1}\left(\frac{x}{x+2}\right)\right]$.

(a) $\frac{1}{3}$ (b) $\frac{1}{2}$
(c) $\frac{1}{4}$ (d) $\frac{1}{6}$

7. $\lim_{h\to 0}\frac{\sin\left(\frac{\pi}{3}+4h\right)-4\sin\left(\frac{\pi}{3}+3h\right)+6\sin\left(\frac{\pi}{3}+2h\right)-4\sin\left(\frac{\pi}{3}+h\right)+\sin\frac{\pi}{3}}{h^4}$ is equal to

(a) $\sin(4260^\circ)$ (b) $\cos(750^\circ)$
(c) $\cos(1500^\circ)$ (d) $\sin(-690^\circ)$

8. If $z_r=\cos\frac{r\alpha}{n^2}+i\sin\frac{r\alpha}{n^2}$, where $r=1,2,3,\ldots,n$, then $\lim_{n\to\infty}z_1z_2z_3\ldots z_n$ is equal to

(a) $\cos\alpha+i\sin\alpha$ (b) $\cos\left(\frac{\alpha}{2}\right)-i\sin\left(\frac{\alpha}{2}\right)$
(c) $e^{\frac{i\alpha}{2}}$ (d) $\sqrt[3]{e^{i\alpha}}$

9. $\lim_{y\to 0}\frac{(x+y)\sec(x+y)-x\sec x}{y}$ is equal to

(a) $\sec x(x\tan x+1)$ (b) $x\tan x+\sec x$
(c) $x\sec x+\tan x$ (d) None of these

10. If $f(x)=\begin{cases}x^n\sin\left(\frac{1}{x^2}\right), & x\neq 0\\ 0, & x=0\end{cases}$, $(n\in I)$, then

(a) $\lim_{x\to 0}f(x)$ exists for $n>1$
(b) $\lim_{x\to 0}f(x)$ exists for $n<0$
(c) $\lim_{x\to 0}f(x)$ does not exist for any value of n
(d) $\lim_{x\to 0}f(x)$ cannot be determined

11. The value of $\lim_{x\to\infty}\frac{(2^{x^n})^{\frac{1}{e^x}}-(3^{x^n})^{\frac{1}{e^x}}}{x^n}$ (where $n\in N$) is

(a) $\log n\left(\frac{2}{3}\right)$ (b) 0
(c) $n\log n\left(\frac{2}{3}\right)$ (d) Not defined

12. $\lim_{x\to 0}\frac{(2^m+x)^{1/m}-(2^n+x)^{1/n}}{x}$ is equal to

(a) $\frac{1}{m2^m}-\frac{1}{n2^n}$ (b) $\frac{1}{m2^m}+\frac{1}{n2^n}$
(c) $\frac{1}{m2^{m-1}}-\frac{1}{n2^{n-1}}$ (d) $\frac{1}{m2^{m-1}}+\frac{1}{n2^{n-1}}$

13. $\lim_{x\to 1}\frac{nx^{n+1}-(n+1)x^n+1}{(e^x-e)\sin\pi x}$, where $n=100$ is equal to

(a) $\frac{5050}{\pi e}$ (b) $\frac{100}{\pi e}$
(c) $-\frac{5050}{\pi e}$ (d) $-\frac{4950}{\pi e}$

14. $\lim_{x\to 0}\frac{e-(1+6x)^{\frac{1}{6x}}}{5x}\cdot(6+x)$ is equal to λe, then λ is equal to

(a) $\frac{9}{5}$ (b) $\frac{18}{5}$ (c) $\frac{7}{5}$ (d) $\frac{19}{5}$

15. $\lim_{x \to \infty} \frac{\cot^{-1}(x^{-a} \log_a x)}{\sec^{-1}(a^x \log_x a)}$ $(a > 1)$ is equal to

(a) 2 (b) 1

(c) $\log_a 2$ (d) 0

16. $\lim_{x \to \frac{\pi}{2}} \left(\tan^2 x \left((2\sin^2 x + 3\sin x + 4)^{\frac{1}{2}} - (\sin^2 x + 6\sin x + 2)^{\frac{1}{2}} \right) \right)$ is equal to

(a) $\frac{1}{12}$ (b) $-\frac{1}{18}$ (c) $-\frac{1}{12}$ (d) $-\frac{1}{6}$

17. If a is non-zero real number and $\lim_{x \to 0} \frac{1 - \cos ax}{x^2} = \lim_{x \to \pi} \frac{\sin x}{\pi - x}$, then sum of the squares of all possible values of a, is

(a) 2 (b) 4 (c) 8 (d) 9

18. Which one of the following limit does not have value unity ?

(a) $\lim_{x \to 0} \frac{\sin(\tan x)}{\sin x}$ (b) $\lim_{x \to \frac{\pi}{2}} \frac{\sin(\cos x)}{\cos x}$

(c) $\lim_{x \to 0} \frac{\sqrt{1+x} - \sqrt{1-x}}{x}$ (d) $\lim_{x \to 0} \left(\frac{\sin x^2}{x} \right)$

19. The value of the

$$\lim_{x \to 0} \frac{30^x - 15^x - 10^x - 6^x + 5^x + 3^x + 2^x - 1}{x \sin x \tan x}$$

$= \lambda \ln 2 \ln k \ln 5$, where $\lambda, k \in N$, then find the value of $\lambda + k$.

20. If $\lim_{x \to 0} \frac{x^a \sin^b x}{\sin^c x}$, where $a, b, c \in R - \{0\}$, exists and has non-zero value if $pa + qb + rc = 0$, then find $p + q + r$.

Answer Key

1. (b)	2. (c)	3. (c)	4. (b)	5. (c)
6. (b)	7. (b)	8. (c)	9. (a)	10. (a)
11. (b)	12. (c)	13. (c)	14. (b)	15. (b)
16. (a)	17. (b)	18. (d)	19. (4)	20. (1)

For Detailed Solution

Milestone 4 Some Special Limits

• Limits Using Expansion • Evaluation of Limits of the form 0^0 and ∞^0 • Limits of the Form 1^∞

In previous session, we discussed about the evaluation of limit of function having indeterminate form like

$\frac{0}{0}, \frac{\infty}{\infty}, 0 \times \infty, \infty - \infty.$

In this section, we will discuss the form 0^0, ∞^0, 1^∞ and limiting value of such function which have algebraic as well as non-algebraic function.

JEE SPIKE

Maclaurin' Theorem

$$f(x) = f(0) + xf'(0) + \frac{x^2}{2!}f''(0) + \frac{x^3}{3!}f''(0) + \ldots + \frac{x^n}{n!}f^n(0) + \ldots$$

Example 56. Expand $\sin x$ in powers of x.

Sol. Here, $f(x) = \sin x$, Hence $f(0) = 0$,

$f'(x) = \cos x$, $f'(0) = 1$,

$f''(x) = -\sin x$, $f''(0) = 0$,

$f'''(x) = -\cos x$, $f'''(0) = -1$

$\vdots \qquad \vdots$

$f^n(x) = \sin\left(x + \frac{n\pi}{2}\right)$, $f^n(0) = \sin \frac{n\pi}{2}$

Thus, $\sin x = x - \frac{x^3}{3!} + \frac{x^5}{5!} - \ldots + \ldots$

3.13 Limits Using Expansion

When two or more different types of algebraic and non-algebraic function are involved in evaluating of limit of function.

Some Series Expansion

1. $e^x = 1 + \frac{x}{1!} + \frac{x^2}{2!} + \frac{x^3}{3!} + \ldots$
2. $a^x = 1 + \frac{x \cdot \log a}{1!} + \frac{(\log a)^2 x^2}{2!} + \ldots$ where, $a \in R^+$
3. $(1+x)^n = 1 + \frac{nx}{1!} + \frac{n(n-1)x^2}{2!} + \frac{n(n-1)(n-2)x^3}{3!} + \ldots n \in R$ and $|x| < 1$
4. $\log(1+x) = x - \frac{x^2}{2} + \frac{x^3}{3} - \frac{x^4}{4} + \ldots$ where, $-1 \le x \le 1$
5. $\frac{x^n - a^n}{x - a} = x^{n-1} + x^{n-2}a + x^{n-3}a^2 + \ldots + a^{n-1}$
6. $(1+x)^{\frac{1}{x}} = e\left(1 - \frac{x}{2} + \frac{11x^2}{24} + \ldots\right)$
7. $\sin x = x - \frac{x^3}{3!} + \frac{x^5}{5!} - \frac{x^7}{7!} + \ldots$
8. $\cos x = 1 - \frac{x^2}{2!} + \frac{x^4}{4!} - \frac{x^6}{6!} + \ldots$
9. $\tan x = x + \frac{x^3}{3} + \frac{2}{15}x^5 + \frac{17}{315}x^7 + \ldots$
10. $\sin^{-1} x = x + \frac{1^2}{3!}x^3 + \frac{1^2 \cdot 3^2}{5!}x^5 + \frac{1^2 \cdot 3^2 \cdot 5^2}{7!}x^7 + \ldots$
11. $\tan^{-1} x = x - \frac{x^3}{3} + \frac{x^5}{5} + \ldots$
12. $\sec^{-1} x = 1 + \frac{x^2}{2!} + \frac{5x^4}{4!} + \frac{61x^6}{6!} + \ldots$
13. $(\sec^{-1} x)^2 = \frac{2}{2!}x^2 + \frac{2 \cdot 2^2}{4!}x^4 + \frac{2 \cdot 2^2 \cdot 4^2}{6!}x^6 + \ldots$
14. $x \cot x = 1 - \frac{x^3}{3} + \frac{x^4}{45} - \frac{2x^6}{945} + \ldots$
15. $\sec x = 1 + \frac{x^2}{2} + \frac{5x^4}{24} + \frac{61x^6}{720} + \ldots$
16. $x \operatorname{cosec} x = 1 + \frac{x^2}{6} + \frac{7x^4}{360} + \frac{31x^6}{15120} + \ldots$

Example 57. Evaluate $\lim_{x \to 0} \frac{\ln(1+x) - \left(\sin x - \frac{x^2}{2}\right)}{x \tan x \sin x}$

Sol. $\lim_{x \to 0} \frac{\ln(1+x) - \sin x + \frac{x^2}{2}}{x \tan x \sin x}$

$$= \lim_{x \to 0} \frac{\left(x - \frac{x^2}{2} + \frac{x^3}{3} \ldots\right) - \left(x - \frac{x^3}{3!} + \frac{x^5}{5!} + \ldots\right) + \frac{x^2}{2}}{x^3 \cdot \frac{\tan x}{x} \cdot \frac{\sin x}{x}}$$

$$= \frac{1}{3} + \frac{1}{6} = \frac{1}{2}$$

Example 58. Find $\lim_{x \to 0} \frac{e^{\sin x} - \sin x - 1}{x^2}$

Sol. $\lim_{x \to 0} \frac{e^{\sin x} - \sin x - 1}{x^2}$

$$= \lim_{x \to 0} \frac{\left(1 + \frac{\sin x}{1!} + \frac{\sin^2 x}{2!} + \frac{\sin^3 x}{3!} + \ldots\right) - \sin x - 1}{x^2}$$

$$= \lim_{x \to 0} \left(\frac{\sin x}{x}\right)^2 \left(\frac{1}{2!} + \frac{\sin x}{3!} + \ldots\right) = \frac{1}{2!} = \frac{1}{2}$$

Example 59. Solve $\lim_{x \to \infty} \left\{x - x^2 \cdot \log\left(1 + \frac{1}{x}\right)\right\}$ is equal to

Sol. Here, on putting $x = \frac{1}{y}$

$$\lim_{y \to 0} \left\{\frac{1}{y} - \frac{\log(1+y)}{y^2}\right\}$$

$$= \lim_{y \to 0} \frac{y - \log(1+y)}{y^2}$$

$$= \lim_{y \to 0} \frac{y - \left\{y - \frac{y^2}{2} + \frac{y^3}{3} - \frac{y^4}{4} + \ldots\right\}}{y^2}$$

$$= \lim_{y \to 0} \frac{y^2 \left\{\frac{1}{2} - \frac{y}{3} + \ldots\right\}}{y^2}$$

$$= \lim_{y \to 0} \left\{\frac{1}{2} - \frac{y}{3} + \ldots\right\} = \frac{1}{2}$$

Example 60. Show that $\lim_{x \to 0} \frac{(1+x)^{1/x} - e + \frac{1}{2} ex}{x^2} = \frac{11e}{24}$.

Sol. Let $y = (1+x)^{1/x}$

$$\therefore \ \ln y = \frac{1}{x} \ln(1+x)$$

$$= \frac{1}{x}\left(x - \frac{1}{2}x^2 + \frac{1}{3}x^3 - \ldots\right) = 1 - \frac{1}{2}x + \frac{1}{3}x^2 - \ldots$$

Now, $y = e^{1 - \frac{1}{2}x + \frac{1}{3}x^2 - \ldots}$

$$= e^1 \cdot e^{-\frac{1}{2}x + \frac{1}{3}x^2 - \ldots}$$

$$= e\left\{1 + \left(-\frac{1}{2}x + \frac{1}{3}x^2 - \ldots\right) + \ldots + \frac{1}{2!}\left(-\frac{1}{2}x + \frac{1}{3}x^2 - \ldots\right)^2 + \ldots\right\}$$

$$= e\left\{1 - \frac{1}{2}x + \left(\frac{1}{3} + \frac{1}{8}\right)x^2 + \ldots\right\}$$

$$= e\left(1 - \frac{1}{2}x + \frac{11}{24}x^2 + \ldots\right)$$

Now, $\lim_{x \to 0} \frac{(1+x)^{1/x} - e + \frac{1}{2} ex}{x^2}$

$$= \lim_{x \to 0} \frac{e\left(1 - \frac{1}{2}x + \frac{11}{24}x^2 + \ldots\right) - e + \frac{1}{2}ex}{x^2} = \frac{11e}{24}$$

JEE SCANNER

Example Similar to PYQ Asked in JEE Main 2023

If $\lim_{t \to 0} \frac{e^{at} - \cos(bt) - \frac{cte^{-ct}}{2}}{1 - \cos(2t)} = 19$, *then* $a^2 + b^2 + c^2$ *is ....*

Sol. (76) Given, $\lim_{t \to 0} \frac{e^{at} - \cos(bt) - \frac{cte^{-ct}}{2}}{1 - \cos 2t} = 19$

On expansion, we get

$$\lim_{t \to 0} \frac{\left(1 + at + \frac{a^2t^2}{2!} + \ldots\right) - \left(1 - \frac{t^2b^2}{2!} + \ldots\right) - \frac{ct}{2}\left(1 - ct + \frac{c^2t^2}{2!} - \ldots\right)}{1 - 1 + \frac{4t^2}{2!} + \ldots} = 19$$

All the heigher terms are negligible

$$\lim_{t \to 0} \frac{\left(a - \frac{c}{2}\right)t + t^2\left(\frac{a^2}{2} + \frac{b^2}{2} + \frac{c^2}{2}\right)}{2t^2} = 19$$

If above limit exist, $a - \frac{c}{2} = 0$

$$a = \frac{c}{2} \Rightarrow c = 2a$$

and $\frac{\frac{a^2}{2} + \frac{b^2}{2} + \frac{c^2}{2}}{2} = 19 \Rightarrow \frac{a^2 + b^2 + c^2}{4} = 19$

$$\therefore \quad a^2 + b^2 + c^2 = 19 \times 4 = 76$$

Skill Builder

If $\lim_{x \to 0} \frac{e^{ax} - \cos(bx) - \frac{cxe^{-cx}}{2}}{1 - \cos(2x)} = 21$, then $\frac{a^2 + b^2 + c^2}{3}$ is ....

For Sol.

■ **For more practice** See Q.6 of Milestone Practice 3.4.

Example 61. Solve $\lim_{x\to 0} \dfrac{a\sin x - bx + cx^2 + x^3}{2x^2 \cdot \log(1+x) - 2x^3 + x^4}$, if it exists and is finite also, then find a, b and c.

Sol. Here, $\lim_{x\to 0} \dfrac{a\sin x - bx + cx^2 + x^3}{2x^2 \log(1+x) - 2x^3 + x^4}$

$$= \lim_{x\to 0} \frac{a\left(x - \frac{x^3}{3!} + \frac{x^5}{5!} - \dots\right) - bx + cx^2 + x^3}{2x^2\left(x - \frac{x^2}{2} + \frac{x^3}{3} - \frac{x^4}{4} + \dots\right) - 2x^3 + x^4}$$

$$\Rightarrow \lim_{x\to 0} \frac{(a-b)x + cx^2 + \left(1 - \frac{a}{3!}\right)x^3 + \frac{a}{5!}x^5 + \dots}{\frac{2}{3}x^5 - \frac{1}{2}x^6 + \dots}$$

For finite limit, $a - b = 0, c = 0, 1 - \frac{a}{3!} = 0$ [i.e. $a = b = 6, c = 0$]

$$= \lim_{x\to 0} \frac{\frac{a}{5!} + \text{higher powers of } x}{2/3 - 1/2x + \dots}$$

$$= \frac{a}{5!}\cdot\frac{3}{2} = \frac{a}{80} = \frac{6}{80} = \frac{3}{40} \quad [\because a = 6]$$

$$\therefore \lim_{x\to 0} \frac{a\sin x - bx + cx^2 + x^3}{2x^2 \log(1+x) - 2x^3 + x^4} = \frac{3}{40},$$

where $a = 6 = b$ and $c = 0$

Example 62. $\lim_{x\to 0} \dfrac{ax^2e^x - b\log_e(1+x) + cxe^{-x}}{x^2 \sin x} = 1$, then $16(a^2 + b^2 + c^2)$ is equal to ....

Sol. (81) $\lim_{x\to 0} \dfrac{ax^2\left(1 + x + \frac{x^2}{2!} + \frac{x^3}{3!} + \dots\right) - b\left(x - \frac{x^2}{2} + \frac{x^3}{3} - \dots\right) + cx\left(1 - x + \frac{x^2}{2!} - \frac{x^3}{3!} + \dots\right)}{x^3 \cdot \frac{\sin x}{x}} = 1$

$$= \lim_{x\to 0} \frac{\left[(c-b)x + \left(\frac{b}{2} - c + a\right)x^2 + \left(a - \frac{b}{3} + \frac{c}{2}\right)x^3 + \dots\right]}{x^3} = 1$$

For finite limit,

$$c - b = 0, \frac{b}{2} - c + a = 0$$

$$a - \frac{b}{3} + \frac{c}{2} = 1$$

$$\Rightarrow \quad a = \frac{3}{4}, b = c = \frac{3}{2}$$

$$\therefore \quad a^2 + b^2 + c^2 = \frac{9}{16} + \frac{9}{4} + \frac{9}{4}$$

$$\therefore \quad 16(a^2 + b^2 + c^2) = 81$$

3.14 Evaluation of limits of the form 0^0 and ∞^0

If $\lim_{x\to a} [f(x)]^{g(x)}$

Case 1 $\lim_{x\to a} f(x) = 0$ and $\lim_{x\to a} g(x) = 0$

Case 2 $\lim_{x\to a} f(x) = \infty$ and $\lim_{x\to a} g(x) = 0$

Method to evaluating limiting value for such type of limits problem we follow the following step:

Step I First of all consider the given limit is equal to L (or accordingly your choice)

Step II Taking logarithm on both sides and then proceed as below

$$L = \lim_{x\to a} [f(x)]^{g(x)}$$

$$\log_e L = \lim_{x\to a} g(x)\cdot \log_e(f(x)) \cdot [0\times\infty \text{ form}]$$

$$\therefore \quad L = e^{\lim_{x\to a} g(x)\cdot \ln f(x)}$$

Example 63. Evaluate $\lim_{x\to 0} (\tan x)^x$.

Sol. Let $L = \lim_{x\to 0} (\tan x)^x$ $[0^0 \text{ form}]$

$$= e^{\lim_{x\to 0} x \ln(\tan x)}$$

$$= e^{\lim_{x\to 0} x \ln(1 + \tan x - 1)}$$

$$= e^{\lim_{x\to 0} x\left((\tan x - 1) - \frac{(\tan x-1)^2}{2} + \frac{(\tan x - 1)^3}{3} - \dots\right)}$$

$$= e^0 = 1$$

$$\therefore \lim_{x\to 0} (\tan x)^x = 1$$

Example 64. Evaluate $\lim_{x\to 0^+} \left(\dfrac{1}{x}\right)^x$.

Sol. $L = \lim_{x\to 0^+} \left(\dfrac{1}{x}\right)^x$ $[\infty^0 \text{ form}]$

$$= e^{\lim_{x\to 0^+} x\cdot\log\frac{1}{x}}$$

$$= e^{\lim_{x \to 0^+} -x \log x}$$

$$= e^{\lim_{x \to 0^+} -x \log[1 + (x-1)]}$$

$$= e^{\lim_{x \to 0^+} -x\left[(x-1) - \frac{(x-1)^2}{2} + \dots\right]}$$

$$= e^0 = 1$$

Example 65. Evaluate $\lim_{x \to 0} |x|^{\sin x}$.

Sol. $L = \lim_{x \to 0} |x|^{\sin x}$ $\qquad [0^0 \text{ form}]$

$$= e^{\lim_{x \to 0} \sin x \log(|x|)}$$

$$= e^{\lim_{x \to 0} \sin x \log\{1 + (|x| - 1)\}}$$

$$= e^{\lim_{x \to 0} \sin x\left[(|x|-1) - \frac{(|x|-1)^2}{2} + \dots\right]}$$

$$= e^0 = 1$$

Example 66. Evaluate $\lim_{n \to 0} (\pi n)^{\frac{2}{n}}$.

Sol. $L = \lim_{n \to \infty} (\pi n)^{\frac{2}{n}}$ $\qquad [\infty^0 \text{ form}]$

$$= e^{\lim_{n \to \infty} \frac{2}{n} \log \pi n}$$

$$= e^{\lim_{n \to \infty} 2\frac{\log \pi + \log n}{n}}$$

$$= e^{\lim_{n \to \infty} 2\left[\frac{\log \pi}{n} + \frac{\log n}{n}\right]}$$

$$= e^0 = 1 \qquad \left[\text{at } n \to \infty, n > \log n, \lim_{n \to \infty} \frac{\log n}{n} = 0\right]$$

3.15 Limit of the form 1^∞

$\lim_{x \to a} f(x)^{g(x)}$, where $\lim_{x \to a} f(x) = 1$ and $\lim_{x \to a} g(x) = \infty$

$$\lim_{x \to a} f(x)^{g(x)} = e^{\lim_{x \to a} [f(x) - 1]\, g(x)}$$

Proof $L = \lim_{x \to a} f(x)^{g(x)}$ $\qquad [1^\infty \text{ form}]$

$$L = e^{\lim_{x \to a} g(x) \log\{f(x)\}}$$

$$= e^{\lim_{x \to a} g(x) \frac{\log[1 + (f(x) - 1)]}{f(x) - 1} \times f(x) - 1}$$

$\because$ $\quad \lim_{x \to a} \dfrac{\log[1 + f(x) - 1]}{f(x) - 1} = 1$

$\therefore$ $\quad L = e^{\lim_{x \to a} g(x)[f(x) - 1]}$

Example 67. Let $P = \lim_{x \to 0^+} (1 + \tan^2 \sqrt{x})^{\frac{1}{2x}}$. Find $\log P$.

Sol. Let $P = \lim_{x \to 0^+} (1 + \tan^2 \sqrt{x})^{\frac{1}{2x}}$ $\qquad [1^\infty \text{ form}]$

If $\quad l = \lim_{x \to a} [f(x)]^{g(x)}$, where $\lim_{x \to a} f(x) \to 1$

and $\quad \lim_{x \to a} g(x) \to \infty$, then $l = e^{\lim_{x \to a} [f(x) - 1] \cdot g(x)}$

$$\Rightarrow \quad P = e^{\lim_{x \to 0^+} (1 + \tan^2 \sqrt{x} - 1) \cdot \frac{1}{2x}} \Rightarrow P = e^{\lim_{x \to 0^+} \frac{1}{2}\left(\frac{\tan \sqrt{x}}{\sqrt{x}}\right)^2}$$

Using $\lim_{x \to 0} \left(\dfrac{\tan x}{x}\right) = 1$, we get

$$P = e^{\frac{1}{2}}$$

$$\Rightarrow \quad \log P = \log\left(e^{\frac{1}{2}}\right) = \frac{1}{2}$$

JEE SCANNER

Example Similar to PYQ Asked in JEE Main 2021

$\lim_{n \to \infty} \left(1 + \dfrac{\frac{1}{1^2} + \frac{1}{2^2} + \frac{1}{3^2} + \dots + \frac{1}{n^2}}{n^3}\right)^{n^2}$ *is equal to ......*

Sol. (1) We have,

$$\lim_{n \to \infty} \left(1 + \frac{\frac{1}{1^2} + \frac{1}{2^2} + \frac{1}{3^2} + \dots + \frac{1}{n^2}}{n^3}\right)^{n^2} \qquad [1^\infty \text{ form}]$$

$$= \lim_{e^{n \to \infty}} \left(\frac{1 + \frac{1}{2^2} + \frac{1}{3^2} + \dots + \frac{1}{n^2}}{n}\right)$$

$$= e^{\lim_{n \to \infty}} \left[\frac{1}{n} + \frac{1}{2^2 n} + \frac{1}{3^2 n} + \dots + \frac{1}{n^3}\right]$$

$$= e^{\lim_{n \to \infty} (0 + 0 + \dots 0)} = e^0 = 1 \qquad [\because e^0 = 1]$$

Skill Builder

$\lim_{n \to \infty} \left[1 + \dfrac{1 + \frac{1}{2^3} + \frac{1}{3^3} + \dots + \frac{1}{n^3}}{n^4}\right]^{n^3}$ is equal to ......

For Sol.

- **For more practice** See Q.15 of Milestone Practice 3.4.

Example 68. $\lim_{n\to\infty}\left(1+\frac{1+\frac{1}{2}+\ldots+\frac{1}{n}}{n^2}\right)^n$ is equal to

Sol. It is 1^∞ form

Let $L = e^{\lim_{n\to\infty}\left(\frac{1+\frac{1}{2}+\frac{1}{3}+\ldots+\frac{1}{n}}{n}\right)}$

$L = e^{\lim_{n\to\infty}\left(\frac{1}{n}+\frac{1}{2n}+\frac{1}{3n}+\ldots+\frac{1}{n^2}\right)}$

$\therefore \quad L = e^{(0+0+0+\ldots+0)} \Rightarrow L = e^0 = 1$

Example 69. Evaluate $\lim_{x\to 0}\left(\frac{\sin x}{x}\right)^{\frac{\sin x}{x-\sin x}}$

Sol. Since, $\lim_{x\to 0}\frac{\sin x}{x} = 1$

and $\lim_{x\to 0}\frac{\sin x}{x-\sin x} = \lim_{x\to 0}\frac{1}{\left(\frac{x}{\sin x}-1\right)} = \frac{1}{1-1} = \infty$

$$\Rightarrow \lim_{x\to 0}\left(\frac{\sin x}{x}\right)^{\left(\frac{\sin x}{x-\sin x}\right)} = e^{\lim_{x\to 0}\left(\frac{\sin x}{x}-1\right)\left(\frac{\sin x}{x-\sin x}\right)}$$

$$= e^{-\lim_{x\to 0}\frac{\sin x}{x}} = e^{-1} = \frac{1}{e}$$

Example 70. Evaluate $\lim_{x\to 0}\left(\frac{a^x+b^x+c^x}{3}\right)^{\frac{2}{x}}$; $(a, b, c > 0)$.

Sol. We have, $\lim_{x\to 0}\left(\frac{a^x+b^x+c^x}{3}\right)^{\frac{2}{x}}$

$$= e^{\lim_{x\to 0}\left(\frac{a^x+b^x+c^x}{3}-1\right)\frac{2}{x}} = e^{\frac{2}{3}\lim_{x\to 0}\left(\frac{a^x+b^x+c^x-3}{x}\right)}$$

$$= e^{\frac{2}{3}\lim_{x\to 0}\left(\frac{a^x-1}{x}+\frac{b^x-1}{x}+\frac{c^x-1}{x}\right)}$$

$$= e^{\frac{2}{3}\left\{\lim_{x\to 0}\frac{a^x-1}{x}+\lim_{x\to 0}\frac{b^x-1}{x}+\lim_{x\to 0}\frac{c^x-1}{x}\right\}}$$

$$= e^{\left(\frac{2}{3}\right)[\ln a+\ln b+\ln c]} = e^{\left(\frac{2}{3}\right)\ln(abc)} = e^{\ln(abc)^{\frac{2}{3}}} = (abc)^{\frac{2}{3}}$$

Example 71. Evaluate $\lim_{x\to\infty}\left(\frac{x^2+5x+4}{x^2-3x+7}\right)^x$.

Sol. By means of division of the numerator of the fraction by the denominator, we isolate the integral part:

$$\frac{x^2+5x+4}{x^2-3x+7} = 1+\frac{8x-3}{x^2-3x+7}$$

Thus, when $x \to \infty$ the given function is a power whose base tends to unity and the exponent, to infinity (an indeterminacy of the form 1^∞).

$$\lim_{x\to\infty}\left(\frac{x^2+5x+4}{x^2-3x+7}\right)^x = \lim_{x\to\infty}\left(1+\frac{8x-3}{x^2-3x+7}\right)^x$$

$$= \lim_{x\to\infty}\left[\left(1+\frac{8x-3}{x^2-3x+7}\right)^{\frac{x^2-3x+7}{8x-3}}\right]^{\frac{x(8x-3)}{x^2-3x+7}}$$

$$= \lim_{x\to\infty}\left[\left(1+\frac{8x-3}{x^2-3x+7}\right)^{\frac{x^2-3x+7}{8x-3}}\right]^{\frac{8-\frac{3}{x}}{1-\frac{3}{x}+\frac{7}{x^2}}}$$

Since, $\frac{8x-3}{x^2-3x+7} \to 0$ and as $x \to \infty$ and we have

$$\lim_{x\to\infty}\left(1+\frac{8x-3}{x^2-3x+7}\right)^{\frac{x^2-3x+7}{8x-3}} = e$$

Taking into account that $\lim_{x\to\infty}\frac{8-\frac{3}{x}}{1-\frac{3}{x}+\frac{7}{x^2}} = 8$, we get

$$\lim_{x\to\infty}\left(\frac{x^2+5x+4}{x^2-3x+7}\right)^x = e^8$$

Example 72. If $\sum_{r=1}^{K}\cos^{-1}\beta r = \frac{K\pi}{2}$ for any $K \ge 1$ and $A = \sum_{r=1}^{K}(\beta r)^r$, then $\lim_{x\to A}\frac{(1+x^2)^{1/3}-(1-2x)^{1/4}}{x+x^2}$ is

(a) 1 (b) -1 (c) $\frac{1}{2}$ (d) $-\frac{1}{2}$

Sol. (c) Since, maximum value of $\cos^{-1}x = \frac{\pi}{2}$

$\sum_{r=1}^{K}\cos^{-1}\beta r = \frac{K\pi}{2}$ is possible if each $\cos^{-1}\beta r = \frac{\pi}{2} \Leftrightarrow \beta r = 0$

$\therefore \quad A = \sum_{r=1}^{K}(\beta r)^r = 0$

$$\therefore \quad \lim_{x\to A}\frac{(1+x^2)^{1/3}-(1-2x)^{1/4}}{x+x^2}$$

$$= \lim_{x\to 0}\frac{(1+x^2)^{1/3}-(1-2x)^{1/4}}{x+x^2}$$

$$= \lim_{x\to 0}\frac{\left(1+\frac{1}{3}x^2+o(x^4)\right)-\left(1-\frac{x}{2}+o(x^2)\right)}{x(1+x)}$$

$$= \lim_{x\to 0}\frac{\frac{1}{2}+\frac{1}{3}x+o(x^2)}{1+x} = \frac{1}{2}$$

[$o(x^2)$ means terms $x, x^2, x^3, x^4, \ldots$]

Example 73. Solve $\lim_{x\to 0} \frac{(1+x)^{1/x}-e}{x}$.

Sol. Let $L = \lim_{x\to 0} \frac{(1+x)^{\frac{1}{x}}-e}{x}$

$$= \lim_{x\to 0} \frac{e^{\log(1+x)^{1/x}}-e}{x}$$

$$= \lim_{x\to 0} \frac{e\left\{e^{\frac{\log(1+x)}{x}-1}-1\right\}}{x}$$

$$= \lim_{x\to 0} \frac{e\{e^M-1\}}{M} \cdot \lim_{x\to 0} \frac{\log(1+x)-x}{x^2}$$

where, $M = \frac{\log(1+x)}{x} - 1$

$$\therefore\ L = \lim_{M\to 0} \frac{e\cdot\{e^M-1\}}{M} \cdot \lim_{x\to 0} \frac{\frac{-x^2}{2}+\frac{x^3}{3}+\dots}{x^2}$$

$$= e \times 1 \times \lim_{x\to 0}\left(\frac{-1}{2}+\frac{x}{3}+\dots\right)$$

$$= -\frac{e}{2} \qquad [\text{as } x\to 0 \Rightarrow M\to 0]$$

Example 74. $\lim_{x\to 0}\left[1^{\frac{1}{\sin^2 x}}+2^{\frac{1}{\sin^2 x}}+\dots+n^{\frac{1}{\sin^2 x}}\right]^{\sin^2 x}$ is equal to

(a) ∞ (b) 0

(c) $\frac{n+1}{2}$ (d) n

Sol. (d) Put $\sin^2 x = y$

$$\lim_{y\to 0}\left(1^{\frac{1}{y}}+2^{\frac{1}{y}}+\dots+n^{\frac{1}{y}}\right)^y$$

$$= \lim_{\frac{1}{y}\to\infty} n\left(\left(\frac{1}{n}\right)^{\frac{1}{y}}+\left(\frac{2}{n}\right)^{\frac{1}{y}}+\dots+1\right)^y = n$$

Example 75. Find the value of $\lim_{x\to 1}\left(\tan\left(\frac{\pi}{4}+\ln x\right)\right)^{\frac{1}{\ln x}}$.

Sol. $\lim_{x\to 1}\left(\tan\left(\frac{\pi}{4}+\ln x\right)\right)^{\frac{1}{\ln x}}$ $[1^\infty \text{ form}]$

$$= \lim_{x\to 1}\left(1+\frac{2\tan(\ln x)}{1-\tan(\ln x)}\right)^{\frac{1}{\ln x}}$$

$$= e^{\lim_{x\to 1}\frac{2\tan(\ln x)}{\{1-\tan(\ln x)\}}\cdot\frac{1}{\ln x}}$$

$$= e^{2\lim_{x\to 1}\frac{\tan(\ln x)}{\ln x}\cdot\frac{1}{1-\tan(\ln x)}}$$

$$= e^{2(1)} = e^2$$

Example 76. Find a polynomial of the least degree, such that $\lim_{x\to 0}\left(1+\frac{x^2+f(x)}{x^2}\right)^{\frac{1}{x}} = e^2$.

Sol. $\lim_{x\to 0}\left(1+\frac{x^2+f(x)}{x^2}\right)^{\frac{1}{x}}$ exists only when it is in 1^∞ form

i.e. $\lim_{x\to 0}\frac{x^2+f(x)}{x^2} = 0$.

So, the term of least degree in $f(x)$ is of degree 2.

i.e. $f(x) = a_2x^2 + a_3x^3 + \dots$

Now, $\lim_{x\to 0}\left(1+\frac{x^2+f(x)}{x^2}\right)^{\frac{1}{x}} = e^2$

$$\Rightarrow\quad e^{\lim_{x\to 0}\left(\frac{x^2+f(x)}{x^2}\right)\frac{1}{x}} = e^2 \Rightarrow e^{\lim_{x\to 0}\frac{x^2+f(x)}{x^3}} = e^2$$

$$\therefore\quad \lim_{x\to 0}\frac{x^2+f(x)}{x^3} = 2$$

$$\Rightarrow \lim_{x\to 0}\frac{x^2+a_2x^2+a_3x^3+\dots}{x^3} = 2$$

$\Rightarrow a_2 = -1$, $a_3 = 2$ and $a_4, a_5, \dots$ are any arbitrary constants. Since, we want a polynomial of the least degree, we choose $f(x) = -x^2 + 2x^3$.

Milestone Practice 3.4

1. Let $f(x)$ be a function such that $\lim_{x\to 0}\frac{f(x)}{x}=1$. If $\lim_{x\to 0}\frac{x(1+a\cos x)-b\sin x}{\{f(x)\}^3}=1$, then $a+b$ is equal to
   (a) -1 (b) 1
   (c) -4 (d) None of these

2. $\lim_{x\to 0}\frac{x\tan 2x-2x\tan x}{(1-\cos 2x)^2}$ is equal to
   (a) 0 (b) $\frac{1}{2}$ (c) 1 (d) 2

3. $\lim_{x\to 0}\frac{\cos x^3-1+\ln(1+x^6)}{x^2(e^{x^2}-1-x^2)}$ is equal to
   (a) 1 (b) 2 (c) 3 (d) 0

4. $\lim_{x\to\infty}\left(\frac{x^2-2x+1}{x^2-4x+2}\right)^x$ is equal to
   (a) 1 (b) 2 (c) e^2 (d) e

5. If $\lim_{x\to 0}[1+x\log(1+b^2)]^{1/x}=2b\sin^2\theta$, $b>0$ and $\theta\in(-\pi,\pi]$, then the value of θ is
   (a) $\pm\frac{\pi}{4}$ (b) $\pm\frac{\pi}{3}$ (c) $\pm\frac{\pi}{6}$ (d) $\pm\frac{\pi}{2}$

6. If $\lim_{x\to 0}\frac{e^{ax}-\cos(bx)-\frac{cx\,e^{-cx}}{2}}{1-\cos 2x}=15$, then $5a^2+b^2$ is
   (a) 65 (b) 60
   (c) 35 (d) 36

7. $\lim_{x\to 0}\left(\cot\left(\frac{\pi}{4}+x\right)\right)^{\operatorname{cosec} x}$ is equal to
   (a) e^{-1} (b) e^2
   (c) e^{-2} (d) e^1

8. $\lim_{x\to\infty}\left(\sin\frac{1}{x}+\cos\frac{1}{x}\right)$ is
   (a) e (b) e^2
   (c) $1/e$ (d) Does not exist

9. $\lim_{n\to\infty}(0.2)^{\log_{\sqrt{5}}(1/4+1/8+1/16+\ldots+n\text{ terms})}$ is equal to
   (a) 2 (b) 4
   (c) 8 (d) 1

10. If α and β are the roots of $ax^2+bx+c=0$, then $\lim_{x\to\alpha}(1+ax^2+bx+c)^{\frac{1}{x-\alpha}}$ is
    (a) $a(\alpha-\beta)$ (b) $\ln|a(\alpha-\beta)|$
    (c) $e^{a(\alpha-\beta)}$ (d) $e^{a|\alpha-\beta|}$

11. $\lim_{x\to 0}\left(\frac{1+\sin x}{1-\sin x}\right)^{\operatorname{cosec} x}$ is equal to
    (a) e (b) 1 (c) e^2 (d) 0

12. The limit $\lim_{x\to 0^+}x^{x^2}$ is equal to
    (a) 0 (b) -1 (c) 1 (d) e

13. The value of $\lim_{x\to\frac{\pi}{2}}[\cos x+\cot x]^{\sin 2x}$ is equal to
    (a) e (b) -1 (c) 1 (d) 0

14. The limit $\lim_{x\to\infty}(\ln x)^{\frac{1}{x}}$ is equal to
    (a) 1 (b) e^2
    (c) 0 (d) e^{-1}

15. $\lim_{x\to\infty}\left[1+\frac{\frac{1}{1^5}+\frac{1}{2^5}+\ldots+\frac{1}{x^5}}{6}\right]^{x^5}$ is
    (a) 2 (b) 1 (c) 0 (d) $\frac{1}{e}$

Answer Key

1. (c)	2. (b)	3. (a)	4. (c)	5. (d)
6. (b)	7. (c)	8. (a)	9. (b)	10. (c)
11. (c)	12. (c)	13. (c)	14. (a)	15. (b)

For Detailed Solution

Milestone 5 Use of Standard Theorem

- Use of Standard Theorems/Results • L'Hospital Rule • Newton Leibnitz's Theorem
- Limit Using Special Type of Function • One Sided Limits • Geometrical Limits

3.16 Use of Standard Theorems/Results

Theorem 1 : Sandwich/Squeeze Play Theorem

General The Squeeze principle is used on limit problems, where the usual algebraic methods, factorisation or algebraic manipulation etc., are not effective.

However, it requires to "squeeze" our problem in between two other simpler function, whose limits can be easily computed and equal. Use of Squeeze principle requires accurate analysis, indepth algebra skills and careful use of inequalities.

Statement If f, g and h are three functions such that $f(x) \le g(x) \le h(x)$ for all x in some interval containing the point $x = c$ and if

$$\lim_{x\to c} f(x) = \lim_{x \to c} h(x) = L$$

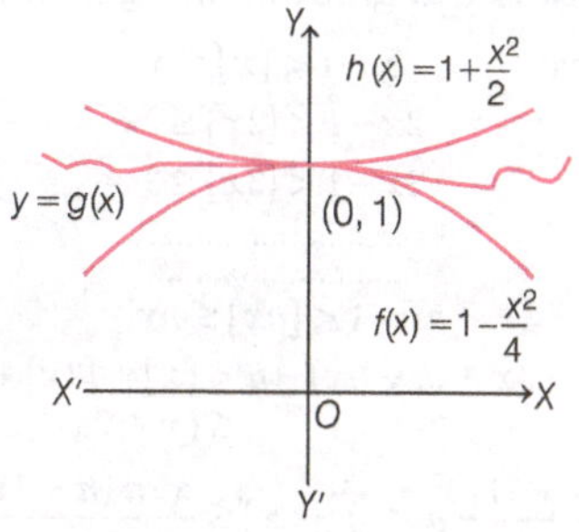

Then, $\lim_{x\to c} g(x) = L$

From the figure, note that $\lim_{x\to 0} g(x) = 1$.

JEE SPIKE

The quantity c may be a finite number, $+\infty$ or $-\infty$.
Similarly, L may also be finite number, $+\infty$ or $-\infty$.

Theorem 2 : Limits of Trigonometric Functions

If x is small and is measured in radians, then

$$\lim_{x\to 0} \frac{\sin x}{x} = 1 = \lim_{x\to 0} \frac{x}{\sin x}$$

$$= \lim_{x\to 0} x \operatorname{cosec} x = \lim_{x\to 0} \frac{\sin^{-1} x}{x} = \lim_{x\to 0} \frac{x}{\sin^{-1} x}$$

Proof Consider a circle with unit radius.

Area of ΔOAP < Area of sector $\widehat{OAP}$ < Area of ΔOAT

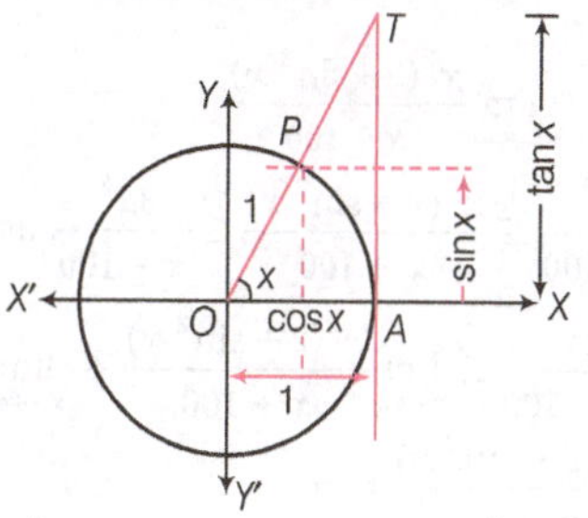

$$\frac{\sin x}{2} < \frac{x}{2} < \frac{\tan x}{2} \Rightarrow 1 < \frac{x}{\sin x} < \frac{1}{\cos x} \quad [\because 0 < x < \pi/2]$$

$$\Rightarrow \cos x < \frac{\sin x}{x} < 1$$

Now, using Sandwich theorem, $\lim_{x\to 0} \cos x < \lim_{x\to 0^+} \frac{\sin x}{x} < 1$

$$1 < \lim_{x\to 0^+} \frac{\sin x}{x} < 1$$

Obviously, we have $\lim_{x\to 0^+} \frac{\sin x}{x} = 1$

Put $x = -y$, $\lim_{y\to 0^-} \frac{\sin y}{y} = 1$

Hence, $\lim_{x\to 0} \frac{\sin x}{x} = 1$

Similarly, $\lim_{x\to 0} \frac{\sin x}{x} = 1 = \lim_{x\to 0} \frac{x}{\sin x} = \lim_{x\to 0} x \operatorname{cosec} x$

$$= \lim_{x\to 0} \frac{\sin^{-1} x}{x} = \lim_{x\to 0} \frac{x}{\sin^{-1} x} \quad \text{...(i)}$$

Using Eq. (i), we can deduce

$$\lim_{x\to 0}\frac{\tan x}{x}=1=\lim_{x\to 0}\frac{x}{\tan x}=\lim_{x\to 0}x\cot x$$

$$=\lim_{x\to 0}\frac{\tan^{-1}x}{x}=\lim_{x\to 0}\frac{x}{\tan^{-1}x}$$

JEE Focus Points

Concept Inside Video

- The $\lim_{x\to 0}\frac{\sin x}{x}$ always approaches 1 from its left hand, i.e. 0.9999....
  $\Rightarrow \lim_{x\to 0}\left[\frac{\sin x}{x}\right]=0$, where $[\cdot]$ denotes greatest integer function. $\left[\because \left(\lim_{x\to 0}\frac{\sin x}{x}\right)=1\right]$
- The $\lim_{x\to 0}\frac{\tan x}{x}$ approaches 1 from RHS.
  $\Rightarrow \lim_{x\to 0}\left[\frac{\tan x}{x}\right]=1$, where $[\cdot]$ denotes greatest integer function.

Example 77. Evaluate $\lim_{x\to\infty}\frac{x^2(2+\sin^2 x)}{x+100}$.

Sol. We have, $\lim_{x\to\infty}\frac{x^2(2+\sin^2 x)}{x+100}$

Now, $\frac{2x^2}{x+100}\le\frac{x^2(2+\sin^2 x)}{x+100}\le\frac{3x^2}{x+100}$, as $0\le\sin^2 x\le 1$

$$\therefore \lim_{x\to\infty}\frac{2x^2}{x+100}\le\lim_{x\to 0}\frac{x^2(2+\sin^2 x)}{x+100}\le\lim_{x\to\infty}\frac{3x^2}{x+100}$$

$$\Rightarrow \lim_{x\to\infty}\frac{x^2(2+\sin^2 x)}{x+100}=\infty$$

$$\left[\because \lim_{x\to\infty}\frac{2x^2}{x+100}=\lim_{x\to\infty}\frac{3x^2}{x+100}=\infty\right]$$

Example 78. Evaluate

$$\lim_{n\to\infty}\left(\frac{n}{n^2+1}+\frac{n}{n^2+2}+\frac{n}{n^2+3}+\ldots+\frac{n}{n^2+n}\right).$$

Sol. Let $f(n)=\frac{n}{n^2+1}+\frac{n}{n^2+2}+\frac{n}{n^2+3}+\ldots+\frac{n}{n^2+n}$

Note that $f(n)$ has n terms which are decreasing.

Suppose,

$$h(n)=\left(\frac{n}{n^2+1}+\frac{n}{n^2+1}+\frac{n}{n^2+1}+\ldots+\frac{n}{n^2+1}\right), n \text{ terms}$$

$$=\frac{n^2}{n^2+1} \qquad [\text{obviously } f(n)<h(n)]$$

and

$$g(n)=\left(\frac{n}{n^2+n}+\frac{n}{n^2+n}+\frac{n}{n^2+n}+\ldots+\frac{n}{n^2+n}\right), n \text{ terms}$$

$$=\frac{n^2}{n^2+n} \qquad [\text{obviously } g(n)<f(n)]$$

Hence, $\lim_{n\to\infty}g(n)<\lim_{n\to\infty}f(n)<\lim_{n\to\infty}h(n)$

Since, $\lim_{n\to\infty}g(n)=1=\lim_{n\to\infty}h(n)$

Hence, using Sandwich theorem, $\lim_{n\to\infty}f(n)=1$.

Example 79. The value of the $\lim_{x\to 0}\frac{x}{a}\left[\frac{b}{x}\right]$ $(a\ne 0)$ (where $[\cdot]$ denotes the greatest integer function) is

(a) a (b) b (c) $\frac{b}{a}$ (d) $1-\frac{b}{a}$

Sol. Since, $\frac{b}{x}-1<\left[\frac{b}{x}\right]\le\frac{b}{x}$

Now, we have two cases depending upon the value of $\frac{x}{a}$.

Case I For $\frac{x}{a}>0$

$$\Rightarrow \lim_{x\to 0}\left(\frac{b}{x}-1\right)\frac{x}{a}<\lim_{x\to 0}\left[\frac{b}{x}\right]\frac{x}{a}\le\lim_{x\to 0}\frac{b}{x}\cdot\frac{x}{a}$$

Using Squeeze play theorem, we have $\lim_{x\to 0}\frac{x}{a}\left[\frac{b}{x}\right]=\frac{b}{a}$

Case II For $\frac{x}{a}<0$

$$\Rightarrow \lim_{x\to 0}\left(\frac{b}{x}-1\right)\frac{x}{a}>\lim_{x\to 0}\left[\frac{b}{x}\right]\frac{x}{a}\ge\lim_{x\to 0}\frac{b}{x}\cdot\frac{x}{a}$$

Using Squeeze play theorem, we have $\lim_{x\to 0}\frac{x}{a}\left[\frac{b}{x}\right]=\frac{b}{a}$

Example 80. Evaluate $\lim_{n\to\infty}\frac{[x]+[2x]+[3x]+\ldots+[nx]}{n^2}$, where $[\cdot]$ denotes the greatest integer function.

Sol. We know that $x-1<[x]\le x$

$$\Rightarrow \quad 2x-1<[2x]\le 2x$$

$$\Rightarrow \quad 3x-1<[3x]\le 3x$$

....

....

$$\Rightarrow \quad nx-1<[nx]\le nx$$

$$\therefore (x+2x+3x+\ldots+nx)-n<[x]+[2x]+\ldots+[nx]\le(x+2x+\ldots+nx)$$

$$\Rightarrow \frac{xn(n+1)}{2}-n<\sum_{r=1}^{n}[rx]\le\frac{x\cdot n(n+1)}{2}$$

Thus, $\lim_{n\to\infty}\frac{[x]+[2x]+\ldots+[nx]}{n^2}$

$$\Rightarrow \lim_{n\to\infty}\frac{x}{2}\left(1+\frac{1}{n}\right)-\frac{1}{n}<\lim_{n\to\infty}\frac{[x]+[2x]+\ldots+[nx]}{n^2}\le\lim_{n\to\infty}\frac{x}{2}\left(1+\frac{1}{n}\right)$$

$$\Rightarrow \frac{x}{2}<\lim_{n\to\infty}\frac{[x]+[2x]+\ldots+[nx]}{n^2}\le\frac{x}{2}$$

$$\therefore \lim_{n\to\infty}\frac{[x]+[2x]+\ldots+[nx]}{n^2}=\frac{x}{2}$$

Alternate Solution

We know that

$$[x] = x - \{x\}$$

$$\sum_{r=1}^{n} rx = [x] + [2x] + \ldots + [nx]$$

$$= x - \{x\} + 2x - \{2x\} + \ldots + nx - \{nx\}$$

$$= (x + 2x + 3x + \ldots + nx) - (\{x\} + \{2x\} + \ldots + \{nx\})$$

$$= \frac{xn(n+1)}{2} - (\{x\} + \{2x\} + \ldots + \{nx\})$$

$$\therefore \quad \frac{1}{n^2}\sum_{r=1}^{n}[rx] = \frac{x}{2}\left(1 + \frac{1}{n}\right) - \frac{\{x\} + \{2x\} + \ldots + \{nx\}}{n^2}$$

Since, $\quad 0 \le \{rx\} < 1$

$$\therefore \quad 0 \le \sum_{r=1}^{n}\{rx\} < n \Rightarrow \lim_{n\to\infty}\frac{\sum_{r=1}^{n}\{rx\}}{n^2} = 0$$

$$\therefore \quad \lim_{n\to\infty}\frac{\sum_{r=1}^{n}[rx]}{n^2} = \lim_{n\to\infty}\frac{x}{2}\left(1 + \frac{1}{n}\right) - \lim_{n\to\infty}\frac{\sum_{r=1}^{n}\{rx\}}{n^2}$$

$$\Rightarrow \quad \lim_{n\to\infty}\frac{\sum_{r=1}^{n}[rx]}{n^2} = \frac{x}{2}$$

3.17 L'Hospital Rule

This rule states that, if $\lim_{x\to a}\frac{f(x)}{g(x)}$, reduces to $\frac{0}{0}$ or $\frac{\infty}{\infty}$.

Then, differentiate numerator and denominator till this form is removed.

i.e. $\lim_{x\to a}\frac{f(x)}{g(x)} = \lim_{x\to a}\frac{f'(x)}{g'(x)}$, provided the later limit exists.

But if it again take form $\left(\frac{0}{0}\text{ or }\frac{\infty}{\infty}\right)$,

then $\lim_{x\to a}\frac{f(x)}{g(x)} = \lim_{x\to a}\frac{f'(x)}{g'(x)} = \lim_{x\to a}\frac{f''(x)}{g''(x)}$

and this process is continued till $\left(\frac{0}{0}\text{ or }\frac{\infty}{\infty}\right)$ form is removed.

Example 81. Evaluate $\lim_{x\to 2}\frac{x^6 - 24x - 16}{x^3 + 2x - 12}$.

Sol. We have, $\lim_{x\to 2}\frac{x^6 - 24x - 16}{x^3 + 2x - 12}$ $\quad\left[\frac{0}{0}\text{ form}\right]$

$$= \lim_{x\to 2}\frac{6x^5 - 24}{3x^2 + 2} \quad \text{[using L'Hospital rule]}$$

$$= \frac{6(2)^5 - 24}{3(2)^2 + 2} = \frac{168}{14} = 12$$

Example 82. Evaluate $\lim_{x\to 0}\log_{\tan^2 x}(\tan^2 2x)$.

Sol. $L = \lim_{x\to 0}\frac{\log(\tan^2 2x)}{\log(\tan^2 x)}$ $\quad\left[\frac{\infty}{\infty}\text{ form}\right]$

Using L'Hospital rule, we have

$$L = \lim_{x\to 0}\frac{\left(\frac{1}{\tan^2 2x}2\tan 2x\sec^2 2x\right)\times 2}{\frac{1}{\tan^2 x}2\tan x\sec^2 x}$$

$$= \lim_{x\to 0}\frac{2\left(\frac{1}{\sin 2x\cos 2x}\right)}{\frac{1}{\sin x\cos x}} = \lim_{x\to 0}\frac{\left(\frac{1}{\sin 2x\cos 2x}\right)}{\left(\frac{1}{\sin 2x}\right)}$$

$$= 1\lim_{x\to 0}\frac{1}{\cos 2x} = 1$$

Example 83. Evaluate $\lim_{x\to 0^+} x^m(\log x)^n$, $m, n \in N$.

Sol. $\lim_{x\to 0^+} x^m(\log x)^n = \lim_{x\to 0^+}\frac{(\log x)^n}{x^{-m}}$ $\quad\left[\frac{\infty}{\infty}\text{ form}\right]$

$$= \lim_{x\to 0^+}\frac{n(\log x)^{(n-1)}\frac{1}{x}}{-mx^{-m-1}} \quad \text{[using L'Hospital rule]}$$

$$= \lim_{x\to 0^+}\frac{n(\log x)^{n-1}}{-mx^{-m}} \quad \left[\frac{\infty}{\infty}\text{ form}\right]$$

$$= \lim_{x\to 0^+}\frac{n(n-1)(\log x)^{(n-2)}\frac{1}{x}}{(-m)^2 x^{-m-1}} \quad \text{[using L'Hospital rule]}$$

$$= \lim_{x\to 0^+}\frac{n(n-1)(\log x)^{(n-2)}}{m^2 x^{-m}} \quad \left[\frac{\infty}{\infty}\text{ form}\right]$$

$$= \lim_{x\to 0^+}\frac{n!}{(-m)^n x^{-m}} = 0$$

[differentiating numerator and denominator n times]

Example 84. Evaluate $\lim_{x\to 0}\frac{\sin^{-1}x - \tan^{-1}x}{x^3}$.

Sol. $\lim_{x\to 0}\frac{\sin^{-1}x - \tan^{-1}x}{x^3}$

$$= \lim_{x\to 0}\frac{(1+x^2) - \sqrt{1-x^2}}{3x^2\sqrt{1-x^2}(1+x^2)} \quad \text{[using L'Hospital rule]}$$

$$= \lim_{x\to 0}\frac{(1+x^2)^2 - (1-x^2)}{3x^2\sqrt{1-x^2}(1+x^2)} \times \frac{1}{(1+x^2)+\sqrt{1-x^2}}$$

[rationalising]

$$= \lim_{x\to 0}\frac{x^4 + 3x^2}{3x^2\sqrt{1-x^2}(1+x^2)} \times \frac{1}{(1+x^2)+\sqrt{1-x^2}}$$

$$= \lim_{x\to 0}\frac{x^2 + 3}{3\sqrt{1-x^2}\,(1+x)^2} \times \frac{1}{(1+x^2)+\sqrt{1-x^2}} = \frac{1}{2}$$

Example 85. If $L = \lim_{x\to 0} \dfrac{\sin 2x + a\sin x}{x^3}$ be finite, then find the value of a and L.

Sol. $L = \lim_{x\to 0} \dfrac{\sin 2x + a\sin x}{x^3}$

$= \lim_{x\to 0} \dfrac{2\sin x\cos x + a\sin x}{x^3}$

$= \lim_{x\to 0} \dfrac{\sin x}{x}\dfrac{(2\cos x + a)}{x^2} = \lim_{x\to 0}\dfrac{2\cos x + a}{x^2}$

Now, denominator tends to 0 when $x \to 0$, then numerator also must tend to zero for which $\lim_{x\to 0}(2\cos x + a) = 0$

$\Rightarrow a = -2.$

Now, $L = \lim_{x\to 0} \dfrac{2\cos x - 2}{x^2} = -2\lim_{x\to 0}\dfrac{2\sin^2\frac{x}{2}}{x^2} = -1$

JEE SCANNER

Example Similar to PYQ Asked in JEE Main 2021

If the value of $\lim_{x\to 0}(3 - \cos x\sqrt{\cos 2x})^{\left(\frac{x+5}{x^2}\right)}$ *is equal to* e^a, *then* $2a$ *is ....*

Sol. (15) $\lim_{x\to 0}(3 - \cos x\sqrt{\cos 2x})^{\left(\frac{x+5}{x^2}\right)}$ $[1^\infty$ form]

$= e^{\lim_{x\to 0}\left(\frac{2-\cos x\sqrt{\cos 2x}}{x^2}\right)(x+5)}$

Now, $\lim_{x\to 0}\left(\dfrac{2-\cos x\sqrt{\cos 2x}}{x^2}\right)$

$= \lim_{x\to 0}\dfrac{\sin x\sqrt{\cos 2x} - \cos x \times \dfrac{1}{2\sqrt{\cos 2x}} \times (-2\sin 2x)}{2x}$

[by L' Hospital rule]

$= \lim_{x\to 0}\dfrac{\sin x\cos 2x + \sin 2x\cos x}{2x}$

$= \lim_{x\to 0}\dfrac{\sin 3x}{2x} = \lim_{x\to 0}\dfrac{\sin 3x}{3x}\times\dfrac{3x}{2x} = \dfrac{3}{2}$

$\therefore e^{\lim_{x\to 0}\left(\frac{2-\cos x\sqrt{\cos 2x}}{x^2}\right)(x+5)} = e^{\frac{3}{2}\times 5} = e^{\frac{15}{2}} = e^a$

$\therefore a = \dfrac{15}{2} \Rightarrow 2a = 15$

Skill Builder

If the value of $\lim_{x\to 0}\dfrac{\sqrt{2}-\sqrt{1+\cos x}}{\sin^2 x}$ is equal to $\dfrac{\sqrt{m}}{n}$, then $(n - m)$ is .... (where m is a prime number)

For Sol.

■ **For more practice** See Q.9 of Milestone Practice 3.5.

Example 86. If $\lim_{x\to 0}\dfrac{\cos 4x + a\cos 2x + b}{x^4}$ is finite, find a and b and limiting value.

Sol. $\lim_{x\to 0}\dfrac{\cos 4x + a\cos 2x + b}{x^4} = L$ [say]

On putting $x = 0 \Rightarrow \dfrac{1+a+b}{0}$, then $1 + a + b = 0$

$a + b = -1$ ...(i)

By L'Hospital rule,

$L = \lim_{x\to 0}\dfrac{-4\sin 4x - 2a\sin 2x}{4x^3}$ $\left[\dfrac{0}{0}\text{ form}\right]$

Again, by L'Hospital rule,

$L = \lim_{x\to 0}\dfrac{-16\cos 4x - 4a\cos 2x}{12x^2}$

$\Rightarrow -16 - 4a = 0 \Rightarrow 4a = -16$

$a = -4$

From Eq. (i), $b = 3$

Again, by L'Hospital rule,

$L = \lim_{x\to 0}\dfrac{64\sin 4x + 8a\sin 2x}{24x}$ $\left[\dfrac{0}{0}\text{ form}\right]$

$L = \lim_{x\to 0}\dfrac{256\cos 4x + 16a\cos 2x}{24}$

$\Rightarrow L = \dfrac{256+16a}{24} = \dfrac{256-64}{24} = \dfrac{192}{24} = 8$

Example 87. Find the values of a and b in order that

$$\lim_{x\to 0}\frac{x(1+a\cos x) - b\sin x}{x^3} = 1$$

[using L'Hospital's rule]

Sol. $\lim_{x\to 0}\dfrac{x(1+a\cos x) - b\sin x}{x^3} = 1$ $\left[\dfrac{0}{0}\text{ form}\right]$

$\Rightarrow \lim_{x\to 0}\dfrac{1(1+a\cos x) + x(-a\sin x) - b\cos x}{3x^2} = 1$

[using L' Hospital's rule]

Here, numerator $\to 1 + a - b$ and denominator $\to 0$ and limit is a finite number 1

$\therefore$ $1 + a - b = 0,$ ...(i)

[if $1 + a - b \neq 0$, then limit will not be finite]

$\Rightarrow \lim_{x\to 0}\dfrac{1 + a\cos x - ax\sin x - b\cos x}{3x^2} = 1$ $\left[\dfrac{0}{0}\text{ form}\right]$

$\Rightarrow \lim_{x\to 0}\dfrac{0 - a\sin x - a\sin x - ax\cos x + b\sin x}{6x} = 1$ $\left[\dfrac{0}{0}\text{ form}\right]$

$\Rightarrow \lim_{x\to 0}\dfrac{-a\cos x - a\cos x - a\cos x + ax\sin x + b\cos x}{6} = 1$

$\Rightarrow \dfrac{-3a+b}{6} = 1 \Rightarrow -3a + b = 6$ ...(ii)

On solving Eqs. (i) and (ii), we get

$a = -\dfrac{5}{2}$ and $b = -\dfrac{3}{2}.$

Example 88. Let $f(a) = g(a) = k$ and their nth derivatives $f^n(a)$, $g^n(a)$ exist and are not equal for some n. Further if $\lim_{x\to a} \dfrac{f(a)g(x) - f(a) - g(a)f(x) + f(a)}{g(x) - f(x)} = 4$, then the value of k is

Sol. $\lim_{x\to a} \dfrac{kg(x) - kf(x)}{g(x) - f(x)} = 4$ [using L'Hospital rule]

$\lim_{x\to a} k\dfrac{g'(x) - f'(x)}{g'(x) - f'(x)} = 4$ or $k = 4$

Example 89. Evaluate $\lim_{x\to\infty} (\pi - 2\tan^{-1} x)\ln x$.

Sol. $\lim_{x\to\infty} \dfrac{(\pi - 2\tan^{-1} x)}{\dfrac{1}{\ln x}}$ $\left[\dfrac{0}{0}\text{ form}\right]$

On applying L'Hospital's rule,

$$\lim_{x\to\infty} \frac{-\dfrac{2}{1+x^2}}{\dfrac{-1}{(\ln x)^2}\times\dfrac{1}{x}}$$

$$= \lim_{x\to\infty} \frac{2x(\ln x)^2}{1+x^2} \quad \left[\frac{\infty}{\infty}\text{ form}\right]$$

$$= \lim_{x\to\infty} \frac{2(\ln x)^2 + 2x\cdot 2\ln x\cdot\dfrac{1}{x}}{2x}$$

$$= \lim_{x\to\infty} \frac{(\ln x)^2 + 2\ln x}{x} \quad \left[\frac{\infty}{\infty}\text{ form}\right]$$

$$= \lim_{x\to\infty} \frac{2\ln x\cdot\dfrac{1}{x} + \dfrac{2}{x}}{x} = \lim_{x\to\infty} \frac{1}{x^2}[2\ln x + 2] = 0$$

Case when L'Hospital rule becomes extremely Exhausted and can be avoided

Let's take an example

Let $I = \lim_{x\to 0} \dfrac{\sin x^2}{x\tan x} = \dfrac{\sin(0)^2}{0\cdot\tan 0} = \dfrac{0}{0}$

Using L'Hospital rule, we get

$$= \lim_{x\to 0} \frac{2x\cos x^2}{x\sec^2 x + \tan x} = \frac{2(0)\cos(0)^2}{0\cdot\sec^2(0) + \tan(0)} = \frac{0}{0}$$

Again, using L'Hospital rule, we get

$$= \lim_{x\to 0} \frac{2x\cdot 2x(-\sin x^2) + 2\cos x^2}{x\cdot 2\sec x\cdot\sec x\tan x + \sec^2 x + \sec^2 x}$$

$$= \lim_{x\to 0} \frac{2\cos x^2 - 4x^2\sin x^2}{2x\sec^2 x\tan x + 2\sec^2 x}$$

$$= \frac{2\cos(0)^2 - 4(0)}{0 + 2\sec^2(0)} = \frac{2-0}{0+2} = 1$$

Here, use of L'Hospital rule becomes exhausted.

So, we can avoid it using this method.

$$I = \lim_{x\to 0} \frac{\sin x^2}{x\tan x} = \lim_{x\to 0} \frac{\sin x^2}{x^2}\cdot\frac{x^2}{x\tan x}$$

$$= \lim_{x\to 0} \frac{\sin x^2}{x^2}\cdot\lim_{x\to 0} \frac{x}{\tan x} = 1\cdot 1 = 1$$

JEE SPIKE

L'Hospital's rule is applicable to only two indeterminate forms $\left(\dfrac{0}{0}\text{ or }\dfrac{\infty}{\infty}\right)$ and indeterminate form $0\times\infty$ have to reduced to $\dfrac{0}{0}$ or $\dfrac{\infty}{\infty}$.

3.18 Newton Leibnitz's Theorem

If $\phi(x)$ and $\psi(x)$ are defined on $[a, b]$ and are differentiable at a point $x \in (a, b)$ and $f(x, t)$ is continuous.

(a) Let $I(x) = \displaystyle\int_{\phi(x)}^{\psi(x)} f(t)\,dt$

$\therefore$ Using Leibnitz rule,

$$\frac{d}{dx}[I(x)] = \psi'(x) f[\psi(x)] - \phi'(x) f[\phi(x)]$$

(b) Let $I(x) = \displaystyle\int_{\phi(x)}^{\psi(x)} f(x, t)\,dt$

$$\therefore \frac{d}{dx}[I(x)] = \int_{\phi(x)}^{\psi(x)} \frac{\partial}{\partial x}[f(x,t)]\,dt + \psi'(x) f[\psi(x)] - \phi'(x) f[\phi(x)]$$

Example 90. Evaluate $\lim_{x\to 0}\left(\dfrac{1}{x^5}\displaystyle\int_0^x e^{-t^2}dt - \dfrac{1}{x^4} + \dfrac{1}{3x^2}\right)$.

Sol. We have, $\lim_{x\to 0}\left(\dfrac{1}{x^5}\displaystyle\int_0^x e^{-t^2}dt - \dfrac{1}{x^4} + \dfrac{1}{3x^2}\right)$

$$= \lim_{x\to 0} \frac{3\int_0^x e^{-t^2}dt - 3x + x^3}{3x^5} \quad \left[\frac{0}{0}\text{ form}\right]$$

$$= \lim_{x\to 0} \frac{3\dfrac{d}{dx}\int_0^x e^{-t^2}dt - 3 + 3x^2}{15x^4}$$

[using L' Hospital's rule]

Applying Newton-Leibnitz's formula,

$$\frac{d}{dx}\int_0^x e^{-t^2}dt = e^{-x^2}\cdot\frac{d}{dx}(x) - e^{-0}\frac{d}{dx}(0) = e^{-x^2}$$

$$\therefore \lim_{x\to 0} \frac{3\dfrac{d}{dx}\int_0^x e^{-t^2}dt - 3 + 3x^2}{15x^4}$$

$$= \lim_{x\to 0} \frac{3e^{-x^2} - 3 + 3x^2}{15x^4} \quad \left[\frac{0}{0}\text{ form}\right]$$

$$= \lim_{x \to 0} \frac{-3(2x)e^{-x^2} + 6x}{60x^3}$$

[again, apply L'Hospital's rule]

$$= \lim_{x \to 0} \frac{-6x(e^{-x^2} - 1)}{60x^3} = \lim_{x \to 0} \frac{-(e^{-x^2} - 1)}{10x^2}$$

$$= \frac{1}{10} \lim_{x \to 0} \left(\frac{e^{-x^2} - 1}{-x^2} \right)$$

$$= \frac{1}{10} \times 1 = \frac{1}{10} \quad \left[\because \lim_{x \to 0} \left(\frac{e^x - 1}{x} \right) = 1 \right]$$

JEE SCANNER

Example Similar to PYQ Asked in JEE Main 2024

$\lim_{x \to 0} \frac{x - \int_0^x \cos t^2 dt}{x^3 - 6x}$ *is equal to ....*

Sol. (0) Let $L = \lim_{x \to 0} \frac{x - \int_0^x \cos t^2 dt}{x^3 - 6x}$ $\left[\frac{0}{0} \text{ form} \right]$

On applying L'Hospital's rule, we get

$$L = \lim_{x \to 0} \frac{1 - \frac{d}{dx} \int_0^x \cos t^2 dt}{3x^2 - 6}$$

On applying Newton-Leibnitz's rule,

$$\frac{d}{dx} \int_0^x (\cos t^2) dt = \cos(x^2) \cdot 1 - 0 = \cos(x^2)$$

$$\therefore \quad L = \lim_{x \to 0} \frac{1 - \frac{d}{dx} \int_0^x \cos t^2 dt}{3x^2 - 6}$$

$$= \lim_{x \to 0} \frac{1 - \cos(x^2)}{3(x^2 - 2)}$$

$$= \frac{1 - \cos 0}{3(0 - 2)}$$

$$= \frac{1 - 1}{3(-2)}$$

$$= \frac{0}{-6} = 0$$

Skill Builder

$\lim_{x \to 0} \frac{x - \int_0^x f(t) dt}{1 - e^{x^2}}$ is equal, when $f(0) = 0$ is ......

For Sol.

■ **For more practice** See Q.10 of Milestone Practice 3.5.

Example 91. $\lim_{x \to \frac{\pi}{2}} \left(\frac{1}{\left(x - \frac{\pi}{2}\right)^2} \int_{x^3}^{(\pi/2)^3} \cos\left(\frac{1}{t^3}\right) dt \right)$ is equal to

Sol. Using L'Hospital rule,

$$= \lim_{x \to \frac{\pi}{2}} \frac{0 - \cos x \times 3x^2}{2\left(x - \frac{\pi}{2}\right)} \quad \text{[Leibnitz rule]}$$

$$= \lim_{x \to \frac{\pi}{2}} \frac{\sin\left(x - \frac{\pi}{2}\right)}{2\left(x - \frac{\pi}{2}\right)} \times 3x^2$$

$$= \frac{3\pi^2}{8}$$

Example 92. Evaluate $\lim_{x \to 3} \left(\frac{x}{x - 3} \int_3^x \frac{\sin t}{t} dt \right)$.

Sol. $\lim_{x \to 3} \left(\frac{x}{x - 3} \int_3^x \frac{\sin t}{t} dt \right)$

$$= 3 \lim_{x \to 3} \frac{\int_3^x \frac{\sin t}{t} dt}{x - 3}$$

$$= 3 \lim_{x \to 3} \frac{F(x) - F(3)}{x - 3}$$

[apply L'Hospital rule and FTCI]

$$= 3F'(3)$$

$$= 3 \frac{\sin 3}{3}$$

$$= \sin 3$$

Example 93. Find $\lim_{x \to \infty} \frac{\int_0^x (\ln(t + \sqrt{1 + t^2}) - \ln(1 + t)) dt}{x + 1}$

Sol. The limit is in (∞ / ∞) form.

Therefore, applying L'Hospital's rule and Leibnitz rule, we get

$$= \lim_{x \to \infty} [\ln(x + \sqrt{1 + x^2}) - \ln(1 + x)]$$

$$= \lim_{x \to \infty} \ln\left(\frac{x + \sqrt{1 + x^2}}{1 + x} \right)$$

$$= \lim_{x \to \infty} \ln \left(\frac{1 + \sqrt{\frac{1}{x^2} + 1}}{\frac{1}{x} + 1} \right) = \ln 2$$

3.19 Limit Using Special Type of Function

Limits Involving GIF and Fractional Part Function

$\because$ $f(x)=[x]$ and $g(x)=\{x\}$ both are piecewise function that changes our values at every integer so limiting value of these function we have to calculate LHL and RHL separately. To understand in better way we are solving some examples.

Example 94. Solve

(i) $\lim_{x\to 0^+}\left[\frac{\tan x}{x}\right]$ (ii) $\lim_{x\to 0^-}\left[\frac{\tan x}{x}\right]$

(where [·] denotes greatest integer function.)

Sol. (i) Here, $\lim_{x\to 0^+}\left[\frac{\tan x}{x}\right]$

On putting $\frac{\tan x}{x}=t \Rightarrow t\to 1^+$ as $x\to 0^+$

$\therefore \lim_{x\to 0^+}[t]=[1+h]=1$ [as $x\to 0+h \Rightarrow t\to 1+h$]

(ii) Here, $\lim_{x\to 0^-}\left[\frac{\tan x}{x}\right]$

On putting $\frac{\tan x}{x}=t \Rightarrow t\to 1^+$ as $x\to 0^-$

$\therefore \lim_{x\to 0^+}[t]=[1+h]=1$ [as $x\to 0-h \Rightarrow t\to 1+h$]

Example 95. Solve

(i) $\lim_{x\to 1^-}[\sin(\sin^{-1}x)]$ (ii) $\lim_{x\to \frac{\pi}{2}}[\sin^{-1}(\sin x)]$

(where [·] denotes greatest integer function.)

Sol. (i) Here, $\lim_{x\to 1^-}[\sin(\sin^{-1}x)]$

$= \lim_{x\to 1^-}[x]$ [as $\sin(\sin^{-1}x)=x$, if $-1\le x\le 1$]

$= \lim_{h\to 0}[1-h]$ [as $x\to 1^- \Rightarrow x=1-h$]

$\therefore \lim_{x\to 1}[\sin(\sin^{-1}x)] = \lim_{x\to 1^-}[\sin(\sin^{-1}x)]$

and no need to check for $\lim_{x\to 1^+}[\sin(\sin^{-1}x)]$

(ii) $\lim_{x\to \frac{\pi}{2}}[\sin^{-1}(\sin x)] = \lim_{x\to \frac{\pi^-}{2}}[\sin^{-1}(\sin x)]$

$= \lim_{x\to \frac{\pi^-}{2}}[x] = \lim_{h\to 0}\left[\frac{\pi}{2}-h\right]=1$

JEE SPIKE

If $\lim_{x\to 1}[\sin(\sin^{-1}x)]$, it means you have to calculate only left hand limit and not right hand limit as for $x>1$, $\sin(\sin^{-1}x)$ is not defined.

Example 96. Solve

(i) $\lim_{x\to 0}[\cot x]$ (ii) $\lim_{x\to +\infty}[\cot^{-1}x]$

(where [·] denotes greatest integer function]

Sol. (i) Here, $\lim_{x\to 0}[\cot x]$

On putting $\cot x=t$, now as $x\to 0$; $\cot x$ exhibits two values for $x\to 0^+$ and $x\to 0^-$. i.e. $\cot x\to +\infty$ and $\cot x\to -\infty$, respectively.

$\therefore$ We should apply right hand and left hand limit.

i.e. $\lim_{x\to 0^+}[\cot x] = \lim_{t\to +\infty}[t]=\infty$

[$\because \cot x=t \Rightarrow t\to +\infty$ as $x\to 0^+$]

and $\lim_{x\to 0^-}[\cot x] = \lim_{x\to -\infty}[t]=-\infty$

[$\because \cot x=t \Rightarrow t\to -\infty$ as $x\to 0^-$]

$\therefore$ Limit does not exist.

(ii) Here, $\lim_{x\to +\infty}[\cot^{-1}x] = \lim_{t\to 0^+}[t]$

[$\because \cot^{-1}x=t \Rightarrow t\to 0^+$ and $x\to +\infty$]

$= \lim_{h\to 0}[0+h]$

$= \lim_{h\to 0} 0=0$

Example 97. Solve $\lim_{x\to 0}\left[\sin\frac{|x|}{x}\right]$, where [·] denotes greatest integer function.

Sol. Here, $\lim_{x\to 0}\left[\sin\frac{|x|}{x}\right]$, since we have greatest integer function, we must define function.

Now, RHL (On putting $x=0+h$)

$= \lim_{h\to 0}\left[\frac{\sin|0+h|}{0+h}\right]$

We know that

$\frac{\sin h}{h}\to 1$ as $h\to 0$ but less than 1.

$\therefore$ RHL $= \lim_{h\to 0} 0=0$ $\left[\because \left(\frac{\sin h}{h}\right)=0 \text{ as } h\to 0\right]$

Again, LHL (On putting $x=0-h$)

$= \lim_{h\to 0}\left[\sin\frac{|0-h|}{0-h}\right]$

We know,

$\frac{\sin h}{-h}\to -1$ as $h\to 0$ but greater than -1

$\therefore$ LHL $= \lim_{h\to 0}[-1]=-1$ $\left[\because \left(\frac{\sin h}{h}\right)=-1 \text{ as } h\to 0\right]$

Thus, limit does not exist,

as RHL = 0 and LHL = − 1.

Example 98. Let $[x]$ denote the greatest integer less than or equal to x. Then,

$$\lim_{x\to 0}\frac{\tan(\pi\sin^2 x)+(|x|-\sin(x[x]))^2}{x^2}$$

(a) equals π (b) equals $\pi+1$

(c) equal 0 (d) Does not exist

Sol. (d) At $x=0$, RHL

$$=\lim_{x\to 0^+}\frac{\tan(\pi\sin^2 x)+(|x|-\sin(x[x]))^2}{x^2}$$

$$=\lim_{x\to 0^+}\frac{\tan(\pi\sin^2 x)+(x-\sin(x\cdot 0))^2}{x^2}$$

$[\because |x|=x \text{ for } x>0 \text{ and } [x]=0 \text{ for } 0<x<1]$

$$=\lim_{x\to 0^+}\frac{\tan(\pi\sin^2 x)+x^2}{x^2}$$

$$=\lim_{x\to 0^+}\left(\frac{\tan(\pi\sin^2 x)}{\pi\sin^2 x}\cdot\frac{\pi\sin^2 x}{x^2}+1\right)$$

$$=\pi\lim_{x\to 0^+}\frac{\tan(\pi\sin^2 x)}{\pi\sin^2 x}\cdot\lim_{x\to 0^+}\frac{\sin^2 x}{x^2}+1$$

$$=\pi+1 \quad \left[\because \lim_{x\to 0}\frac{\tan x}{x}=1 \text{ and } \lim_{x\to 0}\frac{\sin x}{x}=1\right]$$

and LHL $=\lim_{x\to 0^-}\frac{\tan(\pi\sin^2 x)+(|x|-\sin(x[x])^2}{x^2}$

$$=\lim_{x\to 0^-}\frac{\tan(\pi\sin^2 x)+(-x-\sin(x(-1))^2}{x^2}$$

$[\because |x|=-x \text{ for } x<0 \text{ and } [x]=-1 \text{ for } -1<x<0]$

$$=\lim_{x\to 0^-}\frac{\tan(\pi\sin^2 x)+(x+\sin(-x))^2}{x^2}$$

$$=\lim_{x\to 0^-}\frac{\tan(\pi\sin^2 x)+(x-\sin x)^2}{x^2}$$

$[\because \sin(-\theta)=-\sin\theta]$

$$=\lim_{x\to 0^-}\left(\frac{\tan(\pi\sin^2 x)+x^2+\sin^2 x-2x\sin x}{x^2}\right)$$

$$=\lim_{x\to 0^-}\left(\frac{\tan(\pi\sin^2 x)}{x^2}+1+\frac{\sin^2 x}{x^2}-\frac{2x\sin x}{x^2}\right)$$

$$=\lim_{x\to 0^-}\left(\frac{\tan(\pi\sin^2 x)}{\pi\sin^2 x}\cdot\frac{\pi\sin^2 x}{x^2}+1+\frac{\sin^2 x}{x^2}-2\frac{\sin x}{x}\right)$$

$$=\lim_{x\to 0^-}\frac{\tan(\pi\sin^2 x)}{\pi\sin^2 x}\cdot\lim_{x\to 0^-}\frac{\pi\sin^2 x}{x^2}+1+\lim_{x\to 0^-}\frac{\sin^2 x}{x^2}-2\lim_{x\to 0^-}\frac{\sin x}{x}$$

$$=\pi+1+1-2=\pi$$

$\because$ RHL $\neq$ LHL

$\therefore$ Limit does not exist.

Example 99. For each $t\in R$, let $[t]$ be the greatest integer less than or equal to t. Then,

$$\lim_{x\to 1^+}\frac{(1-|x|+\sin|1-x|)\sin\left(\frac{\pi}{2}[1-x]\right)}{|1-x|[1-x]}$$

(a) equals 0 (b) does not exist

(c) equals -1 (d) equals 1

Sol. (a) Given, $\lim_{x\to 1^+}\frac{(1-|x|+\sin|1-x|)\sin\left(\frac{\pi}{2}[1-x]\right)}{|1-x|[1-x]}$

Let $x=1+h$, then $x\to 1^+ \Rightarrow h\to 0^+$

$$\therefore \lim_{x\to 1^+}\frac{(1-|x|+\sin|1-x|)\sin\left(\frac{\pi}{2}[1-x]\right)}{|1-x|[1-x]}$$

$$=\lim_{h\to 0^+}\frac{(1-|h+1|+\sin|-h|)\sin\left(\frac{\pi}{2}[-h]\right)}{|-h|[-h]}$$

$$=\lim_{h\to 0^+}\frac{(1-(h+1)+\sin h)\sin\left(\frac{\pi}{2}[-h]\right)}{h[-h]}$$

$[\because |-h|=h \text{ and } |h+1|=h+1 \text{ as } h>0]$

$$=\lim_{h\to 0^+}\frac{(-h+\sin h)\sin\left(\frac{\pi}{2}(-1)\right)}{h(-1)}$$

$[\because [x]=-1 \text{ for } -1<x<0 \text{ and } h\to 0^+ \Rightarrow -h\to 0^-]$

$$=\lim_{h\to 0^+}\frac{(-h+\sin h)}{-h}\sin\left(\frac{-\pi}{2}\right)$$

$$=\lim_{h\to 0^+}\left(\frac{\sin h}{h}\right)-\lim_{h\to 0^+}\left(\frac{h}{h}\right) \quad \left[\lim_{h\to 0^+}\frac{\sin h}{h}=1\right]$$

$$=1-1=0$$

Example 100. For each $x\in R$, let $[x]$ be the greatest integer less than or equal to x. Then,

$\lim_{x\to 0^-}\frac{x([x]+|x|)\sin[x]}{|x|}$ is equal to

(a) 0 (b) $\sin 1$ (c) $-\sin 1$ (d) 1

Sol. (c) $\lim_{x\to 0^-}\frac{x([x]+|x|)\sin[x]}{|x|}$

$$=\lim_{x\to 0^-}\frac{x([x]-x)\sin[x]}{-x} \quad [\because |x|=-x, \text{ if } x<0]$$

$$=\lim_{x\to 0^-}\frac{x(-1-x)\sin(-1)}{-x} \quad \left[\because \lim_{x\to 0^-}[x]=-1\right]$$

$$=\lim_{x\to 0^-}\frac{-x(x+1)\sin(-1)}{-x}$$

$$=\lim_{x\to 0^-}(x+1)\sin(-1)$$

$$=(0+1)\sin(-1) \quad \text{[by direct substitution]}$$

$$=-\sin 1 \quad [\because \sin(-\theta)=-\sin\theta]$$

Example 101. Let $f(x)=\begin{cases} x-1, & x \text{ is even,} \\ 2x, & x \text{ is odd,} \end{cases} x\in N$. If for some $a \in N, f(f(f(a)))=21$, then $\lim_{x\to a^-}\left\{\frac{|x|^3}{a}-\left[\frac{x}{a}\right]\right\}$, where $[t]$ denotes the greatest integer less than or equal to t, is equal to

(a) 121 (b) 225 (c) 144 (d) 169

Sol. (c) $f(x)=\begin{cases} x-1; x \text{ is even} \\ 2x; x \text{ is odd} \end{cases}$

$f(f(f(a)))=21$

Case I If $a=$ even

$f(a)=a-1=$ odd

$f(f(a))=2(a-1)=$ even

$f(f(f(a)))=2a-3=21 \Rightarrow a=12$

Case II If $a=$ odd

$f(a)=2a=$ even

$f(f(a))=2a-1=$ odd

$f(f(f(a)))=4a-2=21$ [not possible]

Hence, $a=12$

Now, $\lim_{x\to 12^-}\left(\frac{|x|^3}{12}-\left[\frac{x}{12}\right]\right)=\lim_{x\to 12^-}\frac{|x|^3}{12}-\lim_{x\to 12^-}\left[\frac{x}{12}\right]$

$=144-0=144$

Example 102. For each $x\in R$, let $[x]$ be greatest integer less than or equal to x, then $\lim_{x\to 1}\frac{x\sin(x-[x])}{x-1}$ is equal to

(a) 0 (b) -1

(c) Does not exist (d) 1

Sol. (c) $\lim_{x\to 1^+}\frac{x\sin(x-[x])}{x-1}=\lim_{x\to 1^+}\frac{x\sin(x-1)}{x-1}=1(1)=1$

$\lim_{x\to 1^-}\frac{x\sin(x-[x])}{x-1}=\lim_{x\to 1}\frac{x\sin(x-0)}{x-1}$

$=$ not defined $(-\infty)$ [does not exist]

Limit of Functions Which is Defined Differently (having built in limit)

Let $f(x)$ be a function and we want to find

$$\lim_{x\to a} f(x) \text{ but } f(x)=\lim_{y\to x} g(y).$$

So, in this situation, $f(x)$ is self defined by limiting value.

JEE SPIKE

- $\lim_{n\to\infty} a^n=\begin{cases} 0, & 0<a<1 \\ 1, & a=1 \\ \infty, & a>1 \end{cases}$, $\lim_{n\to\infty} a^n=\begin{cases} \infty, & 0<a<1 \\ 1, & a=1 \\ 0, & a>1 \end{cases}$.

Example 103. If $f(x)=\lim_{n\to\infty}\frac{\tan \pi x^2+(x+1)^n \sin x}{x^2+(x+1)^n}$, then find $\lim_{x\to 0} f(x)$.

Sol. $f(x)=\begin{cases} \sin x, & x>0 \\ \frac{\tan \pi x^2}{x^2}, & x<0 \end{cases}$

$\lim_{x\to 0^+} f(x)=\lim_{x\to 0^+}\sin x=0$

$\lim_{x\to 0^-} f(x)=\lim_{x\to 0^-}\frac{\tan \pi x^2}{x^2}=\pi$

$\Rightarrow$ LHL $\neq$ RHL $\Rightarrow \lim_{x\to 0} f(x)=$ Does not exist

Example 104. If $f(x)=\lim_{n\to\infty}\frac{\cos \pi x-x^{2n}\sin(x-1)}{1+x^{2n+1}-x^{2n}}$, then find $\lim_{x\to 1} f(x)$.

Sol. $f(x)=\lim_{n\to\infty}\frac{\cos \pi x-x^{2n}\sin(x-1)}{1+x\cdot x^{2n}-x^{2n}}$

when $0<x^2<1$, $\lim_{n\to\infty} x^{2n}\to 0$

$\therefore$ $f(x)=\cos \pi x$

when $x^2=1$, $\lim_{n\to\infty} x^{2n}\to 1$

$\therefore$ $f(x)=\frac{\cos \pi x-\sin(x-1)}{1+x-1}$

$=\frac{\cos \pi x-\sin(x-1)}{x}$

when $x^2>1$, $\lim_{n\to\infty} x^{2n}\to\infty$

$\therefore$ $\lim_{n\to\infty}\frac{1}{x^{2n}}\to 0$

$f(x)=\lim_{n\to\infty}\frac{\frac{\cos \pi x}{x^{2n}}-\sin(x-1)}{\frac{1}{x^{2n}}+x-1}$

$=\frac{0-\sin(x-1)}{0+x-1}$

$=\frac{-\sin(x-1)}{(x-1)}$

$f(x)=\begin{cases} \cos \pi x, & 0<x^2<1 \\ \frac{\cos \pi x-\sin(x-1)}{x}, & x^2=1 \\ \frac{-\sin(x-1)}{(x-1)}, & x^2>1 \end{cases}$

$\lim_{x\to 1^-} f(x)=\lim_{x\to 1^-}\cos \pi x=-1$,

$\lim_{x\to 1^+} f(x)=\lim_{x\to 1^+}\frac{-\sin(x-1)}{(x-1)}=-1$

$\therefore \lim_{x\to 1} f(x)=-1$

Example 105. Let $f(x)=\min(1, x^{2n}, x^{2n+1})$, $n \in N$.

The value of $\lim\limits_{x \to 0} \dfrac{e^{\tan(f(x))}-e^{\sin(f(x))}}{\tan(f(x))-\sin(f(x))}$, is equal to

(a) 0 (b) 1 (c) 2 (d) Does not exist

Sol. (b) $f(x)=\min(1, x^{2n}, x^{2n+1}), n \in N$

$$= \begin{cases} x^{2n+1}, & x<0 \\ x^{2n+1}, & 0 \le x \le 1 \\ 1, & x \ge 1 \end{cases} = \begin{cases} x^{2n+1}, & x \le 1 \\ 1, & x \ge 1 \end{cases}$$

$$\lim_{x \to 0} \frac{e^{\tan(f(x))}-e^{\sin(f(x))}}{\tan(f(x))-\sin(f(x))}$$

$$= \lim_{x \to 0} \frac{e^{\sin(f(x))}(e^{\tan(f(x))-\sin(f(x))}-1)}{\tan(f(x))-\sin(f(x))}$$

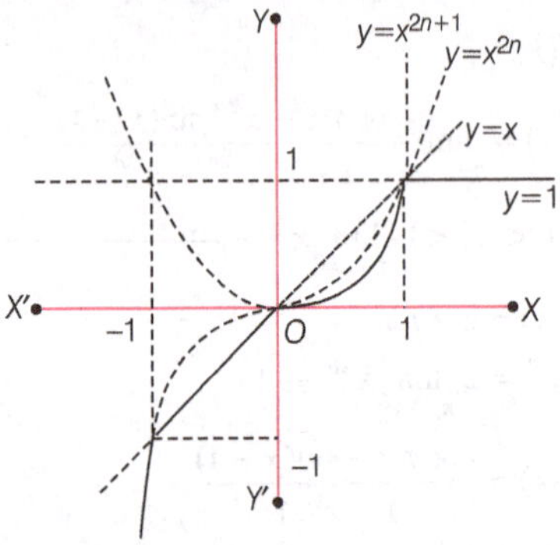

$$= \lim_{x \to 0} \frac{(e^{\tan(x^{2n+1})-\sin(x^{2n+1})}-1)}{\tan(x^{2n+1})-\sin(x^{2n+1})} = \lim_{y \to 0} \frac{e^y-1}{y}=1$$

where, $y=\tan(x^{2n+1})-\sin(x^{2n+1})$

Example 106. Let $f(x)=\lim\limits_{n \to \infty} \dfrac{\sin(\pi x^4)+(x+2)^n \cdot \dfrac{\tan \pi x}{x+1}}{1+(x+2)^n-x^4}$,

then $\lim\limits_{x \to -1} f(x)$ is equal to

(a) π (b) $\dfrac{22}{7}$ (c) 1 (d) non-existent

Sol. (a) Let $f(x)=\lim\limits_{n \to \infty} \dfrac{\sin(\pi x^4)+(x+2)^n \dfrac{\tan \pi x}{(x+1)}}{1+(x+2)^n-x^4}$

$$f(x)=\begin{cases} \dfrac{\sin(\pi x^4)}{1-x^4}, & x<-1 \\ \dfrac{\tan \pi x}{(x+1)}, & x>-1 \end{cases}$$

$$\lim_{x \to -1^+} f(x) = \lim_{x \to -1^+} \frac{\tan \pi x}{(x+1)}$$

$$= \lim_{x \to -1^+} \frac{(\tan \pi(1+x))}{(1+x)} = \pi$$

$$\lim_{x \to -1^-} f(x) = \lim_{x \to -1^-} \frac{\sin(\pi x^4)}{(1-x^4)}$$

$$= \lim_{x \to -1^-} \frac{\sin(\pi(1-x^4))}{(1-x^4)} = \pi$$

$$\lim_{x \to -1^-} f(x)=\pi$$

$$\therefore \quad \lim_{x \to -1} f(x)=\pi$$

3.20 One Sided Limits

Example 107. Evaluate $\lim\limits_{x \to 0} (1+\tan^2 \sqrt{x})^{\frac{1}{x}}$.

Sol. Let $(1+\tan^2 \sqrt{x})^{\frac{1}{x}}$,

$$\log I = \lim_{x \to 0^+} \frac{1}{x} \ln(1+\tan^2 \sqrt{x})$$

$$I = e^{\lim\limits_{x \to 0} \frac{1}{x}\left(\tan^2 \sqrt{x} - \frac{(\tan^2 (\sqrt{x}))^2}{2} + \dots\right)} = e^1 = e$$

$$I = e^{\lim\limits_{x \to 0^-} \frac{1}{x} \ln(1+\tan^2 \sqrt{x})}$$

So, here left hand limit has no significance as $\sqrt{x}$ is not defined for $x<0$.

3.21 Geometrical Limits

When the number of dimensions of a geometrical figure tends to infinity or a process repeats infinitely or any dimension tends to zero or infinity, then to find its limiting area or circumference or any other property.

To understand it we are discussing some examples below.

Example 108. A circular arc of radius 1 subtends an angle of x radians, $0<x<\dfrac{\pi}{2}$ as shown in the figure. The point R is the intersection of the two tangent line at P and Q. Let $T(x)$ be the area of ΔPQR and let $S(x)$ be the area of the shaded region, then find

(i) $T(x)$ (ii) $S(x)$ (iii) $\lim\limits_{x \to 0} \dfrac{T(x)}{S(x)}$

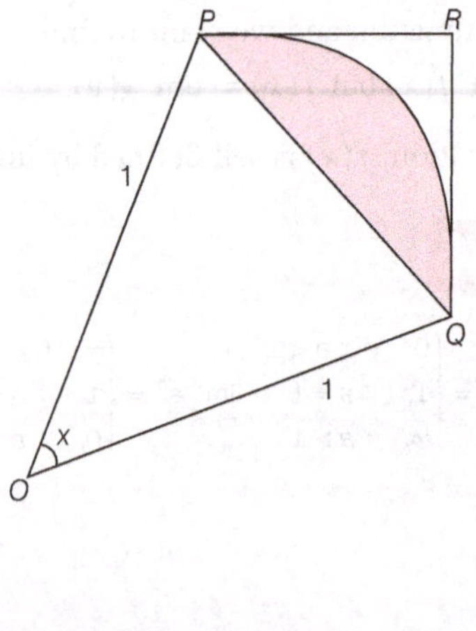

Sol. (i) In ΔPQR, $\tan\left(\frac{x}{2}\right) = \frac{PR}{1}$

$\therefore \quad PR = \tan\frac{x}{2} = RQ$

[$\because$ length of tangent from a point outside the circle are equal]

and $\angle PRQ = (\pi - x)$

$$\therefore \quad T(x) = \text{Area of } \Delta PQR$$

$$= \frac{1}{2}\cdot(PR)(RQ)\sin(\pi - x)$$

$$= \frac{1}{2}\cdot\tan^2\left(\frac{x}{2}\right)\sin x \qquad \text{...(i)}$$

$$= \tan\left(\frac{x}{2}\right) - \frac{\sin x}{2}$$

(ii) $S(x) =$ Area of sector OPQ – Area of ΔOPQ

$$= \frac{1}{2}(1)^2\cdot x - \frac{1}{2}\cdot(1)^2\cdot\sin x$$

$$= \frac{(x - \sin x)}{2}$$

(iii) $$\lim_{x\to 0}\frac{T(x)}{S(x)} = \lim_{x\to 0}\frac{\tan\left(\frac{x}{2}\right) - \frac{\sin x}{2}}{\frac{(x - \sin x)}{2}}$$

$$= \lim_{x\to 0}\frac{\tan^2\left(\frac{x}{2}\right)\sin x}{(x - \sin x)}$$

$$= \lim_{x\to 0}\frac{\left(\frac{\tan\left(\frac{x}{2}\right)}{\frac{x}{2}}\right)^2\left(\frac{\sin x}{x}\right)}{(x - \sin x)}\cdot\frac{x^3}{4}$$

$$= \frac{1}{4}\lim_{x\to 0}\left(\frac{\tan\left(\frac{x}{2}\right)}{\frac{x}{2}}\right)^2 \lim_{x\to 0}\left(\frac{\sin x}{x}\right)$$

$$\cdot\lim_{x\to 0}\frac{x^3}{(x - \sin x)} = \frac{3}{2}.$$

Example 109. A tangent line is drawn to a circle of radius unity at the point A, and a segment AB is laid off whose length is equal to that of the arc AC. A straight line BC is drawn to intersect the extension of the diameter AO at the point P. Prove that:

(i) $PA = \dfrac{\theta(1-\cos\theta)}{\theta - \sin\theta}$

(ii) $\lim\limits_{\theta\to 0} PA = 3$

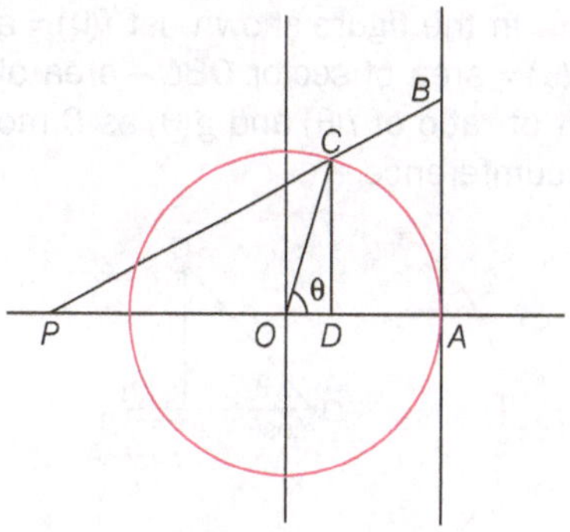

Sol. See the labelled figure below:

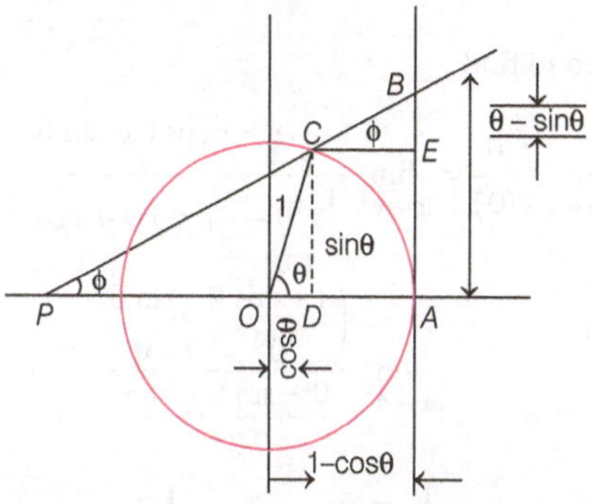

(i) From the figure,

$$\tan\phi = \frac{\theta - \sin\theta}{1 - \cos\theta} \qquad \text{...(i)}$$

Now, in ΔBPA, $\tan\phi = \dfrac{\theta}{PA}$

$$\Rightarrow \qquad PA = \frac{\theta}{\tan\phi} = \frac{\theta(1-\cos\theta)}{\theta - \sin\theta}$$

(ii) $$\lim_{\theta\to 0}\frac{\theta(1-\cos\theta)}{\frac{\theta - \sin\theta}{\theta^3}\cdot\theta^3} = \lim_{\theta\to 0}\frac{1-\cos\theta}{\theta^2}\cdot\lim_{\theta\to 0}\frac{\theta^3}{\theta - \sin\theta}$$

Now, $\lim\limits_{\theta\to 0}\dfrac{1-\cos\theta}{\theta^2} = \dfrac{1}{2}$

Let $\quad l = \lim\limits_{\theta\to 0}\dfrac{\theta - \sin\theta}{\theta^3} = \lim\limits_{t\to 0}\dfrac{3t - \sin 3t}{27t^3}$

where, $\theta = 3t$

$$= \lim_{t\to 0}\frac{3t - (3\sin t - 4\sin^3 t)}{27t^3}$$

$$= \lim_{t\to 0}\frac{t - \sin t}{9t^3} + \frac{4}{27}$$

$$l = \frac{l}{9} + \frac{4}{27} \Rightarrow \frac{8l}{9} = \frac{4}{27} \Rightarrow l = \frac{1}{6}$$

Since, $\lim\limits_{\theta\to 0}\dfrac{\theta^3}{\theta - \sin\theta} = 6$

$$\lim_{\theta\to 0} PA = \frac{1}{2}\cdot 6 = 3$$

Example 110. In the figure shown, let $f(\theta)$ = area of ΔABC and $g(\theta)$ = area of sector OBC – area of ΔOAC. Find the limit of ratio of $f(\theta)$ and $g(\theta)$ as C moves to B along the circumference.

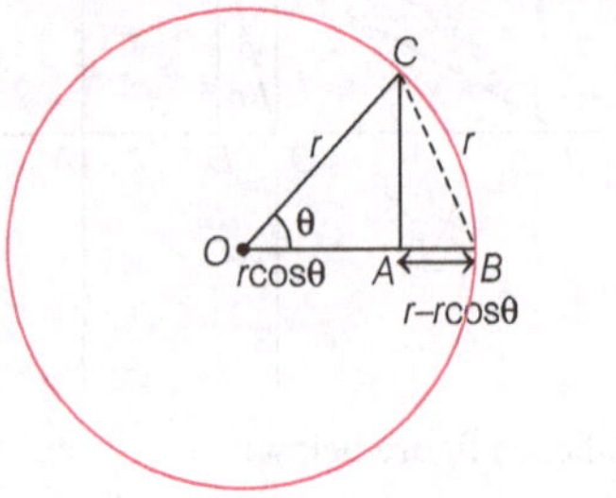

Sol. We need to find

$$\lim_{\theta \to 0^+} \frac{f(\theta)}{g(\theta)} = \lim_{\theta \to 0^+} \frac{\frac{1}{2}(r - r\cos\theta) r \sin\theta}{\frac{1}{2}r^2\theta - \frac{1}{2}r\sin\theta \cdot r\cos\theta}$$

$$= \lim_{\theta \to 0^+} \frac{\left(\frac{1-\cos\theta}{\theta^2}\right)\frac{\sin\theta}{\theta}}{\frac{\theta - \sin\theta\cos\theta}{\theta^3}} \qquad \left[\frac{0}{0}\text{ form}\right]$$

$$= \frac{1}{2}\lim_{\theta \to 0^+} \frac{1}{\frac{\theta - \frac{1}{2}\left(2\theta - \frac{(2\theta)^3}{3!}\ldots\right)}{\theta^3}}$$

$$= \frac{1}{2} \times \frac{12}{8} = \frac{3}{4}$$

Example 111. The figure shows a fixed circle C_1 with equation $(x-1)^2 + y^2 = 1$ and a shrinking circle C_2 with radius r and centre the origin. P is the point $(0, r)$, Q is the upper point of intersection of the two circles, and R is the point of intersection of the line PQ and the X-axis. What happens to R as C_2 shrinks, that is, as $r \to 0$?

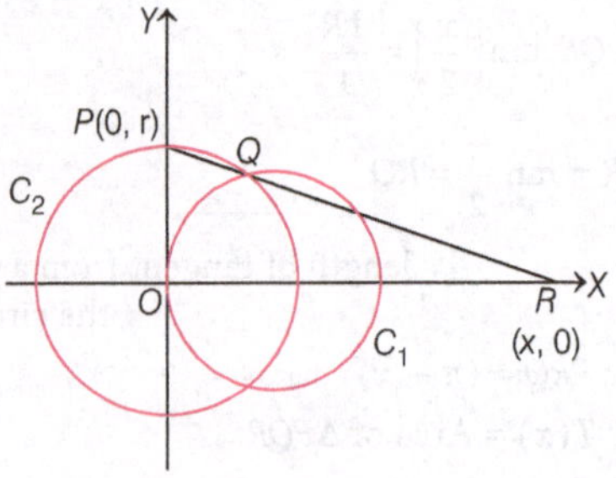

Sol. We find the coordinates of the point Q by solving

$$(x-1)^2 + y^2 = 1$$

and $\qquad x^2 + y^2 = r^2.$

On subtraction, we get

$$x = \frac{r^2}{2}$$

Points P, Q and R are collinear. Hence, $m_{PR} = m_{PQ}$

$$\Rightarrow \quad \frac{r-0}{0-x} = \frac{r\sqrt{1-\frac{r^2}{4}} - r}{\frac{r^2}{2} - 0}$$

$$\Rightarrow \quad x = \frac{\frac{r^2}{2}}{1 - \sqrt{1 - \frac{r^2}{4}}}$$

Now, $\displaystyle \lim_{r \to 0^+} x = \lim_{r \to 0^+} \frac{\frac{r^2}{2}}{1 - \left(1 - \frac{r^2}{4}\right)^{\frac{1}{2}}}$

$$= \lim_{r \to 0^+} \frac{\frac{r^2}{2}}{1 - 1 + \frac{1}{2}\cdot\frac{r^2}{4} + \ldots} = 4$$

Milestone Practice 3.5

1. Evaluate the following limits

(i) $\lim\limits_{x \to \left(\frac{\pi}{2}\right)^+} \dfrac{\{\sin x\} + 1}{\cos\left(\dfrac{\pi}{2} - x\right)}$

(ii) $\lim\limits_{x \to \pi^+} \dfrac{[[\sin x] + [\cos x]]}{|\sin x + \cos x|}$

(iii) $\lim\limits_{x \to \frac{\pi}{2}^-} \dfrac{\sin 3x}{[\sin 3x]}$

2. (i) Evaluate the $\lim\limits_{x \to k} ([k - x] + [x - k] - x)$; where $[x]$ denotes GIF and $k \in Z$.

(ii) Evaluate the above limit if $k \notin Z$.

(iii) Evaluate $\lim\limits_{x \to k} (\{k - x\} + \{x - k\})$; where $k \in Z$ and $\{x\}$ denotes the fractional part of x.

3. Examine whether the following limit exists or not. If exists, find the value of limit. (where [.] denotes greatest integer less than or equal to x and { } denotes fractional part of x).

(i) $\lim\limits_{x \to 0} \left[\dfrac{\sin x}{x}\right]$ (ii) $\lim\limits_{x \to 0} \left[\dfrac{\sin^{-1} x}{x}\right]$

(iii) $\lim\limits_{x \to 0} \left[\dfrac{\tan x}{x}\right]$ (iv) $\lim\limits_{x \to 0} \left[\dfrac{\ln(1+x)}{x}\right]$

4. If $[x]$ denotes the greatest integer $\le x$, then

$\lim\limits_{x \to \infty} \dfrac{1}{n^4} ([1^3 x] + [2^3 x] + \ldots + [n^3 x])$ equals

(a) $\dfrac{x}{2}$ (b) $\dfrac{x}{3}$ (c) $\dfrac{x}{6}$ (d) $\dfrac{x}{4}$

5. $\lim\limits_{x \to 0} \left[(1 - e^x) \dfrac{\sin x}{|x|}\right]$ is (where [.] represents greatest integral part function)

(a) -1 (b) 1
(c) 0 (d) None of these

6. Inscribed in a circle of radius R is a square, a circle is inscribed in the square, a new square in the circle and so on for n times.

Find the limit of the sum of areas of all circles and the limit of the sum of areas of all the squares as $n \to \infty$.

7. Let $f(x) = \left[x^x - (\cot x)^{\sin x} + (\sec x)^{\operatorname{cosec} x} - \dfrac{\ln(\sec x)}{x^2}\right]$, evaluate $\lim\limits_{x \to 0^+} f(x)$.

8. Evaluate the following limits using L' Hospitals rule

(i) $\lim\limits_{x \to 1} \dfrac{x^x - x}{1 - x + \ln x}$ (ii) $\lim\limits_{x \to 0} \dfrac{(1+x)^{\frac{1}{x}} - e + \dfrac{xe}{2}}{x^2}$

(iii) $\lim\limits_{x \to 0} \dfrac{e^x + \ln\left(\dfrac{1-x}{e}\right)}{\tan x - x}$ (iv) $\lim\limits_{x \to \frac{1}{2}} \dfrac{\sec \pi x}{\tan 3\pi x}$

9. If the value of $\lim\limits_{x \to 0} (5 - \cos x\sqrt{\cos 2x})^{\left(\frac{x+3}{x^2}\right)}$ is equal to e^a, then find $4a$.

10. Evaluate

(i) $\lim\limits_{x \to 0} \dfrac{1}{x^3} \displaystyle\int_0^x \dfrac{t^2}{t^4 + 1}\, dt$ (ii) $\lim\limits_{x \to 0} \dfrac{\displaystyle\int_0^x (\cos t)^{\frac{1}{x^2}}\, dt}{x}$

11. Find the limit of the sum of the lengths of ordinates of the curve $y = e^{2x} \cos \pi x$, drawn at the points $x = 0, 1, 2, 3, \ldots$ ..upto ∞.

12. ABC is an isosceles triangle inscribed in a circle of r. If $AB = AC$ and h is the altitude from A to BC and p be the perimeter of ABC, then $\lim\limits_{h \to 0} \dfrac{\Delta}{p^3}$ equals (where Δ is the area of the triangle)

(a) $\dfrac{1}{32r}$ (b) $\dfrac{1}{64r}$

(c) $\dfrac{1}{128r}$ (d) None of these

Answer Key

1. (i) 2 (ii) -2 (iii) 1 **2.** (i) $-1-k$ (ii) $-1-k$ (iii) 1 **3.** (i) 0 (ii) 1 (iii) 1 (iv) Does not exist

4. (d) **5.** (a) **6.** $2\pi R^2, 4R^2$ **7.** $\dfrac{1}{2}$

8. (i) -2 (ii) $\dfrac{11e}{24}$ (iii) $-\dfrac{1}{2}$ (iv) 3 **9.** 18 **10.** (i) $\dfrac{1}{3}$ (ii) $e^{-\frac{1}{2}}$

11. $\dfrac{-1}{e^2 + 1}$ **12.** (c)

For Detailed Solution

JEE Pattern EXAMPLES

Single Option Correct Type Questions

Example 1 ■ *If k is an integer such that*

$$\lim_{n\to\infty}\left(\left(\cos\frac{k\pi}{4}\right)^n-\left(\cos\frac{k\pi}{6}\right)^n\right)=0, \textit{ then}$$

(a) k is divisible neither by 4 nor by 6

(b) k must be divisible by 12, but not necessarily by 24

(c) k must be divisible by 24

(d) either k is divisible by 24 or k is divisible neither by 4 nor by 6

Sol. (d) $\lim_{n\to\infty}\left(\left(\cos\frac{k\pi}{4}\right)^n-\left(\cos\frac{k\pi}{6}\right)^n\right)=0$

This will always hold true if $\cos\frac{k\pi}{4}$ or $\cos\frac{k\pi}{6}$ is not equal to ± 1.

Hence, $k \neq 4k_1$ or $6k_1$

So, k is not divisible by 4 and 6. But k can be a multiple of 24.

Example 2 ■ $\sum_{r=1}^{\infty}\frac{r^3+(r^2+1)^2}{(r^4+r^2+1)(r^2+r)}$ *is equal to*

(a) 3/2 (b) 1

(c) 2 (d) infinite

Sol. (a) $\sum_{r=1}^{\infty}\frac{r^3+(r^2+1)^2}{(r^4+r^2+1)(r^2+r)}$

$$=\sum_{r=1}^{\infty}\frac{r^4+r^2+1+r^3+r^2}{(r^4+r^2+1)(r^2+r)}$$

$$=\sum_{r=1}^{\infty}\frac{1}{r^2+r}+\frac{r}{r^4+r^2+1}$$

$$=\sum_{r=1}^{\infty}\frac{1}{r}-\frac{1}{r+1}+\frac{r}{(r^2+1)^2-r^2}$$

$$=\sum_{r=1}^{\infty}\frac{1}{r}-\frac{1}{r+1}-\frac{1}{2}\left[\frac{1}{r^2+1+r}-\frac{1}{r^2+1-r}\right]$$

$$=\sum_{r=1}^{\infty}\left(\frac{1}{r}-\frac{1}{r+1}\right)-\frac{1}{2}\sum_{r=1}^{\infty}\left(\frac{1}{r^2+1+r}-\frac{1}{r^2+1-r}\right)$$

$$=1-\frac{1}{2}(-1)=\frac{3}{2}$$

JEE SCANNER

Example 3 Similar to PYQ Asked in JEE Main 2023

The value of $\lim_{n\to\infty}\left(\sum_{r=1}^{n}\left(\frac{3r+7}{r^2+r}\right)\left(\frac{4}{7}\right)^{r+1}\right)$ *is equal to*

(a) 0 (b) $\frac{16}{7}$

(c) $\frac{4}{7}$ (d) None of these

Sol. (b) $T_r=\left(\frac{3r+7}{r(r+1)}\right)\left(\frac{4}{7}\right)^{r+1}=\left(\frac{7(r+1)-4x}{r(r+1)}\right)\left(\frac{4}{7}\right)^{r+1}$

$$=4\left(\frac{1}{r}\left(\frac{4}{7}\right)^r-\frac{1}{r+1}\left(\frac{4}{7}\right)^{r+1}\right)$$

$$=4(V_r-V_{r+1})$$

So, $\sum_{r=1}^{n}T_r=4\left[\sum_{r=1}^{n}V_r-\sum_{r=1}^{n}V_{r+1}\right]$

$$S_n=4(V_1-V_{n+1})=\frac{16(n+1)\,7^n-4^{n+2}}{(n+1)\,7^{n+1}}$$

So, $\lim_{n\to\infty}S_n=\lim_{n\to\infty}\frac{16(n+1)7^n-4^{n+2}}{(n+1)\,7^{n+1}}=\frac{16}{7}$

Skill Builder

The value of $\lim_{n\to\infty}\left(\sum_{r=1}^{n}\left(\frac{3r+8}{r^2+r}\right)\left(\frac{5}{8}\right)^{r+1}\right)$ is equal to

(a) 0 (b) $\frac{25}{8}$

(c) $\frac{5}{8}$ (d) None of these

For Sol.

Example 4 ■ *The value of* $\lim_{x\to\infty}\frac{\cot^{-1}(x^{-5}\log_5 x)}{\sec^{-1}(5^x\log_x 5)}$ *is equal to*

(a) 1 (b) 0

(c) $\pi/2$ (d) Does not exist

Sol. (a) $\lim_{x\to\infty}\dfrac{\cot^{-1}(x^{-5}\log_5 x)}{\sec^{-1}(5^x\log_x 5)}$

As, $\lim_{x\to\infty}\dfrac{\log_5 x}{x^5}\to 0$ and $\lim_{x\to\infty}5^x\log_x 5\to\infty$

Thus, $\lim_{x\to\infty}\dfrac{\cot^{-1}(x^{-5}\log_5 x)}{\sec^{-1}(5^x\log_x 5)}=\dfrac{\pi/2}{\pi/2}=1$

Example 5 $\lim_{x\to\infty}\dfrac{\cot^{-1}(\sqrt{x-1}-\sqrt{x})}{\sec^{-1}\left(\left(\dfrac{2x+1}{x-1}\right)^x\right)}$ *is equal to*

(a) 1 (b) 0 (c) $\dfrac{\pi}{2}$ (d) non-existent

Sol. (a) $\lim_{x\to\infty}\dfrac{\cot^{-1}(\sqrt{x-1}-\sqrt{x})}{\sec^{-1}\left(\left(\dfrac{2x+1}{x-1}\right)^x\right)}$

As, $\lim_{x\to\infty}\cot^{-1}(\sqrt{x-1}-\sqrt{x})$

$$=\lim_{x\to\infty}\cot^{-1}\left(\frac{-1}{\sqrt{x-1}+\sqrt{x}}\right)=\frac{\pi}{2}$$

and $\lim_{x\to\infty}\sec^{-1}\left(\left(\dfrac{2x+1}{x-1}\right)^x\right)$

$$=\lim_{x\to\infty}\sec^{-1}\left(\left(\frac{2+1/x}{1-1/x}\right)^x\right)=\frac{\pi}{2}$$

Hence, $\lim_{x\to\infty}\dfrac{\cot^{-1}(\sqrt{x-1}-\sqrt{x})}{\sec^{-1}\left(\left(\dfrac{2x+1}{x-1}\right)^x\right)}=1$

Example 6 $\lim_{n\to\infty}\left\{\dfrac{7}{10}+\dfrac{29}{10^2}+\dfrac{133}{10^3}+\ldots+\dfrac{5^n+2^n}{10^n}\right\}$ *equals*

(a) 3/4 (b) 2 (c) 5/4 (d) 1/2

Sol. (c) $S=\lim_{n\to\infty}\left\{\dfrac{7}{10}+\dfrac{29}{10^2}+\dfrac{133}{10^3}+\ldots+\dfrac{5^n+2^n}{10^n}\right\}$

$$T_r=\frac{5^r+2^r}{10^r}=\left(\frac{1}{2}\right)^r+\left(\frac{1}{5}\right)^r$$

$$S=\lim_{n\to\infty}\sum_{r=1}^{n}\left(\frac{1}{2}\right)^r+\left(\frac{1}{5}\right)^r=\lim_{n\to\infty}\sum_{r=1}^{n}\frac{1}{2^r}+\lim_{n\to\infty}\sum_{r=1}^{n}\frac{1}{5^r}$$

$$=\frac{\frac{1}{2}}{1-\frac{1}{2}}+\frac{\frac{1}{5}}{1-\frac{1}{5}}=1+\frac{1}{4}=\frac{5}{4}$$

Example 7 $\lim_{x\to1}\dfrac{(\ln(1+x)-\ln 2)(3.4^{x-1}-3x)}{[(7+x)^{1/3}-(1+3x)^{1/2}].\sin(x-1)}$ *equals*

(a) $\dfrac{9}{4}\ln\dfrac{4}{e}$ (b) $\dfrac{9}{4}\ln\dfrac{e}{4}$

(c) $\dfrac{4}{9}\ln\dfrac{e}{4}$ (d) None of these

Sol. (b) $\lim_{x\to1}\dfrac{(\ln(1+x)-\ln 2)\,3(4^{x-1}-x)}{[(7+x)^{1/3}-(1+3x)^{1/2}].\sin(x-1)}$

On putting $x=1+h$

$$=3\lim_{h\to0}\frac{(\ln(2+h)-\ln 2)(4^h-(1+h))}{[(8+h)^{1/3}-(4+3h)^{1/2}]\sin h}$$

$$=3\lim_{h\to0}\frac{\ln\left(1+\frac{h}{2}\right)(4^h-1-h)}{[(8+h)^{1/3}-(4+3h)^{1/2}]\sin h}$$

$$=\frac{3\times\frac{1}{2}\times[\ln 4-1]}{\frac{1}{3}(8)^{-2/3}-3\times\frac{1}{2}(4)^{-1/2}}=\frac{3}{2}\frac{\ln 4/e}{\left(\frac{1}{12}-\frac{3}{4}\right)}=\frac{9}{4}\ln\frac{e}{4}$$

Example 8 *Let* $\lim_{x\to\pi}\dfrac{\sin\alpha x}{1-2\cos\beta x}=-\sqrt{3},\alpha\in1^+,\beta>0,$ *then least positive value of* $\alpha\beta$ *is*

(a) $\dfrac{1}{6}$ (b) $\dfrac{1}{3}$ (c) $\dfrac{1}{2}$ (d) 1

Sol. (b) $\cos\beta\pi=\dfrac{1}{2}$

$\Rightarrow\quad \beta=\pm\dfrac{1}{3}+2k,k\in I$

$\Rightarrow\quad \lim_{x\to\pi}\dfrac{\alpha\cos\alpha x}{2\beta\sin(\beta x)}=-\sqrt{3}$

$\Rightarrow\quad \dfrac{(-1)^\alpha.\alpha}{2\beta\frac{\sqrt{3}}{2}}=-\sqrt{3}$

$\Rightarrow\quad \alpha=1$ and $\beta=\dfrac{1}{3}$ for $(\alpha\beta)$ minimum

$\Rightarrow\quad (\alpha\beta)_{\min}=\dfrac{1}{3}$

Example 9 *If* $S_n=3+\dfrac{1+3+3^2}{3!}+\dfrac{1+3+3^2+3^3}{4!}$ ………… *upto n terms. Then, the value of* $[\lim_{n\to\infty}S_n]$ *is, (where* $[\cdot]$ *represent GIF)*

(a) 6 (b) 7 (c) 8 (d) 9

Sol. (c) $S_n=1+\dfrac{1+3}{2!}+\dfrac{1+3+3^2}{3!}+\dfrac{1+3+3^2+3^3}{4!}$ ………

$$=\Sigma\frac{3^n-1}{(3-1)n!}$$

$$\frac{1}{2}\sum_{r=1}^{n}\frac{3^r-1}{r!}=\frac{1}{2}\left[\sum\frac{3^r}{r!}-\frac{1}{r!}\right]$$

$$\lim_{n\to\infty}(S_n)=\frac{1}{2}[(e^3-1)-(e-1)]$$

$$=\frac{1}{2}[e^3-e]\approx 8.59$$

$$[S_n]=8$$

Example 10 $\lim_{x \to 1} \frac{\sin^2(x^3+x^2+x-3)}{1-\cos(x^2-4x+3)}$ *has the value equal to*

(a) 18 (b) $\frac{9}{2}$

(c) 9 (d) Limit does not exist

Decoding the Question

Using L'Hospital rule and property $\lim_{x \to 0} \frac{\sin x}{x} = 1$ and $\cos 2x = 1 - 2\sin^2 x$ to solve this question.

Sol. (a) $L = \lim_{x \to 1} \frac{\sin^2(x^3+x^2+x-3)}{(x^3+x^2+x-3)^2} \cdot \frac{(x^3+x^2+x-3)^2}{1-\cos(x^2-4x+3)}$

$$= (1) \cdot \lim_{x \to 1} \frac{(x^2-4x+3)^2}{1-\cos(x^2-4x+3)} \cdot \frac{(x^3+x^2+x-3)^2}{(x^2-4x+3)^2}$$

$$= (1)(2) \lim_{x \to 1} \left(\frac{x^3+x^2+x-3}{x^2-4x+3} \right)^2 = 2l^2$$

where $l = \lim_{x \to 1} \frac{3x^2+2x+1}{2x-4}$ [using L'Hospital's rule]

$$= \frac{6}{-2} = -3$$

$\therefore \quad L = 2(-3)^2 = 18$

Example 11 $\lim_{x \to 0} \frac{\cos^2(1-\cos^2(1-\cos^2(\ldots\cos^2(x))))}{\sin\left[\pi\left(\frac{\sqrt{x+4}-2}{x}\right)\right]}$

(a) 2 (b) $\sqrt{2}$

(c) $-\sqrt{2}$ (d) None of these

Sol. (b) $\lim_{x \to 0} \frac{\cos^2(1-\cos^2(1-\cos^2(\ldots\cos^2(x))))}{\sin\left[\pi\left(\frac{\sqrt{x+4}-2}{x}\right)\right]}$

$$= \lim_{x \to 0} \frac{\cos^2(1-\cos^2(1-\cos^2(\ldots\cos^2 x)))}{\sin\left[\frac{\pi(\sqrt{x+4}-2)(\sqrt{x+4}+2)}{x(\sqrt{x+4}+2)}\right]}$$

$$= \lim_{x \to 0} \frac{\cos^2(1-\cos^2(1-\cos^2(\ldots\cos^2 x)))}{\sin\left(\frac{\pi}{\sqrt{x+4}+2}\right)} = \sqrt{2}$$

Example 12 *The value of the limit*

$$\lim_{n \to \infty} n^2(\sqrt[n]{a} - \sqrt[n+1]{a})\ (a > 0) \text{ is}$$

(a) $\ln a$ (b) e^a

(c) e^{-a} (d) None of these

Sol. (a) $\lim_{n \to \infty} n^2\left[(a)^{\frac{1}{n}} - (a)^{\frac{1}{n+1}}\right] = \lim_{n \to \infty} n^2 a^{1/n+1}\left[a^{\frac{1}{n}-\frac{1}{n+1}} - 1\right]$

$$= \lim_{n \to \infty} \frac{a^{\frac{1}{n+1}} \times n^2 \times \left[a^{\frac{1}{n(n+1)}} - 1\right]}{\frac{1}{n(n+1)}} \times \frac{1}{n(n+1)}$$

$$= \lim_{n \to \infty} \frac{1}{a^{n+1}} \times \left[\frac{a^{\frac{1}{n(n+1)}} - 1}{1/(n+1)}\right] \times \frac{1}{1+1/n} = \ln a$$

Example 13 *If $\{t_n\}$ be a sequence such that $t_n = \frac{2n}{3n+1}$, S_n denote the sum of the first n terms and $l = \lim_{n \to \infty} \frac{n}{\sqrt{2}} \frac{S_{n+1} - S_n}{\sqrt{\sum_{k=1}^{n} k}}$, then $L = \lim_{n \to \infty} l + 2l^2 + 3l^2 + \ldots + (n+1)l^{n+1}$ equals*

(a) 18 (b) 9 (c) 3 (d) 6

Sol. (d) As, $S_{n+1} - S_n = t_{n+1} = \frac{2(n+1)}{3n+4}$

$$l = \lim_{n \to \infty} n \times \frac{2(n+1)}{(3n+4) \times \sqrt{n(n+1)}} = \frac{2}{3}$$

Now, $L = l + 2l^2 + 3l^3 + \ldots \infty$

$lL = l^2 + 2l^3 + \ldots \infty$

$(1-l)\,L = l + l^2 + l^3 + \ldots \infty$

$$(1-l)L = \frac{l}{1-l}$$

$$L = \frac{l}{(1-l)^2} = \frac{2/3}{1/9} = 6$$

Example 14 *Let $f(x)$ be defined for all $x \in R$ such that $\lim_{x \to 0}\left[f(x) + \ln\left(1 - \frac{1}{e^{f(x)}}\right) - \ln(f(x))\right] = 0$, then $f(0)$ is*

(a) 0 (b) – 1

(c) 2 (d) 1

Sol. (a) $\lim_{x \to 0}\left[f(x) + \ln\left(1 - \frac{1}{e^{f(x)}}\right) - \ln(f(x))\right] = 0$

$$\lim_{x \to 0}[f(x) + \ln(e^{f(x)} - 1) - f(x) - \ln f(x)] = 0$$

$$\lim_{x \to 0} \ln\left(\frac{e^{f(x)} - 1}{f(x)}\right) = 0$$

Hence, $f(x) \to 0$ as $x \to 0$

So, $f(0) = 0$

JEE SCANNER

Example 15 Similar to PYQ Asked in JEE Main 2023

If $f(x)=\frac{1}{2}\left(f(x+5)+\frac{3}{f(x+1)}\right)$ *and* $f(x)>0,\ \forall\ x\in R$, *then* $\lim_{x\to\infty} f(x)$ *is*

(a) 0 (b) $\sqrt{3}$ (c) $\frac{1}{\sqrt{3}}$ (d) ∞

Sol. (b) Here, $\lim_{x\to\infty} f(x)=\lim_{x\to\infty}\frac{1}{2}\left[f(x+5)+\frac{3}{f(x+1)}\right]$

$$\Rightarrow \quad l=\frac{1}{2}\left(l+\frac{3}{l}\right)$$

$$\Rightarrow \quad l^2=\frac{1}{2}(l^2+3)$$

$$\Rightarrow \quad l^2=3$$

$$\Rightarrow \quad l=\sqrt{3}$$

Skill Builder

If $f(x)=\frac{1}{5}\left(f(x+2)+\frac{7}{f(x+3)}\right)$ and $f(x)>0,\ \forall\ x\in R$, then $\lim_{x\to\infty} f(x)$ is

(a) 0 (b) $\frac{\sqrt{7}}{2}$ (c) $\frac{2}{\sqrt{7}}$ (d) ∞

For Sol.

More than One Correct Option Type Questions

Example 16 $\lim_{x\to\infty}\sqrt{x}(\sqrt{x+1}-\sqrt{x})$ *equals*

(a) $\lim_{x\to 0}\frac{\ln(1+x)-x}{x^2}$ (b) $\lim_{x\to 0}\frac{1-\cos x}{x^2}$

(c) $\lim_{x\to 0}\frac{\sqrt{1+x}-1}{x}$ (d) $\lim_{x\to 0}\frac{\sqrt{x}}{\sqrt{x+\sqrt{x^2+2x}}}$

Sol. (b, c) $\lim_{x\to\infty}\sqrt{x}(\sqrt{x+1}-\sqrt{x})$

$$=\lim_{x\to\infty}\frac{\sqrt{x}}{\sqrt{x+1}+\sqrt{x}}=\lim_{x\to\infty}\frac{1}{\sqrt{1+\frac{1}{x}}+1}=\frac{1}{2}$$

Option (a) $\lim_{x\to 0}\frac{\ln(1+x)-x}{x^2}$

$$=\lim_{x\to 0}\frac{\left(x-\frac{x^2}{2}+\frac{x^3}{3}-\dots\right)-x}{x^2}=-\frac{1}{2}$$

Option (b) $\lim_{x\to 0}\frac{1-\cos x}{x^2}=\lim_{x\to 0}\frac{2\sin^2\frac{x}{2}}{4\times\left(\frac{x}{2}\right)^2}=\frac{1}{2}$

Option (c) $\lim_{x\to 0}\frac{\sqrt{1+x}-1}{x}=\lim_{x\to 0}\frac{(1+x)^{1/2}-(1)^{1/2}}{(1+x)-1}=\frac{1}{2}$

Option (d) $\lim_{x\to 0}\frac{\sqrt{x}}{\sqrt{x+\sqrt{x^2+2x}}}=\lim_{x\to 0}\frac{1}{\sqrt{1+\sqrt{1+\frac{2}{x}}}}=\frac{1}{\sqrt{2}}$

Example 17 *If* $f(x)=e^{[\cot x]}$, *where* $[y]$ *denotes the greatest integer less than or equal to* y, *then*

(a) $\lim_{x\to\frac{\pi}{2}^-} f(x)=1$ (b) $\lim_{x\to\frac{\pi}{2}^+} f(x)=\frac{1}{e}$

(c) $\lim_{x\to\frac{\pi}{2}} f(x)=\frac{1}{e}$ (d) $\lim_{x\to\frac{\pi}{2}} f(x)=1$

Sol. (a, b) **Option (a)** As $x\to\frac{\pi}{2}^-$, (cot x is positive (being in Ist quadrant)), thus $[\cot x]=0 \Rightarrow \lim_{x\to\frac{\pi}{2}} f(x)=e^0=1$

Option (b) $f(x)=e^{[\cot x]}$ as cot x is negative in IInd quadrant

and $\cot\frac{\pi}{2}=0\Rightarrow[\cot x]=-1$

$$\lim_{x\to\frac{\pi}{2}^+} f(x)=\frac{1}{e}$$

Example 18 *Let* $g(x)=ax^2+bx+c,\ a,b,c\in N$ *and* $\int_0^1 g(x)\,dx=\frac{11}{6}$. *Let* $f(x)$ *be a continuous and derivable function in* (x_1,x_2). *If* $f(x)\cdot f'(x)\ge x\sqrt{1-(f(x))^4}$ *and* $\lim_{\theta\to x_1^+}(f(x))^2=1$ *and* $\lim_{x\to x_2^-}(f(x))^2=\frac{1}{2}$, *then minimum value of* $[x_1^2-x_2^2]$ *is equal to, where [.] denotes greatest integer function.*

(a) $2-abc$ (b) $a+b-c$ (c) $b-c$ (d) $a-b$

Sol. (a, b) $\int_0^1 g(x)\,dx=\frac{11}{6}$

$$\Rightarrow \quad \frac{a}{3}+\frac{b}{2}+c=\frac{11}{6}$$

$$\Rightarrow \quad 2a+3b+6c=11$$

$$\therefore \quad a=b=c=1 \qquad [\because a,b,c\in N]$$

$$\because \quad \frac{f(x)f'(x)}{\sqrt{1-f(x))^4}}-x\ge 0$$

$\Rightarrow$ $h(x)=\sin^{-1}(f(x)^2)-x^2$ is non-decreasing function

$$\therefore \quad \lim_{x\to x_1^+} h(x)\le\lim_{x\to x_1^-} h(x)\Rightarrow\frac{\pi}{2}-x_1^2\le\frac{\pi}{6}-x_2^2$$

$$\Rightarrow \quad x_1^2-x_2^2\ge\frac{\pi}{3}$$

$$\Rightarrow \quad (x_1^2-x_2^2)\ge 1 \text{ i.e. } [x_1^2-x_2^2]=1$$

Example 19 *If* $f(x)=\dfrac{\cos^{-1}(1-\{x\})\cdot\sin^{-1}(1-\{x\})}{\sqrt{2\{x\}}\cdot(1-\{x\})}$, *here* $\{\cdot\}$ *denotes fractional part of x, then*

(a) $\lim_{x\to0^-} f(x)=\sqrt{2}\lim_{x\to0^-} f(x)$

(b) $\lim_{x\to0^-} f(x)=\sqrt{2}\lim_{x\to0^+} f(x)$

(c) $\lim_{x\to0^-} f(x)=\dfrac{\pi}{2\sqrt{2}}$

(d) $\lim_{x\to0^-} f(x)=\pi\sqrt{2}$

Sol. (a, c) $\because x\to0^-$

$\Rightarrow \{x\}=1+x$

$\therefore \lim_{x\to0^-} f(x)=\lim_{x\to0}\dfrac{\sin^{-1}(-x)\cos^{-1}(-x)}{\sqrt{2(1+x)}\cdot(-x)}=\dfrac{\pi}{2\sqrt{2}}$

and for $x\to0^+\Rightarrow\{x\}=x$

$\lim_{x\to0^+} f(x)=\lim_{x\to0}\dfrac{\sin^{-1}(1-x)\cos^{-1}(1-x)}{\sqrt{2x}(1-x)}=\dfrac{\pi}{2}$

Example 20 Let $f:\left(-\dfrac{\pi}{2},\dfrac{\pi}{2}\right)\to R$,

$$f(x)=\begin{cases}\lim_{n\to\infty}\left(\dfrac{(\tan x)^{2n}+x^2}{\sin^2x+(\tan x)^{2n}}\right); & x\neq0\\ 1; & x=0\end{cases}, n\in N.$$

Which of the following holds good?

(a) $f\left(-\dfrac{\pi^-}{4}\right)=f\left(\dfrac{\pi^+}{4}\right)$ (b) $f\left(-\dfrac{\pi^-}{4}\right)=f\left(-\dfrac{\pi^+}{4}\right)$

(c) $f\left(\dfrac{\pi^-}{4}\right)=f\left(\dfrac{\pi^+}{4}\right)$ (d) $f(0^+)=f(0)=f(0^-)$

Sol. (a, d) $f(x)=\lim_{n\to\infty}\dfrac{(\tan^2x)^n+x^2}{(\sin^2x)+(\tan^2x)^n}$

$\left(\dfrac{\pi}{4}\right)^+\Rightarrow\tan^2x>1$

$\left(-\dfrac{\pi^-}{4}\right)\Rightarrow\tan^2x>1$

$f\left(-\dfrac{\pi^-}{4}\right)=f\left(\dfrac{\pi^+}{4}\right)=\lim_{n\to\infty}\dfrac{1+\dfrac{x^2}{(\tan^2x)^n}}{\dfrac{\sin^2x}{(\tan^2x)^n}+1}=1$

$\left(\dfrac{\pi^-}{4}\right)\Rightarrow\tan^2x<1$

$\left(-\dfrac{\pi^+}{4}\right)\Rightarrow\tan^2x<1$

$f\left(-\dfrac{\pi^+}{4}\right)=f\left(\dfrac{\pi^-}{4}\right)=\lim_{n\to\infty}\dfrac{(\tan^2x)^n+x^2}{\sin^2x+(\tan^2x)^n}=\dfrac{2\times\pi^2}{16}$

Example 21 *Let* $f(x)=\lim_{m\to\infty}\{\lim_{n\to\infty}(\cos^{2m}(n!\pi x))\}$; *where* $x\in R$, *then*

(a) $f(x)=1$ if x is rational

(b) $f(x)=0$ if x is rational

(c) $f(x)=1$ if x is irrational

(d) $f(x)=0$ if x is irrational

Sol. (a, d) $f(x)=\lim_{m\to\infty}\{\lim_{n\to\infty}(\cos^{2m}(n!\pi x))\}$, $x\in R$

Let us discuss two cases for $x\in R$

Case (I) When x is rational

Let $x=\dfrac{p}{q}$, when $p,q\in Z, q\neq0$

when $n\to\infty$, then $n!$ would contain q as one of its factors.

$\Rightarrow n!\pi x$ is multiple of π.

So, $\cos^2(n!\,\pi x)=1$

$\therefore \lim_{m\to\infty}\{\lim_{n\to\infty}(\cos^{2m}(n!\,\pi\,x))\}=1$

Case (II) When x is irrational, then $n!\pi x$ is not multiple of π.

So, $\cos(n!\pi x)$ lie in between -1 to 1

So, $\cos^2(n!\pi x)$ lie in between 0 to 1

$\Rightarrow \lim_{m\to\infty}(\lim_{n\to\infty}\cos^{2m}(n!\pi x)\}=0$

Passage Based Questions

Passage I

(Ex. Nos. 22 to 23)

Let $f(x)=\dfrac{\tan^{-1}(1-\{x\})\cdot\cos^{-1}(1-\{x\})\cdot\sin^{-1}(1-\{x\})}{\sqrt{2\{x\}}\,(1-\{x\})^2}$,

where $\{x\}$ denotes fractional part of x, then

Example 22 $P=\lim_{x\to0^+} f(x)$, *then which is/are correct?*

(a) $\sin\left(\dfrac{2P}{\pi}\right)=\dfrac{1}{2}$ (b) $\cos\left(\dfrac{2P}{\pi}\right)=\dfrac{1}{\sqrt{2}}$

(c) $\tan\left(\dfrac{2P}{\pi}\right)=1$ (d) None of these

Example 23 $Q=\lim_{x\to0^-} f(x)$, *then which is/are correct?*

(a) $\sin\sqrt{2}Q=0$ (b) $\sin\sqrt{2}Q=1$

(c) $\tan\sqrt{2}Q=1$ (d) $\cos\sqrt{2}Q=0$

Sol. (Ex. Nos. 22-24)

22. (b,c) $f(x)=\dfrac{\tan^{-1}(1-\{x\})\cos^{-1}(1-\{x\})\cdot\sin^{-1}(1-\{x\})}{\sqrt{2\{x\}}\,(1-\{x\})^2}$

$$\therefore \quad P = \lim_{x\to 0^+} f(x)$$

$$= \lim_{x\to 0^+} \frac{\tan^{-1}(1-x)\cos^{-1}(1-x)\sin^{-1}(1-x)}{\sqrt{2x}(1-x)^2}$$

$$[\because x \to 0^+ \Rightarrow \{x\} = x]$$

$$= \lim_{x\to 0^+} \frac{\tan^{-1}(1-x)}{(1-x)} \cdot \frac{\sin^{-1}(1-x)}{(1-x)} \cdot \frac{\cos^{-1}(1-x)}{\sqrt{2x}}$$

$$= \frac{\pi}{4}\cdot\frac{\pi}{2} \times \lim_{x\to 0^+} \frac{\cos^{-1}(1-x)}{\sqrt{2}\sqrt{x}}$$

$$= \frac{\pi^2}{8} \times \lim_{\theta\to 0^+} \frac{\theta}{\sqrt{2}\sqrt{1-\cos\theta}} \quad \left[\begin{array}{l}\text{assuming } \cos^{-1}(1-x) = \theta \\ \text{as } x \to 0^+, 1-x \in (0,1) \\ \Rightarrow \theta \in (0, \pi/2) \Rightarrow \sin\theta > 0\end{array}\right]$$

$$= \frac{\pi^2}{8\sqrt{2}} \times \lim_{\theta\to 0^+} \frac{\theta}{\sqrt{2\sin^2\theta/2}}$$

$$= \frac{\pi^2}{8\sqrt{2}} \lim_{\theta\to 0^+} \frac{\theta}{\sqrt{2}|\sin(\theta/2)|}$$

$$= \frac{\pi^2}{16} \lim_{\theta\to 0^+} \frac{\theta}{\sin\theta/2} \quad \left[\because \sin\left(\frac{\theta}{2}\right) > 0\right]$$

$$= \frac{\pi^2}{16} \lim_{\theta\to 0^+} 2\left(\frac{\theta/2}{\sin\theta/2}\right) = \frac{\pi^2}{8}(1) = \frac{\pi^2}{8}$$

$$\Rightarrow \quad P = \frac{\pi^2}{8}$$

$$\Rightarrow \quad \frac{2P}{\pi} = \frac{\pi}{4}$$

$$\Rightarrow \cos\left(\frac{2P}{\pi}\right) = \frac{1}{\sqrt{2}}; \tan\left(\frac{2P}{\pi}\right) = 1$$

23. (b,c) Now, $Q = \lim_{x\to 0^-} f(x)$

$$= \lim_{x\to 0^-} \frac{\tan^{-1}(1-\{x\})\cos^{-1}(1-\{x\})\sin^{-1}(1-\{x\})}{\sqrt{2\{x\}}\,(1-\{x\})^2}$$

$$[\because x \to 0^- \Rightarrow \{x\} = 1 + x]$$

$$= \lim_{x\to 0^-} \tan^{-1}\frac{(1-(1+x))\cos^{-1}(1-(1+x))\sin^{-1}(1-(1+x))}{\sqrt{2(1+x)}(1-(1+x))^2}$$

$$= \lim_{x\to 0^-} \frac{\tan^{-1}(-x)\cos^{-1}(-x)\sin^{-1}(-x)}{\sqrt{2}\sqrt{1+x}(-x)^2}$$

$$= \lim_{x\to 0^+} \frac{(\tan^{-1}x)\cos^{-1}(x)\sin^{-1}x}{\sqrt{2}\sqrt{1-x}x^2}$$

[replacing x by $-x$ and limit $x \to 0^+$]

$$= \lim_{x\to 0^+} \frac{\tan^{-1}x}{x} \cdot \frac{\sin^{-1}x}{x} \cdot \frac{\cos^{-1}x}{\sqrt{2}\sqrt{1-x}}$$

$$= (1)(1)\frac{\pi/2}{\sqrt{2}(1)} = \frac{\pi}{2\sqrt{2}}$$

$$\Rightarrow Q = \frac{\pi}{2\sqrt{2}} \Rightarrow \sqrt{2}Q = \frac{\pi}{2}$$

$\sin\sqrt{2}Q = 1$ and $\cos\sqrt{2}Q = 0$

Passage II

(Ex. Nos. 24 to 25)

Consider two function $f(x) = \lim_{n\to\infty}\left(\cos\frac{x}{\sqrt{n}}\right)^n$ and $g(x) = -x^{4b}$, where $b = \lim_{x\to\infty}(\sqrt{x^2+x+1} - \sqrt{x^2+1})$.

Then,

Example 24 *$f(x)$ is*

(a) e^{-x^2} (b) $e^{\frac{-x^2}{2}}$ (c) e^x (d) $e^{\frac{x^2}{2}}$

Example 25 *$g(x)$ is*

(a) $-x^2$ (b) x^2 (c) x^4 (d) $-x^4$

Sol. (Ex. Nos. 24-25)

24. (b) $f(x) = \lim_{n\to\infty}\left(\cos\frac{x}{\sqrt{n}}\right)^n = e^{\lim_{n\to\infty}\left(\cos\frac{x}{\sqrt{n}}-1\right)\cdot n}$

On substituting $n = \frac{1}{t^2}$, we get

$$f(x) = e^{\lim_{t\to 0}\left(\frac{\cos tx - 1}{t^2}\right)} = e^{\lim_{t\to 0} -x^2\left(\frac{1-\cos tx}{t^2x^2}\right)}$$

$$= e^{\lim_{t\to 0} -x^2\left(\frac{2\sin^2(tx/2)}{4(t^2x^2/4)}\right)} = e^{-\frac{1}{2}x^2}$$

25. (a) Now, $g(x) = -x^{4b}$ (given),

where $b = \lim_{x\to\infty}(\sqrt{x^2+x+1} - \sqrt{x^2+1})$

$$= \lim_{x\to\infty}\left(\frac{x^2+x+1-x^2-1}{\sqrt{x^2+x+1}+\sqrt{x^2+1}}\right) = \frac{1}{2}$$

$$\therefore \; g(x) = -x^{4\left(\frac{1}{2}\right)} = -x^2$$

Passage III

(Ex. Nos. 26 to 27)

$$\text{Let } f(x) = \begin{cases} \dfrac{e^{\{x^2\}}-1}{\sin x - \tan x + \cos x - 1}, & x > 0 \\[2ex] \dfrac{\sin x - \tan x + \cos x - 1}{2x^2 + \ln(2+x) + \tan x}, & x < 0 \\[2ex] 0, & x = 0 \end{cases}$$

where {} represents fractional part function. Suppose lines L_1 and L_2 represent tangent and normal to curve $y = f(x)$ at $x = 0$. Consider the family of circles touching both the lines L_1 and L_2.

Example 26 *Ratio of radii of two circles belonging to this family cutting each other orthogonally is*

(a) $2+\sqrt{3}$ (b) $\sqrt{3}$

(c) $2+\sqrt{2}$ (d) $2-\sqrt{2}$

Example 27 *A circle having radius unity is inscribed in the triangle formed by L_1 and L_2 and a tangent to it. Then, the minimum area of the triangle possible is*

(a) $3+\sqrt{2}$ (b) $2+\sqrt{3}$

(c) $3+2\sqrt{2}$ (d) $3-2\sqrt{2}$

Sol. (Ex. Nos. 26-27)

$$f'(0^-) = \text{LHD} = \lim_{h\to 0} \frac{\dfrac{-\sin h + \tan h + \cos h - 1}{2h^2 + \ln(2-h) - \tan h}}{-h}$$

$$= \lim_{h\to 0} \frac{\dfrac{\sin h}{h} - \dfrac{\tan h}{h} + \dfrac{1-\cos h}{h^2} \times h}{2h^2 + \ln(2-h) - \tan h} = 0$$

$$f'(0^+) = \text{RHD} = \lim_{h\to 0} \frac{e^{h^2} - 1 - 0}{h}$$

$$= h \times \frac{e^{h^2} - 1}{h^2} = 0$$

$L_1 \equiv y = 0$ and $L_2 \equiv x = 0$

26. (a) $(x-r)^2 + (y-r)^2 = r^2$ [family of circle]

$x^2 + y^2 - 2rx - 2ry + r^2 = 0$

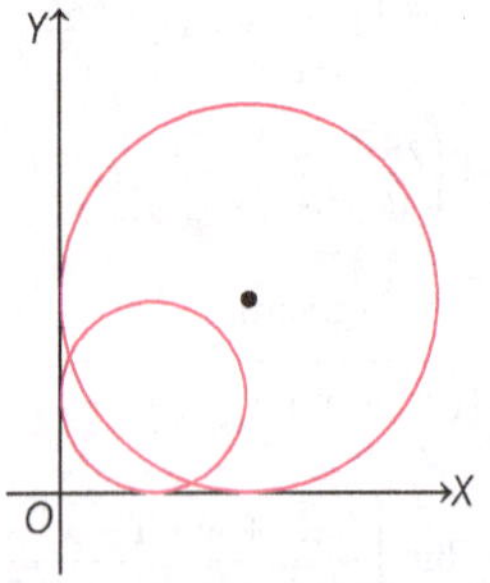

$\because$ $2(r_1r_2 + r_1r_2) = r_1^2 + r_2^2$

or $4r_1r_2 = r_1^2 + r_2^2$

$$\left(\frac{r_2}{r_1}\right)^2 - 4\left(\frac{r_2}{r_1}\right) + 1 = 0$$

$$\Rightarrow \frac{r_2}{r_1} = \frac{4 \pm \sqrt{12}}{2} = 2 \pm \sqrt{3}$$

27. (c) $\Delta = 2[\Delta_1 + \Delta_2 + \Delta_3]$

$$\Delta = 2 \times \frac{1}{2}\left(\cot\left(\frac{\pi}{4} - \frac{\theta}{2}\right) + \cot\frac{\theta}{2} + 1\right) \qquad \left[\text{using, } \frac{1}{2}ab\right]$$

$$\Delta = \frac{\cos\left(\dfrac{\pi}{4} - \dfrac{\theta}{2}\right)}{\sin\left(\dfrac{\pi}{4} - \dfrac{\theta}{2}\right)} + \frac{\cos\dfrac{\theta}{2}}{\sin\dfrac{\theta}{2}} + 1$$

$$\Rightarrow \Delta = 1 + \frac{2\sin\dfrac{\pi}{4}}{2\sin\dfrac{\theta}{2} \cdot \sin\left(\dfrac{\pi}{4} - \dfrac{\theta}{2}\right)}$$

$$\Delta = 1 + \frac{\sqrt{2}}{\cos\left(\theta - \dfrac{\pi}{4}\right) - \cos\left(\dfrac{\pi}{4}\right)}$$

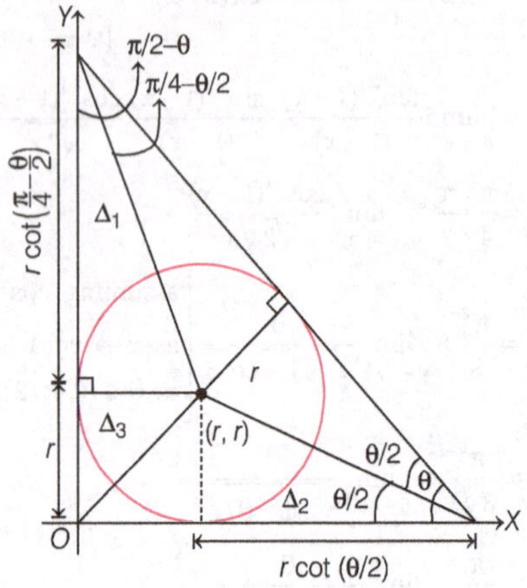

Δ is minimum, if denominator is maximum i.e. $\theta = \dfrac{\pi}{4}$,

$$\Delta_{\min} = 1 + \frac{\sqrt{2}}{1 - \dfrac{1}{\sqrt{2}}} = 1 + \frac{2}{\sqrt{2} - 1} = 1 + 2(\sqrt{2}+1) = 3 + 2\sqrt{2}$$

Stem Based Questions

Stem I

(Ex. Nos. 28 to 29)

It is known that $\lim_{x\to 0}\left(\dfrac{\sin x}{x}\right) = 1 = \lim_{x\to 0}\dfrac{\tan x}{x}$.

Based on this information, answer the following questions.

Example 28 $\lim_{x\to 0} \dfrac{1-\cos x}{x^2}$ *is ....*

Example 29 $\lim_{x\to 0} \dfrac{\sin^3 2x}{x\sin^2 3x}$ *is equal to ....*

Sol. (Ex. Nos. 28-29)

28. $\left(\dfrac{1}{2}\right)$ $\lim_{x\to 0} \dfrac{1-\cos x}{x^2} = \lim_{x\to 0}\left(\dfrac{2\sin^2\dfrac{x}{2}}{x^2}\right)$

$$= \lim_{x\to 0}\left(\frac{\sin\dfrac{x}{2}}{\dfrac{x}{2}}\right)^2 \cdot \frac{1}{2} = 1 \times \frac{1}{2} = \frac{1}{2}$$

29. $\left(\dfrac{8}{9}\right)$ $\lim_{x\to 0} \dfrac{\sin^3 2x}{x\sin^2 3x} = \lim_{x\to 0}\left[\dfrac{\left(\dfrac{\sin 2x}{2x}\right)^3 \cdot 8x^3}{x\left(\dfrac{\sin 3x}{3x}\right)^2 \cdot 9x^2}\right] = \dfrac{8}{9}$

Stem II

(Ex. Nos. 30 to 31)

If $\lim_{x\to 0}\left[\dfrac{\sin 2x + a\cos x + be^{x} + ce^{-x} + c\ln(1+x)}{x^{3}}\right] = L$

(finite real)

Example 30 *The value of $|L|$ is ....*

Example 31 *The value of $a+2b+4c$ equals ....*

Sol. (Ex. Nos. 30-31)

30. (1) $L = \lim_{x\to 0}\left[\dfrac{\sin 2x + a\cos x + be^{x} + ce^{-x} + c\ln(1+x)}{x^{3}}\right]$

$\because$ L is finite and real and denominator = 0

$\Rightarrow \quad \sin 0 + a\cos 0 + b + c + c(0) = 0$

$\Rightarrow \quad a + b + c = 0 \quad$ ...(i)

$$\therefore \quad L = \lim_{x\to 0}\frac{\sin 2x + a\cos x + be^{x} + (-a-b)e^{-x} + (-a-b)\ln(1+x)}{x^{3}}$$

$$= \lim_{x\to 0}\frac{\sin 2x + a(\cos x - e^{-x} - \ln(1+x)) + b(e^{x} - e^{-x} - \ln(1+x))}{x^{3}}$$

$\Rightarrow \quad 2 + a(0) + b(1) = 0 \Rightarrow b = -2$

$$\therefore \quad L = \lim_{x\to 0}\frac{2\cos 2x + a\left(-\sin x + e^{-x} - \dfrac{1}{1+x}\right) - 2\left(e^{x} + e^{-x} - \dfrac{1}{1+x}\right)}{3x^{2}}$$

[using L'Hospitals rule]

$$= \lim_{x\to 0}\frac{-4\sin 2x + a\left(-\cos x - e^{-x} + \dfrac{1}{(1+x)^{2}}\right) - 2\left[e^{x} - e^{-x} + \dfrac{1}{(1+x)^{2}}\right]}{6x}$$

$\Rightarrow \quad a(-1-1+1) - 2(1-1+1) = 0$ as denominator $6x \to 0$

$\Rightarrow \quad -a - 2 = 0 \Rightarrow a = -2$

$\therefore$ From Eq. (i), $c = +4$

$$\therefore \quad L = \lim_{x\to 0}\frac{-4\sin 2x - 2\left[-\cos x - e^{-x} + \dfrac{1}{(1+x)^{2}}\right] - 2\left[e^{x} - e^{-x} + \dfrac{1}{(1+x)^{2}}\right]}{6x}$$

$$= \lim_{x\to 0}\frac{-8\cos 2x - 2\left[\sin x + e^{-x} - \dfrac{2}{(1+x)^{3}}\right] - 2\left[e^{x} + e^{-x} - \dfrac{2}{(1+x)^{3}}\right]}{6}$$

$$= \frac{-8 - 2[0+1-2] - 2[1+1-2]}{6}$$

$$= \frac{-8+2-0}{6}$$

$$= \frac{-6}{6} = -1$$

Hence, $|L| = 1$

31. (10) $a + 2b + 4c = (-2) + 2(-2) + 4(4)$

$= 10$

Single Integer Answer Type Question

Example 32 *For a certain value of c,*

$\lim_{x\to -\infty}[(x^{5} + 7x^{4} + 2)^{c} - x] = \lambda$, is finite and non-zero.

The value of $3c + \lambda$ is ....

Sol. (2) We have, $\lim_{x\to -\infty}[(x^{5} + 7x^{4} + 2)^{c} - x]$

$$= \lim_{x\to -\infty}\left(x^{5c}\left(1 + \frac{7}{x} + \frac{2}{x^{5}}\right)^{c} - x\right)$$

$$= \lim_{x\to -\infty} x\left(x^{5c-1}\left(1 + \frac{7}{x} + \frac{2}{x^{5}}\right)^{c} - 1\right)$$

This will be of the form $\infty \times 0$ only, if

$5c - 1 = 0 \Rightarrow c = \dfrac{1}{5}$, substituting $c = \dfrac{1}{5}$, λ becomes

$\lambda = \lim_{x\to -\infty} x[(1+y)^{1/5} - 1]$, where $y = \dfrac{7}{x} + \dfrac{2}{x^{5}}$

$$= \lim_{x\to -\infty} x\left[1 + \frac{y}{5} + \ldots - 1\right] = \lim_{x\to -\infty} x\left(\frac{7}{x} + \frac{2}{x^{5}}\right)\cdot\frac{1}{5} = \frac{7}{5}$$

Hence, $c = \dfrac{1}{5}$ and $\lambda = \dfrac{7}{5} \Rightarrow 3c + \lambda = 2$

Example 33 *Consider the curve $y = \tan^{-1} x$ and a point $A\left(1, \dfrac{\pi}{4}\right)$ on it. If the variable point $P_i(x_i, y_i)$ moves on the curve for $i = 1, 2, 3, \ldots, n (n \in N)$ such that $y_r = \sum_{m=1}^{r} \tan^{-1}\left(\dfrac{1}{2m^{2}}\right)$ and $B(x, y)$ be the limiting position of variable point P_n as $n \to \infty$, the value of reciprocal of the slope of AB will be ....*

Sol. (2) Here, $y = \lim_{n\to\infty} y_n$

$$= \lim_{n\to\infty}\sum_{m=1}^{n}\tan^{-1}\left(\frac{1}{2m^{2}}\right)$$

$$= \lim_{n\to\infty}\sum_{m=1}^{n}\tan^{-1}\left(\frac{2}{1+(2m+1)(2m-1)}\right)$$

$$= \lim_{n\to\infty}\sum_{m=1}^{n}\tan^{-1}\left[\frac{(2m+1)-(2m-1)}{1+(2m+1)(2m-1)}\right]$$

$$= \lim_{n\to\infty}\sum_{m=1}^{n}(\tan^{-1}(2m+1)-\tan^{-1}(2m-1))$$

$$= \lim_{n\to\infty}(\tan^{-1}3-\tan^{-1}1)+(\tan^{-1}5-\tan^{-1}3)$$
$$+\ldots+(\tan^{-1}(2n+1)-\tan^{-1}(2n-1))$$

$$= \lim_{n\to\infty}(\tan^{-1}(2n+1)-\tan^{-1}(1))$$

$$=\frac{\pi}{2}-\frac{\pi}{4}=\frac{\pi}{4}$$

$\because B\to\left[1,\frac{\pi}{4}\right)$, i.e. coordinates of B approaches towards those of A.

Chord AB approaches to the tangent to $y=f(x)$ at A.

$\therefore$ Slope of $AB=\left(\frac{d}{dx}\tan^{-1}x\right)_{\text{at } x=1}=\left(\frac{1}{1+x^2}\right)_{\text{at } x=1}=\frac{1}{2}$

$\Rightarrow$ (Slope of $AB)^{-1}=2$

Example 34 *If* $\lim_{x\to 0}\int_0^x\frac{2t\,dt}{(e^x-1-x)\sqrt{\frac{2a}{3}-\frac{t}{2}+104}}=\frac{1}{19}$, *then* $\frac{a}{2010}$ *equals* ....

Sol. (1) Here, $\lim_{x\to 0}\dfrac{\int_0^x\frac{2t}{\sqrt{\frac{2a}{3}-\frac{t}{2}+104}}dt}{e^x-1-x}=\frac{1}{19}$

$$\Rightarrow \lim_{x\to 0}\frac{2x}{\sqrt{\frac{2a}{3}-\frac{x}{2}+104}\,(e^x-1)}=\frac{1}{19}$$

[using L' Hospital's rule]

$$\Rightarrow 2\lim_{x\to 0}\frac{1}{\sqrt{\frac{2a}{3}-\frac{x}{2}+104}}\cdot\lim_{x\to 0}\frac{x}{e^x-1}=\frac{1}{19}$$

$$\Rightarrow 2\cdot\frac{1}{\sqrt{\frac{2a}{3}+104}}\cdot 1=\frac{1}{19}$$

$$\Rightarrow \frac{2a}{3}+104=1444$$

$$\Rightarrow 2a=4020$$

$$\Rightarrow \frac{a}{2010}=1$$

Example 35 *If* $T_n=\frac{(2n+1)(2n^2+2n-1)}{(n-1)^2n^2(n+1)^2(n+2)^2}$, $n\in N, n\geq 2$.

If $k=\lim_{n\to\infty}\sum_{r=2}^{n}T$, *then* $27k$ *is equal to* ....

Sol. (3) $T_r=\frac{(2r+1)(2r^2+2r-1)}{(r^2-1)^2(r^2+2r)^2}=\frac{(2r+1)\cdot(2r^2+2r-1)}{(r^2-1)^2((r+1)^2-1)^2}$

$$\therefore T_r=\left[\frac{1}{(r^2-1)^2}-\frac{1}{((r+1)^2-1)^2}\right]$$

$$\therefore k=\lim_{n\to\infty}\sum\left(\left(\frac{1}{(2^2-1)^2}-\frac{1}{(3^2-1)^2}\right)+\left(\frac{1}{(3^2-1)^2}-\frac{1}{(4^2-1)^2}\right)+\ldots+\left(\frac{1}{(n^2-1)^2}-\frac{1}{((n+1)^2-1)^2}\right)\right)$$

$$\therefore k=\frac{1}{9}\Rightarrow 27k=3$$

JEE SCANNER

Example 36 Similar to PYQ Asked in JEE Main 2024

$\lim_{x\to 0}\frac{3\left(\sqrt{3}\sin\left(\frac{\pi}{6}+x\right)-\cos\left(\frac{\pi}{6}+x\right)\right)}{x\sqrt{3}\,(\sqrt{3}\cos x-\sin x)}$ *is* $\frac{m}{n}$, *where* m *and* n *are coprime, then the value of* $m+n$ *is* ....

Sol. (3) $\lim_{x\to 0}\frac{6\left[\frac{\sqrt{3}}{2}\sin\left(\frac{\pi}{6}+x\right)-\frac{1}{2}\cos\left(\frac{\pi}{6}+x\right)\right]}{x\sqrt{3}\,[\sqrt{3}\cos x-\sin x]}$

$$=\lim_{x\to 0}\frac{6\left[\cos\frac{\pi}{6}\sin\left(\frac{\pi}{6}+x\right)-\sin\frac{\pi}{6}\cos\left(\frac{\pi}{6}+x\right)\right]}{\sqrt{3}x\,[\sqrt{3}\cos x-\sin x]}$$

$$=\lim_{x\to 0}\frac{6\sin x}{\sqrt{3}x\,[\sqrt{3}\cos x-\sin x]}$$

$$=\lim_{x\to 0}\frac{\sin x}{x}\cdot\lim_{x\to 0}\frac{6}{\sqrt{3}\,(\sqrt{3}\cos x-\sin x)}=\frac{6}{3}=\frac{2}{1}=\frac{m}{n}\text{ (given)}$$

$\therefore m=2$ and $n=1$

$\therefore m+n=3$

Skill Builder

$\lim_{x\to 0}\frac{5\left(\sqrt{3}\sin\left(\frac{\pi}{6}+x\right)-\cos\left(\frac{\pi}{6}+x\right)\right)}{x\sqrt{3}\,(\sqrt{3}\cos x-\sin x)}$ is $\frac{m}{n}$, where m and n are coprime, then the value of $m+n$ is ....

For Sol.

Example 37 *Let*

$f(x)=\cos 2x\cdot\cos 4x\cdot\cos 6x\cdot\cos 8x\cdot\cos 10x$, *then* $\lim_{x\to 0}\frac{1-(f(x))^3}{55\sin^2 x}$ *equals* ....

Sol. (6) $\lim_{x\to 0}\frac{1-(f(x))^3}{55\sin^2 x}$

$$=\lim_{x\to 0}\frac{1-(f(x))^3}{55x^2}$$

$$=\lim_{x\to 0}\frac{-3[f(x)]^2\cdot f'(x)}{110x}$$

[using L'Hospital rule]

$$= \lim_{x\to 0} \frac{-6f(x)\cdot[f'(x)]^2 - 3[f(x)]^2 f''(x)}{110}$$

$$= \frac{-6f(0)\cdot[f'(0)]^2 - 3f(0)^2\cdot f''(0)}{110}$$

$$f(x) = \cos 2x \cdot \cos 4x \cdot \cos 6x \cos 8x \cos 10x$$

$$f(0) = 1$$

$$f'(0) = 0$$

$$f''(0) = -(2^2 + 4^2 + 6^2 + 8^2 + 10^2)$$

$$= -(4 + 16 + 36 + 64 + 100) = -220$$

$$\therefore \text{ Required limit} = \frac{-6\times 1\times 0 - 3\times 1\times -220}{110} = 3\times 2 = 6$$

Example 38 $\lim_{n\to\infty} \sin\left(\frac{1}{n^2}\right) + \sin\left(\frac{2}{n^2}\right) + \ldots + \sin\left(\frac{n}{n^2}\right)$ *is t, then 2t is equal to ....*

> **Decoding the Question**
> Use Sandwitch theorem,
> If a, b and c are three functions such that $a(x) \le b(x) \le c(x)$ for all x in some interval containing the point $x = \lambda$ and $\lim_{x\to\lambda} a(x) = \lim_{x\to\lambda} c(x) = L$. Then, $\lim_{x\to\lambda} b(x) = L$.

Sol. (1) Let $\sin\left(\frac{1}{n^2}\right) + \sin\left(\frac{2}{n^2}\right) + \ldots + \sin\left(\frac{n}{n^2}\right)$ be S_n

$$\text{So, } \Sigma\frac{1}{n^2} - \frac{1}{6}\Sigma\frac{n^3}{n^6} < S_n < \frac{1}{n^2} + \frac{2}{n^2} + \ldots + \frac{n}{n^2}$$

$$\therefore \lim_{x\to\infty} S_n = \frac{1}{2} = t$$

Example 39 $\lim_{n\to\infty} \dfrac{1 + \frac{1}{2} + \frac{1}{3} + \ldots + \frac{1}{n^7}}{\ln n}$ *is equal to ....*

Sol. (7) $1 + \frac{1}{2} + \frac{1}{3} + \ldots + \frac{1}{n^7} > \int_1^{n^7} \frac{dx}{x} > \frac{1}{2} + \frac{1}{3} + \ldots + \frac{1}{n^7}$

$$\ln^7 - 1 > 1 + \frac{1}{2} + \frac{1}{3} + \ldots + \frac{1}{n^3} > \ln n^7$$

$$\text{So, } \lim_{n\to\infty} \frac{1 + \frac{1}{2} + \frac{1}{3} + \ldots + \frac{1}{n^7}}{\ln n} = 7$$

Example 40 *Let* $P(x) = a_1 x + a_2 x^2 + a_3 x^3 + \ldots + a_{100} x^{100}$, *where* $a_1 = 2$ *and* $a_i \in R, \forall i = 2, 3, 4, \ldots, 100$, *then the value of* $\lim_{x\to 0} \sqrt[50]{1 + P(x)} - \sqrt[100]{1 + P(x)}$ *is equal to L. The value of 250L is ....*

Sol. (5) Using binomial expansion for any index

$$L = \lim_{x\to 0} \frac{\left(1 + \frac{1}{50}P(x) + \ldots\right) - \left(1 + \frac{1}{100}P(x) + \ldots\right)}{x}$$

$$= \frac{1}{50}\cdot a_1 - \frac{1}{100}a_1$$

$$= a_1\left(\frac{1}{50} - \frac{1}{100}\right) = \frac{a_1}{100} = \frac{1}{50} \qquad [\because a_1 = 2]$$

Example 41 *If* $\lim_{n\to\infty}\left(\dfrac{2^{\frac{1}{n}}}{n+1} + \dfrac{2^{\frac{2}{n}}}{n + \frac{1}{2}} + \ldots + \dfrac{2^{\frac{n}{n}}}{n + \frac{1}{n}}\right) = L$, *then the value of* $e^{\frac{1}{L}}$ *is equal to ....*

Sol. (2) $L = \lim_{n\to\infty} \frac{1}{n}\sum_{r=1}^{n} \dfrac{2^{\frac{r}{n}}}{1 + \frac{1}{m}}$

$$\because \quad \frac{2^{\frac{r}{n}}}{1 + \frac{1}{m}} = \frac{2^{\left(\frac{r-1}{n}\right)}2^{\frac{1}{n}}}{1 + \frac{1}{m}} = \frac{2^{\left(\frac{r-1}{n}\right)}e^{\frac{\ln 2}{n}}}{1 + \frac{1}{m}} = \alpha$$

For $r \ge 2$,

$$2^{\frac{r}{n}} > \alpha > 2^{\frac{r-1}{n}}\left(\frac{1 + \frac{\ln 2}{n}}{1 + \frac{1}{m}}\right) > 2^{\frac{r-1}{n}} \qquad [\because e^x > 1 + x]$$

$$\text{So, } \lim_{n\to\infty} \frac{2^{\frac{1}{n}} + 2^{\frac{2}{n}} + \ldots + 2^{\frac{n-1}{n}}}{n} < L < \lim_{n\to\infty} \frac{2^{\frac{2}{n}} + 2^{\frac{3}{n}} + \ldots + 2^{\frac{n}{n}}}{n}$$

$$\text{Hence, } L = \int_0^1 2^x\,dx = \frac{1}{\ln 2}$$

Example 42 *Let* $f:(0, \infty) \to (0, \infty)$ *be a differentiable function and* $g(x)$ *is the anti-derivative of* $f(x)$ *such that* $2(g(x) - f(x)) = (f(x))^2\ \forall\, x \in (0, \infty)$. *Then, the value of* $\lim_{x\to\infty} \frac{f(x)}{x}$ *is ....*

Sol. (1) $2(g'(x) - f'(x)) = 2f(x)f'(x) \qquad [\because g'(x) = f(x)]$

$$\Rightarrow \quad f'(x) = \frac{f(x)}{1 + f(x)}$$

$$\Rightarrow \quad f(x) + \ln f(x) = x + c$$

$$\Rightarrow \quad \frac{f(x)}{x} + \frac{\ln f(x)}{x} = 1 + \frac{c}{x} \Rightarrow \lim_{x\to\infty} \frac{f(x)}{x} = 1$$

Example 43 *Let* $f:(0, \infty) \to (0, \infty)$ *be a function differentiable at* $x = 3$ *and satisfying* $f(3) = 3f'(3)$ *if the value of* $\lim_{x\to\infty}\left(\dfrac{f\left(3 + \frac{3}{x}\right)}{f(3)}\right)^x$ *is L, then* $[L]$ *is equal to ....*

(where $[k]$ *represents greatest integer function).*

Sol. (2) $x = \frac{1}{t}$

$$\lim_{x\to\infty}\left(\frac{f\left(3 + \frac{3}{x}\right)}{f(3)}\right)^x = \lim_{t\to 0}\left(\frac{f(3 + 3t)}{f(3)}\right)^{1/t}$$

$$= e^{\lim_{t\to 0}\left(\frac{f(3+3t)-f(3)}{tf(3)}\right)} \text{ [using L-Hospital's rule]}$$

$$= e^{\lim_{t\to 0}\frac{3f(3+3t)}{f(3)}} = e$$

$$\Rightarrow \quad L = e \Rightarrow [L] = 2$$

Example 44 *If* $\lim_{x\to 1}(1+ax+bx^2)^{\frac{c}{(x-1)}} = e^3$, *then the value of bc is ....*

Sol. (c) $$\lim_{x\to 1}(1+ax+bx^2)^{\frac{c}{(x-1)}} = e^3$$

or $$e^{\lim_{x\to 1}(1+ax+bx^2-1)\frac{c}{(x-1)}} = e^3$$

or $$e^{\lim_{x\to 1}\frac{c(ax+bx^2)}{x-1}} = e^3$$

or $$\lim_{x\to 1}\frac{c(ax+bx^2)}{x-1} = 3$$

or $$\lim_{h\to 0}\frac{c(a(1+h)+b(1+h)^2)}{1+h-1} = 3$$

or $$\lim_{h\to 0}\frac{(ca+b)+(ac+2b)h+bh^2}{h} = 3$$

or $ca+b=0$ and $ac+2b=3$

or $b=3$ and $ac=-3$

Also, the form must be 1^∞ for which $a+b=0$

i.e. $a=-3$ and $c=1$.

Numerical Value Type Questions

Example 45 *The value of* $\lim_{n\to\infty}\sin((2+\sqrt{3})^n\pi), n\in N$ *is equal to P, then P + 50 is ....*

Sol. (50) $(2+\sqrt{3})^n + (2-\sqrt{3})^n = 2m, m\in I^+$

$$\therefore \lim_{n\to\infty}\sin((2+\sqrt{3})^n\pi) = \lim_{n\to\infty}\sin((2m-(2-\sqrt{3})^n)\pi)$$

$$= \lim_{n\to\infty}\sin(2m\pi-(2-\sqrt{3})^n\pi)$$

$$= -\lim_{n\to\infty}\sin((2-\sqrt{3})^n\pi)$$

$$= -\lim_{n\to\infty}\sin\left(\frac{\pi}{(2+\sqrt{3})^n}\right) = 0 = P$$

$\therefore P + 50 = 50$

Example 46 *If*

$$\lim_{x\to\infty}\frac{a(2x^3-x^2)+b(x^3+5x^2-1)-c(3x^3+x^2)}{a(5x^4-x)-bx^4+c(4x^4+1)+2x^2+5x} = 1, \text{ then}$$

the value of (a + b + c) can be expressed in the lowest form as $\frac{p}{q}$. *The value of (p + q) is ....*

Sol. (167) $$\lim_{x\to\infty}\frac{x^3+x^2(5b-a-c)-b}{x^4+2x^2+x(5-a)+c} = 1$$

$$\Rightarrow \left.\begin{aligned} 2a+b-3c&=0 \quad \text{...(i)}\\ 5a-b+4c&=0 \quad \text{...(ii)}\\ 5b-a-c&=2 \quad \text{...(iii)}\end{aligned}\right\}$$

On adding Eqs. (i) and (ii), we get

$$7a+c=0 \Rightarrow c=-7a$$

$$2a+b+21a=0 \Rightarrow b=-23a$$

$$5(-23a)-a+7a=2 \Rightarrow -109a=2 \Rightarrow a=\frac{-2}{109}$$

$$a+b+c = a-23a-7a = -29a$$

$$a+b+c = 29\times\frac{2}{109} = \frac{58}{109}$$

$$p+q = 167$$

Example 47 $\lim_{x\to\infty}x^2\left(\sqrt{\frac{x+2}{x}}-\sqrt[3]{\frac{x+3}{x}}\right) = L$, *then 100 L is equal to ....*

Sol. (50) $$\lim_{x\to\infty}x^2\left[\left(1+\frac{2}{x}\right)^{1/2}-\left(1+\frac{3}{x}\right)^{1/3}\right]$$

$$\lim_{x\to\infty}x^2\left[\left(1+\frac{1}{2}\left(\frac{2}{x}\right)+\frac{\frac{1}{2}\left(\frac{1}{2}-1\right)}{2!}\left(\frac{2}{x}\right)^2\ldots\right)-\left(1+\frac{1}{3}\left(\frac{3}{x}\right)+\frac{\frac{1}{3}\left(\frac{1}{3}-1\right)}{2!}\left(\frac{3}{x}\right)^2-\right)\right]$$

$$\lim_{x\to\infty}x^2\left[\frac{-1}{8}\cdot\frac{4}{x^2}+\frac{1}{x^2}\right]$$

$$\lim_{x\to\infty}x^2\left[\frac{1}{2x^2}\right] = \frac{1}{2} = L$$

$$\therefore \quad 100L = 50$$

Example 48 *Let* $0\le\beta_r\le 1$ *and* $\sum_{r=1}^{k}\cos^{-1}\beta_r = \frac{k\pi}{2}$ *for any* $k\ge 1$ *and* $A = \sum_{r=1}^{k}(\beta_r)^r$, *then* $\lim_{x\to A}498\cdot\frac{(1+x^2)^{1/3}-(1-2x)^{1/4}}{x+x^2}$ *is equal to λ, where* $\frac{5\lambda}{83}$ *is equal to ....*

Sol. (15) Since, maximum value of $\cos^{-1}x$ in $[0, 1] = \frac{\pi}{2}$,

$$\sum_{r=1}^{k}\cos^{-1}\beta_r = \frac{k\pi}{2}$$

is possible if and only if each

$$\cos^{-1}\beta_r = \frac{\pi}{2} \Leftrightarrow \beta_r = 0$$

$$A = \sum_{r=1}^{k}(\beta_r)^r = 0$$

Thus, $\lim_{x\to 0} \frac{(1+x^2)^{1/3}-(1-2x)^{1/4}}{x+x^2}$

$$= \lim_{x\to 0} \frac{\left(1+\frac{x^2}{3}+\ldots\right)-\left(1-\frac{x}{2}+\ldots\right)}{x(1+x)}$$

$$= \lim_{x\to 0} \frac{\frac{1}{2}+\frac{x}{3}+x^n \text{ containing terms}}{1+x} = \frac{1}{2}$$

Thus, the required limit is 249 i.e. $\lambda = 249$

$\therefore \quad \frac{5\lambda}{83} = \frac{1245}{83} = 15$

Example 49 *If* $\lim_{x\to 1^-} \prod_{n=0}^{\infty} \left(\frac{1+x^{n+1}}{1+x^n}\right)^{x^n} = l$, *then* $\left[\frac{1}{l}\right]$ *is equal to m, then m + 100 is ....*

Sol. (100) $\frac{1+x^{n+1}}{1+x^n} = 1 + \frac{x^n(x-1)}{1+x^n}$

So, $\ln\left(\prod_{n=0}^{N}\left(1+\frac{x^n(x-1)}{1+x^n}\right)^{x^n}\right) = \sum_{n=0}^{N} x^n \ln\left(1+\frac{x^n(x-1)}{1+x^n}\right)$

So, $(x-1)\left(\frac{1}{1-x^2}-\frac{1}{1-x^3}+\ldots+\frac{1}{1-x^{2k}}\right) \le \sum_{n=0}^{\infty} x^n\left(\frac{x^n(x-1)}{1+x^n}\right)$

$$\le (x-1)\left(\frac{1}{1-x^2}-\frac{1}{1-x^3}+\ldots-\frac{1}{1-x^{2k+1}}\right)$$

So, limit $= \frac{2}{e} = l$

$\therefore \quad \left[\frac{1}{l}\right] = \left[\frac{e}{2}\right] = 0 = m$

$\therefore \quad m + 100 = 100$

Example 50 $312 \lim_{n\to\infty} (\sqrt[3]{n^2 - n^3} + n)$ *is equal to ....*

Sol. (104) $312 \lim_{n\to\infty} n\left(1+\left(\frac{1}{n}-1\right)^{1/3}\right)$

$$= 312 \lim_{n\to\infty} n\left(1-\left(1-\frac{1}{n}\right)^{1/3}\right)$$

$$= 312 \lim_{n\to\infty} n\left(1-\left(1-\frac{1}{3n}-\frac{2}{9n^2}-\ldots\right)\right)$$

$$= 312\left(\frac{1}{3}\right) = 104$$

Example 51 *If* $\lim_{n\to\infty} \frac{\sqrt[n^2]{1!\ldots n!}}{n^\alpha} = \beta$, *where* β *is a non-zero finite real number, then* $\frac{\left(\frac{\alpha}{2}-\ln\beta\right)}{10}$ *is equal to ....*

Sol. (0.1) $\because \ln\beta = \lim_{n\to\infty} \frac{1}{n^2}$

$[\ln 1 + (\ln 1 + \ln 2) + (\ln 1 + \ln 2 + \ln 3) + \ldots] - \alpha \ln n$

$$= \lim_{n\to\infty} \frac{n\ln\frac{1}{n}+(n-1)\ln\frac{2}{n}+\ldots+\ln\frac{n}{n}+\frac{n(n+1)}{2}\ln n}{n^2} - \alpha\ln n$$

$$= \lim_{n\to\infty} \frac{n+1-2n\alpha}{2n}\ln n + \frac{1}{n}\sum_{r=1}^{n}\frac{n+1-r}{n}\ln\frac{r}{n}$$

$\Rightarrow \quad \alpha = \frac{1}{2}$

and $\quad \ln\beta = \int_0^1 (1-x)\ln x\,dx = -\frac{3}{4}$

Example 52 *If* $f(x) = \frac{\sum_{r=0}^{n}(r+1)\cdot {}^nC_r x^r}{\sum_{r=0}^{n} r^2\,{}^nC_r x^{r-1}}$, *then the value of* $\lim_{n\to\infty}\frac{d}{dx}\left(\frac{n^3 f(x)}{1+x}\right)$ *at* $x = 1$ *is P, then number of non-negative integral solution of the equation* $\alpha+\beta+\gamma = 50P$ *is ....*

Sol. (1326) $\sum_{r=0}^{n}(r+1)\,{}^nC_r x^r = \sum_{r=0}^{n} r \times \frac{n}{r}\,{}^{n-1}C_{r-1} x \cdot x^{r-1} + \sum_{r=0}^{n} {}^nC_r x^r$

$$= (1+x)^{n-1} nx + (1+x)^n$$
$$= (1+x)^{n-1}(1+(n+1)x)$$

$$\sum_{r=1}^{n} r^2\,{}^nC_r x^{r-1} = \sum_{r=1}^{n} r^2 \times \frac{n}{r} \times {}^{n-1}C_{r-1} x^{r-1}$$

$$= n\sum_{r=1}^{n}(r-1+1)^{n-1}C_{r-1}x^{r-1}$$

$$= n\sum_{r=1}^{n}(r\ \ 1) \times \frac{n-1}{r-1}\,{}^{n-2}C_{r-2}x^{r-2} + n\sum_{r=0}^{n}{}^{n-1}C_{r-1}x^{r-1}$$

$$= n(n-1)\times(1+x)^{n-2} + n(1+x)^{n-1}$$
$$= n(1+x)^{n-2}[nx - x + 1 + x]$$
$$= n(1+x)^{n-2}(1+nx)$$

$$\frac{f(x)}{1+x} = \frac{1+(n+1)x}{n(1+nx)}$$

$$\frac{d}{dx}\left(\frac{f(x)}{1+x}\right) \text{at } (x=1) = \frac{1}{n(n+1)^2}$$

$$\lim_{n\to\infty}\frac{d}{dx}\left(\frac{n^3 f(x)}{1+x}\right) = \lim_{n\to\infty}\frac{n^2}{n^2+2n+1} = 1$$

$\therefore \quad \alpha+\beta+\gamma = 50(1)$

$\quad \alpha+\beta+\gamma = 50, \alpha, \beta, \gamma \ge 0$

$\therefore$ Number of solution $= {}^{50+3-1}C_{3-1} = {}^{52}C_2$

$$= \frac{52\times 51}{2} = 26\times 51 = 1326$$

Matching Type Questions

Example 53 *Match the following columns.*

Column I	Column II
(A) $\lim_{x\to\infty}\frac{(1+a^3)+8e^{1/x}}{2+(1-b^3)e^{1/x}}=2$, then (a^3, b^3) lie on line	(p) $x-y+3=0$
(B) If $\lim_{x\to\infty}\sqrt{x^2+x+1}-(ax+b)=0$, then (a, b); $a>0$ lies on the line	(q) $3x+4y-5=0$
(C) If $\lim_{x\to\infty}\sqrt{x^4+x^2-1}-ax^2+b=0$, $a>0$, then (a, b) lies on the line	(r) $x+6y+2=0$
(D) If $\lim_{x\to 0}\frac{\int_0^x\left(\frac{t^2}{\sqrt{b+t}}\right)dt}{ax-\sin x}=1$; $(b\neq 0)$, then (a, b) lies on the line	(s) $x+2y+3=0$

Sol. (A) → (s), (B) → (q), (C) → (r), (D) → (p)

(A) $\lim_{x\to\infty}\frac{(1+a^3)+8e^{1/x}}{2+(1-b^3)e^{1/x}}=2$

As $x\to\infty, \frac{1}{x}\to 0 \Rightarrow e^{1/x}\to e^0\to 1$

$$\Rightarrow \frac{(1+a^2)+8}{2+(1-b^3)}=2$$

$$\Rightarrow \frac{a^3-9}{3-b^3}=2$$

$$\Rightarrow a^3+9=6-2b^3 \Rightarrow a^3+2b^3+3=0$$

$\Rightarrow$ $(a^3\cdot b^3)$ satisfy the line $x+2y+3=0$

(B) $$\lim_{x\to\infty}\sqrt{x^2+x+1}-(ax+b)=0$$

$$\Rightarrow \lim_{x\to\infty}\frac{(x^2+x+1)-(ax+b)^2}{\sqrt{x^2+x+1}+(ax+b)}=0$$

$$\Rightarrow \lim_{x\to\infty}\frac{x^2(1-a^2)+x(1-2ab)+(1-b^2)}{\sqrt{x^2+x+1}+(ax+b)}=0$$

$$\Rightarrow a^2-1=0$$

$$\Rightarrow a=\pm 1 \text{ but } a>0 \Rightarrow a=1$$

$$\Rightarrow \lim_{x\to\infty}\frac{x(1-2b)+(1-b^2)}{\sqrt{x^2+x+1}+(x+b)}=0$$

$$\Rightarrow \lim_{x\to\infty}\frac{(1-2b)+\left(\frac{1-b^2}{x}\right)}{\sqrt{1+\frac{1}{x}+\frac{1}{x^2}}+\left(1+\frac{b}{x}\right)}=0$$

$$\Rightarrow \frac{1-2b}{1+1}=0 \Rightarrow b=\frac{1}{2}$$

$\therefore (a, b)\equiv\left(1, \frac{1}{2}\right)$ which lies on line $3x+4y-5=0$

(C) $$\lim_{x\to\infty}\sqrt{x^4+x^2-1}-ax^2+b=0$$

$$\Rightarrow \lim_{x\to\infty}\frac{x^4+x^2-1-(ax^2-b)^2}{\sqrt{x^4+x^2-1}+(ax^2-b)}=0$$

$$\Rightarrow \lim_{x\to\infty}\frac{x^4(1-a^2)+x^2(1+2ab)+(-1-b^2)}{\sqrt{x^4+x^2-1}+(ax^2-b)}=0$$

$$\Rightarrow (1-a^2)=0$$

$$\Rightarrow a=\pm 1; \text{ but } a>0 \Rightarrow a=1$$

$$\Rightarrow \lim_{x\to\infty}\frac{(1+2b)-\left(\frac{1+b^2}{x^2}\right)}{\sqrt{1+\frac{1}{x^2}+\frac{1}{x^4}}+\left(1-\frac{b}{x^2}\right)}=0$$

$$\Rightarrow \frac{1+2b}{2}=0$$

$$\Rightarrow b=-\frac{1}{2}$$

$\Rightarrow (a, b)\equiv\left(1, -\frac{1}{2}\right)$ which lies on line $x+6y+2=0$.

(D) $$\lim_{x\to 0}\frac{\int_0^x\left(\frac{t^2}{\sqrt{b+t}}\right)dt}{ax-\sin x}=1,$$

$$\Rightarrow \lim_{x\to 0}\frac{\int_0^x\frac{t^2}{\sqrt{b+t}}dt}{ax-\sin x}=1 \qquad \left[\text{limit is of } \frac{0}{0} \text{ form}\right]$$

$$\Rightarrow \lim_{x\to 0}\frac{\frac{d}{dx}\int_0^x\frac{t^2}{\sqrt{b+t}}dt}{(a-\cos x)}=1 \qquad \text{[using L-Hospital's rule]}$$

$$\Rightarrow \lim_{x\to 0}\frac{\frac{x^2}{\sqrt{b+x}}(1)-0}{a-\cos x}=1 \qquad \text{[using Leibinitz's rule]}$$

$$\Rightarrow \lim_{x\to 0}\frac{x^3}{\sqrt{b+x}\,(a-\cos x)}=1$$

$$\Rightarrow \sqrt{b}(a-1)=0 \Rightarrow a=1 \qquad [\because b\neq 0]$$

$$\Rightarrow \lim_{x\to 0}\frac{x^2}{\sqrt{b+x}(1-\cos x)}=1$$

$$\Rightarrow \lim_{x\to 0}\frac{x^2}{\sqrt{b+x}(2\sin^2 x/2)}=1$$

$$\Rightarrow \lim_{x\to 0}\frac{4\left(\frac{x}{2}\right)^2}{2\sqrt{b+x}\sin^2\frac{x}{2}}=1$$

$$\Rightarrow \frac{1}{2\sqrt{b}}(4)(1)^2=1$$

$$\Rightarrow \sqrt{b}=2 \Rightarrow b=4$$

Thus, $a=1$ and $b=4$

$\therefore (a, b)\equiv(1, 4)$ which satisfy the line $x-y+3=0$

Example 54 *Match the following columns.*

Column I		Column II
(A) $\lim_{x\to 0}\left(\left[200\dfrac{\tan x}{x}\right]+\left[200\dfrac{\sin x}{x}\right]\right)$ equals	(p)	1
(B) $\lim_{x\to 0}\left\{100\dfrac{\tan x}{x}\right\}+\left\{100\dfrac{\sin x}{x}\right\}$ equals	(q)	399
(C) $\lim_{x\to 0}\left(100\left[\dfrac{\sin x}{x}\right]+200\left[\dfrac{x}{\tan^{-1}}\right]\right)$ equals	(r)	199
(D) $\lim_{x\to 0}\left\{\dfrac{\sin x^{-1}}{x}\right\}+\left[200\dfrac{\tan^{-1}x}{x}\right]$	(s)	200

Here, [.] and {x} are greatest integer function and fraction part functions, respectively.

Sol. (A) → (q), (B) → (p), (C) → (s), (D) → (r)

(A) $\dfrac{\tan x}{x}>1$ and $\dfrac{\tan x}{x}\to 1$ for $x\to 0$

$$\Rightarrow \frac{\tan x}{x}=1+h,\ h\to 0$$

$$\Rightarrow 200\frac{\tan x}{x}=200+200h;\ h\to 0^+$$

$$\Rightarrow \left[200\frac{\tan}{x}\right]=200$$

Also, $\dfrac{\sin x}{x}<1$ and $\dfrac{\sin x}{x}\to 1$ for $x\to 0$

$$\Rightarrow \frac{\sin x}{x}=1-h,\ h\to 0^+$$

$$\Rightarrow 200\left(\frac{\sin x}{x}\right)=200-200h,\ h\to 0^+$$

$$\Rightarrow \left[200\frac{\sin x}{x}\right]=199$$

$$\therefore \lim_{x\to 0}\left(\left[200\frac{\tan x}{x}\right]+\left[200\frac{\sin x}{x}\right]\right)=399$$

(B) $100\dfrac{\tan x}{x}=100(1+h)=100+100h;\ h\to 0^+$

$$\therefore \left\{100\frac{\tan x}{x}\right\}=100,\ h\to 0 \text{ as } h\to 0^+$$

Also, $\left\{100\dfrac{\sin x}{x}\right\}=\{100(1-h)\}=\{100-100h\}$

$$=\{99+(1-100h)\}=1-100h\to 1 \text{ as } h\to 0^+$$

$$\therefore \lim_{x\to 0}\left\{100\frac{\tan x}{x}\right\}+\left\{100\frac{\sin x}{x}\right\}=0+1=1$$

(C) $\dfrac{\sin x}{x}=1-h;\ h\to 0^+$ as $x\to 0^+$

$$\Rightarrow \left[\frac{\sin x}{x}\right]=[1-h]=0 \text{ and } \frac{x}{\tan^{-1}x}>1 \text{ for } x\to 0$$

$$\Rightarrow \frac{x}{\tan^{-1}x}=1+h;\ h\to 0^+ \Rightarrow \left[\frac{x}{\tan^{-1}x}\right]=1$$

$$\therefore \lim_{x\to 0}\left(100\left[\frac{\sin x}{x}\right]+200\left[\frac{x}{\tan^{-1}x}\right]\right)=0+200=200$$

(D) As, $x\to 0$, $\dfrac{\sin^{-1}x}{x}>1$ and $\dfrac{\sin^{-1}x}{x}\to 1$ as $x\to 0$

$$\Rightarrow \frac{\sin^{-1}x}{x}=1+h;\ h\to 0^+$$

$$\therefore \left\{\frac{\sin^{-1}x}{x}\right\}=h\to 0 \text{ as } h\to 0^+$$

Also, $\dfrac{\tan^{-1}x}{x}<1$ and $\dfrac{\tan^{-1}x}{x}\to 1$ as $x\to 0$

$$\Rightarrow 200\frac{\tan^{-1}x}{x}=200(1-h);\ h\to 0^+$$

$$\Rightarrow \left[200\frac{\tan^{-1}x}{x}\right]=[200-200h]=199$$

$$\therefore \lim_{x\to 0}\left\{\frac{\sin^{-1}x}{x}\right\}+\left[200\frac{\tan^{-1}x}{x}\right]=0+199=199$$

EXERCISE 1

JEE Main Pattern

Single Option Correct Type Questions

1. Consider the function $f(x)=\begin{bmatrix}1-x & , & 0\le x\le 1\\ x+2 & , & 1<x<2.\\ 4-x & , & 2\le x\le 4\end{bmatrix}$

Let $\lim_{x\to 1} f(f(x))=l$ and $\lim_{x\to 2} f(f(x))=m$, then which one of the following hold good?

(a) l exists but m does not (b) m exists but l does not
(c) Both l and m exist (d) Neither l nor m exist

2. $\lim_{x\to 0}\dfrac{\sin(\pi\cos^2(\tan(\sin x)))}{x^2}$ is equal to

(a) π (b) $\dfrac{\pi}{4}$
(c) $\dfrac{\pi}{2}$ (d) None of these

3. $\lim_{x\to 0}\left[\dfrac{\sin(\text{sgn}(x))}{(\text{sgn}(x))}\right]$, where $[\cdot]$ denotes the greatest integer function, is equal to

(a) 0 (b) 1
(c) -1 (d) Does not exist

4. Let $\alpha(a)$ and $\beta(a)$ be the roots of the equation, $(\sqrt[3]{1+a}-1)x^2+(\sqrt{1+a}-1)x-(\sqrt[6]{1+a}-1)=0$, where $a>-1$, then $\lim_{a\to 0^+}\alpha(a)$ and $\lim_{a\to 0^+}\beta(a)$ are

(a) $-\dfrac{5}{2}$ and 1 (b) $-\dfrac{1}{2}$ and -1
(c) $-\dfrac{7}{2}$ and 2 (d) $-\dfrac{9}{2}$ and 3

5. Among (i) $\lim_{x\to\infty}\sec^{-1}\left(\dfrac{x}{\sin x}\right)$ and (ii) $\lim_{x\to\infty}\sec^{-1}\left(\dfrac{\sin x}{x}\right)$

(a) (i) exist and (ii) does not exist
(b) (i) does not exist and (ii) exists
(c) both (i) and (ii) exist
(d) neither (i) nor (ii) exists

6. For $n\in N$, let $f_n(x)=\tan\dfrac{x}{2}(1+\sec x)(1+\sec 2x)$ $(1+\sec 4x)\dots(1+\sec 2^n x)$. Then, $\lim_{x\to 0}\dfrac{f_n(x)}{2x}$ is

(a) 0 (b) 2^n
(c) 2^{n-1} (d) 2^{n+1}

7. $\lim_{x\to 0}\dfrac{\cos(\tan x)-\cos x}{x^4}$ is equal to

(a) $\dfrac{1}{6}$ (b) $\dfrac{1}{3}$ (c) $\dfrac{1}{2}$ (d) 1

8. Let $S_n=1+2+3+\dots+n$ and $P_n=\dfrac{S_2}{S_2-1}\cdot\dfrac{S_3}{S_3-1}\cdot\dfrac{S_4}{S_4-1}\dots\dfrac{S_n}{S_n-1}$ where $n\in N,(n\ge 2)$.

Then, $\lim_{n\to\infty}P_n$ is equal to

(a) 4 (b) 0 (c) 2 (d) 3

9. The value of $\lim_{n\to\infty}\left(\sum_{r=1}^{n}\left(\dfrac{2r+5}{r^2+r}\right)\left(\dfrac{3}{5}\right)^{r+1}\right)$ is equal to

(a) 0 (b) $\dfrac{9}{5}$
(c) $\dfrac{3}{5}$ (d) None of these

10. $\lim_{z\to\infty}\dfrac{\int_{1/2}^{z}[\cot^{-1}x]dx}{\int_{1/2}^{z}\left[1+\dfrac{1}{x}\right]dx}$, where $[\cdot]$ denotes the greatest integer function, equals

(a) 0 (b) 1
(c) cot 1 (d) not defined

11. Let $f:(1,\infty)\to(0,\infty)$ be a continuous decreasing function with $\lim_{x\to\infty}\dfrac{f(4x)}{f(8x)}=1$. Then, $\lim_{x\to\infty}\dfrac{f(6x)}{f(8x)}$ is equal to

(a) $\dfrac{4}{8}$ (b) $\dfrac{4}{6}$ (c) $\dfrac{6}{8}$ (d) 1

12. If $\lim_{x\to 0}\dfrac{x^n-\sin x^n}{x-\sin^n x}$ is non-zero and finite, then n must be equal to

(a) 4 (b) 1 (c) 2 (d) 3

13. If $\lim_{x\to 0}(1+x\ln(1+b^2))^{1/x}=2b\sin^2\theta$, $b>0$ and $\theta\in[-\pi,\pi]$, then θ is

(a) $\pm\dfrac{\pi}{4}$ (b) $\pm\dfrac{\pi}{3}$
(c) $\pm\dfrac{\pi}{6}$ (d) $\pm\dfrac{\pi}{2}$

14. If $\lim_{x\to 0}\dfrac{1-\sqrt{\cos 2x}\cdot\sqrt[3]{\cos 3x}\cdot\sqrt[4]{\cos 4x}\ldots\sqrt[n]{\cos nx}}{x^2}$ has the value equal to 10, the value of n is

(a) 6 (b) 7 (c) 8 (d) 9

15. Let $f(x)$ be a real valued function defined for all $x\ge 1$, satisfying $f(1)=1$ and $f'(x)=\dfrac{1}{x^2+(f(x))}$, then $\lim_{x\to\infty} f(x)$

(a) does not exist

(b) exists and less than $\dfrac{\pi}{4}$

(c) exists and less than $1+\dfrac{\pi}{4}$

(d) exists and equal to 0

16. The quadratic equation whose one root is the minimum value of $\sin^2\theta-\sin\theta+\dfrac{1}{2}$ and other root is $\lim_{x\to\infty}\sqrt{(x+1)(x+2)}-x$ is

(a) $3x^2-7x+3=0$ (b) $8x^2-14x+3=0$

(c) $x^2-7x+3=0$ (d) $2x^2-7x+3=0$

17. Let $f(x)$ be polynomial of degree 4 with roots 1, 2, 3, 4 and leading coefficient is 1 and $g(x)$ be the polynomial of degree 4 with roots $1, \dfrac{1}{2}, \dfrac{1}{3}$ and $\dfrac{1}{4}$ with leading coefficient 1. Then, $\lim_{x\to 1}\dfrac{f(x)}{g(x)}$ equals

(a) $\dfrac{1}{24}$ (b) -24 (c) $\dfrac{1}{12}$ (d) $-\dfrac{1}{12}$

18. If $f(x)=\dfrac{1}{3}\left(f(x+1)+\dfrac{5}{f(x+2)}\right)$ and $f(x)>0, \forall\, x\in R$, then $\lim_{x\to\infty} f(x)$ is

(a) 0 (b) $\sqrt{\dfrac{2}{5}}$ (c) $\sqrt{\dfrac{5}{2}}$ (d) ∞

19. If $f(x+y)=f(x)+f(y)$ for all $x, y\in R$ and $f(1)=1$, then $\lim_{x\to 0}\dfrac{2^{f(\tan x)}-2^{f(\sin x)}}{x^2\, f(\sin x)}$ equals

(a) log 2 (b) log 4 (c) $\log\sqrt{2}$ (d) log 8

20. The polynomial of least degree, such that $\lim_{x\to 0}\left(1+\dfrac{x^2+f(x)}{x^2}\right)^{1/x}=e^2$ is

(a) 1 (b) 3 (c) 2 (d) 0

21. The value of $\lim_{n\to\infty} n^{-n^2}\left[(n+1)\left(n+\dfrac{1}{2}\right)\left(n+\dfrac{1}{2^2}\right)\ldots\left(n+\dfrac{1}{2^{n-1}}\right)\right]^n$ is

(a) e (b) e^2 (c) e^3 (d) e^4

22. Let $(\tan\alpha)\,x+(\sin\alpha)\,y=\alpha$ and $(\alpha\operatorname{cosec}\alpha)\,x+(\cos\alpha)\,y=1$ be two variable straight lines, α being the parameter. Let P be the point of intersection of the lines. In the limiting position, when $\alpha\to 0$, the point of intersection of straight lines is

(a) $(2,-1)$ (b) $(2,1)$ (c) $(-2,1)$ (d) $(-2,-1)$

23. $\lim_{x\to 1}\dfrac{nx^n(x-1)-(x^n-1)}{(e^x-e)\sin\pi x}$, where $n=100$ is equal to

(a) $\dfrac{5050}{\pi e}$ (b) $\dfrac{100}{\pi e}$ (c) $-\dfrac{5050}{\pi e}$ (d) $\dfrac{4950}{\pi e}$

24. Let $f:(1,2)\to R$ satisfies the inequality
$$\frac{\cos(2x+4)-33}{2}\le f(x)\le\frac{x^2|4x-8|}{x-2},\ \forall\, x\in(1,2).$$
Then, $\lim_{x\to 2^-} f(x)$ is

(a) 16 (b) -16

(c) 8 (d) does not exist

25. The value of
$$\left[\lim_{y\to 0}\frac{\lim_{x\to\infty}\exp\left[x\log\left(1+\frac{ay}{x}\right)\right]-\exp\left[x\log\left(1+\frac{by}{x}\right)\right]}{y}\right]$$
is

(a) $a+b$ (b) $a-b$ (c) $b-a$ (d) $-(a+b)$

26. $\lim_{x\to\infty}\dfrac{2+2x+\sin 2x}{(2x+\sin 2x)e^{\sin x}}$ is equal to

(a) 0 (b) 1

(c) -1 (d) Does not exists

27. $\lim_{x\to 0}\left(\dfrac{1^x+2^x+3^x+\ldots+n^x}{n}\right)^{\frac{1}{x}}$ is equal to

(a) $(n!)^n$ (b) $(n!)^{1/n}$ (c) $n!$ (d) $\ln(n!)$

Numerical Value Type Questions

28. $\lim_{x\to 0}\dfrac{\left[\dfrac{x}{\sin x}\right]-\left[\dfrac{\sin x}{x}\right]}{\left[\dfrac{\tan x}{x}\right]}$ is equal to ....

([.] represents the greatest integer function.)

29. For $n\in N$, let $a_n=\sum_{k=1}^{n} 2k$ and $b_n=\sum_{k=1}^{n}(2k-1)$, then $100\lim_{n\to\infty}(\sqrt{a_n}-\sqrt{b_n})$, is equal to ....

30. The value of $\lim_{x\to 0}\dfrac{\sin x^{2012}-x^{2012}\cos x^{2012}+(x^3)^{2012}}{x^{2012}(e^{5x^{2012}}-1-5x^{2012})}$ is λ, then square of sum of digits in $750\,\lambda$ is ....

31. The graph of function f contains the point $P(1, 2)$ and $Q(s, r)$. The equation of secant line through P and Q is $y = \left(\frac{s^2 + 2s - 3}{s - 1}\right)x - 1 - s$. The value of $f'(1)$ is ....

32. The value of $\lim_{x\to 1}\left(\frac{x^3 + 2x^2 + x + 1}{x^2 + 2x + 3}\right)^{\frac{1-\cos(x-1)}{(x-1)^2}}$ is $\left(\frac{\alpha}{\beta}\right)^{1/2}$, then $\alpha + \beta$ is ....

33. $\lim_{x\to 2^+}\left(\frac{|x|^3}{3} - \left[\frac{x}{3}\right]^3\right) = L$, where $[x]$ is the largest integer less than or equal to x, then $\frac{[L]}{10}$ is ....

34. The value of $\lim_{x\to 0^-}(\log(\{x\} + |[x]|))^{\{x\}}$ is P, then $[4P] + 30$ is .... $(\ln 2 = 0.693)$

35. $8\lim_{x\to 0}\frac{\left(\sqrt{(1-\cos x) + \sqrt{(1-\cos x) + \sqrt{(1-\cos x) + \ldots\infty}}}\right) - 1}{x^2}$ is ....

36. $\lim_{x\to 0}\frac{2\left(\sqrt{3}\sin\left(\frac{\pi}{6} + x\right) - \cos\left(\frac{\pi}{6} + x\right)\right)}{x\sqrt{3}(\sqrt{3}\cos x - \sin x)}$ is $\frac{m}{n}$, where m, n are coprime, then the value of $m + n$ is ....

37. Let $\alpha, \beta (\alpha < \beta)$ be two values of m for which the function $f(x) = (m^2 - 4)x + |m|$ is not invertible where $x \in R$, then the absolute value of $\lim_{x\to\frac{\pi}{3}}\frac{(\alpha + \beta + 1)\tan^3 x - (\beta + 1)\tan x}{\cos(x + \pi/6)}$ is equal to ....

38. $\lim_{n\to\infty}\left(\sin\frac{1}{\sqrt{n}}\right)\left(\frac{1}{\sqrt{n+1}} + \frac{1}{\sqrt{n+2}} + \frac{1}{\sqrt{n+3}} + \ldots + \frac{1}{2\sqrt{n}}\right)$, has the value equal to ....

39. The value of $\lim_{x\to 0}\left(\left[\frac{100x}{\sin x}\right] + \left[\frac{99\sin x}{x}\right]\right)$ (where $[\cdot]$ represents the greatest integer function) is m, then exponent of 7 in $\left(\frac{M-2}{4}\right)!$ is ....

40. If $\lim_{x\to 0}(x^{-3}\sin 3x + ax^{-2} + b)$ exists and is equal to 0, then $\left|\frac{2ab}{3}\right|$ is ....

Previous Year Questions

41. $\lim_{x\to 0}\frac{e - (1+2x)^{\frac{1}{2x}}}{x}$ is equal to

[Single Correct Type, 2024 Main]

(a) 0 (b) e (c) $e - e^2$ (d) $\frac{-2}{e}$

42. $\lim_{n\to\infty}\frac{(1^2 - 1)(n-1) + (2^2 - 2)(n-2) + \ldots((n-1)^2 - (n-1))\cdot 1}{(1^3 + 2^3 + \ldots + n^3) - (1^2 + 2^2 + \ldots + n^2)}$ is equal to

[Single Correct Type, 2024 Main]

(a) $\frac{3}{4}$
(b) $\frac{1}{3}$
(c) $\frac{1}{2}$
(d) $\frac{2}{3}$

43. $\lim_{x\to 0}\frac{e^{2|\sin x|} - 2|\sin x| - 1}{x^2}$

[Single Correct Type, 2024 Main]

(a) does not exist
(b) is equal to -1
(c) is equal to 1
(d) is equal to 2

44. If $\lim_{x\to 0}\frac{3 + \alpha\sin x + \beta\cos x + \log_e(1-x)}{3\tan^2 x} = \frac{1}{3}$, then $2\alpha - \beta$ is equal to

[Single Correct Type, 2024 Main]

(a) 2
(b) 5
(c) 7
(d) 1

45. Let $\{x\}$ denote the fractional part of x and $f(x) = \frac{\cos^{-1}(1 - \{x\}^2)\sin^{-1}(1 - \{x\})}{\{x\} - \{x\}^3}$, $x \neq 0$. If L and R respectively denotes the left hand limit and the right hand limit of $f(x)$ at $x = 0$, then $\frac{32}{\pi^2}(L^2 + R^2)$ is equal to ....

[Numerical Value Type, 2024 Main]

46. If $\lim_{x\to 1}\frac{(5x+1)^{\frac{1}{3}} - (x+5)^{\frac{1}{3}}}{(2x+3)^{\frac{1}{2}} - (x+4)^{\frac{1}{2}}} = \frac{m\sqrt{5}}{n(2n)^{\frac{2}{3}}}$, where $gcd(m, n) = 1$, then $8m + 12n$ is equal to......

[Numerical Value Type, 2024 Main]

47. If $\lim_{x\to 0}\frac{ax^2e^x - b\log_e(1+x) + cxe^{-x}}{x^2\sin x} = 1$, then $16(a^2 + b^2 + c^2)$ is equal to ....

[Numerical Value Type, 2024 Main]

48. $\lim_{n\to\infty}\left\{\left(2^{\frac{1}{2}} - 2^{\frac{1}{3}}\right)\left(2^{\frac{1}{2}} - 2^{\frac{1}{5}}\right)\ldots\left(2^{\frac{1}{2}} - 2^{\frac{1}{2n-1}}\right)\right\}$ is equal to

[Single Correct Type, 2023 Main]

(a) $1/\sqrt{2}$
(b) $\sqrt{2}$
(c) 0
(d) 1

49. The set of all values of a for which $\lim_{x\to\infty}[x - 5] - [2x + 2] = 0$, where $[\alpha]$ denotes the greatest integer less than or equal to α is equal to

[Single Correct Type, 2023 Main]

(a) $[-7.5, -6.5)$
(b) $(-7.5, -6.5)$
(c) $(-7.5, -6.5]$
(d) $[-7.5, -6.5]$

50. The value of $\lim_{n\to\infty}\dfrac{(1+2-3)+(4+5-6)+\ldots+(3n-2)+(3n-1)-3n}{\sqrt{2n^4+4n+3}-\sqrt{n^4+5n+4}}$ is

[Single Correct Type, 2023 Main]

(a) $\frac{3}{2}(\sqrt{2}+1)$ (b) $\frac{3}{2\sqrt{2}}$

(c) $3(\sqrt{2}+1)$ (d) $\frac{\sqrt{2}+1}{2}$

51. $\lim_{x\to\infty}\dfrac{(\sqrt{3x+1}+\sqrt{3x-1})^6+(\sqrt{3x+1}-\sqrt{3x-1})^6}{(x+\sqrt{x^2-1})^6+(x-\sqrt{x^2-1})^6}x^3$

[Single Correct Type, 2023 Main]

(a) is equal to $\frac{27}{2}$ (b) does not exist

(c) is equal to 27 (d) is equal to 9

52. $\lim_{x\to\infty}\left(\left(\dfrac{1-\cos^2(3x)}{\cos^3(4x)}\right)\left(\dfrac{\sin^3(4x)}{(\log_e(2x+1))^5}\right)\right)$ is equal to ....

[Single Correct Type, 2023 Main]

(a) 24 (b) 9 (c) 18 (d) 15

53. $\lim_{t\to 0}\left(1^{\frac{1}{\sin^2 t}}+2^{\frac{1}{\sin^2 t}}+\ldots+n^{\frac{1}{\sin^2 t}}\right)^{\sin^2 t}$ is equal to

[Single Correct Type, 2023 Main]

(a) $\frac{n(n+1)}{2}$ (b) n

(c) n^2+n (d) n^2

54. If $\lim_{x\to 0}\dfrac{e^{ax}-\cos(bx)-\dfrac{cxe^{-cx}}{2}}{1-\cos(2x)}=17$, then $5a^2+b^2$ is equal to

[Single Correct Type, 2023 Main]

(a) 76 (b) 72 (c) 64 (d) 68

55. Let $x=2$ be a root of the equation $x^2+px+q=0$ and

$$f(x)=\begin{cases}\dfrac{1-\cos(x^2-4px+q^2+8q+16)}{(x-2p)^4}, & x\neq 2p\\ 0, & x=2p\end{cases}$$

Then, $\lim_{x\to 2p^+}[f(x)]$, where [.] denotes greatest integer function, is

[Single Correct Type, 2023 Main]

(a) 1 (b) -1

(c) 2 (d) 0

56. If $\alpha>\beta>0$ are the roots of the equation $ax^2+bx+1=0$, and $\lim_{x\to\frac{1}{\alpha}}\left(\dfrac{1-\cos(x^2+bx+a)}{2(1-\alpha x)^2}\right)^{1/2}=\dfrac{1}{k}\left(\dfrac{1}{\beta}-\dfrac{1}{\alpha}\right)$, then k is equal to

[Single Correct Type, 2023 Main]

(a) α (b) 2α

(c) 2β (d) β

57. Let f, g and h be the real valued functions defined on R as

$$f(x)=\begin{cases}\dfrac{x}{|x|}, & x\neq 0\\ 1, & x=0\end{cases},\quad g(x)=\begin{cases}\dfrac{\sin(x+1)}{(x+1)}, & x\neq -1\\ 1, & x=-1\end{cases}$$

and $h(x)=2[x]-f(x)$, where $[x]$ is the greatest integer $\leq x$. Then, the value of $\lim_{x\to 1}g(h(x-1))$ is

[Single Correct Type, 2023 Main]

(a) 1 (b) sin(1)

(c) 0 (d) -1

58. Let $\sum_{n=0}^{\infty}\dfrac{n^3((2n)!)+(2n-1)(n!)}{(n!)((2n)!)}=ae+\dfrac{b}{e}+c$, where a, b, $c\in Z$ and $e=\sum_{n=0}^{\infty}\dfrac{1}{n!}$. Then, a^2-b+c is equal to ....

[Numerical Value Type, 2023 Main]

59. Let $\beta=\lim_{x\to 0}\dfrac{\alpha x-(e^{3x}-1)}{\alpha x(e^{3x}-1)}$ for some $\alpha\in R$. Then, the value of $\alpha+\beta$ is

[Single Correct Type, 2022 Main]

(a) $\frac{14}{5}$ (b) $\frac{3}{2}$ (c) $\frac{5}{2}$ (d) $\frac{7}{2}$

60. If $\lim_{n\to\infty}(\sqrt{n^2-n-1}+n\alpha+\beta)=0$, then $8(\alpha+\beta)$ is equal to

[Single Correct Type, 2022 Main]

(a) 4 (b) -8 (c) -4 (d) 8

61. Let a be an integer such that $\lim_{x\to 7}\dfrac{18-[1-x]}{[x]-3a}$ exists, where $[t]$ is greatest integer $\leq t$. Then, a is equal to

[Single Correct Type, 2022 Main]

(a) -6 (b) -2 (c) 2 (d) 6

62. $\lim_{x\to\frac{\pi}{4}}\dfrac{8\sqrt{2}-(\cos x+\sin x)^7}{\sqrt{2}-\sqrt{2}\sin 2x}$ is equal to

[Single Correct Type, 2022 Main]

(a) 14 (b) 7 (c) $14\sqrt{2}$ (d) $7\sqrt{2}$

63. $\lim_{x\to\frac{\pi}{2}}\tan^2 x\left((2\sin^2 x+3\sin x+4)^{\frac{1}{2}}-(\sin^2 x+6\sin x+2)^{\frac{1}{2}}\right)$ is equal to

[Single Correct Type, 2022 Main]

(a) $\frac{1}{12}$ (b) $-\frac{1}{18}$ (c) $-\frac{1}{12}$ (d) $\frac{1}{6}$

64. If $\lim_{x\to 0}\dfrac{\alpha e^x+\beta e^{-x}+\gamma\sin x}{x\sin^2 x}=\dfrac{2}{3}$, where α, β and $\gamma\in R$, then which of the following is not correct?

[Single Correct Type, 2022 Main]

(a) $\alpha^2+\beta^2+\gamma^2=6$

(b) $\alpha\beta+\beta\gamma+\gamma\alpha+1=0$

(c) $\alpha\beta^2+\beta\gamma^2+\gamma\alpha^2+3=0$

(d) $\alpha^2-\beta^2+\gamma^2=4$

65. $\lim_{x\to 0} \frac{\cos(\sin x) - \cos x}{x^4}$ is equal to

[Single Correct Type, 2022 Main]

(a) 1/3 (b) 1/4 (c) 1/6 (d) 1/12

66. $\lim_{x\to 0} \left(\frac{(x+2\cos x)^3 + 2(x+2\cos x)^2 + 3\sin(x+2\cos x)}{(x+2)^3 + 2(x+2)^2 + 3\sin(x+2)} \right)^{100/x}$ is equal to ……… .

[Numerical Value Type, 2022 Main]

67. If $\lim_{x\to 1} \frac{\sin(3x^2 - 4x + 1) - x^2 + 1}{2x^3 - 7x^2 + ax + b} = -2$, then the value of $(a - b)$ is equal to……… .

[Numerical Value Type, 2022 Main]

68. Let $[f]$ denote the greatest integer $\le t$ and $\{t\}$ denote the fractional part of t. Then, integral value of α for which the left hand limit of the function

$$f(x) = [1+x] + \frac{\alpha^{2[x]+\{x\}} + [x] - 1}{2[x] + \{x\}} \text{ at } x = 0 \text{ is equal to}$$

$\alpha - \frac{4}{3}$ is ……… .

[Numerical Value Type, 2022 Main]

69. If $\lim_{x\to\infty} (\sqrt{x^2 - x + 1} - ax) = b$, then the ordered pair (a, b) is

[Single Correct Type, 2021 Main]

(a) $\left(1, \frac{1}{2}\right)$ (b) $\left(1, -\frac{1}{2}\right)$

(c) $\left(-1, \frac{1}{2}\right)$ (d) $\left(-1, -\frac{1}{2}\right)$

70. If α, β are the distinct roots of $x^2 + bx + c = 0$, then

$$\lim_{x\to\beta} \frac{e^{2(x^2+bx+c)} - 1 - 2(x^2 + bx + c)}{(x-\beta)^2} \text{ is equal to}$$

[Single Correct Type, 2021 Main]

(a) $b^2 + 4c$ (b) $2(b^2 + 4c)$

(c) $2(b^2 - 4c)$ (d) $b^2 - 4c$

71. Let $f: R \to R$ be a function such that $f(2) = 4$ and $f'(2) = 1$. Then, the value of $\lim_{x\to 2} \frac{x^2 f(2) - 4f(x)}{x - 2}$ is equal to

[Single Correct Type, 2021 Main]

(a) 4 (b) 8

(c) 16 (d) 12

72. $\lim_{n\to\infty} \left(1 + \frac{1 + \frac{1}{2} + \ldots\ldots + \frac{1}{n}}{n^2}\right)^n$ is equal to

[Single Correct Type, 2021 Main]

(a) 1/2 (b) 0 (c) $1/e$ (d) 1

73. The value of $\lim_{h\to 0} 2\left\{\frac{\sqrt{3}\sin\left(\frac{\pi}{6}+h\right) - \cos\left(\frac{\pi}{6}+h\right)}{\sqrt{3}h(\sqrt{3}\cos h - \sin h)}\right\}$ is

[Single Correct Type, 2021 Main]

(a) $\frac{4}{3}$ (b) $\frac{2}{\sqrt{3}}$ (c) $\frac{3}{4}$ (d) $\frac{2}{3}$

74. The value of $\lim_{n\to\infty} \frac{[r] + [2r] + \ldots\ldots + [nr]}{n^2}$, where r is non-zero real number and $[r]$ denotes the greatest integer less than or equal to r, is equal to

[Single Correct Type, 2021 Main]

(a) $r/2$ (b) r (c) $2r$ (d) 0

75. The value of $\lim_{x\to 0} \left(\frac{x}{\sqrt[8]{1-\sin x} - \sqrt[8]{1+\sin x}}\right)$ is equal to

[Single Correct Type, 2021 Main]

(a) 0 (b) 4 (c) -4 (d) -1

76. The value of the $\lim_{\theta\to 0} \frac{\tan(\pi\cos^2\theta)}{\sin(2\pi\sin^2\theta)}$ is equal to

[Single Correct Type, 2021 Main]

(a) $-1/2$ (b) $-1/4$ (c) 0 (d) 1/4

77. The value of $\lim_{x\to 0^+} \frac{\cos^{-1}(x - [x]^2)\cdot\sin^{-1}(x - [x]^2)}{x - x^3}$, where $[x]$ denotes the greatest integer $\le x$ is

[Single Correct Type, 2021 Main]

(a) π (b) 0 (c) $\pi/4$ (d) $\pi/2$

78. If $\lim_{x\to 0} \frac{\sin^{-1}x - \tan^{-1}x}{3x^3}$ is equal to L, then the value of $(6L + 1)$ is

[Single Correct Type, 2021 Main]

(a) 1/6 (b) 1/2 (c) 6 (d) 2

79. If $\alpha = \lim_{x\to\frac{\pi}{4}} \frac{\tan^3 x - \tan x}{\cos\left(x + \frac{\pi}{4}\right)}$ and $\beta = \lim_{x\to 0} (\cos x)^{\cot x}$ are the roots of the quation, $ax^2 + bx - 4 = 0$, then the ordered pair (a, b) is

[Single Correct Type, 2021 Main]

(a) $(1, -3)$ (b) $(-1, 3)$ (c) $(-1, -3)$ (d) $(1, 3)$

80. If $\lim_{x\to 0} \frac{\alpha x e^x - \beta\log_e(1+x) + \gamma x^2 e^{-x}}{x\sin^2 x} = 10$, $\alpha, \beta, \gamma \in R$, then the value of $\alpha + \beta + \gamma$ is …. .

[Numerical Value Type, 2021 Main]

81. If the value of $\lim_{x\to 0} (2 - \cos x\sqrt{\cos 2x})^{\left(\frac{x+2}{x^2}\right)}$ is equal to e^a, then a is equal to ……… .

[Numerical Value Type, 2021 Main]

82. If $\lim_{x\to 0}\dfrac{ae^{x}-b\cos x+ce^{-x}}{x\sin x}=2$, then $a+b+c$ is equal to .... **[Numerical Value Type, 2021 Main]**

83. $\lim_{x\to a}\dfrac{(a+2x)^{1/3}-(3x)^{1/3}}{(3a+x)^{1/3}-(4x)^{1/3}}$ $(a\neq 0)$ is equal to **[Single Correct Type, 2020 Main]**

(a) $\left(\frac{2}{3}\right)^{4/3}$ (b) $\left(\frac{2}{9}\right)^{4/3}$

(c) $\left(\frac{2}{9}\right)\left(\frac{2}{3}\right)^{1/3}$ (d) $\left(\frac{2}{3}\right)\left(\frac{2}{9}\right)^{1/3}$

84. $\lim_{x\to 0}\dfrac{x\left(e^{(\sqrt{1+x^2+x^4}-1)/x}-1\right)}{\sqrt{1+x^2+x^4}-1}$ **[Single Correct Type, 2020 Main]**

(a) is equal to $\sqrt{e}$ (b) is equal to 1

(c) is equal to 0 (d) does not exist

85. $\lim_{x\to 0}\left(\dfrac{3x^2+2}{7x^2+2}\right)^{1/x^2}$ is equal to **[Single Correct Type, 2020 Main]**

(a) e^2 (b) e

(c) $\dfrac{1}{e^2}$ (d) $\dfrac{1}{e}$

86. $\lim_{x\to 0}\left(\tan\left(\dfrac{\pi}{4}+x\right)\right)^{1/x}$ is equal to **[Single Correct Type, 2020 Main]**

(a) e (b) 2

(c) 1 (d) e^2

87. If $\lim_{x\to 1}\dfrac{x+x^2+x^3+\ldots+x^n-n}{x-1}=820, (n\in N)$ then the value of n is equal to .... **[Numerical Value Type, 2020 Main]**

EXERCISE 2

JEE Advanced Pattern

Single Option Correct Type Questions

1. If $\lim_{x\to 0}(\cos x+a^3\sin(b^6x))^{\frac{1}{x}}=e^{512}$, then the value of ab^2 is equal to

(a) -512 (b) 512 (c) 8 (d) $8\sqrt{8}$

2. $\lim_{x\to\frac{\pi}{4}}\dfrac{1-\tan x}{1-\sqrt{2}\sin x}$

(a) 3 (b) 2 (c) 1 (d) None of these

3. Let $f(x)=\left[\dfrac{\sin x}{x}\right]+\left[\dfrac{2\sin 2x}{x}\right]+\ldots+\left[\dfrac{10\sin 10x}{x}\right]$ (where $[y]$ is the largest integer $\leq y$).

The value of $\lim_{x\to 0}f(x)$ equals

(a) 55 (b) 164 (c) 165 (d) 375

4. $\lim_{x\to 0}\dfrac{6x^2(\cot x)(\operatorname{cosec}2x)}{\sec\left(\cos x+\pi\tan\left(\dfrac{\pi}{4\sec x}\right)-1\right)}$ has the value equal to

(a) 6 (b) -6 (c) 0 (d) -3

5. Suppose that a and b are real positive numbers, then the value of $\lim_{t\to 0}\left(\dfrac{b^{t+1}-a^{t+1}}{b-a}\right)^{1/t}$ is

(a) $\dfrac{a\ln b-b\ln a}{b-a}$ (b) $\dfrac{b\ln b-a\ln a}{b-a}$

(c) $b\ln b-a\ln a$ (d) $\left(\dfrac{b^b}{a^a}\right)^{\frac{1}{b-a}}$

6. Let $P(x)=a_1x+a_2x^2+a_3x^3+\ldots+a_{100}x^{100}$, where $a_1=1$ and $a_i\in R, \forall i=1, 2, 3, 4\ldots 100$, then $\lim_{x\to 0}\dfrac{\sqrt[100]{1+P(x)}-1}{x}$ has the value equal to

(a) 100 (b) $\dfrac{1}{100}$ (c) 1 (d) 5050

7. The value of $\lim_{x\to 0^+}\left(\dfrac{\cot^{-1}(\ln\{x\})}{\pi}\right)^{-\ln\{x\}}$ is equal to

[**Note** where {} denotes fractional part function]

(a) $e^{1/\pi}$ (b) $e^{-1/\pi}$ (c) $e^{-2/\pi}$ (d) $e^{2/\pi}$

8. Let P_k be a point in XY-plane whose x coordinate is $1+\dfrac{k}{n}, (k=1, 2, 3\ldots n)$ on the curve $y=\ln x$. If A is (1, 0), then $\lim_{n\to\infty}\dfrac{1}{n}\sum_{k=1}^{n}(AP_k)^2$ equals

(a) $\dfrac{1}{3}+2\ln^2 2$ (b) $\dfrac{1}{3}+2\ln^2\left(\dfrac{2}{e}\right)$

(c) $\dfrac{1}{3}+\ln^2\left(\dfrac{2}{e}\right)$ (d) $\dfrac{1}{3}+2\ln\left(\dfrac{2}{e}\right)$

9. $f(x)=\lim_{n\to\infty}\dfrac{x^n+\left(\dfrac{\pi}{3}\right)^n}{x^{n-1}+\left(\dfrac{\pi}{3}\right)^{n-1}}$, ($n$ is an even integer), then which of the following is incorrect?

(a) If $f:\left[\dfrac{\pi}{3},\infty\right)\to\left[\dfrac{\pi}{3},\infty\right)$, then function is invertible.

(b) $f(x)=f(-x)$ has infinite number of solutions.

(c) $f(x)=|f(x)|$ has infinite number of solutions.

(d) $f(x)$ is one-one function for all $x\in R$

10. For a certain value of c, $\lim_{x\to\infty}[(x^5+7x^4+2)^c-x]$ is finite and non-zero. Then, the value of limit is

(a) $\dfrac{7}{5}$ (b) 1

(c) $\dfrac{2}{5}$ (d) None of these

11. $\lim_{n\to\infty}\sum_{k=1}^{n}\left(\sin\dfrac{\pi}{2k}-\cos\dfrac{\pi}{2k}-\sin\left(\dfrac{\pi}{2(k+2)}\right)+\cos\dfrac{\pi}{2(k+2)}\right)$ is

(a) 0 (b) 1

(c) 2 (d) 3

12. The value of

$$\lim_{x\to 0}\left((\cos x)^{\frac{1}{\sin^2 x}}+\frac{\sin 2x+2\tan^{-1}3x+3x^2}{\ln(1+3x+\sin^2 x)+xe^x}\right)$$ is

(a) $\sqrt{e}+\dfrac{3}{2}$ (b) $\dfrac{1}{\sqrt{e}}+\dfrac{3}{2}$

(c) $\sqrt{e}+2$ (d) $\dfrac{1}{\sqrt{e}}+2$

13. If $\lim_{x\to 0}\dfrac{(1+a^3)+8e^{1/x}}{1+(1-b^3)e^{1/x}}=2$, then

(a) $a=1, b=2$

(b) $a=1, b=-3^{1/3}$

(c) $a=2, b=3^{1/3}$

(d) $a=-2, b=3^{-1/3}$

14. $\lim_{x\to 0^+}\int_x^{2x}\dfrac{\sin^m t}{t^n}\,dt$ ($m,n\in N$) equals

(a) 0 if $m\ge n$ (b) ln 2 if $n-m=1$

(c) $+\infty$ if $n-m=1$ (d) None of these

15. For each $t\in R$, let $[t]$ be the greatest integer less than or equal to t.

Then, $\lim_{x\to 1^+}\dfrac{(1-|x|+\sin|1-x|)\sin\left(\dfrac{\pi}{2}[1-x]\right)}{|1-x|[1-x]}$ is equal to

(a) 0 (b) -1

(c) 1 (d) Does not exist

More than One Correct Option Type Questions

16. Let $f(x)=\dfrac{1-x(1+|1-x|)}{|1-x|}\cos\left(\dfrac{1}{1-x}\right)$ for $x\neq 1$. Then,

(a) $\lim_{x\to 1^+}f(x)$ does not exist (b) $\lim_{x\to 1^-}f(x)$ does not exist

(c) $\lim_{x\to 1^+}f(x)=0$ (d) $\lim_{x\to 1^-}f(x)=0$

17. Which of the following limits does not exist?

(a) $\lim_{x\to 1^+}([x])^{\frac{1}{x-1}}$ (b) $\lim_{x\to 3}\dfrac{(x^2-9-\sqrt{x^2-6x+9})}{|x-1|-2}$

(c) $\lim_{x\to 0^+}(x)^{\ln x}$ (d) $\lim_{x\to 0^+}\left(\dfrac{1-\cos(\sin^2 x)}{x^2}\right)^{\frac{\ln(1-2x^2)}{\sin^2 x}}$

(where [.] represents greatest integer function).

18. Which of the following statement(s) is (are) incorrect?

(a) If $\lim_{x\to c}f(x)$ and $\lim_{x\to c}g(x)$ both does not exist, then $\lim_{x\to c}f(x)g(x)$ also does not exist.

(b) If $\lim_{x\to c}f(x)$ and $\lim_{x\to c}g(x)$ both does not exist, then $\lim_{x\to c}f(g(x))$ also does not exist.

(c) If $\lim_{x\to c}f(x)$ exist and $\lim_{x\to c}g(x)$ does not exist, then $\lim_{x\to c}g(f(x))$ does not exist.

(d) If $\lim_{x\to c}f(x)$ and $\lim_{x\to c}g(x)$ both exist, then $\lim_{x\to c}f(g(x))$ and $\lim_{x\to c}g(f(x))$ also exist.

19. Which of the following limits equal to $\dfrac{1}{2}$?

(a) $\lim_{n\to\infty}\left(\dfrac{1}{1.3}+\dfrac{1}{3.5}+\ldots+\dfrac{1}{(2n-1)(2n+1)}\right)$

(b) $\lim_{x\to\infty}\left[\dfrac{3x^2}{2x+1}-\dfrac{(2x-1)(3x^2+x+2)}{4x^2}\right]$

(c) $\lim_{n\to\infty}\dfrac{1}{n^2}(1+2+3+\ldots+n)$

(d) $\lim_{n\to\infty}\dfrac{(n+2)!+(n+1)!}{(n+2)!-(n+1)!}$

20. If α is the root of the equation $x-\tan x=3$, where $\alpha\in\left(\dfrac{\pi}{2},\dfrac{3\pi}{2}\right)$; then which of the following is/are correct?, (where [.] denotes the greatest integer function and {.} fractional part function)

(a) $\lim_{x\to\alpha^+}\left[\dfrac{\max(\tan x,\{x\})}{x-3}\right]=1$

(b) $\lim_{x\to\alpha^+}\left[\dfrac{\min(\tan x,\{x\})}{x-3}\right]=1$

(c) $\lim_{x\to\alpha^-}\left[\dfrac{\min(\tan x,\{x\})}{x-3}\right]=0$

(d) $\lim_{x\to\alpha^-}\left[\dfrac{\max(\tan x,\{x\})}{\tan x}\right]=1$

21. If [.] denotes the greatest integer function, then which of the following limit(s) exist(s)?

(a) $\lim_{x\to 0}\left[\frac{1}{\sqrt{2}}\sqrt{1+\cos(\sqrt{2+2\cos(2[x])})}\right]$

(b) $\lim_{x\to 0}\left[\frac{1}{\sqrt{2}}\sqrt{1+\cos(\sqrt{2-2\cos(2[x])})}\right]$

(c) $\lim_{x\to 0}\left[\frac{1}{\sqrt{2}}\sqrt{1-\cos(\sqrt{2+2\cos(2[x])})}\right]$

(d) $\lim_{x\to 0}\left[\frac{1}{\sqrt{2}}\sqrt{1-\cos(\sqrt{2-2\cos(2[x])})}\right]$

22. Let $f(x)=\frac{1-\cos\{x\}}{(x^4+ax^3+bx^2+cx)^2}$. If $l=\lim_{x\to 1^+} f(x)$, $m=\lim_{x\to 2^+} f(x)$ and $n=\lim_{x\to 3^+} f(x)$, where l, m and n are non-zero finite, then [where $\{x\}$ denotes fractional part of x]

(a) $\lim_{x\to 0^+} f(x)=\frac{1}{36}$ (b) $a+b+c=-1$

(c) $l+m+n=\frac{19}{72}$ (d) $\lim_{x\to 4^+} f(x)=0$

23. Let $\lim_{x\to\infty}(2^x+a^x+e^x)^{1/x}=L$

which of the following statement(s) is (are) correct?

(a) If $L=a(a>0)$, then the range of a is $[e,\infty)$.

(b) If $L=2e(a>0)$, then the range of a is $\{2e\}$.

(c) If $L=e(a>0)$, then the range of a is $(0,e]$.

(d) If $L=2a(a>1)$, then the range of a is $\left(\frac{e}{2},\infty\right)$.

24. Which of the following limits tend to unity?

(a) $\lim_{t\to 0}\frac{\sin(\tan t)}{\sin t}$ (b) $\lim_{x\to\pi/2}\frac{\sin(\cos x)}{\cos x}$

(c) $\lim_{x\to 0}\frac{\sqrt{1-x}-\sqrt{1-x}}{x}$ (d) $\lim_{x\to 0}\frac{\sqrt{x^2}}{x}$

25. If $f(x)=\begin{cases}2x-3 & ,-3\le x<0\\ 4-x^2 & ,\ 0\le x\le 5\end{cases}$

and $g(x)=\begin{cases}2x+3 & ,-10\le x<0\\ -1-x & ,\ 0\le x\le 3\end{cases}$, then

(a) $\lim_{x\to 0^+} f(g(x))=-5$ (b) $\lim_{x\to 0^-} f(g(x))=-5$

(c) $\lim_{x\to 0} f(g(x))=-5$ (d) $\lim_{x\to 0} f(g(x))$ exists

26. $\lim_{n\to\infty}\cos^{2n}x$ is equal to

(a) 0, if $x=m\pi$; $m\in Q$ (b) 1, if $x=m\pi$; $m\in Q$

(c) 1, if $x\ne m\pi$; $m\in Q$ (d) 0, if $x\ne m\pi$; $m\in Q$

27. If $f(x)=\left(\frac{|x|}{|x|+2}\right)^{-x}$, then

(a) $\lim_{x\to-\infty} f(x)=0$ (b) $\lim_{x\to 0} f(x)=1$

(c) $\lim_{x\to\infty} f(x)=e^2$ (d) $\lim_{x\to-\infty} f(x)=e^{-2}$

28. Consider the function $f(x)=\left(\frac{ax+1}{bx+2}\right)^x$, where $a^2+b^2\ne 0$, then $\lim_{x\to\infty} f(x)$

(a) exists for all values of a and b

(b) is zero for $a<b$

(c) is non-existent for $a>b$

(d) is $e^{-\left(\frac{1}{a}\right)}$ or $e^{-\left(\frac{1}{b}\right)}$ if $a=b$

29. $\lim_{x\to\infty}\frac{(ax+1)^n}{x^n+A}$ is equal to

(a) a_n if $n\in N$ (b) ∞ if $n\in Z$ and $a=A=0$

(c) $\frac{1}{1+A}$ if $n=0$ (d) a^n if $n\in Z^-$, $A=0$ and $a\ne 0$

30. $\lim_{x\to\infty}\frac{x^n}{e^x}=0$, $n\in$ integer number, is true for

(a) no value of n (b) all values of n

(c) negative values of n (d) positive values of n

Passage Based Questions

Passage I

(Q. Nos. 31 and 32)

▪ Consider the limit $\lim_{x\to 0}\frac{1}{x^3}\left(\frac{1}{\sqrt{1+x}}-\frac{(1+ax)}{(1+bx)}\right)$ exists, finite and has the value equal to l (where a, b are real constants), then

31. $a+b$ is equal to

(a) $\frac{3}{4}$ (b) $\frac{1}{2}$ (c) 1 (d) 0

32. $\left|\frac{b}{l}\right|$ is equal to

(a) 38 (b) 16 (c) 72 (d) 24

Passage II

(Q. Nos. 33 and 34)

▪ Consider a new definition for approximating the values of a function $f(x)$ in the neighbourhood of a point $x=a$ approx $\lim_{x\to a} f(x)=\lim_{x\to a^+} f(x)$ whenever $\left[\left|\lim_{x\to a} f(x)-\lim_{x\to a^+} f(x)\right|\right]\le 1$, otherwise approx $\lim_{x\to a} f(x)$ is said to be non-existent. Here, [.] denotes greatest integer function.

33. The value of Approx $\lim_{x\to 0}\frac{x(e^{[x]+|x|}-2)}{[x]+|x|}$ is

(a) -1 (b) 0

(c) 1 (d) None of these

34. Let $f(x)=\begin{cases}[x^x]+a, & x>0\\ \lim\limits_{t\to\infty}\left(\dfrac{\sin x}{x}\right)^t, & x<0\end{cases}$. The complete set of the values of a for which Approx$_{x\to 0}$ exists is

(a) $(0, 2]$
(b) $(-2, 2)$
(c) $[-1, 1]$
(d) None of these

Stem Based Questions

Stem I

(Q. Nos. 35 and 36)

- Suppose $\lim\limits_{x\to 0}\dfrac{\int_0^x \dfrac{t^2 dt}{(a+t^r)^{1/p}}}{bx-\sin x}=l$, where $p\in N$, $p\geq 2$, $a>0, r>0$ and $b\neq 0$. If l exists and is non-zero.

35. If $p=3$ and $l=1$, then the value of a is equal to ....

36. If $p=2$ and $a=9$, $b=1$ and l exists, then the value of l is equal to ....

Stem II

(Q. Nos. 37 and 38)

- Consider $P(x)=ax^2+bx+c$, where $a,b,c\in R$ and $P(2)=9$. Let α and β be the roots of the equation $P(x)=0$.

37. If $\alpha\to\infty$ and $P'(3)=5$, then $\lim\limits_{x\to\infty}\left(\dfrac{P(x)}{5(x-1)}\right)^x=e^{\frac{M}{N}}$, where M and N are relatively prime positive integers. The value of $M+N$ is equal to ....

38. If α and β both tend to infinity, then $\lim\limits_{x\to 3}\dfrac{\sqrt{P(x)}-3}{\sin(x-3)}$ is equal to ....

Single Integer Type Questions

39. If α,β are two distinct real roots of the equation $ax^3+x-1-a=0, (a\neq -1, 0)$, none of which is equal to unity, then the value of $\lim\limits_{x\to(1/\alpha)}\dfrac{(1+a)x^3-x^2-a}{(e^{1-ax}-1)(x-1)}$ is $\dfrac{al(k\alpha-\beta)}{\alpha}$. The value of kl is ....

40. For $n\in N$, let x_n be defined as $\left(1+\dfrac{1}{n}\right)^{n+x_n}=e$, then $2\lim\limits_{n\to\infty}x_n$ is equal to ....

41. $\lim\limits_{x\to a}$

$$\left[\frac{(x^3-2ax^2-a^2x+2a^3)(x-2a)^{-1}+2a(x+a)}{x^3-a^2x}-\frac{2}{x-a}\right]=l$$

and if l does not exist, then limiting value be least prime.

42. If $\lim\limits_{x\to 1}\dfrac{(3+ax)^{5/2}-b\ln x+c\sin(x-1)}{(x-1)^2}=2$, then the value of the expression $\dfrac{a^2+b^2+c^2}{41}$ is ....

43. If $\lim\limits_{n\to\infty}\dfrac{n\cos^2\frac{1}{2}n\pi+\sin^2\frac{1}{2}n\pi}{n\left(\cos^2\frac{1}{2}n\pi+n\sin^2\frac{1}{2}n\pi\right)}=\begin{cases}\lambda, & \text{when } n \text{ is even integer}\\ \mu, & \text{when } n \text{ is odd integer}\end{cases}$, then $2\lambda+\mu$ is equal to ....

44. $\lim\limits_{x\to 0}\dfrac{\int_0^{\frac{\pi}{4}+x^4e^{1/x^2}}\cos^n t\,dt-\int_0^{\frac{\pi}{4}}\cos^n t\,dt}{x^4e^{\frac{1}{x^2}}}$, $n\in N$ is equal to ....

45. If α,β are two distinct real roots of the equation $ax^3+x-1-a=0, (a\neq -1, 0)$, which are not equal to unity, then $\lim\limits_{x\to 1/\alpha}\dfrac{\ln((1+a)x^3-x^2-a)}{(e^{1-\alpha x}-1)(x-1)}$ is $a\left(\lambda-\dfrac{\beta}{\alpha}\right)$, then 4λ is ....

46. $\lim\limits_{x\to 1}\left[\left(\dfrac{4}{x^2-x^{-1}}-\dfrac{1-3x+x^2}{1-x^3}\right)^{-1}+3\dfrac{x^4-1}{x^3-x^{-1}}\right]$ is equal to ....

47. If $\lim\limits_{x\to 0}\dfrac{e^{-nx}+e^{nx}-2\cos\dfrac{nx}{2}-kx^2}{(\sin x-\tan x)}$ exists and finite $(n,k\in N)$, then the least value of $k+n$ is ....

48. $\lim\limits_{x\to(e^{-1})^+}\dfrac{e^{\frac{\ln(1+\ln x)}{x}}}{x-e^{-1}}$ is equal to ....

49. The value of $\lim\limits_{x\to\pi}\dfrac{1}{(x-\pi)}\left(\sqrt{\dfrac{4\cos^2 x}{2+\cos x}}-2\right)$ is ....

Numerical Value Type Questions

50. $\lim\limits_{n\to\infty}\left(\dfrac{\sqrt{n^2+n}-1}{n}\right)^{2\sqrt{n^2+n}-1}=ke^{-\mu}$, then $\dfrac{5k}{4\mu}$ is ....

51. If $\lim\limits_{x\to\infty}\left(\dfrac{x}{e}-x\left(\dfrac{x}{x+1}\right)^x\right)=\dfrac{-k}{e}$, then k is equal to ....

52. Through a point A on a circle, a chord AP is drawn and on the tangent at A a point T is taken such that $AT=AP$. If TP produced meet the diameter through A at Q, then the limiting value of AO when P moves upto A is k times diameter of the circle, then $\dfrac{7k}{5}$ is equal to ....

53. Evaluate $\lim\limits_{x \to a}\left(\dfrac{(a^{x-a}-1)(x^p-a^p)}{(x-a)^2(\ln a^p)\,a^{p-1}}\right)^{\frac{1}{x-a}} = \dfrac{e^{(p-x)}+a\ln a}{ya}$

where $a > 0$, $p \in Q$, then $\dfrac{x}{y}$ is equal to ....

54. If $a_{n+1} = (a_n + x)^{-1}$, $a_0 = 0$ and $b_{n+1} = (b_n + y)^{-1}$, $b_0 = 0$,

if $\lim\limits_{x \to y}\dfrac{a_n - b_n}{x^2 - y^2}$ for $n = 2, 3$ is $\dfrac{x^p - 1}{(x^q + 1)^r (sx)}$, then

$2p + 3q + r + 4s$ is ....

55. Let $g(x) = f(x-1) + f(x+1)$, where

$f(x) = \begin{cases} 1-|x|, & |x| \le 1 \\ |x|, & |x| > 1 \end{cases}$. Then, $50\lim\limits_{x \to \frac{\pi}{2}} g(\sin x)$ is equal

to ....

56. $\lim\limits_{n \to \infty}\sum\limits_{k=0}^{n}\dfrac{{}^nC_k}{n^k(k+3)} = e - 8p$, then p is equal to ....

57. Let the sequence x_n be defined as

$x_0 = \sqrt{a}$, $x_1 = \sqrt{a+\sqrt{a}}$,

$x_2 = \sqrt{a+\sqrt{a+\sqrt{a}}}$, $x_3 = \sqrt{a+\sqrt{a+\sqrt{a+\sqrt{a}}}}$ ....

If $\lim\limits_{n \to \infty} x_n = p + \sqrt{1+qa}$, then $\dfrac{4p+5}{2q}$ is equal to ....

58. If $f(x) = \lim\limits_{n \to \infty}\{\sin x + 2\sin^2 x + 3\sin^3 x + \ldots n\sin^n x\}$,

then evaluate $\lim\limits_{x \to \pi/2}\{(1-\sin x)^2 f(x)\}^{\frac{1}{(\sin x - 1)}} = e^{4\lambda - 15}$

then 8λ is ....

59. Let $f(x) = \dfrac{\sin^{-1}(1-\{x\})\cdot\cos^{-1}(1-\{x\})}{\sqrt{2\{x\}}\,(1-\{x\})}$, then value of

$\left(\lim\limits_{x \to 0^+} f(x)\right)^2 + \left(\lim\limits_{x \to 0^-} f(x)\right)^2$ is $k\pi^2$, then $k^4 + 2$ is ......

(where {.} denotes the fractional part function)

60. $\lim\limits_{x \to 0}\left(\dfrac{1-\cos x\sqrt{\cos 2x}}{x^2}\right)$ is equal to ....

61. If $f(x) = \sum\limits_{\lambda=1}^{n}\left(x - \dfrac{7}{\lambda}\right)\left(x - \dfrac{5}{4(\lambda+1)}\right)$, then $\lim\limits_{n \to \infty} f(0)$ is

equal to $\dfrac{m}{n}$ (where m and n are coprimes), then the value

of $m + n$ is ....

62. If $\lim\limits_{n \to \infty}\dfrac{n^{98}}{n^x - (n-1)^x} = \dfrac{1}{99}$, then the value of x equals

63. $f_1(x) = \dfrac{x}{2} + 10$, $f_n(x) = f_1(f_{n-1}(x))\, n \ge 2$, then $\lim\limits_{n \to \infty} f_n(x)$

is equal to ....

64. $\lim\limits_{x \to 0}\left(\dfrac{(1+x)^{\frac{1}{x}}}{e}\right)^{\frac{1}{x}} = e^{-4\mu}$, then μ is ....

Matching Type Questions

65. Match the following columns.

	Column I		Column II
(A)	$\lim\limits_{x \to 0}(\sqrt{x+\sqrt{x}} - \sqrt{x-\sqrt{x}})$ equals	(p)	−2
(B)	The value of the, $\lim\limits_{x \to 0}\dfrac{\sin 2x - 2\tan x}{\ln(1+x^3)}$ is	(q)	−1
(C)	$\lim\limits_{x \to 0}(\ln \sin^3 x - \ln(x^4 - ex^3))$ equals	(r)	0
(D)	Let $\tan(2\pi\,\lvert\sin\theta\rvert) = \cot(2\pi\,\lvert\cos\theta\rvert)$, where $\theta \in R$ and $f(x) = (\lvert\sin\theta\rvert + \cos\theta\,\rvert)$. The value of $\lim\limits_{x \to \infty}\left[\dfrac{2}{f(x)}\right]$ equals (here, [.] represents greatest integer function.)	(s)	1

66. Match the following columns.

	Column I		Column II
(A)	If $f(x) = \lvert x-a\rvert + \lvert x-10\rvert + \lvert x-a-10\rvert$, where $a \in (0, 10)$, then the minimum value of f is	(p)	0
(B)	$\lim\limits_{x \to 0}\dfrac{x(1-\cos 2x)^2 - a(\sin x - \tan x)^2}{\tan^5 x + a\sin^8 x}$ is equal to	(q)	1
(C)	$\lim\limits_{n \to \infty}\dfrac{n^a\sin^2(n!)}{n+1}$, $0 < a < 1$, $n \in N$, is equal to	(r)	4
(D)	The number of solutions of the equation $\log_a(2a - x) = \log_a^3 x$, $a > 0$, $a \ne 1$ is	(s)	10
		(t)	depends on a

Previous Year Questions

67. Let α be a positive real number. Let $f : R \to R$ and $g : (\alpha, \infty) \to R$ be the functions defined by $f(x) = \sin\left(\frac{\pi x}{12}\right)$ and $g(x) = \frac{2\log_e(\sqrt{x} - \sqrt{\alpha})}{\log_e(e^{\sqrt{x}} - e^{\sqrt{\alpha}})}$. Then, the value of $\lim_{x \to \alpha^+} f(g(x))$ is ....

[Numerical Value Type, 2022 Adv.]

68. The value of the limit $\lim_{x \to \frac{\pi}{2}} \frac{4\sqrt{2}(\sin 3x + \sin x)}{\left(2 \sin 2x \sin \frac{3x}{2} + \cos \frac{5x}{2}\right) - \left(\sqrt{2} + \sqrt{2} \cos 2x + \cos \frac{3x}{2}\right)}$ is ....

[Numerical Value Type, 2020 Adv.]

69. Let e denote the base of the natural logarithm. The value of the real number a for which the right hand limit $\lim_{x \to 0^+} \frac{(1-x)^{\frac{1}{x}} - e^{-1}}{x^a}$ is equal to a non-zero real number, is ....

[Numerical Value Type, 2020 Adv.]

EXERCISE 3

Challenging Problems

1. Evaluate a, b, c and d, if $\lim_{x \to \infty} \left(\sqrt{x^4 + ax^3 + 3x^2 + bx + 2} - \sqrt{x^4 + 2x^3 - cx^2 + 3x - d}\right) = 4$.

2. If x is a real number in [0, 1]. Find the value of $\lim_{m \to \infty} \lim_{n \to \infty} [1 + \cos^{2m}(n!\,\pi x)]$.

3. If $a_1 = 1$ and $a_{n+1} = \frac{4 + 3a_n}{3 + 2a_n}$, $n \geq 1$, show that $a_{n+2} > a_{n+1}$ and if a_n has a limit l as $n \to \infty$, then evaluate $\lim_{n \to \infty} a_n$.

4. Let $a_1, a_2, \ldots, a_n$ be sequence of real numbers with $a_{n+1} = a_n + \sqrt{1 + a_n^2}$ and $a_0 = 0$. Prove that $\lim_{n \to \infty} \left(\frac{a_n}{2^{n-1}}\right) = \frac{4}{\pi}$.

5. A square is inscribed in a circle of radius R, a circle is inscribed in this square then a square in this circle and so on, n times. Find the limit of the sum of areas of all the squares as $n \to \infty$.

Answer Key

Exercise 1

1. (a)	2. (a)	3. (a)	4. (b)	5. (a)	6. (c)	7. (b)	8. (d)	9. (b)	10. (a)
11. (d)	12. (b)	13. (d)	14. (a)	15. (c)	16. (b)	17. (b)	18. (c)	19. (c)	20. (c)
21. (b)	22. (a)	23. (c)	24. (b)	25. (b)	26. (d)	27. (b)	28. (1)	29. (50)	30. (64)
31. (4)	32. (11)	33. (0.2)	34. (32)	35. (4)	36. (7)	37. (24)	38. (2)	39. (8)	40. (9)
41. (b)	42. (b)	43. (d)	44. (b)	45. (18)	46. (100)	47. (81)	48. (c)	49. (a)	50. (a)
51. (c)	52. (c)	53. (b)	54. (d)	55. (d)	56. (b)	57. (a)	58. (26)	59. (c)	60. (c)
61. (a)	62. (a)	63. (a)	64. (c)	65. (c)	66. (1)	67. (11)	68. (3)	69. (b)	70. (c)
71. (d)	72. (d)	73. (a)	74. (a)	75. (c)	76. (a)	77. (d)	78. (d)	79. (d)	80. (3)
81. (3)	82. (4)	83. (d).	84. (b)	85. (c)	86. (d)	87. (40)			

Exercise 2

1. (c)	2. (b)	3. (d)	4. (d)	5. (d)	6. (b)	7. (b)	8. (b)	9. (d)	10. (a)
11. (d)	12. (d)	13. (b)	14. (a)	15. (a)	16. (a,d)	17. (b,c,d)	18. (a,b,c)	19. (a,c)	20. (a,b,c,d)
21. (a,c,d)	22. (b,c,d)	23. (a,b,c)	24. (a,b,c)	25. (a,b,c,d)	26. (b,d)	27. (b,c,d)	28. (b,c,d)	29. (a,b,c,d)	30. (b,c,d)
31. (c)	32. (d)	33. (a)	34. (b)	35. (8)	36. (2/3)	37. (9)	38. (0)	39. (1)	40. (1)
41. (2)	42. (1)	43. (2)	44. (0)	45. (4)	46. (3)	47. (7)	48. (0)	49. (0)	50. (1.25)
51. (0.5)	52. (2.8)	53. (0.5)	54. (20)	55. (150)	56. (0.25)	57. (1.125)	58. (32)	59. (18)	60. (1.5)
61. (39)	62. (99)	63. (20)	64. (0.125)	65. (A) → (s); (B) → (p); (C) → (q); (D) → (r)					
66. (A) → (s); (B) → (r); (C) → (p); (D) → (q)				67. (0.5)	68. (8)	69. $\left(-\frac{1}{2e}\right)$			

Solutions

Exercise 1 - JEE Main Pattern

1. $f(1) = 0$

$f(1^+) = 1^+ + 2 = 3^+$

$f(1^-) = 1 - (1^-) = 0^+$

$f(2^+) = 4 - (2^+) = 2^-$

$f(2^-) = 2^- + 2 = 4^-$

$l = \lim_{x\to 1} f(f(x))$

$\text{RHL} = \lim_{x\to 1^+} f(f(1^+))$

$= \lim_{x\to 1^+} f(3^+) = 4 - (3^+) = 1$

$\text{LHL} = \lim_{x\to 1^-} f(f(1^-))$

$= \lim_{x\to 1^-} f(0^+) = 1 - 0^+ = 1$

$m = \lim_{x\to 2} f(f(x))$

$\text{RHL} = \lim_{x\to 2^+} f(f(2^+)) = \lim_{x\to 2^+} f(2^-) = 4$

$\text{LHL} = \lim_{x\to 2^-} f(f(2^-)) = \lim_{x\to 2^-} f(4^-)$

$= 4 - (4^-) = 0$

l exists but m does not exist.

2. $$\lim_{x\to 0} \frac{\sin(\pi - \pi\sin^2\tan(\sin x)}{x^2}$$

$$= \lim_{x\to 0} \frac{\sin(\pi\sin^2\tan(\sin x))}{\pi\sin^2\tan(\sin x)}\left(\frac{\pi\sin^2\tan(\sin x)}{\tan^2(\sin x)}\right)\left(\frac{\tan^2(\sin x)}{\sin^2 x}\right)\left(\frac{\sin^2 x}{x^2}\right) = \pi$$

3. $$\text{LHL} = \lim_{x\to 0^-}\left[\frac{\sin(\text{sgn}\,x)}{\text{sgn}(x)}\right] = \lim_{x\to 0^-}\left[\frac{\sin(-1)}{-1}\right] = \lim_{x\to 0^-}[\sin 1] = 0$$

$$\text{RHL} = \lim_{x\to 0^+}\left[\frac{\sin(\text{sgn}\,x)}{\text{sgn}(x)}\right] = \lim_{x\to 0^+}\left[\frac{\sin 1}{1}\right] = 0$$

$$\therefore \lim_{x\to 0}\left[\frac{\sin(\text{sgn}\,x)}{\text{sgn}(x)}\right] = 0$$

4. $$x^2 + \left(\frac{\sqrt{1+a}-1}{\sqrt[3]{1+a}-1}\right)x + \left(\frac{\sqrt[6]{1+a}-1}{\sqrt[3]{1+a}-1}\right) = 0$$

$$\alpha + \beta = \lim_{a\to 0^+} \frac{-((1+a)^{1/2} - 1)}{(1+a)^{1/3} - 1} = \frac{-\left(\frac{1}{2}a\right)}{\frac{1}{3}a} = \frac{-3}{2}$$

$$\alpha\beta = \lim_{a\to 0^+} \frac{(1+a)^{1/6} - 1}{(1+a)^{1/3} - 1}$$

$$= \lim_{a\to 0^+} \frac{(\sqrt[6]{1+a}-1)}{(\sqrt[6]{1+a}-1)(\sqrt[6]{1+a}+1)} = 1/2$$

$$\alpha + \beta = -\frac{3}{2}, \alpha\beta = \frac{1}{2} \Rightarrow \beta = \frac{1}{2\alpha}$$

$$\alpha + \frac{1}{2\alpha} = \frac{-3}{2}$$

$$\Rightarrow (2\alpha^2 + 1) = -3\alpha \Rightarrow 2\alpha^2 + 3\alpha + 1 = 0$$

$$\alpha = -1 \text{ and } \alpha = -\frac{1}{2}$$

when $\alpha = -1, \beta = \frac{1}{2\alpha} = -\frac{1}{2}$

$$\alpha = -\frac{1}{2}, \beta = \frac{1}{2}\times\left(\frac{-2}{1}\right) = -1$$

5. (i) $$\lim_{x\to\infty} \sec^{-1}\left(\frac{x}{\sin x}\right)$$

$$= \sec^{-1}\left(\frac{\infty}{\sin\infty}\right) = \sec^{-1}\left(\frac{\infty}{\text{any value between } -1 \text{ to } 1}\right)$$

$$= \sec^{-1}(\pm\infty) = \frac{\pi}{2}$$

(ii) $$\lim_{x\to\infty} \sec^{-1}\left(\frac{\sin x}{x}\right) = \sec^{-1}\left(\frac{\sin\infty}{\infty}\right)$$

$$= \sec^{-1}\left(\frac{\text{any value between } -1 \text{ to } 1}{\infty}\right)$$

$$= \sec^{-1} 0 = \text{not defined}$$

Hence (i) exists but (ii) does not exist.

6. $$f_n(x) = \tan\frac{x}{2}\left(\frac{1+\cos x}{\cos x}\right)$$

$$(1 + \sec 2x)(1 + \sec 4x)\ldots(1 + \sec 2^n x)$$

$$= \tan x\left(\frac{1+\cos 2x}{\cos 2x}\right)(1 + \sec 4x)\ldots(1 + \sec 2^n x)$$

$$= \tan 2x\,(1 + \sec 2^2 x)\ldots(1 + \sec 2^n x)$$

$$= \tan 2^{n-1} x\,(1 + \sec 2^n x) = \tan 2^n x$$

Now, $$\lim_{x\to 0}\frac{f_n(x)}{2x} = \lim_{x\to 0}\frac{\tan 2^n x}{2^n x}\cdot 2^{n-1} = 2^{n-1}$$

7. $$\cos(\tan x) - \cos x = 2\sin\left(\frac{x+\tan x}{2}\right)\sin\left(\frac{x-\tan x}{2}\right)$$

$$\Rightarrow \lim_{x\to 0}\frac{\cos(\tan x) - \cos x}{x^4} = \lim_{x\to 0}\frac{2\sin\left(\frac{x+\tan x}{2}\right)\sin\left(\frac{x-\tan x}{2}\right)}{x^4}$$

$$= \lim_{x \to 0} \frac{2\sin\left(\frac{x + \tan x}{2}\right)\sin\left(\frac{x - \tan x}{2}\right)}{x^4 \left(\frac{x + \tan x}{2}\right)\left(\frac{x - \tan x}{2}\right)} \left(\frac{x^2 - \tan^2 x}{4}\right)$$

$$= \frac{1}{2} \lim_{x \to 0} \frac{x^2 - \tan^2 x}{x^4}$$

$$= \frac{1}{2} \lim_{x \to 0} \frac{x^2 - \left(x + \frac{x^3}{3} + \frac{2}{15}x^5 + \ldots\right)^2}{x^4}$$

$$= \frac{1}{2} \lim_{x \to 0} \frac{1}{x^2}\left(1 - \left(1 + \frac{x^2}{3} + \frac{2}{15}x^4 + \ldots\right)^2\right) = \frac{1}{3}$$

8. $S_n = \frac{n(n+1)}{2}$ and $S_n - 1 = \frac{(n+2)(n-1)}{2}$

$$\therefore \quad \frac{S_n}{S_n - 1} = \frac{n(n+1)}{2} \cdot \frac{2}{(n+2)(n-1)}$$

$$= \left(\frac{n}{n-1}\right)\left(\frac{n+1}{n+2}\right)$$

$$\therefore \quad P_n = \left(\frac{2}{1} \cdot \frac{3}{2} \cdot \frac{4}{3} \cdot \frac{5}{4} \ldots \frac{n}{n-1}\right)\left(\frac{3}{4} \cdot \frac{4}{5} \cdot \frac{5}{6} \ldots \frac{n+1}{n+2}\right)$$

$$= \left(\frac{n}{1}\right)\left(\frac{3}{n+2}\right)$$

$$\therefore \quad \lim_{n \to \infty} P_n = 3$$

9. $T_r = \left(\frac{2r+5}{r(r+1)}\right)\left(\frac{3}{5}\right)^{r+1} = \left(\frac{5(r+1) - 3r}{r(r+1)}\right)\left(\frac{3}{5}\right)^{r+1}$

$$= 3\left[\frac{1}{r}\left(\frac{3}{5}\right)^r - \frac{1}{r+1}\left(\frac{3}{5}\right)^{r+1}\right] = 3(V_r - V_{r+1})$$

So, $\sum_{r=1}^{n} T_r = 3\left[\sum_{r=1}^{n} V_r - \sum_{r=1}^{n} V_{r+1}\right]$

$$\Rightarrow \quad S_n = 3(V_1 - V_{n+1}) = \left[3\left(\frac{3}{5} - \frac{1}{(n+1)}\left(\frac{3}{5}\right)^{n+1}\right)\right]$$

So, $\lim_{n \to \infty} S_n = \left(\frac{9}{5} - 0\right) = \frac{9}{5}$

10. Here, $\lim_{z \to \infty} \frac{\int_{1/2}^{z} [\cot^{-1} x]\, dx}{\int_{1/2}^{z}\left[1 + \frac{1}{x}\right] dx} = \frac{\int_{1/2}^{\cot 1} 1 \cdot dx + \int_{\cot 1}^{z} 0 \cdot dx}{\int_{1/2}^{1} 2 \cdot dx + \int_{1}^{z} 1 \cdot dx}$

As,

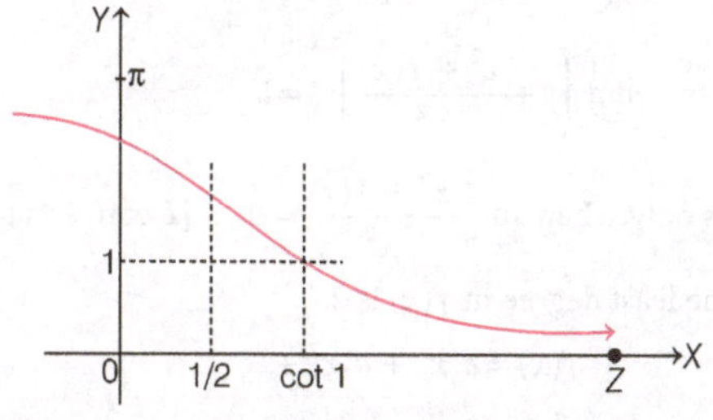

$\because$ $[\cot^{-1} x] = 1$, when $1/2 < x < \cot 1$ and $[\cos^{-1} x] = 0$, when $\cot 1 < x < z$

$$\Rightarrow \quad \lim_{z \to \infty} \frac{\int_{1/2}^{\cot 1} 1 \cdot dx}{\int_{1/2}^{1} 2 \cdot dx + \int_{1}^{z} 1 \cdot dx}$$

$$= \lim_{z \to \infty} \frac{(\cot 1 - 1/2)}{2(1 - 1/2) + (z - 1)} = 0$$

11. As, $f(x)$ is a continuous decreasing positive function on $(1, \infty)$, so

$$0 < f(8x) < f(6x) < f(4x)$$

$$\Rightarrow \quad 0 < 1 < \frac{f(6x)}{f(8x)} < \frac{f(4x)}{f(8x)}$$

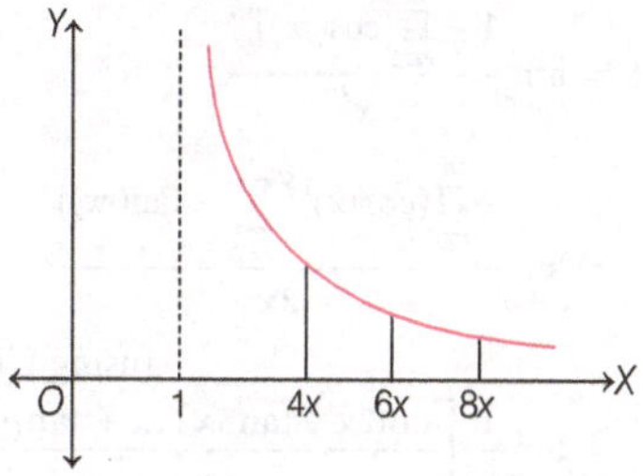

$$\Rightarrow \quad \lim_{x \to \infty} 1 \le \lim_{x \to \infty} \frac{f(6x)}{f(8x)} \le \lim_{x \to \infty} \frac{f(4x)}{f(8x)}$$

$\therefore$ By squeeze theorem,

$$\lim_{x \to \infty} \frac{f(6x)}{f(8x)} = 1$$

12. For $n = 0$, we have

$$\lim_{x \to 0} \frac{1 - \sin 1}{0 - 1} = \sin 1 - 1$$

For $n = 1$, $\lim_{x \to 0} \frac{x - \sin x}{x - \sin x} = 1$

For $n = 2$, $\lim_{x \to 0} \frac{x^2 - \sin^2 x}{x - \sin^2 x} = \lim_{x \to 0} \frac{1 - \frac{\sin^2 x}{x^2}}{\frac{1}{x} - \frac{\sin^2 x}{x^2}}$

This does not exist.

For $n = 3$ also given limit does not exist.

Hence, $n = 0$ or 1

13. $\lim_{x \to 0} (1 + x\ln(1 + b^2))^{1/x} = 2b\sin^2\theta,\ b > 0$

$$\Rightarrow \lim_{x \to 0} e^{\frac{1}{x}(1 + x\ln(1+b^2) - 1)} = 2b\sin^2\theta$$

$$\Rightarrow \quad 1 + b^2 = 2b\sin^2\theta$$

$$\Rightarrow \quad \sin^2\theta = \frac{1}{2}\left[b + \frac{1}{b}\right]$$

$$\sin^2\theta \le 1,\ b + \frac{1}{b} \ge 2$$

$$\Rightarrow \quad \frac{1}{2}\left(b + \frac{1}{b}\right) \ge 1 \Rightarrow \sin^2\theta = 1$$

$$\Rightarrow \quad \theta = \pm\frac{\pi}{2}$$

14. Let $y=\sqrt{\cos 2x}\cdot\sqrt[3]{\cos 3x}\cdot\sqrt[4]{\cos 4x}\ ......\ \sqrt[n]{\cos nx}$

$$\log_e y=\frac{1}{2}\log\cos 2x+\frac{1}{3}\log\cos 3x+\frac{1}{4}\log\cos 4x+\ldots+\frac{1}{n}\log\cos nx$$

On differentiating both sides, we get

$$\frac{1}{y}\cdot\frac{dy}{dx}=\frac{1}{2}\cdot\frac{(-2\sin 2x)}{\cos 2x}+\frac{1}{3}\cdot\left(\frac{-3\sin 3x}{\cos 3x}\right)+\ldots+\frac{1}{n}\left\{\frac{-n\sin nx}{\cos nx}\right\}$$

$$\therefore\quad \frac{dy}{dx}=\prod_{r=2}^{n}(\cos rx)^{1/r}\cdot\sum_{r=2}^{n}[-\tan(rx)] \qquad \ldots\text{(i)}$$

$$\therefore\quad L=\lim_{x\to 0}\frac{1-\prod_{r=2}^{n}[\cos(rx)]^{1/r}}{x^2}$$

$$=\lim_{x\to 0}\frac{-\prod_{r=2}^{n}(\cos rx)^{1/r}\sum_{r=2}^{n}[-\tan(rx)]}{2x}$$

[using L'Hospital's rule]

$$=\lim_{x\to 0}\frac{1}{2}\cdot\left[\frac{\tan 2x+\tan 3x+\ldots+\tan nx}{x}\right]$$

$$=\frac{1}{2}[2+3+\ldots+n]$$

$$=\frac{n^2+n-2}{4}=10 \qquad \text{[given]}$$

$\Rightarrow\quad n^2+n=42$

$\Rightarrow\quad (n+7)(n-6)=0\Rightarrow n=6$

15. As, $f'(x)>0\Rightarrow f(x)$ is increasing.

So, for $t>1$; $f(t)>1$

Now, $\quad f'(t)=\dfrac{1}{t^2+f(t)}<\dfrac{1}{1+t^2}$

$$\therefore\quad f(x)=1+\int_1^x f'(t)\,dt<1+\int_1^x\frac{dt}{1+t^2}$$

$$\Rightarrow\quad \lim_{x\to\infty}f(x)<1+\int_1^\infty\frac{dt}{1+t^2}$$

$$\Rightarrow\quad \lim_{x\to\infty}f(x)<1+\frac{\pi}{4}$$

16. $E=\sin^2\theta-\sin\theta+\dfrac{1}{2}=\left(\sin\theta-\dfrac{1}{2}\right)^2+\dfrac{1}{4}$

$\Rightarrow$ Minimum value is $\dfrac{1}{4}$.

Let $K=\sqrt{(x+1)(x+2)}$, then $K-x=\dfrac{K^2-x^2}{K+x}=\dfrac{3x+2}{K+x}$

$$\lim_{x\to\infty}(K-x)=\lim_{x\to\infty}\frac{3+\frac{2}{x}}{\frac{K}{x}+1}$$

$$\therefore\quad \lim_{x\to\infty}(K-x)=\frac{3+0}{1+1}=\frac{3}{2} \qquad \left[\lim_{x\to\infty}\frac{K}{x}=1\right]$$

The required equation is $x^2-\dfrac{7}{4}x+\dfrac{3}{8}=0$,

i.e. $\quad 8x^2-14x+3=0.$

17. As, $f(x)$ being polynomial having roots 1, 2, 3, 4 and leading coefficient is 1.

$\therefore\quad f(x)=(x-1)(x-2)(x-3)(x-4)$

Similarly, $\quad g(x)=(x-1)\left(x-\dfrac{1}{2}\right)\left(x-\dfrac{1}{3}\right)\left(x-\dfrac{1}{4}\right)$

$$\therefore\quad \lim_{x\to 1}\frac{f(x)}{g(x)}=\lim_{x\to 1}\frac{(x-1)(x-2)(x-3)(x-4)}{(x-1)\left(x-\frac{1}{2}\right)\left(x-\frac{1}{3}\right)\left(x-\frac{1}{4}\right)}$$

$$=\frac{(-1)(-2)(-3)}{\left(\frac{1}{2}\right)\left(\frac{2}{3}\right)\left(\frac{3}{4}\right)}=-24$$

18. Here, $\quad \lim_{x\to\infty}f(x)=\lim_{x\to\infty}\dfrac{1}{3}\left[f(x+1)+\dfrac{5}{f(x+2)}\right]$

$$\Rightarrow\quad l=\frac{1}{3}\cdot\left(l+\frac{5}{l}\right)\Rightarrow l^2=\frac{1}{3}(l^2+5)$$

$$\Rightarrow\quad 2l^2=5\ \Rightarrow l=\sqrt{\frac{5}{2}}$$

19. Here, $\quad f(x+y)=f(x)+f(y)$

$f(2)=f(1)+f(1)=2$

$f(3)=f(1+2)=f(1)+f(2)=3$

$f(4)=f(1+3)=f(1)+f(3)=4$

and so on,

$f(x)=x,$ for all $x\in R$

$\Rightarrow\quad f(\tan x)=\tan x,\quad f(\sin x)=\sin x$

$$\therefore\quad \lim_{x\to 0}\frac{2^{f(\tan x)}-2^{f(\sin x)}}{x^2 f(\sin x)}=\lim_{x\to 0}\frac{2^{\tan x}-2^{\sin x}}{x^2\sin x}$$

$$=\lim_{x\to 0}\frac{2^{\sin x}\cdot\{2^{\tan x-\sin x}-1\}}{\sin x\cdot x^2}\times\frac{\tan x-\sin x}{\tan x-\sin x}$$

$$=\lim_{x\to 0}\frac{\{2^{\tan x-\sin x}-1\}}{\tan x-\sin x}\times\left\{\frac{\tan x-\sin x}{x^2\sin x}\right\}\times 2^{\sin x}$$

$$=\lim_{x\to 0}\frac{2^{\tan x-\sin x}-1}{\tan x-\sin x}\times\frac{1-\cos x}{x^2\cos x}\times 2^{\sin x}$$

$$=\lim_{x\to 0}\frac{2^{\tan x-\sin x}-1}{\tan x-\sin x}\times\frac{2\sin^2 x/2}{4(x/2)^2}\times 2^{\sin x}\times\frac{1}{\cos x}$$

$$=\log 2\times\frac{1}{2}\times 1=\frac{1}{2}\log 2=\log\sqrt{2}$$

20. Here, $\lim_{x\to 0}\left(1+\dfrac{x^2+f(x)}{x^2}\right)^{1/x}$

$$\Rightarrow\quad \lim_{x\to 0}\left(1+\frac{x^2+f(x)}{x^2}\right)^{1/x}=L \qquad \text{(say)}$$

exists only when $\lim_{x\to 0}\dfrac{x^2+f(x)}{x^2}=0 \qquad [L \text{ converts to } 1^\infty \text{ form}]$

So, the least degree in $f(x)$ is 2.

i.e. $\quad f(x)=a_2x^2+a_3x^3+\ldots$

Now, $\quad \lim_{x\to 0}\left(1+\dfrac{x^2+f(x)}{x^2}\right)^{1/x}=e^2$

$$\Rightarrow e^{\lim_{x\to 0}\left(\frac{x^2+f(x)}{x^2}\right)\frac{1}{x}} = e^2 \Rightarrow e^{\lim_{x\to 0}\frac{x^2+f(x)}{x^3}} = e^2$$

$$\therefore \quad \lim_{x\to 0}\frac{x^2+f(x)}{x^3} = 2 \Rightarrow \lim_{x\to 0}\frac{x^2+a_2x^2+a_3x^3+\ldots}{x^3} = 2$$

$\Rightarrow a_2 = -1, a_3 = 2$ and a_4, a_5 are any arbitrary constants. Since, we want polynomial of least degree.

Hence, $f(x) = -x^2 + 2x^3$

21. We have, $\lim_{n\to\infty} n^{-n^2}\left[(n+1)\left(n+\frac{1}{2}\right)\ldots\left(n+\frac{1}{2^{n-1}}\right)\right]^n$

$$= \lim_{n\to\infty}\left[\frac{(n+1)\left(n+\frac{1}{2}\right)\ldots\left(n+\frac{1}{2^{n-1}}\right)}{n^n}\right]^n$$

$$= \lim_{n\to\infty}\left(\frac{n+1}{n}\right)^n\cdot\left(\frac{n+\frac{1}{2}}{n}\right)^n\ldots\left(\frac{n+\frac{1}{2^{n-1}}}{n}\right)^n$$

$$= \lim_{n\to\infty}\left(1+\frac{1}{n}\right)^n\cdot\left(1+\frac{1}{2n}\right)^n\ldots\left(1+\frac{1}{2^{n-1}n}\right)^n \quad [1^\infty \text{ form}]$$

$$= \lim_{n\to\infty}\left(1+\frac{1}{n}\right)^n\cdot\left(1+\frac{1}{2n}\right)^{\frac{2n}{2}}\ldots\left(1+\frac{1}{2^{n-1}n}\right)^{\frac{2^{n-1}\cdot n}{2^{n-1}}}$$

$$= e^1\cdot e^{1/2}\cdot e^{1/4}\ldots e^{1/2^{n-1}} \quad \left[\text{using } \lim_{n\to\infty}\left(1+\frac{1}{n}\right)^{an} = e^a\right]$$

$$= e^{(1+1/2+1/4+\ldots)} = e^{\frac{1}{1-\frac{1}{2}}} = e^2$$

22. Here, two straight lines $(\tan\alpha)\,x + (\sin\alpha)\,y = \alpha$ and $(\alpha\operatorname{cosec}\alpha)\,x + (\cos\alpha)\,y = 1$

have their point of intersection, as

$$x = \frac{\alpha\cos\alpha - \sin\alpha}{\sin\alpha - \alpha} \quad\text{and}\quad y = \frac{\alpha - x\tan\alpha}{\sin\alpha}$$

$\therefore$ When $\alpha \to 0$, we obtain the point P.

i.e. $\lim_{\alpha\to 0} x = \lim_{\alpha\to 0}\frac{\alpha\cos\alpha - \sin\alpha}{\sin\alpha - \alpha} \quad \left[\frac{0}{0}\text{ form}\right]$

$$= \lim_{\alpha\to 0}\frac{-\alpha\sin\alpha + \cos\alpha - \cos\alpha}{\cos\alpha - 1}$$

[applying L'Hospital's rule]

$$= \lim_{\alpha\to 0}\frac{\alpha\left(2\sin\frac{\alpha}{2}\cos\frac{\alpha}{2}\right)}{2\sin^2\frac{\alpha}{2}} = \lim_{\alpha\to 0}\frac{\alpha}{\tan\frac{\alpha}{2}} = \lim_{\alpha\to 0}\frac{\frac{2\alpha}{2}}{\tan\frac{\alpha}{2}} = 2$$

Again, as $\lim_{\alpha\to 0} y = \lim_{\alpha\to 0}\frac{\alpha - x\tan\alpha}{\sin\alpha}$

$$= \lim_{\alpha\to 0}\left(\frac{\alpha}{\sin\alpha} - \frac{x}{\cos\alpha}\right)$$

$$= \lim_{\alpha\to 0}\frac{\alpha}{\sin\alpha} - \lim_{\alpha\to 0}\frac{x}{\cos\alpha}$$

$$= 1 - 2 \quad \left[\text{as } \lim_{\alpha\to 0} x = 2\right]$$

$$\therefore \quad \lim_{\alpha\to 0} y = -1$$

Hence, limiting position P is $(2, -1)$.

23. $l = \lim_{x\to 1}\frac{nx^n(x-1)-(x^n-1)}{(e^x-e)\sin\pi x}$

Put $x = 1 + h$, so that as $x \to 1, h \to 0$

$$\therefore \quad l = -\lim_{h\to 0}\frac{h\cdot n(1+h)^n - \{(1+h)^n - 1\}}{e(e^h-1)\sin\pi h}$$

$$l = -\lim_{h\to 0}\frac{n\cdot h(1+{}^nC_1h+{}^nC_2h^2+{}^nC_3h^3+\ldots) - (1+{}^nC_1h+{}^nC_2h^2+{}^nC_3h^3+\ldots-1)}{\pi e(h^2)\left(\frac{e^h-1}{h}\right)\left(\frac{\sin\pi h}{\pi h}\right)}$$

$$= -\frac{n^2-{}^nC_2}{\pi e} = -\left[\frac{2n^2-n(n-1)}{2\pi e}\right]$$

$$= -\frac{n^2+n}{2(\pi e)} = -\frac{n(n+1)}{2(\pi e)}$$

If $n = 100 \Rightarrow l = -\left(\frac{5050}{\pi e}\right)$

Hence, (c) is the correct answer.

24. $\lim_{x\to 2^-}\frac{\cos(2x+4)-33}{2} = -16$

and $\lim_{x\to 2^-}\frac{x^2|4x-8|}{x-2} = -4(4) = -16$

By Sandwich theorem, $\lim_{x\to 2^-} f(x) = -16$

25. We have,

$$\lim_{y\to 0}\left[\frac{e^{\lim_{x\to\infty}\frac{\ln\left(1+\frac{ay}{x}\right)}{1/x}} - e^{\lim_{x\to\infty}\frac{\ln\left(1+\frac{by}{x}\right)}{1/x}}}{y}\right] \quad \left[\frac{0}{0}\text{form}\right]$$

$$= \lim_{y\to 0}\frac{e^{\lim_{x\to\infty}\frac{\frac{1}{1+ay/x}\cdot ay\left(-\frac{1}{x^2}\right)}{(-1/x^2)}} - e^{\lim_{x\to\infty}\frac{\frac{1}{(1+by/x)}\cdot by\left(-\frac{1}{x^2}\right)}{(-1/x^2)}}}{y}$$

$$= \lim_{y\to 0}\frac{e^{ay}-e^{by}}{y} \quad \left[\frac{0}{0}\text{form}\right]$$

$$= \lim_{y\to 0}\frac{e^{ay}a - be^{by}}{1} = a - b$$

26. We have, $\lim_{x\to\infty}\frac{\frac{2}{x}+2+\frac{\sin 2x}{x}}{\left(2+\frac{\sin 2x}{x}\right)e^{\sin x}}$

$$= \lim_{x\to\infty}\frac{2}{2}e^{-\sin x} \quad \left[\because \lim_{x\to\infty}\frac{\sin 2x}{2x} = 0\right]$$

$$= \lim_{x\to\infty} e^{-\sin x} \quad [\because -1 < \sin x < 1]$$

So, $\frac{1}{e} < l < e$

Hence, limit does not exists.

27. We have, $\lim_{x\to 0} \frac{(1^x + 2^x + \dots + n^x)^{\frac{1}{x}}}{n}$ $[1^\infty \text{ form}]$

$$= e^{\lim_{x\to 0}\left(\frac{1^x + 2^x + \dots + n^x}{n} - 1\right)\frac{1}{x}}$$

$$= e^{\lim_{x\to 0}\left(\frac{1^x - 1}{x} + \frac{2^x - 1}{x} + \frac{3^x - 1}{x} + \dots + \frac{n^x - 1}{x}\right)\frac{1}{n}}$$

$$= e^{\frac{1}{n}(\ln 1 + \ln 2 + \ln 3 + \dots + \ln n)} \quad \left[\because \lim_{x\to 0} \frac{a^x - 1}{x} = \ln a\right]$$

$$= e^{\frac{1}{n}\ln(n!)} = e^{\ln(n!)^{\frac{1}{n}}} = (n!)^{1/n}$$

28. We have, $\lim_{x\to 0}\left[\frac{x}{\sin x}\right] = 1$

and $\lim_{x\to 0}\left[\frac{\sin x}{x}\right] = 0$

$$\lim_{x\to 0}\left[\frac{\tan x}{x}\right] = 1$$

$$\therefore \lim_{x\to 0} \frac{\left[\frac{x}{\sin x}\right] - \left[\frac{\sin x}{x}\right]}{\left[\frac{\tan x}{x}\right]} = 1$$

29. We have, $a_n = \sum_{k=1}^{n} 2k = n(n+1)$

and $b_n = \sum_{k=1}^{n} (2k-1) = n(n+1) - n$

Now, $\lim_{n\to\infty} (\sqrt{a_n} - \sqrt{b_n}) = \lim_{n\to\infty} \sqrt{n(n+1)} - \sqrt{n(n+1) - n}$

$$= \lim_{n\to\infty} \frac{n(n+1) - n(n+1) + n}{\sqrt{n(n+1)} + \sqrt{n(n+1) - n}}$$

$$= \lim_{n\to\infty} \frac{n}{n\left(\sqrt{1 + \frac{1}{n}} + \sqrt{1 + \frac{1}{n} - \frac{1}{n^2}}\right)}$$

$$= \frac{1}{2} = 0.5$$

$\therefore 100 \lim_{n\to\infty} (\sqrt{a_n} - \sqrt{b_n}) = 100 \times 0.5 = 50$

30. Let $x^{2012} = t$, then $t \to 0$ as $x \to 0$

$$\therefore \lim_{t\to 0} \frac{\sin t - t\cos t + t^3}{t(e^{5t} - 1 - 5t)} = \lim_{t\to 0} \frac{\sin t - t\cos t + t^3}{t \cdot 25t^2\left(\frac{e^{5t} - 1 - 5t}{25t^2}\right)}$$

Now, $\lim_{t\to 0} \frac{e^{5t} - 1 - 5t}{25t^2} = \frac{1}{2}$ $\left[\because \lim_{x\to 0} \frac{e^x - 1 - x}{x^2} = \frac{1}{2}\right]$

$$\therefore \frac{2}{25}\lim_{t\to 0} \frac{\sin t - t\cos t + t^3}{t^3}$$

$$= \frac{2}{25}\lim_{t\to 0} \frac{\left(t - \frac{t^3}{3!} + \frac{t^5}{5!} \dots\right) - t\left(1 - \frac{t^2}{2!} + \frac{t^4}{4!} \dots\right) + t^3}{t^3}$$

$$= \frac{2}{25}\left(\frac{1}{2} + 1 - \frac{1}{6}\right) = \frac{8}{75} = 0.106 = \lambda$$

$\therefore \quad 750\lambda = 80$

(Sum of digits)$^2 = (8)^2 = 64$

31. We have, $y = \left(\frac{s^2 + 2s - 3}{s - 1}\right)x - 1 - s$

Slope of line $= \frac{s^2 + 2s - 3}{s - 1}$

$$\therefore \quad f'(1) = \lim_{s\to 1} \frac{s^2 + 2s - 3}{s - 1} = \lim_{s\to 1} \frac{(s+3)(s-1)}{s - 1}$$

$$= \lim_{s\to 1}(s+3) = 4$$

32. We have, $\lim_{x\to 1}\left(\frac{x^3 + 2x^2 + x + 1}{x^2 + 2x + 3}\right)^{\frac{1-\cos(x-1)}{(x-1)^2}}$

$$= \lim_{x\to 1}\left[\frac{x^3 + 2x^2 + x + 1}{x^2 + 2x + 3}\right]^{\lim_{x\to 1}\frac{1-\cos(x-1)}{(x-1)^2}}$$

Now, $\lim_{x\to 1} \frac{1 - \cos(x-1)}{(x-1)^2}$

$$= \lim_{t\to 0} \frac{1 - \cos t}{t^2} = \frac{1}{2} \quad [\text{put } x - 1 = t, \text{ then } t \to 0 \text{ as } x \to 1]$$

$$\therefore \lim_{x\to 1}\left[\frac{x^3 + 2x^2 + x + 1}{x^2 + 2x + 3}\right]^{\frac{1}{2}} = \left(\frac{5}{6}\right)^{\frac{1}{2}}$$

$\therefore \alpha = 5$ and $\beta = 6$

Hence, $\alpha + \beta = 11$

33. We have, $\lim_{x\to 2^+}\left(\frac{|x|^3}{3} - \left[\frac{x}{3}\right]^3\right) = \frac{|2^+|^3}{3} - \left[\frac{2^+}{3}\right]^3$

$$= \frac{8}{3} - 0 = 8/3 = 2.6 = L$$

Hence, $\frac{[L]}{10} = 0.20$

34. We have, $\lim_{x\to 0^-} (\log(\{x\} + |[x]|)^{\{x\}}$

$$= \lim_{h\to 0} \log(\{0 - h\} + |[0 - h]|)^{\{0-h\}}$$

$$= \lim_{h\to 0} \log(1 - h + 1)^{1-h}$$

$$= \lim_{h\to 0} \log(2 - h)^{1-h} = \log 2$$

$$P = \ln 2$$

$$4P = 4\ln 2 = 4 \times 0.693 = 2.772$$

$$[4P] = 2$$

$$[4P] + 30 = 32$$

35. Let $y = \sqrt{(1 - \cos x) + \sqrt{1 - \cos x + \dots \infty}}$

$\therefore \quad y = \sqrt{1 - \cos x + y}$

$\Rightarrow \quad y^2 - y + \cos x - 1 = 0$

When $y > 0$

$$\therefore \quad y = \frac{1 + \sqrt{5 - 4\cos x}}{2}$$

$$\therefore \lim_{x\to 0}\frac{\dfrac{1+\sqrt{5-4\cos x}}{2}-1}{x^2}=\lim_{x\to 0}\frac{\sqrt{5-4\cos x}-1}{2x^2}\quad\left[\frac{0}{0}\text{ form}\right]$$

$$=\lim_{x\to 0}\frac{\dfrac{1}{2\sqrt{5-4\cos x}}(0+4\sin x)}{4x}$$

$$=\lim_{x\to 0}\frac{4\sin x}{8x\sqrt{5-4\cos x}}$$

$$=\frac{1}{2}=0.5\quad\left[\because \lim_{x\to 0}\frac{\sin x}{x}=1\right]$$

$$\therefore 8\lim_{x\to 0}\frac{\left(\sqrt{(1-\cos x)+\sqrt{(1-\cos x)+\sqrt{(1-\cos x)+\ldots\infty}}}\right)-1}{x^2}$$

$$=8\times 0.5=4$$

36. We have, $\lim_{x\to 0}\dfrac{4\left[\dfrac{\sqrt{3}}{2}\sin\left(\dfrac{\pi}{6}+x\right)-\dfrac{1}{2}\cos\left(\dfrac{\pi}{6}+x\right)\right]}{x\sqrt{3}[\sqrt{3}\cos x-\sin x]}$

$$=\lim_{x\to 0}\frac{4\left[\cos\pi/6\sin\left(\dfrac{\pi}{6}+x\right)-\sin\pi/6\cos\left(\dfrac{\pi}{6}+x\right)\right]}{\sqrt{3}x[\sqrt{3}\cos x-\sin x]}$$

$$=\lim_{x\to 0}\frac{4\sin x}{\sqrt{3}\,x(\sqrt{3}\cos x-\sin x)}$$

$$=\lim_{x\to 0}\frac{\sin x}{x}\cdot\frac{4}{\sqrt{3}(\sqrt{3}\cos x-\sin x)}=\frac{4}{3}=\frac{m}{n}\text{ (given)}$$

$\therefore\quad m=4$ and $n=3$

$\therefore\quad m+n=7$

37. For non-invertible, coefficients of x is zero

$$m^2-4=0\Rightarrow m=\pm 2$$

So, $\alpha=-2,\beta=2$ $\quad[\because \alpha<\beta]$

$$\lim_{x\to\frac{\pi}{3}}\frac{\tan^3 x-3\tan x}{\cos(x+\pi/6)}$$

$$=\lim_{x\to\frac{\pi}{3}}\frac{\dfrac{-(3\tan x-\tan^3 x)(1-3\tan^2 x)}{(1-3\tan^2 x)}}{\cos(x+\pi/6)}$$

$$=\lim_{x\to\frac{\pi}{3}}\frac{(-\tan 3x)(1-3\tan^2 x)}{\cos(x+\pi/6)}$$

Put $x=\dfrac{\pi}{3}+h,$

$$=\lim_{h\to 0}\frac{-\tan(\pi+3h)\left(1-3\tan^2\left(\dfrac{\pi}{3}+h\right)\right)}{-\sin h}$$

$$=\lim_{h\to 0}\frac{\tan 3h}{3h}\times\frac{3h}{\sin h}\left(1-3\tan^2\left(\frac{\pi}{3}+h\right)\right)$$

$$=3(-8)=-24$$

38. $\lim_{n\to\infty}\dfrac{\sin\dfrac{1}{\sqrt{n}}}{\dfrac{1}{\sqrt{n}}\times\sqrt{n}}\left(\dfrac{1}{\sqrt{n+1}}+\dfrac{1}{\sqrt{n+2}}+\ldots+\dfrac{1}{\sqrt{n+3n}}\right)$

$$=1\cdot\lim_{n\to\infty}\frac{1}{n}\left(\frac{1}{\sqrt{1+\frac{1}{n}}}+\frac{1}{\sqrt{1+\frac{2}{n}}}+\ldots+\frac{1}{\sqrt{1+\frac{3n}{n}}}\right)$$

$$=\lim_{n\to\infty}\frac{1}{n}\sum_{r=1}^{3n}\frac{1}{\sqrt{1+\frac{r}{n}}}=\int_0^3\frac{dx}{\sqrt{1+x}}$$

$$=\int_0^3(1+x)^{-\frac{1}{2}}dx=2(1+x)^{\frac{1}{2}}\Big|_0^3$$

$$=2(2-1)=2$$

39. We know that

$$\lim_{x\to 0}\frac{\sin x}{x}\to 1^-\text{ and }\lim_{x\to 0}\frac{x}{\sin x}\to 1^+$$

So, $\lim_{x\to 0}\left[100\dfrac{x}{\sin x}\right]+\lim_{x\to 0}\left[99\dfrac{\sin x}{x}\right]=100+98=198$

$$\left(\frac{M-2}{4}\right)!=\left(\frac{196}{4}\right)!=49!$$

Exponent of 7 in 49!

$$=\left[\frac{49}{7}\right]+\left[\frac{49}{7^2}\right]+\left[\frac{49}{7^3}\right]+\ldots$$

$$=7+1=8$$

40. We have, $\lim_{x\to 0}(x^{-3}\sin 3x+ax^{-2}+b)$

$$=\lim_{x\to 0}\frac{\sin 3x}{x^3}+\frac{a}{x^2}+b$$

$$=\lim_{x\to 0}\frac{\sin 3x+ax+bx^3}{x^3}$$

$$=\lim_{x\to 0}\frac{\dfrac{3\sin 3x}{3x}+a+bx^2}{x^2}$$

For existence, of limit $(3+a)=0\Rightarrow a=-3$

$$\therefore\ \lim_{x\to 0}\frac{\sin 3x-3x+bx^3}{x^3}$$

$$=27\lim_{t\to 0}\frac{\sin t-t}{t^3}+b\ (3x=t)$$

$$=-\frac{27}{6}+b=0$$

$\Rightarrow\quad b=9/2$

Now, $\left|\dfrac{2ab}{3}\right|=\left|\dfrac{2(-3)}{3}\dfrac{9}{2}\right|=\left|\dfrac{-27}{3}\right|=9$

41. $\lim_{x\to 0}=\dfrac{e-(1+2x)^{1/2x}}{x}$

$$=\lim_{x\to 0}=\frac{e-e^{\frac{1}{2x}\ln(1+2x)}}{x}=\lim_{x\to 0}(-e)\frac{\left(e^{\frac{\ln(1+2x)}{2x}-1}-1\right)}{x}$$

$$=\lim_{x\to 0}(-e)\frac{e^{\frac{\ln(1+2x)}{2x}-1}-1}{\dfrac{\ln(1+2x)}{2x}-1},\ \frac{\dfrac{\ln(1+2x)}{2x}-1}{x}$$

$$=\lim_{x\to 0}(-e)\frac{\ln(1+2x)-2x}{2x^2}$$

$$=\lim_{x\to 0}(-e)\frac{\left[\left(2x-\dfrac{(2x)^2}{2}+\ldots\right)-2x\right]}{2x^2}=e\times 1=e$$

42. Given expansion can be written as

$$= \lim_{n\to\infty} \frac{\sum_{r=1}^{n-1} (r^2 - r)(n-r)}{\sum_{r=1}^{n} r^3 - \sum_{r=1}^{n} r^2}$$

$$= \lim_{n\to\infty} \frac{\sum_{r=1}^{n-1} (-r^3 + r^2(n+1) - nr)}{\left(\frac{n(n+1)}{2}\right)^2 - \frac{n(n+1)(2n+1)}{6}}$$

$$= \lim_{n\to\infty} \frac{\frac{-n^2(n-1)^2}{4} + \frac{(n+1)(n-1)n(2n-1)}{6} - \frac{n^2}{2}(n-1)}{\frac{n(n+1)}{2}\left(\frac{n(n+1)}{2} - \frac{2n+1}{3}\right)}$$

$$= \lim_{n\to\infty} \frac{\frac{-3n(n-1)^2 + 2(n+1)(n-1)(2n-1) - 6n(n-1)}{12}}{\frac{(n+1)}{2}\frac{[3n(n+1) - 2(2n+1)]}{6}}$$

$$= \lim_{n\to\infty} \frac{(n-1)[-3n(n-1) + 2(2n^2 + 2n - n - 1) - 6n]}{(n+1)[3n^2 + 3n - 4n - 2]}$$

$$= \lim_{n\to\infty} \frac{(n-1)[-3n^2 + 3n + 4n^2 + 2n - 2 - 6n]}{(n+1)(3n^2 - n - 2)}$$

$$= \lim_{n\to\infty} \frac{(n-1)[n^2 - n - 2]}{(n+1)[3n^2 - n - 2]} = \frac{1}{3}$$

43. $\lim_{x\to 0} \frac{e^{2|\sin x|} - 2|\sin x| - 1}{x^2}$

$$e^x = 1 + x + \frac{x^2}{2!} + \frac{x^3}{3!} + \dots$$

$$e^{2|\sin x|} = 1 + 2|\sin x| + \frac{(2|\sin x|)^2}{2!} + \frac{(2|\sin x|)^3}{3!} + \dots$$

$\therefore$

$$\lim_{x\to 0} = \frac{1 + 2|\sin x| + \frac{4|\sin x|^2}{2!} + \frac{8|\sin x|^3}{3!} + \dots - 2|\sin x| - 1}{x^2}$$

$$= \lim_{x\to 0} \frac{|\sin x|^2}{x^2}\left[\frac{4}{2!} + \frac{8}{3!}|\sin x| + \dots\right]$$

$$= \lim_{x\to 0} \frac{\sin^2 x}{x^2}\left[\frac{4}{2!} + \frac{8}{3!}|\sin x| + \dots\right] = \frac{4}{2!} = 2$$

44. Given, $\lim_{x\to 0} \frac{3 + \alpha \sin x + \beta \cos x + \log_e(1-x)}{3\tan^2 x} = \frac{1}{3}$

$$\Rightarrow \quad \lim_{x\to 0} \frac{\frac{3 + \alpha \sin x + \beta \cos x + \log e(1-x)}{x^2}}{\frac{3\tan^2 x}{x^2} \times x^2} = \frac{1}{3}$$

For limit to be exist, $\beta + 3 = 0 \Rightarrow \beta = -3$

$$\text{So, } \lim_{x\to 0} \frac{\alpha \cos x - \beta \sin x - \frac{1}{1-x}}{(2x)} = 1$$

[using L' Hospital rule and $\lim_{x\to 0}\left(\frac{\tan x}{x}\right)^2 = 1$]

For limit to be exist, numerator $\to 0$

$\Rightarrow \quad \alpha - 0 - 1 = 0 \Rightarrow \alpha = 1$

Hence, $2\alpha - \beta = 2 \times 1 - (-3) = 5$

Alternate Solution

$$\lim_{x\to 0} \frac{3 + \alpha \sin x + \beta \cos x + \log_e(1-x)}{3\tan^2 x} = \frac{1}{3}$$

$$\Rightarrow \lim_{x\to 0} \frac{3 + \alpha\left[x - \frac{x^3}{3!} + \dots\right] + \beta\left[1 - \frac{x^2}{2!} + \frac{x^4}{4!} \dots\right] + \left(-x - \frac{x^2}{2} - \frac{x^3}{3} + \dots\right)}{3\tan^2 x} = \frac{1}{3}$$

$$\Rightarrow \lim_{x\to 0} \frac{(3+\beta) + (\alpha - 1)x + \left(-\frac{1}{2} - \frac{\beta}{2}\right)x^2 + \dots}{3x^2} \times \frac{x^2}{\tan^2 x} = \frac{1}{3}$$

$$\Rightarrow \beta + 3 = 0, \alpha - 1 = 0 \text{ and } \frac{-\frac{1}{2} - \frac{\beta}{2}}{3} = \frac{1}{3}$$

$\Rightarrow \quad \beta = -3$ and $\alpha = 1$

$\therefore 2\alpha - \beta = 2 + 3 = 5$

45. Finding right hand limit

$$\lim_{x\to 0^+} f(x) = \lim_{h\to 0} f(0+h) = \lim_{h\to 0} f(h)$$

$$= \lim_{h\to 0} \frac{\cos^{-1}(1-h^2)\sin^{-1}(1-h)}{h(1-h^2)}$$

$$= \lim_{h\to 0} \frac{\cos^{-1}(1-h^2)}{h}\left(\frac{\sin^{-1} 1}{1}\right)$$

Let $\cos^{-1}(1-h^2) = \theta$

$$\Rightarrow \quad \cos\theta = 1 - h^2 = \frac{\pi}{2}\lim_{\theta\to 0} \frac{\theta}{\sqrt{1-\cos\theta}}$$

$$= \frac{\pi}{2}\lim_{\theta\to 0} \frac{1}{\sqrt{\frac{1-\cos\theta}{\theta^2}}} = \frac{\pi}{2}\frac{1}{\sqrt{\frac{1}{2}}}$$

$$\therefore \quad R = \frac{\pi}{\sqrt{2}}$$

$$\therefore \quad L = \lim_{x\to 0^-} f(x) = \lim_{h\to 0} f(-h)$$

$$= \lim_{h\to 0} \frac{\cos^{-1}(1 - \{-h\}^2)\sin^{-1}(1 - \{-h\})}{\{-h\} - \{-h\}^3}$$

$$= \lim_{h\to 0} \frac{\cos^{-1}(1 - (-h+1)^2)\sin^{-1}(1 - (-h+1))}{(-h+1) - (-h+1)^3}$$

$$= \lim_{h\to 0} \frac{\cos^{-1}(-h^2 + 2h)\sin^{-1} h}{(1-h)(1 - (1-h)^2)}$$

$$= \lim_{h\to 0}\left(\frac{\pi}{2}\right)\frac{\sin^{-1} h}{(1 - (1-h)^2)}$$

$$= \frac{\pi}{2}\lim_{h\to 0}\left(\frac{\sin^{-1} h}{-h^2 + 2h}\right)$$

$$= \frac{\pi}{2}\lim_{h\to 0}\left(\frac{\sin^{-1} h}{h}\right)\left(\frac{1}{-h+2}\right)$$

$$\therefore \quad L = \frac{\pi}{4}$$

$$\Rightarrow \quad \frac{32}{\pi^2}(L^2 + R^2) = \frac{32}{\pi^2}\left(\frac{\pi^2}{2} + \frac{\pi^2}{16}\right) = 16 + 2 = 18$$

46. Let $L = \lim_{x \to 1} \dfrac{(5x+1)^{1/3} - (x+5)^{1/3}}{(2x+3)^{1/2} - (x+4)^{1/2}}$ $\left[\text{form } \dfrac{0}{0}\right]$

$$\therefore \quad L = \lim_{x \to 1} \frac{\frac{1}{3}(5x+1)^{\frac{-2}{3}} \cdot 5 - \frac{1}{3}(x+5)^{\frac{-2}{3}}}{\frac{1}{2}(2x+3)^{\frac{-1}{2}} \cdot 2 - \frac{1}{2}(x+4)^{\frac{-1}{2}}}$$

[using L' Hospital rule]

$$= \frac{8\sqrt{5}}{3 \cdot 6^{2/3}} = \frac{m\sqrt{5}}{n(2n)^{2/3}} \quad \text{[given]}$$

On comparing, we get

$$m = 8 \text{ and } n = 3$$

Thus, $\quad 8m + 12n = 100$

47. $\lim_{x \to 0} \dfrac{ax^2e^x - b\log_e(1+x) + cxe^{-x}}{x^2 \sin x} = 1$

$$\lim_{x \to 0} \frac{ax^2\left(1 + x + \frac{x^2}{2!} + \frac{x^3}{3!} + \dots\right) - b\left(x - \frac{x^2}{2} + \frac{x^3}{3} - \dots\right) + cx\left(1 - x + \frac{x^2}{2!} - \frac{x^3}{3!} + \dots\right)}{x^3\left(\frac{\sin x}{x}\right)} = 1$$

$$\lim_{x \to 0} \frac{(c-b)\,x + \left(\frac{b}{2} - c + a\right)x^2 + \left(a - \frac{b}{3} + \frac{c}{2}\right)x^3 + \dots}{x^3} = 1$$

$$c - b = 0 \qquad \text{...(i)}$$

$$\frac{b}{2} - c + a = 0 \qquad \text{...(ii)}$$

$$a - \frac{b}{3} + \frac{c}{2} = 1 \qquad \text{...(iii)}$$

From Eqs. (i), (ii) and (iii), we get

$$a = \frac{3}{4}, b = c = \frac{3}{2}$$

$$\therefore 16(a^2 + b^2 + c^2) = 16\left(\frac{9}{16} + \frac{9}{4} + \frac{9}{4}\right) = 9 + 72 = 81$$

48. Let $L = \lim_{n \to \infty} \{(2^{\frac{1}{2}} - 2^{\frac{1}{3}})(2^{\frac{1}{2}} - 2^{\frac{1}{5}}) \dots (2^{\frac{1}{2}} - 2^{\frac{1}{2n-1}})\}$

Here, $(2^{\frac{1}{2}} - 2^{\frac{1}{3}})^n < (2^{\frac{1}{2}} - 2^{\frac{1}{3}})(2^{\frac{1}{2}} - 2^{\frac{1}{5}}) \dots (2^{\frac{1}{2}} - 2^{\frac{1}{2n-1}}) < (2^{\frac{1}{2}} - 2^{\frac{1}{2n-1}})^n$

$$\Rightarrow \lim_{n \to \infty} (2^{\frac{1}{2}} - 2^{\frac{1}{3}})^n < L < \lim_{n \to \infty} (2^{\frac{1}{2}} - 2^{\frac{1}{2n-1}})^n$$

Since, $\lim_{n \to \infty} (2^{\frac{1}{2}} - 2^{\frac{1}{3}})^n = 0$

and $\lim_{n \to \infty} (2^{\frac{1}{2}} - 2^{\frac{1}{2n-1}})^n = 0$

$$\therefore \quad L = 0$$

49. We have, $\quad \lim_{x \to \alpha} ([x-5] - [2x+2]) = 0$

$$[\alpha - 5] - [2\alpha + 2] = 0$$

$$[\alpha - 5] = [2\alpha + 2] \qquad \text{...(i)}$$

For algebraic calculation,

$$\alpha - 5 = 2\alpha + 2$$

$$\Rightarrow \quad \alpha = -7$$

So, its value will be around -7

For $\alpha = -7.5$ in Eq. (i),

$$[-7.5 - 5] = [-15 + 2]$$

$$\Rightarrow \quad [-12.5] = [-13]$$

$$\Rightarrow \quad -13 = -13 \Rightarrow \text{True}$$

For $\alpha = -6.5$ in Eq. (i),

$$[-6.5 - 5] = [-13 + 2]$$

$$\Rightarrow \quad [-11.5] = [-11]$$

$$\Rightarrow \quad -12 \neq -11$$

$\Rightarrow$ Not satisfies.

$\therefore$ The required range will be $\alpha \in [-7.5, -6.5)$

50. $\lim_{n \to \infty} \dfrac{(1+2-3) + (4+5-6) + \dots + (3n-2) + (3n-1) - 3n}{\sqrt{2n^4 + 4n + 3} - \sqrt{n^4 + 5n + 4}}$

$$= \lim_{n \to \infty} \frac{0 + 3 + 6 + 9 + 12 + \dots + (3n-3)}{\sqrt{2n^4 + 4n + 3} - \sqrt{n^4 + 5n + 4}}$$

$$= \lim_{n \to \infty} \frac{\sum_{r=1}^{n} (3r - 3)}{(\sqrt{2n^4 + 4n + 3} - \sqrt{n^4 + 5n + 4})}$$

$$= \lim_{n \to \infty} \frac{\frac{3 \cdot n(n+1)}{2} - 3}{n^2\left(\sqrt{2 + \frac{4}{n^3} + \frac{3}{n^4}} - \sqrt{1 + \frac{5}{n^3} + \frac{4}{n^4}}\right)}$$

$$= \lim_{n \to \infty} \frac{\frac{3}{2}\left(1 + \frac{1}{n}\right) - \frac{3}{n}}{\left(\sqrt{2 + \frac{4}{n^3} + \frac{3}{n^4}} - \sqrt{1 + \frac{5}{n^3} + \frac{4}{n^4}}\right)}$$

$$= \frac{\frac{3}{2}(1+0) - 0}{(\sqrt{2+0+0} - \sqrt{1+0+0})} = \frac{3}{2(\sqrt{2}-1)} = \frac{3}{2}(\sqrt{2}+1)$$

51. Let $L = \lim_{x \to \infty} \dfrac{(\sqrt{3x+1} + \sqrt{3x-1})^6 + (\sqrt{3x+1} - \sqrt{3x-1})^6}{(x + \sqrt{x^2-1})^6 + (x - \sqrt{x^2-1})^6} x^3$

Now, we know that $(a+b)^6 + (a-b)^6$

$$= 2({}^6C_0a^6 + {}^6C_2a^4b^2 + {}^6C_4a^2b^4 + {}^6C_6b^6)$$

$$\therefore \quad L = \lim_{x \to \infty} x^3\left[\frac{2[{}^6C_0(3x+1)^3 + {}^6C_2(3x+1)^2(3x-1) + {}^6C_4(3x+1)(3x-1)^2 + {}^6C_6(3x-1)^3]}{2[{}^6C_0x^6 + {}^6C_2x^4(x^2-1) + {}^6C_4x^2(x^2-1)^2 + {}^6C_6(x^2-1)^3]}\right]$$

$$= \lim_{x \to \infty} \frac{x^6\left[\left(3 + \frac{1}{x}\right)^3 + 15\left(3 + \frac{1}{x}\right)^2\left(3 - \frac{1}{x}\right) + 15\left(3 + \frac{1}{x}\right)\left(3 - \frac{1}{x}\right)^2 + \left(3 - \frac{1}{x}\right)^3\right]}{x^6\left[1 + 15\left(1 - \frac{1}{x^2}\right) + 15\left(1 - \frac{1}{x^2}\right)^2 + \left(1 - \frac{1}{x^2}\right)^3\right]}$$

$$= \lim_{x \to \infty} \frac{\left[\left(3+\frac{1}{x}\right)^3 + 15\left(3+\frac{1}{x}\right)^2\left(3-\frac{1}{x}\right) + 15\left(3+\frac{1}{x}\right)\left(3-\frac{1}{x}\right)^2 + \left(3-\frac{1}{x}\right)^3\right]}{\left[1 + 15\left(1-\frac{1}{x^2}\right) + 15\left(1-\frac{1}{x^2}\right)^2 + \left(1-\frac{1}{x^2}\right)^3\right]}$$

$$= \frac{(3)^3 + 15(3)^2(3) + 15(3)(3)^2 + (3)^3}{1+15+15+1}$$

$$= \frac{27+405+405+27}{32} = \frac{864}{32} = 27$$

52. $\lim_{x \to 0}\left[\left(\frac{1-\cos^2 3x}{\cos^3 4x}\right)\left(\frac{\sin^3 4x}{[\log_e(2x+1)]^5}\right)\right]$

$$= \lim_{x \to 0}\left[\frac{\sin^2 3x}{(3x)^2} \times \frac{\sin^3 4x}{(4x)^3} \times \frac{1}{\cos^3 4x} \times \frac{1}{\left[\frac{\log(1+2x)}{2x}\right]^5} \times \frac{3^2 \cdot 4^3}{2^5}\right]$$

$$= \frac{3^2 \cdot 4^3}{2^5} = 9 \times 2 = 18$$

53. Let $L = \lim_{t \to 0}\left(1^{\frac{1}{\sin^2 t}} + 2^{\frac{1}{\sin^2 t}} + \ldots + n^{\frac{1}{\sin^2 t}}\right)^{\sin^2 t}$

$$= \lim_{t \to 0} n\left[\left(\frac{1}{n}\right)^{\operatorname{cosec}^2 t} + \left(\frac{2}{n}\right)^{\operatorname{cosec}^2 t} + \left(\frac{3}{n}\right)^{\operatorname{cosec}^2 t} + \ldots + \left(\frac{n-1}{n}\right)^{\operatorname{cosec}^2 t} + \left(\frac{n}{n}\right)^{\operatorname{cosec}^2 t}\right]^{\sin^2 t}$$

$$= \lim_{t \to 0} n \cdot [0+0+0+0+\ldots+0+1]^{\sin^2 t}$$

$[\because a^x \to 0$, when $x \to \infty$; $0 < a < 1]$

$= n \qquad [\because$ (exact 1)$^{\text{(tends to zero)}}$ = always one$]$

54. Given, $\lim_{x \to 0}\frac{e^{ax} - \cos(bx) - \frac{cxe^{-cx}}{2}}{1-\cos 2x} = 17$

On expansion above, we get

$$\Rightarrow \lim_{x \to 0}\frac{\left(1 + ax + \frac{a^2x^2}{2!} + \ldots\right) - \left(1 - \frac{x^2b^2}{2!} + \ldots\right) - \frac{cx}{2}\left(1 - cx + \frac{c^2x^2}{2!}\ldots\right)}{1 - 1 + \frac{4x^2}{2!} + \ldots} = 17$$

[all the neighbour terms are negligible]

$$\Rightarrow \lim_{x \to 0}\frac{\left(a - \frac{c}{2}\right)x + x^2\left(\frac{a^2}{2} + \frac{b^2}{2} + \frac{c^2}{2}\right)}{2x^2} = 17$$

If above limit exist, then $a - \frac{c}{2} = 0$

$$a = \frac{c}{2} \Rightarrow c = 2a \text{ and } \frac{\frac{a^2}{2} + \frac{b^2}{2} + \frac{c^2}{2}}{2} = 17$$

$$\Rightarrow \frac{a^2+b^2+c^2}{4} = 17 \Rightarrow a^2 + b^2 + 4a^2 = 68 \qquad \{\because c = 2a\}$$

$$\Rightarrow 5a^2 + b^2 = 68$$

55. $x = 2$ is a root of $x^2 + px + q = 0$

$$\Rightarrow 2^2 + 2p + q = 0$$

$$\Rightarrow q + 4 = -2p \qquad \text{...(i)}$$

$$\therefore q^2 + 8q + 16 = (q+4)^2 = 4p^2 \qquad \text{...(ii)}$$

and $x^2 - 4px + (q^2 + 8q + 16)$

$$= x^2 - 4px + 4p^2 = (x-2p)^2 \qquad \text{...(iii)}$$

We have, $f(x) = \begin{cases} \dfrac{1-\cos(x^2 - 4px + q^2 + 8q + 16)}{(x-2p)^4}, & x \neq 2p \\ 0 & x = 2p \end{cases}$

$$\Rightarrow f(x) = \begin{cases} \dfrac{1-\cos(x-2p)^2}{(x-2p)^4}, & x \neq 2p \\ 0, & x = 2p \end{cases}$$

Now, as $x \to 2p^+$, $x - 2p \to 0^+$

$$\therefore \lim_{x \to 2p^+} f(x) = \frac{1}{2} \qquad \left[\because \lim_{y \to 0}\frac{1-\cos y}{y^2} = \frac{1}{2}\right]$$

Hence, $\lim_{x \to 2p^+}[f(x)] = 0$, where [.] is the greatest integer function.

56. α, β are the roots of the equation $ax^2 + bx + 1 = 0$

$\Rightarrow$ The roots of the equation $x^2 + bx + a = 0$ are $\frac{1}{\alpha}$ and $\frac{1}{\beta}$.

$$\Rightarrow x^2 + bx + a = \left(x - \frac{1}{\alpha}\right)\left(x - \frac{1}{\beta}\right)$$

$\therefore$ The given limit

$$= \lim_{x \to \frac{1}{\alpha}}\left[\frac{1-\cos\left(x-\frac{1}{\alpha}\right)\left(x-\frac{1}{\beta}\right)}{2\alpha^2\left(x-\frac{1}{\alpha}\right)^2}\right]^{1/2}$$

$$= \lim_{x \to \frac{1}{\alpha}}\left[\frac{1-\cos\left(x-\frac{1}{\alpha}\right)\left(x-\frac{1}{\beta}\right)}{2\alpha^2\left(x-\frac{1}{\alpha}\right)^2\left(x-\frac{1}{\beta}\right)^2}\right]^{1/2} \times \left(x - \frac{1}{\beta}\right)$$

$$= \lim_{x \to \frac{1}{\alpha}}\left[\frac{2\sin^2\left(\frac{\left(x-\frac{1}{\alpha}\right)\left(x-\frac{1}{\beta}\right)}{2}\right)}{2\alpha^2\left\{\frac{\left(x-\frac{1}{\alpha}\right)\left(x-\frac{1}{\beta}\right)}{2}\right\}^2 \times 4}\right]^{1/2}\left(x - \frac{1}{\beta}\right)$$

$$= \frac{1}{2\alpha}\left(\frac{1}{\beta} - \frac{1}{\alpha}\right) = \frac{1}{2\alpha}\left(\frac{1}{\beta} - \frac{1}{\alpha}\right)$$

$$\therefore k = 2\alpha$$

57. Given that $f(x)=\begin{cases}\dfrac{x}{|x|} & x\neq 0\\ 1 & x=0\end{cases}$, $g(x)=\begin{cases}\dfrac{\sin(x+1)}{(x+1)} & x\neq -1\\ 1 & x=-1\end{cases}$

and $h(x)=2[x]-f(x)$

We have to find, $\lim_{x\to 1} g(h(x-1))$

Now, LHL $=\lim_{x\to 1^-}=\lim_{x\to 1^-} g(h(0^-))=\lim_{x\to 1^-} g(2[0^-]-f(0^-))$

$$=\lim_{x\to 1^-} g\left(2(-1)-\frac{0}{|0^-|}\right)=\lim_{x\to 1^-} g(-2+1)=\lim_{x\to 1^-} g(-1)=1$$

RHL $=\lim_{x\to 1^+} g(h(x-1))=\lim_{x\to 1^+} g(h(1^+-1))=\lim_{x\to 1^+} g(h(0^+))$

$$=\lim_{x\to 1^+} g(2[0^+]-f(0^+))=\lim_{x\to 1^+} g\left(2\times 0-\frac{0^+}{|0^+|}\right)$$

$$=\lim_{x\to 1^+} g(-1)=1$$

LHL = RHL So, $\lim_{x\to 1} g(h(x-1))=1$

58. $$\sum_{n=0}^{\infty}\frac{n^3((2n)!)+(2n-1)(n!)}{(n!)((2n)!)}$$

$$=\sum_{n=0}^{\infty}\frac{1}{(n-3)!}+\sum_{n=0}^{\infty}\frac{3}{(n-2)!}+\sum_{n=0}^{\infty}\frac{1}{(n-1)!}+\sum_{n=0}^{\infty}\frac{1}{(2n-1)!}-\sum_{n=0}^{\infty}\frac{1}{(2n)!}$$

$$=e+3e+e+\frac{1}{2}\left(e-\frac{1}{e}\right)-\frac{1}{2}\left(e+\frac{1}{e}\right)=5e-\frac{1}{e}=ae+\frac{b}{e}+c$$

where $a,b,c\in Z$

On comparing $a=5, b=-1, c=0$

$a^2-b+c=25-(-1)+0=26$

59. Given, $\beta=\lim_{x\to 0}\dfrac{\alpha x-(e^{3x}-1)}{\alpha x(e^{3x}-1)}$

$\Rightarrow$ $\beta=\lim_{x\to 0}\dfrac{1}{e^{3x}-1}-\lim_{x\to 0}\dfrac{1}{\alpha x}$

$\Rightarrow$ $\beta=\lim_{x\to 0}\dfrac{3x}{e^{3x}-1}\times\dfrac{1}{3x}-\lim_{x\to 0}\dfrac{1}{\alpha x}$

$\Rightarrow$ $\beta=\lim_{x\to 0}\left[\dfrac{1}{3x}-\dfrac{1}{\alpha x}\right]$ $\left[\because \lim_{x\to 0}\dfrac{e^{3x}-1}{3x}=1\right]$

For the existence of limits, $\alpha=3$ as $\infty-\infty$ is an indeterminant for β.

Now, $\beta=\lim_{x\to 0}\dfrac{3x-(e^{3x}-1)}{3x\cdot(e^{3x}-1)}$

On apply L' Hospital rule, we get

$$\beta=\lim_{x\to 0}\frac{(3-3e^{3x})}{3x\times 3e^{3x}+3(e^{3x}-1)}=\lim_{x\to 0}\frac{3(1-e^{3x})}{9xe^{3x}+3(e^{3x}-1)}$$

Again, applying L' Hospital rule, we get

$$\beta=\lim_{x\to 0}\frac{3(-3e^{3x})}{9x(3e^{3x})+9e^{3x}+3(3e^{3x})}=-\frac{1}{2}$$

$\therefore$ $\alpha+\beta=3+\left(-\dfrac{1}{2}\right)=\dfrac{5}{2}$

60. $\lim_{n\to\infty}\left(\sqrt{n^2-n-1}+n\alpha+\beta\right)=0$

Let $n=\dfrac{1}{t}$ as $n\to\infty \Rightarrow t\to 0$

$\Rightarrow$ $\lim_{t\to 0}\left[\sqrt{\dfrac{1}{t^2}-\dfrac{1}{t}-1}+\dfrac{\alpha}{t}\right]=-\beta$

$\Rightarrow$ $\lim_{t\to 0}\left(\dfrac{\sqrt{1-t-t^2}}{t}+\dfrac{\alpha}{t}\right)=-\beta$

$\Rightarrow$ $\lim_{t\to 0}\left(\dfrac{\sqrt{1-t-t^2}+\alpha}{t}\right)=-\beta$

Since, $\beta\neq 0$, thus clearly from above $\alpha=-1$ otherwise the above explanation is invalid.

Now, $\lim_{t\to 0}\left(\dfrac{\sqrt{1-t-t^2}-1}{t}\right)=-\beta$

$\lim_{t\to 0}\left(\dfrac{1-t-t^2-1}{t(\sqrt{1-t-t^2}+1)}\right)=-\beta$ [by rationalising]

$\Rightarrow$ $\lim_{t\to 0}\dfrac{-t(1+t)}{t(\sqrt{1-t-t^2}+1)}=-\beta$

$\Rightarrow$ $\lim_{t\to 0}\dfrac{-(1+t)}{\sqrt{1-t-t^2}+1}=-\beta$

$\Rightarrow$ $-1/2=-\beta \Rightarrow \beta=1/2$

Thus, $8(\alpha+\beta)=8\left(-1+\dfrac{1}{2}\right)=8\left(-\dfrac{1}{2}\right)=-4$

61. Given function of limit is

$$\lim_{x\to 7}\frac{18-[1-x]}{[x]-3a}$$

$$\text{LHL}=\lim_{x\to 7}\frac{18-[1-x]}{[x]-3a}=\lim_{h\to 0}\frac{18-[1-(7-h)]}{[7-h]-3a}$$

When, $-6\leq x<-5$, then greatest integer function would be -6 and when $6\leq x<7$, then greatest integer would be 6.

$$\text{LHL}=\frac{18-(-6)}{6-3a}=\frac{24}{6-3a}$$

$$\text{RHL}=\lim_{x\to 7}\frac{18-[1-x]}{[x]-3a}=\lim_{h\to 0}\frac{18-[1-(7+h)]}{[7+h]-3a}$$

When, $-7\leq x<-6$, then greatest integer function would be -7 and when $7\leq x<8$, then greatest integer function would be 7.

$$\text{RHL}=\frac{18-(-7)}{7-3a}=\frac{25}{7-3a}$$

Take LHL = RHL

$$\frac{24}{6-3a}=\frac{25}{7-3a}\Rightarrow a=-6$$

62. $\lim_{x\to\frac{\pi}{4}}\dfrac{8\sqrt{2}-(\cos x+\sin x)^7}{\sqrt{2}-\sqrt{2}\sin 2x}$ $\left[\dfrac{0}{0}\text{ form}\right]$

Using L' Hospital rule,

$$=\lim_{x\to\frac{\pi}{4}}\frac{-7(\sin x+\cos x)^6(-\sin x+\cos x)}{-2\sqrt{2}\cos 2x}\quad\left[\frac{0}{0}\text{ form}\right]$$

$$= \frac{-7\left(\frac{1}{\sqrt{2}}+\frac{1}{\sqrt{2}}\right)^6}{-2\sqrt{2}} \cdot \lim_{x\to\frac{\pi}{4}} \frac{(\cos x - \sin x)}{\cos 2x} \quad \left[\frac{0}{0} \text{ form}\right]$$

$$= \frac{7(\sqrt{2})^6}{2\sqrt{2}} \lim_{x\to\frac{\pi}{4}} \frac{(-\sin x - \cos x)}{-2\sin 2x}$$

$$= \frac{56}{2\sqrt{2}} \cdot \frac{1}{2} \lim_{x\to\frac{\pi}{4}} \frac{(\sin x + \cos x)}{\sin 2x} = \frac{56}{4\sqrt{2}} \cdot \frac{\sqrt{2}}{1} = 14$$

63. $\lim_{x\to\frac{\pi}{2}} \left[\tan^2 x \left((2\sin^2 x + 3\sin x + 4)^{\frac{1}{2}} - (\sin^2 x + 6\sin x + 2)^{\frac{1}{2}}\right)\right]$

$$= \lim_{x\to\pi/2} [\tan^2 x [\sqrt{2\sin^2 x + 3\sin x + 4} - \sqrt{\sin^2 x + 6\sin x + 2}]$$

$$= \lim_{x\to\frac{\pi}{2}} \frac{\tan^2 x [(2\sin^2 x + 3\sin x + 4) - (\sin^2 x + 6\sin x + 2)]}{\sqrt{2\sin^2 x + 3\sin x + 4} + \sqrt{\sin^2 x + 6\sin x + 2}}$$

$$= \lim_{x\to\frac{\pi}{2}} \frac{\sin^2 x [\sin^2 x - 3\sin x + 2]}{\cos^2 x [\sqrt{2\sin^2 x + 3\sin x + 4} + \sqrt{\sin^2 x + 6\sin x + 2}]}$$

$$= \lim_{x\to\frac{\pi}{2}} \frac{\sin^2 x (\sin x - 1)(\sin x - 2)}{(1-\sin^2 x)[\sqrt{2\sin^2 x + 3\sin x + 4} + \sqrt{\sin^2 x + 6\sin x + 2}]}$$

$$= \lim_{x\to\frac{\pi}{2}} \frac{\sin^2 x (-1)(\sin x - 2)}{(1+\sin x)[\sqrt{2\sin^2 x + 3\sin x + 4} + \sqrt{\sin^2 x + 6\sin x + 2}]}$$

Substitute $x = \pi/2$

$$= \frac{1(-1)[1-2]}{(2)[\sqrt{9}+\sqrt{9}]} = \frac{1}{2(3+3)} = \frac{1}{12}$$

64. $\lim_{x\to 0} \frac{\alpha e^x + \beta e^{-x} + \gamma \sin x}{x \sin^2 x} = \frac{2}{3}$

$$\lim_{x\to 0} \frac{\alpha\left(1 + x + \frac{x^2}{2!} + \frac{x^3}{3!} + \dots\right) + \beta\left(1 - x + \frac{x^2}{2!} - \frac{x^3}{3!} + \dots\right) + \gamma\left(x - \frac{x^3}{3!} + \frac{x^5}{5!} - \dots\right)}{x\left(x - \frac{x^3}{3!} + \frac{x^5}{5!} - \dots\right)^2} = \frac{2}{3}$$

Now, here constant term = 0

$$\alpha + \beta = 0 \quad \dots\text{(i)}$$

Also coefficient of x should be zero

i.e. $\quad \alpha - \beta + \gamma = 0 \quad \dots$(ii)

and coefficient of x^2 should be zero

$$\frac{\alpha}{2!} + \frac{\beta}{2!} = 0 \Rightarrow \alpha + \beta = 0$$

So, $\lim_{x\to 0} \frac{x^3\left(\frac{\alpha}{3!} - \frac{\beta}{3!} - \frac{\gamma}{3!}\right) + x^4\left(\frac{\alpha}{4!} + \frac{\beta}{4!}\right)}{x^3} = \frac{2}{3}$

$$\frac{\alpha}{3!} - \frac{\beta}{3!} - \frac{\gamma}{3!} = \frac{2}{3} \Rightarrow \alpha - \beta - \gamma = 4 \quad \dots\text{(iii)}$$

On adding Eqs. (ii) and (iii), we get

$$\alpha - \beta = 2 \quad \dots\text{(iv)}$$

From Eqs. (i) and (iv), we get

$$\alpha = 1, \beta = -1, \gamma = -2$$

From option (c),

$$\alpha\beta^2 + \beta\gamma^2 + \gamma\alpha^2 + 3 = 1 - 4 - 2 + 3$$
$$= -2 \neq 0$$

65. $\lim_{x\to 0} \frac{\cos(\sin x) - \cos x}{x^4}$

$$= \lim_{x\to 0} \frac{2\sin\left(\frac{\sin x + x}{2}\right) \cdot \sin\left(\frac{x - \sin x}{2}\right)}{x^4} \quad \left[\frac{0}{0} \text{ form}\right]$$

$$= \lim_{x\to 0} \frac{2\sin\left(\frac{\sin x + x}{2}\right)}{\left(\frac{\sin x + x}{2}\right)} \cdot \frac{\sin\left(\frac{x - \sin x}{2}\right)}{\left(\frac{x - \sin x}{2}\right)} \times \left(\frac{x + \sin x}{2}\right) \times \left(\frac{x - \sin x}{2}\right) \frac{1}{x^4}$$

$$= \lim_{x\to 0} 2\left[\frac{\sin\left(\frac{\sin x + x}{2}\right)}{\left(\frac{\sin x + x}{2}\right)}\right]\left[\frac{\sin\left(\frac{x - \sin x}{2}\right)}{\left(\frac{x - \sin x}{2}\right)}\right]\left(\frac{x^2 - \sin^2 x}{4}\right) \cdot \frac{1}{x^4}$$

We know, $\lim_{t\to 0} \frac{\sin t}{t} = 1$, thus we get

$$\lim_{x\to 0} 2\left(\frac{x^2 - \sin^2 x}{4x^4}\right) \quad \left[\frac{0}{0} \text{ form}\right]$$

Using L' Hospital rule, we get

$$\lim_{x\to 0} 2\left(\frac{2x - 2\sin x \cos x}{16x^3}\right) = \lim_{x\to 0} \frac{2x - \sin 2x}{8x^3} \quad \left[\frac{0}{0} \text{ form}\right]$$

Using L' Hospital rule, we get

$$\lim_{x\to 0} \frac{2 - 2\cos 2x}{24x^2} \quad \left[\frac{0}{0} \text{ form}\right]$$

$$= \lim_{x\to 0} \left(\frac{4\sin 2x}{48x}\right)$$

$$= \frac{1}{6} \lim_{x\to 0} \frac{\sin 2x}{2x} \quad \left[\lim_{x\to 0} \frac{\sin t}{t} = 1\right]$$

$$= \frac{1}{6}$$

66. Given, $\lim_{x\to 0} \left(\frac{(x + 2\cos x)^3 + 2(x + 2\cos x)^2 + 3\sin(x + 2\cos x)}{(x+2)^3 + 2(x+2)^2 + 3\sin(x+2)}\right)^{\frac{100}{x}}$

Let $x + 2\cos x = p$ and $x + 2 = q$

As $x \to 0$, then $p \to 2$ and $q \to 2$

$$\Rightarrow \lim_{x\to 0} \left(\frac{p^3 + 2p^2 + 3\sin p}{q^3 + 2q^2 + 3\sin q}\right)^{\frac{100}{x}}$$

$$= e^{\lim_{x\to 0} \frac{100}{x} \frac{(p^3 - q^3) + 2(p^2 - q^2) + 3(\sin p - \sin q)}{q^3 + 2q^2 + 3\sin q}} \quad [\because \text{we get } 1^\infty \text{ form}]$$

$$= e^0 = 1 \quad \left[\because \lim_{x\to 0} \frac{p - q}{x} = \lim_{x\to 0} \frac{2(\cos x - 1)}{x} = 0\right]$$

67. Given, $\lim_{x\to 1}\frac{\sin(3x^2-4x+1)-x^2+1}{2x^3-7x^2+ax+b}=-2$

$$\Rightarrow \lim_{x\to 1}\frac{\left(\frac{\sin(3x^2-4x+1)}{3x^2-4x+1}\right)(3x^2-4x+1)-x^2+1}{2x^3-7x^2+ax+b}=-2$$

$$\Rightarrow \lim_{x\to 1}\frac{3x^2-4x+1-x^2+1}{2x^3-7x^2+ax+b}=-2$$

$$\Rightarrow \lim_{x\to 1}\frac{2(x-1)^2}{2x^3-7x^2+ax+b}=-2$$

So, $f(x)=2x^3-7x^2+ax+b$ has $x=1$ as repeated root, therefore $f(1)=0$ and $f'(1)=0$ gives $a+b=5$ and $a=8$

$\Rightarrow$ $a=8, b=-3$

So, $a-b=11$

68. Given function is $f(x)=[1+x]+\frac{\alpha^{2[x]+\{x\}}+[x]-1}{2[x]+\{x\}}$

$$\lim_{x\to 0^-}f(x)=\alpha-\frac{4}{3}$$

Here, $0\le x<1$, then $[x]$ is 0 and $-1\le x<0$, then $[x]$ is -1.

$$\Rightarrow 0+\frac{\alpha^{-1}-2}{-1}=\alpha-\frac{4}{3}$$

$$\Rightarrow 2-\frac{1}{\alpha}=\alpha-\frac{4}{3}\Rightarrow \alpha+\frac{1}{\alpha}=\frac{10}{3}$$

$$\Rightarrow 3\alpha^2-10\alpha+3=0\Rightarrow 3\alpha^2-9\alpha-\alpha+3=0$$

$$\Rightarrow 3\alpha(\alpha-3)-1(\alpha-3)=0\Rightarrow(\alpha-3)(3\alpha-1)=0,$$

So, $\alpha=3, \alpha\in I$

69. Given, $\lim_{x\to\infty}(\sqrt{x^2-x+1}-ax)=b$

$$\Rightarrow \lim_{x\to\infty}(\sqrt{x^2-x+1}-ax)\frac{(\sqrt{x^2-x+1})+ax}{(\sqrt{x^2-x+1}+ax)}=b$$

[by rationalising]

$$\Rightarrow \lim_{x\to\infty}\frac{x^2-x+1-a^2x^2}{\sqrt{x^2-x+1}+ax}=b$$

Limit exists only, if $a^2=1\Rightarrow a=\pm 1$

$$\Rightarrow \lim_{x\to\infty}\frac{-x+1}{\sqrt{x^2-x+1}+ax}=b$$

$$\Rightarrow \lim_{x\to\infty}\frac{-1+\frac{1}{x}}{\sqrt{1-\frac{1}{x}+\frac{1}{x^2}}+a}=b\Rightarrow\frac{-1}{1+a}=b$$

But, $a\ne-1\Rightarrow a=1$

$\therefore$ $b=-\frac{1}{2}$, $(a,b)=\left(1,-\frac{1}{2}\right)$

70. $\because$ α and β are distinct roots of $x^2+bx+c=0$

$\Rightarrow x^2+bx+c=(x-\alpha)(x-\beta)=0$

Now, $\lim_{x\to\beta}\frac{e^{2(x^2+bx+c)}-1-2(x^2+bx+c)}{(x-\beta)^2}$

$$=\lim_{x\to\beta}\frac{e^{2(x-\alpha)(x-\beta)}-1-2(x-\alpha)(x-\beta)}{(x-\beta)^2}$$

$$=\lim_{h\to 0}\frac{e^{2(\beta-\alpha+h)h}-1-2(\beta-\alpha+h)h}{h^2}\quad[\because \text{Put } x=\beta+h]$$

$$=\lim_{h\to 0}\frac{1+2(\beta-\alpha+h)h+\frac{|2(\beta-\alpha+h)h|^2}{2!}+\ldots-1-2h(\beta-\alpha+h)}{h^2}$$

$$=\lim_{h\to 0}\frac{2(\beta-\alpha+h)^2h^2+\ldots}{h^2}=2(\beta-\alpha)^2=2(b^2-4c)$$

71. $f(2)=4$, $f'(2)=1$

Now, $\lim_{x\to 2}\frac{x^2f(2)-4f(x)}{x-2}$

On applying L' Hospital rule as 0/0 form on putting $x=2$

So, $\lim_{x\to 2}\frac{2x\,f(2)-4f'(x)}{1}=2\cdot 2\cdot f(2)-4f'(2)$

$$=4\cdot 4-4\cdot 1=12$$

72. Given, limit is of the form 1^∞.

So, $l=\exp\left[\lim_{x\to\infty}\frac{1+\frac{1}{2}+\frac{1}{3}+\ldots+\frac{1}{n}}{n}\right]$

$$\left[\because \lim_{x\to\infty}[f(x)]^{g(x)}=e^{\lim_{x\to a}g(x)[f(x)-1]}\right]$$

Now, $0\le 1+\frac{1}{2}+\frac{1}{3}+\ldots\ldots+\frac{1}{n}\le 1+\frac{1}{\sqrt{2}}+\frac{1}{\sqrt{3}}+\ldots\ldots+\frac{1}{\sqrt{n}}$

$$\le 2\sqrt{n}-1$$

Now $\lim_{x\to\infty}\frac{2\sqrt{n}-1}{n}=\lim_{x\to\infty}\frac{2}{\sqrt{n}}-\frac{1}{n}=0$

$\therefore$ Using Sandwich rule,

$$l=\exp(0)=1$$

73. $\lim_{h\to 0}2\left\{\frac{\sqrt{3}\sin\left(\frac{\pi}{6}+h\right)-\cos\left(\frac{\pi}{6}+h\right)}{\sqrt{3}h(\sqrt{3}\cos h-\sin h)}\right\}$

$$=\lim_{h\to 0}2\left\{\frac{2\left(\frac{\sqrt{3}}{2}\sin\left(\frac{\pi}{6}+h\right)-\frac{1}{2}\cos\left(\frac{\pi}{6}+h\right)\right)}{2\times\sqrt{3}h\left(\frac{\sqrt{3}}{2}\cos h-\frac{1}{2}\sin h\right)}\right\}$$

$$=\lim_{h\to 0}2\left\{\frac{\cos\left(\frac{\pi}{6}\right)\sin\left(\frac{\pi}{6}+h\right)-\sin\left(\frac{\pi}{6}\right)\cos\left(\frac{\pi}{6}+h\right)}{\sqrt{3}h\left(\cos\frac{\pi}{6}\cos h-\sin\frac{\pi}{6}\sin h\right)}\right\}$$

$$=\lim_{h\to 0}2\left[\frac{\sin\left(\frac{\pi}{6}+h-\frac{\pi}{6}\right)}{\sqrt{3}h\cos\left(h+\frac{\pi}{6}\right)}\right]=\lim_{h\to 0}\frac{2}{\sqrt{3}}\left\{\frac{\sin h}{h\cos(h+\pi/6)}\right\}$$

$$=\frac{2}{\sqrt{3}}\cdot\lim_{h\to 0}\frac{\sin h}{h}\cdot\frac{1}{\cos(h+\pi/6)}=\frac{2}{\sqrt{3}}\cdot(1)\cdot\frac{1}{\cos(\pi/6)}$$

$$=\frac{2}{\sqrt{3}}\cdot 1\cdot\frac{2}{\sqrt{3}}=\frac{4}{3}$$

74. **Decoding the Question**

Sandwich Theorem

Let $g(x) \le f(x) \le h(x)$

and $\lim_{x \to a} g(x) = \lim_{x \to a} h(x) = l$

$\therefore \lim_{x \to a} f(x) = l$

As, we know that

$$r \le [r] < r + 1$$
$$2r \le [2r] < 2r + 1$$
$$3r \le [3r] < 3r + 1$$
$$\vdots \quad \vdots \quad \vdots$$
$$nr \le [nr] < nr + 1$$

Adding $(r + 2r + 3r + 4r + \ldots + nr) \le [r] + [2r] + [3r] + [4r] + \ldots [nr] < (r + 1) + (2r + 1) + (3r + 1) + (4r + 1) + \ldots + (nr + 1)$

$\Rightarrow r(1 + 2 + 3 + 4 + \ldots + n) \le [r] + [2r] + [3r] + \ldots + [nr] < (r + 2r + 3r + \ldots + nr) + \underbrace{(1 + 1 + 1 + \ldots + 1)}_{n-\text{times}}$

$$\Rightarrow r \cdot \frac{n(n+1)}{2} \le [r] + [2r] + [3r] + \ldots + [nr] < \frac{r \cdot (n(n+1))}{2} + n$$

$$\Rightarrow \frac{r \cdot \left(\frac{n(n+1)}{2}\right)}{n^2} \le \frac{[r] + [2r] + [3r] + \ldots + [nr]}{n^2} < \frac{r \cdot \left(\frac{n(n+1)}{2}\right) + n}{n^2}$$

Now, $\lim_{n \to \infty} \frac{n(n+1) \cdot r}{2 \cdot n^2} = \lim_{n \to \infty} \frac{n \cdot n(1 + 1/n) \cdot r}{2n^2}$

$$= \frac{(1 + 0) \cdot r}{2} = \frac{r}{2} \quad \ldots(\text{i})$$

and $\lim_{n \to \infty} \frac{\frac{n(n+1)}{2} \cdot r + n}{n^2} = \lim_{n \to \infty} \frac{n(n+1) \cdot r + 2n}{2n^2}$

$$= \lim_{n \to \infty} \frac{n^2 \left\{\left(1 + \frac{1}{n}\right) r + \frac{2}{n}\right\}}{2n^2}$$

$$= \frac{(1 + 0) \cdot r + 0}{2} = \frac{r}{2} \quad \ldots(\text{ii})$$

From Eqs. (i) and (ii), by Sandwich theorem, we conclude that,

$$\lim_{n \to \infty} \frac{[r] + [2r] + [3r] + \ldots + [nr]}{n^2} = \frac{r}{2}$$

75. $\lim_{x \to 0} \left(\frac{x}{\sqrt[8]{1 - \sin x} - \sqrt[8]{1 + \sin x}}\right)$

We get $\frac{0}{0}$ form, using L'Hospital rule, we get

$$\lim_{x \to 0} \frac{1}{\frac{-\cos x}{8(1 - \sin x)^{7/8}} - \frac{\cos x}{8(1 + \sin x)^{7/8}}}$$

$$= \frac{1}{\frac{-\cos 0}{8(1 - \sin 0)^{7/8}} - \frac{\cos 0}{8(1 + \sin 0)^{7/8}}} = -4$$

76. Let $L = \lim_{\theta \to 0} \left(\frac{\tan(\pi \cos^2 \theta)}{\sin(2\pi \sin^2 \theta)}\right) = \lim_{\theta \to 0} \left(\frac{\tan[\pi(1 - \sin^2 \theta)]}{\sin(2\pi \sin^2 \theta)}\right)$

$$= \lim_{\theta \to 0} \left(\frac{\tan(\pi - \pi \sin^2 \theta)}{\sin(2\pi \sin^2 \theta)}\right) = \lim_{\theta \to 0} \left(\frac{-\tan(\pi \sin^2 \theta)}{\sin(2\pi \sin^2 \theta)}\right)$$

$$= \lim_{\theta \to 0} \left[\frac{-\frac{\tan(\pi \sin^2 \theta)}{(\pi \sin^2 \theta)} \times (\pi \sin^2 \theta)}{\frac{\sin(2\pi \sin^2 \theta)}{(2\pi \sin^2 \theta)} \times (2\pi \sin^2 \theta)}\right] = \frac{-1}{2}$$

Alternate Solution

Let $L = \lim_{\theta \to 0} \left[\frac{\tan(\pi \cos^2 \theta)}{\sin(2\pi \sin^2 \theta)}\right] \left(\text{form } \frac{0}{0}\right)$ [using L' Hospital Rule]

$$L = \lim_{\theta \to 0} \frac{\sec^2(\pi \cos^2 \theta)(-2\pi \cos\theta \cdot \sin\theta)}{\cos(2\pi \sin^2 \theta) \cdot (4\pi \sin\theta \cdot \cos\theta)} = \frac{-1}{2} \times \frac{(-1)^2}{1} = \frac{-1}{2}$$

77. $\lim_{x \to 0^+} \frac{\cos^{-1}(x - [x]^2) \cdot \sin^{-1}(x - [x]^2)}{x - x^3}$

Put the value $x \to 0 + h$.

$$\lim_{h \to 0} \frac{\cos^{-1}(h - 0) \cdot \sin^{-1}(h - 0)}{h - h^3} = \lim_{h \to 0} \frac{\cos^{-1} h \cdot \sin^{-1} h}{h(1 - h)(1 + h)}$$

$$= \lim_{h \to 0} \left(\frac{\sin^{-1} h}{h}\right) \left[\frac{\cos^{-1} h}{(1 - h)(1 + h)}\right] = 1 \cdot \frac{\pi}{2} = \frac{\pi}{2}$$

78. Given, $L = \lim_{x \to 0} \frac{\sin^{-1} x - \tan^{-1} x}{3x^3}$

$$\Rightarrow L = \lim_{x \to 0} \frac{\left(x + \frac{1^2 \cdot x^3}{3!} + \frac{1^2 \cdot 3^2 \cdot x^5}{5!} + \ldots\right) - \left(x - \frac{x^3}{3} + \frac{x^5}{5} \ldots\right)}{3x^3}$$

[Using expansion of $\sin^{-1} x$ and $\tan^{-1} x$]

$$\Rightarrow L = \lim_{x \to 0} \frac{\left(\frac{x^3}{3!} + \frac{9x^5}{5!} + \ldots\right) - \left(-\frac{x^3}{3} + \frac{x^5}{5} \ldots\right)}{3x^3}$$

$$\Rightarrow L = \lim_{x \to 0} \frac{x^3\left[\left(\frac{1}{6} + \frac{9x^2}{120} + \ldots\right) + \left(\frac{1}{3} - \frac{x^2}{5} + \ldots\right)\right]}{3x^3}$$

$$\Rightarrow L = \frac{1/6 + 1/3}{3} = \frac{1}{6}$$

$$\therefore 6L + 1 = 6 \times \frac{1}{6} + 1 = 2$$

79. $\alpha = \lim_{x \to \frac{\pi}{4}} \frac{\tan^3 x - \tan x}{\cos\left(x + \frac{\pi}{4}\right)} = \lim_{x \to \frac{\pi}{4}} \frac{\tan x(\tan x + 1)(\tan x - 1)}{\cos\left(x + \frac{\pi}{4}\right)}$

$$= \lim_{x \to \frac{\pi}{4}} \frac{\frac{\sin x}{\cos x} \cdot \left(\frac{\sin x - \cos x}{\cos x}\right)\left(\frac{\sin x + \cos x}{\cos x}\right)}{\frac{1}{\sqrt{2}}(\cos x - \sin x)}$$

$$= \lim_{x \to \frac{\pi}{4}} \frac{-\sqrt{2} \sin x(\sin x + \cos x)}{\cos^3 x} = \frac{-\sqrt{2} \times \frac{1}{\sqrt{2}} \times \sqrt{2}}{\frac{1}{2\sqrt{2}}} = -4$$

and $\beta = \lim_{x \to 0} (\cos x)^{\cot x} = e^{\lim_{x \to 0} \frac{\cos x - 1}{\tan x}}$

Here, we get $\frac{0}{0}$ form, then using L'Hospital rule,

$$e^{\lim_{x\to 0} -\frac{\sin x}{\sec^2 x}} = e^0 = 1$$

Equation whose roots are α and β, is

$$x^2 + 3x - 4 = 0 \Rightarrow \therefore a = 1, b = 3$$

80. Given, $\lim_{x\to 0} \dfrac{\alpha x e^x - \beta \log_e (1+x) + \gamma x^2 e^{-x}}{x \sin^2 x} = 10$

Now, $\lim_{x\to 0} \dfrac{\alpha x e^x - \beta \log_e(1+x) + \gamma x^2 e^{-x}}{x \sin^2 x}$

$$= \lim_{x\to 0} \frac{\alpha x(1 + \frac{x}{1!} + x^2/2! + ..) - \beta\left(x - \frac{x^2}{2} + \frac{x^3}{3} ...\right) + \gamma x^2 (1 - \frac{x}{1!} + x^2/2! ...)}{x \sin^2 x}$$

$$= \lim_{x\to 0} \frac{x(\alpha - \beta) + x^2(\alpha + \beta/2 + \gamma) + x^3\left(\frac{\alpha}{2} - \frac{\beta}{3} - \gamma\right)...}{x \sin^2 x}$$

To exists limit, the numerator must have degree greater than or equal to denominator.

Degree of denominator = 3

$\therefore$ For limit to exist, $\alpha - \beta = 0$ ...(i)

and $\alpha + \frac{\beta}{2} + \gamma = 0$ ...(ii)

Also, for terms greater than degree 3, gives 0 as $x \to 0$

$\therefore$ $\frac{\alpha}{2} - \frac{\beta}{3} - \gamma = 10$ ...(iii)

From Eq. (i), $\beta = \alpha$

From Eq. (ii), $\gamma = -\left(\frac{\alpha}{2} + \alpha\right) = -\frac{3\alpha}{2}$

On putting these in Eq. (iii), we get

$$\frac{\alpha}{2} - \frac{\alpha}{3} + \frac{3\alpha}{2} = 10$$

$\Rightarrow$ $\alpha = 6$

Now, $\alpha = \beta \Rightarrow \beta = 6$

Again, $\gamma = -3\alpha/2 \Rightarrow \gamma = -9$

$\therefore$ $\alpha + \beta + \gamma = 6 + 6 - 9 = 12 - 9 = 3$

81. Let $L = \lim_{x\to 0}(2 - \cos x\sqrt{\cos 2x})^{\frac{x+2}{x^2}}$ is of the form 1^∞.

$$\therefore \quad L = e^{\lim_{x\to 0}(2 - \cos x\sqrt{\cos 2x} - 1)\left(\frac{x+2}{x^2}\right)}$$

$$= e^{\lim_{x\to 0} \frac{(1 - \cos x\sqrt{\cos 2x})}{x^2}.(x+2)} \quad ...(i)$$

Now, $\lim_{x\to 0} \dfrac{1 - \cos x\sqrt{\cos 2x}}{x^2}$ is $\frac{0}{0}$ form.

Using L ' Hospital rule, we get

$$\lim_{x\to 0} \frac{1 - \cos x\sqrt{\cos 2x}}{x^2}$$

$$= \lim_{x\to 0} \frac{\sin x\sqrt{\cos 2x} - \cos x \dfrac{1}{2\sqrt{\cos 2x}} \times (-2\sin 2x)}{2x}$$

$$= \lim_{x\to 0} \frac{\sin x \cos 2x + \cos x \sin 2x}{2x\sqrt{\cos 2x}}$$

$$= \lim_{x\to 0} \frac{\sin(3x)}{2x\sqrt{\cos 2x}} \qquad \left[\frac{0}{0} \text{ form}\right]$$

Using Hospital rule,

$$\lim_{x\to 0} \frac{3\cos(3x)}{2x\sqrt{\cos 2x} + 2x\dfrac{-\sin(2x)}{2\sqrt{\cos 2x}}} = \frac{3}{2}$$

Putting above value in Eq. (i), we get

$$L = e^{\frac{3}{2}\lim_{x\to 0}(x+2)} = e^{3/2\,(0+2)} = e^{(3/2)(2)} = e^3$$

$$\therefore e^a = e^3 \Rightarrow a = 3$$

82. We have, $\lim_{x\to 0} \dfrac{ae^x - b\cos x + ce^{-x}}{x\sin x} = 2$

$$\Rightarrow \lim_{x\to 0} \frac{a\left(1 + x + \frac{x^2}{2!} ...\right) - b\left(1 - \frac{x^2}{2!} + \frac{x^4}{4!} ...\right) + c\left(1 - x + \frac{x^2}{2!} ...\right)}{x\left(x - \frac{x^3}{3!} + ...\right)} = 2$$

$$\Rightarrow \lim_{x\to 0} \frac{(a - b + c) + (a - c)x + \left(\frac{a}{2} + \frac{b}{2} + \frac{c}{2}\right)x^2 + ...}{x^2 - \frac{x^4}{6} + ...} = 2$$

Here, in numerator, all the coefficients of x^k, where $k < 2$ has to be zero, then only limit will exist.

$$a - b + c = 0, \ a - c = 0$$

$\Rightarrow$ $a = c \Rightarrow b = 2a$

After solving limit,

$$\frac{a + b + c}{2} = 2$$

So, $a + 2a + a = 4 \Rightarrow a = 1$

$\Rightarrow$ $a = 1, b = 2$ and $c = 1$

$$a + b + c = 1 + 2 + 1 = 4$$

Alternate Solution

$$\lim_{x\to 0} \frac{ae^x - b\cos x + ce^{-x}}{x\sin x} = 2$$

$$\Rightarrow \lim_{x\to 0} \frac{(a - b + c) + (a - c)x + \left(\frac{a + b + c}{2}\right)x^2 + ...}{x^2\left(\frac{\sin x}{x}\right)} = 2$$

$\Rightarrow$ $a - b + c = 0$ and $a - c = 0$

$\therefore$ $\dfrac{a + b + c}{2} = 2 \Rightarrow a + b + c = 4$

83. $\lim_{x\to a} \dfrac{(a + 2x)^{1/3} - (3x)^{1/3}}{(3a + x)^{1/3} - (4x)^{1/3}}, (a \neq 0)$ $\left[\frac{0}{0} \text{ form}\right]$

Put $x = a + h$

So, $\lim_{h\to 0} \dfrac{(a + 2a + 2h)^{1/3} - (3a + 3h)^{1/3}}{(3a + a + h)^{1/3} - (4a + 4h)^{1/3}}$

$$= \lim_{h\to 0} \frac{(3a)^{1/3}\left[\left(1+\frac{2h}{3a}\right)^{1/3} - \left(1+\frac{3h}{3a}\right)^{1/3}\right]}{(4a)^{1/3}\left[\left(1+\frac{h}{4a}\right)^{1/3} - \left(1+\frac{4h}{4a}\right)^{1/3}\right]}$$

$$= \lim_{h\to 0}\left(\frac{3}{4}\right)^{1/3}\left[\frac{1+\frac{2h}{9a}-1-\frac{3h}{9a}+\text{higher degree terms}}{1+\frac{h}{12a}-1-\frac{4h}{12a}+\text{higher degree terms}}\right]$$

$$= \left(\frac{3}{4}\right)^{1/3}\left(\frac{\frac{2}{9}-\frac{3}{9}}{\frac{1}{12}-\frac{4}{12}}\right) = \left(\frac{3}{4}\right)^{1/3}\left(\frac{\frac{-1}{9}}{\frac{-3}{12}}\right)$$

$$= \left(\frac{3}{4}\right)^{1/3}\frac{4}{(3)^2} = \frac{4^{1-\frac{1}{3}}}{3^{2-\frac{1}{3}}}$$

$$= \frac{4^{2/3}}{3^{5/3}} = \frac{2^{4/3}}{3^{5/3}} = \frac{2}{3}\left(\frac{2}{9}\right)^{1/3}$$

84. $\lim_{x\to 0}\frac{x(e^{(\sqrt{1+x^2+x^4}-1)/x}-1)}{\sqrt{1+x^2+x^4}-1} = \lim_{x\to 0}\frac{e^{(\sqrt{1+x^2+x^4}-1)/x}-1}{(\sqrt{1+x^2+x^4}-1)/x} = 1$

$$\left[\because \lim_{y\to 0}\frac{e^y-1}{y}=1\right]$$

85. Given limit, $\lim_{x\to 0}\left(\frac{3x^2+2}{7x^2+2}\right)^{1/x^2} = P$ (let), having 1^∞ form.

$\therefore \quad P = e^{\lim_{x\to 0}\frac{1}{x^2}\left(\frac{3x^2+2}{7x^2+2}-1\right)}$

[$\because$ if $\lim_{x\to a}(f(x))^{g(x)}$ have indeterminant form 1^∞, then

$$\lim_{x\to a}(f(x))^{g(x)} = e^{\lim_{x\to a} g(x)(f(x)-1)}]$$

$\Rightarrow P = e^{\lim_{x\to 0}\frac{1}{x^2}\left(\frac{3x^2+2-7x^2-2}{7x^2+2}\right)}$

$= e^{\lim_{x\to 0}\frac{1}{x^2}\left(\frac{-4x^2}{7x^2+2}\right)} = e^{\lim_{x\to 0}\frac{-4}{7x^2+2}}$

On applying limit, we get

$$P = e^{-4/2} = e^{-2} = \frac{1}{e^2}$$

86. Given, $\lim_{x\to 0}\left(\tan\left(\frac{\pi}{4}+x\right)\right)^{1/x}$ [having 1^∞ form]

$= e^{\lim_{x\to 0}\left\{\frac{1}{x}\left[\tan\left(\frac{\pi}{4}+x\right)-1\right]\right\}} = e^{\lim_{x\to 0}\left\{\frac{1}{x}\left(\frac{1+\tan x}{1-\tan x}-1\right)\right\}}$

$= e^{\lim_{x\to 0}\left(\frac{1}{x}\times\frac{2\tan x}{1-\tan x}\right)}$

$= e^{\lim_{x\to 0} 2\times\frac{\tan x}{x}\times\frac{1}{1-\tan x}}$

$= e^{2(1)(1)} = e^2$ $\left[\because \lim_{x\to 0}\frac{\tan x}{x}=1\right]$

87. Given, $\lim_{x\to 1}\frac{x+x^2+x^3+\ldots+x^n-n}{x-1} = 820, (n\in N)$

$\Rightarrow \lim_{x\to 1}\left\{\frac{x-1}{x-1}+\frac{x^2-1}{x-1}+\frac{x^3-1}{x-1}+\ldots+\frac{x^n-1}{x-1}\right\} = 820$

$\Rightarrow \quad 1+2+3+\ldots+n = 820$

$\Rightarrow \quad \frac{n(n+1)}{2} = 820$

$\Rightarrow \quad n(n+1) = 1640 = 40\times 41$

$\Rightarrow \quad n = 40$

Exercise 2 - JEE Advanced Pattern

1. $\lim_{x\to 0}(\cos x + a^3\sin b^6 x)^{1/x}$

$= \lim_{x\to 0} e^{\frac{1}{x}(\cos x - 1 + a^3\sin b^6 x)}$

$= \lim_{x\to 0} e^{\left(\frac{-2\sin^2(x/2)}{x}+\frac{a^3\sin b^6 x}{x}\right)}$

$= e^{a^3 b^6} = e^{512}$

$(ab^2)^3 = 512 = 8^3$

$\therefore \quad ab^2 = 8$

2. $\lim_{x\to\frac{\pi}{4}}\frac{1-\frac{\sin x}{\cos x}}{\sqrt{2}\left(\frac{1}{\sqrt{2}}-\sin x\right)}$

$= \lim_{x\to\frac{\pi}{4}}\frac{\left(\cos x\cdot\frac{1}{\sqrt{2}}-\sin x\cdot\frac{1}{\sqrt{2}}\right)}{\cos x\left(\sin\frac{\pi}{4}-\sin x\right)}$

$= \lim_{x\to\frac{\pi}{4}}\frac{\sin\left(\frac{\pi}{4}-x\right)}{\cos x\left(\sin\frac{\pi}{4}-\sin x\right)}\cdot\frac{\left(\sin\frac{\pi}{4}+\sin x\right)}{\left(\sin\frac{\pi}{4}+\sin x\right)}$

$= \lim_{x\to\frac{\pi}{4}}\frac{\sin\left(\frac{\pi}{4}-x\right)\cdot\left(\sin\frac{\pi}{4}+\sin x\right)}{\cos x\cdot\sin\left(\frac{\pi}{4}-x\right)\cdot\sin\left(\frac{\pi}{4}+x\right)}$

$= \frac{2(1/\sqrt{2})}{1/\sqrt{2}} = 2$

3. $\lim_{x\to 0}\frac{\sin x}{x} = 1$

$\lim_{x\to 0}\left[\frac{\sin x}{x}\right] = 0$

and $\lim_{x\to 0}\left[\frac{r\sin rx}{x}\right] = \lim_{x\to 0}\left[r^2\left(\frac{\sin rx}{rx}\right)\right] = r^2-1$

$\lim_{x\to 0}\sum_{r=1}^{10}\left[\frac{r\sin rx}{x}\right] = \sum_{r=1}^{10}(r^2-1)$

$= \frac{10\times 11\times 21}{6} - 10$

$= 5\times 77 - 10 = 385 - 10 = 375$

4. $\lim_{x\to 0} \dfrac{6x^2 \cot x \operatorname{cosec} 2x}{\sec\left(\cos x + \pi \tan\left(\dfrac{\pi}{4\sec x}\right) - 1\right)}$

$$\lim_{x\to 0} \frac{6\dfrac{x}{\tan x}\cdot\dfrac{x}{\sin 2x}}{\sec\left(\cos x + \pi\tan\left(\dfrac{\pi}{4\sec x}\right) - 1\right)} = -3$$

5. $\lim_{t\to 0}\left(\dfrac{b^{t+1} - a^{t+1}}{b-a}\right)^{1/t} = e^{\lim_{t\to 0}\left(\frac{(b^{t+1} - b)}{t} - \frac{(a^{t+1} - a)}{t}\right)\times\frac{1}{b-a}}$

$$= e^{\lim_{t\to 0}\left(\frac{b(b^t - 1)}{t} - \frac{a(a^t - 1)}{t}\right)\times \frac{1}{b-a}}$$

$$= e^{\frac{b\ln b - a\ln a}{b-a}} = e^{\ln\left(\frac{b^b}{a^a}\right)^{1/b-a}}$$

$$= \left(\frac{b^b}{a^a}\right)^{\frac{1}{b-a}}$$

6. $\lim_{x\to 0}\dfrac{(1+P(x))^{\frac{1}{100}} - 1}{x}$

$$= \lim_{x\to 0}\frac{\left(1 + \dfrac{1}{100}P(x) + \ldots\right) - 1}{x}$$

$$= \lim_{x\to 0}\left[\frac{1}{100} + \frac{1}{100}(P(x))^2 + \ldots\right]$$

$$= \frac{1}{100} \qquad [\because P(0) = 0]$$

7. $L = \lim_{x\to 0^+}\left(\dfrac{\cot^{-1}(\ln(x))}{\pi}\right)^{-\ln x}$ $(1^\infty) = e^{\lim_{x\to 0^+}\left(\frac{\cot^{-1}\ln(x)}{\pi}\right)(-\ln x)}$

$$= e^{\lim_{x\to 0^+}\frac{\cot^{-1}(-\ln x)}{\pi}(\ln x)}$$

$$= e^{\lim_{x\to 0^+}\frac{\tan^{-1}\left(-\frac{1}{\ln x}\right)}{\left(-\frac{1}{\ln x}\right)\pi}} = e^{\frac{-1}{\pi}}$$

8. $L = \lim_{n\to\infty}\dfrac{1}{n}\sum_{k=1}^{n}\left(\left(\dfrac{k}{n}\right)^2 + \ln^2\left(1 + \dfrac{k}{n}\right)\right)$

$$= \int_0^1 (x^2 + \ln^2(1+x))\,dx = \frac{1}{3} + 2\ln^2\frac{2}{e}$$

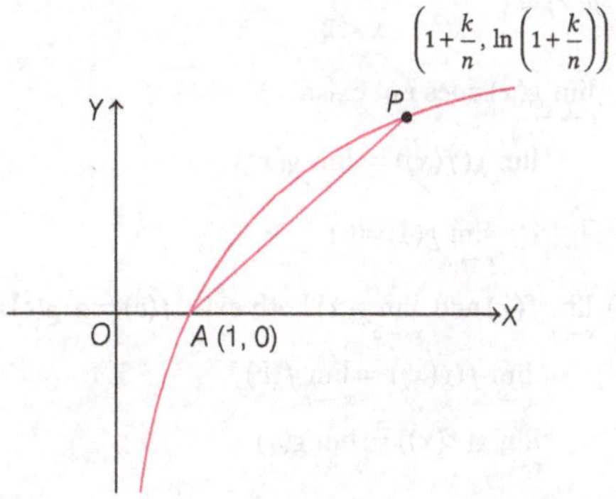

9. $f(x) = \lim_{n\to\infty}\dfrac{x\left(1 + \left(\dfrac{\pi}{3x}\right)^n\right)}{1 + \left(\dfrac{\pi}{3x}\right)^{n-1}} = x,\ x > \dfrac{\pi}{3}$

$$f(x) = \lim_{n\to\infty}\frac{\dfrac{\pi}{3}\left(\left(\dfrac{3x}{\pi}\right)^n + 1\right)}{\left(\left(\dfrac{3x}{\pi}\right)^{n-1} + 1\right)} = \frac{\pi}{3},\ x < \frac{\pi}{3}$$

$$f(x) = \frac{\pi}{3};\ x = \frac{\pi}{3}$$

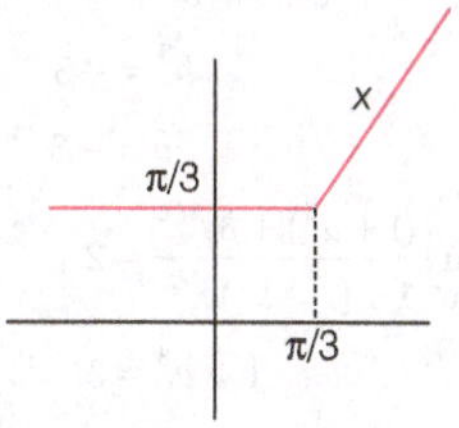

$$f(x) = \begin{cases} x, & x > \dfrac{\pi}{3} \\ \dfrac{\pi}{3}, & x \le \dfrac{\pi}{3}\end{cases}$$

10. $\lim_{x\to\infty} x\left[x^{5c-1}\left(1 + \dfrac{7}{x} + \dfrac{2}{x^5}\right)^c - 1\right] = l$

Case I $5c - 1 > 0$, then $l \to \infty$

Case II $5c - 1 < 0$, then $l \to -\infty$

Since, limit is finite and non-zero, so $5c - 1 = 0 \Rightarrow c = \dfrac{1}{5}$

$$\therefore\quad l = \lim_{x\to\infty} x\left[\left(1 + \frac{7}{x} + \frac{2}{x^5}\right)^{1/5} - 1\right]$$

$$= \lim_{x\to\infty} x\left[1 + \left(\frac{1}{5}\right)\left(\frac{7}{x} + \frac{2}{x^5}\right) + \ldots - 1\right]$$

[by binomial approximation]

$$= \frac{7}{5}$$

11. $\lim_{n\to\infty}\sum_{k=1}^{n}\left(\sin\dfrac{\pi}{2k} - \sin\dfrac{\pi}{2(k+2)}\right)$

$$+ \lim_{n\to\infty}\sum_{k=1}^{n}\left(\cos\frac{\pi}{2(k+2)} - \cos\frac{\pi}{2k}\right)$$

$$= \lim_{n\to\infty}\left(\begin{array}{l}\sin\frac{\pi}{2} - \sin\frac{\pi}{6} + \sin\frac{\pi}{4} - \sin\frac{\pi}{8} + \sin\frac{\pi}{6} - \sin\frac{\pi}{10} \\ + \ldots + \sin\frac{\pi}{2n} - \sin\frac{\pi}{2(n+2)}\end{array}\right)$$

$$+ \lim_{n\to\infty}\left(\begin{array}{l}\cos\frac{\pi}{6} - \cos\frac{\pi}{2} + \cos\frac{\pi}{8} - \cos\frac{\pi}{4} + \cos\frac{\pi}{10} - \cos\frac{\pi}{6} \\ + \ldots + \cos\frac{\pi}{2(n+2)} - \cos\frac{\pi}{2n}\end{array}\right)$$

$$= 1 + \frac{1}{\sqrt{2}} + 2 - \frac{1}{\sqrt{2}} = 3$$

12. $e^{\lim_{x\to 0}\frac{(\cos x-1)}{\sin^2 x}} + \lim_{x\to 0}\dfrac{\frac{\sin 2x}{2x}\cdot 2x+6x\cdot\frac{\tan^{-1}3x}{3x}+3x^2}{\frac{\ln(1+3x+\sin^2 x)}{3x+\sin^2 x}\cdot(3x+\sin^2 x)+xe^x}$

$$=\frac{1}{\sqrt{e}}+2$$

13. On dividing numerator and denominator by $e^{1/x}$, we get

$$\lim_{x\to 0^+}\frac{(1+a^3)e^{-1/x}+8}{e^{-1/x}+(1-b^3)}=2$$

$$\Rightarrow \quad \frac{0+8}{0+1-b^3}=2$$

$$\Rightarrow \quad b^3=-3$$

$$\Rightarrow \quad b=-3^{1/3}$$

$$\lim_{x\to 0^-}\frac{(1+a^3)+8e^{1/x}}{1+(1-b^3)e^{1/x}}=2$$

$$\Rightarrow \quad 1+a^3=2$$

$$\Rightarrow \quad a^3=1$$

$$\Rightarrow \quad a=1$$

14. $I=\lim_{x\to 0^+}\dfrac{\int_x^{2x}\sin^m t\,dt}{x^n}$

Applying L-Hospital rule,

$$I=\lim_{x\to 0^+}\frac{2\sin^m 2x-\sin^m x}{nx^{n-1}}$$

If $m=n-1$

$$I=\frac{2^{m+1}-1}{n}=\frac{2^n-1}{n}$$

If $m\ge n$

$$I=0$$

15. We have, $\lim_{x\to 1^+}\dfrac{(1-|x|+\sin|1-x|)\sin\left(\frac{\pi}{2}[1-x]\right)}{|1-x|[1-x]}$

$$\left[\begin{array}{l}\text{if } x\to 1^+, |1-x|=-(1-x)\\ \text{and } [1-x]=-1\end{array}\right]$$

$$=\lim_{x\to 1^+}\frac{\{1-x+\sin(-(1-x))\}\sin\left(\frac{\pi}{2}(-1)\right)}{-(1-x)(-1)}$$

$$=\lim_{x\to 1^+}\frac{\{1-x-\sin(1-x)\}\sin\left(-\frac{\pi}{2}\right)}{(1-x)}$$

$$=\lim_{x\to 1^+}\frac{(x-1)+\sin(1-x)}{1-x}$$

$$=\lim_{x\to 1^+}\left(\frac{x-1}{1-x}+\frac{\sin(1-x)}{1-x}\right)$$

$$=-1+1=0$$

16. $\lim_{x\to 1^+}f(x)=\lim_{h\to 0}\left(\dfrac{1-(1+h)(1+h)}{h}\right)\cdot\cos\left(\dfrac{1}{-h}\right)$

$$=\lim_{h\to 0}\left(\frac{-2h-h^2}{h}\right)\cos\left(\frac{1}{h}\right)$$

$$=-2\lim_{h\to 0}\cos\left(\frac{1}{h}\right), \text{ oscillatory limit.}$$

At $x=1-h$

$$\lim_{x\to 1^-}f(x)=\lim_{h\to 0}\left(\frac{1-(1-h)(1+h)}{h}\right)\cdot\cos\frac{1}{h}$$

$$=\lim_{h\to 0}\frac{h^2}{h}\cdot\cos\left(\frac{1}{h}\right)$$

$$=\lim_{h\to 0}h\cos\frac{1}{h}$$

$$=0$$

17. (a) $\lim_{x\to 1^+}([x])^{\frac{1}{x-1}}=\lim_{x\to 1^+}(1)^{\frac{1}{x-1}}=1$

(b) $\lim_{x\to 3}\dfrac{(x^2-9)-|x-3|}{(x-3)}$

$$\text{RHL}=\lim_{x\to 3^+}(x+3)-1=5$$

$$\text{LHL}=\lim_{x\to 3^-}(x+3)+1=7$$

(c) $\lim_{x\to 0^+}(x)^{\ln x}\Rightarrow \ln x\to -\infty$

$$(0^+)^{\infty}\Rightarrow 0$$

$$(0^+)^{(-\infty)}=\frac{1}{0}\Rightarrow\infty$$

(d) $\lim_{x\to 0^+}\left(\dfrac{2\sin^2\left(\frac{\sin^2 x}{2}\right)}{x^2}\right)^{\frac{\ln(1-2x^2)}{\sin^2 x}}$

$$\Rightarrow \quad (0)^{(-2)}\Rightarrow\frac{1}{0^2}\Rightarrow\infty$$

18. (a) $f(x)=\begin{cases}1, & x>0\\ 0, & x\le 0\end{cases},\ g(x)=\begin{cases}0, & x>0\\ 1, & x\le 0\end{cases}$

$$f(x)\cdot g(x)=\begin{cases}0, & x>0\\ 0, & x\le 0\end{cases}$$

(b) $\lim_{x\to c}f(x)$ and $\lim_{x\to c}g(x)$

e.g. $f(x)=[x]$, GIF $=2$

$g(x)=\{x\}$, fractional part function $=2$

$$\lim_{x\to 2}f(g(x))=\lim_{x\to 2}[\{x\}]=0$$

(c) $f(x)=x^2,\ c=2$

$$g(x)=\begin{cases}2x+3, & x\ge 2\\ x, & x<2\end{cases}$$

$\lim_{x\to 2}g(x)$ does not exist.

$$\lim_{x\to 2}g(f(x))=\lim_{x\to 2}g(x^2)$$

$$\lim_{x\to 2}g(4)=11$$

(d) $\lim_{x\to c}f(x)$ and $\lim_{x\to c}g(x)$ both exist $f(c)=a,\ g(c)=b$,

$$\lim_{x\to c}f(g(x))=\lim_{x\to c}f(b)$$

$$\lim_{x\to c}g(f(x))=\lim_{x\to c}g(a)$$

19. (a) $\lim_{n\to\infty}\frac{1}{2}\left[\frac{2}{1.3}+\frac{2}{3.5}+\ldots+\frac{2}{(2n-1)(2n+1)}\right]$

$= \lim_{n\to\infty}\frac{1}{2}\left[\frac{3-1}{1.3}+\left(\frac{5-3}{3.5}\right)+\ldots+\frac{(2n+1)-(2n-1)}{(2n-1)(2n+1)}\right]$

$= \lim_{n\to\infty}\frac{1}{2}\left[\left(\frac{1}{1}-\frac{1}{3}\right)+\left(\frac{1}{3}-\frac{1}{5}\right)+\ldots+\left(\frac{1}{2n-1}-\frac{1}{2n+1}\right)\right]$

$= \lim_{n\to\infty}\frac{1}{2}\left[\frac{1}{1}-\frac{1}{2n+1}\right]$

$= \frac{1}{2}$

(b) $\lim_{x\to\infty}\frac{3x^2}{2x+1}-\frac{(2x-1)(3x^2+x+2)}{4x^2}$

$= \lim_{x\to\infty}\frac{12x^4-(4x^2-1)(3x^2+x+2)}{(2x+1)(4x^2)}$

$= \lim_{x\to\infty}\frac{-4x^3-5x^2+\ldots}{8x^3+4x^2}$

$= \frac{-4}{8}=\frac{-1}{2}$

(c) $\lim_{n\to\infty}\frac{1}{n^2}(1+2+3\ldots+n)$

$= \lim_{n\to\infty}\frac{1}{n^2}(n)\frac{(n+1)}{2}$

$= \lim_{n\to\infty}\frac{n^2+n}{2n^2}$

$= \lim_{n\to\infty}\left(\frac{1}{2}+\frac{1}{2n}\right)=\frac{1}{2}$

(d) $\lim_{n\to\infty}\frac{1+\frac{1}{n+2}}{1-\frac{1}{n+2}}=1$

20. Shown in the figure, $\alpha\in(3,4)$

$\because \lim_{x\to\alpha^+}\left[\frac{\max(\tan x,\{x\})}{x-3}\right]=\lim_{x\to\alpha^+}\left[\frac{\{x\}}{x-3}\right]=1$

and $\lim_{x\to\alpha^+}\left[\frac{\min(\tan x,\{x\})}{x-3}\right]=\lim_{x\to\alpha^+}\left[\frac{x-3}{x-3}\right]=1$

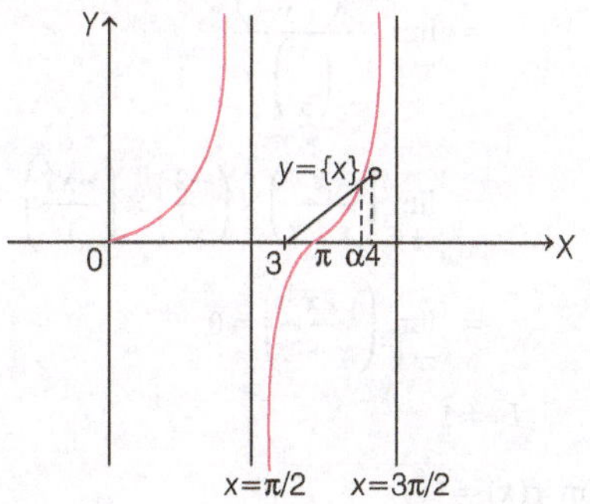

and $\lim_{x\to\alpha^-}\left[\frac{\min(\tan x,\{x\})}{x-3}\right]=\lim_{x\to\alpha^-}\left[\frac{\tan x}{x-3}\right]=0$

and $\lim_{x\to\alpha^-}\left[\frac{\max(\tan x,\{x\})}{\tan x}\right]=\lim_{x\to\alpha^-}\left[\frac{\{x\}}{\tan x}\right]$

$= \lim_{x\to\alpha^-}\left[\frac{x-3}{\tan x}\right]=1$

21. $\lim_{x\to 0}\left[\frac{1}{\sqrt{2}}\sqrt{1+\cos(2+2\cos 2[x])}\right]$

$\lim_{x\to 0}[|\cos|\cos[x]||]=0$

Other cases can also be simplified like this.

22. $f(x)=\frac{1-\cos\{x\}}{x^2(x^3+ax^2+bx+c)^2}$

$x^3+ax^2+bx+c=(x-1)(x-2)(x-3)$

$=x^3-6x^2+11x-6$

$\therefore \quad a+b+c=-1$

$f(x)=\frac{1-\cos\{x\}}{x^2[(x-1)(x-2)(x-3)]^2}$

Now, $l=\frac{1}{8}$, $m=\frac{1}{8}$ and $n=\frac{1}{72}$

$\therefore \quad l+m+n=\frac{19}{72}$

23. $a\ge e\ge 2$

(a) $L=a\lim_{x\to\infty}\left(1+\left(\frac{2}{a}\right)^x+\left(\frac{e}{a}\right)^x\right)^{1/x}$

$\therefore x\to a, \left(\frac{2}{a}\right)\to 0, \left(\frac{e}{a}\right)\to 0, \frac{1}{x}\to 0$

So, $L=a$

(b) If $a=2e>2$

$L=\lim_{x\to\infty}(2^x+(2e)^x+e^x)^{1/x}$

$=2e\lim_{x\to\infty}\left[\left(\frac{1}{e}\right)^x+1+\left(\frac{1}{2}\right)^x\right]^{1/x}$

$=2e(1)=2e$

(c) If $0<a\le e$,

$L=e\left(\lim_{x\to\infty}\left(\left(\frac{2}{e}\right)^x+\left(\frac{a}{e}\right)^x+1\right)^{1/x}\right)=e$

(d) $a>\frac{e}{2}>1$

$L=\lim_{x\to\infty}\left[2^x+\left(\frac{2a}{2}\right)^x+e^x\right]^{1/x}$

$=2a\lim_{x\to\infty}\left(\left(\frac{1}{a}\right)^x+\left(\frac{1}{2}\right)^x+\left(\frac{e}{2a}\right)^x\right)^{1/x}=0$

24. (a) $\lim_{t\to 0}\dfrac{\sin(\tan t)}{\sin t}=\lim_{t\to 0}\dfrac{\sin(\tan t)}{\tan t}\times\dfrac{\tan t}{\sin t}$

$$=\lim_{t\to 0}\frac{1}{\cos t}\left[\frac{\sin(\tan t)}{\tan t}\right]$$

$$=(1)(1)=1$$

(b) $\lim_{t\to \frac{\pi}{2}}\dfrac{\sin(\cos x)}{\cos x}=1$

(c) $\lim_{x\to 0}\dfrac{\sqrt{1+x}-\sqrt{1-x}}{x}=\lim_{x\to 0}\dfrac{1+x-1+x}{x[\sqrt{1+x}+\sqrt{1-x}]}$

$$=\frac{2}{2}=1$$

(d) $\lim_{x\to 0}\dfrac{\sqrt{x^2}}{x}=\lim_{x\to 0}\dfrac{|x|}{x}$

$\Rightarrow$ LHL $=-1$, RHL $=1$

$\Rightarrow$ Limit does not exist.

25. $f(x)=\begin{cases}2x-3; & -3\le x<0\\ 4-x^2; & 0\le x\le 5\end{cases}$

and $g(x)=\begin{cases}2x+3; & -10\le x<0\\ -1-x; & 0\le x\le 3\end{cases}$

$$\lim_{x\to 0^+}f(g(x))=\lim_{x\to 0^+}f(-1-x)$$

$$=\lim_{x\to 0^+}2(-1-x)-3$$

$$=-5$$

and $\lim_{x\to 0^-}f(g(x))=\lim_{x\to 0^-}f(2x+3)$

$$=\lim_{x\to 0^-}[4-(2x+3)^2]$$

$$=4-9$$

$$=-5$$

$\therefore\ \lim_{x\to 0^+}f(g(x))=\lim_{x\to 0^-}f(g(x))$

$\Rightarrow\ \lim_{x\to 0}f(g(x))=-5$

$\lim_{x\to 0}f(g(x))$ exists.

26. $\lim_{x\to\infty}\cos^{2n}x=\lim_{x\to\infty}(\cos^2 x)^n$

As $n\to\infty$, $\cos^2 x\in[0,1)$ for $x\ne m\pi$, $m\in Q$

$\Rightarrow\ (\cos^2 x)^n\to 0$ for $x\ne m\pi$, $n\to\infty$

$\therefore\ \lim_{n\to\infty}\cos^{2n}x=0$ for $x\ne m\pi$, $m\in Q$ and

$\lim_{n\to\infty}(\cos(m\pi))^{2n}=1$

$\therefore\ \lim_{n\to\infty}\cos^{2n}x=1$ for $x=m\pi$, $m\in Q$

27. (a) $\lim_{x\to-\infty}f(x)=\lim_{x\to-\infty}\left(\dfrac{|x|}{|x|+2}\right)^{-x}$

$$=\lim_{x\to-\infty}\left(\frac{-x}{-x+2}\right)^{-x}$$

$$=\lim_{y\to-\infty}\left(\frac{y}{y+2}\right)^{y};\ y=-x$$

$$=\lim_{y\to-\infty}\left(1+\left(\frac{-2}{y+2}\right)\right)^{y}$$

$$=e^{\left(\lim_{x\to\infty}\frac{-2y}{y+2}\right)}=e^{-2}$$

(b) $\lim_{x\to 0}f(x)=\lim_{x\to 0}\left(\dfrac{|x|}{|x|+2}\right)^{-x}$

$\Rightarrow$ LHL $=\lim_{x\to 0^-}\left(\dfrac{-x}{-x+2}\right)^{-x}$

$$=\lim_{h\to 0^+}\left(\frac{h}{h+2}\right)^{h}$$

$$=L_1\text{ (say)}$$

$\Rightarrow\ \ln L_1=\lim_{h\to 0^-}h\ln\left(\dfrac{h}{h+2}\right)$

$$=\lim_{h\to 0^+}\left[\frac{\ln\left(\frac{h}{h+2}\right)}{\left(\frac{1}{h}\right)}\right]$$

$$=\lim_{h\to 0^+}\left(\frac{h+2}{h}\right)\left(\frac{h+2-h}{(h+2)^2}\right)\left(\frac{-h^2}{1}\right)$$

$$=\lim_{h\to 0^+}\frac{-2h}{(h+2)}=0$$

$\Rightarrow\ L_1=e^0=1$

Also, RHL $=\lim_{x\to 0^-}\left(\dfrac{x}{x+2}\right)^{-x}$

$$=\lim_{x\to 0^-}\left(\frac{x+2}{x}\right)^{x}$$

$=L_2$ (say)

$\Rightarrow\ \ln L_2=\lim_{x\to 0^-}x\ln\left(\dfrac{x+2}{x}\right)$

$$=\lim_{x\to 0^-}\frac{\ln\left(\frac{x+2}{x}\right)}{\left(\frac{1}{x}\right)}$$

$$=\lim_{x\to 0^-}\left(\frac{x}{x+2}\right)\times\left(\frac{-2}{x^2}\right)\times\left(\frac{-x^2}{1}\right)$$

$$=\lim_{x\to 0^-}\left(\frac{2x}{x+2}\right)=0$$

$\Rightarrow\ L_2=1$

$\therefore\ \lim_{x\to 0}f(x)=1$

Option (b) is correct.

(c) $\lim_{x\to\infty} f(x) = \lim_{x\to\infty}\left(\frac{|x|}{|x|+2}\right)^{-x}$

$$= \lim_{x\to\infty}\left(\frac{x}{x+2}\right)^{-x}$$

$$= \lim_{x\to\infty}\left(1-\frac{2}{x+2}\right)^{-x}$$

$$= e^{\lim_{x\to\infty}\left(\frac{-2}{x+2}\right)(-x)}$$

$$= e^{\lim_{x\to\infty}\left(\frac{2x}{x+2}\right)}$$

$$= e^2$$

$\Rightarrow$ Option (c) is correct.

28. $L = \lim_{x\to\infty} f(x) = \lim_{x\to\infty}\left(\frac{ax+1}{bx+2}\right)^x = \lim_{x\to\infty}\left(\frac{a+1/x}{b+2/x}\right)^x$

$L = 0$ if $b > a$

$L = \infty$ if $b < a$

If $a = b$

$L = (1)^\infty$ form

$$L = e^{\lim_{x\to\infty}\left(\frac{ax+1}{bx+2}-1\right)x}$$

$$= e^{\lim_{x\to\infty}\left(\frac{ax+1-ax-2}{ax+2}\right)x}$$

$$= e^{\lim_{x\to\infty}\frac{-1}{a+2/x}}$$

$$= e^{-1/a} \text{ or } e^{-1/b}$$

29. $\lim_{x\to\infty}\frac{(ax+1)^n}{x^n+A}$

(a) If $n \in N$

$$\Rightarrow \lim_{x\to\infty}\frac{\left(a+\frac{1}{x}\right)^n}{1+\frac{A}{x^n}} = \frac{(a+0)^n}{1+0} = a^n$$

(b) If $n \in Z$ and $a = A = 0$, then

$$\lim_{x\to\infty}\frac{(ax+1)^n}{x^n+A} = \lim_{x\to\infty}\frac{1}{x^n} = \infty, n \in Z$$

(c) If $n = 0$, then

$$\lim_{x\to\infty}\frac{(ax+1)^n}{x^n+A} = \lim_{x\to\infty}\frac{1}{1+A} = \frac{1}{1+A}$$

(d) If $n \in Z^-$, $A = 0$ and $a \neq 0$, then

$$\lim_{x\to\infty}\frac{(ax+1)^n}{x^n+A} = \lim_{x\to\infty}\frac{(ax+1)^n}{x^n}$$

$$= \lim_{x\to\infty}\left(a+\frac{1}{x}\right)^n$$

$$= (a+0)^n = a^n$$

30. $\lim_{x\to\infty}\frac{x^n}{e^x} = 0$ $\quad [n \in \text{integer}]$

Case (i) When $n = 0$, then

$$\lim_{x\to\infty}\frac{x^n}{e^x} = \lim_{x\to\infty}\frac{1}{e^x} = 0$$

Case (ii) When n is + ve integer.

$$\lim_{x\to\infty}\frac{x^n}{e^x} = \lim_{x\to\infty}\frac{n!}{e^x} = 0 \quad \left(\frac{\infty}{\infty}\text{ form}\right)$$

Case (iii) When n is – ve, $n = -m$, where $m \in Z^+$

$$\lim_{x\to\infty}\frac{x^n}{e^x} = \lim_{x\to\infty}\frac{x^{-m}}{e^x}$$

$$= \lim_{x\to\infty}\frac{1}{x^m\cdot e^x} = 0$$

So, $\lim_{x\to\infty}\frac{x^n}{e^x} = 0$

Sol. (Q. Nos. 31 and 32)

$$\lim_{x\to 0}\frac{[(1+bx)-(1+ax)\sqrt{1+x}]}{x^3}$$

$$= \lim_{x\to 0}\frac{(1+bx)-(1+ax)\left(1+\frac{x}{2}-\frac{x^2}{8}+\frac{x^3}{16}\right)}{x^3}$$

$$= \lim_{x\to 0}\frac{bx-\frac{x}{2}+\frac{x^2}{8}-\frac{x^3}{16}-ax-\frac{ax^2}{2}+\frac{ax^3}{8}}{x^3}$$

$\Rightarrow$ Coefficient of x and $x^2 = 0$

$$\Rightarrow \quad b-a=\frac{1}{2} \text{ and } \frac{a}{2}=\frac{1}{8}$$

$$\Rightarrow \quad a=\frac{1}{4}, b=\frac{3}{4}$$

31. $a + b = 1$

32. $l = \frac{1}{32}; b = \frac{3}{4}$

$$\left|\frac{b}{l}\right| = \left|\frac{\frac{3}{4}}{\frac{1}{32}}\right| = 24$$

Sol. (Q. Nos. 33 and 34)

33. $\lim_{x\to 0^+}\frac{x(e^{[x]+|x|}-2)}{[x]+|x|} = -1$

$$\lim_{x\to 0^-}\frac{x[e^{[x]+|x|}-2)}{[x]+|x|} = \lim_{x\to 0^-}\frac{x(e^{-1-x}-2)}{-1-x} = 0$$

Approx $f(x) = -1$

34. $\lim_{x\to 0^-} f(x) = 0$, $\lim_{x\to 0^+} f(x) = a$

For approx $f(x)$ to exist $[|-a|] \le 1$

$\Rightarrow \quad 0 \le |-a| < 2$

$\Rightarrow \quad -2 < a < 2$

$\Rightarrow \quad a \in (-2, 2)$

Sol. (Q. Nos. 35 and 36)

$$\lim_{x\to 0}\frac{\int_0^x \frac{t^2dt}{(a+t^r)^{1/p}}}{bx-\sin x}$$

$$\Rightarrow \lim_{x\to 0}\frac{x^2}{(a+x^r)^{1/p}}\times\frac{1}{b-\cos x}$$

For limit to exist and non-zero, $b=1$

35. $$\lim_{x\to 0}\frac{x^2}{(1-\cos x)}\times\frac{1}{(a+x^r)^{1/3}}=1$$

$$\Rightarrow \qquad a^{1/3}=2$$

$$\Rightarrow \qquad a=8$$

36. $$\lim_{x\to 0}\left(\frac{x^2}{1-\cos x}\right)\left(\frac{1}{9+x^r}\right)^{1/2}=\frac{2}{3}$$

Sol. (Q. Nos. 37 and 38)

37. If $\alpha\to\infty$, then $a\to 0$

$\therefore \quad P(x)=bx+c$

Now, $P(2)=2b+c=9$

and $P'(3)=b=5$

$\Rightarrow \quad c=-1$

$\Rightarrow \quad P(x)=5x-1$

Now, $\lim_{x\to\infty}\left(\frac{5x-1}{5x-5}\right)^x$ $\qquad [1^\infty \text{ form}]$

$$=e^{\lim_{x\to\infty}\left(\frac{5x-1-5x+5}{5x-5}\right)x}=e^{\frac{4}{5}}$$

$\therefore\ M=4$ and $N=5\Rightarrow M+N=9$

38. When $\alpha,\beta\to\infty$, then $a,b\to 0$

$\therefore\ P(x)=c$ but $P(2)=9$

$\Rightarrow P(x)=9$

Now, $\lim_{x\to 3}\frac{\sqrt{P(x)}-3}{\sin(x-3)}=\lim_{x\to 3}\frac{3-3}{\sin(x-3)}=0$

39. $a(x^3-1)+(x-1)=0$

$(x-1)(ax^2+ax+a+1)=0$

$\alpha,\beta\neq 1$ so, α,β are roots of $ax^2+ax+a+1=0$

$\alpha+\beta=-1,\alpha\beta=\frac{a+1}{a}$

$$\lim_{x\to\frac{1}{\alpha}}\frac{(1+a)x^3-x^2-a}{(e^{1-\alpha x}-1)(x-1)}$$

$$=\lim_{x\to\frac{1}{\alpha}}\frac{(x^3-x^2)+a(x^3-1)}{(e^{1-\alpha x}-1)(x-1)}$$

$$=\lim_{x\to\frac{1}{\alpha}}\frac{[x^2+a(x^2+x+1)]}{(e^{1-\alpha x}-1)}$$

$$=\lim_{x\to\frac{1}{\alpha}}\frac{(1+a)x^2+ax+a}{\left(\frac{e^{1-\alpha x}-1}{1-\alpha x}\right)(1-\alpha x)}$$

$$=\lim_{x\to\frac{1}{\alpha}}a\frac{\left[\left(\frac{1+a}{a}\right)x^2+(1)\,x+1\right]}{(1-\alpha x)}$$

$$=\lim_{x\to\frac{1}{\alpha}}a\frac{(\alpha\beta x^2-(\alpha+\beta)x+1)}{1-\alpha x)}$$

$$=\lim_{x\to\frac{1}{\alpha}}a\frac{(1-(\alpha)x)(1-(\beta)x)}{(1-\alpha x)}$$

$$=\frac{a(\alpha-\beta)}{\alpha}$$

$k=1, l=1$

$lk=1$

40. $$n+x_n=\frac{1}{\ln\left(1+\frac{1}{n}\right)}$$

$$\Rightarrow \qquad x_n=\frac{1}{\ln\left(1+\frac{1}{n}\right)}-n$$

$$\lim_{n\to\infty}x_n=\lim_{t\to 0}\frac{1}{\ln(1+t)}-\frac{1}{t}$$

$$=\frac{t-\ln(1+t)}{t\ln(1+t)}$$

$$=\lim_{t\to 0}\frac{t-\left(t-\frac{t^2}{2}+\dots\right)}{t\ln(1+t)}$$

$$=\frac{1}{2}$$

$\therefore\ 2\lim_{n\to\infty}x_n=2\times\frac{1}{2}=1$

41. $$\lim_{x\to a}\left[\frac{(x^2-2ax^2-a^2x+2a^3)(x-2a)^{-1}+2a(x+a)}{x(x^2-a^2)}-\frac{2}{x-a}\right]$$

$$=\lim_{x\to a}\left[\frac{(x^2-2ax^2-a^2x+2a^3)+2a(x+a)(x-2a)-2x(x+a)(x-2a)}{x(x^2-a^2)(x-2a)}\right]$$

$$=\lim_{x\to a}\left[\frac{x^2-2ax^2-a^2x+2a^3+2ax^2-4a^3-2a^2x-2x^3+4a^2x+2ax}{x(x-a)(x+a)(x-2a)}\right]$$

$$=\lim_{x\to a}\frac{-2x^3+x^2+a^2x+2ax-2a^3}{x(x-a)(x+a)(x-2a)}$$

As $\lim_{x\to a}$ numerator tends to finite value and denominator tends to zero. Hence, limit does not exist.

$\because\ l$ does not exist.

$\therefore$ Least prime number is 2.

42. $\lim_{x\to 1}\frac{(3+ax)^{5/2}-b\ln x-\sin(x-1)}{(x-1)^2}$

For limit to exist, $a=-3$

Now, $\lim_{x\to 1}\frac{-3^{5/2}\frac{5}{2}(1-x)^{3/2}-\frac{b}{x}-c\cos(x-1)}{2(x-1)}$

For limit to exist $\Rightarrow b+c=0$

Now, $\lim_{x\to 1}\frac{+3^{5/2}\frac{15}{4}(1-x)^{1/2}+\frac{b}{x^2}+c\sin(x-1)}{2}=2$

$\Rightarrow \quad b=4$

and $\quad c=-4$

$\frac{a^2+b^2+c^2}{41}=\frac{41}{41}=1$

43. $y=\lim_{n\to\infty}\frac{n\cos^2\frac{n\pi}{2}+\sin^2\frac{n\pi}{2}}{n\left(\cos^2\frac{n\pi}{2}+n\sin^2\frac{n\pi}{2}\right)}$

If n is even integer, then

$$y=\lim_{n\to\infty}\frac{n}{n}=1$$

If n is odd integer, then

$$y=\lim_{n\to\infty}\frac{1}{n^2}=0$$

$$\lambda=1,\mu=0$$

$\therefore \quad 2\lambda+\mu=2$

44. Let $x^4e^{\frac{1}{x^2}}=y$

As $x\to 0, y\to\infty$

If n is odd, $\int_0^{\frac{\pi}{4}+y}\cos^n t\,dt$ is finite

Hence, the limit is zero.

45. α,β are roots of $ax^3+x-1-a=0$

$$\alpha+\beta+1=0$$

$$\alpha\beta+\alpha+\beta=1/a$$

$$\alpha\beta=\frac{1+a}{a}$$

$\Rightarrow\frac{1}{\alpha}$ is a root of $(a+1)x^3-x^2-a=0$

and $(a+1)x^3-x^2-a=(x-1/\alpha)(x-1/\beta)(x-1)(a+1)$

$$\lim_{x\to\frac{1}{\alpha}}\frac{\ln(1+(a+1)x^3-x^2-a)}{((a+1)x^3-x^2-a)}\times\frac{((a+1)x^3-x^2-a)}{\frac{(e^{1-\alpha x}-1)}{1-\alpha x}\times(1-\alpha x)(x-1)}$$

$$=\frac{1}{-\alpha}\left(\frac{1}{\alpha}-\frac{1}{\beta}\right)(a+1)$$

$$=-\frac{a}{\alpha}(\beta-\alpha)=a\left(1-\frac{\beta}{\alpha}\right)$$

$$\lambda=1$$

$$4\lambda=4$$

46. $\lim_{x\to 1}\left[\left(\frac{4}{x^2-x^{-1}}-\frac{1-3x+x^2}{1-x^3}\right)^{-1}+3\left(\frac{x^4-1}{x^3-x^{-1}}\right)\right]$

$$=\lim_{x\to 1}\left[\left(\frac{4x+1-3x+x^2}{x^3-1}\right)^{-1}+3x\right]$$

$$=\lim_{x\to 1}(x-1+3x)=3$$

47. $\lim_{x\to 0}\frac{e^{-nx}+e^{nx}-2\cos\frac{nx}{2}-kx^2}{(\sin x-\tan x)}$

$$=\lim_{x\to 0}\frac{2\left[1+\frac{n^2x^2}{2!}+\frac{n^4x^4}{4!}+\dots\right]-2\left[1-\frac{n^2x^2}{4.2!}+\frac{n^4x^4}{16.4!}-\dots\right]-kx^2}{\left(x-\frac{x^3}{3!}+\dots\right)-\left(x+\frac{x^3}{3}+\frac{2}{15}x^5+\dots\right)}$$

$$=\lim_{x\to 0}\frac{x^2\left(n^2+\frac{n^2}{4}-k\right)+x^4\left(\frac{2n^4}{4!}-\frac{2n^4}{16.4!}\right)}{x^3\left(-\frac{1}{3!}-\frac{1}{3}\right)+\dots}$$

limit exists, if coefficient of x^2 is zero.

$\Rightarrow \quad n^2+\frac{n^2}{4}-k=0$

$\Rightarrow \quad 4k=5n^2$

So, least possible value match that is $n=2,k=5$

$\therefore \quad k+n=7$

48. $\lim_{x\to(e^{-1})^+}\frac{e^{\left(\frac{\ln(1+\ln x)}{x}\right)}}{x-e^{-1}}=\lim_{x\to(e^{-1})^+}\frac{e^{\ln(1+\ln x)^{1/x}}}{x-e^{-1}}$

$$=\lim_{x\to(e^{-1})^+}\frac{(1+\ln x)^{1/x}}{x-e^{-1}}$$

$$=\lim_{x\to(e^{-1})^+}\frac{(1+\ln x)\cdot(1+\ln x)^{\frac{1-x}{x}}}{x-e^{-1}}$$

$$=\lim_{x\to(e^{-1})^+}\frac{e\ln ex}{ex-1}\cdot(1+\ln x)^{\frac{1-x}{x}}=e.1.(0)^{e-1}\left[\because\lim_{x\to 1}\frac{\ln x}{x-1}=1\right]$$

$=0$

49. Let $\quad f(x)=\sqrt{\frac{4\cos^2 x}{2+\cos x}}$

$\Rightarrow \quad f(\pi)=2$

$\therefore \lim_{x\to\pi}\frac{1}{x-\pi}\left(\sqrt{\frac{4\cos^2 x}{2+\cos x}}-2\right)$

$$=\lim_{x\to\pi}\frac{f(x)-f(\pi)}{x-\pi}=f'(\pi)$$

Now,

$$f'(x)=\frac{4}{2\sqrt{\frac{4\cos^2 x}{2+\cos x}}}\cdot\frac{(2+\cos)(-2\cos x\sin x)-\cos^2 x(-\sin x)}{(2+\cos x)^2}$$

$f'(\pi)=0$

50. $\lim\limits_{n\to\infty}\left(\dfrac{\sqrt{n^2+n-1}}{n}\right)^{2\sqrt{n^2+n-1}}$ $[1^\infty \text{ form}]$

$$= \lim_{n\to\infty} e^{(2\sqrt{n^2+n-1})\left(\frac{\sqrt{n^2+n-1}}{n}-1\right)}$$

$$= \lim_{n\to\infty} e^{(2\sqrt{n^2+n}-1)\cdot\left(\frac{\sqrt{n^2+n}-(n+1)}{n}\right)}$$

$$= \lim_{n\to\infty} e^{2(\sqrt{n^2+n}-1)\cdot\left(\frac{n^2+n-(n^2+2n+1)}{n(\sqrt{n^2+n}+(n+1)}\right)}$$

$$= \lim_{n\to\infty} e^{\frac{(2\sqrt{n^2+n}-1)\cdot(-n-1)}{n(\sqrt{n^2+n}+n+1)}}$$

$$= \lim_{n\to\infty} e^{\frac{(2\sqrt{1+1/n}-1/n^2)(-1-1/n)}{1\left(\sqrt{1+\frac{1}{n}}+1+\frac{1}{n}\right)}} = e^{-2/2} = e^{-1}$$

$$k = 1 \text{ and } \mu = 1$$

$$\therefore \quad \frac{5k}{4\mu} = \frac{5}{4} = 1.25$$

51. $\lim\limits_{x\to\infty}\left(\dfrac{x}{e} - xe^{\ln\left(\frac{x}{x+1}\right)^x}\right)$

$$= \lim_{x\to\infty}\left(\frac{x}{e} - xe^{-x\ln\left(\frac{x+1}{x}\right)}\right) = \lim_{x\to\infty}\left(\frac{x}{e} - xe^{-x\ln\left(1+\frac{1}{x}\right)}\right)$$

$$= \lim_{x\to\infty}\frac{x}{e} - xe^{-x\left(\frac{1}{x}-\frac{1}{2x^2}\cdots\right)}$$

$$= \lim_{x\to\infty}\frac{x}{e} - \frac{x}{e}\cdot e^{\frac{1}{2x}} = \lim_{x\to\infty}\frac{x}{e}\left(1-e^{\frac{1}{2x}}\right)$$

$$= \lim_{x\to\infty}\frac{-1}{2e}\cdot\left(\frac{e^{1/2x}-1}{1/2x}\right) = -\frac{1}{2e}$$

$$k = 1/2 = 0.5$$

52.

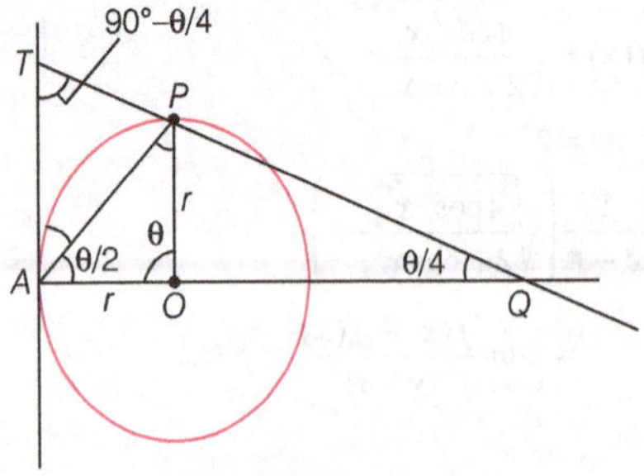

$$P \to A, \theta \to 0$$

$$\angle PAO = 90° - \frac{\theta}{2}$$

$$\angle TAP = \frac{\theta}{2}$$

In ΔOAP, $AP = 2r\sin\theta/2$

$$AT = 2r\sin\theta/2$$

$$\tan\frac{\theta}{4} = \frac{AT}{AQ} \qquad [\text{in } \Delta ATQ]$$

$$AQ = \frac{2r\sin\theta/2}{\tan\theta/4}$$

$$\lim_{\theta\to 0} AQ = 2r\lim_{\theta\to 0}\frac{\sin\theta/2}{\tan\theta/4} = 4r = \text{Double the diameter}$$

$$k = 2$$

Then, $\dfrac{7k}{5} = \dfrac{14}{5} = 2.8$

53. $\lim\limits_{x\to a}\left(\dfrac{(a^{x-a}-1)(x^p-a^p)}{(x-a)^2(\ln a^p)(a^{p-1})}\right)^{\frac{1}{x-a}}$ $[1^\infty \text{ form}]$

$$= e^{\lim\limits_{x\to a}\left(\frac{(a^{x-a}-1)(x^p-a^p)-(x-a)^2\ln a^p(a^{p-1})}{(x-a)^2\ln a^p(a^{p-1})}\right)\times\frac{1}{x-a}}$$

$$= e^{\lim\limits_{x\to a}\frac{(a^{x-a}-1)px^{p-1}+(x^p-a^p)(a^{x-a}\ln a)-2(x-a)\ln a^p(a^{p-1})}{3(x-a)^2(\ln a^p)(a^{p-1})}}$$

$$= e^{\lim\limits_{x\to a}\frac{(a^{x-a}-1)p(p-1)x^{p-2}+(a^{x-a}px^{p-1}\ln a)+p(x^{p-1})(a^{x-a}\ln a)+(x^p-a^p)a^{x-a}(\ln a)^2-2\ln a^p(a^{p-1})}{6(x-a)\ln a^p(a^{p-1})}}$$

$$= e^{\lim\limits_{x\to a}\frac{p\ln a(p-1)(a^{p-2})+p.a^{p-1}(\ln a)^2+2(\ln a^p)a^{(p-1)}\ln a+(p-1)a^{p-2})}{6p\ln a a^{p-1}}}$$

$$= e^{\frac{(p-1)a^{p-2}+a^{p-1}\ln a+2(a^{(p-1)}\ln a+(p-1)a^{p-2})}{6a^{p-1}}} = e^{\frac{(p-1)+a\ln a}{2a}}$$

$$x = 1 \text{ and } y = 2$$

$$\therefore \quad \frac{x}{y} = \frac{1}{2} = 0.5$$

54. $a_{n+1} = (a_n + x)^{-1} = \dfrac{1}{a_n + x}$

$$b_{n+1} = \frac{1}{b_n + y}$$

$$a_{n+1} - b_{n+1} = \frac{b_n - a_n + (y-x)}{(a_n+x)(b_n+y)}$$

On putting $n = 0$,

$$a_1 - b_1 = \frac{y-x}{xy} \qquad \ldots\text{(i)} \; [\because a_0 = b_0 = 0]$$

For $n = 2$, $\lim\limits_{x\to y}\dfrac{a_2 - b_2}{(x-y)(x+y)}$

$$= \lim_{x\to y}\frac{b_1 - a_1 + y - x}{(a_1+x)(b_1+y)(x-y)(x+y)}$$

$$= \lim_{x\to y}\frac{\frac{1}{xy}+1}{(a_1+x)(b_1+y)(x+y)}$$

$$= \lim_{x\to y}\frac{xy-1}{xy\left(\frac{1}{x}+x\right)\left(\frac{1}{y}+y\right)(x+y)}$$

$$= \frac{x^2-1}{(x^2+1)^2(2x)}$$

$\because$ $p = 2, q = 2, r = 2$ and $s = 2$

$\therefore$ $2p + 3q + r + 4s = 4 + 6 + 2 + 8 = 20$

55. $f(x-1)=\begin{cases}1-|x-1|, & |x-1|\le 1\\ |x-1|, & |x-1|>1\end{cases}$

$$=\begin{cases}x, & 0\le x\le 1\\ 2-x, & 1<x\le 2\\ x-1, & x>2\\ 1-x, & x<0\end{cases}$$

$$f(x+1)=\begin{cases}x+2, & -2\le x\le -1\\ -x, & -1<x\le 0\\ x+1, & x>0\\ -x-1, & x<-2\end{cases}$$

$$g(x)=\begin{cases}2x+1, & 0<x\le 1\\ 0 & x=0\\ 3, & 1\le x\le 2\\ 2x & x>2\\ 1-2x & -1<x<0\\ 3 & -2\le x\le -1\\ -2x & x<-2\end{cases}$$

Now, $\lim_{x\to\frac{\pi}{2}} g(\sin x)=g(1)=3$

$\therefore 50\lim_{x\to\frac{\pi}{2}} g(\sin x)=50\times 3=150$

56. $\lim_{n\to\infty}\sum_{k=0}^{n}\frac{{}^nC_k}{n^k(k+3)}$

Now, $(1+x)^n=C_0+C_1x+C_2x^2+\ldots C_nx^n$

On multiplying by x^2 and integrating

$$\int_0^{1/n}x^2(1+x)^n dx=\frac{C_0x^3}{3}+\frac{C_1x^4}{4}+\ldots$$

$$\Rightarrow \frac{1}{n^3}\sum_{k=0}^{n}\frac{{}^nC_k}{n^k(k+3)}=\int_0^{1/n}x^2(1+x)^n dx$$

$$\Rightarrow \lim_{n\to\infty}\sum_{k=0}^{n}\frac{{}^nC_k}{n^k(k+3)}=\lim_{n\to\infty}n^3\int_0^{1/n}x^2(1+x)^n dx \quad \ldots\text{(i)}$$

$$I=\int_0^{1/n}x^2(1+x)^n dx=\frac{x^2(1+x)^{n+1}}{n+1}-\int\frac{2x(1+x)^{n+1}}{n+1}dx$$

$$=\left.\frac{x^2(1+x)^{n+1}}{n+1}-\frac{2x(1+x)^{n+2}}{(n+1)(n+2)}+\frac{2(1+x)^{n+3}}{(n+1)(n+2)(n+3)}\right|_0^{1/n}$$

$$=\frac{(1+n)^n}{n^{n+3}}-\frac{2(n+1)^{n+1}}{n^{n+3}(n+2)}+\frac{2(n+1)^{n+2}}{(n^{n+3})(n+2)(n+3)}-\frac{2}{(n+1)(n+)(n+3)}$$

From Eq. (i),

$$=\lim_{n\to\infty}\left[\left(1+\frac{1}{n}\right)^n-2\left(1+\frac{1}{n}\right)^{n+1}\cdot\frac{n}{n+2}+\frac{2(1+1/n)^{n+2}n^2}{(n+2)(n+3)}-\frac{2n^3}{(n+1)(n+2)(n+3)}\right]$$

$=e-2e+2e-2=e-2$

$8p=2$

$p=\frac{1}{4}=0.25$

57. As, $x_n=\sqrt{a+\sqrt{a+\sqrt{a+}}}\ldots\infty$

$\Rightarrow \quad x_n=\sqrt{a+x_n}\Rightarrow x_n^2-x_n-a=0$

$\Rightarrow \quad x_n=\dfrac{1\pm\sqrt{1+4a}}{2}$

As, x_n is positive $\Rightarrow x_n=1+\sqrt{1+4a}$

$\therefore \quad p=1$ and $q=4$

$\therefore \quad \dfrac{4p+5}{2q}=\dfrac{9}{8}=1.125$

58. Let $y=\sin x+2\sin^2 x+3\sin^3 x+\ldots\infty$

$(\sin x)y=\sin^2 x+2\sin^3 x+\ldots\infty$

$(1-\sin x)\,y=\sin x+\sin^2 x+\sin^3 x+\ldots\infty$

$y=\dfrac{\sin x}{(1-\sin x)^2}$

Now, $\lim_{x\to\frac{\pi}{2}}((1-\sin x)^2 f(x))^{\frac{1}{\sin x-1}}$

$=\lim_{x\to\frac{\pi}{2}}(\sin x)^{1/\sin x-1}$

$=\lim_{x\to\frac{\pi}{2}} e^{(\sin x-1)\times\frac{1}{(\sin x-1)}}=e$

$\therefore \quad 4\lambda-15=1$

$\lambda=4$

$\therefore \quad 8\lambda=32$

59. $\lim_{x\to 0^+}f(x)=\lim_{x\to 0^+}\dfrac{\sin^{-1}(1-\{x\}\cdot\cos^{-1}(1-\{x\})}{\sqrt{2\{x\}}\,(1-\{x\})}$

$$=\lim_{h\to 0}\frac{\sin^{-1}(1-h)\cdot\cos^{-1}(1-h)}{\sqrt{2h}(1-h)}$$

$$=\lim_{h\to 0}\frac{\sin^{-1}(1-h)\sin^{-1}\sqrt{h(2-h)}}{(1-h)\sqrt{2h}}$$

$$=\lim_{h\to 0}\frac{\frac{\pi}{2}}{1}\frac{\sin^{-1}\sqrt{h(2-h)}}{\sqrt{2h-h^2}\sqrt{2h}}\sqrt{2h-h^2}$$

$$=\lim_{h\to 0}\frac{\pi}{2}\cdot 1\cdot\sqrt{1-\frac{h}{2}}=\frac{\pi}{2}$$

$$\lim_{x\to 0^-}f(x)=\lim_{x\to 0^-}\frac{\sin^{-1}(1-\{x\})\cos^{-1}(1-\{x\})}{\sqrt{2\{x\}}\,(1-\{x\})}$$

$$=\lim_{h\to 0}\frac{\sin^{-1}h\cdot\cos^{-1}h}{\sqrt{2(1-h)}\,h}$$

$$=\frac{\frac{\pi}{2}}{\sqrt{2}}=\frac{\pi}{2\sqrt{2}}$$

Then, $4\left(\lim_{x\to 0^+}f(x)\right)^2+8\left(\lim_{x\to 0^-}f(x)\right)^2$

$$=4(\pi/2)^2+8(\pi/2\sqrt{2})^2=2\pi^2$$

Here, $k=2$

$\therefore \quad k^4+2=16+2=18$

60. $\lim_{x\to 0}\dfrac{1-\cos x\sqrt{\cos 2x}}{x^2}$

$$= \lim_{x\to 0}\frac{1-\cos^2 x\cos 2x}{(1+\cos x\sqrt{\cos 2x})x^2}$$

$$= \lim_{x\to 0}\frac{1-\cos^2 x\cos 2x}{x^2}$$

$$= \frac{1}{2}\lim_{x\to 0}\frac{1-\left(\frac{1+\cos 2x}{2}\right)\cos 2x}{x^2}$$

$$= \frac{1}{2}\lim_{x\to 0}\frac{2-\cos 2x-(\cos 2x)^2}{2x^2}$$

$$= \frac{1}{4}\lim_{x\to 0}\left[-\frac{1}{x^2}(\cos 2x+2)(\cos 2x-1)\right]$$

$$= \frac{1}{4}\lim_{x\to 0}(\cos 2x+2)\cdot\lim_{x\to 0}\frac{1-\cos 2x}{x^2}$$

$$= \frac{(1+2)}{4}\cdot\lim_{x\to 0}\frac{2\sin^2 x}{x^2} = \frac{3}{4}\cdot 2\lim_{x\to 0}\left(\frac{\sin x}{x}\right)^2$$

$$= \frac{3}{2} = 1.5$$

61. $f(x) = \sum_{\lambda=1}^{n}\left(x-\frac{7}{\lambda}\right)\left(x-\frac{5}{4(\lambda+1)}\right)$

$$f(0) = \sum_{\lambda=1}^{n}\left(-\frac{7}{\lambda}\right)\left(-\frac{5}{4(\lambda+1)}\right)$$

$$\Rightarrow \quad f(0) = \sum_{\lambda=1}^{n}\left(\frac{35}{4(\lambda)(\lambda+1)}\right)$$

$$\Rightarrow \quad f(0) = \frac{35}{4}\sum_{\lambda=1}^{n}\left(\frac{1}{\lambda}-\frac{1}{\lambda+1}\right)$$

$$\Rightarrow \quad f(0) = \frac{35}{4}\left(1-\frac{1}{n+1}\right)$$

$$\Rightarrow \quad f(0) = \frac{35n}{4(n+1)}$$

Now, $\lim_{n\to\infty} f(0) = \lim_{n\to\infty}\dfrac{35n}{4(n+1)}$

$$= \lim_{n\to\infty}\frac{35}{4\left(1+\frac{1}{n}\right)}$$

$$= \frac{35}{4(1+0)} = \frac{35}{4}$$

Here, $m = 35$, $n = 4$

$\therefore m+n = 39$

62. $\lim_{n\to\infty}\dfrac{n^{98}}{n^{x-1}\left({}^xC_1-\frac{{}^xC_2}{2n}+\frac{{}^xC_3}{6n^2}-\ldots\right)} = \dfrac{1}{99}$

The limit obviously exists if $x-1 = 98$

$\therefore x = 99$

63. $f_2(x) = f_1(f_1(x)) = \dfrac{1}{2}\left(\dfrac{x}{2}+10\right)+10$

$$f_2(x) = \frac{x}{2^2}+\frac{10}{2}+10$$

$$f_n(x) = \frac{x}{2^n}+10+\frac{10}{2}+\frac{10}{2^2}+\ldots+\frac{10}{2^{n-1}}$$

$$\lim_{n\to\infty} f_n(x) = \lim_{n\to\infty}\left(\frac{x}{2^n}+10+\frac{10}{2}+\ldots+\infty\right) = 0+\frac{10}{1-\frac{1}{2}} = 20$$

64. $\lim_{x\to 0}\left(\dfrac{(1+x)^{\frac{1}{x}}}{e}\right)^{\frac{1}{x}} = \lim_{x\to 0}\left(\dfrac{e\left(1-\frac{x}{2}+\frac{11}{24}x^2-\ldots\right)}{e}\right)^{\frac{1}{x}}$

$$= \lim_{x\to 0}\left(1-\frac{x}{2}+\frac{11}{24}x^2-\ldots\right)^{\frac{1}{x}}$$

$$= e^{\lim_{x\to 0}\left(-\frac{x}{2}+\frac{11}{24}x^2-\ldots\right)\frac{1}{x}} = e^{-\frac{1}{2}}$$

$$4\mu = 0.5$$

$$\mu = \frac{0.5}{4} = 0.125$$

65. (A) $\lim_{x\to\infty}\left(\sqrt{x+\sqrt{x}}-\sqrt{x-\sqrt{x}}\right) = \lim_{x\to\infty}\left(\dfrac{2\sqrt{x}}{\sqrt{x+\sqrt{x}}+\sqrt{x-\sqrt{x}}}\right)$

$$= \lim_{x\to\infty}\left(\frac{2}{\sqrt{1+1/\sqrt{x}}+\sqrt{1-1/\sqrt{x}}}\right) = 1$$

(B) $\lim_{x\to 0}\dfrac{\sin 2x-2\tan x}{\ln(1+x^3)}$

$$= \lim_{x\to 0}\frac{-2\sin x}{\cos x}\frac{(\sin^2 x)}{x^3}\times\frac{x^3}{\ln(1+x^3)} = -2$$

(C) $\lim_{x\to 0^+}\ln\sin^3 x-\ln(x^3(x+e))$

$$= \lim_{x\to 0^+}\ln\left(\frac{\sin^3 x}{x^3(x+e)}\right)$$

$$= \ln\left(\frac{1}{e}\right) = -1$$

(D) $2\pi\,|\sin\theta| + 2\pi\,|\cos\theta| = \dfrac{5\pi}{2}$

$$\Rightarrow \quad |\sin\theta|+|\cos\theta| = \frac{5}{4}$$

$$f(x) = \left(\frac{5}{4}\right)^x$$

$$\lim_{x\to\infty}\left[2\times\left(\frac{4}{5}\right)^x\right] = 0$$

66. A-s, B-r, C-p, D-q

(A) $f(x) = |x-a|+|x-10|+|x-a-10|$

At $x = a$, $f(x) = |a-10|+|-10| = 10$ (min value)

At $x = 10$, $f(x) = |10-a|+|-a| = 10$ (min value)

At $x = a+10$, $f(x) = |10|+|a| = 10$ (min value)

(B) $\lim_{x\to 0}\frac{x(1-\cos 2x)^2 - a(\sin x - \tan x)^2}{\tan^5 x + a\sin^8 x}$

$$= \lim_{x\to 0}\frac{\sin^5 x\left(\frac{x}{\sin x}\times 4 - a\frac{(2\sin^2 x/2)^2}{\cos^2 x\sin^3 x}\right)}{\sin^5 x\sin^5 x(\sec^5 x + a\sin^3 x)}$$

$$= \lim_{x\to 0}\left[4\left(\frac{x}{\sin x}\right) - \frac{4a\sin^4 x/2}{\cos^2 x\left(2\sin\frac{x}{2}\cos\frac{x}{2}\right)^3}\right]\Bigg/(\sec^5 x + a\sin^3 x)$$

$= 4$

(C) $\lim_{n\to\infty}\frac{n^a\sin^2 n!}{n+1} = \lim_{n\to\infty}\frac{(\sin^2 n!)n^{a-1}}{1+1/n} = 0$

(D) $\log_a(2a-x) = (\log_a x)^3$ has only one solution at $x = a$

67. Given that $f(x) = \sin\left(\frac{\pi x}{12}\right)$

and $g(x) = \frac{2\log_e(\sqrt{x}-\sqrt{\alpha})}{\log_e(e^{\sqrt{x}} - e^{\sqrt{\alpha}})}$

Now, $\lim_{x\to\alpha^+} g(x)$

$$= \lim_{x\to\alpha^+}\frac{2\log_e(\sqrt{x}-\sqrt{\alpha})}{\log_e(e^{\sqrt{x}}-e^{\sqrt{\alpha}})} \quad \left[\frac{0}{0}\text{ form}\right]$$

$$= \lim_{x\to\alpha^+}\frac{\frac{2}{\sqrt{x}-\sqrt{\alpha}}\left(\frac{1}{2\sqrt{x}}\right)}{\frac{1}{e^{\sqrt{x}}-e^{\sqrt{\alpha}}}\left(\frac{1}{2\sqrt{x}}\times e^{\sqrt{x}}\right)}$$

[using L' Hospital rule]

$$= \lim_{x\to\alpha^+}\frac{e^{\sqrt{x}}-e^{\sqrt{\alpha}}}{\sqrt{x}-\sqrt{\alpha}}\cdot\frac{1}{e^{\sqrt{x}}}\cdot 2 \quad \left[\frac{0}{0}\text{ form}\right]$$

$$= 2\lim_{x\to\alpha^+}\frac{e^{\sqrt{x}}\cdot\frac{1}{2\sqrt{x}}}{\frac{1}{2\sqrt{x}}}\cdot\frac{1}{e^{\sqrt{x}}} \quad \left[\frac{0}{0}\text{ form}\right]$$

$= 2\cdot 1 = 2$

Thus, $\lim_{x\to\alpha^+} g(x) = 2$

$$\therefore \lim_{x\to\alpha^+} f[g(x)] = f\left(\lim_{x\to\alpha^+} g(x)\right) = f(2)$$

$$= \sin\left(\frac{2\pi}{12}\right)$$

$$= \sin\left(\frac{\pi}{6}\right) = \frac{1}{2} = 0.5$$

Hence, the required answer is 0.5.

68. $\lim_{x\to\pi/2}\frac{4\sqrt{2}\cdot 2\sin 2x\cos x}{2\sin 2x\sin\frac{3x}{2} + \left(\cos\frac{5x}{2} - \cos\frac{3x}{2}\right)} - \sqrt{2}(1+\cos 2x)$

$$= \lim_{x\to\frac{\pi}{2}}\frac{8\sqrt{2}\cdot 2\sin x\cos x\cos x}{2\sin 2x\sin\frac{3x}{2} - 2\sin 2x\sin\frac{x}{2}} - 2\sqrt{2}\cos^2 x$$

$$= \lim_{x\to\frac{\pi}{2}}\frac{16\sqrt{2}\sin x\cos^2 x}{2\sin 2x\left(\sin\frac{3x}{2} - \sin\frac{x}{2}\right)} - 2\sqrt{2}\cos^2 x$$

$$= \lim_{x\to\frac{\pi}{2}}\frac{16\sqrt{2}\sin x\cos^2 x}{4\sin x\cos x\left(2\cos x\cdot\sin\frac{x}{2}\right)} - 2\sqrt{2}\cos^2 x$$

$$= \frac{16\sqrt{2}\sin x\cos^2 x}{2\cos^2 x\left(4\sin x\sin\frac{x}{2} - \sqrt{2}\right)}$$

$$= \lim_{x\to\frac{\pi}{2}}\frac{8\sqrt{2}\sin x}{4\sin x\sin\frac{x}{2} - \sqrt{2}} = 8$$

69. The right hand limit $\lim_{x\to 0^+}\frac{(1-x)^{1/x} - e^{-1}}{x^a}$

$$= \lim_{x\to 0^+}\frac{e^{\left\{\frac{1}{x}\log_e(1-x)\right\}} - e^{-1}}{x^a}$$

$$= \lim_{x\to 0^+}\frac{e^{\frac{1}{x}\left(-x-\frac{x^2}{2}-\frac{x^3}{3}-\dots\right)} - e^{-1}}{x^a}$$

$$= \lim_{x\to 0^+}\frac{e^{-1}\cdot e^{\left(-\frac{x}{2}-\frac{x^2}{3}-\frac{x^3}{4}-\dots\dots\right)} - e^{-1}}{x^a}$$

$$= e^{-1}\lim_{x\to 0^+}\frac{e^{-\left(\frac{x}{2}+\frac{x^2}{3}+\frac{x^3}{4}+\dots\right)} - 1}{x^a}$$

The above limit will be non-zero real number, if $a = 1$. And at $a = 1$, the value of the limit is

$$= e^{-1}\left(-\frac{1}{2}\right) = -\frac{1}{2e}$$

Exercise 3 - Challenging Problems

1. Here, $\lim_{x\to\infty}\left(\sqrt{x^4+ax^3+3x^2+bx+2}\right.$

$$\left. - \sqrt{x^4+2x^3-cx^2+3x-d}\right) = 4 \quad [\infty-\infty\text{ form}]$$

Rationalising

$$\lim_{x\to\infty}\frac{(a-2)x^3+(3+c)x^2+(b-3)x+(2+d)}{\left[\sqrt{x^4+ax^3+3x^2+bx+2} + \sqrt{x^4+2x^3-cx^2+3x-d}\right]} = 4$$

Since, limit is finite, the degree of the numerator must be 2. So, $a-2=0$, i.e. $a=2$.

$$\Rightarrow \lim_{x\to\infty} \frac{(3+c)x^2+(b-3)x+(2+d)}{\left[\begin{array}{l}\sqrt{x^4+ax^3+3x^2+bx+2}\\ +\sqrt{x^4+2x^3-cx^2+3x-d}\end{array}\right]}=4$$

On dividing numerator and denominator by x^2, we get

$$\lim_{x\to\infty}\frac{(3+c)+(b-3)/x+(2+d)/x^2}{\sqrt{1+\frac{a}{x}+\frac{3}{x^2}+\frac{b}{x^3}+\frac{2}{x^4}}+\sqrt{1+\frac{2}{x}-\frac{c}{x^2}+\frac{3}{x^3}-\frac{d}{x^4}}}=4$$

$$\Rightarrow \frac{3+c}{2}=4$$

$$\Rightarrow c=5$$

$\therefore \quad c=5,\ a=2$

Hence, $a=2$, $c=5$ and b, d are any real numbers.

2. If x is a real number in [0, 1], then we have two cases either.

***Case* I** $x\in Q$ [rational number]

As $x\in Q$, we have $x=0, \frac{1}{2}, \frac{1}{3}, \frac{1}{4}, \ldots, 1$

which shows $(n!\,\pi x)$ is integral multiple of π for large values of n.

$$\therefore \quad \cos(n!\,\pi x)=\pm 1$$

Thus, $\lim_{m\to\infty}\lim_{n\to\infty}[1+\cos^{2m}(n!\,\pi x)]=\lim_{m\to\infty}\lim_{n\to\infty}(1+1)=2$

***Case* II** $x\notin Q$ [irrational number]

As $x\notin Q$, we have $x=\frac{1}{\sqrt{2}}, \frac{1}{\sqrt{3}}, \frac{1}{\sqrt{5}}, \ldots$

which shows $(n!\,\pi x)$ is not an integral multiple of π and so, $\cos(n!\,\pi x)$ will lie between -1 and $+1$.

Thus, $\lim_{m\to\infty}\lim_{n\to\infty}[1+\cos^{2m}(n!\,\pi x)]$

$$=\lim_{m\to\infty}\lim_{n\to\infty}[1+(\text{a value between }-1\text{ and }+1)^{2m}]$$

$$=\lim_{n\to\infty}[1+0]=1 \qquad [\text{as } 0<x<1\Rightarrow x^\infty=0]$$

Thus, $\lim_{m\to\infty}\lim_{n\to\infty}[1+\cos^{2m}(n!\,\pi x)]=\begin{cases}2, & x\in Q\\ 1, & x\notin Q\end{cases}$

3. Here, $a_1=1$

$$\therefore \quad a_2=\frac{4+3}{3+2}=\frac{7}{5}>1$$

$$\therefore \quad a_2>a_1$$

Assuming $a_{n+1}>a_n$

$$\therefore a_{n+2}-a_{n+1}=\frac{4+3a_{n+1}}{3+2a_{n+1}}-\frac{4+3a_n}{3+2a_n}$$

$$=\frac{(4+3a_{n+1})(3+2a_n)-(4+3a_n)(3+2a_{n+1})}{(3+2a_{n+1})(3+2a_n)}$$

$$=\frac{a_{n+1}-a_n}{(3+2a_{n+1})(3+2a_n)}>0 \qquad [\because a_{n+1}>a_n]$$

$$\therefore \quad a_{n+2}-a_{n+1}>0$$

$$\Rightarrow \quad a_{n+2}>a_{n+1}$$

whenever $a_{n+1}>a_n$.

$\therefore$ The sequence of values a_n is increasing and since $a_1=1$, $a_n>0$, for all n.

Now, let $\quad l=\lim_{n\to\infty}a_n=\lim_{n\to\infty}a_{n+1}$

$$\therefore \quad l=\lim_{n\to\infty}\frac{4+3a_n}{3+2a_n}$$

$$\Rightarrow \quad l=\frac{4+3l}{3+2l} \qquad \left[\because \lim_{n\to\infty}a_n=l\right]$$

$$\Rightarrow \quad 3l+2l^2=4+3l$$

$$\Rightarrow \quad l^2=2$$

$$\therefore \quad l=\sqrt{2} \qquad [\text{neglecting } l=-\sqrt{2}, \text{ as } l>0]$$

4. Here, $\quad a_{n+1}=a_n+\sqrt{1+a_n^2}$, let $a_n=\cot(\alpha_n)$

$$\Rightarrow \quad a_{n+1}=\cot(\alpha_n)+\operatorname{cosec}(\alpha_n)$$

$$\Rightarrow \quad a_{n+1}=\frac{\cos(\alpha_n)+1}{\sin(\alpha_n)}$$

$$=\frac{2\cos^2(\alpha_n/2)}{2\sin(\alpha_n/2)\cos(\alpha_n/2)}$$

$$=\cot\left(\frac{\alpha_n}{2}\right)$$

Putting $n=1$, $a_1=\cot(\alpha_1)$

and $a_1=a_0+\sqrt{1+a_0^2}=1$

$$\Rightarrow \quad \cot(\alpha_1)=1 \text{ or } \alpha_1=\frac{\pi}{4}$$

Again, $\quad a_2=\cot\left(\frac{\alpha_1}{2}\right)=\cot\left(\frac{\pi}{8}\right)$

$$a_3=\cot\left(\frac{\alpha_2}{2}\right)=\cot\left(\frac{\pi}{4\cdot 2^2}\right)$$

$$a_4=\cot\left(\frac{\alpha_3}{2}\right)=\cot\left(\frac{\pi}{4\cdot 2^3}\right)$$

....

....

$$a_n=\cot\left(\frac{\pi}{4\cdot 2^{n-1}}\right);$$

Hence,

$$\lim_{n\to\infty}\left(\frac{a_n}{2^{n-1}}\right)=\lim_{n\to\infty}\frac{\cot\left(\frac{\pi}{4\cdot 2^{n-1}}\right)}{2^{n-1}}=\lim_{x\to 0}\frac{1}{\frac{\tan\left(\frac{\pi}{4}x\right)}{x}}$$

$$\left[\text{put } \frac{1}{2^{n-1}}=x\right]$$

$$\therefore \quad \lim_{n\to\infty}\left(\frac{a_n}{2^{n-1}}\right)=\frac{4}{\pi}$$

5. Let the side of a square, S_1 be a units.

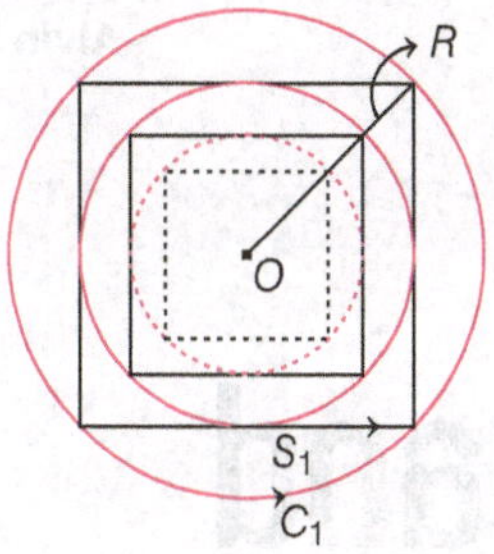

Then, $a\sqrt{2} = 2R \Rightarrow R = \dfrac{a}{\sqrt{2}}$ is radius of circle C_1.

If a_1 be the side of another square, then

$$a_1\sqrt{2} = a$$

$$\Rightarrow \quad a_1 = \frac{a}{\sqrt{2}}$$

$$a_2\sqrt{2} = a_1$$

$$\Rightarrow \quad a_2 = \frac{a_1}{\sqrt{2}} = \frac{a}{2}.$$

....

....

So, sum of areas of all the squares,

$$S_n = a^2 + a_1^2 + a_2^2 + \ldots \text{ upto } n \text{ terms}$$

$$= a^2 + \frac{a^2}{2} + \frac{a^2}{4} + \ldots \text{ upto } n \text{ terms}$$

$$= a^2\left(1 + \frac{1}{2} + \frac{1}{4} + \frac{1}{8} + \ldots \text{ upto } n \text{ terms}\right) = a^2\left\{\frac{1 - \frac{1}{2^n}}{1 - \frac{1}{2}}\right\}$$

$$= 2a^2\left(1 - \frac{1}{2^n}\right)$$

$$\therefore \quad \lim_{n\to\infty} S_n = \lim_{n\to\infty} 2a^2\left(1 - \frac{1}{2^n}\right) = 2\,a^2 = 4\,R^2$$

$$\left[\text{as } n \to \infty \Rightarrow \frac{1}{2^n} \to 0\right]$$

4

I've always been interested in using mathematics to make the world work better.

-Alvin E. Roth

Continuity and Differentiability

Learning Milestones

Milestone 1 Introduction - Continuity
- Continuity of Function

Milestone 2 Types of Discontinuity
- Discontinuity
- Types of Discontinuity
- Points of Discontinuity

Milestone 3 Theorems of Continuity

Milestone 4 Continuity Involving Special Functions
- Continuity of Functions Involving GIF [·]
- Continuity of Functions Involving Fractional Part Function
- Continuity of Functions Involving Signum Function
- Continuity of Composite Functions

Milestone 5 Differentiability
- Differentiability of Function

Milestone 6 Differentiability Over an Interval
- Algebra of Differentiability

Milestone 7 Functional Equation

Practice Milestones

Practice Milestone 1- JEE Main Pattern

Practice Milestone 2 - JEE Advanced Pattern

Practice Milestone 3 - Challenging Problems

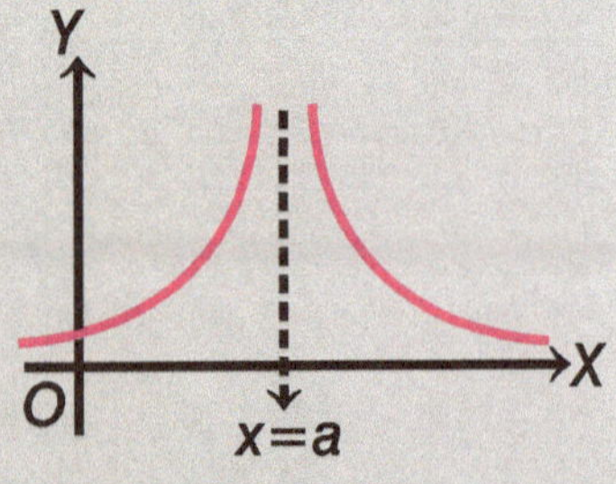

Discontinuous at $x=a$

Milestone 1 Introduction-Continuity

- Continuity of Function

The word 'continue' means the process which goes smoothly without any interruption. In calculus, the continuity refers to no gap, jump and break.A function is said to be continuous function if the graph of that function has no gap, jump and break. This property is known as continuity.

To understand it let us consider the following graphs.

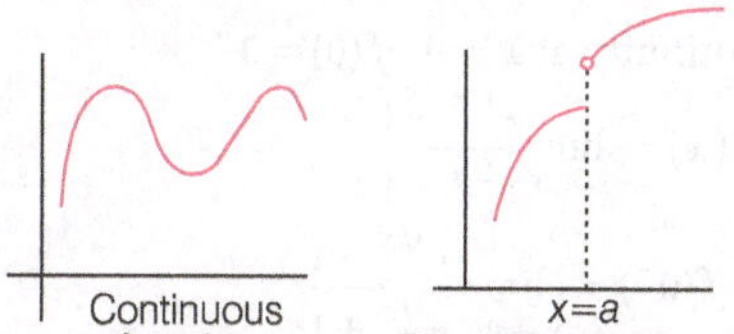

Continuous function (i) | Discontinuous function (jump at x=0) (ii)

(i) Show a continuous function.

(ii) Show a discontinuous function.

JEE Focus Points

- The graph of some discontinuous functions are as follows

(i)

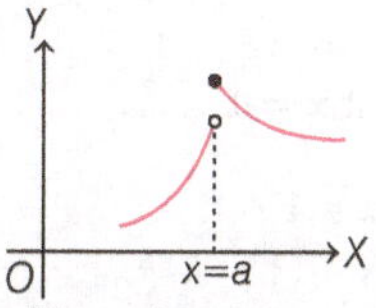

Discontinuous at $x=a$

(ii)

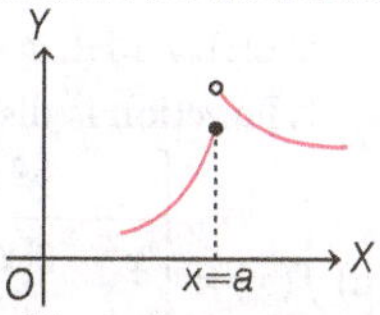

Discontinuous at $x=a$

(iii)

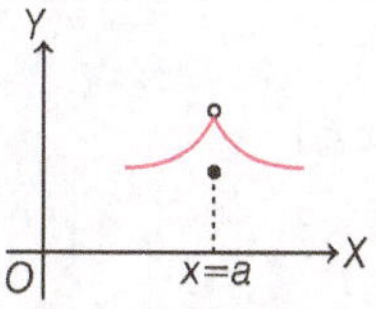

Discontinuous at $x=a$

(iv)

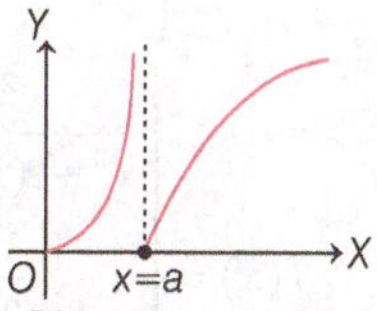

Discontinuous at $x=a$

(v)

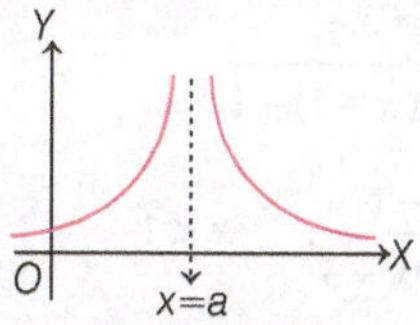

Discontinuous at $x=a$

Symbol $f(a)$ = value of $f(x)$ at $x = a$

$f(a^-)$ = LHL of $f(x)$ at $x = a$

$f(a^+)$ = RHL of $f(x)$ at $x = a$

These graphs are discontinuous because of the following reasons

Graph	Comment about LHL, RHL at $x = a$ and $f(a)$	Comment on continuity
(i)	LHL $\neq$ RHL $= f(a)$	All are discontinuous at $x = a$
(ii)	LHL $= f(a) \neq$ RHL	
(iii)	LHL = RHL $\neq f(a)$	
(iv)	LHL $= \infty$, RHL $= f(a)$	
(v)	LHL $= \infty$, RHL $= \infty$, $f(a)$ = not defined	

4.1 Continuity of Function

Let $y = f(x)$ be a real valued function.

The continuity of $f(x)$ can be discussed in 2 ways.

1. Continuity of function at a point.
2. Continuity of function over an interval.

Continuity of Function At a Point

A function $y = f(x)$ is said to be continuous at a point

$x = a$, if $\quad f(a) = \lim_{x \to a} f(x) =$ finite number

$$\begin{array}{ccc} \text{LHL} & = & \text{RHL} \\ f(a^-) & = & f(a^+) \\ \lim_{x \to a^-} f(x) & = & \lim_{x \to a^+} f(x) \\ \lim_{h \to 0} f(a-h) & = & \lim_{h \to 0} f(a+h) \end{array}$$

Example 1. Check the continuity of function $y = f(x)$ using following graph at $x = 1, 2, 3, 4, 5$

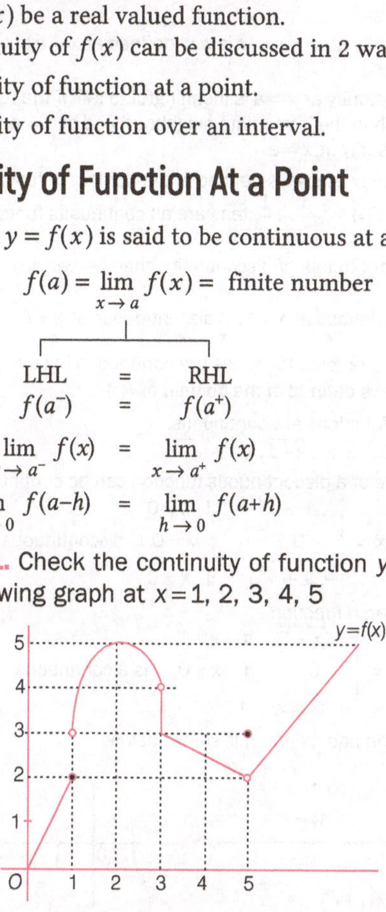

Sol. Continuity at $x=1$, $f(1)=2$

LHL $= \lim_{x\to 1^-} f(x) = 2$ and RHL $= \lim_{x\to 1^+} f(x) = 3$

$\because$ LHL $\neq$ RHL $\Rightarrow f(x)$ is not continuous at $x=1$

Continuity at $x=2$, $f(2)=5$

LHL $= \lim_{x\to 2^-} f(x) = 5$ and RHL $= \lim_{x\to 2^+} f(x) = 5$

$\because$ LHL = RHL $= f(2) = 5$

$\Rightarrow f(x)$ is continuous at $x=2$

Continuity at $x=3$, $f(3)=3$

LHL = 4 and RHL = 3

$\because$ LHL $\neq$ RHL

$\Rightarrow f(x)$ is not continuous at $x=3$

Continuity at $x=4$,

$f(4)$ = LHL = RHL = finite number

$\Rightarrow$ Continuous at $x=4$

Continuity at $x=5$, $f(5)=3$

LHL $= \lim_{x\to 5^-} f(x) = 2$ and RHL $= \lim_{x\to 5^+} f(x) = 2$

$\because$ LHL = RHL $\neq f(5)$

$\Rightarrow f(x)$ is not continuous at $x=5$.

JEE Focus Points

- Continuity at $x=a \Rightarrow$ existence of limit at $x=a$ but not the converse
- Continuity at $x=a \Rightarrow f$ is well defined at $x=a$ but not the converse
- Discontinuity at $x=a$ is meaningful to talk if the function has a graph in the immediate neighbourhood of $x=a$, not necessarily at $x=a$.
- Continuity is always defined in the domain of function and hence $f(x)=\frac{1}{x-1}, \frac{1}{x}$, $\tan x$ are all continuous functions but if you want to talk of discontinuity, then we can say $\frac{1}{x-1}$ is discontinuous at $x=1$, $\frac{1}{x}$ discontinuous at $x=0$.

Note All rational functions are continuous because continuity is always defined in the domain of $f(x)$.

- Point functions are continuous.
  e.g. $\sqrt{1-x}+\sqrt{x-1}$, $\sqrt{x}+\sqrt{-x}$
- Inverse of a discontinuous function can be continuous.

e.g. $f(x)=\begin{cases} 1+x^2 & \text{if } x\neq 0 \\ 0 & \text{if } x=0 \\ -(1+x^2) & \text{if } x\neq 0 \end{cases}$ is discontinuous at $x=0$ but

its inverse function

$f^{-1}(x)=\begin{cases} \sqrt{x-1} & \text{if } x>1 \\ 0 & \text{if } x=0 \\ \sqrt{-(1+x)} & \text{if } x<-1 \end{cases}$, is a continuous

function and its graph is shown below.

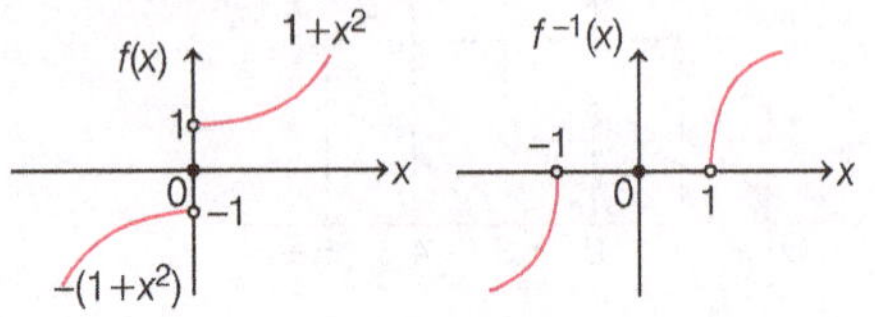

Example 2. Check the continuity of following functions at given points.

(i) $f(x)=\begin{cases} \dfrac{e^{1/x}-1}{e^{1/x}+1}, & x\neq 0 \\ 0, & x=0 \end{cases}$ at $x=0$

(ii) $f(x)=\begin{cases} \dfrac{x^2-1}{x^2-2|x-1|-1}, & x\neq 1 \\ \dfrac{1}{2}, & x=1 \end{cases}$ at $x=1$

(iii) $f(x)=\begin{cases} x\sin\dfrac{1}{x}, & x\neq 0 \\ 0, & x=0 \end{cases}$ at $x=0$

Sol. (i) Given, $f(x)=\begin{cases} \dfrac{e^{1/x}-1}{e^{1/x}+1}, & x\neq 0 \\ 0, & x=0 \end{cases}$

For continuity at $x=0$, $f(0)=0$

$$\lim_{x\to 0} f(x) = \lim_{x\to 0} \frac{e^{1/x}-1}{e^{1/x}+1} \qquad \text{...(i)}$$

$$\text{LHL} = f(0^-) = \lim_{x\to 0^-} \frac{e^{1/x}-1}{e^{1/x}+1}$$

$$\text{Put } x=0^-,\ \frac{e^{-\infty}-1}{e^{-\infty}+1} = \frac{-1}{1} = -1$$

$$\text{RHL} = f(0^+) = \lim_{x\to 0^+} \frac{e^{1/x}-1}{e^{1/x}+1} \qquad \left[\frac{\infty}{\infty} \text{ form}\right]$$

$$= \lim_{x\to 0^+} \frac{1-\dfrac{1}{e^{1/x}}}{1+\dfrac{1}{e^{1/x}}} = \frac{1-0}{1+0} = 1$$

$\because$ LHL $\neq$ RHL $\neq f(0)$

$\therefore$ Function is discontinuous at $x=0$.

(ii) $f(x)=\begin{cases} \dfrac{x^2-1}{x^2-2|x-1|-1}, & x\neq 1 \\ \dfrac{1}{2}, & x=1 \end{cases}$

$$f(x)=\begin{cases} \dfrac{x^2-1}{x^2+2(x-1)-1}, & x<1 \\ \dfrac{1}{2}, & x=1 \\ \dfrac{x^2-1}{x^2-2(x-1)-1}, & x>1 \end{cases}$$

$$=\begin{cases} \dfrac{x^2-1}{x^2+2x-3}, & x<1 \\ \dfrac{1}{2}, & x=1 \\ \dfrac{x^2-1}{x^2-2x+1}, & x>1 \end{cases}$$

Continuity of $f(x)$ at $x=1$, $f(1)=\frac{1}{2}$

$$\text{LHL}=f(1^-)=\lim_{x\to 1^-}\frac{x^2-1}{x^2+2x-3}$$

Put $x=1-h$

$$\lim_{h\to 0}\frac{(1-h)^2-1}{(1-h)^2+2(1-h)-3}=\lim_{h\to 0}\frac{h^2-2h}{h^2-4h}$$

$$=\lim_{h\to 0}\frac{h-2}{h-4}=\frac{1}{2}$$

$$\text{RHL}=f(1^+)=\lim_{x\to 1^+}\frac{x^2-1}{x^2-2x+1}=\lim_{x\to 1^+}\frac{(x-1)(x+1)}{(x-1)^2}$$

$$=\lim_{x\to 1^+}\frac{x+1}{x-1}$$

Put $x=1+h$,

$$\lim_{h\to 0}\frac{2+h}{h}=\infty$$

$\because$ LHL $\neq$ RHL

$\Rightarrow$ Limit does not exist.

$\therefore f(x)$ is discontinuous at $x=1$.

(iii) $f(x)=\begin{cases} x\sin\frac{1}{x}, & x\neq 0\\ 0, & x=0\end{cases}$

Continuity at $x=0$, $f(0)=0$

$$\lim_{x\to 0}f(x)=\lim_{x\to 0}x\sin\frac{1}{x}=0\times\sin\infty \quad \text{[finite number]}$$

$$=0 \quad [\because \sin\theta \text{ lies between } -1 \text{ and } +1]$$

$\because \quad f(0)=\lim_{x\to 0}f(x)=0$

$\therefore f(x)$ is continuous at $x=0$.

Example 3. Let a function $f(x)$ be defined in the neighbourhood of x as $f(x)=\begin{cases}\dfrac{\ln(2-\cos 2x)}{\ln^2(1+\sin 3x)}, & \text{for } x<0\\ \dfrac{e^{\sin 2x}-1}{\ln(1+\tan 9x)}, & \text{for } x>0\end{cases}$

Find whether it is possible to define $f(0)$ so that f may be continuous at $x=0$.

Sol. $$\lim_{h\to 0}f(0+h)=\lim_{h\to 0}\frac{(e^{\sin 2h}-1)\cdot\sin 2h\cdot(2h)}{\ln(1+\tan 9h)\cdot\sin 2h\cdot(2h)}$$

$$=\lim_{h\to 0}\frac{e^{\sin 2h}-1}{\sin 2h}\cdot\lim_{h\to 0}\frac{\sin 2h}{2h}\lim_{h\to 0}\frac{2h}{\ln(1+\tan 9h)}$$

$$=1\cdot 1\cdot\lim_{h\to 0}\frac{2h}{\tan 9h\ln(1+\tan 9h)\cot 9h}$$

$$=\lim_{h\to 0}\frac{2h}{\tan 9h}=\frac{2}{9}$$

Now, $$\lim_{h\to 0}f(0-h)=\lim_{h\to 0}\frac{\ln(1+2\sin^2 h)}{2\sin^2 h}\cdot\lim_{h\to 0}\frac{2\sin^2 h}{\ln^2(1-\sin 3h)}$$

$$=\lim_{h\to 0}\frac{2\sin^2 h}{h^2}\cdot\lim_{h\to 0}\frac{h^2}{\ln^2(1-\sin 3h)}$$

$$=\lim_{h\to 0}\frac{2\cdot h^2(-\sin 3h)^2}{\sin^2 3h\cdot\ln^2(1-\sin 3h)}=\frac{2}{9}$$

Since, $f(0^+)=f(0^-)=\frac{2}{9}\Rightarrow$ limit exists.

Therefore, it is possible to define $f(0)$ such that f is continuous at $x=0$.

$\therefore \quad f(0)=\frac{2}{9}$

Example 4. Given the function,

$f(x)=x\left\{\dfrac{1}{x(1+x)}+\dfrac{1}{(1+x)(1+2x)}+\dfrac{1}{(1+2x)(1+3x)}+\ldots\text{upto }\infty\right\}$. Find $f(0)$, if $f(x)$ is continuous at $x=0$.

Sol. $$f(x)=\frac{1}{1+x}+\frac{(1+2x)-(1+x)}{(1+x)(1+2x)}+\frac{(1+3x)-(1+2x)}{(1+2x)(1+3x)}+\ldots+\frac{(1+nx)-(1+\overline{n-1}\,x)}{(1+\overline{n-1}x)(1+nx)}$$

$$f(x)=\frac{2}{1+x}-\frac{1}{1+nx}\text{ upto } n \text{ terms, when } x\neq 0.$$

Hence, $f(x)=\begin{cases}\dfrac{2}{1+x} & \text{if } x\neq 0 \text{ and } n\to\infty\\ 2 & \text{if } x=0\end{cases}$

$\therefore$ For continuity, $f(0)=2$

Example 5. Let $f(x)=\begin{cases}\dfrac{1+a\cos 2x+b\cos 4x}{x^4}, & \text{if } x\neq 0\\ c, & \text{if } x=0\end{cases}$

be continuous at $x=0$, then find the values of a,b and c.

Sol. $$\lim_{x\to 0}\frac{1+a\cos 2x+b\cos 4x}{x^4}$$

As $x\to 0$, denominator $\to 0$ and numerator $\to 1+a+b$

For existence of limit,

$$a+b+1=0 \quad \text{...(i)}$$

$$\therefore \quad c=\lim_{x\to 0}\frac{a\cos 2x+b\cos 4x-(a+b)}{x^4}$$

$$=-\lim_{x\to 0}\frac{\dfrac{a(1-\cos 2x)}{x^2}+\dfrac{b(1-\cos 4x)}{x^2}}{x^2} \quad \text{...(ii)}$$

The limit of numerator $=4a\left(\frac{1}{2}\right)+16b\left(\frac{1}{2}\right)$

$$\Rightarrow \quad 2a+8b=0\Rightarrow a=-4b \quad \text{...(iii)}$$

From Eqs. (i) and (iii),

$$-4b+b=-1$$

$$\Rightarrow \quad b=\frac{1}{3} \text{ and } a=-\frac{4}{3}$$

From Eq. (ii),

$$c=\lim_{x\to 0}\frac{4(1-\cos 2x)-(1-\cos 4x)}{3x^4}$$

$$=\lim_{x\to 0}\frac{8\sin^2 x-2\sin^2 2x}{3x^4}$$

$$=\lim_{x\to 0}\frac{8\sin^2 x-8\sin^2 x\cos^2 x}{3x^4}$$

$$=\lim_{x\to 0}\frac{8}{3}\cdot\frac{\sin^2 x}{x^2}\cdot\frac{\sin^2 x}{x^2}$$

$$=\frac{8}{3}$$

$$\therefore \quad a=-\frac{4}{3},\ b=\frac{1}{3} \text{ and } c=\frac{8}{3}$$

Example 6. If $f(x)$ is continuous function, for all real values of x and satisfies;
$x^2+\{f(x)-2\}x+2\sqrt{3}-3-\sqrt{3}\cdot f(x)=0,\ \forall\ x\in R.$

Then, find the value of $f(\sqrt{3})$.

Sol. As $f(x)$ is continuous, for all $x\in R$.

Thus, $\lim_{x\to\sqrt{3}} f(x)=f(\sqrt{3})$,

where $f(x)=\dfrac{x^2-2x+2\sqrt{3}-3}{\sqrt{3}-x},\ x\neq\sqrt{3}$

$$\lim_{x\to\sqrt{3}} f(x)=\lim_{x\to\sqrt{3}}\frac{x^2-2x+2\sqrt{3}-3}{\sqrt{3}-x}$$

$$=\lim_{x\to\sqrt{3}}\frac{(2-\sqrt{3}-x)(\sqrt{3}-x)}{(\sqrt{3}-x)}$$

$$=2(1-\sqrt{3})$$

$$\Rightarrow \quad f(\sqrt{3})=2(1-\sqrt{3})$$

JEE SCANNER

Example Similar to PYQ Asked in JEE Main 2021

Let $f(x)=\begin{cases}\dfrac{a(1-x\sin x)+b\cos x+5}{x^2}, & x<0\\ 3, & x=0\\ \left\{1+\left(\dfrac{cx+dx^3}{x^2}\right)\right\}^{1/x}, & x>0\end{cases}$

If f is continuous at $x=0$, *then* $11a+b+c+e^d$ *is equal to*

(a) -12 (b) 7 (c) -8 (d) 5

Sol. (a) $f(0)=3$

$$\text{RHL}=\lim_{x\to 0^+} f(x)=\lim_{h\to 0} f(0+h)=\lim_{h\to 0} f(h)$$

$$=\lim_{h\to 0}\left\{1+\left(\frac{ch+dh^3}{h^2}\right)\right\}^{1/h} \quad \text{...(i)}$$

Since, f is continuous at $x=0$, RHL exists.

For existence of RHL, c must be 0.

$\therefore$ RHL $=\lim_{h\to 0}\{1+dh\}^{1/h}$ [from Eq. (i)]

$$=e^{\lim_{h\to 0}(1+dh-1)1/h}=e^d$$

$$\text{LHL}=\lim_{x\to 0} f(x)=\lim_{h\to 0} f(0-h)$$

$$=\lim_{h\to 0}\frac{a(1-(-h)\sin(-h))+b\cos(-h)+5}{(-h)^2}$$

$$=\lim_{h\to 0}\frac{a(1-h\sin h)+b\cos h+5}{h^2}$$

For finite value of LHL, the numerator must tend to 0 as $h\to 0$.

$$\therefore \quad a+b+5=0$$

$$\text{LHL}=\lim_{h\to 0}\frac{a-ah\sin h-(5+a)\cos h+5}{h^2}$$

$$=\lim_{h\to 0}\frac{(5+a)(1-\cos h)-ah\sin h}{h^2}$$

$$=\lim_{h\to 0}\left\{\frac{(a+5)(1-\cos h)(1+\cos h)}{h^2(1+\cos h)}-\frac{ah\sin h}{h^2}\right\}$$

$$=\lim_{h\to 0}\left\{\frac{(a+5)\sin^2 h}{h^2(1+\cos h)}-\frac{a\sin h}{h}\right\}$$

$$=\frac{(a+5)(1)^2}{1+1}-a\cdot 1=\frac{a+5}{2}-a=\left(\frac{5-a}{2}\right)$$

Now, $f(x)$ is continuous at $x=0$.

$\therefore$ LHL = RHL = $f(0)$

$$\frac{5-a}{2}=e^d=3$$

$$\therefore \quad a=-1,\ d=\ln 3,\ c=0,\ b=-4.$$

$$\Rightarrow 11a+b+c+e^d=11(-1)-4+0+e^{\ln 3}=-11-4+3=-12$$

Skill Builder

If $f(x)=\begin{cases}\dfrac{\sin(a+1)x+\sin x}{x}, & x<0\\ c, & x=0\\ \dfrac{(x+bx^2)^{1/2}-x^{1/2}}{bx^{3/2}}, & x>0\end{cases}$ is continuous at $x=0$, then the value of $a+c$ is equal to

(a) -1 (b) 1
(c) 0 (d) 2

For Sol.

■ **For more practice** See Q.2 of Milestone Practice 4.1.

Example 7. Let $y=f(x)$ be defined parametrically as $y=t^2+t|t|, x=2t-|t|, t \in R$. Then, at $x=0$, find $f(x)$ and discuss continuity.

Sol. As $y=t^2+t|t|$ and $x=2t-|t|$

Thus, when $t \geq 0$

$\Rightarrow \quad x=2t-t=t, y=t^2+t^2=2t^2$

$\therefore \quad x=t$ and $y=2t^2$

$\Rightarrow \quad y=2x^2, \forall\, x \geq 0$

Again, when $t<0$

$\Rightarrow \quad x=2t+t=3t$ and $y=t^2-t^2=0$

$\Rightarrow \quad y=0, \forall\, x<0$

Hence, $f(x)=\begin{cases} 2x^2, & x \geq 0 \\ 0, & x<0 \end{cases}$,

which is clearly continuous for all x as shown graphically.

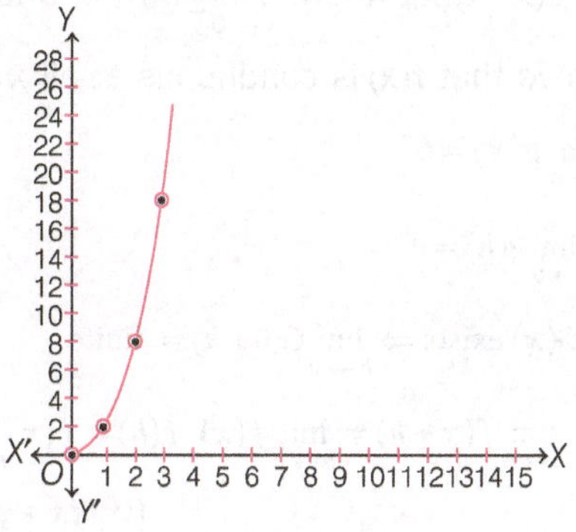

Continuity of Function Over an Interval

1. In an Open Interval

A function f is said to be continuous in an open interval (a, b) if f is continuous at each and every point $\in (a, b)$.

2. In a Closed Interval

A function f is said to be continuous in a closed interval $[a, b]$ if

(a) f is continuous in the open interval (a, b).

(b) f is right continuous at a i.e. $\lim_{x \to a^+} f(x)=f(a)=$ a finite quantity.

(c) f is left continuous at b i.e. $\lim_{x \to b^-} f(x)=f(b)=$ a finite quantity.

JEE SPIKE

- All polynomial, trigonometric, inverse trigonometric, logarithmic and exponential functions are continuous in their respective domain.
- If $f(x)$ is continuous, then $|f(x)|$ is also continuous.

Example 8. Show that the function

$$f(x)=\begin{cases} 2x+3, & -3 \leq x<-2 \\ x+1, & -2 \leq x<0 \\ x+2, & 0 \leq x \leq 1 \end{cases}$$ is continuous at every point in the interval $[-3, 1]$ except 0.

Sol. **Method 1** The graph of $f(x)=\begin{cases} 2x+3, & -3 \leq x<-2 \\ x+1, & -2 \leq x<0 \\ x+2, & 0 \leq x \leq 1 \end{cases}$ is plotted below.

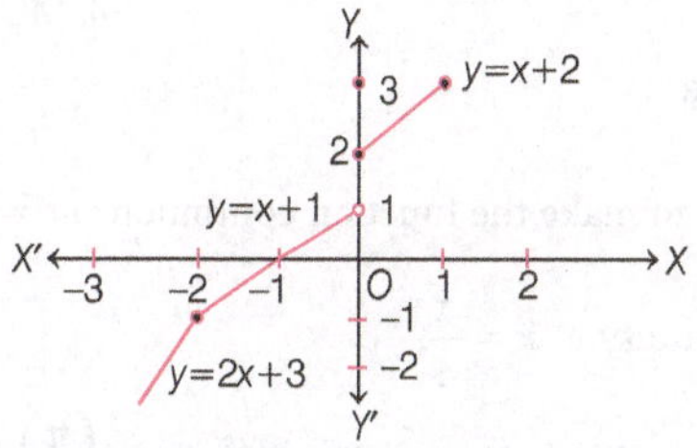

Here, we observe from the graph that at $x=0$,

$\lim_{x \to 0^-} f(x)=1$ and $\lim_{x \to 0^+} f(x)=2$, which shows that the function is not continuous at $x=0$ and continuous at every other point in $[-3, 1]$.

Method 2 $f(x)=\begin{cases} 2x+3, & -3 \leq x<-2 \\ x+1, & -2 \leq x<0 \\ x+2, & 0 \leq x \leq 1 \end{cases}$

$\because 2x+3, x+1, x+2$ all are polynomial functions.

$\therefore f(x)$ is continuous for $-3 \leq x<-2, -2<x<0, 0<x \leq 1$ but we have to check at $x=-2$ and $x=0$.

Continuity at $x=-2$, $f(-2)=-2+1=-1$

$$f(-2^-)=\lim_{x \to -2^-} f(x)=\lim_{x \to -2^-} 2x+3=-4+3=-1$$

$$f(-2^+)=\lim_{x \to -2^+} f(x)=\lim_{x \to -2^+} x+1=-1$$

$\because \quad f(-2)=f(-2^-)=f(-2^+)$

$\therefore \quad$ It is continuous at $x=-2$.

Similarly, continuity at $x=0$,

$$f(0)=0+2=2$$

$$f(0^-)=\lim_{x\to0^-}f(x)=\lim_{x\to0^-}x+1=1$$

$$f(0^+)=\lim_{x\to0^+}f(x)=\lim_{x\to0^+}x+2=2$$

$\because\ f(0^-)\neq f(0^+)$

$\therefore f(x)$ is not continuous at $x=0$.

$\therefore$ The given function $f(x)$ is continuous for $x\in[-3,1]$ except $x=0$.

Example 9. Find the values of a and b so that the function $f(x)=\begin{cases}x+a\sqrt{2}\sin x, & 0\le x<\dfrac{\pi}{4}\\ 2x\cot x+b, & \dfrac{\pi}{4}\le x\le\dfrac{\pi}{2}\\ a\cos 2x-b\sin x, & \dfrac{\pi}{2}<x\le\pi\end{cases}$

is continuous in $[0,\pi]$.

Sol. $f(x)$ is continuous in the interval $0\le x<\dfrac{\pi}{4},\dfrac{\pi}{4}<x<\dfrac{\pi}{2}$, $\dfrac{\pi}{2}<x\le\pi$.

We need to make the function continuous at $x=\dfrac{\pi}{4},\dfrac{\pi}{2}$

For continuity at $x=\dfrac{\pi}{4}$,

$$\lim_{x\to\frac{\pi}{4}^-}f(x)=\lim_{x\to\frac{\pi}{4}^+}f(x)=f\left(\frac{\pi}{4}\right)$$

$$\lim_{x\to\frac{\pi}{4}^-}(x+a\sqrt{2}\sin x)=\lim_{x\to\frac{\pi}{4}^+}(2x\cot x+b)=f\left(\frac{\pi}{4}\right)$$

$$\Rightarrow\quad \frac{\pi}{4}+a\sqrt{2}\sin\left(\frac{\pi}{4}\right)=2\cdot\frac{\pi}{4}\cdot\cot\left(\frac{\pi}{4}\right)+b=2\frac{\pi}{4}\cot\left(\frac{\pi}{4}\right)+b$$

$$\Rightarrow\quad \frac{\pi}{4}+a=\frac{\pi}{2}+b$$

$$\Rightarrow\quad a-b=\frac{\pi}{4}\qquad\text{...(i)}$$

For continuity at $x=\dfrac{\pi}{2}$,

$$\lim_{x\to\frac{\pi}{2}^-}f(x)=\lim_{x\to\frac{\pi}{2}^+}f(x)=f\left(\frac{\pi}{2}\right)$$

$$\Rightarrow\quad \lim_{x\to\frac{\pi}{2}^-}(2x\cot x+b)=\lim_{x\to\frac{\pi}{2}^+}(a\cos 2x-b\sin x)$$

$$=a\cos\pi-b\sin\frac{\pi}{2}$$

$$\Rightarrow\quad 0+b=-a-b$$

$$\Rightarrow\quad a+2b=0\qquad\text{...(ii)}$$

From Eqs. (i) and (ii),

$$a=\frac{\pi}{6},\ b=\frac{-\pi}{12}$$

Example 10. If $f(x+y)=f(x)\cdot f(y)$, for all $x,y\in R$ and $f(x)=1+g(x)\cdot G(x)$, where $\lim_{x\to0}g(x)=0$ and $\lim_{x\to0}G(x)$ exists, prove that $f(x)$ is continuous at all $x\in R$.

Sol. $\lim_{x\to0}g(x)=0$

$$\Rightarrow\quad \lim_{h\to0}g(h)=0\qquad\text{...(i)}$$

$$\lim_{x\to0}G(x)\text{ exists}\Rightarrow\lim_{h\to0}G(0+h)=\text{ finite}\qquad\text{...(ii)}$$

Now, $\lim_{h\to0}f(x+h)=\lim_{h\to0}f(x)\cdot f(h)=f(x)\lim_{h\to0}f(h)$

$[\because f(x+y)=f(x)\cdot f(y)]$

$=f(x)\cdot\lim_{h\to0}\{1+g(h)G(h)\}$ [using the given relation]

$=f(x)\cdot\{1+\lim_{h\to0}g(h)\cdot\lim_{h\to0}G(h)\}$

$=f(x)\cdot\{1+0\cdot\text{finite}\}$[using Eqs. (i) and (ii)]

$=f(x)$

$\because\ \lim_{h\to0}f(x+h)=f(x)$

$\therefore f(x)$ is continuous everywhere.

Milestone Practice 4.1

1. Discuss the continuity of the following functions $f(x)$ at referred points

(i) $f(x) = \begin{cases} \dfrac{[x^2]-1}{x^2-1}, & x^2 \neq 1 \\ 0\ , & x^2 = 1 \end{cases}$ at $x = \pm 1$

(ii) $f(x) = \begin{cases} \dfrac{a^{2[x]+\{x\}}-1}{2[x]+\{x\}}, & x \neq 0 \\ \log_e a\ , & x = 0 \end{cases}$ at $x = 0$,

$[x]$ denotes integer part of x and $\{x\}$ denotes fractional part of x.

2. Let $f(x) = \begin{cases} \dfrac{1-\sin \pi x}{1+\cos 2\pi x}, & x < \dfrac{1}{2} \\ p, & x = \dfrac{1}{2} \\ \dfrac{\sqrt{2x-1}}{\sqrt{4+\sqrt{2x-1}}-2}, & x > \dfrac{1}{2} \end{cases}$.

Determine the value of p if possible so that the function is continuous at $x = \dfrac{1}{2}$.

3. Let

$$f(x) = \begin{cases} \dfrac{\left(\dfrac{\pi}{2} - \sin^{-1}(1-\{x\}^2)\right)\sin^{-1}(1-\{x\})}{\sqrt{2}(\{x\}-\{x\}^3)}, & \text{for } x \neq 0 \\ \dfrac{\pi}{2}, & \text{for } x = 0 \end{cases}$$

where $\{x\}$ is the fractional part of x. Consider another function $g(x)$, such that $g(x) = \begin{cases} f(x), & \text{for } x \geq 0 \\ 2\sqrt{2}f(x), & \text{for } x < 0 \end{cases}$

Discuss the continuity of the functions $f(x)$ and $g(x)$ at $x = 0$.

4. Find the values of a and b so that the functions given below are continuous in their indicated domain

(i) $f(x) = \begin{cases} a\tan^{-1}\left[\dfrac{1}{(x-4)}\right], & 0 \leq x < 4 \\ \dfrac{\pi}{2}, & x = 4 \\ b\tan^{-1}\left[\dfrac{2}{x-4}\right], & 4 < x < 6 \\ \sin^{-1}(7-x) + \dfrac{a\pi}{4}, & 6 \leq x \leq 8 \end{cases}$

(ii) $f(x) = \begin{cases} (1-\sin^3 x)/3\cos^2 x\ , & x < \dfrac{\pi}{2} \\ a, & x = \dfrac{\pi}{2}, \quad x \in (0, \pi) \\ b(1-\sin x)/(\pi - 2x)^2, & x > \dfrac{\pi}{2} \end{cases}$

(iii) $f(x) = \begin{cases} \dfrac{(ae^{1/|x+2|}-1)}{(2-e^{1/|x+2|})}, & -3 < x < -2 \\ b, & x = -2 \\ \dfrac{\sin(x^4-16)}{(x^5+32)}, & -2 < x < 0 \end{cases}$

5. Let $f: R \to R$ be a function which satisfies $f(x+y) = f(x) + (f(y))^3, \forall\ x, y \in R$. If f is continuous at $x = 0$, prove that f is continuous everywhere.

6. The function $f(x)$ is defined by

$f(x) = \begin{cases} \log_{(4x-3)}(x^2-2x+5) & \text{if } \dfrac{3}{4} < x < 1 \text{ or } x > 1 \\ 4 & \text{if } x = 1 \end{cases}$

(a) is continuous at $x = 1$.

(b) is discontinuous at $x = 1$, since $f(1^+)$ does not exist though $f(1^-)$ exists.

(c) is discontinuous at $x = 1$, since $f(1^-)$ does not exist though $f(1^+)$ exists.

(d) is discontinuous, since neither $f(1^-)$ nor $f(1^+)$ exists.

7. The function $f(x) = \begin{cases} [x] + \sqrt{x-[x]}, & \text{for } x \geq 0 \\ \sin x, & \text{for } x < 0 \end{cases}$ is

(a) continuous only, for all non-negative integers.

(b) continuous only, for all positive integers.

(c) discontinuous only, for all negative integers.

(d) continuous, for all real numbers.

8. If $f(x) = \begin{cases} \dfrac{\log(1+2ax) - \log(1-bx)}{x}, & x \neq 0 \\ k, & x = 0 \end{cases}$ is continuous at $x = 0$, then k is equal to

(a) $2a + b$ (b) $2a - b$

(c) $b - 2a$ (d) $a + b$

9. If $f(x) = \begin{cases} [x] + [-x], & x \neq 2 \\ \lambda, & x = 2 \end{cases}$ and f is continuous at $x = 2$, where $[\cdot]$ denotes greatest integer function, then λ is

(a) -1 (b) 0 (c) 1 (d) 2

Answer Key

1. (i) Infinite discontinuity at $x = -1$, removable discontinuity at $x = 1$ (ii) Right continuous, left discontinuous

2. Not possible **3.** f is discontinuous, g is continuous **4.** (i) $a = -1$, $b = 1$ (ii) $a = 1/2$, $b = 4$ (iii) $a = 2/5$, $b = -2/5$

6. (d) **7.** (d) **8.** (a) **9.** (a)

For Detailed Solution

Milestone 2 Types of Discontinuity

• Discontinuity • Types of Discontinuity • Points of Discontinuity

4.2 Discontinuity

A function $f(x)$ is said to be discontinuous at $x = a$ if it is not continuous at $x = a$ and this happens if atleast one of the following conditions holds

(i) $f(a)$ does not exist

(ii) LHL $= f(a^-) = \lim\limits_{h \to a^-} f(x)$ does not exist (i.e. either not defined or infinite)

(iii) RHL $= f(a^+) = \lim\limits_{h \to a^+} f(x)$ does not exist. It may happen that both LHL and RHL are not finite.

(iv) LHL and RHL both exist finitely but LHL $\neq$ RHL

(v) LHL = RHL (a finite real number) $\neq f(a)$

(vi) LHL and RHL or any one of them oscillates i.e. does not tend to a unique real number.

Depending on the above reasons of discontinuity of a function $f(x)$ at a point $x = a$, let us discuss the types of discontinuity of a function at a point $x = a$.

4.3 Types of Discontinuity

Types of Discontinuity

- **On the basis of $f(a)$ (Discontinuity of 1st kind)**
  - **Removable Discontinuity**
    $\lim\limits_{x \to a} f(x)$ = exists
    but
    $\lim\limits_{x \to a} f(x) \neq f(a)$
    or
    $f(a)$ is not defined
    - **Missing point discontinuity**
      limit exist
      but $f(a)$
      not defined
    - **Isolated point discontinuity**
      $\lim\limits_{x \to a} f(x) \neq f(a)$
- **On the basis of $\lim\limits_{x \to a} f(x)$ (Discontinuity of 2nd kind)**
  - **Non-removable Discontinuity**
    $\lim\limits_{x \to a} f(x)$ = Does not exists
    - **Finite type discontinuity**
      LHL $\neq$ RHL
      but both are finite numbers
      1. Jump of discontinuity = | LHL − RHL |
      2. A function having finite number of jumps in a given interval is called a piecewise/sectionally continuous function
    - **Infinite type discontinuity**
      (In LHL and RHL atleast one is infinite)
      Pole discontinuity
      When both LHL and RHL are infinite
    - **Oscillatory type discontinuity**
      In LHL and RHL atleast one limit oscillates between two finite real numbers.

Examples on Type of Discontinuity

Removable Discontinuity

1. Missing Point Discontinuity

(a) $f(x)=\dfrac{(x^2+1)(9-x^2)}{x-1}, x\neq 1$

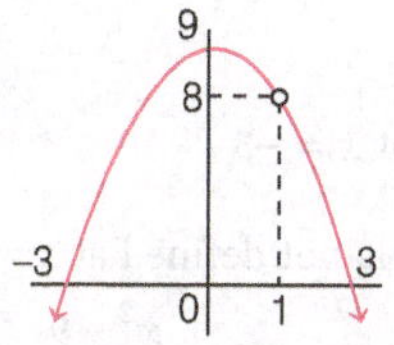

At $x=1$, $f(1)$ is not defined. Hence, $f(x)$ has missing point of discontinuity at $x=1$.

(b) $f(x)=\dfrac{x^2-4}{x-2}, x\neq 2$

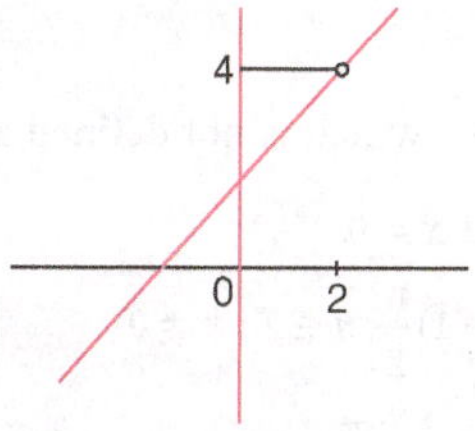

$f(2)$ is not defined. Hence, $f(x)$ has missing point of discontinuity at $x=2$.

(c) $f(x)=\dfrac{\sin x}{x},\ x\neq 0$

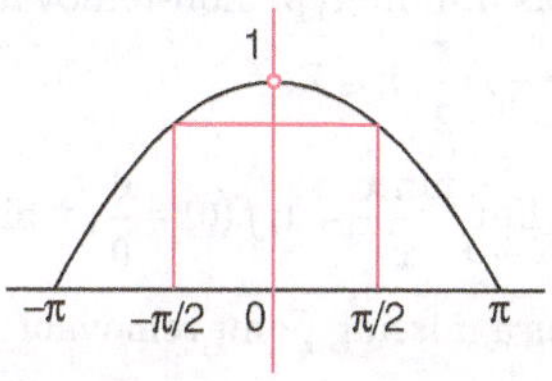

$f(0)$ is not defined. Hence, $f(x)$ has missing point of discontinuity at $x=0$.

2. Isolated Point Discontinuity

(a) $f(x)=[x]+[-x]=\begin{cases}0 & \text{if} \quad x\in I\\ -1 & \text{if} \quad x\notin I\end{cases}$

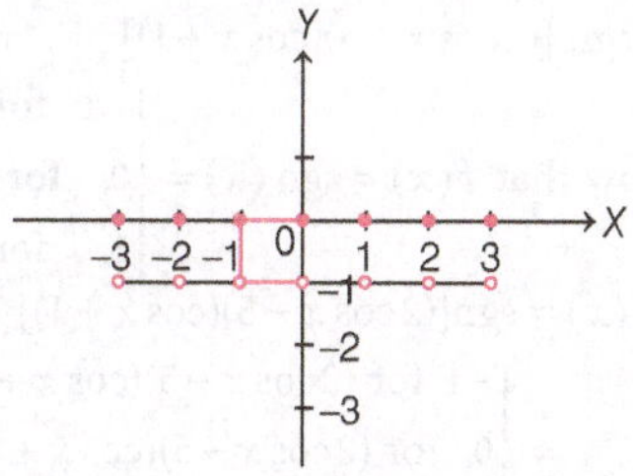

has isolated point of discontinuity at all integral points.

(b) $f(x)=\operatorname{sgn}(\cos 2x-2\sin x+3)$

$=\operatorname{sgn}(2(2+\sin x)(1-\sin x))$

$=\begin{cases}0 & \text{if} \quad x=2n\pi+\dfrac{\pi}{2}\\ +1 & \text{if} \quad x\neq 2n\pi+\dfrac{\pi}{2}\end{cases}$

has an isolated point at $x=0$ discontinuity as $x=2n\pi+\dfrac{\pi}{2}$

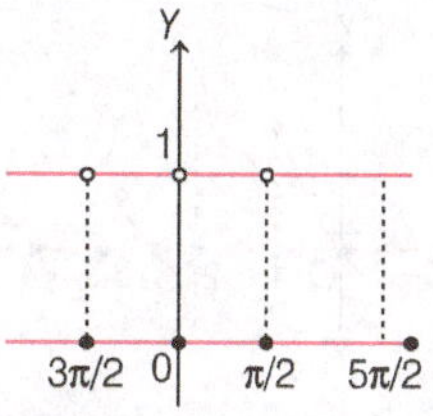

Non-Removable Discontinuity

1. Finite Type Discontinuity

(i) $\lim\limits_{x\to 0}\tan^{-1}\left(\dfrac{1}{x}\right)\begin{cases}f(0^+)=\dfrac{\pi}{2}\\ f(0^-)=-\dfrac{\pi}{2}\end{cases}$; jump $=\pi$

(ii) $\lim\limits_{x\to 0}\dfrac{|\sin x|}{x}\begin{cases}f(0^+)=1\\ f(0^-)=-1\end{cases}$; jump $=2$

(iii) $\lim\limits_{x\to 2}\dfrac{[x]}{2}\begin{cases}f(2^+)=1\\ f(2^-)=\dfrac{1}{2}\end{cases}$; jump $=\dfrac{1}{2}$

2. Infinite Type Discontinuity

(i) $f(x)=\dfrac{x}{1-x}$ at $x=1\begin{cases}f(1^+)=-\infty\\ f(1^-)=+\infty\end{cases}$

(ii) $f(x)=2^{\tan x}$ at $x=\dfrac{\pi}{2}\begin{cases}f\left(\dfrac{\pi^+}{2}\right)=2^{-\infty}\to 0\\ f\left(\dfrac{\pi^-}{2}\right)=2^{\infty}\to\infty\end{cases}$

(iii) $f(x)=\dfrac{1}{x^2}$ at $x=0\begin{cases}f(0^+)=\infty\\ f(0^-)=\infty\end{cases}$

Pole discontinuity.

3. Oscillatory Type Discontinuity

(i) $\left.\begin{array}{l} f(x)=\sin\dfrac{1}{x} \\ \text{or} \\ f(x)=\cos\dfrac{1}{x} \end{array}\right\}$ at $x=0$ oscillates between -1 and 1.

(ii) $f(x)=\left[1+\dfrac{1}{3}\sin(\ln|x|)\right]$ at $x=0$ oscillates between 0 and 1.

Example 11. Observe the following graph and state the type of discontinuity at the following points

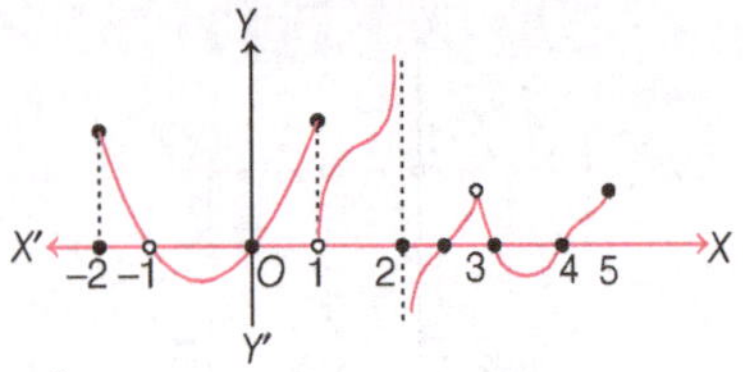

(i) At $x=-1$
(ii) At $x=1$
(iii) At $x=2$
(iv) At $x=3$; where $f(x)$ is defined in domain $[-2,5]$
(v) At $x=-2$
(vi) At $x=5$

Sol. (i) At $x=-1$, $f(-1^-)=f(-1^+)\neq f(-1)$

As image of $f(-1)$ does not exist. Thus, function has a missing point removable discontinuity at $x=-1$.

(ii) At $x=1$, $f(1^-)=f(1)\neq f(1^+)$

$\therefore$ Function has a jump discontinuity at $x=1$, which is non-removable. Hence, $f(x)$ is left continuous but not right discontinuous at $x=1$.

(iii) At $x=2$, $f(2^-)=\infty$ and $f(2^+)=-\infty$

$\therefore$ Function has an infinite discontinuity at $x=2$, which is non-removable.

(iv) At $x=3$, $f(3^-)=f(3^+)\neq f(3)$

$\therefore f(x)$ has isolated removable discontinuity at $x=3$.

(v) Since, no portion of graph lies on the left of $x=-2$, therefore we do not talk about the left hand limit at $x=-2$.

Clearly, $\lim\limits_{x\to(-2)^+} f(x)\neq f(-2)$

$\therefore f(x)$ is discontinuous at $x=-2$ and has isolated point removable discontinuity at $x=-2$.

(vi) Since, no portion of graph lies on the right of $x=5$, therefore we do not talk about the right hand limit at $x=5$. Clearly, $\lim\limits_{x\to 5} f(x)=f(5)$. Thus, $f(x)$ is continuous at $x=5$.

Note If a function is defined on $[a, b]$, then $f(x)$ is said to be continuous at $x=a$ if $f(x)$ is right continuous at $x=a$ and is said to be continuous at $x=b$, if $f(x)$ is left continuous at $x=b$.

Example 12. Mention the nature of discontinuity in the following functions.

(i) $f(x)=\dfrac{x^2-9}{x+3}$, at $x=-3$

(ii) $\dfrac{\tan x}{x}$, at $x=(2n+1)\dfrac{\pi}{2}$; $n\in Z$ and at $x=0$

(iii) $f(x)=\text{sgn}(\cos 2x-3\cos x-4)$, at $x=(2n+1)\pi$; $n\in Z$ and at $x=0$.

Sol. (i) $f(x)=\dfrac{x^2-9}{x+3}$ at $x=-3$

Clearly, $f(x)$ is not defined at $x=-3$

and $\lim\limits_{x\to-3} f(x)=\lim\limits_{x\to-3}\dfrac{x^2-9}{(x+3)}=\lim\limits_{x\to-3}\dfrac{(x+3)(x-3)}{(x+3)}$

$=\lim\limits_{x\to-3}(x-3)=-6$

$\therefore \lim\limits_{x\to-3} f(x)=-6\neq f(-3)$

$\therefore f(x)$ has a missing point removable discontinuity at $x=-3$.

(ii) $f(x)=\dfrac{\tan x}{x}$, which is not defined at $x=(2n+1)\dfrac{\pi}{2}$; $n\in Z$ and at $x=0$.

At $x=(2n+1)\dfrac{\pi}{2}$; $n\in Z$; $x\neq 0$

and $x\to(2n+1)\dfrac{\pi}{2}\Rightarrow \tan x\to\pm\infty$

$\therefore f(x)\to\pm\infty$ and hence $\lim\limits_{x\to(2n+1)\frac{\pi}{2}} f(x)=\pm\infty$

$\therefore f(x)$ has infinite type non-removable discontinuous at $x=(2n+1)\dfrac{\pi}{2}$, $n\in Z$.

At $x=0$, $\lim\limits_{x\to 0}\dfrac{\tan x}{x}=1$; $f(0)=\dfrac{0}{0}$, which is not defined.

$\therefore f(x)$ has a missing point removable discontinuity at $x=0$.

(iii) $f(x)=\text{sgn}(\cos 2x-3\cos x-4)$

$=\text{sgn}(2\cos^2 x-1-3\cos x-4)$

$=\text{sgn}(2\cos^2 x-3\cos x-5)$

$=\text{sgn}[\cos^2 x-5\cos x+2\cos x-5]$

$=\text{sgn}[\cos x(2\cos x-5)+1(2\cos x-5)]$

$=\text{sgn}[(2\cos x-5)(\cos x+1)]$

We know that $f(x)=\text{sgn}(x)=\begin{cases}-1, & \text{for } x<0\\ 0, & \text{for } x=0\\ 1, & \text{for } x>0\end{cases}$

$\therefore f(x)=\text{sgn}[(2\cos x-5)(\cos x+1)]$

$=\begin{cases}-1, & \text{for } (2\cos x-5)(\cos x+1)<0\\ 0, & \text{for } (2\cos x-5)(\cos x+1)=0\\ 1, & \text{for } (2\cos x-5)(\cos x+1)>0\end{cases}$

$$= \begin{cases} -1, & \text{for } -1 < \cos x < \dfrac{5}{2} \\ 0, & \text{for } \cos x = -1, \dfrac{5}{2} \\ 1, & \text{for } \cos x < -1 \text{ or } \cos x > \dfrac{5}{2} \end{cases}$$

But $\cos x \in [-1, 1]$

$$\therefore \quad f(x) = \begin{cases} -1, & \text{for } -1 < \cos x \le 1 \\ 0, & \text{for } \cos x = -1 \end{cases}$$

$$\Rightarrow \quad f(x) = \begin{cases} -1, & \text{for } x \in R - \{(2n+1)\pi; n \in Z\} \\ 0, & \text{for } x = (2n+1)\pi; n \in Z \end{cases}$$

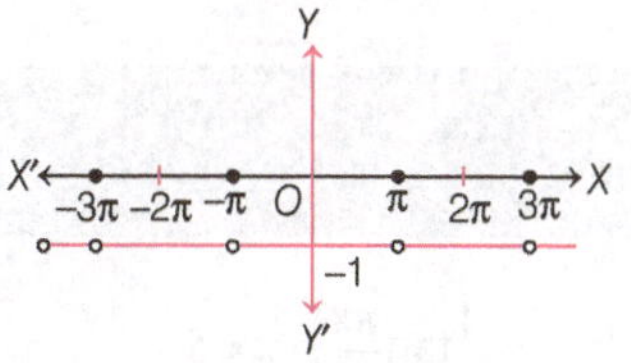

$$\therefore \quad \lim_{x \to (2n+1)\pi} f(x) = \lim_{x \to (2n+1)\pi} (-1) = -1$$

but $f(2n+1)\pi = 0$ and if $k \in R \sim \{(2n-1)\pi; n \in Z\}$,

then $\lim_{x \to k} f(x) = \lim_{x \to k} f(x) = -1$ and $f(k) = -1$.

$\therefore f(x)$ is continuous everywhere except for the point $x = (2n+1)\pi; n \in Z$

and at $x = (2n+1)\pi$, LHL = RHL $= -1 \ne f(2n+1)\pi = 0$

$\therefore f(x)$ has isolated point removable discontinuity at $x = (2n+1)\pi$ i.e. odd integral multiple of π.

4.4 Points of Discontinuity

The values of x at which function is discontinuous are known as points of discontinuity of that function.

Example 13. Find the points of discontinuity of the following functions for $x \in R$.

(i) $f(x) = \dfrac{1}{2\sin x - 1}$ (ii) $f(x) = \dfrac{1}{x^2 - 3|x| + 2}$

(iii) $f(x) = \dfrac{1}{x^4 + x^2 + 1}$ (iv) $f(x) = \dfrac{1}{1 - e^{\frac{x-1}{x-2}}}$

(v) $f(x) = [[x]] - [x-2]$, where [·] represents the greatest integer function.

Sol. A function is discontinuous at all such points where it is undefined.

(i) $f(x) = \dfrac{1}{2\sin x - 1}$, $f(x)$ is discontinuous when

$2\sin x - 1 = 0$ i.e. $\sin x = \dfrac{1}{2}$

$$\Rightarrow \quad x = 2n\pi + \frac{\pi}{6}, 2n\pi + \frac{5\pi}{6}, n \in I$$

(ii) $f(x) = \dfrac{1}{x^2 - 3|x| + 2}$

$f(x)$ is discontinuous when $x^2 - 3|x| + 2 = 0$

$$\Rightarrow \quad |x|^2 - 3|x| + 2 = 0$$

$$\Rightarrow \quad (|x| - 1)(|x| - 2) = 0$$

$$\Rightarrow \quad |x| = 1, 2 \Rightarrow x = \pm 1, \pm 2$$

(iii) $f(x) = \dfrac{1}{x^4 + x^2 + 1} = \dfrac{1}{\left(x^2 + \frac{1}{2}\right)^2 + \frac{3}{4}}$

Now, $x^4 + x^2 + 1 = \left(x^2 + \dfrac{1}{2}\right)^2 + \dfrac{3}{4} \ge 1, \forall x \in R$

$\Rightarrow f(x)$ is continuous, $\forall\ x \in R$.

(iv) $f(x) = \dfrac{1}{1 - e^{\frac{x-1}{x-2}}}$

$f(x)$ is discontinuous, when $x - 2 = 0$ and also when

$$1 - e^{\frac{x-1}{x-2}} = 0 \Rightarrow e^{\frac{x-1}{x-2}} = 1 \Rightarrow \frac{x-1}{x-2} = 0$$

$$\Rightarrow \quad x = 1$$

Thus, $f(x)$ is discontinuous at $x = 1, 2$.

(v) $f(x) = [[x]] - [x-2] = [x] - ([x] - 2) = 2$

$\Rightarrow f(x)$ is continuous, $\forall\ x \in R$.

JEE SCANNER

Example Similar to PYQ Asked in JEE Main 2023

Let $f(x) = x\left[\dfrac{x}{3}\right]$, if $-5 < x < 5$, where [·] denotes the greatest integer function. Then, the number of points of discontinuity of f is ....

Sol. (2) The given function $f(x) = x\left[\dfrac{x}{3}\right]$, for $-5 < x < 5$

may be discontinuous at the points, when $\dfrac{x}{3}$ is an integer,

so possible points of discontinuity are $x = 0, \pm 3$

But at $x = 0$,

$$\lim_{x \to 0^+} f(x) = 0 \text{ and } \lim_{x \to 0^-} f(x) = 0$$

$\therefore$ At $x = 0$, $f(x)$ is continuous.

Hence, $f(x)$ is discontinuous at two points, −3 and 3.

Skill Builder

For Sol.

Let $f(x) = x[x]$, for $-4 < x < 4$, where [·] denotes the greatest integer function. Then, the number of points of discontinuity of f is ......

▪ **For more practice** See Q.13 of Milestone Practice 4.2.

Example 14. Find the points of discontinuity of $y=\dfrac{1}{u^2+u-2}$, where $u=\dfrac{1}{x-1}$.

Sol. The function $u = f(x) = \dfrac{1}{x-1}$ is discontinuous at the point $x = 1$ ...(i)

The function $y = g(x) = \dfrac{1}{u^2+u-2} = \dfrac{1}{(u+2)(u-1)}$

is discontinuous at $u = -2$ and $u = 1$,

when $u = -2 \Rightarrow \dfrac{1}{x-1} = -2$

$\Rightarrow \quad x-1 = -\dfrac{1}{2}$

$\Rightarrow \quad x = \dfrac{1}{2}$ ...(ii)

when $u = 1$, $\dfrac{1}{x-1} = 1$

$\Rightarrow \quad x-1 = 1$

$\Rightarrow \quad x = 2$ ...(iii)

Hence, the composite function $y = g(f(x))$ is discontinuous at three points $x = 1/2, 1, 2$.

Milestone Practice 4.2

1. Mention the nature of discontinuity in the following functions.

(i) $f(x) = 3^{\tan x}$ at $x=(2n+1)\dfrac{\pi}{2}, n \in Z$

(ii) $f(x) = \dfrac{1}{x^4}$ at $x=0$

(iii) $f(x) = \dfrac{|\sin 3x|}{x}$ at $x=0$

(iv) $f(x) = \dfrac{\{x\}}{x}$ at $x=0$

(v) $f(x) = \dfrac{[x]}{x}$ at $x=3$

2. State the type of discontinuity of the following functions at $x=0$.

(i) $f(x) = \dfrac{1}{1+2^{\cot x}}$

(ii) $f(x) = \cos\left(\dfrac{|\sin x|}{x}\right)$

(iii) $f(x) = x\sin\dfrac{\pi}{x}$

(iv) $f(x) = \dfrac{1}{\ln|x|}$

3. If $f(x) = \begin{cases} 1-2x, & x<0 \\ 2, & x=0 \\ x^2+2, & x>0 \end{cases}$, then at $x=0$.

(a) f is continuous.

(b) f is continuous from left.

(c) f has a jump discontinuity.

(d) f has a removable discontinuity.

4. Let $f(x) = \begin{cases} \tan\dfrac{\pi x}{2}, & x<1 \\ x-1, & 1 \le x < 2 \\ \dfrac{1}{2-x}, & x \ge 2 \end{cases}$, then at $x=1$, f has a

(a) jump discontinuity.

(b) removable discontinuity.

(c) infinite discontinuity.

(d) no discontinuity.

5. Let $f(x) = \begin{cases} x^2, & x \le 0 \\ 2, & 0 < x < 1 \\ \dfrac{\sin(x-1)}{x-1}, & x \ge 1 \end{cases}$, then at $x=0$, f has

(a) finite irremovable discontinuity (or jump discontinuity).

(b) removable discontinuity.

(c) infinite discontinuity.

(d) no discontinuity.

6. The function $f(x) = |2\sin 2x| + 2$ has at $x=0$

(a) jump discontinuity

(b) removable discontinuity

(c) infinite discontinuity

(d) no discontinuity

7. Let $f(x) = \sin\dfrac{1}{x}$, then at $x=0$, f has

(a) finite irremovable discontinuity.

(b) removable discontinuity.

(c) oscillatory discontinuity.

(d) no discontinuity.

8. The jump of discontinuity of the function at the point of discontinuity i.e. $x=-2$ of the function $f(x)=\dfrac{|x+2|}{\tan^{-1}(x+2)}$, is

(a) 2 (b) −2 (c) 0 (d) 1

9. Consider $f(x)=\lim\limits_{n\to\infty}\dfrac{x^n-\sin x^n}{x^n+\sin x^n}$, for $x>0$, $x\neq 1$, $f(1)=0$, then

(a) f is continuous at $x=1$.
(b) f has a finite discontinuity at $x=1$.
(c) f has an infinite or oscillatory discontinuity at $x=1$.
(d) f has a removable type of discontinuity at $x=1$.

10. Consider the function $f(x)=\begin{cases}\dfrac{x}{[x]} & \text{if } 1\le x<2\\ 1 & \text{if } x=2\\ \sqrt{6-x} & \text{if } 2<x\le 3\end{cases}$,

where $[x]$ denotes step up function, then at $x=2$, function

(a) has missing point removable discontinuity.
(b) has isolated point removable discontinuity.
(c) has non-removable discontinuity finite type.
(d) is continuous.

11. The set of points of discontinuity of the function

$$f(x)=\frac{\tan x\cdot\tan^{-1}\left(\frac{1}{x-1}\right)}{x(x-3)(x-5)},$$ is equal to

(a) {0, 3, 5}
(b) $\left\{(2n+1)\dfrac{\pi}{2},\ n\in Z\right\}$
(c) $\{0,1,3,5\}\cup\left\{(2n+1)\dfrac{\pi}{2};\ n\in Z\right\}$
(d) None of the above

12. The set of points of discontinuity of the function $f(x)=\sqrt{x}-[\sqrt{x}]$ is (where $[x]$ denotes the greatest integer less than or equal to x contains the set)

(a) {1, 4,9, ..., 100}
(b) $(n^2 : n\in N)$
(c) N
(d) $\{2n : n\in N\}$

13. Let $f(x)=x\left[\dfrac{x}{2}\right]$ if $-4<x<4$, where $[\cdot]$ denotes the greatest integer function. Then, find the number of points of discontinuity of f.

Answer Key

1. (i) Non-removable discontinuity (ii) Non-removable discontinuity (iii) Non-removable discontinuity (iv) Non-removable discontinuity (v) Jump discontinuity
2. (i) Non-removable discontinuity (ii) Removable discontinuity (iii) Removable discontinuity (iv) Removable discontinuity

3. (c)	4. (c)	5. (a)	6. (d)	7. (c)	8. (a)
9. (b)	10. (b)	11. (c)	12. (a, b)	13. (2)	

For Detailed Solution

Milestone 3 Theorems of Continuity

Theorem 1 (Algebra of Continuity)

Let $f(x)$ and $g(x)$ be two functions

Cases	$f+g$	$f-g$	$f \cdot g$	f/g
(i) Both are continuous i.e. $f(x)=$ continuous and $g(x)=$ continuous	Continuous	Continuous	Continuous	Continuous provided $g \neq 0$
(ii) One is continuous and other is discontinuous i.e. $f(x)=$ continuous and $g(x)=$ discontinuous	Discontinuous	Discontinuous	Cannot say	Cannot say
(iii) Both are discontinuous i.e $f(x)=$ discontinuous and $g(x)=$ discontinuous	Cannot say	Cannot say	Cannot say	Cannot say

Cannot say means 'may be continuous or discontinuous'.

e.g. Consider $f(x)=[x]$ and $g(x)=x$ are two functions such that $f(x)$ is discontinuous at $x=0$ and $g(x)$ is continuous at $x=0$, then $f(x) \pm g(x)=[x] \pm x$ will be discontinuous at $x=0$ and $f(x) \cdot g(x)=x[x]\begin{cases}\text{continuous at } x=0 \\ \text{discontinuous at } x=1\end{cases}$.

Let $f(x)=[x]$ be discontinuous at $x=0$ and $g(x)=3-[x]$ is discontinuous at $x=0$, then $f(x)+g(x)=3$ is continuous at $x=0$, $f(x)-g(x)=2[x]-3$ is discontinuous at $x=0$ and $f(x) \cdot g(x)=[x](3-[x])$ is discontinuous at $x=0$.

Let $f(x)=[x]$ and $g(x)=\dfrac{1}{[x]}$ both $f(x)$ and $g(x)$ are discontinuous at $x=1$, then $f(x) \pm g(x)$ is discontinuous at $x=1$ and $f(x) \cdot g(x)$ is continuous at $x=1$.

Theorem 2 (Intermediate Value Theorem)

If f is continuous on $[a, b]$ and $f(a) \neq f(b)$, then for any value $c \in (f(a), f(b))$, there is atleast one number x_0 in (a, b), for which $f(x_0)=c$.

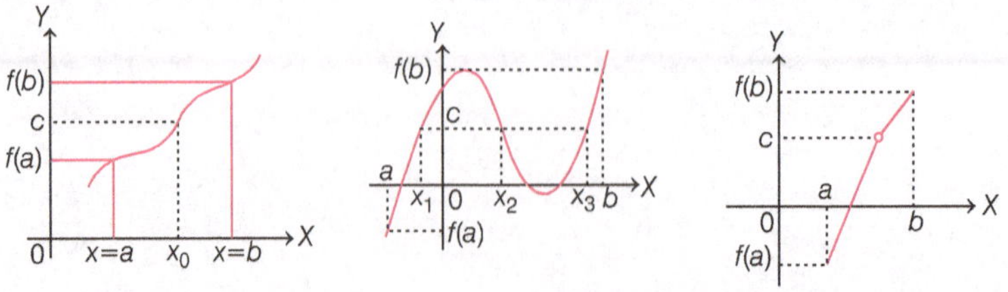

- Continuity over the interval $[a, b]$ is essential for the validity of this theorem.
- In figure-3, $f(a)$ and $f(b)$ are of opposite sign but $f(x)=c$ has no root in (a, b) as f is not continuous.

Example 15. Show that the function $f(x) = 1 - \sin\frac{\pi}{2}x$ attains value 1 in $[-1, 1]$.

Sol. $f(x) = 1 - \sin\frac{\pi}{2}x$ is continuous as 1 being constant, is continuous, $\sin\frac{\pi}{2}x$ is continuous and $1 - \sin\frac{\pi}{2}x$ being the difference of two continuous functions is also continuous.

Further, $f(-1) = 1 - \sin\left(-\frac{\pi}{2}\right) = 2$

and $f(1) = 1 - \sin\left(\frac{\pi}{2}\right) = 0$

By intermediate value theorem, $f(x)$ would attain each and every value between $f(-1)$ and $f(1)$ i.e. of interval $[0, 2]$.

$\therefore f(x)$ also attains value 1 in $[-1, 1]$.

Example 16. Show that the polynomial equation $x^3 - 5x^2 + 17x = 20$ has a solution in [1, 2].

Sol. Let $P(x) = x^3 - 5x^2 + 17x$

$P(x)$ being a polynomial function, is continuous in [1, 2] and $P(1) = 1 - 5 + 17 = 13$; $P(2) = 8 - 20 + 34 = 22$.

By Intermediate value theorem, $f(x)$ would attain each value between 13 and 22 and hence it would also attain value 20 in [1, 2].

Thus, the equation $x^3 - 5x^2 + 17x = 20$ has a solution in [1, 2].

Example 17. Using intermediate value theorem, prove that there exists a number x such that

$$x^{200} + \frac{1}{1 + \sin^2 x} = 200.$$

Sol. Let $f(x) = x^{200} + (1 + \sin^2 x)^{-1}$.

f is continuous and $f(0) = 1 < 200$ and $f(2) > 2^{200}$, which is much greater than 200.

Hence, from the Intermediate value theorem, there exists a number c in (0,2) such that $f(c) = 200$.

Theorem 3 (Extreme Value Theorem)

If f is continuous on $[a, b]$, then f takes a least value m and a greatest value M on this interval.

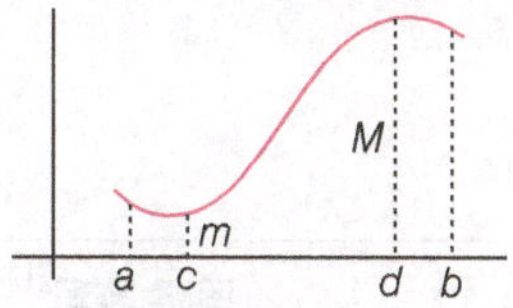

Minimum value m occurs at $x = c$ and maximum value M occurs at $x = d$, where $c, d \in (a, b)$

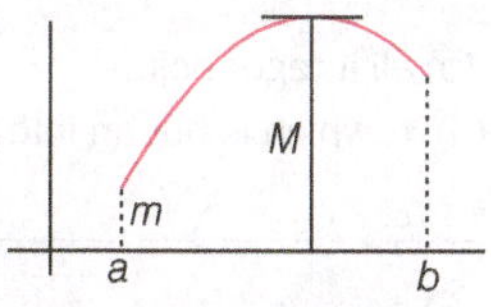

Minimum value m occurs at the end point $x = a$ and the maximum value M occurs inside the interval

JEE SPIKE

- To see that continuity is necessary for the extreme value theorem to be true refer the graph shown.

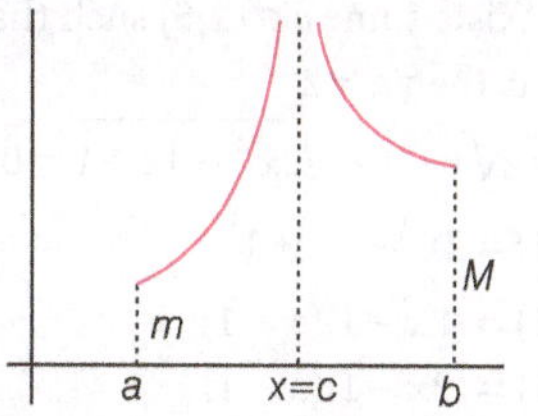

There is a discontinuity at $x = c$. The function has a minimum value at the left end point $x = a$ and f has no maximum value.

- If $f(a)$ and $f(b)$ possess opposite signs, then there exist atleast one solution of the equation $f(x) = 0$ in the open interval (a, b) provided f is continuous in $[a, b]$. It is also known as Bolzano's theorem.

Example 18. Let f be a continuous function defined on [0,1] with range [0, 1]. Show that there is some c in [0, 1] such that $f(c) = 1 - c$.

Sol. Consider $g(x) = f(x) - 1 + x$

$g(0) = f(0) - 1 \le 0$ [as $f(0) \le 1$]

$g(1) = f(1) \ge 0$ [as $f(1) \ge 0$]

$\therefore g(0)$ and $g(1)$ have values of opposite signs.

Hence, there exists at least one $c \in (0, 1)$ such that $g(c) = 0$.

$\therefore \quad g(c) = f(c) - 1 + c = 0 \Rightarrow f(c) = 1 - c$.

Example 19. Let f be continuous on the interval [0, 1] to R such that $f(0) = f(1)$. Prove that there exists a point c in $\left[0, \frac{1}{2}\right]$ such that $f(c) = f\left(c + \frac{1}{2}\right)$.

Sol. Consider a continuous function,

$$g(x) = f\left(x + \frac{1}{2}\right) - f(x) \quad \left(g \text{ is continuous, } \forall\ x \in \left[0, \frac{1}{2}\right]\right)$$

$$\Rightarrow \quad g(0) = f\left(\frac{1}{2}\right) - f(0) = f\left(\frac{1}{2}\right) - f(1) \quad [\text{as } f(0) = f(1)]$$

and $g\left(\frac{1}{2}\right) = f(1) - f\left(\frac{1}{2}\right) = -\left[f\left(\frac{1}{2}\right) - f(1)\right]$

Since, g is continuous and $g(0)$ and $g\left(\frac{1}{2}\right)$ have opposite signs, hence the equation $g(x) = 0$ must have atleast one root in $\left[0, \frac{1}{2}\right]$.

Hence, for some $c \in \left[0, \frac{1}{2}\right]$, $g(c) = 0 \Rightarrow f\left(c + \frac{1}{2}\right) = f(c)$

Example 20. Prove that the function $f(x) = a\sqrt{x - 1} + b\sqrt{2x - 1} - \sqrt{2x^2 - 3x + 1}$, where $a + 2b = 2$ and $a, b \in R$ always has a root in (1, 5), $\forall\ b \in R$.

Sol. There are three cases.

Case I Let $b > 0$, then $f(1) = b > 0$

and $f(5) = 2a + 3b - 6 = 2(a + 2b) - b - 6 \quad [\because a + 2b = 2]$

$= 4 - b - 6 = -(2 + b) < 0$

Hence, there exists some $c \in (1, 5)$ such that $f(c) = 0$.

Case II If $b = 0$, then $a = 2$.

$$f(x) = 2\sqrt{x-1} - \sqrt{2x^2 - 3x + 1} = 0$$

$$\Rightarrow \quad 4(x-1) = 2x^2 - 3x + 1$$

$$\Rightarrow \quad 4(x-1) = (2x-1)(x-1)$$

$$\Rightarrow \quad 4(x-1) = (2x-1)(x-1)$$

$$\Rightarrow \quad (x-1)(4 - 2x + 1) = 0$$

$$\Rightarrow \quad (x-1)(2x-5) = 0 \Rightarrow x = \frac{5}{2}$$

Hence, $f(x) = 0$ if $x = \frac{5}{2}$ which lies in (1, 5).

Case III If $b < 0$, $f(1) = b < 0$ and $f(2) = a + b\sqrt{3} - \sqrt{3}$

$$= (a + 2b) + (\sqrt{3} - 2)b - \sqrt{3}$$

$$= (2 - \sqrt{3}) - (2 - \sqrt{3})b$$

$$= (2 - \sqrt{3})(1 - b) > 0 \text{ (as } b < 0)$$

Thus, $f(1)$ and $f(2)$ have opposite signs.

Hence, there exists some $c \in (1, 2) \subset (1, 5)$, for which $f(c) = 0$.

Example 21. Prove that the equation $\sqrt{x-5} = \frac{1}{x+3}$ has atleast one real root.

Sol. Let $f(x) = \sqrt{x-5} - \frac{1}{x+3}$

The function is continuous on [5, 6].

Also, $f(5) = 0 - \frac{1}{5+3} = -\frac{1}{8} < 0$,

$$f(6) = 1 - \frac{1}{9} = \frac{8}{9} > 0$$

Hence, by Intermediate value theorem, there exists atleast one root $c \in (5, 6)$, for which $f(c) = 0$.

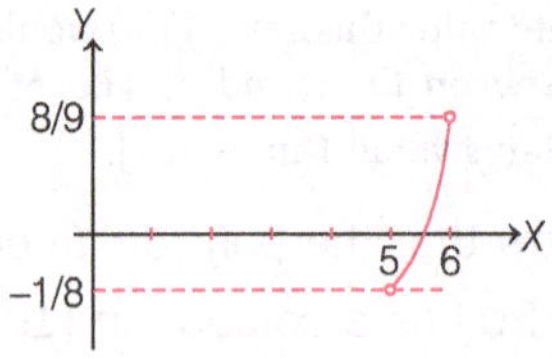

$$\therefore \quad \sqrt{c-5} - \frac{1}{c+3} = 0$$

Thus, c is root of the equation $\sqrt{x-5} = \frac{1}{x+3}$, where $c \in (5, 6)$.

Milestone Practice 4.3

1. Prove that the function $f(x) = \left(\frac{x^3}{4}\right) - \sin\left(\frac{\pi}{x}\right) + 3$ takes the value $\frac{7}{3}$ in the interval [– 2, 2].

2. If $g : [a, b]$ onto $[a, b]$ is continuous show that there is some $c \in [a, b]$ such that $g(c) = c$.

3. Given that $a > b > c > d$, then prove that the equation $(x - a)(x - c) + 2(x - b)(x - d) = 0$ will have two real and distinct roots.

4. If $f(x) = \{x\}$ and $g(x) = [x]$, (where {} and [] denote the fractional part and the integral part functions respectively), then discuss the continuity of

(i) $h(x) = f(x)\, g(x)$, $x = 1$ and 2

(ii) $h(x) = f(x) + g(x)$, $x = 1$

(iii) $h(x) = f(x) - g(x)$, $x = 1$

(iv) $h(x) = g(x) + \sqrt{f(x)}$, $x = 1$ and 2

5. The function $f(x) = [x]\cos\left(\frac{2x-1}{2}\right)\pi$, where [·] denotes the greatest integer function, is discontinuous at

(a) all x

(b) all integer points

(c) no x

(d) x, which is not an integer

Answer Key

4. (i) continuous at $x = 1$, discontinuous at $x = 2$ (ii) continuous (iii) discontinuous (iv) continuous at $x = 1, 2$

5. (c)

For Detailed Solution

Milestone 4 Continuity Involving Special Functions

- Continuity of Functions Involving GIF [·] • Continuity of Functions Involving Fractional Part Function
- Continuity of Functions Involving Signum Function • Continuity of Composite Functions

In this section, we will discuss continuity of some special functions e.g. greatest integer function, fractional part function, etc.

4.5 Continuity of Functions Involving GIF [·]

We know that $f(x)=[x]$ is discontinuous, when x is an integer.

Similarly, $f(x)=[g(x)]$ is discontinuous when $g(x)$ is an integer but this is true only when $g(x)$ is monotonic ($g(x)$ is strictly increasing or decreasing).

e.g. $f(x)=[\sqrt{x}]$ is discontinuous when $\sqrt{x}$ is an integer, as $\sqrt{x}$ is strictly increasing (monotonic function).

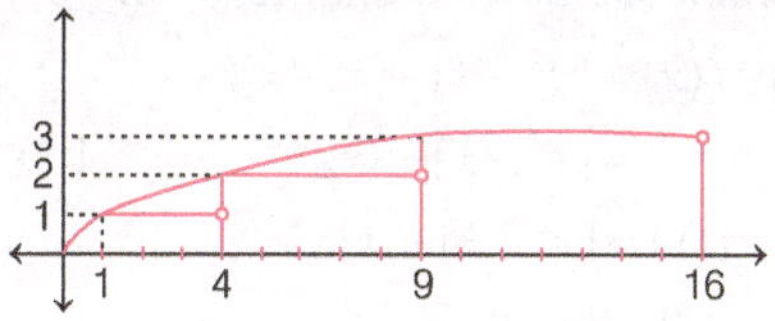

$\Rightarrow f(x)=[x^2]$, $x \geq 0$ is discontinuous, when x^2 is an integer, as x^2 is strictly increasing for $x \geq 0$.

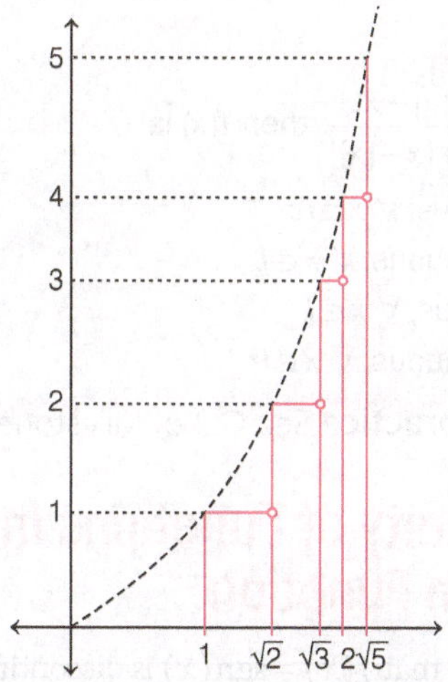

Now, consider $f(x)=[\sin x]$, $x \in [0, 2\pi]$, $g(x)=\sin x$ is not monotonic in $[0, 2\pi]$.

For this type of function, points of discontinuity can be determined easily by graphical methods. We can note that at $x=\frac{3\pi}{2}$, $\sin x$ takes integral value -1 but at $x=\frac{3\pi}{2}$, $f(x)=[\sin x]$ is continuous.

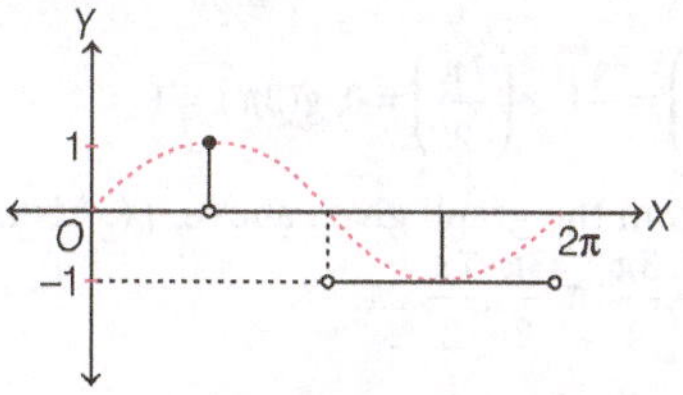

Example 22. Let $[x]$ be the greatest integer less than or equals to x. Then, at which of the following point (s) the function $f(x)=x\cos(\pi(x+[x]))$ is discontinuous?

(a) $x=1$ (b) $x=-1$ (c) $x=0$ (d) $x=2$

Sol. (a,b,d) $f(x)=x\cos(\pi x+[x]\pi) \Rightarrow f(x)=(-1)^{[x]}x\cos(\pi x)$

$[x]$ is discontinuous at all integers and $x \cos \pi x$ is continuous everywhere.

At $x=0$, $f(x)=0$, so it is continuous.

At other integral points, $f(x)$ is discontinuous.

Example 23. Draw the graph and find the points of discontinuity for $f(x)=[2\cos x]$, $x \in [0, 2\pi]$, (where [·] represents the greatest integer function).

Sol. $f(x)=[2\cos x]$

Clearly, from the graph given in figure, $f(x)$ is discontinuous at $x=0$ and when $2\cos x = \pm 1$

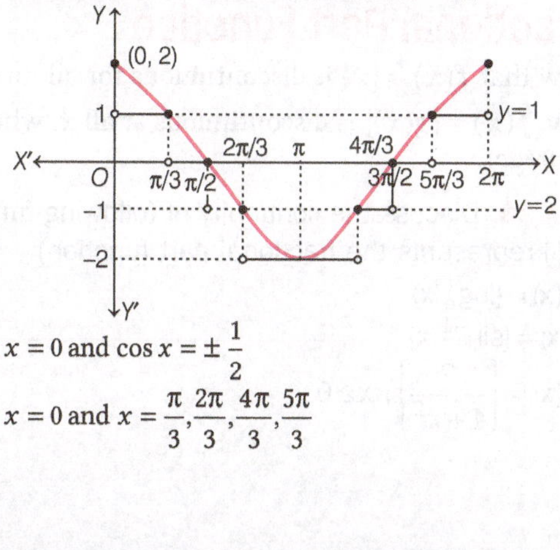

or $x=0$ and $\cos x = \pm\frac{1}{2}$

or $x=0$ and $x=\frac{\pi}{3}, \frac{2\pi}{3}, \frac{4\pi}{3}, \frac{5\pi}{3}$

Example 24. Draw the graph and discuss the continuity of $f(x)=[\sin x+\cos x]$, $x\in[0,2\pi]$, where $[\cdot]$ represents the greatest integer function.

Sol. $f(x)=[\sin x+\cos x]=[g(x)]$,

where $g(x)=\sin x+\cos x$

$$g(0)=1,\ g\left(\frac{\pi}{4}\right)=\sqrt{2},\ g\left(\frac{\pi}{2}\right)=1$$

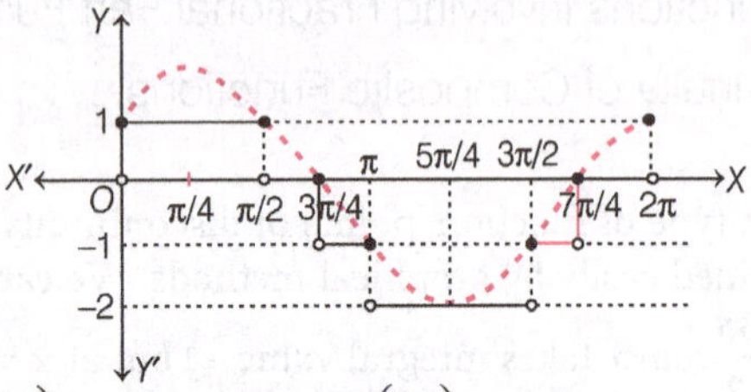

$$g\left(\frac{3\pi}{4}\right)-0 \text{ or } g(\pi)=-1,\ g\left(\frac{5\pi}{2}\right)=\sqrt{2}$$

$$g\left(\frac{3\pi}{2}\right)=-1,\ g\left(\frac{7\pi}{2}\right)=0,\ g(2\pi)=1$$

Clearly, from the graph given above, $f(x)$ is discontinuous at $x=0,\frac{\pi}{2},\frac{3\pi}{4},\pi,\frac{3\pi}{2},\frac{7\pi}{2},2\pi$.

Example 25. If the function

$f(x)=\left[\frac{(x-2)^3}{a}\right]\sin(x-2)+a\cos(x-2)$, where $[\cdot]$ denotes the greatest integer function which is continuous in [4, 6], then find the value of a.

Sol. $\sin(x-2)$ and $\cos(x-2)$ are continuous for all x.

Since, $[x]$ is not continuous at integral point.

So, $f(x)$ is continuous in [4, 6] if $\left[\frac{(x-2)^3}{a}\right]=0,\ \forall\ x\in[4,6]$

Now, $(x-2)^3\in[8,64]$, for $x\in[4,6]$

$\Rightarrow \quad a>64$, for $\left[\frac{(x-2)^3}{a}\right]=0$

$\therefore \quad a\in(64,\infty)$

4.6 Continuity of Functions Involving Fractional Part Function

We know that $f(x)=\{x\}$ is discontinuous for all integers. Similarly, $f(x)=\{g(x)\}$ is discontinuous at all x, where $g(x)=$ integer.

Example 26. Discuss the continuity of following function, (where $\{\cdot\}$ represents the fractional part function)

(i) $f(x)=\{\log_e x\}$

(ii) $f(x)=\{\sin^{-1} x\}$

(iii) $f(x)=\left\{\frac{2}{1+x^2}\right\}$, $x\geq 0$

Sol. (i) $\log_e x$ function is a monotonically increasing function.

Hence, $f(x)=\{\log_e x\}$ is discontinuous, where $\log_e x=k$ or $x=e^k, k\in Z$.

Thus, $f(x)$ is discontinuous at $x=\dots e^{-2},e^{-1},e^0,e^1,e^2,\dots$

(ii) $\sin^{-1} x$ is a monotonically increasing function.

Hence, $f(x)=\{\sin^{-1} x\}$ is discontinuous, where $\sin^{-1} x$ is an integer.

$\Rightarrow \quad \sin^{-1} x=-1,0,1$ or $x=-\sin 1, 0, \sin 1$

(iii) $\left\{\frac{2}{1+x^2}\right\}, x\geq 0$ is a monotonically decreasing function.

Hence, $f(x)=\left\{\frac{2}{1+x^2}\right\}, x\geq 0$ is discontinuous, when $\frac{2}{1+x^2}$ is an integer.

$\Rightarrow \quad \frac{2}{1+x^2}=1,2 \Rightarrow x=1,0$

JEE SCANNER

Example Similar to PYQ Asked in JEE Main 2023

Let $f(x)=[x^2-x]+|x-[x]|$, where $x\in R$ and $[\cdot]$ denotes the greatest integer function. Then, f is

(a) continuous at $x=0$ and $f(0)=-1$.

(b) discontinuous at $x=0$ and $f(0)=0$.

(c) continuous at $x=0$ and $f(0^+)=-1$.

(d) discontinuous at $x=0$ and $f(0)=-1$.

Sol. (b) Given, $f(x)=[x^2-x]+|x-[x]|$

$$=[x^2-x]+|\{x\}| \qquad [\because x-[x]=\{x\}]$$

$$f(x)=[x^2-x]+\{x\} \qquad [\because \{x\}\geq 0]$$

Now, at $x=0$, $f(0)=0$

and $\quad f(0^+)=-1$ {as $x^2-x<0$, for $x\to 0^+$}

So, function is discontinuous at $x=0$.

Skill Builder

Let $f(x)=\frac{[[x]-x]}{1+[x-[x]]}$, then $f(x)$ is

(a) continuous, $\forall\ x\in R$.

(b) discontinuous, $\forall\ x\in I$.

(c) continuous, $\forall\ x\in I$.

(d) discontinuous, $\forall\ x\in R$.

For Sol.

■ **For more practice** See Q.2 of Milestone Practice 4.4.

4.7 Continuity of Functions Involving Signum Function

Since, we know that $f(x)=\text{sgn}(x)$ is discontinuous at $x=0$.

In general, $f(x)=\text{sgn}(g(x))$ is discontinuous at $x=a$ if $g(a)=0$.

Example 27. Discuss the continuity of

(i) $f(x)=\text{sgn}(x^3-x)$

(ii) $f(x)=\text{sgn}(2\cos x-1)$

(iii) $f(x)=\text{sgn}(x^2-2x+3)$

Sol. (i) $f(x)=\text{sgn}(x^3-x)$

Here, $x^3-x=0$

$\Rightarrow \quad x=0,-1,1$

Hence, $f(x)$ is discontinuous at $x=0,-1,1$

(ii) $f(x)=\text{sgn}(2\cos x-1)$

Here, $2\cos x-1=0$

$\Rightarrow \quad \cos x=\dfrac{1}{2}$

$\Rightarrow \quad x=2n\pi+\left(\dfrac{\pi}{3}\right), n\in Z,$

where $f(x)$ is discontinuous.

(iii) $f(x)=\text{sgn}(x^2-2x+3)$

Here, $x^2-2x+3>0$, for all x.

Thus, $f(x)=1$, for all x.

Hence, continuous for all x.

Example 28. If $f(x)=\text{sgn}(2\sin x+a)$ is continuous for all x, then find the possible values of a.

Sol. $f(x)=\text{sgn}(2\sin x+a)$ is continuous for all x.

Then, $2\sin x+a\neq 0$, for any real x.

$\Rightarrow \quad \sin x\neq -\dfrac{a}{2}$

$\Rightarrow \quad \left|\dfrac{a}{2}\right|>1$

$\Rightarrow \quad a<-2$ or $a>2$

Example 29. If $f(x)=\begin{cases}\text{sgn}(x-2)\cdot[\log_e x], & 1\le x\le 3\\ \{x^2\}, & 3<x\le 3.5\end{cases}$,

where [·] denotes the greatest integer function and {·} represents the fractional part function. Find the point where the continuity of $f(x)$ should be checked. Hence, find the points of discontinuity.

Sol. We have, $f(x)=\begin{cases}\text{sgn}(x-2)\cdot[\log_e x], & 1\le x\le 3\\ \{x^2\}, & 3<x\le 3.5\end{cases}$

$$\text{sgn}(x-2)=\begin{cases}-1, & 1\le x<2\\ 0, & x=2\\ 1, & 2<x<3\end{cases}$$

$$[\log_e x]=\begin{cases}0, & 1\le x\le e\\ 1, & e<x\le 3\end{cases}$$

$$\therefore f(x)=\begin{cases}0, & 1\le x\le e\\ 1, & e<x\le 3\\ \{x^2\}, & 3<x\le 3.5\end{cases}$$

Clearly, $f(x)$ is discontinuous at $x=e$.

Now, check at $x=3$

$$\lim_{x\to 3^-} f(x)=\lim_{x\to 3^+} 1=1$$

and $$\lim_{x\to 3^+} f(x)=\lim_{x\to 3^+}\{x^2\}=0$$

$\because \lim_{x\to 3^-} f(x)\neq \lim_{x\to 3^+} f(x)$

Hence, $f(x)$ is discontinuous at $x=3$.

Also, $\{x^2\}$ is discontinuous at $\sqrt{10},\sqrt{11}$ and $\sqrt{12}$

Hence, $f(x)$ is discontinuous at $x=e, 3, \sqrt{10},\sqrt{11},\sqrt{12}$.

4.8 Continuity of Composite Functions

Case 1 If $f(x)$ and $g(x)$ both are continuous functions, then their composite functions fog and gof are also continuous.

Case 2 If $f(x)$ is discontinuous at $x=a$, then $f\{g(x)\}$ is discontinuous at x, where $g(x)=a$ and fog also discontinuous at those points where $g(x)$ is discontinuous.

e.g. $f(x)=\dfrac{1}{1-x}$ is discontinuous at $x=1$.

Now, $f(f(x))=\dfrac{1}{1-\dfrac{1}{1-x}}=\dfrac{x-1}{x}$ is not only discontinuous at $x=0$ but also at $x=1$.

Now, $f(f(f(x)))=\dfrac{\dfrac{x-1}{x}-1}{\dfrac{x-1}{x}}=\dfrac{-1}{x-1}$ seems to be continuous but it is discontinuous at $x=1$ and $x=0$, where $f(x)$ and $f(f(x))$ are discontinuous, respectively.

Example 30. If $f(x)=\dfrac{x+3}{x-1}$ and $g(x)=\dfrac{1}{x-3}$, then discuss the continuity of $f(x)$, $g(x)$ and $fog(x)$.

Sol. $f(x)=\dfrac{x+3}{x-1}$

$f(x)$ is a rational function. It must be continuous in its domain and f is not defined at $x=1$.

$\therefore f$ is discontinuous at $x=1$.

$g(x)=\dfrac{1}{x-3}$

$g(x)$ is also a rational function. It must be continuous in its domain and g is not defined at $x=3$.

$\therefore g$ is discontinuous at $x=3$.

Now, $fog(x)$ will be discontinuous at

(i) $x=3$ (point of discontinuity of $g(x)$).

(ii) $g(x) = 1$, where $g(x)$ = point of discontinuity of $f(x)$)

If $g(x) = 1$

$$\Rightarrow \quad \frac{1}{x-3} = 1 \Rightarrow x = 4$$

$\therefore$ Discontinuity of $fog(x)$ should be checked at $x = 3$ and $x = 4$.

At $x = 3$, $fog(x) = \dfrac{\frac{1}{x-3}+1}{\frac{1}{x-3}-1}$

$fog(3)$ is not defined.

$$\lim_{x\to 3} \log(x) = \lim_{x\to 3} \frac{\frac{1}{x-3}+1}{\frac{1}{x-3}-1} = \lim_{x\to 3} \frac{1+x-3}{1-x+3} = 1$$

$\therefore$ $fog(x)$ is discontinuous at $x = 3$

At $x = 4$,

$fog(4)$ = not defined

$$\lim_{x\to 4^-} fog(x) = \infty \Rightarrow \lim_{x\to 4} fog(x) = -\infty$$

$\therefore$ $fog(x)$ is discontinuous at $x = 4$.

Example 31. $f(x) = \begin{cases} 1+8x^3, & x<0 \\ 4x-1, & x=0 \\ 4x^2-1, & x>0 \end{cases}$

and $g(x) = \begin{cases} (2x-1)^{1/3}, & x<0 \\ 1, & x=0. \\ \sqrt{2x+1}, & x>0 \end{cases}$

Then, define $fog(x)$ and comment on the continuity of $fog(x)$.

Sol. $f(x) = \begin{cases} 1+8x^3, \ x<0; & f \le 1 \\ 4x-1, \ x=0; & f=-1 \\ 4x^2-1, \ x>0; & f<-1 \end{cases}$

$$g(x) = \begin{cases} (2x-1)^{1/3}, & x<0; \ g<-1 \\ 1, & x=0; \ g=1 \\ \sqrt{2x+1}, & x>0; \ g>1 \end{cases}$$

$$fog = \begin{cases} 1+8g^3, & g<0 \\ 4g-1, & g=0 \\ 4g^2-1, & g>0 \end{cases}$$

$$fog(x) = \begin{cases} 1+8(2x-1), & x<0 \\ 4-1, & x=0 \\ 4(2x+1)-1, & x>0 \end{cases}$$

$$fog(x) = \begin{cases} 16x-7, & x<0 \\ 3, & x=0 \\ 8x+3, & x>0 \end{cases}$$

$\because \quad fog(0) = 3$, $fog(0^+) = 3$ and $fog(0^-) = -7$

$\therefore$ It is not continuous at $x = 0$.

$\therefore$ fog is continuous for $x \in R - \{0\}$.

Continuity of Functions in which $f(x)$ is Defined Differently for Rational and Irrational Values of x

To understand this, we are discussing some examples.

Example 32. Discuss the continuity of the following function $f(x) = \begin{cases} 1, & \text{if } x \text{ is rational} \\ 0, & \text{if } x \text{ is irrational} \end{cases}$.

Sol. For any $x = a$,

$$\text{LHL} = \lim_{x\to a^-} f(x) = \lim_{x\to a^-} f(a-h) = 0 \text{ or } 1$$

[as $\lim_{x\to a} (a-h)$ can be rational or irrational]

Similarly, $\text{RHL} = \lim_{x\to a^+} f(x) = \lim_{h\to 0} f(a+h) = 0 \text{ or } 1$

Hence, $f(x)$ oscillates between 0 and 1 for all values of a.

$\therefore$ LHL and RHL do not exist.

$\Rightarrow f(x)$ is discontinuous at a point $x = a$ for all values of a.

Example 33. Find the value of x, where $f(x) = \begin{cases} x, & \text{if } x \text{ is rational} \\ 1-x, & \text{if } x \text{ is irrational} \end{cases}$ is a continuous function.

Sol. $f(x)$ is continuous at some $x = a$, where $x = 1 - x$ or $x = \frac{1}{2}$.

Hence, $f(x)$ is continuous at $x = \frac{1}{2}$

If $x \to \frac{1}{2^+}$, then x may be rational or irrational

$$\Rightarrow \quad f\left(\frac{1}{2^+}\right) = \frac{1}{2} \text{ or } 1 - \frac{1}{2} = \frac{1}{2}$$

If $x \to \frac{1}{2^-}$, then x may be rational or irrational

$$\Rightarrow \quad f\left(\frac{1}{2^-}\right) = \frac{1}{2} \text{ or } 1 - \frac{1}{2} = \frac{1}{2}$$

Hence, $f(x)$ is continuous at $x = \frac{1}{2}$

For other point, $x = 1$ (say)

$$\Rightarrow \quad f(1) = 1$$

If $x \to 1^+$, then x may be rational or irrational.

$$\Rightarrow \quad f(1^+) = 1 \text{ or } 1 - 1 = 0$$

Hence, $f(1^+)$ oscillates between 1 and 0, which causes discontinuity at $x = 1$.

Similarly, $f(x)$ oscillates between 0 and 1 for all $x \in R - \left(\frac{1}{2}\right)$.

JEE Focus Points

Single Point Continuity Following functions are continuous only at one point and defined everywhere (Single point continuity)

- $f(x)=\begin{cases} x & \text{if } x\in Q \\ 0 & \text{if } x\notin Q \end{cases}$, continuous only at $x=0$
- $f(x)=\begin{cases} x & \text{if } x\in Q \\ -x & \text{if } x\notin Q \end{cases}$, continuous only at $x=0$
- $f(x)=\begin{cases} x & \text{if } x\in Q \\ 1-x & \text{if } x\notin Q \end{cases}$, continuous only at $x=\dfrac{1}{2}$
- $f(x)=\begin{cases} x^2 & \text{if } x\in Q \\ 1 & \text{if } x\notin Q \end{cases}$, continuous only at $x=1$ or -1

Continuity of Functions which have Built in Limit

Sometimes functions are defined by a limiting value

$f(x)=\lim\limits_{n\to\infty} g(x,n)$

We are discussing some examples below to understand it.

Example 34. Discuss the continuity of

$$f(x)=\lim_{n\to\infty}\frac{x^{2n}-1}{x^{2n}+1}$$

Sol. $$f(x)=\lim_{n\to\infty}\frac{(x^2)^n-1}{(x^2)^n+1}=\lim_{n\to\infty}\frac{1-\dfrac{1}{(x^2)^n}}{1+\dfrac{1}{(x^2)^n}}$$

$$=\begin{cases} -1, & 0\le x^2<1 \\ 0, & x^2=1 \\ 1, & x^2>1 \end{cases}=\begin{cases} 1, & x<-1 \\ 0, & x=-1 \\ -1, & -1<x<1 \\ 0, & x=1 \\ 1, & x>1 \end{cases}$$

Thus, $f(x)$ is discontinuous at $x=\pm 1$.

Example 35. Discuss the continuity of

$f(x)=\lim\limits_{n\to\infty}\cos^{2n}x$.

Sol. $$f(x)=\lim_{n\to\infty}(\cos^2 x)^n=\begin{cases} 0, & 0\le\cos^2 x<1 \\ 1, & \cos^2 x=1 \end{cases}=\begin{cases} 0, & x\ne n\pi,\ n\in I \\ 1, & x=n\pi,\ n\in I \end{cases}$$

Hence, $f(x)$ is discontinuous, when $x=n\pi, n\in I$.

Example 36. Find the value of $f(1)$ if the function

$$f(x)=\lim_{n\to\infty}\frac{x^{m+1}-(m+1)x+m}{(x-1)^2}, x\ne 1$$ is continuous at

$x=1$.

Sol. We have, $$\lim_{x\to 1}f(x)=\lim_{x\to 0}\frac{x(x^m-1)-m(x-1)}{(x-1)^2}$$

$$=\lim_{x\to 1}\frac{x(x-1)(1+x+x^2+\ldots+x^{m-1})-m(x-1)}{(x-1)^2}$$

$$=\lim_{x\to 1}\frac{(x+x^2+x^3+\ldots+x^m)-(1+1+\ldots m\text{ times})}{x-1}$$

$$=\lim_{x\to 1}\frac{(x-1)+(x^2-1)+(x^3-1)+\ldots+(x^m-1)}{(x-1)}$$

$$=\lim_{x\to 1}\left[1+\frac{x^2-1}{x-1}+\frac{x^3-1}{x-1}+\ldots+\frac{x^m-1}{x-1}\right]$$

$$=1+2+3+\ldots+m=\frac{m(m+1)}{2}$$

Hence, for f to be continuous at $x=1$, we should have $f(1)=\dfrac{m(m+1)}{2}$.

JEE SCANNER

Example Similar to PYQ Asked in JEE Main 2022

$f(x)=\lim\limits_{n\to\infty}\dfrac{\ln(2+x)-x^{2n}\sin x}{1+x^{2n}}$ is

(a) continuous at $x=1$. (b) continuous at $x=0$.
(c) discontinuous at $x=1$. (d) None of the above

Sol. (c) We have, $f(1)=(\ln 3-\sin 1)/2$

and $$\lim_{n\to\infty}x^{2n}=\begin{cases} 0 & \text{if } x^2<1 \\ \infty & \text{if } x^2>1 \end{cases}$$

For $x^2<1$, we get

$$f(x)=\lim\frac{\ln(2+x)-x^{2n}\sin x}{(1+x^{2n})}=-\ln(2+x)$$

Again, for $x^2>1$, we get

$$f(x)=\lim_{n\to\infty}\frac{\dfrac{1}{x^{2n}}\ln(2+x)-\sin x}{1+\dfrac{1}{x^{2n}}}=-\sin(x)$$

Here, as $x\to 1$

$$\lim_{x\to 1^-}f(x)=\ln 3 \text{ and } \lim_{x\to 1^+}f(x)=-\sin 1$$

So, $\lim\limits_{x\to 1^-}f(x)\ne\lim\limits_{x\to 1^+}f(x)$

Therefore, $f(x)$ is discontinuous at $x=1$.

Skill Builder

Let $f(x)=\lim\limits_{m\to\infty}\dfrac{\ln(1+x)-x^{2m}\cos x}{1+x^{2m}}$, then $f(x)$ is

(a) continuous at $x=1$.
(b) continuous at $x=0$.
(c) discontinuous at $x=1$.
(d) None of the above

For Sol.

- **For more practice** See Q.6 of Milestone Practice 4.4.

Example 37. Given $f(x)=\sum_{x=1}^{n}(x^r+x^{-r})^2, x\neq\pm1$ and

$$g(x)=\begin{cases}\lim_{n\to\infty}(f(x)-2n)x^{-2n-2}(1-x^2)), & \text{for } x\neq\pm1\\ -1, & \text{for } x=\pm1\end{cases}.$$

Show that $g(x)$ is continuous for all x in the domain.

Sol. $f(x)=\sum_{r=1}^{n}\left(x^{2r}+\frac{1}{x^{2r}}+2\right)=\sum_{r=1}^{n}x^{2r}+\sum_{r=1}^{n}\frac{1}{x^{2r}}+2n$

$$=(x^2+x^4+\ldots+x^{2n})+\left(\frac{1}{x^2}+\frac{1}{x^4}+\ldots+\frac{1}{x^{2n}}\right)+2n$$

$$=\frac{x^2(1-x^{2n})}{(1-x^2)}+\frac{1}{x^2}\frac{\left(1-\frac{1}{x^{2n}}\right)}{1-\frac{1}{x^2}}+2n$$

Thus, $f(x)=\frac{x^2(1-x^{2n})}{1-x^2}+\frac{(1-x^{2n})}{(1-x^2)x^{2n}}+2n$

$$f(x)=\frac{(1-x^{2n})}{1-x^2}+\left(x^2+\frac{1}{x^{2n}}\right)+2n,\ x\neq\pm1$$

$\therefore\ (f(x)-2n)(1-x^2)=(1-x^{2n})\left(x^2+\frac{1}{x^{2n}}\right)$

Now, consider $g(x)=\lim_{n\to\infty}(f(x)-2n)x^{-2n-2}(1-x^2)),$ for $x\neq\pm1$

$$=\lim_{n\to\infty}(1-x^{2n})\left(x^2+\frac{1}{x^{2n}}\right)\cdot\frac{1}{x^{2n+2}},\ x\neq\pm1$$

$$=\lim_{n\to\infty}\frac{(1-x^{2n})(x^{2n+2}+1)}{(x^{2n})(x^{2n+2})}$$

$$=\lim_{n\to\infty}\left(1+\frac{1}{x^{2n}}\right)\left(1+\frac{1}{x^{2n+2}}\right)$$

Now, $g(x)=\begin{cases}-1, & \text{if } |x|>1\\ \text{undefined}, & \text{if } |x|<1\\ -1, & \text{if } x=\pm1\end{cases}$

The domain of $g(x)$ is $x\in(-\infty,-1]\cup[1,\infty)$.

Now, clearly g is continuous for all x in the domain.

Milestone Practice 4.4

1. Discuss the continuity of $f(x)=\begin{cases}[\cos\pi x], & x\leq1\\ |2x-3|[x-2], & x>1\end{cases}$ in the interval $[0,2]$ if $[x]$ is the integer part and $\{x\}$ is the fractional part of x.

2. Consider $f(x)=\frac{\sqrt{1+x}-\sqrt{1-x}}{\{x\}}$, for $x\neq0$,

$g(x)=\cos2x$, for $-\frac{\pi}{4}<x<0$ and

$$h(x)=\begin{cases}\frac{1}{\sqrt2}f(g(x)), & x<0\\ 1, & x=0,\\ f(x), & x>0\end{cases}$$

where $\{x\}$ denotes fractional part function, then which of the following holds good?

(a) h is continuous at $x=0$.

(b) h is discontinuous at $x=0$.

(c) $f(g(x))$ is an even function.

(d) $f(x)$ is an even function.

3. The number of points, where $f(x)=[\sin x+\cos x]$, (where [ ] denotes the greatest integer function), $x\in(0,2\pi)$ is not continuous, is

(a) 3 (b) 4 (c) 5 (d) 6

4. Number of points where $f(x)=\frac{1}{\ln[x^2-3x+3]}$ is discontinuous, is

(a) 2 (b) 4 (c) 6 (d) 0

5. If $f(x)=\frac{2}{2+x}$, the number of points of discontinuity of $f(f(f(x)))$ is

(a) 1 (b) 2 (c) 3 (d) 4

6. If $g(x)=\lim_{m\to\infty}\frac{x^m f(1)+h(x)+1}{2x^m+3x+3}$ and $g(1)=\lim_{x\to1}\log_e(ex)\}^{2/\log_e x}$ and it is assumed that $f(x)$ and $h(x)$ are continuous at $x=1$, then $2g(1)+3f(1)-h(1)$ equals to

(a) $2e^2-1$ (b) $2e^2+1$

(c) $1+2e^2$ (d) $2+e^2$

7. Number of points of discontinuity of the function $f(x)=\lim_{n\to\infty}\frac{2\sin x}{3^n+(2\cos x)^{2n}}$ is given by

(a) 0 (b) 1

(c) infinite (d) None of these

Answer Key

1. continuous on $[0,2]-\left\{0,\frac{1}{2},2\right\}$ 2. (a) 3. (c) 4. (a) 5. (c) 6. (b) 7. (a)

For Detailed Solution

Milestone 5 Differentiability

- Differentiability of Function

The instantaneous rate of change of y (dependent variable) with respect to change in x (independent variable), when change in x tends to zero is known as derivative of y with respect to x and denoted by $\frac{dy}{dx}$ or $f'(x)$ where $y = f(x)$.

The ability of function whose derivative exist at any point is known differentiability of function at that point.

Let Δf denotes the corresponding change of f, then

$\Delta f = f(x + \Delta x) - f(x)$

$$\frac{\Delta f}{\Delta x} = \frac{f(x + \Delta x) - f(x)}{\Delta x}$$

If $\frac{\Delta f}{\Delta x}$ approaches a limit as Δx approaches to zero, this limit is the derivative of f at the point x. The derivative a function f is denoted by symbols such as $f'(x), \frac{df}{dx}$,

$$\frac{d}{dx} f(x) \text{ or } \frac{df(x)}{dx}$$

$$\Rightarrow \quad \frac{df}{dx} = \lim_{\Delta x \to 0} \frac{\Delta f}{\Delta x}$$

$$= \lim_{\Delta x \to 0} \frac{f(x + \Delta x) - f(x)}{\Delta x}$$

The derivative evaluated at a point a is written as

$$f'(a), \left(\frac{df(x)}{dx}\right)_{x=a}, (f'(x))_{x=a} \text{ etc.}$$

(Two fold meaning of derivability)

Geometrical meaning of derivative	**Physical meaning of derivative**
Slope of the tangent drawn to the curve at $x=a$ if it exists	(functions which are differentiable, Instantaneous rate of change of function)

Note "Tangent at a point *A* is the the limiting case of secant through *A*."

4.9 Differentiability of Function

Differentiability of function is discussed in 2 ways.

1. Differentiability at a point
2. Differentiability in an interval

Differentiability of Function at a Point

The derivative of a function $f(x)$ exists at $x = a$, if

$\lim_{x \to a} \frac{f(x) - f(a)}{(x - a)}$ exists finitely.

or $\lim_{x \to a^-} \frac{f(x) - f(a)}{(x - a)} = \lim_{x \to a+} \frac{f(x) - f(a)}{(x - a)}$

or $\lim_{h \to 0} \frac{f(a - h) - f(a)}{-h} = \lim_{h \to 0} \frac{f(a + h) - f(a)}{h}$

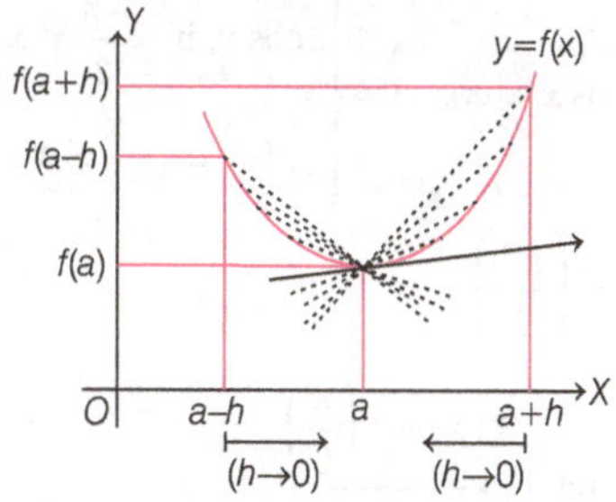

(a) **Right hand derivative** The right hand derivative of $f(x)$ at $x = a$ denoted by $f(a^+)$ is defined as

$f'(a^+) = \lim_{h \to 0} \frac{f(a + h) - f(a)}{h}$, provided the limit exists and is finite $(h > 0)$.

(b) **Left hand derivative** The left hand derivative of $f(x)$ at $x = a$ denoted by $f(a^-)$ is defined as

$f'(a^-) = \lim_{h \to 0} \frac{f(a - h) - f(a)}{-h}$, provided the limit exists and is finite $(h > 0)$. Hence, $f(x)$ is said to be derivable or differentiable at $x = a$.

If $f'(a^+) = f'(a^-)$ = finite quantity and it is denoted by $f'(a)$, where $f'(a) = f'(a^-) = f'(a^+)$ and it is called derivative or differential coefficient of $f(x)$ at $x = a$.

Example 38. Test the differentiability at $x=0$ for the function $f(x)=\begin{cases} x^2, & x<0 \\ \sin x, & x\geq 0 \end{cases}$

Sol. $\text{LHD} = \lim_{h\to 0} \dfrac{f(0)-f(0-h)}{h}$

$= \lim_{h\to 0} \dfrac{\sin(0)-(-h)^2}{h}$

$= \lim_{h\to 0} \dfrac{0-(h)^2}{h}$

$= 0$

and $\text{RHD} = \lim_{h\to 0} \dfrac{\sin(0+h)-\sin(0)}{h}$

$= \lim_{h\to 0} \dfrac{\sinh}{h}$

$= 1$

$\therefore$ LHD $\neq$ RHD

$\Rightarrow f(x)$ is not differentiable at $x=0$

Example 39. Check the differentiability of the function $f(x)=\cos x+|\cos x|$ at $x=\dfrac{\pi}{2}$

Sol. $f(x)=\cos x+|\cos x|$ at $x=\dfrac{\pi}{2}$

We have, $\cos x+|\cos x| = \begin{cases} 2\cos x, \text{ if } & \dfrac{-\pi}{2}<x<\dfrac{\pi}{2} \\ 0, \text{ if } & \dfrac{\pi}{2}\leq x<\dfrac{3\pi}{2} \end{cases}$

$\Rightarrow \text{RHD} = f'\left(\dfrac{\pi^+}{2}\right)$

$= \lim_{\pi\to\frac{\pi^+}{2}} \dfrac{f(x)-f\left(\dfrac{\pi}{2}\right)}{x-\dfrac{\pi}{2}}$

$= \lim_{h\to 0^+} \dfrac{f\left(\dfrac{\pi}{2}+h\right)-f\left(\dfrac{\pi}{2}\right)}{h}$

$= \lim_{h\to 0^+} \dfrac{0-0}{h} = 0$

and $\text{LHD} = f'\left(\dfrac{\pi^-}{2}\right)$

$= \lim_{h\to 0^+} \dfrac{f\left(\dfrac{\pi}{2}-h\right)-f\left(\dfrac{\pi}{2}\right)}{-h}$

$= \dfrac{2\cos\left(\dfrac{\pi}{2}-h\right)-0}{-h} = -2$

JEE Focus Points

- If a function f is derivable at $x=a$, then f is continuous at $x=a$.

Proof

(i) If $f(x)$ is derivable for every point of its domain of definition, then it is continuous in that domain.

The converse of the above result is not true.

For a function f

Differentiability $\Rightarrow$ Continuity;

Continuity $\not\Rightarrow$ Differentiability;

Non differentiability $\not\Rightarrow$ Discontinuous

But discontinuity $\Rightarrow$ Non differentiability

Concept Inside Video

(ii) (a) Let $f'(a^+)=p$ and $f'(a)=q$, where p and q are finite, then

(i) $p=q \Rightarrow f$ is differentiable at $x=a \Rightarrow f$ is continuous at $x=a$

(ii) $p\neq q \Rightarrow f$ is not differentiable at $x=a$.

It is very important to note that f may be still continuous at $x=a$.

(b) If a function f is not differentiable but is continuous at $x=a$ it geometrically implies a sharp corner at $x=a$.

- **How can a function fail to be differentiable** The function $f(x)$ is said to non-differentiable at $x=a$

(a) Both left and right hand derivative exists but are not equal. The function $=|x|$ is not differentiable at 0 as its graph changes direction abrupty when $x=0$. In general, if the graph of a function has a corner or 'kink' in it, then the graph of f has no tangent at this point and f is not differentiable there (To compute $f'(a)$,we find that the left and right limits are different).

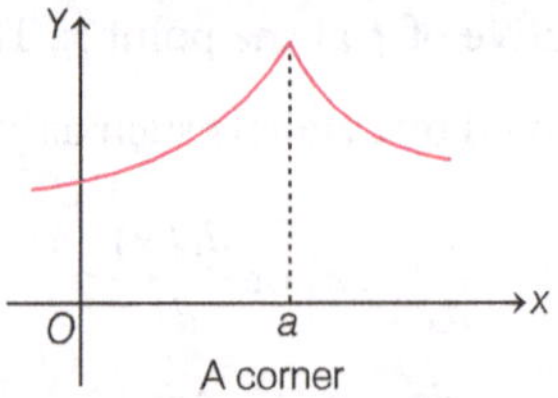

A corner

(b) Function is discontinuous at $x=a$.

If f is not continuous at a, then f is not differentiable at a. So, at any discontinuity (for instance, a jump of discontinuity) f fails to be differentiable.

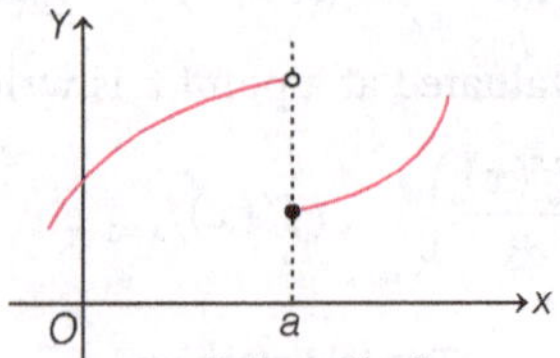

A discontinuity

(c) Either left or right hand derivative or both are not finite. A third possibility is that the curve has a vertical tangent line, when $x=a$, that is f is continuous at a and $\lim_{x\to a} |f'(x)| = \infty$.

This means that the tangents lines becomes steeper and sleeper as $x\to a$..

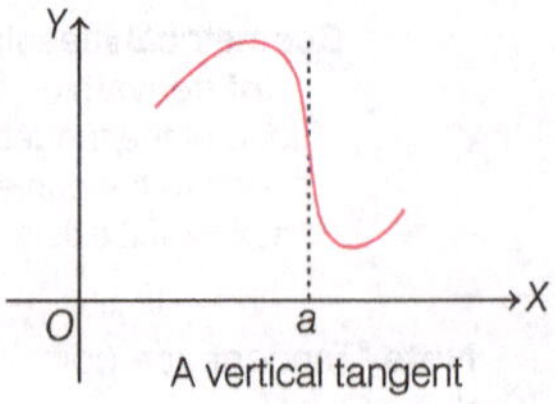

A vertical tangent

Example 40. Check the differentiability at $x=0$. Also, comment on the continuity of $f'(x)$ at $x=0$.

$$f(x)=\begin{cases} x^2\sin\frac{1}{x} & \text{if } x\neq 0 \\ 0 & \text{if } x=0 \end{cases}$$

Sol. $\because \lim_{x\to 0} f(x)=\lim_{x\to 0} x^2\sin\frac{1}{x}=0\times$ (a real number) (oscillating between -1 and 1) $=0=f(0)$

$\therefore f(x)$ is continuous at $x=0$

$$\text{Now, } f'(0^-)=\lim_{h\to 0^+}\frac{-h^2\sin\frac{1}{h}}{-h}=\lim_{h\to 0^+}\left(h\sin\frac{1}{h}\right)=0$$

$$\text{and } f'(0^+)=\lim_{h\to 0^+}\frac{h^2\sin\frac{1}{h}-0}{h}=\lim_{h\to 0^+} h\sin\frac{1}{h}=0$$

$\therefore f(x)$ is differentiable at $x=0$

$$\text{Further, } f'(x)=\begin{cases} -\cos\frac{1}{x}+\left(\sin\frac{1}{x}\right)(2x); & x\neq 0 \\ 0 & ; \quad x=0 \end{cases}$$

$\therefore \lim_{x\to 0} f'(x)=\lim_{x\to 0}\left(2x\sin\frac{1}{x}-\cos\frac{1}{x}\right)$, which does not exist.

$\therefore f'(x)$ is discontinuous at $x=0$.

Example 41. If $f(x)=x\cdot\left(\frac{e^{[x]+|x|}-2}{[x]+|x|}\right)$, $x\neq 0$ and $f(0)=-1$; where $[x]$ denotes greatest integer less than or equal to x. Test the differentiability of $f(x)$ at $x=0$.

$$\textbf{Sol. } \text{Given } f(x)=\begin{cases} x\cdot\left(\frac{e^{[x]+|x|}-2}{[x]+|x|}\right); & x\neq 0 \\ -1\,; & x=0 \end{cases}$$

$$\text{RHD}=\lim_{h\to 0^+}\frac{f(0+h)-f(0)}{h}=\lim_{h\to 0^+}\frac{f(h)+1}{h}$$

$$=\lim_{h\to 0^+}\frac{h\left(\frac{e^{[h]+|h|}-2}{[h]+|h|}\right)+1}{h}=\lim_{h\to 0^+}\frac{\frac{h(e^h-2)}{h}+1}{h}$$

$$=\lim_{h\to 0^+}\frac{e^h-1}{h}=1$$

$$\text{and LHD}=\lim_{h\to 0^+}\frac{f(-h)-f(0)}{-h}$$

$$=\lim_{h\to 0^+}\frac{-h\left(\frac{e^{[-h]+|-h|}-2}{[-h]+|-h|}\right)+1}{-h}=\lim_{h\to 0^+}\frac{-h\left(\frac{e^{-1+h}-2}{-1+h}\right)+1}{-h}$$

$$=\lim_{h\to 0^+}\frac{-he^{-1+h}+2h-1+h}{-h(-1+h)}=\lim_{h\to 0^+}\frac{-he^{-1+h}+3h-1}{-h(-1+h)}$$

which does not exist.

Hence, function is non-differentiable at $x=0$.

JEE SCANNER

Example Similar to PYQ Asked in JEE Main 2021

If $f(x)=\begin{cases} ax^2-b & \text{if } |x|<1 \\ -\frac{1}{|x|} & \text{if } |x|\geq 1 \end{cases}$ *is derivable and continuous at* $x=1$. *Then, the values of a and b are ....*

$$\textbf{Sol. } \text{Given, } f(x)=\begin{cases} ax^2-b & \text{if } |x|<1 \\ -\frac{1}{|x|} & \text{if } |x|\geq 1 \end{cases}$$

$\because f(x)$ is continuous at $x=1$

$$\therefore \quad \lim_{x\to 1} f(x)=f(1)$$

$$\Rightarrow \quad \lim_{x\to 1^-} f(x)=f(1) \Rightarrow \lim_{x\to 1^-} ax^2-b=-1$$

$$\Rightarrow \quad a-b=-1 \qquad \text{...(i)}$$

Also, $f(x)$ is differentiable at $x=1$.

Now, LHD $=f'(1^-)$

$$=\lim_{h\to 0^-}\frac{f(1-h)-f(1)}{-h}=\lim_{h\to 0^-}\frac{a(1-h)^2-b+1}{-h}$$

$$=\lim_{h\to 0^-}\frac{a+ah^2-2ah-b+1}{-h}$$

$$=\lim_{h\to 0^-}\frac{ah^2-2ah}{-h} \qquad [\because a-b=-1 \text{ from Eq. (i)}]$$

$$=\lim_{h\to 0^-}(-ha+2a)=2a$$

$$\text{and RHD } f'(1^+)=\lim_{h\to 0^+}\frac{f(1+h)-f(1)}{h}$$

$$=\lim_{h\to 0^+}\frac{\frac{-1}{|h+1|}+1}{h}=\lim_{h\to 0^+}\frac{\frac{-1+1+h}{1+h}}{h}$$

$$=\lim_{h\to 0^+}\frac{1}{1+h}=1$$

$$\because \quad f'(1^-)=f'(1^+) \Rightarrow 2a=1 \Rightarrow a=\frac{1}{2}$$

$$\Rightarrow \quad b=\frac{3}{2} \qquad [\because a-b=-1]$$

Skill Builder

For Sol.

If $f(x)=\begin{cases} ax^2-b; & |x|<2 \\ -\frac{1}{|x|}; & x\geq 2 \end{cases}$ is derivable and continuous at $x=2$, then the value of $16(a+b)$ is ....

■ **For more practice** See Q.4 of Milestone Practice 4.5.

Example 42. If the function $g(x)$ is differentiable at $x=2$, then find the values of a and b, where $g(x)=\begin{cases} a\sqrt{x+2}, & 0<x<2 \\ bx+2, & 2\le x<5 \end{cases}$.

Sol. Now, LHD $= g'(2^-) = \lim_{h\to 0^-}\dfrac{g(2-h)-g(2)}{-h}$

$$= \lim_{h\to 0^-}\frac{a\sqrt{2-h+2}-2b-2}{-h}$$

$$= \lim_{h\to 0^-}\frac{a\sqrt{4-h}-2b-2}{-h}$$

Above limit is defined if $\lim_{h\to 0} a\sqrt{4-h}-2b-2=0$

$\Rightarrow\ 2a-2b-2=0 \Rightarrow a=b+1$ ...(i)

$\therefore\quad g'(2^-) = \lim_{h\to 0^-}\dfrac{a\sqrt{4-h}-2a}{-h} = \lim_{h\to 0^-}\dfrac{a(2-\sqrt{4-h})}{h}$

$$= \lim_{h\to 0^-}\frac{a}{2+\sqrt{4-h}} = \frac{a}{4} \quad \text{...(ii)}$$

Now, RHD $= g'(2^+) = \lim_{h\to 0^+}\dfrac{f(2+h)-f(2)}{h}$

$$= \lim_{h\to 0^+}\frac{b(2+h)+2-2b-2}{h}$$

$$= \lim_{h\to 0^+}\frac{bh}{h} = b$$

$\because g(x)$ is differentiable at $x=2$

$\Rightarrow\quad g'(2^-)=g'(2^+) \Rightarrow \dfrac{a}{4}=b$

$\Rightarrow\quad a=4b$ ...(iii)

On solving Eqs. (i) and (iii), we get

$$b=\frac{1}{3}, a=\frac{4}{3}$$

Example 43. Let f be differentiable at $x=a$ and let $f(a)\ne 0$. Evaluate $\lim_{n\to\infty}\left\{\dfrac{f(a+1/n)}{f(a)}\right\}^n$

Sol. $\lim_{n\to\infty}\left(\dfrac{f\left(a+\frac{1}{n}\right)}{f(a)}\right)^n = e^{\lim_{n\to\infty}\left(\frac{f\left(a+\frac{1}{n}\right)}{f(a)}-1\right)n}$

$$= e^{\lim_{n\to\infty}\left(\frac{f\left(a+\frac{1}{n}\right)-f(a)}{\left(\frac{1}{n}\right)}\right)\cdot\frac{1}{f(a)}} = e^{\frac{f'(a)}{f(a)}}$$

Example 44. If $f(x)=\begin{cases} x^m\cdot\sin\left(\dfrac{1}{x}\right) & \text{if } x\ne 0 \\ 0 \text{ if } & x=0 \end{cases}$ is continuous but not differentiable at $x=0$, then find m.

Sol. $f(x)=\begin{cases} x^m\sin\left(\dfrac{1}{x}\right), & x\ne 0 \\ 0, & x=0 \end{cases}$

For continuity at $x=0$

$$\lim_{h\to 0} f(0+h)=f(0)$$

$\Rightarrow\quad \lim_{h\to 0} h^m\sin\left(\dfrac{1}{h}\right)=0$

$\Rightarrow\quad m>0$

For function to be not differentiable at $x=0$

$$\lim_{h\to 0}\frac{f(0+h)-f(0)}{h} = \text{Does not exist}$$

$$\lim_{h\to 0}\frac{h^m\sin\left(\frac{1}{h}\right)-0}{h} = \lim_{h\to 0} h^{m-1}\sin\left(\frac{1}{h}\right) = \text{Does not exist}$$

$\Rightarrow\quad m-1\le 0 \Rightarrow m\le 1$

$\therefore\quad m\in[0,1]$ for function $f(x)$ to be continuous and not differentiable at $x=0$.

Differentiability by Differentiation

Short trick to check differentiability

***Step* 1** First of all check continuity at $x=a$ by calculating $f(a), f(a^-), f(a^+)$

***Step* 2** If it is continuous, then differentiate $f(x)$ i.e. $f'(x)$.

***Step* 3** Calculate $f'(a^-)$ and $f'(a^+)$

If $f'(a^-)=f'(a^+)=$ finite number, then $f(x)$ is differentiable at $x=a$.

Example 45. $f(x)=\begin{cases} 4x^3+5x+7 & x<0 \\ x^2-8x+7 & x\ge 0 \end{cases}$

Check the differentiability at $x=0$.

Sol. Using time saving trick

$$f(0=7$$
$$f(0^+)=7$$
$$f(0^-)=7$$

$\because\quad f(0)=f(0^+)=f(0^-)=7$

$\therefore f(x)$ is continuous at $x=7$

Now, differentiate $f(x)$ w.r.t. x, we get

$$f'(x)=\begin{cases} 12x^2+5 & x<0 \\ 2x-8 & x>0 \end{cases}$$

$$f'(0^-)=12(0)+5=5$$
$$f'(0^+)=-8$$

$\because\quad f'(0^-)\ne f'(0^+)$

$\therefore f(x)$ is not differentiable at $x=0$.

Milestone Practice 4.5

1. Draw the graph of the function and discuss the continuity and differentiability at $x=1$ for

$$f(x)=\begin{cases}3^x, & \text{when } -1\le x\le 1\\ 4-x, & \text{when } 1<x<4\end{cases}$$

2. Let $f(x)=\begin{cases} x\exp\left[-\left(\dfrac{1}{|x|}+\dfrac{1}{x}\right)\right], & x\neq 0\\ 0, & x=0\end{cases}$

Test whether

(i) $f(x)$ is continuous at $x=0$

(ii) $f(x)$ is differentiable at $x=0$

3. If $f(x)=\dfrac{xe^{1/x}}{1+e^{1/x}}, x\neq 0$, $f(0)=0$, examine the continuity and differentiability at $x=0$.

4. A function f is defined as,

$$f(x)=\begin{cases}\dfrac{1}{|x|} & \text{if } |x|\ge \dfrac{1}{2}\\ a+bx^2 & \text{if } |x|<\dfrac{1}{2}\end{cases}$$

If $f(x)$ is derivable at $x=\dfrac{1}{2}$ find the values of a and b.

5. If $f(x)=|x-1|.([x]-[-x])$, then find $f'(1^+)$ and $f'(1^-)$, where $[x]$ denotes greatest integer function. Also discuss the differentiability of $f(x)$ at $x=1$.

6. Find the values of a, b and c, if $f(x)=a|\sin x|+be^{|x|}+c|x|^3$ is differentiable at $x=0$.

7. Prove that $f(x)=\dfrac{x}{1+|x|^n}$ is differentiable at $x=0$ for all $n\in[0,\infty)$.

8. The function $f(x)=|2x-3|\,[x], x\ge 1$; and $f(x)=\sin\dfrac{\pi x}{2}, x<1$, ([] denotes the greatest integer function)

(a) is continuous at $x=2$

(b) is differentiable at $x=2$

(c) continuous and differentiable at $x=1$

(d) is continuous but not differentiable at $x=\dfrac{3}{2}$

9. Let the function f, g and h be defined as follows

$$f(x)=\begin{cases}x\sin\left(\dfrac{1}{x}\right) & \text{for } -1\le x\le 1 \text{ and } x\neq 0\\ 0 & \text{for } x=0\end{cases}$$

$$g(x)=\begin{cases}x^2\sin\left(\dfrac{1}{x}\right) & \text{for } -1\le x\le 1 \text{ and } x\neq 0\\ 0 & \text{for } x=0\end{cases}$$

$h(x)=|x|^3$ for $-1\le x\le 1$.

Which of these functions are differentiable at $x=0$?

(a) f and g only

(b) f and h only

(c) g and h only

(d) None of the above

10. If the function $f(x)=\begin{cases}k_1(x-\pi)^2-1, & x\le\pi\\ k_2\cos x, & x>\pi\end{cases}$ is twice differentiable, then the ordered pair (k_1, k_2) is equal to

(a) (1, 1) (b) $\left(\dfrac{1}{2},1\right)$

(c) (1, 0) (d) $\left(\dfrac{1}{2},-1\right)$

Answer Key

1. Continuous but not differentiable **2.** (i) Yes (ii) No **3.** Not continuous, not differentiable

4. $a=3, b=-4$ **5.** $f'(1^-)=-1, f'(1^+)=3$, not differentiable

6. $a+b=0, c\in R$ **8.** (d) **9.** (c) **10.** (b)

For Detailed Solution

Milestone 6 Differentiability Over an Interval

- Algebra of Differentiability

We will discuss it in two ways

1. Differentiability Over an Open Interval

A function $f(x)$ is said to be differentiable in an open interval (a, b) if it is differentiable at all interior points in (a, b).

e.g. $f(x) = |x-1|$ is differentiable in $(0, 1)$.

$y = \sin^{-1} x$ is differentiable in $(-1, 1)$.

2. Differentiability Over a Closed Interval

A function $f(x)$ is said to be differentiable in a closed interval $[a, b]$, if

(i) it is differentiable at all interior points in (a, b).

(ii) RHD $= f'(a^+)$ exists at the left end point a.

(iii) LHD $= f'(a-)$ exists at the right end point b.

e.g. $f(x) = x^{3/2}$ is differentiable in $[0, 1]$.

$f(x) = \sin x$ is differentiable in $[0, 2\pi]$.

JEE Focus Points

- All polynomial, exponential, logarithmic and trigonometric functions (inverse trigonometric not included) are differentiable at each point in their domain.
- Modulus function and signum function are non-differentiable at $x = 0$. Hence, $y = |f(x)|$ and $y = \text{sgn}(f(x))$ should be checked at points, where $f(x) = 0$.
- The inverse trigonometric functions $y = \sin^{-1} x, \cos^{-1} x$, $\text{cosec}^{-1} x$ and $\sec^{-1} x$ are not differentiable at the points $x = \pm 1$. Hence, $y = \sin^{-1}(f(x)), \cos^{-1}(f(x)), \text{cosec}^{-1}(f(x))$ and $\sec^{-1}(f(x))$ should be checked at points, where $f(x) = \pm 1$.
- Greatest integer function and fractional part functions are non-differentiable at all integral x. Hence, $y = [f(x)]$ and $y = \{f(x)\}$ should be checked at points, where $f(x) = n, n \in I$.
- Further, a function should be checked at all those points where discontinuity may arise.
- The points where function is not differentiable are known as points of non-differentiability.

Example 46. Discuss of differentiability of $f(x) = x|x|$.

Sol. $f(x) = \begin{cases} x^2, & x \ge 0 \\ -x^2, & x < 0 \end{cases}$

Now, $f'(x) = \begin{cases} 2x, & x > 0 \\ -2x, & x < 0 \end{cases}$

Now, $f'(0^+) = f'(0^-) = 0$

Also, $f(0^+) = f(0^-) = 0$

Thus, $f(x)$ is differentiable at each real number.

Thus, R is the domain of differentiability of given function.

Example 47. Let $f(x) = \begin{cases} \left\{x + \frac{1}{3}\right\}[\sin \pi x], & 0 \le x < 2 \\ [2x]\,\text{sgn}\left(x - \frac{4}{3}\right), & 1 \le x \le 2 \end{cases}$

where $[\cdot]$ and $\{\cdot\}$ denote the greatest integer function and fractional part function respectively. Find the points at which continuity and differentiability should be checked. Also, check the continuity and differentiability of $f(x)$ at $x = 1$.

Sol. $f(x) = \begin{cases} \left\{x + \frac{1}{3}\right\}[\sin \pi x], & 0 \le x < 1 \\ [2x]\,\text{sgn}\left(x - \frac{4}{3}\right), & 1 \le x \le 2 \end{cases}$

The suspicious points for continuity and differentiability are obtained when

(i) $x + \frac{1}{3}$ becomes an integer for $0 \le x < 1$

$\Rightarrow \quad x = \frac{2}{3}$

(ii) $\sin \pi x$ becomes an integer for $0 \le x < 1$

$\Rightarrow \quad x = 0, \frac{1}{2}$

(iii) The point of change in definition is $x = 1$

(iv) $2x$ becomes an integer for $1 \le x \le 2$

$\Rightarrow \quad x = 1, \frac{3}{2}, 2$

(v) $x-\frac{4}{3}$ becomes zero for $1\leq x\leq 2 \Rightarrow x=\frac{4}{3}$

(vi) The end points of closed domain [0, 2].

$$x=0,2$$

Hence, the points where we should check the continuity and differentiability are

$$x=0,\frac{1}{2},\frac{2}{3},1,\frac{4}{3},\frac{3}{2},2$$

We check continuity at $x=1$

$$\lim_{x\to 1^-} f(x)=\lim_{x\to 1}\left\{x+\frac{1}{3}\right\}[\sin \pi x]=0$$

$$\lim_{x\to 1^+} f(x)=\lim_{x\to 1}[2x]\operatorname{sgn}\left(x-\frac{4}{3}\right)=2\{-1\}=-2$$

Since, LHL $\neq$ RHL.

$f(x)$ is discontinuous at $x=1$

and hence, it is non-differentiable at $x=1$.

Example 48. Check differentiability of $f(x)$ in $[-2,2]$, if $f(x)=\begin{cases}\cos\frac{\pi}{2}(|x|-\{x\}), & x<1\\ \sqrt{4x^2-12x+9\{x\}}, & x\geq 1\end{cases}$, where {·} denotes the fractional part function.

Sol. We have, $f(x)=\begin{cases}\cos\frac{\pi}{2}(|x|-\{x\}), & x<1\\ \sqrt{4x^2-12x+9\{x\}}, & x\geq 1\end{cases}$

i.e. $f(x)=\begin{cases}\cos\frac{\pi}{2}(|x|-\{x\}), & x<1\\ |2x-3|\{x\}, & x\geq 1\end{cases}$

Now, we have $|x|-\{x\}=|x|-x+[x]$

$$=\begin{cases}-2x-2, & -2\leq x<-1\\ -2x-1, & -1\leq x<0\\ 0, & 0\leq x<1\end{cases}$$

and $|2x-3|\{x\}=|2x-3|(x-[x])$

$$=\begin{cases}(3-2x)(x-1), & 1\leq x<3/2\\ (2x-3)(x-1), & 3/2\leq x<2\\ 0, & x=2\end{cases}$$

Thus, $f(x)=\begin{cases}\cos\frac{\pi}{2}(2x+2), & -2\leq x<-1\\ \cos\frac{\pi}{2}(2x+1), & -1\leq x<0\\ \cos 0, & 0\leq x<1\\ (3-2x)(x-1), & 1\leq x<\frac{3}{2}\\ (2x-3)(x-1), & \frac{3}{2}\leq x<2\\ 0, & x=2\end{cases}$

We need to check differentiability of $f(x)$ at $x=-2,-1,0,1,\frac{3}{2},2$. We first check continuity.

At $x=2$, we get

$$f(2)=0 \text{ and } f(2^-)=(2\times 2-3)(2-1)=1$$

Discontinuity at $x=2$.

At $x=\frac{3}{2}$, we get

$$f\left(\frac{3^+}{2}\right)=f\left(\frac{3}{2}\right)=0$$

and $$f\left(\frac{3^-}{2}\right)=\left(3-2\times\frac{3}{2}\right)\left(\frac{3}{2}-1\right)=0$$

$\Rightarrow$ Continuity at $x=\frac{3}{2}$.

At $x=1$, we get $f(1^+)=f(1)=0$ and $f(1^-)=\cos 0=1$

Discontinuity at $x=1$.

At $x=0$, we get

$$f(0^+)=f(0)=\cos 0=1 \text{ and } f(0^-)=\cos\frac{\pi}{2}=0$$

Discontinuity at $x=0$.

At $x=-1$, we get

$$f(-1^+)=f(-1)=\cos\frac{\pi}{2}=0$$

and $$f(-1^-)=\cos 0=1$$

Discontinuity at $x=-1$.

At $x=-2$, we get

$$f(-2^+)=f(-2)$$

Continuity at $x=-2$.

At $x=-2$, we get

$$f(-2^+)=f(-2)$$

$\Rightarrow$ Continuity at $x=-2$.

Hence, we need to check differentiability only at

$$x=-2,\frac{3}{2}$$

At $x=-2$ which is the left end point, we have

$$f'(-2^+)=\lim_{h\to 0}\frac{f(-2+h)-f(-2)}{h}$$

$$=\lim_{h\to 0}\frac{\cos\frac{\pi}{2}(-4+2h+2)-\cos\frac{\pi}{2}(-4+2)}{h}$$

$$=\lim_{h\to 0}\frac{\cos\pi(1-h)+1}{h}=\lim_{h\to 0}\frac{\pi\sin(\pi-\pi h)}{1}=0$$

$\Rightarrow f$ is differentiable at $x=-2$.

At $x=\frac{3}{2}$, we get

$$f'\left(\frac{3^+}{2}\right)=\lim_{h\to 0}\frac{f\left(\frac{3}{2}+h\right)-f\left(\frac{3}{2}\right)}{h}$$

$$= \lim_{h \to 0} \frac{2h\left(\frac{3}{2}+h-1\right)-0}{h} = 1$$

$$f'\left(\frac{3^-}{2}\right) = \lim_{h \to 0} \frac{f\left(\frac{3}{2}\right)-f\left(\frac{3}{2}-h\right)}{h}$$

$$= \lim_{h \to 0} \frac{0-2h\left(\frac{3}{2}-h-1\right)}{h} = -1$$

Non-differentiable at $x = \frac{3}{2}$

Hence, f is differentiable on $[-2, 2]$ except at

$$x = -1, 0, 1, \frac{3}{2}, 2$$

Example 49. If $x + 4|y| = 6y$, then find whether y as a function of x is continuous and derivable or not.

Sol. We have, $x + 4|y| = 6y$

$$\Rightarrow \quad y = f(x) = \begin{cases} \frac{1}{2}x, & x \geq 0 \\ \frac{1}{10}x, & x < 0 \end{cases}$$

$$\lim_{h \to 0} f(x) = \lim_{h \to 0} f(0+h) = \lim_{h \to 0} \frac{1}{2}h = 0$$

$$\lim_{x \to 0} f(x) = \lim_{h \to 0} f(0-h) = \lim_{h \to 0} \frac{1}{10}(0-h) = 0$$

$\Rightarrow f$ is continuous at $x = 0$ and hence for all $x \in R$.

$$f'(0^+) = \lim_{h \to 0} \frac{f(0+h)-f(0)}{h} = \lim_{h \to 0} \frac{\frac{h}{2}-0}{h} = \frac{1}{2}$$

$$f'(0^-) = \lim_{h \to 0} \frac{f(0-h)-f(0)}{-h} = \lim_{h \to 0} \frac{-\frac{h}{10}-0}{-h} = \frac{1}{10}$$

$\therefore f$ is not derivable at $x = 0$.

$\Rightarrow f$ is derivable at all x except $x = 0$.

Example 50. $f(x) = \begin{cases} |1-4x^2|, & 0 \leq x < 1 \\ [x^2-2x], & 1 \leq x \leq 2 \end{cases}$ check differentiability in (0, 2), where [ ] denotes greatest integer function.

Sol. $f(x) = \begin{cases} |1-4x^2|, & 0 \leq x < 1 \\ [x^2-2x], & 1 \leq x \leq 2 \end{cases}$

$$f(x) = \begin{cases} 1-4x^2, & 0 \leq x \leq \frac{1}{2} \\ 4x^2-1, & \frac{1}{2} \leq x < 1 \\ 1, & 1 \leq x < 2 \\ 0, & x = 2 \end{cases}$$

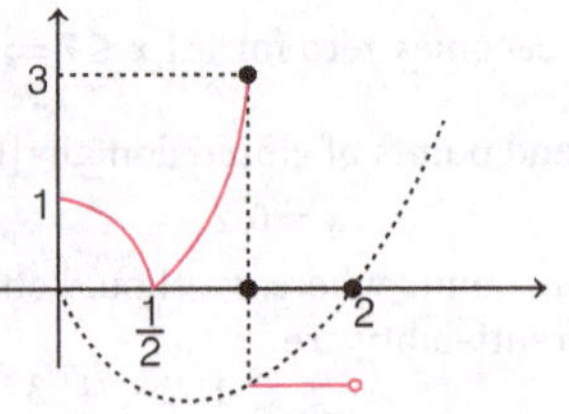

$f(x)$ is not differentiable at $x = \frac{1}{2}$ in $x \in (0, 2)$

JEE SCANNER

Example Similar to PYQ Asked in JEE Main 2020

If $f(x) = \max\{\sin^{-1}|\sin x|, \cos^{-1}|\sin x|\}$, then number of points is ...., where $f(x)$ is not differentiable, where $x \in \left[0, \frac{7\pi}{6}\right]$.

Sol. (5) $\sin^{-1}|\sin x|$ is periodic with period π.

$$\Rightarrow \quad \sin^{-1}|\sin x| = \begin{cases} x, & n\pi \leq x \leq n\pi + \frac{\pi}{2} \\ \pi - x, & n\pi + \frac{\pi}{2} \leq x \leq n\pi + \pi \end{cases}$$

Also, $\cos^{-1}|\sin x| = \frac{\pi}{2} - \sin^{-1}|\sin x|$

$$\Rightarrow f(x) = \max \begin{cases} \left\{x, \frac{\pi}{2} - x\right\}, & n\pi \leq x \leq n\pi + \frac{\pi}{2} \\ \left\{\pi - x, x - \frac{\pi}{2}\right\}, & n\pi + \frac{\pi}{2} \leq x \leq n\pi + \pi \end{cases}$$

$$\Rightarrow f(x) = \begin{cases} \frac{\pi}{2} - x, & n\pi \leq x \leq n\pi + \frac{\pi}{4} \\ x, & n\pi + \frac{\pi}{4} < n\pi + \frac{\pi}{2} \\ \pi - x, & n\pi + \frac{\pi}{2} < x \leq n\pi + \frac{3\pi}{4} \\ x - \frac{\pi}{2}, & n\pi + \frac{3\pi}{4} < x \leq n\pi + \pi \end{cases}$$

$\Rightarrow f(x)$ is not differentiable at

$$x = 0, \frac{\pi}{4}, \frac{\pi}{2}, \frac{3\pi}{4}, \pi \ldots$$

$\Rightarrow f(x)$ is not differentiable at $x = \frac{n\pi}{4}$

$\therefore$ Number of points of non-differentiable = 5

Skill Builder

If $f(x) = \max\{|\tan x|, \cos|x|\}$, then the number of non-differentiable points in the interval $(-\pi, \pi)$ is ....

For Sol.

■ **For more practice** See Q.3 of Milestone Practice 4.6.

Example 51. If $f(x)=\min\{|x|,|x-2|,2-|x-1|\}$, then draw the graph of $f(x)$ and also discuss its continuity and differentiability.

Sol. $f(x)=\min\{|x|,|x-2|,2-|x-1|\}$

We compare the graphs of

$$y=|x|,$$
$$y=|x-2|$$
and $$y=2-|x-1|$$

and choose the least value at each x.

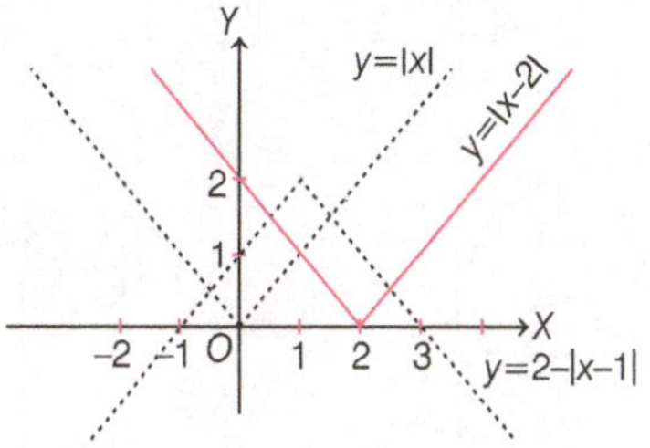

Graph of $y=\min\{|x|,|x-2|,2-|x-1|\}$

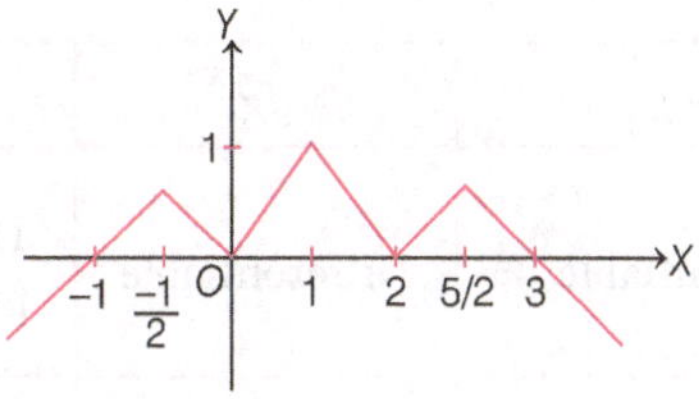

It is clear from the figure that $f(x)$ is continuous $\forall\, x\in R$ and non-differentiable at $x=-\frac{1}{2}, 0, 1, 2, \frac{5}{2}$.

Example 52. Find the number of points at which the function $f(x)=\begin{cases}\max(|x|,x^2), & \text{if } -\infty<x<1\\ \min(2x-1,x^2), & \text{if } x\geq 1\end{cases}$ is not derivable.

Sol. $f(x)=\begin{cases}\max\{|x|,x^2\}, & x<1\\ \min(2x-1,x^2), & x\geq 1\end{cases}$

$\Rightarrow f(x)$ is not differentiable at $x=\pm 1$.

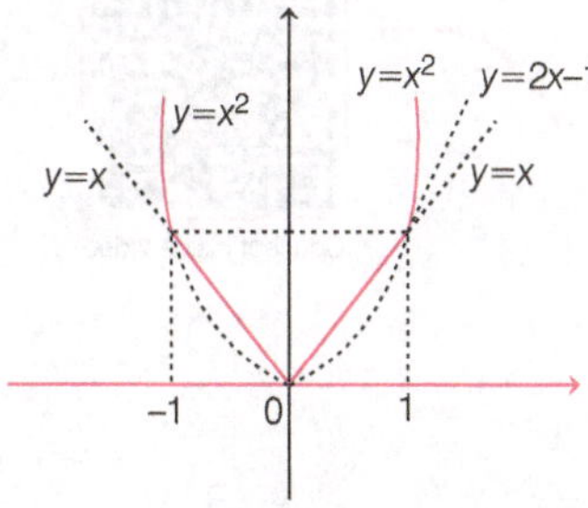

Example 53. Find the interval of values of k for which the function $f(x)=|x^2+(k-1)|x|-k|$ is non-differentiable at five points.

Sol. $f(x)=|x^2+(k-1)|x|-k|=|(|x|-1)(|x|+k)|$

Also, $f(x)$ is an even function and $f(x)$ is not differentiable at five points. So, $|(x-1)(x+k)|$ is non-differentiable for two positive values of x.

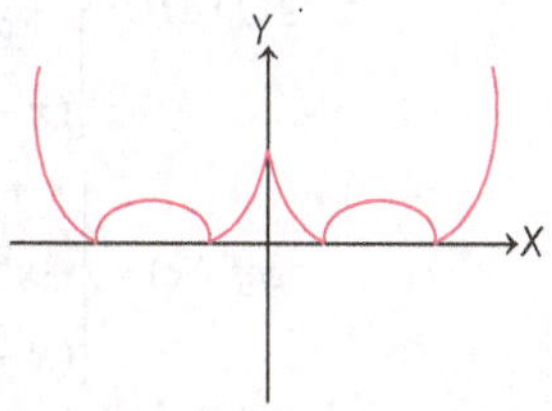

$\Rightarrow$ Both the roots of $(x-1)(x+k)=0$ are positive.

$$\Rightarrow \qquad k<0 \Rightarrow k\in(-\infty,0)$$

Example 54. $f(x)=\begin{cases}x+a, & \text{if } x<0\\ |x-1|, & \text{if } x\geq 0\end{cases}$ and

$g(x)=\begin{cases}x+1, & \text{if } x<0\\ (x-1)^2+b, & \text{if } x\geq 0\end{cases}$, where a and b are non-negative real numbers if gof is differentiable at $x=0$, then

(a) $a^2+b^2=2$ (b) $a^2+b^2=1$
(c) $a^2+b^2=3$ (d) None of these

Sol. (b) $f(x)=\begin{cases}x+a, & \text{if } x<0\\ |x-1|, & \text{if } x\geq 0\end{cases}$

$$\Rightarrow \quad f(x)=\begin{cases}x+a, & \text{if } x<0\\ (x-1), & \text{if } 0\leq x<1\\ (x-1), & \text{if } 1\leq x<\infty\end{cases}$$

$$g(x)=\begin{cases}x+1, & \text{if } x<0\\ (x-1)^2+b, & \text{if } x\geq 0\end{cases}$$

$$g(f(x))=\begin{cases}f(x)+1, & \text{if } f(x)<0\\ (f(x)-1)^2+b, & \text{if } f(x)\geq 0\end{cases}$$

So, $g(f(x))=x+a+1$ if $x+a<0$ and $x<0$

$x<-a$

$=-x+1+1$ if $-x+1<0$

and $0\leq x<1$

$\Rightarrow 1\leq x\leq\infty$

$$g(f(x))=\begin{cases}x+a+1 & \text{if } -\infty<x<-a & \text{...(i)}\\ (x+a-1)^2+b & \text{if } -a\leq x<0 & \text{...(ii)}\\ x^2+b & \text{if } 0\leq x<1 & \text{...(iii)}\\ (x-2)^2+b & \text{if } 1\leq x\leq\infty & \text{...(iv)}\end{cases}$$

$g(f(x))$ is continuous every where so it must be continuous at $x = -a, 0, 1$

From Eqs. (i) and (ii), checking continuity at $x = -a$

$$1 = 1 + b \Rightarrow b = 0$$

Similarly, checking continuity at $x = 0$

$$(0 + a - 1)^2 + b = 0 + b \Rightarrow a = 1$$

$$g(f(x)) = \begin{cases} x+2, & \infty < x < -1 \\ x^2, & -1 \le x < 0 \\ x^2, & 0 \le x < 1 \\ (x-2)^2, & 1 \le x < \infty \end{cases}$$

$$\Rightarrow \quad gof\,(x) = \begin{cases} x+2, & x < -1 \\ -x^2, & -1 \le x < 1 \\ (x-2)^2, & x \ge 1 \end{cases}$$

$\therefore$ $gof(x)$ is differentiable at $x = 0$.

$$\therefore \quad a^2 + b^2 = 0 + 1 = 1$$

4.10 Algebra of Differentiability

Let $f(x)$ and $g(x)$ be two functions

Case	$f+g$	$f-g$	fg	f/g
1. Both are differentiable e.g. $f(x) =$ differentiable and $g(x) =$ differentiable	Differentiable	Differentiable	Differentiable	Differentiable provided $g \ne 0$
2. One differentiable and other non-differentiable e.g. $f(x) =$ differentiable and $g(x) =$ non-differentiable	Non-differentiable	Non-differentiable	Cannot say	Cannot say
3. Both non-differentiable e.g. $f(x) =$ Non-differentiable and $g(x) =$ Non-differentiable	Cannot say	Cannot say	Cannot say	Cannot say

Cannot say means 'may be differentiable or non-differentiable'.

JEE Focus Points

- If $f(x)$ is derivable at $x = a$ and $f(a) = 0$ and $g(x)$ is continuous at $x = a$, then the product function $F(x) = f(x) \cdot g(x)$ will be derivable at $x = a$

$$F'(a^+) = \lim_{h \to 0} \frac{f(a+h)g(a+h) - 0}{h} = f'(a) \cdot g(a)$$

$$F'(a^-) = \lim_{h \to 0} \frac{f(a-h)g(a-h) - 0}{-h} = f'(a) \cdot g(a)$$

Concept Inside Video

- Derivative of a continuous function need not be a continuous function

$$f(x) = \begin{cases} x^2 \sin\frac{1}{x}, & \text{if } x \ne 0 \quad f'(0^+) = 0 \\ 0, & \text{if } x = 0, \quad f'(0^-) = 0 \end{cases}$$

$$f'(x) = \begin{cases} \sin\frac{1}{x} \cdot 2x - x^2 \cos\frac{1}{x}\left(\frac{-1}{x^2}\right), & \text{if } x \ne 0 \\ 0, & \text{if } x = 0 \end{cases}$$

$f'(x)$ is not continuous at $x = 0$. (Refer Example 40)

JEE SCANNER

Example Similar to PYQ Asked in JEE Main 2019

Let $f(x)$ be defined in the interval $[-2, 2]$ such that

$f(x)=\begin{cases}-1; & -2\le x\le 0\\ x-1; & 0<x\le 2\end{cases}$ and $g(x)=f(|x|+|f(x)|)$, then

in interval $(-2, 2)$ $g(x)$ is

(a) differentiable at all points

(b) not continuous

(c) not differentiable at 2 points

(d) None of the above

Sol. (c) $f(x)=\begin{cases}-1, & -2\le x\le 0\\ x-1, & 0<x\le 2\end{cases}$,

$$f(|x|)=\begin{cases}-1, & -2\le |x|\le 0\\ |x|-1, & 0<|x|\le 2\end{cases}$$

and $|f(x)|=\begin{cases}|-1|, & -2\le x\le 0\\ |x-1|, & 0<x\le 2\end{cases}$

$\therefore\quad f(|x|)=\begin{cases}-1, & \text{for } -2\le x\le 0\\ |x|-1, & \text{for } 0<|x|\le 2\end{cases}$

and $|f(x)|=\begin{cases}1, & -2\le x\le 0\\ |x-1|, & 0<x\le 2\end{cases}$

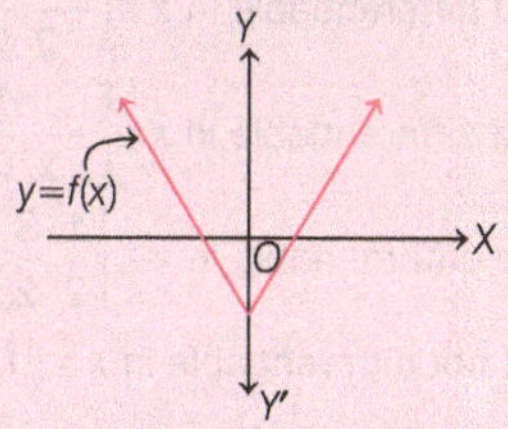

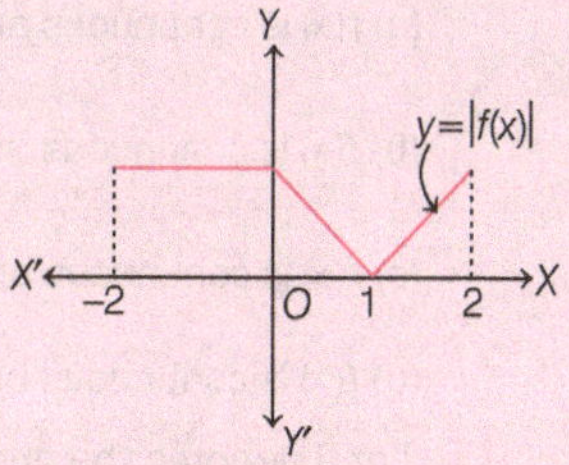

Thus, $y=f(|x|)=\begin{cases}-x-1; & -2\le x<0\\ -1; & x=0\\ x-1; & 0<x\le 2\end{cases}$

and $|f(x)|=\begin{cases}1; & -2<x\le 0\\ -x+1; & 0<x<1\\ x-1; & 1<x\le 2\end{cases}$

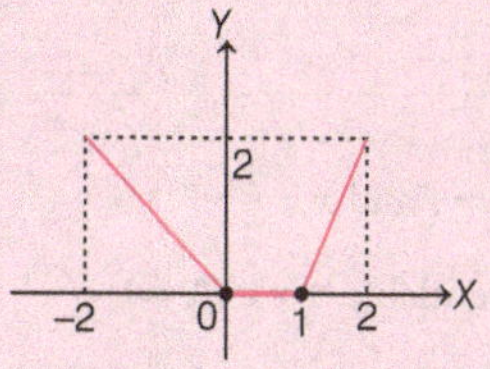

Also, $g(x)=f(|x|)+|f(x)|$

$$=\begin{cases}-x-1+1; & -2\le x\le 0\\ x-1-x+1; & 0<x<1\\ x-1+x-1; & 1\le x\le 2\end{cases}=\begin{cases}-x; & -2\le x\le 0\\ 0; & 0<x<1\\ 2x-2; & 1\le x\le 2\end{cases}$$

$\therefore g(x)$ is non-differentiable at $x=0, 1$.

Skill builder

Let $f(x)$ defined in the interval $[-1, 1]$ such that

$f(x)=\begin{cases}1; & -1\le x<0\\ x-1; & 0\le x\le 1\end{cases}$ and $g(x)=f(|x|)+|f(x)|$, then

$g(x)$ is

(a) continuous at $x=0$ and differentiable at $x=0$

(b) discontinuous at $x=0$

(c) non-differentiable at $x=0$

(d) differentiable at $x=0$

For Sol.

■ **For more practice** See Q.8 of Milestone Practice 4.6.

Example 55. If $f(x)=[x^{-2}[x^2]]$, (where $[\cdot]$ denotes the greatest integer function) $x\ne 0$, then incorrect statement, is/are

(a) $f(x)$ is continuous everywhere

(b) $f(x)$ is discontinuous at $x=\sqrt{2}$

(c) $f(x)$ is non-differentiable at $x=1$

(d) $f(x)$ is discontinuous at infinitely many points

Sol. (b, c, d) Here, $0\le [x^2]\le x^2 \Rightarrow 0\le x^{-2}[x^2]\le 1$

$$\Rightarrow\qquad [x^{-2}[x^2]]=0 \text{ or } 1$$

$f(x)$ is discontinuous at $x^2=n, n\in N \Rightarrow x=\sqrt{n}$

$\therefore f(x)$ is neither continuous nor differentiable at $x=\sqrt{n}$, $n\in N$.

Example 56. If $f(x)=\begin{cases}x^2(\text{sgn}[x])+\{x\}, & 0\le x\le 2\\ \sin x+|x-3|, & 2\le x\le 4\end{cases}$,

where [] and { } represents greatest integer and fractional part function respectively, then

(a) $f(x)$ is differentiable at $x=1$

(b) $f(x)$ is continuous but non-differentiable at $x=2$

(c) $f(x)$ is non-differentiable at $x=2$

(d) $f(x)$ is discontinuous at $x=2$

Sol. (c, d) For continuity at $x=1$

$$\lim_{x\to 1^+} f(x)=\lim_{x\to 1^+} x^2\,\text{sgn}[x]+\{x\}=1+0=1$$

$$\lim_{x\to 1^-} f(x)=\lim_{x\to 1^-} x^2\,\text{sgn}[x]+\{x\}=0+1=1$$

Also, $\quad f(1)=1$

$\therefore f(x)$ is continuous at $x=1$

$$f(x)=\begin{cases}x, & 0\le x<1\\ x^2+x-1, & 1\le x<2\end{cases},$$

non-differentiable at $x=1$

$$\lim_{x\to 2^-} f(x)=\lim_{x\to 2^-} x^2\,\text{sgn}[x]+\{x\}=4\times 1+1=5$$

$$\lim_{x\to 2^+} f(x)=\lim_{x\to 2^+} \sin x+|x-3|=1+\sin 2$$

Thus, $f(x)$ is neither continuous nor differentiable at $x=2$.

Milestone Practice 4.6

1. Discuss the differentiability of the function $f(x)=(x^2-1)|x^2-3x+2|+\cos(|x|)$.

2. If $f(x)=\begin{cases}|1-4x^2|; & 0\le x<1\\ [x^2-2x]; & 1\le x<2\end{cases}$, then discuss the differentiability of f in (0, 2). Here, [] denotes the greatest integer function.

3. The total number of points of non-differentiability of $f(x)=\max\left\{\sin^2 x, \cos^2 x, \frac{3}{4}\right\}$ in $[0, 10\pi]$, is

(a) 40 (b) 30

(c) 20 (d) 10

4. Let $f(x)=\sin x$,

$$g(x)=\begin{cases}\{\max.(f(t)),\ 0\le t\le x\} & \text{for } 0\le x\le\pi\\ (1-\cos x)/2 & \text{for } x>\pi\end{cases}$$

Discuss the continuity and differentiability of $g(x)$ in $(0, \infty)$.

5. Let $f(x)=\begin{cases}-1, & \text{if } -2\le x\le 0\\ |x-1|, & \text{if } 0<x\le 2\end{cases}$ and $g(x)=\int_{-2}^{x} f(t)\,dt$. Test the continuity and differentiability of $g(x)$ in $(-2, 2)$.

6. If $f(x)=\begin{cases}\dfrac{\sin[x^2]\pi}{x^2-3x+8}+ax^3+b, & 0\le x\le 1\\ 2\cos\pi x+\tan^{-1}x, & 1<x\le 2\end{cases}$ is differentiable in [0, 2], find a and b. Here, [x] stands for the greatest integer function.

7. Let $f(x)=x^3-9x^2+15x+6$ and $g(x)=\begin{cases}\min\{f(t);\ 0\le t\le x\}, & 0\le x\le 6\\ x-18, & x>6\end{cases}$. Then, drawn the graph of $g(x)$ and discuss its continuity and differentiability.

8. Let $f(x)$ be defined in the interval $[-2, 2]$ such that $f(x)=\begin{cases}1, & -2\le x<0\\ x+1, & 0\le x\le 2\end{cases}$ and $g(x)=f(|x|)+|f(x)|$.

Test the differentiability of $g(x)$ in $[-2, 2]$.

9. Let $f(x)=\phi(x)+\psi(x)$ and $\phi'(a)$, $\psi'(a)$ are finite and definite. Then,

(a) $f(x)$ is continuous at $x=a$

(b) $f(x)$ is differentiable at $x=a$

(c) $f'(x)$ is continuous at $x=a$

(d) $f'(x)$ is differentiable at $x=a$

10. A real valued function $f(x)$ is given as

$$f(x)=\begin{cases}\int_0^x 2\{x\}\,dx, & x+\{x\}\in I\\ x^2-x+\frac{1}{2}, & \frac{1}{2}<x<\frac{3}{2} \text{ and } x\ne 1\\ x^2-x+\frac{1}{6}, & \text{otherwise}\end{cases}$$

where [] denotes greatest integer less than or equals to x and {} denotes fractional part function of x. Then,

(a) $f(x)$ is continuous and differentiable in $x\in\left(-\frac{1}{2},\frac{1}{2}\right)$

(b) $f(x)$ is continuous and differentiable in $x\in\left[-\frac{1}{2},\frac{1}{2}\right]$

(c) $f(x)$ is continuous and differentiable in $x\in\left[\frac{1}{2},\frac{3}{2}\right]$

(d) $f(x)$ is continuous but not differentiable in $x\in(0, 1)$

11. Let [] denotes the greatest integer function and $f(x)=[\tan^2 x]$, then

(a) $\lim_{x\to 0} f(x)$ does not exist

(b) $f(x)$ is continuous at $x=0$

(c) $f(x)$ is not differentiable at $x=0$

(d) $f'(0)=1$

Answer Key

1. Differentiable at $x=1$, not differentiable at $x=2$

2. Not differentiable at $x=1$ and $x=\frac{1}{2}$

3. (a)

4. Continuous and differentiable $\forall x\in(0,\infty)$

5. Continuous in $(-2, 2)$ but not differentiable at $x=0$

6. $a=\frac{1}{6}, b=\frac{\pi}{4}-\frac{13}{6}$

7. Discontinuous at $x=6$ and not differentiable at $x=\frac{9-\sqrt{21}}{2}, 6$

8. Not differentiable at $x=0$

9. (a,b)

10. (d)

11. (b)

For Detailed Solution

Milestone 7 Functional Equation

4.11 Functional Equation

An equation involving unknown functions is called a functional equation. For example

(i) $f(x)+f(y)=f(x)\cdot f(y)$

(ii) $xf(x)+f\left(\frac{1}{x}\right)=x^2-1$

Determination of Function which are Differentiable and Satisfying the Given Functional Rule

Basic Steps

(i) Write down the expression for $f'(x)$ as $f'(x)=\frac{f(x+h)-f(x)}{h}$

(ii) Manipulate $f(x+h)-f(x)$ in such a way that the given functional rule is applicable. Now apply the functional rule and simplify the RHS to get $f'(x)$ as a function of x along with constants if any.

(iii) Integrate $f'(x)$, get $f(x)$ as a function of x and a constant of integration. In some cases a Differential Equation is formed which can be solved to get $f(x)$.

(iv) Apply the boundary value conditions to determine the value of this constant.

Example 57. Suppose f is a derivable function that satisfies the equation $f(x+y)=f(x)+f(y)+x^2y+xy^2$ for all real numbers x and y. Suppose that $\lim\limits_{x\to 0}\frac{f(x)}{x}=1$, and $f(0)=0$, find

(i) $f'(0)$ (ii) $f'(x)$ (iii) $f(3)$

Sol. $f'(x)=\lim\limits_{x\to 0}\frac{f(x+h)-f(x)}{h}=\lim\limits_{x\to 0}\frac{f(h)+x^2h+xh^2}{h}$

$f'(x)=\lim\limits_{x\to 0}\frac{f(h)}{h}+x^2=1+x^2$

$f(x)=x+\frac{x^3}{3}+c$, as $f(0)=0$ so $c=0$

$f(x)=x+\frac{x^3}{3}$

Now, (i) $f'(0)=1$

(ii) $f'(x)=1+x^2$ (iii) $f(3)=3+9=12$

Example 58. A differentiable function satisfies the relation $f(x+y)=f(x)+f(y)+2xy-1$, $\forall$ $x, y\in R$

If $f'(0)=\sqrt{3+a-a^2}$, find $f(x)$ and prove that $f(x)>0$ $\forall$ $x\in R$.

> **Decoding the Question**
> For a quadratic equation $ax^2+bx+c=0$ discriminant is denoted by D and is given by $D=b^2-4ac$.

Sol. $f'(x)=\lim\limits_{h\to 0}\frac{f(x+h)-f(x)}{h}=\lim\limits_{h\to 0}\frac{f(h)+2xh-1}{h}$

$f(0)=2f(0)-1\Rightarrow f(0)=1$

$f'(x)=\lim\limits_{h\to 0}\frac{f(h)-f(0)}{h}+2x=f'(0)+2x$

$f'(x)=2x+\sqrt{(3+a-a^2)}$

$f(x)=x^2+\sqrt{(3+a-a^2)}x+c$ as $f(0)=1$ so $c=1$

$f(x)=x^2+\sqrt{(3+a-a^2)}x+1$

$D=3+a-a^2-4=a-a^2-1$

$=-(a^2-a+1)<0$

As $a^2-a+1>0\,\forall\, a$

So, $f(x)>0,\forall\, x\in R$

Example 59. If $(x+y)=f(x)+f(y)+xy)(x+y)$ $\forall x, y\in R$; then show that $f(x)=kx+\frac{x^3}{3}$, $\forall x\in R$

Sol. Let $g(x)=f(x)-\frac{x^3}{3}\Rightarrow f(x)=g(x)+\frac{x^3}{3}$

$\Rightarrow g(x+y)=f(x+y)-\frac{(x+y)^3}{3}$

$=f(x)+f(y)+xy(x+y)-\frac{x^3}{3}-\frac{y^3}{3}-\frac{1}{3}(3xy)(x+y)$

$=f(x)-\frac{x^3}{3}+f(y)-\frac{y^3}{3}=g(x)+g(y)$

Thus, $g(x+y)=g(x)+g(y)$

$\Rightarrow$ $g(x)=kx$

[by Cauchy's functional equation]

$\therefore$ $f(x)=kx+\frac{x^3}{3},\forall x\in R$

Example 60. A function $f:(0,\infty)\to(0,\infty)$ satisfy the functional equation $\alpha x^2 f\left(\frac{1}{x}\right)+f(x)=\frac{x}{1+x}$, $\forall\, x\in(0,\infty)$; where $\alpha\in R$. Then, find the function $f(x)$.

Sol. Given functional equation is $\alpha x^2\, f\left(\frac{1}{x}\right)+f(x)=\frac{x}{1+x}$ ...(i)

Replacing x by $\frac{1}{x}$, we get

$$\frac{\alpha}{x^2}\, f(x)+f\left(\frac{1}{x}\right)=\frac{1/x}{1+1/x}=\frac{1}{x+1}$$

$$\Rightarrow \quad \alpha^2 f(x)+\alpha x^2\, f\left(\frac{1}{x}\right)=\frac{ax^2}{1+x}$$

Eliminating $f\left(\frac{1}{x}\right)$ from Eqs. (i) and (ii), we get

$$\frac{x}{1+x}-f(x)=\frac{\alpha x^2}{x+1}-\alpha^2 f(x)$$

$$\Rightarrow \quad (\alpha^2-1)f(x)=\frac{\alpha x^2-x}{x+1}$$

$$\Rightarrow \quad f(x)=\frac{\alpha x^2-x}{(\alpha^2-1)(x+1)}$$

$$\Rightarrow f(x)=\frac{x(1-\alpha x)}{(x+1)(1-\alpha^2)} \text{ if } \alpha^2\neq 1$$

and no solution if $\alpha^2=1$.

Milestone Practice 4.7

1. Find the domain and range of a real valued function $f(x)$ satisfying $2f(\sin x)+f(\cos x)=x$.
2. If f is a polynomial function satisfying $2+f(x)\cdot f(y)=f(x)+f(y)+f(xy)$ for all $x, y\in R$ and if $f(2)=5$, then evaluate $f(f(2))$.
3. Find all continuous functions satisfying $f(x+y)f(x-y)=[f(x)-f(y)]^2$.
4. Find all functions f which are defined for all $x\in R$ and for any x, y satisfy $xf(y)+yf(x)=(x+y)f(x)f(y)$.
5. Let $f(x)$ be a function such that $f(x+y)=f(x)+f(y)$ for all x and y and $f(x)=(2x^2+3x)\cdot g(x)$ for all x, where $g(x)$ is continuous and $g(0)=3$. Then, $f'(x)$ is equal to
   (a) 6 (b) 9
   (c) 8 (d) None of these
6. If a function $g(x)$ which has derivative $g'(x)$ for every real x and which satisfies the following equation $g(x+y)=e^y g(x)+e^x g(y)$ for all x and y and $g'(0)=2$, then the value of $\{g'(x)-g(x)\}$ is equal to
   (a) e^x (b) $\frac{2}{3}e^x$
   (c) $\frac{1}{2}e^x$ (d) $2e^x$
7. Let $f:R\to R$ be a function satisfying $f\left(\frac{xy}{2}\right)=\frac{f(x)\cdot f(y)}{2}, \forall\, x, y\in R$ and $f(1)=f'(1)\neq 0$. Then, $f(x)+f(1-x)$ is (for all non-zero real values of x)
   (a) constant (b) can't be discussed
   (c) x (d) $\frac{1}{x}$
8. Let $f(x)$ be a derivable function at $x=0$ and $f\left(\frac{x+y}{K}\right)=\frac{f(x)+f(y)}{K}$ $(K\in R, K\neq 0, 2)$. Then, $f(x)$ is
   (a) even function
   (b) neither even nor odd function
   (c) either zero or odd function
   (d) either zero or even function
9. Let $f:R\to(-\pi,\pi)$ be a differentiable function such that $f(x)+f(y)=f\left(\frac{x+y}{1-xy}\right)$. If $f(1)=\frac{\pi}{2}$ and $\lim_{x\to 0}\frac{f(x)}{x}=2$. Then, $f(x)$ is equal to
   (a) $2\tan^{-1}x$ (b) $\frac{1}{2}\tan^{-1}x$
   (c) $\frac{\pi}{2}\tan^{-1}x$ (d) $2\pi\tan^{-1}x$

Answer Key

1. Domain $=[-1,1]$, Range $=\left[-\frac{2\pi}{3},\frac{\pi}{3}\right]$ 2. (26) 3. $f(x)=\pm e^{ax^2}$
4. $f(x)=0$, $f(x)=1$ 5. (b) 6. (d) 7. (a)
8. (c) 9. (a)

For Detailed Solution

JEE Pattern EXAMPLES

Single Option Correct Type Questions

Example 1 ■ *For $x > 0$, let $h(x) = \begin{cases} \frac{1}{q}, & \text{if } x = \frac{p}{q} \\ 0, & \text{if } x \text{ is irrational} \end{cases}$;*
where p and $q > 0$ are relatively prime integers, then which one does not hold good?

(a) $h(x)$ is discontinuous for all x in $(0, \infty)$.
(b) $h(x)$ is continuous for each irrational in $(0, \infty)$.
(c) $h(x)$ is discontinuous for each rational in $(0, \infty)$.
(d) $h(x)$ is not derivable for all x in $(0, \infty)$.

> **Decoding the Question**
> For each two rational number there is at least one irrational number between them. If x is a rational number $\left[\frac{p}{q}, q \neq 0, p \text{ and } q \text{ are coprime}\right]$, then x^+ and x^- will be an irrational number. Hence, $\left(\frac{2}{3}\right)^+$ is an irrational.

Sol. (a) Let $x = \frac{2}{3}$, which is rational.

$$\Rightarrow \quad h\left(\frac{2}{3}\right) = \frac{1}{3}$$

$$\lim h \to \left(\frac{2^+}{3}\right) = 0$$

$\Rightarrow$ Discontinuous at $x \in Q$

Let $x = \sqrt{2} \notin Q$

$h(\sqrt{2}) = 0$

Consider $\sqrt{2} = 1.414012358390$

$$h(\sqrt{2}) = h\left(\frac{1414023583}{10^{10}}\right) = \frac{1}{10^{10}} \to 0$$

Hence, h is continuous for all an irrational.

Example 2 ■ *Given $f(x) = b([x]^2 + [x]) + 1$ for $x \geq -1$ $= \sin(\pi(x + a))$ for $x < -1$, where $[x]$ denotes the integral part of x, then for what values of a, b the function is continuous at $x = -1$?*

(a) $a = 2n + \left(\frac{3}{2}\right); b \in R; n \in I$
(b) $a = 4n + 2; b \in R; n \in I$
(c) $a = 4n + \left(\frac{3}{2}\right); b \in R^+; n \in I$
(d) $a = 4n + 1; b \in R^-; n \in I$

Sol. (a) $f(-1) = b(1 - 1) + 1 = 1$

and $\lim\limits_{x \to 1^-} = \lim\limits_{h \to 0} f(-1 - h) = 1$

$$\Rightarrow \lim_{h \to 0} f(-1 - h) = \lim_{h \to 0} \sin(\pi(-1 - h) + \pi a) = 1$$

As, $f(x)$ is continuous at $x = -1$.

$$\Rightarrow \quad \sin \pi a = -1 = \sin\left(2n\pi + \frac{3\pi}{2}\right)$$

$$\Rightarrow \quad \pi a = 2n\pi + \frac{3\pi}{2}$$

$$\Rightarrow \quad a = 2n + \frac{3}{2}$$

Hence, $a = 2n + \frac{3}{2}, n \in I$ and $b \in R$.

Example 3 ■ *Number of points of discontinuity of $f(x) = [2x^3 - 5]$ in [1, 2) is equal to (where $[x]$ denotes greatest integer less than or equal to x).*

(a) 14 (b) 13
(c) 10 (d) 8

Sol. (b) $f(x) = [2x^3 - 5] = [2x^3] - 5$

$$1 \leq x < 2$$

$$1 \leq x^3 < 8$$

$$\Rightarrow \quad 2 \leq 2x^3 < 16$$

$\because [\cdot]$ is discontinuous at integral points.

$$2x^3 = 2, 3, 4, 5, 6, 7, 8, 9, 10, 11, 12, 13, 14, 15$$

$f(x)$ is discontinuous at all above points but we have to check at x, where $2x^3 = 2$

$$\Rightarrow \quad x = 1$$

$$f(1^+) = [2^+ - 5] = -3$$

$$f(1^-) = [2 - 5] = -3$$

$\therefore$ At $x = 1$, f is continuous.

$\therefore$ Total number of points of discontinuity = 13

JEE SCANNER

Example 4 Similar to PYQ Asked in JEE Main 2024

Let $f: R \to R$ be a function defined by

$$f(x)=\begin{cases}\dfrac{1-\cos 4x}{2x^2}, & x<0\\ m, & x=0,\\ \dfrac{n\sqrt{1-\cos x}}{x}, & x>0\end{cases}$$

where $m, n \in R$. If f is continuous at $x=0$, then m^2+n^2 is equal to

(a) 16 (b) 64

(c) 48 (d) 32

Sol. (c) $\lim_{x\to 0^-} f(x)=\lim_{x\to 0^-}\dfrac{1-\cos 4x}{2x^2}$

$$=\lim_{x\to 0^-}\frac{4\sin 4x}{4x}$$

$$=4$$

$\therefore \lim_{x\to 0^-} f(x)=f(0)\Rightarrow m=4$

Now, $\lim_{x\to 0^+} f(x)=\lim_{x\to 0^+}\dfrac{n\sqrt{1-\cos x}}{x}$

$$=\lim_{x\to 0^+}\frac{n\sqrt{2}\ \sin\frac{x}{2}}{x}$$

$$=\lim_{x\to 0^+}\frac{n\sqrt{2}\sin\frac{x}{2}}{2\cdot\left(\frac{x}{2}\right)}$$

$$=\frac{n}{\sqrt{2}}$$

$\therefore \quad m=\dfrac{n}{\sqrt{2}}$ [$\because f(x)$ is continuous]

$n=4\sqrt{2}$ [$\because m=4$]

$m^2+n^2=4^2+(4\sqrt{2})^2$

$=48$

Skill Builder

Let $f: R\to R$ be a function defined by

$$f(x)=\begin{cases}\dfrac{1-\cos 5x}{x^2}, & x<0\\ c, & x=0\\ \dfrac{d\sqrt{1-\cos x}}{x}, & x>0\end{cases}$$

where $c, d\in R$. If $f(x)$ is continuous at $x=0$, then c^2+d^2 is equal to

(a) 468.75 (b) 468

(c) 486 (d) 486.75

For Sol.

Example 5 *Consider*

$$f(x)=\begin{cases}x[x]^2\log_{(1+x)^2}, & \text{for } -1<x<0\\ \dfrac{\ln(e^{x^2}+2\sqrt{\{x\}})}{\tan\sqrt{x}}, & \text{for } 0<x<1\end{cases}$$

where [*] and {} are the greatest integer function and fractional part function respectively, then*

(a) $f(0)=\ln 2 \Rightarrow f$ is continuous at $x=0$

(b) $f(0)=2\Rightarrow f$ is continuous at $x=0$

(c) $f(0)=e^2\Rightarrow f$ is continuous at $x=0$

(d) f has an irremovable discontinuity at $x=0$

Decoding the Question

To solve this problem use properties of greatest integer function as $\lim_{x\to 0^-}$ mean x is less than 0, then its integral value will be – 1 as [– 0.5] = [– 0.6] = ... = – 1.

Sol. (d) $\lim_{x\to 0^-} f(x)=\lim_{h\to 0} -h[-h]^2\log_{(1-h)}2$

$$=\lim_{h\to 0}\frac{-h}{\log_e(1-h)}\cdot\log_e 2$$

$$f(0^-)=\ln 2$$

$$\lim_{x\to 0^+} f(x)=\lim_{h\to 0}\frac{\ln(e^{h^2}+2\sqrt{h})}{\tan\sqrt{h}}$$

$$=\lim_{h\to 0}\frac{\ln(e^{h^2}+2\sqrt{h}-1+1)}{(e^{h^2}+2\sqrt{h}-1)}\cdot\left(\frac{e^{h^2}-1+2\sqrt{h}}{\tan\sqrt{h}}\right)$$

$\Rightarrow \quad 1(0+2)=2$

Example 6 *Let $f:[0,1]\to R$ be a continuous function and assumes only rational values. If $f(0)=2$, then the value of $\tan^{-1}\left(f\left(\frac{1}{2}\right)\right)+\tan^{-1}\left(\frac{3}{2}f\left(\frac{1}{2}\right)\right)$ is*

(a) $\dfrac{\pi}{4}$ (b) $\dfrac{\pi}{6}$

(c) $\dfrac{3\pi}{4}$ (d) π

Sol. (c) $f(0)=2$

$\because f$ is a continuous function and assumes only rational value.

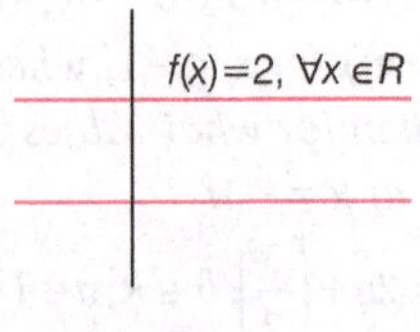

$\therefore\ f(x)=2=$ Constant function

Now, $\tan^{-1}\left(f\left(\frac{1}{2}\right)\right)+\tan^{-1}\left(\frac{3}{2}f\left(\frac{1}{2}\right)\right)$

$\Rightarrow \quad \tan^{-1}2+\tan^{-1}3 \quad [\because xy>1]$

$\Rightarrow \quad \tan^{-1}\left(\frac{2+3}{1-2\times 3}\right)+\pi$

$\Rightarrow \quad \tan^{-1}(-1)+\pi=\pi-\frac{\pi}{4}=\frac{3\pi}{4}$

Example 7 *If* $g(x)=\lim\limits_{m\to\infty}\frac{x^m f(1)+h(x)+1}{2x^m+3x+3}$ *is continuous at* $x=1$ *and* $g(1)=\lim\limits_{x\to 1}\{\log_e(ex)\}^{2/\log_e x}$, *then the value of* $2g(1)+2f(1)-h(1)$ *when* $f(x)$ *and* $h(x)$ *are continuous at* $x=1$, *is*

(a) 0 (b) 1

(c) 2 (d) 3

Sol. (b) Here, $g(1)=\lim\limits_{x\to 1}\{\log e+\log_e x\}^{2/\log_e x}$

$$=\lim_{x\to 1}\{1+\log_e x\}^{2/\log_e x}$$

$$=e^{\lim\limits_{x\to 1}\log_e x\cdot\frac{2}{\log_e x}}$$

$$g(1)=e^2 \quad \text{...(i)}$$

Also, $\lim\limits_{x\to 1^-}g(x)=\lim\limits_{x\to 1^-}\lim\limits_{m\to\infty}\left\{\frac{x^m f(1)+h(x)+1}{2x^m+3x+3}\right\}$

$$=\lim_{m\to\infty}\left\{\lim_{x\to 1^-}\frac{x^m f(1)+h(x)+1}{2x^m+3x+3}\right\}$$

$$=\frac{h(1)+1}{3+3} \quad \left[\text{as } x<1\Rightarrow \lim_{m\to\infty}x^m=0\right]$$

$$\lim_{x\to 1^-}g(x)=\frac{h(1)+1}{6} \quad \text{...(ii)}$$

Again, $\lim\limits_{x\to 1^+}g(x)=\lim\limits_{x\to 1^+}\lim\limits_{m\to\infty}\left\{\frac{x^m f(1)+h(x)+1}{2x^m+3x+3}\right\}$

$$=\lim_{m\to\infty}\left\{\lim_{x\to 1^+}\frac{x^m f(1)+h(x)+1}{2x^m+3x+3}\right\}$$

$$=\lim_{m\to\infty}\lim_{x\to 1^+}\frac{f(1)+h(x)/x^m+1/x^m}{2+3/x^{m-1}+3/x^m}$$

$$=\frac{f(1)}{2}$$

$$\therefore \quad \lim_{x\to 1^+}g(x)=\frac{f(1)}{2} \quad \text{...(iii)}$$

From Eqs. (i), (ii) and (iii), we get

$$e^2=\frac{h(1)+1}{6}=\frac{f(1)}{2} \quad [\text{as } g(x) \text{ is continuous at } x=1]$$

$\Rightarrow h(1)=6e^2-1$ and $f(1)=2e^2$

$\therefore \quad 2g(1)+2f(1)-h(1)=2e^2+4e^2-6e^2+1=1$

$\Rightarrow \quad 2g(1)+2f(1)-h(1)=1$

Example 8 *The equation* $2\tan x+5x-2=0$ *has*

(a) no solution in $[0,\pi/4]$

(b) at least one real solution in $[0,\pi/4]$

(c) two real solutions in $[0,\pi/4]$

(d) None of the above

Sol. (b) Let $f(x)=2\tan x+5x-2$

$$f(0)=-2,\ f\left(\frac{\pi}{4}\right)=2\tan\frac{\pi}{4}+\frac{5\pi}{4}-2=\frac{5\pi}{4}$$

Now, $f(x)\in\left[-2,\frac{5\pi}{4}\right]$ and $f(x)$ is continuous on $[0,\pi/4]$.

$\therefore$ By intermediate value theorem $\exists\, c\in[0,\pi/4]$ for, which $f(c)=0$.

Example 9 *If* $f(x)=\frac{x}{1+(\log x)(\log x)\ldots\infty},\ \forall\, x\in[1,3]$ *is non-differentiable at* $x=k$. *Then, the value of* $[k^2]$, *is (where* $[\cdot]$ *denotes greatest integer function)*

(a) 5 (b) 6 (c) 7 (d) 8

Sol. (c) Let $g(x)=(\log x)\cdot(\log x)\ldots\infty$

$$\therefore \quad g(x)=\begin{cases}1, & x=e\\ 0, & 1\le x<e\\ \infty, & x>e\end{cases}$$

$$\therefore \quad f(x)=\begin{cases}x, & 1\le x<e\\ \frac{x}{2}, & x=e\\ 0, & e<x\le 3\end{cases}$$

$\Rightarrow f(x)$ is neither continuous nor differentiable at $x=e=k$

$\therefore \quad [k^2]=7$

Example 10 *If* $f(x)=\begin{cases}\frac{\sin[x^2]\pi}{x^2-3x-18}+ax^3+b, & \text{for } 0\le x\le 1\\ 2\cos\pi x+\tan^{-1}x, & \text{for } 1<x\le 2\end{cases}$ *differentiable function in [0,2], where [.] denotes the greatest integer function, then*

(a) $a=\frac{1}{6},b=\frac{\pi}{4}-\frac{13}{6}$ (b) $a=-\frac{1}{6},b=\frac{\pi}{4}$

(c) $a=-\frac{1}{6},b=\frac{\pi}{4}-\frac{13}{6}$ (d) None of these

Sol. (a) Here, $[x^2]=0,\ \forall\, 0\le x<1$

and $\quad [x^2]=1$ for $x=1$

$\therefore \quad \sin[x^2]\pi=0$, for $0\le x\le 1$

Hence, $\quad f(x)=\begin{cases}ax^3+b, & 0\le x\le 1\\ 2\cos\pi x+\tan^{-1}x, & 1<x\le 2\end{cases}$

As, $f(x)$ is differentiable in [0, 2].

$\Rightarrow f(x)$ is continuous and differentiable at $x = 1$.

$$\Rightarrow \lim_{x\to 1^-} f(x) = \lim_{x\to 1^+} f(x) = f(1)$$

$$a+b = -2+\frac{\pi}{4} = a+b$$

$$\Rightarrow a+b = -2+\frac{\pi}{4} \quad \text{...(i)}$$

Again, since $f(x)$ is differentiable at $x = 1$.

(LHD at $x = 1$) = (RHD at $x = 1$)

$$\Rightarrow \lim_{x\to 1^-}\frac{f(x)-f(1)}{x-1} = \lim_{x\to 1^+}\frac{f(x)-f(1)}{x-1}$$

$$\Rightarrow \lim_{x\to 1^-}\frac{(ax^3+b)-(a+b)}{x-1}$$

$$= \lim_{x\to 1^+}\frac{(2\cos\pi x+\tan^{-1}x)-(a+b)}{x-1}$$

$$\Rightarrow 3a = \lim_{x\to 1^+}\frac{-2\pi\sin\pi x+\dfrac{1}{1+x^2}}{1}$$

$$\Rightarrow 3a = \frac{1}{2} \text{ or } a = \frac{1}{6} \quad \text{...(ii)}$$

From Eqs. (i) and (ii), we get

$$a = \frac{1}{6} \text{ and } b = \frac{\pi}{4}-\frac{13}{6}$$

Example 11 *Let $g(x) = \log f(x)$, where $f(x)$ is a twice differentiable positive function on $(0, \infty)$ such that $f(x+1) = xf(x)$. Then, for $N = 1, 2, 3, \ldots$, $g''\left(N+\frac{1}{2}\right) - g''\left(\frac{1}{2}\right)$ is equal to*

(a) $-4\left\{1+\frac{1}{9}+\frac{1}{25}+\ldots+\frac{1}{(2N-1)^2}\right\}$

(b) $4\left\{1+\frac{1}{9}+\frac{1}{25}+\ldots+\frac{1}{(2N-1)^2}\right\}$

(c) $-4\left\{1+\frac{1}{9}+\frac{1}{25}+\ldots+\frac{1}{(2N+1)^2}\right\}$

(d) $4\left\{1+\frac{1}{9}+\frac{1}{25}+\ldots+\frac{1}{(2N+1)^2}\right\}$

Sol. (a) We have, $g(x) = \log f(x)$

$$\Rightarrow f(x) = e^{g(x)}$$

$$\Rightarrow f(x+1) = e^{g(x+1)}$$

$$\Rightarrow xf(x) = e^{g(x+1)} \quad \text{[given, } f(x+1) = xf(x)]$$

$$\Rightarrow \log x + \log f(x) = \log e^{g(x+1)} \quad \text{[taking log both sides]}$$

$$\Rightarrow \log x + g(x) = g(x+1) \quad \text{[from Eq. (i)]}$$

i.e. $g(x+1) - g(x) = \log x$ ...(ii)

On replacing x by $x-\frac{1}{2}$ in Eq. (ii), we get

$$g\left(x+\frac{1}{2}\right) - g\left(x-\frac{1}{2}\right) = \log\left(x-\frac{1}{2}\right) = \log(2x-1)-\log 2$$

$$\therefore g''\left(x+\frac{1}{2}\right) - g''\left(x-\frac{1}{2}\right) = \frac{-4}{(2x-1)^2} \quad \text{...(iii)}$$

On substituting $x = 1, 2, 3, \ldots, N$ in Eq. (iii) and adding, we get

$$g''\left(N+\frac{1}{2}\right) - g''\left(\frac{1}{2}\right) = -4\left\{1+\frac{1}{9}+\frac{1}{25}+\ldots+\frac{1}{(2N-1)^2}\right\}$$

Example 12 *Let f be a function such that $f(x+f(y)) = f(x)+y, \forall x, y \in R$, then find $f(0)$. If it is given that there exists a positive real δ, such that $f(h) = h$ for $0 < h < \delta$, then $f'(x)$ is equal to*

(a) 0, 1 (b) – 1, 0 (c) 2, 1 (d) –2, 0

Sol. (a) Let $x = 0, y = 0$ in $f(x+f(y)) = f(x)+y$

$$\Rightarrow f(0+f(0)) = f(0)+0$$

$$\Rightarrow f(f(0)) = f(0)$$

$$\Rightarrow f(a) = a \text{ or } f(0) = 0$$

Given, $f(h) = h$

Then, $f'(x) = \lim_{h\to 0}\frac{f(x+h)-f(x)}{h}$ for $0 < h < \delta$

$$\Rightarrow f'(x) = \lim_{h\to 0}\frac{f(x+f(h))-f(x)}{h} \quad \text{[given, } f(h) = h]$$

$$\Rightarrow f'(x) = \lim_{h\to 0}\frac{f(x)+h-f(x)}{h}$$

$$\Rightarrow f'(x) = \lim_{h\to 0}\frac{h}{h}$$

$$\Rightarrow f'(x) = 1$$

Example 13 *Given*

$$f(x) = \begin{cases} x^2e^{2(x-1)} & ; \quad 0 \le x \le 1 \\ a\,\text{sgn}(x+1)\cos(2x-2)+bx^2; & 1 < x \le 2 \end{cases}$$

is differentiable, then which of the following is correct?

(a) $a = -1, b = 2$ (b) $a = 1, b = -2$

(c) $a = -3, b = 4$ (d) None of these

Sol. (a) LHL $= \lim_{x\to 1^-} f(x) = \lim_{x\to 1^-} x^2e^{2(x-1)} = 1$

Also, $f(1) = 1$

Now, RHL $= \lim_{x\to 1^+} f(x)$

$$= \lim_{x\to 1^+} a\,\text{sgn}(x+1)\cos 2(x-1)+bx^2 = a\cdot 1\cdot 1+b$$

For continuity $a+b = 1$

Also, LHD $(x = 1)$ is

$$\lim_{h\to 0}\frac{(1-h)^2e^{-2h}-1}{h} = \lim_{h\to 0} 2e^{-2h}+he^{-2h}\left(\frac{e^{-2h}-1}{h}\right)$$

$$= 2+0+2 = 4$$

$$\text{RHD}(x=1)=\lim_{h\to 0}\frac{a\,\text{sgn}(2+h)\cos 2h+b(1+h)^2-1}{h}$$

$$=\lim_{h\to 0}\frac{a\cos 2h+b+bh^2+2bh-(a+b)}{h}$$

$$=\lim_{h\to 0}\left(\frac{\cos 2h-1}{h}\right)+bh+2b=2b\quad [\because a+b=1]$$

$f(x)$ is differentiable at $x=1$, if $2b=4$

$\Rightarrow \qquad b=2; a=-1$

Example 14 *Let* $f(x)$

$$=\begin{cases}\lim\limits_{n\to\infty}\dfrac{ax(x-1)\left(\cot\dfrac{\pi x}{4}\right)^n+(px^2+2)}{\left(\cot\dfrac{\pi x}{4}\right)^n+1}, & x\in(0,1)\cup(1,2)\\ 0, & x=1\end{cases}$$

If $f(x)$ *is differentiable for all* $x\in(0,2)$, *then* (a^2+p^2) *equals*

(a) 18 (b) 20 (c) 22 (d) 24

> **Decoding the Question**
>
> First redefine the given function in (0, 1) and (1, 2) using limit $n\to\infty$ such as $f(x)=\begin{cases}ax(x-1), & 0<x<1\\ 0, & x=1\\ px^2+2, & 1<x<2\end{cases}$.

Sol. (b) $f(1^+)=p+2$

$$f(1)=0$$

$$f(1^-)=\frac{a(1)(1-1)}{1}=0\Rightarrow p=-2$$

$$f'(1^+)=\lim_{h\to 0}\frac{p(1+h)^2+2-p-2}{h}=2p$$

$$f'(1^-)=\lim_{h\to 0}\frac{a(1-h)(-h)-0}{-h}=a$$

$$a=2p\Rightarrow a=-4$$

$$a^2+p^2=16+4=20$$

Example 15 *f is a continuous function on the real line. Given that* $x^2+(f(x)-2)x-\sqrt{3}\cdot f(x)+2\sqrt{3}-3=0$. *Then, the value of* $f(\sqrt{3})$ *is*

(a) cannot be determined (b) $2(1-\sqrt{3})$

(c) zero (d) $\dfrac{2(\sqrt{3}-2)}{\sqrt{3}}$

Sol. (b) $x^2+(f(x)-2)x-\sqrt{3}f(x)+2\sqrt{3}-3=0$

$$f(x)(x-\sqrt{3})+x^2-2x+2\sqrt{3}-3=0$$

$$f(x)(x-\sqrt{3})=(2x-2\sqrt{3})-(x^2-3)$$

$$=2(x-\sqrt{3})-(x-\sqrt{3})(x+\sqrt{3})$$

$$f(x)(x-\sqrt{3})=(x-\sqrt{3})(2-x-\sqrt{3})$$

$$f(x)=\frac{(x-\sqrt{3})(2-x-\sqrt{3})}{(x-\sqrt{3})}$$

$$\lim_{x\to\sqrt{3}}f(x)=\lim_{x\to\sqrt{3}}\frac{(x-\sqrt{3})(2-x-\sqrt{3})}{(x-\sqrt{3})}$$

$$=2-2\sqrt{3}$$

$$=2(1-\sqrt{3})$$

More than One Correct Option Type Questions

Example 16 $f(x)=|x[x]|$ *in* $-1\le x\le 2$, *where* $[x]$ *is greatest integer* $\le x$, *then* $f(x)$ *is*

(a) continuous at $x=0$

(b) discontinuous at $x=0$

(c) not differentiable at $x=2$

(d) differentiable at $x=2$

Sol. (a, c) $f(x)=|x[x]|; -1\le x\le 2$

Now, $\lim\limits_{x\to 0^+}f(x)=\lim\limits_{x\to 0^+}|x(0)|=0;$

and $\lim\limits_{x\to 0^-}f(x)=\lim\limits_{x\to 0^-}|x(-1)|=\lim\limits_{x\to 0^-}(-x)=0;\ f(0)=0$

$\Rightarrow f(x)$ is continuous at $x=0$

$$\lim_{x\to 2^+}f(x)=\lim_{x\to 2^+}|x(2)|=\lim_{x\to 2^+}2x=4;$$

$$\lim_{x\to 2^-}f(x)=\lim_{x\to 2^-}|x(1)|=\lim_{x\to 2^-}x=2$$

$\Rightarrow f(x)$ is discontinuous at $x=2$.

Example 17 $f(x)=(\sin^{-1}x)^2\cdot\cos\left(\dfrac{1}{x}\right)$ *if* $x\ne 0$; $f(0)=0$, *then* $f(x)$ *is*

(a) continuous no where in $-1\le x\le 1$

(b) continuous every where in $-1\le x\le 1$

(c) differentiable no where in $-1\le x\le 1$

(d) differentiable every where except at $x=0$

Sol. (b, d) $f(x)=(\sin^{-1}x)^2\cdot\cos\left(\dfrac{1}{x}\right)$ if $x\ne 0$; $f(0)=0$

$$\lim_{x\to 0^-}f(x)=0=\lim_{x\to 0^+}f(x)=f(0)$$

$\Rightarrow f(x)$ is continuous in $[-1,1]$.

$$f'(0^+)=\lim_{h\to 0}\frac{(\sin^{-1}h)^2\cos^{-1}\left(\dfrac{1}{h}\right)-0}{h}$$

$$=\lim_{h\to 0}\frac{\sin^{-1}(h)}{h}\cdot\sin^{-1}(h)\cos^{-1}\left(\frac{1}{h}\right)$$

which does not exist as $\dfrac{1}{h}\to\infty$ as $h\to 0^+$ for which $\cos^{-1}\left(\dfrac{1}{h}\right)$ is not defined.

$\therefore f(x)$ is differentiable every where except at $x=0$.

Example 18 *If* $f(x)=\sum_{r=1}^{n} a_r|x|^r$, *where* a_i*'s are real constants, then* $f(x)$ *is*

(a) continuous at $x=0, \forall\, a_i$

(b) differentiable at $x=0, \forall\, a_i \in R$

(c) differentiable at $x=0, \forall\, a_{2k+1}=0$

(d) None of the above

Sol. (a,c) We know that $|x|^r, r=0, 1, 2, \dots$ are all continuous every where.

$\therefore f(x)=\sum_{r=1}^{n} a_r|x|^r$ is every where continuous.

Since, $|x|, |x|^3, |x|^5, \dots$ are not differentiable at $x=0$, where, as $|x|^2, |x|^4, \dots$ are every where differentiable.

$\therefore f(x)=\sum_{r=1}^{n} a_r|x|^r$ is not differentiable at $x=0$, if anyone of $a_1, a_3, a_5, \dots$ is non-zero.

Thus, for $f(x)$ to be differentiable at $x=0$, we must have $a_1=a_3=a_5 \dots =0$

i.e. $a_{2k+1}=0$

Example 19 *Let* f *be a real valued function defined on the interval* $(0, \infty)$, *by* $f(x)=\ln x+\int_0^x \sqrt{1+\sin t}\,dt$. *Then, which of the following statement(s) is/are true?*

(a) $f''(x)$ exists for all $x \in (0, \infty)$.

(b) $f'(x)$ exists for all $x \in (0, \infty)$ and f' is continuous on $(0, \infty)$ but not differentiable on $(0, \infty)$.

(c) There exists $\alpha > 1$ such that $|f'(x)|<|f(x)|$ for all $x \in (0, \infty)$.

(d) There exists $\beta > 0$ such that $|f(x)|+|f'(x)| \le \beta$ for all $x \in (0, \infty)$.

Decoding the Question

To solve this problem, use the following rule as $f(x)=\int_{g(x)}^{h(x)} F(x)$,

then $f'(x)=h'(x)\,F(h(x))-g'(x)\,F(g(x))$. [Leibnitz rule]

Sol. (b, c) Here, $f'(x)=\frac{1}{x}+\sqrt{1+\sin x}, x>0$ but $f(x)$ is not differentiable in $(0, \infty)$ as $\sin x$ may be -1 and then

$f''(x)=-\frac{1}{x^2}+\frac{1}{2}\frac{\cos x}{\sqrt{1+\sin x}}$ will not exists.

$\Rightarrow f'(x)$ is continuous for all $x \in (0, \infty)$ but $f'(x)$ is not differentiable on $(0, \infty)$.

$\therefore$ Option (b) is true.

Also, $f'(x) \le 3$, if $x>1$ and $f(x)>3$, if $x>e^3$

$\therefore$ Let $\alpha = e^3$

Option (c) is true.

Option (d) is not possible as $f(x) \to \infty$ when $x \to \infty$.

Example 20 *For every pair of continuous functions* $f, g\,[0, 1] \to R$ *such that* $\max(f(x): x \in [0, 1]=\max\{g(x): x \in [0, 1]\}$, *the correct statement(s) is (are)*

(a) $(f(c))^2+3f(c)=(g(c))^2+3g(c)$ for some $c \in [0, 1]$

(b) $(f(c))^2+f(c)=(g(c))^2+3g(c)$ for some $c \in [0, 1]$

(c) $(f(c))^2+3f(c)=(g(c))^2+g(c)$ for some $c \in [0, 1]$

(d) $(f(c))^2=(g(c))^2$ for some $c \in [0, 1]$

Sol. (a, d) Consider $h(x)=f(x)-g(x)$ assume $a<b$

$$h(a)=\lambda-g(a)>0$$
$$h(b)=f(b)-\lambda<0$$

If $a>b, h(a)<0$ and $h(b)>0$.

By intermediate value theorem $\Rightarrow h(c)=0$ ...(i)

(a) $(f(c))^2+3f(c)=(g(c))^2+3g(c)$

$(f(c)-g(c))(f(c)+g(c)+3)=0$

So there exist $a, c: f(c)-g(c)$ [from Eq. (i)]

Hence, option (a) is correct.

(d) Similarly, $(f(c))^2=(g(c))^2$

$(f(c)-g(c))(f(c)+g(c))=0$

Hence, option (d) is correct.

Options (b) and (c) are wrong as by counter.

e.g. If $f(x)=g(x)=\lambda \ne 0$, then

Option (b) $\to \lambda^2+\lambda=\lambda^2+3\lambda$ is not possible

Option (c) $\to \lambda^2+3\lambda=\lambda^2+\lambda$ is not possible

Example 21 *If* f *is defined on an interval* $[a, b]$. *Which of the following statement(s) is/are incorrect?*

(a) If $f(a)$ and $f(b)$ have opposite sign, then there must be a point $c \in (a, b)$ such that $f(c)=0$.

(b) If f is continuous on $[a, b]$, $f(a)<0$ and $f(b)>0$, then there must be a point $c \in (a, b)$ such that $f(c)=0$.

(c) If f is continuous on $[a, b]$ and there is a point c in (a, b) such that $f(c)=0$, then $f(a)$ and $f(b)$ have opposite sign.

(d) If f has no zeroes on $[a, b]$, then $f(a)$ and $f(b)$ have the same sign.

Sol. (a,c,d)

(a) $f(c)=0$, only when f is continuous.

$\therefore$ It is incorrect.

(b) $f(a)<0, f(b)>0$

$\Rightarrow f(c)>0$ (IMVT)

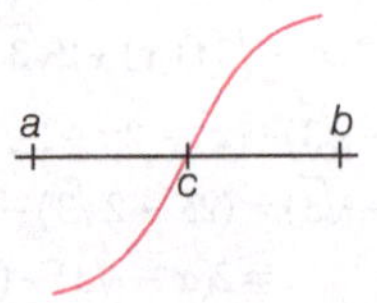

$\therefore$ Option (b) is correct.

(c) It is also incorrect.

e.g.

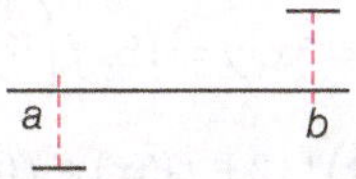

Consider $f(a) < 0$ and $f(b) > 0$.

(d) Converse of IMVT need not be true.

$\therefore$ Option (c) is incorrect.

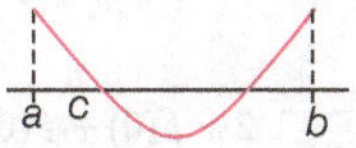

Example 22 *In which of the following cases the given equations has atleast one root in the indicated interval?*

(a) $x - \cos x = 0$ in $\left(0, \frac{\pi}{2}\right)$

(b) $x + \sin x = 1$ in $\left(0, \frac{\pi}{6}\right)$

(c) $\frac{a}{x-1} + \frac{b}{x-3} = 0$, $a, b > 0$ in $(1, 3)$

(d) $f(x) - g(x) = 0$ in (a, b), where f and g are continuous on $[a, b]$ and $f(a) > g(a)$ and $f(b) < g(b)$.

Sol. (a,b,c,d)

(a) $f(x) = x - \cos x$, f is continuous.

$f(0) = 0 - \cos 0 = -1$

$f\left(\frac{\pi}{2}\right) = \frac{\pi}{2}$

(b) $f(x) = x + \sin x - 1$

$f(0) = 0 + \sin 0 - 1 = -1$

$$f\left(\frac{\pi}{6}\right) = \frac{\pi}{6} + \sin\frac{\pi}{6} - 1 = \frac{\pi}{6} - \frac{1}{2} = \left(\frac{\pi - 3}{6}\right) \pi > 3$$

One root in $\left(0, \frac{\pi}{6}\right)$.

(c) $f(x) = \frac{a}{x-1} + \frac{b}{x-3}$

$f(1^+) = \frac{a}{1^+ - 1} + \frac{b}{1^+ - 3} \Rightarrow +\infty$

$f(3^-) = \frac{a}{3^- - 1} + \frac{b}{3^- - 3} \Rightarrow -\infty$

(d) $h(x) = f(x) - g(x)$

$h(a) = f(a) - g(a) > 0$

$h(b) = f(b) - g(b) < 0$

$\therefore$ One root in (a, b).

Example 23 *Which of the following statements is/are correct?*

(a) There exist a function $f : [0, 1] \to R$ which is discontinuous at every point in $[0, 1]$ and $|f(x)|$ is continuous at every point in $[0, 1]$.

(b) Let $F(x) = f(x) \cdot g(x)$. If $f(x)$ is differentiable at $x = a$, $f(a) = 0$ and $g(x)$ is continuous at $x = a$, then $F(x)$ is always differentiable at $x = a$.

(c) If $f'(a^+) = 2$ and $f'(a^-) = 3$, then $f(x)$ is non-differentiable at $x = a$ but will be always continuous at $x = a$.

(d) If $f(a)$ and $f(b)$ possess opposite signs, then there must exist at least one solution of the equation $f(x) = 0$ in (a, b) provided f is continuous on $[a, b]$.

Sol. (a) $f(x) = \begin{cases} x, & x \in Q \\ -x, & x \in Q' \end{cases}$

$|f(x)| = \begin{cases} x, & x \in Q \\ x, & x \in Q \end{cases} = x, x \in [0, 1]$

$\therefore$ Option (a) is correct.

(b) $F(x) = f(x) \cdot g(x)$

Now, $F'(a) = \lim_{h \to 0} \frac{f(a+h) \cdot g(a+h) - f(0) \cdot g(0)}{h}$

$= \lim_{h \to 0} \frac{f(a+h) \cdot g(a+h)}{h}$

$= \lim_{h \to 0} f'(a+h) \cdot g(a+h) + f(a+h) \cdot \frac{d}{dh}[g(a+h)]$

$= h'(a) \cdot g(a)$

$\therefore$ $F'(a)$ exist.

$\Rightarrow F(x)$ is differentiable.

Option (b) is correct.

(c) $f'(a^+)$ and $f'(a^-)$ both exist finitely

$\therefore$ $f(a^-) = f(a^+) = f(a)$

$\therefore$ $f(x)$ is continuous at $x = a$

$\therefore$ Option (c) is correct.

(d) It is statement of IMVT.

$\therefore$ Option (d) is correct.

Example 24 *Let* $f(x) = \sin\left(\frac{\pi}{6}\sin\left(\frac{\pi}{2}\sin x\right)\right) \forall x \in R$ *and* $g(x) = \frac{\pi}{2}\sin x \; \forall x \in R$. *Let* $(fog)(x)$ *denote* $f(g(x))$ *and* $(gof)(x)$ *denotes* $g(f(x))$, *then which of the following is(are) true?*

(a) Range of f is $\left[-\frac{1}{2}, \frac{1}{2}\right]$

(b) Range of fog is $\left[-\frac{1}{2}, \frac{1}{2}\right]$

(c) $\lim_{x \to 0} \frac{f(x)}{g(x)} = \frac{\pi}{6}$

(d) There is an $x \in R$ such that $gof(x) = 1$

Sol. (a,b,c) $f(x) = \sin\left(\frac{\pi}{6}\sin\left(\frac{\pi}{2}\sin x\right)\right)$

Let $\frac{\pi}{2}\sin x = \theta$

$\because$ $\theta \in \left[-\frac{\pi}{2}, \frac{\pi}{2}\right]$

$\therefore \quad f(x)=\sin\left(\frac{\pi}{6}\sin\theta\right)$

Let $\frac{\pi}{6}\sin\theta=\phi$

$\because \quad \phi\in\left[-\frac{\pi}{6},\frac{\pi}{6}\right]$

$\therefore \quad f(x)=\sin\phi\in\left[-\frac{1}{2},\frac{1}{2}\right]$ ...(i)

Now, $fog(x)=\sin\left(\frac{\pi}{6}\sin\left(\frac{\pi}{2}\sin\left(\frac{\pi}{2}\sin x\right)\right)\right)$

Clearly, range of fog is also $\left(-\frac{1}{2},\frac{1}{2}\right)$. ...(ii)

Now, $\lim_{x\to 0}\dfrac{\sin\left(\frac{\pi}{6}\sin\left(\frac{\pi}{2}\sin x\right)\right)}{\frac{\pi}{2}\sin x}$

$=\lim_{x\to 0}\frac{2}{\pi}\dfrac{\sin\left(\frac{\pi}{6}\sin\left(\frac{\pi}{2}\sin x\right)\right)}{\frac{\pi}{6}\sin\left(\frac{\pi}{2}\sin x\right)}\times\dfrac{\frac{\pi}{6}\sin\left(\frac{\pi}{2}\sin x\right)}{\frac{\sin x}{x}\times x}$

$=\lim_{x\to 0}\frac{2}{\pi}\times\frac{\pi}{6}\times\dfrac{\sin\left(\frac{\pi}{2}\sin x\right)}{\frac{\pi}{2}\sin x}\times\dfrac{\frac{\pi}{2}\sin x}{x}=\frac{1}{3}\times\frac{\pi}{2}=\frac{\pi}{6}$ ...(iii)

Now, $gof(x)=1$

$\Rightarrow \quad \frac{\pi}{2}\sin\left(\frac{\pi}{2}\sin\left(\frac{\pi}{2}\sin x\right)\right)=1$

$\Rightarrow \quad \sin\left(\frac{\pi}{6}\sin\left(\frac{\pi}{2}\sin x\right)\right)=\frac{2}{\pi}=\frac{2}{3.14}>\frac{1}{2}$ ...(iv)

Passage Based Questions

Passage I
(Ex. Nos. 25 to 26)

Let $f:R\to R$ be a differentiable function satisfying $f\left(\frac{x+y}{3}\right)=\frac{2+f(x)+f(y)}{3}$ $\forall\ x,y\in R$ and $f'(2)=2$, then answer the following quesitons.

Example 25 *The range of* $g(x)=\left|f\left|\frac{x}{2}\right|\right|$ *is*

(a) $[1,\infty)$
(b) $[2,\infty)$
(c) $[0,\infty)$
(d) None of these

Example 26 *The function* $h(x)=|f(|x|)-4|$ *is*

(a) non-differentiable and discontinuous at $-1, 0, 1$
(b) differentiable for all real numbers
(c) non-differentiable but continuous at $-1, 0, 1$
(d) non-differentiable only at -1 and 1.

Sol. Q. Nos. (25-26)

25. (b) On putting $x=3x$, $y=0$ in $f\left(\frac{x+y}{3}\right)=\frac{2+f(x)+f(y)}{3}$, we get

$f\left(\frac{3x+0}{3}\right)=\frac{2+f(3x)+f(0)}{3}$

$\Rightarrow \quad f(x)=\frac{2+f(3x)+f(0)}{3}$ ...(i)

Put $x=y=0$

$\Rightarrow \quad f(0)=\frac{2+f(0)+f(0)}{3}$

$\Rightarrow \quad 3f(0)=2+2f(0)$

$\Rightarrow \quad f(0)=2$ ...(ii)

$\therefore$ From Eq. (i),

$f(x)=\frac{2+f(3x)+2}{3}$

$\Rightarrow \quad 3f(x)=f(3x)+4$

Now, $f'(x)=\lim_{h\to 0}\frac{f(x+h)-f(x)}{h}$

$=\lim_{h\to 0}\dfrac{f\left(\frac{3x+3h}{3}\right)-f(x)}{h}$

$=\lim_{h\to 0}\left\{\dfrac{\frac{2+f(3x)+f(3h)}{3}-f(x)}{h}\right\}$

$=\lim_{h\to 0}\left\{\frac{2+f(3x)+f(3h)-3f(x)}{3h}\right\}$

$=\lim_{h\to 0}\left\{\frac{2+3f(x)-4+f(3h)-3f(x)}{3h}\right\}$

$f(x)=\lim_{h\to 0}\left[\frac{f(3h)-2}{3h}\right]$

Since, $f(x)$ is differentiable, $\forall\ x$; $\lim_{x\to 0}f(3h)=2$

$\Rightarrow \quad f(0)=2$

$\Rightarrow \quad f(x)=\lim_{x\to 0}\frac{3f'(3h)}{3}=f(0)=k$ (say)

$\Rightarrow \quad f'(x)=k \Rightarrow f(x)=kx+C$

$\Rightarrow \quad f'(x)=k \Rightarrow f'(2)=k$

But $\quad f'(2)=2\Rightarrow k=2$

$\therefore \quad f(x)=2x+C$

Also, $\quad f(0)=2\Rightarrow C=2$

$\therefore \quad f(x)=2x+2$

$\Rightarrow \quad f(|x|)=2|x|+2$

$\Rightarrow \quad f\left(\left|\frac{x}{2}\right|\right)=2\left|\frac{x}{2}\right|+2=|x|+2$

$\Rightarrow \quad g(x)=\left|f\left|\frac{x}{2}\right|\right|=||x|+2|=|x|+2\begin{cases}x+2, & \text{for } x\ge 0\\ -x+2, & \text{for } x<0\end{cases}$

Graph of $||x|+2|$ is shown below

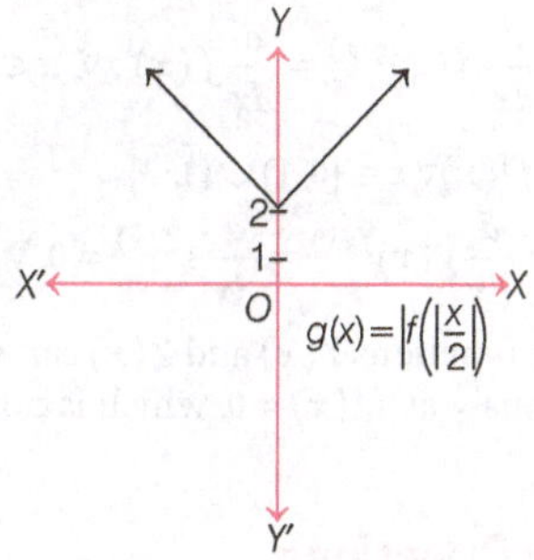

Clearly, the range of $g(x)$ is $[2, \infty)$.

26. (c) $h(x)=|f(|x|)-4|=|2|x|+2-4|=|2|x|-2|$

$$2||x|-1|=\begin{cases}2|x-1|, & \text{for } x\ge 0\\ 2|-x-1|, & \text{for } x<0\end{cases}$$

$$=\begin{cases}2(x-1), & \text{for } x\ge 1\\ 2(-x+1), & \text{for } 0\le x<1\\ 2(x+1), & \text{for } -1\le x<0\\ 2(-x-1), & \text{for } x<-1\end{cases}$$

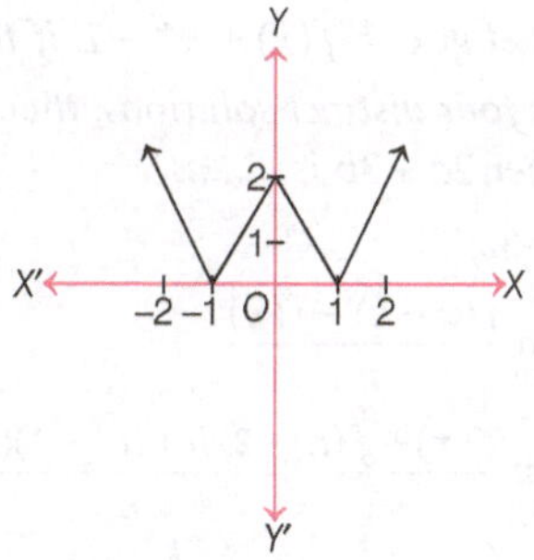

Passage II

(Ex. Nos. 27 to 28)

Let $h(x)=x^2, \phi(x)=(x-1)^2, \psi(x)=2x(1-x)$ suppose $f(x)=\max.\{h(x),\phi(x),\psi(x)\}, 0\le x\le 1$ and $g(x)=\min.\{h(x),\phi(x),\psi(x)\}, 0\le x\le 1$.

Further let $f(x+1)=f(x)$ and $g(x+2)=g(x)$, $g(-x)=g(x), \forall\, x\in R$.

On the above given information, answer the following questions.

Example 27 *For $x\in[0,2]$, $y=[g(x)]$ in discontinuous (where [] stands for greatest integer function) at*

(a) 1 points (b) 2 points

(c) 3 points (d) 4 points

Example 28 *For $x\in(-1,1)$ which of the following is/are true?*

(a) f is non-differentiable at 5 points but g is non-differentiable at 2 points.

(b) f is non-differentiable at 7 points but g is non-differentiable at 2 points

(c) $f(x)+g(x)$ is non-differentiable at 7 points

(d) $f(x)+g(x)$ is non-differentiable at 9 points

Sol. Q. Nos. (27-28)

$$f(x)=\max.\{h(x),\phi(x)\}; 0\le x\le 1 \quad \text{...(i)}$$

$$f(x+1)=f(x)^n, x\in R \quad \text{...(ii)}$$

$$g(x)=\min.\{h(x),\phi(x),\psi(x)\} \text{ for } 0\le x\le 1 \quad \text{...(iii)}$$

$$g(-x)=-g(x) \quad \text{...(iv)}$$

and $$g(x+2)=g(x)^n\ x\in R \quad \text{...(v)}$$

where $h(x)=x^2, \phi(x)=(x-1)^2, \psi(x)-2x(1-x)$

Here, $f(x)$ and $g(x)$ are defined for $x\in[0,1]$ and $f(x)$ and $g(x)$ are given periodic with periods 1 and 2 respectively and $g(x)$ is an odd function.

Let us draw the graphs of given functions

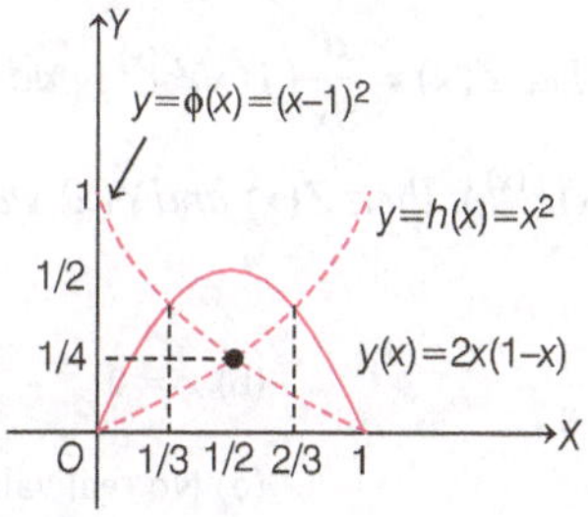

$\therefore$ Graph of $f(x)$ and $g(x)$ would be as shown below.

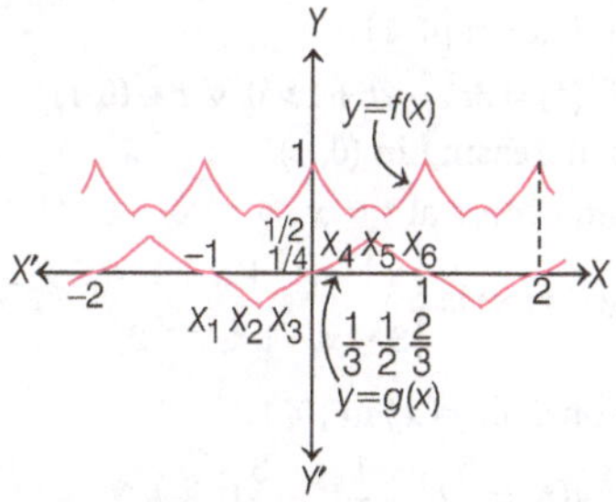

27. (a) Range of $g(x)$ is $\left[-\frac{1}{4},\frac{1}{4}\right]$ which contains only integer value i.e. 0.

In (0, 2), $g(x)$ takes integer value 0 at $x=1$ (only point).

Thus, $[g(x)]$ is discontinuous only at one point in (0, 2).

28. (a,c) In $(-1,1)$ $f(x)$ is non-differentiable at sharp turns which are 5 ponits.

i.e. $x_1, x_2, 0, x_4, x_6$ where as $g(x)$ is non-differentiable at 2 sharp turning points which are x_2 and x_5.

Further there is no common point of non-differentiability of $f(x)$ and $g(x)$. We know that the sum of *a* differentiable and non-differentiable function is always non-differentiable.

So, $f(x)+g(x)$ are non-differentiable at exactly 7 points, which are $x_1, x_2, x_3, 0, x_4, x_5$ and x_6.

Passage III

(Ex. Nos. 29 to 30)

Let $f(x)=\begin{cases}\max.\{t^3-t^2+t+1, 0\le t\le x\}, & 0\le x\le 1\\ \min.\{3-t, 1<t\le x\}, & 1<x\le 2\end{cases}$

and

$$g(x)=\begin{cases}\max.\left\{\frac{3}{8}t^4+\frac{1}{2}t^3-\frac{3}{2}t^2+1, 0\le t\le x\right\}, & 0\le x<1\\ \min.\left\{\frac{3}{8}t+\frac{1}{32}\sin^2\pi t+\frac{5}{8}, 1\le t\le x\right\}, & 1\le x\le 2\end{cases}$$

Example 29 *The function $f(x)$, $\forall\, x\in[0,2]$ is*

(a) continuous and differentiable
(b) continuous but not differentiable
(c) discontinuous and not differentiable
(d) None of the above

Example 30 *Let $Z(x)=\frac{d}{dx}(f(x)^{g(x)})$ and $Y(x)=\frac{d}{dx}(g(x)^{f(x)})$, then $Z(x)$ and $Y(x)$ vanish simultaneously at*

(a) $x=-\frac{1}{3}$ (b) $x=0$
(c) $x=1$ (d) No real value of x

Sol. Q. Nos. (29-30)

Consider $f(x)$ in [0, 1]

$$f'(t)=3t^2-2t+1>0, \forall\, t\in(0,1)$$

$\Rightarrow$ f is increasing in (0, 1).

maximum occurs at $t=x$,

and hence $f(x)$ is $\begin{cases}x^3-x^2+x+1, & 0\le x\le 1\\ 3-x, & 1<x\le 2\end{cases}$

Again, consider $g(x)$ in [0, 1)

$$g(t)=\frac{3}{8}t^4+\frac{1}{2}t^3-\frac{3}{2}t^2+1$$

$$g'(t)=\frac{3}{2}t^3+\frac{3}{2}t^2-3t=\frac{3}{2}t(t^2+t-2)$$

$$=\frac{3}{2}t(t-1)(t+2)$$

$g(t)$ decreases in [0, 1).

Maximum occurs when $t=0$ and $g(0)=1$

Again, consider $g(x)$ function in [1, 2].

$$g(t)=\frac{3}{8}t+\frac{1}{32}\sin^2\pi t+\frac{5}{8}$$

$$g'(t)=\frac{3}{8}+\frac{\pi}{32}\sin(2\pi t)>0, \forall\, t\in R$$

$\therefore$ g is an increasing function in [1, 2].

Minimum occurs when $t=1$ and $g(1)=1$

Hence, $g(x)=\begin{cases}1, & 0\le x<1\\ 1, & 1<x\le 2\end{cases}=1, \forall\, x\in[0,2]$

29. (b) $f(x)$ is continuous but not differentiable at $x=1$.

30. (d) $Z(x)=\frac{d}{dx}f(x)^{g(x)}=\frac{d}{dx}f(x)^1, \forall\, x\in[0,1)\cup(1,2]$

$$=f'(x)\forall x\in[0,1)\cup(1,2]$$

and $Y(x)=\frac{d}{dx}g(x)^{f(x)}=\frac{d}{dx}1^{f(x)}=0, \forall\, x\in[0,1)\cup(1,2]$

Hence, the functions $Y(x)$ and $Z(x)$ can vanish simultaneously at $f'(x)=0$, which is not possible for any real x.

Stem Based Questions

Stem I

(Ex. Nos. 31 to 32)

Let f be a differentiable function satisfying the relation $f(x+y)=f(x)+f(y)-2xy+(e^x-1)(e^y-1), \forall\, x,y\in R$ and $f'(0)=1$.

Example 31 *The value of $\lim_{x\to 0}\frac{f(2x)+4x^2-2x}{x^2}$ is ....*

Example 32 *Let $g(x)=f(x)+x^2-2$. If the equation $|g(|x|)=k$ has four distinct solutions, then the set of values of k is (a,b), then $2a+3b$ is ....*

Sol. Q. Nos. (31-32)

$$f'(x)=\lim_{h\to 0}\frac{f(x+h)-f(x)}{h}$$

$$=\lim_{h\to 0}\frac{f(x)+f(h)-2xh+(e^x-1)(e^h-1)-f(x)}{h}$$

$$=\lim_{h\to 0}\left(\frac{f(h)}{h}+(e^x-1)\frac{(e^h-1)}{h}\right)-2x$$

$$=f'(0)+e^x-1-2x$$

$$=1+e^x-1-2x$$

$$=e^x-2x$$

$$f(x)=e^x-x^2+\lambda$$

$$f(0)=1-0+1$$

$\Rightarrow$ $\lambda=-1$

$\therefore$ $f(x)=e^x-x^2-1$

31. (2) $\lim_{x\to 0}\frac{f(2x)+4x^2-2x}{x^3}$

$$=\lim_{x\to 0}\frac{e^{2x}-4x^2-1+4x^2-2x}{x^2}$$

$$=\lim_{x\to 0}\frac{e^{2x}-2x-1}{x^2}$$

$$=\lim_{x\to 0}\frac{1+2x+\frac{4x^2}{2!}+\ldots-2x-1}{x^2}=2$$

32. (6) $g(x) = f(x) + x^2 - 2 = e^x - x^2 - 1 + x^2 - 2$

$g(x) = e^x - 3$

Graph of $|g(|x|)|$ is

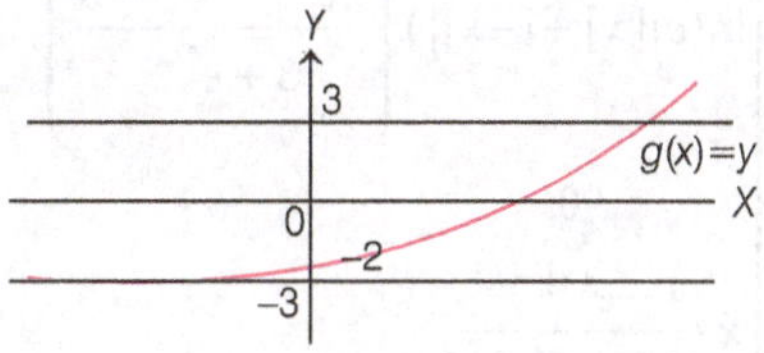

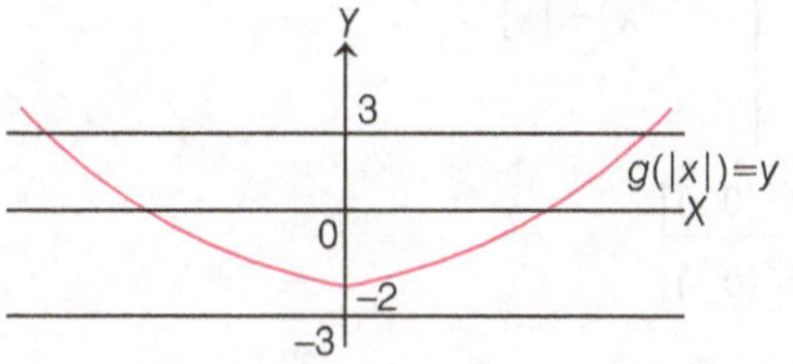

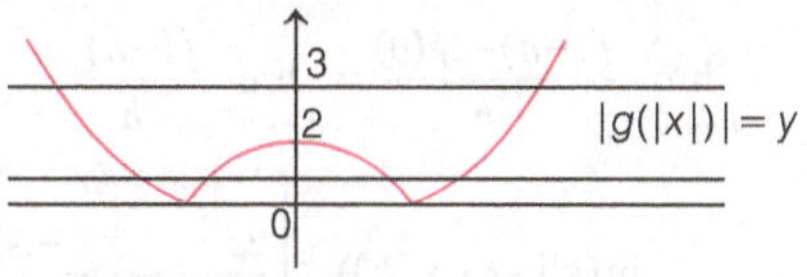

Now, the $|g(|x|)| = k$ has four roots

$\therefore \quad k \in (0, 2)$

$a = 0$ and $b = 2$

$2a + 3b = 6a$

Stem II

(Ex. Nos. 33 to 34)

Let $g(x)$ be a periodic function defined in the interval $[0, 2]$ as $g(x) = |x - 1| - \frac{1}{2}$. Let $h(x)$ be a periodic function with period 2 defined as $h(x) = g(x) + \sin \pi x$.

Further, define a composite function $\psi(x) = f(g(x))$ such that $f(x)$ satisfies the functional equation

$f(mx + ny) = (f(x))^m \, (f(y))^n, \forall\, x, y, m, n \in R$ and $f'(0) = -\ln 2 f(0)$.

Based on the above information, answer the following questions.

Example 33 *The value of* $\lim_{n \to \infty} \int_{-2}^{2} \frac{1}{1 + (f(x))^n} dx$ *is ....*

Example 34 *Number of points where* $f(x)$ *and* $g(x)$ *intersect in* $[-2, 9]$ *is ....*

Sol. Q. Nos. (33-34)

Given, $\psi(x) = f(g(x))$ ...(i)

$f(mx + ny) = (f(x))^m (f(y))^n, \forall\, x, y, m, n \in R$ ...(ii)

$f(0) = -\ln 2 f(0)$ ...(iii)

$g(x)$ is periodic function given by

$g(x) = |x - 1| - \frac{1}{2}, \quad 0 \le x \le 2$ ...(iv)

$h(x) = g(x) + \sin \pi x$ is periodic with period 2

$\Rightarrow \quad h(x + 2) = h(x)$

$\Rightarrow \quad g(x + 2) + \sin \pi(x + 2) = g(x) + \sin \pi x$

$\Rightarrow \quad g(x + 2) + \sin \pi x = g(x) + \sin \pi x$

$\Rightarrow \quad g(x + 2) = g(x)$

$\Rightarrow g(x)$ must be a periodic function with period 2.

$$g(x) = \begin{cases} |x - 1| - \frac{1}{2}, & 0 \le x \le 2 \\ |x - 3| - \frac{1}{2}, & 2 \le x \le 4 \\ |x - 5| - \frac{1}{2}, & 4 \le x \le 6 \\ \text{and so on.} \end{cases}$$

Now, $f(mx + ny) - (f(x))^m (f(y))^n, \forall\, x, y, m, n \in R$

For $m = n = 0$,

$f(0) = 1$;

For $m = n = 1$; $f(x + y) = f(x); f(y)$

$$f(a) = \lim_{h \to 0} \frac{f(x + h) - f(x)}{h} = \lim_{h \to 0} \frac{f(x) f(h) - f(x)}{h}$$

$$= \lim_{h \to 0} f(x) \left[\frac{f(h) - 1}{h}\right]$$

$$= \lim_{h \to 0} f(x) \left[\frac{f(h) - f(0)}{h}\right] \quad [\because f(0) = 1]$$

$$= f(x) f'(0) = f(x)(-\ln 2 \cdot f(0)) = (-\ln 2) f(x))$$

$$\therefore \quad \frac{f'(x)}{f(x)} = -\ln 2$$

$\Rightarrow \ln f(x) + C = -(\ln 2)x \Rightarrow \ln f(x) + x \ln 2 = C$

$\Rightarrow \ln 2^x f(x) = -C$

For $x = 0$, $\ln 1 = -C \Rightarrow C = 0$

$\therefore \ln 2^x f(x) = 0 \Rightarrow 2^x f(x) = 1 \Rightarrow f(x) = 2^{-x}$

$\Rightarrow \quad \psi(x) = (f(g(x)) = 2^{-g(x)} = 2^{1/2 - |x-1|} = \sqrt{2} \cdot 2^{-|x-1|)}$

33. (2) $f(x) = 2^{-x}$

$$\lim_{n \to \infty} \int_{-2}^{2} \frac{1}{1 + 2^{-nx}} dx = \lim_{n \to \infty} \int_{-2}^{2} \frac{2^{nx}}{2^{nx} + 1} dx$$

Putting $2^{nx} + 1 = t$

$$2^{nx} (\ln 2) n \, dx = dt \Rightarrow 2^{nx} dt = \frac{dt}{n \ln 2}$$

when $x = -2, t = 2^{-2n} + 1$ and when $x = 2, t = 2^{-2n} + 1$

$$\therefore \quad I = \lim_{n \to \infty} \int_{1+2^{-2n}}^{1+2^{2n}} \frac{dt}{t n \ln 2} dx$$

$$= \lim_{n \to \infty} \frac{1}{n \ln 2} |\ln t \int_{1+2^{-n}}^{1+2^n} |\ln 4|_{1+2^{-n}}^{1+2^n}$$

$$= \lim_{n \to \infty} \frac{1}{n \ln 2} \left| \ln \left(\frac{1 + 2^n}{1 + 2^{-n}} \right) \right|$$

$$= \lim_{n \to \infty} \frac{1}{n \ln 2} |\ln 2^{2n}| = \lim_{n \to \infty} \frac{1}{n \ln 2} = 2n \ln 2 = 2$$

34. (5) $f(x)=2^{-x}$ and $g(x)=|x-1|-\frac{1}{2}; 0\le x\le 2$ and $g(x)$ is periodic with period 2. The graphs of $f(x)$ and $g(x)$ in $0\le x\le 2$ is shown below.

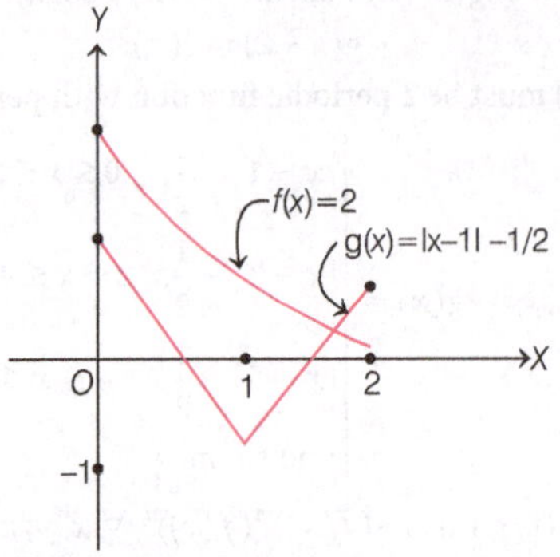

$\therefore$ In [0, 2], $f(x)$ and $g(x)$ intersect only at one point in $[-2, 9]$, $f(x)$ and $g(x)$ would intersect in $[-2, 0]$, [0, 2], [4, 6], [6, 4], [6, 8] i.e. at 5 points.

Single Integer Answer Type Questions

Example 35 *If* $f(x)=\cos x+|\cos x|$, *then the value of* $\left|f'\left(\frac{\pi^+}{2}\right)+f'\left(\frac{\pi^-}{2}\right)\right|$ *is ....*

Sol. (2) $f(x)=\cos x+|\cos x|$

$$=\begin{cases}2\cos x, & \text{for } \frac{-\pi}{2}<x\le\frac{\pi}{2}\\ 0, & \text{for } \frac{\pi}{2}\le x\le\frac{3\pi}{2}\end{cases}$$

$$\therefore \text{LHD}=f'\left(\frac{\pi^-}{2}\right)=\lim_{h\to 0^+}\frac{f\left(\frac{\pi}{2}-h\right)-f\left(\frac{\pi}{2}\right)}{-h}$$

$$=\lim_{h\to 0^+}\frac{2\cos\left(\frac{\pi}{2}-h\right)-0}{-h}$$

$$=\lim_{h\to 0^+}\frac{2\sin h}{-h}=-2$$

$$\text{and RHD}=f'\left(\frac{\pi^+}{2}\right)=\lim_{h\to 0^+}\frac{f\left(\frac{\pi}{2}+h\right)-f\left(\frac{\pi}{2}\right)}{h}$$

$$=\lim_{h\to 0^+}\frac{0-0}{h}$$

$$=0$$

$$\therefore\ |\text{LHD}+\text{RHD}|=\left|f'\left(\frac{\pi^-}{2}\right)+f'\left(\frac{\pi^+}{2}\right)\right|$$

$$=|-2+0|=2$$

Example 36 *For the function*

$$f(x)=\begin{cases}\ln(e|[x]+[-x]|)\left(\dfrac{2e^{\frac{\{x\}+\{-x\}}{x}}-5}{3+e^{1/x}}\right), & \text{for } x<0\\ 0, & \text{for } x=0.\\ x\cdot\dfrac{1-e^{[x]+\{x\}}}{|x|+\{x\}}, & \text{for } x>0\end{cases}$$

Evaluate $\dfrac{|f'(0^-)|}{|f'(0^+)|}$.

Sol. (2) LHD $=f'(0^-)$

$$=\lim_{h\to 0^+}\frac{f(-h)-f(0)}{-h}=\lim_{h\to 0^+}\frac{f(-h)}{-h}$$

$$=\lim_{h\to 0^+}\frac{\ln(e|[-h]+[h]|)^{-h}\left(\dfrac{2e^{\frac{\{-h\}+\{h\}}{h}}-5}{3+e^{1/h}}\right)}{-h}$$

$$=\lim_{h\to 0^+}\frac{\ln(e|-1|)^{-h}\left(\dfrac{2e^{1/h}-5}{3+e^{1/h}}\right)}{-h}$$

$[\because [h]+[-h]=-1 \text{ for } h\notin Z$
and $\{h\}+\{-h\}=1 \text{ for } h\notin Z]$

$$=\lim_{h\to 0^+}\frac{-h\ln e\left(\dfrac{2e^{1/h}-5}{3+e^{1/h}}\right)}{-h}$$

$$=\lim_{h\to 0^+}\left(\frac{2e^{1/h}-5}{3+e^{1/h}}\right)$$

$$=\lim_{h\to 0^+}\left(\frac{2-5e^{-1/h}}{3e^{-1/h}+1}\right)=2$$

$$\text{Now, RHD}=f'(0^+)=\lim_{h\to 0^+}\frac{f(h)-f(0)}{h}$$

$$=\lim_{h\to 0^+}\frac{f(h)}{h}$$

$$=\lim_{h\to 0^+}\frac{h\,\dfrac{1-e^{[h]+\{h\}}}{|h|+\{h\}}}{h}$$

$$=\lim_{h\to 0^+}\frac{1-e^{h+h}}{h+h}$$

$$=\lim_{h\to 0^+}\frac{1-e^{2h}}{2h}=-1$$

$$\therefore\ \frac{|f'(0^-)|}{|f'(0^+)|}=\frac{2}{1}=2$$

Example 37 *The number of points, where $|xf(x)|+||x-2|-1||$ is non-differentiable in $x \in (0, 3\pi)$, where $f(x)=\prod_{k=1}^{\infty}\left(\dfrac{1+2\cos\left(\dfrac{2x}{3^k}\right)}{3}\right)$, is ....*

Sol. (5) We know that

$$\sin 3\theta = 3\sin\theta - 4\sin^3\theta = \sin\theta(1+2\cos 2\theta)$$

$$\therefore \quad \sin 3\theta = \sin\theta(1+2\cos 2\theta) \quad \text{...(i)}$$

Now, on putting $3\theta = x, \dfrac{x}{3}, \dfrac{x}{3^2}, \ldots$ one by one in Eq. (i), we get

$$\sin x = \sin\left(\frac{x}{3}\right)\cdot\left(1+2\cos\frac{2x}{3}\right)$$

and $$\sin\frac{x}{3} = \sin\left(\frac{x}{3^2}\right)\cdot\left(1+2\cos\frac{2x}{3^2}\right)$$

$$\therefore \quad \sin\frac{x}{3^2} = \sin\left(\frac{x}{3^3}\right)\cdot\left(1+2\cos\frac{2x}{3^3}\right) \text{... and so on.}$$

$$\Rightarrow \quad \sin x = \sin\left(\frac{x}{3^n}\right)\cdot\prod_{k=1}^{n}\left(1+2\cos\frac{2x}{3^k}\right)$$

$$\Rightarrow \quad \frac{\sin x}{x} = \lim_{n\to\infty}\frac{\sin x/3^n}{x/3^n}\prod_{k=1}^{n}\frac{\left(1+2\cos\left(\frac{2x}{3^k}\right)\right)}{3^n}$$

$$\Rightarrow \quad \frac{\sin x}{x} = \prod_{k=1}^{\infty}\left(\frac{1+2\cos\left(\frac{2x}{3^k}\right)}{3}\right) = f(x) \quad \text{...(ii)}$$

Thus, $|xf(x)|+||x-2|-1| = \dfrac{|x||\sin x|}{|x|} + ||x-2|-1|$

is not differentiable at $\{\pi, 2\pi, 0, 1, 3\}$.

$\therefore$ Number of points are 5.

Example 38 *Let $f(x)$ be a polynomial function and $(f(\alpha))^2+(f'(\alpha))^2=0$, then find $\lim_{x\to\alpha}\dfrac{f(x)}{f'(x)}\left[\dfrac{f'(x)}{f(x)}\right]$, where $[\cdot]$ denotes greatest integer function, is ......*

Sol. (1) Here, $(f(\alpha))^2+(f'(\alpha))^2=0 \Rightarrow f(\alpha)=f'(\alpha)=0$

$\therefore \alpha$ is repeated root of $f(x)$.

Now, $$\lim_{x\to\alpha}\frac{f(x)}{f'(x)}\left[\frac{f'(x)}{f(x)}\right]$$

$$= \lim_{x\to\alpha}\frac{f(x)}{f'(x)}\left(\frac{f'(x)}{f(x)}-\left\{\frac{f'(x)}{f(x)}\right\}\right)$$

$$= \lim_{x\to\alpha}\left(1-\frac{f(x)}{f'(x)}\cdot\left\{\frac{f'(x)}{f(x)}\right\}\right)$$

[as, $x=\alpha$ is the repeated root and $\left\{\dfrac{f(x)}{f'(x)}\right\}$ is bounded;

$$\therefore \lim_{x\to\alpha}\frac{f(x)}{f'(x)} = 0]$$

$$= 1 - 0 = 1$$

Example 39 *Given $f(x)=\sum_{r=1}^{n}\tan\left(\dfrac{x}{2^r}\right)\sec\left(\dfrac{x}{2^{r-1}}\right)r, n\in N$*

$$g(x)=\lim_{n\to\infty}\frac{\ln\left(f(x)+\tan\frac{x}{2^n}\right)-\left(f(x)+\tan\frac{x}{2^n}\right)^n\left[\sin\left(\tan\frac{x}{2}\right)\right]}{1+\left(f(x)+\tan\frac{x}{2^h}\right)^h}$$ *for*

$x \ne \dfrac{\pi}{4}$, k for $x=\dfrac{\pi}{4}$ and the domain of $g(x)$ is $(0, \pi/2)$.

where [] denotes the greatest integer function. Find the number of possible values of k for which $g(x)$ becomes continuous in its domain.

Sol. (1) $$f(x)=\sum_{r=1}^{n}\frac{\sin\left(\frac{x}{2^{r-1}}-\frac{x}{2^r}\right)}{\cos\frac{x}{2^r}\cdot\cos\frac{x}{2^{r-1}}}$$

$$= \sum_{r=1}^{n}\frac{\sin\left(\frac{x}{2^{r-1}}\right)\cos\left(\frac{x}{2^r}\right)-\left(\cos\frac{x}{2^{r-1}}\right)\left(\sin\frac{x}{2^r}\right)}{\cos\frac{x}{2^r}\cdot\cos\frac{x}{2^{r-1}}}$$

$$= \sum_{r=1}^{n}\tan\left(\frac{x}{2^{r-1}}\right)-\tan\left(\frac{x}{2^r}\right)$$

$$= \left(\tan x - \tan\frac{x}{2}\right)+\left(\tan\frac{x}{2}-\tan\frac{x}{2^r}\right)$$

$$f(x) = \tan x - \tan\left(\frac{x}{2^n}\right)$$

$$g(x) = \lim_{n\to\infty}\frac{\ln\tan x - (\tan x)^n\cdot\left[\sin\left(\tan\frac{x}{2}\right)\right]}{1+(\tan x)^x}, x \ne \frac{\pi}{4}$$

$$g\left(\frac{\pi}{4}\right)=k,\ g\left(\frac{\pi^+}{4}\right)=\lim_{n\to\infty}\frac{\ln\left(\tan\left(\frac{\pi}{4}+h\right)\right)-0}{1+\infty}=0$$

$$g\left(\frac{\pi^-}{4}\right)=\lim_{x\to\infty}\frac{0}{1}=0$$

$$k=0$$

$\therefore$ Number of possible values of k is 1.

Example 40 *The number of points where function*

$$f(x)=\begin{cases}|3x^2-2x-5|, & x\le -1\\ -[3x^2-1], & -1<x<2\\ |3x+4|+|4x-5|, & x\ge 2\end{cases}$$ *where $[t]$ denotes the greatest integer $\le t$, is discontinuous is λ, then $\dfrac{\lambda}{11}$ is ....*

Sol. (2) $|3x^2-2x-5|=|3x^2-5x+3x-5|=|(3x-5)(x+1)|$

$\because \quad x \le -1$

$\therefore |3x^2-2x-5| = -(3x^2-2x-5)$

Now, for $-1<x<2$

$$0<x^2<4$$
$$0<3x^2<12$$
$$-1<3x^2-1<11$$

Point where it will discontinuous when

$$3x^2-1=0,1,2,3,\dots 10$$

$$\Rightarrow \quad x^2=0,\frac{2}{3},\frac{3}{3},\frac{4}{3},\dots,\frac{11}{3}$$

$$\Rightarrow \quad x=0,\pm\sqrt{\frac{2}{3}},\pm 1,\dots,\pm\sqrt{\frac{11}{3}}$$

and for $x\ge 2$

$$|3x+4|+|5x-4|=3x+4+5x-4=8x$$

Now, continuity at $x=-1$ and $x=2$

$$f(-1)=0$$
$$f(-1^-)=0$$
$$f(-1^+)=2$$

$\therefore$ Discontinuous at $x=-1$

Similarly, $f(2)=16$

$$f(2^+)=16 \text{ and } f(2^-)=11$$

$\therefore$ Discontinuous at $x=11$

$\therefore$ Number of points of discontinuity $=\lambda$

$$\left[\begin{array}{l} x=0,\pm\sqrt{\frac{2}{3}},\pm 1,\pm\sqrt{\frac{4}{3}},\pm\sqrt{\frac{5}{3}},\pm\sqrt{2},\pm\sqrt{\frac{7}{3}}, \\ \pm\sqrt{\frac{8}{3}},\pm\sqrt{3},\pm\sqrt{\frac{10}{3}},\pm\sqrt{\frac{11}{3}} \text{ and } n=2 \end{array}\right]$$

$$\therefore \quad \lambda=22 \Rightarrow \frac{\lambda}{11}=2$$

Example 41 *If $f(x)$ is a differentiable function for all $x\in R$ such that $f(x)$ has fundamental period 2. $f(x)=0$ has exactly two solutions in [0, 2], also $f(0)\ne 0$. If minimum number of zeroes of $h(x)=f'(x)\cos x - f(x)\sin x$ in (0, 99) is 120 +k , then k is ....*

Sol. (7) $h(x)=\frac{d}{dx}(f(x)\cdot\cos x)$

First find the minimum number of zeroes of $(f(x)\cdot\cos x)=0$

$f(x)=0$ has minimum 98 roots in [0, 99) and $\cos x=0$ has 31 roots is (0, 99).

Maximum common possible root is only 1.

Hence, minimum number of roots of $f(x)\cos x=0$ is 128.

Thus, $\frac{d}{dx}(f(x)\cos x)=0$ has minimum 127 roots.

$$127=120+7$$

Hence, value of k is 7.

Numerical Value Type Questions

Example 42 *Let $f(x)$ be defined as follows*

$$f(x)=\begin{cases}(\cos x-\sin x)^{\operatorname{cosec} x}, & -\frac{\pi}{2}<x<0\\ a, & x=0\\ \frac{e^{1/x}+e^{2/x}+e^{3/x}}{ae^{2/x}+be^{3/x}}, & 0<x<\frac{\pi}{2}\end{cases}$$

If $f(x)$ is continuous at $x=0$, then find 100 ab.

Sol. (100) Here, $f(x)$ is continuous at $x=0$

$\Rightarrow$ RHL (at $x=0$) = LHL (at $x=0$) = $f(0)$

$\therefore$ RHL (at $x=0$)

$$\lim_{x\to 0^+}\frac{e^{1/x}+e^{2/x}+e^{3/x}}{ae^{2/x}+bx^{3/x}}=\lim_{h\to 0}\frac{e^{3/h}\left\{\frac{1}{e^{2/h}}+\frac{1}{e^{1/h}}+1\right\}}{e^{3/h}\left\{\frac{a}{e^{1/h}}+b\right\}}$$

$$=\frac{1}{b} \quad \dots\text{(i)} \left[\text{as } \lim_{h\to 0}\frac{1}{e^{1/h}}\to 0\right]$$

Again, LHL (at $x=0$) = $\lim_{x\to 0^-}(\cos x-\sin x)^{\operatorname{cosec} x}$

$$=\lim_{h\to 0^-}(\cos h-\sin h)^{\operatorname{cosec} h}$$

$$=\lim_{h\to 0^+}\{1+(\cos h+\sin h-1)\}^{-1/\sin h} \quad [\text{i.e. } (1)^\infty \text{ form}]$$

$$=e^{\lim_{h\to 0^+}(\cos h+\sin h-1)\left(-\frac{1}{\sin h}\right)}$$

$$=e^{\lim_{h\to 0}\left\{-\sin^2\frac{h}{2}+2\sin\frac{h}{2}\cos\frac{h}{2}\right\}\left(-\frac{1}{2\sin h/2\cos h/2}\right)}$$

$$=e^{\lim_{h\to 0}\frac{\sin h/2-\cos h/2}{\cos h/2}}=e^{-1} \quad \dots\text{(ii)}$$

and $f(0)=a$

$$\Rightarrow \quad a=e^{-1}=1/b \Rightarrow a=\frac{1}{e} \text{ and } b=e$$

$\therefore$ $100ab=100$

Example 43 *The function*

$$f(x)=\begin{cases}\left(\frac{6}{5}\right)^{\frac{\tan 6x}{\tan 5x}} & \text{if } 0<x<\frac{\pi}{2}\\ b+2 & \text{if } x=\frac{\pi}{2}\\ (1+|\cos x|)^{\left(\frac{a|\tan x|}{b}\right)} & \text{if } \frac{\pi}{2}<x<\pi\end{cases},$$

if f is continuous at $x=\frac{\pi}{2}$, then $2a+b+11$ is ....

Sol. (10) $f\left(\frac{\pi^-}{2}\right)=\left(\frac{6}{5}\right)^0=1$

$$[\because \tan 6x \to 0, \tan 5x \to \infty, \frac{0}{\infty}=0]$$

$$f\left(\frac{\pi}{2}\right)=b+2$$

$$f\left(\frac{\pi^+}{2}\right)=\lim_{h\to 0}\left(1+\left|\cos\left(\frac{\pi}{2}+h\right)\right|\right)^{\frac{a\left|\tan\left(\frac{\pi}{2}+h\right)\right|}{b}}$$

$$=\lim_{h\to 0}(1+\sin h)^{\frac{a}{b\tan h}}$$

$$=\lim_{h\to 0} e^{\sin h\cdot\frac{a}{b\tan h}}=e^a$$

$$e^a=1$$

$\Rightarrow$ $a=0, b+2=1$

$\Rightarrow$ $b=-1$

$\therefore$ $2a+b+11=0-1+11=10$

Example 44 *Let $f(x)=[x][\sin x]+[-x][-\sin x]+x+[-x][\sin x]+[x][-\sin x]$, where $[\cdot]$ denotes the greatest integer function, then the number of points of discontinuity of $f(x)$ in $(0,\pi)$ is*

Decoding the Question

To solve this problem use properties of greatest integer of x as $[x]=1$ if $x\in I$, $[x]+[-x]=-1$, $x\notin I$

$=0$, $x\in I$.

Sol. (4) We have,

$$f(x)=[x][\sin x]+[-x][-\sin x]+x+[-x][\sin x]+[x][-\sin x],$$

$$=\begin{cases} x, & x\in I \\ x, & x=\frac{n\pi}{2},\ n\in I \\ x+1, & \text{otherwise}\end{cases}$$

$f(x)$ is discontinuous at integers and $\frac{n\pi}{2}$, so in $(0,\pi)$, $f(x)$ is discontinuous at 1, 2, 3 and $\frac{\pi}{2}$.

$\therefore$ Number of points of discontinuity $=4$

Example 45 *The points of discontiuity of $y=g(u)=\frac{1}{u^2+u-2}$, where $u=\frac{1}{x-1}$ are x_1, x_2, x_3, then the value of $x_1+x_2+x_3$ is equal to ....*

Sol. The function $u=f(x)=\frac{1}{x-1}$ is discontinuous at the point $x=1$.

The function $y=g(u)=\frac{1}{u^2+u-2}$

$$=\frac{1}{(u+2)(u-1)}$$

is discontinuous at $u=-2$ and $u=1$,

where $u=-2, \frac{1}{x-1}=4=-2$

$\Rightarrow$ $x=\frac{1}{2}$

when $u=1, \frac{1}{x-1}=1\Rightarrow x=\frac{1}{2}$

when $u=1, \frac{1}{x-1}-1\Rightarrow x=2$

Hence, the composite function $y=g(f(x))$ is discontinuous at three points $x=\frac{1}{2},1,2$

So, $x_1=\frac{1}{2}, x_2=1, x_3=2$

Now, $x_1+x_2+x_3=3.5$

Example 46 $f(x)=\begin{cases}\max g(t), & 0\le t\le x;\ 0\le x<3\\ \min g(t), & x\le t\le 0;\ -3\le x<0\end{cases}$

where $g(x)=x+\sin x$

The number of value of x for which $f(x)$ is not differentiable in $[-3,3]$ is equal to ....

Sol. (0) We have, $g(x)=x+\sin x$

$g'(x)=1+\cos x$

$\therefore$ $g'(x)\ge 0$ and $g'(x)=0$, $\forall\ x\in(2n+1)\pi$

$\Rightarrow$ $g(x)$ is always increasing.

Now, maximum of $g(t)$, $\forall\ t\in[0,x]$ will always occur at x.

$\max(g(t))=g(x)=x+\sin x$

$\min(g(t))$, $\forall\ t\in[x,0]$ will always occur at x.

$\Rightarrow$ $\min(g(t))=g(x)=x+\sin x$

$\Rightarrow$ $f(x)=x+\sin x, -3\le x\le 3$

Hence, f is continuous and differentiable at each and every point $\in[-3,3]$

$\therefore$ Required number is 0.

Example 47 *If $\lim_{x\to 0}\frac{1-\cos\left(1-\cos\frac{x}{2}\right)}{2^m x^n}$ is equal to the left hand derivative of $e^{-|x|}$ at $x=0$, then the value of $(n-10m)$ is ....*

Sol. (74) $f(x)=\begin{cases}e^{x}, & x\le 0\\ e^{-x}, & x>0\end{cases}, f'(0^-)=1$

$$\lim_{x\to 0}\frac{1-\cos\left(2\sin^2\left(\frac{x}{4}\right)\right)}{2^m x^n}=\lim_{x\to 0}\frac{2\sin^2\left(\sin^2\frac{x}{4}\right)}{2^m x^n}=1,\ n=4$$

$$=\lim_{x\to 0}\frac{2\sin^2\left(\sin^2\left(\frac{x}{4}\right)\right)}{2^m\cdot 4^4\left(\frac{x^4}{4^4}\right)}=1$$

$\Rightarrow \quad m+7=0$

$\Rightarrow \quad m=-7$

$\Rightarrow \quad n-10m=4+70=74$

Example 48 *A derivable function $f:R\to R$ satisfies the condition $f(x)-f(y)\ge \ln\left(\frac{x}{y}\right)+x-y$ for every $x,y\in R^+$. If g denotes the derivative of f, then $\sum_{n=1}^{100} g\left(\frac{1}{n}\right)$ is ....*

Sol. (5150) $f(x)-f(y)\ge \ln\left(\frac{x}{y}\right)+x-y$

$\therefore$ Replace x by $x+h$ and y by x

$$f(x+h)-f(x)\ge \ln(x+h)-\ln x+h$$

$$\Rightarrow \quad \frac{(f(x+h)-f(x))}{h}\ge\frac{\ln(x+h)-\ln x}{h}+1$$

For $h\to 0,\quad f'(x)\ge\frac{1}{x}+1$

Now, replace x by $x-h$ and y by x

$$f(x-h)-f(x)\ge \ln\left(\frac{x-h}{x}\right)-h$$

$$\Rightarrow \quad \frac{f(x-h)-f(x)}{-h}\le\frac{\ln\left(1-\frac{h}{x}\right)+1}{-h}$$

$$\Rightarrow \quad f'(x)\le\frac{1}{x}+1$$

$$\Rightarrow \quad f'(x)=\frac{1}{x}+1$$

$$\Rightarrow \quad g(x)=1+x$$

$$\therefore \quad \sum_{n=1}^{100} g\left(\frac{1}{n}\right)=2+3+4+\ldots+101=50\times 103=5150$$

Example 49 *Let f be a real valued continuous function on R and satisfying $f(-x)-f(x)=0, \forall\in R$.*

If $f(-5)=5$, $f(-2)=4$, $f(3)=-2$ and $f(0)=0$, the minimum number of zero's of the equation $f(x)=0$ is α and let β be the number of ponits of discontinuity of the function $f(x)=[5x]+\{3x\}$ in $[0,5]$, where $[y]$ and $\{y\}$ denote largest integer less than or equal to y and fractional part of y respectively, then $\alpha+\beta$ is equal to ....

Sol. (35) $f(x)=f(-x)$

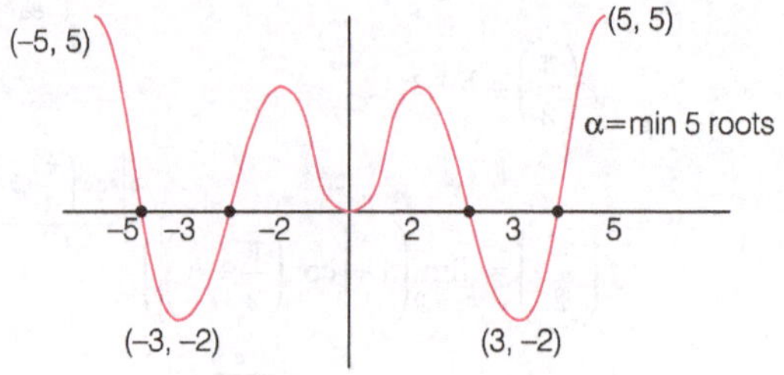

$\because \quad f(x)=[5x]+\{3x\}$ in $[0,5]$

$0\le 5x\le 25$

$$\Rightarrow \quad x=0,\frac{1}{5},\frac{2}{5},\frac{3}{5},\frac{4}{5},1,\frac{6}{5},\frac{7}{5},\frac{8}{5},\frac{9}{5},2,\frac{11}{5},\frac{12}{5},\frac{13}{5},\ldots,\frac{25}{5}$$

$0\le 3x\le 15$

$$\Rightarrow \quad x=0,\frac{1}{3},\frac{2}{3},1,\frac{4}{3},\frac{5}{3}$$

$\left.\begin{array}{l}[5x]=25\text{ points}\\ \{3x\}=15\text{ points}\end{array}\right\}$

$x=1,2,3,4,5$

$[5x]+\{3x\}$ is continuous

$\Rightarrow \quad 25+15-2(5)=30$

Now, $\alpha=5$ and $\beta=30$

$\therefore \quad \alpha+\beta=35$

Example 50 *Let $f:R^+\to R$ satisfies the functional equation $f(xy)=e^{xy-x-y}\{e^y f(x)+e^x f(y)\}\ \forall\ x,y\in R^+$. If $f'(1)=e$. If $f(x)=e^{kx}\ln(lx)$, then $20k+30l$.*

Sol. (50) Given that $f(xy)=e^{xy-x-y}\{e^y f(x)+e^x f(y)\}$,

$\forall\ x,y\in R^+$ ...(i)

On putting $x=y=1$, we get

$$f(1)=e^{-1}\{e^{-1}f(1)+e^{1}f(1)\}$$

$\Rightarrow \quad f(1)=0$ ...(ii)

Now, applying the concept of derivative of function, we get

$$f'(x)=\lim_{h\to 0}\frac{f(x+h)-f(x)}{h}=\lim_{h\to 0}\frac{f\left\{x\left(1+\frac{h}{x}\right)\right\}-f(x)}{h}$$

$$=\lim_{h\to 0}\frac{e^{x\left(1+\frac{h}{x}\right)-x-\left(1+\frac{h}{x}\right)}\left\{e^{1+\frac{h}{x}}f(x)+e^x f\left(1+\frac{h}{x}\right)\right\}-f(x)}{h}$$

$$=\lim_{h\to 0}\frac{e^h f(x)+e^{h-1-\frac{h}{x}+x}\left\{f\left(1+\frac{h}{x}\right)-f(1)\right\}-f(x)}{h}$$

$[\because f(1)=0]$

$$= \lim_{h\to 0} \frac{f(x)(e^h-1)+e^{h-1-\frac{h}{x}+x}\left\{f\left(1+\frac{h}{x}\right)-f(1)\right\}}{h}$$

$$= \lim_{h\to 0} \frac{f(x)(e^h-1)}{h} + \lim_{h\to 0} \frac{e^{h-1-\frac{h}{x}+x}\left\{f\left(1+\frac{h}{x}\right)-f(1)\right\}}{\frac{h}{x}\cdot x}$$

$$= f(x)+\frac{e^{x-1}\cdot f'(1)}{x}$$

$$\left[\because \lim_{h\to 0}\frac{f\left(1+\frac{h}{x}\right)-f(1)}{\frac{h}{x}} = f'(1) \text{ and } \lim_{h\to 0}\frac{e^h-1}{h}=1\right]$$

$$= f(x)+\frac{e^x}{ex}\cdot f'(1) \qquad [\because f(1)=e]$$

$$\therefore \quad f'(x) = f(x)+\frac{e^x}{x}$$

$$\Rightarrow \quad \frac{e^x}{x} = f'(x)-f(x)$$

$$\Rightarrow \quad \frac{1}{x} = \frac{e^x f'(x)-f(x)\cdot e^x}{e^{2x}}$$

$$\left\{\begin{array}{l}\text{as by quotient rule, we can write}\\ \dfrac{e^x f'(x)-f(x)\cdot e^x}{(e^x)^2} = \dfrac{d}{dx}\left\{\dfrac{f(x)}{e^x}\right\}\end{array}\right\}$$

$$\therefore \quad \frac{1}{x} = \frac{d}{dx}\left\{\frac{f(x)}{e^x}\right\}$$

On integrating both sides w.r.t. x, we get

$$\ln|x|+c = \frac{f(x)}{e^x} \text{ or } f(x) = e^x\{\ln|x|+c\}$$

$\because \quad f(1)=0 \Rightarrow c=0$

Thus, $\quad f(x)=e^x\ln|x|$

$\because \quad k=1$ and $l=1$

$\therefore \quad 20k+30l=50$

Example 51 *If $f(x)=||x|-1|$, then the number of points of non-differentiability is λ, then number of positive integral solution of equation $\alpha+\beta+2\gamma=3\lambda$ is equal to ....*

Sol. (56) The graph of $f(x)$ is shown as

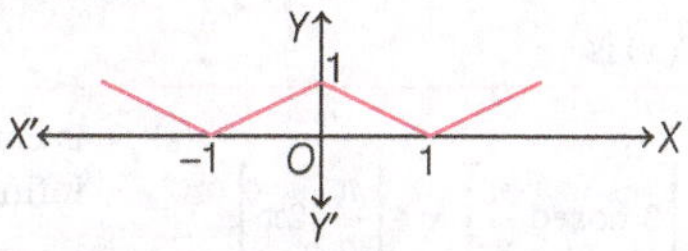

It is clear from the graph that $f(x)$ is continuous for all x, but $f(x)$ is not differentiable at $x=\{-1,0,1\}$.

Now, $fof(x)=||f(x)|-1|=|f(x)-1|$ [as $f(x)\geq 0\ \forall\ x$]

Now, if $f(x)\to f(x)-1$, shift the graph one unit below the X-axis, i.e. as shown

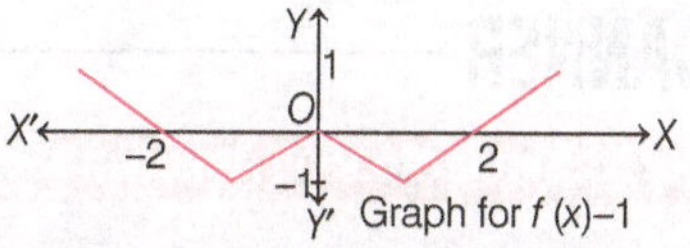

Graph for $f(x)-1$

Thus, for graph of $fof(x)=\{f(x)-1\}$ is taking image of the graph of $f(x)-1$ below X-axis and leaving the portion above Y-axis as it is

$\therefore$ Graph for $fof(x)$ is shown as

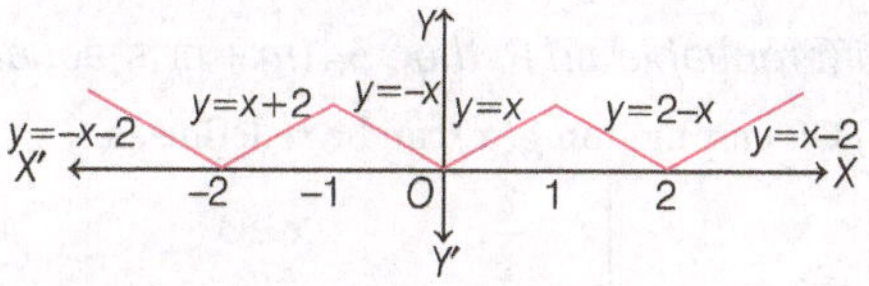

which is clearly continuous for all $x\in R$, but not differentiable at $x=\{-2,-1,0,1,2\}$.

Also, $\quad fof(x)=2-x, 1\leq x\leq 2$

Hence, the total number of points of non-differentiability = 5

$\therefore \quad \alpha+\beta+2\gamma=15$

Number of positive integral solutions is given

$$\alpha+\beta=15-2\gamma$$

$$\sum_{r=0}^{6} {}^{15-2\gamma-1}C_{2-1}$$

[total number positive integral solution is ${}^{n-1}C_{r-1}$]

$$\sum_{r=0}^{6} {}^{14-2\gamma}C_1$$

$$\Rightarrow \quad {}^{14}C_1+{}^{12}C_1+{}^{10}C_1+{}^{8}C_1+{}^{6}C_1+{}^{4}C_1+{}^{2}C_1$$

$$=14+12+10+8+6+4+2$$

$$=56$$

Example 52 *Let $f(x)$ be a differentiable function such that $2f(x+y)+f(x-y)=3f(x)+3f(y)+2xy,\ \forall\ x,y\in R$ and $f(0)=0$, then $f(10)+f'(10)$ is equal to*

Sol. (120) On putting $y=0$, $3f(x)=3f(x)+3f(0)+0$

$$\Rightarrow \quad f(0)=0$$

On putting $y=x$, $2f(2x)=6f(x)+2x^2$

$$\Rightarrow \quad f(2x)=3f(x)+x^2$$

$$\Rightarrow \quad f'(x)=\lim_{h\to 0}\frac{f(x+h)-f(x)}{h}$$

$$\Rightarrow \quad f'(x)=\lim_{h\to 0}\frac{\frac{3f(x)+3f(h)+2hx-f(x-h)}{2}-f(x)}{h}$$

$$=\lim_{h\to 0}\frac{f(x)-f(x-h)}{2h}+\frac{3}{2}\frac{f(h)}{h}+x$$

$$f'(x)=\frac{f'(x)}{2}+x$$

$$\Rightarrow \quad f'(x)=2x \Rightarrow f(x)=x^2$$

$$f(10)+f'(10)=100+20=120$$

JEE SCANNER

Example 53 Similar to PYQ Asked in JEE Main 2024

Let the function g(x) be defined as follows

$$g(x)=\begin{cases}\dfrac{2}{|x|}, & |x|\ge 3\\ mx^2+2n, & |x|<3\end{cases}$$

is differentiable on R, then $54(m+n)$ *is equal to ....*

Sol. (25) Given function $g(x)$ can be redefine as

$$g(x)=\begin{cases}\dfrac{2}{x}, & x\ge 3\\ mx^2+2n, & -3\le x<3\\ -\dfrac{2}{x} & x<-3\end{cases}$$

It is given that $g(x)$ is differentiable on R. So, it will be continuous on R.

Continuous at $x=3$

$$\frac{2}{3}=9m+2n \quad \text{...(i)}$$

and continuous at $x=-3$

$$\frac{2}{3}=9m+2n$$

Since, it is differentiable at $x=3$

$$-\frac{2}{x^2}=2mx$$

At $x=3 \Rightarrow -\dfrac{2}{9}=6m \Rightarrow m=-\dfrac{1}{27}$

From Eq. (i), $\dfrac{2}{3}=-\dfrac{1}{3}+2n \Rightarrow n=\dfrac{1}{2}$

$\therefore \quad 54(m+n)=25$

Skill Builder

If the function $f(x)=\begin{cases}\dfrac{1}{|x|}, & |x|\ge 1\\ cx^2+d, & |x|<1\end{cases}$ is differentiable on R, then $30(c+d)$ is equal to ....

For Sol.

Example 54 *Let* $f:R\to R$ *be a function satisfies condition* $f(x+y^3)=f(x)+[f(y)]^3\ \forall\ x,y\in R$. *If* $f'(0)\ge 0$, *then sum of all possible values of* $f(10)$ *is ....*

Sol. (10) Given, $f(x+y^3)=f(x)+[f(y)]^3$ ...(i)

and $f'(0)\ge 0$

On replacing x, y by 0,

$$f(0)=f(0)+f(0)^3 \Rightarrow f(0)=0 \quad \text{...(ii)}$$

Also, $f'(0)=\lim\limits_{h\to 0}\dfrac{f(0+h)-f(0)}{h}=\lim\limits_{h\to 0}\dfrac{f(h)}{h}$

Let $I=f'(0)=\lim\limits_{h\to 0}\dfrac{f(0+(h^{1/3})^3)-f(0)}{(h^{1/3})^3}$

$$=\lim_{h\to 0}\frac{f(0)+[f(h^{1/3})^3]-f(0)}{(h^{1/3})^3}$$

$$=\lim_{h\to 0}\frac{f(h^{1/3})^3-f(0)}{(h^{1/3})^3}=\lim_{h\to 0}\left(\frac{f(h^{1/3})}{(h^{1/3})}\right)^3=I^3$$

$\Rightarrow I=I^3$

or $I=0,1,-1$ as $f'(0)\ge 0$

$\therefore f'(0)=0,1$ ...(iii)

$$f'(x)=\lim_{h\to 0}\frac{f(x+h)-f(x)}{h}=\lim_{h\to 0}\frac{f(x+(h^{1/3})^3)-f(x)}{(h^{1/3})^3}$$

$$f'(x)=\lim_{h\to 0}\frac{f(x)+(f(h^{1/3}))^3-f(x)}{(h^{1/3})^3} \quad \text{[using Eq. (i)]}$$

$$\Rightarrow f'(x)=\lim_{h\to 0}\left(\frac{f(h^{1/3})}{(h^{1/3})}\right)^3=(f'(0))^3$$

$\Rightarrow f'(x)=0,1$ [as $f'(0)=0,1$, using Eq. (iii)]

On integrating both sides, we get

$f(x)=C$ or $x+C$

as $f(0)=0$

$\Rightarrow \quad C=0 \Rightarrow f(x)=0$ or x

$\Rightarrow \quad f(10)=0$ or 10

$\therefore$ Sum of all possible values $=0+10=10$

Matching Type Questions

Example 55 *Let* [.] *denotes integer function*

	Column I		Column II
(A)	If $P(x)=[2\cos x]$, $x\in[-\pi,\pi]$, then $P(x)$ is	(p)	is discontinous at exactly 7 points
(B)	If $Q(x)=[2\sin x]$, $x\in[-\pi,\pi]$, then $Q(x)$ is	(q)	is discontinous at exactly 4 points
(C)	If $R(x)=[2\tan x/2]$, $x\in\left[-\dfrac{\pi}{2},\dfrac{\pi}{2}\right]$ then $R(x)$ is	(r)	has non-removable discontinous
(D)	If $S(x)=\left[3\ \text{cosec}\ \dfrac{x}{3}\right]$, $x\in\left[\dfrac{\pi}{2},2\pi\right]$ then $S(x)$ is	(s)	is continous at infinitely many value
		(t)	continuous at some odd integer multiple of $\dfrac{\pi}{2}$

Sol. (A) – (p,r,s), (B) – (p,r,s,t), (C) – (q,r,s), (D) – (s,t)

(A) Graph of $2\cos x$ in $[-\pi, \pi]$ is shown below

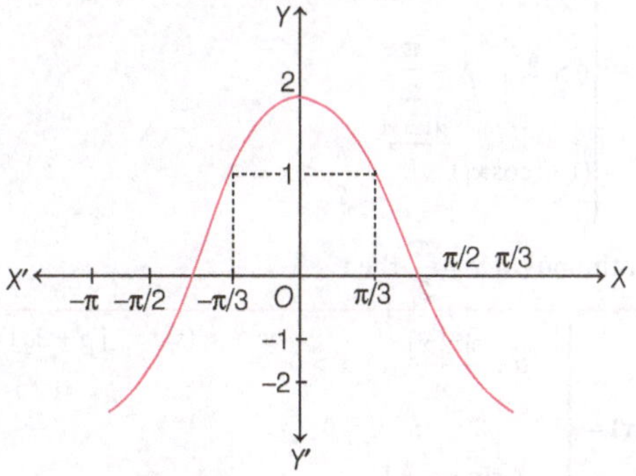

The graph of $P(x) = [2\cos x]$ in $[-\pi, \pi]$ is given below

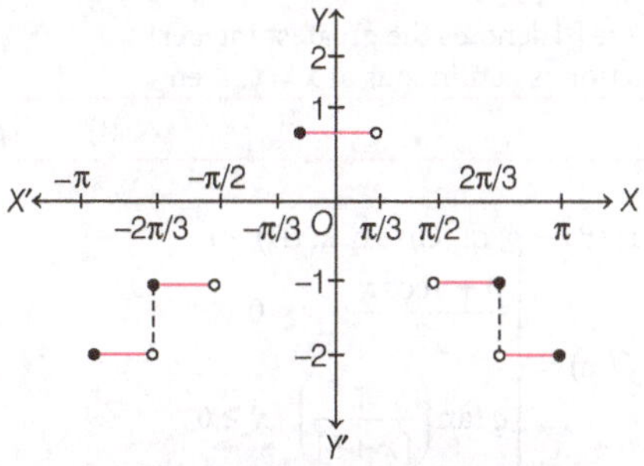

Clearly, $P(x)$ is discontinuous at 7 points i.e.

$$-\frac{2\pi}{3}, -\frac{\pi}{2}, -\frac{\pi}{3}, 0, \frac{\pi}{3}, \frac{\pi}{2}, \frac{2\pi}{3}$$

and hence non-differentiable at 7 points.

Also, $P(x)$ is continuous at infinitely many points except for the above seven points.

(B) Graph of $2\sin x$ in $[-\pi, \pi]$ is shown below

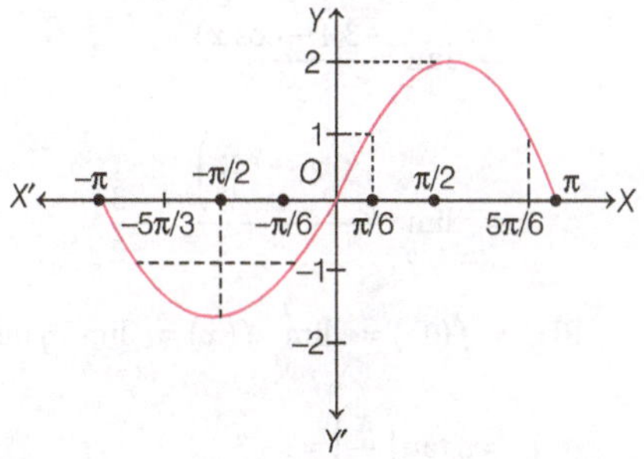

The graph of $Q(x) = [2\sin x]$ is as shown below

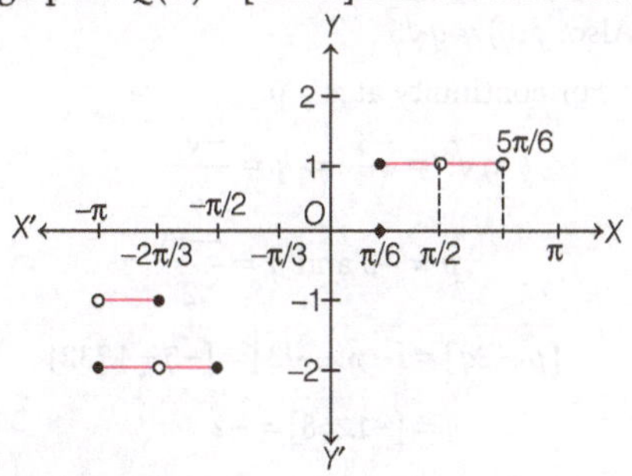

$f(x)$ is discontinuous at 7 points

i.e. $\quad -\pi, \frac{-5\pi}{6}, \frac{-\pi}{6}, 0, \frac{\pi}{6}, \frac{\pi}{2}, \frac{5\pi}{6}$

Also, $f(x)$ has removable discontinuity at $x = \frac{\pi}{2}$ and

$f(x)$ is continuous at infinitely many points in $[-\pi, \pi]$ except for above seven points.

Also, $f(x)$ is continuous at $-\frac{\pi}{2}$

i.e. an odd integer multiple of $\frac{\pi}{2}$.

(C) The graph of $2\tan\frac{x}{2}$ in $\left[-\frac{\pi}{2}, \frac{\pi}{2}\right]$ is as shown below

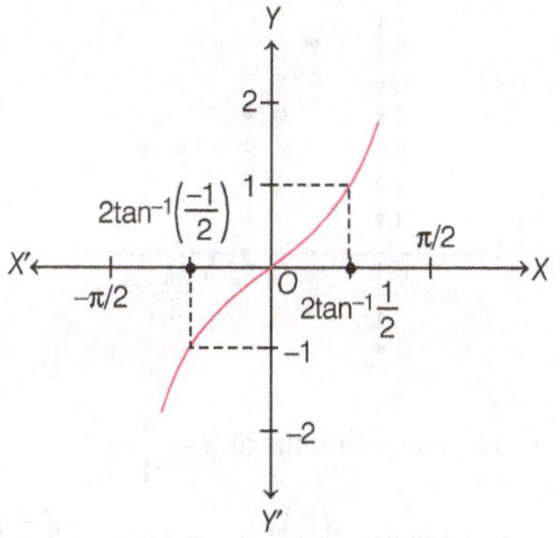

The graph of $R(x) = \left[2\tan\frac{x}{2}\right]$ in $\left[-\frac{\pi}{2}, \frac{\pi}{2}\right]$ is as shown below

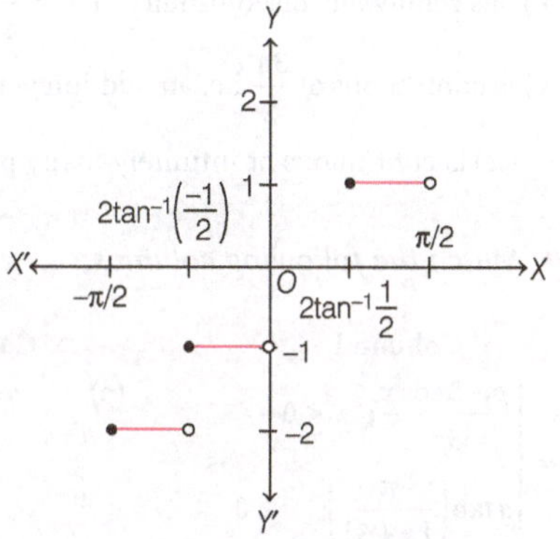

Clearly, $R(x)$ is discontinuous at exactly 4 points

$$2\tan^{-1}\left(-\frac{1}{2}\right), 0, 2\tan^{-1}\left(\frac{1}{2}\right), -\frac{\pi}{2}.$$

Also, $R(x)$ has removable discontinuity at $x = \frac{\pi}{2}$ and

$R(x)$ is continuous at infinitely many points except at above four points.

(D) The graph of $3 \operatorname{cosec} \dfrac{x}{3}$ in $\left[\dfrac{\pi}{2}, 2\pi\right]$ is as shown below.

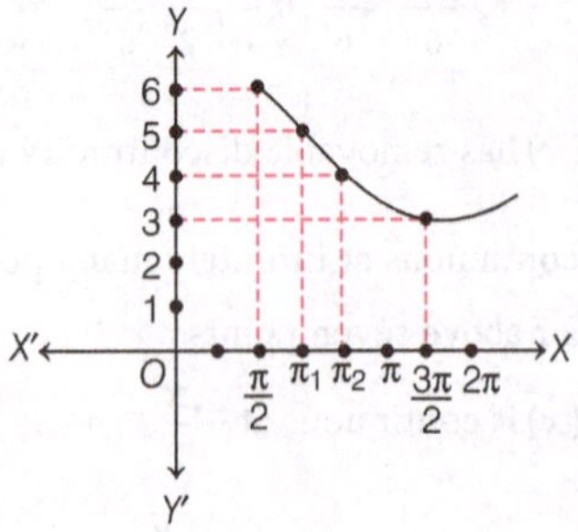

The graph of $S(x) = \left[3 \operatorname{cosec} \dfrac{x}{3}\right]$ in $\left[\dfrac{\pi}{2}, 2\pi\right]$ is as shown below

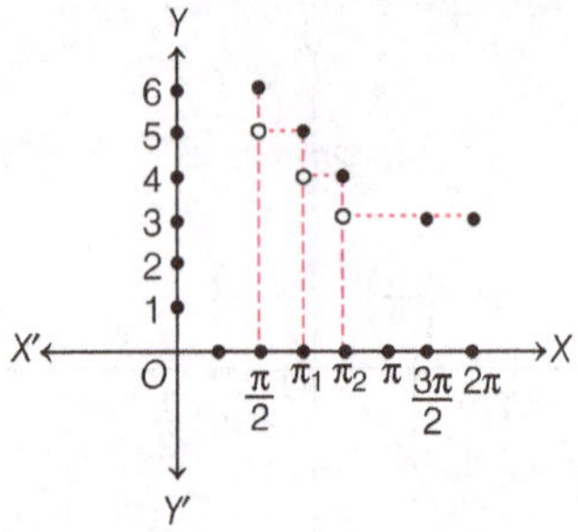

Clearly, $S(x)$ is discontinuous at $x = \dfrac{\pi}{4}$,

$$x_1 = 3 \operatorname{cosec}^{-1}\left(\frac{5}{3}\right), \; x_2 = 3 \operatorname{cosec}^{-1}\left(\frac{4}{3}\right)$$

i.e. at 3 points

Also, $f(x)$ has removable discontinuity at $x = \dfrac{\pi}{4}$.

Also, $f(x)$ is continuous at $\dfrac{3\pi}{2}$ i.e. an odd integer multiple of $\dfrac{\pi}{2}$ and $f(x)$ is continuous at infinitely many points.

Example 56 *Match the following columns.*

Column I	Column II
(A) If $f(x) = \begin{cases} \dfrac{p + 3\cos x}{x^2}; & x < 0 \\ q \tan\left(\dfrac{\pi}{[x+3]}\right); & x \geq 0 \end{cases}$ is continuous at $x = 0$, where $[\cdot]$ denotes the greatest integer function, then	(p) $\lvert p + q \rvert = 0$
(B) If $f(x) = \begin{cases} -2\sin x, & -\pi \leq x \leq -\dfrac{\pi}{2} \\ p\sin x + q, & \dfrac{-\pi}{2} < x < \dfrac{\pi}{2} \\ \cos x, & \dfrac{\pi}{2} \leq x \leq \pi \end{cases}$ is continuous in $[-\pi, \pi]$, then	(q) $\lvert p - q \rvert = 2$
(C) $f(x) = \begin{cases} \left(\dfrac{3}{2}\right)^{\left(\frac{\cos 3x}{\cos 2x}\right)}; & 0 < x < \dfrac{\pi}{2} \\ q + 3 \; ; & x = \dfrac{\pi}{2} \\ (1 + \lvert\cos x\rvert)^{\frac{p\lvert\tan x\rvert}{q}} \; ; & \dfrac{\pi}{2} < x < \pi \end{cases}$ is continuous at $x = \dfrac{\pi}{2}$, then	(r) $[p + 2q] = -2$
(D) If $f(x) = \begin{cases} p + \dfrac{\sin[x]}{x} \; ; & x > 0 \\ 2 \; ; & x = 0 \\ q + \left[\dfrac{\sin x - x}{x^3}\right]; & x < 0 \end{cases}$, where $[\cdot]$ denotes the greatest integer function is continuous at $x = 0$, then	(s) $[p + 2q] = 4$
	(t) $\lvert p - q \rvert = 1$

Sol. (A) – r; (B) – p, q; (C) – q, s; (D) – t

(A) $f(x) = \begin{cases} \dfrac{p + 3\cos x}{x^2}; & x < 0 \\ q \tan\left(\dfrac{\pi}{[x+3]}\right); & x \geq 0 \end{cases}$

$$\text{LHL} = f(0^-) = \lim_{x \to 0^-} f(x) = \lim_{x \to 0^-}\left(\frac{p + 3\cos x}{x^2}\right)$$

∴ Denominator tends to zero, numerator must also tend to zero.

This implies $p = -3$

$$\therefore \quad \text{LHL} = \lim_{x \to 0^-} \frac{-3 + 3\cos x}{x^2}$$

$$= \lim_{x \to 0^-} \frac{-3(1 - \cos x)}{x^2}$$

$$= \lim_{x \to 0^-} \frac{-3\left(2\sin^2 \frac{x}{2}\right)}{x^2} = -\frac{3}{2}$$

$$\text{RHL} = f(0^+) = \lim_{x \to 0^+} f(x) = \lim_{x \to 0^+} q\tan\left(\frac{\pi}{[x+3]}\right)$$

$$= q\tan\left(\frac{\pi}{3}\right) = q\sqrt{3}$$

Also, $f(0) = q\sqrt{3}$

∴ For continuity at $x = 0$

$$q\sqrt{3} = \frac{-3}{2} \Rightarrow q = \frac{-\sqrt{3}}{2}$$

$$p = -3 \text{ and } q = \frac{-\sqrt{3}}{2}$$

$$[p - 2q] = [-3 + \sqrt{3}] = [-3 + 1.732]$$

$$= [-1.268] = -2$$

(B) Possibly $f(x)$ can be discontinuous at $x = \frac{-\pi}{2}$ and $\frac{\pi}{2}$.

So, we shall make $f(x)$ continuous only at

$$x = -\frac{\pi}{2} \text{ and } x = \frac{\pi}{2}.$$

Now, at $x = -\frac{\pi}{2}$,

$$\text{LHL} = \lim_{x \to -\frac{\pi}{2}^-} f(x) = \lim_{x \to -\frac{\pi}{2}^-} (-2\sin x)$$

$$= -2\sin\left(-\frac{\pi}{2}\right) = 2$$

$$\text{RHL} = \lim_{x \to -\frac{\pi}{2}^+} f(x) = \lim_{x \to -\frac{\pi}{2}^-} (p\sin x + q) = -p + q$$

At $x = \frac{\pi}{2}$,

$$\text{LHL} = \lim_{x \to \frac{\pi}{2}^-} f(x) = \lim_{x \to \frac{\pi}{2}^-} (p\sin x + q) = p + q$$

$$\text{RHL} = \lim_{x \to \frac{\pi}{2}^+} f(x) = \lim_{x \to \frac{\pi}{2}^+} \cos x = 0$$

$\therefore$ For continuity at $x = -\frac{\pi}{2}$ and $\frac{\pi}{2}$,

$$-p + q = 2 \text{ and } p + q = 0$$

$$\Rightarrow \quad q = 1 \text{ and } p = -1$$

$$\therefore \quad |p+q| = 0; |p-q| = |-1-1| = 2$$

$$[p-2q] = [-1-2(-1)] = [1] = 1$$

$$[p+2q] = [-1+2(-1)] = [-3] = -3$$

(C) At $x = \frac{\pi}{2}$,

$$\text{LHL} = \lim_{x \to \frac{\pi}{2}^-} f(x)$$

$$= \lim_{x \to \frac{\pi}{2}^-} \left(\frac{3}{2}\right)^{\frac{\cos 3x}{\cos 2x}}$$

$$= \left(\frac{3}{2}\right)^{\lim_{x \to \frac{\pi}{2}^-} \left(\frac{\cos 3x}{\cos 2x}\right)} = \left(\frac{3}{2}\right)^0 = 1$$

$$\text{RHL} = \lim_{x \to \frac{\pi}{2}^+} f(x)$$

$$= \lim_{x \to \frac{\pi}{2}^+} (1 + |\cos x|)^{\frac{p}{q}|\tan x|}$$

$$= \lim_{x \to \frac{\pi}{2}^+} (1 + |\cos x|)^{\frac{1}{(\cos x)}\frac{p}{q}|\sin x|} = e^{p/q}$$

and $f\left(\frac{\pi}{2}\right) = q + 3$

$\therefore$ For continuity at $x = \frac{\pi}{2}$,

$$e^{p/q} = 1 = q + 3$$

$$\Rightarrow \quad p = 0 \text{ and } q = -2$$

$$\therefore \quad |p-q| = 2; |p+2q| = 4$$

(D) At $x = 0$

$$\text{LHL} = \lim_{x \to 0} f(x) = \lim_{x \to 0} q + \left[\frac{\sin x - x}{x^3}\right]$$

$$= \lim_{x \to 0} q + \left[\frac{\left(x - \frac{x^3}{3!} + \frac{x^5}{5!} - \dots\right) - x}{x^3}\right]$$

$$= \lim_{x \to 0} q + \left[-\frac{1}{3!} + \frac{x^2}{5!} - \frac{x^4}{7!} + \frac{x^6}{9!} - \frac{x^8}{11!} + \dots\right]$$

$$= \lim_{x \to 0} q + \left[-\frac{1}{6}\right] = q - 1$$

$$\text{RHL} = \lim_{x \to 0^+} f(x) = \lim_{x \to 0^+} p + \frac{\sin[x]}{x}$$

$$= \lim_{x \to 0^+} p + \frac{\sin[x]}{x} = p$$

Also, $f(0) = 2$

$\therefore$ For continuity at $x = 0$, $p = q - 1 = 2$

$$\Rightarrow \quad p = 2 \text{ and } q = 3$$

$$\therefore \quad |p - q| = 1$$

EXERCISE 1

JEE Main Pattern

Single Option Correct Type Questions

1. The value of p for which the function

$$f(x)=\begin{cases}\dfrac{(4^x-1)^3}{\sin\dfrac{x}{p}\log\left[1+\dfrac{x^2}{3}\right]}, & x\neq 0\\ 12(\log 4)^3, & x=0\end{cases}$$ may be continuous at $x=0$ is

(a) 1 (b) 2
(c) 3 (d) 4

2. The function $f: R-\{0\}\to R$, $f(x)=\dfrac{1}{x}-\dfrac{2}{e^{2x}-1}$ can be made continuous at $x=0$ defining $f(0)$ as

(a) 2 (b) -1
(c) 0 (d) 1

3. If $f(x)=\begin{cases}3(1+|\tan x|)^{\frac{\alpha}{|\tan x|}}; & \dfrac{-1}{2}<x<0\\ \beta\ ; & x=0\\ 3\left(1+\left|\dfrac{\sin x}{3}\right|\right)^{\frac{6}{|\sin x|}}; & 0<x<\dfrac{2}{3}\end{cases}$ is a continuous function at $x=0$, then the ordered pair (α,β) is equal to

(a) $(2, e^2)$ (b) $\left(2, \dfrac{2}{e^2}\right)$
(c) $(2, 3e^2)$ (d) $\left(2, \dfrac{3}{e^2}\right)$

4. Number of points of discontinuity of $f(x)=\left\{\dfrac{x}{5}\right\}+\left[\dfrac{x}{2}\right]$ in $x\in[0, 100]$ is/are (where $[\cdot]$ denotes greatest integer function and $\{\}$ denotes fractional part function)

(a) 50 (b) 51
(c) 52 (d) 61

5. Let $f(x)=\begin{cases}ax+1 & \text{if } x<1\\ 3 & \text{if } x=1\\ bx^2+1 & \text{if } x>1\end{cases}$. If $f(x)$ is continuous at $x=1$, then $(a-b)$ is equal to

(a) 0 (b) 1
(c) 2 (d) 4

6. If $f(x)=\begin{cases}\dfrac{\sin\{\cos x\}}{x-\dfrac{\pi}{2}}, & x\neq\dfrac{\pi}{2}\\ 1, & x=\dfrac{\pi}{2}\end{cases}$, where $\{k\}$ represents the fractional part of k, then

(a) $f(x)$ is continuous at $x=\dfrac{\pi}{2}$

(b) $\lim\limits_{x\to\frac{\pi}{2}} f(x)$ does not exist

(c) $\lim\limits_{x\to\frac{\pi}{2}} f(x)$ exists, but f is not continuous at $x=\dfrac{\pi}{2}$

(d) $\lim\limits_{x\to\frac{\pi}{2}^-} f(x)=1$

7. Let $f(x)=\begin{cases}(1+ax)^{1/x}, & x<0\\ b, & x=0\\ \dfrac{(x+c)^{1/3}-1}{(x+1)^{1/2}-1}, & x>0\end{cases}$, is continuous at $x=0$, then $3(e^a+b+c)$ is equal to

(a) 3 (b) 6 (c) 7 (d) 8

8. If $f(x)=\begin{cases}\dfrac{ae^{\sin x}+be^{-\sin x}-c}{x^2}, & x\neq 0\\ 2, & x=0\end{cases}$ is continuous at $x=0$, then

(a) $a=b=c$ (b) $a=2b=3c$
(c) $a=2c$ (d) $2a=2b=c$

9. Let $f: [0, 1]\xrightarrow{\text{onto}}[0, 1]$ be a continuous function, then $f(x)=x$ holds for

(a) at least one $x\in[0, 1]$ (b) at least one $x\in[1, 2]$
(c) at least one $x\in[-1, 0]$ (d) cannot be discussed

10. Let $y_n(x)=x^2+\dfrac{x^2}{(1+x^2)}+\dfrac{x^2}{(1+x^2)^2}+\ldots+\dfrac{x^2}{(1+x^2)^{n-1}}$ and $y(x)=\lim\limits_{n\to\infty} y_n(x)$, then $y_n(x)$, $n=1, 2, 3, \ldots, n$ and $y(x)$ is

(a) continuous for $x\in R$
(b) continuous for $x\in R-\{0\}$
(c) continuous for $x\in R-\{1\}$
(d) data unsufficient

11. For a differentiable function f $\lim_{h \to 0} \frac{f^2(x+h) - f^2(x)}{2h}$ equals

(a) $(f'(x))^2$ (b) $\frac{1}{2} f(x) f'(x)$

(c) $\frac{1}{2}(f(x))^2$ (d) $f(x) f'(x)$

12. For $x > 0$, let $h(x) = \begin{cases} \frac{1}{q} & \text{if } x = \frac{p}{q} \\ 0 & \text{if } x \text{ is irrational} \end{cases}$, where p and $q > 0$ are relatively prime integers, then which one does not hold good?

(a) $h(x)$ is discontinuous for all x in $(0, \infty)$

(b) $h(x)$ is continuous for each irrational in $(0, \infty)$

(c) $h(x)$ is discontinuous for each rational in $(0, \infty)$

(d) $h(x)$ is not derivable for all x in $(0, \infty)$

13. Let f be a differentiable function on the open interval (a, b). Which of the following statement must be true?

I. f is continuous on the closed interval $[a, b]$

II. f is bounded on the open interval (a, b)

III. If $a < a_1 < b_1 < b$ and $f(a_1) < 0 < f(b_1)$, then there is a number c such that $a_1 < c < b_1$ and $f(c) = 0$

(a) I and II only (b) I and III only

(c) II and III only (d) Only III

14. Which of the following functions defined below are not differentiable at the indicated point?

(a) $f(x) = \begin{cases} x^2 & \text{if } -1 \le x < 0 \\ -x^2 & \text{if } 0 \le x \le 1 \end{cases}$ at $x = 0$

(b) $g(x) = \begin{cases} x & \text{if } -1 \le x < 0 \\ \tan x & \text{if } 0 \le x \le \pi/4 \end{cases}$ at $x = 0$

(c) $h(x) = \begin{cases} \sin 2x & \text{if } x \le 0 \\ 2x & \text{if } x > 0 \end{cases}$ at $x = 0$

(d) $k(x) = \begin{cases} x & \text{if } 0 \le x \le 1 \\ 2 - x & \text{if } 1 < x \le 2 \end{cases}$ at $x = 1$

15. If $f(x) = |1 - x|$, then the number of points where $g(x) = \sin^{-1}(f(|x|))$ is non-differentiable, are

(a) 2 (b) 3 (c) 4 (d) 5

16. If $f(x) = a|\sin x| + be^{|x|} + c|x|^3$ and if $f(x)$ is differentiable at $x = 0$, then

(a) $b = 0$, $c = 0$, a is any real

(b) $a = 0$, $b = 0$, c is any real

(c) $c = 0$, $a = 0$, b is any real

(d) $a + b = 0$

17. The number of values of a for which the function $f(x) = (x+1)|x - a|$ is differentiable, $\forall x \in R$, is

(a) 0 (b) 1

(c) 2 (d) more than 2

18. Let $f(x) = \frac{1}{1 + e^{1/x}}$ for $x \ne 0$ and $f(0) = 0$, then which of the following is true?

(a) $f(0^+)$ does not exist (b) $f(0^-)$ is equal to zero

(c) $f'(0^-)$ is equal to 1 (d) $f'(0^+)$ is equal to 1

19. Let f be a real valued function defined on R given by $f(x) = \{x\} + 2[x]$, where $[y]$ and $\{y\}$ denote largest integer less than or equal to y and fractional part of y respectively. The function $f(x)$ is

(a) continuous and differentiable, $\forall x \in R$

(b) continuous, $\forall x \in R$ but not differentiable at integral points

(c) neither continuous nor derivable at integral points

(d) nowhere differentiable

20. The number of values of x in $(0, 2\pi)$ where the function $f(x) = \frac{\tan x + \cot x}{2} - \left| \frac{\tan x - \cot x}{2} \right|$ is continuous but non-derivable

(a) 3 (b) 4

(c) 0 (d) 1

21. Let $f(x) = \begin{cases} \min(x, x^2), & x \ge 0 \\ \max(2x, x - 1), & x < 0 \end{cases}$, then which of the following is not true?

(a) $f(x)$ is not differentiable at $x = 0$

(b) $f(x)$ is not differentiable at exactly two points

(c) $f(x)$ is continuous everywhere

(d) $f(x)$ is strictly increasing $\forall x \in R$

22. The number of points at which the function,

$$f(x) = \begin{cases} \min\{|x|, x^2\}, & x \in (-\infty, -1) \\ \min\{2x - 1, x^2\}, & \text{otherwise} \end{cases}$$

is not differentiable is

(a) 0 (b) 1

(c) 2 (d) 3

23. If $f(x) = \max\left(x^4, x^2, \frac{1}{81}\right), \forall x \in [0, \infty)$, then the sum of the square of reciprocal of all the values of x where $f(x)$ is non-differentiable, is equal to

(a) 1 (b) 81

(c) 82 (d) $\frac{82}{81}$

24. Let $f(x) = (x^2 - 3x + 2)|(x^3 - 6x^2 - 11x - 6)| + \left|\sin\left(x + \frac{\pi}{4}\right)\right|$.

Number of points at which the function $f(x)$ is non-differentiable in $[0, 2\pi]$ is

(a) 5 (b) 4

(c) 3 (d) 2

25. Let $f(x)=[x]$ and $g(x)=\begin{cases}0, & \text{if } x \text{ is an integer}\\ x^2, & \text{otherwise}\end{cases}$, then

(a) $(gof)'(1)=1$
(b) gof is not continuous
(c) fog is differentiable on $R-I$
(d) fog is a differentiable function

26. Let $f(x)=\begin{cases}x^2, & \text{if } x\le x_0\\ ax+b, & \text{if } x>x_0\end{cases}$

The values of the coefficients a and b for which the function is continuous and has a derivative at x_0, are

(a) $a=x_0, b=-x_0$
(b) $a=2x_0, b=-x_0^2$
(c) $a=x_0^2, b=-x_0$
(d) $a=x_0, b=-x_0^2$

27. Let $f(x)=\begin{cases}x^3\left|\cos\dfrac{\pi}{2x}\right|+x^4\left|\sin\dfrac{\pi}{x}\right|, & x\ne 0\\ 0, & x=0\end{cases}$

then f is

(a) differentiable at $x=0$ and $x=1$
(b) differentiable at $x=0$ not differentiable at $x=2$
(c) differentiable at $x=2$ and not differentiable at $x=1$
(d) differentiable neither at $x=0$ nor at $x=2$

28. If $f(x)=\begin{cases}|x-1|([x]-x), & x\ne 1\\ 0, & x=1\end{cases}$, then

(a) $f'(1^+)=0$
(b) $f'(1^-)=0$
(c) $f'(1^-)=-1$
(d) $f(x)$ is not differentiable at $x=1$

29. If $f(x)=\begin{cases}\left\{x+\dfrac{1}{3}\right\}[\sin \pi x], & 0\le x<1\\ [2x]\operatorname{sgn}\left(x-\dfrac{4}{3}\right), & 1\le x<2\end{cases}$, where $[\cdot]$ and $\{\cdot\}$ denote greatest integer and fractional part of x respectively, then the number of points of non-differentiability, is

(a) 3 (b) 4
(c) 5 (d) 6

30. Let $f(x)=\max\{|x^2-2|x||, |x|\}$ and $g(x)=\min\{|x^2-2|x||, |x|\}$, then

(a) both $f(x)$ and $g(x)$ are non-differentiable at 5 points
(b) $f(x)$ is not differentiable at 5 points whether $g(x)$ is non-differentiable at 7 points
(c) number of points of non-differentiability for $f(x)$ and $g(x)$ are 7 and 5 points, respectively
(d) both $f(x)$ and $g(x)$ are non-differentiable at 3 and 5 points, respectively

31. If $f(x)=\begin{cases}b([x]^2+[x])+1, & \text{for } x\ge -1\\ \sin(\pi(x+a)), & \text{for } x<-1\end{cases}$, where $[x]$ denotes the integral part of x, then for what values of a, b the function is continuous at $x=-1$?

(a) $a=2n+(3/2);\ b\in R; n\in I$
(b) $a=4n+2;\ b\in R;\ n\in I$
(c) $a=4n+(3/2);\ b\in R^+;\ n\in I$
(d) $a=4n+1;\ b\in R^+;\ n\in I$

32. If $f(x)=\dfrac{\{x\}g(x)}{\{x\}g(x)}$ is a periodic function with period $\dfrac{1}{4}$, where $g(x)$ is a differential function, then (where $\{\cdot\}$ denotes fractional part of x)

(a) $g'(x)$ has exactly three roots in $\left(\dfrac{1}{4},\dfrac{5}{4}\right)$
(b) $g(x)=0$ at $x=\dfrac{k}{4}$, where $k\in I$
(c) $g(x)$ must be non-zero function
(d) $g(x)$ must be periodic function

Numerical Value Type Questions

33. If $f(x)=\begin{cases}\dfrac{\sin 2x-\tan 2x}{(e^x-1)x^2}, & \text{if } x\ne 0\\ k, & \text{if } x=0\end{cases}$ is continuous at $x=0$, then the absolute value of k is ....

34. Let $f(x)=\begin{cases}(\sin x+\cos x)^{\operatorname{cosec} x}, & \dfrac{-\pi}{2}<x<0\\ a, & x=0\\ \dfrac{e^{1/x}+e^{2/x}+e^{3/|x|}}{ae^{2/x}+be^{3/|x|}}, & 0<x<\dfrac{\pi}{2}\end{cases}$

If $f(x)$ is continuous at $x=0$, then the value of $\dfrac{\lambda}{4\mu}$ is ..., if $(a^2+b^2)=\dfrac{\lambda}{4}e^2+\mu e^{-2}$.

35. Let $f(x)=\begin{cases}ax(x-1)+b, & x<1\\ x+2, & 1\le x\le 3\\ px^2+qx+2, & x>3\end{cases}$ is continuous $\forall\ x\in R$ except $x=1$ but $|f(x)|$ is differentiable everywhere and $f'(x)$ is continuous at $x=3$ and $|a+p+b+q|=k$, then k is equal to ....

36. If $f(x)=\begin{cases}\cos x^3, & x<0\\ \sin x^3-|x^3-1|, & x\ge 0\end{cases}$

Then, number of points where $g(x)=f(|x|)$ is non-differentiable is ....

37. If the function $f(x)=\dfrac{\tan(\tan x)-\sin(\sin x)}{\tan x-\sin x}$ $(x\ne 0)$ is continuous at $x=0$, then the value of $f(0)$ is ....

38. Let $f(x)=\begin{cases}2-x, & -3\le x\le 0\\ x-2, & 0<x<4\end{cases}$

Then, $f^{-1}(x)$ is discontinuous at $x=$ ....

39. Let $f(x)=\text{sgn}(x)$ and $g(x)=x(x^2-10x+21)$, then the number of points of discontinuity of $f[g(x)]$ is ....

40. The value of x, $x\in(2,\infty)$, where $f(x)=\sqrt{x+\sqrt{8x-16}}+\sqrt{x-\sqrt{8x-16}}$ is not differentiable is ....

41. The number of non-differentiability points of function $f(x)=\min\left([x],\{x\},\left|x-\frac{3}{2}\right|\right)$ for $x\in(0,2)$, where $[\cdot]$ and $\{\cdot\}$ denote greatest integer function and fractional part function respectively, is ....

42. Given a function g which has derivative $g'(x)$ for all x satisfying $g'(0)=2$ and $g(x+y)=e^y g(x)+e^x g(y)$ for all $x,y\in R$, $g(5)=32$. The value of $1/4\,(g'(5)-2e^5)$ is ....

43. Number of point(s) of discontinuity of the function $f(x)=[x^{1/x}]$, $x>0$, (where [] denotes the greatest integral function) is ....

44. Let $f_1(x)$ and $f_2(x)$ be twice differentiable function, where $F(x)=f_1(x)+f_2(x)$ and $G(x)=f_1(x)-f_2(x)$, $\forall\, x\in R$, $f_1(0)=2$ and $f_2(0)=1$. If $f_1'(x)=f_2(x)$ and $f_2'(x)=f_1(x)$, $\forall\, x\in R$, then the number of solutions of the equation $(F(x))^2=\dfrac{9x^4}{G(x)}$ is ....

45. In a ΔABC, angles A, B, C are in AP.

If $f(x)=\lim\limits_{A\to C}\dfrac{\sqrt{3-4\sin A\sin C}}{|A-C|}$, then $f'(x)$ is equal to ....

46. The number of points at which the function $f(x)=(x-|x|)^2\,(1-x+|x|)^2$ is not differentiable in the interval $(-3,4)$ is ....

Previous Year Questions

47. Let $f(x)=|2x^2+5|x|-3|$, $x\in R$. If m and n denote the number of points where f is not continuous and not differentiable respectively, then $m+n$ is equal to **[Single Correct Type, 2024 Main]**

(a) 5
(b) 2
(c) 0
(d) 3

48. Let $f:R\to R$ be defined as

$$f(x)=\begin{cases}\dfrac{a-b\cos 2x}{x^2}; & x<0\\ x^2+cx+2; & 0\le x\le 1\\ 2x+1; & x>1\end{cases}$$

If f is continuous everywhere in R and m is the number of points where f is not differential, then $m+a+b+c$ equals **[Single Correct Type, 2024 Main]**

(a) 1 (b) 4
(c) 3 (d) 2

49. Consider the function $f:(0,2)\to R$ defined by $f(x)=\dfrac{x}{2}+\dfrac{2}{x}$ and the function $g(x)$ defined by

$$g(x)=\begin{cases}\min\{f(t)\}, & 0<t\le x \text{ and } 0<x\le 1\\ \dfrac{3}{2}+x, & 1<x<2\end{cases}$$

Then, **[Single Correct Type, 2024 Main]**

(a) g is continuous but not differentiable at $x=1$
(b) g is not continuous for all $x\in(0,2)$
(c) g is neither continuous nor differentiable at $x=1$
(d) g is continuous and differentiable for all $x\in(0,2)$

50. Consider the function $f(x)=\begin{cases}\dfrac{a(7x-12-x^2)}{b|x^2-7x+12|}, & x<3\\ 2^{\frac{\sin x}{x}}, & x>3\\ b, & x=3\end{cases}$

where $[x]$ denotes the greatest integer less than or equal to x. If S denote the set of all ordered pairs (a,b) such that $f(x)$ is continuous at $x=3$, then the number of elements in S is **[Single Correct Type, 2024 Main]**

(a) 2 (b) infinitely many
(c) 4 (d) 1

51. Let $g(x)$ be a linear function and

$$f(x)=\begin{cases}g(x), & x\le 0\\ \left(\dfrac{1+x}{2+x}\right)^{1/2}, & x>0\end{cases}$$, is continuous at $x=0$

If $f'(1)=f(-1)$, then the value of $g(3)$ is **[Single Correct Type, 2024 Main]**

(a) $\frac{1}{2}\log_e\left(\frac{1}{9e^{1/3}}\right)$ (b) $\frac{1}{3}\log_e\left(\frac{4}{9}\right)+1$

(c) $\log_e\left(\frac{4}{9}\right)-1$ (d) $\log_e\left(\frac{4}{9e^{1/3}}\right)$

52. If the function $f(x)=\begin{cases}\dfrac{1}{|x|}, & |x|\ge 2\\ ax^2+2b, & |x|<2\end{cases}$ is differentiable on R, then $48(a+b)$ is equal to

[Single Correct Type, 2024 Main]

53. Let $f(x)=[x^2-x]+|-x+[x]|$, where $x\in R$ and $[t]$ denotes the greatest integer less than or equal to t. Then, f is **[Single Correct Type, 2023 Main]**

(a) continuous at $x=0$ and $x=1$
(b) continuous at $x=1$ but not continuous at $x=0$
(c) not continuous at $x=0$ and $x=1$
(d) continuous at $x=0$ but not continuous at $x=1$

54. If the function $f(x)=\begin{cases}(1+|\cos x|)^{\frac{\lambda}{|\cos x|}}, & 0<x<\dfrac{\pi}{2}\\ \mu, & x=\dfrac{\pi}{2}\\ e^{\frac{\cot 6x}{\cot 4x}}, & \dfrac{\pi}{2}<x<\pi\end{cases}$

is continuous at $x=\dfrac{\pi}{2}$, then $9\lambda+6\log_e\mu+\mu^6-e^{6\lambda}$ is equal to **[Single Correct Type, 2023 Main]**

(a) 10
(b) $2e^4+8$
(c) 8
(d) 11

55. Let $[x]$ denotes the greatest integer function and $f(x)=\max\{1+x+[x], 2+x, x+2[x]\}, 0\le x\le 2$. Let m be the number of points in [0, 2], where f is not continuous and n be the number of points in (0, 2), where f is not differentiable. Then, $(m+n)^2+2$ is equal to

[Single Correct Type, 2023 Main]

(a) 6
(b) 3
(c) 11
(d) 2

56. For the differentiable function $f:R-\{0\}\to R$, let $3f(x)+2f\left(\dfrac{1}{x}\right)=\dfrac{1}{x}-10$, then $\left|f(3)+f'\left(\dfrac{1}{4}\right)\right|$ is equal to

[Single Correct Type, 2023 Main]

(a) $\dfrac{33}{5}$
(b) $\dfrac{29}{5}$
(c) 7
(d) 13

57. Let f and g be two functions defined by

$f(x)=\begin{cases}x+1, & x<0\\ |x-1|, & x\ge 0\end{cases}$ and $g(x)=\begin{cases}x+1, & x<0\\ 1, & x\ge 0\end{cases}$

Then, $(gof)(x)$ is **[Single Correct Type, 2023 Main]**

(a) Continuous everywhere but not differentiable exactly at one point
(b) continuous everywhere but not differentiable at $x=1$
(c) differentiable everywhere
(d) not continuous at $x=-1$

58. Let $f:[2,4]\to R$ be a differentiable function such that $(x\log_e x)f'(x)+(\log_e x)f(x)+f(x)\ge 1$, $x\in[2,4]$ with $f(2)=\dfrac{1}{2}$ and $f(4)=\dfrac{1}{4}$.

Consider the following two statements

(A) $f(x)\le 1, \forall x\in[2,4]$
(B) $f(x)\ge\dfrac{1}{8}, \forall x\in[,2\ 4]$

Then, **[Single Correct Type, 2023 Main]**

(a) Both the statements (A) and (B) are true
(b) Neither statement (A) nor statement (B) is true
(c) Only statement (A) is true
(d) Only statement (B) is true

59. Let $f(x)=\begin{cases}x^2\sin\left(\dfrac{1}{x}\right), & x\ne 0\\ 0, & x=0\end{cases}$

Then, at $x=0$ **[Single Correct Type, 2023 Main]**

(a) f and f' both are continuous
(b) f is continuous but f' is not continuous
(c) f is continuous but not differentiable
(d) f' is continuous but not differentiable

60. Let f and g be twice differentiable functions on R such that $f''(x)=g''(x)+6x$; $f'(1)=4g'(1)-3=9$
$f(2)=3g(2)=12$

Then, which of the following is not true?

[Single Correct Type, 2023 Main]

(a) There exists $x_0\in\left(1,\dfrac{3}{2}\right)$ such that $f(x_0)=g(x_0)$
(b) $g(-2)-f(-2)=20$
(c) If $-1<x<2$, then $|f(x)-g(x)|<8$
(d) $|f'(x)-g'(x)|<6\Rightarrow -1<x<1$

61. Let $[x]$ be the greatest integer less than or equal to x. Then, the number of points in the interval $(-2, 1)$, where the function $f(x)=|[x]|+\sqrt{x-[x]}$ is discontinuous is ...... **[Numerical Value Type, 2023 Main]**

62. Let $f:(-2,2)\to R$ be defined by

$f(x)=\begin{cases}x[x], & -2<x<0\\ (x-1)[x], & 0\le x<2\end{cases}$

where $[x]$ denotes the greatest integer function. If m and n respectively are the number of points $(-2, 2)$ at which $y=|f(x)|$ is not continuous and in not differentiable, then $m+n$ is equal to ....

[Numerical Value Type, 2023 Main]

63. Let k and m be positive real numbers such that the function $f(x)=\begin{cases}3x^2+k\sqrt{x+1}, & 0<x<1\\ mx^2+k^2, & x\ge 1\end{cases}$ is differentiable for all $x>0$. Then, $\dfrac{8f'(8)}{f'\left(\dfrac{1}{8}\right)}$ is equal to ....

[Numerical Value Type, 2023 Main]

64. Let $a \in Z$ and $[t]$ be the greatest integer $\leq t$. Then, the number of points,where the function $f(x)=[a+13\sin x]$, $x \in (0, \pi)$ is not differentiable, is ...... **[Numerical Value Type, 2023 Main]**

65. The number of points, where the function $f: R \to R$, $f(x)=|x-1|\cos|x-2|\sin|x-1| + (x-3)|x^2-5x+4|$, is not differentiable, is **[Single Correct Type, 2022 Main]**

(a) 1 (b) 2
(c) 3 (d) 4

66. Let $f, g: R \to R$ be functions defined by

$$f(x)=\begin{cases}[x], & x<0\\ |1-x|, & x\geq 0\end{cases} \text{ and } g(x)=\begin{cases}e^x-x, & x<0\\ (x-1)^2-1, & x\geq 0\end{cases}$$

where $[x]$ denotes the greatest integer less than or equal to x. Then, the function fog is discontinuous at exactly **[Single Correct Type, 2022 Main]**

(a) one point
(b) two points
(c) three points
(d) four points

67. Let $f(x)=\min\{1, 1+x\sin x\}$, $0\leq x\leq 2\pi$. If m is the number of points, where f is not differentiable and n is the number of points, where f is not continuous, then the ordered pair (m, n) is equal to **[Single Correct Type, 2022 Main]**

(a) (2, 0) (b) (1, 0)
(c) (1, 1) (d) (2, 1)

68. $f, g: R \to R$ be two real valued functions defined as

$$f(x)=\begin{cases}-|x+3|, & x<0\\ e^x, & x\geq 0\end{cases} \text{ and } g(x)=\begin{cases}x^2+k_1x, & x<0\\ 4x+k_2, & x\geq 0\end{cases},$$

where k_1 and k_2 are real constants. If (gof) is differentiable at $x=0$, then $(gof)(-4)+(gof)(4)$ is equal to **[Single Correct Type, 2022 Main]**

(a) $4(e^4+1)$
(b) $2(2e^4+1)$
(c) $4e^4$
(d) $2(2e^4-1)$]

69. Let $f: R \to R$ be defined as

$$f(x)=\begin{cases}[e^x], & x<0\\ ae^x+[x-1], & 0\leq x<1\\ b+[\sin(\pi x)], & 1\leq x<2\\ [e^{-x}]-c, & x\geq 2\end{cases}$$

where $a, b, c, \in R$ and $[t]$ denotes greatest integer less than or equal to t. Then, which of the following statement is true? **[Single Correct Type, 2022 Main]**

(a) There exists $a, b, c \in R$ such that f is continuous on R
(b) If f is discontinuous at exactly one point,then $a+b+c=1$
(c) If f is discontinuous at exactly one point,then $a+b+c\neq 1$
(d) f is discontinuous at atleast two points, for any values of a, b and c

70. If $[t]$ denotes the greatest integer less than or equal to t, then number of points,at which the function $f(x)=4|2x+3|+9\left[x+\frac{1}{2}\right]-12[x+20]$ is not differentiable in the open interval $(-20, 20)$, is .... **[Numerical Value Type, 2022 Main]**

71. Let f and g be twice differentiable even functions on $(-2, 2)$ such that $f\left(\frac{1}{4}\right)=0$, $f\left(\frac{1}{2}\right)=0$, $f(1)=1$ and $g\left(\frac{3}{4}\right)=0$, $g(1)=2$. Then, the minimum number of solutions of $f(x)g''(x)+f'(x)g'(x)=0$ in $(-2, 2)$ is equal to .... **[Numerical Value Type, 2022 Main]**

72. Let $f(x)=[2x^2+1]$ and $g(x)=\begin{cases}2x-3, & x<0\\ 2x=3, & x\geq 0\end{cases}$, where $[t]$ is the greatest integer less than or equal to t. Then, in the open interval $(-1, 1)$,the number of points where fog is discontinuous is equal to ...... **[Numerical Value Type, 2022 Main]**

73. The number of points where the function

$$f(x)=\begin{cases}|2x^2-3x-7|, & \text{if } x\leq -1\\ [4x^2-1], & \text{if } -1<x<1,\\ |x+1|+|x-2|, & \text{if } x\geq 1\end{cases}$$

$[t]$ denotes the greatest integer less than or equal to t, is discontinuous, is ...... **[Numerical Value Type, 2022 Main]**

74. If the function $f(x)=\begin{cases}\frac{1}{x}\log_e\left(\frac{1+\frac{x}{a}}{1-\frac{x}{b}}\right), & x<0\\ k, & x=0\\ \frac{\cos^2 x-\sin^2 x-1}{\sqrt{x^2+1}-1}, & x>0\end{cases}$

is continuous at $x=0$, then $\frac{1}{a}+\frac{1}{b}+\frac{4}{k}$ is equal to **[Single Correct Type, 2021 Main]**

(a) -5 (b) 5
(c) -4 (d) 4

75. Let $f : R \to R$ be defined as

$$f(x)=\begin{cases}\dfrac{\lambda|x^2-5x+6|}{\mu(5x-x^2-6)}, & x<2\\ e^{\frac{\tan(x-2)}{x-[x]}}, & x>2\\ \mu, & x=2\end{cases}$$

where, $[x]$ is the greatest integer less than or equal to x. If f is continuous at $x=2$, then $\lambda+\mu$ is equal to

[Single Correct Type, 2021 Main]

(a) $e(-e+1)$
(b) $e(e-2)$
(c) 1
(d) $2e-1$

76. Let a function $f : R \to R$ be defined as

$$f(x)=\begin{cases}\sin x - e^x & \text{if } x\le 0\\ a+[-x] & \text{if } 0<x<1\\ 2x-b & \text{if } x\ge 1\end{cases}$$

where, $[x]$ is the greatest integer less than or equal to x. If f is continuous on R, then $(a+b)$ is equal to

[Single Correct Type, 2021 Main]

(a) 4
(b) 3
(c) 2
(d) 5

77. Let $f : R \to R$ be a function defined as

$$f(x)=\begin{cases}\dfrac{\sin(a+1)x+\sin 2x}{2x} & \text{if } x<0\\ b & \text{if } x<0\\ \dfrac{\sqrt{x+bx^3}-\sqrt{x}}{bx^{5/2}} & \text{if } x>0\end{cases}$$

If f is continuous at $x=0$, then the value of $a+b$ is equal to

[Single Correct Type, 2021 Main]

(a) $-\frac{5}{2}$
(b) -2
(c) -3
(d) $-\frac{3}{2}$

78. Let $\alpha \in R$ be such that the function

$$f(x)=\begin{cases}\dfrac{\cos^{-1}(1-\{x\}^2)\sin^{-1}(1-\{x\})}{\{x\}-\{x\}^3}, & x\ne 0\\ \alpha, & x=0\end{cases}$$

is continuous at $x=0$, where $\{x\}=x-[x]$, $[x]$ is the greatest integer less than or equal to x. Then,

[Single Correct Type, 2021 Main]

(a) $\alpha=\frac{\pi}{\sqrt{2}}$
(b) $\alpha=0$
(c) No such α exists
(d) $\alpha=\frac{\pi}{4}$

79. Let $f : R \to R$ be defined as

$$f(x)=\begin{cases}2\sin\left(-\dfrac{\pi x}{2}\right), & \text{if } x<-1\\ |ax^2+x+b|, & \text{if } -1\le x\le 1\\ \sin(\pi x), & \text{if } x>1\end{cases}$$

If $f(x)$ is continuous on R, then $a+b$ equals

[Single Correct Type, 2021 Main]

(a) -3
(b) -1
(c) 3
(d) 1

80. If $f : R \to R$ is a function defined by $f(x)=[x-1]\cos\left(\dfrac{2x-1}{2}\right)\pi$, where $[\cdot]$ denotes the greatest integer function, then f is

[Single Correct Type, 2021 Main]

(a) discontinuous only at $x=1$
(b) discontinuous at all integral values of x except at $x=1$
(c) continuous only at $x=1$
(d) continuous for every real x

81. Let $f : (a, b) \to R$ be twice differentiable function such that $f(x)=\int_a^x g(t)\,dt$ for a differentiable function $g(x)$. If $f(x)=0$ has exactly five distinct roots in (a, b), then $g(x)g'(x)=0$ has atleast **[Single Correct Type, 2021 Main]**

(a) twelve roots in (a, b)
(b) five roots in (a, b)
(c) seven roots in (a, b)
(d) three roots in (a, b)

82. Let $f : [0, \infty) \to [0, \infty)$ be defined as $f(x)=\int_0^x [y]\,dy$ where, $[x]$ is the greatest integer less than or equal to x. Which of the following is true?

[Single Correct Type, 2021 Main]

(a) f is continuous at every point in $[0, \infty)$ and differentiable except at the integer points
(b) f is both continuous and differentiable except at the integer points in $[0, \infty)$
(c) f is continuous everywhere except at the integer points in $[0, \infty)$
(d) f is differentiable at every point in $[0, \infty)$

83. The function $f(x)=|x^2-2x-3|e^{|9x^2-12x+4|}$ is not differentiable at exactly **[Single Correct Type, 2021 Main]**

(a) four points
(b) three points
(c) two points
(d) one point

84. Let $[t]$ denotes the greatest integer less than or equal to t. Let $f(x)=x-[x]$, $g(x)=1-x+[x]$ and $h(x)=\min\{f(x), g(x)\}$, $x\in[-2, 2]$. Then, h is

[Single Correct Type, 2021 Main]

(a) continuous in $[-2, 2]$ but not differentiable at more than four points in $(-2, 2)$
(b) not continuous at exactly three points in $[-2, 2]$
(c) continuous in $[-2, 2]$ but not differentiable at exactly three points in $(-2, 2)$
(d) not continuous at exactly four point in $[-2, 2]$

85. Let $f:[0,\infty)\to[0,3]$ be a function defined by

$$f(x)=\begin{cases}\max\{\sin t: 0\le t\le x\}, & 0\le x<\pi\\ 2+\cos x, & x>\pi\end{cases}$$

Then, which of the following is true? **[Single Correct Type, 2021 Main]**

(a) f it continuous everywhere but not differentiable exactly at one point in $(0,\infty)$
(b) f is differentiable everywhere in $(0,\infty)$
(c) f is not continuous exactly at two points in $(0,\infty)$
(d) f is continuous everywhere but not differentiable exactly at two points in $(0,\infty)$

86. Let $[t]$ denotes the greatest integer less than or equal to t. The number of points where the function

$$f(x)=[x]|x^2-1|+\sin\left(\frac{\pi}{[x]+3}\right)-[x+1],\ x\in(-2,2)\text{ is}$$

not continuous, is ...... **[Numerical Value Type, 2021 Main]**

87. Let $f:[0,3]\to R$ be defined by

$f(x)=\min\{x-[x], 1+[x]-x\}$,

where $[x]$ is the greatest integer less than or equal to x. Let P denotes the set containing all $x\in(0,3)$, where f is discontinuous and Q denotes the set containing all $x\in(0,3)$, where f is not differentiable.

Then, the sum of number of elements in P and Q is equal to ...... **[Numerical Value Type, 2021 Main]**

88. Let a function $g:[0,4]\to R$ be defined as

$$g(x)=\begin{cases}\max\limits_{0<t\le x}(t^3-6t^2+9t-3), & 0\le x\le 3\\ 4-x, & 3<x\le 4\end{cases},$$

then the number of points in the interval (0,4), where $g(x)$ is not differentiable, is ...... **[Numerical Value Type, 2021 Main]**

EXERCISE 2

JEE Advanced Pattern

Single Option Correct Type Questions

1. Given $f(x)=\begin{cases}\dfrac{[\{|x|\}]e^{x^2}\{[x+\{x\}]\}}{(e^{1/x^2}-1)\operatorname{sgn}(\sin x)}, & \text{for } x\ne 0\\ 0, & \text{for } x=0\end{cases}$, then

$f(x)$ (where $\{x\}$ is the fractional part function; $[x]$ is the step up function and $\operatorname{sgn}(x)$ is the signum function of x)

(a) is continuous at $x=0$
(b) is discontinuous at $x=0$
(c) has a removable discontinuity at $x=0$
(d) has an irremovable discontinuity at $x=0$

2. Consider $f(x)=\begin{cases}x[x]^2\log_{(1+x)}2, & \text{for } -1<x<0\\ \dfrac{\ln(e^{x^2}+2\sqrt{\{x\}})}{\tan\sqrt{x}}, & \text{for } 0<x<1\end{cases}$,

then (where $[*]$ and $\{*\}$ are the greatest integer function and fractional part function respectively)

(a) $f(0)=\ln 2\Rightarrow f$ is continuous at $x=0$
(b) $f(0)=2\Rightarrow f$ is continuous at $x=0$
(c) $f(0)=e^2\Rightarrow f$ is continuous at $x=0$
(d) f has an irremovable discontinuity at $x=0$

3. The function f defined by $f(x)=\lim\limits_{t\to\infty}\left\{\dfrac{(1+\sin\pi x)^t-1}{(1+\sin\pi x)^t+1}\right\}$ is

(a) everywhere continuous
(b) discontinuous at all integer values of x
(c) continuous at $x=0$
(d) continuous at $x=1$

4. Let $g(x)=\tan^{-1}|x|-\cot^{-1}|x|$, $f(x)=\dfrac{[x]}{[x+1]}\{x\}$, $h(x)=|g(f(x))|$, then which of the following holds good?

(where $\{*\}$ denotes fractional part and $[*]$ denotes the integral part)

(a) h is continuous at $x=0$ (b) h is discontinuous at $x=0$
(c) $h(0^-)=\pi$ (d) $h(0^+)=-\dfrac{\pi}{2}$

5. Let f be a real valued differentiable function on R such that $f'(1)=6$ and $f'(2)=2$.

Then, $\lim\limits_{h\to 0}\dfrac{f(3\cos h+4\sin h-2)-f(1)}{f(3e^h-5\sec h+4)-f(2)}$ is equal to

(a) 24 (b) 8 (c) 4 (d) 2

6. Given $f(x)=\sum_{k=1}^{n}\tan\left(\frac{x}{2^k}\right)\sec\left(\frac{x}{2^{k-1}}\right); k, n\in N$

and $g(x)=\lim_{n\to\infty}\prod_{r=1}^{n}\left(1-\tan^2\frac{x}{2^r}\right): r, n\in N$

If $h(x)=\begin{cases}\dfrac{\ln\left(1+f(x)+\tan\dfrac{x}{2^n}\right)}{x}, & x<0\\ g(x), & x>0\\ k, & x=0\end{cases}$, then

(a) if $k=0$, $f(x)$ is continuous at $x=0$
(b) if $k=1$, $h(x)$ is continuous at $x=0$
(c) if $k\in R$, $h(x)$ is continuous at $x=0$
(d) $h(x)$ can not be made continuous at $x=0$ for any k

7. Let $f(x)$, $f:R\to R$ be a non-constant continuous function such that $(e^x-1)f(2x)=(e^{2x}-1)f(x)$.

If $f'(0)=1$, then $\lim_{x\to 0}\left(\frac{f(x)}{x}\right)^{1/x}$ equal to

(a) e (b) $e^{1/2}$
(c) e^2 (d) e^{-2}

8. Let f be an injective function with domain $[a, b]$ and range $[c, d]$. If α is a point in (a, b) such that f has left hand derivative l and right hand derivative r at $x=\alpha$ with both l and r non-zero different and negative, then left hand derivative and right hand derivative of f^{-1} at $x=f(\alpha)$ respectively, is

(a) $\frac{1}{r}\cdot\frac{1}{l}$ (b) r, l (c) $\frac{1}{l},\frac{1}{r}$ (d) l, r

9. If $f(x)$ is defined, $\forall\ x\in R$ and is discontinuous only at $x=0$, such that $f^3(x)-6f^2(x)+11f(x)-3=3, \forall\ x\in R$, then the number of such functions is equal to

(a) 4 (b) 8 (c) 16 (d) 24

10. Let $f:R^+\to R^+$ be a differentiable function such that $f(x^n)=2f(x^{n-1}), n\in N, n\geq 2$. If $k\cdot f'(2^n)=f'(2)$, then the value of k is

(a) $n!$ (b) $\frac{1}{n!}$ (c) n (d) $\frac{1}{n}$

11. Let $f(x)$ be continuous function, $\forall\ x\in R$ except at $x=1$ such that $f'(x)>0\ \forall\ x\in(1,\infty)$ and $f'(x)<0, \forall\ x\in(-\infty, 1)$ such that $f(1^+)=\frac{1}{2}$ and $f(1^-)=2$, $f(1)=1$, then $\lim_{x\to 0}f(\cos^3 x+\sin^2 x)$ is equal to

(a) $\frac{1}{2}$ (b) 1
(c) 2 (d) 0

12. If graphs of $|y|=f(x)$ and $y=|f(x)|$ are given as below $(a, b>0)$

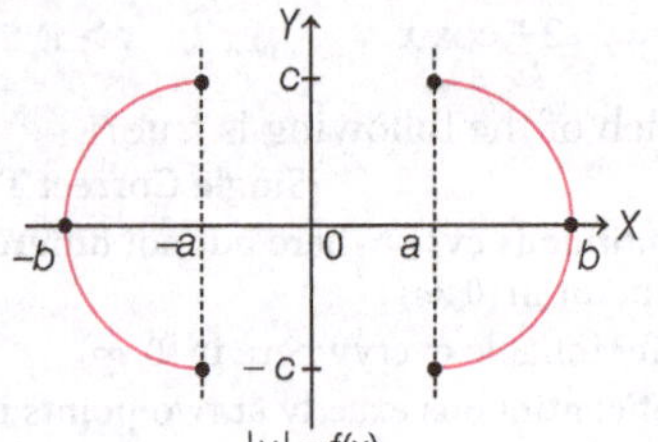

$|y|=f(x)$

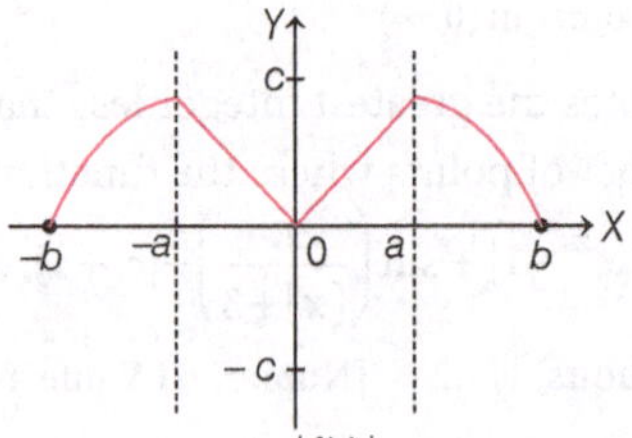

$y=|f(x)|$

Then, identify the correct statement.

(a) $f(x)$ is discontinuous at 2 points in $[-b, b]$ and non-differentiable at 2 points in $(-b, b)$.
(b) $f(x)$ is discontinuous at 2 points in $[-b, b]$ and non-differentiable at 3 points in $(-b, b)$.
(c) $f(x)$ is discontinuous at 3 points in $[-b, b]$ and non-differentiable at 3 points in $(-b, b)$.
(d) $f(x)$ is discontinuous at 3 points in $[-b, b]$ and non-differentiable at 4 points in $(-b, b)$.

13. If A, B and C are angles of an acute angled triangle with $A<B<C$ and

$f(x)=\begin{cases}(1+(\sin A)^{1/x})^{(\operatorname{cosec} B\sin C)^{1/x}}, & x>0\\ k, & x=0\end{cases}$

is right continuous at $x=0$, then the value of k is equal to

(a) $e^{\frac{\sin A\sin C}{\sin B}}$ (b) e^{ABC}
(c) e (d) 1

14. Let $f(x)=\begin{cases}\dfrac{\pi^2}{e}(1-x)\dfrac{(x^{1/x-1}-e)}{(1+\cos\pi x)}, & x\neq 1\\ k, & x=1\end{cases}$

If $f(x)$ is continuous at $x=1$, then the value of k, is

(a) 1 (b) 2 (c) 3 (d) 4

15. If $f(x)$ is a continuous function from $R\to R$ and attains only irrational values, then $\sum_{r=1}^{100}f(r)$ equals

(a) $\sum_{r=1}^{99}f(r)$ (b) $\sum_{r=1}^{100}f(2r)$
(c) $\sum_{r=1}^{100}(f(2r)+1)$ (d) $\sum_{r=1}^{101}f(2r)$

16. Let $f(x)=\begin{cases}\dfrac{\tan\left(\dfrac{\pi}{4}+2x\right)-2\tan\left(\dfrac{\pi}{4}+x\right)+\tan\dfrac{\pi}{4}}{\sin\left(\dfrac{\pi}{4}+2x\right)-2\sin\left(\dfrac{\pi}{4}+x\right)+\sin\dfrac{\pi}{4}}, & x\neq 0\\ k, & x=0\end{cases}$.

If $f(x)$ is continuous at $x=0$, then k is equal to

(a) $4\sqrt{2}$ (b) $2\sqrt{2}$
(c) $-4\sqrt{2}$ (d) $-2\sqrt{2}$

17. If $f(x)=\dfrac{6}{\pi}\tan^{-1}\left(\dfrac{2x}{1-x^2}\right)$, then number of points where $y=[f(x)]$ is discontinuous in its domain, is

(a) 3 (b) 5
(c) 7 (d) 9

[**Note** $[k]$ denotes greatest integer less than or equal to k]

18. A continuous even periodic function f with period 8 is such that $f(0)=0$, $f(1)=-2$, $f(2)=1$, $f(3)=2$, $f(4)=3$, then the value of

$\tan^{-1}(\tan(f(-5)+f(20)+\cos^{-1}(f(-10))+f(17)))$ is equal to

(a) $2\pi-3$ (b) $3-2\pi$
(c) $2\pi+3$ (d) $3-\pi$

19. Let f be a differentiable function on $(0,\infty)$ and suppose that $\lim_{x\to\infty}(f(x)+f'(x))=L$, where L is a finite quantity, then which of the following must be true?

(a) $\lim_{x\to\infty}f(x)=0$ and $\lim_{x\to\infty}f'(x)=L$

(b) $\lim_{x\to\infty}f(x)=\dfrac{L}{2}$ and $\lim_{x\to\infty}f'(x)=\dfrac{L}{2}$

(c) $\lim_{x\to\infty}f(x)=L$ and $\lim_{x\to\infty}f'(x)=0$

(d) nothing definite can be said

20. Consider

$f(x)=\min\left\{x^3-1,-\dfrac{1}{4}(|x-2|+|x+2|),7-x^3\right\}$

p and q denotes number of points, where $f(x)$ is discontinuous and non-derivable in $[-2,3]$ respectively, then $p+q$ is

(a) 0 (b) 2 (c) 3 (d) 4

21. Let $f:R\to R$ be a derivable function satisfying $f(y)f(x-y)=f(x),\forall\, x,y\in R$. If $f'(0)=p$, $f'(5)=q\ (p,q\neq 0)$, then $f(5)$ is equal to

(a) $\dfrac{p}{q}$ (b) $\dfrac{q}{p}$ (c) $\dfrac{p^2}{q}$ (d) $\dfrac{q^2}{p}$

22. Let $f(x)$ be a function continuous for all $x\in R$ except at $x=0$ such that $f'(x)<0,\forall\, x\in(-\infty,0)$ and $f'(x)>0$, $\forall\, x\in(0,\infty)$. If $\lim_{x\to 0^+}f(x)=3$, $\lim_{x\to 0^-}f(x)=4$ and $f(0)=5$, then the image of the point $(0,1)$ about the line, $y\cdot\lim_{x\to 0}f(\cos^3x-\cos^2x)=x\cdot\lim_{x\to 0}f(\sin^2x-\sin^3x)$, is

(a) $\left(\dfrac{12}{25},\dfrac{-9}{25}\right)$ (b) $\left(\dfrac{12}{25},\dfrac{9}{25}\right)$
(c) $\left(\dfrac{16}{25},\dfrac{-8}{25}\right)$ (d) $\left(\dfrac{24}{25},\dfrac{-7}{25}\right)$

23. Consider the following statements

S_1 : Number of points where $f(x)=|x\operatorname{sgn}(1-x^2)|$ is non-differentiable is 3.

S_2 : Defined $f(x)=\begin{cases}a\sin\dfrac{\pi}{2}(x+1) & ; \ x\leq 0\\ \dfrac{\tan x-\sin x}{x^2} & ; \ x>0\end{cases}$, in order that $f(x)$ be continuous at $x=0$, a should be equal to $\dfrac{1}{2}$.

S_3 : The set of all points, where the function $\sqrt[3]{x^2|x|}$ is differentiable is $(-\infty,0)\cup(0,\infty)$

S_4 : Number of points where $f(x)=\dfrac{1}{\sin^{-1}(\sin x)}$ is non-differentiable in the interval $(0,3\pi)$ is 3.

State in order whether S_1,S_2,S_3 and S_4 are true or false

(a) TTTF (b) TTTT (c) FTTF (d) TFTT

24. Consider the following statements

S_1 : Let $f(x)=\dfrac{\sin(\pi[x-\pi])}{1+[x]^2}$, where $[\cdot]$ stands for the greatest integer function. Then, $f(x)$ is discontinuous at $x=n+\pi, n\in I$.

S_2 : The function $f(x)=p[x+1]+q[x-1]$, (where $[\cdot]$ denotes the greatest integer function) is continuous at $x=1$ if $p+q=0$.

S_3 : Let $f(x)=|[x]x|$ for $-1\leq x\leq 2$, where $[\cdot]$ denotes greatest integer function,then f is not differentiable at $x=2$

S_4 : If $f(x)$ takes only rational values for all real x and is continuous, then $f'(10)=10$

(a) FTTT (b) FTTF (c) FTFT (d) FTFF

More than One Correct Option Type Questions

25. Let $f(x)=\dfrac{1-\sin x}{(\pi-2x)^2}\cdot\dfrac{\ln(\sin x)}{\ln(1+\pi^2-4\pi x+4x^2)}$, $x\neq\dfrac{\pi}{2}$. The value of $f\left(\dfrac{\pi}{2}\right)$ so that the function is continuous at $x=\dfrac{\pi}{2}$ is less than

(a) $\dfrac{1}{16}$ (b) $\dfrac{1}{32}$ (c) $\dfrac{-1}{64}$ (d) $\dfrac{1}{128}$

26. Given $f(x)=\begin{cases}\left[3-\left[\cot^{-1}\left(\dfrac{2x^3-3}{x^2}\right)\right]\right], & \text{for } x>0\\ \{x^2\}\cos(e^{1/x}), & \text{for } x<0\end{cases}$,

then which of the following statement does not hold good?

(where $\{*\}$ and $[*]$ denote the fractional part and the integral part function respectively)

(a) $f(0^-)=0$

(b) $f(0^+)=3$

(c) $f(0)=0 \Rightarrow$ continuity of f at $x=0$

(d) irremovable discontinuity of f at $x=0$

27. In which of the following cases the given equations have atleast one root in the indicated interval?

(a) $x-\cos x=0$ in $\left(0,\dfrac{\pi}{2}\right)$

(b) $x+\sin x=1$ in $\left(0,\dfrac{\pi}{6}\right)$

(c) $\dfrac{a}{x-1}+\dfrac{b}{x-3}=0$, $a, b>0$ in $(1, 3)$

(d) $f(x)-g(x)=0$ in (a, b), where f and g are continuous on $[a, b]$ and $f(a)>g(a)$ and $f(b)<g(b)$.

28. Let $f(x)=\dfrac{1}{[\sin x]}$, then

(where $[\cdot]$ denotes the greatest integer function)

(a) domain of $f(x)$ is $2n\pi+\pi, 2n\pi+2\pi)\cup\{2n\pi+\pi/2\}$

(b) $f(x)$ is continuous when $x\in(2n\pi+\pi, 2n\pi+2\pi)$

(c) $f(x)$ is continuous at $x=2n\pi+\pi/2$

(d) $f(x)$ has the period 2π

29. The graph of a function $y=f(x)$ is shown in the figure. One more function $y=g(x)$ is defined as

$$g(x)=\begin{cases}f(x)-2 & , \quad x<0\\ f(x) & , \quad x=0\\ \dfrac{-1}{f(x)}-\dfrac{1}{2} & , \quad 0<x<\dfrac{3}{2}\\ -f(x) & , \quad x\ge\dfrac{3}{2}\end{cases}$$

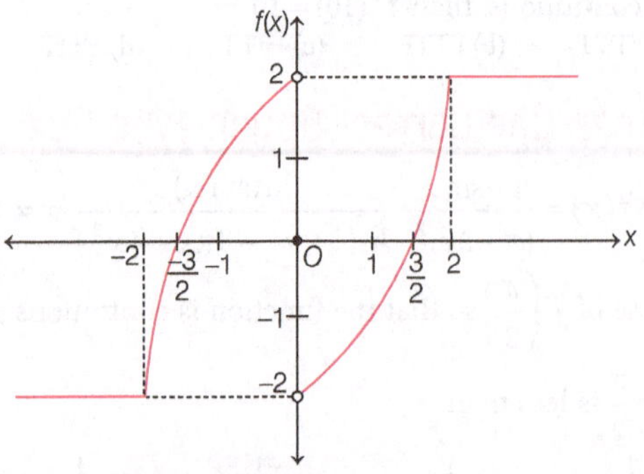

Identify the correct statement(s)?

[**Note** $[k]$ denotes greatest integer less than or equal to k]

(a) Range of $g(x)$ is $[-4, \infty)$

(b) $\lim\limits_{x\to 0^-}[g(x)]=-1$

(c) $g(x)$ is continuous at $x=0$

(d) $g(x)$ is discontinuous at $x=\pm\dfrac{3}{2}$

30. Let $f(x)$ be a differentiable function satisfying the relation $\left|f(x)-\sum\limits_{k=1}^{n}x^k-f(y)+\sum\limits_{k=1}^{n}y^k\right|\le(x-y)^2$, for all $x, y\in R$ and $f(0)=1$

(a) $\lim\limits_{n\to\infty}f\left(\dfrac{1}{2}\right)=2$

(b) For $n=100$, $\lim\limits_{x\to 1}\dfrac{f(x)-f(1)}{x-1}=5050$

(c) For $n=3$, sgn $(f(x))$ is discontinuous at exactly one point

(d) For $n=4$, sgn $(f'(x))$ is discontinuous at exactly one point

31. Let α be the number of solution of $3^{\{x\}}+[x^2-2x+3]=0$ and $f(x)=\dfrac{xa^x+bx\cos x+c\sin x}{x^5}$, $x\ne\alpha (a\ge 1)$ is continuous at $x=\alpha$, then

(a) $f(\alpha)=\dfrac{1}{120}$

(b) $a+b+c=0$

(c) $4abc=-3$

(d) $a-c=5b$

[**Note** $\{y\}$ and $[y]$ denote fractional part of function and greatest integer function of y.]

32. Consider the function $f:R\to A$ given by $f(x)=x+[x]$, where $[x]$ denotes greatest integer less than or equal to x and A is the range of the function. Then, which of the following is/are correct?

(a) $f^{-1}(x)$ exists and is given by $f^{-1}(x)=x-\dfrac{[x]}{2}, \forall\, x\in A$

(b) $f^{-1}(x)$ exists and is given by $f^{-1}(x)=x-[x], \forall\, x\in A$

(c) $f(x)$ is a continuous function

(d) $f^{-1}(x)$ is a continuous function

33. Let $g(x)$ and $h(x)$ be two quadratic polynomials with leading coefficients as unity.

If $g(0)=c$, $h(0)=b$, $g(1)=0$, $h(1)=0$ and $b+c=-1$, also $f(x)=\dfrac{g([x])}{h([x])}$, then which of the following holds good?

($[\cdot]$ represents greatest integer function).

(a) domain of $f(x)$ is $R-[1, 2)$ if $b\notin 1$

(b) domain of $f(x)$ is $R-[1, 2)\cup[b, b+1)$ if $b\in 1$

(c) $\lim\limits_{x\to 1^-}f(x)=\dfrac{c}{b}$ if $b\ne 0$

(d) $f(x)$ is continuous if $b=c=-\dfrac{1}{2}$

34. Let $f(x)=\sum_{r=1}^{n}(x^r+x^{-r})^2,\ x\neq\pm1$

and $g(x)=\begin{cases}\lim_{n\to\infty}(f(x)-2n)x^{-2n-2}(1-x^2), & x\neq 0,\pm1\\ -1, & x=0,\pm1\end{cases}$,

then $g(x)$
(a) is discontinuous at $x=-1$.
(b) is continuous at $x=2$.
(c) has a removable discontinuity at $x=1$.
(d) has an irremovable discontinuity at $x=1$.

35. If $f(x)=\sqrt{x+2\sqrt{2x-4}}+\sqrt{x-2\sqrt{2x-4}}$, then which of the following is/are correct?
(a) $f(x)$ is continuous at all points in its domain
(b) $f(x)$ is differentiable at all points in its domain
(c) $f'(x)=0$, for all $x\in[2,4)$
(d) Range of function is $[2\sqrt{2},\infty)$

36. Let two lines be $f_1(t)x+f_2(t)y=5$ and $g_1(t)x+g_2(t)y=4,\ t\in[0,1]$, where f_1,f_2,g_1,g_2 are continuous functions, $f_1(0)=g_2(0)=f_2(1)=g_1(1)=2$, $f_2(0)=g_1(0)=3$ and $f_1(1)=g_2(1)=4$, then both the lines
(a) are parallel for some $t\in[0,1]$.
(b) are perpendicular for some $t\in[0,1]$.
(c) make complimentary angles with positive X-axis for some $t\in[0,1]$.
(d) None of the above

37. The number of points of discontinuity of function $f(x)=\lim_{n\to\infty}\dfrac{x^{2n}-2\sin x^{2n}}{x^{2n}+2\sin x^{2n}}$ is equal to number of points of non-differentiability of which of the following function(s)?
(a) $g(x)=\text{sgn}(x^2-1)$ (b) $h(x)=\sin^{-1}\left(\dfrac{2x}{1+x^2}\right)$
(c) $k(x)=\cos^{-1}\left(\dfrac{1-x^2}{1+x^2}\right)$ (d) $l(x)=\text{sgn}(|x|-1)$

38. If $f(x)$ be such that $f(x)=\max(|3-x|,3-x^3)$, then
(a) $f(x)$ is continuous, $\forall\ x\in R$
(b) $f(x)$ is differentiable, $\forall\ x\in R$
(c) $f(x)$ is non-differentiable at three points only
(d) $f(x)$ is non-differentiable at four points only

39. Consider the function $f:\left[0,\dfrac{5}{2}\right)\to\left(\dfrac{1}{2},3\right]$ defined by

$f(x)=\dfrac{[x]+1}{\{x\}+1}$, when $[\cdot]$ represents the greatest integer function and $\{\}$ represents the fractional part function. Then, which of the following is/are true?
(a) $f(x)$ is injective discontinuous function
(b) $f(x)$ is surjective non-differentiable function
(c) $\min.(\lim_{x\to1^-}f(x),\ \lim_{x\to1^+}f(x))\neq f(2)$
(d) Number of points of discontinuity of $f(x)$ in its domain is 3

40. If $f(x)=\begin{cases}\int_0^x(1+|1-t|)\,dt, & x>2\\ 5x+1, & x\leq 2\end{cases}$, then
(a) $f(x)$ is not continuous at $x=2$
(b) $f(x)$ is continuous but not differentiable at $x=2$
(c) $f(x)$ is differentiable everywhere
(d) the right derivative of $f(x)$ at $x=2$ does not exist

Passage Based Questions

Passage I

(Q. Nos. 41 to 42)

- Let f be a differentiable function satisfying the relation $f(x+y)=f(x)+f(y)-2xy+(e^x-1)(e^y-1)$, $\forall\ x,y\in R$ and $f'(0)=1$

41. The value of $\lim_{x\to0}\dfrac{f(2x)+4x^2-2x}{x^2}$ is
(a) 2 (b) 4 (c) 8 (d) 16

42. Let $g(x)=f(x)+x^2-2$. If the equation $|g(|x|)|=k$ has four distinct solutions, then the set of values of k is
(a) (0, 1) (b) (− 2, 2) (c) (0, 3) (d) (0, 2)

Passage II

(Q. Nos. 43 to 44)

- Let $f(x)=\begin{cases}\max.\{t^3-t^2+t+1,\ 0\leq t\leq x\}, & 0\leq x\leq 1\\ \min.\{3-t, 1<t\leq x\}, & 1<x\leq 2\end{cases}$

and

$g(x)=\begin{cases}\max.\left\{\dfrac{3}{8}t^4+\dfrac{1}{2}t^3-\dfrac{3}{2}t^2+1,\ 0\leq t\leq x\right\}, & 0\leq x<1\\ \min.\left\{\dfrac{3}{8}t+\dfrac{1}{32}\sin^2\pi t+\dfrac{5}{8}, 1\leq t\leq x\right\}, & 1\leq x\leq 2\end{cases}$

43. The function $f(x),\forall\ x\in[0,2]$ is
(a) continuous and differentiable
(b) continuous but not differentiable
(c) discontinuous and not differentiable
(d) None of the above

44. Which of the following is true?
(a) $\lim_{x\to1^-}fog(x)>\lim_{x\to1^+}gof(x)$
(b) $\lim_{x\to1^-}fog(x)<\lim_{x\to1^+}gof(x)$
(c) $\lim_{x\to1^-}fog(x)=\lim_{x\to1^+}gof(x)$
(d) None of the above

Passage III

(Q. Nos. 45 to 46)

- A function $f(x)$ is said to be differentiable at $x=c$, if $f'(c^+)=f'(c^-)=$ a finite quantity. Also, $f(x)$ is said to be bounded if $|f(x)|<n,\forall\ x$ for which $f(x)$ is defined (where n is finite)

45. Let $f : R \to R$ and $c \in R$ such that

$$\lim_{n\to\infty} n\left(f\left(c+\frac{1}{n}\right)-f(c)\right) = a (a \in R), \text{ then}$$

(a) $f'(c)$ exists and is equal to a
(b) $f'(c)$ does not exist
(c) $f'(c)$ exists but is not equal to a
(d) $f'(c)$ may or may not exist

46. $f(x)$ is defined on [0, 1] and

$$f(x) = \begin{cases} x^a \sin(x^{-c}), & x \neq 0 \\ 0, & x = 0 \end{cases}, \text{ where } a, c \in R \text{ and } c > 0$$

(a) $f'(0)$ exists if $0 < a < 1$
(b) $f(x)$ is continuous if $a < 0$
(c) $f'(x)$ is bounded and continuous if $a > c$
(d) $f(x)$ and $f'(x)$ are continuous if $a > 1 + c$

Passage IV
(Q. Nos. 47 and 48)

- Let $f : \left(\frac{-\pi}{2}, \frac{\pi}{2}\right) \to R$ such that $f(x)$ is differentiable at $x = 0$ and $f(x) = \begin{cases} \frac{1}{2}(1+\sec x)\, f\left(\frac{x}{2}\right), & x \neq 0 \\ 2, & x = 0 \end{cases}$

47. The value of $f\left(\frac{\pi}{4}\right) + f'\left(\frac{\pi}{4}\right)$ is

(a) $\frac{24\pi - 16}{\pi}$ (b) $\frac{24\pi + 16}{\pi^2}$
(c) $\frac{8(3\pi - 4)}{\pi^2}$ (d) $\frac{8(3\pi + 4)}{\pi}$

48. The value of $\lim_{x\to 0}\left[\left\{\frac{f(x)-2}{x^2}\right\} + \left[\frac{f(x)-2\cos x}{x^2}\right]\right]$ is

[**Note** where $[y]$ denotes greatest integer function less than or equal to y and $\{y\}$ denotes fractional part function of y]

(a) $\frac{3}{5}$ (b) $\frac{5}{3}$
(c) $\frac{2}{3}$ (d) $\frac{3}{2}$

Stem Based Questions

Stem I
(Q. Nos. 49 and 50)

- Let f be a real valued function defined on R (the set of all real numbers), where $y = f(x)$ is defined parametrically as $x = 5t - |2 - t|, y = -3t + 2|t - 1|, \forall t \in R$.

49. The function $f(x)$ is non-differentiable at $x = 2$, then sum of all possible values of α is ....

50. The value of $|[f'(\pi)]|$ is equal to ....

Stem II
(Q. Nos. 51 and 52)

- Let $f(x)$ be a polynomial satisfying $\lim_{x\to\infty}\frac{x^4 f(x)}{x^8+1} = 3$, $f(2) = 5$, $f(3) = 10$, $f(-1) = 2$ and $f(-6) = 37$.

51. The value of $\left|\lim_{x\to -6}\frac{f(x)-x^2-1}{3(x+6)}\right|$ is equal to ....

52. The number of points of discontinuity of $g(x) = \frac{1}{x^2+1-f(x)}$ in $\left[\frac{-15}{2}, \frac{5}{2}\right]$ is equal to ....

Single Integer Type Questions

53. Let $f(x) = \text{cosec } 2x + \text{cosec } 2^2 x + \text{cosec } 2^3 x + \ldots \text{cosec } 2^n x, x \in (0, \pi/2)$ and $g(x) = f(x) + \cot 2^n x$

$$\text{If } H(x) = \begin{cases} (\cos x)^{g(x)} + (\sec x)^{\text{cosec } x} & \text{if } x > 0 \\ p & \text{if } x = 0, \\ \frac{e^x + e^{-x} - 2\cos x}{x \sin x} & \text{if } x < 0 \end{cases}$$

then the value of p is, if possible to make the function $H(x)$ continuous at $x = 0$.

54. If for a differentiable function $y = f(x), (f'(x) > 0)$

$$\lim_{x\to 1}\frac{e^{2f(x)} - 2e^{f(x)+1} + e^2\cos(x-1)}{\sec^2(x-1)-1} = \frac{7}{2}e^2$$ and area of the triangle formed by the tangent drawn to the curve $= f(x)$ at $(1, f(1))$ and coordinate axes is Δ, then the value of $\frac{1}{\Delta}$ is equal to ....

55. Let $f(x) = \begin{cases} \lim_{t\to 0}\left[\frac{q\tan t}{t}\right]\frac{(1-\sin x)}{(\pi-2x)^2}, & x > \frac{\pi}{2} \\ \frac{1}{2}\lim_{\alpha\to 0}\left(\left[\frac{p\sin\alpha}{\alpha}\right]\right), & x = \frac{\pi}{2}, \\ \frac{1-\sin^3 x}{3\cos^2 x}, & x < \frac{\pi}{2} \end{cases}$

where p, q are natural numbers and [] denotes greatest integer function. If $f(x)$ is continuous at $x = \frac{\pi}{2}$, then the value of $(p+q)$ is ....

56. Let $f'(x^2) = \frac{1}{x}$ for $x > 0$, $f(1) = 1$ and $g'(\sin^2 x - 1) = \cos^2 x + p, \forall x \in R$, $g(-1) = 0$.

If $h(x) = \begin{cases} f(x), & x > 0 \\ g(x), & -1 \leq x \leq 0 \end{cases}$ is a continuous function, then the absolute value of $2p$ is ....

57. Let n_1, n_2 and n_3 denote the number of points of non-derivability of functions $f(x) = \cot^2 x - \operatorname{cosec}^2 x$ in $(0, 2\pi)$, $g(x) = \cot^{-1} x + \sin^{-1} x + \tan^{-1} x$ in $(-1, 1)$ and $h(x) = [5 + \cos x]$ in $[0, 2\pi)$, respectively. The value of $n_1 + n_2 + n_3$ is ....

Note $[y]$ denotes largest integer less than or equal to y.

58. Let $P(x)$ be a polynomial satisfying $P(x) - 2P'(x) = 3x^3 - 27x^2 + 38x + 1$.

If the function

$$f(x) = \begin{cases} \dfrac{P''(x) + 18}{6}, & x \neq \dfrac{\pi}{2} \\ \sin^{-1}(ab) + \cos^{-1}(a + b - 3ab), & x = \dfrac{\pi}{2} \end{cases}$$

is continuous at $x = \dfrac{\pi}{2}$, then $(a + b)$ is ....

59. Let $f(x) = [x] + |1 - x|$, then the number of points, where $f(x)$ is not differentiable in $(-1, 3)$ is ....

60. Let $f(x)$ be a function satisfying

$$2(f(x))^2 - \frac{d^2 f(x)}{dx^2} f(x) + \left(\frac{df(x)}{dx}\right)^2 = 0 \text{ and}$$

$|\ln |f(x)|| = g(x)$. If $f(0) = 1$ and $f(1) < e$, where e is Euler's constant (base of natural logarithm), then the number of points where $g(x)$ is non-differentiable is equal to ....

61. Let $f(x)$ be a function defined in $[0, 5]$ such that $f^2(x) = 1, \forall\, x \in [0, 5]$ and $f(x)$ is discontinuous only at all integers in $[0, 5]$. If total number of possible functions is λ, then sum of digits at odd places in λ is ....

62. Consider a function

$$f(x) = \begin{cases} \dfrac{\ln\left(1 - ax\left[\dfrac{4x^2}{x^4 + 1}\right] + a\right)}{e^{bx} - e^{b\left[\frac{4x^2}{x^4+1}\right]}}, & -1 < x < 1,\ x \neq 0 \\ \dfrac{(\tan bx - \tan b)(1 + \cos 2bx)}{2(x - 1)}, & 1 < x < 2 \end{cases},$$

where $[k]$ denotes greatest integer less than or equal to k. If $f(x)$ is continuous in $(-1, 0) \cup (0, 2)$ and passing through the point $(1, \ln 2)$, then the value of $(1 + a + 2b^2)$ is ....

63. If

$$f(x) = \begin{cases} f(x) = \ln(1 + |x| + (b - 2)|x + 1|) + a \tan^{-1} x + 2, & -2 < x < 0 \\ b, & x = 0 \\ \dfrac{(c + 2)\sin^{-1}\sqrt{\{x\}} + e^{2x} - e^{\ln\left(4\left\{\frac{x}{2}\right\}\right)} - 1}{x^2}, & 0 < x < 2 \end{cases}$$

is derivable in $(-2, 2)$, then the value of $\dfrac{(9a^2 + b^2 + c^2)}{19}$ is ....

[**Note** $\{y\}$ denotes fractional part of y]

64. Consider the function f defined as

$$f(x) = \begin{cases} \dfrac{e^{[3\cot x - 1]} + \sin 2x - a + [\cos x - \sin x]}{\left(x - \dfrac{\pi}{4}\right)^2}, & x > \dfrac{\pi}{4} \\ P([P] - 2) - 2, & x = \dfrac{\pi}{4} \\ b\left[\dfrac{2}{3} - \dfrac{1 + \sin 2x}{1 + \sin 2x + \sin^2 2x}\right], & x < \dfrac{\pi}{4} \end{cases}$$

If $f(x)$ is continuous $x = \dfrac{\pi}{4}$, then the value of $[a + b + n]$, where n is number of integral values of P, is ....

[**Note** $[y]$ denotes greatest integer less than or equal to y]

65. Let $f : \left[0, \dfrac{\pi}{2}\right] \to [-1, 1]$ and $g : \left[0, \dfrac{\pi}{2}\right] \to [-1, 1]$ be two functions defined as $f(x) = \sin\left(\dfrac{\pi}{2}[x^2] - x^2\right)$ and $g(x) = \cos\left(\dfrac{\pi}{2}[x^3] - x^3\right)$ respectively, where $[x]$ denotes greatest integer function of x and p denotes number of points of discontinuity of $f(x)$ and q denotes number of points of non-differentiability of $g(x)$, then the value of $(p^2 + q^2 - 10)$ is ....

66. If $f(x) = \lim\limits_{n \to \infty} \dfrac{(1 + \sin x)^n + e^x}{1 + (1 + \sin x)^n}$, where $x \in [-2\pi, 2\pi]$, then the total number of points of discontinuity of $f(x)$ is ....

Numerical Value Type Questions

67. If $f(x) = \begin{cases} \dfrac{a^x - 1}{x^n \sin x}\left(\dfrac{b\sin x - \sin bx}{\cos x - \cos bx}\right)^n, & x > 0 \\ \dfrac{a^x \sin bx - b^x \sin ax}{\tan bx - \tan ax}, & x < 0 \end{cases}$

is continuous at $x = 0$ $(a, b > 0, b \neq 1, a \neq b)$, if

$f(0^+) = (\ln xa)\left(\dfrac{b}{y}\right)^{2n}$ and $f(0^+) = x$, then $5x + 7y + 9z$ is equal to ....

68. The function $f(x) = \left(\dfrac{2 + \cos x}{x^3 \sin x} - \dfrac{3}{x^4}\right)$ is not defined at $x = 0$. If function is continuous, then $3f(0)$ is ....

69. For $x \in (0, \infty)$, let $f(x) = \ln x + x + 1$.

If $g(x) = \begin{cases} \left(1 + \dfrac{15(x-2)}{x^2+1}\right)^{\frac{\ln(3e)}{\tan(x-2)}}, & 1 \le x < 2 \\ 27e^3, & x = 2 \\ \lambda\left(\dfrac{e^{f(x)} - 2e^3}{\sin x \cos 2 - \cos x \sin 2}\right), & 2 < x \le 3 \end{cases}$

is continuous in [1, 3], then the value of λ^2 is equal to ....

70. Let α be the number of possible integral values of a for which $ax - x^2 < 1, \forall x \in R$. Number of points of non-derivability of the function $g(x) = [3 + 4\alpha \sin x]$ in $(0, \pi)$ is ....

[**Note** $[k]$ denotes largest integer less than or equal to k]

71. A derivable function $f : R^+ \to R$ satisfies the condition $f(x) - f(y) \ge \ln\left(\dfrac{x}{y}\right) + x - y$ for every $x, y \in R^+$. If g denotes the derivative of f', then $g'\left(\dfrac{1}{3}\right)$ is equal to ......

72. Let $X = \{1, 2, 3, 4, 5, 6\}$ and a, c are natural numbers selected from set X with replacement

Let $f(x) = \begin{cases} x^2 + x, & x \le 1 \\ x^2 - ax, & x > 1 \end{cases}$, $g(x) = \begin{cases} x^2 - cx, & x \le 2 \\ x^2 - 4x, & x > 2 \end{cases}$

and $h(x) = f(x) \cdot g(x), x \in R$

N_1 = Number of function $h(x)$ such that $f(x)$ and $g(x)$ both are discontinuous.

N_2 = Number of function $h(x)$ such that $h(x)$ is continuous at $x = 1$ and discontinuous at $x = 2$ but $f(x)$ and $g(x)$ both are discontinuous.

N_3 = Number of function $h(x)$ such that $h(x)$ is discontinuous at $x = 1$ and continuous at $x = 2$.

The value of $(N_1 + N_2 + N_3)$ is ....

73. Let $f(x)$ be a continuous function satisfying $f^3(x) - 5f^2(x) + 10f(x) - 12 \le 0$, $f^2(x) - 4f(x) + 3 \ge 0$ and $f^2(x) - 6f(x) + 8 \le 0$ and A is the area bounded by the line $y = x$, $y = f(x)$ and $x = 0$, then the value of $10A$ is ....

74. Let $f(x) = x^2 + ax + 3$ and $g(x) = x + b$, where $F(x) = \lim\limits_{n \to \infty} \dfrac{f(x) + x^{2n} g(x)}{1 + x^{2n}}$. If $F(x)$ is continuous at $x = 1$ and $x = -1$, then the value of $(a^2 + b^2)$ is ....

75. Let $f(x)$ be a differentiable function satisfying $f(xy) = f(x) + f(y) + xy - x - y - 1, \forall x, y > 0$ and $\lim\limits_{h \to 0} \dfrac{2 - f(1-h)}{h} = 2$. If $L = \lim\limits_{x \to \infty} \dfrac{2 + \frac{2}{x} - f\left(\frac{x+1}{x}\right)}{1 - \sqrt{\cos\frac{1}{3x}}}$, then the absolute value of 1 is ....

76. Let $f(x) = \begin{cases} \sqrt{(2n+1)x - x^2 - (n^2+n)}, & n \le x < n + \frac{1}{2} \\ n + 1 - x, & n + \frac{1}{2} \le x < n + 1 \end{cases}$

$(n \in I)$, then the number of values of x, where $f(x)$ is non-derivable in $(-5, 5)$ is ....

77. Let $f(x) = \lim\limits_{n \to \infty} ((a^n + b^n)^{1/n} \sin x + \{e^x\}^n)$ $\left(\left[\dfrac{1}{n \cot^{-1} n}\right] + 1\right), \forall x \in R$, where $a > b > 0$.

If $H(x) = \operatorname{sgn}(f(x) - 3)$ has exactly one point of discontinuity, $\forall x \in [0, 2\pi]$, then the value of $24a$ is ....

[**Note** $\{k\}$ and $[k]$ denote fractional part of k and greatest integer less than or equal to k respectively and sgn α denotes signum function of α]

78. Let $f(x) = \begin{cases} \lim\limits_{n \to \infty} \dfrac{|\log_e |x|| - e^{nx}\{\sin x\}}{2x + e^{(n+1)x}}, & x \in (-\pi, \pi) - \{0\} \\ 0, & x = 0 \end{cases}$

If l and m are number of points, where $f(x)$ is discontinuous and non-differentiable in $(-\pi, \pi)$ respectively, then the value of $(l + m)^2$ is equal to ......

(**Note** $\{y\}$ denotes fractional part of y)

79. If $\sum\limits_{r=1}^{n} \sin^{-1} \alpha_r = \dfrac{n\pi}{2}$, for any $n \in N$ and $p = \prod\limits_{r=1}^{n} (\alpha_r)^r$.

If $f(x) = \begin{cases} \dfrac{x^{1/3} - (3-2x)^{1/4}}{x^2 - x}, & x \ne p \\ k, & x = p \end{cases}$ is continuous at $x = p$, then the value of $6(k + p)$ is ....

80. Let $f(x) = ax^9 + b \sin x + cx^2 \operatorname{sgn}(x) + \dfrac{(e^x - e^{-x})}{(e^x + e^{-x})}$ be defined on set of real numbers, $(a > 0, b, c \in R)$. If $f(-5) = 5$, $f(-2) = -3$. If the minimum number of zeroes of the equation $f(x) = 0$ is α, then number of positive integral solutions of the equation $x_1 + x_2 + x_3 = 3\alpha$ is ....

81. If $f(x)$ and $g(x)$ are two differentiable functions and graph of $y = g(x)$ is reflection of graph of $y = f(x)$ with respect to line $y = x$. If point (a, b) lies on curve $y = f(x)$ and $f'(a) = 3$, then the value of $\dfrac{670}{\gamma}$ (where γ is ordinate of the point on the curve $y = g'(x)$ whose abscissa is b) is ....

Matching Type Questions

82. Match the following columns.

Column I	Column II
(A) Let $f(x)=\begin{cases} x\dfrac{\left(\frac{4}{5}\right)^{1/x}-\left(\frac{4}{5}\right)^{-1/x}}{\left(\frac{4}{5}\right)^{1/x}+\left(\frac{4}{5}\right)^{-1/x}}, & x\neq 0 \\ 0, & x=0\end{cases}$ If $\alpha = f'(0^-)-f'(0^+)$, then $\lim\limits_{x\to\alpha}\dfrac{(\exp((x+2)\ln 4))^{\frac{\lvert x+0.5\rvert}{4}}-16}{(2)^{2x}-16}$ is less than or equal to	(p) 3
(B) If $f(x)=[2+5\mid n\mid \sin x]$, where $n\in Z$ has exactly 19 points of non-differentiability in $(0,\pi)$, then the possible values of n are ([·]) is greatest integer function)	(q) 2
(C) If $f(x)=\begin{cases}\dfrac{\left(\frac{\pi}{2}-\sin^{-1}(1-\{x\}^2)\right)\sin^{-1}(1-\{x\})}{\sqrt{2}(\{x\}-\{x\}^3)}, & x>0 \\ \lambda, & x=0 \\ \dfrac{\mu\sin^{-1}(1-\{x\})\cos^{-1}(1-\{x\})}{\sqrt{2\{x\}}(1-\{x\})}, & x<0\end{cases}$ is continuous at $x=0$, then the value of $\sin^2\lambda+\cos^2\left(\dfrac{\mu\pi}{\sqrt{2}}\right)$ is ({·} denotes fractional part function)	(r) −3
(D) If $f(x)=\dfrac{1}{1+\frac{2}{x}}$, then the number of points in R at which $g(x)=\dfrac{1}{1+\frac{3}{f(x)}}$ is non-differentiable, is	(s) 5
	(t) −2

83. Match the function in Column I with its behaviour at $x=0$ in Column II, where [·] denote greatest integer function and sgn (x) denotes signum function

Column I	Column II
(A) $f(x)=[x][1+x]$	(p) LHL exists at $x=0$
(B) $f(x)=[-x][1+x]$	(q) RHL exist at $x=0$
(C) $f(x=(\text{sgn}(x))(2-x)$ $[1+\lvert x\rvert]$	(r) Continuous at $x=0$
(D) $f(x)=[\cos x]$	(s) $\lim\limits_{x\to 0} f(x)$ exists but function is discontinuous at $x=0$
	(t) $\lim\limits_{x\to 0} f(x)$ does not exist

84. Matching the following columns.

Column I	Column II
(A) If $f(xy)=f(x), f(y)$ and f is differentiable at $x=1$, such that $f'(1)=1$ also, $f(1)\neq 0$, then $f'(7)$ equals	(p) 13
(B) The number of points, where $f(x)=\lvert x^2-3x+2\rvert+\lvert\sin x\rvert$; $-[x-1/2], -\pi\le x\le\pi$ is non-differentiable is ([·] denotes greatest integer function)	(q) 9
(C) The number of points at which $f(x)=[a+7\sin x]; x\in[0,\pi], a\in Z$ is non-differentiable is ([·] denotes greatest integer function)	(r) 2
(D) If for a continuous function $f, f(0)=f(1)=0, f'(1)=2$ and $g(x)=f(e^x)\cdot e^{f(x)}$, then $g'(0)$ equals	(s) 3
	(t) 1

Previous Year Questions

85. Let $f:R\to R$ and $g:R\to R$ be functions defined by

$$f(x)=\begin{cases} x\lvert x\rvert\sin\left(\dfrac{1}{x}\right), & x\neq 0, \\ 0, & x=0,\end{cases}$$

and $g(x)=\begin{cases}1-2x, & 0\le x\le\dfrac{1}{2}, \\ 0, & \text{otherwise}\end{cases}$

Let $a,b,c,d\in R$. Define the function $h:R\to R$ by

$$h(x)=af(x)+b\left(g(x)+g\left(\frac{1}{2}-x\right)\right)+c\,(x-g(x))+dg(x),\ x\in R.$$

Match each entry in List-I to the correct entry in List-II.

List I	List II
(P) If $a=0, b=1, c=0$ and $d=0$, then	(1) h is one-one.
(Q) If $a=1, b=0, c=0$ and $d=0$, then	(2) h is onto.
(R) If $a=0, b=0, c=1$ and $d=0$, then	(3) h is differentiable on R.
(S) If $a=0, b=0, c=0$ and $d=1$, then	(4) the range of h is [0, 1].
	(5) the range of h is {0, 1}

The correct options is **[Single Correct Type, 2024 Adv.]**

(a) (P) → (4), (Q) → (3), (R) → (1), (S) → (2)
(b) (P) → (5), (Q) → (2), (R) → (4), (S) → (3)
(c) (P) → (5), (Q) → (3), (R) → (2), (S) → (4)
(d) (P) → (4), (Q) → (2), (R) → (1), (S) → (3)

86. Let $S=(0,1)\cup(1,2)\cup(3,4)$ and $T=\{0,1,2,3\}$. Then, which of the following statements is (are) true?

[More than Correct Type, 2023 Adv.]

(a) There are infinitely many functions from S to T

(b) There are infinitely many strictly increasing functions from S to T

(c) The number of continuous functions from S to T is at most 120

(d) Every continuous function from S to T is differentiable

87. Let $f: R\to R$ and $g: R\to R$ be functions satisfying $f(x+y)=f(x)+f(y)+f(x)f(y)$ and $f(x)=xg(x)$ for all $x, y\in R$. If $\lim_{x\to 0} g(x)=1$, then which of the following statements is/are true?

[More than Correct Type, 2020 Adv.]

(a) f is differentiable at every $x\in R$

(b) If $g(0)=1$, then g is differentiable at every $x\in R$

(c) The derivative $f'(1)$ is equal to 1

(d) The derivative $f'(0)$ is equal to 1

88. Let the function $f: R\to R$ be defined by $f(x)=x^3-x^2+(x-1)\sin x$ and let $g: R\to R$ be an arbitrary function. Let $fg: R\to R$ be the product function defined by $(fg)(x)=f(x)g(x)$. Then which of the following statements is/are TRUE?

[More than Correct Type, 2020 Adv.]

(a) If g is continuous at $x=1$, then fg is differentiable at $x=1$

(b) If fg is differentiable at $x=1$, then g is continuous at $x=1$

(c) If g is differentiable at $x=1$, then fg is differentiable at $x=1$

(d) If fg is differentiable at $x=1$, then g is differentiable at $x=1$

89. Let the functions $f:(-1,1)\to R$ and $g:(-1,1)\to(-1,1)$ be defined by $f(x)=|2x-1|+|2x+1|$ and $g(x)=x-[x]$, where $[x]$ denotes the greatest integer less than or equal to x. Let $fog:(-1,1)\to R$ be the composite function defined by $(fog)(x)=f(g(x))$. Suppose c is the number of points in the interval $(-1,1)$ at which fog is not continuous, and suppose d is the number of points in the interval $(-1,1)$ at which fog is not differentiable. Then the value of $c+d$ is ....

[Numerical Value Type, 2020 Adv.]

EXERCISE 3

Challenging Problems

1. If $f(x)=\begin{cases} x-[x], & x\notin I \\ 1, & x\in I\end{cases}$, where I is an integer and $[\cdot]$ represents the greatest integer function and

$$g(x)=\lim_{n\to\infty}\frac{\{f(x)\}^{2n}-1}{\{f(x)\}^{2n}+1}, \text{ then}$$

(i) draw graphs of $f(2x)$, $g(x)$ and $g\{g(x)\}$.

(ii) find the domain and range of these functions.

(iii) are these functions periodic? If yes, find their periods.

2. Prove that $f(x)=[\tan x]+\sqrt{\tan x-[\tan x]}$, (where $[\cdot]$ denotes greatest integer function) is continuous in $\left[0,\frac{\pi}{2}\right)$.

3. Discuss the continuity on $0\le x\le 1$ and differentiability at $x=0$ for the function.

$$f(x)=x\cdot\sin\frac{1}{x}\cdot\sin\frac{1}{x\sin\frac{1}{x}}, \text{ where } x\ne 0,\ x\ne 1/r\pi \text{ and}$$

$$f(0)=f(1/r\pi)=0, r=1,2,3,\ldots$$

4. Discuss the continuity and the derivability of f at $x=\sqrt{2}$, where $f(x)=$ degree of $(u^{x^2}+u^2+2u-3)$.

5. Discuss the continuity and differentiability of the function $y=f(x)$ defined parametrically; $x=2t-|t-1|$ and $y=2t^2+t|t|$.

6. Let $f(x)=$ maximum $\{2\sin x, 1-\cos x\}$, for all $x\in(0,\pi)$, then discuss differentiability of $f(x)$ in $(0,\pi)$.

7. If $f(x)=x^2-2|x|$ and

$$g(x)=\begin{cases}\min.\{f(t), & -2\le t\le x, \quad -2\le x<0\} \\ \max.\{f(t), & 0\le t\le x, \quad 0\le x\le 2\} \\ f(x) & , \quad x>2\end{cases}$$

(i) Draw the graph of $f(x)$ and discuss its continuity and differentiability.

(ii) Find and draw the graph of $g(x)$. Also, discuss the continuity and differentiability.

8. Let $f(x)=x^4-8x^3+22x^2-24x$

and $g(x)=\begin{cases}\min. f(t), & x\le t\le x+1,\ -1\le x\le 1\\ x-10, & x>1\end{cases}$ discuss

the continuity and differentiability of $g(x)$ in $[-1,\infty)$.

9. Let f be a continuous function from R to R such that f is differentiable at 0. Suppose that $f\left(\frac{1}{n}\right)=0$, for all $n\in N$.

(i) Prove that $f(0)=0$. (this fact does not require the differentiability of f)

(ii) Prove that $f'(0)=0$

10. Let $f\left(\frac{x_1+x_2+x_3+\ldots+x_n}{n}\right)$

$$=\left(\frac{f(x_1)+f(x_2)+f(x_3)+\ldots+f(x_n)}{n}\right),$$

where x_i are any real numbers and $n\in N$. If $f(x)$ is differentiable and $f'(0)=a$ and $f(0)=b$, find $f(x)$.

11. If $g(x)$ is continuous function in $[0,\infty)$ satisfying $g(1)=1$. If $\int_0^x 2x\cdot g^2(t)\,dt=\left(\int_0^x 2g(x-t)dt\right)^2$, find $g(x)$.

12. If $|f(p+q)-f(q)|\le\frac{p}{q}$, for all p and $q\in Q^+$, show that

$$\sum_{i=1}^{k}|f(2^k)-f(2^i)|\le\frac{k(k-1)}{2}$$

13. Let $g(x)$ be a polynomial of degree one and $f(x)$ be defined by $f(x)=\begin{cases}g(x)<0\\ \left(\frac{1+x}{2+x}\right)^{1/x}, & x>0\end{cases}$. Find the continuous function $f(x)$ satisfying $f'(1)=f(-1)$

14. Let $(a_1 f(a))$ and $(b_1 f(b))$ are any two points on the graph of a differentiable function $y=f(x)$. Let chord AB always intersects Y-axis at $(0, 2ab)$.

If $\lim_{x\to 0}\left(\frac{f(x)}{2x}\right)^{1/x}=e^{-1}$, then number of points at which $|f(x-1)|$ is non differentiable is equal to

15. If $f(x)=[x+[x^3+1)]^{x^2+\sin x}$, find the derivative when $x\in(1, 3/2)$ and indicate the points where it does not exist, (where $[\cdot]$ denotes the greatest integer function)

16. Let $f(0)=0$ and $f'(0)=1$. For a positive integer k, show that

$$\lim_{x\to 0}\frac{1}{x}\left(f(x)+f\left(\frac{x}{2}\right)+\ldots+f\left(\frac{x}{k}\right)\right)=1+\frac{1}{2}+\frac{1}{3}+\ldots+\frac{1}{k}$$

Answer Key

Exercise 1

1. (d)	2. (d)	3. (c)	4. (a)	5. (a)	6. (b)	7. (c)	8. (d)	9. (a)	10. (b)
11. (d)	12. (a)	13. (d)	14. (d)	15. (d)	16. (d)	17. (b)	18. (c)	19. (c)	20. (b)
21. (b)	22. (b)	23. (c)	24. (c)	25. (c)	26. (b)	27. (c)	28. (d)	29. (c)	30. (b)
31. (a)	32. (b)	33. (4)	34. (1)	35. (3)	36. (2)	37. (2)	38. (2)	39. (3)	40. (4)
41. (3)	42. (8)	43. (1)	44. (2)	45. (0)	46. (0)	47. (d)	48. (d)	49. (a)	50. (d)
51. (d)	52. (15)	53. (b)	54. (a)	55. (b)	56. (d)	57. (a)	58. (a)	59. (b)	60. (c)
61. (2)	62. (4)	63. (309)	64. (25)	65. (b)	66. (b)	67. (b)	68. (d)	69. (c)	70. (79)
71. (4)	72. (62)	73. (7)	74. (a)	75. (a)	76. (b)	77. (d)	78. (c)	79. (b)	80. (d)
81. (c)	82. (a)	83. (c)	84. (a)	85. (b)	86. (2)	87. (5)	88. (1)		

Exercise 2

1. (a)	2. (d)	3. (b)	4. (a)	5. (c)	6. (b)	7. (b)	8. (a)	9. (d)	10. (c)
11. (b)	12. (b)	13. (d)	14. (a)	15. (c)	16. (c)	17. (d)	18. (d)	19. (c)	20. (b)
21. (b)	22. (d)	23. (a)	24. (b)	25. (a,b,d)	26. (b,d)	27. (a,b,c,d)	28. (a,b,d)	29. (a,b,c)	30. (a,b,c)
31. (a,b,c,d)	32. (a,d)	33. (a,b,d)	34. (a,b,d)	35. (a,c,d)	36. (a,b,c)	37. (a,b,d)	38. (a,d)	39. (a,b,c)	40. (a,d)
41. (a)	42. (d)	43. (a)	44. (a)	45. (d)	46. (d)	47. (c)	48. (b)	49. (14)	50. (1)
51. (360)	52. (3)	53. (2)	54. (4)	55. (6)	56. (3)	57. (4)	58. (2)	59. (3)	60. (3)
61. (3)	62. (1)	63. (3)	64. (6)	65. (3)	66. (4)	67. (53)	68. (0.05)	69. (81)	70. (23)
71. (54)	72. (45)	73. (45)	74. (17)	75. (18)	76. (19)	77. (36)	78. (25)	79. (11)	80. (91)

81. (2010) 82. (A) → (p,q,s), (B) → (q,t), (C) → (q), (D) → (p) 83. (A) → (p,q,r), (B) → (p,q,t), (C) → (p,q,t), (D) → (p,q,s)

84. (A) → (t), (B) → (q), (C) → (p), (D) → (r) 85. (c) 86. (a,c,d) 87. (a,b,d) 88. (a,c) 89. (4)

Solutions

Exercise 1 - JEE Main Pattern

1. For $f(x)$ to be continuous at $x = 0$, we should have

$$\lim_{x\to 0} f(x) = f(0) = 12(\log 4)^3$$

$$\lim_{x\to 0} f(x) = \lim_{x\to 0}\left(\frac{4^x-1}{x}\right)^3 \times \frac{\left(\frac{x}{p}\right)}{\left(\sin\frac{x}{p}\right)} \cdot \frac{px^2}{\log\left(1+\frac{1}{3}x^2\right)}$$

$$= \log(4)^3 \cdot 1 \cdot p \cdot \lim_{x\to 0}\left(\frac{x^2}{\frac{1}{3}x^2 - \frac{1}{18}x^4 + \ldots}\right)$$

$$= 3p\,(\log 4)^3.$$

Hence, $p = 4$

2. $$\lim_{x\to 0}\left(\frac{1}{x} - \frac{2}{e^{2x}-1}\right) = \lim_{x\to 0}\frac{e^{2x}-1-2x}{x(e^{2x}-1)}$$

$$= \lim_{x\to 0}\frac{\left\{\left(1+2x+\frac{4x^2}{2!}+\frac{8x^3}{3!}+\ldots\right)-1-2x\right\}}{x\left\{\left(1+2x+\frac{4x^2}{2!}+\frac{8x^3}{3!}+\ldots\right)-1\right\}}$$

$$= f(0) = 1$$

3. We have, $$f(x) = \begin{cases} 3(1+|\tan x|)^{\frac{\alpha}{|\tan x|}}; & \frac{-1}{2} < x < 0 \\ \beta; & x = 0 \\ 3\left(1+\left|\frac{\sin x}{3}\right|\right)^{\frac{6}{|\sin x|}}; & 0 < x < \frac{2}{3} \end{cases}$$

Now, RHL $= f(0^+) = \lim_{x\to 0^+} f(x) = \lim_{x\to 0^+} 3\left(1+\frac{|\sin x|}{3}\right)^{6/|\sin x|}$

$$= 3e^2$$

Similarly, LHL $= f(0^-) = \lim_{x\to 0^-} f(x) = 3e^{\alpha}$

So, for the function $f(x)$ to be continuous at $x = 0$, we must have

$$f(0^+) = f(0^-) = f(0)$$

$$\Rightarrow \quad 3e^{\alpha} = 3e^2 = \beta, \text{ So, } \alpha = 2,\ \beta = 3e^2$$

4. $\frac{x}{5}$ is integer at 21 points in [0, 100]

$\frac{x}{2}$ is integer at 51 points in [0, 100]

$\therefore$ But when x is a multiple of 10, then $f(x)$ is continuous.

So that respective points should be subtract from both i.e. multiple of 10 are 11 points in [0,100].

$$21+51-11-11 = 72-22 = 50$$

5. LHL $= a+1$

RHL $= b+1$

$\therefore$ They are continuous LHL = RHL $= f(1)$

$$a+1 = b+1 = 3$$

$$\Rightarrow \quad a = 2,\ b = 2$$

$$\Rightarrow \quad a - b = 0$$

6. $$f\left(\frac{\pi^-}{2}\right) = \lim_{x\to\frac{\pi^-}{2}}\frac{\sin\{\cos x\}}{x-\frac{\pi}{2}} = \lim_{x\to\frac{\pi^-}{2}}\frac{\sin(\cos x)}{x-\frac{\pi}{2}} = -1$$

$$f\left(\frac{\pi^+}{2}\right) = \lim_{x\to\frac{\pi^+}{2}}\frac{\sin\{\cos x\}}{x-\frac{\pi}{2}} = \lim_{x\to\frac{\pi^+}{2}}\frac{\sin(\cos x+1)}{x-\frac{\pi}{2}} = \infty$$

7. $$f(0^-) = e^a$$

$$f(0) = b$$

$$c = 1$$

$$f(0^+) = \frac{2}{3} \Rightarrow b = e^a = \frac{2}{3}$$

$$\therefore\ 3(e^a+b+c) = 3\left(\frac{2}{3}+\frac{2}{3}+1\right) = 7$$

8. $$\lim_{x\to 0}\frac{ae^{\sin x}+be^{-\sin x}-c}{x^2} = 2$$

Limit exist only when $a+b-c = 0$

On applying L'Hospital rule, we get

$$\lim_{x\to 0}\frac{ae^{\sin x}\cdot\cos x - be^{-\sin x}\cdot\cos x}{2x} = 2$$

Limit exist only when $a - b = 0$

$$a = b$$

Again, on applying L'Hospital rule, we get

$$\lim_{x\to 0}\frac{ae^{\sin x}\cdot(-\sin x) + a\cos^2 xe^{\sin x} + be^{-\sin x}\cdot\sin x + be^{-\sin x}\cdot\cos^2 x}{2} = 2$$

$$\therefore \quad a+b = 2$$

$$a = 1 = b$$

$$\therefore \quad c = 2 \Rightarrow 2a = 2b = c$$

9. Consider $g(x) = f(x) - x$

$$g(0) = f(0) - 0 = f(0) \ge 0 \qquad [\because 0 \le f(x) \le 1]$$

$$g(1) = f(1) - 1 \le 0 \Rightarrow g(0)\cdot g(1) \le 0$$

$\Rightarrow$ $g(x) = 0$ has at least one root in [0, 1]

$\Rightarrow$ $f(x) = x$ has at least one root in [0, 1]

10. Here, $y_n(x) = \begin{cases} \dfrac{x^2\left[\dfrac{1}{(1+x^2)^n}-1\right]}{\dfrac{1}{1+x^2}-1} = (1+x^2)\cdot\left[1-\dfrac{1}{(1+x^2)^n}\right], & \text{when } x \neq 0,\ n \in N \\ 0, & \text{when } x = 0,\ n \in N \end{cases}$

$\therefore \quad y(x) = \lim_{n\to\infty} y_n(x) = \begin{cases} (1+x^2), & x \neq 0 \\ 0, & x = 0 \end{cases}$

$\therefore$ $y(x)$ is discontinuous at $x = 0$.

Hence, $y(x)$ is continuous for $x \in R - \{0\}$.

11. $\lim_{h\to 0} \dfrac{f^2(x+h)-f^2(x)}{2h} = \lim_{h\to 0} \dfrac{f(x+h)-f(x)}{h} \times \dfrac{f(x+h)+f(x)}{2}$

$= f'(x)\,f(x)$

12. Let $x = \dfrac{2}{3}$, which is rational

$\Rightarrow \quad h\left(\dfrac{2}{3}\right) = \dfrac{1}{3}$

$\lim_{t\to 0} h\left(\dfrac{2}{3}+t\right) = 0$

$\Rightarrow$ discontinuous at $x \in Q$

Let $x = \sqrt{2} \notin Q$

$h(\sqrt{2}) = 0$

If consider $\sqrt{2} = 1.4140123583$, then

$h(\sqrt{2}) = h\left(\dfrac{1.4140123583}{10^{10}}\right) = \dfrac{1}{10^{10}} \to 0$

Hence, h is continuous for all irrational.

13. I and II are false.

The function $f(x) = \dfrac{1}{x}$, $0 < x < 1$ is a counter example.

Statement III is true. Apply the Intermediate value theorem on f on the closed interval $[a_1, b_1]$

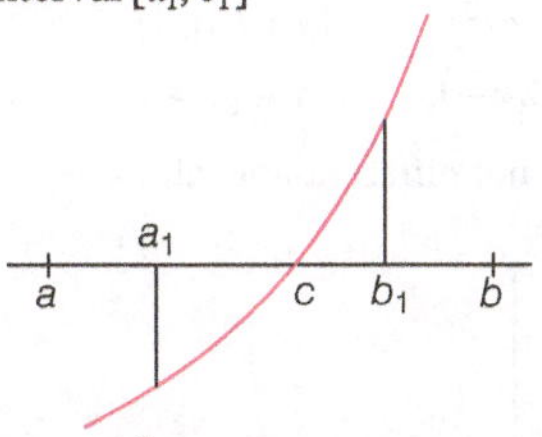

14. From option (a), $f(x) = \begin{cases} x^2 & \text{if } -1 \le x < 0 \\ -x^2 & \text{if } 0 \le x \le 1 \end{cases}$

$\Rightarrow$ continuous at $x = 0$

$f'(x) = \begin{cases} 2x, & -1 \le x < 0 \\ -2x, & 0 \le x \le 1 \end{cases}$

$\Rightarrow$ differentiable at $x = 0$

From option (b), $g(x) = \begin{cases} x & \text{if } -1 \le x < 0 \\ \tan x & \text{if } 0 \le x \le \dfrac{\pi}{4} \end{cases}$

$\Rightarrow$ continuous at $x = 0$

$f'(x) = \begin{cases} 1, & -1 \le x < 0 \\ \sec^2 x, & 0 \le x \le \dfrac{\pi}{4} \end{cases}$

$\Rightarrow$ differentiable at $x = 0$

From option (c), $h(x) = \begin{cases} \sin 2x, & x \le 0 \\ 2x, & x > 0 \end{cases}$

$\Rightarrow$ continuous at $x = 0$

$h'(x) = \begin{cases} 2\cos 2x, & x \le 0 \\ 2, & x > 0 \end{cases}$

$\Rightarrow$ differentiable at $x = 0$

From option (d), $k(x) = \begin{cases} x, & 0 \le x \le 1 \\ 2-x, & 1 < x \le 2 \end{cases}$

$\Rightarrow$ continuous at $x = 1$

$k'(x) = \begin{cases} 1, & 1-h < x < 1 \\ -1, & 1 < x < 1+4 \end{cases}$

$\Rightarrow$ not differentiable at $x = 1$

15. Clearly, the domain of $g(x) = \sin^{-1}(f(|x|))$ is $[-2, 2]$

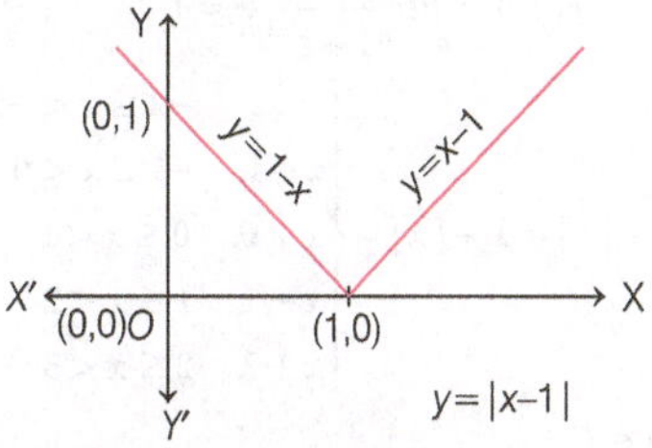

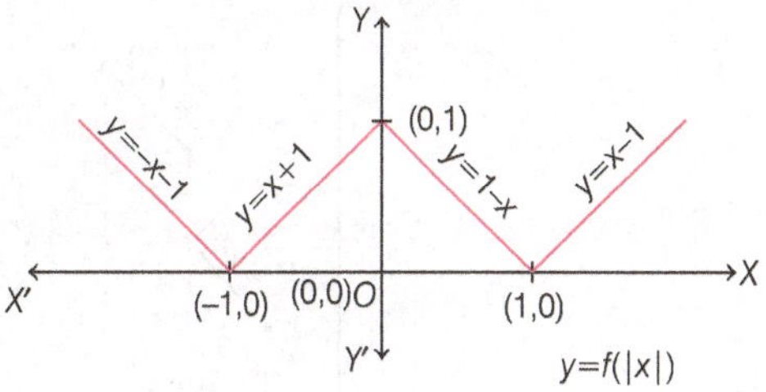

$\Rightarrow g(x)$ is non-differentiable at $x = -2, -1, 0, 1, 2$.

$\therefore$ Number of non-derivable points are 5.

16. $f'(0^-) = \lim_{h\to 0} \dfrac{a\sin h + be^h + ch^3 - b}{-h} = -(a+b)$

$f'(0^+) = \lim_{h\to 0} \dfrac{a\sin h + be^h + ch^3 - b}{h}$

$= \dfrac{a(\sin h)}{h} + \dfrac{b(e^h-1)}{h} + \dfrac{ch^3}{h} = a+b$

Hence, $a + b = -(a+b)$

$\Rightarrow \quad (a+b) = 0$

17. If function is differentiable in R, then it must be differentiable at $x_0 = a$

$f'(a^+) = \lim_{h\to 0} \dfrac{(a+h+1)|h| - 0}{h} = a+1$

$f'(a^-) = \lim_{h\to 0} \dfrac{(a-h+1)|-h|}{-h} = -(a+1)$

$\therefore \quad f'(a^+) = f'(a^-)$

$\Rightarrow \quad a = -1$

18. $f(x)=\begin{cases}\dfrac{1}{1+e^{1/x}}, & x\neq 0\\ 0, & x=0\end{cases}$

$$f'(0^+)=\lim_{h\to 0}\frac{\dfrac{1}{1+e^{1/h}}}{h}$$

$$=\lim_{h\to 0}\frac{1/h}{1+e^{1/h}}$$

$$=\lim_{h\to 0}\frac{-1/h^2}{e^{1/h}(1/h^2)}=0$$

$$f'(0^-)=\lim_{h\to 0}\frac{\dfrac{1}{1+e^{-1/h}}}{-h}\to -\infty,$$

$$f(0^+)=\lim_{h\to 0}\frac{1}{1+e^{1/h}}=0;$$

$$f(0^-)=\lim_{h\to 0}\frac{1}{1+e^{-1/h}}=1$$

19. $f(x)=\{x\}+[x]=x+[x]=\begin{cases}x-2, & -2\le x<-1\\ x-1, & -1\le x<0\\ x+0, & 0\le x<1\\ x+1, & 1\le x<2\\ x+2, & 2\le x<3\end{cases}$

At $x=n, n\in I$

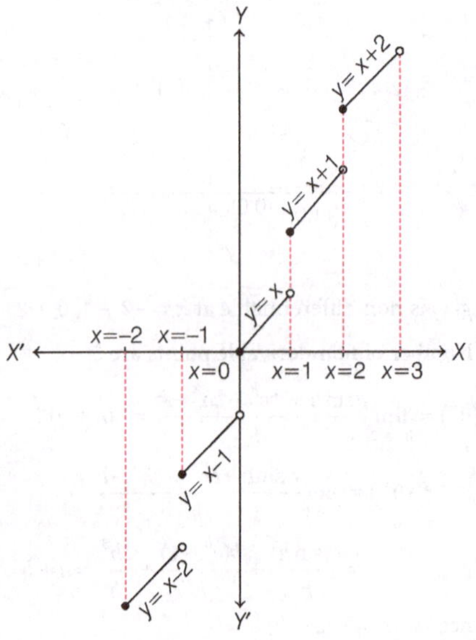

LHL $= n+(n-1)=2n-1$

and RHL $=n+n=2n=f(n)$

$\therefore f(x)$ is discontinuous at all integral points.

As discontinuity $\Rightarrow$ non-derivability

So, $f(x)$ is neither continuous nor derivable at integral points.

20. $f(x)=\begin{cases}\tan x, & \tan x<\cot x\\ \cot x, & \tan x\ge \cot x\end{cases}$

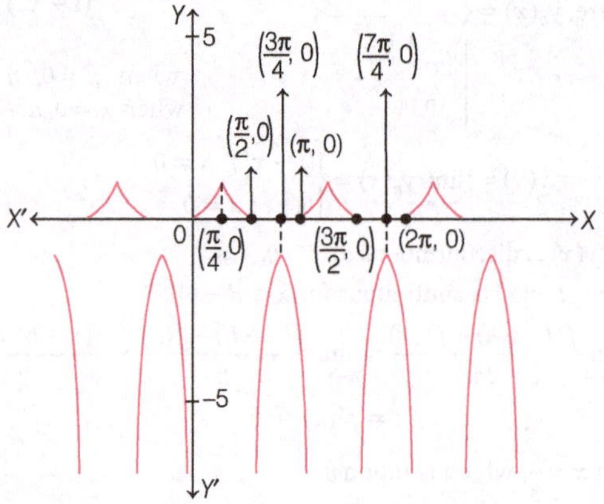

Points of non-derivability $=\dfrac{\pi}{4},\dfrac{3\pi}{4},\dfrac{5\pi}{4},\dfrac{7\pi}{4}$

21. $f(x)=\begin{cases}x^2 & x\ge 1\\ x & 0\le x\le 1\\ 2x & -1\le x\le 0\\ x-1 & x\le -1\end{cases}$

$\because$ $f(x)$ is continuous for all $x\in R$

$\therefore f'(x)=\begin{cases}2x & x>1\\ 1 & 0<x<1\\ 2 & -1<x<0\\ 1 & x<-1\end{cases}$

$\therefore$ Clearly, it is non-differentiable at $x=0,-1$ and 1.

$\therefore$ Option (b) is not true.

22. $f(x)=\begin{cases}|x|, & x\in(-\infty,-1)\\ x^2, & x\in(-1,1)\\ 2x-1, & x\in[1,\infty)\end{cases}$

Function is not differentiable at $x=-1$.

23.

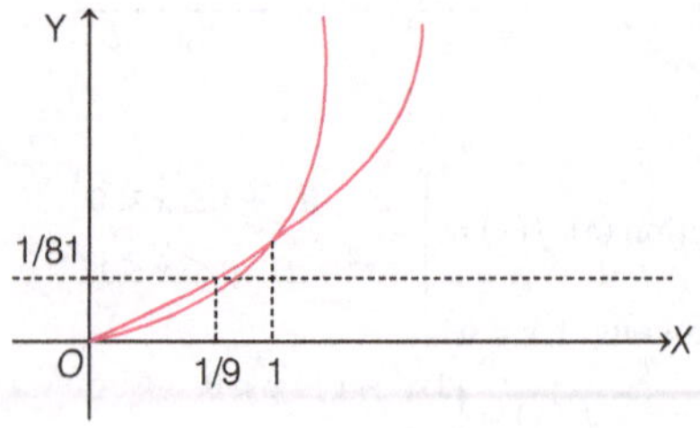

$f(x)=\text{maximum}\left(x^4,x^2,\dfrac{1}{81}\right)=\begin{cases}1/81, & x\le 1/9\\ x^2, & 1/9<x<1\\ x^4, & x\ge 1\end{cases}$

$f(x)$ is non-differentiable at $x=\dfrac{1}{9},1$

$\therefore$ Sum of square of reciprocal of all the values of $x=81+1=82$

24. $f(x) = (x^2 - 3x + 2)\,|(x-1)(x-2)(x-3)| + \left|\sin\left(x + \frac{\pi}{4}\right)\right|$

$f(x) = (x-3)(x-1)|(x-1)(x-2)(x-3)| + |\sin(x + \pi/4)|$

Let $g(x) = \left|\sin\left(x + \frac{\pi}{4}\right)\right|$

$h(x) = (x-3)(x-1)(x-1)(x-2)(x-3)$

$\because$ $|g(x)|$ is not differentiable,

where $g(x) = 0$

but $h(x) + |g(x)|$ is not differentiable at those point $g(x) = 0$ but $h(x) \neq 0$

$\therefore$ $(x-3)(x-1)|(x-1)(x-2)(x-3)|$

is not differentiable at $x = 3$ only,

where $\left|\sin\left(x + \frac{\pi}{4}\right)\right|$ is not differentiable at $x = \frac{3\pi}{4}$ and $x = \frac{7\pi}{4}$

$\therefore$ Total number of points of non-differentiability = 3

25. $gof(x) = 0$ for all $x \in R$

and $fog(x) = \begin{cases} 0, \text{ if } x \text{ is an integer} \\ n, \text{ if } x \in R^+ \text{ and } \sqrt{n} < x < \sqrt{n+1} \text{ or} \\ x \in R^- \text{ and } -\sqrt{n+1} < x < -\sqrt{n} \end{cases}$

So, fog is differentiable on $R - I$.

26. For f to be continuous everywhere, we must have

$$x_0^2 = f(x_0) = \lim_{x \to x_0^+} f(x) = ax_0 + b$$

Also, f has a derivative at x_0 if $f'(x_0^+) = f(x_0^-)$

Now, $f'(x_0^+) = \lim_{h \to 0^+} \frac{f(x_0 + h) - f(x_0)}{h}$

$= \lim_{h \to 0^+} \frac{a(x_0 + h) + b - x_0^2}{h}$

$= \lim_{h \to 0^+} \left(\frac{ax_0 + b - x_0^2}{h} + a\right)$

$= \lim_{h \to 0^+} a = a$ $\quad [\because x_0^2 = ax_0 + b]$

and $f'(x_0^-) = \lim_{h \to 0^-} \frac{f(x_0 + h) - f(x_0)}{h}$

$= \lim_{h \to 0^-} \frac{(x_0 + h)^2 - x_0^2}{h}$

$= \lim_{h \to 0^-} \frac{x_0^2 + h^2 + 2x_0 h - x_0^2}{h}$

$= \lim_{h \to 0^-} (h + 2x_0) = 2x_0$

i.e. $a = 2x_0$ and hence $b = x_0^2 - ax_0 = x_0^2 - 2x_0^2 = -x_0^2$

27. $\lim_{x \to 0} \frac{f(x) - f(0)}{x - 0} = \lim_{x \to 0} \frac{x^3\left|\cos\frac{\pi}{2x}\right| + x^4\left|\sin\frac{\pi}{x}\right|}{x}$

$= \lim_{x \to 0} x^2\left|\cos\frac{\pi}{2x}\right| + x^3\left|\sin\frac{\pi}{x}\right|$

For $x \neq 0$, $\quad 0 \le \left|\cos\frac{\pi}{2x}\right| \le 1,\ 0 \le \left|\sin\frac{\pi}{x}\right| \le 1$

$\Rightarrow \quad 0 \le x^2\left|\cos\frac{\pi}{2x}\right| \le x^2.$

If $x > 0$, then $0 \le x^3\left|\sin\frac{\pi}{x}\right| \le x^3$ and

If $x < 0$, then $x^3 \le x^3\left|\sin\frac{\pi}{x}\right| \le 0.$

Thus, the last limit is zero.

For $1 \le x \le 2$, $\quad \frac{1}{2} \le \frac{1}{x} \le 1$

$\Rightarrow \quad \frac{1}{4} \le \frac{1}{2x} \le \frac{1}{2} \Rightarrow \cos\frac{\pi}{2x} \ge 0$

$3 > x > 2, \frac{1}{3} < \frac{1}{x} < \frac{1}{2}$

$\Rightarrow \quad \frac{\pi}{6} < \frac{\pi}{2x} < \frac{\pi}{4}$

$\Rightarrow \quad \cos\frac{\pi}{2x} \ge 0$

Similarly, for $1 \le x \le 2$ and $2 < x < 3$; $\sin\frac{\pi}{x} \ge 0$

Thus, $f(x) = x^3\cos\frac{\pi}{2x} + x^4\sin\frac{\pi}{x}$,

$f'(x) = 3x^2\cos\frac{\pi}{2x} - x\frac{\pi}{2}\sin\frac{\pi}{2x} + 4x^3\sin\frac{\pi}{x} - \pi x^2\sin\frac{\pi}{x}$ $f'(2)$

exist.

For $\frac{1}{2} < x \le 1 \Rightarrow 1 \le \frac{1}{x} < 2$

$\Rightarrow \quad \frac{1}{2} \le \frac{1}{2x} < 1$

$\Rightarrow \quad \cos\frac{\pi}{2x} \le 0, \sin\frac{\pi}{x} < 0$

For $1 < x < 2$,

$\Rightarrow \quad \frac{1}{2} < \frac{1}{x} < 1, \frac{1}{4} < \frac{1}{2x} < \frac{1}{2}$

$\Rightarrow \quad \cos\frac{\pi}{2x} > 0, \sin\frac{\pi}{x} > 0$

Hence, $f(x) = \begin{cases} -x^3\cos\frac{\pi}{2x} - x^4\sin\frac{\pi}{x}, & \frac{1}{2} < x \le 1 \\ x^3\cos\frac{\pi}{2x} + x^4\sin\frac{\pi}{x}, & 1 < x < 2 \end{cases}$

$f'(1^+) = \lim_{h \to 0^+} \frac{f(1+h) - f(1)}{h}$

$= \lim_{h \to 0^+} \frac{(1+h)^3\cos\frac{\pi}{2(1+h)} + (1+h)^4\sin\frac{\pi}{1+h}}{h}$

$= \lim_{h \to 0^+} 3(1+h)^2\cos\frac{\pi}{2(1+h)} - \frac{\pi}{2}(1+h)\sin\frac{\pi}{2(1+h)}$

$+4(1+h)^3\sin\frac{\pi}{1+h} - \pi(1+h)^3\cos\frac{\pi}{1+h}$

$= -\frac{\pi}{2} + \pi = \frac{\pi}{2}$

$f'(1^-) = -\frac{\pi}{2}$

28. $f'(1^+) = \lim_{h\to 0} \frac{f(1+h)-f(1)}{h}$

$= \lim_{h\to 0} \frac{|1+h-1|([1+h]-(1+h))}{h} = 0$

$= \lim_{h\to 0} \frac{h(1-1-h)}{h} = 0$

$f'(1^-) = \lim_{h\to 0} \frac{f(1-h)-f(1)}{-h}$

$= \lim_{h\to 0} \frac{|-h|([1-h]-(1-h))}{-h}$

$= \lim_{h\to 0} \frac{h(0-1+h)}{-h} = 1$

$\Rightarrow \quad f'(1^+) = 0, f'(1^-) = 1$

$\therefore$ $f(x)$ is not differentiable at $x = 1$.

29. $f(x) = \begin{cases} 0, & 0 \le x < 1/2 \\ 5/6, & x = 1/2 \\ 0, & 1/2 < x < 1 \\ -2, & 1 \le x < 4/3 \\ 0, & x = 4/3 \\ 2, & 4/3 < x < 3/2 \\ 3, & 3/2 \le x < 2 \\ 4, & x = 2 \end{cases}$

Hence, $f(x)$ is neither continuous non differentiable at $x = \frac{1}{2}, 1, \frac{4}{3}, \frac{3}{2}, 2$

$\therefore$ Number of ponits is 5.

30. $f(x)$ is non-differentiable at $x = \alpha, \beta, 0, \gamma, \delta$

and $g(x)$ is non-differentiable at $x = \alpha, -2, \beta, 0, \gamma, 2, \delta$

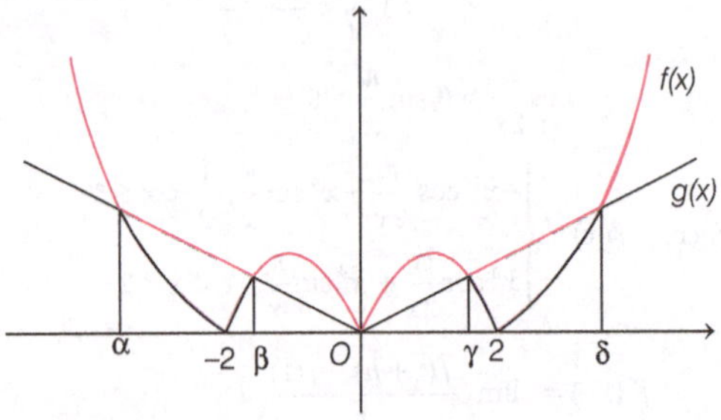

31. $f(-1) = b(1-1)+1 = 1$ and RHL $= \lim_{h\to 0} f(-1+h) = 1$

and LHL $= \lim_{h\to 0} f(-1-h) = \lim_{h\to 0} \sin((-1-h+a)\pi) = -\sin \pi a$

For continuity, $\sin \pi a = -1 = \sin\left(2n\pi + \frac{3\pi}{2}\right)$

$\Rightarrow \quad \pi a = 2n\pi + \frac{3\pi}{2}$

$\Rightarrow \quad a = 2n + \frac{3}{2}$

Hence, $a = 2n + \frac{3}{2}, n \in I$ and $b \in R$

32. Here, $f(x) = \frac{\{x\}g(x)}{\{x\}g(x)} = 1$, when $\{x\}\, g(x) \ne 0$

If $f(x)$ is periodic with period $\frac{1}{4}$, then

$\{x\}g(x) \ne 0$ with period $\frac{1}{4}$

$\Rightarrow \quad g(x) = 0$ at $x = \frac{k}{4}$, where $k \in I$

33. For $f(x)$ to be continuous at $x = 0$, $\lim_{x\to 0} f(x) = f(0)$

Hence, $k = \lim_{x\to 0} \frac{\sin 2x - \tan 2x}{(e^x-1)\cdot x^2}$

or $\quad \lim_{x\to 0}\left[\left(\frac{\sin 2x}{2x}\right)\frac{(1-\cos 2x)}{(2x)^2}\left(\frac{x}{(e^x-1)}\right)\cdot 8\right]$

or $\quad -(1)\cdot\left(\frac{1}{2}\right)\cdot(1)\cdot(8) = -4$

$\Rightarrow$ absolute value = 4

34. $f(0^-) = \lim_{h\to 0}(-\sin h + \cos h)^{-\operatorname{cosec} h} = e^{\lim_{h\to 0} \frac{-\sin h + \cos h - 1}{-\sin h}}$

$= e^1 = e = f(0) = a$

$\Rightarrow \quad a = e$

$f(0^+) = \lim_{h\to 0} \frac{e^{1/h}+e^{2/h}+e^{3/h}}{ae^{2/h}+be^{3/h}}$

$= \lim_{h\to 0} \frac{e^{-2/h}+e^{-1/h}+1}{ae^{-1/h}+b} = \frac{1}{b}$

$\therefore \quad a = e, b = \frac{1}{e}$

Hence, $(a^2+b^2) = e^2 + e^{-2}$

$\therefore \quad \lambda = 4, \mu = 1$

$\therefore \quad \frac{\lambda}{4\mu} = 1$

35. $f(x)$ is discontinuous at $x = 1$, $|f(x)|$ is differential everywhere

$f(1) = -f(1^+) = -f(1^-)$

$\Rightarrow \quad 3 = -(0+b)$

$\Rightarrow \quad b = -3$

$f'(1^+) = -f'(1^-)$

[as $|f(x)|$ is differentiable everywhere]

$\therefore \quad 1 = -(2a-a)$

$\Rightarrow \quad a = -1$

Continuous at $x = 3$,

So, $\quad 5 = 9p + 3q + 2$

$\Rightarrow \quad 3p + q = 1$

$f'(x)$ is continuous at $x = 3$

So, $\quad f'(3^-) = f'(3^+)$

$\Rightarrow \quad 6p + q = 1$

On solving Eqs. (i) and (ii), we get

$p = 0, q = 1$

So, $|a+b+p+q| = |-1-3+0+1| = 3$

36. $g(x)=\begin{cases}\sin x^3 - x^3 + 1, & x \ge 1\\ \sin x^3 + x^3 - 1, & 0 \le x < 1\\ \sin x^3 - x^3 - 1, & -1 \le x < 0\\ \sin x^3 + x^3 + 1, & x \le -1\end{cases}$

Function is not differentiable at $x = -1, 1$

$\therefore$ Number of points of non-differentiability = 2

37. $$f(0) = \lim_{x\to 0}\frac{\tan(\tan x) - \sin(\sin x)}{\tan x - \sin x}$$

$$= \lim_{x\to 0}\frac{\tan(\tan x) - \sin(\sin x)}{\frac{\tan x}{x}\left(\frac{1-\cos x}{x^2}\right)x^3}$$

$$= 2\lim_{x\to 0}\frac{\tan(\tan x) - \sin(\sin x)}{x^3}$$

$$= 2\lim_{x\to 0}\frac{\left(\tan x + \frac{\tan^3 x}{3} + \frac{2}{15}\tan^5 x + \dots\right) - \left(\sin x + \frac{\sin^3 x}{3!} + \frac{\sin^5 x}{5!} - \dots\right)}{x^3}$$

$$= 2\lim_{x\to 0}\left(\left(\frac{\tan x - \sin x}{x^3}\right) + \frac{\left(\frac{\tan^3 x}{3} + \frac{\sin^3 x}{3!}\right)}{x^3} + \dots\right)$$

$$= 2\lim_{x\to 0}\left(\left(\frac{\tan x}{x}\right)\left(\frac{1-\cos x}{x^2}\right) + \frac{1}{3} + \frac{1}{6}\right)$$

$$= 2\left[\frac{1}{2} + \frac{1}{2}\right] = 2$$

38. For inverse put $f(x) = y$

$$y = \begin{cases} 2-x, & -3 \le x \le 0 \Rightarrow 2 \le 2-x \le 5\\ x-2, & 0 < x < 4 \Rightarrow -2 < x-2 < 2\end{cases}$$

$$\therefore \quad x = \begin{cases} 2-y, & 2 \le y \le 5\\ y+2, & -2 < y < 2\end{cases}$$

$$\therefore \quad f^{-1}(y) = \begin{cases} 2-y, & 2 \le y \le 5\\ y+2, & -2 < y < 2\end{cases}$$

$$f^{-1}(x) = \begin{cases} 2-x, & 2 \le x \le 5\\ 2+x, & -2 < x < 2\end{cases}$$

$\therefore$ It is discontinuous at $x = 2$.

39. $g(x) = x(x-3)(x-7)$

$$f(g(x)) = \text{sgn}\,(x(x-3)(x-7))$$

$\because$ Signum $(g(x))$ is discontinuous at points where $g(x) = 0$

$\therefore$ Points of discontinuity will be $x = 0, 3, 7$

40. Let $8x - 16 = t^2$

$$\Rightarrow \sqrt{\frac{t^2+16+8t}{8}} + \sqrt{\frac{t^2+16-8t}{8}} = \frac{|t+4| + |t-4|}{2\sqrt{2}}$$

$\therefore$ $f(x)$ is not differentiable when $t = \pm 4$

$$\therefore \quad 8x - 16 = (\pm 4)^2$$

$$\Rightarrow \quad 8x = 32$$

$$\Rightarrow \quad x = 4$$

41. $f(x)=\begin{cases}[x], & 0 < x < 1\\ \{x\}, & 1 \le x < \frac{5}{4}\\ \left|x - \frac{3}{2}\right|, & \frac{5}{4} \le x < 2\end{cases}$

Number of points where $f(x)$ is non-differentiable are three $x = 1, \frac{5}{4}, \frac{3}{2}$

42. On putting $x = y = 0$ in $g(x+y) = e^y g(x) + e^x g(y)$, we get

$$g(0) = g(0) + g(0) = 2g(0)$$

$$\Rightarrow \quad g(0) = 0$$

So, $$2 = g'(0) = \lim_{h\to 0}\frac{g(h) - g(0)}{h} = \lim_{h\to 0}\frac{g(h)}{h}$$

Also, $$g'(x) = \lim_{h\to 0}\frac{g(x+h) - g(x)}{h}$$

$$= \lim_{h\to 0}\frac{e^x g(h) + e^h g(x) - g(x)}{h}$$

$$= \lim_{h\to 0}\left(e^x\frac{g(h)}{h} + \frac{e^h - 1}{h}g(x)\right)$$

$$= e^x \lim_{h\to 0}\frac{g(h)}{h} + 1\cdot g(x)$$

$$= 2e^x + g(x)$$

$$\Rightarrow \quad g'(x) = 2e^x + g(x)$$

Thus, $g'(5) - 2e^5 = g(5) = 32$

$$\therefore \quad \frac{1}{4}(g'(5) - 2e^5) = 8$$

43. Let $g(x) = x^{1/x}, g'(x) = x^{1/x}\left(\frac{1 - \ln x}{x^2}\right)$

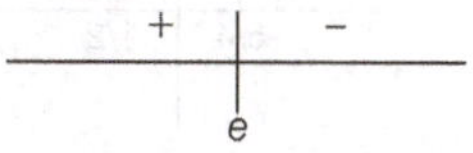

$$\Rightarrow \quad g_{\max} = e^{1/e} \in (1, 2)$$

$$\Rightarrow \quad \lim_{x\to 0} x^{1/x} = 0, \ \lim_{x\to\infty} x^{1/x} = 1$$

So, $$f(x) = \begin{cases}0, & 0 < x < 1\\ 1, & 1 \le x < \infty\end{cases}$$

which is not continuous at $x = 1$.

44. $F(x) = 3e^x$ and $G(x) = e^{-x}$

The equation $9x^4 = (F(x))^2 G(x)$ becomes $x^4 = e^x$

Hence, number of solutions = 2

45. A, B, C are in AP

$$\therefore \quad 2B = A + C \text{ and } A + B + C = 180^\circ$$

$$\therefore \quad B = 60^\circ$$

$$\therefore \quad \cos B = \frac{1}{2} = \frac{a^2 + c^2 - b^2}{2ac}$$

$$\Rightarrow \quad a^2 + c^2 = b^2 + ac$$

$$\Rightarrow \quad (a-c)^2 = b^2 - ac$$

or $|\sin A - \sin C| = \sqrt{\sin^2 B \sin A \sin C}$

$$\Rightarrow 2\cos\left(\frac{A+C}{2}\right)\left|\sin\left(\frac{A-C}{2}\right)\right| = \sqrt{\frac{3}{4} - \sin A \sin C}$$

$$\Rightarrow 2\left|\sin\left(\frac{A-C}{2}\right)\right| = \sqrt{3 - 4\sin A \sin C}$$

$$\therefore \lim_{A\to C}\frac{\sqrt{3-4\sin A\sin C}}{|A-C|} = \lim_{A\to C}\frac{2\left|\sin\left(\frac{A-C}{2}\right)\right|}{|A-C|}$$

$$= \lim_{A\to C}\left|\frac{\sin\left(\frac{A-C}{2}\right)}{\left(\frac{A-C}{2}\right)}\right| = |1| = 1$$

$$\Rightarrow f(x) = 1$$

$$\therefore f'(x) = 0$$

46. We have, $f(x) = (x - |x|)^2 (1 - x + |x|)^2$

$$\Rightarrow f(x) = \begin{cases}(2x)^2(1-2x)^2, & x < 0\\ 0, & x \ge 0\end{cases}$$

$$= \begin{cases}16x^4 - 16x^3 + 4x^2, & x < 0\\ 0, & x \ge 0\end{cases}$$

Clearly, $f(x)$ is continuous as well as derivable for all $x \in R$.

$\therefore$ Number of points of non-differentiability = 0

47. $f(x) = |2x^2 + 5|x| - 3|$

Graph of $y = 2x^2 + 5x - 3$

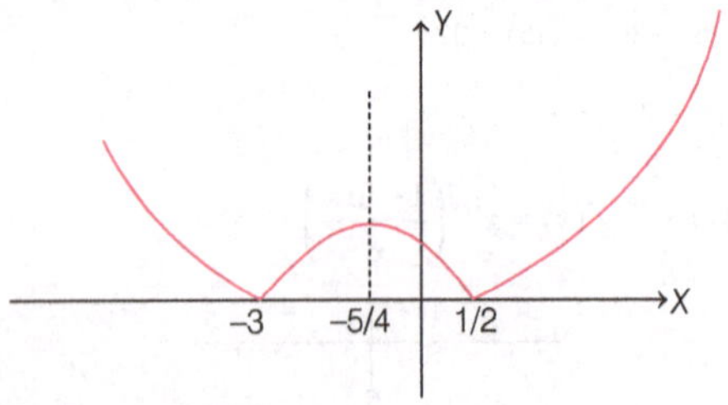

Graph of $f(x)$

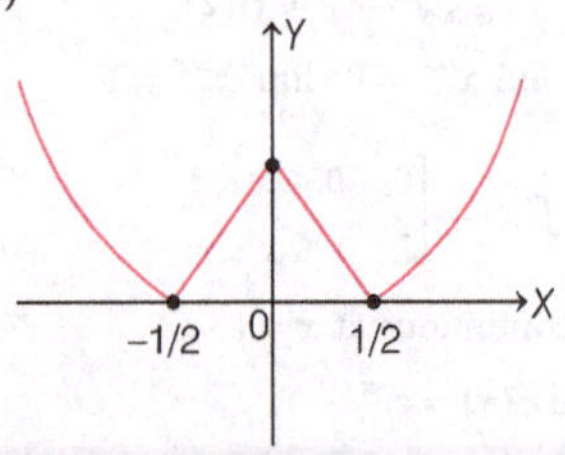

Number of points of discontinuity = 0 = m

Number of points of non-differentiability = 3 = n

48. At $x = 1$, $f(x)$ is continuous, therefore

$$f(1^-) = f(1) = f(1^+)$$

$$f(1) = 3 + c \quad \text{...(i)}$$

$$f(1^+) = \lim_{h\to 0} 2(1+h) + 1$$

$$f(1^+) = \lim_{h\to 0} 3 + 2h = 3 \quad \text{...(ii)}$$

From Eqs. (i) and (ii), we get

$$c = 0$$

at $x = 0$, $f(x)$ is continuous, therefore

$$f(0^-) = f(0) = f(0^+)$$

$$f(0) = f(0^+) = 2 \quad \text{...(iii)}$$

$f(0^-)$ has to be equal to 2

$$\lim_{h\to 0}\frac{a - b\cos(2h)}{h^2}$$

$$\lim_{h\to 0}\frac{a - b\left(1 - \frac{4h^2}{2!} + \frac{16h^4}{4!} + \dots\right)}{h^2}$$

$$\lim_{h\to 0}\frac{a - b + b\left\{2h^2 - \frac{2}{3}h^4 \dots\right\}}{h^2}$$

for limit to be exist $a - b = 0$ ...(iv)

limit is $2b$ ...(v)

$$a = b = 1$$

Checking differentiability at $x = 0$

$$\text{LHD} = \lim_{h\to 0}\frac{\frac{1-\cos 2h}{h^2} - 2}{-h}$$

$$\lim_{h\to 0}\frac{1 - \left(1 - \frac{4h^2}{2!} + \frac{16h^4}{4!} \dots\right) - 2h^2}{-h^3} = 0$$

$$\text{RHD} = \lim_{h\to 0}\frac{(0+h)^2 + 2 - 2}{h} = 0$$

Function is differentiable at every point in its domain

$$\therefore m = 0$$

$$m + a + b + c = 0 + 1 + 1 + 0 = 2$$

49. $f : (0, 2) \to R;\quad f(x) = \frac{x}{2} + \frac{2}{x}$

$$f'(x) = \frac{1}{2} - \frac{2}{x^2}$$

$\therefore f(x)$ is decreasing in domain

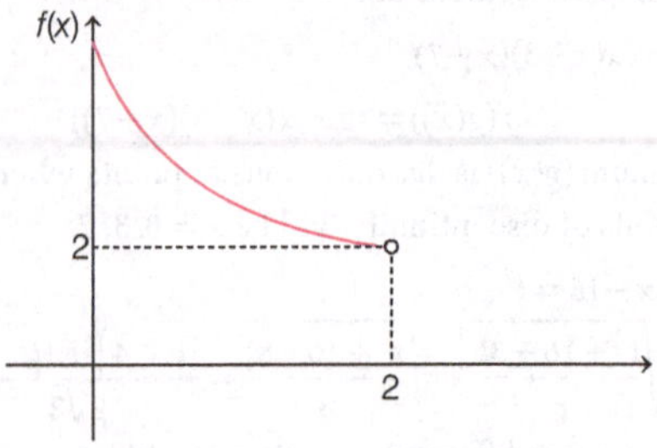

$$g(x)=\begin{cases}\dfrac{x}{2}+\dfrac{2}{x} & 0<x\le 1\\ \dfrac{3}{2}+x & 1<x<2\end{cases}$$

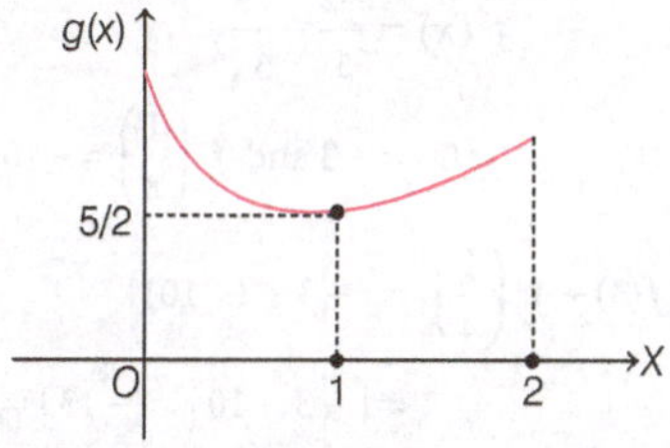

From graph $g(x)$ is not differentiable at $x=1$.

50. $f(3^-)=\dfrac{a\,(7x-12-x^2)}{b\,|x^2-7x+12|}$ (for $f(x)$ to be continuous)

$$\Rightarrow \quad f(3^-)=\frac{-a}{b}\frac{(x-3)(x-4)}{(x-3)(x-4)},\ x<3 \ \Rightarrow\ \frac{-a}{b}$$

Hence, $\quad f(3^-)=\dfrac{-a}{b}$

Then, $f(3^+)=2^{\lim_{x\to 3^+}\left(\frac{\sin(x-3)}{x-3}\right)}=2$ and $f(3)=b$

Hence, $f(3)=f(3^+)=f(3^-)$

$$\Rightarrow \quad b=2=-\frac{a}{b}$$

$$b=2,\ a=-4$$

Hence, only 1 ordered pair $(-4,2)$.

51. Let $g(x)=ax+b$

Now, function $f(x)$ is continuous at $x=0$

$$\therefore \quad \lim_{x\to 0^+} f(x)=f(0)$$

$$\Rightarrow \quad \lim_{x\to 0}\left(\frac{1+x}{2+x}\right)^{1/x}=b \Rightarrow 0=b$$

$$\therefore \quad g(x)=ax$$

Now, for $x>0$

$$f'(x)=\frac{1}{x}\cdot\left(\frac{1+x}{2+x}\right)^{\frac{1}{x}-1}\cdot\frac{1}{(2+x)^2}+\left(\frac{1+x}{2+x}\right)^{1/x}\cdot\ln\left(\frac{1+x}{2+x}\right)\cdot\left(-\frac{1}{x^2}\right)$$

$$\therefore\ f'(1)=\frac{1}{9}-\frac{2}{3}\cdot\ln\left(\frac{2}{3}\right) \text{ and } f(-1)=g(-1)=-a$$

$$\therefore \quad a=\frac{2}{3}\ln\left(\frac{2}{3}\right)-\frac{1}{9}$$

$$\therefore\ g(3)=2\ln\left(\frac{2}{3}\right)-\frac{1}{3}=\ln\left(\frac{4}{9\cdot e^{1/3}}\right)$$

52. $f(x)=\begin{cases}\dfrac{1}{x}, & x\ge 2\\ ax^2+2b, & -2<x<2\\ -\dfrac{1}{x}, & x\le -2\end{cases}$

Continuous at $x=2$

$$\Rightarrow \quad \frac{1}{2}=\frac{a}{4}+2b$$

Continuous at $x=-2$

$$\Rightarrow \quad \frac{1}{2}=\frac{a}{4}+2b$$

Since, it is differentiable at $x=2$

$$-\frac{1}{x^2}=2ax$$

Differentiable at $x=2$

$$\Rightarrow \quad \frac{-1}{4}=4a \Rightarrow a=\frac{-1}{16}, b=\frac{3}{8}$$

$$48(a+b)=48\left(-\frac{1}{16}+\frac{3}{8}\right) \Rightarrow 48\times\frac{5}{16}=15$$

53. We have, $f(x)=[x^2-x]+|-x+[x]|=[x(x-1)]+\{x\}$

$$f(x)=\begin{cases}x+1, & -0.5<x<0\\ 0, & x=0\\ -1+x, & 0<x<1\\ 0, & x=1\\ x-1, & 1<x<1.5\end{cases}$$

At $x=0$,

LHL $=\lim_{x\to 0^-} f(x)=1$

RHL $\lim_{x\to 0^+} f(x)=-1$

$$f(0)=0$$

$\therefore f(x)$ is not continuous at $x=0$

At $x=1$,

LHL $=\lim_{x\to 1^-} f(x)=-1+1=0$

RHL $=\lim_{x\to 1^+} f(x)=1-1=0$

$$f(1)=0$$

$\therefore f(x)$ is continuous at $x=1$

Hence, $f(x)$ is continuous at $x=1$ but not continuous at $x=0$.

54. Let $f(x)=\begin{cases}(1+|\cos x|)^{\frac{\lambda}{|\cos x|}}, & 0<x<\dfrac{\pi}{2}\\ \mu, & x=\dfrac{\pi}{2}\\ e^{\left(\frac{\cot 6x}{\cot 4x}\right)}, & \dfrac{\pi}{2}<x<\pi\end{cases}$

Now, LHL $=\lim_{x\to\frac{\pi}{2}^-} f(x)=\lim_{x\to\frac{\pi}{2}^-}(1+|\cos x|)^{\frac{\lambda}{|\cos x|}}$ $\quad [1^\infty$ form$]$

So, LHL $=e^{\left(\lim_{x\to\frac{\pi}{2}^-}\lambda\right)}=e^{\lambda}$

Now, RHL $=\lim_{x\to\frac{\pi}{2}^+} f(x)=\lim_{x\to\frac{\pi}{2}^+} e^{\left(\frac{\cot 6x}{\cot 4x}\right)}$

$$\text{RHL}=e^{\lim_{x\to\frac{\pi}{2}^+}\frac{\cot 6x}{\cot 4x}}$$

So, $\text{RHL} = e^{\lim_{x \to \frac{\pi}{2}^+} \left(\frac{\tan 4x}{\tan 6x}\right)}$

$\text{RHL} = e^{\lim_{h \to 0} \left(\frac{\tan 4\left(\frac{\pi}{2}+h\right)}{\tan 6\left(\frac{\pi}{2}+h\right)}\right)}$

So, $\text{RHL} = e^{\lim_{h \to 0} \left[\frac{\tan 4h}{\tan 6h}\right]}$

Now, multiplying and dividing $4h$ and $6h$ in power of e.

$$\text{RHL} = \lim_{e^h \to 0} \left[\left(\frac{\tan 4h}{4h}\right)\left(\frac{6h}{\tan 6h}\right)\left(\frac{4h}{6h}\right)\right] \qquad \left[\because \lim_{x \to 0} \frac{\tan x}{x} = 1\right]$$

So, $\text{RHL} = e^{2/3}$

For continuity of a function

LHL = RHL = Functional value

$$e^{\lambda} = e^{2/3} = \mu$$

By comparison, $\lambda = \frac{2}{3}$ and $\mu = e^{2/3}$

Now, $9\lambda + 6\log_e \mu + \mu^6 - e^{6\lambda} = 6 + 6\left(\frac{2}{3}\right) + e^4 - e^4 = 10$

55. Given, $f(x) = \max\{1 + x + [x], 2 + x, x + 2[x]\}$

$0 \le x \le 2$

Given, m be the number of points in [0, 2], where f is not continuous and n be denotes the number of point in [0, 2] where f is not differentiable.

Let $f_1(x) = 1 + x + [x] = \begin{cases} 1+x &, x \in [0,1) \\ 2+x &, x \in [1,2) \\ 5 &, x = 2 \end{cases}$

$f_2(x) = 2 + x,\ 0 \le x \le 2$

$f_3(x) = x + 2[x] = \begin{cases} x &, x \in [0,1] \\ 2+x &, x \in [3,2) \\ 6 &, x = 2 \end{cases}$

So, $f(x) = \max\{f_1(x), f_2(x), f_3(x)\}$ in $0 \le x \le 2$.

Then, $f(x) = \begin{cases} 2+x, & x \in [0, 2) \\ 6, & x = 2 \end{cases}$

Clearly, $f(x)$ is discontinuous only at $x = 2$

So, $m = 1$

and $f(x)$ is differentiable in (0, 2) so, $n = 0$

$\therefore \quad (m+n)^2 + 2 = (1+0)^2 + 2 = 1 + 2 = 3$

56. Given, $3f(x) + 2f\left(\frac{1}{x}\right) = \frac{1}{x} - 10$ ...(i)

Change x by $1/x$, we get

$$3f\left(\frac{1}{x}\right) + 2f(x) = x - 10$$

$\Rightarrow \frac{3}{2}\left[\frac{1}{x} - 10 - 3f(x)\right] + 2f(x) = x - 10$ [from Eq. (i)]

$\Rightarrow \frac{3}{2x} - 15 - \frac{9}{2}f(x) + 2f(x) = x - 10$

$\Rightarrow -\frac{5}{2}f(x) - 15 + \frac{3}{2x} = x - 10$

$\Rightarrow -\frac{5}{2}f(x) = x - \frac{3}{2x} + 5$

$\Rightarrow f(x) = -\frac{2}{5}x + \frac{3}{5x} - 2$

$\Rightarrow f'(x) = \frac{-2}{5} - \frac{3}{5x^2}$

$\therefore f(3) = -3$ and $f'\left(\frac{1}{4}\right) = -10$

$$\left|f(3) + f'\left(\frac{1}{4}\right)\right| = |-3 + (-10)|$$

$$= |-3 - 10| = |-13| = 13$$

57. Given, $f(x) = \begin{cases} x+1, & x < 0 \\ |x-1|, & x \ge 0 \end{cases}$

and $g(x) = \begin{cases} x+1, & x < 0 \\ 1, & x \ge 0 \end{cases}$

Then, $gof(x) = g(f(x)) = \begin{cases} f(x)+1, & f(x) < 0 \\ 1, & f(x) \ge 0 \end{cases}$

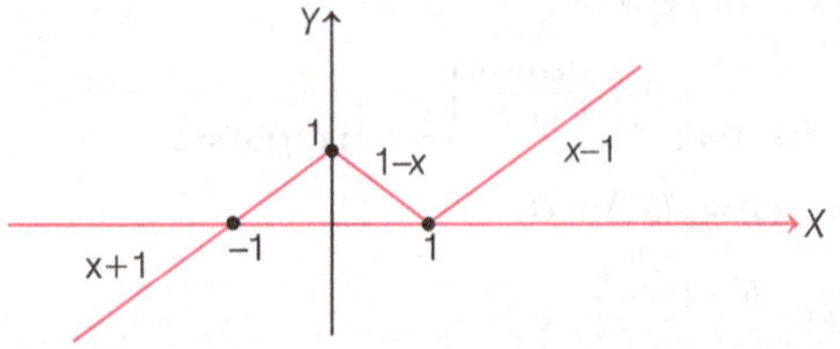

Here, $f(x) < 0$ for $x \in (-\infty, -1]$ and $f(x) \ge 0$ for $x \in [-1, \infty)$

Now, $g(f(x)) = \begin{cases} (x+1)+1, & x < -1 \\ 1, & x \ge -1 \end{cases}$

$g(f(x)) = \begin{cases} x+2, & x < -1 \\ 1, & x \ge -1 \end{cases}$

Check continuity at $x = -1$

$\text{LHL} = g(f(-1)) = -1 + 2 = 1$

$\text{RHL} = g(f(-1^+)) = 1$

Continuous at $x = -1$

$g'(f(x)) = \begin{cases} 1, & x < -1 \\ 0, & x \ge -1 \end{cases}$

For differentiability at $x = -1$

$\text{LHD} = g'(f(-1^-)) = 1$

$\text{RHD} = g'(f(-1^+)) = 0$

$\text{LHD} \ne \text{RHD}$

$\Rightarrow$ not differentiable at $x = -1$

Hence, $gof(x)$ is continuous everywhere but not differentiable at $x = -1$ (exactly at one point)

58. We have, $(x\log_e x)f'(x) + (\log_e x)f(x) + f(x) \ge 1,\ x \in [2, 4]$

$(x\log_e x)f'(x) + f(x)[\log_e x + 1] \ge 1$

$\frac{d}{dx}[x\log_e xf(x)] \ge 1$

$\frac{d}{dx}[x\log_e xf(x) - x] \ge 0 \qquad \left[\because \frac{d}{dx}(v) = 1\right]$

$\forall\ x \in [2, 4]$

Let $g(x) = x\log_e xf(x) - x$

As $g(x) \geq 0, \forall x \in [2,4], g(x)$ is an increasing function in [2, 4].

$$g(2) = 2\log_e 2 f(2) - 2 = \log_e 2 - 2 \qquad \left[\because f(x) = \frac{1}{2}\right]$$

$$g(4) = 4\log_e 4 f(4) - 4 = \log_e 4 - 4 \qquad \left[\because f(4) = \frac{1}{4}\right]$$

$$= 2(\log_e 2 - 2)$$

As, $g(x)$ is an increasing function,

$$g(2) \leq g(x) \leq g(4)$$

$$\log_e 2 - 2 \leq g(x) \leq 2(\log_e 2 - 2)$$

$$\log_e 2 - 2 \leq x\log_e xf(x) - x \leq 2(\log_e 2 - 2)$$

$$\frac{\log_e 2 - 2 + x}{x\log_e x} \leq f(x) \leq \frac{2(\log_e 2 - 2) + x}{x\log_e x}$$

For $x \in [2,4]$,

$$\frac{\log_e 2 - 2 + x}{x\log_e x} \leq \frac{2(\log_e 2 - 2) + e^2}{2\log_e 2} = 1 - \frac{1}{\log_e 2} < 1$$

$$\therefore \quad f(x) \leq 1, \forall x \in [2,4]$$

Now, $\dfrac{2(\log_e 2 - 2) + 2}{2\log_e 2} \geq \dfrac{\log_e 2 - 2 + 4}{4\log_e 4} = \dfrac{1}{8} + \dfrac{1}{2\log_e 2} > \dfrac{1}{8}$

$$\therefore \quad f(x) \geq \frac{1}{8}, \forall x \in [2,4]$$

Hence, both statements A and B are true.

59. Given function,

$$f(x) = \begin{cases} x^2 \sin\left(\frac{1}{x}\right), & x \neq 0 \\ 0, & x = 0 \end{cases}$$

To check continuity at $x = 0$

$$\text{LHL} = \lim_{x \to 0^-} f(x) = \lim_{h \to 0} f(0-h) = \lim_{h \to 0} (-h)^2 \cdot \sin\left(-\frac{1}{h}\right) = 0$$

$$\text{RHL} = \lim_{x \to 0^+} f(x) = \lim_{h \to 0} f(0+h) = \lim_{h \to 0} h^2 \sin\left(\frac{1}{h}\right) = 0$$

The value of function $= f(0) = 0$

Here, LHL = RHL = $f(0)$

$= f(x)$ is continuous at $x = 0$

To check differentiability of $f(x)$ at $x = 0$

$$\text{RHD} = f'(0^+) = \lim_{h \to 0} \frac{f(0+h) - f(0)}{h} = \lim_{h \to 0} h\sin\left(\frac{1}{h}\right) = 0$$

$$\text{LHD} = f'(0^-) = \lim_{h \to 0} \frac{f(0-h) - f(0)}{-h}$$

$$= \lim_{h \to 0} h \sin\frac{1}{h} = 0$$

Here, LHD = RHD = 0

$\therefore f(x)$ is differentiable at $x = 0$.

Now, we differentiate $f(x)$

$$\Rightarrow \quad f'(x) = \begin{cases} 2x\sin\left(\frac{1}{x}\right) - \cos\left(\frac{1}{x}\right), & x \neq 0 \\ 0, & x = 0 \end{cases}$$

As, we know that $\cos\left(\dfrac{1}{x}\right)$ is highly oscillating at $x = 0$.

So, $f'(x)$ is not continuous at $x = 0$.

60. Given that $f''(x) = g''(x) + 6x$

$$f'(1) = 4g'(1) - 3 = 9$$

$$f(2) = 3g(2) = 12$$

Here, $f''(x) = g''(x) + 6x$

On integrating both sides, we get

$$f'(x) = g'(x) + 3x^2 + C_1 \qquad \text{...(i)}$$

Again, on integrating both sides, we get

$$f(x) = g(x) + x^3 + C_1 x + C_2 \qquad \text{...(ii)}$$

where C_1 and C_2 are constant of integration.

Now, use $f'(1) = 4g'(1) - 3 = 9$ in Eq. (i), we get

$$\therefore \quad 9 = 3 + 3 + C_1$$

$$\Rightarrow \quad C_1 = 3$$

Again, use $f(2) = 3g(2) = 12$ in Eq. (ii), we get

$$12 = 4 + 8 + 6 + C_2$$

$$\Rightarrow \quad C_2 = -6$$

So, $f(x) = g(x) + x^3 + 3x - 6$

Now, $f(x) - g(x) = x^3 + 3x - 6$

Let at $x = x_0, f(x_0) = g(x_0)$

So, $\quad x_0^3 + 3x_0 - 6 = 0$

Now, let $h(x) = x^3 + 3x - 6$

In the interval $\left(1, \dfrac{3}{2}\right), h(1) = -2$(–ve)

$$h\left(\frac{3}{2}\right) = \frac{15}{8}(\text{+ve})$$

So, $h(x)$ has a root between (1, 3/2)

$$\Rightarrow \quad f(x_0) \in \left(1, \frac{3}{2}\right) \text{ such that } f(x_0) = g(x_0)$$

Option (a) is true.

$$h(-2) = f(-2) - g(-2) = -20$$

$$g(-2) - f(-2) = 20$$

Option (b) is true.

Now, $|f'(x) - g'(x)| < 6$

$$|3x^2 + 3| < 6$$

$$\Rightarrow \quad -6 < 3x^2 + 3 < 6$$

$$\Rightarrow \quad 3x^2 + 3 < 6$$

$$[\because 3x^2 + 3 > -6 \text{ is true}, \forall x \in R]$$

$$\Rightarrow \quad x^2 - 1 < 0$$

$$\Rightarrow \quad |x| < 1$$

$$\Rightarrow \quad x \in (-1, 1)$$

Option (d) is true.

61. We have, $f(x) = |[x]| + \sqrt{x - [x]}, x \in (-2,1)$

$$\text{Now,} \quad [x] = \begin{cases} -2, & x \in (-2,-1) \\ -1, & x \in [-1,0) \\ 0, & x \in (0,1) \end{cases}$$

$$\therefore \quad f(x) = \begin{cases} 2 + \sqrt{x+2}, & x \in (-2,-1) \\ 1 + \sqrt{x+1}, & x \in [-1,0) \\ \sqrt{x}, & x \in (0,1) \end{cases}$$

Since, square root function is continuous, we need to check on end points of intervals.

$$f(-1^-) = \lim_{x \to 1^-} f(x) = 2 + \sqrt{-1+2} = 3$$

$$\lim_{x \to -1^+} f(x) = 1 + \sqrt{-1+1} = 1$$

Since, LHL $\neq$ RHL at $x = -1$, it is a point of discontinuity.

$$\lim_{x \to 0^-} f(x) = 1 + \sqrt{0+1} = 2$$

$$\lim_{x \to 0^+} f(x) = \sqrt{0} = 0$$

Since, LHL $\neq$ RHL at $x = 0$, it is a point of discontinuity.

$\therefore$ Total 2 points of discontinuity of $f(x)$ in $(-2, 1)$.

62. Given function is

$$f(x) = \begin{cases} x[x], & -2 < x < 0 \\ (x-1)[x], & 0 \le x < 2 \end{cases}$$

where $[x]$ denotes greatest integer function.

$$f(x) = \begin{cases} -2x & , -2 < x < -1 \\ -x & , -1 \le x < 0 \\ 0 & , 0 \le x < 1 \\ x-1 & , 1 \le x < 2 \end{cases}$$

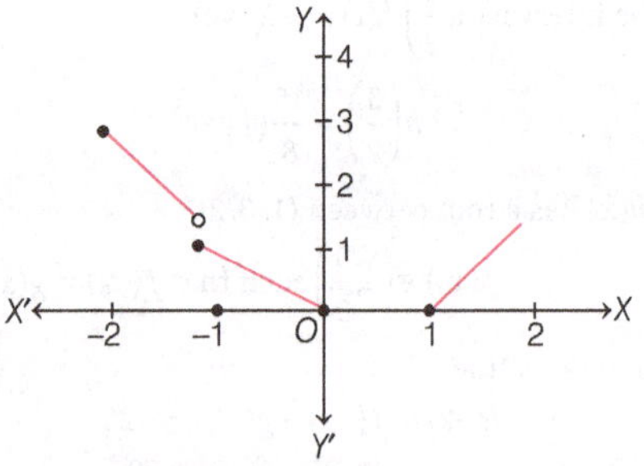

Clearly, $|f(x)|$ remains same.

Given that m and n respectively the number of points in $(-2, 2)$ at which $y = |f(x)|$ is not continuous and not differentiable.

So, $m = 1$, where $y = |f(x)|$ not continuous and $n = 3$, when $|f(x)|$ is not differentiable.

Thus, $m + n = 4$

63. $\because f(x)$ is continuous at $x = 1$

$\therefore$ $$f(1^-) = f(1^+) \Rightarrow 3 + k\sqrt{2} = m + k^2 \quad \text{...(i)}$$

$$f'(1^-) = \left[6x + \frac{k}{2\sqrt{x+1}}\right]_{x=1^-} = 6 + \frac{k}{2\sqrt{2}}$$

$$f'(1^+) = [2mx]_{x=1^+} = 2m$$

$f(x)$ is differentiable at $x = 1$

$$6 + \frac{k}{2\sqrt{2}} = 2m \quad \text{...(ii)}$$

From Eqs. (i) and (ii), we get

$$k = \frac{7}{4\sqrt{2}} \text{ and } m = \frac{103}{32}$$

$$f'(8) = |2mx|_{x=8} = 16m = 16 \times \frac{103}{32} = \frac{103}{2}$$

$$f'\left(\frac{1}{8}\right) = \left[6x + \frac{k}{2\sqrt{x+1}}\right]_{x=\frac{1}{8}}$$

$$= \left[6 \times \frac{1}{8} + \frac{k}{2\sqrt{\frac{1}{8}+1}}\right]$$

$$= \frac{3}{4} + \frac{7}{4\sqrt{2}} \times \frac{\sqrt{2}}{3} = \frac{4}{3}$$

$$\frac{8f'(8)}{f'\left(\frac{1}{8}\right)} = \frac{8 \times \frac{103}{2}}{\frac{4}{3}}$$

$$= 4 \times 103 \times \frac{3}{4} = 309$$

64. We have, $f(x) = [a + 13\sin x]$, $x \in (0, \pi)$

$[13\sin x]$ is not differentiable, where $13\sin x$ is an integer.

$\therefore$ Total number of point where $f(x)$ is not differential

$$= 2 \times 13 - 1 = 25$$

[$\because f(x) = [n + p\sin x]$, $0 < x < \pi$, $n \in I$ and p is a prime number, then the number of points where $f(x)$ is not differentiable $= 2p - 1$].

65. $f : R \to R$

$$f(x) = |x-1| \cos|x-2| \sin|x-1| + (x-3)|x^2 - 5x + 4|$$

$$f(x) = |x-1| \cos|x-2| \sin|x-1| + (x-3)\ |x-1||x-4|$$

$$|x-1|\,|\cos|x-2| \sin|x-1| + (x-3)|x-4|$$

So, there are only two points $x = 1$ and $x = 4$, where $f(x)$ is not differentiable.

66. We have, $$f(x) = \begin{cases} [x], & x < 0 \\ |1-x|, & x \ge 0 \end{cases}$$

and $$g(x) = \begin{cases} e^x - x, & x < 0 \\ (x-1)^2 - 1, & x \ge 0 \end{cases}$$

Now, $$fog(x) = \begin{cases} [g(x)], & g(x) < 0 \\ |1 - g(x)|, & g(x) \ge 0 \end{cases}$$

$$= \begin{cases} 1 + x - e^x, & x < 0 \\ 1, & x = 0 \\ [(x-1)^3 - 1], & 0 < x < 2 \\ |2 - (x-1)^2|, & x \ge 2 \end{cases}$$

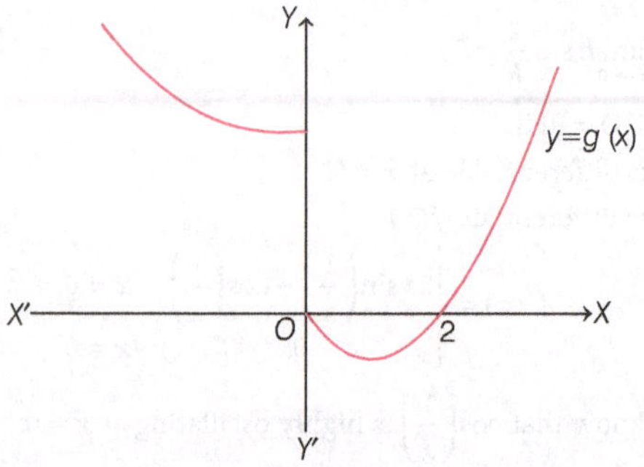

So, $x = 0, 2$ are the two points, where fog is discontinuous.

67. Given, $f(x) = \min[1, 1 + x\sin x], 0 \le x \le 2\pi$

Number of non-differentiable points = 1 (m)

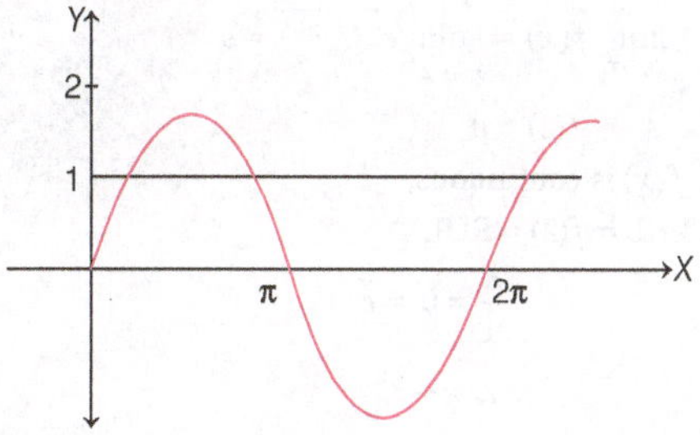

Number of non-continuous point = 0(n)

$\therefore \quad (m, n) = (1, 0)$

68. Given, $f(x) = \begin{cases} -|x+3|, & x < 0 \\ e^x, & x \ge 0 \end{cases}$

$\Rightarrow \quad f(x) = \begin{cases} x+3, & x < -3 \\ -(x+3), & -3 \le x < 0 \\ e^x, & x \ge 0 \end{cases}$

and $\quad g(x) = \begin{cases} x^2 + k_1 x, & x < 0 \\ 4x + k_2, & x \ge 0 \end{cases}$

For $x < 0$, $(gof)(x) = [-(x+3)]^2 + k_1(-(x+3))$

$= (x+3)^2 - k_1(x+3)$

For $x \ge 0, (gof)(x) = 4e^x + k_2$

It is given that $gof(x)$ is differentiable at $x = 0$

$gof(0^-) = gof(0^+)$

$\Rightarrow \quad (0+3)^2 - k_1(0+3) = 4e^0 + k_2$

$\Rightarrow \quad 9 - 3k_1 = 4 + k_2 \quad$ ...(i)

Also, LHD = RHD

$\Rightarrow \quad 2(x+3) - k_1 = 4e^x$

$\Rightarrow \quad 2(0+3) - k_1 = 4 \times e^0 = 4$

$\Rightarrow \quad k_1 = 2$

On putting $k_1 = 2$ in Eq. (i), we get

$9 - 6 = 4 + k_2$

$\Rightarrow \quad k_2 = -1$

Now, $\quad gof((-4) = (x+3)^2 + k_1(x+3) \quad [\because -4 < -3]$

$= (-4+3)^2 + 2(-4+3)$

$= 1 - 2 = -1$

and $\quad (gof)(4) = 4e^4 - 1$

Then, $(gof)(4) + (gof)(-4) = 4e^4 - 1 - 1$

$= 4e^4 - 2$

$= 2(2e^4 - 1)$

69. $f(x) = \begin{cases} 0, & x < 0 \\ ae^x - 1, & 0 \le x < 1 \\ b, & x = 1 \\ b - 1, & 1 < x < 2 \\ -c, & x \ge 2 \end{cases}$

To be continuous at $x = 0$

$\Rightarrow \quad a - 1 = 0 \Leftrightarrow a = 1$

To be continuous at $x = 1$

$\Rightarrow \; ae - 1 = b \Rightarrow b = -1$ not possible.

and to be continuous at $x = 2$

$b - 1 = -c$

$\Rightarrow \quad b + c = 1$

If $a = 1$ and $b + c = 1$, then $f(x)$ is discontinuous at exactly one point.

70. $f(x) = 4|2x+3| + 9\left[x + \frac{1}{2}\right] - 12[x+20], x \in (-20, 2)$

$f(x)$ is not differentiating at

$x = I \in [-19, -18, \ldots 0, \ldots 19]$ i.e. 39 points

At $x = I + \frac{1}{2}, f(x)$ is non-differentiating at 39 points.

Also, $f \times N$ is non-differentiating at $x = -\frac{3}{2}$.

So, total points of non-differentiability = 39 + 39 + 1 = 79

71. Given, f and g are twice differentiable even functions,

$\therefore \quad f\left(\frac{1}{4}\right) = f\left(-\frac{1}{4}\right) = f\left(\frac{1}{2}\right) = f\left(-\frac{1}{2}\right) = 0$

$g\left(\frac{3}{4}\right) = g\left(-\frac{3}{4}\right) = 0$

It means $f(x)$ has atleast 4 roots and $g(x)$ has atleast 2 roots as per the given information

Let $h(x) = f(x)g''(x) \to 4$ roots

Let $p(x) = f'(x)g'(x) \to 4$ roots

$[\because f'(x)$ has atleast 3 roots, $g'(x)$ has atleast 1 root$]$

Hence, the given expression $f(x)g''(x) + f'(x)g'(x)$ has atleast 4 roots.

72. $f(x) = [2x^2 + 1], g(x) = \begin{cases} 2x - 3, & x < 0 \\ 2x + 3, & x \ge 0 \end{cases}$

$fog\,(x) = \begin{cases} [2(2x-3)^2] + 1, & x < 0 \\ [2(2x+3)^2] + 1, & x \ge 0 \end{cases}$

The function is continuous at $x = 0$

$fog(x)$ is discontinuous when

(i) $2(2x-3)^2 \in I$ and $x \in (-1, 0)$

(ii) $2(2x+3)^2 \in I$ and $x \in (0, 1)$

Now, when $-1 < x < 0$

$-5 < 2x - 3 < -3$

$9 < (2x-3)^2 < 25$

$18 < 2(2x-3)^2 < 50$

$\therefore$ There are total 31 discontinuous points.

When $\quad 0 < x < 1$

$3 < 2x + 3 < 5$

$9 < (2x+3)^2 < 25$

$18 < 2(2x+3)^2 < 50$

$\therefore$ There are 31 points of discontinuous in this case

Hence, there are total 62 points of discontinuity.

73. The given function is

$$f(x)=\begin{cases} |2x^2-3x-7| & \text{if } x\le -1 \\ [4x^2-1] & \text{if } -1<x<1 \\ |x+1|+|x-2| & \text{if } x\ge 1 \end{cases}$$

Since, clearly $f(-1)=2$ and $f(1)=3$

For $x\in(-1,1)$, $(4x^2-1)\in[-1,3)$

Hence, $f(x)$ will be discontinuous at $x=1$ and also whenever $4x^2-1=0$, 1 or 2

$$\Rightarrow \quad 4x^2-1=0 \Rightarrow x=\pm\frac{1}{2}$$

and $\quad 4x^2=2$

$$\Rightarrow \quad x=\pm\frac{1}{\sqrt{2}}$$

and $\quad 4x^2=3 \Rightarrow x=\pm\frac{\sqrt{3}}{2}$

Thus, all points of discontinuity of $f(x)$ are $1, \pm\frac{1}{2}, \pm\frac{1}{\sqrt{2}}, \pm\frac{\sqrt{3}}{2}$.

74. $f(x)$ is continuous at $x=0$.

LHL (at $x=0$) $=f(0)=$ RHL (at $x=0$)

$$\lim_{x\to 0^-}\frac{\ln\left(\dfrac{1+\frac{x}{a}}{1-\frac{x}{b}}\right)}{x}=\frac{\lim\limits_{x\to 0^-}\left(\frac{1}{a}\right)\ln\left(1+\frac{x}{a}\right)}{\left(\frac{1}{a}\right)x}$$

$$-\frac{\lim\limits_{x\to 0^-}\left(-\frac{1}{b}\right)\ln\left(1-\frac{x}{b}\right)}{\left(-\frac{1}{b}\right)x}=\left(\frac{1}{a}+\frac{1}{b}\right)$$

and $\quad f(0)=k$

$$\Rightarrow \quad \lim_{x\to 0^+}\frac{\cos^2 x-\sin^2 x-1}{\sqrt{x^2+1}-1}$$

$$\Rightarrow \quad \lim_{x\to 0^+}\frac{-2\sin^2 x}{\sqrt{x^2+1}-1}=\lim_{x\to 0^+}-\left(\frac{2\sin^2 x}{x^2}\right)$$

$$(\sqrt{x^2+1}+1)=-4$$

$$\Rightarrow \quad \frac{1}{a}+\frac{1}{b}=-4=k$$

$$\left(\frac{1}{a}+\frac{1}{b}\right)+\left(\frac{4}{k}\right)=-4-1=-5$$

75. We have, $f(x)=\begin{cases} \dfrac{\lambda|x^2-5x+6|}{\mu(5x-x^2-6)}, & x<2 \\ e^{\frac{\tan(x-2)}{x-[x]}}, & x>2 \\ \mu, & x=2 \end{cases}$

$f(x)$ is continuous at $x=2$.

$$\therefore \quad \lim_{x\to 2^-}f(x)=\lim_{x\to 2^+}f(x)=f(2)$$

$$\therefore \quad \lim_{x\to 2^-}f(x)=\lim_{x\to 2^-}\frac{\lambda|(x-3)(x-2)|}{\mu(x-3)(x-2)}=-\frac{\lambda}{\mu}$$

$$\lim_{x\to 2^+}f(x)=\lim_{x\to 2^+}e^{\frac{\tan(x-2)}{x-2}}=e$$

$$f(2)=\mu$$

As, $f(x)$ is continuous,

So, LHL $=f(2)=$ RHL

$$-\frac{\lambda}{\mu}=\mu=e$$

$$\lambda=-e^2$$

$$\mu=e$$

$$\lambda+\mu=e(-e+1)$$

76. $f(x)=\begin{cases} \sin x-e^x, & x<0 \\ a+[-x], & 0<x<1 \\ 2x-b, & x\ge 1 \end{cases}$

given $f(x)$ is continuous.

So, $\quad f(0^-)=0-e^0=-1$

$$f(0^+)=a-1 \Rightarrow a-1=-1 \Rightarrow a=0$$

$$f(1^-)=\lim_{h\to 0}a+[-1-h]=a-1$$

$$f(1^+)=2(1+h)-b=2-b$$

$$2-b=a-1 \Rightarrow b=2+1=3$$

$$a+b=3$$

77. Given, $f(x)=\begin{cases} \dfrac{\sin(a+1)x+\sin 2x}{2x}, & x<0 \\ b, & x=0 \\ \dfrac{\sqrt{x+bx^3}-\sqrt{x}}{bx^{5/2}}, & x>0 \end{cases}$

$f(x)$ is continuous at $x=0$

$$\lim_{x\to 0^-}f(x)=\lim_{x\to 0^+}f(x)=f(0) \quad \text{...(i)}$$

$$\because \quad f(0)=b \quad \text{...(ii)}$$

Now, $\lim\limits_{x\to 0^-}f(x)=\lim\limits_{x\to 0^-}\left(\dfrac{\sin(a+1)x+\sin 2x}{2x}\right)$

$$=\lim_{x\to 0^-}\left(\frac{\sin(a+1)x}{(a+1)x}\times\left(\frac{a+1}{2}\right)+\frac{\sin 2x}{2x}\right)$$

$$=\frac{a+1}{2}+1 \quad \text{...(iii)}$$

Again, $\lim\limits_{x\to 0^+}f(x)=\lim\limits_{x\to 0^+}\left(\dfrac{\sqrt{x+bx^3}-\sqrt{x}}{bx^{5/2}}\right)$

$$=\lim_{x\to 0^+}\frac{(\sqrt{x+bx^3}-\sqrt{x})(\sqrt{x+bx^3}+\sqrt{x})}{bx^{5/2}(\sqrt{x+bx^3}+\sqrt{x})}$$

$$=\lim_{x\to 0^+}\frac{(x+bx^3-x)}{bx^{5/2}(\sqrt{x+bx^3}+\sqrt{x})}$$

$$=\lim_{x\to 0^+}\frac{\sqrt{x}}{\sqrt{x}(\sqrt{1-bx^2}+1)}$$

$$\Rightarrow \quad \lim_{x\to 0^+}f(x)=\frac{1}{2} \quad \text{...(iv)}$$

From Eqs. (i), (ii), (iii) and (iv), we get

$$\frac{1}{2} = b = \frac{a+1}{2} + 1$$

$$\Rightarrow \quad b = \frac{1}{2} \text{ and } a = -2$$

$$\therefore \quad a + b = \frac{-3}{2}$$

78. Given, $f(x) = \begin{cases} \dfrac{\cos^{-1}(1-\{x\}^2 \sin^{-1}(1-\{x\})}{\{x\}-\{x\}^3}, & x \neq 0 \\ \alpha, & x = 0 \end{cases}$

$$\{x\} = x - [x]$$

So, when $x \to 0^+ \Rightarrow \{x\} = x - 0 = x$

and when $x \to 0^- \Rightarrow \{x\} = x + 1$

$$\text{LHL} = \lim_{x \to 0^-} f(x)$$

$$= \lim_{x \to 0} \frac{\cos^{-1}[1-(1+x)^2|\sin^{-1}[1-(1+x)]}{(1+x)-(1+x)^3}$$

$$= \lim_{x \to 0} \frac{\cos^{-1}(-x^2-2x)\sin^{-1}(-x)}{(1+x)(x+2)(-x)}$$

$$= \lim_{x \to 0} \frac{\cos^{-1}(-x^2-2x)}{(1+x)(x+2)} = \frac{\cos^{-1}(0)}{2} = \frac{\pi}{4}$$

$$\text{RHL} = \lim_{x \to 0^+} f(x)$$

$$= \lim_{x \to 0} \frac{\cos^{-1}(1-x^2)\sin^1(1-x)}{x(1-x)(1+x)}$$

$$= \frac{\pi}{2} \lim_{x \to 0} \frac{\cos^{-1}(1-x^2)}{x}$$

On applying L-Hospital rule, we get

$$\frac{\pi}{2} \lim_{x \to 0} \frac{(-1)(-2x)}{\sqrt{1-(1-x^2)^2}} = \frac{\pi}{2} \cdot 2 \lim_{x \to 0} \frac{x}{\sqrt{2x^2 - x^4}}$$

$$= \pi \lim_{x \to 0} \frac{1}{\sqrt{2-x^2}} = \frac{\pi}{\sqrt{2}}$$

$$\text{LHL} = \frac{\pi}{4} \text{ and RHL} = \frac{\pi}{\sqrt{2}}$$

Hence, LHL $\neq$ RHL

So, the function will be discontinuous for every value of $\alpha \in R$.

$\therefore$ No such α exists.

79. Given, $f(x)$ is continuous on R.

If $f(x)$ is continuous, then

f is continuous at $x = 1$

$$\Rightarrow \quad \lim_{x \to 1^-} f(x) = f(1) = \lim_{x \to 1^+} f(x)$$

$$|a + 1 + b| = \sin \pi = 0$$

$$a + b = -1$$

Also, f is continuous at $x = -1$

$$\lim_{x \to 1^-} f(x) = f(-1) = \lim_{x \to -1^+} f(x)$$

$$\Rightarrow \quad 2\sin\left(\frac{-\pi}{2}(-1)\right) = |a - 1 + b| \Rightarrow 2 = |a + b - 1| \quad \text{...(ii)}$$

Eq. (ii) is satisfied, when

$$a + b = -1$$

80. Given, $f(x) = [x-1]\cos\left(\frac{2x-1}{2}\right)\pi$, where $[\cdot]$ denotes greatest integer function and $f : R \to R$

$\because$ It is a greatest integer function, then we need to check its continuity at $x = I$ except these it is continuous.

Let $x = n$, where $n \in I$

$$\text{Then, LHL} = \lim_{x \to n^-} [x-1]\cos\left(\frac{2x-1}{2}\right)\pi = 0$$

$$\text{RHL} = \lim_{x \to n^+} [x-1]\cos\left(\frac{2x-1}{2}\right)\pi \text{ and } f(n) = 0$$

Here, $\lim_{x \to n^-} f(x) = \lim_{x \to n^-} f(x) = f(n)$

$\therefore$ It is continuous at every integers.

Therefore, the given function is continuous for all real x.

81. We have, $f(x) = \int_a^x g(t)\,dt$

So, $\quad f'(x) = g(x)$ and $f''(x) = g'(x)$

$$\left[\begin{array}{l} \because \; f(x) = \int_{g(x)}^{h(x)} h(x)(t) \cdot dt \\ \Rightarrow f'(x) = f[h(x)] \cdot h'(x) - f[g(x)] \cdot g'(x) \end{array}\right]$$

Now, $g'(x)g(x) = 0 \Rightarrow f''(x)f'(x) = 0$

If $f(x)$ has five roots, then $f'(x)$ has atleast 4 roots and $f''(x)$ has atleast 3 roots.

So, $f''(x) \cdot f'(x) = 0$ has atleast 7 roots.

Hence, the minimum number of roots of the equation $g'(x)g(x) = 0$ is 7.

82. $f : [0, \infty) \to [0, \infty)$

$$f(x) = \int_0^x [y]\,dy$$

Let $x = I + f, \quad 0 < f < 1$

$$f(x) = \int_0^1 [y]dy + \int_1^2 [y]dy + \int_2^3 [y]dy + \dots \int_{I-1}^{I} [y]dy + \int_I^{I+f} [y]dy$$

$$f(x) = 0 + 1 + 2 + \dots (I-1) + I \cdot f$$

$$= \frac{(I-1)(I-1+1)}{2} + I \cdot f$$

$$= \frac{I(I-1)}{2} + I \cdot f$$

$$f(x) = \frac{[x]([x]-1)}{2} + [x]\{x\}$$

$$f(x) = \frac{[x]([x]-1)}{2} + [x](x - [x])$$

$$f(I) = \frac{I(I-1)}{2}$$

$$\lim_{x \to I^-} f(x) = \lim_{h \to 0} \frac{I(I-1)}{2} + I(I + h - I) = \frac{I(I-1)}{2}$$

$$\lim_{x \to I^-} f(x) = \lim_{h \to 0} \frac{I(I-1)(I-2)}{2} + (I-1)(I + h - I + 1)$$

$$= \frac{(I-1)(I-2)}{2} + (I-1) = \frac{(I-1)I}{2}$$

$\therefore f(x)$ is continuous and differentiable.

83. $f(x)=\begin{cases}(x-3)(x+1)e^{(3x-2)^2}, & x>3\\ -(x-3)(x+1)e^{(3x-2)^2}, & -1\le x\le 3\\ (x-3)(x+1)e^{(3x-2)^2}, & x<-1\end{cases}$

At $x=-1$, let LHD be α, then its clear that RHD be $-\alpha$.
Similarly, at $x=3$, if LHD is β, then RHD at $x=3$ will be $-\beta$.
So, $f(x)$ is not differentiable at $x=-1$, $x=3$.
At all other points $f(x)$ will be differentiable.

84. We have, $f(x)=x-[x]=[x]$

and $\qquad g(x)=1-x+[x]=1-[x]$

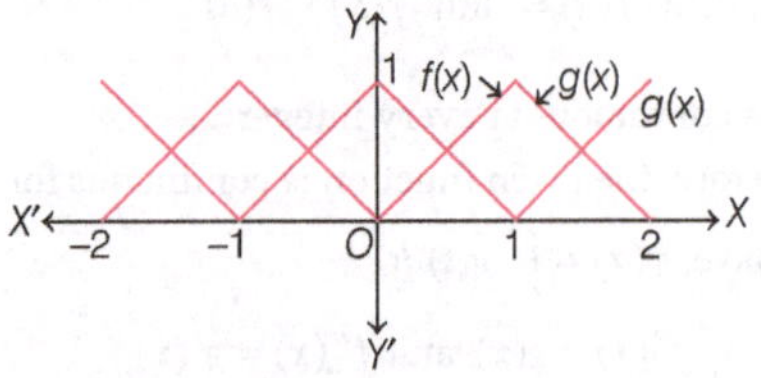

Again, $h(x)=\min[f(x),g(x)]$, so graph of $h(x)$ will be
Point of non-differentiability

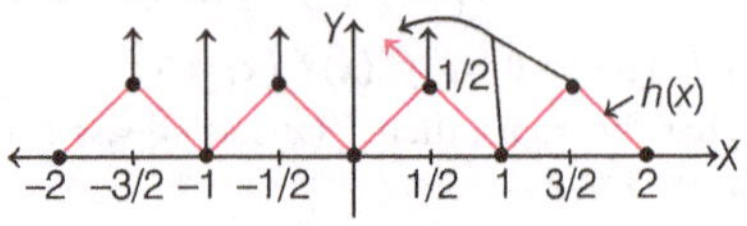

From graph, it is clear that $h(x)$ is continuous in $[-2,2]$ but not differentiable at $x=\frac{-3}{2},-1,\frac{-1}{2},0,\frac{1}{2},1,\frac{3}{2}$ in $(-2,2)$.

85. Graph of max $(\sin t: 0\le t\le x)$ in $x\in[0,\pi]$

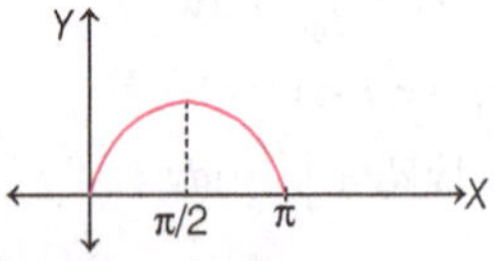

and graph of $2+\cos x$ for $x\in[\pi,\infty]$

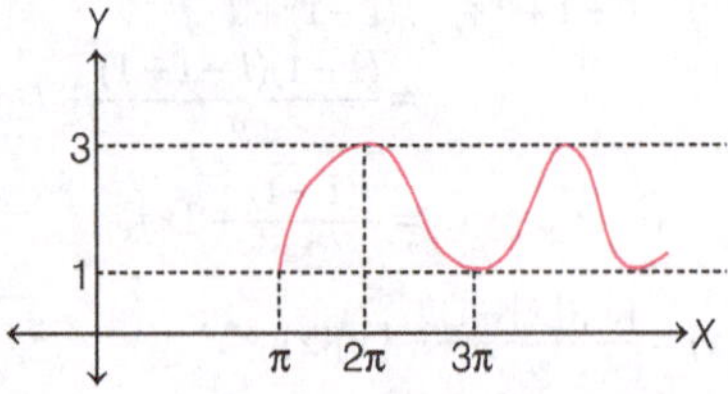

So, graph of

$f(x)=\begin{cases}\max[\sin t: 0\le t\le x], & 0\le x\le R\\ 2+\cos x, & x>\pi\end{cases}$

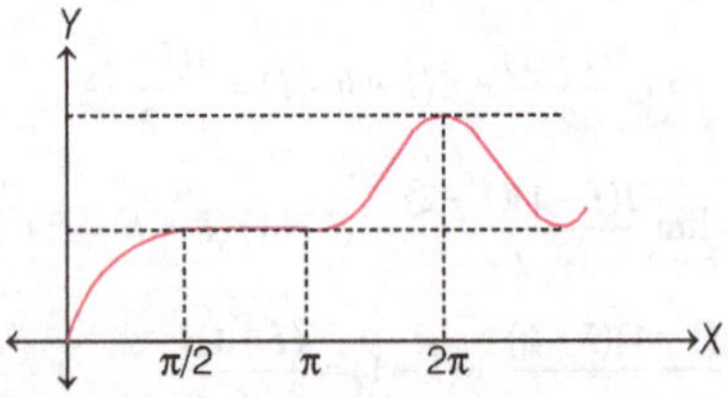

So, $f(x)$ is differentiable everywhere in $(0,\infty)$.

86. For $-2<x<-1$

$f(x)=-2\times(x^2-1)+\sin(\pi)-(-2+1)=(3-2x^2)$

For $-1\le x<0$,

$f(x)=-1\times(1-x^2)+\sin\left(\frac{\pi}{2}\right)-(-1+1)=1-(-1-x^2)=x^2$

For $0\le x<1$,

$f(x)=0\cdot|x^2-1|+\sin\left(\frac{\pi}{3}\right)-(0+1)=\sin\frac{\pi}{3}-1=\frac{\sqrt{3}}{2}-1$

For $1\le x<2$,

$$f(x)=(x^2-1)+\sin\left(\frac{\pi}{1+3}\right)-(1+1)$$
$$=x^2-1+\frac{1}{\sqrt{2}}-2=x^2-3+\frac{1}{\sqrt{2}}$$

$\therefore f(x)$ is defines as

$$f(x)=\begin{cases}3-2x^2, & x\in(-2,-1)\\ x^2, & x\in[-1,0)\\ \frac{\sqrt{3}}{2}-1, & x\in[0,1)\\ \frac{1}{\sqrt{2}}-3+x^2, & x\in[1,2)\end{cases}$$

Now, $\lim_{x\to-1^-}f(x)=1=f(-1)$ and $\lim_{x\to-1^+}f(x)=1$

$\therefore f(x)$ is continuous at $x=-1$

$$\lim_{x\to0^-}f(x)=0 \text{ and } \lim_{x\to0^+}f(x)=\frac{\sqrt{3}}{2}-1$$

$\therefore f(x)$ is discontinuous at $x=0$,

$$\lim_{x\to1^-}f(x)=\frac{\sqrt{3}}{2}-1 \text{ and } \lim_{x\to1^+}f(x)=\frac{1}{\sqrt{2}}-2$$

$\therefore f(x)$ is discontinuous at $x=1$

$\Rightarrow$ $f(x)$ is discontinuous at 2 points.

87. $\therefore$ $f(x)=\min(\{x\},1-\{x\})$

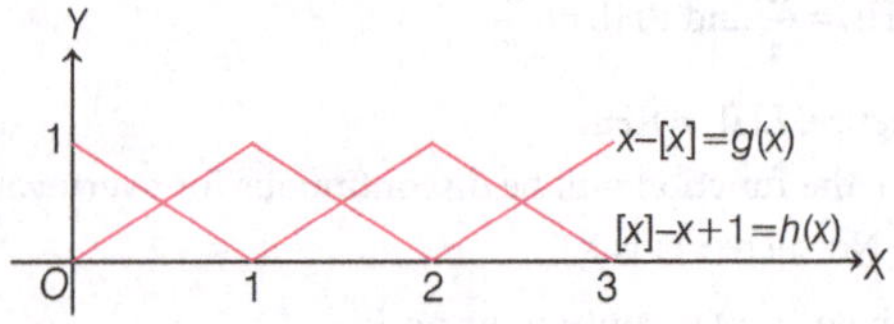

So, the graph of $f(x)$ will be

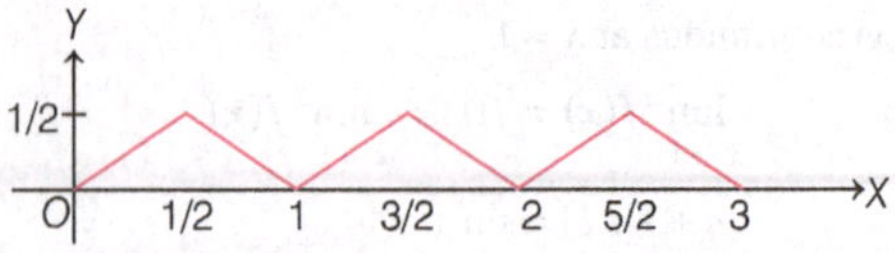

f is continuous everywhere for $0\le x\le 3$.

But f is non-differentiable at $x=\frac{1}{2},\frac{3}{2},\frac{5}{2}$ and $x=1,2$. So, if set P denotes the points of discontinuity, then $n(P)=0$.

and if set Q denotes the points of non-differentiable, then $n(Q)=5$

$\therefore$ $m(P)+n(Q)=0+5=5$

88. Let $f(x) = x^3 - 6x^2 + 9x - 3$

$$f'(x) = 3x^2 - 12x + 9$$

$$f'(x) = 0 \quad \text{[given]}$$

$$3x^2 - 12x + 9 = 0 \Rightarrow 3(x-1)(x-3) = 0$$

$$\therefore \quad x = 1 \text{ or } x = 3$$

Now, $f(1) = 1$ and $f(3) = -3$

+   −   +
(1, 3 marked on the number line)

$$g(x) = \begin{cases} f(x) & , \ 0 \le x \le 1 \\ 1 & , \ 1 \le x \le 3 \\ 4 - x & , \ 3 < x \le 4 \end{cases}$$

$g(x)$ is continuous.

$$g'(x) = \begin{cases} 3(x-1)(x-3) & , \ 0 \le x \le 1 \\ 0 & , \ 1 \le x \le 3 \\ -1 & , \ 3 < x \le 4 \end{cases}$$

$g(x)$ is non-differentiable at $x = 3$.

So, the number of points in (0,4), where $g(x)$ is not differentiable is 1.

Exercise 2 - JEE Advanced Pattern

1. LHL $= \lim_{x \to 0^-} \dfrac{[\{|x|\}]e^{x^2}\{[x + \{x\}]\}}{(e^{1/x^2} - 1)\cdot \operatorname{sgn}(\sin x)}$

$$\because \quad [\{|x|\}] = 0, \qquad [\because \{x\} \in [0, 1) \Rightarrow [\{x\}] = 0]$$

$$e^{x^2} = 1, \ \{[x + \{x\}]\} = 0$$

$$e^{1/x^2} - 1 = \infty, \ \operatorname{sgn}(\sin x) = -1$$

$$\text{LHL} = \frac{0 \times 1 \times 0}{\infty \times -1} = 0$$

Similarly, RHL $= \lim_{x \to 0^+} \dfrac{[\{|x|\}]e^{x^2}\{[x + \{x\}]\}}{(e^{1/x^2} - 1)\operatorname{sgn}(\sin x)}$

Fraction part of greatest integer is always zero.

So, RHL = LHL = 0

So, continuous at $x = 0$.

2. LHL $= f(0^-)$

$$= \lim_{x \to 0^-} \frac{x[x]^2 \ln 2}{\ln(x+1)}$$

$$= \lim_{x \to 0^-} \frac{x \ln 2}{\ln(x+1)}$$

$$= \lim_{x \to 0^-} \frac{\ln 2}{\dfrac{\ln(1+x)}{x}}$$

$$= \frac{\ln 2}{1} = \ln 2$$

$$\text{RHL} = \lim_{x \to 0^+} \frac{\ln(e^{x^2} + 2\sqrt{x} + 1 - 1)(e^{x^2} + 2\sqrt{x} - 1)}{(e^{x^2} + 2\sqrt{x} - 1)(\tan\sqrt{x})} = 2$$

$$\because \quad \text{LHL} \ne \text{RHL}$$

Hence, non-removable discontinuity at $x = 0$.

3. $f(x) = \lim_{t \to \infty} \left\{ \dfrac{|(1 + \sin \pi x)^t - 1|}{|(1 + \sin \pi x)^t + 1|} \right\}$

$$\lim_{t \to \infty} \frac{(1 + \sin \pi x)^t - 1}{(1 + \sin \pi x)^t + 1} \begin{cases} 0, & \begin{array}{l} 1 + \sin \pi x = 1 \\ \sin \pi x = 0 \\ \pi x = n\pi \\ x = n, n = 0, 1, 2, \ldots \end{array} \\ -1, & \begin{array}{l} 1 + \sin \pi x > 1 \\ \sin \pi x > \sin 0 \\ x > n \\ 1 > 1 + \sin \pi x > 0 \end{array} \\ -1, & \begin{array}{l} \pi x > -\dfrac{\pi}{2} \\ 0 > x > -\dfrac{n}{2} \end{array} \end{cases}$$

Now, $$f(x) = \begin{cases} 0, & x = n, n = 1, 2, 3 \ldots \\ -1, & x > n \\ -1, & -\dfrac{n}{2} < n < 0 \end{cases}$$

(i) $f(0^-) = -1$, $f(0^+) = -1$, $f(0) = 0$

(ii) $f(1^+) = -1$, $f(1^-) = -1$, $f(1) = 0$

$\therefore$ Similarly, for all integer the function will be discontinuous.

4. $g(x) = \tan^{-1}|x| - \cot^{-1}|x|$

$$f(x) = \frac{[x]}{[x+1]}\{x\}$$

$$h(x) = |g(f(x))|$$

$$\lim_{x \to 0^-} |g(f(0^-))| = \frac{\pi}{2}$$

$$\lim_{x \to 0^+} |g(f(0^+))| = \frac{\pi}{2}$$

$\therefore$ h is continuous at $x = 0$.

5. $\lim_{h \to 0} \dfrac{f(3\cosh + 4\sin h - 2) - f(1)}{f(3e^h - 5\sec h + 4) - f(2)}$ $\left[\dfrac{0}{0} \text{ form}\right]$

$$= \lim_{h \to 0} \frac{(-3\sin h + 4\cos h) f'(3\cos h + 4\sin h - 2)}{(3e^h - 5\sec h \tan h) f'(3e^h - 5\sec h + 4)}$$

$$= \frac{4}{3} \times \frac{f'(1)}{f'(2)} = \frac{4 \times 6}{3 \times 2}$$

$$= \frac{24}{6} = 4$$

6. $f(x) = \sum_{k=1}^{n} \tan\left(\dfrac{x}{2^k}\right) \sec\left(\dfrac{x}{2^{k-1}}\right)$

$$= \sum_{k=1}^{n} \frac{\sin\left(\dfrac{x}{2^k}\right)}{\cos\left(\dfrac{x}{2^k}\right)\cos\left(\dfrac{x}{2^{k-1}}\right)}$$

$$= \sum_{k=1}^{n} \left(\tan\frac{x}{2^{k-1}} - \tan\frac{x}{2^k} \right) = \tan x - \tan\frac{x}{2^n}$$

$\therefore$ LHL (at $x=0$) $= \lim_{x\to 0^-} \dfrac{\ln(1+\tan x)}{x} = 1 = h(0^-)$

$$g(x) = \lim_{n\to\infty} \prod_{r=1}^{n} \left(\frac{\cos^2 \frac{x}{2^r} - \sin^2 \frac{x}{2^r}}{\cos^2 \frac{x}{2^r}} \right)$$

$$\lim_{n\to\infty} \prod_{r=1}^{n} \frac{2\tan \frac{x}{2^r}}{\tan \frac{x}{2^{r-1}}} = \frac{x}{\tan x}$$

RHL (at $x=0$) $= \lim_{x\to 0^+} g(x) = 1 = h(0^+)$

$\therefore \quad k = \text{LHL} = \text{RHL} = 1$

7. $\dfrac{f(2x)}{e^{2x}-1} = \dfrac{f(x)}{e^x - 1}$ (given)

$$\Rightarrow \quad \frac{f(x)}{e^x-1} = \frac{f\left(\frac{x}{2}\right)}{e^{x/2}-1} = \frac{f\left(\frac{x}{4}\right)}{e^{x/2^2}-1} = \dots = \frac{f\left(\frac{x}{2^n}\right)}{e^{x/2^n}-1}$$

$$\Rightarrow \quad \frac{f(x)}{e^x-1} = \lim_{n\to\infty} \frac{f\left(\frac{x}{2^n}\right)}{e^{x/2^n}-1} = \lim_{h\to 0} \frac{f(h)}{e^h - 1}$$

$$= \lim_{h\to 0} \frac{f(h)}{h} = \lim_{h\to 0} \frac{f(h)-f(0)}{h} = f'(0)$$

$\therefore \quad f(x) = e^x - 1$

$$\lim_{x\to 0} \left(\frac{f(x)}{x} \right)^{1/x} = \lim_{x\to 0} \left(\frac{e^x - 1}{x} \right)^{1/x} = e^{\lim_{x\to 0} \frac{e^x - 1 - x}{x^2}} = e^{1/2}$$

8. Let $f(\alpha) = b \Rightarrow f^{-1}(b) = \alpha$

$f(\alpha+h) = b - k \Rightarrow f^{-1}(b-k) = \alpha + h$

$f(\alpha-h) = b + k \Rightarrow f^{-1}(b+k) = \alpha - h$

Now, LHD of $f^{-1}(x)$ at $x = f(\alpha) = b$

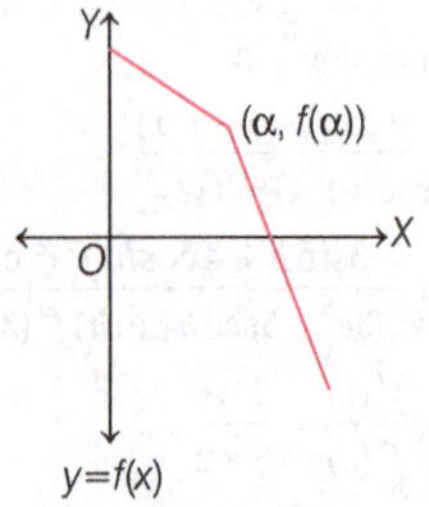

$$(f^{-1})'(b^-) = \lim_{k\to 0} \frac{f^{-1}(b-k) - f^{-1}(b)}{(b-k)-b}$$

$$= \lim_{h\to 0} \frac{\alpha + h - \alpha}{f(\alpha+h) - f(\alpha)} = \lim_{h\to 0} \frac{1}{\frac{f(\alpha+h)-f(\alpha)}{h}}$$

$$= \frac{1}{f'(\alpha^+)} = \frac{1}{r}$$

Perpendicularly now RHD of $f^{-1}(x)$ at $x = f(\alpha) = b$

$$(f^{-1})'(b^+) = \lim_{k\to 0} \frac{f^{-1}(b+k) - f^{-1}(b)}{(b-k)-b}$$

$$= \lim_{h\to 0} \frac{(\alpha-h)-\alpha}{f(\alpha-h)-f(\alpha)}$$

$$= \lim_{h\to 0} \frac{1}{\frac{f(\alpha-h)-f(\alpha)}{-h}} = \frac{1}{f'(\alpha^-)} = \frac{1}{l}$$

Alternate Solution

Verification by taking an example

$$y = f(x) = \begin{cases} -3x, & \text{for } x \le 0 \\ -2x, & \text{for } x > 0 \end{cases}$$

$f'(0^-) = -3 = l$

$f'(0^+) = -2 = r$

$$g(y) = x = f^{-1}(y) = \begin{cases} \frac{-y}{3}, & \text{for } y \ge 0 \\ \frac{-y}{2}, & \text{for } y < 0 \end{cases}$$

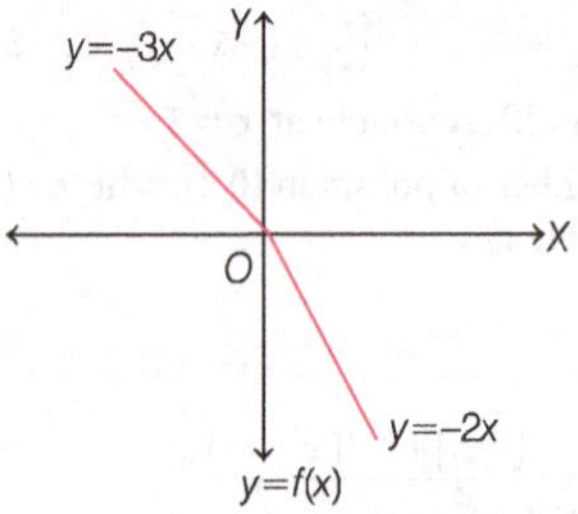

$$g'(0^+) = f'(0^+) = \frac{-1}{3} = \frac{1}{l}$$

$$g'(0^-) = f'(0^+) = \frac{-1}{2} = \frac{1}{r}$$

Note If l and r are positive, then LHD and RHD of f^{-1} are $\frac{1}{l}$ and $\frac{1}{r}$ and if l and r are negative, then LHD and RHD are $\frac{1}{r}$ and $\frac{1}{l} \cdot r$.

9. $\because \quad f^3(x) - 6f^2(x) + 11f(x) - 6 = 0$

$\Rightarrow (f^2(x) - 3f(x) + 2)(f(x) - 3) = 0$

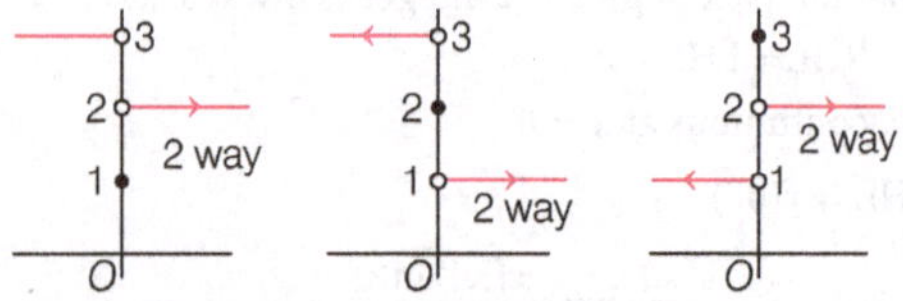

$\Rightarrow \quad (f(x)-1)(f(x)-2)(f(x)-3) = 0$

$\Rightarrow \quad f(x) = 1$ or 2 or 3

(i) If LHL $\ne$ RHL $\ne f(0)$,
then number of such functions $= 3! = 6$, (see figure)

(ii) If any two of LHL $f(0^-)$, RHL $f(0^+)$ and $f(0)$ are equal and third one is not equal, then number of such functions
$= {}^3C_2 \times {}^3C_2 \times {}^2C_1 = 18$
$\therefore$ Number of such function $= 24$

(iii) Out of 1, 2, 3 we can select any two of ${}^3C_2$ say 1 and 2 and out of $f(0^+)$, $f(0^-)$ and $f(0)$ we can select any two which are equal in ${}^3C_2$ ways.

Now, total ways ${}^3C_2 \cdot {}^3C_2 \cdot 2 = 18$

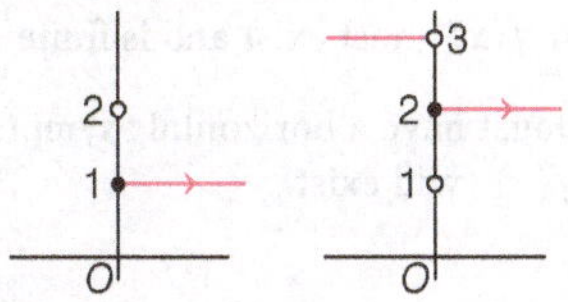

Alternate Solution

Total number of function = $3^3 = 27$

Total number of continuous function = 3

Hence, total number of discontinuous function = 27 − 3 = 24

10. $f(x^n) = 2f(x^{n-1})$

$$f'(x^n)\cdot nx^{n-1} = 2f'(x^{n-1})\cdot(n-1)x^{n-2}$$

On putting $x = 2$, $f'(2^n)\cdot n\cdot 2^{n-1} = 2\cdot f'(2^{n-1})\cdot(n-1)2^{n-2}$

$$\Rightarrow \quad f'(2^n) = \frac{(n-1)}{(n)} f'(2^{n-1})$$

$$\Rightarrow \quad f'(2^n) = \frac{(n-1)}{n}\times\frac{(n-2)}{(n-1)}\cdots\frac{1}{2}\cdot f'(2)$$

$$\Rightarrow \quad f'(2^n) = \frac{f'(2)}{n} \Rightarrow n\cdot f'(2^n) = f'(2)$$

$$\therefore \quad k = n$$

11. $\lim_{x\to 0} f(\cos^3 x + \sin^2 x)$

$$x\to 0 \ \cos^3 x - \cos^2 x < 0$$

$$\therefore \quad 1 + \cos^3 x - \cos^2 x < 1$$

$$\therefore \quad \lim_{x\to 0} f(\cos^3 x + \sin^2 x) = \lim_{x\to 0} f(1 + \cos^3 x - \cos^2 x) = 1$$

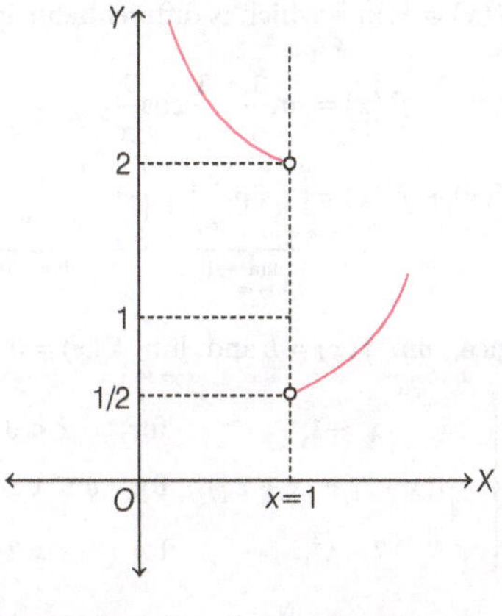

12. From the Ist graph if $x \in (-a, a)$, then number value of y and hence $f(x)$ must be negative in $(-a, a)$. Also, from the above two graph if $x \in [-b, -a] \cup [a, b]$, then $f(x)$ is positive and hence from the given graphs, graph of $f(x)$ is as follows

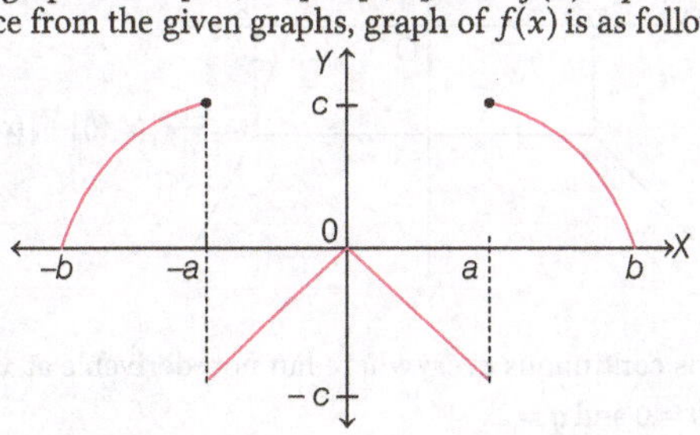

Clearly, $f(x)$ is discontinuous at 2 points and non-differentiable at 3 points.

13. $k = \lim_{x\to 0^+} (1 + (\sin A)^{1/x})^{(\operatorname{cosec} B \sin C)^{1/x}}$ $\qquad (1^\infty$ form)

$[\because C > B \Rightarrow \sin C > \sin B \Rightarrow \sin C \operatorname{cosec} B > 1]$

$$= e^{\lim_{x\to 0^+} (\operatorname{cosec} B \sin C)^{1/x} (\sin A)^{1/x}}$$

$$= e^{\lim_{x\to 0^+}\left(\frac{\sin C \sin A}{\sin B}\right)^{1/x}} = e^0 = 1$$

$$\left[\because \quad A < B < C < \frac{\pi}{2}\right.$$

$$\sin A < \sin B < \sin C < 1$$

$$\therefore \quad 0 < \frac{\sin A}{\sin B} < 1$$

$$\text{and} \quad 0 < \sin C < 1$$

$$\left.\Rightarrow \quad 0 < \frac{\sin A \sin C}{\sin B} < 1\right]$$

14. $x = 1 + h$

$$\lim_{h\to 0} \frac{\pi^2}{e}(-h)\frac{((1+h)^{1/h} - e)}{(1 + \cos(\pi + \pi h))}$$

$$= \lim_{h\to 0} -\frac{\pi^2}{e} h \frac{((1+h)^{1/h} - e)}{(1 - \cos \pi h)}$$

$$= \lim_{h\to 0} -\frac{\pi^2}{e} h \frac{(e^{1/h \ln(1+h)} - e)}{\left(2\sin^2\left(\frac{\pi h}{2}\right)\right)}$$

$$= \lim_{h\to 0} -\frac{\pi^2}{e} h \frac{\left(e^{\frac{1}{h}\left(h - \frac{h^2}{2} + \frac{h^3}{3} + \ldots\right)} - e\right)}{\dfrac{2\sin^2\left(\frac{\pi h}{2}\right)}{\left(\frac{\pi h}{2}\right)^2}\dfrac{\pi^2 h^2}{4}}$$

$$\Rightarrow \quad \lim_{h\to 0} -\frac{2}{e}\frac{e}{h}\left(e^{\frac{-h}{2} + \frac{h^2}{3} + \ldots} - 1\right) = 1$$

15. Continuity

$\Rightarrow f(1) = f(2) = \ldots = f(100) =$ a fixed irrational value if option (a) is correct, then

$$f(1) + f(2) + \ldots + f(100) = f(1) + f(2) + \ldots + f(99)$$

$\Rightarrow f(100) = 0$

which is not possible as $f(100)$ must be irrational if option (b) is correct, then

$$f(1) + f(2) + \ldots + f(100) = f(2) + f(4) + \ldots + f(100) + f(102) + \ldots + f(200)$$

$$\therefore \quad \underbrace{f(1) + f(3) + \ldots + f(99)}_{50 \text{ terms}} = \underbrace{f(102) + f(104) + \ldots + f(200)}_{50 \text{ terms}}$$

equality holds.

16. $f(0)=k=\lim_{x\to 0} f(x)$

$$=\lim_{x\to 0}\frac{\tan\left(\frac{\pi}{4}+2x\right)-2\tan\left(\frac{\pi}{4}+x\right)+\tan\frac{\pi}{4}}{\sin\left(\frac{\pi}{4}+2x\right)-2\sin\left(\frac{\pi}{4}+x\right)+\sin\frac{\pi}{4}}$$

$$=\lim_{x\to 0}\frac{\left(\tan\left(\frac{\pi}{4}+2x\right)-\tan\left(\frac{\pi}{4}+x\right)\right)+\left(\tan\frac{\pi}{4}-\tan\left(\frac{\pi}{4}+x\right)\right)}{\left(\sin\left(\frac{\pi}{4}+2x\right)+\sin\frac{\pi}{4}\right)-2\sin\left(\frac{\pi}{4}+x\right)}$$

$$=\lim_{x\to 0}\frac{\tan x\left(1+\tan\left(\frac{\pi}{4}+2x\right)\tan\left(\frac{\pi}{4}+x\right)\right)-\tan x\left(1+\tan\left(\frac{\pi}{4}+x\right)\tan\frac{\pi}{4}\right)}{2\sin\left(\frac{\pi}{4}+x\right)\cos x-2\sin\left(\frac{\pi}{4}+x\right)}$$

$$=\lim_{x\to 0}\frac{\tan x\tan\left(\frac{\pi}{4}+x\right)\left(\tan\left(\frac{\pi}{4}+2x\right)-\tan\frac{\pi}{4}\right)}{-2\sin\left(\frac{\pi}{4}+x\right)\left(\frac{1-\cos x}{x^2}\right)x^2}$$

$$=\lim_{x\to 0}\frac{\tan x\tan\left(\frac{\pi}{4}+x\right)\tan 2x\left(1+\tan\left(\frac{\pi}{4}+2x\right)\tan\frac{\pi}{4}\right)}{-2\sin\left(\frac{\pi}{4}+x\right)\left(\frac{1-\cos x}{x^2}\right)x^2}$$

$=-4\sqrt{2}$

Hence, $k=-4\sqrt{2}$

17. Graph of $f(x)=\frac{6}{\pi}\tan^{-1}\left(\frac{2x}{1-x^2}\right)$

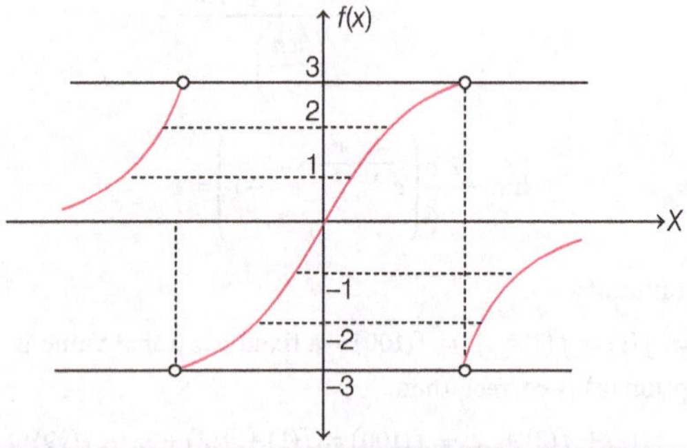

Range of $f(x)$ is $(-3, 3)$ integral values of $f(x)$ are $-2, -1, 0, 1, 2$.

For each integral value of $f(x)$ (except zero)there are exactly two values of x and for $f(x)=0$, there is exactly are value of x, $x=0$.

$\therefore$ Total number of points where $f(x)$ is an integer and where $[f(x)]$ is discontinuous is 9.

18. $f(-5)=2, f(20)=f(4)=3, f(-10)=1, f(17)=-2$

$\therefore$ Given expression $=\tan^{-1}\tan\{2+3+0-2\}=3-\pi$

19. $f(x)$ is differentiable in $(0, \infty)$.

Hence, $\lim_{x\to\infty} f(x)$ must exist and is finite

$\therefore y=f(x)$ must have a horizontal asymptote as $x\to\infty$, then only $\lim_{x\to\infty} f(x)$ will exist.

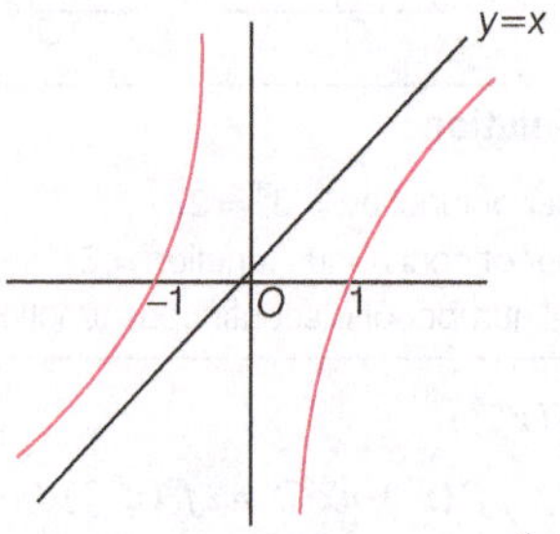

If $f(x)$ has an inclined asymptotes as $y=x-\frac{1}{x}$, then $\lim_{x\to\infty} f(x)\to\infty$

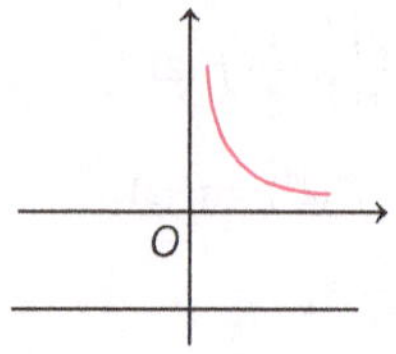

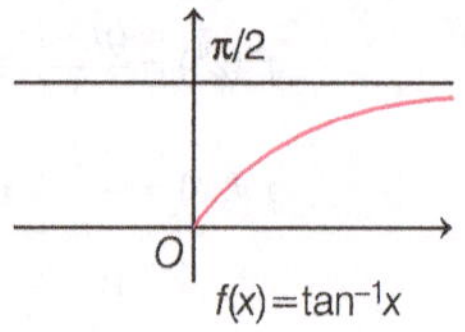

$\therefore f(x)$ has a horizontal asymptote hence $\lim_{x\to\infty} f'(x)\to 0$

(c) (also see figure for $f(x)=\tan^{-1}x$)

e.g. Take the example given

(i) Let $f(x)=x\sin\frac{1}{x}$ which is differentiable in $(0, \infty)$

$$f'(x)=\sin\frac{1}{x}-\frac{1}{x}\cos\frac{1}{x}$$

$$f(x)+f'(x)=\underbrace{\left(x\sin\frac{1}{x}\right)}_{\lim_{x\to\infty}\to 1}+\underbrace{\left(\sin\frac{1}{x}-\frac{1}{x}\cos\frac{1}{x}\right)}_{\lim_{x\to\infty}\to 0}$$

Hence, $\lim_{x\to\infty} f(x)=L$ and $\lim_{x\to\infty} f'(x)=0$.

20. $$f(x)=\begin{cases} x^3-1, & \text{for } x<0 \\ -\frac{1}{4}(|x-2|+|x+2|), & \text{for } 0\le x\le 2 \\ 7-x^3, & \text{for } x>2\end{cases}$$

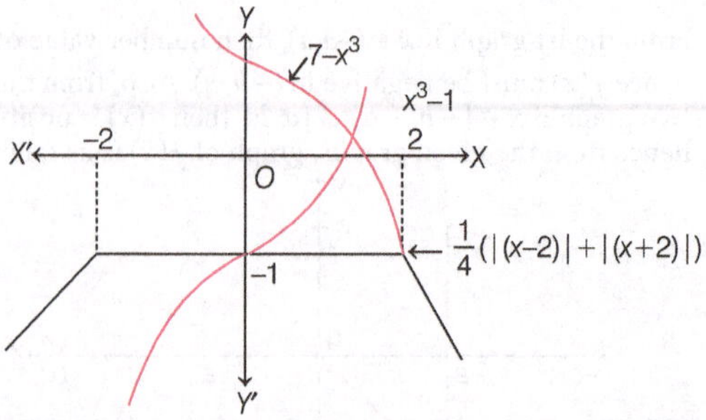

$f(x)$ is continuous everywhere but non-derivable at $x=0, 2$.

$\therefore\quad p=0$ and $q=2$

21. Put $x \to x+h$ and $y \to h$

$$f(x)\cdot f(h) = f(x+h)$$

$$\therefore \quad f'(x) = \lim_{h\to 0}\frac{f(x+h)-f(x)}{h}$$

$$= \lim_{h\to 0}\frac{f(x)[f(h)-1]}{h},$$

$$[x=0, y=0; f(0)=0 \text{ not possible}, f(0)=1]$$

$$f'(x) = f(x)\cdot f'(0) \Rightarrow f'(5) = f(5)\cdot f'(0)$$

$$q = f(5)\cdot p$$

$$\Rightarrow \quad f(5) = \frac{q}{p}$$

22. We have,

$$y\cdot \lim_{x\to 0} f(\cos^3 x - \cos^2 x) = x\cdot \lim_{x\to 0} f(\sin^2 x - \sin^3 x)$$

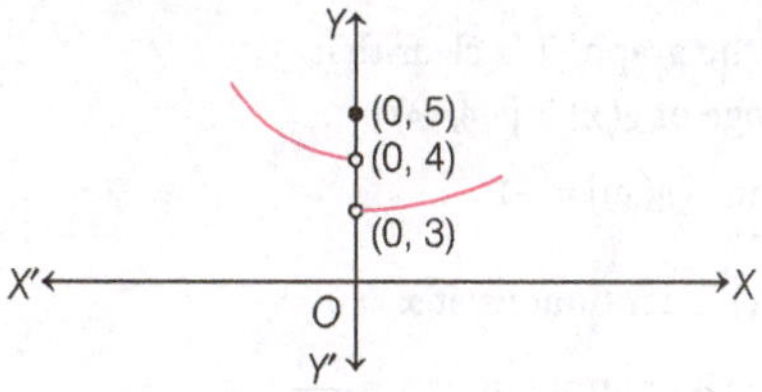

Here, $\cos^3 x - \cos x \to 0$ from LHS

$$\therefore \quad \lim_{x\to 0} f(\cos^3 x - \cos x) = 4$$

$\sin^2 x - \sin^3 x \to 0$ from RHS

$$\therefore \quad \lim_{x\to 0} f(\sin^2 x - \sin^3 x) \to 3$$

$\therefore$ Equation of straight line is $4y = 3x$ ...(i)

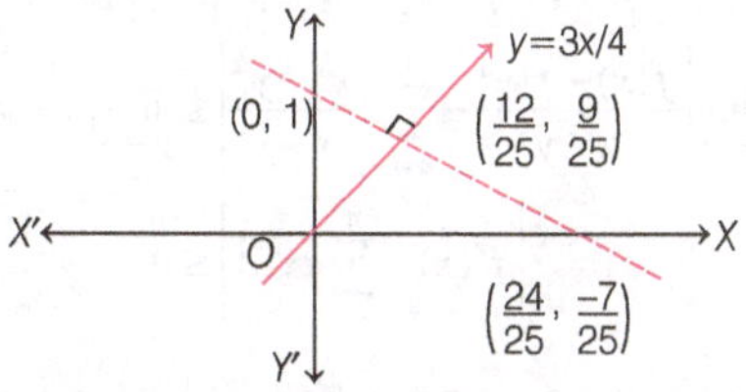

Equation of line perpendicular to $y = \frac{3}{4}x$ and passing through $(0,1)$ is $(y-1) = \frac{-4}{3}(x-0)$

$$\Rightarrow \quad y - 1 = \frac{-4}{3}x \quad \text{...(ii)}$$

On solving Eqs. (i) and (ii), we get

$$x = \frac{12}{25}, y = \frac{9}{25}$$

Hence, image point is $\left(\frac{24}{25}, \frac{-7}{25}\right)$.

23. $S_1 : f(x) = |x \operatorname{sgn}(1-x^2)|$

$$= \begin{cases} -x, & x \in (-\infty,-1)\cup(-1,0) \\ 0, & x = -1, 0, 1 \\ x, & x \in (0,1)\cup(1,\infty) \end{cases}$$

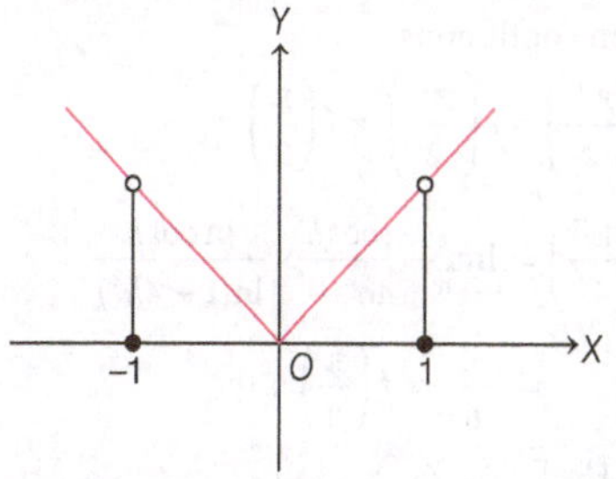

Function is discontinuous at $x = -1, 1$

and non-differentiable at $x = -1, 0, 1$

$$S_2 = \lim_{x\to 0^-} f(x) = \lim_{x\to 0^-} a\sin\frac{\pi}{2}(x+1) = a$$

$$\lim_{x\to 0^+} f(x) = \lim_{x\to 0^+}\frac{\tan x - \sin x}{x^3} = \lim_{x\to 0^+}\frac{\tan x(1-\cos x)}{x^3} = \frac{1}{2}$$

$$\therefore \quad a = \frac{1}{2}$$

$$S_3 : f(x) = (x^2|x|)^{1/3} = \begin{cases} (x^3)^{1/3} = x, & x \ge 0 \\ (-x^5)^{1/3} = (-1)^{1/3}x = -x, & x < 0 \end{cases}$$

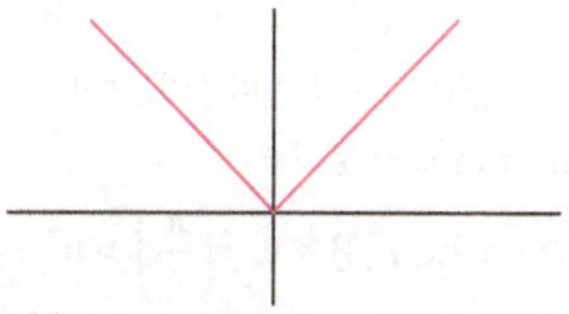

$f(x)$ is differentiable everywhere except at $x = 0$

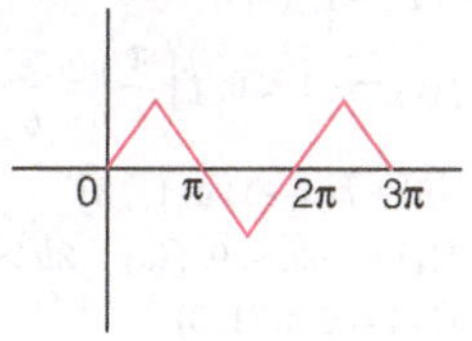

$S_4 : f(x)$ will be non-differentiable if $\sin^{-1}(\sin x) = 0$ or graph of $f(x)$ has a sharp point.

Hence, number of points of non-differentiable will be 5.

24. $S_1 : f(x) = \dfrac{\sin(\pi[x-\pi])}{1+[x]^2}$, where $[x-\pi]$ is an integer for $x \in R$

$\therefore \quad f(x) = 0, \forall x \in R$

Hence, $f(x)$ is always continuous. (False)

$S_2 : f(x) = p[x+1] + q[x-1] = (p+q)[x] + p - q$

$f(1) = 2p, f(1^+) = 2p, f(1^-) = p - q$

But $f(x)$ is continuous at $x = 1$

$$2p = p - q \Rightarrow p + q = 0 \text{ (True)}$$

$$S_3 : f(x) = |[x]\,x| = \begin{cases} -x, & -1 \le x < 0 \\ 0, & 0 \le x < 1 \\ x, & 1 \le x < 2 \\ 4, & x = 2 \end{cases}$$

$\because$ Function is not continuous at $x = 2$

$\therefore$ Non-differentiable also (True)

$S_4 : f(0) = \text{constant}$

$f'(0) = 0, \forall x \in R$

$f'(10) = 0$ (False)

25. Function continuous

$$\Rightarrow f\left(\frac{\pi^+}{2}\right)=f\left(\frac{\pi^-}{2}\right)=f\left(\frac{\pi}{2}\right)$$

$$\Rightarrow f\left(\frac{\pi^-}{2}\right)=\lim_{h\to 0}\frac{1-\cos h}{4h^2}\times\frac{\ln\cos h}{\ln(1+4h^2)}$$

$$=-\frac{1}{64}=f\left(\frac{\pi}{2}\right)$$

26. $$f(x)=\begin{cases}3-\left[\cot^{-1}\left(\dfrac{2x^3-3}{x^2}\right)\right], & \text{for } x>0\\ \{x^2\}\cos(e^{1/x}), & \text{for } x<0\end{cases}$$

$$\text{RHL}=\lim_{x\to 0^+}3-\left[\cot^{-1}\frac{2x^3-3}{x^2}\right]=3-3=0$$

$$[\because \cot^{-1}(-\infty)\to[\pi]=3]$$

$$\text{LHL}=\lim_{x\to 0^-}\{x^2\}\cos e^{1/x}$$

$$x=0-h$$

$$\lim_{h\to 0}\underbrace{\{h^2\}}_{0}\times\underbrace{\cos e^{-1/h}}_{1}=0$$

$\therefore$ $f(0^-)=0$ and $f(0)=0$

$\Rightarrow$ f is continuous at $x=0$

27. (a) $f(x)=x-\cos x$, $f(0)<0$, $f\left(\frac{\pi}{2}\right)>0$

(b) $f(x)=x+\sin x-1$,

$$f(0)=-1<0;\ f\left(\frac{\pi}{6}\right)=\frac{\pi}{6}+\frac{1}{2}-1>0$$

(c) $f(x)=a(x-3)+b(x-1)$ in $[1, 3]$

$$f(1)=-2a<0;\ f(3)=2b>0$$

$\Rightarrow$ $f(x)=0$ in $(1, 3)$

(d) $h(x)=f(x)-g(x)$

$\Rightarrow h(a)=f(a)-g(a)>0$

$h(b)=f(b)-g(b)<0$

Hence, using Intermediate value theorem all the four have at least one root in indicated interval.

28. $$f(x)=\frac{1}{[\sin x]}$$

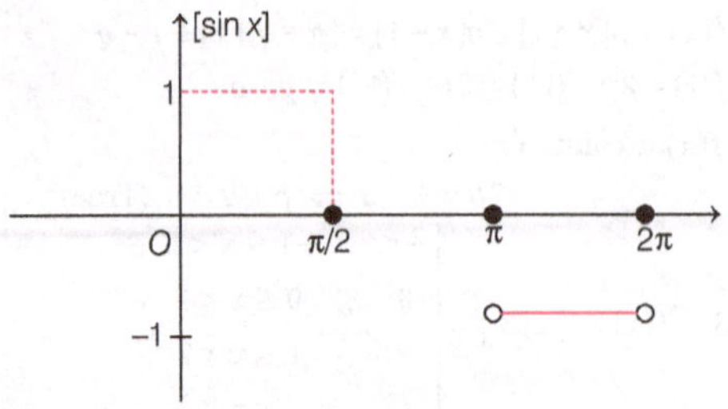

$D_f:[\sin x]\neq 0$

$$x\in(2n\pi+\pi,2n\pi+2\pi)\cup\left\{2n\pi+\frac{\pi}{2}\right\}$$

continuous, when $x\in(2n\pi+\pi,2n\pi+2\pi)$

$\therefore$ $f(x)$ has the period of 2π.

29. Graph of $y=g(x)$

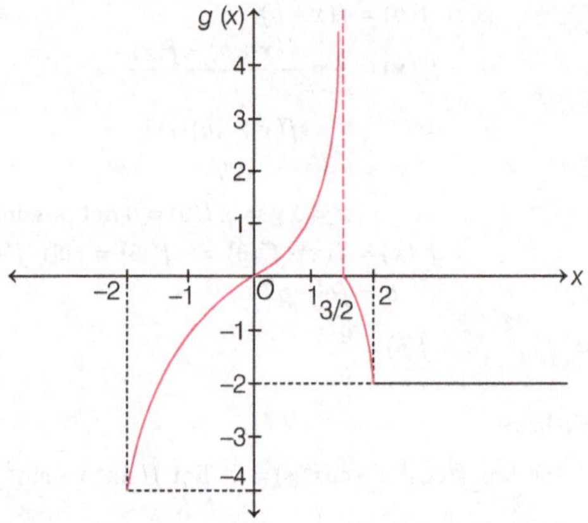

From the graph, it is clear that

(a) range of $g(x)$ is $[-4,\infty)$

(b) $\lim_{x\to 0^-}[g(x)]=-1$

(c) $g(x)$ is continuous at $x=0$

(d) $g(x)$ is continuous at $x=\frac{-3}{2}$

but discontinuous at $x=\frac{3}{2}$

30. $$\left|f(x)-f(y)-\sum_{k=1}^{n}(x^k-y^k)\right|\le|x-y|^2$$

$$\left|\frac{f(x)-f(y)}{x-y}-\sum_{k=1}^{n}\frac{x^k-y^k}{x-y}\right|\le|x-y|$$

$$\lim_{y\to x}\left|\frac{f(x)-f(y)}{x-y}-\sum_{k=1}^{n}\frac{x^k-y^k}{x-y}\right|\le\lim_{y\to x}|x-y|$$

$$\left|f'(x)-\sum_{k=1}^{n}kx^{k-1}\right|\le 0$$

$$f'(x)=\sum_{k=1}^{n}kx^{k-1}=1+2x+3x^2+\ldots+nx^{n-1}$$

$$f(x)=x+x^2+x^3+\ldots+x^n+c$$

$$f(0)=1$$

$$\therefore\ f(x)=1+x+x^2+\ldots+x^n$$

$$\lim_{n\to\infty}f\left(\frac{1}{2}\right)=1+\frac{1}{2}+\left(\frac{1}{2}\right)^2+\ldots+\infty=\frac{1}{1-\frac{1}{2}}=2$$

For $n=100$, $$\lim_{x\to 1}\frac{(1+x+x^2+\ldots+x^{100})-101}{(x-1)}$$

$$=\lim_{x\to 1}\frac{(x-1)}{(x-1)}+\frac{(x^2-1)}{(x-1)}+\ldots+\frac{(x^{100}-1)}{(x-1)}$$

$$=1+2+3+\ldots+100=5050$$

For $n=3$,

$$\operatorname{sgn}(f(x))=\operatorname{sgn}(1+x+x^2+x^3)=\operatorname{sgn}((1+x)(1+x^2))$$

$(1+x)(1+x^2)=0$, when $x=-1$

For $n=4$, $\operatorname{sgn}(f'(x))=\operatorname{sgn}(1+2x+3x^2+4x^3)$

Let $F(x)=1+2x+3x^2+4x^3$

$F'(x)=2+6x+12x^2>0$

$\Rightarrow F(x)$ has exactly one real zero

$\operatorname{sgn}\{f'(x)\}=1$

$\therefore$Number point of discontinuity

31. $\alpha=0$

$$f(0)=\lim_{x\to 0}\frac{xa^x+bx\cos x+c\sin x}{x^5}$$

$$=\lim_{x\to 0}\frac{x\left(1+x\ln a+\frac{x^2(\ln a)^2}{2!}+\dots\right)+bx\left(1-\frac{x^2}{2!}+\frac{x^4}{4!}\right)+c\left(x-\frac{x^3}{3!}+\frac{x^5}{5!}\right)}{x^5}$$

$$=\lim_{x\to 0}\frac{x(1+b+c)+x^2\ln a+x^3\left[\frac{(\ln a)^2}{2}-\frac{b}{2}-\frac{c}{6}\right]+x^5\left[\frac{b}{24}+\frac{c}{120}\right]}{x^5}$$

To exist, $1+b+c=0$, $\ln a=0\Rightarrow a=1$

$$-\frac{b}{2}-\frac{c}{6}=0\Rightarrow 3b+c=0$$

$$\Rightarrow\quad b=\frac{1}{2}, c=\frac{-3}{2}$$

$$f(0)=\frac{1}{120}\text{ and }f'(0)=0$$

$$\therefore\quad f(\alpha)=\frac{1}{120}$$

$$a+b+c=1+\frac{1}{2}-\frac{3}{2}=0,\ 4abc=4\times 1\times\frac{1}{2}\times-\frac{3}{2}=-3$$

and $\quad a-c=1+\frac{3}{2}=\frac{5}{2}=5b$

32. Let $x\in[m,m+1)$, where $m\in I$, then $f(x)=x+[x]=x+m$

$\because\ f'(x)=1>0,\ \forall\ x\in(m,m+1)$

$\therefore\ f(x)$ is strictly increasing.

$\therefore\ f^{-1}(x)$ exists.

$\therefore\quad y=f(x)=x+m\Rightarrow x=y-m$

but $m\le x<m+1$

$\therefore\quad 2m\le x+m<2m+1$

$\therefore\quad 2m\le y<2m+1$

$\therefore\quad [y]=2m$

$\therefore\quad m=\frac{[y]}{2}$

$\therefore\quad x=y-m=y-\frac{[y]}{2}=f^{-1}(y)$

$\therefore\quad f^{-1}(x)=x-\frac{[x]}{2}, \forall\ x\in[2m,2m+1]$, where $m\in I$

Now, $f(x)=x+[x]=\begin{cases}x, & \forall\ x\in[0,1)\\ x+1, & \forall x\in[1,2)\\ x+2, & \forall x\in[2,3)\end{cases}$,

which is discontinuous at every integer point.

Consider $f^{-1}(x)=x-\frac{[x]}{2}$, where $x\in[2m,2m+1)$

$$=\begin{cases}x, & \forall\ x\in[0,1)\\ x-1, & \forall\ x\in[2,3)\\ x-2, & \forall\ x\in[4,5)\end{cases}$$

Clearly, $f^{-1}(x)$ is continuous, $\forall\ x\in[2m,2m+1)$, where $m\in I$

Considering $\lim_{x\to 2m}f^{-1}(x)$, only RHL exists and is equal to $f^{-1}(2m)$.

$\therefore f^{-1}(x)$ is continuous, $\forall\ x\in[2m,2m+1)(m\in I)$ i.e. $f^{-1}(x)$ is continuous in its domain.

33. $\quad g(0)=c$

$\therefore\quad g(x)=x^2+k_1x+c$

$\Rightarrow\quad g(1)=1+k_1+c$

$\because\quad h(0)=b$

$\therefore\quad h(x)=x^2+k_2x+b\Rightarrow h(1)=1+k_2+b$

$f(x)=0$ and $h(x)=0$ have one common root.

$g(1)=h(1)=0$, if $k_1=b$ and $k_2=c$ $\quad(\because 1+b+c=0)$ ...(i)

$\therefore\quad g(x)=x^2+bx+c$

$h(x)=x^2+cx+b$

$$f(x)=\frac{[x]^2+b[x]+c}{[x]^2+c[x]+b}=\frac{([x]-1)([x]-c)}{([x]-1)([x]-b)}$$

$$f(x)=\frac{([x]-c)}{([x]-b)},\ ([x]\ne 1)\Rightarrow x\ne(1,2)$$

Now, if b is not an integer, then denominator cannot be zero and hence domain of $f(x)$ is $R-[1,2)$ if $b\notin I$.

If b is an integer, then domain of $f(x)$ is $R-[1,2)\cup[b,b+1)$ if $b\in I$

$f(x)$ is continuous only iff $b=c=-\frac{1}{2}$ i.e. when $f(x)$ becomes constant because if $b\ne c$, then limit of $f(x)=\frac{([x]-c)}{([x]-b)}$ will not exists at any x in the domain of $f(x)$.

34. We have, $f(x)=\sum_{r=1}^{n}\left(x^{2r}+\frac{1}{x^{2r}}+2\right)$

$$=\sum_{r=1}^{n}x^{2r}+\sum_{r=1}^{n}\frac{1}{x^{2r}}+2n$$

$$=(x^2+x^4+\dots+x^{2n})+\left(\frac{1}{x^2}+\frac{1}{x^4}+\dots+\frac{1}{x^{2n}}\right)+2n$$

$$=\frac{x^2(1-x^{2n})}{(1-x^2)}+\frac{1}{x^2}\frac{\left(1-\frac{1}{x^{2n}}\right)}{1-\frac{1}{x^2}}+2n$$

$$f(x)=\frac{x^2(1-x^{2n})}{(1-x^2)}+\frac{(1-x^{2n})}{(1-x^2)x^{2n}}+2n$$

$$f(x)=\frac{(1-x^{2n})}{(1-x^2)}\left(x^2+\frac{1}{x^{2n}}\right)+2n,\ x\ne\pm 1$$

$$\therefore\ (f(x)-2n)(1-x^2)=(1-x^{2n})\left(x^2+\frac{1}{x^{2n}}\right)$$

Now, consider $g(x) = \lim_{n\to\infty} (f(x) - 2n)x^{-2n-2}(1 - x^2))$

For $x \neq \pm 1, 0 = \lim_{n\to\infty} (1 - x^{2n})\left(x^2 + \frac{1}{x^{2n}}\right)\cdot\frac{1}{x^{2n+2}}, x \neq \pm 1, 0$

$$= \lim_{n\to\infty} \frac{(1 - x^{2n})(x^{2n+2} + 1)}{(x^{2n})(x^{2n+2})}$$

$$= \lim_{n\to\infty} \left(-1 + \frac{1}{x^{2n}}\right)\left(1 + \frac{1}{x^{2n+2}}\right)$$

Now, $g(x) = \begin{bmatrix} -1 & \text{if} & |x| > 1 \\ +\infty & \text{if} & |x| < 1 - \{0\} \\ -1 & \text{if} & x = \pm 1, 0 \end{bmatrix}$

Now, clearly g has non-removable infinite type of discontinuity at $x = 1$ and -1.

Also, g is continuous at $x = 2$.

35. $f(x) = \sqrt{x + 2\sqrt{2x-4}} + \sqrt{x - 2\sqrt{2x-4}}$

Its domain is $[2, \infty)$

Let $t = \sqrt{2x-4}$

$$f(x) = \sqrt{\frac{t^2}{2} + 2 + 2t} + \sqrt{\frac{t^2}{2} + 2 - 2t} = \frac{1}{\sqrt{2}}(t + 2 + |t - 2|)$$

$$= \begin{cases} 2\sqrt{2} & \text{if} \quad t < 2 \\ \sqrt{2}t & \text{if} \quad t \geq 2 \end{cases} = \begin{cases} 2\sqrt{2} & \text{if} \quad x \in [2, 4) \\ 2\sqrt{x-2} & \text{if} \quad x \in [4, \infty) \end{cases}$$

$$f'(x) = \begin{cases} 0 & \text{if} \quad x \in [2, 4) \\ \dfrac{1}{\sqrt{x-2}} & \text{if} \quad x \in [4, \infty) \end{cases},$$

$f(x)$ is not derivable at $x = 4$ and range of $f(x) = [2\sqrt{2}, \infty)$.

36. (a) If lines are parallel for some $t \in (0,1)$, then we have to prove

$$\frac{-f_1(t)}{f_2(t)} = \frac{-g_1(t)}{g_2(t)} \Rightarrow f_1(t)g_2(t) - f_2(t)g_1(t) = 0$$

Let $\phi(t) = f_1(t)g_2(t) - f_2(t)g_1(t)$

$\because$ f_1, f_2, g_1, g_2 are continuous functions

$\therefore \phi(t)$ is continuous function

$$\phi(0) = f_1(0)g_2(0) - f_2(0)g_1(0) = 2 \times 2 - 3 \times 3 = -5$$

and $\quad \phi(1) = f_1(1)g_2(1) - f_2(1)g_1(1) = 4 \times 4 - 2 \times 2 = 12$

$\therefore$ According to Intermediate value theorem $\phi(t) = 0$, for some $t \in (0, 1)$

$\therefore$ Lines are parallel for some $t \in (0, 1)$.

(b) If lines are perpendicular, then

$$\left(\frac{-f_1(t)}{f_2(t)}\right)\left(\frac{-g_1(t)}{g_2(t)}\right) = -1$$

$\Rightarrow \quad f_1(t)g_1(t) + f_2(t)g_2(t) = 0$

Let $\quad h(t) = f_1(t)g_1(t) + f_2(t)g_2(t)$

$\Rightarrow \quad h(0) = 12$ and $h(1) = 16$

(c) If lines make complimentary angles, then

$$\left(\frac{-f_1(t)}{f_2(t)}\right)\left(\frac{-g_1(t)}{g_2(t)}\right) = 1$$

$\Rightarrow \quad f_1(t)g_1(t) - f_2(t)g_2(t) = 0$

Let $k(t) = f_1(t)g_1(t) - f_2(t)g_2(t)$

Here, $k(0) = 0$ and $k(1) = 0$

37. $f(x) = \lim_{n\to\infty} \dfrac{x^{2n} - 2\sin x^{2n}}{x^{2n} + 2\sin x^{2n}}$

$$= \begin{cases} 1 & , \quad |x| > 1 \\ -\dfrac{1}{3} & , \quad 0 \leq |x| < 1 \\ \dfrac{1 - 2\sin 1}{2 + 2\sin 1} & , \quad |x| = 1 \end{cases}$$

$\therefore$Number of points of discontinuity = 2.

(a) $g(x) = \text{sgn}(x^2 - 1) = \begin{cases} 1, & |x| > 1 \\ -1, & |x| < 1 \\ 0, & |x| = 1 \end{cases}$

$\therefore$Number of points of non-differentiability = 2.

(b) $h(x) = \sin^{-1}\dfrac{2x}{1+x^2} = \begin{cases} 2\tan^{-1}x & , \quad -1 \leq x \leq 1 \\ \pi - 2\tan^{-1}x & , \quad x > 1 \\ -\pi - 2\tan^{-1}x & , \quad x < -1 \end{cases}$

Clearly, $h(x)$ is non-differentiable at $x = 1, -1$

$\therefore$ $h(x)$ is non-differentiable at two points.

(c) $k(x) = \cos^{-1}\left(\dfrac{1 - x^2}{1 + x^2}\right) = \begin{cases} 2\tan^{-1}x, & x \geq 0 \\ -2\tan^{-1}x, & x < 0 \end{cases}$

$\therefore$ $k(x)$ is non-differentiable at only one point.

(d) $l(x) = \text{sgn}(|x| - 1) = \begin{cases} 1, & |x| > 1 \\ -1, & |x| < 1 \\ 0, & |x| = 1 \end{cases}$

$\therefore$ Function $l(x)$ is non-differentiable at $x = 1, -1$

$\therefore$ $l(x)$ is non-differentiable at two points.

38. Firstly, we draw the graph of $f(x) = \max.(|3 - x|, 3 - x^3)$

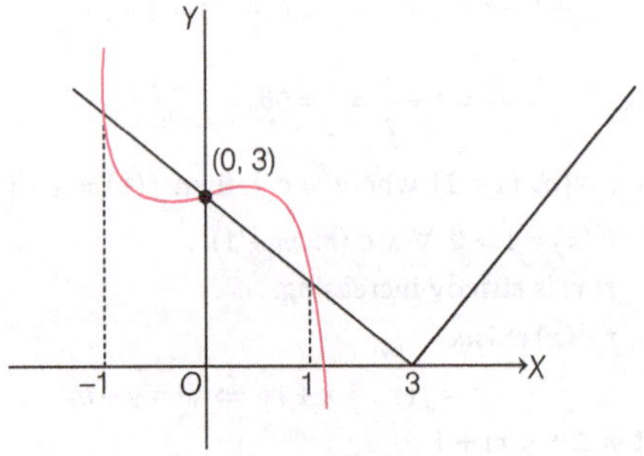

From the graph, clearly we can see that

$f(x)$ is continuous, $\forall\ x \in R$

and $f(x)$ is non-differentiable at $x = -1, 0, 1$ and 3.

39. Here, $f(x) = \dfrac{[x] + 1}{x - [x] + 1}$

$$= \left\{\frac{0 + 1}{x - 0 + 1} \text{ if } 0 \leq x < 1\right.$$

$$= \left\{\frac{1 + 1}{x - 1 + 1}, \quad 1 \leq x < 2\right.$$

$$= \left\{\frac{2 + 1}{x - 2 + 1}, \quad 2 \leq x < \frac{5}{2}\right.$$

$$= \begin{cases} \dfrac{1}{x+1}, & 0 \le x < 1 \\ \dfrac{2}{x}, & 1 \le x < 2 \\ \dfrac{3}{x-1}, & 2 \le x < \dfrac{5}{2} \end{cases}$$

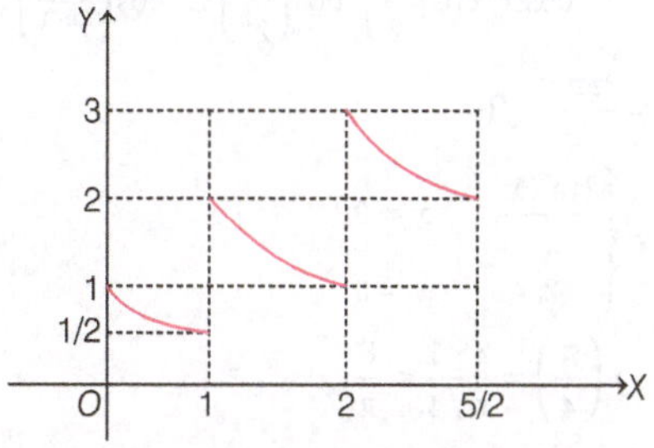

From graph, it is discontinuous at the poitns $x = 1, 2$

$\Rightarrow f(x)$ is discontinuous as well as non-differentiable

Also, $R_f = \left(\dfrac{1}{2}, 3\right] =$ codomain of $f(x)$

$\Rightarrow f(x)$ is subjective

Also, $\lim\limits_{x \to 1^-} f(x) = \lim\limits_{x \to 1^-} \dfrac{1}{x+1} = \lim\limits_{h \to 0}\left(\dfrac{1}{1-h+1}\right) = \dfrac{1}{2}$

and $\lim\limits_{x \to 1^+} f(x) = \lim\limits_{x \to 1^+} \dfrac{2}{x} = \lim\limits_{h \to 0} \dfrac{2}{1+h} = \dfrac{2}{1+0} = 2$

$\therefore$ min. $\left(\lim\limits_{x \to 1^-} f(x), \lim\limits_{x \to 1^+} f(x)\right) = \text{min.}\left(\dfrac{1}{2}, 2\right)$

40. For $x > 2$,

$$f(x) = \int_0^x (1 + |1-t|)\, dt = \int_0^1 (2-t)dt + \int_1^x t \cdot dt = \frac{1}{2}x^2 + 1$$

We have, $f(x) = \begin{cases} \dfrac{1}{2}x^2 + 1, & x > 2 \\ 5x + 1, & x \le 2 \end{cases}$

$\therefore \lim\limits_{x \to 2^+} f(x) = 3$ and $\lim\limits_{x \to 2^-} f(x) = 11$

Hence, $f(x)$ is not continuous at $x = 2$.

Now, $Rf'(2) = \lim\limits_{h \to 0} \dfrac{f(2+h) - f(2)}{h} = \lim\limits_{h \to 0} \dfrac{\frac{1}{2}(2+h)^2 - 10}{h}$

$$= \lim_{h \to 0} \frac{(2+h)^2 - 20}{2h} \to \pm\infty$$

Sol. Q. Nos. (41 to 42)

Given, $f(x+y) = f(x) + f(y) - 2xy + (e^x - 1)(e^y - 1)$

$$f'(x) = \lim_{h \to 0} \frac{f(x+h) - f(x)}{h}$$

$$= \lim_{h \to 0} \frac{f(x) + f(h) - 2xh + (e^x-1)(e^h-1) - f(x)}{h}$$

$$= \lim_{h \to 0}\left(\frac{f(h)}{h} + (e^x - 1)\frac{(e^x-1)}{h}\right) - 2x$$

$$= f'(0) + e^x - 1 - 2x = 1 + e^x - 1 - 2x = e^x - 2x$$

$$f(x) = e^x - x^2 + \lambda$$

$$f(0) = 1 - 0 + 1 \Rightarrow \lambda = -1$$

$$\therefore \quad f(x) = e^x - x^2 - 1$$

41. $\lim\limits_{x \to 0} \dfrac{f(2x) + 4x^2 - 2x}{x^2}$

$$= \lim_{x \to 0} \frac{e^{2x} - 4x^2 - 1 + 4x^2 - 2x}{x^2}$$

$$= \lim_{x \to 0} \frac{e^{2x} - 2x - 1}{x^2}$$

$$= \lim_{x \to 0} \frac{1 + 2x + \frac{4x^2}{2!} + \ldots - 2x - 1}{x^2} = 2$$

42. $g(x) = f(x) + x^2 - 2 = e^x - x^2 - 1 + x^2 - 2$

$g(x) = e^x - 3$

graph $= |g(|x|)|$ is

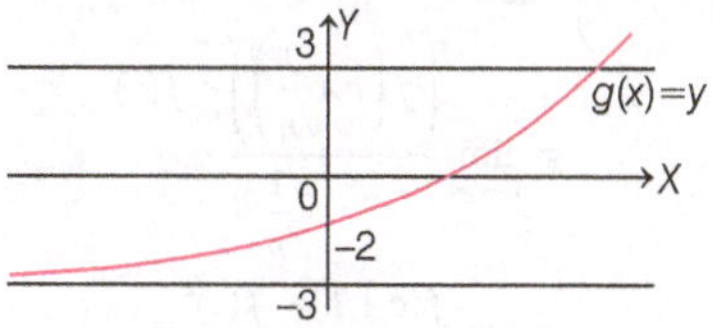

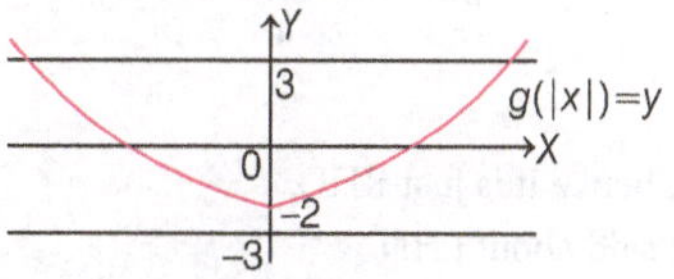

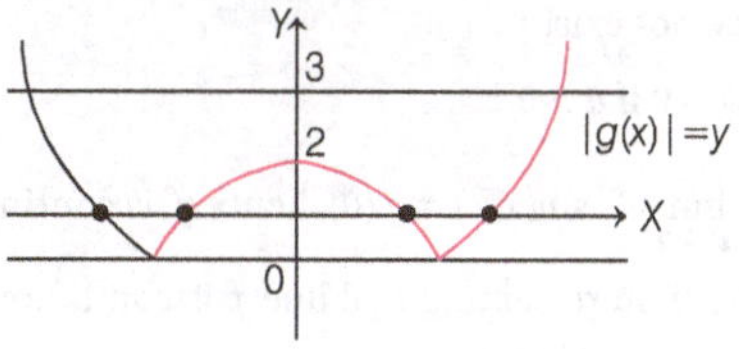

Now, $|g(|x|)| = k$ has four roots

$\therefore \quad k \in (0, 2)$

Sol. Q. Nos. (43 to 44)

Consider $f(x)$ in $[0, 1]$

$f'(t) = 3t^2 - 2t + 1 > 0, \forall\, t \in (0, 1)$

$\Rightarrow f$ is increasing in $(0, 1)$

maximum occurs at $t = x$

and hence $f(x)$ is $\begin{cases} x^3 - x^2 + x + 1, & 0 \le x \le 1 \\ 3 - x, & 1 < x \le 2 \end{cases}$

Again, consider $g(x)$ in $[0, 1)$

$$g(t) = \frac{3}{8}t^4 + \frac{1}{2}t^3 - \frac{3}{2}t^2 + 1$$

$$g'(t) = \frac{3}{2}t^3 + \frac{3}{2}t^2 - 3t = \frac{3}{2}t(t^2 + t - 2)$$

$$= \frac{3}{2}t(t-1)(t+2)$$

$g(t)$ decreases in $[0, 1)$

$\Rightarrow$ maximum occurs, when $t = 0$ and $g(0) = 1$

Again, consider $g(x)$ function in [1, 2]

$$g(t) = \frac{3}{8}t + \frac{1}{32}\sin^2 \pi t + \frac{5}{8}$$

$$g'(t) = \frac{3}{8} + \frac{\pi}{32}\sin(2\pi t) > 0, \forall t \in R$$

$\therefore$ g is an increasing function in [1, 2]

$\Rightarrow$ Minimum occurs, when $t = 1$ and $g(1) = 1$

Hence, $g(x) = \begin{cases} 1, & 0 \le x < 1 \\ 1, & 1 < x \le 2 \end{cases} = 1, \forall x \in [0, 2]$

43. $f(x)$ is continuous but not differentiable at $x = 1$

44. $\lim_{x\to 1^-} fog(x) = f(1)$ and $\lim_{x\to 1^+} gof(x) = 1$,

also $f(1) > 1$

Sol. Q. Nos. (45 to 46)

45. $\lim_{n\to\infty} n\left(f\left(c+\frac{1}{n}\right) - f(c)\right) = a$

$$= \lim_{n\to\infty} \frac{\left(f\left(c+\frac{1}{n}\right)\right) - f(c)}{\frac{1}{n}}$$

$$= \lim_{h\to 0} \frac{f(c+h) - f(c)}{h} = a,$$

where $\frac{1}{n} = h$

$h \to 0$ from RHS, hence it is just RHD.

$\therefore$Nothing can be said about LHD.

$f'(c)$ may or may not exist.

46. $\lim_{x\to\infty} x^{+a}\sin(x^{-c}) = 0$ if $a > 0$

Hence, if $a > 0$, $\lim_{x\to 0} x^{+a}\sin(x^{-c}) = f(0)$, hence f is continuous at $x = 0$ and clearly on remaining real line f is continuous.

Hence, f is continuous if $a > 0$ ...(i)

Now, $f'(0^+) = \lim_{h\to 0} \frac{h^a \sin(h^{-c})}{h} = \lim_{h\to 0} h^{a-1}\sin(h^{-c})$,

which exists if $a - 1 > 0$ i.e. $a > 1$ ...(ii)

Now, $f'(x) = \begin{cases} 0, & x = 0 \\ ax^{a-1}\sin(x^{-c}) + x^a\cos(x^{-c})(cx^{-c-1}), & x \ne 0 \end{cases}$

Clearly, f' is continuous in (0, 1]

But at $x = 0$,

$\lim_{h\to 0} f'(0+h) = \lim_{h\to 0} ah^{a-1}\sin(h^{-c}) + h^a\cos(h^{-c})(-ch^{-c-1})$,

$= \lim_{h\to 0} ah^{a-1}\sin(h^{-c}) + h^{a-c-1}(-c)\cos(h^{-c})$

which exists if $a - c - 1 > 0$

$\Rightarrow$ $a > 1 + c$ ...(iii)

Sol. Q. Nos. (47 to 48)

Let $f: \left(\frac{-\pi}{2}, \frac{\pi}{2}\right) \to R$ such that $f(x)$ is differentiable at $x = 0$

and $f(x) = \begin{cases} \frac{1}{2}(1 + \sec x)\, f\left(\frac{x}{2}\right), & x \ne 0 \\ 2, & x = 0 \end{cases}$

$$f(x) = \frac{(1+\cos x)}{2\cos x} f\left(\frac{x}{2}\right) = \frac{\cos^2\frac{x}{2}}{\cos x} f\left(\frac{x}{2}\right)$$

$$= \frac{\cos^2\left(\frac{x}{2}\right)\cdot\cos^2\left(\frac{x}{2^2}\right)\cdot\cos^2\left(\frac{x}{2^3}\right)\ldots\cos^2\left(\frac{x}{2^n}\right)}{\cos x\cdot\cos\left(\frac{x}{2}\right)\cdot\cos\left(\frac{x}{2^2}\right)\ldots\cos\left(\frac{x}{2^{n-1}}\right)}\cdot f\left(\frac{x}{2^n}\right)$$

$$= \frac{\tan x}{x}\cdot f(0)$$

$$f(x) = \begin{cases} \frac{2\tan x}{x}, & x \ne 0 \\ 2, & x = 0 \end{cases}$$

$$\therefore \quad f\left(\frac{\pi}{4}\right) = \frac{2\times 1}{\pi/4} = \frac{8}{\pi}$$

47. $f'(x) = \frac{2[x\sec^2 x - \tan x]}{x^2}$, $x \ne 0$

$$\Rightarrow f'\left(\frac{\pi}{4}\right) = \frac{2\left(\frac{\pi}{2}-1\right)}{\frac{\pi}{4}\cdot\frac{\pi}{4}} = \frac{32}{\pi^2}\left(\frac{\pi}{2}-1\right) = \frac{16(\pi-2)}{\pi^2}$$

$$\Rightarrow f\left(\frac{\pi}{4}\right) + f'\left(\frac{\pi}{4}\right) = \frac{8(3\pi-4)}{\pi^2}$$

48. $\lim_{x\to 0}\left\{\frac{f(x)-2}{x^2}\right\} + \left[\frac{f(x)-2\cos x}{x^2}\right]$

$$= \lim_{x\to 0}\left\{\frac{\frac{2\tan x}{x} - 2}{x^2}\right\} + \left[\frac{\frac{2\tan x}{x} - 2\cos x}{x^2}\right]$$

$$= \lim_{x\to 0}\left\{\frac{2(\tan x - x)}{x^3}\right\} + \left[\frac{2(\tan x - x\cos x)}{x^3}\right]$$

$$= \lim_{x\to 0}\left\{\frac{2x^3\left(\frac{1}{3} + \frac{2x^2}{15} + \ldots\right)}{x^3}\right\} + \left[\frac{2\left(x + \frac{x^3}{3} + \frac{2x^5}{15} - x\left(1 - \frac{x^2}{2!} + \frac{x^4}{4!}\right)\right)}{x^3}\right]$$

$$= \lim_{x\to 0}\left\{\frac{2}{3} + \frac{4x^2}{15} + \ldots\right\} + \left[\frac{5}{3} + \left(\frac{4}{15} - \frac{1}{4!}\right)x^2 + \ldots\right] = \frac{2}{3} + 1 = \frac{5}{3}$$

Sol. Q. Nos. (49 to 50)

We have, $x = 5t - |t-2|$, $y = -3t + 2|t-1|$, $\forall t \in R$

Case I $-\infty < t < 1$

Now, $x = 5t + (t-2) = 6t - 2$

$$\Rightarrow \quad t = \frac{x+2}{6} \text{ and } y = -3t - 2(t-1) = -5t + 2$$

$$\Rightarrow \quad y = \frac{-5}{6}(x+2) + 2 = \frac{-5x+2}{6}$$

As $t < 1 \Rightarrow \frac{x+2}{6} < 1 \Rightarrow x < 4$

Case II $1 \le t < 2$

Now, $x = 5t + (t-2) = 6t - 2$

$$\Rightarrow \quad t = \frac{x+2}{6} \text{ and } y = -3t + 2(t-1) = -1-2$$

$$\Rightarrow \quad y = -\frac{(x+2)}{6} - 2 = \frac{-x-14}{6}$$

As $1 \le t < 2 \Rightarrow 1 \le \frac{x+2}{6} < 2 \Rightarrow 4 \le x < 10$

Case III $t \ge 2$

Now, $x = 5t - (t-2) - 4t + 2 \Rightarrow t = \left(\frac{x-2}{4}\right)$

and $\quad y = -3t + 2(t-1) = -t - 2$

$$\Rightarrow \quad y = -\left(\frac{x-2}{4}\right) - 2 = \frac{-x-6}{4}$$

As $t \ge 2 \Rightarrow \frac{x-2}{4} \ge 2 \Rightarrow x \ge 10$

$$\therefore \quad y = f(x) = \begin{cases} \frac{-5x+2}{6}, & -\infty < x < 4 \\ \frac{-14-x}{6}, & 4 \le x < 10 \\ \frac{-x-6}{4}, & 10 \le x < \infty \end{cases}$$

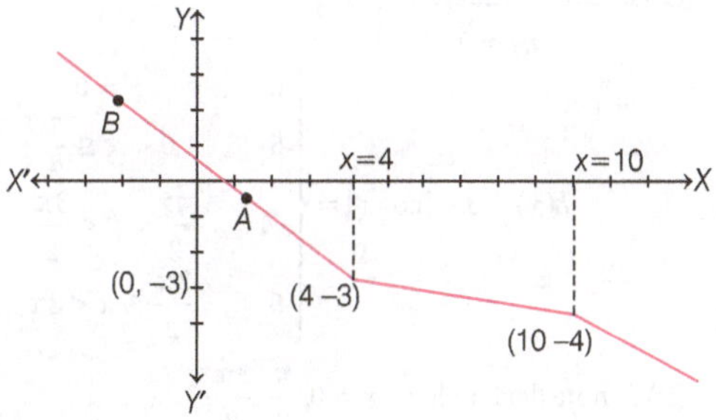

49. Clearly, from above graph,

$f(x)$ is continuous everywhere on R but not derivable at $x = 4$ and $x = 10$.

$\therefore$ Sum of all possible values of $\alpha = 4 + 10 = 14$

50. Clearly, $f'(\pi) = \frac{-5}{6}$

$$\therefore \quad |[f'(\pi)]| = \left|\left[\frac{-5}{6}\right]\right| = 1$$

Sol. Q. Nos. (51 to 52)

According to given information, we must have $f(x)$ a polynomial of degree 4 with leading coefficient 3.

So, $f(x) = 3(x-2)(x-3)(x+1)(x+6) + (x^2+1)$

51. $\left|\lim_{x \to -6} \frac{f(x) - x^2 - 1}{3(x+6)}\right| = \lim_{x \to -6} \frac{3(x-2)(x-3)(x+1)(x+6)}{3(x+6)}$

$$= (-8)(-9)(-5) = |-360| = 360$$

52. We have, $g(x) = \frac{1}{x^2 + 1 - f(x)}$

$$= \frac{1}{(x^2+1) - 3(x-2)(x-3)(x+1)(x+6) - (x^2+1)}$$

$$= \frac{-1}{3(x-2)(x-3)(x+1)(x+6)}, x \ne -6, -1, 2, 3$$

But $x \in \left[\frac{-15}{2}, \frac{5}{2}\right]$, so points of discontinuity are three

i.e. $x = -6, -1, 2$

$\therefore$ Number of points of discontinuity = 3

53. $f(x) = \text{cosec } 2x + \text{cosec } 2^2 x + \ldots + \text{cosec } 2^n x$

Now, $\text{cosec } 2x = \frac{1}{\sin 2x} = \frac{\sin(2x - x)}{\sin x \sin 2x} = \cot x - \cot 2x$

Perpendicularly, $\text{cosec } 2^2 x = \cot 2x - \cot 2^2 x$

$$\text{cosec} 2^3 x = \cot 2^2 x - \cot 2^3 x$$

$$\vdots$$

$$\text{cosec } 2^n x = \cot 2^{n-1} x - \cot 2^n x$$

$$\therefore \quad f(x) = \cot x - \cot 2^n x$$

$$\therefore \quad g(x) = f(x) + \cot 2^n x = \cot x$$

Now, $H(0+h) = \lim_{h \to 0} ((\cos h)^{\coth} + (\sec h)^{\text{cosech}})$

$$= e^{\lim_{h \to 0} \coth(\cos h - 1)} + e^{\lim_{h \to 0} \text{cosech}\,(\sec h - 1)}$$

$$= 1 + 1 = 2 \quad \ldots \text{(i)}$$

$$H(0-h) = \lim_{h \to 0} \frac{e^{-h} + e^h - 2\cos h}{h \sin h}$$

$$= \lim_{h \to 0} \left\{\frac{e^h + e^{-h} - 2}{h^2} + \frac{2(1 - \cos h)}{h^2}\right\} = 2 \quad \ldots \text{(ii)}$$

From Eqs. (i) and (ii), we get

$H(x)$ will be continuous if $p = 2$.

54. $\lim_{x \to 1} \frac{e^{2f(x)} - 2e^{f(x)+1} + e^2 \cos(x-1)}{\sec^2(x-1) - 1} = \frac{7}{2} e^2$

Here, limit exists.

Therefore, as $x \to 1$, Numerator $\to 0$

[$\because$ denominator also tends to zero]

$$e^{2f(1)} - 2 \cdot e \cdot e^{f(1)} + e^2 = 0$$

$$(e^{f(1)} - e)^2 = 0 \Rightarrow e^{f(1)} = e \Rightarrow f(1) = 1$$

$$\lim_{x \to 1} \frac{e^{2f(x)} - 2 \cdot e \cdot e^{f(x)} + e^2 - e^2(1 - \cos(x-1))}{\tan^2(x-1)} = \frac{7}{2} e^2$$

$$\lim_{x \to 1} \frac{(e^{f(x)} - e)^2 - e^2(1 - \cos(x-1))}{\frac{\tan^2(x-1)}{(x-1)^2}(x-1)^2} = \frac{7}{2} e^2$$

$$\lim_{x \to 1} \left(\frac{e^2(e^{f(x)-1} - 1)^2}{(f(x)-1)^2} \cdot \left(\frac{f(x)-1}{x-1}\right)^2 - e^2 \frac{(1 - \cos(x-1))}{(x-1)^2}\right) = \frac{7}{2} e^2$$

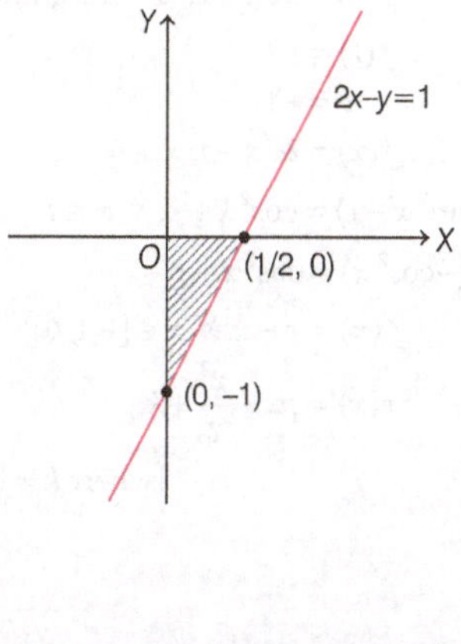

$$e^2 \cdot 1 \cdot (f'(1))^2 - e^2 \cdot \frac{1}{2} = \frac{7}{2}e^2$$

$$(f'(1))^2 = 4 \Rightarrow f'(1) = \pm 2$$

$$\Rightarrow \quad f'(1) = 2 \qquad [\because f'(x) > 0]$$

Now, equation of tangent at (1, $f(1)$) is

$$y - 1 = 2(x-1)$$

$$2x - y = 1$$

$$\therefore \quad \Delta = \frac{1}{2} \times \frac{1}{2} \times 1 = \frac{1}{4} \Rightarrow \frac{1}{\Delta} = 4$$

55. $f\left(\frac{\pi}{2}\right) = \frac{1}{2} \lim_{\alpha \to 0}\left[\frac{p\sin\alpha}{\alpha}\right] = \left(\frac{p-1}{2}\right)$

$$\left[\begin{array}{l}\because \frac{\sin\alpha}{\alpha} \text{ is little less than 1 as } \alpha \to 0 \\ \therefore p - 1 < \frac{p\sin\alpha}{\alpha} < p, \text{ where } p \in I^+\end{array}\right]$$

$$\text{LHL at } x = \frac{\pi}{2} = \lim_{x \to \frac{\pi}{2}^-} \frac{1 - \sin^3 x}{3\cos^2 x}$$

$$= \lim_{x \to \frac{\pi}{2}^-} \frac{(1-\sin x)(1 + \sin^2 x + \sin x)}{3(1-\sin x)(1+\sin x)} = \frac{1}{2}$$

$$\text{RHL at } x = \frac{\pi}{2} = \lim_{x \to \frac{\pi}{2}^+} \left\{\lim_{t \to 0}\left[\frac{q\tan t}{t}\right]\frac{1-\sin x}{(\pi - 2x)^2}\right\}$$

$$\left[\begin{array}{l}\because \frac{\tan t}{t} \text{ is little greater than 1 as } t \to 0 \\ \therefore q < \frac{q\tan t}{t} < q+1, \text{ for } q \in I^+\end{array}\right]$$

$$= \lim_{x \to \frac{\pi}{2}^+} \frac{q(1-\sin x)}{(\pi - 2x)^2} = \lim_{h \to 0} \frac{q(1-\cos h)}{4h^2} = \frac{q}{8}\left(x = \frac{\pi}{2} + h\right)$$

$\because$ Function is continuous.

$$\therefore \quad \text{LHL} = \text{RHL} = f\left(\frac{\pi}{2}\right) \Rightarrow \frac{q}{8} = \frac{1}{2} \Rightarrow q = 4$$

$$\frac{p-1}{2} = \frac{1}{2} \Rightarrow p = 2$$

$$\therefore \quad p + q = 6$$

56. $f'(x^2) = \frac{1}{x}$

$$\Rightarrow \quad f'(x) = \frac{1}{\sqrt{x}}, x > 0$$

$$\Rightarrow \quad f(x) = 2\sqrt{x} + c, \ (c = \text{integration constant})$$

$$\because \quad f(1) = 1$$

$$\Rightarrow \quad c = -1$$

$$\therefore \quad f(x) = 2\sqrt{x} - 1, \ x > 0$$

and $g'(\sin^2 x - 1) = \cos^2 x + p, \ \forall \ x \in R$

$$\Rightarrow \quad g'(-\cos^2 x) = \cos^2 x + p$$

$$\Rightarrow \quad g'(x) = p - x, \ \forall \ x \in [-1, 0]$$

$$\Rightarrow \quad g(x) = px - \frac{x^2}{2} + k,$$

[where k = integration constant]

$$\because \quad g(-1) = 0 \Rightarrow 0 = -p - \frac{1}{2} + k$$

$$\Rightarrow \quad k = \frac{1}{2} + p$$

$$\therefore \quad g(x) = px - \frac{x^2}{2} + \frac{1}{2} + p$$

$$\therefore \quad h(x) = \begin{cases} 2\sqrt{x} - 1, & x > 0 \\ px - \frac{x^2}{2} + \frac{1}{2} + p, & -1 \le x \le 0 \end{cases}$$

At $x = 0$, LHL = RHL = $f(0)$

$$\Rightarrow \quad -1 = \frac{1}{2} + p \Rightarrow p = \frac{-3}{2}$$

Hence, $2p = -3$

$\therefore$ Absolute value of $2p$ is 3.

57. $f(x) = \cot^2 x - \text{cosec}^2 x$

Clearly, $f(x)$ is discontinuous at $x = \pi$

$$n_1 = 1$$

$$g(x) = \frac{\pi}{2} + \sin^{-1} x$$

$\therefore$ $g(x)$ is differentiable in $(-1, 1)$

$$n_2 = 0$$

$$h(x) = 5 + [\cos x] = \begin{cases} 6, & x = 0 \\ 5, & 0 < x \le \frac{\pi}{2} \\ +4, & \frac{\pi}{2} < x < \frac{3\pi}{2} \\ 5, & \frac{3\pi}{2} \le x < 2\pi \end{cases}$$

$\Rightarrow$ $h(x)$ is non-derivable at $x = 0, \frac{\pi}{2}, \frac{3\pi}{2}$

$$\therefore \quad n_3 = 3$$

Hence, $n_1 + n_2 + n_3 = 1 + 0 + 3 = 4$

58. Let $P(x) = Ax^3 + Bx^2 + Cx + D$

So, $P'(x) = 3Ax^2 + 2Bx + C$

Now, on putting above result in

$$P(x) - 2P'(x) = 3x^3 - 27x^2 + 38x + 1$$

We have, $A = 3, B = -9, C = 2, D = 5$

$$\therefore \quad P(x) = (3x^3 - 9x^2 + 2x + 5)$$

$$P'(x) = 9x^2 - 18x + 2$$

$$P''(x) = 18x - 18$$

$$\text{So, } f(x) = \begin{cases} 3x, & x \ne \frac{\pi}{2} \\ \sin^{-1}(ab) + \cos^{-1}(a + b - 3ab), & x = \frac{\pi}{2} \end{cases}$$

As $f(x)$ is continuous at $x = \frac{\pi}{2}$,

$$\text{so } \frac{3\pi}{2} = (\sin^{-1}(ab) + \cos^{-1}(a + b - 3ab))$$

$\therefore$ $ab = 1$ and $a + b - 3ab = -1$

$$\therefore \quad a = 1, \ b = 1$$

Hence, $(a + b) = 2$

59. Let $g(x) = |1-x|, -1 \le x \le 3$

$$[x] = -1, \quad -1 \le x < 0$$
$$= 0, \quad 0 \le x < 1$$
$$= 1, \quad 1 \le x < 2$$
$$= 2, \quad 2 \le x < 3$$

Now, we will draw the graph of $f(x)$ with the help of graph transformation, we can draw $y = g(x) \pm C$ from the graph

$$y = g(x)$$

For $-1 \le x < 0, [x] = -1$

$\therefore \quad f(x) = -1 + |1-x|$

Hence, the graph of $f(x)$ is obtained by shifting downward the AB portion of the curve by 1 unit.

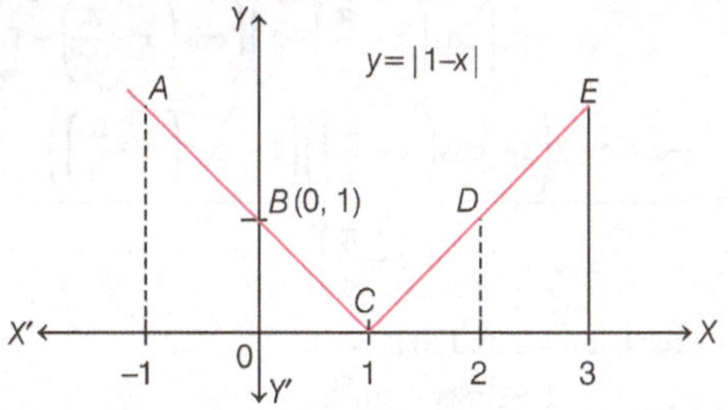

But there is a blank dot at the right end due to inequality at $x = 0$.

For $0 \le x < 1, [x] = 0$

$\therefore \quad f(x) = |1-x|$

i.e. The graph of $f(x)$ is same as that of y_1 which is BC for $1 \le x < 2, [x] = 1$

$\therefore f(x) = 1 + |1-x|$, which is obtained by the upward shifting of $|1-x|$ i.e. portion CD through 1 unit.

For $2 \le x < 3, [x] = 2$

$\therefore \quad f(x) = 2 + |1-x|$, which can be obtained by shifting the DE portion by 2 units lastly.

$$f(3) = [3] + |1-3| = 5$$

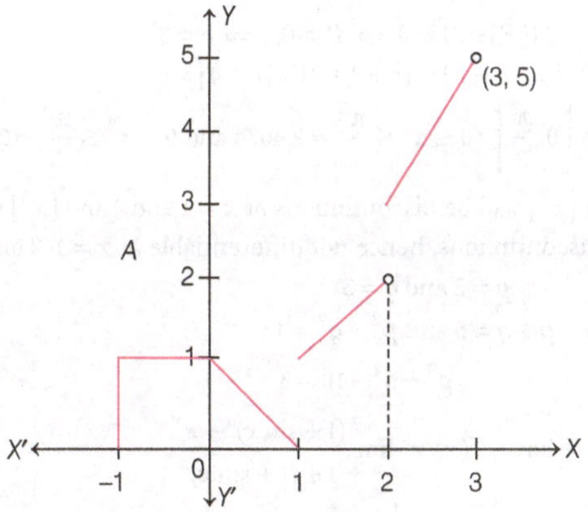

$\therefore$Number of points of non-differentiability = 3

60. We have, $2(f(x))^2 - f''(x)f(x) + (f'(x))^2 = 0$

$$\Rightarrow \quad \frac{f''(x)f(x) - (f'(x))^2}{(f(x))^2} = 2$$

$$\Rightarrow \quad \frac{d}{dx}\left(\frac{f'(x)}{f(x)}\right) = 2$$

$$\Rightarrow \quad \frac{f'(x)}{f(x)} = 2x + a \Rightarrow \frac{df(x)}{f(x)} = (2x+a)dx$$

$$\Rightarrow \quad \ln|f(x)| = x^2 + ax + b$$

$$\Rightarrow \quad |f(x)| = e^{x^2+ax+b}$$

$$f(0) = 1 \Rightarrow b = 0$$
$$f(1) < e \Rightarrow a < 0$$

Hence, $g(x) = ||x|^2 + a|x| + b|$ is non-differentiable at 3 points.

61. $f(0)$ can be taken in 2 ways $\begin{cases} f(0) = 1 \\ f(0) = -1 \end{cases}$

Perpendicularly at $x = 1, 2, 3, 4$ 3 possibilities think!

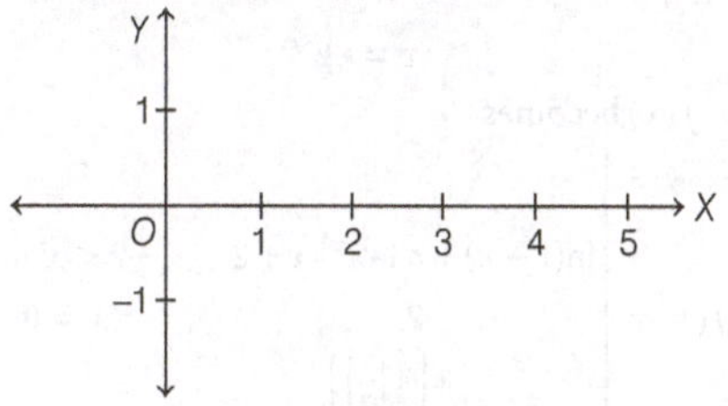

and at $x = 5$ only one possibilities.

$\therefore$ Total number of functions $= 2 \times 3^4 \times 1 = 162$

$$\lambda = 162$$

Sum of digits at odd places $= 1 + 2 = 3$

62. For $-1 < x < 1$,

$$\frac{4x^2}{x^4+1} = \begin{cases} 0, & \text{when } x = 0 \\ \dfrac{4}{x^2 + \dfrac{1}{x^2}}, & \text{when } x \ne 0 \end{cases}$$

$$\therefore \quad \frac{4x^2}{x^4+1} \le 2 \qquad \left[\because x^2 + \frac{1}{x^2} \ge 2\right]$$

Sign of equality holds at $x = \pm 1$ but $x \in (-1, 1) - \{0\}$

$$\therefore \quad \frac{4x^2}{x^4+1} < 2$$

$$\Rightarrow \quad \left[\frac{4x^2}{x^4+1}\right] = 1$$

as $x \to 1$ from LHS

$$\text{Now, } \lim_{x \to 1^-} \frac{\ln(1 - ax + a)}{e^{bx} - e^b} = \lim_{x \to 1^-} \frac{\ln(1 + a(1-x))a(1-x)}{e^b \dfrac{(e^{b(x-1)} - 1)}{b(x-1)} b(x-1)a(1-x)}$$

$$= -\frac{a}{be^b}$$

$$\text{Again, } \lim_{x \to 1^+} \frac{(\tan bx - \tan b)(1 + \cos 2bx)}{2(x-1)}$$

$$= \lim_{x \to 1^+} \frac{\tan(b(x-1))(1 + \tan bx \tan b) \cdot 2\cos^2 bx}{2b(x-1)} \cdot b$$

$$= (1 + \tan^2 b)(\cos^2 b) \cdot b = b$$

$\because f(x)$ is continuous at $x = 1$

$$\therefore \quad \frac{-a}{be^b} = b = \ln 2 \Rightarrow b = \ln 2$$

and $\frac{-a}{be^b} = \ln 2 \Rightarrow -a = (\ln 2)^2 \cdot 2$

$\Rightarrow \quad a = -2(\ln 2)^2$

$a + 2b^2 = -2(\ln 2)^2 + 2(\ln 2)^2 = 0$

$\therefore \quad 1 + a + 2b^2 = 1$

63. Since, $f(x)$ is derivable in $(-2, 2)$

Derivability of $f(x)$ at $x = -1$ is possible only when $b - 2 = 0$

$\Rightarrow \quad b = 2$

$[\because |x+1| \text{ is non-derivable at } x = -1]$

Similarly, derivability of $f(x)$ at $x = 1$ is possible only when $c + 2 = 0$

$\Rightarrow \quad c = -2$

Now, $f(x)$ becomes

$$f(x) = \begin{cases} \ln(1-x) + a\tan^{-1}x + 2 &, \quad -2 < x < 0 \\ 2 &, \quad x = 0 \\ \dfrac{e^{2x} - e^{\ln\left(4\left\{\frac{x}{2}\right\}\right)} - 1}{x^2} &, \quad 0 < x < 2 \end{cases}$$

$$f(x) = \begin{cases} \ln(1-x) + a\tan^{-1}x + 2, & -2 < x < 0 \\ 2, & x = 0 \\ \dfrac{e^{2x} - 2x - 1}{x^2}, & 0 < x < 2 \end{cases}$$

$$\left[\because 0 < \frac{x}{2} < 1 \Rightarrow \left\{\frac{x}{2}\right\} = \frac{x}{2}\right]$$

$$= \lim_{x \to 0^+} \frac{e^{2x} - 2x - 1}{4x^2} \cdot 4 = \frac{1}{2} \times 4 = 2$$

$$\therefore \quad \lim_{x \to 0^-} \ln(1-x) + a\tan^{-1}x + 2 = 2$$

$$f'(0^-) = \lim_{h \to 0} \frac{\ln(1+h) + a\tan^{-1}(-h) + 2 - 2}{-h}$$

$$\lim_{h \to 0} \frac{\ln(1+h)}{-h} + \frac{a\tan^{-1}(-h)}{-h} = -1 + a$$

$$f'(0^+) = \lim_{h \to 0} \frac{\frac{e^{2h} - 2h - 1}{h^2} - 2}{h}$$

$$= \lim_{h \to 0} \frac{e^{2h} - 2h - 1 - 2h^2}{h^3} = \frac{4}{3}$$

$$\therefore \quad a - 1 = \frac{4}{3} \Rightarrow a = \frac{7}{3}$$

$$\Rightarrow \quad 9a^2 + b^2 + c^2 = 9 \cdot \frac{49}{9} + 4 + 4 = \frac{57}{19} = 3$$

$$\therefore \quad \frac{9a^2 + b^2 + c^2}{19} = \frac{57}{19} = 3$$

64. $$\text{RHL} = \lim_{x \to \frac{\pi^+}{4}} \frac{e^{[3\cot x - 1]} + \cos\left(2x - \frac{\pi}{2}\right) - a + [\cos x - \sin x]}{\left(x - \frac{\pi}{4}\right)^2}$$

$\cot x < 1$ in $x \in \frac{\pi^+}{4} \Rightarrow e^{[3\cot x - 1]} = e$ in $x \in \frac{\pi^+}{4}$

Also, $\cos x < \sin x$ in $x \in \frac{\pi^+}{4}$

$\Rightarrow \quad [\cos x - \sin x] = -1$ in $x \in \frac{\pi^+}{4}$

$$\text{Also, } \cos\left(2x - \frac{\pi}{2}\right) = 2\cos^2\left(x - \frac{\pi}{4}\right) - 1$$

$$= 2\left(\cos\left(x - \frac{\pi}{4}\right) - 1\right)\left(\cos\left(x - \frac{\pi}{4}\right) + 1\right) + 1$$

$$\therefore \quad \lim_{x \to \frac{\pi^+}{4}} \frac{-a + e - 2\left(1 - \cos\left(x - \frac{\pi}{4}\right)\right)\left(1 + \cos\left(x - \frac{\pi}{4}\right)\right)}{\left(x - \frac{\pi}{4}\right)^2}$$

If limit exists, if $a = e$ and RHL $= -2$

For LHL, let $y = \dfrac{1 + \sin 2x + \sin^2 2x}{1 + \sin 2x}$

$$y = 1 + \frac{\sin^2 2x}{1 + \sin 2x} = 1 + \frac{1}{\frac{1}{\sin 2x} + \frac{1}{\sin 2x}}$$

$$< 1 + \frac{1}{2} = \frac{3}{2}, \quad \frac{1}{y} > \frac{2}{3}$$

$$\lim_{x \to -\frac{\pi}{4}} \left[\frac{2}{3} - \frac{1 + \sin 2x}{1 + \sin x + \sin^2 2x}\right] = -1$$

$\therefore \quad -b = -2 \Rightarrow b = 2$

Also, $f\left(\frac{\pi}{4}\right) = P([P] - 2) - 2 = -2$

$P([P] - 2) = 0 \Rightarrow P = 0, 2 \Rightarrow n = 2$

$\therefore \quad [a + b + n] = [e + 2 + 2] = [e + 4] = 6$

65. $\ln\left[0, \frac{\pi}{2}\right]$, $0 \le x^2 \le \frac{\pi^2}{4} \approx 2.4674$ and $0 \le x^3 \le \frac{\pi^3}{8} \approx 3.8758$

$\therefore [x^2]$ will be discontinuous at $x = 1$ and 2 and $[x^3]$ will be discontinuous, hence not differentiable at $x = 1, 2$ and 3.

$\therefore \quad p = 2$ and $q = 3$

$\therefore \quad p + q = 5$ and $p^2 + q^2 = 13$

$\therefore \quad p^2 + q^2 - 10 = 3$

66. We have, $f(x) = \lim_{n \to \infty} \dfrac{(1 + \sin x)^n + e^x}{1 + (1 + \sin x)^n}$

$$= \begin{cases} e^x, & x \in ((2n-1)\pi, 2n\pi) \\ \dfrac{1 + e^x}{2}, & x = n\pi \\ 1, & x \in (2n\pi, (2n+1)\pi) \end{cases}, \text{ where } n \in I$$

$\because$ When $x \in (2n\pi, (2n+1)\pi)$

$\Rightarrow$ $0 < \sin x \le 1$ and $x \in ((2n-1)\pi, 2n\pi) \Rightarrow -1 \le \sin x < 0$

So,
$$f(x) = \begin{cases} \dfrac{1+e^{-2\pi}}{2}, & x = -2\pi \\ 1, & -2\pi < x < -\pi \\ \dfrac{1+e^{-\pi}}{2}, & x = -\pi \\ e^x, & -\pi < x < 0 \\ 1, & x = 0 \\ 1, & 0 < x < \pi \\ \dfrac{1+e^x}{2}, & x = \pi \\ e^x, & \pi < x < 2\pi \\ \dfrac{1+e^x}{2}, & x = 2\pi \end{cases}$$

Clearly, number of points of discontinuity of $f(x)$ in $[-2\pi, 2\pi] = 4$

i.e. $x = -2\pi, -\pi, \pi, 2\pi$

Note The function $f(x)$ is continuous at $x = 0$.

67. $\lim_{h\to 0} f(0+h) = \lim_{h\to 0} \dfrac{a^h - 1}{\sinh \cdot h^n}\left[\dfrac{b\sin h - \sin bh}{\cos h - \cos bh}\right]^n$

$$= \lim_{h\to 0} \frac{a^h-1}{h}\cdot\frac{h}{\sin h}\left[\left(\frac{b\sin(h)-\sin(bh)}{h\cdot h^2}\right)\cdot\frac{h^2}{\cos h - \cos bh}\right]^n$$

$= \ln a \cdot l^n$

Using expansion here to get $\ln(a)\cdot\left(\dfrac{b}{3}\right)^n = 1,$

where $l = \lim_{h\to 0}\dfrac{b\sin h - \sin bh}{h^3}\cdot\dfrac{h^2}{\cos h - \cos bh} = \dfrac{l_1}{l_2},$

and $l_1 = \dfrac{b\sin h - \sin bh}{h^3}$ and $l_2 = \dfrac{\cos h - \cos bh}{h^2}$

$$= \lim_{h\to 0}\left[\frac{b(\sin h - h) - (\sin bh - bh)}{h^3}\right]\left[b^2\left(\frac{1-\cos bh}{b^2h^2}\right) - \left(\frac{1-\cosh}{h^2}\right)\right]^{-1}$$

$$= \lim_{h\to 0}\left[b\left(\frac{\sin h - h}{h^3}\right) - \left(\frac{\sin bh - bh}{b^3h^3}\right)b^3\right]\left[\left(\frac{b^2}{2} - \frac{1}{2}\right)\right]^{-1}$$

$$= \lim_{h\to 0}\left[b\left(-\frac{1}{6}\right) - b^3\left(-\frac{1}{6}\right)\right]\cdot\frac{2}{(b^2-1)}\left[\lim_{h\to 0}\frac{\sin x - x}{x^3} = -\frac{1}{6}\right]$$

$$= \lim_{h\to 0}\frac{b(b^2-1)}{6}\cdot\frac{2}{(b^2-1)} = \left(\frac{b}{3}\right),$$

hence $f(0^+) = \ln a \cdot \left(\dfrac{b}{3}\right)^n$

$$f(0^-) = \lim_{h\to 0} f(0-h) = \lim_{h\to 0}\frac{a^{-h}\sin(-bh) - b^{-h}\sin(-ah)}{\tan(-bh) - \tan(-ah)}$$

(multiply D' and N' by $a^h - b^h$)

$$= \lim_{h\to 0}\frac{a^h\sin ah - b^h \sin bh}{a^n\cdot b^h[\tan ah - \tan bh]}$$

$$= \lim_{h\to 0}\frac{ah\cdot\dfrac{a^h\sin(ah)}{ah} - \dfrac{b^h\sin(bh)}{bh}\cdot bh}{ah\cdot\dfrac{\tan(ah)}{ah} - bh\cdot\dfrac{\tan(bh)}{bh}}$$

$$f(0^-) = \lim_{h\to 0}\frac{(a-b)}{(a-b)} = 1$$

$\because$ $f(0^+) = \ln a\left(\dfrac{b}{3}\right)^n \Rightarrow x = 1, y = 3,\ z = 3$

$f(0^-) = 1 = x$

$\therefore$ $5x + 7y + 9z = 5 + 21 + 27 = 53$

68. $l = \lim_{x\to 0}\dfrac{2x + x\cos x - 3\sin x}{x^4\sin x}$

$$= \lim_{x\to 0}\frac{2x + x\cos x - 3\sin x}{x^4}$$

$$= \lim_{t\to 0}\frac{6t + 3t\cos 3t + 3\sin 3t}{243t^5}\ (\text{put } x = 3t)$$

$$= \frac{2t + t(4\cos^3 t - 3\cos t) - (3\sin t - 4\sin^3 t)}{81\cdot t^5}\quad(\text{cancelling by 3})$$

$$= \frac{2t + t\cos t(1 - 4\sin^2 t) - (3\sin t - 4\sin^3 t)}{81\cdot t^5}$$

$$= \frac{(2t + t\cos t - 3\sin t)}{81t^5} + \frac{4\sin^2 t(\sin t - t\cos t)}{81t^5}$$

$$l = \frac{l}{81} + \frac{4}{81}\lim_{t\to 0}\frac{\sin^2 t}{t^2}\lim_{t\to 0}\frac{\cos t(\tan t - t)}{t^3}$$

$$l = \frac{l}{81} + \frac{4}{81}\lim_{t\to 0}\frac{\tan t - t}{t^3} = \frac{l}{81} + \frac{4}{81}\cdot\frac{1}{3}$$

[**Note** l can be checked using expansion of $\sin x$ and $\cos x$ as]

$$\frac{80l}{81} = \frac{4}{81\cdot 3} \Rightarrow l = \frac{1}{60}$$

$\Rightarrow$ $f(0) = \dfrac{1}{60} \Rightarrow 3f(6) = 0.05$

Alternate Solution

$\cos x = 1 - \dfrac{x^2}{2!} + \dfrac{x^4}{4!}\ldots$ and $\sin x = x - \dfrac{x^3}{3!} + \dfrac{x^5}{5!}\ldots$

$$\lim_{x\to 0}\frac{x(2 + \cos x) - 3\sin x}{x^5}$$

$$= \frac{x\left[2 + 1 - \dfrac{x^2}{2!} + \dfrac{x^4}{4!} - \dfrac{x^6}{6!} + \ldots\right] - 3\left[x - \dfrac{x^3}{3!} + \dfrac{x^5}{5!}\ldots\right]}{x^5}$$

$$= \frac{1}{4!} - \frac{3}{5!} = \frac{1}{24} - \frac{3}{120} = \frac{5-3}{120} = \frac{1}{60}$$

$\therefore 3f(0) = \dfrac{1}{20} = 0.05$

69. $f(x) = \ln x + x + 1$

$$g(2^-) = e^l \text{ where } l = \lim_{x\to 2^-}\frac{\ln(3e)}{\tan(x-2)}\left(1 + \frac{15(x-2)}{x^2+1} - 1\right)$$

$$= \ln(3e)\lim_{x\to 2^-}\frac{15(x-2)}{\tan(x-2)}\left(\frac{1}{1+x^2}\right) l - 3\ln(3e) - \ln(27e^3)$$

$$g(2^-) = e^{\ln(27e^3)} = 27e^3 = g(2)$$

Again, $g(2^+) = \lim_{x \to 2^+} \dfrac{\lambda(e^{f(2^+)} - 2e^3)}{\left(\dfrac{\sin(x-2)}{x-2}\right)(x-2)}$

$$= \lim_{h \to 0} \lambda \left[\frac{e^{\ln(1+h)+3+h} - 2e^3}{h}\right]$$

$$= \lambda\left[e^3\left\{\frac{e^{\ln h(2+h)} - 2}{h}\right\}\right] - \lambda e^3\left(\frac{(2+h)e^h - 2)}{h}\right)$$

$$= \lambda e^3\left[\lim_{h \to 0} \frac{2(e^h - 1)}{h} + e^h\right]$$

For continuous $3e^3\lambda = 27e^3$

$\Rightarrow \quad 3\lambda = 27 \Rightarrow \lambda = 9$

$\Rightarrow \quad \lambda^2 = 81$

70. As $-1 + ax - x^2 < 0, \forall x \in R$

$\Rightarrow \quad x^2 - ax + 1 > 0, \forall x \in R$

$\Rightarrow \quad a^2 - 4 < 0 \Rightarrow -2 < a < 2$

So, number of integral values of $\alpha = 3$

$\therefore \quad g(x) = [3 + 4\alpha \sin x] = [3 + 12\sin x] = 3 + [12\sin x]$

So, in $(0, \pi)$, number of points of discontinuity

$$= (2 \times 11) + 1 = 23$$

Hence, number of points of non-derivability = 23

71. $f(x) - f(y) \geq \ln x - \ln y + x - y$ ...(i)

$x \to y$ and $y \to x$

$f(y) - f(x) \geq \ln y - \ln x + y - x$

i.e. $f(x) - f(y) \leq \ln x - \ln y + x - y$ ...(ii)

From Eqs. (i) and (ii), we get

$f(x) - f(y) = \ln x - \ln y + x - y$ ...(iii)

$\therefore \quad f(x) - f(y) = (\ln x + x) - (\ln y + y)$

Hence, $f(x) = \ln x + x$

Alternate Solution

$f'(x) = \lim_{h \to 0} \dfrac{f(x+h) - f(x)}{h}$ $\quad [x \to x+h, y \to x \text{ in Eq. (iii)}]$

$$= \lim_{h \to 0} \frac{\ln(x+h) - \ln x + h}{h}$$

$$= \lim_{h \to 0} \frac{\ln\left(\dfrac{x+h}{x}\right) + h}{h}$$

$$= \lim_{h \to 0}\left[1 + \frac{\ln(1 + (h/x))}{x(h/x)}\right]$$

$$= 1 + \frac{1}{x}\lim_{t \to 0} \frac{\ln(1+t)}{t}$$

$$f'(x) = 1 + \frac{1}{x}$$

$$g(x) = \text{derivative of } f'(x) = -\frac{1}{x^2}$$

$$g'(x) = \frac{2}{x^3}$$

$$g'\left(\frac{1}{3}\right) = \frac{2}{\left(\dfrac{1}{3}\right)^3} = 27 \times 2 = 54$$

72. Given, $f(x) = \begin{cases} x^2 + x, & x \leq 1 \\ x^2 - ax, & x > 1 \end{cases}$, $g(x) = \begin{cases} x^2 - cx, & x \leq 2 \\ x^2 - 4x, & x > 2 \end{cases}$

and $h(x) = f(x) \cdot g(x), x \in R$

Now, define $h(x)$ in the neighbourhood of $x = 1$ and $x = 2$.

$$h(x) = f(x) \cdot g(x) = \begin{cases} (x^2 + x)(x^2 - cx), & x \leq 1 \\ (x^2 - ax)(x^2 - cx), & x > 1 \end{cases}$$

and $$h(x) = \begin{cases} (x^2 - ax)(x^2 - cx), & x \leq 2 \\ (x^2 - ax)(x^2 - 4x), & x > 2 \end{cases}$$

Note $f(x)$ is discontinuous, $\forall a \in \{1, 2, 3, 4, 5, 6\}$

$g(x)$ is discontinuous if $c \neq 4$.

N_1 : given both $f(x)$ and $g(x)$ are discontinuous.

Hence, $a \to 6$ ways

$\therefore \quad N_1 = 6 \times 5 = 30$

$c \to 5$ ways

N_2 : since $g(x)$ is discontinuous.

$\therefore \quad c \neq 4$

Now, $h(x)$ is continuous at $x = 1$

$$h(1^-) = h(1^+)$$

$\Rightarrow \quad 2(1-c) = (1-a)(1-c) \Rightarrow (1-c)(1+a) = 0$

$\therefore \quad 1 - c = 0 \; (a \neq -1)$ (given)

$\Rightarrow \quad c = 1$

Also, given $h(x)$ is discontinuous at $x = 2$

$$(4-2a)(4-2c) \neq (4-2a)(-4)$$

$$(4-2a)(8-2c) \neq 0$$

$$(2-a)(4-c) \neq 0$$

Since, $c = 1$

$\therefore \quad a \neq 2$

$a \to 5$ ways

$c \to 1$ way

$\therefore \quad N_2 = 5$

Now, N_3 : given $h(x)$ is discontinuous at $x = 1$

$\Rightarrow \quad (1-c)(a+1) \neq 0$

$\therefore \quad c \neq 1$

and given $h(x)$ is continuous at $x = 2$

$\Rightarrow \quad (2-a)(4-c) = 0$

If $c = 4$, then $a \to 6$ ways

If $a = 2$, then $c \to 4$ ways

Total 10 ways.

$\therefore \quad N_1 = 30$

$N_2 = 5$

$N_3 = 10$

Total $N_1 + N_2 + N_3 = 45$

73. Let $f(x) = y$

$\therefore \quad y^2 - 4y + 3 \geq 0$

$(y-1)(y-3) \geq 0$ ...(i)

$y^2 - 6y + 8 \leq 0$

$(y-4)(y-2) \leq 0$ ...(ii)

$y^3 - 5y^2 + 10y - 12 \leq 0$

$(y-3)(y^2 - 2y + 4) \leq 0$ ...(iii)

On combining Eqs. (i), (ii) and (iii), we get

$$f(x) = 3 \text{ i.e. constant function}$$

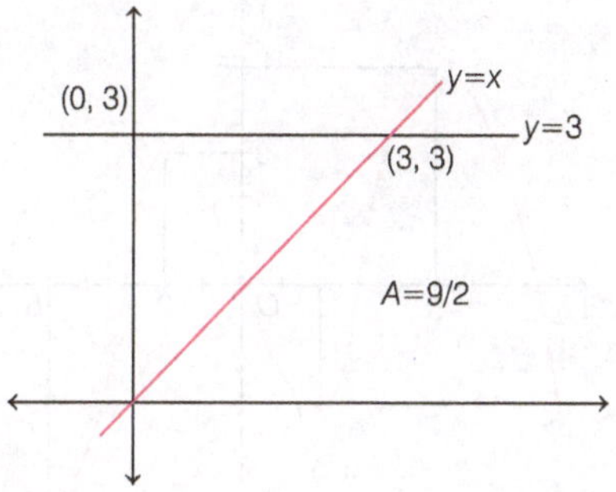

Hence, $10A = 45$ sq units

74. $$F(x) = \begin{cases} f(x), & -1 < x < 1 \\ g(x), & x \in (-\infty, -1) \cup (1, \infty) \\ \dfrac{f(1) + g(1)}{2}, & x = 1 \\ \dfrac{f(-1) + g(-1)}{2}, & x = -1 \end{cases}$$

Continuous at $x = 1$

$$\Rightarrow \quad F(1^-) = F(1^+) = F(1)$$

$$\Rightarrow \quad f(1^-) = g(1^+) = \frac{f(1) + g(1)}{2}$$

$$\Rightarrow \quad 4 + a = 1 + b = \frac{(4 + a) + (1 + b)}{2} = \frac{5 + a + b}{2}$$

$$\therefore \quad b - a = 3 \qquad \text{...(i)}$$

Continuous at $x = -1$

$$\Rightarrow \quad F(-1^-) = F(-1^+) = F(-1)$$

$$\Rightarrow \quad b - 1 = 4 - a = \frac{(4 - a) + (b - 1)}{2}$$

$$\Rightarrow \quad b - 1 = 4 - a = \frac{3 + b - a}{2}$$

$$\therefore \quad a + b = 5 \qquad \text{...(ii)}$$

From Eqs. (i) and (ii), we get

$$\Rightarrow \quad a = 1, b = 4$$

$$\Rightarrow \quad a^2 + b^2 = 17$$

75. $(xy) = f(x) + f(y) + xy - x - y - 1$

$$x = y = 1$$

$$f(1) = 2f(1) + 1 - 1 - 1 - 1$$

$$\Rightarrow \quad f(1) = 2$$

$$\lim_{h \to 0} \frac{2 - f(1 - h)}{h} = 2$$

$$\Rightarrow \quad \lim_{h \to 0} \frac{f(1 - h) - (1)}{-h} = 2$$

$$\Rightarrow \quad f'(1) = 2$$

Now, $f'(x) = \lim_{h \to 0} \dfrac{f(x + h) - f(x)}{h} = \lim_{h \to 0} \dfrac{f\left(x\left(1 + \frac{h}{x}\right)\right) - f(x)}{h}$

$$= \lim_{h \to 0} \frac{f(x) + \left(1 + \frac{h}{x}\right) + x\left(1 + \frac{h}{x}\right) - x - \left(1 + \frac{h}{x}\right) - 1 - f(x)}{h}$$

$$= \lim_{h \to 0} \frac{f\left(1 + \frac{h}{x}\right) - 2}{x \frac{h}{x}} + 1 - \frac{1}{x}$$

$$= \frac{1}{x} \cdot f'(1) + 1 - \frac{1}{x} = \frac{2}{x} + 1 - \frac{1}{x} = \frac{1}{x} + 1$$

$$f(x) = \ln x + x + C$$

On putting $x = 1$,

$$2 = 0 + 1 + c$$

$$\Rightarrow \quad c = 1$$

$$\therefore \quad f(x) = \ln x + x + 1$$

$$L = \lim_{x \to \infty} \frac{2 + \frac{2}{x} - f\left(1 + \frac{1}{x}\right)}{1 - \sqrt{\cos \frac{1}{3x}}}$$

$$= \lim_{h \to 0} \frac{2 + 2t - f(1 + t)}{1 - \sqrt{\cos \frac{t}{3}}}, \text{ where } x = \frac{1}{t}$$

$$= \lim_{t \to 0} \frac{2 + 2t - \{\ln(1 + t) + 1 + t + 1\}}{1 - \cos \frac{t}{3}} \left(1 + \sqrt{\cos \frac{t}{3}}\right)$$

$$= \lim_{t \to 0} \frac{t - \left(t - \frac{t^2}{2} + \frac{t^3}{3} \ldots\right)}{\frac{t - \cos \frac{t}{3}}{\frac{t^2}{9}} \cdot \frac{t^2}{9}} \cdot \left(1 + \sqrt{\cos \frac{t}{3}}\right)$$

$$= \frac{1}{2} \times \frac{9 \times 2}{1/2} = 18$$

76. $$f(x) = \begin{cases} \sqrt{\frac{1}{4} - \left\{x - \left(n + \frac{1}{2}\right)\right\}^2}, & n \le x < n + \frac{1}{2} \\ n + 1 - x, & n + \frac{1}{2} \le x < n + 1 \end{cases}$$

$\therefore$ Graph of $f(x)$ will be

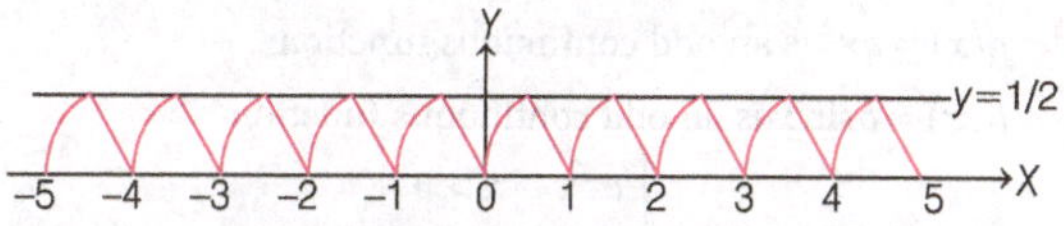

Clearly, $f(x)$ is continuous in R but not differentiable at $x = n + \frac{1}{2}$ and n, $\forall\, n \in I$

$\therefore$ Not differentiable at 19 points in $(-5, 5)$.

Also, $f(x)$ is periodic with fundamental period 1.

$\Rightarrow$ 19 points

77. $$f(x) = \lim_{n \to \infty} \left(\left(a\left(1 + \left(\frac{b}{a}\right)^n\right)\right)^{1/n} \sin x + \{e^x\}^n\right) \left(\left[\frac{\frac{1}{n}}{\tan^{-1} \frac{1}{n}}\right] + 1\right)$$

$$\therefore \quad f(x) = (a \sin x + 0)(1 + 1)$$

$$\therefore \quad f(x) = 2a \sin x$$

$H(x)=\text{sgn}(2a\sin x-3)$ has exactly one point of discontinuity in $[0, 2\pi]$, then $2a\sin x-3=0$ must have one real root in $[0, 2\pi]$, $\sin x=\dfrac{3}{2a}$

$\therefore \quad a=\dfrac{3}{2}$ only $\Rightarrow 24a=36$

78. $f(x)=\begin{cases}\dfrac{|\log_e|x||}{2x}, & -\pi<x<0\\ 0, & x=0\\ \dfrac{-\{\sin x\}}{e^x}, & 0<x<\pi\end{cases}$

$f(x)$ is discontinuous at $x=0, \dfrac{\pi}{2}$ and non-differentiable at $x=0, \dfrac{\pi}{2}$ and -1; $(l+m)^2=5^2=25$

79. As, $\sin^{-1}\alpha_1+\sin^{-1}\alpha_2 \dots +\sin^{-1}\alpha_n=\dfrac{n\pi}{2}$

$\Rightarrow \quad \sin^{-1}\alpha_1=\sin^{-1}\alpha_2=\dots=\sin^{-1}\alpha_n=\dfrac{\pi}{2}$

$\left[\because -\dfrac{\pi}{2}\le \sin^{-1}\alpha \le \dfrac{\pi}{2}\right]$

$\Rightarrow \quad \alpha_1=\alpha_2=\dots\alpha_n=1$

So, $\quad p=\prod_{r=1}^{n}(1)^r=1$

Hence, $f(x)=\begin{cases}\dfrac{x^{1/3}-(3-2x)^{1/4}}{x^2-x}, & x\ne 1\\ k, & x=1\end{cases}$

Clearly, $f(x)$ is continuous at $x=1$

$\therefore \quad k=\dfrac{x^{1/3}-(3-2x)^{1/4}}{x^2-x}=\lim_{h\to 0}\dfrac{(1+h)^{1/3}-(1-2h)^{1/4}}{(1+h)^2-(1+h)}$

(put $x=1+h$)

$=\dfrac{1}{3}+\dfrac{1}{2}=\dfrac{5}{6}$

Hence, $6(k+p)=6\left(\dfrac{5}{6}+1\right)=11$

80. $f_1(x)=ax^9$ is an odd continuous function

$f_2(x)=b\sin x$ is an odd continuous function

$f_3(x)=cx^2\text{sgn}(x)=\begin{cases}cx^2, & x>0\\ 0, & x=0\\ -cx^2, & x<0\end{cases}$ is an odd continuous function.

$f_4(x)=\dfrac{d(e^x-e^{-x})}{(e^x+e^{-x})}$

$f_4(-x)=\dfrac{(e^{-x}-e^{-x})}{(e^{-x}+e^{x})}=-f_4(x)$

$\therefore f_4(x)$ is an odd function and continuous, $\forall\, x\in R$

[$\because$ denominator is never zero]

$\therefore$ $f(x)$ will be an odd continuous.

$\Rightarrow \quad f(-x)=-f(x)$

$\therefore \quad f(5)=-5$ and $f(2)=+3$, $f(0)=0$

If $a>0$, then when $x\to-\infty$, $f(x)\to-\infty$ and when $x\to+\infty$, $f(x)\to+\infty$

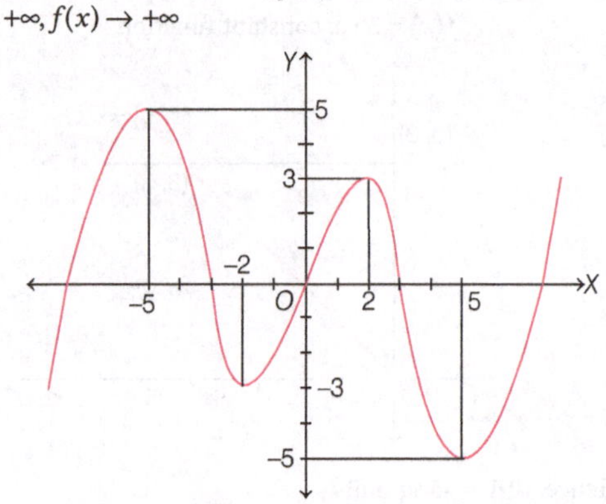

Clearly, $f(x)=0$ will have minimum five roots, $\alpha=5$

$\therefore \quad x_1+x_2+x_3=15$

$\therefore$Number of positive integral solution

${}^{15-1}C_{3-1}={}^{14}C_2=91$

81. $\because$ Graph of $y=g(x)$ is reflection of graph of $y=f(x)$ with respect to line $y=x$.

$g(x)$ is inverse function of $f(x)$.

$\because \quad (a, b)$ lies on $y=f(x)$

$f(a)=b$

$g(f(x))=x$

$\Rightarrow \quad g'(f(x))f'(x)=1$

$\Rightarrow \quad g'(f(x))=\dfrac{1}{f'(x)}$

$\Rightarrow \quad g'(f(a))=\dfrac{1}{f'(a)}$

$\Rightarrow \quad g'(b)=\dfrac{1}{3}$

$\Rightarrow \quad \gamma=\dfrac{1}{3}$

$\Rightarrow \quad \dfrac{670}{\gamma}=2010$

82. (A) $f(x)=\begin{cases}x\dfrac{\left(\frac{4}{5}\right)^{1/x}-\left(\frac{4}{5}\right)^{-1/x}}{\left(\frac{4}{5}\right)^{1/x}+\left(\frac{4}{5}\right)^{-1/x}}, & x\ne 0\\ 0, & x=0\end{cases}$

Now, $f'(0^-)=\lim_{h\to 0^+}\dfrac{f(0-h)-f(0)}{-h}=\lim_{h\to 0^+}\dfrac{f(-h)}{-h}$

$=\lim_{h\to 0^+}\dfrac{\left(\frac{4}{5}\right)^{-1/h}-\left(\frac{4}{5}\right)^{1/h}}{\left(\frac{4}{5}\right)^{-1/h}+\left(\frac{4}{5}\right)^{1/h}}$

$=\lim_{h\to 0^+}\left(\dfrac{1-\left(\frac{4}{5}\right)^{2/h}}{1+\left(\frac{4}{5}\right)^{2/h}}\right)=1$

and $f'(0^+) = \lim_{h\to 0^+} \frac{f(0+h)-f(0)}{h} = \lim_{h\to 0^+} \frac{f(h)}{h}$

$$= \lim_{h\to 0^+} \frac{(4/5)^{1/h} - (4/5)^{-1/h}}{(4/5)^{1/h} + (4/5)^{-1/h}}$$

$$= \lim_{h\to 0^+} \frac{\left(\frac{4}{5}\right)^{2/h} - 1}{\left(\frac{4}{5}\right)^{2/h} + 1} = -1$$

$\therefore \quad \alpha = f'(0^-) - f'(0^+) = 1-(-1) = 2$

$$\therefore \lim_{h\to 2}\left(\frac{(\exp(x+2)\ln 4)^{\frac{[x+0.5]}{4}} - 16}{(2)^{2x} - 16}\right)$$

$$= \lim_{x\to 2} \frac{(4^{(x+2)})^{2/4} - 16}{(4)^x - 16} = \lim_{x\to 2} \frac{(4)^{\frac{x+2}{2}} - 16}{4^x - 16}$$

$$= \lim_{x\to 2} \frac{(4)^{\frac{x}{2}+1-2}}{(4)^{x-2} - 1} = \lim_{x\to 2} \frac{(4)^{\frac{x}{2}} - 1}{4^{x-2} - 1}$$

$$= \lim_{x\to 2} \frac{(4)^{\frac{x}{2}-1} - 1}{(4)^{x-2} - 1} \times \frac{(x-2)}{\left(\frac{x}{2}-1\right)} = \frac{\ln(4)}{\ln(4)} \cdot (2) = 2$$

which is less than or equal to 2, 3 and 5.

(B) $f(x) = [2 + 5|n| \sin x]$, $n \in Z$ and $x \in (0, \pi)$.

For non-differentiability of $f(x) = 2 + 5|n|\sin x \in Z$.

$\Rightarrow 5|n|\sin x \in Z$

$\Rightarrow 5|n|\sin x = k; k \in Z$

$\Rightarrow \sin x = \frac{k}{5|n|}; k \in Z$

But $\sin x \in (0,1]$ for $x \in \left(0, \frac{\pi}{2}\right]$

$\Rightarrow 0 < \frac{k}{5|n|} < 1$

$\Rightarrow k \in (0, 5|n|]$

$\because$ $f(x)$ is non-differentiable at exactly 10 points in $\left(0, \frac{\pi}{2}\right)$.

$\Rightarrow k \in \{1, 2, 3, 4, \dots, 5|n|\}$ and $k = 10$ and $\frac{k}{5|n|} = 1$

$\Rightarrow \quad 5|n| = 10$

$\Rightarrow \quad |n| = \frac{10}{5} = 2$

$\Rightarrow \quad n = \pm 2$

In $(0, \pi)$; $\sin x - 1$ at $x = \frac{\pi}{2}$ common value in $\left(0, \frac{\pi}{2}\right]$ and $\left[\frac{\pi}{2}, \pi\right)$ and hence non-differentiability at exactly 19 points means differentiability at 9 points in each quadrant $\left(0, \frac{\pi}{2}\right)$ and $\left(\frac{\pi}{2}, \pi\right)$ and once at $x = \frac{\pi}{2}$.

(C) $\text{LHL} = \lim_{x\to 0^-} f(x)$

$$= \lim_{x\to 0^-} \frac{\mu \sin^{-1}(1-\{x\})\cos^{-1}(1-\{x\})}{\sqrt{2\{x\}}(1-\{x\})}$$

$$= \lim_{x\to 0^-} \frac{\mu \sin^{-1}(\{-x\})\cos^{-1}(-\{x\})}{\sqrt{2(1-\{x\})}(\{-x\})}$$

$$= \lim_{x\to 0^-} \frac{\mu \sin^{-1} h \cos^{-1} h}{\sqrt{2(1-h)}(h)} = \frac{\mu \cos^{-1}(0)}{\sqrt{2}} = \frac{\mu\pi}{2\sqrt{2}}$$

$[\because \{x\} + \{-x\} = 1 \text{ for } x \notin Z]$

and $\text{RHL} = \lim_{x\to 0^+} f(x)$

$$= \lim_{x\to 0^+} \frac{\left(\frac{\pi}{2} - \sin^{-1}(1-\{x\}^2)\right)\sin^{-1}(1-\{x\})}{\sqrt{2}(\{x\} - \{x\}^2)}$$

$$= \lim_{x\to 0^+} \frac{\cos^{-1}(1-x^2)\sin^{-1}(1-x)}{\sqrt{2}\,x(1-x^2)}$$

$$= \lim_{x\to 0^+} \frac{\cos^{-1}(1-x^2)}{x} \cdot \frac{1}{\sqrt{2}} \cdot \frac{\sin^{-1}(1-x)}{(1-x^2)}$$

$$= \lim_{x\to 0^+} \frac{-1}{\sqrt{1-(1-x^2)^2}}(-2x)\frac{\pi}{2\sqrt{2}}$$

[by L'Hospital rule]

$$= \lim_{x\to 0^+} \frac{2x}{\sqrt{2x^2 - x^4}} \cdot \frac{\pi}{\sqrt{2}\cdot 2}$$

$$= \lim_{x\to 0^+} \frac{\pi}{\sqrt{2-x^2}} \cdot \frac{1}{2} = \frac{\pi}{\sqrt{2}} \cdot \frac{1}{\sqrt{2}} = \frac{\pi}{2}$$

$\therefore$ For continuity at $x = 0$,

$$\lim_{x\to 0^-} f(x) = \lim_{x\to 0^+} f(x) = f(0) = \lambda$$

$\Rightarrow \quad \frac{\mu\pi}{2\sqrt{2}} = \frac{\pi}{2} = \lambda$

$\Rightarrow \quad \lambda = \frac{\pi}{2}; \mu = \sqrt{2}$

$\therefore \sin^2 \lambda + \cos^2\left(\mu \frac{\pi}{\sqrt{2}}\right) = \sin^2 \frac{\pi}{2} + \cos^2(\pi) = 1 + 1 = 2$

(D) $g(x) = \frac{1}{1 + \frac{3}{f(x)}}$; $f(x) = \frac{1}{1 + \frac{2}{x}} \Rightarrow g(x) = \frac{x}{6+4x}$

$g(x)$ being a rational expression can be non-differentiable only where $g(x)$ is not defined i.e. where $f(x) = 0, -3$ and $f(x)$ is not defined.

But $f(x) = \frac{1}{1+\frac{2}{x}} \neq 0, \forall x \in R$ and $f(x)$ is not defined at $x = 0$ and at $x = -2$; $f(x) = -3$

$\Rightarrow \quad \frac{x}{2+x} = -3 \Rightarrow x = -6 - 3x$

$\Rightarrow \quad 4x = -6 \Rightarrow x = -\frac{3}{2}$

$\therefore$ Domain of $g(x) = R - \{0, -2, -3/2\}$

$\therefore$ $g(x)$ is non-differentiable at exactly 3 real number.

83. (A) $f(x)=[x][1+x]$

$f(0^+)=0,\ f(0^-)=(-1)(0)=f(0)=0$

(B) $f(x)=[-x][1+x]$

$f(0^+)=(-1)(1)=-1,$

$f(0^-)=0,\ f(0)=0$

(C) $f(x)=\operatorname{sgn} x[2-x][1+|x|]$

$f(0^+)=1[2-0^+][1+|0^+|]=1$

$f(0^-)=(-1)(2)(1)=-2$

$f(0)=0$

(D) $f(x)=[\cos x]$

$f(0^+)=0,\ f(0^-)=0,\ f(0)=1$

84. (A) $f'(x)=\lim_{h\to 0}\dfrac{f(x+h)-f(x)}{h}$

$$=\lim_{h\to 0}\frac{f\left[x\left(1+\frac{h}{x}\right)\right]-f(x)}{h}$$

$$=\lim_{h\to 0}\frac{f(x)f\left(1+\frac{h}{x}\right)-f(x)}{h}$$

$$=\lim_{h\to 0} f(x)\left\{\frac{f\left(1+\frac{h}{x}\right)-1}{h}\right\}$$

$$\therefore f'(1)=f(1)\lim_{h\to 0}\left\{\frac{f(1+h)-1}{h}\right\}$$

$\because f'(1)$ exist finitely and $f(1)\neq 0$ and denominator is approaching to zero, numerator must approach to zero

$$\Rightarrow \lim_{h\to 0}\{f(1+h)-1\}=0 \Rightarrow f(1)=1$$

$$f'(x)=f(x)\lim_{h\to 0}\left\{\frac{f\left(1+\frac{h}{x}\right)-1}{h}\right\}$$

$$\Rightarrow f'(x)=f(x)\lim_{h\to 0}\left\{\frac{f\left(1+\frac{h}{x}\right)-f(1)}{h}\right\}$$

$$=f(x)\lim_{h\to 0}\left\{\frac{1}{x}\frac{f\left(1+\frac{h}{x}\right)-f(1)}{h/x}\right\}$$

$$f'(x)=\frac{f(x)}{x}, f'(1)=\frac{f(x)}{x}\ [\because f'(1)=1]$$

$$\frac{f'(x)}{f(x)}=\frac{1}{x}$$

$$\Rightarrow \ln|f(x)|=\ln|x|+C$$

$$\Rightarrow \ln|f'(1)|=\ln 1+C$$

$$\Rightarrow \ln 1=\ln 1+C \Rightarrow C=0$$

$$\therefore \ln|f(x)|-\ln|x|$$

$$\Rightarrow f(x)=\pm x$$

But $f(1)=1$

$$\Rightarrow f(x)=\pm x$$

$$\therefore f'(x)=1$$

$$\Rightarrow f'(7)=1$$

(B) $f(x)=|x^2-3x+2|+|\sin x|-\left[x-\frac{1}{2}\right]; -\pi\le x\le\pi$

$$=|(x-1)(x-2)|+|\sin x|-\left[x-\frac{1}{2}\right]$$

Clearly, $|(x-1)(x-2)|$ is non-differentiable at $x=1$, $x=2$, $|\sin x|$ non-differentiable at $n\pi;\ n\in Z$

But, here $x\in[-\pi,\pi]$

$\Rightarrow$ $|\sin x|$ is non-differentiable only at $x=0$

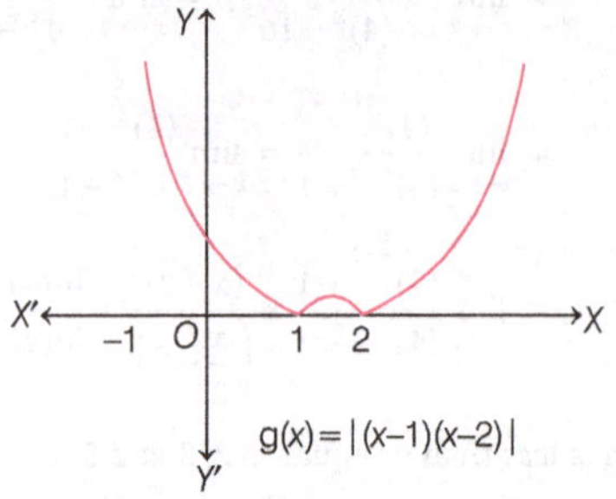

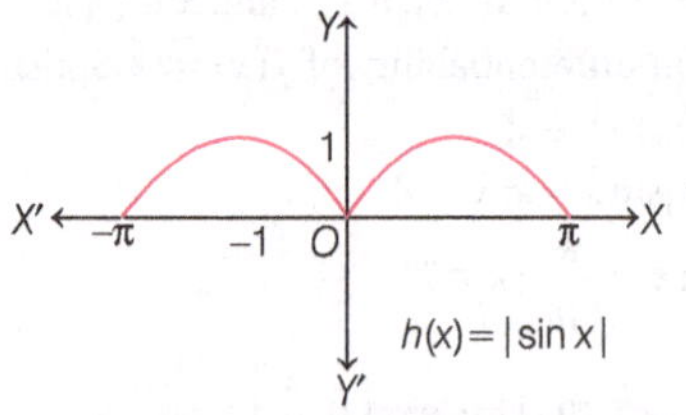

Also, $[x-1/2]$ is non-differentiable at integer points for $x\in[-\pi,\pi]$.

i.e. for $\left(x-\frac{1}{2}\right)\in\left[-\pi-\frac{1}{2},\pi-\frac{1}{2}\right]$

i.e. for $x-\frac{1}{2}=-3,-2,-1,0,1,2\Rightarrow x=\frac{-5}{2},\frac{-3}{2},\frac{-1}{2},\frac{1}{2},\frac{3}{2},\frac{5}{2}$

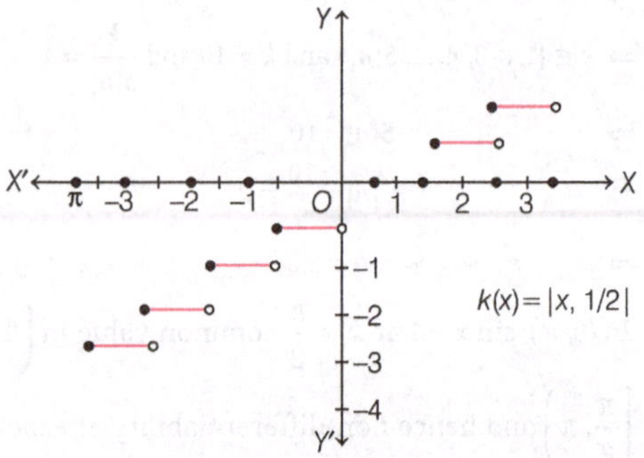

We observe that among the given three functions, no two have any common point of non-differentiability and by algebra of differentiability, we know that the sum of a differentiable and non-differentiable function is non-differentiable.

So, $\frac{-5}{2}, \frac{-3}{2}, \frac{-1}{2}, 0, \frac{1}{2}, 1, \frac{3}{2}, 2, \frac{5}{2}$ are the points, where $f(x)$ is non-differentiable at exactly 9 points.

(C) $f(x) = [a + 7\sin x]$; $x \in [0, \pi]$, $a \in Z$ (fixed integer) for non-differentiability $a + 7\sin x$ must be an integer.

As $a \in Z, 7\sin x \in Z$

$$\Rightarrow \quad 7\sin x = k, k \in Z$$

$$\Rightarrow \quad \sin x = k/7, k \in Z$$

But $\sin x$ has its range $[-1, 1]$

$$\Rightarrow \quad -1 \le \frac{k}{7} \le 1$$

$$\Rightarrow \quad k \in [-7, 7]$$

and $\quad k \in Z$

$$\Rightarrow k \in \{-7, -6, -5, -4, -3, -2, -1, 0, 1, 2, 3, 4, 5, 6, 7\}.$$

But in $[0, \pi]$, $\sin x \ge 0$

$$\Rightarrow \quad k \in \{0, 1, 2, 3, 4, 5, 6, 7\}$$

$$\Rightarrow \quad \sin x = 0, \frac{1}{7}, \frac{2}{7}, \frac{3}{7}, \frac{4}{7}, \frac{5}{7}, \frac{6}{7}, 1$$

But $x \in [0, \pi]$ (closed interval)

$$\Rightarrow \quad \sin x = \frac{1}{7}, \frac{2}{7}, \frac{3}{7}, \frac{4}{7}, \frac{5}{7}, \frac{6}{7}, 1$$

and $\sin x$ would repeat these values twice, once in $[0, \pi/2]$ and secondly in $[\pi/2, \pi]$, but 1 is common value in two quadrants.

Thus, total number of points of non-differentiability will be $7 \times 2 - 1 = 13$

(D) $g(x) = f(e^x) \cdot e^{f(x)}$

$$g'(x) = f(e^x) \cdot e^{f(x)} \cdot f'(x) + e^{f(x)} \cdot f'(e^x) \cdot e^x$$

$$\Rightarrow \quad g'(0) = f(1) \cdot e^{f(0)} \cdot f'(0) + e^{f(0)} \cdot f'(1) \cdot 1$$

$$= 0 \cdot e^{(0)} \cdot f'(0) + e^0 (2) \cdot 1$$

$$= 2$$

85. Given, $f(x) = \begin{cases} x|x| \sin\left(\frac{1}{x}\right), & x \ne 0 \\ 0. & x = 0 \end{cases}$

$$g(x) = \begin{cases} 1 - 2x, & 0 \le x \le \frac{1}{2} \\ 0, & \text{otherwise} \end{cases} \quad \text{...(i)}$$

$$\text{and } g\left(\frac{1}{2} - x\right) = \begin{cases} 2x, & 0 \le x \le \frac{1}{2} \\ 0, & \text{otherwise} \end{cases} \quad \text{...(ii)}$$

On adding Eqs. (i) and (ii), we get

$$g(x) + g\left(\frac{1}{2} - x\right) = \begin{cases} 1, & 0 \le x \le \frac{1}{2} \\ 0, & \text{otherwise} \end{cases}$$

Lets check options

(P) Now, $a = 0, b = 1, c = 0, d = 0$

$$\because \quad h(x) = g(x) + g\left(\frac{1}{2} - x\right) = \begin{cases} 1, & 0 \le x \le \frac{1}{2} \\ 0, & \text{otherwise} \end{cases}$$

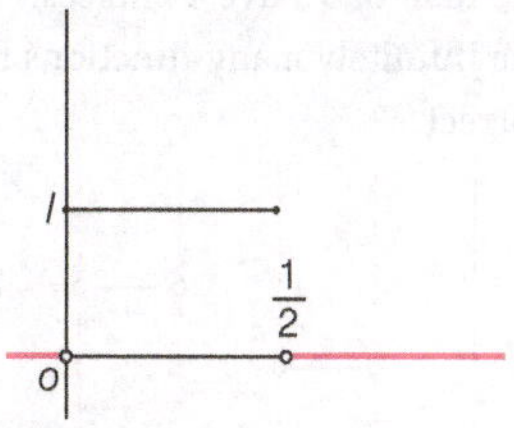

Hence, range of $h(x)$ is $\{0, 1\}$.

(Q) $\quad a = 1, b = 0, c = 0, d = 0$

$$h(x) = f(x) = \begin{cases} x|x| \sin\left(\frac{1}{x}\right), & x \ne 0 \\ 0, & x = 0 \end{cases}$$

$$\text{RHD} = \lim_{x \to 0^+} \frac{x^2 \sin\frac{1}{x} - 0}{x} = 0$$

$$\text{LHD} = \lim_{x \to 0^-} \frac{-x^2 \sin\frac{1}{x} - 0}{x} = 0$$

Since, RHD = LHD

$\therefore$ $h(x)$ is differentiable on R

(R) $\quad a = 0, b = 0, c = 1, d = 0$

$$h(x) = x - g(x) = \begin{cases} 3x - 1, & 0 \le x \le \frac{1}{2} \\ 0, & \text{otherwise} \end{cases}$$

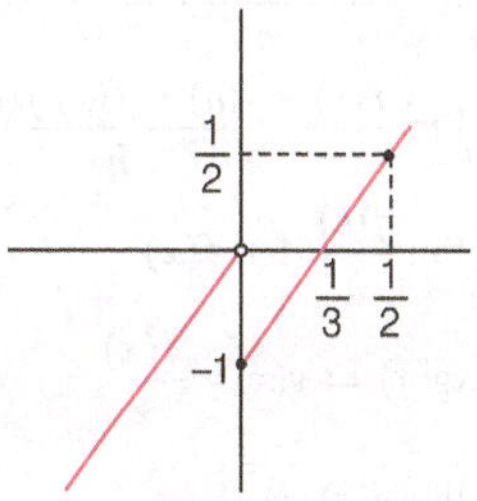

Hence, $h(x)$ is onto.

(S) $a = 0, b = 0, c = 0$ and $d = 1$

$$h(x) = g(x) = \begin{cases} 1 - 2x, & 0 \le x \le \frac{1}{2} \\ 0, & \text{otherwise} \end{cases}$$

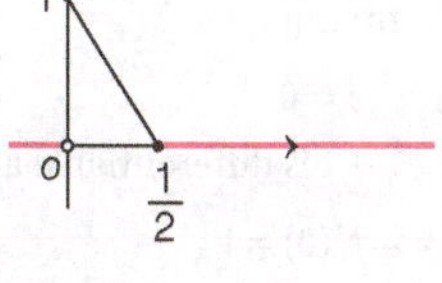

$\therefore$ Range of $h(x)$ is $[0, 1]$.

86. Given, $S = (0, 1) \cup (1, 2) \cup (3, 4)$ and $T = \{0, 1, 2, 3\}$

We observe that there are infinitely many elements in S and 4 elements in set T.

So, total number of functions from S to T is 4^m where $m \to \infty$ because each element of S have 4 choices.

Hence, there are infinitely many functions from S to T.

Option (a) is correct.

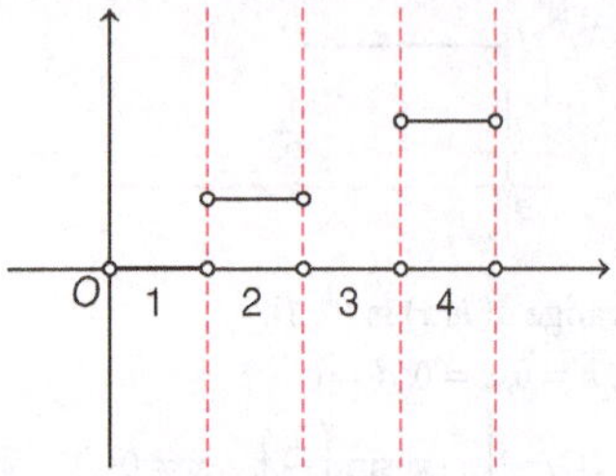

From figure, option (b) is obviously incorrect or you can also observe that number of elements in domain (S) is greater than the number of elements in co-domain (T), then the number of strictly increasing function is zero.

For continuous function, we see that each interval of S have 4 choices.

$\therefore$Maximum number of continuous functions $= 4 \times 4 \times 4 = 64 < 120$

Hence, option (c) is also correct.

For option (d), we see that for every point at which function is continuous, its derivative will be zero.

So, every continuous function from S to T is differentiable.

87. The given function $f : R \to R$ is satisfying as

$$f(x + y) = f(x) + f(y) + f(x)\, f(y).$$

So, $$f'(x) = \lim_{h \to 0} \frac{f(x+h) - f(x)}{h}$$

$$= \lim_{h \to 0} \frac{f(x) + f(h) + f(x)\, f(h) - f(x)}{h}$$

$$= \lim_{h \to 0} \frac{f(h)}{h} (1 + f(x)$$

$\because$ $$f(x) = xg(x) \Rightarrow g(x) = \frac{f(x)}{x}$$

$\therefore$ $$\lim_{x \to 0} \frac{f(x)}{x} = \lim_{x \to 0} g(x) = 1 \quad \text{[given]}$$

$\therefore$ $$f'(x) = 1 + f(x) \Rightarrow \frac{f'(x)}{1 + f(x)} = 1$$

$\Rightarrow$ $$\log_e(1 + f(x)) = x + c$$

$\Rightarrow$ $$1 + f(x) = e^{x+c}$$

$\Rightarrow$ $$f(x) = e^{x+c} - 1$$

$\because$ $$f(0) = 0$$

$\therefore$ $$c = 0$$

Therefore, $f(x) = e^x - 1$ is differentiable at every $x \in R$.

And $f'(x) = e^x \Rightarrow f'(0) = 1$

Now, $g(x) = \dfrac{f(x)}{x} = \dfrac{e^x - 1}{x}$ and if $g(0) = 1$

LHD (at $x = 0$) of

$$g(x) = \lim_{h \to 0} \frac{g(0-h) - g(0)}{-h}$$

$$= \lim_{h \to 0} \frac{\dfrac{e^{-h} - 1}{-h} - 1}{-h} = \lim_{h \to 0} \frac{e^{-h} - 1 + h}{h^2} = \frac{1}{2}$$

and RHD (at $x = 0$) if

$$g(x) = \lim_{h \to 0} \frac{g(0+h) - g(0)}{h} = \lim_{h \to 0} \frac{e^h - 1 - h}{h^2} = \frac{1}{2}$$

So, if $g(0) = 1$, then g is differentiable at every $x \in R$.

88. Given functions $f : R \to R$ be defined by $f(x) = x^3 - x^2 + (x - 1)\sin x$ and $g : R \to R$ be an arbitrary function.

Now, let g is continuous at $x = 1$, then

$$\lim_{x \to 1^-} \frac{(fg)(x) - (fg)(1)}{x - 1} = \lim_{h \to 0} \frac{(fg)(1-h) - (fg)(1)}{1 - h - 1}$$

$\because$ $$(fg)(x) = f(x) \cdot g(x) \quad \text{[given]}$$

$$= \lim_{h \to 0} \frac{f(1-h) \cdot g(1-h) - f(1) \cdot g(1)}{-h}$$

$$= \lim_{h \to 0} \frac{f(1-h) \cdot g(1)}{-h}$$

{$\because f(1) = 0$ and g is continuous at $x = 1$, so $g(1-h) = g(1)$ as $h \to 0$}

$$= g(1) \lim_{h \to 0} \frac{(1-h)^2(-h) + (-h)\sin(1-h)}{-h}$$

$$= (1 + \sin 1) g(1)$$

Similarly, $$\lim_{x \to 1^+} \frac{(fg)(x) - (fg)(1)}{x - 1} = \lim_{h \to 0} \frac{f(1+h) \cdot g(1)}{h}$$

$$= g(1) \lim_{h \to 0} \frac{(1+h)^2(h) + h\sin(1+h)}{h}$$

$$= (1 + \sin 1) g(1)$$

$\because$ RHD and LHD of function fg at $x = 1$ finitely exists and equal, so fg is differentiable at $x = 1$

Now, $(fg)(x)$ is differentiable at $x = 1$, so

$$\lim_{x \to 1^-} \frac{(fg)(x) - (fg)(1)}{x - 1} = \lim_{x \to 1^+} \frac{(fg)(x) - (fg)(1)}{x - 1}$$

$$\Rightarrow \lim_{x \to 1^-} \frac{f(x)g(x) - f(1)g(1)}{x - 1} = \lim_{x \to 1^+} \frac{f(x)g(x) - f(1)g(1)}{x - 1}$$

$$\Rightarrow \lim_{x \to 1^-} \frac{f(x)\, g(x)}{x - 1} = \lim_{x \to 1^+} \frac{f(x)\, g(x)}{x - 1} \quad [\because f(1) = 0]$$

$$\Rightarrow \lim_{h \to 0} \frac{f(1-h)g(1-h)}{-h} = \lim_{h \to 0} \frac{f(1+h)g(1+h)}{h}$$

$$\Rightarrow \lim_{h \to 0} \frac{[(1-h)^2(-h) + (-h)\sin(1-h)]g(1-h)}{-h}$$

$$= \lim_{h \to 0} \frac{[(1+h)^2(h) + (h)\sin(1+h)]g(1+h)}{h}$$

$$\Rightarrow \lim_{h \to 0} [(1-h)^2 + \sin(1-h)]g(1-h)$$

$$= \lim_{h \to 0} [(1+h)^2 + \sin(1+h)]g(1+h)$$

It does not mean that $g(x)$ is continuous or differentiable at $x = 1$.

But if g is differentiable at $x = 1$, then it must be continuous at $x = 1$ and so fg is differentiable at $x = 1$.

89. The given functions $f : (-1, 1) \to R$ and $g : (-1, 1) \to (-1, 1)$ be defined by

$$f(x) = |2x - 1| + |2x + 1| \text{ and } g(x) = x - [x].$$

As, we know the composite function $(fog)(x)$ is discontinuous at the points, where $g(x)$ is discontinuous for given domain and since $g(x)$ is discontinuous at $x = 0$ lies in interval $(-1, 1)$, so $c = 1$.

And, since $(fog)(x)$ is not differentiable at the point where $g(x)$ is not differentiable as well as at those points also where $g(x)$ attains the values so that $f(g(x))$ is non-differentiable.

Since, $g(x)$ is not continuous at $x = 0 \in (-1, 1)$, so $fog(x)$ is not differentiable and as $f(x) = |2x - 1| + |2x + 1|$ is not differentiable at $x = -1/2$ and $1/2$, so $(fog)(x)$ is not differentiable for those x, for which $g(x) = -1/2$ or $1/2$.

But $g(x) \geq 0$, so $g(x)$ can be $1/2$ only and for $x = -1/2$ and $1/2$, $g(x) = \frac{1}{2}$.

So, $(fog)(x)$ is not differentiable at $x = -1/2, 0, 1/2$, therefore $d = 3$

$\therefore \quad c + d = 1 + 3 = 4$

Exercise 3 - Challenging Problems

1. Here, $f(x) = \begin{cases} x - [x], & x \notin I \\ 1, & x \in I \end{cases}$

(i) **Graph of $f(2x)$**

As $f(2x) = \begin{cases} 2x - [2x], & 2x \notin I \\ 1, & 2x \in I \end{cases}$

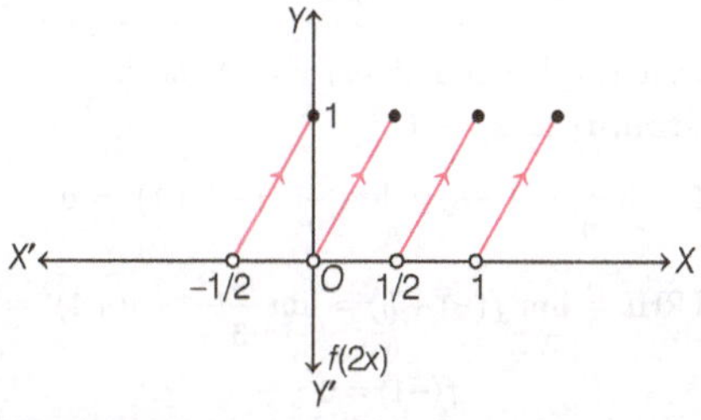

Graph of $g(x)$

Here, $\quad g(x) = \lim_{n \to \infty} \frac{\{f(x)\}^{2n} - 1}{\{f(x)\}^{2n} + 1}$

$$g(x) = \begin{cases} 0, & x \in I \\ -1, & x \notin I \end{cases}, \text{ as } \lim_{n \to \infty} \{f(x)\}^{2n} = 0$$

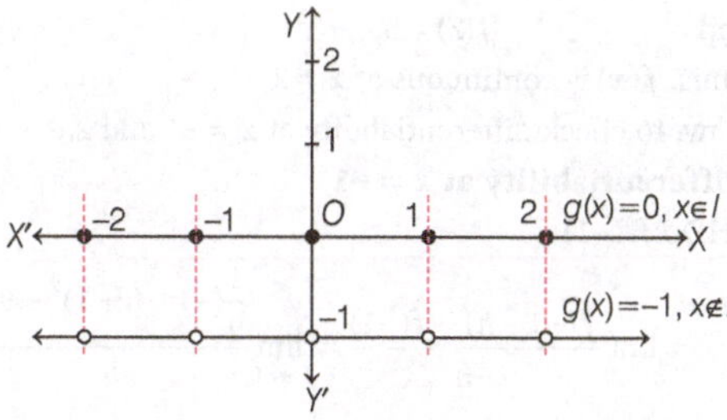

Graph of $g\{(g(x)\}$

We have, $g(x) = \begin{cases} 0, & x \in I \\ -1, & x \notin I \end{cases} \Rightarrow g\{g(x)\} = \begin{cases} 0, & g(x) \in I \\ -1, & g(x) \notin I \end{cases}$,

where $g(x) \in \{0, -1\}$

and thus $g(x) \notin I$, should be neglected.

$\Rightarrow g\{g(x)\} = 0, x \in R$ and could be plotted as

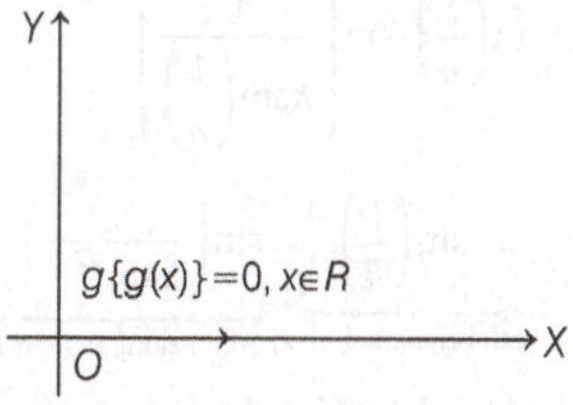

(ii) From the above three graphs, we get
domain of $f(2x) \in R$ and range of $f(2x) \in (0, 1]$,
domain of $g(x) \in R$ and range of $g(x) \in \{0, -1\}$
and domain of $g(g(x)) \in R$ and range of $g(g(x)) \in \{0\}$

(iii) Here, $f(2x)$ and $g(x)$ are periodic with period 1/2 and 1.
Also, $g\{g(x)\}$ is constant function.
Therefore, periodic and its period is undetermined.

2. Here, $f(x) = [\tan x] + \sqrt{\tan x - [\tan x]}$

or $\quad g(x) = [x] + \sqrt{x - [x]}$, where $x = \tan x \geq 0$

Then, for $a \in N$.

We discuss continuity of $f(x)$ as LHL (at $x = a$)

$$= \lim_{x \to a^-} g(x) = \lim_{h \to 0}([a - h] + \sqrt{a - h - [a - h]})$$

$$= \lim_{h \to 0}((a - 1) + \sqrt{a - h - a + 1}) = a - 1 + 1 = a,$$

$$[\text{where } a - 1 < a - h < a, \therefore [a - h] = a - 1]$$

Now, RHL (at $x = a$)

$$= \lim_{x \to a^+} g(x) = \lim_{h \to 0}([a + h] + \sqrt{a + h - [a + h]})$$

$$= \lim_{h \to 0}(a + \sqrt{a + h - a}) = a$$

$$[\because a < a + h < a + 1 \Rightarrow [a + h] = a]$$

and $\quad g(a) = [a] + \sqrt{a - [a]} = a$ as $a \in N$

So, $g(x)$ is continuous, $\forall\, a \in N$, now $g(x)$ is clearly continuous in $(a - 1, a), \forall\, a \in N$.

Hence, $g(x)$ is continuous in $[0, \infty)$.

Now, let $\phi(x) = \tan x$, which is continuous in $[0, \pi/2]$.

So, $g\{\phi(x)\}$ is continuous in $[0, \pi/2)$.

Hence, $f(x) = [\tan x] + \sqrt{\tan x - [\tan x]}$ is continuous in $[0, \pi/2)$.

3. Given, $f(x) = \begin{cases} x \cdot \sin\frac{1}{x} \cdot \sin\frac{1}{x \cdot \sin\frac{1}{x}}, & x \neq 0, 1/r\pi, r = 1,2,3 \\ 0, \quad \text{for } x = 0, \; x = \frac{1}{r\pi}, & r = 1,2,3... \end{cases}$

$$f'(0) = \lim_{h \to 0} \frac{f(h + 0) - f(0)}{h} = \lim_{h \to 0} \frac{h\sin\left(\frac{1}{h}\right) \cdot \sin\left(\frac{1}{h\sin\left(\frac{1}{h}\right)}\right) - 0}{h}$$

$$= \lim_{h\to 0} \frac{h\sin\left(\frac{1}{h}\right)\cdot\sin\left(\frac{1}{h\sin\left(\frac{1}{h}\right)}\right)}{h}$$

$$= \lim_{h\to 0} \sin\left(\frac{1}{h}\right)\cdot\sin\left(\frac{1}{h\sin\left(\frac{1}{h}\right)}\right)$$

$$= \lim_{h\to 0} \underbrace{\sin\left(\frac{1}{h}\right)}_{\text{both belong to }[-1,1]} \underbrace{\sin\left(\frac{1}{h\sin(1/h)}\right)}_{\text{both belong to }[-1,1]}$$

which does not exist uniquely.

So, $f(x)$ is not differentiable at $x=0$

$$\lim_{x\to 0} f(x) = \lim_{x\to 0} x\sin\left(\frac{1}{x}\right)\cdot\sin\left(\frac{1}{x\sin(1/x)}\right)$$

$$= \lim_{x\to 0} \underbrace{x}_{\to 0} \underbrace{\sin(1/x)}_{\text{both belong to }[-1,1]} \cdot \underbrace{\sin\left(\frac{1}{x\sin(1/x)}\right)}_{\text{both belong to }[-1,1]} = 0 = f(0)$$

$\Rightarrow$ $f(x)$ is continuous at $x=0$

$$\lim_{x\to \frac{1}{r\pi}} f(x) = \lim_{x\to \frac{1}{r\pi}} x\sin\left(\frac{1}{x}\right)\cdot\sin\left(\frac{1}{x\sin\left(\frac{1}{x}\right)}\right)$$

$$= \lim_{x\to \frac{1}{r\pi}} \underbrace{x\cdot\sin\left(\frac{1}{x}\right)}_{\to 0} \cdot \underbrace{\sin\left(\frac{1}{x\sin\left(\frac{1}{x}\right)}\right)}_{\text{both belong to }[-1,1]}$$

$$= 0 = f\left(\frac{1}{r\pi}\right)$$

Hence, function is continuous, $\forall\ x \in [0, 1]$.

4. $f(x) = \text{degree of }(u^{x^2} + u^2 + 2u - 3) = \begin{cases} 2, & x \le \sqrt{2} \\ x^2, & x > \sqrt{2} \end{cases}$

$$f(\sqrt{2}) = \lim_{h\to 0} \frac{f(\sqrt{2}+h) - f(\sqrt{2})}{h}$$

$$= \begin{cases} \lim_{h\to 0^+} \frac{f(h+\sqrt{2}) - f(\sqrt{2})}{h} \\ \lim_{h\to 0^-} \frac{f(h+\sqrt{2}) - f(\sqrt{2})}{h} \end{cases}$$

$$= \begin{cases} \lim_{h\to 0^+} \frac{(h+\sqrt{2})^2 - 2}{h} \\ \lim_{h\to 0^-} \frac{2-2}{h} \end{cases}$$

$$= \begin{cases} \lim_{h\to 0^+} \frac{2+2\sqrt{2}h + h^2 - 2}{h} \\ 0 \end{cases}$$

$$= \begin{cases} \lim_{h\to 0^+} \frac{h^2 + 2\sqrt{2}h}{h} \\ 0 \end{cases}$$

$$= \begin{cases} \lim_{h\to 0^+} (h + 2\sqrt{2}) \\ 0 \end{cases} = \begin{cases} 2\sqrt{2} \\ 0 \end{cases}$$

$\therefore$ $f'(\sqrt{2}^-) \ne f'(\sqrt{2}^+)$

Hence, $f(x)$ is non-differentiable at $x=\sqrt{2}$

$$\lim_{x\to \sqrt{2}^+} f(x) = \lim_{x\to \sqrt{2}^+} x^2 = 2 = f(\sqrt{2}) = \lim_{x\to \sqrt{2}^-} (2)$$

$$\Rightarrow \quad f(\sqrt{2}) = \lim_{x\to \sqrt{2}} f(x) = 2$$

Hence, $f(x)$ is continuous at $x=\sqrt{2}$.

5. Here, $x = 2t - |t-1|$ and $y = 2t^2 + t|t|$

Now, when $t < 0$, $x = 2t - \{-(t-1)\} = 3t - 1$

and $\quad y = 2t^2 - t^2 = t^2$

$$\Rightarrow \quad y = \frac{1}{9}(x+1)^2$$

When $0 \le t < 1$, $x = 2t - (-(t-1)) = 3t - 1$

and $\quad y = 2t^2 + t^2 = 3t^2 \Rightarrow y = \frac{1}{3}(x-1)^2$

When $t \ge 1$, $x = 2t - (t-1) = t + 1$

and $\quad y = 2t^2 + t^2 = 3t^2 \Rightarrow y = 3(x-1)^2$

Thus, $$y = f(x) = \begin{cases} \frac{1}{9}(x+1)^2, & x < -1 \\ \frac{1}{3}(x+1)^2, & -1 \le x < 2 \\ 3(x-1)^2, & x \ge 2 \end{cases}$$

Now, to check continuity at $x=-1$ and 2.

Continuity at $x = -1$

$$\text{LHL} = \lim_{h\to 0} f(-1-h) = \lim_{h\to 0} \frac{1}{9}(-1-h+1)^2 = 0$$

$$\text{and RHL} = \lim_{h\to 0} f(-1+h) = \lim_{h\to 0} \frac{1}{3}(-1+h+1)^2 = 0$$

$$f(-1) = 0$$

$\therefore f(x)$ is continuous at $x=-1$.

Now, to check continuity at $x = 2$

$$\text{LHL} = \lim_{h\to 0} f(2-h) = \lim_{h\to 0} \frac{1}{3}(2-h+1)^2 = 3$$

$$\text{and RHL}, \lim_{h\to 0} f(2+h) = \lim_{h\to 0} 3(2+h-1)^2 = 3;$$

and $\quad f(2) = 3.$

Thus, $f(x)$ is continuous at $x=2$.

Now, to check differentiability at $x=-1$ and 2.

Differentiability at $x = -1$

LHD $Lf'(-1)$

$$= \lim_{h\to 0} \frac{f(-1-h) - f(-1)}{-h} = \lim_{h\to 0} \frac{\frac{1}{9}(-1-h+1)^2 - 0}{-h} = 0$$

and RHD $= Rf'(-1)$

$$= \lim_{h\to 0} \frac{f(-1+h)-f(-1)}{h}$$

$$= \lim_{h\to 0} \frac{\frac{1}{3}(-1+h+1)^2 - 0}{h} = 0$$

Hence, $f(x)$ is differentiable at $x = -1$.

Differentiability at $x = 2$

LHD $Lf'(2) = \lim_{h\to 0} \frac{f(2-h)-f(2)}{-h}$

$$= \lim_{h\to 0} \frac{\frac{1}{3}(2-h+1)^2 - 3}{-h} = 2$$

RHD $Rf'(2) = \lim_{h\to 0} \frac{f(2+h)-f(2)}{h}$

$$= \lim_{h\to 0} \frac{3(2+h-1)^2 - 3}{h} = 6$$

Hence, $f(x)$ is not differentiable at $x = 2$.

$\therefore f(x)$ is continuous for all x and differentiable for all x except for $x = 2$.

6. $f(x) = \text{maximum } \{2\sin x, 1-\cos x\}$ may not be differentiable, when $2\sin x = 1 - \cos x$.

$\Rightarrow \quad 4\sin^2 x = (1-\cos x)^2$

$\Rightarrow \quad 4(1+\cos x) = (1-\cos x)$

$\Rightarrow \quad 4 + 4\cos x = 1 - \cos x$

$\Rightarrow \quad 4(1-\cos^2 x) - (1-\cos x)^2 = 0$

$\Rightarrow \quad (1-\cos x)[4 + 4\cos x - 1 + \cos x] = 0$

$\Rightarrow \quad \cos x = 1 \text{ or } \cos x = -\frac{3}{5}$

But for $x \in (0, \pi)$, $\cos x \neq 1$

$\Rightarrow \quad x = \cos^{-1}\left(-\frac{3}{5}\right) \Rightarrow x = \pi - \cos^{-1}\left(\frac{3}{5}\right)$

Graphically, $f(x)$ maximum $\{2\sin x, 1-\cos x\}$ can be represented as shown below (thick curve)

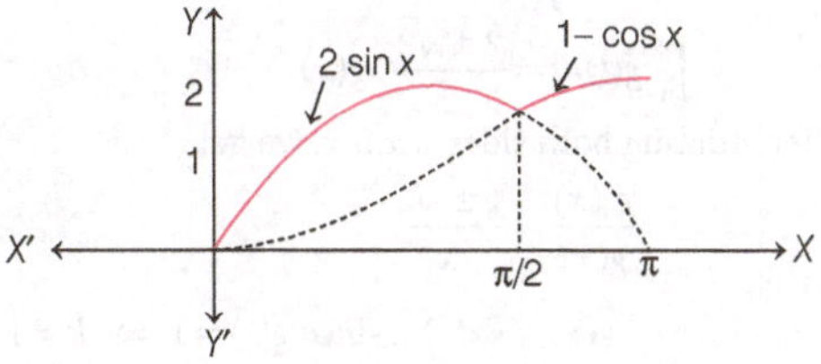

Clearly, $f(x) = \begin{cases} 2\sin x, & 0 < x < \theta \\ 1-\cos x, & 0 \leq x < \pi \end{cases}$, where $\theta = \pi - \cos^{-1}\left(\frac{3}{5}\right)$

$\therefore \quad f'(x) = \begin{cases} 2\cos x, & 0 < x < \theta \\ \sin x, & \theta < x < \pi \end{cases}$

$\therefore \quad f'(0^-) = 2\cos\theta = -\frac{6}{5}$

and $\quad f'(0^+) = \sin\theta = \sin\left(\cos^{-1}\frac{3}{5}\right)$

$$= \sin\left(\sin^{-1}\frac{4}{5}\right) = \frac{4}{5}$$

$\therefore \quad$ LHD $\neq$ RHD at $x = -\cos^{-1}\left(\frac{3}{5}\right)$

Thus, $f(x)$ is differentiable at all $x \in (0, \pi)$ except for $x = \pi - \cos^{-1}\left(\frac{3}{5}\right)$.

7. (i) $f(x) = \begin{cases} x^2 - 2x, & x \geq 0 \\ x^2 + 2x, & x < 0 \end{cases}$

The graph of $f(x)$ is shown below

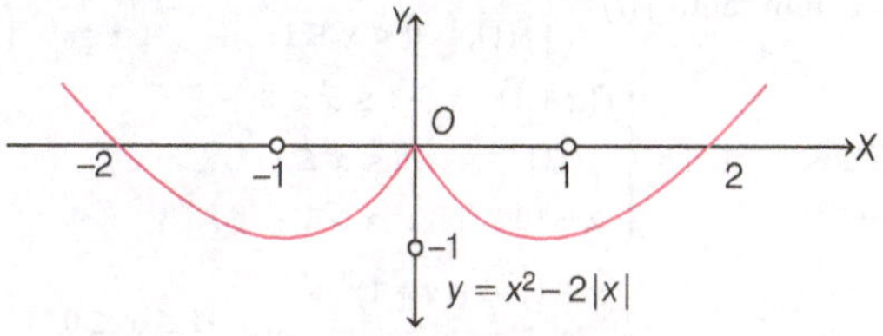

which shows $f(x)$ is continuous for all $x \in R$ but not differentiable at $x = 0$ i.e. differentiable an $R - \{0\}$.

(ii) If $f(x)$ is an increasing function on $[a, b]$, then

max. $\{f(t) : a \leq t \leq x, \ a \leq x \leq b\} = f(x)$

min. $\{f(t) : a \leq t \leq x, \ a \leq x \leq b\} = f(a)$

If $f(x)$ is decreasing function on $[a, b]$, then

max. $\{f(t) : a \leq t \leq x, \ a \leq x \leq b\} = f(a)$

min. $\{f(t) : a \leq t \leq x, \ a \leq x \leq b\} = f(x)$

Clearly, $f(x)$ decreases on $(-\infty, -1]$ and $[0, 1]$, where as increase on $[-1, 0]$ and $[1, \infty)$

$$\therefore \quad g(x) = \begin{cases} f(x), & -2 \leq x \leq -1 \\ f(-1), & -1 \leq x < 0 \\ f(0), & 0 \leq x \leq 1 \\ f(2), & 1 \leq x \leq 2 \end{cases}$$

$$\Rightarrow \quad g(x) = \begin{cases} x^2 + 2x, & -2 \leq x \leq -1 \\ -1, & -1 \leq x < 0 \\ 0, & 0 \leq x < 2 \\ x^2 - 2x, & x > 2 \end{cases}$$

$$\Rightarrow \quad g'(x) = \begin{cases} 2x + 2, & -2 \leq x < -1 \\ 0, & -1 < x < 0 \\ 0, & 0 < x < 2 \\ 2x - 2, & x > 2 \end{cases}$$

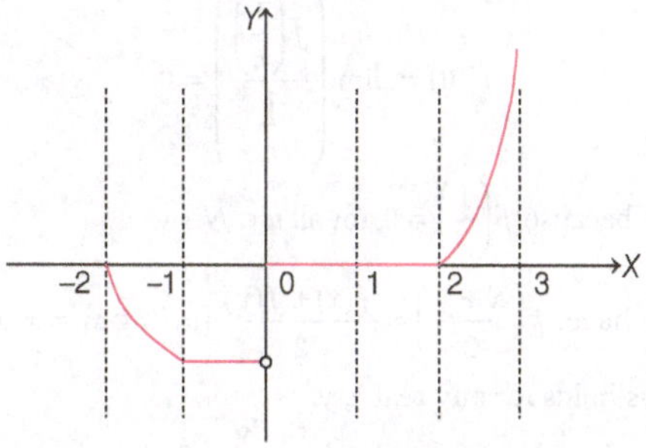

Thus, graph of $g(x)$ is as shown above

From above figure, it is clear that $g(x)$ is not continuous at $x = 0$ and from $g'(x)$, $g(x)$ is non-differentiable at $x = -1$, 0 and 2.

8. Here, $f(x) = x^4 - 8x^3 + 22x^2 - 24x$

$\Rightarrow \quad f'(x) = 4x^3 - 24x^2 + 44x - 24$

or $\quad f'(x) = 4(x-1)(x-2)(x-3)$

$\quad = 4(x^3 - 6x^2 + 11x - 6)$

which shows $f(x)$ is increasing in $[1, 2] \cup [3, \infty)$ and decreasing in $(-\infty, 1] \cup [2, 3]$.

Thus, minimum $f(t), x \le t \le x+1, -1 \le x \le 1$ is given by

$$\Rightarrow \text{minimum } f(t) = \begin{cases} f(x+1), & -1 \le x \le 0 \\ f(1), & 0 < x \le 1 \end{cases}$$

Thus, $$g(x) = \begin{cases} f(x+1), & -1 \le x \le 0 \\ f(1), & 0 < x \le 1 \\ x - 10, & x > 1 \end{cases}$$

$$= \begin{cases} (x+1)^4 - 8(x+1)^3 + 22(x+1)^2 - 24(x+1), & -1 \le x \le 0 \\ 1 - 8 + 22 - 24, & 0 < x \le 1 \\ x - 10, & x > 1 \end{cases}$$

$$g(x) = \begin{cases} x^4 - 4x^3 + 4x^2 - 9, & -1 \le x \le 0 \\ -9, & 0 < x \le 1 \\ x - 10, & x > 1 \end{cases}$$

Also, $$g'(x) = \begin{cases} 4x^3 - 12x^2 + 8x, & -1 \le x \le 0 \\ 0, & 0 < x \le 1 \\ +1, & x > 1 \end{cases}$$

$\Rightarrow g(x)$ is continuous on $[-1, \infty)$ but non-differentiable at $x = 1$

9. (i) Since, f is continuous at 0 and $\lim_{n \to \infty} \left(\frac{1}{n}\right) = 0$,

we must have, $f(0) = \lim_{n \to \infty} f\left(\frac{1}{n}\right) = 0$,

since we are given that $f\left(\frac{1}{n}\right) = 0$, for all $n \in N$.

(ii) By part (i), we have $f(0) = 0$ and so

$$f'(0) = \lim_{x \to 0}\left(\frac{f(x) - f(0)}{x - 0}\right) = \lim_{x \to 0}\left(\frac{f(x)}{x}\right)$$

Thus, since $\frac{1}{n} \ne 0$ and $\frac{1}{n} \to 0$ as $n \to \infty$

$$f'(0) = \lim_{n \to \infty}\left(\frac{f\left(\frac{1}{n}\right)}{\frac{1}{n}}\right) = 0$$

because $f\left(\frac{1}{n}\right) = 0$, for all $n \in N$.

10. We have, $f\left(\frac{x+y}{2}\right) = \frac{f(x) + f(y)}{2}$ [taking $x_1 = x, x_2 = y, n = 2$]

This holds for any real x, y.

So, y is independent of x i.e. $\frac{dy}{dx} = 0$

On differentiating w.r.t. x, we get

$$f'\left(\frac{x+y}{2}\right) \cdot \frac{1}{2}\left(1 + \frac{dy}{dx}\right) = \frac{1}{2}\left\{f'(x) + f'(y)\frac{dy}{dx}\right\}$$

$$\therefore \quad \frac{1}{2} f'\left(\frac{x+y}{2}\right) = \frac{1}{2} f'(x)$$

On taking $x = 0$ and x in place of y, we get

$$\frac{1}{2} f'\left(\frac{0+x}{2}\right) = \frac{1}{2} f'(0)$$

$$\therefore \quad f'\left(\frac{x}{2}\right) = f'(0) = a \qquad \text{[given]}$$

On integrating w.r.t. $\frac{x}{2}, f\left(\frac{x}{2}\right) = a \cdot \frac{x}{2} + c$

When $x = 0$, $f(0) = 0 + c$ i.e. $b = c$ $\quad [\because f(0) = b \text{ (given)}]$

Thus, $$f\left(\frac{x}{2}\right) = \frac{ax}{2} + b \qquad \text{...(i)}$$

Again, on putting $y = 0$ in $f\left(\frac{x+y}{2}\right) = \frac{f(x) + f(y)}{2}$, we get

$$f\left(\frac{x}{2}\right) = \frac{f(x) + f(0)}{2} = \frac{f(x) + b}{2}$$

$\therefore$ From Eq. (i), $\frac{f(x) + b}{2} = \frac{ax}{2} + b$

Hence, $f(x) = ax + b$

11. Here, $\int_0^x g(t)dt = 2\left(\int_0^x g(x-t)\right)dt$, the given equation could be written as

$$x\int_0^x g^2(t)dt = 2\left(\int_0^x g(t)dt\right)^2 \qquad \text{...(i)}$$

On differentiating both sides w.r.t. x, we get

$$\int_0^x g^2(t)dt + xg^2(x) = 4g(x)\left\{\int_0^x g(t)dt\right\}$$

or $$x\int_0^x g^2(t)dt + x^2g^2(x) = 4xg(x)\int_0^x g(t)dt \qquad \text{...(ii)}$$

Using Eq. (i), we get

$$2\left(\int_0^x g(t)dt\right)^2 + x^2g^2(x) = 4xg(x)\int_0^x g(t)dt$$

$$\Rightarrow 2\left(\int_0^x g(t)dt\right)^2 - 4xg(x)\int_0^x g(t)dt + x^2g^2(x) = 0,$$

which is quadratic in $\int_0^x g(t)dt$.

$$\therefore \quad \int_0^x g(t)dt = \frac{2 \pm \sqrt{2}}{2} xg(x)$$

On differentiating both sides w.r.t. x, we get

$$\frac{g'(x)}{g(x)} = \frac{1 \pm \sqrt{2}}{x}$$

$$\Rightarrow \quad g(x) = kx^{1 \pm \sqrt{2}}, \text{ since } g(1) = 1 \Rightarrow k = 1$$

$$\therefore \quad g(x) = x^{1 \pm \sqrt{2}}$$

which is continuous in $[0, \infty)$.

12. $|f(2^k) - f(2^i)| = |f(2^k) - f(2^{k-1})$

$\qquad + f(2^{k-1}) - f(2^{k-2}) \dots f(2^{i+1}) - f(2^i)|$

$\le |f(2^k) - f(2^{k-1})| + |f(2^{k-1}) - f(2^{k-2})| + \dots |f(2^{i+1}) - f(2^i)|$

Consider $|f(2^{k-1} + 2^{k-1})| - |f(2^{k-1})| \le 1$

So, $|f(2^k) - f(2^i)| \le 1 + 1 + \dots (k-i)$ term

$$\le \sum |f(2^k) - f(2^i)| \le \sum_{i=1}^{k} (k-i) \le \frac{k \cdot (k-1)}{2}$$ **Hence proved.**

13. Since, $g(x)$ is a polynomial of degree one.

$\therefore\ g(x) = ax + b$

because $f(x)$ is continuous function, thus it is continuous at $x = 0$.

$$\therefore \quad f(0) = \text{RHL}$$

$$\Rightarrow \quad a \cdot 0 + b = \lim_{x \to 0+h} \left(\frac{1+x}{2+x}\right)^{1/x} \quad [\because f(0) = g(0)]$$

$$\Rightarrow \quad b = \left(\frac{1}{2}\right)^{\infty} = 0$$

$$\text{Hence,} \quad f(x) = \begin{cases} ax + 0, & x \le 0 \\ \left(\dfrac{1+x}{2+x}\right)^{1/x}, & x > 0 \end{cases}$$

Now, $\quad f(-1) = a(-1) = -a$ and for $x > 0$,

$$f(x) = \left(\frac{1+x}{2+x}\right)^{1/x} = e^{\frac{1}{x}\log\left(\frac{1+x}{2+x}\right)}$$

$$\therefore \quad f'(x) = e^{\frac{1}{x}\{\log(1+x) - \log(2+x)\}} \times \left\{\frac{1}{x}\left(\frac{1}{1+x} - \frac{1}{2+x}\right) + \{\log(1+x) - \log(2+x)\}\left(-\frac{1}{x^2}\right)\right\}$$

$$\therefore \quad f'(1) = e^{\log\frac{2}{3}} \cdot \left\{\frac{1}{6} - \log\frac{2}{3}\right\} = \frac{2}{3}\left\{\frac{1}{6} - \log\left(\frac{2}{3}\right)\right\}$$

Since, $\quad f(-1) = f'(1)$

$$-a = \frac{2}{3}\left\{\frac{1}{6} - \log\left(\frac{2}{3}\right)\right\} \Rightarrow a = -\frac{1}{9} + \frac{2}{3}\log\left(\frac{2}{3}\right)$$

Thus, $g(x) = ax = \left\{-\dfrac{1}{a} + \dfrac{2}{3}\log\left(\dfrac{2}{3}\right)\right\} \cdot x$

14. Equation of chord AB

$$y - f(a) = \frac{f(b) - f(a)}{b - a}(x - a)$$

This line passes through $(0, 2ab)$.

Therefore, $\quad 2ab - f(a) = \dfrac{f(a) - f(b)}{b - a} \times a$

$$2ab(b - a) - (b - a)f(a) = af(a) - af(b)$$

$$2(b - a) = \frac{f(a)}{a} - \frac{f(b)}{b}$$

$$\frac{f(a)}{a} + 2a = \frac{f(b)}{b} + 2b = k \text{ (let)}$$

Therefore, $\dfrac{f(x)}{x} + 2x = k$

$$f(x) = -2x^2 + kx$$

$$\lim_{x \to 0}\left(\frac{f(x)}{2x}\right)^{1/x} = \frac{1}{e}$$

$$\lim_{x \to 0}\left(\frac{-2x^2 + kx}{2x}\right)^{1/x} = \frac{1}{e} \Rightarrow k = 2$$

$$f(x) = -2x^2 + 2x$$

$$f(x-1) = -2(x-1)(x-2)$$

$|f(x-1)|$ is non-differentiable at 3 points.

15. Here, $\quad f(x) = (x + [x^3 + 1])^{x^2 + \sin x}$

$$\Rightarrow \quad f(x) = \begin{cases} (x+2)^{x^2+\sin x}, & 1 < x < 2^{1/3} \\ (x+3)^{x^2+\sin x}, & 2^{1/3} \le x < 3^{1/3} \\ (x+4)^{x^2+\sin x}, & 3^{1/3} \le x < 3/2 \end{cases}$$

$$\text{As } [x^3 + 1] = \begin{cases} 2, & 1 < x < 2^{1/3} \\ 3, & 2^{1/3} \le x < x^{1/3} \\ 4, & 3^{1/3} \le x < 3/2 \end{cases}$$

which shows $f(x)$ is discontinuous at $x = 2^{1/3}$ and $3^{1/3}$ and not differentiable at $x = 2^{1/3}$ and $3^{1/3}$.

Also,

$$f(x) = \begin{cases} (x+2)^{x^2+\sin x}\left\{\begin{matrix}(2x + \cos x)\ln(x+2) \\ + \dfrac{x^2 + \sin x}{x+2}\end{matrix}\right\}, & x \in (1, 2^{1/3}) \\ (x+3)^{x^2+\sin x}, \left\{\begin{matrix}(2x + \cos x)\ln(x+3) \\ + \dfrac{x^2 + \sin x}{x+3}\end{matrix}\right\}, & x \in (2^{1/3}, 3^{1/3}) \\ (x+4)^{x^2+\sin x}, \left\{\begin{matrix}(2x + \cos x)\ln(x+4) \\ + \dfrac{x^2 + \sin x}{x+4}\end{matrix}\right\}, & x \in (3^{1/3}, 3/2) \end{cases}$$

as $\dfrac{d}{dx}(f(x)g(x)) = f(x)g(x)\left\{\dfrac{g(x)}{g(x)}f'(x) + g'(x)\ln f(x)\right\}$

Clearly, $f(x)$ is discontinuous at $x = 2^{1/3}$ and $x = 3^{1/3}$

16. $\displaystyle\lim_{x \to 0}\frac{1}{x}\left[f(x) + f\left(\frac{x}{2}\right) + \ldots + f\left(\frac{x}{k}\right)\right]$

$$= \lim_{x \to 0}\frac{f(x)}{x} + \frac{f\left(\frac{x}{2}\right)}{x} + \ldots + \frac{f\left(\frac{x}{k}\right)}{x}$$

$$= \lim_{x \to 0}\frac{f(x+0) - f(0)}{x} + \lim_{x \to 0}\frac{f\left(\frac{x}{2} + 0\right) - f(0)}{\frac{x}{2}} \cdot \frac{1}{2} + \ldots + \lim_{x \to 0^+}\frac{f\left(\frac{x}{k} + 0\right) - f(0)}{\frac{x}{k}} \cdot \frac{1}{k}$$

$$= f'(0) + \frac{1}{2}f'(0) + \ldots + \frac{1}{k}f'(0)$$

$$= 1 + \frac{1}{2} + \ldots + \frac{1}{k}$$

Hence proved.

5

> “Mathematics is the most beautiful and most powerful creation of the human spirit.*
>
> **-Stefan Banach**

Differentiation

Learning Milestones

Milestone 1 Derivative and Its Geometrical Meaning
- Meaning of Derivatives
- Geometrical Meaning of Derivatives
- Derivative of *f*(*x*) by First Principle
- Some Standard Formulae
- Rules for Differentiation

Milestone 2 Differentiation of Implicit Functions
- Chain Rule
- Differentiation of Implicit Function

Milestone 3 Differentiation of Inverse Function
- Derivatives of Invertible Function
- Geometrical Interpretation
- Derivatives Involving Inverse Trigonometric Function (ITF)

Milestone 4 Logarithmic Differentiation

Milestone 5 Differentiation of Parametric Function
- Parametric Differentiation
- Differentiation of One Function with respect to Other Function

Milestone 6 Higher Order Derivatives

Milestone 7 Special Points
- Differentiation of a Function in the form of Determinant
- Sum of Special Series Obtained by Differentiation

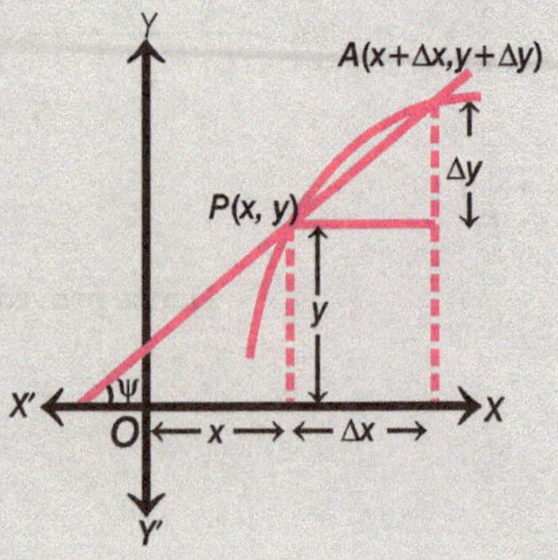

Practice Milestones

Practice Milestone 1- JEE Main Pattern

Practice Milestone 2 - JEE Advanced Pattern

Practice Milestone 3 - Challenging Problems

Milestone 1 Derivative and Its Geometrical Meaning

- Meaning of Derivatives • Geometrical Meaning of Derivatives • Derivative of $f(x)$ by First Principle
- Some Standard Formulae • Rules for Differentiation

In calculus 'Differentiation' plays very important role. Differentiation is a process of finding derivatives and derivatives represent the rate of change of quantities.

5.1 Meaning of Derivatives

The rate of change of dependent variable y with respect to change in independent variable x is known as derivative of y with respect to x and denoted by $\frac{dy}{dx}$.

In case of function $y = f(x)$, derivative is denoted by $\frac{dy}{dx}, f'(x)$ or y_1.

5.2 Geometrical Meaning of Derivatives

Let us consider a function $y = f(x)$ in a rectangular coordinate system. We also consider a point $P(x, y)$ on the curve. If a point corresponding to an increased value of the argument $x + \Delta x$ is considered, its ordinate value is given by $y + \Delta y = f(x + \Delta x)$.

In figure, the point $(x + \Delta x, y + \Delta y)$ is represented by A.

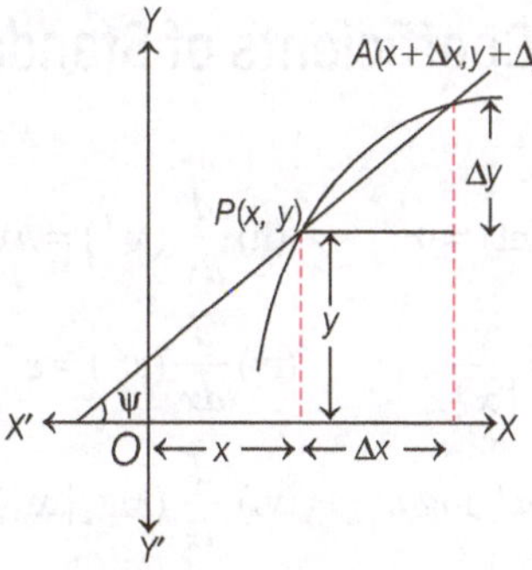

Here, PA is the secant to the curve.

Now, as $\Delta x \to 0, \Delta y \to 0 \Rightarrow PA \to 0$

(i.e. the distance PA tends to zero or to a single point P)

$\Rightarrow \lim_{\Delta x \to 0}$ (slope of chord PA) $\to$ (slope of tangent at P).

or $$\lim_{\Delta x \to 0} \tan \psi = \tan \theta$$

$$\Rightarrow \quad \lim_{\Delta x \to 0} \frac{\Delta y}{\Delta x} = \frac{dy}{dx} \text{ or } f'(x)$$

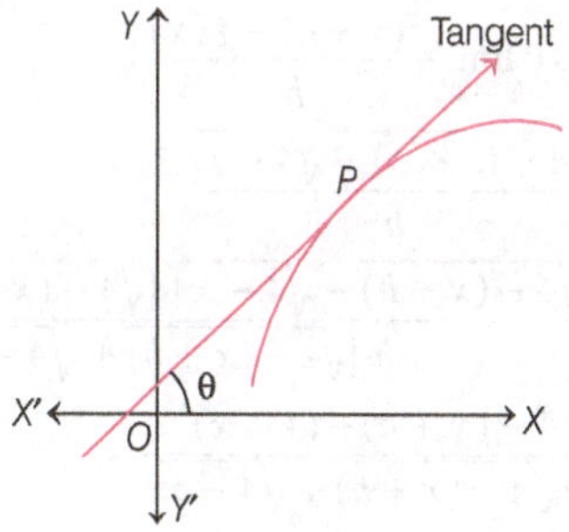

which means that the value of the derivative $f'(x)$ for a given value of x is equal to the tangent of the angle formed by the tangent line to the graph of the function $y = f(x)$ at the point $P(x, y)$ with the positive X-axis.

JEE Focus Points

Concept Inside Video

Relation between dy/dx and dx/dy

Let x and y be two variables connected by a relation of the form $f(x, y) = 0$.

Let Δx be a small change in x and Δy be a small change in y, then

$$\frac{dy}{dx} = \lim_{\Delta x \to 0} \frac{\Delta y}{\Delta x} \text{ and } \frac{dx}{dy} = \lim_{\Delta y \to 0} \frac{\Delta x}{\Delta y}$$

Now, $$\frac{\Delta y}{\Delta x} \cdot \frac{\Delta x}{\Delta y} = 1 \Rightarrow \lim_{\Delta x \to 0} \left(\frac{\Delta y}{\Delta x} \cdot \frac{\Delta x}{\Delta y} \right) = 1$$

$$\Rightarrow \quad \lim_{\Delta x \to 0} \frac{\Delta y}{\Delta x} \cdot \lim_{\Delta y \to 0} \frac{\Delta x}{\Delta y} = 1 \qquad [\because \Delta x \to 0 \Leftrightarrow \Delta y \to 0]$$

$$\Rightarrow \quad \frac{dy}{dx} \cdot \frac{dx}{dy} = 1$$

So, $$\frac{dy}{dx} = \frac{1}{dx/dy}$$

$\frac{dy}{dx}$ is also known as differential coefficient.

5.3 Derivative of $f(x)$ by First Principle

(Ab-Initio Method/Delta Method (by definition))

Statement Let $y = f(x)$ be any differentiable function, then its derivative is given by

$$\frac{dy}{dx} = \lim_{\Delta x \to 0} \frac{\Delta y}{\Delta x}$$

$$= \lim_{\Delta x \to 0} \frac{f(x+\Delta x) - f(x)}{\Delta x}$$

$$= \lim_{h \to 0} \frac{f(x+h) - f(x)}{h} = f'(x)$$

Example 1. Find the derivatives of the following functions using first principle.

(i) $\sqrt{4-x}$ (ii) $x^3 - 2x - 4$

(iii) $\ln^2 x$ (iv) e^{x^2}

Sol. (i) Let $f(x) = \sqrt{4-x}$, then $f(x+h) = \sqrt{4-(x+h)}$

$$\therefore \frac{d}{dx}(f(x)) = \lim_{h \to 0} \frac{f(x+h) - f(x)}{h}$$

$$= \lim_{h \to 0} \frac{\sqrt{4-(x+h)} - \sqrt{4-x}}{h}$$

$$= \lim_{h \to 0} \frac{\{\sqrt{4-(x+h)} - \sqrt{4-x}\}\{\sqrt{4-(x+h)} + \sqrt{4-x}\}}{h\{\sqrt{4-(x+h)} + \sqrt{4-x}\}}$$

$$= \lim_{h \to 0} \frac{4-(x+h)-(4-x)}{h\{\sqrt{4-(x+h)} + \sqrt{4-x}\}}$$

$$= \lim_{h \to 0} \frac{-h}{h\{\sqrt{4-x-h} + \sqrt{4-x}\}}$$

$$= \frac{-1}{2\sqrt{4-x}}$$

(ii) On substituting $x + \Delta x$ for x, we get

$$y + \Delta y = (x+\Delta x)^3 - 2(x+\Delta x) - 4$$

$$= x^3 + 3x^2\Delta x + 3x(\Delta x)^2 + (\Delta x)^3 - 2x - 2\Delta x - 4$$

On subtracting y from $y + \Delta y$, we get

$$\Delta y = 3x^2\Delta x + 3x(\Delta x)^2 + (\Delta x)^3 - 2\Delta x$$

On dividing by Δx,

$$\frac{\Delta y}{\Delta x} = 3x^2 + 3x\,\Delta x + (\Delta x)^2 - 2$$

Let $\Delta x \to 0$

The second and third terms of $\frac{\Delta y}{\Delta x}$ will evidently approach 0, therefore $\frac{dy}{dx} = 3x^2 - 2$.

(iii) $y = f(x) = \ln^2 x$

$$\frac{dy}{dx} = \lim_{h \to 0} \frac{f(x+h) - f(x)}{h}$$

$$= \lim_{h \to 0} \frac{\ln^2(x+h) - \ln^2 x}{h}$$

$$= \lim_{h \to 0} \left(\frac{\ln(x+h) - \ln x}{h}\right)(\ln(x+h) + \ln x)$$

$$= \lim_{h \to 0} \frac{\ln\left(1+\frac{h}{x}\right)}{h}(\ln(x+h) + \ln x)$$

$$= \frac{2\ln x}{x}$$

(iv) Let $f(x) = e^{x^2} \Rightarrow f(x+h) = e^{(x+h)^2}$

$$\therefore \frac{d}{dx} f(x) = \lim_{h \to 0} \frac{f(x+h) - f(x)}{h}$$

$$= \lim_{h \to 0} \frac{e^{(x+h)^2} - e^{x^2}}{h}$$

$$= \lim_{h \to 0} \frac{e^{x^2 + h^2 + 2hx} - e^{x^2}}{h}$$

$$= \lim_{h \to 0} \frac{e^{x^2} \cdot e^{h^2 + 2hx} - e^{x^2}}{h}$$

$$= \lim_{h \to 0} e^{x^2}\left(\frac{e^{h^2+2hx} - 1}{h}\right)$$

$$= e^{x^2} \lim_{h \to 0}\left(\frac{e^{h^2+2hx} - 1}{h^2 + 2hx}\right) \times \left(\frac{h^2 + 2hx}{h}\right)$$

$$= e^{x^2} \lim_{t \to 0}\left(\frac{e^t - 1}{t}\right) \lim_{h \to 0}(h + 2x),$$

where $t = h^2 + 2hx$

$$= e^{x^2} \times 1 \times \lim_{h \to 0}(h + 2x)\left[\because \lim_{x \to 0} \frac{e^x - 1}{x} = 1\right]$$

$$= e^{x^2} \times 2x = 2xe^{x^2}$$

5.4 Some Standard Formulae

Differential Coefficients of Standard Functions

(i) $\frac{d}{dx}(\text{constant}) = 0$ (ii) $\frac{d}{dx}(x^n) = nx^{n-1}$

(iii) $\frac{d}{dx}(|x|) = \frac{x}{|x|}$ (iv) $\frac{d}{dx}(e^x) = e^x$

(v) $\frac{d}{dx}(a^x) = a^x \log a$ (vi) $\frac{d}{dx}(\log_e |x|) = \frac{1}{x}$

(vii) $\frac{d}{dx}(\log_a |x|) = \frac{1}{x \log_e a}$

(viii) $\frac{d}{dx}(\sin x) = \cos x$ (ix) $\frac{d}{dx}(\cos x) = -\sin x$

(x) $\frac{d}{dx}(\tan x)=\sec^2 x$ (xi) $\frac{d}{dx}(\cot x)=-\operatorname{cosec}^2 x$

(xii) $\frac{d}{dx}(\sec x)=\sec x\tan x$

(xiii) $\frac{d}{dx}(\operatorname{cosec} x)=-\operatorname{cosec} x\cot x$

(xiv) $\frac{d}{dx}(\sin^{-1} x)=\frac{1}{\sqrt{1-x^2}}, \ -1<x<1 \text{ or } |x|<1$

(xv) $\frac{d}{dx}(\cos^{-1} x)=\frac{-1}{\sqrt{1-x^2}}, -1<x<1 \text{ or } |x|<1$

(xvi) $\frac{d}{dx}(\tan^{-1} x)=\frac{1}{1+x^2}, \ -\infty<x<\infty \text{ or } x\in R$

(xvii) $\frac{d}{dx}(\sec^{-1} x)=\frac{1}{|x|\sqrt{x^2-1}}, |x|>1 \text{ or } x\in R-[-1,1]$

(xviii) $\frac{d}{dx}(\cot^{-1} x)=\frac{-1}{1+x^2}, \ -\infty<x<\infty \text{ or } x\in R$

(xix) $\frac{d}{dx}(\operatorname{cosec}^{-1} x)=\frac{-1}{|x|\sqrt{x^2-1}}, |x|>1 \text{ or } x\in R-[-1,1]$

Example 2. Find $\frac{dy}{dx}$ of the following.

(i) $y=(1+x^{1/4})(1+x^{1/2})(1-x^{1/4})$

(ii) $y=x|x|$

(iii) $y=\sqrt{\frac{1-\cos 2x}{1+\cos 2x}}, x\in\left(0,\frac{\pi}{2}\right)\cup\left(\frac{\pi}{2},\pi\right)$

Sol. (i) $y=(1-x^{1/2})(1+x^{1/2})=(1)^2-(x^{1/2})^2$

$$=1-x$$

$$y=1-x$$

$$\frac{dy}{dx}=-1$$

(ii) $y=x|x|=\begin{cases}-x^2, & x\le 0\\ x^2, & x>0\end{cases}$

$$\frac{dy}{dx}=\begin{cases}-2x & x\le 0\\ 2x & x>0\end{cases}$$

(iii) $y=\sqrt{\frac{1-\cos 2x}{1+\cos 2x}}=\sqrt{\frac{2\sin^2 x}{2\cos^2 x}}=\sqrt{\tan^2 x}=|\tan x|$

$$y=\begin{cases}\tan x, & 0<x<\frac{\pi}{2}\\ -\tan x, & \frac{\pi}{2}<x<\pi\end{cases}$$

$$\frac{dy}{dx}=\begin{cases}\sec^2 x, & 0<x<\frac{\pi}{2}\\ -\sec^2 x, & \frac{\pi}{2}<x<\pi\end{cases}$$

JEE Focus Points

- Always keep a point in your mind that we are differentiating with respect to x or any other variables.
- When we are finding derivative of a function first of all simplify it, if it is possible.
- The value of derivative at $x=a$ is denoted by $f'(a)$ or $\left.\frac{dy}{dx}\right|_{x=a}$.

Example 3. Find $\frac{dy}{da}$ and $\frac{dy}{dx}$ where

$y=a^x+e^a+\sin x+\log_e a$

Sol. $y=a^x+e^a+\sin x+\log_e a$

On differentiating both sides w.r.t. a, we get

$$\frac{dy}{da}=x\cdot a^{x-1}+e^a+\frac{1}{a}$$

and differentiating both sides w.r.t. x, we get

$$\frac{dy}{dx}=a^x\ln a+\cos x$$

Example 4. Let $y=\frac{2^{\log_{2^{1/4}} x}-3^{\log_{27}(x^2+1)^3}-2x}{7^{4\log_{49} x}-x-1}$ and $\frac{dy}{dx}=ax+b$, find the value of a and b.

Sol. $y=\frac{x^4-(x^2+2x+1)}{x^2-x-1}=x^2+x+1$

$$\left[\begin{array}{l}\because a^{\log_c b}=b^{\log_c a}\\ \therefore 2^{\log_{2^{1/4}} x}=x^4, 3^{\log_{27}(x^2+1)^3}=x^2+1 \text{ and } 7^{4\log_{49} x}=x^2\end{array}\right]$$

$$\therefore \frac{dy}{dx}=2x+1=ax+b$$

Hence, $a=2$ and $b=1$

Example 5. Find $\frac{dy}{dx}$ and its value at $x=\frac{\pi}{4}$

$$y=\frac{4\tan(x/4)-4\tan^3(x/4)}{1-6\tan^2(x/4)+\tan^4(x/4)}+\frac{1-\cot^2 x/2}{2\cot x/2}$$

Sol. $y=\frac{4\tan(x/4)-4\tan^3(x/4)}{1-6\tan^2(x/4)+\tan^4(x/4)}+\frac{1-\cot^2(x/2)}{2\cot(x/2)}$

$$=\tan(4(x/4))-\cot(2(x/2))$$

$$=\tan x-\cot x$$

$$\frac{dy}{dx}=\sec^2 x+\operatorname{cosec}^2 x$$

$$\left.\frac{dy}{dx}\right|_{x=\frac{\pi}{4}}=\sec^2\frac{\pi}{4}+\operatorname{cosec}^2\frac{\pi}{4}$$

$$=2+2$$

$$=4$$

5.5 Rules for Differentiation

1. **Addition and Subtraction Rule** Let $f(x)$ and $g(x)$ are two differentiable functions, then $\frac{d}{dx}[f(x) \pm g(x)]$

$$= \frac{d}{dx}[f(x)] \pm \frac{d}{dx}[g(x)]$$

In general, $\frac{d}{dx}[f_1(x) \pm f_2(x) \pm \ldots \pm f_n(x)]$

$$= \frac{d}{dx}(f_1(x)) \pm \frac{d}{dx}(f_2(x)) \pm \ldots \pm \frac{d}{dx}(f_n(x))$$

Example 6. Find derivative of following.

(i) $y = x^2 + \sin^{-1} x - \log_e x$

(ii) $y = \log_e x + \log_e 10 - \log_x x - \log_{10} 10$

(iii) $y = \frac{1}{\sqrt{x}} + e^x - \frac{\sin x}{\cos x} - 2^x$

Sol. (i) $y = x^2 + \sin^{-1} x - \log_e x$

On differentiating both sides w.r.t. x, we get

$$\frac{dy}{dx} = \frac{d}{dx}(x^2 + \sin^{-1} x - \log_e x)$$

$$= \frac{d}{dx}(x^2) + \frac{d}{dx}(\sin^{-1} x) - \frac{d}{dx}(\log_e x) \quad \text{[using rule 1]}$$

$$= 2x + \frac{1}{\sqrt{1-x^2}} - \frac{1}{x}$$

(ii) $y = \log_e x + \log_e 10 - \log_x x - \log_{10} 10$

$\because \quad \log_a a = 1$

$\therefore \quad y = \log_e x + \log_e 10 - 1 - 1$

$= \log_e x + \log_e 10 - 2$

On differentiating both sides w.r.t. x, we get

$$\frac{dy}{dx} = \frac{d}{dx}(\log_e x + \log_e 10 - 2)$$

$$= \frac{d}{dx}(\log_e x) + \frac{d}{dx}(\log_e 10) - \frac{d}{dx}(2)$$

$$= \frac{1}{x} + 0 - 0$$

$$= \frac{1}{x}$$

(iii) $y = \frac{1}{\sqrt{x}} + e^x - \frac{\sin x}{\cos x} - 2^x = x^{-1/2} + e^x - \tan x - 2^x$

On differentiating both sides w.r.t. x, we get

$$\frac{dy}{dx} = \frac{d}{dx}(x^{-1/2}) + \frac{d}{dx}(e^x) - \frac{d}{dx}(\tan x) - \frac{d}{dx}(2^x)$$

$$= -\frac{1}{2}x^{-1/2-1} + e^x - \sec^2 x - 2^x \ln 2$$

$$= -\frac{1}{2}x^{-3/2} + e^x - \sec^2 x - 2^x \ln 2$$

2. **Scalar Multiplication Rule** Let $f(x)$ be any differentiable function and K be any scalar, then

$$\frac{d}{dx}[Kf(x)] = K\frac{d}{dx}[f(x)]$$

In general, $\frac{d}{dx}[K_1 f_1(x) + K_2 f_2(x) + \ldots K_n f_n(x)]$

$$= K_1 \frac{d}{dx}[f_1(x)] + K_2 \frac{d}{dx}[f_2(x)] + \ldots + K_n \frac{d}{dx}[f_n(x)]$$

3. **Product Rule** Let $f(x)$ and $g(x)$ be two differentiable functions, then

$$\frac{d}{dx}[f(x) \cdot g(x)] = f(x) \cdot \frac{d}{dx}[g(x)] + g(x) \cdot \frac{d}{dx}[f(x)],$$

In other way, $(uv)' = uv' + vu'$

JEE Focus Points

- $(uvw)' = uvw' + uv'w + u'vw$
- $(f_1 f_2 f_3 \ldots f_n)' = f'_1 f_2 f_3 \ldots f_n + f_1 f'_2 f_3 \ldots f_n + \ldots + f_1 f_2 f_3 \ldots f'_n$

Example 7. Find $f'(x)$ for the following functions.

(i) $f(x) = 5xe^x + \sin 2x - 6\ln^2 x$

(ii) $f(x) = 7x^3 \cos x - 5^x \cdot \ln x + 8e^{2x}$

Sol. (i) $f(x) = 5xe^x + \sin 2x - 6\ln^2 x$

$= 5xe^x + 2\sin x \cos x - 6(\ln x)(\ln x)$

On differentiating both sides w.r.t. x,

$$f'(x) = \frac{d}{dx}(5xe^x) + \frac{d}{dx}(2\sin x \cos x) - \frac{d}{dx}(6\ln x \cdot \ln x)$$

$$= 5\frac{d}{dx}(xe^x) + 2\frac{d}{dx}(\sin x \cos x) - 6\frac{d}{dx}(\ln x \cdot \ln x)$$

$$= 5\left[x\frac{d}{dx}e^x + e^x\frac{d}{dx}(x)\right] + 2\left[\sin x \frac{d}{dx}(\cos x) + \cos x \frac{d}{dx}(\sin x)\right] - 6\left[\ln x \frac{d}{dx}(\ln x) + \ln x \frac{d}{dx}(\ln x)\right]$$

$$= 5[xe^x + e^x] + 2[-\sin^2 x + \cos^2 x] - 6\left(\frac{\ln x}{x} + \frac{\ln x}{x}\right)$$

$$= 5e^x(x+1) + 2\cos 2x - \frac{12\ln x}{x}$$

(ii) $f(x) = 7x^3 \cos x - 5^x \ln x + 8e^{2x}$

On differentiating both sides w.r.t. x, we get

$$f'(x) = 7\left[x^3\frac{d}{dx}(\cos x) + \cos x \frac{d}{dx}(x^3)\right] - \left[5^x\frac{d}{dx}(\ln x) + \ln x \frac{d}{dx}(5^x)\right] + 8\left[e^x\frac{d}{dx}(e^x) + e^x\frac{d}{dx}(e^x)\right]$$

$$= 7(-x^3 \sin x + 3x^2 \cos x) - \left[5^x \cdot \frac{1}{x} + \ln x \cdot 5^x \cdot \ln 5\right] + 8\,[2e^{2x}]$$

$$= 7x^2\,[3\cos x - x\sin x] - 5^x\left[\frac{1}{x} + \ln x \cdot \ln 5\right] + 16e^{2x}$$

Example 8. Let $F(x) = f(x)\cdot g(x)\cdot h(x)$. If for some $x = x_0$, $F'(x_0) = 21F(x_0)$, $f'(x_0) = 4f(x_0)$, $g'(x_0) = -7g(x_0)$ and $h'(x_0) = kh(x_0)$, then find k.

Sol. $F(x) = f(x)\,g(x)\,h(x)$

Given that

$$F'(x_0) = 21F(x_0),\ f'(x_0) = 4f(x_0);$$
$$g'(x_0) = -7g(x_0) \text{ and } h'(x_0) = kh(x_0)$$
$$F'(x_0) = f'(x_0)\,g(x_0)\,h(x_0) + f(x_0)\,g'(x_0)\,h(x_0) + f(x_0)\,g(x_0)\,h'(x_0)$$
$$21F(x_0) = (4 - 7 + k)\,f(x_0)\,g(x_0)\,h(x_0)$$
$$\Rightarrow \quad 21 = -3 + k \Rightarrow k = 24$$

Example 9. Let f, g and h are differentiable functions. If $f(0) = 1$; $g(0) = 2$; $h(0) = 3$ and the derivatives of their pairwise products at $x = 0$ are $(fg)'(0) = 6$; $(gh)'(0) = 4$ and $(hf)'(0) = 5$, then compute the value of $(fgh)'(0)$.

Sol. Let $\quad w(x) = f(x)\,g(x)\,h(x)$

$$\frac{d}{dx}(w(x)) = f'(x)\,g(x)\,h(x) + f(x)\,g'(x)\,h(x) + f(x)\,g(x)\,h'(x)$$

$$2\frac{d}{dx}(w(x)) = 2f'(x)\,g(x)\,h(x) + 2f(x)\,g'(x)\,h(x) + 2f(x)\,g(x)\,h'(x)$$

$$= h(x)\frac{d}{dx}(f(x)\,g(x)) + g(x)\frac{d}{dx}(f(x)\,h(x)) + f(x)\frac{d}{dx}(g(x)\,h(x))$$

$$2\frac{d}{dx}(w(0)) = (3)(6) + (2)(5) + (1)(4) = 32$$

$$\frac{d}{dx}(w(0)) = 16$$

4. **Quotient Rule** Let $f(x)$ and $g(x)$ be two differentiable functions, then $\frac{d}{dx}\left[\frac{f(x)}{g(x)}\right]$

$$= \frac{g(x)\frac{d}{dx}[f(x)] - f(x)\frac{d}{dx}[g(x)]}{[g(x)]^2}$$

Example 10. Find $\frac{dy}{dx}$ where $y = \frac{2x^3 - 7x^2 + 4x + 1}{4x^2 - 3x - 1}$.

Sol. $y = \dfrac{2x^3 - 7x^2 + 4x + 1}{4x^2 - 3x - 1}$

$$y = \frac{(x-1)(2x^2 - 5x - 1)}{(x-1)(4x+1)} = \frac{2x^2 - 5x - 1}{4x + 1}$$

On differentiation both sides, we get

$$\frac{dy}{dx} = \frac{\left(\frac{d}{dx}(2x^2 - 5x - 1)\right)(4x+1) - \left(\frac{d}{dx}(4x+1)\right) \times (2x^2 - 5x - 1)}{(4x+1)^2}$$

$$= \frac{(4x-5)(4x+1) - 4(2x^2 - 5x - 1)}{(4x+1)^2}$$

$$= \frac{(16x^2 - 20x + 4x - 5) + (-8x^2 + 20x + 4)}{(4x+1)^2}$$

$$= \frac{8x^2 + 4x - 1}{(4x+1)^2}$$

Example 11. Find the derivative with respect to x of the function $(\log_{\cos x} \sin x)(\log_{\sin x} \cos x)^{-1} + \arcsin \frac{2x}{1+x^2}$ at $x = \frac{\pi}{4}$.

Sol. $\quad y = (\log_{\cos x} \sin x)(\log_{\sin x} \cos x)^{-1} + \text{arc}\sin\frac{2x}{1+x^2}$

$$= \frac{\ln \sin x}{\ln \cos x}\cdot\left(\frac{\ln \cos x}{\ln \sin x}\right)^{-1} + 2\tan^{-1} x$$

$$\Rightarrow \quad y = \left(\frac{\ln \sin x}{\ln \cos x}\right)^2 + 2\tan^{-1} x$$

$$\Rightarrow \quad \frac{dy}{dx} = 2\left(\frac{\ln \sin x}{\ln \cos x}\right)\frac{(\ln \cos x)\frac{\cos x}{\sin x} - (\ln \sin x)\left(-\frac{\sin x}{\cos x}\right)}{(\ln \cos x)^2} + \frac{2}{1+x^2}$$

$$\Rightarrow \quad \left.\frac{dy}{dx}\right|_{\frac{\pi}{4}} = 2\frac{(1+1)}{\left(\ln\frac{1}{\sqrt{2}}\right)} + \frac{2}{1+\left(\frac{\pi}{4}\right)^2}$$

$$= \frac{2\times 2}{\left(\frac{-1}{2}\right)\ln 2} + \frac{2}{1+\left(\frac{\pi}{4}\right)^2} = -\frac{8}{\ln 2} + \frac{32}{16+\pi^2}$$

Example 12. Find $\frac{dy}{dx}$ where

$$y = \frac{\sin 8x + 3\sin 6x + 4\sin 4x - 3\sin 2x}{\cos 7x + 4\cos 5x + 8\cos 3x + 5\cos x}$$

Sol. $y = \dfrac{\sin 8x + 3\sin 6x + 4\sin 4x - 3\sin 2x}{\cos 7x + 4\cos 5x + 8\cos 3x + 5\cos x}$

Let $y = \dfrac{\text{Numerator}}{\text{Denominator}}$

Now, considering numerator

$$= \sin 8x + 3\sin 6x + 4\sin 4x - 3\sin 2x$$
$$= (\sin 8x - \sin 6x) + (4\sin 6x - 4\sin 4x) + (8\sin 4x - 8\sin 2x) + 5\sin 2x$$

$$= 2\sin x \cos 7x + 4 \times 2\sin x \times \cos 5x$$
$$+ 8 \times 2\sin x \cos 3x + 5 \times 2\sin x \cos x$$
$$= 2\sin x\,[\cos 7x + 4\cos 5x + 8\cos 3x + 5\cos x]$$

$$\therefore \quad y = \frac{\text{Numerator}}{\text{Denominator}} = 2\sin x, \frac{dy}{dx} = 2\cos x$$

JEE SPIKE

We do not use the quotient rule every time we see a quotient. Sometimes it's easier to rewrite a quotient in a form that is simpler for the purpose of differentiation.

For instance, although it is possible to differentiate the function $F(x) = \dfrac{3x^2 + 2\sqrt{x}}{x}$.

Using the quotient rule, it is much easier to perform the division first and write the function as $F(x) = 3x + 2x^{-1/2}$ before differentiating.

Example 13. Find the derivative of $y = \dfrac{(x-1)(x^2-2x)}{x^4}$

Sol. Rather than using the quotient rule to find the derivative of

$$y = \frac{(x-1)(x^2-2x)}{x^4}$$

We expand the numerator and divide by x^4,

$$y = \frac{(x-1)(x^2-2x)}{x^4}$$
$$= \frac{x^3 - 3x^2 + 2x}{x^4}$$
$$= x^{-1} - 3x^{-2} + 2x^{-3}$$

Then, we use the sum and power rules,

$$\frac{dy}{dx} = -x^{-2} - 3(-2)x^{-3} + 2(-3)x^{-4} = -\frac{1}{x^2} + \frac{6}{x^3} - \frac{6}{x^4}$$

Milestone Practice 5.1

1. Find the derivative of the following functions with respect to x using first principle.

(i) $y = \dfrac{x}{x^2+1}$ (ii) $y = \cos^2 x$ (iii) $y = \sin 3x$

(iv) $y = x^3 - 3^x$ (v) $y = \ln^2 x$

2. Find a and b, if given $y = \dfrac{5^{\log_{5^{1/4}} x} - 9^{\log_{729}(x+1)^6}}{49^{4\log_{2401} x} - x - 1}$ and $\dfrac{dy}{dx} = 2ax - b$.

3. If $y = (1 - 2\tan x)(5 + 4\sin x)$, then $\dfrac{dy}{dx}$ is

(a) $4\cos x(1 - 2\tan x) - 2\sec^2 x(5 + 4\sin x)$
(b) $4\sin x(1 - 2\tan x) + 2\sec^2 x(5 + 4\sin x)$
(c) $4\sin x - 8\sin^2 x \sec x + 10\sec^2 x + 8\sin x \sec^2 x$
(d) None of the above

4. If $f(x) = \cos x \cdot \cos 2x \cdot \cos 4x \cdot \cos 8x \cdot \cos 16x$, then $f'\left(\dfrac{\pi}{4}\right)$ is

(a) $\sqrt{2}$ (b) $\dfrac{1}{\sqrt{2}}$
(c) 1 (d) None of these

5. If $y = \dfrac{1}{1 + x^{n-m} + x^{p-m}} + \dfrac{1}{1 + x^{m-n} + x^{p-n}} + \dfrac{1}{1 + x^{m-p} + x^{n-p}}$, then $\dfrac{dy}{dx}$ is equal to

(a) 1 (b) 0
(c) $m + n + p$ (d) $m - n + p$

6. If $y = \dfrac{\cos 6x + 6\cos 4x + 15\cos 2x + 10}{\cos 5x + 5\cos 3x + 10\cos x}$, then $\dfrac{dy}{dx}$ is equal to

(a) $2\sin x + \cos x$ (b) $-2\sin x$
(c) $\cos 2x$ (d) $\sin 2x$

7. If $f(x) = \left(\dfrac{x^a}{x^b}\right)^{a+b} \cdot \left(\dfrac{x^b}{x^c}\right)^{b+c} \cdot \left(\dfrac{x^c}{x^a}\right)^{c+a}$, then $f'(x)$ is equal to

(a) 1 (b) 0
(c) x^{a+b+c} (d) None of these

8. Let $f(x) = \dfrac{\sqrt{x - 2\sqrt{x-1}}}{\sqrt{x-1} - 1} \cdot x$, then

(a) $f'(10) = 1$ (b) $f'\left(\dfrac{3}{2}\right) = -1$
(c) domain of $f(x)$ is $x \ge 1$ (d) All of these

Answer Key

1. (i) $\dfrac{1-x^2}{(x^2+1)^2}$ (ii) $-\sin 2x$ (iii) $3\cos 3x$ (iv) $3x^2 - 3^x \ln 3$ (v) $\dfrac{2\ln x}{x}$ **2.** $a = 1$ and $b = -1$

3. (a) **4.** (a) **5.** (b) **6.** (b)
7. (b) **8.** (d)

For Detailed Solution

Milestone 2 Differentiation of Implicit Functions

• Chain Rule • Differentiation of Implicit Function

5.6 Chain Rule (Differentiation of Composite Function)

Let $f(x)$ and $g(x)$ are two function and their comopsite function are $fog(x)$ and $gof(x)$, then their derivatives is given by

$$\frac{d}{dx}[fog(x)] = \frac{d}{dx}[f\{g(x)\}] = f'\{g(x)\} \cdot g'(x)$$

$$\frac{d}{dx}[gof(x)] = \frac{d}{dx}[g\{f(x)\}] = g'\{f(x)\} \cdot f'(x)$$

Proof Let $y = f(u)$, $u = g(v)$ and $v = h(x)$ are three function, then $\frac{dy}{dx}$ is given by

$$\frac{dy}{dx} = \frac{d}{dx} f(u) = f'(u) \cdot \frac{du}{dx}$$

$$= f'(u) \cdot \frac{d}{dx}(g(v)) = f'(u) \cdot g'(v) \cdot \frac{dv}{dx}$$

$$= f'(u) \cdot g'(v) \cdot \frac{d}{dx}(h(x)) = f'(u) \cdot g'(v) \cdot h'(x)$$

In short $\frac{dy}{dx} = \frac{dy}{du} \cdot \frac{du}{dv} \cdot \frac{dv}{dx}$

due to this chain process it is called chain rule.

Example 14. Find derivatives of the following function.

(i) $y = e^{(\tan^{-1} x)^3}$ (ii) $y = \log_e(\tan^{-1}\sqrt{1+x^2})$

(iii) $y = \sqrt{\log\left\{\sin\left(\frac{x^2}{3} - 1\right)\right\}}$

(iv) $y = \log_e\left(\frac{x + \sqrt{x^2 - a^2}}{x - \sqrt{x^2 - a^2}}\right)$

(v) $y = 2^{\ln \sin e^{(\tan^{-1}\sqrt{x^2-1})}}$

Sol. (i) Here, $y = e^{(\tan^{-1} x)^3}$

On differentiating, we get

$$\frac{dy}{dx} = \frac{d\{e^{(\tan^{-1} x)^3}\}}{d\{(\tan^{-1} x)^3\}} \cdot \frac{d\{(\tan^{-1} x)^3\}}{d(\tan^{-1} x)} \cdot \frac{d(\tan^{-1} x)}{dx}$$

$$= e^{(\tan^{-1} x)^3} \cdot 3(\tan^{-1} x)^2 \cdot \frac{1}{1+x^2} \quad \text{[by chain rule]}$$

Alternate Solution

Here, $y = e^{(\tan^{-1} x)^3}$

On putting $(\tan^{-1} x) = v$ and $(\tan^{-1} x)^3 = u \Rightarrow u = v^3$

$\therefore\ y = e^u, u = v^3$ and $v = \tan^{-1} x$

On differentiating, we get

$$\frac{dy}{dx} = \frac{dy}{du} \cdot \frac{du}{dv} \cdot \frac{dv}{dx}$$

$$\frac{dy}{dx} = \frac{d}{du} e^u \times \frac{d(v)^3}{dv} \times \frac{d}{dx} \tan^{-1} x$$

$$= e^u \cdot 3v^2 \cdot \frac{1}{1+x^2} = e^{(\tan^{-1} x)^3} \cdot (3\tan^{-1} x)^2 \cdot \frac{1}{1+x^2}$$

(ii) Here, $y = \log_e(\tan^{-1}\sqrt{1+x^2})$

On differentiating, we get

$$\frac{dy}{dx} = \frac{d\,[\log_e(\tan^{-1}\sqrt{1+x^2})]}{d(\tan^{-1}\sqrt{1+x^2})} \cdot \frac{d(\tan^{-1}\sqrt{1+x^2})}{d(\sqrt{1+x^2})} \cdot \frac{d(\sqrt{1+x^2})}{d(1+x^2)} \cdot \frac{d(1+x^2)}{dx}$$

$$= \frac{1}{\tan^{-1}(\sqrt{1+x^2})} \cdot \frac{1}{1+(\sqrt{1+x^2})^2} \cdot \frac{1}{2\sqrt{1+x^2}} \cdot 2x$$

$$= \frac{x}{\tan^{-1}(\sqrt{1+x^2})(2+x^2)\sqrt{1+x^2}}$$

(iii) Let $y = \sqrt{\log\left\{\sin\left(\frac{x^2}{3} - 1\right)\right\}}$

On differentiating, we get

$$\frac{dy}{dx} = \frac{1}{2\sqrt{\log\left\{\sin\left(\frac{x^2}{3} - 1\right)\right\}}} \times \frac{1}{\sin\left(\frac{x^2}{3} - 1\right)} \times \cos\left(\frac{x^2}{3} - 1\right) \times \frac{2x}{3}$$

$$= \frac{x \cot\left(\frac{x^2}{3} - 1\right)}{3\sqrt{\log\left\{\sin\left(\frac{x^2}{3} - 1\right)\right\}}}$$

(iv) Let $y = \log_e \left(\dfrac{x + \sqrt{x^2 - a^2}}{x - \sqrt{x^2 - a^2}} \right)$

$\Rightarrow y = \log(x + \sqrt{x^2 - a^2}) - \log(x - \sqrt{x^2 - a^2})$

$\left[\because \log \dfrac{a}{b} = \log a - \log b \right]$

On differentiating, we get

$$\frac{dy}{dx} = \left(\frac{1}{x + \sqrt{x^2 - a^2}} \right) \left(1 + \frac{2x}{2\sqrt{x^2 - a^2}} \right) - \left[\left(\frac{1}{x - \sqrt{x^2 - a^2}} \right) \left(1 - \frac{2x}{2\sqrt{x^2 - a^2}} \right) \right]$$

$$= \frac{1}{\sqrt{x^2 - a^2}} + \frac{1}{\sqrt{x^2 - a^2}} = \frac{2}{\sqrt{x^2 - a^2}}$$

(v) $y = 2^{\ln \sin e^{\tan^{-1}\sqrt{x^2-1}}}$

$$\frac{dy}{dx} = 2^{\ln \sin e^{\tan^{-1}\sqrt{x^2-1}}} \ln 2 \cdot \frac{1}{\sin (e^{\tan^{-1}\sqrt{x^2-1}})} \cos (e^{\tan^{-1}\sqrt{x^2-1}}) \cdot e^{\tan^{-1}\sqrt{x^2-1}} \cdot \frac{1}{1 + (x^2 - 1)} \cdot \frac{1}{2\sqrt{x^2 - 1}} \cdot 2x$$

$$= 2^{\ln \sin e^{\tan^{-1}\sqrt{x^2-1}}} \ln 2 \cdot \frac{1}{\sin (e^{\tan^{-1}\sqrt{x^2-1}})} \cos (e^{\tan^{-1}\sqrt{x^2-1}}) \cdot e^{\tan^{-1}\sqrt{x^2-1}} \cdot \frac{1}{x\sqrt{x^2 - 1}}$$

JEE SCANNER

Example Similar to PYQ Asked in JEE Mains 2019

If $f(2) = 2$, $f'(2) = 4$, then value of derivative of $f\{f\{f(x)\}\} + (f(x))^2$ at $x = 2$ is ....

Sol. Let $y = f\{f\{f(x)\}\} + \{f(x)\}^2$

$$\frac{dy}{dx} = f'\{f\{f(x) \cdot f'\{f(x) \cdot f'(x)\} + 2f(x) \cdot f'(x)$$

$$\left.\frac{dy}{dx}\right|_{x=2} = f'\{f\{f(2)\} \cdot f'\{f(2)\} \cdot f'(2) + 2f(2) \cdot f'(2)\}$$

$$= f'\{f(2)\} \cdot f'(2) \cdot f'(2) + 2f(2) \cdot f'(2)$$

$$= f'(2) \cdot f'(2)\, f'(2) + 2f(2)\, f'(2)$$

$$= 4 \times 4 \times 4 + 2 \times 2 \times 4 = 64 + 16 = 80$$

Skill Builder

Let f be a differentiable function $f(0) = -1$ and $f'(0) = -1$. Let $g(x) = [f(2f(x) + 2)]^2$ and $g'(0)$ is equal to $-\lambda$, then λ is equal to ......

For Sol.

■ **For more practice** See Q.3 of Milestone Practice 5.2.

5.7 Differentiation of Implicit Function

Implicit Function An equation $f(x, y) = 0$ represents an implicit function, when y can not be easily expressed in terms of x or *vice-versa*. Otherwise function is known as explicitly function.

To find $\dfrac{dy}{dx}$ in this situation, we simply differentiate the complete equation with respect to x and separate the $\dfrac{dy}{dx}$ containing terms in LHS, remaining in RHS.

Shortcut for Differentiation of Implicit Function

Given $f(x, y) = 0$

Then, $\dfrac{dy}{dx} = \dfrac{-\partial f / \partial x}{\partial f / \partial y}$

$$f = \frac{\text{Partial derivative of } f \text{ w.r.t. } x \text{ (taking } y \text{ as constant)}}{\text{Partial derivative of } f \text{ w.r.t. } x \text{ (taking } x \text{ as constant)}}$$

JEE Focus Points

- Differentiation of y w.r.t. $x = \dfrac{dy}{dx}$
- Differentiation of y^2 w.r.t. $x = 2y \cdot \dfrac{dy}{dx}$
- Differentiation of $\sin y$ w.r.t. $x = \cos y \cdot \dfrac{dy}{dx}$
- Differentiation of $\ln y$ w.r.t. $x = \dfrac{1}{y} \cdot \dfrac{dy}{dx}$

Example 15. Find $\dfrac{dy}{dx}$.

(i) $x^3 + y^3 = 3axy$ (ii) $\log(x^2 + y^2) = 2\tan^{-1}\left(\dfrac{y}{x}\right)$

(iii) $y = x\cos y + y\sin x$

Sol. (i) $x^3 + y^3 = 3axy$

On differentiating both sides w.r.t. x

$$\frac{d}{dx}(x^3) + \frac{d}{dx}(y^3) = 3a\frac{d}{dx}(xy)$$

$$3x^2 + 3y^2\frac{dy}{dx} = 3a\left(x\frac{dy}{dx} + y(1)\right)$$

$$y^2\frac{dy}{dx} - ax\frac{dy}{dx} = ay - x^2$$

$$\frac{dy}{dx}(y^2 - ax) = ay - x^2 \Rightarrow \frac{dy}{dx} = \frac{ay - x^2}{y^2 - ax}$$

Alternate Solution

$f(x, y): x^3 + y^3 - 3axy = 0$

$$\frac{dy}{dx} = -\frac{\frac{\partial}{\partial x}(x^3 + y^3 - 3axy)}{\frac{\partial}{\partial y}(x^3 + y^3 - 3axy)} = -\frac{(3x^2 - 3ay)}{(3y^2 - 3ax)} = \frac{ay - x^2}{y^2 - ax}$$

(ii) Given, $\log(x^2+y^2) = 2\tan^{-1}\left(\frac{y}{x}\right)$

On differentiating both sides of the given relation w.r.t. x, we get

$$\frac{d}{dx}\{\log(x^2+y^2)\} = 2\frac{d}{dx}\left\{\tan^{-1}\left(\frac{y}{x}\right)\right\}$$

$$\frac{1}{x^2+y^2}\times\frac{d}{dx}(x^2+y^2) = 2\times\frac{1}{1+(y/x)^2}\times\frac{d}{dx}\left(\frac{y}{x}\right)$$

$$\frac{1}{x^2+y^2}\left\{\frac{d}{dx}(x^2)+\frac{d}{dx}(y^2)\right\}$$

$$= 2\times\frac{x^2}{x^2+y^2}\left\{\frac{x\frac{dy}{dx}-y\times 1}{x^2}\right\}$$

$$\Rightarrow \frac{1}{x^2+y^2}\left\{2x+2y\frac{dy}{dx}\right\} = \frac{2}{x^2+y^2}\left\{x\frac{dy}{dx}-y\right\}$$

$$\Rightarrow 2\left\{x+y\frac{dy}{dx}\right\} = 2\left\{x\frac{dy}{dx}-y\right\}$$

$$\Rightarrow x+y\frac{dy}{dx} = x\frac{dy}{dx}-y$$

$$\Rightarrow \frac{dy}{dx}(y-x) = -(x+y) \Rightarrow \frac{dy}{dx} = \frac{x+y}{x-y}$$

(iii) Given, $f(x, y): x\cos y + y\sin x - y = 0$

$$\frac{dy}{dx} = \frac{-\frac{\partial}{\partial x}(x\cos y + y\sin x - y)}{\frac{\partial}{\partial y}(x\cos y + y\sin x - y)}$$

$$= -\frac{(\cos y + y\cos x)}{(-x\sin y + \sin x - 1)} = \frac{\cos y + y\cos x}{x\sin y - \sin x + 1}$$

Example 16. If $\sin y = x\sin(a+y)$, then prove that $\frac{dy}{dx} = \frac{\sin^2(a+y)}{\sin a}$.

Sol. Given, $\sin y = x\sin(a+y)$

On differentiating both sides w.r.t. x, we get

$$\cos y\cdot\frac{dy}{dx} = \sin(a+y) + x\cos(a+y)\cdot\left(0+\frac{dy}{dx}\right)$$

$$\Rightarrow \frac{dy}{dx}(\cos y - x\cos(a+y)) = \sin(a+y)$$

$$\Rightarrow \frac{dy}{dx} = \frac{\sin(a+y)}{\cos y - x\cos(a+y)}$$

$$= \frac{\sin(a+y)}{\cos y - \frac{\sin y}{\sin(a+y)}\cos(a+y)}$$

$$= \frac{\sin^2(a+y)}{\sin(a+y)\cos y - \sin y\cos(a+y)}$$

$$= \frac{\sin^2(a+y)}{\sin a}$$

Example 17. If $y = \sqrt{\sin x + \sqrt{\sin x + \sqrt{\sin x + \ldots\infty}}}$, then find $\frac{dy}{dx}$ $(\sin x > 0)$.

Sol. $y = \sqrt{\sin x + \sqrt{\sin x + \sqrt{\sin x + \ldots\infty}}}$

$$\Rightarrow y = \sqrt{\sin x + y}$$

$$\Rightarrow y^2 - y = \sin x$$

On differentiating both sides w.r.t. x, we get

$$2y\frac{dy}{dx} - \frac{dy}{dx} = \cos x \Rightarrow \frac{dy}{dx} = \left(\frac{\cos x}{2y-1}\right)$$

JEE SCANNER

Example Similar to PYQ Asked in JEE Mains 2020

If $(\alpha+\sqrt{3}\beta\sin x)(\alpha-\sqrt{3}\beta\sin y) = \alpha^2 - 2\beta^2$, where $\alpha > \beta > 0$, then $\frac{dx}{dy}$ at $\left(\frac{\pi}{3}, \frac{\pi}{6}\right)$ in terms of α and β is

(a) $\frac{\sqrt{3}(2\alpha+3\beta)}{2\alpha-\sqrt{3}\beta}$ (b) $\frac{\sqrt{3}(3\alpha+2\beta)}{3\alpha-2\beta}$

(c) $\frac{\sqrt{3}(2\alpha-3\beta)}{3\alpha+2\beta}$ (d) None of these

Sol. (a) $(\alpha+\sqrt{3}\beta\sin x)(\alpha-\sqrt{3}\beta\sin y) - \alpha^2 + 2\beta^2 = 0$

Now, $\frac{dy}{dx} = -\frac{\partial f/\partial x}{\partial f/\partial y}$

$$= -\frac{(\alpha-\sqrt{3}\beta\sin y)(\sqrt{3}\beta\cos x)}{(\alpha+\sqrt{3}\beta\sin x)(-\sqrt{3}\beta\cos y)}$$

$$= \frac{(\alpha-\sqrt{3}\beta\sin y)\cos x}{(\alpha+\sqrt{3}\beta\sin x)\cos y}$$

$$\because \frac{dx}{dy} = \frac{1}{dy/dx} = \frac{(\alpha+\sqrt{3}\beta\sin x)\cos y}{(\alpha-\sqrt{3}\beta\sin y)\cos x}$$

$$\left.\frac{dx}{dy}\right|_{\left(\frac{\pi}{3},\frac{\pi}{6}\right)} = \frac{\left[\alpha+\sqrt{3}\beta\left(\frac{\sqrt{3}}{2}\right)\right]\cdot\frac{\sqrt{3}}{2}}{\left[\alpha-\sqrt{3}\beta\left(\frac{1}{2}\right)\right]\cdot\frac{1}{2}} = \frac{\sqrt{3}(2\alpha+3\beta)}{(2\alpha-\sqrt{3}\beta)}$$

Skill Builder

For Sol.

If $(a - b\tan x)(a + b\tan y) = a^2 - b^2$, then $\left.\frac{dy}{dx}\right|_{(\pi/4,\pi/4)}$ is

(a) $\left.\frac{dy}{dx}\right|_{(\pi/4,\pi/4)} = \frac{a-b}{a+b}$ (b) $\left.\frac{dy}{dx}\right|_{(3\pi/4,\pi/4)} = \frac{a+b}{a-b}$

(c) $\left.\frac{dy}{dx}\right|_{(\pi/4,\pi/4)} = \frac{a^2-b^2}{a+b}$ (d) $\left.\frac{dy}{dx}\right|_{(\pi/4,\pi/4)} = \frac{a^2+b^2}{a-b}$

■ **For more practice** See Q.5 of Milestone Practice 5.2.

Example 18. If $\sqrt{1-x^6}+\sqrt{1-y^6}=a^3(x^3-y^3)$, then prove that $\frac{dy}{dx}=\frac{x^2}{y^2}\sqrt{\frac{1-y^6}{1-x^6}}$.

Sol. Here, $\sqrt{1-x^6}+\sqrt{1-y^6}=a^3(x^3-y^3)$

Let $x^3=\sin\theta$, $y^3=\sin\phi$. Then, we get

$$\sqrt{1-\sin^2\theta}+\sqrt{1-\sin^2\phi}=a^3(\sin\theta-\sin\phi)$$

$$\Rightarrow \quad \cos\theta+\cos\phi=a^3(\sin\theta-\sin\phi)$$

$$\Rightarrow 2\cos\left(\frac{\theta+\phi}{2}\right)\cdot\cos\left(\frac{\theta-\phi}{2}\right)=a^3\left[2\cos\left(\frac{\theta+\phi}{2}\right)\sin\left(\frac{\theta-\phi}{2}\right)\right]$$

$$\Rightarrow \quad \cos\left(\frac{\theta-\phi}{2}\right)=a^3\sin\left(\frac{\theta-\phi}{2}\right)$$

$$\Rightarrow \quad \cot\left(\frac{\theta-\phi}{2}\right)=a^3$$

$$\Rightarrow \quad \theta-\phi=2\cot^{-1}(a^3) \text{ or } \sin^{-1}x^3-\sin^{-1}y^3=2\cot^{-1}(a^3)$$

On differentiating both sides, we get

$$\frac{1}{\sqrt{1-x^6}}\cdot 3x^2-\frac{1}{\sqrt{1-y^6}}\cdot 3y^2\cdot\frac{dy}{dx}=0$$

Hence, $\frac{dy}{dx}=\frac{x^2\sqrt{1-y^6}}{y^2\sqrt{1-x^6}}$

Example 19. If $y\sqrt{1-x^2}+x\sqrt{1-y^2}=1$, when $|x|<1$ and $|y|<1$, then find $\frac{dy}{dx}$.

Sol. Here, $y\sqrt{1-x^2}+x\sqrt{1-y^2}=1, |x|<1$ and $|y|<1$

Let $\quad x=\sin\theta, y=\sin\phi$

Then, $\sin\phi\sqrt{1-\sin^2\theta}+\sin\theta\sqrt{1-\sin^2\phi}=1$

$$\Rightarrow \quad \sin\phi\cos\theta+\sin\theta\cos\phi=1$$

$$\Rightarrow \quad \sin(\theta+\phi)=1 \Rightarrow \theta+\phi=\sin^{-1}(1)$$

$$\Rightarrow \quad \sin^{-1}x+\sin^{-1}y=\sin^{-1}(1)$$

$$\left[\because \sin\theta=x\Rightarrow\theta=\sin^{-1}x \text{ and } \sin\phi=y\Rightarrow\phi=\sin^{-1}y\right]$$

On differentiating both the sides, we get

$$\frac{1}{\sqrt{1-x^2}}+\frac{1}{\sqrt{1-y^2}}\cdot\frac{dy}{dx}=0$$

Hence, $\frac{dy}{dx}=-\sqrt{\frac{1-y^2}{1-x^2}}$

Milestone Practice 5.2

1. Find $\frac{dy}{dx}$.

 (i) $y=\ln\sqrt{\frac{1+\sin x}{1-\sin x}}$ (ii) $y=\ln\{\cot^{-1}(a^{5x+3})\}$

 (iii) $y=\cos^{-1}(e^{\sqrt{\tan x}})$ (iv) $y=[\ln\{\ln(\sin x)\}]^7$

 (v) $y=\sin^{-1}\left(\frac{a+b\cos x}{b+a\cos x}\right), b>a$

 (vi) $y=e^{\sqrt{\sin^{-1}(x^2)}}$ (vii) $y=\sqrt[3]{2e^x+2^x+1}+\ln^5 x$

 (viii) $y=\sqrt{x+\sqrt{x+\sqrt{x}}}$ (ix) $y=\tan^{-1}\left(\frac{5ax}{a^2-6x^2}\right)$

2. If $y=f\left(\frac{3x+4}{5x+6}\right)$ and $f'(x)=\tan x^2$, then find $\frac{dy}{dx}$.

3. If $f(1)=1, f'(1)=2$, then the value of derivative of $f[f\{f(x)\}]+\{f(x)\}^2$ at $x=1$ is ....

4. If $f'(x)=\sin x+\sin 4x\cdot\cos x$, then $f'\left(2x^2+\frac{\pi}{2}\right)$ is

 (a) $4x\{\cos(2x^2)-\sin 8x^2\cdot\sin 2x^2\}$
 (b) $4x\{\cos(2x^2)+\sin 8x^2\cdot\cos 2x^2\}$
 (c) $\{\cos(2x^2)-\sin 8x^2\cdot\sin 2x^2\}$
 (d) None of the above

5. If $y=|\cos x|+|\sin x|$, then $\frac{dy}{dx}$ at $x=\frac{2\pi}{3}$ is

 (a) $\frac{1}{2}(\sqrt{3}+1)$ (b) $2(\sqrt{3}-1)$
 (c) $\frac{1}{2}(\sqrt{3}-1)$ (d) None of these

Answer Key

1. (i) $\sec x$ (ii) $\frac{1}{\cot^{-1}(a^{5x+3})}\cdot\frac{-1}{1+(a^{5x+3})^2}\cdot a^{5x+3}\cdot\log a\cdot 5$ (iii) $\frac{-e^{\sqrt{\tan x}}\cdot\sec^2 x}{2\sqrt{\tan x}\cdot\sqrt{1-e^{2\sqrt{\tan x}}}}$ (iv) $\frac{7\cos x(\ln(\ln(\sin x)))^6}{\sin x\ln\sin x}$

(v) $-\frac{\sqrt{b^2-a^2}}{b+a\cos x}$ (vi) $\frac{xe^{\sqrt{\sin^{-1}x^2}}}{\sqrt{\sin^{-1}x^2(1-x^4)}}$ (vii) $\frac{(2e^x+2^x\ln 2)}{3(2^x+2^x+1)^{2/3}}+5\ln^4 x\frac{1}{x}$

(viii) $\frac{1}{4(\sqrt{x+\sqrt{x+\sqrt{x}}})}\left(2+\frac{1+\frac{1}{2\sqrt{x}}}{\sqrt{x+\sqrt{x}}}\right)$ (ix) $\frac{2a}{a^2+4x^2}+\frac{3a}{a^2+9x^2}$ 2. $-2\tan\left(\frac{3x+4}{5x+6}\right)^2\cdot\frac{1}{(5x+6)^2}$ 3. 12 4. (c) 5. (c)

For Detailed Solution

Milestone 3 Differentiation of Inverse Function

- Derivatives of Invertible Function • Geometrical Interpretation
- Derivatives Involving Inverse Trigonometric Function (ITF)

Here, we will discuss the derivatives of invertible functions (functions which are bijective). There are two type of situation,

Type 1 Derivatives of invertible functions.

Type 2 Derivatives involving inverse trigonometric functions.

5.8 Derivatives of Invertible Function

If $f(x)$ is any one-one onto function, then its inverse function (say $g(x)$) is also a differentiable function (except where its tangents are parallel to Y-axis).

$$y = f(x) \Leftrightarrow x = g(y)$$

Differentiating both sides of $y = f(x)$ w.r.t. x, we get

$$\frac{dy}{dx} = f'(x)$$

And differentiating both sides of $x = g(y)$ w.r.t. y, we get

$$\frac{dx}{dy} = g'(y)$$

$$\frac{dy}{dx} = \lim_{\Delta x \to 0} \times \frac{\Delta y}{\Delta x} \text{ if it exists finitely}$$

$$= \lim_{\Delta x \to 0} \times \frac{\Delta y}{\Delta x} \quad [\because \Delta x \to 0 \Rightarrow \Delta y \to 0]$$

$$= \lim_{\Delta y \to 0} \left(\frac{1}{\frac{\Delta x}{\Delta y}} \right) = \frac{1}{\lim_{\Delta y \to 0} \left(\frac{\Delta x}{\Delta y} \right)} = \frac{1}{\frac{dx}{dy}}$$

$$\therefore \quad f'(x) = \frac{1}{g'(y)} \text{ (provided } g'(y) \neq 0)$$

This is more evident by taking differentiation of two composite functions.

If $\quad g(x) = f^{-1}(x) \Rightarrow f(g(x)) = f(f^{-1}(x)) = x$

Differentiation both sides w.r.t. x, we get

$$f'(g(x)) \times g'(x) = 1 \Rightarrow g'(x) = \frac{1}{f'(g(x))}$$

i.e. derivative of f^{-1} at $x = x_0$ is equal to reciprocal of the derivative of $f(x)$ at $x = f^{-1}(x_0)$.

5.9 Geometrical Interpretation

If the tangent T_1 (tangent to $y = f(x)$ at $x = (a, f(a))$) makes an angle of α with positive X-axis, then the line T_2 (tangent to $y = f'(x)$ or $x = f(y)$ at $(f(a), a)$ makes an angle α with positive y-axis.

For $0 < \alpha < \pi/2$

As is evident from the diagram 'β', i.e. the angle that the line T_2 makes with positive X-axis is equal to $\pi/2 - \alpha$.

$\therefore \quad f(x) = \tan\alpha$ and $g'(y) = \tan\beta$

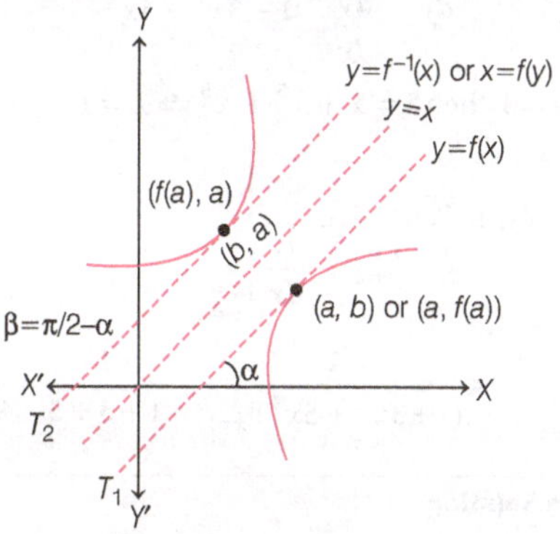

We need to prove that $\tan\alpha = \frac{1}{\tan\beta}$ or $\tan\alpha \cdot \tan\beta = 1$ or $\tan\alpha \tan\left(\frac{\pi}{2} - \alpha\right) = 1$ or $\tan\alpha \cdot \cot\alpha = 1$ which is obviously true and hence $\tan\alpha = \frac{1}{\tan\beta}$ or $\frac{dy}{dx} = \frac{1}{\frac{dx}{dy}}$ or $f'(x) = \frac{1}{g'(y)}$

Similarly, for $\pi/2 < \alpha < \pi, \beta = 3\pi/2 - \alpha$.

$$\therefore \quad \tan\alpha \cdot \tan\beta = \tan\alpha \times \tan\left(\frac{3\pi}{2} - \alpha\right)$$

$$= \tan\alpha \times \cot\alpha = 1$$

$\therefore \quad \tan\alpha = \dfrac{1}{\tan\beta}$

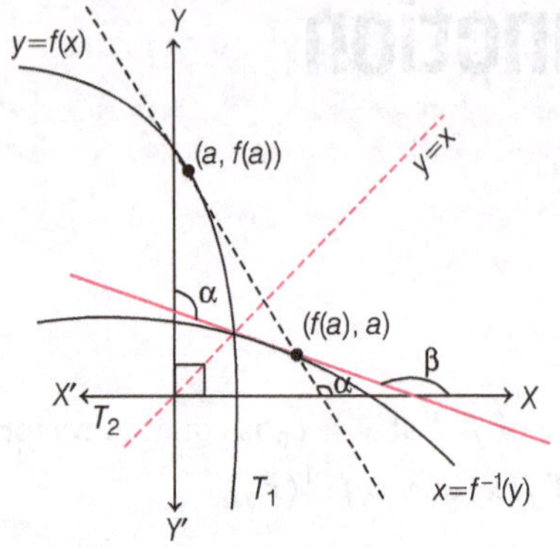

And hence again, we get

$$f'(x) = \frac{1}{g'(y)}$$

Example 20. If $y = f(x) = x + x^3 + x^5$ and g is the inverse function of f, then find $g'(3)$.

Sol. $\dfrac{dy}{dx} = 1 + 3x^2 + 5x^4 > 0$

Therefore, $f(x)$ is an one-one function.

Now, $g'(y) = \dfrac{dx}{dy} = \dfrac{1}{\frac{dy}{dx}} = \dfrac{1}{1 + 3x^2 + 5x^4}$

When $y = 3$, then $3 = x + x^3 + x^5 \Rightarrow x = 1$

$$\therefore \quad g'(3) = \left.\frac{dx}{dy}\right|_{\substack{x=1\\y=3}} = \frac{1}{\left.\frac{dy}{dx}\right|_{\substack{x=1\\y=3}}}$$

$$= \frac{1}{(1 + 3x^2 + 5x^4)|_{x=1}} = \frac{1}{1+3+5} = \frac{1}{9}$$

Alternate Solution

$$g(f(x)) = x = g'(f(x)) \times f'(x) = 1$$

Now, when $f(x) = 3$; $x = 1$,

$\Rightarrow \quad g'(3) \times f'(1) = 1$

$\Rightarrow \quad g'(3) = \dfrac{1}{f'(1)} = \dfrac{1}{1+3+5} = \dfrac{1}{9}$

Example 21. If the function $f(x) = \dfrac{7}{4} e^{\frac{2-x}{3}} + 3x + 5x^2$ and $f(x) = g^{-1}(x)$, then find the value of $g'\left(\dfrac{111}{4}\right)$.

Sol. Let $y = \dfrac{7}{4} e^{\frac{2-x}{3}} + 3x + 5x^2$

Now, $y = \dfrac{111}{4}$ when $x = 2$

$$\frac{dy}{dx} = \frac{-7}{12} e^{\frac{2-x}{3}} + 3 + 10x$$

$$g'(y) = \frac{dx}{dy} = \frac{1}{\frac{dy}{dx}} = \frac{1}{\frac{-7}{12} e^{\frac{2-x}{3}} + 3 + 10x}$$

$$\therefore \quad g'\left(\frac{111}{4}\right) = \frac{1}{\left.\frac{dy}{dx}\right|_{x=2}} = \frac{1}{\frac{-7}{12} e^{\frac{2-2}{3}} + 3 + 10 \times 2}$$

$$= \frac{1}{\frac{-7}{12} + 3 + 20} = \frac{1}{\frac{269}{12}} = \frac{12}{269}$$

Example 22. If the function $f(x) = x^3 + e^{x/2}$ and $g(x) = f^{-1}(x)$, then find the value of $g'(x)$ at $x = 1$.

Sol. $\because g'\{f(x)\} = \dfrac{1}{f'(x)}$

For $g'(1) \Rightarrow f(x) = 1$

$$x^3 + e^{x/2} = 1$$

$$x = 0$$

$$\therefore \quad g'(1) = \frac{1}{f'(0)}$$

$$\because \quad f(x) = x^3 + e^{x/2}$$

$$f'(x) = 3x^2 + \frac{1}{2} e^{x/2}$$

$$f'(0) = \frac{1}{2}$$

$$\therefore \quad g'(1) = 2$$

Example 23. $\dfrac{d^2x}{dy^2}$ is equal to

(a) $\left(\dfrac{d^2y}{dx^2}\right)^{-1}$ (b) $\left(\dfrac{d^2y}{dx^2}\right)^{-1}\left(\dfrac{dy}{dx}\right)^{-3}$

(c) $\left(\dfrac{d^2y}{dx^2}\right)\left(\dfrac{dy}{dx}\right)^{-2}$ (d) $-\left(\dfrac{d^2y}{dx^2}\right)\left(\dfrac{dy}{dx}\right)^{-3}$

Sol. (d) $\dfrac{dx}{dy} = \dfrac{1}{\left(\frac{dy}{dx}\right)}$

$$\frac{d^2x}{dy^2} = \frac{d}{dy}\frac{1}{\left(\frac{dy}{dx}\right)} = \frac{d}{dx}\frac{1}{\left(\frac{dy}{dx}\right)} \cdot \frac{dx}{dy}$$

$$= -\frac{1}{\left(\frac{dy}{dx}\right)^2} \cdot \frac{d^2y}{dx^2} \cdot \frac{1}{\left(\frac{dy}{dx}\right)}$$

$$= -\frac{1}{\left(\frac{dy}{dx}\right)^3} \frac{d^2y}{dx^2}$$

Example 24. Let $f:R\to R, g:R\to R$ and $h:R\to R$ be differentiable functions such that $f(x)=x^3+3x+2$, $g\{f(x)\}=x$ and $h\{g(g(x))\}=x\ \forall\ x\in R$, then

(a) $g'(2)=\dfrac{1}{15}$ (b) $h'(1)=666$

(c) $h(0)=18$ (d) $h\{g(3)\}=36$

Sol. (b) $f(x)=x^3+3x+2$

$$g\{f(x)\}=x \Rightarrow f(x) \text{ is inverse of } g(x)$$

and $h\{g\{g(x)\}\}=x$

$\Rightarrow gog\,(x)$ is inverse of $h(x)$

Now, $f(x)=x^3+3x+2$

$$f'(x)=3x^2+3$$

$\because$ $g'\{f(x)\}=\dfrac{1}{f'(x)}=\dfrac{1}{3x^2+3}$

For $g'(2)\Rightarrow f(x)=2\Rightarrow x=0$

$\therefore$ $g'(2)=\dfrac{1}{f'(0)}=\dfrac{1}{3}$

Similarly,

$$h'\{g(g(x))\}=\frac{1}{[g\{g(x)\}]'}=\frac{1}{g'\{g(x)\}\cdot g'(x)}$$

For $h'(1)\Rightarrow g\{g(x)\}=1$

$\Rightarrow$ $g(x)=g^{-1}(1)$ ...(i)

$\because$ $g\{f(x)\}=x$

$\Rightarrow$ $f(x)=g^{-1}(x)$

$\Rightarrow$ $f(1)=g^{-1}(1)$ ...(ii)

From Eqs. (i) and (ii), we get

$$g(x)=f(1)$$
$$g(x)=6$$

and $f^{-1}(x)=6\Rightarrow x=f(6)=236$

$\because$ $h'(1)=\dfrac{1}{g'(6)\cdot g'(236)}$

$$=\frac{1}{\dfrac{1}{f'(1)}\cdot\dfrac{1}{f'(6)}}=\frac{1}{\dfrac{1}{6}\cdot\dfrac{1}{111}}=666,$$

$\therefore$ $h'(1)=666$

For $h(0)$

$\Rightarrow$ $g\{g(x)\}=0$

$\Rightarrow$ $g(x)=g^{-1}(0)=f(0)=2$

$\Rightarrow$ $g(x)=2$

$\Rightarrow$ $x=g^{-1}(2)=f(2)=16$

$\therefore$ $h(0)=16$

For $h\{g(3)\}$

$\Rightarrow$ $h\{g(g(x)\}=x$, then $g(x)=3$

$$x=g^{-1}(3)=f(3)$$
$$=3^3+3\times3+2=38$$

$\therefore$ $h\{g(3)\}=38$

5.10 Derivatives Involving Inverse Trigonometric Function (ITF)

- Some formulae of derivatives of inverse trigonometric functions are already discussed in milestone 1.
- Here, we discuss some advance concepts of finding derivatives when ITF is involved.

JEE Focus Points

- When inverse trigonometric functions are involved, then sometimes we have to simplify these functions before finding the derivatives.
- For simplification of ITF we use two basic approach.
  - Using properties,
  - Using trigonometric substitution,

Some Standard Trigonometric Substitution

Expression	Substitutions
$\sqrt{a^2-x^2}$	$x=a\sin\theta$ or $a\cos\theta$
$\sqrt{a^2+x^2}$	$x=a\tan\theta$ or $a\cot\theta$
$\sqrt{x^2-a^2}$	$x=a\sec\theta$ or $a\,\text{cosec}\,\theta$
$\sqrt{\dfrac{a+x}{a-x}}$ or $\sqrt{\dfrac{a-x}{a+x}}$	$x=a\cos\theta$ or $a\cos2\theta$
$\sqrt{(a-x)(x-b)}$ or $\sqrt{\dfrac{a-x}{x-b}}$ or $\sqrt{\dfrac{x-b}{a-x}}$	$x=a\cos^2\theta+b\sin^2\theta$
$\sqrt{(x-a)(x-b)}$ or $\sqrt{\dfrac{x-a}{x-b}}$ or $\sqrt{\dfrac{x-b}{x-a}}$	$x=a\sec^2\theta-b\tan^2\theta$
$\sqrt{2ax-x^2}$	$x=a(1-\cos\theta)$

Example 25. Find $\dfrac{dy}{dx}$ for the following functions

$$y=\cos^{-1}\left[\frac{2\cos x+3\sin x}{\sqrt{13}}\right]$$

Sol. $y=\cos^{-1}\left[\dfrac{2\cos x+3\sin x}{\sqrt{13}}\right]$

$$=\cos^{-1}\left[\frac{2}{\sqrt{13}}\cos x+\frac{3}{\sqrt{13}}\sin x\right]$$

Let $\dfrac{2}{\sqrt{13}}=\cos\theta$ and $\dfrac{3}{\sqrt{13}}=\sin\theta$

$$\therefore \quad y = \cos^{-1}[\cos\theta\cos x + \sin\theta\sin x]$$
$$= \cos^{-1}[\cos(x-\theta)]$$
$$y = x - \theta, \theta \text{ is a constant w.r.t. } x$$
$$\frac{dy}{dx} = 1 - 0$$
$$= 1$$

Example 26. If $y = \sec^{-1}(\sqrt{1+x^2})$, when $-1 < x < 1$, then find $\frac{dy}{dx}$.

Sol. Here, $y = \sec^{-1}(\sqrt{1+x^2})$, put $x = \tan\theta$

$$\Rightarrow \quad y = \sec^{-1}(\sqrt{\sec^2\theta})$$
$$= \sec^{-1}(\sec\theta)$$
$$= \theta = \tan^{-1} x$$
$$\therefore \quad \frac{dy}{dx} = \frac{1}{1+x^2}$$

Example 27. If $y = \tan^{-1}\sqrt{\frac{1-x}{1+x}}$, then find $\frac{dy}{dx}$, when $-1 < x < 1$.

Sol. Here, $y = \tan^{-1}\sqrt{\frac{1-x}{1+x}}$, put

$$x = \cos\theta$$
$$\Rightarrow \quad y = \tan^{-1}\sqrt{\frac{1-\cos\theta}{1+\cos\theta}}$$
$$\Rightarrow \quad y = \tan^{-1}\sqrt{\frac{2\sin^2\theta/2}{2\cos^2\theta/2}}$$
$$\Rightarrow \quad y = \tan^{-1}|\tan\theta/2|$$
$$\left[\because -1 < \cos\theta < 1 \Rightarrow 0 < \theta < \pi \quad \therefore 0 < \frac{\theta}{2} < \frac{\pi}{2}\right]$$
$$\therefore \quad y = \tan^{-1}\left(\tan\frac{\theta}{2}\right)$$
$$[\because \tan^{-1}(\tan x) = x, -\pi/2 < x < \pi/2]$$
$$\Rightarrow \quad y = \frac{\theta}{2}$$
$$\Rightarrow \quad y = \frac{1}{2}\cos^{-1} x$$
$$\therefore \quad \frac{dy}{dx} = -\frac{1}{2\sqrt{1-x^2}}$$

Example 28. Find $\frac{dy}{dx}$, for $y = \tan^{-1}\sqrt{\frac{a-x}{a+x}}$, where $-a < x < a$.

Sol. Here, $y = \tan^{-1}\sqrt{\frac{a-x}{a+x}}$, where $-a < x < a$

Put $x = a\cos\theta \Rightarrow \theta = \cos^{-1}\frac{x}{a}$

$$\therefore \quad y = \tan^{-1}\left\{\sqrt{\frac{a - a\cos\theta}{a + a\cos\theta}}\right\}$$
$$\Rightarrow \quad y = \tan^{-1}\left\{\sqrt{\frac{1-\cos\theta}{1+\cos\theta}}\right\}$$
$$\Rightarrow \quad y = \tan^{-1}\left\{\sqrt{\tan^2\frac{\theta}{2}}\right\}$$
$$\Rightarrow \quad y = \tan^{-1}\left|\tan\frac{\theta}{2}\right|$$

Also, $-a < x < a \Rightarrow -1 < \cos\theta < 1$

$$\Rightarrow \quad \theta \in (0, \pi) \Rightarrow \frac{\theta}{2} \in \left(0, \frac{\pi}{2}\right)$$
$$\therefore \quad y = \tan^{-1}\left|\tan\frac{\theta}{2}\right|$$
$$= \tan^{-1}\left(\tan\frac{\theta}{2}\right) = \frac{\theta}{2}$$
$$\Rightarrow \quad y = \frac{1}{2}\cos^{-1}\frac{x}{a}$$
$$\therefore \quad \frac{dy}{dx} = -\frac{1}{2} \times \frac{1}{\sqrt{1-\frac{x^2}{a^2}}}\frac{d}{dx}\left(\frac{x}{a}\right)$$
$$= -\frac{1}{2\sqrt{a^2-x^2}}$$

Example 29. Find the derivative of $y = \sin^{-1}\left(\frac{2x}{1+x^2}\right)$ and mention the points of non-differentiability.

Sol. $y = f(x) = \sin^{-1}\left(\frac{2x}{1+x^2}\right)$

$$= \begin{cases} 2\tan^{-1} x, & |x| \le 1 \\ \pi - 2\tan^{-1} x, & x > 1 \\ -(\pi + 2\tan^{-1} x), & x < -1 \end{cases}$$

$$\Rightarrow \quad \frac{dy}{dx} = \begin{cases} \frac{2}{1+x^2}, & \text{for } |x| < 1 \\ \text{not exist}, & \text{for } |x| = 1 \\ -\frac{2}{1+x^2}, & \text{for } |x| > 1 \end{cases}$$

f is continuous for all x but not differentiable at $x = 1, -1$.

JEE SCANNER

Example Similar to PYQ Asked in JEE Mains 2021

If $y=\cot^{-1}\left(\dfrac{\sqrt{1+\cos x}+\sqrt{1-\cos x}}{\sqrt{1+\cos x}-\sqrt{1-\cos x}}\right)$, $x\in\left(\dfrac{\pi}{2},\pi\right)$, then $\dfrac{dy}{dx}$ at $x=\dfrac{2\pi}{3}$ is

(a) $\frac{1}{2}$ (b) -1 (c) 0 (d) $-\frac{1}{2}$

Sol. (d) We have,

$$y=\cot^{-1}\left(\frac{\sqrt{1+\cos x}+\sqrt{1-\cos x}}{\sqrt{1+\cos x}-\sqrt{1-\cos x}}\right)$$

$$=\cot^{-1}\left[\frac{\sqrt{1+2\cos^2\frac{x}{2}-1}+\sqrt{1-1+2\sin^2\frac{x}{2}}}{\sqrt{1+2\cos^2\frac{x}{2}-1}-\sqrt{1-1+2\sin^2\frac{x}{2}}}\right]$$

$$=\cot^{-1}\left[\frac{\cos\frac{x}{2}+\sin\frac{x}{2}}{\cos\frac{x}{2}-\sin\frac{x}{2}}\right]$$

$$=\cot^{-1}\left[\frac{1+\tan\frac{x}{2}}{1-\tan\frac{x}{2}}\right]$$

$$=\cot^{-1}\left[\tan\left(\frac{\pi}{4}+\frac{x}{2}\right)\right]=\frac{\pi}{2}-\tan^{-1}\left[\tan\left(\frac{\pi}{4}+\frac{x}{2}\right)\right]$$

$$\because \frac{\pi}{4}+\frac{x}{2}\in\left(\frac{\pi}{2},\frac{3\pi}{4}\right)$$

$$=\frac{5\pi}{4}-\frac{x}{2}$$

$$\therefore \frac{dy}{dx}=-\frac{1}{2}$$

Skill Builder

If $y=\tan^{-1}\left[\dfrac{\sqrt{1+\cos x}+\sqrt{1-\cos x}}{\sqrt{1+\cos x}-\sqrt{1-\cos x}}\right]$, $x\in\left(\dfrac{\pi}{2},\pi\right)$, then $\dfrac{dy}{dx}$ is equal to

(a) $-\frac{1}{2}$ (b) $\frac{3}{2}$

(c) $\frac{1}{2}$ (d) $\frac{5}{2}$

For Sol.

■ **For more practice** See Q.10 of Milestone Practice 5.3.

Example 30. If $y=\sqrt{(a-x)(x-b)}-(a-b)\tan^{-1}\sqrt{\dfrac{a-x}{x-b}}$, then find $\dfrac{dy}{dx}$.

Sol. Let $x=a\cos^2\theta+b\sin^2\theta$

$\therefore \quad a-x=a-a\cos^2\theta-b\sin^2\theta=(a-b)\sin^2\theta$

and $x-b=a\cos^2\theta+b\sin^2\theta-b=(a-b)\cos^2\theta$

$$\therefore \quad y=(a-b)\sin\theta\cos\theta-(a-b)\tan^{-1}\tan\theta$$

$$=\frac{a-b}{2}\sin 2\theta-(a-b)\theta$$

$$\therefore \quad \frac{dy}{dx}=\frac{dy/d\theta}{dx/d\theta}=\frac{(a-b)\cos 2\theta-(a-b)}{(b-a)\sin 2\theta}$$

$$=\frac{1-\cos 2\theta}{\sin 2\theta}=\tan\theta=\sqrt{\frac{a-x}{x-b}}$$

Example 31. If $y=\tan^{-1}\dfrac{1}{x^2+x+1}+\tan^{-1}\dfrac{1}{x^2+3x+3}+\tan^{-1}\dfrac{1}{x^2+5x+7}+\tan^{-1}\dfrac{1}{x^2+7x+13}+\ldots$ to n terms, show that $\dfrac{dy}{dx}=\dfrac{1}{1+(x+n)^2}-\dfrac{1}{1+x^2}$.

Sol. Let
$$t_1=\tan^{-1}\frac{1}{x^2+x+1}$$

$$=\tan^{-1}\frac{1}{1+x(x+1)}=\tan^{-1}\frac{x+1-x}{1+(x+1)x}$$

$$=\tan^{-1}(x+1)-\tan^{-1}x$$

and
$$t_2=\tan^{-1}\frac{1}{1+(x+1)(x+2)}$$

$$=\tan^{-1}\frac{(x+2)-(x+1)}{1+(x+1)(x+2)}$$

$$=\tan^{-1}(x+2)-\tan^{-1}(x+1)$$

Thus, $t_1=\tan^{-1}(x+1)-\tan^{-1}x$

$t_2=\tan^{-1}(x+2)-\tan^{-1}(x+1)$

Similarly, $t_3=\tan^{-1}(x+3)-\tan^{-1}(x+2)$

....

....

$t_n=\tan^{-1}(x+n)-\tan^{-1}(x+n-1)$

Adding, we get

$$y=t_1+t_2+\ldots+t_n=\tan^{-1}(x+n)-\tan^{-1}x$$

$$\therefore \quad \frac{dy}{dx}=\frac{1}{1+(x+n)^2}-\frac{1}{1+x^2}$$

Milestone Practice 5.3

1. Let $f: R \to R$ be defined as $f(x) = x^3 + 3x^2 + 6x - 5 + 4e^{2x}$ and $g(x) = f^{-1}(x)$, then find $g'(-1)$.

2. The function $f(x) = e^x + x$ being differentiable and one to one, has a differentiable inverse $f^{-1}(x)$. Find $\frac{d}{dx}(f^{-1}(x))$ at point $f(\log 2)$.

3. Find $\frac{dy}{dx}$.

   (i) $y = \tan^{-1}\left(\frac{\sqrt{1+x} - \sqrt{1-x}}{\sqrt{1+x} + \sqrt{1-x}}\right)$

   (ii) $y = \tan^{-1}\left(\frac{\sqrt{1+x^2} - 1}{x}\right)$

   (iii) $y = \sin^{-1}\left(\frac{2^{x+1}}{1+4^x}\right)$

4. If $y = \sqrt{a^2 - x^2} + \frac{a}{2}\log\left(\frac{a - \sqrt{a^2 - x^2}}{a + \sqrt{a^2 - x^2}}\right)$, then show that $\frac{dy}{dx} = \frac{\sqrt{a^2 - x^2}}{x}$.

5. If $f(x) = x + \tan x$ and f is inverse of g, then $g'(x)$ equals

   (a) $\frac{1}{1 + (g(x) - x)^2}$ (b) $\frac{1}{2 - (g(x) - x)^2}$

   (c) $\frac{1}{2 + (g(x) - x)^2}$ (d) None of these

6. Let $f(x) = \exp(x^3 + x^2 + x)$ for any real number x and let g be the inverse function for f. The value of $g'(e^3)$ is

   (a) $\frac{1}{6e^3}$ (b) $\frac{1}{6}$

   (c) $\frac{1}{34e^{39}}$ (d) 6

7. If $y = \frac{(a-x)\sqrt{a-x} - (b-x)\sqrt{x-b}}{\sqrt{a-x} + \sqrt{x-b}}$, then $\frac{dy}{dx}$ wherever it is defined is equal to

   (a) $\frac{x + (a+b)}{\sqrt{(a-x)(x-b)}}$ (b) $\frac{2x - (a+b)}{2\sqrt{(a-x)(x-b)}}$

   (c) $\frac{(a+b)}{2\sqrt{(a-x)(x-b)}}$ (d) $\frac{2x + (a+b)}{2\sqrt{(a-x)(x-b)}}$

8. If $\frac{-1}{\sqrt{3}} < x < \frac{1}{\sqrt{3}}$, then find the derivative of $\tan^{-1}\left(\frac{3x - x^3}{1 - 3x^2}\right)$ w.r.t. x

   (a) $\pi - \frac{3}{1+x^2}$ (b) $\frac{3}{1+x^2}$

   (c) $\pi + \frac{3}{1+x^2}$ (d) None of these

9. If $y = \tan^{-1}\sqrt{\frac{x+1}{x-1}}$, then $\frac{dy}{dx}$ is equal to

   (a) $\frac{-1}{2|x|\sqrt{x^2-1}}$ (b) $\frac{-1}{2x\sqrt{x^2-1}}$

   (c) $\frac{1}{2x\sqrt{x^2-1}}$ (d) None of these

10. If $y = \tan^{-1}\frac{2^x}{1 + 2^{2x+1}}$, then $\frac{dy}{dx}$ at $x = 0$ is

    (a) 1 (b) 2

    (c) $-\frac{1}{10}\ln 2$ (d) None of these

11. If $y = 2\sin^{-1}\sqrt{1-x} + \sin^{-1}2\sqrt{x(1-x)}$, then for $x \in \left(0, \frac{1}{2}\right)$, $\frac{dy}{dx}$ is equal to

    (a) $\frac{2}{x\sqrt{1-x}}$ (b) $\sqrt{\frac{1-x}{x}}$

    (c) $\frac{-1}{\sqrt{x(1-x)}}$ (d) Zero

Answer Key

1. $\frac{1}{14}$
2. $\frac{1}{2e^2 + 1}$
3. (i) $\frac{1}{2\sqrt{1-x^2}}$ (ii) $\frac{1}{2(1+x^2)}$ (iii) $\frac{1}{1+2^{2x}}(2^{x+1}\ln 2)$
5. (c)
6. (a)
7. (b)
8. (b)
9. (a)
10. (c)
11. (d)

For Detailed Solution

Milestone 4 Logarithmic Differentiation

The logarithmic indices is generally used to simplify exponent, product and division of different functions. Here, we discuss 3 types of situations in differentiation using logarithm.

Type 1 When two or more function are having relation of product or division

Let $y=\dfrac{f_1(x)\cdot f_2(x)\cdot f_3(x)\ldots f_n(x)}{g_1(x)\cdot g_2(x)\cdot g_3(x)\ldots g_m(x)}$

$\therefore$ Taking logarithm both sides

$$\log y=\log\left[\frac{f_1(x)\cdot f_2(x)\ldots f_n(x)}{g_1(x)\cdot g_2(x)\ldots g_m(x)}\right]$$

$$=[\log f_1(x)+\log f_2(x)+\ldots\log f_n(x)]-[\log g_1(x)+\log g_2(x)+\ldots\log g_m(x)]$$

On differentiating both sides, we get

$$\frac{1}{y}\frac{dy}{dx}=\left[\frac{f'_1(x)}{f_1(x)}+\frac{f'_2(x)}{f_2(x)}+\ldots\frac{f'_n(x)}{f_n(x)}\right]-\left[\frac{g'_1(x)}{g_1(x)}+\frac{g'_2(x)}{g_2(x)}+\ldots\frac{g'_m(x)}{g_m(x)}\right]$$

Example 32. Find $\dfrac{dy}{dx}$

(i) $y=\sin x\cdot\sin 2x\cdot\sin 3x\ldots\sin nx$

(ii) $y=(\sin x)(e^{\sqrt{\sin x}})(\ln x)(x^x)$

(iii) $y=(x^{\ln x})(\sec x)^{3x}$

Sol. (i) $y=\sin x\sin 2x\sin 3x\ldots\sin nx$

Taking logarithm on both sides

$$\ln y=\ln(\sin x)+\ln(\sin 2x)+\ln(\sin 3x)+\ldots+\ln(\sin nx)$$

$$\frac{1}{y}\frac{dy}{dx}=\frac{\cos x}{\sin x}+\frac{2\cos 2x}{\sin 2x}+\frac{3\cos 3x}{\sin 3x}+\ldots+\frac{n\cos nx}{\sin nx}$$

$$y'=y(\cot x+2\cot 2x+3\cot 3x+\ldots+n\cot nx)$$

(ii) $y=(\sin x)(e^{\sqrt{\sin x}})(\ln x)(x^x)$

Taking logarithm on both sides

$$\ln y=\ln(\sin x)+\sqrt{\sin x}+\ln(\ln x)+x\ln x$$

$$\frac{1}{y}\frac{dy}{dx}=\frac{\cos x}{\sin x}+\frac{(\cos x)}{2\sqrt{\sin x}}+\frac{1}{(\ln x)}\cdot\frac{1}{x}+\ln x+1$$

$$\frac{dy}{dx}=y\left(\cot x+\frac{1}{2}\frac{\cos x}{\sqrt{\sin x}}+\frac{1}{x\ln x}+\ln x+1\right)$$

(iii) $y=x^{\ln x}(\sec x)^{3x}$

$$\ln y=(\ln x)^2+3x\ln(\sec x)$$

$$\frac{1}{y}\frac{dy}{dx}=\frac{2\ln x}{x}+3\ln(\sec x)+\frac{3x}{(\sec x)}(\sec x\tan x)$$

$$\frac{dy}{dx}=y\left(\frac{2\ln x}{x}+3\ln(\sec x)+3x\tan x\right)$$

Example 33. If $f(x)=\prod_{n=1}^{100}(x-n)^{n(101-n)}$, then find $\dfrac{f(101)}{f'(101)}$.

Sol. On applying log both sides, we get

$$\ln f(x)=\sum_{n=1}^{100}n(101-n)\ln(x-n)$$

Note that Π changes to Σ.

On differentiating w.r.t. x, we get

$$\frac{f'(x)}{f(x)}=\sum_{n=1}^{100}\frac{n(101-n)}{(x-n)}$$

$$\frac{f'(101)}{f(101)}=\sum_{n=1}^{100}\frac{n(101-n)}{(101-n)}=\sum_{n=1}^{100}n=5050$$

$$\therefore\quad\frac{f(101)}{f'(101)}=\frac{1}{5050}$$

Example 34. Given that $\cos\dfrac{x}{2}\cdot\cos\dfrac{x}{4}\cdot\cos\dfrac{x}{8}\ldots=\dfrac{\sin x}{x}$, prove that $\dfrac{1}{2^2}\sec^2\dfrac{x}{2}+\dfrac{1}{2^4}\sec^2\dfrac{x}{4}+\ldots=\operatorname{cosec}^2x-\dfrac{1}{x^2}$.

Sol. We have,

$$\cos\frac{x}{2}\cdot\cos\frac{x}{4}\cdot\cos\frac{x}{8}\ldots=\frac{\sin x}{x}$$

Taking log on both sides, we get

$$\log\cos\frac{x}{2}+\log\cos\frac{x}{4}+\log\cos\frac{x}{8}\ldots=\log\sin x-\log x$$

On differentiating both sides with respect to x, we get

$$\Rightarrow\quad-\frac{1}{2}\frac{\sin\frac{x}{2}}{\cos\frac{x}{2}}-\frac{1}{4}\frac{\sin\frac{x}{4}}{\cos\frac{x}{4}}-\frac{1}{8}\frac{\sin\frac{x}{8}}{\cos\frac{x}{8}}\ldots=\frac{\cos x}{\sin x}-\frac{1}{x}$$

$$\Rightarrow\quad-\frac{1}{2}\tan\frac{x}{2}-\frac{1}{4}\tan\frac{x}{4}-\frac{1}{8}\tan\frac{x}{8}\ldots=\cot x-\frac{1}{x}$$

On differentiating both sides with respect to x, we get

$$-\frac{1}{2^2}\sec^2\frac{x}{2}-\frac{1}{4^2}\sec^2\frac{x}{4}-\frac{1}{8^2}\sec^2\frac{x}{8}\ldots$$

$$=-\operatorname{cosec}^2 x+\frac{1}{x^2}$$

$$\Rightarrow \frac{1}{2^2}\sec^2\frac{x}{2}+\frac{1}{4^2}\sec^2\frac{x}{4}+\frac{1}{8^2}\sec^2\frac{x}{8}\ldots$$

$$=\operatorname{cosec}^2 x-\frac{1}{x^2}$$

Hence, $\frac{1}{2^2}\sec^2\frac{x}{2}+\frac{1}{2^4}\sec^2\frac{x}{4}+\ldots=\operatorname{cosec}^2 x-\frac{1}{x^2}$

Type 2 In the form $f(x)^{g(x)}$

Case I When $y=f(x)^{g(x)}$

Taking logarithm on both sides

$$\log y=\log[f(x)]^{g(x)}$$

$$=g(x)\cdot\log f(x)$$

On differentiating both sides w.r.t. x, we get

$$\frac{1}{y}\cdot\frac{dy}{dx}=g(x)\frac{1}{f(x)}\cdot f'(x)+\log f(x)\cdot g'(x)$$

$$\Rightarrow \frac{dy}{dx}=y\left[\frac{g(x)\,f'(x)}{f(x)}+g'(x)\cdot\log f(x)\right]$$

$$=[f(x)]^{g(x)}\left[\frac{g(x)\,f'(x)}{f(x)}+g'(x)\log f(x)\right]$$

JEE SPIKE

(For Quickly Solving Objective MCQs)

If $y=\{f(x)\}^{\phi(x)}$, then $\frac{dy}{dx}$ = Differentiation of y taking $f(x)$ as constant + Differentiation of y taking $\phi(x)$ as constant.

Example 35. If $y=x^{\sin x}$, then find $\frac{dy}{dx}$.

Sol. $y=x^{\sin x}$

Taking log on both sides, we get

$$\log y=\sin x\log x$$

On differentiating both sides, we get

$$\frac{1}{y}\frac{dy}{dx}=\sin x\cdot\left(\frac{1}{x}\right)+\log x\cdot(\cos x)$$

$$\Rightarrow \frac{dy}{dx}=y\left[\frac{\sin x}{x}+(\cos x)\log x\right]$$

$$\therefore \frac{dy}{dx}=x^{\sin x}\left[\frac{\sin x}{x}+(\cos x)\log x\right]$$

Example 36. If $x^y\cdot y^x=1$, then find $\frac{dy}{dx}$.

Sol. Taking log on both sides, we get

$$y\log x+x\log y=\log 1$$

On differentiating both the sides, we get

$$y\cdot\frac{d}{dx}(\log x)+\left\{\frac{d}{dx}y\right\}\cdot\log x+\left\{\frac{d}{dx}x\right\}\cdot\log y+x\left\{\frac{d}{dx}\log y\right\}=0$$

$$\Rightarrow y\cdot\frac{1}{x}+\log x\cdot\frac{dy}{dx}+1\cdot\log y+x\cdot\frac{1}{y}\cdot\frac{dy}{dx}=0$$

$$\Rightarrow \left[\log x+\frac{x}{y}\right]\frac{dy}{dx}=-\left[\frac{y}{x}+\log y\right]$$

$$\Rightarrow \frac{dy}{dx}=-\frac{(y+x\log y)}{(x+y\log x)}\cdot\frac{y}{x}$$

JEE SCANNER

Example Similar to PYQ Asked in JEE Main 2023

If $y(x)=(x^x)^x$, $x>0$, then $\frac{dy}{dx}+5y(x)$ at $x=1$ is equal to ....

Sol. (2) Given, $y(x)=(x^x)^x$

$$\Rightarrow y(1)=1$$

$$\ln y=x^2\ln x$$

On differentiating both sides, we get

$$\frac{1}{y}\frac{dy}{dx}=2x\ln x+\frac{x^2}{x}$$

$$=x+2x\ln x$$

$$\Rightarrow \frac{dy}{dx}=y(x+2x\ln x)$$

$$\Rightarrow \left.\frac{dy}{dx}\right|_{x=1}=1$$

$$\therefore \left.\left[\frac{dy}{dx}+5y(x)\right]\right|_{x=1}=1+5(1)=6$$

Skill Builder

If $y(x)=x^x$, $x>0$, then $\frac{dy}{dx}+10$ at $x=1$ is equal to ....

For Sol.

■ **For more practice** See Q.3 of Milestone Practice 5.4.

Case II When $y = [f(x)]^{g(x)} + h(x)$

In this we cannot take logarithm both sides first of all we assume

$$u = [f(x)]^{g(x)} \text{ and } v = h(x)$$

$$\therefore \quad y = u + v$$

On differentiating both sides w.r.t. x, we get

$$\frac{dy}{dx} = \frac{du}{dx} + \frac{dv}{dx} \quad \text{...(i)}$$

For $\frac{du}{dx}$, $\quad u = [f(x)]^{g(x)}$

$$\log u = g(x) \log f(x)$$

$$\frac{du}{dx} = [f(x)]^{g(x)} \left[\frac{g(x) f'(x)}{f(x)} + g'(x) \log f(x)\right]$$

and $\quad v = h(x)$

$$\frac{dv}{dx} = h'(x)$$

$$\therefore \quad \frac{dy}{dx} = [f(x)]^{g(x)} \left[\frac{g(x) f'(x)}{f(x)} + g'(x) \log f(x)\right] + h'(x)$$

Example 37. If $y^{\cot x} + (\tan^{-1} x)^y = 1$, then find $\frac{dy}{dx}$.

Sol. Let $u = y^{\cot x}$ and $v = (\tan^{-1} x)^y$, then we get

$$u + v = 1 \quad \text{...(i)}$$

Taking log on both sides for u and v, we get

$$\log u = \cot x \log y$$

and $\quad \log v = y \log (\tan^{-1} x)$

On differentiating both sides, we get

$$\frac{1}{u} \cdot \frac{du}{dx} = \cot x \cdot \frac{1}{y} \frac{dy}{dx} + \log y \cdot (-\operatorname{cosec}^2 x)$$

$$\Rightarrow \quad \frac{du}{dx} = y^{\cot x} \left[\frac{\cot x}{y} \cdot \frac{dy}{dx} - (\operatorname{cosec}^2 x) \log y\right] \quad \text{...(ii)}$$

Again, on differentiating $\log v = y \log (\tan^{-1} x)$, we get

$$\frac{1}{v} \cdot \frac{dv}{dx} = y \cdot \frac{1}{\tan^{-1} x} \cdot \frac{1}{1 + x^2} + \log (\tan^{-1} x) \cdot \frac{dy}{dx}$$

$$\Rightarrow \quad \frac{dv}{dx} = (\tan^{-1} x)^y \left[\frac{y}{(1 + x^2) \tan^{-1} x} + \log (\tan^{-1} x) \cdot \frac{dy}{dx}\right] \quad \text{...(iii)}$$

From Eq. (i), we get $\frac{du}{dx} + \frac{dv}{dx} = 0$

$$\Rightarrow y^{\cot x} \left\{\frac{\cot x}{y} \cdot \frac{dy}{dx} - (\operatorname{cosec}^2 x) \log y\right\} + (\tan^{-1} x)^y \left[\frac{y}{(1 + x^2) \tan^{-1} x} + \log (\tan^{-1} x) \cdot \frac{dy}{dx}\right] = 0$$

$$\Rightarrow \quad \left\{\frac{y^{\cot x} \cdot \cot x}{y} + (\tan^{-1} x)^y \cdot \log (\tan^{-1} x)\right\} \frac{dy}{dx} = \left\{y^{\cot x} \cdot (\operatorname{cosec}^2 x) \log y - \frac{(\tan^{-1} x)^y \cdot y}{(1 + x^2) \tan^{-1} x}\right\}$$

$$\text{Hence, } \frac{dy}{dx} = \frac{(y^{\cot x} \cdot \operatorname{cosec}^2 x \cdot \log y) - \left\{\frac{(\tan^{-1} x)^{y-1} \cdot y}{1 + x^2}\right\}}{(y^{\cot x - 1} \cdot \cot x) + \{(\tan^{-1} x)^y \cdot \log (\tan^{-1} x)\}}$$

Example 38. Find $\frac{dy}{dx}$ for

(i) $y = (\sin x)^{\log x}$ (ii) $y = x^{\tan x} + (\sin x)^{\cos x}$

Sol. (i) Given, $y = (\sin x)^{\log x}$ [Based on Case I]

Then, $y = e^{\log x \log \sin x}$

On differentiating both sides w.r.t. x, we get

$$\frac{dy}{dx} = e^{\log x \log \sin x} \frac{d}{dx} \{\log x \log \sin x\}$$

$$\Rightarrow \frac{dy}{dx} = (\sin x)^{\log x} \left\{\log \sin x \frac{d}{dx} (\log x) + \log x \frac{d}{dx} (\log \sin x)\right\}$$

$$\Rightarrow \frac{dy}{dx} = (\sin x)^{\log x} \left\{\frac{\log \sin x}{x} + \log x \frac{1}{\sin x} \cos x\right\}$$

$$\Rightarrow \frac{dy}{dx} = (\sin x)^{\log x} \left\{\frac{\log \sin x}{x} + \cot x \log x\right\}$$

(ii) $y = x^{\tan x} + (\sin x)^{\cos x}$ [Based on Case II]

Let $u = x^{\tan x}$, $v = (\sin x)^{\cos x}$

$\therefore \ln u = \tan x \ln x$

$$\therefore \quad \frac{d}{dx} (\ln u) = \frac{d}{dx} (\tan x \cdot \ln x)$$

$$\frac{1}{u} \cdot \frac{du}{dx} = \tan x \left(\frac{1}{x}\right) + \sec^2 x \cdot \ln x$$

$$\frac{du}{dx} = x^{\tan x} \left(\frac{\tan x}{x} + \sec^2 x \cdot \ln x\right) \quad \text{...(i)}$$

Now, $v = (\sin x)^{\cos x}$

$\ln v = \cos x \cdot \ln \sin x$

$$\Rightarrow \quad \frac{d}{dx} \ln v = \frac{d}{dx} (\cos x \ln \sin x)$$

$$\frac{1}{v} \frac{dv}{dx} = \left(\cos x \cdot \frac{\cos x}{\sin x}\right) + \ln \sin x \cdot (-\sin x)$$

$$\frac{dv}{dx} = (\sin x)^{\cos x} \left(\frac{\cos^2 x}{\sin x} - \sin x \ln (\sin x)\right) \quad \text{...(ii)}$$

$$\because \quad y = u + v$$

$$\therefore \quad \frac{dy}{dx} = \frac{du}{dx} + \frac{dv}{dx}$$

From Eqs. (i) and (ii), we get

$$\Rightarrow \frac{dy}{dx} = x^{\tan x}\left(\frac{\tan x}{x} + \sec^2 x \cdot \ln x\right) + (\sin x)^{\cos x}\left(\frac{\cos^2 x}{\sin x} - \sin x \cdot \ln(\sin x)\right)$$

Type 3 In Infinite Series

To understand this we are discussing some examples below

Example 39. Find $\frac{dy}{dx}$

(i) $y = x^{x^{x^{\cdots\infty}}}$ (ii) $y = (\ln x)^{(\ln x)^{(\ln x)^{\cdots\infty}}}$

Sol. (i) $y = x^{x^{x\ldots\infty}}$

$$\Rightarrow y = x^y$$

$$\Rightarrow \ln y = y \ln x$$

$$\Rightarrow \frac{1}{y}\cdot\frac{dy}{dx} = \frac{y}{x} + \ln x \frac{dy}{dx}$$

$$\Rightarrow \frac{dy}{dx}\left(\frac{1}{y} - \ln x\right) = \frac{y}{x}$$

$$\Rightarrow \frac{dy}{dx} = \frac{\frac{y}{x}}{\frac{(1 - y\ln x)}{y}} = \frac{y^2}{x(1 - y\ln x)}$$

(ii) $y = (\ln x)^{(\ln x)^{(\ln x)^{\cdots\infty}}}$

$$y = (\ln x)^y$$

$$\Rightarrow \ln y = y \ln(\ln x)$$

$$\Rightarrow \frac{1}{y}\frac{dy}{dx} = \frac{y}{x\ln x} + \ln(\ln x)\frac{dy}{dx}$$

$$\Rightarrow \frac{dy}{dx}\left(\frac{1}{y} - \ln(\ln x)\right) = \frac{y}{x\ln x}$$

$$\Rightarrow \frac{dy}{dx} = \frac{\frac{y}{x\ln x}}{\frac{(1 - y\ln(\ln x))}{y}} = \frac{y^2}{x\ln x\,(1 - y\ln(\ln x))}$$

Some Other Type of Examples of Infinite Series

Example 40. If $y = x + \cfrac{1}{x + \cfrac{1}{x + \cfrac{1}{x + \ldots}}}$, then prove that $\frac{dy}{dx} = \frac{y}{2y - x}$.

Sol. We have, $y = x + \cfrac{1}{x + \cfrac{1}{x + \cfrac{1}{x + \ldots}}}$

$$\Rightarrow y = x + \frac{1}{y} \Rightarrow y^2 = xy + 1$$

$$\Rightarrow 2y\frac{dy}{dx} = y + x\frac{dy}{dx} + 0$$

[on differentiating both sides with respect to x]

$$\Rightarrow \frac{dy}{dx}(2y - x) = y \Rightarrow \frac{dy}{dx} = \frac{y}{2y - x}$$

Example 41. Let $f(x) = x + \cfrac{1}{2x + \cfrac{1}{2x + \cfrac{1}{2x + \ldots\infty}}}$. Compute the value of $f(100)\cdot f'(100)$.

Sol. We have, $f(x) = x + \cfrac{1}{2x + \cfrac{1}{2x + \cfrac{1}{2x + \ldots\infty}}}$

$$\Rightarrow y = x + \frac{1}{x + y} = \frac{x^2 + xy + 1}{x + y}$$

$$\Rightarrow xy + y^2 = xy + x^2 + 1 \Rightarrow y^2 = 1 + x^2$$

$$\Rightarrow y = \pm\sqrt{1 + x^2} \Rightarrow y = \sqrt{1 + x^2}$$

[$\because$ y cannot be negative as x is positive]

$$\Rightarrow \frac{dy}{dx} = \frac{2x}{2\sqrt{1 + x^2}} = \frac{x}{\sqrt{1 + x^2}}$$

$$\Rightarrow \left.\frac{dy}{dx}\right|_{100} = \frac{100}{\sqrt{1 + 100^2}}$$

and $y|_{100} = \sqrt{1 + 100^2}$

$\therefore$ $f(100)\cdot f'(100) = 100$

Milestone Practice 5.4

1. Find the derivative w.r.t. x

(i) $y=\sqrt[5]{\dfrac{x(x^2+1)}{\sqrt[3]{1-x}}}$ (ii) $y=\sqrt{\dfrac{1-x}{1+x}}\dfrac{\sin^3 x}{\cos x}$

(iii) $y=\sqrt[3]{\dfrac{1-\cos 3x}{1+\sin 3x}}$

2. If $y=x^{(\ln x)^{\ln(\ln x)}}$, then $\dfrac{dy}{dx}$ is equal to

(a) $\dfrac{y}{x}(\ln x^{\ln x-1}+2\ln x\ln(\ln x))$

(b) $\dfrac{y}{x}(\ln x)^{\ln(\ln x)}(2\ln(\ln x)+1)$

(c) $\dfrac{y}{x\ln x}((\ln x)^2+2\ln(\ln x))$

(d) $\dfrac{y\ln y}{x\ln x}(2\ln(\ln x)+1)$

3. If $y=2^{\log_2 x^{2x}}+\left(\tan\dfrac{\pi x}{4}\right)^{\frac{4}{\pi x}}$, then $\left.\dfrac{dy}{dx}\right]_{x=1}$ is

(a) 4 (b) $\dfrac{5}{2}$

(c) 3 (d) not defined

4. If $[x+y]^{a+b}=x^a\cdot y^b$, then $\dfrac{dy}{dx}=$

(a) $\dfrac{y}{x}$

(b) $\dfrac{x}{y}$

(c) $\dfrac{y}{a+x}$

(d) $\dfrac{x}{(b+y)}$

5. If $f(x)=|x|^{|\sin x|}$, then $f'\left(\dfrac{\pi}{4}\right)$ equals

(a) $\left(\dfrac{\pi}{4}\right)^{1/\sqrt{2}}\left(\dfrac{\sqrt{2}}{2}\ln\dfrac{4}{\pi}-\dfrac{2\sqrt{2}}{\pi}\right)$

(b) $\left(\dfrac{\pi}{4}\right)^{1/\sqrt{2}}\left(\dfrac{\sqrt{2}}{2}\ln\dfrac{4}{\pi}+\dfrac{2\sqrt{2}}{\pi}\right)$

(c) $\left(\dfrac{\pi}{4}\right)^{1/\sqrt{2}}\left(\dfrac{\sqrt{2}}{2}\ln\dfrac{4}{\pi}-\dfrac{2\sqrt{2}}{\pi}\right)$

(d) $\left(\dfrac{\pi}{4}\right)^{1/\sqrt{2}}\left(\dfrac{\sqrt{2}}{2}\ln\dfrac{\pi}{4}+\dfrac{2\sqrt{2}}{\pi}\right)$

Answer Key

1. (i) $\sqrt[5]{\dfrac{x(x^2+1)}{\sqrt[3]{1-x}}}\cdot\dfrac{8x^3-9x^2+2x-3}{15x(x-1)(x^2+1)}$ (ii) $\sqrt{\dfrac{1-x}{1+x}}\dfrac{\sin^3 x}{\cos x}\left[\dfrac{1}{x^2-1}+3\cot x+\tan x\right]$

(iii) $\sqrt[3]{\dfrac{|1-\cos 3x|}{1+\sin 3x}}\;\dfrac{1+\sin 3x-\cos 3x}{(1-\cos 3x)(1+\sin 3x)}$

2. (b) 3. (a) 4. (a) 5. (d)

For Detailed Solution

Milestone 5 Differentiation of Parametric Function

• Parametric Differentiation • Differentiation of One Function with respect to Other Function

5.11 Parametric Differentiation

Differentiation of a Function in Parametric Form

Until now we have differentiate the variable y w.r.t. x, but what can we do if the variable x and y are depend on third variable 't' (say) i.e. $x = g(t), y = f(t)$. In such case x and y are called parametric functions and t is called parameter.

In this case to find $\frac{dy}{dx}$, we first obtain the relationship between x and y by eliminating the parameter t, then we differentiate w.r.t. x. But always, it is not possible to eliminate t, then we use the following formula

$$\frac{dy}{dx} = \frac{\frac{dy}{dt}}{\frac{dx}{dt}} = \frac{f'(t)}{g'(t)}$$

Example 42. Find $\frac{dy}{dx}$ of the following parametric form

(i) $y = a(\cos t + t \sin t)$ and $x = a(\sin t - t\cos t)$

(ii) $y = \sin t - t\cos t - \frac{t^2}{2}\sin t$

and $x = \cos t + t\sin t - \frac{t^2}{2}\cos t$

Sol. (i) Given, $y = a(\cos t + t\sin t)$ and $x = a(\sin t - t\cos t)$

$$\therefore \quad \frac{dy}{dt} = a[-\sin t + t(\cos t) + \sin t(1)] = at\cos t$$

Similarly, $\frac{dx}{dt} = a[\cos t - t(-\sin t)] - \cos t(1)] = at\sin t$

$$\therefore \quad \frac{dy}{dx} = \frac{dy/dt}{dx/dt} = \frac{at\cos t}{at\sin t} = \cot t$$

(ii) Given, $y = \sin t - t\cos t - \frac{t^2}{2}\sin t$

$$\frac{dy}{dt} = \cos t + t\sin t - \cos t - t\sin t - \frac{t^2}{2}\cos t = -\frac{t^2}{2}\cos t$$

and $x = \cos t + t\sin t - \frac{t^2}{2}\cos t$

$$\frac{dx}{dt} = -\sin t + \sin t + t\cos t - t\cos t + \frac{t^2}{2}\sin t = \frac{t^2}{2}\sin t$$

$$\therefore \quad \frac{dy}{dx} = \frac{dy/dt}{dx/dt} = \frac{-\frac{t^2}{2}\cos t}{\frac{t^2}{2}\sin t} = -\cot t$$

JEE SCANNER

Example Similar to PYQ Asked in JEE Main 2022

Let $x = 3\tan t$ and $y = 3\sec t$, then the value of $\dfrac{1+\left(\frac{dy}{dx}\right)^2}{\frac{d^2y}{dx^2}}$ at $t = \frac{\pi}{4}$ is equal to

(a) $9\sqrt{2}$ (b) $6\sqrt{2}$ (c) $3\sqrt{2}$ (d) $\sqrt{2}$

Sol. (a) Given, $x = 3\tan t \Rightarrow \frac{dx}{dt} = 3\sec^2 t$

and $y = 3\sec t \Rightarrow \frac{dy}{dt} = 3\sec t\tan t$

$$\therefore \quad \frac{dy}{dx} = \frac{\frac{dy}{dt}}{\frac{dx}{dt}} = \frac{3\sec t\tan t}{3\sec^2 t} = \sin t$$

and $\frac{d^2y}{dx^2} = \cos t\,\frac{dt}{dx} = \cos t \times \frac{1}{3\sec^2 t} = \frac{\cos^3 t}{3}$

$$\therefore \quad \frac{1+\left(\frac{dy}{dx}\right)^2}{\frac{d^2y}{dx^2}} \text{ at } t = \frac{\pi}{4} = \frac{1+\left(\sin\frac{\pi}{4}\right)^2}{\frac{1}{3}\left(\cos^3\frac{\pi}{4}\right)} = 9\sqrt{2}$$

Skill Builder

Let $x = \cos t - \cos^3 t$ and $y = \sin t - \sin^3 t$, then $\frac{dy}{dx}$ at $t = \frac{\pi}{4}$ is equal to

(a) 1 (b) 0

(c) −1 (d) 2

For Sol.

■ **For more practice** See Q.1 of Milestone Practice 5.5.

Example 43. If $x = a\sec^3\theta$ and $y = a\tan^3\theta$, find $\frac{dy}{dx}$ at $\theta = \frac{\pi}{3}$.

Sol. We have, $x = a\sec^3\theta$ and $y = a\tan^3\theta$

$$\frac{dx}{d\theta} = 3a\sec^2\theta\,\frac{d}{d\theta}(\sec\theta) = 3a\sec^3\theta\tan\theta$$

and $\dfrac{dy}{d\theta} = 3a\tan^2\theta \dfrac{d}{d\theta}(\tan\theta) = 3a\tan^2\theta\sec^2\theta$

$$\Rightarrow \frac{dy}{dx} = \frac{dy/d\theta}{dx/d\theta} = \frac{3a\tan^2\theta\sec^2\theta}{3a\sec^3\theta\tan\theta} = \frac{\tan\theta}{\sec\theta} = \sin\theta$$

$$\Rightarrow \left(\frac{dy}{dx}\right)_{\theta=\pi/3} = \sin\frac{\pi}{3} = \frac{\sqrt{3}}{2}$$

Example 44. If $x = a\left(\cos t + \log\tan\dfrac{t}{2}\right)$ and $y = a\sin t$, then find $\dfrac{dy}{dx}$ at $t = \dfrac{\pi}{4}$.

Sol. Here, $x = a\left(\cos t + \log\tan\dfrac{t}{2}\right)$ and $y = a\sin t$

On differentiating both equations w.r.t. t, we get

$$\frac{dx}{dt} = a\left(-\sin t + \frac{1}{\tan\frac{t}{2}}\sec^2\frac{t}{2}\times\frac{1}{2}\right)$$

$$\Rightarrow \frac{dx}{dt} = a\left(-\sin t + \frac{1}{2\sin\frac{t}{2}\cos\frac{t}{2}}\right)$$

$$\Rightarrow \frac{dx}{dt} = a\left(-\sin t + \frac{1}{\sin t}\right) = \frac{a\cos^2 t}{\sin t} \text{ and } \frac{dy}{dt} = a\cos t$$

So, $$\frac{dy}{dx} = \frac{dy}{dt}\Big/\frac{dx}{dt} = \frac{a\cos t}{\frac{a\cos^2 t}{\sin t}} = \tan t$$

$$\Rightarrow \left(\frac{dy}{dx}\right)_{t=\frac{\pi}{4}} = \tan\frac{\pi}{4} = 1$$

5.12 Differentiation of One Function with respect to Other Function

Suppose it is required to differentiate a function $f(x)$ with respect to another function $g(x)$. Let $y = f(x)$ and $z = g(x)$.

Here, both functions are different but both are in same variable x.

Then, to find the derivative of $f(x)$ with respect to $g(x)$ or derivative of $g(x)$ with respect to $f(x)$, i.e. to find $\dfrac{dy}{dz}$ or $\dfrac{dz}{dy}$. We firstly differentiate both functions $f(x)$ and $g(x)$ with respect to x separately and then put these values in the following formulae:

$$\frac{dy}{dz} = \frac{dy/dx}{dz/dx} \text{ or } \frac{dz}{dy} = \frac{dz/dx}{dy/dx}$$

Example 45. If $x = \sqrt{a^{\sin^{-1}t}}$, $y = \sqrt{a^{\cos^{-1}t}}$, $a > 0$ and $-1 < t < 1$. Show that $\dfrac{dy}{dx} = -\dfrac{y}{x}$.

Sol. Given, $x = \sqrt{a^{\sin^{-1}t}}$ and $y = \sqrt{a^{\cos^{-1}t}}$

$$\Rightarrow \frac{dx}{dt} = \frac{1}{2}(a^{\sin^{-1}t})^{-\frac{1}{2}}\frac{d}{dt}(a^{\sin^{-1}t})$$

$$\Rightarrow \frac{dx}{dt} = \frac{1}{2}(a^{\sin^{-1}t})^{-\frac{1}{2}}\cdot a^{\sin^{-1}t}\log_e a\times\frac{1}{\sqrt{1-t^2}} = \frac{x\log_e a}{2\sqrt{1-t^2}}$$

Again, $$\frac{dy}{dt} = \frac{1}{2}(a^{\cos^{-1}t})^{-1/2}\frac{d}{dt}(a^{\cos^{-1}t})$$

$$= \frac{1}{2}(a^{\cos^{-1}t})^{-1/2}\cdot a^{\cos^{-1}t}\log_e a\times\left(\frac{-1}{\sqrt{1-t^2}}\right)$$

$$= \frac{-y\log_e a}{2\sqrt{1-t^2}}$$

So, $$\frac{dy}{dx} = \frac{\frac{dy}{dt}}{\frac{dx}{dt}} = -\frac{y}{x}$$

Alternate Solution

We have, $xy = \sqrt{a^{\sin^{-1}t}}\cdot\sqrt{a^{\cos^{-1}t}}$

$$= \sqrt{a^{\sin^{-1}t+\cos^{-1}t}} = \sqrt{a^{\pi/2}}$$

$\Rightarrow x^2y^2 = a^{\pi/2}$ $\left[\because \sin^{-1}x + \cos^{-1}x = \dfrac{\pi}{2}\right]$

On differentiating, we get

$$y + x\cdot\frac{dy}{dx} = 0 \Rightarrow \frac{dy}{dx} = -\frac{y}{x}$$

Example 46. Find derivative of $(\ln x)^{\tan x}$ w.r.t. x^x.

Sol. $u = (\ln x)^{\tan x}$; $v = x^x$ and $\ln(u) = \tan x\ln(\ln x)$

$$\Rightarrow \frac{1}{u}\left(\frac{du}{dx}\right) = (\sec^2 x)\ln(\ln x) + \tan x\left(\frac{1}{\ln x}\cdot\frac{1}{x}\right)$$

$$\frac{du}{dx} = \frac{u((x\ln x)\ln(\ln x)\sec^2 x + \tan x)}{(x\ln x)}$$

$\ln v = x\ln x$

$$\Rightarrow \frac{1}{v}\left(\frac{dv}{dx}\right) = (\ln x + 1) \Rightarrow \frac{dv}{dx} = x^x(\ln x + 1)$$

$$\therefore \frac{du}{dv} = \frac{(\ln x)^{\tan x}}{x^x}\left(\frac{x\ln x\ln(\ln x)\sec^2 x + \tan x}{(x\ln x)(\ln x + 1)}\right)$$

Example 47. Differentiate $\sin^{-1}\left(\dfrac{2x}{1+x^2}\right)$ w.r.t. $\tan^{-1}x$, $-1 < x < 1$.

Sol. Let $u=\sin^{-1}\left(\frac{2x}{1+x^2}\right)$ and $v=\tan^{-1}x$

On putting $x=\tan\theta \Rightarrow \theta=\tan^{-1}x$

$$\Rightarrow \quad u=\sin^{-1}\left(\frac{2\tan\theta}{1+\tan^2\theta}\right)$$

$$\Rightarrow \quad u=\sin^{-1}(\sin 2\theta) \qquad \left[\because \sin 2\theta=\frac{2\tan\theta}{1+\tan^2\theta}\right]$$

$$\Rightarrow \quad u=2\theta \Rightarrow u=2\tan^{-1}x$$

$$\Rightarrow \quad \frac{du}{dx}=\frac{2}{1+x^2} \qquad \text{...(i)}$$

Again, $v=\tan^{-1}x \Rightarrow \frac{dv}{dx}=\frac{1}{1+x^2}$ ...(ii)

Now, $\frac{du}{dv}=\frac{du/dx}{dv/dx}=\frac{\frac{2}{1+x^2}}{\frac{1}{1+x^2}}=2$ [from Eqs. (i) and (ii)]

Example 48. Find the derivative of $\sec^{-1}\left(\frac{1}{2x^2-1}\right)$ w.r.t. $\sqrt{1-x^2}$ at $x=\frac{1}{2}$.

Sol. Let $u=\sec^{-1}\left(\frac{1}{2x^2-1}\right)$ and $v=\sqrt{1-x^2}$

Put $x=\cos\theta$

$\therefore$ $u=\sec^{-1}(\sec 2\theta)=2\theta$

and $v=\sqrt{1-\cos^2\theta}=\sin\theta$

$$\Rightarrow \quad \frac{du}{d\theta}=2$$

and $\frac{dv}{d\theta}=\cos\theta$

$$\Rightarrow \quad \frac{du}{dv}=\frac{du/d\theta}{dv/d\theta}=\frac{2}{\cos\theta}=\frac{2}{x}$$

Now, $\left(\frac{du}{dv}\right)_{\text{at } x=\frac{1}{2}}=\frac{2}{\frac{1}{2}}=4$

Example 49. If $x\in\left(\frac{1}{\sqrt{2}},1\right)$. Differentiate $\tan^{-1}\left(\frac{\sqrt{1-x^2}}{x}\right)$ w.r.t. $\cos^{-1}(2x\sqrt{1-x^2})$.

Sol. Let $u=\tan^{-1}\left(\frac{\sqrt{1-x^2}}{x}\right)$

and $v=\cos^{-1}(2x\sqrt{1-x^2})$

Putting $x=\sin\theta$, then $x\in\left(\frac{1}{\sqrt{2}},1\right)$

$$\Rightarrow \quad \frac{1}{\sqrt{2}}<\sin\theta<1$$

$$\Rightarrow \quad \frac{\pi}{4}<\theta<\frac{\pi}{2}$$

Now, $u=\tan^{-1}\left(\frac{\sqrt{1-x^2}}{x}\right) \Rightarrow u=\tan^{-1}\left(\frac{\sqrt{1-\sin^2\theta}}{\sin\theta}\right)$

$$\Rightarrow \quad u=\tan^{-1}\left(\frac{\cos\theta}{\sin\theta}\right) \Rightarrow u=\tan^{-1}(\cot\theta)$$

$$\Rightarrow \quad u=\tan^{-1}\left\{\tan\left(\frac{\pi}{2}-\theta\right)\right\}$$

$$\left[\because \frac{\pi}{4}<\theta<\frac{\pi}{2} \Rightarrow 0<\frac{\pi}{2}-\theta<\frac{\pi}{4}\right]$$

$$\Rightarrow \quad u=\frac{\pi}{2}-\theta \Rightarrow u=\frac{\pi}{2}-\sin^{-1}x$$

$$\Rightarrow \quad \frac{du}{dx}=-\frac{1}{\sqrt{1-x^2}} \qquad \text{...(i)}$$

Again, $v=\cos^{-1}(2x\sqrt{1-x^2})$

$$\Rightarrow \quad v=\frac{\pi}{2}-\sin^{-1}(2x\sqrt{1-x^2})$$

$$\Rightarrow \quad v=\frac{\pi}{2}-\sin^{-1}(\sin 2\theta), \text{ where } x=\sin\theta$$

$$\Rightarrow \quad v=\frac{\pi}{2}-\sin^{-1}(\sin(\pi-2\theta)) \Rightarrow v=\frac{\pi}{2}-(\pi-2\theta)$$

$$\left[\because \frac{\pi}{4}<\theta<\frac{\pi}{2} \Rightarrow 0<\pi-2\theta<\frac{\pi}{2}\right]$$

$$\Rightarrow \quad v=-\frac{\pi}{2}+2\theta$$

$$\Rightarrow \quad v=-\frac{\pi}{2}+2\sin^{-1}x$$

$$\Rightarrow \quad \frac{dv}{dx}=\frac{2}{\sqrt{1-x^2}} \qquad \text{...(ii)}$$

$$\therefore \quad \frac{du}{dv}=\frac{\frac{du}{dx}}{\frac{dv}{dx}}=\frac{-\frac{1}{\sqrt{1-x^2}}}{\frac{2}{\sqrt{1-x^2}}}=-\frac{1}{2}$$

Example 50. Find the derivative of $f(\sin^{-1}x)$ w.r.t. $g(x^2+x)$ at $x=0$ if $f'(0)=2g'(0)$.

Sol. We have, $\frac{d}{dx}\{f(\sin^{-1}x)\}=f'(\sin^{-1}x)\cdot\frac{1}{\sqrt{1-x^2}}$

and $\frac{d}{dx}\{g(x^2+x)\}=g'(x^2+x)\cdot(2x+1)$

$$\Rightarrow \quad \frac{d\{f(\sin^{-1}x)\}}{d\{g(x^2+x)\}}=\frac{f'(\sin^{-1}x)}{g'(x^2+x)}\cdot\frac{1}{(2x+1)\sqrt{1-x^2}}$$

Hence, the value of the derivative at $x=0$ is

$$=\frac{f'(0)}{g'(0)}=2 \qquad [\because f'(0)=2g'(0)]$$

Example 51. Find the derivative of $f(\tan x)$ w.r.t. $g(\sec x)$ at $x=\frac{\pi}{4}$, where $f'(1)=2$ and $g'(\sqrt{2})=4$.

Sol. Let $u=f(\tan x)$ and $v=g(\sec x)$

$$\Rightarrow \quad \frac{du}{dx}=f'(\tan x)\sec^2 x$$

and
$$\frac{dv}{dx}=g'(\sec x)\sec x\tan x$$

$$\Rightarrow \quad \frac{du}{dv}=\frac{du/dx}{dv/dx}=\frac{f'(\tan x)\sec^2 x}{g'(\sec x)\sec x\tan x}$$

$$\Rightarrow \quad \left[\frac{du}{dv}\right]_{x=\frac{\pi}{4}}=\frac{f'\left(\tan\frac{\pi}{4}\right)}{g'\left(\sec\frac{\pi}{4}\right)\sin\frac{\pi}{4}}$$

$$=\frac{f'(1)\sqrt{2}}{g'(\sqrt{2})}=\frac{2\sqrt{2}}{4}=\frac{1}{\sqrt{2}}$$

Milestone Practice 5.5

1. Find $\frac{dy}{dx}$ at $t=\frac{\pi}{6}$, where $x=\frac{\sin^3 t}{\sqrt{\cos 2t}}$; $y=\frac{\cos^3 t}{\sqrt{\cos 2t}}$.

2. If $x=\sin^{-1}\left(\frac{2t}{1+t^2}\right)$ and $y=\tan^{-1}\left(\frac{2t}{1-t^2}\right)$, then prove that $\frac{dy}{dx}=1$.

3. If $x=\sec\theta-\cos\theta$ and $y=\sec^n\theta-\cos^n\theta$, then show that $(x^2+4)\left(\frac{dy}{dx}\right)^2=n^2(y^2+4)$.

4. Differentiate $\sin^{-1}(4x\sqrt{1-4x^2})$ w.r.t. $\sqrt{1-4x^2}$, if

(i) $x\in\left(\frac{-1}{2\sqrt{2}},\frac{1}{2\sqrt{2}}\right)$ (ii) $x\in\left(\frac{1}{2\sqrt{2}},\frac{1}{2}\right)$

(iii) $x\in\left(-\frac{1}{2},-\frac{1}{2\sqrt{2}}\right)$

5. Differentiate $\tan^{-1}\left(\frac{2x}{1-x^2}\right)$ with respect to $\sin^{-1}\left(\frac{2x}{1+x^2}\right)$, if

(i) $x\in(-1,1)$ (ii) $x\in(1,\infty)$

(iii) $x\in(-\infty,-1)$

6. Obtain differential coefficients of $\tan^{-1}\frac{\sqrt{1+x^2}-1}{x}$ with respect to $\cos^{-1}\sqrt{\frac{1+\sqrt{1+x^2}}{2\sqrt{1+x^2}}}$.

7. If $y=\frac{\sqrt{(1+t^2)}-\sqrt{(1-t^2)}}{\sqrt{(1+t^2)}+\sqrt{(1-t^2)}}$ and $x=\sqrt{(1-t^4)}$, then $\frac{dy}{dx}$ is

(a) $\frac{-1}{t^2[1+\sqrt{(1-t^4)}]}$ (b) $\frac{[\sqrt{(1-t^4)}-1]}{t^6}$

(c) $\frac{1}{t^2[1+\sqrt{(1-t^4)}]}$ (d) $\frac{[1-\sqrt{(1-t^4)}]}{t^6}$

8. If $x=\frac{1+t}{t^3}$, $y=\frac{3}{2t^2}+\frac{2}{t}$, then, $x\left(\frac{dy}{dx}\right)^3-\frac{dy}{dx}=$

(a) 0 (b) −1 (c) 1 (d) 2

Answer Key

1. 0 **4.** (i) $-\frac{1}{x}$ (ii) $\frac{1}{x}$ (iii) $-\frac{1}{x}$ **5.** (i) 1 (ii) −1 (iii) −1

6. 1 **7.** (a, b) **8.** (c)

For Detailed Solution

Milestone 6 Higher Order Derivatives

Let $y = f(x)$ be a differentiable function. Then,

$\frac{dy}{dx} / f'(x) / y' / y_1$ – First order derivative

$\frac{d^2y}{dx^2} / f''(x) / y'' / y_2$ – 2nd order derivative

$\frac{d^3y}{dx^3} / f'''(x) / y''' / y_3$ – 3rd order derivative

JEE SPIKE

If y is a function of x, given parametrically by $x = \phi(t)$, $y = \psi(t)$, then

$$\frac{d^2y}{dx^2} = \frac{d}{dx}\left(\frac{dy}{dx}\right) = \frac{d}{dx}\left(\frac{\psi'(t)}{\phi'(t)}\right) = \frac{d}{dt}\cdot\left(\frac{\psi'(t)}{\phi'(t)}\right) \times \frac{dt}{dx}$$

$$\frac{d^ny}{dx^n} = \frac{d}{dx}\left(\frac{d^{n-1}y}{dx^{n-1}}\right)$$

Example 52. Find y_n, if

(i) $y = \sin x$ (ii) $y = e^{x+a}$

(iii) $y = e^{ax+b}$ (iv) $y = \frac{1}{ax+b}$

(v) $y = \ln(ax+b)$ (vi) $y = \frac{3x^2-1}{x^3-x}$

Sol. (i) $y = \sin x \Rightarrow y_1 = \cos x = \sin\left(x + \frac{\pi}{2}\right)$

$\Rightarrow \quad y_2 = -\sin x = \sin\left(x + \frac{2\pi}{2}\right)$

$\Rightarrow \quad y_3 = -\cos x = \sin\left(x + \frac{3\pi}{2}\right)$

$\Rightarrow \quad y_4 = \sin x = \sin(x + 2\pi)$

....

$\Rightarrow \quad y_n = \sin\left(x + \frac{n\pi}{2}\right), n \in N$

(ii) $y = e^{x+a} \Rightarrow y_1 = e^{x+a}$

$\Rightarrow \quad y_2 = e^{x+a}$

$\Rightarrow \quad y_n = e^{x+a}$

(iii) $y = e^{ax+b}$

$\Rightarrow \quad y_1 = ae^{ax+b}$

$\Rightarrow \quad y_2 = a^2e^{ax+b}$

$\Rightarrow \quad y_n = a^ne^{ax+b}$

(iv) $y = \frac{1}{ax+b} \Rightarrow y_1 = \frac{-1 \times a}{(ax+b)^2}$

$\Rightarrow \quad y_2 = \frac{-1 \times -2 \times a^2}{(ax+b)^3} \Rightarrow y_n = \frac{(-1)^n \times n! \times a^n}{(ax+b)^{n+1}}$

(v) $y = \ln(ax+b) \Rightarrow y_1 = \frac{a}{ax+b}$

$\Rightarrow \quad y_2 = \frac{-1 \times a^2}{(ax+b)^2} \Rightarrow y_n = \frac{(-1)^{n-1} \times (n-1)! \times a^n}{(ax+b)^n}$

(vi) $y = \frac{3x^2-1}{x^3-x} = \frac{3x^2-1}{(x-1)\,x(x+1)} = \frac{A}{x-1} + \frac{B}{x} + \frac{C}{x+1}$

$\Rightarrow 3x^2 - 1 = Ax(x+1) + B(x-1)(x+1) + C(x-1)\,x$

On solving, we get $A = B = C = 1$

$\Rightarrow \quad y = \frac{1}{x-1} + \frac{1}{x} + \frac{1}{x+1}$

$\Rightarrow \quad y_1 = \frac{-1}{(x-1)^2} + \frac{-1}{x^2} + \frac{-1}{(x+1)^2}$

$\Rightarrow \quad y_2 = \frac{-1 \times -2}{(x-1)^3} + \frac{-1 \times -2}{x^3} + \frac{-1 \times -2}{(x+1)^3}$

....

$\Rightarrow \quad y_n = (-1)^n \cdot n!\left[\frac{1}{(x-1)^{n+1}} + \frac{1}{x^{n+1}} + \frac{1}{(x+1)^{n+1}}\right]$

Example 53. If $x = a(t + \sin t)$ and $y = a(1 - \cos t)$, then find $\frac{d^2y}{dx^2}$.

Sol. Here, $x = a(t + \sin t)$ and $y = a(1 - \cos t)$

On differentiating both sides w.r.t. t, we get

$$\frac{dx}{dt} = a(1 + \cos t) \text{ and } \frac{dy}{dt} = a(\sin t)$$

$$\therefore \quad \frac{dy}{dx} = \frac{a \sin t}{a(1+\cos t)} = \frac{2\sin\frac{t}{2}\cdot\cos\frac{t}{2}}{2\cos^2\frac{t}{2}} = \tan\left(\frac{t}{2}\right)$$

Again, differentiating both sides, we get

$$\frac{d^2y}{dx^2} = \sec^2\left(\frac{t}{2}\right)\cdot\frac{1}{2}\cdot\frac{dt}{dx} = \frac{1}{2}\sec^2\left(\frac{t}{2}\right)\cdot\frac{1}{a(1+\cos t)}$$

$$= \frac{1}{2a}\cdot\frac{\sec^2\left(\frac{t}{2}\right)}{2\left(\cos^2\frac{t}{2}\right)}$$

Hence, $\frac{d^2y}{dx^2} = \frac{1}{4a}\cdot\sec^4\left(\frac{t}{2}\right)$

Example 54. If $y = e^{a\cos^{-1}x}$, then prove that $(1 - x^2)y_2 - xy_1 - a^2y = 0$

Sol. $y = e^{a\cos^{-1}x}$

$$\frac{dy}{dx} = e^{a\cos^{-1}x}\left(\frac{-a}{\sqrt{1-x^2}}\right) = y_1 \Rightarrow y_1 = \frac{-ay}{\sqrt{1-x^2}}$$

$$\Rightarrow (1 - x^2)(y_1)^2 = a^2y^2$$

Now, on differentiating w.r.t. x, we get

$$(1 - x^2)\cdot 2y_1y_2 - 2x(y_1)^2 = a^2(2yy_1)$$

$$\Rightarrow (1 - x^2)y_2 - xy_1 = a^2y.$$

Hence, $(1 - x^2)y_2 - xy_1 - a^2y = 0.$

Example 55. If $y^{1/m} + y^{-1/m} = 2x$, then prove that $(x^2 - 1)y_3 + 3xy_2 + (1 - m^2)y_1 = 0$

Sol. $y^{1/m} + y^{-1/m} = 2x \Rightarrow y^{2/m} - 2xy^{1/m} + 1 = 0$

$$\Rightarrow y^{1/m} = \frac{2x \pm \sqrt{4x^2 - 4}}{2} = (x \pm \sqrt{x^2 - 1})$$

$$\Rightarrow y = (x \pm \sqrt{x^2 - 1})^m$$

$$\Rightarrow y_1 = m(x \pm \sqrt{x^2 - 1})^{m-1}\left(1 \pm \frac{x}{\sqrt{x^2 - 1}}\right)$$

$$\Rightarrow y_1 = \frac{m}{\sqrt{x^2 - 1}}(x \pm \sqrt{x^2 - 1})^{m-1}(\sqrt{x^2 - 1} \pm x)$$

$$\Rightarrow y_1 = \frac{my}{\sqrt{x^2 - 1}}$$

$$\Rightarrow (x^2 - 1)(y_1)^2 = m^2y^2$$

$$\Rightarrow (x^2 - 1)2y_1y_2 + (y_1)^2 2x = 2m^2yy_1$$

$$\Rightarrow (x^2 - 1)y_2 + xy_1 = m^2y$$

$$\Rightarrow (x^2 - 1)y_3 + 2xy_2 + xy_2 + y_1 = m^2y_1$$

$$\Rightarrow (x^2 - 1)y_3 + 3xy_2 + (1 - m^2)y_1 = 0$$

Example 56. If $(x - a)^2 + (y - b)^2 = c^2$ $(c > 0)$, then $\dfrac{\left[1 + \left(\dfrac{dy}{dx}\right)^2\right]^{3/2}}{\dfrac{d^2y}{dx^2}}$ equals

(a) c (b) c^2 (c) c^3 (d) c^4

Sol. (a) $(x - a)^2 + (y - b)^2 = c^2 \ (c > 0)$ ...(i)

Now, differentiating w.r.t. x, we get

$$2(x - a) + 2(y - b)y_1 = 0$$

$$\Rightarrow (x - a) + (y - b)y_1 = 0 \quad \text{...(ii)}$$

$$\Rightarrow 1 + (y - b)y_2 + (y_1)^2 = 0 \quad \text{...(iii)}$$

$$1 + (y_1)^2 = 1 + \frac{(x - a)^2}{(y - b)^2} \quad \text{[from Eq. (ii)]}$$

$$\Rightarrow 1 + (y_1)^2 = \frac{c^2}{(y - b)^2}$$

$$\Rightarrow \frac{(1 + (y_1)^2)^{3/2}}{y_2} = \frac{\left(\dfrac{c^2}{(y - b)^2}\right)^{3/2}}{\dfrac{-(1 + (y_1)^2)}{(y - b)}} \quad \text{[from Eq. (iii)]}$$

$$= \frac{|c^3/(y - b)^3|}{-c^2/(y - b)^3} = \pm c$$

JEE SCANNER

Example Similar to PYQ Asked in JEE Mains 2024

Let $f: R \to R$ be a function such that $f(x) = x^3 + x^2f'(1) + xf''(2) + f'''(3) \ \forall \ x \in R$, then the equation $f(x) = 0$ has α number of real roots and $f(1) = \beta$, then $\alpha + \beta$ is ....

Sol. (7) We have, $f(x) = x^3 + x^2f'(1) + xf''(2) + f'''(3)$

$$f'(x) = 3x^2 + 2xf'(1) + f''(2)$$

$$\Rightarrow f'(1) = 3 + 2f'(1) + f''(2)$$

$$\Rightarrow f'(1) + f''(2) + 3 = 0$$

$$f''(x) = 6x + 2f'(1) \Rightarrow f''(2) = 12 + 2f'(1)$$

$$f'''(x) = 6 \Rightarrow f'''(3) = 6$$

$$f'(1) = -5$$

$$f''(2) = 2$$

Hence, $f(x) = x^3 - 5x^2 + 2x + 6$

Now, $f(-1) = -1 - 5 - 2 + 6 = -2$

$f(0) = 6 \Rightarrow$ one root $\in (-1, 0)$

$f(2) = 8 - 20 + 4 + 6 = -2$

$\Rightarrow$ One root $\in (0, 2)$.

$\Rightarrow$ Two roots are real.

$\Rightarrow$ All three roots are real.

Also, $f(5) = 125 - 125 + 10 + 6 = 16$

$\Rightarrow$ One root $\in (2, 5)$

$\therefore$ One root lies in each of the intervals $(-1, 0)$, $(0, 2)$, $(2, 5)$

Hence, all roots are real and distinct.

$\therefore \ \alpha = 3$ and $\beta = f(1) = 1 - 5 + 2 + 6 = 4$

$\therefore \ \alpha + \beta = 7$

Skill Builder

Let $f: R \to R$ be a function such that $f(x) = x^2 + 2xf'(1) + f''(2) \ \forall \ x \in R$, then equation $f(x) = 0$, has α number of real root and $f(1) = \beta$, then $\alpha - \beta$ is ....

For Sol.

■ **For more practice** See Q.4 of Milestone Practice 5.6.

Example 57. Use the substitution $x = \tan\theta$ to show that the equation $\dfrac{d^2y}{dx^2} + \dfrac{2x}{1 + x^2}\dfrac{dy}{dx} + \dfrac{y}{(1 + x^2)^2} = 0$ changes to $\dfrac{d^2y}{d\theta^2} + y = 0.$

Sol. $$\frac{d^2y}{dx^2}+\frac{2x}{1+x^2}\left(\frac{dy}{dx}\right)+\frac{y}{(1+x^2)^2}=0 \quad \text{...(i)}$$

$$x=\tan\theta$$

$$\Rightarrow \quad dx=\sec^2\theta\, d\theta$$

$$\Rightarrow \quad \frac{d\theta}{dx}=\frac{1}{\sec^2\theta}=\cos^2\theta$$

$$\frac{dy}{dx}=\frac{dy}{d\theta}\left(\frac{d\theta}{dx}\right)$$

$$=\frac{1}{\sec^2\theta}\left(\frac{dy}{d\theta}\right)=\cos^2\theta\left(\frac{dy}{d\theta}\right)$$

$$\frac{d^2y}{dx^2}=\frac{d}{dx}\left(\frac{1}{\sec^2\theta}\cdot\frac{dy}{d\theta}\right)=\frac{d}{d\theta}\left(\cos^2\theta\frac{dy}{d\theta}\right)\cdot\frac{d\theta}{dx}$$

$$=\left(\cos^2\theta\frac{d^2y}{d\theta^2}-2\cos\theta\sin\theta\frac{dy}{d\theta}\right)\cos^2\theta$$

From Eq. (i) putting $x=\tan\theta$

$$\cos^2\theta\left(\cos^2\theta\frac{d^2y}{d\theta^2}-2\cos\theta\sin\theta\frac{dy}{d\theta}\right)+\left(\frac{2\tan\theta}{1+\tan^2\theta}\right)\left(\cos^2\theta\frac{dy}{d\theta}\right)+\left(\frac{y}{(1+\tan^2\theta)^2}\right)=0$$

$$\Rightarrow \quad \left(\frac{d^2y}{d\theta^2}-2\tan\theta\frac{dy}{d\theta}\right)+\left(2\tan\theta\frac{dy}{d\theta}\right)+y=0$$

$$\Rightarrow \quad \frac{d^2y}{d\theta^2}+y=0$$

Example 58. If $y^2=P(x)$, a polynomial of degree $n>3$, show that $2\frac{d}{dx}\left(y^3\frac{d^2y}{dx^2}\right)=P(x)\cdot P'''(x)$

Sol. Given, $y^2=P(x)$ ...(i)

$$\therefore \quad 2y\frac{dy}{dx}=P'(x) \quad \text{...(ii)}$$

On differentiating again w.r.t. x, we get

$$2\frac{dy}{dx}\cdot\frac{dy}{dx}+2y\cdot\frac{d^2y}{dx^2}=P''(x)$$

or $$2y^2\left(\frac{dy}{dx}\right)^2+2y^3\frac{d^2y}{dx^2}=y^2P''(x)$$

or $$2y^3\frac{d^2y}{dx^2}=y^2P''(x)-2y^2\left(\frac{dy}{dx}\right)^2$$

$$=y^2P''(x)-\frac{1}{2}[P'(x)]^2$$

On differentiating again w.r.t. x, we get

$$2\frac{d}{dx}\left(y^3\frac{d^2y}{dx^2}\right)$$

$$=2y\frac{dy}{dx}P''(x)+y^2P'''(x)-\frac{1}{2}2(P'(x)P''(x)$$

$$=P'(x)P''(x)+y^2P'''(x)-P'(x)P''(x) \quad \left[\because 2y\frac{dy}{dx}=P'(x)\right]$$

$$=y^2P'''(x)$$

$$=P(x)P'''(x) \quad [\because y^2=P(x)]$$

Theorem If $y=fg$, where f and g are functions of x having derivatives of nth order, then

$$y_n=\sum_{r=0}^{n}{}^nC_rf_{n-r}g_r$$

i.e. $y_n=f_ng+{}^nC_1f_{n-1}g_1+\ +{}^nC_2f_{n-2}g_2$
$+\ldots\ {}^nC_rf^{n-r}g_r+\ldots\ {}^nC_nfg_n$

where suffixes denote order of derivatives with respect to x.

Example 59. Find the general expressions for derivatives of order n of the following functions

(i) $y=e^{-x}$ (ii) $y=\sin^2 x$
(iii) $y=x\ln x$ (iv) $y=\sin^4 x+\cos^4 x$

Sol. (i) Given, $y=e^{-x}$

$$\Rightarrow \quad \frac{dy}{dx}=(-1)e^{-x}\Rightarrow\frac{d^ny}{dx^n}=(-1)^ne^{-x}$$

(ii) Let $y=\sin^2 x$

$$\Rightarrow \quad \frac{dy}{dx}=2\sin x\cos x=\sin 2x$$

$$\Rightarrow \quad \frac{d^2y}{dx^2}=2\cos 2x=2\sin\left(2x+\frac{\pi}{2}\right)$$

$$\Rightarrow \quad \frac{d^3y}{dx^3}=4\sin\left(2x+2\cdot\frac{\pi}{2}\right)$$

$$\Rightarrow \quad \frac{d^ny}{dx^n}=2^{n-1}\sin\left(2x+(n-1)\frac{\pi}{2}\right)$$

(iii) Let $y=x\ln x$

$$\Rightarrow \quad \frac{dy}{dx}=x\cdot\frac{1}{x}+\ln x=1+\ln x$$

$$\Rightarrow \quad \frac{d^2y}{dx^2}=\frac{1}{x}\text{ and }\frac{d^3y}{dx^3}=-\frac{1}{x^2}$$

$$\Rightarrow \quad \frac{d^ny}{dx^n}=\frac{(-1)(-2)\ldots(n-2)}{x^{n-1}};n\geq 2$$

$$=\frac{(-1)^n(n-2)!}{x^{n-1}};n>2$$

(iv) $y=\sin^4 x+\cos^4 x$

$$=(\sin^2 x+\cos^2 x)^2-2\sin^2 x\cos^2 x$$

$$y=1-\frac{1}{2}\sin^2 2x$$

$$\Rightarrow \quad \frac{dy}{dx}=-\frac{1}{2}\cdot 2\sin 2x\cdot\cos 2x$$

$$\Rightarrow \quad \frac{dy}{dx}=-\sin 4x$$

$$\Rightarrow \quad \frac{d^ny}{dx^n}=4^{n-1}\cos\left(4x+\frac{n\pi}{2}\right)$$

Example 60. Using mathematical induction

(i) If $y = e^{\tan^{-1} x}$, then prove that

$$(1+x^2)\, y_{n+1} + (2nx - 1)\, y_n + n(n-1)\, y_{n-1} = 0$$

(ii) If $y = \sin(m \sin^{-1} x)$, then show that

$$(1-x^2)\, y_{n+2} = (2n+1)\, xy_{n+1} + (n^2 - m^2)\, y_n$$

Sol. (i) $y = e^{\tan^{-1} x}$, then

$$(1+x^2)\, y_{n+1} + (2nx - 1)\, y_n + n(n-1)\, y_{n-1} = 0$$

$$\frac{dy}{dx} = \frac{e^{\tan^{-1} x}}{(1+x^2)} \Rightarrow (1+x^2)\, y_1 = e^{\tan^{-1} x} = y$$

On differentiating again, $(1+x^2)\, y_2 + 2xy_1 = y_1$

So, at $n = 1$; $(1+x^2)\, y_2 + (2x-1)\, y_1 + 0 = 0$

Let this equation is true for n; then

$$(1+x^2)\, y_{n+1} + (2nx-1)\, y_n + n(n-1)\, y_{n-1} = 0$$

Now, again differentiating w.r.t. x,

$$(1+x^2)\, y_{n+2} + 2xy_{n+1} + (2nx-1)\, y_{n+1} + 2ny_n + n(n-1)\, y_n = 0$$

$$(1+x^2)\, y_{n+2} + [2x(n+1) - 1]\, y_{n+1} + n(n+1)\, y_n = 0$$

So, the equation is valid for $(n+1)$ also

So, from M.I. $(1+x^2)\, y_{n+1} + (2nx-1)\, y_n + n(n+1)\, y_{n-1} = 0$ is valid for all n.

(ii) $y = \sin(m \sin^{-1} x)$, then

$$(1-x^2)\, y_{n+2} = (2n+1)\, xy_{n+1} + (n^2 - m^2)\, y_n$$

Now, differentiating w.r.t. x, we get

$$\frac{dy}{dx} = \cos(m \sin^{-1} x) \frac{m}{\sqrt{(1-x^2)}}$$

$$y_1 = \sqrt{(1-y^2)} \frac{m}{\sqrt{(1-x^2)}}$$

Now, on squaring, we get

$$y_1^2 = m^2 \frac{1-y^2}{1-x^2} \Rightarrow (1-x^2)\, y_1^2 = m^2(1-y^2)$$

$$(1-x^2)\, 2y_1y_2 - 2xy_1^2 = -m^2 2yy_1$$

$$\Rightarrow \quad (1-x^2)\, y_2 - xy_1 + m^2 y = 0$$

So, for $n = 0$; $(1-x^2)\, y_2 - xy_1 + m^2 y = 0$

Let the equation $(1-x^2)\, y_{n+2} = (2n+1)\, xy_{n+1} + (n^2 - m^2)\, y_n$ is true for any n, then again differentiating

$$(1-x^2)\, y_{n+3} - 2xy_{n+2} = (2n+1)\, xy_{n+2} + (2n+1)\, y_{n+1} + (n^2 - m^2)\, y_{n+1}$$

$$\Rightarrow (1-x^2) y_{n+3} - 2xy_{n+2} - (2n+1)\, xy_{n+2} = [(n+1)^2 - m^2]\, y_{n+1}$$

$$\Rightarrow (1-x^2)\, y_{n+3} = [2(n+1)+1]\, xy_{n+2} + [(n+1)^2 - m^2]\, y_{n+1}$$

So, the equation is valid for $(n+1)$ also

from mathematical induction

$$(1-x^2)\, y_{n+2} = (2n+1)\, xy_{n+1} + (n^2 - m^2)\, y_n$$

Milestone Practice 5.6

1. $y = x \log\left(\frac{x}{a+bx}\right)$, then show that

$$x^3 \frac{d^2y}{dx^2} = \left[x\frac{dy}{dx} - y\right]^2$$

2. If $y = (ax+b)/(x^2+c)$, then show that $(2xy' + y)\, y''' = 3(xy'' + y')\, y''$, where a, b, c are constants and dashes denote differentiation w.r.t. x.

3. Show that the function $y = f(x)$ defined by the parametric equations $x = e^t \cdot \sin t$, $y = e^t \cdot \cos t$, satisfies the relation $y''(x+y)^2 = 2(xy' - y)$

4. Let $P(x)$ be a polynomial of degree 4, with $P(2) = -1$, $P'(2) = 0$, $P''(2) = 2$, $P'''(2) = -12$ and $P''''(2) = 24$. Find the value of $P''(1)$.

5. If $x = 2\cos t - \cos 2t$ and $y = 2\sin t - \sin 2t$, find the value of $\left(\frac{d^2y}{dx^2}\right)$, when $t = \left(\frac{\pi}{2}\right)$.

6. If $x = t^3 + t + 5$ and $y = \sin t$, then $\frac{d^2y}{dx^2}$ is equal to

(a) $-\frac{(3t^2+1)\sin t + 6t\cos t}{(3t^2+1)^3}$

(b) $\frac{(3t^2+1)\sin t + 6t\cos t}{(3t^2+1)^2}$

(c) $-\frac{(3t^2+1)\sin t + 6t\cos t}{(3t^2+1)^2}$

(d) $\frac{\cos t}{3t^2+1}$

7. If $y = \left[\ln\left(\frac{x+\sqrt{x^2-a^2}}{a}\right)\right] + k\ln(x+\sqrt{x^2-a^2})$, then find the value of $(x^2-a^2)\frac{d^2y}{dx^2} + x\frac{dy}{dx}$

(a) 1 (b) 2

(c) 3 (d) None of these

Answer Key

4. 26 **5.** $-\frac{3}{2}$ **6.** (a) **7.** (d)

For Detailed Solution

Milestone 7 Special Points

• Differentiation of a Function in the form of Determinant • Sum of Special Series Obtained by Differentiation

5.13 Differentiation of a Function in the Form of Determinant

To find the derivative of a determinant, we differentiate the row (or columns) keeping other rows (or columns) unchanged,

i.e.

If $y = \begin{vmatrix} u(x) & v(x) & w(x) \\ p(x) & q(x) & r(x) \\ \lambda(x) & \mu(x) & \gamma(x) \end{vmatrix}$,

then $\dfrac{dy}{dx} = \begin{vmatrix} u'(x) & v'(x) & w'(x) \\ p(x) & q(x) & r(x) \\ \lambda(x) & \mu(x) & \gamma(x) \end{vmatrix}$

$$+\begin{vmatrix} u(x) & v(x) & w(x) \\ p'(x) & q'(x) & r'(x) \\ \lambda(x) & \mu(x) & \gamma(x) \end{vmatrix} + \begin{vmatrix} u(x) & v(x) & w(x) \\ p(x) & q(x) & r(x) \\ \lambda'(x) & \mu'(x) & \gamma'(x) \end{vmatrix}$$

The differentiation can also be done column-wise.

Example 61. If $f(x) = \begin{vmatrix} x+a^2 & ab & ac \\ ab & x+b^2 & bc \\ ac & bc & x+c^2 \end{vmatrix}$, then find $f'(x)$.

Sol. We have, $f(x) = \begin{vmatrix} x+a^2 & ab & ac \\ ab & x+b^2 & bc \\ ac & bc & x+c^2 \end{vmatrix}$

$$\therefore f'(x) = \begin{vmatrix} 1 & 0 & 0 \\ ab & x+b^2 & bc \\ ac & bc & x+c^2 \end{vmatrix} + \begin{vmatrix} x+a^2 & ab & ac \\ 0 & 1 & 0 \\ ac & bc & x+c^2 \end{vmatrix}$$

$$+\begin{vmatrix} x+a^2 & ab & ac \\ ab & x+b^2 & bc \\ 0 & 0 & 1 \end{vmatrix}$$

$$= \{(x+b^2)(x+c^2) - b^2c^2\} + \{(x+a^2)(x+c^2) - a^2c^2\}$$
$$+ \{(x+a^2)(x+b^2) - a^2b^2\}$$
$$= 3x^2 + 2x(a^2+b^2+c^2)$$

Example 62. If

$f(x) = \begin{vmatrix} \cos(x+x^2) & \sin(x+x^2) & -\cos(x+x^2) \\ \sin(x-x^2) & \cos(x-x^2) & \sin(x-x^2) \\ \sin 2x & 0 & \sin 2x^2 \end{vmatrix}$, then find $f'(x)$.

Sol. $f(x) = \begin{vmatrix} \cos(x+x^2) & \sin(x+x^2) & -\cos(x+x^2) \\ \sin(x-x^2) & \cos(x-x^2) & \sin(x-x^2) \\ \sin 2x & 0 & \sin 2x^2 \end{vmatrix}$

$$= \sin 2x\,[\sin(x+x^2)\sin(x-x^2)$$
$$+ \cos(x-x^2)\cos(x+x^2)] + \sin 2x^2[\cos(x+x^2)$$
$$\cos(x-x^2) - \sin(x+x^2)\sin(x-x^2)]$$
$$= \sin 2x \cos(x+x^2-x+x^2) + \sin 2x^2 \cos 2x$$
$$= \sin 2x \cdot \cos 2x^2 + \sin 2x^2 \cdot \cos 2x$$
$$\Rightarrow f(x) = \sin(2x+2x^2) \Rightarrow f'(x) = \cos(2x+2x^2)(2+4x)$$

Example 63. If $f(x) = \begin{vmatrix} (x-a)^4 & (x-a)^3 & 1 \\ (x-b)^4 & (x-b)^3 & 1 \\ (x-c)^4 & (x-c)^3 & 1 \end{vmatrix}$, then

$f'(x) = \lambda \begin{vmatrix} (x-a)^4 & (x-a)^2 & 1 \\ (x-b)^4 & (x-b)^2 & 1 \\ (x-c)^4 & (x-c)^2 & 1 \end{vmatrix}$. Find the value of λ.

Sol. $f(x) = \begin{vmatrix} (x-a)^4 & (x-a)^3 & 1 \\ (x-b)^4 & (x-b)^3 & 1 \\ (x-c)^4 & (x-c)^3 & 1 \end{vmatrix}$

$$f'(x) = \begin{vmatrix} 4(x-a)^3 & (x-a)^3 & 1 \\ 4(x-b)^3 & (x-b)^3 & 1 \\ 4(x-c)^3 & (x-c)^3 & 1 \end{vmatrix} + \begin{vmatrix} (x-a)^4 & 3(x-a)^2 & 1 \\ (x-b)^4 & 3(x-b)^2 & 1 \\ (x-c)^4 & 3(x-c)^2 & 1 \end{vmatrix}$$

$$+\begin{vmatrix} (x-a)^4 & (x-a)^3 & 0 \\ (x-b)^4 & (x-b)^3 & 0 \\ (x-c)^4 & (x-c)^3 & 0 \end{vmatrix}$$

$$\Rightarrow \quad f'(x) = 3\begin{vmatrix} (x-a)^4 & (x-a)^2 & 1 \\ (x-b)^4 & (x-b)^2 & 1 \\ (x-c)^4 & (x-c)^2 & 1 \end{vmatrix}$$

$\therefore \quad \lambda = 3$

Example 64. If α be the repeated root of a quadratic equation $f(x)=0$ and $A(x), B(x), C(x)$ be the polynomials of degree 3, 4 and 5 respectively, then show that $\begin{vmatrix} A(x) & B(x) & C(x) \\ A(\alpha) & B(\alpha) & C(\alpha) \\ A'(\alpha) & B'(\alpha) & C'(\alpha) \end{vmatrix}$ is divisible by $f(x)$, where dash denotes the derivative.

Sol. $f(x)=a(x-\alpha)^2$

$$\text{Let } g(x)=\begin{vmatrix} A(x) & B(x) & C(x) \\ A(\alpha) & B(\alpha) & C(\alpha) \\ A'(\alpha) & B'(\alpha) & C'(\alpha) \end{vmatrix}$$

$$g(\alpha)=\begin{vmatrix} A(\alpha) & B(\alpha) & C(\alpha) \\ A(\alpha) & B(\alpha) & C(\alpha) \\ A'(\alpha) & B'(\alpha) & C'(\alpha) \end{vmatrix}=0$$

$\Rightarrow \alpha$ is the root of $g(x)$

and $$g'(\alpha)=\begin{vmatrix} A'(\alpha) & B'(\alpha) & C'(\alpha) \\ A(\alpha) & B(\alpha) & C(\alpha) \\ A'(\alpha) & B'(\alpha) & C'(\alpha) \end{vmatrix}=0$$

$\Rightarrow \alpha$ is the root of $g'(x)$

$\Rightarrow \alpha$ is the repeated root of $g(x)$ and, hence $g(x)$ is divisible by $f(x)$.

Example 65. If $Y=SX$ and $Z=tX$, where all the letters denotes the functions of x and suffixes denotes the differentiation w.r.t. x, then prove that

$$\begin{vmatrix} X & Y & Z \\ X_1 & Y_1 & Z_1 \\ X_2 & Y_2 & Z_2 \end{vmatrix}=X^3\begin{vmatrix} S_1 & t_1 \\ S_2 & t_2 \end{vmatrix}.$$

Sol. $Y=SX; Z=tX$

$Y_1=S_1X+SX_1; Z_1=t_1X+tX_1$

$Y_2=S_2X+2S_1X_1+SX_2;$

$Z_2=t_2X+tX_2+2t_1X_1$

$$\text{Now, }\begin{vmatrix} X & Y & Z \\ X_1 & Y_1 & Z_1 \\ X_2 & Y_2 & Z_2 \end{vmatrix}$$

$$=\begin{vmatrix} X & SX & tX \\ X_1 & S_1X+SX_1 & t_1X+tX_1 \\ X_2 & S_2X+SX_2+2S_1X_1 & t_2X+tX_2+2t_1X_1 \end{vmatrix}$$

On applying the transformation $\begin{cases} C_2 \Rightarrow C_2-SC_1 \\ C_3 \Rightarrow C_3-tC_1 \end{cases}$, we get

$$\begin{vmatrix} X & 0 & 0 \\ X_1 & S_1X & t_1X \\ X_2 & S_2X+2S_1X_1 & t_2X+2t_1X_1 \end{vmatrix}$$

$$=X\begin{vmatrix} S_1X & t_1X \\ S_2X+2S_1X_1 & t_2X+2t_1X_1 \end{vmatrix}$$

$$=X^2\begin{vmatrix} S_1 & t_1 \\ 2S_1X_1+S_2X & 2t_1X_1+t_2X \end{vmatrix}$$

Applying $R_2 \to R_2-2X_1R_1$

$$=X^2\begin{vmatrix} S_1 & t_1 \\ S_2X & t_2X \end{vmatrix}$$

$$=X^3\begin{vmatrix} S_1 & t_1 \\ S_2 & t_2 \end{vmatrix}$$

Example 66. If $f(x)=\begin{vmatrix} (1+x)^a & (1+2x)^b & 1 \\ 1 & (1+x)^a & (1+2x)^b \\ (1+2x)^b & 1 & (1+x)^a \end{vmatrix}$

$=A+Bx+Cx^2+\ldots$, then find

(i) constant term

(ii) coefficient of x

Sol. Here, $$f(x)=\begin{vmatrix} (1+x)^a & (1+2x)^b & 1 \\ 1 & (1+x)^a & (1+2x)^b \\ (1+2x)^b & 1 & (1+x)^a \end{vmatrix}$$

$$=A+Bx+Cx^2+ \qquad \ldots\text{(i)}$$

On putting $x=0$, we get

$$f(0)=\begin{vmatrix} 1 & 1 & 1 \\ 1 & 1 & 1 \\ 1 & 1 & 1 \end{vmatrix}$$

$$=A+B(0)+C(0)^2+\ldots$$

$$\Rightarrow \quad A=0$$

Again, on differentiating Eq. (i) w.r.t. x, we get

$$f'(x)=\begin{vmatrix} a(1+x)^{a-1} & 2b(1+2x)^{b-1} & 0 \\ 1 & (1+x)^a & (1+2x)^b \\ (1+2x)^b & 1 & (1+x)^a \end{vmatrix}$$

$$+\begin{vmatrix} (1+x)^a & (1+2x)^b & 1 \\ 0 & a(1+x)^{a-1} & 2b(1+2x)^{b-1} \\ (1+2x)^b & 1 & (1+x)^a \end{vmatrix}$$

$$+\begin{vmatrix} (1+x)^a & (1+2x)^b & 1 \\ 1 & (1+x)^a & (1+2x)^b \\ 2b(1+2x)^{b-1} & 0 & a(1+x)^{a-1} \end{vmatrix}$$

$$=B+2Cx+\ldots$$

$$f'(0)=\begin{vmatrix} a & 2b & 0 \\ 1 & 1 & 1 \\ 1 & 1 & 1 \end{vmatrix}+\begin{vmatrix} 1 & 1 & 1 \\ 0 & a & 2b \\ 1 & 1 & 1 \end{vmatrix}+\begin{vmatrix} 1 & 1 & 1 \\ 1 & 1 & 1 \\ 2b & 0 & a \end{vmatrix}=B$$

$$\Rightarrow \quad B=0 \qquad \ldots\text{(ii)}$$

$\therefore$ Coefficient of constant term = Coefficient of $x=0$

JEE SCANNER

Example Similar to PYQ Asked in JEE Mains 2024

If $f(x)=\begin{vmatrix} x^2 & 3x^2+1 & 1+2x \\ 2x^2 & 2x & x^2+4 \\ x^2-x & 8 & -x \end{vmatrix}$, $\forall\, x\in R$, then

$3f(0)+f'(0)$ is equal to

(a) −4 (b) 4 (c) 8 (d) 0

Sol. (a) Given, $f(x)=\begin{vmatrix} x^2 & 3x^2+1 & 1+2x \\ 2x^2 & 2x & x^2+4 \\ x^2-x & 8 & -x \end{vmatrix}$

$$f(0)=\begin{vmatrix} 0 & 1 & 1 \\ 0 & 0 & 4 \\ 0 & 8 & 0 \end{vmatrix}=0$$

Now, $f'(x)=\begin{vmatrix} 2x & 6x & 2 \\ 2x^2 & 2x & x^2+4 \\ x^2-x & 8 & -x \end{vmatrix}$

$$+\begin{vmatrix} x^2 & 3x^2+1 & 1+2x \\ 4x & 2 & 2x \\ x^2-x & 8 & -x \end{vmatrix}$$

$$+\begin{vmatrix} x^2 & 3x^2+1 & 1+2x \\ 2x^2 & 2x & x^2+4 \\ 2x-1 & 0 & -1 \end{vmatrix}$$

and $f'(0)=\begin{vmatrix} 0 & 0 & 2 \\ 0 & 0 & 4 \\ 0 & 8 & 0 \end{vmatrix}+\begin{vmatrix} 0 & 1 & 1 \\ 0 & 2 & 0 \\ 0 & 8 & 0 \end{vmatrix}+\begin{vmatrix} 0 & 1 & 1 \\ 0 & 0 & 4 \\ -1 & 0 & -1 \end{vmatrix}$

$$=0+0-1(4-0)=-4$$

$\therefore \quad 3f(0)+f'(0)=-4$

Skill Builder

If $f(x)=\begin{vmatrix} \sin x & \cos x & x^3 \\ x^2+2 & \sin x & -\cos x \\ \cos x & -\sin x & x^3-1 \end{vmatrix}$

For Sol.

$\forall\, x\in R$ then $3f(0)+5f'(0)$ is equal to

(a) 0 (b) 3 (c) −3 (d) 1

■ **For more practice** See Q.7 of Milestone Practice 5.7.

Example 67. If $y=\cos ax$, then prove that

$$\begin{vmatrix} y & y_1 & y_2 \\ y_3 & y_4 & y_5 \\ y_6 & y_7 & y_8 \end{vmatrix}=0, \text{ where } y_r=\frac{d^r}{dx^r}y.$$

Sol. Given, $y=\cos(ax)$

Then, $y_1=-a\sin(ax)=a\cos\left(\frac{\pi}{2}+ax\right)$

$$y_2=-a^2\cos(ax)=a^2\cos\left(\frac{2\pi}{2}+ax\right)$$

$$y_3=+a^3\sin(ax)=a^3\cos\left(\frac{3\pi}{2}+ax\right)$$

....

$$y_n=a^n\cos\left(\frac{n\pi}{2}+ax\right)$$

$\therefore$ The determinant $\Delta(x)=\begin{vmatrix} y & y_1 & y_2 \\ y_3 & y_4 & y_5 \\ y_6 & y_7 & y_8 \end{vmatrix}$

$$\Delta(x)=\begin{vmatrix} \cos ax & a\cos\left(\frac{\pi}{2}+ax\right) & a^2\cos\left(\frac{2\pi}{2}+ax\right) \\ a^3\cos\left(\frac{3\pi}{2}+ax\right) & a^4\cos\left(\frac{4\pi}{2}+ax\right) & a^5\cos\left(\frac{5\pi}{2}+ax\right) \\ a^6\cos\left(\frac{6\pi}{2}+ax\right) & a^7\cos\left(\frac{7\pi}{2}+ax\right) & a^8\cos\left(\frac{8\pi}{2}+ax\right) \end{vmatrix}$$

$$\Delta(x)=a^3\times a^6\begin{vmatrix} \cos(ax) & -a\sin(ax) & -a^2\cos(ax) \\ \sin(ax) & a\cos(ax) & -a^2\sin(ax) \\ -\cos(ax) & a\sin(ax) & a^2\cos(ax) \end{vmatrix}$$

$\Delta(x)=a^9\times(0)$ $\quad [R_1\to R_1+R_3]$

Hence, $\Delta(x)=0$

5.14 Sum of Special Series Obtained by Differentiation

If $f(x)$ is a sum of series the using derivatives we can obtained different types of summation of series.

To understand it we are considering some examples given below.

Example 68. Prove the identity

$$\cos x+\cos 3x+\ldots+\cos(2n-1)x=\frac{\sin 2nx}{2\sin x}\ (x\neq k\pi)$$

Hence, prove that

$$\sin x+3\sin 3x+\ldots+(2n-1)\sin(2n-1)x$$
$$=\frac{(2n+1)\sin(2n-1)x-(2n-1)\sin(2n+1)x}{4\sin^2 x}$$

Sol. We have,

$$\text{LHS}=\cos x+\cos 3x+\cos 5x+\ldots+\cos(2n-1)x$$
$$=\frac{1}{\sin x}[\sin x\cos x+\sin x\cos 3x$$
$$+\sin x\cos 5x+\ldots+\sin x\cos(2n-1)x]$$

$$= \frac{1}{\sin x}\left[\frac{\sin 2x}{2} + \frac{\sin 4x - \sin 2x}{2} + \frac{\sin 6x - \sin 4x}{2} + \ldots + \frac{\sin 2nx - \sin(2n-2)x}{2}\right]$$

$$= \frac{\sin 2nx}{2\sin x} = \text{RHS}$$

On differentiating both sides w.r.t. x, we get

$$-\sin x - 3\sin 3x - \ldots - (2n-1)\sin(2n-1)x = \frac{(2\sin x)(2n\cos 2nx) - (2\cos x)(\sin 2nx)}{4\sin^2 x}$$

$$\Rightarrow \sin x + 3\sin 3x + \ldots + (2n-1)\sin(2n-1)x = \frac{(2\sin 2nx\cos x) - 2n(2\sin x\cos 2nx)}{4\sin^2 x}$$

$$= \frac{[\sin(2n+1)x + \sin(2n-1)x] - 2n[\sin(2n+1)x - \sin(2n-1)x]}{4\sin^2 x}$$

$$= \frac{(2n+1)\sin(2n-1)x - (2n-1)\sin(2n+1)x}{4\sin^2 x}$$

which is the desired result.

Example 69. If $0 < x < 1$, then prove that

$$\frac{1-2x}{1-x+x^2} + \frac{2x-4x^3}{1-x^2+x^4} + \frac{4x^3-8x^7}{1-x^4+x^8} + \ldots \infty = \frac{1+2x}{1+x+x^2}$$

Sol. We have, $(1+x+x^2)(1-x+x^2)$

$$= (1+x^2)^2 - x^2 = 1 + x^2 + x^4$$

Now, $(1+x+x^2)(1-x+x^2)(1-x^2+x^4)$

$$= (1+x^2+x^4)(1-x^2+x^4) = 1 + x^4 + x^8$$

Continuing in this way, we have

$$(1+x+x^2)(1-x+x^2)(1-x^2+x^4)(1-x^4+x^8)\ldots(1-x^{2^{n-1}}+x^{2^n})$$

$$= (1 + x^{2^n} + x^{2^{n+1}}) \quad \ldots(i)$$

Now, for $0 < x < 1$, $x^m \to 0$ as $m \to \infty$.

Taking limit $n \to \infty$ in Eq. (i), we get

$$(1+x+x^2)(1-x+x^2)(1-x^2+x^4)(1-x^4+x^8)\ldots = 1$$

Taking logarithm on both sides, we get

$$\Rightarrow \ln(1+x+x^2) + \ln(1-x+x^2) + \ln(1-x^2+x^4) + \ln(1-x^4+x^8) + \ldots = 0$$

On differentiating both sides w.r.t. x, we get

$$\frac{1+2x}{1+x+x^2} + \frac{-1+2x}{1-x+x^2} + \frac{-2x+4x^3}{1-x^2+x^4} + \frac{-4x^3+8x^7}{1-x^4+x^8}\ldots = 0$$

Hence, $$\frac{1-2x}{1-x+x^2} + \frac{2x-4x^3}{1-x^2+x^4} + \frac{4x^3-8x^7}{1-x^4+x^8} + \ldots = \frac{1+2x}{1+x+x^2}$$

Example 70. If $(1+x)^n = C_0 + C_1x + C_2x^2 + \ldots + C_nx^n$, then prove that $C_1 + 2C_2 + 3C_3 + \ldots + nC_n = n2^{n-1}$ and $C_0 + 2C_1 + 3C_2 + \ldots + (n+1)C_n = (n+2)2^{n-1}$

Sol. Given, $(1+x)^n = C_0 + C_1x + C_2x^2 + \ldots + C_nx^n \quad \ldots(i)$

Differentiating Eq. (i) w.r.t. x, we get

$$n(1+x)^{n-1} = C_1 + 2C_2x + 3C_3x^2 + \ldots + nC_nx^{n-1}$$

On putting $x = 1$, we get

$$n2^{n-1} = C_1 + 2C_2 + 3C_3 + \ldots + nC_n$$

Now, multiplying x on both sides of Eq. (i), we get

$$x(1+x)^n = C_0x + C_1x^2 + C_2x^3 + \ldots + C_nx^{n+1}$$

On differentiating Eq. (i) w.r.t. x, we get

$$(1+x)^n + nx(1+x)^{n-1} = C_0 + 2C_1x + 3C_2x^2 + \ldots + (n+1)C_nx^n$$

On putting $x = 1$, we get

$$2^n + n2^{n-1} = C_0 + 2C_1 + 3C_2 + \ldots + (n+1)C_n$$

$$2^{n-1}(n+2) = C_0 + 2C_1 + 3C_2 + \ldots + (n+1)C_n$$

Milestone Practice 5.7

1. If $f(x)=\begin{vmatrix} x^3 & \sin x & \cos x \\ 6 & -1 & 0 \\ p & p^2 & p^3 \end{vmatrix}$, then prove that $\dfrac{d^3}{dx^3}[f(x)]=0$ at $x=0$ (where p is constant).

2. If $\begin{vmatrix} e^x & \sin x \\ \cos x & \log(1+x^2) \end{vmatrix} = A + Bx + Cx^2 + \dots$, then find A and B.

3. If $y=\dfrac{u}{v}$, where u and v are functions of x show that,

$$v^3\frac{d^2y}{dx^2}=\begin{vmatrix} u & v & 0 \\ u' & v' & v \\ u'' & v'' & 2v' \end{vmatrix}$$

4. The coefficient of x in the expansion of

$$f(x)=\begin{vmatrix} (x+2)^2 & (x+3)^2 & (x+4)^2 \\ x & x^2 & x^3 \\ 1 & 2x & 3x^2 \end{vmatrix}$$

(a) 1 (b) 2

(c) 3 (d) 0

5. If $\Delta(x)=\begin{vmatrix} x & 1+x^2 & x^3 \\ \log(1+x^2) & e^x & \sin x \\ \cos x & \tan x & \sin^2 x \end{vmatrix}$, then

(a) $\Delta(x)$ is divisible by x

(b) $\Delta(x)=0$

(c) $\Delta'(x)=0$

(d) None of the above

6. If $f(x)=\begin{vmatrix} x^n & \sin x & -\cos x \\ n! & \sin(n\pi/2) & \cos(n\pi/2) \\ a & a^2 & a^3 \end{vmatrix}$, then the value of $\dfrac{d^n}{dx^n}(f(x))$ at $x=0$ for $n=2m+1$ is

(a) -1 (b) 0

(c) 1 (d) independent of a

7. Let $f(x)=\begin{vmatrix} \cos x & x & 1 \\ 2\sin x & x^2 & 2x \\ \tan x & x & 1 \end{vmatrix}$. Then, $\lim\limits_{x\to 0}\dfrac{f'(x)}{x}$ is equal to

(a) 2 (b) -2

(c) -1 (d) 1

Answer Key

1. 0	**2.** $A=0$ and $B=-1$	**4.** (d)
5. (a)	**6.** (b, d)	**7.** (b)

For Detailed Solution

JEE Pattern EXAMPLES

Single Option Correct Type Questions

Example 1 *If $f(x) = 4x^3 - 6x^2 \cdot \cos 2a + 3x \cdot \sin 2a \cdot \sin 6a + \sqrt{\log(2a - a^2)}$, then*

(a) $f'\left(\frac{1}{2}\right) < 0$ (b) $f'\left(\frac{1}{2}\right) \le 0$

(c) $f'\left(\frac{1}{2}\right) > 0$ (d) None of these

Sol. (c) Here, $f(x) = 4x^3 - 6x^2 \cdot \cos 2a + 3x \sin 2a \cdot \sin 6a + \sqrt{\log(2a - a^2)}$

For $f(x)$ to exist, $\log(2a - a^2) \ge 0 \Rightarrow (2a - a^2) \ge e^0$

i.e. $2a - a^2 \ge 1$ or $a^2 - 2a + 1 \le 0 \Rightarrow (a-1)^2 \le 0$

which is only possible, if $(a-1)^2 = 0$ i.e. $a = 1$.

$\therefore \quad f(x) = 4x^3 - 6x^2 \cos 2 + 3x \sin 2 \cdot \sin 6$

$\Rightarrow \quad f'(x) = 12x^2 - 12x \cos 2 + 3 \sin 2 \sin 6$

$\Rightarrow \quad f'\left(\frac{1}{2}\right) = 3 - 6\cos 2 + 3 \sin 2 \sin 6$

$= 3(1 + \sin 2 \sin 6) - 6 \cos 2$

$\Rightarrow \quad f'\left(\frac{1}{2}\right) > 0$

Note $\cos 2 < 0$ and $1 + \sin 2 \sin 6 > 0$

Example 2 *If $\frac{\cos^4\theta}{x} + \frac{\sin^4\theta}{y} = \frac{1}{x+y}$, then $\frac{dy}{dx}$ is equal to*

(a) xy (b) $\tan^2\theta$

(c) 0 (d) $(x^2 + y^2)\sec^2\theta$

Sol. (b) $(x+y)\left(\frac{\cos^4\theta}{x} + \frac{\sin^4\theta}{y}\right) = [\cos^2\theta + \sin^2\theta]^2$

$\therefore \quad \frac{y}{x}\cos^4\theta + \frac{x}{y}\sin^4\theta - 2\sin^2\theta\cos^2\theta = 0$

or $\quad \left(\sqrt{\frac{y}{x}}\cos^2\theta - \sqrt{\frac{x}{y}}\sin^2\theta\right)^2 = 0$

$\therefore \quad \tan^2\theta = \frac{y}{x}$ or $y = x\tan^2\theta$

$\therefore \quad \frac{dy}{dx} = \tan^2\theta$

Example 3 *If $f(x) = e^x - e^{-x} - 2\sin x - \frac{2}{3}x^3$, then the least value of n for which $\frac{d^n}{dx^n}f(x)$ at $x = 0$ is non-zero, is*

(a) 2 (b) 1

(c) 7 (d) either 1 or 2

Sol. (c) $f(x) = e^x - e^{-x} - 2\sin x - \frac{2}{3}x^3$

Now, $e^x = 1 + \frac{x}{1!} + \frac{x^2}{2!} + \frac{x^3}{3!} + \frac{x^4}{4!} + \dots \infty$

$e^{-x} = 1 - \frac{x}{1!} + \frac{x^2}{2!} - \frac{x^3}{3!} + \frac{x^4}{4!} - \dots \infty$

$\Rightarrow f(x) = 2\left[x + \frac{x^3}{3!} + \frac{x^5}{5!} + \frac{x^7}{7!} + \dots\right] - 2\left[x - \frac{x^3}{3!} + \frac{x^5}{5!} - \frac{x^7}{7!}\dots\right] - \frac{2}{3}x^3$

$\therefore \quad f(x) = 4\left(\frac{x^7}{7!} + \frac{x^{11}}{11!} + \frac{x^{15}}{15!} + \dots \infty\right)$

$f'(x) = 4\left(\frac{7 \times x^6}{7!} + \frac{11x^{10}}{11!} + \dots\right)$

$f''(x) = 4\left(\frac{6 \times x^5}{6!} + \frac{10 \times x^9}{10!} + \dots\right)$

....

....

$f^7(x) = 4\left(x^0 + \frac{x^4}{4!} + \frac{x^8}{8!} + \dots\right)$

$f^7(0) = 4$ i.e. a non-zero constant.

Hence, at $x = 0$, it will be non-zero

$\therefore \quad n = 7$

Example 4 *If $f(0)=0$, $f'(0)=3$, then the derivative of $y=f(f(f(f(x))))$ at $x=0$ is*

(a) 2 (b) 81

(c) 16 (d) 4

Sol. (b) $y'(x)=f'(f(f(f(x))))$

$f'(f(f(x)))f'(f(x))\,f'(x)$

So, $y'(0)=f'(f(f(f(0))))$,

$f'(f(f(0)))\,f'(f(0))\,f'(0)$

$\Rightarrow \quad f'(f(f(0)))\,f'(f(0))\,f'(0)\,f'(0)$

$=(f'(0))^4$

$=3^4=81$

Example 5 *If $f(x)=\cot^{-1}\left(\dfrac{x^x-x^{-x}}{2}\right)$, then $f'(1)$ equals to*

(a) −1 (b) 1

(c) log 2 (d) − log 2

Sol. (a) If $u=x^x$ and using logarithmic differentiation, we get

$$\log u = x\log x$$

$$\Rightarrow \quad \frac{1}{u}\frac{du}{dx}=x\cdot\frac{1}{x}+\log x$$

$$\Rightarrow \quad \frac{du}{dx}=x^x(1+\log x)$$

Similarly, if $v=x^{-x}$, we get

$$\frac{dv}{dx}=-x^{-x}(1+\log x)$$

$$f'(x)=-\frac{1}{1+\left(\dfrac{x^x-x^{-x}}{2}\right)^2}\frac{d}{dx}\left(\frac{x^x-x^{-x}}{2}\right)$$

$$=-\frac{4}{x^{2x}+x^{-2x}+2}\left[\frac{1}{2}(x^x+x^{-x})(1+\log x)\right]$$

$$\Rightarrow \quad f'(1)=-\frac{2}{1+1+2}[2(1+\log 1)]$$

$$=-1$$

Example 6 *If $y=\cos^{-1}\dfrac{x^n-x^{-n}}{x^n+x^{-n}}$, then $y'(x)$ is equal to*

(a) $\dfrac{2nx^{n-1}}{x^{2n}+1}$ if n is even

(b) $\dfrac{2nx^n}{|x|(x^{2n}+1)}$ if n is odd

(c) $-\dfrac{2nx^n}{|x|(x^{2n}+1)}$ if n is odd

(d) $\dfrac{2nx^{n-1}}{(x^{2n}+1)}$

Sol. (c) Given, $y=\cos^{-1}\dfrac{x^n-x^{-n}}{x^n+x^{-n}}$

On differentiating both sides w.r.t. x, we get

$$y'(x)=-\frac{1}{\sqrt{1-\left(\dfrac{x^{2n}-1}{x^{2n}+1}\right)^2}}\frac{d}{dx}\left(\frac{x^{2n}-1}{x^{2n}+1}\right)$$

$$=\frac{x^{2n}+1}{\sqrt{(x^{2n}+1)^2-(x^{2n}-1)^2}}\times\frac{2nx^{2n-1}(x^{2n}+1)-2nx^{2n-1}(x^{2n}-1)}{(x^{2n}+1)^2}$$

$$=-\frac{1}{\sqrt{4x^{2n}}}\cdot\frac{4nx^{2n-1}}{(x^{2n}+1)}$$

$$=\frac{-2nx^{2n-1}}{|x^n|(x^{2n}+1)}$$

$$=-\frac{2n(|x|^2)^n}{x|x|^n(x^{2n}+1)}=-\frac{2n|x|^n}{x(x^{2n}+1)}$$

$$=\begin{cases}-\dfrac{2nx^{n-1}}{x^{2n}+1} & \text{if } n \text{ is even}\\[2ex] -\dfrac{2nx^n}{|x|(x^{2n}+1)} & \text{if } n \text{ is odd}\end{cases}$$

Example 7 *If $x=\cos\theta$, $y=\sin^3\theta$, then $\left(\dfrac{dy}{dx}\right)^2+y\dfrac{d^2y}{dx^2}$ at $\theta=\dfrac{\pi}{2}$ is*

(a) 1 (b) 2 (c) −2 (d) −3

Sol. (d) $\dfrac{dx}{d\theta}=-\sin\theta$, $\dfrac{dy}{d\theta}=3\sin^2\theta\cos\theta$

So, that $\dfrac{dy}{dx}=-3\sin\theta\cos\theta=-\dfrac{3}{2}\sin 2\theta$

On differentiating again, we get

$$\frac{d^2y}{dx^2}=-3\cos 2\theta\cdot\frac{d\theta}{dx}=\frac{3\cos 2\theta}{\sin\theta}$$

Now, $\left(\dfrac{dy}{dx}\right)^2+y\dfrac{d^2y}{dx^2}=9\sin^2\theta\cos^2\theta+\sin^3\theta\dfrac{3\cos 2\theta}{\sin\theta}$

$$=9\sin^2\theta\cos^2\theta+3\sin^2\theta\cos 2\theta$$

On putting $\theta=\dfrac{\pi}{2}$, we get $\left(\dfrac{dy}{dx}\right)^2+y\dfrac{d^2y}{dx^2}=-3$

Example 8 *If $r=[2\phi+\cos^2(2\phi+\pi/4)]^{1/2}$, then what is the value of the derivative $dr/d\phi$ at $\phi=\pi/4$?*

(a) $2\left(\dfrac{1}{\pi+1}\right)^{1/2}$ (b) $2\left(\dfrac{2}{\pi+1}\right)^{2}$

(c) $\left(\dfrac{2}{\pi+1}\right)^{1/2}$ (d) $2\left(\dfrac{2}{\pi+1}\right)^{1/2}$

Sol. (d) Given, $r = \left[2\phi + \cos^2\left(2\phi + \frac{\pi}{4}\right)\right]^{1/2}$

On differentiating both sides w.r.t. ϕ, we get

$$\frac{dr}{d\phi} = \frac{\left[2 - 2\cos\left(2\phi + \frac{\pi}{4}\right)\sin\left(2\phi + \frac{\pi}{4}\right)\cdot 2\right]}{2\sqrt{2\phi + \cos^2\left(2\phi + \frac{\pi}{4}\right)}}$$

$$= \frac{\left[1 - \sin\left(4\phi + \frac{\pi}{2}\right)\right]}{\sqrt{2\phi + \cos^2\left(2\phi + \frac{\pi}{4}\right)}}$$

$$\therefore \quad \left(\frac{dr}{d\phi}\right)_{\phi = \pi/4} = \frac{\left[1 - \sin\left(\pi + \frac{\pi}{2}\right)\right]}{\sqrt{2\cdot\frac{\pi}{4} + \cos^2\left(\frac{\pi}{2} + \frac{\pi}{4}\right)}}$$

$$= \frac{1+1}{\sqrt{\frac{\pi}{2} + \frac{1}{2}}} = 2\sqrt{\frac{2}{1+\pi}}$$

Example 9 *If $x = \cos\theta$, $y = \sin 5\theta$, then the value of $(1 - x^2)\frac{d^2y}{dx^2} - x\frac{dy}{dx}$ is given by*

(a) $-5y$ (b) $5y$

(c) $-9y$ (d) $-25y$

Sol. (d) Given, $x = \cos\theta$, $y = \sin 5\theta$

$$\Rightarrow \quad \frac{dx}{d\theta} = -\sin\theta, \frac{dy}{d\theta} = 5\cos 5\theta$$

$$\therefore \quad \frac{dy}{dx} = \frac{dy/d\theta}{dx/d\theta} = -\frac{5\cos 5\theta}{\sin\theta}$$

On differentiating again w.r.t. x, we get

$$\frac{d^2y}{dx^2} = \frac{d}{d\theta}\left(\frac{dy}{dx}\right)\cdot\frac{d\theta}{dx} = \frac{d}{d\theta}\left(\frac{-5\cos 5\theta}{\sin\theta}\right)\frac{1}{-\sin\theta}$$

$$= \left(\frac{\sin\theta\sin 5\theta\cdot 25 + 5\cos 5\theta\cos\theta}{\sin^2\theta}\right)\frac{1}{-\sin\theta}$$

$$= -\frac{25\sin 5\theta}{\sin^2\theta} - \frac{5\cos 5\theta\cos\theta}{\sin^3\theta}$$

$$\therefore (1 - x^2)\frac{d^2y}{dx^2} - x\frac{dy}{dx}$$

$$= (1 - \cos^2\theta)\left(\frac{-25\sin 5\theta}{\sin^2\theta} - \frac{5\cos 5\theta\cos\theta}{\sin^3\theta}\right) - \cos\theta\left(\frac{-5\cos 5\theta}{\sin\theta}\right)$$

$$= \sin^2\theta\left(\frac{-25\sin 5\theta}{\sin^2\theta} - \frac{5\cos\theta\cos 5\theta}{\sin^3\theta}\right) + \frac{5\cos\theta\cos 5\theta}{\sin\theta}$$

$$= -25\sin 5\theta - \frac{5\cos\theta\cos 5\theta}{\sin\theta} + \frac{5\cos\theta\cos 5\theta}{\sin\theta} = -25y$$

JEE SCANNER

Example 10 Similar to PYQ Asked in JEE Main 2024

Let $f(x) = x^4 + 4e^{\frac{x}{2}}$, $\forall\ x \in R$. Consider a function $g(x)$ such that $g(f(x)) = x$, $\forall\ x \in R$. Then, the value of $16g'(4)$ is

(a) 8 (b) 4 (c) 16 (d) 6

Sol. (a) We have, $f(x) = x^4 + 4e^{\frac{x}{2}}$ ...(i)

Now, as $x = 0$, $f(0) = 4$

$$\therefore \quad g'(f(x))\cdot f'(x) = 1$$

$$g'(4) = \frac{1}{f'(0)}$$

$$f'(x) = 4x^3 + 4\cdot e^{\frac{x}{2}}\cdot\frac{1}{2} \Rightarrow f'(0) = 2$$

$$g'(4) = \frac{1}{2}$$

$$\therefore \quad 16g'(4) = 8$$

Skill Builder

Let $f(x) = 3x^{10} + 6e^{x/3}, \forall\ x \in R$. Consider a function $g(x)$ such that $g(f(x)) = x$, $\forall\ x \in R$, then the value of $10\,g'(6)$ is equal to

(a) 10 (b) 4

(c) 5 (d) 6

For Sol.

Example 11 *Let $f(x) = x^3 + 3x^2 - 33x - 33$ for $x > 0$ and g be its inverse, then the value of k such that $kg'(2) = 1$ is*

(a) -36 (c) -42

(c) 12 (d) All of these

Sol. (a) $g(f(x)) = x$

On differentiating both sides w.r.t. x, we get

$$\Rightarrow \quad g'(f(x))\,f'(x) = 1 \Rightarrow g'(f(x)) = \frac{1}{f'(x)}$$

Now, $f(x) = 2$

$$\Rightarrow \quad x^3 + 3x^2 - 33x - 33 = 2$$

$$\Rightarrow \quad x^3 + 3x^2 - 33x - 35 = 0$$

$$\Rightarrow \quad x^3 - 5x^2 + 8x^2 - 40x + 7x - 35 = 0$$

$$\text{or} \quad (x - 5)(x^2 + 8x + 7) = 0$$

$$\Rightarrow \quad (x - 5)(x + 1)(x + 7) = 0$$

$$\Rightarrow \quad x = -7, -1, 5$$

Now, since g is the inverse function of $f(x)$

$$\therefore \quad f(g(x)) = x$$

Again, on differentiating both sides w.r.t. x, we get

$$f'(g(x))\cdot g'(x) = 1 \Rightarrow g'(x) = \frac{1}{f'(g(x))}$$

Also, on putting $x = 2$, we get

$$g'(2) = \frac{1}{f'(g(2))}$$

Also, since $f(x) = 2$ has solutions $x = -7, -1, 5$

$\therefore x = f'(x)$ or $x = g(2)$ also has solutions $x = -7, -1, 5$

$\therefore f'(g(2))$ is equal to either $f'(-7)$ or $f'(-1)$ or $f'(5)$

Now, $f'(-1) = 3(1)^2 + 6(-1) - 33 = 3 - 6 - 33 = -36$

$$f'(-7) = 3(7)^2 + 6(-7)^2 + 6(-7) - 33$$
$$= 147 - 63 - 33 - 51$$
$$f'(5) = 3 \cdot 5^2 + 6 \cdot 5 - 33 = 75 + 30 - 33 = 72$$

Now, $kg'(2) = 1 \Rightarrow g'(2) = \frac{1}{k}$

$$\Rightarrow \quad \frac{1}{k} = \frac{1}{f'(g(2))}$$

$$\Rightarrow \quad k = f'(g(2))$$

$\Rightarrow k$ is equal to either $f'(-7)$ or $f'(-1)$ or $f'(5)$

$\therefore k \in \{36, -51, 72\}$

Example 12 *A function $f(x)$ satisfies the condition,*

$f(x) = f'(x) + f''(x) + f'''(x) + \ldots \infty$

where $f(x)$ is an indefinitely differentiable function and dash denotes the order of derivatives. If $f(0) = 1$, then $f(x)$ is

(a) $e^{x/2}$ (b) e^x

(c) e^{2x} (d) e^{4x}

Sol. (a) $f(x) = f'(x) + f''(x) + f'''(x) + \ldots \infty$

$$f'(x) = f''(x) + f'''(x) + f''''(x) + \ldots \infty$$

$\therefore \; 2f'(x) = f'(x) + f''(x) + f'''(x) + \ldots$

$\Rightarrow 2f'(x) = f(x) \Rightarrow \frac{f'(x)}{f(x)} = \frac{1}{2}$

On integrating w.r.t. x, we get

$\ln f(x) = \frac{1}{2} x + c$

If $x = 0$, $f(0) = 1 \Rightarrow c = 0$

Hence, $\ln f(x) = \frac{x}{2} \Rightarrow f(x) = e^{x/2}$

Example 13 *Let f be a twice differentiable function such that $f''(x) = -f(x)$ and $f'(x) = g(x)$. If $h(x) = \{f(x)\}^2 + \{g(x)\}^2$, where $h(5) = 11$. Find $h(10)$.*

(a) 0 (b) 9

(c) 11 (d) None of these

Sol. (c) Given, $h(x) = \{f(x)\}^2 + \{g(x)\}^2$

On differentiating both sides w.r.t. x, we get

$$h'(x) = 2f(x) \cdot f'(x) + 2g(x) \cdot g'(x) \quad \text{...(i)}$$

Now, $f'(x) = g(x)$

Then, $f''(x) = g'(x) \Rightarrow -f(x) = g'(x)$ ...(ii)

$[\because f''(x) = -f(x)$, given$]$

From Eqs. (i) and (ii), we get

$$h'(x) = 2f(x) \cdot g(x) + 2g(x) \cdot \{-f(x)\}$$

[using $f'(x) = g(x)$ and $g'(x) = -f(x)$]

$\therefore \quad h'(x) = 0$

So, $h(x)$ must be constant $\left[\because \frac{d}{dx}(\text{constant}) = 0\right]$

But $h(5) = 11$

$h(x) = 11$

So, $h(10) = 11$

Example 14 *Let $f(x)$ be a real valued differentiable function not identically zero such that $f(x + y^{2n+1}) = f(x) + \{f(y)\}^{2n+1}$, $n \in N$ and x, y are any real numbers and $f'(0) \geq 0$. Find the values of $f(5)$ and $f'(10)$.*

(a) 3, 2

(b) 0, 1

(c) 1, 5

(d) 5, 1

Sol. (d) Here, $f(x + y^{2n+1}) = f(x) + \{f(y)\}^{2n+1}$ ...(i)

On putting $x = 0$ and $y = 0$, we get

$$f(0) = f(0) + \{f(0)\}^{2n+1} \Rightarrow f(0) = 0$$

$f'(0) \geq 0$ [given]

$$\Rightarrow \quad \lim_{x \to 0} \frac{f(x) - f(0)}{x - 0} \geq 0$$

$$\Rightarrow \quad \lim_{x \to 0} \frac{f(x)}{x} \geq 0$$

Now, if $x > 0 \Rightarrow f(x) \geq 0$ ...(ii)

On putting $x = 0$ and $y = 1$ in Eq. (i), we get

$$f(1) = f(0) + \{f(1)\}^{2n+1}$$

or $f(1)[1 - \{f(1)\}^{2n}] = 0$

$\therefore \quad f(1) = 0$ or 1 [using Eq. (ii)]

On putting $y = 1$ in Eq. (i), for all real x.

$$f(x + 1) = f(x) + \{f(1)\}^{2n+1} \quad \text{...(iii)}$$

Now, two cases arise either $f(1) = 0$ or 1

Case I If $f(1) = 0$

$\Rightarrow \quad f(x + 1) = f(x)$ [using Eq. (iii)]

$\Rightarrow \quad f(1) = f(2) = f(3) = \ldots = 0$

$\therefore f(x)$ is identically zero. (which is not possible)

Case II If $f(1) = 1$

$\Rightarrow \quad f(x + 1) = f(x) + 1$ [using Eq. (iii)]

$\therefore \quad f(2) = f(1) + 1 = 1 + 1 = 2$

$f(3) = f(2) + 1 = 2 + 1 = 3$

$f(4) = f(3) + 1 = 3 + 1 = 4$

$f(5) = f(4) + 1 = 4 + 1 = 5$

Proceeding in same way, we get

$$f(x) = x \text{ and } f'(x) = 1 \Rightarrow f'(10) = 1$$

So, $f(5) = 5$ and $f'(10) = 1$

Example 15 *Let* $f\left(\frac{x+y}{2}\right)=\frac{f(x)+f(y)}{2}$ *and* $f'(0)=a$ *and* $f(0)=b$. *Find* $f''(x)$ *(where y is independent of x), when* $f(x)$ *is differentiable.*

(a) 0 (b) 1

(c) a (d) None of these

Sol. (a) Here, $f\left(\frac{x+y}{2}\right)=\frac{f(x)+f(y)}{2}$, this holds for any real x, y and y is independent of x, i.e. $\frac{dy}{dx}=0$

On differentiating w.r.t. x, we get

$$f'\left(\frac{x+y}{2}\right)\cdot\frac{1}{2}\left(1+\frac{dy}{dx}\right)=\frac{1}{2}\left\{f'(x)+f'(y)\cdot\frac{dy}{dx}\right\}$$

$$\therefore \quad \frac{1}{2}f'\left(\frac{x+y}{2}\right)=\frac{1}{2}f'(x) \qquad \left[\text{as } \frac{dy}{dx}=0\right]$$

$$\Rightarrow \quad f'\left(\frac{x+y}{2}\right)=f'(x) \qquad \text{...(i)}$$

On putting $x=0$ and $y=x$ in Eq. (i), we get

$$f'\left(\frac{0+x}{2}\right)=f'(0)$$

$$\Rightarrow \quad f'\left(\frac{x}{2}\right)=a \qquad [\because f'(0)=a, \text{ given}]$$

which shows $f\left(\frac{x}{2}\right)=a\left(\frac{x}{2}\right)+c$ [using integration]

$$\therefore \quad f(x)=ax+c$$

Let $x=0$

$$\Rightarrow \quad f(0)=b=c$$

$$\therefore \quad f(x)=ax+b$$

On differentiating,

$$f'(x)=a \text{ and } f''(x)=0$$

Example 16 *If* $x^2+y^2=R^2$ $(R>0)$, *then* $K=\frac{y''}{\sqrt{(1+(y')^2)^3}}$. *Find K in terms of R.*

(a) $\frac{1}{R}$ (b) $-\frac{1}{R}$ (c) R (d) $\frac{1}{2R}$

Sol. (b) Here, $x^2+y^2=R^2$

On differentiating w.r.t. x, we get

$$2x+2yy'=0$$

$$\Rightarrow \quad x+yy'=0$$

$$\Rightarrow \quad y'=-\frac{x}{y} \qquad \text{...(i)}$$

Again, on differentiating both sides,

$$1+yy''+(y')^2=0$$

$$\therefore \quad y''=-\frac{(1+(y')^2)}{y} \qquad \text{...(ii)}$$

Now, $K=\frac{y''}{\sqrt{(1+(y')^2)^3}}=-\frac{(1+(y')^2)}{y\cdot(1+(y')^2)^{3/2}}$

$$=-\frac{1}{y\sqrt{1+(y')^2}}=-\frac{1}{y\sqrt{1+\frac{x^2}{y^2}}} \qquad \text{[from Eq. (i)]}$$

$$=-\frac{1}{\sqrt{x^2+y^2}}=-\frac{1}{R}$$

$$\therefore \quad K=-\frac{1}{R}$$

More than One Correct Option Type Questions

Example 17 *Two functions f and g have first and second derivatives at* $x=0$ *and satisfy the relations* $f(0)=\frac{2}{g(0)}$, $f'(0)=2g'(0)=4g(0)$, $g''(0)=5f''(0)=6f(0)=3$. *Then,*

(a) If $h(x)=\frac{f(x)}{g(x)}$, then $h'(0)=\frac{15}{4}$

(b) If $k(x)=f(x)\cdot g(x)\cdot\sin x$, then $k'(0)=2$

(c) $\lim_{x\to 0}\frac{g'(x)}{f'(x)}=\frac{1}{2}$

(d) None of the above

Sol. (a, b, c) We have, $f(0)=\frac{2}{g(0)}$,

$$f'(0)=2g'(0)=4g(0)$$

$$g''(0)=5f''(0)=6f(0)=3$$

Now, on solving these equations, we get

$$f(0)=\frac{1}{2},\ g(0)=4,\ f'(0)=16,\ g'(0)=8$$

$$f''(0)=\frac{3}{5},\ g''(0)=3$$

(a) We have, $h(x)=\frac{f(x)}{g(x)}$,

$$h'(x)=\frac{g(x)f'(x)-g'(x)f(x)}{[g(x)]^2}$$

$$\therefore \quad h'(0)=\frac{g(0)f'(0)-g'(0)f(0)}{[g(0)]^2}$$

$$=\frac{4\times16-8\times\frac{1}{2}}{(4)^2}=\frac{15}{4}$$

(b) $k(x)=f(x)\cdot g(x)\cdot\sin x$

$$k'(x)=f(x)\,g(x)\cos x + f(x)\sin x\cdot g'(x)+g(x)\sin x f'(x)$$

$$k'(0)=f(0)\,g(0)\cos 0 + f(0)\sin 0\cdot g'(0)+g(0)\sin 0\cdot f'(0)$$

$$k'(0)=\frac{1}{2}\times4\times1+0+0=2$$

(c) $\lim_{x\to 0}\frac{g'(x)}{f'(x)}=\frac{g'(0)}{f'(0)}=\frac{1}{2}$

Example 18 *If $f(x)=|x^2-3|x|+2|$, then which of the following is/are true?*

(a) $f'(x)=2x-3$ for $x\in(0,1)\cup(2,\infty)$
(b) $f'(x)=2x+3$ for $x\in(-\infty,-2)\cup(-1,0)$
(c) $f'(x)=-2x-3$ for $x\in(-2,-1)$
(d) None of the above

Sol. (a, b, c) We have, $f(x)=|x^2-3|x|+2|$

$$=\begin{cases}|x^2-3x+2|, & x\ge 0\\ |x^2+3x+2|, & x<0\end{cases}$$

$$\Rightarrow f(x)=\begin{cases}x^2-3x+2, & x^2-3x+2\ge 0, & x\ge 0\\ -x^2+3x-2, & x^2-3x+2<0, & x\ge 0\\ x^2+3x+2, & x^3+3x+2\ge 0, & x<0\\ -x^2-3x-2, & x^2+3x+2<0, & x<0\end{cases}$$

$$\Rightarrow f(x)=\begin{cases}x^2-3x+2, & x\in[0,1]\cup[2,\infty)\\ -x^2+3x+2, & x\in(1,2)\\ x^2+3x+2, & x\in(-\infty,-2]\cup[-1,0)\\ -x^2-3x+2, & x\in(-2,-1)\end{cases}$$

$$\Rightarrow f'(x)=\begin{cases}2x-3, & x\in(0,1)\cup(2,\infty)\\ -2x+3, & x\in(1,2)\\ 2x+3, & x\in(-\infty,-2)\cup(-1,0)\\ -2x-3, & x\in(-2,-1)\end{cases}$$

Example 19 *If $f(x)=(2x-3\pi)^5+\frac{4}{3}x+\cos x$ and g is the inverse function of f, then*

(a) $g'(2\pi)=\frac{7}{3}$ (b) $g'(2\pi)=\frac{3}{7}$
(c) $g''(2\pi)=\frac{7}{3}$ (d) $g''(2\pi)=0$

Sol. (b, d) $g(f(x))=x \Rightarrow g'(f(x))\,f'(x)=1$

$$\Rightarrow \quad g'(f(x))=\frac{1}{f'(x)}$$

$$f\left(\frac{3\pi}{2}\right)=2\pi,\ g(2\pi)=\frac{3\pi}{2}$$

$$\Rightarrow \quad g'(f(x))=\frac{1}{10(2x-3\pi)^4+\frac{4}{3}-\sin x}$$

$$\Rightarrow \quad g'\left(f\left(\frac{3\pi}{2}\right)\right)=\frac{1}{\frac{4}{3}+1}=\frac{3}{7}$$

$$\Rightarrow \quad g''(f(x))\cdot f'(x)=\frac{-1}{(f'(x))^2}\cdot f''(x)$$

$$\Rightarrow \quad g''(f(x))=\frac{-f''(x)}{(f'(x))^3}$$

$$\therefore \quad g''\left(f\left(\frac{3\pi}{2}\right)\right)=g''(2\pi)=0$$

Example 20 *Which of the following statements are true?*

(a) If $xe^{xy}=y+\sin^2 x$, then at $x=0$, $\left(\frac{dy}{dx}\right)=1$.

(b) If $f(x)=a_0x^{2m+1}+a_1x^{2m}+a_3x^{2m-1}+\ldots+a_{2m+1}=0\ (a_0\ne 0)$ is a polynomial equation with rational coefficients then the equation $f'(x)=0$ must have a real root $(m\in N)$.

(c) If $(x-r)$ is a factor of the polynomial $f(x)=a_nx^n+a_{n-1}x^{n-1}+a_{n-2}x^{n-2}+\ldots+a_0$ repeated m times where $1\le m\le n$, then r is a root of the equation $f'(x)=0$ repeated $(m-1)$ times.

(d) If $y=\sin^{-1}(\cos\sin^{-1}x)+\cos^{-1}(\sin\cos^{-1}x)$, then $\frac{dy}{dx}$ is dependent on x.

Sol. (a, c) (a) $xe^{xy}=y+\sin^2 x$

$$\Rightarrow e^{xy}+xe^{xy}\left(y+x\frac{dy}{dx}\right)=\frac{dy}{dx}+\sin 2x$$

At $x=0$, $\frac{dy}{dx}=1$

(b) $f(x)=a_0x^{2m+1}+a_1x^{2m}+a_3x^{2m-1}+\ldots+a_{2m+1}=0$

$f'(x)=(2m+1)\,a_0x^{2m}+a_1x^{2m-1}+\ldots$

Even degree polynomial may not have a real root.

(c) $f(x)=P(x)(x-r)^m$

$$\Rightarrow \quad f'(x)=P'(x)(x-r)^m+mP(x)(x-r)^{m-1}$$

$$f'(x)=(x-r)^{m-1}[P'(x)(x-r)+mP(x)]$$

(d) $y=\frac{\pi}{2}-\cos^{-1}(\cos\sin^{-1}x)+\frac{\pi}{2}-\sin^{-1}(\sin\cos^{-1}x)$

$$=\pi-\sin^{-1}x-\cos^{-1}x=\frac{\pi}{2}$$

$$\frac{dy}{dx}=0$$

Example 21 *Let f be a differentiable function satisfying $f(x+y)=f(x)+f(y)+xy(x+y)$ for all $x, y\in R$. If $f'(0)=2$, then*

(a) f is a polynomial function
(b) f is a exponential function
(c) f is thrice differentiable
(d) f is a polynomial of degree 3 whose roots are $0, \pm i\sqrt{2}$

Sol. (a, c, d)

We have, $f(x+y)=f(x)+f(y)+xy(x+y)$

On differentiating w.r.t. x, keeping y as a constant,

$$f'(x+y)=f'(x)+0+y(x+y)+xy$$

Put $x=0$

$$f'(y)=f'(0)+y^2=y^2+2 \Rightarrow f(y)=y^3+2y+c$$

Putting $x=0=y$

$$f(0)=f(0)+f(0)+0 \Rightarrow f(0)=0$$

Thus, $f(y)=y^3+2y=y(y^2+2)$

Passage Based Questions

Passage I

(Ex. Nos. 22 to 23)

A differentiable function satisfy the relation $\ln(f(x+y)) = \ln(f(x)) \cdot \ln(f(y))\ \forall\ x, y \in R$, $f(0) \neq 1, f'(0) = e$ and g be the inverse of f.

Example 22 *The value of $g''(e)$ is equal to*

(a) $\frac{-2}{e^2}$ (b) $\frac{-1}{2e^2}$ (c) $-2e^2$ (d) $\frac{2}{e^2}$

Example 23 *The number of solution(s) of the equation*

$\ln[\ln f(x)] = g^2[f(x)] - 3g[f(x)] - 5$ is(are)

(a) 0 (b) 1 (c) 2 (d) Infinite

Solutions (Q. 22 and 23)

$$\frac{1}{f(x+y)} f'(x+y) = \frac{1}{f(x)} f'(x) \ln f(y)$$

On putting $x = 0$, $\frac{f'(x)}{f(y)} = \frac{f'(0)}{f(0)} \ln f(y)$

$\Rightarrow \quad \frac{f'(y)}{f(y)\ln f(y)} = 1 \qquad [\because f(0) = e, f'(0) = e]$

$\Rightarrow \quad \ln(\ln f(y)) = y + c \Rightarrow c = 0$

$\Rightarrow \quad f(y) = e^{e^y} \Rightarrow f(x) = e^{e^x}$

22. (a) Now, $g(x) = \ln(\ln(x))$

and $\quad g'(x) = \frac{1}{\ln x} \cdot \frac{1}{x} = \frac{1}{x \ln x}$

$$g''(x) = -\frac{x \cdot \frac{1}{x} + \ln x}{(x\ln x)^2} = -\frac{1+\ln x}{(x \ln x)^2}$$

$\therefore \quad g''(e) = -\frac{1+1}{e^2} = \frac{-2}{e^2}$

23. (c) $\ln(\ln f(x)) = g^2(f(x) - 3g(f(x))) - 5$

$\Rightarrow \quad x = x^2 - 3x - 5 \Rightarrow x^2 - 4x - 5 = 0$

$\Rightarrow \quad (x-5)(x+1) = 0 \Rightarrow x = -1, 5$

Passage II

(Ex. Nos. 24 to 25)

A curve is represented parametrically by the equations $x = f(t) = a^{\ln(b^t)}$ and $y = g(t) = b^{-\ln(a^t)}$ where $a, b > 0$ and $a \neq 1, b \neq 1$ where $t \in R$.

Example 24 *Which of the following is a correct expression for $\frac{dy}{dx}$?*

(a) $\frac{-1}{f(t)^2}$ (b) $-(g(t))^2$ (c) $\frac{-g(t)}{f(t)}$ (d) $\frac{-f(t)}{g(t)}$

Example 25 *The value of $\frac{d^2y}{dx^2}$ at the point where $f(t) = g(t)$ is*

(a) 0 (b) $\frac{1}{2}$

(c) 1 (d) 2

Solutions (Q. No. 24 and 25)

24. (c) Given, $\quad x = f(t) = a^{\ln(b^t)}$

and $\quad y = g(t) = b^{-\ln(a^t)}$

$x = f(t) = a^{\ln(b^t)}$

$\Rightarrow \quad \ln x = \ln(b^t) \cdot \ln a$

$\Rightarrow \quad \frac{1}{x}\frac{dx}{dt} = \ln(b) \cdot \ln(a)$

$\Rightarrow \quad \frac{dx}{dt} = x \ln(b) \cdot \ln(a)$

Similarly, $\quad \frac{dy}{dt} = -y \ln(b) \cdot \ln(a)$

$\therefore \quad \frac{dy}{dx} = \frac{dy/dt}{dx/dt} = \frac{-y}{x}$ or $\frac{dy}{dx} = -\frac{g(t)}{f(t)}$

25. (d) From previous solution 23, we have

$$\frac{dy}{dx} = -\frac{y}{x}$$

On differentiating w.r.t. x, we get

$$\frac{d^2y}{dx^2} = -\left[\frac{x\frac{dy}{dx} - y}{x^2}\right] = -\left[\frac{x \times \frac{-y}{x} - y}{x^2}\right]$$

$$= -\left[-\frac{2y}{x^2}\right] = \frac{2y}{x^2} = \frac{2}{x}$$

Now, $\quad f(t) = g(t)$

$a^{\ln(b^t)} = b^{-\ln(a^t)}$

$\Rightarrow \quad t\ln(a)\ln(b) = -t\ln(a)\ln(b)$

$\Rightarrow \quad 2t\ln(a)\ln(b) = 0$

$\Rightarrow \quad t = 0$

So, $\quad x = a^{\ln b^t} = a^0 = 1$

$\therefore \quad \frac{d^2y}{dx^2} = 2$

Passage III

(Ex. Nos. 26 to 27)

If f and g both are differentiable functions and $F = fog$ is the composite function defined by $F(x) = f(g(x))$, then f is differentiable and F' is given by the product

$$F'(x) = f'(g(x)) \cdot g'(x)$$

Example 26 *Let $f(x)=\sin x$, $g(x)=[x+1]$ and $g\{f(x)\}=\phi(x)$, where $[\cdot]$ is the GIF, then the value of $\phi'\left(\frac{\pi}{2}\right)$ is*

(a) non-existent (b) 1
(c) -1 (d) None of these

Example 27 *If $f(x)=|3-x|$ and $g(x)=f\{f(x)\}$, then $g'(2)$ is*

(a) 1 (b) -1 (c) 3 (d) -3

Solutions (Q. No. 26 and 27)

26. (a) Given, $f(x)=\sin x,\ g(x)=[x+1]$

and $g(f(x))=\phi(x)$

$$\phi(x)=g(f(x))=g(\sin x)$$

or $\phi(x)=[\sin x+1]$

Now, $$\lim_{h\to 0}\phi\left(\frac{\pi}{2}-h\right)=\lim_{h\to 0}\left[\sin\left(\frac{\pi}{2}-h\right)\right]+1$$

$$=\lim_{h\to 0}[\cos h]+1=0+1=1$$

and $$\lim_{h\to 0}\phi\left(\frac{\pi}{2}+h\right)=\lim_{h\to 0}\left[\sin\left(\frac{\pi}{2}+h\right)\right]+1$$

$$=\lim_{h\to 0}[\cos h]+1=1$$

and $$\phi\left(\frac{\pi}{2}\right)=\left[\sin\frac{\pi}{2}+1\right]=2$$

Hence, LHS = RHS $\neq$ Value of function

$\therefore$ $\phi(x)$ is not continuous at $x=\frac{\pi}{2}$

Hence, $\phi'\left(\frac{\pi}{2}\right)$ is non-existent.

27. (a) If $f(x)=|3-x|$ and $g(x)=f(f(x))$

Now $g(x)=|3-f(x)|=|3-|3-x||$

$$g'(x)=\frac{d}{dx}(||x-3|-3|)$$

$$=\frac{|x-3|-3}{||x-3|-3|}\cdot\frac{d}{dx}(|x-3|-3)$$

$$=\frac{\left(\frac{d}{dx}(|x-3|)+\frac{d}{dx}(-3)\right)(|x-3|-3)}{||x-3|-3|}$$

$$=\frac{\left(\frac{x-3}{|x-3|}\cdot\frac{d}{dx}(x-3)+0\right)(|x-3|-3)}{||x-3|-3|}$$

$$=\frac{\left(\frac{d}{dx}(x)+\frac{d}{dx}(-3)\right)(|x-3|-3)(x-3)}{||x-3|-3||x-3|}$$

$$=\frac{(1+0)(|x-3|-3)(x-3)}{||x-3|-3||x-3|}$$

$$=\frac{(|x-3|-3)(x-3)}{||x-3|-3||x-3|}$$

$\therefore$ $g'(2)=1$

Stem Based Questions

Stem I

(Ex. Nos. 28 to 29)

The figure of $y=P(x)=ax^5+bx^4+cx^3+dx^2+ex+f$ is given below

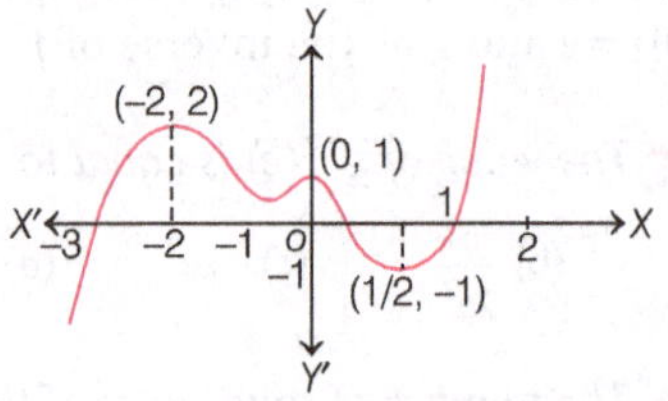

Example 28 *If $P''(x)$ has real roots α, β and γ. Then, $|[\alpha]+[\beta]+[\gamma]|$ (where $[\cdot]$ is greatest integer function) is ......*

Sol. (3) Here, $P'(x)=0$ at $x=-2,-1,0,\frac{1}{2}$.

$\Rightarrow$ $P''(x)$ will have real roots belong to $(-2,-1),(-1,0),\left(0,\frac{1}{2}\right)$.

[$\because$ between any two roots of a function, atleast one root of its derivative exist]

$\therefore$ $|[\alpha]+[\beta]+[\gamma]|=|-3|=3$

Example 29 *The minimum number of real roots of equation $(P''(x))^2+P'(x)\cdot P'''(x)=0$ is ....*

Sol. (6) Let $f(x)=(P''(x))^2+P'(x)\cdot P'''(x)$

$$\Rightarrow\quad f(x)=\frac{d}{dx}(P'(x)\cdot P''(x))$$

Since, $P'(x)$ has 4 real roots.

So, $P''(x)$ has 3 real roots.

$\Rightarrow f(x)$ has 6 real roots.

Stem II

(Ex. Nos. 30 to 31)

A non-zero polynomial with real coefficients has the property that $f''(x)\cdot f'(x)=f(x)$. Then,

Example 30 *The leading coefficients of $f(x)$ is, then value of 90λ is ....*

Example 31 *The value of $f'''(x)$ is $\frac{p}{q}$ where p and q are co-prime, then $p+q$ is ....*

Solutions (Q. No. 30 and 31)

Let degree of $f(x)=n$

$\therefore$ Degree of $f'(x)=n-1$,

Degree of $f''(x)=n-2$

Since, $f''(x)\cdot f'(x)=f(x)$ [given]

$\because$ $(n-1)+(n-2)=n\ \Rightarrow\ 2n-3=n\Rightarrow n=3$

$\therefore$ Degree of $f(x)=3$

Hence, $f(x)=ax^3+bx^2+cx+d$

$\Rightarrow \quad f'(x)=3ax^2+2bx+c$

$\Rightarrow \quad f''(x)=6ax+2b$

$f'''(x)=6a$

As, $f''(x)\cdot f'(x)=f(x)$

$\Rightarrow (6ax+2b)(3ax^2+2bx+c)=(ax^3+bx^2+cx+d)$

On comparing coefficients of x^3, we get

$18a^2=a$

$\Rightarrow \quad a=0,\frac{1}{18}$

$\therefore \quad a=\frac{1}{18} \quad [\because a\neq 0]$

The leading coefficient of $f(x)=\frac{1}{18}$ and $f'''(x)=6a=\frac{1}{3}$

30. $\lambda=\frac{1}{18} \Rightarrow 90\lambda=5$

31. $\frac{p}{q}=\frac{1}{3} \Rightarrow p+q=4$

Single Integer Answer Type Questions

Example 32 *The function $f:R\to R$ satisfies $f(x^2)\cdot f''(x)=f'(x)\cdot f'(x^2)$ for all real x. Given that $f(1)=1$ and $f'''(1)=8$, then the value of $f'(1)+f''(1)$ is ......*

Sol. (6) $f(x^2)\cdot f''(x)=f'(x)\cdot f'(x^2)$ ...(i)

$\Rightarrow f(x^2)f'''(x)+f''(x)\cdot f'(x^2)2x$

$=f''(x)f'(x^2)+2xf'(x)f''(x^2)$ ...(ii)

Put $x=1$ in Eq. (i), we get

$f(1)f''(1)=(f'(1))^2 \Rightarrow f''(1)=(f'(1))^2$

Put $x=1$ in Eq. (ii), we get

$\Rightarrow f(1)f'''(1)+f''(1)f'(1)2$

$=f''(1)f'(1)+2f'(1)f''(1)$

$\Rightarrow f(1)f'''(1)=f''(1)f'(1)$

$8=f'(1)f''(1)$

$\Rightarrow f'(1)=2$

$f''(1)=4$

$\therefore f'(1)+f''(1)=6$

Example 33 *Suppose f and g are two functions such that $f,g:R\to R$, $f(x)=\ln(1+\sqrt{1+x^2})$ and $g(x)=\ln(x+\sqrt{1+x^2})$, then the value of $xe^{g(x)}\left(f\left(\frac{1}{x}\right)\right)'+g'(x)$ at $x=1$ is equal to ....*

Sol. (0) $f'(x)=\left(\frac{1}{1+\sqrt{1+x^2}}\right)\cdot\frac{x}{\sqrt{1+x^2}}$

$\Rightarrow \left(f\left(\frac{1}{x}\right)\right)'=\left(\frac{x}{x+\sqrt{1+x^2}}\right)\frac{1}{\sqrt{x^2+1}}\cdot\left(-\frac{1}{x^2}\right)$

$=\frac{-1}{x(x+\sqrt{1+x^2})\sqrt{x^2+1}}$

$xe^{g(x)}\cdot\left(f\left(\frac{1}{x}\right)\right)'=\frac{-1}{\sqrt{x^2+1}}$

$g'(x)=\frac{1}{(x+\sqrt{1+x^2})}\left(1+\frac{x}{\sqrt{x^2+1}}\right)=\frac{1}{\sqrt{x^2+1}}$

$\therefore \quad xe^{g(x)}\cdot\left(f\left(\frac{1}{x}\right)\right)'+g'(x)=0$

Example 34 *If $y=\sqrt{(x-\sin x)+\sqrt{(x-\sin x)+\ldots}}$, then $\left|\left|\frac{dx}{dy}\right|^2_{x=\frac{\pi}{2}}-2\pi\right|$ is equal to ....*

Sol. (3) Here, $y=\sqrt{(x-\sin x)+\sqrt{(x-\sin x)+\ldots\infty}}$

So, $=\sqrt{(x-\sin x)+y}$

$\therefore \quad y^2=x-\sin x+y$

On differentiating w.r.t. x, we get

$2y\frac{dy}{dx}=1-\cos x+\frac{dy}{dx}$ ...(i)

At $x=\frac{\pi}{2}, y^2-y=\frac{\pi}{2}-1 \Rightarrow y^2-y+\frac{1}{4}=\frac{\pi}{2}-\frac{3}{4}$

$\Rightarrow \left(y-\frac{1}{2}\right)^2=\frac{2\pi-3}{4}$

$\Rightarrow (2y-1)=\pm\sqrt{2\pi-3}$

From Eq. (i), we get

$(2y-1)\frac{dy}{dx}=1-\cos x$

$\Rightarrow \left|\frac{dy}{dx}\right|_{x=\frac{\pi}{2}}=\frac{1}{\sqrt{2\pi-3}}$

$\therefore \left|\left|\frac{dx}{dy}\right|^2_{x=\frac{\pi}{2}}-2\pi\right|=3$

Example 35 *If $f(x)=(x-a)(x-b)$ for $a,b\in R$. Then, the minimum number of roots of equation $\pi(f'(x))^2\cos(\pi f(x))+\sin(\pi f(x))f''(x)=0$ in (α,β), where $f(\alpha)=3=f(\beta)$, is ...... (where $\alpha<a<b<\beta$).*

Sol. (4) Let $g(x) = f'(x)\sin(\pi f(x))$

$$= 2\left[x - \left(\frac{a+b}{2}\right)\right]\sin(\pi f(x))$$

$$g'(x) = \pi(f'(x))^2\cos(\pi f(x)) + \sin(\pi f(x))\,g''(x) = 0$$

$$g(a) = 0 = g(b) = g\left(\frac{a+b}{2}\right) = g(\alpha) = g(\beta)$$

$\therefore g'(x)$ must have atleast one root in the intervals (α, a), $\left(a, \frac{a+b}{2}\right), \left(\frac{a+b}{2}, b\right)$ and (b, β) i.e. minimum 4 roots.

Example 36 *Let $f(x) = \int_{-2}^{x} e^{(1+t)^2}\,dt$ and $g(x) = f(h(x))$, where $h(x)$ is defined for all $x \in R$. If $g'(2) = e^4$ and $h'(2) = 1$, then absolute value of sum of all possible values of $h(2)$, is ......*

Decoding the Question

Let $f(x) = \int_{g(x)}^{h(x)} F(x)dx \Rightarrow f'(x) = h'(x)\,F(h(x)) - g'(x)\,F(g(x))$

Sol. (2) Here,

$$f(x) = \int_{-2}^{x} e^{(1+t)^2}\,dt$$

$$g(x) = \int_{-2}^{h(x)} e^{(1+t)^2}\,dt$$

$$\Rightarrow \quad g'(x) = h'(x)\cdot e^{(1+h(x))^2} \quad \text{[by Leibnitz rule]}$$

$$\Rightarrow \quad g'(2) = h'(2)\cdot e^{(1+h(2))^2}$$

$$\Rightarrow \quad e^4 = 1\cdot e^{(1+h(2))^2}$$

[given $g'(2) = e^4$ and $h'(2) = 1$)]

$$\Rightarrow \quad (1+h(2))^2 = 4 \Rightarrow h(2) = -3, 1$$

$\therefore$ Absolute value of sum of all possible values of $h(2) = |-3+1| = 2$.

Example 37 *If the derivative with respect to x of the function $(\log_{\cos x}\sin x)(\log_{\sin x}\cos x)^{-1} + \sin^{-1}\frac{2x}{1+x^2}$ at $x = \frac{\pi}{4}$ is $\frac{a}{\ln b} + \frac{c}{d+\pi e}$, then $c - a - b - d - e$ is ....*

Sol. (4) $(\log_{\cos x}\sin x)^2 + \sin^{-1}\left(\frac{2x}{1+x^2}\right)$

$$\Rightarrow \quad y = \left(\frac{\ln\sin x}{\ln\cos x}\right)^2 + 2\tan^{-1}x$$

$$\frac{dy}{dx} = 2\left(\frac{\ln\sin x}{\ln\cos x}\right)\cdot\left[\frac{(\ln\cos x)\cdot\cot x + (\ln\sin x)\cdot\tan x}{\ln^2\cos x}\right] + \frac{2}{1+x^2}$$

$$\Rightarrow \quad f'\left(\frac{\pi}{4}\right) = 2\left[\frac{2}{\ln\left(\frac{1}{\sqrt{2}}\right)}\right] + \frac{2}{1+\frac{\pi^2}{16}} = \frac{-8}{\ln 2} + \frac{32}{16+\pi^2}$$

$$a = 8, b = 2, c = 32, d = 16, e = 2$$

$$\therefore \quad c - a - b - d - e = 32 - 28 = 4$$

Example 38 *If $f(x) = \begin{vmatrix} (x+1)^6 & (x+1)^5 & 1 \\ (x+2)^6 & (x+2)^5 & 1 \\ (x+3)^6 & (x+3)^5 & 1 \end{vmatrix}$, then*

$f'(x) = \lambda\cdot\begin{vmatrix} (x+1)^6 & (x+1)^4 & 1 \\ (x+2)^6 & (x+2)^4 & 1 \\ (x+3)^6 & (x+3)^4 & 1 \end{vmatrix}$, then the value of λ is ...

Sol. (3) We have, $f(x) = \begin{vmatrix} (x+1)^6 & (x+1)^5 & 1 \\ (x+2)^6 & (x+2)^5 & 1 \\ (x+3)^6 & (x+3)^5 & 1 \end{vmatrix}$

$$f'(x) = 6\begin{vmatrix} (x+1)^5 & (x+1)^5 & 1 \\ (x+2)^5 & (x+2)^5 & 1 \\ (x+3)^5 & (x+3)^5 & 1 \end{vmatrix} + 5\begin{vmatrix} (x+1)^6 & (x+1)^4 & 1 \\ (x+2)^6 & (x+2)^4 & 1 \\ (x+3)^6 & (x+3)^4 & 1 \end{vmatrix} + 0$$

$$f'(x) = 5\begin{vmatrix} (x+1)^6 & (x+1)^4 & 1 \\ (x+2)^6 & (x+2)^4 & 1 \\ (x+3)^6 & (x+3)^4 & 1 \end{vmatrix}$$

$$\therefore \quad \lambda = 5$$

Example 39 *If $y = \sin^{-1}\ln\left(\frac{x^2}{2}\right)$, then the absolute value of $(xy')^2\left\{\left(\ln\frac{x^2}{2}\right)^2 - 1\right\}$ is equal to ....*

Sol. (4)

$$y = \sin^{-1}\left(\ln\frac{x^2}{2}\right) \quad \text{...(i)}$$

$$\Rightarrow \quad \sin y = \ln\left(\frac{x^2}{2}\right) \quad \text{...(ii)}$$

$$\Rightarrow (\cos y)\,y' = \frac{2}{x^2}(x) \Rightarrow y' = \frac{2}{x\cos y} \Rightarrow (xy')^2 = \frac{4}{\cos^2 y} \quad \text{...(iii)}$$

$$\Rightarrow \quad (xy')^2\cdot\left\{\left(\ln\left(\frac{x^2}{2}\right)\right)^2 - 1\right\} = \frac{4}{\cos^2 y}\{\sin^2 y - 1\} = -4$$

$\therefore$ Absolute value $= 4$

Example 40 *If f and g are two functions having derivative of order three for all x satisfying $f(x)\,g(x) = C$ (constant) and $\frac{f'''}{f'} - A\frac{f''}{f} - \frac{g'''}{g'} + \frac{3g''}{g} = 0$. Then, A is equal to ....*

Sol. (3) $f(x)\cdot g(x) = C \Rightarrow f(x)\cdot g'(x) + g(x)\cdot f'(x) = 0$ ...(i)

$$\Rightarrow \quad \frac{g'(x)}{g(x)} = -\frac{f'(x)}{f(x)} \Rightarrow \frac{g'(x)}{g(x)} + \frac{f'(x)}{f(x)} = 0 \quad \text{...(ii)}$$

On differentiating Eq. (i) again, we get

$$f(x)\,g''(x)+g'(x)\cdot f'(x) + g(x)\,f''(x)+f'(x)\cdot g'(x)=0$$

$$\Rightarrow \quad f(x)\cdot g''(x)+g(x)\cdot f''(x)+2f'(x)\cdot g'(x)=0 \quad \text{...(iii)}$$

$$\Rightarrow \quad \frac{g''(x)}{g(x)}+\frac{f''(x)}{f(x)}+\frac{2f'(x)\cdot g'(x)}{f(x)\cdot g(x)} \quad \text{...(iv)}$$

On differentiating Eq. (iii) again, we get

$$f(x)\,g'''(x)+g''(x)\,f'(x)+g(x)\,f'''(x)+f''(x)\,g'(x) + 2f'(x)\,g''(x)+2g'(x)\,f''(x)=0$$

$$\Rightarrow f(x)\cdot g'''(x)+g(x)\cdot f'''(x) + 3f'(x)\cdot g''(x)+3g'(x)\,f''(x)=0$$

$$\Rightarrow \quad \frac{g'''(x)}{g(x)}+\frac{f'''(x)}{f(x)}+\frac{3f'(x)\,g''(x)}{f(x)\cdot g(x)} + \frac{3g'(x)\cdot f''(x)}{g(x)\,f(x)}=0 \quad \text{...(v)}$$

$$\Rightarrow \quad \frac{g'''(x)}{g'(x)}\cdot\frac{g'(x)}{g(x)}+\frac{f'''(x)}{f'(x)}\cdot\frac{f'(x)}{f(x)} + \frac{3g''(x)}{g(x)}\cdot\frac{f'(x)}{f(x)}+\frac{3f''(x)}{f(x)}\cdot\frac{g'(x)}{g(x)}=0 \quad \text{...(vi)}$$

From Eq. (ii), using $\frac{g'(x)}{g(x)}=-\frac{f'(x)}{f(x)}$ in Eq. (vi), we get

$$\Rightarrow \quad -\frac{g'''(x)}{g'(x)}+\frac{f'''(x)}{f'(x)}+\frac{3g''(x)}{g(x)}-\frac{3f''(x)}{f(x)}=0$$

$$\Rightarrow \quad \frac{f'''(x)}{f'(x)}-\frac{3f''(x)}{f(x)}-\frac{g'''(x)}{g'(x)}+\frac{3g''(x)}{g(x)}=0$$

$\therefore \quad A=3$ (on comparing)

Numerical Value Type Questions

Example 41 ■ *Let $f:R\to R$ be a function defined by $f(x)=x^3+2x^2+3x+2$ and g be the inverse of f. If $\frac{d}{dx}(g(g(g(x))))_{x=24}=\frac{a}{b}$ where a and b are co-prime, then the value of $(a+b)$ is ....*

Sol. (277) $f(-1)=0$, $f(0)=2$ and $f(2)=24$

$$\frac{d}{dx}(g(g(g(x))))=g'(g(x)g(x))\cdot g'(g(x))\cdot g'(x)$$

$$=g'(g(g(24)))\cdot g'(g(24))\cdot g'(24)$$

$$=g'(g(2))\cdot g'(2)\frac{1}{f'(2)}$$

$[\because g(24)=2,\ g(2)=0]$

$$=g'(0)\cdot\frac{1}{f'(0)}\cdot\frac{1}{f'(2)}=\frac{1}{f'(-1)}\cdot\frac{1}{f'(0)}\cdot\frac{1}{f'(2)}$$

Now, $\quad f'(x)=3x^2+4x+3$

$$f'(-1)=3-4+3=4$$

$$f'(0)=3$$

$$f'(2)=12+8+3=23$$

$$\therefore \quad \frac{1}{f'(-1)}\cdot\frac{1}{f'(0)}\cdot\frac{1}{f'(2)}=\frac{1}{4}\times\frac{1}{3}\times\frac{1}{23}=\frac{1}{276}$$

$\therefore \quad a=1, b=276$

$\therefore \quad a+b=277$

Example 42 ■ *If $x\in\left(0,\frac{\pi}{2}\right)$ and*

$$\frac{d}{dx}\cos^{-1}\left\{\frac{7}{2}(1+\cos 2x)+\sqrt{(\sin^2 x-48\cos^2 x)}\sin x\right\}$$

$$=\alpha+\frac{\beta\sin x}{\sqrt{\sin^2 x-\gamma\cos^2 x}},\ \textit{then}\ \alpha+\beta+\gamma\ \textit{is ....}$$

Decoding the Question

To solve this problem use the formula given as

$$\cos^{-1}x-\cos^{-1}y=\cos^{-1}[xy+\sqrt{1-x^2}\sqrt{1-y^2}]$$

Sol. (42) $\cos^{-1}\left(\frac{7}{2}(1+\cos 2x)+\sqrt{(\sin^2 x-48\cos^2 x)}\sin x\right)$

$$=\cos^{-1}(7\cos^2 x+\sqrt{(1-7\cos x)(1+7\cos x)}\sin x)$$

$$=\cos^{-1}(\cos x\cdot 7\cos x+\sqrt{1-\cos^2 x}\sqrt{1-49\cos^2 x})$$

$$=\cos^{-1}(\cos x)-\cos^{-1}(7\cos x)=x-\cos^{-1}(7\cos x)$$

Now, on differentiating w.r.t. x, we get

$$=1+\frac{-7\sin x}{\sqrt{1-49\cos^2 x}}=1-\frac{7\sin x}{\sqrt{\sin^2 x-48\cos^2 x}}$$

On comparing, we get

$$\alpha=1, \beta=-7 \text{ and } \gamma=48$$

$$\therefore \quad \alpha+\beta+\gamma=42$$

Example 43 ■ *If $y=\cos^{-1}\sqrt{\frac{\cos 3x}{\cos^3 x}}$ and this derivative $\frac{dy}{dx}=\sqrt{\frac{p}{\cos qx+\cos rx}}$, where p, q and r are even number, then $p+q+r$ is ....*

Sol. (12) $\quad y=\cos^{-1}\sqrt{\frac{\cos 3x}{\cos^3 x}} \Rightarrow \cos^2 y=4-3\sec^2 x$

$$\Rightarrow 2\cos y\sin y\frac{dy}{dx}=6\sec^2 x\tan x$$

$$\Rightarrow \frac{dy}{dx}=\frac{6\sec^2 x\tan x}{\sin 2y}=\frac{6\sin x}{\cos^3 x\,[2\sqrt{4-3\sec^2 x}\sqrt{3\sec^2 x-3}]}$$

$$=\frac{\sqrt{3}}{\sqrt{(4\cos^2 x-3)\cdot\cos^2 x}}=\frac{\sqrt{6}}{\sqrt{2\cos 3x\cdot\cos x}}$$

$$\frac{dy}{dx}=\frac{\sqrt{6}}{\sqrt{\cos 4x+\cos 2x}}$$

$$p=6, q=4, r=2$$

$$\therefore \quad p+q+r=12$$

Example 44 *Given* $z=\cos^7 x$; $y=\sin x$ *and* $\dfrac{d^3z}{dy^3}=\dfrac{\alpha}{\beta}\sin\gamma x$, *then* $\alpha+\beta-4\gamma$ *is ....*

Sol. (93) We have, $z=\cos^7 x,\ y=\sin x$

On differentiating above equations w.r.t. x

$$\frac{dz}{dx}=-7\cos^6 x\sin x,$$

$$\frac{dy}{dx}=\cos x$$

$$\frac{dz}{dy}=-7y(z)^{5/7}$$

$$\frac{d^2z}{dy^2}=-7(z)^{5/7}-5y(z)^{-2/7}\frac{dz}{dy}$$

$$\frac{d^2z}{dy^2}=-7(z)^{5/7}+35y^2(z)^{3/7}$$

$$\frac{d^3z}{dy^3}=-5(z)^{-2/7}\frac{dz}{dy}+70y(z)^{3/7}+15y^2\cdot z^{-4/7}\frac{dz}{dy}$$

$$=35y(z)^{3/7}+70y(z)^{3/7}-105y^3z^{1/7}$$

$$=35\sin x\cos^3 x+70\sin x\cos^3 x-105\sin^3 x\cos x$$

$$=105\sin x\cos x\,[\cos 2x]=\frac{105}{4}\sin 4x$$

$$\alpha=105$$

$$\beta=4$$

$$\gamma=4$$

$\therefore\ \alpha+\beta-4\gamma=109-16=93$

Example 45 *Let* $F(x)=f(x)\,g(x)\,h(x)$ *for all real x, where* $f(x)$, $g(x)$ *and* $h(x)$, *are differentiable functions. At some point* x_0 $F'(x_0)=21F(x_0)$, $f'(x_0)=4f(x_0)$, $g'(x_0)=-7g(x_0)$, $h'(x_0)=kh(x_0)$.

Then, k is equal to ....

Sol. (24) $F(x)=f(x)\,g(x)\,h(x)$

$$F'(x)=f'(x)\,g(x)\,h(x)+f(x)\,g'(x)\,h(x)+f(x)\,g(x)\,h'(x)$$

$$F'(x_0)=(k-3)\,f(x_0)\,g(x_0)\,h(x_0)$$

$\therefore\quad k-3=21$

$$k=24$$

Example 46 *If* $\dfrac{dy}{dx}$ *at* $x=-1$, *when*

$$(\sin y)^{\sin(\pi x/2)}+\left(\frac{\sqrt{3}}{2}\right)\sec^{-1}(2x)+2^x\tan\{\ln(x+2)\}=0 \text{ is } \lambda,$$

then number of even natural number less than 90 divides 4λ, *is ....*

Sol. (45) $(\sin y)^{\sin\frac{\pi x}{2}}+\dfrac{\sqrt{3}}{2}\sec^{-1}(2x)+2^x\tan(\ln(x+2))=0$

On differentiating w.r.t. x, we get

$$(\sin y)^{\sin\frac{\pi x}{2}}\left[\frac{\pi}{2}\cos\frac{\pi x}{2}\ln\sin y+\sin\frac{\pi x}{2}\cot y\frac{dy}{dx}\right]$$

$$+\sqrt{3}\times\frac{1}{2x\sqrt{4x^2-1}}+2^x\ln 2\tan\ln(x+2)$$

$$+\frac{2^x\sec^2\ln(x+2)}{x+2}=0$$

Put $x=-1$, $\sin y=\dfrac{-\sqrt{3}}{\pi}\ \Rightarrow\ y'=0$

$\therefore\quad \lambda=0\Rightarrow 4\lambda=0$

$\therefore$ Total number of even natural number less than 90 divides 4λ is $=45$.

JEE SCANNER

Example 47 Similar to PYQ Asked in JEE Main 2024

Let $f(x)=\dfrac{1}{3}x^3+x^2f'(1)+xf''(2)+f'''(3)$, $x\in R$. Then, $f'(6)$ is equal to .....

Sol. (16.67) We have, $f(x)=\dfrac{1}{3}x^3+x^2f'(1)+xf''(2)+f'''(3)$ ...(i)

$$f'(x)=x^2+2xf'(1)+f''(2) \quad \text{...(ii)}$$

$$f''(x)=2x+2f'(1) \quad \text{...(iii)}$$

$$f'''(x)=2 \quad \text{...(iv)}$$

Now, $\quad f'''(3)=2$

From Eqs. (ii) and (iii), we get

$$f'(1)=1+2f'(1)+f''(2)$$

$$f''(2)=4+2f'(1)$$

$$f'(1)=1+2f'(1)+4+2f'(1)$$

$$f'(1)=-\frac{5}{3} \quad \text{...(v)}$$

$$f''(2)=4-\frac{10}{3}=\frac{2}{3}$$

From Eq. (i), we get

$$f(x)=\frac{1}{3}x^3-\frac{5}{3}x^2+\frac{2x}{3}+2$$

$$f'(x)=x^2-\frac{10}{3}x+\frac{2}{3}$$

$$f'(6)=36-20+\frac{2}{3}=\frac{50}{3}=16.67$$

Skill Builder

Let $f(x)=x^3+x^2f''(1)+xf''(2)-4f'''(3)$, $x\in R$. Then, $f'(5)$ is equal to ....

For Sol.

Matching Type Questions

Example 48 *Match the following columns.*

Column I	Column II
(A) $y = 2\sin^{-1}\sqrt{\dfrac{x-\beta}{\alpha-\beta}}$	(p) $\dfrac{dy}{dx} = \dfrac{4}{\sqrt{(\alpha-x)(x-\beta)}}$
(B) $y = 4\sin^{-1}\sqrt{\dfrac{x-\beta}{\alpha-x}}$	(q) $\dfrac{dy}{dx} = \dfrac{1}{\sqrt{(\alpha-x)(x-\beta)}}$
(C) $y = 4\sin^{-1}\theta$, where $\theta = \dfrac{2\sqrt{(\alpha-x)(x-\beta)}}{\alpha-\beta}$	(r) $\dfrac{dy}{dx} = \dfrac{2}{\sqrt{(\alpha-x)(x-\beta)}}$
(D) $y = 2\cos^{-1}\sqrt{\dfrac{x-\beta}{\alpha-\beta}}$	(s) $\dfrac{dy}{dx} = -\dfrac{1}{\sqrt{(\alpha-x)(x-\beta)}}$

Sol. (A) → (q), (B) → (r), (C) → (p), (D) → (s)

If y is as in (a), then $y'(x)$

$$= \frac{2}{\sqrt{1-\dfrac{(x-\beta)}{(\alpha-\beta)}}}\,\frac{1}{2}\sqrt{\frac{\alpha-\beta}{x-\beta}}\times\frac{1}{\alpha-\beta}$$

$$= \frac{1}{\sqrt{\dfrac{(\alpha-x)}{(x-\beta)}}}$$

If y is as in (b), then

$$y'(x) = \frac{4}{\sqrt{1+(x-\beta)/(\alpha-x)}}$$

$$\cdot\frac{1}{2}\sqrt{\frac{\alpha-x}{x-\beta}}\cdot\frac{\alpha-\beta}{(\alpha-x)^2}$$

$$= \frac{2}{\sqrt{(\alpha-x)(x-\beta)}}$$

If y is as in (c), we have

$$y'(x) = \frac{4}{\sqrt{1-\dfrac{4(\alpha-x)(x-\beta)}{(\alpha-\beta)^2}}}$$

$$\times\frac{2}{\alpha-\beta}\,\frac{1}{2}\,\frac{4}{\sqrt{\dfrac{(\alpha-x)}{(x-\beta)}}}[-x+\beta+\alpha-x]$$

$$= \frac{4}{\sqrt{(\alpha-x)/(x-\beta)}}$$

Since, $\sin^{-1}x + \sin^{-1}x = \dfrac{\pi}{2}$, from (a) and (d), so (d) is clear.

Example 49 *Match the following columns.*

Column I	Column II
(A) If $f'(x) = \sqrt{3x^2+6}$ and $y = f(x^3)$, then at $x = 1$, $\dfrac{dy}{dx}$ is	(p) -2
(B) If f is a differentiable function such that $f(xy) = f(x) + f(y) : x, y \in R$, then $f(e) + f(1/e)$ is	(q) -1
(C) If f is a twice differentiable function such that $f''(x) = -f(x)$ and $f'(x) = g(x)$. If $h(x) = [f(x)]^2 + [g(x)]^2$ and $h(5) = 9$, then $h(10)$ is	(r) 0
(D) $y = \tan^{-1}(\cot x) + \cot^{-1}(\tan x)$, $\dfrac{\pi}{2} < x < \pi$, then $\dfrac{dy}{dx}$ is	(s) 9

Ans. (A) → (s), (B) → (r), (C) → (s), (D) → (p)

Sol. (A) $\because y = f(x^3)$

$$\therefore \quad \frac{dy}{dx} = f'(x^3)\cdot 3x^2$$

$$\left(\frac{dy}{dx}\right)_{x=1} = f'(1)\cdot 3 = 9$$

(B) $\because f(xy) = f(x) + f(y)$

Put $x = y = 1$, $f(1) = f(1) + f(1)$

$\therefore \quad f(1) = 0$

Also, $\quad f(1) = f(e) + f\left(\dfrac{1}{e}\right)$

i.e. $x = e, y = \dfrac{1}{e}$

$\therefore f(e) + f\left(\dfrac{1}{e}\right) = 0$

(C) $\because f''(x) = -f(x)$ and $g(x) = f'(x)$

$\therefore \quad g'(x) = f''(x) = -f(x) \quad$ ...(i)

Also, $h(x) = [f(x)]^2 + [g(x)]^2$

$\therefore \quad h'(x) = 2f(x)\,f'(x) + 2g(x)\,g'(x)$

$= 2f(x)\,g(x) - 2g(x)\,f(x) = 0$

$\therefore \quad h(x) = c, \forall\, x \in R$

Here, $h(5) = 9$

$\Rightarrow \quad h(10) = 9$

(D) $\because y = \tan^{-1}(\cot x) + \cot^{-1}(\tan x)\ \dfrac{\pi}{2} < x < \pi$

$$\therefore \frac{dy}{dx} = \frac{-\operatorname{cosec}^2 x}{1+\cot^2 x} + \frac{(-1)\sec^2 x}{1+\tan^2 x} = -1-1 = -2$$

EXERCISE 1

JEE Main Pattern

Single Option Correct Type Questions

1. If $y = \sin^{-1}(x\sqrt{1-x} + \sqrt{x}\sqrt{1-x^2})$ and $\frac{dy}{dx} = \frac{1}{2\sqrt{x(1-x)}} + p'$, then p is equal to

(a) 0 (b) $\sin^{-1} x + C$
(c) $\sin^{-1}\sqrt{x} + C$ (d) None of these

2. Let y be an implicit function of x defined by $x^{2x} - 2x^x \cot y - 1 = 0$. Then, $y'(1)$ equals to

(a) -1 (b) 1
(c) $\log 2$ (d) $-\log 2$

3. Let $f(x) = 2^{2x-1}$ and $\phi(x) = -2^x + 2x \log 2$. If $f'(x) > \phi'(x)$, then

(a) $0 < x < 1$ (b) $0 \le x < 1$
(c) $x < 0$ (d) $x \ge 0$

4. If $f(x) = \left(1+\frac{1}{x}\right)\left(1+\frac{2}{x}\right)\left(1+\frac{3}{x}\right)\ldots\left(1+\frac{1}{x}\right)$ and $x \ne 0$, then $\frac{dy}{dx}$, when $x = -1$, is

(a) $n!$ (b) $(n-1)!$
(c) $(-1)^n (n-1)!$ (d) $(1)^n n!$

5. If $y = \log^n x$, where $\log^n$ means log log log ...... (repeated n times), then $x \log x \log^2 x \log^3 x \ldots \log^{n-1} x \log^n x \frac{dy}{dx}$ is equal to

(a) $\log x$ (b) x
(c) $\frac{1}{\log x}$ (d) $\log^n x$

6. Let $u(x)$ and $v(x)$ are differentiable functions such that $\frac{u(x)}{v(x)} = 7$. If $\frac{u'(x)}{v'(x)} = p$ and $\left(\frac{u(x)}{v(x)}\right)' = q$, then $\frac{p+q}{p-q}$ has the value equals to

(a) 1 (b) 0 (c) 7 (d) -7

7. The equation $y^2 e^{xy} = 9e^{-3} \cdot x^2$ defines y as a differentiable function of x. The value of $\frac{dy}{dx}$ for $x = -1$ and $y = 3$ is

(a) $-\frac{15}{2}$ (b) $-\frac{9}{5}$
(c) 3 (d) 15

8. If $y = \frac{x}{\sqrt{a^2-1}} - \frac{2}{\sqrt{a^2-1}} \tan^{-1}\left(\frac{\sin x}{a + \sqrt{a^2-1} + \cos x}\right)$, where $a \in (-\infty, -1) \cup (1, \infty)$, then $y'\left(\frac{\pi}{2}\right)$ equals to

(a) $\frac{1}{a}$ (b) $\frac{2}{a}$ (c) $\frac{1}{2a}$ (d) a

9. The derivative of the function,
$f(x) = \cos^{-1}\left\{\frac{1}{\sqrt{13}}(2\cos x - 3\sin x)\right\} + \sin^{-1}\left\{\frac{1}{\sqrt{13}}(2\cos x + 3\sin x)\right\}$ w.r.t. $\sqrt{1+x^2}$ at $x = \frac{3}{4}$ is

(a) $\frac{3}{2}$ (b) $\frac{5}{2}$ (c) $\frac{10}{3}$ (d) 0

10. If $f(x) = \sin^{-1}\{[3x+2] - \{3x + (x - \{2x\})\}\}$, $x \in \left(0, \frac{\pi}{12}\right)$ and $gof(x) = x, \forall x \in \left(0, \frac{\pi}{12}\right)$, then $g'\left(\frac{\pi}{6}\right)$ is equal to

Note $\{y\}$ and $[y]$ denote fractional part function and greatest integer function, respectively.

(a) $\frac{\sqrt{3}}{8}$ (b) $\frac{-1}{4}$ (c) $\frac{1}{8}$ (d) $\frac{-\sqrt{3}}{4}$

11. Given $f(x) = -\frac{x^3}{3} + x^2 \sin 1.5a - x \sin a \cdot \sin 2a - 5 \text{ arc} \sin(a^2 - 8a + 17)$, then

(a) $f(x)$ is not defined at $x = \sin 8$
(b) $f'(\sin 8) > 0$
(c) $f'(x)$ is not defined at $x = \sin 8$
(d) $f'(\sin 8) < 0$

12. If $f(x) = \sin(\log x)$ and $y = f\left(\frac{2x+3}{3-2x}\right)$, then $\frac{dy}{dx}$ equals to

(a) $\frac{12}{9-4x^2} \cos\left[\log\left(\frac{2x+3}{3-2x}\right)\right]$
(b) $-\frac{12}{9-4x^2} \cos\left[\log\left(\frac{2x+3}{3-2x}\right)\right]$
(c) $\frac{12}{9-4x^2} \log\left[\cos\left(\frac{2x+3}{3-2x}\right)\right]$
(d) None of the above

13. If $f(x)=\dfrac{x}{1+e^{1/x}}, x\neq 0$, then

(a) $x^3f'(x)-x^2f(x)-e^{1/x}(f(x))^2=0$

(b) $x^3f'(x)+x^2f(x)-e^{1/x}(f(x))^2=0$

(c) $xf'(x)-f(x)+e^{1/x}(f(x))^2=0$

(d) $xf'(x)-f(x)-e^{1/x}(f(x))^2=0$

14. If g is the inverse of f and $f'(x)=\cos 2x$, then $g'(x)$ equals to

(a) $2\sec[2\{g(x)\}]$ (b) $\dfrac{\sec[2\{g(x)\}]}{2}$

(c) $\sec 2(g(x))$ (d) None of these

15. Let $f:R\to R$ be a differentiable function satisfying $f(y)\cdot f(x-y)=f(x), \forall\, x,y\in R$ and $f'(5)=q$ and $\dfrac{f(0)}{f'(0)}=\dfrac{1}{p}$, then $f(5)$ is

(a) $\dfrac{p^2}{q}$ (b) $\dfrac{p}{q}$

(c) $\dfrac{q}{p}$ (d) q

16. Suppose $f(x)=e^{ax}+e^{bx}$, where $a\neq b$ and that $f''(x)-2f'(x)-15f(x)=0$ for all x. Then, the product ab is

(a) 25 (b) 9

(c) −15 (d) −9

17. If $f(x)=(|x|)^{|\sin x|}$, then $f'\left(-\dfrac{\pi}{4}\right)$ is equal to

(a) $\left(\dfrac{\pi}{4}\right)^{1/\sqrt{2}}\cdot\left(\dfrac{\sqrt{2}}{2}\log\dfrac{4}{\pi}-\dfrac{2\sqrt{2}}{\pi}\right)$

(b) $\left(\dfrac{\pi}{4}\right)^{1/\sqrt{2}}\cdot\left(\dfrac{\sqrt{2}}{2}\log\dfrac{4}{\pi}+\dfrac{2\sqrt{2}}{\pi}\right)$

(c) $\left(\dfrac{\pi}{4}\right)^{1/\sqrt{2}}\cdot\left(\dfrac{\sqrt{2}}{2}\log\dfrac{\pi}{4}-\dfrac{2\sqrt{2}}{\pi}\right)$

(d) $\left(\dfrac{\pi}{4}\right)^{1/\sqrt{2}}\cdot\left(\dfrac{\sqrt{2}}{2}\log\dfrac{\pi}{4}+\dfrac{2\sqrt{2}}{\pi}\right)$

18. If f and g are the functions whose graphs are as shown below.

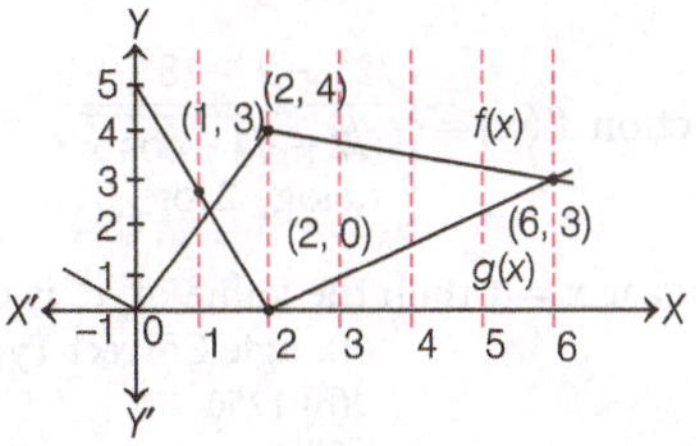

Let $u(x)=f(g(x)), w(x)=g(g(x))$.

Then, the value of $u'(1)+w'(1)$ is

(a) $-\dfrac{1}{2}$ (b) $-\dfrac{3}{2}$

(c) $-\dfrac{5}{4}$ (d) does not exist

19. If $y=\sqrt{x+\sqrt{y+\sqrt{x+\sqrt{y+\ldots\infty}}}}$, then $\dfrac{dy}{dx}$ is equal to

(a) $\dfrac{y+x}{y^2-2x}$ (b) $\dfrac{y^3-x}{2y^2-2xy-1}$

(c) $\dfrac{y^3+x}{2y^2-x}$ (d) None of these

20. If $f(x)$ is given by $f(x)=(\cos x+i\sin x)(\cos 3x+i\sin 3x)\ldots(\cos(2n-1)x+i\sin(2n-1)x)$, then $f''(x)$ is equal to

(a) $n^3f(x)$ (b) $-n^4f(x)$

(c) $-n^2f(x)$ (d) $n^4f(x)$

21. Let $f(x)=x^2+xg'(1)+g''(2)$ and $g(x)=x^2+xf'(2)+f''(3)$. Then,

(a) $f'(1)=4+f'(2)$ (b) $g'(2)=8+g'(1)$

(c) $g''(2)+f''(3)=4$ (d) All of these

22. If $f(x)=x^n$, then the value of

$$f(1)-\frac{f'(1)}{1!}+\frac{f''(1)}{2!}-\frac{f'''(1)}{3!}+\frac{f''''(1)}{4!}-\ldots+\frac{(-1)^nf^n(1)}{n!}$$ is

(a) 1 (b) 2^n (c) 2^{n-1} (d) 0

23. Let $f(x)=e^x-e^{-x}-2\sin x-\dfrac{2}{3}x^3$, then the least value of n for which $\left.\dfrac{d^n}{dx^n}f(x)\right|_{x=0}$ is non-zero, is

(a) 4 (b) 5 (c) 7 (d) 3

24. If $f(x)=1+nx+\dfrac{n(n-1)}{2}x^2+\dfrac{n(n-1)(n-2)}{6}x^3+\ldots+x^n$, then $f''(1)$ is equal to

(a) $n(n-1)2^{n-1}$ (b) $(n-1)2^{n-2}$

(c) $n(n-1)2^{n-2}$ (d) $n(n-1)2^n$

25. If $y=Ae^{x^2}+Be^{x^2/2}$ satisfies the relation $\dfrac{d^2y}{dx^2}+\left(kx-\dfrac{1}{x}\right)\dfrac{dy}{dx}+2x^2y=0$, then find the value of k.

(a) 2 (b) 1

(c) −3 (d) None of these

26. If $f(x)=\tan^{-1}\left(\frac{1}{\cos^2 x+\cos x+1}\right)$ $+\tan^{-1}\left(\frac{1}{\cos^2 x+3\cos x+3}\right)+\tan^{-1}\left(\frac{1}{\cos^2 x+5\cos x+7}\right)$ $+\tan^{-1}\left(\frac{1}{\cos^2 x+7\cos x+13}\right)+\ldots$ to n terms, then find $f'(x)$.

(a) $-\frac{\sin x}{1+\cos^2 x}+\frac{\sin x}{1+\cos(x+n))^2}$

(b) $\frac{\sin x}{1+\cos^2 x}-\frac{\sin x}{1+(\cos x+n)^2}$

(c) $\frac{\sin x}{1+\cos^2 x}-\frac{\sin(x+n-1)}{1+\cos^2(x+n-1)}$

(d) None of the above

27. If a, b, c are the angles of a triangle such that $\sin B\cdot\sin C+\sin C\cdot\sin A+\sin A\cdot\sin B=k$ (where k is a constant), then $\frac{dB}{dA}$ can be written as

(a) $\frac{\sin(C+A)+\sin B(\cos A+\cos C)}{\sin(B+C)+\sin A(\cos C+\cos B)}$

(b) $\frac{\sin(C-A)+\sin B(\cos A-\cos C)}{\sin(B-C)+\sin A(\cos C-\cos B)}$

(c) $\frac{\sin(C+A)+\sin B(\cos A-\cos C)}{\sin(B+C)+\sin A(\cos C-\cos B)}$

(d) None of the above

Numerical Value Type Questions

28. Suppose $A=\frac{dy}{dx}$ when $x^2+y^2=4$ at $(\sqrt{2},\sqrt{2})$, $B=\frac{dy}{dx}$ when $\sin y+\sin x=\sin x\cdot\sin y$ at (π,π) and $C=\frac{dy}{dx}$ when $2e^{xy}+e^xe^y-e^x-e^y=e^{xy+1}$ at (1, 1), then $|A+B+C|$ has the value equal to ....

29. Let $f(x)=\sin^{-1}\left(\frac{2x+2}{\sqrt{4x^2+8x+13}}\right)$, then the value of $\frac{d(\tan f(x))}{d(\tan^{-1}x)}$, when $x=\frac{1}{2}$, is ....

30. Let $P(x)$ be a polynomial of degree 4 such that $P(1)=P(3)=P(5)=P(7)=0$. If the real number $x\neq 1,3,5$ is such that $P(x)=0$ can be expressed as $x=\frac{p}{q}$, where p and q are relatively prime, then $(p-8q)$ is ....

31. Let $h(x)$ be differentiable for all x and let $f(x)=(kx+e^x)h(x)$, where k is some constant. If $h(0)=5$, $h'(0)=-2$ and $f'(0)=18$, then the value of k is equal to ....

32. Let $x_1, x_1, x_1, x_2, x_3, x_4, \ldots, x_8$ be 10 real zeroes of the polynomial $P(x)=x^{10}+ax^2+bx+c$, where $a, b, c\in R$. If the value of $Q(x_1)=\frac{p}{q}$, where p and q are co-prime to each other. If $Q(x)=(x-x_2)(x-x_3)\ldots(x-x_8)$ and $x_1=\frac{1}{2}$, then the value of $q-p$ is ....

Previous Year Questions

33. For $a, b>0$, let

$$f(x)=\begin{cases}\frac{\tan((a+1)x)+b\tan x}{x}, & x<0\\ 3, & x=0\\ \frac{\sqrt{ax+b^2x^2}-\sqrt{ax}}{b\sqrt{ax}\cdot\sqrt{x}}, & x>0\end{cases}$$

be a continuous function at $x=0$. Then, $\frac{b}{a}$ is equal to

[Single Correct Type, 2024 Main]

(a) 4 (b) 5
(c) 8 (d) 6

34. Let $f:[-1,2]\to R$ be given by $f(x)=2x^2+x+[x^2]-[x]$, where $[t]$ denotes the greatest integer less than or equal to t. The number of points, where f is not continuous, is

[Single Correct Type, 2024 Main]

(a) 3 (b) 6
(c) 4 (d) 5

35. If the function $f(x)=\frac{\sin 3x+\alpha\sin x-\beta\cos 3x}{x^3}$, $x\in R$, is continuous at $x=0$, then $f(0)$ is equal to

[Single Correct Type, 2024 Main]

(a) 2 (b) −2
(c) 4 (d) −4

36. If the function $f(x)=\begin{cases}\frac{72^x-9^x-8^x+1}{\sqrt{2}-\sqrt{1+\cos x}}, & x\neq 0\\ a\log_e 2\log_e 3, & x=0\end{cases}$ is continuous at $x=0$, then the value of a^2 is equal to

[Single Correct Type, 2024 Main]

(a) 1152 (b) 1250
(c) 968 (d) 746

37. Let $f : R \to R$ be a function given by

$$f(x) = \begin{cases} \dfrac{1-\cos 2x}{x^2}, & x<0 \\ \alpha, & x=0 \\ \dfrac{\beta\sqrt{1-\cos x}}{x}, & x>0 \end{cases}$$

where $\alpha, \beta \in R$. If f is continuous at $x = 0$, then $\alpha^2 + \beta^2$ is equal to **[Single Correct Type, 2024 Main]**

(a) 3 (b) 12 (c) 48 (d) 6

38. Consider the function

$$f(x) = \begin{cases} \dfrac{a(7x-12-x^2)}{b|x^2-7x+12|}, & x<3 \\ 2^{\frac{\sin(x-3)}{x-[x]}}, & x>3, \\ b, & x=3 \end{cases}$$

where $[x]$ denotes the greatest integer less than or equal to x. If S denotes the set of all ordered pairs (a, b) such that $f(x)$ is continuous at $x = 3$, then the number of elements in S, is **[Single Correct Type, 2024 Main]**

(a) 4 (b) 2
(c) 1 (d) Infinitely many

39. Let $f(x) = |2x^2 + 5|x| - 3|$, $x \in R$. If m and n denote the number of points where f is not continuous and not differentiable respectively, then $m + n$ is equal to **[Single Correct Type, 2024 Main]**

(a) 3 (b) 0 (c) 2 (d) 5

40. Let $f : R \to R$ be defined as

$$f(x) = \begin{cases} \dfrac{a-b\cos 2x}{x^2}, & x<0 \\ x^2+cx+2, & 0 \le x \le 1 \\ 2x+1, & x>1 \end{cases}$$

If f is continuous everywhere in R and m is the number of points where f is not differential, then $m + a + b + c$ equals **[Single Correct Type, 2024 Main]**

(a) 4 (b) 2 (c) 3 (d) 1

41. Consider the function $f : (0, \infty) \to R$, defined by $f(x) = e^{-|\log_e x|}$. If m and n are respectively, the number of points at which f is not continuous and f is not differentiable, then $m + n$ is **[Single Correct Type, 2024 Main]**

(a) 1 (b) 2 (c) 3 (d) 0

42. Consider the function $f : (0, 2) \to R$ defined by $f(x) = \dfrac{x}{2} + \dfrac{2}{x}$ and the function $g(x)$ defined by

$$g(x) = \begin{cases} \min\{f(t)\}, & 0 < t \le x \text{ and } 0 < x \le 1 \\ \dfrac{3}{2} + x, & 1 < x < 2 \end{cases}$$. Then,

[Single Correct Type, 2024 Main]

(a) g is neither continuous nor differentiable at $x = 1$
(b) g is not continuous for all $x \in (0, 2)$
(c) g is continuous but not differentiable at $x = 1$
(d) g is continuous and differentiable for all $x \in (0, 2)$

43. Let $f : (-\infty, \infty) - \{0\} \to R$ be a differentiable function such that $f'(1) = \lim\limits_{a \to \infty} a^2 f\left(\dfrac{1}{a}\right)$. Then,

$$\lim_{a \to \infty} \frac{a(a+1)}{2} \tan^{-1}\left(\frac{1}{a}\right) + a^2 - 2\log_e a$$

is equal to **[Single Correct Type, 2024 Main]**

(a) $\dfrac{5}{2} + \dfrac{\pi}{8}$ (b) $\dfrac{3}{2} + \dfrac{\pi}{4}$ (c) $\dfrac{3}{4} + \dfrac{\pi}{8}$ (d) $\dfrac{3}{8} + \dfrac{\pi}{4}$

44. Suppose for a differentiable function h, $h(0) = 0$, $h(1) = 1$ and $h'(0) = h'(1) = 2$. If $g(x) = h(e^x)e^{h(x)}$, then $g'(0)$ is equal to **[Single Correct Type, 2024 Main]**

(a) 3 (b) 5 (c) 4 (d) 8

45. Let $f(x) = x^5 + 2x^3 + 3x + 1$, $x \in R$ and $g(x)$ be a function such that $g(f(x)) = x$, for all $x \in R$, then $g(7)/g'(7)$ is equal to **[Single Correct Type, 2024 Main]**

(a) 1 (b) 7 (c) 42 (d) 14

46. Let $f(x) = x^5 + 2e^{x/4}$ for all $x \in R$. Consider a function $g(x)$ such that $(gof)(x) = x$ for all $x \in R$. Then, the value of $8g'(2)$ is **[Single Correct Type, 2024 Main]**

(a) 4 (b) 2 (c) 8 (d) 16

47. If $f(x) = \begin{vmatrix} x^3 & 2x^2+1 & 1+3x \\ 3x^2+2 & 2x & x^3+6 \\ x^3-x & 4 & x^2-2 \end{vmatrix}$ for all $x \in R$, then $2f(0) + f'(0)$ is equal to **[Single Correct Type, 2024 Main]**

(a) 42 (b) 24 (c) 18 (d) 48

48. Let $g(x)$ be a linear function and

$$f(x) = \begin{cases} g(x), & x \le 0 \\ \left(\dfrac{1+x}{2+x}\right)^{\frac{1}{x}}, & x>0 \end{cases}$$, is continuous at $x = 0$.

If $f'(1) = f(-1)$, then the value $g(3)$ is **[Single Correct Type, 2024 Main]**

(a) $\log_e\left(\dfrac{4}{9}\right) - 1$ (b) $\log_e\left(\dfrac{4}{9e^{1/3}}\right)$

(c) $\dfrac{1}{3}\log_e\left(\dfrac{4}{9e^{1/3}}\right)$ (d) $\dfrac{1}{3}\log_e\left(\dfrac{4}{9}\right) + 1$

49. Let $f : R - \{0\} \to R$ be a function satisfying $f\left(\dfrac{x}{y}\right) = \dfrac{f(x)}{f(y)}$ for all x, y, $f(y) = 0$. If $f'(1) = 2024$, then **[Single Correct Type, 2024 Main]**

(a) $xf'(x) + f(x) = 2024$ (b) $xf'(x) - 2023\, f(x) = 0$
(c) $xf'(x) + 2024\, f(x) = 0$ (d) $xf'(x) - 2024\, f(x) = 0$

50. Suppose $f(x)=\dfrac{(2^x+2^{-x})\tan x\sqrt{\tan^{-1}(x^2-x+1)}}{(7x^2+3x+1)^3}$.

Then, the value of $f'(0)$ is equal to

[Single Correct Type, 2024 Main]

(a) 0 (b) $\pi/2$ (c) π (d) $\sqrt{\pi}$

51. If $\log_e y=3\sin^{-1}x$, then $(1-x^2)y''-xy'$ at $x=\dfrac{1}{2}$ is equal to **[Single Correct Type, 2024 Main]**

(a) $3e^{\pi/6}$ (b) $9e^{\pi/6}$ (c) $9e^{\pi/2}$ (d) $3e^{\pi/2}$

52. Let $f(x)=ax^3+bx^2+cx+41$ be such that $f(1)=40$, $f'(1)=2$ and $f''(1)=4$. Then, $a^2+b^2+c^2$ is equal to

[Single Correct Type, 2024 Main]

(a) 73 (b) 54 (c) 62 (d) 51

53. If $f(x)=\begin{cases} x^3\sin\left(\dfrac{1}{x}\right), & x\neq 0\\ 0, & x=0\end{cases}$, then

[Single Correct Type, 2024 Main]

(a) $f''(0)=1$ (b) $f''(0)=0$

(c) $f''\left(\dfrac{2}{\pi}\right)=\dfrac{12-\pi^2}{2\pi}$ (d) $f''\left(\dfrac{2}{\pi}\right)=\dfrac{24-\pi^2}{2\pi}$

54. If $y(\theta)=\dfrac{2\cos\theta+\cos 2\theta}{\cos 3\theta+4\cos 2\theta+5\cos\theta+2}$, then at $\theta=\dfrac{\pi}{2}$, $y''+y'+y$ is equal to **[Single Correct Type, 2024 Main]**

(a) 3/2 (b) 1/2 (c) 1 (d) 2

55. Let $y=\log_e\left(\dfrac{1-x^2}{1+x^2}\right)$, $-1<x<1$. Then, at $x=\dfrac{1}{2}$, the value of $225(y'-y'')$ is equal to

[Single Correct Type, 2024 Main]

(a) 736 (b) 742 (c) 732 (d) 746

56. Let $g:R\to R$ be a non-constant twice differentiable function such that $g'\left(\dfrac{1}{2}\right)=g'\left(\dfrac{3}{2}\right)$. If a real valued function f is defined as $f(x)=\dfrac{1}{2}[g(x)+g(2-x)]$, then

[Single Correct Type, 2024 Main]

(a) $f''(x)=0$ for exactly one x in $(0,1)$

(b) $f''(x)=0$ for atleast two x in $(0,2)$

(c) $f''(x)=0$ for no x in $(0,1)$

(d) $f'\left(\dfrac{3}{2}\right)+f'\left(\dfrac{1}{2}\right)=1$

57. Let $f:(0,\pi)\to R$ be a function given by

$$f(x)=\begin{cases}\left(\dfrac{8}{7}\right)^{\frac{\tan 8x}{\tan 7x}}, & 0<x<\dfrac{\pi}{2}\\ a-8, & x=\dfrac{\pi}{2}\\ (1+|\cot x|)^{\frac{b}{a}|\tan x|}, & \dfrac{\pi}{2}<x<\pi\end{cases}$$

where $a,b\in Z$. If f is continuous at $x=\dfrac{\pi}{2}$, then a^2+b^2 is equal to .... **[Numerical Value Type, 2024 Main]**

58. Let $[t]$ denote the greatest integer less than or equal to t. Let $f:[0,\infty]\to R$ be a function defined by $f(x)=\left[\dfrac{x}{2}+3\right]-[\sqrt{x}]$. Let S be the set of all points in the interval $[0, 8]$ at which f is not continuous. Then, $\sum_{a\in S} a$ is equal to ....

[Numerical Value Type, 2024 Main]

59. The value of

$$\lim_{x\to 0} 2\left(\frac{1-\cos x\sqrt{\cos 2x}\sqrt[3]{\cos 3x}\ldots\sqrt[10]{\cos 10x}}{x^2}\right)$$ is ....

[Numerical Value Type, 2024 Main]

60. If $y=\dfrac{(\sqrt{x}+1)(x^2-\sqrt{x})}{x\sqrt{x}+x+\sqrt{x}}+\dfrac{1}{15}(3\cos^2 x-5)\cos^3 x$, then $96y'(\pi/6)$ is equal to ....

[Numerical Value Type, 2024 Main]

61. Let $f(x)=2^x-x^2$, $x\in R$. If m and n are respectively the number of points at which the curves $y=f(x)$ and $y=f'(x)$ intersect the X-axis, then the value of $m+n$ is .... **[Numerical Value Type, 2024 Main]**

62. Let $f:R\to R$ be a thrice differentiable function such that $f(0)=0$, $f(1)=1$, $f(2)=-1$, $f(3)=2$ and $f(4)=-2$. Then, the minimum number of zeroes of $(3f'f''+ff''')(x)$ is .... **[Numerical Value Type, 2024 Main]**

63. Let $f(x)=x^3+x^2f'(1)+xf''(2)+f'''(3)$, $x\in R$. Then, $f'(10)$ is equal to .... **[Numerical Value Type, 2024 Main]**

64. Let $f(x)=[x^2-x]+|-x+[x]|$, where $x\in R$ and $[t]$ denotes the greatest integer less than or equal to t. Then, f is **[Single Correct Type, 2023 Main]**

(a) continuous at $x=0$ and $x=1$

(b) continuous at $x=1$, but not continuous at $x=0$

(c) not continuous at $x=0$ and $x=1$

(d) continuous at $x=0$, but not continuous at $x=1$

65. If the function $f(x)=\begin{cases}(1+|\cos x|)^{\frac{\lambda}{|\cos x|}}, & 0<x<\dfrac{\pi}{2}\\ \mu, & x=\dfrac{\pi}{2}\\ e^{\frac{\cot 6x}{\cot 4x}}, & \dfrac{\pi}{2}<x<\pi\end{cases}$

is continuous at $x=\dfrac{\pi}{2}$, then $9\lambda+6\log_e\mu+\mu^6-e^{6\lambda}$ is equal to **[Single Correct Type, 2023 Main]**

(a) 10 (b) $2e^4+8$

(c) 8 (d) 11

66. Let $[x]$ denote the greatest integer function and $f(x)=\max\{1+x+[x], 2+x, x+2[x]\}, 0\le x\le 2$. Let m be the number of points in $[0, 2]$, where f is not continuous and n be the number of points in $(0, 2)$, where f is not differentiable. Then, $(m+n)^2+2$ is equal to

[Single Correct Type, 2023 Main]

(a) 6 (b) 3
(c) 11 (d) 2

67. For the differentiable function $f: R-\{0\}\to R$, let $3f(x)+2f\left(\frac{1}{x}\right)=\frac{1}{x}-10$, then $\left|f(3)+f'\left(\frac{1}{4}\right)\right|$ is equal to

[Single Correct Type, 2023 Main]

(a) $\frac{33}{5}$ (b) $\frac{29}{5}$
(c) 7 (d) 13

68. Let f and g be two functions defined by

$$f(x)=\begin{cases} x+1, & x<0 \\ |x-1|, & x\ge 0\end{cases} \text{ and } g(x)=\begin{cases} x+1, & x<0 \\ 1, & x\ge 0\end{cases}$$

Then, $(gof)(x)$ is **[Single Correct Type, 2023 Main]**

(a) continuous everywhere but not differentiable exactly at one point
(b) continuous everywhere but not differentiable at $x=1$
(c) differentiable everywhere
(d) not continuous at $x=-1$

69. Let $f(x)=\begin{cases} x^2\sin\left(\frac{1}{x}\right), & x\ne 0 \\ 0, & x=0\end{cases}$

Then, at $x=0$ **[Single Correct Type, 2023 Main]**

(a) f and f' both are continuous
(b) f is continuous but f' is not continuous
(c) f is continuous but not differentiable
(d) f' is continuous but not differentiable

70. Let $y=f(x)=\sin^3\left(\frac{\pi}{3}\left(\cos\left(\frac{\pi}{3\sqrt{2}}(-4x^3+5x^2+1)^{\frac{3}{2}}\right)\right)\right)$.

Then, at $x=1$ **[Single Correct Type, 2023 Main]**

(a) $2y'+3\pi^2y=0$ (b) $2y'+\sqrt{3}\pi^2y=0$
(c) $y'+3\pi^2y=0$ (d) $\sqrt{2}y'-3\pi^2y=0$

71. Let $f(\theta)=3\left(\sin^4\left(\frac{3\pi}{2}-\theta\right)+\sin^4(3\pi+\theta)\right)$ $-2(1-\sin^2 2\theta)$ and $S=\left\{\theta\in[0,\pi]: f'(\theta)=-\frac{\sqrt{3}}{2}\right\}$.

If $4\beta=\sum_{\theta\in S}\theta$, then $f(\beta)$ is equal to

[Single Correct Type, 2023 Main]

(a) 5/4 (b) 3/2
(c) 11/8 (d) 9/8

72. Let $f(x)=\frac{\sin x+\cos x-\sqrt{2}}{\sin x-\cos x}, x\in[0,\pi]-\left\{\frac{\pi}{4}\right\}$.

Then, $f\left(\frac{7\pi}{12}\right)\cdot f''\left(\frac{7\pi}{12}\right)$ is equal to

[Single Correct Type, 2023 Main]

(a) $\frac{2}{9}$ (b) $\frac{-1}{3\sqrt{3}}$ (c) $\frac{-2}{3}$ (d) $\frac{2}{3\sqrt{3}}$

73. If $y(x)=x^x, x>0$, then $y''(2)-2y'(2)$ is equal to

[Single Correct Type, 2023 Main]

(a) $4(\log_e 2)^2-2$ (b) $4\log_e 2+2$
(c) $8\log_e 2-2$ (d) $4(\log_e 2)^2+2$

74. Let f and g be twice differentiable functions on R such that $f''(x)=g''(x)+6x; f'(1)=4g'(1)-3=9$

$f(2)=3g(2)=12$.

Then, which of the following is not true?

[Single Correct Type, 2023 Main]

(a) There exists $x_0\in\left(1,\frac{3}{2}\right)$ such that $f(x_0)=g(x_0)$
(b) $g(-2)-f(-2)=20$
(c) If $-1<x<2$, then $|f(x)-g(x)|<8$
(d) $|f'(x)-g'(x)|<6 \Rightarrow -1<x<1$

75. Let $y(x)=(1+x)(1+x^2)(1+x^4)(1+x^8)(1+x^{16})$. Then, $y'-y''$ at $x=-1$ is equal to

[Single Correct Type, 2023 Main]

(a) 496 (b) 464 (c) 976 (d) 944

76. Let $[x]$ be the greatest integer $\le x$. Then, the number of points in the interval $(-2, 1)$, where the function $f(x)=|[x]|+\sqrt{x-[x]}$ is discontinuous, is ....

[Numerical Value Type, 2023 Main]

77. Let k and m be positive real numbers such that the function $f(x)=\begin{cases} 3x^2+k\sqrt{x+1}, & 0<x<1 \\ mx^2+k^2, & x\ge 1\end{cases}$ is differentiable for all $x>0$. Then, $\frac{8f'(8)}{f'(1/8)}$ is equal to ....

[Numerical Value Type, 2023 Main]

78. Let $f:(-2,2)\to R$ be defined by

$$f(x)=\begin{cases} x[x], & -2<x<0 \\ (x-1)[x], & 0\le x<2\end{cases}$$

where $[x]$ denotes the greatest integer function. If m and n respectively are the number of points in $(-2, 2)$ at which $y=|f(x)|$ is not continuous and not differentiable, then $m+n$ is equal to ......

[Numerical Value Type, 2023 Main]

79. Let $a\in Z$ and $[t]$ be the greatest integer $\le t$. Then, the number of points, where the function $f(x)=[a+13\sin x], x\in(0,\pi)$ is not differentiable, is ....

[Numerical Value Type, 2023 Main]

80. Let $f(x) = \sum_{k=1}^{10} kx^k, x \in R$. If $2f(2) + f'(2) = 119(2)^n + 1$, then n is equal to ....

[Numerical Value Type, 2023 Main]

81. Let the function

$$f(x) = \begin{cases} \dfrac{\log_e(1+5x) - \log_e(1+\alpha x)}{x}; & \text{if } x \neq 0 \\ 10 & ; \text{if } x = 0 \end{cases}$$

be continuous at $x = 0$. Then, α is equal to

[Single Correct Type, 2022 Main]

(a) 10 (b) – 10 (c) 5 (d) –5

82. The function $f : R \to R$ defined by

$f(x) = \lim_{n \to \infty} \dfrac{\cos(2\pi x) - x^{2n} \sin(x-1)}{1 + x^{2n+1} - x^{2n}}$ is continuous for all x in **[Single Correct Type, 2022 Main]**

(a) $R - \{-1\}$ (b) $R - \{-1, 1\}$ (c) $R - \{1\}$ (d) $R - \{0\}$

83. If for $p \neq q \neq 0$, then function $f(x) = \dfrac{\sqrt[7]{p(729 + x)} - 3}{\sqrt[3]{(729 + qx)} - 9}$ is continuous at $x = 0$, then **[Single Correct Type, 2022 Main]**

(a) $7pqf(0) - 1 = 0$ (b) $63qf(0) - p^2 = 0$
(c) $21qf(0) - p^2 = 0$ (d) $7pqf(0) - 9 = 0$

84. If $f(x) = \begin{cases} x + a, & x \leq 0 \\ |x - 4|, & x > 0 \end{cases}$ and

$$g(x) = \begin{cases} x + 1, & x < 0 \\ (x-4)^2 + b, & x \geq 0 \end{cases}$$

are continuous on R, then $(gof)(2) + (fog)(-2)$ is equal to **[Single Correct Type, 2022 Main]**

(a) – 10 (b) 10 (c) 8 (d) – 8

85. Let $f, g : R \to R$ be functions defined by

$$f(x) = \begin{cases} [x], & x < 0 \\ |1 - x|, & x \geq 0 \end{cases} \text{ and } g(x) = \begin{cases} e^x - x, & x < 0 \\ (x-1)^2 - 1, & x \geq 0 \end{cases}$$

where, $[x]$ denotes the greatest integer less than or equal to x. Then, the function fog is discontinuous at exactly.

[Single Correct Type, 2022 Main]

(a) one point (b) two points
(c) three points (d) four points

86. Let $f : R \to R$ be defined as

$$f(x) = \begin{cases} [e^x], & x < 0 \\ ae^x + [x - 1], & 0 \leq x < 1 \\ b + [\sin(\pi x)], & 1 \leq x < 2 \\ [e^{-x}] - c, & x \geq 2 \end{cases}$$

where $a, b, c \in R$ and $[t]$ denotes greatest integer less than or equal to t. Then, which of the following statement is true? **[Single Correct Type, 2022 Main]**

(a) There exists $a, b, c \in R$ such that f is continuous of R
(b) If f is discontinuous at exactly one point, then $a + b + c = 1$
(c) If f is discontinuous at exactly one point, then $a + b + c = 2$
(d) f is discontinuous at atleast two points, for any values of a, b and c

87. The number of points, where the function $f : R \to R$,
$f(x) = |x - 1| \cos|x - 2| \sin|x - 1| + (x - 3)|x^2 - 5x + 4|$, is not differentiable, is

[Single Correct Type, 2022 Main]

(a) 1 (b) 2 (c) 3 (d) 4

88. Let $f(x) = \min\{1, 1 + x\sin x\}, 0 \leq x \leq 2\pi$. If m is the number of points, where f is not differentiable and n is the number of points, where f is not continuous, then the ordered pair (m, n) is equal to

[Single Correct Type, 2022 Main]

(a) (2, 0) (b) (1, 0)
(c) (1, 1) (d) (2, 1)

89. Let $\dfrac{dy}{dx} = \dfrac{ax - by + a}{bx + cy + a}$, where a, b, c are constants represent a circle passing through the point (2, 5). Then, the shortest distance of the point (11, 6) from this circle is **[Single Correct Type, 2022 Main]**

(a) 10 (b) 8 (c) 7 (d) 5

90. If $\cos^{-1}\left(\dfrac{y}{2}\right) = \log_e\left(\dfrac{x}{5}\right)^5, |y| < 2$, then

[Single Correct Type, 2022 Main]

(a) $x^2y'' + xy' - 25y = 0$ (b) $x^2y'' - xy' - 25y = 0$
(c) $x^2y'' - xy' + 25y = 0$ (d) $x^2y'' + xy' + 25y = 0$

91. If $y = \tan^{-1}(\sec x^3 - \tan x^3) \cdot \dfrac{\pi}{2} < x^3 < \dfrac{3\pi}{2}$, then

[Single Correct Type, 2022 Main]

(a) $xy'' + 2y' = 0$ (b) $x^2y'' - 6y + \dfrac{3\pi}{2} = 0$
(c) $x^2y'' - 6y + \pi = 0$ (d) $xy'' - 4' = 0$

92. Let $f(x) = [2x^2 + 1]$ and $g(x) = \begin{cases} 2x - 3, & x < 0 \\ 2x + 3, & x \geq 0 \end{cases}$, where $[t]$ is the greatest integer $\leq t$. Then, in the open interval $(-1, 1)$, the number of points where fog is discontinuous is equal to ....

[Numerical Value Type, 2022 Main]

93. The number of points where the function

$$f(x) = \begin{cases} |2x^2 - 3x - 7| & \text{if } x \leq -1 \\ [4x^2 - 1] & \text{if } -1 < x < 1 \\ |x + 1||x - 2| & \text{if } x \geq 1 \end{cases}$$

$[t]$ denotes the greatest integer $\leq t$, is discontinuous is ....

[Numerical Value Type, 2022 Main]

94. Let $f: R \to R$ satisfy the equation $f(x+y) = f(x) \cdot f(y)$ for all $x, y \in R$ and $f(x) \neq 0$ for any $x \in R$. If the function f is differentiable at $x = 0$ and $f'(0) = 3$, then $\lim_{h \to 0} \frac{1}{h}(f(h) - 1)$ is equal to ...... **[Numerical Value Type, 2022 Main]**

95. Let $f: \left(-\frac{\pi}{4}, \frac{\pi}{4}\right) \to R$ be defined as

$$f(x) = \begin{cases} (1 + |\sin x|)^{\frac{3a}{|\sin x|}}, & \frac{-\pi}{4} < x < 0 \\ b, & x = 0 \\ e^{\frac{\cot 4x}{\cot 2x}}, & 0 < x < \frac{\pi}{4} \end{cases}$$

If f is continuous at $x = 0$, then the value of $6a + b^2$ is equal to **[Single Correct Type, 2021 Main]**

(a) $1 - e$ (b) $e - 1$ (c) $1 + e$ (d) e

96. Let $f: R \to R$ be defined as

$$f(x) = \begin{cases} \frac{\lambda |x^2 - 5x + 6|}{\mu(5x - x^2 - 6)}, & x < 2 \\ e^{\frac{\tan(x-2)}{x - [x]}}, & x > 2 \\ \mu, & x = 2 \end{cases}$$

where, $[x]$ is the greatest integer less than or equal to x. If f is continuous at $x = 2$, then $\lambda + \mu$ is equal to **[Single Correct Type, 2021 Main]**

(a) $e(-e + 1)$ (b) $e(e - 2)$ (c) 1 (d) $2e - 1$

97. The function $f(x) = |x^2 - 2x - 3| \cdot e^{|9x^2 - 12x + 4|}$ is not differentiable at exactly **[Single Correct Type, 2021 Main]**

(a) four points (b) three points
(c) two points (d) one point

98. If $y(x) = \cot^{-1}\left(\frac{\sqrt{1 + \sin x} + \sqrt{1 - \sin x}}{\sqrt{1 + \sin x} - \sqrt{1 - \sin x}}\right), x \in \left(\frac{\pi}{2}, \pi\right)$, then $\frac{dy}{dx}$ at $x = \frac{5\pi}{6}$ is **[Single Correct Type, 2021 Main]**

(a) $-\frac{1}{2}$ (b) -1
(c) $\frac{1}{2}$ (d) 0

99. Let $f(x)$ be a differentiable function at $x = a$ with $f'(a) = 2$ and $f(a) = 4$. Then, $\lim_{x \to a} \frac{xf(a) - af(x)}{x - a}$ equals **[Single Correct Type, 2021 Main]**

(a) $4 - 2a$ (b) $a + 4$ (c) $2a - 4$ (d) $2a + 4$

100. Let $[t]$ denotes the greatest integer $\leq t$. The number of points where the function

$f(x) = [x]|x^2 - 1| + \sin\left(\frac{\pi}{[x] + 3}\right) - [x + 1], x \in (-2, 2)$ is not continuous is .... **[Numerical Value Type, 2021 Main]**

101. If $y = y(x)$ is an implicit function of x such that $\log_e(x + y) = 4xy$, then $\frac{d^2y}{dx^2}$ at $x = 0$ is equal to .... **[Numerical Value Type, 2021 Main]**

EXERCISE 2

— JEE Advanced Pattern

Single Option Correct Type Questions

1. If $y^2 = P(x)$ is a polynomial of degree 3. Then, $2\frac{d}{dx}\left[y^3 \frac{d^2y}{dx^2}\right]$ is equal to

(a) $P(x) + P''(x)$ (b) $P(x) + P'''(x)$
(c) $P(x)\, P'''(x)$ (d) None of these

2. If $e^x = \frac{\sqrt{1+t} - \sqrt{1-t}}{\sqrt{1+t} + \sqrt{1-t}}$ and $\tan\frac{y}{2} = \sqrt{\frac{1-t}{1+t}}$, then $\frac{dy}{dx}$ at $t = \frac{1}{2}$ is

(a) $-\frac{1}{2}$ (b) $\frac{1}{2}$ (c) 0 (d) None of these

3. For $x > 1$, if $(2x)^{2y} = 4e^{2x - 2y}$, then $(1 + \log_e 2x)^2 \frac{dy}{dx}$ is equal to

(a) $\log_e 2x$ (b) $\frac{x \log_e 2x + \log_e 2}{x}$
(c) $x \log_e 2x$ (d) $\frac{x \log_e 2x - \log_e 2}{x}$

4. Consider the function $f: R \to R$ defined by

$$f(x) = \begin{cases} \left(2 - \sin\left(\frac{1}{x}\right)\right)|x|, & x \neq 0 \\ 0, & x = 0 \end{cases}$$

Then, f is

(a) monotonic on $(-\infty, 0) \cup (0, \infty)$
(b) non-monotonic on $(-\infty, 0)$ and $(0, \infty)$
(c) monotonic on $(0, \infty)$ only
(d) monotonic on $(-\infty, 0)$ only

5. Let $f(x)$ be a polynomial of degree 4 with $f(2)=-1$, $f'(2)=0$, $f''(2)=2$, $f'''(2)=-12$, $f''''(2)=24$, then the value of $f''(1)$ is
(a) 24 (b) 26 (c) 28 (d) 30

More than One Correct Option Type Questions

6. Let $f: R \to R$ be a thrice differentiable function such that $f(x), f'(x), f''(x)$ and $f'''(x)$ are positive, $\forall x \in R$. Moreover, $f'''(x) < f(x), \forall x \in R$, then
(a) $f'(x) < 2f(x), \forall x \in R$ (b) $f'(x) < \left(\frac{3}{2}\right)^{\frac{1}{3}} f(x), \forall x \in R$
(c) $f'(x) < \frac{5}{2} f(x), \forall x \in R$ (d) $f'(x) < 3f(x), \forall x \in R$

7. Let $f(x)$ be a differentiable function for $x > -1$ and $f(0) = 1$, $f'(0) > 0$. Also, $f'(x)(1+f(x)) = 1+x$. If $f'(2) = \frac{3}{\sqrt{m}}$ and $f'(3) = \frac{4}{\sqrt{n}}$, then which of the following statement(s) is/are true?
(a) $m+n=31$ (b) $|m-2n|=26$
(c) $3m-n=2$ (d) $m=n$

8. If $f(\theta) = \tan\left(\sin^{-1}\sqrt{\frac{2}{3+\cos 2\theta}}\right)$, then
(a) $f'\left(\frac{\pi}{4}\right) = \sqrt{2}$ (b) $f\left(\frac{\pi}{4}\right) = \sqrt{2}$
(c) $\frac{d(f(\theta))}{d(\cos\theta)}$ at $\theta = \frac{\pi}{4}$ is $-\sqrt{2}$ (d) $\frac{d(f(\theta))}{d(\cos\theta)}$ at $\theta = \frac{\pi}{4}$ is -2

9. If $f(x) = \int \frac{x}{2}\, d\left(\frac{x^2-1}{x^2}\right)$ and $f(2) = \frac{1}{2}$ and $g_r(x) = \underbrace{f[f\{f(\ldots f(x)\ldots)\}]}_{r\text{-times}}$ i.e. $g_1(x) = f(x)$, $g_2(x) = f[f(x)]$ and so on, then identify the correct statement(s).
(a) $\frac{d}{dx}(g_{(3n-2)}(x)) = 1$ whenever exists $n \in N$
(b) $\frac{d}{dx}(g_{3n}(x)) = 1$ whenever exists $n \in N$
(c) $\lim\limits_{x\to 1} \frac{\sum_{r=1}^{100} (g_{3r}(x))^r + x - 101}{x-1} = 5050$
(d) Slope of the tangent to the graph of the function $y = g_{80}(x)$ at $x = \frac{1}{2}$ is 4

10. Let $P(x)$ be the polynomial $x^3 + ax^2 + bx + c$, where $a, b, c \in R$. If $P(-3) = P(+2) = 0$ and $P'(-3) < 0$. Which of the following is a possible value of c?
(a) −27 (b) −19 (c) −6 (d) −3

11. For the function $y = f(x) = (x^2 + bx + c)e^x$, which of the following holds?
(a) if $f(x) > 0, \forall x \not\Rightarrow f'(x) > 0$
(b) if $f(x) > 0, \forall x \Rightarrow f'(x) > 0$
(c) if $f'(x) > 0, \forall x \Rightarrow f(x) > 0$
(d) if $f'(x) > 0, \forall x \not\Rightarrow f(x) > 0$

12. Which of the following statements are true?
(a) If $xe^{xy} = y + \sin^2 x$, then at $x = 0$, $\left(\frac{dy}{dx}\right) = 1$.
(b) If $f(x) \equiv a_0 x^{2m+1} + a_1 x^{2m} + a_2 x^{2m-1} + \ldots + a_{3n+1} = 0$ $(a \neq 0)$ is a polynomial equation with rational coefficient, then the equation $f'(x) = 0$ must have a real root $(m \in N)$.
(c) If $(x-r)$ is a factor of the polynomial $f(x) = a_n x^n + a_{n-1}x^{n-1} + a_{n-2}x^{n-2} + \ldots + a_0$ repeated m times, where $1 \le m \le n$, then r is a root of the equation $f'(x) = 0$ repeated $(m-1)$ times.
(d) If $y = \sin^{-1}(\cos \sin^{-1} x) + \cos^{-1}(\sin \cos^{-1} x)$, then $\frac{dy}{dx}$ is dependent on x.

13. If $f_n(x) = e^{f_{n-1}(x)}, \forall n \in N$ and $f_0(x) = x$, then $\frac{d}{dx} f_n(x)$ is equal to
(a) $f_n(x) \frac{d}{dx}(f_{n-1}(x))$
(b) $f_n(x)\, f_{n-1}(x)$
(c) $f_n(x)\, f_{n-1}(x) \ldots f_2(x)\, f_1(x)$
(d) None of the above

14. Let $y = \sqrt{(\sin x + \sin 2x + \sin 3x)^2 + (\cos x + \cos 2x + \cos 3x)^2}$
Then, which of the following is correct?
(a) $\frac{dy}{dx}$ when $x = \frac{\pi}{2}$ is -2
(b) Value of y when $x = \frac{\pi}{5}$ is $\frac{3+\sqrt{5}}{2}$
(c) Value of y when $x = \frac{\pi}{12}$ is $\frac{\sqrt{1}+\sqrt{2}+\sqrt{3}}{2}$
(d) y simplifies to $(1 + 2\cos x)$ in $[0, \pi]$

Paragraph Based Questions

Passage I

(Q. Nos. 15 to 16)

- Consider f and g be two real-valued differentiable functions on R (the set of all real numbers).
Let $f(x) = x^2 + g'(0)\, x + g''(3)$ and
$g(y) = f(-2)\, y^2 + yf''(y) + f'(y) - 2$

15. $f(1)$ is equal to
(a) 0 (b) 5 (c) 13 (d) 1

16. If $f(\alpha)\, g(\beta) \le 4$, where $\alpha, \beta \in [-3, 3]$, then the number of non-positive ordered pairs (α, β) is equal to
(a) 0 (b) 1 (c) 2 (d) more than two

Stem Based Questions

Stem I

(Q. Nos. 17 and 18)

- Let $f: R \to R$ be a differentiable function such that $f(1) = 1$, $f(2) = 20$, $f(-4) = -4$, $f'(0) = 0$ and $f(x + y) = f(x) + f(y) + axy(x + y) + bxy + c(x + y) + 4$, $\forall\, x, y \in R$, where a, b, c are constants.

17. The value of $(b + c)$ is equal to ....

18. Number of solutions of th equation $f(x) = x^3 + 4e^x$ is equal to ....

Stem II

(Q. Nos. 19 and 20)

- Consider a function $y = f(x)$. Let the functional rule for $y = f(x)$ is same as the functional rule for the height h (dependent variable) of a ΔABC from the vertex A to the base BC (where $\angle A$ is independent variable). The ΔABC is inscribed in a circle of radius 6 and the area of the ΔABC is 12.

19. The least value of $f(x)$ is equal to ....

20. If $g(x) = f(\sin^{-1} x)$, then $\left| g'\left(\frac{4}{5}\right) \times 8 \right|$ is equal to ....

Single Integer Type Questions

21. $y = f(x)$, where f satisfies the relation $f(x + y) = 2f(x) + xf(y) + y\sqrt{f(x)}$, $\forall\, x, y \in R$ and $f'(0) = 0$, then $f(6)$ is equal to ....

22. If the function $f(x) = -4e^{\frac{1-x}{2}} + 1 + x + \frac{x^2}{2} + \frac{x^3}{3}$ and $g(x) = f^{-1}(x)$, then the reciprocal of $g'\left(\frac{-7}{6}\right)$ is ....

23. Let $g(x) = \begin{cases} \dfrac{x^2 + x \tan x - x \tan 2x}{ax + \tan x - \tan 3x}, & x \neq 0 \\ 0, & x = 0 \end{cases}$. If $g'(0)$ exists and is equal to non-zero value b, then $52\frac{b}{a}$ is equal to ......

24. Let the equation $(a - 1)\,x^2 = x(2b + 3)$ be satisfied by three distinct values of x, where $a, b \in R$. If $f(x) = (a - 1)\,x^3 + (2b + 3)\,x^2 + 2x + 1$ and $f\,[g(x)] = 6x - 7$, where $g(x)$ is a linear function, then the value of $g'(2012)$ is equal to ....

25. Let $f(x) = 2\tan^{-1} x$ and $g(x)$ be a differentiable function satisfying $g\left(\frac{x + 2y}{3}\right) = \frac{g(x) + 2g(y)}{3}$, $\forall\, x, y \in R$ and $g'(0) = 1$, $g(0) = 2$. The number of integers satisfying $f^2(g(x)) - 5f(g(x)) + 4 > 0$, where $x \in (-10, 10)$ is equal to ....

26. Let $f(x)$ and $g(x)$ be twice differentiable functions satisfying $f(x) = xg(x)$ and $g'(x) = f(x)$, where $g(x) \neq 0$, $\forall\, x \in R$. If $f'(x) = g(x) \cdot h(x)$, then the number of roots of the equation $h(x) = e^x$ is ....

27. Let f be a function defined implicitly by the equation $\frac{1 - e^{f(x)}}{1 + e^{f(x)}} = x$ and g be the inverse of f.

If $g''(\ln 3) - g'(\ln 3) = \frac{p}{q}$, where p and q relative prime numbers, then the value of $\sqrt{(p + q)}$ is ....

Numerical Value Type Questions

28. If $y = x^5[\cos(\ln x) + \sin(\ln x)]$, then the value of $(a + b)$ in the relation $x^2 y_2 + axy_1 + by = 0$ is equal to ....

29. If $f(x) = \ln(1 + x^2) + \tan^{-1} x$, $x > 0$ and $g(x) = f^{-1}(x)$, then the value of $\left| \frac{81 g''\left(\ln 2e^{\frac{\pi}{4}}\right)}{20} \right|$, where $g''(x)$ denotes second derivative of $g(x)$ is equal to ....

30. For the curve $\sin x + \sin y = 1$ lying on the first quadrant, if $\lim\limits_{x \to 0} x^\alpha \cdot \frac{d^2y}{dx^2}$ exists and has the non-zero value equal to L, then the value of $\left(\frac{\alpha}{L}\right)^2$ is ....

31. Let $f(x) = \tan[\sin\{\cos^{-1}(\sin(\cos^{-1}(x))\} + \cos\{\sin^{-1}(\cos(\sin^{-1} x))\}]$, $x \in (0, 1)$ and $g(x) = \tan x$, $x \in \left(0, \frac{\pi}{2}\right)$, then the value of $\frac{d(f(x))}{d(g(x))}$ at $x = \frac{\pi}{6}$ is 100λ, then λ is ....

32. Let $g(x)$ is the only invertible function from $R \to R$ which satisfy the equation $g^3(x) - (x^3 + 2)\,g^2(x) + (2x^3 + 1)\,g(x) - x^3 = 0$, then the value of $g'(8) \cdot (g^{-1})'(8)$ is equal to ....

33. If $\frac{dy}{dx}$ at $x = -1$, when $(\sin y)^{\sin\left(\frac{\pi}{2} x\right)} + \frac{\sqrt{3}}{2}\sec^{-1}(2x) + 2^x \tan(\log(x + 2)) = 0$ is $\lambda - 5$, then the number of diagonal in polygon having 20λ number of vertices is ....

34. If $x = \tan\frac{y}{2} - \ln\left[\frac{\left(1+\tan\frac{y}{2}\right)^2}{\tan\frac{y}{2}}\right]$ and $\frac{dy}{dx} = \frac{1}{\lambda}\sin y\,(\mu + \sin y + \cos y)$, then $\frac{50\lambda}{4\mu}$ is equal to ....

35. If a curve is represented parametrically by the equations $x = \sin\left(t + \frac{7\pi}{12}\right) + \sin\left(t - \frac{\pi}{12}\right) + \sin\left(t + \frac{3\pi}{12}\right)$, $y = \cos\left(t + \frac{7\pi}{12}\right) + \cos\left(t - \frac{\pi}{12}\right) + \cos\left(t + \frac{3\pi}{12}\right)$, then the value of $\frac{d}{dt}\left(\frac{x}{y} - \frac{y}{x}\right)$ at $t = \frac{\pi}{8}$ is μ, then 11μ is ....

36. Let $f : R \to R$ be a function defined by $f(x) = x^3 - 3x^2 - 9x + 27$. If $x \in (a, b) \cup (c, d)$, then $f^3(x) - 3f^2(x) - 9f(x) + 27 < f(x^3 - 4x^2 - 3x + 19)$. Then, $(b - a) + (c + d)$ is ....

37. Let $f(x)$ be a non-constant thrice differential function defined on $(-\infty, \infty)$ such that $f\left(\frac{x+13}{2}\right) = f\left(\frac{3-x}{2}\right)$ and $f'(0) = f'\left(\frac{1}{2}\right) = f'(2) = f'(3) = f'\left(\frac{9}{2}\right) = 0$, then the minimum number of zeroes of $h(x) = (f''(x))^2 + f'(x)\,f'''(x)$ in the interval $[0, 9]$ is $2k$, then k^2 is equal to ....

38. Let $f(x)$ be a differentiable function $f'(0) = 2$ and $f(0) = 3$ such that $f'(x) = \frac{f(x+n) - f(x)}{n}$, $\forall\, x \in R$ and $n \in N$, then $10 \cdot \frac{f(5)}{f(1)}$ is equal to ....

39. If the function $f(x) = \sin(x - 1) + \left[\frac{x}{2}\right] + x^3 + 4x$ and $g(x) = f^{-1}(x)$, then the value of $\left(\frac{1}{g'(5)}\right)^2$ equals ....
(where [.] represents the greatest integer function)

Matching Type Questions

40. Match the following column.

	Column I		Column II
(A)	Suppose that the function $F(x)$ and $G(x)$ satisfy the following properties $F(3) = 2$, $G(3) = 4$, $G(0) = 3$, $F'(3) = -1$, $G'(3) = 0$; $G'(0) = 2$. If $T(x) = F(G(x))$ and $U(x) = \ln(F(x))$, then $T'(0) + 6U'(3)$ has the value equal to	(p)	-1
(B)	$\lim_{x \to -\infty} (x + \sqrt{x^2 + 2x})$	(q)	$3\sqrt{2}$
(C)	If $y = t^2$ at $x = t + t^2$, then $\frac{d^2y}{dx^2}$ at $t = -1$ is	(r)	-2
(D)	If $f(x) = x + x^n$, a value of n for which $f(x)$ is invertible for all $x \in R$, is	(s)	3
		(t)	-5

41. Match the following column.

	Column I		Column II
(A)	If $\lvert g(x) - g(y)\rvert \le \lvert x - y\rvert^{99}$, $(n \in N)$, then $g'(x)$ equals	(p)	-2
(B)	Differential coefficient of $\sin^{-1}\frac{2x}{1+x^2}$ with respect to $\cos^{-1}\frac{1-x^2}{1+x^2}$ in the domain of $f(x) = \frac{1}{\sqrt{1-x^2}}$ is	(q)	-1
(C)	If $y = \cot^{-1}(\tan x) + \tan^{-1}(\cot x)$, $\pi/2 < x < \pi$, then dy/dx equals	(r)	0
(D)	If $y = y(x)$ and it follows the relation $4xe^{xy} = y + 5\sin^2 x$, then $y'(0)$ is equal to	(s)	1
		(t)	4

42. Find $\frac{dy}{dx}$.

	Column I		Column II
(A)	$\sin^{-1}(2x\sqrt{1-x^2})$, $\left(x < -\frac{1}{\sqrt{2}}\right)$	(p)	0
(B)	$2\sin^{-1}(\sqrt{1-x} + \sin^{-1}(2\sqrt{x(1-x)})$, $\left(0 < x < \frac{1}{2}\right)$	(q)	$-\frac{2}{1+x^2}$
(C)	$\sin^{-1}(3x - 4x^3)$, $0 < x < \frac{1}{2}$	(r)	$\frac{3}{\sqrt{1-x^2}}$
(D)	$\cos^{-1}\frac{2x}{1+x^2}$ for $\lvert x\rvert > 1$	(s)	$-\frac{2}{\sqrt{1-x^2}}$

43. Three functions, f_1, f_2 and f_3 are given as

$$f_1(x) = \sin^{-1}\left(\frac{1-x^2}{1+x^2}\right),$$

$$f_2(x) = x - \cos^{-1}\left(\frac{2x}{1+x^2}\right)$$

and $$f_3(x) = 4\left\{\frac{\tan^{-1} x}{2}\right\} - \{x\}.$$

[**Note** $\{k\}$ denotes fractional part function of k.]

	Column I		Column II
(A)	The differential coefficient of $f_1(x)$ with respect to $f_2(x)$ at $x = \tan 1$, is	(p)	-1
(B)	$\left.\frac{d[f_3(x)]}{d[f_2(x)]}\right\vert_{x=\tan 1}$ is equal to	(q)	2
(C)	$\frac{d}{dx}\left(\int (f_2(x) - f_1(x)\, dx)\right)\vert_{x=\tan 1}$ is equal to	(r)	$1 + \sec 2$
(D)	The slope of the normal to the curve $y = f_3(x)$ at $x = \sqrt{3}$ is	(s)	$\tan 1$

44. Match the following.

	Column I		Column II
(A)	$y = \sin^{-1}\left(\frac{2x}{1+x^2}\right)$, then $\frac{dy}{dx} = -\frac{2}{1+x^2}$	(p)	for $x < 0$
(B)	$y = \cos^{-1}\left(\frac{1}{\sqrt{1+x^2}}\right)$, then $\frac{dy}{dx} = -\frac{1}{1+x^2}$	(q)	for $x > 1$
(C)	$y = \vert e^{\vert x\vert} - e\vert$, then $\frac{dy}{dx} > 0$	(r)	for $x < -1$
(D)	$u = \log\vert 2x\vert$, $v = \vert\tan^{-1} x\vert$, then $\frac{du}{dv} > 2$	(s)	for $-1 < x < 0$

Previous Years Questions

45. Let $f: R \to R$, $g: R \to R$ and $h: R \to R$ be differentiable functions such that $f(x) = x^3 + 3x + 2$, $g(f(x)) = x$ and $h(g(g(x))) = x$, for all $x \in R$. Then,

(a) $g'(2) = \frac{1}{15}$ (b) $h'(1) = 666$

(c) $h(0) = 16$ (d) $h(g(3)) = 36$

EXERCISE 3

Challenging Problems

1. If $x = \frac{1 + \ln t}{t^2}$ and $y = \frac{3 + 2\ln t}{t}$, show that

$$y\frac{dy}{dx} = 2x\left(\frac{dy}{dx}\right)^2 + 1.$$

2. (i) If $y = y(x)$ and it follows the relation $e^{xy} + y\cos x = 2$, then find (a) $y'(0)$ and (b) $y''(0)$.

(ii) A twice differentiable function $f(x)$ is defined for all real numbers and satisfies the following equations. $f(0) = -2$, $f'(0) = -5$ and $f''(0) = 3$

The function $g(x)$ is defined by $g(x) = e^{ax} + f(x)$, $\forall x \in R$, where a is any constant. If $g'(0) + g''(0) = 0$. Find the value(s) of a.

3. Find a polynomial function $f(x)$ such that $f(2x) = f'(x) f''(x)$.

4. Given, $F(x) = f(x)\cdot\phi(x)$ and $f'(x)\cdot f'(x)\cdot f'(x) = c$, then prove that $\frac{F'''}{F} = \frac{f'''}{f} + \frac{\phi'''}{\phi}$, where $c \in$ constant, when $f(x), \phi(x), F(x)$ are differentiable.

5. Let $f(x) = e^{-1/x^2}\sin(1/x)$, when $x \neq 0$ and $f(0) = 0$. Show that at every point f has a differential coefficient and this is continuous at $x = 0$. The differential coefficients vanishes at $x = 0$ and at infinite number of points in the neighbourhood of $x = 0$. Show that the function f' like f makes an infinite number of oscillations.

6. If $x_1, x_1, x_2, x_3, \ldots, x_{n-1}$ be n zeros of the polynomial $P(x) = x^n + \alpha x + \beta$, where $x_i \neq x_j$, $\forall\, i$ and $j = 1, 2, 3, \ldots, (n-1)$. Show that the value of $Q(x) = (x_1 - x_2)(x_1 - x_3)(x_1 - x_4)\ldots(x_1 - x_{n-1})$, is ${}^nC_2 x_1^{n-2}$

7. If $y = 1 + \dfrac{x_1}{x - x_1} + \dfrac{x_2 \cdot x}{(x - x_1)(x - x_2)} + \dfrac{x_3 \cdot x^2}{(x - x_1)(x - x_2)(x - x_3)} + \ldots$ upto $(n+1)$ terms, then prove that

$$\frac{dy}{dx} = \frac{y}{x}\left[\frac{x_1}{x_1 - x} + \frac{x_2}{x_2 - x} + \frac{x_3}{x_3 - x} + \ldots + \frac{x_n}{x_n - x}\right].$$

8. Find $\left.\dfrac{dy}{dx}\right|_{x=1}$ if $y = \dfrac{{}^nC_0 + 2\,{}^nC_1 x + 3\,{}^nC_2 x^2 + \ldots + (n+1)\,{}^nC_n x^n}{{}^nC_1 + (2^2)\,{}^nC_2 + (3^2)\,{}^nC_3 x^2 + \ldots (n^2)\,{}^nC_n x^{n-1}}$.

9. If $y = \dfrac{1}{\sqrt{a^2 - b^2 - c^2}} \cos^{-1}\left\{\dfrac{a\theta - a^2 + b^2 + c^2}{\theta\sqrt{b^2 + c^2}}\right\}$ and $\theta = a + b\cos x + c\sin x$, then prove that $\dfrac{dy}{dx} = \dfrac{1}{\theta}$.

Answer Key

Exercise 1

1. (b)	2. (a)	3. (c)	4. (c)	5. (d)	6. (a)	7. (d)	8. (a)	9. (c)	10. (d)
11. (d)	12. (a)	13. (a)	14. (c)	15. (c)	16. (c)	17. (a)	18. (b)	19. (d)	20. (b)
21. (d)	22. (d)	23. (c)	24. (c)	25. (c)	26. (b)	27. (b)	28. (3)	29. (1)	30. (1)
31. (3)	32. (1)	33. (d)	34. (c)	35. (d)	36. (a)	37. (b)	38. (c)	39. (a)	40. (b)
41. (a)	42. (c)	43. (a)	44. (c)	45. (d)	46. (d)	47. (a)	48. (b)	49. (d)	50. (d)
51. (c)	52. (d)	53. (d)	54. (d)	55. (a)	56. (b)	57. (81)	58. (17)	59. (55)	60. (105)
61. (5)	62. (5)	63. (202)	64. (b)	65. (a)	66. (b)	67. (d)	68. (a)	69. (b)	70. (a)
71. (a)	72. (a)	73. (a)	74. (c)	75. (a)	76. (2)	77. (309)	78. (4)	79. (25)	80. (10)
81. (d)	82. (b)	83. (b)	84. (d)	85. (b)	86. (c)	87. (b)	88. (b)	89. (b)	90. (d)
91. (b)	92. (62)	93. (6)	94. (3)	95. (c)	96. (a)	97. (c)	98. (a)	99. (a)	100. (2)
101. (40)									

Exercise 2

1. (c)	2. (a)	3. (d)	4. (b)	5. (b)	6. (a,b,c,d)	7. (a,b)	8. (a,b,d)	9. (b,d)	10. (a,b)
11. (a,c)	12. (a,c)	13. (a,c)	14. (a,b)	15. (c)	16. (b)	17. (8)	18. (2)	19. (2)	20. (25)
21. (9)	22. (5)	23. (7)	24. (3)	25. (8)	26. (1)	27. (5)	28. (17)	29. (0.15)	30. (18)
31. (0.06)	32. (16)	33. (4850)	34. (25)	35. (88)	36. (10)	37. (81)	38. (26)	39. (64)	

40. (A)→ (t), (B)→ (p), (C)→ (r), (D)→ (s)
41. (A)→ (r), (B)→ (q), (C)→ (p), (D)→ (t)
42. (A)→ (s), (B)→ (p), (C)→ (r), (D)→ (q)
43. (A)→ (r), (B)→ (p), (C)→ (s), (D)→ (q)
44. (A)→ (q,r), (B)→ (p), (C)→ (q,s), (D)→ (q,r)
45. (b,c)

Solutions

Exercise 1 - JEE Main Pattern

1. $y = \sin^{-1}(x\sqrt{1-x} + \sqrt{x}\sqrt{1-x^2})$

Clearly, $0 \le x \le 1$

Now, $y = \sin^{-1}(x\sqrt{1-(\sqrt{x})^2} + \sqrt{x}\sqrt{1-x^2})$

Put $\sqrt{x} = y \in [0, 1]$

$$\Rightarrow \quad y = \sin^{-1}(x\sqrt{1-y^2} + y\sqrt{1-x^2})$$

$$= \sin^{-1} x + \sin^{-1} y = \sin^{-1} x + \sin^{-1}\sqrt{x}$$

$$\Rightarrow \quad \frac{dy}{dx} = \frac{1}{\sqrt{1-x^2}} + \frac{1}{\sqrt{1-x}}\cdot\frac{1}{2\sqrt{x}}$$

$$= \frac{1}{\sqrt{1-x^2}} + \frac{1}{2\sqrt{x(1-x)}}$$

$$= p' + \frac{1}{2\sqrt{x(1-x)}} \qquad \text{[given]}$$

Also, $\frac{d}{dx}(\sin^{-1} x + C) = \frac{1}{\sqrt{1-x^2}}$

$$\Rightarrow \quad p = \sin^{-1} x + C$$

2. $x^{2x} - 2x^x \cot y - 1 = 0$ ...(i)

Let $P = x^{2x}$

Taking log both sides, we get

$\ln P = 2x \ln x$

$$\Rightarrow \quad \frac{1}{P}\frac{dP}{dx} = 2 + 2\ln x$$

$$\Rightarrow \quad \frac{dP}{dx} = x^{2x}(2 + 2\ln x) \qquad \text{...(ii)}$$

Let $Q = x^x$

On taking log both side, we get $\ln Q = x \ln x$

$$\Rightarrow \quad \frac{1}{Q}\cdot\frac{dQ}{dx} = 1 + \ln x$$

$$\Rightarrow \quad \frac{dQ}{dx} = x^x(1 + \ln x) \qquad \text{...(iii)}$$

On differentiating Eq. (i), we get

$$x^{2x}(2 + 2\ln x) - 2x^x(1 + \ln x)\cot y + 2x^x(\text{cosec}^2 y)\cdot y' = 0$$

At $x = 1$, $\quad 2 - 2(1)(\cot y) + 2(\text{cosec}^2 y)\, y'(1) = 0$

$$\Rightarrow \quad 2 - 2(0) + 2(1)\, y'(1) = 0$$

$$\Rightarrow \quad y'(1) = -1$$

3. $f(x) = 2^{2x-1}$

$\ln(f(x)) = (2x - 1)\ln 2$

$$\Rightarrow \quad \frac{f'(x)}{f(x)} = 2\ln 2$$

$$\Rightarrow \quad f'(x) = f(x)\, 2\ln 2 = 2^{2x}\cdot\ln 2 \qquad \text{...(i)}$$

Now, $\quad \phi(x) = -2^x + 2x\ln 2$

$$\Rightarrow \quad \phi'(x) = -2^x \ln 2 + 2\ln 2$$

$$\Rightarrow \quad 2^{2x}\ln 2 > -2^x \ln 2 + 2\ln 2 \quad [\because f'(x) > \phi'(x), \text{ given}]$$

$$\Rightarrow \quad 2^x \ln 2(2^x + 1) > 2\ln 2$$

$$\Rightarrow \quad 2^x(2^x + 1) > 2 \Rightarrow (2^x)^2 + 2^x - 2 > 0$$

$$\Rightarrow (2^x + 2)(2^x - 1) > 0 \Rightarrow -2 < 2^x < 1$$

$$\Rightarrow \quad 0 < 2^x < 1$$

$$\Rightarrow \quad -\infty < x < 0 \text{ i.e. } x < 0$$

4. $y = \left(1 + \frac{1}{x}\right)\left(1 + \frac{2}{x}\right)\ldots\left(1 + \frac{n}{x}\right)$

$$\Rightarrow \ln y = \ln(x + 1) + \ln(x + 2) + \ldots + \ln(x + n) - n\ln x$$

$$\Rightarrow \quad \frac{1}{y}\frac{dy}{dx} = \left(\frac{1}{x+1} + \frac{1}{x+2} + \ldots + \frac{1}{x+n} - \frac{n}{x}\right)$$

$$\Rightarrow \quad \frac{dy}{dx} = \frac{(x+1)(x+2)\ldots(x+n)}{x^n}\left[\left(\frac{1}{x+1} + \frac{1}{x+2} + \ldots + \frac{1}{x+n}\right) - \frac{n}{x}\right]$$

$$\Rightarrow \quad \frac{dy}{dx} = \frac{(x+2)(x+3)\ldots(x+n)}{x^n}\left(\left(1 + \frac{x+1}{x+2} + \ldots + \frac{x+1}{x+n}\right) - \frac{n}{x}(x+1)\right)$$

$$\Rightarrow \quad \left(\frac{dy}{dx}\right)_{x=-1} = \frac{(1)(2)(3)\cdot(n-1)}{(-1)^n}\cdot 1$$

$$\Rightarrow \quad \left.\frac{dy}{dx}\right|_{x=-1} = (n-1)!\,(-1)^n$$

5. Given, $\quad y = \log^n x$

$$\Rightarrow \quad \frac{dy}{dx} = \frac{1}{\log^{n-1} x \log^{n-2} x \ldots x}$$

$$\Rightarrow \quad x\cdot\log x\cdot\log^2 x \ldots \log^n x\,\frac{dy}{dx} = \log^n x$$

6. $u(x) = 7v(x) \Rightarrow u'(x) = 7v'(x)$

$$\Rightarrow \quad p = 7 \qquad \text{[given]}$$

Again, $\frac{u(x)}{v(x)} = 7 \Rightarrow \left(\frac{u(x)}{v(x)}\right)' = 0 \Rightarrow q = 0$

Now, $\frac{p+q}{p-q} = \frac{7+0}{7-0} = 1$

7. Using product rule

$$y^2\left(e^{xy}\left(x\frac{dy}{dx} + y\right)\right) + e^{xy}\cdot 2y\frac{dy}{dx} = 9e^{-3}\cdot 2x$$

Put $x = -1$ and $y = 3$

$$9\left(e^{-3}\left(-1\frac{dy}{dx}+3\right)\right)+e^{-3}\cdot 6\frac{dy}{dx}=-9e^{-3}\cdot 2$$

$$\Rightarrow \quad -9\left(\frac{dy}{dx}-3\right)+6\frac{dy}{dx}=-18$$

$$\Rightarrow \quad 3\frac{dy}{dx}=45 \Rightarrow \frac{dy}{dx}=15$$

8. Let $\sqrt{a^2-1}=C_1$ and $a+\sqrt{a^2-1}=C_2 \Rightarrow C_2-C_1=a$

$$\therefore \quad y=\frac{x}{C_1}-\frac{2}{C_1}\tan^{-1}\left(\frac{\sin x}{C_2+\cos x}\right)$$

$$\frac{dy}{dx}=\frac{1}{C_1}-\frac{2}{C_1}\frac{[(C_2+\cos x)\cos x+\sin^2 x]}{\left[1+\left(\frac{\sin x}{C_2+\cos x}\right)^2\right]\cdot(C_2+\cos x)^2}$$

$$=\frac{1}{C_1}-\frac{2}{C_1}\cdot\frac{C_2\cos x+1}{(C_2+\cos x)^2+\sin^2 x}$$

$$\left.\frac{dy}{dx}\right|_{x=\frac{\pi}{2}}=\frac{1}{C_1}-\frac{2}{C_1}\cdot\frac{1}{C_2^2+1}$$

$$=\frac{1}{C_1}\left[\frac{C_2^2+1-2}{C_2^2+1}\right]=\frac{1}{C_1}\cdot\frac{C_2^2-1}{C_2^2+1}$$

$$\therefore \quad \left.\frac{dy}{dx}\right|_{x=\frac{\pi}{2}}=\frac{2a^2+2a\sqrt{a^2-1}-2}{\sqrt{a^2-1}\,(2a^2-1+2a\sqrt{a^2-1}+1)}$$

$$=\frac{2a^2+2a\sqrt{a^2-1}-2}{\sqrt{a^2-1}\,(2a(a+\sqrt{a^2-1}))}$$

$$=\frac{2(a^2-1)+2a\sqrt{a^2-1}}{\sqrt{a^2-1}\,(2a(a+\sqrt{a^2-1}))}$$

$$=\frac{2\sqrt{a^2-1}\,(\sqrt{a^2-1}+a)}{(\sqrt{a^2-1})\,(2a)\,(a+\sqrt{a^2-1})}=\frac{1}{a}$$

9. **Decoding the Question**

Put $\cos\phi=\frac{2}{\sqrt{13}}$, $\sin\phi=\frac{3}{\sqrt{13}}$ and use chain rule.

Put $\cos\phi=\frac{2}{\sqrt{13}}$, $\sin\phi=\frac{3}{\sqrt{13}}$

$$y=\cos^{-1}\{\cos(x+\phi)\}+\sin^{-1}\{\cos(x-\phi)\}$$

$$=\cos^{-1}\{\cos(x+\phi)\}+\frac{\pi}{2}-\cos^{-1}\{\cos(\phi-x)\}$$

$$=x+\phi+\frac{\pi}{2}-\phi+x$$

$$y=2x+\frac{\pi}{2}, \quad z=\sqrt{1+x^2}$$

Now, compute $\frac{dy}{dz}=\frac{dy/dx}{dz/dx}$

$$=\frac{2}{\frac{2x}{2\sqrt{1+x^2}}}=\frac{2\sqrt{1+x^2}}{x}$$

At $x=\frac{3}{4}$, $\frac{dy}{dz}=\frac{10}{3}$

10. $f(x)=\sin^{-1}\{[3x+2]-\{3x+(x-\{2x\})\}\}$

$$\because \quad x\in\left(0,\frac{\pi}{12}\right)\Rightarrow 2x\in\left(0,\frac{\pi}{6}\right)$$

$$\therefore \quad \{2x\}=2x \text{ and } 3x\in\left(0,\frac{\pi}{4}\right)$$

$$f(x)=\sin^{-1}\{2-\{3x-x\}\}$$

$$=\sin^{-1}\{2-2x\}$$

$$f(x)=\sin^{-1}(1-2x)=y\text{ (say)} \quad [\text{as }\{2-2x\}=1-2x]$$

$$\Rightarrow \quad 1-2x=\sin y \Rightarrow x=\frac{1-\sin y}{2}=f^{-1}(y)$$

$$\therefore \quad f^{-1}(x)=\frac{1-\sin x}{2}=g(x) \Rightarrow g'(x)=\frac{-1}{2}\cos x$$

$$\therefore \quad g'\left(\frac{\pi}{6}\right)=\frac{-1}{2}\left(\frac{\sqrt{3}}{2}\right)=\frac{-\sqrt{3}}{4}$$

11. $f(x)=-\frac{x^3}{3}+x^2\sin 6-x\sin 4\cdot\sin 8-5\sin^{-1}((a-4)^2+1)$

$$f'(x)=-x^2+2x\sin 6-\sin 4\sin 8\,(a=4)$$

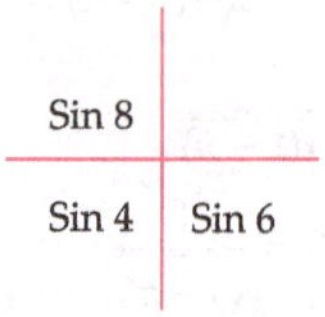

$$f'(\sin 8)=-\sin^2 8+2\sin 6\sin 8-\sin 4\sin 8$$

$$=\sin 8\,[-\sin 8+2\sin 6-\sin 4]$$

$$=-\sin 8\,[\sin 8+\sin 4-2\sin 6]$$

$$=-\sin 8\,[2\sin 6\cos 2-2\sin 6]$$

$$=2\sin 8\sin 6\,[1-\cos 2]<0$$

12. $\frac{dy}{dt}=f'\left(\frac{2x+3}{3-2x}\right)\left(\frac{2x+3}{3-2x}\right)=\frac{12}{9-4x^2}\cos\left(\ln\left(\frac{2x+3}{3-2x}\right)\right)$

13. $f(x)=\frac{x}{1+e^{1/x}}$

$$f(x)(1+e^{1/x})-x=0$$

$$f'(x)(1+e^{1/x})-\frac{f(x)\,e^{1/x}}{x^2}-1=0$$

$$x^2f'(x)\frac{(x)}{f(x)}-f(x)\,e^{1/x}-x^2=0$$

$$\Rightarrow \quad x^3f'(x)-x^2f(x)-e^{1/x}(f(x))^2=0$$

14. $\because g(x)$ is inverse of $f(x)$

$$\therefore \quad g'(x)=\frac{1}{f'(g(x))}=\frac{1}{\cos(2g(x))}=\sec(2g(x))$$

15. Put $x=y=0$, $f(0)=1$

$$\Rightarrow \quad f'(0)=p,\ f'(5)=q$$

$$f(y)\,f'(x-y)=f'(x)$$

Put $y=5=x$

$$f(5)\,f'(0)=f'(5)$$

$$f(5)=\frac{q}{p}$$

16. **Decoding the Question**

If α and β are roots of equation $ax^2 + bx + c = 0$, then $\alpha + \beta = \frac{-b}{a}$ and $\alpha\beta = \frac{c}{a}$.

$$f(x) = e^{ax} + e^{bx}$$
$$f'(x) = ae^{ax} + be^{bx}$$
$$f''(x) = a^2e^{ax} + b^2e^{bx}$$

Now, $\quad f''(x) - 2f'(x) - 15f(x) = 0$

$\Rightarrow \quad (a^2 - 2a - 15)\, e^{ax} + (b^2 - 2b - 15)\, e^{bx} = 0$

$\Rightarrow \quad a^2 - 2a - 15 = 0$ and $b^2 - 2b - 15 = 0$

a, b are two roots of $x^2 - 2x - 15 = 0$

$$ab = -15$$

17. Here, $f(x) = (|\, x\,|)^{|\sin x|}$

As, $x \to \frac{-\pi}{4} \Rightarrow f(x) = (-x)^{-\sin x}$

Taking logarithm on both sides, we get

$$\log(f(x)) = (-\sin x)\log(-x)$$

On differentiating both sides, we get

$$\frac{1}{f(x)} \cdot f'(x) = (-\sin x)\frac{1}{x} + \log(-x) \cdot (-\cos x)$$

At $x = -\frac{\pi}{4}$, $f'\left(-\frac{\pi}{4}\right) = f\left(-\frac{\pi}{4}\right)\left[\frac{-\frac{1}{\sqrt{2}}}{\frac{\pi}{4}} + \log\left(\frac{\pi}{4}\right)\cdot\left(-\frac{1}{\sqrt{2}}\right)\right]$

$$= \left(\frac{\pi}{4}\right)^{\frac{1}{\sqrt{2}}}\left[\frac{\sqrt{2}}{2}\log\frac{4}{\pi} - \frac{2\sqrt{2}}{\pi}\right]$$

18. Here, $u'(x) = f'(g(x)) \cdot g'(x)$

$\Rightarrow \quad u'(1) = f'(g(1)) \cdot g'(1)$

$= f'(3) \cdot g'(1)$

$= \left(-\frac{1}{4}\right) \cdot (-3) = \frac{3}{4}$

and $\quad w'(x) = g'(g(x)) \cdot g'(x)$

$\Rightarrow \quad w'(1) = g'(g(1)) \cdot g'(1) = g'(3) \cdot g'(1)$

$= \frac{3}{4} \cdot (-3) = -\frac{9}{4}$

$\therefore u'(1) + w'(1) = \frac{3}{4} - \frac{9}{4} = -\frac{6}{4} = -\frac{3}{2}$

19. We have,

$$y = \sqrt{x + \sqrt{y + \sqrt{x + \sqrt{y + \dots \infty}}}}$$

$\Rightarrow \quad y^2 = x + \sqrt{y + \sqrt{x + \sqrt{y + \dots \infty}}}$

$\Rightarrow \quad y^2 = x + \sqrt{y + y}$

$\Rightarrow \quad (y^2 - x)^2 = 2y$

On differentiating both sides w.r.t. x, we get

$$2(y^2 - x)\left(2y\frac{dy}{dx} - 1\right) = 2\frac{dy}{dx}$$

$\Rightarrow \quad \frac{dy}{dx} = \frac{y^2 - x}{2y^3 - 2xy - 1}$

20. We have, $f(x) = \cos\{x + 3x + \dots + (2n-1)\,x\}$
$\quad + i\sin\{x + 3x + 5x + \dots + (2n-1)\,x\}$

$\Rightarrow \quad f(x) = \cos n^2x + i\sin n^2x$

$\Rightarrow \quad f'(x) = -n^2(\sin n^2x) + n^2(i\cos n^2x)$

$\Rightarrow \quad f''(x) = -n^4\cos n^2x - n^4 i\sin n^2x$

$\Rightarrow \quad f''(x) = -n^4(\cos n^2x + i\sin n^2x)$

$\Rightarrow \quad f''(x) = -n^4 f(x)$

21. We have, $f(x) = x^2 + xg'(1) + g''(2)$

and $\quad g(x) = x^2 + xf'(2) + f''(3)$

$\Rightarrow \quad f'(x) = 2x + g'(1)$ and $g'(x) = 2x + f'(2) \quad$ ...(i)

On putting $x = 1$ in Eq. (i), we get

$f'(1) = 2 + g'(1)$ and $g'(1) = 2 + f'(2)$

$\Rightarrow \quad f'(1) = 4 + f'(2)$

Putting $x = 2$ in Eq. (i), we get

$f'(2) = 4 + g'(1)$ and $g'(2) = 4 + f'(2)$

$\Rightarrow \quad g'(2) = 4 + 4 + g'(1) = 8 + g'(1)$

On differentiating Eq. (i) w.r.t. x, we get

$f''(x) = 2$ and $g''(x) = 2$ for all x

$\Rightarrow \quad f''(3) = 2$ and $g''(2) = 2$

$\Rightarrow \quad g''(2) + f''(3) = 2 + 2 = 4$

22. We have, $f(x) = x^n$

$f^r(x) = n(n-1)(n-2)\dots\{n-(r-1)\}\,x^{n-r}$

$\Rightarrow \quad f^r(x) = \frac{n!}{(n-r)!}x^{n-r}$

$\Rightarrow \quad f^r(1) = \frac{n!}{(n-r)!}$

$\therefore \quad f(1) - \frac{f'(1)}{1!} + \frac{f''(1)}{2!} - \frac{f'''(1)}{3!} + \dots + \frac{(-1)^n f^n(1)}{n!}$

$= \sum_{r=0}^{n}(-1)^r\frac{f^r(1)}{r!}$, where $f^0(1) = f(1)$

$= \sum_{r=0}^{n}(-1)^r\frac{n!}{(n-r)!\,r!} = \sum_{r=0}^{n}(-1)^r\,{}^nC_r = 0$

23. $f(x) = e^x - e^{-x} - 2\sin x - \frac{2}{3}x^3$

$f'(x) = e^x + e^{-x} - 2\cos x - 2x^2$

$f''(x) = e^x - e^{-x} + 2\sin x - 4x$

$f'''(x) = e^x + e^{-x} + 2\cos x - 4$

$f^{iv}(x) = e^x - e^{-x} - 2\sin x$

$f^{v}(x) = e^x + e^{-x} - 2\cos x$

$f^{vi}(x) = e^x - e^{-x} + 2\sin x$

$f^{vii}(x) = e^x + e^{-x} + 2\cos x$

24. $f(x) = 1 + nx + \frac{n(n-1)}{2}x^2 + \frac{n(n-1)(n-2)}{6}x^2 + \dots + x^n$

$f(x)$ can be written as

$f(x) = 1 + {}^nC_1x + {}^nC_2x^2 + {}^nC_3x^3 + \dots {}^nC_nx^n$

$\Rightarrow \quad f(x) = (1+x)^n$

$\Rightarrow \quad f'(x) = n(1+x)^{n-1}$

$\Rightarrow \quad f''(x) = n(n-1)(1+x)^{n-2}$

$\Rightarrow \quad f''(1) = n(n-1)\cdot 2^{n-2}$

25. $$y = Ae^{x^2} + Be^{x^2/2}$$

$$\Rightarrow \frac{dy}{dx} = Ae^{x^2}(2x) + Be^{x^2/2}(x)$$

$$\Rightarrow \frac{d^2y}{dx^2} = 2Axe^{x^2}(2x) + 2Ae^{x^2} + Bxe^{x^2/2}(2x) + Be^{x^2/2}$$

$$\Rightarrow \frac{d^2y}{dx^2} = 4Ax^2e^{x^2} + 2Ae^{x^2} + 2Bx^2e^{x^2/2} + 2Be^{x^2/2}$$

$$\Rightarrow \frac{d^2y}{dx^2} + 2x^2y = 4Ax^2e^{x^2} + 2Bx^2e^{x^2/2} + 2Ae^{x^2} + 2Be^{x^2/2} + 2x^2Ae^{x^2} + Bx^2e^{x^2/2}$$

$$= 6x^2Ae^{x^2} + 3Bx^2e^{x^2/2} + 2Ae^{x^2} + Be^{x^2/2}$$

$$= 3x\left(\frac{dy}{dx}\right) + \frac{1}{x}\frac{dy}{dx}$$

$$\Rightarrow \frac{d^2y}{dx^2} + \left(-3x\frac{dy}{dx} - \frac{1}{x}\right)\frac{dy}{dx} + 2x^2y = 0$$

$$\Rightarrow \qquad k = -3$$

26. $$f(x) = \tan^{-1}\left(\frac{1}{\cos^2 x + \cos x + 1}\right) + \tan^{-1}\left(\frac{1}{\cos^2 x + 3\cos x + 3}\right) + \tan^{-1}\left(\frac{1}{\cos^2 x + 5\cos x + 7}\right) + \tan^{-1}\left(\frac{1}{\cos^2 x + 7\cos x + 13}\right) + \ldots + \text{to } n \text{ terms}$$

$$= [\tan^{-1}(\cos x + 1) - \tan^{-1}(\cos x)] + [\tan^{-1}(\cos x + 2) - \tan^{-1}(\cos x + 1)] + [\tan^{-1}(\cos x + 3) - \tan^{-1}(\cos x + 2)] + \ldots + [\tan^{-1}(\cos x + n) - \tan^{-1}(\cos x + n - 1)]$$

$$= \tan^{-1}(\cos x + n) - \tan^{-1}(\cos x)$$

$$\Rightarrow f'(x) = \frac{1}{1 + (\cos x + n)^2}[-\sin x] - \frac{1}{1 + \cos^2 x}(-\sin x)$$

$$= \frac{-\sin x}{1 + (\cos x + n)^2} + \frac{\sin x}{1 + \cos^2 x}$$

27. Given, $(\sin B + \sin A)\sin C + \sin A \cdot \sin B = k$

$$\Rightarrow \qquad (\sin B + \sin A)\sin(A + B) + \sin A \cdot \sin B = k$$

On differentiating both sides w.r.t. A, we get

$$(\sin B + \sin A)\cdot\cos(A + B)\left(1 + \frac{dB}{dA}\right) + \sin(A + B)\left(\cos B \cdot \frac{dB}{dA} + \cos A\right) + \sin A \cdot \cos B \cdot \frac{dB}{dA} + \sin B \cdot \cos A = 0$$

$$\Rightarrow \frac{dB}{dA} = \frac{-(\sin A + \sin B)\cos(A + B) - \sin(A + B)\cdot\cos A - \sin B\cos A}{(\sin A + \sin B)\cos(A + B) + \cos B \cdot \sin(A + B) + \sin A\cos B}$$

$$= \frac{(\sin A + \sin B)\cos C - \sin C\cos A - \sin B\cos A}{-(\sin A + \sin B)\cos C + \cos B\sin C + \sin A\cos B}$$

$$= \frac{-(\sin C\cos A - \cos C\sin A) - \sin B(\cos A - \cos C)}{(\sin C\cos B - \cos C\sin B) + \sin A(\cos B - \cos C)}$$

$$= \frac{-\sin(C - A) - \sin B(\cos A - \cos C)}{\sin(C - B) + \sin A(\cos B - \cos C)}$$

$$A = \frac{\sin(C - A) + \sin B(\cos A - \cos C)}{\sin(B - C) + \sin A(\cos C - \cos B)}$$

28. Differentiate $x^2 + y^2 = 4$

We get $A = -1$

Differentiate $\sin y + \sin x = \sin x \cdot \sin y$

We get $B = -1$

Differentiate $2e^{xy} + e^x \cdot e^y - e^x - e^y = e^{xy+1}$

We get $C = -1$

So, $|A + B + C| = 3$

29. Let $y = \tan\left(\sin^{-1}\left(\frac{2x + 2}{\sqrt{4x^2 + 8x + 13}}\right)\right)$ and $z = \tan^{-1} x$

$$\Rightarrow y = \tan\left(\sin^{-1}\left(\frac{2x + 2}{\sqrt{(2x + 2)^2 + 9}}\right)\right)$$

$$= \tan\left(\tan^{-1}\left(\frac{2x + 3}{3}\right)\right) = \frac{2x + 3}{3}$$

$$\Rightarrow \frac{dy}{dx} = \frac{2}{3} \text{ and } \frac{dz}{dx} = \frac{1}{1 + x^2}$$

$$\therefore \frac{dy}{dz} = \frac{\frac{dy}{dx}}{\frac{dz}{dx}} = \frac{2}{3}(1 + x^2)$$

$$\Rightarrow \left(\frac{dy}{dz}\right)_{x = \frac{1}{\sqrt{2}}} = \frac{2}{3}\left(1 + \frac{1}{2}\right) = \frac{2}{3} \times \frac{3}{2} = 1$$

30. Let $P(x) = a(x - 1)(x - 3)(x - 5)(x - \lambda)$

$$\Rightarrow \log P(x) = \log a + \log(x - 1) + \log(x - 3) + \log(x - 5) + \log(x - \lambda)$$

On differentiating both sides, we get

$$\frac{1}{P(x)}\cdot P'(x) = \frac{1}{x - 1} + \frac{1}{x - 3} + \frac{1}{x - 5} + \frac{1}{x - \lambda}$$

As, $P'(7) = 0$ $\quad [\because P(x) = 0 \Rightarrow P'(x) = 0 \Rightarrow P'(7) = 0]$

$$\Rightarrow 0 = \frac{1}{6} + \frac{1}{4} + \frac{1}{2} + \frac{1}{7 - \lambda} \Rightarrow \lambda = \frac{89}{11} = \frac{p}{q}$$

$\therefore \; p - 8q = 1$

31. $f'(x) = (kx + e^x)h'(x) + h(x)(k + e^x)$

$$\therefore \qquad f'(0) = h'(0) + h(0)(k + 1)$$

$$\Rightarrow \qquad 18 = -2 + 5(k + 1) \Rightarrow k = 3$$

32. $P(x) = (x - x_1)^3(x - x_2)(x - x_3)\ldots(x - x_8)$

$$\Rightarrow \qquad P(x) = (x - x_1)^3 \cdot Q(x)$$

$$\therefore \qquad Q(x) = \frac{P(x)}{(x - x_1)^3}$$

As, $Q(x)$ is polynomial.

$\therefore Q(x)$ must be continuous at $x = x_1$.

$$\therefore Q(x_1) = \lim_{x \to x_1} Q(x) = \lim_{x \to x_1} \frac{x^{10} + ax^2 + bx + c}{(x - x_1)^3}$$

By L' Hospital's rule, we have

$$Q(x_1)=\frac{10\times9\times8\times x_1^7}{3\times2\times1}$$

$$\therefore\quad Q\left(\frac{1}{2}\right)=\frac{10\times9\times8\times\left(\frac{1}{2}\right)^7}{3\times2\times1}=\frac{15}{16}=\frac{p}{q}$$

$$\therefore\quad q-p=1$$

33. $f(x)=\begin{cases}\dfrac{\tan((a+1)x)+b\tan x}{x}, & x<0\\ 3, & x=0\\ \dfrac{\sqrt{ax+b^2x^2}-\sqrt{ax}}{b\sqrt{a}\cdot x\sqrt{x}}, & x>0\end{cases}$

$\because f(x)$ is continuous at $x=0$

So, $$\lim_{x\to0}f(x)=f(0)=3$$

$$\Rightarrow\quad \lim_{x\to0^+}\frac{\sqrt{ax+b^2x^2}-\sqrt{ax}}{b\sqrt{a}\cdot x\sqrt{x}}=3$$

$$\Rightarrow\quad \lim_{x\to0^+}\frac{(\sqrt{ax+b^2x^2}-\sqrt{ax})(\sqrt{ax+b^2x^2}+\sqrt{ax})}{b\sqrt{a}\cdot x\sqrt{x}\,(\sqrt{ax+b^2x^2}+\sqrt{ax})}=3$$

$$\Rightarrow\quad \lim_{x\to0^+}\frac{ax+b^2x^2-ax}{b\sqrt{a}\,x^{3/2}(\sqrt{ax+b^2x^2}+\sqrt{ax})}=3$$

$$\Rightarrow\quad \lim_{x\to0^+}\frac{b^2x^2}{b\sqrt{a}\,x^2(\sqrt{a+b^2x}+\sqrt{a})}=3$$

$$\Rightarrow\quad \lim_{x\to0^+}\frac{b}{\sqrt{a}(\sqrt{a+b^2x}+\sqrt{a})}=3$$

$$\Rightarrow\quad \frac{b}{\sqrt{a}(\sqrt{a}+\sqrt{a})}=3$$

$$\Rightarrow\quad \frac{b}{2a}=3\Rightarrow\frac{b}{a}=6$$

34. $f(x)=2x^2+x+[x^2]-[x]$

$$f:[-1,2]\to R$$

$\because$ $[x]$ is discontinuous at integral point

$$-1\le x\le2,\quad 0\le x^2\le4$$

$\therefore$Point where $f(x)$ can be discontinuous are

$$x=1,0,1,\sqrt{2},\sqrt{3},2$$

At end points we have to check

At $x=-1$,

$$f(-1)=3$$

$$f(-1^+)=2-1+0-(-1)=2$$

$\therefore$Discontinuous at $x=-1$

At $x=0$,

$$f(0)=0 \text{ and } f(0^-)=0+0+0-(-1)=1$$

$\therefore$ Discontinuous at $x=0$

At $x=2$,

$$f(2)=8+2+4-2=12$$

$$f(2^-)=8+2+3-1=12$$

$$f(2^+)=8+2+4-2=12$$

$\therefore$ Continuous at $x=2$

At $x=1$,

$$f(1)=3-1+1=3$$

$$f(1^+)=2+1-1+1=3$$

$$f(1^-)=2+1-0-0=3$$

$\therefore$ Continuous at $x=1$

Similarly, $f(x)$ will be discontinuous at $x=\sqrt{2}$ and $\sqrt{3}$ also.

Number of points of discontinuity = 4

35. Given, $f(x)=\dfrac{\sin3x+\alpha\sin x-\beta\cos3x}{x^3}$, $x\in R$ is continuous at $x=0$

$$\therefore\quad \lim_{x\to0}f(x)=f(0)$$

$$\Rightarrow \lim_{x\to0}\left[\frac{3x-\frac{(3x)^3}{3!}+\frac{(3x)^5}{5!}+\ldots+\alpha\left(x-\frac{x^3}{3!}+\frac{x^5}{5!}\ldots\right)-\beta\left(1-\frac{(3x)^2}{2!}+\frac{(3x)^4}{4!}\ldots\right)}{x^3}\right]=f(0)$$

$$\Rightarrow \lim_{x\to0}\frac{-\beta+x(3+\alpha)+\frac{9\beta x^2}{2!}+\left(-\frac{27}{3!}-\frac{\alpha}{3!}\right)x^3\ldots}{x^3}=f(0)$$

Limit will exist, if

$$\beta=0,\ 3+\alpha=0 \text{ and } \frac{-27}{3!}-\frac{\alpha}{3!}=f(0)$$

$$\Rightarrow\quad \beta=0,\ \alpha=-3$$

$$\therefore\quad f(0)=\frac{-27}{6}+\frac{3}{6}=\frac{-27+3}{6}=-4$$

36. Given, $f(x)=\begin{cases}\dfrac{72^x-9^x-8^x+1}{\sqrt{2}-\sqrt{1+\cos x}}, & x\ne0\\ a\log_e2\log3, & x=0\end{cases}$

$\because f(x)$ is continuous at $x=0$

$$\therefore\quad \lim_{x\to0}f(x)=f(0)$$

$$\Rightarrow\quad \lim_{x\to0}\frac{72^x-9^x-8^x+1}{\sqrt{2}-\sqrt{1+\cos x}}=a\ln2\cdot\ln3$$

$$\Rightarrow\quad \lim_{x\to0}\frac{(8^x-1)(9^x-1)}{\sqrt{2}-\sqrt{1+\cos x}}\times\frac{\sqrt{2}+\sqrt{1+\cos x}}{\sqrt{2}+\sqrt{1+\cos x}}=a\ln2\cdot\ln3$$

$$\Rightarrow \lim_{x\to0}\frac{(8^x-1)(9^x-1)}{1-\cos x}\times(\sqrt{2}+\sqrt{1+\cos x})=a\ln2\cdot\ln3$$

$$\Rightarrow \lim_{x\to0}\left(\frac{8^x-1}{x}\right)\left(\frac{9^x-1}{x}\right)\frac{x^2(\sqrt{2}+\sqrt{1+\cos x})}{\frac{2\sin^2\frac{x}{2}}{(x/2)^2}\times\frac{x^2}{4}}=a\ln2\ln3$$

$$\Rightarrow\quad \ln8\cdot\ln9\cdot2\cdot2\sqrt{2}=a\ln2\cdot\ln3$$

$$\Rightarrow\quad a=\frac{3\ln2\cdot2\ln3\times4\sqrt{2}}{\ln2\cdot\ln3}$$

$$\Rightarrow\quad a=24\sqrt{2}\ \Rightarrow\ a^2=576\times2=1152$$

37. Given, $f(x)=\begin{cases}\dfrac{1-\cos 2x}{x^2}, & x<0\\ \alpha, & x=0\\ \dfrac{\beta\sqrt{1-\cos x}}{x}, & x>0\end{cases}$ where, $\alpha, \beta \in R$

Since, $f(x)$ is continuous at $x=0$.

So, LHL = RHL = Value of function ... (i)

Now, $f(0^-)=\lim_{x\to 0^-}\dfrac{2\sin^2 x}{x^2}=2$ [using $1-\cos 2x=2\sin^2 x$]

$$f(0^+)=\lim_{x\to 0^+}\beta\times\sqrt{2}\,\frac{\sin\frac{x}{2}}{2.\frac{x}{2}}=\frac{\beta}{\sqrt{2}}$$

[$\because$ for $x\to 0^+$, $|\sin x/2|=\sin x/2$]

and $f(0)=\alpha$

From Eq. (i), $\alpha=2$ and $\beta=2\sqrt{2}$

Hence, $\alpha^2+\beta^2=4+8=12$

38. Given, $f(x)=\begin{cases}\dfrac{a(7x-12-x^2)}{b|x^2-7x+12|}, & x<3\\ 2^{\frac{\sin(x-3)}{x-[x]}}, & x>3\\ b, & x=3\end{cases}$

Also, given $f(x)$ is continuous at $x=3$.

So, LHL $=f(3^-)=\lim_{x\to 3^-}\left\{\dfrac{a(7x-12-x^2)}{b|x^2-7x+12|}\right\}$

$$=\lim_{x\to 3^-}\frac{-a(x-3)(x-4)}{b(x-3)(x-4)}$$

[$\because$ when $x<3$, then $|x^2-7x+12|$ $=x^2-7x+12$ as $x^2-7x+12>0\ \forall\ x<3$]

$$=-\frac{a}{b}$$

RHL $=f(3^+)=\lim_{x\to 3^+}f(x)$

$$=\lim_{x\to 3^+}\left(2^{\frac{\sin(x-3)}{x-[x]}}\right)$$

$$=2^{\lim_{x\to 3^+}\left\{\frac{\sin(x-3)}{x-[x]}\right\}}=2^{\lim_{x\to 3^+}\frac{\sin(x-3)}{(x-3)}}\quad\left[\because \lim_{x\to 3^+}[x]=3\right]$$

$=2$

$f(3)=b=$ value of function

For $f(x)$ to be continuous at $x=3$;

$$f(3^-)=f(3^+)=f(3)$$

$\Rightarrow\quad -\dfrac{a}{b}=b=2$

$\Rightarrow\quad b=2$ and $-\dfrac{a}{2}=2\Rightarrow a=-4$

Hence, only one ordered pair $(-4, 2)$.

$\therefore$ $n(S)=$ Number of elements in the set $S=1$

39. We have, $f(x)=\left|2x^2+5|x|-3\right|$

Firstly we draw the graph of $f(x)$

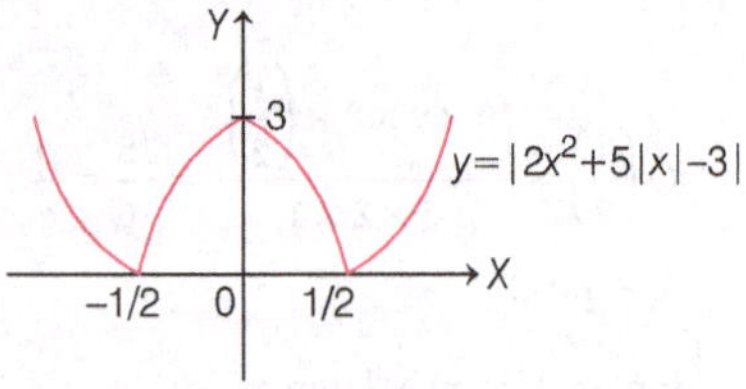

Clearly, by graph of y, $f(x)$ is continuous for every $x\in R$ and not differentiable at $x=-\frac{1}{2},\frac{1}{2}$ and 0 i.e. 3 points

$m=0$ and $n=3$

$\Rightarrow\quad m+n=3$

40. At $x=0$,

RHL $=2$

LHL $=\lim_{x\to 0}\dfrac{a-b\cos 2x}{x^2}$

$$=\lim_{x\to 0}\frac{a-b\left(1-\frac{(2x)^2}{2!}+\frac{(2x)^4}{4!}\dots\infty\right)}{x^2}=2$$

For LHL = RHL

$\Rightarrow\quad a-b=0$

$\Rightarrow\quad a=b\Rightarrow 2b=2$

$\Rightarrow\quad b=1\Rightarrow a=b=1$

At $x=1$, $f(x)$ is continuous, therefore

$$f(1^-)=f(1)=f(1^+)$$

$\Rightarrow\quad f(1)=3+c$

$\Rightarrow\quad f(1^+)=\lim_{h\to 0}(2(1+h)+1)$

$\Rightarrow\quad f(1^+)=\lim_{h\to 0}3+2h=3$

$\Rightarrow\quad 3+c=3$

$\therefore\quad c=0$

$$f(x)=\begin{cases}\dfrac{1-\cos 2x}{x^2}, & x<0\\ x^2+2, & 0\le x\le 1\\ 2x+1, & x>1\end{cases}$$

At $x=1$, LHD $=2=$ RHD

$\Rightarrow f$ is differentiable at $x=1$

At $x=0$, RHD $=0$

$$\text{LHD}=\lim_{x\to 0}\frac{1-\cos 2x}{x^2}=\lim_{h\to 0}\frac{\frac{1-\cos 2h}{h^2}-2}{-h}$$

$$=\lim_{h\to 0}\frac{1-\left(1-\frac{4h^2}{2!}+\frac{16h^2}{4!}\dots\right)2h^2}{-h^3}=0$$

$\Rightarrow$ LHD = RHD

$\Rightarrow f$ is differentiable at $x=0$

$\Rightarrow\quad m=0$

$\therefore\quad m+a+b+c=0+1+1+0=2$

41. $f:(0,\infty)\to R,\ f(x)=e^{-|\log_e x|}$

$$f(x)=\begin{cases}\dfrac{1}{e^{-\ln x}}=\dfrac{1}{e^{\ln\frac{1}{x}}}=\dfrac{1}{1/x}=x, & 0<x<1\\[2mm] \dfrac{1}{e^{\ln x}}=\dfrac{1}{x}, & x\geq 1\end{cases}$$

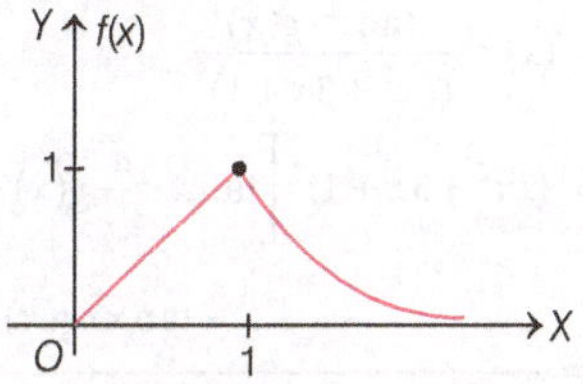

[no point at which function is not continuous]

$n=1,$ [not differentiable]

$\therefore\quad m+n=1$

42. Given, $f:(0,2)\to R$ such that

$$f(x)=\frac{x}{2}+\frac{2}{x}\Rightarrow f'(x)=\frac{1}{2}-\frac{2}{x^2}$$

For $x\in(0,2)$, $f(x)$ is decreasing.

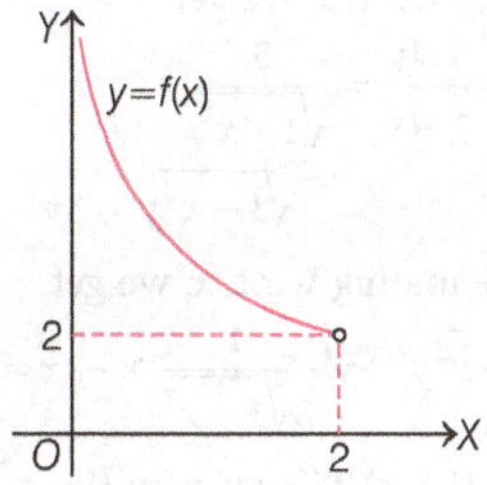

$$g(x)=\begin{cases}\dfrac{x}{2}+\dfrac{2}{x}, & 0<x\leq 1\\[2mm] \dfrac{3}{2}+x, & 1<x<2\end{cases}$$

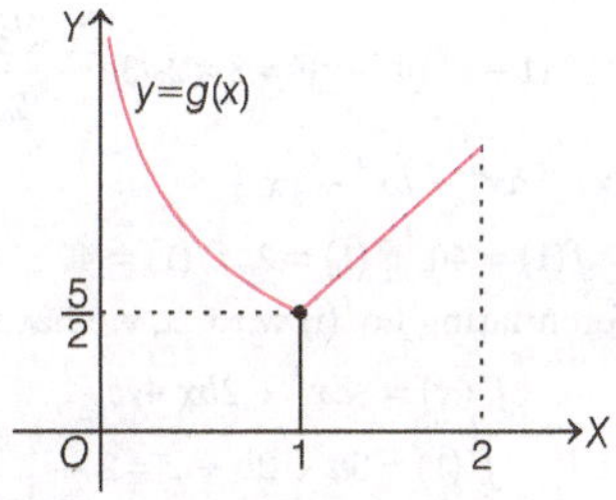

43. Given, $f:(-\infty,\infty)-\{0\}\to R$

$$f'(1)=\lim_{a\to\infty}a^2 f\left(\frac{1}{a}\right)$$

Now, we have to find

$$\lim_{a\to\infty}\frac{a(a+1)}{2}\tan^{-1}\left(\frac{1}{a}\right)+a^2-2\ln(a)$$

$$=\lim_{a\to\infty}a^2\left(\frac{\left(1+\frac{1}{a}\right)}{2}\tan^{-1}\left(\frac{1}{a}\right)+1+\frac{2}{a^2}\ln\frac{1}{a}\right)$$

$$\Rightarrow\quad f(x)=\frac{1}{x^2}(1+x)\tan^{-1}x+1+2x^2\ln(x)$$

$$\Rightarrow\quad f'(x)=\frac{1}{x^2}\left(\frac{1+x}{1+x^2}+\tan^{-1}x\right)+4x\ln x+2x$$

$$\Rightarrow\quad f'(1)=\frac{1}{2}\left(1+\frac{\pi}{4}\right)+2$$

$$\Rightarrow\quad f'(1)=\frac{5}{2}+\frac{\pi}{8}$$

44. According to the question,

$$g(x)=h(e^x)\cdot e^{h(x)}$$

$$\Rightarrow\quad g'(x)=h(e^x)\cdot e^{h(x)}\cdot h'(x)+e^{h(x)}\cdot h'(e^x)\cdot e^x$$

$$\Rightarrow\quad g'(0)=h(1)\,e^{h(0)}\,h'(0)+e^{h(0)}\,h'(1)=2+2=4$$

45. We have, $f(x)=x^5+2x^3+3x+1$

$\Rightarrow\quad f'(x)=5x^4+6x^2+3$

$\Rightarrow\quad f'(1)=5(1)+6(1)+3=14$

Also, $g(f(x))=x$

$\Rightarrow\quad g'(f(x))\,f'(x)=1$

Now, for $f(x)=7$

$\Rightarrow\quad x^5+2x^3+3x+1=7\Rightarrow x=1$

$\therefore\quad g'(7)\,f'(1)=1\Rightarrow g'(7)=\dfrac{1}{f'(1)}=\dfrac{1}{14}$

and $\quad g(7)=g(f(1))=1$

$\therefore\quad \dfrac{g(7)}{g'(7)}=\dfrac{1}{1/14}=14$

46. Given, $f(x)=x^5+2e^{x/4}$ ... (i)

and $\quad g(f(x))=x$ ... (ii)

Here, $\quad f(0)=0+2\times1=2$ ...(iii)

Differentiating w.r.t. x, we get

$$g'(f(x))\cdot f'(x)=1$$

$\Rightarrow\quad g'(f(x))=1/f'(x)$

Putting $x=0$, we get

$$g'(f(0))=\frac{1}{f'(0)}\Rightarrow g'(2)=\frac{1}{f'(0)}\qquad\text{...(iv)}$$

Now, $\quad f'(x)=5x^4+\dfrac{2}{4}.e^{x/4}=5x^4+\dfrac{1}{2}e^{x/4}$

$\therefore\quad f'(0)=0+\dfrac{1}{2}\times1=\dfrac{1}{2}\Rightarrow g'(2)=2$

Hence, $8g'(2)=8\times2=16$

47. Given, $\quad f(x)=\begin{vmatrix}x^3 & 2x^2+1 & 1+3x\\ 3x^2+2 & 2x & x^3+6\\ x^3-x & 4 & x^2-2\end{vmatrix}$

$$f(0)=\begin{vmatrix}0 & 1 & 1\\ 2 & 0 & 6\\ 0 & 4 & -2\end{vmatrix}=-1(-4)+1(8)=12$$

$$f'(x)=\begin{vmatrix}3x^2 & 4x & 3\\ 3x^2+2 & 2x & x^3+6\\ x^3-x & 4 & x^2-2\end{vmatrix}$$

$$+\begin{vmatrix}x^3 & 2x^2+1 & 1+3x\\ 6x & 2 & 3x^2\\ x^3-x & 4 & x^2-2\end{vmatrix}+\begin{vmatrix}x^3 & 2x^2+1 & 1+3x\\ 3x^2+2 & 2x & x^3+6\\ 3x^2-1 & 0 & 2x\end{vmatrix}$$

$$f'(0)=\begin{vmatrix}0&0&3\\2&0&6\\0&4&-2\end{vmatrix}+\begin{vmatrix}0&1&1\\0&2&0\\0&4&-2\end{vmatrix}+\begin{vmatrix}0&1&1\\2&0&6\\-1&0&0\end{vmatrix}$$

$$=3(8)+2(0)+(-1)(6)=24-6=18$$

$\therefore$ $$2f(0)+f'(0)=24+18=42$$

48. $g(x)=$ linear function $=ax+b$ [let]

$$f(x)=\begin{cases}g(x), & x\le 0\\ \left(\dfrac{1+x}{2+x}\right)^{\frac{1}{x}}, & x>0\end{cases}=\begin{cases}ax+b, & x\le 0\\ \left(\dfrac{1+x}{2+x}\right)^{\frac{1}{x}}, & x>0\end{cases}$$

$\because$ $f(x)$ is continuous at $x=0$

$\therefore$ $$f(0^+)=f(0)=f(0^-)\Rightarrow 0=b$$

Let $y=f(x)=\left(\dfrac{1+x}{2+x}\right)^{1/x}$

$$\ln y=\frac{1}{x}\ln\frac{1+x}{2+x}$$

$$\Rightarrow \frac{1}{y}\frac{dy}{dx}=\frac{1}{x}\cdot\frac{1}{\frac{1+x}{2+x}}\cdot\frac{2+x-1-x}{(2+x)^2}+\ln\left(\frac{1+x}{2+x}\right)\left(\frac{-1}{x^2}\right)$$

$$\Rightarrow \frac{dy}{dx}=y\left[\frac{1}{x(1+x)(2+x)}-\frac{1}{x^2}\ln\left(\frac{1+x}{2+x}\right)\right]$$

$$f'(1)=\left.\frac{dy}{dx}\right|_{x=1}=y(1)\left[\frac{1}{6}-\ln\left(\frac{2}{3}\right)\right]=\left(\frac{2}{3}\right)\left(\frac{1}{6}-\ln\frac{2}{3}\right)$$

Let $f(-1)=-a$

$\because$ $f'(1)=f(-1)$

$$a=\frac{2}{3}\left(\ln\frac{2}{3}-\frac{1}{6}\right)$$

$$g(3)=3a=2\left[\ln\left(\frac{2}{3}\right)-\frac{1}{6}\right]$$

$$=\ln\left(\frac{4}{9}\right)-\frac{1}{3}$$

$$=\ln\frac{4}{3}-\ln e^{1/3}=\ln\left(\frac{4}{9e^{1/3}}\right)$$

49. $f\left(\dfrac{x}{y}\right)=\dfrac{f(x)}{f(y)}$, $f'(1)=2024$

Put $x=y$

$f(1)=1$

On differentiating given equation w.r.t. x, taking y as constant, we get

$$f'\left(\frac{x}{y}\right)\cdot\frac{1}{y}=\frac{f'(x)}{f(y)}$$

Put $x=y$

$$f'(1)\frac{1}{x}=\frac{f'(x)}{f(x)}$$

$$\Rightarrow \frac{2024}{x}=\frac{f'(x)}{f(x)}$$

$$\Rightarrow 2024f(x)=xf'(x)$$

$$\Rightarrow xf'(x)-2024f(x)=0$$

50. We have, $f(x)=\dfrac{(2^x+2^{-x})\tan x\sqrt{\tan^{-1}(x^2-x+1)}}{(7x^2+3x+1)^3}$

$$f(x)=\frac{(\tan x)[(2^x+2^{-x})\sqrt{\tan^{-1}(x^2-x+1)}]}{(7x^2+3x+1)^3}$$

Let $g(x)=(2^x+2^{-x})\sqrt{\tan^{-1}(x^2-x+1)}$

$\therefore$ $$f(x)=\frac{\tan x\cdot g(x)}{(7x^2+3x+1)^3}$$

$$\therefore f'(x)=\frac{(7x^2+3x+1)^3\left[\tan x\cdot\frac{d}{dx}g(x)+g(x)\cdot\sec^2 x\right]-\tan x\cdot g(x)\frac{d}{dx}(7x^2+3x+1)^3}{(7x^2+3x+1)^6}$$

$$\therefore f'(0)=\frac{(1)^3g(0)\sec^2(0)-0}{(1)^6}$$

$$f'(0)=(1+1)\sqrt{\tan^{-1}(1)}=2\sqrt{\frac{\pi}{4}}=\frac{2\sqrt{\pi}}{2}=\sqrt{\pi}$$

51. $\ln y=3\sin^{-1}x$

Differentiating w.r.t. x, we get

$$\frac{1}{y}\frac{dy}{dx}=\frac{3}{\sqrt{1-x^2}}$$

$$\sqrt{1-x^2}y'=3y$$

Again, differentiating w.r.t. x, we get

$$\sqrt{1-x^2}y''+y'\frac{1}{2\sqrt{1-x^2}}\times -2x=3y'$$

$$(1-x^2)y''-xy'=3y'(1-x^2)^{1/2}$$

At $x=1/2$,

$$y=e^{\pi/2}$$

$$\Rightarrow y'=2\sqrt{3}e^{\pi/2}$$

$$\therefore (1-x^2)y''-xy'=3\times 2\sqrt{3}e^{\frac{\pi}{2}}\cdot\frac{\sqrt{3}}{2}=9e^{\pi/2}$$

52. Given, $f(x)=ax^3+bx^2+cx+41$ ...(i)

$$f(1)=40,\ f'(1)=2,\ f''(1)=4$$

Now, differentiating Eq. (i) w.r.t. x, we have

$$f'(x)=3ax^2+2bx+c$$

$\therefore$ $f'(1)=3a+2b+c=2$ [given] ...(ii)

Again, differentiating,

$$f''(x)=6ax+2b$$

$\therefore$ $f''(1)=6a+2b=4$ [given]

$\Rightarrow$ $3a+b=2$ ...(iii)

Subtracting in Eqs. (ii) and (iii), we get

$\Rightarrow$ $b+c=0$ ...(iv)

Now, $f(1)=40\Rightarrow a+b+c+41=40$

$\Rightarrow$ $a+0=40-41$

$\Rightarrow$ $a=-1$ [using Eq. (iv)]

From Eq. (iii), $3\times(-1)+b=2\Rightarrow b=5$

From Eq. (ii), $3\times(-1)+2\times 5+c=2\Rightarrow c=-5$

Hence, $a^2+b^2+c^2=1+25+25=51$

53. According to the question,

$$f(x) = x^3 \sin\left(\frac{1}{x}\right)$$

Let's find first derivative

$$f'(x) = 3x^2 \sin\frac{1}{x} + x^3 \cos\frac{1}{x} \times \left(-\frac{1}{x^2}\right)$$

$$= 3x^2 \sin\frac{1}{x} - x\cos\frac{1}{x}$$

Now, $f''(x) = 6x \sin\frac{1}{x} + 3x^2 \cos\frac{1}{x} \times \left(-\frac{1}{x^2}\right)$

$$- \cos\frac{1}{x} - x \times \left(-\sin\frac{1}{x}\right)\left(-\frac{1}{x^2}\right)$$

$$= 6x \sin\frac{1}{x} - 4\cos\frac{1}{x} - \frac{1}{x}\sin\frac{1}{x};\ x \neq 0$$

Now, $f''(0) =$ Not defined,

$$f''\left(\frac{2}{\pi}\right) = 6 \times \frac{2}{\pi} \sin\left(\frac{\pi}{2}\right) - 4\cos\frac{\pi}{2} - \frac{\pi}{2}\sin\frac{\pi}{2}$$

$$= \frac{12}{\pi} - \frac{\pi}{2} = \frac{24 - \pi^2}{2\pi}$$

54. $y = \dfrac{2\cos\theta + \cos 2\theta}{\cos 3\theta + 4\cos 2\theta + 5\cos\theta + 2}$

$[\because \cos 2\theta = 2\cos^2\theta - 1 \text{ and } \cos 3\theta = 4\cos^3\theta - 3\cos\theta]$

$$= \frac{(2\cos^2\theta + 2\cos\theta - 1)}{4\cos^3\theta - 3\cos\theta + 8\cos^2\theta - 4 + 5\cos\theta + 2}$$

$$= \frac{(2\cos^2\theta + 2\cos\theta - 1)}{(2\cos^2\theta + 2\cos\theta - 1)(2\cos\theta + 2)}$$

$$\Rightarrow \quad y = \frac{1}{2\cos\theta + 2}$$

$$y = \frac{1}{2}\left(\frac{1}{\cos\theta + 1}\right) = \frac{1}{4}\cdot\sec^2\frac{\theta}{2}$$

$$\Rightarrow [y]_{\theta = \frac{\pi}{2}} = \frac{1}{4} \times 2 = \frac{1}{2}$$

$$\Rightarrow \quad y' = \frac{1}{4} \times 2 \cdot \sec\frac{\theta}{2} \cdot \sec\frac{\theta}{2} \cdot \tan\frac{\theta}{2} \times \frac{1}{2} = \frac{1}{2}\sec^2\frac{\theta}{2} \cdot \tan\frac{\theta}{2} \cdot \frac{1}{2}$$

$$[y']_{\theta = \frac{\pi}{2}} = \frac{1}{2} \times 2 \times \frac{1}{2} = \frac{1}{2}$$

$$y'' = \frac{1}{2}\left[\frac{1}{2}\left(2\sec\frac{\theta}{2} \cdot \sec\frac{\theta}{2} \cdot \tan\frac{\theta}{2}\right) + \frac{1}{2}\sec^2\frac{\theta}{2} \cdot \sec^2\frac{\theta}{2}\right]$$

$$\Rightarrow \quad [y'']_{\theta = \pi/2} = 1$$

$$\therefore \quad y'' + y' + y = 2$$

55. $y = \log_e\left(\dfrac{1 - x^2}{1 + x^2}\right), -1 < x < 1$

$$y' = \frac{1}{\left(\frac{1 - x^2}{1 + x^2}\right)} \cdot \frac{(1 + x^2)(-2x) - (1 - x^2)(2x)}{(1 + x^2)^2}$$

$$= \frac{2x(-1 - x^2 - 1 + x^2)}{(1 - x^2)(1 + x^2)} = \frac{-4x}{1 - x^4}$$

$$y'' = \frac{(1 - x^4)(-4) - (-4x)(-4x^3)}{(1 - x^4)^2}$$

$$= 4\frac{(-3x^4 - 1)}{(1 - x^4)^2} = -4\left[\frac{3x^4 + 1}{(1 - x^4)^2}\right]$$

At $x = \dfrac{1}{2}$, $y' = \dfrac{-4 \times \frac{1}{2}}{1 - \frac{1}{16}} = \dfrac{-2 \times 16}{15} = \dfrac{-32}{15}$

and $\quad y'' = \dfrac{-4\left(\frac{3}{16} + 1\right)}{\left(1 - \frac{1}{16}\right)^2} = \dfrac{-4 \times 19}{16} \times \dfrac{16 \times 16}{15 \times 15} = \dfrac{-64 \times 19}{225}$

Now, $225(y' - y'') = 225\left(\dfrac{-32}{15} + \dfrac{64 \times 19}{225}\right)$

$$= 32(-15 + 38) = 736$$

56. Given, $g'\left(\dfrac{1}{2}\right) = g'\left(\dfrac{3}{2}\right)$

Now, $\quad f(x) = \dfrac{1}{2}[g(x) + g(2 - x)]$

$$f'(x) = \frac{1}{2}(g'(x) - g'(2 - x)]$$

Now, $\quad f'\left(\dfrac{1}{2}\right) = \dfrac{1}{2}\left[g'\left(\dfrac{1}{2}\right) - g'\left(\dfrac{3}{2}\right)\right] = 0 \quad \left[\because g'\left(\dfrac{1}{2}\right) = g'\left(\dfrac{3}{2}\right)\right]$

Now, $\quad f'\left(\dfrac{3}{2}\right) = \dfrac{1}{2}\left[g'\left(\dfrac{3}{2}\right) - g'\left(\dfrac{1}{2}\right)\right] = 0$

$$\therefore \quad f'\left(\frac{3}{2}\right) = f'\left(\frac{1}{2}\right) = 0$$

So, roots in $\left(\dfrac{1}{2}, 1\right)$ and $\left(\dfrac{1}{2}, \dfrac{3}{2}\right)$.

$\Rightarrow f''(x) = 0$ at least two x in $(1/2, 3/2)$

So, $f''(x) = 0$ for atleast two x in $(0, 2)$.

57. Given, $f(x) = \begin{cases} \left(\dfrac{8}{7}\right)^{\frac{\tan 8x}{\tan 7x}}, & 0 < x < \dfrac{\pi}{2} \\ a - 8, & x = \dfrac{\pi}{2} \\ (1 + |\cot x|)^{\frac{b}{a}|\tan x|}, & \dfrac{\pi}{2} < x < \pi \end{cases}$

LHL at $x = \dfrac{\pi}{2}$ i.e. $f\left(\dfrac{\pi^-}{2}\right) = \lim\limits_{x \to \frac{\pi^-}{2}} \left(\dfrac{8}{7}\right)^{\frac{\tan 8x}{\tan 7x}}$

Putting $x = \dfrac{\pi}{2} - h$, as $x \to \dfrac{\pi^-}{2}$, then $h \to 0$

So, LHL $= \lim\limits_{h \to 0}\left(\dfrac{8}{7}\right)^{\frac{\tan\left[8\left(\frac{\pi}{2} - h\right)\right]}{\tan\left[7\left(\frac{\pi}{2} - h\right)\right]}} = \lim\limits_{h \to 0}\left(\dfrac{8}{7}\right)^{\frac{-\tan 8h}{\cot h}} = \left(\dfrac{8}{7}\right)^0 = 1$

$$f\left(\frac{\pi}{2}\right) = a - 8$$

$$\text{RHL} = \lim_{x\to \frac{\pi}{2}^+} (1+|\cot x|)^{\frac{b}{a}|\tan x|}$$

$$= e^{\lim_{x\to \frac{\pi}{2}^+} |\cot x|\cdot\frac{b}{a}|\tan x|} = e^{\frac{b}{a}}$$

Since, $f(x)$ is continuous at $x = \frac{\pi}{2}$

So, $a - 8 = 1 = e^{b/a} \Rightarrow a = 9$ and $b = 0$

Hence, $a^2 + b^2 = (9)^2 + (0)^2 = 81$

58. $\left[\frac{x}{2}+3\right]$ is discontinuous at $x = 2, 4, 6, 8$

$\sqrt{x}$ is discontinuous at $x = 1, 4$

$F(x)$ is discontinuous at $x = 1, 2, 6, 8$

$$\Sigma a = 1 + 2 + 6 + 8 = 17$$

59. $L = \lim_{x\to 0} 2\left(\frac{1-\cos x\,(\cos 2x)^{1/2}\,(\cos 3x)^{1/3}\ldots(\cos 10x)^{1/10}}{x^2}\right)$

At $x = 0$, L makes $\frac{0}{0}$ form

So, we will use L-Hospital's rule

$\because \quad \frac{d}{dx}(x^2) = 2x$ and $\frac{d}{dx}(1) = 0$

Let $y = \cos x\,(\cos 2x)^{\frac{1}{2}} \ldots (\cos 10x)^{\frac{1}{10}}$

Let $\log(y) = \log(\cos x) + \frac{1}{2}\log\cos(2x) + \ldots + \frac{1}{10}\log(\cos 10x)$

$$\frac{1}{y}\left(\frac{dy}{dx}\right) = \tan x + \frac{1}{2}\times 2\tan 2x + \ldots + \frac{1}{10}\times 10\tan 10x$$

$$\frac{dy}{dx} = y(\tan x + \tan 2x + \ldots + \tan 10x)$$

So, $L = \lim_{x\to 0} 2\left(\frac{y(\tan x + \tan 2x + \ldots + \tan 10x)}{2x}\right)$

$$\left[\because \lim_{x\to 0} \cos x\,(\cos 2x)^{\frac{1}{2}} \ldots (\cos 10x)^{\frac{1}{10}} = 1\right]$$

$$= \lim_{x\to 0} 1\times\left(\frac{\tan x}{x} + \frac{2\tan 2x}{2x} + \ldots + \frac{10\tan 10x}{10x}\right)$$

$$= 1 + 2 + 3 + \ldots + 10$$

$$= \frac{10\times 11}{2} = 55$$

60. We have, $y = \frac{(\sqrt{x}+1)(x^2-\sqrt{x})}{x\sqrt{x}+x+\sqrt{x}} + \frac{1}{15}(3\cos^2 x - 5)\cos^3 x$

$$y = \frac{(\sqrt{x}+1)\cdot\sqrt{x}(x\sqrt{x}-1)}{x\sqrt{x}+x+\sqrt{x}} + \frac{1}{15}(3\cos^2 x - 5)\cos^3 x$$

$$y = \frac{(\sqrt{x}+1)\cdot(\sqrt{x}((\sqrt{x})^3 - 1^3)}{x\sqrt{x}+x+\sqrt{x}} + \frac{1}{15}(3\cos^5 x - 5\cos^3 x)$$

$$y = \frac{(\sqrt{x}+1)\cdot\sqrt{x}(\sqrt{x}-1)(x+\sqrt{x}+1)}{\sqrt{x}\,(x+\sqrt{x}+1)} + \frac{1}{15}(3\cos^5 x - 5\cos^3 x)$$

$$y = (x-1) + \frac{1}{15}(3\cos^5 x - 5\cos^3 x)$$

Now, differentiate w.r.t. x, we get

$$y' = 1 - 0 + \frac{1}{15}[15\cos^4 x(-\sin x) - 15\cos^2 x(-\sin x)]$$

$$y' = 1 - \sin x(\cos^4 x - \cos^2 x)$$

$$y'\left(\frac{\pi}{6}\right) = 1 - \sin\frac{\pi}{6}\left(\cos^4\frac{\pi}{6} - \cos^2\frac{\pi}{6}\right)$$

$$= 1 - \frac{1}{2}\left(\frac{9}{16} - \frac{3}{4}\right) = 1 - \frac{1}{2}\left(\frac{9-12}{16}\right) = 1 + \frac{3}{32} = \frac{35}{32}$$

$$\therefore \quad 96y'\left(\frac{\pi}{6}\right) = 96\times\frac{35}{32} = 105$$

61. $f(x) = 2^x - x^2 \Rightarrow f'(x) = 2^x\log 2 - 2x$

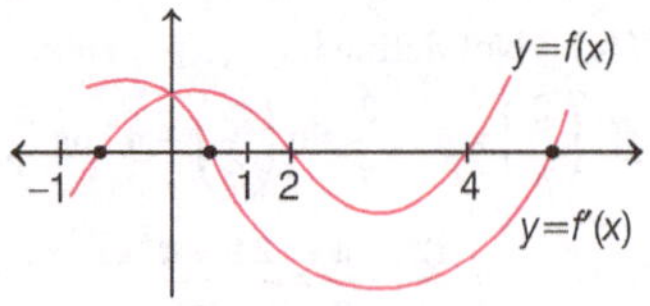

Clearly, $\quad m = 3$ and $n = 2$

$\therefore \quad m + n = 5$

62. $(3f'f'' + ff''')(x) = [(ff'' + (f')^2)(x)]'$

$$= (f'(f'(x))' = (f(x) - f'(x))''$$

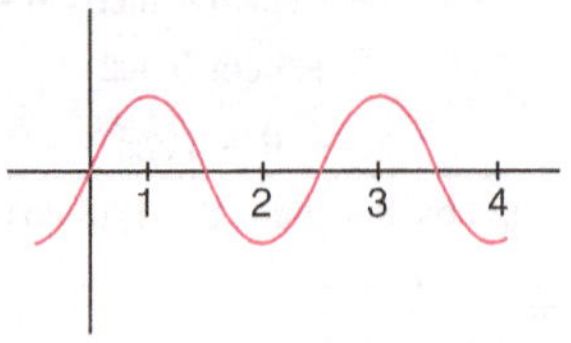

Minimum number of roots of $f(x) = 4$

Minimum number of root of $f'(x) = 3$

Minimum number of root of $f(x)\cdot f'(x) = 7$

Minimum number of roots of $[f(x)\cdot f'(x)]' = 5$

63. Given equation is

$$f(x) = x^3 + x^2 f'(1) + xf''(2) + f'''(3),\ x\in R \quad \ldots\text{(i)}$$

Differentiating

$$f'(x) = 3x^2 + 2xf'(1) + f''(2) \quad \ldots\text{(ii)}$$

Again, differentiating

$$f''(x) = 6x + 2f'(1) \quad \ldots\text{(iii)}$$

Again, differentiating,

$$f'''(x) = 6 \quad \ldots\text{(iv)}$$

Now, $f(1) = -5$, $f''(2) = 2$, $f'''(3) = 6$

[with the help of above Eqs. (ii), (iii) and (iv)]

$$f(x) = x^3 + x^2(-5) + x(2) + 6$$

$$\Rightarrow \quad f'(x) = 3x^2 - 10x + 2$$

Hence, $f'(10) = 300 - 100 + 2$

$$= 202$$

64. We have, $f(x)=[x^2-x]+|-x+[x]|=[x(x-1)]+\{x\}$

$$f(x)=\begin{cases} x+1 & ; & -0.5<x<0 \\ 0 & ; & x=0 \\ -1+x & ; & 0<x<1 \\ 0 & ; & x=1 \\ x-1 & ; & 1<x<1.5 \end{cases}$$

At $x=0$,

$$\text{LHL}=\lim_{x\to 0^-} f(x)=1$$

$$\text{RHL}=\lim_{x\to 0^+} f(x)=-1 \text{ and } f(0)=0$$

$\therefore f(x)$ is not continuous at $x=0$

At $x=1$, LHL $=\lim_{x\to 1^-} f(x)=-1+1=0$

$$\text{RHL}=\lim_{x\to 1^+} f(x)=1-1=0$$

$$f(1)=0$$

$\therefore f(x)$ is continuous at $x=1$

Hence, $f(x)$ is continuous at $x=1$,

but not continuous at $x=0$.

65. Let $f(x)=\begin{cases} (1+|\cos x|)^{\frac{\lambda}{|\cos x|}}, & 0<x<\dfrac{\pi}{2} \\ \mu \quad , & x=\dfrac{\pi}{2} \\ e^{\left(\frac{\cot 6x}{\cot 4x}\right)} \quad , & \dfrac{\pi}{2}<x<\pi \end{cases}$

Now, LHL $=\lim_{x\to \frac{\pi}{2}^-} f(x)=\lim_{x\to \frac{\pi}{2}^-} (1+|\cos x|)^{\frac{\lambda}{|\cos x|}}$

[it's of 1^∞ form]

So, LHL $=e^{\left(\lim_{x\to \frac{\pi}{2}^-} \lambda\right)}=e^{\lambda}$

Now, RHL $=\lim_{x\to \frac{\pi}{2}^+} f(x)=\lim_{x\to \frac{\pi}{2}^+} e^{\left(\frac{\cot 6x}{\cot 4x}\right)}$

$$\text{RHL}=e^{\lim_{x\to \frac{\pi}{2}^+} \frac{\cot 6x}{\cot 4x}}$$

So, $\quad \text{RHL}=e^{\lim_{x\to \frac{\pi}{2}^+}\left(\frac{\tan 4x}{\tan 6x}\right)}$

$$\text{RHL}=e^{\lim_{h\to 0}\left(\frac{\tan 4\left(\frac{\pi}{2}+h\right)}{\tan 6\left(\frac{\pi}{2}+h\right)}\right)}$$

So, $\quad \text{RHL}=e^{\lim_{h\to 0}\left[\frac{\tan 4h}{\tan 6h}\right]}$

Now, multiplying and divide $4h$ and $6h$ in power of e

$$\text{RHL}=\lim_{e^{h\to 0}}\left[\left(\frac{\tan 4h}{4h}\right)\left(\frac{6h}{\tan 6h}\right)\left(\frac{4h}{6h}\right)\right] \quad \left[\because \lim_{x\to 0}\frac{\tan x}{x}=1\right]$$

So, RHL $=e^{2/3}$

For continuity of a function

LHL = RHL = Functional value

$$e^{\lambda}=e^{2/3}=\mu$$

By comparison, $\lambda=2/3$ and $\mu=e^{2/3}$

Now, $9\lambda+6\log_e\mu+\mu^6-e^{6\lambda}=6+6\left(\frac{2}{3}\right)+e^4-e^4=10$

66. Given, $f(x)=\max\{1+x+[x]; 2+x, x+2[x]\}\ 0\le x\le 2$

Given that, m denoter the number of points in $[0, 2]$, where f is not continuous and n be denote the number of point in $(0, 2)$, where f is not differentiable.

Let $f_1(r)=1+x+[x]=\begin{bmatrix} 1+x, & x\in[0,1) \\ 2+x, & x\in[1,2) \\ 5 & x=2 \end{bmatrix}$

$$f_2=2+x,\quad 0\le x\le 2$$

$$f_3(x)=x+2[x]=\begin{cases} x, & x\in[0,1) \\ 2+x, & x\in[1,2] \\ 6, & x=2 \end{cases}$$

So, $f(x)=\max\{f_1(x), f_2(x), f_3(x)\}$ in $0\le x\le 2$

Then, $f(x)=\begin{cases} 2+x, & x\in[0,2) \\ 6, & x=2 \end{cases}$

Clearly, $f(x)$ is discontinuous only at $x=2$

So, $\qquad m=1$

and $f(x)$ is differentiable in $(0, 2)$ so $n=0$

$\therefore \qquad (m+n)^2+2=(1+0)+2=1+2=3$

67. Given, $3f(x)+2f\left(\frac{1}{x}\right)=\frac{1}{x}-10$ ...(i)

Change x to $1/x$, we get

$$3f\left(\frac{1}{x}\right)+2f(x)=x-10$$

$\Rightarrow \quad \frac{3}{2}\left[\frac{1}{x}-10-3f(x)\right]+2f(x)=x-10$ [from Eq. (i)]

$$\Rightarrow \quad \frac{3}{2x}-15-\frac{9}{2}f(x)+2f(x)=x-10$$

$$\Rightarrow \quad -\frac{5}{2}f(x)-15+\frac{3}{2x}=x-10$$

$$\Rightarrow \quad -\frac{5}{2}f(x)=x-\frac{3}{2x}+5$$

$$\Rightarrow \quad f(x)=-\frac{2}{5}x+\frac{3}{5x}-2$$

$$\Rightarrow \quad f'(x)=\frac{-2}{5}-\frac{3}{5x^2}$$

$\therefore \qquad f(3)=-3$ and $f'\left(\frac{1}{4}\right)=-10$

$$\left|f(3)+f'\left(\frac{1}{4}\right)\right|=|-3+(-10)|$$

$$=|-3-10|$$

$$=|-13|=13$$

68. Given, $f(x)=\begin{cases} x+1, & x<0 \\ |x-1|, & x\ge 0\end{cases}$

and $g(x)=\begin{cases} x+1, & x<0 \\ 1, & x\ge 0\end{cases}$

Then, $gof(x)=g(f(x))=\begin{cases} f(x)+1, & f(x)<0 \\ 1, & f(x)\ge 0\end{cases}$

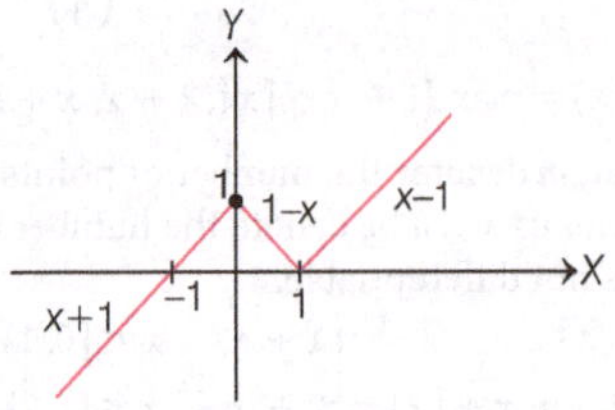

Here, $f(x)<0$ for $x\in(-\infty,-1]$ and $f(x)\ge 0$ for $x\in[-1,\infty)$

Now, $g(f(x))=\begin{cases}(x+1)+1, & x<-1\\ 1, & x\ge -1\end{cases}$

$g(f(x))=\begin{cases}x+2, & x<-1\\ 1, & x\ge -1\end{cases}$

Check continuity at $x=-1$

$\text{LHL}=g(f(-1))=-1+2=1$

$\text{RHL}=g(f(-1^+))=1$

$\therefore$ Continuous at $x=-1$

$(g((f(x)))'=\begin{cases}1, & x<-1\\ 0, & x\ge -1\end{cases}$

For differentiability at $x=-1$

$\text{LHD}=g'(f(-1^-))=1$

$\text{RHD}=g'(f(-1^+))=0$

$\text{LHD}\ne\text{RHD}$

$\Rightarrow$ not differentiable at $x=-1$

Hence, $gof(x)$ is continuous everywhere but not differentiable at $x=-1$ (exactly at one point).

69. Given function,

$$f(x)=\begin{cases}x^2\sin\left(\dfrac{1}{x}\right), & x\ne 0\\ 0, & x=0\end{cases}$$

To check continuity at $x=0$

$\text{LHL}\ \lim\limits_{x\to 0^-} f(x)=\lim\limits_{h\to 0} f(0-h)$

$=\lim\limits_{h\to 0}(-h)^2\cdot\sin\left(-\dfrac{1}{h}\right)=0$

$\text{RHL}=\lim\limits_{x\to 0^+} f(x)=\lim\limits_{h\to 0} f(0+h)=\lim\limits_{h\to 0} h^2\sin\left(\dfrac{1}{h}\right)=0$

Value of function $=f(0)=0$

Here, $\text{LHL}=\text{RHL}=f(0)$

$\Rightarrow f(x)$ is continuous at $x=0$.

To check differentiability of $f(x)$ at $x=0$

$\text{RHD}=f'(0^+)=\lim\limits_{h\to 0}\dfrac{f(0+h)-f(0)}{h}=\lim\limits_{h\to 0} h\sin\left(\dfrac{1}{h}\right)=0$

$\text{LHD}=f'(0^-)=\lim\limits_{h\to 0}\dfrac{f(0-h)-f(0)}{-h}=\lim\limits_{h\to 0}-h\sin\left(\dfrac{1}{h}\right)=0$

Here, $\text{LHD}=\text{RHD}=0$

$\therefore f(x)$ is differentiable at $x=0$.

Now, we differentiate $f(x)$,

$$\Rightarrow\quad f'(x)=\begin{cases}2x\sin\left(\dfrac{1}{x}\right)-\cos\left(\dfrac{1}{x}\right), & x\ne 0\\ 0, & x=0\end{cases}$$

As, we know that $\cos\left(\dfrac{1}{x}\right)$ is highly oscillating at $x=0$.

So, $f'(x)$ is not continuous at $x=0$.

70. We have, $y=f(x)=\sin^3\left(\dfrac{\pi}{3}\left(\cos\left(\dfrac{\pi}{3\sqrt{2}}(-4x^3+5x^2+1)^{3/2}\right)\right)\right)$

$$\frac{dy}{dx}=3\sin^2\left(\frac{\pi}{3}\left(\cos\left(\frac{\pi}{3\sqrt{2}}(-4x^3+5x^2+1)^{3/2}\right)\right)\right)\times\cos\left(\frac{\pi}{3}\left(\cos\left(\frac{\pi}{3\sqrt{2}}(-4x^3+5x^2+1)^{3/2}\right)\right)\right)\times\frac{\pi}{3}\times\left(-\sin\left(\frac{\pi}{3\sqrt{2}}(-4x^3+5x^2+1)^{3/2}\right)\right)\times\frac{\pi}{3\sqrt{2}}\times\frac{3}{2}\times(-4x^3+5x^2+1)^{1/2}\times(-12x^2+10x)$$

Now, at $x=1$ $\quad y=f(1)=\sin^3\left(\dfrac{\pi}{3}\cos\left(\dfrac{\pi}{3\sqrt{2}}(-4+5+1)^{3/2}\right)\right)$

$$=\sin^3\left(\frac{\pi}{3}\left(\cos\frac{2\pi}{3}\right)\right)=\sin^3\left(\frac{\pi}{3}\times\left(-\frac{1}{2}\right)\right)$$

$$=\left(-\frac{1}{2}\right)^3=-\frac{1}{8}$$

and $\quad y'(1)=3\left(-\dfrac{1}{2}\right)^2\cdot\left(\dfrac{\sqrt{3}}{2}\right)\left(-\dfrac{\pi}{3}\right)\left(\dfrac{\sqrt{3}}{2}\right)\cdot\dfrac{\pi}{3\sqrt{2}}\left(\dfrac{3}{2}\sqrt{2}\right)(-2)=\dfrac{3\pi^2}{16}$

Now, $2y'+3\pi^2 y$

$$=2\left(\frac{3\pi^2}{16}\right)+3\pi^2\left(-\frac{1}{8}\right)=\frac{3\pi^2}{8}-\frac{3\pi^2}{8}=0$$

71. We have, $f(\theta)=3\left\{\sin^4\left(\dfrac{3\pi}{2}-\theta\right)+\sin^4(3\pi+\theta)\right\}-2(1-\sin^2(2\theta))$

Using $\sin\left(\dfrac{3\pi}{2}-\theta\right)=-\cos\theta$

and $\quad(\sin(3\pi+\theta)=\sin\theta)$, we get

$$f(\theta)=3(\cos^4\theta+\sin^4\theta)-2(1-\sin^2(2\theta))$$

$$=3[(\cos^2\theta+\sin^2\theta)^2-2\sin^2\theta\cos^2\theta]-2[(1-\sin^2(2\theta)]$$

$$=3\left[1-\frac{(2\sin\theta\cos\theta)^2}{2}\right]-2+2\sin^2(2\theta)\ [\because \sin^2\theta+\cos^2\theta=1]$$

$$= 3 - \frac{3\sin^2(2\theta)}{2} - 2 + 2\sin^2(2\theta) \quad [\because 2\sin A\cos A = \sin 2A]$$

$$= 1 + \frac{\sin^2(2\theta)}{2} \quad \text{... (i)}$$

Now, $S = \left\{\theta \in [0, \pi] : f'(\theta) = -\frac{\sqrt{3}}{2}\right\}$

Now, $f'(\theta) = \left[1 + \frac{\sin^2(2\theta)}{2}\right]' = \frac{1}{2} \times [\sin^2(2\theta)]'$

$$= \frac{1}{2} \times 2\sin(2\theta) \cdot [\sin(2\theta)]'$$

$$= \sin(2\theta) \cdot \cos(2\theta) \cdot 2 = \sin(4\theta)$$

$\theta \in [0, \pi] \Rightarrow 4\theta \in [0, 4\pi]$

According to question,

$$\sin(4\theta) = -\frac{\sqrt{3}}{2} \text{ in } [0, 4\pi] \Rightarrow 4\theta = \frac{4\pi}{3}, \frac{5\pi}{3}, \frac{10\pi}{3}, \frac{11\pi}{3}$$

$$\Rightarrow \quad \theta = \frac{\pi}{3}, \frac{5\pi}{12}, \frac{5\pi}{6}, \frac{11\pi}{12}$$

Given, $4\beta = \sum_{\theta \in S} \theta = \frac{\pi}{3} + \frac{5\pi}{12} + \frac{5\pi}{6} + \frac{11\pi}{12}$

$$= \frac{4\pi + 5\pi + 10\pi + 11\pi}{12} = \frac{5\pi}{2} \Rightarrow \beta = \frac{5\pi}{8}$$

$$\therefore \quad f(\beta) = 1 + \frac{\sin^2(2\beta)}{2} = 1 + \frac{\sin^2\left(\frac{5\pi}{4}\right)}{2} = 1 + \frac{\sin^2\left(\pi + \frac{\pi}{4}\right)}{2}$$

[using $\sin(\pi + x) = -\sin x$]

$$= 1 + \frac{\sin^2\left(\frac{\pi}{4}\right)}{2} = 1 + \frac{\left(\frac{1}{\sqrt{2}}\right)^2}{2} = 1 + \frac{1}{4} = \frac{5}{4}$$

72. $f(x) = \dfrac{\sin x + \cos x - \sqrt{2}}{\sin x - \cos x}$

On dividing numerator and denominator by $\sqrt{2}$,

$$f(x) = \frac{\frac{1}{\sqrt{2}}\sin x + \frac{1}{\sqrt{2}}\cos x - 1}{\frac{1}{\sqrt{2}}\sin x - \frac{1}{\sqrt{2}}\cos x}$$

$$f(x) = \frac{\sin\left(x + \frac{\pi}{4}\right) - 1}{\sin\left(x - \frac{\pi}{4}\right)}$$

Differentiating $f(x)$ w.r.t. x, we get

$$f'(x) = \frac{\sin\left(x - \frac{\pi}{4}\right)\cos\left(x + \frac{\pi}{4}\right) - \cos\left(x - \frac{\pi}{4}\right)\left\{\sin\left(x + \frac{\pi}{4}\right) - 1\right\}}{\sin^2\left(x - \frac{\pi}{4}\right)}$$

$$= \frac{\cos\left(x - \frac{\pi}{4}\right) - 1}{\sin^2\left(x - \frac{\pi}{4}\right)} = \frac{-1}{1 + \cos\left(x - \frac{\pi}{4}\right)}$$

Again differentiating $f(x)$ w.r.t. x, we get

$$f''(x) = \frac{-\sin\left(x - \frac{\pi}{4}\right)}{\left[1 + \cos\left(x - \frac{\pi}{4}\right)\right]^2}$$

Now, $f\left(\frac{7\pi}{12}\right) = -\frac{1}{\sqrt{3}}$ and $f''\left(\frac{7\pi}{12}\right) = -\frac{2\sqrt{3}}{9}$

$$\therefore \quad f\left(\frac{7\pi}{12}\right) f''\left(\frac{7\pi}{12}\right) = \frac{2}{9}$$

73. We have, $y = x^x$

$\Rightarrow \quad \log y = x\log x$

On differentiating both sides w.r.t. x, we get

$$\frac{1}{y}y' = \log x + \frac{x}{x}$$

$$\Rightarrow \quad y' = y(\log x + 1) \quad \text{...(i)}$$

Again, differentiating both sides w.r.t. x, we get

$$y'' = y'(\log x + 1) + \frac{y}{x} \quad \text{...(ii)}$$

Now, $y'(2) = y(2)(\log 2 + 1) = 2^2(\log 2 + 1) = 4(\log 2 + 1)$

and $y''(2) = y'(2)(\log 2 + 1) + \frac{y(2)}{2} = 4(\log 2 + 1)^2 + 2$

Now, $y''(2) - 2y'(2) = 4(\log 2 + 1)^2 + 2 - 8(\log 2 + 1)$

$$= 4(\log 2 + 1)[\log 2 + 1 - 2] + 2$$
$$= 4(\log 2 + 1)(\log 2 - 1) + 2$$
$$= 4((\log 2)^2 - 1) + 2$$
$$= 4(\log 2)^2 - 4 + 2 = 4(\log 2)^2 - 2$$

74. Given that $f''(x) = g''(x) + 6x$

$$f'(1) = 4g'(1) - 3 = 9$$
$$f(2) = 3g(2) = 12$$

Here, $f''(x) = g''(x) + 6x$

Integrating both sides, we get

$$f'(x) = g'(x) + 3x^2 + c_1 \quad \text{...(i)}$$

Again integrating both sides, we get

$$f(x) = g(x) + x^3 + c_1x + c_2 \quad \text{...(ii)}$$

where, c_1 and c_2 are constant of integration.

Now, use $f'(1) = 4g'(1) - 3 = 9$ in Eq. (i), we get

$$9 = 3 + 3 + c_1 \Rightarrow c_1 = 3$$

Again use $f(2) = 3g(2) = 12$ in Eq. (ii), we get

$$12 = 4 + 8 + 6 + c_2 \Rightarrow c_2 = -6$$

So, $f(x) = g(x) = + x^3 + 3x - 6$

Now, $f(x) - g(x) = x^3 + 3x - 6$

Let at $x = x_0$, $f(x_0) = g(x_0)$

So, $x_0^3 + 3x_0 - 6 = 0$

Now, let $h(x) = x^3 + 3x - 6$

In the interval $\left(1, \frac{3}{2}\right)$, $h(1) = -2(-\text{ve})$

$$h\left(\frac{3}{2}\right) = \frac{15}{8}(+\text{ve})$$

So, $h(x)$ has a root between $(1, 3/2)$.

$\Rightarrow \quad x_0 \in \left(1, \frac{3}{2}\right)$ such that $f(x_0) = g(x_0)$

Option (a) is true.

$$h(-2) = f(-2) - g(-2) = -20$$

$$\Rightarrow \quad g(-2) - f(-2) = 20$$

Option (b) is true.

Now, $|f'(x) - g'(x)| < 6$

$$\Rightarrow \quad |3x^2 + 3| < 6$$

$$\Rightarrow \quad -6 < 3x^2 + 3 < 6$$

$$\Rightarrow \quad 3x^2 + 3 < 6 \quad [\because 3x^2 + 3 > -6 \text{ is true for all } x \in R]$$

$$\Rightarrow \quad x^2 - 1 < 0$$

$$\Rightarrow \quad |x| < 1$$

$$\Rightarrow \quad x \in (-1, 1)$$

Option (d) is true.

75. $y = (1 + x)(1 + x^2)(1 + x^4)(1 + x^8)(1 + x^{16})$

$$\Rightarrow y = \frac{(1 - x)(1 + x)(1 + x^2)(1 + x^4)(1 + x^8)(1 + x^{16})}{(1 - x)}$$

$$\Rightarrow y = \frac{(1 - x^2)(1 + x^2)(1 + x^4)(1 + x^8)(1 + x^{16})}{(1 - x)}$$

$$\Rightarrow y = \frac{(1 - x^4)(1 + x^4)(1 + x^8)(1 + x^{16})}{(1 - x)}$$

$$\Rightarrow y = \frac{(1 - x^8)(1 + x^8)(1 + x^{16})}{(1 - x)}$$

$$\Rightarrow y = \frac{(1 - x^{16})(1 + x^{16})}{1 - x} \Rightarrow y = \frac{1 - x^{32}}{1 - x}$$

$$\Rightarrow y(1 - x) = 1 - x^{32}$$

On differentiating w.r.t. x, we get

$$y'(1 - x) + y(-1) = -32x^{31}$$

Again differentiating w.r.t. x, we get

$$y''(1 - x) + y'(-1) - y' = -32 \times 31\, x^{30}$$

At $x = -1$,

$$2y'' - 2y' = -32 \times 31$$

Hence, $y' - y'' = 16 \times 31 = 496$

76. We have, $f(x) = |[x]| + \sqrt{x - [x]},\ x \in (-2, 1)$

$$\text{Now, } [x] = \begin{cases} -2, & x \in (-2, -1) \\ -1, & x \in [-1, 0) \\ 0, & x \in (0, 1) \end{cases}$$

$$\therefore \quad f(x) = \begin{cases} 2 + \sqrt{x + 2}, & x \in (-2, -1) \\ 1 + \sqrt{x + 1}, & x \in [-1, 0) \\ \sqrt{x}, & x \in (0, 1) \end{cases}$$

Since square root function is continuous, we need to check on end points of intervals.

$$f(-1^-) = \lim_{x \to 1^-} f(x) = 2 + \sqrt{-1 + 2} = 3$$

$$\lim_{x \to -1^+} f(x) = 1 + \sqrt{-1 + 1} = 1$$

Since, LHL $\neq$ RHL at $x = -1$, it is a point of discontinuity.

$$\lim_{x \to 0^-} f(x) = 1 + \sqrt{0 + 1} = 2$$

$$\lim_{x \to 0^+} f(x) = \sqrt{0} = 0$$

Since, LHL $\neq$ RHL at $x = 0$, it is a point of discontinuity.

So, total 2 points of discontinuity of $f(x)$ in $(-2, 1)$.

77. $\because f(x)$ is continuous at $x = 1$

$$\therefore \quad f(1^-) = f(1^+) \Rightarrow 3 + k\sqrt{2} = m + k^2 \quad \text{... (i)}$$

$$f'(1^-) = \left[6x + \frac{k}{2\sqrt{x + 1}}\right]_{x = 1^-} = 6 + \frac{k}{2\sqrt{2}}$$

$$f'(1^+) = [2mx]_{x = 1^+} = 2m$$

$f(x)$ is differentiability at $x = 1$

$$6 + \frac{k}{2\sqrt{2}} = 2m \quad \text{... (ii)}$$

From Eqs. (i) and (ii),

$$k = \frac{7}{4\sqrt{2}} \text{ and } m = \frac{103}{32}$$

$$f'(8) = [2mx]_{x = 8} = 16m = 16 \times \frac{103}{32} = \frac{103}{2}$$

$$f'\left(\frac{1}{8}\right) = \left[6x + \frac{k}{2\sqrt{x + 1}}\right]_{x = \frac{1}{8}} = \left[6 \times \frac{1}{8} + \frac{k}{2\sqrt{\frac{1}{8} + 1}}\right]$$

$$= \frac{3}{4} + \frac{7}{4\sqrt{2}} \times \frac{\sqrt{2}}{3} = \frac{4}{3}$$

$$\therefore \quad \frac{8f'(8)}{f'\left(\frac{1}{8}\right)} = \frac{8 \times \frac{103}{2}}{\frac{4}{3}} = 4 \times 103 \times \frac{3}{4} = 309$$

78. Given function is $f(x) = \begin{cases} x[x], & -2 < x < 0 \\ (x - 1)[x], & 0 \le x < 2 \end{cases}$

When $[x]$ denotes greatest integer function

$$f(x) = \begin{cases} -2x; & -2 < x < -1 \\ -x; & -1 \le x < 0 \\ 0; & 0 \le x < 1 \\ x - 1; & 1 \le x < 2 \end{cases}$$

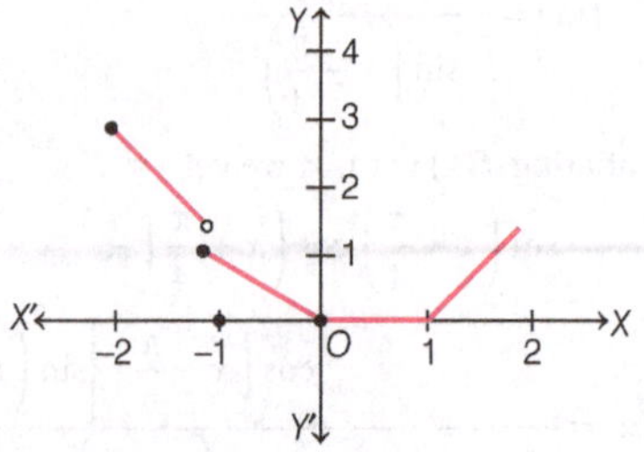

Clearly $|f(x)|$ remains same.

Given that, m and n respectively the number points in $(-2, 2)$ at which $y = |f(x)|$ is not continuous and not differentiable.

So, $m = 1$ where $y = |f(x)|$ not continuous

and $n = 3$ where $|f(x)|$ is not differentiable.

Thus, $m + n = 4$

79. We have, $f(x)=[a+13\sin x], x\in(0,\pi)$

$[13\sin x]$ is not differentiable, where $13\sin x$ is an integer.

$\therefore$ Total number of point where $f(x)$ is not differential

$$=2\times 13-1$$
$$=25$$

[$\because f(x)=[n+p\sin x], 0<x<\pi, n\in I$. and p is a prime number, then the number of points where $f(x)$ is not differentiable $=2p-1$]

80. Given, $f(x)=\sum_{k=1}^{10} k\cdot x^{k}, x\in R$

Now, $f(x)=x+2x^2+\ldots+10x^{10}$

$$\Rightarrow\quad x\cdot f(x)=x^2+2x^3+\ldots+9x^{10}+10x^{11}$$
$$\Rightarrow (1-x)f(x)=(x+2x^2+\ldots+10x^{10})-(x^2+2x^3+\ldots+9x^{10}+10x^{11})$$
$$=x+x^2+x^3+\ldots+x^{10}-10x^{11}$$
$$=\frac{x(1-x^{10})}{(1-x)}-10x^{11}$$
$$\Rightarrow f(x)=\frac{x(1-x^{10})}{(1-x)^2}-\frac{10x^{11}}{(1-x)}$$
$$=\frac{x-x^{11}-10x^{11}+10x^{12}}{(1-x)^2}=\frac{10x^{12}-11x^{11}+x}{(1-x)^2}$$
$$f'(x)=\frac{(10x^{12}-11x^{11}+x)\cdot 2\cdot(1-x)+(120x^{11}-121x^{10}+1)\cdot(1-x)^2}{(1-x)^4}$$
$$=\frac{20x^{12}-22x^{11}+2x+(120x^{11}-121x^{10}+1)(1-x)}{(1-x)^3}$$

Thus, $2f(2)+f'(2)=119\cdot 2^{10}+1$

So, $\quad n=10$

81. $f(x)=\begin{cases}\dfrac{\log_e(1+5x)-\log_e(1+\alpha x)}{x} & ;\text{ if } x\neq 0\\ 10 & ; x=0\end{cases}$

is continuous at $x=0$

Then, $\lim_{x\to 0} f(x)=10$

$$\lim_{x\to 0}\frac{\log_e(1+5x)-\log_e(1+\alpha x)}{x}=10$$
$$\lim_{x\to 0}\frac{\log(1+5x)}{5x}\times 5-\frac{\log(1+\alpha x)}{\alpha x}\times\alpha=10$$
$$\Rightarrow\quad 5-\alpha=10$$
$$\Rightarrow\quad \alpha=-5$$

82. $f(x)=\lim_{n\to\infty}\dfrac{\cos(2\pi x)-x^{2n}\sin(x-1)}{1+x^{2n+1}-x^{2n}}$

Case I $|x|<1$

If $|x|<1$, then $x\in(-1,1)$

$$\lim_{n\to\infty}|x|^{2n+1}=\lim_{n\to\infty}|x|^{2n}=0$$
$$f(x)=\lim_{n\to\infty}\cos 2\pi x$$

$f(x)$ is continuous everywhere .

Case II $|x|>1$

If $|x|>1$, then $x\in(-\infty,-1)\cup(1,\infty)$

$$\lim_{n\to\infty}|x|^{2n+1}=\infty$$
$$=\lim_{n\to\infty}\frac{\cos 2\pi x-x^{2n}\sin(x-1)}{1+x^{2n+1}-x^{2n}}$$
$$=\lim_{n\to\infty}\frac{|x|^{2n+1}\left[\dfrac{\cos 2\pi x}{|x|^{2n+1}}-\dfrac{\sin(x-1)}{|x|}\right]}{|x|^{2n+1}\left[\dfrac{1}{|x|^{2n+1}}+1-\dfrac{1}{|x|}\right]}$$
$$=\lim_{n\to\infty}\frac{-\sin(x-1)}{|x|-1}\text{ which is continuous.}$$

Case III When $|x|=1$

$$f(x)=\begin{cases}1 & ;\ \text{if } x=1\\ -(1+\sin 2) & ;\ \text{if } x=-1\end{cases}$$

Now, $\lim_{x\to 1^+} f(x)=\lim_{x\to 1^+}-\dfrac{\sin(x-1)}{|x|-1}\quad\left[\dfrac{0}{0}\text{ form}\right]$

$$\lim_{x\to 1^+}-\frac{\cos(x-1)}{1}=-1$$
$$\Rightarrow\quad \lim_{x\to 1^-} f(x)=\lim_{x\to 1^-}\cos 2\pi x=1$$

As $\quad\lim_{x\to 1^+} f(x)\neq\lim_{x\to 1^-} f(x)$

$\therefore f(x)$ is discontinuous at $x=1$

Similarly, $f(x)$ is also discontinuous at $x=-1$. Hence, the function $f(x)$ is continuous at $R-\{-1,1\}$.

83. Given that function is continuous.

Then, $f(0)=\lim_{x\to 0} f(x)$

Limit should be $\frac{0}{0}$ form.

So, $\quad\sqrt[7]{p(729)}-3=0$

$$\Rightarrow\quad p\cdot 3^6=3^7$$
$$\Rightarrow\quad p=3$$

Now, $f(0)=\lim_{x\to 0}\dfrac{\sqrt[7]{3(3^6+x)}-3}{\sqrt[3]{3^6+qx}-9}$

$$\lim_{x\to 0}\frac{3\left[\left(1+\dfrac{x}{3^6}\right)^{\frac{1}{7}}-1\right]}{9\left[\left(1+\dfrac{qx}{3^6}\right)^{\frac{1}{3}}-1\right]}=\frac{3}{9}\times\frac{\dfrac{1}{7\cdot 3^6}}{\dfrac{q}{3\cdot 3^6}}$$
$$\Rightarrow\quad f(0)=\frac{1}{3}\times\frac{3}{7q}=\frac{1}{7q}$$
$$\Rightarrow\quad 7qf(0)-1=0$$
$$\Rightarrow\quad 7\cdot p^2\cdot qf(0)-p^2=0$$
$$\Rightarrow\quad 63qf(0)-p^2=0$$

84. Given, $f(x)=\begin{cases} x+a, & x\le 0 \\ |x-4|, & x>0 \end{cases}$

$$g(x)=\begin{cases} x+1, & x<0 \\ (x-4)^2+b, & x\ge 0 \end{cases}$$

Function is continuous at R, and it is defined at $x=0$

Then, LHL = RHL = $f(0)$.

$$\lim_{x\to 0^+} f(x)=\lim_{x\to 0^-} f(x)$$

$$\lim_{x\to 0^+} |x-4| = \lim_{x\to 0} (x+a)$$

$$\lim_{h\to 0} |(0+h)-4| = (0+a) \Rightarrow a=4$$

and $\lim_{x\to 0^+} g(x)=\lim_{x\to 0^-} g(x)$

$$\lim_{x\to 0^+} [(x-4)^2+b]=\lim_{x\to 0^-}(x+1)$$

$$16+b=1 \Rightarrow b=-15$$

Now, $(gof)(2)+(fog)(-2)$

$$g(f(2))+f(g(-2))=g|2-4|+f(-2+1)$$

$$=g(2)+f(-1)$$

$$=(2-4)^2-15+(-1)+4$$

$$=4-15-1+4=8-16=-8$$

85. We are given that

$f, g: R\to R$ such that

$$f(x)=\begin{bmatrix} [x]; & x<0 \\ |1-x|; & x\ge 0 \end{bmatrix}$$

and $$g(x)=\begin{bmatrix} e^x-x; & x<0 \\ (x-1)^2-1; & x\ge 0 \end{bmatrix}$$

Here $fog(x)=f[g(x)]$

$$=\begin{cases} [g(x)]; & g(x)<0 \\ |1-g(x)|; & g(x)\ge 0 \end{cases}$$

$$=\begin{cases} |1+x-e^x|; & x<0 \\ 1; & x=0 \\ [(x-1)^2-1]; & 0<x<2 \\ |2-(x-1)^2|; & x\ge 2 \end{cases}$$

Here $x=0, 2$ are two point of discontinuities of $fog(x)$.

86. Given, function is

$$f(x)=\begin{cases} 0; & x<0 \\ ae^x-1; & 0\le x<1 \\ b; & x=1 \\ b-1; & 1<x<2 \\ -c; & x\ge 2 \end{cases}$$

$f(x)$ is discontinuous at $x=1$ because $ae-1$, b and $(b-1)$ cannot be equal.

If f is continuous at $x=0$, then $a-1=0 \Rightarrow a=1$

If f is continuous at $x=2$, then $b-1=-c$, $b+c=1$

Here, if f is discontinuous only at one point.

Then, $a+b+c=2$.

87. Given, $f(x)=|x-1|\cos|x-2|$

$$\sin|x-1|+(x-3)|x^2-5x+4|$$

$$=|x-1|\cos|x-2|\sin|x-1|$$
$$+(x-3)|x-1||x-4|$$
$$=|x-1|[\cos|x-2|\sin|x-1|+(x-3)|x-4|]$$

So, given function is not differentiable at $x=1$ and $x=4$.

88.

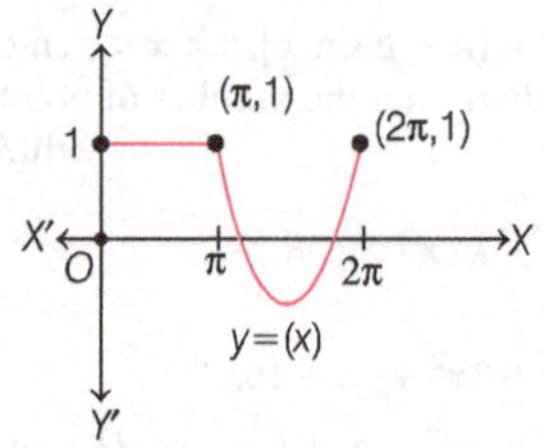

From the above graph you can see from 0 to 2π there is one non-differentiable point and discontinuous point is none.

89. Let the equation of circle be

$$x^2+y^2+2gx+2fy+k=0$$

Differentiate w.r.t. x, $\dfrac{dy}{dx}=\dfrac{-(2x+2g)}{(2y+2f)}$

Comparing with $\dfrac{dy}{dx}=\dfrac{ax-by+a}{bx+cy+a}$

$\Rightarrow$ $b=0, a=-2, c=2$

$\Rightarrow$ $-2g=-2 \Rightarrow g=1$

and $2f=-2 \Rightarrow f=-1$

Now, circle will be

$$x^2+y^2+2x-2y+c=0$$

Substitute (2, 5) in the above equation.

Then, $c=-23$

So, circle will be $x^2+y^2+2x-2y-23=0$ with centre $C=(-1, 1)$ and radius 5.

So, the minimum distance of $P(11, 6)$ from circle will be

$$=\sqrt{(11+1)^2+(6-1)^2}-5=13-5=8$$

90. From given,

$$\cos^{-1}\left(\frac{y}{2}\right)=\log_e\left(\frac{x}{5}\right)^5 \Rightarrow \cos^{-1}\left(\frac{y}{2}\right)=5\log_e\left(\frac{x}{5}\right)$$

Differentiate w.r.t. x, we get

$$\frac{-1}{\sqrt{1-\frac{y^2}{4}}}\cdot\frac{y'}{2}=5\cdot\frac{1}{\frac{x}{5}}\times\frac{1}{5}\Rightarrow\frac{-y'}{\sqrt{4-y^2}}=\frac{5}{x} \quad \text{...(i)}$$

$\Rightarrow$ $-xy'=5\sqrt{4-y^2}$

Again, differentiate w.r.t. x, we get

$$-xy''-y'=5\cdot\frac{1}{2\sqrt{4-y^2}}(-2yy')$$

$\Rightarrow$ $$xy''+y'=\frac{5y'\cdot y}{\sqrt{4-y^2}}\Rightarrow xy''+y'=5\cdot\left(\frac{-5}{x}\right)y$$

[From Eq. (i)]

$\Rightarrow$ $x^2y''+xy'=-25y$

So, required differential equation is

$$x^2y''+xy'=-25y$$

91. Given, function is

$$y = \tan^{-1}(\sec x^3 - \tan x^3) = \tan^{-1}\left(\frac{1 - \sin x^3}{\cos x^3}\right)$$

$$= \tan^{-1}\left(\frac{1 - \cos\left(\frac{\pi}{2} - x^3\right)}{\sin\left(\frac{\pi}{2} - x^3\right)}\right)$$

$$= \tan^{-1}\left(\tan\left(\frac{\pi}{4} - \frac{x^3}{2}\right)\right)$$

We have, $\frac{\pi}{4} - \frac{x^3}{2} \in \left(-\frac{\pi}{2}, 0\right)$

Let $y = \left(\frac{\pi}{4} - \frac{x^3}{2}\right)$ ...(i)

Differentiating w.r.t. x, we get

$$y' = \frac{-3x^2}{2}, y'' = -3x \quad \text{[From Eq. (i)]}$$

$$4y = \pi - 2x^3$$

$$\Rightarrow \quad 4y = \pi - 2x^2\left(\frac{-y''}{3}\right)$$

$$12y = 3\pi + 2x^2y''$$

So, the required equation, $x^2y'' - 6y + \frac{3\pi}{2} = 0$

92. Now, $fog(x) = f(g(x)) = [2g^2(x)] + 1$

$$f(g(x)) = \begin{cases} [2(2x-3)^2] + 1; & x < 0 \\ [2(2x+3)^2] + 1; & x \geq 0 \end{cases}$$

As, greatest integer is discontinuous at integers values, therefore, fog is discontinuous, whenever $2(2x-3)^2$ or $2(2x+3)^2$ belongs to integer except $x = 0$.

Take, $-1 < x < 0$ and find interval of functions $2(2x-3)^2$.

So, $\quad -2 < 2x < 0 \Rightarrow -5 < (2x-3) < -3$

$\Rightarrow \quad 9 < (2x-3)^2 < 25$

$\Rightarrow \quad 18 < 2(2x-3)^2 < 50$

$\therefore$ Point of discontinuity $= 31 + 31 = 62$

93. Let's draw the graph of the given function.

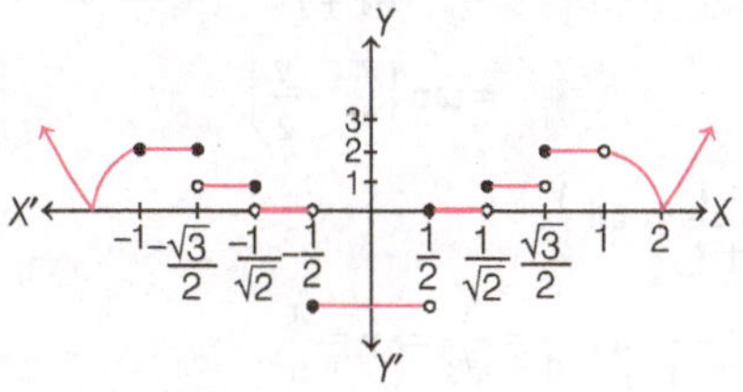

Hence, there are 6 points $\pm\frac{1}{2}, \pm\frac{1}{\sqrt{2}}$ and $\pm\frac{\sqrt{3}}{2}$ at which function is discontinuous.

94. Given, $f(x+y) = f(x)\, f(y), \forall x, y \in R$

Put $x = y = 0 \Rightarrow f(0) = (f(0))^2 \Rightarrow f(0) = 0$

$\because f(x) \neq 0$ for any $x \in R \Rightarrow f(0) = 1$

$$\because \quad f'(0) = 3 \quad \text{[given]}$$

$$\Rightarrow \quad \lim_{h \to 0} \frac{f(0+h) - f(0)}{h} = 3$$

$$\Rightarrow \quad \lim_{h \to 0} \frac{f(h) - 1}{h} = 3$$

95. $f: \left(-\frac{\pi}{4}, \frac{\pi}{4}\right) \to R$

$$f(x) = \begin{cases} (1 + |\sin x|)^{\frac{3a}{|\sin x|}}, & -\frac{\pi}{4} < x < 0 \\ b, & x = 0 \\ e^{\frac{\cot 4x}{\cot 2x}}, & 0 < x < \frac{\pi}{4} \end{cases}$$

Given, $f(x)$ is continuous at $x = 0$

LHL at $x = 0 = \lim_{x \to 0^-} (1 + |\sin x|)^{\frac{3a}{|\sin x|}}$

On putting $x = 0 - h$, we get

$$\text{LHL} = \lim_{h \to 0} (1 + |\sin h|)^{\frac{3a}{|\sin h|}} = e^{\lim |\sin h| \frac{3a}{|\sin h|}} = e^{3a}$$

$$\left[\because \text{If } \lim_{x \to a} f(x) = 0 \text{ and } \lim_{x \to a} g(x) = \infty, \text{ then } \lim_{x \to a} (1 + f(x))^{g(x)} = e^{\lim_{x \to a}[f(x)g(x)]}\right]$$

RHL at $x = 0 = \lim_{x \to 0^+} e^{\frac{\cot 4x}{\cot 2x}}$

On putting $x = 0 + h$, we get

$$\text{RHL} = \lim_{h \to 0} e^{\frac{\cot 4h}{\cot 2h}} = \lim_{h \to 0} e^{\frac{\cos 4h}{\cos 2h} \times \frac{\sin 2h}{\sin 4h}} = \lim_{h \to 0} e^{\frac{\cos 4h}{\cos 2h} \times \frac{\frac{\sin 2h}{2h} \times 2h}{\frac{\sin 4h}{4h} \times 4h}}$$

$$= e^{1/2}$$

As, $f(x)$ is continuous at $x = 0$.

So, LHL $= f(0) =$ RHL

$$e^{3a} = b = e^{1/2}$$

$$\therefore \quad a = 1/6, b = \sqrt{e}$$

$$\therefore \quad 6a + b^2 = 6\left(\frac{1}{6}\right) + (\sqrt{e})^2 = 1 + e$$

96. We have, $f(x) = \begin{cases} \dfrac{\lambda|x^2 - 5x + 6|}{\mu(5x - x^2 - 6)}, & x < 2 \\ e^{\frac{\tan(x-2)}{x - [x]}}, & x > 2 \\ \mu, & x = 2 \end{cases}$

Since, $f(x)$ is continuous at $x = 2$.

$$\therefore \quad \lim_{x \to 2^-} f(x) = \lim_{x \to 2^+} f(x) = f(2)$$

$$\therefore \quad \lim_{x \to 2^-} f(x) = \lim_{x \to 2^-} \frac{\lambda}{-\mu} \frac{|(x-3)(x-2)|}{(x-3)(x-2)}$$

$$= \lim_{x \to 2^-} \frac{\lambda}{-\mu} \frac{(x-3)(x-2)}{(x-3)(x-2)} = -\frac{\lambda}{\mu}$$

$$\lim_{x\to 2^+} f(x) = \lim_{x\to 2^+} e^{\frac{\tan(x-2)}{x-2}} = e$$

$$f(2) = \mu$$

As, $f(x)$ is continuous.

So, LHL $= f(2) =$ RHL $-\dfrac{\lambda}{\mu} = \mu = e$

$$\Rightarrow \quad \lambda = -e^2$$

$$\mu = e \Rightarrow \lambda + \mu = e(-e+1)$$

97. $f(x) = \begin{cases} (x-3)(x+1)e^{(3x-2)^2}; & x > 3 \\ -(x-3)(x+1)e^{(3x-2)^2}; & -1 \le x \le 3 \\ (x-3)(x+1)e^{(3x-2)^2}; & x < -1 \end{cases}$

At $x = -1$, let LHD be α, then its clear that RHD be $-\alpha$.
Similarly, at $x = 3$, if LHD is β, then RHD at $x = 3$ will be $-\beta$.
So, $f(x)$ is not differentiable at $x = -1$, $x = 3$
At all other points, $f(x)$ will be differentiable.

98. $y(x) = \cot^{-1}\left(\dfrac{\sqrt{1+\sin x}+\sqrt{1-\sin x}}{\sqrt{1+\sin x}-\sqrt{1-\sin x}}\right), x \in \left(\dfrac{\pi}{2}, \pi\right)$

$$= \cot^{-1}\frac{\left|\cos\frac{x}{2}+\sin\frac{x}{2}\right| + \left|\cos\frac{x}{2}-\sin\frac{x}{2}\right|}{\left|\cos\frac{x}{2}+\sin\frac{x}{2}\right| - \left|\cos\frac{x}{2}-\sin\frac{x}{2}\right|}$$

$$= \cot^{-1}\left(\frac{\cos\frac{x}{2}+\sin\frac{x}{2}+\sin\frac{x}{2}-\cos\frac{x}{2}}{\cos\frac{x}{2}+\sin\frac{x}{2}-\sin\frac{x}{2}+\cos\frac{x}{2}}\right) \quad \left[\because \frac{x}{2} \in \left(\frac{\pi}{4}, \frac{\pi}{2}\right)\right]$$

$$= \cot^{-1}\left(\frac{\sin\frac{x}{2}}{\cos\frac{x}{2}}\right) = \cot^{-1}\left(\tan\frac{x}{2}\right)$$

$$= \cot^{-1}\left(\cot\left(\frac{\pi}{2}-\frac{x}{2}\right)\right)$$

$$\Rightarrow \quad y(x) = \frac{\pi}{2} - \frac{x}{2}$$

$$\therefore \quad y'(x) = \frac{-1}{2}$$

99. $\lim\limits_{x\to a} \dfrac{xf(a) - af(x)}{x-a} \qquad \left[\dfrac{0}{0} \text{ form}\right]$

On applying L' Hospital rule, we get

$$= \lim_{x\to a} \frac{f(a) - af'(x)}{1}$$

$$f(a) - af'(a) = 4 - 2a \qquad [\because f'(a) = 2 \text{ and } f(a) = 4]$$

100. Given that,

$$f(x) = [x]\,|x^2-1| + \sin\frac{\pi}{[x]+3} - [x+1]$$

$$f(x) = \begin{cases} 3-2x^2; & -2 < x < -1 \\ x^2; & -1 \le x < 0 \\ \dfrac{\sqrt{3}}{2} - 1; & 0 \le x < 1 \\ x^2 - 3 + \dfrac{1}{\sqrt{2}}; & 1 \le x < 2 \end{cases}$$

$\therefore f(x)$ is discontinuous at $x = 0, 1$.

101. Given, $\log_e(x+y) = 4xy$

On differentiating w.r.t. x, we get

$$\frac{1}{x+y}\left(1+\frac{dy}{dx}\right) = 4\left(\frac{dy}{dx} + x\frac{dy}{dx}\right)$$

At $x = 0$, $y = 1 \Rightarrow \dfrac{dy}{dx} = 3$

$$1 + \frac{dy}{dx} = 4(x+y)\left(x\frac{dy}{dx} + y\right) \qquad \text{...(ii)}$$

On differentiating Eq. (ii), w.r.t. x, we get

$$\frac{d^2y}{dx^2} = 40$$

Exercise 2 - JEE Advanced Pattern

1. Given, $y^2 = P(x)$ ...(i)

On differentiating, we get

$$2y\frac{dy}{dx} = P'(x) \qquad \text{...(ii)}$$

Again, on differentiating, we get

$$2\left(\frac{dy}{dx}\right)^2 + 2y\cdot\frac{d^2y}{dx^2} = P''(x) \qquad \text{...(iii)}$$

On multiplying by y^2 in Eq. (iii), we get

$$2y^2\left(\frac{dy}{dx}\right)^2 + 2y^3\frac{d^2y}{dx^2} = P(x)\cdot P''(x)$$

$$\Rightarrow \quad \frac{(P'(x))^2}{2} + 2y^3\frac{d^2y}{dx^2} = P(x)\cdot P''(x) \qquad \text{[from Eq. (ii)]}$$

$$\Rightarrow \quad 2y^3\frac{d^2y}{dx^2} = P(x)\cdot P''(x) - \frac{(P'(x))^2}{2} \qquad \text{...(iv)}$$

On differentiating Eq. (iv), we get

$$\frac{d}{dx}\left(2y^3\frac{d^2y}{dx^2}\right) = P(x)\cdot P'''(x) + P'(x)\cdot P''(x) - P'(x)\cdot P''(x)$$

$$\Rightarrow \quad 2\frac{d}{dx}\left(y^3\frac{d^2y}{dx^2}\right) = P(x)\cdot P'''(x)$$

2. $e^x = \dfrac{\sqrt{1+t}-\sqrt{1-t}}{\sqrt{1+t}+\sqrt{1-t}} = \dfrac{1-\dfrac{\sqrt{1-t}}{\sqrt{1+t}}}{1+\dfrac{\sqrt{1-t}}{\sqrt{1+t}}} = \dfrac{1-\tan\frac{y}{2}}{1+\tan\frac{y}{2}}$

$$= \tan\left(\frac{\pi}{4} - \frac{y}{2}\right) \qquad \text{...(i)}$$

As, $\dfrac{\sqrt{1-t}}{\sqrt{1+t}} = \tan\dfrac{y}{2}$

Also at $t = \dfrac{1}{2}$, $\tan\dfrac{y}{2} = \dfrac{1}{\sqrt{3}} \Rightarrow y = \dfrac{\pi}{3}$ ...(ii)

Now, on differentiating both sides of Eq. (i) w.r.t. x

$$e^x = \sec^2\left(\frac{\pi}{4}-\frac{y}{2}\right) \times -\frac{1}{2} \times \frac{dy}{dx}$$

$$\Rightarrow \quad \frac{dy}{dx} = \frac{-2e^x}{\sec^2\left(\frac{\pi}{4}-\frac{y}{2}\right)}$$

$$\Rightarrow \quad \frac{dy}{dx} = \frac{-2\tan\left(\frac{\pi}{4}-\frac{y}{2}\right)}{\sec^2\left(\frac{\pi}{4}-\frac{y}{2}\right)} \qquad \text{[from Eq. (i)]}$$

$$\Rightarrow \quad \frac{dy}{dx} = -\sin 2\left(\frac{\pi}{4}-\frac{y}{2}\right) = -\sin\left(\frac{\pi}{2}-y\right) = -\cos y$$

Hence, $\frac{dy}{dx}$ (at $t = \frac{1}{2}$ i.e. $y = \frac{\pi}{3}$) [from Eq. (ii))]

$$= -\cos\frac{\pi}{3} = -\frac{1}{2}$$

3. $\because \quad (2x)^{2y} = 4e^{2x-2y}$

$\Rightarrow 2y \ln 2x = \ln 4 + 2x - 2y$

$$\Rightarrow y = \frac{x+\ln 2}{1+\ln 2x} \Rightarrow y' = \frac{(1+\ln 2x) - (x+\ln 2)\frac{1}{x}}{(1+\ln 2x)^2}$$

$$\Rightarrow \quad y'(1+\ln 2x)^2 = \left[\frac{x\ln 2x - \ln 2}{x}\right]$$

4.
$$f(x) = \begin{cases} -x\left(2-\sin\left(\frac{1}{x}\right)\right), & x<0 \\ 0, & x=0 \\ x\left(2-\sin\left(\frac{1}{x}\right)\right), & x>0 \end{cases}$$

$$f'(x) = \begin{cases} -\left(2-\sin\frac{1}{x}\right) - x\left(-\cos\frac{1}{x}\cdot\left(-\frac{1}{x^2}\right)\right) & x<0 \\ \left(2-\sin\frac{1}{x}\right) + x\left(-\cos\frac{1}{x}\left(-\frac{1}{x^2}\right)\right) & x>0 \end{cases}$$

$$f'(x) = \begin{cases} -2+\sin\frac{1}{x} - \frac{1}{x}\cos\frac{1}{x} & x<0 \\ 2-\sin\frac{1}{x} + \frac{1}{x}\cos\frac{1}{x} & x>0 \end{cases}$$

$f'(x)$ is an oscillating function which is non-monotonic in $(-\infty, 0) \cup (0, \infty)$.

5. Let $f(x) = a(x-2)^4 + b(x-2)^3 + c(x-2)^2 + d(x-2) - 1$

$f'(x) = 4a(x-2)^3 + 3b(x-2)^2 + 2c(x-2) + d$

$f'(2) = 0 \Rightarrow d = 0$

Similarly, $f''(x) = 12a(x-2)^2 + 6b(x-2) + 2c$

$f''(2) = 2 \Rightarrow c = 1$

$f'''(x) = 24a(x-2) \Rightarrow 6b = -12 \Rightarrow b = -2$

$f''''(x) = 24a \Rightarrow a = 1$

$f(x) = 12(x-2)^2 - 12(x-2) + 2$

$f''(1) = 26$

6. $f''(x)\, f'''(x) \le f''(x)\, f(x) < f''(x)\, f(x) + (f'(x))^2, \forall x \in R$

$$\Rightarrow \quad \frac{1}{2}(f''(x))^2 < f(x)\, f'(x), \forall x \in R$$

$$\left[\because \lim_{x\to-\infty} \frac{1}{2}(f''(x))^2 - f(x)\, f'(x) = 0\right]$$

$$\frac{1}{2}(f''(x))^2 + \frac{1}{2} f'(x)\, f'''(x)$$

$$< f(x)\cdot f'(x) + \frac{1}{2} f'(x)\, f''(x)$$

$$< f(x)\cdot f'(x) + \frac{1}{2} f'(x)\, f(x)$$

$$\frac{1}{2} f'(x)\, f''(x) < \frac{3}{4} f^2(x), \forall x \in R$$

$$\Rightarrow \quad \frac{1}{2}(f'(x))^2\, f''(x) < \frac{3}{4} f^2(x)\, f'(x), \forall x \in R$$

$$\Rightarrow \quad \frac{1}{6} f'^3(x) < \frac{1}{4} f^3(x), \forall x \in R$$

$$\Rightarrow \quad f'(x) < \left(\frac{3}{2}\right)^{\frac{1}{3}} f(x), \forall x \in R$$

7. $\int f'(x)(1+f(x))\,dx = \int (1+x)\,dx$

$$\frac{(1+f(x))^2}{2} = \frac{(1+x)^2}{2} + C$$

Given, $f(0) = 1$

$$\frac{(1+1)^2}{2} = \frac{1}{2} + C$$

$$\therefore \quad \frac{3}{2} = C$$

$$\frac{(1+f(x))^2}{2} = \frac{(1+x)^2}{2} + \frac{3}{2}$$

$$(1+f(x))^2 = (1+x)^2 + 3$$

$$1 + f(x) = \pm\sqrt{(1+x)^2+3}$$

$$f(x) = -1 \pm \sqrt{(1+x)^2+3}$$

$\because \quad f(0) = 1$

$\therefore \quad f(x) = -1 + \sqrt{(1+x)^2+3}$

$f(x) = -1 + \sqrt{(1+x)^2+3}$

$\Rightarrow \quad f(x) > -1, \forall x > 0$

$$f'(x) = \frac{(1+x)}{\sqrt{(1+x)^2+3}}$$

$$\Rightarrow \quad f'(2) = \frac{3}{\sqrt{12}},\ f'(3) = \frac{4}{\sqrt{19}}$$

$\therefore \quad m = 12, n = 19$

8. $f(\theta) = \tan\left(\sin^{-1}\sqrt{\frac{2}{3+\cos 2\theta}}\right)$

$$f(\theta) = \sqrt{\frac{2}{1+\cos 2\theta}} = \sec\theta \Rightarrow f\left(\frac{\pi}{4}\right) = \sqrt{2}$$

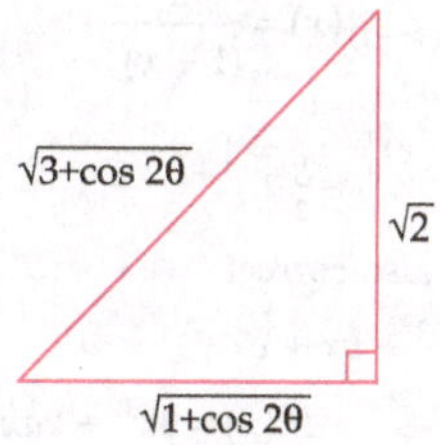

$$f'(\theta) = \sec\theta\tan\theta$$

$$f'\left(\frac{\pi}{4}\right) = \sqrt{2}$$

$$\left.\frac{d(f(\theta))}{d(\cos\theta)}\right|_{\theta=\frac{\pi}{4}} = \left(\frac{-1}{\cos^2\theta}\right)_{\theta=\frac{\pi}{4}} = -2$$

9. $f(x)=\int \frac{x}{2}\, d\left(1-\frac{1}{x^2}\right)=\int \frac{x}{2}\,\frac{2}{x^3}\,dx=\int \frac{1}{x^2}\,dx=-\frac{1}{x}+C$

$f(2)=-\frac{1}{2}+C=\frac{1}{2} \Rightarrow C=1$

$\therefore \quad f(x)=\frac{x-1}{x}$

$g_1(x)=f(x)=\frac{x-1}{x},$

$g_2(x)=f(f(x))=\frac{\frac{x-1}{x}-1}{\frac{x-1}{x}}=\frac{-1}{x-1}=\frac{1}{1-x},$

$g_3(x)=f(f(f(x)))=\frac{1}{1-\left(\frac{x-1}{x}\right)}=x$

$g_4(x)=g_1(x)=\frac{x-1}{x},\ g_5(x)=g_2(x)=\frac{1}{1-x},$

$g_6(x)=g_3(x)=x$ and so on

$\therefore \quad g_{(3n-2)}(x)=\frac{x-1}{x},$

$g_{(3n-1)}(x)=\frac{1}{1-x},\ g_{3n}(x)=x$

$\frac{d}{dx}(g_{(3n-2)}(x))=\frac{d}{dx}\left(1-\frac{1}{x}\right)=\frac{1}{x^2}$

$\therefore$ Option (a) is wrong.

$\frac{d}{dx}(g_{(3n)}(x))=\frac{d}{dx}(x)=1$

$\therefore$ Option (b) is correct.

$$\lim_{x\to 1}\frac{x+x^2+\ldots+x^{100}+x-101}{x-1}$$

On applying L'Hospital's rule

$$\lim_{x\to 1}\frac{1+2x+\ldots+100x^{99}+1}{1}$$
$$=1+2+\ldots+100+1=5051$$

$\therefore$ Option (c) is wrong.

$$y=g_{80}(x)=g_{(3n-1)}(x)=\frac{1}{1-x}$$

$\therefore \quad g'_{(3n-1)}(x)=\frac{1}{(1-x)^2}$

$g'_{(3n-1)}(x)\big|_{x=\frac{1}{2}}=4$

$\therefore$ Option (d) is also correct.

10. $P(x)=x^3+ax^2+bx+c$

$P'(x)=3x^2+2ax+b$

$P(-3)=0$

$\Rightarrow \quad -27+9a-3b+c=0 \quad$ ...(i)

$P(2)=0$

$\Rightarrow \quad 8+4a+2b+c=0 \quad$ ...(ii)

Here, on subtracting Eq. (ii) from Eq. (i), we get

$5a-5b-35=0$

$a-b=7 \quad$ ...(iii)

$P'(-3)=27-6a+b<0$

$\Rightarrow \quad 27-6(a-b)-5b<0 \Rightarrow 27-42-5b<0$

$\Rightarrow \quad -15-5b<0 \Rightarrow 3+b>0 \Rightarrow b>-3$

Hence, $a-7=b>-3$

$a-7>-3 \quad$ [from Eq. (iii)]

$a>4 \quad$ ...(iv)

$\therefore$ From Eq. (ii), we get

$8+16-6+c_{max}=0$

$c_{max}=-18 \Rightarrow c<-18$

11. $f(x)=(x^2+bx+c)e^x$

$\therefore \quad f'(x)=(x^2+(b+2)x+(b+c))e^x$

$f(x)>0$ iff $D=b^2-4c<0$

Now, $f'(x)>0$

iff $D'=(b+2)^2-4(b+c)=D+4<0$

Thus, for $f'(x)>0$

$D+4<0$ holds.

$\Rightarrow \quad D<0 \Rightarrow f(x)>0$

Note that the converse need not be true.

e.g. $b=c=1$, $f(x)>0$ but $f'(-1)=0$.

12. (a) $\frac{dy}{dx}=1$ (b) It is false

(c) It is correct (d) y reduces to $\frac{\pi}{2} \Rightarrow$ false

13. $\frac{d}{dx}f_n(x)=\frac{d}{dx}\{e^{f_{n-1}(x)}\}=e^{f_{n-1}(x)}\frac{d}{dx}f_{n-1}(x)$

$=f_n(x)\frac{d}{dx}(f_{n-1}(x))$

$=f_n(x)\frac{d}{dx}(e^{f_{n-2}(x)})$

$=f_n(x)\,e^{f_{n-2}(x)}\frac{d}{dx}f_{n-2}(x)$

$=f_n(x)\,f_{n-1}(x)\frac{d}{dx}f_{n-2}(x)$

$=f_n(x)\,f_{n-1}(x)\ldots f_2(x)\frac{d}{dx}f_1(x)$

$=f_n(x)\,f_{n-1}(x)\ldots f_2(x)\,e^{f_0(x)}\frac{d}{dx}f_0(x)$

14. $y=\sqrt{\begin{array}{l}3+2\,[\sin x\sin 2x+\sin x\sin 3x\\ \quad+\sin 2x\sin 3x+\cos x\cos 2x\\ \quad\quad+\cos x\cos 3x+\cos 2x\cos 3x]\end{array}}$

$=\sqrt{3+2\,[\cos x+\cos 2x+\cos x]}$

$=\sqrt{3+4\cos x+4\cos^2 x-2}$

$=\sqrt{4\cos^2 x+4\cos x+1}$

$y=|2\cos x+1|$

At $x=\frac{\pi}{2}$, $\quad y=2\cos x+1$

$y'=-2\sin x$

$y'=-2$

15. $\because f(x) = x^2 + g'(0)\, x + g''(3)$

Let $g'(0) = a$ and $g''(3) = b$

$\therefore \quad f(x) = x^2 + ax + b$

$f(-2) = 4 - 2a + b,$

$f'(x) = 2x + a$ and $f''(x) = 2$

$\because \quad g(y) = f(-2)\, y^2 + yf''(y) + f'(y) - 2$

$= (4 - 2a + b)\, y^2 + 2y + 2y + (a - 2)$

$= (4 - 2a + b)\, y^2 + 4y + (a - 2)$

$\Rightarrow \quad g'(y) = 2(4 - 2a + b)\, y + 4$

and $\quad g''(y) = 2(4 - 2a + b)$

$\because \quad g''(3) = b \Rightarrow 2(4 - 2a + b) = b \Rightarrow 4a - b = 8$

$g'(0) = a \Rightarrow 4 = a$

$\therefore \quad 16 - b = 8 \Rightarrow b = 8$

$\therefore \quad f(x) = x^2 + 4x + 8$ and $g(y) = 4y^2 + 4y + 2$

$\therefore \quad f(1) = 1 + 4 + 8 = 13$

16. $f(\alpha) = \alpha^2 + 4\alpha + 8 = (\alpha + 2)^2 + 4 \ge 4$

and $g(\beta) = 4\beta^2 + 4\beta + 2 = (2\beta + 1)^2 + 1 \ge 1$

$\Rightarrow \quad f(\alpha)\, g(\beta) \ge 4$

But given $f(\alpha)\, g(\beta) \le 4$

So, $f(\alpha)\, g(\beta) = 4 \Rightarrow \alpha = -2$ and $\beta = \frac{-1}{2}$

Hence, number of non-positive ordered pairs = 1.

17. Given, $\quad f(1) = 1,\ f(2) = 20,\ f(-4) = -4$

and $f(x + y) = f(x) + f(y) + axy(x + y)$
$+ bxy + c(x + y) + 4, \forall\, x, y \in R$, where a, b are constants.

Put $x = y = 0$

$\Rightarrow \quad f(0) = 2f(0) + 4 \Rightarrow f(0) = -4$

Now, put $x = 1$ and $y = 0$, we get $c = 0$

Put $x = 1$ and $y = 1$, we get

$f(2) = 2f(1) + 6 + b + 4$

$\Rightarrow \quad 20 = 2(1) + 6 + b + 4$

$\Rightarrow \quad 14 = 6 + b \Rightarrow b = 8$

Hence, $b = 8$ and $c = 0 \Rightarrow b + c = 8$

18. $f(x + y) = f(x) + f(y) + 3xy(x + y) + 8xy + 4$

Now, $\quad f'(x) = \lim_{h \to 0} \frac{f(x + h) - f(x)}{h}$

$= \lim_{h \to 0} \frac{f(h) + 3xh\,(x + h) + 8xh + 4}{h}$

$= \lim_{h \to 0} \frac{f(h) + 3xh(x + h) + 8xh - f(0)}{h}$

$= f'(0) + 3x^2 + 8x = 3x^2 + 8x$

On integrating both sides w.r.t. x, we get

$f(x) = x^3 + 4x^2 + C$

$f(0) = -4 \Rightarrow C = -4$

Hence, $f(x) = x^3 + 4x^2 - 4$

$\therefore \quad f(x) = x^3 + 4e^x$

$x^3 + 4x^2 - 4 = x^3 + 4e^x$

$x^2 - 1 = e^x$

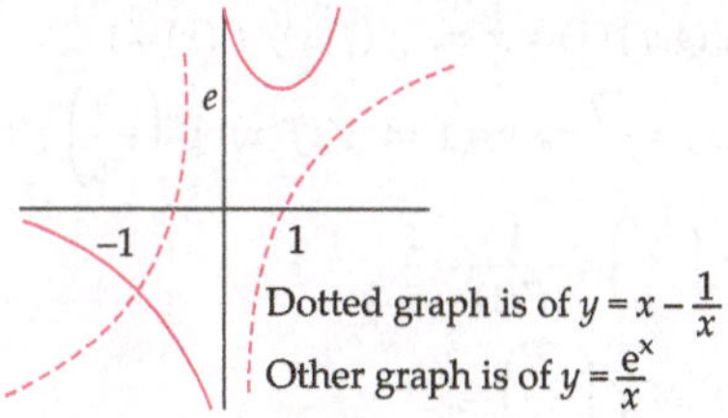

On dividing by x, we get $x - \frac{1}{x} = \frac{e^x}{x}$

Hence, the above equation will have two solutions.

19. Area of ΔABC

We have, $\Delta = \frac{1}{2}\, ah = 12$

$\Rightarrow \quad ah = 24 \Rightarrow h = \frac{24}{a} = \frac{24}{2R \sin A}$

$\Rightarrow \quad h = \frac{24}{2 \times 6 \times \sin A} \Rightarrow h = 2 \operatorname{cosec} A$

So, $\quad y = f(x) = 2 \operatorname{cosec} A$

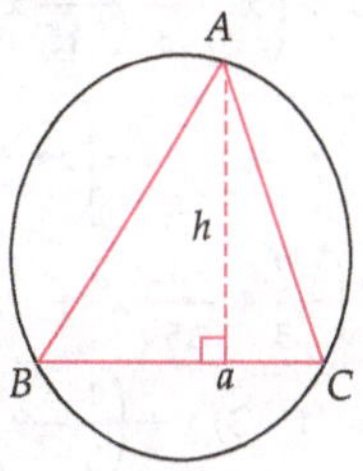

Clearly, the least value of $f(x)$ is 2.

20. We have, $g(x) = f(\sin^{-1} x) = 2 \operatorname{cosec} (\sin^{-1} x) = \frac{2}{x}$

$g'(x) = \frac{-2}{x^2}$

$\Rightarrow \quad g'\left(\frac{4}{5}\right) = \frac{-2 \cdot 25}{16} = \frac{-25}{8}$

$\therefore \quad \left| 8g'\left(\frac{4}{5}\right) \right| = |-25| = 25$

21. $f'(x) = \lim_{h \to 0} \frac{f(x + h) - f(x + 0)}{h}$

$2f(x) + xf(h) + h\sqrt{f(x)}$

$\Rightarrow \quad \lim_{h \to 0} \frac{-2f(x) - xf(0) - 0\sqrt{f(x)}}{h}$

As $f(0) = 0,$

$\Rightarrow \lim_{h \to 0} x\left(\frac{f(h) - f(0)}{h - 0}\right) + \sqrt{f(x)} = f'(0) + \sqrt{f(x)}$

$\Rightarrow \quad f'(x) = \sqrt{f(x)} \quad [\because f'(0) = 0]$

$\Rightarrow \quad \int \frac{f'(x)}{\sqrt{f(x)}}\, dx = \int dx$

$\Rightarrow \quad 2\sqrt{f(x)} = x + C$

$\Rightarrow \quad f(x) = \frac{x^2}{4} \quad [\because f(0) = 0]$

$\therefore \quad f(6) = \frac{36}{4} = 9$

22. We have, $(gof)(x) = x \Rightarrow g'(f(x))\, f'(x) = 1$

When $f(x) = -\frac{7}{6} \Rightarrow x = 1 \Rightarrow g'(f(x))\, g'\left(-\frac{7}{6}\right) f'(1) = 1$

Hence, $g'\left(-\frac{7}{6}\right) = \frac{1}{f'(1)} = \frac{1}{5}$

Reciprocal of $g'\left(-\frac{7}{6}\right) = 5$

23. $g'(0) = b = \lim_{x \to 0} \frac{x^2 + x\tan x - x\tan 2x}{x(ax + \tan x - \tan 3x)}$

$$= \lim_{x \to 0} \frac{x + \tan x - \tan 2x}{ax + \tan x - \tan 3x}$$

$$= \lim_{x \to 0} \frac{x + \left(x + \frac{x^3}{3} + \frac{2}{15}x^5 + \dots \infty\right) - \left(2x + \frac{8x^3}{3} + \frac{2}{15}\cdot 32x^5 + \dots \infty\right)}{ax + \left(x + \frac{x^3}{3} + \frac{2}{15}x^5 + \dots \infty\right) - \left(3x + \frac{27x^3}{3} + \frac{2}{15}243x^5 + \dots \infty\right)}$$

$$= \lim_{x \to 0} \frac{x^3\left(-\frac{7}{3} + \frac{-62}{15}x^2 + \dots \infty\right)}{(a + 1 - 3)\,x + \left(\frac{1}{3} - 9\right)x^3} + \frac{2}{15}(-242)\,x^5 + \dots \infty$$

b can be finite if $a + 1 - 3 = 0$

$\therefore \quad a = 2$ and $b = \frac{-\frac{7}{3}}{\frac{1}{3} - 9} = \left(\frac{-7}{3}\right)\left(\frac{3}{-26}\right) = \frac{7}{26} \Rightarrow 52\,\frac{b}{a} = 7$

24. $(a - 1)\,x^2 = x(2b + 3)$

The above equation is satisfied by three distinct values of x, therefore it is a identity.

$\therefore \quad 2 - 2a = 0$

$\Rightarrow \quad a = 1$ and $2b + 3 = 0$

$\Rightarrow \quad b = \frac{-3}{2}$

Now, $f(x) = 2x + 1$

Let $g(x) = px + q \Rightarrow g'(x) = p$

$f(g(x)) = 6x - 7$

$\Rightarrow \quad 2(px + q) + 1 = 6x - 7$

$\Rightarrow \quad 2px + 2q + 1 = 6x - 7$

$\Rightarrow \quad 2p = 6$

$\Rightarrow \quad p = 3$ and $q = -4$

$\therefore \quad g'(2012) = 3$

25. $f(x) = 2\tan^{-1} x$ and $g(x) = x + 2$

$\Rightarrow f(g(x)) = 2\tan^{-1}(x + 2)$ solution of inequality

$f^2(g(x)) - 5f(g(x)) + 4 > 0$ is $f(g(x)) < 1$ or $f(g(x)) > 4$

$\Rightarrow \quad \tan^{-1}(x + 2) < \frac{1}{2}$ or $\tan^{-1}(x + 2) > 2$

$\Rightarrow \quad \tan^{-1}(x + 2) < \frac{1}{2} \qquad \left[\text{As } \tan^{-1}(x + 2) < \frac{1}{2}\right]$

or $\quad x + 2 < \tan\left(\frac{1}{2}\right) \Rightarrow x \in \left(-10, \tan\left(\frac{1}{2}\right) - 2\right)$

As $\frac{1}{2} < \frac{\pi}{6} \Rightarrow \tan\frac{1}{2} < \frac{1}{\sqrt{3}} \Rightarrow \tan\frac{1}{2} - 2 < \frac{1}{\sqrt{3}} - 2$

Hence, total integers in the range are

$(-9, -8, -7, -6, -5, -4, -3, -2) \Rightarrow 8$ integers

26. $g'(x) = f(x) = xg(x)$

$$\frac{g'(x)}{g(x)} = x \Rightarrow \ln(g(x)) = \frac{x^2}{2} + C \Rightarrow g(x) = k \cdot e^{\frac{x^2}{2}}$$

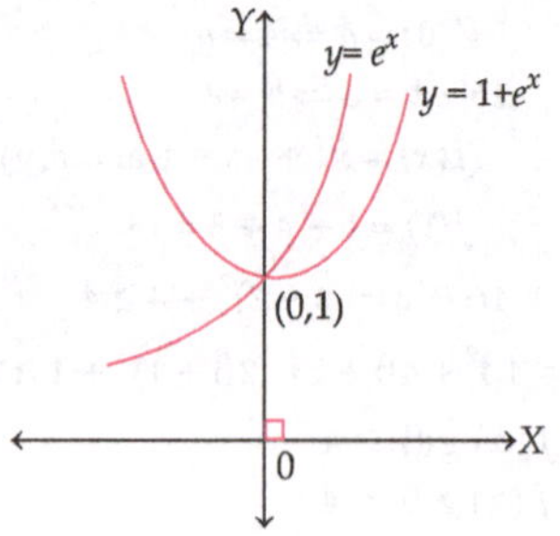

$$f(x) = xg(x) = kxe^{\frac{x^2}{2}}$$

$\therefore \quad f'(x) = ke^{\frac{x^2}{2}}(1 + x^2) = g(x)\,h(x)$

$\therefore \; h(x) = 1 + x^2$

Now, $1 + x^2 = e^x$

Only one solution

Alternate Solution

$f(x) = xg(x)$

$f'(x) = xg'(x) + g(x)$

$f'(x) = xf(x) + g(x)$

$g(x)\,h(x) = x^2 g(x) + g(x)$

$\Rightarrow \quad h(x) = x^2 + 1 \qquad [g(x) \neq 0]$

27. $\frac{1 - e^{f(x)}}{1 + e^{f(x)}} = x$

$\Rightarrow \quad f(x) = \ln\left(\frac{1 - x}{1 + x}\right)$ domain of $f(x)$ is $(-1, 1)$

$$f'(x) = -\frac{1}{1 - x} - \frac{1}{1 + x} = \frac{2}{x^2 - 1} < 0$$

$\Rightarrow f(x)$ is decreasing

$$f(x) = \ln 3 \Rightarrow x = \frac{-1}{2}$$

$$g'(y) = \frac{1}{f'(x)} \Rightarrow g'(\ln 2) = \frac{1}{f'\left(\frac{-1}{2}\right)} = \frac{1}{\frac{-8}{3}} = \frac{-3}{8}$$

$$g''(y) = -\frac{f''(x)}{(f'(x))^3} \Rightarrow g''(\ln 2) = -\frac{f''\left(\frac{-1}{2}\right)}{\left(f'\left(\frac{-1}{2}\right)\right)^3}$$

$$f''(x) = -\frac{4x}{(x^2-1)^2}$$

$$f''\left(\frac{-1}{2}\right) = \frac{-4\cdot\left(\frac{-1}{2}\right)}{\frac{9}{16}} = \frac{32}{9}$$

$$g''(\ln 2) = -\frac{\left(\frac{32}{9}\right)}{\left(\frac{-8}{3}\right)^3} = \frac{32\times 3}{2^9} = \frac{3}{16}$$

$$g''(\ln 2) - g'(\ln 2) = \frac{3}{16} - \left(\frac{-3}{8}\right) = \frac{9}{16}$$

$$p+q = 25 \Rightarrow \sqrt{p+q} = \sqrt{25} = 5$$

28. We have, $\frac{dy}{dx} = 5x^4(\cos(\ln x) + \sin(\ln x))$

$$+ x^5\left(\frac{-\sin(\ln x)}{x} + \frac{\cos(\ln x)}{x}\right)$$

$$\Rightarrow \quad xy_1 = 5y + x^5(\cos(\ln x) - \sin(\ln x))$$

$$\Rightarrow \quad xy_2 + y_1 = 5y_1 + 5x^4(\cos(\ln x)$$

$$-\sin(\ln x)) + x^5\left(\frac{-\sin(\ln x)}{x} - \frac{\cos(\ln x)}{x}\right)$$

$$\Rightarrow \quad x^2y_2 + xy_1 = 5xy_1 + 5x^5(\cos(\ln x) - \sin(\ln x))$$

$$- x^5(\sin(\ln x) + \cos(\ln x))$$

$$\Rightarrow \quad x^2y_2 - 4xy_1 = 5(xy_1 - 5y) - y$$

$$\Rightarrow \quad x^2y_2 - 4xy_1 = 5xy_1 - 26y$$

$$\Rightarrow x^2y_2 - 9xy_1 + 26y = 0 = x^2y_2 + axy_1 + by = 0$$

$\therefore \quad a = -9$ and $b = 26$

Hence, $(a+b) = 17$

29. $f(x) = \ln(1+x^2) + \tan^{-1} x$

$$g(f(x)) = x$$

$$g'(f(x))\, f'(x) = 1$$

$$\Rightarrow \quad g'(f(x)) = \frac{1}{f'(x)}$$

$$\Rightarrow \quad g''(f(x))\, f'(x) = -\frac{f''(x)}{(f'(x))^2} \Rightarrow g''(f(x)) = -\frac{f''(x)}{(f'(x))^3}$$

$$f(x) = \ln(2e^{\frac{\pi}{4}}) = \ln(1+x^2) + \tan^{-1} x$$

$$\Rightarrow \quad \ln 2 + \frac{\pi}{4} = \ln(1+x^2) + \tan^{-1} x$$

$$\Rightarrow \quad x = 1$$

$$g''\left(\ln\left(2e^{\frac{\pi}{4}}\right)\right) = \frac{-f''(1)}{(f'(1))^3}$$

$$f'(x) = \frac{1}{1+x^2} + \frac{2x}{1+x^2} = \frac{2x+1}{1+x^2}$$

$$\Rightarrow \quad f'(1) = \frac{3}{2}$$

$$f''(x) = \frac{(1+x^2)\,2 - (2x+1)\,2x}{(1+x^2)^2} = \frac{2(1-x-x^2)}{(1+x^2)^2}$$

$$\Rightarrow \quad f''(1) = \frac{-1}{2}$$

$$g''\left(\ln(2e^{\frac{\pi}{4}})\right) = \frac{\frac{-1}{2}}{\frac{27}{8}} = \frac{-4}{27}$$

$$\left|\frac{81 g''\left(\ln\left(2e^{\frac{\pi}{4}}\right)\right)}{20}\right| = \left|\frac{81}{20}\times\frac{-4}{27}\right| = \frac{3}{20} = 0.15$$

Alternate Solution

$$\frac{d^2x}{dy^2} = -\frac{\frac{d^2y}{dx^2}}{\left(\frac{dy}{dx}\right)^3}$$

Hence, $g''(y) = -\frac{f''(x)}{(f(x))^3}$

30. Given, $\sin x + \sin y = 1$

$$\cos x + \cos y\,\frac{dy}{dx} = 0 \quad \text{...(i)}$$

Again, $-\sin x + \cos y\,\frac{d^2y}{dx^2} - \left(\frac{dy}{dx}\right)^2 \sin y = 0$

or $\cos y\,\frac{d^2y}{dx^2} = \sin x + \sin y\left(\frac{dy}{dx}\right)^2 = \sin x + \sin y\left(\frac{\cos x}{\cos y}\right)^2$

$$\cos^3 y\,\frac{d^2y}{dx^2} = \sin x\cos^2 y + \sin y\cos^2 x$$

$$\frac{d^2y}{dx^2} = \frac{\sin x(1-\sin^2 y) + \sin y(1-\sin^2 x)}{(1-\sin^2 y)\sqrt{1-\sin^2 y}}$$

Using $\sin x + \sin y = 1$

$$\frac{d^2y}{dx^2} = \lim_{x\to 0}\frac{\sin x(1-(1-\sin x)^2) + (1-\sin x)(1-\sin^2 x)}{(1-(1-\sin x)^2)\sqrt{1-(1-\sin x)^2}}$$

$$= \frac{\sin x(2\sin x - \sin^2 x) + (1-\sin x)(1-\sin^2 x)}{(2\sin x - \sin^2 x)\sqrt{2\sin x - \sin^2 x}}$$

$$= \frac{\sin^2 x(2-\sin x) + 1 - \sin^2 x - \sin x + \sin^3 x}{(\sin x)^{3/2}(2-\sin x)^{3/2}}$$

$$\frac{d^2y}{dx^2} = \frac{\sin^2 x - \sin x + 1}{(\sin x)^{3/2}(2-\cos x)^{3/2}}$$

$$\lim_{x\to 0} x^\alpha \frac{d^2y}{dx^2} = \frac{x^\alpha}{(\sin x)^{3/2}}\cdot\frac{\sin^2 x - \sin x + 1}{(2-\sin x)^{3/2}}$$

For non-zero existence of limit $\alpha = \frac{3}{2}$

(if $a > \frac{3}{2}$, then limit will be zero)

and $\quad L = \frac{1}{2\sqrt{2}}$

$$\therefore \quad \frac{\alpha}{L} = \frac{3}{2}\cdot\frac{2\sqrt{2}}{1} = 3\sqrt{2} \Rightarrow \left(\frac{\alpha}{L}\right)^2 = 18$$

31. $\because \cos^{-1} x = \frac{\pi}{2} - \sin^{-1} x,$

$$\sin(\cos^{-1} x) = \cos(\sin^{-1} x)$$

$$\sin(\cos^{-1}(\sin(\cos^{-1} x))) = \cos(\sin^{-1}(\cos(\sin^{-1} x))) = x$$

$$f(x) = \tan 2x$$

$$\frac{d(\tan 2x)}{d(\tan x)} = \frac{2\sec^2 2x}{\sec^2 x}$$

$$\therefore \quad \left.\frac{df(x)}{dg(x)}\right|_{x=\frac{\pi}{6}} = \frac{2\times \sec^2\frac{\pi}{3}}{\sec^2\frac{\pi}{6}} = \frac{2\times 4\times 3}{4} = 6$$

$$\therefore \quad 100\lambda = 6$$

$$\lambda = 0.06$$

32. $g^3(x) - (x^3+2)\, g^2(x) + (2x^3+1)\, g(x) - x^3 = 0$

$$\Rightarrow \quad (g(x)-1)^2\,(g(x)-x^3) = 0$$

So, invertible function is

$$g(x) = x^3$$

$$g^{-1}(x) = x^{1/3}$$

$$g'(8)\cdot(g^{-1})'(8) = 16$$

33. Given, $(\sin y)^{\sin\left(\frac{\pi x}{2}\right)} + \frac{\sqrt{3}}{2}\sec^{-1}(2x)$

$$+ 2^x \tan[\log(x+2)] = 0 \quad \text{...(i)}$$

For $x = -1$, we have

$$(\sin y)^{\sin\left(\frac{-\pi}{2}\right)} + \frac{\sqrt{3}}{2}\sec^{-1}(-2) + 2^{-1}\tan[\log(-1+2)] = 0$$

$$\Rightarrow \quad (\sin y)^{-1} + \frac{\sqrt{3}}{2}\left(\frac{2\pi}{3}\right) + \frac{1}{2}\tan 0 = 0$$

$$\Rightarrow \quad \frac{1}{\sin y} = -\frac{\pi}{\sqrt{3}} \Rightarrow \sin y = -\frac{\sqrt{3}}{\pi}, \text{ when } x = -1 \quad \text{...(ii)}$$

Now, let $u = (\sin y)^{\sin\left(\frac{\pi x}{2}\right)}$

Taking log on both sides, we get

$$\log u = \sin\left(\frac{\pi x}{2}\right)\log \sin y$$

On differentiating both sides w.r.t. x, we get

$$\frac{1}{u}\frac{du}{dx} = \frac{\pi}{2}\cos\left(\frac{\pi x}{2}\right)\log \sin y + \cot y\,\frac{dy}{dx}\sin\left(\frac{\pi x}{2}\right)$$

$$\Rightarrow \quad \frac{du}{dx} = (\sin y)^{\sin\left(\frac{\pi x}{2}\right)}\left[\frac{\pi}{2}\cos\left(\frac{\pi x}{2}\right)\log \sin y\right.$$

$$\left. + \sin\left(\frac{\pi x}{2}\right)\cot y\,\frac{dy}{dx}\right] \quad \text{...(iii)}$$

Now, differentiating Eq. (i), we get

$$\Rightarrow (\sin y)^{\sin\left(\frac{\pi x}{2}\right)}\left[\frac{\pi}{2}\cos\left(\frac{\pi x}{2}\right)\log \sin y\right.$$

$$\left. + \sin\left(\frac{\pi x}{2}\right)\cot y\,\frac{dy}{dx}\right] + \frac{\sqrt{3}}{2x\sqrt{4x^2-1}} + 2^x(\log 2)$$

$$\tan(\log(x+2)) + \frac{2^x\sec^2[\log(x+2)]}{x+2} = 0$$

At $x = -1$ and $\sin y = -\frac{\sqrt{3}}{\pi}$, we get

$$\Rightarrow \left(-\frac{\sqrt{3}}{\pi}\right)^{-1}\left[0 + (-1)\sqrt{\frac{\pi^2}{3} - 1}\left(\frac{dy}{dx}\right)_{x=-1}\right]$$

$$+ \frac{\sqrt{3}}{-2\sqrt{3}} + 0 + 2^{-1} = 0$$

$$\Rightarrow \quad \frac{\pi}{\sqrt{3}\,\sqrt{3}}\sqrt{\pi^2 - 3}\left(\frac{dy}{dx}\right)_{x=-1} - \frac{1}{2} + \frac{1}{2} = 0$$

$$\Rightarrow \quad \frac{dy}{dx} = 0$$

$$\therefore \quad \lambda - 5 = 0 \Rightarrow \lambda = 5$$

Number of diagonal in polygon having 20λ i.e. 100 vertices are

$$= {}^{100}C_2 - 100 = 4950 - 100 = 4850$$

34. $x = \tan\frac{y}{2} - 2\ln\left(1 + \tan\frac{y}{2}\right) + \ln\tan\frac{y}{2}$

$$\frac{dx}{dy} = \frac{1}{2}\sec^2\frac{y}{2} - \frac{\sec^2 y/2}{1 + \tan y/2} + \frac{1}{2}\frac{\sec^2 y/2}{\tan y/2}$$

$$= \frac{\sec^2 y/2}{2}\left[\frac{1 + \tan y/2}{\tan y/2}\right] - \frac{\sec^2 y/2}{1 + \tan y/2}$$

$$\Rightarrow \quad \frac{\sec^2 y}{2}\left[\frac{(1+\tan y/2)}{2\tan y/2} - \frac{1}{1+\tan y/2}\right]$$

$$\Rightarrow \quad \frac{\sec^2 y}{2}\left[\frac{(1+\tan y/2)^2 - 2\tan y/2}{2\tan y/2\,(1+\tan y/2)}\right]$$

$$\frac{dx}{dy} \Rightarrow \frac{\sec^2 y/2}{2\sin y/2\,(\sin y/2 + \cos y/2)}$$

$$\frac{dy}{dx} = 2\sin\frac{y}{2}\cos^2\frac{y}{2}\left[\sin\frac{y}{2} + \cos\frac{y}{2}\right]$$

$$\Rightarrow \quad \frac{\sin y}{2}[\sin y + 1 + \cos y]$$

$$\therefore \lambda = 2, \mu = 1 \Rightarrow \frac{50\lambda}{4\mu} = \frac{100}{4} = 25$$

35. $X = 2\sin\left(t + \frac{\pi}{4}\right)\cos\frac{\pi}{3} + \sin\left(t + \frac{3\pi}{12}\right)$

$$X = 2\sin\left(t + \frac{\pi}{4}\right)$$

$$Y = 2\cos\left(t + \frac{\pi}{4}\right)\cos\frac{\pi}{3} + \cos\left(t + \frac{3\pi}{12}\right)$$

$$Y = 2\cos\left(t + \frac{\pi}{4}\right)$$

$$\Rightarrow \frac{d}{dt}\left[\frac{x}{y} - \frac{y}{x}\right] = \frac{d}{dt}\left[\tan\left(t + \frac{\pi}{4}\right) - \cot\left(t + \frac{\pi}{4}\right)\right]$$

$$= \frac{d}{dt}\left[\frac{1+\tan t}{1-\tan t} - \frac{1-\tan t}{1+\tan t}\right]$$

$$= \frac{d}{dt}\frac{4\tan t}{1-\tan^2 t} = \frac{d}{dt}(2\tan 2t)$$

$$= 4\sec^2 2t = 4\times 2 = 8$$

$$\therefore \quad \mu = 8 \Rightarrow 11\mu = 88$$

36. $f'(x) = 3(x^2 - 2x - 3) = 3(x+1)(x-3)$

Case I $f'(x) > 0$ i.e. $f(x)$ is increasing, then $x > 3$ or $x < -1$

$$f(f(x)) < f(x^3 - 4x^2 - 3x + 19)$$

$$\Rightarrow \quad f(x) < x^3 - 4x^2 - 3x + 19$$

$$\Rightarrow \quad x^2 - 6x + 8 < 0 \Rightarrow x \in (2, 4)$$

$$\therefore \quad x \in (3, 4)$$

Case II $f'(x) < 0$ i.e. $f(x)$ is decreasing, then $-1 < x < 3$

$$f(x) > x^3 - 4x^2 - 3x + 19$$

$$\Rightarrow x^2 - 6x + 8 > 0 \Rightarrow (x-2)(x-4) > 0$$

$$\Rightarrow \quad x < 2 \text{ or } x > 4$$

$$\therefore \quad x \in (-1, 2)$$

$$\therefore \quad x \in (-1, 2) \cup (3, 4)$$

$\therefore b - a + c + d = 2 + 1 + 3 + 4 = 10$

37. $f\left(\dfrac{x+13}{2}\right) = f\left(\dfrac{3-x}{2}\right)$

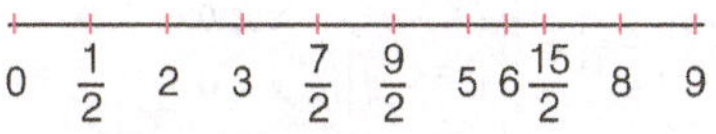

$$f(x) = f(8-x) \Rightarrow f'(x) = -f'(8-x)$$

$$f'\left(\frac{1}{2}\right) = -f'\left(\frac{15}{2}\right) = 0$$

$$f'(2) = -f'(6) = 0 \Rightarrow f'(3) = -f'(5) = 0$$

$$f'\left(\frac{9}{2}\right) = -f'\left(\frac{7}{2}\right) = 0$$

$$f'(0) = -f'(8),\ h(x) = \frac{d}{dx}(f'(x)\, f''(x))$$

Clearly, $h(x)$ has minimum 18 zeroes

$$2k = 18 \Rightarrow k = 9 \Rightarrow k^2 = 81$$

38. Put $n = 1$; $f(x) = f(x+1) - f(x)$, $n = 2$;

$$f'(x) = \frac{f(x+2) - f(x)}{2}$$

So, $$f'(x) = \frac{f(x+2) - f(x+1) + f(x+1) - f(x)}{2}$$

$$f'(x) = \frac{1}{2} f'(x+1) + \frac{1}{2} f'(x)$$

$$\Rightarrow \quad f(x) = f'(x+1),\ \forall\, x \in R$$

$$\Rightarrow \quad (f(x+1) - f(x))' = 0,\ \forall\, x \in R$$

$$\Rightarrow f(x+1) - f(x) = c \text{ for a constant } c \in R$$

$$\Rightarrow \quad f'(x) = c \Rightarrow f(x) = cx + d$$

$$\Rightarrow \quad f(0) = 3 \Rightarrow d = 3 \text{ and } f'(0) = c = 2$$

$$f(x) = 2x + 3$$

$$\therefore \quad 10\,\frac{f(5)}{f(1)} = 10\,\frac{(13)}{5} = 26$$

39. $g(f(x)) = x$

$$f'(x) = \cos(x-1) + 0 + 3x^2 + 4$$

$$g'(f(x)) \cdot f'(x) = 1$$

Put $x = 1$, $\quad g'(5) \cdot f'(1) = 1$

$$g'(5) = \frac{1}{1+3+4} = \frac{1}{8}$$

$$\therefore \quad \left(\frac{1}{g'(5)}\right)^2 = 8^2 = 64$$

40. (A) $T'(x) = F'(G(x) \times G'(x))$

$$T'(0) = F'(G(0))G'(0) = -2$$

$$U(x) = \ln F(x)$$

$$U'(x) = \frac{F'(x)}{F(x)}$$

$$U'(3) = \frac{F'(3)}{F(3)} = -\frac{1}{2}$$

$$T'(0) + 6U'(3) = -5$$

(B) Put $x = -\dfrac{1}{y}$, $\lim\limits_{y\to 0}\left(\dfrac{-1}{y} + \dfrac{\sqrt{1-2y}}{y}\right) = \lim\limits_{y\to 0} \dfrac{-2y}{y(\sqrt{1-2y}+1)} = -1$

(C) $y = t^2$

$$\frac{dy}{dt} = 2t,\ \frac{d^2y}{dt^2} = 2$$

$$x = t + t^2$$

$$\Rightarrow \quad \frac{dx}{dt} = 1 + 2t,\ \frac{d^2x}{dt^2} = 2$$

$$\frac{dy}{dx} = \frac{2t}{1+2t} = 1 - \frac{1}{1+2t}$$

$$\frac{d^2y}{dx^2} = \frac{\dfrac{dx}{dt}\dfrac{d^2y}{dt^2} - \dfrac{dy}{dt}\dfrac{d^2x}{dt^2}}{\left(\dfrac{dx}{dt}\right)^3} = \frac{2(1+2t) - 2t(2)}{(1+2t)^3}$$

$$= \frac{2}{(1+2t)^3}$$

$$\frac{d^2y}{dx^2} = -2$$

(D) $f(x) = x + x^n = x(1 + x^{n-1})$

For invertible, $\dfrac{dy}{dx}$ is > 0 or < 0

$$f'(x) = 1 + nx^{n-1}$$

$$\Rightarrow \quad n - 1 = 2$$

$$\Rightarrow \quad n = 3$$

41. (A) $\left|\dfrac{g(x) - g(y)}{x - y}\right| \le |x - y|^{98}$

$$\lim_{x\to y}\left|\frac{g(x) - g(y)}{(x-y)}\right| \le \lim_{x\to y} |x-y|^{98}$$

$$\Rightarrow \quad |g'(x)| \le 0$$

$$\Rightarrow \quad g'(x) = 0$$

(B) Derivative of $\sin^{-1}\dfrac{2x}{1+x^2}$ with respect to $\cos^{-1}\dfrac{(1-x^2)}{1+x^2}$ is -1.

(C) $y = \cot^{-1}(\tan x) + \tan^{-1}(\cot x)$

$$y = \pi - \tan^{-1}(\tan x) - \cot^{-1}(\cot x)$$

$$= \pi - (x - \pi) - x = 2\pi - 2x$$

$$y' = -2$$

(D) $4xe^{xy} = y + 5\sin^2 x$

$$4e^{xy} = 4xe^{xy}(y + xy') = y' + 5\sin 2x$$

Put $x = y = 0$

$$y' = 4$$

42. (A) $y = \sin^{-1} 2x\sqrt{1-x^2} = -\pi - 2\sin^{-1} x$

$$y' = \frac{-2}{\sqrt{1-x^2}}$$

(B) $y = 2\sin^{-1}\sqrt{1-x} + \sin^{-1} 2\sqrt{x(1-x)} = \pi$

$$y' = 0$$

(C) $y = \sin^{-1}(3x - 4x^3) = 3\sin^{-1} x$

$$y' = \frac{3}{\sqrt{1-x^2}}$$

(D) $y = \cos^{-1}\frac{2x}{1+x^2} = \frac{\pi}{2} - \sin^{-1}\frac{2x}{1+x^2}$

$$y = \frac{\pi}{2} - 2\tan^{-1} x$$

$$y' = \frac{-2}{1+x^2}$$

43. $f_1(x) = \frac{\pi}{2} - \cos^{-1}\left(\frac{1-x^2}{1+x^2}\right) = \frac{\pi}{2} - 2\tan^{-1} x,\ x \geq 0$

$$f_2(x) = x - \frac{\pi}{2} + \sin^{-1}\left(\frac{2x}{1+x^2}\right)$$

$$= \begin{cases} x - \dfrac{\pi}{2} + 2\tan^{-1} x, & -1 \leq x \leq 1 \\ x - \dfrac{\pi}{2} + \pi - 2\tan^{-1} x, & x > 1 \end{cases}$$

$$f_3(x) = 2\tan^{-1} x - x + [x]$$

$$= 2\tan^{-1} x - x + 1,\ 1 \leq x < 2$$

$\because$ $\tan 1 > 1$

(A) $\dfrac{d(f_1(x))}{d(f_2(x))} = \dfrac{\dfrac{-2}{1+x^2}}{1 - \dfrac{2}{1+x^2}} = \dfrac{d(f_1(x))}{d(f_2(x))}\Bigg|_{x-\tan 1} = 1 + \sec 2$

(B) $\dfrac{d(f_3(x))}{d(f_2(x))} = \dfrac{\dfrac{2}{1+x^2} - 1}{1 - \dfrac{2}{1+x^2}} = -1$

(C) $f_2(x) - f_1(x) = x$ for $x > 1$

$$\int (f_2(x) - f_1(x))\,dx = \int x\,dx = \frac{x^2}{2} + c$$

$$\Rightarrow \frac{d}{dx}\left(\int (f_2(x) - f_1(x))\,dx\right) = x$$

$$\Rightarrow \frac{d}{dx}\left(\int (f_2(x) - f_1(x))\,dx\right)\Bigg|_{x = \tan 1} = \tan 1$$

(D) $\dfrac{d}{dx}(f_3(x)) = \dfrac{2}{1+x^2} - 1$

$$\frac{d}{dx}(f_3(x))\Bigg|_{x=\sqrt{3}} = \frac{2}{4} - 1$$

$$= \frac{-1}{2}$$

$\therefore$ Slope of the normal = 2

44. (A) We know that,

$$2\tan^{-1} x = \begin{cases} \sin^{-1}\left(\dfrac{2x}{1+x^2}\right), & \text{if } -1 \leq x \leq 1 \\ \pi - \sin^{-1}\left(\dfrac{2x}{1+x^2}\right), & \text{if } x > 1 \\ -\pi - \sin^{-1}\left(\dfrac{2x}{1+x^2}\right), & \text{if } x < -1 \end{cases}$$

$$\Rightarrow \quad \frac{dy}{dx} = -\frac{2}{1+x^2}, \text{ if } x < -1 \text{ or } x > 1$$

(B) $\cos^{-1}\left(\dfrac{1}{\sqrt{1+x^2}}\right) = \begin{cases} \tan^{-1} x, & x \geq 0 \\ -\tan^{-1} x, & x < 0 \end{cases}$

$$\Rightarrow \quad \frac{dy}{dx} = -\frac{1}{1+x^2}, \text{ if } x < 0$$

(C) $y = |e^{|x|} - e| = \begin{cases} |e^x - e|, & x \geq 0 \\ |e^{-x} - e|, & x < 0 \end{cases}$

$$= \begin{cases} e^x - e, & x \geq 1 \\ e - e^x, & 0 \leq x < 1 \\ e - e^{-x}, & -1 \leq x < 0 \\ e^{-x} - e, & x < -1 \end{cases}$$

$$\Rightarrow \frac{dy}{dx} > 0, \text{ if } x > 1 \text{ or } -1 < x < 0$$

(D) $\dfrac{du}{dx} = \dfrac{1}{x}$ and $\dfrac{dv}{dx} = \begin{cases} \dfrac{1}{1+x^2}, & x > 0 \\ -\dfrac{1}{1+x^2}, & x < 0 \end{cases}$

$$\Rightarrow \frac{du}{dv} = \begin{cases} \dfrac{1+x^2}{x}, & x > 0 \\ -\dfrac{1+x^2}{x}, & x < 0 \end{cases}$$

Now, we know that

$$\frac{1+x^2}{x} = x + \frac{1}{x} > 2, \text{ if } x > 1$$

and $\qquad < -2, \text{ if } x < -1$

$$\Rightarrow \quad \frac{du}{dv} > 2, \text{ if } x < -1 \text{ or } x > 1$$

45. If $f'(x) = 3x^2 + 3$

$$\Rightarrow \quad g(f(x)) = x$$

$$\Rightarrow \quad g'(f(x)) = \frac{1}{f'(x)}$$

Also, $f(0) = 2$ [put $x = 0$]

So, $\quad g'(2) = \dfrac{1}{f'(0)} \Rightarrow g'(2) = \dfrac{1}{3}$

If $h(g(g(x))) = x$

$$h'(g(g(x))) = \frac{1}{g'(g(x)) \cdot g'(x)}$$

If $g(g(x)) = 1$

$$g(f(x)) = x$$

$\Rightarrow$ $g^{-1}(x) = f(x) \Rightarrow g(x) = g^{-1}(1)$

$\Rightarrow$ $g(x) = f(1) = 6$

To find, $g'(6)$ use $x = 1$ in $g'(f(x)) = \dfrac{1}{f'(1)}$ as $f(1) = 6$

To find, $g'(236)$, use $x = 6$ as

$$f(6) = 236$$

$\therefore$ $h'(1) = \dfrac{1}{g'(6) \cdot g'(236)} = \dfrac{1}{\frac{1}{6} \cdot \frac{1}{111}} \Rightarrow h'(1) = 666$

If $g(g(x)) = 0$

$\therefore$ $g(x) = g^{-1}(0) \Rightarrow g(x) = f(0)$

$\Rightarrow$ $g(x) = 2 \Rightarrow x = g^{-1}(2)$

$\Rightarrow$ $x = f(2) \Rightarrow x = 16$

$\therefore$ $h(0) = 16$

$g(x) = 3 \Rightarrow x = g^{-1}(3)$

$\Rightarrow$ $x = f(3) \Rightarrow x = 38$

So, $h(g(3)) = 38$

Exercise 3 - Challenging Problems

1. $\dfrac{dx}{dt} = \dfrac{t^2\left(\frac{1}{t}\right) - (1 + \ln t)\, 2t}{t^4}$

$\Rightarrow$ $\dfrac{dx}{dt} = \dfrac{-1 - 2\ln t}{t^3}$

$$\frac{dy}{dt} = \frac{t\left(\frac{2}{t}\right) - (3 + 2\ln t)}{t^2} = \frac{-1 - 2\ln t}{t^2} \Rightarrow \frac{dy}{dx} = t$$

$\Rightarrow \ln t = t^2 x - 1 = \dfrac{ty - 3}{2}$

$\Rightarrow$ $x\left(\dfrac{dy}{dx}\right)^2 - 1 = \dfrac{y\dfrac{dy}{dx} - 3}{2} \Rightarrow y\dfrac{dy}{dx} = 2x\left(\dfrac{dy}{dx}\right)^2 + 1$

2. (i) (a) $e^{xy} + y\cos x = 2 \Rightarrow y(0) = 1$

$$e^{xy}\left(y + x\frac{dy}{dx}\right) + \frac{dy}{dx}\cos x - y\sin x = 0$$

$$\left(\frac{dy}{dx}\right)_{x=0} = -1$$

(b) $\dfrac{dy}{dx}(xe^{xy} + \cos x) = y\sin x - ye^{xy}$

$\Rightarrow$ $e^{xy}\left(x\dfrac{dy}{dx} + y\right) = y\sin x - \cos x\dfrac{dy}{dx}$

$\Rightarrow$ $e^{xy}\left(x\dfrac{d^2y}{dx^2} + 2\dfrac{dy}{dx}\right) + \left(x\dfrac{dy}{dx} + y\right)e^{xy}\left(y + x\dfrac{dy}{dx}\right)$

$$= y\cos x + \sin x\frac{dy}{dx} - \cos x\frac{d^2y}{dx^2} + \sin x\frac{dy}{dx}$$

$\Rightarrow$ $2y'(0) + 1 = 1 - y''(0)$

$\Rightarrow$ $y''(0) = 2$

(ii) $g(x) = e^{ax} + f(x)$

$$f(0) = 2,\ f'(0) = -5,\ f''(0) = 3$$

$\Rightarrow$ $g'(x) = ae^{ax} + f'(x) \Rightarrow g''(x) = a^2e^{ax} + f''(x)$

$\Rightarrow$ $g'(0) + g''(0) = a + a^2 + f'(0) + f''(0)$

$$= a^2 + a - 2 = 0$$

$\Rightarrow$ $(a + 2)(a - 1) = 0 \Rightarrow a = -2, 1$

3. $f(2x) = f'(x) \cdot f''(x)$

Let $f(x) = a_n x^n + a_{n-1}x^{n-1} + \dots$

Degree of LHS is n

Degree of RHS is $(n - 1 + n - 2)$

$\Rightarrow$ $n = 2n - 3 \Rightarrow n = 3$

$\Rightarrow$ $f(x) = a_3x^3 + a_2x^2 + a_1x + a_0$

$\Rightarrow$ $f(2x) = 8a_3x^3 + 4a_2x^2 + 2a_1x + a_0$

$\Rightarrow$ $f'(x) = 3a_3x^2 + 2a_2x + a_1$

$\Rightarrow$ $f''(x) = 6a_3x + 2a_2$

$\Rightarrow$ $8a_3 = 18a_3^2 \Rightarrow a_3 = \dfrac{4}{9}$

$\Rightarrow$ $\left(\dfrac{32}{9}x^3 + 4a_2x^2 + 2a_1x + a_0\right)$

$$= \left(\frac{4}{3}x^2 + 2a_2x + a_1\right)\left(\frac{8}{3}x + 2a_2\right)$$

$$4a_2 = \frac{8}{3}a_2 + \frac{16}{3}a_2 \Rightarrow a_2 = 0$$

$$a_1 = 4a_2^2 + \frac{8}{3}a_1$$

$\Rightarrow$ $a_1 = 0, a_0 = 0 \Rightarrow f(x) = \dfrac{4x^3}{9}$

4. Given, $F(x) = f(x) \cdot \phi(x)$ ...(i)

and $f'(x) = f(x) \cdot \phi'(x) + f'(x) \cdot \phi(x)$ ...(ii)

On differentiating Eq. (i) w.r.t. x, we get

$$F'(x) = f(x) \cdot \phi'(x) + f'(x) \cdot \phi(x)$$

Again, differentiating;

$$F''(x) = \{f(x)\,\phi''(x) + f'(x)\,\phi'(x)\}$$
$$+ \{f'(x) \cdot \phi'(x) + f''(x)\,\phi(x)\}$$

$$F''(x) = f(x)\,\phi''(x) + 2f'(x)\,\phi'(x)\} + \{f'(x) \cdot \phi'(x)\}$$

or $F''(x) = f(x)\,\phi''(x) + f'(x)\,\phi(x) + 2c$ [using Eq. (ii)]

Now, again differentiating w.r.t. x, we get

$$F'''(x) = f(x) \cdot \phi'''(x) + f'(x) \cdot \phi''(x)$$
$$+ f''(x) \cdot \phi'(x) + f'''(x) \cdot \phi(x) \quad \text{...(iii)}$$

On differentiating Eq. (ii) w.r.t. x, we get

$$f'(x) \cdot \phi''(x) + \phi'(x) \cdot f''(x) = 0 \quad \text{...(iv)}$$

From Eqs. (iii) and (iv), we get,

$$F'''(x) = f(x)\,\phi'''(x) + \phi(x) \cdot f'''(x) + 0$$

or $\dfrac{F'''(x)}{F(x)} = \dfrac{f(x) \cdot \phi'''(x)}{F(x)} + \dfrac{\phi(x) \cdot f'''(x)}{F(x)}$

$\dfrac{F'''(x)}{F(x)} = \dfrac{\phi'''(x)}{\phi(x)} + \dfrac{f'''(x)}{f(x)}$ [$\because F(x) = f(x)\,\phi(x)$]

or $\dfrac{F'''}{F} = \dfrac{\phi'''}{\phi} + \dfrac{f'''}{f}$

5. At $x = 0$, we have

$$f'(0^+) = \lim_{h\to 0} \frac{e^{-1/h^2}\sin(1/h) - 0}{h}$$

$$= \lim_{h\to 0} \frac{\sin(1/h)}{he^{1/h^2}}$$

$$= \lim_{h\to 0} \frac{\sin(1/h)}{\left\{1 + \frac{1}{h^2} + \frac{1}{2!}\cdot\frac{1}{h^4} + \dots\right\}h}$$

$$= \lim_{h\to 0} \frac{\sin(1/h)}{h + \frac{1}{h} + \frac{1}{2!}\cdot\frac{1}{h^3} + \dots} = 0$$

Similarly, $f'(0^-) = 0$

Hence, $f'(0) = 0$.

At any point other than zero,

$$f'(x) = \left(\frac{2}{x^3}\right)e^{-1/x^2}\sin\left(\frac{1}{x}\right) - \left(\frac{1}{x^2}\right)e^{-1/x^4}\cos\left(\frac{1}{x}\right)$$

$$= \left\{\left(\frac{2}{x}\right)\cdot\sin\left(\frac{1}{x}\right) - \cos\left(\frac{1}{x}\right)\right\}\left(\frac{1}{x^2}\right)\left(\frac{1}{e^{1/x^2}}\right) \quad \text{...(i)}$$

Then, $f'(0^+) = \lim_{h\to 0}\left(\frac{2}{h}\sin\frac{1}{h} - \cos\frac{1}{h}\right)\cdot\frac{1}{h^2e^{1/h^2}}$

$$= \lim_{h\to 0}\left(\frac{2\sin(1/h)}{h^3e^{1/h^2}} - \frac{\cos(1/h)}{h^2e^{1/h^2}}\right)$$

$$= \lim_{h\to 0}\left(\frac{2\sin(1/h)}{h^3\left(1 + \frac{1}{h^2} + \frac{1}{2!}\cdot\frac{1}{h^4} + \dots\right)} - \frac{\cos(1/h)}{h^2\left(1 + \frac{1}{h^2} + \frac{1}{2!}\cdot\frac{1}{h^4} + \dots\right)}\right)$$

$$= \frac{\text{some finite quantity}}{\infty} - \frac{\text{some finite quantity}}{\infty} = 0$$

Similarly, $f'(0^-) = 0$.

Hence, f' is continuous at $x = 0$.

Now, if $x = \frac{1}{2n\pi}$, then $f'\left(\frac{1}{2n\pi}\right)$

$$= (0 - 1)\cdot e^{4n^2\pi^2/4n^2\pi^2}$$

$= -e < 0$ and similarly at

$$x = \frac{1}{(4n+1)\pi},\ f'\left(\frac{1}{(2n+1)\pi}\right) > 0$$

Hence, between $\frac{1}{2n\pi}$ and $\frac{1}{(2n+1)\pi}$, $f'(x)$ changes from negative to positive values and since f' is continuous in $\left[\frac{1}{2n\pi}, \frac{1}{(2n+1)\pi}\right]$

It follows that f' must take all values between

$$f'\left(\frac{1}{2n\pi}\right) \text{ and } f'\left(\frac{1}{(2n+1)\pi}\right)$$

Giving successively large values to n, we see that f' changes from negative to positive, taking all intermediate values in the neighbourhood of zero an infinite number of times. It follows that f' makes an infinite number of oscillations like f (which can be easily proved) in the neighbourhood of the origin.

6. Let $P(x) = x^n + \alpha x + \beta$

As $x_1, x_1, x_2, x_3, \dots, x_{n-1}$ be zeroes of $P(x)$

$$\therefore \quad P(x) = (x - x_1)^2(x - x_2)(x - x_3)(x - x_4) \dots (x - x_{n-1}) = x^n + \alpha x + \beta$$

Let $Q(x) = (x - x_2)(x - x_3)(x - x_4)\dots(x - x_{n-1}) = \frac{P(x)}{(x - x_1)^2}$

Then, $Q(x_1) = (x_1 - x_2)(x_1 - x_3)(x_1 - x_4)\dots(x_1 - x_{n-1})$

As $Q(x)$ is a polynomial function, hence it is continuous and differentiable at $x = x_1$

$$\therefore \quad Q(x_1) = \lim_{x\to x_1}\frac{P(x)}{(x - x_1)^2} = \lim_{x\to x_1}\frac{x^n + \alpha x + \beta}{(x - x_1)^2}$$

Applying L'Hospital's rule twice or otherwise

$$Q(x_1) = \frac{n(n-1)}{2}x_1^{n-2} = {}^nC_2\cdot x_1^{n-2}$$

7. $y = 1 + \frac{x_1}{x - x_1} + \frac{x_2\cdot x}{(x - x_1)(x - x_2)} + \dots + \frac{x_n x^{n-1}}{(x - x_1)(x - x_2)\dots(x - x_n)}$

$$= \frac{x}{x - x_1} + \frac{x_2 x}{(x - x_1)(x - x_2)} = \dots + \frac{x_n x^{n-1}}{(x - x_1)(x - x_2)\dots(x - x_n)}$$

$$= \frac{x(x)}{(x - x_1)(x - x_2)} + \frac{x_2 x^2}{(x - x_1)(x - x_2)(x - x_3)} + \dots + \frac{x_n x^{n-1}}{(x - x_1)(x - x_2)\dots(x - x_n)}$$

$$= \frac{x^n}{(x - x_1)(x - x_2)\dots(x - x_n)}$$

$$\Rightarrow y = \frac{x^n}{(x - x_1)(x - x_2)\dots(x - x_n)}$$

On taking $\log_e$ on both sides, we get

$$\ln y = n\ln x - \ln(x - x_1) - \ln(x - x_2)\dots\ln(x - x_n)$$

$$\Rightarrow \frac{1}{y}\frac{dy}{dx} = \left(\frac{n}{x} - \frac{1}{x - x_1} - \frac{1}{x - x_2} + \dots + \frac{1}{x - x_n}\right]$$

$$= \left(\frac{n}{x} + \frac{1}{x_1 - x} + \frac{1}{x_2 - x} + \dots + \frac{1}{x_n - x}\right)$$

$$= \left(\left(\frac{1}{x} + \frac{1}{x_1 - x}\right) + \left(\frac{1}{x} + \frac{1}{x_2 - x}\right) + \dots + \left(\frac{1}{x} + \frac{1}{x_n - x}\right)\right)$$

$$= \frac{1}{x}\left(\frac{x_1}{x_1 - x} + \frac{x_2}{x_2 - x} + \frac{x_3}{x_3 - x} + \dots + \frac{x_n}{x_n - x}\right)$$

$$\Rightarrow \quad \frac{dy}{dx} = \frac{y}{x}\left(\frac{x_1}{x_1 - x} + \frac{x_2}{x_2 - x} + \frac{x_3}{x_3 - x} + \dots + \frac{x_n}{x_n - x}\right)$$

8. First all let us try the simplify the RHS

Now, $N^r = {}^nC_0 + 2\,{}^nC_1 x + 3\,{}^nC_3 x^2 + \ldots + (n+1)\,{}^nC_n x^n$

We already know that

$$(1+x)^n = {}^nC_0 + {}^nC_1\,x + {}^nC_2 x^2 \ldots + {}^nC_n x^n$$

Multiplying both sides by x, we get

$$x(1+x)^n = C_0 x + C_1 x^2 + c_2 x^3 + \ldots + C_n x^{n+1}$$

On differentiating both sides, w.r.t. x, we get

$$n(1+x)^{n-1} + (1+n)^n \cdot 1 = C_0 + 2C_1 x + 3C_2 x^2 + \ldots C_n x^n$$

$$\therefore \quad N^r = x \cdot n(1+x)^{n-1} + (1+x)^n \cdot 1$$

$$= (1+x)^{n-1}[nx + 1 + x] = (1+x)^{n-1}[(1 + (n+1)x]$$

Similarly for D^r; we have

$$(1+x)^n = {}^nC_0 + {}^nC_1 x + {}^nC_2 x^2 + \ldots + {}^nC_n x^n$$

On differentiating both sides w.r.t. x, we get

$$n(1+x)^{n-1} = C_1 + 2C_2 x + 3C_3 x^2 + \ldots + nC_n x^{n-1}$$

Multiplying both sides by x, we get

$$nx(1+x)^{n-1} = C_1 x + 2C_2 x^2 + 3C_3 x^3 + \ldots + nC_n x^n$$

Again, differentiating w.r.t. x, we get

$$nx(1+x)^{n-1} + n(n-1)\,x(1+x)^{n-2}$$

$$= C_1 + 2^2 C_2 x + 3^2 C_3 x^2 + \ldots + n^2 C_n x^{n-1}$$

$$\therefore \quad D^r = n(1+x)^{n-1} + n(n-1)\,x(1+x)\,n-2$$

$$= n(1+x)^{x-2}[(1+x) + (n-1)\,x]$$

$$= n(1+x)^{n-2}[1+nx]$$

$$\therefore \quad y = \frac{N^r}{D^r} = \frac{(1+x)^{n-1}[1+(n+1)\,x]}{n(1+x)^{n-2}[1+n^x]}$$

$$= \frac{(1+x)(1+(n+1)\,x)}{n(1+nx)}$$

To obtain $\frac{dy}{dx}$, we differentiate both sides w.r.t. x, we get

$$[(1+(n+1)\,x) + ((n+1)(1+x))]$$

$$\Rightarrow \quad \frac{dy}{dx} = \frac{(n(1+nx)) - [n^2(1+x)(1+(n+1)\,x)]}{(n(1+nx))^2}$$

On substituting $x = 1$, we get

$$\frac{dy}{dx} = \frac{(2+n) \times 2(n+1) \times n(n+1) - 2n^2 \times (2+n)}{n^2(1+n)^2}$$

$$= \frac{2(2+n)[n(n+1)^2 - n^2]}{n^2(1+n)^2}$$

$$= \frac{2(2+n) \times n[n^2 + 1 + 2n - n]}{n^2(1+n)^2}$$

$$= \frac{2(2+n)(n^2+n+1)}{n(1+n)^2}$$

9. $\frac{1}{A}\cos^{-1}\left(\frac{a\theta - A^2}{B\theta}\right)$,

where $A = \sqrt{a^2 - b^2 - c^2}$ and $B = \sqrt{b^2 + c^2}$

$$\frac{dy}{d\theta} = \frac{1}{A}\left[\frac{-1}{\sqrt{1 - \left(\frac{a\theta - A^2}{B\theta}\right)^2}} \cdot \frac{B\theta a - (a\theta - A^2)\,B}{B^2\theta^2}\right]$$

$$= -\frac{1}{A}\left[\frac{B\theta}{\sqrt{B^2\theta^2 - (a\theta - A^2)^2}} \cdot \frac{A^2 B}{B^2\theta^2}\right]$$

$$\frac{dy}{d\theta} = \frac{-A}{\theta\sqrt{B^2\theta^2 - (a\theta - A^2)^2}} \quad \ldots\text{(i)}$$

$$\frac{d\theta}{dx} = -b\sin x + c\cos x \quad \ldots\text{(ii)}$$

$$\frac{dy}{dx} = \frac{dy}{d\theta}\,\frac{d\theta}{dx} = \frac{-A}{\theta\sqrt{B^2\theta^2 - (a\theta - A^2)^2}}$$

From Eqs. (i) and (ii), we get

$$\left[\frac{A(-c\cos x + b\sin x)}{\sqrt{B^2\theta^2 - a^2\theta^2 - A^4 + 2aA^2\theta}}\right]\frac{1}{\theta}$$

$$\left[\frac{A(-c\cos x + b\sin x)}{\sqrt{(b^2 + c^2)\,\theta^2 - a^2\theta^2 - (a^2 - b^2 - c^2)^2 + 2a\theta\,(a^2 - b^2 - c^2)}}\right]\frac{1}{\theta}$$

$$\left[\frac{A(-c\cos x + b\sin x)}{\sqrt{-(a^2 + b^2 - c^2)(\theta^2 + a^2 - b^2 - c^2) + 2a\theta\,(a^2 - b^2 - c^2)}}\right]\frac{1}{\theta}$$

$$\left[\frac{A(-c\cos x + b\sin x)}{\sqrt{a^2 - b^2 - c^2}\sqrt{(b^2 - c^2) - (\theta^2 - 2a\theta + a^2)}}\right]\frac{1}{\theta}$$

$$\left[\frac{A(-c\cos x + b\sin x)}{\sqrt{a^2 - b^2 - c^2}\sqrt{(b^2 - c^2) - (\theta - a)^2}}\right]\frac{1}{\theta}$$

Now, $(\theta - a)^2 = b^2\cos^2 x + c^2\sin^2 x$

$$+ 2bc\sin x\cos x\,(b^2 + c^2) - (\theta - a)^2$$

$$= b^2\sin^2 x + c^2\cos^2 x - 2bc\sin x\cos x$$

$$= (c\cos x - b\sin x)^2$$

$$\therefore \quad \frac{dy}{dx} = \left\{\frac{A(-c\cos x + b\sin x)}{A(-c\cos x + b\sin x)}\right\}\frac{1}{\theta}$$

$$\frac{dy}{dx} = \frac{1}{\theta}$$

6

> *There are two ways to do great mathematics. The first is to be smarter than everybody else. The second way is to be stupider than everybody else — but persistent.*
>
> **-Raoul Bott**

Application of Derivatives-I (Derivatives as a Rate Measure, Tangent & Normal, Theorems)

Learning Milestones

Milestone 1 Derivative as a Rate Measure, Velocity and Acceleration
- Derivative as a Rate Measure
- Velocity and Acceleration

Milestone 2 Differential and Approximation
- Differential and Approximation
- Geometrical Meaning of Δx, Δy, dx and dy
- Errors

Milestone 3 Tangent and Normal
- Slope of Tangent
- Slope of Normal
- Equation of Tangent
- Equation of Normal

Milestone 4 Angle of Intersection Between Curves
- Angle of Intersection Between Two Curves
- Length of Tangent, Sub-tangent, Normal and Sub-normal
- Shortest Distance Between Two Curves

Milestone 5 Rolle's Theorem, Lagrange's Mean Value Theorem
- Rolle's Theorem and Its Geometrical Interpretation
- Lagrange's Mean Value Theorem and Its Geometrical Interpretation

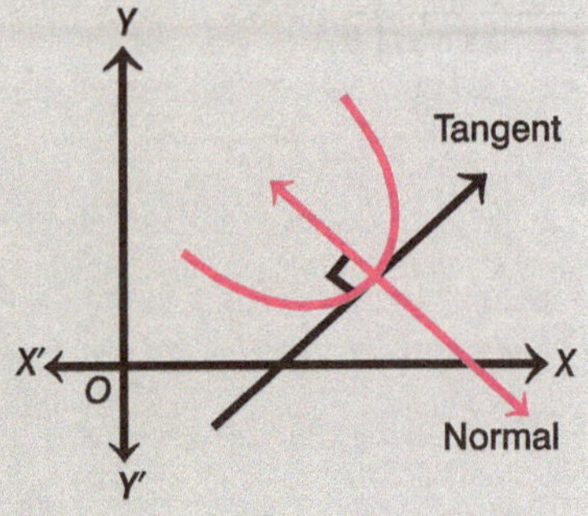

Practice Milestones

Practice Milestone 1- JEE Main Pattern
Practice Milestone 2 - JEE Advanced Pattern
Practice Milestone 3 - Challenging Problems

Milestone 1 Derivative as a Rate Measure, Velocity and Acceleration

• Derivative as a Rate Measure • Velocity and Acceleration

6.1 Derivative as a Rate Measure

If a variable quantity y is some function of time t, i.e. $y = f(t)$, then small change in time Δt have a corresponding change Δy in y.

Thus, the average rate of change $= \dfrac{\Delta y}{\Delta t}$

When limit $\Delta t \to 0$ is applied, the rate of change becomes instantaneous and we get the rate of change of y with respect to the instant t.

i.e.
$$\lim_{\Delta t \to 0} \frac{\Delta y}{\Delta t} = \frac{dy}{dt}$$

Hence, it is clear that the rate of change of any variable with respect to some other variable is the derivative of first variable with respect to other variable.

The differential coefficient of y with respect to x i.e. $\dfrac{dy}{dx}$ is nothing but the instantaneous rate of change of y relative to x.

JEE Focus Points

- $\dfrac{dy}{dx} = \dfrac{(dy/dt)}{(dx/dt)} = \dfrac{\text{rate of change of } y}{\text{rate of change of } x}$
  i.e. derivative of y w.r.t. x is equal to the ratio of the rate change of y w.r.t. time is to the rate of change of x w.r.t. time.
- Suppose $a + b^2 + c^2 + s^4 = 2h^2$ be an equation, where a, b, c, h are constants and s is the function of t, then differentiating both sides with respect to t, we get
  $$0 + 0 + 0 + 4s^3\frac{ds}{dt} = 0$$
  $$\therefore \quad \frac{ds}{dt} = 0 \text{ (is a wrong process)}$$
  Instead technically correct way of performing the operation is
  $$\frac{da}{dt} + 2b\frac{db}{dt} + 2c\frac{dc}{dt} + 4s^3\frac{ds}{dt} = 4h\frac{dh}{dt}$$
  i.e.
  $$0 + 0 + 0 + 4s^3\frac{ds}{dt} = 0$$
  $$\Rightarrow \quad \frac{ds}{dt} = 0$$

Example 1. A cube of ice melts without changing shape at the uniform rate of 4 cm^3/min. The rate of change of the surface area of the cube (in cm^2/min) when the volume of the cube is 125 cm^3, is

(a) -4 (b) $-\dfrac{16}{5}$ (c) $-\dfrac{16}{6}$ (d) $-\dfrac{8}{15}$

Sol. (b) Given, $\dfrac{dV}{dt} = -4 \text{ cm}^3/\text{min}$ and $V = 125 \text{ cm}^3$

$$V = x^3 \Rightarrow \frac{dV}{dt} = 3x^2\frac{dx}{dt} \Rightarrow -4 = 3x^2\frac{dx}{dt}$$

and
$$S = 6x^2 \Rightarrow \frac{dS}{dt} = 12x\frac{dx}{dt}$$

$$\Rightarrow \quad -4 = 3x^2\frac{dS}{dt}\cdot\frac{1}{12x} \Rightarrow \frac{dS}{dt} = -\frac{16}{x} \left[\because \frac{dx}{dt} = \frac{1}{12x}\cdot\frac{dS}{dt}\right]$$

Now, $V = 125 = x^3 \Rightarrow x = 5$

$$\therefore \quad \frac{dS}{dt} = -\frac{16}{x} \text{ cm}^2/\text{min}$$

$$\Rightarrow \left(\frac{dS}{dt}\right)_{x=5} = -\frac{16}{5} \text{ cm}^2/\text{min}$$

Example 2. The radius of a right circular cylinder increases at the rate of 0.1 cm/min and the height decrease at the rate of 0.2 cm/min. The rate of change of the volume of the cylinders (in cm^3/min) when the radius is 2 cm and the height is 3 cm, is

(a) -2π (b) $-\dfrac{8\pi}{5}$ (c) $-\dfrac{3\pi}{5}$ (d) $\dfrac{2\pi}{5}$

Sol. (d) Given, $V = \pi r^2 h$

On differentiating both sides, we get

$$\frac{dV}{dt} = \pi\left(r^2\frac{dh}{dt} + 2r\frac{dr}{dt}h\right) = \pi r\left(r\frac{dh}{dt} + 2h\frac{dr}{dt}\right)$$

Given, $\dfrac{dr}{dt} = \dfrac{1}{10}$ and $\dfrac{dh}{dt} = -\dfrac{2}{10}$

$$\frac{dV}{dt} = \pi r\left(r\left(-\frac{2}{10}\right) + 2h\left(\frac{1}{10}\right)\right) = \frac{\pi r}{5}(-r + h)$$

Thus, when $r = 2$ and $h = 3$,

$$\frac{dV}{dt} = \frac{\pi(2)}{5}(-2 + 3) = \frac{2\pi}{5} \text{ cm}^3/\text{min}$$

JEE SCANNER

Example Similar to PYQ Asked in JEE Main 2022

A water tank has the shape of an inverted circular cone with base radius 2 m and height 4 m. If water is being pumped into the tank at a rate of 2 m^3/min, then the rate at which the water level is rising when the water is 3 m deep is

(a) 0.38 m/min (b) 0.28 m/min
(c) 0.48 m/min (d) 0.18 m/min

Sol. (b) We first sketch the cone and label it as in the figure. Let V, r and h be the volume of the water, the radius of the surface and the height at time t, where t is measured in minutes.

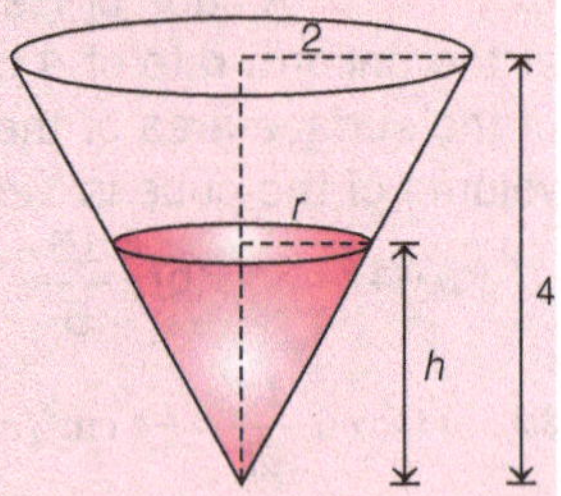

We are given that $\frac{dV}{dt} = 2\ \text{m}^3/\text{min}$ and we are asked to find $\frac{dh}{dt}$, when h is 3 m.

The quantities V and h are related by the equation $V = \frac{1}{3}\pi r^2 h$. But it is the very useful to express V as a function of h alone. In order to eliminate r, we use the similar triangles in the figure to write

$$\frac{r}{h} = \frac{2}{4} \Rightarrow r = \frac{h}{2}$$

and the expression for V becomes

$$V = \frac{1}{3}\pi\left(\frac{h}{2}\right)^2 h = \frac{\pi}{12}h^3$$

Now, we differentiate each side with respect to t,

$$\frac{dV}{dt} = \frac{\pi}{4}h^2\frac{dh}{dt}$$

So,
$$\frac{dh}{dt} = \frac{4}{\pi h^2}\frac{dV}{dt}$$

On substituting $h = 3$ m and $\frac{dV}{dt} = 2\ \text{m}^3/\text{min}$, we get

$$\frac{dh}{dt} = \frac{4}{\pi(3)^2}\cdot 2 = \frac{8}{9\pi}$$

The water level is rising at a rate of $\frac{8}{9\pi} \approx 0.28$ m/min

Skill Builder

From a tank full of water shaped in inverted cone with radius 4 m and height 20 m, water is pouring out a speed of 9 m^3/sec, then the rate of depth is decreasing when radius of cone is 1 m is

(a) 2.8 m/sec (b) 3.8 m/s
(c) 4.8 m/sec (d) 5.8 m/s

For Sol.

■ **For more practice** See Q.1 of Milestone Practice 6.1.

Example 3. Sand is draining from a conical filter, where height and diameter are both 15 cm, into a cylindrical sand pot of diameter 15 cm. The rate at which sand drains from the filter into the pot is 100 cu cm/min. The rate in cm/min at which the level in the pot is rising at the instant when the sand in the pot is 10 cm, is

(a) $\frac{9}{16\pi}$ (b) $\frac{25}{9\pi}$
(c) $\frac{5}{3\pi}$ (d) $\frac{16}{9\pi}$

Sol. (d) For cylindrical pot, $V = \pi r^2 h$

$$\frac{dV}{dt} = \pi r^2\frac{dh}{dt} \qquad \left[r = \text{constant}, \frac{dr}{dt} = 0\right]$$

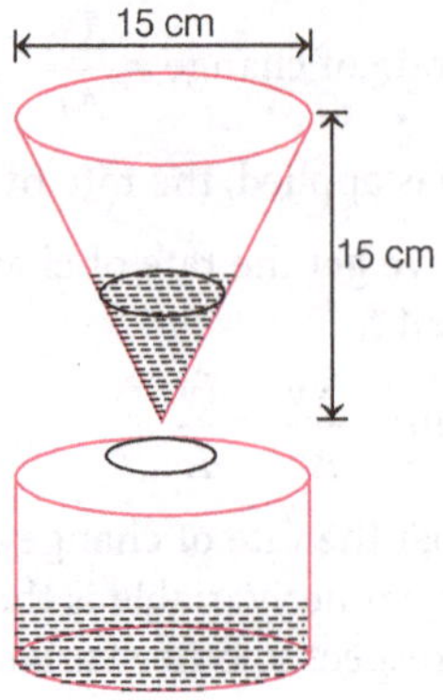

Hence, $100 = \pi r^2 \frac{dh}{dt}$

$\Rightarrow$ $100 = \pi\cdot\frac{225}{4}\cdot\frac{dh}{dt}$ $\quad\left[\because r = \frac{15}{2}\text{cm}\right]$

$\Rightarrow$ $\frac{dh}{dt} = \frac{400}{225\pi} = \frac{16}{9\pi}$ cm/min

JEE Focus Points

- Marginal Cost (MC) is the instantaneous rate of change of total cost with respect to the number of items produced at an instant.
- If total cost when x units is produced is $C(x)$, then marginal cost $= \frac{d(C(x))}{dx} = \frac{dC}{dx}$
- Marginal Revenue (MR) is the instantaneous rate of change of total revenue with respect to the number of items sold at an instant.
- If $R(x)$ be the total revenue when x units are sold, then marginal revenue $= \frac{d}{dx}\{R(x)\} = \frac{dR}{dx}$

Example 4. The total cost $C(x)$ associated with the production of x units of an item is given by $C(x) = 0.007x^3 + 0.003x^2 + 15x + 4000$. Find the marginal cost when 17 units are produced.

Sol. Given, $C(x) = 0.007x^3 + 0.003x^2 + 15x + 4000$

Marginal cost is given by

$$MC(x) = \frac{dC}{dx}$$

$$= (0.007)3x^2 + (0.003)2x + 15$$

$$= 0.021x^2 + 0.006x + 15$$

When $x = 17$,

$$MC(x) = 0.021(17)^2 + 0.006 \times 17 + 15$$

Hence, $MC(17) = 0.021 \times 289 + 0.102 + 15$

$$= 6.069 + 0.102 + 15$$

$$= 21.171$$

6.2 Velocity and Acceleration

Let a particle start moving in a straight line from O and in time t it reaches P having covered a distance s and in $t + \delta t$ it reaches Q having covered a distance $s + \delta s$.

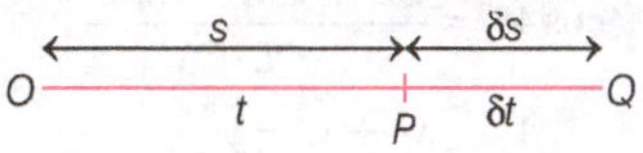

Now, $OP = s, OQ = s + \delta s$

In time δt, average rate of displacement $= \dfrac{\delta s}{\delta t}$

When $\delta t \to 0, \dfrac{\delta s}{\delta t}$ gives the rate of displacement at time t and it is the velocity at time t.

$\therefore$ Velocity at time, $t = \lim\limits_{\delta t \to 0} \dfrac{\delta s}{\delta t} = \dfrac{ds}{dt}$

Hence, $v = \dfrac{ds}{dt}$

Now, let $v =$ velocity at time t and $v + \delta v =$ velocity at time $t + \delta t$.

$\therefore$ In time δt, change in velocity $= v + \delta v - v = \delta v$

$\therefore$ In time δt, average rate of change in velocity $= \dfrac{\delta v}{\delta t}$

But when $\delta t \to 0, \dfrac{\delta s}{\delta t}$ gives the rate of change of velocity at time t and it is the acceleration at time t.

$\therefore$ Acceleration at time, $t = \lim\limits_{\delta t \to 0} \dfrac{\delta v}{\delta t}$

$$= \frac{dv}{dt} = \frac{d}{dt}(v)$$

$$= \frac{d}{dt}\left(\frac{ds}{dt}\right)$$

$$= \frac{d^2 s}{dt^2}$$

Hence, acceleration $(a) = \dfrac{dv}{dt} = \dfrac{d^2 s}{dt^2}$

$$a = \frac{d^2 s}{dt^2} \text{ or } \frac{dv}{dt} = \frac{dv}{ds} \times \frac{ds}{dt} = v\frac{dv}{ds}$$

JEE SCANNER

Example Similar to PYQ Asked in JEE Main 2020

The position of a moving car at time t is given by $f(t) = 3t^2 + 2t + 4, t > 0$. The average speed of the car over the time interval $[t_1, t_2]$ is (attained at the point)

(a) $a(t_2 - t_1) + b$ (b) $\dfrac{t_2 - t_1}{2}$

(c) $2a(t_1 + t_2) + b$ (d) $\dfrac{t_1 + t_2}{2}$

Sol. (d) $\dfrac{f(t_2) - f(t_1)}{t_2 - t_1} = f'(t)$

$$\Rightarrow \frac{3(t_2^2 - t_1^2) + 2(t_2 - t_1)}{(t_2 - t_1)} = 6t + 2$$

$$\Rightarrow 3(t_2 + t_1) + 2 = 6t + 2$$

$$\Rightarrow t = \frac{3(t_1 + t_2)}{6} = \frac{t_1 + t_2}{2}$$

Skill Builder

The position of a moving car at time t is given by $f(t) = 6t^2 + 3t, t > 0$. Then, the average speed of the car over the time interval $[t_1, t_2]$ is (attained at the point)

(a) $a(t_2 - t_1) + b$ (b) $\dfrac{t_1 + t_2}{2}$

(c) $\dfrac{t_2 - t_1}{2}$ (d) $a(t_1 + t_2) + 6$

For Sol.

■ **For more practice** See Q.12 of Milestone Practice 6.1.

Example 5. If the displacement of a particle is given by $s = \left(\dfrac{1}{2}t^2 + 4\sqrt{t}\right)$ m. Find the velocity and acceleration at $t = 4$ sec.

Sol. We have, the displacement of particle is given by,

$$s = \left(\frac{1}{2}t^2 + 4\sqrt{t}\right) \text{m}$$

As, we know velocity, $v = \dfrac{ds}{dt} = \left(t + \dfrac{2}{\sqrt{t}}\right)$ m/s ...(i)

and acceleration, $a = \dfrac{d^2 s}{dt^2} = \dfrac{dv}{dt} = \left(1 - \dfrac{1}{t^{3/2}}\right)$ m/s ...(ii)

Now, velocity when $t = 4$, is

$$v = \left(4 + \frac{2}{\sqrt{4}}\right) \text{m/s} \qquad \text{[from Eq. (i)]}$$

$$\Rightarrow \quad v = 5 \text{ m/s}$$

and acceleration when $t = 4$, is

$$a = \left(1 - \frac{1}{4^{3/2}}\right) \text{m/s}^2 \qquad \text{[from Eq. (i)]}$$

$$\Rightarrow \quad a = \left(1 - \frac{1}{8}\right) \text{m/s}^2$$

$$\Rightarrow \quad a = \frac{7}{8} \text{ m/s}^2$$

Example 6. If $s = \frac{1}{2}t^3 - 6t$, then find the acceleration at time when the velocity tends to zero.

Sol. We have, the displacement s given by,

$$s = \frac{1}{2}t^3 - 6t$$

Now, velocity, $v = \dfrac{ds}{dt} = \left(\dfrac{3t^2}{2} - 6\right)$ ...(i)

and acceleration, $a = \dfrac{dv}{dt} = \dfrac{d^2s}{dt^2} = (3t)$ ...(ii)

To find acceleration, when velocity tends to 0.

Now, when velocity tends to 0, then

$$\frac{3t^2}{2} - 6 = 0 \qquad \text{[from Eq. (i)]}$$

$$\Rightarrow \quad t^2 = 4$$

$$\Rightarrow \quad t = 2$$

Thus, acceleration when velocity tends to zero, is

$$a = 3t = 6 \qquad \text{[from Eq. (ii)]}$$

Example 7. Two men A and B start with velocities v at the same time from the junction of two roads inclined at 45° to each other. If they travel by different roads, find the rate at which they are being separated.

Sol. Let L and M be the positions of men A and B at any time t.

Since, velocities are same $OL = OM = x$ (say)

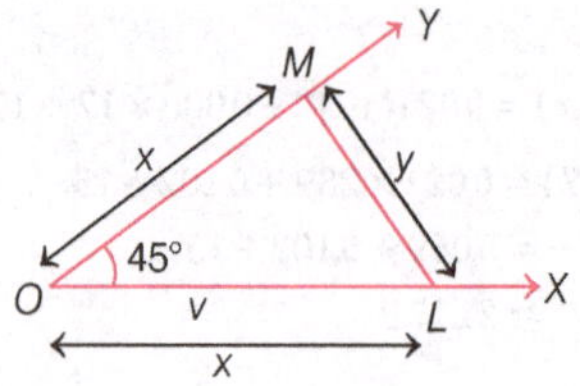

Let $LM = y$

Then, $OM = x$.

It is given that $\dfrac{dx}{dt} = v$ and we need to find $\dfrac{dy}{dt}$ from ΔLOM.

$$\cos 45° = \frac{OL^2 + OM^2 - LM^2}{2 \cdot OL \cdot OM}$$

$$\Rightarrow \quad \frac{1}{\sqrt{2}} = \frac{x^2 + x^2 - y^2}{2 \cdot x \cdot x}$$

$$\Rightarrow \quad \frac{1}{\sqrt{2}} = \frac{2x^2 - y^2}{2x^2}$$

$$\Rightarrow \quad \sqrt{2}x^2 = 2x^2 - y^2$$

$$\Rightarrow \quad (2 - \sqrt{2})x^2 = y^2$$

$$\therefore \quad y = \sqrt{2 - \sqrt{2}}\, x$$

On differentiating w.r.t. t, we get

$$\frac{dy}{dt} = \sqrt{2 - \sqrt{2}} \frac{dx}{dt} = \sqrt{2 - \sqrt{2}}\, v \qquad \left[\because \frac{dx}{dt} = v\right]$$

$\therefore$ The two men are being separated from each other at the rate of $\sqrt{2 - \sqrt{2}}\, v$.

Milestone Practice 6.1

1. The radius of the base of the cone is increasing at the rate of 3 cm/min and the altitude is decreasing at the rate of 4 cm/min. Find the rate of change of lateral surface area, when the radius is 7 cm and altitude is 24 cm

2. The length x of a rectangle is decreasing at the rate of 5 cm/min and the width y is increasing at the rate of 4 cm/min. When $x = 8$ cm and $y = 6$ cm, find the rate of change of (i) the perimeter (ii) the area of the rectangle.

3. A circular disc of radius 3 m is being heated. Due to expansion, its radius increases at the rate of 0.05 cm/sec. Find the rate which its area is increasing when radius is 3.2 cm.

4. A car starts from a point P at time $t = 0$ seconds and stops at a point Q. The distance x, in metres, covered by it, in t seconds is given by $x = t^2\left(2 - \frac{t}{3}\right)$.

Find the time taken by it to reach Q and also find distance PQ.

5. An edge of a variable cube is increasing at the rate of 10 cm/s. How fast the volume of the cube will increase when the edge is 5 cm long?

(a) 750 cm^3/s (b) 75 cm^3/s
(c) 300 cm^3/s (d) 150 cm^3/s

6. A stone is thrown vertically upwards from the top of a tower 64 m high according to the law $s = 48t - 16t^2$. The greatest height attained by the stone above ground is

(a) 36 m (b) 32 m (c) 100 m (d) 64 m

7. A particle is moving in a straight line. At time t, the distance between the particle from its starting point is given by $x = t - 6t^2 + t^3$. Its acceleration will be zero at

(a) $t = 1$ unit time (b) $t = 2$ units time
(c) $t = 3$ units time (d) $t = 4$ units time

8. The distance covered by a particle in t seconds is given by $x = 3 + 8t - 4t^2$. After 1 s its velocity will be

(a) 0 unit (b) 3 units
(c) 4 units (d) 7 units

9. The distance travelled by a motor car in t seconds after the brakes are applied is s feet, where $s = 22t - 12t^2$. The distance travelled by the car before it stops, is

(a) 10.08 ft (b) 10 ft (c) 11 ft (d) 11.5 ft

10. The radius of a circle is increasing at the rate of 0.1 cm/s. When the radius of the circle is 5 cm, the rate of change of its area is

(a) $-\pi$ cm^2/s (b) 10π cm^2/s
(c) $0.1\,\pi$ cm^2/s (d) π cm^2/s

11. A particle describes an ellipse whose semi-axes are 4 m and 3 m with a constant speed of 1 m/sec. The velocity of the foot of the perpendicular from the particle on the major axis, when the particle is at a distance of 1 m from the major axis is equal to

(a) $\frac{2}{11}$ m/s (b) $\frac{11}{2}$ m/s
(c) $-\sqrt{\left(\frac{2}{11}\right)}$ m/s (d) None of these

12. The position of a moving car at time t is given by $f(t) = \frac{3}{2}t^2 + \frac{5}{2}t,\ t > 0$. Then, the average speed of the car over the time interval $[t_1, t_2]$ is (attained at the point)

(a) $a(t_2 - t_1) + b$ (b) $\frac{t_2 - t_1}{2}$
(c) $\frac{t_1 + t_2}{2}$ (d) $a(t_1 + t_2) + b$

13. If the distance s covered by a particle in time t is proportional to the cube root of its velocity, then the acceleration is

(a) a constant (b) $\propto s^3$ (c) $\propto \frac{1}{s^3}$ (d) $\propto s^5$

14. A particle moves in a straight line so that $s \propto \sqrt{t}$, then its acceleration is proportional to

(a) $(\text{velocity})^3$ (b) velocity
(c) $(\text{velocity})^2$ (d) $(\text{velocity})^{3/2}$

15. If a particle moves such that the displacement is proportional to the square of the velocity acquired, then its acceleration is

(a) proportional to s^2 (b) proportional to $\frac{1}{s^2}$
(c) proportional to $\frac{1}{s}$ (d) a constant

Answer Key

1. $54\,\pi$ cm^2/min	2. (i) Perimeter decreases at the rate of 2 cm/min (ii) Area increases at the rate of 2 cm^2/min			
3. $(0.32\,\pi$ cm^2/s)	4. 4 s, 32/3 m	5. (a)	6. (c)	7. (b)
8. (a)	9. (a)	10. (d)	11. (c)	12. (c)
13. (d)	14. (a)	15. (d)		

For Detailed Solution

Milestone 2 Differential and Approximation

• Differential and Approximation • Geometrical Meaning of Δx, Δy, dx and dy • Errors

6.3 Differential and Approximation

We are familiar with the symbol $\frac{dy}{dx}$ representing derivative of y w.r.t. x.

Now, we shall give meaning to the symbols dx and dy such that the symbol $\frac{dy}{dx}$ represents the **quotient of dy and dx.**

Let $y = f(x)$ be a function of x.

Let Δx denotes small change in x and let the corresponding change in y be Δy.

Then, $\lim_{\Delta x \to 0} \frac{\Delta y}{\Delta x} = \frac{dy}{dx}$

$\Rightarrow \quad \frac{\Delta y}{\Delta x} = \frac{dy}{dx}$ (approx.)

$\Rightarrow \quad \frac{\Delta y}{\Delta x} = \frac{dy}{dx} + \varepsilon,$

where $\varepsilon \to 0$ as $\Delta x \to 0$

$\Rightarrow \quad \Delta y = \frac{dy}{dx} \cdot \Delta x + \varepsilon \cdot \Delta x$ ...(i)

Now, Δy consists of two parts. The part $\varepsilon \cdot \Delta x$ is very small and hence negligible. The part of $\frac{dy}{dx} \cdot \Delta x$ is called **principal part of Δy** and is denoted by **dy** and is called **differential of y.**

Thus, $dy = \frac{dy}{dx} \cdot \Delta x$ ...(ii)

$\Rightarrow \quad dx = \frac{dx}{dy} \cdot \Delta x = (1)\,\Delta x = \Delta x$ ...(iii)

From Eqs. (ii) and (iii), we get

$$dy = \frac{dy}{dx} \cdot dx$$

$\Rightarrow$ (Differential of y) = (Differential coefficient of y w.r.t. x) $\cdot$ (Differential of x)

$\Rightarrow \quad \frac{\text{Differential of } y}{\text{Differential of } x}$ = (Differential coefficient of y w.r.t. x)

From Eq. (i), $\Delta y = \frac{dy}{dx} \cdot \Delta x$ (approx.)

$\Rightarrow \quad \Delta y = dy$ (approx.)

Hence, approximately

$$dy = \Delta y = (y + \Delta y) - y = f(x + \Delta x) - f(x)$$

$\Rightarrow \quad \frac{dy}{dx} \cdot dx = f(x + \Delta x) - f(x)$ (approx.)

$$f(x + \Delta x) - f(x) = f'(x) \cdot \Delta x \text{ (approx.)}$$

6.4 Geometrical Meaning of Δx, Δy, dx and dy

Let us take a point $A(x, y)$ on the curve $y = f(x)$, where $f(x)$ is differentiable real function.

Let $B(x + \Delta x, y + \Delta y)$ be a neighbouring point on the curve, where Δx denotes a small change in x and Δy is the corresponding change in y.

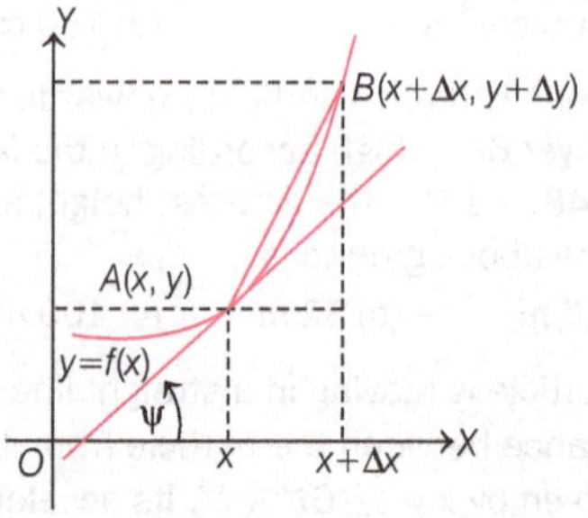

From the figure, it is clear that if Δx and Δy are sufficiently small quantities, then

$$\frac{\Delta y}{\Delta x} = \tan \psi \cong \frac{dy}{dx} = f'(x)$$

Hence, approximate change in the value of y, called its differential, is given by $\Delta y = f'(x) \cdot \Delta x$.

Example 8. Using differentials find the approximate value of the following

(i) $82^{1/4}$ (ii) $\sqrt{25.2}$ (iii) $(0.007)^{1/3}$ (iv) $(1.999)^6$

(v) $\tan 46°$, where $1° = 0.01745$ radian

(vi) $[(3.92)^2 + 3(2.1)^4]^{1/6}$

Sol. (i) Let $f(x) = x^{1/4}$

$\therefore \quad f'(x) = \frac{1}{4}(x)^{-3/4} = \frac{1}{4x^{3/4}}$

Also, $\quad f(x + \Delta x) = (x + \Delta x)^{1/4}$

Now, $\quad f(x + \Delta x) = f(x) + \Delta x\, f'(x)$ (approx.)

$$f(x+\Delta x)^{1/4} = x^{1/4} + \Delta x \cdot \frac{1}{4x^{3/4}} \qquad \text{...(i)}$$

We have to find $(82)^{1/4}$ and we know the value of $(81)^{1/4}$ which is equal to 3.

On putting $x = 81$, $x + \Delta x = 82$ so that $\Delta x = 1$ in Eq. (i), we get

$$(82)^{1/4} = (81)^{1/4} + 1 \cdot \frac{1}{4(81)^{3/4}}$$

$$= 3 + \frac{1}{4 \times 3^3} = 3 + \frac{1}{108} = 3.009$$

(ii) Let $f(x) = \sqrt{x} \Rightarrow f'(x) = \frac{1}{2\sqrt{x}}$

$\because \quad f(x + \Delta x) - f(x) = f'(x) \cdot \Delta x$

Therefore, $f(x + \Delta x) - f(x) = \frac{\Delta x}{2\sqrt{x}}$

So, we may write as $25.2 = 25 + 0.2$

Taking $x = 25$ and $\Delta x = 0.2$, we get

$$f(25.2) - f(25) = \frac{0.2}{2\sqrt{25}}$$

$$\Rightarrow \quad f(25.2) - f(25) = \frac{0.2}{10} = 0.02$$

$$\Rightarrow \quad f(25.2) = 5.02 \Rightarrow \sqrt{25.2} = 5.02$$

(iii) Let $f(x) = x^{1/3} \Rightarrow f'(x) = \frac{1}{3}x^{-2/3}$

Now, $f(x + \Delta x) - f(x) = f'(x) \cdot \Delta x = \frac{\Delta x}{3(x^{2/3})}$

We may write $0.007 = 0.008 - 0.001$, taking $x = 0.008$ and $\Delta x = -0.001$, we get

$$f(0.007) - f(0.008) = -\frac{0.001}{3(0.008)^{2/3}}$$

$$\Rightarrow f(0.007) - (0.008)^{1/3} = -\frac{0.001}{3(0.2)^2}$$

$$\Rightarrow \quad f(0.007) = 0.2 - \frac{0.001}{3(0.04)} = 0.2 - \frac{1}{120} = \frac{23}{120}$$

Hence, $(0.007)^{1/3} = \frac{23}{120}$

(iv) Let $f(x) = x^6$

Now, $f(x + \Delta x) - f(x) = f'(x) \cdot \Delta x = 6x^5 \Delta x$

We may write $1.999 = 2 - 0.001$

Taking $x = 2$ and $\Delta x = -0.001$, we get

$$f(1.999) - f(2) = 6(2)^5 \times -0.001$$

$$\Rightarrow \quad f(1.999) = f(2) - 6 \times 32 \times 0.001$$

$$= 64 - 64 \times 0.003 = 64 \times 0.997$$

$$= 63.808 \text{ (approx.)}$$

(v) Let $y = f(x) = \tan x$, $x = 45° = \left(\frac{\pi}{4}\right)^c$ and $x + \Delta x = 46°$.

Then, $\Delta x = 1° = 0.01745$ radians

For $x = \frac{\pi}{4}$, $\quad y = f\left(\frac{\pi}{4}\right) = \tan\frac{\pi}{4} = 1$

Let $\quad dx = \Delta x = 0.01745$

Now, $\quad y = \tan x \Rightarrow \frac{dy}{dx} = \sec^2 x$

$$\Rightarrow \quad \left(\frac{dy}{dx}\right)_{x=\pi/4} = \sec^2\frac{\pi}{4} = 2$$

$$\therefore \quad \Delta y = \frac{dy}{dx}\Delta x$$

$$\Rightarrow \quad dy = 2(0.01745) = 0.03490$$

$$\Rightarrow \quad \Delta y = 0.03490 \qquad [\because \Delta y \cong dy]$$

Hence, $\tan 46° = y + \Delta y = 1 + 0.03490 = 1.03490$

(vi) Let $f(x, y) = (x^2 + 3y^4)^{1/6}$ ...(i)

Taking $x = 4$, $\Delta x = -0.08$ and $y = 2$, $\Delta y = 0.1$

On differentiating Eq. (i) wr.t. x, treating y as constant,

$$\frac{\Delta f}{\Delta x} = \frac{1}{6}(x^2 + 3y^4)^{-5/6}(2x)$$

$$= \frac{8}{6}(16 + 48)^{-5/6} = \frac{4}{3} \times 2^{-5} = \frac{1}{24}$$

and differentiating Eq. (i) w.r.t. y, treating x as consant,

$$\therefore \quad \frac{\Delta f}{\Delta y} = \frac{1}{6}(x^2 + 3y^4)^{-5/6}(12y^3)$$

$$= \frac{12(8)}{6}(64)^{-5/6} = 16(2)^{-5} = \frac{1}{2}$$

$$\therefore \quad df = \frac{\Delta f}{\Delta x} \cdot \Delta x + \frac{\Delta f}{\Delta y}\Delta y$$

$$= \frac{1}{24} \times -0.08 + \frac{1}{2} \times 0.1 = -\frac{0.01}{3} + \frac{0.1}{2} = 0.466$$

$\therefore [(3.92)^2 + 3(2.1)^4]^{1/6} = f(4, 2) + df = 2 + 0.466 = 2.466$

6.5 Errors

Definition of Absolute Error

Δx or dx is called absolute error in x.

Definition of Relative Error

$\frac{\Delta x}{x}$ or $\frac{dx}{x}$ is called relative error in x.

Definition of Percentage Error

$\left(\frac{\Delta x}{x}\right) \cdot 100$ or $\left(\frac{dx}{x}\right) \cdot 100$ is called percentage error in x.

Example 9. If there is an error of $k\%$ in measuring the edge of a cube, then the percent error in estimating its volume is

(a) k (b) $3k$

(c) $\frac{k}{3}$ (d) None of these

Sol. (b) $V = x^3$ and the percent error in measuring $x = \frac{dx}{x} \times 100$

The percent error in measuring volume $= \frac{dV}{V} \times 100$

Now, $\frac{dV}{dx} = 3x^2$

$\Rightarrow \quad dV = 3x^2 dx$

$\Rightarrow \quad \frac{dV}{V} = \frac{3x^2 dx}{x^3} = 3\frac{dx}{x}$

$\therefore \quad \frac{dV}{V} \times 100 = 3\frac{dx}{x} \times 100 = 3k\%$

Example 10. Find the possible percentage error in computing the parallel resistance R of three resistances R_1, R_2, R_3 from the formula $\frac{1}{R} = \frac{1}{R_1} + \frac{1}{R_2} + \frac{1}{R_3}$, if R_1, R_2, R_3 are each in error by plus 1.2%.

Sol. Given, $\frac{1}{R} = \frac{1}{R_1} + \frac{1}{R_2} + \frac{1}{R_3}$ ...(i)

On differentiating both sides, we get

$$-\frac{1}{R^2} dR = -\frac{1}{R_1^2} dR_1 - \frac{1}{R_2^2} dR_2 - \frac{1}{R_3^2} dR_3$$

$$\Rightarrow \frac{1}{R}\left(\frac{dR}{R} \times 100\right) = \frac{1}{R_1}\left(\frac{dR_1}{R_1} \times 100\right) + \frac{1}{R_2}\left(\frac{dR_2}{R_2} \times 100\right) + \frac{1}{R_3}\left(\frac{dR_3}{R_3} \times 100\right)$$

$$= \frac{1}{R_1}(1.2) + \frac{1}{R_2}(1.2) + \frac{1}{R_3}(1.2)$$

$$\left[\because \frac{dR_i}{R_i} \times 100 = 1.2, \forall i \in \{1,2,3\}\right]$$

$$= 1.2\left(\frac{1}{R_1} + \frac{1}{R_2} + \frac{1}{R_3}\right) = 1.2\left(\frac{1}{R}\right)$$

[from Eq. (i)]

$\therefore \quad \frac{dR}{R} \times 100 = 1.2\%$

Example 11. The time T of a complete oscillation of a simple pendulum of length l is given by the equation $T = 2\pi\sqrt{\frac{l}{g}}$, where g is constant. What is the percentage error in T when l is increased by 1%?

Sol. Let Δl be the change in l and ΔT be the corresponding error in T.

Then, $\frac{\Delta l}{l} \times 100 = 1$ [given]

$\Rightarrow \quad \frac{dl}{l} \times 100 = 1$

Now, $T = 2\pi\sqrt{\frac{l}{g}}$

$\Rightarrow \quad \ln T = \ln 2\pi + \left(\frac{1}{2}\right)\ln l - \frac{1}{2}\ln g$

$\Rightarrow \quad \frac{1}{T}\frac{dT}{dl} = \frac{1}{2} \cdot \frac{1}{l}$

$\Rightarrow \quad \frac{dT}{dl} = \frac{T}{2l}$

$\Rightarrow \quad \frac{dT}{T} = \frac{1}{2l} dl$

$\Rightarrow \quad \frac{dT}{T} \times 100 = \frac{1}{2}\left(\frac{dl}{l} \times 100\right)$

$\Rightarrow \quad \frac{dT}{T} \times 100 = \frac{1}{2}$ $\left[\because \frac{dl}{l} \times 100 = 1\right]$

So, there is (1/2)% error in calculating the time period T.

Example 12. The pressure p and the volume V of a gas are connected by the relation $pV^{1.4}$ = const. Find the percentage error in p corresponiding to a decrease of 1.2% in V.

Sol. We have, $pV^{1.4} = k$ (constant)

$\Rightarrow \quad \log p + 1.4 \log V = \log k$

$\Rightarrow \quad \frac{1}{p}\frac{dp}{dV} + \frac{1.4}{V} = 0$

$\Rightarrow \quad \frac{dp}{dV} = -\frac{1.4p}{V}$

Now, $\Delta p = \frac{dp}{dV} \Delta V$

$\Rightarrow \quad \Delta p = -\frac{1.4p}{V} \Delta V$

$\Rightarrow \quad \frac{\Delta p}{p} = -1.4\frac{\Delta V}{V}$

$\Rightarrow \quad \frac{\Delta p}{p} \times 100 = -1.4\left(\frac{\Delta V}{V} \times 100\right)$

$\Rightarrow \quad \frac{\Delta p}{p} \times 100 = -1.4(-1.2) = 1.68$

$\left[\because \frac{\Delta V}{V} \times 100 = 1.2 \text{ (given)}\right]$

Milestone Practice 6.2

1. Using differentials, find the approximate values of the following
   (i) $\sqrt{26}$ (ii) $\sqrt{0.48}$
2. Find the approximate value of $f(5.001)$, where $f(x) = x^3 - 7x^2 + 15$.
3. If the radius of a sphere is measured as 9 m with an error of 0.03 m, find the approximate error in calculating its surface area.
4. If the radius of a sphere is measured as 7 m with an error of 0.02 m, find the approximate error in calculating its volume.
5. If there is 2% error in measuring the radius of sphere, then what will be the percentage error in the surface area?
   (a) 3% (b) 1%
   (c) 4% (d) 2%
6. The height of a cylinder is equal to the radius. If an error of k% is made in the height, then percentage error in its volume is
   (a) k% (b) $2k$%
   (c) $k/2$% (d) $3k$%
7. If the ratio of base radius and height of a cone is 1 : 2 and percentage error in radius is k%, then the error in its volume is
   (a) k% (b) $2k$%
   (c) $3k$% (d) None of these
8. The pressure P and volume V of a gas are connected by the relation $PV^{1/4}$ = constant. The percentage increase in the pressure corresponding to a reduction of (1/2)% in the volume is
   (a) $\frac{1}{2}$% (b) $\frac{1}{4}$%
   (c) $\frac{1}{8}$% (d) None of these
9. If $y = x^n$, then the ratio of relative errors in y and x is
   (a) 1 : 1 (b) 2 : 1
   (c) 1 : n (d) n : 1

Answer Key

1. (i) 5.1 (ii) 0.693	2. (−34.995)	3. ($2.16\pi\ m^2$)	4. ($3.92\pi\ m^3$)	5. (c)
6. (d)	7. (c)	8. (c)	9. (d)	

For Detailed Solution

Milestone 3 Tangent and Normal

• Slope of Tangent • Slope of Normal • Equation of Tangent • Equation of Normal

6.6 Slope of Tangent

Let $y = f(x)$ be a continuous curve and let $P(x_1, y_1)$ be a point on it.

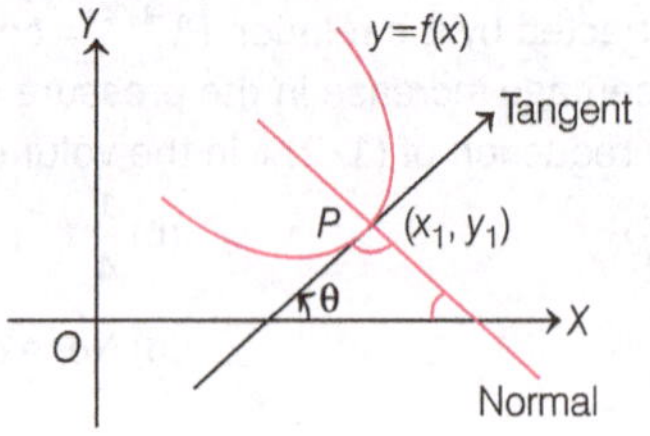

Then, $\left(\frac{dy}{dx}\right)_{(x_1, y_1)}$ is the slope of tangent to the curve $y = f(x)$ at a point $P(x_1, y_1)$.

$$\Rightarrow \quad \left(\frac{dy}{dx}\right)_P = \tan\theta$$

$$= \text{Slope of tangent at } P$$

where, θ is the angle which the tangent at $P(x_1, y_1)$ forms with the positive direction of X-axis in anti-clockwise sense as shown in the figure.

6.7 Slope of Normal

We know that the normal to the curve at $P(x_1, y_1)$ is a line perpendicular to tangent at $P(x_1, y_1)$ and passes through P.

$$\therefore \text{ Slope of the normal at } P = -\frac{1}{\text{Slope of the tangent at } P}$$

$$\Rightarrow \text{Slope of normal at } P(x_1, y_1) = -\frac{1}{\left(\frac{dy}{dx}\right)_{(x_1, y_1)}}$$

$$\text{or slope of normal at } P(x_1, y_1) = -\left(\frac{dx}{dy}\right)_{(x_1, y_1)}$$

JEE Focus Points

- If $\left.\frac{dy}{dx}\right|_{(x_1, y_1)} = 0$, then tangent is parallel to X-axis and converse. If tangent is parallel to $ax + by + c = 0$, then $\frac{dy}{dx} = -\frac{a}{b}$

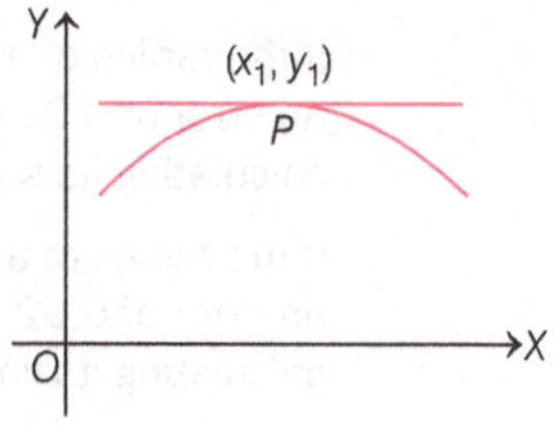

- If $\left.\frac{dy}{dx}\right|_{(x_1, y_1)} \to \infty$ or $\left.\frac{dx}{dy}\right|_{(x_1, y_1)} = 0$, then tangent is perpendicular to X-axis. If tangent with a finite slope is perpendicular to $ax + by + c = 0$, then $\left.\frac{dy}{dx}\right|_{(x_1, y_1)} \times \left(-\frac{a}{b}\right) = -1$

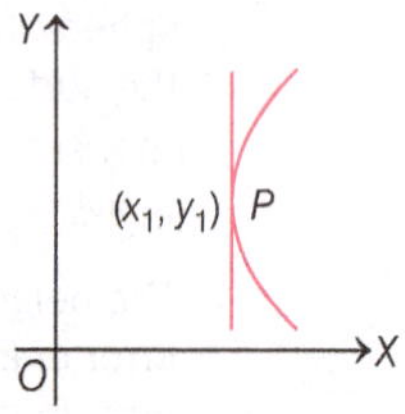

- If the tangent at $P(x_1, y_1)$ on the curve is equally inclined to the coordinate axes, then $\left.\frac{dy}{dx}\right|_{(x_1, y_1)} = \pm 1$

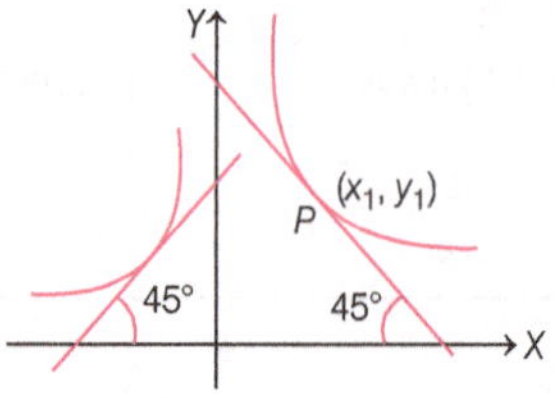

- If the tangent makes equal non-zero intercept on the coordinate axes, then $\left.\frac{dy}{dx}\right|_{(x_1, y_1)} = -1$

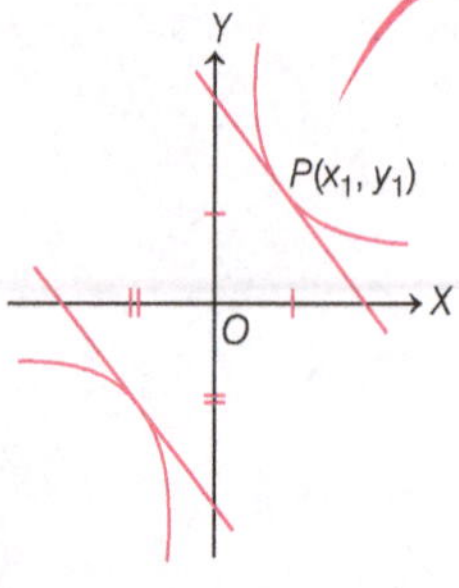

Concept Inside Video

- If tangent cuts off from the coordinate axes equal distance from the origin, then $\frac{dy}{dx} = \pm 1$

Example 13. Find the slopes of the tangent and normal to the curve $x^3 + 3xy + y^3 = 2$ at (1, 1).

Sol. Given equation of curve is $x^3 + 3xy + y^3 = 2$

On differentiating w.r.t. x, we get

$$3x^2 + 3x\frac{dy}{dx} + 3y + 3y^2\frac{dy}{dx} = 0$$

$$\Rightarrow \quad \frac{dy}{dx} = -\frac{(3x^2 + 3y)}{(3x + 3y^2)}$$

$$\Rightarrow \quad \frac{dy}{dx} = -\frac{(x^2 + y)}{(x + y^2)}$$

$$\Rightarrow \quad \left(\frac{dy}{dx}\right)_{(1,1)} = -\left(\frac{2}{2}\right) = -1$$

$\therefore$ Slope of tangent at (1, 1) $= \left(\frac{dy}{dx}\right)_{(1,1)} = -1$

and slope of normal at (1, 1) $= -\dfrac{1}{\left(\frac{dy}{dx}\right)_{(1,1)}} = \dfrac{-1}{-1} = 1$

Example 14. Find the point on the the curve $y = x^3 - 3x$ at which tangent is parallel to X-axis.

Sol. Let the point at which tangent is parallel to X-axis be $P(x_1, y_1)$.

Then, it must lie on curve.

Therefore, we have $y_1 = x_1^3 - 3x_1$ ...(i)

On differentiating $y = x^3 - 3x$ w.r.t. x, we get

$$\frac{dy}{dx} = 3x^2 - 3$$

$$\Rightarrow \quad \left(\frac{dy}{dx}\right)_{(x_1, y_1)} = 3x_1^2 - 3$$

Since, the tangent is parallel to X-axis.

$$\therefore \quad \left(\frac{dy}{dx}\right)_{(x_1, y_1)} = 0$$

$$\Rightarrow \quad 3x_1^2 - 3 = 0$$

$$\Rightarrow \quad x_1 = \pm 1 \quad \text{...(ii)}$$

From Eqs. (i) and (ii), we get

When $x_1 = 1$, then $y_1 = 1 - 3 = -2$

When $x_1 = -1$, then $y_1 = -1 + 3 = 2$

$\therefore$ Points at which tangent is parallel to X-axis are $(1, -2)$ and $(-1, 2)$.

Example 15. Find the point on the curve $y = x^3 - 2x^2 - x$ at which the tangent line is parallel to the line $y = 3x - 2$.

Sol. Let $P(x_1, y_1)$ be the required point.

Then, we have $y_1 = x_1^3 - 2x_1^2 - x_1$ ...(i)

On differentiating the curve $y = x^3 - 2x^2 - x$ w.r.t. x, we get

$$\frac{dy}{dx} = 3x^2 - 4x - 1$$

$$\Rightarrow \quad \left(\frac{dy}{dx}\right)_{(x_1, y_1)} = 3x_1^2 - 4x_1 - 1$$

Since, tangent at (x_1, y_1) is parallel to the line $y = 3x - 2$.

$\therefore$ Slope of the tangent at $P(x_1, y_1)$

= Slope of the line $y = 3x - 2$

$$\Rightarrow \quad \left(\frac{dy}{dx}\right)_{(x_1, y_1)} = 3$$

$$\Rightarrow \quad 3x_1^2 - 4x_1 - 1 = 3$$

$$\Rightarrow \quad 3x_1^2 - 4x_1 - 4 = 0$$

$$\Rightarrow \quad (x_1 - 2)(3x_1 + 2) = 0$$

$$\Rightarrow \quad x_1 = 2, -\frac{2}{3} \quad \text{...(ii)}$$

From Eqs. (i) and (ii), we get

When $x_1 = 2$, then

$$y_1 = 8 - 8 - 2$$

$$\Rightarrow \quad y_1 = -2$$

When $x_1 = -\frac{2}{3}$, then $y_1 = x_1^3 - 2x_1^2 - x_1$

$$\Rightarrow \quad y_1 = \frac{-8}{27} - \frac{8}{9} + \frac{2}{3}$$

$$\Rightarrow \quad y_1 = \frac{-14}{27}$$

Thus, the point at which tangent is parallel to $y = 3x - 2$ are $(2, -2)$ and $\left(-\frac{2}{3}, -\frac{14}{27}\right)$.

Example 16. In which of the following cases, the function $f(x)$ has a vertical tangent at $x = 0$?

(i) $f(x) = x^{1/3}$

(ii) $f(x) = \text{sgn } x$

(iii) $f(x) = x^{2/3}$

(iv) $f(x) = \sqrt{|x|}$

(v) $f(x) = \begin{cases} 0, & \text{if } x < 0 \\ 1, & \text{if } x \geq 0 \end{cases}$

Decoding the Question

Vertical Tangent

$y = f(x)$ has a vertical tangent at the points $x = x_0$, if $\lim_{h \to 0} \dfrac{f(x_0 + h) - f(x_0)}{h} = \infty$ or $-\infty$ but not both.

Sol. (i) $f(x) = x^{1/3}$

$$f'(0^+) = \lim_{h \to 0} \frac{h^{1/3}}{h} = \frac{1}{h^{2/3}} \to \infty$$

$$f'(0^-) = \lim_{h \to 0} \frac{(-h)^{1/3}}{-h} = \frac{1}{(-h)^{2/3}} = \frac{1}{h^{2/3}} \to \infty$$

$\Rightarrow$ $f(x)$ has a vertical tangent at $x = 0$.

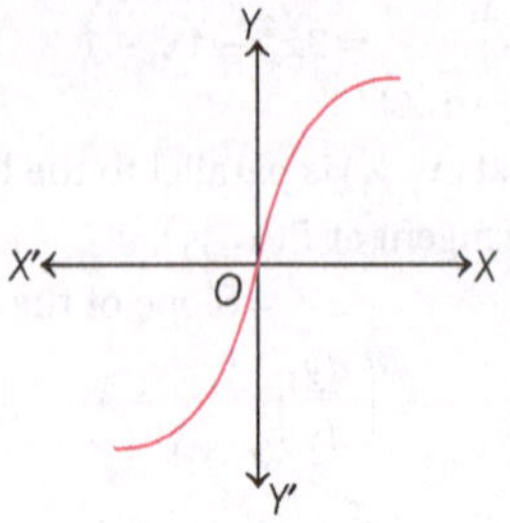

(ii) $f(x) = \text{sgn } x = \begin{cases} 1, & \text{if } x > 0 \\ 0, & \text{if } x = 0 \\ -1, & \text{if } x < 0 \end{cases}$

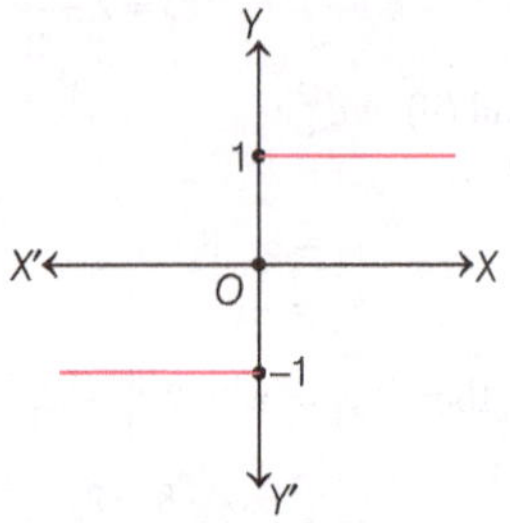

$$\left.\begin{aligned} f'(0^+) &= \lim_{h \to 0} \frac{1-0}{h} \to \infty \\ f'(0^-) &= \lim_{h \to 0} \frac{-1}{-h} \to \infty \end{aligned}\right\}$$

$\Rightarrow$ $f(x)$ has a vertical tangent at $x = 0$.

(iii) $f(x) = x^{2/3}$

$$\left.\begin{aligned} f'(0^+) &= \lim_{h \to 0} \frac{h^{2/3}}{h} \to \infty \\ f'(0^-) &= \lim_{h \to 0} \frac{(-h)^{2/3}}{-h} = -\frac{1}{h^{1/3}} \to -\infty \end{aligned}\right\}$$

$\Rightarrow$ No vertical tangent at $x = 0$.

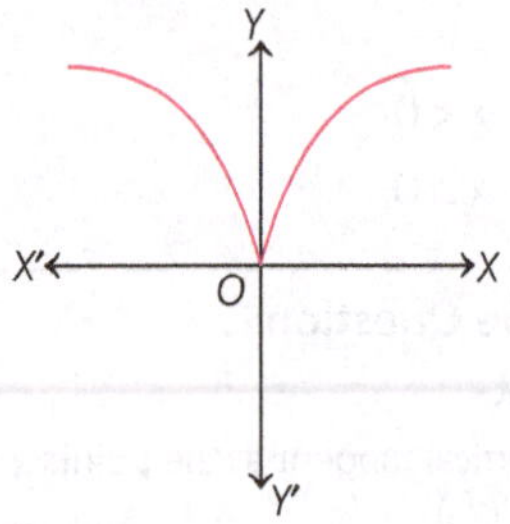

(iv) $f(x) = \sqrt{|x|} = \begin{bmatrix} \sqrt{x}, & \text{if } x \geq 0 \\ \sqrt{-x}, & \text{if } x < 0 \end{bmatrix}$

$$\left.\begin{aligned} f'(0^+) &= \lim_{h \to 0} \frac{\sqrt{h}-0}{h} \to \infty \\ f'(0^-) &= \lim_{h \to 0} \frac{\sqrt{h}}{-h} \to -\infty \end{aligned}\right\}$$

$\Rightarrow$ No vertical tangent at $x = 0$.

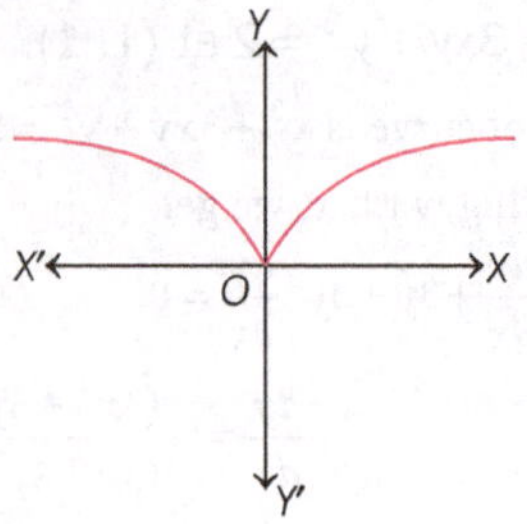

(v) $f(x) = \begin{cases} 0, & \text{if } x < 0 \\ 1, & \text{if } x \geq 0 \end{cases}$

$$\left.\begin{aligned} f'(0^+) &= \lim_{h \to 0} \frac{1-1}{h} = 0 \\ f'(0^-) &= \lim_{h \to 0} \frac{0-1}{h} \to -\infty \end{aligned}\right\}$$

$\Rightarrow$ No vertical tangent at $x = 0$.

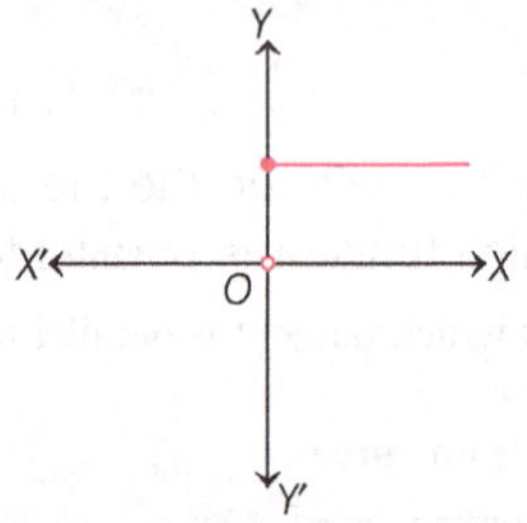

6.8 Equation of Tangent

Let $y = f(x)$ be the equation of curve and point (x_1, y_1) be any point on the curve.

Let PT be the tangent at point $P(x_1, y_1)$.

Since, tangent is a line passing through the point $P(x_1, y_1)$ and having slope, $m = \left(\frac{dy}{dx}\right)_{(x_1, y_1)}$.

Therefore, by coordinate geometry, the equation of tangent is

$$y - y_1 = m(x - x_1)$$

$$\Rightarrow \quad y - y_1 = \left(\frac{dy}{dx}\right)_{(x_1, y_1)} \cdot (x - x_1)$$

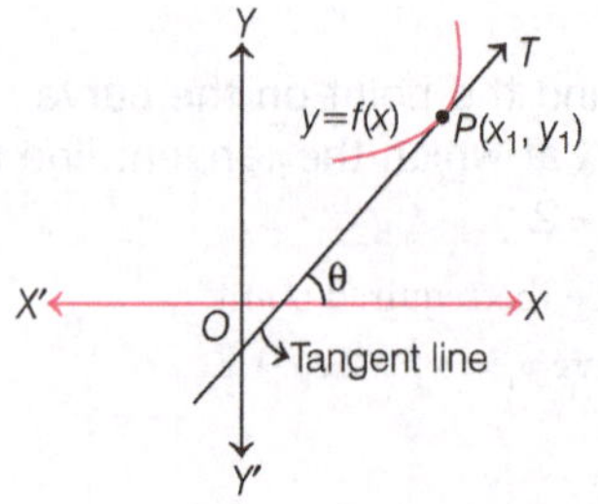

JEE SPIKE

Tangent from External Point If a point $P(a, b)$ does not lie on the curve $y = f(x)$, then the equation of all possible tangents to the curve $y = f(x)$, passing through (a, b), can be found by solving for the point of contact Q.

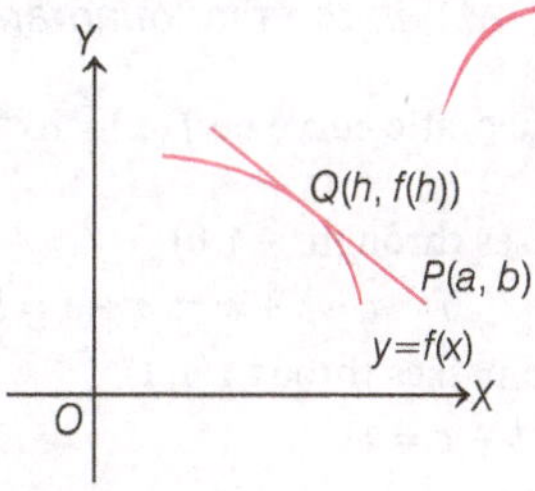

Concept Inside Video

Then, $f'(h) = \dfrac{f(h) - b}{h - a}$

and equation of tangent is $y - b = \dfrac{f(h) - b}{h - a} \cdot (x - a)$

6.9 Equation of Normal

We know that normal to curve at any point is a straight line passes through that point and is perpendicular to the tangent to the curve at that point.

Since, the slope of tangent at $P(x_1, y_1) = \left(\dfrac{dy}{dx}\right)_{(x_1, y_1)}$.

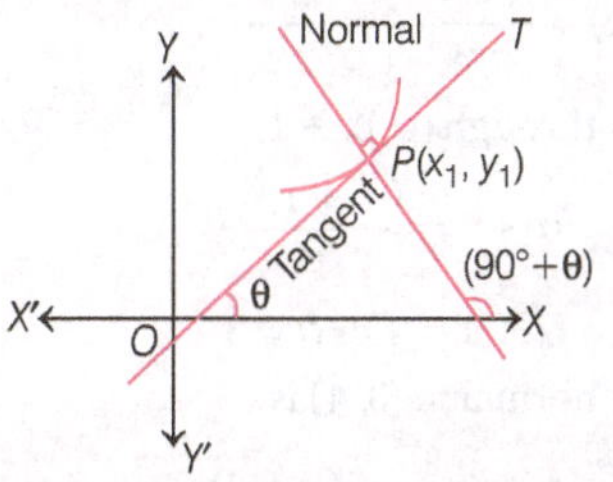

Now, as normal is perpendicular to the tangent.

$\therefore$ Slope of normal at $P(x_1, y_1) = \dfrac{-1}{\left(\dfrac{dy}{dx}\right)_{(x_1, y_1)}}$

Hence, from coordinate geometry equation of normal is

$$y - y_1 = -\frac{1}{\left(\dfrac{dy}{dx}\right)_{(x_1, y_1)}}(x - x_1)$$

or $$y - y_1 = -\left(\frac{dx}{dy}\right)_{(x_1, y_1)}(x - x_1)$$

When point of contact is not given in the question. Assume it (x_1, y_1) or can be assume it in parametric form.

e.g.

(i) **Circle** $x^2 + y^2 = a^2$ point of contact $(a\cos\theta, a\sin\theta)$

(ii) **Parabola** $y^2 = 4ax$ point of contact $(at^2, 2at)$

(iii) **Ellipse** $\dfrac{x^2}{a^2} + \dfrac{y^2}{b^2} = 1$ point of contact $(a\cos\theta, b\sin\theta)$

(iv) **Hyperbola** $\dfrac{x^2}{a^2} - \dfrac{y^2}{b^2} = 1$ point of contact $(a\sec\theta, b\tan\theta)$

Example 17. Find the equation of tangent and normal to the curve $x^2 = 8y + 8$ at the point $(0, -1)$.

Sol. Equation of the curve is $x^2 = 8y + 8 \Rightarrow y = \dfrac{x^2 - 8}{8}$

Slope of the tangent to the curve at $(0, -1)$ is $\left(\dfrac{dy}{dx}\right)$ at that point.

$\because \quad \dfrac{dy}{dx} = \dfrac{2x}{8} = \dfrac{x}{4}$ at $(0, -1)$

$\Rightarrow \quad \left(\dfrac{dy}{dx}\right)_{(0, -1)} = 0$

$\therefore$ Equation of tangent at $(0, -1)$ is given by

$$y - (-1) = 0(x - 0)$$

$\Rightarrow \quad y + 1 = 0(x - 0)$

$\Rightarrow \quad y + 1 = 0$

Normal is perpendicular to tangent, so slope of normal

$$= \frac{-1}{dy/dx} = \infty$$

Since, $\dfrac{dy}{dx} = 0$

Hence, the normal will be a line parallel to Y-axis and will pass through $(0, -1)$.

Therefore, the equation of normal at $(0, -1)$ is given by $x = 0$.

Example 18. The tangent to the curve $y = x^2 + 3x$ will pass through the point $(0, -9)$ if it is drawn at the point.

(a) (3, 18) (b) (1, 4)

(c) (- 4, 4) (d) (- 3, 0)

Sol. (a, d) Let (x_1, y_1) be the point of contact from $(0, -9)$ to the curve $y = x^2 + 3x$.

Then, the slope of the tangent can be given by $\dfrac{y_1 + 9}{x_1}$.

Also, $\left.\dfrac{dy}{dx}\right|_{(x_1, y_1)} = (2x_1 + 3)$

$\Rightarrow \quad \dfrac{y_1 + 9}{x_1} = 2x_1 + 3$

$\Rightarrow \quad y_1 = 2x_1^2 + 3x_1 - 9 \quad$ ...(i)

Also, since x_1, y_1 satisfies the equation of the curve.

$\therefore \qquad y_1 = x_1^2 + 3x_1 \qquad$ ...(ii)

On comparing Eqs. (i) and (ii), we get

$$x_1^2 + 3x_1 = 2x_1^2 + 3x_1 - 9$$

$$x_1^2 = 9 \Rightarrow x_1 = \pm 3$$

Point of contact are (3, 18) and (–3, 0).

Example 19. Find all the lines that pass through the point (1, 1) and are tangent to the curve represented parametrically as $x = 2t - t^2$ and $y = t + t^2$.

Sol. We have, $x = 2t - t^2 \qquad$ ...(i)

and $\qquad y = t + t^2 \qquad$ ...(ii)

$$\frac{dx}{dt} = 2 - 2t \text{ and } \frac{dy}{dt} = 1 + 2t$$

$$\Rightarrow \frac{dy}{dx} = \frac{dy/dt}{dx/dt} = \frac{1+2t}{2-2t} \qquad \text{...(iii)}$$

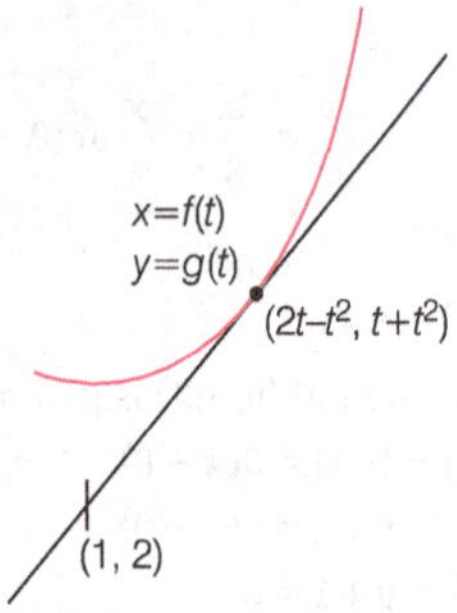

Slope of the line passing through the ponits (1, 1) and $(2t - t^2, t + t^2)$ is given by $m = \dfrac{t + t^2 - 1}{2t - t^2 - 1} \qquad$ ...(iv)

On equating Eqs. (iii) and (iv), we get

$$\frac{dy}{dx} = \frac{t + t^2 - 1}{2t - t^2 - 1}$$

$$\Rightarrow \frac{1+2t}{2-2t} = \frac{t+t^2-1}{2t-t^2-1}$$

$$\Rightarrow 2t - t^2 - 1 + 4t^2 - 2t^3 - 2t = 2t + 2t^2 - 2 - 2t^2 - 2t^3 + 2t$$

$$\Rightarrow 3t^2 - 4t + 1 = 0$$

$$\Rightarrow 3t^2 - 3t - t + 1 = 0$$

$$\Rightarrow (3t-1)(t-1) = 0 \Rightarrow t = 1 \text{ or } t = \frac{1}{3}$$

Now, when $t = 1$, then point $(2t - t^2, t + t^2)$ becomes (1, 2)

when $t = 1$, then point will be (1, 2) when $t = \frac{1}{3}$, then point will be $\left(\frac{5}{9}, \frac{4}{9}\right)$ and $\frac{dy}{dx} = \frac{3}{0}$ for $t = 1$ and $\frac{dy}{dx} = \frac{5}{4}$ for $t = \frac{1}{3}$

$\therefore$ Equations of tangents will be $y - 2 = \frac{1}{0}(x - 1)$ and

$$y - \frac{4}{9} = \frac{5}{4}\left(x - \frac{5}{9}\right),$$

$$x = 1 \text{ and } 5x - 4y - 1$$

JEE SCANNER

Example Similar to PYQ Asked in JEE Main 2023

Let the quadratic curve passing through the point (– 1, 0) and touching the line y = x at (1, 1) be y = f(x). Then, the y-intercept of the normal to the curve at the point (α, α + 1) in the first quadrant is ....

Sol. $\left(\frac{11}{2}\right)$ Let the quadratic curve be $f(x) = ax^2 + bx + c$

The curve passes through (– 1, 0)

$$0 = a - b + c \Rightarrow a + c = b$$

The curve also passes through (1, 1)

$$a + b + c = 1$$

$$2b = 1 \Rightarrow b = \frac{1}{2}$$

$$f'(x) = 2ax + b$$

Slope of tangent of curve $= f'(x)$ at (1, 1)

$$= 2a + b$$

Slope of line $y = x$ is 1.

$$\therefore \quad 2a + b = 1$$

$$\Rightarrow \quad 2a + \frac{1}{2} = 1 \Rightarrow a = \frac{1}{4}$$

$$\therefore \quad c = \frac{1}{4}$$

$$f(x) = \frac{1}{4}x^2 + \frac{1}{2}x + \frac{1}{4} = \frac{(x+1)^2}{4}$$

$$f'(x) = \frac{2(x+1)}{4} = \frac{x+1}{2}$$

$f(x)$ passes through $(\alpha, \alpha + 1)$

$$\alpha + 1 = \frac{(\alpha+1)^2}{4}$$

$$\Rightarrow \quad \alpha + 1 = 4 \text{ or } \alpha = 3$$

Equation of normal at (3, 4) is

$$y - 4 = -\frac{1}{2}(x - 3)$$

For y-intercept, $\quad x = 0$

$$y - 4 = \frac{3}{2}$$

$$\Rightarrow \quad y = \frac{3}{2} + 4 = \frac{11}{2}$$

Skill Builder

Let the quadratic curve passing through the point (– 1, 0) and touching the line y = x at (1, 1) be y = f(x). Then, the square of x-intercept of the normal to the curve at the point (α, α + 1) in the first quadrant is ....

For Sol.

▪ **For more practice** See Q.8 of Milestone Practice 6.3.

1. For standard curves students are advised to use direct method of finding equation of tangent. (valid for second degree curves)

For the curve of the form

$ax^2 + 2hxy + by^2 + 2gx + 2fy + c = 0$, replace

x^2 by xx_1 : $2x$ by $x + x_1$;

y^2 by yy_1 : $2y$ by $y + y_1$

and xy by $\dfrac{xy_1 + x_1y}{2}$

Then, equation of tangent is

$$axx_1 + h(xy_1 + yx_1) + byy_1 + g(x + x_1) + f(y + y_1) + c = 0$$

e.g.

(i) Find equation of tangent to the curve $2y = x^2 + 3$ at (x_1, y_1).

Sol. On replacing $2y$ by $y + y_1$ and x^2 by xx_1, we get

$$(y + y_1) = xx_1 + 3,$$

which is the required equation of tangent.

(ii) Find equation of tangent to the curve $y^2 = 4ax$ at $(at^2, 2at)$.

Sol. Clearly, the equation of curve $y^2 = 4ax$ is a standard equation of curve.

Therefore, on replacing y^2 by yy_1 and we can get the equation of tangent.

Thus, the required equation is given by

$$yy_1 = 2a(x + x_1)$$

where, $(x_1, y_1) = (at^2, 2at)$

Hence, the requried equation of tangent is

$$y(2at) = 2a(x + at^2)$$

$$\Rightarrow \quad yt = x + at^2$$

(iii) Find the equation of tangent at point $P(x_1, y_1)$ to the curve $\dfrac{x^2}{a^2} + \dfrac{y^2}{b^2} = 1$.

Sol. Clearly, the equatioan of curve $\dfrac{x^2}{a^2} + \dfrac{y^2}{b^2} = 1$ is a standard equation of curve.

Therefore, equation of the tangent can be obtained by replacing x^2 by xx_1 and y^2 by yy_1.

i.e. $$\frac{xx_1}{a^2} + \frac{yy_1}{b^2} = 1$$

2. If a curve passes through the origin, then the equation of the tangent at the origin can be directly written by equating the lowest degree terms appearing in the equation of the curve to zero.

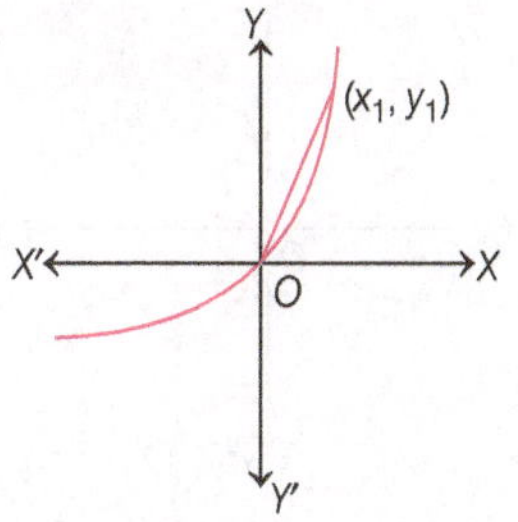

Proof Let the equation of the curve be

$$a_1x + b_1y + a_2x^2 + b_2xy + c_2y^2 = 0 \quad \text{...(i)}$$

Tangent $y - 0 = \lim\limits_{\substack{x_1 \to 0 \\ y_1 \to 0}} \dfrac{y_1}{x_1}(x - 0)$

Now, Eq. (i) becomes

$$a_1 + b_1\frac{y_1}{x_1} + a_2x_1 + b_2\frac{y_1}{x_1} \cdot x_1 + c_2\frac{y_1}{x_1} \cdot y_1 = 0 \quad \text{...(ii)}$$

At $x_1 \to 0$ and $y_1 \to 0, \dfrac{y_1}{x_1} \to m$

From Eq. (ii), $a_1 + b_1m = 0$ $\left[\because m = -\dfrac{a_1}{b_1}\right]$

Hence, tangent is $y = -\dfrac{a_1}{b_1} \cdot x \Rightarrow a_1x + b_1y = 0$

e.g.

(i) Equation of tangent at origin, to the curve $x^2 + y^2 + 2gx + 2fy = 0$ is $gx + fy = 0$.

(ii) Equation of tangent at origin to the curve $x^3 + y^3 - 3x^2y + 3xy^2 + x^2 - y^2 = 0$ is $x^2 - y^2 = 0$.

(iii) Equation of tangent at origin to the curve $x^3 + y^3 - 3xy = 0$ is $xy = 0$.

3. If the curve is $x^4 + y^4 = x^2 + y^2$, then the equation of the tangent would be $x^2 + y^2 = 0$ which would indicate that the origin is an isolated point on the graph.

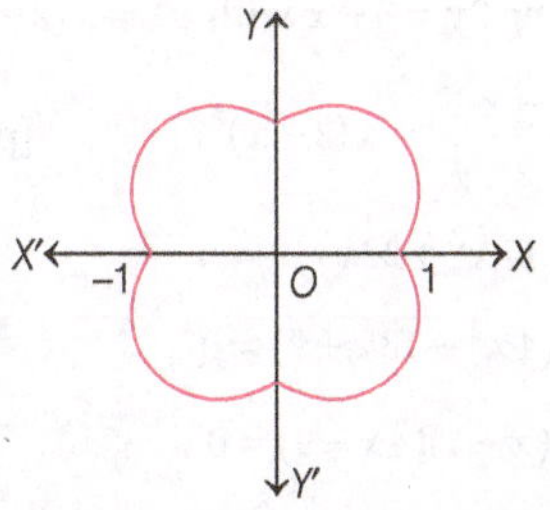

4. Same line could be the tangent as well as normal to a given curve at a given point.

e.g. In $x^3 + y^3 - 3xy = 0$ [folium of descartes]

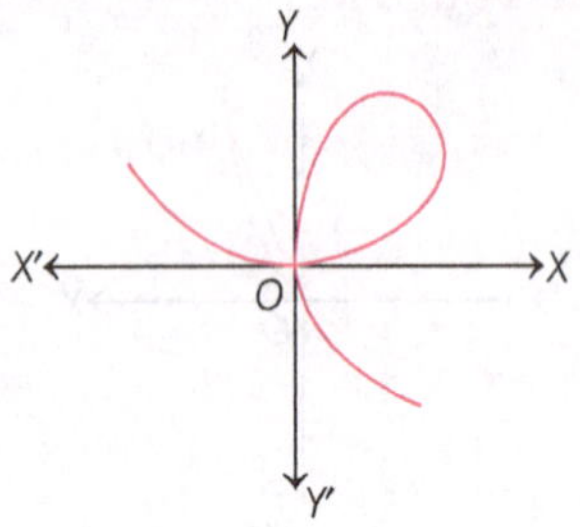

The line pair $xy = 0$ is both the tangent as well as normal at $x = 0$.

5. Some common parametric coordiantes on a curve are

(i) For $x^{2/3} + y^{2/3} = a^{2/3}$, take parametric coordinate $x = a\cos^3\theta$ and $y = a\sin^3\theta$.

(ii) For $\sqrt{x} + \sqrt{y} = \sqrt{a}$, take $x = a\cos^4\theta$ and $y = a\sin^4\theta$.

(iii) For $\frac{x^n}{a^n} + \frac{y^n}{b^n} = 1$, take $x = a(\cos\theta)^{2/n}$ and $y = b(\sin\theta)^{2/n}$

(iv) For $c^2(x^2 + y^2) = x^2y^2$, take $x = c\sec\theta$ and $y = c\,\text{cosec}\,\theta$

(v) For $y^2 = x^3$, take $x = t^2$ and $y = t^3$.

Example 20. If the tangent at $P(1,1)$ on $y^2 = x(2-x)^2$ meets the curve again at Q, then the point Q is

(a) $(-1, 2)$ (b) $\left(\frac{9}{4}, \frac{3}{8}\right)$

(c) $(4, 4)$ (d) None of these

Sol. (b) Given, $y^2 = x(2-x)^2$

On differentiating both sides w.r.t. x, we get

$$2yy' = (2-x)^2 - 2x(2-x)$$

$$\therefore \quad \frac{dy}{dx} \text{ at } (1,1) = \frac{1-2}{2} = -\frac{1}{2}$$

$\therefore$ Tangent is $y - 1 = -\frac{1}{2}(x-1)$ or $2y = 3 - x$

Now, on solving $2y = 3 - x$ with $y^2 = x(2-x)^2$, we get

$$\left(\frac{3-x}{2}\right)^2 = x(2-x)^2 \quad \text{[put the value of } y\text{]}$$

or $\quad 4x^3 - 17x^2 + 22x - 9 = 0$

$\Rightarrow \quad (x-1)(4x^2 - 13x + 9) = 0$

$\Rightarrow \quad (x-1)(x-1)(4x-9) = 0$

$\Rightarrow \quad x = 1 \text{ or } x = \frac{9}{4}$

Then, $y = \frac{3-x}{2} = \frac{3-\frac{9}{4}}{2} = \frac{12-9}{4\times 2} = \frac{3}{8}$

Hence, Q is $\left(\frac{9}{4}, \frac{3}{8}\right)$.

Also, when $x = 1, y = 1$

Hence, (1, 1) point is rejected, since it is the point P from where tangent is drawn.

Example 21. The normal to the curve $x = a(\cos\theta + \theta\sin\theta)$, $y = a(\sin\theta - \theta\cos\theta)$ at any θ is such that

(a) it makes a constant angle with X-axis

(b) it passes through the origin

(c) it is at a constant distance from the origin

(d) None of the above

Sol. (c) We have, $x = a(\cos\theta + \theta\sin\theta)$ and $y = a(\sin\theta - \theta\cos\theta)$

$$\frac{dx}{d\theta} = -a\sin\theta + a\theta\cos\theta + a\sin\theta = a\theta\cos\theta$$

$$\frac{dy}{d\theta} = a\cos\theta - a\cos\theta + a\theta\sin\theta = a\theta\sin\theta$$

$$\therefore \frac{dy}{dx} = \frac{y}{x} = \frac{\sin\theta}{\cos\theta} = \text{Slope of tangent}$$

$$\therefore \text{Slope of normal} = -\frac{\cos\theta}{\sin\theta}$$

Now, since slope $= -\cot\theta$

$\therefore$ Slope is dependent upon θ.

Hence, it does not make a constant angle with X-axis.

$\therefore$ Normal is $[y - (a\sin\theta - a\theta\cos\theta)]$

$$= -\frac{\cos\theta}{\sin\theta} \times [x - (a\cos\theta + a\theta\sin\theta)]$$

or $\quad y\sin\theta + x\cos\theta = a(\cos^2\theta + \sin^2\theta) = a$

Since, the constant term in the equation of the normal is not equal to zero.

$\therefore$ The normal does not pass through (0, 0).

Now, its distance from the origin is given by

$$\frac{a}{\sqrt{(\cos^2\theta + \sin^2\theta)}} = a, \text{ i.e. constant.}$$

Example 22. The tangent represented by the graph of the function $y = f(x)$ at the point with abscissa $x = 1$ form an angle of $\pi/6$, at the point $x = 2$ form an angle of $\pi/3$ and at the point $x = 3$ form an angle of $\pi/4$. Then, find the value of $\int_1^3 f'(x)f''(x)dx + \int_2^3 f''(x)dx$.

Sol. Given, at $x = 1, \frac{dy}{dx} = \tan\frac{\pi}{6} = \frac{1}{\sqrt{3}}$

or at $x = 1, f'(1) = \tan\frac{\pi}{6} = \frac{1}{\sqrt{3}}$

Also, at $x = 2$, $f'(2) = \tan\frac{\pi}{3} = \sqrt{3}$

and at $x = 3$, $f'(3) = \tan\frac{\pi}{4} = 1$

Then, $\int_1^3 f'(x)f''(x)dx + \int_2^3 f''(x)dx = \int_{f'(1)}^{f'(3)} t\,dt + (f'(x))_2^3$

[put $f'(x) = t \Rightarrow f''(x)dx = dt$]

$$= \frac{1}{2}(t^2)_{f'(1)}^{f'(3)} + \{f'(3) - f'(2)\}$$

$$= \frac{1}{2}\{(f'(3))^2 - (f'(1))^2\} + \{f'(3) - f'(2)\}$$

$$= \frac{1}{2}\left\{(1)^2 - \left(\frac{1}{\sqrt{3}}\right)^2\right\} + (1 - \sqrt{3}) = \frac{1}{2}\left(1 - \frac{1}{3}\right) + (1 - \sqrt{3})$$

$$= \frac{4}{3} - \sqrt{3} = \frac{4 - 3\sqrt{3}}{3}$$

Example 23. Find the equation for family of curves for which the length of normal is equal to the radius vector.

Sol. Let $P(x, y)$ be the point on the curve.

OP = Radius vector $= \sqrt{x^2 + y^2}$

PN = Length of normal

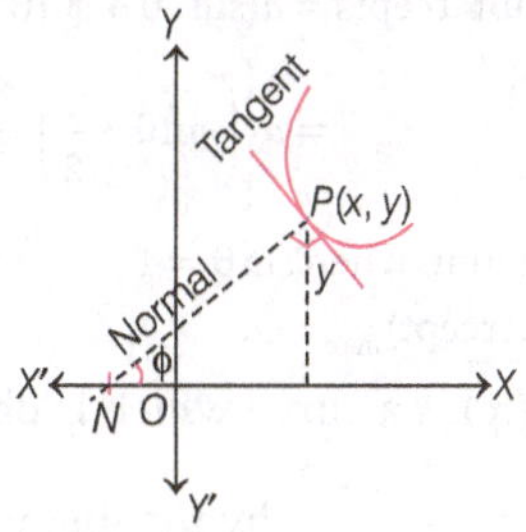

Now, $\tan\phi = -\frac{1}{\left(\frac{dy}{dx}\right)}$ and $PN = \frac{y}{\sin\phi}$

It is given that $OP = PN$,

$$\sqrt{x^2 + y^2} = y\sqrt{1 + \left(\frac{dy}{dx}\right)^2}$$

On squaring both sides, we get

$$x^2 + y^2 = y^2\left[1 + \left(\frac{dy}{dx}\right)^2\right]$$

$$\Rightarrow \quad x^2 = y^2\left(\frac{dy}{dx}\right)^2$$

$$\Rightarrow \quad \frac{dy}{dx} = \pm\frac{x}{y} \text{ or } y\,dy = \pm x\,dy$$

On integrating both the sides, we get

$$y^2 = \pm x^2 + C,$$

which is the required family of curves.

JEE SCANNER

Example Similar to PYQ Asked in JEE Main 2023

If the tangent at a point P on the parabola $y^2 = 6x$ is parallel to the line $x + 2y = 1$ and the tangents at the points Q and R on the ellipse $\frac{x^2}{4} + \frac{y^2}{1} = 1$ are perpendicular to the line $x - y = 2$, then the area of the ΔPQR is

(a) $5\sqrt{3}$ (b) $\frac{3}{2}\sqrt{5}$ (c) $\frac{9}{\sqrt{5}}$ (d) $6\sqrt{5}$

Sol. (d) Tangent at $P(x_1, y_1)$ on $y^2 = 6x$ is given by

$$y - y_1 = m_1(x - x_1)$$

which is parallel to $x + 2y = 1$.

Now, $y^2 = 6x$

On differentiating, we get

$$2yy' = 6 \Rightarrow y' = \frac{3}{y} \Rightarrow m_1 = y' = \frac{3}{y}$$

$\therefore \quad \frac{3}{y_1} = -\frac{1}{2}$ [slope of $x + 2y = 1$]

$\Rightarrow \quad y_1 = -6$

$\therefore \quad x_1 = 6$ [$\because y^2 = 6x$ and (x_1, y_1) lies on it]

$\therefore$ Point P is $(6, -6)$.

Tangent at point $Q(x_2, y_2)$ on $\frac{x^2}{4} + \frac{y^2}{1} = 1$ is given by

$$y - y_1 = m_2(x - x_2)$$

which is perpendicular to the line $x - y = 2$.

On differentiating the equation of ellipse,

$$\frac{2x}{4} + \frac{2yy'}{1} = 0 \Rightarrow y' = \frac{-x}{4y} \Rightarrow m_2 = \frac{-x_2}{4y_2}$$

$\therefore \quad \frac{-x_2}{4y_2} = -1$ [slope of $x - y = 2$ is 1]

$\Rightarrow \quad 4y_2 = x_2$

$\therefore$ On putting this is equation of ellipse, we get

$$Q(x_2, y_2) = \left(\frac{4}{\sqrt{5}}, \frac{1}{\sqrt{5}}\right), \; R(x_3, y_3) = \left(\frac{-4}{\sqrt{5}}, \frac{-1}{\sqrt{5}}\right)$$

$$\therefore \text{Area of } \Delta PQR = \frac{1}{2}\begin{vmatrix} x_1 & y_1 & 1 \\ x_2 & y_2 & 1 \\ x_3 & y_3 & 1 \end{vmatrix} = \frac{1}{2}\begin{vmatrix} 6 & -6 & 1 \\ \frac{4}{\sqrt{5}} & \frac{1}{\sqrt{5}} & 1 \\ \frac{-4}{\sqrt{5}} & \frac{-1}{\sqrt{5}} & 1 \end{vmatrix} = 6\sqrt{5}$$

Skill Builder

If the tangent at a point P on the parabola $y^2 = 9x$ is parallel to the line $x + 2y = 1$ and the tangents at the points Q and R on the ellipse $\frac{x^2}{4} + \frac{y^2}{1} = 1$ are perpendicular to the line $x - y = 2$, then the area of the ΔPQR is

(a) $5\sqrt{3}$ (b) $\frac{3}{2}\sqrt{5}$

(c) $9\sqrt{5}$ (d) $6\sqrt{5}$

For Sol.

■ **For more practice** See Q.20 of Milestone Practice 6.3.

Example 24. Find the condition that the line $x\cos\alpha + y\sin\alpha = p$ may touch the curve $\left(\frac{x}{a}\right)^m + \left(\frac{y}{b}\right)^m = 1$.

Sol. Given equation of curve is $\left(\frac{x}{a}\right)^m + \left(\frac{y}{b}\right)^m = 1$

On differentiating the equation of curve w.r.t. x, we get

$$m\left(\frac{x}{a}\right)^{m-1}\cdot\frac{1}{a} + m\left(\frac{y}{b}\right)^{m-1}\cdot\frac{1}{b}\cdot\frac{dy}{dx} = 0$$

On simplifying, we get $\frac{dy}{dx} = \frac{-b^m x^{m-1}}{a^m y^{m-1}}$

Now, at any point $P(x_1, y_1)$ on the curve.

$$\text{Slope of tangent} = \left(\frac{dy}{dx}\right)_{(x_1, y_1)} = \frac{-b^m x_1^{m-1}}{a^m y_1^{m-1}}$$

$\therefore$ Equation of tangent at P is

$$y - y_1 = \frac{-b^m x_1^{m-1}}{a^m y_1^{m-1}}(x - x_1)$$

$$\Rightarrow \quad \frac{yy_1^{m-1}}{b^m} - \frac{y_1^m}{b^m} = -\frac{xx_1^{m-1}}{a^m} + \frac{x_1^m}{a^m}$$

i.e. $\frac{x}{a}\left(\frac{x_1}{a}\right)^{m-1} + \frac{y}{b}\left(\frac{y_1}{b}\right)^{m-1} = \left(\frac{x_1}{a}\right)^m + \left(\frac{y_1}{b}\right)^m = 1$

Since, P lies on the curve. Therefore, the equation of tangent at $P(x_1, y_1)$ on the curve is

$$\frac{x}{a}\left(\frac{x_1}{a}\right)^{m-1} + \frac{y}{b}\left(\frac{y_1}{b}\right)^{m-1} = 1 \quad \text{...(i)}$$

Also, we have $\quad x\cos\alpha + y\sin\alpha = p \quad$ ...(ii)

If Eq. (ii) is the equation of tangent, then coefficients of Eqs. (i) and (ii) must be proportional for point (x_1, y_1).

i.e. $\frac{\cos\alpha}{\frac{1}{a}\left(\frac{x_1}{a}\right)^{m-1}} = \frac{\sin\alpha}{\frac{1}{b}\left(\frac{y_1}{b}\right)^{m-1}} = \frac{p}{1}$

This gives $\frac{x_1}{a} = \left(\frac{a\cos\alpha}{p}\right)^{\frac{1}{m-1}}, \frac{y_1}{b} = \left(\frac{b\sin\alpha}{p}\right)^{\frac{1}{m-1}}$

Since, point $P(x_1, y_1)$ lies on the curve.

Therefore, we have $\left(\frac{x_1}{a}\right)^m + \left(\frac{y_1}{b}\right)^m = 1$

i.e. $\left(\frac{a\cos\alpha}{p}\right)^{\frac{m}{m-1}} + \left(\frac{b\sin\alpha}{p}\right)^{\frac{m}{m-1}} = 1$

$$\therefore \quad (a\cos\alpha)^{\frac{m}{m-1}} + (b\sin\alpha)^{\frac{m}{m-1}} = p^{\frac{m}{m-1}}$$

which is the required condition.

Example 25. If tangent and normal to the curve $y = 2\sin x + \sin 2x$ are drawn at $P\left(x = \frac{\pi}{3}\right)$, then area of the quadrilateral formed by the tangent, the normal at P and the coordinate axes is

(a) $\frac{\pi}{3}$ (b) 3π (c) $\frac{\pi\sqrt{3}}{2}$ (d) None of these

Sol. (c) Here, $\frac{dy}{dx} = 0$ at $\left(x = \frac{\pi}{3}, y = \frac{3\sqrt{3}}{2}\right)$

Then, tangent at $x = \frac{\pi}{3}$ is parallel to X-axis.

$\therefore$ Equation of tangent is $y = \frac{3\sqrt{3}}{2}$

Also, equation of normal is $x = \frac{\pi}{3}$

Now, area of quadrilateral $= \frac{\pi}{3}\cdot\frac{3\sqrt{3}}{2} = \frac{\pi\sqrt{3}}{2}$ sq units

Example 26. The maximum value of the sum of the intercepts made by any tangent to the curve $(a\sin^2\theta, 2a\sin\theta)$ with the axes is

(a) $2a$ (b) $\frac{a}{4}$ (c) $\frac{a}{2}$ (d) a

Sol. (a) The curve is $(a\sin^2\theta, 2a\sin\theta)$

$\Rightarrow \quad x = a\sin^2\theta, y = 2a\sin\theta$

Now, the equation of any tangent to the curve is

$$\frac{y - 2a\sin\theta}{x - a\sin^2\theta} = \frac{1}{\sin\theta} \Rightarrow y\sin\theta = x + a\sin^2\theta$$

$$\Rightarrow \quad \frac{x}{-a\sin^2\theta} + \frac{y}{a\sin\theta} = 1$$

$\Rightarrow \quad$ Sum of intercepts $= a(\sin^2\theta + \sin\theta)$

$$= a\left\{\left(\sin\theta + \frac{1}{2}\right)^2 - \frac{1}{4}\right\}$$

which is maximum, when $\sin\theta = 1$

i.e. $(\text{Sum of intercept})_{\max} = 2a$

Example 27. If $g(x)$ is a curve which is obtained by the reflection of $f(x) = \frac{e^x - e^{-x}}{2}$ by the line $y = x$, then

(a) $g(x)$ has more than one tangent parallel to X-axis.
(b) $g(x)$ has more than one tangent parallel to Y-axis.
(c) $y = -x$ is a tangent to $g(x)$ at $(0, 0)$.
(d) $g(x)$ has no extremum.

Sol. (d) As $g(x)$ is a curve, obtained by the reflection of $f(x) = \frac{e^x - e^{-x}}{2}$ on $y = x$.

So, $g(x)$ is inverse of $f(x)$.

$\therefore g(x) = \log(x + \sqrt{1 + x^2}) = f^{-1}(x)$

$$g'(x) = \frac{1}{x + \sqrt{1 + x^2}}\cdot\left(1 + \frac{2x}{2\sqrt{1 + x^2}}\right) = \frac{1}{\sqrt{1 + x^2}} \neq 0, \forall\ x \in R$$

$g(x)$ has no tangent parallel to X-axis.

Also, $g'(x)$ is always defined, $\forall\ x \in R$.

$\Rightarrow g(x)$ has no tangent parallel to Y-axis.

Since, $g'(x) > 0 \forall x \in R$.

Therefore, $g(x)$ does not have any extremum.

Milestone Practice 6.3

1. Find the tangents to the curve $y=(x^3-1)(x-2)$ at the points, where the curve cuts the X-axis.

2. Find the equation of the normal to the curve $y=(1+x)^y+\sin^{-1}(\sin^2 x)$ at the point $x=0$.

3. Find the points where the tangent is parallel to X-axis and where it is parallel to Y-axis, for the curve $25x^2+12xy+4y^2=1$.

4. Find the equation of the tangent line to the curve $y=\sqrt{5x-3}-2$ which is
   (i) parallel to the line $2x-y+9=0$.
   (ii) perpendicular to the line $5y+2\sqrt{2}x=13$.

5. Prove that the sum of the intercepts on the coordinate axes of any tangent to $\sqrt{x}+\sqrt{y}=\sqrt{a}$ is constant.

6. Find the equations of tangent and normal to the curve $x+y=x^y$, where the curve cuts X-axis.

7. For the curve $y=4x^3-2x^5$, find all the points at which the tangent passes through the origin.

8. The slope of the tangent to the curve $y=x^2-x$ at the point where the line $y=2$ cuts the curve in the first quadrant is
   (a) 2 (b) 3
   (c) −3 (d) None of these

9. If at each point of the curve $y=x^3-ax^2+x+1$, the tangent is inclined at an acute angle with the positive direction of the X-axis, then
   (a) $a>0$ (b) $a\le\sqrt{3}$
   (c) $-\sqrt{3}<a<\sqrt{3}$ (d) None of these

10. The points at which the tangent to the curve $ax^2+2hxy+by^2=1$ is parallel to Y-axis are
   (a) (0, 0)
   (b) where $hx+by=0$ meet it.
   (c) where $ax+hy=0$ meet it.
   (d) None of the above

11. The point of contact at which tangent to $y=e^{-x}$ cuts off equal intercepts, is
   (a) $(1, e^{-1})$ (b) (0, 1)
   (c) $(-1, e)$ (d) None of these

12. The slope of the tangent to the locus $y=\cos^{-1}(\cos x)$ at $x=-\dfrac{\pi}{4}$ is
   (a) 1 (b) 0
   (c) 2 (d) −1

13. If the tangent to the curve $2y^3=ax^2+x^3$ at the point (a, a) cuts off intercepts α, β on coordinate axes, where $\alpha^2+\beta^2=61$, then the value of a is
   (a) 20 (b) 25
   (c) 30 (d) −30

14. The equation of the tangent to the curve $\left(\dfrac{x}{a}\right)^n+\left(\dfrac{y}{b}\right)^n=2, (n\in N)$ at the point with abscissa equal to a is
   (a) $\left(\dfrac{x}{a}\right)+\left(\dfrac{y}{b}\right)=2$
   (b) $\left(\dfrac{x}{a}\right)-\left(\dfrac{y}{b}\right)=2$
   (c) $\left(\dfrac{x}{a}\right)-\left(\dfrac{y}{b}\right)=0$
   (d) $\left(\dfrac{x}{a}\right)+\left(\dfrac{y}{b}\right)=0$

15. The point on the curve $y^3+3x^2=12y$, where the tangent is vertical, is
   (a) $\left(\pm\dfrac{4}{\sqrt{3}}, -2\right)$ (b) $\left(\pm\dfrac{11}{\sqrt{3}}, 1\right)$
   (c) (0, 0) (d) $\left(\pm\dfrac{4}{\sqrt{3}}, 2\right)$

16. If a variable tangent to the curve $x^2y=c^3$ makes intercepts a, b on X and Y-axes respectively, then the value of a^2b is
   (a) $27c^3$ (b) $\dfrac{4}{27}c^3$
   (c) $\dfrac{27}{4}c^3$ (d) $\dfrac{4}{9}c^3$

17. The x-intercept of the tangent at any arbitrary point of the curve $\dfrac{a}{x^2}+\dfrac{b}{y^2}=1$ is proportional to
   (a) square of the abscissa of the point of tangency.
   (b) square root of the abscissa of the point of tangency.
   (c) cube of the abscissa of the point of tangency.
   (d) cube root of the abscissa of the point of tangency.

18. The tangent to the curve $3xy^2-2x^2y=1$ at (1, 1) meets the curve again at the point.
   (a) $\left(-\dfrac{16}{5}, -\dfrac{1}{20}\right)$ (b) $\left(\dfrac{16}{5}, \dfrac{1}{20}\right)$
   (c) $\left(\dfrac{1}{20}, \dfrac{16}{5}\right)$ (d) $\left(-\dfrac{1}{20}, \dfrac{16}{1}\right)$

19. If the tangent at P of the curve $y^2 = x^3$ intersects the curve again at Q and the straight lines OP, OQ make angles α, β with the X-axis where O is the origin, then $\frac{\tan\alpha}{\tan\beta}$ has the value, equal to

(a) -1 (b) -2
(c) 2 (d) $\sqrt{2}$

20. The lines $y = -\frac{3}{2}x$ and $y = -\frac{2}{5}x$ intersect the curve $3x^2 + 4xy + 5y^2 - 4 = 0$ at the points P and Q, respectively. The tangents drawn to the curve at P and Q

(a) intersect each other at angle of 45°.
(b) are parallel to each other.
(c) are perpendicular to each other.
(d) None of the above

21. Normal to the curve $x = a(2 + \cos\theta)$ and $y = a\sin\theta$ at θ always passes through the point

(a) $(2a, 0)$
(b) $(0, a)$
(c) (a, a)
(d) $(a, 0)$

22. Let C be the curve $y = x^3$ (where, x takes all real values). The tangent at A meets the curve again at B. If the gradient at B is k times the gradient at A, then k is equal to

(a) 4 (b) 2
(c) -2 (d) $\frac{1}{4}$

23. A curve is represented by the equations $x = \sec^2 t$ and $y = \cot t$, where t is a parameter. If the tangent at the point P on the curve, where $t = \frac{\pi}{4}$ meets the curve again at the point Q, then $|PQ|$ is equal to

(a) $\frac{5\sqrt{3}}{2}$ (b) $\frac{5\sqrt{5}}{2}$
(c) $\frac{2\sqrt{5}}{3}$ (d) $\frac{3\sqrt{5}}{2}$

Answer Key

1. $3x + y - 3 = 0, -7x + y + 14 = 0$ **2.** $x + y = 1$ **3.** $\left(\frac{1}{4}, \frac{-3}{8}\right)$ and $\left(\frac{-1}{4}, \frac{3}{8}\right)$

4. (i) $80x - 40y = 103$ (ii) $2\sqrt{2}y - 5x + 4\sqrt{2} + 1 = 0$

6. Tangent to the curve $= y + x - 1 = 0$, normal to the curve $= y - x + 1 = 0$

7. (0, 0), (1, 2), (−1, − 2)	**8.** (b)	**9.** (c)	**10.** (b)	
11. (b)	**12.** (d)	**13.** (c,d)	**14.** (a,b)	**15.** (d)
16. (c)	**17.** (c)	**18.** (a)	**19.** (b)	**20.** (c)
21. (a)	**22.** (a)	**23.** (d)		

For Detailed Solution

Milestone 4 Angle of Intersection Between Curves

- Angle of Intersection Between Two Curves • Length of Tangent, Sub-tangent, Normal and Sub-normal
- Shortest Distance Between Two Curves

6.10 Angle of Intersection between Two Curves

The angle of intersection of two curves is defined as the angle between the tangents to the two curves at their point of intersection.

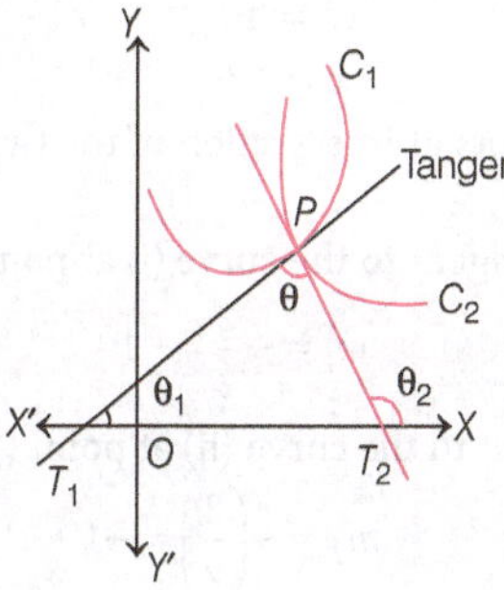

Let C_1 and C_2 be two curves having equations $y = f(x)$ and $y = g(x)$, respectively.

Let PT_1 and PT_2 be tangents to the curves C_1 and C_2 at their point of intersection.

Let θ be the angle between the two tangents PT_1 and PT_2 and θ_1 and θ_2 are the angles made by tangents with the positive direction of X-axis in anti-clockwise sense.

Then, $m_1 = \tan\theta_1 = \left(\dfrac{dy}{dx}\right)_{C_1}$

$$m_2 = \tan\theta_2 = \left(\frac{dy}{dx}\right)_{C_2}$$

From the figure, it follows, $\theta = \theta_2 - \theta_1$

$$\Rightarrow \tan\theta = \tan(\theta_2 - \theta_1) = \frac{\tan\theta_2 - \tan\theta_1}{1 + \tan\theta_2 \tan\theta_1}$$

$$\Rightarrow \tan\theta = \left| \frac{\left(\frac{dy}{dx}\right)_{C_2} - \left(\frac{dy}{dx}\right)_{C_1}}{1 + \left(\frac{dy}{dx}\right)_{C_2}\left(\frac{dy}{dx}\right)_{C_1}} \right|$$

Angle of intersection of these curves is defined as an acute angle between the tangents.

Orthogonal Curves

If the angle of intersection of two curves is a right angle, then the two curves are said to be orthogonal and the curves are called orthogonal curves.

$\therefore$ If the curves are orthogonal, then $\theta = \dfrac{\pi}{2}$

$$\Rightarrow \quad 1 + \left(\frac{dy}{dx}\right)_{C_1}\left(\frac{dy}{dx}\right)_{C_2} = 0$$

$$\Rightarrow \quad \left(\frac{dy}{dx}\right)_{C_1}\left(\frac{dy}{dx}\right)_{C_2} = -1$$

Condition for Two Curves to Touch

If two curves touch each other, then

$$\theta = 0$$

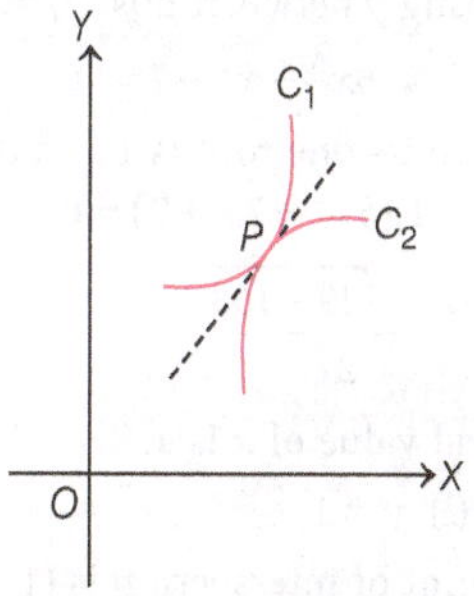

$$\Rightarrow \quad \tan\theta = 0$$

$$\Rightarrow \quad \left(\frac{dy}{dx}\right)_{C_1} - \left(\frac{dy}{dx}\right)_{C_2} = 0$$

$$\Rightarrow \quad \left(\frac{dy}{dx}\right)_{C_1} = \left(\frac{dy}{dx}\right)_{C_2}$$

Example 28. Find the angle of intersection between the curves

(i) $y^2 = 2x$ and $x^2 + y^2 = 8$

(ii) $y = x^3$ and $6y = 7 - x^2$

Sol. (i) Equation of the curve are $y^2 = 2x$ ...(i)

and $x^2 + y^2 = 8$ ...(ii)

On eliminating y between Eqs. (i) and (ii), we get

$$x^2 + 2x - 8 = 0$$

or $(x + 4)(x - 2) = 0$

$\therefore$ $x = -4, 2$

where $x = -4$ gives imaginary values of y and is rejected.

When $x = 2$, $y^2 = 4$

$\therefore$ $y = \pm 2$

$\therefore$ Points of intersection are (2,2) and (2, − 2).

For the curve (i), $2y\dfrac{dy}{dx} = 2$

$\therefore$ $\dfrac{dy}{dx} = \dfrac{1}{y}$

For the curve (ii), $2x + 2y\dfrac{dy}{dx} = 0$

$\therefore$ $\dfrac{dy}{dx} = -\dfrac{x}{y}$

At (2, 2) slopes of tangents are $\dfrac{1}{2}$ and -1.

$$\therefore \tan\theta = \frac{\frac{1}{2} - (-1)}{1 + \frac{1}{2}(-1)} = \frac{3/2}{1/2} = 3 \Rightarrow \theta = \tan^{-1} 3$$

(b) Equation of the curve are $y = x^3$ ...(i)

and $6y = 7 - x^2$ ...(ii)

On eliminating y between Eqs. (i) and (ii), we get

$$6x^3 + x^2 - 7 = 0 \quad \text{...(iii)}$$

By inspection its one root is 1 and therefore Eq. (iii) becomes $(x - 1)(6x^2 + 7x + 7) = 0$

$$\therefore \quad x = 1, \frac{-7 \pm \sqrt{49 - 168}}{2}$$

The only real value of x is 1.

$\therefore$ From Eq. (i), $y = 1$

The only point of intersection is (1, 1)

For the curve (i), $\dfrac{dy}{dx} = 3x^2$

For the curve (ii), $6\dfrac{dy}{dx} = -2x$ or $\dfrac{dy}{dx} = -\dfrac{x}{3}$

At (1, 1) slopes of tangents are 3 and $-\dfrac{1}{3}$.

Since, these slopes are negative reciprocals of each other. Hence, the curves cut orthogonally.

Example 29. Prove that the curves $xy = 4$ and $x^2 + y^2 = 8$ touch each other.

Sol. Equation of the given curves are $xy = 4$ ...(i)

and $x^2 + y^2 = 8$ ...(ii)

From Eq. (i), $1y + x\dfrac{dy}{dx} = 0$

$\therefore$ $\dfrac{dy}{dx} = -\dfrac{y}{x}$ ...(iii)

From Eq. (ii), $2x + 2y\dfrac{dy}{dx} = 0$

$\therefore$ $\dfrac{dy}{dx} = -\dfrac{x}{y}$ ...(iv)

On putting the value of y from Eq. (i) in Eq. (ii), we get

$$x^2 + \frac{16}{x^2} = 8 \qquad \left[\because y = \frac{4}{x}\right]$$

$\Rightarrow$ $x^4 + 16 = 8x^2$

$\Rightarrow$ $x^4 - 8x^2 + 16 = 0$

$\Rightarrow$ $(x^2 - 4)^2 = 0$

$\Rightarrow$ $x^2 - 4 = 0$

$\Rightarrow$ $x^2 - 4 = 0$

$\Rightarrow$ $x^2 = 4$

$\therefore$ $x = \pm 2$

Hence, the points of intersection of the two curves are (2, 2) and (−2, − 2).

Slope of the tangent to the curve (i) at point (2, 2)

$$m_1 = -\frac{2}{2} = -1 \qquad \text{[from Eq. (iii)]}$$

Slope of tangent to the curve (ii) at point (2, 2)

$$m_2 = -\left(\frac{2}{2}\right) = -1 \qquad \text{[from Eq. (iv)]}$$

$\because m_1 = m_2$, therefore the curves have a common tangent at (2, 2) i.e. they touch each other at (2, 2).

At point (−2, − 2),

Slope of tangent to the curve (i),

$$m_3 = -\left(\frac{-2}{-2}\right) = -1$$

Slope of tangent to the curve (ii),

$$m_4 = -\left(\frac{-2}{-2}\right) = -1$$

Since, $m_3 = m_4$, hence the two curves touch each other at (−2, − 2). Thus, curves (i) and (ii) touch each other.

Example 30. Which of the following pair(s) of curves is/are orthogonal?

(a) $y^2 = 4ax; y = e^{-x/2a}$ (b) $y^2 = 4ax; x^2 = 4ay$

(c) $xy = a^2, x^2 - y^2 = b^2$ (d) $y = ax; x^2 + y^2 = c^2$

Sol. (a,c,d) (a) $y^2 = 4ax, \dfrac{dy}{dx} = \dfrac{4a}{2y} = m_1$

$$y = e^{-x/2a}, \frac{dy}{dx} = \frac{-1}{2a}y = m_2$$

$$\therefore m_1 m_2 = \frac{4a}{2y} \times \left(-\frac{1}{2a}\right) y = -1$$

(b) $y^2 = 4ax, \dfrac{dy}{dx} = \dfrac{4a}{2y} = m_1$

$x^2 = 4ay, \dfrac{dy}{dx} = \dfrac{2x}{4a} = m_2$

$\therefore \quad m_1 m_2 = \dfrac{x}{y}$

(c) $xy = a^2, y + x\dfrac{dy}{dx} = 0 \Rightarrow \dfrac{dy}{dx} = -\dfrac{y}{x} = m_1$

$x^2 - y^2 = b^2 \Rightarrow \dfrac{dy}{dx} = \dfrac{x}{y} = m_2$

$\therefore \quad m_1 m_2 = -1$

(d) $y = ax, \dfrac{dy}{dx} = a = m_1$

$x^2 + y^2 = c^2$

$2x + 2y\dfrac{dy}{dx} = 0 \Rightarrow \dfrac{dy}{dx} = -\dfrac{x}{y} = m_2$

$\therefore \quad m_1 m_2 = -\dfrac{ax}{y} = -1$

JEE SCANNER

Example Similar to PYQ Asked in JEE Main 2021

In the two curves $c_1 : x = y^2$ and $c_2 : xy = k$ cut at right angles. The value of $32k^2$ is ....

Sol. Given, $x = y^2$ ...(i)

and $xy = k$ ...(ii)

$y^3 = k \Rightarrow y = k^{1/3}$

Then, $x = k^{2/3}$

Point of intersection $(k^{2/3}, k^{1/3})$.

Using Eq. (i), $\dfrac{dy}{dx} = \dfrac{1}{2y}$

$$\left.\frac{dy}{dx}\right|_{(k^{2/3}, k^{1/3})} = \frac{1}{2k^{1/3}} \Rightarrow m_1 = \frac{1}{2k^{1/3}}$$

Using Eq. (ii), $\dfrac{dy}{dx} = -\dfrac{y}{x}$

$$\left.\frac{dy}{dx}\right|_{(k^{2/3}, k^{1/3})} = -\frac{k^{1/3}}{k^{2/3}} \Rightarrow m_2 = -\frac{1}{k^{1/3}}$$

For orthogonality, $m_1 m_2 = -1$

$$-\frac{1}{2 \cdot k^{1/3} \cdot k^{1/3}} = -1 \Rightarrow k^{2/3} = \frac{1}{2} \Rightarrow (k^2) = \left(\frac{1}{2}\right)^3 \Rightarrow k^2 = \frac{1}{8}$$

$\therefore \quad 32k^2 = \dfrac{1}{8} \times 32 = 4$

Skill Builder

If the curves $y^2 = 4ax$ and $xy = c^2$ cut orthogononally, then $\dfrac{c^4}{a^4}$ equals ....

For Sol.

■ **For more practice** See Q.12 of Milestone Practice 6.4.

6.11 Length of Tangent, Subtangent, Normal and Subnormal

Length of Tangent

The length of the segment PT, i.e. the portion of the tangent intercepted between the point of contact and X-axis is called the length of tangent.

Subtangent and Its Length

The projection of the segment PT along X-axis is called the subtangent. Here, ST is the length of subtangent.

Length of Normal

The length of segment PN, i.e. the portion of the normal intercepted between the point on the curve and X-axis is called the length of normal.

Subnormal and Its Length

The projection of the segment PN along X-axis is called the subnormal. Here, SN is the length of subnormal.

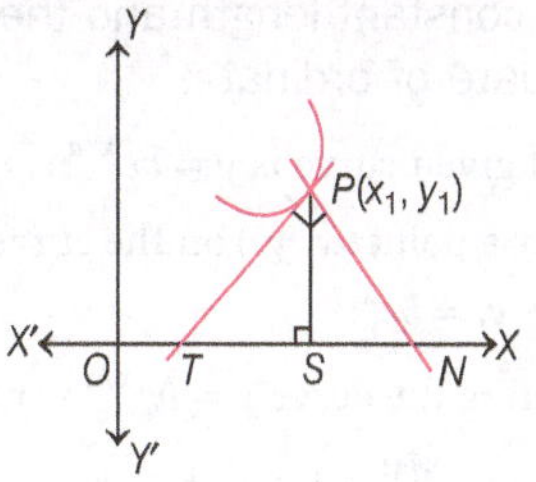

From the figure, if PT makes an angle θ with X-axis, then

$$\tan\theta = \left(\frac{dy}{dx}\right)_{(x_1, y_1)}.$$

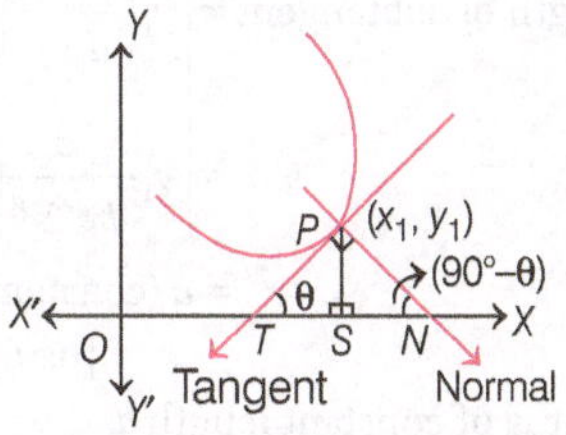

Also, we have

$$\frac{ST}{PS} = \cot\theta$$

$\Rightarrow \quad ST = PS \cot\theta$

or $\quad$ subtangent $= ST = \left| y_1 \left(\dfrac{dx}{dy}\right)_{(x_1, y_1)} \right|$

Similarly, $\frac{SN}{PS} = \cot(90° - \theta)$

$\Rightarrow$ Subnormal $= SN = PS \tan\theta$

$\Rightarrow$ Subnormal $= SN = \left| y_1 \left(\frac{dy}{dx}\right)_{(x_1, y_1)} \right|$

Now, length of tangent, $PT = \left| \sqrt{y_1^2 + y_1^2 \left(\frac{dx}{dy}\right)^2_{(x_1, y_1)}} \right|$

$$PT = \left| y_1 \sqrt{1 + \left(\frac{dx}{dy}\right)^2_{(x_1, y_1)}} \right|$$

and length of normal, $PN = \left| \sqrt{y_1^2 + y_1^2 \left(\frac{dy}{dx}\right)^2_{(x_1, y_1)}} \right|$

$$\Rightarrow \quad PN = \left| y_1 \sqrt{1 + \left(\frac{dy}{dx}\right)^2_{(x_1, y_1)}} \right|$$

Example 31. Show that for the curve $y = be^{x/a}$, the subtangent is of constant length and the subnormal varies as the square of ordinate.

Sol. The equation of given curve is $y = be^{x/a}$

Let us consider a point (x_1, y_1) on the curve.

Then, we have $y_1 = be^{x_1/a}$ ...(i)

On differentiating the curve $y = be^{x/a}$ w.r.t. x, we get

$$\frac{dy}{dx} = be^{x/a} \cdot \frac{1}{a}$$

$$\therefore \quad \left(\frac{dy}{dx}\right)_{(x_1, y_1)} = \frac{b}{a} e^{x_1/a} \quad \text{...(ii)}$$

Thus, the length of subtangent $= \left| y_1 \left(\frac{dx}{dy}\right)_{(x_1, y_1)} \right|$

$$= \left| y_1 \cdot \frac{a}{be^{x_1/a}} \right| = \left| be^{x_1/a} \cdot \frac{a}{be^{x_1/a}} \right|$$

$= a$ (constant) [using Eqs. (i) and (ii)]

$\Rightarrow$ Subtangent is of constant length a.

Again, length of subnormal $= \left| y_1 \left(\frac{dy}{dx}\right)_{(x_1, y_1)} \right|$

$$= \left| be^{x_1/a} \cdot \frac{be^{x_1/a}}{a} \right| = \frac{1}{a}(be^{x_1/a})^2$$

$= \frac{1}{a} y^2$ [using Eq. (i)]

Therefore, subnormal varies as the square of ordinate.

Example 32. Find the length of tangent, subtangent, normal and subnormal to $y^2 = 4ax$ at $(at^2, 2at)$.

Sol. The equation of given curve is

$$y^2 = 4ax \quad \text{...(i)}$$

On differentiating Eq. (i) w.r.t. x, we get

$$2y\frac{dy}{dx} = 4a$$

$$\Rightarrow \quad \left[\frac{dy}{dx}\right]_{(at^2, 2at)} = \frac{4a}{4at} = \frac{1}{t} \quad \text{...(ii)}$$

Now, the length of tangent at $(at^2, 2at)$ is

$$= y_1 \sqrt{1 + \left(\frac{dx}{dy}\right)^2_{(x_1, y_1)}}$$

$= 2at\sqrt{1 + t^2}$ [using Eq. (ii)]

Length of normal at $(at^2, 2at)$ is

$$= y_1 \sqrt{1 + \left(\frac{dy}{dx}\right)^2_{(x_1, y_1)}}$$

$$= 2at\sqrt{1 + 1/t^2}$$

$$= 2a\sqrt{t^2 + 1}$$

Length of subtangent is

$$\frac{y_1}{\left(\frac{dy}{dx}\right)_{(x_1, y_1)}} = \frac{2at}{1/t} = 2at^2$$

Example 33. Find the equations of the tangent and normal, the length of the tangent and the sub-tangent, the length of the normal and sub-normal for the ellipse $x = a\cos t$, $y = b\sin t$, at the point $M(x_1, y_1)$ for which $t = \frac{\pi}{4}$.

Sol. From the given equations, we find that

$$\frac{dx}{dt} = -a\sin t, \quad \frac{dy}{dt} = b\cos t$$

$$\frac{dy}{dx} = -\frac{b}{a}\cot t; \left(\frac{dy}{dx}\right)_{t=\pi/4} = -\frac{b}{a}$$

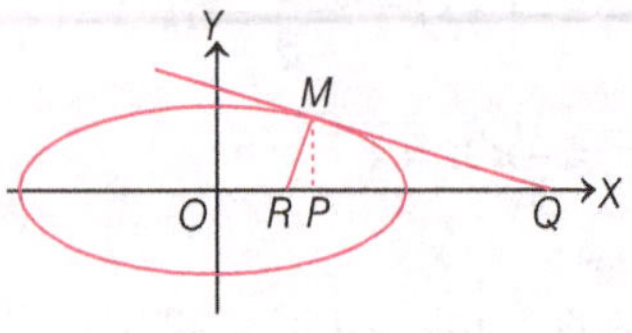

We find the coordinates of the point of tangency

$$M : x_1 = (x)_{t=\pi/4} = \frac{a}{\sqrt{2}}, \; y_1 = (y)_{t=\pi/4} = \frac{b}{\sqrt{2}}$$

The equation of the tangent is

$$y-\frac{b}{\sqrt{2}}=-\frac{b}{a}\left(x-\frac{a}{\sqrt{2}}\right) \Rightarrow bx+ay-ab\sqrt{2}=0$$

The equation of the normal is

$$y-\frac{b}{\sqrt{2}}=\frac{a}{b}\left(x-\frac{a}{\sqrt{2}}\right) \Rightarrow (ax-by)\sqrt{2}-a^2+b^2=0$$

The lengths of the sub-tangent and sub-normal are

$$S_T=\left[\frac{b/\sqrt{2}}{-b/a}\right]=\frac{a}{\sqrt{2}} \text{ and } S_N=\left|\frac{b}{\sqrt{2}}\left(-\frac{b}{a}\right)\right|=\frac{b^2}{a\sqrt{2}}$$

The lengths of the tangent and the normal are

$$T=\left|\frac{b/\sqrt{2}}{-b/a}\sqrt{(-b/a)^2+1}\right|=\frac{1}{\sqrt{2}}\sqrt{a^2+b^2}$$

and $$N=\left|\frac{b}{\sqrt{2}}\sqrt{1+(-b/a)^2}\right|=\frac{b}{a\sqrt{2}}\sqrt{a^2+b^2}$$

Example 34. Show that in the curve $y=a\ln(x^2-a^2)$, sum of the length of tangent and sub-tangent varies as the product of the coordinates of the point of contact.

Sol. $$y=a\ln(x^2-a^2)$$

$$\frac{dy}{dx}=\frac{a\cdot 2x}{x^2-a^2}$$

$$\text{Length of tangent}=\frac{y\sqrt{1+\left(\frac{dy}{dx}\right)^2}}{dy/dx}$$

$$=\frac{y\sqrt{1+\left(\frac{2ax}{x^2-a^2}\right)^2}}{\left(\frac{2ax}{x^2-a^2}\right)}$$

$$=\frac{y\sqrt{x^4+a^4-2a^2x^2+4a^2x^2}}{2ax}$$

$$=\frac{y(x^2+a^2)}{2ax}$$

$$\text{Length of sub-tangent}=\frac{y}{dy/dx}=\frac{y(x^2-a^2)}{2ax}$$

$$LT+ST=\frac{y(x^2+a^2)}{2ax}+\frac{y(x^2-a^2)}{2ax}$$

$$=y\cdot\frac{2x^2}{2ax}=\frac{yx}{a}$$

Example 35. If the length of subnormal is equal to length of subtangent at any point (3, 4) on the curve $y=f(x)$ and the tangent at (3, 4) to $y=f(x)$ meets the coordinate axes at A and B, then maximum area of the ΔOAB, where O is origin, is

(a) $\frac{45}{2}$ (b) $\frac{49}{2}$ (c) $\frac{25}{2}$ (d) $\frac{81}{2}$

Sol. (b) Length of subnormal = Length of subtangent

$$\Rightarrow \quad \frac{dy}{dx}=\pm 1$$

If $\frac{dy}{dx}=1$, then equation of tangent is

$$y-4=x-3$$

$$\Rightarrow \quad y-x=1$$

$$\therefore \quad \text{Area of } \Delta OAB=\frac{1}{2}\times 1\times 1=\frac{1}{2} \quad \text{...(i)}$$

If $\frac{dy}{dx}=-1$, then equation of tangent is

$$y-4=-x+3$$

$$\Rightarrow \quad x+y=7$$

$$\therefore \quad \text{Area of } \Delta OAB=\frac{1}{2}\times 7\times 7=\frac{49}{2} \quad \text{...(ii)}$$

Clearly, maximum area $=\frac{49}{2}$

6.12 Shortest Distance Between Two Curves

The shortest distance between two non-intersecting curves is found along the common normal to the two curves. In fact, if the two curves also have the largest distance between them, then it is also found along the common normal to the two curves. This can be established with the help the concept of maximum and minima.

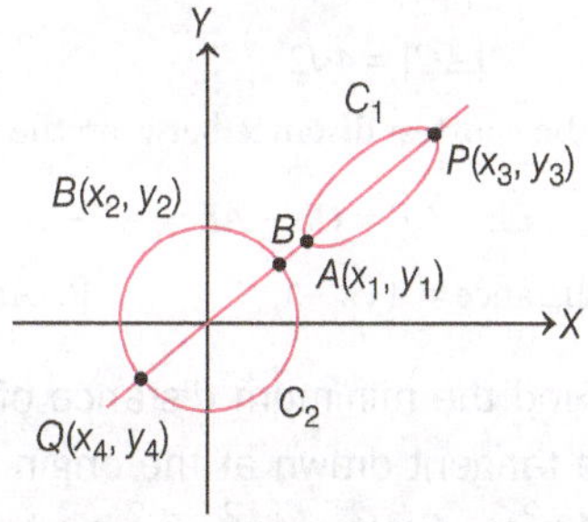

In the figure, we notice that the shortest distance between the curves is AB and the largest distance between them is PQ both of which are found along a common normal.

Example 36. Find the shortest distance between the curves $y^2=8x$ and $(x-6)^2+y^2=1$.

Sol. First of all, let us drawn the two curves.

Now, since we know that the shortest and the longest distance are along the common normal, hence we need to find the normals common to the two curves.

The normal to a curve passes through the centre and hence, every line passing though (6, 0) will be a normal to the circle.

Now, we need to find the normal from (6, 0) to $y^2 = 8x$

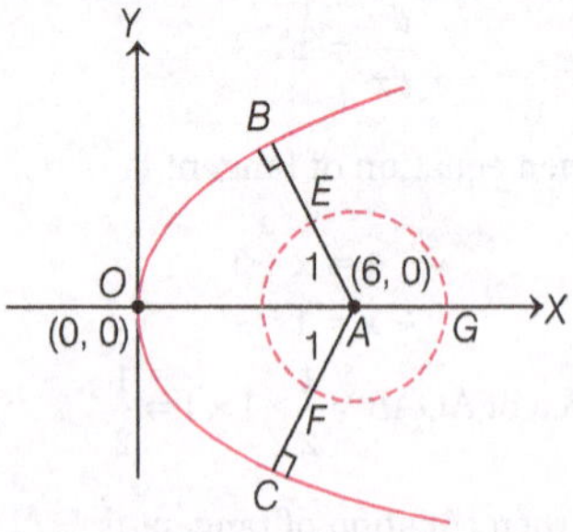

Equation of normals on parabola from a point (x_1, y_1) is

$$y_1 = mx_1 - 2am - am^3$$

where $(x_1, y_1) = (6, 0)$ and $a = 2$

$$\Rightarrow \quad 0 = 6m - 4m - 2m^3$$

$$\Rightarrow \quad 2m^3 + 4m - 6m = 0$$

$$\Rightarrow \quad 2m(m^2 - 1) = 0$$

$$\Rightarrow \quad m(m-1)(m+1) = 0$$

$$\Rightarrow \quad m = 0 \text{ or } 1 \text{ or } -1$$

Now, any parametric form of the parabola $y^2 = 4ax$ can be written in the terms of slope of the normal as $(am^2, -2am)$.

$\therefore$ Points on the parabola $O \to (0, 0)$ at $m = 0$

i.e. $O \equiv (0, 0)$

$B \to (a, 2a)$ at $m = -1$ i.e. $B \equiv (2, 4)$

$C \to (a, -2a)$ at $m = 1$ i.e. $C \equiv (2, -4)$

Now, $\quad |OA| = 6,$

$\quad |AB| = 4\sqrt{2}$

and $\quad |AC| = 4\sqrt{2}$

Therefore, the shortest distance between the two curves is given by

$$BE = CF = OB - AE = AC - AF$$

$\therefore$ Shortest distance $= 4\sqrt{2} - 1 \quad [\because AF = AE = r = 1]$

Example 37. Find the minimum distance of the point (0, 3) from the tangent drawn at the origin to the curve $3x^3 + 7x^3 + 11x^2y + 9xy^2 - 4x^2 - y^2 + xy + 2x - 3y = 0$

Sol. It is important to note that the curve passes through (0, 0) and hence the equation of the tangent at (0, 0) will be $2x - 3y = 0$.

Now, minimum distance from (0, 3) to $2x - 3y = 0$ is the perpendicular distance from (0, 3) to $2x - 3y = 0$

$$= \frac{|2 \times 0 - 3 \times 3|}{\sqrt{2^2 + 3^2}} = \frac{9}{\sqrt{13}}$$

Example 38. Find the shortest distance between the line $y = x - 2$ and the parabola $y = x^2 + 3x + 2$.

Sol. Let $P(x_1, y_1)$ be a point closest to the line $y = x - 2$.

Then, $\left.\frac{dy}{dx}\right|_{(x_1, y_1)} = $ Slope of line

$$\Rightarrow \quad 2x_1 + 3 = 1 \Rightarrow x_1 = -1 \Rightarrow y_1 = 0$$

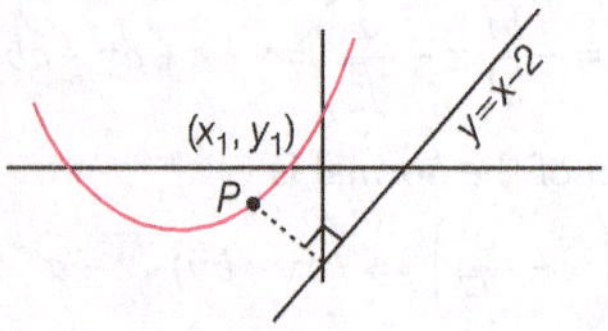

Hence, point $(-1, 0)$ is the closest and its perpendicular distance from the line $y = x - 2$ will give the shortest distance

$$\Rightarrow \quad p = \frac{3}{\sqrt{2}}$$

JEE SCANNER

Example Similar to PYQ Asked in JEE Main 2021

The shortest distance between the line $y - x = 1$ and the curve $x = y^2$ is

(a) $\frac{2\sqrt{3}}{8}$ (b) $\frac{3\sqrt{5}}{8}$ (c) $\frac{\sqrt{3}}{4}$ (d) $\frac{3\sqrt{2}}{8}$

Sol. (d) General point on curve is (a^2, a).

Distance of it form the line $y - x - 1 = 0$

$$d = \left|\frac{a - a^2 - 1}{\sqrt{2}}\right| = \left|\frac{a^2 - a + 1}{\sqrt{2}}\right|$$

$$\frac{d}{da}(d) = \frac{2a - 1}{\sqrt{2}},$$ for minimum distance it is equal to zero.

$$\Rightarrow \quad a = \frac{1}{2}$$

$$\Rightarrow \quad d = \left|\frac{\frac{1}{4} - \frac{1}{2} + 1}{\sqrt{2}}\right| = \left|\frac{1 - \frac{1}{4}}{\sqrt{2}}\right| = \frac{3}{4\sqrt{2}}$$

Hence, $d = \frac{3\sqrt{2}}{8}$

Skill Builder

The shortest distance between the line $x - y = 2$ and the curve $y^2 = 4x$ is

(a) $\frac{3\sqrt{2}}{2}$ (b) $\frac{3\sqrt{2}}{4}$

(c) $\frac{3\sqrt{2}}{8}$ (d) $3\sqrt{2}$

For Sol.

- **For more practice** See Q.6 of Milestone Practice 6.4.

Example 39. Find the shortest distance between the curve $(x - 6)^2 + y^2 = 1$ and the tangent at (0, 0) in the curve $x^3 + y^2 + x^2 = 0$.

Sol. The tangent at (0, 0) on the curve $x^3 + y^2 + x^2 = 0$ will be given by $x^2 + y^2 = 0$ which denotes the point (0, 0) only. Hence, we need to find the shortest and the longest distance from the point (0, 0) to the curve $(x - 6)^2 + y^2 = 1$.

Common normal to (0, 0) and $(x - 6)^2 + y^2 = 1$ will be $y = 0$ and hence shortest distance = 5.

Milestone Practice 6.4

1. Find the angle of intersection of curves $y = x^2$ and $6y = 7 - x^3$ at (1, 1).
2. Find the angle of intersection of the ellipse $\frac{x^2}{a^2} + \frac{y^2}{b^2} = 1$ and the circle $x^2 + y^2 = ab$ at their point of intersection.
3. Find the angle of intersection of curves $y = [|\sin x| + |\cos x|]$ and $x^2 + y^2 = 5$, where $[x]$ denotes the integral part of number x.
4. Find the minimum and maximum values of $[(x+2)^2 + (y-1)^2]^{1/2}$, if $(x-2)^2 + (y+1)^2 \le 4$.
5. Find the coordinates of the point on the curve $x^2 = 4y$ which is at least distance from the line $y = x - 4$.
6. Find the shortest distance between curves $xy = 9$ and $x^2 + y^2 = 1$.
7. Find the point on hyperbola $3x^2 - 4y^2 = 72$ which is nearest to the straight line $3x + 2y + 1 = 0$
8. Show that the curve $ay^2 = (x+b)^3$, the sub-normal varies as the square of the sub-tangent.
9. Show that the sub-tangent and sub-normal of the curve $y^n = a^{n-1}x$ are nx and $\frac{y^2}{nx}$.
10. Prove that the sub-normal at any point of the curve $y^2x^2 = a^2(x^2 - a^2)$ varies inversely as the cube of its abscissa.
11. The angle of intersection of the two curves $xy = a^2$ and $x^2 + y^2 = 2b^2$ is
    (a) $\frac{\pi}{3}$ (b) $\frac{\pi}{6}$
    (c) $\frac{\pi}{4}$ (d) None of these
12. The curves $x^3 + pxy^2 = -2$ and $3x^2y - y^3 = 2$ are orthogonal for
    (a) $p = 3$ (b) $p = -3$
    (c) no value of p (d) $p = \pm 3$
13. If the curves $a_1x^3 + b_1y^3 = 1$ and $a_2x^3 + b_2y^3 = 1$ are orthogonal, then
    (a) $a_1a_2(b_1 - b_2)^{4/3} + b_1b_2(a_1 - a_2)^{4/3} = 0$
    (b) $a_1a_2(b_1 - b_2)^{4/3} - b_1b_2(a_1 - a_2)^{4/3} = 0$
    (c) $a_1a_2(a_1 - a_2)^{4/3} + b_1b_2(b_1 - b_2)^{4/3} = 0$
    (d) $a_1a_2(a_1 - a_2)^{4/3} - b_1b_2(b_1 - b_2)^{4/3} = 0$
14. If two curves $y = a^x$ and $y = e^x$ intersect at an angle α, then $\tan\alpha$ equals
    (a) $\left|\frac{1-\log a}{1+\log a}\right|$ (b) $\left|\frac{1+\log a}{1-\log a}\right|$
    (c) $\left|\frac{\log a - 1}{\log a + 1}\right|$ (d) None of these
15. The equation of the common tangent to the curves $y^2 = 8x$ and $xy = -1$ is
    (a) $3y = 9x + 2$ (b) $y = 2x + 1$
    (c) $2y = x + 8$ (d) $y = x + 2$
16. Point on the line $y = 2x + 11$ that is nearest to the circle $16x^2 + 16y^2 + 32x - 8y - 50 = 0$, is
    (a) $\left(-\frac{7}{2}, 4\right)$ (b) $\left(-\frac{9}{2}, 2\right)$
    (c) $(-3, 5)$ (d) $\left(\frac{1}{2}, 12\right)$
17. The coordinates of a point on the parabola $2y = x^2$ which is nearest to the point (0, 3) is
    (a) (2, 2) (b) $(-\sqrt{2}, 1)$ (c) $(\sqrt{2}, 1)$ (d) $(-2, 2)$
18. Area of triangle formed by the positive X-axis and the normal and the tangent to $x^2 + y^2 = 4$ at $(1, \sqrt{3})$ is
    (a) $2\sqrt{3}$ sq units (b) $\sqrt{3}$ sq unit
    (c) $4\sqrt{3}$ sq units (d) None of these
19. The sub-normal at any point on the curve $xy^n = a^{n+1}$ is constant for
    (a) $n = 0$ (b) $n = 1$
    (c) $n = -2$ (d) no value of n
20. If the sub-normal at any point on $y^n = a^{1-n} \cdot x^{n-1}$ is of constant length, then the value of n is
    (a) -2 (b) $\frac{1}{2}$
    (c) 1 (d) 2
21. The length of the normal at t on the curve $x = a(t + \sin t), y = a(1 - \cos t)$ is
    (a) $a\sin t$ (b) $2a\sin^3\left(\frac{t}{2}\right)\sec\left(\frac{t}{2}\right)$
    (c) $2a\sin\left(\frac{t}{2}\right)$ (d) $2a\sin\left(\frac{t}{2}\right)\tan\left(\frac{t}{2}\right)$

Answer Key

1. $\pi/2$ 2. $\tan^{-1}\left|\frac{b-a}{\sqrt{ab}}\right|$ 3. $\tan^{-1}2$ 4. $(2\sqrt{5}-2), (2\sqrt{5}+2)$ 5. (2, 1)
6. $(3\sqrt{2}-1)$ units 7. (− 6, 3) 11. (c) 12. (b) 13. (a)
14. (a,c) 15. (d) 16. (b) 17. (a,d) 18. (a)
19. (c) 20. (d) 21. (d)

For Detailed Solution

Milestone 5 Rolle's Theorem, Lagrange's Mean Value Theorem

- Rolle's Theorem and Its Geometrical Interpretation
- Lagrange's Mean Value Theorem and Its Geometrical Interpretation

6.13 Rolle's Theorem and Its Geometrical Interpretation

The theorem was named after the French Mathematician Michel Rolle (1652–1719). Who first gave it in his book *Methode pour resoudre lesegalites* (1691).

Statement

Let f be a real-valued function defined on the closed interval $[a, b]$ such that

(i) $f(x)$ is continuous in the closed interval $[a, b]$

(ii) $f(x)$ is differentiable in the open interval $]a, b[$ and

(iii) $f(a) = f(b)$

Then, there is atleast one value c of x in open interval $]a, b[$ for which $f'(c) = 0$.

Geometrical Proof

Consider the portion AB of the curve $y = f(x)$, lying between $x = a$ and $x = b$ such that

(i) it goes continuously from A to B

(ii) it has tangent at every point between A and B

(iii) ordinate of A = ordinate of B

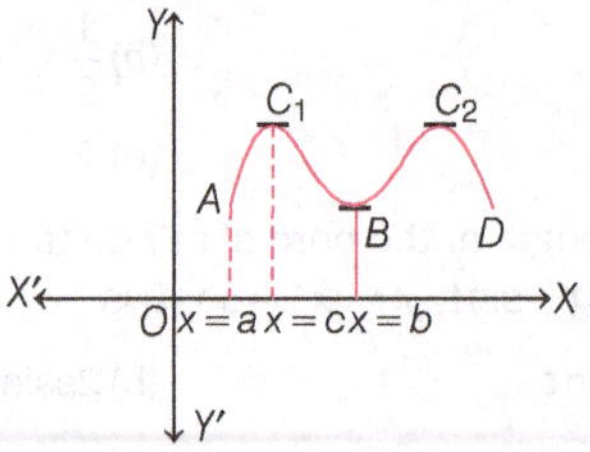

From the figure, it is clear that $f(x)$ **increases in the interval AC_1**, which implies that $f'(x) > 0$ in this region and decreases in the interval C_1B which implies $f'(x) < 0$ in this region. Now, **since there is unique tangent to be drawn on the curve lying in between A and B and since each of them has a unique slope i.e. unique value of $f'(x)$.**

So, due to continuity and differentiability of the function $f(x)$ in the region A to B, there is a point $x = c$, where $f'(c)$ should be zero.

Hence, $f'(c) = 0$, where $a < c < b$

Thus, Rolle's theorem is proved.

JEE Focus Points

Generally, two types of problems are formulated on Rolle's theorem.

- To check the applicability of Rolle's theorem to a given function on a given interval
- To verify Rolle's theorem for a given function in a given interval. In both the types of problems, first we check whether $f(x)$ satisfies the conditions of Rolle's theorem or not.

Some Important Results Regarding Rolle's Theorem

(i) A polynomial function is everywhere continuous and differentiable.

(ii) The exponential function, sine and cosine functions are everywhere continuous and differentiable.

(iii) Logarithmic function is continuous and differentiable in its domain.

(iv) $\tan x$ is not continuous and differentiable at $x = \pm\pi/2, \pm 3\pi/2, \pm 5\pi/2, \ldots\ldots\ldots$

(v) $|x|$ is not differentiable at $x = 0$.

(vi) If $f'(x)$ tends to $\pm\infty$ as $x \to k$, then $f(x)$ is not differentiable at $x = k$.

e.g. If $f(x) = (2x-1)^{1/2}$, then $f'(x) = \dfrac{1}{\sqrt{2x-1}}$ is such that as

$$x \to \left(\frac{1}{2}\right)^+ \Rightarrow f'(x) \to \infty$$

So, $f(x)$ is not differentiable at $x = 1/2$.

Example 40. Verify Rolle's theorem for the function $f(x) = x^3 - 3x^2 + 2x$ in the interval $[0, 2]$.

Sol. Here, we observe that

(i) $f(x)$ is polynomial and since polynomials are always continuous, so $f(x)$ is continuous in the interval $[0, 2]$.

(ii) $f'(x) = 3x^2 - 6x + 2$, which exists for all $x \in (0, 2)$. So, $f(x)$ is differentiable, for all $x \in (0, 2)$ and

(iii) $f(0) = 0$, $f(2) = 2^3 - 3 \cdot (2)^2 + 2(2) = 0$

$\therefore \quad f(0) = f(2)$

Thus, all the conditions of Rolle's theorem are satisfied.

So, there must exists some $c \in (0, 2)$ such that $f'(c) = 0$

$\Rightarrow \quad f'(c) = 3c^2 - 6c + 2 = 0 \Rightarrow c = 1 \pm \dfrac{1}{\sqrt{3}}.$

Where, $c = 1 \pm \dfrac{1}{\sqrt{3}} \in (0, 2)$, thus Rolle's theorem is verified.

Example 41. If $ax^2 + bx + c = 0$, $a, b, c \in R$, then find the condition that this equation would have at least one root in $(0, 1)$.

Sol. Let $f'(x) = ax^2 + bx + c$

On integrating both sides, we get

$$f(x) = \frac{ax^3}{3} + \frac{bx^2}{2} + cx + d$$

$$\Rightarrow \quad f(0) = d \text{ and } f(1) = \frac{a}{3} + \frac{b}{2} + c + d$$

Now, for Rolle's theorem to be applicable, we should have

$$f(0) = f(1)$$

$$\Rightarrow \quad d = \frac{a}{3} + \frac{b}{2} + c + d$$

$$\Rightarrow \quad 2a + 3b + 6c = 0$$

Here, the required condition is $2a + 3b + 6c = 0$.

Example 42. If $f(x)$ and $g(x)$ are continuous functions in $[a, b]$ and they are differentiable in (a, b), then prove that there exists $c \in (a, b)$ such that

$$\begin{vmatrix} f(a) & f(b) \\ g(a) & g(b) \end{vmatrix} = (b-a) \begin{vmatrix} f(a) & f'(c) \\ g(a) & g'(c) \end{vmatrix}$$

Sol. Consider a function, $\phi(x) = f(a)\, g(x) - f(x)\, g(a)$, for all $x \in [a, b]$.

As $\phi(x)$ is continuous and differentiable on (a, b).

$$\therefore \quad \phi'(c) = \frac{\phi(b) - \phi(a)}{b - a}, \text{ for some } c \in (a, b). \quad \ldots(i)$$

Now, as $\quad \phi(x) = f(a)\, g(x) - f(x)\, g(a)$

$\therefore \quad \phi'(x) = f(a)\, g'(x) - f'(x)\, g(a)$

$\Rightarrow \quad \phi'(c) = f(a)\, g'(c) - f'(c)\, g(a)$

$$\Rightarrow \quad \phi'(c) = \begin{vmatrix} f(a) & f'(c) \\ g(a) & g'(c) \end{vmatrix}$$

Also, $\phi(b) = f(a)\, g(b) - f(b)\, g(a) = \begin{vmatrix} f(a) & f(b) \\ g(a) & g(b) \end{vmatrix}$

and $\quad \phi(a) = f(a)\, g(a) - f(a)\, g(a) = 0$

$\therefore$ Eq. (i) reduces to;

$$\begin{vmatrix} f(a) & f'(c) \\ g(a) & g'(c) \end{vmatrix} = \frac{1}{(b-a)} \begin{vmatrix} f(a) & f(b) \\ g(a) & g(b) \end{vmatrix}$$

or

$$\begin{vmatrix} f(a) & f(b) \\ g(a) & g(b) \end{vmatrix} = (b-a) \begin{vmatrix} f(a) & f'(c) \\ g(a) & g'(c) \end{vmatrix}$$

Example 43. Use Rolle's theorem to find the condition for the polynomial equation $f(x) = 0$ have a repeated real roots. Hence, or otherwise prove that the equation; $1 + \dfrac{x}{1!} + \dfrac{x^2}{2!} + \ldots + \dfrac{x^n}{n!} = 0$, cannot have repeated roots.

Sol. By Rolle's theorem, we can say that between any two roots of a polynomial there is always a root of its derivative. Thus, if α is a repeated root of a polynomial $f(x)$, then there must be a root of $f'(x)$ in the interval.

$\Rightarrow \quad f'(\alpha) = 0$

i.e. $\quad f(\alpha) = f'(\alpha) = 0$, for α to be a repeated root.

Let $\quad \phi(x) = 1 + \dfrac{x}{1!} + \dfrac{x^2}{2!} + \ldots + \dfrac{x^n}{n!}$ has a repeated root α.

$$\Rightarrow \quad \phi(\alpha) = 0 \text{ and } \phi'(\alpha) = 0$$

$$\Rightarrow \quad 1 + \frac{\alpha}{1!} + \frac{\alpha^2}{2!} + \ldots + \frac{\alpha^n}{n!} = 0$$

and $\quad 1 + \alpha + \dfrac{\alpha^2}{2!} + \ldots + \dfrac{\alpha^{n-1}}{(n-1)!} = 0$

On solving above equations, we get $\dfrac{\alpha^n}{n!} = 0$

or $\alpha = 0$, thus 0 is the repeated root of $\phi(x) = 0$.

But, 0 does not satisfy $\phi(x)$.

$\therefore$ There is no repeated root of $\phi(x) = 0$.

Example 44. Let $f(x)$ and $g(x)$ be differentiable functions such that $f'(x)g(x) \neq f(x)g'(x)$, for any real x. Show that between any two real solutions of $f(x) = 0$, there is atleast one real solution of $g(x) = 0$.

Sol. Let a, b be the solutions of $f(x) = 0$.

Suppose $g(x)$ is not equal to zero, for any x belonging to $[a, b]$.

Now, consider $\quad h(x) = f(x) / g(x)$

Since, $g(x)$ is not equal to zero, therefore $h(x)$ is differentiable and continuous in $[a, b]$.

Also, $\quad h(a) = h(b) = 0$

[as $f(a) = 0$ and $f(b) = 0$ but $g(a)$ and $g(b) \neq 0$]

On applying Rolle's theorem for $h(x)$ in $[a, b]$, we get

$h'(c) = 0$, for some c belonging to (a, b)

$\Rightarrow \quad f(c)g'(c) = f'(c)g(c)$, for some $c \in (a, b)$.

This gives the contradiction. **Hence proved.**

Example 45. Consider the function

$$f(x)=\begin{cases} x\sin\dfrac{\pi}{x}, & \text{for } x>0 \\ 0, & \text{for } x=0 \end{cases}$$, then the number of points in (0, 1), where the derivative $f'(x)$ tends to zero is

(a) 0 (b) 1 (c) 2 (d) infinite

Sol. (d) $f(x)$ tends to zero at points, where $\sin\dfrac{\pi}{x}=0$

i.e. $\dfrac{\pi}{x}=k\pi,\ k=1,2,3,4,\ldots$

Hence, $x=\dfrac{1}{k}$.

Also, $f'(x)=\sin\dfrac{\pi}{x}-\dfrac{\pi}{x}\cos\dfrac{\pi}{x}$, if $x\neq 0$

Since, the function has a derivative at any interior point of the interval (0, 1), also continuous in [0, 1] and $f(0)=f(1)$, therefore Rolle's theorem is applicable to any one of the intervals $\left[\dfrac{1}{2},1\right],\left[\dfrac{1}{3},\dfrac{1}{2}\right],\ldots,\left[\dfrac{1}{k+1},\dfrac{1}{k}\right]$.

Hence, there exists some c in each of these intervals, where $f'(c)=0\Rightarrow$ Infinite points.

Example 46. A continuous and differentiable function $y=f(x)$ is such that its graph cuts the line $y=px+q$ at m distinct points. Find the minimum number of points at which $f''(x)=0$.

Sol. If line cuts the graph at m points, then using LMVT, there exists atleast $(m-1)$ points, where $f'(x)=p$ (slope of the line)

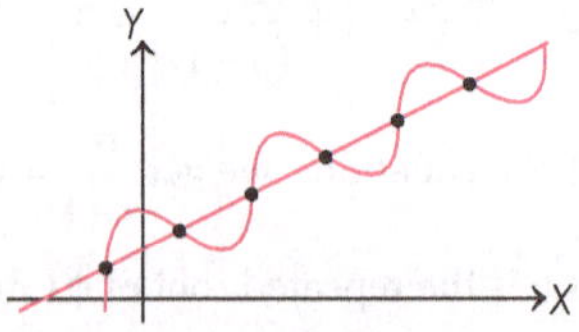

$\therefore$ Using Rolle's theorem, there exists atleast $(m-2)$ points, where $f''(x)=0$.

6.14 Lagrange's Mean Value Theorem and Its Geometrical Interpretation

First Form

If a function $f(x)$,

(i) is continuous in the closed interval $[a,b]$ and

(ii) is differentiable in the open interval $]a,b[$

Then, there is at least one value $c\in(a,b)$ such that

$$f'(c)=\frac{f(b)-f(a)}{b-a}$$

Second Form

If we write $b=a+h$, then $c=a+\theta h$, where $0<\theta<1$.

$[\because\ a<c<b]$

Thus, the mean value theorem can be stated as follows:

If (i) $f(x)$ is continuous in closed interval $[a,a+h]$.

(ii) $f'(x)$ exists in the open interval $]a,a+h[$, then there exists at least one number $\theta\ (0<\theta<1)$, such that

$f(a+h)=f(a)+hf'(a+\theta h)$

Geometrical Interpretation of Lagrange's Theorem

Let A, B be the points on the curve $y=f(x)$ corresponding to $x=a$ and $x=b$, so that $A=(a,f(a))$ and $B=(b,f(b))$

Now, slope of chord $AB=\dfrac{f(b)-f(a)}{b-a}$

The slope of the chord $AB=f'(c)$, the slope of the tangent to the curve at $x=c$.

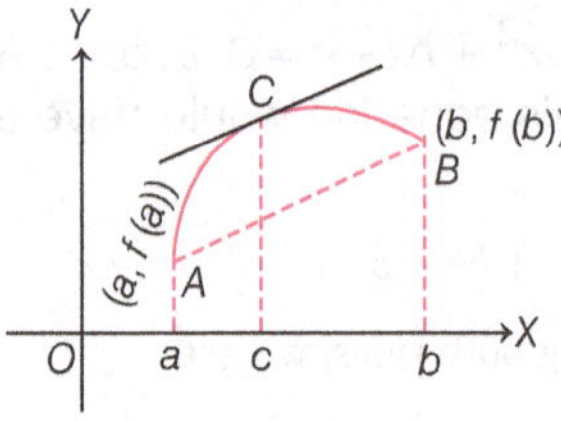

Hence, the Lagrange's mean value theorem asserts that if a curve has a tangent at each of its points, then there is a point c on this curve in between A and B, the tangent at which is parallel to the chord AB.

Example 47. Find c of the Lagrange's mean value theorem, for which $f(x)=\sqrt{25-x^2}$ in $[1,5]$.

Sol. It is clear that $f(x)$ has a definite and unique value, for each $x\in[1,5]$.

Thus, for every point in the interval [1, 5], the value of $f(x)$ is equal to the limit of $f(x)$.

So, $f(x)$ is continuous in the interval [1, 5].

Also, $f'(x)=\dfrac{-x}{\sqrt{25-x^2}}$, which clearly exists for all x in open interval (1, 5)

Hence, $f(x)$ is differentiable in (1, 5).

So, there must be a value $c\in(1,5)$ such that,

$$f'(c)=\frac{f(5)-f(1)}{5-1}=\frac{0-\sqrt{24}}{4}=\frac{-\sqrt{6}}{2}$$

But $f'(c)=\dfrac{-c}{\sqrt{25-c^2}}$

$\therefore$ $\dfrac{-c}{\sqrt{25-c^2}}=\dfrac{-\sqrt{6}}{2}\Rightarrow 4c^2=6(25-c^2)$

$\Rightarrow$ $c=\pm\sqrt{15}$

Clearly, $c=\sqrt{15}\in(1,5)$. So, for $c=\sqrt{15}$ Lagrange's theorem is satisfied.

Example 48. Let $f(x)$ and $g(x)$ be differentiable for $0 \le x \le 2$ such that $f(0)=2, g(0)=1$ and $f(2)=8$. Let there exists a real number c in [0, 2] such that $f'(c)=3g'(c)$, then the value of $g(2)$ must be

(a) 2 (b) 3 (c) 4 (d) 5

Sol. (b) As $f(x)$ and $g(x)$ are continuous and differentiable in [0, 2], therefore there exists atleast one value c such that

$$\frac{f'(c)}{g'(c)} = \frac{f(2)-f(0)}{g(2)-g(0)} \Rightarrow \frac{8-2}{g(2)-1} = 3$$

$$\Rightarrow \quad g(2)-1=2 \Rightarrow g(2)=3$$

Example 49. If $f(x)=\log_e x$, $g(x)=x^2$ and $c \in (4,5)$, then $c \log\left(\frac{4^{25}}{5^{16}}\right)$ is equal to

(a) $c\log_e 5-8$ (b) $2(c^2\log_e 4-8)$

(c) $2(c^2\log_e 5-8)$ (d) $c\log_e 4-8$

Sol. (b) Let $\phi(x)=x^2(\log_e 4)-16\log_e x$, which is continuous in [4, 5] and differentiable in (4, 5).

Then, by Lagrange's theorem, we get

$$\frac{\phi(5)-\phi(4)}{5-4} = \phi'(c), \text{ for some } c \in (4,5)$$

Now, $\phi(5)-\phi(4)=\log_e\left(\frac{4^{25}}{5^{16}}\right)$

Also, $\phi'(c)=\frac{2}{c}(c^2\log_e 4-8)$

$\therefore \quad \phi'(c)=\frac{\phi(5)-\phi(4)}{5-4}$

$\Rightarrow \quad \frac{2}{c}(c^2\log_e 4-8)=\log_e\left(\frac{4^{25}}{5^{16}}\right)$

or $\quad c\log\left(\frac{4^{25}}{5^{16}}\right)=2(c^2\log 4-8)$

Example 50. If $0<a<b<\frac{\pi}{2}$ and $f(a,b)=\frac{\tan b-\tan a}{b-a}$, then

(a) $f(a,b)\ge 2$ (b) $f(a,b)>1$

(c) $f(a,b)\le 1$ (d) None of these

Sol. (b) Consider the function $f(x)=\tan x$, defined on $[a,b]$ such that $a, b \in \left(0, \frac{\pi}{2}\right)$.

On applying Lagrange's mean value theorem, we have

$$f'(c)=\frac{f(b)-f(a)}{b-a}, \text{ for some } c \in (a,b)$$

$\Rightarrow \quad \sec^2 c=\frac{\tan b-\tan a}{b-a}$

$\Rightarrow \quad f(a,b)=\sec^2 c$

$\Rightarrow \quad f(a,b)>1 \qquad [\because \sec^2 c>1 \text{ as } c\in(0,\pi/2)]$

Example 51. In [0, 1] Lagrange's mean value theorem is not applicable to

(a) $f(x)=\begin{cases}\frac{1}{2}-x, & x<\frac{1}{2}\\ \left(\frac{1}{2}-x\right)^2, & x\ge\frac{1}{2}\end{cases}$

(b) $f(x)=\begin{cases}\frac{\sin x}{x}, & x\ne 0\\ 1, & x=0\end{cases}$

(c) $f(x)=x|x|$

(d) $f(x)=|x|$

Sol. (a) For the function $f(x)$ given in option (a), we have LHD (at $x=1/2$) $=-1$ and RHD (at $x=1/2$) $=0$.

So, it is not differentiable at $x=1/2 \in (0,1)$.

$\therefore$ Lagrange's mean value theorem is not applicable.

Example 52. Let $f(x)$ satisfy the requirements of Lagrange's mean value theorem in [0, 2]. If $f(0)=0$ and $|f'(x)|\le 1/2$, for all $x\in[0,2]$, then

(a) $f(x)\le 2$

(b) $|f(x)|\le 2x$

(c) $|f(x)|\le 1$

(d) $f(x)=3$, for atleast one $x\in[0,2]$

Sol. (c) Let $x\in[0,2]$. Since, $f(x)$ satisfies the requirements of Lagrange's mean value theorem in [0, 2]. So, it also satisfies in $[0,x]$.

Consequently, there exists $c\in(0,x)$ such that

$$f'(c)=\frac{f(x)-f(0)}{x-0} \Rightarrow f'(c)=\frac{f(x)}{x}$$

$\Rightarrow \quad \left|\frac{f(x)}{x}\right|=|f'(c)|\le 1/2 \qquad [\because |f'(x)|\le 1/2]$

$\Rightarrow \quad |f(x)|\le\frac{x}{2}$

$\Rightarrow \quad |f(x)|\le 1 \qquad [\because x\in[0,2], \therefore x\le 2]$

Example 53. Let $f:[2,7]\to[0,\infty)$ be a continuous and differentiable function. Then, the value of $(f(7)-f(2))\frac{(f(7))^2+(f(2))^2+f(2)\cdot f(7)}{3}$ is (where $c\in(2,7)$)

(a) $3f^2(c)f'(c)$ (b) $5f^2(c)\cdot f(c)$

(c) $5f^2(c)\cdot f'(c)$ (d) None of these

Sol. (c) Let $g(x)=f^3(x) \Rightarrow g'(x)=3f^2(x)\cdot f'(x)$

$\because \quad f:[2,7]\to[0,\infty)$

$\therefore \quad g:[2,7]\to[0,\infty)$

Using Lagrange's mean value theorem on $g(x)$, we get

$$g'(c)=\frac{g(7)-g(2)}{5}, c\in(2,7)$$

$$\Rightarrow 3f^2(c)f'(c) = \frac{f^3(7) - f^3(2)}{5}$$

$$\Rightarrow 5f^2(c)\cdot f'(c)$$

$$= \frac{(f(7) - f(2))(f^2(7) + f^2(2) + f(7)\cdot f(2))}{3}$$

Example 54. Let $f(x)$ be twice differentiable function such that $f''(x) < 0$ in $[0, 2]$. Then, prove that

(i) $f(0) + f(2) = 2f(c)$, $0 < c < 2$

(ii) $f(0) + f(2) < 2f(1)$

Sol. By intermediate value theorem,

$$\frac{f(0) + f(2)}{2} = f(c), 0 < c < 2$$

By mean value theorem,

$$f(1) - f(0) = f'(c_1), 0 < c_1 < 1 \quad \text{...(i)}$$

$$f(2) - f(1) = f'(c_2), 1 < c_2 < 2 \quad \text{...(ii)}$$

By subtracting Eq. (i) from Eq. (ii), we get

$$f(0) + f(2) - 2f(1) = f'(c_2) - f'(c_1)$$

$$= (c_2 - c_1)f''(c), c_1 < c < c_2$$

$$\Rightarrow f(0) + f(2) - 2f(1) < 0$$

$$\Rightarrow f(0) + f(2) < 2f(1)$$

Example 55. If $y = f(x)$ is twice differentiable function such that $f(a) = f(b) = 0$ and $f(x) > 0\ \forall\ x \in (a, b)$, then prove that $f''(c) < 0$ for some $c \in (a, b)$.

Sol. Applying LMVT to $f(x)$ for $x \in \left[a, \frac{a+b}{2}\right]$

$$f'(c_1) = \frac{f\left(\frac{a+b}{2}\right) - f(a)}{\left(\frac{b-a}{2}\right)} = \frac{2}{(b-a)}\cdot f\left(\frac{a+b}{2}\right),$$

for some $c_1 \in \left(a, \frac{a+b}{2}\right)$.

Applying LMVT again on $f(x)$ for $x \in \left[\frac{a+b}{2}, b\right]$,

$$f'(c_2) = -\frac{2f\left(\frac{a+b}{2}\right)}{b - \frac{a+b}{2}}, \text{ for some } c_2 \in \left(\frac{a+b}{2}, b\right)$$

On applying LMVT to $y = f'(x)$ in $[c_1, c_2]$,

$$f''(x) = \frac{f'(c_2) - f'(c_1)}{c_2 - c_1} = \frac{-\frac{4}{(b-a)}\cdot f\left(\frac{a+b}{2}\right)}{c_2 - c_1} < 0,$$

where $x \in (c_1, c_2)$.

JEE SCANNER

Example 6 Similar to PYQ Asked in JEE Main 2024

Let $g: R \to R$ be a non-constant twice differentiable function such that $g'\left(\frac{1}{4}\right) = g'\left(\frac{3}{4}\right)$. If a real valued function f is defined as $f(x) = \frac{1}{2}[g(x) + g(1-x)]$, then

(a) $f''(x) = 0$, for atleast two x in $(0, 1)$

(b) $f''(x) = 0$, for exactly one x in $(0, 1)$

(c) $f''(x) = 0$, for no x in $(0, 1)$

(d) $f'\left(\frac{1}{4}\right) + f'\left(\frac{3}{4}\right) = 1$

Sol. (a) $f'(x) = \dfrac{g'(x) - g'(1-x)}{2}$

$$\Rightarrow f'\left(\frac{1}{4}\right) = \frac{g'\left(\frac{1}{4}\right) - g'\left(\frac{3}{4}\right)}{2} = 0,$$

$$f'\left(\frac{1}{2}\right) = \frac{g'\left(\frac{1}{2}\right) - g'\left(\frac{1}{2}\right)}{2} = 0$$

and $$f'\left(\frac{3}{4}\right) = \frac{g'\left(\frac{3}{4}\right) - g'\left(\frac{1}{4}\right)}{2} = 0$$

$$\because f'\left(\frac{1}{4}\right) = f'\left(\frac{3}{4}\right) = 0 = f'\left(\frac{1}{2}\right)$$

$\therefore$ Roots in $\left(\frac{1}{4}, \frac{1}{2}\right)$ and $\left(\frac{1}{2}, \frac{3}{4}\right)$

$\Rightarrow f''(x)$ is zero atleast twice in $\left(\frac{1}{4}, \frac{3}{4}\right)$.

Skill Builder

Let $f(x)$ be a non-constant thrice differentiable function defined on $(-\infty, \infty)$ such that $f(x) = f(6-x)$ and $f'(0) = 0 = f'(2) = f'(5)$ and $g(x) = (f'(x))^2 + f'(x)f'''(x)$, then

(a) $g(x) = 0$ has atleast 12 roots in $[0, 6]$

(b) $g(x) = 0$ has atleast 14 roots in $[0, 6]$

(c) $g(x) = 0$ has atleast 15 roots in $[0, 6]$

(d) None of the above

For Sol.

■ **For more practice** See Q.19 of Milestone Practice 6.5.

Milestone Practice 6.5

1. Are the conditions of Rolle's theorem satisfied for the following functions?
   (i) $f(x) = |9 - x^2|$ in $[-3, 3]$
   (ii) $f(x) = \ln\{(x^2 + ab)/[(a+b)x]\}$ in $[a, b]$, $ab > 0$
   (iii) $f(x) = x^3 - 3x^2 + 2x$ in $[0, 2]$
   (iv) $f(x) = e^x(\sin x - \cos x)$ in $[\pi/4, 5\pi/4]$
2. Using Lagrange's mean value theorem or otherwise, prove that
   (i) $|\sin x - \sin y| \le |x - y| \ \forall \ x, y \in R$
   (ii) $\frac{\beta - \alpha}{1+\beta^2} < \tan^{-1}\beta - \tan^{-1}\alpha < \frac{\beta - \alpha}{1+\alpha^2}$, where $\beta > \alpha > 0$.
   (iii) $(b-a)\sec^2 a < \tan b - \tan a < (b-a)\sec^2 b$, where $0 < a < b < \frac{\pi}{2}$.
3. Suppose that the second derivative of f exists everywhere and that $f(x_1) = f(x_2) = f(x_3) = 0$, where $x_1 < x_2 < x_3$. Show that $f''(c) = 0$, for some numbers c with $x_1 < c < x_3$.
4. If $f(x)$ is differentiable function, $\forall \ x \in [a, b]$ such that a and b are both positive, then show that there exists atleast one $c \in (a, b)$, where $2\sqrt{c}\, f'(c) = \frac{f(b) - f(a)}{\sqrt{b} - \sqrt{a}}$.
5. Prove that the equation $3x^5 + 15x - 8 = 0$ has only one real root.
6. Discuss the nature of roots of the equation $x^3 - 6x^2 + 9x - 2 = 0$ and locate them.
7. Let f'' exists, for all $x \in [a, b]$. Let $\phi(x) = f(x) + (b - x) f'(x) + A(b - x)^2$, where A is constant, so chosen that $\phi(b) = \phi(a)$. Apply Rolle's theorem to calculate that $f(b) = f(a) + (b-a)f'(a) + [f''(c)/2](b-a)^2$, for some $c \in (a, b)$.
8. Polynomial $x^3 + 3x - 10$ has
   (a) at least one real root
   (b) exactly one real root
   (c) two real roots
   (d) all the three roots are equal
9. The function in which Rolle's theorem is verified, is
   (a) $f(x) = \log\left(\frac{x^2 + ab}{(a+b)x}\right)$ in $[a, b]$, where $0 < a < b$
   (b) $f(x) = (x-1)(2x-3)$ in $(1, 3)$
   (c) $f(x) = 2 + (x-1)^{2/3}$ in $[0, 2]$
   (d) $f(x) = \cos\left(\frac{1}{x}\right)$ in $[-1, 1]$
10. If $a + b + c = 0$, then the quadratic equation $3ax^2 + 2bx + c = 0$ has
    (a) imaginary roots
    (b) at least one real root in (0, 1)
    (c) one root in [2, 3] and other in [3, 6]
    (d) None of the above
11. Of the equation $x^4 - x^3 - x + 1 = 0$, 1 is a
    (a) double root (b) simple root
    (c) triple root (d) None of these
12. The equation $3x^2 + 4ax + b = 0$ has at least one root in (0, 1), if
    (a) $4a + b + 3 = 0$ (b) $2a + b + 1 = 0$
    (c) $b = 0, a = -\frac{4}{3}$ (d) None of these
13. Let $f(x)$ and $g(x)$ be differentiable in $[0, 1]$ such that $f(0) = 2$, $g(0) = 0$, $f(1) = 6$ by LMVT. Let there exists a real number c in $(0, 1)$ such that $f'(c) = 2g'(c)$, then $g(1)$ is equal to
    (a) 1 (b) −1
    (c) 2 (d) −2
14. Let $f(x) = \frac{1}{x^2}$, $g = \frac{1}{x}$ on $[a, b]$, $0 < a < b$. Let $\frac{f(b) - f(a)}{g(b) - g(a)} = \frac{f'(c)}{g'(c)}$, for some $a < c < b$.Then, c is
    (a) AM of a and b (b) GM of a and b
    (c) HM of a and b (d) None of these
15. If $f(x)$ is twice differentiable polynomial function such that $f(1) = 1$, $f(2) = 4$, $f(3) = 9$, then
    (a) $f''(x) = 2 \ \forall \ x \in R$
    (b) there exist at least one $x \in (1, 2)$ such that $f'(x) = 3$
    (c) there exist at least one $x \in (2, 3)$ such that $f'(x) = 5 = f''(x)$
    (d) there exist at least one $x \in (1, 3)$ such that $f'(x) = 2$

16. If the mean value theorem is $f(b) - f(a) = (b-a)f'(c)$. Then, for the function $x^2 - 2x + 3$ in $\left[1, \frac{3}{2}\right]$, the value of c is

(a) $\frac{6}{5}$ (b) $\frac{5}{4}$
(c) $\frac{4}{3}$ (d) $\frac{7}{6}$

17. If $f(x) = \frac{\sin x}{e^x}$ in $[0, \pi]$, then $f(x)$

(a) satisfies Rolle's theorem and $c = \frac{\pi}{4}$ so that $f'\left(\frac{\pi}{4}\right) = 4$
(b) does not satisfy Rolle's theorem but $f'\left(\frac{\pi}{4}\right) > 0$
(c) satisfies Rolle's theorem and $f'\left(\frac{\pi}{4}\right) = 0$
(d) satisfies Lagrange's mean value theorem but $f'\left(\frac{\pi}{4}\right) \neq 0$

18. If $f(x) = x^2 - 2x + 4$ on $[1, 5]$, then the value of a constant c such that $\frac{f(5) - f(1)}{5-1} = f'(c)$, is

(a) 0 (b) 1 (c) 2 (d) 3

19. Let $f(x)$ be a non-constant twice differentiable function defined on $(-\infty, \infty)$ such that $f(x) = f(1-x)$ and $f'\left(\frac{1}{4}\right) = 0$. Consider the following statements

(i) $f'(x)$ vanishes at least twice on $[0, 1]$
(ii) $f'\left(\frac{1}{2}\right) = 0$, $f''(x) = 0$ at least once in $\left(\frac{1}{4}, \frac{1}{2}\right)$ and $\left(\frac{1}{2}, \frac{3}{4}\right)$
(iii) $\int_{-1/2}^{1/2} f\left(x + \frac{1}{2}\right) \sin x \, dx = 0$
(iv) $\int_{-1/2}^{1/2} f(t) e^{\sin \pi t} dt = \int_{1/2}^{1} f(1-t) e^{\sin \pi t} dt$, then only

(a) (i) and (ii) are true (b) (ii) and (iii) are true
(c) (i), (ii) and (iii) are true (d) All of these are true

Answer Key

1. (i) satisfied (ii) satisfied (iii) satisfied (iv) satisfied
8. (b) 9. (a)
10. (b) 11. (a) 12. (b) 13. (c) 14. (c)
15. (b) 16. (b) 17. (c) 18. (d) 19. (d)

For Detailed Solution

JEE Pattern EXAMPLES

Single Option Correct Type Questions

Example 1 *With the usual meaning for a, b, c and s, if Δ is the area of a triangle, if then the error in Δ, i.e. $(\delta \Delta)$ resulting from a small error in the measurement of c i.e. (δc) is given by $\delta\Delta = \frac{\Delta}{k}\left(\frac{1}{s} + \frac{1}{s-a} + \frac{1}{s-b} - \frac{1}{s-c}\right)\delta c$, then the value of k is*

(a) 1 (b) 2 (c) 3 (d) 4

Sol. (d) Since, $\Delta = \sqrt{s(s-a)(s-b)(s-c)}$

$$= \{s(s-a)(s-b)(s-c)\}^{1/2}$$

On taking logarithm both sides, we get

$$\ln \Delta = \frac{1}{2}\{\ln s + \ln(s-a) + \ln(s-b) + \ln(s-c)\}$$

On differentiating both sides w.r.t. c, we get

$$\frac{1}{\Delta}\frac{d\Delta}{dc} = \frac{1}{2}\left[\frac{1}{s}\cdot\frac{ds}{dc} + \frac{1}{(s-a)}\cdot\frac{d(s-a)}{dc} + \frac{1}{(s-b)}\cdot\frac{d(s-b)}{dc} + \frac{1}{(s-c)}\cdot\frac{d(s-c)}{dc}\right] \quad \text{...(i)}$$

But $s = \frac{1}{2}(a+b+c)$

$$\therefore \frac{ds}{dc} = \frac{1}{2}\left(\frac{da}{dc} + \frac{db}{dc} + \frac{dc}{dc}\right)$$

$$\because \frac{da}{dc} = \frac{db}{dc} = 0 \Rightarrow \frac{dc}{dc} = 1 \Rightarrow \frac{ds}{dc} = \frac{1}{2}$$

Similarly, $\frac{d(s-a)}{dc} = \frac{ds}{dc} - \frac{da}{dc} = \frac{1}{2}$

and $\frac{d(s-b)}{dc} = \frac{ds}{dc} - \frac{db}{dc} = \frac{1}{2}$

and $\frac{d(s-c)}{dc} = \frac{ds}{dc} - \frac{dc}{dc} = -\frac{1}{2}$

Therefore, from Eq. (i),

$$\frac{1}{\Delta}\cdot\frac{\delta\Delta}{\delta c} = \frac{1}{2}\left\{\frac{1}{s}\cdot\frac{1}{2} + \frac{1}{(s-a)}\cdot\frac{1}{2} + \frac{1}{(s-b)}\frac{1}{2} - \frac{1}{(s-c)}\frac{1}{2}\right\}$$

$$\Rightarrow \frac{1}{\Delta}\cdot\frac{\delta\Delta}{\delta c} = \frac{1}{4}\left\{\frac{1}{s} + \frac{1}{(s-a)} + \frac{1}{(s-b)} - \frac{1}{(s-c)}\right\}$$

Therefore, $\delta\Delta = \frac{\Delta}{4}\left(\frac{1}{s} + \frac{1}{s-a} + \frac{1}{s-b} - \frac{1}{s-c}\right)\delta c$

Example 2 *If tangent at any point on the curve $e^y = 1 + x^2$ makes an angle θ with positive direction of X-axis, then*

(a) $|\tan\theta| > 1$ (b) $|\tan\theta| < 1$
(c) $\tan\theta > 1$ (d) $|\tan\theta| \le 1$

Sol. (d) Given, $e^y = (1 + x^2)$

On taking $\log_e$ both the sides, we get

$$y = \ln(1 + x^2)$$

Now, $m = \tan\theta = \frac{dy}{dx} = \frac{2x}{1+x^2}$

$$\Rightarrow |\tan\theta| = \left|\frac{2x}{1+x^2}\right| = \frac{2|x|}{1+|x|^2} \le 1$$

But we already know that $1 + |x|^2 \ge 2|x|$ [$\because$ AM $\ge$ GM]

$$\therefore \frac{2|x|}{1+|x|^2} \le 1$$

Example 3 *The value of n for which the area of the triangle formed by the axes of coodinates and any tangent to the curve $x^n y = a^n$ is constant is*

(a) $\frac{1}{2}$ (b) 2 (c) $\frac{3}{2}$ (d) 1

Sol. (d) Given, $x^n y = a^n$

On differentiating both sides w.r.t. x, we get

$$nx^{n-1}y + x^n y' = 0 \Rightarrow \frac{dy}{dx} = -\frac{nx^{n-1}y}{x^n} = -\frac{ny}{x}$$

Equation of tangent is $Y - y = -\frac{ny}{x}(X - x)$

If the tangent meets the X-axis at $(A, 0)$, then putting $y = 0$ we can find the value of A

i.e. $A = x\frac{(1+x)}{x}$

Similarly, if the tangent meets the Y-axis at $(0, B)$, then putting $x = 0$, we get

$$B = Y(1 + x)$$

$$\therefore \Delta = \frac{1}{2}AB = \frac{1}{2}\frac{(1+n)^2}{n}xy = \frac{1}{2}\frac{(1+n)^2}{n}x\cdot\frac{a^n}{x^n}$$

It will be constant if $x^{n-1} = 1$

i.e. $n - 1 = 0$ or $n = 1$

JEE SCANNER

Example 4 Similar to PYQ Asked in JEE Main 2022

A water tank has the shape of an inverted right circular cone, whose semi-vertical angle is $\tan^{-1}\left(\frac{1}{2}\right)$. *Water is poured into it at a constant rate of 5 m^3/min. Then, the rate (in m/min) at which the level of water is rising at the instant when the depth of water in the tank is 10 m, is*

(a) $\frac{2}{\pi}$ (b) $\frac{1}{5\pi}$

(c) $\frac{1}{15\pi}$ (d) $\frac{1}{10\pi}$

Sol. (b) Given, semi-vertical angle of right circular cone

$$=\tan^{-1}\left(\frac{1}{2}\right)$$

Let $\alpha = \tan^{-1}\left(\frac{1}{2}\right) \Rightarrow \tan\alpha = \frac{1}{2} \Rightarrow \frac{r}{h} = \frac{1}{2}$

$\left[\text{from figure, } \tan\alpha = \frac{r}{h}\right]$

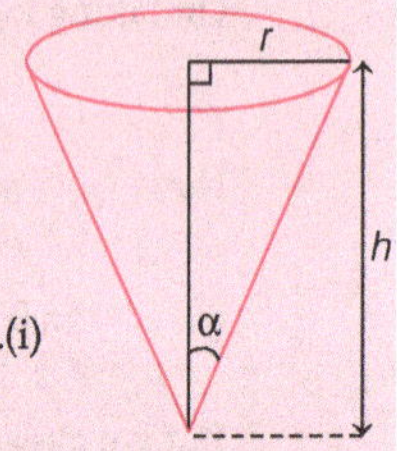

$$r = \frac{1}{2}h \quad \text{...(i)}$$

$\because$ Volume of cone is $(V) = \frac{1}{3}\pi r^2 h$

$$\therefore \quad V = \frac{1}{3}\pi\left(\frac{1}{2}h\right)^2 (h) = \frac{1}{12}\pi h^3 \quad \text{[from Eq. (i)]}$$

On differentiating both sides, w.r.t. t, we get

$$\frac{dV}{dt} = \frac{1}{12}\pi(3h^2)\frac{dh}{dt}$$

$$\Rightarrow \quad \frac{dh}{dt} = \frac{4}{\pi h^2}\frac{dV}{dt}$$

$$\Rightarrow \quad \frac{dh}{dt} = \frac{4}{\pi h^2} \times 5 \quad \left[\because \text{given } \frac{dV}{dt} = 5 \text{ m}^3/\text{min}\right]$$

Now, at $h = 10$ m, the rate at which height of water level is rising $= \left.\frac{dh}{dt}\right|_{h=10} = \frac{4}{\pi(10)^2} \times 5 = \frac{1}{5\pi}$ m/min

Skill Builder

A water tank has shape of an inverted circular cone with circular top opening of radius 2m and height 4 m. If water is being pumped into tank at rate of 2 m^3/min, then the rate at which water level is rising, when water is 3m deep, is

(a) $\frac{4}{9\pi}$ m/min (b) $\frac{2}{3\pi}$ m/min

(c) $\frac{8}{3\pi}$ m/min (d) $\frac{8}{9\pi}$ m/min

For Sol.

Example 5 *The point P on the curve* $y = x\tan\alpha - \frac{1}{2}\frac{x^2}{u^2\cos^2\alpha}, \alpha \in \left(0, \frac{\pi}{2}\right)$ *has a tangent parallel to* $y = x + 5$. *If the ordiante of P is* $\frac{u^2}{4}$, *then* α *is equal to*

(a) 15° (b) 30° (c) 45° (d) 60°

Sol. (d) Given, $y = x\tan x - \frac{1}{2}\frac{x^2}{u^2\cos^2\alpha}$

$$\frac{dy}{dx} = \tan\alpha - \frac{x}{u^2}\sec^2\alpha \quad \text{...(i)}$$

Now, since it is parallel to $y = x + 5$, then $\frac{dy}{dx} = 1$

$$\therefore \quad \tan x - \frac{x}{u^2}\sec^2\alpha = 1$$

$$\Rightarrow \quad x = (\tan\alpha - 1)u^2\cos^2\alpha$$

and $\quad y = \frac{u^2}{4}$ [given]

On putting the values of x and y in given equation

$$y = x\left[\tan\alpha - \frac{1}{2}\frac{x}{u^2\cos^2\alpha}\right]$$

$$\frac{u^2}{4} = (\tan\alpha - 1)u^2\cos^2\alpha\left[\tan\alpha - \frac{1}{2}(\tan\alpha - 1)\right]$$

$$\Rightarrow \quad \frac{1}{4} = (\tan\alpha - 1)\cos^2\alpha\left[\frac{\tan\alpha + 1}{2}\right]$$

$$\Rightarrow \quad \frac{1}{2} = \cos^2\alpha \cdot (\tan^2\alpha - 1) = \sin^2\alpha - \cos^2\alpha$$

$$\Rightarrow \quad \frac{1}{2} = 1 - 2\cos^2\alpha \text{ or } \frac{1}{4} = \cos^2\alpha$$

$$\therefore \cos\alpha = \frac{1}{2} \text{ only as } \alpha \in \left(0, \frac{\pi}{2}\right)$$

$$\Rightarrow \quad \alpha = \frac{\pi}{3} = 60°$$

Example 6 *The tangent and normal at the point* $P(at^2, 2at)$ *to the parabola* $y^2 = 4ax$ *meet the X-axis in T and N respectively, then the angle at which the tangent at P to the parabola is inclined to the tangent at P to the circle through T, P and N is*

(a) $\tan^{-1}t^2$

(b) $\cot^{-1}t^2$

(c) $\tan^{-1}|t|$

(d) $\cot^{-1}|t|$

Sol. (c) The tangent to the parabola $y^2 = 4ax$ at (x_1, y_1) i.e. a point on the conic is given by $yy_1 = 2a(x + x_1)$

$$\Rightarrow \quad T_p \text{ is } ty = x + at^2 \quad \text{...(i)}$$

and N_p is $\quad y = -tx + 2at + at^3$

Both meet X-axis i.e. $y = 0$ in $T \equiv (-at^2, 0)$ and $N \equiv (2a + at^2, 0)$

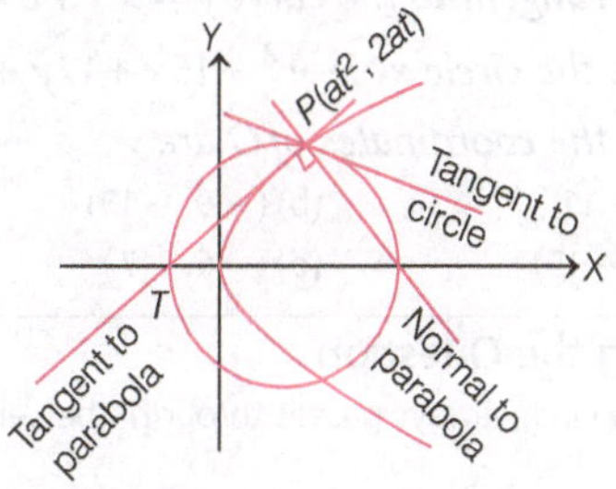

Circle through T, P and N where TP and NP are perpendicular (being tangent and normal), is a circle on TN as diameter.

$\therefore$ Equation of the circle in diametric form can be written as

and $$(x + at^2)(x - 2a - at^2) + y^2 = 0$$

$$x^2 + y^2 - 2ax - at^2(2a + at^2) = 0$$

Now, tangent to the circle at point (x_1, y_1) can be given as $xx_1 + yy_1 - a(x + x_1) - at^2(2a + at^2) = 0$

Slope of tangent $-\dfrac{x_1 - a}{y_1} = -\dfrac{at^2 - a}{2at} = \dfrac{1 - t^2}{2t}$

Also, from Eq. (i), slope of tangent to parabola is $1/t$.

$$\therefore \quad \tan\theta = \left|\frac{\left(\frac{1}{t} - \frac{1 - t^2}{2t}\right)}{\left(1 + \frac{1 - t^2}{2t^2}\right)}\right| = |t|$$

$$\therefore \quad \theta = \tan^{-1}|t|$$

Example 7 *The tangent to $y = ax^2 + bx + \frac{7}{2}$ at (1, 2) is parallel to the normal at the point $(-2, 2)$ on the curve $y = x^2 + 6x + 10$. Then, the value of $\frac{a}{2} - b$ is*

(a) 2 (b) 0 (c) 3 (d) 1

Sol. (c) $m_1 = \left.\dfrac{dy}{dx}\right]_{\text{at } (1, 2)} = 2a + b$

$$m_2 = g'(x) = \left.\frac{dy}{dx}\right]_{\text{at } (-2, 2)} = 2$$

$$\Rightarrow \quad 2a + b = -\frac{1}{2} \quad \text{...(i)}$$

Also, $$2 = a + b + \frac{7}{2}$$

$$\Rightarrow \quad a + b = -\frac{3}{2} \quad \text{...(ii)}$$

From Eqs. (i) and (ii), we get

$$a = 7$$

and $$b = \frac{-5}{2}$$

$$\therefore \quad \frac{a}{2} - b = \frac{1}{2} + \frac{5}{2} = \frac{6}{2} = 3$$

Example 8 *Let A be the point where the curve $5\alpha^2x^3 + 10\alpha x^2 + x + 2y - 4 = 0\ (\alpha \in R, \alpha \neq 0)$ meets the Y-axis, then the equation of tangent to the curve at the point where normal at A meets the curve again, is*

(a) $x - \alpha y + 2\alpha = 0$ (b) $\alpha x + y - 2 = 0$
(c) $2x - y + 2 = 0$ (d) $x + 2y - 4 = 0$

Sol. (c) Curve $5\alpha^2x^3 + 10\alpha x^2 + x + 2y - 4 = 0$ ...(i)

$\because$ $A(0, 2)$ point on Y-axis.

On differentiating Eq. (i) w.r.t. x, we get

$$5\alpha^2(3x^2) + 10\alpha(2x) + 1 + 2\frac{dy}{dx} = 0$$

$$\Rightarrow \quad \frac{dy}{dx} = \frac{-15\alpha^2x^2 - 20\alpha x - 1}{2}$$

$$\Rightarrow \quad \frac{dy}{dx} \text{ at } A = -\frac{1}{2}$$

Equation of normal at A is $y = 2x + 2$

Let normal meets the curve at B

$$5\alpha^2x^3 + 10\alpha x^2 + x + 4x + 4 - 4 = 0$$

$$\Rightarrow \quad 5x(\alpha x + 1)^2 = 0$$

$$\Rightarrow \quad x = -\frac{1}{\alpha}$$

So, $B\left(\dfrac{-1}{\alpha}, \dfrac{-2}{\alpha} + 2\right)$

$\therefore$ Slope of tangent at $B = \dfrac{-15 + 20 - 1}{2} = 2$

$\therefore$ Equation of tangent at B is

$$\left(y + \frac{2}{\alpha} - 2\right) = 2\left(x + \frac{1}{\alpha}\right)$$

$$\Rightarrow \quad \alpha y + 2 - 2\alpha = 2x\alpha + 2$$

$$\Rightarrow \quad 2x - y + 2 = 0$$

Example 9 *If the line $x\cos\alpha + y\sin\alpha = P$ touches the curve $4x^3 = 27ay^2$, then $\frac{P}{a}$ is equal to*

(a) $\cot^2\alpha\cos\alpha$ (b) $\cot^2\alpha\sin\alpha$
(c) $\tan^2\alpha\cos\alpha$ (d) $\tan^2\alpha\sin\alpha$

Sol. (a) Let $x = \dfrac{3at}{2^{2/3}}$, $y = at^{3/2}$

$$\frac{dy}{dx} = \frac{2\left(\frac{9a^2t^2}{2^{4/3}}\right)}{9a^2t^{3/2}} = -\cot\alpha \qquad \left[\because \frac{dy}{dx} = \frac{dy/dt}{dx/dt}\right]$$

$$\Rightarrow \quad \sqrt{t} = -2^{1/3}\cot\alpha$$

and $$P = \cos\alpha\left(\frac{3at}{2^{2/3}} - \frac{at^{3/2}}{-\cot\alpha}\right)$$

$$\Rightarrow \quad \frac{P}{a} = \cos\alpha\cot^2\alpha$$

Example 10 *If the tangent to the curve $2y^3 = ax^2 + x^3$ at a point (a, a) cuts off intercepts p and q on the coordinates axes, where $p^2 + q^2 = 61$, then a equals*

(a) 40 (b) −60 (c) 0 (d) ± 30

Sol. (d) Given, $2y^3 = ax^2 + x^3$

$$\Rightarrow \quad 6y^2 \frac{dy}{dx} = 2ax + 3x^2$$

$$\Rightarrow \quad \frac{dy}{dx} = \frac{5}{6} \text{ at } (a, a)$$

$$\Rightarrow \quad y - a = \frac{5}{6}(x - a)$$

$$\Rightarrow \quad 6y - 5x = a$$

$$\Rightarrow \quad p = -\frac{a}{5}, q = \frac{a}{6}$$

$$\Rightarrow \quad \frac{a^2}{25} + \frac{a^2}{36} = 61$$

$$\Rightarrow \quad a^2 = 25 \times 36 \Rightarrow a = \pm 30$$

JEE SCANNER

Example 11 Similar to PYQ Asked in JEE Main 2023

If the equation of tangent to the curve $y^2 = ax^3 + b$ at point $(2, 3)$ is $y = 4x - 5$, then the value of $a + b$ is

(a) −7 (b) 2

(c) 5 (d) −5

Sol. (d) We have, $y^2 = ax^3 + b$ ...(i)

On differentiating w.r.t. x, we get

$$2yy' = 3ax^2$$

$$\Rightarrow \quad y' = \frac{3ax^2}{2y}$$

Now, y' at $(2, 3)$ $\quad y' = \frac{3a(4)}{6}$

$$\Rightarrow \quad y' = 2a$$

It is given that $y = 4x - 5$ is a tangent to curve (i)

$$2a = 4$$

$$\Rightarrow \quad a = 2$$

Also $(2, 3)$ lies on $y^2 = ax^3 + b$

i.e. $\quad 9 = 8a + b \Rightarrow b = -7$

$$\therefore \quad a + b = -5$$

Skill Builder

If equation of tangent to curve $y^2 = 4ax^2 + b$ at $(1, 2)$ is $y = 4x + 7$, then the value of $a + b$ is

(a) −4

(b) −2

(c) −5

(d) 2

For Sol.

Example 12 *Tangent to the curve $y = x^2 + 6$ at a point $P(1, 7)$ touches the circle $x^2 + y^2 + 16x + 12y + c = 0$ at a point Q. Then, the coordinates of Q are*

(a) (−6, −11) (b) (−9, −13)

(c) (−10, −15) (d) (−6, −7)

Decoding the Question

Normal to a circle always passes through the centre of that circle.

Sol. (d) Given, $y = x^2 + 6$

$$\frac{dy}{dx} = 2x \Rightarrow m = 2$$

$$y - 7 = 2(x - 1) \Rightarrow 2x - y + 5 = 0 \quad \text{...(i)}$$

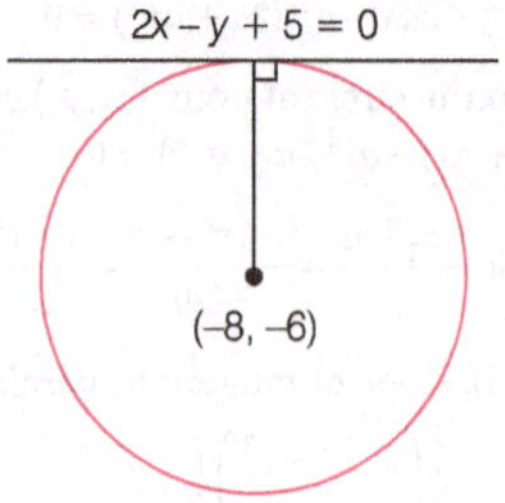

Equation of normal is

$$y + 6 = \frac{-1}{2}(x + 8)$$

$$\Rightarrow \quad x + 2y + 20 = 0 \quad \text{...(ii)}$$

On solving Eqs. (i) and (ii), we get

$$x + 2(2x + 5) + 20 = 0 \Rightarrow 5x = -30$$

$$\therefore \quad x = -6, \; y = -7$$

Example 13 *The angle of intersection of curves $y = [|\sin x| + |\cos x|]$ and $x^2 + y^2 = 5$, where $[\cdot]$ denotes the greatest integer function, is*

(a) $\tan^{-1}(2)$ (b) $\tan^{-1}\left(\frac{1}{2}\right)$

(c) $\tan^{-1}(\sqrt{2})$ (d) $\frac{\pi}{2}$

Sol. (a) Since, $(|\sin x| + |\cos x|)^2 = \sin^2 x + \cos^2 x + 2|\sin x| \times |\cos x| = 1 + |\sin 2x| \geq 1$

and $\quad 1 + |\sin 2x| \leq 2$

and therefore $\quad 1 \leq |\sin x| + |\cos x| \leq \sqrt{2}$

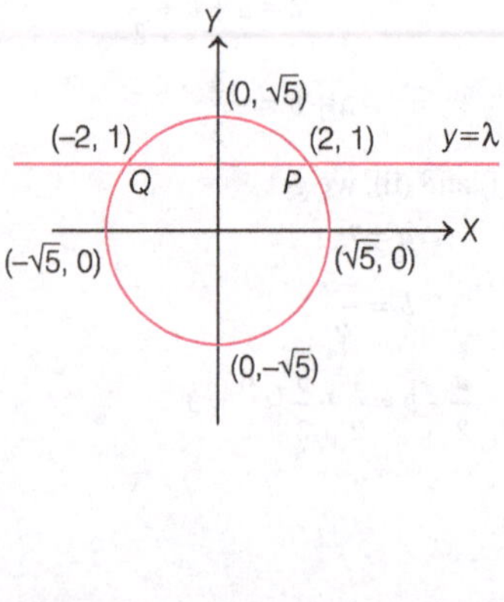

$\therefore \quad y = [|\sin x| + |\cos x|] = 1, \forall x \in R$

Let P and Q be the points of intersection of given curves.

Clearly, the given curves meet at points where $y = 1$ so, we get

$$x^2 + 1 = 5 \Rightarrow x = \pm 2$$

Now, $P(2, 1)$ and $Q(-2, 1)$

Now, $x^2 + y^2 = 5$

On differentiating the above equation w.r.t. x, we get

$$2x + 2y\frac{dy}{dx} = 0$$

$$\Rightarrow \quad \frac{dy}{dx} = -\frac{x}{y}$$

$$\therefore \quad \left(\frac{dy}{dx}\right)_{(2,1)} = -2 \text{ and } \left(\frac{dy}{dx}\right)_{(-2,1)} = 2$$

Clearly, slope of line $y = 1$ is zero and the slope of the tangents at P and Q are -2 and 2, respectively.

Thus, the angle of intersection is $\tan^{-1}(2)$.

Example 14 *The tangent to the curve $y = e^x$ drawn at the point (c, e^c) intersects the line joining the points $(c-1, e^{c-1})$ and $(c+1, e^{c+1})$*

(a) on the left of $x = c$ (b) on the right of $x = c$

(c) at no point (d) at all points

Sol. (a) Slope of the line joniing the points $(c-1, e^{c-1})$ and $(c+1, e^{c+1})$ is equal to $\frac{e^{c+1} - e^{c-1}}{2} > e^c$

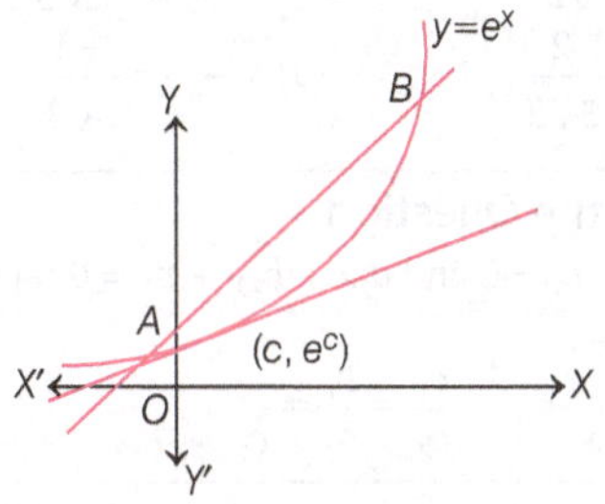

$\Rightarrow$ Tangent to the curve $y = e^x$ will intersect the given line to the left of the line $x = c$.

Alternate Solution

The equation of the tangent to the curve $y = e^x$ at (c, e^c) is

$$y - e^c = e^c(x - c) \quad \text{...(i)}$$

Equation of the line joining the given points is

$$y - e^{c-1} = \frac{e^c(e - e^{-1})}{2}[x - (c-1)] \quad \text{...(ii)}$$

On eliminating y from Eqs. (i) and (ii), we get

$$[x - (c-1)][2 - (e - e^{-1})] = 2e^{-1}$$

or $$x - c = \frac{e + e^{-1} - 2}{2 - (e - e^{-1})} < 0$$

$$\Rightarrow \quad x < c$$

Example 15 *Let for the function*

$$f(x) = \begin{cases} \cos^{-1} x; & -1 \le x \le 0 \\ mx + c; & 0 < x \le 1 \end{cases}$$ *. Lagrange's mean value theorem is applicable in $[-1, 1]$, then ordered pair (m, c) is*

(a) $\left(1, -\frac{\pi}{2}\right)$ (b) $\left(1, \frac{\pi}{2}\right)$

(c) $\left(-1, -\frac{\pi}{2}\right)$ (d) $\left(-1, \frac{\pi}{2}\right)$

Sol. (d) $f(x)$ is continuous and differentiable in $[-1, 1]$.

$$\because \quad f(0^-) = f(0^+) \Rightarrow \frac{\pi}{2} = c$$

$$f'(x) = \begin{cases} \frac{-1}{\sqrt{1-x^2}}, & -1 < x < 0 \\ m, & 0 < x < 1 \end{cases}$$

$$f'(0^+) = f'(0^-)$$

$$\Rightarrow \quad -1 = m$$

$$\Rightarrow \quad m = -1$$

$$\therefore \quad (m, c) = \left(-1, \frac{\pi}{2}\right)$$

Example 16 *If $f(x) = x^3 - 6x^2 + ax + b$ is defined on [1, 3] satisfies Rolle's theorem for $c = \frac{2\sqrt{3}+1}{\sqrt{3}}$, then*

(a) $a = -11, \ b = 6$ (b) $a = -11, \ b = -6$

(c) $a = 11, \ b \in R$ (d) $a = 22, \ b = -6$

Sol. (c) $\because$ Rolle's theorem is applicable.

$$f(1) = f(3)$$

$$\Rightarrow \quad a + b - 5 = 3a + b - 27$$

$$\Rightarrow \quad a = 11$$

$$\Rightarrow \quad f'(c) = 3c^2 - 12c + a = 0$$

$$\Rightarrow \quad b \in R$$

More than One Correct Option Type Questions

Example 17 *If the side of a triangle vary slightly in such a way that its circum radius remains constant, then $\frac{da}{\cos A} + \frac{db}{\cos B} + \frac{dc}{\cos C}$ is equal to*

(a) $6R$ (b) $2R$

(c) 0 (d) $2R(dA + dB + dC)$

Sol. (c, d) Given, $\frac{a}{\sin A} = \frac{b}{\sin B} = \frac{c}{\sin C} = 2R$ (say)

$$\therefore \quad da = 2R\cos A\, dA, db = 2R\cos B\, dB$$

and $$dc = 2R\cos C\, dC$$

$$\therefore \quad \frac{da}{\cos A} + \frac{db}{\cos B} + \frac{dc}{\cos C} = 2R(dA + dB + dC) \quad \text{...(i)}$$

Also, $A+B+C=\pi$

So, $dA+dB+dC=0$ ...(ii)

From Eqs. (i) and (ii), we get

$$\frac{da}{\cos A}+\frac{db}{\cos B}+\frac{dc}{\cos C}=0$$

Example 18 *If tangent drawn to the curve $f(x)=x^3-9x-1$ at $P(x_0, f(x_0))$ meets the curve again at Q, m_A denotes the slope of the tangent at A and m_{OB} denotes the slope of the line joining O origin and a point B on the curve, then*

(a) $m_Q-4m_P=27$

(b) $m_Q-4m_P=9$

(c) $\frac{m_{OP}}{m_{OQ}}=2$, where $x_0=1$

(d) $\frac{m_{OP}}{m_{OQ}}=\frac{1}{2}$, where $x_0=1$

Sol. (a, c) $f(x)=x^3-9x-1$

Let $Q(x_1, f(x_1)) \Rightarrow f'(x)=3x^2-9$

$$m_P=3x_0^2-9,\ m_Q=3x_1^2-9$$

$$\Rightarrow\quad m_P=m_{PQ}$$

$$\Rightarrow\quad 3x_0^2-9=\frac{(x_0^3-9x_0)-(x_1^3-9x_1)}{(x_0-x_1)}$$

$$\Rightarrow\quad 3x_0^2-9=x_0^2+x_1^2+x_0x_1-9$$

$$\Rightarrow\quad 2x_0^2-x_0x_1-x_1^2=0$$

$$\Rightarrow\quad (x_0-x_1)(2x_0+x_1)=0 \qquad [x_0-x_1\neq 0]$$

$$\Rightarrow\quad x_1=-2x_0$$

$$m_Q-4m_P=(3x_1^2-9)-4(3x_0^2-9)=-9+36=27$$

For $x_0=1$, $x_1=-2$,

$$m_{OP}=\frac{x_0^3-9x_0-1}{x_0}=-9$$

$$m_{OQ}=\frac{x_1^3-9x_1-1}{x_1}$$

$$=\frac{-8+18-1}{-2}=\frac{-9}{2}$$

$$\Rightarrow\quad \frac{m_{OP}}{m_{OQ}}=2$$

Example 19 *If $f(x)$ is continuous and derivable, $\forall\, x\in R$ and $f'(c)=0$ for exactly 2 real values of c, then the number of real and distinct values of d for which $f(d)=0$ can be*

(a) 1 (b) 2

(c) 3 (d) 4

Sol. (a, b, c) If $f'(x)=0$ has n real roots, then

$f(x)=0$ has atmost $(n+1)$ real roots.

Now, if $f'(c)=0$ for exactly 2 real values of c.

Then, following cases may arise

(a)

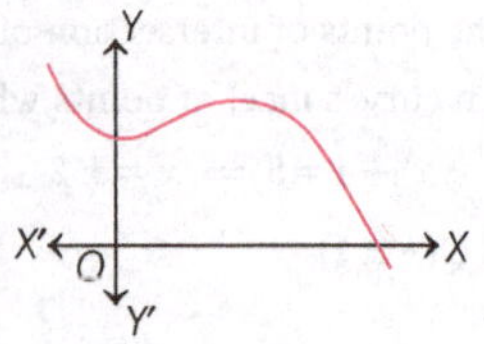

$\Rightarrow f(x)=0$ have 1 real root.

(b)

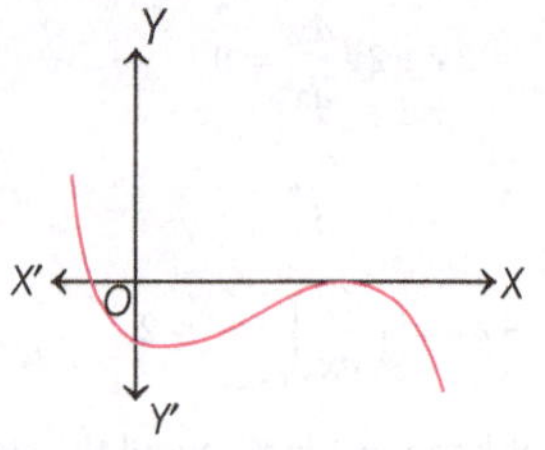

$\Rightarrow f(x)=0$ has 2 real roots.

(c)

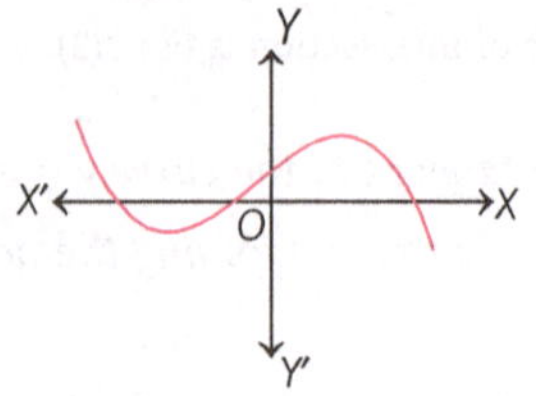

$\Rightarrow f(x)=0$ has 3 real roots.

Example 20 *Common tangent (s) to $y=x^3$ and $x=y^3$ is/are*

(a) $x-y=\frac{1}{\sqrt{3}}$ (b) $x-y=-\frac{1}{\sqrt{3}}$

(c) $x-y=\frac{2}{3\sqrt{3}}$ (d) $x-y=\frac{-2}{3\sqrt{3}}$

Decoding the Question

If $a_1x+b_1y+c_1=0$ and $a_2x+b_2y+c_2=0$ represent the same line, then

$$\frac{a_1}{a_2}=\frac{b_1}{b_2}=\frac{c_1}{c_2}$$

Sol. (c, d) Equation of tangent to $y=x^3$

$$y-x_1^3=3x_1^2(x-x_1)$$

Equation of tangent to $y=x^{1/3}$ is

$$y-x_2^{1/3}=\frac{1}{3x_2^{2/3}}(x-x_2)$$

If these tangents represent same line, then

$$\frac{1}{1}=\frac{9x_1^2x_2^{2/3}}{1}=\frac{-2x_1^3}{\frac{2}{3}x_2^{1/3}} \Rightarrow x_1=\pm\frac{1}{\sqrt{3}}$$

For $x_1=\frac{1}{\sqrt{3}}$, $y_1=\frac{1}{3\sqrt{3}}$

From $y=x^3 \Rightarrow \frac{dy}{dx}=3x^2$

$$\left.\frac{dy}{dx}\right]_{\left(\frac{1}{\sqrt{3}},\frac{1}{3\sqrt{3}}\right)}=3\left(\frac{1}{3}\right)=1$$

Equation of common tangent is

$$y-\frac{1}{3\sqrt{3}}=1\left(x-\frac{1}{\sqrt{3}}\right)$$

$$\Rightarrow \quad x-y=\frac{2}{3\sqrt{3}}$$

For $x_1=-\frac{1}{\sqrt{3}}, y_1=-\frac{1}{3\sqrt{3}}$

Equation of common tangent

$$y+\frac{1}{3\sqrt{3}}=+1\left(x+\frac{1}{\sqrt{3}}\right)$$

$$x-y=\frac{-2}{3\sqrt{3}}$$

Example 21 *Let $f:[0,8]\to R$ be differentiable function such that $f(0)=0$, $f(4)=1$, $f(8)=1$, then which of the following hold(s) good?*

(a) There exist some $c_1\in(0,4)$, where $f'(c_1)=\frac{1}{4}$

(b) There exist some $c_2\in(4,8)$, where $f'(c_2)=0$

(c) There exist $c_1, c_2\in[0,8]$, where $8f'(c_1)f(c_2)=1$

(d) There exist some $\alpha,\beta\in(0,2)$ such that

$$\int_0^8 f(t)\,dt=3(\alpha^2 f(\alpha^3)+\beta^2 f(\beta^3))$$

Sol. (a,b,d) (a) $f'(c_1)=\frac{f(4)-f(0)}{4-0}=\frac{1}{4};\ c_1\in(0,4)$

(b) $f'(c_2)=\frac{f(8)-f(4)}{8-4}=c_2\in(4,8)$

$$f'(c_2)=0$$

(d) Let $g(x)=\int_0^{x^3} f(t)\,dt$

$$\Rightarrow g(0)=0,\ g(2)=\int_0^8 f(t)\,dt$$

$$g'(\alpha)=3\alpha^2 f(\alpha^3)=\frac{g(2)-g(0)}{2},\ \alpha\in(0,2)$$

$$\text{and } g'(\beta)=3\beta^2 f(\beta^3)=\frac{g(2)-g(0)}{2},\ \beta\in(0,2)$$

$$g'(\alpha)+g'(\beta)=g(2)=\int_0^8 f(t)\,dt$$

Example 22 *Given that $f(x)$ is a non-constant linear function. Then, the curves*

(a) $y=f(x)$ and $y=f^{-1}(x)$ are orthogonal.

(b) $y=f(x)$ and $y=f^{-1}(-x)$ are orthogonal.

(c) $y=f(-x)$ and $y=f^{-1}(x)$ are orthogonal.

(d) $y=f(-x)$ and $y=f^{-1}(-x)$ are orthogonal.

Sol. (b, c) Let $y=ax+b=f(x),\ a\neq 0$

$$f^{-1}(x)=\frac{x-b}{a}$$

(a) $m_1=a,\ m_2=\frac{1}{a}\Rightarrow m_1m_2=1$

(b) $m_1=a,\ m_2=\frac{-1}{a}\Rightarrow m_1m_2=-1$

(c) $m_1=-a,\ m_2=\frac{1}{a}\Rightarrow m_1m_2=-1$

(d) $m_1=-a,\ m_2=\frac{-1}{a}\Rightarrow m_1m_2=1$

Passage Based Questions

Passage I

(Ex. Nos. 23 to 24)

Let f and g be two functions such that f and g are continuous in $[a,b]$ and differentiable in (a,b), then $\exists$ at least one $c\in(a,b)$ such that

(i) $f'(c)=\frac{f(b)-f(a)}{b-a}$

(ii) if $f(a)=f(b)$ but $a\neq b$, then $f'(x)=0$

(iii) If $g'(x)\neq 0$, then $\frac{f(b)-f(a)}{g(b)-g(a)}=\frac{f'(c)}{g'(c)}$

(Cauchy theorem)

Example 23 *The set of values of k, for which equation $x^3-3x+k=0$ has two distinct roots in (0, 1) is*

(a) $k\in(1,4)$ (b) $k\in(0,\infty)$
(c) $k\in(0,1)$ (d) $k\in\phi$

Example 24 *Which of the following is true?*

(a) $|\tan^{-1}x-\tan^{-1}y|\le|x-y|,\ \forall\ x,y\in R$

(b) $|\tan^{-1}x-\tan^{-1}y|\ge|x-y|,\ \forall\ x,y\in R$

(c) $|\sin x-\sin y|\ge|x-y|,\ \forall\ x,y\in R$

(d) None of the above

Sol. (Ex. Nos. 23 to 24)

23. (d) Let $0<\alpha<\theta<\beta<1$ and α,β be the roots of $f(x)=x^3-3x+k=0$

$$\Rightarrow \quad f(\alpha)=f(\beta)=0$$

$\Rightarrow f(x)$ satisfies LMVT

$$\Rightarrow \quad f'(c)=0\Rightarrow 3c^2-3=0\Rightarrow c=\pm 1$$

But c must be lies between α and β.

Hence, $k\in\phi$

24. (a) Let $f(x)=\tan^{-1}x$

Then, for some $\alpha\in(x,y)$,

$$f'(\alpha)=\frac{\tan^{-1}y-\tan^{-1}x}{y-x} \quad \text{[LMVT]}$$

$$\Rightarrow \quad \left|\frac{1}{1+\alpha^2}\right|=\left|\frac{\tan^{-1}x-\tan^{-1}y}{x-y}\right|\le 1$$

$$\Rightarrow \quad |\tan^{-1}x-\tan^{-1}y|\le|x-y|$$

Stem Based Questions

Stem I

(Ex. Nos. 25 to 26)

Consider a cubic, $f(x) = ax^3 + bx^2 + cx + 4, a, b, c \in R$ and $f''\left(\frac{-2}{3}\right) = 0$ and tangent drawn to the graph of the function $y = f(x)$ at $x = \frac{-2}{3}$ is $y = \frac{5x}{3} + \frac{100}{27}$.

Example 25 *The value of $(a + b + c)$ is equal to ....*

Example 26 *If g is the inverse of f, then $\left\{\frac{d}{dx}(g(x) \cdot f\{g(x)\}\right\}$ at $x = 4$ is equal to ....*

Sol. (Ex. Nos. 25 to 26)

25. (6) We have, $f''\left(-\frac{2}{3}\right) = 0$

$$f(x) = ax^3 + bx^2 + cx + 4$$

Solving with tangent $y = \frac{5x}{3} + \frac{100}{27}$

$$ax^3 + bx^2 + cx + 4 - \left(\frac{5x}{3} + \frac{100}{27}\right) = k\left(x + \frac{2}{3}\right)^3 \quad \text{...(i)}$$

Put $x = 0$, $\quad 4 - \frac{100}{27} = k \times \frac{8}{27} \Rightarrow k = 1$

Put $x = 1$, $\quad a + b + c + 4 - \left(\frac{5}{3} + \frac{100}{27}\right) = \frac{125}{27}$

$\therefore \quad a + b + c = 6$

26. $\left(\frac{4}{3}\right)$ $g = f^{-1} \because f(0) = 4$

$\therefore g(4) = 0$

Now,

$$\frac{d}{dx}(g(x) \cdot f\{g(x)\}) = g'(x) \cdot f(g(x)) + g(x) \cdot f'(g(x)) \cdot g'(x)$$

$$= g'(4) \cdot f(g(4)) + g(4) \cdot f'(g(4)) \cdot g'(4) \quad [\text{at } x = 4]$$

$$= g'(4) \cdot f(0) = \frac{4}{f'(0)} = \frac{4}{3}$$

$$\left[\because f(g(x)) = x \therefore g'(x) = \frac{1}{f'(g(x))}\right]$$

Stem II

(Ex. Nos. 27 to 28)

If $y = f(x)$ is a curve and if there exists two points $A(x_1, f(x_1))$ and $B(x_2, f(x_2))$ on it such that

$f'(x_1) = -\frac{1}{f'(x_2)} = \frac{f(x_2) - f(x_1)}{x_2 - x_1}$, then the tangent at x_1 is normal at x_2 for that curve. Now, answer the following questions.

Example 27 *Number of such lines on the curve $y = \sin x$ is ....*

Sol. (0) Let $f(x) = y = \sin x$

Then, $f'(x) = \frac{dy}{dx} = \cos x$

$\therefore \quad \cos x_1 = -\frac{1}{\cos x_2} = \frac{\sin x_2 - \sin x_1}{x_2 - x_1}$

i.e. $\quad \cos x_1 \cos x_2 = -1$

$\therefore \quad \sin x_1 = \sin x_2 = 0$

$\therefore$ There is no solution.

Example 28 *Number of such lines on the curve $y = |\ln x|$ is ....*

Sol. (0) $f(x) = y = |\ln x|$

$$f'(x_1) = -\frac{1}{f'(x_2)} = \frac{f(x_2) - f(x_1)}{x_2 - x_1}$$

$$\Rightarrow \quad \frac{\ln x_1}{x_1|\ln x_1|} = -\frac{x_2|\ln x_2|}{\ln x_2} = \frac{|\ln x_2| - |\ln x_1|}{x_2 - x_1} \quad \text{...(i)}$$

$$\Rightarrow \quad \ln x_1 \cdot \ln x_2 < 0$$

Let $0 < x_1 < 1$, then $1 < x_2$ and $x_1 \cdot x_2 = 1$

From Eq. (i), we get

$$-\frac{1}{x_1} = -x_2 = \frac{\ln x_2 + \ln x_1}{x_2 - x_1} = \frac{\ln x_1 x_2}{x_2 - x_1} = 0,$$

which is not possible.

$\therefore$ There is no solution.

Single Integer Answer Type Questions

Example 29 *For a cubic function $y = f(x)$, $f''(x) = 4x$ at each point (x, y) on it and it crosses the X-axis at $(-2, 0)$ at an angle of 45° with positive direction of the X-axis. Then, the value of $\left|\frac{f(1)}{5}\right|$ is ....*

Sol. (3) $f''(x) = 4x$

$$f'(x) = 2x^2 + C$$

Given, $\quad f'(-2) = 1$

$\Rightarrow \quad C = -7$

$\therefore \quad f'(x) = 2x^2 - 7$

$$f(x) = \frac{2}{3}x^3 - 7x + C, \ f(-2) = 0$$

$\Rightarrow \quad 0 = -\frac{16}{3} + 14 + C$

$\Rightarrow \quad C = -\frac{26}{3}$

$\therefore \quad f(x) = \frac{2}{3}x^3 - 7x - \frac{26}{3} = \frac{1}{3}(2x^3 - 21x - 26)$

$\therefore \quad f(1) = -15$

Example 30 *If the point (α, β) on the curve $4x^2 + a^2y^2 = 4a^2, 4 < a^2 < 8$ that is farthest from the point $(0, -2)$, then $\alpha + \beta$ is ....*

Sol. (2) Given curve is $4x^2 + a^2y^2 = 4a^2$

$$\Rightarrow \quad \frac{x^2}{a^2} + \frac{y^2}{4} = 1 \quad \text{...(i)}$$

Let point $P(a \cos \phi, 2 \sin \phi)$ be on Eq. (i), also given a point $Q(0, -2)$.

Let $u = (PQ)^2 = (a\cos\phi)^2 + (2\sin\phi + 2)^2$

On differentiating both sides w.r.t. ϕ, we get

$$\frac{du}{d\phi} = \cos\phi[(8 - 2a^2)\sin\phi + 8]$$

For the extremum value of u, $\frac{du}{d\phi} = 0$

$$\Rightarrow \quad \phi = \frac{\pi}{2} \text{ and } \sin\phi = \frac{4}{a^2 - 4}$$

$$\because \quad 4 < a^2 < 8 \Rightarrow 0 < a^2 - 4 < 4$$

$$\Rightarrow \quad \frac{a^2 - 4}{4} < 1 \Rightarrow \frac{4}{a^2 - 4} > 1$$

$$\Rightarrow \quad \sin\phi > 1 \quad \text{[not possible]}$$

$$\therefore \quad \phi = \frac{\pi}{2}$$

Again, $\frac{d^2u}{d\phi^2} = (8 - 2a^2)\cos^2\phi + (2a^2 - 8)\sin^2\phi - 8\sin\phi$

$$\therefore \left.\frac{d^2u}{d\phi^2}\right|_{\phi = \pi/2} = 0 + (2a^2 - 8) - 8 = 2(a^2 - 8) < 0 \quad [\because 4 < a^2 < 8]$$

$\therefore$ u is maximum at $\phi = \pi / 2$.

So, $\sqrt{PQ}$ is also maximum at $\phi = \frac{\pi}{2}$.

Hence, coordinates of required point P are (0, 2).

$$\alpha = 0, \beta = 2 \Rightarrow \alpha + \beta = 2$$

Example 31 *A curve is given by the equations $x = \sec^2\theta$, $y = \cot\theta$. If the tangent at P, where $\theta = \frac{\pi}{4}$ meets the curve again at Q, then length $PQ = \frac{a\sqrt{b}}{2}$. When a and b are prime number, then $2a - b$ is ....*

Sol. (1) $\frac{dy}{dx} = \frac{dy / d\theta}{dx / d\theta} = -\frac{1}{2}\cot^3\theta$

When $\theta = \frac{\pi}{4}, \frac{dy}{dx} = -\frac{1}{2}\cot^3\left(\frac{\pi}{4}\right) = -\frac{1}{2}$

Now, when $\theta = \frac{\pi}{4}$, $x = \sec^2\left(\frac{\pi}{4}\right) = 2$ and $y = \cot\frac{\pi}{4} = 1$

$$\therefore \quad P \equiv (2, 1)$$

$$T_p \equiv y - 1 = -1/2(x - 2) \text{ or } x + 2y - 4 = 0 \quad \text{...(i)}$$

Now, the cartesian equation of the parametric function can be obtained by eliminating θ using the identify $\sec^2\theta - \tan^2\theta = 1$, we get

$$y^2 = \frac{1}{x - 1} \quad \text{...(ii)}$$

From Eq. (i), we get

$$y = \frac{4 - x}{2}$$

On substituting this value of y in Eq. (ii), we get

$$\left(\frac{4 - x}{2}\right)^2 = \frac{1}{x - 1} \Rightarrow x = 2, 5$$

$\Rightarrow y = 1$, when $x = 2$ and $y = \frac{1}{2}$, when $x = 5$

Hence, P is (2, 1) (given) and Q is $\left(5, \frac{1}{2}\right)$.

$$\therefore \quad PQ = \sqrt{(5 - 2)^2 + \left(1 - \frac{1}{2}\right)^2} = \sqrt{\frac{45}{4}} = \frac{3\sqrt{5}}{2}$$

$$\Rightarrow \quad a = 3 \text{ and } b = 5$$

$$\Rightarrow \quad 2a - b = 1$$

Example 32 *A curve passes through the point $(2, -8)$ and the slope of tangent at any point (x, y) is given by $\frac{x^2}{2} - 6x$. The maximum ordinate on the curve is given by λ, then (3λ) is ....*

Sol. (8) $\frac{dy}{dx}$ = slope of tangent at $P(x, y)$

$$= \frac{x^2}{2} - 6x = \frac{d}{dx}\left(\frac{x^3}{6} - 3x^2 + C\right)$$

$$\Rightarrow y = \frac{x^3}{6} - 3x^2 + C$$

Since, it passes through $(2, -8)$.

$$\therefore \quad -8 = \frac{4}{3} - 12 + C \Rightarrow C = \frac{8}{3} \Rightarrow y = \frac{x^3}{6} - 3x^2 + \frac{8}{3}$$

Now, $\frac{dy}{dx} = 0 \Rightarrow \frac{x^2}{2} - 6x = 0$

$$\Rightarrow \quad x = 0 \text{ or } x = 12 \text{ and } \frac{d^2y}{dx^2} = x - 6$$

$$\Rightarrow \left(\frac{d^2y}{dx^2}\right)_{x=0} = -6 \text{ and } \left(\frac{d^2y}{dx^2}\right)_{x=12} = 6$$

$\Rightarrow$ Ordinate y is maximum at $x = 0$, given by $\lambda = \frac{8}{3} \Rightarrow 3\lambda = 8$

Example 33 *The abscissa of the point on the curve $4y^2 = x^3$, the normal at which cuts intercepts (x intercept and y intercept) in the ratio 3 : 4, is ....*

Sol. (1) $4y^2 = x^3 \Rightarrow$ RHS ≥ 0

$$\Rightarrow \quad x \geq 0 \text{ and } y = \pm\sqrt{\frac{x^3}{4}} = \pm\frac{\sqrt{x^3}}{2}$$

Let $x = t^2 \Rightarrow y = \pm\frac{\sqrt{t^6}}{2} \Rightarrow y = \pm\frac{t^3}{2}$

Equation of normal to curve at point $\left(t^2, \pm\frac{t^3}{2}\right)$ is

$$\left(Y - \left(\pm\frac{t^3}{2}\right)\right) = \left(\mp\frac{4}{3t}\right)(X - t^2)$$

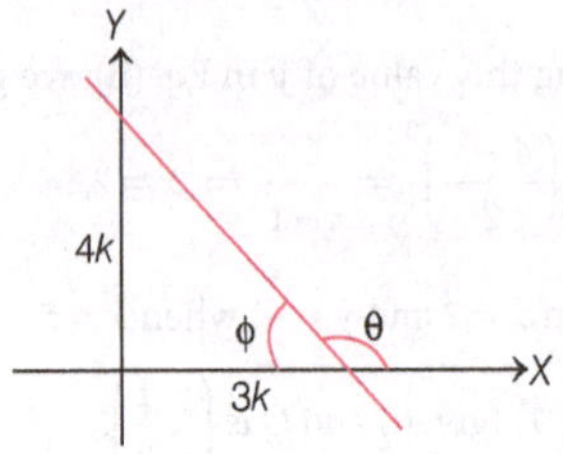

$$\tan\theta = \tan(180° - \phi) = -\tan\phi = -\frac{4}{3}$$

$\Rightarrow \quad \mp\frac{4}{3t} = \frac{-4}{3} \Rightarrow t = \pm 1 \Rightarrow t^2 = 1$

$\therefore$ Abscissa of point is $x = t^2 = 1$

Example 34 *The least positive integer value of α for which Rolle's theorem is applicable to function*

$$f(x) = \begin{cases} x^{(\alpha^2-4\alpha+3)} \cdot \log x & \text{if } x > 0 \\ 0 & \text{if } x = 0 \end{cases} \text{ in [0, 1] is ....}$$

Sol. (4) $f(0) = 0$ and $f(1) = 0$

Thus, $f(0) = f(1)$

Also, $f'(x) = x^{\alpha^2-4\alpha+2} + (\alpha^2 - 4\alpha + 3)\, x^{\alpha^2-4\alpha+2} \log x$, which exists finitely in (0, 1), $\forall\, x \in R$.

Also, $f(x)$ is continuous, $\forall x \in (0, 1)$.

Thus, Rolle's theorem will be applicable to $f(x)$ in [0, 1], if

$$\lim_{x \to 0^+} f(x) = f(0) = 0$$

$$\lim_{x \to 0^+} x^{(\alpha^2-4\alpha+3)} \cdot \log x = 0$$

If $\alpha^2 - 4\alpha + 3 = 0$, then above is false.

If $\alpha^2 - 4\alpha + 3 < 0$, then $\lim_{x \to 0^+} x^{(\alpha^2-4\alpha+3)} \cdot \log x = -\infty \neq 0$

If $\alpha^2 - 4\alpha + 3 > 0$, then

$$\lim_{x \to 0^+} \frac{\log x}{x^{-(\alpha^2-4\alpha+3)}} = \lim_{x \to 0^+} \frac{\frac{1}{x}}{-(\alpha^2 - 4\alpha + 3)\, x^{-(\alpha^2-4\alpha+4)}}$$

$$= \lim_{x \to 0^+} \frac{x^{(\alpha^2-4\alpha+4)}}{-(\alpha^2 - 4\alpha + 3)} = 0$$

$\therefore \quad \alpha^2 - 4\alpha + 3 > 0$

$(\alpha - 1)(\alpha - 3) > 0$

$\alpha \in (-\infty, 1) \cup (3, \infty)$

$\therefore$ Least positive integer value of α is 4.

Example 35 *The volume of a moth ball decreases at a rate proportional to its instantaneous surface area. If the diameter of ball decreases from 3 cm to 1 cm in 4 month, then t is time taken for complete disappear, then t − 1 is, (t is in months)*

Sol. (5) Given, $\frac{dV}{dt} \propto -\pi r^2$

$\Rightarrow \quad \frac{dV}{dt} = -k\pi r^2$

$\Rightarrow \quad \frac{d}{dt}\left(\frac{4}{3}\pi r^3\right) = -k\pi r^2$

$\Rightarrow \quad \frac{4}{3}\pi\left(3r^2\frac{dr}{dt}\right) = -k\pi r^2$

$\Rightarrow \quad 4\frac{dr}{dt} = -k$

$\Rightarrow \quad \frac{dr}{dt} = \frac{-k}{4} \Rightarrow \frac{d}{dt}\left(\frac{D}{2}\right) = \frac{-k}{4}$

$\Rightarrow \quad dD = \frac{-k}{2}dt \Rightarrow D = \frac{-k}{2}t + C$

According to question,

when $t = 0$, then $D = 3$ and when $t = 4$, then $D = 1$

$\Rightarrow 3 = C$ and $1 = -2k + C \Rightarrow k = 1$

$\therefore \quad D = \frac{-t}{2} + 3$

$\therefore$ For $D = 0$, $\frac{t}{2} = 3 \Rightarrow t = 6$

$\therefore \quad t - 1 = 5$

Example 36 *A tangent at a point P_1 on the curve $y = x^3$ meets the curve again at P_2 and the tangent at P_2 meets the curve again at P_3 and so on. If coordinates of P_1 are (2, 8), then sum of digits of the abscissa of point P_5 is ...*

Sol. (5) The parametric equation of curve is (t, t^3).

$\Rightarrow$ Slope tangent $= 3t^2$

$\therefore$ Equation of tangent to curve at $P_1(t)$ is given by

$$(y - t^3) = 3t^2(x - t)$$

It meets curve $y = x^3$, where $x^3 - t^3 = 3t^2(x - t)$.

$\Rightarrow \quad (x - t)(x^2 + tx + t^2) = 3t^2(x - t)$

$\Rightarrow \quad (x - t)(x^2 + tx + t^2 - 3t^2) = 0$

$\Rightarrow \quad (x - t)(x^2 + tx - 2t^2) = 0$

$\Rightarrow \quad (x - t)[(x - t)(x + 2t)] = 0$

$\Rightarrow \quad x = t$ or $x = -2t$

If $P_1 \equiv (t, t^3)$

$\Rightarrow \quad P_2 \equiv (-2t, -2^3t^3), P_3 \equiv ((-2)^2t, (-2)^6t^3)$

$P_4 \equiv ((-2)^3t, (-2)^9t^3)$

and $P_5 \equiv ((-2)^4t, (-2)^{12}t^3) \equiv (16t, 2^{12}t^3)$

Now, if $P_1 \equiv (2, 8) = (t, t^3)$

$\Rightarrow \quad t = 2 \Rightarrow P_5 = (32, 2^{15})$

$\therefore$ Abscissa of $P_5 = 32$

Hence, the sum of digits of the abscissa of point P_5 is $3 + 2 = 5$.

Example 37 *A and B are two tanks such that the capacity of A is 3 times that of B. Both tanks are completely filled and their inlets are closed. Now, water is released from the tanks. The rate of flow of water from each tank is proportional to the water in the tank at that instant. If after 1 hour, the water in tank A is 2 times the water in tank B. If both tanks have same quantity of water after time* $(\log_{2m}(m))$, *then* $\left(\frac{1}{m}\right)$ *is ....*

Sol. (3) Let V_A and V_B be volume of water in tank at an instant t.

Then, $\frac{dV_A}{dt} = -k_1 V_A$

and $\frac{dV_B}{dt} = -k_2 V_B$

$\Rightarrow \ln V_A = -k_1 t + C_1$

and $\ln V_B = -k_2 t + C_2$

Now, initially $t = 0$, $V_A = v_a$ and $V_B = v_b$

$\Rightarrow \ln v_a = C_1$ and $\ln v_b = C_2$

$\Rightarrow \ln\left(\frac{V_A}{v_a}\right) = -k_1 t$

and $\ln\left(\frac{V_B}{v_b}\right) = -k_2 t$

$\Rightarrow V_A = v_a e^{-k_1 t}$ and $V_B = v_b \cdot e^{-k_2 t}$

After 1 hour, $V_A = 2V_B$

$\Rightarrow \frac{V_A}{V_B} = 2$

$\Rightarrow 2 = \frac{v_a}{v_b} \cdot \frac{e^{-k_1}}{e^{-k_2}}$

$\Rightarrow 2 = 3\frac{e^{-k_1}}{e^{-k_2}}$ $\quad [\because v_a = 3v_b]$

$\Rightarrow \frac{2}{3} = e^{(k_2 - k_1)}$ $\quad$ ...(i)

Now, if both tanks have same quantity of water after time t, then $V_A = V_B$

$\Rightarrow v_{a \cdot e^{-k_1 t}} = v_{b \cdot e^{-k_2 t}}$

$\Rightarrow 3(e^{(k_2 - k_1)t}) = 1$

$\Rightarrow 3\left(\frac{2}{3}\right)^t = 1$ $\quad$ [using Eq. (i)]

$\Rightarrow \left(\frac{2}{3}\right)^t = \left(\frac{1}{3}\right)$

$\Rightarrow t = \log_{2/3}\left(\frac{1}{3}\right) = \log_{2m}(m)$ $\quad$ [given]

$\Rightarrow m = \frac{1}{3}$

$\Rightarrow \frac{1}{m} = 3$

Example 38 *From a point P on the curve* $a^4 x + 2b^2 y^2 = 0$, *tangent PQ and PR are drawn to hyperbola* $\frac{x^2}{b^2} - \frac{y^2}{a^2} = 1$. *If QR touches a fixed parabola, then the length of latus rectum of that parabola is ....*

Sol. (8) Given curve is $y^2 = \frac{-a^4}{2b^2}x$, which is a parabola having parametric equation $P\left(-\frac{a^4}{8b^2}t^2, \frac{a^4}{4b^2}t\right)$.

Slope of tangent $= \frac{-a^4/4b^2}{-2a^{4t}/8b^2} = \frac{1}{t}$

The tangent to hyperbola $\frac{x^2}{b^2} - \frac{y^2}{a^2} = 1$ have points of contact Q and R.

QR is the chord of contact of point P.

Equation of QR will be

$$\frac{\frac{-a^4}{8b^2}t^2 x}{b^2} - \frac{\left(\frac{-a^2}{4b^2}t\right)y}{a^2} = 1 \text{ or } \frac{a^2}{4b^2}ty = 1 + \frac{a^4}{8b^4}t^2 x$$

$$\Rightarrow \quad y = \frac{1}{\left(\frac{a^2}{4b^2}t\right)} + \frac{\frac{a^4}{8b^4}t^2 x}{\left(\frac{a^2}{4b^2}t\right)}$$

$$\text{or} \quad y = \frac{1}{\frac{a^2}{4b^2}t} + \frac{a^2 tx}{2b^2}$$

$$\text{or} \quad y = \frac{a^2 t}{2b^2}x + \frac{2}{\frac{a^2}{2b^2}t}$$

On comparing with $y = mx + \frac{a'}{m}$,

Length of latusrectum $= 4a' = 4(2) = 8$

Example 39 *A lamp post is of height 50 m. A ball is dropped from same height and falls under gravity* ($g = 10\ m/s^2$). *If the horizontal distance between the ball and shadow of ball is moving along the ground* $\frac{1}{2}$ *s after the ball is dropped is 20 m and the speed of shadow of ball is decrease with λ m/sec, then* $\sqrt{\frac{\lambda}{50}}$ *is ....*

Sol. (8) Ball is falling under gravity, $g = 10$ m/sec^2

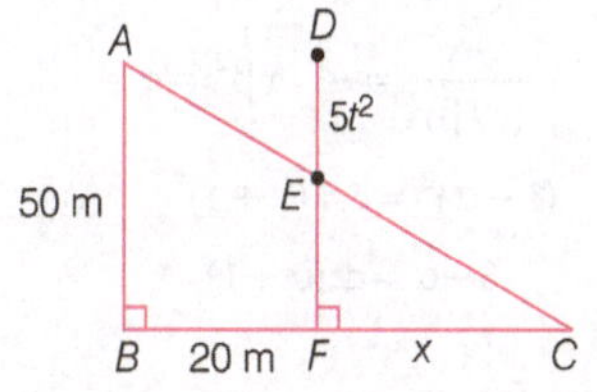

$\therefore \quad s = ut + \frac{1}{2}gt^2, u = 0$

$\Rightarrow \quad s = 5t^2$

is the displacement travelled by ball in t seconds.

$\Rightarrow \quad DE = 5t^2$

$\therefore \quad EF = 50 - 5t^2$

In similar ΔABC and ΔEFC,

$$\frac{AB}{EF} = \frac{BC}{FC}$$

$$\Rightarrow \quad \frac{50}{50-5t^2} = \frac{20+x}{x}$$

$$\Rightarrow \quad 50x = 1000 - 100t^2 + 50x - 5t^2x$$

$$\Rightarrow \quad x = \frac{200}{t^2} - 20$$

$$\Rightarrow \quad \frac{dx}{dt} = -\frac{400}{t^3} \text{ m/sec}$$

$$\Rightarrow \quad \left(\frac{dx}{dt}\right)_{t=\frac{1}{2}s} = -400 \times 8 = -3200 \text{ m/s}$$

Here, negative sign indicates that the image distance from point F is decreasing with time.

Thus, in magnitude, shadow of ball is moving with 3200 m/s.

$\therefore \quad \lambda = 3200$

$$\Rightarrow \quad \sqrt{\frac{\lambda}{50}} = \sqrt{\frac{3200}{50}} = \sqrt{64} = 8$$

Numerical Value Type Questions

Example 40 *If the line joining the points (0, 3)and (5, – 2) is a tangent to the curve $y = \frac{c}{x+1}$, then the value of c^3 is ....*

Sol. (64) The equation of the line is $y - 3 = \frac{3+2}{0-5}(x-0)$,

i.e. $x + y - 3 = 0$

$$\Rightarrow \quad y = \frac{c}{x+1}$$

$$\Rightarrow \quad \frac{dy}{dx} = \frac{-c}{(x+1)^2}$$

Let the line touches the curve at (α, β).

$\therefore \quad \alpha + \beta - 3 = 0$

$\Rightarrow \quad \beta = 3 - \alpha$

$$\Rightarrow \quad \left.\frac{dy}{dx}\right]_{\alpha,\beta} = \frac{-c}{(\alpha+1)^2} = -1 \text{ and } \beta = \frac{c}{\alpha+1}$$

$$\therefore \quad \frac{-c}{(c/\beta)^2} = -1 \text{ or } \beta^2 = c$$

or $\quad (3-\alpha)^2 = c = (\alpha+1)^2$

$\quad 3 - \alpha = \pm(\alpha+1)$

or $\quad 3 - \alpha = \alpha + 1$

$\therefore \quad \alpha = 1$

So, $\quad c = (1+1)^2 = 4$

$\therefore \quad c^3 = (4)^3 = 64$

Example 41 *The radius of a right circular cylinder increases of a constant rate. Its altitude is a linear function of the radius and increases three times as fast as radius. When the radius is 1 cm and the altitude is 6 cm. When the radius is 6 cm, the volume is increasing at the rate of 1 cu cm/sec. When the radius is 36 cm, the volume is increasing at a rate of n cu cm/sec. The value of n is equal to*

Sol. (33) If h and r denotes the height and radius of the cylinder, then $h = ar + b$, where a, b are consant.

Also, $\quad \frac{dh}{dt} = 3\frac{dr}{dt}$ [given]

$\therefore \quad a\frac{dr}{dt} = 3\frac{dr}{dt}$

$\Rightarrow \quad a = 3$

Hence, $h = 3r + b$, when $r = 1, h = 6$

$\Rightarrow \quad 6 = 3 + b$

$\Rightarrow \quad b = 3$

$\therefore \quad h = 3(r+1)$

$$V = \pi r^2 h = 3\pi r^2(r+1) = 3\pi(r^3 + r^2)$$

$$\Rightarrow \quad \frac{dV}{dt} = 3\pi(3r^2 + 2r)\frac{dr}{dt}$$

When $r = 6$, $\frac{dV}{dt} = 1$ cc/sec

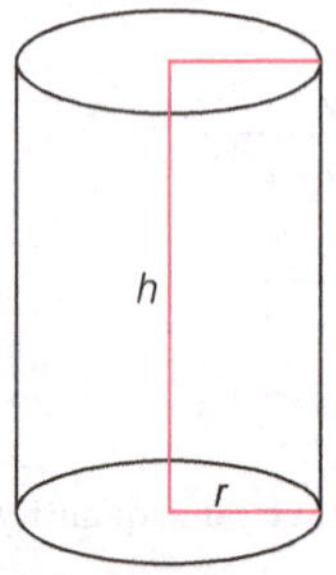

$$\therefore \quad 1 = 3\pi(108 + 12)\frac{dr}{dt}$$

$$\Rightarrow \quad 360\pi\frac{dr}{dt} = 1$$

$$\Rightarrow \quad \frac{dr}{dt} = \frac{1}{360\pi}$$

Again, when $r = 36$, $\frac{dV}{dt} = n$

$$\therefore \quad n = 3\pi(3 \cdot (36)^2 + 2 \cdot 36)\frac{dr}{dt}$$

$$n = 3\pi \cdot 36(110) \cdot \frac{1}{360\pi} = 33$$

Example 42 *Two men A and B start with velocities v at the same time from the junction of the two roads inclined at 45° to each other. If they travel by different roads if the rate at which they are being separated is $\sqrt{\alpha-\sqrt{\alpha}}v$, then find α^4.*

Decoding the Question

In ΔABC, cosine rule $\cos A=\dfrac{b^2+c^2-a^2}{2bc}$.

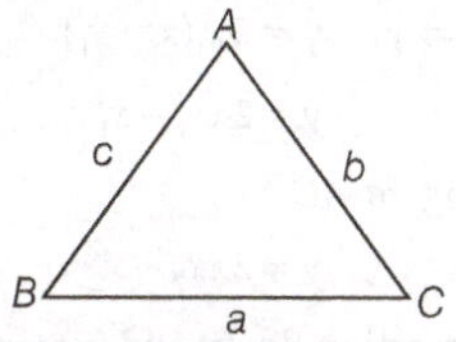

Sol. (16) Let L and M be the positions of men A and B at any time t after start.

Let $OL=x$ and $LM=y$.

Then, $OM=x$ and so $\dfrac{dx}{dt}=v$ [given]

From ΔLOM, $\cos 45°=\dfrac{OL^2+OM^2-LM^2}{2\cdot OL\cdot OM}$

or $$\frac{1}{\sqrt{2}}=\frac{x^2+x^2-y^2}{2\cdot x\cdot x}=\frac{2x^2-y^2}{2x^2}$$

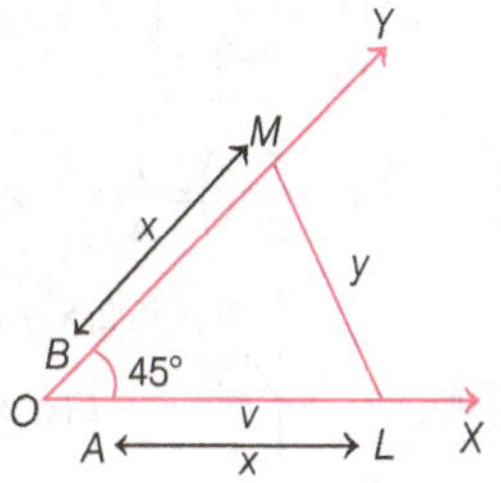

$$\sqrt{2}x^2=2x^2-y^2 \text{ or } (2-\sqrt{2})x^2=y^2$$

$$\Rightarrow \quad y=\sqrt{2-\sqrt{2}}\,x$$

On differentiating w.r.t. x, we get $\dfrac{dy}{dx}=\sqrt{2-\sqrt{2}}$

Now, $\dfrac{dy}{dt}=\dfrac{dy}{dx}\cdot\dfrac{dx}{dt}=(\sqrt{2-\sqrt{2}})v$

$\therefore$ They are being separated from each other at the rate $\sqrt{2-\sqrt{2}}v$.

$$\Rightarrow \quad \alpha=2$$

$$\therefore \quad \alpha^4=16$$

Example 43 *A balloon is in the form of right circular cylinder of radius 1.5 m and length 4 m and is surrounded by hemispherical ends. If the radius is increased by 0.01 m and the length by 0.05 m. The percentage change in the volume of the balloon is P%, where [·] denotes greatest integer function, then $\dfrac{[P]}{100}$ is ....*

Sol. (0.02) Let r be the radius and h be the height of the cylinder

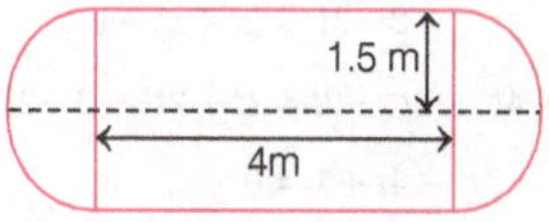

Volume, $V=\pi r^2h+\dfrac{2}{3}\pi r^3+\dfrac{2}{3}\pi r^3=\pi r^2h+\dfrac{4}{3}\pi r^3$

$$\delta V=(\pi r^2)\delta h+h(2\pi r\delta r)+\frac{4}{3}\pi(3r^2)\delta r$$

$$\therefore \quad \frac{\delta V}{V}=\frac{\pi r(r\delta h+2h\delta r+4r\delta r)}{\pi r\left(rh+\frac{4}{3}r^2\right)}=\frac{r\delta h+2h\delta r+4r\delta r}{rh+\frac{4}{3}r^2}$$

$$=\frac{1.5\times 0.05+2\times 4\times 0.01+4\times 1.5\times 0.01}{1.5\times 4+\frac{4}{3}(1.5)^2}=\frac{0.215}{9}$$

$$\therefore \quad \frac{\delta V}{V}\times 100=\frac{0.215}{9}\times 100=\frac{21.5}{9}=2.389\%$$

$$\Rightarrow \quad P=2.389 \Rightarrow \frac{[P]}{100}=\frac{2}{100}=0.02$$

Example 44 *If all the lines that pass through the point (1, 1) and are tangent to the curve represented parametrically as $x=2t-t^2$ and $y=t+t^2$ are $\alpha_i x+\beta_i y+\gamma=0$, where $\gamma>0$, then $10\left[\sum_{i=1}^{4}\alpha_i+\beta_i\right]^2$ is ....*

Sol. (20) $\qquad x=2t-t^2 \qquad$ ...(i)

$$y=t+t^2 \qquad \text{...(ii)}$$

$$\frac{dx}{dt}=2-2t$$

$$\Rightarrow \quad \frac{dy}{dt}=1+2t$$

$$\Rightarrow \quad \frac{dy}{dx}=\frac{dy/dt}{dx/dt}=\frac{1+2t}{2-2t} \qquad \text{...(iii)}$$

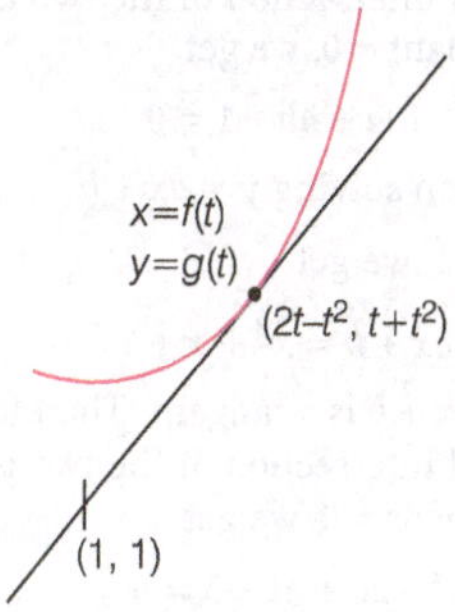

Slope of the line passing through the points (1, 1) and $(2t-t^2, t+t^2)$ is given by $m=\dfrac{t+t^2-1}{2t-t^2-1}$ ...(iv)

On equating Eqs. (iii) and (iv), we get

$$\frac{dy}{dx}=\frac{t+t^2-1}{2t-t^2-1}$$

$$\Rightarrow \quad \frac{1+2t}{2-2t} = \frac{t+t^2-1}{2t-t^2-1}$$

$$\Rightarrow \quad 2t-t^2-1+4t^2-2t^3-2t = 2t+2t^2-2-2t^2-2t^3+2t$$

$$\Rightarrow \quad 3t^2-4t+1=0$$

$$\Rightarrow \quad 3t^2-3t-t+1=0$$

$$\Rightarrow \quad (3t-1)(t-1)=0$$

$$\Rightarrow \quad t=1 \text{ or } t=1/3$$

Now, when $t=1$, point $(2t-t^2, t+t^2)$ becomes (1, 1).

When $t=1$, then point will be (1, 2), when $t=1/3$, then point will be $\left(\frac{5}{9}, \frac{4}{9}\right)$

and $\frac{dy}{dx}=\frac{3}{0}$, for $t=1$ and $\frac{dy}{dx}=\frac{5}{4}$, for $t=1/3$

∴ Equations of tangents will be $x=1$

and $y-\frac{4}{9}=\frac{5}{4}\left(x-\frac{5}{9}\right)$, $x=1$; $5x-4y-1=0$

$$L_1: -x+1=0$$

$$L_2: -5x+4y+1=0$$

$$\therefore \quad 10\left[\sum_{i=1}^{4} \alpha_i+\beta_i\right]^2 = 10[(1+0)^2+(-5+4)]$$

$$= 10(2) = 20$$

Example 45 *If the gradient of the common tangent to the two curves $y=x^2-5x+6$ and $y=x^2+x+1$ is α, then $|96\alpha|$ is equal to ....*

Sol. (32) Let us suppose that $y=ax+b$ is the common tangent to both the curves.

Simultaneously, on solving $y=ax+b$ and $y=x^2-5x+6$, we get

$$ax+b=x^2-5x+6$$

Now, since $y=ax+b$ is a tangent. Therefore, there will be only one point of intersection of the two graphs and hence putting discriminant = 0, we get

$$a^2+10a+4b+1=0 \quad \text{...(i)}$$

Simultaneously, on solving $y=ax+b$

and $y=x^2+x+1$, we get

$$ax+b=x^2+x+1$$

Now, since $y=ax+b$ is a tangent. Therefore, there will be only one point of intersection of the two graphs and hence putting discriminant = 0, we get

$$a^2-2a+4b-3=0 \quad \text{...(ii)}$$

On solving the Eqs. (i) and (ii), we get

$$a=-\frac{1}{3} \text{ and } b=\frac{5}{9}$$

⇒ $3x+9y=5$ is the equation of the common tangent.

Then, gradient is $-\frac{1}{3}=\alpha$

∴ $|96\alpha|=32$

Example 46 *A and B are points of the parabola $y=x^2$. The tangents at A and B meet at C. The median of the ΔABC from C has length m units. If the area of the triangle in terms of m is $\frac{m^\alpha}{2^\beta}$, then $6\alpha+8\beta$ is ....*

Sol. (13) $y=x^2 \Rightarrow \frac{dy}{dx}=2x$

Tangent $BC \Rightarrow y-x_1^2=2x_1(x-x_1)$

$$y=2xx_1-x_1^2 \quad \text{...(i)}$$

Similarly, tangent AC

$$y=2xx_2-x_2^2 \quad \text{...(ii)}$$

Point of intersection Eq. (i) and (ii) is C.

$$2xx_1-x_1^2=2xx_2-x_2^2$$

$$x=\frac{x_1+x_2}{2} \text{ and } y=x_1x_2$$

$$\Delta=\frac{1}{2}\begin{vmatrix} x_1 & x_1^2 & 1 \\ x_2 & x_2^2 & 1 \\ \frac{x_1+x_2}{2} & x_1x_2 & 1 \end{vmatrix} = \frac{1}{2}\begin{vmatrix} x_1 & x_1^2 & 1 \\ x_2-x_1 & x_2^2-x_1^2 & 0 \\ \frac{x_2-x_1}{2} & x_1x_2-x_1^2 & 0 \end{vmatrix}$$

$$=-(x_2-x_1)(x_2-x_1)\begin{vmatrix} 1 & x_2-x_1 \\ \frac{1}{2} & x_1 \end{vmatrix}$$

$$=\frac{1}{2}(x_2-x_1)^2\left(x_1-\frac{1}{2}x_2-\frac{1}{2}x_1\right)=\frac{1}{4}(x_2-x_1)^3$$

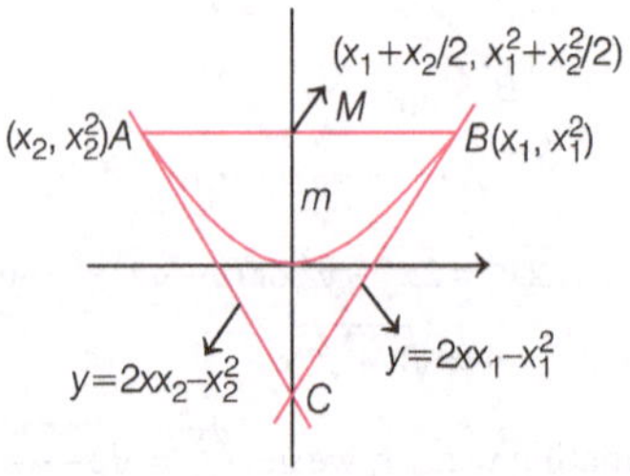

Now, $CM=m$

$$\frac{x_1^2+x_2^2}{2}-x_1x_2=m$$

$$\Rightarrow \quad \frac{(x_1-x_2)^2}{2}=m$$

$$\Rightarrow \quad (x_1-x_2)^2=2m$$

$$=\frac{1}{4}(2m)^{3/2}$$

$$=\frac{m^{3/2}}{\sqrt{2}}=\frac{m^{3/2}}{2^{1/2}}$$

$$\Rightarrow \quad \alpha=\frac{3}{2}, \beta=\frac{1}{2}$$

$$\Rightarrow \quad 6\alpha+8\beta=9+4=13$$

Matching Type Questions

Example 47 *Match the following columns.*

	Column I		Column II
(A)	Circular plate is expanded by heat from radius 5 cm to 5.06 cm. The approximate increase in area is	(p)	4
(B)	Sides of a cube increasing by 1%, then the percentage increase in volume is	(q)	$0.6\ \pi$
(C)	If the rate of decrease of $\frac{x^2}{2}-2x+5$ is twice the rate of decrease of x, then x is equal to	(r)	3
(D)	Rate of increase in area of equilateral triangle of side 15 cm, when each side is increasing at the rate of 0.1 cm/s, is	(s)	$\frac{3\sqrt{3}}{4}$

Sol. (A) → q; (B) → r; (C) → p; (D) → s

(A) Given, $r = 5$ cm, $\delta r = 0.06$

$\therefore \quad A = \pi r^2$

$\Rightarrow \quad \delta A = 2\pi r \delta r = 10\pi \times 0.06 = 0.6\pi$

(B) Let $V = x^3 \Rightarrow \delta V = 3x^2 \delta x$

$\therefore \quad \frac{\delta V}{V} \times 100 = 3\frac{\delta x}{x} \times 100 = 3 \times 1 = 3$

(C) Since, $(x-2)\frac{dx}{dt} = 2\frac{dx}{dt}$

$\Rightarrow \quad x = 4$

(D) $A = \frac{\sqrt{3}}{4}x^2$

$\Rightarrow \frac{dA}{dt} = \frac{\sqrt{3}}{2}x \times \frac{dx}{dt} = \frac{\sqrt{3}}{2}\cdot 15 \cdot \frac{1}{10} = \frac{3\sqrt{3}}{4}\ \text{cm}^2/\text{s}$

Example 48 Match the following columns.

	Column I		Column II
(A)	If $f(x)$ is a quadratic expression in x and $6\int_0^1 f(x)\,dx = kf(1) + f(0) + 4f(1/2)$, then k is	(p)	1
(B)	If the sum of the squares of the intercepts on the axes cut off by the tangents to the curve $x^{1/3} + y^{1/3} = a^{1/3}, (a > 0)$ at $\left(\frac{a}{8}, \frac{a}{8}\right)$ is 2, then a is	(q)	4
(C)	The distance of the point on $y = x^4 + 3x^2 + 2x$, which is nearest to the line $y = 2x - 1$ is r, then $\sqrt{5}\ r$ is	(r)	3
(D)	If $f(x) = -2\ \lvert\sin x\rvert + ae^{\lvert x\rvert} + 5\lvert\tan x\rvert^3$ is differentiable at $x = 0$, then a is	(s)	2

Sol. (A) → p; (B) → q; (C) → p; (D) → s

(A) $6\int_0^1 (ax^2 + bx + c)dx = 2a + 3b + 6c$

$$= k(a+b+c) + c + 4\left(\frac{a}{4} + \frac{b}{2} + c\right)$$

$\therefore \quad k = 1$

(B) $\frac{1}{3}x^{2/3} + \frac{1}{3}y^{2/3}\frac{dy}{dx} = 0$

$\frac{dy}{dx} = -1$ at $x = \frac{a}{8}, y = \frac{a}{8}$

Equation of tangent is $y + x = \frac{a}{4}$

$\Rightarrow \quad \frac{x}{a/4} + \frac{y}{a/4} = 1$

$\therefore \quad \frac{a^2}{16} + \frac{a^2}{16} = 2$

$\Rightarrow \quad a^2 = 16 \Rightarrow a = 4 \quad [\because a > 0]$

(C) $\frac{dy}{dx} = 4x^3 + 6x + 2 = 2$

$\Rightarrow \quad 2x^3 + 3x = 0$

$\Rightarrow \quad x = 0,\ y = 0$

∴Point on the curve at the least distance from the line $y = 2x - 1$ is (0, 0).

⇒Least distance, $r = \frac{1}{\sqrt{5}} \Rightarrow \sqrt{5}r = 1$

(D) $f'(0^+) = f'(0^-)$

$\Rightarrow \quad -2 + a = 2 - a$

$\Rightarrow \quad a = 2$

Example 49 *Let $x = a\cos t + at\sin t$ and $y = a\sin t - at\cos t$. Match the column for $t = \pi/4$.*

	Column I		Column II
(A)	Length of sub-tangent	(p)	$\frac{a\pi}{2}$
(B)	Length of normal	(q)	$\frac{a}{\sqrt{2}}\left(1 - \frac{\pi}{4}\right)$
(C)	Length of intercepts by tangent between coordinate axes.	(r)	$\frac{a\pi}{4}$
(D)	Perpendicular distance of tangent from origin.	(s)	$a\left(1 - \frac{\pi}{4}\right)$

Sol. (A) → q; (B) → s; (C) → p; (D) → r

$x = a\cos t + at\sin t,\ y = a\sin t - at\cos t$

$\Rightarrow \quad \frac{dy}{dx} = \frac{a\cos t + at\sin t - a\cos t}{-a\sin t + at\cos t + a\sin t}$

$\Rightarrow \quad \frac{dy}{dx} = \tan t$

(A) Length of sub tangent $= \frac{y}{y'} = (a\sin t - at\cos t)\cdot\cot t$

$= a\cos t - at\cos t\cot t$

$\therefore$ At $t = \frac{\pi}{4}$,

Length of sub tangent $= \frac{a}{\sqrt{2}} - a\left(\frac{\pi}{4}\right)\cdot\frac{1}{\sqrt{2}}(1) = \frac{a}{\sqrt{2}}\left(1-\frac{\pi}{4}\right)$

(B) Length of normal $= y\sqrt{1+\left(\frac{dy}{dx}\right)^2} = \left(\frac{a}{\sqrt{2}} - \frac{a\pi}{4\sqrt{2}}\right)\sqrt{1+(1)^2}$

$= \left(\frac{a}{\sqrt{2}} - \frac{a\pi}{4\sqrt{2}}\right)(\sqrt{2}) = a\left(1-\frac{\pi}{4}\right)$

(C) Equation of tangnet at $t = \frac{\pi}{4}$ will be

$Y - \left(\frac{a}{\sqrt{2}} - \frac{a\pi}{4\sqrt{2}}\right) = 1\left(X - \left(\frac{a}{\sqrt{2}} + \frac{a\pi}{4\sqrt{2}}\right)\right)$ on X-axis, $Y = 0$

$\Rightarrow \quad X = \frac{a\pi}{2\sqrt{2}}$

On Y-axis, $\quad X = 0$

$\Rightarrow \quad Y = \frac{-a\pi}{2\sqrt{2}}$

$\Rightarrow$ Length of intersect of tangent between the axis $= \frac{a\pi}{2}$

(D) Perpendicular distance of tangent from origin

$$d = \frac{\left|0 - 0 - \frac{a\pi}{2\sqrt{2}}\right|}{\sqrt{2}} = \frac{a\pi}{4}$$

Example 50 Match the following columns.

	Column I		Column II
(A)	The angle of intersection of $y^2 = 4x$ and $x^2 = 4y$ is 90° and $\tan^{-1}\left(\frac{m}{n}\right)$, then $\|m+n\|$ is equal to (m and n are coprime)	(p)	0
(B)	The area of triangle formed by normal at the point (1, 0) on the curve $x = e^{\sin y}$ with axes is	(q)	1/2
(C)	The angle between curve $x^2y = 1$ and $y = e^{2(1-x)}$	(r)	7
(D)	The length of sub-tangent at any point on the curve $y = be^{x/3}$ is equal to	(s)	3

Sol. (A) $\to$ r; (B) $\to$ q; (C) $\to$ p; (D) $\to$ s

(A) Let the point of intersection be (x_0, y_0).

Now, $x^2 = 4y \Rightarrow \frac{dy}{dx} = \frac{x}{2}$

$\therefore \quad m_1 = \left(\frac{dy}{dx}\right)_{(x_0, y_0)} = \frac{x_0}{2}$

and for $y^2 = 4x, \quad \frac{dy}{dx} = \frac{2}{y}$

$\therefore \quad m_2 = \left(\frac{dy}{dx}\right)_{(x_0, y_0)} = \frac{2}{y_0}$

$\therefore \quad \theta = \tan^{-1}\left|\frac{\frac{x_0}{2} - \frac{2}{y_0}}{1 + \frac{x_0}{2}\cdot\frac{2}{y_0}}\right| = \tan^{-1}\left|\frac{x_0y_0 - 4}{2(x_0 + y_0)}\right|$

Clearly, $\theta = 90°$ at $x_0 + y_0 = 0$.

At the point of intersection, $y_0 = \frac{x_0^2}{4}$ and $y_0^2 = 4x_0$

$\Rightarrow \quad \frac{x_0^4}{16} = 4x_0$

$\Rightarrow \quad x_0 = 0$ or $x_0 = 4, y_0 = 4$

$\Rightarrow \quad \theta = \tan^{-1}\left|\frac{6}{8}\right| = \tan^{-1}\left|\frac{3}{4}\right| \Rightarrow |m+n| = 7$

(B) Given curve is $x = e^{\sin y}$

$\Rightarrow \quad \ln x = \sin y$

$\Rightarrow \quad \frac{1}{x} = (\cos y)\frac{dy}{dx} \Rightarrow \frac{dy}{dx} = \frac{1}{x}\sec y$

$\Rightarrow \quad \left(\frac{dy}{dx}\right)_{(1,0)} = 1$

$\therefore$ Equation of normal at (1, 0) is

$(y - 0) = -1(x - 1) \Rightarrow x + y = 1$

Area of triangle $= \frac{1}{2}(1)(1) = \frac{1}{2}$ sq unit

(C) Given curve is $x^2y = 1$.

$\Rightarrow \quad x^2y' + y(2x) = 0$

$\Rightarrow \quad y' = \frac{-2y}{x}$

$\Rightarrow \quad m_1 = \frac{-2y_0}{x_0}$ ...(i)

Also, second curve is $y = e^{2(1-x)}$

$\Rightarrow \quad y' = -2e^{2(1-x)}$

$\Rightarrow \quad m_2 = -2e^{2(1-x_0)}$ ...(ii)

$\therefore \quad \theta = \tan^{-1}\left|\frac{\frac{-2y_0}{x_0} + 2e^{2(1-x_0)}}{1 + \frac{4y_0e^{2(1-x_0)}}{x_0}}\right| = \tan^{-1}\left|\frac{2x_0e^{2(1-x_0)} - 2y_0}{x_0 + 4y_0e^{2(1-x_0)}}\right|$

At the point of intersection,

$x_0^2y_0 = 1$ and $y_0 = e^{2(1-x_0)}$

$\Rightarrow \quad x_0 = y_0 = 1$

$\therefore \quad \theta = \tan^{-1}\left|\frac{2x_0y_0 - 2y_0}{x_0 + 4y_0^2}\right| = 0$

(D) Given curve is $y = be^{x/3}$

$\Rightarrow \quad y' = \frac{b}{3}e^{x/3}$

$\Rightarrow \quad \frac{y}{y'} = \frac{y}{\frac{b}{3}e^{x/3}} = \frac{3be^{x/3}}{be^{x/3}} = 3$

EXERCISE 1

JEE Main Pattern

Single Option Correct Type Questions

1. Let
$$f(x)=\begin{cases}\dfrac{x^3-2x^2-5x+6}{x-1}, & \text{if } x\neq 1 \text{ and } x\in[-2,3]\\ -6, & \text{if } x=1\end{cases}.$$
Then, value of c in the Rolle's theorem for the function $f(x)$ on $[-2, 3]$ is
(a) 1 (b) 2 (c) $-\frac{1}{2}$ (d) $\frac{1}{2}$

2. If $f(x)$ is a polynomial of degree 5 with real coefficients such that $f(|x|)=0$ has 8 real roots, then $f(x)=0$ has
(a) 4 real roots (b) 5 real roots
(c) 3 real roots (d) nothing can be said

3. The normal to the curve $x^2+2xy-3y^2=0$, at (1, 1)
(a) meets the curve again in the third quadrant
(b) meets the curve again in the fourth quadrant
(c) does not meet the curve again
(d) meets the curve again in the second quadrant

4. If a variable tangent to the curve $x^2y=c^3$ makes intercepts a, b on X and Y-axes respectively, then the value of a^2b is
(a) $27c^3$ (b) $\frac{4}{27}c^3$ (c) $\frac{27}{4}c^3$ (d) $\frac{4}{9}c^3$

5. If the normal of $y=f(x)$ at (0, 0) is given by $y-x=0$, then $\lim\limits_{x\to 0}\dfrac{x^2}{f(x^2)-20f(9x^2)+2f(99x^2)}$ is equal to
(a) $\frac{1}{19}$ (b) $\frac{-1}{19}$
(c) $\frac{1}{2}$ (d) non-existent

6. Let P be the point on the curve $4x^2+\alpha^2y^2=4\alpha^2$, $0<\alpha^2<8$ whose distance from $Q(0,-2)$ is greatest. If R is the reflection of P in the X-axis, then find the least distance of R from the line $3x-4y+7=0$ is
(a) 1 (b) 2 (c) 3 (d) 4

7. Let $f:[0,\infty)\to R$ be a continuous, strictly increasing function such that $f^3(x)=\int_0^x tf^2(t)\,dt$. If a normal is drawn to the curve $y=f(x)$ with gradient $\frac{-1}{2}$, then the intercept made by it on the Y-axis is
(a) 5 (b) 7 (c) 9 (d) 11

8. In which one of the following intervals Rolle's theorem hold(s) good for $y=x^2\sin\frac{1}{x}+x^3\cos\frac{1}{2x}$?
(a) $\left[\frac{1}{\pi},\frac{2}{\pi}\right]$ (b) $\left[\frac{1}{3\pi},\frac{1}{\pi}\right]$ (c) $\left[\frac{1}{2\pi},\frac{1}{\pi}\right]$ (d) $\left[\frac{1}{\pi},\frac{3}{\pi}\right]$

9. The length of the normal to the curve at (x, y) $y=a\left(\dfrac{e^{x/a}+e^{-x/a}}{2}\right)$ at any point varies as
(a) x (b) x^2 (c) y (d) y^2

10. The equation $e^{x-1}+x-2=0$ as
(a) one real root (b) two real roots
(c) three real roots (d) four real roots

11. The normal to the curve $x=a(\cos\theta+\theta\sin\theta)$, $y=a(\sin\theta-\theta\cos\theta)$ at any point θ is such that
(a) it makes a constant angle with the X-axis
(b) it passes through the origin
(c) it is at a constant distance from the origin
(d) None of the above

12. Tangent to the curve $y=x^2+6$ at a piont $P(1, 7)$ touches the curve $x^2+y^2+16x+12y+c=0$ at a point Q. Then, the coordinates of Q are
(a) $(-9,-13)$ (b) $(-10,-15)$
(c) $(-6,-7)$ (d) $(6,-7)$

13. The acute angles between the curves $y=2x^2-x$ and $y^2=x$ at (0, 0) and (1, 1) are α and β respectively, then
(a) $\alpha-\beta=0$ (b) $\alpha+\beta=0$
(c) $\alpha>\beta$ (d) $\alpha<\beta$

14. The slope of the tangent to the curve $y=\int_x^{x^2}(\cos^{-1}t^2)\,dt$ at $x=\frac{1}{\sqrt{2}}$ is equal to
(a) $\cos^{-1}\left(\frac{1}{4}\right)-\frac{\pi}{3}$ (b) $\cos^{-1}\left(\frac{1}{4}\right)+\frac{\pi}{3}$
(c) $\sqrt{2}\cos^{-1}\left(\frac{1}{4}\right)-\frac{\pi}{3}$ (d) $\sqrt{2}\cos^{-1}\left(\frac{1}{4}\right)+\frac{\pi}{3}$

15. The tangent at any point on the curve $xy=4$ makes intercepts on the coordinate axes as a and b. Then, the value of ab is
(a) 8 (b) 16
(c) 32 (d) 64

16. If $y = f(x)$ satisfies the conditions of Rolle's theorem in $[2, 6]$, then $\int_2^6 f'(x)\,dx$ is equal to

(a) 2 (b) 0 (c) 4 (d) 6

17. A differentiable function $f(x)$ satisfies $f(0) = 0$ and $f(1) = \sin 1$, then (where f' represents derivative of f)

(a) $f'(c) = \cos c, \forall c \in [0, 1]$
(b) $f'(c) = \cos c$, for some $c \in [0, 1]$
(c) $f'(c) = -\cos c, \forall c \in [0, 1]$
(d) $f'(c) = 2\cos c, \forall c \in [0, 1]$

18. Two persons start from the junction of two perpendicular roads with velocities 3 m/sec and 4 m/sec. The rate at which the two persons separate is

(a) 5 m/sec (b) 25 m/sec (c) 4 m/sec (d) 3 m/sec

19. The volume of a cube is increasing at the rate of 18 cm^3 per second. When the edge of the cube is 12 cm, then the rate in cm^2/s at which the surface area of the cube increases, is

(a) 3 (b) 0
(c) 2 (d) None of these

20. The number of tangents with positive slope that can be drawn from the origin to the curve $y = \sin x$ is

(a) 0 (b) 2
(c) 4 (d) infinitely many solutions

21. A function $y = f(x)$ has a second order derivative $f''(x) = 6(x-1)$. If its graph passes through the point (2, 1) and at that point tangent to the graph is $y = 3x - 5$, then the value of $f(0)$ is

(a) 1 (b) −1
(c) 2 (d) 0

22. At any point on the curve $2x^2y^2 - x^4 = c$, the mean proportional between the abscissa and the difference between the abscissa and the sub-normal drawn to the curve at the same point is equal to

(a) ordinate (b) radius vector
(c) x-intercept of tangent (d) sub-tangent

23. If the length of sub-normal is equal to the length of sub-tangent at any point (3, 4) on the curve $y = f(x)$ and the tangent at (3, 4) to $y = f(x)$ meets the coordinate axes at A and B, then the maximum area of the ΔOAB, where O is origin, is

(a) $\frac{45}{2}$ (b) $\frac{49}{2}$ (c) $\frac{25}{2}$ (d) $\frac{81}{2}$

24. If $f(x) = x^3 + 7x - 1$, then $f(x)$ has a zero between $x = 0$ and $x = 1$. The theorem that best describes this is

(a) mean value theorem
(b) maximum-minimum value theorem
(c) intermediate value theorem
(d) None of the above

25. Let $f(x)$ and $g(x)$ be differentiable for $0 \le x \le 1$ such that $f(0) = 0$, $g(0) = 0$, $f(1) = 6$. Let there exists a real number c in (0, 1) such that $f'(c) = 2g'(c)$, then the value of $g(1)$ must be

(a) 1 (b) 3 (c) −2 (d) −1

26. Let $f(x)$ be a twice differentiable function for all real values of x and satisfies $f(1) = 1$, $f(2) = 4$, $f(3) = 9$. Then, which of the following is definitely true?

(a) $f''(x) = 2, \forall\, x \in (1, 3)$
(b) $f''(x) = f'(x) = 5$, for some $x \in (2, 3)$
(c) $f''(x) = 3, \forall\, x \in (2, 3)$
(d) $f''(x) = 2$, for some $x \in (1, 3)$

27. A lamp of negligible height is placed on the ground l_1 m away from a wall. A man l_2 m tall is walking at a speed of $\frac{l_1}{10}$ m/s from the lamp to the nearest point on the wall. When he is midway between the lamp and the wall,the rate of change in the length of this shadow on the wall is

(a) $-\frac{5l_2}{2}$ m/s (b) $-\frac{2l_2}{5}$ m/s
(c) $-\frac{l_2}{2}$ m/s (d) $-\frac{l_2}{5}$ m/s

28. The radius of a right circular cylinder increases at the rate of 0.1 cm/min and the height decreases at the rate of 0.2 cm/min. The rate of change of the volume of the cylinder in cm^3/min, when the radius is 2 cm and the height is 3 cm, is

(a) $-2p$ (b) $-\frac{8\pi}{5}$ (c) $-\frac{3\pi}{5}$ (d) $\frac{2\pi}{5}$

29. A cube of ice melts without changing its shape at the uniform rate of 4 cm^3/min. The rate of change of the surface area of the cube in cm^2/min, when the volume of the cube is 125cm^3, is

(a) −4 (b) $-\frac{16}{5}$ (c) $-\frac{16}{6}$ (d) $-\frac{8}{15}$

Numerical Value Type Questions

30. Let $x^3 - 2kx^2 - 4kx + k^2 = 0$. If one root is less than 1 and the other is in (1, 4) and the third root is greater than 4 such that $k \in (m + \sqrt{n}, n(m + \sqrt{n}))$, then the value of $2(m + n - 1)^3 + 17$ is ……..

31. The sum of integral value of a for which the equation $x^3 - 3x + a = 0$ would have two distinct roots in $(-1, 1)$ is ……..

32. The value of k such that Rolle's theorem is applicable to the function $f(x) = x^3 - 2x^2 - 4x + 7$ in the interval $[0, k]$ is ……..

33. If the tangent at any point $P(4m^2, 8m^3)$ of $x^3 - y^2 = 0$ is a normal also the curve $x^3 - y^2 = 0$, then the value of $(9m^2 + 2)$ is ....

34. The sum of the intercepts made on the axes of coordinates by any tangent to the curve $\sqrt{x} + \sqrt{y} = 2$ is ....

35. If m is the length of the sub-normal to the curve $y^2 = x^3$ at the point (4, 8), then the value of $(\sqrt{m+1})^3$ is ....

36. The curve $(x+y) - \ln(x+y) = 2x + 5$ has a vertical tangent at the point (α, β), then the value of $(|\alpha + \beta| + 4)^{-1}$ is ....

37. If $x + y = a$ be a tangent to the ellipse $\frac{x^2}{9} + \frac{y^2}{16} = 1$, then the value of $(|a| + 1)^3$ is ....

38. If m is the number of points on the curve $xy = 2$, where the tangent makes an acute angle with the X-axis, then the value of $(m+4)^2$ is ....

39. If the coordinates of the point $y^2 = 8x$ which is nearest to the circle $x^2 + (y+6)^2 = 1$ is (α, β), then the value of $(|\alpha + \beta| + 3)$ is ....

40. If m is the slope of the common tangents $y = x^2 - x + 1$ and $y = x^2 - 3x + 1$, then the value of $(|m| + 3)$ is ....

Previous Year Questions

41. Let $g: R \to R$ be a non-constant twice differentiable such that $g'\left(\frac{1}{2}\right) = g'\left(\frac{3}{2}\right)$. If a real values function f is defined as $f(x) = \frac{1}{2}|g(x) + g(2-x)|$, then

[Single Correct Type, 2024 Main]

(a) $f''(x) = 0$ for atleast two x in (0, 2)
(b) $f''(x) = 0$ for exactly one x in (0, 1)
(c) $f''(x) = 0$ for no x in (0, 1)
(d) $f'\left(\frac{3}{2}\right) + f'\left(\frac{1}{2}\right) = 1$

42. If the tangent at a point P on the parabola $y^2 = 3x$ is parallel to the line $x + 2y = 1$ and the tangents at the points Q and R on the ellipse $(x^2/4) + (y^2/1) = 1$ are perpendicular to the line $x - y = 2$, then the area of the ΔPQR is **[Single Correct Type, 2023 Main]**

(a) $5\sqrt{3}$
(b) $\frac{3}{2}\sqrt{5}$
(c) $\frac{9}{\sqrt{5}}$
(d) $3\sqrt{5}$

43. Let the quadratic curve passing through the point (– 1, 0) and touching the line $y = x$ at (1, 1) be $y = f(x)$. Then, the x-intercept of the normal to the curve at the point $(\alpha, \alpha + 1)$ in the first quadrant is .... **[Numerical Value Type, 2023 Main]**

44. Let a curve $y = f(x)$, $x \in (0, \infty)$ pass through the points $P\left(1, \frac{3}{2}\right)$ and $Q\left(a, \frac{1}{2}\right)$. If the tangent at any point $R(b, f(b))$ to the given curve cuts the Y-axis at the point $S(0, c)$ such that $bc = 3$, then $(PQ)^2$ is equal to ....

[Numerical Value Type, 2023 Main]

45. Let S be the set of all the natural number, for which the line $\frac{x}{a} + \frac{y}{b} = 2$ is a tangent to the curve $\left(\frac{x}{a}\right)^n + \left(\frac{y}{b}\right)^n = 2$ at the point (a, b), $ab \neq 0$. Then,

[Single Correct Type, 2022 Main]

(a) $S = \phi$
(b) $n(S) = 1$
(c) $S = \{2k : k \in N\}$
(d) $S = N$

46. If the line $y = 4 + kx$, $k > 0$, is the tangent to the parabola $y = x - x^2$ at the point P and V is the vertex of the parabola, then the slope of the line through P and V is

[Single Correct Type, 2022 Main]

(a) $\frac{3}{2}$
(b) $\frac{26}{9}$
(c) $\frac{5}{2}$
(d) $\frac{23}{6}$

47. If the angle made by the tangent at the point (x_0, y_0) on the curve $x = 12(t + \sin t \cos t)$, $y = 12(1 + \sin t)^2$, $0 < t < \frac{\pi}{2}$, with the positive X-axis is $\frac{\pi}{3}$, then y_0 is equal to **[Single Correct Type, 2022 Main]**

(a) $6(3 + 2\sqrt{2})$
(b) $3(7 + 4\sqrt{3})$
(c) 27
(d) 48

48. Water is being filled at the rate of 1 cm^3/s in a right circular conical vessel (vertex downwards) of height 35 cm and diameter 14 cm. When the height of the water level is 10 cm, the rate (in cm^2/ s) at which the wet conical surface area of the vessel increases is

[Single Correct Type, 2022 Main]

(a) 5
(b) $\frac{\sqrt{21}}{5}$
(c) $\frac{\sqrt{26}}{5}$
(d) $\frac{\sqrt{26}}{10}$

49. The surface area of a balloon of spherical shape being inflated, increases at a constant rate. If initially, the radius of balloon is 3 units and after 5 sec, it becomes 7 units, then its radius after 9 sec is

[Single Correct Type, 2022 Main]

(a) 9
(b) 10
(c) 11
(d) 12

50. Let M and N be the number of points on the curve $y^5 - 9xy + 2x = 0$, where the tangents to the curve are parallel to X-axis and Y-axis, respectively. Then, the value of $M + N$ equals .... **[Numerical Value Type, 2022 Main]**

51. Let the function $f(x) = 2x^2 - \log_e x, x > 0$ be decreasing in $(0, a)$ and increasing in $(a, 4)$. A tangent to the parabola $y^2 = 4ax$ at a point P on it passes through the point $(8a, 8a - 1)$ but does not pass through the point $\left(-\frac{1}{a}, 0\right)$. If the equation of the normal at P is $\frac{x}{\alpha} + \frac{y}{\beta} = 1$, then $\alpha + \beta$ is equal to .... **[Numerical Value Type, 2022 Main]**

52. A water tank has the shape of a right circular cone with axis vertical and vertex downwards. Its semi-vertical angle is $\tan^{-1}(3/4)$. Water is poured in it at a constant rate of 6 cu m/h. The rate (in sq m/h), at which the wet curved surface area of the tank is increasing, when the depth of water in the tank is 4 m, is .... **[Numerical Value Type, 2022 Main]**

53. A spherical iron ball of radius 10 cm is coated with a layer of ice of uniform thickness that melts at a rate of 50 cm^3/min. When the thickness of the ice is 5 cm, then the rate at which the thickness (in cm/min) of the ice decreases, is **[Single Correct Type, 2021 Main]**
(a) $\frac{1}{9\pi}$ (b) $\frac{5}{6\pi}$
(c) $\frac{1}{36\pi}$ (d) $\frac{1}{18\pi}$

54. Let the normals at all the points on a given curve pass through a fixed point (a, b). If the curve passes through $(3, -3)$ and $(4, -2\sqrt{2})$ and given that $a - 2\sqrt{2}b = 3$, then $(a^2 + b^2 + ab)$ is equal to .... **[Numerical Value Type, 2021 Main]**

55. If the surface area of a cube is increasing at a rate of 3.6 cm^2/sec, retaining its shape, then the rate of change of its volume (in cm^3/sec), when the length of a side of the cube is 10 cm, is **[Single Correct Type, 2020 Main]**
(a) 18 (b) 10
(c) 20 (d) 9

EXERCISE 2

JEE Advanced Pattern

Single Option Correct Type Questions

1. The normal to the curve $5x^5 - 10x^3 + x + 2y + 6 = 0$ at $P(0, -3)$ meets the curve again at two points, then the equations of the tangents to the curve at these points is/are
(a) $2x - y - 3 = 0$ (b) $2x + y - 3 = 0$
(c) $2x + y + 3 = 0$ (d) $2x - y + 3 = 0$

2. If $|f''(x)| \le 1, \forall x \in R$ and $f(0) = 0 = f'(0)$, then which of the following can be true?
(a) $f\left(\frac{1}{3}\right) = \frac{1}{5}$ (b) $f\left(-\frac{1}{3}\right) = \frac{1}{4}$
(c) $f(-3) = \frac{1}{3}$ (d) None of these

3. Let S be a sphere with radius r. If we approximate the change of volume of S by $h \cdot A|_{r=r_0} + \frac{h^2}{2}\frac{dA}{dr}\Big|_{r=r_0}$, where A is surface area, when radius is changed from r_0 to $(r_0 + h)$, then the absolute value of error in our approximation is
(a) h^3 (b) $4\pi h r_0^2$ (c) $4\pi r_0 h^2$ (d) $\frac{4\pi}{3}h^3$

4. A curve is represented parametrically by the equations $x = t + e^{at}$ and $y = -t + e^{at}$, when $t \in R$ and $a > 0$. If the curve touches the axis of X at the point A, then the coordinates of the point A are
(a) (1, 0) (b) $(1/e, 0)$ (c) $(e, 0)$ (d) $(2e, 0)$

5. The area of triangle formed by tangent at (1, 1) on $y = x^2 + bx + c$ with coordinate axis is equal to 2. Then, the integral value of b is
(a) -3 (b) 3 (c) 2 (d) -2

6. Number of tangents drawn from the point $\left(-\frac{1}{2}, 0\right)$ to the curve $y = e^{\{x\}}$. (here, {} denotes fractional part function).
(a) 2 (b) 1 (c) 3 (d) 4

7. Let $f(x) = \begin{cases} -x^2, & x < 0 \\ x^2 + 8, & x \ge 0 \end{cases}$. Equation of tangent line touching both branches of $y = f(x)$ is
(a) $y = 4x + 1$ (b) $y = 4x + 4$
(c) $y = x + 4$ (d) $y = x + 1$

8. Let $f(x)=\begin{cases}(1-x)^{\alpha}\cdot x\cdot(1-\cos(2\pi x)), & 0<x\le 1\\ 0, & x=0\end{cases}$. If Rolle's theorem is applicable to $f(x)$ for $x\in(0,1)$, then α can be

(a) -2 (b) -1 (c) $\frac{1}{2}$ (d) 1

9. Let x be the length of one of the equal sides of an isosceles triangle and let θ be the angle between them. If x is increasing at the rate (1/12) m/h and θ is increasing at the rate of $\pi/180$ radians/h, then the rate in m^2/h at which the area of the triangle is increasing, when $x=12$ m and $\theta=\frac{\pi}{4}$, is

(a) $2^{1/2}\left(1+\frac{2\pi}{5}\right)$ (b) $\frac{73}{2}\sqrt{2}$

(c) $\frac{3^{1/2}}{2}+\frac{\pi}{5}$ (d) $2^{1/2}\left(\frac{1}{2}+\frac{\pi}{5}\right)$

10. A flu epidemic hits Pune. Health officers estimate that that number of persons sick with the flu at time t (measured in days from the beginning of the epidemic) is estimated by $P(t)=60t^2-t^3, 0\le t\le 40$. At what time t is the flu spreading at the rate of 900 people per day?

(a) $t=10$ or 30 (b) t=10 only

(c) $t=38$ (d) $t=25$ and 32

11. Tangent and normal to the curve $y=2\sin x+\sin 2x$ are drawn at $P\left(x=\frac{\pi}{3}\right)$. The area of the quadrilateral formed by the tangent, the normal and the coordinate axes, is

(a) $\frac{\pi\sqrt{3}}{2}$ (b) $\frac{\pi}{2}$

(c) $\frac{\sqrt{3}}{2}$ (d) None of these

More than One Correct Option Type Questions

12. If $f(x)=\int\frac{x}{2}\,d\left(\frac{x^2-1}{x^2}\right)$ and $f(2)=\frac{1}{2}$ and $g_r(x)=\underbrace{f[f\{f(\ldots f(x)\ldots)\}]}_{r\text{-times}}$ i.e. $g_1(x)=f(x)$, $g_2(x)=f[f(x)]$ and so on, then identify the correct statement(s).

(a) $\frac{d}{dx}(g_{(3n-2)}(x))=1$ whenever exists, $n\in N$

(b) $\frac{d}{dx}(g_{3n}(x))=1$ whenever exists, $n\in N$

(c) $\lim_{x\to 1}\frac{\sum_{r=1}^{100}(g_{3r}(x))^r+x-101}{x-1}=5050$

(d) Slope of the tangent to the graph of the function $y=g_{80}(x)$ at $x=\frac{1}{2}$ is 4.

13. If f is an odd continuous function in $[-1,1]$ and differentiable in $(-1,1)$, then which of the following statement(s) is (are) correct?

(a) $f'(a)=f(1)$ for some $a\in(-1,0)$

(b) $f'(b)=f(1)$ for some $b\in(0,1)$

(c) $n(f(\alpha))^{n-1}f'(\alpha)=(f(1))^n$ for some $a\in(-1,0)$, $\forall\, n\in N$

(d) $n(f(\beta))^{n-1}f'(\beta)=(f(1))^n$ for some $\beta\in(1,0)$, $\forall\, n\in N$

14. Let the function $f(x)$ be thrice differentiable and satisfies $f(f(x))=1-x, \forall\, x\in[0,1]$. If $J=\int_0^1 f(x)\,dx$ and $f''\left(\frac{4}{5}\right)=0$, then which of the following is(are) true?

(a) $f\left(\frac{1}{3}\right)+f\left(\frac{2}{3}\right)=1$

(b) $J=\frac{1}{2}$

(c) $f''(x)=0$ has atleast one root in $x\in\left(\frac{1}{4},\frac{3}{4}\right)$.

(d) $f'''(x)=0$ has atleast one root in $x\in\left(\frac{1}{2},\frac{4}{5}\right)$.

15. If $ab>0$ and $3a+5b+15c=0$, then which of the following statement is correct?

(a) There exist exactly one root of equation $ax^4+bx^2+c=0$ in $(-1,0)$.

(b) There exist exactly one root of equation $ax^4+bx^2+c=0$ in $(0,1)$.

(c) There exist exactly two roots of equation $ax^4+bx^2+c=0$ in $(-1,1)$.

(d) Number of roots of equation $ax^4+bx^2+c=0$ can be two in $(-1,0)$.

16. Let $f,g:[-1,2]\to R$ be continuous functions which are twice differentiable on the interval $(-1,2)$. Let the values of f and g at the points -1, 0 and 2 be as given in the following table:

	$x=-1$	$x=0$	$x=2$
$f(x)$	3	6	0
$g(x)$	0	1	-1

In each of the intervals $(-1,0)$ and $(0,2)$, the function $(f-3g)''$ never vanishes. Then, the correct statement(s) is (are)

(a) $f'(x)-3g'(x)=0$ has exactly three solutions in $(-1,0)\cup(0,2)$

(b) $f'(x)-3g'(x)=0$ has exactly one solution in $(-1,0)$

(c) $f'(x)-3g'(x)=0$ has exactly one solution in $(0,2)$

(d) $f'(x)-3g'(x)=0$ has exactly two solutions in $(-1,0)$ and exactly two solutions in $(0,2)$

Passage Based Questions

Passage I

(Q. Nos. 17 to 18)

- The sales S of a new product after it has been on the market for t years is $S = 30(1 - e^{kt})$.

17. The value of the constant k if 5 units have been sold after 1 yr, is

(a) $\ln \frac{6}{5}$ (b) $\ln \frac{5}{6}$

(c) $\ln \frac{4}{5}$ (d) None of these

18. The number of units which will saturate the market is

(a) 30 (b) 31

(c) 150 (d) None of these

Passage II

(Q. Nos. 19 to 20)

- Consider the two quadratic polynomials

$$C_a : y = \frac{x^2}{4} - ax + a^2 + a - 2 \text{ and } C : y = 2 - \frac{x^2}{4}$$

19. If the origin lies between the zeroes of the polynomial C_a, then the number of integral value (s) of a is

(a) 1 (b) 2

(c) 3 (d) more than 3

20. If a varies, then the equation of the locus of the vertex of C_a, is

(a) $x - 2y - 4 = 0$ (b) $2x - y - 4 = 0$

(c) $x - 2y + 4 = 0$ (d) $2x + y - 4 = 0$

Passage III

(Q. Nos. 21 to 22)

- To find the point of contact $P \equiv (x_1, y_1)$ of a tangent to the graph of $y = f(x)$ passing through origin O, we equate the slope of tangent to $y = f(x)$ at p to the slope of OP. Hence, we solve the equation $f'(x_1) = \frac{f(x_1)}{x_1}$ to get x_1 and y_1.

21. The equation $|\ln mx| = px$, where m is a positive constant, has a single root for

(a) $0 < p < \frac{m}{e}$ (b) $p < \frac{e}{m}$

(c) $0 < p < \frac{e}{m}$ (d) $p > \frac{m}{e}$

22. The equation $|\ln mx| = px$, where m is a positive constant, has exactly two roots for

(a) $p = \frac{m}{e}$ (b) $p = \frac{e}{m}$

(c) $0 < p \le \frac{e}{m}$ (d) $0 < p \le \frac{m}{e}$

Passage IV

(Q. Nos. 23 to 24)

- Consider the family of circles : $x^2 + y^2 - 3x - 4y - c_i = 0, c_i \in N (i = 1, 2, 3, ..., n)$

Also, let all circles intersect X-axis at integral points only and $c_1 < c_2 < c_3 < c_4 \ldots < c_n$. A point (x, y) is said to be integral point if both coordinates x and y are integers.

23. If circle $x^2 + y^2 - 3x - 4y - (c_2 - c_1) = 0$ and circle $x^2 + y^2 = r^2$ have only one common tangent, then

(a) $r = \frac{1}{2}$

(b) tangent passes through (10, 0)

(c) (3, 4) lies outside the circle $x^2 + y^2 = r^2$

(d) $c_2 = 2r = c_1$

24. The ellipse $4x^2 + 9y^2 = 36$ and hyperbola $a^2x^2 - y^2 = 4$ intersect orthogonally, then the equation of circle through the points of intersection of two conics is

(a) $x^2 + y^2 = (c_5)^2$ (b) $x^2 + y^2 = \frac{c_4}{7}$

(c) $x^2 + y^2 = c_3 - 2c_1$ (d) $x^2 + y^2 = \frac{c_7}{14}$

Stem Based Questions

Stem I

(Q. Nos. 25 to 26)

- $a(t)$ is a function of t such that $\frac{da}{dt} = 2$, for all values of t and $a = 0$, when $t = 0$. Further $y = m(t)x + c(t)$ is tangent to the curve $y = x^2 - 2ax + a^2 + a$ at the point whose abscissa 0. Then,

25. If the rate of change distance of vertex from the origin with respect to t is k, then k^2 is equal to ....

26. If the rate of change of $c(t)$ with respect to t, when $t = k$ is l and $l = a\sqrt{2} + b$, then $a + b$ is ....

Stem II

(Q. Nos. 27 to 28)

- If $f(x)$ is a differentiable function wherever it is continuous and $f'(c_1) = f'(c_2) = 0$, $f''(c_1) \cdot f''(c_2) < 0$, $f(c_1) = 5$, $f(c_2) = 0$ and $(c_1 < c_2)$.

27. If $f(x)$ is continuous in $[c_1, c_2]$ and $f''(c_1) - f''(c_2) > 0$, then minimum number of roots of $f'(x) = 0$ in $[c_1 - 1, c_2 + 1]$ is ....

28. If $f(x)$ is continuous in $[c_1, c_2]$ and $f''(c_1) - f''(c_2) < 0$, then minimum number of roots of $f'(x) = 0$ in $[c_1 - 1, c_2 + 1]$ is ....

Single Integer Type Questions

29. The length of the shortest path that begins at the point (2, 5), touches the X-axis and then ends at a point on the circle $x^2+y^2+12x-20y+120=0$ is ab metre, then $a+b$ is ......

30. Let the function $f(x)=ax^6+bx^5+cx^4+dx^3+ex^2+fx+g(a\neq 0)$ touches the line $y=g(x)=x+p$ at $x=1, 2$ and 3 and $h(x)=f(x)-g(x)$. If $\int_1^3 h(x)\,dx=\frac{32}{105}$, the value of a is ....

31. There is a point (p, q) on the graph of $f(x)=x^2$ and a point (r, s) on the graph of $g(x)=\frac{-8}{x}$, where $p>0$ and $r>0$. If the line through (p, q) and (r, s) is also tangent to both the curves at these points respectively, then the value of $p+r$ is ....

32. A curve is given by the equations $x=\sec^2\theta, y=\cot\theta$. If the tangent at P, where $\theta=\frac{\pi}{4}$ meets the curve again at Q, then $[PQ]$ is ....
(where $[\cdot]$ represents the greatest integer function)

33. Water is dropped at the rate of $2\text{m}^3/\text{s}$ into a cone of semi-vertical angle 45°. If the rate at which periphery of water surface changes when the height of the water in the cone is 2 m is d, then the value of $5d$ is ....

34. Let C be a curve defined by $y=e^{a+bx^2}$. The curve C passes through the point $P(1, 1)$ and the slope of the tangent at P is (-2). Then, the value of $2a-3b$ is ....

35. If the curve C in the XY-plane has the equation $x^2+xy+y^2=1$, then the fourth power of the greatest distance of a point on C from the origin, is ....

36. If at each point of the curve $y=x^3-ax^2+x+1$, the tangent is inclined at an acute angle with the positive direction of the X-axis, then sum of all possible integral values of a is ....

37. The tangent at a point P to the rectangular hyperbola $xy=c^2$ meets the lines $x-y=0, x+y=0$ at Q and R, Δ_1 is the area of the ΔOQR, where O is the origin. The normal at P meets the X-axis at M and Y-axis at N. If Δ_2 is the area of the ΔOMN and Δ_2 varies $\Delta_1 k$, then k is equal to ....

Numerical Value Type Questions

38. The normal at the point $P\left(2, \frac{1}{2}\right)$ on the curve $xy=1$ meets the curve again at Q. If m is the slope of the curve at Q, then $|m|$ is equal to ....

39. If equation of tangent drawn to the curve $y=f(x)$ at its point $P(3, 5)$ is $5x-4y+5=0$ and
$$\lim_{x\to 3}\frac{(3^{4f(x)}-2(1+3^2+\ldots+3^{19})-1)^2}{1-\cos(\ln(4-x))}=2(a3^b\ln c)^2,$$
where a and c are prime numbers and $b\in N$, then the value of $(a+b+c)$ is ....

40. The equation of the normal to the curve $y=(1+x)^y+\sin^{-1}(\sin^2 x)$ at $x=0$ is $ax+by+cz=0$, then $20a^2+30b^2-4c$ is ....

41. A dynamite blast blows a heavy rock straight up with a launch velocity of 160 m/sec. It reaches a height of $s=160t-16t^2$ after t sec. The velocity of the rock when it is 256 m above the ground on the way up is ....

42. A line is tangent to the curve $f(x)=\frac{41x^3}{3}$ at the point P in the first quadrant and has a slope of 2009. This line intersects the Y-axis at $(0, b)$. Then, $\left|\frac{3b}{82}\right|$ is ....

Matching Type Questions

43. Match the following columns.

	Column I		Column II
(A)	If curves $y^2=4ax$ and $y=e^{-\frac{x}{2a}}$ are orthogonal, then a can take value	(p)	3
(B)	If θ is angle between the curves $y=[\lvert\sin x\rvert+\lvert\cos x\rvert]$, ($[\cdot]$ denote GIF) and $x^2+y^2=5$, then $\text{cosec}^2\theta$ is	(q)	1
(C)	If curves $y^2=4a(x+a)$ and $y^2=4b(x+b)$ intersects each other orthogonally, then $\left\lvert\frac{a}{b}\right\rvert$ can be equal to	(r)	5/4
(D)	If $y=x^2+3x+c$ and $x=y^2+3y+c$ has only one common point (h, k), then $\lvert h+k+c\rvert$ can be equal to ...	(s)	2

44. Match the following columns.

Column I	Column II
(A) $f(x)=\frac{\sin x}{e^x}, x \in [0, \pi]$	(p) Conditions in Rolle's theorem are satisfied.
(B) $f(x)=\text{sgn}((e^x-1)\ln x), x \in \left[\frac{1}{2}, \frac{3}{2}\right]$	(q) Coditions in LMVT are satisfied.
(C) $f(x)=(x-1)^{2/5}, x \in [0, 3]$	(r) At least one condition in Rolle's theorem is not satisfied.
(D) $f(x)=\begin{cases} x\left(\frac{e^{1/x}-1}{e^{1/x}+1}\right), & x \in [-1, 1]-\{0\} \\ 0, & x=0 \end{cases}$	(s) At least one condition in LMVT is not satisfied.

45. Match the following columns.

Column I	Column II
(A) The sides of a triangle vary slightly in such a way that its circumradius remains constant. If $\frac{da}{\cos A}+\frac{db}{\cos B}+\frac{dc}{\cos C}+1=\|m\|$, then the values of m is/are	(p) 1
(B) The sub-tangent to the curve $x^2y^2=16$ at the point $(-2, 2)$ is $\|k\|$. Then, the value of k is	(q) -1
(C) The curve $y=2e^{2x}$ intersects the Y-axis at an angle $\cot^{-1}\|(8n-4)/3\|$, then the value of n is	(r) 2
(D) The area of a triangle formed by normal at the point $(1, 0)$ on the curve $x=e^{\sin y}$ with axes is $\|2t+1\|/6$ sq. units. Then, the value of t is	(s) -2

EXERCISE 3

Challenging Problems

1. The tangent represented by the graph of the function $y=f(x)$ at the point with abscissa $x=1$ form an angle $\frac{\pi}{6}$ and at the point $x=2$ an angle of $\frac{\pi}{3}$ and at the point $x=3$ an angle of $\frac{\pi}{4}$. Then, find the value of $\int_1^3 f'(x)f''(x)\,dx+\int_2^3 f''(x)\,dx$.

2. Find a point M on the curve $y=\frac{3}{\sqrt{2}}x\ln x, x \in (e^{-1.5}, \infty)$ such that the segment of the tangent at M intercepted between M and the Y-axis is shortest.

3. Show that the curve $\frac{x^2}{a^2+K_1}+\frac{y^2}{b^2+K_1}=1$ and $\frac{x^2}{a^2+K_2}+\frac{y^2}{b^2+K_2}=1$ intersect orthogonally.

4. Water is flowing out at the rate of $6\,m^3$/min from a reservoir shaped like a hemispherical bowl of radius $R=13$ m. The volume of water in the hemispherical bowl is given by $V=\frac{\pi}{3}y^2(3R-y)$ when the water is y meter deep. Find

(i) at what rate is the water level changing when the water is 8 m deep.

(ii) at what rate is the radius of the water surface changing when the water is 8 m deep.

5. The angles of a triangle are calculated from the sides a, b, c. If small changes $\delta a, \delta b, \delta c$ are made in sides show that approximately $\delta A=\frac{a}{2\Delta}\{\delta a-\delta b\cdot\cos C-\delta c\cdot\cos B\}$, where Δ is the area of the triangle and A, B, C are the angles opposite to a, b, c, respectively. Verify that $\delta A+\delta B+\delta C=0$.

6. Find the possible values of 'a' such that the inequality $3-x^2>|x-a|$ has atleast one negative solution.

7. A straight line is drawn through the origin and parallel to the tangent to a curve $\frac{x+\sqrt{a^2-y^2}}{a}=\ln\left(\frac{a+\sqrt{a^2+y^2}}{y}\right)$ at an arbitrary point M. Show that the locus of the point p of intersection of the straight line through the origin and the straight line parallel to the X-axis and passing through the point M is $x^2+y^2=a^2$.

8. The chord of the parabola $y=-a^2x^2+5ax-4$ touches the curve $y=\frac{1}{1-x}$ at the point $x=2$ and is bisected by that point. Find a.

9. Let $f(x)=\text{Max.}\{x^2,(1-x)^2,2x(1-x)\}$, where $x\in[0,1]$. If Rolle's theorem is applicable for $f(x)$ on largest possible interval $[a,b]$, then the value of $(4a+6b+11c)$, when $c\in(a,b)$ such that $f'(c)=0$, is ......

10. A particle moving on a curve has the position at time t given by $x=f'(t)\sin t+f''(t)\cos t$, $y=f'(t)\cos t-f''(t)\sin t$, where f is a thrice differentiable function. Then, prove that the velocity of the particle at time t is $f'(t)+f'''(t)$.

11. If $\phi(x)$ is a differentiable function $x\in R$ and $a\in R$ such that $\phi(0)=\phi(2a)$, $\phi(a)=\phi(3a)$ and $\phi(0)=\phi(a)$, then show that there is at least one root of equation $\phi'(x+a)=\phi'(x)$ in $(0,2a)$.

12. $f:[0,4]\to R$ is a differentiable function. Then, prove that for some $a,b\in(0,4)$, $f^2(4)-f^2(0)=8f'(a)\cdot f(b)$.

13. Show that the distance from the origin of the normal at any point of the curve $x=ae^{\theta}\left(\sin\frac{\theta}{2}+2\cos\frac{\theta}{2}\right)$ and $y=ae^{\theta}\left(\cos\frac{\theta}{2}-2\sin\frac{\theta}{2}\right)$ is twice the distance of the tangent at the point from the origin.

14. If the cubic function $f(x)=x^3+px+q$ has 3 distinct real roots, then prove that $4p^3+27q^2<0$.

15. A container in the shape of an inverted cone has height 16 cm and radius 5 cm at the top. It is partially filled with a liquid that oozes through the sides at a rate proportional to the area of the container that is in contact with the liquid. If we pour the liquid into the container at a rate of 2 cm^3/min, then the height of the liquid decreases at a rate of 0.3 cm/min when the height is 10 cm. If our goal is to keep the liquid at a constant height of 10 cm, then at what rate should be pour the liquid into the container?

16. Prove that the portion of the tangent to the curve

$$x=\sqrt{a^2-y^2}+\frac{a}{2}\log\frac{a-\sqrt{a^2-y^2}}{a+\sqrt{a^2-y^2}}$$ between the point of contact and the X-axis is of length a.

17. (i) Consider the curve the equation
$$y(y^2-1)(y-2)=x(x-1)(x-2)$$
At how many points does this curve have horizontal tangents? Find the x-coordinats of these points.

(ii) Find equations of the tangent lines at the points (0, 1) and (0, 2).

Answer Key

Exercise 1

1. (d)	2. (b)	3. (b)	4. (c)	5. (b)	6. (c)	7. (c)	8. (b)	9. (d)	10. (a)
11. (c)	12. (c)	13. (a)	14. (c)	15. (b)	16. (b)	17. (b)	18. (a)	19. (d)	20. (d)
21. (b)	22. (a)	23. (b)	24. (c)	25. (b)	26. (d)	27. (b)	28. (d)	29. (b)	30. (2017)
31. (0)	32. (2)	33. (4)	34. (4)	35. (125)	36. (0.2)	37. (216)	38. (16)	39. (5)	40. (5)
41. (a)	42. (d)	43. (11)	44. (5)	45. (d)	46. (c)	47. (c)	48. (c)	49. (a)	50. (2)
51. (45)	52. (5)	53. (d)	54. (9)	55. (d)					

Exercise 2

1. (a)	2. (c)	3. (d)	4. (d)	5. (a)	6. (b)	7. (b)	8. (a)	9. (d)	10. (a)
11. (a)	12. (b,d)	13. (a,b,d)	14. (a,b,c,d)	15. (a,b,c)	16. (b,c)	17. (b)	18. (a)	19. (b)	20. (a)
21. (d)	22. (a)	23. (b)	24. (d)	25. (8)	26. (18)	27. (4)	28. (2)	29. (4)	30. (2)
31. (5)	32. (3)	33. (5)	34. (5)	35. (4)	36. (0)	37. (2)	38. (64)	39. (28)	40. (54)

41. (96) 42. (343) 43. (A) → (p,q,r,s), (B) → (r), (C) → (p,q,r,s), (D) → (q)

44. (A) → (p,q), (B) → (r,s), (C) → (r,s), (D) → (r,s) 45. (A) → (p,q), (B) → (r,s), (C) → (q,r), (D) → (p,s)

Solutions

Exercise 1 - JEE Main Pattern

1. We have,

$$f(x) = \begin{cases} x^2 - x - 6, & \text{if } x \neq 1 \text{ and } x \in [-2, 3] \\ -6, & \text{if } x = 1 \end{cases}$$

Clearly, $\lim_{x \to 1} f(x) = -6 = f(1)$

$\Rightarrow f$ is continuous at $x = 1$

and hence f is continuous on $[-2, 3]$. f is also differentiable in $(-2, 3)$.

Further, $f(-2) = 4 + 2 - 6 = 0$

and $f(3) = 9 - 3 - 6 = 0$

Thus, $f(-2) = 0 = f(3)$.

Hence, $f'(c) = 0$ for some $c \in (-2, 3)$.

Therefore, $f'(c) = 0$ implies

$$2c - 1 = 0 \text{ or } c = \frac{1}{2} \in [-2, 3]$$

2. Given that $f(|x|) = 0$ has 8 real roots.

$\Rightarrow f(x) = 0$ has 4 positive roots.

Since, $f(x)$ is a polynomial of degree 5, $f(x)$ cannot have even number of real roots.

$\Rightarrow f(x)$ has all the five roots real, in which four positive and one root is negative.

3. **Decoding the Question**

Find the equation of normal using the formula $y - y_1 = -\frac{dx}{dy}(x - x_1)$, then solve it with given curves.

$$2x + 2x\frac{dy}{dx} + 2y - 6y\frac{dy}{dx} = 0$$

$$\Rightarrow \frac{dy}{dx}(2x - 6y) = -(2x + 2y)$$

$$\Rightarrow \frac{dy}{dx} = 1 \quad \text{[at (1, 1)]}$$

Equation of normal

$$y - 1 = -1(x - 1)$$

$$\Rightarrow x + y = 2$$

Equation of curve $x^2 + 2xy - 3y^2 = 0$

$$\Rightarrow (x - y)(x + 3y) = 0$$

$$\Rightarrow x + y = 2$$

$$\Rightarrow x + 3y = 0$$

$$\Rightarrow y = -1 \Rightarrow x = 3$$

Normal meets curve at (3, – 1) again in IVth quadrant.

4. $x^2 y = c^3$

On differentiating w.r.t. x, we get

$$2xy + x^2\frac{dy}{dx} = 0$$

$$\Rightarrow \frac{dy}{dx} = -\frac{2y}{x}$$

Let a point P on curve $\left(ct, \frac{c}{t^2}\right)$.

Slope of tangent at $P = m_T = \dfrac{-2 \times \frac{c}{t^2}}{ct} = -\frac{2}{t^3}$

Equation of tangent, $\left(y - \frac{c}{t^2}\right) = -\frac{2}{t^3}(x - ct)$

For x-intercept $\Rightarrow$ put $y = 0 \Rightarrow x = \frac{3ct}{2} = a$

For y-intercept $\Rightarrow$ put $x = 0$

$$\Rightarrow y = \frac{3c}{t^2} = b$$

$$\therefore \quad a^2 b = \frac{9c^2t^2}{4} \times \frac{3c}{t^2} = \frac{27c^3}{4}$$

5. The form being $\frac{0}{0}$, so the required limit by L'Hospital rule is

$$\lim_{x \to 0} \frac{2x}{2xf'(x^2) - 360x\, f'(9x^2) + 396x\, f'(99x^2)}$$

$$= \lim_{x \to 0} \frac{1}{f'(x^2) - 180f'(9x^2) + 198f'(99x^2)}$$

For $f(x) = 0$, the slope of tangent is $f'(x)$ and slope of normal at $x = 0$ is $\frac{-1}{f'(0)} = 1$ (given)

$$\Rightarrow f'(0) = -1$$

$$\therefore \text{Limit} = \frac{1}{f'(0) - 180f'(0) + 198f'(0)}$$

$$= \frac{-1}{(1 - 180 + 198)}$$

$$= \frac{-1}{19}$$

6. The given equation can be written as $\frac{x^2}{\alpha^2} + \frac{y^2}{4} = 1$

Any point on the curve is $P(\alpha \cos\theta, 2\sin\theta)$

$$\therefore \quad PQ = \sqrt{\alpha^2\cos^2\theta + 4(1 + \sin\theta)^2}$$

Let $S(\theta) = \alpha^2\cos^2\theta + 4(1 + \sin\theta)^2$

$$= (4 + \alpha^2) + 8\sin\theta + (4 - \alpha^2)\sin^2\theta$$

Now, $\frac{dS}{d\theta} = 2\cos\theta[4 + (4 - \alpha^2)\sin\theta]$

$\therefore \quad \frac{dS}{d\theta} = 0$ gives $\theta = \frac{\pi}{2}, \frac{3\pi}{2}$ or $\sin\theta = \frac{4}{\alpha^2 - 4}$

But $0 < \alpha^2 < 8$ and $|\sin\theta| \le 1$, so $\sin\theta = \frac{4}{\alpha^2 - 4}$ is not possible.

Also, at $\theta = \frac{3\pi}{2}$, P becomes $(0, -2)$, which is same as point Q.

So, $PQ = 0$.

Also, $\left.\frac{d^2S}{d\theta^2}\right]_{\theta = \frac{\pi}{2}} = -8\sin\theta + 2(4 - \alpha^2)\cos 2\theta = -8 + 2(4 - \alpha^2)(-1)$

$= -2(8 - \alpha^2) < 0$ [as $0 < \alpha^2 < 8$]

Hence, $\theta = \frac{\pi}{2}$ corresponds to the maximum values of S.

So, P is $(0, 2)$.

Clearly, reflection of $P(0, 2)$ in the X-axis is $R\ (0, -2)$.

So, least distance of $R(0, -2)$ from the line $3x - 4y + 7 = 0$ is

$$\frac{|3(0) - 4(-2) + 7|}{\sqrt{(3)^2 + (-4)^2}} = \frac{15}{5} = 3$$

7.

> **Decoding the Question**
>
> Use Leibnitz rule as
>
> $f(x) = \int_{g(x)}^{h(x)} F(x)dx \Rightarrow f'(x) = F(h(x)) \cdot h'(x) - F(g(x)) \cdot g'(x)$

Given, $f^3(x) = \int_0^x tf^2(t)\,dt$ ...(i)

On differentiating both sides of Eq. (i) and using Leibnitz rule, we get

$$3f^2(x)f'(x) = xf^2(x)$$

As, $f(x)$ is strictly increasing, so $f(x) = 0$

$$\therefore \quad 3f'(x) = x \Rightarrow f'(x) = \frac{x}{3}$$

$$\therefore \quad f(x) = \frac{x^2}{6} + C$$

[intergrate both sides w.r.t. x]

But $f(0) = 0 \Rightarrow C = 0$

$$\therefore \quad f(x) = \frac{x^2}{6}, x \ge 0$$

Slope of the tangent at $P(x_1, y_1)$ to the curve $f(x) = \frac{x_1}{3}$.

$\therefore$ Slope of normal $= \frac{-3}{x_1}$ i.e. $\frac{-1}{2} = \frac{-3}{x_1}$ [given]

$$\Rightarrow \quad x_1 = 6 \text{ and } y_1 = 6$$

So, equation of normal is $(y - 6) = \frac{-1}{2}(x - 6)$

For y-intercept, put $x = 0$, we get

$$y = 9$$

8. We have, $f(x) = x^2 \sin\frac{1}{x} + x^3 \cos\frac{1}{2x}$;

$f'(x)$ has opposite signs in $\left[\frac{1}{2\pi}, \frac{1}{\pi}\right]$

$\Rightarrow f'(x) = 0$ atleast once

Clearly, $f(x)$ is continuous as well as differentiable in $\left[\frac{1}{3\pi}, \frac{1}{\pi}\right]$

Also, $f\left(\frac{1}{3\pi}\right) = 0 = f\left(\frac{1}{\pi}\right)$

[only in this interval this will be true]

So, $f(x)$ satisfies Rolle's theorem.

Hence, there exist some $c \in \left(\frac{1}{3\pi}, \frac{1}{\pi}\right)$ such that $f'(c) = 0$.

9. $$y = a\frac{(e^{x/a} + e^{-x/a})}{2}$$

$$\frac{dy}{dx} = a\frac{(e^{x/a} - e^{-x/a})}{2} \times \frac{1}{a} = \frac{e^{x/a} - e^{-x/a}}{2}$$

Length of normal $= y\sqrt{1 + \left(\frac{dy}{dx}\right)^2}$

$$= \frac{a(e^{x/a} + e^{-x/a})}{2} \times \sqrt{1 + \left(\frac{e^{x/a} - e^{-x/a}}{2}\right)^2}$$

$$= \frac{a(e^{x/a} + e^{-x/a})}{2} \cdot \frac{e^{x/a} + e^{-x/a}}{2}$$

$$= a\left(\frac{e^{x/a} + e^{-x/a}}{2}\right)^2 = a \times \frac{y^2}{a^2} = \frac{y^2}{a}$$

$\therefore$ Point varies as y^2.

10. Clearly, $x = 1$ satisfies the given equation.

Assume that $f(x) = e^{x-1} + x - 2 = 0$ has a real root α other than $x = 1$.

We may suppose that $\alpha > 1$ (the case $\alpha < 1$ is exactly similar).

Applying Rolle's theorem on $[1, \alpha]$ (if $\alpha < 1$ apply the theorem on $[\alpha, 1]$), we get

$$\beta \in (1, \alpha) \text{ such that } f'(\beta) = 0.$$

But $f'(\beta) = e^{\beta - 1} + 1$, so that $e^{\beta - 1} = -1$,

which is not possible.

Hence, there is no real root other than 1.

11. Given, $x = a(\cos\theta + \theta\sin\theta)$

$$\frac{dx}{d\theta} = a(-\sin\theta + \sin\theta + \theta\cos\theta) = a\theta\cos\theta$$

Also, $y = a(\sin\theta - \theta\cos\theta)$

$$\frac{dy}{d\theta} = a(\cos\theta - \cos\theta + \theta\sin\theta) = a\theta\sin\theta$$

$$\frac{dy}{dx} = \tan\theta$$

Slope of normal $= -\cot\theta$

Equation of normal at θ is

$y - a(a(\cos\theta - \theta\cos\theta))$

$= -\cot\theta(x - a(\cos\theta + \theta\sin\theta)) \cdot (\cos\theta)x + (\sin\theta)y$

$= a$

Length of perpendicular from the origin is

$$= \left|\frac{a}{\sqrt{\cos^2 + \sin^2\theta}}\right| = a = \text{constant}$$

12. Given parabola is $y = x^2 + 6 \Rightarrow \frac{dy}{dx} = 2x$

Slope of the tangent, $m = 2$ at (1, 7)

Equation of the tangent at $P(1, 7)$ is

$$y - 7 = 2(x-1) \Rightarrow 2x - y + 5 = 0 \quad \text{...(i)}$$

Given circle is $x^2 + y^2 + 16x + 12y + c = 0$

$$(x+8)^2 + (y+6)^2 = r^2,$$

where $r = \sqrt{100 - c}$

Here, CQ is perpendicular to the tangent.

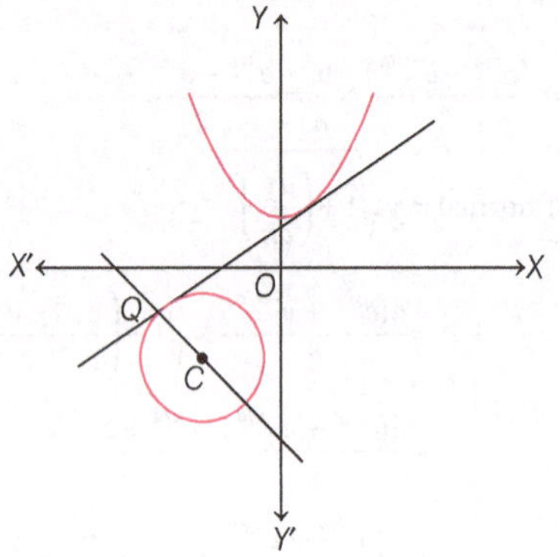

Thus, slope of $CQ = -\frac{1}{2}$

Equation of CQ is

$$y + 6 = -\frac{1}{2}(x+8) \Rightarrow x + 2y = -20 \quad \text{...(ii)}$$

On solving Eqs. (i) and (ii), we get

$$x = -6 \text{ and } y = -7$$

Hence, the point Q is $(-6, -7)$.

13. $y = 2x^2 - x \Rightarrow \frac{dy}{dx} = 4x - 1$

Let $m_1 = 4x - 1$

Now, $y^2 = x \Rightarrow 2y\frac{dy}{dx} = 1$

Let $m_2 = \frac{dy}{dx} = \frac{1}{2y}$

At $P(0, 0)$, $m_1 = -1$, $m_2 \to$ not defined

Angle $\alpha = \frac{\pi}{4}$

At $Q(1, 1)$, $m_1 = 3$, $m_2 = \frac{1}{2}$

$$\beta = \tan^{-1}\left(\frac{3 - \frac{1}{2}}{1 + \frac{3}{2}}\right) = \frac{\pi}{4}$$

14. $\frac{dy}{dx} = \cos^{-1}(x^4) \cdot 2x - \cos^{-1}(x^2) \cdot 1$

$$\left(\frac{dy}{dx}\right)_{x=\frac{1}{\sqrt{2}}} = \cos^{-1}\left(\frac{1}{4}\right) \cdot \sqrt{2} - \cos^{-1}\left(\frac{1}{2}\right)$$

$$= \sqrt{2}\cos^{-1}\left(\frac{1}{4}\right) - \frac{\pi}{3}$$

15. Let $P(h, k)$ be a point on curve $xy = 4$

$$\Rightarrow \quad hk = 4 \quad \text{...(i)}$$

On differentiating $xy = 4$ w.r.t. x, we get

$$\frac{xdy}{dx} + y = 0 \Rightarrow \frac{dy}{dx} = \frac{-y}{x}$$

The slope of the tangent at $P(h, k) = \frac{-k}{h}$

So, the equation of the tangent is

$$kx + hy = 2hk$$

$$\Rightarrow \quad kx + hy = 8 \quad \text{[from Eq. (i)]}$$

$$x\text{-intercept} = \frac{-8}{k},$$

$$y\text{-intercept} = \frac{-8}{h}$$

Hence, $ab = \frac{64}{hk} = \frac{64}{4} = 16$

16. Since, $f(x)$ satisfies the conditions of Rolle's theorem,

so $f(2) = f(6)$

Now, given integral $= (f(x))_2^6 = f(6) - f(2) = 0$

17. Let $g(x) = f(x) - \sin x$

Now, $g(0) = f(0) - 0 = 0$

and $g(1) = f(1) - \sin 1 = 0$

As, $g(x)$ is differentiable, so by Rolle's theorem,

$$g'(c) = 0, \text{ for some } c \in [0, 1]$$

i.e. $f'(c) - \cos c = 0$

$\Rightarrow f'(c) = \cos c$, for some $c \in [0, 1]$

18. Let at time t, the distance between the two persons be x m

$$\Rightarrow \quad x = \sqrt{(3t)^2 + (4t)^2}$$

$$\Rightarrow \quad x = 5t$$

$$\Rightarrow \quad \frac{dx}{dt} = 5 \text{ m/sec}$$

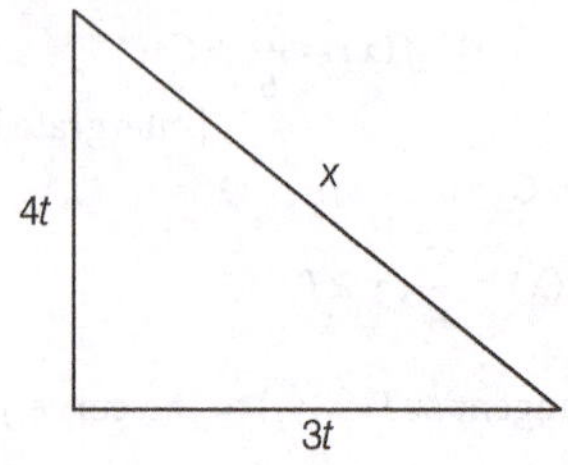

19. Let x be the length of an edge, V be the volume and S be the surface area of the cube.

$$\frac{dV}{dt} = 18,\ V = x^3$$

$$\Rightarrow \quad \frac{dV}{dt} = 18 = 3x^2\frac{dx}{dt}$$

$$\Rightarrow \quad \frac{dx}{dt} = \frac{6}{x^2} \quad \text{...(i)}$$

$$S = 6x^2$$

$$\Rightarrow \quad \frac{dS}{dt} = 12x\frac{dx}{dt} \quad \text{[from Eq. (i)]}$$

$$\Rightarrow \quad \frac{dS}{dt} = 12x \times \frac{6}{x^2}$$

$$\Rightarrow \quad \frac{dS}{dt} = 12 \times \frac{6}{x} = 6 \quad \text{[given } x = 12\text{]}$$

$$\therefore \quad \frac{dS}{dt} = 6 \text{ cm}^2/\text{sec}$$

20. Slope of $OP = \cos\alpha = \dfrac{\sin\alpha}{\alpha}$

$\Rightarrow \quad \tan\alpha = \alpha,$

(which is true for infinitely many positive values of α)

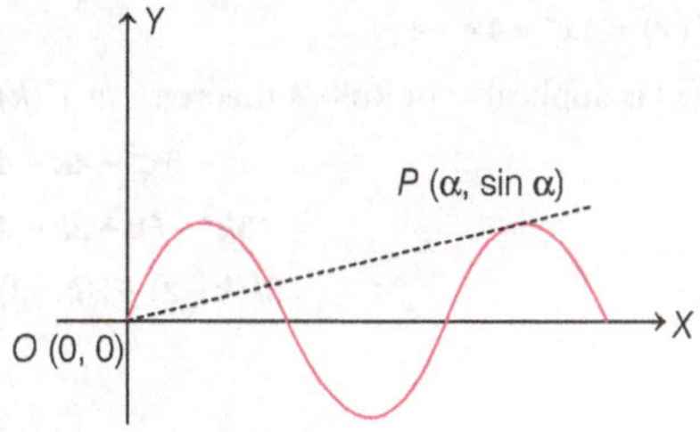

21. We have, $f'''(x) = 6(x-1)$

On integrating, we get

$$f''(x) = 3(x-1)^2 + C \quad \text{...(i)}$$

At (2, 1), $y = 3x - 5$ is tangent to $y = f(x)$

$\therefore \quad f''(2) = 3$

From Eq. (i), we get

$$3 = 3(2-1)^2 + C$$

$$\Rightarrow \quad 3 = 3 + C \Rightarrow C = 0$$

$$\therefore \quad f'(x) = 3(x-1)^2$$

On integrating, we get

$$f(x) = (x-1)^3 + C'$$

Since, the curve passes through (2, 1)

$$\therefore \quad 1 = (2-1)^3 + C' \Rightarrow C' = 0$$

$$\therefore \quad f(x) = (x-1)^3$$

$$\therefore \quad f(0) = -1$$

22. Given curve is $2x^2y^2 - x^4 = c$ ...(i)

Sub-normal at $P(x, y) = y\dfrac{dy}{dx}$ ...(ii)

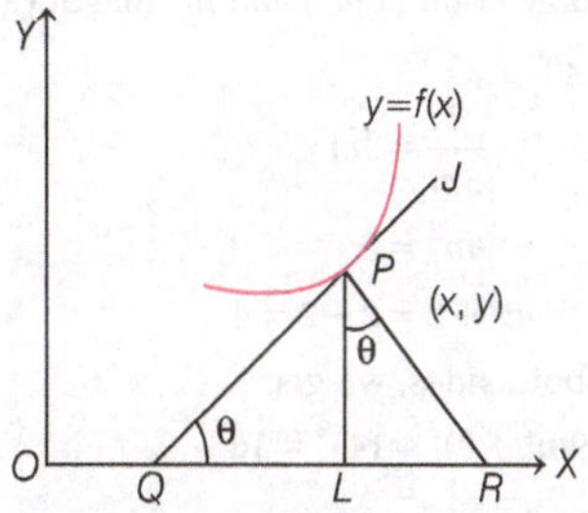

On differentiating Eq. (i), we get

$$2\left(x^2 2y\frac{dy}{dx} + 2xy^2\right) - 4x^3 = 0$$

$$\Rightarrow \quad \frac{dy}{dx} = \frac{x(x^2 - y^2)}{x^2 y} \quad \text{...(iii)}$$

Now, $x(x - yy') = x^2 - xy\dfrac{dy}{dx}$

$$= x^2 - (x^2 - y^2) \quad \text{[from Eq. (iii)]}$$

$$= y^2$$

Mean proportion $= \sqrt{x(x - yy')} = y$

23. Length of sub-normal = length of sub-tangent

$$\Rightarrow \quad \frac{dy}{dx} = \pm 1$$

If $\dfrac{dy}{dx} = 1$, equation of the tangent is

$$y - 4 = x - 3$$

$$\Rightarrow \quad y - x = 1$$

Area of $\Delta OAB = \dfrac{1}{2} \times 1 \times = \dfrac{1}{2}$

If $\dfrac{dy}{dx} = -1$, equation of tangent is $y - 4 = -x + 3$

$$\Rightarrow \quad y + x = 7, \text{ area} = \frac{1}{2} \times 7 \times 7 = \frac{49}{2}$$

24. $f(0) = -1$; $f(1) = 7$.

So, $f(0)$ and $f(1)$ have opposite signs.

25. Applying Rolle's theorem to $F(x) = f(x) - 2g(x)$, we get

$$F(0) = 0$$

$$F(1) = f(1) - 2g(1)$$

$$\Rightarrow \quad 0 = 6 - 2g(1) \Rightarrow g(1) = 3$$

26. Let $g(x) = f(x) - x^2$.

We have, $g(1) = 0$, $g(2) = 0$, $g(3) = 0$

$$[\because f(1) = 1, f(2) = 4, f(3) = 9]$$

From Rolle's theorem on $g(x)$, $g'(x) = 0$ for at least $x \in (1, 2)$.

Let $g'(c_1) = 0$, where $c_1 \in (1, 2)$.

Similarly, $g(x) = 0$, for at least one $x \in (2, 3)$.

Let $g'(c_2) = 0$, where $c_2 \in (2, 3)$

$$\therefore \quad g'(c_1) = g'(c_2) = 0$$

By Rolle's theorem, at least one $x \in (c_1, c_2)$ such that

$$g''(x) = 0 \Rightarrow f''(x) = 2 \text{ for some } x \in (1, 3).$$

27. Let $BP = x$

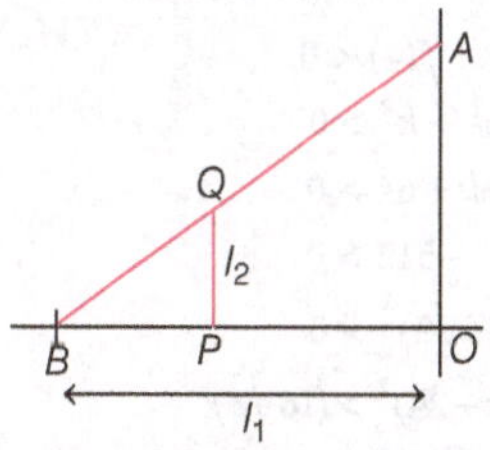

From similar triangle property, we get

$$\frac{AO}{l_1} = \frac{l_2}{x} \Rightarrow AO = \frac{l_1 l_2}{x} = \frac{d(AO)}{dt} = \frac{-l_1 l_2}{x^2}\frac{dx}{dt}$$

When $x = \dfrac{l_1}{2}, \dfrac{d(AO)}{dt} = -\dfrac{2l_2}{5}$ m/s

28. Given, $V = \pi r^2 h$

On differentiating both sides, we get

$$\frac{dV}{dt} = \pi\left(r^2\frac{dh}{dt} + 2r\frac{dr}{dt}h\right) = \pi r\left(r\frac{dh}{dt} + 2h\frac{dr}{dt}\right)$$

$$\frac{dr}{dt} = \frac{1}{10} \text{ and } \frac{dh}{dt} = -\frac{2}{10}$$

$$\frac{dV}{dt} = \pi r\left(r\left(-\frac{2}{10}\right) + 2h\left(\frac{1}{10}\right)\right) = \frac{\pi r}{5}(-r+h)$$

Thus, when $r = 2$ and $h = 3$,

$$\frac{dV}{dt} = \frac{\pi(2)}{5}(-2+3) = \frac{2\pi}{5}$$

29. $\frac{dV}{dt} = -4 \text{ cm}^3/\text{min}$,

$\frac{dS}{dt} = ?$ when $V = 125 \text{ cm}^3$

$$V = x^3; S = 6x^2$$

$$\Rightarrow \quad \frac{dV}{dt} = 3x^2\frac{dx}{dt}$$

$$\Rightarrow \quad -4 = 3x^2\frac{dx}{dt} \Rightarrow \frac{dx}{dt} = -\frac{4}{3x^2} \quad \text{...(i)}$$

Also, $\frac{dS}{dt} = 12x\frac{dx}{dt}$

$$\frac{dS}{dt} = -\frac{16}{x}$$

When $V = 125 = x^3$, then $x = 5$

$$\Rightarrow \quad \left(\frac{dS}{dt}\right)_{x=5} = -\frac{16}{5} \text{ cm}^2/\text{min}$$

30. Let $f(x) = x^3 - 2kx^2 - 4kx + k^2$, where $f(0) = k^2 \geq 0$

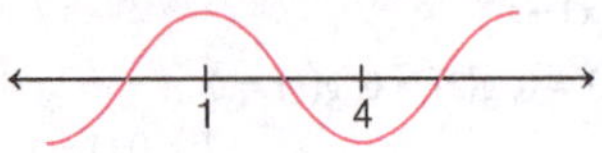

Clearly, $f(1) > 0$

$$\Rightarrow \quad k^2 - 6k + 1 > 0$$

$$\Rightarrow \quad (k-3)^2 - (2\sqrt{2})^2 > 0$$

$$\Rightarrow \quad (k-3)^2 > (2\sqrt{2})^2$$

$$\Rightarrow \quad |(k-3)| > (2\sqrt{2})$$

$$\Rightarrow \quad (k-3) > (2\sqrt{2}), (k-3) < -2\sqrt{2}$$

$$\Rightarrow \quad k > (3+2\sqrt{2}), k < 3-2\sqrt{2} \quad \text{...(i)}$$

Also, $f(4) < 0$

$$64 - 32k - 16k + k^2 > 0$$

$$\Rightarrow \quad k^2 - 48k + 64 > 0$$

$$\Rightarrow \quad (k-24)^2 - 512 > 0$$

$$\Rightarrow \quad (k-24)^2 - (16\sqrt{2})^2 > 0$$

$$\Rightarrow \quad (k-24)^2 > (16\sqrt{2})^2$$

$$\Rightarrow \quad |(k-24)| > (16\sqrt{2})$$

$$\Rightarrow \quad (k-24) > (16\sqrt{2}), (k-24) < -16\sqrt{2}$$

$$\Rightarrow \quad k > (24+16\sqrt{2}), k < 24 - 16\sqrt{2} \quad \text{...(ii)}$$

From Eqs. (i) and (ii), we get

$$3 + 2\sqrt{2} < k < 24 + 16\sqrt{2}$$

$$\Rightarrow \quad 3 + \sqrt{8} < k < 8(3+\sqrt{8})$$

Thus, $m = 3$ and $n = 8$

Hence, the value of $2(m+n-1)^3 + 17 = 2(3+8-1)^3 + 17$

$$= 2017$$

31. Let $\quad f(x) = x^3 - 3x + a$

$$\Rightarrow \quad f'(x) = 3x^2 - 3$$

Now, $f'(x) = 0$ gives $x = \pm 1$

Since, it has two distinct roots in $(-1, 1)$, so $f(-1)f(1) < 0$

$$\Rightarrow \quad (-1+3+a)(1-3+a) < 0$$

$$\Rightarrow \quad (a+2)(a-2) < 0$$

$$\Rightarrow \quad -2 < a < 2$$

Hence, the sum of integral values of $a = -1 + 1 + 0 = 0$

32. Given, $f(x) = x^3 - 2x^2 - 4x + 7$

$$\Rightarrow \quad f'(x) = 3x^2 - 4x - 4$$

Since, $f(x)$ is applicable of Rolle's theorem, so $f'(k) = 0$

$$\Rightarrow \quad 3k^2 - 4k - 4 = 0$$

$$\Rightarrow \quad 3k^2 - 6k + 2k - 4 = 0$$

$$\Rightarrow \quad 3k(k-2) + 2(k-2) = 0$$

$$\Rightarrow \quad k = 2, -\frac{2}{3}$$

Hence, the value of k is 2.

33. Given curve is $x^3 - y^2 = 0$ ...(i)

$$\Rightarrow \quad 3x^2 - 2y\frac{dy}{dx} = 0$$

$$\Rightarrow \quad \frac{dy}{dx} = \frac{3x^2}{2y}$$

Slope of the tangent $= \left(\frac{dy}{dx}\right)_{(4m^2, 8m^3)} = \frac{3 \times 16m^4}{2 \times 8m^3} = 3m$

Hence, the equation of the tangent is

$$y - 8m^3 = 3m(x - 4m^2)$$

$$\Rightarrow \quad y = 3mx - 4m^3 \quad \text{...(ii)}$$

On solving Eqs. (i) and (ii), we get

$$x = 4m^2, m^2$$

Thus,the new point is $Q(m^2, -m^3)$.

Slope of the tangent at $Q(m^2, -m^3)$ is $-\frac{3m}{2}$.

Slope of the normal at $Q(m^2, -m^3)$ is $\frac{2}{3m}$.

Since, tangent at $P(4m^2, 8m^2)$ and normal at $Q(m^2, -m^3)$ coincide, we get

$$\frac{2}{3m} = 3m$$

$$\Rightarrow \quad 9m^2 = 2$$

$$\Rightarrow \quad 9m^2 + 2 = 2 + 2 = 4$$

On squaring both sides, we get

$$(9m^2 + 2)^2 = (4)^2 = 16$$

34. Given curve is $\sqrt{x} + \sqrt{y} = 2$

Let $P(\alpha, \beta)$ be a variable point on the given curve.

Equation of tangent at $P(\alpha, \beta)$ is

$$y - \beta = -\frac{\sqrt{\beta}}{\sqrt{\alpha}}(x - \alpha)$$

$$\Rightarrow \quad \frac{y-\beta}{\sqrt{\beta}} = -\frac{(x-\alpha)}{\sqrt{\alpha}}$$

$$\Rightarrow \quad \frac{y}{\sqrt{\beta}} - \sqrt{\beta} = -\frac{x}{\sqrt{\alpha}} + \sqrt{\alpha}$$

$$\Rightarrow \quad \frac{x}{\sqrt{\alpha}} + \frac{y}{\sqrt{\beta}} = \sqrt{\alpha} + \sqrt{\beta} \Rightarrow \frac{x}{\sqrt{\alpha}} + \frac{y}{\sqrt{\beta}} = 2$$

Thus, the sum of the intercepts $= 2(\sqrt{\alpha} + \sqrt{\beta})$

$$= 2 \times 2 = 4$$

35. Given curve is $\quad y^2 = x^3$

$$\Rightarrow \quad 2y\frac{dy}{dx} = 3x^2 \Rightarrow \frac{dy}{dx} = \frac{3x^2}{2y}$$

Now, $\quad \left(\frac{dy}{dx}\right)_{(4,\,8)} = \frac{3 \times 16}{16} = 3$

Hence, the length of the sub-normal $= y\frac{dy}{dx} = 8 \times 3 = 24$

Thus, $m = 24$

Hence, the value of $(\sqrt{m+1})^3$ is 125.

36. The given curve is

$$(x+y) - \ln(x+y) = 2x + 5$$

$$\Rightarrow \quad 1 + \frac{dy}{dx} - \frac{1}{(x+y)}\left(1 + \frac{dy}{dx}\right) = 2$$

$$\Rightarrow \quad \left(1 + \frac{dy}{dx}\right) - \frac{1}{(x+y)}\left(1 + \frac{dy}{dx}\right) = 2$$

$$\Rightarrow \quad \left(1 + \frac{dy}{dx}\right)\left(1 - \frac{1}{(x+y)}\right) = 2$$

$$\Rightarrow \quad \left(1 + \frac{dy}{dx}\right)\left(\frac{x+y-1}{(x+y)}\right) = 2 \Rightarrow \left(1 + \frac{dy}{dx}\right) = \frac{2(x+y)}{x+y-1}$$

$$\Rightarrow \quad \frac{dy}{dx} = \frac{2(x+y)}{x+y-1} - 1 = \frac{2x+2y-x-y+1}{x+y-1}$$

$$\Rightarrow \quad \frac{dy}{dx} = \frac{x+y+1}{x+y-1}$$

Since, it has a vertical tangent, so $\frac{dy}{dx} = \infty$

$$\Rightarrow \quad \frac{x+y-1}{x+y+1} = 0 \qquad \left[\because \frac{dx}{dy} = 0\right]$$

$$\Rightarrow \quad x + y - 1 = 0$$

$$\Rightarrow \quad x + y = 1$$

$$\Rightarrow \quad \alpha + \beta = 1$$

Hence, the value of $(|\alpha + \beta| + 4)^{-1}$ is 0.2.

37. The line $y = mx + c$ will be a tangent to the ellipse $\frac{x^2}{a^2} + \frac{y^2}{b^2} = 1$,

then $c^2 = a^2m^2 + b^2$

Here, $c = a, \quad m = -1, a^2 = 9$ and $b^2 = 16$

Thus, $a^2 = 16 + 9 = 25$

$$\Rightarrow \quad a = \pm 5$$

$$\Rightarrow \quad (|a| + 1)^3 = (|\pm 5| + 1)^3 = 6^3 = 216$$

38. We have, $\quad xy = 2$

$$y = \frac{2}{x}$$

$$\frac{dy}{dx} = -\frac{2}{x^2} < 0$$

So, the tangent makes obtuse angle with the X-axis.

Thus, the number of points is zero i.e. $m = 0$

Hence, the value of $(m+4)^2$ is 16.

39. Given curves are

$$y^2 = 8x \text{ and } x^2 + (y+6)^2 = 1$$

$$\Rightarrow \quad 2y\frac{dy}{dx} = 8\,;\, 2x + 2(y+6)\frac{dy}{dx} = 0$$

$$\Rightarrow \quad \frac{dy}{dx} = \frac{4}{y};\, \frac{dy}{dx} = -\frac{x}{(y+6)}$$

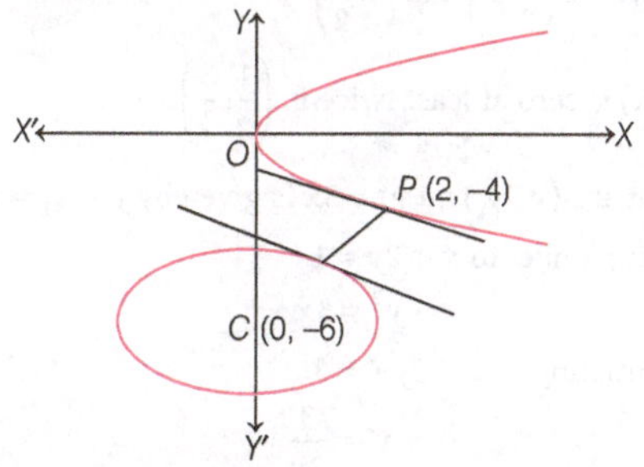

Since, the tangents are parallel, so their slopes are same

$$\frac{4}{y} = -\frac{x}{(y+6)}$$

$$\Rightarrow \quad 4y + 24 + xy = 0$$

$$\Rightarrow \quad 4y + 24 + y \cdot \frac{y^2}{8} = 0$$

$$\Rightarrow \quad y^3 + 32y + 192 = 0$$

$$\Rightarrow \quad y^3 + 4y^2 - 4y^2 - 16y + 48y + 192 = 0$$

$$\Rightarrow \quad y^2(y+4) - 4y(y+4) + 48(y+4) = 0$$

$$\Rightarrow \quad (y^2 - 4y + 48)(y+4) = 0$$

$$\Rightarrow \quad (y+4) = 0 \Rightarrow y = -4$$

When $y = -4$, then $8x = 16$

$$x = 2$$

Hence, the nearest point is $(2, -4)$.

Thus, $(\alpha, \beta) = (2, -4)$.

Hence, the value of $(|\alpha + \beta|) + 3$ is $2 + 3 = 5$.

40. Let the common tangent be $y = ax + b$

On solving with both the curves.

$$x^2 - x + 1 = ax + b$$

$$\Rightarrow \quad x^2 - 3x + 1 = ax + b$$

$$\Rightarrow \quad x^2 - (1+a)x + (1-b) = 0$$

$$\Rightarrow \quad x^2 - (a+3)x + (1-b) = 0$$

On putting $D = 0$, we get

$$(a+1)^2 - 4(1-b) = 0 \qquad \text{...(i)}$$

$\Rightarrow \quad (a+3)^2 - 4(1-b) = 0 \quad$ ...(ii)

On solving Eqs. (i) and (ii), we get

$$a = -2$$

Thus, slope of the common tangent $= m = -2$

Hence, the value of $(|m| + 3)$ is 5.

41. $f'(x) = \dfrac{g'(x) - g'(2-x)}{2}$, $f'\left(\dfrac{3}{2}\right) = \dfrac{g'\left(\dfrac{3}{2}\right) - g'\left(\dfrac{1}{2}\right)}{2} = 0$

Also, $f'\left(\dfrac{1}{2}\right) = \dfrac{g'\left(\dfrac{1}{2}\right) - g'\left(\dfrac{3}{2}\right)}{2} = 0$, $f'\left(\dfrac{1}{2}\right) = 0$

$\Rightarrow f'\left(\dfrac{3}{2}\right) = f'\left(\dfrac{1}{2}\right) = 0$

$\Rightarrow$ Roots are $\left(\dfrac{1}{2}, 1\right)$ and $\left(1, \dfrac{3}{2}\right)$.

$\Rightarrow f''(x)$ is zero at least twice in $\left(\dfrac{1}{2}, \dfrac{3}{2}\right)$.

42. Tangent at $P(x_1, y_1)$ on $y^2 = 3x$ is given by $y - y_1 = m_1(x - x_1)$ which is parallel to $x + 2y = 1$

Now, $\quad y^2 = 3x$

Differentiating, $\quad 2yy' = 3$

$$y' = \frac{3}{2y}$$

$\Rightarrow \quad m_1 = y' = \dfrac{3}{2y_1}$

$\therefore \quad \dfrac{3}{2y_1} = -\dfrac{1}{2} \quad \left[\text{slope of } x + 2y = \dfrac{1}{2}\right]$

$\Rightarrow \quad y_1 = -3$

$\therefore \quad x_1 = 3 \quad [\because (x_1, y_1) \text{ lies on } y^2 = 3x]$

$\therefore$ Point P is $(3, -3)$.

Tangent at point $Q(x_2, y_2)$ on $\dfrac{x^2}{4} + \dfrac{y^2}{1} = 1$ is given by

$y - y_1 = m_2(x - x_2)$ which is perpendicular to the line

$$x - y = 2$$

$\therefore$ Differentiating the equation of ellipse,

$$\frac{2x}{4} + \frac{2yy'}{1} = 0$$

$\Rightarrow \quad y' = \dfrac{-x}{4y}$

$\Rightarrow \quad m_2 = -\dfrac{x_2}{4y_2}$

$\therefore \quad \dfrac{-x_2}{4y_2} = -1 \quad$ [slope of $x - y = 2$ is $1 = m_3$]

(But $m_2 m_3 = -1 \Rightarrow m_2 = -1$)

$\Rightarrow \quad 4y_2 = x_2$

$\therefore$ On putting this in equation of ellipse, we get

$$Q(x_2, y_2) = \left(\frac{4}{\sqrt{5}}, \frac{1}{\sqrt{5}}\right)$$

$$R(x_3, y_3) = \left(-\frac{4}{\sqrt{5}}, -\frac{1}{\sqrt{5}}\right)$$

$$\therefore \text{Area of } \Delta PQR = \frac{1}{2}\begin{vmatrix} x_1 & y_1 & 1 \\ x_2 & y_2 & 1 \\ x_3 & y_3 & 1 \end{vmatrix} = \frac{1}{2}\begin{vmatrix} 3 & -3 & 1 \\ \frac{4}{\sqrt{5}} & \frac{1}{\sqrt{5}} & 1 \\ -\frac{4}{\sqrt{5}} & -\frac{1}{\sqrt{5}} & 1 \end{vmatrix} = 3\sqrt{5}$$

43. Let the quadratic curve be $f(x) = ax^2 + bx + c$.

The curve passes through $(-1, 0)$

$$0 = a - b + c \Rightarrow a + c = b \quad \text{...(i)}$$

The curve also passes through $(1, 1)$

$$a + b + c = 1 \quad \text{...(ii)}$$

$$2b = 1 \Rightarrow b = 1/2$$

$$f'(x) = 2ax + b$$

Slope tangent of curve $= f'(x)$ at $(1, 1)$

$$= 2a + b$$

Slope of line $y = x$ is 1.

$\therefore \quad 2a + b = 1$

$\Rightarrow \quad 2a + \dfrac{1}{2} = 1 \Rightarrow a = \dfrac{1}{4}$

$\therefore \quad c = \dfrac{1}{4}$

$$f(x) = \frac{1}{4}x^2 + \frac{1}{2}x + \frac{1}{4} = \frac{(x+1)^2}{4}$$

$$f'(x) = \frac{2(x+1)}{4} = \frac{x+1}{2}$$

$f(x)$ passes through $(\alpha, \alpha + 1)$

$$\alpha + 1 = \frac{(\alpha+1)^2}{4}$$

$$\alpha + 1 = 4 \text{ or } \alpha = 3$$

Equation of normal at $(3, 4)$ is

$$y - 4 = -\frac{1}{2}(x - 3)$$

For x, intercept, $y = 0$

$$x - 3 = 8 \text{ or } x = 11$$

Hence, the required x intercept is 11.

44. Equation of tangent at $R(b, f(b))$

$$y - f(b) = f'(b)(x - b),$$

which passes through $S(0, c)$.

$\therefore \quad c - f(b) = f'(b)(0 - b)$

$\Rightarrow \quad bf'(b) - f(b) = -c$

$\Rightarrow \quad bf'(b) - f(b) = \dfrac{-3}{b} \quad [\because bc = 3]$

$\Rightarrow \quad \dfrac{bf'(b) - f(b)}{b^2} = \dfrac{-3}{b^3}$

$\Rightarrow \quad d\left(\dfrac{f(b)}{b}\right) = \dfrac{-3}{b^3} \Rightarrow \dfrac{f(b)}{b} = \dfrac{3}{2b^2} + c$

which passes through $P\left(1, \dfrac{3}{2}\right)$

$\Rightarrow \quad \dfrac{3/2}{1} = \dfrac{3}{2} + c \Rightarrow c = 0$

$\therefore \quad f(b) = \dfrac{3}{2b^2} \times b \Rightarrow f(b) = \dfrac{3}{2b}$

It passes through $\left(a, \dfrac{1}{2}\right)$.

$\therefore \quad \dfrac{1}{2} = \dfrac{3}{2a} \Rightarrow a = 3$

$P \equiv \left(1, \dfrac{3}{2}\right)$ and $Q \equiv \left(3, \dfrac{1}{2}\right)$

$\therefore \quad (PQ)^2 = (3-1)^2 + \left(\dfrac{1}{2} - \dfrac{3}{2}\right)^2 = 4 + 1 = 5$

45. Given, curve is $\left(\dfrac{x}{a}\right)^n + \left(\dfrac{y}{b}\right)^n = 2$.

Now, slope of tangent at (a, b)

$$n \cdot \left(\frac{x}{a}\right)^{n-1} \cdot \frac{1}{a} + n\left(\frac{x}{b}\right)^{n-1} \cdot \frac{1}{b}\frac{dy}{dx} = 0$$

$$\left.\frac{dy}{dx}\right|_{(a,b)} = -\frac{b}{a}$$

$\therefore$ Equation of tangent

$$y - b = -\frac{b}{a}(x - a)$$

$\Rightarrow \quad ay - ab = -bx + ab$

$\Rightarrow \quad bx + ay = 2ab$

$\Rightarrow \quad \dfrac{x}{a} + \dfrac{y}{b} = 2, \forall n \in N$

$\therefore \quad S = N$

46. **Decoding the Question**

Find vertex at parabola $y = x - x^2$, using concept given as

$\therefore \quad \dfrac{dy}{dx} = 0 \Rightarrow 1 - 2x = 0$ or $x = \dfrac{1}{2}$

For $x = \dfrac{1}{2}, y = \dfrac{1}{4}$, so coordinate of vertex $\equiv \left(\dfrac{1}{2}, \dfrac{1}{4}\right)$.

Point P satisfies the equation of curve.

Let abscissa of point P be α, then $y = \alpha - \alpha^2$.

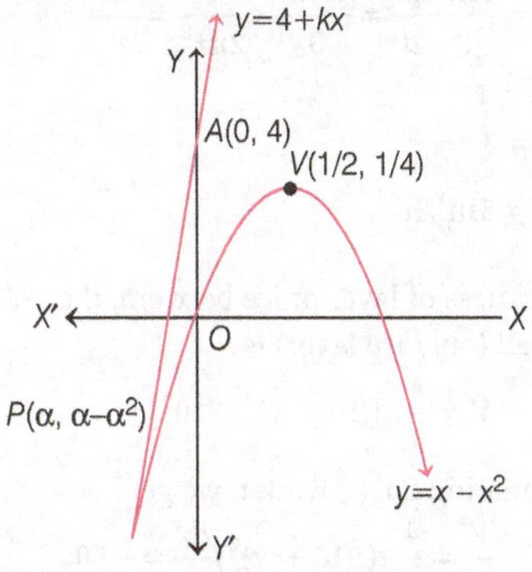

Slope of tangent at P = Slope of line AP

$$(1 - 2x)\big|_{(\alpha, \alpha - \alpha^2)} = (1 - 2\alpha) = \frac{\alpha - \alpha^2 - 4}{\alpha}$$

$\Rightarrow \quad \alpha - 2\alpha^2 = \alpha - \alpha^2 - 4 \Rightarrow \alpha = \pm 2$

Take $\alpha = -2, x = -2, y = -6$

$\Rightarrow \quad P(-2, -6)$

$$\text{Slope of } PV = \frac{\frac{1}{4} + 6}{\frac{1}{2} + 2} = \frac{5}{2}$$

47. Given equation of curve

$$x = 12(t + \sin t \cos t), y = 12(1 + \sin t)^2$$

On differentiate w.r.t. t, we get

$$\frac{dx}{dt} = 12(1 + \cos^2 t - \sin^2 t) = 12(1 + \cos 2t)$$

$$\frac{dx}{dt} = 12(1 + \cos 2t) \text{ and } \frac{dy}{dt} = 24(1 + \sin t)\cos t$$

$$\frac{dy}{dx} = \frac{2(1 + \sin t) \times \cos t}{1 + \cos 2t}$$

$$= \frac{2(1 + \sin t)\cos t}{2\cos^2 t} = \left(\tan\left(\frac{\pi}{3}\right)\right)$$

Thus, $\quad t = \pi/6$

So, $\quad y_0 = 12\left(1 + \sin\dfrac{\pi}{6}\right)^2 = 12\left(1 + \dfrac{1}{2}\right)^2 = 12 \times \dfrac{9}{4} = 27$

48. Ratio of radius to height $(r : h)$ is $7 : 35$ or $1 : 5$

$\Rightarrow \quad r = \dfrac{h}{5}$

Volume of cone $(V) = \dfrac{1}{3}\pi r^2 h = \dfrac{1}{75}\pi h^3$

$\therefore \quad \dfrac{dV}{dt} = \dfrac{1}{75}\pi 3h^2 \dfrac{dh}{dt}$

$\Rightarrow \quad 1 = \dfrac{1}{75}\pi \times 3 \times h^2 \times \dfrac{dh}{dt} \quad \left[\because \dfrac{dV}{dt} = 1\,\text{cm}^3/\text{s}\right]$

$\Rightarrow \quad \dfrac{dh}{dt} = \dfrac{25}{\pi h^2}$

Conical Surface Area $(S) = \pi r l = \pi r\left(\sqrt{r^2 + h^2}\right)$

$$= \pi\frac{h}{5}\sqrt{\frac{h^2}{25} + h^2} = \pi\frac{h^2}{25}\sqrt{26}$$

$\therefore \quad \dfrac{dS}{dt} = \dfrac{\pi \times 2h\sqrt{26}}{25}\dfrac{dh}{dt}$

$$\left(\frac{dS}{dt}\right)_{h=10} = \frac{2\pi h\sqrt{26}}{25} \times \frac{25}{\pi h^2} = \frac{2\sqrt{26}}{h} = \frac{\sqrt{26}}{5}\,\text{cm}^2/\text{s}$$

49. Let r be the radius of spherical balloon and S is surface area $= 4\pi r^2$

On differentiating both sides w.r.t. t, we get

$$\frac{dS}{dt} = 8\pi r \times \frac{dr}{dt} = k \text{ (constant)} \quad \text{[given]}$$

Taking integral on both sides, we get

$$4\pi r^2 = k_1 t + C \text{ (C is constant of an integration)} \quad \text{...(i)}$$

On putting the values of t and r in Eq. (i), we get

At $t = 0, r = 3 \Rightarrow 36\pi = C$

At $t = 5, r = 7 \Rightarrow k_1 = 32\pi$

On putting the values of C and k_1 in Eq. (i), we get

$$4\pi r^2 = 32\pi t + 36\pi$$

$$\Rightarrow \quad r^2 = 8t + 9$$

On putting $t = 9$, $\quad r^2 = 81 \Rightarrow r = 9$

50. We have, $y^5 - 9xy + 2x = 0$

On differentiating w.r.t. x, we get

Now, $5y^4 \dfrac{dy}{dx} - 9x\dfrac{dy}{dx} - 9y + 2 = 0$

$$\frac{dy}{dx}(5y^4 - 9x) = 9y - 2$$

$$\Rightarrow \quad \frac{dy}{dx} = \frac{9y-2}{5y^4 - 9x}$$

For horizontal tangent,

$$\frac{dy}{dx} = \frac{9y-2}{5y^4 - 9x} = 0 \Rightarrow y = \frac{2}{9}$$

which does not satisfy the given equation.

So, $\quad M = 0$

Now, $5y^4 - 9x = 0$ $\quad$ [for vertical tangent]

$$5y^4(9y-2) - 9y^5 = 0$$

$$\Rightarrow \quad y^4[45y - 10 - 9y] = 0$$

Either $\quad y = 0$ or $36y = 10$

So, $y = 0$ or $y = \dfrac{5}{18}$

Thus, $y = 0 \Rightarrow x = 0$ and $y = \dfrac{5}{18}$

$\Rightarrow$ (0, 0) and $\left(x, \dfrac{5}{18}\right)$

$$N = 2 \text{ and } M + N = 2$$

51. Given function, $f(x) = 2x^2 - \log_e x$

On differentiating w.r.t. x, we get

$$f'(x) = 4x - \frac{1}{x}$$

Now, $\quad f'(x) = 0$

$$\Rightarrow \quad 4x - \frac{1}{x} = 0 \Rightarrow 4x^2 - 1 = 0$$

$$\Rightarrow \quad x = \pm\frac{1}{2}.$$

According to given interval $(0, a)$ and $(a, 4)$, a must be positive.

Then, $x = \dfrac{1}{2}$. So, $a = \dfrac{1}{2}$ $\quad$ [$\because x > 0$]

Let $p(h, k)$ on parabola $y^2 = 4ax$.

So, that it passes the point $(8a, 8a - 1)$

$$\rightarrow \left(8 \times \frac{1}{2}, 8 \times \frac{1}{2} - 1\right) \rightarrow (4, 3)$$

$$\frac{1}{k} = \frac{3-k}{4-h} \Rightarrow k^2 - 6k + 8 = 0$$

$$k = 2, 4$$

Satisfy point $p(h, k)$ on equation of parabola $k^2 = 2h$.

So, $k = 4 \Rightarrow h = 8$

Equation of normal,

$$p(y - 4) = -4(x - 8)$$

$$\Rightarrow \quad y - 4 = -4x + 32$$

$$\Rightarrow \quad 4x + y = 36$$

$$\Rightarrow \quad \frac{x}{9} + \frac{y}{36} = 1$$

Here, $\alpha = 9, \beta = 36$

So, $\alpha + \beta = 9 + 36 = 45$

52. We have, $\quad \tan\theta = \dfrac{3}{4} \Rightarrow \dfrac{r}{h} = \dfrac{3}{4}$

[$\because \theta$ is semi-vertical angle]

$$\therefore \quad h = \frac{4r}{3}$$

$$\Rightarrow \quad l = \sqrt{r^2 + \frac{16r^2}{9}} = \frac{5r}{3}$$

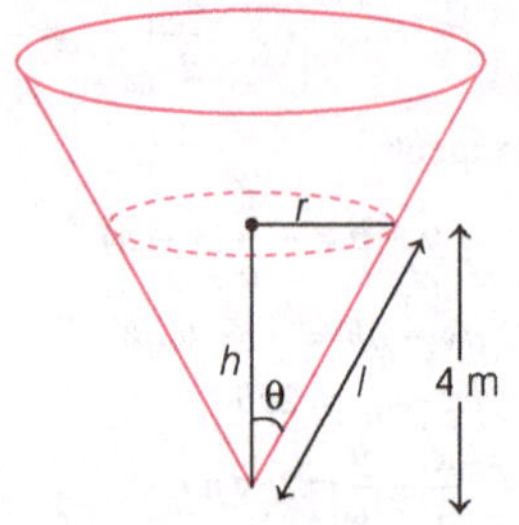

Volume of water $= V = \dfrac{1}{3}\pi r^2 h = \dfrac{4\pi(r)^3}{9}$

$$\frac{dV}{dt} = \frac{4\pi r^2}{3} \cdot \frac{dr}{dt} = 6$$

$$\therefore \quad \frac{dr}{dt} = \frac{9}{2\pi r^2}$$

Now, curved surface area $= S = \pi r l$

$$\therefore \quad S = \frac{5\pi r^2}{3}$$

$$\therefore \quad \frac{dS}{dt} = \frac{10\pi r}{3}\frac{dr}{dt} = \frac{10\pi r}{3} \times \frac{9}{2\pi r^2} = \frac{15}{r}$$

Now, $\quad h = 4$

$\therefore \quad r = 3$

$$\frac{dS}{dt} = 5\text{m}^2/\text{h}$$

53. Let the thickness of layer of ice be x cm, the volume of spherical ball (only ice layer) is

$$V = \frac{4}{3}\pi[(10 + x)^3 - 10^3] \quad \text{...(i)}$$

On differentiating Eq. (i) w.r.t. t, we get

$$\frac{dV}{dt} = \frac{4}{3}\pi(3(10 + x)^2)\frac{dx}{dt} = -50 \quad \text{[given]}$$

[– ve sign indicate that volume is decreasing as time passes]

$$\Rightarrow \quad 4\pi(10 + x)^2\frac{dx}{dt} = -50$$

At $x = 5$ cm,

$$\frac{dx}{dt}[4\pi(10+5)^2] = -50$$

$$\Rightarrow \quad \frac{dx}{dt} = -\frac{50}{225(4\pi)}$$

$$= -\frac{1}{9(2\pi)} = -\frac{1}{18\pi} \text{ cm/min}$$

So, the thickness of the ice decreases at the rate of $\frac{1}{18\pi}$ cm/min.

54. Since, all normals of circle passes through centre. Therefore, curve is a circle with centre (a, b) and passes through $(3, -3)$ and $(4, -2\sqrt{2})$.

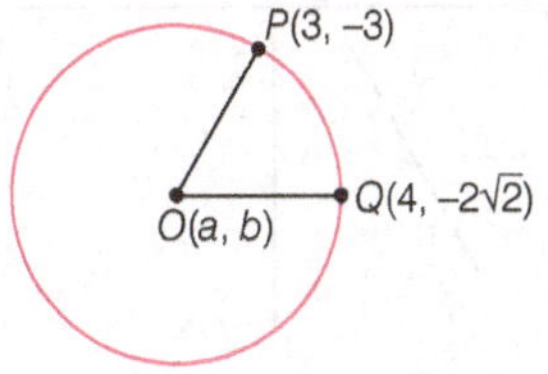

Since, $OP = OQ \Rightarrow OP^2 = OQ^2$ [squaring on both sides]

$$(a-3)^2 + (b+3)^2 = (a-4)^2 + (b+2\sqrt{2})^2$$

$$\Rightarrow \quad a + (3 - 2\sqrt{2})b = 3 \quad \text{...(i)}$$

Now, $\quad a - 2\sqrt{2}\,b = 3 \quad$ (given) ...(ii)

From Eqs. (i) and (ii), we get

$$b = 0, a = 3$$

$$\therefore \quad a^2 + b^2 + ab = 9 + 0 + 0 = 9$$

55. Let the side of cube be a and S be the surface area of cube.

$$S = 6a^2$$

$$\Rightarrow \quad \frac{dS}{dt} = 12a \cdot \frac{da}{dt} \Rightarrow 3.6 = 12a \cdot \frac{da}{dt}$$

$$\Rightarrow \quad 12(10)\frac{da}{dt} = 3.6 \Rightarrow \frac{da}{dt} = 0.03$$

$\therefore$ Volume, $V = a^3$

$$\Rightarrow \quad \frac{dV}{dt} = 3a^2 \cdot \frac{da}{dt} = 3(10)^2 \cdot \left(\frac{3}{100}\right) = 9$$

Exercise 2 - JEE Advanced Pattern

1. $5x^5 - 10x^3 + x + 2y + 6 = 0 \quad$ ...(i)

On differentiating w.r.t. x, we get

$$25x^4 - 30x^2 + 1 + 2\frac{dy}{dx} = 0$$

$$\frac{dy}{dx} = -\frac{1}{2}(25x^4 - 30x^2 + 1)$$

$$\left(\frac{dy}{dx}\right)_{(0,-3)} = -\frac{1}{2}(0 - 0 + 1) = -\frac{1}{2}$$

$\therefore$ Equation of the normal at $P(0, -3)$ is

$$y + 3 = 2(x - 0)$$

$$\Rightarrow \quad y = 2x - 3 \quad \text{...(ii)}$$

On solving Eqs. (i) and (ii),

$$5x^5 - 10x^3 + x + 4x - 6 + 6 = 0$$

$$5x(x^4 - 2x^2 + 1) = 0$$

$$5x(x^2 - 1)^2 = 0$$

$$\therefore \quad x = 0, 1, -1$$

$$\text{and} \quad y = -3, -1, -5$$

$\therefore$ Normal at point $P(0, -3)$ meets the curve again at two points $(1, -1)$ and $(-1, -5)$.

Now, equation of tangent at point $(1, -1)$ is

$$y + 1 = \left(\frac{dy}{dx}\right)_{(1,-1)}(x - 1)$$

$$\Rightarrow \quad y + 1 = 2(x - 1)$$

$$\Rightarrow \quad 2x - y - 3 = 0 \quad \text{...(iii)}$$

Equation of tangent at point $(-1, -5)$ is

$$y + 5 = \left(\frac{dy}{dx}\right)_{(-1,-5)}(x + 1)$$

$$\Rightarrow \quad y + 5 = 2(x + 1)$$

$$\Rightarrow \quad 2x - y - 3 = 0$$

2. According to LMVT,

$$\left|\frac{f'(x) - f'(0)}{x}\right| = |f''(C_1)| \le 1$$

$$\Rightarrow \quad |f'(x)| \le |x|$$

Again, by LMVT

$$\left|\frac{f(x) - f(0)}{x}\right| = |f'(C_2)| \le |x|$$

$$\Rightarrow \quad f(x) \le x^2$$

3. We have, volume of sphere, $S = \frac{4}{3}\pi r^2 \quad$ ...(i)

Change in volume, $\Delta S = hA\,|_{r=r_0} + \frac{h^2}{2}\cdot\frac{dA}{dr}\Big|_{r=r_0}$

$$\text{Area, } A = 4\pi r^2 \quad \text{...(ii)}$$

On differentiating w.r.t. r, we get

$$\frac{dA}{dr} = 8\pi r$$

From Eq. (i), we get

$$\Delta S = h \times 4\pi r_0^2 + \frac{h^2}{2} 8\pi r$$

$$\Delta S = 4\pi r_0^2 h + 4\pi r_0 h^2$$

New volume $= S + \Delta S$

$$= \frac{4}{3}\pi r_0^3 + 4\pi h r_0^2 + 4\pi r_0 h^2$$

As, it is given that radius is change from r_0 to $r_0 + h$.

So, actual volume will be

$$\frac{4}{3}\pi(r_0 + h)^3 \text{ or } \frac{4\pi}{3}[r_0^3 + h^3 + 3r_0^2 h + 3r_0 h^2]$$

Change in volume $= (S + \Delta S) - \frac{4}{3}\pi(r_0 + h)^3$

$$= -\frac{4}{3}\pi h^3$$

4. We have, $x = t + e^{at}, y = -t + e^{at}$

Let curve touches X-axis at $(x_1, 0)$, then slope of tangent at this point will be zero.

Now, $\frac{dx}{dt} = 1 + ae^{at}$ and $\frac{dy}{dt} = -1 + ae^{at}$

$\therefore \quad \frac{dy}{dx} = \frac{-1 + ae^{at}}{1 + ae^{at}}$

Now, slope at $(x_1, 0)$, $\frac{-1 + ae^{at_1}}{1 + ae^{at_1}} = 0$

$\Rightarrow \quad ae^{at_1} = 1 \quad$ ...(i)

Also, at X-axis $y = 0$,

so $\quad -t_1 + e^{at_1} = 0 \quad$ ...(ii)

From Eqs. (i) and (ii), we get

$$t_1 = \frac{1}{a}$$

Again from Eq. (i), $ae = 1 \Rightarrow a = \frac{1}{e}$

$\therefore \quad t_1 = e$

So, $x_1 = t_1 + e^{at_1}$ or $x = e + e = 2e$

Hence, the required point is $(2e, 0)$.

5. $1 = 1 + b + c \Rightarrow c = -b$

$$\frac{dy}{dx} = 2x + b = 2 + b \text{ at } (1, 1)$$

Equation of tangent is $y - 1 = (2 + b)(x - 1)$

$\Rightarrow$ x-intercept $= \frac{b+1}{b+2}$

y-intercept $= -(b + 1)$

$\Rightarrow \quad \left| \frac{1}{2} \times \left(\frac{b+1}{b+2} \right) \times (b + 1) \right| = 2$

$$b^2 + 2b + 1 = 4b + 8 \text{ or } -4b - 8$$

$$b^2 - 2b - 7 = 0 \text{ or } b^2 + 6b + 9 = 0$$

$\Rightarrow$ Integral $b = -3$

6. $y = e^{\{x\}} = e^{x-a}$ in $x \in [a, a + 1)$

$\frac{dy}{dx} = e^{x-a} = e^{\{x\}}$

Equation of tangent, $(Y - y) = \frac{dy}{dx}(X - x)$ passing through $\left(-\frac{1}{2}, 0\right)$, Then,

$$(0 - y) = e^{\{x\}}\left(-\frac{1}{2} - x\right)$$

$\Rightarrow \quad -1 = -\frac{1}{2} - x$

$\Rightarrow \quad x = \frac{1}{2}$

$\therefore$ Point $\left(\frac{1}{2}, e^{1/2}\right)$

So, number of tangent $= 1$

7. Let $y = mx + c$ be tangent touching both branches.

$$f(x) = -x^2, y = mx + c, x < 0$$

$x^2 + mx + c = 0, m > 0 \quad$ [$\because x < 0$, negative roots]

$$D = 0 \Rightarrow m^2 = 4c$$

$$f(x) = x^2 + 8, y = mx + c, x > 0$$

$x^2 - mx + 8 - c = 0, m > 0 \quad$ [positive roots]

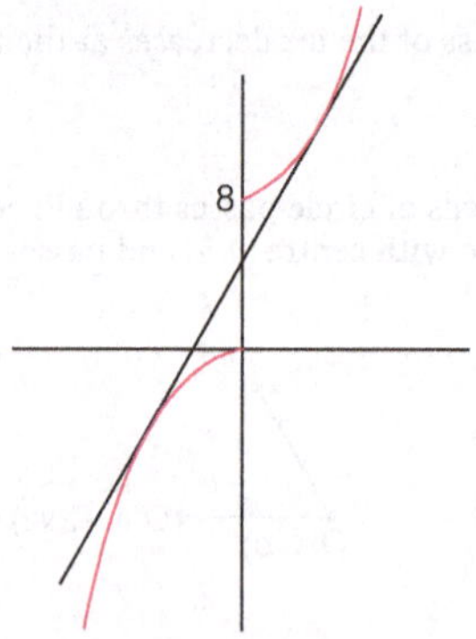

$$D = 0 \Rightarrow m^2 = 32 - 4c$$

$\Rightarrow \quad c = 4, m^2 = 16 \Rightarrow c = 4, m = 4$

$\therefore$ Equation of tangent line is $y = 4x + 4$.

8. **Decoding the Question**

If $x = a$ is the right most point of the domain, then for function to continuous at $x = a$

$\lim_{x \to a^-} f(x) = f(a)$, i.e LHL$|_{x=a} = f(a)$

Given, $f(x) = \begin{cases} (1 - x)^\alpha \cdot x \cdot (1 - \cos(2\pi x)), & 0 < x \le 1 \\ 0, & x = 0 \end{cases}$

$f(x)$ is not defined at $x = 1$ for $\alpha \le 0 \quad$ ...(i)

$f(x)$ is continuous at $x = 0$ but for continuous at $x = 1$

$$f(1^-) = f(1)$$

$\therefore \quad 2 \lim_{h \to 0} h^\alpha \sin^2 \pi h = 0$

$\Rightarrow \quad \lim_{h \to 0} h^{\alpha+2} = 0$

$\therefore \quad \alpha + 2 > 0 \Rightarrow \alpha > -2 \quad$ ...(ii)

Hence, $(1) \cap (2) \Rightarrow \alpha > 0$

$f(x)$ is differentiable in $(0, 1)$.

9.

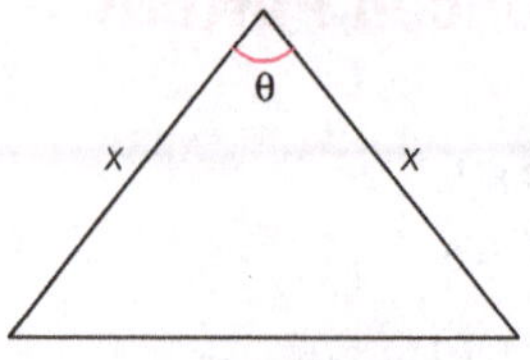

$$A = \frac{1}{2}x^2 \sin\theta$$

$$\frac{dA}{dt} = x\sin\theta \frac{dx}{dt} + \frac{x^2}{2}\cos\theta \frac{d\theta}{dt}$$

$$= 12 \times \frac{1}{\sqrt{2}} \times \frac{1}{12} + \frac{144}{2} \times \frac{1}{\sqrt{2}} \times \frac{\pi}{180} = 2^{1/2}\left(\frac{1}{2} + \frac{\pi}{5}\right)$$

10. $$P(t) = 60t^2 - t^3$$
$$P'(t) = 120t - 3t^2 = 900$$
$$\Rightarrow \quad t^2 - 40t + 300 = 0 \Rightarrow t = 10, 30$$

11. At $x = \dfrac{\pi}{3}, y = \dfrac{3\sqrt{3}}{2}$

$$\frac{dy}{dx} = 2\cos x + 2\cos 2x \Rightarrow \frac{dy}{dx} = 0$$

Tangent $\Rightarrow y = \dfrac{3\sqrt{3}}{2}$

Normal $\Rightarrow x = \dfrac{\pi}{3}$

$\therefore$ Area $= \dfrac{\pi}{3} \times \dfrac{3\sqrt{3}}{2} = \dfrac{\sqrt{3}\pi}{2}$

12. $f(x) = \int \dfrac{x}{2} d\left(1 - \dfrac{1}{x^2}\right) = \int \dfrac{x}{2} \dfrac{2}{x^3} dx = \int \dfrac{1}{x^2} dx = -\dfrac{1}{x} + C$

$f(2) = -\dfrac{1}{2} + C = \dfrac{1}{2} \Rightarrow C = 1$

$$\therefore \quad f(x) = \frac{x-1}{x}$$

$$g_1(x) = f(x) = \frac{x-1}{x};$$

$$g_2(x) = f(f(x)) = \frac{\frac{x-1}{x} - 1}{\frac{x-1}{x}} = \frac{-1}{x-1} = \frac{1}{1-x}$$

$$g_3(x) = f(f(f(x))) = f\left(\frac{1}{1-x}\right) = \frac{\frac{1}{1-x} - 1}{\frac{1}{1-x}} = x$$

$$g_3(x) = x$$

$$\therefore \quad \frac{d}{dx}(g_{3x}(x)) = 1 \text{ and } g_{80}(x) = g_2(x) = \frac{1}{1-x}$$

$$\Rightarrow \quad \frac{d}{dx}(g_2(x)) = \frac{1}{(1-x)^2} \Rightarrow \frac{d}{dx}(g_2 x)_{x=\frac{1}{2}} = 4$$

13. $f(-1) = -f(-1)$ and $f(0) = 0$ as is odd.

Consider the interval $x \in [-1, 0]$

Slope of chord joining $(-1, f(-1))$

and $(0, f(0)) = \dfrac{(f(-1) - f(0))}{-1-0} = \dfrac{-f(1) - 0}{-1-0} = f(1)$

So, applying LMVT, we get

$$\exists\, a \in (-1, 0) \text{ such that } f'(a) = f(1)$$

Similarly, considering the interval $x \in [0, 1]$ and applying LMVT, we get

$$\exists\, b \in (0, 1) \text{ such that } f'(b) = f(1)$$

Now, consider the function $g(x) = f^n(x), x \in [-1, 1]$

Consider the interval $x \in [-1, 0]$

Slope of chord joining $(-1, g(-1))$

and $(0, g(0)) = \dfrac{g(-1) - g(0)}{-1-0} = \dfrac{f^n(-1)}{-1} = \dfrac{(-1)^n f^n(1)}{-1}$

$$= (-1)^{n-1} f^n(1) = \begin{cases} f^n(1), & \text{if } n \text{ is odd} \\ -f^n(1), & \text{if } n \text{ is even} \end{cases}$$

So, option (c) is correct only when n is odd.

But in the interval $x \in [0, 1]$: slope of chord joining $(0, g(0))$ and $(1, g(1)) = \dfrac{g(1) - g(0)}{1-0} = f^n(1)$

So, LMVT $\Rightarrow \exists\, \beta \in (0, 1)$ such that $g'(\beta) = f^n(1)$

14. Given, $f(f(x)) = -x + 1$

Replacing $x \to f(x)$,

$$f(f(f(x))) = -f(x) + 1$$
$$\Rightarrow \quad f(1-x) = -f(x) + 1$$
$$\Rightarrow \quad f(x) + f(1-x) = 1 \quad \text{...(i)}$$

Now, $J = \int_0^1 f(x)dx = \int_0^1 f(1-x)dx$ [using $(a-x)$ property]

$$\Rightarrow \quad 2J = \int_0^1 (f(x) + f(1-x))dx \Rightarrow J = \frac{1}{2}$$

Also, from Eq. (i), we get

$$f''(x) + f''(1-x) = 0 \Rightarrow f''\left(\frac{1}{2}\right) = 0$$

So, $$f''\left(\frac{1}{2}\right) = f''\left(\frac{4}{5}\right)$$

Hence, by Rolle's theorem,

$$f'''(x) = 0 \Rightarrow x \in \left(\frac{1}{2}, \frac{4}{5}\right)$$

Also, $$f'(x) = f'(1-x) \Rightarrow f'\left(\frac{1}{4}\right) = f'\left(\frac{3}{4}\right)$$

So, by Rolle's theorem, $f''(x) = 0 \Rightarrow x \in \left(\dfrac{1}{4}, \dfrac{3}{4}\right)$

15. Let $f(x) = \dfrac{ax^5}{5} + \dfrac{bx^3}{3} + cx$, then $f(1) = 0, f(-1) = 0, f(0) = 0$

$\Rightarrow$ There exist atleast one root of equation $ax^4 + bx^2 + c = 0$ in $(-1, 0)$ and there exist atleast one root of equation $f'(x) = 0$ in $(0, 1)$.

But $\dfrac{-b}{a}$ equals to negative, so equation $ax^4 + bx^2 + c = 0$ has two real and two non-real roots.

Hence, there exist exactly one root of equation $ax^4 + bx^2 + c = 0$ in $(-1, 0)$ and there exist exactly one root of equation $f'(x) = 0$ in $(0, 1)$.

16. Let $h(x) = f(x) - 3g(x)$

$$h(-1) = f(-1) - 3g(-1) = 3 - 0 = 3$$
$$h(0) = f(0) - 3g(0) = 6 - 3 = 3$$
$$h(2) = f(2) - 3g(2) = 0 - (-3) = 3$$

Thus, $h'(x) = 0$ has atleast one root in $(-1, 0)$ and atleast one root in $(0, 2)$.

But since $h''(x) = 0$ has no root in $(-1, 0)$ and $(0, 2)$.

Therefore, $h'(x) = 0$ has exactly 1 root in $(-1, 0)$ and exactly 1 root in $(0, 2)$.

Sol. (Q. Nos. 17 to 18)

17. $$s = 30(1 - e^{kt})$$
$$5 = 30(1 - e^k)$$
$$e^k = \frac{5}{6}$$
$$k = \ln\left(\frac{5}{6}\right)$$

18. $S = 30(1 - e^{kt})$

$\frac{dS}{dt} = -30ke^{kt} > 0,$ [as $k < 0$]

Max S, when $t \to \infty$

Max $S = 30$

Sol. (Q. Nos. 19 to 20)

19. $f(0) < 0$

$\Rightarrow \quad a^2 + a - 2 < 0$

$\Rightarrow \quad a \in (-2, 1)$

Integral values of a are -1, 0.

20. $y = \left(\frac{x}{2} - a\right)^2 + a - 2$

$4(y - (a-2)) = (x - 2a)^2$

Vertex $\Rightarrow h = 2a, k = a - 2$

Locus of vertex $\Rightarrow y = \frac{x}{2} - 2$

$\Rightarrow \quad 2y = x - 4$

Sol. (Q. Nos. 21 to 22)

Slope of tangent at P = Slope of OP

$\Rightarrow \quad \frac{1}{t} = \frac{\ln mt}{t}$

$\Rightarrow \quad t = \frac{e}{m}$

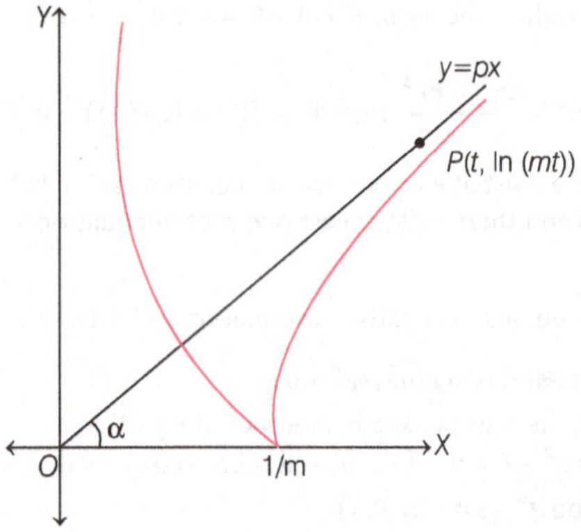

$\Rightarrow \quad P \equiv \left(\frac{e}{m}, 1\right)$

$\Rightarrow \quad \tan\alpha = p = \frac{m}{e}$

21. (d) **22.** (a)

Sol. (Q. Nos. 23 and 24)

23. On putting $y = 0$, we get

$$x^2 - 3x - c_i = 0$$

As roots are integers and $D = 9 + 4c_i$ must be perfect square.

Therefore, $9 + 4c_i = (2\lambda + 1)^2, \lambda \in I$.

$\Rightarrow \quad c_i = \lambda^2 + \lambda - 2$

$\Rightarrow \quad c_k = k(k+3), k = 1, 2, 3, \ldots$

$\therefore \quad c_1 = 4, c_2 = 10, \ldots$

$\Rightarrow \quad x^2 + y^2 - 3x - 4y - (c_2 - c_1) = 0$

or $\quad x^2 + y^2 - 3x - 4y - 6 = 0$

and $x^2 + y^2 = r^2$ will touch each other if

$$\sqrt{\frac{9}{4} + 4} = r - \left|\sqrt{\frac{9}{4} + 10}\right|$$

$\Rightarrow \quad \left|r - \frac{7}{2}\right| = \frac{5}{2} \Rightarrow r = 6$

$\therefore$ Common tangent is $3x + 4y - 30 = 0$ and passes through (10, 0).

24. An ellipse and hyperbola intersect orthogonally. They must be confocal.

$\therefore \quad a = 2$

Let point $P(\alpha, \beta)$ lies on both the curves, then

$4\alpha^2 + 9\beta^2 = 36$ ...(i)

and $\quad 4\alpha^2 - \beta^2 = 4$ ...(ii)

On adding Eqs. (i) and (ii), we get

$$8\alpha^2 + 8\beta^2 = 40$$

$\Rightarrow \quad \alpha^2 + \beta^2 = 5$

or $\quad x^2 + y^2 = \frac{c_7}{14}$, as $c_7 = 70$

Sol. (Q. Nos. 25 to 26)

25. $\frac{da}{dt} = 2 \Rightarrow a = 2t + C$

$C = 0$ [$\because a = 0$, when $t = 0$]

$\Rightarrow a = 2t$

$\therefore$ The curve $y = x^2 - 2ax + a^2 + a$ becomes

$$y = x^2 - 4tx + 4t^2 + 2t$$

If $x = 0$, then $y = 4t^2 + 2t$

$\frac{dy}{dx} = 2x - 4t$

$\therefore \quad \left.\frac{dy}{dx}\right|_{at\ x=0} = -4t$

$\therefore$ Equation of the tangent

$$y - (4t^2 + 2t) = -4t(x - 0)$$

i.e. $\quad y = -4tx + 4t^2 + 2t$

Vertex of $y = x^2 - 4tx + 4t^2 + 2t$ is $(2t, 2t)$.

$\therefore$ Distance of vertex from the origin $= 2\sqrt{2}t$

$\therefore$ Rate of change with respect to $t = 2\sqrt{2}$

i.e. $\quad k = 2\sqrt{2} \Rightarrow k^2 = 8$

26. $c(t) = 4t^2 + 2t$

$\therefore \quad \frac{dc}{dt} = 8t + 2$

$\Rightarrow \quad \left.\frac{dc}{dt}\right|_{at\ (t = 2\sqrt{2})} = 16\sqrt{2} + 2$

$\Rightarrow \quad a = 16, b = 2$

$\Rightarrow \quad a + b = 18$

Sol. (Q. Nos. 27 to 28)

27. $f''(c_2)\, f''(c_1) < 0$ and $f'(c_1) = f'(c_2) = 0$

$\Rightarrow f''(c_1) - f''(c_2) > 0$

$\Rightarrow f''(c_1) > 0$ and $f''(c_2) < 0$

$\Rightarrow c_2$ is local maximum and c_1 is local minimum for $f(x)$.

$\Rightarrow f'(x) = 0$ atleast four times in $[c_1 - 1, c_2 + 1]$.

28. Here, c_1 is local maximum and c_2 is local minimum.

$\Rightarrow f'(x) = 0$ has atleast two roots in $[c_1 - 1, c_2 + 1]$.

29. Circle with centre $(-6, 10)$ and radius $= \sqrt{36 + 100 - 120} = 4$

Now, let $(a, 0)$ be a point on the X-axis.

If y is the distance from A to P and P to M

$$y = \sqrt{(a-2)^2 + 25} + \sqrt{(a+6)^2 + 100} - 4$$

y will be minimum when $(-6, 10)$, $(a, 0)$ and $(2, -5)$ are collinear.

$\therefore$ Straight line which is passing through $(-6, 10)$ and $(2, -5)$ is

$$y + 5 = \frac{10+5}{-6-2}(x-2)$$

$$-8y - 40 = 15x - 30$$

$$15x + 8y + 10 = 0$$

$\therefore$ $(a, 0)$ must lie on this line for y minimum.

$$15a = -10$$

$$a = -\frac{2}{3}$$

$$y_{\min} = \sqrt{\left(-\frac{2}{3} - 2\right)^2 + 25} + \sqrt{\left(-\frac{2}{3} + 6\right)^2 + 100} - 4$$

$$= 13$$

$\therefore \quad a + b = 4$

30. Since, the line touches the graph of $f(x)$ at 1, 2, 3.

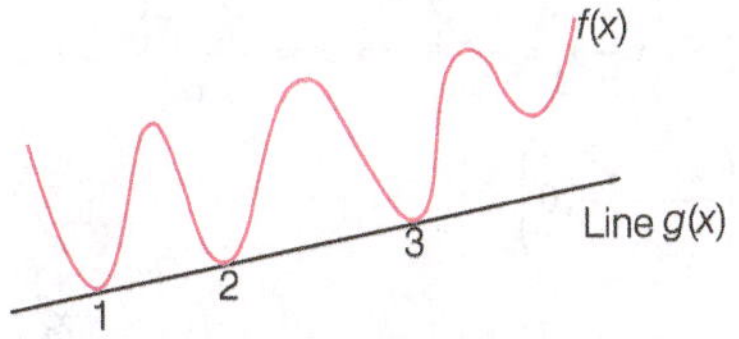

$\therefore \quad h(x) = f(x) - g(x)$ has a double root at 1, 2, 3.

$\Rightarrow h(x) = a(x-1)^2(x-2)^2(x-3)^2$

$$I = a\int_1^3 (x-1)^2(x-2)^2(x-3)^2\, dx = \frac{32}{105}$$

$$a \times \frac{16}{105} = \frac{32}{105}$$

$\therefore \quad a = 2$

31. $y = x^2$ and $y = -\frac{8}{x}$, $q = p^2$ and $s = -\frac{8}{r}$

On equating $\frac{dy}{dx}$ at A and B, we get

$$2p = \frac{8}{r^2}$$

$$\Rightarrow \quad pr^2 = 4$$

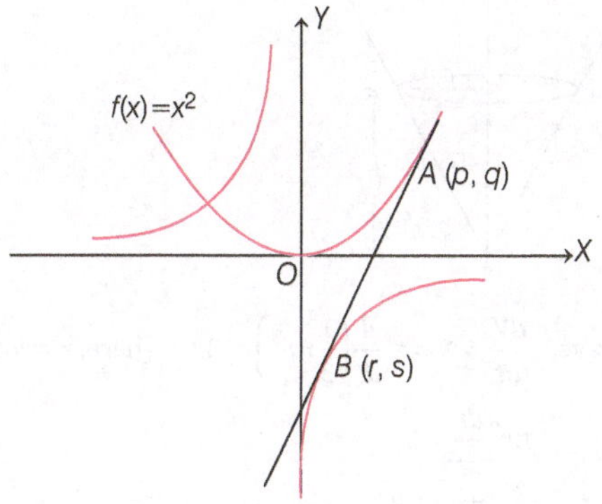

Now, $\quad m_{AB} = \frac{q-s}{p-r}$

$$\Rightarrow \quad 2p = \frac{p^2 + \frac{8}{r}}{p-r}$$

$$\Rightarrow \quad p^2 = 2pr + \frac{8}{r}$$

$$\Rightarrow \quad p^2 = \frac{16}{r}$$

$$\Rightarrow \quad \frac{16}{r^4} = \frac{16}{r}$$

$$\Rightarrow \quad r = 1\ (r \neq 0)$$

$$\Rightarrow \quad p = r$$

$$\therefore \quad r = 1, p = 4$$

Hence, $p + r = 5$

32. $\frac{dy}{dx} = \frac{dy/dt}{dx/dt} = -\frac{1}{2}\cot^3\theta = -\frac{1}{2}$ at $\theta = \frac{\pi}{4}$

Also, the point P for $\theta = \frac{\pi}{4}$ is $(2, 1)$.

Equation of tangent is $y - 1 = -\frac{1}{2}(x-2)$

or $\quad x + 2y - 4 = 0 \quad$ ...(i)

This meets the curve whose cartesian equation on eliminating θ by $\sec^2\theta - \tan^2\theta = 1$ is

$$y^2 = \frac{1}{x-1} \quad \text{...(ii)}$$

On solving Eqs. (i) and (ii), we get

$$y = 1, -\frac{1}{2}$$

$$\therefore \quad x = 2, 5$$

Hence, P is $(2, 1)$ as given and Q is $\left(5, -\frac{1}{2}\right)$.

$$\therefore \quad PQ = \sqrt{\frac{45}{4}} = \frac{3\sqrt{5}}{2}$$

33.

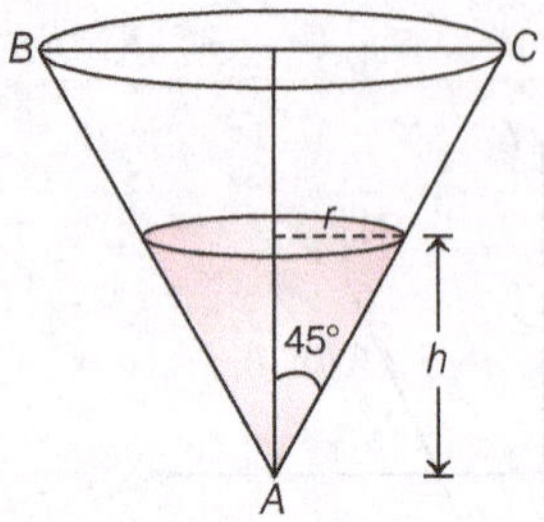

We have, $\frac{dV}{dt} = 2 \Rightarrow \frac{d}{dt}\left(\frac{1}{3}\pi r^3\right) = 2$ [here, $r = h$ as $\theta = 45°$]

$\Rightarrow \quad \pi r^2 \frac{dr}{dt} = 2$

$\Rightarrow \quad \frac{dr}{dt} = \frac{2}{\pi r^2}$ ...(i)

Now, perimeter $= 2\pi r = p$ (let)

$\Rightarrow \quad \frac{d}{dt}(2\pi r) = 2\pi\left(\frac{2}{\pi r^2}\right) = \frac{4}{r^2}$ ...(ii)

[using Eq. (i)]

When $h = 2\,\text{m} \Rightarrow r = 2\,\text{m}$

Hence, $\frac{dp}{dt} = \frac{4}{4} = 1\,\text{m/s}$

$\therefore \quad d = 1$ or $5d = 5$

34. $y = e^{a+bx^2}$ passes through (1, 1).

$\Rightarrow \quad 1 = e^{a+b}$

$\Rightarrow \quad a + b = 0$

Also, $\left(\frac{dy}{dx}\right)_{(1,1)} = -2$

$\Rightarrow \quad e^{a+bx^2} \cdot 2bx = -2$

$\Rightarrow \quad e^{a+b} \cdot 2b(1) = -2$

$\Rightarrow \quad b = -1$ and $a = 1$

$\Rightarrow \quad 2a - 3b = 5$

35. **Decoding the Question**

We know that $\sin\theta \in [-1, 1]$.

So, minimum value of $\sin\theta$ is -1.

$\therefore$ Minimum value of $\sin 2\theta$ is also -1.

For maximum value of $\frac{2}{2 + \sin 2\theta}$,

$\sin 2\theta$ should be minimum i.e. -1.

Let $x = r\cos\theta$, $y = r\sin\theta$

$\Rightarrow r^2(1 + \cos\theta\sin\theta) = 1$

$\Rightarrow \quad r^2 = \frac{2}{2 + \sin 2\theta}$

$\Rightarrow \quad r^2_{\max} = \frac{2}{1}$

36. As, $y = x^3 - ax^2 + x + 1$ and the tangent is inclined at an acute angle with the positive direction of X-axis.

$\therefore \quad \frac{dy}{dx} \geq 0$

$\Rightarrow 3x^2 - 2ax + 1 \geq 0, \forall x \in R$

[we know that $ax^2 + bx + c \geq 0$, $\forall x \in R \Rightarrow a > 0$ and $D \leq 0$]

$\Rightarrow \quad (2a)^2 - 4(3)(1) \leq 0$

$\Rightarrow \quad 4(a^2 - 3) \leq 0$

$\Rightarrow \quad (a - \sqrt{3})(a + \sqrt{3}) \leq 0$

$\therefore \quad -\sqrt{3} \leq a \leq \sqrt{3}$

$\therefore$ Sum of all possible integral values of a is 0.

37. Tangent at $P(x_1, y_1)$ is $xy_1 + yx_1 = 2c^2$

The point of intersection of this line with $x - y = 0$ is given by $x(x_1 + y_1) = 2c^2$ i.e. $x = 2c^2/(x_1 + y_1)$

$\therefore \quad Q$ is $\left(\frac{2c^2}{x_1 + y_1}, \frac{2c^2}{x_1 + y_1}\right)$

The point of intersection of the tangent with $x + y = 0$ is given by

$$x(y_1 - x_1) = 2c^2 \Rightarrow x = \frac{2c^2}{y_1 - x_1}$$

$\therefore \quad R$ is $\left(\frac{2c^2}{y_1 - x_1}, \frac{2c^2}{x_1 - y_1}\right)$

Now, $\Delta_1 = \frac{1}{2}\{a_1b_2 - a_2b_1\} = \frac{1}{2}\{-a_1a_2 - a_2a_1\} = -a_1a_2$

$$\Delta_1 = \frac{4c^4}{x_1^2 - y_1^2}$$

The normal at (x_1, y_1) is $y - y_1 = \frac{x_1}{y_1}(x - x_1)$

Intersection with $y = 0$ is given by

$$x - x_1 = -\frac{y_1^2}{x_1} \Rightarrow x = \frac{x_1^2 - y_1^2}{x_1}$$

$\therefore \quad M$ is $\left(\frac{x_1^2 - y_1^2}{x_1}, 0\right)$.

Intersection with $x = 0$ is given by $y - y_1 = -\frac{x_1^2}{y_1}$

$\Rightarrow \quad y = \frac{y_1^2 - x_1^2}{y_1}$

$\therefore N$ is $\left(0, \frac{y_1^2 - x_1^2}{y_1}\right)$.

Now, $\Delta_2 = \frac{1}{2}\frac{(x_1^2 - y_1^2)}{x_1} \cdot \frac{(y_1^2 - x_1^2)}{y_1}$

$$= -\frac{1}{2}\frac{(x_1^2 - y_1^2)^2}{x_1y_1} = -\frac{1}{2}\frac{(x_1^2 - y_1^2)^2}{c^2}$$

$\therefore \quad \Delta_1^2\Delta_2 = \frac{16c^8}{(x_1^2 - y_1^2)^2}\left(-\frac{1}{2}\right)\frac{(x_1^2 - y_1^2)^2}{c^2}$

$= -8c^6 =$ Constant

$\Rightarrow \quad \Delta_2 \propto \frac{1}{\Delta_1^2}$

$\therefore \quad k = 2$

38. We have, $y = \frac{1}{x}$

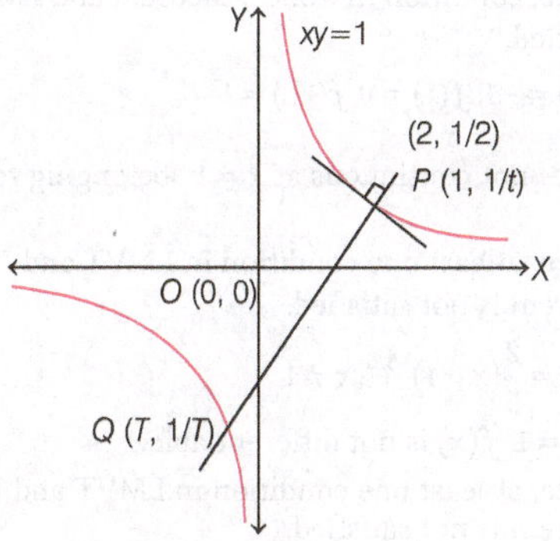

$$\frac{dy}{dx} = \frac{-1}{x^2} = \text{Slope of the tangent}$$

Slope of normal at $P = x^2 = t^2$

$$\therefore \quad t^2 = \frac{\frac{1}{t} - \frac{1}{T}}{t - T} = \frac{T-t}{tT} \cdot \frac{1}{t-T} = \frac{-1}{tT} \Rightarrow T = \frac{-1}{t^3}$$

Hence, slope of the curve at $Q = \frac{-1}{x^2} = \frac{-1}{T^2} = -\left(\frac{1}{\left(\frac{-1}{t^3}\right)^2}\right) = -t^6$

Let $t = 2$

Slope of the curve at $Q = -2^6 = -64 = m$ [given]

Hence, $|m| = |-64| = 64$

39. Given, $f(3) = 5$ and $f'(3) = \frac{5}{4}$ ...(i)

$$L = \lim_{x \to 3} \frac{\left(3^{4f(x)} - 2 \cdot \left(\frac{3^{20}-1}{2}\right) - 1\right)^2}{\frac{1 - \cos(\ln(4-x))}{\ln^2(4-x)} \ln^2(4-x)}$$

$$= \lim_{x \to 3} \frac{(3^{4f(x)} - 3^{20})^2}{\frac{1}{2} \frac{\ln^2(1+3-x)}{(3-x)^2}(3-x)^2}$$

$$L = \lim_{x \to 3} 2\left(\frac{3^{4f(x)} - 3^{20}}{x-3}\right)^2 \quad \text{...(ii)}$$

Let $l = \lim_{x \to 3}\left(\frac{3^{4f(x)} - 3^{20}}{x-3}\right)$ $\left[\frac{0}{0} \text{ form}\right]$

Using L'Hospital rule,

$$l = \lim_{x \to 3} \frac{(3^{4f(x)} \ln 3)(4f'(x))}{1}$$

$$= \frac{(3^{4f(3)} \ln 3) 4f'(3)}{1} = (3^{20} \ln 3) \times 4\left(\frac{5}{4}\right)$$

$$= 5(3^{20} \ln 3)$$

Hence, $l = 2(5 \cdot 3^{20} \cdot \ln 3)^2 = 2(a \cdot 3^b \ln c)^2$ [given]

So, $a = 5, b = 20, c = 3$

Hence, $(a + b + c) = 5 + 20 + 3 = 28$

40. $y = (1+x)^y + \sin^{-1}(\sin^2 x)$

If $x = 0, y = 1$

Now, $y = e^{y \ln(1+x)} + \sin^{-1}(\sin^2 x)$

On differentiating, we get

$$\frac{dy}{dx} = (1+x)^y \left[\frac{y}{1+x} + \ln(1+x)\frac{dy}{dx}\right] + \frac{\sin 2x}{\sqrt{1 - \sin^4 x}}$$

Put $x = 0$ and $y = 1$,

$$\frac{dy}{dx} = 1$$

Slope of normal $= -1$

$$y - 1 = -1(x - 0)$$

$$x + y - 1 = 0$$

$$a = 1, \ b = 1, \ c = -1$$

$$20a^2 + 30b^2 - 4c = 50 + 4 = 54$$

41. $v = \frac{ds}{dt} = 160 - 32t.$

Now, we find values of t for which $s(t) = 256$

So, $160t - 16t^2 = 256$

$\Rightarrow 16(t^2 - 10t + 16) = 0$

$\Rightarrow (t-2)(t-8) = 0$

$\Rightarrow t = 2, t = 8$

So, $v(2) = 160 - 32.2 = 96$

$v(8) = 160 - 256 = -96$

Hence, the velocity on the way up is 96 m/s.

42. $f(x) = \frac{41x^3}{3}$

$f'(x) = 41x^2$

$f'(x)|_{x_1, y_1} = 41x_1^2$

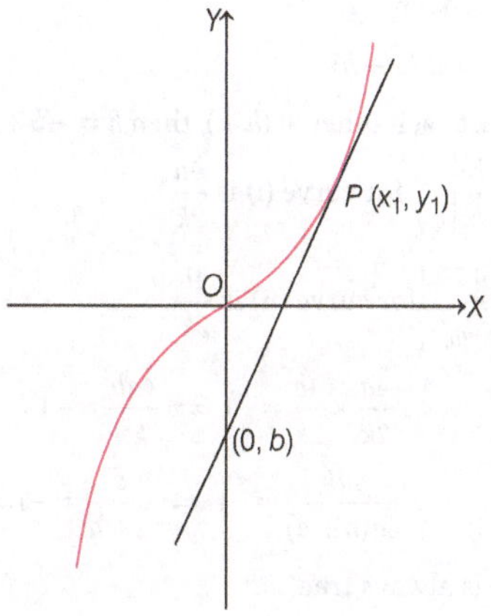

$\therefore \quad 41x_1^2 = 2009 = 7^2 \cdot 41$

$\Rightarrow \quad x_1^2 = 49$

$\Rightarrow \quad x_1 = 7, y_1 = \frac{41 \cdot 7^3}{3}$ [$x_1 \neq -7$, P lies in Ist quadrant]

Now, $\frac{y_1 - b}{x_1 - 0} = 2009$

$\Rightarrow \quad y_1 - b = 7 \cdot 2009 = 7^3 \cdot 41$

$$b = \frac{41 \cdot 7^3}{3} - 7^3 \cdot 41 = \frac{41 \cdot 7^3}{3}(-2) = -\frac{82 \cdot 7^3}{3}$$

$$= \frac{3b}{82} = -7^3 = -343$$

$$\left|\frac{3b}{82}\right| = 343$$

43. **(A)** $y^2 = 4ax \Rightarrow \frac{dy}{dx} = \frac{2a}{y}$

$$y = e^{-x/2a} \Rightarrow \frac{dy}{dx} = \frac{-1}{2a}e^{-x/2a} = \frac{-1}{2a}y$$

$$\text{Product of slopes} = \left(\frac{2a}{y}\right)\left(\frac{-y}{2a}\right) = -1$$

So, a can take any value.

(B) $1 \le |\sin x| + |\cos x| \le \sqrt{2}$

$$y = [|\sin x|] + |\cos x|] \Rightarrow y = 1$$

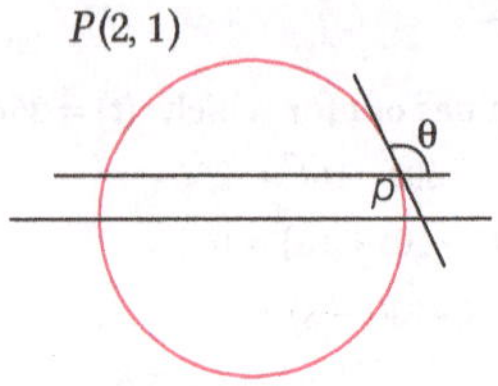

$$x^2 + y^2 = 5$$

$$\frac{dy}{dx} = \frac{-x}{y}$$

$$\tan\theta = \left|\frac{-2-0}{1+0}\right|$$

$$\operatorname{cosec}^2\theta = \frac{5}{4}$$

(C) Let $y^2 = 4a(x+a)$ ...(i)

and $y^2 = 4b(x+b)$ ...(ii)

Intersect each other at (h, k), then $h = -(b+a)$

Now, $\left.\frac{dy}{dx}\right|_{h,k}$ for curve (i) is $\frac{4a}{2k}$

and $\left.\frac{dy}{dx}\right|_{(h,k)}$ for curve (ii) is $\frac{4b}{2k}$

$$\Rightarrow \frac{4a}{2k} \times \frac{4b}{2k} = -1 \Rightarrow \frac{4ab}{k^2} = -1$$

$$\Rightarrow \frac{4ab}{4a(h+a)} = -1 \Rightarrow \frac{b}{h+a} = -1 \Rightarrow \frac{b}{-b} = -1,$$

which is always true.

$\Rightarrow \frac{a}{b}$ can take any value from interval.

$R - \{0\}$

(D) Inverse curves touches each other at line $y = x$.

$\Rightarrow$ $y = x$ is tangent to both curves

$\Rightarrow$ Equation $x = x^2 + 3x + c$ has both equal roots.

$\Rightarrow$ $c = 1$ and $x = -1 = h$ and $y = -1 = k$

$$\Rightarrow |h + k + c| = 1$$

44. **(A)** $f(x)$ is continuous and differentiable $f(0) = f(\pi)$

Hence, condition in Rolle's theorem and LMVT are satisfied.

(B) $f(1^-) = -1, f(1) = 0, f(1^+) = 1$

$f(x)$ is not continuous at $x = 1$, belonging to $\left[\frac{1}{2}, \frac{3}{2}\right]$.

Hence, atleast one condition in LMVT and Rolle's theorem is not satisfied.

(C) $f'(x) = \frac{2}{5}(x-1)^{-3/5}, x \ne 1$

At $x = 1$, $f(x)$ is not differentiable.

Hence, at least one condition in LMVT and Rolle's theorem is not satisfied.

(D) At $x = 0$,

$$\text{LHD} = \lim_{x \to 0^-} t\frac{x\left(\frac{e^{1/x}-1}{e^{1/x}+1}\right) - 0}{x - 0} = \frac{0-1}{0+1} = -1$$

RHD = 1

At $x = 0$, $f(x)$ is not differentiable.

Hence, at least one condition in LMVT and Rolle's theorem is not satisfied.

45. **(A)** As, $\frac{a}{\sin A} = \frac{b}{\sin B} = \frac{c}{\sin C} = 2R$

$$\Rightarrow a = 2R\sin A$$

$$\Rightarrow \frac{da}{dA} = 2R\cos A$$

$$\Rightarrow \frac{da}{\cos A} = 2R dA$$

Similarly, $\frac{db}{\cos B} = 2R dB$, $\frac{dc}{\cos C} = 2R dC$

$$= \frac{da}{\cos A} + \frac{db}{\cos B} + \frac{dc}{\cos C} + 1$$

$$= 2R(dA + dB + dC) + 1 \quad \text{...(i)}$$

As, $A + B + C = \pi \Rightarrow dA + dB + dC = 0$

Using Eq. (i),

$$|m| = 1 \Rightarrow m = \pm 1$$

(B) $x^2y^2 = 16$

$$2x^2y\frac{dy}{dx} + 2xy^2 = 0$$

$$\frac{dy}{dx} = -\frac{y}{x} = 1$$

Subtangent $= y / dy / dx = 2 = |k|$

$$\Rightarrow k = \pm 2$$

(C) $y = 2e^{2x}$

$$\frac{dy}{dx} = 4e^{2x} = 4 \text{ for } Y\text{-axis}$$

$$\tan^{-1} 4 = \frac{\pi}{2} - \cot^{-1}\left(\frac{8n-4}{3}\right) = \tan^{-1}\left|\left(\frac{8n-4}{3}\right)\right|$$

$$12 = |8n - 4|$$

$$n = 2 \text{ or } -1$$

(D) $x = e^{\sin y}$

$$1 = e^{\sin y}\cos y\frac{dy}{dx}$$

At (1, 0), $\frac{dy}{dx} = 1$

Equation of normal is $y = -(x-1)$

$$y + x - 1 = 0$$

$$\text{Area of triangle} = \frac{1}{2}\times 1\times 1 = \frac{1}{2} \Rightarrow |2t+1| = 3$$

$$2t+1 = \pm 3 \Rightarrow t = 1 \text{ or } -2$$

Exercise 3 - Challenging Problems

1. Given, at $x = 1$, $\frac{dy}{dx} = \tan\frac{\pi}{6} = \frac{1}{\sqrt{3}}$

or at $x = 1$, $f'(1) = \tan\frac{\pi}{6} = \frac{1}{\sqrt{3}}$

Also, at $x = 2$, $f'(2) = \tan\frac{\pi}{3} = \sqrt{3}$

and at $x = 3$, $f'(3) = \tan\frac{\pi}{4} = 1$

Then, $\int_1^3 f'(x)f''(x)dx + \int_2^3 f''(x)dx$

Let $f'(x) = t$, $f''(x)dx = dt$

$$= \int_{f'(1)}^{f'(3)} t\,dt + [f'(x)]_2^3$$

$$= \frac{1}{2}[t^2]_{f'(1)}^{f'(3)} + \{f'(3) - f'(2)\}$$

$$= \frac{1}{2}\{(f'(3))^2 - (f'(1))^2\} + \{f'(3) - f'(2)\}$$

$$= \frac{1}{2}\left\{(1)^3 - \left(\frac{1}{\sqrt{3}}\right)^2\right\} + \{1 - \sqrt{3}\}$$

$$= \frac{1}{2}\left(1 - \frac{1}{3}\right) + (1 - \sqrt{3})$$

$$= \frac{4}{3} - \sqrt{3}$$

$$= \frac{4 - 3\sqrt{3}}{3}$$

2. We have, $y = \frac{3}{\sqrt{2}}x\ln x$, $x \in (e^{-1.5}, \infty)$

and $y' = \frac{3}{\sqrt{2}}(1 + \ln x), x \in (e^{-1.5}, \infty)$ ...(i)

Any point on the curve can be chosen as $M = \left(h, \frac{3}{\sqrt{2}}h\ln h\right)$

Slope of the tangent at $M = \frac{3}{\sqrt{2}}(1 + \ln h)$ [using Eq. (i)]

Equation of the tangent at M is given by

$$y - \frac{3}{\sqrt{2}}h\ln h = \frac{3}{\sqrt{2}}(1 + \ln h)(x - h) \quad \text{...(ii)}$$

The tangent cuts the Y-axis at

$$N \equiv \left(0, \frac{-3h}{\sqrt{2}}\right) \quad \text{[put } x = 0 \text{ in Eq. (ii)]}$$

Length l of the tangent segment MN, is given by

$$l^2 = h^2 + \left\{\frac{3}{\sqrt{2}}h(1 + \ln h)\right\}^2 = h^2 + \frac{9}{2}h^2(1 + \ln h)^2$$

The value of h at which l^2 attains minima, is given by the equation

$$\frac{d}{dh}(l^2) = 0$$

i.e. $2h + 9h(1 + \ln h)^2 + 9h^2(1 + \ln h)\left(\frac{1}{h}\right) = 0$

i.e. $h\left[(1 + \ln h)^2 + (1 + \ln h) + \frac{2}{9}\right] = 0$

i.e. $1 + \ln h = \dfrac{-1 \pm \sqrt{1 - \frac{8}{9}}}{2} = \frac{-2}{3}, \frac{-1}{3}$

[$h = 0$ does not lie in $(e^{-1.5}, \infty)$]

gives $h = e^{-5/3}, e^{-4/3}$

Only $h = e^{-4/3}$ is acceptable, since $e^{-5/3}$ does not lie in $(e^{-1.5}, \infty)$.

Hence, the required point is $M \equiv (e^{-4/3}, -2\sqrt{2}e^{-4/3})$.

3. $\frac{2x}{a^2 + K_1} + \frac{2yy'}{b^2 + K_1} = 0$

$$m_1 = \frac{dy}{dx} = -\frac{x_1}{y_1}\left(\frac{b^2 + K_1}{a^2 + K_1}\right)$$

$$m_2 = \frac{dy}{dx} = -\frac{x_1}{y_1}\left(\frac{b^2 + K_2}{a^2 + K_2}\right)$$

Point of intersection of two curves (x_1, y_1),

$$x_1^2\left[\frac{1}{a^2 + K_1} - \frac{1}{a^2 + K_2}\right] + y_1^2\left[\frac{1}{b^2 + K_1} - \frac{1}{b^2 + K_2}\right] = 0$$

$$\Rightarrow x_1^2\left[\frac{(K_2 - K_1)}{(a^2 + K_1)(a^2 + K_2)}\right] + y_1^2\left[\frac{(K_2 - K_1)}{(b^2 + K_1)(b^2 + K_2)}\right] = 0$$

$$\Rightarrow \frac{x_1^2(b^2 + K_1)(b^2 + K_2)}{y_1^2(a^2 + K_1)(a^2 + K_2)} = -1$$

Also, $m_1m_2 = \dfrac{x_1^2(b^2 + K_1)(b^2 + K_2)}{y_1^2(a^2 + K_1)(a^2 + K_2)} = -1$

Hence, curves are orthogonal.

4. $\frac{dV}{dt} = -6$

$$V = \frac{\pi}{3}y^2(3R - y)$$

$$\frac{dV}{dt} = \frac{\pi}{3}(6yR - 3y^2)\frac{dy}{dt} = -6$$

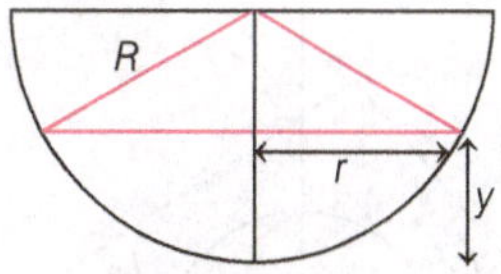

(i) $\frac{\pi}{3}(6\times 8\times 13 - 3\times 8^2)\frac{dy}{dt} = -6$

$$\Rightarrow \frac{dy}{dt} = -\frac{18}{\pi\times 432} = \frac{-1}{24\pi}$$

(ii) $(R-y)^2+r^2=R^2$, at $y=8, r=12$

$$\Rightarrow \quad r^2=2Ry-y^2$$

$$\Rightarrow \quad 2r\frac{dr}{dt}=2(R-y)\frac{dy}{dt}$$

$$\Rightarrow \quad 12\frac{dr}{dt}=-5\times\frac{1}{24\pi} \Rightarrow \frac{dr}{dt}=-\frac{5}{288\pi}$$

5. From cosine rule, $\cos A=\dfrac{b^2+c^2-a^2}{2bc}$

or $$2\cos A=\frac{b^2+c^2-a^2}{bc} \quad \text{...(i)}$$

On differentiating both sides, we get

$$-2\sin A\,\delta A=\frac{bc\{2b\delta b+2c\delta c-2a\delta a\}-(b^2+c^2-a^2)(b\delta c+c\delta b)}{(bc)^2}$$

$\Rightarrow -2bc\sin A\cdot\delta A$

$$=\frac{(b^2c-c^3+a^2c)\delta b+(bc^2-b^3+a^2b)\delta c-2abc\delta a}{bc}$$

$$\Rightarrow -2bc\left(\frac{2\Delta}{bc}\right)\cdot\delta A$$

$$=\frac{c(a^2+b^2-c^2)\delta b+b(a^2+c^2-b^2)\delta c-2abc\delta a}{bc}$$

$$\left[\Delta=\frac{1}{2}bc\sin A\right]$$

$$\Rightarrow -4\Delta\cdot\delta A=\frac{c(2ab\cos C)\delta b+b(2ac\cos B)\delta c-2abc\,\delta a}{bc}$$

$$\therefore \quad \delta A=\frac{a}{2\Delta}\{\delta a-\delta b\cdot\cos C-\delta c\cdot\cos B\} \quad \text{...(ii)}$$

Similarly, $$\delta B=\frac{b}{2\Delta}\{\delta b-\delta c\cdot\cos A-\delta a\cdot\cos C\} \quad \text{...(iii)}$$

and $$\delta C=\frac{c}{2\Delta}\{\delta C-\delta a\cdot\cos B-\delta b\cdot\cos A\} \quad \text{...(iv)}$$

On adding Eqs. (ii), (iii) and (iv), we get

$$\delta A+\delta B+\delta C=\frac{\delta a}{2\Delta}\{a-b\cos C-c\cdot\cos B\}$$

$$+\frac{\delta b}{2\Delta}\{b-a\cos C-c\cdot\cos A\}$$

$$+\frac{\delta c}{2\Delta}\{c-a\cos B-b\cos A\}$$

$$=\frac{\delta c}{2\Delta}(a-a)+\frac{\delta b}{2\Delta}(b-b)+\frac{\delta c}{2\Delta}(c-c)=0$$

Hence, $\delta A+\delta B+\delta C=0$

6. If $a<a_{\min}$, then the curve $y=|x-a|$ will be above than $y=-x^2+3$

Similarly, if $a>a_{\max}$.

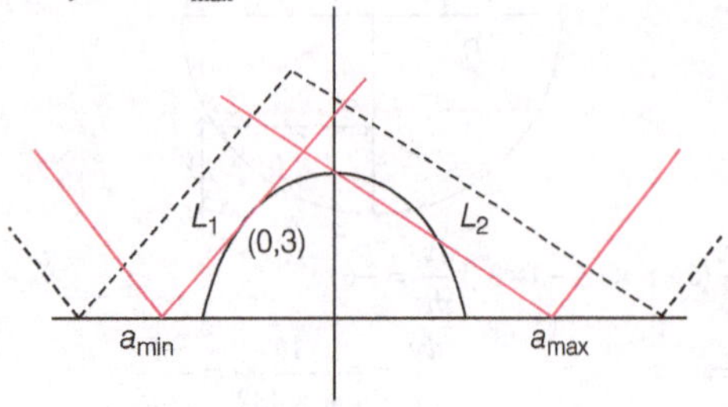

Case I L_1 is tangent to $y=-x^2+3$ and its equation of $y=x-a$

$$\therefore \quad \frac{dy}{dx}=-2x=1 \text{ i.e. } x=-\frac{1}{2}$$

$$\therefore \quad \left(-\frac{1}{2},\frac{11}{4}\right) \text{ lies on } y=x-a$$

$\therefore$ Point of contact is $\left(-\dfrac{1}{2},\dfrac{11}{4}\right)$.

Since, it lies on $y=x-a$

$$\therefore a_{\min}=-\frac{13}{4}$$

$\Rightarrow$ The inequality has a negative solution, if $-\dfrac{13}{4}<a<0$ ...(i)

Case II Line L_2 is $y=a-x$ and passes through (0, 3), if $a=3$

$\Rightarrow$ The inequality has a negative $-\sqrt{3}<a<3$ ...(ii)

From Eqs. (i) and (ii), we get

The inequation has atleast one negative solution if $-\dfrac{13}{4}<a<3$.

7. $$\frac{x+\sqrt{a^2-y^2}}{a}=\ln\left(\frac{a+\sqrt{a^2-y^2}}{y}\right)$$

Put $y=a\sin\theta$ ...(i)

$$\frac{x+a\cos\theta}{a}=\ln\left(\frac{a+a\cos\theta}{a\sin\theta}\right)$$

$$\frac{x+a\cos\theta}{a}=\ln\left(\frac{2\cos^2\frac{\theta}{2}}{2\sin\frac{\theta}{2}\cos\frac{\theta}{2}}\right)$$

$$x=a\ln\left(\cot\frac{\theta}{2}\right)-a\cos\theta \quad \text{...(ii)}$$

$$\frac{dy}{dx}=\frac{a\cos\theta}{\frac{1}{2\cot\frac{\theta}{2}}\left(-\text{cosec}^2\frac{\theta}{2}\right)+a\sin\theta}$$

$$\frac{dy}{dx}=\frac{\cos\theta}{-\frac{1}{\sin\theta}+\sin\theta} \Rightarrow \frac{dy}{dx}=-\tan\theta$$

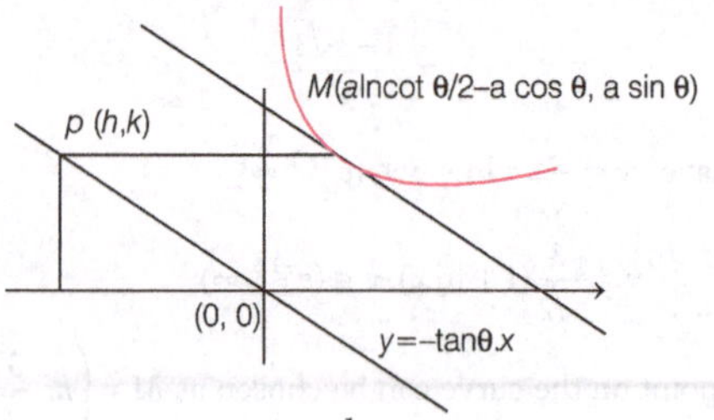

Now, $k=-\tan\theta\, h, k=-\dfrac{k}{\sqrt{a^2-k^2}}\cdot h \Rightarrow -h=\sqrt{a^2-k^2}$

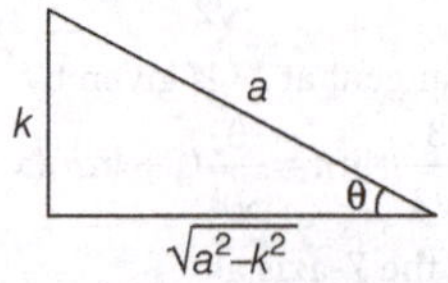

$$a^2-k^2=h^2$$

$$x^2+y^2=a^2$$

8. $y = -a^2x^2 + 5ax - 4$

$$y = \frac{1}{1-x} \Rightarrow \frac{dy}{dx} = \frac{1}{(1-x)^2}$$

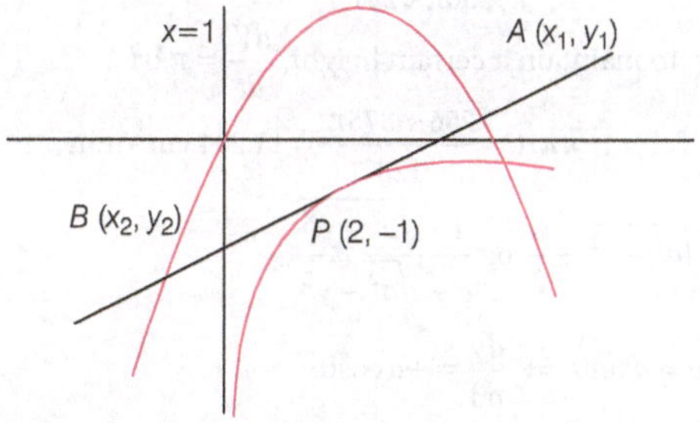

Equation of tangent at $x = 2$,

$$y + 1 = 1(x - 2) \Rightarrow y = x - 3$$

Point of intersection of $y = x - 3$ with $y = -a^2x^2 + 5ax - 4$

$$\Rightarrow \quad x - 3 = -a^2x^2 + 5ax - 4$$

$$\Rightarrow \quad -a^2x^2 + x(5a - 1) - 1 = 0$$

$$x_1 + x_2 = \frac{1-5a}{-a^2} = 4, (P(2, -1)) \quad \text{[bisects } AB\text{]}$$

$$\Rightarrow \quad 4a^2 - 5a + 1 = 0 \Rightarrow a = 1, \frac{1}{4}$$

For $a = \frac{1}{4}$, $D < 0$

Hence, $a = 1$

9.

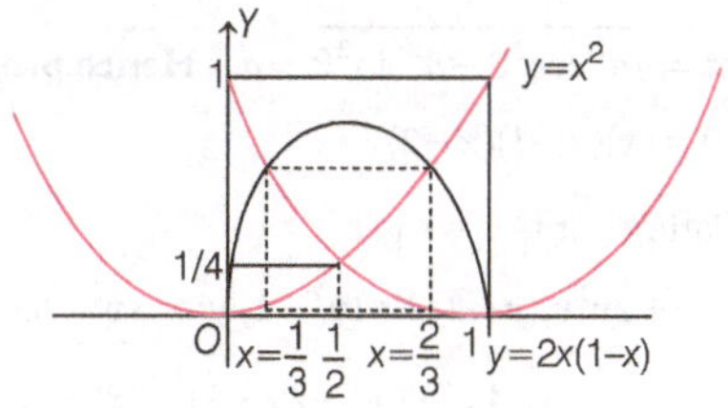

From figure, we can see Rolle's theorem is applicable for $x \in \left[\frac{1}{3}, \frac{2}{3}\right]$ and $f'(c) = 0 = 2 - 4c$

$$\Rightarrow \quad c = \frac{1}{2}$$

$$4a + 6b + 11c = \frac{4}{3} + 4 + \frac{11}{2} = \frac{8 + 24 + 33}{6} = \frac{65}{6}$$

10. Given, $x = f'(t)\sin t + f''(t)\cos t$

$$y = f'(t)\cos t - f''(t)\sin t$$

From given equation,

$$\frac{dx}{dt} = \{f'(t) + f'''(t)\}\cos t$$

and $\frac{dy}{dt} = -\{f'(t) + f'''(t)\}\sin t$

$$\text{Velocity} = \sqrt{\left(\frac{dx}{dt}\right)^2 + \left(\frac{dy}{dt}\right)^2}$$

$$= \sqrt{\{f'(t) + f'''(t)\}^2\cos^2 t + \{f'(t) + f'''(t)\}^2\sin^2 t}$$

$$= f'(t) + f'''(t)$$

Hence proved.

11. Let $f'(x) = \phi'(x + a) - \phi'(x)$

$$\Rightarrow \quad f(x) = \phi(x + a) - \phi(x) + k$$

$$f(0) = \phi(a) - \phi(0) + k$$

$$f(2a) = \phi(3a) - \phi(2a) + k$$

$$\Rightarrow \quad f(0) = f(2a)$$

By Rolle's theorem on $[0, 2a]$, $f'(c) = 0$ for at least one $c \in (0, 2a)$.

$\Rightarrow$ $\phi'(x + a) = \phi'(x)$ has at least one root in $(0, 2a)$.

12. Here, f is differentiable function, then f is continuous function.

So, by LMVT theorem for any $a \in (0, 4)$,

$$f'(a) = \frac{f(4) - f(0)}{4 - 0} \quad \text{...(i)}$$

Again, from mean value for any $b \in (0, 4)$,

$$f(b) = \frac{f(4) + f(0)}{2} \quad \text{...(ii)}$$

Now, on multiplying Eqs. (i) and (ii), we get

$$\frac{f^2(4) - f^2(0)}{8} = f'(a) \cdot f(b)$$

$$\Rightarrow \quad f^2(4) - f^2(0) = 8f'(a) \cdot f(b)$$

13. $\frac{dy}{dx} = \frac{dy/d\theta}{dx/d\theta}$

$$= \frac{a\left[e^\theta\left(-\sin\frac{\theta}{2}\cdot\frac{1}{2} - 2\cos\frac{\theta}{2}\cdot\frac{1}{2}\right) + \left(\cos\frac{\theta}{2} - 2\sin\frac{\theta}{2}\right)e^\theta\right]}{a\left[e^\theta\left(\cos\frac{\theta}{2}\cdot\frac{1}{2} - 2\sin\frac{\theta}{2}\cdot\frac{1}{2}\right) + \left(\sin\frac{\theta}{2} + 2\cos\frac{\theta}{2}\right)e^\theta\right]}$$

$$= \frac{e^\theta\left[-\frac{1}{2}\sin\frac{\theta}{2} - \cos\frac{\theta}{2} + \cos\frac{\theta}{2} - 2\sin\frac{\theta}{2}\right]}{e^\theta\left[\frac{1}{2}\cos\frac{\theta}{2} - \sin\frac{\theta}{2} + \sin\frac{\theta}{2} + 2\cos\frac{\theta}{2}\right]} = -\frac{\frac{5}{2}\sin\frac{\theta}{2}}{\frac{5}{2}\cos\frac{\theta}{2}}$$

$$= -\tan\frac{\theta}{2}$$

Equation of normal is

$$y - ae^\theta\left(\cos\frac{\theta}{2} - 2\sin\frac{\theta}{2}\right) = \frac{\cos\frac{\theta}{2}}{\sin\frac{\theta}{2}}\left(x - ae^\theta\left(\sin\frac{\theta}{2} + 2\cos\frac{\theta}{2}\right)\right)$$

$$\Rightarrow \quad y \cdot \sin\frac{\theta}{2} - ae^\theta\cos\frac{\theta}{2}\sin\frac{\theta}{2} + 2ae^\theta\sin^2\frac{\theta}{2}$$

$$= x\cos\frac{\theta}{2} - ae^\theta\sin\frac{\theta}{2}\cdot\cos\frac{\theta}{2} - 2ae^\theta\cos^2\frac{\theta}{2}$$

$$\Rightarrow \quad x\cos\frac{\theta}{2} - y\sin\frac{\theta}{2} = 2ae^\theta$$

$$\Rightarrow \quad x\cos\frac{\theta}{2} - y\sin\frac{\theta}{2} - 2ae^\theta = 0$$

Its distance from origin,

$$P_1 = \left|\frac{0 + 0 - 2ae^\theta}{\sqrt{\cos^2\frac{\theta}{2} + \sin^2\frac{\theta}{2}}}\right| = 2ae^\theta$$

Equation of tangent

$$y - ae^{\theta}\left(\cos\frac{\theta}{2} - 2\sin\frac{\theta}{2}\right) = \frac{-\sin\frac{\theta}{2}}{\cos\frac{\theta}{2}}\left(x - ae^{\theta}\left(\sin\frac{\theta}{2} + 2\cos\frac{\theta}{2}\right)\right)$$

$$\Rightarrow y\cos\frac{\theta}{2} - ae^{\theta}\cos^2\frac{\theta}{2} + 2ae^{\theta}\sin\frac{\theta}{2}\cos\frac{\theta}{2}$$

$$= -x\sin\frac{\theta}{2} + ae^{\theta}\sin^2\frac{\theta}{2} + 2ae^{\theta}\sin\frac{\theta}{2}\cos\frac{\theta}{2}$$

$$= x\sin\frac{\theta}{2} - y\cos\frac{\theta}{2} + ae^{\theta}\left(\cos^2\frac{\theta}{2} + \sin^2\frac{\theta}{2}\right) = 0$$

$$\Rightarrow x\sin\frac{\theta}{2} - y\cos\frac{\theta}{2} + ae^{\theta} = 0$$

$\therefore$ Distance from origin,

$$P_2 = \left|\frac{0 - 0 + ae^{\theta}}{\sqrt{\sin^2\frac{\theta}{2} + \cos^2\frac{\theta}{2}}}\right|$$

$$P_2 = ae^{\theta}$$

$$\therefore \quad P_1 = 2P_2$$ **Hence proved.**

14. $f'(x) = 3x^2 + p = 3x^2 + 0 \cdot x + p$

Now, we have $x_1 + x_2 = 0$ and $x_1x_2 = \frac{p}{3}$,

where x_1, x_2 are roots of $f'(x) = 0$

According to given conditions, we have

$$(x_1^3 + px_1 + q)(x_2^3 + px_2 + q) < 0$$

$$\Rightarrow x_1^3 \cdot x_2^3 + px_1^3x_2 + qx_1^3 + p^2x_1x_2 + px_1x_2^3 + qx_2^3 + pqx_1 + q^2 + pqx_2 < 0$$

$$\Rightarrow (x_1x_2)^3 + px_1x_2(x_1^2 + x_2^2) + q(x_1^3 + x_2^3) + q\{(x_1 + x_2)^3 + pq(x_1 + x_2) + p^2x_1x_2 + q^2 < 0$$

$$\Rightarrow (x_1x_2)^3 + px_1x_2\{(x_1 + x_2)^2 - 2x_1x_2\} + q\{(x_1 + x_2)^3$$

$$\Rightarrow \frac{p^3}{27} + \frac{p^2}{3}\left\{-\frac{2p}{3}\right\} + p^2\left\{\frac{p}{3}\right\} + q^2 < 0$$

$$\Rightarrow 4p^3 + 27q^2 < 0$$

15. Volume of cone $= \frac{1}{3}\pi r^2 h$

$$V = \frac{1}{3}\pi \times \frac{25}{256}h^3 \Rightarrow \frac{dV}{dt} = \frac{25\pi}{3 \times 256} \times 3h^2\frac{dh}{dt} \quad \text{...(i)}$$

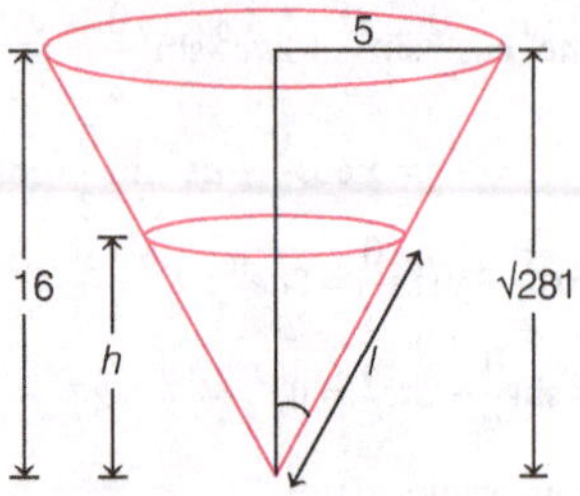

As, $$\frac{dV}{dt} = 2 - k\pi rl \quad \text{...(ii)}$$

On equating Eqs. (i) and (ii) and $h = 10$,

$$\frac{dh}{dt} = 0.3,\ r = \frac{25}{8}, \frac{1}{\sqrt{281}} = \frac{10}{16}, \text{ we get}$$

$$k = \frac{256 + 375\pi}{250\pi\sqrt{281}}$$

Now, to maintain a certain height, $\frac{dV}{dt} = \pi krl$

$$\Rightarrow \quad k\pi rl = \frac{256 + 375\pi}{128} = 11.204 \text{ cm}^3\text{/min}$$

16. $x = \sqrt{a^2 - y^2} + \frac{a}{2}\log\frac{a - \sqrt{a^2 - y^2}}{a + \sqrt{a^2 - y^2}}$

Put $y = a\sin\theta \Rightarrow \frac{dy}{d\theta} = +a\cos\theta$

$$\Rightarrow x = a\cos\theta + \frac{a}{2}\log\left(\frac{1 - \cos\theta}{1 + \cos\theta}\right)$$

$$\Rightarrow x = a\cos\theta + a\log\tan\frac{\theta}{2}$$

$$\frac{dx}{d\theta} = -a\sin\theta + \frac{a}{\sin\theta} \Rightarrow \frac{dy}{dx} = \frac{\cos\theta\sin\theta}{1 - \sin^2\theta} = \tan\theta$$

Equation of tangent $\Rightarrow y - a\sin\theta$

$$= \tan\theta\left(x - \left(a\cos\theta + a\log\tan\frac{\theta}{2}\right)\right)$$

$$\Rightarrow \quad y = x\tan\theta - a\tan\theta\log\tan\frac{\theta}{2} \quad \text{...(i)}$$

Put $y = 0,\ x = +a\log\tan\frac{\theta}{2}$

Portion of tangent $= \sqrt{a^2\cos^2\theta + a^2\sin^2\theta} = a$ **Hence proved.**

17. As, $y(y^2 - 1)(y - 2) = (x)(x - 1)(x - 2)$

(i) On differentiating w.r.t. x, we get

$$y_1(y^2 - 1)(y - 2) + 2y^2y_1(y - 2) + y(y^2 - 1)y_1 = 3x^2 - 6x + 2$$

$$\Rightarrow \quad y_1[4y^3 - 6y^2 - 2y + 2] = 3x^2 - 6x + 2$$

For horizontal tangent, $y_1 = 0$

$$\Rightarrow \quad 3x^2 - 6x + 2 = 0$$

$$\Rightarrow \quad x = \frac{6 \pm 2\sqrt{3}}{6}$$

$$= 1 \pm \frac{\sqrt{3}}{3}$$

For each value of x, there are four values of y on the curve.

Hence, total number of 8 horizontal tangents.

(ii) $\frac{dy}{dx} = \frac{3x^2 - 6x + 2}{4y^3 - 6y^2 - 2y + 2}$

For point (0, 1), $\frac{dy}{dx} = -1$

Equation $\rightarrow y - 1 = -x$

For point (0, 2), $\frac{dy}{dx} = \frac{1}{3}$

Equation $\Rightarrow y - 2 = \frac{1}{3}x$

7

"Go down deep enough into anything and you will find mathematics.

-Dean Schlicter

Application of Derivatives-II (Monotonicity and Maxima-Minima)

Learning Milestones

Milestone 1 Monotonicity and Its Critical Points

- Monotonicity at a Point
- Monotonicity in an Interval
- Application of Derivatives in Monotonicity
- Critical Points

Milestone 2 Application of Monotonicity

- Establishing Inequalitites
- Comparison of Constants
- Greatest and Least Value of a Function
- Solution of Equations
- Jenson Inequality

Milestone 3 Introduction of Maxima and Minima

- Local (Relative) Maxima and Minima
- Maxima and Minima Using Derivatives
- Concept of Global Maximum/Minimum Values
- Maxima and Minima of Discontinuous Functions

Milestone 4 Application of Maxima and Minima

- Application of Maxima and Minima
- Convexity/Concavity and Point of Inflection
- Relation of Concavity with the Derivative
- Nature of Roots of Cubic Polynomials
- Graphical Representation of Roots of Cubic Polynomials

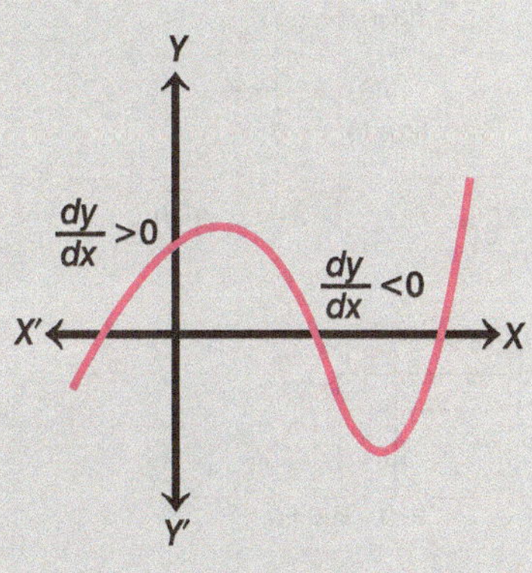

Practice Milestones

Practice Milestone 1- JEE Main Pattern
Practice Milestone 2 - JEE Advanced Pattern
Practice Milestone 3 - Challenging Problems

Milestone 1 Monotonicity and Its Critical Points

- Monotonicity at a Point
- Application of Derivatives in Monotonicity
- Monotonicity in an Interval
- Critical Points

The word 'monotonicity' derives from the word 'monotonous' which means without variation so 'monotonic functions' are functions which are either strictly increasing or strictly decreasing throughout.

Monotonocity will be discussed in 2 ways

(i) Monotonocity at a point

(ii) Monotonocity in an interval

7.1 Monotonicity at a Point

If a function $f(x)$ follows any one of the four natures given below, then it is said to be monotonic at $x = a$. Following four terms shall be clearly defined in order to understand monotonicity of $f(x)$ in an interval.

(i) Strictly increasing

(ii) Increasing (non-decreasing)

(iii) Strictly decreasing

(iv) Decreasing (non-increasing)

To understand monotonocity at a point we are considering some example below

(i) Strictly Increasing Function

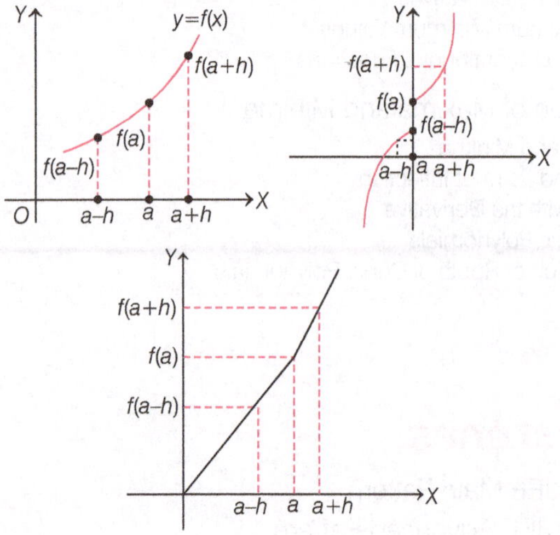

Strictly increasing at $x = a$, if $f(a-h) < f(a) < f(a+h)$

(ii) Increasing (non-decreasing) Function

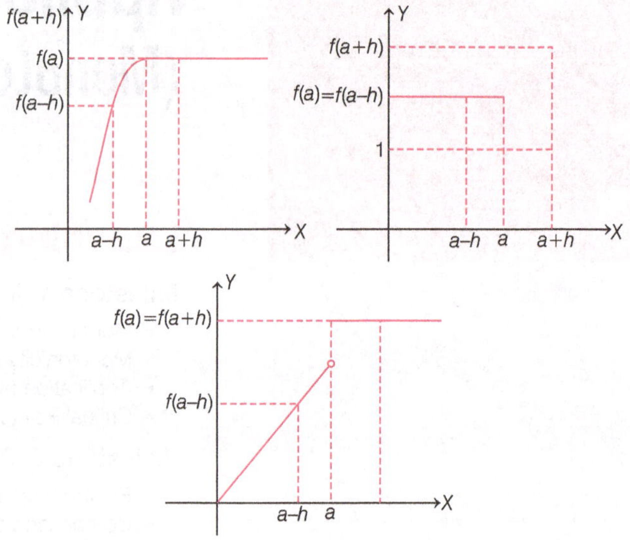

Increasing at $x = a$,
iff $f(a-h) \le f(a) \le f(a+h)$.

(iii) Strictly Decreasing Function

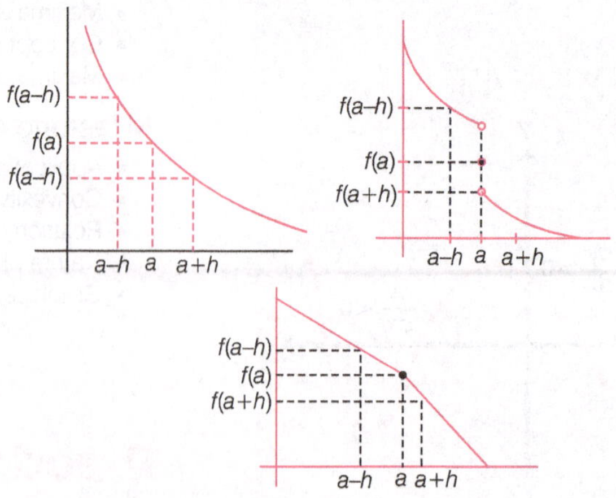

Strictly decreasing at $x = a$,
if $f(a+h) < f(a) < f(a-h)$.

(iv) Decreasing (non-increasing) Function

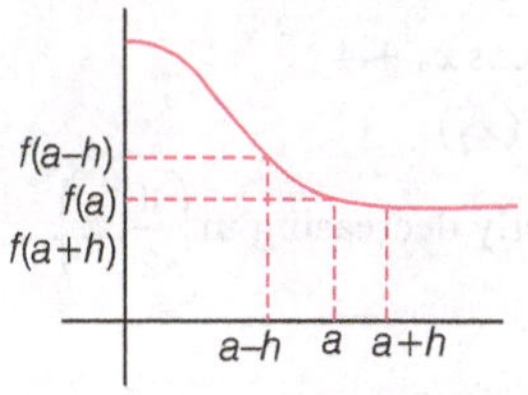

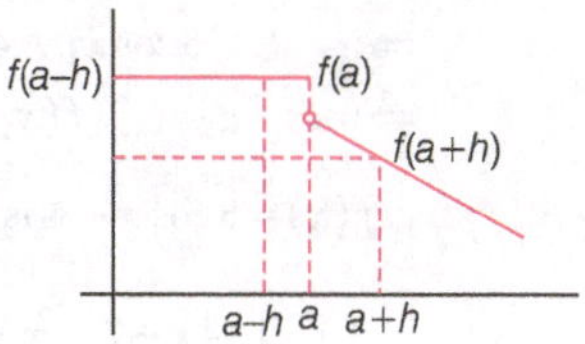

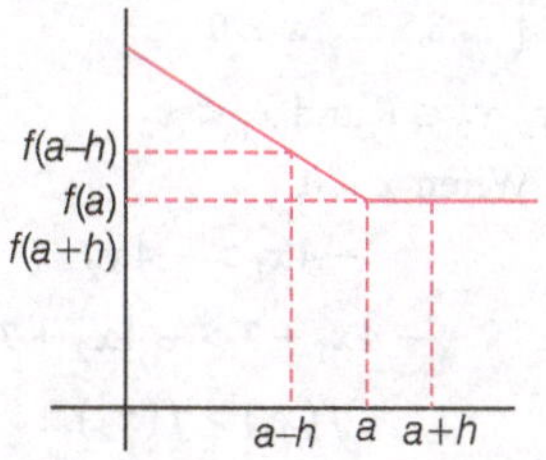

Decreasing at $x = a$, iff $f(a+h) \le f(a) \le f(a-h)$

JEE SPIKE

A discontinuous or non-differentiable function can be monotonic function at a point.

Example 1. Examine the behaviour of the function $f(x)$, when

(i) $f(x) = x^3$ at the point $x = 0$

(ii) $f(x) = \dfrac{1}{2+x}$ at the point $x = 0$

(iii) $f(x) = \dfrac{1}{1-x^2}$ at the point $x = 0$

(iv) $f(x) = [\sin x]$ at the point $x = \dfrac{\pi}{2}$

Sol. (i) We have, $f(x) = x^3$

$$f(0-h) = (-h)^3 = -h^3 < 0 \qquad [\text{where, } h > 0]$$

$$f(0) = (0)^3 = 0$$

$$f(0+h) = h^3 > 0$$

Since, $f(0-h) < f(0) < f(0+h)$

Hence, $f(x)$ is a strictly increasing function at $x = 0$.

For $y = x^3$, $\dfrac{dy}{dx} = 3x^2$

At $x = 0$, $\dfrac{dy}{dx} = 0$

$\therefore$ If the derivative at a point is zero, then the function can be monotonic. i.e. derivatives can be the criterion for determining monotonicity but it is not the sole criterion.

(ii) We have, $f(x) = \dfrac{1}{2+x}$

$$f(0-h) = \frac{1}{2+(-h)} = \frac{1}{2-h} > \frac{1}{2}$$

$$\left[\because \text{if } h > 0, \text{ then } 2-h < 2 \Rightarrow \frac{1}{2-h} > \frac{1}{2}\right]$$

$$f(0) = \frac{1}{2+0} = \frac{1}{2}$$

$$f(0+h) = \frac{1}{2+(h)} = \frac{1}{2+h} = \frac{1}{2+h} < \frac{1}{2}$$

$$\left[\because \text{if } h > 0, \text{ then } 2+h > 2 \Rightarrow \frac{1}{2+h} < \frac{1}{2}\right]$$

Since, $f(0-h) > f(0) > f(0+h)$

Hence, $f(x)$ is a strictly decreasing function at $x = 0$.

(iii) $f(x) = \dfrac{1}{1-x^2}$

$$f(0-h) = \frac{1}{1-h^2} > 1, \; f(0) = \frac{1}{1-0} = 1$$

$$f(0+h) = \frac{1}{1-h^2} > 1$$

Now, $f(0-h) > f(0)$ and $f(0) < f(0+h)$, therefore the function is neither increasing nor decreasing at $x = 0$.

(iv) $g(x) = \sin x$

$f(x) = [g(x)] = [\sin x]$

$$f\left(\frac{\pi}{2} - h\right) = \left[\sin\left(\frac{\pi}{2} - h\right)\right] = 0$$

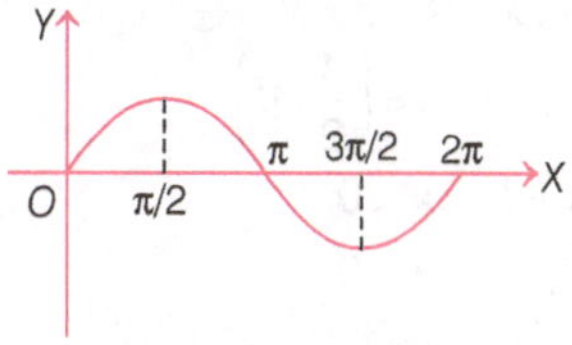

$$f\left(\frac{\pi}{2}\right) = \left[\sin\left(\frac{\pi}{2}\right)\right] = 1$$

$$f\left(\frac{\pi}{2} + h\right) = \left[\sin\left(\frac{\pi}{2} + h\right)\right] = 0$$

Now, since $f\left(\dfrac{\pi}{2} - h\right) < f\left(\dfrac{\pi}{2}\right)$ and $f\left(\dfrac{\pi}{2}\right) > f\left(\dfrac{\pi}{2} + h\right)$

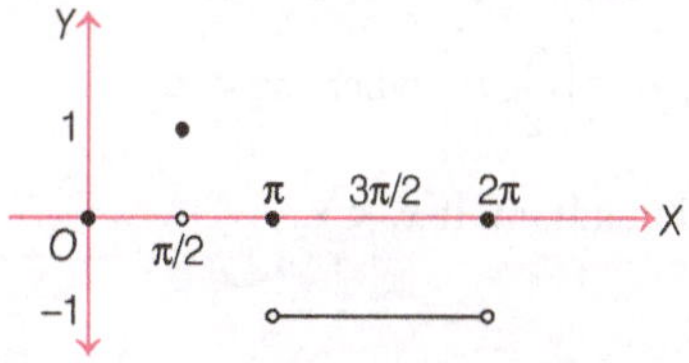

$\therefore$ The function is neither increasing nor decreasing at $x = \dfrac{\pi}{2}$.

7.2 Monotonocity in an Interval

Let $f(x)$ be any real valued function and I be an interval, then $f(x)$ is said to be strictly increasing in interval I if it is strictly increasing at every point in the interval I.

Similarly, we can conclude same about the strictly decreasing, increasing and decreasing also.

Concept Inside Video

JEE Focus Points

Let $f(x)$ be a function and x_1, x_2 are any two arbitrary constant where x_1, x_2 belong to domain of x, then

- A function $f(x)$ is said to be strictly increasing, when $f(x_1) < f(x_2) \Leftrightarrow x_1 < x_2$
- A function $f(x)$ is said to be non-decreasing or increasing, when $f(x_1) \le f(x_2) \Leftrightarrow x_1 < x_2$
- A function $f(x)$ is said to be strictly decreasing, when $f(x_1) > f(x_2) \Leftrightarrow x_1 < x_2$
- A function $f(x)$ is said to be non-increasing or decreasing, when $f(x_1) \ge f(x_2) \Leftrightarrow x_1 < x_2$

Strictly increasing　Increasing　Strictly decreasing　Decreasing

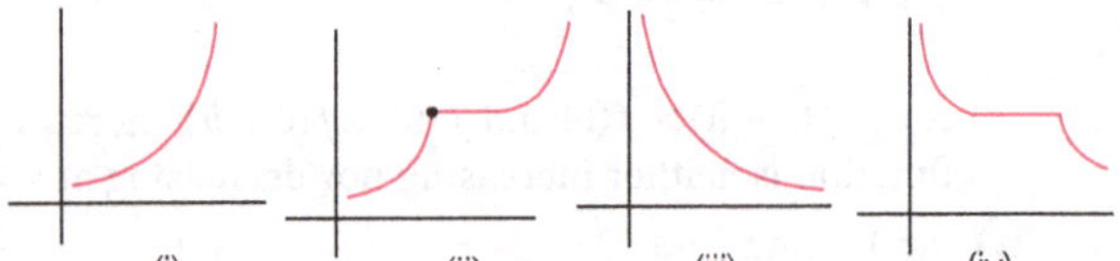

(i)　(ii)　(iii)　(iv)

Example 2. Comment on monotonocity of the following function in their domain.

(i) $f(x) = 3x + 7,\ x \in R$

(ii) $f(x) = 5\cos x + 4,\ x \in \left(\frac{\pi}{2}, \pi\right)$

(iii) $f(x) = \begin{cases} -4x + 7, & x < 0 \\ 3, & x \ge 0 \end{cases}$

Sol. (i) $f(x) = 3x + 7$

Let $x_1, x_2 \in R$, where $x_1 < x_2$

$\Rightarrow \quad 3x_1 < 3x_2$

$\Rightarrow 3x_1 + 7 < 3x_2 + 7$

$\Rightarrow \quad f(x_1) < f(x_2)$

$\therefore f(x) = 3x + 7$ is strictly increasing function.

(ii) $f(x) = 5\cos x + 4$

Let $x_1, x_2 \in \left(\frac{\pi}{2}, \pi\right)$, where $x_1 < x_2$

In IInd quadrant, if $x_1 < x_2$

$\Rightarrow \quad \cos x_1 > \cos x_2$

$\Rightarrow \quad 5\cos x_1 > 5\cos x_2$

$\Rightarrow \quad 5\cos x_1 + 4 > 5\cos x_2 + 4$

$\Rightarrow \quad f(x_1) > f(x_2)$

$\therefore f(x) = 5\cos x + 4$ is strictly decreasing in $\left(\frac{\pi}{2}, \pi\right)$.

(iii) $f(x) = \begin{cases} -4x + 7, & x < 0 \\ 3, & x \ge 0 \end{cases}$

$\because$ Let $x_1, x_2 \in R$ and $x_1 < x_2$

Case I When $x < 0$,

$\therefore \quad -4x_1 > -4x_2$

$\Rightarrow \quad -4x_1 + 7 > -4x_2 + 7$

$\Rightarrow \quad f(x_1) > f(x_2)$

Case II When $x \ge 0$,

$f(x_1) = f(x_2)$

$\therefore \quad f(x_1) \ge f(x_2)\ \forall\ x_1, x_2 \in R$

$\therefore f(x)$ will be decreasing or non increasing function.

Example 3. Let f(x) be an increasing function defined on $(0, \infty)$. If $f(2a^2 + a + 1) > f(3a^2 - 4a + 1)$. Find the range of a.

Sol. Given that $f(x)$ is increasing on $(0, \infty)$ and $f(2a^2 + a + 1) > f(3a^2 - 4a + 1)$.

Now, $2a^2 + a + 1 > 0,\ \forall\ a \in R$ ...(i)

[$\because$ discriminant $< 0,\ \forall\ a \in R$]

Also, $3a^2 - 4a + 1 > 0$ [$\because 3a^2 - 4a + 1 \in D_f$]

$\Rightarrow \quad (a - 1)(3a - 1) > 0$

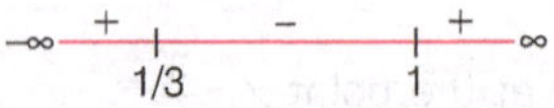

$\Rightarrow \quad a \in (-\infty, 1/3) \cup (1, \infty)$ ...(ii)

And given that $f(x)$ is increasing on $(0, \infty)$.

Therefore, $f(2a^2 + a + 1) > f(3a^2 - 4a + 1)$

$\Rightarrow \quad 2a^2 + a + 1 > 3a^2 - 4a + 1$

$\Rightarrow \quad a^2 - 5a < 0$

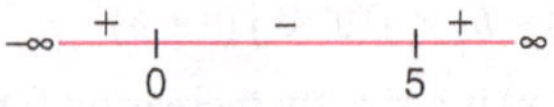

$\Rightarrow \quad a \in (0, 5)$ ...(iii)

From the intersection of Eqs. (ii) and (iii), we get

$$a \in (0, 1/3) \cup (1, 5)$$

Behaviour of Some Function in Different Interval

Examples of functions and their behaviour in different intervals.

Functions	Behaviour
$f(x)=x$	Strictly increasing on R
$f(x)=x^2$	Strictly decreasing on $(-\infty,0]$ Strictly increasing on $[0,\infty)$
$f(x)=\sqrt{x}$	Strictly increasing on $[0,\infty)$
$f(x)=x^3$	Strictly increasing on R
$f(x)=\|x\|$	Strictly decreasing on $(-\infty,0]$ Strictly increasing on $[0,\infty)$
$f(x)=\frac{1}{x}$	Neither decreasing nor increasing on R. Strictly decreasing on $(-\infty,0)$. Strictly decreasing on $(0,\infty)$
$f(x)=[x]$	Increasing on R
$f(x)=\{x\}$	Neither increasing nor decreasing on R. However, strictly increasing on $[n,n+1)$, where $n\in Z$
$f(x)=\sin x$	Neither increasing nor decreasing on R. Strictly increasing on $\left[\left(2n-\frac{1}{2}\right)\pi,\left(2n+\frac{1}{2}\right)\pi\right];n\in Z$ Strictly decreasing on $\left[\left(2n+\frac{1}{2}\right)\pi,\left(2n+\frac{3}{2}\right)\pi\right];n\in Z$
$f(x)=\cos x$	Neither increasing nor decreasing on R. Strictly increasing on $[(2n-1)\pi,2n\pi]$; $n\in Z$ Strictly decreasing on $[2n\pi,(2n+1)\pi]$; $n\in Z$
$f(x)=\tan x$	Neither increasing or decreasing on R Strictly increasing on $\left[\left(n-\frac{1}{2}\right)\pi,\left(n+\frac{1}{2}\right)\pi\right];n\in Z$
$f(x)=e^x$	Strictly increasing on R
$f(x)=e^{-x}$	Strictly decreasing on R
$f(x)=\ln x$	Strictly increasing on $(0,\infty)$

7.3 Application of Derivatives in Monotonicity

Let us now deduce the condition(s) on the derivative of a function $f(x)$ which determines whether $f(x)$ is increasing/decreasing on a given interval. We are assuming that $f(x)$ is everywhere differentiable.

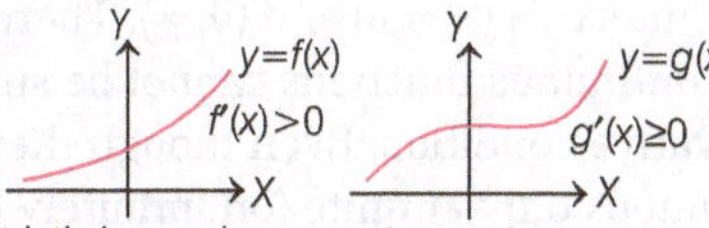

Strictly increasing function (i) Increasing function (ii)

In figure (i), the function $y=f(x)$ is strictly increasing function. Notice that the slope of the tangent drawn at any point on this curve is always positive.

Hence, a sufficient condition for $f(x)$ to be **strictly increasing** on a given domain D is $\boldsymbol{f'(x)>0,\ \forall\ x\in D}$ (later on, we will see that this is not a necessary condition for a function to be strictly increasing).

In figure (ii), the function $y=g(x)$ is not strictly increasing though it is increasing. Notice that $g'(x)>0$ or $g'(x)=0,\forall\ x$. $g'(x)$ is never negative.

Hence, a sufficient condition for $g(x)$ to be **increasing** on a given domain D is $\boldsymbol{g'(x)\geq 0,\ \forall\ x\in D}$. Now, consider $f(x)$ and $g(x)$ in given figure.

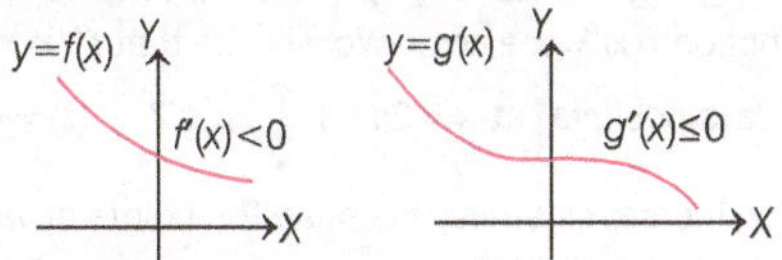

Strictly decreasing function Decreasing function

Extending as above, we get the conditions for a **strictly decreasing and decreasing** functions.

Strictly decreasing $f'(x)<0,\forall\ x\in D$

Decreasing $g'(x)\leq 0,\forall\ x\in D$

(i) Above conditions on the derivatives to be applied, the function must be differentiable in the given domain. However, these conditions will hold good even if the function is non differentiable, at a finite number (or infinitely countable number) of points

e.g. $f(x)=[x]+\sqrt{\{x\}}$ is strictly increasing on R. However, $f(x)$ is non differentiable at all integers (a countable set).

(ii) A function must be continuous for above conditions to be applied. Consider $y=\{x\}$. This is non differentiable (due to discontinuities) at all integers. At all other points, $y'=1>0$. However, we know that $y=\{x\}$ is not strictly increasing.

Similarly, $y = \frac{1}{x}$ is non-differentiable (and non-continuous) at $x = 0$. At all other points, $y' = \frac{-1}{x^2} < 0$, so y should be strictly decreasing on $R - \{0\}$. However, it is not strictly decreasing on $R - \{0\}$ although it is strictly decreasing in the separate intervals $(-\infty, 0)$ and $(0, \infty)$. Therefore, we see that discontinuous functions cannot be subjected to the derivative condition. Even though they may be discontinuous only at finite (on infinitely countable) number of points.

Concept Inside Video

JEE Focus Points

- If $f(x)$ is strictly increasing, then $f^{-1}(x)$ is also strictly increasing. Similarly, if $f(x)$ is strictly decreasing, then $f^{-1}(x)$ is also strictly decreasing.
- If $f(x)$ and $g(x)$ have the same monotonicity (both increasing or decreasing) on $[a, b]$, then $f(g(x))$ and $g(f(x))$ are monotonically increasing on $[a, b]$.
- If $f(x)$ and $g(x)$ have opposite monotonicity on $[a, b]$, then $f(g(x))$ and $g(f(x))$ are strictly decreasing on $[a, b]$.
- The inverse of a continuous function is continuous
- If $f'(x) > 0, \forall\ x \in (a, b)$ except for a finite (or an infinitely countable) number of points, where $f'(x) = 0$, $f(x)$ is still strictly increasing on (a, b). That is why, we said earlier that $f'(x) > 0, \forall\ x \in$ domain is not necessary condition for strictly increasing. e.g. In later example, we will consider the graph of the function $f(x) = x + \cos x$. We will see that $f'(x) = 1 - \sin x$ is not always positive $\left(\text{at } x = 2n\pi + \frac{\pi}{2}, n \in Z, f'(x) = 0\right)$, even, then $f(x)$ increases strictly because the points at which $f'(x) = 0$ are countable.
- Similarly, if $f'(x) < 0, \forall\ x \in (a, b)$ except for a finite (or an infinitely countable) number of points, where $f'(x) = 0$, $f(x)$ is still strictly decreasing on (a, b).

Classification of Strictly Increasing Functions

Increasing functions can be classified as

(i) **Concave up** When $f'(x) > 0$ and $f''(x) > 0$, $\forall x \in$ domain.

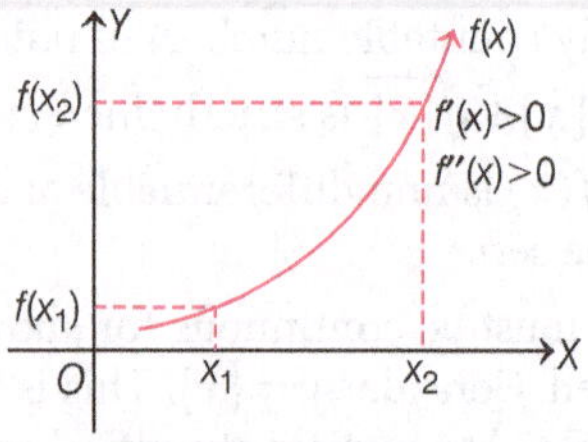

From the figure, it is clear that the graph of $f(x)$ is concave up and increases as x increases.

(ii) **Concave down** When $f'(x) > 0$ and $f''(x) < 0$, $\forall\ x \in$ domain.

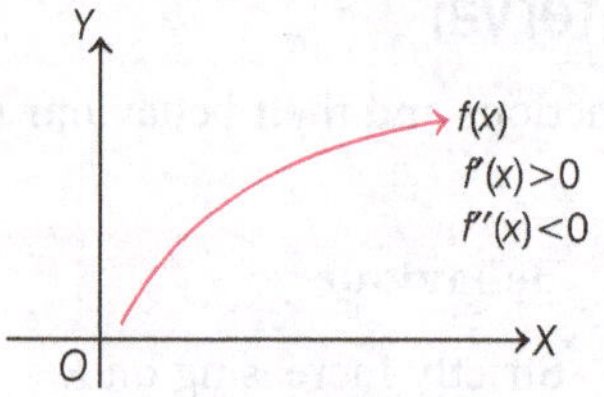

From the figure, it is clear that the graph of $f(x)$ is concave down and increases as x increases.

(iii) When $f'(x) > 0$ and $f''(x) = 0, \forall\ x \in$ domain.

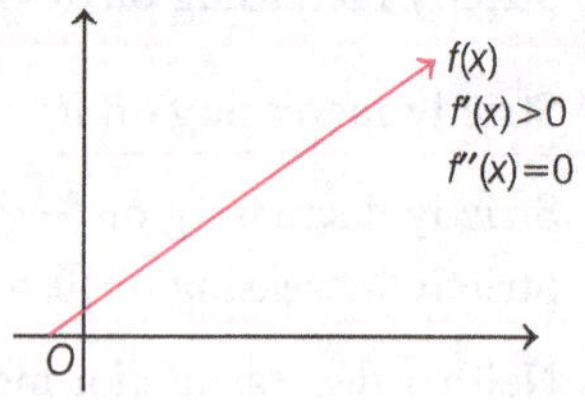

From the figure, it is clear that the graph of $f(x)$ is neither concave up nor concave down but still increases as x increases.

Classification of Strictly Decreasing Functions

Decreasing functions can be classified as follows

(i) **Concave up** When $f'(x) < 0$ and $f''(x) > 0$, $\forall x \in$ domain.

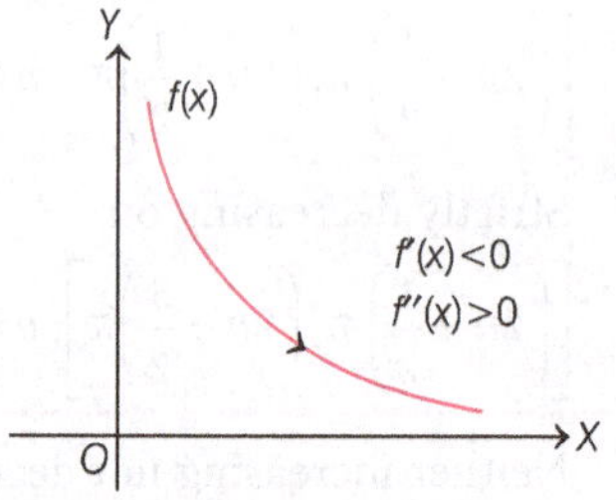

From the figure, it is clear that the graph of the function $f(x)$ is concave up and decreases as x increases.

(ii) **Concave down** When $f'(x) < 0$ and $f''(x) < 0$, $\forall\ x \in$ domain.

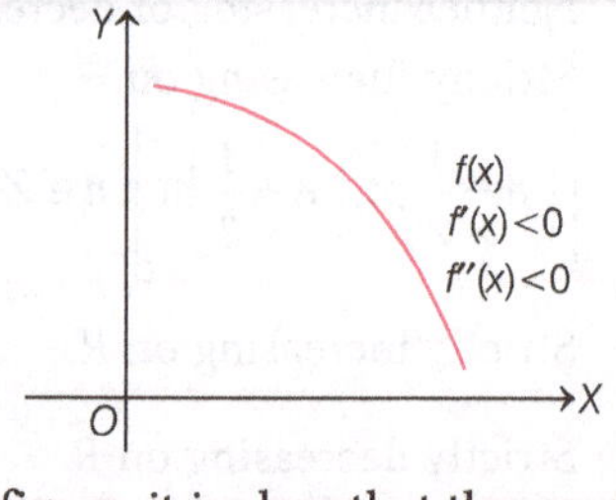

From the figure, it is clear that the graph of $f(x)$ is concave down and $f(x)$ decreases as x increases.

(iii) When $f'(x) < 0$ and $f''(x) = 0, \forall\ x \in$ domain.

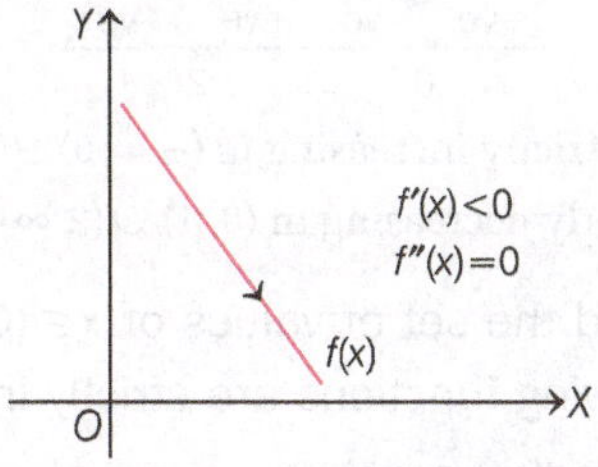

From the figure, it is clear that the graph of $f(x)$ is neither concave up nor concave down but $f(x)$ is decreasing as x increases.

We are discussing some examples below.

Example 4. Find the interval where given functions are strictly increasing, increasing, strictly decreasing and decreasing.

(i) $f(x) = 2x^3 + 3x^2 - 12x + 1$

(ii) $f(x) = 2 \cdot e^{x^2 - 4x}$

Sol. (i) Given, $f(x) = 2x^3 + 3x^2 - 12x + 1$

On differentiating both sides, we get

$$f'(x) = 6x^2 + 6x - 12$$

$\Rightarrow \quad f'(x) = 6(x^2 + x - 2)$

$\Rightarrow \quad f'(x) = 6(x + 2)(x - 1)$

Using number line rule, we have

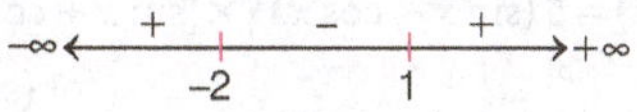

Hence, strictly increasing for $f'(x) > 0$

$\Rightarrow \quad x \in (-\infty, -2) \cup (1, \infty)$

Strictly decreasing, $f'(x) < 0 \Rightarrow x \in (-2, 1)$

Increasing, $f'(x) \geq 0$

$\Rightarrow \quad x \in (-\infty, -2] \cup [1, \infty)$

Decreasing, $f'(x) \leq 0 \Rightarrow x \in [-2, 1]$

(ii) Given, $f(x) = 2e^{x^2 - 4x}$

$\Rightarrow \quad f'(x) = 2e^{x^2 - 4x}(2x - 4) = 4e^{x^2 - 4x}(x - 2)$

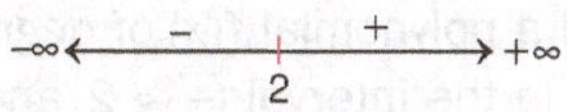

$\therefore$ Strictly increasing, $f'(x) > 0$

$\Rightarrow \quad x \in (2, \infty)$

Strictly decreasing, $f'(x) < 0$

$\Rightarrow \quad x \in (-\infty, 2)$

Increasing, $f'(x) \geq 0$

$\Rightarrow \quad x \in [2, \infty)$

Decreasing, $f'(x) \leq 0$

$\Rightarrow \quad x \in (-\infty, 2]$

Example 5. Prove that

(i) $f(x) = -x - \cot^{-1} x$ is strictly decreasing function.

(ii) $f(x) = \begin{cases} x^2 + 2x, & -1 \leq x < 0 \\ 3x, & 0 \leq x \leq 1 \end{cases}$ is strictly increasing in $[-1, 1]$ but $g(x) = \begin{cases} x^2 + 2x, & -1 \leq x < 0 \\ 3x, & 0 \leq x < 1 \\ 1, & x = 1 \end{cases}$ is not strictly increasing in $[-1, 1]$.

Sol. (i) Given, $f(x) = -x - \cot^{-1} x$

$\Rightarrow \quad f'(x) = -1 + \dfrac{1}{1 + x^2} = -\dfrac{x^2}{1 + x^2}$

We have, $f'(x) \leq 0$, for all x.

$f'(x) = 0$, at $x = 0$ only.

Now, $f'(x) < 0$ everywhere except at $x = 0$. Hence, we can conclude that $f(x)$ is strictly decreasing for all x.

(ii) We have, $f'(x) = \begin{cases} 2x + 2, & -1 \leq x < 0 \\ 3, & 0 < x \leq 1 \end{cases}$

For all $x \neq 0$, $f'(x) > 0$, f is continuous at $x = 0$ and $f'(0^-) > 0$ and $f'(0^+) > 0$.

Hence, $f(x)$ is strictly increasing at $x = 0$.

At $x = -1$, $f'(-1^+) > 0$ and $f'(-1^-) > 0$

At $x = 1$, $f'(1^-) > 0$ and $f'(1^+) > 0$

Hence, $f(x)$ is strictly increasing at both the end points.

Finally, $f(x)$ is strictly increasing in $[-1, 1]$.

Now, $g'(x) = \begin{cases} 2x + 2, & -1 \leq x < 0 \\ 3, & 0 < x < 1 \end{cases}$

For all $x \neq 0, 1$, $g'(x) > 0$.

At $x = 0$ and -1, $g(x)$ is strictly increasing like $f(x)$.

At $x = 1$, $g(x)$ is discontinuous, since $g(1^-) = 3$ while $g(1) = 1$

Hence, $g(x)$ is not strictly increasing at $x = 1$.

Thus, $g(x)$ is not strictly increasing in $[-1, 1]$.

However, $g(x)$ is strictly increasing in $[-1, 1)$.

Example 6. Find intervals of monotonicity of following functions.

(i) $f(x) = x^4 - 8x^3 + 22x^2 - 24x + 7$

(ii) $f(x) = \dfrac{2x}{1 + x^2}$

(iii) $f(x) = \ln(x^2 - 2x)$

(iv) $f(x) = \dfrac{|x - 1|}{x^2}$

Sol. (i) We have, $f(x) = x^4 - 8x^3 + 22x^2 - 24x + 7, x \in R$

and $\quad f'(x) = 4x^3 - 24x^2 + 44x - 24$

$= 4(x - 1)(x - 2)(x - 3)$

From the sign scheme for $f'(x)$, we can see that

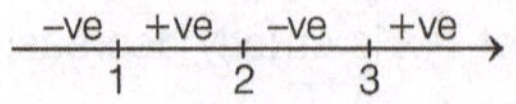

The shape of the curve is drawn below.

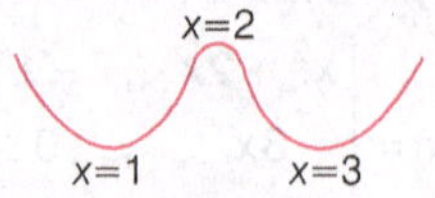

$f(x)$ is strictly decreasing in $(-\infty, 1) \cup (2, 3)$ and strictly increasing in $(1, 2) \cup (3, \infty)$.

(ii) We have, $f(x) = \dfrac{2x}{1+x^2}, x \in R$

and $f'(x) = \dfrac{(1+x^2)2 - 2x(2x)}{(1+x^2)^2}$

$= \dfrac{-2(x^2-1)}{(1+x^2)^2} = \dfrac{-2(x+1)(x-1)}{(1+x^2)^2}$

From the sign scheme for $f'(x)$, we can see that

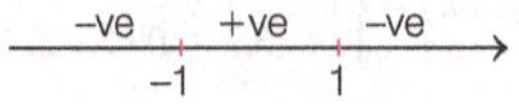

The shape of the curve is shown below.

$f(x)$ is strictly decreasing in $(-\infty, -1) \cup (1, \infty)$ and strictly increasing in $(-1, 1)$.

(iii) We have, $f(x) = \ln(x^2 - 2x), x \in (-\infty, 0) \cup (2, \infty)$

and $f'(x) = \dfrac{2x-2}{x^2-2x} = \dfrac{2(x-1)}{x(x-2)}$

From the sign scheme for $f'(x)$, we can see that

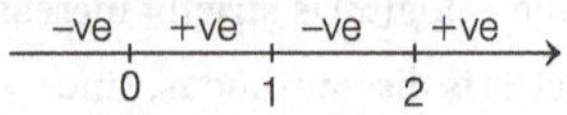

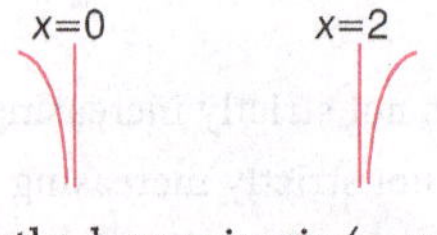

$f(x)$ is strictly decreasing in $(-\infty, 0) \cup (1, 2)$ and strictly increasing in $(0, 1) \cup (2, \infty)$.

Also, we can see that $f(0^-) = -\infty$ and $f(2^+) = -\infty$.

(iv) We have, $f(x) = -\dfrac{(x-1)}{x^2}, x < 1$

and $f(x) = \dfrac{x-1}{x^2}, x \geq 1$

$\Rightarrow \quad f'(x) = \dfrac{-2}{x^3} + \dfrac{1}{x^2} = \dfrac{x-2}{x^3}, x < 1$

and $f'(x) = \dfrac{2-x}{x^3}, x > 1$

Now, from the sign scheme for $f'(x)$, we get

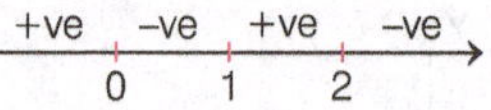

$f(x)$ is strictly increasing in $(-\infty, 0) \cup (1, 2)$ and strictly decreasing in $(0, 1) \cup (2, \infty)$.

Example 7. Find the set of values of $x \in (0, 2\pi)$, for which the following functions are strictly increasing.

(i) $2^{x - \sin x} + \log(x + \cos x)$

(ii) $(\sin x - \cos x)^5$

Sol. (i) Let $f(x) = x - \sin x$ and $g(x) = (x + \cos x)$

$\Rightarrow f'(x) = 1 - \cos x \geq 0, \forall x \in R$

$\Rightarrow f(x)$ is an increasing function, $\forall x \in R$

$\Rightarrow f(x) > f(0) = 0, \forall x > 0$

$\Rightarrow 2^{f(x)}$ is increasing on $x \in (0, 2\pi)$

and $g(x) = x + \cos x$

$\Rightarrow g'(x) = 1 - \sin x \geq 0, \forall x \in R$

$\Rightarrow g(x)$ is an increasing function, $\forall x \in R$

$\Rightarrow g(x) > g(0) = 1, \forall x > 0$

$\Rightarrow \ln(g(x))$ is an increasing function, $\forall x \in (0, 2\pi)$

$\Rightarrow y = 2^{f(x)} + \ln(g(x))$ is an increasing function, $\forall x \in (0, 2\pi)$.

(ii) $f(x) = (\sin x - \cos x)^5$

$\Rightarrow f'(x) = 5(\sin x - \cos x)^4 \times [\sin x + \cos x] \geq 0,$ for $(\sin x + \cos x) \geq 0$

$\Rightarrow \quad \sqrt{2}\sin\left(x + \dfrac{\pi}{4}\right) \geq 0$

$\Rightarrow \quad \sin\left(x + \dfrac{\pi}{4}\right) \geq 0, \forall x \in (0, 2\pi)$

$\Rightarrow \quad x + \dfrac{\pi}{4} \in \left(\dfrac{\pi}{4}, \pi\right] \cup \left[2\pi, \dfrac{9\pi}{4}\right)$

$\Rightarrow \quad x \in \left(0, \dfrac{3\pi}{4}\right] \cup \left[\dfrac{7\pi}{4}, 2\pi\right)$

Example 8. Find a polynomial $f(x)$ of degree 5 which increases in the interval $(-\infty, 2]$ and $[6, \infty)$ and decreases in the interval $[2, 6]$. Given that $f(0) = 3$ and $f'(4) = 0$.

Sol. Since, $f'(4) = 0$; therefore $x = 4$ is a repeated root of the polynomial $f(x)$, hence $f'(x)$ contains $(x-4)^2$.

Also, since $x = 2$ and $x = 6$ are critical points, therefore $f'(x)$ must contain $(x-2)$ and $(x-6)$.

$\Rightarrow f'(x) = k(x-2)(x-4)^2(x-6)$ and $k>0$

$\Rightarrow f(x) = k\int(x^2-8x+12)(x^2-8x+16)dx$

$\Rightarrow f(x) = k\int(x^4-16x^3+64x^2+28(x^2-8x)+192)\,dx$

$\Rightarrow f(x) = k\left(\frac{x^5}{5}-4x^4+\frac{92}{3}x^3-112x^2+192x\right)+c$

The wavy curve of derivative will be like

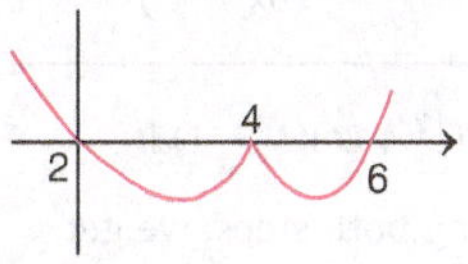

Now, as $f(0)=3 \Rightarrow C=3$

$\Rightarrow f(x) = k\left[\frac{x^5}{5}-4x^4+\frac{92}{3}x^3-112x^2+192x\right]+3,\ k>0$

JEE SCANNER

Example Similar to PYQ Asked in JEE Main 2021-22

If the function $f(x)=(a+2)x^3-3ax^2+9ax-1$ is always decreasing, $\forall\ x\in R$, then a is

(a) $(-\infty,-2)$ (b) $(-2,\infty)$

(c) $(-\infty,-3]$ (d) $(-3,\infty)$

Sol. (c) $f'(x)=3(a+2)x^2-6ax+9a\le 0,\ \forall\ x\in R$

$\Rightarrow\ 3(a+2)<0$ and $36a^2-4\cdot 3(a+2)\cdot 9a\le 0$

$\Rightarrow\ a<-2$ and $a^2-3a(a+2)\le 0$

$\Rightarrow\ a<-2$ and $a^2+3a\ge 0$ ...(i)

$\Rightarrow\ a\in(-\infty,-3]\cup[0,\infty)$ ...(ii)

From Eqs. (i) and (ii), we get

$a\le -3$

$\therefore\ a\in(-\infty,-3]$

Skill Builder

If function $f(x)=(a+1)x^3-2ax^2+4ax-1$ is always decreasing, $\forall\ x\in R$, then a is

(a) $\left(-\infty,\frac{3}{2}\right]$ (b) $\left(-\infty,\frac{-3}{2}\right]$

(c) $\left(\infty,\frac{3}{2}\right]$ (d) $\left(0,\frac{3}{2}\right]$

For Sol.

■ **For more practice** See Q.8 of Milestone Practice 7.1.

Example 9. Let $\phi(x)=\sin(\cos x)$, then check whether it is increasing or decreasing in $[0,\pi/2]$.

Sol. Given, $\phi(x)=\sin(\cos x) \Rightarrow \phi'(x)=\cos(\cos x)\cdot(-\sin x)$

$\Rightarrow\ \phi'(x)=-\cos(\cos x)\cdot\sin x$

Therefore, it is clearly decreasing, for $x\in[0,\pi/2]$ as $\phi'(x)\le 0$.

$\left[\because \cos(\cos x)>0 \text{ and } \sin x>0, \forall x\in\left(0,\frac{\pi}{2}\right)\right]$

Alternate Solution

Here, $f(x)=\sin x$ and $g(x)=\cos x$ are increasing and decreasing in $[0,\pi/2]$ respectively.

$\Rightarrow fog(x)=\phi(x)=\sin(\cos x)$ is decreasing.

Example 10. If $f(x)$ is a decreasing function and attains positive values, then the set of value of k, for which the major axis of the ellipse $\frac{x^2}{f(k^2+2k+5)}+\frac{y^2}{f(k+11)}=1$, is the X-axis, is the interval $(-a,b)$, then find $(a+b)$.

Sol. Here, $f(x)$ is decreasing function and major axis is X-axis.

$\Rightarrow\ f(k^2+2k+5)>f(k+11)$

$\left[\because \text{for the ellipse } \frac{x^2}{a^2}+\frac{y^2}{b^2}=1 \text{ major axis lies along } X\text{-axis, then } a^2>b^2\right]$

As, $f(x)$ is decreasing, therefore

$k^2+2k+5<k+11$

$\Rightarrow\ k^2+k-6<0$

$\Rightarrow\ (k+3)(k-2)<0$

$\Rightarrow\ k\in(-3,2)=(-a,b)$ [given]

$\therefore\ a+b=5$

Example 11. If $\phi(x)=f(x)+f(1-x)$ and $f''(x)<0$ in $(-1,1)$, then show that $\phi(x)$ strictly increases in $\left(0,\frac{1}{2}\right)$.

Sol. We have, $\phi(x)=f(x)+f(1-x)$

and $\phi'(x)=f'(x)-f'(1-x)$,

which vanishes at points given by $x=1-x$ i.e. $x=\frac{1}{2}$

$f''(x)<0 \Rightarrow f'(x)$ is decreasing for $x\in\left(0,\frac{1}{2}\right)$

i.e. $1-x>x$

$\Rightarrow\ f'(1-x)<f'(x)$

$\Rightarrow\ \phi'(x)>0,\ \forall x\in\left(0,\frac{1}{2}\right)$

$\therefore\ \phi(x)$ strictly increases in $\left(0,\frac{1}{2}\right)$

Example 12. The function $f(x)=\sin^4 x+\cos^4 x$ increasing, if

(a) $0<x<\pi/8$ (b) $\pi/4<x<3\pi/8$

(c) $3\pi/8<x<5\pi/8$ (d) $3\pi/8<x<3\pi/4$

Sol. (b) Here, $f(x)=\sin^4 x+\cos^4 x$

$\Rightarrow\ f'(x)=4\sin^3 x\cdot\cos x+4\cos^3 x(-\sin x)$

$f'(x)=4\sin x\cos x(\sin^2 x-\cos^2 x)$

$$f'(x) = 2(\sin 2x)(-\cos 2x)$$

$$\Rightarrow \quad f'(x) = -\sin 4x$$

Now, $f'(x) \geq 0$, if $\sin 4x \leq 0$

$$\Rightarrow \quad \pi \leq 4x \leq 2\pi$$

$$\Rightarrow \quad \pi/4 \leq x \leq \pi/2$$

Here, $\left(\frac{\pi}{4}, \frac{3\pi}{8}\right)$ is only subset of $\left[\frac{\pi}{4}, \frac{\pi}{2}\right]$.

JEE SCANNER

Example Similar to PYQ Asked in JEE Main 2021

Let $f(x) = \begin{cases} xe^{ax}, & x \leq 0 \\ x + ax^2 - x^3, & x > 0 \end{cases}$, *where a is positive constant. The interval in which $f'(x)$ is increasing, is*

(a) $\left[-\frac{2}{a}, \frac{a}{3}\right]$ (b) $\left[\frac{-a}{3}, \frac{2}{3a}\right]$

(c) $\left(\frac{-2}{a}, \frac{a}{6}\right)$ (d) $(0, -a]$

Sol. (a) Given, $f(x) = \begin{cases} xe^{ax}, & x \leq 0 \\ x + ax^2 - x^3, & x > 0 \end{cases}$

On differentiating both sides, we get

$$f'(x) = \begin{cases} axe^{ax} + e^{ax}, & x < 0 \\ 1 + 2ax - 3x^2, & x > 0 \end{cases}$$

Again, on differentiating both sides, we get

$$f''(x) = \begin{cases} 2ae^{ax} + a^2xe^{ax}, & x < 0 \\ 2a - 6x, & x > 0 \end{cases}$$

Now, $f''(x) = 0$, then in the interval $x \leq 0$, the root is $x = -\frac{2}{a}$ and in interval $x > 0$, root is $x = \frac{a}{3}$.

Using sign scheme or number line rule as shown in figure, we get

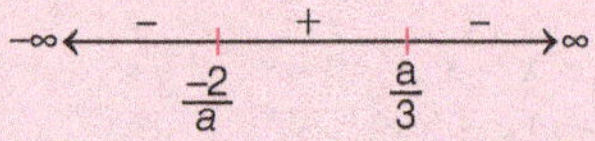

$f'(x)$ decreases on $\left(-\infty, -\frac{2}{a}\right] \cup \left[\frac{a}{3}, \infty\right)$ and increases on $\left[-\frac{2}{a}, \frac{a}{3}\right]$.

Skill Builder

Let $f(x) = \begin{cases} xe^{bx}, & x \leq 0 \\ bx^2 - 2x^3, & x > 0 \end{cases}$, where b is positive constant, then the interval in which $f'(x)$ is increasing, is

(a) $\left[\frac{-2}{a}, a\right]$ (b) $\left[-a, \frac{2}{3b}\right]$

(c) $\left(\frac{-2}{b}, \frac{b}{6}\right)$ (d) $(0, -b]$

For Sol.

■ **For more practice** See Q.16 of Milestone Practice 7.1.

Example 13. Find the interval of increasing or decreasing of the $f(x) = \int_{-1}^{x} (t^2 + 2t)(t^2 - 1)\, dt$.

Decoding the Question

Use Leibnitz rule, which is stated as

$$\frac{d}{dx}\left[\int_{\phi(x)}^{\psi(x)} f(t)\, dt\right] = f(\psi(x)) \left\{\frac{d}{dx}\psi(x)\right\} - f(\phi(x)) \left\{\frac{d}{dx}\phi(x)\right\}.$$

Sol. Given, $f(x) = \int_{-1}^{x} (t^2 + 2t)(t^2 - 1) dt$

On differentiating both sides, we get

$$f'(x) = (x^2 + 2x)(x^2 - 1)\left\{\frac{d}{dx}(x)\right\} - (1-2)(1-1)\left\{\frac{d}{dx}(-1)\right\}$$

[Leibnitz integral rule]

$$\Rightarrow f'(x) = (x^2 + 2x)(x^2 - 1)$$

$$\Rightarrow f'(x) = x(x+2)(x+1)(x-1)$$

Using number line rule as shown in figure,

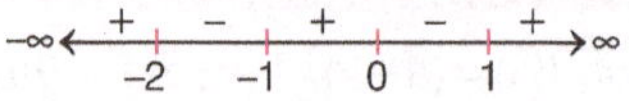

Clearly, $f'(x) \geq 0$, when $x \in (-\infty, -2) \cup (-1, 0) \cup (1, \infty)$

and $f'(x) \leq 0$, when $x \in (-2, -1) \cup (0, 1)$

Hence, $f(x)$ is increasing, when $x \in (-\infty, -2) \cup (-1, 0) \cup (1, \infty)$ and $f(x)$ is decreasing, when $x \in (-2, -1) \cup (0, 1)$.

Example 14. If $0 < \alpha < \frac{\pi}{6}$, then the value of $(\alpha \operatorname{cosec} \alpha)$ is

(a) less than $\frac{\pi}{3}$ (b) more than $\frac{\pi}{3}$

(c) less than $\frac{\pi}{6}$ (d) more than $\frac{\pi}{6}$

Sol. (a) From the figure, we can say

Slope of OA > Slope of OB,

where $A = (\alpha, \sin \alpha)$ and $B\left(\frac{\pi}{6}, \sin\frac{\pi}{6}\right)$

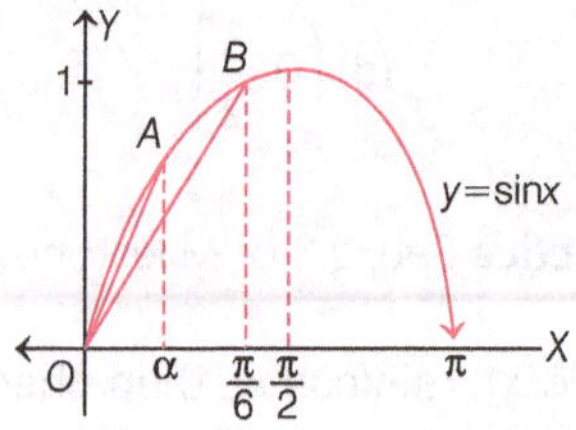

$$\Rightarrow \quad \frac{\sin \alpha - 0}{\alpha - 0} > \frac{\sin\frac{\pi}{6} - 0}{\frac{\pi}{6} - 0}$$

$$\Rightarrow \quad \frac{\sin \alpha}{\alpha} > \frac{3}{\pi} \text{ or } \frac{\alpha}{\sin \alpha} < \frac{\pi}{3} \Rightarrow \alpha \operatorname{cosec} \alpha < \frac{\pi}{3}$$

Example 15. If $f(x) = ax^3 + bx^2 + cx + d$, where a, b, c and d are real numbers and $3b^2 < c^2$, is an increasing cubic function and $g(x) = af'(x) + bf''(x) + c^2$, then

(a) $\int_a^x g(t)dt$ is a decreasing function.

(b) $\int_a^x g(t)\,dt$ is an increasing function.

(c) $\int_a^x g(t)\,dt$ is a neither increasing nor a decreasing function.

(d) None of the above

Sol. (b) $f'(x) = 3ax^2 + 2bx + c > 0$ [$\because f(x)$ is increasing]

$\Rightarrow a > 0$ and $b^2 - 3ac < 0$

$\Rightarrow a > 0$ and $b^2 < 3ac$

Also, $g(x) = af'(x) + bf''(x) + c^2$

$$g(x) = 3a^2x^2 + 2abx + ac + 6abx + 2b^2 + c^2$$

$$g(x) = 3a^2x^2 + 8abx + (2b^2 + c^2 + ac)$$

Now, $D = 64a^2b^2 - 4 \cdot 3a^2 \cdot (2b^2 + c^2 + ac)$

$= 4a^2(16b^2 - 6b^2 - 3c^2 - 3ac)$

$= 4a^2(10b^2 - 3c^2 - 3ac) < 4a^2(10b^2 - 3c^2 - b^2)$ [as $3ac > b^2 \Rightarrow -3ac < -b^2$]

$= 4a^2(9b^2 - 3c^2)$

$= 12a^2(3b^2 - c^2)$

$\therefore D < 0$ [given $3b^2 < c^2$]

$\Rightarrow g(x) > 0, \forall x \in R$

$\therefore \int_a^x g(t)\,dt$ is an increasing function.

$$\left[\because \frac{d}{dx}\left(\int_a^x g(t)\,dt\right) = g(x) > 0\right]$$

Example 16. If $f(x)$ and $g(x)$ are two positive and increasing functions, then

(a) $(f(x))^{g(x)}$ is always increasing.

(b) if $(f(x))^{g(x)}$ is decreasing, then $f(x) < 1$.

(c) if $(f(x))^{g(x)}$ is increasing, then $f(x) > 1$.

(d) if $f(x) > 1$, then $(f(x))^{g(x)}$ is increasing.

Sol. (d) Let $h(x) = (f(x))^{g(x)}$

$\Rightarrow \log(h(x)) = g(x)\{\log f(x)\}$

$\Rightarrow \dfrac{1}{h(x)} \cdot h'(x) = \dfrac{g(x)}{f(x)} \cdot f'(x) + \{\log f(x)\}\, g'(x)$

and $h(x)$ is increasing, if $\log(f(x)) > 0$

$\Rightarrow f(x) > 1$

Example 17. If $f''(x) > 0$ and $f'(1) = 0$ such that $g(x) = f(\cot^2 x + 2\cot x + 2)$, where $0 < x < \pi$, then the interval in which $g(x)$ is decreasing, is

(a) $(0, \pi)$ (b) $\left(\dfrac{\pi}{2}, \pi\right)$

(c) $\left(\dfrac{3\pi}{4}, \pi\right)$ (d) $\left(0, \dfrac{3\pi}{4}\right)$

Sol. (d) Here, $g(x) = f(\cot^2 x + 2\cot x + 2)$

$\Rightarrow g'(x) = f'(\cot^2 x + 2\cot x + 2) \cdot \{-2\cot x \operatorname{cosec}^2 x - 2\operatorname{cosec}^2 x\}$

For $g(x)$ to be decreasing, $g'(x) < 0$

$\Rightarrow f'\{(\cot x + 1)^2 + 1\} \cdot (-2\operatorname{cosec}^2 x)(\cot x + 1) < 0$

$\Rightarrow f'\{(\cot x + 1)^2 + 1\} \cdot (\cot x + 1) > 0$ ...(i)

As $f''(x) > 0 \Rightarrow f'(x)$ is increasing, then

$f'\{(\cot x + 1)^2 + 1\} > f'(1) = 0, \forall x \in \left(0, \dfrac{3\pi}{4}\right) \cup \left(\dfrac{3\pi}{4}, \pi\right)$

Thus, Eq. (i) holds, if $\cot x + 1 > 0$

$\Rightarrow \cot x > -1, \forall x \in \left(0, \dfrac{3\pi}{4}\right)$

1. Test for Finding Monotonicity at an Endpoint

If $x = a$ is an endpoint, then we use the sign of the appropriate one-sided derivative to test the monotonicity of $f(x)$ at $x = a$. Assume that the function f is differentiable at $x = a$.

If $x = a$ is the left endpoint, we check as follows

(i) If $f'(a^+) > 0$, then $f(x)$ is strictly increasing at $x = a$.

(ii) If $f'(a^+) < 0$, then $f(x)$ is strictly decreasing at $x = a$.

(iii) If $f'(a^+) = 0$ but $f'(a+h) > 0$, then $f(x)$ is strictly increasing at $x = a$.

(iv) If $f'(a^+) = 0$ but $f'(a+h) < 0$, then $f(x)$ is strictly decreasing at $x = a$.

If $x = a$ is the right endpoint, we check as follows

(i) If $f'(a^-) > 0$, then $f(x)$ is strictly increasing at $x = a$.

(ii) If $f'(a^-) < 0$, then $f(x)$ is strictly decreasing at $x = a$.

(iii) If $f'(a^-) = 0$ but $f'(a-h) > 0$, then $f(x)$ is strictly increasing at $x = a$.

(iv) If $f'(a^-) = 0$ but $f'(a-h) < 0$, then $f(x)$ is strictly decreasing at $x = a$.

e.g. consider the function $f(x) = (x-1)^{3/2}$.

$x = 1$ is the left endpoint of the domain $[1, \infty)$.

$$f'(x) = \frac{3}{2}(x-1)^{1/2}$$

$$f'(1^+) = 0$$

but $f'(1+h) = \dfrac{3}{2}h^{1/2} > 0$.

Hence, $f(x)$ is strictly increasing at $x = 1$.

2. Test for Finding Monotonicity at Points where $f'(x)$, does not exist

Consider a continuous function $f(x)$ whose derivative $f'(x)$ does not exist at $x=c$ but exists in the neighbourhood of c.

(i) If $f'(c^-)>0$ and $f'(c^+)>0$, then $f(x)$ is strictly increasing at $x=c$.

(ii) If $f'(c-h)>0, f'(c^-)\geq 0, f'(c^+)\geq 0, f'(c+h)>0$, then $f(x)$ is strictly increasing at $x=c$.

(iii) If $f'(c^-)<0$ and $f'(c^+)<0$, then $f(x)$ is strictly decreasing at $x=c$.

(iv) If $f'(c-h)>0, f'(c^-)\leq 0, f'(c^+)\leq 0, f'(c+h)>0$, then $f(x)$ is strictly increasing at $x=c$.

Now, consider a function $f(x)$ which is discontinuous at $x=c$ but its derivative exists in the neighbourhood of c.

(i) If $f'(c-h)>0, f(c^-)\leq f(c), f(c)\leq f(c^+)$, $f'(c+h)>0$, then $f(x)$ is strictly increasing at $x=c$.

(ii) If $f'(c-h)<0, f(c^-)\geq f(c), f(c)\geq f(c^+)$, $f'(c+h)<0$, then $f(x)$ is strictly decreasing at $x=c$.

Example 18. Let $f(x)=\begin{cases} x^2+2x, & -2\leq x<0 \\ \sin^{-1}x, & 0\leq x<1 \end{cases}$. Investigate the behaviour of the function at $x=-2, 0$ and 1.

Sol. We have, $f'(x)=\begin{cases} 2x+2, & -2\leq x<0 \\ \dfrac{1}{\sqrt{1-x^2}}, & 0<x<1 \end{cases}$

At $x=-2$, $f'(-2^+)<0$.

Hence, $f(x)$ is strictly decreasing at $x=-2$.

At $x=0$, $f'(0^-)=2>0$, $f'(0^+)=1>0$.

Hence, $f(x)$ is strictly increasing at $x=0$.

At $x=1$, $f'(1^-)=\infty$, f is continuous at $x=1$.

The infinite (positive) derivative implies that $f(x)$ is strictly increasing at $x=1$.

Example 19. Let $f(x)=\begin{cases} x^3+x^2+10x, & x<0 \\ x^2e^x, & x\geq 0 \end{cases}$.

Investigate the behaviour of the function for $x\in R$.

Sol. We have, $f'(x)=\begin{cases} 3x^2+2x+10, & x<0 \\ x(x+2)e^x, & x>0 \end{cases}$

For $x<0$, $f'(x)$ is a quadratic expression whose discriminant is positive, with coefficient of x^2 positive. Hence, it is positive.

Clearly, $f'(x)>0$, for $x>0$.

Thus, $f'(x)>0$, for all $x\neq 0$.

Now, consider the point $x=0$ where $f(x)$ is continuous but non differentiable at $x=0$.

Here, $f'(0^-)=10>0$, $f'(0^+)=0$, $f'(0+h)>0$.

This means that f is strictly increasing at $x=0$.

Finally, $f(x)$ is strictly increasing function for $x\in R$.

JEE SCANNER

Example Similar to PYQ Asked in JEE Main 2024

Let $g(x)=2f\left(\dfrac{x^2}{2}\right)+f(6-x^2)$, $\forall\ x\in R$ given that $f''(x)>0$, $\forall\ x\in R$. Then, $g(x)$ is

(a) increasing in $(-2, 0)$ only.

(b) decreasing in $(-\infty, -1)$.

(c) increasing in $(-2,0)\cup(2,\infty)$.

(d) decreasing in $(-\infty,-2)\cup(2,\infty)$.

Sol. (c) $g(x)=2f\left(\dfrac{x^2}{2}\right)+f(6-x^2)$

$$\Rightarrow g'(x)=2xf'\left(\frac{x^2}{2}\right)-2xf'(6-x^2)$$

$$=2x\left\{f'\left(\frac{x^2}{2}\right)-f'(6-x^2)\right\} \quad ...(i)$$

But given that $f''(x)>0 \Rightarrow f'(x)$ is increasing, for all $x\in R$.

Case I Let $\dfrac{x^2}{2}>(6-x^2)\Rightarrow x^2>4\Rightarrow x\in(-\infty,-2)\cup(2,\infty)$

$$\therefore f'\left(\frac{x^2}{2}\right)>f'(6-x^2)\Rightarrow f'\left(\frac{x^2}{2}\right)-f'(6-x^2)>0,$$

for $x\in(-\infty,-2)$ and $(2,\infty)$ ...(ii)

From Eqs. (i) and (ii), we get

$g'(x)>0$, for $x\in(2,\infty)$ and $g'(x)<0$, for $x\in(-\infty,-2)$.

Case II Let $\dfrac{x^2}{2}<(6-x^2)\Rightarrow x^2<4\Rightarrow x\in(-2,2)$

$$\therefore \quad f'\left(\frac{x^2}{2}\right)<f'(6-x^2)$$

$$\Rightarrow f'\left(\frac{x^2}{2}\right)-f'(6-x^2)<0, \text{ for } x\in(-2,2) \quad ...(iii)$$

From Eqs. (i) and (iii), we get

$g'(x)<0$, for $x\in(0,2)$ and $g'(x)>0$, for $x\in(-2,0)$

On combining both cases, $g(x)$ is increasing in $x\in(-2,0)$ and $(2,\infty)$.

Skill Builder

Let $g(x)=3f\left(\dfrac{x^2}{3}\right)+f(12-x^2)$, $\forall\ x\in R$

Given that $f''(x)>0$, $\forall\ x\in R$, then $g(x)$ is

(a) decreasing in $(-\infty, 3]$.

(b) decreasing in $(-\infty,-2)$.

(c) increasing in $(-3,0)$ only.

(d) increasing in $(-3,0)\cup(3,\infty)$.

For Sol.

■ **For more practice** See Q.13 of Milestone Practice 7.1.

Example 20. Let the function $g: R \to \left(-\frac{\pi}{2}, \frac{\pi}{2}\right)$ be given by $g(t) = \frac{\pi}{2} - 2\cot^{-1}(3^{-t})$. Prove that g is odd and is strictly decreasing in $(-\infty, \infty)$.

Sol. We have, $g(t) = \frac{\pi}{2} - 2\cot^{-1}(3^{-t})$

$$\therefore \quad g(-t) = \frac{\pi}{2} - 2\cot^{-1}(3^{t}) = \frac{\pi}{2} - 2\tan^{-1}(3^{-t})$$

$$\left[\text{as } \cot^{-1} x = \tan^{-1}\frac{1}{x}, x > 0\right]$$

$$= \frac{\pi}{2} - 2\left(\frac{\pi}{2} - \cot^{-1}(3^{-t})\right) = -\frac{\pi}{2} + 2\cot^{-1}(3^{-t})$$

$$\left[\text{as } \cot^{-1} x + \tan^{-1} x = \frac{\pi}{2}, \forall x \in R\right]$$

$$= -g(t)$$

Hence, $g(-t) = -g(t)$

$\Rightarrow g$ is an odd function.

Also, $g'(t) = \frac{-2 \cdot 3^{-t} \cdot \ln 3}{(1 + (3^{-t})^2)}$

$\therefore \quad g'(t) < 0, \forall t \in R$

$\Rightarrow g$ is strictly decreasing in $(-\infty, \infty)$.

7.4 Critical Points

It is a collection of points for which,

(i) $f(x)$ does not exist.

(ii) $f'(x)$ does not exist.

(iii) $f'(x) = 0$

All the values of x obtained from above conditions are said to be the critical points.

It should be noted that critical points are the interior points of an interval.

Example 21. Find the critical points for $f(x) = (x-2)^{2/3}(2x+1)$.

Sol. Given, $f(x) = (x-2)^{2/3}(2x+1)$

$$\Rightarrow \quad f'(x) = \frac{2}{3}(x-2)^{-1/3}(2x+1) + (x-2)^{2/3} 2$$

$$\text{or} \quad f'(x) = 2\left[\frac{(2x+1)}{3(x-2)^{1/3}} + \frac{(x-2)^{2/3}}{1}\right]$$

Clearly, $f'(x)$ is not defined at $x = 2$, so $x = 2$ is a critical point.

Another critical point is given by $f'(x) = 0$

$$\text{i.e.} \quad 2\left[\frac{(2x+1) + 3(x-2)}{(x-2)^{1/3}}\right] = 0$$

$$\Rightarrow \quad 5x - 5 = 0 \Rightarrow x = 1$$

Hence, $x = 1$ and $x = 2$ are two critical points of $f(x)$.

Example 22. Find all the values of a, for which the function $f(x) = (a^2 - 3a + 2)\cos\left(\frac{x}{2}\right) + (a-1)x$, possesses critical points.

Decoding the Question

All stationary points are critical point. At stationary points, $f'(x) = 0$.

Sol. Given, $f(x) = (a^2 - 3a + 2)\cos\left(\frac{x}{2}\right) + (a-1)x$

$$\Rightarrow \quad f'(x) = -\frac{1}{2}(a-1)(a-2)\sin\left(\frac{x}{2}\right) + (a-1)$$

$$\Rightarrow \quad f'(x) = (a-1)\left[1 - \frac{1}{2}(a-2)\sin\left(\frac{x}{2}\right)\right]$$

If $f(x)$ possesses critical points, then

$$f'(x) = 0$$

$$\Rightarrow \quad (a-1)\left[1 - \left(\frac{a-2}{2}\right)\sin\frac{x}{2}\right] = 0$$

$$\Rightarrow \quad a = 1 \text{ and } 1 - \left(\frac{a-2}{2}\right)\sin\frac{x}{2} = 0$$

But at $a = 1 \Rightarrow f(x) = 0$

$$\text{Thus,} \quad \sin\left(\frac{x}{2}\right) = \frac{2}{a-2} \Rightarrow \left|\frac{2}{a-2}\right| \le 1$$

$$\Rightarrow \quad |a-2| \ge 2 \Rightarrow a - 2 \ge 2 \text{ or } a - 2 \le -2$$

$$a \ge 4 \text{ or } a \le 0$$

Therefore, $a \in (-\infty, 0] \cup [4, \infty)$

Example 23. The set of all values of b, for which the function $f(x) = (b^2 - 3b + 2)(\cos^2 x - \sin^2 x) + (b-1)x + \sin 2$ does not possess stationary points, is

(a) $[1, \infty)$ (b) $(0, 1) \cup (1, 4)$

(c) $\left(\frac{3}{2}, \frac{5}{2}\right)$ (d) None of these

Sol. (c) Here, $f(x) = (b^2 - 3b + 2)(\cos^2 x - \sin^2 x) + (b-1)x + \sin 2$

$$= (b^2 - 3b + 2)\cos 2x + (b-1)x + \sin 2$$

$$\Rightarrow \quad f'(x) = (b^2 - 3b + 2) \cdot (-2\sin 2x) + (b-1)$$

As $f(x)$ does not possess stationary points

$$\Rightarrow \quad f'(x) \ne 0$$

$$\Rightarrow \quad (b-1)(b-2)(-2\sin 2x) + (b-1) \ne 0,$$

for any $x \in R$

$$\Rightarrow \quad (b-1)\{1 - 2(b-2)\sin 2x\} \ne 0$$

$$\Rightarrow \quad \left|\frac{1}{2(b-2)}\right| > 1 \text{ and } b \ne 1$$

$$\Rightarrow \quad -\frac{1}{2} < b - 2 < \frac{1}{2} \text{ and } b \ne 1$$

$$\Rightarrow \quad \frac{3}{2} < b < \frac{5}{2} \Rightarrow b \in \left(\frac{3}{2}, \frac{5}{2}\right)$$

Example 24. Find the set of critical points of the function $f(x) = x - \log x + \int_2^x \left(\frac{1}{z} - 2 - 2\cos 4z\right) dz.$

Sol. Here, $f(x) = x - \log x + \int_2^x \left(\frac{1}{z} - 2 - 2\cos 4z\right) dz$

$$\Rightarrow \quad f'(x) = 1 - \frac{1}{x} + \left(\frac{1}{x} - 2 - 2\cos 4x\right)(1) - 0$$

$$= -1 - 2\cos 4x \qquad \text{[using Leibnitz rule]}$$

Put $f'(x) = 0$,

$$\Rightarrow \quad \cos 4x = -\frac{1}{2}$$

$$\Rightarrow \quad \cos 4x = \cos\left(\pi - \frac{\pi}{3}\right)$$

$$\Rightarrow \quad 4x = 2n\pi + \frac{2\pi}{3}, n \in \text{Integer}$$

$$\Rightarrow \quad x = \frac{n\pi}{2} \pm \frac{\pi}{6}, n \in I$$

But $\log x$ is defined for $x > 0$

For $n = 0$, $\quad x = \pm\frac{\pi}{6} \Rightarrow x = \frac{\pi}{6} \qquad$ [neglecting $x = -\pi/6$]

$\therefore$ Set of critical points $= \left\{\frac{\pi}{6}, \frac{n\pi}{2} \pm \frac{\pi}{6}\right\}$, where $n \in N$.

Example 25. Find all possible b, for which $f(x) = \sin 2x - 8(b+2)\cos x - (4b^2 + 16b + 6)\,x$ is monotonic decreasing, for all $x \in R$ and has no critical point.

Sol. $f'(x) = 2\cos 2x + 8(b+2)\sin x - (4b^2 + 16b + 6)$

$$= 2(1 - 2\sin^2 x) + 8(b+2)\sin x - (4b^2 + 16b + 6)$$

$$= -4\,[\sin^2 x - 2(b+2)\sin x + (b^2 + 4b + 1)]$$

For monotonic decreasing and no critical points,

$$f'(x) < 0, \forall\, x \in R$$

Hence, $\quad \sin^2 x - 2(b+2)\sin x + b^2 + 4b + 1 > 0$

$$\Rightarrow \quad [\sin x - (b+2)]^2 - (b+2)^2 + 4b + b^2 + 1 > 0$$

$$\Rightarrow \quad [\sin x - (b+2)]^2 - (\sqrt{3})^2 > 0$$

$$\Rightarrow \quad [\sin x - b - 2 - \sqrt{3}][\sin x - b - 2 + \sqrt{3}] > 0$$

$$\Rightarrow [\sin x - (b + 2 + \sqrt{3})][\sin x - (b + 2 - \sqrt{3})] > 0$$

$$\Rightarrow [\sin x - (b + 2 + \sqrt{3})][\sin x - (b + 2 - \sqrt{3})] > 0$$

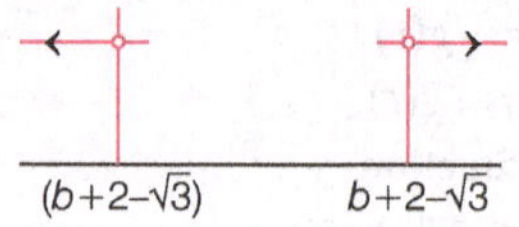

Hence, $\sin x > b + (2 + \sqrt{3})$ or $\sin x < (b + 2 - \sqrt{3})$

$$\Rightarrow \quad b + (2 + \sqrt{3}) < \sin x, \forall\, x \in R$$

or $\quad (b + 2 - \sqrt{3}) > \sin x, \forall\, x \in R$

$$\Rightarrow \quad b + (2 + \sqrt{3}) < -1$$

or $\quad (b + 2 - \sqrt{3}) > 1$

$$\Rightarrow \quad b < -(3 + \sqrt{3}) \text{ or } b > \sqrt{3} - 1$$

$$\Rightarrow \quad b \in (-\infty, -(3 + \sqrt{3})) \cup (\sqrt{3} - 1, \infty)$$

Milestone Practice 7.1

1. Find the interval in which $f(x) = x^4 - 14x^2 + 24x - 3$ is strictly increasing or strictly decreasing.

2. Find the intervals in which the function $f(x) = 3\cos^4 x + 10\cos^3 x + 6\cos^2 x - 3, 0 \le x \le \pi$ is monotonically increasing and decreasing.

3. Find the range of values of a, for which the function $f(x) = x^3 + (2a+3)x^2 + 3(2a+1)x + 5$ is monotonic in R. Hence, find the set of values of a, for which $f(x)$ is invertible.

4. Let $g(x) = 2f\left(\frac{x}{2}\right) + f(2-x)$ and $f'(x) < 0, \forall\ x \in (0, 2)$.

Find the intervals of increase and decrease of $g(x)$.

5. Find the possible set of values of k, for which the function $f(x) = \begin{cases} x+1, & x<1 \\ k, & x=1 \\ x^2+x+3, & x>1 \end{cases}$

is strictly increasing at $x = 1$.

(a) [1, 3] (b) [2, 5]
(c) [1, 2] (d) None of these

6. Let $x_i, \forall\ i \in N$ be the values of x, for which the function $f(x) = \max.\{x^2, (1-x)^2, 2x(1-x)\}$ is non monotonic, then find Σx_i

(a) 2 (b) $\frac{3}{2}$
(c) 1 (d) None of these

7. The function $f(x) = 2\log(x-2) - x^2 + 4x + 1$ increases in the interval

(a) (1, 2) (b) (2, 3) (c) $\left(\frac{5}{2}, 3\right)$ (d) (2, 4)

8. If $f(x) = \sin x + a^2 x + b$ is a decreasing function, for all values of x, then

(a) $a \in (-\infty, -1)$ (b) $a \in R$
(c) $a \in R - (-1, 1)$ (d) None of these

9. If $f(x) = kx^3 - 9x^2 + 9x + 3$ is monotonically increasing in each interval, then

(a) $k < 3$ (b) $k \le 3$
(c) $k \ge 3$ (d) None of these

10. The number of critical points of $f(x) = (x-1)(x-2) + (x-2)|x-1|$, is

(a) 2 (b) 3
(c) 4 (d) None of these

11. The function $f(x) = 2\ln|x| - x|x|$ decreases over the interval

(a) $(-\infty, -1)$ (b) $(-1, 0)$ (c) $(0, 1)$ (d) $(1, \infty)$

12. The function f defined by $f(x) = (x+2)e^{-x}$ is

(a) decreasing for all x.
(b) decreasing in $(-\infty, -1)$ and increasing $(-1, \infty)$.
(c) increasing for all x.
(d) decreasing in $[-1, \infty)$ and increasing $(-\infty, -1]$.

13. Let $g(x) = 2f(x/2) + f(1-x)$ and $f''(x) < 0$ in $0 \le x \le 1$, then $g(x)$

(a) decreases in [0, 2/3]. (b) decreases in (2/3, 1].
(c) increases in [0, 2/3]. (d) increases in (2/3, 1].

14. If $\phi(x) = f(x) + f(2a - x)$ and $f''(x) > 0, a > 0, 0 \le x \le 2a$, then

(a) $\phi(x)$ increases in $(a, 2a)$.
(b) $\phi(x)$ increases in $(0, a)$.
(c) $\phi(x)$ decreases in $(0, a)$.
(d) $\phi(x)$ decreases in $(a, 2a)$.

15. If $\phi(x) = 3f\left(\frac{x^2}{3}\right) + f(3 - x^2)$, for all $x \in (-3, 4)$, where $f''(x) > 0$, for all $x \in (-3, 4)$, then $\phi(x)$ is

(a) increasing in [3/2, 4).
(b) decreasing in (−3, −3/2].
(c) increasing in [−3/2, 0].
(d) decreasing in [0, 3/2].

16. If $f(x) = \begin{cases} xe^{ax}, & x \le 0 \\ x + ax^2 - 2x^3, & x > 0 \end{cases}$, where a is positive constant. The interval in which $f'(x)$ is increasing is

(a) $\left[\frac{-2}{a}, \frac{a}{6}\right]$ (b) $\left[\frac{-2}{a}, a\right]$
(c) $[a, -b]$ (d) $\left(\frac{-2}{b}, \frac{b}{6}\right)$

Answer Key

1. $x \in [-3, 1]$ and $[2, \infty)$; $x \in (-\infty, -3]$ and $[1, 2]$ **2.** $\left[\frac{\pi}{2}, \frac{2\pi}{3}\right]; \left[0, \frac{\pi}{2}\right]$ and $\left[\frac{2\pi}{3}, \pi\right]$ **3.** $a \in [0, 3/2]$
4. $\left(0, \frac{4}{3}\right); \left(\frac{4}{3}, 2\right)$ **5.** (b) **6.** (b) **7.** (b,c) **8.** (c)
9. (c) **10.** (d) **11.** (a,b,d) **12.** (d) **13.** (b,c)
14. (a,c) **15.** (a,b,c,d) **16.** (a)

For Detailed Solution

Milestone 2 Application of Monotonicity

• Establishing Inequalitites • Comparison of Constants • Greatest and Least Value of a Function
• Solution of Equations • Jenson Inequality

In this milestone, we will discuss the use of monotonocity in calculus.

7.5 Establishing Inequalities

Knowledge of monotonicity helps us establishing variety of inequalities involving algebraic and transcedental functions with much greater ease.

If $f(x) \geq g(x)$ or $f(x) \leq g(x)$ is to be shown in some interval we create a new function $h(x) = f(x) - g(x)$ and using monotonicity check whether $h(x) \geq 0$ or $h(x) \leq 0$ in the given interval.

Example 26. Prove that $\dfrac{\tan x}{x} > \dfrac{x}{\sin x}$ for $0 < x < \dfrac{\pi}{2}$.

Sol. We have to show that $\dfrac{\tan x}{x} > \dfrac{x}{\sin x}$ for $x \in \left(0, \dfrac{\pi}{2}\right)$

i.e. $\dfrac{\tan x \sin x - x^2}{x \sin x} > 0$ for $0 < x < \dfrac{\pi}{2}$.

Since, $x \sin x > 0$ for $0 < x < \dfrac{\pi}{2}$,

it is enough to show that $\tan x \cdot \sin x - x^2 > 0$ for $0 < x < \dfrac{\pi}{2}$.

Let $f(x) = \tan x \sin x - x^2$ for $0 < x < \dfrac{\pi}{2}$

$$f'(x) = \sin x \sec^2 x + \tan x \cos x - 2x$$
$$= \sin x \sec^2 x + \sin x - 2x$$
$$f''(x) = \cos x \sec^2 x + \sin x \cdot 2 \sec^2 x \tan x + \cos x - 2$$
$$= \sec x + \cos x - 2 + 2 \sin x \tan x \sec^2 x$$
$$= (\sqrt{\sec x} - \sqrt{\cos x})^2 + 2 \sin x \tan x \sec^2 x > 0 \text{ for } 0 < x < \frac{\pi}{2}$$

$\therefore$ f' is strictly increasing in $[0, \pi/2)$. Also, $f'(0) = 0$

$\Rightarrow f'(x) > 0$ for $0 < x < \dfrac{\pi}{2}$

$\Rightarrow f$ is strictly increasing in $[0, \pi/2)$.

Also, $f(0) = 0 \Rightarrow f(x) > 0$, for $0 < x < \dfrac{\pi}{2}$

$\Rightarrow \tan x \sin x - x^2 > 0$ for $0 < x < \dfrac{\pi}{2}$

$\therefore \dfrac{\tan x \sin x - x^2}{x \sin x} > 0, 0 < x < \dfrac{\pi}{2}$

$\Rightarrow \dfrac{\tan x}{x} > \dfrac{x}{\sin x}$ for $0 < x < \dfrac{\pi}{2}$

Example 27. Find the set of values of x for which the inequality $\ln(1 + x) > x / (1 + x)$ is valid.

Sol. Let $f(x) = \ln(1 + x) - \dfrac{x}{x+1}$; $x \in (-1, \infty) = D_f$

$f'(x) = \dfrac{x}{(x+1)^2}$

$\because f'(x) > 0 \, \forall \, x \in (0, \infty)$

So, $f(x)$ is increasing on $(0, \infty)$.

$f(x) > f(\text{min}) = 0$ at $x \to 0$

$\Rightarrow f(x) > 0, \forall \, x \in (0, \infty)$ ...(i)

$\Rightarrow \ln(1 + x) > \dfrac{x}{x+1}, \forall \, x \in (0, \infty)$

Also, $f'(x) < 0, \forall \, x \in (-1, 0)$

$f(x)$ is decreasing on $x \in (-1, 0)$

So, $f(x) > f(\text{min}) = 0$ at $x \to 0^-$

$f(x) > 0, \forall \, x \in (-1, 0)$ ...(ii)

From Eqs. (i) and (ii), we get

$f(x) > 0, \forall \, x \in (-1, 0) \cup (0, \infty)$

$\therefore \ln(1 + x) > \dfrac{x}{1+x} \forall \, x \in (-1, 0) \cup (0, \infty)$

Example 28. For all $x \in (0, 1)$, which one is correct?

(a) $e^x < 1 + x$ (b) $\ln(1 + x) < x$
(c) $\sin x > x$ (d) $\ln x > x$

Sol. (b) (a) Let $f(x) = e^x - 1 - x$

$\Rightarrow f'(x) = e^x - 1 > 0, \forall \, x \in (0, 1)$

So, $f(x)$ is increasing, when $0 < x < 1$

$\Rightarrow \quad f(x) > f(0)$

or $\quad e^x - 1 - x > 0 \Rightarrow e^x > 1 + x$

Hence, option (a) is false.

(b) Let $g(x) = \ln(1+x) - x$

$$\Rightarrow g'(x) = \frac{1}{1+x} - 1 = \frac{-x}{1+x} < 0, \forall\, x \in (0,1)$$

So, $g(x)$ is decreasing, when $0 < x < 1$

$$\Rightarrow \quad g(0) > g(x)$$

$$\Rightarrow \quad \ln(1+x) < x$$

Therefore, option (b) is correct.

(c) Let $h(x) = \sin x - x$

$$\Rightarrow h'(x) = \cos x - 1 < 0, \forall\, x \in (0,1)$$

So, $h(x)$ is decreasing, when $0 < x < 1$

$$\Rightarrow \quad h(x) < h(0) \Rightarrow \sin x < x$$

Hence, option (c) is false.

(d) Let $g(x) = \ln x - x$

$$\Rightarrow g'(x) = \frac{1}{x} - 1 = \frac{1-x}{x} > 0 \text{ for } x \in (0,1)$$

$$\therefore g'(x) > 0, \forall\, x \in (0,1)$$

$\Rightarrow g(x)$ is increasing for $x \in (0,1)$

$$\Rightarrow \quad g(x) < g(0)$$

$$\Rightarrow \quad \log x - x < 0 \Rightarrow \log x < x$$

Hence, option (d) is false.

Example 29. Show that

(i) $\sin x < x - \dfrac{x^3}{6} + \dfrac{x^5}{120}$ for $x > 0$

(ii) $e^x + e^{-x} > 2 + x^2$ for $x \neq 0$

Sol. (i) Let $f(x) = \sin x - x + \dfrac{x^3}{6} - \dfrac{x^5}{120}$

$$\Rightarrow \quad f'(x) = \cos x - 1 + \frac{x^2}{2} - \frac{x^4}{24}$$

$$\Rightarrow \quad f''(x) = -\sin x + x - \frac{x^3}{6}$$

$$\Rightarrow \quad f'''(x) = 1 - \cos x - \frac{x^2}{2}$$

$$\Rightarrow f''''(x) = \sin x - x$$

For $x > 0$, $f''''(x)$ is always negative.

$\Rightarrow f'''(x)$ is decreasing and $f'''(0) = 0$

$\Rightarrow f'''(x) < 0$ for $x > 0$

$\Rightarrow f''(x)$ is decreasing for $x > 0$ and $f''(0) = 0$

$\Rightarrow f''(x) < 0$ for $x > 0$

$\Rightarrow f'(x)$ is decreasing for $x > 0$ and $f'(0) = 0$

$\Rightarrow f'(x) < 0$ for $x > 0$

$\Rightarrow f(x)$ is decreasing for $x > 0$ and $f(0) = 0$

$\Rightarrow f(x) < f(0) = 0$ for $x > 0$

$$\Rightarrow \sin x < x - \frac{x^3}{6} + \frac{x^5}{120} \text{ for } x > 0$$

(ii) $e^x + e^{-x} > 2 + x^2$ for $x \neq 0$

$$f(x) = e^x + e^{-x} - 2 - x^2$$

$$\Rightarrow f'(x) = e^x - e^{-x} - 2x$$

$$= \left[1 + x + \frac{x^2}{2!} + \frac{x^3}{3!} + \frac{x^4}{4!} + \frac{x^5}{5!} + \ldots\right] - \left[1 - x + \frac{x^2}{2!} - \frac{x^3}{3!} + \frac{x^4}{4!} - \frac{x^5}{5!} + \ldots\right] - 2x$$

$$= 2\left[\frac{x^3}{3!} + \frac{x^5}{5!} + \ldots\right] \qquad \ldots\text{(i)}$$

$\Rightarrow f'(x)$ is positive, for $x > 0$ [from Eq. (i)]

$\Rightarrow f(x)$ is increasing, for $x > 0$

$\Rightarrow f(x) > f(0)$, for $x > 0$

$\Rightarrow e^x + e^{-x} - 2 - x^2 > 0$

$\Rightarrow e^x + e^{-x} > 2 + x^2$, for $x > 0$ ...(ii)

Also, $f'(x) =$ negative, for all $x < 0$ [from Eq. (i)]

$\Rightarrow f(x)$ is decreasing, for all $x < 0$

$\Rightarrow f(x) > f(0)$, for all $x < 0$

$\Rightarrow e^x + e^{-x} - 2 - x^2 > 0$, for all $x < 0$

$\therefore \quad e^x + e^{-x} > 2 + x^2$ ...(iii)

From Eqs. (ii) and (iii), we get

for all $x \neq 0$; $e^x + e^{-x} > 2 + x^2$.

Example 30. If $f(x) = \ln(\ln x)$, where $x > e$, prove that $\dfrac{1}{(m+1)\ln(m+1)} \le f(m+1) - f(m) \le \dfrac{1}{m \cdot \ln(m)}$, for $m > e$.

Sol. $f(x) = \ln(\ln x)$

$$g(x) = f'(x) = \frac{1}{x \ln x}$$

$$g'(x) = \frac{1}{-(x \ln x)^2}[\ln x + 1]$$

$$= -\left[\frac{1}{x^2 \ln^2 x} + \frac{1}{x^2 \ln x}\right] < 0, \text{ for } x > e$$

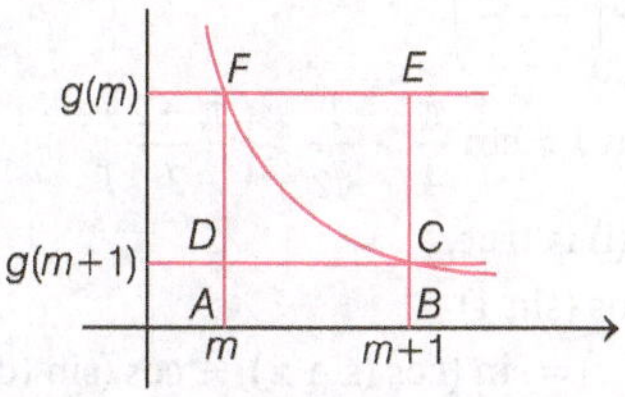

Hence, $g(x)$ is decreasing function for $x > e$ and hence $g(m) > g(m+1)$ for $m > e$.

From the graph of $y = g(x)$;

It can be inferred that area of $ABCD <$ area of $ABCF$ $<$ area of $ABEF$

$$\Rightarrow g(m+1)(m+1-m) < \int_m^{m+1} g(x)\,dx < g(m)[m+1-m]$$

$$\Rightarrow g(m+1) \le \int_m^{m+1} f'(x)\,dx \le g(m)$$

$$\Rightarrow \frac{1}{(m+1)\ln(m+1)} \le f(m+1) - f(m) \le \frac{1}{m \cdot \ln(m)}$$

Example 31. Show that $1 + x\ln(x+\sqrt{x^2+1}) \geq \sqrt{1+x^2}$ for all $x \geq 0$.

Sol. Let $f(x) = 1 + x\ln(x+\sqrt{x^2+1}) - \sqrt{1+x^2}$ for all $x \geq 0$.

$$\therefore f'(x) = 0 + x\frac{1}{(x+\sqrt{x^2+1})}\left(1+\frac{1}{2\sqrt{x^2+1}}2x\right) + \ln(x+\sqrt{x^2+1})\cdot 1 - \frac{1}{2\sqrt{x^2+1}}\cdot 2x$$

$$= \frac{x}{(x+\sqrt{x^2+1})}\left(\frac{\sqrt{x^2+1}+x}{\sqrt{x^2+1}}\right) + \ln(x+\sqrt{x^2+1}) - \frac{x}{\sqrt{1+x^2}}$$

$$= \ln(x+\sqrt{x^2+1}) + \frac{x}{\sqrt{1+x^2}} - \frac{x}{\sqrt{x^2+1}}$$

$$= \ln(x+\sqrt{x^2+1})$$

Since, $x+\sqrt{x^2+1} > 1$ for $x > 0$.

$\ln(x+\sqrt{x^2+1}) > \ln 1$ i.e. $f'(x) > 0$, for all $x > 0$.

i.e. $f(x)$ increases for $x > 0$.

$\therefore\ x \geq 0 \Rightarrow f(x) \geq f(0)$

$\Rightarrow 1 + x\ln(x+\sqrt{x^2+1}) - \sqrt{1+x^2} \geq 0$

$\Rightarrow\quad 1 + x\ln(x+\sqrt{x^2+1}) \geq \sqrt{1+x^2}$

Hence proved.

Example 32. Prove that $\sin 1 > \cos(\sin 1)$. Also, show that the equation $\sin(\cos(\sin x)) = \cos(\sin(\cos x))$ has only one solution in $x \in (0, \pi/2)$.

Sol. $\sin 1 > \cos(\sin 1)$, if $\cos\left(\frac{\pi}{2}-1\right) > \cos(\sin 1)$

i.e. if $\frac{\pi}{2} - 1 < \sin 1$

i.e. if $\sin 1 > \left(\frac{\pi-2}{2}\right)$ ...(i)

We have, $\sin 1 > \sin\frac{\pi}{4} > \frac{1}{\sqrt{2}} > \left(\frac{\pi-2}{2}\right)$

Hence, Eq. (i) is true.

$\Rightarrow \sin 1 > \cos(\sin 1)$

Now, let $f(x) = \sin(\cos(\sin x)) - \cos(\sin(\cos x))$

$$f'(x) = -\cos(\cos(\sin x))\sin(\sin x)\cos x - \sin(\sin(\cos x))\cos(\cos x)\cdot\sin x$$

$\Rightarrow\quad f'(x) < 0, \forall\ x \in (0, \pi/2)$

$\Rightarrow\quad f(x)$ is decreasing in $(0, \pi/2)$

and $f(0) = \sin 1 - \cos(\sin 1) > 0$

$f\left(\frac{\pi}{2}\right) = \sin(\cos(1)) - 1 < 0$

$\because\ f(0)$ is positive and $f\left(\frac{\pi}{2}\right)$ is negative.

$f(x) = 0$ has one solution in $x \in (0, \pi/2)$.

7.6 Comparision of Constants

Example 33. Compare which of the two is greater $(100)^{1/100}$ or $(101)^{1/101}$.

Sol. Assume $f(x) = x^{1/x}$ and let us examine monotonic behaviour of $f(x)$

$$f'(x) = x^{1/x}\cdot\left(\frac{1-\ln x}{x^2}\right)$$

$f'(x) > 0 \Rightarrow x \in (0, e)$

and $f'(x) < 0 \Rightarrow x \in (e, \infty)$

Hence, $f(x)$ is strictly decreasing for $x \geq e$.

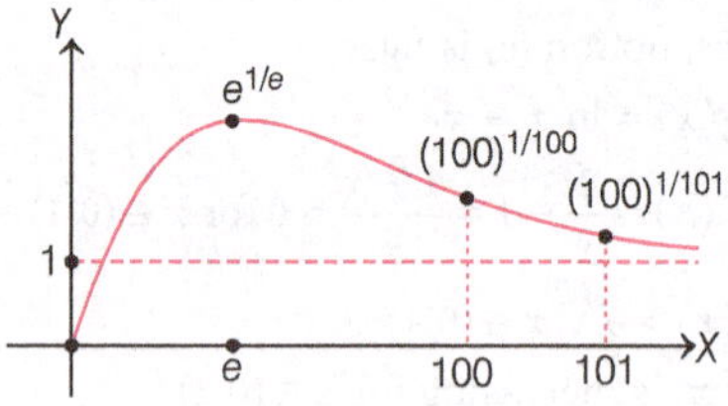

and since $e < 100 < 101$

$\Rightarrow\quad f(100) > f(101)$

$\Rightarrow\quad (100)^{1/100} > (101)^{1/101}$

7.7 Greatest and Least Value of a Function

Case I

If a continuous function $y = f(x)$ is strictly increasing in the closed interval $[a, b]$, then $f(a)$ is the least value (as shown figure) and $f(b)$ is greatest value.

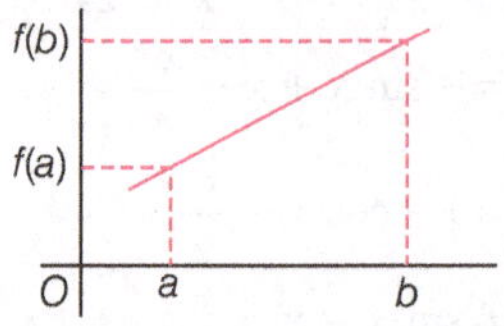

Case II

If $f(x)$ is decreasing in $[a, b]$, then $f(b)$ is the least and $f(a)$ is the greatest value of $f(x)$ in $[a, b]$.

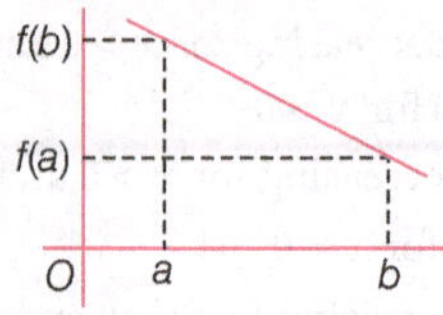

Case III

If $f(x)$ is non-monotonic in $[a, b]$ and is continuous, then the greatest and least value of $f(x)$ in $[a, b]$ are those where $f(x) = 0$ or $f'(x)$ does not exist or at the extreme values.

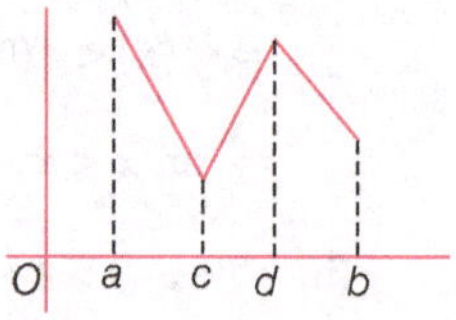

Example 34. Find least and greatest value of $f(x) = e^{x^2 - 4x + 3}$ in $[-5, 5]$.

Sol. $f(x) = e^{x^2 - 4x + 3}$

For $f(x)$ max $\rightarrow x^2 - 4x + 3$ be maximum in $[-5, 5]$

$x^2 - 4x + 3$ will be maximum at $x = -5$ in the given interval.

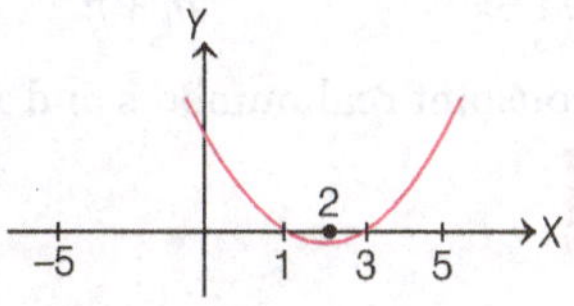

i.e. $25 + 20 + 3 = 48$

$\therefore$ Max $f(x) = e^{48}$ at $x = -5$

$x^2 - 4x + 3$ will be minimum at $x = 2$.

i.e. $4 - 8 + 3 = -1$

$\therefore$ Min. $f(x) = e^{-1}$ at $x = 2$

Example 35. Find the range of the following function $f(x) = \dfrac{x^4 - x^2 - 2x + 8}{x^4 - x^2 - 2x + 4}$.

Sol. We have, $f(x) = \dfrac{x^4 - x^2 - 2x + 8}{x^4 - x^2 - 2x + 4}$

$$= 1 + \frac{4}{x^4 - x^2 - 2x + 4}$$

$$= 1 + \frac{4}{(x^2 - 1)^2 + (x - 1)^2 + 2}$$

Let $g(x) = (x^2 - 1)^2 + (x - 1)^2 + 2$ whose least value $= 2$

and greatest value $= \infty$

Thus, greatest value of $f(x) = 1 + \dfrac{4}{2} = 3$

and least value $= 1 + \dfrac{4}{\infty} = 1$.

Also, $f(x)$ is continuous and defined on R.

Hence, the range of $f(x)$ is $y \in (1, 3]$.

7.8 Solution of Equations

Suppose that

(i) f is continuous on $[a, b]$ and differentiable on (a, b),

(ii) $f(a)$ and $f(b)$ have opposite signs,

(iii) $f'(x) > 0$ on (a, b) or $f'(x) < 0$ on (a, b), then f has exactly one root between a and b.

It cannot have more than one root because it is either increasing on $[a, b]$ or decreasing on $[a, b]$. Yet it has atleast one root, by the Intermediate value theorem.

e.g. $f(x) = x^3 + 3x + 1$ has exactly one zero on $[-1, 1]$ because

(i) f is differentiable on $[-1, 1]$,

(ii) $f(-1) = -3$ and $f(1) = 5$ have opposite signs and

(iii) $f'(x) = 3x^2 + 3 > 0$ for all x in $[-1, 1]$.

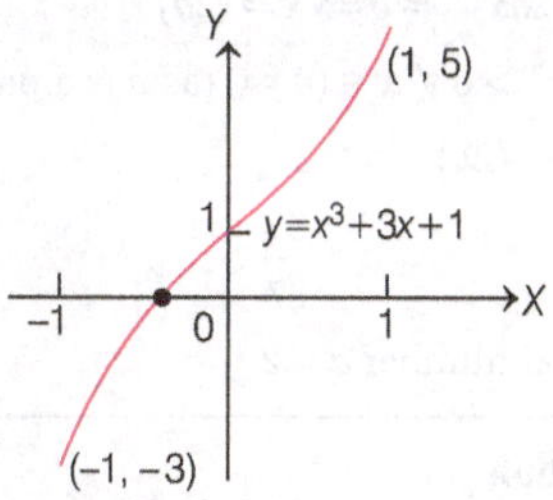

Consider another example.

Let us take the equation

$$f(x) = x^3 + 1.1x^2 + 0.9x - 1.4 = 0$$

$\because f'(x) = 3x^2 + 2.2x + 0.9 > 0$ for all the values of x, the function $f(x)$ is strictly increasing, and hence its graph cuts the X-axis only once.

Besides, $f(0) = -1.4$ and $f(1) = 1.6$, which means that there is a single real root located within the interval [0, 1].

Let us compute $f(0.5) = -0.55$ and then $f(0.7) = 0.112$. This shows that [0.5, 0.7] is a reduced interval of isolation of the sought-for root.

JEE SCANNER

Example Similar to PYQ Asked in JEE Main 2022

The number of real roots of the equation $x^5 - 3x - 1 = 0$ in [1, 2] is

(a) 1 (b) 2 (c) 3 (d) 4

Sol. (a) Consider the function

$$f(x) = x^5 - 3x - 1,\ x \in [1, 2]$$

and $f'(x) = 5x^4 - 3 > 0\ \forall\ x \in (1, 2)$

$\Rightarrow f(x)$ is strictly increasing in (1, 2).

Also, we have

$f(1) = 1 - 3 - 1 = -3$

and $f(2) = 32 - 6 - 1 = 25$

Hence, $y = f(x)$ will cut the X-axis exactly once in [1, 2]

i.e. $f(x)$ will have a unique root in [1, 2].

Skill Builder

The number of real roots of the equation $x^4 - 2x - 1 = 0$ in [1, 2] is

(a) 2 (b) 1

(c) 0 (d) 4

For Sol.

■ **For more practice** See Q.10 of Milestone Practice 7.2.

Example 36. Find the least natural number a for which $x + ax^{-2} > 2 \;\forall\; x \in (0, \infty)$.

Sol. Let $f(x) = x + ax^{-2}$

$$f'(x) = 1 - 2ax^{-3} = 0 \Rightarrow x = (2a)^{1/3}$$

$$f''(x) = 6ax^{4} > 0 \;\forall\; x \in (0, \infty) \text{ (as } a \text{ is a natural number)}$$

Thus, $(2a)^{1/3} + a(2a)^{-2/3} > 2$

$$\Rightarrow \quad a > \frac{32}{27}$$

$\Rightarrow$ least natural number $a = 2$

Alternate Solution

$$x + ax^{-2} > 2 \Rightarrow x^3 - 2x^2 + a > 0$$

Let $f(x) = x^3 - 2x^2 + a$

$\because$ $f(x) > 0, \forall\; x \in (0, \infty) \Rightarrow \min f(x) > 0$

For minimum $f(x)$,

$$f'(x) = 3x^2 - 4x = 0$$

$$\Rightarrow \quad x = 0, \frac{4}{3}$$

$$\Rightarrow \quad f\left(\frac{4}{3}\right) > 0 \Rightarrow a > \frac{32}{27}$$

The least natural number a for which $x + ax^{-2} > 2$ is 2.

Example 37. If $ax^2 + \dfrac{b}{x} \ge c, \;\forall\; x \in R^+$ where a, b, c are positive constants then prove that $27ab^2 \ge 4c^3$.

Sol. Let $f(x) = ax^2 + \dfrac{b}{x} - c$

$$\therefore f'(x) = 2ax - \frac{b}{x^2}$$

If $f'(x) = 0$, then $x = \left(\dfrac{b}{2a}\right)^{1/3}$,

which is a positive critical point.

We can find that the least value of $f(x)$ occurs at

$$x = \left(\frac{b}{2a}\right)^{1/3}.$$

$\because$ $ax^2 + \dfrac{b}{x} \ge c, \forall\; x \in R^+$ we should have $f\left(\dfrac{b}{2a}\right)^{1/3} \ge 0.$

$$\Rightarrow \quad a\left\{\frac{b}{2a}\right\}^{2/3} + \frac{b}{\left\{\frac{b}{2a}\right\}^{1/3}} \ge c$$

$$\Rightarrow \quad a\left(\frac{b}{2a}\right) + b \ge c\left(\frac{b}{2a}\right)^{1/3}$$

$$\Rightarrow \quad \left(\frac{3b}{2}\right)^3 \ge \frac{b}{2a} \cdot c^3$$

$$\Rightarrow \quad \frac{27b^3}{8} \ge \frac{b}{2a} \cdot c^3$$

or $\quad 27b^2 a \ge 4c^3 \Rightarrow 27ab^2 \ge 4c^3.$

7.9 Jenson Inequality

Jenson observed that for the function $f(x)$ which are either increasing with a constant rate of increase or decreasing with a constant rate of decrease follows the equation

$$f\left(\frac{mx_1 + nx_2}{m+n}\right) = \frac{mf(x_1) + nf(x_2)}{m+n};$$

where m, n are constant real numbers and $x_1, x_2 \in D_f$.

JEE SPIKE

For concave up curve,we have

$$f\left(\frac{mx_1 + nx_2}{m+n}\right) < \frac{mf(x_1) + nf(x_2)}{m+n}$$

and for concave down curve, we have

$$f\left(\frac{mx_1 + nx_2}{m+n}\right) > \frac{mf(x_1) + nf(x_2)}{m+n}.$$

Concept Inside Video

Example 38. Prove that for any two numbers x_1 and x_2,

$$\frac{2e^{x_1} + e^{x_2}}{3} > e^{\frac{2x_1 + x_2}{3}}.$$

Sol. Assume $f(x) = e^x$ and let x_1 and x_2 be two points on the curve $y = e^x$.

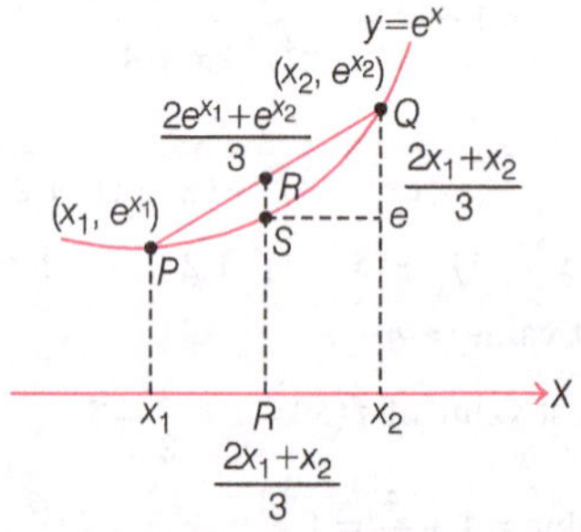

Let R be another point which divides P and Q in ratio 1 : 2. The y-coordinate of point R is $\dfrac{2e^{x_1} + e^{x_2}}{3}$ and y-coordinate of point S is $e^{\frac{2x_1 + x_2}{3}}$.

$\because$ $f(x) = e^x$ is always concave up, hence point R will always be above point S.

$$\Rightarrow \quad \frac{2e^{x_1} + e^{x_2}}{3} > e^{\frac{2x_1 + x_2}{3}}$$

Example 39. If $0 < x_1 < x_2 < x_3 < \pi$, then prove that $\sin\left(\dfrac{x_1 + x_2 + x_3}{3}\right) > \dfrac{\sin x_1 + \sin x_2 + \sin x_3}{3}$. Hence or otherwise prove that if A, B, C are angles of triangle then maximum value of $\sin A + \sin B + \sin C$ is $\dfrac{3\sqrt{3}}{2}$.

Sol. Let points A, B, C form a triangle, y-coordinate of centroid G is $\dfrac{\sin x_1 + \sin x_2 + \sin x_3}{3}$ and y-coordinate of point F is $\sin\left(\dfrac{x_1 + x_2 + x_3}{3}\right)$.

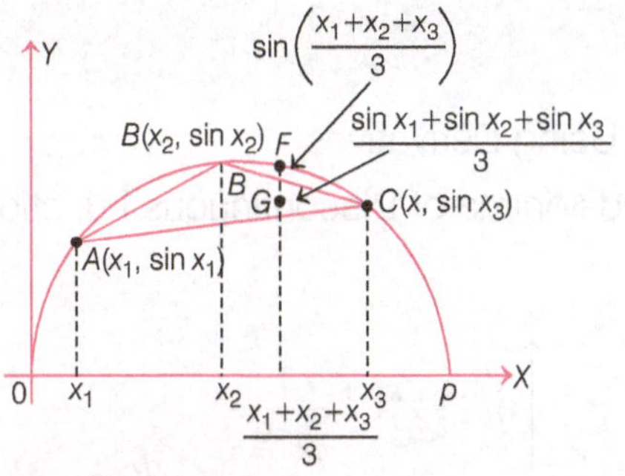

Hence, $\sin\left(\dfrac{x_1 + x_2 + x_3}{3}\right) > \dfrac{\sin x_1 + \sin x_2 + \sin x_3}{3}$

If $A + B + C = \pi$, then

$$\sin\left(\frac{A+B+C}{3}\right) > \frac{\sin A + \sin B + \sin C}{3}$$

$$\Rightarrow \quad \sin\frac{\pi}{3} > \frac{\sin A + \sin B + \sin C}{3}$$

$$\Rightarrow \quad \frac{3\sqrt{3}}{2} > \sin A + \sin B + \sin C$$

$\Rightarrow$ Maximum value of $(\sin A + \sin B + \sin C) = \dfrac{3\sqrt{3}}{2}$.

It is attained if $A = B = C$

Milestone Practice 7.2

1. Prove the following results

(i) $e^{\cos x - \sin x} < \dfrac{1 - \sin x}{1 - \cos x}, \forall x \in (0, \pi/4)$

(ii) $\sin^2 x < x \sin(\sin x), (0 < x < \pi/2)$

(iii) $x \ge \tan^{-1} x, \forall x \in [0, \infty)$

(iv) $\left(\tan^{-1}\dfrac{1}{e}\right)^2 + \dfrac{2e}{\sqrt{e^2+1}} < (\tan^{-1} e)^2 + \dfrac{2}{\sqrt{e^2+1}}$

(v) $\cos(\sin x) > \sin(\cos x), \forall x \in (0, 3\pi/2)$

(vi) $(2\sin x + \tan x) \ge 3x; 0 \le x < \pi/2$

(vii) $e^{\tan^{-1} x}(x + \sqrt{1 + x^2}) < e^{2x}, \forall x \in (0, \infty)$

2. For an acute angle ΔABC, prove that

(i) $\sin A + \sin B + \sin C > 2$ for any triangle

(ii) $\cos(\pi/4 + A/4) + \cos(\pi/4 + B/4) + \cos(\pi/4 + C/4) \le 3/2$ for any triangle

(iii) $\cos A + \cos B + \cos C \le \dfrac{3}{2}$ for any triangle

3. Prove the following inequalities

(i) $\dfrac{x^2 + y^2}{2} \ge \left(\dfrac{x+y}{2}\right)^2$

(ii) $\dfrac{x^2 + y^2 + z^2}{3} \ge \left(\dfrac{x+y+z}{3}\right)^2$

4. Find the set of value(s) a for which the function $f(x) = \dfrac{ax^3}{3} + (a+2)x^2 + (a-1)x + 2$ possesses negative point of inflection.

5. For $x \in (0, \pi/2)$, which of the following is correct?

(a) $0 < x\sin x - (1/2)\sin^2 x$

(b) $x\sin x - \dfrac{1}{2}\sin^2 x < \dfrac{\pi - 1}{2}$

(c) Both (a) and (b)

(d) None of the above

6. Find the range of $y = \ln(\sin x^{\sin x} + 1)$

(a) $[\ln(e^{-1/e} + 1), \ln 2]$ (b) $[\ln e^{-1/e}, \ln 2]$
(c) $[\ln e^{-1/e}, \ln 2e]$ (d) None of these

7. Find the range of $y = \ln(x^x + 1)$

(a) $[\ln(e^{-1/e} + 1), \ln 2]$ (b) $[\ln e^{-1/e}, \ln 2]$
(c) $[\ln e^{-1/e}, \ln 2e]$ (d) None of these

8. Let $f(x) = \dfrac{\sin x}{x}$, where $0 < x < \dfrac{\pi}{2}$, then

(a) $\sin^2 x < x\sin(\sin x)$ (b) $\sin^2 x > x\sin(\sin x)$
(c) $\sin^2 x > 1 + x\sin(\sin x)$ (d) None of these

9. If $f(x)$ is monotonically decreasing function and have concavity up, then its inverse $f^{-1}(x)$ will be

(a) decreasing and has concavity upwards

(b) decreasing and has concavity downwards

(c) increasing and has concavity downwards

(d) increasing and has concavity upwards

10. The number of real roots of the equation $x^5 + x^3 + 5x + 7 = 0$ is

(a) 3 (b) 2
(c) 1 (d) None of these

Answer Key

4. $a \in (-\infty, -2) \cup (0, \infty)$	**5.** (a,b)	**6.** (a)	**7.** (a)
8. (a)	**9.** (a)	**10.** (c)	

For Detailed Solution

Milestone 3 Introduction of Maxima and Minima

• Local (Relative) Maxima and Minima • Maxima and Minima Using Derivatives
• Concept of Global Maximum/Minimum Values • Maxima and Minima of Discontinuous Functions

For finding optimised value of any expression, we introduce concept of extremum i.e. maxima or minima.

Concept of maxima and minima will be discuss in two types

1. Local (relative) maxima and minima.
2. Global (absolute) maxima and minima.

7.10 Local (Relative) Maxima and Minima

A function $f(x)$ is said to have a local maxima at $x = a$ if $f(a)$ is greater than every other value assumed by $f(x)$ in the immediate neighbourhood of $x = a$.

$$\left.\begin{array}{l} f(a) \geq f(a+h) \\ f(a) \geq f(a-h) \end{array}\right\} \text{for a sufficiently small positive } h.$$

$\Rightarrow x = a$ gives maxima

In other words, a function $f(x)$ is said to have a local maxima at $x = a$ if $f(a) \geq f(x)$, $\forall\, x \in (a-h, a+h)$, where h is a small positive arbitrary number.

A function $f(x)$ is said to have a minima at $x = b$ if

$$\left.\begin{array}{l} f(b) \leq f(b+h) \\ f(b) \leq f(b-h) \end{array}\right\} \text{for a sufficiently small positive } h.$$

In other words, a function $f(x)$ is said to have a local minima at $x = b$ if $f(b) \leq f(x)$, $\forall\, x \in (b-h, b+h)$, where h is a small positive arbitrary number.

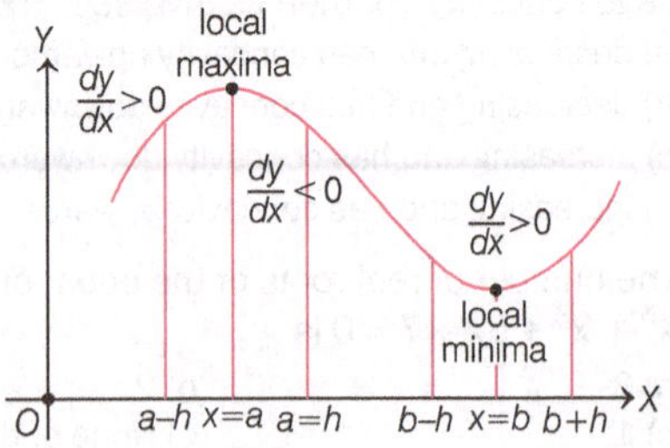

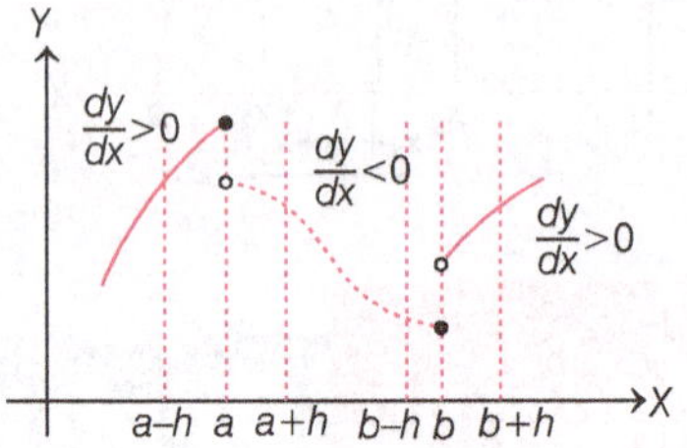

Being the greatest and least values of the function in the neighbourhood of the point in question, these are also known as local/relative extrema.

- The term 'extremum' or 'extremal' or 'turning value' is used both for maximum/minimum value.
- The above definition is applicable to all functions continuous or discontinuous, differentiable or non-differentiable at $x = a$.
- If the graph of a function f attains a local maximum at the point $(a, f(a))$, then $x = a$ is called the point of local maximum and $f(a)$ is called the local maximum value. A similar terminology is used for local minimum.
- A function can have several local maximum and minimum values.
- If a function is strictly increasing or strictly decreasing at an interior point $x = a$, it cannot have an extremum at $x = a$ and *vice-versa*.

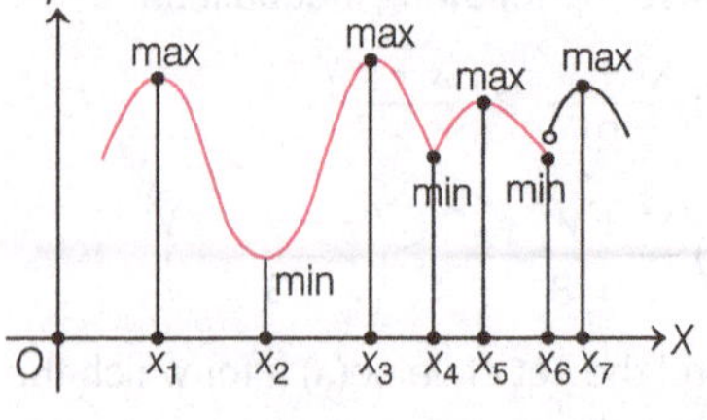

Here, x_1, x_3, x_5 and x_7 are the points of local maxima and x_2, x_4 and x_6 are the points of local minima.

- A local maximum (local minimum) value of a function may not be the greatest (least) value in a finite interval. A local minimum value may be greater than a local maximum value.

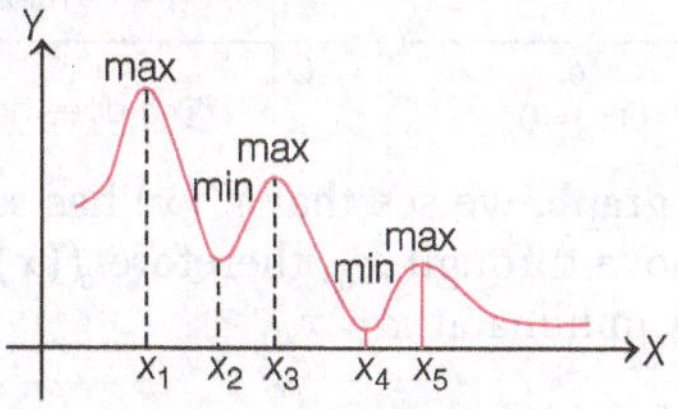

Here, $f(x)$ at x_2 (point of local minima) is more than $f(x)$ at x_5 (point of local maxima).

For continuous function there must exist one local minima between any two local maxima and *vice-versa*. However this may or may not be the case for discontinuous functions.

Example 40. Let $f(x)=\begin{cases} |x|, & 0<|x|\le 2 \\ \dfrac{1}{2}, & x=0 \end{cases}$. Examine the behaviour of $f(x)$ at $x=0$.

Sol. The graph of $y=f(x)$ is shown below

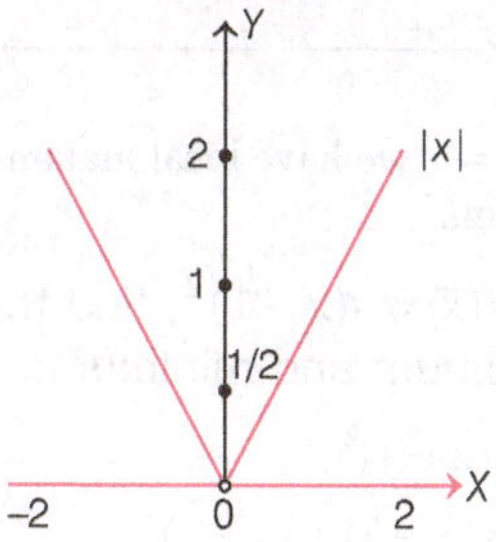

$f(x)$ has local maxima at $x=0$ because $f(0)=\dfrac{1}{2}$ is greater than every other values assumed by $f(x)$ in the immediate neighborhood of $x=0$.

Example 41. Let $f(x)=\begin{cases} |x-1|+a, & \text{if } x\le 1 \\ 2x+3, & \text{if } x>1 \end{cases}$. If $f(x)$ has local minimum at $x=1$, then a is less than or equal to

(a) 2 (b) 3 (c) 5 (d) None of these

Sol. (c) We have, $f(x)=\begin{cases} 1-x+a, & \text{if } x\le 1 \\ 2x+3, & \text{if } x>1 \end{cases}$

Since, $y=1-x+a$ is decreasing function and $y=2x+3$ is increasing function $f(x)$ will have a local minimum at $x=1$.

If $f(1)\le f(x)$ for $x>1$

or if $a\le 2x+3$ for $x>1 \Rightarrow a\le 5$

Example 42. Find the points of local maxima/minima for $x\in[0, 4.5]$ for the function $y=|x-1|+|x-2|+|x-3|+|x-4|$, where $x\in[0, 9/2]$.

Sol. $y=|x-1|+|x-2|+|x-3|+|x-4|$

$$y=\begin{cases} 10-4x; & x<1 \\ 8-2x; & 1\le x<2 \\ 4; & 2\le x<3 \\ 2x-2; & 3\le x<4 \\ 4x-10; & x\ge 4 \end{cases}$$

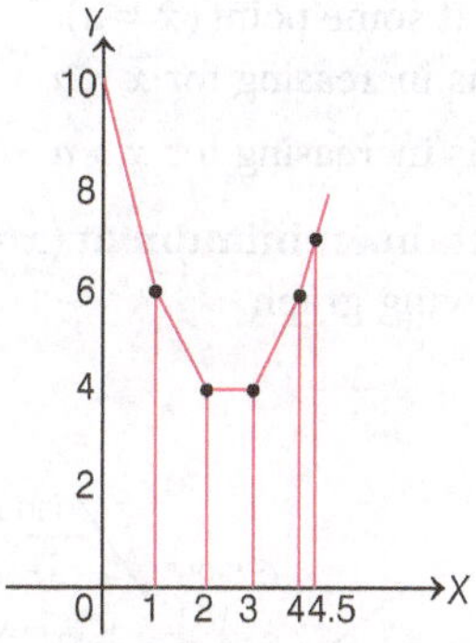

Now, $x=0$ and $x=4.5$ are the points of local maxima and points $x=2, 3$ are points of local minima.

The points in the interval (2, 3) can be referred to as neither the points of local maxima nor the pionts of local minima, since the function $f(x)$ is constant for $x\in(2, 3)$.

7.11 Maxima and Minima using Derivatives

Let $f(x)$ be a continuous and differentiable function. Then, for extremum value of function two methods are given as

1. First order derivative test
2. Higher order derivative test

First Order Derivative Test

As we know the function attains maximum when it has assumed its maximum value and attains minimum, when it has assumed its minimum value which could be shown as

At a Critical Point $x=a$

(i) When $f(x)$ attains maximum at $(x=a)$

Consider the following graph

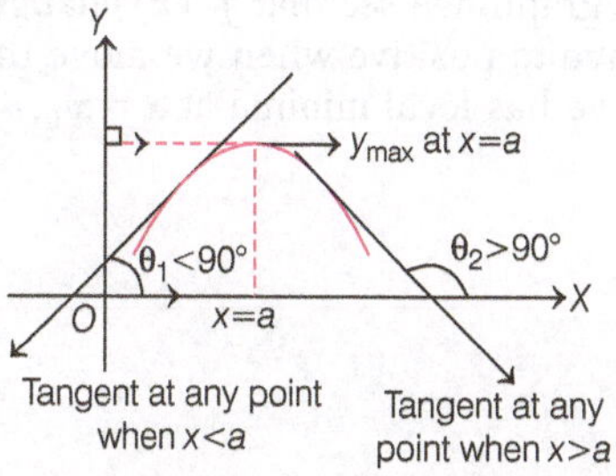

From above graph,

For $x < a, \theta_1 < 90° \Rightarrow \tan\theta_1 > 0$ or increasing for $x < a$

For $x = a, \tan\theta = 0 \Rightarrow$ neither increasing nor decreasing for $x = a$

For $x > a, \theta_2 > 90° \Rightarrow \tan\theta_2 < 0$ or decreasing for $x > a$

Thus, we can say

$f(x)$ is maximum at some point $(x = a)$.

$$\Rightarrow \begin{cases} f(x) \text{ is increasing for } x < a \\ f(x) \text{ is increasing for } x > a \end{cases}$$

(ii) **When $f(x)$ attains minimum at $(x = a)$**

Consider the following graph

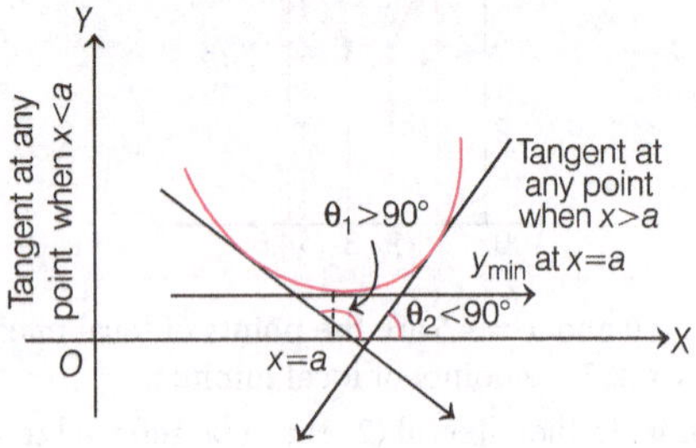

From the above graph,

For $x < a, \theta_1 > 90° \Rightarrow \tan\theta_1 < 0$ or decreasing when $x < a$

For $x = a, \tan\theta = 0 \Rightarrow$ neither increasing nor decreasing for $x = a$

For $x > a, \theta_2 < 90° \Rightarrow \tan\theta_2 > 0$ or increasing when $x > a$

Thus, we can say

$f(x)$ is minimum at some points $x = a$,

$$\Rightarrow \begin{cases} f(x) \text{ is decreasing for } x < a \\ f(x) \text{ is increasing for } x > a \end{cases}$$

- In both the graph, we see that $f'(x)$ changes its sign from positive to negative when we move through x_0 and the function has local maxima at $x = x_0$.

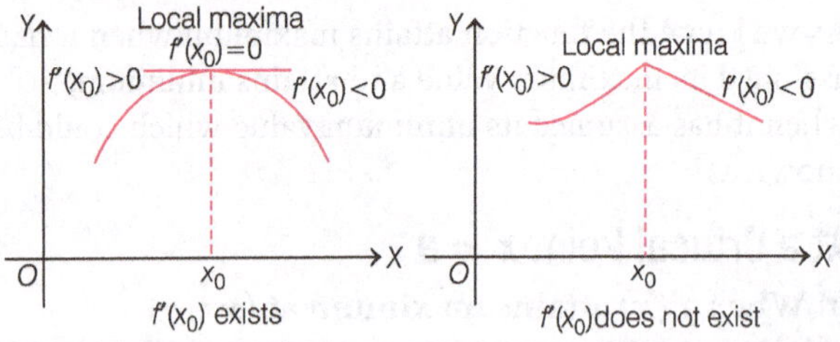

- In both the graph, we see that $f'(x)$ changes its sign from negative to positive when we move through x_0 and the curve has local minima at $x = x_0$.

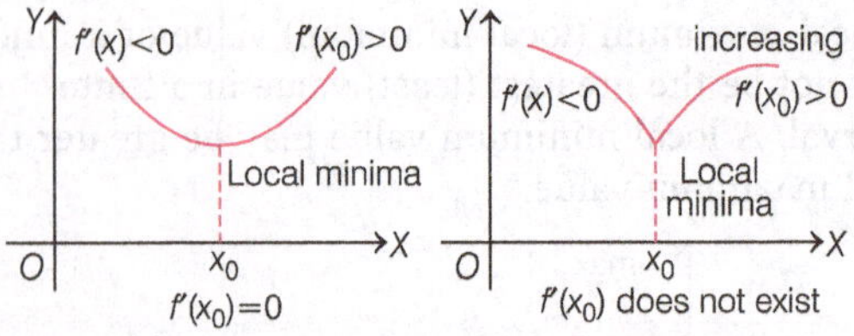

- In both the graph, we see that $f'(x)$ has same sign when we move through x_0, therefore $f(x)$ has neither maxima nor minima at $x = x_0$.

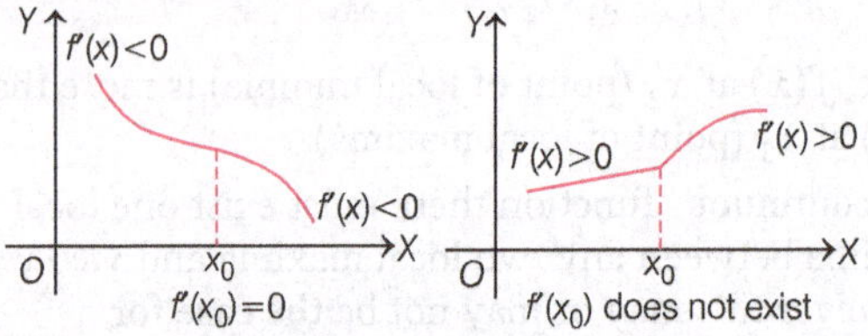

Example 43. Let $f(x) = x^3 - 3x^2 + 6$. Find the point at which $f(x)$ assumes local maximum and local minimum.

Sol. Given, $f(x) = x^3 - 3x^2 + 6 \Rightarrow f'(x) = 3x^2 - 6x = 3x(x - 2)$

Using number line rule,

$f'(x)$ changes sign from positive to negative at $x = 0$ and $f'(x)$ changes sign from positive to negative at $x = 2$.

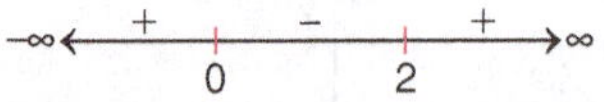

Therefore, at $x = 0$, we have local maxima and at $x = 2$, we have local minima.

Example 44. Let $f(x) = x(x - 1)^2$, find the point at which $f(x)$ assumes maximum and minimum.

Sol. Given, $f(x) = x(x - 1)^2$

$$f'(x) = 2x(x - 1) + (x - 1)^2$$

$$f'(x) = (x - 1)[2x + x - 1]$$

$$f'(x) = (x - 1)(3x - 1)$$

Using number line rule for $f'(x)$, we have the following figure which shows $f'(x)$ changes sign from positive to negative at $x = \frac{1}{3}$.

Hence, at $x = \frac{1}{3}$, we have maximum and $f'(x)$ changes sign from negative to positive at $x = 1$.

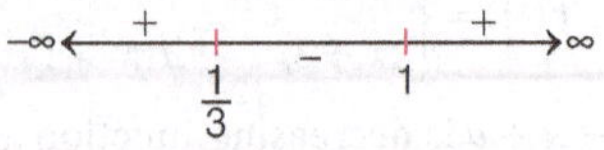

Hence, $f(x)$ is minimum at $x = 1$.

JEE SCANNER

Example Similar to PYQ Asked in JEE Main 2022

The function $f(x)=\int_{-1}^{x} t(e^t-1)(t-1)(t-2)^3(t-3)^5\,dt$ *has m number of local maxima and n number at local minima, then* $|m-n|$ *is*

(a) 0 (b) 1 (c) 2 (d) 3

Sol. (b) Given, $f(x)=\int_{-1}^{x} t(e^t-1)(t-1)(t-2)^3(t-3)^5\,dt$

$$f'(x)=x(e^x-1)(x-1)(x-2)^3(x-3)^5$$

[using Leibnitz rule]

Using number line rule for $f'(x)$, we get the following figure which shows local maxima at $x=2$ as $f'(x)$ changes from positive to negative and local minima at $x=1$ and $x=3$ as $f'(x)$ changes from negative to positive.

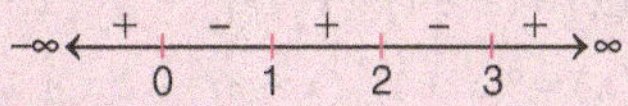

$\therefore$ Local minima at $x=1, 3$ and local maxima at $x=2$.

$\therefore$ $m=1$ and $n=2$

$\therefore$ $|m-n|=1$

Skill Builder

The function $f(x)=\int_{-1}^{x} t(e^{2t}-1)(t+1)(t-2)(t-3)^3\,dt$ has m number of local maxima and n number of local minima, then $|m+n|$ is

For Sol.

(a) 4 (b) −3

(c) 3 (d) 2

■ **For more practice** See Q. 18 of Milestone Practice 7.3.

At Left end Point *a* and Right end Point *b* in $[a, b]$

Let $f(x)$ be defined on $[a, b]$ and if $f'(x)<0$ for $x>a$, then $f(x)$ has local maximum at $x=a$ and local minimum at $x=b$.

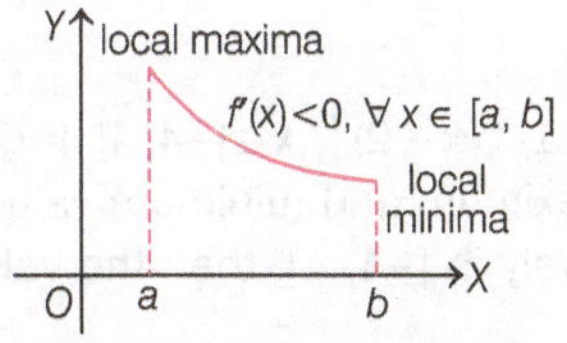

Again, if $f'(x)>0$ for $x>a$, then $f(x)$ has local minimum at $x=a$ and local maximum at $x=b$.

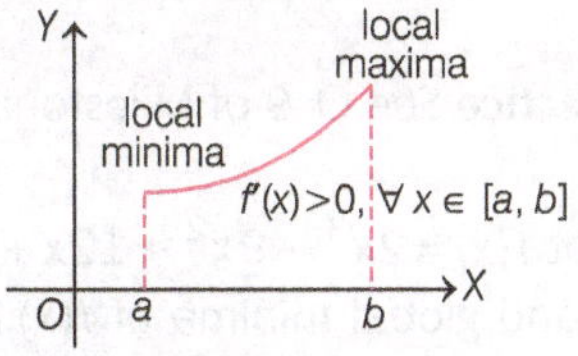

We can summarise above results as

(i) If a function is strictly increasing in $[a, b]$, then

$$\begin{cases} f(a) \text{ is local minimum} \\ f(b) \text{ is local maximum} \end{cases}$$

(ii) If a function is strictly decreasing in $[a, b]$, then

$$\begin{cases} f(a) \text{ is local maximum} \\ f(b) \text{ is local minimum} \end{cases}$$

Example 45. Find the local maximum and local minimum of $f(x)=x^3+3x$ in $[-2,4]$.

Sol. Given, $f(x)=x^3+3x \Rightarrow f'(x)=3x^2+3$

which is strictly increasing for all $x\in R$ and thus increasing for $[-2, 4]$.

Hence, local minimum is $f(-2)=(-2)^3+3(-2)=-14$

and local maximum is $f(4)=(4)^3+3(4)=76$.

Higher Order Derivative Test (*n*th Derivative Test)

First we find the root of $f'(x)=0$. Suppose, $x=a$ is one of the roots of $f'(x)=0$.

Now, find $f''(x)$ at $x=a$

(i) If $f''(a)=$ negative, then $f(x)$ is maximum at $x=a$.

(ii) If $f''(a)=$ positive, then $f(x)$ is minimum at $x=a$.

(iii) If $f''(a)=$ zero

Then, we find $f'''(x)$ at $x=a$

If $f'''(a)\neq 0$, then $f(x)$ has neither maximum nor minimum (inflexion point), at $x=a$.

But, if $f'''(a)=0$, then find $s^{iv}(a)$.

If $f^{iv}(a)=$ positive, then $f(x)$ is minimum at $x=a$.

If $f^{iv}(a)=$ negative, then $f(x)$ is maximum at $x=a$.

and so on process is repeated till point is discussed.

Example 46. Let $f(x)=(x-1)^4$ discuss the point at which $f(x)$ assumes maximum or minimum value.

Sol. Given, $f(x)=(x-1)^4$

$$f'(x)=4(x-1)^3$$

Using number line rule,

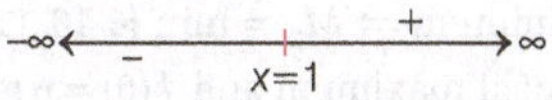

Shows $f'(x)$ changes sign from negative to positive.

Therefore, $f(x)$ assumes minimum at $x=1$.

Alternate Solution

Given, $f(x)=(x-1)^4 \Rightarrow f'(x)=4(x-1)^3$

Let $f'(x)=0 \Rightarrow x=1$

Now, $f''(x)=12(x-1)^2$ which is zero at $x=1$

i.e. $f''(1)=0$

Thus, finding $f'''(x)=24(x-1)$ which is again zero at $x=1$

i.e. $f'''(1)=0$

Again, finding $f^{iv}(x)=24$ which is positive at $x=1$ i.e. $f^{iv}(1)>0$

Therefore, minimum at $x=1$.

7.12 Concept of Global Maximum/Minimum Values

Let $y = f(x)$ be a given function with domain D.

Let $[a, b] \subseteq D$, then global maximum/minimum values of $f(x)$ in $[a, b]$ is basically the greatest/least value of $f(x)$ in $[a, b]$.

Global maxima/minima in $[a, b]$ would always occur at critical points of $f(x)$ within $[a, b]$ or at the end points of the interval.

Global Maximum/Minimum values in [a, b]

In order to find the global maximum and minimum values of $f(x)$ in $[a, b]$, find out all critical points of $f(x)$ in $[a, b]$ (i.e. all points at which $f'(x) = 0$).

Let $c_1, c_2, c_3, \ldots, c_n$ be the points at which $f'(x) = 0$ and let $f(c_1), f(c_2), \ldots, f(c_n)$ be the values of the function at these points,

$\max\{f(a), f(c_1), f(c_2), \ldots, f(c_n), f(b)\} = M_1$ (say)

$\min\{f(a), f(c_1), f(c_2), \ldots, f(c_n), f(b)\} = M_2$ (say)

Then, M_1 is the greatest value or global maxima in $[a, b]$ and M_2 is the least value or global minima in $[a, b]$.

Example 47. Let $f(x) = 2x^3 - 9x^2 + 12x + 6$. Discuss the global maxima and minima of $f(x)$ in $[0, 2]$.

Sol. Given, $f(x) = 2x^3 - 9x^2 + 12x + 6$

$\Rightarrow \quad f'(x) = 6x^2 - 18x + 12$

$\Rightarrow \quad f'(x) = 6(x^2 - 3x + 2)$

$\Rightarrow \quad f'(x) = 6(x-1)(x-2)$

Put $f'(x) = 0$

$\therefore \quad x = 1, 2$ [say c_1 and c_2]

Then, for global maximum or global minimum.

We have, $f(0) = 6, f(1) = 11, f(2) = 10$

$\therefore$ Global maximum $\Rightarrow M_1 = \max\{6, 10, 11\} = 11$

and global minimum $\Rightarrow M_2 = \min\{6, 10, 11\} = 6$

$\therefore f(1) = 11$ global maximum and $f(0) = 6$ global minimum.

Global Maximum/Minimum Values in (a, b)

Method for obtaining the greatest and least values of $f(x)$ in (a, b) is almost the same as the method used for obtaining the greatest and least values in $[a, b]$.

However a caution may be exercised

Let $M_1 = \max\{f(c_1), f(c_2), \ldots, f(c_n)\}$

and $M_2 = \min\{f(c_1), f(c_2), \ldots, f(c_n)\}$

Now, M_1 and M_2 are global maximum and global minimum, respectively.

But if $\lim_{x \to a^+} f(x) > M_1$ or $\lim_{x \to b^-} f(x) < M_2$

$\Rightarrow f(x)$ would not possess global maximum or global minimum in (a, b).

This means that if **limiting values at the end points are greater than M_1 or less than M_2, then global maximum or global minimum does not exist in (a, b).**

JEE SCANNER

Example Similar to PYQ Asked in JEE Main 2024

Let $f(x) = (x+1)^3 (x-3)^2$, $x \in [-5, 5]$. Q and q are the maximum and minimum values of f respectively in [-5, 5], then the value of $Q - q$ is

(a) 1220 (b) 1120

(c) 1320 (d) None of these

Sol. (b) Given, $f(x) = (x+1)^3 (x-3)^2$

$$f'(x) = 3(x+1)^2 (x-3)^2 + 2(x+1)^3 (x-3)$$
$$= (x+1)^2 (x-3)[3x - 9 + 2x + 2]$$
$$= (x+1)^2 (x-3)(5x-7)$$

$$f'(x) = 0 \Rightarrow x = -1, 3, \frac{7}{5}$$

Sign of $f'(x)$: $+$ on $(-\infty, -1)$, $+$ on $(-1, \frac{7}{5})$, $-$ on $(\frac{7}{5}, 3)$, $+$ on $(3, \infty)$

$\therefore \quad f(-5) = -64 \times 4 = -256$

$$f\left(\frac{7}{5}\right) = \frac{(12)^3}{5^3} \times \frac{8^2}{5^2} = \frac{12^3 \times 8^2}{5^5}$$

$f(3) = 0$

$f(5) = 6^3 \cdot 2^2 = 864$

$\therefore \quad Q = 864$ and $q = -256$

$Q - q = 864 + 256 = 1120$

Skill Builder

Let $f(x) = (x+1)^3 (x-2)^2$, $x \in [-4, 4]$. If Q and P are maximum and minimum values of f, respectively in [-4, 4], then the value of $Q + P$ is

(a) −472 (b) 572

(c) 500 (d) −972

For Sol.

■ **For more practice** See Q. 9 of Milestone Practice 7.3.

Example 48. Let $f(x) = 2x^3 - 9x^2 + 12x + 6$. Discuss the global maxima and global minima of $f(x)$ in $(1, 3)$.

Sol. Given, $f(x) = 2x^3 - 9x^2 + 12x + 6$

$\Rightarrow \quad f'(x) = 6x^2 - 18x + 12$

$\Rightarrow \quad f'(x) = 6(x-1)(x-2)$

Put $f'(x) = 0 \Rightarrow x = 1, 2$

$\therefore \quad f(1) = 11$ and $f(2) = 10$ ...(i)

Let us consider the given interval (1, 3).

Clearly, $x = 2$ is the only point in (1, 3)

and $f(2) = 10$ [from Eq. (i)]

Now, $\lim_{x \to 1^+} f(x) = \lim_{h \to 0} f(1+h)$

$= \lim_{h \to 0} 2(1+h)^3 - 9(1+h)^2 + 12(1+h) + 6$

$= 11$

and $\lim_{x \to 3^-} f(x) = \lim_{h \to 0} f(3-h)$

$= \lim_{h \to 0} 2(3-h)^3 - 9(3-h)^2 + 12(3-h) + 6$

$= 15$

Thus, $x = 2$ is the point of global minima in (1, 3) and global maxima does not exist in (1, 3).

Example 49. Find the greatest and least values of the following functions on the indicated intervals

(i) $f(x) = 2x^3 - 3x^2 - 12x + 1$ on [-2, 5/2].

(ii) $f(x) = x^2 \ln x$ on [1, e].

Sol. (i) Let $f(x) = 2x^3 - 3x^2 - 12x + 1$

$\Rightarrow f'(x) = 6x^2 - 6x - 12$

It vanishes at two points $x_1 = -1$ and $x_2 = 2$.

They both lie inside the indicated interval [−2, 5/2], consequently both of them must be taken into consideration.

To find the extreme values of the function it is necessary to compute its values at the points x_1 and x_2 and also at the end pionts of the segment.

$$f(-2) = -3,\ f(-1) = 8;\ f(2) = -19,\ f(5/2) = -16\frac{1}{2}$$

Hence, the greatest value is $f(-1) = 8$ and least $f(2) = -19$.

(ii) Find the critical points of $f'(x) = x(1 + 2\ln x)$. The derivative $f'(x)$ does not vanish inside the given interval $[1, e]$.

Therefore, there are no critical points inside the indicated interval. It now remains to compute the values of the function at the end points of the interval $[1, e]$, $f(1) = 0$; $f(e) = e^2$.

Thus, $f(1) = 0$ is the least value of the function and $f(e) = e^2$, is the greatest.

Example 50. Find the maximum value of $f(x) = \left(\frac{1}{x}\right)^x$.

Sol. $f(x) = \left(\frac{1}{x}\right)^x \Rightarrow f'(x) = \left(\frac{1}{x}\right)^x \left(\ln \frac{1}{x} - 1\right)$

$f'(x) = 0 \Rightarrow \ln \frac{1}{x} = 1 \Rightarrow \frac{1}{x} = e \Rightarrow x = \frac{1}{e}$

Also, for $x < \frac{1}{e}$, $f'(x)$ is positive and for $x > \frac{1}{e}$, $f'(x)$ is negative.

Hence, $x = \frac{1}{e}$ is point of maxima.

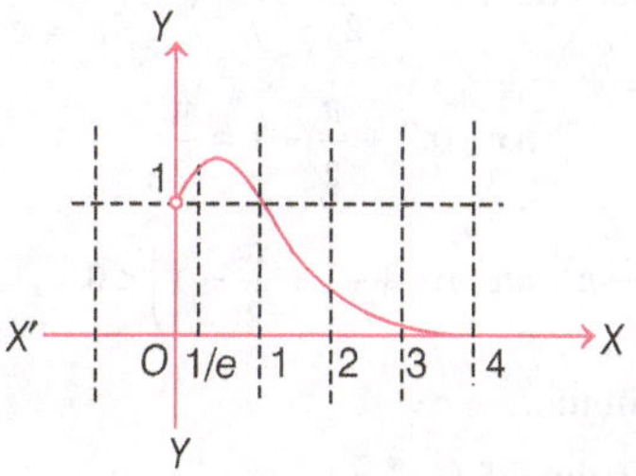

Therefore, the maximum value of function is $e^{1/e}$.

Example 51. Find greatest and least value of $f(x) = \frac{a^2}{x} + \frac{b^2}{1-x}$, $x \in (0, 1)$ $(a, b > 0)$.

Sol. We have, $f(x) = \frac{a^2}{x} + \frac{b^2}{1-x}$, $x \in (0, 1)$

and $f'(x) = \frac{-a^2}{x^2} + \frac{b^2}{(1-x)^2}$

which exists everywhere in (0, 1) and vanishes at points, given by

$$\frac{b^2}{(1-x)^2} = \frac{a^2}{x^2}$$

$$a^2(1-x)^2 = b^2x^2$$

i.e. $a(1-x) = bx \Rightarrow x = \frac{a}{a+b}$

To find the greatest and least value, we need to check the values of $f(x)$ at $x = 0^+, I^-, \frac{a}{a+b}$.

We have, $f(0^+) \to +\infty$, $f(I^-) \to +\infty$

and $f\left(\frac{a}{a+b}\right) = (a+b)^2$

Hence, least value $= (a+b)^2$ and greatest value not exist.

Example 52. The greatest value of

$f(x) = \sin\left\{x[x] + e^{[x]} + \frac{\pi}{2} - 1\right\}$, $\forall\ x \in [0, \infty)$ is

(where [·] represent greatest integer function)

(a) −1 (b) 0

(c) 1 (d) 2

Sol. Let $[x] = n$

$$\therefore\ f(x) = \sin\left(nx + e^n + \frac{\pi}{2} - 1\right)$$

$$f'(x) = n\cos\left(nx + e^n + \frac{\pi}{2} - 1\right)$$

$$f'(x) = \cos\left(nx + e^n + \frac{\pi}{2} - 1\right) = 0$$

$$nx + e^n + \frac{\pi}{2} - 1 = \frac{\pi}{2}$$

$$f''(x) = -n^2 \sin\left(nx + e^n + \frac{\pi}{2} - 1\right) < 0$$

f has maximum.

Maximum value of $f(x) = 1$ $[\because \sin x \le 1]$

JEE SCANNER

Example Similar to PYQ Asked in JEE Main 2023

If the largest term in the sequence $a_n = \dfrac{n^2}{n^3 + 200}$ *is* a_α, *then* α *is ....*

Sol. Consider the function $f(x) = \dfrac{x^2}{x^3 + 200}$ in the interval $(1, \infty)$.

Since, the derivative $f'(x) = \dfrac{x(400 - x^3)}{(x^3 + 200)^2}$

It is positive at $0 < x < \sqrt[3]{400}$ and negative at $x > \sqrt[3]{400}$, the function $f(x)$ increases at $0 < x < \sqrt[3]{400}$ and decreases at $x > \sqrt[3]{400}$.

From the inequality $7 < \sqrt[3]{400} < 8$ it follows that the largest term in the sequence can be either a_7 or a_8.

Since, $a_7 = \dfrac{49}{543} > a_8 = \dfrac{8}{89}$, the largest term in the given sequence is $a_7 = \dfrac{49}{543}$

$\therefore \qquad \alpha = 7$

Skill Builder

If the largest term in the sequence $a_n = \dfrac{n^2}{(n^3 + 400)^2}$ is a_α, then α is ......

For Sol.

■ **For more practice** See Q. 17 of Milestone Practice 7.3.

7.13 Maxima and Minima of Discontinuous Functions

In discontinuous functions, we do not apply any of the methods discussed earlier but we observe certain conditions and their graphs which would give you more clear picture.

Minimum of Discontinuous Functions

Let $f(x)$ be a function discontinuous or not differentiable at $x = a$, then the following four cases arise for minimum at $x = a$

***Case* I** From figure (i),

$$f(a) < f(a+h) \qquad f(a) < f(a-h)$$

***Case* II** From figure (ii),

$$f(a) < f(a+h) \qquad f(a) < f(a-h)$$

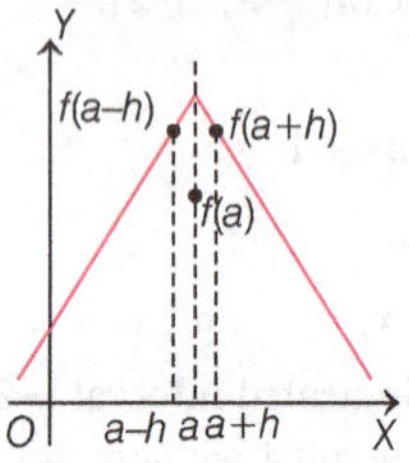

(i)

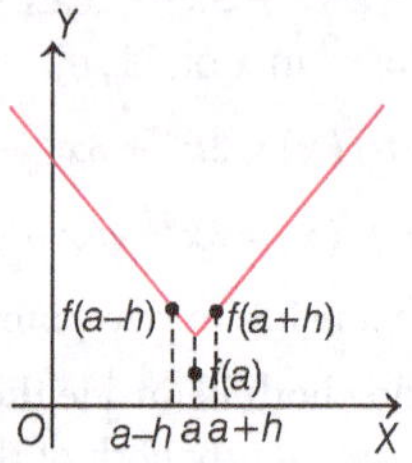

(ii)

***Case* III** From figure (iii),

$$f(a) < f(a+h) \qquad f(a) \le f(a-h)$$

***Case* IV** From figure (iv),

$$f(a) \le f(a+h) \qquad f(a) < f(a-h)$$

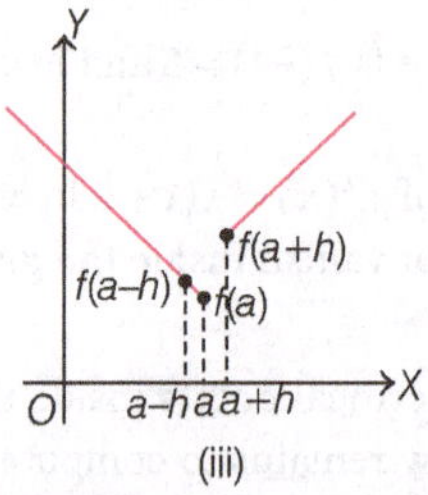

(iii)

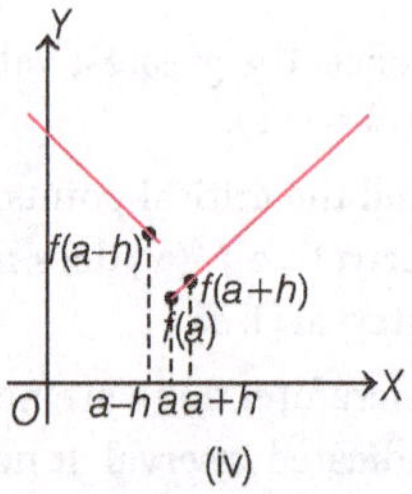

(iv)

from all the four above mentioned cases for minimum of discontinuous functions, we have

$$f(a) \le f(a+h) \text{ and } f(a) \le f(a-h)$$

Example 53. Discuss the minima of $f(x) = \{x\}$, (where $\{.\}$ denotes the fractional part of x) for $x = 6$.

Sol. As we have discussed for discontinuous functions, minimum at $x = a$ is attained when,

$f(a) \le f(a+h)$ and $f(a) \le f(a-h) \Rightarrow f(x)$ is minimum at $x = a$.

Here, $f(x) = \{x\}$ is discontinuous function at $x = 6$

where, $f(6) = 0$

$$f(6+h) > 0 \text{ and } f(6-h) > 0$$

So, $f(6) < f(6+h)$ and $f(6) < f(6-h)$

$\Rightarrow$ $f(x)$ is minimum at $x = 6$.

$\therefore$ $f(x)$ attains local minima for $x = 6$.

Example 54. Let $f(x) = \begin{cases} |x-2| + a^2 - 9a - 9, & \text{if } x < 2 \\ 2x - 3, & \text{if } x \geq 2 \end{cases}$.

Then, find the value of a for which $f(x)$ has local minimum at $x = 2$.

Sol. We have, $f(x) = \begin{cases} |x-2| + a^2 - 9a - 9, & \text{if } x < 2 \\ 2x - 3, & \text{if } x \geq 2 \end{cases}$

$f(x)$ has local minima at $x = 2$.

Since, $f(x) = 2x - 3$ for $x \geq 2$ [is strictly increasing]

$\therefore$ $\lim_{x \to 2^-} f(x) \geq f(2)$ or $\lim_{h \to 0} f(2-h) \geq f(2)$

$\Rightarrow$ $\lim_{h \to 0} \{|2-h-2| + a^2 - 9a - 9\} \geq 1$ [$\because f(2) = 2 \times 2 - 3 = 1$]

$\Rightarrow$ $a^2 - 9a - 10 \geq 0$

$\Rightarrow$ $(a+1)(a-10) \geq 0$

+   −   − (sign scheme with points −1 and 10)

$\Rightarrow$ $a \leq -1$ or $a \geq 10$

Maximum of Discontinuous Functions

Let $f(x)$ be a function discontinuous or not differentiable at $x = a$, then the following four cases arise for maximum at $x = a$.

(i) From figure (i)

$f(a) > f(a+h)$

$f(a) > f(a-h)$

(ii) From figure (ii)

$f(a) > f(a+h)$

$f(a) > f(a-h)$

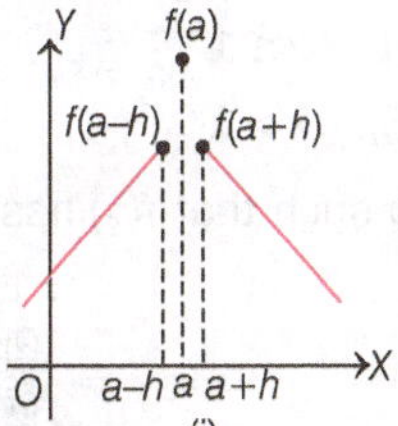

(i)

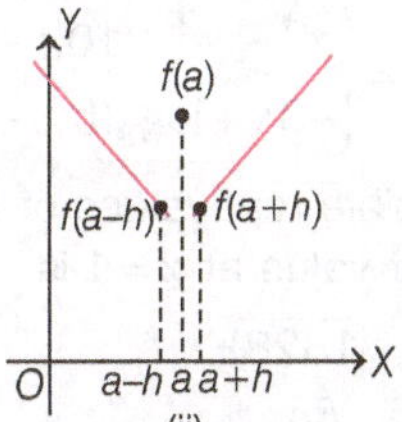

(ii)

(iii) From figure (iii)

$f(a) > f(a+h)$

$f(a) \geq f(a-h)$

(iv) From figure (iv)

$f(a) \geq f(a+h)$

$f(a) > f(a-h)$

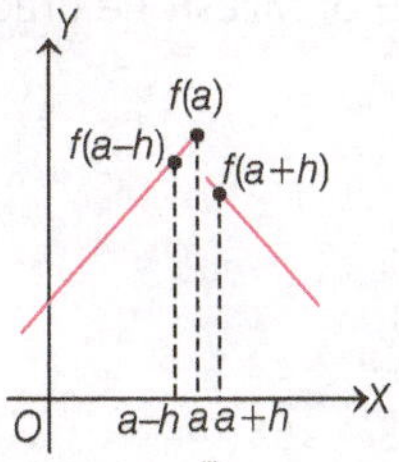

(i)

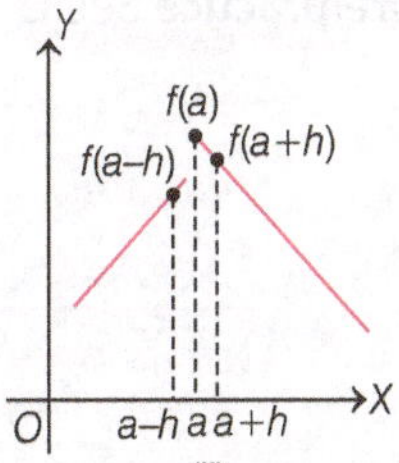

(ii)

From all the above four mentioned cases for maximum of discontinuous functions, we have

$$f(a) \geq f(a+h),\ f(a) \geq f(a-h)$$

Neither Maximum Nor Minimum for Discontinuous Functions

Let $f(x)$ be a function discontinuous or not differentiable at $x = a$, then the following cases arise for neither maximum nor minimum at $x = a$

(i) $f(a) < f(a-h)$

$f(a) \geq f(a+h)$

(ii) $f(a) \leq f(a+h)$

$f(a) > f(a-h)$

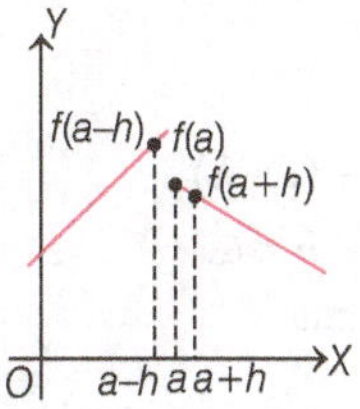

(i)

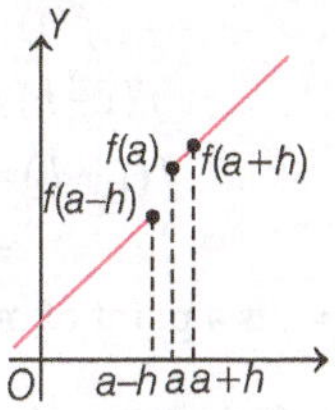

(ii)

(iii) $f(a) < f(a+h)$

$f(a) \geq f(a-h)$

(iv) $f(a) \leq f(a-h)$

$f(a) > f(a+h)$

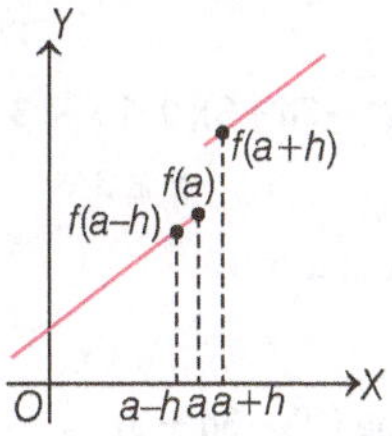

(iii)

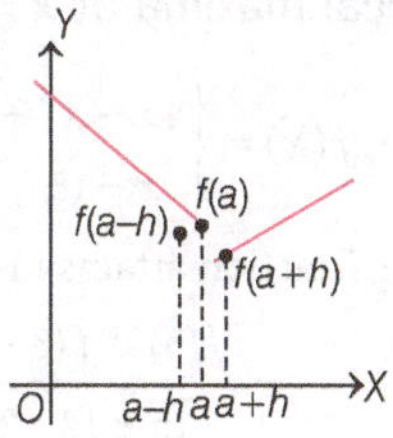

(iv)

(v) $f(a) < f(a-h)$

$f(a) > f(a+h)$

(vi) $f(a) < f(a-h)$

$f(a) \geq f(a+h)$

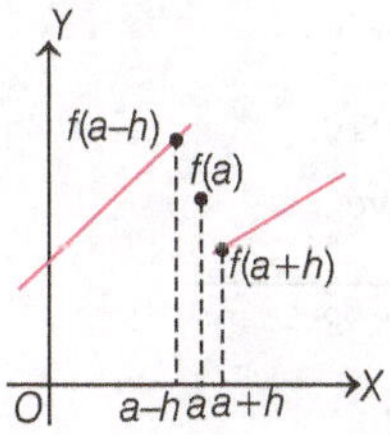

(v)

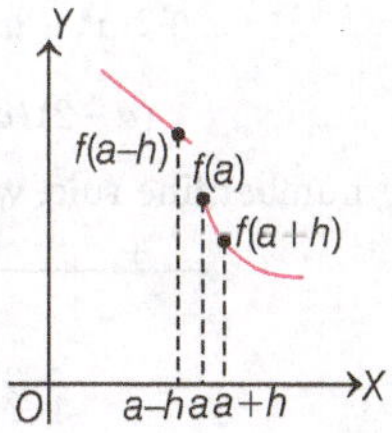

(vi)

In all above cases no extremum exist.

Example 55. Let $f(x) = \begin{cases} 6, & x \leq 1 \\ 7 - x, & x > 1 \end{cases}$, then for $f(x)$ at $x = 1$ discuss maxima and minima.

Sol. Here, $f(x)=\begin{cases}6, & x\le 1\\ 7-x, & x>1\end{cases}$

Clearly, $f(x)$ is not differentiable at $x=1$.

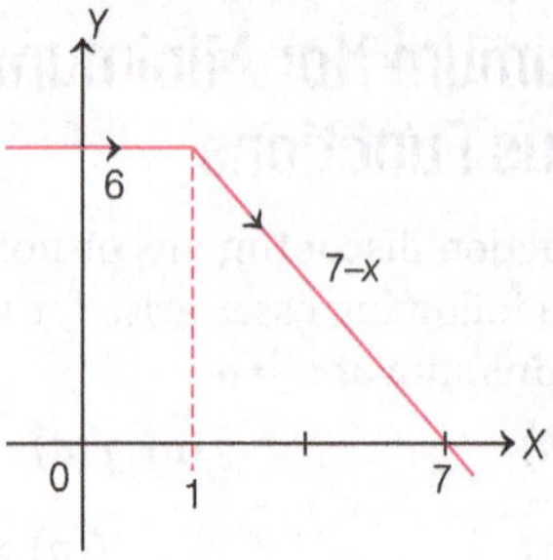

$\Rightarrow \quad f(1)=6$

$\Rightarrow \quad f(1-h)=6$

and $\quad f(1+h)=7-(1+h)$

$\quad =6-h<6$

Thus, $x=1$ is a point of maxima.

Example 56. Find the values of a for which,

$$f(x)=\begin{cases}4x-x^3+\log(a^2-3a+3), & 0\le x<3\\ x-18, & x\ge 3\end{cases}$$

has a local maxima at $x=3$.

Sol. Given, $f(x)=\begin{cases}4x-x^3+\log(a^2-3a+3), & 0\le x<3\\ x-18, & x\ge 3\end{cases}$

Since, function attains maxima at $x=3$

$\Rightarrow \quad f(3)\ge f(3-0)$

$\Rightarrow \quad -15\ge 12-27+\log(a^2-3a+3)$

$\Rightarrow \quad \log(a^2-3a+3)\le 0$

where for log to exists,

$a^2-3a+3>0$ and $\log(a^2-3a+3)\le 0$

$\Rightarrow \quad 0<a^2-3a+3\le 1$

i.e. $\quad (a-2)(a-1)\le 0$

Using number line rule, we have

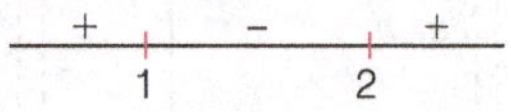

i.e. $\quad 1\le a\le 2$

$\therefore$ $f(x)$ attains local maxima at $x=3$, when $a\in[1,2]$.

JEE SCANNER

Example Similar to PYQ Asked in JEE Main 2024

Let $f(x)=\begin{cases}x^3-x^2+10x-5, & x\le 1\\ -2x+\log_2(b^2-2), & x>1\end{cases}$*. All possible real values of b such that f(x) has greatest value at x = 1 is*

(a) $[-\sqrt{130},-\sqrt{2})\cup(\sqrt{2},\sqrt{130}]$

(b) $(-\sqrt{2},\sqrt{2})$

(c) $(-\sqrt{120},\sqrt{3})\cup(\sqrt{3},\sqrt{120})$

(d) None of the above

Sol. (a) $f'(x)=3x^2-2x+10$

$$=3\left\{x^2-\frac{2x}{3}+\frac{10}{3}\right\}=3\left\{\left(x-\frac{1}{3}\right)^2+\frac{29}{9}\right\}>0$$

$\therefore f(x)$ is increasing for $x\le 1$.

Now, for $x>1$, $f'(x)=-2<0$

So, $f(x)$ is decreasing for $x>1$.

Now, $f(x)$ will have greatest value at $x=1$, if

$$\lim_{x\to 1} f(x)\le f(1)$$

$\Rightarrow \quad \lim_{h\to 0} f(1+h)\le 5$

$\Rightarrow \quad \lim_{h\to 0}\{-2(1+h)+\log_2(b^2-2)\}\le 5$

$\Rightarrow \quad -2+\log_2(b^2-2)\le 5$

$\Rightarrow \quad \log_2(b^2-2)\le 7$

$\Rightarrow \quad 2<b^2\le 130$

$\therefore \quad b\in[-\sqrt{130},-\sqrt{2})\cup(\sqrt{2},\sqrt{130}]$

Skill Builder

Let $f(x)=\begin{cases}x^3-x^2+10x-1, & x\le 1\\ -3x+\log_3(b^2-3), & x>1\end{cases}$

All possible real values of b such that $f(x)$ has greatest value at $x=1$ is

(a) $(\sqrt{3},\sqrt{1328})$

(b) $(-\sqrt{3},\sqrt{3})$

(c) $(-\sqrt{3},2\sqrt{13281}]$

(d) $[-2\sqrt{132861},-\sqrt{3})\cup(\sqrt{3},2\sqrt{132861}]$

For Sol.

■ **For more practice** See Q. 19 of Milestone Practice 7.3.

Milestone Practice 7.3

1. Find the greatest (M) and least (m) values of the following functions in the indicated intervals

(i) $f(x) = xe^{-x}$ on $[0, \infty)$

(ii) $f(x) = \sqrt{(1 - x^2)(1 + 2x^2)}$ on $[-1, 1]$

2. Find the greatest least values of the functions

(i) $f(x) = \text{arc tan } x - \frac{1}{2} \ln x$ on $\left[\frac{1}{\sqrt{3}}, \sqrt{3}\right]$

(ii) $f(x) = 2 \sin x + \sin 2x$ on $\left[0, \frac{3\pi}{2}\right]$

(iii) $f(x) = \begin{cases} 2x^2 + \dfrac{2}{x^2}; & -2 \le x < 0; 0 < x \le 2 \\ 1; & x = 0 \end{cases}$

(iv) $f(x) = x - 2 \ln x$ on $[1, e]$

3. Find the local maxima/local minima of the function $f(x)$ and also the image of interval

(i) $[0, 3]$ (ii) $[0, 4]$

under the mapping $f(x) = x^5 - 5x^4 + 5x^3 + 1$.

4. Find the points of local maxima and local minima of the function $f(x) = (x - 1)^3 (x + 1)^2$. Find also the local maximum and local minimum values.

5. Using the first derivative, find the extrema of the function $f(x) = \dfrac{x^2 - 3x + 2}{x^2 + 2x + 1}$.

6. Find the extrema of function $f(x) = \sqrt[3]{(x - 1)^2} + \sqrt[3]{(x + 1)^2}$.

7. The function $f(x) = x^3 + ax^2 + bx + c$, $a^2 \le 3b$ has

(a) one maximum value
(b) one minimum value
(c) no extreme value
(d) one maximum and one minimum value

8. If $y = \dfrac{\sin (x + a)}{\sin (x + b)}$, $a \ne b$, then y has

(a) minima at $x = 0$
(b) maxima at $x = 0$
(c) neither minima nor maxima at $x = 0$
(d) None of the above

9. The difference between the greatest and least values of function $f(x) = \cos x + \frac{1}{2} \cos 2x - \frac{1}{3} \cos 3x$ is

(a) $\frac{2}{3}$ (b) $\frac{8}{7}$ (c) $\frac{3}{8}$ (d) $\frac{9}{4}$

10. The minimum value of $x^2 + \dfrac{1}{1 + x^2}$ is at

(a) $x = 0$ (b) $x = 1$ (c) $x = 4$ (d) $x = 3$

11. The minimum value of $e^{(2x^2 - 2x + 1) \sin^2 x}$ is

(a) 0 (b) 1 (c) 2 (d) 3

12. The absolute maximum of $x^{40} - x^{20}$ on the interval $[0, 1]$ is

(a) $-\frac{1}{4}$ (b) 0 (c) $\frac{1}{4}$ (d) $\frac{1}{2}$

13. The extreme values of $4 \cos (x^2) \cos \left(\frac{\pi}{3} + x^2\right) \cos \left(\frac{\pi}{3} - x^2\right)$ over R, are

(a) $-1, 1$ (b) $-2, 2$ (c) $-3, 3$ (d) $-4, 4$

14. The maximum value $x^{1/x}$ is

(a) $1 / e^e$ (b) e (c) $e^{1/e}$ (d) $1 / e$

15. The largest value of $2x^3 - 3x^2 - 12x + 5$ for $-2 \le x \le 4$ occurs at x equals to

(a) -4 (b) 0 (c) 1 (d) 4

16. The minimum value of $4e^{2x} + 9e^{-2x}$ is

(a) 11 (b) 12 (c) 10 (d) 14

17. If the largest term in the sequence $a_n = \dfrac{n^2}{(n^3 + 100)^2}$ is a_α, then α is ....

18. The function $f(x) = \int_{-1}^{x} t(e^t - 1)(t - 1)(t - 2)^3 dt$ has m number of local maxima and n number at local minima, then $|m - n|$ is

(a) 1 (b) 2 (c) 3 (d) 4

19. Let the function $f(x)$ be defined as $f(x) = \begin{cases} \tan^{-1}\alpha - 3x^2, & 0 < x < 1 \\ -6x, & x \ge 1 \end{cases}$. $f(x)$ can have a maximum at $x = 1$. If the value of α is

(a) 0 (b) 2
(c) 1 (d) None of these

Answer Key

1. (i) $M = \frac{1}{e}$, $m =$ does not exist (ii) $M = \frac{3}{\sqrt{8}}$, $m = 0$ **2.** (i) $M = \frac{\pi}{6} - \frac{1}{4} \ln 3$, $m = \frac{\pi}{3} - \frac{1}{4} \ln 3$ (ii) $M = \frac{3\sqrt{3}}{2}$, $m = -2$ (iii) $M = \frac{17}{2}$, $m = 1$ (iv) $M = 1$, $m = 2 - \ln 4$ **3.** 2, 26; (i) $[-26, 2]$ (ii) $[-26, 65]$ **4.** $0, \frac{-3456}{3125}$ **5.** $-\frac{1}{24}$ **6.** $4^{1/3}$

7. (c) **8.** (c) **9.** (d) **10.** (a) **11.** (b)
12. (b) **13.** (a) **14.** (c) **15.** (d) **16.** (b)
17. (4) **18.** (a) **19.** (d)

For Detailed Solution

Milestone 4 Application of Maxima and Minima

• Application of Maxima and Minima • Convexity/Concavity and Point of Inflection • Relation of Concavity with the Derivative • Nature of Roots of Cubic Polynomials • Graphical Representation of Roots of Cubic Polynomials

7.14 Application of Maxima and Minima

In this milestone, we will discuss practical use of maxima and minima.

To understand we are discussing some examples.

Example 57. What is the radius of the smallest circular disc large enough to cover every isosceles triangle of a given perimeter L?

Sol. $AB = (R + R\cos\theta)\sec\dfrac{\theta}{2}$

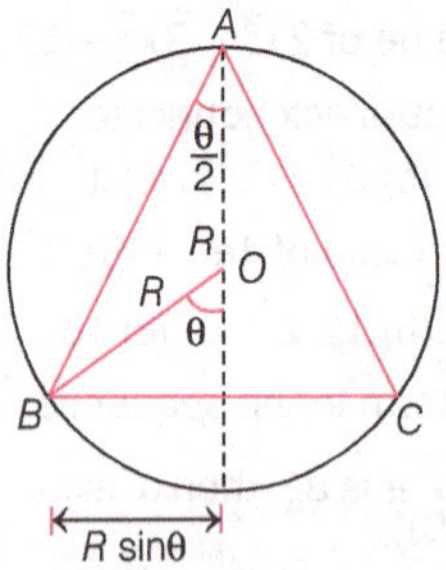

Hence, $L = 2AB + BC$

$$= 2R\left[(1+\cos\theta)\sec\frac{\theta}{2} + \sin\theta\right]$$

$$= 2R\left[2\cos\frac{\theta}{2} + 2\sin\frac{\theta}{2}\cos\frac{\theta}{2}\right]$$

$$L = 4R\cos\frac{\theta}{2}\left(1+\sin\frac{\theta}{2}\right)$$

$$R = \frac{L}{4\cos\frac{\theta}{2}\left(1+\sin\frac{\theta}{2}\right)}$$

Let $f(\theta) = \cos\dfrac{\theta}{2}\left(1+\sin\dfrac{\theta}{2}\right)$

For R to be minimum, $f(\theta)$ should be maximum.

$$\Rightarrow f'(\theta) = -\frac{1}{2}\sin\frac{\theta}{2}\left(1+\sin\frac{\theta}{2}\right) + \frac{1}{2}\cos^2\frac{\theta}{2}$$

$$\Rightarrow f'(\theta) = \frac{1}{2}\cos\theta - \frac{1}{2}\sin\frac{\theta}{2} = 0 \Rightarrow \theta = \frac{\pi}{3}$$

But $0 < \theta \le \dfrac{\pi}{2}$

So, $f(0) = 1$ (maximum)

$$f\left(\frac{\pi}{3}\right) = \frac{1}{2} + \frac{\sqrt{3}}{4} = \frac{2+\sqrt{3}}{4}$$

$$f\left(\frac{\pi}{2}\right) = 0.207$$

If $\theta = 0$, $R = \dfrac{L}{4}$ is the smallest required radius.

Though $\theta = 0$ is not possible, practically $R = \dfrac{L}{4}$ is the radius of the smallest area.

Example 58. Suppose that you need to cut a beam with maximal rectangular cross section from a circular log of radius 1 ft. What are the shape and cross-sectional area of such a beam?

Sol. Let x and y denotes half the base and half the height, respectively of inscribed rectangle $x^2 + y^2 = 1$, so $y = \sqrt{1-x^2}$

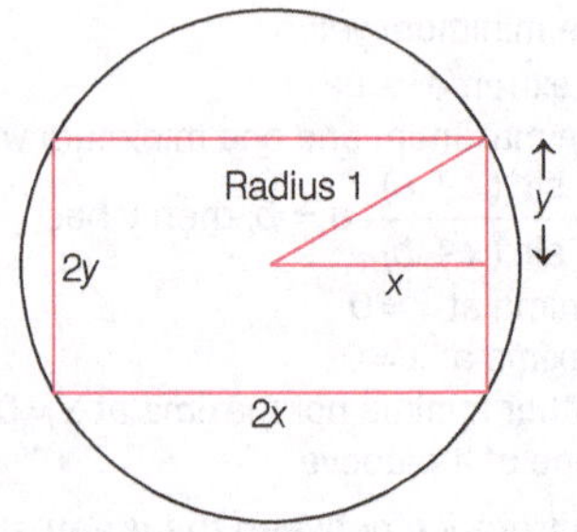

The area of the inscribed rectangle is $A = (2x)(2y) = 4xy$.

We may now express A as a function of x alone

$$A(x) = 4x\sqrt{1-x^2}$$

The practical domain of definition of A is $(0, 1)$.

$$\frac{dA}{dx} = 4\cdot(1-x^2)^{1/2} + 2x(1-x^2)^{-1/2}(-2x)$$

$$= \frac{4-8x^2}{(1-x^2)^{1/2}}$$

We observe that $A'(1)$ does not exist, but this causes no trouble, because $x = 1$ is an end point.

$$A'(x) = 0 \text{ when } 4 - 8x^2 = 0.$$

Thus, only critical point of A in the open interval (0, 1) is

$$x = \sqrt{\frac{1}{2}} = \frac{1}{2}\sqrt{2} \qquad [\because 2x = 2y = \sqrt{2}]$$

We evaluate A here and at the two end points to find that

$$A(0^+) = 0 = A(1^-),$$

$$A\left(\frac{1}{2}\sqrt{2}\right) = 2$$

This is the absolute maximum.

Therefore, the beam with rectangular cross section of maximal area is square, with edges $\sqrt{2}$ ft along and with cross-sectional area 2 ft^2.

Example 59. Rectangles are inscribed inside a semi-circle of radius r. Find the rectangle with maximum area.

Sol. Let the sides of rectangle be x and y.

$$\Rightarrow \qquad A = xy$$

Here, x and y are not independent variables and are related by Pythagoras theorem with r.

$$\frac{x^2}{4} + y^2 = r^2$$

$$\Rightarrow \qquad y = \sqrt{r^2 - \frac{x^2}{4}}$$

$$\Rightarrow \qquad A(x) = x\sqrt{r^2 - \frac{x^2}{4}}$$

$$\Rightarrow \qquad A(x) = \sqrt{x^2r^2 - \frac{x^4}{4}}$$

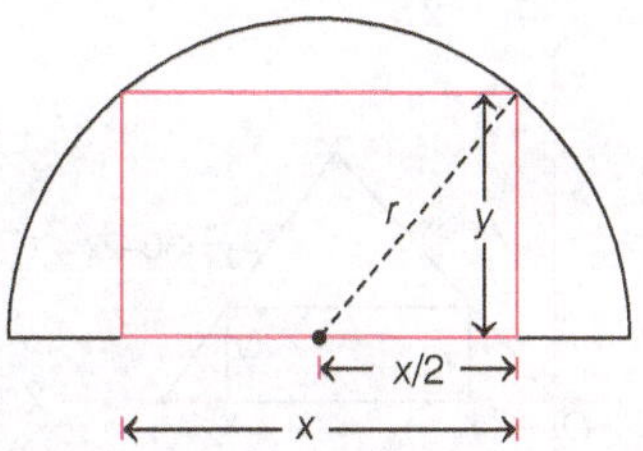

Let $f(x) = r^2x^2 - \frac{x^4}{4}$; $x \in (0, r)$

$A(x)$ is maximum when $f(x)$ is maximum.

Hence, $f'(x) = x(2r^2 - x^2) = 0 \Rightarrow x = r\sqrt{2}$

and $f''(x) = 2r^2 - 3x^2$

$$f''(r\sqrt{2}) = 2r^2 - 6r^2 < 0$$

and $f'(r\sqrt{2^-}) > 0$

$\therefore$ Confirming that $f(x)$ is maximum when $x = r\sqrt{2}$ and $y = \frac{r}{\sqrt{2}}$.

Example 60. Find the volume of the greatest cylinder which can be inscribed in a cone of height h and semi-vertical angle α.

Sol. Let x be the radius of the cylinder $A'B'EF$.

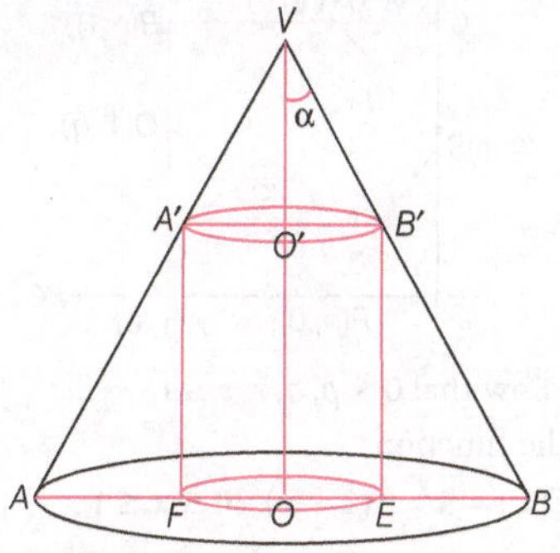

In $\Delta VO'B'$, $VO' = x \cot \alpha$

$\therefore$ Height of cylinder $= OO'$

$$= h - VO' = (h - x \cot \alpha)$$

$\therefore$ Volume of cylinder, $V = \pi \cdot x^2 \cdot OO'$

$$= \pi x^2(h - x \cot \alpha)$$

$$= \pi(x^2h - x^3 \cot \alpha) \qquad \text{...(i)}$$

$$\therefore \qquad \frac{dV}{dx} = \pi(2xh - 3x^2 \cot \alpha)$$

$$\frac{dV}{dx} = 0 \Rightarrow x = \frac{2}{3}h \tan \alpha$$

Since, $\frac{d^2V}{dx^2} = \pi(2h - 6x \cot \alpha)$

$$= -2\pi h < 0$$

at the critical point, V has a local maximum.

Since, $x = \frac{2}{3}h \tan \alpha$ is the only critical point, V has an absolute maximum at this point.

From Eq. (i), the maximum volume of cylinder

$$= \pi \cdot \frac{4}{9}h^2 \tan^2 \alpha \left(h - \frac{2h}{3}\right)$$

$$= \left(\frac{4}{27}\right)\pi h^3 \tan^2 \alpha$$

Example 61. Let S be a square of unit area. Consider any quadrilateral which has one vertex on each side of S. If a, b, c and d denote the lengths of the sides of the quadrilateral, prove that $2 \le a^2 + b^2 + c^2 + d^2 \le 4$.

Sol. Consider the quadrilateral $PQRS$, where coordinates P, Q, R and S are $(p, 0)$, $(1, q)$, $(r, 1)$ and $(0, s)$, respectively.

$$\therefore \qquad a^2 = p^2 + s^2,$$

$$b^2 = (1 - p)^2 + q^2,$$

$$c^2 = (1 - r)^2 + (1 - q)^2$$

and $$d^2 = r^2 + (1 - s)^2$$

So, $a^2+b^2+c^2+d^2 = p^2+(1-p)^2+q^2+(1-q)^2$
$$+r^2+(1-r)^2+s^2+(1-s)^2$$

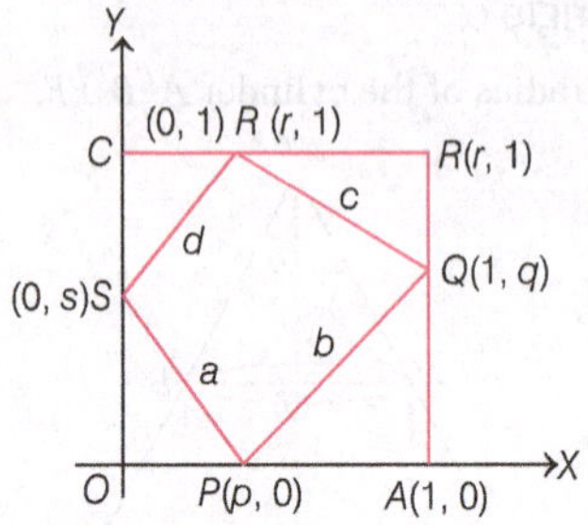

Now, we know that $0 \le p, q, r, s \le 1$

Consider the function

$$f(x) = x^2+(1-x)^2, 0 \le x \le 1$$
$$f'(x) = 2x - 2(1-x)$$
$$f'(x) = 0 \Rightarrow x = \frac{1}{2}$$
$$f\left(\frac{1}{2}\right) = \frac{1}{2}, f(0) = 1, f(1) = 1$$

$\therefore$ The minimum value of $f(x) = \frac{1}{2}$ and the maximum value of $f(x) = 1$.

$$\Rightarrow \quad \frac{1}{2} \le p^2+(1-p)^2 \le 1;$$
$$\frac{1}{2} \le q^2+(1-q)^2 \le 1$$
$$\frac{1}{2} \le r^2+(1-r)^2 \le 1;$$
$$\frac{1}{2} \le s^2+(1-s)^2 \le 1$$

On adding these inequalities, we get
$$2 \le a^2+b^2+c^2+d^2 \le 4.$$

Example 62. Find the minimum distance between $x^2+y^2 = 2$ and $xy = 9$.

Sol. Given, $xy = 9 \Rightarrow y = \frac{9}{x}$
$$\frac{dy}{dx} = -\frac{9}{x^2}$$

Slope of the normal at the point $P(3t, 3/t)$.

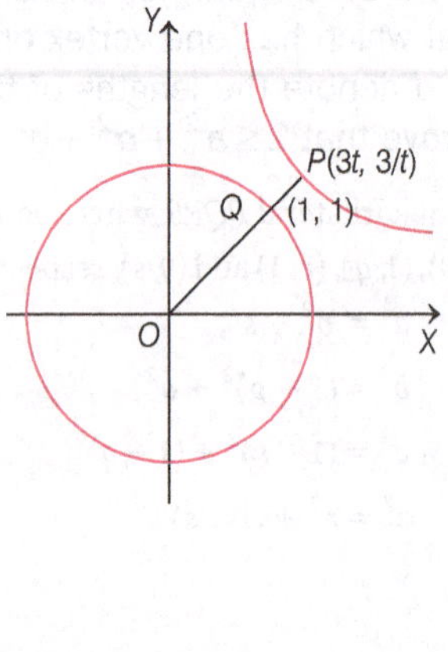

Equation of normal at P is
$$y - \frac{3}{t} = t^2(x - 3t) \quad \text{...(i)}$$

The minimum distance PQ is found along the common normal.

$\therefore$ Eq. (i) must pass through origin (the centre of the circle)

$$\Rightarrow \quad -\frac{3}{t} = -3t^2 \Rightarrow t^4 = 1$$
$$\Rightarrow \quad t = 1 \text{ or } -1$$

[$t = -1$ corresponds to a point $xy = 9$ in the IIIrd quadrant]

$$\therefore \quad t = 1$$

Hence, P is $(3, 3) \Rightarrow$ Slope of $OP = 1$

Equation of OP is $y = x \Rightarrow Q(1, 1)$

Hence, $d_{\min} = \sqrt{4+4} = 2\sqrt{2}$

Example 63. A rectangle with one side lying along the X-axis is the to be inscribed in the closed region of XY-plane bounded by the line $y = 0, y = 3x$ and $y = 30 - 2x$. If M is the largest area of such a rectangle, then the value of $\frac{2M}{27}$ is

(a) 5 (b) 2 (c) 4 (d) 6

Sol. (a) $A = (x_2 - x_1)y$

$y = 3x_1$ and $y = 30 - 2x_2$

$$A(y) = \left(\frac{30-y}{2} - \frac{y}{3}\right)y$$
$$6A(y) = (90 - 3y - 2y)y = 90y - 5y^2$$
$$6A'(y) = 90 - 10y = 0$$
$$\text{or} \quad y = 9;\ A''(y) = -10 < 0$$
$$x_1 = 3 \text{ and } x_2 = \frac{21}{2}$$

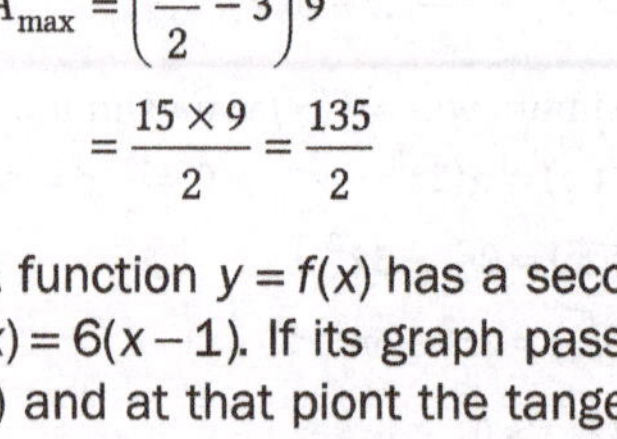

$$\therefore \quad A_{\max} = \left(\frac{21}{2} - 3\right)9$$
$$= \frac{15 \times 9}{2} = \frac{135}{2}$$

Example 64. A function $y = f(x)$ has a second order derivative $f''(x) = 6(x-1)$. If its graph passes through the point (2, 1) and at that piont the tangent to the graph is $y = 3x - 5$, then the function is

(a) $(x+1)^2$ (b) $(x-1)^3$
(c) $(x+1)^3$ (d) $(x-1)^2$

Sol. (b) We have, $f''(x) = 6(x-1)$

On integrating both sides, we get

$$f'(x) = \frac{6(x-1)^2}{2} + C$$

$$f'(2) = 3 \Rightarrow 3(2-1)^2 + C = 3$$

$$C = 0$$

$$\therefore \quad f'(x) = 3(x-1)^2$$

On integrating both sides, we get

$$f(x) = (x-1)^3 + C_1$$

$$f(2) = 1$$

$$1 + C_1 = 1$$

$$C_1 = 0$$

$$\therefore \quad f(x) = (x-1)^3$$

7.15 Convexity/Concavity and Point of Inflection

Observe the two graphs sketched in the figure below. What is the difference between them? Although they are both increasing, the first graph's rate of increase in itself increasing whereas the rate of increase is decreasing in case of the second graph.

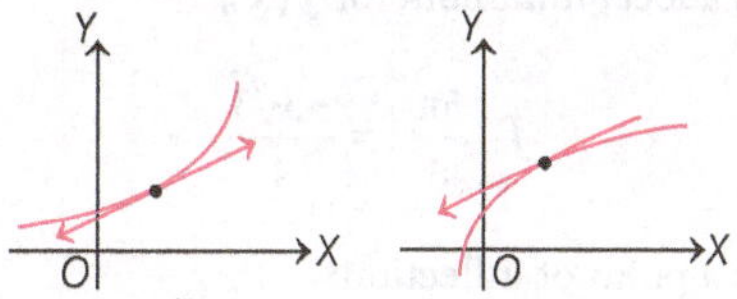

On graph (i), if you draw a tangent any where, the entire curve will lie above this tangent. Such a curve is called a **concave upwards curve.**

For graph (ii), the entire curve will lie below any tangent drawn to itself. Such a curve is called a **concave downwards curve.**

The concavity's nature can of course be restricted to particular intervals.

e.g. A graph might be concave upwards in some interval while concave downwards in another shown in figure.

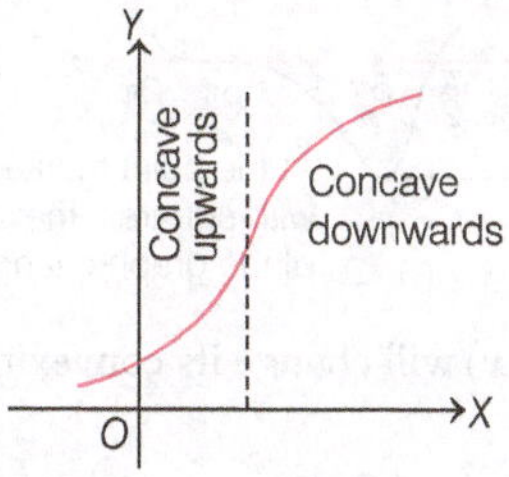

7.16 Relation of Concavity with the Derivative

Let us again consider a graph in figure. This is a concave upwards curve. We see that the rate of increase of the graph itself increases with increasing x, i.e. rate of increase of slope is positive.

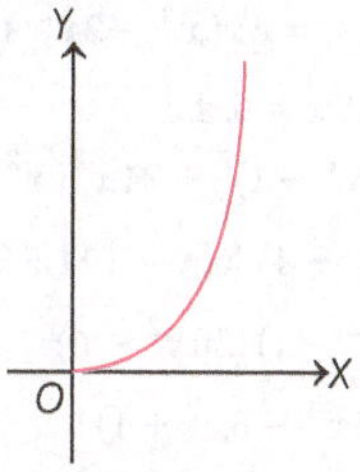

$$\frac{d}{dx}\left(\frac{dy}{dx}\right) > 0$$

$$\Rightarrow \quad \frac{d^2y}{dx^2} > 0$$

Similarly, for a **concave downwards curve,** $\boldsymbol{\frac{d^2y}{dx^2} < 0}$

The nature of concavity is simply related to the sign of the second derivative.

We now finally come to what we mean by point of inflection.

Consider $f(x) = x^3$

Again, $\quad f'(0) = f''(0) = 0$

$\quad f''(x) < 0$ for $x < 0$

and $\quad > 0$ for $x > 0$

$\Rightarrow f''(x)$ changes sign as x crosses 0.

$\Rightarrow f(x)$ changes the nature of its concavity as x crosses 0.

Such a point is called a **point of inflection,** a point at which the concavity of the graph changes.

Notice that $f''(a) = 0$ alone is not sufficient to guarantee a point of inflection at $x = a$. $f''(x)$ must also change sign as x crosses a.

e.g. In $f(x) = x^4, f''(0) = 0$, but $x = 0$ is not a point of inflection, since $f''(x)$ does not change its sign as x crosses 0.

From the higher order derivative test, we know that $x = 0$ is a local minimum for $f(x) = x^4$.

Example 65. Discuss the function $f(x) = x^6 - 3x^4 + 3x^2 - 5$ and plot the graph.

Sol. The domain is obviously R.

$f(x)$ is an even function.

Since, $f(x)$ is a polynomial function, it is continuous and differentiable on R.

$$f'(x) = 6x^5 - 12x^2 + 6x$$
$$= 6x(x^4 - 2x^2 + 1) = 6x(x^2 - 1)^2$$

$f'(x) = 0$ at $x = 0, \pm 1$

$$f''(x) = 6(x^2 - 1)^2 + 24x^2(x^2 - 1)$$
$$= (x^2 - 1)\{6(x^2 - 1) + 24x^2\}$$
$$= (x^2 - 1)(30x^2 - 6) \quad \text{...(i)}$$
$$= 6(5x^4 - 6x^2 + 1)$$

$f''(0) = 6, f''(\pm 1) = 0$

$\Rightarrow x = 0$ is a point of local minimum and $x = \pm 1$ are points of inflection.

[verify that $f''(x)$ does not change sign as x crosses ± 1]

Now, $f'(x) > 0$ if $x > 0$ and $f'(x) < 0$ if $x < 0$.

Therefore, $f(x)$ decreases on $(-\infty, 0)$ and increases on $(0, -\infty)$.

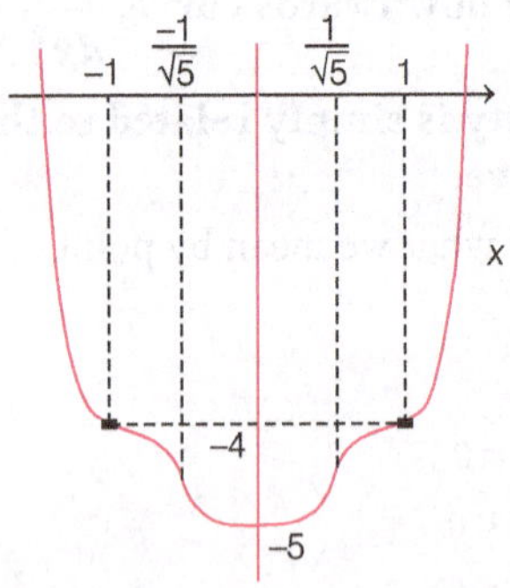

There is one more important fact we must take into account.

$f''(x)$ has roots ± 1 and additionally, $\pm \frac{1}{\sqrt{5}}$. [from Eq. (i)]

Therefore, at these four points the convexity of the graph changes.

$\Rightarrow f''(x) > 0 \, \forall \, x \in (-\infty, -1) \cup \left(\frac{-1}{\sqrt{5}}, \frac{1}{\sqrt{5}}\right) \cup (1, \infty)$ so that $f(x)$ is concave upwards in these intervals.

$\Rightarrow f''(x) < 0 \, \forall \, x \in \left(-1, \frac{-1}{\sqrt{5}}\right) \cup \left(\frac{1}{\sqrt{5}}, 1\right)$ so that $f(x)$ is concave downwards in these intervals.

$$f(0) = -5, f(\pm 1) = -4, f(\pm 2) = 23$$

Therefore, one root each of $f(x)$ lies in $(-2, -1)$ and $(1, 2)$.

This information is sufficient to accurately draw the graph of the given function.

Example 66. Discuss the function $f(x) = \frac{1}{2}\sin 2x + \cos x$, and plot its graph.

Sol. The domain of $f(x)$ is R.

$f(x)$ is periodic with period 2π and therefore we need to analyse it only in $[0, 2\pi]$.

$f(x)$ is continuous and differentiable on R.

$$f'(x) = \cos 2x - \sin x$$
$$= 1 - 2\sin^2 x - \sin x$$
$$= (1 + \sin x)(1 - 2\sin x)$$

This is 0 in $[0, 2\pi]$ when $x = \frac{\pi}{6}, \frac{5\pi}{6}, \frac{3\pi}{2}$

$f''(x) = -2\sin 2x - \cos x$

Now, $f''\left(\frac{\pi}{6}\right) < 0, f''\left(\frac{5\pi}{6}\right) > 0$

and $f''\left(\frac{3\pi}{2}\right) = 0$

$\Rightarrow x = \frac{\pi}{6}$ is a local maximum for $f(x)$;

$$f\left(\frac{\pi}{6}\right) = \frac{3\sqrt{3}}{4}$$

$x = \frac{5\pi}{6}$ is a local minimum for $f(x)$;

$$f\left(\frac{5\pi}{6}\right) = \frac{-3\sqrt{3}}{4}$$

$x = \frac{3\pi}{2}$ is a point of inflection;

$$f\left(\frac{3\pi}{2}\right) = 0$$

We now need to analyse the sign of $f''(x)$.

$$f''(x) = -2\sin 2x - \cos x$$
$$= -4\sin x\cos x - \cos x$$
$$= -\cos x(1 + 4\sin x)$$

This is 0 in $[0, 2\pi]$ when

$$x = \frac{\pi}{2}, \pi + \sin^{-1}\frac{1}{4}, \frac{3\pi}{2}, 2\pi - \sin^{-1}\frac{1}{4}$$

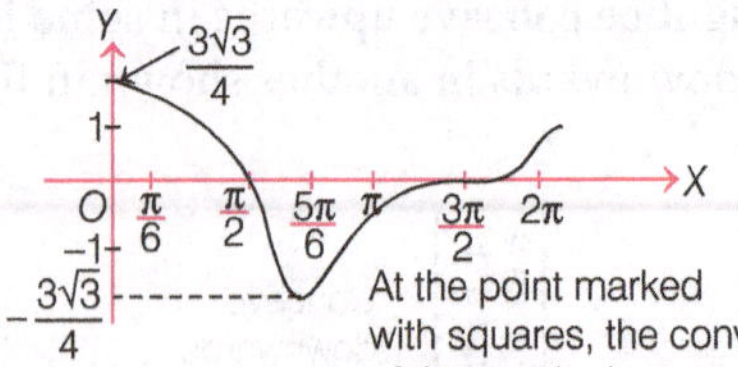

We see that $f(x)$ will change its convexity at four different points.

$\Rightarrow f''(x) > 0, \forall \, x \in \left(\frac{\pi}{2}, \pi + \sin^{-1}\frac{1}{4}\right) \cup \left(\frac{3\pi}{2}, 2\pi - \sin^{-1}\frac{1}{4}\right)$

So that $f(x)$ is concave upwards in these intervals.

$$\Rightarrow f''(x) < 0, \forall\ x \in \left(0, \frac{\pi}{2}\right) \cup \left(\pi + \sin^{-1}\frac{1}{4}, \frac{3\pi}{2}\right)$$
$$\cup \left(2\pi - \sin^{-1}\frac{1}{4}, 2\pi\right)$$

So that $f(x)$ is concave downwards in these intervals.

$$f(0) = 1,\ f\left(\frac{\pi}{2}\right) = 0 \text{ and } f(2\pi) = 1$$

The graph has been plotted below for $[0, 2\pi]$.

7.17 Nature of Roots of Cubic Polynomials

Let $f(x) = ax^3 + bx^2 + cx + d$ be the given cubic polynomial and $f(x) = 0$ be the corresponding cubic equations, where $a, b, c, d \in R$ and $a > 0$.

Now, $f'(x) = 3ax^2 + 2bx + c$

Let $D = 4b^2 - 12ac = 4(b^2 - 3ac)$ be the discriminant of the equations $f'(x) = 0$.

Now, we have the following three cases

***Case* I** If $D < 0 \Rightarrow f'(x) > 0, \forall x \in R,$

i.e. $f(x)$ would be an increasing function of x.

Also, $\lim\limits_{x \to \infty} f(x) = \infty$

and $\lim\limits_{x \to -\infty} f(x) = -\infty.$

Since, $f(x)$ is an increasing function, so it will intersect the X-axis at only once.

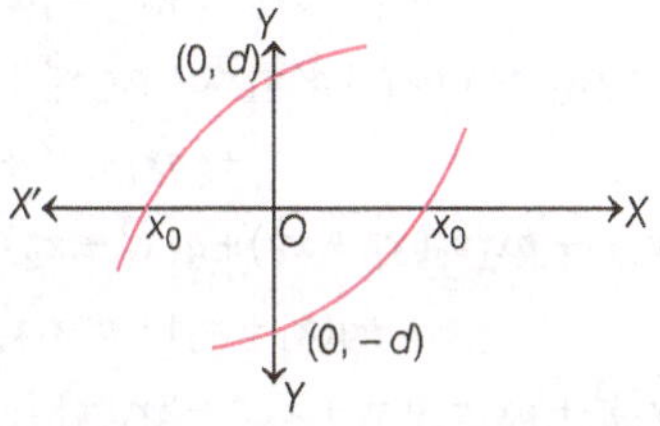

Clearly, $x_0 > 0$, if $d < 0$

and $x_0 < 0$, if $d > 0$

***Case* II** If $D > 0, f'(x) = 0$ would have two real roots (say) α and β (where $\alpha < \beta$)

$$\Rightarrow \quad f'(x) = 3a(x - \alpha)(x - \beta)$$

$$\Rightarrow \begin{cases} f'(x) < 0, x \in (\alpha, \beta) \\ f'(x) > 0, x \in (-\infty, \alpha) \cup (\beta, \infty) \\ f'(x) = 0, x \in \{\alpha, \beta\} \end{cases}$$

+   –   +
α   β

Here, $x = \alpha$, will be point of local maxima and $x = \beta$ will be point of local minima.

***Case* III** If $D = 0$, $f'(x) = 3a(x - \alpha)^2$, where α is a root of $f'(x) = 0$, then $f(x) = a(x - \alpha)^3 + K.$

If $K = 0$, then $f(x) = 0$ has three equal real roots. if $K \neq 0$, then $f(x) = 0$ has one real root.

7.18 Graphical Representation of Roots of Cubic Polynomials

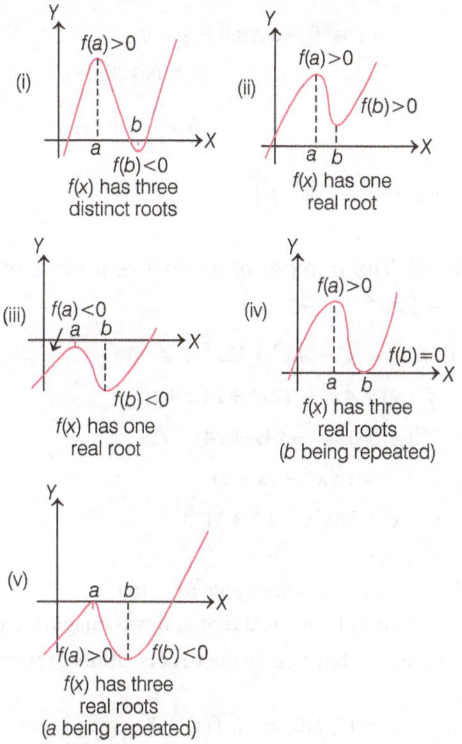

Conclusions

(i) If $f(a) \cdot f(b) < 0$, then $f(x)$ has three distinct roots (see figure (i)).

(ii) If $f(a) \cdot f(b) > 0$, then $f(x)$ has one real and two imaginary roots (see figure (ii) and (iii)).

(iii) If $f(a) \cdot f(b) = 0$, then $f(x)$ has three roots but two roots are identical (see figure (iv) and (v)).

Example 67. If $4x^3 - 3x - p = 0$, where $-1 \leq p \leq 1$ has unique root in $\left[\frac{1}{2}, 1\right]$, then the root is

(a) $\frac{\cos^{-1} p}{3}$ (b) $\cos\left(\frac{1}{3}\cos^{-1} p\right)$

(c) $\cos(\cos^{-1} p)$ (d) None of these

Sol. (b) Given that $-1 \le p \le 1$

Let $f(x) = 4x^3 - 3x - p$

Now, $f\left(\frac{1}{2}\right) = \frac{1}{2} - \frac{3}{2} - p = -1 - p \le 0$ $\quad [\because p \ge -1]$

and $\quad f(1) = 4 - 3 - p = 1 - p \ge 0$ $\quad [\because p \le 1]$

$\therefore$ $f(x)$ has atleast one real root between $\left[\frac{1}{2}, 1\right]$.

To find a root we observe $f(x)$ contains $4x^3 - 3x$, which is multiple angle formula for $\cos 3\theta$.

$\therefore$ On putting $x = \cos\theta$, then

$$4\cos^3\theta - 3\cos\theta - p = 0$$

$$\Rightarrow \quad p = \cos 3\theta$$

$$\Rightarrow \quad \theta = \frac{1}{3}\cos^{-1}(p)$$

$\therefore$ Root is $\cos\left(\frac{1}{3}\cos^{-1} p\right)$.

Example 68. The number of distinct real roots of $x^4 - 4x^3 + 12x^2 + x - 1 = 0$.

Sol. Given, $f(x) = x^4 - 4x^3 + 12x^2 + x - 1$

$\Rightarrow \quad f'(x) = 4x^3 - 12x^2 + 24x + 1$

$\Rightarrow \quad f''(x) = 12x^2 - 24x + 24$

$\Rightarrow \quad f''(x) = 12(x^2 - 2x + 2)$

$\Rightarrow \quad f''(x) = 12((x-1)^2 + 1)$

$\Rightarrow \quad f''(x) > 0$

$\Rightarrow f'(x)$ is an increasing cubic function.

$\Rightarrow f'(x)$ has only one real root and two imaginary root.

$\therefore$ $f(x)$ cannot have all distinct roots, atmost two real roots.

Now, $f(-1) = 15$, $f(0) = -1$, $f(1) = 9$

$\therefore f(x)$ must have one root in $(-1, 0)$ and other in $(0, 1)$.

Hence, there are 2 real roots.

Example 69. Find the set of value of m for the cubic $x^3 - \frac{3}{2}x^2 + \frac{5}{2} = \log_{4^{-1}}(m)$ has 3 distinct solutions.

Sol. Consider $\quad y = x^3 - \frac{3}{2}x^2 + \frac{5}{2}$

$$\frac{dy}{dx} = 3x^2 - 3x = 3x(x-1) = 0 \Rightarrow x = 0 \text{ or } 1$$

$$\frac{d^2y}{dx^2} = 6x - 3$$

$$\left.\frac{d^2y}{dx^2}\right|_{x=0} = -3 \text{ i.e.} < 0$$

$\therefore$ Maximum at $x = 0$

$$\left.\frac{d^2y}{dx^2}\right|_{x=t} = 3 \text{ i.e.} > 0 \Rightarrow \text{minimum}$$

Hence, the graph of the cubic has 3 distinct roots.

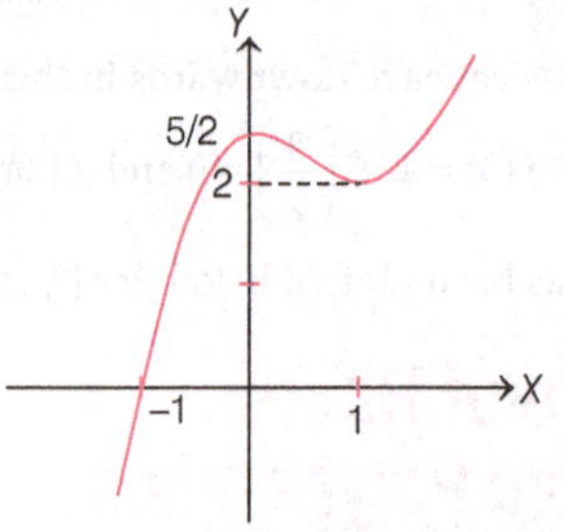

$$2 < \log_{1/4}(m) < \frac{5}{2}$$

$$2 < -\log_4(m) < \frac{5}{2}$$

$$-\frac{5}{2} < \log_4(m) < -2$$

$$\frac{1}{32} < m < \frac{1}{16}$$

Example 70. If the cubic function $f(x) = x^3 + px + q$ has 3 distinct real roots, then prove that $4p^3 + 27q^2 < 0$.

Sol. $f'(x) = 3x^2 + p = 3x^2 + 0 \cdot x + p$

Now, we have, $x_1 + x_2 = 0$ and $x_1 x_2 = \frac{p}{3}$,

where x_1, x_2 are roots of $f'(x) = 0$.

According to given condition, we have

$$(x_1^3 + px_1 + q)(x_2^3 + px_2 + q) < 0$$

$$\Rightarrow \quad x_1^3 \cdot x_2^3 + px_1^3 x_2 + qx_1^3 + p^2 x_1 x_2 + px_1 x_2^3 + qx_2^3 + pqx_1 + q^2 + pqx_2 < 0$$

$$\Rightarrow \quad (x_1x_2)^3 + px_1x_2(x_1^2 + x_2^2) + q(x_1^3 + x_2^3) + pq(x_1 + x_2) + p^2 x_1 x_2 + q^2 < 0$$

$$\Rightarrow \quad (x_1x_2)^3 + px_1x_2\{(x_1 + x_2)^2 - 2x_1x_2\} + q\{(x_1 + x_2)^3 - 3(x_1x_2)(x_1 + x_2)\} + pq(x_1 + x_2) + p^2 x_1 x_2 + q^2 < 0$$

$$\Rightarrow \quad \frac{p^3}{27} + \frac{p^2}{3}\left\{-\frac{2p}{3}\right\} + p^2\left\{\frac{p}{3}\right\} + q^2 < 0$$

$$\Rightarrow \quad 4p^3 + 27q^2 < 0$$

Example 71. If $f(x)$ is a polynomial of degree 5 with real coefficients such that $f(|x|) = 0$ has 8 real roots, then $f(x) = 0$ has

(a) 4 real roots (b) 5 real roots

(c) 3 real roots (d) Nothing can be said

Sol. (b) Given that $f(|x|) = 0$ has 8 real roots.

$\Rightarrow f(x) = 0$ has 4 positive roots.

Since, $f(x)$ is a polynomial of degree 5.

So, $f(x)$ cannot have even number of real roots.

$\Rightarrow f(x)$ has all the five roots real in which four positive and one root is negative.

Example 72. If the function $f(x) = x^3 - 9x^2 + 24x + C$ has three real and distinct roots α, β and γ, then the value of $[\alpha] + [\beta] + [\gamma]$ are

(a) 5, 6 (b) 6, 7

(c) 7, 8 (d) None of these

Sol. (c) Take $y = x^3 - 9x^2 + 24x$

$$\Rightarrow \frac{dy}{dx} = 3x^2 - 18x + 24 = 3(x^2 - 6x + 8) = 3(x-2)(x-4)$$

+ 2 4 +

For three real roots of

$$f(x) = x^3 - 9x^2 + 24x + C,$$

$$f(2)f(4) < 0$$

$$\therefore \quad (C+20)(C+16) < 0$$

$$C \in (-20, -16)$$

Now, if $C \in (-20, -18)$,

$\alpha \in (1, 2), \beta \in (2, 3), \gamma \in (4, 5)$

$\Rightarrow \quad [\alpha] + [\beta] + [\gamma] = 7$

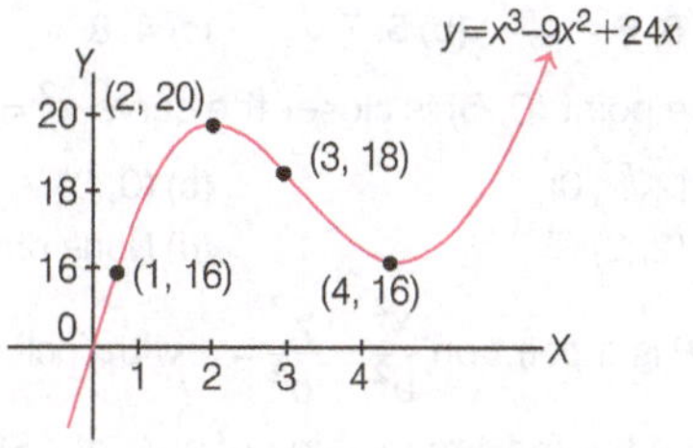

If $C \in (-18, -16)$

$\Rightarrow \alpha \in (1, 2), \beta \in (3, 4), \gamma \in (4, 5)$

$\Rightarrow [\alpha] + [\beta] + [\gamma] = 8$

Milestone Practice 7.4

1. A manufacturer plans to construct a cylindrical cane to hold one cubic meter of liquid. If the cost of constructing the top and bottom of the cane is twice the cost of constructing the sides, what are the dimensions of the most economical cane?

2. The shape of a hole bored by a drill is cone surmounted by a cylinder. If the cylinder be of height h and radius r and semi-vertical angle of the cone be α, where $\tan \alpha = h/r$, show that for a total height H of the hole, volume removed is maximum if $h = H(\sqrt{7} + 1)/6$.

3. A factory D is to be connected by a road with a straight railway line on which a town A is situated. The distance DB of the factory to the railway line is $5\sqrt{3}$ km, length AB of the railway line is 20 km. Freight charges on road are twice the charges on the railway. At what point $P(AP < AB)$ on the railway line should be road DP be so as to ensure minimum freight charges from the factory to the town?

4. Find the coordinates of a point on the parabola $y = x^2 + 7x + 2$ which is closest to the straight line $y = 3x - 3$.

5. Find the point on the hyperbola $\frac{x^2}{24} - \frac{y^2}{18} = 1$ which is closest to the straight line $3x + 2y + 1 = 0$. Compute the distance between the point and the line.

6. Find the point on $p^2x^2 + 9y^2 = 9p^2, 9 < p^2 < 18$ that is farthest from the point (–3, 0).

7. Prove that the minimum intercept made by the axes on the tangent to the ellipse $\frac{x^2}{a^2} + \frac{y^2}{b^2} = 1$ is $a + b$.

8. The shortest distance between the line $y - x = 1$ and the curve $x = y^2$ is

(a) $\frac{3\sqrt{2}}{8}$ (b) $\frac{2\sqrt{3}}{8}$

(c) $\frac{3\sqrt{2}}{5}$ (d) $\frac{\sqrt{3}}{4}$

9. If θ is the semi-vertical angle of a cone of maximum volume and given slant height, then $\tan \theta$ is given by

(a) 2 (b) 1 (c) $\sqrt{2}$ (d) $\sqrt{3}$

10. A circular sector of perimeter 60 m with maximum area is to be construted. The radius the circular arc in metre must be

(a) 20 (b) 5 (c) 15 (d) 10

11. Divide 12 into two parts such that the product of the square of one part and fourth power of the second part is maximum, are

(a) 6, 6 (b) 5, 7 (c) 4, 8 (d) 3, 9

12. The point (0, 5) is closer the curve $x^2 = 2y$ at

(a) $(2\sqrt{2}, 0)$ (b) (0, 0)

(c) (2, 2) (d) None of these

13. If P is a point on $\frac{x^2}{a^2} + \frac{y^2}{b^2} = 1$ with focii S and S', then the maximum value of area of $\Delta SPS'$ is

(a) ab (b) abe^2 (c) abe (d) $\frac{ab}{e}$

14. The graph of the derivative f' of a continuous function f is shown with $f(0) = 0$

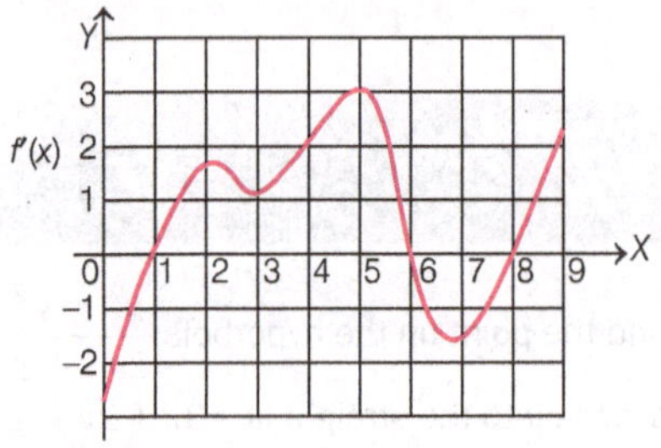

(i) On what intervals is f increasing and decresing?

(ii) At what values of x does f have a local maximum or minimum?

(iii) On what intervals is f concave upward or downward?

(iv) State the x- coordinate(s) of the point(s) of inflection.

(v) Assuming that $f(0) = 0$, sketch a graph of f.

15. The set of value(s) of a, for which the function $f(x) = \frac{ax^3}{3} + (a+2)x^2 + (a-1)x + 2$ possesses a negative point inflection, is

(a) $(-\infty, -2)$ (b) $\left\{-\frac{4}{5}\right\}$

(c) $(-2, 0)$ (d) empty set

16. The number of values of k, for which the equation $x^3 - 3x + k = 0$ has two distinct roots lying in the interval (0, 1), is

(a) three

(b) two

(c) infinitely many

(d) zero

17. For the function $f(x) = x^4(12\log_e x - 7)$

(a) there is no point of inflection.

(b) $x = e^{1/3}$ is the point of minima.

(c) the graph is concave upwards in (0, 1).

(d) the graph is concave downwards in $(1, \infty)$.

Answer Key

1. $\left(\frac{1}{4\pi}\right)^{1/3}$ m, $\left(\frac{16}{\pi}\right)^{1/3}$ m **3.** 5 km from B **4.** $(-2, -8)$

5. $(-6, 3), \frac{11}{\sqrt{13}}$ **6.** $p \equiv (3, 0)$ **8.** (a) **9.** (c)

10. (c) **11.** (c) **12.** (d) **13.** (c)

14. (i) $x \in (1, 6) \cup (8, 9)$; $x \in (-2, -1) \cup (6, 8)$ (ii) $x = 1, 8$; $x = 6$

(iii) $x \in (0, 2) \cup (3, 5) \cup (7, 9)$; $x \in (2, 3) \cup (5, 7)$ (iv) $x = 2, 3, 5, 7$

15. (a) **16.** (d) **17.** (b)

For Detailed Solution

JEE Pattern EXAMPLES

Single Option Correct Type Questions

Example 1 ■ *Let three degree polynomial function $f(x)$ has local maxima at $x=-1$ and $f(-1)=2$, $f(3)=18$, $f'(x)$ has a minima at $x=0$, then*

(a) the distance between $(-1, 2)$ and $(a, f(a))$, where a denotes point where function has local max./min. is $2\sqrt{5}$.

(b) the function decreases from 1 to $2\sqrt{5}$.

(c) the function increases from 1 to $2\sqrt{5}$.

(d) the function decreases from -1 to 1.

Sol. (a) Let $f(x) = ax^3 + bx^2 + cx + d$

$f(-1) = 2$, $f(3) = 18$, $f'(x)$ has a min. at $x = 0$ so that $f''(x) = 0$ at $x = 0$, $f(x)$ has a local max. at $x = -1$.

$\therefore\ f'(-1) = 0$

$\therefore$ These conditions imply

$$-a + b - c + d = 2$$

$$27a + 9b + 3c + d = 18$$

$$\therefore \quad 28a + 8b + 4c = 16$$

$$f'(x) = 3ax^2 + 2bx + c,$$

$$f''(x) = 6ax + 2b$$

$$f'(-1) = 0$$

$$\Rightarrow \quad 3a - 2b + c = 0,\ f''(0) = 0$$

$$\Rightarrow \quad b = 0$$

On putting $\quad b = 0, 7a + c = 4, 3a + c = 0$

$$\therefore \quad a = 1, c = -3, b = 0$$

$$\Rightarrow \quad d = 0$$

Hence, $f(x) = x^3 - 3x$

$$\therefore \quad f'(x) = 3(x^2 - 1),\ f''(x) = 6x$$

Now, $\ f'(x) = 0$

$$\Rightarrow \quad x = 1, -1;\ y = -2, 2$$

$\therefore\ (1, -2)$ or $(-1, 2) = (a, f(a))$

Now, at $x = 1$, $f''(x) = 6x = 6$

and at $x = -1$, $f''(x) = 6x = -6$

$\therefore$ At $(1, -2)$, $f(x)$ is min. and at $(-1, 2)$, $f(x)$ is max.

$$\therefore \quad \text{Distance} = \sqrt{4 + 16} = 2\sqrt{5}$$

JEE SCANNER

Example 2 Similar to PYQ Asked in JEE Main 2024

The function $f(x) = \dfrac{x}{x^2 - 5x - 6}$, $x \in R - \{-1, 6\}$ is

(a) decreases in $(-\infty, -1)$ and increases in $(6, \infty)$.

(b) increases in $(-\infty, -1) \cup (-1, 6) \cup (6, \infty)$.

(c) decreases in $(-\infty, -1) \cup (-1, 6) \cup (6, \infty)$.

(d) decreases in $(-1, 6)$ and increases in $(-\infty, -1) \cup (6, \infty)$.

Sol. (c) $f(x) = \dfrac{x}{x^2 - 5x - 6}$, $x \in R - \{-1, 6\}$

$$f'(x) = \frac{(x^2 - 5x - 6)(1) - x(2x - 5)}{(x^2 - 5x - 6)^2}$$

$$= \frac{x^2 - 5x - 6 - 2x^2 + 5x}{(x^2 - 5x - 6)^2}$$

$$= \frac{-x^2 - 6}{(x^2 - 5x - 6)^2} = \frac{-(x^2 + 6)}{(x^2 - 5x - 6)^2} < 0$$

$\because\ f'(x) < 0$ for $x \in$ domain

$\therefore$ It is decreasing function in its domain.

$x \in (-\infty, -1) \cup (-1, 6) \cup (6, \infty)$.

Skill Builder

For Sol.

The function $f(x) = \dfrac{x}{x^2 + x - 6}$,

$x \in R - \{-3, 2\}$ is

(a) decreases in $(-\infty, -3)$ and increases in $(2, \infty)$.

(b) increases in $(-\infty, -3) \cup (-3, 2) \cup (2, \infty)$.

(c) decreases in $(-\infty, -3) \cup (-3, 2) \cup (2, \infty)$.

(d) decreases in $(-3, 2)$ and increases in $(-\infty, -3) \cup (2, \infty)$.

Example 3 ■ *Global minimum value of $f(x) = x^8 + x^6 - x^4 - 2x^3 - x^2 - 2x + 9$ is*

(a) 0 (b) 1 (c) 5 (d) 9

Sol. (c) $f(x) = x^8 + x^6 - x^4 - 2x^3 - x^2 - 2x + 9$

If we represent $f(x) = (\text{real number})^2 + c$.

Then, c will be minimum.

$$f(x) = (x^8 - 2x^4 + 1) + (x^6 - 2x^3 + 1) + (x^4 - 2x^2 + 1) + (x^2 - 2x + 1) + 5$$
$$= (x^4 - 1)^2 + (x^3 - 1)^2 + (x^2 - 1)^2 + (x - 1)^2 + 5$$

Obviously at $x = 1$, all square terms will be zero

$\Rightarrow \quad f(x)_{\min} = 5$, at $x = 1$

JEE SCANNER

Example 4 Similar to PYQ Asked in JEE Main 2024

The values of K for which the point of minimum of the function $f(x) = 1 + K^2x - x^3$ satisfy the inequality $\dfrac{(x^2 + x + 2)}{(x^2 + 5x + 6)} < 0$, belongs

(a) $(-3\sqrt{3}, \infty)$
(b) $(-3\sqrt{3}, -2\sqrt{3}) \cup (0, \infty)$
(c) $(-3\sqrt{3}, -2\sqrt{3}) \cup (2\sqrt{3}, 3\sqrt{3})$
(d) $(0, \infty)$

Sol. (c) Here, $\dfrac{x^2 + x + 2}{x^2 + 5x + 6} < 0 \Rightarrow \dfrac{\left(x + \frac{1}{2}\right)^2 + \frac{7}{4}}{(x + 2)(x + 3)} < 0.$

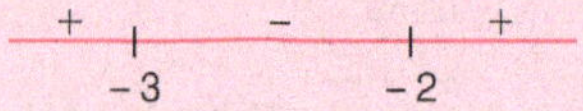

where $\left(x + \frac{1}{2}\right)^2 + \frac{7}{4}$ is always positive.

$\therefore$ Using number line rule for $(x + 2)(x + 3)$ as shown above, we get

$$\frac{x^2 + x + 2}{x^2 + 5x + 6} < 0 \Rightarrow -3 < x < -2 \qquad \text{...(i)}$$

Now, consider $f(x) = 1 + K^2x - x^3$

$$f'(x) = K^2 - 3x^2, \; f''(x) = -6x$$

For maximum/minimum, put $f'(x) = 0 \Rightarrow x = \pm \dfrac{|K|}{\sqrt{3}}$

Let $x_1 = \dfrac{|K|}{\sqrt{3}}$ and $x_2 = -\dfrac{|K|}{\sqrt{3}}$

$\therefore f''(x_1) < 0$ and $f''(x_2) > 0$

$\Rightarrow f(x)$ is maximum at $x = x_1$ and $f(x)$ is minimum at $x = x_2$.

$\therefore \quad -3 < x_2 < -2$

$\Rightarrow \quad -3 < \dfrac{-|K|}{\sqrt{3}} < -2 \qquad$ [from Eq. (i)]

$\Rightarrow \quad 3\sqrt{3} > |K| > 2\sqrt{3}$

$\Rightarrow \quad K \in (-3\sqrt{3}, -2\sqrt{3}) \cup (2\sqrt{3}, 3\sqrt{3})$

Skill Builder

Let the set of all positive values of λ, for which the point of local minimum of the function $(1 + x(\lambda^2 - x^2))$ satisfies $\dfrac{x^2 - x + 4}{x^2 - 5x + 6} < 0$, be (α, β). Then, $\alpha^2 + \beta^2$ is equal to

(a) 13 (b) 12 (c) 27 (d) 39

For Sol.

Example 5 *The values of a and b for which all the extrema of the function, $f(x) = a^2x^3 - 0.5ax^2 - 2x - b$ is positive and the minimum is at the point $x_0 = \frac{1}{3}$, are*

(a) when $a = -2 \Rightarrow b < -\frac{11}{27}$ and when $a = 3 \Rightarrow b < -\frac{1}{2}$
(b) when $a = 3 \Rightarrow b < -\frac{11}{27}$ and when $a = 2 \Rightarrow b < -\frac{1}{2}$
(c) when $a = -2 \Rightarrow b < -\frac{1}{2}$ and when $a = 3 \Rightarrow b < -\frac{11}{27}$
(d) None of the above

Sol. (a) Given, $f(x) = a^2x^3 - 0.5ax^2 - 2x - b$

$\Rightarrow \quad f'(x) = 3a^2x^2 - ax - 2$

For extrema, $f'(x) = 0$,

$\Rightarrow 3a^2x^2 - ax - 2 = 0$, at $x = \frac{1}{3}$

$\left[\text{as at } x = \frac{1}{3}, \text{ function is minimum}\right]$

$\therefore \quad 3a^2\left(\frac{1}{3}\right)^2 - a\left(\frac{1}{3}\right) - 2 = 0$

$\Rightarrow \quad \dfrac{a^2}{3} - \dfrac{a}{3} - 2 = 0$

$\Rightarrow \quad a^2 - a - 6 = 0$ or $a = -2, 3$

So, their arise two cases as

Case I At $a = 3$, if function attains minimum and is positive.

Then, $9\left(\frac{1}{3}\right)^3 - (0.5)(3)\left(\frac{1}{3}\right)^2 - 2\left(\frac{1}{3}\right) - b > 0$

$\left[\because \text{minimum at } x = \frac{1}{3} \text{ and } a = 3 \Rightarrow f\left(\frac{1}{3}\right) > 0, \text{ when } a = 3\right]$

$\Rightarrow \quad b < \frac{1}{3} - \frac{1.5}{9} - \frac{2}{3} \Rightarrow b < -\frac{1}{2}$

Case II At $a = -2$, if function attains minimum and is positive.

Then, $(-2)^2\left(\frac{1}{3}\right)^3 - (0.5)(-2)\left(\frac{1}{3}\right)^2 - 2\left(\frac{1}{3}\right) - b > 0$

$\left[\because \text{minimum at } x = \frac{1}{3}, \text{ when } a = -2 \Rightarrow f\left(\frac{1}{3}\right) > 0, \text{ when } a = -2\right]$

$\Rightarrow \quad b < \frac{4}{27} + \frac{1}{9} - \frac{2}{3}$ or $b < -\frac{11}{27}$

$\therefore$ When $a = 3 \Rightarrow b < -\frac{1}{2}$ and when $a = -2 \Rightarrow b < -\frac{11}{27}$

Example 6 *Suppose x_1 and x_2 are the point of maximum and the point of minimum respectively of the function $f(x) = 2x^3 - 9ax^2 + 12a^2x + 1$, then for the equality $x_1^2 = x_2$ to be true, the value of a must be*

(a) 0 (b) 2 (c) 1 (d) 1/4

Sol. (b) $f'(x) = 6(x^2 - 3ax + 2a^2)$

$$= 6(x - 2a)(x - a) = 0 \Rightarrow x = 2a \text{ or } a$$

$$f''(x) = 6(2x - 3a)$$

$$\left.\begin{array}{l} f''(2a) = a \\ f''(a) = -a \end{array}\right];$$

Now,

Case I If $a > 0$, then $x_1 = a \Rightarrow x_2 = 2a$

Now, $x_1^2 = x_2 \Rightarrow a^2 = 2a \Rightarrow a = 2$

Case II If $a < 0$, then $x_1 = 2a \Rightarrow x_2 = a$

Now, $x_1^2 = x_2$ but LHS > 0 and RHS < 0

$\therefore$ Not possible

Example 7 *If $P(x)$ is a polynomial of degree less than or equal to 2 and S is the set of all such polynomials so that $P(0) = 0$, $P(1) = 1$ and $P'(x) > 0, \forall\, x \in [0, 1]$, then*

(a) $S = \phi$

(b) $S = ax + 1(1 - a)\, x^2, \forall\, a \in (0, 2)$

(c) $S = ax + (1 - a)\, x^2, \forall\, a \in (0, \infty)$

(d) $S = ax + (1 - a)\, x^2, \forall\, a \in (0, 1)$

Sol. (b) Let the polynomial be

$$P(x) = ax^2 + bx + c$$

Given, $P(0) = 0$ and $P(1) = 1$

$\Rightarrow \quad c = 0$ and $a + b = 1 \Rightarrow a = 1 - b$

$\therefore \quad P(x) = (1 - b)\, x^2 + bx$

$\Rightarrow \quad P'(x) = 2(1 - b)\, x + b$

Given, $P'(x) > 0, \forall\, x \in [0, 1] \Rightarrow 2(1 - b)\, x + b > 0$

When $x = 0$, $b > 0$ and when $x = 1$, $b < 2 \Rightarrow 0 < b < 2$

$\therefore \quad S = \{(1 - a)\, x^2 + ax, a \in (0, 2)\}$

Example 8 *The minimum value of the function, $f(x) = x^{3/2} + x^{-3/2} - 4\left(x + \dfrac{1}{x}\right)$ for all permissible real values of x, is*

(a) −10 (b) −6 (c) −7 (d) −8

Sol. (a) Here, $f(x) = x^{3/2} + x^{-3/2} - 4\left(x + \dfrac{1}{x}\right)$

$$f(x) = \left(\sqrt{x} + \frac{1}{\sqrt{x}}\right)^3 - 3\left(\sqrt{x} + \frac{1}{\sqrt{x}}\right) - 4\left(\left(\sqrt{x} + \frac{1}{\sqrt{x}}\right)^2 - 2\right)$$

Let $\sqrt{x} + \dfrac{1}{\sqrt{x}} = t \qquad [x > 0]$

$\therefore \quad g(t) = t^3 - 3t - 4(t^2 - 2)$

Now, $g(t) = t^3 - 4t^2 - 3t + 8$, where $t \in [2, \infty)$

$$g'(t) = 3t^2 - 8t - 3 = (t - 3)(3t + 1)$$

$$g'(t) = 0 \Rightarrow t = 3 \left(t \neq \frac{-1}{3}\right)$$

$$g''(t) = 6t - 8$$

$\Rightarrow g''(3) = 10 > 0$

$\therefore$ Minimum value is $g(3) = 27 - 36 - 9 + 8 = -10$

Example 9 *The least value of a for which the equation $\dfrac{4}{\sin x} + \dfrac{1}{1 - \sin x} = a$ has at least one solution on the interval $(0, \pi/2)$, is*

(a) 9 (b) 4 (c) 8 (d) 1

Sol. (a) Since, $a = \left(\dfrac{4}{\sin x} + \dfrac{1}{1 - \sin x}\right)$, a is least

$$\therefore \quad \frac{da}{dx} = \left[-\frac{4}{\sin^2 x} + \frac{1}{(1 - \sin x)^2}\right] \cos x = 0$$

We have to find the values of x in the interval $(0, \pi/2)$.

$\therefore$ $\cos x \neq 0$ and the other factor when equated to zero give

$$\sin x = \frac{2}{3}$$

$$\therefore \quad \frac{d^2a}{dx^2} = \left[\frac{8}{\sin^3 x} + \frac{2}{(1 - \sin x)^3}\right]$$

Put $\sin x = \dfrac{2}{3}$

$$\therefore \quad \frac{d^2a}{dx^2} = \left[\frac{8}{8/27} + 2 \times 27\right] = 81$$

$\therefore$ a is minimum and its value is

$$\frac{4}{2/3} + \frac{1}{1 - (2/3)} = 6 + 3 = 9$$

Example 10 *The set of all values of k for which the function $f(x) = (k^2 - 3k + 2)\left(\cos^2 \dfrac{x}{4} - \sin^2 \dfrac{x}{4}\right) + (k - 1)\, x - \sin 1$ does not posses critical points, is*

(a) $[1, \infty)$ (b) $(0, 1) \cup (1, 4)$

(c) $(-2, 4)$ (d) $(1, 3) \cup (3, 5)$

Sol. (b) On replacing $\cos^2 \dfrac{x}{4} - \sin^2 \dfrac{x}{4}$ by $\cos \dfrac{x}{2}$, we get

$$\frac{dy}{dx} = -\frac{1}{2}(k^2 - 3k + 2) \sin \frac{x}{2} + (k - 1)$$

$$= -\frac{1}{2}(k - 1)(k - 2) \sin \frac{x}{2} + (k - 1)$$

$$= -\frac{(k - 1)}{2}\left[(k - 2) \sin \frac{x}{2} - 2\right] \neq 0$$

because the function does not posses critical points

$k - 1 \neq 0$ and $\sin \dfrac{x}{2} = \dfrac{2}{k - 2}$ does not posses any solution

$$\Rightarrow \quad k \neq 1 \text{ and } \left|\frac{2}{k - 2}\right| > 1 \text{ as } \left|\sin \frac{x}{2}\right| \leq 1$$

$\Rightarrow \quad k \neq 1$ and $|k-2| < 2$

$\Rightarrow \quad k \neq 1$ and $-2 < (k-2) < 2$

or $\quad 0 < k < 4$

Thus, k lies in the interval $(0, 4)$ but $k \neq 1$

i.e. $k \in (0, 1) \cup (1, 4)$.

Example 11 *The minimum value of* $\left(1+\frac{1}{\sin^n \alpha}\right)\left(1+\frac{1}{\cos^n \alpha}\right)$, *for* $\alpha \in \left(0, \frac{\pi}{2}\right)$ *is given by*

(a) 1 (b) 2

(c) $(1+2^{n/2})^2$ (d) None of these

Sol. (c) Let $f(\alpha) = \left(1+\frac{1}{\sin^n \alpha}\right)\left(1+\frac{1}{\cos^n \alpha}\right)$

$$f(\alpha) = (1+\text{cosec}^n \alpha)(1+\sec^n \alpha)$$

$$\Rightarrow f'(\alpha) = -n\, \text{cosec}^n \alpha \cdot \cot \alpha)(1+\sec^n \alpha) + (1+\text{cosec}^n \alpha)\cdot n \sec^n \alpha \cdot \tan \alpha$$

$$f'(\alpha) = 0$$

$$\Rightarrow n\,\text{cosec}^n \alpha \cdot \cot \alpha (1+\sec^n \alpha) = (1+\text{cosec}^n \alpha)\cdot n\sec^n \alpha \cdot \tan \alpha$$

$$\Rightarrow \frac{1}{\sin^n \alpha}\cdot\frac{\cos \alpha}{\sin \alpha}\cdot\left(1+\frac{1}{\cos^n \alpha}\right) = \left(1+\frac{1}{\sin^n \alpha}\right)\cdot\frac{1}{\cos^n \alpha}\cdot\frac{\sin \alpha}{\cos \alpha}$$

$$\Rightarrow \frac{\cos^2 \alpha}{\sin^2 \alpha}\cdot(1+\cos^n \alpha) = (1+\sin^n \alpha)$$

$$\Rightarrow \cos \alpha - \sin \alpha = 0$$

$$\Rightarrow \alpha = \frac{\pi}{4}$$

For $\alpha \to \left(\frac{\pi}{4}\right)^-$, $\cos \alpha - \sin \alpha > 0$

$$\Rightarrow f'(\alpha) < 0$$

and $\alpha \to \left(\frac{\pi}{4}\right)^+$, $\cos \alpha - \sin \alpha < 0$

$$\Rightarrow f'(\alpha) > 0$$

$\therefore \quad \alpha = \frac{\pi}{4}$ is a point of minima

and $f\left(\frac{\pi}{4}\right) = (1+2^{n/2})^2$

Example 12 *If* $\sin \theta + \cos \theta = 1$, *then the minimum value of* $(1+\text{cosec}\,\theta)(1+\sec\theta)$ *is*

(a) 3 (b) 4

(c) 6 (d) 9

Sol. (d) We know that AM $\geq$ GM

$$\Rightarrow \frac{\sin \theta + \cos \theta}{2} \geq \sqrt{\sin \theta \cos \theta}$$

$$\Rightarrow \sin \theta \cos \theta \leq \frac{1}{4} \qquad [\because \sin\theta + \cos\theta = 1]$$

Now, let $\sin \theta = x$, $\cos \theta = y$

and $(1+\text{cosec}\,\theta)(1+\sec \theta) \geq p$

$$\Rightarrow \left(1+\frac{1}{x}\right)\left(1+\frac{1}{y}\right) \geq p$$

$$\Rightarrow \left(\frac{1+x}{x}\right)\left(\frac{1+y}{y}\right) \geq p$$

$$\Rightarrow xy + x + y + 1 \geq pxy$$

$$\Rightarrow x + y + 1 \geq (p-1)\,xy$$

$$\Rightarrow 2 \geq (p-1)\,xy \qquad [\because x + y = 1]$$

$$\Rightarrow xy \leq \frac{2}{p-1}$$

$$\Rightarrow \frac{2}{p-1} = \frac{1}{4}$$

$$\Rightarrow p - 1 = 8$$

$$\Rightarrow p = 9$$

Example 13 *If* $k \sin^2 x + \frac{1}{k}\text{cosec}^2 x = 2$, $x \in \left(0, \frac{\pi}{2}\right)$, *then* $\cos^2 x + 5 \sin x \cos x + 6 \sin^2 x$ *is equal to*

(a) $\frac{k^2+5k+6}{k^2}$

(b) $\frac{k^2-5k+6}{k^2}$

(c) 6

(d) None of the above

Sol. (d) Given, $k \sin^2 x + \frac{1}{k \sin^2 x} = 2$

$$\Rightarrow \left(\sqrt{k}\sin x - \frac{1}{\sqrt{k}\sin x}\right)^2 = 0$$

$$\Rightarrow \sin^2 x = \frac{1}{k}$$

So, $\cos^2 x + 5 \sin x \cos x + 6 \sin^2 x$

$$= \frac{k-1}{k} + \frac{5\sqrt{k-1}}{k} + \frac{6}{k}$$

$$= \frac{k+5+5\sqrt{k-1}}{k}$$

Example 14 *Let* $f(x) = \int_0^x \cos\left(\frac{t^2 + 2t + 1}{5}\right) dt, 0 < x < 2,$ *then* $f(x)$

(a) increases monotonically.
(b) decreases monotonically.
(c) has one point of local maxima.
(d) has one point of local minima.

Sol. (c) We have, $f'(x) = \cos\left(\frac{x^2 + 2x + 1}{5}\right) \times 1 = \cos\left(\frac{(x+1)^2}{5}\right)$

Since, $0 < x < 2 \Rightarrow \frac{1}{5} < \frac{(x+1)^2}{5} < \frac{9}{5}$

Now, $\cos\left(\frac{(x+1)^2}{5}\right) = 0$

$$\Rightarrow \quad \frac{(x+1)^2}{5} = \frac{\pi}{2}$$

$f'(x) > 0$, if $0 < x < (\sqrt{5\pi/2} - 1)$

and $f'(x) < 0$, if $(\sqrt{5\pi/2} - 1) < x < 2$

$\therefore \quad x = (\sqrt{5\pi/2} - 1)$ is a point of local maxima.

Example 15 *As x ranges over the interval* $(0, \infty)$, *the function* $f(x) = \sqrt{9x^2 + 173x + 900} - \sqrt{9x^2 + 77x + 900}$, *ranges over*

(a) (0, 4) (b) (0, 8) (c) (0, 12) (d) (0, 16)

Sol. (d) $\because \sqrt{9x^2 + 173x + 900} > \sqrt{9x^2 + 77x + 900}, \forall x \in (0, \infty)$

$\Rightarrow f(x) > 0, \forall x \in (0, \infty)$

Now, $f(x) = \frac{96x}{\sqrt{9x^2 + 173x + 900} + \sqrt{9x^2 + 77x + 900}}$ [rationalise]

$$\therefore \lim_{x \to \infty} f(x) = \lim_{x \to \infty} \frac{96}{\sqrt{9 + \frac{173}{x} + \frac{900}{x^2}} + \sqrt{9 + \frac{77}{x} + \frac{900}{x^2}}} = \frac{96}{6} = 16$$

$\therefore$ Range of $f(x) \in (0, 16)$.

Example 16 *Let* $f(x) = \frac{\tan^n x}{\sum_{r=0}^{2n} \tan^r x}$, $n \in N$, *where* $x \in \left[0, \frac{\pi}{2}\right)$

(a) $f(x)$ is bounded and it takes both of it's bounds and the range of $f(x)$ contains exactly one integral point.
(b) $f(x)$ is bounded and it takes both of it's bounds and the range of $f(x)$ contains more than one integral point.
(c) $f(x)$ is bounded but minimum and maximum do not exist.
(d) $f(x)$ is not bounded as the upper bound does not exist.

Sol. (a) Let $\tan x = t$

$$\Rightarrow \quad f(x) = \frac{t^n}{1 + t + \ldots + t^4 + \ldots + t^{2n}}$$

$$= \frac{1}{\left(t^n + \frac{1}{t^n}\right) + \left(t^{n-1} + \frac{1}{t^{n-1}}\right) + \ldots + \left(t + \frac{1}{t}\right) + 1}$$

$$\le \frac{1}{2n+1}$$

[equality holds at $x = \pi/4$]

Also, $f(0) = 0$

$\Rightarrow$ Range of $f(x)$ is $\left[0, \frac{1}{2n+1}\right]$.

Example 17 *The function* $f(x) = \frac{\log(\pi + x)}{\log(e + x)}$ *is*

(a) increasing on $[0, \infty)$.
(b) decreasing on $[0, \infty)$.
(c) increasing on $[0, \pi/e]$ and decreasing on $[\pi/e, \infty)$.
(d) decreasing on $[0, \pi/e]$ and decreasing on $[\pi/e, \infty)$.

Sol. (b) $f(x) = \frac{\log(\pi + x)}{\log(e + x)}$

$$\therefore \quad f'(x) = \frac{\left(\frac{1}{\pi + x}\right) \times \log(e + x) - \left(\frac{1}{e + x}\right) \times \log(\pi + x)}{(\log(e + x))^2}$$

Let $h(x) = \frac{\log(e + x)}{\pi + x} - \frac{\log(\pi + x)}{e + x}$

Let us consider $g(x) = x \ln x$

$$\Rightarrow \quad g'(x) = x \times \frac{1}{x} + \ln x = 1 + \ln x$$

$g'(x) > 0, \forall x \in (1/e, \infty)$

and $g'(x) < 0, \forall x \in (0, 1/e)$

Now, $e < \pi \Rightarrow e + x < \pi + x, \forall x \in (0, \infty)$

$\Rightarrow \quad g(e + x) < g(\pi + x)$

[$\because g(x)$ is an increasing function, for $x > 1/e$]

$\Rightarrow (e + x) \log(e + x) < (\pi + x) \log(\pi + x)$

$$\Rightarrow \quad \frac{\log(e + x)}{\pi + x} < \frac{\log(\pi + x)}{e + x}$$

$$\Rightarrow \quad \frac{\ln(e + x)}{\pi + x} - \frac{\ln(\pi + x)}{e + x} < 0$$

$$\Rightarrow \quad h(x) < 0$$

$$\therefore \quad f'(x) = \frac{h(x)}{(\ln(e + x))^2} < 0, \forall x \in [0, \infty)$$

Hence, $f(x)$ decreases for $[0, \infty)$.

Example 18 *The tangent to the curve* $y = 1 - x^2$ *at* $x = \alpha$, *where* $0 < \alpha < 1$, *meets the axes at P and Q. If* α *varies and the minimum value of the area of the* ΔOPQ *is k times the area bounded by the axes and the part of the curve for* $0 < x < 1$, *then k is equal to*

(a) $\frac{2}{\sqrt{3}}$ (b) $\frac{75}{16}$ (c) $\frac{25}{18}$ (d) $\frac{2}{3}$

Sol. (a) Given, $y = 1 - x^2$

$$\frac{dy}{dx} = -2x$$

Slope of tangent, $m = -2\alpha$

Then, equation of tangent, $y - (1 - \alpha^2) = -2\alpha(x - \alpha)$

$$y + 2\alpha x = \alpha^2 + 1 \quad \text{...(i)}$$

From Eq. (i) intersect the axes at

$$P\left(\frac{\alpha^2 + 1}{2\alpha}, 0\right) \text{ and } Q(0, \alpha^2 + 1)$$

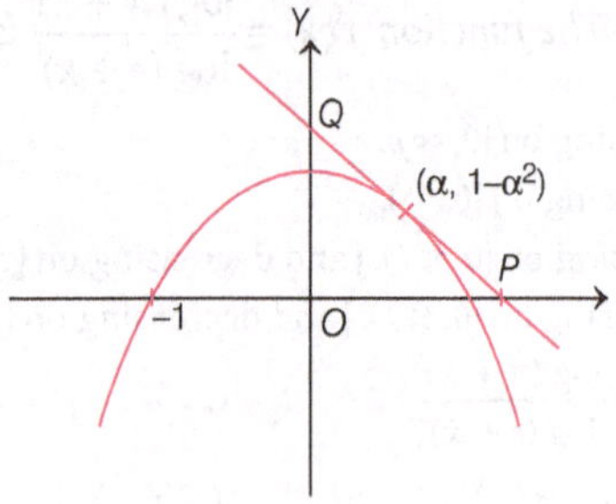

$$\therefore \text{ Area of } \Delta OPQ = \frac{1}{2} \cdot \frac{(\alpha^2 + 1)^2}{2\alpha}$$

$$= \frac{(\alpha^2 + 1)^2}{4\alpha}$$

$$f(\alpha) = \frac{1}{4}\left(\alpha^3 + 2\alpha + \frac{1}{\alpha}\right)$$

$$f'(\alpha) = \frac{1}{4}\left(3\alpha^2 + 2 - \frac{1}{\alpha^2}\right)$$

$$= \frac{1}{4} \frac{(3\alpha^4 + 2\alpha^2 - 1)}{\alpha^2}$$

$$= \frac{1}{4} \cdot \frac{(\alpha^2 + 1)(3\alpha^2 - 1)}{\alpha^2}$$

$$= \frac{1}{4} \frac{(\alpha^2 + 1)(\sqrt{3}\alpha - 1)(\sqrt{3}\alpha + 1)}{\alpha^2}$$

Using number line rule, we have

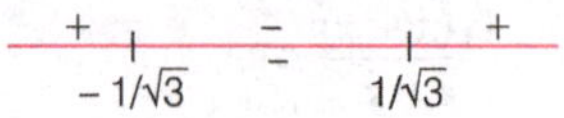

$$\therefore \text{ Minimum, when } \alpha = \frac{1}{\sqrt{3}}$$

Thus, minimum area of triangle $= \dfrac{4}{3\sqrt{3}}$

Given, $\dfrac{4}{3\sqrt{3}} = k \int_0^1 (1 - x^2)\, dx = k\left(x - \dfrac{x^3}{3}\right)_0^1 = \dfrac{2k}{3} \Rightarrow k = \dfrac{2}{\sqrt{3}}$

Example 19 *The least value of the expression* $x^2 + 4y^2 + 3z^2 - 2x - 12y - 6z + 14$ *is*

(a) 0 (b) 1
(c) no least value (d) None of these

Sol. (b) Let $f(x, y, z) = x^2 + 4y^2 + 3z^2 - 2x - 12y - 6z + 14$

$$= (x - 1)^2 + (2y - 3)^2 + 3(z - 1)^2 + 1$$

For least value of $f(x, y, z)$,

$$x - 1 = 0, 2y - 3 = 0 \text{ and } z - 1 = 0$$

$$\therefore x = 1, y = \frac{3}{2}, z = 1$$

Hence, least value of $f(x, y, z)$ is $f\left(1, \dfrac{3}{2}, 1\right) = 1$

Example 20 *The coordinates of the point on the curve* $x^3 = y(x - a)^2$, $a > 0$ *for which function has minimum value.*

(a) $(2a, 8a)$ (b) $\left(-2a, \dfrac{-8a}{9}\right)$
(c) $\left(3a, \dfrac{27a}{4}\right)$ (d) $\left(-3a, \dfrac{-27a}{16}\right)$

Sol. (c) The ordinate of any point on the curve is given by

$$y = \frac{x^3}{(x - a)^2}$$

$$\frac{dy}{dx} = \frac{x^2(x - 3a)}{(x - a)^3}$$

Now, $\dfrac{dy}{dx} = 0 \Rightarrow x = 0$ or $x = 3a$

$$\left[\frac{d^2y}{dx^2}\right]_{x = 0} = 0$$

and $$\left[\frac{d^2y}{dx^2}\right]_{x = 3a} = \frac{72a^5}{(2a)^6} > 0$$

So, y is minimum at $x = 3a$ and y is equal to $\dfrac{27a}{4}$.

Example 21 *If* $a > b > 0$ *and* $f(\theta) = \dfrac{(a^2 - b^2)\cos\theta}{a - b\sin\theta}$, *then the maximum value of* $f(\theta)$ *is*

(a) $2\sqrt{a^2 + b^2}$

(b) $\sqrt{a^2 + b^2}$

(c) $\sqrt{a^2 - b^2}$

(d) $\sqrt{b^2 - a^2}$

Sol. (c) Here, $f(\theta) = \dfrac{(a^2 - b^2)\cos\theta}{a - b\sin\theta}$

$$= \frac{(a^2 - b^2)}{a\sec\theta - b\tan\theta}$$

or $$f(\theta) = \frac{a^2 - b^2}{h(\theta)},$$

where $h(\theta) = a\sec\theta - b\tan\theta$

$\therefore\ f(\theta)$ is maximum and minimum as $h(\theta)$ is minimum and maximum, respectively.

$\Rightarrow\quad h(\theta) = a\sec\theta - b\tan\theta$

$\Rightarrow\quad h'(\theta) = \sec\theta\,(a\tan\theta - b\sec\theta)$

For maximum and minimum, put $h'(\theta) = 0$,

$\Rightarrow\quad \sin\theta = \dfrac{b}{a}\ [\sec\theta \neq 0]$ ...(i)

Also, $h''(\theta) = a\sec^3\theta + a\sec\theta\cdot\tan^2\theta - 2b\sec^2\theta\tan\theta$

or $\quad h''(\theta) = \dfrac{a + a\sin^2\theta - 2b\sin\theta}{\cos^3\theta}$

When $\sin\theta = \dfrac{b}{a}$,

$$(h''(\theta)) = \frac{a + a\cdot\dfrac{b^2}{a^2} - 2b\cdot\dfrac{b}{a}}{\left(1 - \dfrac{b^2}{a^2}\right)^{3/2}}$$

$$= \frac{a^2 - b^2}{a\left(\dfrac{a^2 - b^2}{a^2}\right)^{3/2}} > 0$$

[as $a > b > 0$]

$\Rightarrow h(\theta)$ is minimum, when $\sin\theta = \dfrac{b}{a}$

$\therefore\ f(\theta)$ is maximum, when $\sin\theta = \dfrac{b}{a}$

$\Rightarrow\quad f_{\max}(\theta) = \sqrt{a^2 - b^2}$

Example 22 *If composite function $f_1(f_2(f_3(\ldots(f_n(x)))))$ n times, is an increasing function and if r of f_i's are decreasing function while rest are increasing, then maximum value of function is*

(a) $\dfrac{n^2 - 1}{4}$, when n is an even number.

(b) $\dfrac{n^2}{4}$, when n is an odd number.

(c) $\dfrac{n^2 - 1}{4}$, when n is an odd number.

(d) None of the above

Sol. (c) r must be an even integer because two decreasing functions are required to make it increasing function.

Let $y = r(n - r)$

When n is odd,

$$r = \frac{n-1}{2} \text{ or } \frac{n+1}{2}, \text{ for maximum value of } y.$$

When n is even,

$$r = \frac{n}{2}, \text{ for maximum value of } y.$$

$\therefore$ Maximum $(y) = \dfrac{n^2 - 1}{4}$, when n is odd and $\dfrac{n^2}{4}$, when n is even.

JEE SCANNER

Example 23 Similar to PYQ Asked in JEE Main 2024

Let a rectangle ABCD of sides be inscribed in another rectangle PQRS such that the vertices of the rectangle ABCD lie on the sides of the rectangle PQRS. Let a and b be the sides of the rectangle PQRS when its area is maximum. Then, $(a + b)^2$ is equal to

(a) 2 (b) 484 (c) 121 (d) 242

Sol. (d) Given, rectangle $ABCD$ of sides inscribed in another rectangle $PQRS$.

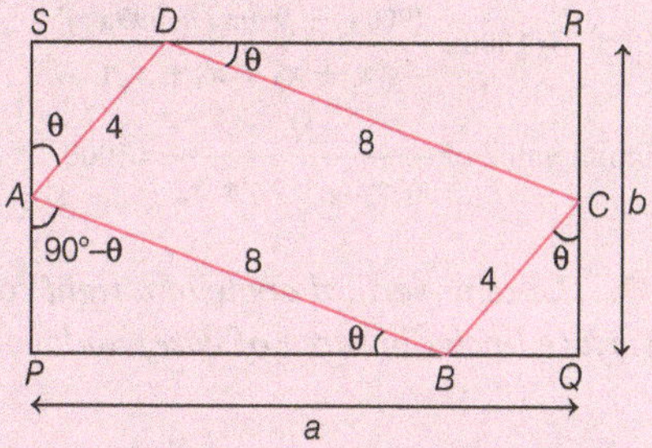

Let $\angle ABP = \theta$

$\because\quad \angle DAS = \angle CDR = \angle BCQ = \theta$

Now, $\quad PB = 8\cos\theta$ and $BQ = 4\sin\theta$

$\therefore\quad PQ = 8\cos\theta + 4\sin\theta$

Also, $\quad AP = 8\sin\theta$ and $AS = 4\cos\theta$

$\because\quad PS = 8\sin\theta + 4\cos\theta$

$\therefore$ Area of rectangle $PQRS$

$= (8\cos\theta + 4\sin\theta)(8\sin\theta + 4\cos\theta)$

$= 32\cos^2\theta + 32\sin^2\theta + 80\sin\theta\cos\theta$

$= 16(2 + 5\sin\theta\cos\theta) = 32 + 40\sin 2\theta$

Area will be maximum, when $\sin 2\theta = 1 \Rightarrow \theta = 45°$

$\because$ Maximum area $= 32 + 40 = 72$ sq units

$\therefore\quad a = PQ = 8\cos 45° + 4\sin 45° = \dfrac{8}{\sqrt{2}} + \dfrac{4}{\sqrt{2}} = \dfrac{12}{\sqrt{2}} = 6\sqrt{2}$

and $b = PS = 8\sin 45° + 2\cos 45°$

$= \dfrac{8}{\sqrt{2}} + \dfrac{2}{\sqrt{2}} = \dfrac{10}{\sqrt{2}} = 5\sqrt{2}$

$\because\ (a + b)^2 = (6\sqrt{2} + 5\sqrt{2})^2 = (11\sqrt{2})^2 = 242$

Skill Builder

Rectangle of maximum area that can be inscribed in an equilateral triangle of side a will have area is equal to

(a) $\dfrac{a^2\sqrt{3}}{2}$ (b) $\dfrac{a^2\sqrt{3}}{4}$

(c) $\dfrac{a^2\sqrt{3}}{8}$ (d) None of these

For Sol.

Example 24 *Let N be any four digit number say $x_1x_2x_3x_4$. Then, maximum value of $\dfrac{N}{x_1+x_2+x_3+x_4}$ is equal to*

(a) 1000 (b) $\dfrac{1111}{4}$

(c) 800 (d) None of these

Sol. (a) $\dfrac{N}{x_1+x_2+x_3+x_4}$

$$= \frac{1000x_1+100x_2+10x_3+x_4}{x_1+x_2+x_3+x_4}$$

$$= 1000 - \frac{(900x_2+990x_3+999x_4)}{(x_1+x_2+x_3+x_4)}$$

$\Rightarrow$ maximum value of $\dfrac{N}{x_1+x_2+x_2+x_4} = 1000$

Example 25 *The semi-vertical angle of a right cone of given total surface (including area of base) and max. volume, is*

(a) $\sin^{-1}\dfrac{1}{3}$ (b) $\sin^{-1}\left(\dfrac{1}{\sqrt{3}}\right)$

(c) 45° (d) 30°

Sol. (a) $S = \pi r(r+l) = \text{constant}$ ...(i)

$V = \dfrac{1}{3}\pi r^2 h$ ...(ii)

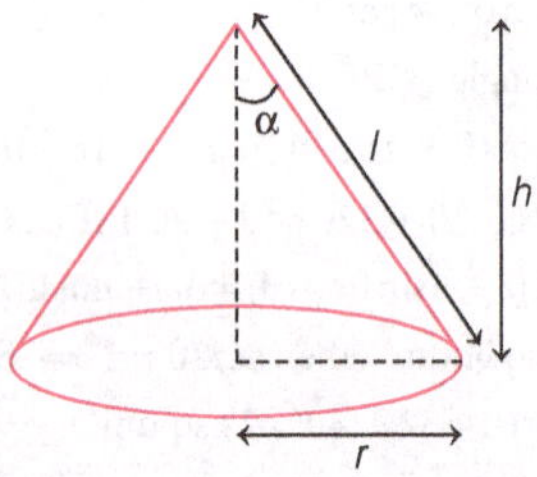

$\therefore \quad z = V^2 = \dfrac{1}{9}\pi^2 r^4 h^2$ or $z = \dfrac{1}{9}\pi^2 r^4 (l^2 - r^2)$

Hence, z is a function of two variables r and l and we will eliminate l with the help of (2) in order to make z (i.e. V^2) a function of a single variable.

From (2), $[(S/\pi r) - r] = l$

$\therefore \quad z = \dfrac{1}{9}\pi^2 r^4 [((S/\pi r) - r)^2 - r^2]$

or $\quad z = \dfrac{1}{9}\pi^2 r^4 \left[\dfrac{S^2}{\pi^2 r^2} - \dfrac{2S}{\pi}\right]$

or $\quad z = \dfrac{1}{9}\pi^2 \left[\dfrac{S^2}{\pi^2} r^2 - \dfrac{2S}{\pi} r^4\right] = \dfrac{S}{9}[Sr^2 - 2\pi r^4]$

Now, V is max, when V^2 i.e. z is max.

$\therefore \quad \dfrac{dz}{dr} = \left(\dfrac{S}{9}\right)[2Sr - 8\pi r^3] = 0$

$\therefore \quad r = 0$ or $r^2 S/4\pi$

$r = 0$ is obviously rejected

Now, $\dfrac{d^2z}{dr^2} = \left(\dfrac{S}{9}\right)[2S - 24\pi r^2] = \left(\dfrac{S}{9}\right)[2S - 6S] = -\left(\dfrac{4S^2}{9}\right) < 0$

When $r^2 = \dfrac{S}{4\pi}$, z i.e. V^2 is max. or V is max.

Now, $r^2 = \dfrac{S}{4\pi}$

or $\quad 4\pi r^2 = S = \pi r^2 + \pi r l$

$3\pi r^2 = \pi r l$

$\therefore \quad \dfrac{r}{l} = \dfrac{1}{3}$ or $\sin\alpha = \dfrac{1}{3}$

$\therefore \quad \alpha = \sin^{-1}\dfrac{1}{3}$

More than One Correct Option Type Questions

Example 26 *$f(x)$ is cubic polynomial which has local maxima at $x = -1$, If $f(2) = 18$, $f(1) = -1$ and $f'(x)$ has local minima at $x = 0$, then*

(a) the distance between points of maxima and minima is $2\sqrt{5}$.

(b) $f(x)$ is increasing, for $x \in [1, 2\sqrt{5}]$.

(c) $f(x)$ has local minima at $x = 1$.

(d) the value of $f(0) = 5$.

Sol. (b), (c) Since, $f(x)$ has local maxima at $x = -1$ and $f'(x)$ has local minima at $x = 0$.

$\therefore \quad f''(x) = \lambda x$

$f'(x) = \lambda \dfrac{x^2}{2} + c$ $\quad [f'(-1) = 0]$

$\Rightarrow \dfrac{\lambda}{2} + c = 0 \Rightarrow \lambda = -2c$ ...(i)

Again, on integrating both sides, we get

$$f(x) = \lambda \frac{x^3}{6} + cx + d$$

$f(2) = \lambda\left(\dfrac{8}{6}\right) + 2c + d = 18$ ...(ii)

and $\quad f(1) = \dfrac{\lambda}{6} + c + d = -1$ ...(iii)

$\therefore$ Using Eqs. (i), (ii) and (iii), we get

$$f(x) = \frac{1}{4}(19x^3 - 57x + 34)$$

$\therefore \quad f'(x) = \dfrac{1}{4}(57x^2 - 57) = \dfrac{57}{4}(x-1)(x+1)$

[using number line rule]

$\therefore$ $f(x)$ is increasing for $[1, 2\sqrt{5}]$

and $f(x)$ has local maxima at $x = -1$ and $f(x)$ has local minima at $x = 1$

Also, $f(0) = \dfrac{34}{4}$

Example 27 *Suppose $f'(x)$ exists for each x and $h(x) = f(x) - (f(x))^2 + (f(x))^3$ for every real number x. Then,*

(a) h is increasing whenever f is increasing.
(b) h is increasing whenever f is decreasing.
(c) h is decreasing whenever f is decreasing.
(d) nothing can be said in general.

Sol. (a, c) We have,

$$h'(x) = f'(x) - 2f'(x)\, f(x) + 3f'(x)\, f(x)^2$$
$$= 3f'(x)\left[f(x)^2 - \frac{2}{3}f(x) + \frac{1}{3}\right]$$
$$= 3f'(x)\left[\left(f(x) - \frac{1}{3}\right)^2 + \frac{2}{9}\right]$$

Thus, $h'(x) > 0$ if $f'(x) > 0$
and $h'(x) < 0$ if $f'(x) < 0$
Therefore, h increases (decreases) whenever f increases (decreases).

Example 28 *If $a > 0, b > 0, c > 0$ and $a + b + c = abc$, then atleast one of the numbers a, b, c exceeds*

(a) $\frac{3}{2}$ (b) $\frac{17}{10}$
(c) 2 (d) $\frac{13}{10}$

Sol. (a, b, c) We may suppose $a \ge b \ge c$

$$abc = a + b + c \ge 3c$$

So, $ab \ge 3$, $a \ge b$ and $a \ge \sqrt{3} > \frac{17}{10}$

Alternate Solution

$$(a + b + c)^3 \ge 27abc \ge 27(a + b + c)$$
$$\therefore \quad a + b + c \ge 3\sqrt{3}$$
$\Rightarrow$ Atleast one of them $\ge \sqrt{3}$

Example 29 *Let $f(x, y) = x^2 + 2xy + 3y^2 - 6x - 2y$, where $x, y \in R$, then*

(a) $f(x, y) \ge -11$ (b) $f(x, y) \ge -10$
(c) $f(x, y) > -11$ (d) $f(x, y) > -12$

Sol. (a, c, d) Let $z = x^2 + 2xy + 3y^2 - 6x - 2y$

$\Rightarrow x^2 + 2xy + 3y^2 - 6x - 2y - z = 0$ as $x \in R$
$\therefore \quad D \ge 0$
$\Rightarrow 4(y - 3)^2 - 4(3y^2 - 2y - z) \ge 0$
$\Rightarrow y^2 + 9 - 6y - 3y^2 + 2y + z \ge 0$
$\Rightarrow \quad -2y^2 - 4y + 9 + z \ge 0$
$\Rightarrow \quad z \ge 2(y^2 + 2y + 1) - 11 = 2(y + 1)^2 - 11$
$\Rightarrow \quad z \ge -11$

Example 30 *Let $g(x) = f(\tan x) + f(\cot x), \forall x \in \left(\frac{\pi}{2}, \pi\right)$. If $f''(x) < 0, \forall x \in \left(\frac{\pi}{2}, \pi\right)$, then*

(a) $g(x)$ is increasing in $\left(\frac{\pi}{2}, \frac{3\pi}{4}\right)$.
(b) $g(x)$ has local minima at $x = \frac{3\pi}{4}$.
(c) $g(x)$ is decreasing in $\left(\frac{3\pi}{4}, \pi\right)$.
(d) $g(x)$ has local maxima at $x = \frac{3\pi}{4}$.

Sol. (a, c, d) Given, $g(x) = f(\tan x) + f(\cot x)$

$$g'(x) = f'(\tan x)\sec^2 x - f'(\cot x)\operatorname{cosec}^2 x$$

For increasing $g'(x) > 0$,

$$f'(\tan x) > f'(\cot x)$$

$[\because f''(x) < 0$ and $\tan x < \cot x, \forall x \in \left(\frac{\pi}{4}, \frac{\pi}{2}\right)]$

Also, $\sec^2 x > \operatorname{cosec}^2 x$, $x \in \left(\frac{\pi}{2}, \frac{3\pi}{4}\right)$

$g'(x) > 0 \Rightarrow g(x)$ is increasing in $\left(\frac{\pi}{2}, \frac{3\pi}{4}\right)$

Similarly, $g(x)$ is decreasing in $\left(\frac{3\pi}{4}, \pi\right)$

Also, $g(x)$ has local maxima at $x = \frac{3\pi}{4}$.

Example 31 *The function $f(x) = \int_0^x \sqrt{1 - t^4}\, dt$ is such that*

(a) it is defined on the interval $[-1, 1]$.
(b) it is an increasing function.
(c) it is an odd function.
(d) the point (0, 0) is the point of inflection.

Sol. (a, b, c, d) $f'(x) = \sqrt{1 - x^4} > 0$ in $(-1, 1)$

$\Rightarrow f$ is increasing

Now, $f(x) + f(-x)$

$$= \int_0^x \sqrt{1 - t^4}\, dt + \int_0^{-x} \sqrt{1 - t^4}\, dt$$

$$\Rightarrow \int_0^x \sqrt{1 - t^4}\, dt + \left(-\int_0^x \sqrt{1 - y^4}\, dy\right) = 0 \qquad [t = -y]$$

$\Rightarrow f(x)$ is odd

Again, $f''(x) = \dfrac{-4x^3}{2\sqrt{1 - x^4}}$,

which vanished at $x = 0$ and changes sign $\Rightarrow$ (0, 0) is point of inflection, since, f is well defined in $[-1, 1]$.

Example 32 *The function* $\dfrac{\sin(x+a)}{\sin(x+b)}$ *has no maxima or minima if*

(a) $b-a=n\pi, n\in I$ (b) $b-a=(2n+1)\pi, n\in I$
(c) $b-a=2n\pi, n\in I$ (d) None of these

Sol. (a, b, c) Given, $f(x)=\dfrac{\sin(x+a)}{\sin(x+b)}$

$$f'(x)=\frac{\sin(x+b)\times\cos(x+a)-\sin(x+a)\cos(x+b)}{\sin^2(x+b)}$$

$$=\frac{\sin(b-a)}{\sin^2(x+b)}$$

If $\sin(b-a)=0$, then $f'(x)=0$

$\Rightarrow f(x)$ will be constant.

i.e. $b-a=n\pi$

or $b-a=(2n+1)\pi$

or $b-a=2n\pi$,

then $f(x)$ has no minima.

Example 33 *The function* $f(x)=x^{1/3}(x-1)$

(a) has 2 inflection points.

(b) is strictly increasing for $x>\frac{1}{4}$ and strictly decreasing for $x<\frac{1}{4}$.

(c) is concave down in $\left(-\frac{1}{2},0\right)$.

(d) are enclosed by the curve lying in the fourth quadrant is $\frac{9}{28}$.

Sol. (a, b, c, d) $y=x^{1/3}(x-1)$

$$\frac{dy}{dx}=\frac{4}{3}x^{1/3}-\frac{1}{3}\cdot\frac{1}{x^{2/3}}=\frac{1}{3x^{2/3}}[4x-1]$$

$x^{2/3}$ is always positive and $x=\frac{1}{4}$ has a local minima.

Hence, f is increasing for $x>\frac{1}{4}$

and f is decreasing for $x<\frac{1}{4}$.

Now, $f'(x)=\frac{4}{3}x^{1/3}-\frac{1}{3}\cdot x^{-2/3}$

[non-existence at $x=0$, vertical tangent]

$$f''(x)=\frac{4}{9}\cdot\frac{1}{x^{2/3}}+\frac{1}{3}\cdot\frac{2}{3}\cdot\frac{1}{x^{5/3}}$$

$$=\frac{2}{9x^{2/3}}\left[2+\frac{1}{x}\right]$$

$$=\frac{2}{9x^{2/3}}\left[\frac{2x+1}{x}\right]$$

$\therefore$ $f''(x)=0$ at $x=-\frac{1}{2}$ [inflection point]

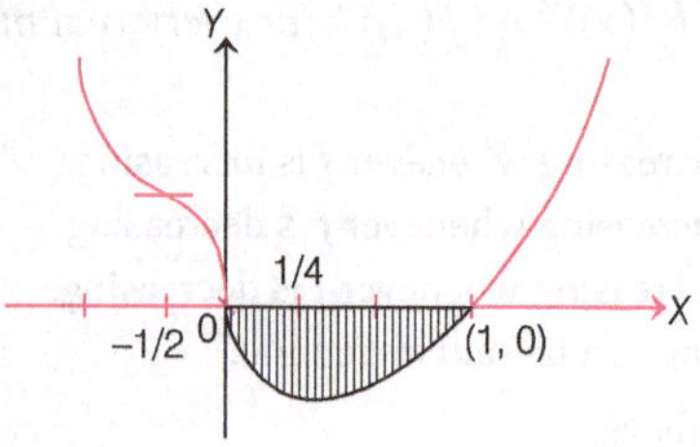

Graph of $f(x)$ is as

$$A=\int_0^1(x^{4/3}-x^{1/3})\,dx$$

$$=\left[\frac{3}{7}x^{3/7}-\frac{3}{4}x^{4/3}\right]_0^1$$

$$=\left|\frac{3}{7}-\frac{3}{4}\right|$$

$$=3\left|\frac{4-7}{28}\right|=\frac{9}{28}$$

Example 34 *Assume that inverse of the function f is denoted by g, then which of the following statements hold good?*

(a) If f is increasing, then g is also increasing.
(b) If f is decreasing, then g is increasing.
(c) The function f is injective.
(d) The function g is onto.

Sol. (a, c, d) If f and g are inverse, then $fog(x)=x$

$f'[g(x)]\,g'(x)=1$

If f is increasing $\Rightarrow f'>0$

$\Rightarrow$ sign of g' is also positive.

Therefore, option (a) is correct.

If f is decreasing $\Rightarrow f'<0$

$\Rightarrow$ sign of g' is negative.

Therefore, option (b) is false.

Since, f has an inverse.

$\Rightarrow f$ is bijective $\Rightarrow f$ is injective

Therefore, option (c) is correct.

Inverse of a bijective mapping is bijective.

$\Rightarrow g$ is also bijective $\Rightarrow g$ is onto

Therefore, option (d) is correct.

Example 35 *If* $f(x)=\begin{cases}3x^2+12x-1, & -1\le x\le 2\\ 37-x, & 2<x\le 3\end{cases}$

Then,

(a) $f(x)$ is increasing on $[-1, 2]$.
(b) $f(x)$ is continuous on $[-1, 3]$.
(c) $f'(2)$ does not exist.
(d) $f(x)$ has the maximum value at $x=2$.

Sol. (a, b, c, d) For $x \in [-1, 2)$, $f'(x) = 6x + 12 > 0$ on $(-1, 2)$, so f increases on $[-1, 2]$. f is trivially continuous on $[-1, 3]$ except possibly $x = 2$.

At point $x = 2$, $f(2) = 35$ and

$$\lim_{x \to 2^+} f(x) = \lim_{x \to 2^+} (37 - x) = 35,$$

$$\lim_{x \to 2^-} f(x) = \lim_{x \to 2^-} (3x^2 + 12x - 1)$$

$$= 3 \times 4 + 12 \times 2 - 1 = 35$$

Thus, f is continuous at $x = 2$ as well.

Now, $$f'(2^+) = \lim_{h \to 0^+} \frac{f(2+h) - f(2)}{h}$$

$$= \lim_{h \to 0^-} \frac{37 - (2+h) - 35}{h} = -1$$

Similarly, $f'(2^-) = 24 \neq f'(2^+)$

$$f'(2^+) < f(2) \text{ and } f'(2^-) < f(2)$$

$f(x)$ is non-differentiable at $x = 2$.

As f increases on $[-1, 2]$ and decreases on $[2, 3]$, so f has a maximum at $x = 2$.

Example 36 *If $f(x) = \tan^{-1} x - (1/2) \log x$. Then,*

(a) the greatest value of $f(x)$ on $[1/\sqrt{3}, \sqrt{3}]$ is $\pi/6 + (1/4) \log 3$.

(b) the least value of $f(x)$ on $[1/\sqrt{3}, \sqrt{3}]$ is $\pi/3 - (1/4) \log 3$.

(c) $f(x)$ decreases on $(0, \infty)$.

(d) $f(x)$ increases on $(-\infty, 0)$.

Sol. (a, b, c) The domain of $f(x)$ is $(0, \infty)$.

For $x > 0$,

$$f'(x) = \frac{1}{1+x^2} - \frac{1}{2x} = \frac{2x - (1+x^2)}{(1+x^2)\,2x} = -\frac{(1-x)^2}{(1+x^2)\,2x}$$

Thus, $f'(x) < 0$ i.e. $f(x)$ decreases on $(0, \infty)$.

Also, $f'(x) = 0$ if $x = 1$ and $f(1) = \pi/4$,

$f(1/\sqrt{3}) = \pi/6 + (1/4) \log 3$, $f(\sqrt{3}) = \pi/3 - (1/4) \log 3$.

Thus, the greatest value is $\pi/6 + \left(\frac{1}{4}\right) \log 3$ and the least value is $\pi/3 - (1/4) \log 3$.

Passage Based Questions

Passage I

(Ex. Nos. 37 and 38)

For the cubic $f(x) = \frac{x^3}{3} - (m-3)\frac{x^2}{2} + mx + 3 = 0$, find the value of m for which it has

Example 37 *positive point of maximum*

(a) (0, 1]
(b) $(-\infty, 1] \cup [9, \infty)$
(c) $[9, \infty)$
(d) None of these

Example 38 *negative point of minimum*

(a) (0, 1]
(b) $(-\infty, 1] \cup [9, \infty)$
(c) $[9, \infty)$
(d) None of these

Sol. (Ex. Nos. 37 and 38)

Given, $f(x) = \frac{x^3}{3} - (m-3)\frac{x^2}{2} + mx + 3$

$\Rightarrow \quad f'(x) = x^2 - (m-3)x + m$ and $f''(x) = 2x - (m-3)$

37. (c) For positive point of maximum, both roots of $f'(x) = 0$ must be positive.

$\therefore$ Discriminant of $f'(x) = 0$ must be ≥ 0 and sum of roots > 0 and product of roots > 0

$\Rightarrow D \geq 0 \Rightarrow m \in (-\infty, 1] \cup [9, \infty)$

Sum $> 0 \Rightarrow m > 3$

Product $> 0 \Rightarrow m > 0$

On taking intersection, we get $m \in [9, \infty)$

38. (a) For negative point of minimum, both roots of $f'(x) = 0$ must be negative.

$\therefore$ Discriminant of $f'(x) = 0$ must be ≥ 0 and sum of roots < 0 and product of roots > 0

$\Rightarrow D \geq 0 \Rightarrow m \in (-\infty, 1] \cup [9, \infty)$ and $m - 3 < 0$ and $m > 0$

$\Rightarrow m \in (0, 1]$

Passage II

(Ex. Nos. 39 to 40)

Let $f'(\sin x) < 0$ and $f''(\sin x) > 0$, $\forall\, x \in \left(0, \frac{\pi}{2}\right)$

Now, consider a function $g(x) = f(\sin x) + f(\cos x)$

Example 39 *$g(x)$ decreases if x belongs to*

(a) $\left(0, \frac{\pi}{4}\right)$
(b) $\left(\frac{\pi}{4}, \frac{\pi}{2}\right)$
(c) $\left(\frac{\pi}{6}, \frac{\pi}{3}\right)$
(d) None of these

Example 40 *$g(x)$ increases if x belongs to*

(a) $\left(0, \frac{\pi}{4}\right)$
(b) $\left(\frac{\pi}{4}, \frac{\pi}{2}\right)$
(c) $\left(\frac{\pi}{8}, \frac{\pi}{3}\right)$
(d) $\left(\frac{\pi}{6}, \frac{\pi}{3}\right)$

Sol. (Ex. Nos. 39 and 40)

$$f'(\sin x) < 0, \forall\, x \in \left(0, \frac{\pi}{2}\right) \quad \text{...(i)}$$

$$\Rightarrow \quad f'\left(\sin\left(\frac{\pi}{2} - x\right)\right) < 0, \forall\, x \in \left(0, \frac{\pi}{2}\right) \quad \text{...(ii)}$$

Similarly as $f''(\sin x) > 0$ ...(iii)

$$\Rightarrow \quad f''(\cos x) > 0, \forall\, x \in \left(0, \frac{\pi}{2}\right) \quad \text{...(iv)}$$

Now, $g'(x) = f'(\sin x) \cdot \cos x - f'(\cos x) \cdot \sin x$

$\Rightarrow \quad g''(x) = f''(\sin x) \cdot \cos^2 x - f'(\sin x) \cdot \sin x$

$\quad - f''(\cos x)(-\sin^2 x) - f'(\cos x) \cos x$

$\Rightarrow \quad g''(x) > 0, \forall x \in \left(0, \frac{\pi}{2}\right)$ [using Eqs. (i), (ii), (iii) and (iv)]

$\Rightarrow g'(x)$ is increasing function $x \in \left(0, \frac{\pi}{2}\right), g'(x) = 0 \Rightarrow x = \frac{\pi}{4}$

$\Rightarrow g'(x) < 0, \forall x \in \left(0, \frac{\pi}{4}\right)$

$\Rightarrow g(x)$ is decreasing for $\left(0, \frac{\pi}{4}\right)$

and $g'(x) > 0$, for $x \in \left(\frac{\pi}{4}, \frac{\pi}{2}\right)$

$\Rightarrow g(x)$ is increasing for $\left(\frac{\pi}{4}, \frac{\pi}{2}\right)$.

39. (a) **40.** (b)

Passage III

(Ex. Nos. 41 and 42)

Let x_1, x_2, x_3, x_4 be the roots (real or complex) of the equation $x^4 + ax^3 + bx^2 + cx + d = 0$. If $x_1 + x_2 = x_3 + x_4$ and $a, b, c, d \in R$. Then,

Example 41 *If $a = 2$, then the value of $b - c$ is*

(a) -1 (b) 1
(c) -2 (d) 2

Example 42 *If $b < 0$, then how many different values of a, we may have*

(a) 3 (b) 2
(c) 1 (d) 0

Sol. (Ex. Nos. 41-42)

Let $x^4 + ax^3 + bx^2 + cx + d = (x - x_1)(x - x_2)(x - x_3)(x - x_4)$

Let $(x - x_1)(x - x_2) = x^2 + px + q$

and $(x - x_3)(x - x_4) = x^2 + px + r$

$\therefore \quad q = x_1 x_2$ and $r = x_3 x_4$

$$x^4 + ax^3 + bx^2 + cx + d$$
$$= x^4 + 2px^3 + (p^2 + q + r)x^2 + p(q + r)x + qr$$

$\therefore \quad a = 2p, b = p^2 + q + r, c = p(q + r), d = qr$

Clearly, $a^3 - 4ab + 8c = 0$ ...(i)

41. (b) If $a = 2 \Rightarrow b - c = 1$

42. (c) Investigating the nature of the cubic equation of a.

Let $f(a) = a^3 - 4ab + 8c$

$f'(a) = 3a^2 - 4b$

If $\quad b < 0$

$\Rightarrow \quad f'(a) > 0$

$\therefore$ The equation $a^3 - 4ab + 8c = 0$,

has only one real root.

Passage IV

(Ex. Nos. 43 and 44)

Let $f(x) = \begin{cases} \max \{t^3 - t^2 + t + 1, 0 \le t \le x\}, 0 \le x \le 1 \\ \min \{3 - t, 1 < t \le x\}, 1 < x \le 2 \end{cases}$

and $g(x) = \begin{cases} \max \left\{\frac{3}{8t^4} + \frac{1}{2t^3} - \frac{3}{2t^2} + 1, 0 \le t \le x\right\}, 0 \le x \le 1 \\ \min \left\{\frac{3}{8t} + \frac{1}{32 \sin^2 \pi t} + \frac{5}{8}, 1 \le t \le x\right\}, 1 \le x \le 2 \end{cases}$

Define $f(x)$ and $g(x)$ expilicitly and then answer the following questions.

Example 43 *The function $f(x), \forall x \in [0, 2]$ is*

(a) continuous and differentiable.
(b) continuous but not differentiable.
(c) discontinuous and not differentiable.
(d) None of the above

Example 44 *Which of the following is true?*

(a) $\lim_{x \to 1^-} (fog)(x) > \lim_{x \to 1^+} (gof)(x)$
(b) $\lim_{x \to 1^-} (fog)(x) < \lim_{x \to 1^+} (gof)(x)$
(c) $\lim_{x \to 1^-} (fog)(x) = \lim_{x \to 1^+} (gof)(x)$
(d) None of the above

Sol. (Ex. Nos. 43-44)

Consider $f(x)$ in $[0, 1]$

$f'(t) = 3t^2 - 2t + 1 > 0, \forall t \in (0, 1)$

$\Rightarrow f(t)$ is increasing on $(0, 1)$.

Maximum occurs at $t = x$

and $\quad f(x) = \begin{cases} x^3 - x^2 + x + 1, & 0 \le x \le 1 \\ 3 - x, & 1 \le x \le 2 \end{cases}$

Again, consider $g(x)$ in $(0, 1)$.

$$g(t) = \frac{3}{8t^4} + \frac{1}{2t^3} - \frac{3}{2t^2} + 1$$

$$g'(t) = \frac{-3}{2t^5} - \frac{3}{2t^4} + \frac{3}{t^3}$$

$g(t)$ decreases in $[0, 1) \Rightarrow$ maximum occurs, when $t = 0$ and $g(0) = 1$, again consider $g(x)$ function in $[1, 2]$.

$$g(t) = \frac{3}{8t} + \frac{1}{32 \sin^2 \pi t} + \frac{5}{8}$$

$$g'(t) = \frac{-3}{8t^2} - \frac{\pi \sin 2\pi t}{32 \sin^4 \pi t}, \forall t \in R$$

$\therefore g(t)$ is an increasing function in $[1, 2]$.

$\Rightarrow$ Minimum occurs, when $t = 1$ and $g(1) = 1$

Hence, $g(x) = \begin{cases} 1, & 0 \le x \le 1 \\ 1, & 1 < x \le 2 \end{cases} = 1$

$\Rightarrow \quad g(x) = 1, \forall x \in [0, 2]$

43. (b) $f(x)$ is continuous but not differentiable at $x = 1$.

44. (a) $\lim_{x \to 1^-} fog(x) = f(1)$ and $\lim_{x \to 1^+} gof(x) = 1$.

Also, $f(1) > 1$.

Passage V

(Ex. Nos. 45 and 46)

A window of fixed perimeter (including the base of the arch) is in the form of a rectangle surmounted by a semi-circle. The semi-circular portion is fitted with coloured glass, while the rectangular portion is fitted with clear glass. The clear glass transmits three times as much light per square metre as the coloured glass.

Suppose that y is the length and x is the breadth of the rectangular portion and p the perimeter.

Example 45 *The ratio of the sides $y : x$ of the rectangle so that the window transmit the maximum light is*

(a) $3 : 2$ (b) $6 : 6 + \pi$ (c) $6 + \pi : 6$ (d) $1 : 2$

Example 46 *If μ is the amount of light per square metre for the coloured: glass and L is the total light transmitted, then $\left.\frac{dL}{dy}\right|_{y=1}$ is equal to*

(a) $\frac{\mu}{2}\left[3p - 12 - \frac{5\pi}{2}\right]$ (b) $\mu\left[2p - 6 - \frac{3\pi}{2}\right]$

(c) $\mu\left[p - 2 - \frac{\pi}{2}\right]$ (d) $2\mu\left[3p - \frac{\pi}{2}\right]$

Sol. (Ex. Nos. 45 and 46)

Let y be the length and x be the breadth of the rectangular portion. Total perimeter of the window is

$2x + 2y + \left(\frac{1}{2}\right)\pi y = p$ (say). Let amount of light per square metre for the coloured glass be μ. If L is the total light transmitted, then

$$L = 3\mu \times \text{Area of rectangular portion} + \mu \times \text{Area of semi-circular portion}$$

$$= 3\mu xy + \frac{1}{8}\mu\pi y^2$$

$$= \mu\left[\frac{3}{2}y\left(p - \left(2 + \frac{\pi}{2}\right)y\right) + \frac{1}{8}\pi y^2\right]$$

$$\frac{dL}{dy} = \frac{\mu}{2}\left[3p - 6\left(2 + \frac{\pi}{2}\right)y + \frac{\pi}{2}y\right]$$

$$\left.\frac{dL}{dy}\right|_{y=1} = \frac{\mu}{2}\left[3p - 12 - \frac{5\pi}{2}\right]$$

$$\frac{dL}{dy} = 0$$

$$\Rightarrow \quad y = \frac{3p}{12 + \frac{5\pi}{2}}$$

$$\frac{d^2L}{dy^2} = \frac{\mu}{2}\left(-12 - \frac{5\pi}{2}\right) < 0.$$

Therefore, for $y = \frac{3p}{\left[12 + \left(\frac{5\pi}{2}\right)\right]}$, there will be maximum light transmission.

$$\frac{y}{x} = \frac{2 \cdot \frac{3p}{12 + \frac{5\pi}{2}}}{p - \left(2 + \frac{\pi}{2}\right)\frac{3p}{12 + \frac{5\pi}{2}}}$$

$$= \frac{6}{\left(12 + \frac{5\pi}{2}\right) - 3\left(2 + \frac{\pi}{2}\right)} = \frac{6}{6 + \pi}$$

45. (b) **46.** (a)

Stem Based Questions

Stem I

(Ex. Nos. 47 and 48)

Let $f(x) = \left(1 + \frac{1}{x}\right)^x \quad (x > 0)$

and $g(x) = \begin{cases} x \ln\left(1 + \left(\frac{1}{x}\right)\right), & \text{if } 0 < x \le 1 \\ 0, & \text{if } x = 0 \end{cases}$

Example 47 $\lim_{x \to 0^+} g(x) = k$, *then k^2 is ....*

Example 48 $\lim_{n \to \infty}\left\{f\left(\frac{1}{n}\right) \cdot f\left(\frac{2}{n}\right) \cdot f\left(\frac{3}{n}\right) \ldots f\left(\frac{n}{n}\right)\right\}^{\frac{1}{n}} = e^{\lambda}$, *then 4λ is ....*

Sol. (Ex. Nos. 47 and 48)

47. (0) $\lim_{x \to 0^+} x \ln\left(1 + \frac{1}{x}\right) = \lim_{x \to 0^+} \frac{\ln\left(\frac{x+1}{x}\right)}{\frac{1}{x}} \quad \left[\frac{\infty}{\infty} \text{ form}\right]$

Using L' Hospital's rule,

$$l = \lim_{x \to 0} -\left(\frac{1}{x+1} - \frac{1}{x}\right)x^2 = \lim_{x \to 0}\left(\frac{1}{x} - \frac{1}{x+1}\right)x^2$$

$$= \lim_{x \to 0} \frac{1}{x(x+1)} \cdot x^2 = \lim_{x \to 0} \frac{x}{(x+1)} = 0 = k$$

$\therefore k^2 = 0$

48. (2) Given, $\lim_{n\to\infty}\left(f\left(\frac{1}{n}\right)f\left(\frac{2}{n}\right)\cdots f\left(\frac{n}{n}\right)\right)^{\frac{1}{n}}$

$$l=\left(\prod_{k=1}^{n}\left(1+\frac{n}{k}\right)^{\frac{k}{n}}\right)^{\frac{1}{n}}$$

$$\left[\text{given } f(x)=\left(1+\frac{1}{x}\right)^{x} \text{ and } f\left(\frac{k}{n}\right)=\left(1+\frac{n}{k}\right)^{\frac{k}{n}}\right]$$

On taking log both sides, we get

$$\ln l=\lim_{n\to\infty}\frac{1}{n}\cdot\sum_{k=1}^{n}\ln\left(1+\frac{n}{k}\right)^{\frac{k}{n}}$$

$$=\lim_{n\to\infty}\frac{1}{n}\cdot\sum_{k=1}^{n}\frac{k}{n}\ln\left(1+\frac{1}{\frac{k}{n}}\right)$$

$$=\int_0^1 \underset{\text{II}}{x}\ \underset{\text{I}}{\ln\left(1+\frac{1}{x}\right)}dx=\left[\ln\left(1+\frac{1}{x}\right)\cdot\frac{x^2}{2}\right]_0^1+\int_0^1\left(\frac{1}{x}-\frac{1}{x+1}\right)\cdot\frac{x^2}{2}dx$$

$$=\left(\frac{1}{2}\ln 2-0\right)+\frac{1}{2}\int_0^1\frac{x+1-1}{x+1}dx$$

$$=\frac{1}{2}\ln 2+\frac{1}{2}[x-ln(x+1)]_0^1$$

$$=\frac{1}{2}\ln+\frac{1}{2}[(1-\ln 2)-0]=\frac{1}{2}$$

$\Rightarrow$ $l=\sqrt{e}=e^{\lambda}$

$\Rightarrow$ $\lambda=\frac{1}{2}\Rightarrow 4\lambda=2$

Stem II

(Ex. Nos. 49 and 50)

There is a parabola $y=x^2+x+a$, where a be a parameter which changes at a constant rate such that $\frac{da}{dt}=5$. If $a=0$, when $t=0$. Let $A(t)$ be the area bounded by $y=x^2+x+a$, X-axis, Y-axis and $x=a$ at the time t.

Example 49 *$A(2)=\lambda$, then 3λ is ………*

Example 50 *6 times of maximum value of $A(t)$, when $t\in[0,2]$, is ………*

Sol. (Ex. Nos. 49-50)

$\frac{da}{dt}=5$

$\therefore$ $a=5t+C$

$\therefore$ $a=5t$ $\quad [a=0, \text{ when } t=0]$

$\therefore$ $y=x^2+x+5t$

Now $I=\int_0^{10}(x^2+x+10)dx$

$$\Rightarrow \quad I=\left(\frac{x^3}{3}+\frac{x^2}{2}+10x\right)\Bigg|_0^{10}=\frac{1000}{3}+\frac{100}{2}+100$$

$$=\frac{1000+450}{3}=\frac{1450}{3}$$

$$\int_0^{5t}(x^2+x+5t)dt=\left(\frac{x^3}{3}+\frac{x^2}{2}+5tx\right)_0^{5t}$$

49. (1450) $A(t)=\frac{125t^3}{3}+\frac{25t^2}{2}+25t^2$

$\therefore$ $A(2)=\frac{1000}{3}+50+100=\frac{1450}{3}=\lambda\Rightarrow 3\lambda=1450$

50. (2900) $A'(t)=125t^2+25t+50t>0$

$\therefore$ Maximum value of $A(t)=\frac{1000}{3}+\frac{1000}{2}+100=\frac{1450}{3}$

So, 6 times maximum value of $A(t)=6\times\frac{1450}{3}=2900$

Stem III

(Ex. Nos. 51 and 52)

We are given the curves $y=\int_{-\infty}^{x}f(t)\,dt$ through the point $\left(0,\frac{1}{2}\right)$ and $y=f(x)$, where $f(x)>0$ and $f(x)$ is differentiable, $\forall\, x\in R$ through (0, 1). If tangents drawn to both the curves at the points with equal abscissae intersect on the same point on the X-axis, then

Example 51 *Number of solutions $f(x)=2ex$ is equal to ………*

Example 52 $\lim_{x\to\infty}(f(x))^{f(-x)}$ *is ………*

Sol. (Ex. Nos. 51 and 52)

51. (1) We have, the equations of the tangents to the curves $y=\int_{-\infty}^{x}f(t)dt$ and $y=f(x)$ at arbitrary points on them are

$$Y-\int_{-\infty}^{x}f(t)dt=f(x)(X-x) \quad \text{...(i)}$$

and $\quad Y-f(x)=f'(x)(X-x)$ ...(ii)

As Eqs. (i) and (ii), intersect at the same point on X-axis.

On putting $Y=0$ and equating x-coordinates, we have

$$x-\frac{f(x)}{f'(x)}=x-\frac{\int_{-\infty}^{x}f(t)dt}{f(x)}\Rightarrow\frac{f(x)}{\int_{-\infty}^{x}f(t)dt}=\frac{f'(x)}{f(x)}$$

$$\Rightarrow \quad \int_{-\infty}^{x}f(t)=cf(x) \quad \text{...(iii)}$$

As, $f(0)=1 \Rightarrow \int_{-\infty}^{0} f(t)dt = \frac{1}{2} = c \times 1 \Rightarrow c = \frac{1}{2}$

$\Rightarrow \int_{-\infty}^{x} f(t)dt = \frac{1}{2} f(x)$, differentiating both the sides and on integrating and using boundary condition, we get

$$f(x) = e^{2x}, y = 2ex \text{ is tangent to } y = e^{2x}$$

$\Rightarrow$ Number of solutions = 1

52. (1) Clearly, $f(x)$ is increasing for all x.

$$\lim_{x \to \infty} (e^{2x})^{e^{-2x}} = 1 \quad [\infty^0 \text{ form}]$$

Single Integer Answer Type Questions

Example 53 *The radius of a right circular cylinder increases at a constant rate. Its altitude is a linear function of the radius and increases three times as fast as radius. When the radius is 1 cm the altitude is 6 cm. When the radius is 6 cm, the volume is increasing at the rate of 1 cu cm/s, when the radius is 36 cm, the volume is increasing at a rate of n cu cm/s. The value of n / 11 is equal to ....*

Sol. (3) Here, $\frac{dr}{dt} = c$ and $h = ar + b$

Also, $\frac{dh}{dt} = 3\frac{dr}{dt}$ [given]

$\therefore \quad a\frac{dr}{dt} = 3\frac{dr}{dt} \Rightarrow a = 3$

Hence, $h = 3r + b$

When, $r = 1, h = 6 \Rightarrow 6 = 3 + b \Rightarrow b = 3$

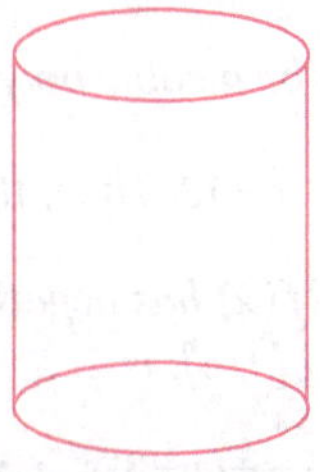

$\therefore h = 3(r+1)$

$$V = \pi r^2 h = 3\pi r^2(r+1) = 3\pi(r^3 + r^2)$$

$$\frac{dV}{dt} = 3\pi(3r^2 + 2r)\frac{dr}{dt}$$

Where $r = 6, \frac{dV}{dt} = 1$ cu/s

$\therefore \quad 1 = 3\pi(108 + 12)\frac{dr}{dt} \Rightarrow 360\pi \frac{dr}{dt} = 1$

Again, when $r = 23, \frac{dV}{dt} = n$

$$n = 3\pi((3.36)^2 + 2.36)\frac{dr}{dt}$$

$$n = 3\pi \cdot 36(110) \cdot \frac{1}{360\pi} \Rightarrow n = 33$$

$$\Rightarrow \frac{n}{11} = \frac{33}{11} = 3$$

Example 54 *The set of all points where $f(x)$ is increasing is $(a, b) \cup (c, \infty)$, then find $[a+b+c]$ (where $[\cdot]$ denotes GIF). Given that $f(x) = 2f\left(\frac{x^2}{2}\right) + f(6-x^2), \forall x \in R$ and $f''(x) > 0, \forall x \in R$.*

Sol. (0) Here, $f(x) = 2f\left(\frac{x^2}{2}\right) + f(6-x^2)$

$$f'(x) = 2f'\left(\frac{x^2}{2}\right) \cdot x - 2xf'(6-x^2)$$

$$f'(x) = 2x\left(f'\left(\frac{x^2}{2}\right) - f'(6-x^2)\right)$$

$$f'\left(\frac{x^2}{2}\right) > f'(6-x)^2, \text{ if } \frac{x^2}{2} > 6 - x^2$$

[$\because f'(x)$ is increasing]

$$\frac{x^2}{2} > 6 - x^2 \Rightarrow x^2 > 4$$

$$\Rightarrow \quad f'\left(\frac{x^2}{2}\right) - f'(6-x^2) > 0$$

When $x < -2$ or $x > 2 \Rightarrow f'(x) > 0$

When $x(-2, 0) \cup (2, \infty)$

$\therefore \quad a + b + c = 0 \Rightarrow [a+b+c] = 0$

Example 55 *The graphs $y = 2x^3 - 4x + 2$ and $y = x^3 + 2x - 1$ intersect at exactly 3 distinct points. The slope of the line passing through two of these points is equal to.....*

Sol. (8) Let (x_1, y_1) and (x_2, y_2) be two of these points.

Given, $y = x^3 + 2x - 1$ and $y = 2x^3 - 4x + 2$

$\therefore \quad y_1 = 2x_1^3 - 4x_1 + 2$ ...(i)

and $2y_1 = 2x_1^3 + 4x_1 - 2$ ...(ii)

On subtracting Eq. (i) from Eq (ii), we get

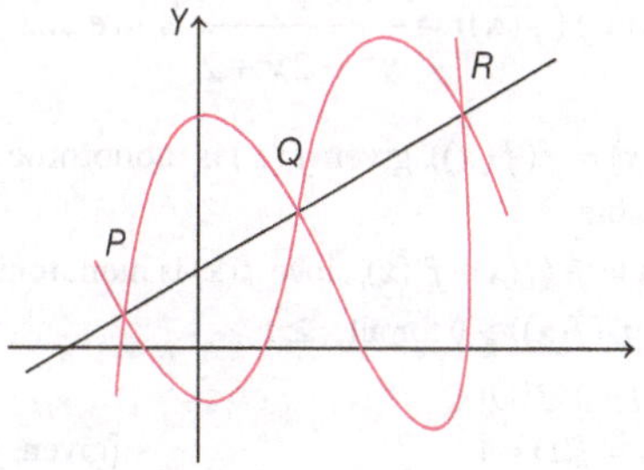

$y_1 = 8x_1 - 4$ ...(iii)

Similarly, $y_2 = 8x_2 - 4$ ...(iv)

$$y_2 - y_1 = 8(x_2 - x_1)$$

$$\frac{y_2 - y_1}{x_2 - x_1} = 8$$

Example 56 *The length of the shortest path that begins at the point (2, 5), touches the X-axis and then ends at a point on the circle $x^2+y^2+12x-20y+120=0$, is λ, then $\frac{2\lambda}{13}$ is ......*

Sol. (2) Circles with centre $(-6, 10)$ and radius $=\sqrt{36+100-120}=4$

Now, let $(a, 0)$ be a point on the X-axis. If y is the distance from A to P and P to M

$$y=\sqrt{(a-2)^2+25}+\sqrt{(a+6)^2+100}-4$$

$$\frac{dy}{da}=\frac{2(a-2)}{2\sqrt{(a-2)^2+25}}+\frac{2(a+6)}{2\sqrt{(a+6)^2+100}}$$

$\frac{dy}{da}$ can be zero only if $a-2>0$ and $a+6<0$ not possible or $a-2<0$ and $a+6>0$, hence $a\in(-6, 2)$

Solving $\frac{dy}{da}=0$ gives $a=10$ (rejected) or $a=-\frac{2}{3}$

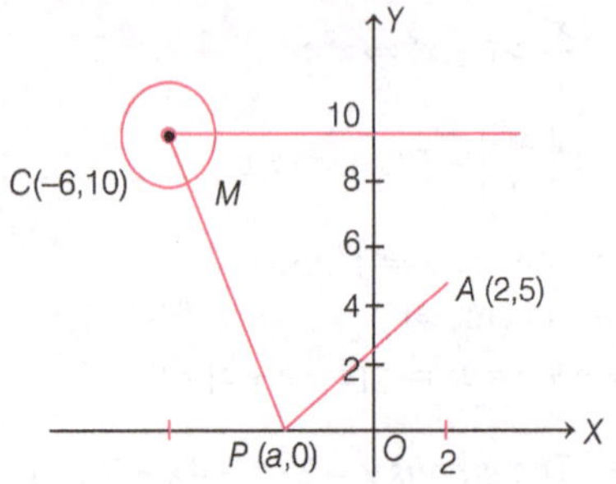

Hence, $y_{\min}=\sqrt{\frac{64}{9}+25}+\sqrt{\frac{256}{9}+100}-4$

$$=\frac{17}{3}+\frac{\sqrt{1156}}{3}-4=\frac{17}{3}+\frac{34}{3}-4=17-4=13=\lambda$$

$\therefore \quad \frac{2\lambda}{13}=2$

Example 57 *If $f:[1,\infty)\to R$: $f(x)$ is monotonic and differentiable function and $f(1)=1$, then number of solutions of the equation $f(f(x))=\frac{1}{x^2-2x+2}$ is/are ......*

Sol. (1) Let $g(x)=f(f(x))$, given $f(x)$ is monotonic and differentiable

$\therefore \quad g'(x)=f'(f(x))\cdot f'(x)$, since $f(x)$ is monotonic

$\Rightarrow f'(x)\cdot f'(f(x))>0$ for all $x\geq 1$

Here, $g(1)=f(f(1))$

$\therefore \quad g(1)=f(1)=1 \qquad$ [given, $f(1)=1$)] ...(i)

Since, $g(x)$ is increasing for $x\geq 1$.

$\therefore \quad g(x)\geq g(1)\Rightarrow \frac{1}{x^2-2x+2}\geq 1$

$\Rightarrow \frac{1}{(x-1)^2+1}\geq 1$, i.e. only possible, when $x=1$.

$\therefore$ Number of solutions of $f(f(x))$ is 1.

Example 58 *The set of values of a for which the equation $x^4+4x^3+ax^2+4x+1=0$ has all its roots real is given by $(a_1, a_2)\cup\{a_3\}$. Then, $|a_3+a_2|$ is ......*

Sol. (4) Here, $x^4+4x^3+ax^2+4x+1=0$

On dividing by x^2 $\left(x^2+\frac{1}{x^2}\right)+4\left(x+\frac{1}{x}\right)+a=0$

$$\left(x+\frac{1}{x}\right)^2+4\left(x+\frac{1}{x}\right)+(a-2)=0$$

Put $x+\frac{1}{x}=y, \qquad [y\geq 2 \text{ or } \leq -2]$

$\therefore \quad y^2+4y+(a-2)=0$

For y to be real $D\geq 0$.

$16-4(a-2)\geq 0\Rightarrow a\leq 6 \qquad$ ...(i)

Also, if $f(y)=y^2+4y+(a-2)\Rightarrow f(-2)\cdot f(2)\geq 0$

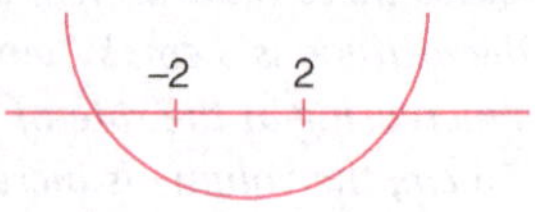

$\Rightarrow (4+8+a-2)(4-8+a-2)\geq 0$

$\Rightarrow \qquad (a+10)(a-6)\geq 0 \qquad$ ...(ii)

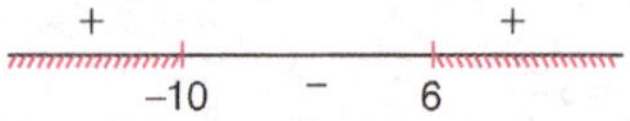

From Eqs. (i) and (ii), we get $a\in(-\infty,-10)\cup\{6\}$

When $a=6$, $y^2+4y+4=0\Rightarrow y=-2$

$\therefore \quad a\in(-\infty,-10]\cup P\{6\}$

$a_2=-10, a_3=6\Rightarrow |a_2+a_3|=4$

Example 59 *Let $f(x)$ be a cubic polynomial defined by $f(x)=\frac{x^3}{3}+(a-3)x^2+x-13$. Then, the sum of all possible value(s) of 'a' for which $f(x)$ has negative point of local minimum in the interval [1, 5], is ......*

Sol. (5) We have, $f(x)=\frac{x^3}{3}+(a-3)x^2+x-13$

$\therefore$ For $f(x)$ have negative point of local minimum, the equation $f'(x)=0$ must have two distinct negative roots.

Now, $f'(x)=x^2+2(a-3)x+1$

$\therefore$ Following condition(s) must be satisfied simultaneously

(i) $D>0$ (ii) $\alpha+\beta<0$ (iii) $\alpha\beta>0$

Now, $D>0\Rightarrow 4(a-3)^2-4>0\Rightarrow (a-2)(a-4)>0$

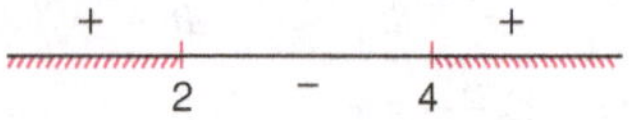

$\therefore \quad a\in(-\infty, 2)\cup(4,\infty) \qquad$ ...(i)

Also, $-2(a-3)<0\Rightarrow a-3>0\Rightarrow a>3 \qquad$ ...(ii)

and product of root(s) $=1>0$, $\forall\, a\in R$

$\therefore$ (i) $\cap$ (ii) $\cap$ (iii) $\Rightarrow a\in(4,\infty) \qquad$ ...(iii)

$\therefore \quad a=5$, as $a\in[1, 5]$

Thus, sum of all possible values is 5.

Example 60 *Consider a polynomial $P(x)$ of the least degree that has a maximum equal to 6 at $x=1$ and a minimum equal to 2 at $x=3$. Then, the value of $P(2)+P'(0)-7$, is ......*

Sol. (6) The polynomial is an everywhere differentiable function. Therefore, the points of extremum can only be roots of derivative, Further more, the derivative of a polynomial is a polynomial.

The polynomial of the least degree with roots $x_1=1$ and $x_2=3$ has the form $a(x-1)(x-3)$.

Hence, $P'(x)=a(x-1)(x-3)=a(x^2-4x+3)$

Since, at $x=1$, there must be $P(1)=6$, we have

$$P(x)=\int_1^x P'(x)dx+6=a\int_1^x (x^2-4x+3)dx+6$$

$$=a\left(\frac{x^3}{3}-2x^2+3x-\frac{4}{3}\right)+6$$

Also, $P(3)=2 \Rightarrow a=3$

Hence, $P(x)=x^3-6x^2+9x+2$

Now, $P(2)=8+24+18+2=4$, also

$$P'(x)=3(x^2-4x+3) \Rightarrow P'(0)=9$$

$\therefore P(2)+P'(0)-7=6$

Example 61 *The function $y=\dfrac{ax+b}{(x-1)(x-4)}$ has turning point at $P(2,-1)$ then sum of values of a and b and that y is maximum at P is ......*

Sol. (1) We have, $y=\dfrac{ax+b}{(x-1)(x-4)}$ ...(i)

So that $\dfrac{dy}{dx}=\dfrac{a(x^2-5x+4)-(ax+b)(2x-5)}{(x^2-5x+4)^2}$ ...(iii)

Since $P(2,-1)$ is the turning point,

$\therefore$ P lies on (i) and at P, $\dfrac{dy}{dx}=0$ $\because$ $P(2,-1)$ lies on (i)

On substituting $x=2, y=-1$ in (i)

Also, at $P(2,-1) \Rightarrow \dfrac{dy}{dx}=\dfrac{-2a+(2a+b)}{4}=0 \Rightarrow b=0$

From Eq. (iii), we get $a=1$

Hence, $a=1, b=0$

On putting $a=1, b=0$ in (i), we get

$$y=\frac{x}{x^2-5x+4}=\frac{1}{x-5+\frac{4}{x}}=\frac{1}{z} \quad \text{[say]}$$

where $z=x-5+\dfrac{4}{x}$

$$\Rightarrow \frac{dz}{dx}=1-\frac{4}{x^2}, \frac{d^2z}{dx^2}=\frac{8}{x^3}$$

For maximum or minimum of $z \cdot \dfrac{dz}{dx}=0 \Rightarrow x=\pm 2$

When $x=2, y=-1$ and $\dfrac{d^2z}{dx^2}=1(+ve)$

$\Rightarrow z$ is minimum at $P(2,-1)$ $\quad \therefore a+b=1.$

Hence, $y=\dfrac{1}{z}$ is maximum at $P(2,-1)$.

Numerical Value Type Questions

Example 62 *$f(x)=\left(\alpha-\dfrac{1}{\alpha}-x\right)(4-3x^2)$ has just one maximum and one minimum value, then the difference between them is $\dfrac{p}{q}\left(\dfrac{\alpha+1}{\alpha}\right)^3$ where p, q are co-prime number. The $2p+3q$ is ....*

Sol. (35) Let $f(x)=\left(\alpha-\dfrac{1}{\alpha}-x\right)(4-3x^2)$

$$\therefore f'(x)=9x^2-6\left(\alpha-\frac{1}{\alpha}\right)x-4$$

This is a quadratic in x and hence $f(x)=0$ gives one value, which is maximum and another value which is minimum. The two roots are

$$\therefore \quad x=\frac{6\left(\alpha-\frac{1}{\alpha}\right)\pm\sqrt{36\left(\alpha-\frac{1}{\alpha}\right)^2+144}}{18}$$

$$=\frac{2\alpha}{3} \text{ or } -\frac{2}{3\alpha}$$

The difference between the values of $f(x)$ at $x=-\dfrac{2}{3\alpha}$ and $x=\dfrac{2\alpha}{3}$ is

$$=\left(\alpha-\frac{1}{\alpha}+\frac{2}{3\alpha}\right)\left(4-\frac{4}{3\alpha^2}\right)-\left(\alpha-\frac{1}{\alpha}-\frac{2\alpha}{3}\right)\left(4-\frac{4\alpha^2}{3}\right)$$

$$=4\left(\alpha-\frac{1}{\alpha}\right)-\frac{4}{3\alpha^2}\left(\alpha-\frac{1}{\alpha}\right)+\frac{8}{3\alpha}-\frac{8}{9\alpha^3}-4\left(\alpha-\frac{1}{\alpha}\right)$$

$$+\frac{4\alpha^2}{3}\left(\alpha-\frac{1}{\alpha}\right)+\frac{8\alpha}{3}-\frac{8\alpha^3}{9}$$

$$=\frac{8}{3}\left(\alpha+\frac{1}{\alpha}\right)+\frac{4}{3}\left(\alpha-\frac{1}{\alpha}\right)\left(\alpha^2-\frac{1}{\alpha^2}\right)-\frac{8}{9}\left(\alpha^3+\frac{1}{\alpha^3}\right)$$

$$=\frac{1}{9}\left(\alpha+\frac{1}{\alpha}\right)\left[24+12\left(\alpha-\frac{1}{\alpha}\right)^2-8\left(\alpha^2+\frac{1}{\alpha^2}-1\right)\right]$$

$$=\frac{4}{9}\left(\alpha+\frac{1}{\alpha}\right)^3$$

$\therefore \quad p=4, q=9$

Hence, $2p+3q=35$

Example 63 *Let two non-collinear vectors **a** and **b** inclined at an angle $\dfrac{2\pi}{3}$ be such that $|\mathbf{a}|=3$ and $|\mathbf{b}|=4$. A point P moves so that at any time t the position vector **OP**, where O is the origin) is given as $\mathbf{OP}=(e^t+e^{-t})\mathbf{a}+(e^t-e^{-t})\mathbf{b}$. If the least distance of P from origin is $\sqrt{2}\sqrt{\sqrt{a}-b}$ where a, $b \in N$, then the value of $(a+b)$ is ....*

Sol. (72) We have, $(\mathbf{OP})^2 = (e^t + e^{-t})^2(\mathbf{a})^2$

$$+ (e^t - e^{-t})^2(\mathbf{b})^2 + 2(e^t + e^{-t})(e^t - e^{-t})(\mathbf{a}\cdot\mathbf{b})$$

$$\left[\begin{array}{l}(\mathbf{a})^2 = |\,a\,|^2 = 9, (\mathbf{b})^2 = |\,\mathbf{b}\,|^2 = 16 \\ \text{and } \mathbf{a}\cdot\mathbf{b} = |\,\mathbf{a}\,|\,|\,\mathbf{b}\,| \cos\dfrac{2\pi}{3}\end{array}\right]$$

$$\Rightarrow \quad |\,OP\,|^2 = 9(e^t + e^{-t})^2 + 16(e^t - e^{-t})^2$$

$$+ 2(e^{2t} - e^{-2t})\cdot 3\cdot 4\cdot\left(-\frac{1}{2}\right)$$

$$= 13e^{2t} + 5e^{-2t} - 14$$

Now, $\dfrac{d}{dt}|\,OP\,|^2 = 0 \Rightarrow 26e^{2t} - 10e^{-2t} = 0$

$$\Rightarrow \quad e^{4t} = \frac{5}{13}, \text{ so } e^{2t} = \frac{\sqrt{5}}{\sqrt{13}}$$

$$\therefore \quad |\,OP\,|^2_{\min} = 13\left(\frac{\sqrt{5}}{\sqrt{13}}\right) + 5\left(\frac{\sqrt{13}}{\sqrt{5}}\right) - 14$$

$$\Rightarrow \quad |\,OP\,|^2_{\min} = 2\sqrt{65} - 14$$

$$\Rightarrow \quad |\,OP\,|_{\min} = \sqrt{2}\,\sqrt{\sqrt{65} - 7} = \sqrt{2}\,\sqrt{\sqrt{a} - b}.$$

So, $a = 65, b = 7$

Hence, $(a + b) = 72$.

Example 64 *Let $x, y \in R$ in the interval $(0, 1)$ and $x + y = 1$. If the minimum value of the expression $x^x + y^y$ is ....*

Sol. (12) Let $Z = x^x + (1 - x)^{1 - x}$

$$Z = f(x) + f(1 - x), \text{ where } f(x) = x^x$$

$$\frac{dZ}{dx} = f'(x) - f'(1 - x) = 0$$

For maxima and minima, $\dfrac{dZ}{dx} = 0$

$$\Rightarrow \quad f'(x) = f'(1 - x) \Rightarrow x = \frac{1}{2}$$

$$Z\big|_{x = \frac{1}{x}} = f\left(\frac{1}{2}\right) + f\left(\frac{1}{2}\right) = 2f\left(\frac{1}{2}\right) = 2\cdot\left(\frac{1}{2}\right)^{\frac{1}{2}} = \sqrt{2}$$

$$\frac{d^2Z}{dx^2} = f''(x) + f''(1 - x)$$

$$\left.\frac{d^2Z}{dx^2}\right|_{x = \frac{1}{2}} = 2f''\left(\frac{1}{2}\right) > 0,$$

$$\left[\begin{array}{l}\because \quad f'(x) = x^x(1 + \ln x) \\ \Rightarrow \quad f''(x) = x^x\cdot\dfrac{1}{x} + (1 + \ln x)^2 x^x \\ \Rightarrow f''\left(\dfrac{1}{2}\right) > 0\end{array}\right]$$

$\therefore$ Minimum value of $Z = \sqrt{2} = k$

Hence, $5k^2 + 2 = 12$

Example 65 *If the function $y = f(x)$ is represented parametrically by $x = t^5 - 5t^3 - 20t + 7$ and $y = 4t^3 - 3t^2 - 18t + 3 (-2 < t < 2)$, then find the maximum value of $y = f(x)$.*

Sol. (14) Given, $x = \phi(t) = t^5 - 5t^3 - 20t + 7$

$$\Rightarrow \quad \frac{dx}{dt} = \phi'(t) = 5t^4 - 15t^2 - 20$$

$$= 5(t^4 - 3t^2 - 4)$$

$$= 5(t^2 - 4)(t^2 + 1) \neq 0, \text{ if } -2 < t < 2$$

and $\quad y = \psi(t) = 4t^3 - 3t^2 - 18t + 3$

$$\frac{dy}{dt} = \psi'(t) = 12t^2 - 6t - 18$$

For maxima and minima $\dfrac{dy}{dt} = 0$

$$\Rightarrow \quad 12t^2 - 6t - 18 = 0$$

$$\Rightarrow \quad 6(2t^2 - t - 3) = 0 \Rightarrow t = -1, \frac{3}{2}$$

Both values of $t \in (-2, 2)$.

Now, $\dfrac{d^2y}{dt^2} = \psi''(t) = 24t - 6$

$\therefore$ $\psi''(-1) = -24 - 6 = -30 < 0, t = 1$ is the point of maxima.

and $\psi''\left(\dfrac{3}{2}\right) = 36 - 6 = 30 > 0$

Hence, $t = \dfrac{3}{2}$ is the point of minima.

$\therefore$ Maximum value of $y = 14$ at $t = -1$.

Example 66 *Given that $S = |\sqrt{x^2 + 4x + 5} - \sqrt{x^2 + 2x + 5}\,|$ for all real x, then the maximum value of S is P, then $4P^2 + 17$ is*

Sol. (25) Here, $S = \left|\sqrt{(x + 2)^2 + 1} - \sqrt{(x + 1)^2 + 4}\right|$

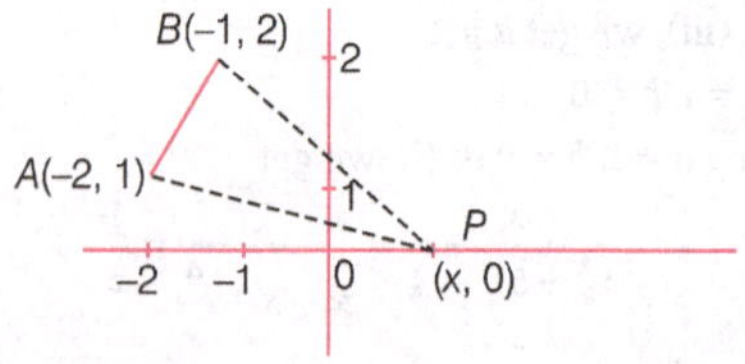

$$\therefore \quad S = \left|\sqrt{(x - (-2))^2 + (1 - 0)^2} - \sqrt{(x - (-1))^2 + (2 - 0)^2}\right|$$

$$= |\,PA - PB\,| \qquad \text{...(i)}$$

Since, $|\,PA - PB\,| \leq AB$, using triangle law

$$\therefore |\,PA - PB\,|_{\max} = \sqrt{1 + 1} = \sqrt{2}$$

$$[\because AB = \sqrt{-1 + 2^2 + (2 - 1)^2} = \sqrt{2}] \text{ ...(ii)}$$

$$\therefore \quad S_{\max} = \sqrt{2} \Rightarrow P = \sqrt{2}$$

$\therefore$ $4P^2 + 17 = 8 + 17 = 25$

JEE SCANNER

Example 67 Similar to PYQ Asked in JEE Main 2024

Find the maximum and minimum value of $f(x)=\dfrac{40}{3x^4+8x^3-18x^2+60}$ is $\dfrac{p}{q}$, where p and q are co-prime, then $p+q$ is ....

Sol. (385) Given, $f(x)=\dfrac{40}{3x^4+8x^3-18x^2+60}$ is maximum or minimum. According by $3x^4+8x^3-18x^2+60$ is minimum or maximum.

Then, f_{max} if $3x^4+8x^3-18x^2+60$ is minimum.

f_{min} if $3x^4+8x^3-18x^2+60$ is maximum.

Let $g(x)=3x^4+8x^3-18x^2+60$

$\Rightarrow g'(x)=12x(x^2+2x-3)$

$\Rightarrow g'(x)=12x(x+3)(x-1)$

Using number line rule,

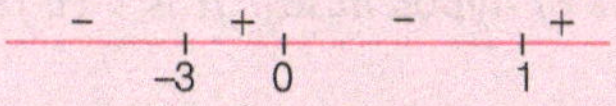

which indicates $g'(x)$ changes sign from negative to positive at $x=-3, 1$.

$\therefore$ Local minimum at $x=-3, 1$

and local maximum at $x=0$

[as changes from positive to negative]

$\Rightarrow g(x)$ is maximum at $x=0$

i.e. $g_{max}(0)=60$ and for $g(x)$ to be minimum,

$g_{min}(-3)=243-216-162+60=-75$

$g_{min}(1)=3+8-18+60=53$

On substituting these values in Eq. (i), we get

$f_{max}(x)$, when g_{min} i.e. $f(x)=\dfrac{40}{-75}$ and $\dfrac{40}{53}$

Maximum value $=\dfrac{40}{53}, \dfrac{-8}{15}$

$f_{min}(x)$, when g_{max} i. e. $f(x)=\dfrac{40}{60}=\dfrac{2}{3}$

Minimum value $=\dfrac{2}{3}$

$$\text{Sum}=\frac{40}{53}+\frac{2}{3}=\frac{120+106}{159}=\frac{226}{159}$$

$\therefore \quad p=226, q=159$

Hence, $p+q=385$

Skill Builder

Let $f(x)=3\sqrt{x-3}+\sqrt{9-x}$ be a real valued function. If α and β are respectively the minimum and the maximum values of f, then $(\alpha^2+\beta^2)$ is equal to ....

For Sol.

Example 68 *In the graph of the function $y=\dfrac{3}{\sqrt{2}}x\log x$, where $x\in[e^{-1.5}, \infty]$ and the point $P(x, y)$ such that the segment of the tangent to the graph of the function at the point, intercepted between the point P and Y-axis, is shortest, then $(3\ln x)^4$ is ....*

Sol. (16) Given, $y=\dfrac{3}{\sqrt{2}}x\log x$

On differentiating w.r.t. x the given function, we have

$$\frac{dy}{dx}=\frac{3}{\sqrt{2}}\left(x\cdot\frac{1}{x}+\log_e x\right)=\frac{3}{\sqrt{2}}(1+\log_e x)$$

Let the point $P(x, y)\Rightarrow P\left(x, \dfrac{3}{\sqrt{2}}x\log_e x\right)$

Hence, the equation of tangent to the curve at the point $P\left(x, \dfrac{3}{\sqrt{2}}x\log_e x\right)$ is

$$Y-\frac{3}{\sqrt{2}}x\log_e x=\frac{3}{\sqrt{2}}(1+\log_e x)(X-x)$$

When it cuts Y-axis, $X=0$

Thus, $y=\dfrac{3}{\sqrt{2}}x\log_e x-\dfrac{3}{\sqrt{2}}(1+\log_e x)x$

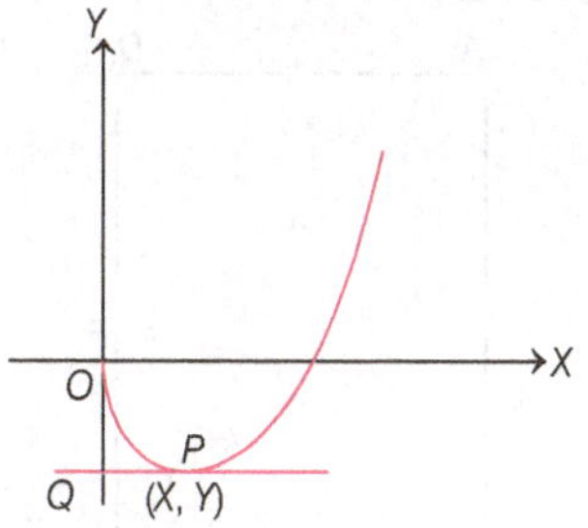

So, $y=-\dfrac{3}{\sqrt{2}}x$

Hence, the given tangent intersects axis at $Q\left(0, -\dfrac{3}{\sqrt{2}}x\right)$.

Now, $PQ^2=x^2+\left(y+\dfrac{3}{\sqrt{2}}x\right)^2=x^2+\left(\dfrac{3}{\sqrt{2}}x(1+\log_e x)\right)^2$

$$PQ^2=x^2\left[1+\frac{9}{2}(1+\log_e x)^2\right]$$

On differentiating w.r.t. x, we have

$$\frac{d(PQ)^2}{dx}=x^2\left[\frac{9}{2}\cdot 2(1+\log_e x)\cdot\frac{1}{x}\right]+\left[1+\frac{9}{2}(1+\log_e x)^2\right]2x$$

$$=x\,[9(1+\log_e x)+2+9(1+\log_e x)^2]$$

For extremum, $\dfrac{d(PQ)^2}{dx}=0$

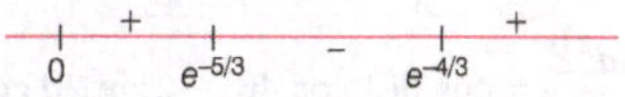

Since, $x\neq 0, 9(1+\log x)^2+9(1+\log x)+2=0$

$$\Rightarrow \quad (1+\log x) = -\frac{1}{3}, -\frac{2}{3}$$

$$\Rightarrow \quad \log x = -\frac{4}{3}, -\frac{5}{3} \Rightarrow x = e^{-\frac{4}{3}}, e^{-\frac{5}{3}}$$

$x = e^{-\frac{5}{3}}$ lie outside the interval $(e^{-1.5}, \infty)$.

The sign scheme for $\frac{d(PQ)^2}{dx}$ is shown in figure which shows that PQ is minimum.

Therefore, PQ is minimum when $x = e^{-\frac{4}{3}}$.

$$\therefore \quad (3\ln x)^2 = \left[3\cdot\left(-\frac{4}{3}\right)\right]^2 = 16$$

Example 69 *One corner of a long rectangular sheet of paper of width 1 unit is folded over so as to reach the opposite edge of the sheet. The minimum length of the crease is k, the $(4k^2)$ is ....*

Sol. (27) Let $ABCD$ be the rectangular sheet whose corner C is folded over along EF so as to reach the edge AB at C'.

Let $EF = x$

$\angle FEC = \theta = \angle FEC'$

$\therefore \; EC = x\cos\theta = EC'$

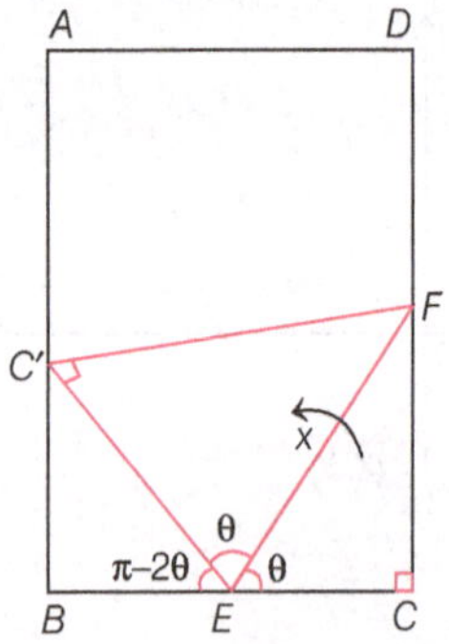

From $\Delta BEC'$, we have

$$BE = C'E\cos(\pi - 2\theta)$$

$$\Rightarrow \quad BE = -x\cos\theta\cdot\cos 2\theta$$

$$\therefore \quad BC = BE + EC$$

$$1 = -x\cos\theta\cos 2\theta + x\cos\theta$$

$$\Rightarrow \quad x = \frac{1}{\cos\theta(1-\cos 2\theta)} \quad \text{...(i)}$$

Let $Z = \cos\theta(1-\cos 2\theta)$ to be minimum, Z has to be maximum.

$$Z = \cos\theta(1-\cos 2\theta) \quad \text{...(ii)}$$

On differentiating Eq. (ii) w.r.t. θ, we get

$$\frac{dZ}{d\theta} = \cos\theta(0 + 2\sin 2\theta) - \sin\theta(1-\cos 2\theta)$$

and
$$\frac{d^2Z}{d\theta^2} = \cos\theta(4\cos 4\theta) - 2\sin 2\theta\cos\theta\sin\theta - \sin\theta(2\sin 2\theta) - \cos\theta(1-\cos 2\theta)$$

For maximum or minimum,

$$\frac{dZ}{d\theta} = 0 \Rightarrow 2\sin\theta(2 - 3\sin^2\theta) = 0$$

$$\therefore \quad \sin\theta = +\sqrt{\frac{2}{3}} \quad [\because \sin\theta \neq 0]$$

When $\sin\theta = \sqrt{\frac{2}{3}} \Rightarrow \frac{d^2Z}{d\theta^2} = -\frac{5}{5\sqrt{3}} - \frac{16}{3\sqrt{3}} - \frac{1}{\sqrt{3}} = -\frac{8}{\sqrt{3}} < 0$

Hence, Z is maximum.

$$\Rightarrow \quad x = \frac{1}{Z} \text{ is minimum} \quad \text{[from Eq. (i)]}$$

$\therefore$ x is minimum.

$$\Rightarrow \quad x_{\min} \Rightarrow \frac{1}{Z} = \frac{1}{\left(\frac{1}{\sqrt{3}}\right)\left(1+\frac{1}{3}\right)} = \frac{3\sqrt{3}}{4} \text{ unit}$$

$$\therefore \quad k = \frac{3\sqrt{3}}{4} \Rightarrow 4k = 3\sqrt{3} \Rightarrow (4k)^2 = 27$$

Example 70 *The volume of the greatest right circular cone that can be described by the revolution about a side of a right angled triangle of hypotenuse 1 ft is V cu ft, then $81\sqrt{3}\,V$ is ....*

Sol. (18) Let ΔABC be right angled triangle.

Let the cone be revolved about AB.

$$AC = 1 \text{ ft} \quad \text{[given]}$$

Let $AB = a$ = Height of cone

$\therefore \; BC = \sqrt{1-a^2}$ = Radius of cone

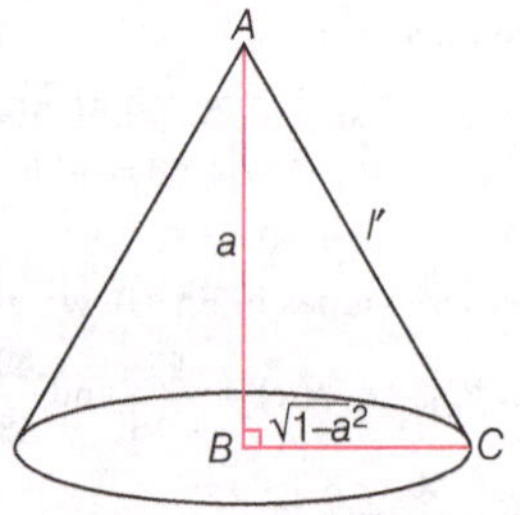

$$\text{Volume of cone} = \frac{1}{3}\pi(1-a^2)a$$

$$V = \frac{1}{3}\pi(a - a^3)$$

$$\Rightarrow \quad \frac{dV}{da} = \frac{1}{3}\pi(1-3a^2)$$

and
$$\frac{d^2V}{da^2} = \frac{1}{3}\pi(-6a) < 0$$

$\therefore$ Maximum volume when $\frac{dV}{da} = 0$ i.e. when $a = \frac{1}{\sqrt{3}}$

On putting $a = \frac{1}{\sqrt{3}}$, we get

$$V_{\max} = \frac{2\sqrt{3}}{27}\pi \text{ cu ft}$$

$$81\sqrt{3}\,V = 81\times\sqrt{3}\times\frac{2\sqrt{3}}{27} = 18 \text{ cu ft}$$

Example 71 *The circle $x^2+y^2=1$ intersects the X-axis at P and Q. Another circle with centre at Q and variable radius intersects the first circle at R above the X-axis and the line segment PQ at S. If the maximum area of the ΔQSR is A, then $(9\sqrt{3}\ A)^2+17$ is ....*

Sol. (161) The centre of the circle $x^2+y^2=1$ ...(i)

is (0, 0) and radius $OP=1=OQ$

So, coordinates of Q are (1,0).

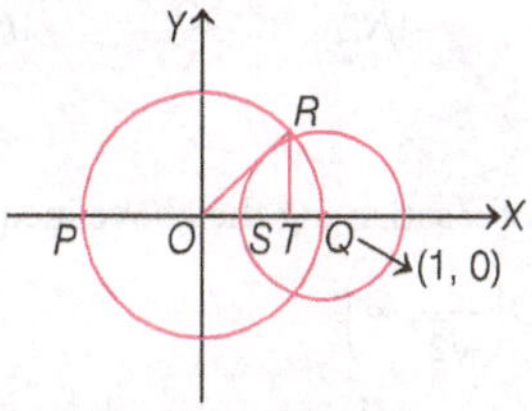

Let the radius of the variable circle be r.

Hence, its equation is $(x-1)^2+(y)^2=r^2$ ...(ii)

On subtracting Eq. (ii) from Eq (i), we get

$$2x-1=1-r^2 \Rightarrow x=1-\frac{r^2}{2}=OT \quad \text{...(iii)}$$

Now, $RT=\sqrt{OR^2-OT^2}=\sqrt{1-\left(1-\frac{r^2}{2}\right)^2}=\sqrt{r^2-\frac{r^2}{4}}$ ...(iv)

Now, the area of ΔQSR is,

$$A=\frac{1}{2}\cdot QS\cdot RT$$

$$\therefore \quad A^2=\frac{1}{4}(QS^2)\cdot(RT^2) \Rightarrow A^2=\frac{1}{4}r^2\left(r^2-\frac{r^4}{4}\right)$$

[using Eqs. (ii) and (iv)]

$$\Rightarrow \quad A^2=\frac{1}{16}(4r^4-r^6)=f(r) \quad \text{[say]}$$

Thus, $\frac{df(r)}{dr}=\frac{1}{16}(16r^3-6r^5)=0$ [for extremum]

$$\Rightarrow \quad r=2\sqrt{\frac{2}{3}}$$

Also, $\frac{d^2f(r)}{dr^2}=\frac{1}{16}(48r^2-30r^4)=-\frac{16}{3}<0$, where $r=2\sqrt{\frac{2}{3}}$

Hence, area is maximum at $r=2\sqrt{\frac{2}{3}}$ and $A_{\max}=\frac{4}{3\sqrt{3}}$ sq unit.

$\therefore \ (9\sqrt{3}\ A)^2+17=(12)^2+17=161$

Example 72 *Suppose $f(x)$ is a real valued polynomial function of degree 6 satisfying the following conditions.*

(i) f has minimum value at $x=0$ and 2

(ii) f has maximum value at $x=1$

(iii) for all x, $\lim_{x\to 0}\frac{1}{x}\ln\begin{vmatrix}\frac{f(x)}{x} & 1 & 0\\ 0 & \frac{1}{x} & 1\\ 1 & 0 & \frac{1}{x}\end{vmatrix}=2$, *then*

$18[f(1)+f(-1)]$ *is ....*

Sol. (96) $\lim_{x\to 0}\frac{1}{x}\log_e\begin{vmatrix}\frac{f(x)}{x} & 1 & 0\\ 0 & \frac{1}{x} & 1\\ 1 & 0 & \frac{1}{x}\end{vmatrix}=2$

$$\Rightarrow \quad \lim_{x\to 0}\frac{1}{x}\log_e\left\{\frac{f(x)}{x^3}+1\right\}=2$$

$$\Rightarrow \quad \lim_{x\to 0}\log_e\left\{\frac{f(x)}{x^3}+1\right\}^{\frac{1}{x}}=2$$

Let $f(x)=ax^6+bx^5+cx^4+dx^3+ex^2+fx+g$

For the $\lim_{x\to 0}\log_e\left(\frac{f(x)}{x^3}+1\right)^{\frac{1}{x}}$ to be finite $\lim_{x\to 0}\frac{f(x)}{x^3}$ must be zero.

$$\Rightarrow \lim_{x\to 0}ax^3+bx^2+cx+d+\frac{e}{x}+\frac{f}{x^2}+\frac{g}{x^3}=0$$

$$\Rightarrow \quad d=e=f=g=0$$

$$\Rightarrow \quad f(x)=ax^6+bx^5+cx^4$$

Now, $\lim_{x\to 0}\log_e\left[\frac{f(x)}{x^3}+1\right]^{\frac{1}{x}}$

$$\Rightarrow \quad \lim_{x\to 0}\log_e\left(1+\frac{f(x)}{x^3}\right)^{\frac{1}{\frac{f(x)}{x^3}}\times\frac{\frac{f(x)}{x^3}}{x}}$$

$$\Rightarrow \quad \lim_{x\to 0}\log_e e^{\frac{f(x)}{x^4}}=\lim_{x\to 0}\frac{f(x)}{x^4}$$

$$\Rightarrow \quad \lim_{x\to 0}\frac{f(x)}{x^4}=2$$

$$\Rightarrow \quad \lim_{x\to 0}ax^2+bx+c=2$$

$$\Rightarrow \quad c=2$$

$$\Rightarrow \quad f(x)=ax^6+bx^5+2x^4$$

$$\Rightarrow \quad f'(x)=6ax^5+5bx^4+8x^3$$

Now, given that $f'(1)=0$ and $f'(2)=0$

$$\Rightarrow \quad 6a+5b=-8 \quad \text{...(i)}$$

$$\text{and} \quad 24a+10b=-8 \quad \text{...(ii)}$$

On solving, we get

$$a=\frac{2}{3} \text{ and } b=-\frac{12}{5}$$

$$\Rightarrow \quad f(x)=\frac{2}{3}x^6-\frac{12}{5}x^5+2x^4$$

$$f(1)=\frac{2}{3}-\frac{12}{5}+2$$

$$f(-1)=\frac{2}{3}+\frac{12}{5}+2$$

$$\therefore \quad 18[f(1)+f(-1)]=18\left(\frac{4}{3}+4\right)$$

$$\Rightarrow \quad 16\times 6=96$$

Example 73 *Let* $f(x)=\frac{2}{\sqrt{3}}\tan^{-1}\left(\frac{2x+1}{\sqrt{3}}\right)$

$$-\log(x^2+x+1)+(b^2-5b+3)x+C$$

If $f(x)$ is a decreasing function of x for all $x \in R$, then square the sum of are positive integral permissible values of parameter b is ....

Sol. (36) $f'(x)=\frac{2}{\sqrt{3}}\left\{\frac{1}{1+\left(\frac{(2x+1)}{\sqrt{3}}\right)^2}\right\}$

$$\times\left(\frac{2}{\sqrt{3}}\right)-\frac{(2x+1)}{x^2+x+1}+(b^2-5b+3)$$

$$=\frac{4}{3}\left(\frac{3}{4x^2+4x+4}\right)-\frac{(2x+1)}{x^2+x+1}+(b^2-5b+3)$$

$$=\frac{-2x}{x^2+x+1}+(b^2-5b+3)$$

$$f'(x)<0, \forall\, x \in R$$

$$\Rightarrow \quad b^2-5b+3<\frac{2x}{x^2+x+1}$$

Let $\quad \frac{2x}{x^2+x+1}=y$

$$\Rightarrow \quad yx^2+(y-2)x+y=0$$

$$\Rightarrow \quad (y-2)^2-4y^2 \ge 0 \qquad [\because x \in R]$$

$$\Rightarrow \quad (3y-2)(y+2)\le 0$$

$$\Rightarrow \quad -2 \le y \le \frac{2}{3}$$

$$\Rightarrow \quad \left.\frac{2x}{x^2+x+1}\right]_{\min}=-2$$

$$\therefore \quad b^2-5b+3<-2 \Rightarrow b^2-5b+5<0$$

$$\Rightarrow \quad b \in \left(\frac{5-\sqrt{5}}{2}, \frac{5+\sqrt{5}}{2}\right)$$

Permissible positive integral values of $b = 1, 2, 3$

$\therefore$ Square the sum $=(1+2+3)^2=36$

Example 74 *Let $f(x)=1-x-4x^3$. If values of x satisfying the inequality $1-f(x)-4(f(x))^3>f(1-3x)$ is $(a, b)\cup(c, d)$, then $196\left(a^2+b^2+c^2+\left(\frac{1}{d}\right)^2\right)$ is ....*

Sol. (196) $f(x)=1-x-4x^3$

$\Rightarrow f(f(x))=1-f(x)-4(f(x))^3$

Also, $f'(x)=-1-12x^2<0$

$\therefore$ $f(x)$ is strictly decreasing for $x \in R$

$\therefore$ $f(f(x))>f(1-3x)$

$\therefore$ $f(x)<1-3x \qquad [\because f(x)$ is a decreasing function$]$

$$\Rightarrow \quad 1-x-4x^3<1-3x \Rightarrow 2x-4x^3<0$$

$$\Rightarrow \quad 2x(1-2x^2)<0 \Rightarrow x(2x^2-1)>0$$

$$\Rightarrow x\left(x-\frac{1}{\sqrt{2}}\right)\left(x+\frac{1}{\sqrt{2}}\right)>0$$

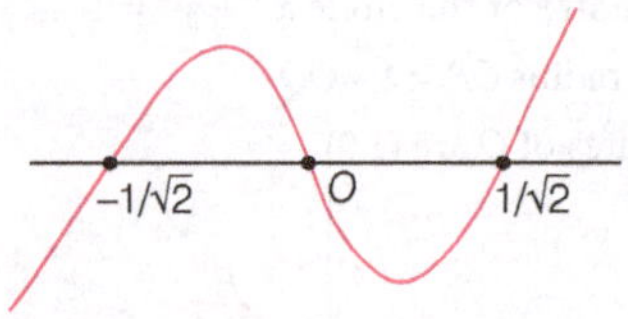

The values of x satisfying the above inequality at $\left(-\frac{1}{\sqrt{2}}, 0\right)\cup\left(\frac{1}{\sqrt{2}}, \infty\right)$.

$$a=-\frac{1}{\sqrt{2}}, b=0, c=\frac{1}{\sqrt{2}}, d=\infty$$

$$\therefore\ 196\left(a^2+b^2+c^2+\left(\frac{1}{d}\right)^2\right)=196\left(\frac{1}{2}+\frac{1}{2}\right)=196$$

Example 75 *The set of all values of a for which $f(x)=\left(\frac{\sqrt{a+8}}{2-a}-1\right)x^5-7x+\log_3 4$ decreases for all x, is $(\lambda, b)\cup(c, \infty)$. Then, $\lambda^2+(2b+\sqrt{41})^2+c^2$ is ....*

Sol. (93) $f'(x)=5\left(\frac{\sqrt{a+8}}{2-a}-1\right)x^4-7$

Since, $f(x)$ decreases for all x, $f'(x)\le 0$

$$\Rightarrow \quad 5\left(\frac{\sqrt{a+8}}{2-a}-1\right)x^4-7\le 0$$

$$\Rightarrow \quad 5\left(\frac{\sqrt{a+8}}{2-a}-1\right)\le\frac{7}{x^4}$$

The LHS should be less than equal to the least values of RHS.

$$\Rightarrow \quad 5\left(\frac{\sqrt{a+8}}{2-a}-1\right)\le 0 \Rightarrow \frac{\sqrt{a+8}}{2-a}\le 1$$

Now, $\quad a+8\ge 0 \Rightarrow a \ge -8 \qquad$ ...(i)

Case I If $2-a>0$, then $a<2$ and $\sqrt{a+8}\le 2-a \qquad$ ...(ii)

On squaring both sides, we get

$$a+8\le 4+a^2-4a \Rightarrow a^2-5a-4\ge 0$$

$$a=\frac{5\pm\sqrt{25+16}}{2}=\frac{5\pm\sqrt{41}}{2}$$

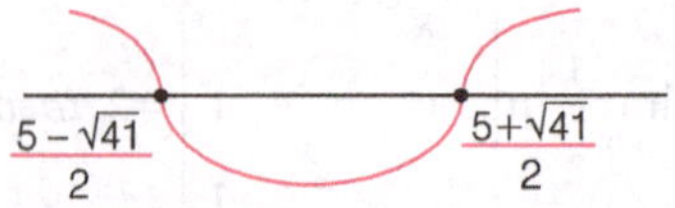

$$\Rightarrow \quad a \in \left(-\infty, \frac{5-\sqrt{41}}{2}\right]\cup\left[\frac{5+\sqrt{41}}{2}, \infty\right) \qquad \text{...(iii)}$$

On taking intersection of Eqs. (i), (ii) and (iii), we get

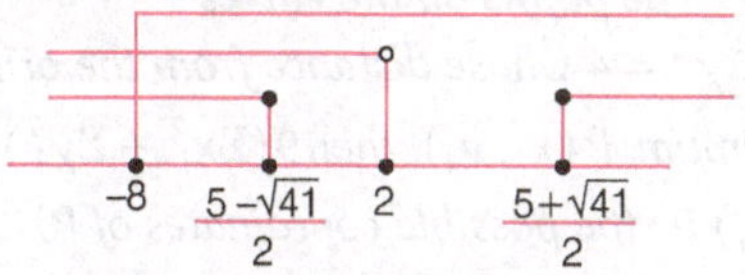

$$a \in \left[-8, \frac{5-\sqrt{41}}{2}\right] \quad \text{...(iv)}$$

Case II If $2 - a < 0 \Rightarrow a > 2$ ...(v)

Then, $\dfrac{\sqrt{a+8}}{2-a} \le 1$ is always true, since LHS < 0 and RHS ≥ 1

On taking intersection of Eqs. (iv) and (v), we get

$$a \in \left[-8, \frac{5-\sqrt{41}}{2}\right] \text{ and } (2, \infty)$$

$$\lambda = -8, b = \frac{5-\sqrt{41}}{2}, c = 2$$

$$\therefore \ \lambda^2 + (2b + \sqrt{41})^2 + c^2 = 64 + 25 + 4 = 93$$

Example 76 *A cylinder is obtained by revolving a rectangle about the X-axis, the base of the rectangle lying on the X-axis and the entire rectangle lying in the region between the curve* $y = \dfrac{x}{x^2+1}$ *and the X-axis. The maximum possible volume of the cylinder is* $k\pi$*. if the value of* $16k + 17$ *is ....*

Sol. (21) $y = \dfrac{x}{x^2+1}, \dfrac{dy}{dx} = \dfrac{(x^2+1) - 2x^2}{(x^2+1)^2} = \dfrac{1-x^2}{(1+x^2)^2}$

Now, $\dfrac{dy}{dx} = 0 \Rightarrow x = 1$ or -1

Now, $v = \pi y^2 (x_2 - x_1)$

Since, the ordinate at A and B (vertices other than those lying on the X-axis) have to be equal.

$$\therefore \ \frac{x_1}{x_1^2 + 1} = \frac{x_2}{x_2^2 + 1}$$

or $\quad x_1 x_2^2 + x_1 = x_2 x_1^2 + x_2$

or $\quad x_1 x_2 (x_2 - x_1) - (x_2 - x_1) = 0$

$\Rightarrow \quad (x_2 - x_1)(x_1 x_2 - 1) = 0$

$\Rightarrow \quad x_2 = \dfrac{1}{x_1}$ as $(x_1 \ne x_2)$

Hence, $v = \dfrac{\pi x_1^2}{(1 + x_1^2)^2}\left(\dfrac{1}{x_1} - x_1\right) = \dfrac{\pi x_1 (1 - x_1^2)}{(1 + x_1^2)^2}$

$$\therefore \ v(x) = \frac{\pi x (1 - x^2)}{(1 + x^2)^2}$$

$$v'(x) = \pi[(1 + x^2)^2 (1 - 3x^2) - (x - x^3)(1 + x^2)4x] = 0$$

On simplifying, we get $x^6 - 5x^4 - 5x^2 + 1 = 0$

$(x^2 + 1)(x^4 - 6x^2 + 1) = 0, \ x^2 = \dfrac{6 \pm \sqrt{32}}{2} = 3 \pm 2\sqrt{2} \ [\because x^2 + 1 \ne 0]$

Positive sign is rejected as $x = \sqrt{3 + 2\sqrt{2}} = \sqrt{2} + 1$ which is greater than 1.

Hence, $x = \sqrt{3 - 2\sqrt{2}} = \sqrt{2} - 1$

$$\therefore \ v_{max} = \frac{\pi(\sqrt{2} - 1)(1 - (3 - 2\sqrt{2}))}{(1 + 3 - 2\sqrt{2})^2}$$

$$= \frac{\pi(\sqrt{2} - 1)(2\sqrt{2} - 2)}{(4 - 2\sqrt{2})^2} = \frac{2\pi(3 - 2\sqrt{2})}{4(2 - \sqrt{2})^2}$$

$$= \frac{2\pi}{8} \frac{3 - 2\sqrt{2}}{(\sqrt{2} - 1)^2} = \frac{\pi}{4}$$

$$\therefore \ k\pi = \frac{\pi}{4} \Rightarrow k = \frac{1}{4}$$

$\therefore \ 16k + 17 = 4 + 17 = 21$

Example 77 *The shortest distance between the curves* $y^2 = x^3$ *and* $9x^2 + 9y^2 - 30y + 16 = 0$ *is* λ*. Then, the value of* $[-8\lambda]^2 + 18$ *is, where* $[\cdot] =$ *GIF.*

Sol. (22) We have, $9x^2 + 9y^2 - 30y + 16 = 0$ which is a circle, having

centre $= \left(0, \dfrac{5}{3}\right)$ and radius $= \sqrt{\left(\dfrac{5}{3}\right)^2 - \dfrac{16}{9}} = 1$.

Let us choose any point on the curve $y^2 = x^3$ as $A(t^2, t^3)$. If B is the point on the circle and nearest to A(see figure), then

$$AB = AC - \text{Radius} = \sqrt{(t^2 - 0)^2 + \left(t^3 - \frac{5}{3}\right)^2} - 1$$

Let $f(t) = t^4 + \left(t^3 - \dfrac{5}{3}\right)^2$

and $f'(t) = 4t^3 + 2\left(t^3 - \dfrac{5}{3}\right) \cdot 3t^2 = 2t^2\left[2t + 3\left(t^3 - \dfrac{5}{3}\right)\right]$

$$= 2t^2(3t^3 + 2t - 5) = 2t^2(t - 1)(3t^2 + 3t + 5)$$

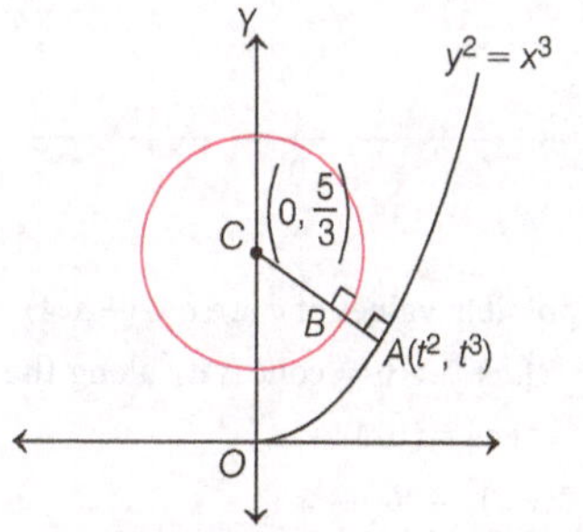

The value of t at which AB attains minima is given by the equation $f'(t) = 0$ gives $t = 0, 1$

But $t = 0$ is not a point of extrema, since $f'(1)$ does not change sign in the neighbourhood of $t = 0$.

However, $t = 1$ is a point of minima, since $f(1^-) < 0$ and $f'(1^+) > 0$. Hence, the minimum value of AB is

$$\sqrt{1 + \left(1 - \frac{5}{3}\right)^2} - 1 \simeq 0.2 = \lambda$$

$$\therefore \qquad [-8\lambda]^2 + 18 = (-2)^2 + 18 = 22$$

JEE SCANNER

Example 78 Similar to PYQ Asked in JEE Main 2023

If the function $f(x)=(a+3)x^3+(a-3)x^2+4(a-4)x+5$ has maxima at some $x\in R^-$ and a minima at some $x\in R^+$, then square of possible integral values of $|a|$ is ....

Sol. (36) We have, $f(x)=(a+3)x^3+(a-3)x^2+4(a-4)x+5$

and $f'(x)=3(a+3)x^2+2(a-3)x+4(a-4)$

According to the given condition,

$f'(x)$ must vanish at two real and distinct points say α,β such that $\alpha<0$ and $\beta>0$.

Thus, we have $f'(x)=3(a+3)(x-\alpha)(x-\beta)$

and $f''(x)=3(a+3)[2x-(\alpha+\beta)]$

According to the given condition, α is to be a maxima

i.e. $f''(\alpha)<0$

$\Rightarrow$ $3(a+3)(\alpha-\beta)<0$

i.e. $a+3>0$ $[\alpha-\beta<0]$

$\Rightarrow$ $a>-3$ and β is to be a minima

i.e. $f''(\beta)>0$

$\Rightarrow$ $3(a+3)(\beta-\alpha)>0$

$\Rightarrow$ $a+3>0$ $[\beta-\alpha>0]$

$\Rightarrow$ $a>-3$

Thus, on taking together all the above results $(a+3>0)$, the graph of

$$y=3(a+3)x^2+2(a-3)x+4(a-4)$$

must look as shown alongside. For the curve to look like this, the necessary and sufficient condition is

$y(0)<0$

i.e. $4(a-4)<0\Rightarrow a<4$

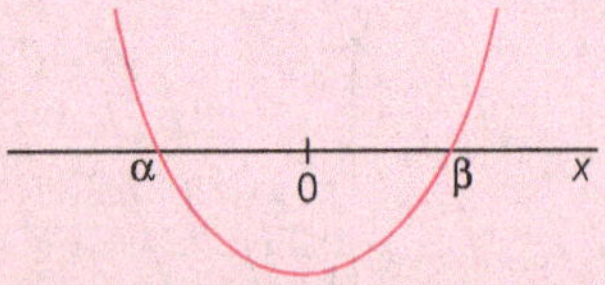

Hence, the possible values of a are $a\in(-3,4)$.

$[a+3>0\Rightarrow$ concavity along the positive Y-axis$]$

$\therefore$ $|a|=[0,4)$

$\therefore$ $(0+1+2+3)^2=36$

Skill Builder

Let the function $f(x)=2x^3+(p-7)x^2+2(2p-6)x-6$ have a maxima, for some value of $x<0$ and a minima for some value of $x>0$ and the set of $p\in(-\infty,k)$. Then, $5k$ is equal to ....

For Sol.

Example 79 *The points on the curves $5x^2-8xy+5y^2=4$ whose distance from the origin is maximum or minimum. $P(x_i,y_i)$, then $9(\Sigma x_i^2+\Sigma y_i^2)$ is ...... (where (x_i,y_i) be the possible coordinates of P)*

Sol. (80) Let (r,θ) be the polar coordinates of any point P on the curve, where r is the distance of the point from the origin.

$\Rightarrow$ $r^2[5(\cos^2\theta+\sin^2\theta)-8\sin\theta\cos\theta]=4$

$\Rightarrow$ r^2 is maximum when $5-4\sin2\theta$ is minimum $=5-4=1$ [when $\sin2\theta=1$]

$\Rightarrow$ $2\theta=90^\circ\Rightarrow\theta=45^\circ\Rightarrow r=\pm2,\theta=45^\circ$ ...(i)

Again, r^2 is minimum when $5-4\sin2\theta$ is maximum

$=5+4=9$, when $\sin2\theta=-1\Rightarrow2\theta=\dfrac{3\pi}{2}\Rightarrow\theta=\dfrac{3\pi}{4}$

$\Rightarrow$ $r=\pm\dfrac{2}{3},\theta=\dfrac{3\pi}{4}$ ...(ii)

Hence, the points are $(r\cos\theta,r\sin\theta)$, where r and θ are given by Eqs. (i) and (ii).

Thus, we get four points

$(\sqrt{2},\sqrt{2}),(-\sqrt{2},-\sqrt{2}),\left(\dfrac{\sqrt{2}}{3},-\dfrac{\sqrt{2}}{3}\right)$ and $\left(-\dfrac{\sqrt{2}}{3},\dfrac{\sqrt{2}}{3}\right)$.

$\therefore 9(\Sigma x_i^2+\Sigma y_i^2)=9\left(8+\dfrac{8}{9}\right)=80$

Matching Type Questions

Example 80 *Match the statements of Column I with value of Column II.*

	Column I		Column I
A.	Number of the values of x lying in $\left(0,\dfrac{\pi}{2}\right)$ at which $f(x)=\ln(\sin x)$ is not monotonic, is	p.	0
B.	If the greatest interval of decrease of the function $f(x)=x^3-3x+2$ is $[a,b]$, then $a+b$ equals	q.	2
C.	Let $f(x)=\dfrac{x^2+2}{[x]}$, $1\le x\le3$, where $[\cdot]$ greatest integer function, then least value of $f(x)$ is	r.	-3
D.	Set of all possible values of a such that $f(x)=e^{2x}-(a+1)e^x+2x$ is monotonically increasing for all $x\in R$ is $(-\infty,a]$, then a equals	s.	3

Sol. (A) $\to$ (p), (B) $\to$ (p), (C) $\to$ (s), D $\to$ (s)

(A) $f(x)=\ln(\sin x)\Rightarrow f'(x)=\dfrac{\cos x}{\sin x}>0$

$\therefore$ Required number of values of x is 0.

(B) $f'(x) = 3x^2 - 3 \le 0$, if $-1 \le x \le 1$

$\therefore \quad a = -1, b = 1$

$\therefore \quad a + b = 0$

(C) $f(x) = \begin{cases} x^2 + 2, & 1 \le x < 2 \\ \dfrac{x^2+2}{2}, & 2 \le x < 3 \\ \dfrac{x^2+2}{3}, & x = 3 \end{cases} \Rightarrow f'(x) = \begin{cases} 2x, & 1 < x < 2 \\ x, & 2 < x < 3 \end{cases}$

$\therefore$ Least value of $f(x)$ in [1, 2] is 3.

Least value of $f(x)$ in [2, 3] is 3.

$$f(3) = \frac{11}{3}$$

$\therefore$ Least value of $f(x)$ is 3.

(D) $f(x) = e^{2x} - (a+1)e^x + 2x$

$f'(x) = 2e^{2x} - (a+1)e^x + 2$

Now, $2e^{2x} - (a+1)e^x + 2 \ge 0$, for all $x \in R$

$\Rightarrow 2\left(e^x + \dfrac{1}{e^x}\right) - (a+1) \ge 0$, for all $x \in R$

$\Rightarrow \quad 4 - (a+1) \ge 0 \Rightarrow a \le 3$

$\therefore \quad a = 3$

Example 81 *Match the statements of Column I with value of Column II.*

	Column I		Column I
A.	A rectangle is inscribed in an equilateral triangle of side 4 cm. Maximum area of such a rectangle is	p.	$2\sqrt{3}$
B.	The greatest distance between $x^2 + y^2 - 2x - 2y + 1 = 0$, $x^2 + y^2 - 10x + 4y + 20 = 0$ is 3λ, then λ is	q.	0
C.	Maximum value of $x^3 - 3x^2 - x + 3$ when $x \in [0, 4]$ is $5k$, then value of k is	r.	32
D.	Minimum value of $\cos^4 x - 6\cos^2 x + 5$ is	s.	3

Sol. A $\to$ (p), B $\to$ (s), C $\to$ (s), D $\to$ (q)

(A) Let $PQ = x$. Then, $BP = \dfrac{4-x}{2}$

In ΔBPS, $PS = \dfrac{4-x}{2}$, $\tan 60° = \dfrac{\sqrt{3}(4-x)}{2}$

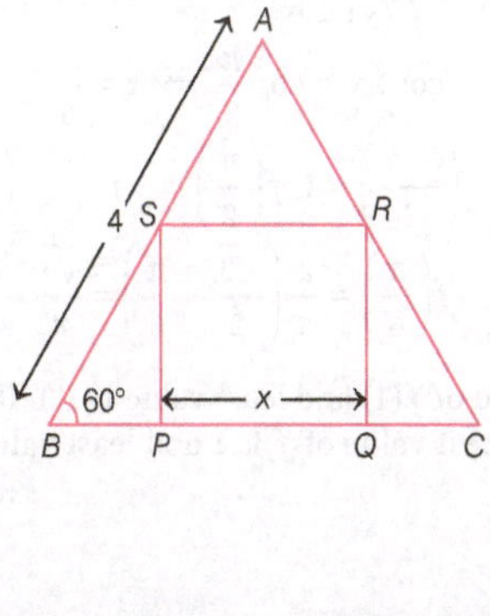

$\therefore$ Area A of rectangle $= PS \cdot PQ = \dfrac{\sqrt{3}}{2}(4-x)x$

$$\frac{dA}{dx} = \frac{\sqrt{3}}{2}(4-2x) = 0$$

$\Rightarrow \quad x = 2$

$$\frac{d^2A}{dx^2} = -\sqrt{3} < 0$$

$\therefore$ A is maximum, when $x = 2$

$\therefore$ Maximum area $= \dfrac{\sqrt{3}}{2} \times 2 \times 2 = 2\sqrt{3}$

(B) $S_1 = x^2 + y^2 - 2x - 2y + 1 = 0$

$\Rightarrow C_1 : (1, 1), R_1 = 1$

$S_2 = x^2 + y^2 - 10x + 4y + 20 = 0$

$\Rightarrow C_2 : (5, -2), R_2 : 3$

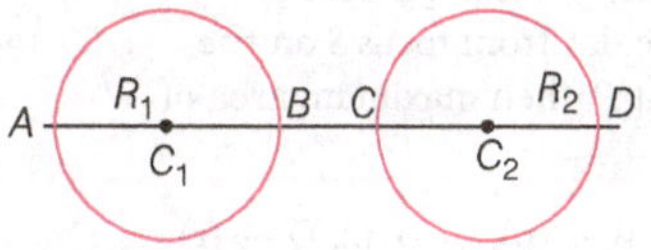

Greatest distance is

$$AD = C_1C_2 + R_1 + R_2 = 5 + 1 + 3 = 9$$

(C) $y = x^3 - 3x^2 - x + 3 \Rightarrow y' = 3x^2 - 6x - 1$

$y' = 0$, we get

$$3x^2 - 6x - 1 = 0$$

On equating $y' = 0$, we get

$$3x^2 - 6x - 1 = 0$$

$\Rightarrow \quad x = \dfrac{6 + 4\sqrt{3}}{6}, \dfrac{6 - 4\sqrt{3}}{6}$

Now, $y' = 3\left(x - \left(\dfrac{6+4\sqrt{3}}{6}\right)\right)\left(x - \left(\dfrac{6-4\sqrt{3}}{6}\right)\right)$

wavy curve of y is as shown below.

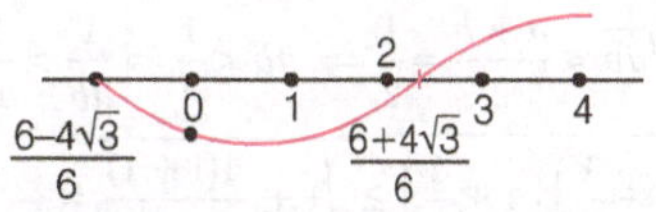

Hence, we see that y attains its maximum values at the end points only.

$$f(0) = 3, f(4) = 15$$

$\Rightarrow$ Maximum is 15.

$\Rightarrow \quad 5k = 15$

$\Rightarrow \quad k = 3$

(D) $y = \cos^4 x - 6\cos^2 x + 5$.

Let $\cos^2 x = t$

$$y = t^2 - 6t + 5, \ 0 \le t \le 1$$

For $t \in [0, 1]$ min occurs at $t = 1$

$$y \text{ min} = 0$$

Example 82 *Match the following columns.*

	Column I		Column I
A.	If x is real, then the greatest and least value of the expression $\frac{x+2}{2x^2+3x+6}$ is	p.	3
B.	If $a+b=1, a>0, b>0$, then the minimum value of $\sqrt{\left(1+\frac{1}{a}\right)\left(1+\frac{1}{b}\right)}$ is	q.	$\frac{1}{3}$
C.	The maximum value obtained by $y=10-\|x-10\|, -9\le x\le 9$ is λ, then $\frac{\lambda}{3}$ is	r.	5
D.	If $P(t^2, 2t)$, $t[0,2]$ is an arbitrary point on parabola $y-4x$. Q is foot of perpendicular from focus S on the tangent at P, then maximum area of ΔPQS is	s.	$\frac{-1}{13}$

Sol. A → (q, s), B → (p), C → (p), D → (r)

(A) $y=\frac{x+2}{2x^2+3x+6}$

$$\Rightarrow 2yx^2+3xy+6y=x+2$$
$$2yx^2+x(3y-1)+6y-2=0$$
$$D\ge 0$$
$$\Rightarrow (3y-1)^2-8y(6y-2)\ge 0$$
$$9y^2-6y+1-48y^2+16y\ge 0$$
$$\Rightarrow -39y^2+10y+1\ge 0 \Rightarrow 39y^2-10y-1\le 0$$
$$\Rightarrow (13y+1)(3y-1)\le 0$$
$$\frac{-1}{13}\le y\le\frac{1}{3}$$

(B) $a+b=1$

Now, $\sqrt{\left(1+\frac{1}{a}\right)\left(1+\frac{1}{b}\right)}=\sqrt{1+\frac{1}{a}+\frac{1}{b}+\frac{1}{ab}}=\sqrt{1+\frac{1+1}{ab}}$

Also, $\sqrt{ab}<\frac{a+b}{2}=\frac{1}{2}\Rightarrow ab<\frac{1}{4}\Rightarrow\frac{1}{ab}>\frac{4}{1}$

$$\therefore \sqrt{\left(1+\frac{1}{a}\right)\left(1+\frac{1}{b}\right)}\ge\sqrt{1+\frac{4(1+1)}{1}}=3$$

(C) $y=10-|x-10|$

$$-9\le x\le 9$$
$$-19x-10-1<0$$
$$\therefore y=10-(10-x)=x$$
$\therefore$ Maximum value of $y=9$

(D) Equation of tangent at P is $ty=x+t^2$

It intersects the line $x=0$ at Q.

$\therefore$ Coordinates of Q are $(0, t)$.

$$\text{Area of } \Delta PQS=\frac{1}{2}\begin{vmatrix}0 & t & 1\\ 1 & 0 & 1\\ t^2 & 2t & 1\end{vmatrix}$$
$$=\frac{1}{2}[-t(1-t^2)+2t]=\frac{1}{2}(t+t^3)$$
$$\frac{dA}{dt}=\frac{1}{2}(3t^2+1)>0, \forall t\in[0,2]$$

Area is maximum at $t=2$

So, maximum area $=\frac{1}{2}[2+8]=5$

Example 83 *Match the following columns.*

	Column-I		Column-I
A.	If $f(x)=\frac{1-x+x^2}{1+x-x^2}$ on $[0,1]$	p.	Greatest value of $f=1$
B.	If $f(x)=2\tan x-\tan^2 x$ on $\left[0,\frac{\pi}{2}\right)$	q.	Least value of $f=\frac{3}{5}$
C.	$f(x)=\frac{2}{\pi}(\sin 2x-x)$ on $\left[-\frac{\pi}{2},\frac{\pi}{2}\right]$	r.	Least value of $f=-1$
D.	$f(x)=\frac{1}{2}(x^3-3x^2+6x-2)$ on $[-1,1]$	s.	Least value of $f=-6$

Sol. A → (p,q), B → (p), C → (p,r), D → (p,s)

If f is as in (A) above, then

$$f'(x)=\frac{(1+x-x^2)(2x-1)-(1-x+x^2)(1-2x)}{(1+x-x^2)^2}$$
$$=\frac{2(2x-1)}{(1+x-x^2)^2}=0$$
$$\Rightarrow x=\frac{1}{2}$$

$f(0)=1$, $f(1)=1$ and $f\left(\frac{1}{2}\right)=\frac{3}{5}$, so the greatest value of $f=1$ and the least value is $\frac{3}{5}$.

If f is an in (B) then $f'(x)=2\sec^2 x-2\tan x\sec^2 x$ and so $f'(x)=0\Rightarrow x=\frac{\pi}{4}$.

But $f(0)=0$ and $f\left(\frac{\pi}{4}\right)=1$, so greatest value is 1 and has no least value.

Similarly, if f is as in (C)

$$f'(x)=\frac{2}{\pi}(2\cos 2x-1)$$
$$f'(x)=0$$
$$\Rightarrow \cos 2x=\cos\frac{\pi}{3}\Rightarrow x=\frac{\pi}{6}$$
$$f\left(\frac{-\pi}{2}\right)=1, f\left(\frac{\pi}{2}\right)=-1$$

and $$f\left(\frac{\pi}{6}\right)=\frac{2}{\pi}\left(\frac{\sqrt{3}}{2}-\frac{\pi}{6}\right)=\frac{\sqrt{3}}{\pi}-\frac{1}{3}<1$$

Greatest value of $f(1)$ and least value is -1. If f is as in (D), then the greatest value of f is 1 and least value is -6.

EXERCISE 1
— JEE Main Pattern

Single Option Correct Type Questions

1. Let $f(x)=\sin^2 x-(2a+1)\sin x+(a-3)$. If $f(x)\le 0$, for all $x\in\left[0,\frac{\pi}{2}\right]$, then range of values of a is
(a) $[-3, 0]$ (b) $[3, \infty)$ (c) $[-3, 3]$ (d) $(-\infty, 3]$

2. If $f(x)$ is a differentiable real valued function satisfying $f''(x)-3f'(x)>3, \forall\ x\ge 0$ and $f'(0)=-1$, then $f(x)+x, \forall\ x>0$ is
(a) decreasing function of x (b) increasing function of x
(c) constant function (d) None of these

3. If $\tan(\pi\cos\theta)=\cot(\pi\sin\theta), 0<\theta<\frac{\pi}{2}$ and $f(x)=(\cos\theta+\sin\theta)^x$, then f is
(a) increasing, for all $x\in R$. (b) decreasing, for all $x\in R$.
(c) increasing in $(0,\infty)$. (d) decreasing in $(0,\infty)$.

4. $f:R\to R$ be a differentiable function, $\forall\ x\in R$. If a tangent drawn to the curve at any point $x\in(a, b)$ always lies below the curve. Then,
(a) $f'(x)<0$ and $f''(x)>0, \forall\in(a,b)$
(b) $f'(x)>0$ and $f''(x)<0, \forall\ x\in(a, b)$
(c) $f'(x)$ can have any value and $f''(x)>0, \forall\ x\in(a, b)$
(d) None of the above

5. Let $f''(x)>0, \forall\ x\in R$ and $g(x)=f(2-x)+f(4+x)$. Then, $g(x)$ is increasing in
(a) $(-\infty,-1)$ (b) $(-\infty, 0)$
(c) $(-1,\infty)$ (d) None of these

6. Let f, g and h are differentiable functions such that $g(x)=f(x)-x$ and $h(x)=f(x)-x^3$ are both strictly increasing functions. Then, the function
$F(x)=f(x)-\frac{\sqrt{3}x^2}{2}$ is
(a) strictly increasing, $\forall\ x\in R$.
(b) strictly decreasing, $\forall x\in R$.
(c) strictly decreasing on $\left(-\infty,\frac{1}{\sqrt{3}}\right)$ and strictly increasing on $\left(\frac{1}{\sqrt{3}},\infty\right)$.
(d) strictly increasing on $\left(-\infty,\frac{1}{\sqrt{3}}\right)$ and strictly decreasing on $\left(\frac{1}{\sqrt{3}},\infty\right)$.

7. Let $f(x)=x\sqrt{4ax-x^2}, (a>0)$. Then, $f(x)$ is
(a) increasing in $(0, 3a)$, decreasing in $(-\infty, 0)$ and $(3a, 4a)$.
(b) increasing in $(a, 4a)$, decreasing in $(4a,\infty)$.
(c) increasing in $(0, 4a)$, decreasing in $(-\infty, 0)$.
(d) None of the above

8. Let f be a function such that $f'(x)=\log_{1/3}(\log_3(\sin x+a))$. If f is decreasing for all real values of x, then
(a) $a\in(1, 4)$ (b) $a\in(4,\infty)$
(c) $a\in(2, 3)$ (d) $a\in(2,\infty)$

9. Let $f(x)$ be an increasing function and $g(\theta)=\int_0^{\sin^2\theta} f(x)dx+\int_0^{\cos^2\theta} f(x)dx$, $x\in\left(-\frac{\pi}{2},\frac{\pi}{2}\right)$, then $g(\theta)$ is increasing in the interval
(a) $\left(-\frac{\pi}{2}, 0\right)$ (b) $\left(-\frac{\pi}{2},-\frac{\pi}{4}\right)$
(c) $\left(0,\frac{\pi}{4}\right)$ (d) $\left(-\frac{\pi}{4}, 0\right)$

10. If $f(x)=ax^3+bx^2+cx+d$, where a, b, c, d are real numbers and $3b^2<c^2$, is an increasing cubic function and $g(x)=af'(x)+bf''(x)+c^2$, then
(a) $\int_a^x g(t)dt$ is a decreasing function.
(b) $\int_a^x g(t)\,dt$ is an increasing function.
(c) $\int_a^x g(t)\,dt$ is neither increasing nor decreasing function.
(d) None of the above

11. The intervals in which $f(x)=3\cos^4 x+10\cos^3 x+6\cos^2 x-3, x\in(0,\pi)$, decreases and increases, are
(a) decreases on $\left(\frac{\pi}{2},\frac{2\pi}{3}\right)$ and increases on $\left(0,\frac{\pi}{2}\right)\cup\left(\frac{2\pi}{3},\pi\right)$.
(b) decreases on $\left(\frac{\pi}{2},\pi\right)$ and increases on $\left(0,\frac{\pi}{2}\right)$.
(c) decreases on $\left(0,\frac{\pi}{2}\right)\cup\left(\frac{2\pi}{3},\pi\right)$ and increases on $\left(\frac{\pi}{2},\frac{2\pi}{3}\right)$.
(d) decreases on $\left(0,\frac{\pi}{2}\right)$ and increases on $\left(\frac{\pi}{2},\pi\right)$.

12. Let $f^1(x)$ denotes $g(x)$, $f^2(x)$ denotes $g(g(x))$, $f^3(x)$ denotes $g(g(g(x)))$ and so on. If $g(x)$ is an increasing function and lies between $(0, \infty)$, $\forall\ x \in R$, then $\lim_{n \to \infty} \left(\frac{1}{f^n(x)}\right)$ is equal to

(a) 0 (b) 1
(c) Does not exist (d) None of these

13. $f(x)$ is increasing, concave up function for all $x \in [a, b]$, then for any $\lambda > 0$, f is invertible if

(a) $\left(\frac{b + a\lambda}{1 + \lambda}\right) > f^{-1}\left(\frac{f(b) + \lambda f(a)}{1 + \lambda}\right)$

(b) $\left(\frac{b + a\lambda}{1 + \lambda}\right) \le f^{-1}\left(\frac{f(b) + \lambda f(a)}{1 + \lambda}\right)$

(c) $\left(\frac{b + a\lambda}{1 + \lambda}\right) < f^{-1}\left(\frac{f(b) + \lambda f(a)}{1 + \lambda}\right)$

(d) $\left(\frac{b + a\lambda}{1 + \lambda}\right) \ge f^{-1}\left(\frac{f(b) + \lambda f(a)}{1 + \lambda}\right)$

14. If $g(x) = 2f(2x^3 - 3x^2) + f(6x^2 - 4x^3 - 3)$, $\forall\ x \in R$ and $f''(x) > 0$, $\forall\ x \in R$, then $g(x)$ is increasing in the interval

(a) $\left(-\infty, -\frac{1}{2}\right) \cup (0, 1)$ (b) $\left(-\frac{1}{2}, 0\right) \cup (1, \infty)$
(c) $(0, \infty)$ (d) None of these

15. Let $f : [2, 7] \to [R]$ be a continuous and differentiable function. Then, the value of $(f(7) - f(2)) \cdot \frac{((f(7))^2 + (f(2))^2 + f(2) \cdot f(7))}{3}$, is (where $c \in (2, 7)$)

(a) $3f^2(c)\ f'(c)$ (b) $5f^2(c)\ f'(c)$
(c) $5f^2(c)\ f'(c)$ (d) None of these

16. If $f(x)$ is a polynomial of degree 5 with real coefficients such that $f(|x|) = 0$ has 8 real roots, then $f(x) = 0$ has

(a) 4 real roots only
(b) 5 real roots (one negative, others positive)
(c) 3 real roots
(d) Nothing can be said

17. If $f(x) = (ab - b^2 - 2)x + \int_0^x (\cos^4 \theta + \sin^4 \theta) d\theta$ is a decreasing function of x for all $x \in R$ and $b \in R$, b being independent of x, then

(a) $a \in (0, \sqrt{2}]$ (b) $a \in [-2, 2]$
(c) $a \in [-\sqrt{2}, 0)$ (d) None of these

18. Let $f(x) = \int_1^x \left(t \ln(t) - \frac{\ln t}{t}\right) dt; (x > 1)$, then

(a) $f(x)$ has one point of maxima and no point of minima.
(b) $f'(x)$ has two distinct roots.
(c) $f(x)$ has one point of minima and no point of maxima.
(d) $f(x)$ is monotonic.

19. Let $f : [a, b] \to R$ be a function such that $c \in (a, b)$, $f'(c) = f''(c) = f'''(c) = f^{iv}(c) = f^{v}(c) = 0$, then

(a) f has local extrema at $x = c$.
(b) f has neither local maxima nor local minima at $x = c$.
(c) f is necessarily a constant function.
(d) it is difficult to say whether (a) or (b)

20. In the interval $\left[\frac{5\pi}{4}, \frac{4\pi}{3}\right]$, the least value of the function $f(x) = \int_{\frac{5\pi}{4}}^{x} (3 \sin t + 4 \cos t) dt$ is equal to

(a) 0 (b) $-2\sqrt{3} + \frac{3}{2} + \frac{1}{\sqrt{2}}$
(c) $-2\sqrt{2} + \frac{2}{3} + \frac{1}{\sqrt{3}}$ (d) None of these

21. The function $f(x) = (4 \sin^2 x - 1)^n (e^x - x + 1)$, $n \in N$, has a local minima at $x = \frac{\pi}{6}$, then

(a) n can be any even natural number.
(b) n can be an odd natural number.
(c) n can be an odd prime number.
(d) n can be any natural number.

22. The global minimum value of $e^{(2x^2 - 2x + 1)\sin^2 x}$ is

(a) e (b) $\frac{1}{3}$
(c) 1 (d) 0

23. The global maximum value of $f(x) = \log_{10}(4x^3 - 12x^2 + 11x - 3)$, $x \in [2, 3]$ is

(a) $-\frac{3}{2}\log_{10}3$ (b) $1 + \log_{10}3$
(c) $\log_{10}3$ (d) $\frac{3}{2}\log_{10}3$

24. If $a > b > 0$, then the maximum value of $\frac{ab(a^2 - b^2)\sin x \cos x}{a^2 \sin^2 x + b^2 \cos^2 x}$ in $\left(0, \frac{\pi}{2}\right)$ is

(a) $a^2 - b^2$ (b) $\frac{a^2 - b^2}{2}$
(c) $\frac{a^2 + b^2}{2}$ (d) None of these

25. If the function $f(x) = \frac{t + 3x - x^2}{x - 4}$, where t is a parameter, has minima and maxima, then the range of values of t is

(a) $(0, 4)$
(b) $(0, \infty)$
(c) $(-\infty, 4)$
(d) $(4, \infty)$

26. A wire of length a is cut into two parts which are bent respectively in the form of a square and a circle. The least value of the sum of the areas so formed is

(a) $\frac{a^2}{\pi+4}$ (b) $\frac{a}{\pi+4}$

(c) $\frac{a}{4(\pi+4)}$ (d) $\frac{a^2}{4(\pi+4)}$

27. The maximum value of the expression $|\sqrt{\sin^2 x + 2a^2} - \sqrt{2a^2 - 1 - \cos^2 x}|$, where a and x are real numbers, is

(a) $\sqrt{2}$ (b) 1

(c) $\sqrt{3}$ (d) None of these

28. A box constructed from a rectangular metal sheet is 21×16 cm by cutting equal squares of sides x from the corners of the sheet and then turning up the projected portions. The value of x so that volume of the box is maximum, is

(a) 1 (b) 2 (c) 3 (d) 4

29. The set of critical points of the function

$$f(x) = x - \log x + \int_2^x (1/z - 2 - 2\cos 4z)dz \text{ is}$$

(a) $\left\{\frac{\pi}{6}, \frac{n\pi}{2} + \frac{\pi}{6}\right\}, n \in N$ (b) $\{n\pi\}, n \in N$

(c) $\left\{\frac{\pi}{2}, n\pi + \frac{\pi}{6}\right\}, n \in N$ (d) None of these

30. If $f(\theta) = \dfrac{\sin^4\frac{\theta}{n} - \sin^2\frac{\theta}{n} + 1}{\sin^4\frac{\theta}{n} + \sin^2\frac{\theta}{n} + 1}$, where $\theta \neq kn\pi, k \in I$, then range of $f(\theta)$ is

(a) $\left(\frac{1}{3}, 1\right]$ (b) $\left[\frac{1}{3}, 1\right]$

(c) $\left[\frac{1}{3}, 1\right)$ (d) $\left(\frac{1}{3}, 1\right)$

Numerical Value Type Questions

31. Let $f: [-1, 2] \to (-\infty, \infty)$ be given by $f(x) = \dfrac{x^4 + 3x^2 + 1}{x^2 + 1}$, then value of $[f_{max}]^2$ in $[-1, 2]$; where $[\cdot]$ is greatest integer function, is ....

32. The interval to which λ belongs so that the function $f(x) = \left(1 - \dfrac{\sqrt{21 - 4\lambda - \lambda^2}}{\lambda + 1}\right)x^3 + 5x + 7$ is increasing at every point of its domain is $(a, b) \cup [c, d]$, then $|a + b + c + d|^2 + 8$ is ....

33. The perimeter of a rectangle is 20 cm (constant). If length l of rectangle is increasing at rate 2cm/sec, then the length l beyond which if length is increased, area of rectangle decreases is ....

34. A circular sheet has radius $\sqrt{6}$ units. A sector is cut and the remaining part of sheet is used to form a cone by joining the edges. Let V_0 be the maximum volume of which the cone can be formed, then $\tan^4 \dfrac{V_0}{8\sqrt{2}}$ is ....

35. Let $f(x)$ be a function such that $f(x + y) = f(x) + f(y) + 2xy - 1, \forall x, \in R$ and $f'(0) = 2$. Further, let $g(x) = \int_0^x f(t)dt$, then find maximum value of $g(x)$ in $[1, 3]$ is ....

36. If $y = ax^4 + bx^3 + cx^2 + dx + e$ has critical points and $\log[-3b^4 + 12b^2 - 32ac + 8ab^2c]$ is defined, then the greatest possible value of b is equal to ....

37. If $f(x)$ is a twice differentiable function in R such that $f(a) = 0, f(b) = -2, f(c) = 3, f(d) = -1, f(e) = 0; a < b < c,$ then square of the minimum number of roots of equation $g(x) = 0$, where $g(x) = (f'(x))^2 + f(x) \cdot f''(x)$ is ....

38. An enemy's helicopter is flying on a curve having its equation given by $y = x^2 + 4$. A soldier is waiting at a point (3, 4) to hit the helicopter as soon as it is at nearest distance to him. The distance between the helicopter and the soldier at the time, he hits the helicopter is d. Then $[d]^6$ is .... (where $[\cdot]$ is greatest integer function)

39. If $a, b > 0$ such that $a^2 + b = 2^{\frac{5}{3}} \cdot 3^{\frac{1}{3}}$, then double of the maximum value of term independent of x in the expansion of $\left(\frac{a}{2}x^{\frac{1}{6}} + \frac{b}{3}x^{\frac{-1}{3}}\right)^9$, is ....

40. If $f(x) = \begin{cases} 5\tan^{-1}\alpha - 3x^2, & 0 < x < 1 \\ 5x - 3, & x \geq 1 \end{cases}$, then the least integer value of α for which $f(x)$ has minima at $x = 1$ is ....

41. For x to be real, cube of the maximum value of $f(x) = 6(\cos x - x)(x + \sqrt{x^2 + \sin^2 x})$ is ....

42. From a given solid cone of height H, another cone of height h is carved out such that its volume is maximum, then $8(H:h)$ is ....

43. Consider $P(x)$ be a polynomial of degree 5 having extremum at $x=-1, 1$ and $\lim_{x\to 0}\left(\frac{P(x)}{x^3}-2\right)=4$. Then, the value of $[P(1)]$ is ....
(where [·] represents greatest integer function)

44. If m is the minimum value of $f(x, y)=x^2-4x+y^2+6y$ when x and y are subjected to the restrictions $0\le x\le 1$ and $0\le y\le 1$, then the value of $|m|$ is ....

45. For a cubic function $y=f(x)$, $f''(x)=4x$ at each point (x, y) on it and it crosses the X-axis at $(-2, 0)$ at an angle of 45° with positive direction of the X-axis. Then, the value of $\left|\frac{f(1)}{5}\right|$ is ....

46. Number of integral values of b for which the equation $\frac{x^3}{3}-x=b$ has 3 distinct solutions, is ....

47. Let $f(x)=\begin{cases} x+2, & x<-1 \\ x^2, & -1\le x<1 \\ (x-2)^2, & x\ge 1\end{cases}$, then number of times $f'(x)$ changes its sign in $(-\infty, \infty)$ is ....

48. A right triangle is drawn in a semicircle of radius $\frac{1}{2}$ with one of its legs along the diameter. If the maximum area of the triangle is M, then the value of $32M$ is ....

49. A rectangle with one side lying along the X-axis is to be inscribed in the closed region of the XY-plane bounded by the lines $y=0$, $y=3x$ and $y=30-2x$. If M is the largest area of such a rectangle, then the value of $\frac{2M}{27}$ is ....

50. The least integral value of x, where $f(x)=\log_{1/2}(x^2-2x-3)$ is monotonically decreasing, is ....

51. The least area of a circle circumscribing any right triangle of area $\frac{9}{\pi}$ is ....

Previous Year Questions

52. For the function $f(x)=(\cos x)-x+1$, $x\in R$, between the following two statements

(S1) $f(x)=0$ for only one value of x in $[0, \pi]$.

(S2) $f(x)$ is decreasing in $\left[0, \frac{\pi}{2}\right]$ and increasing in $\left[\frac{\pi}{2}, \pi\right]$.

[Single Correct Type, 2024 Main]

(a) Only (S2) is correct.
(b) Both (S1) and (S2) are correct.
(c) Both (S1) and (S2) are incorrect.
(d) Only (S1) is correct.

53. The interval in which the function $f(x)=x^x$, $x>0$, is strictly increasing is **[Single Correct Type, 2024 Main]**

(a) $\left[\frac{1}{e}, \infty\right)$ (b) $\left(0, \frac{1}{e}\right]$
(c) $(0, \infty)$ (d) $\left[\frac{1}{e^2}, 1\right)$

54. The function $f(x)=\frac{x}{x^2-6x-16}$, $x\in R-\{-2, 8\}$

[Single Correct Type, 2024 Main]

(a) decreases in $(-\infty, -2)$ and increases in $(8, \infty)$
(b) increases in $(-\infty, -2)\cup(-2, 8)\cup(8, \infty)$
(c) decreases in $(-\infty, -2)\cup(-2, 8)\cup(8, \infty)$
(d) decreases in $(-2, 8)$ and increases in $(-\infty, -2)\cup(8, \infty)$

55. The number of critical points of the function $f(x)=(x-2)^{2/3}(2x+1)$ is

[Single Correct Type, 2024 Main]

(a) 1 (b) 3
(c) 0 (d) 2

56. For the function $f(x)=\sin x+3x-\frac{2}{\pi}(x^2+x)$, where $x\in\left[0, \frac{\pi}{2}\right]$, consider the following two statements:

[Single Correct Type, 2024 Main]

I. f is increasing in $\left(0, \frac{\pi}{2}\right)$.

II. f' is decreasing in $\left(0, \frac{\pi}{2}\right)$.

Between the above two statements,
(a) Neither I nor II is true (b) Both I and II are true
(c) Only I is true (d) Only II is true

57. Let $f: R\to(0, \infty)$ be strictly increasing function such that $\lim_{x\to\infty}\frac{f(7x)}{f(x)}=1$. Then, the value of $\lim_{x\to\infty}\left[\frac{f(5x)}{f(x)}-1\right]$ is equal to **[Single Correct Type, 2024 Main]**

(a) 7/5 (b) 1
(c) 0 (d) 4

58. Let $g(x)=3f\left(\frac{x}{3}\right)+f(3-x)$ and $f''(x)>0$, for all $x\in(0, 3)$. If g is decreasing in $(0, \alpha)$ and increasing in $(\alpha, 3)$, then 8α is **[Single Correct Type, 2024 Main]**

(a) 0 (b) 20 (c) 18 (d) 24

59. If $5f(x)+4f\left(\frac{1}{x}\right)=x^2-2, \forall x \neq 0$ and $y=9x^2 f(x)$, then y is strictly increasing in **[Single Correct Type, 2024 Main]**

(a) $\left(0, \frac{1}{\sqrt{5}}\right) \cup \left(\frac{1}{\sqrt{5}}, \infty\right)$ (b) $\left(-\frac{1}{\sqrt{5}}, 0\right) \cup \left(\frac{1}{\sqrt{5}}, \infty\right)$

(c) $\left(-\frac{1}{\sqrt{5}}, 0\right) \cup \left(0, \frac{1}{\sqrt{5}}\right)$ (d) $\left(-\infty, \frac{1}{\sqrt{5}}\right) \cup \left(0, \frac{1}{\sqrt{5}}\right)$

60. Let the sum of the maximum and the minimum values of the function $f(x)=\frac{2x^2-3x+8}{2x^2+3x+8}$ be $\frac{m}{n}$, where $gcd\,(m, n)=1$. Then, $m+n$ is equal to **[Single Correct Type, 2024 Main]**

(a) 201 (b) 217

(c) 195 (d) 182

61. Let $f(x)=(x+3)^2(x-2)^3, x \in [-4, 4]$. If M and m are the maximum and minimum values of f, respectively in $[-4, 4]$, then the value of $M-m$ is **[Single Correct Type, 2024 Main]**

(a) 392 (b) 108

(c) 608 (d) 600

62. The function $f(x)=2x+3(x)^{2/3}, x \in R$ has **[Single Correct Type, 2024 Main]**

(a) exactly one point of local minima and no point of local maxima

(b) exactly two points of local maxima and exactly one point of local minima

(c) exactly one point of local maxima and exactly one point of local minima

(d) exactly one point of local maxima and no point of local minima

63. Let $f(x)=4\cos^3 x+3\sqrt{3}\cos^2 x-10$. The number of points of local maxima of f in interval $(0, 2\pi)$ is **[Single Correct Type, 2024 Main]**

(a) 3 (b) 1

(c) 2 (d) 4

64. If the function $f(x)=\left(\frac{1}{x}\right)^{2x}; x>0$ attains the maximum value at $x=\frac{1}{e}$, then **[Single Correct Type, 2024 Main]**

(a) $e^{2\pi}<(2\pi)^e$ (b) $e^{\pi}>\pi^e$

(c) $e^{\pi}<\pi^e$ (d) $(2e)^{\pi}>\pi^{(2e)}$

65. Let a rectangle $ABCD$ of sides 2 and 4 be inscribed in another rectangle $PQRS$ such that the vertices of the rectangle $ABCD$ lie on the sides of the rectangle $PQRS$. Let a and b be the sides of the rectangle $PQRS$ when its area is maximum. Then, $(a+b)^2$ is equal to **[Single Correct Type, 2024 Main]**

(a) 72 (b) 64

(c) 60 (d) 80

66. Let $f(x)=3\sqrt{x-2}+\sqrt{4-x}$ be a real valued function. If α and β are respectively the minimum and the maximum values of f, then $\alpha^2+2\beta^2$ is equal to **[Single Correct Type, 2024 Main]**

(a) 42 (b) 38 (c) 44 (d) 24

67. A variable line L passes through the point (3, 5) and intersects the positive coordinate axes at the points A and B. The minimum area of the ΔOAB, where O is the origin, is **[Single Correct Type, 2024 Main]**

(a) 35 (b) 30 (c) 25 (d) 40

68. If the function $f(x)=2x^3-9ax^2+12a^2x+1, a>0$ has a local maximum at $x=\alpha$ and a local minimum at $x=\alpha^2$, then α and α^2 are the roots of the equation **[Single Correct Type, 2024 Main]**

(a) $x^2-6x+8=0$ (b) $8x^2-6x+1=0$

(c) $8x^2+6x-1=0$ (d) $x^2+6x+8=0$

69. Let the set of all values of p, for which $f(x)=(p^2-6p+8)(\sin^2 2x-\cos^2 2x)+2(2-p)x+7$ does not have any critical point, be the interval (a, b). Then, $16ab$ is equal to .... **[Numerical Value Type, 2024 Main]**

70. Let the set of all positive values of λ, for which the point of local minimum of the function $(1+x(\lambda^2-x^2))$ satisfies $\frac{x^2+x+2}{x^2+5x+6}<0$, be (α, β). Then, $\alpha^2+\beta^2$ is equal to .... **[Numerical Value Type, 2024 Main]**

71. Let A be the region enclosed by the parabola $y^2=2x$ and the line $x=24$. Then, the maximum area of the rectangle inscribed in the region A is .... **[Numerical Value Type, 2024 Main]**

72. Let the maximum and minimum values of $(\sqrt{8x-x^2-12}-4)^2+(x-7)^2, x \in R$ be M and m, respectively. Then, M^2-m^2 is equal to .... **[Numerical Value Type, 2024 Main]**

73. Let $S=\{\sin^2 2\theta : (\sin^4\theta+\cos^4\theta)x^2+(\sin 2\theta)x+(\sin^6\theta+\cos^6\theta)=0$ has real roots$\}$. If α and β are the smallest and largest elements of the set S, respectively, then $3((\alpha-2)^2+(\beta-1)^2)$ equals .... **[Numerical Value Type, 2024 Main]**

74. Let $g(x)=f(x)+f(1-x)$ and $f''(x)>0, x \in (0, 1)$. If g is decreasing in the interval $(0, \alpha)$ and increasing in the interval $(\alpha, 1)$, then $\tan^{-1}(2\alpha)+\tan^{-1}\left(\frac{1}{\alpha}\right)+\tan^{-1}\left(\frac{\alpha+1}{\alpha}\right)$ is equal to **[Single Correct Type, 2023 Main]**

(a) $\frac{5\pi}{4}$ (b) $\frac{3\pi}{4}$ (c) $\frac{3\pi}{2}$ (d) π

75. Let $f(x) = 2x + \tan^{-1} x$ and $g(x) = \log_e(\sqrt{1 + x^2} + x)$, $x \in [0, 3]$. Then, **[Single Correct Type, 2023 Main]**

(a) there exists $x \in [0, 3]$ such that $f'(x) < g'(x)$

(b) there exist $0 < x_1 < x_2 < 3$ such that $f(x) < g(x)$, $\forall x \in (x_1, x_2)$

(c) $\max f(x) > \max g(x)$

(d) $\min f'(x) = 1 + \max g'(x)$

76. Let $f : (0, 1) \to R$ be a function defined by $f(x) = \dfrac{1}{1 - e^{-x}}$ and $g(x) = (f(-x) - f(x))$. Consider two statements

(I) g is an increasing function in $(0, 1)$.

(II) g is one-one in $(0, 1)$.

Then, **[Single Correct Type, 2023 Main]**

(a) only (II) is true

(b) Both (I) and (II) are true

(c) only (I) is true

(d) Neither (I) nor (II) is true

77. The sum of the absolute maximum and minimum values of the function $f(x) = |x^2 - 5x + 6| - 3x + 2$ in the interval $[-1, 3]$ is equal to **[Single Correct Type, 2023 Main]**

(a) 12 (b) 24 (c) 13 (d) 10

78. The abolute minimum value of the function $f(x) = |x^2 - x + 1| + [x^2 - x + 1]$, which $[t]$ denotes the greatest integer function, in the interval $[-1, 2]$, is **[2023, 31 Jan Shift-II]**

(a) 3/2 (b) 5/4 (c) 3/4 (d) 1/4

79. If the functions $f(x) = \dfrac{x^3}{3} + 2bx + \dfrac{ax^2}{2}$ and $g(x) = \dfrac{x^3}{3} + ax + bx^2$, $a \neq 2b$ have a common extreme point, then $a + 2b + 7$ is equal to **[Single Correct Type, 2023 Main]**

(a) 3 (b) $\dfrac{3}{2}$ (c) 6 (d) 4

80. Let the function $f(x) = 2x^3 + (2p - 7)x^2 + 3(2p - 9)x - 6$ have a maxima, for some value of $x < 0$ and a minima for some value of $x > 0$. Then, the set of all values of p is **[Single Correct Type, 2023 Main]**

(a) $\left(0, \dfrac{9}{2}\right)$ (b) $\left(-\infty, \dfrac{9}{2}\right)$ (c) $\left(\dfrac{9}{2}, \infty\right)$ (d) $\left(-\dfrac{9}{2}, \dfrac{9}{2}\right)$

81. Let $x = 2$ be a local minima of the function $f(x) = 2x^4 - 18x^2 + 8x + 12$, $x \in (-4, 4)$. If M is local maximum value of the function f in $(-4, 4)$, then $M =$ **[Single Correct Type, 2023 Main]**

(a) $12\sqrt{6} - \dfrac{33}{2}$ (b) $18\sqrt{6} - \dfrac{33}{2}$

(c) $18\sqrt{6} - \dfrac{31}{2}$ (d) $12\sqrt{6} - \dfrac{31}{2}$

82. $\max\limits_{0 \le x \le \pi} \left\{x - 2\sin x \cos x + \dfrac{1}{3}\sin 3x\right\}$ is equal to **[Single Correct Type, 2023 Main]**

(a) $\dfrac{5\pi + 2 + 3\sqrt{3}}{6}$ (b) $\dfrac{\pi + 2 - 3\sqrt{3}}{6}$

(c) π (d) 0

83. If the local maximum value of the function $f(x) = \left(\dfrac{\sqrt{3e}}{2\sin x}\right)^{\sin^2 x}$, $x \in \left(0, \dfrac{\pi}{2}\right)$ is $\dfrac{k}{e}$, then $\left(\dfrac{k}{e}\right)^8 + \dfrac{k^8}{e^5} + k^8$ is equal to **[Single Correct Type, 2023 Main]**

(a) $e^3 + e^6 + e^{10}$ (b) $e^3 + e^6 + e^{11}$

(c) $e^5 + e^6 + e^{11}$ (d) $e^3 + e^5 + e^{11}$

84. A square piece of tin of side 30 cm is to be made into a box without top by cutting a square from each corner and folding up the flaps to form a box. If the volume of the box is maximum, then its surface area (in cm^2) is equal to **[Single Correct Type, 2023 Main]**

(a) 800 (b) 900

(c) 1025 (d) 675

85. If a_a is the greatest term in the sequence $a_n = \dfrac{n^3}{n^4 + 147} \cdot n = 1, 2, 3\ldots$, then α is equal to .... **[Single Correct Type, 2023 Main]**

86. If the absolute maximum value of the function $f(x) = (x^2 - 2x + 7)e^{(4x^3 - 12x^2 - 180x + 31)}$ in the interval $[-3, 0]$ is $f(\alpha)$, then **[Single Correct Type, 2022 Main]**

(a) $\alpha = 0$ (b) $\alpha = -3$

(c) $\alpha \in (-1, 0)$ (d) $\alpha \in (-3, -1]$

87. Let $f : R \to R$ be a function defined by $f(x) = (x - 3)^{n_1}(x - 5)^{n_2}$, $n_1, n_2 \in N$. Then, which of the following is not true? **[Single Correct Type, 2022 Main]**

(a) For $n_1 = 3, n_2 = 4$, there exists $\alpha \in (3, 5)$, where f attains local maxima

(b) For $n_1 = 4, n_2 = 3$, there exists $\alpha \in (3, 5)$, where f attains local minima

(c) For $n_1 = 3, n_2 = 5$, there exists $\alpha \in (3, 5)$ where, f attains local maxima

(d) For $n_1 = 4, n_2 = 6$, there exists $\alpha \in (3, 5)$ where, f attains local maxima

88. The lengths of the sides of a triangle are $10 + x^2$, $10 + x^2$ and $20 - 2x^2$. If for $x = k$, the area of the triangle is maximum, then $3k^2$ is equal to **[Single Correct Type, 2022 Main]**

(a) 5 (b) 8

(c) 10 (d) 12

89. The sum of the absolute minimum and the absolute maximum values of the function $f(x)=|3x-x^2+2|-x$ in the interval $[-1, 2]$ is **[Single Correct Type, 2022 Main]**

(a) $\frac{\sqrt{17}+3}{2}$ (b) $\frac{\sqrt{17}+5}{2}$

(c) 5 (d) $\frac{9-\sqrt{17}}{2}$

90. Let $f(x)=|(x-1)(x^2-2x-3)|+x-3$, $x \in R$. If m and M are respectively the number of points of local minima and local maxima of f in the interval $(0, 4)$, then $m+M$ is equal to .... **[Single Correct Type, 2022 Main]**

91. Let A be the set of all points (α, β) such that the area of triangle formed by the points (5, 6), (3, 2) and (α, β) is 12 sq units. Then, the least possible length of a line segment joining the origin to a point in A, is **[Single Correct Type, 2021 Main]**

(a) $4/\sqrt{5}$ (b) $16/\sqrt{5}$

(c) $8/\sqrt{5}$ (d) $12/\sqrt{5}$

92. The sum of all the local minimum values of the twice diffrentiable function $f: R \to R$ defined by $f(x)=x^3-3x^2-\frac{3f''(2)}{2}x+f''(1)$ is **[Single Correct Type, 2021 Main]**

(a) -22 (b) 5

(c) -27 (d) 0

93. Let a be a real number such that the function $f(x)=ax^2+6x-15$, $x \in R$ is increasing in $\left(-\infty, \frac{3}{4}\right)$ and decreasing in $\left(\frac{3}{4}, \infty\right)$. Then, the function $g(x)=ax^2-6x+15$, $x \in R$ has a **[Single Correct Type, 2021 Main]**

(a) local maxima at $x=-3/4$

(b) local minima at $x=-3/4$

(c) local maxima at $x=3/4$

(d) local minima at $x=3/4$

94. If the curves, $\frac{x^2}{a}+\frac{y^2}{b}=1$ and $\frac{x^2}{c}+\frac{y^2}{d}=1$ intersect each other at an angle of 90°, then which of the following relations is TRUE? **[Single Correct Type, 2021 Main]**

(a) $ab=\frac{c+d}{a+b}$ (b) $a-b=c-d$

(c) $a-c=b+d$ (d) $a+b=c+d$

95. The number of distinct real roots of the equation $3x^4+4x^3-12x^2+4=0$ is ... . **[Numerical Value Type, 2021 Main]**

96. The minimum value of α for which the equation $\frac{4}{\sin x}+\frac{1}{1-\sin x}=\alpha$ has at least one solution in $(0, \pi/2)$ is .... **[Numerical Value Type, 2021 Main]**

EXERCISE 2

JEE Advanced Pattern

Single Option Correct Type Questions

1. The set of value(s) of a for which the function $f(x)=\frac{ax^3}{3}+(a+2)x^2+(a-1)x+2$ possesses a negative point of inflection, is

(a) $(-\infty,-2)\cup(0,\infty)$ (b) $\left\{\frac{-4}{5}\right\}$

(c) $(-2,0)$ (d) empty set

2. Let $f(x)=e^{\left|x^2-4x+3\right|}$, then

(a) $f(x)$ decreases in the interval $(1, 2)\cup(3,\infty)$.

(b) $f(x)$ increases in the interval $(-\infty, 1)\cup(2, 3)$.

(c) $f(x)$ has one local maximum point and two local minimum points.

(d) $f(x)$ has one local minimum point and two local maximum points.

3. The value of t for which $\dfrac{\int_0^{\frac{\pi}{2}}(\sin x+t\cos x)dx}{\sqrt{\int_0^{\frac{\pi}{2}}(\sin x+t\cos x)^2dx}}$ is maximum, lies in the interval

(a) $\left(0,\frac{1}{2}\right)$ (b) $\left(\frac{1}{2},\frac{3}{4}\right)$

(c) $\left(\frac{3}{4},\frac{3}{2}\right)$ (d) $\left(\frac{3}{2},\frac{5}{2}\right)$

4. Let α be a fixed constant number such that $0<\alpha<\frac{\pi}{2}$. The function F is defined by $F(\theta)=\int_0^{\theta}x\cos(x+\alpha)dx$. If θ lies in the range of $\left[0,\frac{\pi}{2}\right]$, then the maximum value of $F(\theta)$ is

(a) $\frac{\pi}{2}-\alpha+\sin\alpha$ (b) $\frac{\pi}{2}-\alpha+\cos\alpha$

(c) $\frac{\pi}{2}-\alpha-\sin\alpha$ (d) $\frac{\pi}{2}-\alpha-\cos\alpha$

5. If $f(x)=\int_0^1 e^{|t-x|}\,dt$, where $(0\le x\le 1)$, then maximum value of $f(x)$ is

(a) $e-2$ (b) $e-3$ (c) $e-1$ (d) $2(\sqrt{e}-1)$

6. If $\alpha,\beta\in\left(\frac{\pi}{2},\pi\right)$ and $\alpha<\beta$, then which one of the following is true?

(a) $e^{\cos\alpha-\cos\beta}<\frac{\alpha}{\beta}$ (b) $e^{\cos\beta-\cos\alpha}<\frac{\beta}{\alpha}$

(c) $e^{\cos\alpha-\cos\beta}<\frac{\beta}{\alpha}$ (d) $e^{\cos\beta-\cos\alpha}<\frac{\alpha}{\beta}$

7. The maximum value of $(\cos\alpha_1)\cdot(\cos\alpha_2)\ldots(\cos\alpha_n)$ under the restrictions $0\le\alpha_1,\alpha_2,\ldots,\alpha_n\le\frac{\pi}{2}$ and $\cot\alpha_1\cdot\cot\alpha_2\cdot\ldots\cdot\cot\alpha_n=1$, is

(a) $\frac{1}{2^{\frac{n}{2}}}$ (b) $\frac{1}{2^n}$ (c) $\frac{1}{2n}$ (d) 1

8. If $a_1,a_2,\ldots,a_n$ are positive real numbers whose product is a fixed number e, then minimum value of $a_1+a_2+a_3+\ldots+a_{n-1}+2a_n$ is

(a) $n(2e)^{\frac{1}{n}}$ (b) $(n+1)e^{1/n}$

(c) $2ne^{\frac{1}{n}}$ (d) $(n+1)(2e)^{\frac{1}{n}}$

9. If $p\in(p_1,p_2)$ satisfies the condition that the point of local minima and point of local maxima is less than 4 and greater than -2 respectively for the function $f(x)=x^3-3px^2+3(p^2-1)x+1$, then the value of (p_2-p_1) is equal to

(a) -1 (b) 3 (c) 0 (d) 4

10. The smallest natural number c for which the equation $e^x=cx^2$ has exactly three real and distinct solutions, is

(a) 1 (b) 2 (c) 3 (d) 4

11. Let $f(x)=(pq-q^2-2)x+\int_0^x(\cos^4\theta+\sin^4\theta)\,d\theta$. If $f(x)$ is strictly decreasing, $\forall\ q$ and $x\in R$, then p may belong to

(a) $(-\sqrt{6},\sqrt{6})$ (b) $(-\sqrt{3},\sqrt{3})$

(c) $(-\sqrt{5},\sqrt{5})$ (d) $(-1,1)$

12. Let $f(x)=|x-1|+|x-2|$, $I=\int_0^3 f(x)dx$, $M=$ the minimum value of f, $N=f'(x)$, for $x<-4$ and $C=$ the value of $f''(4)$. Then, the value of $\frac{M^2-N^2+IC}{2}$ is

(a) $\frac{-3}{2}$ (b) $\frac{-5}{2}$ (c) $\frac{3}{2}$ (d) $\frac{5}{2}$

13. Let $f: R \to R$ be a function defined by $f(x)=2x^3-21x^2+78x+24$. Number of integers in the solutions set of x satisfying the inequality $f(f(f(x)-2x^3)) \geq f(f(2x^3-f(x)))$ is

(a) 3 (b) 4 (c) 5 (d) 6

14. Consider the three linear equations with respect to X, Y, Z as

$$(x)X+Y+2Z=0,\ (f(x))X+3Y+x^2Z=0$$

and $(5x)X+6Y+Z=0$

having non-trivial solution for X, Y, Z. The curve $f(x)$

(a) is always increasing
(b) is always decreasing
(c) has exactly one critical point
(a) has three critical points

15. For a certain curve $\frac{d^2y}{dx^2}=6x-4$ and curve has local minimum value 5 at $x=1$. Let the global maximum and global minimum values, where $0 \leq x \leq 2$; are M and m. Then, the value of $(M-m)$ equals to

(a) -2 (b) 2
(c) 12 (d) -12

16. The difference between the greatest and the least value of the function $f(x)=\cos x+\frac{1}{2}\cos 2x-\frac{1}{3}\cos 3x$ is

(a) $\frac{11}{5}$ (b) $\frac{13}{6}$ (c) $\frac{9}{4}$ (d) $\frac{7}{3}$

17. Let $f(x)=\int_{x^2}^{x^3}\frac{dt}{\ln t}$, for $x>1$ and $g(x)=\int_1^x (2t^2-\ln t)\, f(t)\, dt (x>1)$, then

(a) g is increasing on $(1, \infty)$
(b) g is decreasing on $(1, \infty)$
(c) g is increasing on (1, 2) and decreasing on $(2, \infty)$
(d) g is decreasing on (1, 2) and increasing on $(2, \infty)$

18. On the curve $y=\frac{1}{1+x^2}$, the point at which $\left|\frac{dy}{dx}\right|$ is greatest in the first quadrant is

(a) $\left(\frac{1}{2}, \frac{4}{5}\right)$ (b) $\left(1, \frac{1}{2}\right)$
(c) $\left(\frac{1}{\sqrt{2}}, \frac{2}{3}\right)$ (d) $\left(\frac{1}{\sqrt{3}}, \frac{3}{4}\right)$

19. $f(x)=x^6-x-1$, $x \in [1, 2]$. Consider the following statements.

(i) f is increasing on [1,2]
(ii) f has a root in [1, 2]
(iii) f is decreasing on [1,2]
(iv) f has no root in [1, 2]

Which of the above are correct?

(a) (i) and (ii) (b) (i) and (iv)
(c) (ii) and (iii) (d) (iii) and (iv)

20. The function $f(x)=\sin^3 x-m\sin x$ is defined on open interval $\left(-\frac{\pi}{2}, \frac{\pi}{2}\right)$ and it assumes only one maximum value and only one minimum value on this interval. Then, which one of the following must be correct ?

(a) $0<m<3$ (b) $-3<m<0$
(c) $m>3$ (d) $m<-3$

21. If $g(x)$ is twice differentiable real valued function satisfying $g''(x)-3g'(x)>3, \forall\, x \geq 0$ and $g'(0)=-1$, then $h(x)=g(x)+x, \forall x>0$ is

(a) strictly increasing (b) strictly decreasing
(c) non monotonic (d) data insufficient

22. For any real number b, let $f(b)$ denotes the maximum of $\left|\sin x+\frac{2}{3+\sin x}+b\right|, \forall\, x \in R$. Then, the minimum value of $f(b), \forall\, b \in R$ is

(a) $\frac{1}{2}$ (b) $\frac{3}{2}$ (c) $\frac{1}{4}$ (d) 1

23. Which of the following are correct?

(a) $x^4+2x^2-6x+2=0$ has exactly four real solutions.
(b) $x^5+5x+1=0$ has exactly three real solutions.
(c) $x^n+ax+b=0$, where n is an even natural number, has atmost two real solutions $a, b \in R$.
(d) $x^3-3x+c=0$, $c>0$ has two real solutions, for $x \in (0, 1)$.

24. Point A lies on the curve $y=e^{-x^2}$ and has the coordinate (x, e^{-x^2}), where $x>0$. Point B has the coordinates $(x, 0)$. If O is the origin, then the maximum area of the triangle AOB is

(a) $\frac{1}{\sqrt{2e}}$ (b) $\frac{1}{\sqrt{4e}}$
(c) $\frac{1}{\sqrt{e}}$ (d) $\frac{1}{\sqrt{8e}}$

25. Let h be a continuous twice differentiable positive function on an open interval J. Let $g(x)=\ln(h(x))$, for each $x \in J$. Suppose $(h'(x))^2>h''(x)\,h(x)$, for exch $x \in J$. Then,

(a) g is increasing on J (b) g is decreasing on J
(c) g is concave up on J (d) g is concave down on J

26. If $f(x)=1+2x^2+4x^4+6x^6+\ldots+100x^{100}$ is a polynomial in a real variable x, then $f(x)$ has
(a) neither a maximum nor a minimum
(b) only one maximum
(c) only one minimum
(d) one maximum and one minimum

27. The minimum value of

$$f(x)=\frac{(x-2)^{10}+(x-2)^{11}+3(x-2)^{12}+(x-2)^{15}+(x-2)^{23}+(x-2)^{25}}{(x-2)^{15}},\ \forall\ x>2 \text{ is}$$

(a) 2 (b) 4 (c) 6 (d) 8

28. Four points A, B, C and D lie in that order on the parabola $y=ax^2+bx+c$. The coordinates of A, B and D are known as $A(-2, 3)$; $B(-1, 1)$ and $D(2, 7)$. The coordinates of C for which the area of the quadrilateral $ABCD$ is greatest, is
(a) $\left(\frac{1}{2}, \frac{7}{4}\right)$ (b) $\left(\frac{1}{2}, \frac{-7}{4}\right)$ (c) $\left(\frac{-1}{2}, \frac{7}{4}\right)$ (d) $\left(\frac{-1}{2}, \frac{-7}{4}\right)$

More than One Correct Option Type Questions

29. If $4\sin\alpha\cos\beta+2\cos\beta-\sqrt{3}=2\sqrt{3}\sin\alpha$, where $\alpha, \beta\in[0, 2\pi]$ and $L=\alpha-\beta$, then
(a) maximum value of L is $\frac{11\pi}{6}$.
(b) minimum value of L is $-\frac{5\pi}{6}$.
(c) maximum value of L is $\frac{5\pi}{3}$.
(d) minimum value of L is $\frac{-11\pi}{6}$.

30. Let $f:[1, \infty)\to R$ is a differentiable function such that $f'(x)=\frac{1}{x^2+f^2(x)}$ and $f(1)=1$, then which of the following is/are correct?
(a) $f(x)$ is strictly increasing in $(1, \infty)$
(b) $\lim\limits_{x\to\infty} f(x)<2$
(c) The number of solution of $f(x)=1+2x$ is 0
(d) $f(3)<2$

31. If ABC is a triangle inscribed in an ellipse $\frac{x^2}{4}+\frac{y^2}{2}=1$, then
(a) area of ΔABC is maximum when the eccentric angles of the vertices differ by $\frac{2\pi}{3}$.
(b) area of ΔABC is maximum when the eccentric angles of the vertices differ by $\frac{5\pi}{9}$.
(c) maximum area of $\Delta ABC=3\sqrt{\frac{3}{2}}$
(d) if area of ΔABC is maximum, then normals at A, B and C are concurrent.

32. Let $f(x)$ be a differentiable function satisfying $f(x)=x+\int_0^1(xt^2+x^2t)f(t)\,dt$ and $g(x)$ be a polynomial satisfying $g(x)+g\left(\frac{1}{x}\right)=g(x)\cdot g\left(\frac{1}{x}\right)$, $g(2)=9$, then which of the following is/are false?
(a) $y=f(x)$ and $y=g(x)$ intersect at only two points.
(b) $y=f(x)$ is even function.
(c) $y=g(x)$ is odd function.
(d) $f(x)$ and $g(x)$ do not have a global minima, $\forall\ x\in R-\{0\}$.

33. If $f(x)=\big|\,|x-1|+|x-3|-|2x-1|\,\big|+\big|\,|x-1|+|x-3|+|2x-1|\,\big|$, then
(a) $f(x)$ is non-differentiable at $x=1$.
(b) $f(x)$ is non-differentiable at $x=\frac{3}{2}$.
(c) $f(x)$ has minimum value is 2.
(d) $x=1$ is point of local minima.

34. If $f(x)=\{b^2+(a-1)b+2\}x-\int(\sin^2 x+\cos^4 x)dx$ be an increasing function of $x\in R$ and $b\in R$, then a can take value(s)
(a) 0 (b) 1 (c) 2 (d) 4

35. Let $f(x)$ be a continuous function which takes positive values for $x\geq 0$ and satisfy $\int_0^x f(t)\,dt=x\sqrt{f(x)}$ with $f(1)=\frac{1}{2}$. Then,
(a) $f(x)$ is increasing function in domain.
(b) $f(x)$ is decreasing function in domain.
(c) $f(\sqrt{2}+1)=\frac{1}{2\sqrt{2}}$.
(d) $f(\sqrt{2}+1)=\frac{1}{4}$.

36. $f(x)=\tan^{-1}(\sin x+\cos x)$, then $f(x)$ is increasing in
(a) $\left(-\frac{\pi}{2}, \frac{\pi}{4}\right)$ (b) $\left(-\frac{\pi}{4}, \frac{\pi}{4}\right)$ (c) $\left(\frac{5\pi}{4}, \frac{3\pi}{4}\right)$ (d) $\left(-2\pi, -\frac{7\pi}{4}\right)$

37. If the global maximum value of $f(x)=x^2+ax-a^2-2a-2$ for $x\in[0, 1]$ be -5, then a can take the value
(a) $\frac{-4+2\sqrt{13}}{3}$ (b) $\frac{-4-2\sqrt{13}}{3}$
(c) 1 (d) -3

38. If $f(x)=a^{\{a^{|x|}\operatorname{sgn} x\}}$: $g(x)=a^{[a^{|x|}\operatorname{sgn} x]}$, for $a>0$, $a\neq 1$ and $x\in R$, where { } and [ ] denote the fractional part and integral part functions respectively, then which of the following statements can hold good for the function $h(x)$, where $(\ln a)\,h(x)=(\ln f(x)+\ln g(x))$.
(a) h is even and increasing.
(b) h is odd and decreasing.
(c) h is even and decreasing.
(d) h is odd and increasing.

39. Which of the following function(s) cannot exist?

(a) $f''(x) > 0, \forall x \in R, f'(0) = 1$ and $f'(1) = 1$

(b) $f''(x) > 0, \forall x \in R, f'(0) = 1$ and $f'(1) = 2$

(c) $f''(x) \ge 0, \forall x \in R, f'(0) = 1$ and $f(x) \le 100$, for all $x > 0$.

(d) $f''(x) > 0, \forall x \in R, f'(0) = 1$ and $f(x) \le 1$, for all $x < 0$

40. The interval to which b may belong so that the derivative of function $f(x) = \left(1 - \sqrt{\dfrac{21 - 4b - b^2}{b+1}}\right)x^3 + 5x + \sqrt{6}$ is always positive, is

(a) $[-7, 1)$

(b) $[-6, -2]$

(c) $\left[2, \dfrac{5}{2}\right]$

(d) $[2, 3]$

41. Let $f(x)$ be twice differentiable function such that $f''(x) > 0$ in $[0, 2]$. Then,

(a) $f(0) + f(2) = 2f(c)$, for atleast one $c, c \in (0, 2)$

(b) $f(0) + f(2) < 2f(1)$

(c) $f(0) + f(2) > 2f(1)$

(d) $2f(0) + f(2) > 3f\left(\dfrac{2}{3}\right)$

42. Let m and n be positive integers and $x, y > 0$ and $x + y = k$, where k is a constant. Let $f(x, y) = x^m y^n$. Then,

(a) $f(x, y)$ is maximum when $x = \dfrac{mk}{m+n}$

(b) $f(x, y)$ is maximum where $x = y$

(c) maximum value of $f(x, y)$ is $\dfrac{m^n n^m k^{m+n}}{(m+n)^{m+n}}$

(d) maximum value of $f(x, y)$ is $\dfrac{k^{m+n} m^m n^n}{(m+n)^{m+n}}$

43. Let $f(x) = \int_0^x e^{t^3}(t^2 - 1)t^2(t+1)^{2011}(t-2)^{2012}$ at $(x > 0)$, then

(a) the number of point of inflections is atleast 1.

(b) the number of point of inflections is 0.

(c) the number of point of local maxima is 1.

(d) the number of point of local minima is 1.

44. Consider $f(x) = \sin^5 x + \cos^5 x - 1, x \in \left[0, \dfrac{\pi}{2}\right]$, which of the following is/are correct ?

(a) f is strictly decreasing in $\left[0, \dfrac{\pi}{4}\right]$

(b) f is strictly increasing in $\left[\dfrac{\pi}{4}, \dfrac{\pi}{2}\right]$

(c) There exist a number c in $\left(0, \dfrac{\pi}{2}\right)$ such that $f'(c) = 0$.

(d) The equation $f(x) = 0$ has only two roots in $\left[0, \dfrac{\pi}{2}\right]$.

45. If $(f(x) - 1)(x^2 + x + 1)^2 - (f(x) + 1)(x^4 + x^2 + 1) = 0$, $\forall x \in R - \{0\}$ and $f(x) \ne \pm 1$, then which of the following statement (s) is/are correct ?

(a) $|f(x)| \ge 2, \forall x \in R - \{0\}$.

(b) $f(x)$ has a local maxima at $x = -1$.

(c) $f(x)$ has a local minima at $x = 1$.

(d) $\int_{-\pi}^{\pi} (\cos x)\, f(x) dx = 0$.

46. If f is an odd continuous function in $[-1, 1]$ and differentiable in $(-1, 1)$, then which of the following statements) is(are) correct?

(a) $f'(a) = f(1)$, for some $a \in (-1, 0)$

(b) $f'(b) = f(1)$, for some $b \in (0, 1)$

(c) $n(f(\alpha))^{n-1} f'(\alpha) = (f(1))^n$, for some $\alpha \in (-1, 0)$ and $\forall n \in N$

(d) $n(f(\beta))^{n-1} f'(\beta) = (f(1))^n$, for some $\beta \in (0, 1)$ and $n \in N$

47. Let the function $f(x)$ be thrice differentiable and satisfies $f(f(x)) = 1 - x, \forall x \in [0, 1]$. If $J = \int_0^1 f(x)dx$ and $f''\left(\dfrac{4}{5}\right) = 0$, then which of the following is (are) true?

(a) $f\left(\dfrac{1}{3}\right) + f\left(\dfrac{2}{3}\right) = 1$

(b) $J = \dfrac{1}{2}$

(c) $f''(x) = 0$ has atleast one root in $x \in \left(\dfrac{1}{4}, \dfrac{3}{4}\right)$

(d) $f'''(x) = 0$ has at least one root in $x \in \left(\dfrac{1}{2}, \dfrac{4}{5}\right)$

48. Let $f(x) = \cot x - \tan x - 2\tan 2x - 4\tan 4x - 8\cot 8x$, $x \ne \dfrac{n\pi}{8}, n \in I$ and $g(x) = x^3 + 6x - 1$. One more function $h(x)$ is defined as $h : R - \left\{\dfrac{n\pi}{8}, n \in I\right\} \to R$, $h(x) = f(x) + g(x)$, then identify the correct statement(s).

(a) $h''\left(\dfrac{\pi}{24}\right) = \dfrac{\pi}{4}$

(b) $h(x)$ is odd function.

(c) $h(x)$ is increasing in the domain.

(d) If the equation $h(x) = \lambda$ has a solution in $(0, 3)$, then number of integral values of λ is 7.

49. Let $f(x)=\cos^2 x\cdot e^{\tan x}, x\in\left(\frac{-\pi}{2},\frac{\pi}{2}\right)$, then

(a) $f'(x)$ has a point of local minima at $x=\frac{\pi}{4}$.

(b) $f'(x)$ has a point of local maxima in $\left(\frac{-\pi}{4},0\right)$.

(c) $f'(x)$ has exactly two points of local maxima/minima in $\left(\frac{-\pi}{2},\frac{\pi}{2}\right)$.

(d) $f''(x)=0$ has no roots in $\left(\frac{-\pi}{2},\frac{\pi}{2}\right)$.

Passage Based Questions

Passage I

(Q. Nos. 50 and 51)

- Consider the cubic $f(x)=8x^3+4ax^2+2bx+a$, where $a, b\in R$.

50. For $a=1$ if $y=f(x)$ is strictly increasing, $\forall\ x\in R$, then maximum range of values of b is

(a) $\left(-\infty,\frac{1}{3}\right]$ (b) $\left(\frac{1}{3},\infty\right)$ (c) $\left[\frac{1}{3},\infty\right)$ (d) $(-\infty,\infty)$

51. For $b=1$, if $y=f(x)$ is non monotonic, then the sum of all the integral values of $a\in[1, 100]$ is

(a) 4950 (b) 5049 (c) 5050 (d) 5047

Passage II

(Q. Nos. 52 and 53)

- Consider f, g and h be three real-valued differentiable functions defined on R.
Let $g(x)=x^3+g''(1)x^2+(3g'(1)-g''(1)-1)x+3g'(1)$, $f(x)=x\,g(x)-12x+1$ and $f(x)=(h(x))^2$, where $h(0)=1$.

52. The function $y=f(x)$ has

(a) exactly one local minima and no local maxima
(b) exactly one local maxima and no local minima
(c) exactly one local maxima and two local minima
(d) exactly two local maxima and one local minima

53. Which of the following is/are true for the function $y=g(x)$?

(a) $g(x)$ monotonically decreases in $\left(-\infty,2-\frac{1}{\sqrt{3}}\right)\cup\left(2+\frac{1}{\sqrt{3}},\infty\right)$

(b) $g(x)$ monotonically increases in $\left(2-\frac{1}{\sqrt{3}},2+\frac{1}{\sqrt{3}}\right)$

(c) There exists exactly one tangent to $y=g(x)$ which is parallel to the chord joining the points $(1, g(1))$ and $(3, g(3))$

(d) There exists exactly two distinct Lagrange's mean value in $(0, 4)$ for the function $y=g(x)$.

Passage III

(Q. Nos. 54 and 55)

- Consider the functions $f(x)$ and $g(x)$ such that $f(x)=\frac{x^3}{2}+1-x\int_0^x g(t)\,dt$ and $g(x)=x-\int_0^1 f(t)\,dt$.
Both $f(x)$ and $g(x)$ are defined from $R\to R$.

54. Which one of the following holds good for $f(x)$?

(a) $f(x)$ is bounded
(b) $f(x)$ has exactly one maxima and one minima
(c) $f(x)$ has a maxima but no minima
(d) $f(x)$ has a minima but no maxima

55. Minimum distance between the functions $f(x)$ and $g(x)$ is

(a) $\frac{4}{3\sqrt{2}}$ (b) $\frac{7}{6\sqrt{2}}$
(c) $\frac{7}{3\sqrt{2}}$ (d) $\frac{8}{3\sqrt{2}}$

Passage IV

(Q. Nos. 56 and 57)

- Let f be a real-valued function on R defined by $f(x)=xe^{-x}$. Suppose a line parallel to the X-axis has distinct intersection points P, Q with the curve $y=f(x)$. Denote the length of the line segment PQ equal to L. Also β is the value of x for which $y=f(x)$ has a local maximum and R be the intersection point of the line $x=\beta$ and the line PQ.

56. If p and q are the abscissa's of the points P and Q respectively, then the ordered pair (p, q) is

(a) $\left(\frac{L}{e^L-1},\frac{e^L}{e^L-1}\right)$ (b) $\left(\frac{e^L}{e^L-1},\frac{L}{e^L-1}\right)$
(c) $\left(\frac{L}{e^L-1},\frac{Le^L}{e^L-1}\right)$ (d) $\left(\frac{e^L}{e^L-1},\frac{e^L}{e^L-1}\right)$

57. If α denotes the x-coordinate of the point of inflection, then $(\alpha-\beta)$ equals to

(a) $e-1$ (b) $e-2$
(c) 2 (d) 1

Passage V

(Q. Nos. 58 and 59)

- $f(x)=x+\log_e x-x\log_e x, x\in(0,\infty)$.
List I contains information about zero of $f(x)$, $f'(x)$ and $f''(x)$.
List II contains information about the limiting behavior of $f(x)$, $f'(x)$ and $f''(x)$ at infinity.
List III contains information about increasing/decreasing nature of $f(x)$ and $f'(x)$.

	Column 1		Column 2		Column 3
(I)	$f(x)=0$ for some $x \in (1, e^2)$	(i)	$\lim_{x\to\infty} f(x)=0$	(P)	f is increasing in (0, 1)
(II)	$f'(x)=0$ for some $x \in (1, e)$	(ii)	$\lim_{x\to\infty} f(x)=-\infty$	(Q)	f is decreasing in (e, e^2)
(III)	$f'(x)=0$ for some $x \in (0, 1)$	(iii)	$\lim_{x\to\infty} f'(x)=0$	(R)	f' is increasing in (0, 1)
(IV)	$f''(x)=0$ for some $x \in (1, e)$	(iv)	$\lim_{x\to\infty} f''(x)=0$	(S)	f' is decreasing in (e, e^2)

58. Which of the following option is the only correct combination?
(a) (IV) (i) (S)
(b) (I) (ii) (R)
(c) (III) (iv) (P)
(d) (II) (iii) (S)

59. Which of the following option is the only correct combination?
(a) (III) (iii) (R)
(b) (I) (i) (R)
(c) (IV) (iv) (S)
(d) (II) (ii) (Q)

Stem Based Questions

Stem I

(Q. Nos. 60 and 61)

■ Let $f(x)=\begin{cases} 2\ln(-x-1), & -e-1 \le x \le -2 \\ \frac{1}{2}(4-x^2), & -2 < x < 0 \\ 0, & x=0 \\ \frac{1}{2}(x^2-4), & 0 < x < 2 \\ 2\ln(x-1), & 2 \le x \le e+1 \end{cases}$

and graph of $f(x)$ is as shown.

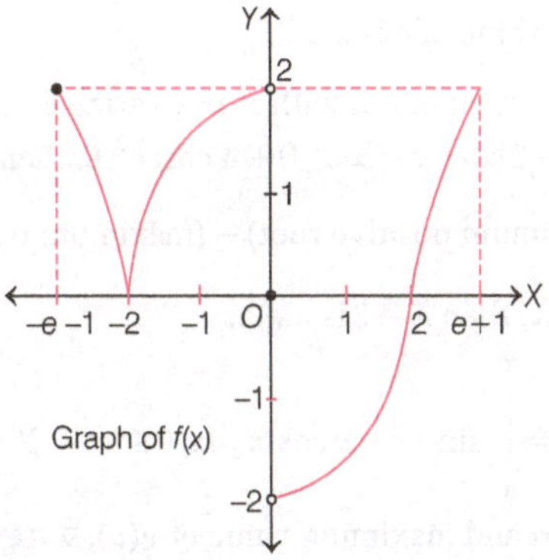

Also, $g(x)=\begin{cases} \min\{f(t): -e-1 \le t \le x\}, & -e-1 \le x < 0 \\ \max\{f(t): 0 \le t \le x\}, & 0 \le x \le e+1 \end{cases}$

60. If range of $g(x)$ is $[a, b]$, then the number of positive integral solutions of equation $\alpha+\beta+\gamma=5a+7b$ is ....

61. If the equation $g(x)=k$ has exactly two distinct solutions in $[-e-1, e+1]$, then the sum of all possible integral values of k is ....

Stem II

(Q. Nos. 62 and 63)

■ Let $f(x)$ be function defined on the set of real numbers to real numbers, such it is continuous on R.

62. The equation $k\cdot e^x = 5+x+\frac{x^2}{2}$, where k is a positive constant has number of real roots, then λ^2 is ....

63. If $f(x)=x^3-(9-a)x^2+3(9-a^2)x+7$ has points of extrema which are of opposite sign, then the values of parameter a is $(a, b)\cup(c, d)$, then (b^2+c^2) is ....

Single Integer Type Questions

64. Let $f(x)=\frac{x^3}{3}+\frac{x^2}{2}+x+2$ and $g'(x)=(x^2-9)(x^2-4x+3)(x^2-3x+2)(x^2-2x-3)$. If n_1, n_2 and n_3 denote number of points of local minima, number of points of local maxima and number of points of inflection of the function $f[g(x)]$, then the value of $(n_1+n_2+n_3)$ is ....

65. Let f be a continuous function and satisfies $f'(x)>0$ on $(-\infty, \infty)$ and the value of $f''(x), \forall x\,(0,\infty)$ is equal to minimum value of $\min_{x\in R}\{e^{-|x|}+2, |x|+2\}$.

If $L=\lim_{x\to\infty}\frac{3x^2-\frac{3}{x^2+1}-4f'(x)}{f(x)}$, then the value of $[L^2]$ is ....

[**Note** $[k]$ denotes greatest integer less than or equal to k]

66. If $a^2+b^2=1$ and u is the minimum value of $\frac{b+1}{a+b-2}$, then the value of u^2 is ....

67. Let $f(x)$ be a continuous and differentiable function satisfying the following conditions

(i) $\prod_{r=1}^{6} f(r)<0$, $\prod_{r=1}^{3} f(2r)<0$, $\prod_{r=1}^{2} f(3r)<0$

(ii) $f(6)>0$

(iii) $f(x)$ is monotonic in $(n, n+1)$, $n\in I$

Let A denotes the set consisting of number of distinct possible roots of $f(x)=0$ in $x\in(1, 6)$ and the sum of all the elements of set A is λ, then $\lambda-3$ is ....

68. A circle of radius 1 unit touches the positive X-axis and positive Y-axis at P and Q, respectively. A variable line L passing through the origin intersects the circle in two points M and N. If m is the slope of the line L for which the area of the triangle MNQ is maximum, then the value of $2010(m^2)-666$ is ....

69. For constant number a, consider the function $f(x)=ax+\cos 2x+\sin x+\cos x$ on R (the set of real numbers) such that $f(u)<f(v)$ for $u<v$. If the range of a for any real numbers u, v is $\left[\frac{m}{n}, \infty\right)$, then the minimum value of $\frac{(m+n)}{5}$ is ....

70. Let $a_n (n\geq 1)$ be the value of x for which $\int_x^{2x} e^{-t^n}\,dt\,(x>0)$ is maximum. If $L=\lim_{n\to\infty}\ln(a_n)$, then the value of e^{-L} is ....

71. The absolute value of $k\,(k\in R)$ for which $f(k)=\int_{-\pi}^{\pi}(x+1+k\sin x)^2\,dx$ is minimum, is ....

72. Let $f(x)=\begin{cases}(x+2)^3, & -3<x\leq -1\\ x^{\frac{2}{3}}, & -1<x<2\end{cases}$ and $g(x)=\int_{-3}^{x} f(t)dt$, $-3<x<2$, then the number of extremum points of $g'(x)$ is ....

73. If the exhaustive set of all possible values of c such that $f(x)=e^{2x}-(c+1)e^x+2x+\cos 2+\sin 1$, is monotonically increasing for all $x\in R$, is $(-\infty, \lambda]$, then the value of λ is ....

74. Let f be a twice differentiable function defined in $[-3,3]$ such that $f(0)=-4$, $f'(3)=0$, $f'(-3)=12$ and $f''(x)\geq -2, \forall\, x\in[-3,3]$. If $g(x)=\int_0^x f(t)\,dt$, then number of prime factor of maximum value of $g(x)$ is ......

75. Let $f(x)=\int_x^{x+\frac{\pi}{3}}|\sin\theta|\,d\theta, 0\leq x\leq \pi$. If m and M are minimum and maximum values of $f(x)$ and $m+M=\sqrt{p}-\sqrt{q}$, where $p, q\in N$, then the value of $\frac{(p+q)}{2}$ is ....

76. If $f(x)=a|\cos x|+b|\sin x|\,(a, b\in R)$ has a local minima at $x=\frac{-\pi}{3}$ and satisfies $\int_{-\frac{\pi}{2}}^{\frac{\pi}{2}}(f(x))^2\,dx=2$, hence $\frac{b^2}{a^2}$ is ......

77. If the maximum value of the expression $y=\frac{x^4-x^2}{x^6+2x^3-1}$, for $x>1$, is $\frac{p}{q}$ and it occurs at $x=\frac{a+\sqrt{b}}{c}$, where p and q are in their lowest terms and a, b, c are pairwise relatively prime positive numbers, the value of $\frac{(a+b+c+p+q)}{3}$ is ....

78. The square root of the sum of all integral values of a such that $a(x^2+x-1)\leq(x^2+x+1)^2, \forall\, x\in R$ is ......

79. Let f be a real function defined on R (the set of real numbers) such that $f'(x)=100(x-1)(x-2)^2(x-3)^3\,....(x-100)^{100}$, for all $x\in R$. If g is a function defined on R such that $\int_a^x e^{f(t)}dt=\int_0^x g(x-t)dt+2x+3$, then sum of digits of the sum of all the values of x for which $g(x)$ has a local extrema is ....

80. Let $f(x)$ be a differentiable function on R defined by $f(x)=5-(x+1)^2$ and A be the point of intersection where the tangent line drawn to the graph of $y=f(x)$ at the point $P(x, f(x))$ intersects with X-axis and B be the intersection point where the tangent line intersects with Y-axis. If $S(x)$ denotes the area of ΔOAB, where O is the origin, then the minimum value of $S(x)$ in the interval $(0, 1)$ is equal to $\frac{p}{q}$, (where p and q are in their lowest form), then the value of $\frac{(p+q)}{107}$ is ....

81. Let the function $f(x)=ax^6+bx^5+cx^4+dx^3+ex^2+fx+g\,(a\neq 0)$ touches the line $y=g(x)=x+p$ at $x=1$, 2 and 3 and $h(x)=f(x)-g(x)$. If $\int_1^3 h(x)dx=\frac{32}{105}$, then the value of a is ....

82. Consider an equation with x as a variable $7\sin 3x-2\sin 9x=\sec^2\theta+4\,\mathrm{cosec}^2\,\theta$, then the value of $\frac{15}{\pi}$[(minimum positive root) – (maximum negative root)] $=\lambda$, then $\lambda-2$ is ....

83. Let $g(a)=\int_0^{\frac{\pi}{2}}|\sin 2x-a\cos x|\,dx, 0\leq a\leq 1$. If m and M is minimum and maximum value of $g(a), \forall\, a\in[0,1]$, then the value of $2(M+m)$ is ....

84. If $9+f''(x)+f'(x)=x^2+f^2(x)$, where $f(x)$ is twice differentiable function such that $f''(x)\neq 0, \forall\, x\in R$ and let P be the point of maxima of $f(x)$, then the number of tangents which can be drawn from P to the circle $x^2+y^2=9$ is ....

Numerical Value Type Questions

85. A conical vessel is to be prepared out of a circular sheet of metal of unit radius. In order that the vessel has maximum volume, the sectorial area that must be removed from the sheet is A_1 and the area of the given sheet is A_2. If $\frac{A_2}{A_1} = m + \sqrt{n}$, where $m, n \in N$, then $(m+n)^2$ is equal to ....

86. On $[1, e]$, the least and greatest values of $f(x) = x^2 \ln x$ are m and M respectively, then $[\sqrt{M+m}]^5$ is .... (where [·] denotes greatest integer function)

87. If $f(x) = \frac{px}{e^x} - \frac{x^2}{2} + x$ is a decreasing function for every $x \le 0$, then the least value of $\frac{p^2}{4}$ is ....

88. Let $f(x) = \begin{cases} xe^{ax}, & x \le 0 \\ x + ax^2 - x^3, & x > 0 \end{cases}$, where a is a positive constant. The interval in which $f'(x)$ is increasing is $\left[\frac{k}{a}, \frac{a}{l}\right]$. Then, $(k-l)^4$ is equal to ....

89. The sum of all possible values of the real parameter b if the difference between the largest and smallest values of the function $f(x) = x^2 - 2bx + 1$ in the interval $[0, 1]$ is 4 is λ, then $9\lambda + 11$ is ....

90. Let set of all possible values of λ such that $f(x) = e^{2x} - (\lambda + 1)e^x + 2x$ is monotonically increasing for $\forall\, x \in R$ is $(-\infty, k]$. Then, the value of $\frac{38}{3}k$ is ....

91. There is a point (p, q) on the graph of $f(x) = x^2$ and a point (r, s) on the graph of $g(x) = -\frac{8}{x}$, where $p > 0$ and $r < 0$. If the line through (p, d) and (r, s) is also tangent to both the curves at these points respectively, then find the value of $(p + r) + 30$ is ....

92. $f(x) = \max |2 \sin y - x|$, where $y \in R$. If the minimum value of $f(x)$ is α, then number of diagonals in polygon having vertices 5α is ....

93. Let $f(x) = \int_0^x ((a-1)(t^2 + t + 1)^2 - (a+1)(t^4 + t^2 + 1))dt$. Then, the total number of integral values of a for which $f'(x) = 0$ has no real roots is γ, then $2\gamma + 7$ is ....

94. The number of real roots of the equation $x^{2013} + e^{2014x} = 0$ is r, then $3r + 19$ is ....

95. Let $f(x) = x^2 + 2x - t^2$ and $f(x) = 0$ has two roots $\alpha(t)$ and $\beta(t)$ $(\alpha < \beta)$, where t is a real parameter. Let $I(t) = \int_\alpha^\beta f(x)dx$. If the maximum value of $I(t)$ be λ and $|\lambda| = \frac{p}{q}$, where p and q are relatively prime positive integers, then the product pq is ....

96. If $f(x)$ is continuous and differentiable in $[-3, 9]$ and $f'(x) \in [-2, 8]$, $\forall\, x \in (-3, 9)$. Let N be the number of divisors of the greatest possible value of $f(9) - f(-3)$, then the sum of digits of N is ......

97. The number of real root(s) of the equation $ae^x = 1 + x + \frac{x^2}{2}$, where a is positive constant, is λ, then sum of infinite terms having λ as first term and $\frac{\lambda}{3}$ as common ratio, is ....

Matching Type Questions

98. Match the following columns.

	Column I		Column I
A.	If $\Pi\, b$ denotes the product of all possible values of b and $\Sigma\, b$ denotes the sum of all possible values of b, for which a line tangent to the graph of $f(x) = x^3 - \frac{11x}{3}$ at the point $M(b, f(b))$ passes through the point $N(3, 0)$, then $\Sigma\, b - \Pi\, b$ has the value equals to	(p)	1
B.	The real value of a for which the integral $\int_{a-1}^{a+1} e^{-(x-1)^2} dx$ attains its maximum value is equal to	(q)	4
C.	Line l is tangent to the curve $y = e^x$ and is parallel to the line $x - 4y = 1$. If x intercept of the line is $-\ln(ke)$, $k \in N$, then k is equal to	(r)	6
		(s)	10

99. Consider $f(x) = |\ln|x|| - kx^2, x \neq 0$.
Match the column I with the value of k in column II.

Column I		Column II
A. $f(x) = 0$ has two distinct solutions	(p)	$k = 0$
B. $f(x) = 0$ has four distinct solutions	(q)	$k = \frac{1}{2e}$
C. $f(x) = 0$ has six distinct solutions	(r)	$k \in \left(\frac{1}{2e}, \infty\right)$
D. $f(x) = 0$ has no solution	(s)	$k \in (-\infty, 0)$
	(t)	$k \in \left(0, \frac{1}{2e}\right)$

100. The function $f(x) = \sqrt{ax^3 + bx^2 + cx + d}$ has its non-zero local minimum and maximum values at $x = -2$ and $x = 2$, respectively. If a is one of the root of $x^2 - x - 6 = 0$, then match the following

Column I	Column II
A. The value of a is	(p) 0
B. The value of b is	(q) 24
C. The value of c is	(r) greater than 32
D. The value of d is	(s) -2

101. Match the following columns.

Column I		Column II
A. The ratio of altitude to the radius of the cylinder of maximum volume that can be inscribed in a given sphere is	(p)	$\frac{1}{\sqrt{2}}$
B. The ratio of radius to the altitude of the cone of the greatest volume which can be inscribed in a given sphere is	(q)	$\sqrt{2}$
C. The cone circumscribing the sphere of radius r has the maximum volume if its semi vertical angle is θ, then $33 \sin\theta =$	(r)	$\frac{32}{3}$
D. The greatest value of x^3y^4 if $2x + 3y = 7$, $x \geq 0, y \geq 0$ is	(s)	11

Previous Year Questions

102. Let the function $f : R \to R$ be defined by

$$f(x) = \frac{\sin x}{e^{\pi x}} \frac{(x^{2023} + 2024x + 2025)}{(x^2 - x + 3)} + \frac{2}{e^{\pi x}} \frac{(x^{2023} + 2024x + 2025)}{(x^2 - x + 3)}$$

Then, the number of solutions of $f(x) = 0$ in R is ....
[Numerical Value Type, 2024 Adv.]

103. Let S be the set of all twice differentiable functions f from R to R such that $\frac{d^2 f}{dx^2}(x) > 0$ for all $x \in (-1, 1)$. For $f \in S$, let X_f be the number of points $x \in (-1, 1)$ for which $f(x) = x$. Then, which of the following statements is(are) true? **[More than Correct Type, 2023 Adv.]**

(a) There exists a function $f \in S$ such that $X_f = 0$
(b) For every function $f \in S$, we have $X_f \leq 2$
(c) There exists a function $f \in S$ such that $X_f = 2$
(d) There does not exist any function f in S such that $X_f = 1$

104. Let $f : (0, 1) \to R$ be the function defined as $f(x) = [4x]\left(x - \frac{1}{4}\right)^2\left(x - \frac{1}{2}\right)$, where $[x]$ denotes the greatest integer less than or equal to x. Then, which of the following statements is(are) true?
[More than Correct Type, 2023 Adv.]

(a) The function f is discontinuous exactly at one point in (0, 1)
(b) There is exactly one point in (0, 1) at which the function f is continuous but not differentiable
(c) The function f is not differentiable at more than three points in (0, 1)
(d) The minimum value of the function f is $-\frac{1}{512}$

105. Let $\alpha = \sum_{k=1}^{\infty} \sin^{2k}\left(\frac{\pi}{6}\right)$. Let $g : [0, 1] \to R$ be the function defined by $g(x) = 2^{\alpha x} + 2^{\alpha(1-x)}$. Then, which of the following statements is/are true?
[More than Correct Type, 2022 Adv.]

(a) The minimum value of $g(x)$ is $2^{7/6}$
(b) The maximum value of $g(x)$ is $1 + 2^{1/3}$
(c) The function $g(x)$ attains its maximum at more than one point
(d) The function $g(x)$ attains its minimum at more than one point

106. Let $f : R \to R$ be defined by $f(x) = \frac{x^2 - 3x - 6}{x^2 + 2x + 4}$. Then, which of the following statements is(are) true?
[More than Correct Type, 2021 Adv.]

(a) f is decreasing in the interval $(-2, -1)$
(b) f is increasing in the interval (1, 2)
(c) f is onto
(d) Range of f is $\left[-\frac{3}{2}, 2\right]$

Stem

(Q. Nos. 107 and 108)

- Let $f_1:(0,\infty)\to R$ and $f_2:(0,\infty)\to R$ be defined by $f_1(x)=\int_0^x \prod_{j=1}^{21}(t-j)^j\,dt,\ x>0$ and $f_2(x)=98(x-1)^{50}-600(x-1)^{49}+2450,\ x>0$, where for any positive integer n and real numbers $a_1,a_2,\ldots,a_n$, $\prod_{i=1}^{n}a_i$ denotes the product of $a_1,a_2,\ldots,a_n$. Let m_i and n_i, respectively, denote the number of points of local minima and the number of points of local maxima of function f_i, $i=1,2$ in the interval $(0,\infty)$.

[Stem Type, 2021 Adv.]

107. The value of $2m_1+3n_1+m_1n_1$ is ....

108. The value of $6m_2+4n_2+8m_2n_2$ is ....

109. Consider the rectangles lying in the region

$$\left\{(x,y)\in R\times R: 0\le x\le\frac{\pi}{2}\text{ and } 0\le y\le 2\sin(2x)\right\}$$

and having one side on the X-axis. The area of the rectangle which has the maximum perimeter among all such rectangles, is **[Single Correct Type, 2020 Adv.]**

(a) $\frac{3\pi}{2}$ (b) π

(c) $\frac{\pi}{2\sqrt{3}}$ (d) $\frac{\pi\sqrt{3}}{2}$

110. Let the function $f:(0,\pi)\to R$ be defined by $f(\theta)=(\sin\theta+\cos\theta)^2+(\sin\theta-\cos\theta)^4$. Suppose, the function f has a local minimum at θ precisely when $\theta\in\{\lambda_1\pi,\ldots,\lambda_r\pi\}$, where $0<\lambda_1<\ldots\lambda_r<1$. Then, the value of $\lambda_1+\ldots+\lambda_r$ is ....

[Numerical Value Type, 2020 Adv.]

111. For a polynomial $g(x)$ with real coefficients, let m_g denote the number of distinct real roots of $g(x)$. Suppose, S is the set of polynomials with real coefficients defined by

$$S=\{(x^2-1)^2(a_0+a_1x+a_2x^2+a_3x^3):\ a_0,a_1,a_2,a_3\in R\};$$

For a polynomial f, let f' and f'' denote its first and second order derivatives, respectively. Then, the minimum possible value of $(m_{f'}+m_{f''})$, where $f\in S$, is .... **[Numerical Value Type, 2020 Adv.]**

EXERCISE 3

Challenging Problems

1. Find the values of x for which $f(x)+g(x)$ is strictly increasing/decreasing for $0 < x < 1$, where

$$f(x)=\frac{x^2}{2-2\cos x} \text{ and } g(x)=\frac{x^2}{6x-6\sin x}$$

2. If $f(0)=0$ and $f''(x)$ exists on $[0,\infty]$, show that

$$f'(x)-\frac{f(x)}{x}=\frac{1}{2}xf''(\xi), 0<\xi<x$$

and deduce that if $f''(x)$ is positive for positive values of x, then $\frac{f(x)}{x}$ strictly increases in $(0, \infty)$.

3. If $f(x)=\{-c^2+(b-1)c-2\}x+\int_0^x(\sin^2 x+\cos^4 x)dx$ is an increasing function, $\forall \in R$. Then, find all possible values of b, for any $c \in R$.

4. Find the number of real roots of the equation

$$\sum_{i=1}^{n}\frac{a_i^2}{x-b_i}=c, \text{ where } b_1<b_2<\ldots<b_n.$$

5. Consider the function,

$$f(x)=x^3-9x^2+15x+6, \text{ for } 1\le x\le 6$$

and $g(x)=\begin{cases}\text{minimum } f(t), & \text{for } 1\le t\le x, 1\le x\le 6\\ x-18, & \text{for } x>6\end{cases}$,

then prove that

(i) $g(x)$ is differentiable at $x=1$

(ii) $g(x)$ is discontinuous at $x=6$

(iii) $g(x)$ is continuous and derivable at $x=5$

(iv) $g(x)$ is monotonic in (1, 5)

6. Given $f:[0,\infty)\to R$ be a strictly increasing function such that the functions $g(x)=f(x)-3x$ and $h(x)=f(x)-x^3$ are both strictly increasing function. Then, prove that the function $F(x)=f(x)-x^2-x$ is increasing throughout $(0, \infty)$.

7. If $H(x_0)=0$ for some $x=x_0$ and $\frac{d}{dx}H(x)>2cx\,H(x)$ for all $x\ge x_0$, where $c>0$, then prove that $H(x)$ cannot be zero for any $x>x_0$.

8. Using calculus establish the inequality.

$$(x^b+y^b)^{\frac{1}{b}}<(x^a+y^a)^{\frac{1}{a}}, \text{ where } x>0, y>0 \text{ and } b>a>0.$$

9. Prove that $f(x)=\left(1+\frac{1}{x}\right)^x$ is strictly increasing in its domain. Hence, draw the graph of $f(x)$ and find its range.

10. Let R^+ be the set of positive real numbers. Find all functions $f:R^+\to R^+$ such that for all $x, y\in R^+$, $f(x)\,f(yf(x))=f(x+y)$.

11. Let $f\in c'[a,b]$, $f(a)=0$ and suppose that $\lambda\in R, \lambda>0$ is such that $|f'(x)|\le\lambda|f(x)|$ for all $x\in[a,b]$. Is it true that $f(x)=0$ for all $x\in[a,b]$?

12. Prove the inequality

$$\sin x+2x\ge\frac{3x(x+1)}{\pi}, \forall\, x\in\left(0,\frac{\pi}{2}\right).$$

13. If $0<x<1$, show that

$$2x<\ln\frac{1+x}{1-x}<2x\left(1+\frac{1}{3}\cdot\frac{x^2}{1-x^2}\right).$$

Hence, deduce that

$$e<\left(1+\frac{1}{n}\right)^{n+\frac{1}{2}}<e\cdot e^{\frac{1}{12\,n(n+1)}}.$$

14. If x is increasing at the rate of 2 cm/s at the instant, when $x=3$ cm and $y=1$ cm, at what rate y must be changing in order that the quantity $(2xy-3x^2y)$ shall be neither increasing nor decreasing.

If $S=\{(a,b)\in R\times R: x=a, y=b, 2xy-3x^2y=\text{constant} \Rightarrow \frac{dy}{dx}>0\}$

$S'=\{(x,y)\in A\times B: -1\le A\le 1 \text{ and } -1\le B\le 1\}$, then find the area $S\cap S'$.

15. Consider a square with vertices at (1, 1) (− 1, 1) (− 1, − 1) and (1, − 1). Let S be the region consisting of all points inside the square which are nearer to the origin than to any edge. Sketch the region S and find its area.

16. Find the maximum value of $f(x)=|x|^p\,|x-1|^q$, for all $x\in$ where $p, q, \in$ $f(x)=\begin{cases}(-1)^{p+q}x^p(x-1)^q, & x<0\\ 0, & x=0\\ (-1)^q x^p(x-1)^q, & 0<x<1\\ 0, & x=1\\ x^p(x-1)^q, & x>1\end{cases}$

17. Obtain the maximum and minimum values of the expression $\dfrac{x^2-2x\cos\alpha+1}{x^2-2x\cos\beta+1}$, $x\in R$ and $0<\beta<\dfrac{\pi}{2}$.

18. Determine the points of maxima and minima of the function $f(x)=\dfrac{1}{8}\ln x-bx+x^2$, $x>0$, where $b\geq 0$ is constant.

Answer Key

Exercise 1

1. (c)	2. (b)	3. (b)	4. (c)	5. (c)	6. (a)	7. (d)	8. (b)	9. (d)	10. (b)
11. (c)	12. (a)	13. (c)	14. (b)	15. (c)	16. (b)	17. (b)	18. (d)	19. (d)	20. (b)
21. (a)	22. (c)	23. (b)	24. (b)	25. (c)	26. (d)	27. (a)	28. (c)	29. (a)	30. (c)
31. (25)	32. (17)	33. (5)	34. (9)	35. (21)	36. (2)	37. (36)	38. (64)	39. (14)	40. (2)
41. (27)	42. (24)	43. (2)	44. (3)	45. (3)	46. (1)	47. (4)	48. (8)	49. (5)	50. (4)
51. (9)	52. (d)	53. (a)	54. (c)	55. (d)	56. (b)	57. (c)	58. (c)	59. (b)	60. (a)
61. (c)	62. (c)	63. (c)	64. (b)	65. (a)	66. (a)	67. (b)	68. (a)	69. (252)	70. (39)
71. (128)	72. (1600)	73. (4)	74. (d)	75. (c)	76. (b)	77. (d)	78. (c)	79. (c)	80. (b)
81. (a)	82. (a)	83. (b)	84. (a)	85. (5)	86. (b)	87. (c)	88. (c)	89. (a)	90. (3)
91. (c)	92. (c)	93. (a)	94. (b)	95. (4)	96. (9)				

Exercise 2

1. (a)	2. (c)	3. (c)	4. (d)	5. (c)	6. (b)	7. (a)	8. (a)	9. (d)	10. (b)
11. (a)	12. (a)	13. (c)	14. (a)	15. (b)	16. (c)	17. (a)	18. (d)	19. (a)	20. (a)
21. (a)	22. (b)	23. (c)	24. (d)	25. (d)	26. (c)	27. (d)	28. (a)	29. (a,d)	30. (a,b,c,d)
31. (a,c)	32. (a,b,c)	33. (a,b,d)	34. (a,b,c)	35. (a,d)	36. (a,b,c,d)	37. (a,d)	38. (d)	39. (a,c)	40. (a,b,c,d)
41. (c,d)	42. (a,d)	43. (a,d)	44. (a,b,c,d)	45. (a,b,c,d)	46. (a,b,d)	47. (a,b,c,d)	48. (a,c)	49. (a,b,c)	50. (c)
51. (b)	52. (c)	53. (d)	54. (d)	55. (c)	56. (c)	57. (d)	58. (d)	59. (d)	60. (78)
61. (3)	62. (1)	63. (18)	64. (5)	65. (9)	66. (9)	67. (7)	68. (3)	69. (5)	70. (2)
71. (2)	72. (2)	73. (3)	74. (2)	75. (6)	76. (3)	77. (5)	78. (6)	79. (7)	80. (1)
81. (2)	82. (8)	83. (3)	84. (0)	85. (81)	86. (32)	87. (0.25)	88. (625)	89. (20)	90. (38)
91. (35)	92. (35)	93. (13)	94. (22)	95. (12)	96. (15)	97. (1.5)			

98. (A) → (s); (B) → (p); (C) → (q)
99. (A) → (r,p); (B) → (q); (C) → (t); (D) → (s)
100. (A) → (s); (B) → (p); (C) → (q); (D) → (r)
101. (A) → (q); (B) → (p); (C) → (s); (D) → (r)

102. (1) 103. (a,b,c) 104. (a,b) 105. (a,b,c) 106. (a,b) 107. (57) 108. (6) 109. (c) 110. (0.50) 111. (5)

Solutions

Exercise 1 - JEE Main Pattern

1. $f(x) = \sin^2 x - (2a + 1)\sin x + (a - 3)$

$f'(x) = \cos x(2\sin x - 1 - 2a) = 0$

$\Rightarrow \cos x = 0 \text{ or } 2\sin x - 1 - 2a = 0$

$\Rightarrow x = \dfrac{\pi}{2} \text{ or } \sin x = \dfrac{2a+1}{2}$

At $\sin x = \dfrac{2a+1}{2}, \left(\dfrac{2a+1}{2}\right)^2 - (2a+1)\dfrac{(2a+1)}{2} + (a-3)$

$= \dfrac{(2a+1)^2}{2}\left[\dfrac{1}{2} - 1\right] + a - 3$

$= \dfrac{-(4a^2 + 4a + 1) + 4a - 12}{4}$

$= \dfrac{-4a^2 - 13}{4}$

$= -\left(a^2 + \dfrac{13}{4}\right) \le 0$

$\therefore a \in R$

At $x = 0$, $f(x) = a - 3 \le 0$

$\Rightarrow a \le 3$

At $x = \dfrac{\pi}{2}$, $f(x) = -a - 3 \le 0$

$\Rightarrow -3 \le a$

2. $f''(x) - 3f'(x) > 3, f'(0) = -1$

Let us consider, $g(x) = f(x) + x$

$g'(x) = f'(x) + 1$

$g''(x) = f''(x)$

Now, $f''(x) > 3(f'(x) + 1)$

$\dfrac{f''(x)}{f'(x) + 1} > 3$

On integrating, $f'(x) + 1 > e^{3x + C} > 0$

$\Rightarrow g'(x) > 0$

3. $\tan(\pi \cos\theta) = \cot(\pi \sin\theta), 0 < \theta \le \dfrac{\pi}{2}$

$\Rightarrow \pi\cos\theta = \dfrac{\pi}{2} - \pi\sin\theta$

$\Rightarrow \cos\theta + \sin\theta = \dfrac{1}{2}$

$\Rightarrow f(x) = 2^{-x}$

$f'(x) = -2^{-x} < 0$

4. $\because f : R \to R$ be a differentiable function and tangent drawn to the curve at any point $x \in (a, b)$ always lie below the curve.

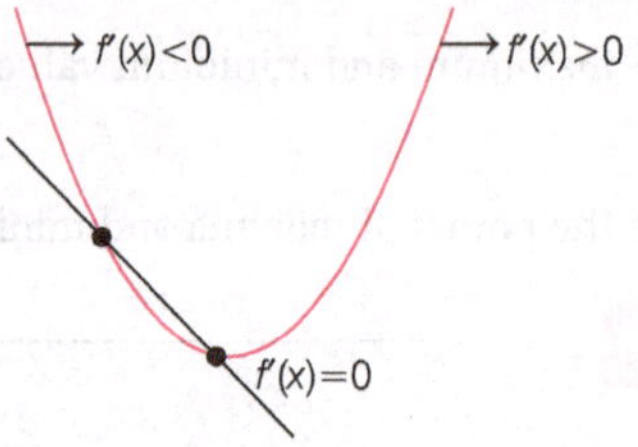

From figure,

$f''(x) > 0$ [$\because f'(x)$ is increasing]

5. If $f''(x) > 0$

$\Rightarrow f'(x)$ is increasing function.

$g(x) = f(2 - x) + f(4 + x)$

$g'(x) = f'(4 + x) - f'(2 - x) > 0$

$\Rightarrow 4 + x > 2 - x$

$\Rightarrow 2x > -2$

$\therefore x > -1$

6. $F(x) = f(x) - \dfrac{\sqrt{3}x^2}{2}$

$\Rightarrow F'(x) = f'(x) - \sqrt{3}x$ ...(i)

Now, $g(x) = f(x) - x$

$g'(x) = f'(x) - 1 > 0$ ...(ii)

As, $h(x) = f(x) - x^3$

$h'(x) = f'(x) - 3x^2 = f'(x) - 3x^2 > 0$ ...(iii)

Now, for $x \in R$, $\sqrt{3}x < 1$ or $3x^2$

Hence, $f'(x) - \sqrt{3}x > 0$

7. $f(x) = x\sqrt{4ax - x^2}$

$f'(x) = \sqrt{4ax - x^2} + \dfrac{x(2a - x)}{\sqrt{4ax - x^2}} = \dfrac{6ax - 2x^2}{\sqrt{4ax - x^2}} = \dfrac{2x(3a - x)}{\sqrt{x(4a - x)}}$

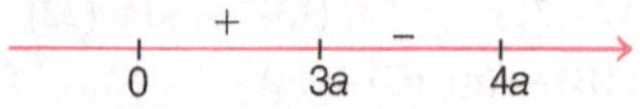

So, increasing in $(0, 3a)$ and decreasing in $(3a, 4a)$.

8. $f'(x) = \log_{1/3} \log_3(\sin(x) + a)) < 0$

$\log_3(\sin(x) + a)) > 1$

$\sin(x) + a > 3$

$a > 3 - \sin x$

$a > 4$

9. $g'(\theta) = (f(\sin^2\theta) - f(\cos^2\theta))\sin 2\theta$

In $\left(-\frac{\pi}{4}, 0\right)$, $\sin 2\theta < 0$ and $\sin^2\theta > \cos^2\theta$

and $f(\sin^2\theta) > f(\cos^2\theta)$

So, $g'(\theta) > 0$.

10. $f(x) = ax^3 + bx^2 + cx + d$

$f(x)$ is increasing cubic function, $a > 0$.

$f'(x) = 3ax^2 + 2bx + c > 0$

$\Rightarrow \quad 4b^2 - 12ac < 0$ and $a > 0 \Rightarrow b^2 - 3ac < 0$

$b^2 < 3ac$ and $a > 0, 3b^2 < c^2$

Now, $h(x) = \int_a^x g(t)\,dt$

$$h'(x) = g(x)$$
$$= a(3ax^2 + 2bx + c) + b(6ax + 2b) + c^2$$
$$= 3a^2x^2 + 2abx + \frac{b^2}{3} + 6abx + 2b^2 + 3b^2$$
$$> \left(\sqrt{3}ax + \frac{4b}{\sqrt{3}}\right)^2 > 0.$$

11. $f(x) = 3\cos^4 x + 10\cos^3 x + 6\cos^2 x - 3$

$$f'(x) = -6\sin x(2\cos^3 x + 5\cos^2 x + 2\cos x)$$
$$= -3\sin 2x(2\cos^2 x + 5\cos x + 2)$$
$$= -3\sin 2x(\cos x + 2)(2\cos x + 1) = 0$$

$\therefore \ x = \frac{\pi}{2}, \frac{2\pi}{3}$

Now, $f'(x) > 0$ in interval $\left(\frac{\pi}{2}, \frac{2\pi}{3}\right)$

and $f'(x) < 0$ in interval $\left(0, \frac{\pi}{2}\right)$ and $\left(\frac{2\pi}{3}, \pi\right)$.

12. $\lim_{n\to\infty} \frac{1}{f^n(x)} = \lim_{n\to\infty} \frac{1}{g\cdot g\cdot \ldots g(x)}$

As, $g(x)$ is increasing function from $(0, \infty)$.

$\lim_{n\to\infty} g(x) \to \infty$

$\therefore \ \lim_{n\to\infty} \frac{1}{f^n(x)} = 0$

13. $f'(x) > 0$ and $f''(x) < 0$

Let point p that divides a and b in ratio $1 : \lambda$.

Point $p \to \frac{b + a\lambda}{1+\lambda}$.

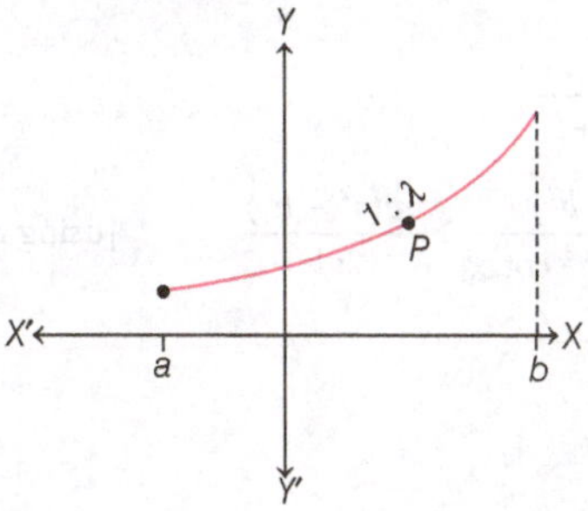

Their corresponding $f(x) = \frac{f(b) + \lambda f(a)}{1+\lambda}$

$\Rightarrow \quad$ Value at point $p = f\left(\frac{b + a\lambda}{1+\lambda}\right)$

$\Rightarrow \quad f\left(\frac{b + a\lambda}{1+\lambda}\right) < \frac{f(b) + \lambda f(a)}{1+\lambda}$

14. $g'(x) = 2(6x^2 - 6x) \times f'(2x^3 - 3x^2)$

$$+ (12x - 12x^2) \times f'(6x^2 - 4x^3 - 3)$$
$$g'(x) = (12x^2 - 12x)[f'(2x^3 - 3x^2) - f'(6x^2 - 4x^3 - 3)]$$
$$= 12x(x-1)[f'(2x^3 - 3x^2) - f'(6x^2 - 4x^3 - 3)]$$

For increasing,

If $x \in (1, \infty)$

$$2x^3 - 3x^2 > 6x^2 - 4x^3 - 3$$
$$6x^3 - 9x^2 + 3 > 0$$
$$\Rightarrow \quad 2x^3 - 3x^2 + 1 > 0$$

$\therefore \ x \in (1, \infty)$

If $x \in (0, 1)$, then

$$6x^2 - 4x^3 - 3 > 2x^3 - 3x^2$$
$$2x^3 - 3x^2 + 1 < 0$$

No solution.

If $x < 0$, then

$$2x^3 - 3x^2 + 1 > 0$$
$$x \in \left(-\frac{1}{2}, 0\right)$$

15. $\frac{(f(7) - f(2))}{1} \cdot \frac{(f(7)^2 + f(2)^2 + f(2)\cdot(7)}{3} = \frac{(f(7))^3 - (f(2))^3}{3}$

Let $\quad g(x) = (f(x))^3$

$\Rightarrow \quad g'(c) = \frac{(f(7))^3 - (f(2))^3}{(7-2)}$

$\Rightarrow \quad 3(f(c))^2 \cdot f'(c) = \frac{(f(7))^3 - (f(2))^3}{5}$

$\Rightarrow \quad \frac{(f(7))^3 - (f(2))^3}{3} = 5(f(c))^2 f'(c)$

16. Given that $f(|x|) = 0$ has eight real roots

i.e. $\pm\alpha_1, \pm\alpha_2, \pm\alpha_3, \pm\alpha_4$ (say) where $\alpha_1 > 0$

$\Rightarrow f(x) = 0$ has 4 positive real roots $\alpha_1, \alpha_2, \alpha_3, \alpha_4$ and 1 negative.

17. $f(x) = (ab - b^2 - 2)x + \int_0^x (\cos^4\theta + \sin^4\theta)\,d\theta$

$\Rightarrow f'(x) = (ab - b^2 - 2) + (\cos^4 x + \sin^4 x) \le 0$

$\Rightarrow \cos^4 x + \sin^4 x + ab - b^2 - 2 \le 0, \ \forall \ x \in R$ and $b \in R$

$\Rightarrow 1 - 2\sin^2 x\cos^2 x + ab - b^2 - 2 \le 0$

$\Rightarrow -b^2 + ab - 1 \le \frac{1}{2}\sin^2 2x, \ \forall \ x, b \in R$

$\Rightarrow \quad b^2 - ab + 1 \ge \frac{-1}{2}\sin^2 2x, \ \forall \ x, b \in R$

$\Rightarrow \quad b^2 - ab + 1 \geq 0, \forall\, b \in R$

$\Rightarrow \quad (-a)^2 - 4 \leq 0$

$\therefore \quad a \in [-2, 2]$

18. $f(x) = \int_1^x \left(t \ln t - \dfrac{\ln t}{t} \right) dx, x > 1$

$\Rightarrow \quad f'(x) = x \ln x - \dfrac{\ln x}{x}$

$\therefore \quad f'(x) = 0$

$\Rightarrow (\ln x)\left(x - \dfrac{1}{x} \right) = 0$

$\Rightarrow \quad \ln x = 0 \text{ or } x - \dfrac{1}{x} = 0$

$\Rightarrow \quad x = 1 \text{ or } x^2 - 1 = 0$

$\Rightarrow \quad x = 1 \text{ or } x = \pm 1$

But $x > 1$

$\Rightarrow f$ has no stationary point.

$\because \quad \left(x - \dfrac{1}{x} \right) = \dfrac{x^2 - 1}{x} > 0$

$\Rightarrow \quad (x^2 - 1) > 0$

$\Rightarrow \quad x^2 - 1 > 0 \text{ as } x > 1$

$\Rightarrow \quad (x + 1)(x - 1) > 0 \Rightarrow x > 1$

Also, $\ln x$ for $x > 1$

$\therefore \quad f'(x) > 0, \forall\, x > 1$

$\Rightarrow f(x)$ is monotonically increasing function for $x > 1$.

19. $\because f'(c) = 0$

$f''(c) > 0$

$\Rightarrow c$ is a point of local minima.

$f''(c) < 0$

$\Rightarrow c$ is a point of local maxima.

If $f''(c) = 0$, then we find $f'''(c)$, if $f'''(c) \neq 0$, then $x = c$ is a point of inflexion i.e. neither maxima, nor minima and if $f'''(c) = 0$, then we find $f^{iv}(c)$, if $f^{iv}(c) > 0$

$\Rightarrow x = c$ is a part minima and if $f^{iv}(c) < 0$

$\Rightarrow x = c$ is a part of maxima and so on.

So, $f'(c) = f''(c) = f'''(c) = f^{v}(c) = 0$

$\Rightarrow x = c$ may be a point of extremum or point of inflection.

20. $x \in \left[\dfrac{5\pi}{4}, \dfrac{4\pi}{3} \right], f(x) = \int_{\frac{5\pi}{4}}^{x} (3 \sin t + 4 \cos t)\, dt$

$f'(x) = (3 \sin x + 4 \cos x)$

$\because \; x \in \left[\dfrac{5\pi}{4}, \dfrac{4\pi}{3} \right]$, $\sin x < 0$ and $\cos x < 0$

$\Rightarrow f'(x) < 0, \forall\, x \in \left(\dfrac{5\pi}{4}, \dfrac{4\pi}{3} \right)$

$\Rightarrow f(x)$ is a decreasing function on $\left[\dfrac{5\pi}{4}, \dfrac{4\pi}{3} \right]$.

$\Rightarrow f(x)$ has its least value at $x = \dfrac{4\pi}{3}$ given by $f\left(\dfrac{4\pi}{3} \right)$.

$$= \int_{\frac{5\pi}{4}}^{\frac{4\pi}{3}} (3 \sin t + 4 \cos t)\, dt = [3(-\cos t)]_{\frac{5\pi}{4}}^{\frac{4\pi}{3}} + 4[\sin t]_{\frac{5\pi}{4}}^{\frac{4\pi}{3}}$$

$$= -3\left[\left(-\frac{1}{2} \right) - \left(-\frac{1}{\sqrt{2}} \right) \right] + 4\left[\frac{-\sqrt{3}}{2} + \frac{1}{\sqrt{2}} \right]$$

$$= \frac{3}{2} - \frac{3}{\sqrt{2}} - \frac{4\sqrt{3}}{2} + \frac{4}{\sqrt{2}} = \frac{3}{2} - 2\sqrt{3} + \frac{1}{\sqrt{2}}$$

21. $f(x) = (4 \sin^2 x - 1)^n (e^x - x + 1)$

At $x = \dfrac{\pi}{6} + h, \sin^2 x = \dfrac{1}{4} + h$

and at $x = \dfrac{\pi}{6} - h, \; \sin^2 x = \dfrac{1}{4} - h$

$$f\left(\frac{\pi}{6} + h \right) = (4h)^n \left(e^{\frac{\pi}{6} + h} - \frac{\pi}{6} - h - 1 \right)$$

$$f\left(\frac{\pi}{6} - h \right) = (-4h)^n \left(e^{\frac{\pi}{6} - h} - \frac{\pi}{6} + h - 1 \right)$$

For $f\left(\dfrac{\pi}{6} - h \right) > f\left(\dfrac{\pi}{6} \right) < f\left(\dfrac{\pi}{6} + h \right)$

Hence, n needs to be even natural number.

22. Let $y = e^{(2x^2 - 2x + 1) \sin^2 x}$

Now, $f(x) = 2x^2 - 2x + 1$ has minima at

$$x = \frac{1}{2} \text{ and } f\left(\frac{1}{2} \right) = \frac{1}{2}$$

So, minimum value of y occurs when

$(2x^2 - 2x + 1) \sin^2 x = 0 \Rightarrow y = e^0 = 1$

23. $y = 4x^3 - 12x^2 + 11x - 3$

$\dfrac{dy}{dx} = 12x^2 - 24x + 11 = 0$

$$x = \frac{24 \pm \sqrt{48}}{24} = \frac{6 \pm \sqrt{3}}{6}$$

$+ \quad \dfrac{6 - \sqrt{3}}{6} \quad - \quad \dfrac{6 + \sqrt{3}}{6} \quad +$

For $x \in [2, 3]$, y is an increasing function.

Maximum value of $f(x)$ is at $x = 3$.

$= \log_{10}(4(3)^3 - 12(3)^2 + 33 - 3)$

$= 1 + \log_{10} 3$

24. $y = \dfrac{ab(a^2 - b^2) \sin 2x}{2(a^2 \sin^2 x + b^2 \cos^2 x)}$

$$= \frac{ab(a^2 - b^2) \tan x}{a^2 \tan^2 x + b^2}$$

$$y = \frac{ab(a^2 - b^2)}{a^2 \tan x + b^2 \cot x} \geq \frac{ab(a^2 - b^2)}{2ab} \qquad \text{[using AM} \geq \text{GM]}$$

$$y_{\max} = \frac{a^2 - b^2}{2}$$

25. $f(x) = \dfrac{t + 3x - x^2}{x - 4}$

$$\Rightarrow f'(x) = \frac{(x-4)(3-2x) - (t + 3x - x^2)}{(x-4)^2}$$

$$= \frac{-x^2 + 8x - (12 + t)}{(x-4)^2} = 0$$

$\Rightarrow \quad 64 - 4(12 + t) > 0$

$\Rightarrow \quad 4 - t > 0$

$\Rightarrow \quad t < 4$

26. Let say x, $a - x$ are two length.

Side of square $= \dfrac{a - x}{4}$

Radius of circle $= \dfrac{x}{2\pi}$

$$\text{Area, } A = \frac{(a-x)^2}{16} + \pi \frac{x^2}{4\pi^2}$$

$$\frac{dA}{dx} = \frac{-1}{8}(a - x) + \frac{x}{2\pi} = 0$$

$\Rightarrow \quad \dfrac{a}{8} = \dfrac{x}{2\pi} + \dfrac{x}{8}$

$\Rightarrow \quad \pi a = 4x + \pi x$

$\Rightarrow \quad x = \dfrac{\pi a}{4 + \pi}$

Now, $\quad a - x = \dfrac{4a}{4 + \pi}$

$$A = \frac{a^2}{(4+\pi)^2} + \frac{1}{4}\frac{\pi a^2}{(4+\pi)^2}$$

$$= \frac{a^2}{4(4+\pi)}$$

27. $y = \sqrt{\sin^2 x + 2a^2} - \sqrt{2a^2 - 2 + \sin^2 x}$

On rationalising the expression

$$y = \frac{2}{\sqrt{\sin^2 x + 2a^2} + \sqrt{2a^2 - 2 + \sin^2 x}}$$

For maximum value, denominator should be minimum.

$\Rightarrow \quad \sin x = 0$

$$y = \frac{\sqrt{2}}{a + \sqrt{a^2 - 1}}$$

$\Rightarrow \quad a = 1$ (for y to be maximum)

$y_{max} = \sqrt{2}$

28.

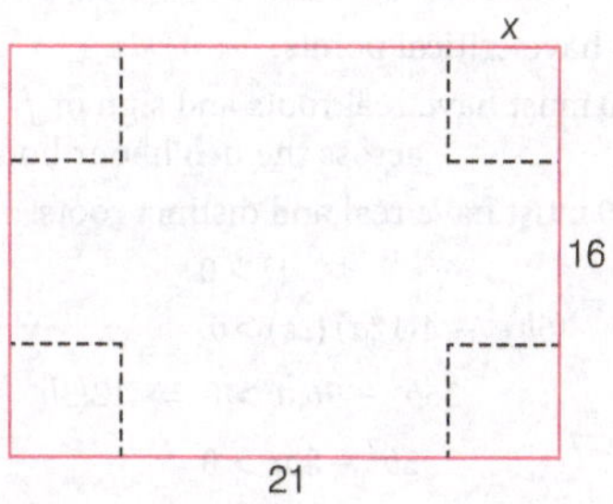

Volume $= (21 - 2x)(16 - 2x)x$

$$\frac{dv}{dx} = -2(16 - 2x)x - 2(21 - 2x)x + (21 - 2x)(16 - 2x)$$

$\Rightarrow \quad -32x + 4x^2 - 42x + 4x^2 + 4x^2 - 74x + 336 = 0$

$\Rightarrow \quad 12x^2 - 148x + 336 = 0$

$\Rightarrow \quad 3x^2 - 37x + 84 = 0$

$\Rightarrow \quad (x - 3)(3x - 28) = 0$

$x = 3$ or $\dfrac{28}{3}$

29. $f(x) = x - \log x + \displaystyle\int_2^x \left(\frac{1}{z} - 2 - 2\cos 4z\right) dz$

$$f'(x) = 1 - \frac{1}{x} + \frac{1}{x} - 2 - 2\cos 4x = 0$$

$\Rightarrow \quad \cos 4x = \dfrac{-1}{2}$

$\Rightarrow \quad 4x = \dfrac{2\pi}{3}$ or $2n\pi + \dfrac{2\pi}{3}$

$\Rightarrow \quad x = \dfrac{\pi}{6}$ or $\dfrac{n\pi}{2} + \dfrac{\pi}{6}$

30. Put $\sin^2\left(\dfrac{\theta}{n}\right) = x$

$$y = \frac{x^2 - x + 1}{x^2 + x + 1} = 1 - \frac{2}{\left(x + \dfrac{1}{x}\right) + 1}$$

As, $x + \dfrac{1}{x} \geq 2$ [as $x > 0$]

$$y \in \left[\frac{1}{3}, 1\right)$$

31. Let $x^2 = t$, $y = g(t)$ and $t = h(x)$,

where $g(t) = \dfrac{t^2 + 3t + 1}{t + 1}$, $t = x^2$

$$\therefore \frac{dy}{dx} = \frac{dg}{dt} \times \frac{dt}{dx} = \frac{(t+1)(2t+3) - (t^2 + 3t + 1)}{(t+1)^2} \times 2x$$

$$\therefore \frac{dy}{dx} = \frac{t^2 + 2t + 2}{(t+1)^2} \times (2x) = 0$$

$\Leftrightarrow \quad x = 0$ and $\dfrac{dy}{dx} < 0$ for $x < 0$ and $\dfrac{dy}{dx} > 0$ for $x > 0$

$\Rightarrow f(x)$ decreases on $[-1, 0)$ and increases on $[0, 2]$

Also, $f(x)$ is even function.

$\Rightarrow \quad f_{max} = f_{max}$ is $[0, 2] = f(2) = \dfrac{16 + 12 + 1}{4 + 1} = \dfrac{29}{5}$

$$\therefore [f_{max}]^2 = \left[\frac{29}{5}\right]^2 = 5^2 = 25$$

32. $f'(x) = 3\left(1 - \dfrac{\sqrt{21 - 4\lambda - \lambda^2}}{\lambda + 1}\right)x^2 + 5 \geq 0$

$\Leftrightarrow \quad 0 - 60\left(1 - \dfrac{\sqrt{24 - 4\lambda - \lambda^2}}{\lambda + 1}\right) \leq 0$ [i.e. $D \leq 0$]

$\Rightarrow \quad \left(1 - \dfrac{\sqrt{24 - 4\lambda - \lambda^2}}{\lambda + 1}\right) \geq 0$

It is trivially true for $\lambda + 1 < 0$.

i.e. $\lambda \in (-\infty, -1)$ and $\lambda^2 + 4\lambda - 21 \leq 0$

$\Rightarrow \lambda \in (-\infty, -1)$ and $\lambda \in [-7, 3]$

$\Rightarrow \lambda \in [-7, -1)$

For $\lambda + 1 > 0$ and $\lambda \in [-7, 3]$ i.e. $\lambda \in (-1, 3]$,

$$1 \geq \frac{\sqrt{21 - 4\lambda - \lambda^2}}{\lambda + 1}$$

$\Rightarrow \quad \lambda + 1 \geq \sqrt{21 - 4\lambda - \lambda^2}$

$\Rightarrow \quad \lambda^2 + 2\lambda + 1 \geq 21 - 4\lambda - \lambda^2 \Rightarrow 2\lambda^2 + 6\lambda - 20 \geq 0$

$\Rightarrow \lambda^2 + 3\lambda - 10 \geq 0 \Rightarrow (\lambda + 5)(\lambda - 2) \geq 0$

$\Rightarrow \quad \lambda \in (-\infty, -5] \cup [2, \infty)$, but $\lambda \in (2, 3]$

$\Rightarrow \quad \lambda \in (2, 3]$

$\therefore$ $f(x)$ increases for $\lambda \in [-7, -1) \cup [2, 3] = [a, b) \cup [c, d]$

$\Rightarrow \quad a = -7, b = -1, c = 2, d = 3$

$\therefore \quad |a + b + c + d| = |-7 - 1 + 2 + 3| = 3$

$\Rightarrow \quad |a + b + c + d|^2 + 8 = 9 + 8 = 17$

33. Perimeter $= 2(l + b) = 20$

$\Rightarrow \quad l + b = 10$

$\Rightarrow \quad \dfrac{dl}{dt} + \dfrac{db}{dt} = 0 \Rightarrow \dfrac{db}{dt} = -\dfrac{dl}{dt} = -2$ cm/sec

Now, $A = l \cdot b$

$\Rightarrow \quad \dfrac{dA}{dt} = l\dfrac{db}{dt} + b \cdot \dfrac{dl}{dt} \Rightarrow l(-2) + b(2) = -2(l - b)$

Now, $\quad \dfrac{dA}{dt} \leq 0$

$\Rightarrow \quad -2(l - b) \leq 0 \Rightarrow l \geq b$

$\Rightarrow \quad l \geq (10 - l) \qquad [\because l + b = 10]$

$\Rightarrow \quad 2l \geq 10 \Rightarrow l \geq 5$

$\therefore$ When $l = 5$ cm, area of rectangle start decreasing.

34. Let h be the height of cone and r be its radius.

Clearly, $\sqrt{6}$ will be the slant height of the cone.

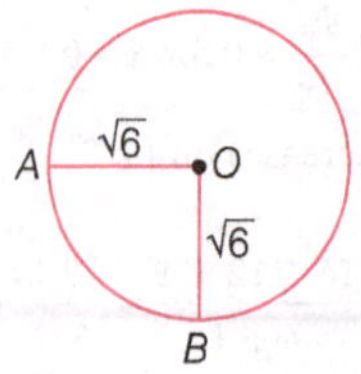

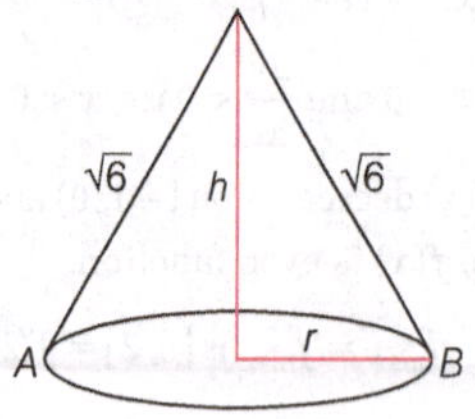

Thus, $\quad h^2 + r^2 = 6 \qquad$ ...(i)

Now, volume of cone is given by

$$V = \frac{4}{3}\pi r^2 h = \frac{4}{3}\pi(6 - h^2)h$$

$\therefore \quad \dfrac{dV}{dh} = \dfrac{4}{3}\pi(6 - 3h^2) = 0 \Rightarrow h^2 = 2$

$\Rightarrow \quad \dfrac{d^2V}{dh^2} = \dfrac{4}{3}\pi(-6h) = -8\pi h < 0$

$\Rightarrow V$ will be maximum for $h = \sqrt{2}$

$\therefore \quad V_{max} = V_0 = \dfrac{4}{3}\pi(6 - 2)\sqrt{2}$

$\Rightarrow \quad V_0 = \dfrac{16\sqrt{2}\pi}{3} = 8\sqrt{2}\left(\dfrac{2\pi}{3}\right) \Rightarrow \dfrac{V_0}{8\sqrt{2}} = \dfrac{2\pi}{3}$

$\Rightarrow \quad \tan^4\left(\dfrac{V_0}{8\sqrt{2}}\right) = \tan^4\left(\dfrac{2\pi}{3}\right) = \tan^4 \dfrac{\pi}{3} = 3^2 = 9$

35. $g(x) = \int_0^x f(t)\,dt$

$\Rightarrow g'(x) = f(x) \qquad$ ...(i)

and $g(0) = 0 \qquad$ ...(ii)

Now, $f'(x) = \lim\limits_{h \to 0} \dfrac{f(x + h) - f(x)}{h}$

$= \lim\limits_{h \to 0} \dfrac{f(x) + f(h) + 2xh - 1 - f(x)}{h}$

$= \lim\limits_{h \to 0} \dfrac{f(h) + 2xh - 1}{h} = 2x + \lim\limits_{h \to 0} \dfrac{f(h) - 1}{h}$

$= 2x + \lim\limits_{h \to 0} \dfrac{f(h) - f(0)}{h} = 2x + f'(0) = 2x + 2$

$\left[\begin{array}{l}\because \text{put } x = y = 0 \\ \Rightarrow f(0) = f(0) + f(0) - 1 \\ \Rightarrow f(0) = 1\end{array}\right]$

$\therefore \quad f'(x) = 2(x + 1)$

$\Rightarrow \quad f(x) = 2\left[\dfrac{x^2}{2} + x\right] + C$

$\Rightarrow \quad f(x) = x^2 + 2x + C$

$\because \quad f(0) = 1$

$\Rightarrow \quad C = 1$

$\Rightarrow \quad f(x) = (x + 1)^2 \qquad$ ...(iii)

Now, from Eqs. (i) and (iii), $g'(x) = (x + 1)^2 \geq 0, \forall x \in R$

$\Rightarrow g(x)$ is an increasing function and $g(x) = \int (x + 1)^2 dx$

$\Rightarrow \quad g(x) = \dfrac{(x + 1)^2}{3} + C_1$

Also, $g(0) = 0$

$\Rightarrow \quad C_1 = -\dfrac{1}{3} \Rightarrow g(x) = \dfrac{(x + 1)^3}{3} - \dfrac{1}{3}$

$\Rightarrow g$ maximum is $[1, 3] = g(3) = \dfrac{(4)^3}{3} - \dfrac{1}{3} = \dfrac{63}{3} = 21$

36. Let $\quad f(x) = ax^4 + bx^3 + cx^2 + dx + e$

$\Rightarrow \quad f'(x) = 4ax^3 + 3bx^2 + 2cx + d$

$\Rightarrow \quad f''(x) = 12ax^2 + 6bx + 2c$

For $f(x)$ to have critical points.

$f''(x) = 0$ must have real roots and sign of $f''(x)$ must change across the neighbour hood of these roots.

$f''(x) = 0$ must have real and distinct roots.

$$D > 0$$

$\Rightarrow \quad (6b)^2 - 4(12a)(2c) > 0$

$\Rightarrow \quad 36b^2 - 96ac > 0 \Rightarrow 12(3b^2 - 8ac) > 0$

$\Rightarrow \quad 3b^2 - 8ac > 0 \qquad$ ...(i)

Now, $\log[-3b^4 + 12b^2 - 32ac + 8ab^2c]$ is defined.

$\Rightarrow -3b^4 + 12b^2 - 32ac + 8ab^2c > 0$

$\Rightarrow \quad -3b^2(b^2-4) - 8ac(4-b^2) > 0$

$\Rightarrow \quad (b^2-4)(8ac-3b^2) > 0$

$\Rightarrow \quad (b^2-4)(3b^2-8ac) < 0$ ...(ii)

From Eq. (i) and (ii), $\quad b^2 - 4 < 0$

$\Rightarrow \quad b \in [-2, 2]$

$\Rightarrow$ Greatest possible value of $b = 2$

37. Since, $f(x)$ is twice differentiable, $f(x)$ and $f'(x)$ are continuous function and by the given information, the rough graph will be as shown below.

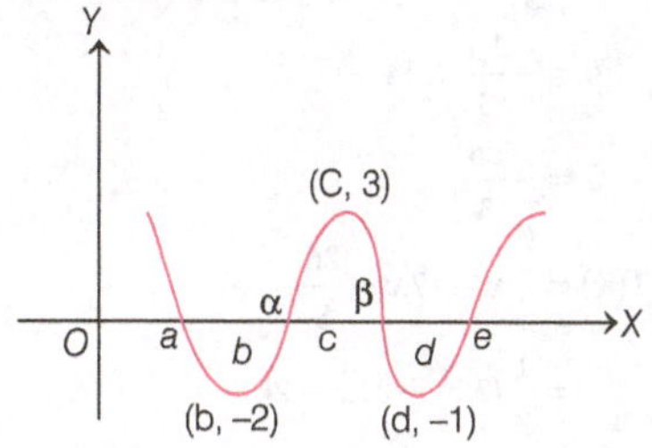

$$g(x) = (f'(x))^2 + f(x)\cdot f''(x) = \frac{d}{dx}(f(x)\cdot f'(x)) = \frac{dh}{dx} \quad ...(i)$$

where, $h(x) = f(x)\cdot f'(x)$

Clearly, $f(x) = 0$ has at least 4 roots $a, \alpha \in (b, c), \beta \in (c, d), e$ and $f'(x) = 0$ has at least 3 roots (3 stationary points).

$\Rightarrow h(x) = f(x)\cdot f'(x) = 0$ has at least 7 roots as roots of $f(x) = 0$ and that of $f'(x) = 0$ are different.

$\Rightarrow$ By Rolle's theorem, $h'(x) = g(x) = 0$ has at least 6 roots, at least one root between two consecutive roots of $h(x) = 0$

$\therefore$ Required answer $= 6^2 = 36$

38. Equation of parabola is $y = x^2 + 4$. Its parametric equation is $\left(\frac{1}{2}t, 4 + \frac{1}{2}t^2\right)$, let it be Q (nearest point to P).

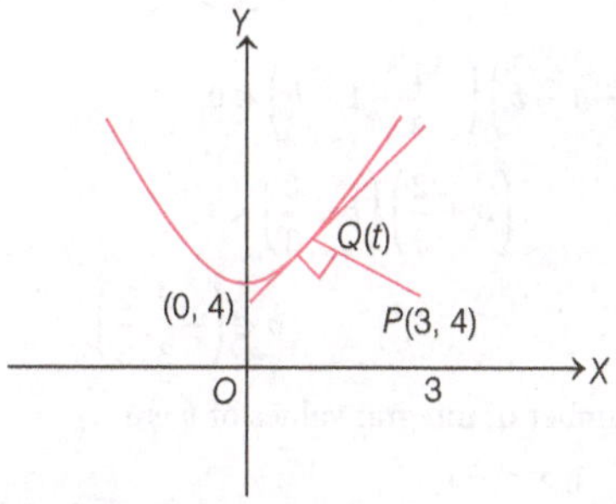

$\Rightarrow$ (Slope of tangent at Q) $\times$ (Slope of PQ) $= -1$

$$\Rightarrow \quad (t) \times \left(\frac{\frac{1}{4}t^2}{\frac{1}{2}t - 3}\right) = -1$$

$$\Rightarrow \quad \frac{t^3}{t-6} = -2$$

$$\Rightarrow \quad t^3 + 2t - 12 = 0 \Rightarrow t = 2$$

$\Rightarrow \quad Q \equiv (1, 5)$

$\Rightarrow \quad PQ = \sqrt{(3-1)^2 + (4-5)^2} = \sqrt{5}$

$\Rightarrow \quad d = \sqrt{5} \Rightarrow [d] = 2$

$\therefore \quad [d]^6 = 2^6 = 64$

39. $$T_{r+1} = {}^9C_r\left(\frac{a}{2}x^{1/6}\right)^{9-r}\cdot\left(\frac{b}{3}x^{\frac{-1}{3}}\right)^r$$

$$= {}^9C_r = \frac{(a)^{9-r}}{(2)^{9-r}}\cdot\frac{(b)^r}{(3)^r}\cdot(x)^{\frac{9-r}{6}-\frac{r}{3}}$$

For term independent of x,

$$\frac{9-r}{6} - \frac{r}{3} = 0 \Rightarrow r = 3$$

$$\therefore \quad T_4 = {}^9C_3\frac{(a)^6}{(2)^6}\cdot\frac{(b)^3}{(3)^3} = \frac{9\times8\times7}{6\times(2)^6(3)^3}\cdot a^6\cdot b^3$$

$$= \frac{7}{144}a^6b^3 = \frac{7}{144}(a^2b)^3 = \frac{7}{144}(\sqrt{a^2b})^6$$

$$\leq \frac{7}{144}\left(\frac{a^2+b}{2}\right)^6$$

$$= \frac{7}{144}\left(\frac{(2)^{\frac{5}{3}}\cdot(3)^{\frac{1}{3}}}{2}\right)^6 = \frac{7}{144}((2)^{2/3}\cdot(3)^{1/3})^6$$

$\therefore \quad T_4 \leq \frac{7}{144}\times(2)^4(3)^2 \Rightarrow T_4 \leq 7$

$\therefore$ Maximum value of $T_4 = 7$

$\therefore$ Required value $= 14$

40. For $0 < x < 1$, $f'(x) = -6x < 0$ and for $x > 1$, $f'(x) = 5 > 0$

$\Rightarrow f(x)$ is decreasing for $x \in (0, 1)$ and increasing for $x \in (1, \infty)$.

$\therefore$ For $f(x)$ to be minima at $x = 1$, $5\tan^{-1}\alpha - 3 \geq f(1)$

$\Rightarrow \quad 5\tan^{-1}\alpha - 3 \geq 2$

$\Rightarrow \quad \alpha \geq \tan 1 > \tan\frac{\pi}{4} = 1 \Rightarrow \alpha > 1$

$\Rightarrow$ Least integer value of $\alpha = 2$

41. Let $x + \sqrt{x^2 + \sin^2 x} = p$ ...(i)

$\Rightarrow \quad -\sin^2 x = P(x - \sqrt{x^2 + \sin^2 x})$

$\Rightarrow \quad x - \sqrt{x^2 + \sin^2 x} = -\frac{\sin^2 x}{p}$ ...(ii)

On adding Eqs. (i) and (ii), we get

$$2x = p - \frac{\sin^2 x}{p} \quad ...(iii)$$

$$\therefore \quad f(x) = 6\left(\cos x - \frac{p}{2} + \frac{\sin^2 x}{2p}\right)p$$

$\Rightarrow f(x) = 3(2p\cos x - p^2 + \sin^2 x)$

$= 3(2p\cos x - p^2 + 1 - \cos^2 x)$

$= 3[1 - (p^2 + \cos^2 x - 2p\cos x)]$

$= 3[1 - (p - \cos x)^2] \leq 3$

$\Rightarrow$ Maximum value of $f(x) = 3 \Rightarrow$ Its cube $= 27$

42. In similar, ΔADE and ΔAFC, $\frac{r}{R} = \frac{H-h}{H}$

$\Rightarrow \quad r = \frac{R}{H}(H-h) \quad$ ...(i)

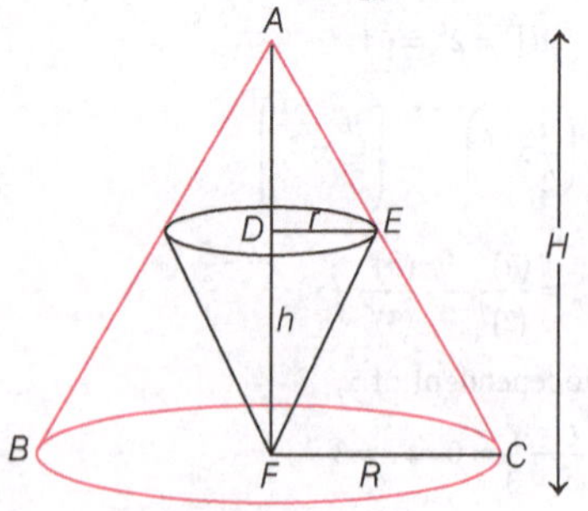

Now, volume of small cone,

$$V = \frac{1}{3}\pi r^2 h = \frac{1}{3}\pi \frac{R^2}{H^2}(H-h)^2 h$$

$$\Rightarrow \quad V = \frac{\pi R^2}{3H^2}(H^2 h + h^3 - 2Hh^2)$$

$$\Rightarrow \quad \frac{dV}{dh} = \frac{\pi R^2}{3H^2}(H^2 + 3h^2 - 4Hh)$$

$\therefore$ For maximum volume, $\frac{dV}{dh} = 0$

$\Rightarrow \quad H^2 + 3h^2 - 4Hh = 0$

$\Rightarrow \quad H^2 - 3hH - hH + 3h^2 = 0$

$\Rightarrow \quad H(H-3h) - h(H-3h) = 0$

$\Rightarrow \quad (H-h)(H-3h) = 0$

$\Rightarrow \quad H = h$ or $H = 3h$

But $H = h$ is impossible, hence $H = 3h$ for maximum volume.

Thus, $H : h = 3$

$\therefore$ Required value $= 8 \times 3 = 24$

43. Given, $\lim_{x \to 0}\left(\frac{P(x)}{x^3} - 2\right) = 4$

$$\therefore \quad \lim_{x \to 0} \frac{P(x)}{x^3} = 6$$

Consider $P(x) = ax^5 + bx^4 + 6x^3$

$\Rightarrow \quad P'(x) = 5ax^4 + 4bx^3 + 18x^2$

Now, $P'(-1) = 0 \Rightarrow 5a - 4b = -18$

and $\quad P'(1) = 0 \Rightarrow 5a + 4b = -18$

$\therefore$ On solving, we get $a = \frac{-18}{5}, b = 0$

Hence, $P(x) = \frac{-18}{5}x^5 + 6x^3 \Rightarrow [P(1)] = \left[\frac{12}{5}\right] = [2.4] = 2$

44. We have, $f(x, y) = x^2 + y^2 - 4x + 6y$

Let $(x, y) = (\cos\theta, \sin\theta)$, then $\theta \in \left[0, \frac{\pi}{2}\right]$ and

$$f(x, y) = f(\theta) = \cos^2\theta + \sin^2\theta - 4\cos\theta + 6\sin\theta$$

$$f'(\theta) = 6\cos\theta + 4\sin\theta > 0, \forall\, \theta \in \left[0, \frac{\pi}{2}\right]$$

$\therefore$ $f'(\theta)$ is strictly increasing in $\left[0, \frac{\pi}{2}\right]$.

$\therefore \quad f(\theta)_{\min} = f(0) = 1 - 4 + 0 = -3$

$\therefore \quad |m| = 3$

45. $f''(x) = 4x$

$f'(x) = 2x^2 + C$

Given, $f'(-2) = 1$

$\Rightarrow \quad C = -7$

$\therefore \quad f'(x) = 2x^2 - 7$

$f(x) = \frac{2}{3}x^3 - 7x + C, f(-2) = 0$

$0 = -\frac{16}{3} + 14 + C$

$\Rightarrow \quad C = -\frac{26}{3}$

$\therefore \quad f(x) = \frac{2}{3}x^3 - 7x - \frac{26}{3}$

$= \frac{1}{3}(2x^3 - 21x - 26)$

$\therefore \quad f(1) = -15$

$\therefore \quad \left|\frac{-15}{5}\right| = 3$

46. $f(x) = \frac{x^3}{3} - x - b,$

$f'(x) = x^2 - 1 = 0$

$\therefore \quad x = 1$ or -1

For three distinct roots, $f(x_1) \cdot f(x_2) < 0$, where x_1 and x_2 are the roots $f'(x) = 0$.

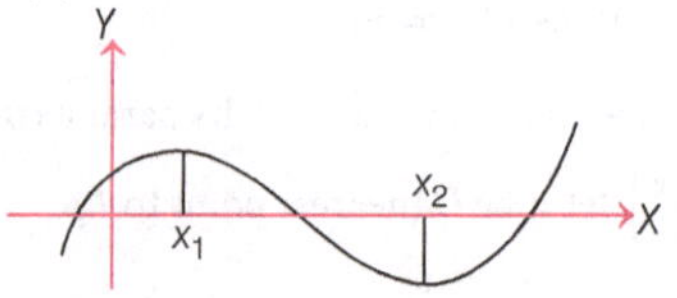

$$\Rightarrow \quad \left(\frac{1}{3} - 1 - b\right)\left(-\frac{1}{3} + 1 - b\right) < 0$$

$$\Rightarrow \quad \left(b + \frac{2}{3}\right)\left(b - \frac{2}{3}\right) < 0$$

$$\Rightarrow \quad b \in \left(-\frac{2}{3}, \frac{2}{3}\right)$$

Hence, number of integral values of b is 1.

47. $f'(x) = \begin{cases} 1, & x < -1 \\ 2x, & -1 < x < 1 \\ 2(x-2), & x > 1 \end{cases}$ $f'(x)$ changes sign at $x = -1, 0, 1, 2$

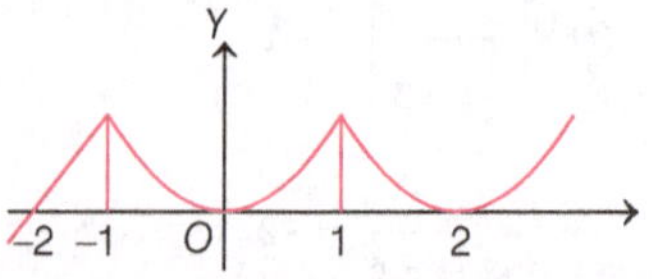

48. We know, in semicircle $AB \perp BC$

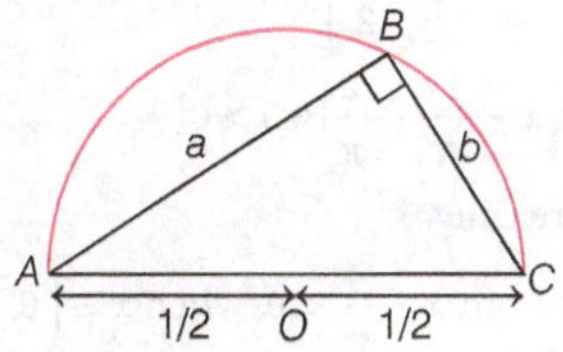

Let $AB = a$ units and $BC = b$ units

$$AC = \sqrt{a^2 + b^2}$$

$$AC = 1 \text{ unit}$$

or $$a^2 + b^2 = 1$$

We know that

$$\text{AM} \ge \text{GM}$$

$$\Rightarrow \frac{a^2+b^2}{2} \ge \sqrt{a^2b^2}$$

$$\Rightarrow \frac{1}{2} \ge ab$$

$$\text{Area of triangle} = \frac{1}{2} a \times b$$

$$\because \quad ab = \frac{1}{2}$$

$$\text{Area of triangle} = \frac{1}{2} \times \frac{1}{2} = \frac{1}{4}$$

Now, the value of $32\text{ M} = 32 \times \frac{1}{4} = 8$

49.

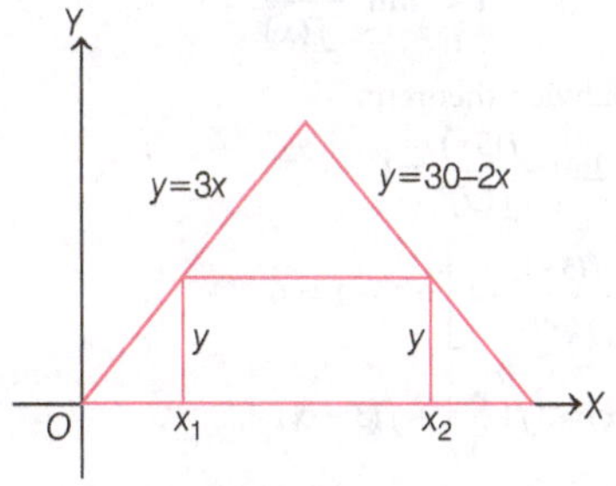

$$A = (x_2 - x_1)y$$

$$y = 3x_1 \text{ and } y = 30 - 2x_2$$

$$A(y) = \left(\frac{30-y}{2} - \frac{y}{3}\right)y$$

$$6A(y) = (90 - 3y - 2y)y = 90y - 5y^2$$

$$6A'(y) = 90 - 10y = 0$$

$$\Rightarrow y = 9, A''(y) = -10 < 0$$

$$x_1 = 3, x_2 = \frac{21}{2}$$

$$\Rightarrow M = A_{\max} = \left(\frac{21}{2} - 3\right)9 = \frac{15 \cdot 9}{2} = \frac{135}{2}$$

$$\therefore \frac{2M}{27} = \frac{2 \times 135}{2 \times 27} = 5$$

50. $$x^2 - 2x - 3 > 0$$

$$\Rightarrow (x-3)(x+1) > 0$$

$$\Rightarrow x < -1 \text{ or } x > 3 \quad \text{...(i)}$$

Now, $f(x) = \log_{1/2}(x^2 - 2x - 3)$

$$= \frac{\log_e(x^2 - 2x - 3)}{\log_e\left(\frac{1}{2}\right)}$$

$$f'(x) = \frac{2x-2}{(\log_e(1/2))(x^2 - 2x - 3)}$$

For $f(x)$ to be decreasing, $f'(x) < 0$

$$\Rightarrow \frac{x-1}{(\log_e(1/2))(x-3)(x+1)} < 0$$

$$\Rightarrow x > 1 \quad \text{...(ii)}$$

From Eqs. (i) and (ii), $x > 3$

$\therefore$ The least integral value is 4.

51.

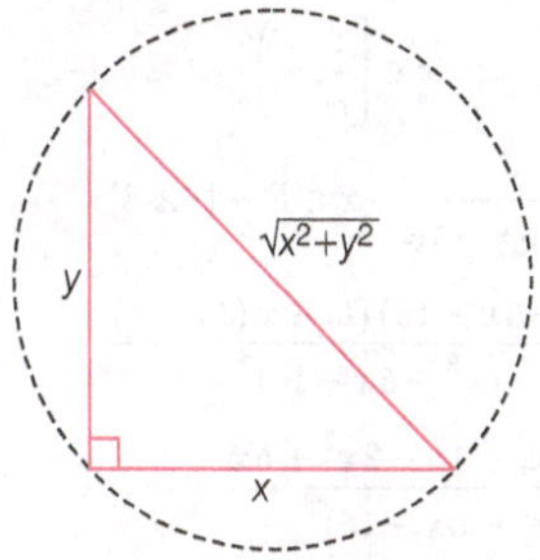

$$\frac{9}{\pi} = S = \frac{xy}{2} = \text{Constant}$$

Area of the circle $A(x) = \pi r^2$

$$= \frac{\pi(x^2+y^2)}{4}, (x^2 + y^2 = 4r^2)$$

$$A(x) = \frac{\pi}{4}\left[x^2 + \left(\frac{2S}{x}\right)^2\right]$$

$$A'(x) = \frac{\pi x}{2} - \frac{2\pi S^2}{x^3} = 0$$

$$\Rightarrow x^4 = 4S^2$$

$$\Rightarrow x^2 = 2S$$

$$\Rightarrow S^2 = \frac{x^2y^2}{4} = \frac{2Sy^2}{4}$$

$$\Rightarrow y^2 = 2S$$

Therefore, least area of circle $= \pi r^2 = \frac{\pi}{4}(x^2 + y^2)$

$$= \pi S = 9 \text{ sq units}$$

52. $f(x) = \cos x - x + 1$

So, $f'(x) = -\sin x - 1$

Put $f'(x) = 0 \Rightarrow -\sin x = 1 \Rightarrow \sin x = -1$

In $x \in [0, \pi]$, $\sin x = -1$ is not possible.

So, there is no critical point in $[0, \pi]$.

Now, $f(0) = 2 > 0$

$$f(\pi) = -1 - \pi + 1 = -\pi < 0$$

That means, $f(x)$ will have only one zero in $[0, \pi]$.

and $f(x)$ is decreasing in $[0, \pi]$.

Hence, only (SI) is correct.

53. Firstly find $\frac{dy}{dx}$, then use $f'(x) > 0$ for strictly increasing function.

$$f(x) = x^x; x > 0$$

$$\Rightarrow \quad \ln y = x \ln x$$

On differentiating w.r.t. x, we get

$$\Rightarrow \quad \frac{1}{y} f'(x) = \frac{x}{x} + \ln x$$

$$\Rightarrow \quad f'(x) = x^x(1 + \ln x)$$

For strictly increasing,

$$\Rightarrow \quad f'(x) \geq 0$$

$$\Rightarrow \quad x^x(1 + \ln x) \geq 0$$

$$\Rightarrow \quad x \geq e^{-1}$$

$$\therefore \quad x \in \left[\frac{1}{e}, \infty\right)$$

54. $f(x) = \dfrac{x}{x^2 - 6x - 16}$, $x \in R - \{-2, 8\}$

$$f'(x) = \frac{(x^2 - 6x - 16)(1) - x(2x - 6)}{(x^2 - 6x - 16)^2}$$

$$= \frac{x^2 - 6x - 16 - 2x^2 + 6x}{(x^2 - 6x - 16)^2}$$

$$= \frac{-x^2 - 16}{(x^2 - 6x - 16)^2} = \frac{-(x^2 + 16)}{(x^2 - 6x - 16)^2} < 0$$

$\because$ $f'(x) < 0$ for $x \in$ domain.

$\therefore$ It is a decreasing function in its domain.

$x \in (-\infty, -2) \cup (-2, 8) \cup (8, \infty)$

55. $f(x) = (x - 2)^{2/3}(2x + 1)$

For critical points,

Put $f'(x) = 0$

So, $f'(x) = \dfrac{d}{dx}[(x - 2)^{2/3}(2x + 1)]$

$$= 2(x - 2)^{2/3} + (2x + 1)\left(\frac{2}{3}(x - 2)^{-1/3}\right)$$

$$= \frac{6(x-2)^{2/3} \cdot (x-2)^{1/3} + 2(2x+1)}{3(x-2)^{1/3}} \{x \neq 2\}$$

So, $x = 2$ is critical point.

Put $f'(x) = 0$

$$\Rightarrow \quad \frac{2(3(x-2) + (2x+1))}{3(x-2)^{1/3}} = 0$$

$$\Rightarrow \quad 3x - 6 + 2x + 1 = 0 \Rightarrow 5x = 5 \Rightarrow x = 1$$

Hence, there is only two critical points.

56. Given, $f(x) = \sin x + 3x - \dfrac{2}{\pi}(x^2 + x)$

$$\Rightarrow \quad f'(x) = \cos x + 3 - \frac{2}{\pi}(2x + 1) = \cos x - \frac{4x}{\pi} - \frac{2}{\pi} + 3$$

When $x \in \left[0, \dfrac{\pi}{2}\right]$

$$\Rightarrow \quad 4x \in [0, 2\pi] \Rightarrow \frac{4x}{\pi} \in [0, 2],$$

$\cos x > 0$, when $x \in \left[0, \dfrac{\pi}{2}\right]$

$\therefore$ $f'(x) = \cos x - \dfrac{4x}{\pi} - \dfrac{2}{\pi} + 3 > 0$

$\Rightarrow$ $f(x)$ is increasing.

Now, $f''(x) = -\sin x - \dfrac{4}{\pi} < 0$, when $x \in \left(0, \dfrac{\pi}{2}\right)$.

$\Rightarrow f'(x)$ is decreasing.

Hence, both statements are true.

57.

> **Decoding the Question**
>
> **Sandwich theorem** Let $f(x)$, $g(x)$ and $h(x)$ be real functions such that $f(x) \leq g(x) \leq h(x)$, $\forall\, x$ in the common domain, If $\lim_{x \to a} f(x) = l = \lim_{x \to a} h(x)$
>
> Then, $\lim_{x \to a} f(x) = l$

$$f : R \to (0, \infty), \lim_{x \to \infty} \frac{f(7x)}{f(x)} = 1$$

Since, $f(x)$ is strictly increasing function.

$$f(x) < f(5x) < f(7x)$$

$$\frac{f(x)}{f(x)} < \frac{f(5x)}{f(x)} < \frac{f(7x)}{f(x)}$$

$$\lim_{x \to \infty} 1 < \lim_{x \to \infty} \frac{f(5x)}{f(x)} < \lim_{x \to \infty} \frac{f(7x)}{f(x)}$$

$$1 < \lim_{x \to \infty} \frac{f(5x)}{f(x)} < 1$$

So, by Sandwich theorem,

$$\lim_{x \to \infty} \frac{f(5x)}{f(x)} = 1$$

Or $\lim_{x \to \infty} \left[\dfrac{f(5x)}{f(x)} - 1\right] = 1 - 1 = 0$

58. Given, $g(x) = 3f\left(\dfrac{x}{3}\right) + f(3 - x)$

On differentiating both sides w.r.t. x, we get

$$g'(x) = 3 \times \frac{1}{3} f'\left(\frac{x}{3}\right) - f'(3 - x)$$

$$= f'\left(\frac{x}{3}\right) - f'(3 - x) \quad \text{...(i)}$$

Given, $g(x)$ is decreasing in $(0, \alpha)$.

So, $\quad g'(x) < 0$

$$\Rightarrow \quad f'\left(\frac{x}{3}\right) < f'(3 - x) \quad \text{[from Eq. (i)] ...(ii)}$$

$$\because \quad f''(x) > 0 \quad \text{[given]}$$

i.e. $f'(x)$ is an increasing function.

From Eq. (ii),

$$\frac{x}{3} < 3 - x \Rightarrow \frac{4x}{3} < 3 \Rightarrow x < \frac{9}{4}$$

So, $\alpha = \dfrac{9}{4}$

Hence, $8\alpha = 8 \times \dfrac{9}{4} = 18$

59. Given, $5f(x) + 4f\left(\frac{1}{x}\right) = x^2 - 2$ ...(i)

Substitute $x \to \frac{1}{x}$, we get

$$5f\left(\frac{1}{x}\right) + 4f(x) = \frac{1}{x^2} - 2 \quad \text{...(ii)}$$

On solving Eqs. (i) and (ii), we get

$$9f(x) = 5x^2 - \frac{4}{x^2} - 2$$

$\because \quad y = 9x^2 f(x)$

$$y = x^2\left(5x^2 - \frac{4}{x^2} - 2\right)$$

$$y = 5x^4 - 4 - 2x^2$$

$$\frac{dy}{dx} = 20x^3 - 4x = 4x(5x^2 - 1)$$

For increasing, $4x(5x^2 - 1) > 0$

$$x = 0, \frac{1}{\sqrt{5}}, \frac{-1}{\sqrt{5}}$$

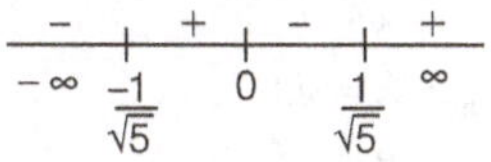

$$x \in \left(\frac{-1}{\sqrt{5}}, 0\right) \cup \left(\frac{1}{\sqrt{5}}, \infty\right)$$

60. First convert $y = \frac{2x^2 - 3x + 8}{2x^2 + 3x + 8}$ into quadratic equation in x where, y is constant. Then, use $D \ge 0$ to find minimum and maximum value of y.

Let $y = \frac{2x^2 - 3x + 8}{2x^2 + 3x + 8}$ ... (i)

Here, we observe that

$$2x^2 + 3x + 8 > 0, \forall x \in R \quad [\because a > 0 \text{ and } D < 0]$$

Now, Eq. (i)

$\Rightarrow \quad 2x^2y + 3xy + 8y = 2x^2 - 3x + 8$

$\Rightarrow \quad x^2(2y - 2) + x(3y + 3) + 8y - 8 = 0$

$\because x \in R$, so the equation has real roots.

i.e. $D \ge 0$

$\Rightarrow (3y + 3)^2 - 4(2y - 2)(8y - 8) \ge 0$

$\Rightarrow \quad (11y - 5)(5y - 11) \le 0$

$\Rightarrow \quad y \in \left[\frac{5}{11}, \frac{11}{5}\right]$

Hence, sum of y_{max} and $y_{min} = \frac{11}{5} + \frac{5}{11} = \frac{121 + 25}{55} = \frac{146}{55} = \frac{m}{n}$ [given]

$\therefore \quad m + n = 146 + 55 = 201$

61. $f(x) = (x+3)^2(x-2)^3, x \in [-4, 4]$

$\therefore \quad f'(x) = (x+3)^2 \, 3(x-2)^2 + (x-2)^3 \cdot 2(x+3)$

$= (x+3)(x-2)^2 [3(x+3) + 2(x-2)]$

$= (x-2)^2 (x+3)(5x+5) = 5(x-2)^2(x+3)(x+1)$

$\because \quad f'(x) = 0$

$\Rightarrow \quad x = 2, -3, -1$

$\therefore \quad f(2) = 0, \; f(-3) = 0,$

$f(-1) = -4 \times 27 = -108,$

$f(-4) = -216$ and $f(4) = 392$

$\Rightarrow \quad M = 392, m = -216$

$\therefore \quad M - m = 392 + 216 = 608$

62. $f(x) = 2x + 3x^{2/3}$

$$f'(x) = 2 + 2x^{\frac{-1}{3}} = 2 + \frac{2}{x^{1/3}}$$

$$= 2\left(\frac{x^{\frac{1}{3}} + 1}{x^{\frac{1}{3}}}\right)$$

$f'(x) = 0$

$x^{1/3} + 1 = 0$

$x = -1$

Critical point $x = 0, -1$

Also, at $x = 0$, $f(x) = 0$

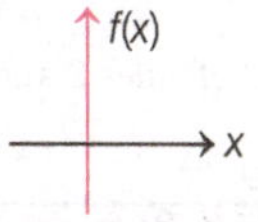

Using first order derivative test

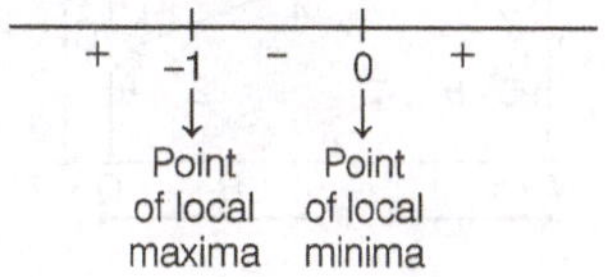

$\therefore f(x)$ has exactly one point local maxima and exactly one point local minima.

63. $f(x) = 4 \cdot \cos^3 x + 3\sqrt{3} \cos^2 x - 10$ and $x \in (0, 2\pi)$

So, $f'(x) = 12 \cos^2 x(-\sin x) + 6\sqrt{3} \cos x(-\sin x)$

$= -6 \sin x \cdot \cos x(2 \cos x + \sqrt{3})$

$= -3\sin(2x)(2 \cos x + \sqrt{3})$

Now, $-3 \sin(2x) = 0, x = \frac{\pi}{2}, \frac{3\pi}{2}, \pi, 2\pi$

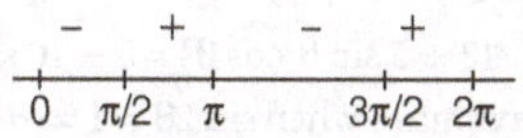

and $(2 \cos x + \sqrt{3}) = 0$

$\Rightarrow \quad \cos x = -\frac{\sqrt{3}}{2} \Rightarrow x = \frac{5\pi}{6}, \frac{7\pi}{6}$

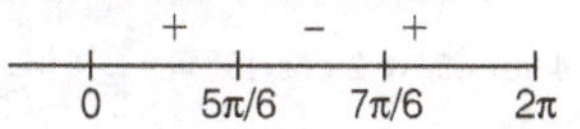

Now, $-3 \sin(2x)(2\cos x + \sqrt{3})$

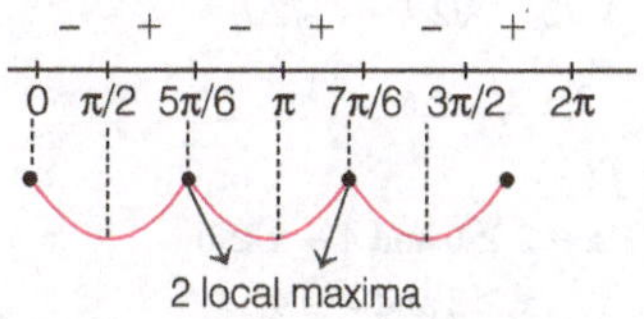

64. We know, $e < \pi$

$\Rightarrow \quad \frac{1}{e} > \frac{1}{\pi}$

Then, according to the question,

If $f(x)$ attains maximum value at $x = 1/e$, then

$$f(x)\big|_{x=\frac{1}{\pi}} < f(x)\big|_{x=\frac{1}{e}}$$

$$\Rightarrow \quad f\left(\frac{1}{\pi}\right) < f\left(\frac{1}{e}\right)$$

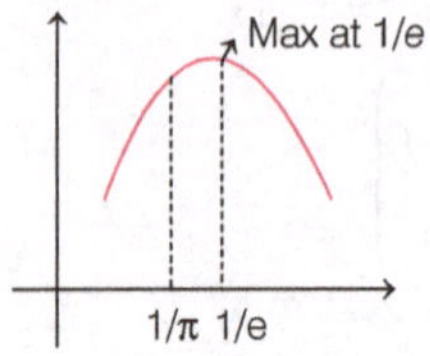

$$\Rightarrow \quad (\pi)^{\frac{2}{\pi}} < e^{\frac{2}{e}}$$

$$\Rightarrow \quad (\pi)^{2e} < e^{2\pi}$$

$$\Rightarrow \quad \pi^e < e^\pi$$

65. Given, rectangle $ABCD$ of sides 2 and 4 be inscribed in another rectangle $PQRS$.

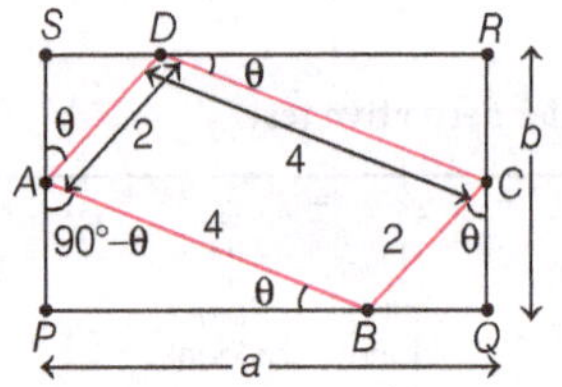

Let $\angle ABP = \theta$

$\therefore \quad \angle DAS = \angle CDR = \angle BCQ = \theta$

Now, $PB = 4\cos\theta$ and $BQ = 2\sin\theta$

$\therefore \quad PQ = 4\cos\theta + 2\sin\theta$

Also, $AP = 4\sin\theta$, $AS = 2\cos\theta$

$\therefore \quad PS = 4\sin\theta + 2\cos\theta$

$\therefore$ Area of rectangle $PQRS$

$$= (4\cos\theta + 2\sin\theta)(4\sin\theta + 2\cos\theta)$$

$$= 4(2\cos^2\theta + 2\sin^2\theta + 5\sin\theta\cos\theta)$$

$$= 4(2 + 5\sin\theta\cos\theta) = 8 + 10\sin 2\theta$$

Area will be maximum, when $\sin 2\theta = 1 \Rightarrow \theta = 45°$

$\therefore$ Maximum area $= 8 + 10 = 18$ sq units

$\therefore a = PQ = 4\cos 45° + 2\sin 45° = \frac{4}{\sqrt{2}} + \frac{2}{\sqrt{2}} = \frac{6}{\sqrt{2}}$

and $b = PS = 4\sin 45° + 2\cos 45° = \frac{4}{\sqrt{2}} + \frac{2}{\sqrt{2}} = \frac{6}{\sqrt{2}}$

$$\therefore \ (a+b)^2 = \left(\frac{6}{\sqrt{2}} + \frac{6}{\sqrt{2}}\right)^2 = \left(\frac{12}{\sqrt{2}}\right)^2 = 72$$

66. $f(x) = 3\sqrt{x-2} + \sqrt{4-x}$

Domain of $f(x)$

$$x - 2 \ge 0 \text{ and } 4 - x \ge 0$$

$$\Rightarrow \quad x \ge 2 \text{ and } x \le 4$$

$$\Rightarrow \quad x \in [2, 4]$$

$$f'(x) = \frac{3}{2\sqrt{x-2}} + \frac{1}{2\sqrt{4-x}}(-1)$$

$$\Rightarrow \quad f'(x) = 0$$

$$\frac{3}{\sqrt{x-2}} = \frac{1}{\sqrt{4-x}}$$

$$\Rightarrow \quad \frac{9}{x-2} = \frac{1}{4-x}$$

$$\Rightarrow \quad 36 - 9x = x - 2$$

$$\Rightarrow \quad 10x = 38$$

$$\Rightarrow \quad x = \frac{38}{10} = \frac{19}{5}$$

$$\therefore \quad f(2) = \sqrt{2},\ f(4) = 3\sqrt{2}$$

and $$f\left(\frac{19}{5}\right) = 3\sqrt{\frac{19}{5} - 2} + \sqrt{4 - \frac{19}{5}}$$

$$= 3 \times \frac{3}{\sqrt{5}} + \frac{1}{\sqrt{5}}$$

$$= \frac{10}{\sqrt{5}} = 2\sqrt{5}$$

$$f_{\min} = \alpha = \sqrt{2}$$

$$f_{\max} = \beta = 2\sqrt{5}$$

$\therefore \quad \alpha^2 + 2\beta^2 = 2 + 40 = 42$

67. Equation of line in intercept form is

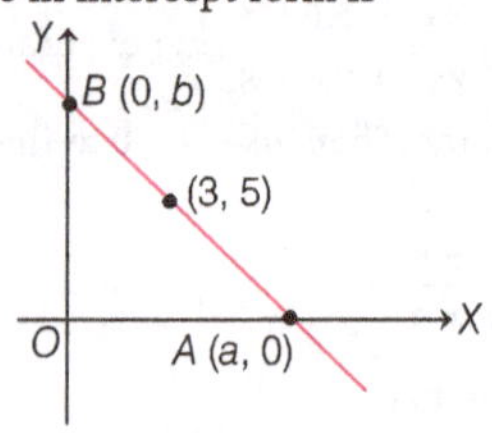

$$\frac{x}{a} + \frac{y}{b} = 1 \quad \text{...(i)}$$

Since, Eq. (i) passes through (3, 5), then

$$\frac{3}{a} + \frac{5}{b} = 1$$

$\Rightarrow b = \frac{5a}{a-3}$, $a - 3 > 0$ is $a > 3$

Now, area of $\Delta OAB = \Delta = \frac{1}{2}ab$

$$\Rightarrow \quad \Delta = \frac{1}{2} \cdot a \cdot \frac{5a}{a-3} = \frac{5}{2} \cdot \frac{a^2}{a-3} = \frac{5}{2}\left(\frac{a^2 - 9 + 9}{a-3}\right)$$

$$\Delta = \frac{5}{2}\left(a + 3 + \frac{9}{a-3}\right)$$

On differentiating both sides, we get

Now, $$\frac{d\Delta}{da} = \frac{5}{2}\left[1 + 0 - \frac{9}{(a-3)^2}\right] = 0$$

$$\Rightarrow \quad (a-3)^2 = 9$$

$$\Rightarrow \quad a - 3 = \pm 3$$

$$\Rightarrow \quad a = 0, 6$$

Again, on differentiating, $\dfrac{d^2\Delta}{da^2} = \dfrac{5}{2}\left[0 + \dfrac{9 \times 2}{(a-3)^3}\right]$

Here, when $a = 0$, then $\dfrac{d^2\Delta}{da^2} < 0$ which gives maximum area

and when $a = 6$, then $\dfrac{d^2\Delta}{da^2} > 0$ which gives minimum area

$$\therefore \quad \Delta\big|_{a=6} = \frac{5}{2} \times \frac{(6)^2}{(6-3)} = \frac{5}{2} \times \frac{6 \times 6}{3} = 30$$

68. We know that if $y = f(x)$, then

for local maxima and minima $f'(x) = 0$

at $x < a, b$,

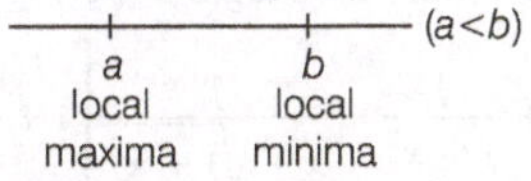

Now, on differentiating w.r.t. x, we get

$$f'(x) = 6x^2 - 18ax + 12a^2$$

For local maxima and minima

$$6x^2 - 18ax + 12a^2 = 0$$
$$(x-a)(x-2a) = 0$$
$$x = a \text{ and } x = 2a$$

Now, local maxima, $\quad x = \alpha = a \quad$ ...(i)

Local minima, $\quad x = \alpha^2 = 2a \quad$ ...(ii)

From Eqs. (i) and (ii), we get

$$\alpha^2 = 2\alpha$$
$$\alpha = 0 \text{ and } \alpha = 2$$

Now, consider $\alpha = 2$, roots of equation α and α^2 are 2 and 4.

So, the equation we get

$$x^2 - 6x + 8 = 0$$

69. $f(x) = (p^2 - 6p + 8)(\sin^2 2x - \cos^2 2x) + 2(2-p)x + 7$

$$f(x) = (p^2 - 6p + 8)(-\cos 4x) + 2(2-p)x + 7$$
$$f'(x) = (p^2 - 6p + 8)(\sin 4x)(4) + 2(2-p) \neq 0$$

$$\sin 4x \neq \frac{2p-4}{4(p-4)(p-2)}$$

$$\sin 4x \neq \frac{1}{2(p-4)}, \text{ where } p \neq 2$$

$$\therefore \quad \left(\frac{1}{2(p-4)}\right) > 1$$

$$|2(p-4)| < 1$$
$$-1 < 2(p-4) < 1$$
$$-\frac{1}{2} < p - 4 < \frac{1}{2}$$
$$\frac{7}{2} < p < \frac{9}{2}$$
$$a = \frac{7}{2}, b = \frac{9}{2}$$
$$16ab = 16 \times \frac{7}{2} \times \frac{9}{2} = 252$$

70. Given, $\dfrac{x^2 + x + 2}{x^2 + 5x + 6} < 0$

$\Rightarrow \quad \dfrac{1}{(x+2)(x+3)} < 0 \quad [\because x^2 + x + 2 > 0, \forall x \in R]$

$\Rightarrow \quad x \in (-3, -2) \quad$ ...(i)

Also, $f(x) = 1 + x(\lambda^2 - x^2)$

$\Rightarrow \quad f'(x) = (\lambda^2 - x^2) + (-2x)x$

For finding local minima, we put $f'(x) = 0$

$$\lambda^2 = 3x^2$$

$\Rightarrow \quad x = \pm \dfrac{\lambda}{\sqrt{3}}$

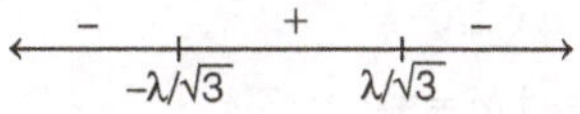

$\therefore$ Local minima at $x = \dfrac{-\lambda}{\sqrt{3}}$

So, from Eq. (i),

$$-3 < x < -2$$

$\Rightarrow \quad -3 < -\dfrac{\lambda}{\sqrt{3}} < -2$

$\Rightarrow \quad 3\sqrt{3} > \lambda > 2\sqrt{3}$

$\Rightarrow \quad 2\sqrt{3} < \lambda < 3\sqrt{3}$

$\therefore \quad \alpha = 2\sqrt{3}$ and $\beta = 3\sqrt{3}$

Hence, $\alpha^2 + \beta^2 = 12 + 27 = 39$

71.

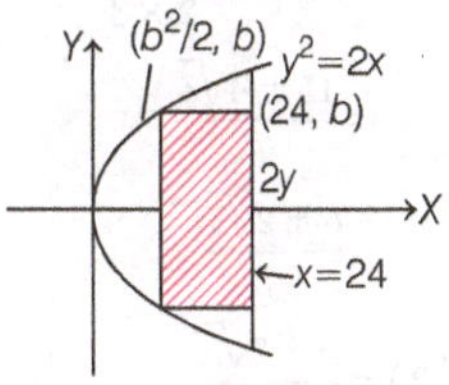

So, $A = \left(24 - \dfrac{b^2}{2}\right) \times 2b$

Then, for maximum area $\dfrac{dA}{db} = 0$

$\Rightarrow 2b\left(0 - \dfrac{2b}{2}\right) + \left(24 - \dfrac{b^2}{2}\right) \times 2 = 0$

$\Rightarrow \quad -b^2 + 48 - 2b^2 = 0$

$\Rightarrow \quad 3b^2 = 48$

$\Rightarrow \quad b = 4$

Hence, $\quad A = \left(24 - \dfrac{16}{2}\right) \times 2 \times 4$

$$= 16 \times 8 = 128$$

72. Let $\; y = \sqrt{8x - x^2 - 12}$

$\Rightarrow y^2 = 8x - x^2 - 12$

$$(x-4)^2 + y^2 = 4 \quad \text{...(i)}$$

Centre (4, 0) and radius = 2

$\therefore$ Let $P = (x-7)^2 + (y-4)^2$ ...(ii)

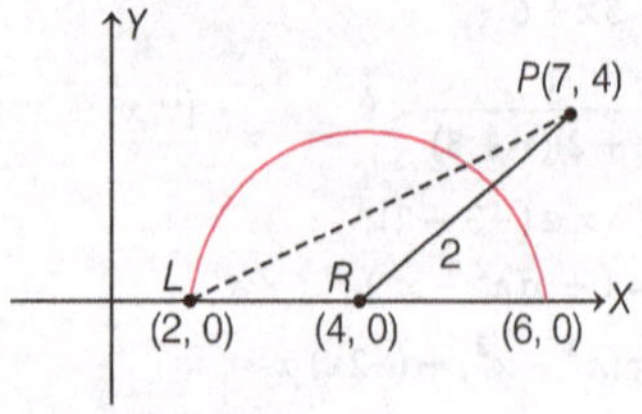

$M = PL^2 = (7-2)^2 + (4-0)^2 = 25 + 16 = 41$

and $m = PR^2 = \sqrt{(7-4)^2 + (4-0)^2}$

$= (\sqrt{9+16} - 2)^2$

$= (5-2)^2 = 9$

$\therefore \quad m = 9$ and $M = 41$

Then, $M^2 - m^2 = (41-9)(41+9) = 1600$

73. $D = \sin^2 2\theta - 4\left(1 - \dfrac{\sin^2 2\theta}{2}\right)\left(1 - \dfrac{3}{4}\sin^2 2\theta\right)$

$= (\sin 2\theta)^2 - 4\left(1 - \dfrac{5}{4}\sin^2 2\theta + \dfrac{3}{8}\sin^4 2\theta\right)$

$\Rightarrow D = -\dfrac{3}{2}\sin^4 2\theta + 6\sin^2 2\theta - 4 > 0$

$\Rightarrow \quad 3\sin^4 2\theta - 12\sin^2 2\theta + 8 < 0$

Critical point

$$\sin^2 2\theta = \frac{12 \pm \sqrt{(12)^2 - 4(3)(8)}}{2 \times 3}$$

$$= \frac{12 \pm 4\sqrt{3}}{6}$$

$$= \frac{6 \pm 2\sqrt{3}}{3}$$

$$\sin^2 2\theta = \frac{6 \pm 2\sqrt{3}}{3} \qquad [\because \sin^2 2\theta \in [0, 1]]$$

$$\therefore \quad \sin^2 2\theta \in \left[2 - \frac{2}{\sqrt{3}}, 1\right]$$

$$\alpha = 2 - \frac{2}{\sqrt{3}}, \beta = 1$$

$$(\alpha - 2)^2 = \frac{4}{3}, (\beta - 1)^2 = 0$$

$\therefore 3(\alpha - 2)^2 + (\beta - 1)^2 = 4$

74. We have, $g(x) = f(x) + f(1-x)$

On differentiating both sides, we get

$$g'(x) = f'(x) - f'(1-x)$$

As $f''(x) > 0$, $f'(x)$ is an increasing function.

Also, $g(x) = f(x) + f(2a - x)$ is always symmetric about $x = a$

So, $g(x) = f(x) + f(1-x)$ is also symmetric about $x = 1/2$

$\therefore$ g is decreasing in the interval $(0, 1/2)$ and increasing in the interval $(1/2, 1)$.

$\therefore \quad \alpha = 1/2$

Now, $\tan^{-1} 2\alpha + \tan^{-1}\left(\dfrac{1}{\alpha}\right) + \tan^{-1}\left(\dfrac{\alpha + 1}{\alpha}\right)$

$= \tan^{-1} 1 + \tan^{-1}(2) + \tan^{-1} 3 = \pi$

$[\because \tan^{-1} x + \tan^{-1} y + \tan^{-1} z = \pi$ if $(x + y + z = xyz)]$

75. We have, $f(x) = 2x + \tan^{-1} x$

and $\quad g(x) = \log(x + \sqrt{1 + x^2})$

Let $\quad h(x) = f(x) - g(x)$

$= 2x + \tan^{-1} x - \log(x + \sqrt{1 + x^2})$

$\therefore \quad h'(x) = 2 + \dfrac{1}{1+x^2} - \dfrac{1}{x + \sqrt{1+x^2}}\left[1 + \dfrac{1}{2\sqrt{1+x^2}}(2x)\right]$

$= 2 + \dfrac{1}{1+x^2} - \dfrac{1}{x + \sqrt{1+x^2}}\left[\dfrac{\sqrt{1+x^2} + x}{\sqrt{1+x^2}}\right]$

$= 2 + \dfrac{1}{1+x^2} - \dfrac{1}{\sqrt{1+x^2}}$

Now, $\quad 1 + x^2 \ge 1$

$\Rightarrow \quad \sqrt{1+x^2} \ge 1$

$\Rightarrow \quad \dfrac{1}{\sqrt{1+x^2}} \le 1$

$\therefore h'(x) = 2 + \dfrac{1}{1+x^2} - \dfrac{1}{\sqrt{1+x^2}} \ge 0$

So, $h'(x)$ is increasing on R.

$\therefore \quad h(x) > h(0)$

$\Rightarrow \quad h(x) > f(0) - g(0)$

$\Rightarrow \quad h(x) > 2(0) + \tan^{-1} 0 - \log(0 + \sqrt{1+0})$

$\Rightarrow \quad h(x) > 0$

$\Rightarrow \quad f(x) - g(x) > 0$

$\Rightarrow \quad f(x) > g(x)$

So, $\quad f_{\max}(x) > g_{\max}(x)$

76. Given, $f : (0, 1) \to R$, $f(x) = \dfrac{1}{1 - e^{-x}}$

$g(x) = f(-x) - f(x) = \dfrac{1}{1 - e^x} - \dfrac{1}{1 - e^{-x}}$

$= \dfrac{1}{1 - e^x} - \dfrac{1}{1 - \dfrac{1}{e^x}}$

$g(x) = \dfrac{1}{1 - e^x} - \dfrac{e^x}{e^x - 1} = \dfrac{1 + e^x}{1 - e^x}$

Now, on differentiating w.r.t. x, we get

$g'(x) = \dfrac{(1 - e^x)e^x - (1 + e^x)(-e^x)}{(1 - e^x)^2} = \dfrac{2e^x}{(1 - e^x)^2}$

Now, $g'(x) = \dfrac{2e^x}{(1-e^x)^2} > 0$

So, g is increasing in (0, 1).

Now, for one-one or not $g(x_1) = g(x_2)$

$$\Rightarrow \quad \frac{1+e^{x_1}}{1-e^{x_1}} = \frac{1+e^{x_2}}{1-e^{x_2}}$$

$$\Rightarrow \quad 1 + e^{x_1} - e^{x_2} - e^{x_1} \cdot e^{x_2}$$

$$= 1 + e^{x_2} - e^{x_1} - e^{x_1} \cdot e^{x_2}$$

$$\Rightarrow \quad 2e^{x_1} = 2e^{x_2}$$

$$\Rightarrow \quad x_1 = x_2$$

So, $g(x)$ is one-one also.

77. We have, $f(x) = |x^2 - 5x + 6| - 3x + 2$

$$= \begin{cases} (x^2-5x+6)-3x+2, & x \in [-1, 2] \\ -(x^2-5x+6)-3x+2, & x \in [2, 3] \end{cases}$$

$$= \begin{cases} x^2 - 8x + 8, & x \in [-1, 2] \\ -x^2 + 2x - 4, & x \in [2, 3] \end{cases}$$

Now, we have to check in the interval $[-1, 3]$ only

$\therefore$ Absolute maximum $= f(-1) = (-1)^2 - 8(-1) + 8 = 17$

and absolute minimum $= f(3) = (3)^2 - 8(3) + 8 = -7$

$\therefore$ Required sum $= 17 - 7 = 10$

78. We have, $f(x) = |x^2 - x + 1| + [x^2 - x + 1]$

Let $g(x) = x^2 - x + 1$

$$= \left(x - \frac{1}{2}\right)^2 + \frac{3}{4}$$

$\therefore$ $g(x)$ attains minimum value at $x = \dfrac{1}{2}$.

So, $f(x)$ attains minimum value at $x = \dfrac{1}{2}$.

$$\therefore f_{\min} = f\left(\frac{1}{2}\right) = \left|\frac{3}{4}\right| + \left[\frac{3}{4}\right] = \frac{3}{4}$$

79. Given, $f(x) = \dfrac{x^3}{3} + 2bx + \dfrac{ax^2}{2}$ and $g(x) = \dfrac{x^3}{3} + ax + bx^2$

For extreme points,

$$f'(x) = x^2 + 2b + ax = 0 \qquad \text{...(i)}$$

and $g'(x) = x^2 + a + 2bx = 0 \qquad$ ...(ii)

From Eqs. (i) and (ii), we get

$x = 1$ will be common root, then put $x = 1$

$$\Rightarrow \quad (1)^2 + 2b + a(1) = 0$$

$$\Rightarrow \quad 2b + a + 1 = 0$$

On adding 6 both sides, we get

$$2b + a + 1 + 6 = 0 + 6 = 6$$

$$\therefore \quad 2b + a + 7 = 6$$

80. $f(x) = 2x^3 + (2p - 7)x^2 + 3(2p - 9)x - 6$

On differentiating $f(x)$ w.r.t. x, we get

$$f'(x) = 6x^2 + 2(2p - 7)x + 3(2p - 9)$$

$f'(x)$ is a quadratic function.

So, Product of root's $= \dfrac{\text{Constant}}{\text{Lead coefficient}}$

if sign of maxima or minima are opposite, then

Product of roots < 0

$$\frac{3(2p-9)}{6} < 0$$

$$\Rightarrow \quad 2p - 9 < 0 \Rightarrow p < \frac{9}{2}$$

or $\quad p \in \left(-\infty, \dfrac{9}{2}\right)$

81. $f(x) = 2x^4 - 18x^2 + 8x + 12;\ x \in (-4, 4)$

On differentiating $f(x)$ w.r.t. x, we get

$$f'(x) = 8x^3 - 36x + 8$$

$$f'(x) = 0 = 4(2x^3 - 9x + 2)$$

$$\Rightarrow \quad 2x^3 - 9x + 2 = 0$$

$$(x - 2)(2x^2 + 4x - 1) = 0$$

$$x = 2,\ x = \frac{-4 \pm \sqrt{16+8}}{2 \times 2} = \frac{\pm\sqrt{6} - 2}{2} \in (-4, 4)$$

Now, $f(x) = 2x^4 - 18x^2 + 8x + 12$

– + – +
$-1-\sqrt{3/2}$ $\quad -1+\sqrt{3/2}$ $\quad 2$

$\because f'(x)$ changes sign from positive to negative when passing through $-1 + \dfrac{\sqrt{3}}{2}$.

$\therefore\ x = -1 + \sqrt{\dfrac{3}{2}}$ is point of local maxima.

$$\therefore M = f\left(-1 + \sqrt{\frac{3}{2}}\right)$$

$$= 2\left(-1 + \sqrt{\frac{3}{2}}\right)^4 - 18\left(-1 + \sqrt{\frac{3}{2}}\right)^2 + 8\left(-1 + \sqrt{\frac{3}{2}}\right) + 12$$

$$= 2 - 4\sqrt{6} + 18 - 6\sqrt{6} + \frac{4}{2} - 18 + 18\sqrt{6} - 27 - 8 + 4\sqrt{6} + 12$$

$$= 12\sqrt{6} - \frac{33}{2}$$

82. Let $\quad f(x) = x - 2\sin x \cos x + \dfrac{1}{3}\sin 3x,\ 0 \le x \le \pi$

$$= x - \sin 2x + \frac{1}{3}\sin 3x$$

$$\Rightarrow \quad f'(x) = 1 - 2\cos 2x + \cos 3x$$

$$\Rightarrow \quad f''(x) = 4\sin 2x - 3\sin 3x$$

Now, $f'(x) = 0$

$$\Rightarrow 1 - 2\cos 2x + \cos 3x = 0$$

$$\Rightarrow 1 - 2(2\cos^2 x - 1) + 4\cos^3 x - 3\cos x = 0$$

$$\Rightarrow \quad 1 - 4\cos^2 x + 2 + 4\cos^3 x - 3\cos x = 0$$

$$\Rightarrow \quad 4\cos^3 x - 4\cos^2 x - 3\cos x + 3 = 0$$

$$\Rightarrow \quad 4\cos^2 x(\cos x - 1) - 3(\cos x - 1) = 0$$

$$\Rightarrow \quad (\cos x - 1)(4\cos^2 x - 3) = 0$$

$\Rightarrow (\cos x - 1)(2\cos x + \sqrt{3})(2\cos x - \sqrt{3}) = 0$

$\therefore \quad \cos x = -\dfrac{\sqrt{3}}{2}, \cos x = \dfrac{\sqrt{3}}{2}, \cos x = 1$

$\therefore \quad x = \dfrac{5\pi}{6}, x = \dfrac{\pi}{6}, x = 0$

$f''\left(\dfrac{5\pi}{6}\right) = 4\sin\dfrac{5\pi}{3} - 3\sin\dfrac{5\pi}{2} = -2\sqrt{3} - 3 < 0$

$f''\left(\dfrac{\pi}{6}\right) = 4\sin\dfrac{\pi}{3} - 3\sin\dfrac{\pi}{2} = 2\sqrt{3} - 3 > 0$

$f''(0) = 0$

So, $x = \dfrac{5\pi}{6}$ is point of maxima.

$\therefore f\left(\dfrac{5\pi}{6}\right) = \dfrac{5\pi}{6} - \sin\dfrac{5\pi}{3} + \dfrac{1}{3}\sin\dfrac{5\pi}{2}$

$= \dfrac{5\pi}{6} + \dfrac{\sqrt{3}}{2} + \dfrac{1}{3} = \dfrac{5\pi + 3\sqrt{3} + 2}{6}$

83. Let $P(x) = y = \left(\dfrac{\sqrt{3e}}{2\sin x}\right)^{\sin^2 x}, x \in \left(0, \dfrac{\pi}{2}\right)$

$\Rightarrow \ln(y) = (\sin^2 x)\ln\left(\dfrac{\sqrt{3e}}{2\sin x}\right) = (\sin^2 x)(\ln\sqrt{3e} - \ln(2\sin x))$

On differentiating w.r.t. x, we get

$\dfrac{1}{y} \times y' = (\sin^2 x)(\ln\sqrt{3e} - \ln(2\sin x))'$
$\quad + (\sin^2 x)'(\ln\sqrt{3e} - \ln(2\sin x))$

$= (\sin^2 x)\left(0 - \dfrac{1}{2\sin x} \times 2\cos x\right)$
$\quad + 2\sin x\cos x(\ln\sqrt{3e} - \ln(2\sin x))$

$\Rightarrow \dfrac{y'}{y} = \sin x\cos x(2\ln\sqrt{3e} - 2\ln(2\sin x) - 1)$

For local maxima, $y' = 0$

$\Rightarrow \sin x\cos x(2\ln\sqrt{3e} - 2\ln(2\sin x) - 1) = 0$

$\Rightarrow 2\ln\sqrt{3e} - 2\ln(2\sin x) - 1 = 0 \quad \left[\because x \in \left(0, \dfrac{\pi}{2}\right)\right]$

$\Rightarrow \ln\left(\dfrac{3e}{e}\right) = 2\ln(2\sin x)$

$\Rightarrow \dfrac{1}{2}\ln(3) = \ln(2\sin x) \Rightarrow \sin x = \dfrac{\sqrt{3}}{2}$

$\therefore$ Local maximum value $= \left(\dfrac{\sqrt{3e}}{2 \times \left(\dfrac{\sqrt{3}}{2}\right)}\right)^{\frac{3}{4}}$

$= (\sqrt{e})^{\frac{3}{4}} = e^{\frac{3}{8}} = \dfrac{k}{e}$ [given]

$\Rightarrow \quad k = e^{\frac{11}{8}}$

$\therefore \left(\dfrac{k}{e}\right)^8 + \dfrac{k^8}{e^5} + k^8 = e^3 + e^6 + e^{11}$

84. Given length of square sheet of side is 30 cm.

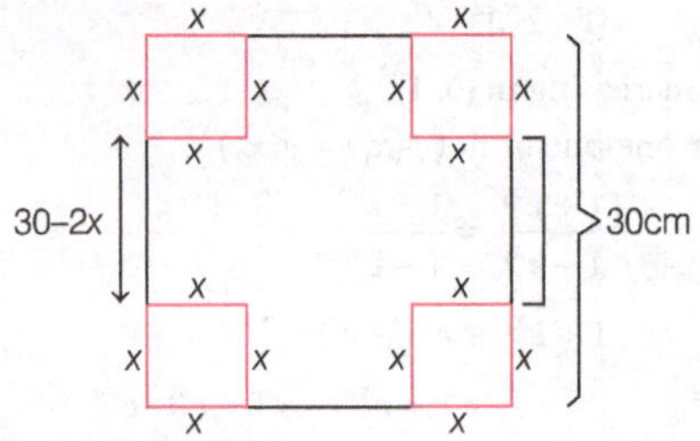

Let side of small square be x cm. Since, a square piece of tin is to be made into a box without top by cutting square from each convex and folding up the flaps to from a box. Then, this shape framed a cuboidal shape.

Their, volume of the box (V)

$= (30 - 2x)(30 - 2x)x$

$\Rightarrow \quad V = x(30 - 2x)^2$

On differentiating both sides w.r.t. x, we get

$\dfrac{dV}{dx} = (30 - 2x)^2 + x\{2(30 - 2x)\cdot(-2)\}$

$= (30 - 2x)^2 - 4x(30 - 2x)$

$= (30 - 2x)\{30 - 6x\}$

Therefore, maximum of V, $\dfrac{dV}{dx} = 0$

$(30 - 2x)(30 - 6x) = 0$

$\Rightarrow \quad x = 15$ or $x = 5$

$\because x = 15$ is not possible $x = 5$

So, the surface area is

$= 4 \times (30 - 2x) \times x + (30 - 2x)^2$

$= 4 \times (30 - 10) \times 5 + (30 - 10)^2$ [put $x = 5$]

$= 400 + 400 = 800$

85. Let $f(n) = \dfrac{n^3}{n^4 + 147}$

So, $f'(n) = \dfrac{3n^2(n^4 + 147) - n^3(4n^3)}{(n^4 + 147)^2}$

For maxima, $f'(n) = 0$

$\Rightarrow \quad 3n^2(n^4 + 147) - n^3(4n^3) = 0 \Rightarrow n = \sqrt{21}$

$\because \quad 4 < \sqrt{21} < 5$

$\Rightarrow f(5) > f(4)$ or $a_5 > a_4$

For $n = 5$, $f(n)$ or a_n is maximum.

$\therefore a_\alpha$ is maximum at $\alpha = 5$

86. Given, $f(x) = (x^2 - 2x + 7) \cdot e^{(4x^3 - 12x^2 - 180x + 31)}$

Let $f_1(x) = (x^2 - 2x + 7) > 0, \forall x \in R$

$f_1'(x) = 2x - 2 = 0 \Rightarrow x = 1$

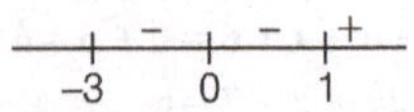

Thus, $f_1(x)$ is decreasing on $[-3, 0]$.

Also, let $f_2(x) = e^{4x^3 - 12x^2 - 180x + 31}$

$\Rightarrow \quad f_2'(x) = e^{4x^3 - 12x^2 - 180x + 31} \cdot (12x^2 - 24x - 180)$

$$= 12(x^2 - 2x - 15) \cdot e^{4x^3 - 12x^2 - 180x + 31}$$

$$= 12(x + 3)(x - 5)\, e^{4x^3 - 12x^2 - 180x + 31}$$

Thus,

+ − − +
−3 0 5

$\therefore$ Clearly, $f_2(x)$ is also decreasing in $[-3, 0]$ and also positive, $\forall\, x \in R$.

$\therefore$ Absolute maximum value of $f(x)$ occurs at $x = -3$

Given that, absolute maximum value of the above function in $[-3, 0]$ is $f(\alpha)$.

Thus, $\alpha = -3$.

87. (i) Find $f'(x)$ using product rule of differentiation and expression for $f'(x)$ for different value of n_1 and n_2 as per options and solve further using first derivative test.

(ii) $(uv)' = u'v + v'u$

$$f(x) = (x-3)^{n_1}(x-5)^{n_2}$$

On differentiating w.r.t. x, we get

$$f'(x) = n_1(x-3)^{n_1 - 1}(x-5)^{n_2} + (x-3)^{n_1} \cdot n_2(x-5)^{n_2 - 1}$$

$$= (x-3)^{n_1 - 1}(x-5)^{n_2 - 1}[n_1(x-5) + n_2(x-3)]$$

$$= (x-3)^{n_1 - 1}(x-5)^{n_1 - 1}[n_1 x + n_2 x - 5n_1 - 3n_2]$$

$$= (x-3)^{n_1 - 1}(x-5)^{n_2 - 1}[x(n_1 + n_2) - (5n_1 + 3n_2)]$$

$$= (x-3)^{n_1 - 1}(x-5)^{n_2 - 1}(n_1 + n_2)\left[x - \frac{5n_1 + 3n_2}{n_1 + n_2}\right]$$

Option (c) is incorrect.

For $n_1 = 3, n_2 = 5$

$$f'(x) = 8(x-3)^2(x-5)^4\left(x - \frac{30}{8}\right)$$

By $f'(x) = 0$

Critical point : $x = 30/8$

$$f''(x) = 8\left[2(x-3)(x-5)^4\left(x - \frac{30}{8}\right) + (x-3)^2 \cdot 4(x-5)^3\left(x - \frac{30}{8}\right) + (x-3)^2(x-5)^4(1-0)\right]$$

At $x = \frac{30}{8}$, $f''(x) = 8$ [0 + 0 + positive value]

= positive

$\therefore$ f attains local minima at $x = \alpha = 30/8$

88. Let $a = 20 - 2x^2$

and $b = 10 + x^2, c = 10 + x^2$

$$s = \frac{a + b + c}{2} = 20$$

$$\Delta = \sqrt{20(2x^2)(10 - x^2)(10 - x^2)}$$

$$\Delta = 2\sqrt{10}\sqrt{x^2(10 - x^2)^2}$$

$$\Delta = 2\sqrt{10}|10x - x^3|$$

Let $p = 10x - x^3$

$dp/dx = 10 - 3x^2$

For Δ to be maximum

$$\frac{dp}{dx} = 0 \Rightarrow 10 - 3x^2 = 0$$

$$\Rightarrow \quad x^2 = \frac{10}{3} \Rightarrow x = \pm\sqrt{\frac{10}{3}}$$

$$\frac{d^2p}{dx^2} = -6x$$

At $x = \sqrt{\frac{10}{3}}$, $\frac{d^2p}{dx^2} = -6\sqrt{\frac{10}{3}} < 0$

So, $x = \sqrt{\frac{10}{3}}$ is point of maxima.

So, $k = \sqrt{\frac{10}{3}}$

$$3k^2 = 3 \times \frac{10}{3} = 10$$

89. $f(x) = |x^2 - 3x - 2| - x,\ x \in [-1, 2]$

For $x^2 - 3x - 2$, $-\frac{b}{2a} = \frac{3}{2}$ and $\frac{D}{4a} = \frac{17}{4}$

where, $D = b^2 - 4ac = 9 + 8 = 17$

and roots are $x = \frac{3 \pm \sqrt{17}}{2}$ out of which only

$$x = \frac{3 - \sqrt{17}}{2} \in [-1, 2]$$

$$\text{So, } f(x) = \begin{cases} x^2 - 4x - 2, & -1 \le x \le \frac{3 - \sqrt{17}}{2} \\ -x^2 + 2x + 2, & \frac{3 - \sqrt{17}}{2} \le x \le 2 \end{cases}$$

$$f\left(\frac{3 - \sqrt{17}}{2}\right) = 0 + \frac{\sqrt{17} - 3}{2}$$

$$= \frac{\sqrt{17} - 3}{2} = f(x)_{\min} \quad \text{[absolute minimum value]}$$

$$f'(x) = -2x + 2 = 0$$

$$\Rightarrow \quad x = 1 \in \left[\frac{3 - \sqrt{17}}{2} \le x \le 2\right]$$

$\therefore$ $f(x)_{\max} = f(1) = -1 + 2 + 2 = 3$ [absolute maximum value]

So, $\frac{\sqrt{17} - 3}{2} + 3 = \frac{\sqrt{17} + 3}{2}$

90. $f(x) = |(x-1)(x^2 - 2x - 3)| + x - 3,\ x \in R$

$= |(x-1)(x+1)(x-3)| + x - 3,\ x \in R$

$= |(x^2 - 1)(x - 3)| + (x - 3),\ x \in R$

$$f(x) = \begin{cases} (x^2 - 1)(x - 3) + (x - 3), & 3 \le x < 4 \\ -(x^2 - 1)(x - 3) + (x - 3), & 1 \le x < 3 \\ (x^2 - 1)(x - 3) + (x - 3), & 0 < x < 1 \end{cases}$$

$$f(x) = \begin{cases} (x - 3)x^2, & 3 \le x < 4 \\ (2 - x^2)(x - 3), & 1 \le x < 3 \\ (x - 3)x^2, & 0 < x < 1 \end{cases}$$

$$f'(x) = \begin{cases} 3x^2 - 6x, & 3 \le x < 4 \\ -3x^2 + 6x + 2, & 1 \le x < 3 \\ 3x^2 - 6x, & 0 < x < 1 \end{cases}$$

Clearly, $f'(3^+) > 0$ and $f(3^-) < 0$

$\therefore$ 3 is local minima.

$f'(1^+) > 0$ and $f'(1^{-1}) < 0$

$\therefore$ 1 is local minima.

When $x \in (1, 3)$

$f'(x) = 0$

$-3x^2 + 6x + 2 = 0$

$$x = \frac{-6 \pm \sqrt{36+24}}{2 \times (-3)} = \frac{-6 \pm \sqrt{60}}{-6} = 1 \pm \sqrt{\frac{5}{3}}$$

$\therefore$ There are two minimum and one maximum point.

$\therefore m + M = 2 + 1 = 3$

91. Area = 12 sq units

$$\Rightarrow \begin{vmatrix} \alpha & \beta & 1 \\ 5 & 6 & 1 \\ 3 & 2 & 1 \end{vmatrix} = \pm 24$$

$\Rightarrow \quad 4\alpha - 2\beta - 8 = \pm 24$

$\Rightarrow \quad 4\alpha - 2\beta = 32,\ 4\alpha - 2\beta + 16 = 0$

$\Rightarrow \quad 2\alpha - \beta - 16 = 0,\ 2\alpha - \beta + 8 = 0$

Distance from origin when $\beta = 2\alpha + 8$ is

$$D = \sqrt{\alpha^2 + (2\alpha + 8)^2} = \sqrt{5\alpha^2 + 32\alpha + 64}$$

$\Rightarrow \quad D^2 = 5\alpha^2 + 32\alpha + 64$

Now, $\frac{d}{d\alpha}(D^2) = 0 \Rightarrow 10\alpha + 32 = 0 \Rightarrow \alpha = -\frac{16}{5}$

$\Rightarrow \quad \beta = -\frac{32}{5} + 8 = \frac{8}{5}$

$$\therefore \quad D = \sqrt{\left(\frac{-16}{5}\right)^2 + \left(\frac{8}{5}\right)^2} = \frac{8}{5}\sqrt{5} = \frac{8}{\sqrt{5}}$$

Similarly, if $\beta = 2\alpha - 16$, then $D = \frac{16}{\sqrt{5}}$

So, least possible length of line segment $= \frac{8}{\sqrt{5}}$

92. Given, $f(x) = x^3 - 3x^2 - \frac{3}{2}f''(2) \cdot x + f''(1)$

Then, $f'(x) = 3x^2 - 6x - \frac{3}{2}f''(2)$

$f''(x) = 6x - 6$

Put $\quad x = 1$ and $x = 2$,

$f''(2) = 12 - 6 = 6$ and $f''(1) = 0$

Therefore, $\quad f(x) = x^3 - 3x^2 - 9x$ ...(i)

and $\quad f'(x) = 3x^2 - 6x - 9$

and $\quad f''(x) = 6x - 6$

Equate $f'(x) = 0$ gives,

$\Rightarrow \quad 3x^2 - 6x - 9 = 0$

$3(x + 1)(x - 3) = 0$

$\Rightarrow \quad x = -1, x = 3$

Now, $f''(-1) = 6(-1) - 6 = -12 < 0$

$f''(3) = 6(3) - 6 = 12 > 0$

$\therefore (-1)$ is maxima and 3 is minima.

Local minimum value $= f(3)$

$f(3) = (3)^3 - 3(3)^2 - 9(3)$ [using Eq. (i)]

$= 27 - 27 - 27$

$\therefore$ Sum of all the local minimum values is -27.

93. $f(x) = ax^2 + 6x - 15$

$f'(x) = 2ax + 6$

$f'(x) = 2(ax + 3)$

$f(x)$ is increasing for $\left(-\infty, \frac{3}{4}\right)$.

So, $x = -\frac{3}{a} = \frac{3}{4}$

$\Rightarrow \quad a = -4$

$g(x) = ax^2 - 6x + 15$

$g'(x) = 2(ax - 3)$

For local maxima, $g'(x) = 0$

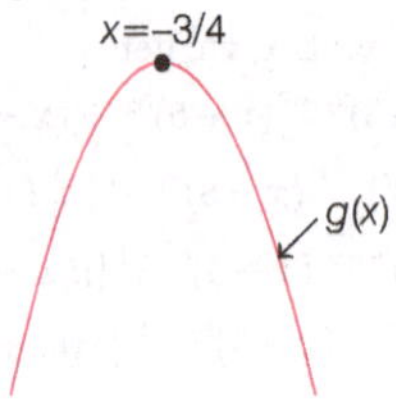

$x = \frac{3}{a} = -\frac{3}{4}$

$g(x)$ has local maxima at $x = -\frac{3}{4}$.

94. We have, $\frac{x^2}{a} + \frac{y^2}{b} = 1$ ...(i)

On differentiating Eq. (i) w.r.t. x, we get

$$\frac{dy}{dx} = -\frac{bx}{ay} = m_1 \text{ (say)}$$

Also, $\frac{x^2}{c} + \frac{y^2}{d} = 1$ ...(ii)

Differentiating Eq. (ii) w.r.t. x, we get

$$\frac{dy}{dx} = -\frac{dx}{cy} = m_2 \text{ (say)}$$

Now, $m_1 m_2 = -1$ [given]

$\Rightarrow \left(-\frac{bx}{ay}\right)\left(\frac{-dx}{cy}\right) = -1$

$\Rightarrow \quad bdx^2 = -acy^2$ ...(iii)

Now, subtracting Eq.(ii) from Eq. (i), we get

$$\left(\frac{1}{a} - \frac{1}{c}\right)x^2 + \left(\frac{1}{b} - \frac{1}{d}\right)y^2 = 0$$

$\Rightarrow \quad \left(\frac{c-a}{ac}\right)x^2 + \left(\frac{d-b}{bd}\right)y^2 = 0$

$\Rightarrow \quad \frac{(c-a)}{ac}x^2 + \left(\frac{d-b}{bd}\right)\left(\frac{-bdx^2}{ac}\right) = 0$ [using Eq. (iii)]

$\Rightarrow \quad (c - a) - (d - b) = 0$

$\Rightarrow \quad c - d = a - b$

95. Let $f(x) = 3x^4 + 4x^3 - 12x^2 + 4$

On differentiating w.r.t. x, we get

$$f'(x) = 12x^3 + 12x^2 - 24x$$
$$= 12x(x^2 + x - 2) = 12x(x+2)(x-1)$$

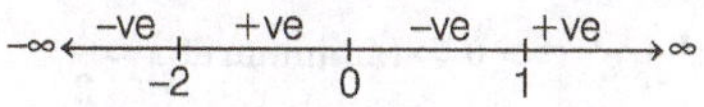

Sign of $f'(x)$

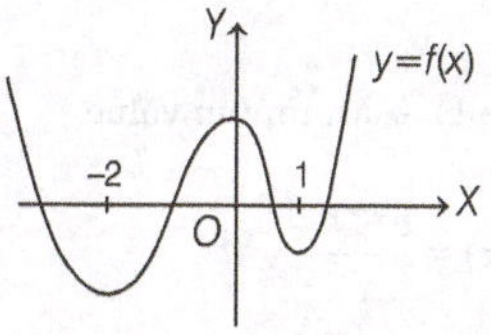

$$f(0) = 4,\ f(-2) = -28,\ f(1) = -1$$

From graph, we observe that $f(x)$ has minima at $x = -2$ and $x = 1$ and maxima at $x = 0$.

$\Rightarrow f(x)$ cuts the X-axis at 4 distinct points.

So, there are 4 distinct real roots of the given equation.

96. Let $y = \dfrac{4}{\sin x} + \dfrac{1}{1 - \sin x} = \dfrac{4 - 3\sin x}{\sin x(1 - \sin x)}$

Let $\sin x = t$, where $t \in (0, 1)$

$\therefore \quad y = \dfrac{4 - 3t}{t - t^2}$

Now, putting $dy/dt = 0$

$$\frac{dy}{dt} = \frac{(t - t^2)(-3) - (4 - 3t)(1 - 2t)}{(t - t^2)^2} = 0$$

$\Rightarrow \quad 3t^2 - 3t - (4 - 11t + 6t^2) = 0$

$\Rightarrow \quad 3t^2 - 8t + 4 = 0$

$\Rightarrow \quad (3t - 2)(t - 2) = 0 \Rightarrow t = \dfrac{2}{3}$

[$t = 2$ discarded because $t \in (0, 1)$ only]

$\Rightarrow \quad \sin x = \dfrac{2}{3}$

$\therefore \quad y_{\min} = \dfrac{4}{2/3} + \dfrac{1}{1 - 2/3} = 9 \qquad [\because y_{\max} \to \infty]$

$\Rightarrow \quad \alpha_{\min} = 9$

Exercise 2 - JEE Advanced Pattern

1. For negative point of inflection $-\dfrac{b}{2a} < 0$,

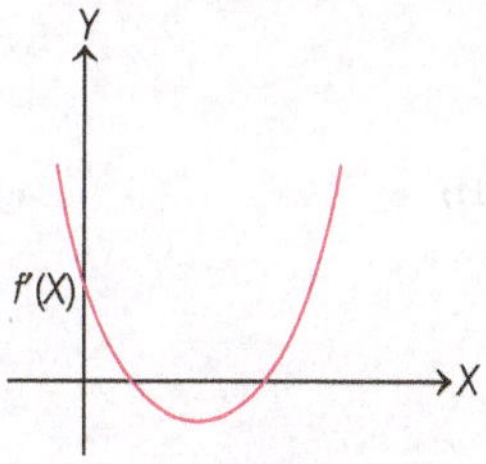

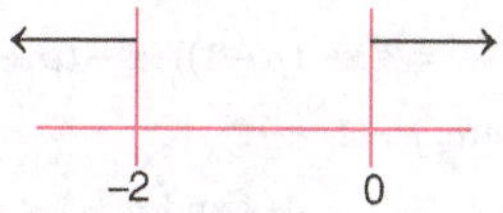

Alternatively $\dfrac{d^2y}{dx^2} = 0$, get x and put $x < 0$

$$f'(x) = ax^2 + 2(a+2)x + (a-1)$$

$$f''(x) = 2ax + 2(a+2) = 0$$

$\Rightarrow \quad x = -\dfrac{a+2}{a} < 0 \Rightarrow \dfrac{a+2}{a} > 0$

$\therefore a \in (-\infty, -2) \cup (0, \infty)$

2. Since, $f(x) = e^{g(x)}$

$$f'(x) = e^{g(x)} \cdot g'(x)$$

$\therefore$ Check the nature of $g(x)$, $g(x)$ is increasing ($\uparrow$) in $(1, 2) \cup (3, \infty)$ and decreasing ($\downarrow$) in $(-\infty, 1) \cup (2, 3)$

$g(x)$ is continuous, $\forall\ x \in R$. But non-derivable at $x = 1, 3$

$g(x)$ has local maximum at $x = 2$ and local minimum at $x = 1, 3$.

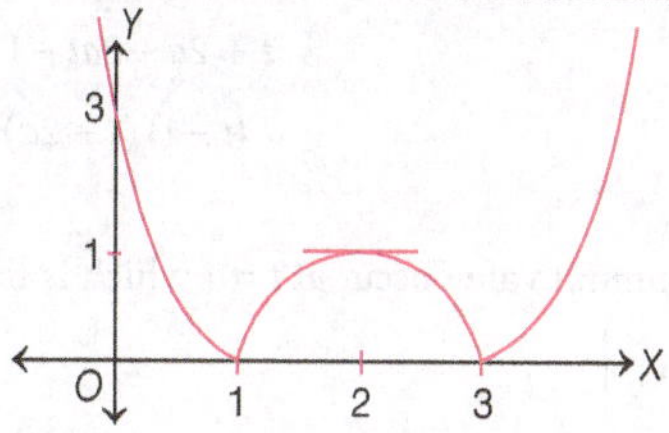

Graph of $g(x) = |x^2 - 4x + 3| = |(x-3)(x-1)|$

Alternate Solution

We have, $f(x) = e^{|x^2 - 4x + 3|}$

$$= \begin{cases} e^{(x^2 - 4x + 3)}, & x \in (-\infty, 1) \cup (3, \infty) \\ e^{-(x^2 - 4x + 3)}, & x \in [1, 3] \end{cases}$$

$$\Rightarrow \quad f'(x) = \begin{cases} 2(x-2) \cdot e^{(x^2 - 4x + 3)}, & x \in (-\infty, 1) \cup (3, \infty) \\ -2(x-2) \cdot e^{-(x^2 - 4x + 3)}, & x \in [1, 3] \end{cases}$$

Clearly, $f(x)$ is continuous for every $x \in R$ but non-derivable at $x = 1, 3$.

Also, $f'(2^+) = 0 = f'(2^-)$.

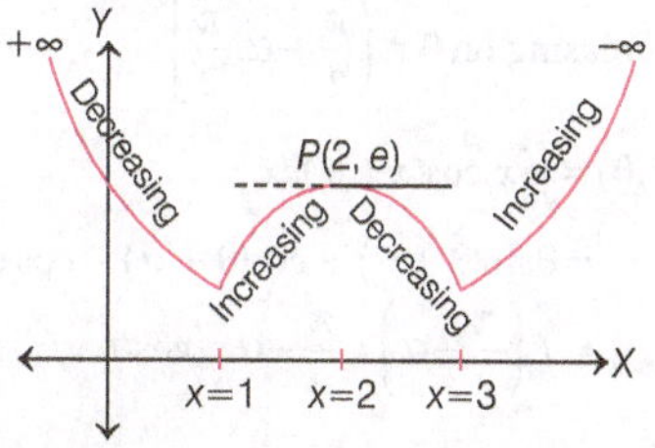

Graph of $y = f(x) = e^{|x^2 - 4x - 3|}$

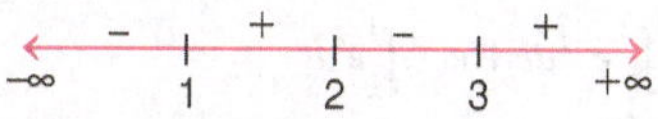

Sign scheme of $y = f'(x)$

Clearly, $f(x)$ increasing ($\uparrow$) in $(1, 2) \cup (3, \infty)$ and $f(x)$ decreases ($\downarrow$) in $(-\infty, 1) \cup (2, 3)$.

Also, $f(x)$ has relative minima at $r = 1$ and $x = 3$.

$f(x)$ has relative maxima at $x = 2$.

3. We have, $\int_0^{\frac{\pi}{2}} (\sin x + t \cos x) dx = 1 + t$

and $\quad I = \int_0^{\frac{\pi}{2}} (\sin x + t \cos x)^2 dx$

$$= \int_0^{\frac{\pi}{2}} (\sin^2 x + t^2 \cos^2 x + t \sin 2x) dx$$

$$= \frac{\pi}{4} + t^2 \frac{\pi}{4} + t = \frac{\pi}{4} t^2 + t + \frac{\pi}{4}$$

So, let $y = f(t) = \dfrac{t+1}{\sqrt{at^2 + t + a}}$,

where $a = \dfrac{\pi}{4}$ (say)

For maximum or minimum, $f'(t) = 0$

$$f'(t) = \sqrt{at^2 + t + a} - \frac{t+1}{2\sqrt{at^2 + t + a}}(2at + 1) = 0$$

$\therefore \quad 2(at^2 + t + a) - (t + 1)(2at + 1) = 0$

$\Rightarrow \quad (2at^2 + 2t + 2a) - (2at^2 + t + 2at + 1) = 0$

$\Rightarrow \quad t + 2a - 2at - 1 = 0$

$\Rightarrow \quad (t - 1)(1 - 2a) = 0$

$\therefore \quad t = 1$

Hence, maximum value occur at $t = 1$ which is lies in the interval $\left(\dfrac{3}{4}, \dfrac{3}{2}\right)$.

4. As $F'(\theta) = \theta\cos(\theta + \alpha)$, where $\theta + \alpha \in (0, \pi)$

For maximum $F'(\theta) = 0$

$\Rightarrow \quad \theta = 0$ or $\theta = \dfrac{\pi}{2} - \alpha$

$F''(\theta) = \cos(\theta + \alpha) - \theta\sin(\theta + \alpha)$

$F''(0) > 0$ and $F''\left(\dfrac{\pi}{2} - \alpha\right) < 0 \Rightarrow$ Maxima at $x = \dfrac{\pi}{2} - \alpha$

Now, F is increasing on $\theta \in \left[0, \dfrac{\pi}{2} - \alpha\right)$

$$\left[\text{as } 0 < \theta + \alpha < \pi, \text{ so } \theta + \alpha = \frac{\pi}{2} \Rightarrow \theta = \left(\frac{\pi}{2} - \alpha\right)\right]$$

and F is decreasing on $\theta \in \left(\dfrac{\pi}{2} - \alpha, \dfrac{\pi}{2}\right]$

We have, $F(\theta) = \int_0^\theta x\cos(x + \alpha)dx$

$= \theta\sin(\theta + \alpha) + \cos(\theta + \alpha) - \cos\alpha$

$$F_{\max} = F\left(\frac{\pi}{2} - \alpha\right) = \frac{\pi}{2} - \alpha - \cos\alpha$$

5. $f(x) = \int_0^x e^{x-t}dt + \int_x^1 e^{t-x}dx$

$f(x) = e^x\int_0^x e^{-t}dt + e^{-x}\int_x^1 e^t dt$

$f(x) = e^x(1 - e^{-x}) + e^{-x}(e - e^x)$

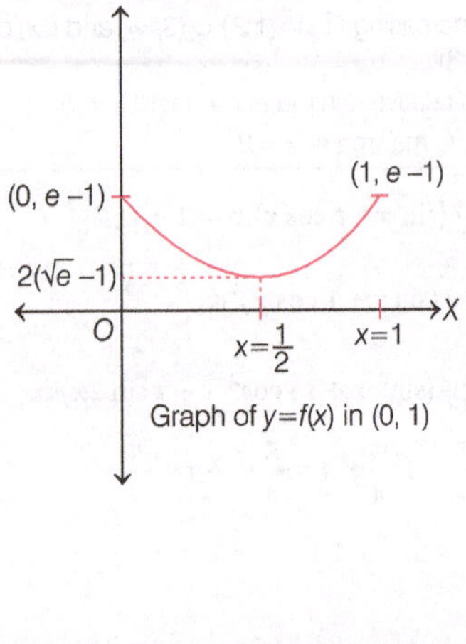

Graph of $y=f(x)$ in (0, 1)

$\therefore \quad f(x) = e^x + e^{1-x} - 2$

$f'(x) = e^x - e^{1-x} = 0$

$\therefore \quad x = \dfrac{1}{2}$

$f''(x) = e^x + e^{1-x} > 0 \Rightarrow$ Minimum at $x = \dfrac{1}{2}$

$\left.\begin{array}{l} f(0) = e - 1 \\ f(1) = e - 1 \end{array}\right\}$ Maximum value

$f\left(\dfrac{1}{2}\right) = 2(\sqrt{e} - 1) \rightarrow$ Minimum value

6. (b) Consider $f(x) = \dfrac{e^{\cos x}}{x}$

Now, $\quad f'(x) = \dfrac{-e^{\cos x}(1 + x\sin x)}{x^2}$

As $\quad f'(x) < 0 \Rightarrow f(\alpha) > f(\beta)$

So, $\quad \dfrac{e^{\cos\alpha}}{\alpha} > \dfrac{e^{\cos\beta}}{\beta}$

$\Rightarrow e^{\cos\alpha - \cos\beta} > \dfrac{\alpha}{\beta} \Rightarrow e^{\cos\beta - \cos\alpha} < \dfrac{\beta}{\alpha}$

7. We have, $\prod_{i=1}^{n}\cot\alpha_i = 1$

$\Rightarrow \quad \prod_{i=1}^{n}\cos\alpha_i = 1 = \prod_{i=1}^{n}\sin\alpha_i$

$\Rightarrow \quad \prod_{i=1}^{n}\cos^2\alpha_i = \prod_{i=1}^{n}\cos\alpha_i\sin\alpha_i$

$= \prod_{i=1}^{n}\left(\dfrac{\sin 2\alpha_i}{2}\right)$

$= \dfrac{1}{2^n}$ [for maximum value, $\sin 2\alpha_i = 1$]

$\Rightarrow \quad \prod_{i=1}^{n}\cos\alpha_i = \dfrac{1}{2^{n/2}}$

8. Given, $a_1 a_2 \ldots a_n = e$

Consider $a_1 a_2 \ldots a_n = e$

$AM \geq GM$

$$\frac{a_1 + a_2 + \ldots + 2a_n}{n} \geq (a_1 a_2 a_3 \ldots 2a_n)^{\frac{1}{n}} = (2e)^{\frac{1}{n}}$$

$\therefore a_1 + a_2 + \ldots + a_{n-1} + 2a_n \geq n(2e)^{1/n}$

9. $f'(x) = 3x^2 - 6px + 3(p^2 - 1)$

$= 3(x^2 - 2px + p^2 - 1)$

$= 3(x - (p - 1))(x - (p + 1))$

Here, $p - 1 > -2$

$\Rightarrow \quad p > -1$ and $p + 1 < 4$

$\Rightarrow \quad p < 3$

$\therefore \quad p \in (-1, 3)$

So, $(p_2 - p_1) = 3 - (-1) = 4$

10. Let $f(x)=\frac{e^x}{x^2}$, $f'(x)=\frac{(x-2)e^x}{x^3}$

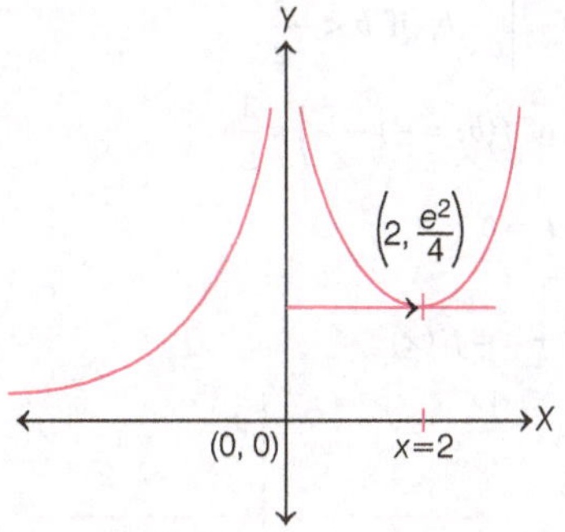

So, from the graph, $c>\frac{e^2}{4}$

So, $c_{min}=2$

11. $f'(x)=(pq-q^2-2)+(\cos^4 x+\sin^4 x)<0$

$\Rightarrow \quad pq-q^2-1<\frac{\sin^2 2x}{2} \Rightarrow pq-q^2-1<\frac{1}{2}$

$\Rightarrow \quad 2q^2-2pq+3>0 \Rightarrow 4p^2-24<0$

$\Rightarrow \quad -\sqrt{6}<p<\sqrt{6}$

12. $f(x)=\begin{cases}-2x+3, & x<1\\ 1, & x\in[1,2)\\ 2x-3, & x\geq 2\end{cases}$

$I=\int_0^1(-2x+3)dx+\int_1^2 dx+\int_2^3(2x-3)dx$

$=(-x^2+3x)_0^1+(x)_1^2+(x^2-3x)_2^3=2+1+2=5$

$M=1, N=-2, C=0$

$\therefore \frac{M^2-N^2+IC}{2}=\frac{-3}{2}$

13. $f(x)=2x^3-21x^2+78x+24$

$f'(x)=6(x^2-7x+13)$

$\Rightarrow f'(x)>0, \forall x\in R$

$\Rightarrow f(x)$ is increasing function

Now, $f(f(f(x)-2x^3))\geq f(f(2x^3-f(x)))$

$\Rightarrow \quad f(f(x)-2x^3)\geq f(2x^3-f(x))$

$\Rightarrow \quad f(x)-2x^3\geq 2x^3-f(x)$

$\Rightarrow \quad f(x)\geq 2x^3 \Rightarrow 7x^2-26x-8\leq 0$

$\Rightarrow x\in\left[-\frac{2}{7}, 4\right] \Rightarrow$ number of integers $=5$

14. We must have, $\begin{vmatrix} x & 1 & 2\\ f(x) & 3 & x^2\\ 5x & 6 & 1\end{vmatrix}=0$

$\therefore x(3-6x^2)-1(f(x)-5x^3)+2(6f(x)-15x)=0$

$\therefore \quad f(x)=\frac{x^3+27x}{11}$

$\Rightarrow \quad f'(x)=\frac{3x^2+27}{11}>0, \forall x\in R$

15. $\frac{dy}{dx}=3x^2-4x+C_1$

$y=x^3-2x^2+C_1x+C_2$

Also, $\left.\frac{dy}{dx}\right]_{at\ x=1}=0$

and $y]_{at\ x=1}=5$

$\Rightarrow \quad 3-4+C_1=0$

$1-2+C_1+C_2=5$

$C_1=1, C_2=5$

$\therefore \quad y=x^3-2x^2+x+5$

For $x\in[0,2] \Rightarrow f(0)=5=m \Rightarrow M-m=2$

$\because \quad f(1)=5$

$f(2)=2+5=7=M$

16. $f(x)=\cos x+\frac{1}{2}\cos 2x-\frac{1}{3}\cos 3x$

$f'(x)=-\sin x-\sin 2x+\sin 3x=2\sin x(2\cos x+1)(\cos x-1)=0$

$\sin x=0$

$\cos x=-\frac{1}{2}, \cos x=1$

For $x\in[0,2\pi] \Rightarrow x=0, \frac{2\pi}{3}, \frac{4\pi}{3}, 2\pi$

Now, for maximum and minimum

$f(0)=1+\frac{1}{2}-\frac{1}{3}=\frac{7}{6}$

$f\left(\frac{2\pi}{3}\right)=-\frac{1}{2}-\frac{1}{4}-\frac{1}{3}=\frac{-6-3-4}{12}=\frac{-13}{12}$

$f\left(\frac{4\pi}{3}\right)=\frac{-1}{2}-\frac{1}{4}-\frac{1}{3}=\frac{-13}{12}$

$f(2\pi)=\frac{7}{6}$

$\therefore$ Difference of maximum and minimum

$=\frac{7}{6}+\frac{13}{12}=\frac{14+13}{12}=\frac{27}{12}=\frac{9}{4}$

17. $g'(x)=(2x^2-\ln x)\, f(x)$

$f'(x)=\frac{1}{\ln x^3}3x^2-\frac{1}{\ln x^2}2x$

$f'(x)=\frac{x^2-x}{\ln x}$

$f'(x)=\frac{x(x-1)}{\ln x}>0, \forall x>1; f(x)>f(1)$

$\Rightarrow f(x)>0, \forall x>1$

For $g(x)$ is increasing

$g'(x)>0 \Rightarrow 2x^2-\ln x>0$, as $(f(x)>0)$

Let $H(x)=2x^2-\ln x$

$H'(x)=4x-\frac{1}{x}=\frac{4x^2-1}{x}>0$, when $x>1$

$H(x)>H(1) \Rightarrow H(x)>2$

$\therefore g'(x)>0\ \forall\ x\in(1,\infty)$

$\therefore g(x)$ is increasing on $(1,\infty)$.

18. $y = \dfrac{1}{1+x^2}$

Let $x = \tan\theta$, then $y = \cos^2\theta$

$\left|\dfrac{dy}{dx}\right| = \left|2\sin\theta\cos^3\theta\right|$

$\left|\dfrac{dy}{dx}\right|_{max}$ at $\theta = \dfrac{\pi}{6} \Rightarrow x = \dfrac{1}{\sqrt{3}}, y = \dfrac{3}{4}$

$\therefore \left(\dfrac{1}{\sqrt{3}}, \dfrac{3}{4}\right)$

19. $f(x) = x^6 - x - 1$

$f'(x) = 6x^5 - 1 > 0 \ \forall\ x \in [1, 2] \Rightarrow$ increasing on $[1, 2]$

If $f(1) = -1 < 0$ and $f(2) = 2^6 - 3 > 0$, then $f(x)$ has one root in $[1, 2]$.

20. $f'(x) = \cos x(3\sin^2 x - m) = 0$

$\sin^2 x = \dfrac{m}{3} \Rightarrow 0 < \dfrac{m}{3} < 1$

$0 < m < 3$

21. $h(x) = g(x) + x$

$\Rightarrow h'(x) = g'(x) + 1$

$\Rightarrow g'(x) = h'(x) - 1$

$\Rightarrow g''(x) = h''(x)$

$\Rightarrow h''(x) - 3(h'(x) - 1) > 3$

$\Rightarrow \quad h''(x) - 3h'(x) > 0$

$\Rightarrow \quad \dfrac{d}{dx}(e^{-3x}h'(x)) > 0$

Let $P(x) = e^{-3x}h'(x)$

$\Rightarrow P'(x) > 0$

$\Rightarrow P(x)$ is an increasing function.

$P(0) = h'(0) = 0$

$\Rightarrow \quad P(x) > 0, \forall\ x > 0$

$\Rightarrow \quad h'(x) > 0, \forall\ x > 0$

$\Rightarrow h(x)$ is an increasing function, $\forall\ x > 0$

22. $f(b) = \left|\sin x + \dfrac{2}{3+\sin x} + b\right|_{max}, \forall\ x \in R$

$\sin x = t$ (let)

$g(t) = t + \dfrac{2}{3+t}, t \in [-1, 1]$

$g'(t) = 1 - \dfrac{2}{(3+t)^2} > 0$

$(3+t)^2 - 2 > 0$

$(3 + t - \sqrt{2})(3 + t + \sqrt{2}) > 0$

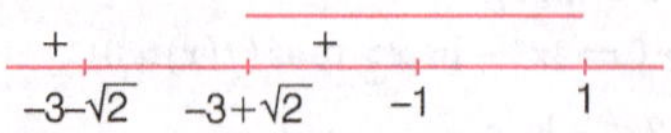

$g(t) = t + \dfrac{2}{3+t}$ increasing, $\forall\ t \in [-1, 1]$

$g(t)_{max} = \dfrac{3}{2}$

$g(t)_{min} = 0$

$f(b) = \begin{cases} \dfrac{3}{2} + b & \text{if } b \geq -\dfrac{3}{2} \\ -b, & \text{if } b < -\dfrac{3}{2} \end{cases}$

Minimum of $f(b) = -\left(\dfrac{-3}{2}\right) = \dfrac{3}{2}$

23. $x^n + ax + b = 0$

x is even.

$nx^{n-1} + a = f'(x)$

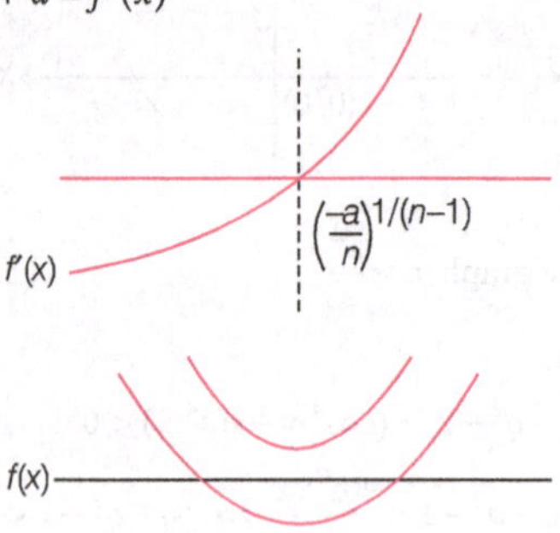

24. $A = \dfrac{xe^{-x^2}}{2}; A' = \dfrac{1}{2}\left[e^{-x^2} - 2x^2e^{-x^2}\right]$

$= \dfrac{e^{-x^2}}{2}[1 - 2x^2] = 0 \Rightarrow x = \dfrac{1}{\sqrt{2}}$ gives A_{max}

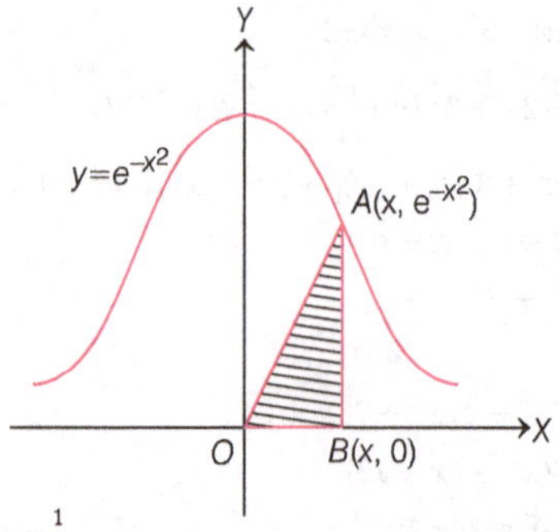

$\therefore A_{max} = \dfrac{e^{-\frac{1}{2}}}{2\sqrt{2}} = \dfrac{1}{\sqrt{8e}}$

25. Given, $g(x) = \ln(h(x))$

$g'(x) = \dfrac{h'(x)}{h(x)}$

$g''(x) = \dfrac{h(x)\,h''(x) - (h'(x))^2}{h^2(x)} < 0$ (given)

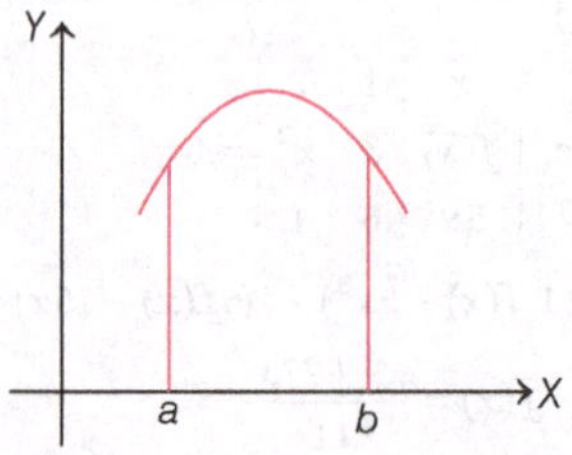

$\therefore g''(x) < 0 \Rightarrow g(x)$ is concave down.

26. $f'(x) = (2^2 + 4^2x^2 + 6^2x^4 + \ldots + 100^2x^{98})x$

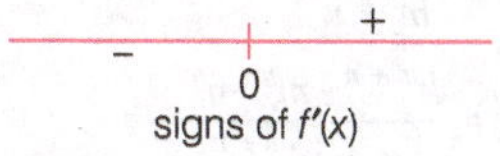

Minimum at $x = 0$

27. $f(x) = (x-2)^{-5} + (x-2)^{-4} + 3(x-2)^{-3} + 1 + (x-2)^8 + (x-2)^{10}$

Say $x - 2 = t\,(>0)$

$f(x) = t^{-5} + t^{-4} + 3t^{-3} + 1 + t^8 + t^{10}.$

Now, apply AM $\geq$ GM

$$\frac{t^{-5} + t^{-4} + t^{-3} + t^{-3} + t^{-3} + 1 + t^8 + t^{10}}{8} \geq (t^{-5}\cdot t^{-4}\cdot t^{-3}\cdot t^{-3}\cdot t^{-3}\cdot 1\cdot t^8\cdot t^{10})^{\frac{1}{8}}$$

$\Rightarrow f(x) \geq 8,\ \forall\ x > 2$ minimum value of $f(x)$ is 8.

28. $A(-2, 3) \Rightarrow 3 = 4a - 2b + c$

$B(-1, 1) \Rightarrow 1 = a - b + c$

$D(2, 7) \Rightarrow 7 = 4a + 2b + c$

$\Rightarrow \quad y = x^2 + x + 1$

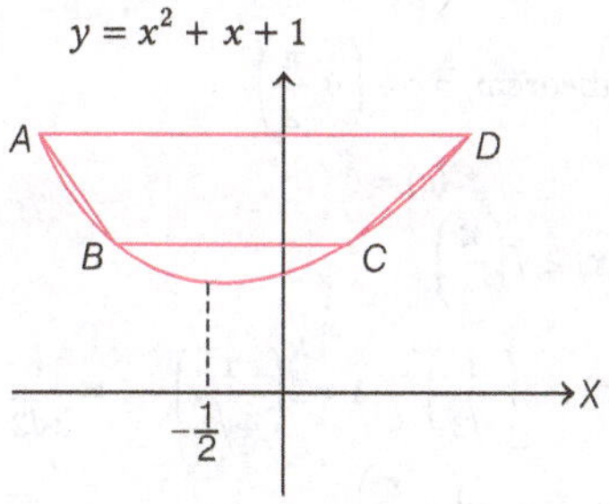

$C(h, h^2 + h + 1),\ -1 < h < 2$

$\text{Area} = \frac{3}{2}(-h^2 + h + 6)$

Maximum at $h = \frac{1}{2}$

$\Rightarrow \quad C\left(\frac{1}{2}, \frac{7}{4}\right)$

29. $(2\cos\beta - \sqrt{3})(2\sin\alpha + 1) = 0$

$\therefore \quad \cos\beta = \frac{\sqrt{3}}{2}$ or $\sin\alpha = -\frac{1}{2}$

$\beta = \frac{\pi}{6}, \frac{11\pi}{6}$ or $\alpha = \frac{7\pi}{6}, \frac{11\pi}{6}$

$\therefore \quad L = \alpha - \beta$

$$= \begin{cases} \text{maximum where } \alpha = \frac{11\pi}{6} \text{ and } \beta = 0 \\ \text{minimum when } \alpha = 0,\ \beta = \frac{11\pi}{6} \end{cases}$$

$L_{\max} = \frac{11\pi}{6};\ L_{\min} = \frac{-11\pi}{6}$

30. $f'(x) > 0,\ \forall\ x \in (1, \infty)$, so $f(x)$ strictly increasing.

So, $f(x) \geq f(1),\ \forall\ x \in (1, \infty) \Rightarrow f'(x) \leq \frac{1}{x^2+1}$

So, $f(x) = 1 + \int_1^x f'(t)dt \leq 1 + \int_1^x \frac{1}{t^2+1}dt \leq 1 + |\tan^{-1} t|_1^x \leq 1 + \tan^{-1} x - \frac{\pi}{4}$

$x \to \infty,\ f(x) \to 1 + \frac{\pi}{4}$

31. $\text{ar}(\Delta ABC) = \frac{\text{ar}(\Delta A'B'C')}{\sqrt{2}}$

Hence, two areas are maximum simultaneously.

Thus, $A'B'C'$ is equilateral.

So, $|\alpha - \beta| = |\beta - \gamma| = |\gamma - \alpha| = \frac{2\pi}{3},\ \Delta(ABC) = 3\sqrt{\frac{3}{2}}$

Hence, let $\alpha < \beta < \gamma$, $\sin(\alpha + \beta) + \sin(\beta + \gamma) + \sin(\gamma + \alpha)$

$$= \sin\left(\frac{2\pi}{3} + 2\alpha\right) + \sin(2\pi + 2\alpha) + \sin\left(\frac{4\pi}{3} + 2\alpha\right)$$

$$= 2\sin(\pi + 2\alpha)\cos\frac{\pi}{3} + \sin 2\alpha = 0$$

32. $f(x) = x + x\int_0^1 t^2 f(t)dt + x^2\int_0^1 tf(t)dt$

$\Rightarrow \quad f(x) = (a+1)x + bx^2$, where $a = \int_0^1((a+1)t^3 + bt^4)dt$

and $\quad b = \int_0^1((a+1)t^2 + bt^3)dt$

$\Rightarrow \quad f(x) = \frac{180x}{119} + \frac{80x^2}{119}$ and $g(x) = 1 + x^3$

33. Since, $f(x) = 2 \times \max\{|x-1| + |x-3|, |2x-1|\}$

$\therefore x = 1, \frac{3}{2}$ points of non-differentiability and $x = 1$ is point of local minima.

34. Since, $f'(x) = b^2 + (a-1)b + 2 - (\sin^2 x + \cos^4 x) \geq 0$

$(f'(x))_{\min} = b^2 + (a-1)b + 1 \geq 0$

$\therefore \quad (a-1)^2 - 4 < 0 \Rightarrow a \in (-1, 3)$

35. Since, $f(x) = \frac{xf'(x)}{2\sqrt{f(x)}} + \sqrt{f(x)}$

$\Rightarrow \quad \sqrt{f(x)} = \frac{1}{1 - cx} \Rightarrow f(x) = \frac{1}{(1-cx)^2}$

$\because \quad f(1) = \frac{1}{2}$

$\therefore \quad c = 1 - \sqrt{2}$

$\Rightarrow \quad f(x) = \frac{1}{[1 + (\sqrt{2} - 1)x]^2}$

36. $f'(x) = \frac{\cos x - \sin x}{1 + (\sin x + \cos x)^2} > 0$

$\Rightarrow \quad \cos x > \sin x$

$\Rightarrow \quad x \in \left(-2\pi, -\frac{7\pi}{4}\right) \cup \left(-\frac{3\pi}{4}, \frac{\pi}{4}\right) \cup \left(\frac{5\pi}{4}, 2\pi\right)$

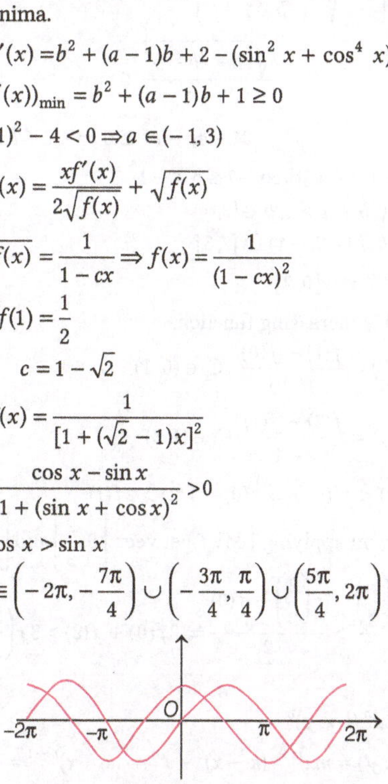

37. Vertex of $f(x)$ will be at $x = \frac{a}{2}$

Case I If $a < 0$, then maximum value of $f(x)$ is at $x = 0$,

$$f(0) = -5 \Rightarrow a^2 + 2a - 3 = 0$$

$$\Rightarrow \quad a = -3 \text{ or } 1$$

$$\Rightarrow \quad a = -3$$

Case II If $a > 2$, then maximum value of $f(x)$ is at $x = 1$,

$$f(1) = -5 \Rightarrow a^2 + a - 2 = 0$$

$\Rightarrow \quad a = -2$ or 1 which is not possible.

Case III If $0 < a < 2$, then maximum value is at $x = \frac{a}{2}$,

$$f\left(\frac{a}{2}\right) = -5 \Rightarrow 3a^2 + 8a - 12 = 0$$

$\Rightarrow \quad a = \frac{-4 \pm 2\sqrt{13}}{3} \Rightarrow a = \frac{-4 + 2\sqrt{13}}{3}$ is possible.

38. $h(x) = \frac{\ln(f(x) \cdot g(x))}{\ln a} = \frac{\ln a^{\{a^{|x|} \cdot \operatorname{sgn} x\} + [a^{|x|} \cdot \operatorname{sgn} x]}}{\ln a}$ $[\{y\} + [y] = y]$

$$= \begin{cases} a^x, & \text{for } x > 0 \\ 0, & \text{for } x = 0 \\ -a^{-x}, & \text{for } x < 0 \end{cases} \Rightarrow h(x) \text{ is an odd function.}$$

39. (a) $f''(x) > 0, \forall x \in R \Rightarrow f'(x)$ is a strictly increasing function, hence $f'(1) > f'(0)$, but given $f'(1) = f'(0) = 1$ which is not possible.

(b) $f''(x) > 0, \forall x \in R \Rightarrow f'(x)$ is increasing $f'(1) > f'(0)$, which is true.

40. $f'(x) = 3\left(1 - \sqrt{\frac{21 - 4b - b^2}{b + 1}}\right)x^2 + 5 > 0$

$$\Rightarrow \quad \frac{\sqrt{21 - 4b - b^2}}{b + 1} \le 1$$

$$\Rightarrow \quad 21 - 4b - b^2 \ge 0 \Rightarrow -7 \le b \le 3$$

Case I $b + 1 < 0$, then $-7 \le b < -1$ ...(i)

Case II If $b + 1 > 0$, $b \in [2, \infty)$ ...(ii)

$\Rightarrow \quad b \in [-7, -1) \cup [2, 3]$

41. $f''(x) > 0, \forall x \in [0, 2]$

$\Rightarrow f'(x)$ is increasing function.

$$f'(C_1) = \frac{f(1) - f(0)}{1 - 0}, C_1 \in (0, 1)$$

and $f'(C_2) = \frac{f(2) - f(1)}{2 - 1}, C_2 \in (1, 2)$

$$f'(C_1) < f'(C_2) \Rightarrow f(0) + f(2) > 2f(1)$$

Similarly, on applying LMVT between $\left[0, \frac{2}{3}\right]$ and $\left[\frac{2}{3}, 2\right]$, we get

$$\frac{f(2) - f\left(\frac{2}{3}\right)}{\frac{4}{3}} > \frac{f\left(\frac{2}{3}\right) - f(0)}{\frac{2}{3}} \Rightarrow 2f(0) + f(2) > 3f\left(\frac{2}{3}\right)$$

42. $f(x, y) = x^m(k - x)^n$

$$f'(x, y) = mx^{m-1}(k - x)^n - x^m n \cdot (k - x)^{n-1} = 0$$

$$\Rightarrow \quad x = \frac{mk}{m + n}$$

$$\text{Maximum value} = \frac{k^{m+n} \cdot m^m \cdot n^n}{(m + n)^{m+n}}$$

43. $f'(x) = e^{x^3}(x^2 - 1)x^2(x + 1)^{2011}(x - 2)^{2012}$

$$= e^{x^3} x^2 (x + 1)^{2012} (x - 1)(x - 2)^{2012}$$

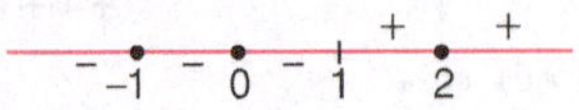

$x = -1, 0, 2$ are points of inflections and might be more points in (1, 2).

$x = 1$ is point of minima

44. $f'(x) = 5 \sin x \cos x (\sin x - \cos x)(1 + \sin x \cos x)$

Clearly, $f'(x) > 0, \forall x \in \left(\frac{\pi}{4}, \frac{\pi}{2}\right)$

$$f'(x) < 0, \forall x \in \left(0, \frac{\pi}{4}\right)$$

$$f(0) = 0, f\left(\frac{\pi}{2}\right) = 0$$

By Rolle's theorem, $\exists c \in \left(0, \frac{\pi}{2}\right)$

$$\Rightarrow \quad f'(c) = 0$$

Clearly, $f(x) \ge f\left(\frac{\pi}{4}\right)$

$$f(x) \ge 2\left(\frac{1}{\sqrt{2}}\right)^5 - 1 = 2\left(\frac{1}{4\sqrt{2}}\right) - 1 = \frac{1}{2\sqrt{2}} - 1$$

and $f(x) < 0, \forall x \in \left(0, \frac{\pi}{4}\right)$

45. $\frac{f(x) - 1}{f(x) + 1} = \frac{x^4 + x^2 + 1}{(x^2 + x + 1)^2} = \frac{x^2 - x + 1}{x^2 + x + 1}$

$$\Rightarrow \quad f(x) = \frac{x^2 + 1}{x}$$

$$\therefore \quad f(x) = x + \frac{1}{x}$$

$\Rightarrow \quad |f(x)| = \left|x + \frac{1}{x}\right| \ge 2$ [from AM and GM]

Now, on differentiating of $f(x)$ w.r.t x, we get

$$f'(x) = 1 - \frac{1}{x^2}$$

$$f'(x) = 0 \Rightarrow x = \pm 1$$

$$f''(x) = \frac{2}{x^3}$$

$\therefore \ f''(1) > 0 \Rightarrow$ Point of minima

$f''(-1) < 0 \Rightarrow$ Point of maxima

$$\because \quad I = \int_{-\pi}^{\pi} \cos x \cdot f(x) dx = \int_{-\pi}^{\pi} \cos x \left(\frac{x^2 + 1}{x}\right) dx$$

$$g(x) = \cos x \left(\frac{x^2 + 1}{x}\right)$$

$\Rightarrow \quad g(-x) = -\cos x \cdot \left(\frac{x^2+1}{x}\right) = -g(x)$

$\Rightarrow -g(x)$ is odd function.

$\therefore -\int_{-\pi}^{\pi} \left(\frac{x^2+1}{x}\right)\cos x\, dx = 0$

46. Clearly, $f(-1) = -f(1)$, $f(0) = 0$

For option (a) and (b), apply LMVT for the function $y = f(x)$ in $[-1, 0]$ and $[0, 1]$, respectively.

For option (d), apply LMVT to the function $y = (f(x))^n$ in $[0, 1]$.

47. Given, $f(f(x)) = -x + 1$

Replacing $x \to f(x)$

$\Rightarrow \quad f(f(f(x))) = -f(x) + 1$

$\Rightarrow \quad f(1-x) = -f(x) + 1$

$\Rightarrow \quad f(x) + f(1-x) = 1 \quad$ ...(i)

Now, $\mathcal{J} = \int_0^1 f(x)dx = \int_0^1 f(1-x)dx$

$\Rightarrow \; 2\mathcal{J} = \int_0^1 (f(x) + f(1-x))dx \Rightarrow \mathcal{J} = \frac{1}{2}$

Also, from Eq. (i), we get

$f''(x) + f''(1-x) = 0$

$\Rightarrow \quad f''\left(\frac{1}{2}\right) = 0$

So, $\quad f''\left(\frac{1}{2}\right) = f''\left(\frac{4}{5}\right)$

Hence, by Rolle's theorem, $f'''(x) = 0 \Rightarrow x \in \left(\frac{1}{2}, \frac{4}{5}\right)$

Also, $f'(x) = f'(1-x)$

$\Rightarrow \; f'\left(\frac{1}{4}\right) = f'\left(\frac{3}{4}\right)$

So, by Rolle's theorem

$f''(x) = 0 \Rightarrow x \in \left(\frac{1}{4}, \frac{3}{4}\right)$

48. $f(x) = \cot x - \tan x - 2\tan 2x - 4\tan 4x - 8\cot 8x = 0$

$[\because \cot x - \tan x = 2\cot 2x]$

$h(x) = f(x) + g(x)$

$h(x) = x^3 + 6x - 1, \; x \in R - \left\{\frac{n\pi}{8}, n \in I\right\}$

(a) $h'(x) = 3x^2 + 6$, $h''(x) = 6x$

$\therefore h''\left(\frac{\pi}{24}\right) = \frac{\pi}{4}$

(b) $h(x) = x^3 + 6x - 1$ which is not an odd function.

(c) $h'(x) = 3x^2 + 6 > 0 \Rightarrow h(x)$ is increasing

(d) $h(x) = \lambda$, values of λ in (0, 3) for which equation has a solution if $\lambda \in (-1, 8)$.

49. $f(x) = \cos^2 x \cdot e^{\tan x}$

$\Rightarrow f'(x) = e^{\tan x} \cdot (1 - \sin 2x) \geq 0, \; \forall \; x \in \left(\frac{-\pi}{2}, \frac{\pi}{2}\right)$

$\Rightarrow f(x)$ is an increasing on $\left(\frac{-\pi}{2}, \frac{\pi}{2}\right)$

$\Rightarrow f''(x) = e^{\tan x}(-2\cos 2x) + e^{\tan x} \cdot \sec^2 x \cdot (1 - \sin 2x)$

$\therefore \; f''(x) = e^{\tan x}\left(\frac{2(\tan^2 x - 1)}{1 + \tan^2 x} + (\sec^2 x - 2\tan x)\right)$

$= f(x) \cdot (\tan x - 1)(\tan^3 x - \tan^2 x + 3\tan x + 1)$

Now, let $g(x) = \tan^3 x - \tan^2 x + 3\tan x + 1$

$\Rightarrow g'(x) = (3\tan^2 x - 2\tan x + 3)\sec^2 x > 0 \; \forall \; x \in \left(\frac{-\pi}{2}, \frac{\pi}{2}\right)$.

So, $g(x)$ is an increasing function.

Also, $g\left(\frac{-\pi}{4}\right) g(0) < 0$

So, $g(x) = 0$ has exactly one root $\left(-\frac{\pi}{2}, \frac{\pi}{2}\right)$ in where one root is $\frac{\pi}{4}$ and other root lies in $\left(\frac{-\pi}{4}, 0\right)$.

So, $f''(x) = 0$ has exactly two roots in $\left(-\frac{\pi}{2}, \frac{\pi}{2}\right)$

At $x = \frac{\pi}{4}$, $f'(x)$ has a local minima.

Sol. (Q.Nos. 50 and 51)

50. $a = 1$

$f(x) = 8x^3 + 4x^2 + 2bx + 1$

$f'(x) = 24x^2 + 8x + 2b = 2(12x^2 + 4x + b)$

For increasing function, $f'(x) \geq 0 \; \forall \; x \in R$

$\therefore \; D \leq 0 \Rightarrow 16 - 48b \leq 0 \Rightarrow b \geq \frac{1}{3}$

51. If $b = 1$

$f(x) = 8x^3 + 4ax^2 + 2x + a$

$f'(x) = 24x^2 + 8ax + 2$ or $f'(x) = 2(12x^2 + 4ax + 1)$

For non-montonic $f'(x) = 0$ must have distinct roots.

Hence, $D > 0$ i.e. $16a^2 - 48 > 0 \Rightarrow a^2 < 3$;

$\therefore a > \sqrt{3}$ or $a < -\sqrt{3}$

$\therefore a \in \{2, 3, 4, ..., 100\}$

Sum $= 5050 - 1 = 5049$

Sol. (Q.Nos. 52 and 53)

We have, $g(x) = x^3 + g''(1)x^2 + (3g'(1) - g''(1) - 1)x + 3g'(1)$

Let $g'(1) = a$ and $g''(1) = b$ then

$g(x) = x^3 + bx^2 + (3a - b - 1)x + 3a$

On differentiating both sides w.r.t. x, we get

$g'(x) = 3x^2 + 2bx + (3a - b - 1)$

Put $x = 1 \Rightarrow g'(1) = 3 + 2b + 3a - b - 1$

$\Rightarrow \; a = b + 3a + 2 \Rightarrow 2a + b = -2 \quad$ ...(i)

$g''(x) = 6x + 2b$

Put $x = 1$, we get

$g''(1) = 6 + 2b \Rightarrow b = 6 + 2b \Rightarrow b = -6$

From Eq. (i), we get $a = 2$

$\therefore \quad g(x) = x^3 - 6x^2 + 11x + 6$

Given, $f(x) = xg(x) - 12x + 1 = x^4 - 6x^3 + 11x^2 - 6x + 1$

$$= (x^2+1)^2 - 2x^2 + 11x^2 - 6x^4 - 6x$$
$$= (x^2+1)^2 - 6x(x^2+1) + (3x)^2$$

$f(x) = (x^2 - 3x + 1)^2 = (h(x))^2$ [given]

$\because \quad h(0) = 1$

$\therefore \quad h(x) = x^2 - 3x + 1$

52. $f(x) = (x^2 - 3x + 1)^2$

$\Rightarrow f'(x) = 2(x^2 - 3x + 1)(2x - 3) = 0$

$\Rightarrow \quad x = \dfrac{3-\sqrt{5}}{2}, \dfrac{3}{2}$ and $\dfrac{3+\sqrt{5}}{2}$

Sign scheme for $f'(x)$ will be

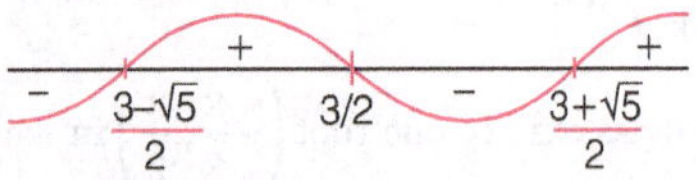

Clearly, $f(x)$ has local maxima at $x = \dfrac{3}{2}$ and local minima at $x = \dfrac{3 \pm \sqrt{5}}{2}$.

$\therefore f(x)$ has exactly one local maxima and two local minima.

53. We have, $g(x) = x^3 - 6x^2 + 11x + 6$

$$g'(x) = 3x^2 - 12x + 11 = 3(x-2)^2 - 1 = 3\left[(x-2)^2 - \frac{1}{3}\right]$$

$\therefore \; g'(x) > 0 \Rightarrow x \in \left(-\infty, 2 - \dfrac{1}{\sqrt{3}}\right) \cup \left(2 + \dfrac{1}{\sqrt{3}}, \infty\right)$ and $g'(x) < 0$

$\Rightarrow x \in \left(2 - \dfrac{1}{\sqrt{3}}, 2 + \dfrac{1}{\sqrt{3}}\right)$

$\therefore \; g(x)$ monotonically increases for $x \in \left(-\infty, 2 - \dfrac{1}{\sqrt{3}}\right) \cup \left(2 + \dfrac{1}{\sqrt{3}}, \infty\right)$ and monotonically decreases for $x \in \left(2 - \dfrac{1}{\sqrt{3}}, 2 + \dfrac{1}{\sqrt{3}}\right)$

For $x \in [1, 3]$,

$g(x) = (x-1)(x-2)(x-3) + 12$

$\Rightarrow \quad g(1) = 12$ and $g(3) = 12$

$\therefore$ By Rolle's theorem in $[1, 3]$ we have, $g'(c) = 0$

$\Rightarrow \quad c = 2 \pm \dfrac{1}{\sqrt{3}}$ [both $\in (1, 3)$]

$\therefore$ There exists two distinct tangents to the curve $y = g(x)$ which are parallel to the chord joining $(1, g(1))$ and $(3, g(3))$.

For $x \in [0, 4]$,

$g(0) = 6$ and $g(4) = 18$

$\therefore$ By LMVT

$$g'(c) = \frac{(18-6)}{4-0}$$

$\Rightarrow \quad 3c^2 - 12c + 11 = 3 \Rightarrow 3c^2 - 12c + 8 = 0$

$\Rightarrow \quad c = 2 \pm \dfrac{2}{\sqrt{3}}$ [both $\in (0, 4)$]

$\therefore$ There exists exactly two distinct Lagrange's mean value in $(0, 4)$ for $y = g(x)$.

Sol. (Q.Nos. 54 and 55)

$$g(x) = x - k \text{ where } k = \int_0^1 f(t)dt \quad \text{...(i)}$$

$$f(x) = \frac{x^3}{2} + 1 - x\int_0^x g(t)dt = \frac{x^2}{2} + 1 - x\int_0^x (t-k)dt$$

$$= \frac{x^3}{2} + 1 - x\left(\frac{t^2}{2} - kt\right)\Bigg|_0^x$$

$$= \frac{x^3}{2} + 1 - x\left(\frac{x^2}{2} - kx\right) = 1 + kx^2 \quad \text{...(ii)}$$

From Eq. (i),

$$k = \int_0^1 (1 + kt^2)dt = t + \frac{kt^3}{3}\Bigg|_0^1 = 1 + \frac{k}{3} \Rightarrow \frac{2k}{3} = 1 \Rightarrow k = \frac{3}{2}$$

54. Also, $f(x) = 1 + \dfrac{3x^2}{2}$ which is a quadratic polynomial.

55. Now, $f'(x)\big|_p = 3x_1 = 1$

$\Rightarrow \quad x_1 = \dfrac{1}{3} \Rightarrow y_1 = 1 + \dfrac{3}{2} \cdot \dfrac{1}{9} = 1 + \dfrac{1}{6} = \dfrac{7}{6}$

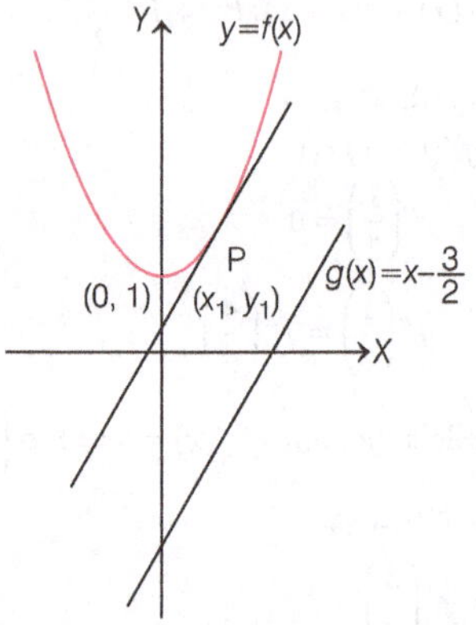

Hence, $P\left(\dfrac{1}{3}, \dfrac{7}{9}\right)$

Perpendicular distance from P on the line $y = x - \dfrac{3}{2}$ is

$$d = \left|\frac{\frac{1}{3} - \frac{7}{6} - \frac{3}{2}}{\sqrt{2}}\right| = \left|\frac{-\frac{5}{6} - \frac{3}{2}}{\sqrt{2}}\right| = \left|\frac{-7}{3\sqrt{2}}\right| = \frac{7}{3\sqrt{2}}$$

Sol. (Q.Nos. 56 and 57)

56. $f(x) = xe^{-x}$

$f'(x) = e^{-x}(1 - x) = 0 \Rightarrow x = 1 \Rightarrow \beta = 1$

Also, $q - p = L$ ...(i)

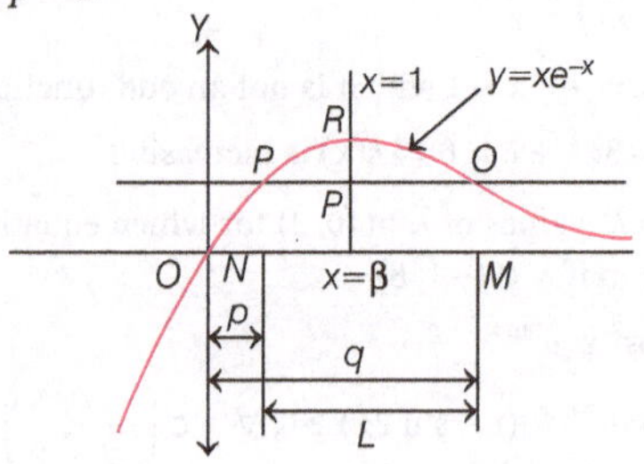

Now, $\quad PN = QM$

$$pe^{-p} = qe^{-q}$$

$$p \cdot e^{q-p} = q$$

$$pe^{L} = q \qquad \text{...(ii)}$$

From Eqs. (i) and (ii), we get

$$p = \frac{L}{e^L - 1} \text{ and } q = \frac{Le^L}{e^L - 1}$$

57. Also, maxima occurs at $x = 1 \Rightarrow \beta = 1$

and $f''(x) = -e^{-x} - (1-x)e^{-x}$

$$= e^{-x}(-1-1+x) = e^{-x}(x-2)$$

$f''(x) = 0 \Rightarrow x = 2$ (which is the point of inflection)

Hence, $\alpha = 2$

$\therefore \ \alpha - \beta = 1$

Sol. (Q.Nos. 58 and 59)

58. $f(x) = x + \log_e x - x \log_e x$

$$f'(x) = 1 + \frac{1}{x} - \left(x \times \frac{1}{x} + \log x\right) = \frac{1}{x} - \log_e x$$

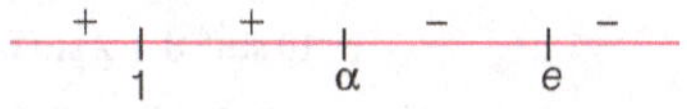

$f''(x) = -\frac{1}{x^2} - \frac{1}{x} < 0, \ \forall \ x \in (0, \infty).$

Thus, $f'(x)$ is strictly decreasing function for $x \in (0, \infty)$.

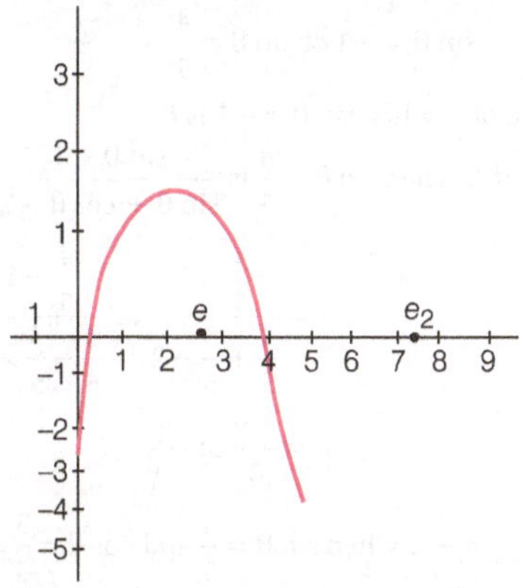

$$\left.\begin{array}{l}\lim\limits_{x \to \infty}\left(\frac{1}{x} - \log_e x\right) = \lim\limits_{x \to \infty} f'(x) = -\infty \\ \lim\limits_{x \to 0^+}\left(\frac{1}{x} - \log_e x\right) = \lim\limits_{x \to 0^-} f'(x) = \infty\end{array}\right]$$

i.e. $\quad f'(x) =$ has only one real root in $(0, \infty)$

$f'(1) = 1 > 0$

$f'(e) = \frac{1}{e} - 1 < 0$

so, $f'(x) = 0$ has one root in $(1, e)$,

Let $f'(\alpha) = 0$, where $\alpha \in (1, e)$

Therefore, $f(x)$ is increasing in $(0, \alpha)$ and decreasing in (α, ∞).

$f(1) = 1$ and $f(e^2) = e^2 + 2 - 2e = 2 - e^2 < 0$

The graph of the function is as shown in the given figure.

So, $f(x) = 0$ has one root in $(1, e^2)$.

From Column I: I and II are correct.

From Column II: (ii), (iii) and (iv) are correct.

From Column III : P, Q and S are correct.

59. $f(x) = 1 + \frac{1}{x} - \left(x \times \frac{1}{x} + \log x\right) = \frac{1}{x} - \log x$

Sol. (Q.Nos. 60 and 61)

$$\text{Given, } f(x) = \begin{cases} 2\ln(-x-1), & -e-1 \le x \le -2 \\ \frac{1}{2}(4 - x^2), & -2 < x < 0 \\ 0, & x = 0 \\ \frac{1}{2}(x^2 - 4), & 0 < x < 2 \\ 2\ln(x-1), & 2 \le x \le e+1 \end{cases}$$

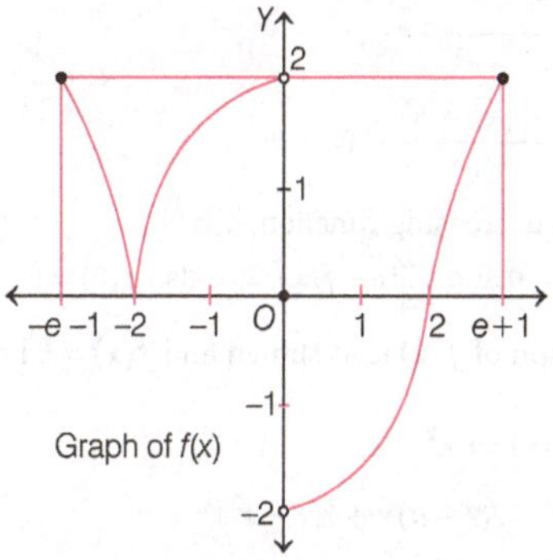

Graph of $f(x)$

$$\text{Clearly, } g(x) = \begin{cases} 2\ln(-x-1), & -e-1 \le x < -2 \\ 0, & -2 \le x \le 2 \\ 2\ln(x-1), & 2 < x \le e+1 \end{cases}$$

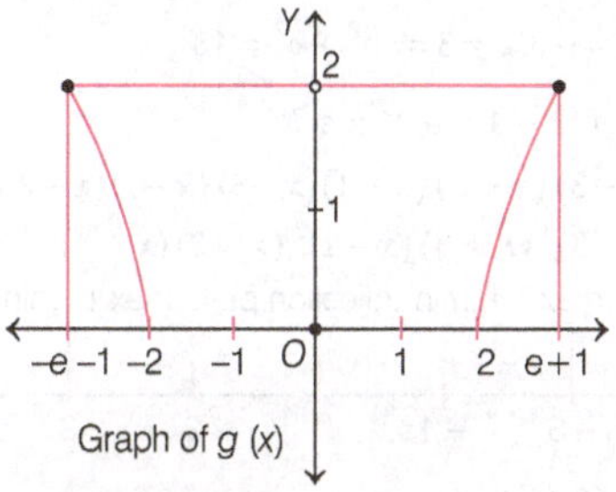

Graph of $g(x)$

60. Also, $g(x)$ is an even continuous function.

$\therefore$ Range of $g(x) = [0, 2]$

$\therefore \ a = 0, b = 2$

$\therefore$ For positive integer solution of equation

$\Rightarrow \qquad \alpha + \beta + \gamma = 5a + 7b = 14.$

$\because \qquad \alpha, \beta, \gamma \ge 1$

$\therefore$ Required number of solution $= {}^{14-1}C_{3-1} = {}^{13}C_2$

$$= \frac{13 \times 12}{2} = 78$$

61. Clearly, $g(x)$ is non-differentiable at $x = -2, 2$

$\Rightarrow$ absolute sum = 0.

Clearly, $g(x) = k$ has exactly two distinct solutions, then integral value of k is either 1 or 2. So, sum of all possible integral values of $k = 1 + 2 = 3$.

Sol. (Q.Nos. 62 and 63)

62. $k = \dfrac{5 + x + \dfrac{x^2}{2}}{e^x}$

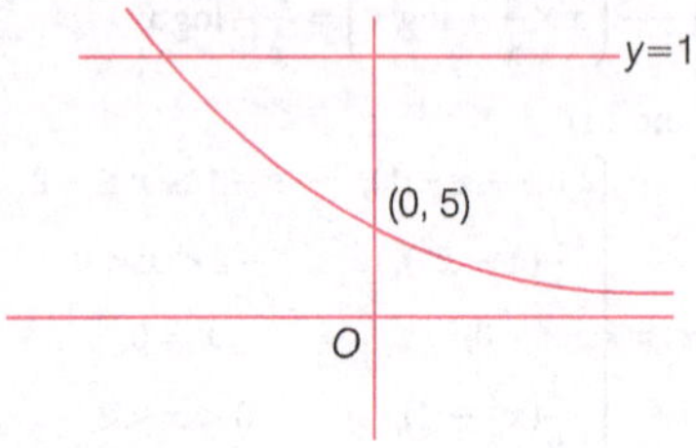

Let $f(x) = \dfrac{5 + x + \dfrac{x^2}{2}}{e^x}$

$f'(x) = \dfrac{-(x^2 + 8)}{2e^x} < 0$

$\therefore$ $f(x)$ is a decreasing function, $\forall\ x$

$\lim\limits_{x \to \infty} f(x) = 0$ and $\lim\limits_{x \to -\infty} f(x) = \infty$ also $f(0) = 5$

Hence, graph of $f(x)$ is as shown and $f(x) = k$ has exactly one root.

$\Rightarrow \quad \lambda = 1 \Rightarrow \lambda^2 = 1$

63. $g'(x) = 3x^2 - 2(9 - a)x + 3(9 - a^2) \begin{smallmatrix} x_1 \\ x_2 \end{smallmatrix}$

Since, x_1 and x_2 have opposite signs.

$\therefore$ Product < 0

Product of roots $9 - a^2 < 0$

$a^2 > 9 \Rightarrow a \in (-\infty, -3) \cup (3, \infty)$

$b = -3, c = 3 \Rightarrow b^2 + c^2 = 18$

64. $f'(x) = x^2 + x + 1 > 0,\ \forall\ x \in R$

$g'(x) = (x-3)(x+3)(x-1)(x-3)(x-1)(x-2)(x-3)(x+1)$
$= (x-3)^3 (x+3)(x-1)^2 (x-2)(x+1)$

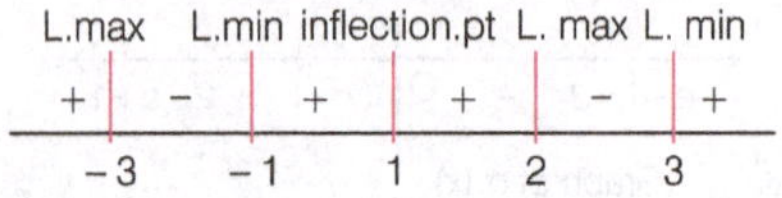

$n(x) = f(g(x))$

$f'(x) = \underset{+\text{ve}}{f'(g(x))}\, g'(x)$

$\therefore \quad n_1 = 2, n_2 = 2, n_3 = 1 \Rightarrow n_1 + n_2 + n_3 = 5$

65. $f''(x) = 2 \Rightarrow$ graph of $f(x)$ is concave upward on $(0, \infty)$.

As $x \to \infty$, $f(x) \to \infty$ and $f'(\infty) \to \infty$

$$L = \lim_{x \to \infty} \left(\frac{3x^2}{f(x)} - \frac{3}{(x^2+1)\, f(x)} + \frac{4f'(x)}{f(x)} \right)$$

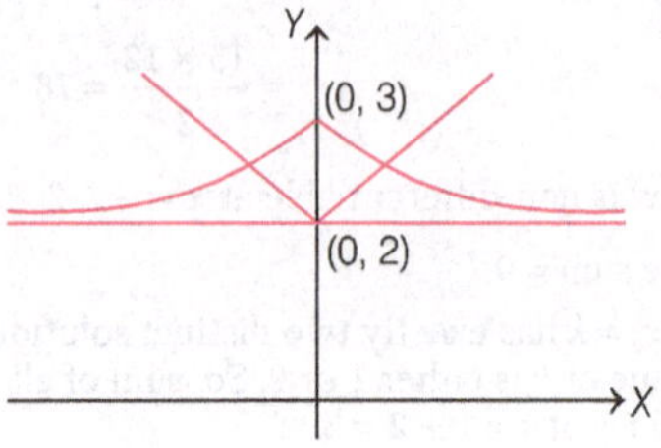

$$= \lim_{x \to \infty} \left(\frac{6x}{f'(x)} - \frac{4f''(x)}{f'(x)} \right)$$

$$= \lim_{x \to \infty} \left(\frac{6}{f''(x)} \right) = 3$$

$\therefore \quad [L^2] = 9$

66. Put $a = \cos\theta$ and $b = \sin\theta$, we get

$$E = \frac{b+1}{a+b-2} = \frac{\sin\theta + 1}{\sin\theta + \cos\theta - 2} = f(\theta)$$

For maxima/minima,

$f'(\theta) = 0$

$\Rightarrow (\sin\theta + \cos\theta - 2)(\cos\theta) - (\sin\theta + 1)(\cos\theta - \sin\theta) = 0$

$\Rightarrow \sin\theta\cos\theta + \cos^2\theta - 2\cos\theta - \sin\theta\cos\theta$
$+ \sin^2\theta - \cos\theta + \sin\theta = 0$

$\Rightarrow \quad \cos^2\theta - 2\cos\theta + \sin^2\theta - \cos\theta + \sin\theta = 0$

$\Rightarrow \quad 1 - 3\cos\theta + \sin\theta = 0$

$\Rightarrow \quad 1 + \sin\theta = 3\cos\theta$

$\Rightarrow \quad (1 + \sin\theta)^2 = 9\cos^2\theta = 9 - 9\sin^2\theta$

$\Rightarrow \quad 10\sin^2\theta + 2\sin\theta - 8 = 0$

$\Rightarrow \quad 5\sin^2\theta + \sin\theta - 4 = 0$

$\Rightarrow \quad 5\sin^2\theta + 5\sin\theta - 4\sin\theta - 4 = 0$

$\Rightarrow \quad (\sin\theta + 1)(5\sin\theta - 4) = 0$

$\Rightarrow \quad \sin\theta = -1$ or $\sin\theta = \dfrac{4}{5}$

Now, value of E when $\sin\theta = -1$ is 0.

and value of E when $\sin\theta = \dfrac{4}{5}$ is $\dfrac{\sin\theta + 1}{\sin\theta + \cos\theta - 2}$

$$= \frac{\frac{4}{5} + 1}{\frac{4}{5} + \frac{3}{5} - 2} \text{ or } \frac{\frac{4}{5} + 1}{\frac{4}{5} - \frac{3}{5} - 2}$$

i.e. $\quad E = \dfrac{-9}{3}$ or $\dfrac{9}{-9}$

$\therefore\ E\,|_{\text{minimum}} = -3$, when $\sin\theta = \dfrac{4}{5}$ and $\cos\theta = \dfrac{3}{5} \Rightarrow u = -3$

Hence, $u^2 = 9$.

67. $f(6) > 0$, $f(3) < 0$, $f(2)$, $f(4)$ will be of opposite sign. $f(1)$, $f(5)$ will be opposite sign. Following 4 possibilities are as

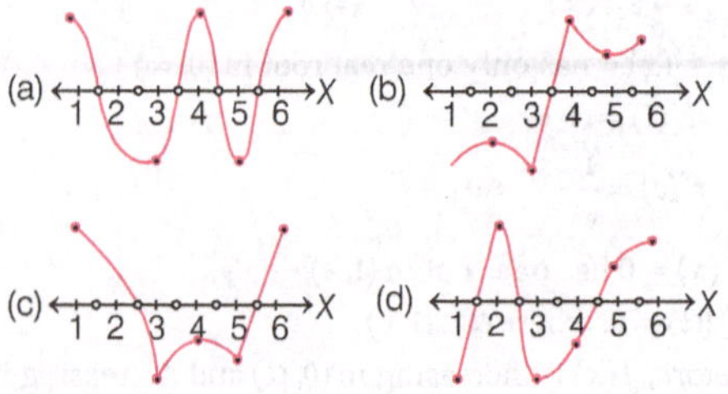

Number of possible roots 1, 2, 3, 4.

$A = \{1, 2, 3, 4\}$

Hence, $\Sigma n(A) = 10 = \lambda \Rightarrow \lambda - 3 = 7$

68. Clearly, equation of the circle is

$$(x-1)^2+(y-1)^2=1$$

$$\Rightarrow \quad x^2+y^2-2x-2y+1=0$$

Let the equation of the line be $y = mx$.

$$\therefore \quad mx - y = 0$$

So, $p=\left|\dfrac{m-1}{\sqrt{1+m^2}}\right|$

(where p is the length of the perpendicular form C on MN)

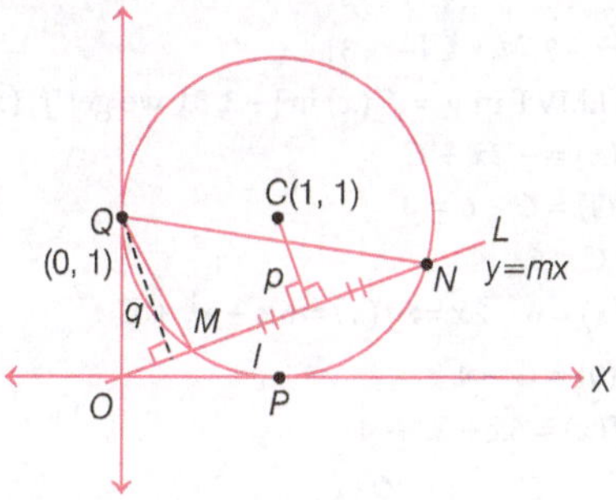

Now, $l^2 = 1 - p^2 = 1 - \dfrac{(m-1)^2}{1+m^2}$

$$\Rightarrow \quad l^2 = \frac{2m}{1+m^2}$$

$$\Rightarrow \quad l = \frac{\sqrt{2m}}{\sqrt{1+m^2}}$$

$$\Rightarrow \quad 2l = MN = \frac{2\sqrt{2m}}{\sqrt{1+m^2}}$$

Perpendicular from (0, 1) on $mx - y = 0$, is

$$q=\left|\frac{-1}{\sqrt{1+m^2}}\right|=\frac{1}{\sqrt{1+m^2}}$$

Hence, area of the ΔQPN is $\left(\dfrac{1}{2}\cdot 2l\cdot q\right)$.

$$A=\frac{1}{2}\,\frac{2\sqrt{2m}}{\sqrt{1+m^2}}\cdot\left(\frac{1}{\sqrt{1+m^2}}\right)$$

$$A=\frac{\sqrt{2m}}{(1+m^2)}=f(m)\text{ (say)}$$

Hence, $f'(m)=\sqrt{2}\left|\dfrac{\dfrac{(1+m^2)}{2\sqrt{m}}-\sqrt{m}\cdot 2m}{(1+m^2)^2}\right|=0$

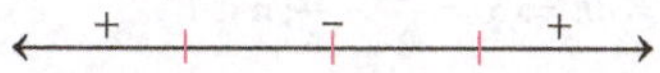

$$m=\frac{1}{\sqrt{3}}$$

(Point of maximum) sign of $f'(m)$

or $(1+m^2)-4m^2=0$

Also, $3m^2=1 \Rightarrow m=\dfrac{1}{\sqrt{3}}$

Hence, $2010(m^2)-666=670-666=3$

69. We have, $f(x)=ax+\cos 2x+\sin x+\cos x$

$$\Rightarrow \quad f'(x)=a-2\sin 2x+\cos x-\sin x$$

As $f'(x)\ge 0$ for any real number x

$\Rightarrow a \ge 2\sin 2x+\sin x-\cos x$

Let $t=\sin x-\cos x=\sqrt{2}\sin\left(x-\dfrac{\pi}{4}\right)$

$\Rightarrow -\sqrt{2}\le t\le\sqrt{2}$

So, the inequality can be written as $a\ge -2t^2+t+2$

Let $g(t)=-2t^2+t+2=-2\left(t-\dfrac{1}{4}\right)^2+\dfrac{17}{8}$

Then, range of $g(t)$ for $-\sqrt{2}\le t\le\sqrt{2}$ is $g(-\sqrt{2})\le g\left(\dfrac{1}{4}\right)$

$$\Rightarrow \quad -2-\sqrt{2}\le g(t)\le\frac{17}{8}$$

So, the range of a can be found $a\ge \max_{|t|\ge\sqrt{2}}$

$$\Rightarrow \quad a\ge\frac{17}{8}$$

$$\Rightarrow \quad a\in\left[\frac{17}{8},\infty\right)$$

Hence, $\dfrac{(m+n)}{5}$ least $=\dfrac{17+8}{5}$

$$=\frac{25}{5}=5$$

70. Let $f_n(x)=\displaystyle\int_x^{2x} e^{-t^n}\,dt$

$$f'_n(x)=2\cdot e^{-(2x)^n}-e^{-x^n}$$

For maxima and minima,

$$f'_n(x)=0 \Rightarrow 2e^{-(2x)^n}=e^{-x^n}\Rightarrow 2\cdot e^{-(2^n x^n)}=e^{-x^n}$$

On taking log both sides, we get

$\ln 2-2^n x^n=-x^n \Rightarrow \ln 2 = x^n(2^n-1)$

$$\Rightarrow \quad x^n=\frac{\ln 2}{2^n-1}$$

$$\Rightarrow \quad x=\left(\frac{\ln 2}{2^n-1}\right)^{\frac{1}{n}}=a_n$$

Also, $f''_n\left(x=\left(\dfrac{\ln 2}{2^n-1}\right)^{\frac{1}{n}}\right)<0 \Rightarrow f_n(x)$ is maximum at

$$x=\left(\frac{\ln 2}{2^n-1}\right)^{\frac{1}{n}}$$

Now, $\ln a_n=\dfrac{\ln\left(\dfrac{\ln 2}{2^n-1}\right)}{n}$

$$=\frac{\ln(\ln 2)-\ln(2^n-1)}{n}$$

Hence, $L=\lim\limits_{n\to\infty}\ln(a_n)=\lim\limits_{n\to\infty}\dfrac{\ln(\ln 2)-\ln(2^n-1)}{n}$

$$= \lim_{n\to\infty}\left(\frac{\ln(\ln 2)}{n} - \frac{\ln\left(2^n\left(1-\frac{1}{2^n}\right)\right)}{n}\right)$$

$$L = \lim_{n\to\infty}\left(0 - \frac{n\cdot\ln 2 + \ln\left(1-\frac{1}{2^n}\right)}{n}\right) = -\ln 2$$

Hence, $e^{-L} = 2$

71. $f(x) = \int_{-\pi}^{\pi}(x^2 + 1 + k^2\sin^2 x + 2x + 2k\sin x + 2kx\sin x)dx$

$$= 2\int_0^{\pi}(x^2 + 1 + k^2\sin^2 x + 2kx\sin x)dx$$

$$= \frac{2\pi^3}{3} + 2\pi + 2k^2\int_0^{\pi}\sin^2 x\,dx + 4k\int_0^{\pi}x\sin x\,dx$$

$$= \frac{2\pi^3}{3} + 2\pi + 2k^2\cdot 2\cdot\frac{\pi}{4} + 4k\pi$$

$$f(k) = \frac{2\pi^3}{3} + \pi(k^2 + 4k + 2)$$

Minimum at $k = \frac{-b}{2a} = \frac{-4\pi}{2\pi} = -2$

Note Minimum value $f(-2) = \frac{2\pi^3}{3} - 2\pi$

72. Clearly, $g'(x) = f(x) = \begin{cases}(x+2)^3, & -3 < x \le -1\\ x^{\frac{2}{3}}, & -1 < x < 2\end{cases}$

$\Rightarrow g'(x)$ is a continuous function.

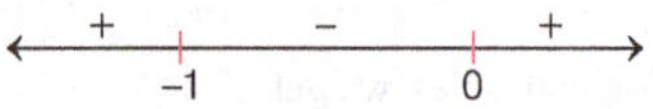

sign scheme of $g''(x)$

$\Rightarrow g'(x)$ has a local maximum at $x = -1$

and local minimum at $x = 0$.

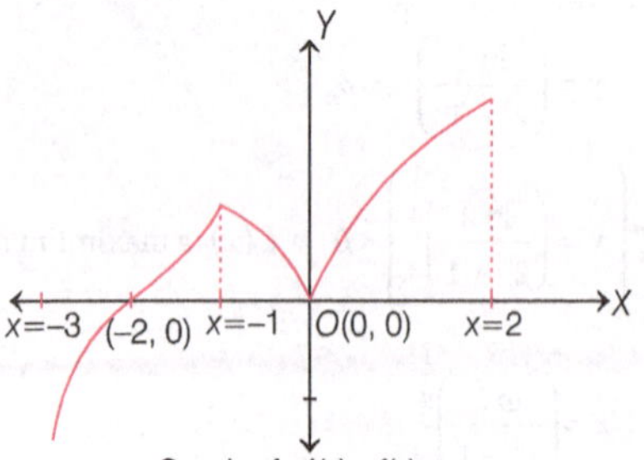

Graph of $g'(x)=f(x)$

Hence, $g'(x)$ has two extremum points.

73. We have, $f(x) = e^{2x} - (c+1)e^x + 2x + \cos 2 + \sin 1$

$\therefore \quad f'(x) = 2e^{2x} - (c+1)e^x + 2$

Now, $f'(x) \ge 0, \forall x \in R$

i.e. $2\left(e^x + \frac{1}{e^x}\right) - (c+1) \ge 0, \forall x \in R$

$\Rightarrow \quad (c+1) \le 2\left(e^x + \frac{1}{e^x}\right), \forall x \in R$

$\therefore \quad c + 1 \le 4 \Rightarrow c \le 3 \qquad \left[\because e^x + \frac{1}{e^x} \ge 2\right]$

$\therefore \quad c \in (-\infty, 3] \equiv (-\infty, \lambda]$

$\lambda = 3$

74. Given, $f''(x) \ge -2, \forall x \in [-3, 3]$

$\therefore \int_{-3}^{3} f''(x)\,dx \ge -2\int_{-3}^{3} dx \Rightarrow f'(x)]_{-3}^{3} \ge -12 \Rightarrow -12 \ge -12$

$\therefore f''(x) = -2, \forall x \in [-3, 3]$

or apply LMVT in $y = f'(x)$ in $[-3, 3]$, we get $f''(x) = -2$.

Now, $f'(x) = -2x + C$

$f'(3) = C - 6 = 0$

$\Rightarrow \quad C = 6$

$f'(x) = 6 - 2x \Rightarrow f(x) = 6x - x^2 + C$

$f(0) = C - 4$

Hence, $f(x) = 6x - x^2 - 4$

Now, $g(x) = \int_0^x f(t)dt = \int_0^x(-t^2 + 6t - 4)dt$

$\therefore \quad g(x) = \frac{-x^3}{3} + 3x^2 - 4x$ in $[-3, 3]$

$g'(x) = -x^2 + 6x - 4$

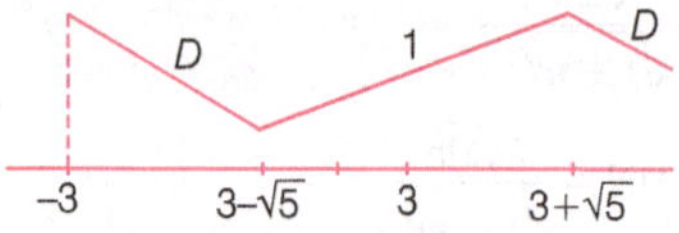

$g(-3) = 48$ which is maximum value in $[-3, 3]$.

$\therefore$ Number of prime factor of $48 = 2$

75. $f(x) = \int_x^{x+\frac{\pi}{3}} |\sin\theta|\,d\theta; x \in [0, \pi]$

For maximum/minimum, put $f'(x) = 0$,

$$f'(x) = \left|\sin\left(x + \frac{\pi}{3}\right)\right| - |\sin x| = 0$$

$$\therefore \quad \sin^2\left(x + \frac{\pi}{3}\right) = \sin^2 x = 0$$

$$\sin^2\left(x + \frac{\pi}{3}\right) - \sin^2 x = 0$$

$$\sin\left(2x + \frac{\pi}{3}\right)\cdot\sin\frac{\pi}{3} = 0$$

$$\therefore \quad 2x + \frac{\pi}{3} = n\pi \Rightarrow x = \frac{n\pi}{2} - \frac{\pi}{6}; n \in I$$

$$\therefore \quad \ln[0, \pi],\ x = \frac{\pi}{3} \text{ or } \frac{5\pi}{6}$$

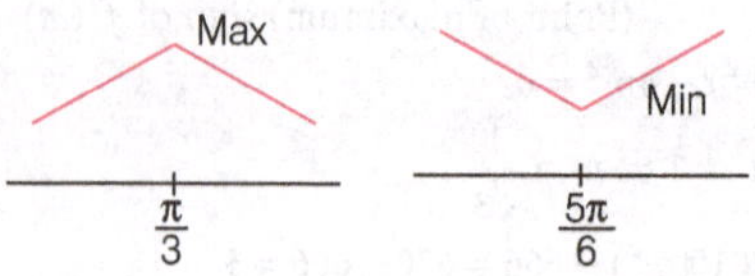

Now, $f(0) = \int_0^{\frac{\pi}{3}} |\sin\theta| d\theta = \cos\theta \Big]_{\frac{\pi}{3}}^{0} = 1 - \frac{1}{2} = \frac{1}{2}$

$$f(\pi) = \int_0^{\pi + \frac{\pi}{3}} |\sin\theta| d\theta$$

$$= \int_\pi^{\frac{4\pi}{3}} -\sin\theta\, d\theta$$

$\therefore$ $f(\pi) = \cos\theta\Big]_\pi^{\frac{4\pi}{3}}$

$$= \frac{-1}{2} + 1 = \frac{1}{2}$$

$$f\left(\frac{\pi}{3}\right) = \int_{\frac{\pi}{3}}^{\frac{2\pi}{3}} |\sin\theta| d\theta = \cos\theta\Big]_{\frac{2\pi}{3}}^{\frac{\pi}{3}} = \frac{1}{2} - \left(\frac{-1}{2}\right) = 1$$

$$f\left(\frac{5\pi}{6}\right) = \int_{\frac{5\pi}{6}}^{\frac{7\pi}{6}} |\sin\theta| d\theta = \int_{\frac{5\pi}{6}}^{\pi} \sin\theta\, d\theta + \int_\pi^{\frac{7\pi}{6}} -\sin\theta\, d\theta$$

$$= 2 - \sqrt{3}$$

Hence, minimum value $m = 2 - \sqrt{3}$ and maximum value $M = 1$

$\therefore$ $m + M = 3 - \sqrt{3} = \sqrt{9} - \sqrt{3} = \sqrt{p} - \sqrt{q}$

$\therefore$ $p = 9; q = 3 \Rightarrow p + q = 12$

$\Rightarrow$ $\frac{p+q}{2} = 6$

76. $f(x) = \begin{cases} a\cos x + b\sin x, & \text{if } 0 \le x \le \frac{\pi}{2} \\ a\cos x - b\sin x, & \text{if } -\frac{\pi}{2} \le x \le 0 \end{cases}$

For $-\frac{\pi}{2} < x < 0$

$$f'(x) = -a\sin x - b\cos x \quad \text{...(i)}$$

and $f''(x) = -a\cos x + b\sin x$ ...(ii)

Since, $f(x)$ has a minima at $x = \frac{-\pi}{3}$

Hence, $f'\left(\frac{-\pi}{3}\right) = 0$ and $f''(x) = \left(\frac{-\pi}{3}\right) > 0$

Now, $f'\left(\frac{-\pi}{3}\right) = +a \cdot \frac{\sqrt{3}}{2} - \frac{b}{2} = 0$

$$= \sqrt{3}a - b = 0$$

and $f''\left(\frac{-\pi}{3}\right) = -\frac{a}{2} - b \cdot \frac{\sqrt{3}}{2} = -\frac{1}{2}[a + b\sqrt{3}]$

$$= -2a > 0$$

Hence, $a < 0$ and $b < 0$.

Now, $I = \int_{\frac{-\pi}{2}}^{\frac{\pi}{2}} (f(x))^2 dx$

$$= \int_{\frac{-\pi}{2}}^{0} f^2(x)dx + \int_0^{\frac{\pi}{2}} f^2(x)dx$$

$$= \int_{\frac{-\pi}{2}}^{0} (a^2\cos^2 x - 2ab\sin x\cos x + b^2\sin^2 x)dx$$

$$+ \int_0^{\frac{\pi}{2}} (a^2\cos^2 x + 2ab\sin x\cos x + b^2\sin^2 x)dx$$

Hence, $I = \frac{\pi a^2}{2} + \frac{\pi b^2}{2} + 2ab = 2$

$$2(\sqrt{3} + \pi)a^2 = 2$$

$\Rightarrow$ $a = -\frac{1}{\sqrt{\pi + \sqrt{3}}}$

and $b = -\frac{\sqrt{3}}{\sqrt{\pi + \sqrt{3}}}$

$\Rightarrow$ $\frac{b^2}{a^2} = 3$

77. $y = \frac{x^4 - x^2}{x^6 + 2x^3 - 1} = \frac{x - \frac{1}{x}}{x^3 + 2 - \frac{1}{x^3}}$ [taking x^3 common]

$$y = \frac{x - \frac{1}{x}}{\left(x - \frac{1}{x}\right)^3 + 3\left(x - \frac{1}{x}\right) + 2} \quad \text{...(i)}$$

Let $\left(x - \frac{1}{x}\right) = t$

$$y = \frac{t}{t^3 + 3t + 2}; \frac{dy}{dx} = (t^3 + 3t + 2) - t(3t^2 + 3)$$

$$= -2t^2 + 2 = 0$$

$\Rightarrow$ $t = 1$

$$\left.\frac{d^2y}{dx^2}\right]_{t=1} = -4t = -4 < 0 \Rightarrow \text{maxima at } t = 1$$

Maximum value $= \frac{1}{6} = \frac{p}{q} \Rightarrow p = 1$ and $q = 6$

It occurs when $t = 1 \Rightarrow x - \frac{1}{x} = 1$

$\Rightarrow$ $x^2 - x - 1 = 0$

$$x = \frac{1 \pm \sqrt{5}}{2} \Rightarrow \frac{1 + \sqrt{5}}{2} \text{ as } x > 1$$

$\therefore$ $p = 1; q = 6; a = 1; b = 5; c = 2$

$\therefore$ $p + q + a + b + c = 15$

$\therefore$ Required value $= \frac{15}{3} = 5$

78. Let $x^2 + x + 1 = t$

$$\therefore \quad t \in \left[\frac{3}{4}, \infty\right) \Rightarrow t^2 - at + 2a \geq 0, \forall t \in \left[\frac{3}{4}, \infty\right]$$

Let $f(t) = t^2 - at + 2a \Rightarrow f'(t) = 2t - a$

Case I If $\frac{a}{2} \leq \frac{3}{4} \Rightarrow a \leq \frac{3}{2}$

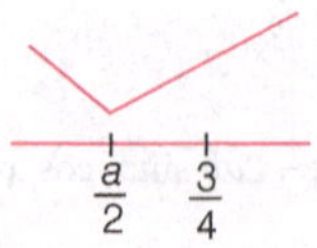

In this case, for $t \in \left[\frac{3}{4}, \infty\right)$, minimum value occur at $t = \frac{3}{4}$.

$$\therefore \quad f\left(\frac{3}{4}\right) \geq 0 \Rightarrow \frac{9}{16} - \frac{3a}{4} + 2a \geq 0$$

$$\Rightarrow \quad \frac{9}{16} + \frac{5a}{4} \geq 0 \Rightarrow 9 + 20a \geq 0 \Rightarrow a \geq \frac{-9}{20}$$

$$\therefore \quad a \in \left[\frac{-9}{20}, \frac{3}{2}\right] \qquad \text{...(ii)}$$

Case II If $\frac{a}{2} \geq \frac{3}{4} \Rightarrow a \geq \frac{3}{2}$

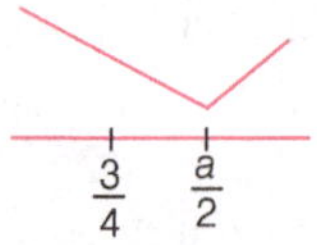

Then, for $t \in \left[\frac{3}{4}, \infty\right)$, minimum value occur at $t = \frac{a}{2}$.

$$\therefore \quad f\left(\frac{a}{2}\right) \geq 0 \Rightarrow \frac{a^2}{4} - \frac{a^2}{4} + 2a \geq 0$$

$$\Rightarrow -\frac{a^2}{4} + 2a \geq 0 \Rightarrow a\left(2 - \frac{a}{4}\right) \geq 0 \Rightarrow a \in (0, 8)$$

$$\therefore \quad a \in \left(\frac{3}{2}, 8\right] \qquad \text{...(ii)}$$

$$\text{(i)} \cup \text{(ii)} \Rightarrow a \in \left[-\frac{9}{20}, 8\right]$$

$\therefore$ Sum of all integral values

$$S = 1 + 2 + \ldots + 8 = \frac{8 \times 9}{2} = 36$$

$\therefore$ Required value $= \sqrt{36} = 6$

79. $\int_a^x e^{f(t)} dt = \int_0^x g(x - t) dt + 2x + 3$

$$\Rightarrow \int_a^x e^{f(t)} dt = \int_0^x g(t) dt + 2x + 3 \qquad \text{[using King Property]}$$

On differentiating both sides, we get

$$e^{f(x)} = g(x) + 2$$

$$\Rightarrow \quad g(x) = e^{f(x)} - 2$$

$$\Rightarrow \quad g'(x) = e^{f(x)} \cdot f'(x)$$

$\because e^{f(x)}$ is always greater than zero.

$\therefore$ Sign of $g'(x)$ is same as sign of $f'(x)$.

$\therefore$ Sign of $g'(x)$

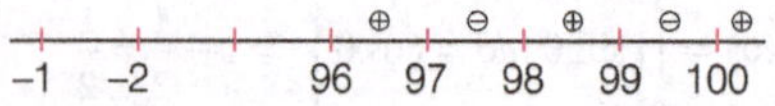

Clearly, local extermum (maximum or minimum) will occur at

$$x = 99, 97, 95, \ldots, 3, 1$$

$\therefore$ Sum of all the values $= 1 + 3 + 5 + \ldots + 99$

$$= \frac{50}{2} [2 \times 1 + (50 - 1) \times 2]$$

$$= 2500$$

$\therefore$ Sum of digits $= 7$

80. Equation of tangent

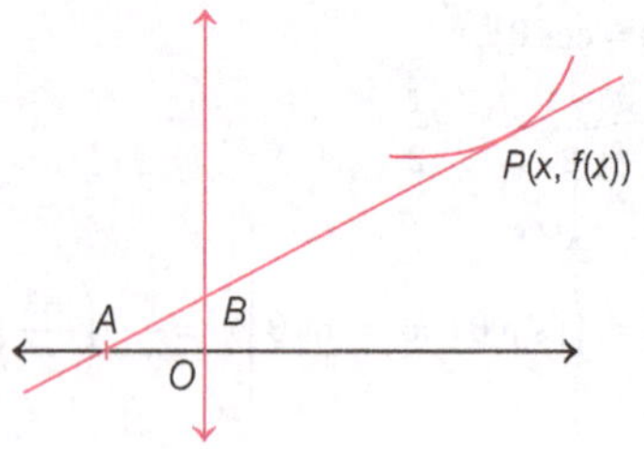

$$Y - f(x) = f'(x)(X - x)$$

$$A \equiv \left(x - \frac{f(x)}{f'(x)}, 0\right)$$

$$B \equiv (0, f(x) - xf'(x))$$

Area of ΔOAB, $S(x) = \frac{1}{2} \times OA \times OB$

$$\Rightarrow \quad S(x) = \frac{1}{2}\left(x - \frac{f(x)}{f'(x)}\right)(f(x) - xf'(x))$$

$$= -\frac{1}{2} \frac{(f(x) - xf'(x))^2}{f'(x)}$$

$$= \frac{\{(5 - (x+1)^2 + 2x(x+1)\}^2}{4(x+1)}$$

$$= \frac{\{5 - x^2 - 2x - 1 + 2x^2 + 2x\}^2}{4(x+1)}$$

$$= \frac{(x^2 + 4)^2}{4(x+1)}$$

$$S'(x) = \frac{2(x+1)(x^2+4) \cdot 2x - (x^2+4)^2}{4(x+1)^2} = 0$$

$$\Rightarrow 4x^2 + 4x - x^2 - 4 = 0$$

$$\Rightarrow \quad 3x^2 + 4x - 4 = 0 \Rightarrow 3x^2 + 6x - 2x - 4 = 0$$

$$\Rightarrow \quad (x+2)(3x-2) = 0 \Rightarrow x = \frac{2}{3} \qquad [\because 0 < x < 1]$$

$\therefore$ Minimum value of $S(x) = \frac{80}{27} \Rightarrow (p + q) = 107 \Rightarrow \frac{p+q}{107} = 1$

81. Since, the line touches the graph of $f(x)$ at 1, 2, 3.

$\therefore \quad h(x) = f(x) - g(x)$ has a double root at 1, 2, 3

$\therefore \quad h(x) = a(x-1)^2 (x-2)^2 (x-3)^2$

$$I = a\int_1^3 (x-1)^2 (x-2)^2 (x-3)^2 dx = \frac{32}{105}$$

$$a \times \frac{16}{105} = \frac{32}{105}$$

$\therefore$ $a = 2$

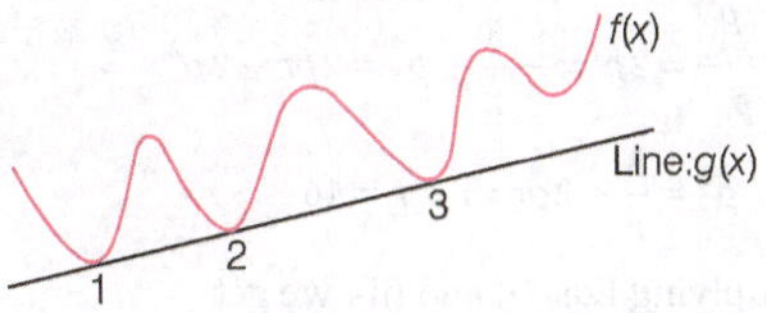

82. Given, $7 \sin 3x - 2(3 \sin 3x - 4 \sin^3 3x)$
$= (1 + \tan^2 \theta) + 4(1 + \cot^2 \theta)$

Put $\sin 3x = y$, we get
$y(8y^2 + 1) = 9 + (\tan \theta - 2 \cot \theta)^2$
LHS min occurs when $y = -1$ and minimum value $= -9$
Maximum occurs when $y = 1$ and maximum value $= 9$ when $\tan^2 \theta = 2$.

Hence, maximum of L.H.S. = maximum value of RHS.

$\therefore \sin 3x = 1 = \sin \frac{\pi}{2} \Rightarrow x = \frac{\pi}{6}$ (minimum positive root)

or $\sin 3x = \sin\left(\frac{-3\pi}{2}\right) \Rightarrow x = \frac{-\pi}{2}$ (maximum negative root)

$\text{Sum} = \frac{\pi}{6} + \frac{\pi}{2} = \frac{\pi + 3\pi}{6} = \frac{2\pi}{3}$

Hence, $\frac{15}{\pi}$ (minimum positive root – maximum negative root)

$$= \left(\frac{15}{\pi}\right)\left(\frac{2\pi}{3}\right) = 10$$

$\therefore$ $\lambda = 10 \Rightarrow \lambda - 2 = 8$

83. $g(a) = \int_0^{\frac{\pi}{2}} |2 \sin x - a| \cos x \, dx, 0 \le a \le 1$

$2 \sin x - a = t$

$\therefore$ $2 \cos x \, dx = dt$

$$g(a) = \frac{1}{2} \int_0^{2-a} |t| \, dt; a \in [0, 1]$$

$$2g(a) = \int_{-a}^{0} (-t) dt + \int_0^{2-a} t \, dt$$

$$2g(a) = \frac{1}{2} t^2 \Big]_0^{a} + \frac{t^2}{2}\Big]_0^{2-a}$$

$$4g(a) = a^2 + (a - 2)^2$$

$$4g(a) = 2a^2 - 4a + 4$$

$$g(a) = \frac{a^2}{2} - a + 1$$

$\therefore$ $g(a) = \frac{1}{2}(a^2 - 2a + 2)$

$$= \frac{1}{2}[(a-1)^2 + 1], 0 \le a \le 1$$

$$m = \frac{1}{2}, M = 1$$

Hence, $2(M + m) = 3$

84. Given, $9 + f''(x) + f'(x) = x^2 + f^2(x)$

or $9 + \frac{d^2y}{dx^2} + \frac{dy}{dx} = x^2 + y^2$

As, P be the point of maxima of $f(x)$, so $\frac{dy}{dx} = 0$ and $\frac{d^2y}{dx^2} < 0$.

$\Rightarrow x^2 + y^2 = 9 + \frac{d^2y}{dx^2}$

So, $P(x, y)$ will lie inside the circle $x^2 + y^2 = 9$.

Hence, no tangent is possible.

85. $\frac{A_2}{A_1} = \frac{\pi r^2}{\left(\frac{2\pi - \theta}{2\pi}\right) \cdot \pi r^2} = \frac{2\pi}{2\pi - \theta}$

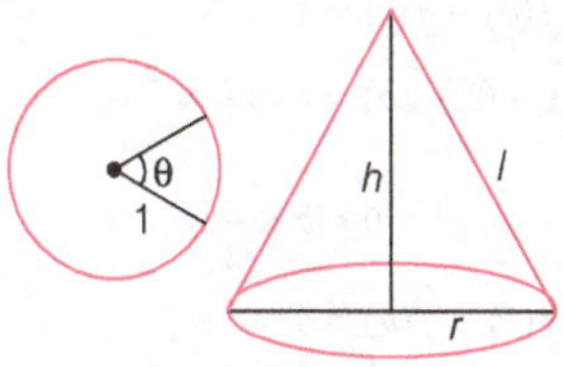

$$V = \frac{\pi}{3}\left(\frac{\theta}{2\pi}\right)^2 \sqrt{1^2 - \left(\frac{\theta}{2\pi}\right)^2}$$

$$\frac{dV}{d\theta} = 0 \Rightarrow \theta = \sqrt{\frac{8}{3}}\pi$$

$$\frac{A_2}{A_1} = \frac{\sqrt{3}}{\sqrt{3} - \sqrt{2}} = 3 + \sqrt{6}$$

$\Rightarrow$ $m = 3, n = 6$

$\therefore$ $(m + n)^2 = (3 + 6)^2 = 81$

86. $f(x) = x^2 \ln x$

$\Rightarrow f'(x) = x(1 + 2 \ln x)$

and $f'(x) > 0$ for $\in [1, e]$

$\therefore f(x)$ is continuously increasing on $[1, e]$ with the least value zero at $x = 1$ and the greatest value e^2 at $x = e$.

$\therefore$ $[\sqrt{0 + e}]^5 = [e]^5 = 2^5 = 32$

87. $f(x) = pxe^{-x} - \frac{x^2}{2} + x$

$$f'(x) = (1 - x)[pe^{-x} + 1] \le 0$$

$\Rightarrow$ $p \le -1$

$\therefore$ $p^2 \ge 1 \Rightarrow \frac{p^2}{4} \ge \frac{1}{4}$

$\therefore$ Least value of $\frac{p^2}{4} = \frac{1}{4} = 0.25$

88. $f'(x) = \begin{cases} ax\, e^{ax} + e^{ax}, & x \le 0 \\ 1 + 2ax - 3x^2, & x > 0 \end{cases}$

Clearly, $f'(x)$ is continuous at $x = 0$

$\Rightarrow$ $f''(x) = \begin{cases} a^2xe^{ax} + 2ae^{ax}, & x \le 0 \\ 2a - 6x, & x > 0 \end{cases}$, $f'(x)$ increasing if

$(ax + 2)ae^{ax} \ge 0$ and $2a - 6x \ge 0$

For $x \le 0$, $a(ax+2) \ge 0 \Rightarrow x \ge \frac{-2}{a}$

and for $x > 0$, $2a - 6x \ge 0$

$$6x \le 2a$$

$$x \le \frac{a}{3}$$

$$\therefore \quad x \ge \left[\frac{-2}{a}, \frac{a}{3}\right]$$

$$\Rightarrow \quad k = -2, l = 3$$

$$(k-l)^4 = 5^4 = 625$$

89. $f(x) = x^2 - 2bx + 1$

Case I $\quad b > 1$

$$\Rightarrow \quad f(0) - f(1) = 4$$

$$\Rightarrow \quad 1 - (2 - 2b) = 4 \Rightarrow b = \frac{5}{2}$$

Case II $\quad 0 < b < \frac{1}{2}$

$$\Rightarrow \quad f(1) - f(b) = 4$$

$$\Rightarrow \quad b = 3, -1 \quad \text{[not possible]}$$

Case III $\quad \frac{1}{2} < b < 1$

$$\Rightarrow \quad f(0) - f(b) = 4$$

$$b = \pm 2 \quad \text{[not possible]}$$

Case IV $\quad b < 0$

$$\Rightarrow \quad f(1) - f(0) = 4$$

$$\Rightarrow \quad b = -\frac{3}{2}$$

$$\therefore \quad \lambda = \frac{5}{2} - \frac{3}{2} = 1$$

$$\Rightarrow \quad 9\lambda + 11 = 9 + 11 = 20$$

90. $f'(x) = 2e^{2x} - (\lambda+1)e^x + 2 \ge 0, \forall x \in R$

i.e. $\quad 2e^{2x} + 2 - (\lambda+1)e^x$

$$\lambda + 1 \le (e^x + e^{-x})$$

$$\frac{\lambda+1}{2} \le (e^x + e^{-x}), \forall x \in R$$

$$\Rightarrow \quad \frac{\lambda+1}{2} \le (e^x + e^{-x})_{\min}, \forall x \in R$$

So, $\quad \frac{\lambda+1}{2} \le 2$

$$\lambda + 1 \le 4$$

$$\lambda \le 3$$

$$\lambda \in (-\infty, 3]$$

$$\therefore \quad k = 3 \Rightarrow \frac{38}{3}k = 38$$

91. $f(x) = x^2, g(x) = -\frac{8}{x}$

$$\Rightarrow \quad q = p^2 \Rightarrow s = -\frac{8}{r}$$

Also, $\frac{s-q}{r-p} = 2p$ and $2p = \frac{8}{r^2}$

$$pr^2 = 4 \qquad \text{...(i)}$$

$$\frac{s-q}{r-p} = 2p$$

$$\Rightarrow \frac{-\frac{8}{r} - p^2}{r-p} = 2p \Rightarrow -\frac{8}{r} - p^2 = 2pr - 2p^2$$

$$p^2 = \frac{8}{r} + 2pr \Rightarrow p^2 r = 16 \qquad \text{...(ii)}$$

On multiplying Eqs. (i) and (ii), we get

$$pr = 4 \Rightarrow r = 1, p = 4$$

$$\Rightarrow \quad p + r + 30 = 35$$

92. $f(x) = \begin{cases} |x+2|, & x \ge 0 \\ |x-2|, & x < 0 \end{cases}$

Minimum value of $f(x)$ is $2 = \alpha$

$\therefore$ Number of diagonals in polygon having 10 vertices are $= {}^{10}C_2 - 10 = 45 - 10 = 35$

93. $f(x) = \int_0^x [(a-1)(t^2+t+1)^2 - (a+1)(t^4+t^2+1)]dt$

$$= 2\int_0^x (t^2+t+1)(at - t^2 - 1)dt$$

$$\Rightarrow \quad f'(x) = 2(x^2+x+1)(ax - x^2 - 1) = 0$$

$$D < 0 \Rightarrow a^2 - 4 < 0$$

$$a \in (-2, 2) \Rightarrow \gamma = 3 \Rightarrow 2\gamma + 7 = 13$$

94. $f(x) = x^{2013} + e^{2014x}$

$$f'(x) = 2013x^{2012} + 2014e^{2014x} > 0$$

$\Rightarrow f(x)$ is increasing function.

$$f(-\infty) = -\infty$$

$$f(0) = 1$$

$$f(\infty) = \infty$$

$\therefore$ Number of real roots $= 1 = r$

$\therefore 3r + 19 = 22$

95. $I(t) = \int_\alpha^\beta (x^2 + 2x - t^2)dx = \left[\frac{x^3}{3} + x^2 - t^2x + x\right]_\alpha^\beta$

$$I(t) = \frac{\beta^3 - \alpha^3}{3} + (\beta^2 - \alpha^2) - t^2(\beta - \alpha)$$

$$I'(t) = -2t(\beta - \alpha) = 0$$

$$I(t) \le I(0)$$

$$\therefore \quad I(0) = \int_{-2}^0 (x^2 + 2x)dx = -\frac{4}{3} \Rightarrow \frac{p}{q} = |I(0)| = \frac{4}{3}$$

$$pq = 4 \times 3 = 12$$

96. Let $f'(x) = K$

$\Rightarrow \quad f(x) = Kx + c \Rightarrow f(9) - f(-3) = 12K$

Maximum value of $f(9) - f(-3) = 96$

$\therefore$ Sum of digits $= 15$

97. $e^{-x}\left(\frac{x^2}{2} + x + 1\right) = a$

Let $f(x) = e^{-x}\left(\frac{x^2}{2} + x + 1\right)$

$$f'(x) = e^{-x}\left(-\frac{x^2}{2}\right) < 0$$

$$f(-\infty) = \infty$$

$$f(\infty) = \lim_{x\to\infty} e^{-x}\left(\frac{x^2}{2} + x + 1\right)$$

$$= \lim_{x\to\infty} \frac{x^2 + 2x + 2}{2e^x}$$

Using L'Hospital Rule

$$\Rightarrow \lim_{x\to\infty} \frac{2x+2}{2e^x}$$

Using L'Hospital Rule

$$\Rightarrow \lim_{x\to\infty} = \frac{2}{2e^x} = 0$$

$$\therefore \quad f(x) = (0, \infty)$$

$\therefore$ $y = a$ cuts $y = f(x)$ at one point, then $\lambda = 1$

$$S_\infty = \frac{\lambda}{1 - \frac{\lambda}{3}}$$

$$= \frac{1}{1 - \frac{1}{3}} = \frac{3}{2} = 1.5$$

98. (A) Given, $f(x) = x^3 - \frac{11x}{3}$.

We have, $\frac{f(b)}{b-3} = f'(b) = 3b^2 - \frac{11}{3}$

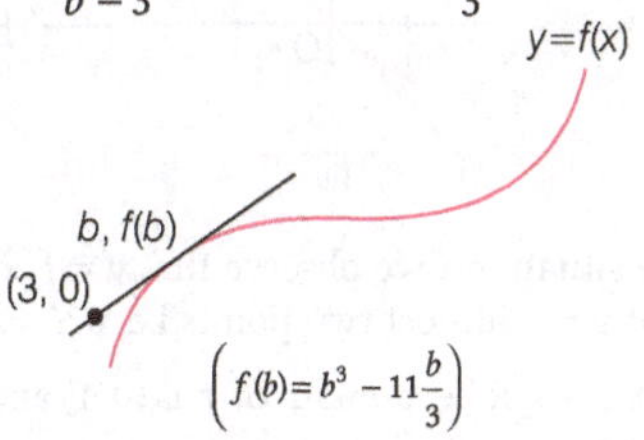

$$\Rightarrow b^3 - \frac{11b}{3} = (b-3)\left(3b^2 - \frac{11}{3}\right)$$

or $b^3 - \frac{11b}{3} = 3b^3 - \frac{11b}{3} - 9b^2 + 11$

or $2b^3 - 9b^2 + 11 = 0$

$$\therefore \quad \Sigma b = \frac{9}{2}; \Pi\, b = -\frac{11}{2}$$

$$\Rightarrow \Sigma\, b - \Pi\, b = 10$$

(B) Let $I(a) = \int_{a-1}^{a+1} e^{-(x-1)^2} dx$

$$\Rightarrow I'(a) = e^{-a^2} - e^{-(a-2)^2}$$

Now, for maximum or minimum value of $I(a)$, we must have $I'(a) = 0$.

$$\Rightarrow \quad e^{-a^2} = e^{-(a-2)^2 - a^2} = 1 = e^0$$

$$\Rightarrow \quad e^{(a-2)^2 - a^2} = 1 = e^0$$

$$\Rightarrow \quad (a-2)^2 - a^2 = 0$$

$$\Rightarrow \quad -4a + 4 = 0$$

$$\Rightarrow \quad a = 1$$

Also, $I''(a) = -2ae^{-a^2} + 2e^{-(a-2)^2}(a-2)$

$$= 2[(a-2)\,e^{-(a-2)^2} - ae^{-a^2}]$$

Clearly $I''(a = 1) = 2[-e^{-1} - e^{-1}]$

$$= 2\left(\frac{-2}{e}\right)$$

$$= \frac{-4}{e} < 0$$

So, $I(a)$ will be maximum for $a = 1$

(C) We have, $\frac{dy}{dx} = e^{x_1} = \frac{1}{4}$

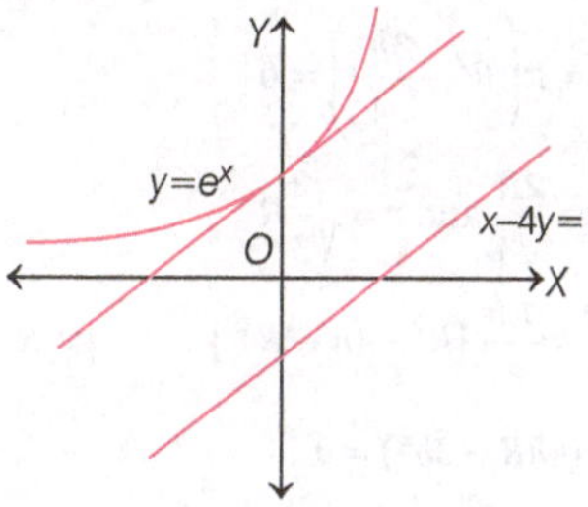

$$\Rightarrow x_1 = \ln 4 \text{ and } y_1 = e^{-\ln 4} = \frac{1}{e^{\ln 4}} = \frac{1}{4}$$

Equation of l is $\left(y - \frac{1}{4}\right) = \frac{1}{4}(x + \ln 4)$

$$\Rightarrow \quad 4y - 1 = x + \ln 4 \quad \text{...(i)}$$

Put $y = 0$ in Eq. (i), we get

$$x = -(1 + \ln 4) = -\ln(4e) = \ln\left(\frac{1}{4e}\right)$$

$$= -\ln(4e)$$

$$\Rightarrow \quad k = 4$$

99. $f(x) = |\ln|x|| - kx^2 = 0$

$$\Rightarrow k = \frac{|\ln|x||}{x^2}$$

Consider $g(x) = \frac{\ln x}{x^2}$, $x > 0$

$g(x)$ is increasing in $(1, \sqrt{e})$ and decreasing $(\sqrt{e}, \infty)$.

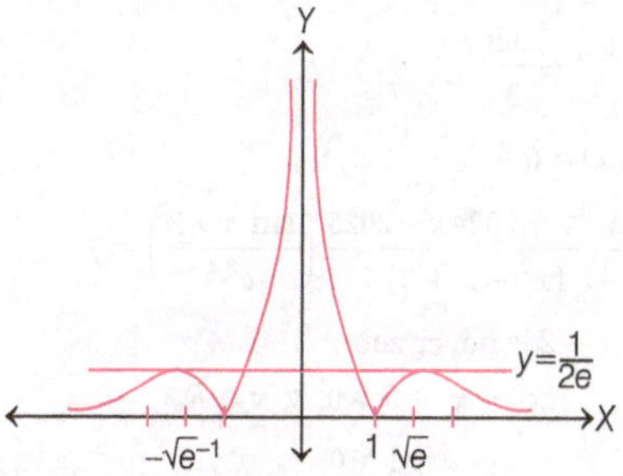

100. Let $g(x) = ax^3 + bx^2 + cx + d$

$$f(x) = \sqrt{g(x)}$$

$f(x)$ has local minima and local maxima at $x = -2$ and $x = 2$.

$g(x)$ has same local minima and maxima and $x = -2$ and 2.

$\Rightarrow \quad a < 0;\ a = -2$

$$f'(x) = \frac{3ax^2 + 2bx + c}{2\sqrt{ax^3 + bx^2 + cx + d}} = 0$$

$f'(-2) = 0$ and $f'(2) = 0$

$\Rightarrow \quad b = 0, c = 24$

Also, $g(2) > 0$ and $g(-2) > 0$

$\Rightarrow -16 + 48 + d > 0$ and $16 - 48 + d > 0$

$d > -32$ and $d > 32$

$\Rightarrow \quad d > 32$

101. (A) $V = \pi r^2 h = \pi h \cdot \left(R^2 - \frac{h^2}{4}\right) \quad \left[\because R^2 = r^2 + \frac{h^2}{4}\right]$

$$\frac{dV}{dh} = \pi\left(R^2 - \frac{3h^2}{4}\right) = 0$$

$$\Rightarrow \quad h = \frac{2R}{\sqrt{3}} \text{ and } r = \sqrt{\frac{2}{3}}R$$

(B) $V = \frac{\pi r^2 h}{3} = \frac{\pi h}{3}\{R^2 - (h - R)^2\} \quad [\because R^2 = r^2 + (h - R)^2]$

$$\frac{dV}{dh} = \frac{\pi}{3}(4hR - 3h^2) = 0$$

$$\Rightarrow h = \frac{4R}{3} \text{ and } r = \frac{2\sqrt{2}R}{3}$$

(C) $\sin\theta = \frac{r}{h - r} = \frac{R}{\sqrt{R^2 + h^2}}$

$$\Rightarrow R^2 = \frac{h^2 r^2}{h^2 - 2hr}$$

Volume of cone $= \frac{\pi}{3}R^2 h = \frac{\pi}{3}\left(\frac{h^2 r^2}{h - 2r}\right)$

$$\frac{dV}{dh} = \frac{\pi}{3}r^2\left(\frac{(h - 2r)\,2h - h^2}{(h - 2r)^2}\right) = 0$$

$\Rightarrow \quad h = 4r$

(D) $$\frac{\left(\frac{2x}{3} + \frac{2x}{3} + \frac{2x}{3}\right) + \left(\frac{3y}{4} + \frac{3y}{4} + \frac{3y}{4} + \frac{3y}{4}\right)}{7} \geq \left(\frac{8x^3}{27} \cdot \frac{81y^4}{256}\right)^{\frac{1}{7}}$$

$$\Rightarrow x^3 y^4 \leq \frac{32}{3}$$

102. Given, $f(x) = 0$

$$\Rightarrow \quad \frac{x^{2023} + 2024x + 2025}{(x^2 - x + 3)}\left(\frac{\sin x + 2}{e^{\pi x}}\right) = 0 \quad \text{...(i)}$$

Here, $\sin x + 2$ is never zero.

and $\quad x^2 - x + 3 > 0, \forall x \in R,$

$\because \quad a = 1 > 0$

and $\quad D = (-1)^2 - 4 \times 1 \times 3 = -11 < 0$

and $\quad e^{\pi x} > 0, \forall x \in R$

So, Eq. (i) $\Rightarrow x^{2023} + 2024x + 2025 = 0$

Consider, $g(x) = x^{2023} + 2024x + 2025$

$\Rightarrow \quad g'(x) = 2023x^{2022} + 2024,$

which is strictly positive for every real value of x.

i.e., $g'(x) > 0, \forall x \in R$

So, $g(x)$ is a strictly increasing function.

$\therefore \quad g(x) = 0$ for exactly one value of x.

$\therefore \quad f(x) = 0$ has one solution.

103. **Method I** Given, S = Set of all twice differentiable functions from R to R.

$$\frac{d^2 f}{dx^2} > 0, \forall x \in (-1, 1)$$

So, graph is concave upward.

Let $\quad h(x) = f(x) - x$

$\therefore \quad h'(x) = f'(x) - 1, \; h''(x) = f''(x) > 0$

$\therefore \quad h'(x) = 0$ has atmost one root in $x \in (-1, 1)$

$\therefore \quad h(x) = 0$ has atmost two roots in $x \in (-1, 1)$.

$\therefore \quad x_f \leq 2$

Method II (Graphical Approach) As $\frac{d^2 y}{dx^2} > 0$ in $(-1, 1)$.

$\therefore f$ is concave upward.

Three situations : so that, number of solution of $f(x) = x \rightarrow x_f$

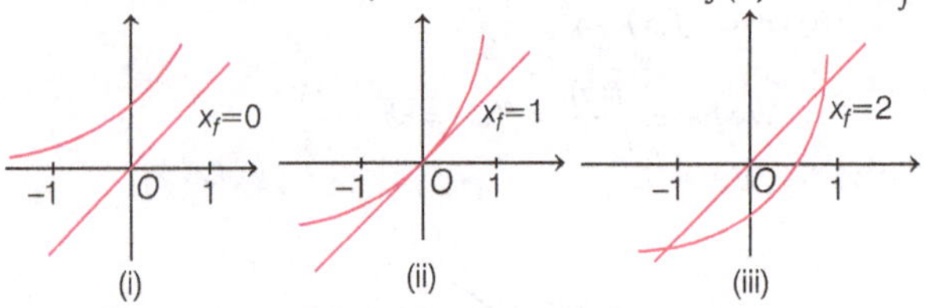

From above situations, we observe that $y = f(x)$ can intersect the graph of $y = x$ atmost two points i.e. $0 \leq x_f \leq 2$.

104. Given, $f : (0, 1) \rightarrow R$ i.e. domain of f is $(0, 1)$ and codomain is $(-\infty, \infty)$.

Also, given $f(x) = [4x]\left(x - \frac{1}{4}\right)^2\left(x - \frac{1}{2}\right)$, where $[\cdot]$ = GIF

[concept interval breaking for $[4x]$]

Since, $\quad 0 < x < 1 \Rightarrow 0 < 4x < 4$

$\Rightarrow \quad 0 < 4x < 1$ or $1 \leq 4x < 2$

or $\quad 2 \leq 4x < 3$ or $3 \leq 4x < 4$

$\Rightarrow \quad 0 < x < \frac{1}{4}$ or $\frac{1}{4} \leq x < \frac{1}{2}$

or $\quad \frac{1}{2} \leq x < \frac{3}{4}$ or $\frac{3}{4} \leq x < 1$

So, $\quad [4x] = 0$, if $0 < x < \frac{1}{4}$

$[4x] = 1$, if $\frac{1}{4} \leq x < \frac{1}{2}$

$[4x] = 2$, if $\frac{1}{2} \leq x < \frac{3}{4}$

$[4x] = 3$, if $\frac{3}{4} \leq x < 1$

$$\therefore f(x)=\begin{cases}0, & 0<x<\frac{1}{4}\\ \left(x-\frac{1}{4}\right)^2\left(x-\frac{1}{2}\right), & \frac{1}{4}\le x<\frac{1}{2}\\ 2\left(x-\frac{1}{4}\right)^2\left(x-\frac{1}{2}\right), & \frac{1}{2}\le x<\frac{3}{4}\\ 3\left(x-\frac{1}{4}\right)^2\left(x-\frac{1}{2}\right), & \frac{3}{4}\le x<1\end{cases}$$

From above piecewise defined function, we observe that critical points/change points are $x=\frac{1}{4},\frac{1}{2},\frac{3}{4}$.

As we know that a function $f(x)$ is continuous at $x=a$ if left hand limit, right hand limit and value of function at $x=a$ are equal, otherwise it is discontinuous.

So, at $x=\frac{1}{4}$ and at $x=\frac{1}{2}$, $f(x)$ is continuous but at $x=\frac{3}{4}$, $f(x)$ will be discontinuous.

So, option (a) is correct.

$$\text{Now, } f'(x)=\begin{cases}0, & 0<x<\frac{1}{4}\\ 2\left(x-\frac{1}{4}\right)\left(x-\frac{1}{2}\right)+\left(x-\frac{1}{4}\right)^2, & \frac{1}{4}<x<\frac{1}{2}\\ 4\left(x-\frac{1}{4}\right)\left(x-\frac{1}{2}\right)+2\left(x-\frac{1}{4}\right)^2, & \frac{1}{2}<x<\frac{3}{4}\\ 6\left(x-\frac{1}{4}\right)\left(x-\frac{1}{2}\right)+3\left(x-\frac{1}{4}\right)^2, & \frac{3}{4}<x<1\end{cases}$$

From above, we see that $f(x)$ is not differentiable at $x=1/2, \frac{3}{4}$.

Since, maximum value of $f(x)$ exist between 1/4 and 1/2, i.e. minimum value of $f(x)$ occurs at $x=\frac{5}{12}$.

$$\therefore f\left(\frac{5}{12}\right)=\left(\frac{5}{12}-\frac{1}{4}\right)^2\left(\frac{5}{12}-\frac{1}{2}\right)$$

$$=\frac{1}{36}\times\frac{(-1)}{12}=\frac{-1}{432}$$

105. $\alpha=\sum_{k=1}^{\infty}\sin^{2k}\left(\frac{\pi}{6}\right)=\sum_{k=1}^{\infty}\left(\sin^2\frac{\pi}{6}\right)^k=\sum_{k=1}^{\infty}\left(\frac{1}{4}\right)^k$

$$\alpha=\frac{1}{4}+\left(\frac{1}{4}\right)^2+\left(\frac{1}{4}\right)^3+\ldots\quad \alpha=\frac{\frac{1}{4}}{1-\frac{1}{4}}=\frac{\frac{1}{4}}{\frac{3}{4}}=\frac{1}{3}$$

Now, $g:[0,1]\to R$

$$\Rightarrow g(x)=2^{\alpha x}+2^{\alpha(1-x)}$$

$$\Rightarrow g(x)=2^{\frac{x}{3}}+2^{\frac{1}{3}(1-x)}=2^{\frac{x}{3}}+2^{\frac{1}{3}}\cdot 2^{\frac{-x}{3}}$$

$$\Rightarrow g'(x)=\left(\frac{1}{3}2^{\frac{x}{3}}-\frac{1}{3}2^{\frac{1}{3}}\cdot 2^{-\frac{x}{3}}\right)\log 2=0$$

$$\Rightarrow \frac{1}{3}2^{x/3}=\frac{1}{3}2^{1/3}2^{-x/3}$$

$$\Rightarrow 2^{2x/3}=2^{1/3}$$

$$\Rightarrow \frac{2x}{3}=\frac{1}{3}\Rightarrow x=\frac{1}{2}$$

So, $x=\frac{1}{2}$ is critical point.

Also, $g(0)=1+2^{1/3}$, $g(1)=1+2^{1/3}$

$$g\left(\frac{1}{2}\right)=2^{1/6}+2^{1/6}=2\cdot 2^{1/6}=2^{7/6}$$

So, graph of $g(x)$ in [0, 1].

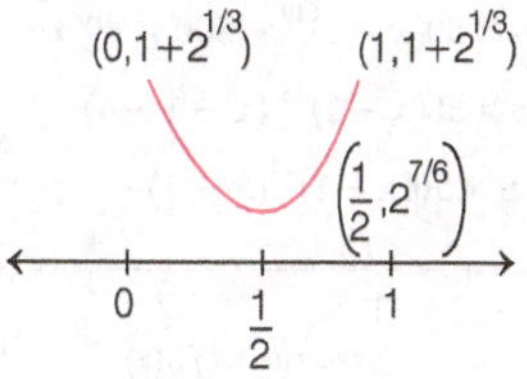

So, maximum value of function in [0, 1] is $1+2^{1/3}$. Minimum value of function in [0, 1] is $2^{7/6}$.

$g(x)$ attains its maximum value at 0 and 1.

106. Given, $f(x)=\frac{x^2-3x-6}{x^2+2x+4}$ ... (i)

$$\Rightarrow \quad f'(x)=\frac{(x^2+2x+4)(2x-3)-(x^2-3x-6)(2x+2)}{(x^2+2x+4)^2}$$

$$\Rightarrow \quad f'(x)=\frac{5x(x+4)}{(x^2+2x+4)^2}$$

Sign scheme for $f'(x)$

Here, f is decreasing in the interval $(-2,-1)$ and f is increasing in the interval (1, 2).

Now, $f(-4)=11/6, f(0)=-3/2$ [from Eq. (i)]

and $\lim_{x\to\pm\infty} f(x)=1$

$$\therefore \text{Range}=\left[\frac{-3}{2},\frac{11}{6}\right]$$

Hence, $f(x)$ is into.

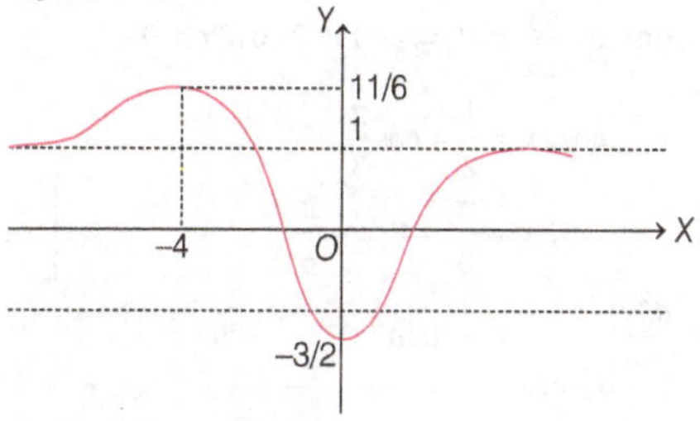

$f(x)$ has local maxima at $x=-4$ and local minima at $x=0$.

Sol. (Q.Nos. 107-108)

$$f_1(x)=\int_0^x (t-1)^1(t-2)^2(t-3)^3(t-4)^4\ldots(t-21)^{21}dt$$

$$\Rightarrow f_1'(x)=(x-1)(x-2)^2(x-3)^3(x-4)^4\ldots(x-21)^{21}$$

Sign Scheme for $f_1'(x)$

From sign scheme of $f_1'(x)$, we observe that $f(x)$ has local minima at $x = 4k + 1, k \in W$ i.e. $f_1'(x)$ changes sign from – ve to + ve which are $x = 1, 5, 9, 13, 17, 21$ and $f(x)$ has local maxima at $x = 4k + 3, k \in W$ i.e. $f_1'(x)$ changes sign from +ve to –ve, which are $x = 3, 7, 11, 15, 19$.

So, m_1 = number of local minima points = 6 and n_1 = number of local maxima points = 5

Hence, $2m_1 + 3n_1 + m_1n_1 = 2 \times 6 + 3 \times 5 + 6 \times 5 = 57$

Also, $f_2(x) = 98(x-1)^{50} - 600(x-1)^{49} + 2450$

$\Rightarrow \quad f_2'(x) = 98 \times 50(x-1)^{49} - 600 \times 49(x-1)^{48}$

$\Rightarrow \quad f_2'(x) = 98 \times 50(x-1)^{48}(x-1-6)$

$\Rightarrow \quad f_2'(x) = 98 \times 50(x-1)^{48}(x-7)$

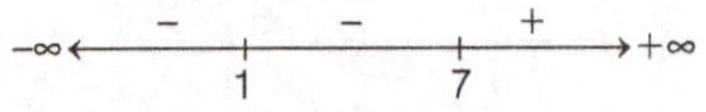

Sign scheme for $f_2'(x)$

Clearly, $m_2 = 1$ and $n_2 = 0$

So, $6m_2 + 4n_2 + 8m_2n_2 = 6 + 0 + 0 = 6$

107. 57 **108.** 6

109. Given region is

$\{(x, y) \in R \times R : 0 \le x \le \pi/2 \text{ and } 0 \le y \le 2\sin(2x)\}$

On drawing the diagram,

Let the side PS on the X-axis, such that $P(x, 0)$, and $Q(x, 2\sin(2x))$, so length of the sides $PS = QR = 2\left(\dfrac{\pi}{4} - x\right)$

and $PQ = RS = 2\sin 2x$

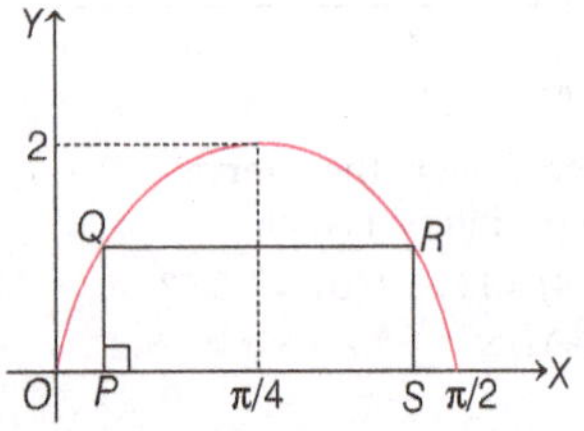

$\therefore$ Perimeter of the rectangle, $y = 4\left[\dfrac{\pi}{4} - x + \sin 2x\right]$

For maximum, $\dfrac{dy}{dx} = 0 \Rightarrow -1 + 2\cos 2x = 0$

$\Rightarrow \quad \cos 2x = \dfrac{1}{2} = \cos\dfrac{\pi}{3}$

$\Rightarrow \quad 2x = \dfrac{\pi}{3} \Rightarrow x = \dfrac{\pi}{6} \quad \left[\because x \in \left[0, \dfrac{\pi}{2}\right]\right]$

and $\left.\dfrac{d^2y}{dx^2}\right|_{x=\pi/6} = -4\sin 2x\Big|_{x=\frac{\pi}{6}} < 0$

$\therefore$ At $x = \dfrac{\pi}{6}$, the rectangle $PQRS$ have maximum perimeter.

So, length of sides, $PS = QR = 2\left(\dfrac{\pi}{4} - \dfrac{\pi}{6}\right) = \dfrac{\pi}{6}$

and $PQ = RS = 2\sin\left(\dfrac{\pi}{3}\right) = \sqrt{3}$

$\therefore$ Required area $(PS \times QR) = \dfrac{\pi}{6} \times \sqrt{3} = \dfrac{\pi}{2\sqrt{3}}$

110. The given function $f : R \to R$ be defined by

$$f(\theta) = (\sin\theta + \cos\theta)^2 + (\sin\theta - \cos\theta)^4$$
$$= 1 + \sin 2\theta + (1 - \sin 2\theta)^2$$
$$= 1 + \sin 2\theta + 1 + \sin^2 2\theta - 2\sin 2\theta$$
$$= \sin^2 2\theta - \sin 2\theta + 2 = \left(\sin 2\theta - \frac{1}{2}\right)^2 + \frac{7}{4}$$

The local minimum of function 'f' occurs when

$\sin 2\theta = \dfrac{1}{2} \Rightarrow 2\theta = \dfrac{\pi}{6}, \dfrac{5\pi}{6}, \dfrac{13\pi}{6} \ldots$

$\Rightarrow \quad \theta = \dfrac{\pi}{12}, \dfrac{5\pi}{12}, \dfrac{13\pi}{12}, \ldots$

but $\theta \in \{\lambda_1\pi, \lambda_2\pi, \ldots \lambda_r\pi\}$, where $0 < \lambda_1 < \ldots < \lambda_r < 1$.

$\therefore \quad \theta = \dfrac{\pi}{12}, \dfrac{5\pi}{12}$

So, $\lambda_1 + \ldots + \lambda_r = \dfrac{1}{12} + \dfrac{5}{12} = 0.5$

111. Given set S of polynomials with real coefficients

$S = \{(x^2 - 1)^2(a_0 + a_1x + a_2x^2 + a_3x^3) : a_0, a_1, a_2, a_3 \in R\}$

and for a polynomial $f \in S$,

Let $f(x) = (x^2 - 1)^2 (a_0 + a_1x + a_2x^2 + a_3x^3)$

it have – 1 and 1 as repeated roots twice, so graph of $f(x)$ touches the X-axis at $x = -1$ and $x = 1$, so $f'(x)$ having at least three roots $x = -1, 1$ and α. Where $\alpha \in (-1, 1)$ and $f''(x)$ having at least two roots in interval $(-1, 1)$

So, $m_{f'} = 3$ and $m_{f''} = 2$

$\therefore$ Minimum possible value of $(m_{f'} + m_{f''}) = 5$

Exercise 3 - Challenging Problem

1. $f'(x) = \dfrac{1}{2}\left[\dfrac{(1 - \cos x)2x - x^2 \sin x}{(1 - \cos x)^2}\right]$

Now, consider the numerator as

$p(x) = 2(1 - \cos x) - x\sin x$

$$= 4\sin^2\frac{x}{2} - 2x\sin\frac{x}{2}\cos\frac{x}{2}$$

$$= 2x\sin\frac{x}{2}\cos\frac{x}{2}\left(\frac{\tan\frac{x}{2}}{\frac{x}{2}} - 1\right) > 0 \Rightarrow f'(x) > 0$$

$\Rightarrow f$ is strictly increasing

Now, $g'(x) = \dfrac{1}{6}\left[\dfrac{(x - \sin x)2x - x^2(1 - \cos x)}{(x - \sin x)^2}\right]$

Again, consider the numerator as

$q(x) = x - 2\sin x + x\cos x$

$$= 2x\cos^2\frac{x}{2} - 4\sin\frac{x}{2}\cdot\cos\frac{x}{2}$$

$$\Rightarrow \quad 2x\cos^2\frac{x}{2}\left[1 - \frac{\tan\frac{x}{2}}{\frac{x}{2}}\right] < 0$$

$\Rightarrow g'(x) < 0 \Rightarrow g$ is strictly decreasing

Now, $f'(x)+g'(x)$

$$=2x\left(1-\frac{\tan\frac{x}{2}}{\frac{x}{2}}\right)\times\cos\frac{x}{2}\times\left(\cos\frac{x}{2}-\sin\frac{x}{2}\right)$$

$x>0,\ \forall\ x\in(0,1)$

and $\tan x > x,\ \forall\ x\in\left(0,\frac{\pi}{2}\right)$

For $x\in(0,1),\ \frac{x}{2}\in\left(0,\frac{1}{2}\right)$

$$\Rightarrow \quad \tan\frac{x}{2}>\frac{x}{2}$$

$$\Rightarrow \quad \frac{\tan\left(\frac{x}{2}\right)}{\frac{x}{2}}>1 \Rightarrow 1-\frac{\tan\left(\frac{x}{2}\right)}{x/2}<0$$

Now, for $x\in\left(0,\frac{\pi}{2}\right),\ \cos\frac{x}{2}>\frac{\sin x}{2}$

$\Rightarrow$ for $x\in(0,1),\ \cos\frac{x}{2}>\sin\frac{x}{2}$

Now, $f'(x)+g'(x)<0,\ \forall\ x\in(0,1)$

and hence $f(x)+g(x)$ is strictly decreasing in $(0,1)$.

2. $f'(x)-\frac{f(x)}{x}=\frac{1}{2}xf''(\xi),\ 0<\xi<x$ ...(i)

The relation in Eq. (i) can be rearranged in the form

$$f(x)-xf'(x)+\frac{1}{2}x^2f''(\xi)=0 \quad \text{...(ii)}$$

We may consider the function F defined as

$$F(x)=f(x)-xf'(x)+\frac{1}{2}Ax^2, \quad \text{...(iii)}$$

where A is a constant to be suitably chosen.

Let c be any positive real number.

Choosing A in Eq. (iii) so that $F(c)=0$, we find that F satisfies the hypothesis of Rolle's theorem on $[0,c]$.

Therefore, there exists ξ such that $0<\xi<c$ and $F'(\xi)=0$.

Since, $F''(x)=-xf''(x)+Ax$, therefore $F'(\xi)=0$ yields

$$A=f''(\xi) \quad \text{...(iv)}$$

Also, $F(c)=0$ yields

$$f(c)-cf'(c)+\frac{1}{2}Ac^2=0 \quad \text{...(v)}$$

From Eqs. (iv) and (v), we get

$$f(c)-cf'(c)+\frac{1}{2}c^2f''(\xi)=0$$

or

$$f'(c)-\frac{f(c)}{c}=\frac{1}{2}cf''(\xi) \quad \text{...(vi)}$$

Since, Eq. (vi) is true for each $c>0$, therefore Eq. (i) is established.

Also, if G be defined by setting

$$G(x)=\frac{f(x)}{x}, \text{ whenever } x<0, \text{ then}$$

$$G'(x)=\frac{xf'(x)-f(x)}{x^2}=\frac{1}{2}f''(\xi) \quad \text{[by Eq. (i)]}$$

Assuming that $f''(x)>0$ whenever $x>0$, it follows that $G'(x)>0$, whenever $x>0$.

If x_1 and x_2 be any two positive real numbers such that $x_2<x_1$, then by applying the Mean value theorem to G in $[x_1,x_2]$ it follows that

$$G(x_2)-G(x_1)=(x_2-x_1)G'(\gamma),$$

where γ is some real number in (x_1,x_2).

Since, $G'(\gamma)>0$, therefore it follows that $G(x_2)<G(x_1)$.

Hence, $\frac{f(x)}{x}$ is strictly increasing in $(0,\infty)$.

3. Given, $f(x)=\{-c^2+(b-1)c-2\}x+\int_0^x(\sin^2x+\cos^4x)dx$

$$\therefore \quad f'(x)=-c^2+(b-1)c-2+\sin^2x+\cos^4x$$

$$\Rightarrow \quad f'(x)=(1-\sin^2x)^2+\sin^2x-c^2+(b-1)c-2$$

$$=\sin^4x-\sin^2x-c^2+(b-1)c-1$$

$$=\left(\sin^2x-\frac{1}{2}\right)^2-c^2+(b-1)c-\frac{5}{4}$$

We should have, $f'(x)\ge 0,\ \forall\ x\in R$

$$\therefore \quad \left(\sin^2x-\frac{1}{2}\right)^2-c^2+(b-1)c-\frac{5}{4}\ge 0$$

$$0-c^2+(b-1)c-\frac{5}{4}\ge 0$$

[$\because$ the least value of $(\sin^2x-1/2)^2$ is 0]

or $c^2-(b-1)c+\frac{5}{4}\le 0$, for all c.

$$\therefore \quad D\le 0\Rightarrow (b-1)^2\le 5$$

$$\Rightarrow \quad -\sqrt{5}\le b-1\le +\sqrt{5}$$

$$\Rightarrow \quad 1-\sqrt{5}\le b\le 1+\sqrt{5}$$

Hence, $b\in[1-\sqrt{5},1+\sqrt{5}]$.

4. Consider the function,

$$f(x)=\sum_{i=1}^{n}\frac{a_i^2}{x-b_i}-c$$

$$=\frac{a_1^2}{x-b_1}+\frac{a_2^2}{x-b_2}+\ldots+\frac{a_n^2}{x-b_n}-c$$

and $f'(x)=-\left[\frac{a_1^2}{(x-b_1)^2}+\frac{a_2^2}{(x-b_2)^2}+\ldots+\frac{a_n^2}{(x-b_n)^2}\right]$

$$<0,\ \forall\ x\in R-\{b_1,b_2,\ldots,b_n\}$$

$\Rightarrow f(x)$ strictly decreases in $(-\infty,b_1),(b_1,b_2),\ldots,(b_{n-1},b_n)$

Now, we have

$$f(-\infty)=-c=f(\infty)$$

$$f(b_1^-)=-\infty \text{ and } f(b_1^+)=\infty$$

$$f(b_2^-)=-\infty \text{ and } f(b_2^+)=\infty$$

......

......

$$f(b_n^-)=-\infty \text{ and } f(b_n^+)=\infty$$

The plot of the curve $y = f(x)$ is shown alongside.

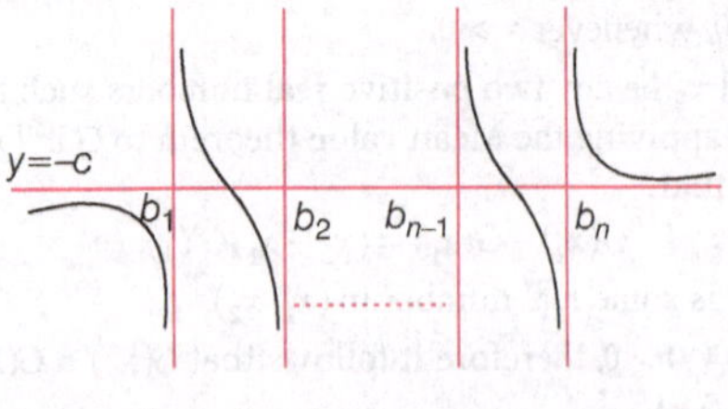

Hence, the number of real roots of the equation is $n-1$.

5. $f(x) = x^3 - 9x^2 + 15x + 6$

$$f(t) = t^3 - 9t^2 + 15t + 6$$

$$f'(t) = 3t^2 - 18t + 15 = 3[t^2 - 6t + 5]$$

$$= 3(t-5)(t-1)$$

Hence, f is increasing in (5, 6) and f is decreasing in (1, 5).

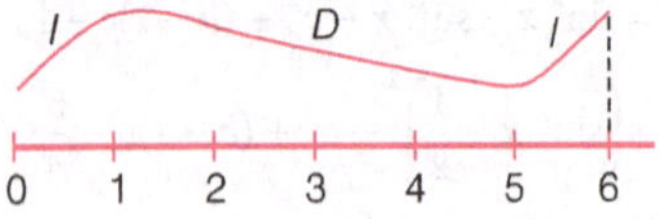

$$\text{Now, } g(x) = \begin{cases} f(x) = x^3 - 9x^2 + 15x + 6, & 1 \le x < 5 \\ f(5) = -19, & 5 \le x \le 6 \\ x - 18, & x > 6 \end{cases}$$

$$\therefore \quad g(x) = \begin{cases} x^3 - 9x^2 + 15x + 6, & 1 \le x < 5 \\ -19, & 5 \le x \le 6 \\ x - 18, & x > 6 \end{cases}$$

Hence, g is continuous and differentiable at $x = 1$.

g is continuous and differentiable at $x = 5$.

g is neither continuous nor derivable at $x = 6$.

$g(x)$ is monotonic in (1, 5).

6. $3F(x) = 3[f(x) - x^2 - x]$

$$= 2\underbrace{[f(x) - 3x]}_{g(x)} + \underbrace{(f(x) - x^3)}_{h(x)} + x^3 - 3x^2 + 3x - 1 + 1$$

$$3F(x) = 2g(x) + h(x) + (x-1)^3 + 1$$

$\Rightarrow F(x)$ is increasing, $\forall\ x \in [0, \infty]$.

Alternative

Given $f(x)$ is increasing

$$\Rightarrow \quad f'(x) > 0$$

$$g(x) = f(x) - 3x$$

$$g'(x) = f'(x) - 3 > 0 \Rightarrow f'(x) > 3$$

Also, $h(x) = f(x) - x^3$

$$h'(x) = f'(x) - 3x^2 > 0 \Rightarrow f'(x) > 3x^2$$

To prove that $F(x) = f(x) - x^2 - x$ is increasing.

i.e. $\quad F'(x) = f'(x) - 2x - 1 > 0$

$$F'(x) > 0$$

$$f'(x) > 2x + 1$$

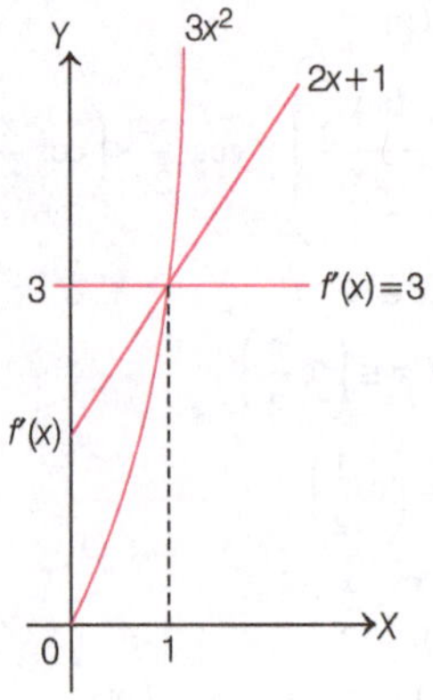

For in [0, 1), obviously $f'(x) > 3 > 2x + 1$ and in (1, 2), $3x^2 > 2x + 1$.

Hence proved.

7. Given that $\dfrac{d}{dx} H(x) > 2cx\, H(x)$

$$\Rightarrow \quad \frac{d}{dx} H(x) - 2\,cx\,H(x) > 0$$

$$\Rightarrow \left\{\frac{d}{dx} H(x)\right\} e^{-cx^2} - 2cxe^{-cx^2}\ a \cdot H(x) > 0$$

$$\Rightarrow \left\{\frac{d}{dx} H(x)\right\} e^{-cx^2} - H(x)\left\{\frac{d}{dx} e^{-cx^2}\right\} > 0$$

$$\Rightarrow \quad \left\{\frac{d}{dx} H(x) \cdot e^{-cx^2}\right\} > 0$$

$\therefore\ H(x)e^{-cx^2}$ is an increasing function.

But $H(x_0) = 0$ and e^{-cx^2} is always positive.

$\Rightarrow H(x_0) > 0$, for all $x > x_0$.

$\Rightarrow H(x)$ cannot be zero for any $x > x_0$.

8. $(x^b + y^b)^{\frac{1}{b}} < (x^a + y^a)^{\frac{1}{a}}$

$$\Rightarrow \quad \left(\left(\frac{x}{y}\right)^b + 1\right)^{\frac{1}{b}} < \left(\left(\frac{x}{y}\right)^a + 1\right)^{\frac{1}{a}} \qquad [\because y > 0]$$

To prove that $(t^b + 1)^{\frac{a}{b}} < t^a + 1 \left[\dfrac{x}{y} = t > 0\right]$

Let $f(t) = (t^b + 1)^{\frac{a}{b}} - t^a - 1$

$$\Rightarrow f'(t) = \frac{a}{b}(t^b + 1)^{\frac{a}{b} - 1} \cdot bt^{b-1} - at^{a-1}$$

$$\Rightarrow f'(t) = at^{a-1}\left[t^{b-a}(t^b + 1)^{\frac{a}{b} - 1} - 1\right]$$

$$= at^{a-1}\left[\left(1 + \frac{1}{t^b}\right)^{\frac{a}{b} - 1} - 1\right]$$

Now, since $1 + \dfrac{1}{t^b} > 1$ and $\dfrac{a}{b} - 1 < 0$

Therefore, $\left(1+\frac{1}{t^b}\right)^{\frac{a}{b}-1} < 1.$

Hence, $f'(t) < 0$ i.e. $f(t)$ is decreasing function

So, $f(t) < f(0)$ but $f(0) = 0$

$\Rightarrow \quad (t^b+1)^{\frac{a}{b}} < t^a + 1.$ **Hence proved.**

9. $f(x) = \left(1+\frac{1}{x}\right)^x$

Domain of $f(x)$, $1+\frac{1}{x} > 0$

$\Rightarrow \quad \frac{x+1}{x} > 0 \Rightarrow (-\infty, -1) \cup (0, \infty)$

Consider $f'(x) = \left(1+\frac{1}{x}\right)^x \left[\ln\left(1+\frac{1}{x}\right) + \frac{x}{1+\frac{1}{x}}\left(\frac{-1}{x^2}\right)\right]$

$\Rightarrow \quad f'(x) = \left(1+\frac{1}{x}\right)^x \left[\ln\left(1+\frac{1}{x}\right) - \frac{1}{x+1}\right]$

Now, $\left(1+\frac{1}{x}\right)^x$ is always positive, hence the sign of $f'(x)$ depends on sign of $\ln\left(1+\frac{1}{x}\right) - \frac{1}{1+x}$

i.e. we have to compare $\ln\left(1+\frac{1}{x}\right)$ and $\frac{1}{1+x}$

So, let us assume $g(x) = \ln\left(1+\frac{1}{x}\right) - \frac{1}{1+x}$

$$g'(x) = \frac{1}{1+\frac{1}{x}}\left(\frac{-1}{x^2}\right) + \frac{1}{(x+1)^2}$$

$\Rightarrow \quad g'(x) = \frac{-1}{x(x+1)^2},$

for $x \in (0, \infty)$, $g'(x) < 0$ ...(i)

$\Rightarrow g(x)$ is strictly decreasing for $x \in (0, \infty)$

$g(x) > \lim_{x \to \infty} g(x)$

$g(x) > 0$

and since $g(x) > 0 \Rightarrow f'(x) > 0$

For $x \in (-\infty, -1)$, $g'(x) > 0$ ...(iii)

$\Rightarrow g(x)$ is strictly increasing for $x \in (-\infty, -1)$

$\Rightarrow \quad g(x) > \lim_{x \to \infty} g(x)$

$\Rightarrow \quad g(x) > 0 \Rightarrow f'(x) > 0$

From Eqs. (i) and (ii), we get

$f'(x) > 0$, for all $x \in (-\infty, -1) \cup (0, \infty)$

$\Rightarrow f(x)$ is strictly increasing in its domain

For drawing the graph of $f(x)$, its important to find the value of $f(x)$ at endpoints $\pm\infty, 0, -1$.

$$\lim_{x \to \pm\infty}\left(1+\frac{1}{x}\right)^x = e$$

$$\lim_{x \to 0^-}\left(1+\frac{1}{x}\right)^x = 1 \text{ and } \lim_{x \to -1}\left(1+\frac{1}{x}\right)^x = \infty$$

So, the graph of $f(x)$ is

From the graph, the range is $y \in (1, \infty) - \{e\}$.

10. First, if we assume that $f(x) > 1$, for some $x \in R^+$, setting $y = \frac{x}{f(x)-1}$ gives the contradiction $f(x) = 1$.

Hence, $f(x) \le 1$, for each $x \in R^+$, which implies that f is a decreasing function.

If $f(x) = 1$, for some $x \in R^+$, then $f(x+y) = f(y)$ for each $y \in R^+$ and by the monotonicity of f it follows that $f \equiv 1$.

Now, let $f(x) < 1$ for each $x \in R^+$. Then, f is strictly decreasing function in particular injective. By the equalities,

$$f(x)\,f(yf(x)) = f(x+y) = f(yf(x) + x + y(1-f))$$
$$= f(yf(x))\,f((x+y)(1-f(x))\,f(yf(x)))$$

We obtain that $x = (x + y(1-f(x)))f(yf(x))$.

Setting $x = 1$, $z = xf(1)$ and $a = \frac{1-f(1)}{f(1)}$, we get $f(z) = \frac{1}{1+az}$.

Combining the two cases, we conclude that $f(x) = \frac{1}{1+ax}$ for each $x \in R^+$, where $a \ge 0$. Conversely, a direct verification shows that the function of this form satisfy the initial equality.

Alternative

As in the first solution, we get that f is a decreasing function in particular differentiable almost everywhere. Write the initial equality in the form

$$\frac{f(x+y)-f(x)}{y} = f^2(x) = \frac{f(yf(x))-1}{yf(x)}$$

It follows that if f is differentiable at the point $x \in R^+$, then there exists the limit $\lim_{z \to 0^+}\frac{f(z)-1}{z} = -a$. Therefore,

$f'(x) = -af^2(x)$ for each $x \in R^+$ i.e. $\left(\frac{1}{f(x)}\right) = a$, which means that $f(x) = \frac{1}{ax+b}$.

On substituting in the initial relation, we find that $b = 1$ and $a \ge 0$.

11. Assume that there is $y \in (a, b]$ such that $f(y) \ne 0$. Without loss of generality, we have $f(y) > 0$.

In view of the continuity of f there exists $c \in [a, y)$ such that $f(c) = 0$ and $f(x) > 0$, for $x \in (c, y]$.

For $x \in (c, y]$, we have $|f'(x)| \le \lambda f(x)$. This implies that the function $g(x) = \ln f(x) - \lambda x$ is not increasing in $(c, y]$ because of $g'(x) = \frac{f'(x)}{f(x)} - \lambda \le 0$.

Thus, $\ln f(c) - \lambda x \ge \ln f(y) - \lambda y$ and $f(x) \ge e^{\lambda x - \lambda y} f(y)$ for $x \in (c, y]$.

Thus, $0 = f(c) = f(c+0) \ge e^{\lambda c - \lambda y} f(y) > 0$ a contradiction.

Hence, one has $f(x) = 0$, for $x \in [a, b]$.

Suppose that $f(x)$ is a real valued function defined for real values of x. Suppose that both $f(x) - 3x$ and $f(x) - x^3$ are increasing functions. Must $f(x) - x - x^2$, also be.

12. $f(x) = \sin x + 2x$

$$g(x) = \frac{3(x^2+x)}{\pi}$$

$f'(x) = \cos x + 2 > 0,\ f''(x) = -\sin x < 0$

Hence, f is concave down and increasing.

$$g'(x) = \frac{3}{\pi}(2x+1),\ g''(x) = \frac{3}{\pi}(2) > 0$$

$\Rightarrow g$ is concave up and increasing.

$$f\left(\frac{\pi}{2}\right) = \pi + 1$$

$$g\left(\frac{\pi}{2}\right) = 3\frac{\pi}{2\pi}\left(\frac{\pi}{2}+1\right)$$

$$= \frac{3}{2}\left(\frac{\pi}{2}+1\right] = \frac{3\pi}{4} + \frac{3}{2} = \pi + \frac{3}{4} - \frac{\pi}{4}.$$

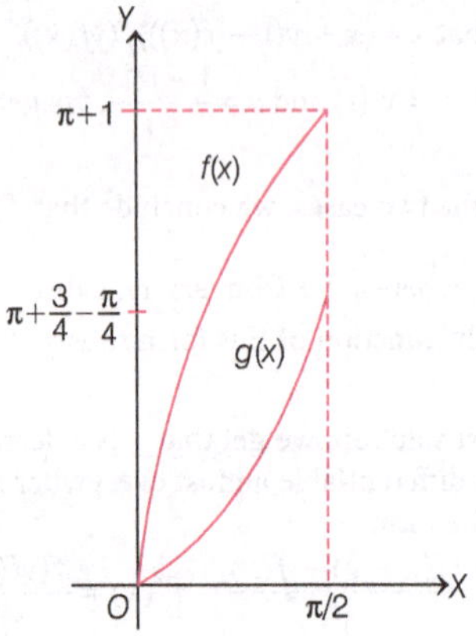

From the graph, it is clear that $f(x) \ge g(x),\ \forall\ x \in \left(0, \frac{\pi}{2}\right)$.

13. To show that $2x < \ln\frac{1+x}{1-x}$,

consider the function f defined on (0, 1] as

$$f(x) = 2x - \ln\frac{1+x}{1-x}.$$

Let c be any real number in [0, 1]. Then, f is continuous in [0, c] and derivable in (0, c).

Also, $f'(x) = \frac{-2x^2}{1-x^2}$,

so that $f'(x) < 0$ in [0, c). This shows that f is strictly decreasing in [0, c].

In particular, $f(c) < f(0)$.

Since, $f(0) = 0$, this means that

$$2x - \ln\frac{1+x}{1-x} < 0, \text{ when } x = c.$$

Since, c is any real number in (0, 1),it follows that

$$2x < \ln\frac{1+x}{1-x}, \text{ whenever } 0 < x < 1. \quad \text{...(i)}$$

To show that

$$\ln\frac{1+x}{1-x} < 2x\left(1 + \frac{1}{3}\cdot\frac{x^2}{1-x^2}\right).$$

Consider the function g defined by setting

$$g(x) = \ln\frac{1+x}{1-x} - 2x\left(1 + \frac{1}{3}\,dt\,\frac{x^2}{1-x^2}\right)$$

Then, $g'(x) = -\frac{4}{3}\cdot\frac{x^4}{(1-x^2)^2}$

Since, $g'(x) < 0$ for all x in (0, 1) and since $g(0) = 0$, therefore it follows in the same manner as above that $g(x) < 0$, whenever $0 < x < 1$,

$$\text{that is } \ln\frac{1+x}{1-x} < 2x\left(1 + \frac{1}{3}\frac{x^2}{1-x^2}\right), \quad \text{...(ii)}$$

whenever $0 < x < 1$.

From Eqs. (i) and (ii), we get

$$2x < \ln\frac{1+x}{1-x} < 2x\left(1 + \frac{1}{3}\cdot\frac{x^2}{1-x^2}\right), \quad \text{...(iii)}$$

whenever $0 < x < 1$.

On putting $x = \frac{1}{2n+1}$ in Eq. (iii), we get

$$\frac{2}{2n+1} < \ln\frac{n+1}{n} < \frac{2}{2n+1}\left(1 + \frac{1}{12n(n+1)}\right),$$

or $$1 < \left(n + \frac{1}{2}\right)\ln\left(1 + \frac{1}{n}\right) < 1 + \frac{1}{12n(n+1)},$$

so that $$e < \left(1 + \frac{1}{n}\right)^{n+\frac{1}{2}} < e^{1+\frac{1}{12n(n+1)}}$$

which is the desired inequality.

14. Here, $x = 3$ cm, $y = 1$ cm and $\frac{dx}{dt} = 2$ cm/s

Let $f = 2xy - 3x^2y$

$$\Rightarrow \frac{df}{dt} = 2y\frac{dx}{dt} + 2x\frac{dy}{dt} - 3x^2\frac{dy}{dt} - 6xy\frac{dx}{dt}$$

$$= (2x - 3x^2)\frac{dy}{dx} + (2y - 6xy)\frac{dx}{dt} \quad \text{...(i)}$$

$\because f$ is neither increasing nor decreasing.

$$\therefore \left(\frac{df}{dt}\right)_{(3,1)} = 0$$

$$\Rightarrow (2\times 3 - 27)\frac{dy}{dt} + (2 - 18)2 = 0 \Rightarrow \frac{dy}{dt} = -\frac{32}{21}$$

Now, for S, f = constant

$$\Rightarrow \quad 0 = (2x - 3x^2)\frac{dy}{dt} + (2y - 6xy)\frac{dx}{dt}$$

$$\Rightarrow \quad \frac{dy}{dx} = \frac{6xy - 2y}{2x - 3x^2}$$

$$\Rightarrow \quad \frac{dy}{dx} > 0 \Rightarrow \frac{6xy - 2y}{2x - 3x^2} > 0 \Rightarrow \frac{y(3x-1)}{x(3x-2)} < 0.$$

Thus, there arise two cases

Case I $y(3x-1) > 0$ and $x(3x-2) < 0$

$$\Rightarrow (y > 0 \text{ and } x > 1/3) \text{ or } (y < 0 \text{ and } x < 1/3) \text{ and } \left(0 < x < \frac{2}{3}\right)$$

$$\Rightarrow \left(y > 0 \text{ and } \frac{1}{3} < x < \frac{2}{3}\right) \text{ or } \left(y < 0 \text{ and } 0 < x < \frac{1}{3}\right)$$

Case II $y(3x-1)<0$ and $x(3x-2)>0$

$\Rightarrow$ $(y>0 \text{ and } x<1/3)$ or $(y<0 \text{ and } x>1/3)$

and $(x<0 \text{ or } x>2/3)$

$\Rightarrow$ $(y>0 \text{ and } x<0)$ or $(y<0 \text{ and } x>2/3)$

Thus, S is shaded portion shown in figure (i).

Also, S' represents the portion shown in figure (ii).

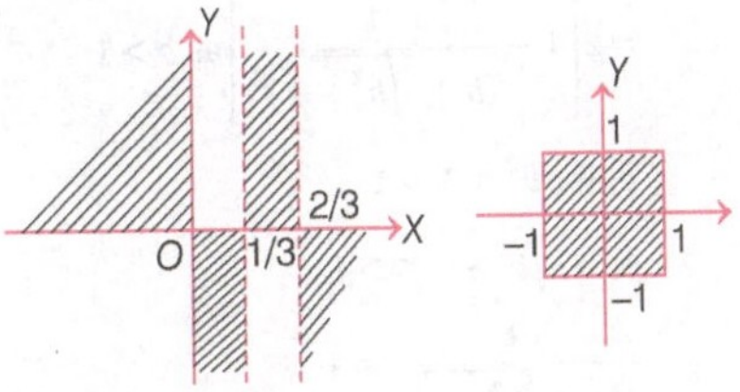

(i) (ii)

Thus, area for $S \cap S'$ is shown in figure (iii).

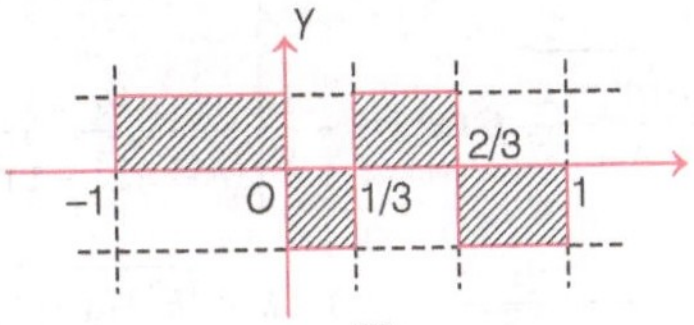

(iii)

Hence, the area of $S \cap S' = 2$

15. Let the square $ABCD$ and the equations of the sides of the square are as follows.

$AB: y=1$, $BC: x=-1$, $CD: y=-1$, $DA: x=1$

Let the region be S and (x, y) be any point inside it. Then, according to given conditions,

$$\sqrt{x^2+y^2}<|1-x|, |1+x|, |1-y|, |1+y|$$

$$\Rightarrow (x^2+y^2)<x^2-2x+1, x^2+2x+1, y^2-2y+1, y^2+2y+1$$

$$\Rightarrow \quad y^2<1-2x, y^2<1+2x, x^2<1-2y \text{ and } x^2<2y+1$$

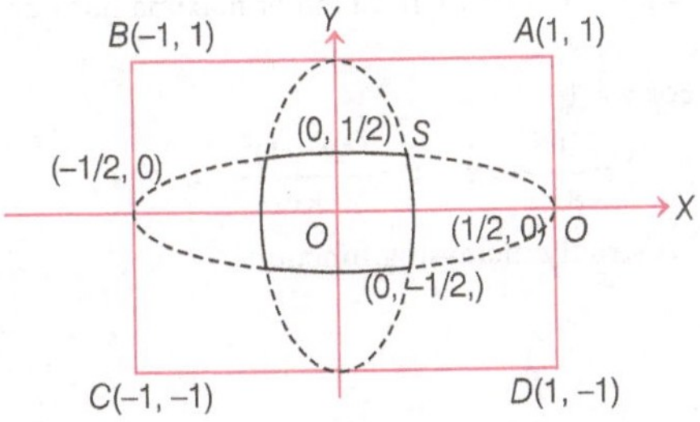

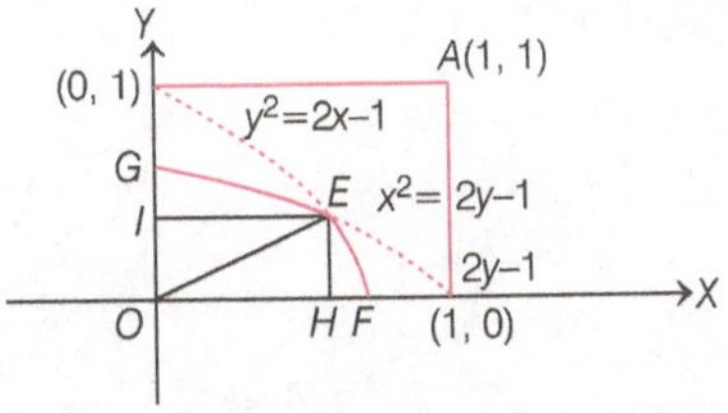

Now, in $y^2=1-2x$ and $y^2=2x+1$, the first equation represents a parabola with vertex $\left(\frac{1}{2}, 0\right)$ and second equation represents a parabola with vertex $\left(\frac{-1}{2}, 0\right)$ and in $x^2=1-2y$ and $x^2=1+2y$, the first equation represents parabola with vertex at $\left(0, \frac{1}{2}\right)$ and second equation represents a parabola with vertex at $\left(0, \frac{-1}{2}\right)$.

So, the region S is the region lying inside the four parabolas

$$y^2=1-2x$$
$$y^2=1+2x$$
$$x^2=1-2y$$
$$x^2=1+2y$$

Now, S is symmetrical in all four quadrants.

$\therefore \quad S = 4 \times$ area lying in first quadrant.

Now, $y^2=1-2x$ and $x^2=1-2y$ intersect on $y=x$.

The point of intersection is $E(\sqrt{2}-1, \sqrt{2}-1)$.

$\therefore$ Area of region $OEFO$ = Area of ΔOEH + Area of region $HEFH$

$$=\frac{1}{2}(\sqrt{2}-1)^2+\int_{\sqrt{2}-1}^{1/2}\sqrt{1-2x}\,dx$$

$$=\frac{1}{2}(2+1-2\sqrt{2})+\frac{2}{3}\left[(1-2x)^{3/2}\right]_{\sqrt{2}-1}^{1/2}$$

$$=\frac{1}{2}(3-2\sqrt{2})+\frac{1}{3}(3-2\sqrt{2})^{\frac{3}{2}}$$

$$=\frac{1}{2}(3-2\sqrt{2})+\frac{1}{3}(\sqrt{2}-1)^3$$

$$=\frac{1}{2}(3-2\sqrt{2})+\frac{1}{3}(5\sqrt{2}-7)$$

$$=\frac{1}{6}[4\sqrt{2}-5]$$

Similarly, area of region $OEGO=\frac{1}{6}(4\sqrt{2}-5)$

So, area of S lying in first quadrant $=\frac{2}{6}(4\sqrt{2}-5)$

Hence, $S=\frac{4}{3}(4\sqrt{2}-5)$

16. $f(x)=$

$$\begin{cases} (-1)^{p+q}[x^{p-1}(p)(x-1)^q+qx^p(x-1)^{q-1}, & x<0 \\ 0 & , \quad x=0 \\ (-1)^q[px^{p-1}(x-1)^q+qx^p(x-1)^{q-1}] & , \quad 0<x<1 \\ 0 & , \quad x=1 \\ px^{p-1}(x-1)^q+qx^p(x-1)^{q-1}, & x>1 \end{cases}$$

$\therefore \quad f'(x)=0$

$\Rightarrow ((x^{p-1})(x-1)^{q-1})(p(x-1)+qx)=0$

Now, $x=0$ (rejected) or $x=1$ (rejected)

or $\quad (p+q)x=p$

$\Rightarrow \quad x=\frac{p}{p+q}$ (accepted)

$\therefore$ For maxima,

$$f\left(\frac{p}{p+q}\right)=\left(\frac{p}{p+q}\right)^p\left|\frac{p}{p+q}\right|^2$$

$$\left[\because \frac{p}{p+q}>0 \text{ and } \frac{p}{p+q}-1<0\right]$$

$$\Rightarrow \quad f\left(\frac{p}{p+q}\right)=\frac{p^p+q^q}{(p+q)^{p+q}}$$

17. Let $f(x)=\dfrac{x^2-2x\cos\alpha+1}{x^2-2x\cos\beta+1}$

$$\Rightarrow f'(x)=\frac{2(x^2-1)(\cos\alpha-\cos\beta)}{(x^2-2x\cos\beta+1)^2}$$

$$=\frac{2(1-x^2)(\cos\beta-\cos\alpha)}{(x^2-2x\cos\beta+1)^2} \quad [\because 0<\beta<\alpha<\pi/2]$$

For maximum or minimum of $f(x)$, $f'(x)=0$

$\therefore \quad x=\pm 1$

$$\therefore f''(x)=\frac{4(\cos\beta-\cos\alpha)(x^3-3x+2\cos\beta)}{(x^2-2x\cos\beta+1)^3}$$

$f''(1)<0$ and $f''(-1)>0$

$\Rightarrow f(x)$ is maximum at $x=1$ and minimum at $x=-1$.

Hence, maximum and minimum values of $f(x)$ are $f(1)$ and $f(-1)$.

or $\quad \dfrac{2-2\cos\alpha}{2-2\cos\beta}$ and $\dfrac{2+2\cos\alpha}{2+2\cos\beta}$

i.e. $\quad \dfrac{\sin^2\frac{\alpha}{2}}{\sin^2\frac{\beta}{2}}$ and $\dfrac{\cos^2\frac{\alpha}{2}}{\cos^2\frac{\beta}{2}}$

18. Note that $f(x)$ is differentiable for each $x>0$.

Thus, critical points of $f'(x)=0$ are solutions, we have

$$f'(x)=\frac{1}{8x}-b+2x$$

For critical points, we solve $f'(x)=0$

Now, since equation $f'(x)=0$ is quadratic in x, so on solving

$\dfrac{1}{8x}-b+2x=0$, we get $x=\dfrac{b\pm\sqrt{b^2-1}}{4}$

For x to be real, $b^2-1\geq 0$, $b\leq -1$ or $b\geq 1$

but $b\geq 0$ is given, so $b\geq 1$

$$f''(x)=-\frac{1}{8x^2}+2$$

At $x=\dfrac{b+\sqrt{b^2-1}}{4}$, $f''(x)=2-\dfrac{1}{8}\left[\dfrac{+16}{(b+\sqrt{(b^2-1)})^2}\right]$

$$=2\left[1-\frac{1}{(b+\sqrt{b^2-1})^2}\right] \text{ as } b>1$$

$\Rightarrow \quad b+\sqrt{b^2+1}>1$

$\Rightarrow \quad (b+\sqrt{b^2-1})^2>1$

$$\frac{1}{(b+\sqrt{b^2-1})^2}<1$$

$f''(x)=$ positive for $x=\dfrac{b+\sqrt{b^2-1}}{4}$, for $b>1$

At $x=\dfrac{b-\sqrt{b^2-1}}{4}$, $f''(x)=2-\dfrac{1}{8}\left[\dfrac{16}{(b-\sqrt{b^2-1})^2}\right]$

$$=2\left[1-\frac{1}{(b-\sqrt{b^2-1})^2}\right], 0<b-\sqrt{b^2-1}<1, \text{ for } b>1$$

$f''(x)=$ negative

(i) For $b>1$, $f''(x)$ has maxima at $x=\dfrac{b-\sqrt{b^2-1}}{4}$ and minima at $x=\dfrac{b+\sqrt{b^2-1}}{4}$

For $b=1$, $f''(x)=0$, $f'''(x)=\dfrac{2}{8x^3}=\dfrac{1}{4x^3}$

So, $f'''(x)=\dfrac{1}{4\left(\frac{1}{4}\right)^3}\neq 0$, for $b=1$, $x=\dfrac{1}{4}$

$\therefore$ If $b=1$, then function has neither maxima nor minima at any x.

Note For $b=1$

$$f'(x)=\frac{1}{8x}+2x-1=\frac{(4x-1)^2}{8x}>0, \forall x>0$$

$\therefore f(x)$ is strictly increasing function.